MW00824116

Literature & Composition

Essential Voices, Essential Skills

for the AP® Course

Third Edition

Literature & Composition

Essential Voices, Essential Skills for the AP® Course

Renée H. Shea
Bowie State University, Maryland

Robin Dissin Aufses
Lycée Français de New York

Lawrence Scanlon
Brewster High School, New York

Katherine E. Cordes
Skyview High School, Montana

Carlos A. Escobar
Felix Varela Senior High School, Florida

Carol Jago
Santa Monica High School, California

bedford, freeman & worth
high school publishers
Boston | New York

Senior Vice President, Humanities, Social Sciences, and High School: Chuck Linsmeier
Executive Program Director, High School: Ann Heath
Executive Program Manager, High School Humanities: Nathan Odell
Senior Development Editor: Caitlin Kaufman
Associate Editor: Kelly Noll
Editorial Assistant: Meghan Kelly
Director of Media Editorial: Adam Whitehurst
Media Editor: Gina Forsythe
Executive Marketing Manager, High School: Lisa Erdely
Assistant Marketing Manager, High School: Tiffani Tang
Senior Director, Content Management Enhancement: Tracey Kuehn
Senior Managing Editor: Michael Granger
Senior Manager of Publishing Services: Andrea Cava
Senior Workflow Project Manager: Lisa McDowell
Production Supervisor: Robin Besofsky
Senior Design Services Manager: Natasha A. S. Wolfe
Interior Design: Jerilyn DiCarlo
Cover Design: William Boardman
Icon Credits: (numbers) KRAHOVNET/Shutterstock; (lightbulb) PureSolution/Shutterstock; (arrows) Palsur/Shutterstock
Director, Rights and Permissions: Hilary Newman
Text Permissions Project Manager: Elaine Kosta, Lumina Datamatics, Inc.
Photo Permissions Project Manager: Krystyna Borgen, Lumina Datamatics, Inc.
Photo Researcher: Danniel Schoonebeek
Director of Digital Production: Keri deManigold
Lead Media Project Manager: Jodi Isman
Project Management: Vanavan Jayaraman, Lumina Datamatics, Inc.
Copyeditor: Nancy Benjamin
Editorial Services: Lumina Datamatics, Inc.
Composition: Lumina Datamatics, Inc.
Cover Image: Viviana Gonzalez/Media Bakery
Printing and Binding: Transcontinental

Library of Congress Control Number: 2021941857
ISBN 978-1-319-28114-4 (Student Edition)
ISBN 978-1-319-40437-6 (Teacher's Edition)

Printed in Canada.
1 2 3 4 5 6 26 25 24 23 22 21

Acknowledgments
Text acknowledgments and copyrights appear at the back of the book on pages 1370–1375, which constitute an extension of the copyright page. Art acknowledgments and copyrights appear on the same page as the art selections they cover.

For information, write: BFW Publishers, 120 Broadway, 25th Floor, New York, NY 10271
hsmarketing@bfwpub.com

To Bertha Vogelsang Bahn;

Kate and Michael Aufses;

Aidan and Annie Prezzano and Eliza Gadway;

John Cordes;

Alejandro and Maria Eugenia Escobar;

Michael and James Jago;

and to students and teachers everywhere for their courage, commitment, and creativity during the COVID-19 pandemic.

About the Authors

Renée H. Shea was professor of English and Modern Languages and director of freshman composition at Bowie State University in Maryland. A College Board faculty consultant for more than thirty years in AP® Language and Literature, and Pre-AP® English, she has been a reader and question leader for both AP® English exams. Renée served as a member on three committees for the College Board: the AP® Language and Composition Development Committee, the English Academic Advisory Committee, and the SAT Critical Reading Test Development Committee. She is co-author of *American Literature & Rhetoric*, *The Language of Composition*, *Conversations in American Literature*, *Advanced Language & Literature*, and *Foundations of Language & Literature*, as well as volumes on Amy Tan and Zora Neale Hurston for the NCTE High School Literature Series. Renée continues to write about contemporary authors for publications such as *World Literature Today*, *Poets & Writers*, and *Kenyon Review*. Her recent profiles focused on Imbolo Mbue, Natalie Handal, Lan Cao, and Ohio's current poet laureate Kari Gunter-Seymour.

Robin Dissin Aufses is director of English Studies at Lycée Français de New York, where she teaches AP® English Language and Composition. Previous to this position, Robin was the English department chair and a teacher at John F. Kennedy High School in Bellmore, New York, and prior to that she taught English at Paul D. Schreiber High School in Port Washington, New York. She taught AP® English Literature and AP® English Language at both schools. She is co-author of *American Literature & Rhetoric*, *The Language of Composition*, and *Conversations in American Literature* and has published articles for the College Board on novelist Chang-rae Lee and the novel *All the King's Men*.

Lawrence Scanlon taught at Brewster High School for more than thirty years and then for another ten years at Iona College in New York. For twenty-five years he was a Reader and Question Leader for the AP® Language and Composition Exam. Over that same period of time, he has conducted AP® workshops and institutes in both AP® English Language and AP® English Literature throughout the United States and also in South America, Asia, Europe, and the Middle East as a College Board® consultant. He has served as a private consultant for many school districts. In addition, he also served on the AP® English Language Test Development Committee. Larry is co-author of *American Literature & Rhetoric*, *The Language of Composition*, and *Conversations in American Literature* and has published articles on curriculum and method for the College Board, *Business Insider*, and other publications.

©2021 Macmillan, Photo by Steven Lemon

Katherine E. Cordes is a National Board-certified English teacher with a BA in English, psychology, and medieval studies; an MEd in curriculum and instruction; more than nineteen years of experience in the secondary English Language Arts classroom; and six years of experience working with NBCT candidates through the National Education Association. She currently teaches tenth-grade English and AP® English Literature at Skyview High School in Billings, Montana. As part of the College Board's Instructional Design Team, Katherine contributed to the development, review, and dissemination of the 2019 AP® English Literature Course and Exam Description, and she has been an AP® Reader for the AP® English Literature exam for nine years. A co-author of *American Literature & Rhetoric*, she has also authored teacher resource materials for *Conversations in American Literature* and *The Language of Composition*.

©2021 Macmillan, Photo by Steven Lemon

Carlos A. Escobar teaches tenth-grade English and AP® English Literature and Composition at Felix Varela Senior High School in Miami, Florida, where he is also the AP® Program Director. Carlos has been the College Board Advisor for AP® English Literature, an AP® Reader, and a member of the AP® English Literature Test Development Committee. He has mentored new AP® English teachers and presented at numerous local and national AP® workshops and conferences. As part of the College Board's Instructional Design Team, Carlos contributed to the development, review, and dissemination of the 2019 AP® English Literature and Composition Course and Exam Description. He designed and delivered daily live YouTube lessons streamed globally by the College Board and was the Lead Instructor for AP® Daily, the College Board's skill-based, on-demand video series. Carlos has co-authored the Teacher's Editions for *Literature & Composition*, Second Edition; *Advanced Language & Literature*; and *Foundations of Language & Literature*. He is also a co-author of the second edition of *Advanced Language & Literature*.

Courtesy of Carol Jago

Carol Jago has taught English in middle and high school for thirty-two years and is associate director of the California Reading and Literature Project at UCLA. She is a past president of the National Council of Teachers of English and in 2021 was elected to the International Reading Association Executive Board. She also served as AP® Literature content advisor for the College Board. She has published seven books with Heinemann, including *With Rigor for All*; *Papers, Papers, Papers*; and most recently *The Book in Question: Why and How Reading Is in Crisis.* She has also published four books on contemporary multicultural authors for NCTE's High School Literature series. Carol was an education columnist for the *Los Angeles Times*, and her essays have appeared in *English Journal, Language Arts, NEA Today*, as well as in other newspapers across the nation. She edits the journal of the California Association of Teachers of English, *California English*, and served on the planning committee for the 2009 NAEP Reading Framework and the 2011 NAEP Writing Framework. Carol also served a four-year term on the National Assessment Governing Board. In 2020 she was awarded a Lifetime Achievement Award from the California Association of Teachers of English.

Dear Colleagues:

Welcome to *Literature & Composition: Essential Voices, Essential Skills for the AP® Course*, Third Edition, the newest edition of our book designed for the AP® English Literature and Composition course and the one most aligned to the College Board's Course and Exam Description (CED). As AP® Literature teachers ourselves, we know the joys of teaching the course as well as the pressure of the challenging exam that always looms. With this in mind, the third edition includes new features that provide you and your students with as many tools for success as possible, from on-the-spot AP® exam tips, to strategies for scoring as many points as possible on their essays, to AP® multiple-choice practice in every chapter and a full practice exam at the back of the book. Still, the main focus of *Literature & Composition* remains its instructional guidance for reading and writing, its thoughtfully curated text selections, and the reading questions students encounter as they build their literary analysis skills throughout the year. We have carefully crafted the reading questions in this edition to align with the Skills and Big Ideas of the AP® Literature CED; but more than that, they help deepen understanding, require close reading and analysis, and provide engaging prompts that begin with AP® exam FRQ practice before moving outward to research topics, creative writing opportunities, speaking and listening discussion starters, and more. We are confident that this book — with its step-by-step writing instruction, its diverse and provocative reading selections, and its underpinning of scaffolded reading questions — will be just what you need to enjoy an exciting year with your students and prepare them well for the exam.

Beyond the AP® course and the exam, though, we believe that literature must be a part of our students' — and our — everyday lives. Some say that today's students need preparation for the "real world," but in the push for practical college and career preparedness we don't want to overlook the importance of cultivating students' critical thinking skills and imaginations. The study of literature offers a chance to think deeply about ourselves and others, to study human nature, and to write about complex and compelling ideas. Literature helps us find our place in the world and understand our responsibility to others. Study after study show that people who read are happier in their work, in their relationships, in their engagement with their communities and cultures. Above all, this wider view of the power of literature animates our approach to everything in this textbook.

We welcome you to *Literature & Composition*, Third Edition, with the promise that you and your students will find joy in the literature and that you will all be well prepared for the exam.

Best of luck,

Renée H. Shea

Robin Dissin Aufses

Lawrence Scanlon

Katherine E. Cordes

Carlos A. Escobar

Carol Jago

GUIDED TOUR OF

Literature & Composition, Third Edition

Flexibility and alignment: The best of both worlds.

Since its first edition, *Literature & Composition* was designed specifically for the AP® English Literature course. Its unique structure of skill-building opening chapters combined with an engaging thematic anthology provides the ultimate flexibility to customize the course and ensure targeted skill development. In this edition, the book you know and love now fully aligns to the new AP® Course and Exam Description.

Chapters 1–3 cover the reading and writing skills key to success in the course and on the AP® Exam. Chapters 4–9 are anthology chapters arranged by timeless themes, such as Identity and Culture, that help bring our readings to life. Each of these thematic chapters offers a wide variety of classic and contemporary writing — including fiction, poetry, drama, nonfiction, visual texts, and several full-length works — with guidance and support to think critically and write insightfully about great literature.

NEW! 9 Chapters, 9 AP® Units: Making the AP® Course easy to navigate.

Nine chapters in this edition make it easy to align to the new AP® Course and Exam Description's nine units. **Yet the flexible structure you know and love hasn't changed:** Skill-building opening chapters and an engaging thematic anthology of some of the best literature through the ages. We know that not every school, teacher, or classroom is the same — and you need a book that's right for you. Now, you don't have to use a one-size-fits-all option. *Literature & Composition*, Third Edition, is flexible enough to make it your own, with enough structure and guidance to adhere closely to the AP® Course and Exam Description if you so choose.

Take a look at how we've incorporated the course units without sacrificing any of the flexibility that is key to an effective AP® Literature course.

A Year with the AP® Literature Units

AP® Unit	1	2	3	4	5	6	7	8	9
Opening Chapters	**Ch. 1** Section 1	**Ch. 2** Section 1	**Ch. 3** Section 1	**Ch. 1** Section 2	**Ch. 2** Section 2	**Ch. 3** Section 2	**Ch. 1** Section 3	**Ch. 2** Section 3	**Ch. 3** Section 3
Thematic Chapters				**Ch. 4**	**Ch. 5**	**Ch. 6**	**Ch. 7**	**Ch. 8**	**Ch. 9**

Opening chapters provide targeted instruction covering *all* the AP® course skills.

The opening chapters develop key reading and writing skills for the three literary genres of the course:

- Chapter 1, *Analyzing Short Fiction* (**Units 1-4-7**), cover the AP® Prose Fiction Analysis Essay (FRQ 1)
- Chapter 2, *Analyzing Poetry* (**Units 2-5-8**), covers the AP® Poetry Analysis Essay (FRQ 2)
- Chapter 3, *Analyzing Longer Fiction and Drama* (**Units 3-6-9**), covers the AP® Literary Argument Essay (FRQ 3)

With **scaffolded step-by-step instruction**, **AP® Tips, activities**, **AP®-style FRQ prompts, guidance for revising**, and **model student essays**, these chapters help develop the reading and writing skills of the AP® Literature course from the ground up. Each chapter is divided into three distinct sections that end with **Culminating Activities aligned to the AP® Units and Personal Progress Checks.** Designed with flexibility in mind, these chapters can be read straight through in the beginning of the year, or used in close alignment with the new course framework.

AP® Literature Short Fiction Strand

		AP® Skills Instruction	Formative Assessment	Further AP® Skills Practice
CHAPTER 1	AP® Unit 1	Section 1	Section 1 Culminating Activity	
	AP® Unit 4	Section 2	Section 2 Culminating Activity	Chapter 4
	AP® Unit 7	Section 3	Section 3 Culminating Activity	Chapter 7

AP® Literature Poetry Strand

		AP® Skills Instruction	Formative Assessment	Further AP® Skills Practice
CHAPTER 2	AP® Unit 2	Section 1	Section 1 Culminating Activity	
	AP® Unit 5	Section 2	Section 2 Culminating Activity	Chapter 5
	AP® Unit 8	Section 3	Section 3 Culminating Activity	Chapter 8

AP® Literature Longer Works of Fiction or Drama Strand

		AP® Skills Instruction	Formative Assessment	Further AP® Skills Practice
CHAPTER 3	AP® Unit 3	Section 1	Section 1 Culminating Activity	
	AP® Unit 6	Section 2	Section 2 Culminating Activity	Chapter 6
	AP® Unit 9	Section 3	Section 3 Culminating Activity	Chapter 9

Thematic anthology chapters have built-in alignment to the AP® course.

Each thematic chapter includes the following key elements:

NEW! Each **chapter** has a genre focus aligned to the AP® Literature course units. Chs. 4 and 7 emphasize short fiction, Chs. 5 and 8 emphasize poetry, and Chs. 6 and 9 emphasize longer works.

NEW! AP® Unit Chapter Introductions give an overview of the AP® Unit Skills and Essential Knowledge.

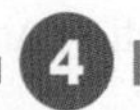

Identity and Culture 165

A **universal theme** designed to focus students' interpretation of the literature in the chapter.

A **Central Text** — an exemplar of the AP® Unit genre by a twentieth-century or contemporary author — opens and anchors the chapter.

A **Classic Text** — a major work from the AP® Unit genre by a world-renowned author — is perfect for practicing AP® reading and writing skills on challenging, beloved literature.

Texts in Context explore intriguing interpretations and insights into the Classic Text. Designed to help with incorporating sophistication into literary arguments, these sections illuminate the complexities within and around a work of literature.

A collection of **Short Fiction** in each chapter showcases classics like Herman Melville's "Bartleby, the Scrivener" and fresh new voices like Weike Wang's "The Trip."

A diverse collection of **Poetry**, spanning the sixteenth century to the present day, all exploring different angles of the chapter's theme.

NEW! TalkBacks in each chapter pair challenging pieces of literature with thought-provoking responses that explore new and nuanced ways of interpreting a work.

NEW! An **AP® Multiple-Choice Practice** section with a set of questions on the Central and Classic Texts in that chapter.

Suggestions for Writing — from AP®-style Exam FRQs to longer multimodal assignments, research projects, creative writing ideas, and more — these prompts offer plenty of practice to hone AP® reading and writing skills.

A diverse range of essential voices from the past and present bring literature to life.

Central and Classic Texts spark discussion and foster critical thinking.

A Central Text and a Classic Text from the corresponding AP® Unit genre begin and anchor each thematic chapter. These works offer ways to delve deeply into the theme, forming a foundation for interpreting the stories and poems in the rest of the chapter. The Classic Texts are challenging works of literature from an earlier time, often written for a very different audience than today's, with syntax and vocabulary that may be unfamiliar. These Classic Texts, which include such works as William Shakespeare's *Hamlet*, Mary Shelley's *Frankenstein*, Marianne Moore's "The Steeple-Jack," and Ralph Ellison's "Boy on a Train," are ideal for practicing the reading and writing that will be on the AP® exam. Central Texts range from selections written by celebrated twentieth-century and contemporary authors, including Nella Larsen, August Wilson, Jhumpa Lahiri, and Terrance Hayes.

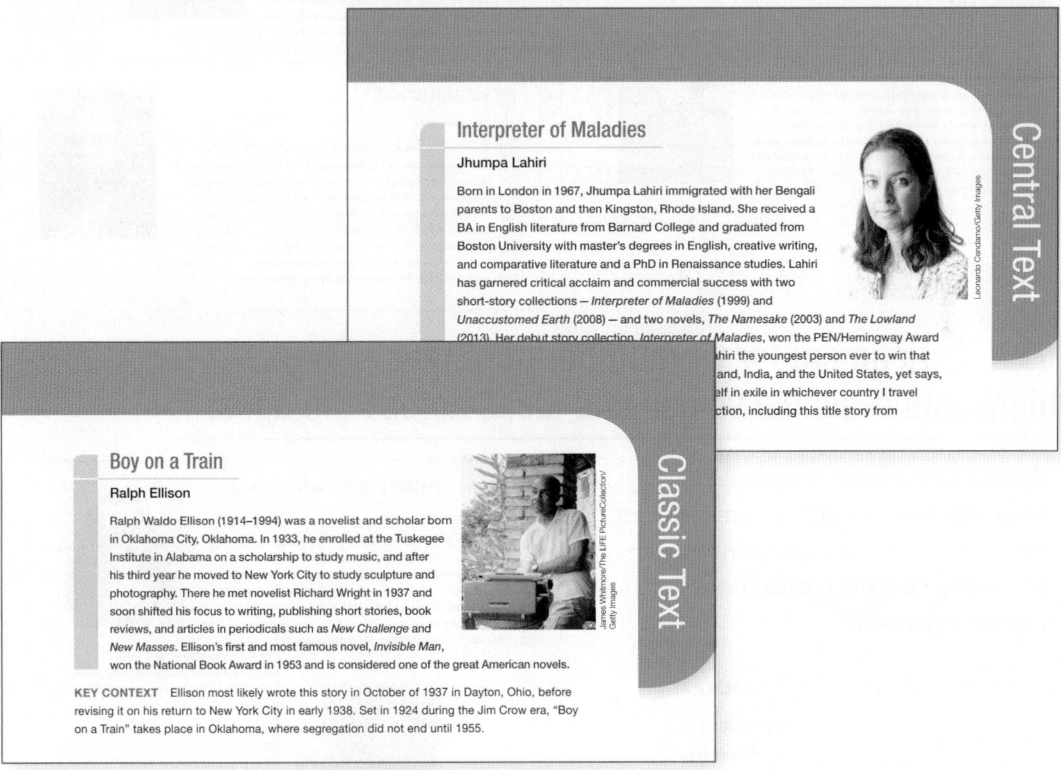

Central Text
Interpreter of Maladies
Jhumpa Lahiri
Born in London in 1967, Jhumpa Lahiri immigrated with her Bengali parents to Boston and then Kingston, Rhode Island. She received a BA in English literature from Barnard College and graduated from Boston University with master's degrees in English, creative writing, and comparative literature and a PhD in Renaissance studies. Lahiri has garnered critical acclaim and commercial success with two short-story collections — Interpreter of Maladies (1999) and Unaccustomed Earth (2008) — and two novels, The Namesake (2003) and The Lowland
hiri the youngest person ever to win that
and, India, and the United States, yet says,
elf in exile in whichever country I travel
ction, including this title story from
Leonardo Cendamo/Getty Images
Classic Text
Boy on a Train
Ralph Ellison
Ralph Waldo Ellison (1914–1994) was a novelist and scholar born in Oklahoma City, Oklahoma. In 1933, he enrolled at the Tuskegee Institute in Alabama on a scholarship to study music, and after his third year he moved to New York City to study sculpture and photography. There he met novelist Richard Wright in 1937 and soon shifted his focus to writing, publishing short stories, book reviews, and articles in periodicals such as New Challenge and New Masses. Ellison's first and most famous novel, Invisible Man, won the National Book Award in 1953 and is considered one of the great American novels.
KEY CONTEXT Ellison most likely wrote this story in October of 1937 in Dayton, Ohio, before revising it on his return to New York City in early 1938. Set in 1924 during the Jim Crow era, "Boy on a Train" takes place in Oklahoma, where segregation did not end until 1955.
James Whitmore/The LIFE PictureCollection/Getty Images

Fresh and familiar fiction and poetry readings center diverse voices.

The Central Texts and Classic Texts are followed by a collection of rich, rigorous short stories and poems that are engaging and appealing. These texts span several centuries, drawing from work both familiar and fresh, building on classics by writers such as Emily Dickinson and Nathaniel Hawthorne but also offering literature by a wealth of new voices, including Chimamanda Ngozi Adichie, Juan Felipe Herrera, Te-Ping Chen, Laura van den Berg, Jason Reynolds, Natalie Diaz, Jericho Brown, and many more. Bridging the old and the new emphasizes that many questions and issues — about the nature of war or the concept of identity, for example — have captivated and puzzled humanity through the ages and across cultures. Contemporary writers, such as Richard Blanco, Ada Limón, and Tracy K. Smith, continue to explore these issues.

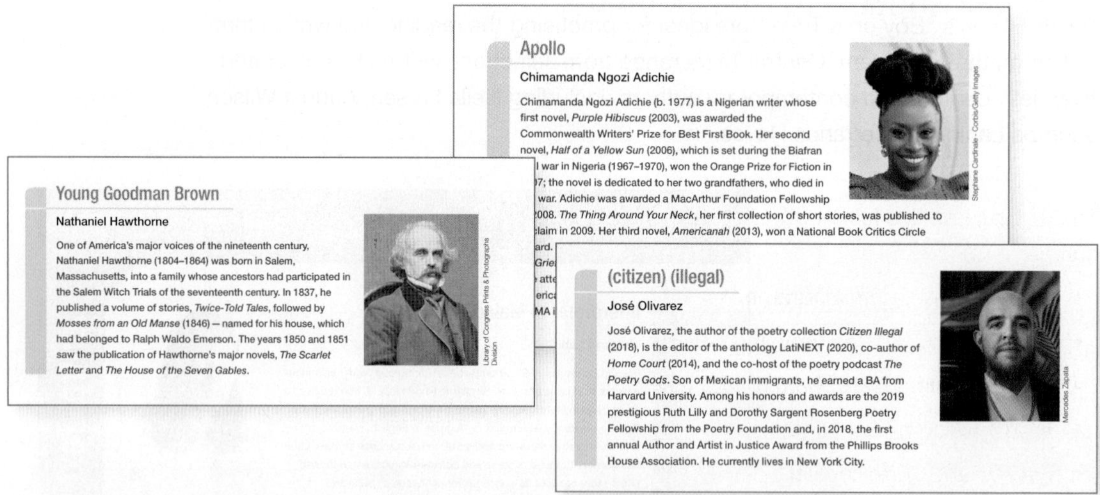

NEW! Enrichment for vibrant literature that highlights essential voices and ideas across the ages.

TalkBacks threaded throughout the book pair challenging pieces of literature with thought-provoking responses, presenting new and nuanced ways of interpreting a work.

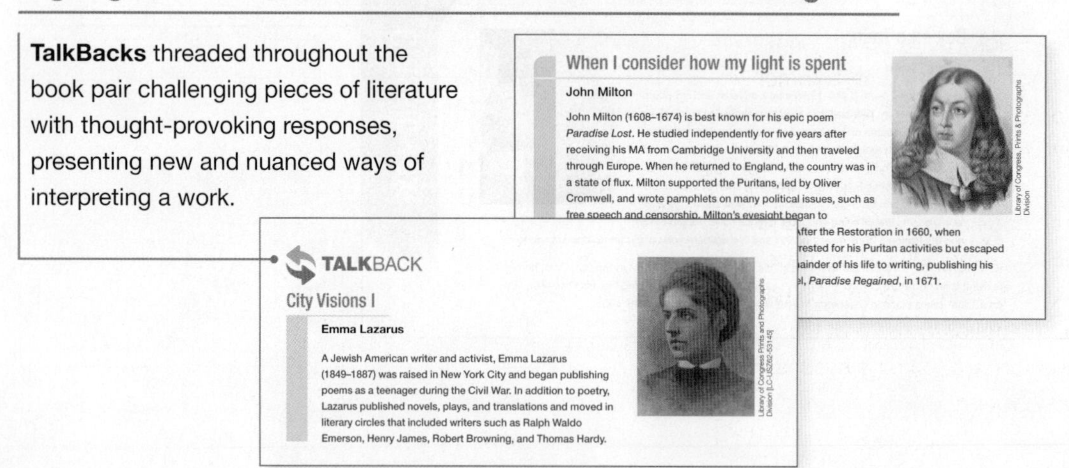

Key Context notes accompanying most texts help with navigating unfamiliar contexts that come with literature from other time periods or cultural traditions, providing a sense of the bigger picture. This support is key for developing readers and English Language Learners.

The Facts of Art

Natalie Diaz

Natalie Diaz (b. 1978) is an American poet and language activist. She is Mojave and an enrolled member of the Gila River Indian community. After attending Old Dominion University in Norfolk, Virginia, on an athletic scholarship as a Division 1 basketball player, Diaz went on to play professional basketball in Austria, Portugal, Spain, Sweden, and Turkey. She returned to Old Dominion University and earned an MFA in writing. A recipient of the MacArthur Foundation "Genius" Grant, she has authored two books of poetry: *When My Brother Was an Aztec* (2012) and *Post-Colonial Love Poem* (2020), which won the Pulitzer Prize for poetry. She is part of the Institute of American Indian Arts low-residency MFA faculty in Santa Fe, New Mexico, and currently splits her time between Princeton, New Jersey, and Mohave Valley, Arizona, where she works with the last speakers of the Mojave language to teach and revitalize the Mojave language.

Courtesy Natalie Diaz

KEY CONTEXT This poem is set during the Great Depression of the 1930s. The government, headed by President Franklin Delano Roosevelt, created the Civilian Conservation Corps (CCC) to generate jobs for the many unemployed across the nation. A division of this program, known as the CCC-ID, employed American Indians on public works projects, including roads, on their reservations. However, most local roads were not built on reservations until the 1970s.

Essential support for developing sophisticated literary arguments.

An emphasis on the full-length works that are integral to the AP® course.

This edition has five full-length works carefully chosen to support the AP® Literature course:

- Susan Glaspell, *Trifles* (drama)
- Nella Larsen, *Passing* (novel)
- William Shakespeare, *Hamlet* (drama)
- August Wilson, *Fences* (drama)
- Mary Shelley, *Frankenstein* (novel)

NEW! An extensive digital library of full-length works gives you freedom to approach AP® Literature your way.

Almost one hundred full-length works, many of which commonly appear on the AP® exam, are available at your fingertips in the e-book. It's easy and intuitive to add bookmarks, highlight, and annotate the texts. With these works to choose from, you have all the options and all of the support needed for a successful school year.

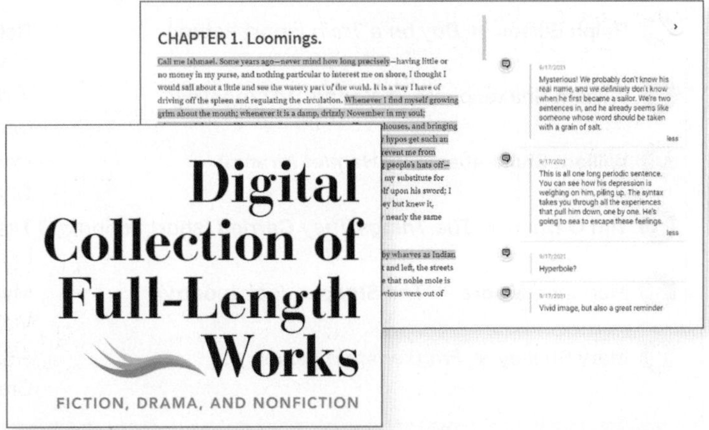

Texts in Context provide support for developing nuanced interpretations of Classic Texts.

Designed specifically to broaden understanding of complex, classic works of literature, Texts in Context sections present a collection of fiction, poetry, nonfiction, and visual texts that provide new insights into the chapter's Classic Text. Exploring connections between, among, and beyond the Texts in Context allows the Classic Text to be seen from new angles — and guides readers to deeper, more nuanced interpretations of meaning that take into account a variety of literary, artistic, cultural, political, and historical issues. A series of questions and writing prompts offer ways to enter the literary conversation and express individual viewpoints on the big ideas reflected in these readings.

Texts in Context

Ralph Ellison and the Influence of the Harlem Renaissance

...ure, the **Harlem Renaissance** continues to be a ...ussion among literary critics and historians. Even the ...that the movement began after the 1919 "Red ...throughout the United States; scholar Henry Louis ...of World War II. All agree, however, that the period of ...of extraordinary creativity that centered around New ...od, called "more a spirit than a movement" by critic ...ide range of ideas and writing styles, exploration ...eritages, protests against racial discrimination, ... The intellectual and artistic productivity of this era ...nkers, musicians, and visual artists whose work

4 / Identity and Culture

UPDATED EDITION HARLEM RENAISSANCE NATHAN IRVIN HUGGINS FOREWORD BY ARNOLD RAMPERSAD

This cover of scholar Nathan Irvin Huggins's book *Harlem Renaissance* features work by artist Aaron Douglas.
How does Douglas situate the cultural values of the Harlem Renaissance within American society? How do the composition, perspective, and the images themselves contribute to your interpretation?

unlike refugees in other part of the world fleeing famine, war, and pestilence."

Yet the denizens of the Great Migration often encountered racism and inequality similar to that of the South they had fled. While more jobs were available in the cities of the north and west, pay was often low and barriers to employment high; the work itself was typically menial labor. Fair housing was nearly nonexistent, and educational opportunities were far from guaranteed — while segregated schools were not a function of the law in the north, they were often the status quo.

Despite these obstacles and continuing inequities, the literature, art, and music created by Black people underwent profound changes and found wider audiences during the 1920s and 30s, especially in New York City. The uptown neighborhood of Harlem was not only a destination for many migrant African Americans and Black immigrants seeking work and economic opport... it was home to a new Black middle class. It was the nucleus of an artistic movement that center... Black experiences and celebrated various cultu... and traditions of Black people throughout the U... Writers and thinkers such as Alain Locke, Langs... Hughes, Countee Cullen, and Zora Neale Hurst... found more mainstream publishers receptive to... work and found a broad audience. Artists such... Augusta Savage, Aaron Douglass, and Jacob

...EXTS IN CONTEXT

1. **Alain Locke** ■ **from *The New Negro* (nonfiction)**
2. **Countee Cullen** ■ ***Heritage* (poetry)**
3. **Zora Neale Hurston** ■ ***Spunk* (short fiction)**
4. **Langston Hughes** ■ ***I look at the world* (poetry)**
5. **Jacob Lawrence** ■ **From *every southern town migrants left by the hundreds to travel north (Migration Series #3)* (painting)**

Classic Text	Texts in Context
4 **Ralph Ellison** ■ ***Boy on a Train* (short fiction)**	Ralph Ellison and the Influence of the Harlem Renaissance
5 **William Shakespeare** ■ ***Sonnet 147* (poetry)**	William Shakespeare and the Sonnet Form
6 **William Shakespeare** ■ ***Hamlet* (drama)**	*Hamlet* and the Evolution of Character
7 **Tim O'Brien** ■ ***The Things They Carried* (short fiction)**	*The Things They Carried* and Voices of the Vietnam Conflict
8 **Marianne Moore** ■ ***The Steeple-Jack* (poetry)**	Marianne Moore and the Modernist Vision
9 **Mary Shelley** ■ ***Frankenstein* (novel)**	*Frankenstein* and the Ethics of Creation

NEW! Even more engaging visuals and outside texts enrich the study of challenging literature.

Extending Beyond the Text features encourage exploration and inspire new ideas. This feature provides extension opportunities to explore how the ideas of a piece connect with real-world issues and other texts.

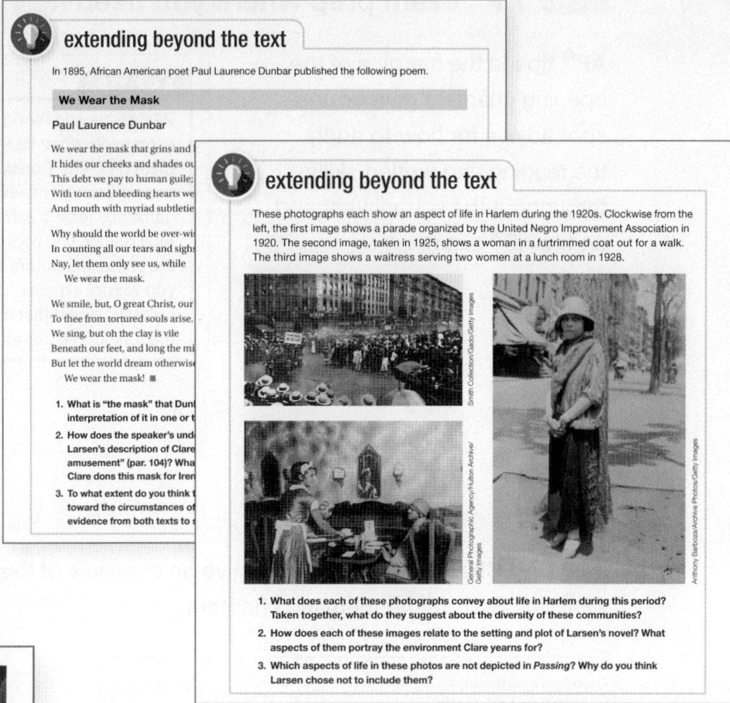

extending beyond the text

In 1895, African American poet Paul Laurence Dunbar published the following poem.

We Wear the Mask

Paul Laurence Dunbar

We wear the mask that grins and
It hides our cheeks and shades ou
This debt we pay to human guile;
With torn and bleeding hearts we
And mouth with myriad subtletie

Why should the world be over-wi
In counting all our tears and sigh
Nay, let them only see us, while
We wear the mask.

We smile, but, O great Christ, our
To thee from tortured souls arise.
We sing, but oh the clay is vile
Beneath our feet, and long the mi
But let the world dream otherwis
We wear the mask! ■

1. What is "the mask" that Dunl interpretation of it in one or t
2. How does the speaker's und Larsen's description of Clare amusement" (par. 104)? Wha Clare dons this mask for Iren
3. To what extent do you think toward the circumstances of evidence from both texts to

extending beyond the text

These photographs each show an aspect of life in Harlem during the 1920s. Clockwise from the left, the first image shows a parade organized by the United Negro Improvement Association in 1920. The second image, taken in 1925, shows a woman in a furtrimmed coat out for a walk. The third image shows a waitress serving two women at a lunch room in 1928.

Smith Collection/Gado/Getty Images

Anthony Barboza/Archive Photos/Getty Images

General Photographic Agency/Hulton Archive/Getty Images

1. What does each of these photographs convey about life in Harlem during this period? Taken together, what do they suggest about the diversity of these communities?
2. How does each of these images relate to the setting and plot of Larsen's novel? What aspects of them portray the environment Clare yearns for?
3. Which aspects of life in these photos are not depicted in *Passing*? Why do you think Larsen chose not to include them?

©Dee Conway/Bridgeman Images

In this photo from the National Beijing Opera's 2005 production of *The Legend of the White Snake*, two singers play the roles of the white and green snakes.

How do you interpret the women's posture and facial expressions? What parallels do you see between this depiction of the legend and the discussions the protagonist, his wife, and her cousin have about the characters in the legend?

Emphasizing visual analysis: Images with a purpose. We believe that visual literacy is an important scaffold for textual literacy as well as a bridge between the readings in this book and the contemporary world, which is why *Literature & Composition* includes visual texts that accompany the fiction and drama in the thematic chapters. These images are carefully chosen — each one has a clear, authentic pedagogical purpose and a critical thinking question. We made it our goal to carefully select images that inform the reading of a print text, suggest new ideas, or provide additional context.

CORR/AFP/Getty Images

In this December 1967 photo, two American soldiers relax beside a Christmas tree that has been set up in a trench surrounded by sandbags.

How does this image reflect the surreal experiences O'Brien describes in his story?

Continuous reinforcement of AP® Skills.

NEW! AP® exam prep where you need it.

AP® tips in the margins of the opening chapters give on-the-spot advice for how to apply the reading and writing skills throughout the school year and on the AP® exam.

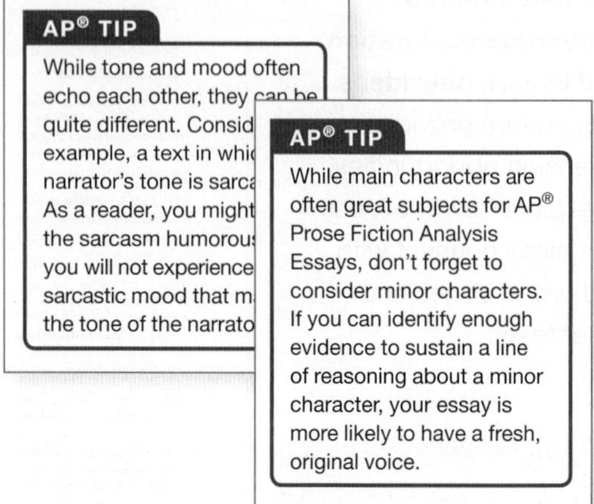

AP® TIP

While tone and mood often echo each other, they can be quite different. Consid example, a text in whic narrator's tone is sarca As a reader, you might the sarcasm humorous you will not experience sarcastic mood that m the tone of the narrato

AP® TIP

While main characters are often great subjects for AP® Prose Fiction Analysis Essays, don't forget to consider minor characters. If you can identify enough evidence to sustain a line of reasoning about a minor character, your essay is more likely to have a fresh, original voice.

AP® Unit Chapter Introductions give an overview of Essential Knowledge and AP® Unit Skills in the thematic chapters.

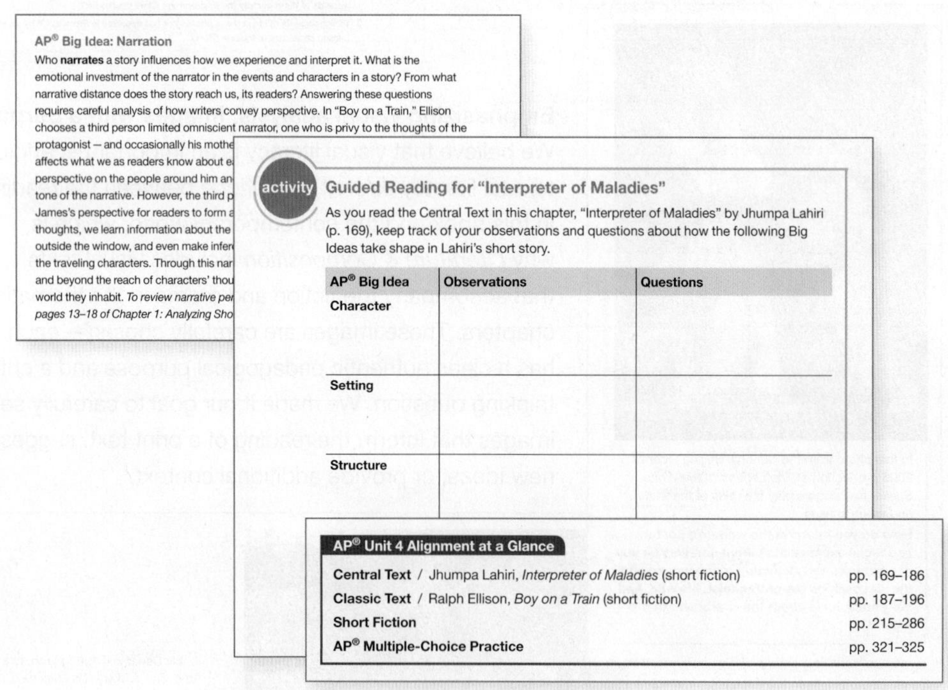

AP® Big Idea: Narration

Who **narrates** a story influences how we experience and interpret it. What is the emotional investment of the narrator in the events and characters in a story? From what narrative distance does the story reach us, its readers? Answering these questions requires careful analysis of how writers convey perspective. In "Boy on a Train," Ellison chooses a third person limited omniscient narrator, one who is privy to the thoughts of the protagonist — and occasionally his mothe affects what we as readers know about e perspective on the people around him an tone of the narrative. However, the third p James's perspective for readers to form a thoughts, we learn information about the outside the window, and even make infer the traveling characters. Through this nar and beyond the reach of characters' thou world they inhabit. *To review narrative per pages 13–18 of Chapter 1: Analyzing Sho*

activity **Guided Reading for "Interpreter of Maladies"**

As you read the Central Text in this chapter, "Interpreter of Maladies" by Jhumpa Lahiri (p. 169), keep track of your observations and questions about how the following Big Ideas take shape in Lahiri's short story.

AP® Big Idea	Observations	Questions
Character		
Setting		
Structure		

AP® Unit 4 Alignment at a Glance

Central Text / Jhumpa Lahiri, *Interpreter of Maladies* (short fiction)	pp. 169–186
Classic Text / Ralph Ellison, *Boy on a Train* (short fiction)	pp. 187–196
Short Fiction	pp. 215–286
AP® Multiple-Choice Practice	pp. 321–325

AP® Exam FRQ prompts accompany all readings in the thematic chapters. No matter what readings are covered during the year, there will always be ample opportunity to practice writing for the AP® exam.

1. AP® FRQ **Poetry Analysis.** In Gwendolyn Brooks's "We Real Cool," published in 1960, the speakers share the way they see themselves at a particular moment in their lives. Read the poem carefully. Then, in a well-written essay, analyze how Brooks uses literary elements and techniques to conv

1. AP® FRQ **Prose Fiction Analysis.** The following question refers to paragraphs 27–49 of Weike Wang's "The Trip," published in 2019. In this passage, a husband and wife react to the expectations of others in ways that reveal important dynamics in their marriage. Read the passage carefully. Then, in a well-written essay, analyze how Wang uses literary elements and techni

2. AP® FRQ **Literary Argument.** Many works of literature feature characters who undertake a journey, both literal and figurative, that depicts their growing complexity as human beings. In some cases, the journey results in greater maturity; in others, disillusionment; in some, a better understanding of the self. In "Young Goodman Brown" by Nathaniel Hawthorne, the main character, Goodman Brown experiences such a journey. In a well-written essay, analyze how his journey into the wilderness contributes to an interpretation of the work as a whole. Do not merely summarize the plot.

AP® multiple-choice practice at the end of each thematic chapter provides opportunities for formative assessment, class discussion, group work, and other in-class activities.

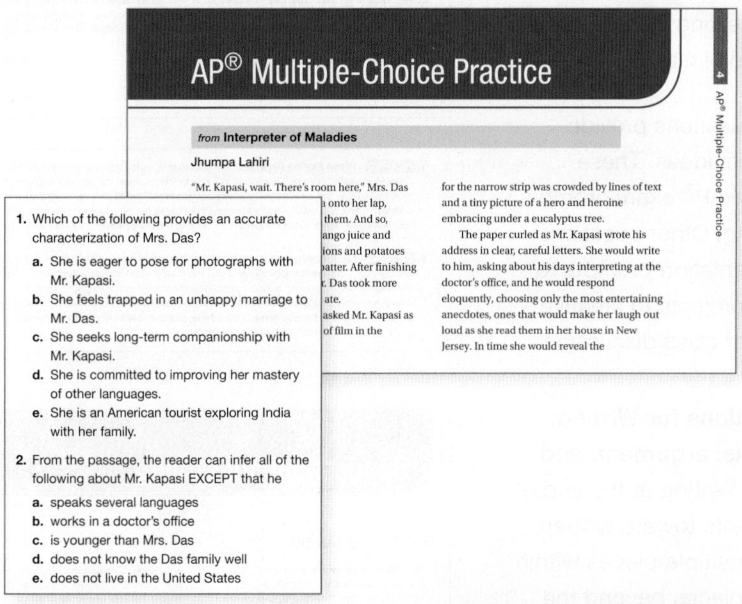

AP® Multiple-Choice Practice

from **Interpreter of Maladies**

Jhumpa Lahiri

"Mr. Kapasi, wait. There's room here," Mrs. Das … onto her lap, … them. And so, … ango juice and … ions and potatoes … batter. After finishing … Das took more … ate. … asked Mr. Kapasi as … of film in the

for the narrow strip was crowded by lines of text and a tiny picture of a hero and heroine embracing under a eucalyptus tree.

The paper curled as Mr. Kapasi wrote his address in clear, careful letters. She would write to him, asking about his days interpreting at the doctor's office, and he would respond eloquently, choosing only the most entertaining anecdotes, ones that would make her laugh out loud as she read them in her house in New Jersey. In time she would reveal the

1. Which of the following provides an accurate characterization of Mrs. Das?
   a. She is eager to pose for photographs with Mr. Kapasi.
   b. She feels trapped in an unhappy marriage to Mr. Das.
   c. She seeks long-term companionship with Mr. Kapasi.
   d. She is committed to improving her mastery of other languages.
   e. She is an American tourist exploring India with her family.
2. From the passage, the reader can infer all of the following about Mr. Kapasi EXCEPT that he
   a. speaks several languages
   b. works in a doctor's office
   c. is younger than Mrs. Das
   d. does not know the Das family well
   e. does not live in the United States

A practice AP® exam at the back of the book offers practice taking a full exam.

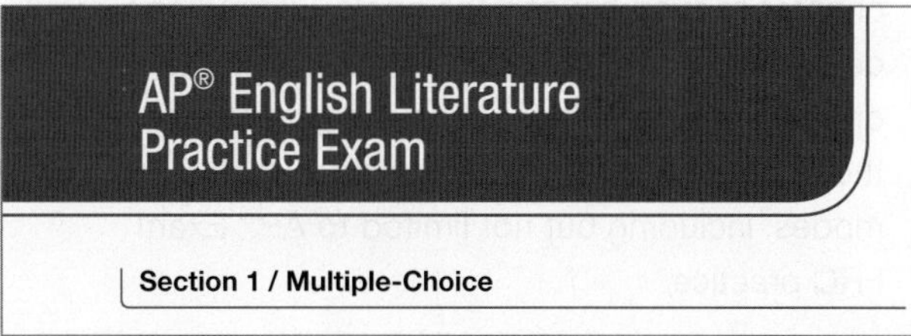

NEW! Expanded question sets provide targeted practice for key AP® Literature skills.

The comprehensive, in-depth questions and writing prompts that follow each reading enable students to link reading with writing, guiding students from understanding what a text is about to analysis of how the content is presented and why — close literary analysis. Questions are tagged to the AP® Big Ideas to help you strategically choose which AP® Essential Knowledge and Skills to emphasize.

Understanding and Interpreting questions lay the foundation for analysis. All tagged to specific AP® Big Ideas, these questions guide students to an understanding of the content and move them toward an interpretation.

> **Understanding and Interpreting**
>
> 1. **AP® Character and Narration.** At one point, Mr. Kapasi thinks that Mr. and Mrs. Das act more as "siblings" (par. 45) than parents to their children. Why does he draw that conclusion? What does that conclusion suggest about the Das family?
> 2. **AP® Setting.** "Interpreter of Maladies" explores the impact of immigration, including the result of an imagined rather than an experienced homeland. How does the Das family imagine India? Why does Jhumpa Lahiri emphasize the taking of photographs during the family's vacation?
> 3. **AP® Character and Narration.** What do we normally think of when considering the job of an "interpreter," and how does Mr. Kapasi's job at the infirmary expand this definition? How does he view his role as an interpreter?

Analyzing Language, Style, and Structure questions ask students to look at craft — how the writer's choices create meaning. Also tagged to specific AP® Big Ideas, these questions are excellent scaffolding for creating literary analysis to support an interpretation of a text.

> **Analyzing Language, Style, and Structure**
>
> 1. **Vocabulary in Context.** When Goodman Brown returns to Salem, he "shrank from the venerable saint [his minister] as if to avoid an anathema" (par. 70). The common meaning of *anathema* is something or someone that is vehemently disliked. The word also carries a religious connotation of being cursed, even excommunicated. How do the denotative and connotative meanings of this word add a layer of meaning to this scene?
> 2. **AP® Character and Figurative Language.** Is Faith a fully developed character or a symbol? Explain in terms of her appearance, behavior, and influence on her husband. Support your response with textual evidence, starting with Goodman Brown's statement, "Faith kept me back a while" (par. 12).

Topics for Composing questions provide extended essay and project ideas. These always begin with practice AP® exam prompts with stable prompt wording. Other questions range from literary argumentation prompts to research and multimodal projects to creative writing and suggestions for class discussion.

> **Topics for Composing**
>
> 1. AP® FRQ **Prose Fiction Analysis.** The following question refers to paragraphs 5–11 of Sakinah Hofler's "Erasure," published in 2020. In this passage, the narrator explains how the world adjusts to the unexplained disappearances of millions of people. Read the passage carefully. Then, in a well-written essay, analyze how Hofler uses literary elements and techniques to convey what people's responses to the disappearances reveal about the fabric of our society.
> 2. AP® FRQ **Literary Argument.** Works of literature often explore the ways in which people are divided — both philosophically and geographically — into social, cultural, and religious communities. In "Erasure," division exists on a literal level as the setting divides the characters who disappear from those who remain, and the divisions occur on deeper levels, too. In a well-written essay, analyze how these divisions contribute to an interpretation of the story as a whole. Do not merely summarize the plot.

End-of-chapter Suggestions for Writing: Prompts for AP® analysis, argument, and beyond. Suggestions for Writing at the end of each chapter guide students toward written responses that connect multiple pieces within the chapter or extend to pieces beyond the chapter or even beyond the book. Expanding on the AP® Literature skills introduced in the opening chapters, these prompts give students the opportunity to practice writing in many modes, including but not limited to AP® Exam FRQ practice.

> **Suggestions for Writing**
>
> **Identity and Culture**
>
> 1. **AP® Literary Argumentation.** In many works of literature, characters find their identities by stepping away from their culture. Choose one of the works in this chapter and analyze how this break contributes to an interpretation of the work as a whole. Do not merely summarize the plot.
> 2. **Connections.** In Nathaniel Hawthorne's novel *The Scarlet Letter* (1850), the narrator says,
>
> experience." Discuss this quotation by referring to at least one of the texts you've read in this chapter and your own experience.
>
> 6. **Connections.** Most Americans believe that they are the master of their own destiny and that anyone can create and re-create a sense of self. To what extent do you believe that identity is the result of free choice rather than something determined by factors out of

Student and teacher resources for *Literature & Composition* offer unmatched student and instructor support.

Teacher's Edition

The wraparound **Teacher's Edition** for *Literature & Composition* is an invaluable resource for both experienced and new AP® English Literature teachers. Written by seasoned teachers, the Teacher's Edition includes thoughtful instruction for planning, pacing, differentiating, and enlivening an AP® English Literature course.

Teacher's Resource Materials

The Teacher's Resource Materials accompany the Teacher's Edition and contain materials to effectively plan the course, including a detailed suggested pacing guide, handouts, suggested responses to questions, activities, and more.

Digital Collection of Full-Length Works

With nearly 100 classic and commonly taught works of literature, including several works that have appeared on past AP® exams, this resource is perfect for building a unique AP® Literature course. It's easy and intuitive to highlight, bookmark, and annotate the texts.

Digital Options

Literature & Composition is available in our fully interactive **digital platform**. In this platform, students can read, highlight, and take notes on any device, online or offline. You have the ability to assign every question from the book as well as supplemental quizzes and activities, and students' results automatically sync to your gradebook. You can also access the Teacher's Resource Materials, test bank, adaptive quizzing, and more.

LearningCurve

LearningCurve, an adaptive quizzing engine, formatively assesses and improves students' language and analysis skills. Through their responses, the program determines any areas of weakness and offers additional questions and links to e-book content to strengthen understanding and build mastery.

Test Bank

The Test Bank includes practice AP® Literature exam multiple-choice questions for every unit and several AP®-style FRQ prompts. Get the most out of the course with ample practice for success on the AP® exam.

Acknowledgments

We would like to thank the talented team at Bedford, Freeman, and Worth. We've relied on their expertise, enjoyed their enthusiasm, and appreciated their encouragement more than we can say. We have had the stunningly good luck to work with two remarkable Bedford editors. To Nathan Odell, who has been with us since the start of *Literature & Composition*, we send a thankful praise song for being a cheerleader, a taskmaster, a diplomat, at once an advocate and a chief skeptic, a perfectionist, and the best of friends — as well as our "dear reader." To Caitlin Kaufman, who led the team for this revision, we send continuous applause for her knowledge of contemporary writers, generous work ethic, commitment to ensuring that all students see themselves in the literature they study, and — most of all — her unfaltering vision for how to improve this book for students and teachers alike.

Since it does indeed take a village, we are grateful for the efforts of a supportive team. Our associate editor, Kelly Noll, and our editorial assistant, Meghan Kelly, are fine researchers and general problem solvers. Our gifted and innovative media editor, Gina Forsythe, keeps us in the third decade of the twenty-first century. We are enormously thankful to Andrea Cava, senior manager of publishing services; Vanavan Jayaraman, senior project manager; and Nancy Benjamin, copyeditor, for their meticulous and tireless attention to details of language and design. To say a simple thanks to Lisa Erdely, executive marketing manager, and Tiffani Tang, assistant marketing manager, is to deal in understatement. Their unflagging determination, faith in the project, and creativity sustained us throughout this revision.

We are fortunate to have had the assistance of some amazing teachers at key times in this project, especially with the development of the Teacher's Edition and Teacher's Resource Materials. Our thanks to contributors Christine Carson, Nancy Dickinson, Natalie Fallert, Kimberly Frazier-Booth, Ellen Greenblatt, Charise Hallberg, David Hillis, Julie Horger, Maura Kelly, Steve Klinge, Mark Leidner, Tamara Schoen, Tom Tucker, and Nikki Wilson.

Thank you to the students who contributed sample essays included in this edition of the textbook and its teacher resource materials: Anette Aponte, Clara Asseily, Brian Carbajal, Isabella Ganfield, Yanis Koutoupes Guessous, Caroline Ho, Maeva Kounga, Fabiana Martinez, Luigi Onorato, Alyssa Pierangeli, Alexis Rendel, Sara Sam, Selin Selcuker, and Aislinn Smeader. We appreciate their insights into the literature in this book, and their work was integral to the writing instruction in the opening chapters.

We are grateful to the reviewers who always kept us anchored in the world of the classroom reality and generously shared their amazing experience and expertise for each edition of *Literature & Composition*. Our thanks to Megan Adams, Lance Balla, Maren Baum, Barbara Bloy, Helen Boyd, Hannah Broich, Barbra A. Brooks-Barker, Brian Burnett, Chasidy Burton, Betsy Butler, Mary Calkin, Caryl Catzlaff, Jolinda Collins, Shirley Counsil, Cathy A. D'Agostino, Peter Drewniany, Jennifer Dooley, Carol Elsen, Heather Ewing, Denise Ferguson, Michael Feuer,

Andrew Foster, Amy Gallagher, Elizabeth Gonsalves, Tammy Guehne, Kelly E. Guilfoil, James Hausman III, Maggie Henderson, David Herring, Jennifer Hiller, Allyson Howard, Suzanne Hunt, Erica Jacobs, Jan Kelly, Billie Krasniqi, Carol Krause, Tom Lippi, Joan Mangan, Kelsey Mapes, Marie Leone Meyer, Nancy Monroe, Tracy Mosca, Skip Nicholson, Jeffrey Nienaber, Sherlayne Nuckols, Frazier L. O'Leary Jr., Susan Oswalt, Deborah Parker, Julia Parsons, Linda A. Pavich, Bill Pell, Catherine Pfaff, Sally P. Pfeifer, John Przyborowski, Amy Regis, Kyle Reynolds, Stacia Richmond, Linda Rood, Jaclynn Rozansky, Heidi Rubin de la Borbolla, Edward Schmieder, Kimberly Schuenemann, Bobbi Scott, Conni Shelnut, Deborah Shepard, Pat Sherbert, William Smith, Larissa Snyder, Danielle Sorrells, Virginia Allen Speaks, Al Stout, Doranna Tindle, Karen Van Duyn, Johnny Walters, Deb Ward, Addison Welp, Luke Wiseman, Carol Yoakley-Terrell, and David Youngblood. We are deeply grateful for spouses, children, friends, and family who have supported our efforts, given up their weekends and evenings to advise us, and kept the faith that this project was absolutely worthwhile and would eventually be finished!

Finally, we would like to thank our students over the years, including more than a few who have become admirable teachers themselves, for honoring the tradition of reading and writing that gives meaning to our lives.

This is the book we committed ourselves to developing for you and your students. We've brought to the task our many years of working with high school and college students as well as our deep love of literature, reading, and writing. We hope *Literature & Composition* helps you and your students and that you enjoy using it as much as we enjoyed writing it.

Contents

Analyzing Short Fiction 1

4 Identity and Culture 165

5 Love and Relationships 329

6 Conformity and Rebellion 483

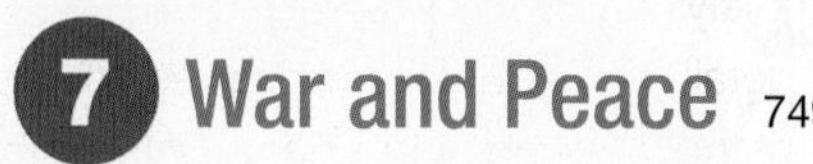

7 War and Peace 749

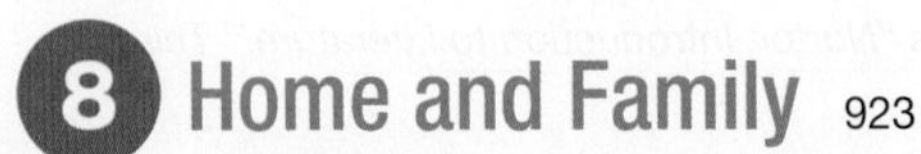

9 Tradition and Progress 1043

Literature & Composition

Essential Voices, Essential Skills

for the AP® Course

The Observer Book of Birds © 2018 Art-work by Su Blackwell. Photography by John Reynolds

Analyzing Short Fiction

While several characteristics distinguish humans from other animals, one of the most profound is our ability to tell stories. In fact, we have been doing so for tens of thousands of years. Plenty of nonhuman species and organisms communicate with each other — think of the waggle dance honeybees perform, the song chickadees sing, the tails dogs wag, and even the chemical signals plants send — but none of them tell stories about anything but the here and now. Whether with cave paintings in France, an epic poem in Anglo-Saxon England, or the trickster stories of American Indians, humans have been communicating about food sources, common enemies, and life lessons in ways that not only educate but that also entertain. And once humans could rely less on communication as a means for survival, storytellers became revered for their abilities to transfix audiences and preserve the immortality of heroes. In fact, stories are so important to every human culture that you are now embarking on a journey to discover and analyze the art of storytelling on the page.

In Section 1 of this chapter, we will look at the big-picture elements of storytelling, including characters, setting, plot, point of view, and perspective. You will experience each of these in Edward P. Jones's short story "The First Day" as well as in excerpts from other works. Section 2 provides an opportunity to examine the more detailed elements of this art form through close reading, and we will explore how a writer's word choice and sentence structure shape a story and how figurative language, imagery, tone, and mood convey meaning. By engaging in this work, you are participating in a uniquely human experience that really is magical. Welcome.

When someone asks us about a short story, novel, or play, we usually describe it by retelling the plot in our own words. After all, who doesn't enjoy a good page-turner? But the way the author tells the story and the ideas the story explores are often just as important as what happens in it. In these stories, events may occur because of internal conflicts within a character or external conflicts between characters or between a character and other forces, such as those found in nature. Particular settings also influence both events and conflicts in different ways. As readers, we pick up on all of these details to help us understand characters' relationships with each other and with the environment around them. We also experience the story's characters, setting, and plot through a narrator's point of view, and both the narrator and the characters within the story have their own perspectives and understanding of the world around them.

Elements of Fiction

By studying how these literary elements work individually and together, we begin to understand how they shape readers' interpretations of a story's meaning. To explore these elements, let's take a look at the short story "The First Day" by Edward P. Jones. As you read, notice the ways the characters respond to the changes in the setting, think about how the plot introduces and resolves the conflicts characters experience, and consider the narrator's role in the story.

The First Day

Edward P. Jones

On an otherwise unremarkable September morning, long before I learned to be ashamed of my mother, she takes my hand and we set off down New Jersey Avenue to begin my very first day of school. I am wearing a checkeredlike blue-and-green cotton dress, and scattered about these colors are bits of yellow and white and brown. My mother has uncharacteristically spent nearly an hour on my hair that morning, plaiting and replaiting so that now my scalp tingles. Whenever I turn my head quickly, my nose fills with the faint smell of Dixie Peach hair grease. The smell is somehow a soothing one now and I will reach for it time and time again before the morning ends. All the plaits, each with a blue barrette near the tip and each twisted into an uncommon sturdiness, will last until I go to bed that night, something that has never happened before. My stomach is full of milk and oatmeal sweetened with brown sugar. Like everything else I have on, my pale green slip and underwear are new, the underwear having come three to a plastic package with a little girl on the front who appears to be dancing. Behind my ears, my mother, to stop my whining, has dabbed the stingiest bit of her gardenia perfume, the last present my father gave her before he disappeared into memory. Because I cannot smell it, I have only her word that the perfume is there. I am also wearing yellow socks trimmed with thin lines of black and white around the tops. My shoes are my greatest joy, black patent-leather miracles, and when one is nicked at the toe later that morning in class, my heart will break.

I am carrying a pencil, a pencil sharpener, and a small ten-cent tablet with a black-and-white speckled cover. My mother does not believe that a girl in kindergarten needs such things, so I am taking them only because of my insistent whining and because they are presents from our neighbors, Mary Keith and Blondelle Harris. Miss Mary and Miss Blondelle are watching my two younger sisters until my mother returns. The women are as precious to me as my mother and sisters. Out playing one day, I have overheard an older child, speaking to another child, call Miss Mary and Miss Blondelle a word that is brand new to me. This is my mother: When I say the word in fun to one of my sisters, my mother slaps me across the mouth and the word is lost for years and years.

All the way down New Jersey Avenue, the sidewalks are teeming with children. In my neighborhood, I have many friends, but I see none of them as my mother and I walk. We cross New York Avenue, we cross Pierce Street, and we cross L and K, and still I see no one who knows my name. At I Street, between New Jersey Avenue and Third Street, we enter Seaton Elementary School, a timeworn, sad-faced building across the street from my mother's church, Mt. Carmel Baptist.

Just inside the front door, women out of the advertisements in *Ebony* are greeting other parents and children. The woman who greets us has pearls thick as jumbo marbles that come down almost to her navel, and she acts as if she had known me all my life, touching my shoulder, cupping her hand under my chin. She is enveloped in a perfume that I only know is not gardenia. When, in answer to her question, my mother tells her that we live at 1227 New Jersey Avenue, the woman first seems to be picturing in her head where we live. Then she shakes her head and says that we are at the wrong school, that we should be at Walker-Jones.

5 My mother shakes her head vigorously. “I want her to go here,” my mother says. “If I'da wanted her someplace else, I'da took her there.” The woman continues to act as if she has known me all my life, but she tells my mother that we live beyond the area that Seaton serves. My mother is not convinced and for several more minutes she questions the woman about why I cannot attend Seaton. For as many Sundays as I can remember, perhaps even Sundays when I was in her womb, my mother has pointed across I Street to Seaton as we come and go to Mt. Carmel. “You gonna go there and learn about the whole world.” But one of the guardians of that place is saying no, and no again. I am learning this about my mother: The higher up on the scale of respectability a person is — and teachers are rather high up in her eyes — the less she is liable to let them push her around. But finally, I see in her eyes the closing gate, and she takes my hand and we leave the building. On the steps, she stops as people move past us on either side.

“Mama, I can't go to school?”

She says nothing at first, then takes my hand again and we are down the steps quickly and nearing New Jersey Avenue before I can blink. This is my mother: She says, “One monkey don't stop no show.”

Walker-Jones is a larger, newer school and I immediately like it because of that. But it is not across the street from my mother's church, her rock, one of her connections to God, and I sense her doubts as she absently rubs her thumb over the back of her hand. We find our way to the crowded auditorium where gray metal chairs are set up in the middle of the room. Along the wall to the left are tables and other chairs. Every chair seems occupied by a child or adult. Somewhere in the room a child is crying, a cry that rises above the buzz-talk of so many people. Strewn about the floor are dozens and dozens of pieces of white paper, and people are walking over them without any thought of picking them up. And seeing this lack of concern, I am all of a sudden afraid.

"Is this where they register for school?" my mother asks a woman at one of the tables.

The woman looks up slowly as if she has heard this question once too often. She nods. She is tiny, almost as small as the girl standing beside her. The woman's hair is set in a mass of curlers and all of those curlers are made of paper money, here a dollar bill, there a five-dollar bill. The girl's hair is arrayed in curls, but some of them are beginning to droop and this makes me happy. On the table beside the woman's pocketbook is a large notebook, worthy of someone in high school, and looking at me looking at the notebook, the girl places her hand possessively on it. In her other hand she holds several pencils with thick crowns of additional erasers.

"These the forms you gotta use?" my mother asks the woman, picking up a few pieces of the paper from the table. "Is this what you have to fill out?"

The woman tells her yes, but that she need fill out only one.

"I see," my mother says, looking about the room. Then: "Would you help me with this form? That is, if you don't mind."

The woman asks my mother what she means.

"This form. Would you mind helpin me fill it out?"

The woman still seems not to understand.

"I can't read it. I don't know how to read or write, and I'm askin you to help me." My mother looks at me, then looks away. I know almost all of her looks, but this one is brand new to me. "Would you help me, then?"

The woman says Why sure, and suddenly she appears happier, so much more satisfied with everything. She finishes the form for her daughter and my mother and I step aside to wait for her. We find two chairs nearby and sit. My mother is now diseased, according to the girl's eyes, and until the moment her mother takes her and the form to the front of the auditorium, the girl never stops looking at my mother. I stare back at her. "Don't stare," my mother says to me. "You know better than that."

Another woman out of the *Ebony* ads takes the woman's child away. Now, the woman says upon returning, let's see what we can do for you two.

My mother answers the questions the woman reads off the form. They start with my last name, and then on to the first and middle names. This is school, I think. This is going to school. My mother slowly enunciates each word of my name. This is my mother: As the questions go on, she takes from her pocketbook document after document, as if they will support my right to attend school, as if she has been saving them up for just this moment. Indeed, she takes out more papers than I have ever seen her do in other places: my birth certificate, my baptismal record, a doctor's letter concerning my bout with chicken pox, rent receipts, records of immunization, a letter about our public assistance payments, even her marriage license — every single paper that has anything even remotely to do with my five-year-old life. Few of the papers are needed here, but it does not matter and my mother continues to pull out the documents with the purposefulness of a magician pulling out a long string of scarves. She has learned that money is the beginning and end of everything in this world, and when the woman finishes, my mother offers her fifty cents, and the woman accepts it without hesitation. My mother and I are just about the last parent and child in the room.

My mother presents the form to a woman sitting in front of the stage, and the woman looks at it and writes something on a white card, which she gives to my mother. Before long, the woman who has taken the girl with the drooping curls appears from behind us, speaks to the sitting woman, and introduces herself to my mother and me. She's to be my teacher, she tells my mother. My mother stares.

We go into the hall, where my mother kneels down to me. Her lips are quivering. "I'll be back to pick you up at twelve o'clock. I don't want you to go nowhere. You just wait right here. And listen to every word she say." I touch her lips and press them together. It is an old, old game between us. She puts my hand down at my side, which is not part of the game. She stands and looks a second at the teacher, then she turns and walks away. I see where she has darned one of her socks the night before. Her shoes make loud sounds in the hall. She passes through the doors and I can still hear the loud sounds of her shoes. And even when the teacher turns me toward the classrooms and I hear what must be the singing and talking of all the children in the world, I can still hear my mother's footsteps above it all. ■

1992

Character

Characters are key to shaping a narrative. In a story with an external conflict, the main character is usually the **protagonist**, who is in conflict with another person, called the **antagonist**. A conflict may also be internal, such as those in which a character struggles with temptation or tries to reconcile two incompatible values or beliefs. The main character in a literary work also usually grows or changes over the course of the story; in fact, that change often structures the narrative. The clearest example of character change structuring a narrative happens in a **coming-of-age story**, also called a **bildungsroman**, which chronicles how a young character transitions from a state of innocence to one of experience. Sometimes the change is gradual and sometimes it is sudden, as with an **epiphany**, a term Irish author James Joyce used to describe when a character suddenly realizes something significant about life. Regardless of how quickly a character changes, the growth must be believable, and it must be clearly motivated by the circumstances of the story.

Authors reveal character through descriptions and through characters' dialogue and behavior. Considering how and why certain details are included in a story is key to interpreting who the characters are, what they believe, and what motivates them. Let's take a look at the main characters of "The First Day": the mother and the daughter. The daughter, who tells us this story, serves as the protagonist, and we can learn about her by paying attention to what she chooses to share with us. For example, she describes in great detail the clothing she is wearing on her first day of school. Why are these details important? What do they communicate about the daughter's personality? It seems clear that she appreciates the clothes and shoes she gets to wear because they are new — in fact, the sadness she experiences when one of her new shoes gets nicked conveys how important they are to her. These details reveal that new clothing is not an everyday experience for the daughter, and perhaps they provide some insight into what she values about appearances: clothing shows the world who we are and influences how others see us. This attention to appearances also extends to the world around her — her fearful response to the paper strewn across the floor at her new school contrasts with others' apparent lack of awareness or concern.

Similarly, the mother values money, or at least the security it can bring, whether in the form of proper clothing, adequate school supplies, or access to services and opportunities. Finally, the way both mother and daughter interact indicates the close relationship they have. From her recognition of Mt. Carmel Baptist Church as her mother's "rock," we know the daughter has a keen sense of what matters to her mom and, therefore, what should matter to her. Her insistence on wearing her mother's perfume — which she must trust is behind her ears because she cannot smell it — also shows how the daughter's sense of who she is rests in large part with what her mother thinks and does.

Character Development

Authors can develop characterization either directly or indirectly. **Direct characterization** occurs when a narrator explicitly describes the background, motivation, temperament, or appearance of a character. While "The First Day" provides few details about the physical descriptions of the characters, there are some details that serve to directly characterize the daughter. In two instances, she refers directly to her own "whining" (pars. 1 and 2). In the first, the daughter explains that her mother gives in to her requests to wear some of her mother's perfume. In the second, she wants to take supplies given to her by the neighbors to school even though her mother believes they are unnecessary. The daughter also tells us directly she cares so much for Miss Mary and Miss Blondelle that "the women are as precious to [her] as [her] mother and sisters" (par. 2).

Indirect characterization occurs when an author requires the audience to infer what a character is like through what the character says, does, or thinks, or what others say about the character. Edward P. Jones uses indirect characterization in "The First Day" to emphasize how perceptive the daughter is of other peoples' shifting attitudes without the daughter explicitly telling us about her ability. For example, the daughter perceives her mother's reluctance to believe the staff member at Seaton Elementary who insists her daughter has to go to Walker-Jones, and the daughter also notices

AP® TIP

While main characters are often great subjects for AP® Prose Fiction Analysis Essays, don't forget to consider minor characters. If you can identify enough evidence to sustain a line of reasoning about a minor character, your essay is more likely to have a fresh, original voice.

when her mother accepts this reality only moments later. The daughter's ability to "see in her [mother's] eyes the closing gate" (par. 5) allows readers to make an inference about the daughter's awareness of others even at such a young age.

KEY QUESTIONS

Analyzing Character

- Who are the main characters? Who is the protagonist, and who is the antagonist? How do minor characters function in the story?
- What do specific details reveal about characters' values, beliefs, assumptions, biases, and cultural norms?
- Are the descriptions and characterizations direct or indirect?
- How do characters' relationships with each other inform your understanding of them?
- How do characters change throughout the story?
- Do you see some characters differently from the way they see themselves?

Analyzing Character

activity

Fools Crow, by Great Plains Indian writer James Welch, begins by introducing the protagonist, White Man's Dog, who later earns the name Fools Crow. Discuss the direct and indirect methods Welch uses to characterize him in the following passage.

from Fools Crow

James Welch

Now that the weather had changed, the moon of the falling leaves turned white in the blackening sky and White Man's Dog was restless. He chewed the stick of dry meat and watched Cold Maker gather his forces. The black clouds moved in the north in circles, their dance a slow deliberate fury. It was almost night, and he looked back down into the flats along the Two Medicine River. The lodges of the Lone Eaters were illuminated by cooking fires within. It was that time of evening when even the dogs rest and the horses graze undisturbed along the grassy banks.

White Man's Dog raised his eyes to the west and followed the Backbone of the World from south to north until he could pick out Chief Mountain. It stood a little apart from the other mountains, not as tall as some but strong, its square granite face a landmark to all who passed. But it was more than a landmark to the Pikunis, Kainahs, and Siksikas, the three tribes of the Blackfeet, for it was on top of Chief Mountain that the blackhorn skull pillows of the great warriors still lay. On those skulls Eagle Head and Iron Breast had dreamed their visions in the long-ago, and the animal helpers had

(*continued*)

made them strong in spirit and fortunate in war.

Not so lucky was White Man's Dog. He had little to show for his eighteen winters. His father, Rides-at-the-door, had many horses and three wives. He himself had three horses and no wives. His animals were puny, not a blackhorn runner among them. He owned a musket and no powder and his animal helper was weak. ■

1986

Setting

On a literal level, **setting** indicates the time and place, or the when and where, of a literary text. This physical sense of time and place also contributes to the tone, mood, and meaning of a literary work. Writer Eudora Welty described setting as "the named, identified, concrete, exact and exacting, and therefore credible, gathering spot of all that has been felt, is about to be experienced." Writer and retired musician Marcia Butler likened setting to the "bedrock" or "harmony" of a narrative, on top of which "characters or soloists of the story will be maneuvered." Writer Alice McDermott explained the relationship between setting and meaning in literature very succinctly: "setting illuminates character, not the other way around." All of these explanations of setting are valid.

Setting also includes such objective facts as the community and nation, date and time, and weather and season in which the story occurs. If events occur on a dark and stormy night, we can reasonably expect a dark and stormy tale. If the action opens on a spring morning in a sunlit meadow, it is likely the author is preparing us for a lighter tale. The author may also contrast the character's emotions and the setting or even establish a contrast between different settings in the story. In order to understand how setting relates to the short story as a whole, you will have to consider the significance of elements that might at first seem merely physical and objective. For example, a story that takes place as winter transitions into spring could signify new beginnings. The most important thing is that you pay attention to the details — the sights and sounds, textures and tones, colors and shapes — because they will convey more about the setting than just when and where the story takes place.

The setting of "The First Day" is a poor neighborhood of Washington, D.C., and we're given details about the school the mother wants her daughter to attend — the school that is directly across from her church. Why is the proximity of the church important to the setting? What do these details reveal about the mother and her values? The narrator tells us that the church is very important to her mother — it is her "rock" — so it's clear the mother wants the daughter to go to the nearby school because it is familiar and in a community she trusts. The physical details of both schools in the story contribute somewhat to the setting, too, because while Seaton Elementary is older and worn down, the newer looking exterior of Walker-Jones Elementary appeals to the daughter. What, then, does the daughter's perception of the schools convey about the communities and their inhabitants' circumstances? We might read these contrasting descriptions of the settings of each elementary school as an expression of both mother and daughter's desire for stability and belonging.

KEY QUESTIONS

Analyzing Setting

- What is the geographical setting? Urban or rural? The United States or a foreign country? What is the weather like?
- When does the story take place? How are these details important to the story?
- How does the author use details to convey the story's setting? How do these details create atmosphere or mood?
- In what ways does a story's setting reveal important information about its characters?

Analyzing Setting

activity

Authors often use setting as another means of developing a character. Khaled Hosseini's novel *The Kite Runner* features Amir, a young man from Kabul, Afghanistan, as its protagonist. In the following passage, Amir describes traveling to Peshawar, a city in Pakistan, after having visited it as a child. Read the passage carefully. How does Hosseini use details of the setting to convey the experience Amir has returning to a place he knew in his youth?

from The Kite Runner

Khaled Hosseini

I remembered Peshawar pretty well from the few months Baba and I had spent there in 1981. We were heading west now on Jamrud road, past the Cantonment[1] and its lavish, high-walled homes. The bustle of the city blurring past me reminded me of a busier, more crowded version of the Kabul I knew, particularly of the *Kocheh-Morgha*, or Chicken Bazaar, where Hassan and I used to buy chutney-dipped potatoes and cherry water. The streets were clogged with bicycle riders, milling pedestrians, and rickshaws popping blue smoke, all weaving through a maze of narrow lanes and alleys. Bearded vendors draped in thin blankets sold animal-skin lampshades, carpets, embroidered shawls, and copper goods from rows of small, tightly jammed stalls. The city was bursting with sounds; the shouts of vendors rang in my ears mingled with the blare of Hindi music, the sputtering of rickshaws, and the jingling bells of horse-drawn carts. Rich scents, both pleasant and not so pleasant, drifted to me through the passenger window, the spicy aroma of pakora and the nihari Baba had loved so much blended with the sting of diesel fumes, the stench of rot, garbage, and feces.

A little past the redbrick buildings of Peshawar University, we entered an area my garrulous driver referred to as "Afghan Town." I saw sweetshops and carpet vendors, kabob stalls, kids with dirt-caked hands selling

[1] Military quarters. — Eds.

(continued)

cigarettes, tiny restaurants — maps of Afghanistan painted on their windows — all interlaced with backstreet aid agencies. "Many of your brothers in this area, *yar*. They are opening businesses, but most of them are very poor." He *tsk*'ed his tongue and sighed. "Anyway, we're getting close now." ■

2003

Plot

Essentially, **plot** is what happens in a **narrative**. Yet plot is more than a series of events because authors must arrange **conflicts** and **resolutions** to create logical patterns of cause-and-effect and to develop characters' relationships with each other. The conflicts characters experience often arise because of these relationships, so character and plot go hand in hand. This means readers must understand not just *what* is happening but also *why* it's happening as well as how plot elements work together to create meaning. Additionally, a plot must be believable even though it does not have to be realistic.

A conventional narrative, especially in short stories, typically involves five main stages:

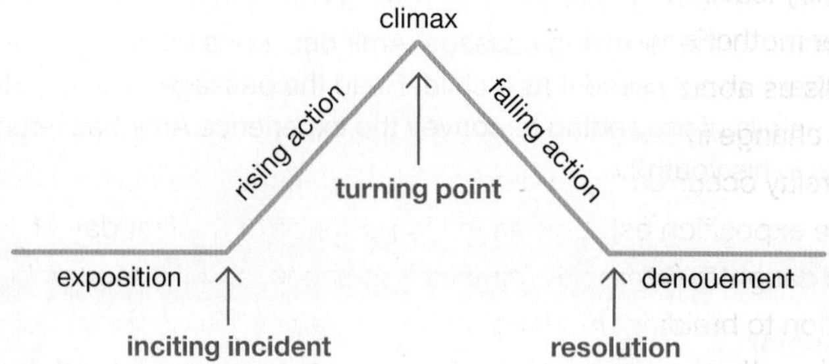

- **Exposition:** This opening section of a story provides background information about the characters, the setting, and the basic situation. The exposition also describes the nature of key conflicts generally creating an unstable situation.
- **Rising action:** After an inciting incident or event, the conflict and complications the main character experiences begin to build.
- **Climax:** The climax occurs when the emotional tension or **suspense** of the plot reaches its peak. It may include a turning point where the fortunes of the protagonist improve or worsen. Building to the climax usually occupies most of a story, and what follows is comparatively brief.
- **Falling action:** This section details the result (or fallout) of the climax or turning point. In this phase, conflicts often get resolved.
- **Denouement** (pronounced *day-noo-mah*): This French word means "untying the knot." In this often very brief phase, the conflict has been resolved, and balance is restored to the world of the story. Fairy tales often abbreviate this phase further: "And they lived happily ever after." Traditionally, the denouement was also used to tell "the moral of the story," but writers in the twentieth and twenty-first centuries

frequently close without this final resolution and leave readers to construct the meaning of the story's end on their own.

While plot may follow a chronological sequence, particularly in realistic fiction and drama, sometimes writers deliberately present events in a manner that requires readers to assemble them into a cohesive pattern. A story may begin ***in medias res***, a Latin term meaning "in the middle of the action" — that is, just as an important event is about to take place. Homer's *Iliad*, for example, opens not in the first year of the Trojan War but after nine years of fighting. Writers may also employ **flashbacks** to describe events that have taken place before the story begins, or **foreshadowing** to hint at things that will happen later in the story.

The basic plot of "The First Day" is pretty straightforward: a mother takes her daughter to the first day of kindergarten; the daughter is refused admission to one school and has to go to another, where another parent helps the mother fill out the necessary forms; the mother leaves her daughter at school, telling her to pay close attention to the teacher. That's pretty much it. Along the way, however, we gain insight into the mother and daughter as characters, we learn about the challenges they face from the time they leave home until they part, and we experience the daughter's discovery of her mother's inability to read. The daughter, who is the narrator and protagonist, tells us about her first day of school as a flashback. The exposition also foreshadows a change in the daughter's opinions of her mother by telling us the events she's about to relay occurred "long before I learned to be ashamed of my mother." Additionally, the exposition establishes the importance of the first day of school to both characters: the daughter wears new clothes and shoes, and the mother has given extra time and attention to braiding the daughter's hair. As we take a closer look, we also sense early on how the daughter's nervousness hints at her innocence in the beginning of the story, and we become aware of the potential learning experiences ahead of her as she leaves home to venture around the city with her mother.

During the rising action of the story, the complications begin when the daughter recognizes none of the children around her as she and her mother near the first school. Upon arrival, the physical condition of Seaton Elementary disappoints her, and then, of course, they learn she will not be allowed to attend this school based on where they live. We witness the daughter's increasing anxiety as her mother challenges the school staff and insists they admit her daughter. Eventually, however, the mother realizes her efforts are futile, and the pair sets out again, this time to find the correct school, Walker-Jones Elementary. Take a moment and identify the additional complications the mother and daughter experience when they arrive at Walker-Jones. How do the characters' immediate responses differ, and how do both characters' interactions with others contribute to internal and external conflicts? For example, you have probably noticed how the daughter picks up on her mother's anxiety about the less-familiar location of Walker-Jones. She recognizes that its distance from her mother's church creates a conflict for her mother even as she herself experiences fear over everyone else's lack of concern about the paper strewn everywhere at Walker-Jones, which is a detail her mother appears not to notice.

The rising action culminates in the mother's admission: "I don't know how to read or write" (par. 17). This moment, the climax of the story, reveals to us why the daughter's first day of school is such a momentous occasion for both mother and daughter. Even the mother's care in grooming and dressing her daughter for school takes on a new dimension — education is important to the mother because she did not have the opportunity to attain it for herself, and she wants to make sure her daughter has more opportunities than she has had. This information also complicates the daughter's understanding of the woman who has raised her. While the daughter's sense of excitement and anxiety about the first day of school before this point in the story seems to stem from the idea that everything about the day — from her attire to the school building itself — is fresh and new, she starts to understand more about why her mother also feels the day is important. Emphasizing this turning point in the story, the mother looks at her daughter before looking away with an expression that the daughter has never seen before.

The falling action begins when another parent agrees to help the mother. Seemingly, this woman does so out of kindness, but the daughter recognizes a subtle shift in the other mother's attitude as well as a more pronounced feeling of superiority now coming from the other woman's daughter, who stares at them as the required paperwork gets completed. Toward the end of the falling action, the daughter attempts to share a familiar, physical exchange with her mother, but her mother's reaction signals a shift in their relationship because she responds in a way that "is not a part of the game" (par. 22) they have long played. The story's brief denouement establishes the daughter's new understanding of her mother as someone who not only cannot read and write but also as someone who darns her socks and wears noisy shoes, both of which cause the daughter to feel disappointed at this insight into how the world sees her mother and, perhaps, appreciative of the lengths to which her mother goes to ensure she will have more opportunities in life.

KEY QUESTIONS

Analyzing Plot

- Is the plot arranged in chronological order? If not, how would you describe the arrangement and structure of the plot elements?
- Does the plot involve foreshadowing? A flashback? If so, what is the purpose of this choice, and how does it contribute to your interpretation of the story?
- Are the key conflicts internal or external? What complications intensify them?
- What is the turning point or climax of the story?
- How are the conflicts resolved? If there is no resolution, why not?

Analyzing Plot

Choose a fairy tale, myth, or movie and analyze its plot. Identify specific parts of the plot, such as the exposition, rising action, climax, falling action, and denouement, and examine whether the plot is chronological or whether it employs flashbacks. Consider the guiding questions on plot to explore how the plot contributes to the meaning of the story. How would the meaning of the story change if the plot handled one of these aspects differently — for instance, if the plot is chronological, what would be the effect of the protagonist narrating it as a flashback?

Narrative Perspective and Point of View

Narration, point of view, and perspective all focus on who tells the story, how they tell it, and how they — and we, as readers — understand their roles in the narrative. In literature, **point of view** is the position from which a narrator relates the events of a narrative. Imagine for a moment that you have been watching a championship soccer game, and the ref makes a controversial call that ultimately affects the final score. Consider the differences between the ways opposing players would describe the call or the differences between the way you and other fans would describe it. Whether the ref's call was valid is, to the fans and players at least, in the eye of the beholder. Each witness and participant in the game, if asked to recall the incident, would convey a unique point of view, and it's probable that many of these points of view would be in direct conflict. Narrative **perspective**, though similar to point of view, describes how narrators or characters see and experience their individual circumstances. In the soccer game we just discussed, your perspective as a spectator is your individual experience of watching the ref make the controversial call. When you share your perspective with others, you are sharing it from your point of view as a fan. The varying perspectives of fans and players determine which details they share when they tell the story of the game, and each of the varying points of view that come across in the telling make for different stories about the same moment and its effect on the game's outcome. In a later discussion of the game, point of view and perspective would also explain the role each of you plays in portraying what happened, and this portrayal would influence what others believe about the game's outcome.

When it comes to writing fiction, authors must consider the point of view they want to use as well as the narrator's perspective. For example, should they tell a story about a championship soccer game from the point of view and perspective of a fan, a ref, a player, or even a coach? Most commonly, writers use first-person and third-person narrators, but sometimes you will come across stories told by second-person narrators.

First-Person Point of View

A first-person narrator tells a story using first-person pronouns such as *I* and *we*. From this point of view, we see the world from a single character's perspective. Usually,

first-person point of view is the main character's, though it can be a minor character's instead. Regardless, the first-person narrator gives us a vivid on-the-spot account of events and internal thoughts. In most cases, a first-person narrator is every bit as much a creation of the writer's imagination as any other character, so be careful not to confuse a first-person narrator with the author.

Edward P. Jones uses an unnamed first-person narrator in "The First Day" — the daughter — and she recalls the events of the story as an adult from the perspective of a flashback. She says that these events occurred "long before [she] learned to be ashamed of [her] mother" (par. 1). Yet as she's telling this story, she does not seem ashamed; she instead seems proud of her mother's heroic journey and proud that her mother overcame so many obstacles to make sure her daughter had a bright future. As a result, the flashback provides the daughter an opportunity to share a more mature, developed understanding of the day than she could have as a child experiencing it, or even as an older child who has "learned" to feel ashamed of her mother's lack of education.

Second-Person Point of View

Second-person narrators are rare but not unheard of. **Second-person point of view** puts the reader right in the story, but it is rarely used (and is often viewed as a gimmick), perhaps because it makes the reading experience too literal — you are not just asked to imagine a character, you are told that you *are* the character. However, it can be very effective at involving the reader in the story and creating intimacy, as in the following example from Italo Calvino's novel *If on a Winter's Night a Traveler*.

from If on a Winter's Night a Traveler

Italo Calvino

You are about to begin reading Italo Calvino's new novel, *If on a winter's night a traveler.* Relax. Concentrate. Dispel every other thought. Let the world around you fade. Best to close the door; the TV is always on in the next room. Tell the others right away, "No, I don't want to watch TV!" Raise your voice — they won't hear you otherwise — "I'm reading! I don't want to be disturbed!" Maybe they haven't heard you, with all that racket; speak louder, yell: "I'm beginning to read Italo Calvino's new novel!" *Or* if you prefer, don't say anything; just hope they'll leave you alone.

Find the most comfortable position: seated, stretched out, curled up, or lying flat. Flat on your back, on your side, on your stomach. In an easy chair, on the sofa, in the rocker, the deck chair, on the hassock. In the hammock, if you have a hammock. On top of your bed, of course, or in the bed. You can even stand on your hands, head down, the yoga position. With the book upside down, naturally. ■

1979

In this example, the narrator of the novel *If on a Winter's Night a Traveler* involves readers in the story by acknowledging exactly what the readers are doing in real time. While some authors create a more fictional world in which to immerse readers, Calvino's novel begins inside the reader's world instead, forging an immediate bond between the reader and the story.

Third-Person Point of View

A third-person narrator tells the story using the third-person pronouns *he*, *she*, and *it*. This type of narrator views all events in a story from a distance and does not play a role in the actual plot. A third-person narrator with a limited point of view tells us what just one major or minor character is thinking and feeling. This perspective both conceals and reveals. While it restricts how much readers know, it can also give readers insight into who a character is and how that character sees the world. In "Miss Brill" by Katherine Mansfield, we see through the eyes of an aging woman sitting in a park in a vacation town in France and observing others around her. We experience all of the action and characters through her perspective.

from Miss Brill

Katherine Mansfield

Oh, how fascinating it was! How she enjoyed it! How she loved sitting here, watching it all! It was like a play. It was exactly like a play. Who could believe the sky at the back wasn't painted? But it wasn't till a little brown dog trotted on solemn and then slowly trotted off, like a little "theatre" dog, a little dog that had been drugged, that Miss Brill discovered what it was that made it so exciting. They were all on the stage. They weren't only the audience, not only looking on; they were acting. Even she had a part and came every Sunday. No doubt somebody would have noticed if she hadn't been there; she was part of the performance after all. How strange she'd never thought of it like that before! And yet it explained why she made such a point of starting from home at just the same time each week — so as not to be late for the performance — and it also explained why she had quite a queer, shy feeling at telling her English pupils how she spent her Sunday afternoons. No wonder! Miss Brill nearly laughed out loud. She was on the stage. She thought of the old invalid gentleman to whom she read the newspaper four afternoons a week while he slept in the garden. She had got quite used to the frail head on the cotton pillow, the hollowed eyes, the open mouth, and the high pinched nose. If he'd been dead she mightn't have noticed for weeks; she wouldn't have minded. But suddenly he knew he was having the paper read to him by an actress! "An actress!" The old head lifted; two points of light quivered in the old eyes. "An actress — are ye?" And Miss Brill smoothed the newspaper as though it were the manuscript of her part and said gently: "Yes, I have been an actress for a long time." ■

1920

AP® TIP

Remember, point of view creates meaning because it reflects what the author wants to convey. For instance, first-person offers a sense of immediacy, drawing the reader in, while third-person narration can seem honest and less biased.

In this passage, Miss Brill (whose first name is never revealed) feels like part of the world she is observing. Priding herself on her ability to notice the rich details all around her, she does not see herself as a solitary or pitiful figure. We get to know her as a vibrant, joyful, appreciative, perhaps even contemplative person. Soon after, however, she overhears a young couple laughing at her, a slight that causes her to question whether she really has a part in this world that belongs to the young. We never know the motivation or level of awareness of any other character because the third-person **limited omniscient point of view** is that of Miss Brill. As you consider the excerpt from "Miss Brill," think about how much more connected we would feel to Miss Brill as a character were she the one sharing her story with us. We would, however, also be trapped within her perspective, and we would only experience what she experiences. A third person limited perspective, such as the one Mansfield chooses here, means the narrator can zoom in to share more details and zoom out to share the larger picture.

Another variation on the third-person perspective involves an **omniscient narrator**. This perspective gives readers access to what multiple characters are thinking and feeling. Some omniscient narrators remain objective, recount only what characters say and do, and offer no analysis of events or insight into characters' thinking. As a result, all interpretations are left to the reader. Other omniscient narrators provide subjective interpretations in addition to relating events in the narrative. In the novel *Pride and Prejudice*, for example, the omniscient narrator adds commentary while describing characters, such as in the passage below when the narrator offers details about Mr. Bingley's physical appearance and personality before introducing Bingley's sisters, brother-in-law, and friend. As you read the passage, look for additional places the narrator infuses the commentary with a more personal, subjective tone than an impartial, objective one.

from Pride and Prejudice

Jane Austen

Mr. Bingley was good-looking and gentlemanlike; he had a pleasant countenance, and easy, unaffected manners. His sisters were fine women, with an air of decided fashion. His brother-in-law, Mr. Hurst, merely looked the gentleman; but his friend Mr. Darcy soon drew the attention of the room by his fine, tall person, handsome features, noble mien, and the report which was in general circulation within five minutes after his entrance, of his having ten thousand a year. The gentlemen pronounced him to be a fine figure of a man, the ladies declared he was much handsomer than Mr. Bingley, and he was looked at with great admiration for about half the evening, till his manners gave a disgust which turned the tide of his popularity; for he was discovered to be proud; to be above his company, and above being pleased; and not all his large estate in

Derbyshire could then save him from having a most forbidding, disagreeable countenance, and being unworthy to be compared with his friend.

Mr. Bingley had soon made himself acquainted with all the principal people in the room; he was lively and unreserved, danced every dance, was angry that the ball closed so early, and talked of giving one himself at Netherfield. Such amiable qualities must speak for themselves. What a contrast between him and his friend! Mr. Darcy danced only once with Mrs. Hurst and once with Miss Bingley, declined being introduced to any other lady, and spent the rest of the evening in walking about the room, speaking occasionally to one of his own party. His character was decided. He was the proudest, most disagreeable man in the world, and everybody hoped that he would never come there again. Amongst the most violent against him was Mrs. Bennet, whose dislike of his general behaviour was sharpened into particular resentment by his having slighted one of her daughters. ■

1813

Consider, too, places where the narrator of *Pride and Prejudice* provides more objective commentary that merely recounts other characters' interpretations of each other. For example, the first details we read about Mr. Darcy largely come from others in attendance at the ball even if through the narrator. While we know as readers that the information is being conveyed from the point of view of other people, the details and vivid language that describe Mr. Darcy encourage readers to share that same first impression.

KEY QUESTIONS

Analyzing Narrative Perspective and Point of View

- Is the point of view first person (I, we) or third person (he, she, it)?
- Is the narrator a participant or an observer in the story?
- How does the narrator's perspective influence readers' experiences of the story?
- Does the point of view or perspective ever shift? If so, what is the effect?
- How do the point of view and perspective shape what you learn about the story's characters and setting, and how do they affect the story's structure and plot?

Analyzing Narrative Perspective and Point of View

The following excerpt is from the opening of *The Round House* by Louise Erdrich. Joe Coutts, the main character, is helping his father do yard work around their home on an unnamed American Indian reservation in North Dakota. What effect does first-person point of view have on this passage? What does it reveal about Joe's perspective?

(*continued*)

from The Round House

Louise Erdrich

Small trees had attacked my parents' house at the foundation. They were just seedlings with one or two rigid, healthy leaves. Nevertheless, the stalky shoots had managed to squeeze through knife cracks in the decorative brown shingles covering the cement blocks. They had grown into the unseen wall and it was difficult to pry them loose. My father wiped his palm across his forehead and damned their toughness. I was using a rusted old dandelion fork with a splintered handle; he wielded a long, slim iron fireplace poker that was probably doing more harm than good. As my father prodded away blindly at the places where he sensed roots might have penetrated, he was surely making convenient holes in the mortar for next year's seedlings.

Whenever I succeeded in working loose a tiny tree, I placed it like a trophy beside me on the narrow sidewalk that surrounded the house. There were ash shoots, elm, maple, box elder, even a good-sized catalpa, which my father placed in an ice cream bucket and watered, thinking that he might find a place to replant it. I thought it was a wonder the treelets had persisted through a North Dakota winter. They'd had water perhaps, but only feeble light and a few crumbs of earth. Yet each seed had managed to sink the hasp of a root deep and a probing tendril outward. ■

2012

Putting It All Together: Interpreting Major Elements of Fiction

As you analyze literature, you have not only the challenge of comprehending what happens in the story but also of understanding how characters, plot, setting, point of view, and perspective come together to raise questions, explore issues, and ultimately convey meaning. When you put forth your understanding of the text, you are making a **claim** about its deeper meaning, or **theme**(s). A claim must be arguable, which is where your interpretation will come in. If the plot, characters, and setting are the *what* of a story, then your interpretation is the *so what.* Developing an interpretation is not a simple process, and you might even feel as though you have to make it up by using your imagination — but that's not necessarily a bad thing. In fact, literary critic Northrop Frye used the term "the educated imagination" to describe the intersection of skills and knowledge with creativity. In a way, this chapter so far has educated your imagination — what you've learned about the basic building blocks of stories such as character, perspective, point of view, plot, and setting all give you ways to exercise your imagination as you think about what these stories mean. The complexity of this process of interpretation means that while others may develop similar interpretations, yours is still unique. That is why you will also need to provide **evidence** from the text to back the claims you make as you explain and support your interpretation. All of these pieces, when put together, essentially form a literary argument.

To find solid evidence, you will have to rely on your observations, find portions of the work that seem significant, and then explain why and how you think they are meaningful. Sometimes this process happens naturally as you reflect on a story you immediately connected with and enjoyed, but sometimes a work of literature can seem like it's just a wall of words you have to climb. In such situations, the basic elements of fiction are tools you can use to make the ascent. This approach to developing an interpretation is relatively systematic, but it will always get you where you need to go. Let's look at how you might go element by element in "The First Day" by Edward P. Jones to develop your interpretation of the story.

AP® TIP

Try to use language that conveys certainty in your claims. Instead of writing, "I think the daughter in 'The First Day' finds it ironic. . . " or even, "The daughter seems to find it ironic . . ." you might instead write, "The daughter in 'The First Day' finds it ironic. . . ."

Let's start with character. Who are the characters in this story? The main characters are the mother and the daughter. All of the other characters are female — where are the men in this story? Their absence could speak to the importance and complexity of women's relationships with each other, particularly mothers and daughters. What else do you know about the protagonist of the story, the daughter? How does she change or develop because of the action in the plot? Consider, for example, the title of the text: "The First Day." We can ask, "The first day of what?" Literally, it's the first day of school, but what else does this day signify? The daughter is leaving her family and entering society as a whole. It's the first day that her education and her fate are being transferred from her mother to the adults at the school, who are minor but important characters in this story. These observations suggest a number of interpretations, especially the importance of community in raising a child.

The setting of the story also offers opportunities for interpretation. In our earlier discussion of setting, we focused on what the neighborhood reveals about the lives of the narrator and her mother, as well as what significance the mother's church holds as a symbol of community. But the setting also speaks to the mother's anxiety about letting her daughter go and the daughter's readiness to have new experiences on her own. This creates a bit of tension in the story: while the mother sees the school near the church as an extension of a community she trusts to protect her daughter, the fact that it's familiar ground might ultimately limit the daughter's opportunities to establish herself on her own terms. Regardless of which school the daughter attends, the general setting of schools also reinforces our earlier interpretation of the roles wider communities play in raising children.

The plot of the story is pretty straightforward: an illiterate mother takes her daughter to the first day of kindergarten; they are refused admission to one school and have to go to another, where another parent assists the mother in filling out the necessary forms. The mother then leaves the daughter at school, telling her to pay close attention to the teacher. That basic sequence of events is a summary of the plot, but an interpretation of it requires a deeper exploration that moves beyond what happens and looks at how the order of events and the overall structure of the story communicate meaning. Within the plot of "The First Day," some of the events take on deeper significance as we re-examine them. For instance, why would a mother who has not had the opportunity to receive a formal education work so hard and overcome multiple obstacles to make sure her daughter is enrolled in school? A possible interpretation could be that the people who best understand the importance of an education are those who didn't have the benefit of one.

Point of view can often be a difficult angle to analyze and interpret, but in this story, it is especially interesting. The narrator is the daughter, yet she recalls the incident from the vantage point of adulthood. We learn some details about how the daughter's understanding of her mother has changed over the years, and we also know quite a bit about the daughter's understanding of her mother at the time. Consider how your knowledge of your own parents' strength and fallibility has changed as you've grown up. As you experienced people outside of your family and became part of the larger world, you likely began to see your parents as humans capable of imperfection. This brings us to a more specific aspect of the narrator's point of view. She says that these events occurred "long before [she] learned to be ashamed of [her] mother" (par. 1). The word "learned" seems significant, given this story's focus on formal education. We think of education as being "book learning," but it's clear that some part of the narrator's education eventually involves "learning" to be ashamed of her mother. Yet as she's telling this story, she does not seem ashamed; she seems proud of her mother's heroic journey, proud that her mother overcame so many obstacles in order to make sure her daughter had a bright future. So one interpretation of "The First Day" might be that the story illustrates how our perspectives of our parents' identities change over time and shape our appreciation for the sacrifices they make. Only later in life can we fully reflect upon all the things our parents have done on our behalf.

As you can see, an interpretation of a text moves beyond an understanding of what happens in the story to draw conclusions about the real world. "The First Day," for example, suggests something about the role of education in our lives that goes beyond this particular five-year-old's first day in kindergarten. Isn't this story really about the role education can play in parent-child relationships and about the opportunities and experiences children might have that their parents did not have? Maybe Jones is asking us to think about what happened later in the narrator's life as she aged, was successful at school, and went on to college. Her mother may be one hundred percent supportive of her daughter's education. Yet as the daughter's experiences diverge from those of her mother, those very opportunities can divide and separate the two. The narrator looks back with obvious love and appreciation for her mother, but Jones does not give us the story of what took place between "the first day" and the point from which the narrator remembers it. Recall, however, that the daughter tells us that this "first day" is not just about school—it's also a day she views in relation to her own perception of her mother, who she later "learn[s]" to be "ashamed" of. Perhaps the narrator's education began not just with her first day at school but also this first day of experiencing her mother's infallibility and her own first sense of shame. In looking back, the daughter also realizes so much more about the bravery and love in her mother's actions on the first day of school. In revealing her inability to read and in facing public humiliation, her mother ensures that the daughter doesn't ever have to be similarly dependent on others.

section 1 / culminating activity

Interpreting Short Fiction: Defending a Claim with Evidence

The following is Lydia Davis's 2001 short story "Blind Date." In this story, the speaker relates a friend's teenage experience with being set up on a date with a boy she did not know. Write a paragraph in which you make a defensible claim regarding how Davis uses characterization to express the friend's complex attitude toward the experience. In your paragraph, you should incorporate at least one piece of evidence from the text to support your claim.

Blind Date

Lydia Davis

"There isn't really much to tell," she said, but she would tell it if I liked. We were sitting in a midtown luncheonette. "I've only had one blind date in my life. And I didn't really have it. I can think of more interesting situations that are like a blind date — say, when someone gives you a book as a present, when they fix you up with that book. I was once given a book of essays about reading, writing, book collecting. I felt it was a perfect match. I started reading it right away, in the backseat of the car. I stopped listening to the conversation in the front. I like to read about how other people read and collect books, even how they shelve their books. But by the time I was done with the book, I had taken a strong dislike to the author's personality. I won't have another date with her!" She laughed. Here we were interrupted by the waiter, and then a series of incidents followed that kept us from resuming our conversation that day.

The next time the subject came up, we were sitting in two Adirondack chairs looking out over a lake in, in fact, the Adirondacks. We were content to sit in silence at first. We were tired. We had been to the Adirondack Museum that day and seen many things of interest, including old guide boats and good examples of the original Adirondack chair. Now we watched the water and the edge of the woods, each thinking, I was sure, about James Fenimore Cooper. After some parties of canoers had gone by, older people in canvas boating hats, their quiet voices carrying far over the water to us, we went on talking. These were precious days of holiday together, and we were finishing many unfinished conversations.

"I was fifteen or sixteen, I guess," she said. "I was home from boarding school. Maybe it was summer. I don't know where my parents were. They were often away. They often left me alone there, sometimes for the evening, sometimes for weeks at a time. The phone rang. It was a boy I didn't know. He said he was a friend of a boy from school — I can't remember who. We talked a little and then he asked me if I wanted to have dinner with him. He sounded nice enough so I said I would, and we agreed on a day and a time and I told him where I lived.

"But after I got off the phone, I began thinking, worrying. What had this other boy said about me? What had the two of them said about me? Maybe I had some kind of a reputation. Even now I can't imagine that what they said was completely pure or innocent — for instance, that I was pretty and fun to be with. There had to be something nasty about it, two boys talking

(continued)

privately about a girl. The awful word that began to occur to me was fast. She's fast. I wasn't actually very fast. I was faster than some but not as fast as others. The more I imagined the two boys talking about me the worse I felt.

"I liked boys. I liked the boys I knew in a way that was much more innocent than they probably thought. I trusted them more than girls. Girls hurt my feelings, girls ganged up on me. I always had boys who were my friends, starting back when I was nine and ten and eleven. I didn't like this feeling that two boys were talking about me.

"Well, when the day came, I didn't want to go out to dinner with this boy. I just didn't want the difficulty of this date. It scared me — not because there was anything scary about the boy but because he was a stranger, I didn't know him. I didn't want to sit there face-to-face in some restaurant and start from the very beginning, knowing nothing. It didn't feel right. And there was the burden of that recommendation — 'Give her a try.'

"Then again, maybe there were other reasons. Maybe I had been alone in that apartment so much by then that I had retreated into some kind of inner, unsociable space that was hard to come out of. Maybe I felt I had disappeared and I was comfortable that way and did not want to be forced back into existence. I don't know.

"At six o'clock, the buzzer rang. The boy was there, downstairs. I didn't answer it. It rang again. Still I did not answer it. I don't know how many times it rang or how long he leaned on it. I let it ring. At some point, I walked the length of the living room to the balcony. The apartment was four stories up. Across the street and down a flight of stone steps was a park. From the balcony on a clear day you could look out over the park and see all the way across town, maybe a mile, to the other river. At this point I think I ducked down or got down on my hands and knees and inched my way to the edge of the balcony. I think I looked over far enough to see him down there on the sidewalk below — looking up, as I remember it. Or he had gone across the street and was looking up. He didn't see me.

"I know that as I crouched there on the balcony or just back from it I had some impression of him being puzzled, disconcerted, disappointed, at a loss what to do now, not prepared for this — prepared for all sorts of other ways the date might go, other difficulties, but not for no date at all. Maybe he also felt angry or insulted, if it occurred to him then or later that maybe he hadn't made a mistake but that I had deliberately stood him up, and not the way I did it — alone up there in the apartment, uncomfortable and embarrassed, chickening out, hiding out — but, he would imagine, in collusion with someone else, a girlfriend or boyfriend, confiding in them, snickering over him.

"I don't know if he called me, or if I answered the phone if it rang. I could have given some excuse — I could have said I had gotten sick or had to go out suddenly. Or maybe I hung up when I heard his voice. In those days I did a lot of avoiding that I don't do now — avoiding confrontations, avoiding difficult encounters. And I did a fair amount of lying that I also don't do now.

"What was strange was how awful this felt. I was treating a person like a thing. And I was betraying not just him but something larger, some social contract. When you knew a decent person was waiting downstairs, someone you had made an appointment with, you did not just not answer the buzzer. What was even more surprising to me was what I felt about myself in that instant. I was behaving as though I had no responsibility to anyone or anything, and that made me feel as though I existed outside society, some kind of criminal, or didn't exist at all. I was annihilating myself even more than him. It was an awful violation."

She paused, thoughtful. We were sitting inside now, because it was raining. We had come inside to sit in a sort of lounge or recreation room provided for guests of that lakeside camp. The rain fell every afternoon there, sometimes for minutes, sometimes for hours. Across the water, the white pines and spruces were very still against the gray sky. The water was silver. We did not see any of the waterbirds we sometimes saw paddling around the edges of the lake — teals and loons. Inside, a fire burned in the fireplace. Over our heads hung a chandelier made of antlers. Between us stood a table constructed of a rough slab of wood resting on the legs of a deer, complete with hooves. On the table stood a lamp made from an old gun. She looked away from the lake and around the room. "In that book about the Adirondacks I was reading last night," she remarked, "he says this was what the Adirondacks was all about, I mean the Adirondacks style: things made from things."

A month or so later, when I was home again and she was back in the city, we were talking on the telephone and she said she had been hunting through one of the old diaries she had on her shelf there, which might say exactly what had happened — though of course, she said, she would just be filling in the details of something that did not actually happen. But she couldn't find this incident written down anywhere, which of course made her wonder if she had gotten the dates really wrong and she wasn't even in boarding school anymore by then. Maybe she was in college by then. But she decided to believe what she had told me. "But I'd forgotten how much I wrote about boys," she added. "Boys and books. What I wanted more than anything else at the age of sixteen was a great library." ■

2001

Section 2

So far in the chapter, we have explored some of the larger elements of fiction — that is, how character, plot, setting, perspective, and point of view all contribute to the meaning of an entire work. In this section, we'll discuss *how* a writer expresses these elements in prose, analyzing ways that language choices work together to create meaning. By looking at the various parts of a short passage of fiction, we begin to appreciate different writers' artistry and understand how they use various literary elements to make a statement, suggest an emotion, or convey an idea. In short, we are moving from a panoramic view to a close-up.

Close reading, sometimes called explication of text, means developing an understanding of a work that is based on its small details and the larger ideas those details evoke, add up to, or suggest. Essential to close reading is observation — taking note of what catches your attention as you read and then asking questions about why a phrase or scene strikes you. The texts you are asked to read closely are often not that

AP® TIP

You will likely encounter unfamiliar words in the AP® Exam texts. Remember to look for context clues that point to what a word or phrase means. If you don't find any, consider the overall mood of the passage to get the gist of things.

long, which means you can read them several times. Each time you read a passage, you will notice more and more. This section will offer ways to deepen your awareness of the specific literary elements authors use to express their ideas. We'll move from identifying these elements to analyzing their effect on us as readers, and then show you how to approach writing a close analysis essay that shares your insights. For now, though, let's concentrate on the first impressions you have when you read a short passage of fiction by taking a look at an excerpt from *Americanah*, a 2013 novel by Chimamanda Ngozi Adichie. The novel tells the story of a young Nigerian woman, Ifemelu, who emigrates to America to attend college. As you read this passage, pay careful attention to the specific language Adichie uses to set the scene and jot down your first impressions. You should also note any unfamiliar vocabulary, and, if possible, look up words you don't know. If you are able to work only with the passage itself, do your best to use the surrounding context to figure out words, phrases, or usages that confuse you. Finally, try and tune in to the way the language of the passage affects you as you read; for instance, do specific words or phrases carry an emotional meaning? Do they create a certain feeling or atmosphere?

from Americanah

Chimamanda Ngozi Adichie

Ifemelu had grown up in the shadow of her mother's hair. It was black-black, so thick it drank two containers of relaxer at the salon, so full it took hours under the hooded dryer, and when finally released from pink plastic rollers, sprang free and full, flowing down her back like a celebration. Her father called it a crown of glory. "Is it your real hair?" strangers would ask and then reach out to touch it reverently. Others would say "Are you from Jamaica?" as though only foreign blood could explain such bounteous hair that did not thin at the temples. Through the years of childhood, Ifemelu would often look in the mirror and pull at her own hair, separate the coils, will it to become like her mother's, but it remained bristly and grew reluctantly; braiders said it cut them like a knife. ■

2013

You probably noticed, first of all, that the very idea of Ifemelu growing up not simply in the shadow of her mother, but "in the shadow of her mother's hair" is striking. But it's the description of the hair that tells us why. Instead of just writing "black" or "very black" or using another qualifier, Adichie repeats "black-black," which instantly gains our attention because of the unusual repetition. This is hair that is "full, flowing down [her mother's] back like a celebration." That comparison to a celebration — a party, a joyous occasion — gives us a visual image at the same time it evokes the awe that Ifemelu feels. This is "bounteous" hair, a word that suggests more than quantity but both luxurious quantity and quality. The expression "a crown of glory," not the more common "crowning glory," suggests the mother is royalty, which makes the idea of her having "foreign blood" sound downright foolish. Further, this is hair that seems to have a will of its own. Adichie gives it human qualities when she tells us that it "drank" the relaxer solution. No wonder strangers wanted to touch it "reverently," a word we usually associate with religion or spirituality.

Imagine how different this passage would have been had Adichie simply said that Ifemelu had grown up envying her mother's beautiful hair. The careful choices of details and the language used to convey them make the difference. That skill — the writer's art and craft — is the subject of this section. By paying attention to striking language choices and asking questions, we have gathered textual evidence to begin interpreting the passage. In this case, we see this scene as one that reveals something deeper about the relationship between mother and daughter, perhaps one of admiration tinged with a bit of envy.

By exploring what catches your attention, you're already starting to develop a kind of interior conversation with the text that explores what the writer is doing and why. One important point to keep in mind is that your goal is not simply to identify and list literary elements — although you may spot and even name some — but to analyze their effect. In other words, how do the writer's choices help craft the meaning of the work? You may find the following approaches helpful to keep in mind as you read any text for the first time.

KEY QUESTIONS

Close Reading

- Pose questions about things that confuse you — are there aspects of the setting that do not seem to fit with the rest of the narrative? Are characters behaving in ways that appear unusual, particularly in light of what else the author has revealed about them?
- Make connections within the passage or story — where do you spot repetitions, patterns, contrasts, or points of tension, especially between and among characters?
- Note striking, unusual, or distinctive word choices — where do the language choices signal a change of some sort in the narrative?

Close Reading: Analyzing Literary Elements and Techniques

The point of close reading is to go from the *what* to the *how* by examining details: that is, to go beyond merely summarizing what happens or identifying the literary techniques the writer employs in a piece of prose. To perform close analysis, we must understand how a writer's style choices, such as figurative language, convey a work's meaning. Once you begin to analyze literature closely, you will see how all of the parts of a piece of literature work together, from large elements like characterization and setting to the details revealed by individual word choices, sentence structure, and tone.

Let's look closely at an excerpt from *My Ántonia* by Willa Cather, a novel about early settlers in the American West, narrated by a young boy who moves from Virginia to Nebraska to be brought up by his grandparents.

from My Ántonia

Willa Cather

I sat down in the middle of the garden, where snakes could scarcely approach unseen, and leaned my back against a warm yellow pumpkin. There were some ground-cherry bushes growing along the furrows, full of fruit. I turned back the papery triangular sheaths that protected the berries and ate a few. All about me giant grasshoppers, twice as big as any I had ever seen, were doing acrobatic feats among the dried vines. The gophers scurried up and down the ploughed ground. There in the sheltered draw-bottom the wind did not blow very hard, but I could hear it singing its humming tune up on the level, and I could see the tall grasses wave. The earth was warm under me, and warm as I crumbled it through my fingers. Queer little red bugs came out and moved in slow squadrons around me. Their backs were polished vermilion, with black spots. I kept as still as I could. Nothing happened. I did not expect anything to happen. I was something that lay under the sun and felt it, like the pumpkins, and I did not want to be anything more. I was entirely happy. Perhaps we feel like that when we die and become a part of something entire, whether it is sun and air, or goodness and knowledge. At any rate, that is happiness; to be dissolved into something complete and great. When it comes to one, it comes as naturally as sleep. ■

1918

After even an initial reading of such a descriptive passage, you probably have a sense of how comfortable the narrator feels in this natural environment. But how does Cather convey that feeling? To answer that question, we need to get more specific about exactly what literary elements and techniques are at work. Understanding these concepts will give you things to be on the lookout for as you read closely, as well as the vocabulary to help you describe what you see. Most important, these elements provide essential evidence for close literary analysis and help you support your interpretation. It's likely you know some of these terms, but others may be new to you. Examples of all of these concepts, and more, are available in the Glossary/Glosario at the back of this book (p. 1340).

Diction

Authors choose their words carefully to convey precise meanings. We call these word choices the author's **diction**. A word can have more than one dictionary definition, or **denotation**, so when you analyze diction, you must consider all of a word's possible meanings. If some words have associations, or **connotations**, beyond the dictionary definitions, you should ask how those contribute to the meaning of the piece, too. Sometimes a word's connotations will reveal another layer of meaning in terms of **formal** or **informal diction**, which is sometimes called **slang**, or **colloquial** language. For instance, "fake" and "artificial" have basically the same denotation of "not authentic," but "fake" is more conversational; when referring to a person, it carries a negative connotation. "Artificial" is more formal, suggesting a lack of originality but not intentional deception. Diction can also be **abstract** or **concrete**. Concrete words are generally those you can perceive through your senses because they are part of the physical world; abstract words are less tangible and refer to a concept or an idea. For example, Cather includes several concrete nouns in the first part of this excerpt such as the "pumpkin" and the "grasshoppers." Later in the paragraph, she mentions much more abstract concepts, including "goodness" and "happiness."

While the passage from *My Ántonia* is entirely narrative, it's important to note the function diction serves as part of dialogue in prose. The characters' spoken words are also the author's language choices, and you should think critically about their effect on the reader.

Let's look at some of the diction choices Cather makes. The passage begins in a garden where it would be hard for a snake to "approach unseen." The narrator is outdoors on a sheltered part of a prairie farm, so the garden and the snake are examples of concrete details. But snakes and gardens also carry other meanings. It is hard not to think of the Garden of Eden and a sheltered, childlike innocence. Perhaps the most striking detail is the narrator leaning back "against a warm yellow pumpkin" and slowly eating berries after "turn[ing] back the papery triangular sheaths that protected [them]." The language itself conveys a sense of ease and trust.

KEY QUESTIONS

Analyzing Diction

- Which of the verbs, nouns, adjectives, and adverbs are general and abstract, and which are specific and concrete?
- Are important words and phrases formal, informal, colloquial, or slang?
- Do any of the words have multiple denotations, and if so, which of the definitions apply?
- Do any words have strong connotations or seem "loaded"? What are those connotations?

Analyzing Diction

activity

Following is a passage from *The Great Gatsby* by F. Scott Fitzgerald. The book takes place on and around Long Island, New York, in the 1920s and is narrated by Nick Carraway, a young man of relatively modest means whose wealthy friends and family treat him as a confidant. In this passage, Nick goes to visit Tom Buchanan, his cousin's

(continued)

husband and a former classmate from their years together at Yale University. Analyze the effect of the diction Fitzgerald uses in this scene, being sure to pay particular attention to the connotations of the words he chooses. How do those choices set the scene? What do they reveal about the characters?

from The Great Gatsby

F. Scott Fitzgerald

And so it happened that on a warm windy evening I drove over to East Egg to see two old friends whom I scarcely knew at all. Their house was even more elaborate than I expected, a cheerful red-and-white Georgian Colonial mansion, overlooking the bay. The lawn started at the beach and ran toward the front door for a quarter of a mile, jumping over sun-dials and brick walks and burning gardens — finally when it reached the house drifting up the side in bright vines as though from the momentum of its run. The front was broken by a line of French windows, glowing now with reflected gold and wide open to the warm windy afternoon, and Tom Buchanan in riding clothes was standing with his legs apart on the front porch.

He had changed since his New Haven years. Now he was a sturdy straw-haired man of thirty with a rather hard mouth and a supercilious manner. Two shining arrogant eyes had established dominance over his face and gave him the appearance of always leaning aggressively forward. Not even the effeminate swank of his riding clothes could hide the enormous power of that body — he seemed to fill those glistening boots until he strained the top lacing, and you could see a great pack of muscle shifting when his shoulder moved under his thin coat. It was a body capable of enormous leverage — a cruel body.

His speaking voice, a gruff husky tenor, added to the impression of fractiousness he conveyed. There was a touch of paternal contempt in it, even toward people he liked — and there were men at New Haven who had hated his guts.

"Now, don't think my opinion on these matters is final," he seemed to say, "just because I'm stronger and more of a man than you are." We were in the same senior society, and while we were never intimate I always had the impression that he approved of me and wanted me to like him with some harsh, defiant wistfulness of his own.

5 We talked for a few minutes on the sunny porch.

"I've got a nice place here," he said, his eyes flashing about restlessly.

Turning me around by one arm, he moved a broad flat hand along the front vista, including in its sweep a sunken Italian garden, a half acre of deep, pungent roses, and a snub-nosed motor-boat that bumped the tide offshore.

"It belonged to Demaine, the oil man." He turned me around again, politely and abruptly. "We'll go inside."

We walked through a high hallway into a bright rosy-colored space, fragilely bound into the house by French windows at either end. The windows were ajar and gleaming white against the fresh grass outside that seemed to grow a little way into the house. A breeze blew through the room, blew curtains in at one end and out the other like pale flags, twisting them up toward the frosted wedding-cake of the ceiling, and then rippled over the wine-colored rug, making a shadow on it as wind does on the sea.

10 The only completely stationary object in the room was an enormous couch on which two

young women were buoyed up as though upon an anchored balloon. They were both in white, and their dresses were rippling and fluttering as if they had just been blown back in after a short flight around the house. I must have stood for a few moments listening to the whip and snap of the curtains and the groan of a picture on the wall. Then there was a boom as Tom Buchanan shut the rear windows and the caught wind died out about the room, and the curtains and the rugs and the two young women ballooned slowly to the floor. ■

1925

Figurative Language

Language that is not literal is called **figurative**, as in a **figure of speech**. Sometimes this kind of language is called *metaphorical* because it explains or expands on an idea by comparing it to something else. **Similes** make such comparisons by using the words *like*, *as*, or *than* (e.g., *love is like a rose*; *love is lighter than air*), while **metaphors** directly state that one thing is another (e.g., *love is a battlefield*). **Personification** is a figure of speech in which a concept, an object, or an animal is given human characteristics (e.g., *love is blind*).

Personification prevails in the passage from *My Ántonia*. The narrator describes the grasshoppers "doing acrobatic feats" as though they are people, and hears the wind "singing its humming tune" as the tall grasses "wave." Taken together, all these examples from the natural world seem to the narrator like friendly companions, suggesting his comfort and perhaps even that he believes he is a part of their world. In the next sentence, when he "crumble[s]" the earth between his fingers, the line between human and natural worlds blurs.

Keep in mind that good writers do not choose figurative language merely to decorate their work. These choices are not icing on the cake, but instead work together to convey something central to literature: a deeper meaning or a broader context, particularly when it comes to character and setting. Like descriptive words in general, figurative language conveys a unique perspective toward an event, a place, a character, an idea, and so forth.

AP® TIP

For more on figurative language, see the Glossary/Glosario (p. 1340).

Imagery

Imagery is also figurative language. Like similes and metaphors, imagery relies on associations the reader might have. It is typically developed and sustained throughout a passage of prose, whereas metaphors and similes are often just a single phrase or sentence. Imagery creates a vivid mental picture or a physical sensation by appealing to one or more of the five senses: that is, how something looks, feels, sounds, smells, or tastes. In considering imagery, look carefully at how the sense impressions are created. Also pay attention to patterns of images that are repeated throughout a work. Often, writers use figurative language to make their descriptions even more vivid. In the Cather passage, the narrator hears the wind and feels the warmth of the earth, but the keenest

AP® TIP

Although imagery often makes prose more vivid, that's not its sole purpose. Make sure you can explain what vivid imagery conveys about the narrator, the characters, the setting, and so on.

images are visual: he sees the grasshoppers jumping and the tall grasses waving. Let's take a closer look at this description in particular:

> Queer little red bugs came out and moved in slow squadrons around me. Their backs were polished vermilion, with black spots.

The imagery tells us that these are little red bugs with black spots, but consider what is added with the words "squadrons" and "polished vermilion," both figurative descriptions. Our imagination is piqued by the self-sufficiency of an army of bugs, painted bright red, going about their business, oblivious to the human presence of the narrator. With such striking images, the narrator suggests a heightened sensory awareness of his experience.

KEY QUESTIONS

Analyzing Figurative Language

- Which words and/or phrases are used literally, and which are used figuratively?
- What images do you find? How do they convey a larger meaning?
- In what ways does the figurative language evoke a specific feeling or mood?
- Is the figurative language consistent throughout the passage, or does it shift? If you detect a shift, how does it develop meaning?

Analyzing Figurative Language

Following is an excerpt from the novel *Monkey Bridge* by Lan Cao. In this passage, the main character, a young refugee from Vietnam who has come to the United States to live with her adoptive family, describes the experience of learning English. Identify the figurative language in the passage and discuss what it conveys about the narrator's complex attitude toward her newly acquired language skills.

from Monkey Bridge

Lan Cao

I followed Aunt Mary around the house, collecting words like a beggar gathering rain with an earthen pan. She opened her mouth and out came a constellation of gorgeous sounds. Each word she uttered was a round stone, with the smoothness of something that had been rubbed and polished by the waves of a warm summer beach. She could swim straight through her syllables. On days when we studied together, I almost convinced myself that we would continue that way forever, playing with the movement of sound itself. I would listen as she tried to inspire me into replicating the "th" sound with the seductive powers of her voice. . . . Once I made it past the fourth or fifth week in Connecticut, the new language began gathering momentum, like tumbleweed in a storm. This was my realization: we have only to let one thing go — the language we think in, or the composition of our dream, the grass roots clinging underneath its rocks — and all at once everything goes. It had astonished me, the ease with which continents shift and planets change course, the casual way in which the earth goes about shedding the laborious folds of its memories. Suddenly out of that difficult space between here and there, English revealed itself to me with the ease of thread unspooled. I began to understand the levity and weight of its sentences. First base, second base, home run. New terminologies were not difficult to master, and gradually the possibility of perfection began edging its ways into my life. How did those numerous Chinatowns and Little Italys sustain the will to maintain a distance, the desire to inhabit the edge and margin of American life? A mere eight weeks into Farmington, and the American Dream was exerting a sly but seductive pull. ■

1997

Syntax

Syntax is the arrangement of words into phrases, clauses, and sentences. When we read closely, we consider whether the sentences in a work are long or short, **simple** or **complex**. The most common type of syntax is a sentence with a subject-verb-object pattern, usually with a single clause. More complex sentences have two or more clauses. A **cumulative** sentence begins with an independent clause that is followed by subordinate clauses or phrases that add detail; often, this sentence pattern conveys detailed descriptions or qualifications. Another type of a longer complex sentence is **periodic**: it begins with subordinate clauses or phrases that build toward the main clause. Most sentences follow the traditional subject-verb-object order, though some are **inverted**: that is, the verb may appear before the subject. You might also look at syntactic patterns, such as several long sentences followed by a short sentence. In some cases, a writer will choose to use a sentence fragment, which in most academic writing is considered an error. But in fiction, a short phrase or even a single word followed by a period can deliberately slow the pace of the passage down or emphasize a point.

The Cather passage is almost entirely composed of straightforward, declarative sentences that follow a subject-verb-object pattern. Only in the last three sentences, when Cather departs from the concrete natural world, does she deviate from this structure. Note the immediate contrast between short, perhaps even abrupt sentences — for instance, "Nothing happened," and "I was entirely happy" — and the longer ones that follow: "Perhaps we feel like that when we die and become a part of something entire, whether it is sun and air, or goodness and knowledge. At any rate, that is happiness; to be dissolved into something complete and great." Those two sentences, which accumulate details as part of the speaker's natural thought processes, almost seem like an incantation. The syntax itself reinforces the narrator's progress from observation to reflection or even meditation. By the end of the passage, we have a sense of the narrator's ease as he seems to float from idea to idea. Note, too, that the shifts in syntax parallel shifts in diction. In the shorter, more straightforward sentences, the narrator is a keen observer of details in the natural world; as he moves into longer, more reflective thoughts, his language becomes more abstract. He has moved from the external physical world to the interior realm of thought.

KEY QUESTIONS

Analyzing Syntax

- What is the order of the words in the sentences? Are they inverted?
- How do the sentences connect words, phrases, and clauses?
- How do the sentences build on each other to create meaning?
- How is the passage organized? Is it chronological? Does it move from concrete to abstract language, or vice versa? Do you see any other patterns?

Analyzing Syntax

Carefully read the following passage from *There There* by Tommy Orange. In this excerpt the young narrator, Dene, describes reading to Maxine, who is his guardian. Analyze how Orange uses syntax to reveal Dene's understanding of his experience of reading.

from There There

Tommy Orange

Maxine makes me read to her. . . . I don't like it because I read slow. The letters move on me sometimes like bugs. Just whenever they want, they switch places. But then sometimes the words don't move. When they stay still like that I have to wait to be sure they're not gonna move, so it ends up taking longer for me to read them than the ones I can put back together after they scramble. Maxine makes me read her Indian stuff that I don't always get. I like it, though, because when I do get it, I get it way down at that place where it hurts but feels better because you feel it, something you couldn't feel before reading it, that makes you feel less alone, and like it's not gonna hurt as much anymore. One time she used the word *devastating* after I finished reading a passage from her favorite author — Louise Erdrich. It was something about how life will break you. How that's the reason we're here, and to go sit by an apple tree and listen to the apples fall and pile around you, wasting all that sweetness. I didn't know what it meant then, and she saw that I didn't. She didn't explain it either. But we read the passage, that whole book, another time, and I got it.

Maxine's always known me and been able to read me like no one else can, better than myself even, like I don't even know all that I'm showing to the world like I'm reading my own reality slow, because of the way things switch around on me, how people look at me and treat me, and how long it takes me to figure out if I have to put it all back together. ■

2018

Tone and Mood

Tone reflects the attitude of the narrator or a character toward an idea, situation, character, or overall subject of the work. **Mood** is the feeling the reader experiences as a result of the tone and other details in the text. Closely related, tone and mood evoke emotions and are created by the writer's style choices. To discern tone and mood, keep in mind that you must consider how all of the literary elements we've discussed in this chapter work together, not just individually. When you describe the tone and mood of a work, try to use at least two precise words, rather than words that are vague and general, such as *happy*, *sad*, or *different*. Though there are many possibilities, a pair of adjectives with similar connotations (e.g., *detached and bitter*), a pair of contrasting adjectives (e.g., *detached but optimistic*), and an adverb-adjective combination (e.g., *bitterly detached*) are all effective and versatile. When analyzing the Cather passage, for instance, you might say that the joyful and contented tone creates a reflective, peaceful mood.

> **AP® TIP**
>
> While tone and mood often echo each other, they can be quite different. Consider, for example, a text in which the narrator's tone is sarcastic. As a reader, you might find the sarcasm humorous, but you will not experience a sarcastic mood that matches the tone of the narrator.

Let's consider the opening passage from *Bleak House*, an 1853 novel by the British author Charles Dickens. This excerpt is set in the city of London, specifically on the route leading to the Chancery Court, a high court of justice in England.

from Bleak House

Charles Dickens

London. Michaelmas term lately over, and the Lord Chancellor sitting in Lincoln's Inn Hall. Implacable November weather. As much mud in the streets as if the waters had but newly retired from the face of the earth, and it would not be wonderful to meet a Megalosaurus, forty feet long or so, waddling like an elephantine lizard up Holborn Hill. Smoke lowering down from chimney-pots, making a soft black drizzle, with flakes of soot in it as big as full-grown snowflakes — gone into mourning, one might imagine, for the death of the sun. Dogs, undistinguishable in mire. Horses, scarcely better; splashed to their very blinkers.[1] Foot passengers, jostling one another's umbrellas in a general infection of ill temper, and losing their foot-hold at street-corners, where tens of thousands of

[1] Also known as blinders, these shields over horses' eyes prevent them from being able to see (and be frightened by) anything except what is right in front of them. — Eds.

(*continued*)

other foot passengers have been slipping and sliding since the day broke (if this day ever broke), adding new deposits to the crust upon crust of mud, sticking at those points tenaciously to the pavement, and accumulating at compound interest.

Fog everywhere. Fog up the river, where it flows among green aits[2] and meadows; fog down the river, where it rolls defiled among the tiers of shipping and the waterside pollutions of a great (and dirty) city. Fog on the Essex marshes, fog on the Kentish heights. Fog creeping into the cabooses of collier-brigs; fog lying out on the yards and hovering in the rigging of great ships; fog drooping on the gunwales of barges and small boats. Fog in the eyes and throats of ancient Greenwich pensioners,[3] wheezing by the firesides of their wards; fog in the stem and bowl of the afternoon pipe of the wrathful skipper, down in his close cabin; fog cruelly pinching the toes and fingers of his shivering little 'prentice boy on deck. Chance people on the bridges peeping over the parapets into a nether sky of fog, with fog all round them, as if they were up in a balloon and hanging in the misty clouds. ■

1853

[2] Small islands. — Eds.

[3] Retirees. — Eds.

The diction in the beginning of the passage sets the time and place: the city of London, in November, in weather described as "implacable," an example of personification that implies it cannot be pacified. From there, descriptions of mud and fog take over most of the passage. Similes abound, with the mud accumulating "as if the waters had but newly retired from the face of the earth." Soot comes out of chimneys like snowflakes that have "gone into mourning . . . for the death of the sun." Pedestrians walk "in a general infection of ill temper."

Everything that follows describes where the fog is — everywhere — and how it insinuates itself into everyone's lives. An unrelenting force, it is not only in the physical environment but in "the eyes and throats of elderly . . . pensioners." Dickens repeats the word "fog" at the start of nearly every sentence, building a sense of its inescapable nature. The syntax in this paragraph is interesting, too — all of the sentences are actually fragments. This choice could suggest the ways in which fog interrupts people's everyday lives and how the inconvenience of it is something they have to overcome. Again using personification, Dickens writes that the fog operates "cruelly" and envelops people "as if they were up in a balloon and hanging in the misty clouds." Taken together, the descriptive language, figures of speech, and unusual syntax combine to create a sense of being unable to see clearly ahead, let alone around the next corner.

As we've analyzed some literary elements in this passage, you've probably noted that some descriptions at first don't seem to make sense or fit together. Writers often use overstatement or **hyperbole** to exaggerate and signal to the reader that something is important, often because it is wrong or out of place. That giant "Megalosaurus" at the outset, for instance, is clearly hyperbole. Why would Dickens include that — what does it mean about the setting? And while the presence of fog in general isn't totally out of place for a street in London, the way that Dickens personifies it as cruel, overpowering, even sinister is definitely hyperbolic. When you consider the specific setting — a street where a court of justice is located — the exaggerated description of fog takes on other possibilities. Why not bright sunshine to signal the clarity that justice is supposed to bring? Perhaps Dickens is suggesting that what initially seems contradictory — the murkiness, the difficulty in seeing clearly near a place where truth should rule — is the reality: a system of justice that is not just. This would be a **paradox**: a statement or situation that seems contradictory but actually reveals a surprising truth.

Since tone and mood are matters of interpretation based on evidence in a text, let's step back and consider what we've just observed. The overall mood of the passage is melancholy, even oppressive. As readers, we have the sense that whatever is about to come next in the story won't be fun for the characters. If we return to our definition of tone as a narrator or character's attitude toward a subject or idea, then how do Dickens's style choices add up? We're on a street leading to a place where justice is supposed to be served, the Chancery Court, but Dickens characterizes it as murky and possibly even dangerous. We might describe the tone as somber, perhaps even funereal, since much of life seems obscured by fog, smoke, and mud. It would be fair to go even further and claim that the literary elements and techniques Dickens employs reveal his attitude and the narrator's toward the high court as a challenge to the very concept of justice — a suggestion with pretty sinister implications. To expand on our description of tone, it might be described as somber and ominous.

AP® TIP

Some common tone words: *anxious*, *bitter*, *bittersweet*, *bold*, *callous*, *confident*, *contemptuous*, *cynical*, *detached*, *hopeful*, *humorous*, *impassioned*, *indifferent*, *indignant*, *lighthearted*, *mysterious*, *nostalgic*, *restrained*, *sentimental*, *somber*, *violent*. Remember, you can and should use more than just these words to describe tone.

KEY QUESTIONS

Interpreting Tone and Mood

- On first read, how do you experience the text on an emotional level?
- What is the attitude of the narrator toward events or characters? How do you know?
- How do specific word choices contribute to tone?
- How do the sentence structures contribute to tone?
- Does the mood match the tone? Does either shift over the course of the passage? If so, what is the effect of each shift?

Analyzing Tone and Mood

In the following excerpt from *Their Eyes Were Watching God* by Zora Neale Hurston, the main character Janie is preparing to attend her husband's funeral. What are the tone and mood of the passage? Consider how literary elements of diction, including figurative language, and syntax work together to develop the tone. How does that tone characterize Janie?

from Their Eyes Were Watching God

Zora Neale Hurston

Janie starched and ironed her face and came set in the funeral behind her veil. It was like a wall of stone and steel. . . . All things concerning death and burial were said and done. Finish. End. Never-more. Darkness. Deep hole. Dissolution. Eternity. Weeping and wailing outside. Inside the expensive black folds were resurrection and life. She did not reach outside for anything, nor did the things of death reach inside to disturb her calm. She sent her face to Joe's funeral, and herself went rollicking with the springtime across the world. . . .

Most of the day she was at the store, but at night she was there in the big house and sometimes it creaked and cried all night under the weight of lonesomeness. Then she'd lie awake in bed asking lonesomeness some questions. . . . She had been getting ready for her great journey to the horizons in search of *people*; it was important to all the world that she should find them and they find her. But she had been whipped like a cur dog. . . . [Her grandmother] had taken the biggest thing God ever made, the horizon — for no matter how far a person can go the horizon is still way beyond you — and pinched it in to such a little bit of a thing that she could tie it about her granddaughter's neck tight enough to choke her. She hated the old woman who had twisted her so in the name of love. Most humans didn't love one another nohow, and this mislove was so strong that even common blood couldn't overcome it all the time. She had found a jewel down inside herself and she had wanted to walk where people could see her and gleam it around. But she had been set in the market-place to sell. ■

1937

From Reading to Writing: Crafting an AP® Prose Fiction Analysis Essay

Most of the time you will analyze literature in response to an assignment that provides both a fiction passage and a prompt for writing about it. Frequently, you will be asked to analyze how a writer uses literary elements and techniques to reveal some element or elements of complexity about a central character's identity or relationship with another character. Other writing prompts might ask you to focus on the effect of a setting (like the landscape or the cultural environment) or how a specific plot event (such as another character's death or a dramatic revelation) affects a character. The point of view — who tells the story — is tied to character in myriad ways, as you've seen in the discussion of "The First Day" earlier in this chapter. We've also discussed how significant the language a writer chooses to convey these elements is to interpretive analysis. Now, we'll go through a step-by-step process of formulating and supporting an interpretation of meaning in prose fiction.

In our discussion, we'll focus on "Girl," a short story written in 1978 by Jamaica Kincaid, a Caribbean writer who grew up on the island of Antigua. It is presented primarily as a monologue of a mother to her daughter. Start out by perusing the entire story just to get an initial sense of what's going on. Use the following questions to help focus your reading.

KEY QUESTIONS

Preparing to Write about Short Fiction

- From whose viewpoint is the story being told? What beliefs or biases might the narrator have?
- Who are the characters, and how are they described? Can you sense any conflicts or contradictions within or between individuals?
- Where and when does the story take place? What is striking about the language the author uses to present the time and setting?
- What are the major events that occur during the story or that are referenced from the past?

Girl

Jamaica Kincaid

Wash the white clothes on Monday and put them on the stone heap; wash the color clothes on Tuesday and put them on the clothesline to dry; don't walk bare-head in the hot sun; cook pumpkin fritters in very hot sweet oil; soak your little cloths right after you take them off; when buying cotton to make yourself a nice blouse, be sure that it doesn't have gum in it, because that way it won't hold up well after a wash; soak salt fish overnight before you cook it; is it true that you sing benna[1] in Sunday school?; always eat your food in such a way that it won't turn someone else's stomach; on Sundays try to walk like a lady and not like the slut you are so bent on becoming; don't sing benna in Sunday school; you mustn't speak to wharf-rat boys, not even to give directions; don't eat fruits on the street — flies will follow you; *but I don't sing benna on Sundays at all and never in Sunday school*; this is how to sew on a button; this is how to make a buttonhole for the button you have just sewed on; this is how to hem a dress when you see the hem coming down and so to prevent yourself from looking like the slut I know you are so bent on becoming; this is how you iron your father's khaki shirt so that it doesn't have a crease; this is how you iron your father's khaki

(*continued*)

[1] Antiguan and Barbudan music that spreads local gossip and rumors. — Eds.

pants so that they don't have a crease; this is how you grow okra—far from the house, because okra tree harbors red ants; when you are growing dasheen, make sure it gets plenty of water or else it makes your throat itch when you are eating it; this is how you sweep a corner; this is how you sweep a whole house; this is how you sweep a yard; this is how you smile to someone you don't like too much; this is how you smile to someone you don't like at all; this is how you smile to someone you like completely; this is how you set a table for tea; this is how you set a table for dinner; this is how you set a table for dinner with an important guest; this is how you set a table for lunch; this is how you set a table for breakfast; this is how to behave in the presence of men who don't know you very well, and this way they won't recognize immediately the slut I have warned you against becoming; be sure to wash every day, even if it is with your own spit; don't squat down to play marbles—you are not a boy, you know; don't pick people's flowers—you might catch something; don't throw stones at blackbirds, because it might not be a blackbird at all; this is how to make a bread pudding; this is how to make doukona;[2] this is how to make pepper pot; this is how to make a good medicine for a cold; this is how to make a good medicine to throw away a child before it even becomes a child; this is how to catch a fish; this is how to throw back a fish you don't like, and that way something bad won't fall on you; this is how to bully a man; this is how a man bullies you; this is how to love a man, and if this doesn't work there are other ways, and if they don't work don't feel too bad about giving up; this is how to spit up in the air if you feel like it, and this is how to move quick so that it doesn't fall on you; this is how to make ends meet; always squeeze bread to make sure it's fresh; but what if the baker won't let me feel the bread?; you mean to say that after all you are really going to be the kind of woman who the baker won't let near the bread? ■

1978

[2] An Antiguan dish, doukona is a starchy pudding wrapped in a banana or plantain leaf and boiled like a dumpling.—Eds.

Preparing to Write: Annotating Short Fiction

Most of the time, you'll be given a prompt or a writing assignment that will focus your interpretation. For instance, in this case, your teacher might assign the following prompt:

> The following question refers to Jamaica Kincaid's "Girl," published in 1978. In this story, a mother addresses her daughter by imparting expectations for proper behavior. Read the story carefully. Then, in a well-written essay, analyze how Kincaid uses literary elements and techniques to convey how social values and traditions shape the complex relationship between the mother and her daughter.

Before starting to analyze at a deeper level and beginning your written response, it's helpful to put into a sentence or two just what is going on in this story. We might sum up

"Girl," which is only 650 words long, as the story of a mother giving her daughter advice and instruction about how to become a respectable woman in their community. That's actually it — the outline of what happens in the story. But the emotional wallop, the part that makes us feel the experience and think about it, comes from the details, language, and structure that Kincaid uses to tell this brief tale. To get to the deeper layer required by such a task, you will need to reread the story, annotating as you do so. Why bother with annotation? In *How to Read a Book*, scholars and avid readers Mortimer Adler and Charles van Doren sum it up:

> Why is marking a book indispensable to reading it? First, it keeps you awake — not merely conscious, but wide awake. Second, reading, if it is active, is thinking, and thinking tends to express itself in words, spoken or written. The person who says he knows what he thinks but cannot express it usually does not know what he thinks. Third, writing your reactions down helps you to remember the thoughts of the author.

Annotation is probably the most important strategy and habit of mind to develop as you read closely and analytically. It is the process of noting, right on the text itself, words that strike you, phrases that confuse or thrill you, or places where you want to talk back to the speaker, a character, or even the author. In other words, annotation is your running commentary as the reader. That commentary need not be full sentences about literary elements, though some of your observations might be. You can also ask questions or write brief remarks about your emotional reactions. Try to avoid simply highlighting, though, because it doesn't require you to respond in words. While highlighting can call attention to details of a text, it doesn't fully engage you as a reader because it is merely a way of recognizing how the text is speaking to you; it doesn't allow you to talk back to the text about what you think of it. What you as a reader want to get from annotation is a deeper understanding, and one that is more likely to stick in your memory. You can then use that knowledge to help inform your discussions with others or plan your writing about the text.

AP® TIP

Even in a timed situation, annotation is useful because it focuses your reading, engages you physically with the text, and can be a form of planning. When annotation isn't an option, sticky notes also work.

Once you finish, your annotation might look like a jumble of ideas. Sometimes it is helpful to make annotation a two-step process: annotate directly onto the text first, and then write a paragraph summing up your observations and questions. This informal writing can help you explore your thoughts and bring together the observations you made during the process. Let's practice with the first half or so of the clauses that make up the story — which is a single long sentence. From your pre and initial reading, you already know who the author is, that the speaker is the mother, and that the setting is the Caribbean. This context will help you start to make your observations and develop an interpretation.

Wash the white clothes on Monday and put them on the stone heap; wash the color clothes on Tuesday and put them on the clothesline to dry; don't walk bare-head in the hot sun; cook pumpkin fritters in very hot sweet oil; soak your little cloths right after you take them off; when buying cotton to make yourself a nice blouse, be sure that it doesn't have gum in it, because that way it won't hold up well after a wash; soak salt fish overnight before you cook it; is it true that you sing benna in Sunday school?; always eat your food in such a way that it won't turn someone else's stomach; on Sundays try to walk like a lady and not like the slut you are so bent on becoming; don't sing benna in Sunday school; you mustn't speak to wharf-rat boys, not even to give directions; don't eat fruits on the street — flies will follow you; *but I don't sing benna on Sundays at all and never in Sunday school*; this is how to sew on a button; this is how to make a buttonhole for the button you have just sewed on; this is how to hem a dress when you see the hem coming down and so to prevent yourself from looking like the slut I know you are so bent on becoming;

First the mother tells what to do about laundry, now cooking — like a servant?

Why not? Is that about appearance? Health?

Reference to her period? How old is this girl?

Emphasis on cleanliness and washing again.

Based on the footnote it seems like a tradition from a tight-knit community.

More focus on appearances. She's expected to behave a certain way.

Feminine rules! Being "a lady" seems to involve a lot of cleaning, washing, and silence.

Wow, an ugly term. "[B]ent on becoming" one makes it sound like it's her goal somehow.

Lots of commands ("mustn't" and "don't") here!

Repetition of benna, church. Religion must be a big part of life in the community. But focus on gossip seems almost paranoid.

Is the "girl" talking? At last! But no name, doesn't even get to finish her sentence.

Telling her who she can associate with. Controlling?

While the mother issues a lot of orders, sometimes she shares knowledge and tradition, too.

Is the whole story one long sentence? Unusual syntax. The mother is basically steamrolling the reader!

This ugly phrase is repeated, making the mother sound paranoid, since her daughter denies singing benna.

While this annotation definitely shows an active, engaged reader, there are so many insights and ideas and questions and observations — it's a bit of a noisy process. So, to begin sorting through to figure out what you need to do next to deepen your understanding, let's write a paragraph of exploratory writing. Doing so should help you sift through your observations and order your thoughts.

> So far in "Girl," the mother seems really bossy. This is kind of like a rant, but it's not clear if the mother is angry or what caused it. The things she is telling her daughter to do are mainly domestic chores, so she's very traditional or at least she wants her daughter to follow a traditional path, perhaps becoming a wife and mother in the future. The daughter speaks up in the italicized section, defending herself against her mother's accusation that she sings "benna" in church. Benna is popular music that includes gossip, so the mom probably finds it offensive or dangerous. The mother tells her daughter that she is "bent on" becoming a "slut," which is a pretty harsh word. Maybe she's afraid her daughter will rebel, perhaps in ways that wind up hurting her. Is the mother angry that she's losing control of her daughter, or is she afraid that she won't be able to protect her daughter?

Notice that the language of such a paragraph is not formal, but more conversational. It also poses open-ended questions — it's okay at this point if you don't know how to answer them. Some of the ideas are subjective, even judgmental (e.g., the mother is "bossy"), and while this kind of language probably shouldn't make it into a more academic analysis, it's an honest representation of first impressions and an interpretation of the text you'll want to return to and reconsider. In general, though, this kind of informal writing helps bridge the gap between annotating a text with your thoughts and writing an analysis that crafts a literary argument to support your interpretation of the text's meaning. In this case, focusing on the way the mother speaks to the daughter may lead to some ideas about the mother's motivations.

activity

Annotating Short Fiction

Annotate the remainder of "Girl." Consider whether some of the patterns noted in the opening paragraphs continue, but also look for different ways in which Kincaid uses literary elements and techniques to convey the complex relationship between mother and daughter.

Developing a Thesis Statement

Annotation helps you prepare to write, but you won't be able to use every idea you've noted in a focused, coherent close analysis — especially if you have time or length constraints. Even with an assignment as specific as our sample prompt, there's no "right answer" and certainly more than one way to write an effective response. Keep in mind that, as we discussed earlier in the chapter, to interpret a specific aspect of a text you must make an arguable claim about what you think it means and support that claim with evidence from the text. In this case, the prompt is asking you to make a claim about the complex relationship between a mother and her daughter. But, as the prompt states, your essay must link your interpretation of the mother-daughter relationship to literary elements of style. It may help to think of these elements as evidence to support your claim.

In effect, you are building a kind of literary argument with references from the text that show how the language and structure of this story develop and reflect the complexities of the relationship between the narrator, who is a mother, and her daughter. This means that a **thesis statement** that merely restates the prompt will not be effective:

> In "Girl," Jamaica Kincaid uses several literary elements and techniques to convey how social values and traditions shape the complex relationship between the mother and her daughter.

This thesis acknowledges the prompt, but it does not make any progress toward conveying an understanding, much less an interpretation, of how Kincaid develops that complex relationship. A strong thesis also goes beyond a summary of the story:

> In "Girl," by Jamaica Kincaid, the narrator delivers a long list of instructions and rules about the proper behavior expected of her daughter.

The thesis above tells what happens in "Girl" in a general way but fails to identify any literary elements or techniques that Kincaid employs — it's missing insight into the meaning of the story. This is why pure plot description does not leave room for you to develop an analysis.

Furthermore, developing a defensible interpretation by reading a passage closely does not involve your personal opinion about the topic: it focuses on the craft of writing. Thus, a thesis such as this one is inappropriate:

> The way the mother in "Girl" lectures her daughter tells me that she is more concerned about appearances than she is in getting to know her own daughter.

Part of that thesis — the part about the mother's concern for appearances — could develop into an interpretation of the story, but the judgment about the mother is personal opinion and speculation that is difficult to support with evidence from the text. In addition, the use of first person ("tells me") is typically not useful in this kind of analysis because it pulls attention away from the focus of the analysis: the text itself.

An effective thesis will focus on specific characteristics of the story's literary elements of style, so that in the body of the essay you can analyze how they help convey your interpretation of the mother-daughter relationship. However, you must be careful not to make your thesis so narrow that you'll run out of things to say about it as you write your essay:

> In "Girl," Jamaica Kincaid uses a series of clauses that form a single sentence to show how social values and traditions shape the mother's attitude toward her daughter.

Although this thesis identifies a literary element — a syntactical pattern — it's short on analysis. It does not go far enough because there's no interpretation of what that pattern reveals about the story or its characters. What is the mother's "attitude," for instance? The fact that the story is one long complex sentence doesn't automatically tell us the answer to that question. An interpretation of what that syntax is doing — perhaps setting a frantic pace that reveals the mother's anxiety about her daughter coming into her own as a young woman — is key to an effective response to the prompt.

> **AP® TIP**
>
> You can find a copy of the rubric that will be used to score your essay on the AP® Exam at College Board's AP® Central website. It provides a detailed description of what to include—and what not to include—in your thesis statement.

Before you determine what literary elements or techniques you'll discuss, you need to decide on your interpretation of the relationship of the narrator and her daughter: what makes it "complex"? Otherwise, your essay will likely boil down to a list of literary elements that don't relate to each other or convey a larger insight into the story. In this case, let's consider one way to characterize the mother-daughter relationship. Here's the start of a thesis that captures that idea:

> In "Girl," Jamaica Kincaid shows a mother's fierce determination to mold her daughter according to the traditions of their community through the dominating presence of first-person narration, a barrage of scolding commands, and a pattern of syntax that emphasizes accepted norms and values.

This thesis predicts the development of a defensible interpretation of "Girl." One way to read the story is to view the narrator, who values her own community and culture, as someone who wants to prepare her daughter to become an integral part of both things. It also draws on specific aspects of the story's style and structure to back this claim, and if we look at each element the thesis addresses, we see that it has set up an essay that will explore how three different literary elements work together to convey this interpretation.

Supporting Your Thesis

Keep in mind that your initial thesis — what we call a "working thesis" — isn't set in stone and may change as you draft your essay. But a clear working thesis can guide you and serve as a solid essay outline. Your essay can be organized around literary elements and techniques, with one body paragraph on point of view, another on the scolding list of dos and don'ts, another on how syntax reveals the mother's anxiety about how well prepared her daughter will be for adulthood. In each paragraph, make sure you discuss both the element and its effect; do not simply define and illustrate the literary element or technique but explain how it also conveys meaning. Of course, the best thesis in the world is no good unless you have evidence from the text in your body paragraphs to support it.

Writing Topic Sentences

If you've developed a strong thesis statement, you've already hinted at the evidence you plan to gather. Each of the points you make in your thesis will become a topic sentence for your body paragraphs. For example, the topic sentence of the first body paragraph might look like this:

> By presenting the mother as the narrator of the story, and presenting her perspective in what is essentially a monologue, Kincaid emphasizes the mother's authority over her daughter, a "girl" who seems to be coming of age.

This topic sentence links to the thesis without merely repeating it. It also takes a literary technique from the sample thesis and connects it to meaning — in this case, the character of a mother who wants to maintain control over her daughter's behavior, especially because the girl is on the precipice of becoming an independent young adult.

Developing a Line of Reasoning with Evidence from the Text

Once you have the focus of a topic sentence, you can plan the development of the rest of your paragraph. Prose fiction analysis, as you know, requires textual references, either via direct quotations or paraphrased references to the story. When you're writing an analysis or interpretation of a work, the text is your evidence. Quotations that are carefully chosen and incorporated into your own writing provide persuasive support for your thesis.

Take care to avoid quoting big chunks of text because your voice (not the author's) should prevail in a close analysis — that is, you must offer thoughtful commentary on what you quote. One way you might check to make sure that you're analyzing a work is to highlight all your quotations from the text. The following paragraph incorporates quotations from "Girl."

> By presenting the mother as the narrator of the story, and presenting her perspective in what is essentially a monologue, Kincaid emphasizes the mother's authority over her daughter, a "girl," who seems to be coming of age. She says, "Wash the white clothes on Monday and put them on the stone heap; wash the color clothes on Tuesday . . . don't walk barehead in the hot sun; cook pumpkin fritters in very hot sweet oil." The mother asks, "is it true that you sing benna in Sunday school?" and then tells her, "on Sundays try to walk like a lady and not like the slut you are so bent on becoming." The daughter responds by saying, *"but I don't sing benna on Sundays at all and never in Sunday school,"* but her mother doesn't even acknowledge hearing her.

It's true that the quotations from the story are accurate, and they are all — or could be — relevant to the topic sentence. However, except for that topic sentence, this paragraph is almost entirely made up of quotations from "Girl." In fact, it probably feels as though you're rereading the story itself. There is almost no commentary, which leaves the reader without a clear understanding of the paragraph writer's interpretation.

Compare that paragraph with the one that follows. While they share a similar structure and even use some of the same quotations, the original commentary is what moves the following paragraph toward analysis. Notice how the writer interprets the effect and function of the literary elements and techniques that Kincaid has chosen.

> By presenting the mother as the narrator of the story, and presenting her perspective in what is essentially a monologue, Kincaid emphasizes the mother's authority over her daughter, a "girl," who seems to be coming of age. From the first word, the mother is the voice readers hear as she issues one instruction after another: "Wash the white clothes on Monday and put them on the stone heap; wash the color clothes on Tuesday . . . don't

walk barehead in the hot sun." In one of the rare times she shifts from listing instructions and the rules of her community, the mother asks her daughter a question — "is it true that you sing benna in Sunday school?" — but she does not pause a moment to wait for an answer, a point Kincaid emphasizes with a semicolon as her questions to her daughter continue relentlessly. In fact, the mother persists, making a harsh accusation: "on Sundays try to walk like a lady and not like the slut you are so bent on becoming." Kincaid puts the daughter's response in italics, almost as if she is whispering *"but I don't sing benna on Sundays at all and never in Sunday school."* The mother does not respond to her daughter's protests; instead, she continues to hold center stage — a clear signal to the reader that the story isn't about the daughter's behavior so much as it is about the mother's concern that her daughter may not grow up to follow the rules, stated or unstated, of the community.

Notice how the highlighted parts of the paragraph are spread out, and the paragraph is no longer overrun by the quotations. Instead, the essay writer's commentary shines through. The writer's explanations of why those quotations support the topic sentence of the paragraph form a line of reasoning that supports the writer's interpretation of the story. The evidence that quotations provide is always important — you can't perform a close analysis without going back into the text in this way — but evidence on its own is not convincing. Readers need you to explain why it matters.

Writing a Body Paragraph of an AP® Prose Fiction Analysis Essay

Choose one of the other two points in our sample thesis (p. 43). Then, write a body paragraph that uses textual evidence from "Girl" and commentary to support the overall interpretation of the story as a study of the complex relationships between the mother and daughter.

Revising an AP® Prose Fiction Analysis Essay

Revision is a vital step in the writing process. While at times it can seem difficult, it is always worthwhile — taking time to reflect on your work can provide new insight. It also doesn't have to be a task you grapple with alone. With the benefit of feedback from a good critical reader, whether peer or teacher, you will also be able to see your work with fresh eyes. Revising from that vantage point will give you a leg up for your next draft, and your argument will emerge stronger than before. Keep in mind that you don't have to follow every suggestion for revision you are given, but most are worth considering.

The process of revision is more than proofreading. Of course, it's absolutely essential that you reread carefully to catch grammatical errors and learn to edit yourself by scrutinizing the language you're using — your own diction and syntax. But this is revising at the micro level. The most satisfying revision comes from taking the word literally: *re-vision* — that is, looking at your entire essay in a new light.

Rethinking basic parts of your argument, including your presentation of that argument, is where the real work comes in. You may find the following questions helpful for guiding your revision of a prose fiction analysis essay:

- **Reread the entire essay for comprehension.** Is there a clear line of reasoning that puts forth an argument for your interpretation of the passage or story?
- **Reread your introduction and thesis statement.** Is the thesis clear? Have you taken a position that goes beyond summary or paraphrase? Does it respond to the prompt by presenting an argument for how literary elements and techniques create meaning?
- **Reread each topic sentence.** Does it accurately reflect a claim in your thesis? Does it provide a bridge between the line of reasoning in your thesis and the evidence in the paragraph?
- **Check your evidence.** Do the quotations you've chosen to use clearly support the claim in the topic sentence of each body paragraph?
- **Evaluate your commentary.** Does it explain the relationship between the textual evidence you've selected and the topic sentence in the body paragraphs?
- **Reread for spelling and grammar.** Do you have run-ons? Misspelled words?
- **Read your writing aloud to yourself.** Does it sound right? Can you tighten anything up?
- **If possible, step away from it.** Clear your mind for a few hours — a day if you can. Return to your work with fresh eyes as a reader instead of as the writer.
- **Reread one final time with a clear head.** Just a tune-up. Are there small changes you can make to improve word choice and sentence structure?

Analyzing a Sample AP® Prose Fiction Analysis Essay

The following student essay responds to the prompt we introduced on page 38. As you read it, think about how you would provide feedback to help this student revise her draft.

"Girl"

Selin Selcuker

In her short story "Girl," Jamaica Kincaid comments on society's values through a mother's expectations for her daughter. Her words offer a series of demonstrations of how to act like a proper woman of society, placing femininity as a top priority for young girls. Kincaid's short story shapes the complex relationship between the mother and her daughter by the usage of informal diction that contrasts the formality of the mother's expectations, the accusatory tone of the mother, and the parallel structure evoking the strong feelings of the mother toward her daughter's success.

A mother's role is to provide her daughter with the tools she needs to succeed in society without her. The mother in the story does just that: she offers clear, demonstrative directions to her daughter aiming to implement proper behavior. Yet, this is done so using informal diction and in a conversational manner. Adding in elements such as "you know" and "if you feel like it" creates a casual tone in the mother's voice that actually contradicts what the mother is saying. The picture painted by the mother of social values through her expectations is very proper. The mother goes as far as to demonstrate "how you smile to someone you don't like too much" suggesting that societal values are just for show. The mother's contradiction of herself from her actions to her words amplifies the external importance of tradition within society. As a result, the daughter is led to confusion, as she is told to act proper and presentable at all times yet is being shown the hidden reality of society by her mother.

The mother and daughter's tense relationship is illustrated by the accusatory tone of the mother. As she continuously barks out instructions to her daughter, the mother occasionally interrupts herself to accuse her daughter of something. These accusations often ring on the idea of being a "slut." The mother is so insistent on the idea that her daughter is "so bent on becoming" a "slut," yet offers no examples of times that her daughter acted as one. Their society is defined by a right and a wrong, and to be a "slut" is categorized in the wrong. The accusations created by the mother highlight the tensions between the mother and the daughter in which the conversation is very limited. The mother asks "is it true that you sing benna in Sunday school?," yet is not really expecting a response as she doesn't offer time for her daughter to respond and actually ignores her daughter's short interjected response. Given that the daughter is not given a true chance to explain herself, the relationship between the mother and daughter is thus a very hierarchical relationship in which "Mother is always right" and what is said by the mother goes.

The mother's passion for her daughter's success is exemplified by the parallel structure used at the start of her instructions, amplifying her desires for her daughter's future. The words "this is" repeat very often in the mother's instructions. The repeated usage of these demonstratives highlights not only the knowledge of the mother being shared with the daughter but also stress of the importance of her being able to do these actions as well. Societal tradition clearly puts emphasis on specifics, and the mother wants her daughter to adhere to these specifics as well. A sonic effect is created by the structure with a very sharp rhythm, indicating the mother is not pausing and is almost going through a list. The mother does not steer away from her goal of educating her daughter at any point by consecutively demonstrating tasks to her daughter, highlighting the image of herself she wants her daughter to portray.

The future actions of her daughter reflect on the mother's teachings. The mother's emphasis on her daughter's future suggests their society's focus on women staying home for the cooking and for the kids. It is likely that once her daughter grows up, she will have the same expectations for her future daughter. Her final sentence, "you mean to say that after all you are really going to be the kind of woman who the baker won't let near the bread?" emphasizes that the mother has a precise plan for her daughter and that each of her demonstrations had a specific intent: to paint society's "perfect" woman.

Providing Peer Feedback for Revision

Carefully read the student sample essay on "Girl" and answer the following questions for revision.

Questions for Revision

1. What is the greatest strength of this literary interpretation? Why?
2. In what ways is the thesis strong enough to preview and sustain the argument? How might it be improved?
3. Which paragraph do you think has the most persuasive analysis? Why?
4. What is one place where the writer incorporates textual evidence well and provides effective commentary?
5. Where does the writer's textual evidence and commentary need more development? Explain why the additions would improve the clarity and persuasiveness of the argument.
6. To what extent does the concluding paragraph answer the "so what?" question about the student's interpretation of the story? How might that paragraph be improved to leave a lasting impression?

section 2 / culminating activity

Crafting an AP® Prose Fiction Analysis Essay

The following question refers to an excerpt from Edith Wharton's *The House of Mirth*, published in 1905. In this passage, Lily Bart, a woman determined to ensure her position in upper-class society by marrying a wealthy man, is meeting with Lawrence Selden, an intellectual with modest resources. Read the passage carefully. Then, in a well-written essay, analyze how Wharton uses literary elements and techniques to depict Lily's complex and conflicting emotions about her relationship with Selden.

from The House of Mirth

Edith Wharton

The afternoon was perfect. A deeper stillness possessed the air, and the glitter of the American autumn was tempered by a haze which diffused the brightness without dulling it.

In the woody hollows of the park there was already a faint chill; but as the ground rose the air grew lighter, and ascending the long slopes beyond the high-road, Lily and her companion reached a zone of lingering summer. The path wound across a meadow with scattered trees; then it dipped into a lane plumed with asters and purpling sprays of bramble, whence, through the light quiver of ash-leaves, the country unrolled itself in pastoral distances. . . .

Lily had no real intimacy with nature, but she had a passion for the appropriate and could be keenly sensitive to a scene which was the fitting background of her own sensations. The landscape outspread below her seemed an enlargement of her present mood, and she found something of herself in its calmness, its breadth, its long free reaches. On the nearer slopes the sugar-maples wavered like pyres of light; lower down was a massing of grey orchards, and here and there the lingering green of an oak-grove. Two or three red farm-houses dozed under the apple-trees, and the white wooden spire of a village church showed beyond the shoulder of the hill; while far below, in a haze of dust, the high-road ran between the fields.

"Let us sit here," Selden suggested, as they reached an open ledge of rock above which the beeches rose steeply between mossy boulders.

Lily dropped down on the rock, glowing with her long climb. She sat quiet, her lips parted by the stress of the ascent, her eyes wandering peacefully over the broken ranges of the landscape. Selden stretched himself on the grass at her feet, tilting his hat against the level sun-rays, and clasping his hands behind his head, which rested against the side of the rock. He had no wish to make her talk; her quick-breathing silence seemed a part of the general hush and harmony of things. In his own mind there was only a lazy sense of pleasure, veiling the sharp edges of sensation as the September haze veiled the scene at their feet. But Lily, though her attitude was as calm as his, was throbbing inwardly with a rush of thoughts. There were in her at the moment two beings, one drawing deep breaths of freedom and exhilaration, the other gasping for air in a little black prison-house of fears. But gradually the captive's gasps grew fainter, or the other paid less heed to them: the horizon expanded, the air grew stronger, and the free spirit quivered for flight.

She could not herself have explained the sense of buoyancy which seemed to lift and swing her above the sun-suffused world at her feet. Was it love, she wondered, or a mere fortuitous combination of happy thoughts and sensations? How much of it was owing to the spell of the perfect afternoon, the scent of the fading woods, the thought of the dullness she had fled from? Lily had no definite experience by which to test the quality of her feelings. She had several times been in love with fortunes or careers, but only once with a man. . . . If Lily recalled this early emotion it was not to compare it with that which now possessed her; the only point of comparison was the sense of lightness, of emancipation, which she remembered feeling, in the whirl of a waltz or the seclusion of a conservatory, during the brief course of her youthful romance. She had not known again till today that lightness, that glow of freedom; but now it was something more than a blind groping of the blood. The peculiar charm of her feeling for Selden was that she understood it; she could put her finger on every link of the chain that was drawing them together. ■

1905

Developing Sophistication in an AP® Prose Fiction Analysis Essay

Throughout this chapter, we have emphasized that rarely, if ever, is there only one defensible interpretation of a literary work. To interpret fiction and craft literary arguments, we examine the text carefully to uncover its meaning and cite concrete details from the text to support our interpretation of that meaning. As you have likely noticed, some interpretations arise from a deep and creative reading of the text, while others are more straightforward. A straightforward reading that reveals a basic understanding of the text is an important component of analysis — without this level of engagement with the text, you don't have solid ground underneath you to build on. The strongest literary arguments, however, show a more sophisticated understanding of the text at hand. What makes a literary argument sophisticated? The answer to this question can be both frustrating and freeing. There's no single "right" way to develop a sophisticated and nuanced interpretation of a work of literature — but there are several approaches you can apply to your own reading and writing that will help you do so. In this section we'll take a look at one way to develop sophistication in a prose fiction analysis essay: by recognizing the complexities and tensions within a work.

AP® TIP

Developing sophistication in your writing is not a skill you're expected to master immediately. It requires practice and even some risk-taking, especially because "sophistication" is an abstract concept. Throughout the school year, experiment with the suggestions provided in this textbook as you work on incorporating sophistication into your essays.

Keep in mind that developing sophistication in literary analysis takes practice in reading literature, reading writing about that literature, and writing about that literature yourself. Like any skill, it is one you can work on and eventually master. Another important building block of sophisticated analysis is rereading, perhaps multiple times, to keep working at an understanding of the ideas the writer is exploring in a passage or short story. Above all, sophistication involves approaching literature less as a place to find "answers" and more as a source of questions and possibilities.

Analyzing Complexities and Tensions within a Text

A solid interpretation of a passage or short story may analyze how the author's choices of literary elements and techniques reveal one aspect of, or one way of seeing, a character's motivations, for instance. This approach still requires you to read closely and think critically to arrive at a unique interpretation of a character in a narrative. A more sophisticated approach looks for how literary elements reveal multiple, often conflicting or even contradictory, aspects of characters' motivations and relationship dynamics. A more sophisticated interpretation could identify and explore stresses and strains within the character and connect those complications to your overall interpretation of the text. Often, this kind of re-evaluation of a text leads you to revise or expand your original interpretation. It can introduce ambiguity to your argument, and it should add another layer to your first reading of the text.

Keep in mind that when you have the opportunity to reread or discuss a text with others, you may notice what at first appear to be inconsistencies in a character's motivations, or even just thoughts and behavior that strike you as out of place. These are the places to look closer. Often, such spots are where the author has introduced tensions in the text — and these tensions both reveal a character's conflicting feelings or motivations and shape that character's relationships with others. Such ambivalence adds depth and interest to a character; in fact, it also often makes characters seem more like real people, since our lives and relationships are rich and complex, too. What the author could be doing, for instance, is exploring what happens to us when an inclination for duty exists along with a desire for freedom. Seeing how a character resolves or fails to resolve such tensions is often the basis of a sophisticated interpretation of fiction.

Qualifying Your Argument

If you're revising an essay you've already written, this doesn't mean you have to throw your work out and start over. Developing sophistication is about expanding and deepening your existing argument throughout the entire essay. The most reliable way to ensure you develop a more sophisticated interpretation when you revise is to start with the thesis. Once you have done this, you can proceed paragraph by paragraph to incorporate new commentary on the textual evidence you've selected to support your thesis. A word of caution: waiting until the conclusion to add this additional layer of depth to your analysis will not give you enough of an opportunity to develop your interpretation thoroughly — while it may provoke thought and provide new insight into the text, you won't be able to demonstrate how your nuanced view applies to the text itself. Think of it as a cliffhanger: engaging, but unfulfilling without anything to follow it.

Let's walk through how you might revise the sample working thesis for Kincaid's story, "Girl," to better incorporate sophistication. The original thesis reads:

> In "Girl," Jamaica Kincaid shows a mother's fierce determination to mold her daughter according to the traditions of their community through the dominating presence of first-person narration, a barrage of scolding commands, and a pattern of syntax that emphasizes accepted norms and values.

This thesis is strong: it provides an outline for a defensible interpretation of how literary elements and techniques reveal the complexity of the relationship between a mother and her daughter, who is coming of age. It focuses solely, however, on the mother's motivation to provide her daughter with strict guidelines for conventional behavior, specifically behavior expected of women. How might we use this as a starting point for a more sophisticated and nuanced argument?

Let's first revisit the idea that interpretations are arguable — which means that any interpretation you've developed can lead to other possibilities, too. One approach to deepening your interpretation is to argue with yourself, maybe even pretend to disagree with your thesis, and see where that takes you. Keep in mind, though, that the goal is not necessarily to abandon or reject your interpretation outright but rather to add nuance to it. In a way, you're asking, "What if . . .?" Doing this qualifies your argument—that is, it shows you're considering multiple ways to approach and ultimately interpret a text.

The original thesis presents the mother through the lens of domination, a desire to make her daughter follow a certain path to respectability as the mother defines it. But what about that overwhelming love that we usually associate with motherhood? How does that translate into the "domination"? If you explore that question, you might start to see the mother's motivation, in telling her daughter how to become a certain kind of woman, is to protect her daughter, maybe even to nurture a certain kind of independence. Maybe the mother herself feels the tension between wanting to offer love and protection and the urgency of telling the daughter important rules of behavior in the society where she lives. Let's take a look at how we can adjust the original example thesis to allow for a more nuanced view of the mother:

> In "Girl" by Jamaica Kincaid, a mother's dominating presence, barrage of scolding commands, and a pattern of syntax that emphasize accepted norms and values show a mother's determination to mold the "girl" into traditional gender roles; a closer look, however, reveals a protective mother's determination to encourage her daughter's independent spirit.

This revised thesis goes right to the heart of two sets of tensions in "Girl": love vs. domination and conformity vs. independence. Each of these tensions feels on the surface like a binary conflict where one or the other should prevail (or "win"), although that's rarely the case. In fact, body paragraphs that follow from this thesis would analyze how the mother's actions (and her words) embody what appear to be contrasts. Exploring these tensions requires a sophistication of thought about the short story — especially the character of the mother.

Here, for instance, is a possible body paragraph in an essay guided by the thesis we've just discussed.

> Throughout the story, the mother issues stern directives that provide advice about how her daughter should behave in order to take her place as a vital part of her community. She delivers a barrage of imperative verbs of what to do and not to do: "Wash the white clothes on Monday . . . cook pumpkin fritters in very hot sweet oil . . . sew on a button . . ." — all chores requiring the conformity expected of women in the traditional role of housekeepers and likely of wives and mothers. However, the mother also advises her daughter on ways to take control of her life by, for instance, knowing how to "smile to

someone you don't like at all" and "how you smile to someone you like completely." She reminds her daughter "how to love a man," yet reassures her that if it doesn't work, "don't feel too bad about giving up." Perhaps ironically, while this girl's mother sounds as though she's trying to assert her power over her daughter, she's modeling, in her own way, the power she wants her daughter to have. Thus, when she expresses shock that her daughter might become "the kind of woman who the baker won't let near the bread," it's clear that her goal is not a compliant daughter. Paradoxically, as she seems to drown out her daughter's voice, she is actually challenging her to become a confident, self-reliant woman.

While not everyone would agree with this interpretation, the paragraph draws on textual evidence to support a complex reading of the mother's behavior and language, and the essay writer's commentary thoughtfully defends this line of reasoning. Kincaid doesn't give us a back story for the mother, nor does she offer details of the mother's experiences in her earlier life. We see one glimpse in "Girl," and an interpretation has to be based on what we know from the narrative voice, the form of a monologue that is one long sentence, and the choices of diction and syntax. By focusing on tensions that ask "what if?" rather than explaining a single motivation, this essay paragraph develops into a more complex literary argument. It's an argument that recognizes and explores the skill of the author, Jamaica Kincaid, to draw her readers in to consider some unexpected possibilities.

section 3 / culminating activity

Developing Sophistication in an AP® Prose Fiction Analysis Essay

Revise the essay that you wrote on the passage from *The House of Mirth* by Edith Wharton (p. 48) to develop a more sophisticated line of reasoning in your interpretation. As you revise, focus on identifying and exploring complexities or tensions within the passage.

2

Analyzing Poetry

The language and structure of poetry are often more compressed than prose; most poems say a lot in a small amount of space. While both forms of writing convey meaning that runs deeper than the literal, the stories, emotions, and ideas that poetry expresses often seem much less straightforward. However, many poems do contain familiar narrative arcs, and all poetry uses language that is rich and rewards an active reader. Every word matters, which is why it's a good idea to read a poem more than once in a sitting. Of course, the most important step — even before the ones we offer in this chapter — is to open your heart and mind to the emotional effects of the work, which will be both satisfying and helpful in getting you started.

As you read poetry, keep in mind some of the ways you will be asked to respond to it. Nearly always, you will be asked to analyze a poem — in other words, you must interpret not just *what* a poem means, but *how* that meaning is created. Often, this will involve analyzing the speaker's attitude toward an idea expressed in the poem. You may also be asked to examine how elements of the poem connect to a larger meaning or to analyze the relationship between two ideas in a single poem. Another common objective of close analysis is to study more than one poem at a time, typically through comparison and contrast of the ways each work treats a common theme or idea. Above all, the key to close analysis is making connections between style and meaning.

In this chapter, we suggest three steps you can use to help you begin the study of a new poem:

1. First, we recommend reading a poem at its most literal level to form a basic understanding of it — this will help you discover the poem's main subject and provide the foundation for your analysis.

2. Second, we will show you how to identify and characterize the speaker of a poem, along with how to explore relationships among ideas, such as contrasts, that help signal the speaker's attitude toward the subject. This will help form the basis of your interpretation of a poem's meaning.
3. Third, we will walk you through how to read a poem for its style details, demonstrating how each of the major poetic elements of style contributes to a poem's meaning. This last step is crucial: it connects style to meaning by providing evidence for your interpretation of the poem — no close analysis is complete without it.

Usually, you will be asked to put your analysis in writing, and this process directly connects to how we approach reading poetry in this chapter. When you write a close analysis essay, you start with the larger ideas you've discovered and use the small details — the words themselves and how they're arranged — to support your interpretation of the meaning of the piece. Later in the chapter, we illustrate how to craft a thesis statement and write an effective close analysis essay, including strategies for organizing the essay and guidance on how to integrate quotations seamlessly into your writing. Let's start with some strategies for approaching a poem on your first read-through.

Section 1

Reading for Literal Meaning

Before you can begin to analyze a poem, you must identify its subject. In other words, what is the poem about? Your answer should distill the poem's main idea or ideas into a sentence, phrase, or even just a word — this short summary will provide the foundation for your interpretation of its meaning.

While they can be easy to overlook, titles often provide key words that help reveal a poem's subject. A poem's title sometimes even serves as its first line, and untitled poems also raise questions about why the poet made such a choice. Keep in mind, too, that titles can be misleading, ironic, or indirect. Taking note of the title is just one of many approaches to understanding a poem, and it should happen alongside the other reading strategies we include here, including considering questions such as the following.

KEY QUESTIONS

Reading Poetry for Literal Meaning

- What is happening in the poem?
- What do you visualize as you read?
- What does it make you think about?
- What is your emotional reaction?

With those questions in mind, let's take a look at "Digging," by Nobel Laureate Seamus Heaney.

Digging

Seamus Heaney

Between my finger and my thumb
The squat pen rests; snug as a gun.

Under my window, a clean rasping sound
When the spade sinks into gravelly ground:
My father, digging. I look down

Till his straining rump among the flowerbeds
Bends low, comes up twenty years away
Stooping in rhythm through potato drills
Where he was digging.

The coarse boot nestled on the lug, the shaft
Against the inside knee was levered firmly.
He rooted out tall tops, buried the bright edge deep
To scatter new potatoes that we picked
Loving their cool hardness in our hands.

By God, the old man could handle a spade.
Just like his old man.

My grandfather cut more turf in a day
Than any other man on Toner's bog.
Once I carried him milk in a bottle
Corked sloppily with paper. He straightened up
To drink it, then fell to right away
Nicking and slicing neatly, heaving sods
Over his shoulder, going down and down
For the good turf. Digging.

The cold smell of potato mould, the squelch and slap
Of soggy peat, the curt cuts of an edge
Through living roots awaken in my head.
But I've no spade to follow men like them.

Between my finger and my thumb
The squat pen rests.
I'll dig with it. ■

1966

As you begin to think about "Digging," remember to consider the title; it provides a useful clue about the poem's subject. In "Digging," the title is only part of the story — we know by the second line that the poem's speaker is holding a pen, not a shovel — but it gives us a way into the poem by raising questions for the reader to explore: who's digging, and why?

While it can often feel natural to pause at the end of each line of a poem as you would at the end of a sentence in prose, you should check for full sentences that extend past the line and stanza breaks — especially if you find that the poem is confusing or difficult to follow. These full sentences may reveal a story that you didn't see at first. Notice that, in "Digging," the poem's first stanza (see p. 57) can be read as one sentence:

> Between my finger and my thumb the squat pen rests; snug as a gun.

The poem's second sentence ends in the middle of line 5:

> Under my window, a clean rasping sound when the spade sinks into gravelly ground: my father, digging.

The next sentence goes on until line 9:

> I look down till his straining rump among the flowerbeds bends low, comes up twenty years away stooping in rhythm through potato drills where he was digging.

Follow the pattern yourself on your next read-through. After one or two readings, you've probably noticed that "Digging" is about more than just digging. In fact, there's a story here — one that spans generations but is compressed into just fifteen sentences:

> Between my finger and my thumb the squat pen rests; snug as a gun. Under my window, a clean rasping sound when the spade sinks into gravelly ground: my father, digging. I look down till his straining rump among the flowerbeds bends low, comes up twenty years away stooping in rhythm through potato drills where he was digging. The coarse boot nestled on the lug, the shaft against the inside knee was levered firmly. He rooted out tall tops, buried the bright edge deep to scatter new potatoes that we picked, loving their cool hardness in our hands. By God, the old man could handle a spade. Just like his old man. My grandfather cut more turf in a day than any other man on Toner's bog. Once I carried him milk in a bottle corked sloppily with paper. He straightened up to drink it, then fell to right away nicking and slicing neatly, heaving sods over his shoulder, going down and down for the good turf. Digging. The cold smell of potato mould, the squelch and slap of soggy peat, the curt cuts of an edge through living roots awaken in my head. But I've no spade to follow men like them. Between my finger and my thumb the squat pen rests. I'll dig with it.

You may discover, after breaking a poem down into sentences, that you can immediately identify its subject. However, if this is not the case, another useful exercise to try — particularly when a poem's narrative does not appear to be linear, or when it does not appear to follow any narrative pattern whatsoever — is paraphrasing. Putting the poem in your own words may make it easier to spot whether it has a narrative arc, and if so, to identify its most important aspects. This will help clarify the poem's subject. A paraphrase of "Digging," for example, may look something like this:

> **AP® TIP**
> Since the AP® exam is timed, you can't stop to paraphrase or to reread a poem as often as you'd like. Practicing these processes during the year, however, will help you gain the skills and confidence to develop an analysis quickly.

> The speaker is holding a pen and looks out his window, maybe taking a break from writing, where he sees his father in the garden. The speaker then remembers his father digging potatoes twenty years earlier. His father was very good at digging potatoes. This observation brings to mind his grandfather cutting turf and a time that the speaker brought him some milk. The speaker remembers the smells he associates with digging potatoes and turf. The speaker doesn't dig turf or potatoes. He is a writer and uses a pen to dig.

Once you've paraphrased a poem, you can take a step back and look at the bigger picture. What stands out most in this paraphrase? In this case, we can see that the poem's subject is more complex than the simple act of digging. The speaker's connection to his family, and his family's connection to the land, is clear: the bulk of the paragraph is about his observation of his father and grandfather physically digging into the earth in a few different outdoor settings. In this paraphrase the speaker's present-day actions come into focus only in the first sentence and again in the final two. The contrast between what the speaker is doing and what he is observing is stark. In both places, the speaker is clearly not performing manual labor; instead, he carries a pen. When he uses his pen to dig, he does not mean in the literal sense. Based on this information, here's one way you might phrase the subject of the poem:

> In "Digging," the speaker's thoughts about his father and grandfather lead him to contemplate different ways of digging.

Reading a Poem for Literal Meaning

Read Christina Rossetti's "Promises like Pie-Crust," keeping in mind that the title reflects an old English proverb: "Promises are like pie-crust, made to be broken." Paraphrase the poem and identify its subject.

(*continued*)

Promises like Pie-Crust

Christina Georgina Rossetti

Promise me no promises,
So will I not promise you;
Keep we both our liberties,
Never false and never true:
Let us hold the die uncast,
Free to come as free to go;
For I cannot know your past,
And of mine what can you know?

You, so warm, may once have been
Warmer towards another one;
I, so cold, may once have seen
Sunlight, once have felt the sun:
Who shall show us if it was
Thus indeed in time of old?
Fades the image from the glass
And the fortune is not told.

If you promised, you might grieve
For lost liberty again;
If I promised, I believe
I should fret to break the chain:
Let us be the friends we were,
Nothing more but nothing less;
Many thrive on frugal fare
Who would perish of excess. ■

1861

Considering the Speaker: Analyzing Contrasts

Once you have identified the subject of a poem, the next step is to think about who the **speaker** is. A poem's speaker provides its "voice"; when we read a poem, we are viewing the world from the speaker's perspective. It may be tempting to jump to the conclusion that the speaker and poet are the same, but most often the speaker is a **persona**, or character, created by the poet. And even when the speaker is the poet, it's often the poet in a particular mood, with a particular purpose or attitude, telling a particular story at a particular time. In "Digging," we can guess that the speaker is a writer — he's got a pen in his hand. The poem begins with him at his desk looking out the window. By the end of the poem we know the speaker wants to communicate something more than that he is taking a break from writing; interestingly, the focus comes back to the pen he uses to do his work.

> **AP® TIP**
> Keep in mind that the poet is not the same as the speaker. The poet uses the voice of the speaker — sometimes called a persona — to communicate ideas or emotions about a particular topic.

Developing a clear view or understanding of the speaker is the first step toward clarifying his or her attitude toward the poem's subject. You can do this in the same way you learn about character in prose: what the speaker says, what the speaker does, what the other figures present in a poem say or think about the speaker all reveal the speaker's perspective. Your understanding of the speaker's perspective on the poem's subject will form the basis for your interpretation of the poem's meaning.

The speaker's attitude toward the subject of a poem is sometimes revealed through contrasts. This is because poetry as a genre often deals with ambiguities and nuances of human experience. In other words, the speaker often has mixed feelings about the subject of the poem — even if those feelings aren't directly in conflict, they're still layered and complex. Thus, being on the lookout for contrasts helps us fully consider the complexity of a poem's meaning. How do we spot contrasts? Look for words, phrases, or ideas that strike you as contradictory, at least on first read. From there, you can use some of the approaches we discuss in the following section to arrive at an interpretation of what those contrasts mean.

One final thing to keep in mind as we begin to close read poetry is that a poem can be interpreted in several ways — because meaning is complex, and because every reader is a unique person, there is no single "right" way to approach deciphering the speaker's attitude toward the subject. Your job is to defend your interpretation of a poem's meaning with evidence from the work itself. Let's look at "Digging" again as a poem, not just a group of sentences or a short paraphrase. How does the subject — family and different ways of digging — connect with the speaker's perspective? What contrasts stand out, and what do they reveal about the speaker? Let's discuss some elements that are key to understanding the speaker's attitude.

Diction

Writers of poetry make conscious word choices, depending on the connotations and denotations of the words they choose. **Denotation** refers to a word's explicit meaning, while **connotation** refers to the associations a word carries. Together, these word choices work in concert to create **diction**. Literary language is richer than everyday language, so reading poetry requires bringing those associations to the surface, while at the same time remaining alert to the concrete meanings of the words in the poem.

A poem's diction provides a direct link to the speaker's attitude, and, in turn, some of the poem's more profound ideas. As you consider diction, try to locate the words with strong connotations and think about how these added layers affect the poem's meaning.

> **AP® TIP**
>
> Remember, the writer's language choices don't merely help you understand the speaker's experiences. These choices come together to convey a larger message.

If you're not sure how to find the diction that gives a poem its depth and power, look for word choices that appeal to one or more of your five senses. In "Digging," for instance, Heaney uses words that create rich, immediate visual images for the reader: the "squat pen" (l. 2), the "gravelly ground" (l. 4), his father's "straining rump" (l. 6), the "bright edge" of the shovel (l. 12), and the recurrence of the "squat pen" at the end of the poem (l. 30). Consider how those words develop the character of the speaker and affect how we see his father and grandfather. They are typically associated with hard, sharp, and solid surfaces; they not only point to the difficulty of manual labor, but also highlight the physical strength of the speaker's father and grandfather.

Many of Heaney's other word choices relate to sound: the "clean rasping sound" (l. 3) of the speaker's father digging in the garden mirrors the "nicking and slicing" (l. 22) of his grandfather's shovel as it cuts through turf. The "squelch and slap" (l. 25) made by the soggy peat when his grandfather heaved it over his shoulder is less mechanical, but no less vivid — all of these sounds remind the reader that the digging the speaker's family has traditionally done is physically demanding.

Throughout the poem, Heaney's diction emphasizes the speaker's connections to rural Irish life and conveys what are, for him, the familiar sounds of home. His language choices portray the speaker as a man who admires his father and grandfather and has deep respect for the grueling work they have done. The title, "Digging," a word used several times in the poem, has connotations as well — such as depth or discovery — and invites us to consider how a poet could dig.

> **KEY QUESTIONS**
>
> **Analyzing Diction**
>
> - Which of the important words (verbs, nouns, adjectives, and adverbs) in the poem are general and abstract, and which are specific and concrete?
> - Are important words and phrases formal, informal, colloquial, or slang?
> - Are there words with strong connotations, words we might refer to as "loaded"? What are those connotations?
> - How do the poet's word choices appeal to one or more of your senses?

Juxtaposition, Antithesis, and Paradox

The contrasts that are usually easiest to spot are the ones that appear right next to each other. Poetry often contains such **juxtapositions** — placing two words or concepts side by side, often to emphasize their incongruity — that reveal the speaker's attitude toward the subject. The juxtaposition of the speaker's pen and his father's and grandfather's shovels in "Digging," for instance, draws our attention to the relationship between these men and how their work shapes the speaker's understanding of their lives, and his own. It places questions about the speaker's relationship to his family and the past front and center in the reader's mind.

Sometimes juxtapositions create **antithesis**, revealing contradictory ideas that often by using parallel grammatical construction. For instance, in Christina Rossetti's "Promises like Pie-Crust" (p. 60), the following lines present antithesis:

> If you promised, you might grieve
>   For lost liberty again;
> If I promised, I believe
>   I should fret to break the chain:

Here, the speaker uses parallel structure to juxtapose the "lost liberty" of a romantic relationship with the anguish that "break[ing] the chain" would bring her. The only course of action guaranteed to bring both the speaker and the person she is addressing happiness is to remain just friends.

Finally, you might spot juxtaposed ideas that at first appear to contradict each other. Instead, these elements reveal a deeper meaning. This is called a **paradox**. A paradox made of two seemingly contradictory words—such as "deafening silence" or "sweet sorrow" — is called an **oxymoron**.

KEY QUESTIONS

Analyzing Juxtaposition, Antithesis, and Paradox

- Where do you spot contrasts in close proximity to each other?
- How do these contrasts reveal a deeper meaning, especially in terms of the speaker's attitude toward the subject of the poem?
- Are there any juxtaposed words or concepts that at first appear to contradict each other? If so, what message do they convey to the reader?

Shifts

When we think about the speaker's attitude toward the subject of a poem, it can also be helpful to look at the **shifts**, which indicate some kind of change, often in the speaker's perspective. If you're not immediately clear on where shifts are occurring in a poem, try looking for words, such as qualifiers, which set parameters for the things they're describing. Poetry is unlikely to use the qualifiers you might find in expository writing, such as *whereas* or *however*, but be on the lookout for words such as *but* and *yet*. Another thing to keep an eye out for is punctuation — an unexpected question mark, for example, can be a clue that the speaker is changing tack. You might see a shift in verb tense, such as a shift from past to present. Or there might be a shift in tone — from exuberant to melancholy, maybe — or even a change in speaker or perspective. Spotting these shifts can help focus your analysis.

AP® TIP

As you read the poems on the exam, you may want to circle words like *yet*, *but*, *still*, and *though*. These words often signal a shift in tone, mood, perspective, and/or meaning.

You'll notice that "Digging" starts in the present tense, with the speaker looking out the window and seeing his father digging in the flowerbeds. But when his father "comes up twenty years away," the tense changes to the past and stays there for the next three stanzas. The second-to-last stanza of the poem moves back to the present, and the final line is in the future tense. The speaker has, perhaps, used these memories to consider his own vocation and its connection to the work done by his father and grandfather.

You might also have seen another series of shifts: from reality (the speaker looking out his window) to memory (those cool hard potatoes) and imagination (from the flowerbeds to the potato drills) and even to legend ("My grandfather cut more turf in a day / Than any other man on Toner's bog"). The speaker sifts through these memories and myths to see where he fits. These shifts in tenses might suggest that despite the passing of time and the flexibility of memory, the speaker feels close to his father and grandfather, and can conjure their presence when he needs to.

You may detect yet another shift in the tone of the second-to-last stanza, which begins with describing a sort of unpleasant quality to the grandfather's digging: "the squelch and slap / Of soggy peat, the curt cuts of an edge." Line 28, however, begins with the qualifier *but*: "But I've no spade to follow men like them." Could there be a sense of relief? The speaker, unlike the other men in his family, will work indoors, at a desk, looking out a window.

KEY QUESTIONS

Analyzing Shifts

- What words in the poem are qualifiers? How do these affect meaning?
- Do any punctuation choices, such as question marks, stand out to you? How might these signal a shift in the speaker's perspective?
- Does the tone change as the poem progresses, or does it remain the same?

Analyzing Contrasts

The following poem by Lucille Clifton was published posthumously in 2020. Read the poem carefully and analyze how the diction and contrasts convey the speaker's attitude toward her coat.

poem to my yellow coat

Lucille Clifton

today i mourn my coat.
my old potato.
my yellow mother.
my horse with buttons.

my rind.
today she split her skin
like a snake,
refusing to excuse my back
for being big
for being old
for reaching toward other
cuffs and sleeves.
she cracked like a whip and
fell apart,
my terrible teacher to the end;
to hell with the arms you want
she hissed,
be glad when you're cold
for the arms you have. ■

2020

Tone and Mood

The speaker's attitude toward the subject of a poem is expressed by the poem's tone and mood. **Tone** provides the emotional coloring of a work and is a direct reflection of the speaker's attitude; diction is often the primary contributor to a poem's tone, but all of the writer's style choices affect it. **Mood** is the feeling the reader experiences as a result of the tone. If you are unsure of how to read a poem's tone, its mood — the way you feel about it — will help point you in the right direction. For instance, the speaker's description of his memories in "Digging" might call to mind your own childhood or family history and the nostalgia typically associated with times past. The fact that both you and the speaker are sitting comfortably (you are reading; the speaker is writing) while his family labors outside may sharpen your view of the contrast between the speaker's occupation and that of his forebears. And that contrast may help you identify the tone of the poem.

There are many other ways to identify the tone of a work, and if you have a solid understanding of the poem's subject and the identity of its speaker, the tone may be clear to you before you begin to look closely at the poet's language choices. But, as we mentioned earlier, examining a poem's diction is an excellent place to start, and "Digging" is no exception. Throughout the poem, the speaker uses words that connote strength and ruggedness to describe his father and grandfather — these choices suggest he admires them, and his admiration implies he may be nostalgic for an earlier time. This same language also communicates the difficulty of the work, and the phrases that appeal to the reader's sense of sound bring home the fact that the men in the speaker's family have traditionally made their living from arduous physical labor. Despite the fact that the speaker describes his pen as a blunt, "squat" instrument — not unlike a shovel — the contrast between the digging his father and grandfather have done and the digging the speaker plans to do with his pen is striking. We can feel the speaker's nostalgia as he thinks wistfully about his father and grandfather. But we also sense some ambivalence: the speaker's deep respect for the tradition of manual labor in his family seems a bit at odds with the idea that writing is a worthwhile pursuit.

KEY QUESTIONS

Interpreting Tone and Mood

- How does the poem make you feel on your first read?
- What is the speaker's attitude toward the subject of the poem? How do you know?
- How do specific word choices contribute to tone?
- Does the tone change over the course of the poem? If so, what is the effect of that shift?

Irony

Irony is an incongruity between expectation and reality. It helps to know that there are several kinds: **verbal irony**, in which there is a difference between what the speaker says and what he or she means; **situational irony**, in which there is a discrepancy between what seems fitting and what actually happens; and **dramatic irony**, in which the contrast is between what a character or speaker says or thinks and what the audience (or readers) know to be true. In all of these cases, the reader or observer plays a key role. Irony only occurs if the audience perceives the discrepancy. If a writer makes an ironic comment and the audience takes it at face value, the attempt at irony has failed.

Examining specific techniques writers use to create irony is a helpful step toward understanding both what irony is and how an author develops an ironic tone. There are many ways to create irony, but the following are two common techniques. **Hyperbole**, or overstatement, is more than simple exaggeration or a lie: it is exaggeration in the service of truth, and, like a well-crafted metaphor, it suggests a deeper meaning. Hyperbole can be ironic because it highlights an incongruity between the exaggeration and the subject of that exaggeration. The opposite of hyperbole — **understatement** — has a similar effect. Both elements draw the reader's attention to the speaker's perspective on the idea that is being downplayed or overemphasized. The close reader must ask: why is the speaker distorting the "facts," and how does that distortion contribute to meaning?

Analyzing Tone and Mood

Read "My Heart and I" by Elizabeth Barrett Browning. What is the speaker's situation in this poem? How does her repeated reference to "my heart and I," as though her heart were separate from her, reveal her attitude toward her experiences? Consider how the poem's tone and mood reflect the speaker's perspective.

My Heart and I

Elizabeth Barrett Browning

Enough! we're tired, my heart and I;
We sit beside the headstone thus,
And wish the name were carved for us;
The moss reprints more tenderly
The hard types of the mason's knife,
As Heaven's sweet life renews earth's life,
With which we're tired, my heart and I.

You see we're tired, my heart and I;
We dealt with books, we trusted men,
And in our own blood drenched the pen,
As if such colors could not fly.
We walked too straight for fortune's end,
We loved too true to keep a friend;
At last we're tired, my heart and I.

How tired we feel, my heart and I;
We seem of no use in the world;
Our fancies hang gray and uncurled
About men's eyes indifferently;
Our voice, which thrilled you so, will let
You sleep; our tears are only wet;
What do we here, my heart and I?

So tired, so tired, my heart and I;
It was not thus in that old time
When Ralph sat with me 'neath the lime
To watch the sun set from the sky:
"Dear Love, you're looking tired," he said;
I, smiling at him, shook my head;
'Tis now we're tired, my heart and I.

(continued)

So tired, so tired, my heart and I!
    Though now none takes me on his arm
    To fold me close and kiss me warm,
Till each quick breath ends in a sigh
    Of happy languor. Now, alone
    We lean upon his graveyard stone,
Uncheered, unkissed, my heart and I.

Tired out we are, my heart and I.
    Suppose the world brought diadems
    To tempt us, crusted with loose gems
Of powers and pleasures? Let it try.
    We scarcely care to look at even
    A pretty child, o' God's blue heaven,
We feel so tired, my heart and I.

Yet, who complains? My heart and I?
    In this abundant earth no doubt
    Is little room for things worn out;
Disdain them, break them, throw them by;
    And if before the days grew rough,
    We once were loved, then — well enough
I think we've fared, my heart and I. ■

1862

Close Reading: Analyzing Poetic Elements and Techniques

Determining the subject of a poem and the speaker's attitude toward it will help you form an original opinion about the meaning of the work. However, a truly effective close analysis incorporates support from the text itself — that is, you must show *how* the poem's meaning is created, using the poet's language, style, and structure choices as evidence.

AP® TIP

The terms *literary elements*, *literary techniques*, *elements of style*, and *poetic devices* are used interchangeably in this course. They all refer to the resources of language a writer uses to convey meaningful ideas.

You may be familiar with many of the terms used to analyze poetry, sometimes called the elements of style or poetic devices. As you strengthen your familiarity with them, keep in mind that close analysis is more than just a treasure hunt for those elements. Remember, all style elements help convey the speaker's attitude and perspective, and successful close analysis considers the effect that each style element has on the tone and meaning of the poem. Here, we'll work with "To an Athlete Dying Young," by

A. E. Housman, to examine how several of its style elements help create and reinforce meaning. Examples for all of these concepts, and more, are available in the glossary at the back of the book.

To an Athlete Dying Young

A. E. Housman

The time you won your town the race
We chaired you through the market-place;
Man and boy stood cheering by,
And home we brought you shoulder-high.

To-day, the road all runners come,
Shoulder-high we bring you home,
And set you at your threshold down,
Townsman of a stiller town.

Smart lad, to slip betimes away
From fields where glory does not stay
And early though the laurel grows
It withers quicker than the rose.

Eyes the shady night has shut
Cannot see the record cut,
And silence sounds no worse than cheers
After earth has stopped the ears:

Now you will not swell the rout
Of lads that wore their honours out,
Runners whom renown outran
And the name died before the man.

So set, before its echoes fade,
The fleet foot on the sill of shade,
And hold to the low lintel up
The still-defended challenge-cup.

And round that early-laurelled head
Will flock to gaze the strengthless dead,
And find unwithered on its curls
The garland briefer than a girl's. ■

1896

Figurative Language

As we discussed in Chapter 1, language that is not literal is called figurative. Sometimes a poet will **personify** an object or idea, giving it human qualities. A good example of this can be found in the fourth stanza of Housman's poem:

> Eyes the shady night has shut
> Cannot see the record cut,
> And silence sounds no worse than cheers
> After earth has stopped the ears:

Here, "the shady night" — death — "has shut" the eyes of the young athlete. Personifying death in this way gives it a gentler quality, in keeping with the idea of death as a blessing.

Figurative language is often called *metaphorical* because it explains or expands on an idea by making a direct comparison between unlike things. **Similes** make such comparisons by using the words *like*, *as*, or *than* (e.g., *cold as ice*), while **metaphors** directly state that one thing is another (e.g., *an icy glare*). An **extended metaphor** is one that spans several lines of a work, expanding the comparison through additional details. Let's look back at the poem's last two stanzas:

> So set, before its echoes fade,
> The fleet foot on the sill of shade,
> And hold to the low lintel up
> The still-defended challenge cup.
>
> And round that early-laurelled head
> Will flock to gaze the strengthless dead,
> And find unwithered on its curls
> The garland briefer than a girl's.

Here, Housman develops a metaphor in which the speaker compares the burial of the young athlete to walking through a door — the "sill of shade." His trophy will be displayed at the "low lintel" (the beam across the top of a door), a metaphor for the edge of his coffin. In the next stanza his "garland briefer than a girl's" will be admired by the "strengthless dead," the crowd he will meet in the afterlife. This metaphor implies that dying young is a blessing because it keeps youthful achievements alive — the athlete will never know when the cheering stops or that his records have been broken.

AP® TIP

When discussing metaphors, be sure to identify both variables: the object or concept being compared and the object or concept to which it is being compared.

Some extended metaphors are **conceits**, complex comparisons developed through the juxtaposition or association of unexpected or paradoxical ideas. Poets sometimes use a conceit to illustrate the complex relationship between the speaker and the natural world. For example, in John Donne's 1633 poem "The Flea" (p. 413), the speaker uses the conceit of a flea that has bit both the speaker and his love interest to argue that the couple is essentially married because their bloods have combined in the body of the flea. Fleas are often associated with disease and death, and this reminder of the uncertainty of life serves as an implicit argument that the couple should enjoy life, and each other, while they can.

Another type of figurative language that relies on comparison is **allusion**, which is a reference to another work of literature, art, famous people and places, history, or current events. As with irony, allusion is only effective when the audience understands the reference. Common allusions involve references to sacred texts such as the Bible. While Housman's poem is short on allusion, Seamus Heaney's "Digging" does contain a subtle example. In Heaney's poem, the descriptions of digging for potatoes, including the "cold smell of potato mould" (l. 25) and its connection to "living roots" that "awaken in my head" (l. 27) may allude to a major event in Irish history: the great potato famine of the nineteenth century. Referencing this period of hardship not only extends the universe of the poem beyond just three generations of Heaney men to evoke a long and rich tradition, but it also further connects the strength and resilience of the men the speaker is descended from with the resolve he has to "dig" into — and draw from — that legacy with his pen.

AP® TIP

Keep in mind that a successful analysis of allusion goes beyond simply identifying what the allusion is. You must also address its significance — what does the event, idea, or work referenced in the allusion mean to the speaker? How does it contribute to the meaning of the poem?

Symbol

Literary texts sometimes include objects, places, events, or even characters that carry meanings or associations beyond the literal. These **symbols** allow the author to signify the speaker's attitude toward the subject of a poem without stating it outright. A symbol usually begins as something literal that takes on metaphorical significance throughout the poem to represent an idea or attitude. In "Digging" the pen comes to mean quite a bit more than a writing implement. It becomes a symbol of upward mobility — the speaker works indoors at his desk, not out in the cold. At the same time, the speaker connects it to the shovels used by his father and grandfather; all are used for digging, but what the pen digs for is a way to make meaning out of history, tradition, culture, and experience. Of course, another meaning is that it helps create the character of the speaker, but that is a literal meaning rather than a symbolic one; he's a poet so he works with a pen. None of these claims about the meaning of the pen is wrong; in fact, each of them is plausible. Like all poetic elements and devices, symbols offer many opportunities for interpretation.

Imagery

As we discussed in Chapter 1, **imagery** is language that appeals to any of the five senses. When you read poetry, it's important to think about how poets create impressions of sensory experiences. These are often revealed in patterns of images repeated throughout a poem, not just in a single stanza. As you consider poetic imagery, it may be helpful to begin by asking yourself whether the images are concrete, or whether they depend on figurative language to come alive. Two of the strongest images in "To an Athlete Dying Young" are of the young athlete on two different days. In the first stanza he is held shoulder-high in a chair and marched before the cheering crowd, having just won a race:

> The time you won your town the race
> We chaired you through the market-place;
> Man and boy stood cheering by,
> And home we brought you shoulder-high.

In the second stanza he is also held shoulder-high, but this time in his coffin by pallbearers:

> To-day, the road all runners come,
> Shoulder-high we bring you home,
> And set you at your threshold down,
> Townsman of a stiller town.

Let's think about what the mirroring of these two images suggests. The first image is quite concrete — the speaker remembers the cheers when the young athlete was carried home "shoulder-high" after his success in the race. The second image, of the athlete in a coffin held "shoulder-high," is more abstract. He is lowered into a much "stiller town": a grave. That he is carried shoulder-high in both a victory parade and his funeral march suggests that an early death has preserved his glory; he will always be remembered as a young athlete in his prime.

KEY QUESTIONS

Analyzing Figurative Language

- Which words and phrases are used literally, and which are used figuratively?
- How does the figurative language evoke a specific feeling or mood?
- Is the figurative language consistent throughout the poem, or does it shift? If you detect a shift, how does it develop meaning?

activity

Analyzing Figurative Language

Read "When I Became La Promesa" by Peggy Robles-Alvarado and discuss how the poem's figurative language, including imagery and symbols, conveys the significance of the event the speaker describes in the fourth stanza.

When I Became La Promesa

Peggy Robles-Alvarado

For every unexpected illness that required medical insurance,
every second-trimester miscarriage, every chaos unemployment
caused, every looming eviction, every arrest warrant gone
unanswered, the women in my family made promesas[1] to plaster
cast statues worshipped in overcrowded apartments with rum
poured over linoleum, nine-day candles coughing black soot
until the wick surrendered, Florida water perfuming doorways
and the backs of necks.

Promesas: barters/contracts with a God they didn't vow to
change for but always appeased/ bowls of fruit/ paper bags filled
with coconut candy and caserolas de ajiaco/ left at busy intersections,
an oak tree in High bridge park, the doorway of the 34th precinct,
and when mar pacifico and rompe saraguey refused to grow on
Washington Heights windowsills, the youngest became part of
the trade.

Unsullied and unaware: cousin Mari pissed about having to dress
in green and red for twenty-one days to keep Tío Pablo out of jail/
Luisito scratching at an anklet made of braided corn silk to help
Tía Lorna find a new job/ and my hair not to be cut until Papi's
tumor was removed.

Gathered in tight buns or sectioned pigtails, falling long past my
waist when asymmetrical bobs were in fashion, unaware my crown
had the necessary coercion to dislodge a mass from a colon, I grabbed
my older brother's clippers, ran thirsty blades across my right temple
to the back of my ear, massaged the softness that emerged as strands
surrendered on bathroom tiles. My desire to mimic freestyle icons,
whose albums my cousins and I scratched on old record players,
wagered against Papi's large intestine.

My unsteady hand: a fist
in the face of God. ■

2020

---

[1] *Promesas* are promises or vows made in prayer. — Eds.

Structure

Like fiction, poetry has specific structural elements that shape and reveal the perspective of the speaker. Poems are made up of **stanzas**, comprised of lines that are grouped together. Paragraphs in prose are roughly comparable, though not exactly equivalent. The arrangement of lines and stanzas — including their shape and length — often speaks to the relationship between ideas within a poem, signals their relative importance to the speaker, and helps develop meaning. For instance, a poem with three stanzas might tell you, at a basic level, that the poem has a clear and linear narrative arc with a beginning, middle, and end. Considering these basic elements of structure as you begin to read a poem will help direct your focus. Now, let's discuss how examining specific aspects of poetic structure will help you generate a deeper, more complex analysis.

AP® TIP

Prior to reading the poetry analysis prompt on the AP® exam, spend a few moments observing the structure of the poem. It's often easiest to make these general observations before you start reading and interpreting a text.

Poetic Syntax

Syntax — the arrangement of words into phrases, clauses, and sentences — is another style element that applies to both prose and poetry. For example, Housman uses **inversion** in several places, perhaps to maintain the rhyme scheme but also to emphasize a point. When he writes, "And home we brought you shoulder-high" (l. 4), the shift in expected word order ("We brought you home") emphasizes "home," which is further reinforced through repetition two lines later: "Shoulder-high we bring you home." The first home is the triumphant return of the living athlete; the second is the home he will inhabit in the cemetery.

When you analyze poetry, you will want to be on the lookout for **enjambment** (also called a run-on line, when one line ends without a pause and must continue into the next line to complete its meaning) and **caesura** (a pause within a line of poetry, signaled by punctuation or unusual spacing between words). You can see an example of enjambment in lines 17–18 of "To an Athlete Dying Young":

> Now you will not swell the route
> Of lads that wore their honours out,

There is also an instance of caesura in line 9:

> Smart lad, to slip betimes away

You can see how the continuation of the sentence in the first example echoes the procession winding through the town. The caesura in the second example reflects the unexpected death of the athlete.

You will also want to pay attention to syntactic patterns such as line length: are the poem's lines long, short, or a combination of the two? The lines in Housman's poem are generally short, which could be seen as a comment on the short life of the athlete.

Meter

The lines in structured poems often follow a regular pattern of **rhythm** called a **meter**. Literally, meter counts the measure of a line, referring to the pattern of stressed or unstressed syllables, combinations of which we call **feet**. Iambic meter is by far the most common in English. An **iamb** is a poetic foot of two syllables with the stress, or accent, on the second, as in the word *again*, or the phrase "by far." The two most common metric patterns are **iambic pentameter**, in which a line consists of five iambic feet, and **iambic tetrameter**, which measures four iambic feet. "To an Athlete Dying Young," is in iambic tetrameter. Each of its lines follows a rhythm of four beats, each one an iambic foot with the emphasis on the second syllable:

> The tĭme | yŏu wón | yŏur tówn | thĕ ráce
> Wĕ cháired | yŏu thróugh | thĕ már | kĕt-pláce.

You can probably see and even feel how the meter, with its steadily flowing pace, mimics a procession or march. It would sound odd and halting if you were to emphasize the first syllable instead:

> Thé time | yóu won | yóur town | thé race

You might also notice a break in the pattern early in the poem, which can also be significant. In the third line, "Man and boy stood cheering by" has only seven metrical feet instead of the expected eight. In this way, the interruption to the expected meter, especially so early in the poem, mirrors the jarring interruption of a young and healthy athlete's life cut short.

Form

Poetry is sometimes written in conventional or traditional forms, known as **closed forms**, that can give you hints about how the structure relates to the meaning of the poem. When you recognize a traditional form, consider whether it maintains the conventions or defies them. Notice interruptions to the form as well, which can point to ideas or contrasts that the poet wishes to emphasize. Another way to approach an analysis of a poem written in a closed form is to ask yourself whether the poem's content strikes you as traditional or unusual. Looking for the connections — and contrasts — between form and content through this lens will help inform your analysis. "To an Athlete Dying Young," for instance, is quite traditional: it has four-line stanzas that rhyme, its narrative is chronological, and it develops a particular idea metaphorically. The poem addresses the age-old question of how to make meaning from the death of a young person, and this traditional form suits Housman's purpose.

Not all poetry is written to follow a traditional or conventional pattern. When you look at the structure of a poem written in an **open form**, try to figure out how it is organized. Is it a narrative, in which the action dictates the structure? Are the stanzas chronological, cause and effect, or question and answer? What is the relationship between them? Look for word or sentence patterns or patterns of imagery that might reveal the relationships among the stanzas. Ultimately, what you should be on the lookout for is how the patterns you see in a poem's structure — or absence of them — reinforce its meaning.

Although poetry has many closed forms, the most common is the **sonnet**. Traditionally written as love poems, the sonnet form has been used for a wide variety of purposes, including war poems, protest poems, and parodies. Sonnets generally consist of fourteen lines, usually in iambic pentameter, as you may observe in the opening lines of Shakespeare's famous Sonnet 29:

> Whĕn, ín| dĭs- gráce | wĭth fór- | tŭne ánd | mĕn's éyes
> Ĭ áll | ă- lóne | bĕ - wéep | mў óut- | căst státe.

The two most common types of sonnet are the Italian, or Petrarchan, sonnet and the English, or Shakespearean sonnet. The **Petrarchan sonnet** is divided into an **octet** (eight lines) rhyming *abba*, *abba* and a **sestet** (six lines) with a variety of different rhyme schemes: *cdcdcd*, *cdecde*, or *cddcdd*. Traditionally, the octet raises an issue or expresses a doubt, and the sestet resolves the issue or doubt. The shift from the first to the second section is called the "turn." The **Shakespearean sonnet** consists of three **quatrains** (four lines) and a **couplet** (two lines) at the end. This type of sonnet rhymes *abab*, *cdcd*, *efef*, *gg*. The third quatrain often provides the turn, or **volta**, in which the speaker shifts his or her perspective in some way. The last two lines sometimes close the sonnet with a witty remark.

Other common traditional forms include:

- **Elegy.** A contemplative poem, usually for someone who has died.
- **Lyric.** A short poem expressing the personal thoughts or feelings of a first-person speaker.
- **Ode.** A form of poetry used to meditate on or address a single object or condition. It originally followed strict rules of rhythm and rhyme, but by the Romantic period it was more flexible.
- **Villanelle.** A form of poetry in which five **tercets**, or three-line stanzas (rhyme scheme *aba*), are followed by a quatrain (rhyme scheme *abaa*). At the end of tercets two and four, the first line of tercet one is repeated. At the end of tercets three and five, the last line of tercet one is repeated. These two repeated lines, called *refrain lines*, are repeated again to conclude the quatrain. Much of the power of this form lies in its repeated lines and their subtly shifting sense or meaning over the course of the poem.

AP® TIP

The AP® exam won't require you to name specific rhyme schemes, meter, or forms. If you're ever stumped as to what some aspect of a poem's structure is technically called, let it go and focus instead on what meaning that structural pattern conveys, or what it reveals about the speaker's perspective.

KEY QUESTIONS

Analyzing Structure

- What is the order of the words in the poem? Are they in the usual subject-verb-object order, or are they inverted?
- What are the lines of the poem like? Do their meanings build periodically or cumulatively?
- What do you notice about the rhythm and meter? How does each relate to the speaker's perspective?
- What form does the poem take? How is this form suited to the meaning of the poem?

Analyzing Structure

Read the poem "Sonnet" by Alice Moore Dunbar-Nelson and consider the relationship between form and meaning. Describe the ways the poem's content does and does not conform to the traditions of the sonnet form. Next, explain how the poem's form reflects the speaker's attitude toward springtime.

Sonnet

Alice Moore Dunbar-Nelson

I had no thought of violets of late,
The wild, shy kind that spring beneath your feet
In wistful April days, when lovers mate
And wander through the fields in raptures sweet.
The thought of violets meant florists' shops,
And bows and pins, and perfumed papers fine;
And garish lights, and mincing little fops
And cabarets and songs, and deadening wine.
So far from sweet real things my thoughts had strayed,
I had forgot wide fields, and clear brown streams;
The perfect loveliness that God has made,—
Wild violets shy and Heaven-mounting dreams.
And now—unwittingly, you've made me dream
Of violets, and my soul's forgotten gleam. ■

1922

Sound

Sound is the musical quality of poetry. It can be created through some of the other techniques we discuss, such as rhyme, enjambment, and caesura. It can also be created by word choice, especially through **alliteration** (the repetition of initial consonant sounds in a sequence of words or syllables), **assonance** (the repetition of vowel sounds in a sequence of words or syllables), **consonance** (identical consonant sounds in nearby words), and **onomatopoeia** (use of a word that refers to a sound and whose pronunciation mimics that sound). Sound can also be created by rhythm and **cadence** (similar to rhythm but related to the rise and fall of the voice). As with all of the elements of style, the key to analyzing sound is to connect it to the poem's overall meaning. Take a look at the alliteration in stanzas 4 and 5 of "To an Athlete Dying Young":

> Eyes the shady night has shut
> Cannot see the record cut,
> And silence sounds no worse than cheers
> After earth has stopped the ears:
>
> Now you will not swell the rout
> Of lads that wore their honours out,
> Runners whom renown outran
> And the name died before the man.

Within these stanzas, consider these two lines in particular: "And silence sounds no worse than cheers" (l. 15) and "Runners whom renown outran" (l. 19). The repetition of the *s* and *r* sounds quiet the poem, evoking the sound of somber, lowered voices at a funeral. You'll also see how the rhythm, created by the poem's meter, marches the poem forward, much like a funeral procession.

Rhyme

As you know, some poems **rhyme** and some — those written in **free verse** — do not. Rhyme at the end of a line is called **end rhyme**, while rhyme within a line of poetry is called **internal rhyme**. There is an example of both in the first two lines of "To an Athlete Dying Young":

> The time you won your town the race
> We chaired you through the market-place;

End rhyme

Internal rhyme

The last word of each line, "race" and "market-place," are end rhymes, while "you" and "through" in the second line is an instance of internal rhyme.

Sometimes a rhyme is visual; you can see it although the sounds of the two words don't rhyme. When an author uses poetic license to rhyme words that do not sound quite the same, it is called **near rhyme**, also known as **slant rhyme**. Lines 5 and 6 of Housman's poem contain a good example:

> To-day, the road all runners come,
> Shoulder-high we bring you home,

Even though *come* and *home* don't sound exactly the same, they sound — and look — close enough to draw our attention. This particular near rhyme calls our attention both to the fact that dying is an expected part of our life cycle but also reminds us that this particular death is untimely.

Rhyme is usually notated using letters of the alphabet; you use one letter for each sound that rhymes. For instance, a simple quatrain (set of four lines) might rhyme *abab*, meaning that every other line rhymes. Or it might be arranged as couplets that rhyme *aabb*; the first two lines rhyme with each other and the second two lines rhyme with each other. The pattern of rhyme for an entire poem is called its **rhyme scheme**. It can be useful to consider the effects of rhyme in a poem by charting its rhyme scheme; reading a rhyming poem out loud is also helpful. Notice how the consistent *aabb* rhyme scheme in "To an Athlete Dying Young" contributes to the rhythm of the procession — the young athlete's funeral march.

It is also important to notice disruptions to an established rhyme scheme and consider the effect of the change or disruption. As with interruptions to established conventions of form, these inconsistencies can provide insight into the speaker's perspective. As you know, many poems don't rhyme or may contain only sections that rhyme. This doesn't mean that you're off the hook when it comes to considering rhyme, though. An absence of rhyme, like an interruption to it, tells its own story. As the poet Ilya Kaminsky has said, "Silence is the invention of the hearing" — in the case of poetry, the omission of a particular style element is a choice that holds meaning. Just because something is missing doesn't mean that nothing is there. Many of the selections you'll encounter in this book will ask you to take a closer look at the ways that the presence — or absence — of style elements such as rhyme shapes and reflects the speaker's perspective and contributes to the complexity of the work.

KEY QUESTIONS

Analyzing Sound

- What qualities of the poem strike you as "musical"?
- Where do you see patterns of repeated or contrasting sounds?
- Is the poem written in free verse, or does it follow a traditional rhyme scheme? How does the rhyme (or lack of it) relate to the meaning of the poem?

Analyzing Sound

Read "The Century Quilt" by Marilyn Nelson. Describe how the poem's sound helps convey the importance of the quilt to the speaker.

(*continued*)

The Century Quilt

Marilyn Nelson

My sister and I were in love
with Meema's Indian blanket.
We fell asleep under army green
issued to Daddy by Supply.
When Meema came to live with us
she brought her medicines, her cane,
and the blanket I found on my sister's bed
the last time I visited her.
I remembered how I'd planned to inherit
that blanket, how we used to wrap ourselves
at play in its folds and be chieftains
and princesses.

Now I've found a quilt
I'd like to die under;
Six Van Dyke brown squares,
two white ones, and one square
the yellowbrown of Mama's cheeks.
Each square holds a sweet gum leaf
whose fingers I imagine
would caress me into the silence.

I think I'd have good dreams
for a hundred years under this quilt,
as Meema must have, under her blanket,
dreamed she was a girl again in Kentucky
among her yellow sisters,
their grandfather's white family
nodding at them when they met.
When their father came home from his store
they cranked up the pianola
and all of the beautiful sisters
giggled and danced.
She must have dreamed about Mama
when the dancing was over:
a lanky girl trailing after her father
through his Oklahoma field.

Perhaps under this quilt
I'd dream of myself,
of my childhood of miracles,
of my father's burnt umber pride,
my mother's ochre gentleness.
Within the dream of myself
perhaps I'd meet my son
or my other child, as yet unconceived.
I'd call it The Century Quilt,
after its pattern of leaves. ■

1985

Putting It All Together: Interpreting Major Elements of Poetry

When you read poetry, you read not only to get a sense of what takes place at the literal level but also to gain an understanding of how the language, structure, and tone of a poem come together to raise questions, explore issues, reveal the speaker's perspective, and ultimately convey meaning. As we discussed in Chapter 1, to effectively express your individual interpretation of meaning in literature is to make — and defend — a **claim**. A claim you make about what you think a poem means must be arguable; otherwise, there's nothing to distinguish it from fact or personal opinion. If the various poetic elements such as figurative language, form, sound, and so on make up the *what* of a poem, then your interpretation is the *so what.* In other words, what do those elements add up to, and why does that meaning matter? Keep in mind that while others may develop similar interpretations, yours is still unique. You are making the leap from the text on the page to a statement of what you think it is telling you. That is why you need to provide **evidence** from the poem to support the claims that make up your interpretation.

AP® TIP

To maximize your score on the AP® exam's Poetry Analysis Essay, you must support each of the claims you make with specific textual evidence.

To find solid evidence you will have to rely on your observations, find features of the poem that stand out to you, and then explain why and how you think they are meaningful. This process may come naturally, especially when you feel moved by it. On the other hand, sometimes reading a poem can make you feel like you've been locked out of a room where something important is happening. In situations like that, try the steps we've suggested so far: reading the poem for literal meaning, paraphrasing, identifying the speaker, and taking a close look at the poetic elements we've introduced in this chapter. Now that we've considered some of the specific techniques poets use to convey meaning, let's look at a poem by Robert Herrick, "Delight in Disorder," in which the speaker describes the appeal of dressing in a way that is careless — or seemingly so. We'll walk through how you can use annotation, a pre-writing strategy we introduced in Chapter 1, to notice poetic elements and begin to form an interpretation of how they come together to create meaning.

Delight in Disorder

Robert Herrick

A sweet disorder in the dress
Kindles in clothes a wantonness.
A lawn[1] about the shoulders thrown
Into a fine distraction;
An erring lace, which here and there
Enthralls the crimson stomacher,[2]
A cuff neglectful, and thereby
Ribbons to flow confusedly;
A winning wave, deserving note,
In the tempestuous petticoat;
A careless shoestring, in whose tie
I see a wild civility;
Do more bewitch me than when art
Is too precise in every part. ■

1648

[1] Linen scarf. — Eds.
[2] A piece of stiff, embroidered cloth worn over the stomach. — Eds.

This is a great poem for practicing close reading. Written over 350 years ago, it may seem difficult at first. Some of the vocabulary, such as *lawn* and *stomacher*, is unfamiliar to readers today. Other words, such as *petticoat*, may be **archaic**, but you have probably come across them before. As always, if you don't know what something means, you should look it up. Let's look at how you might briefly annotate the poem as you read:

A sweet disorder in the dress
Kindles in clothes a wantonness.
A lawn about the shoulders thrown
Into a fine distraction;
An erring lace, which here and there
Enthralls the crimson stomacher,
A cuff neglectful, and thereby
Ribbons to flow confusedly;
A winning wave, deserving note,
In the tempestuous petticoat;
A careless shoestring, in whose tie
I see a wild civility;
Do more bewitch me than when art
Is too precise in every part.

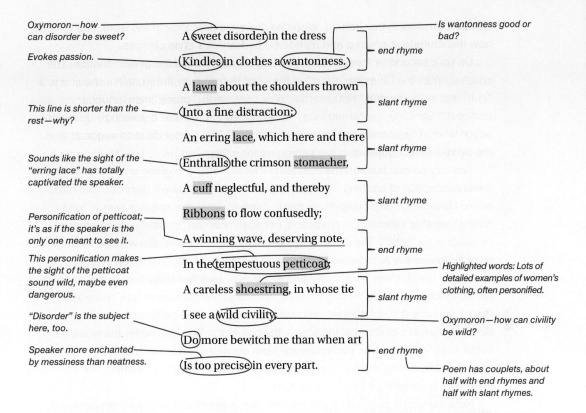

Oxymoron—how can disorder be sweet?

Evokes passion.

This line is shorter than the rest—why?

Sounds like the sight of the "erring lace" has totally captivated the speaker.

Personification of petticoat; it's as if the speaker is the only one meant to see it.

This personification makes the sight of the petticoat sound wild, maybe even dangerous.

"Disorder" is the subject here, too.

Speaker more enchanted by messiness than neatness.

Is wantonness good or bad?

end rhyme

slant rhyme

slant rhyme

slant rhyme

end rhyme

Highlighted words: Lots of detailed examples of women's clothing, often personified.

slant rhyme

Oxymoron—how can civility be wild?

end rhyme

Poem has couplets, about half with end rhymes and half with slant rhymes.

If we take this poem a line at a time, we see that the speaker uses the first two lines (which form a full sentence) to make a kind of argument. He says that "sweet disorder" in the way someone dresses "[k]indles . . . a wantonness." The verb "kindles" means to light up, awaken, or arouse, and "wantonness" can mean flirting or even lewdness. By the next line, it's clear that the speaker is talking about women's clothing in particular: "A lawn about the shoulders thrown." He continues to describe in detail a woman's clothing – style, color, and fabric. Every example he gives is different: lawn, lace, crimson stomacher, cuff, ribbons, petticoat, and shoestring. Together, they could almost form an outfit – the only thing missing is the actual dress. The last two lines break from description, however, as the speaker notes the effect such clothing has on him.

It may take a couple of readings to realize that the speaker is giving his views on messiness in women's clothing and that he finds it attractive. He seems at first a bit ambivalent – is the "wantonness" good or bad? Wanton dress calls to mind wanton behavior, which has mostly negative connotations, but the speaker is obviously inspired by it. As the poem's title suggests, he finds "delight in disorder" though he waits until very close to the end of the poem to give his final verdict: dress that appears careless is bewitching. When you take a closer look at the work, you will see how this attitude is created and reinforced by Herrick's style choices.

On your second or third reading, you might have noticed the personification. The speaker notes the "fine distraction" of the scarf thrown over the woman's shoulders, a "cuff" that is "neglectful," ribbons that "flow confusedly," and a "tempestuous petticoat." Similarly, the "erring lace," a mere decoration, takes surprisingly deliberate action when it "[e]nthralls the crimson stomacher." This personification suggests that the clothes reflect qualities of the person wearing them.

Two oxymorons support the possibility that something is going on other than just a literal description of clothing. The opening line refers to a "sweet disorder," but most would consider disorder unsettling, hardly "sweet"; later, the speaker sees a "wild civility," another seeming contradiction, because how can "civility" — or courteous behavior — be "wild"? The clothing he describes hints at finery; the woman wearing it is most likely wealthy and dresses with a certain amount of decorum. However, the way she wears her clothing is wild: the lawn is "thrown" over her shoulders, and the lace on her stomacher is "erring" — it "[e]nthralls," or holds, the stomacher only "here and there," implying it is not securely fastened to the dress. The petticoat is another typical detail of women's clothing at the time — the bigger the skirt, the better the woman's social standing. However, petticoats are worn beneath a dress and not meant to be seen in public. Using them to give the speaker a "wave" he finds "winning," or charming, is definitely a flirtatious gesture.

Note the words suggesting passion: *kindles*, *wantonness*, *crimson*, *tempestuous*, and *bewitch*. Is this poem actually about seduction? If so, its indirect manner is not overtly sexual or vulgar but flirtatious, sly, even mischievous. Alliteration adds a teasing singsong quality: "Delight . . . Disorder," "winning wave," and "precise . . . part." Further, the symmetry of the alliteration brings a bit of order into the description of disorder — but only a bit.

We might look to the structure of the poem for further evidence of the playful tone. The structure seems regular and predictable. The fourteen lines are presented in seven rhymed pairs, or couplets, most having eight syllables. The opening and closing couplets have exactly rhyming final syllables ("dress" / "wantonness" and "art" / "part"). Notice the neatly repeating **parallel structure** of lines 3, 5, 7, 9, and 11. However, there are inconsistencies within the poem. Some of the rhymes are only near rhymes (e.g., ll. 11 and 12: "tie" does not rhyme with "civility"). The poem's lines are in iambic tetrameter, but the rhythm is not always even. The evenness of the opening line, for instance ("A sweet disorder in the dress") is violated by line 10 ("In the tempestuous petticoat"). It seems Herrick's contention that "disorder" can be "sweet" is reflected in the structure of the poem.

Or, put in more thematic terms, Herrick might be reminding us that appearances can be deceiving, that perfection may not be as appealing as charming imperfections. Or, since the cultural values of his time dictated strict outward propriety, he might be telling his readers that passion lurks just beneath the veneer of polite society.

section 1 / culminating activity

Interpreting Poetry: Defending a Claim with Evidence

In the following poem by Paisley Rekdal, the speaker uses the experience of cultivating a garden to understand hardships she has weathered. Write a paragraph in which you make a defensible claim about how Rekdal uses literary elements to express the speaker's complex attitude toward her experiences. In your paragraph, you should incorporate at least one piece of evidence from the text to support your claim.

Happiness

Paisley Rekdal

I have been taught never to brag but now
I cannot help it: I keep
a beautiful garden, all abundance,
indiscriminate, pulling itself
from the stubborn earth: does it offend you
to watch me working in it,
touching my hands to the greening tips or
tearing the yellow stalks back, so wild
the living and the dead both
snap off in my hands?
The neighbor with his stuttering
fingers, the neighbor with his broken
love: each comes up my drive
to receive his pitying,
accustomed consolations, watches me
work in silence awhile, rises in anger,
walks back. Does it offend them to watch me
not mourning with them but working
fitfully, fruitlessly, working
the way the bees work, which is to say
by instinct alone, which looks like pleasure?
I can stand for hours among the sweet
narcissus, silent as a point of bone.
I can wait longer than sadness. I can wait longer
than your grief. It is such a small thing
to be proud of, a garden. Today
there were scrub jays, quail,
a woodpecker knocking at the white-
and-black shapes of trees, and someone's lost rabbit

(continued)

scratching under the barberry: is it
indiscriminate? Should it shrink back, wither,
and expurgate? Should I, too, not be loved?
It is only a little time, a little space.
Why not watch the grasses take up their colors in a rush
like a stream of kerosene being lit?
If I could not have made this garden beautiful
I wouldn't understand your suffering,
nor care for each the same, inflamed way.
I would have to stay only like the bees,
beyond consciousness, beyond
self-reproach, fingers dug down hard
into stone, and growing nothing.
There is no end to ego,
with its museum of disappointments.
I want to take my neighbors into the garden
and show them: Here is consolation.
Here is your pity. Look how much seed it drops
around the sparrows as they fight.
It lives alongside their misery.
It glows each evening with a violent light. ■

2012

Section 2

Earlier in this chapter, we outlined steps to help you read a poem. We suggested identifying its subject, determining the speaker's attitude toward that subject, and then looking at how the language of the poem conveys that attitude to create meaning. This kind of close reading is good preparation for writing about poetry. In this section, we will show you how to use the observations you've made in your close reading to put together a clear, effective analysis essay.

From Reading to Writing: Crafting an AP® Poetry Analysis Essay

The purpose of a close analysis essay is to examine how a poem's style helps convey its meaning. Often, the key to achieving this lies in analyzing the speaker's attitude toward an idea or theme expressed by the poem — typically, the poem's subject — or examining the relationship between two ideas within a poem. Regardless of the specific task you are asked to perform, a successful close analysis essay always connects a poem's style elements to its meaning.

Let's take a look at "Woodchucks" by Maxine Kumin. Begin by following the steps we outlined earlier in the chapter: read the poem literally to identify the subject, establish the speaker's attitude toward that subject, and read it again to consider how the style elements convey the speaker's attitude.

Woodchucks

Maxine Kumin

Gassing the woodchucks didn't turn out right.
The knockout bomb from the Feed and Grain Exchange
was featured as merciful, quick at the bone
and the case we had against them was airtight,
both exits shoehorned shut with puddingstone,
but they had a sub-sub-basement out of range.

Next morning they turned up again, no worse
for the cyanide than we for our cigarettes
and state-store Scotch, all of us up to scratch.
They brought down the marigolds as a matter of course
and then took over the vegetable patch
nipping the broccoli shoots, beheading the carrots.

The food from our mouths, I said, righteously thrilling
to the feel of the .22, the bullets' neat noses.
I, a lapsed pacifist fallen from grace
puffed with Darwinian pieties for killing,
now drew a bead on the littlest woodchuck's face.
He died down in the everbearing roses.

Ten minutes later I dropped the mother. She
flipflopped in the air and fell, her needle teeth
still hooked in a leaf of early Swiss chard.
Another baby next. O one-two-three
the murderer inside me rose up hard,
the hawkeye killer came on stage forthwith.

There's one chuck left. Old wily fellow, he keeps
me cocked and ready day after day after day.
All night I hunt his humped-up form. I dream
I sight along the barrel in my sleep.
If only they'd all consented to die unseen
gassed underground the quiet Nazi way. ■

1972

Preparing to Write: Creating a Graphic Organizer

Let's start by summarizing the work in one sentence, just to be sure you know what's going on.

> In "Woodchucks" the speaker is stymied and disturbed by the difficulty of exterminating the woodchucks that are taking over her garden.

Even this quick paraphrase engages in a certain level of interpretation — not only does it state that the poem is about killing woodchucks, but it also draws the inference that the speaker has some ambivalence about her situation.

Now that we've clarified the subject of the poem, our next consideration should be deepening our understanding of the speaker. Who is she, and what is her attitude toward killing the woodchucks in her garden? She has already tried one method of getting rid of the woodchucks, and now she's making the case for escalating her efforts. You'll probably notice a sense of "us against them" as she justifies her actions. The speaker describes the crimes committed by the woodchucks, how they "took over the vegetable patch / nipping the broccoli shoots, beheading the carrots." She describes herself as "righteously thrilling" when she picks up her gun; you may find her quite self-righteous. It's clear that her attitude toward the woodchucks is anger and frustration, but you might also get a hint of mixed feelings about her actions against them.

You have probably noticed some things about the poem as a whole, such as its short lines, strong verbs, and vivid images. Keep those things in mind as you take a look at the following graphic organizer, where we examine the way specific elements of style and structure add layers of meaning to Kumin's poem and support one interpretation of the work.

Creating a graphic organizer is a way to approach deciding which style elements to focus on in your analysis. This pre-writing strategy will help you break the poem down into specific areas for commentary — line or stanza divisions provide natural breaking points. The graphic organizer that follows first paraphrases what the poem is saying, then identifies a style element by name or description, and finally considers its effect: how does it help establish the speaker's attitude? How does it help convey meaning? Setting up your close reading in such a structured way guides you through an analysis that does not stop with simple restatement or even identification of elements of style but links them to effect and meaning.

There is no denying that completing a detailed graphic organizer like this one takes time. But understanding a text with layers of meaning requires time and attention to detail, especially if you are preparing to write about it. Plus, once you have examined the work so closely, you'll have already found ideas and evidence to use in your essay.

Lines	Paraphrase	Element of Style	Effect or Function
"Gassing the woodchucks didn't turn out right."	Killing the woodchucks didn't work.	Informal, conversational diction — concrete and straightforward.	Introduces the poem's subject, draws the reader into the speaker's world immediately.
"The knockout bomb from the Feed and Grain Exchange / was featured as merciful, quick at the bone / and the case we had against them was airtight, / both exits shoehorned shut with puddingstone, / but they had a sub-sub-basement out of range."	The gas was supposed to give the woodchucks a quick and painless death, but never reached them.	Play on words: the "case" against the woodchucks is "airtight," much as the woodchucks' underground home is made airtight to poison them.	Dark humor downplays the fact that the speaker is killing living creatures.
		The "case" and the "sub-sub-basement" ascribe human behavior to the woodchucks.	Humanizing the woodchucks could hint at ambivalence, or it could suggest that the speaker believes it's fair to wage war against them because they aren't simply defenseless animals.
"Next morning they turned up again, no worse / for the cyanide than we for our cigarettes / and state-store Scotch, all of us up to scratch."	The next morning, the woodchucks were in the garden again.	More informal diction — also clarifies point of view: "we," rather than just first-person "I."	Use of "we" makes reader complicit in everything the speaker does.
		Comparison: "cyanide" to "state-store Scotch" — neither has an apparent effect on woodchucks or speaker.	Comparison of poison to alcohol again downplays the fact that the speaker was trying to kill the woodchucks.
		The only instance in which "us" describes both humans and woodchucks.	Grouping the woodchucks and humans together suggests that woodchucks are as hardy as humans.

(continued)

Lines	Paraphrase	Element of Style	Effect or Function
"They brought down the marigolds as a matter of course / and then took over the vegetable patch / nipping the broccoli shoots, beheading the carrots."	The woodchucks destroyed the flowers and the vegetable patch.	Use of "they" and repeated dependent clauses with strong and/or violent verbs: "brought down," "took over," "nipping," and "beheading."	Portrays woodchucks as an enemy army, evoking speaker's feelings of anger and indignation.
"The food from our mouths, I said, righteously thrilling / to the feel of the .22, the bullets' neat noses."	The speaker picked up a gun to shoot the woodchucks.	Concrete imagery: "the .22" and "the bullets' neat noses." The speaker is "thrilling."	Heightens visceral thrill of contemplating violent action.
		Sentence fragment: "The food from our mouths."	The speaker justifies killing by suggesting the woodchucks are taking the food from the mouths of her own family.
"I, a lapsed pacifist fallen from grace / puffed with Darwinian pieties for killing, / now drew a bead on the littlest woodchuck's face."	The speaker used to be a pacifist. But she had reasons for killing the woodchucks. She aimed at the smallest woodchuck.	The speaker uses abstract diction to describe herself as a "lapsed pacifist fallen from grace" whose new "Darwinian pieties" compel her to pick up a gun.	Abstractions could mean the speaker is viewing her actions from a critical distance and is self-aware — or they could simply cloak the speaker's delight in violence with rhetoric that justifies killing the woodchucks.
		Diction: "puffed"	The verb "puffed" hints at speaker's sense of self-righteousness.
		Violent imagery: the speaker "drew a bead," aiming her gun at a woodchuck.	The speaker is not sugarcoating her actions; the woodchucks are the enemy, and she is at war with them.

Lines	Paraphrase	Element of Style	Effect or Function
"He died down in the everbearing roses."	The smallest woodchuck died.	Short, declarative sentence. Diction: "everbearing"	The brevity of the sentence echoes the finality of death; perhaps the speaker enjoys the irony, as everbearing roses bloom all season long.
"Ten minutes later I dropped the mother. She / flipflopped in the air and fell, her needle teeth / still hooked in a leaf of early Swiss chard."	The speaker shot an adult woodchuck next. The bullet knocked the woodchuck off the ground. The woodchuck still had food in its teeth.	Concrete, brutal imagery used to describe woodchuck: "flipflopped," "needle teeth," "hooked." Informal diction: "dropped"	The woodchucks are portrayed as increasingly aggressive and tenacious opponents. This informal word choice implies that the killing is casual and comes easily to the speaker. It also draws the reader into the scene.
"Another baby next. O one-two-three / the murderer inside me rose up hard, / the hawkeye killer came on stage forthwith."	The speaker shot another small woodchuck next. The speaker began to feel like a murderer.	Theatrical diction describes the speaker's actions: "murderer inside me" and "hawkeye killer" who "came on stage."	Speaker distances herself from the killings. It wasn't her essential self; it was something "inside her," performing the deed "on stage." This suggests her ambivalence about her behavior.
"There's one chuck left. Old wily fellow, he keeps / me cocked and ready day after day after day."	Only one old woodchuck is still alive. The speaker looks for it every day.	Repetition of "day"; the speaker is "cocked and ready."	There is a sense of the need for eternal vigilance, on guard for the enemy.

(*continued*)

Lines	Paraphrase	Element of Style	Effect or Function
"All night I hunt his humped-up form. I dream / I sight along the barrel in my sleep."	The speaker dreams of shooting the oldest woodchuck.	Violent diction used to describe the speaker's dreams about the last woodchuck standing: "hunt" and "sight along the barrel."	The "dream" could point to the speaker's obsession with killing the woodchucks, or it could indicate her actions have begun to haunt her.
"If only they'd all consented to die unseen / gassed underground the quiet Nazi way."	The speaker wishes the gas had worked, and that the woodchucks had died somewhere out of sight.	Draws a parallel between killing rodents and Nazi war crimes of gassing people.	Emphasizes speaker's uneasiness with having to kill the woodchucks in an active fashion, leaving her obsessed with doing it and feeling repulsed by her actions.

Creating a graphic organizer is good preparation for writing, but it's important to remember that you won't be able to use every single idea in a clear and cohesive close analysis essay. Our sample graphic organizer identifies more style elements than you could likely use in a single essay — particularly if there are limits on time and length. As you begin to plan to write an essay, you must decide which style elements best support your thesis.

Preparing to Write about Poetry

Read the following poem by Major Jackson and either create a graphic organizer or annotate the poem in preparation for writing an analysis.

Mighty Pawns

Major Jackson

If I told you Earl, the toughest kid
on my block in North Philadelphia,
bow-legged and ominous, could beat
any man or woman in ten moves playing white,
or that he traveled to Yugoslavia to frustrate the bearded
masters at the Belgrade Chess Association,
you'd think I was given to hyperbole,
and if, at dinnertime, I took you

into the faint light of his Section 8 home
reeking of onions, liver, and gravy,
his six little brothers fighting on a broken love-seat
for room in front of a cracked flat-screen,
one whose diaper sags it's a wonder
it hasn't fallen to his ankles,
the walls behind doors exposing the sheetrock
the perfect O of a handle, and the slats
of stairs missing where Baby-boy gets stuck
trying to ascend to a dominion foreign to you and me
with its loud timbales and drums blasting down
from the closed room of his cousin whose mother
stands on a corner on the other side of town
all times of day and night, except when her relief
check arrives at the beginning of the month,
you'd get a better picture of Earl's ferocity
after-school on the board in Mr. Sherman's class,
but not necessarily when he stands near you
at a downtown bus-stop in a jacket a size too
small, hunching his shoulders around his ears,
as you imagine the checkered squares of his poverty
and anger, and pray he does not turn his precise gaze
too long in your direction for fear he blames
you and proceeds to take your Queen. ■

2015

Developing a Thesis Statement

When it comes time to write a close analysis essay, the first thing to do is formulate a **thesis statement**. Your thesis statement will reflect your interpretation of the meaning of the work and should incorporate the style elements you plan to use to support it. It should be defensible — that is, it should not be a statement of fact or just a personal opinion but an arguable claim that you are planning to defend in the body of your essay, using evidence from the poem. Part of your job will be to show a line of reasoning that connects to your thesis and your examples. That is the way you will prove your argument about your interpretation of the poem. You may end up changing your thesis statement as you go but having an idea of your argument will help you stay focused. Your teacher will likely have provided you with a prompt or an assignment, and if you've done a thorough job of reading and taking notes in the form of annotation or a graphic organizer, you will probably have more ideas than you can actually use in the essay. For example, your reading may have revealed the vivid imagery and sense of irony in "Woodchucks." You may have also noticed allusions to history, and underlying themes — like guilt and violence — that highlight the speaker's ambivalence and self-doubt. Another prominent feature of the poem is its syntax: the long conversational sentences interspersed with short simple ones. Does this pattern suggest self-justification? There are several ways to approach this poem and many possible interpretations.

Let's say your teacher has assigned you the following prompt:

> In Maxine Kumin's "Woodchucks," published in 1972, the speaker takes increasingly extreme measures to rid her garden of woodchucks. Read the poem carefully. Then, in a well-written essay, analyze how Kumin uses literary elements and techniques to develop the speaker's complex perspective on her actions.

Remember, your thesis must be an interpretation of the meaning of the poem that you will support with evidence from the text, using a clear line of reasoning. You should avoid creating a thesis statement that is so broad that it just restates the prompt:

> Maxine Kumin uses literary techniques to convey the speaker's complex perspective on her killing of the woodchucks in her poem "Woodchucks."

Not only does this thesis fail to mention the specific elements the writer plans to discuss, it also fails to provide any insight into what the speaker's perspective on killing the woodchucks actually is. This thesis does not give any indication of whether the essay writer believes Kumin's speaker is proud or ashamed of herself — or anything in between. Remember, too, that an effective thesis needs to focus on specific characteristics of the poem's style and structure, so that in the body of the essay you can analyze how these elements help convey your interpretation of the speaker's attitude.

However, it is important not to narrow your thesis so much that there is nothing to say about it:

> In "Woodchucks" the speaker's diction is violent and defensive.

Although this thesis isolates a style element — violent and defensive diction — it, too, fails to express any interpretation of the speaker's complex perspective on her own behavior. Thus, it does not recognize or begin to grapple with the complexity of the poem. You could not discuss a thesis like this for long before running out of things to say. A good thesis should be expressed clearly and should inform the reader of the essay's purpose. It is the backbone of your essay, and everything will connect to it.

Working with our example prompt, let's consider how Kumin develops the speaker's persona and how that voice conveys the speaker's complex perspective on killing the woodchucks in her garden. Looking back at what we've noted about "Woodchucks" in the graphic organizer, there is a feeling of mounting aggression as the speaker demonizes the woodchucks. But first she expresses her disappointment that the "knockout bomb from the Feed and Grain Exchange" was ineffective. You'll have noted that the end of the poem comes back to the gas, with the speaker lamenting that the woodchucks didn't "die unseen / gassed underground the quiet Nazi way." That may make us rethink what we first saw as a progression in the speaker's aggression. What does this regret suggest about the speaker's feelings toward her own actions? Is killing with gas really any different from killing with a gun?

We might also look at Kumin's diction choices. Her word choices are conversational; we get the sense that the speaker is a weekend gardener, annoyed that the woodchucks are getting in the way of her hobby. After all, she and her friends are smokers and drinkers, not subsistence farmers. The language of killing is hard and unambiguous: she "dropped" and "drew a bead" on each woodchuck with the rifle; her "murderer inside . . . rose up hard." But she also considers the woodchucks fair game: they are taking the "food from our mouths," "nipping the broccoli shoots," and "beheading the carrots." These language choices suggest that aggression is close to the surface and can rise quickly when people feel their interests are threatened.

The rhyme scheme is interesting too: *abc*, *acb*, which sounds like just enough of a sing-song to soothe a troubled soul. There's a funny sort of delay in the second set of three lines when the *b* rhyme becomes the *c* rhyme. That hesitation may reflect the speaker's self-doubt:

> Gassing the woodchucks didn't turn out right. *a*
> The knockout bomb from the Feed and Grain Exchange *b*
> was featured as merciful, quick at the bone *c*
> and the case we had against them was airtight, *a*
> both exits shoehorned shut with puddingstone, *c*
> but they had a sub-sub-basement out of range. *b*

Remembering that it is always important to address a work's complexity, we might develop the following thesis statement in response to the original prompt:

> In "Woodchucks" the diction, imagery, and rhyme scheme help convey the speaker's ambivalence about her own violent behavior, illuminating her uneasiness with how quickly she resorts to harsher measures.

Supporting Your Thesis

Once you have an idea for a thesis statement — and, remember, this "working thesis" can change at any time — look back at the text and your notes, keeping in mind the ideas that inspired your thesis as you prepare to support it. Your essay might be organized around the style elements, with a paragraph each on diction, imagery, and rhyme scheme, for example. Or you could approach it a different way: you might group your ideas according to the ways Kumin shows the changes in the speaker's

AP® TIP

To earn three or more points for Evidence and Commentary on the AP® Exam Scoring Guideline, you have to discuss how each literary element or technique you mention contributes to meaning.

attitude toward her actions, with one paragraph on her justifications, one on her ambivalence and self-doubt, and another on what's implied by her actions.

You've probably noticed that the thesis statement we've suggested is likely to lead to a five-paragraph essay. Perhaps you've been warned to stay away from this organization because it is formulaic or prescriptive. We agree: stay away from the formulaic or prescriptive. However, the five-paragraph essay may or may not fall into that category. There's no rule that says that every question or topic will fit neatly into an introduction, three body (or developmental) paragraphs, and a conclusion. Yet if you happen to have three points to make, you'll end up with five paragraphs that could form a cogent and insightful essay.

Writing Topic Sentences

If you've developed a strong thesis statement, you've already created your claims, each of which will become a topic sentence for a different body paragraph. The following topic sentence links to the thesis point about diction without simply repeating the claim stated in the thesis:

> **AP® TIP**
>
> Establishing a line of reasoning in your essay is important. To do this, make sure to link a specific claim in your thesis statement with the topic sentence that opens each body paragraph.

> The violent word choices in "Woodchucks" help create a battle scene in the poem, not only illustrating the carnage of a war between human and nature but illuminating the speaker's increasing uneasiness with her capacity for violence.

Developing a Line of Reasoning with Evidence from the Poem

Close analysis, as you know, requires references to the text, and you should think of the language of a poem as evidence to support the claims you make in your thesis. When you quote directly from a poem in your analysis, use a forward slash mark to indicate a line break. The key is to choose quotations carefully and integrate them as seamlessly as possible into your own writing, avoiding big chunks of text. Just remember that your voice should prevail in a close analysis essay — that is, you must offer thoughtful commentary on what you quote. One way you might check to make sure that you're providing sufficient analysis of a work is to highlight all your quotations from the text. Here's an example of a paragraph that quotes from "Woodchucks."

> The violent word choices in "Woodchucks" help create a battle scene in the poem, not only illustrating the carnage of a war between human and nature but illuminating the speaker's increasing uneasiness with her capacity for violence. The woodchucks are "no worse / for the cyanide," still "nipping the broccoli shoots, beheading the carrots." The speaker references World War II, including "the quiet Nazi way" and "gassing." She also takes up arms, "thrilling / to the feel of the .22," "[draws] a bead" on a baby woodchuck, then triumphs again as she "drop[s] the mother," whose body "flipflop[s] in the air." She feels the

"murderer inside" and begins to see herself as a "hawkeye killer." She stays "cocked and ready day after day after day" as she "hunts [the old woodchuck's] humped-up form."

Apart from the topic sentence, the paragraph consists primarily of a string of quotations. There is no commentary on the text and, as a result, very little to guide the reader to an understanding of the essay writer's interpretation. Instead, this paragraph reads more like a list that catalogs instances of violent language throughout the poem.

Compare that paragraph to the one below. While the structure and some of the quotations remain essentially the same, original commentary develops a line of reasoning that moves the paragraph beyond a string of quotes to a discussion of the effect of Kumin's language choices.

> The violent word choices in "Woodchucks" help create a battle scene in the poem, not only illustrating the carnage of a war between human and nature but illuminating the speaker's increasing uneasiness with her capacity for violence. The woodchucks, on a rampage, are "nipping the broccoli shoots" and "beheading the carrots." Their actions against the speaker's garden, as well as the speaker's response, are acts of war, and casualties follow. The speaker's references to World War II bring the battle to a new level, as words like "gassing" and "Nazi" remind us that wartime atrocities take place both seen and unseen. This suggests the speaker sees herself as a soldier who must accomplish her mission, though she is aware that her actions are over the top. There is, however, no denying a certain sense of glee as the speaker prepares to fight. She finds the .22 "thrilling" and is proud of being able to "[draw] a bead" as she "dropped the mother." She believes she is an even match for the woodchucks and assumes that the playing field is level because they attacked her first. Her sense of ambivalence toward her behavior grows as she realizes that there is a "murderer inside" her, but she's not quite self-aware enough to know that the war against the old woodchuck, which keeps her "cocked and ready day after day after day," has dehumanized her. Both through her actions and the language used to describe them, the speaker's uneasy relationship with nature — most important, her own — is made clear.

Documenting Sources

In a close analysis essay, you are likely only writing about one text, so you won't need a formal Works Cited page. Your teacher may ask you to use line numbers to identify where your quotations can be found, but with a short poem it may be unnecessary. If you do add line numbers, they should go in parentheses after the quotation mark and before your punctuation, like this:

> The youngest woodchuck dies in the "everbearing roses" (l. 18).

> The speaker seems to feel no remorse as she sees "the littlest woodchuck's face. / He died down in the everbearing roses" (ll. 19–20).

Writing a Body Paragraph of an AP® Poetry Analysis Essay

Write a body paragraph that supports the claim in our model thesis that imagery helps convey the speaker's ambivalence toward killing the woodchucks. Be mindful of keeping your own voice central by choosing quotations carefully and commenting more than you quote.

Revising an AP® Poetry Analysis Essay

Don't forget that giving yourself the opportunity to revisit, edit, and revise your essay is a key component of the writing process when you are not in a timed environment, such as an exam or in-class essay. You may find the following questions helpful for guiding your revision.

- **Reread the entire essay for comprehension.** Is there a clear line of reasoning that puts forth an argument for your interpretation of the poem?
- **Reread your introduction and thesis statement.** Is the thesis clear? Have you taken a position that goes beyond summary or paraphrase? Does your thesis respond to the prompt by presenting an argument for how poetic elements and techniques create meaning and/or reveal the speaker's perspective?
- **Reread each topic sentence.** Does it accurately reflect a claim in your thesis? Does it provide a bridge between the line of reasoning in your thesis and the evidence in the paragraph?
- **Check your evidence.** Do the quotations you've chosen to use clearly support the claim in the topic sentence of each body paragraph?
- **Evaluate your commentary.** Does it explain the relationship between the textual evidence you've selected and the central claim in the topic sentence in each body paragraph?
- **Reread for spelling and grammar.** Do you have run-ons? Misspelled words?
- **Read your writing aloud to yourself.** Does it sound right? Can you tighten anything up?
- **If possible, step away from it.** Clear your mind for a few hours — a day if you can. Return to your work with fresh eyes.
- **Reread one final time with a clear head.** Just a tune-up. Are there small changes you can make to improve word choice and sentence structure that will further clarify your argument?

Analyzing a Sample AP® Poetry Analysis Essay

The following student essay responds to the prompt we introduced on page 94. As you read it, think about how you would provide feedback to help this student revise her draft.

A Fall from Grace

Alyssa Pierangeli

What struggle can prompt a man to lose his humanity? Maxine Kumin explores this complex idea and human cruelty in her poem "Woodchucks." The poem describes the speaker's violent attempts to kill off pesky creatures invading her garden. As the story progresses, the speaker grows irritable and even more determined to exterminate the trespassers using brutality. Though the speaker attempts to justify her hostility, her self-righteous front begins to fade as she recognizes the aggression's deleterious effects — turning the speaker into something that she is not. In "Woodchucks," Kumin employs dark humor, macabre images, and a regretful tone to illustrate the speaker's ambivalence about her violent behavior, which also perhaps demonstrates the speaker's inordinate power over the enemy.

To begin, the poem's dark humor and colloquialism consistently minimize the speaker's cruel nature and play it off as casual. These tactics also demonstrate the speaker's conflict with her callous decisions as they downplay her misdeeds. After the speaker realizes that "gassing" the woodchucks failed — this line in itself, offered conversationally, reflects the speaker's nonchalance in regards to killing — the play on words, "case" and "airtight," resembling the woodchucks' underground airtight home intended to poison them, downplays what has actually occurred: the murder of living creatures (l. 4). Kumin also humanizes the woodchucks in the same sentence: the words "case" and "sub-sub-basement" show the speaker's ambivalence because in her mind, at this point, they are not defenseless creatures; instead, they are attributed human traits and belongings. With this idea in mind, the speaker finds it easier to view the creatures as equals. Hence the speaker can delude herself that she is the victim. Of course, in dramatic irony, the reader understands the reality that the balance of power is anything but even. The poem's informal diction illustrates the speaker's nonchalance when it comes to killing. "Ten minutes later I dropped the mother," the speaker admits with ease. She almost boasts it. The colloquial word choice, "dropped," further implies that the speaker holds no guilt or shame for her behavior. She is unsympathetic toward the woodchucks at this point in the poem. However, in the lines "I, a lapsed pacifist fallen from grace / puffed with Darwinian pieties for killing, / now drew a bead on the littlest woodchuck's face," the speaker, from a critical standpoint, now speaks with abstract and colloquial diction as she grows self-aware of her behavior (ll. 15–17). The word "puffed" reveals her self-righteous attitude that will, at a moment's notice, turn into regret. Upon reflection, the speaker ruminates about her pacifist beliefs and states that she has "fallen from grace." Here the speaker recognizes the immorality of her ruthlessness. The poem's overall tone smacks of tongue-in-cheek, revealing a sense of insincerity and antithesis to the severity of the encounter. Through Kumin's colloquialism and dark humor, the reader recognizes the speaker's unease and ambivalence through the downplaying of her violent behavior toward the creatures.

The poem's macabre imagery paints a clearer picture of the speaker's remorse as she deals with the fallout of her choices. She now thinks of herself differently; she is shamefaced. The speaker's drawing a "bead" on the "littlest woodchuck's face" who died in "everbearing roses" vividly summons infanticide and laments the pacifism she so casually surrendered. Describing herself later on in the poem as a "hawkeye killer" (l. 24) and having a "murderer inside [her]" (l. 23), the speaker recognizes not only the mayhem her actions cause but also their gravity. In calling herself a "hawkeye killer," the speaker compares herself to a stalking predator ready to attack, further signifying the unbalanced power dynamic and her initial ambivalence about her violence. She has, in her mind, fallen from grace.

In effect, the speaker takes on several moments of reflection illustrated through the poem's regretful tone, demonstrating her ambivalent attitude even more in her wistfulness. The speaker wishes that the woodchucks had "consented to die unseen / gassed underground the quiet Nazi way" (ll. 29–30). In stating that she had high hopes for the gas to work and that they would die somewhere out of sight, the speaker's hopes mirrors those of Nazi Germany, which circles back to the opening line: "Gassing the woodchucks didn't turn out right" (l. 1). That she draws a parallel between killing rodents and Nazi war crimes discloses that she now feels guilty and repulsed by her savagery. This regretful tone illustrates the speaker's mixed feelings about whether the rodents deserved to die so violently. The oldest rodent that she has yet to kill leaves her feeling that her capabilities are subpar, and her actions begin to haunt her. "All night I hunt his humped-up form. I dream / I sight along the barrel in my sleep" (ll. 27–28). The speaker's nihilistic brutality toward the rodents has finally brought her to the point of obsession and abhorrence. It is this regretful tone that clarifies how the speaker is conflicted by her abhorrent decisions.

When the speaker declares her falling from grace, the poem's mood alters significantly so as to transition the poem from woodchuck mischief to woodchuck holocaust. The speaker has almost absolute power over the animals and yet tries to downplay this fact to assume an egalitarian relationship. Her downplaying of her preponderance of power increases her willingness to go through with her actions. In some ways the story portrayed in "Woodchucks" perhaps acts as an extended metaphor intended to reflect not only warfare but also the potential evil within all of us. The speaker likely acted in such a way that she, prior to the rodents, would never have considered before; they triggered her worst behavior. When she confronts them, her alacrity to violence and disregard for its effects reveal how low she can stoop, how much she can disappoint herself in her fall from grace. The lone rodent winds up haunting her, like the rest of her merciless actions.

Providing Peer Feedback for Revision

Carefully read the student sample essay on "Woodchucks" and answer the following questions for revision.

Questions for Revision

1. Examine the relationship between the thesis and the topic sentences. Do you think the basic structure of the essay is effective or ineffective? Why?
2. How does the essay support its argument with evidence from the text? Cite evidence that you find especially effective and explain why.
3. The writer argues that the poem's dark humor, macabre images, and a regretful tone illustrate the speaker's ambivalence. To what extent do you think that the textual evidence supports this interpretation?
4. What is another argument you might make based on a close reading of "Woodchucks"? It does not have to contradict this writer's interpretation entirely but rather offer another way to read the poem or a different conclusion from the one drawn in this sample essay.

section 2 / culminating activity

Crafting an AP® Poetry Analysis Essay

In Major Jackson's "Mighty Pawns," published in 2015, the speaker comments on the way expectations can mislead us. Read the poem carefully. Then, in a well-written essay, analyze how Jackson uses literary elements and techniques to develop the speaker's attitude toward Earl.

Mighty Pawns

Major Jackson

If I told you Earl, the toughest kid
on my block in North Philadelphia,
bow-legged and ominous, could beat
any man or woman in ten moves playing white,
or that he traveled to Yugoslavia to frustrate the bearded
masters at the Belgrade Chess Association,
you'd think I was given to hyperbole,
and if, at dinnertime, I took you
into the faint light of his Section 8 home
reeking of onions, liver, and gravy,
his six little brothers fighting on a broken love-seat
for room in front of a cracked flat-screen,

(continued)

one whose diaper sags it's a wonder
it hasn't fallen to his ankles,
the walls behind doors exposing the sheetrock
the perfect O of a handle, and the slats
of stairs missing where Baby-boy gets stuck
trying to ascend to a dominion foreign to you and me
with its loud timbales and drums blasting down
from the closed room of his cousin whose mother
stands on a corner on the other side of town
all times of day and night, except when her relief
check arrives at the beginning of the month,
you'd get a better picture of Earl's ferocity
after-school on the board in Mr. Sherman's class,
but not necessarily when he stands near you
at a downtown bus-stop in a jacket a size too
small, hunching his shoulders around his ears,
as you imagine the checkered squares of his poverty
and anger, and pray he does not turn his precise gaze
too long in your direction for fear he blames
you and proceeds to take your Queen. ■

2015

Section 3

Developing Sophistication in an AP® Poetry Analysis Essay

In Sections 1 and 2 of this chapter, we examined how to read a poem for literal meaning, explored what contrasts reveal about the speaker's perspective, and walked through how to interpret the ways specific poetic elements contribute to meaning. We also went one step further than simply dissecting individual elements of poetry—we examined how all of these elements work together to convey meaning in a sample analysis and an example student essay. If you completed the Culminating Activity for Section 2, you also got to try this entire process out for yourself with Major Jackson's poem "Mighty Pawns." But how do we continue to improve our analytical skills once we begin to gain confidence with interpreting poetry and writing literary arguments? In this section, we're going to walk through one way to adjust how to approach poetry that will help you move from an effective analysis to a sophisticated one.

But first, let's discuss what sophistication means when it comes to writing about literature. You can develop it through the quality of your writing, the quality of your ideas, or a combination of both. The language you use to convey your interpretation of a poem should be vivid and specific, and your commentary on the evidence you use from the text should reflect your own unique voice and thoughts. This takes practice — like any other skill, this one will develop through repetition and variety. The more poetry you read and the more you write about it, the more sophisticated your writing and analysis will be.

> **AP® TIP**
>
> Sophistication must be woven throughout your essay rather than resting on a single section, sentence, or word. You must add more than one or two sentences to an essay when you revise it.

There's no magic formula for developing sophisticated ideas, but there are strategies you can use to help organize and deepen your thinking. One approach that works particularly well for poetry analysis essays is to situate your interpretation of the poem in a broader context. Let's take a closer look at how this works. Sophisticated analyses don't typically emerge from a single reading of a text. Rereading literature with an active and open mind is essential to analyzing and writing about it with a degree of sophistication.

Considering Broader Contexts

Interpreting the nature of a poem's speaker or determining how the poetic devices contribute to the meaning of a poem — especially within a timed essay — is quite an achievement. Providing a defensible thesis and supporting it with relevant and specific textual evidence and commentary are key ingredients that you can't omit. Once you're ready to make your analysis more sophisticated, it's important to shift your focus from the individual components of the poem to looking at its overall meaning within a broader context — history, culture, and/or society as a whole. This broader view invites two questions: 1) How does the poem extend beyond the speaker's situation and into the life and context of the poet? and 2) How does the poem address concerns that extend across time and place? For instance, if we're reading a sixteenth-century sonnet written by William Shakespeare, we might focus our essay exclusively on the speaker, his intended audience, and their situation. However, we could elevate our analysis by using the sonnet to draw conclusions about both individuals living during the 1500s *and* modern-day readers.

By considering these additional questions, we are actually focusing on why reading literature matters. Our engagement with text helps us understand how those who came before us thought and functioned; in doing so, we also learn about ourselves.

If we reread Maxine Kumin's "Woodchucks," what can we determine about the poem's relation to Kumin's experiences and worldview? How might the poem serve as commentary for all of humanity? The analysis derived from these two questions can help you add layers to your understanding and writing about the poem. For example, we might make the following observations:

1. The poem's allusion to Nazis and its publication in the midst of the conflict in Vietnam suggests that "Woodchucks" could reflect the carnage that characterized global affairs during Kumin's lifetime: 1925–2014.

2. The speaker, who becomes obsessed with killing the woodchucks, might represent all human beings. Once we abandon civility and become "lapsed pacifist[s]," we are each capable of becoming a "murderer" or a "hawkeye killer."
3. Perhaps Kumin is not necessarily telling us that all humans are capable of murder. The speaker's obsession with killing the woodchucks might be hyperbolic. Maybe it represents a more general capacity for cruelty or a natural tendency to seek dominance or victory at any cost.

Situating Your Argument in a Broader Context

Now that we have considered how a few broader contexts for the poem affect our interpretation of its meaning, it's time to return to the model thesis on "Woodchucks" (p. 87) with these ideas in mind. Keep in mind that developing sophistication through revision does not discredit what you've written so far. Nothing in an essay's thesis or body paragraphs has to be discarded as you develop additional sophistication in an existing argument. However, because the thesis is basically home base for your argument, any changes you make to it will have to also be addressed in the body of your essay. Again, this doesn't mean your evidence and commentary need to be thrown out; it does mean that you need to extend and deepen your commentary, and perhaps add additional evidence from the text.

Let's walk through how we might revise our example working thesis for Kumin's poem, "Woodchucks," to incorporate sophistication. The original thesis reads:

> In "Woodchucks" the diction, imagery, and rhyme scheme help convey the speaker's ambivalence about her own violent behavior, illuminating her uneasiness with how quickly she resorts to harsher measures.

This thesis already provides a defensible interpretation of the speaker's perspective on her actions, and it delineates the literary elements and techniques that serve to convey this perspective. Notice, however, that it doesn't address the broader context that we are now thinking about.

So far, our thesis centers exclusively on the speaker. Kumin, however, might be using the speaker's actions to comment on humanity as a whole. If one person is able to forego nonviolence and begin to shoot woodchucks in the face, then couldn't we all turn such aggression toward each other? And hasn't the allusion to the Nazis not, in fact, suggested that humanity's capacity for cruelty and murder is frighteningly vast? Our thesis, however, is already quite long—but there's no reason to stick to just one sentence in a thesis, especially as you develop sophistication in your argument. It is perfectly acceptable to add an additional sentence to our thesis, like so:

> In "Woodchucks" the diction, imagery, and rhyme scheme help convey the speaker's ambivalence about her own violent behavior, illuminating her uneasiness with how quickly she resorts to harsher measures. This rapid descent from civility to savagery is Maxine Kumin's ultimate commentary and admonition: if left unrestrained, human beings' capacity for violence can quickly supplant morality.

This addition to our thesis stems from situating "Woodchucks" within a broader context. Notice that the thesis not only focuses on the speaker and her perspective, but also encompasses an interpretation of Kumin's broader commentary about humanity. Remember, simply adding a sentence to our thesis statement does not suddenly mean the essay is sophisticated. This change does, however, provide us with other opportunities to build upon the sophistication introduced by the revised thesis. We can address this new dimension to the argument in at least one of two ways in the remainder of the essay. We can either add commentary about the broader context to the paragraphs we already have—see Chapter 1, Section 3 for a closer look at how to do so—or we can add an entirely new body paragraph to the revised essay. Here, for instance, is a possible new body paragraph of an essay guided by the thesis we've just developed:

AP® TIP

Remember that there's no magic formula for writing about literature. Avoid using canned phrases and repeating memorized statements. Your own authentic voice needs to come through in your commentary on a text.

> Kumin's reference to World War II situates the poem within the known world, as opposed to a fictional poetic landscape; as such, the speaker's show of violence is not just a reflection of her own character, but of the capacity for violence that is inherent in all of humanity. Like many personal and political conflicts, this poem hinges upon trying to make things "right," as noted in the first line. This attempt quickly leads to "cyanide" in the second stanza, ".22" caliber bullets in the third, and the death of a "mother" and "baby" in the fourth. Such decline can only lead to the final sentence of this poem, one that simultaneously hints at regret and alludes to "the quiet Nazi way." If art is said to hold up a mirror to nature, then this poem reveals an ugly reality. Kumin laments what we're capable of turning into — and all because of the inconvenience presented by a few "woodchucks."

This interpretation is not necessarily infallible — nor is it the only plausible one. Interpreting literature in a sophisticated way, however, demands that we take risks. Yes, we need to answer the prompt — we need to discuss the speaker's perspective and the poet's language — but that does not mean that we cannot situate the poem within a broader context. Not everyone has to agree with your interpretation, and it's even possible that you might be wrong about some of your claims. But by taking these risks, you are pursuing a more complex understanding of literature which, in turn, could lead to writing that is rewarded for its sophistication.

section 3 / culminating activity

Developing Sophistication in an AP® Poetry Analysis Essay

Revise the essay that you wrote on "Mighty Pawns" by Major Jackson (p. 101) to develop a more sophisticated line of reasoning in your interpretation. As you revise, focus on situating your interpretation of the poem in a broader context.

E INSPECTION!
REMODELING &
FENCES
CALENDAR ITEMS:
Low maintenance
hours at

James Gooch

3

Analyzing Longer Fiction and Drama

Reading longer works takes time, but it also gives you time — time to encounter characters and ideas in depth. You get to visit places and worlds, real or imagined, that you might never otherwise have known. You experience vicariously the struggles, challenges, and triumphs of characters — some with backgrounds or viewpoints different from yours, others who remind you of yourself. When you immerse yourself in these worlds, you'll see how complex characters change and grow as plot lines intertwine and diverge. In longer works of fiction and drama, settings may change several times, and the point of view might even shift. All of these features of full-length texts allow a novelist or playwright to explore timeless ideas and values, what we call the human condition, from many angles throughout the narrative. As we become engaged in the times, places, lives, and issues these authors portray, we can also see alternative ways of being in the world. The French novelist Albert Camus characterized fiction as "the lie through which we tell the truth." In this paradoxical statement, he referred not to deliberate falsehoods, but imagined stories and events that allow us to reflect on what constitutes the truth in our own lives. The distance that we are granted by the fact that a novel or play is not "real" gives us freedom to interpret motivation and meaning.

In this chapter, we'll continue to discuss the literary elements and techniques that you analyzed in short fiction and poetry, but we'll consider how they work in a full-length novel or play. You'll likely find that analyzing drama is familiar: like fiction, it also requires consideration of plot, character, setting, symbol, and theme. There is, however, one major difference: a novel is intended as a private experience, whether you're reading a paper book or on an electronic device, while a play can be a social and a literary experience. Even if we're just reading a play, we imagine the performance: the actors creating the characters and reading the lines, the director interpreting the atmosphere and physical setting on stage, and especially the interaction between the performers and the audience. When we see a play on stage, we literally see how other people read, imagine, and interpret that play, and that inevitably adds to the meaning of the work.

Literary Elements of Longer Fiction and Drama

Character

In longer works, characters commonly fall into two categories: round (also called *dynamic*) or flat (also called *static*). The protagonist is typically a round, or **dynamic, character**, one who exhibits a range of emotions and personality traits and changes over the course of the story — much like real people are affected by their experiences and relationships. Round characters are, as the author E. M. Forster wrote, "capable of surprising in a convincing way." As readers, we can infer what these characters think and feel based on how they behave. Likewise, we can predict how they will act based on an author's description of their thoughts, feelings, and behavior. Our interpretations of these characters often depend on whether or not they meet our expectations of them as the plot progresses.

Round characters typically grow and change, often by experiencing conflicts and facing obstacles throughout the narrative, and the actions they take as a result typically either directly or indirectly move the plot through its climax and to a conclusion. These changes can be inward or outward, or a combination of the two — for instance, a dynamic character can experience psychological or emotional changes as a result of changes in their circumstances, such as their health and wealth. Keep in mind, too, that *growth* and *change* are not the same thing; round characters can change for the worse. In addition, round characters sometimes may not change over the course of the narrative, and this lack of change provides important insight into the meaning of the work as a whole.

Character development in longer works is often enriched by characters' inconsistent behavior — often, dynamic characters will act unpredictably, or in ways that seem to contradict their values. In fact, a character's perspective may shift during the course of a novel because of such changes. These inconsistencies often lead to major narrative conflicts and highlight what makes dynamic characters so compelling. Whether heroes or villains, likable or despicable, these characters are complex — that is, they come across as real people with flaws as well as virtues. When we enter worlds populated with such characters, we can see how their differing perspectives and values offer us various ways to interpret the meaning of the work.

Flat characters are two-dimensional, embodying only one or two traits; they usually provide a background for the protagonist's actions. Flat characters are predictable, never changing appreciably throughout the narrative, and more of a type than an individual. Some of these characters are known as **stock characters**, who may represent predictable stereotypes — such as the absent-minded professor or the town drunk — and occasionally provide comic relief. Such characters may only be part of the narrative of a novel or play to advance the plot or to illuminate major characters' motivations and development.

Another common type of character is the **foil**, a contrasting character who shines a spotlight on the protagonist through contrasting traits. This allows the protagonist to stand out more distinctly and points to how the contrasts between the characters' values and attitudes contribute to the meaning of the work as a whole. Foils are often, but not always, flat characters. In Shakespeare's play *Romeo and Juliet*, for instance, Mercutio is a dynamic character and a foil to Romeo. Mercutio's more casual approach to love and romance makes Romeo's seriousness, some may say obsessiveness, stand out.

AP® TIP

Keep in mind that not all foils are flat characters, and dynamic foils can be excellent characters for analysis in the Literary Argument essay on the exam. Even if a foil is flat, discussing this character in relation to the protagonist can help you develop a nuanced interpretation of a work.

Dialogue between characters in fiction is a key way that authors develop their characters — what is said, how it is said, and what the nature of the interaction tells us are all important. Often in a novel, dialogue and narration are interspersed, thus giving context and commentary about the actual words characters speak (generally signaled by quotation marks). In a play, **dialogue**, or the conversation between two or more characters, becomes an essential way to reveal character. Though playwrights attempt to represent normal speech patterns and usage, dramatic dialogue is usually different from normal human conversation. Every minute on stage must be used to the greatest advantage, so conversations must be pointed and charged with meaning. When reading drama, you should try to isolate three elements of dialogue: (1) the content of what is being said; (2) the way it is being said, including both the language and the stage directions for delivering the line; and (3) the reaction and response from other characters.

In *Pygmalion* by George Bernard Shaw, the two central characters, Eliza Doolittle and Henry Higgins, come from different worlds: she is a Cockney flower girl, and he is a professor of phonetics (pronunciation). Higgins bets that he can "make a duchess of this draggle-tailed guttersnipe" in six months, and he wins the bet. The following dialogue takes place as Eliza realizes that she's a fish out of water in both her new world and her old world. In this exchange, notice how the dialogue characterizes Eliza and Henry. You might want to read the lines aloud to get a better sense of the pacing and rhythm, noting that Shaw uses spacing to emphasize some words.

from Pygmalion

George Bernard Shaw

ELIZA *tries to control herself and feel indifferent as she rises and walks across to the hearth to switch off the lights. By the time she gets there she is on the point of screaming. She sits down in Higgins's chair and holds on hard to the arms. Finally she gives way and flings herself furiously on the floor raging.*

HIGGINS *[in despairing wrath outside]:* What the devil have I done with my slippers? *[He appears at the door].*

LIZA *[snatching up the slippers, and hurling them at him one after the other with all her force]:* There are your slippers. And there. Take your slippers; and may you never have a day's luck with them!

HIGGINS *[astounded]*: What on earth —! *[He comes to her]*. Whats the matter? Get up. *[He pulls her up]*. Anything wrong?

LIZA *[breathless]*: Nothing wrong — with y o u. Ive won your bet for you, havnt I? Thats enough for you. *I* dont matter, I suppose.

HIGGINS Y o u won my bet! You! Presumptuous insect! *I* won it. What did you throw those slippers at me for?

LIZA Because I wanted to smash your face. Id like to kill you, you selfish brute. Why didnt you leave me where you picked me out of — in the gutter? You thank God its all over, and that now you can throw me back again there, do you? *[She crisps her fingers frantically]*.

HIGGINS *[looking at her in cool wonder]:* The creature i s nervous, after all.

LIZA *[gives a suffocated scream of fury, and instinctively darts her nails at his face]:* !!

HIGGINS *[catching her wrists]:* Ah! would you? Claws in, you cat. How dare you shew your temper to me? Sit down and be quiet. *[He throws her roughly into the easy-chair].*

LIZA *[crushed by superior strength and weight]:* Whats to become of me? Whats to become of me?

HIGGINS How the devil do I know whats to become of you? What does it matter what becomes of you?

LIZA You dont care. I know you dont care. You wouldnt care if I was dead. I'm nothing to you — not so much as them slippers.

HIGGINS *[thundering]:* T h o s e slippers.

LIZA *[with bitter submission]:* Those slippers. I didnt think it made any difference now.

A pause. **ELIZA** *hopeless and crushed.* **HIGGINS** *a little uneasy.*

HIGGINS *[in his loftiest manner]:* Why have you begun going on like this? May I ask whether you complain of your treatment here?

LIZA No.

HIGGINS Has anybody behaved badly to you? Colonel Pickering? Mrs. Pearce? Any of the servants?

LIZA No.

HIGGINS I presume you dont pretend that I have treated you badly.

LIZA No.

HIGGINS I am glad to hear it. *[He moderates his tone]*. Perhaps youre tired after the strain of the day. Will you have a glass of champagne? *[He moves towards the door]*.

LIZA No. *[Recollecting her manners]* Thank you.

HIGGINS *[good-humored again]*: This has been coming on you for some days. I suppose it was natural for you to be anxious about the garden party. But thats all over now. *[He pats her kindly on the shoulder. She writhes]*. Theres nothing more to worry about.

LIZA No. Nothing more for y o u to worry about. *[She suddenly rises and gets away from him by going to the piano bench, where she sits and hides her face]*. Oh God! I wish I was dead.

HIGGINS *[staring after her in sincere surprise]*: Why? in heaven's name, why? *[Reasonably, going to her]* Listen to me, Eliza. All this irritation is purely subjective.

LIZA I dont understand. Im too ignorant.

HIGGINS Its only imagination. Low spirits and nothing else. Nobodys hurting you. Nothings wrong. You go to bed like a good girl and sleep it off. Have a little cry and say your prayers: that will make you comfortable.

LIZA I heard y o u r prayers. "Thank God its all over!"

HIGGINS *[impatiently]*: Well, dont you thank God its all over? Now you are free and can do what you like.

LIZA *[pulling herself together in desperation]*: What am I fit for? What have you left me fit for? Where am I to go? What am I to do? What's to become of me? ■

1913

Perhaps what is most striking in this dialogue is that Higgins never really hears Liza. She is despondent and trying to figure out how she's going to live the rest of her life, while he's trying to find his slippers. When she hurls the slippers at him along with the wish that they never bring him anything good, he responds with utter surprise, asking, "Anything wrong?" The understatement in this scene is humorous, yet as the dialogue continues, we realize that Higgins completely lacks empathy for the young woman, who is his student — and his subject. In the face of her anger, he responds indignantly that she has stepped out of her place: "Presumptuous insect," he calls her. She accuses him of not caring at all about her, and he responds by correcting her diction. He counters her emotion with sheer logic, asking her if she has been treated badly by anyone during her stay with him. Since she cannot point to any concrete act of mistreatment, he concludes that her problem is simply stress, which he dismisses as "purely subjective." Ultimately, he treats her as if she were a child, sending her off to bed to have a good cry and get some rest. The dialogue has not only shown us the quintessential failure to communicate but also characterized Higgins as intellectual and detached and Liza as a woman in the midst of an identity crisis.

AP® TIP

When you analyze scenes from a play, be sure to consider varying ways an actor might deliver lines. For example, how might the meaning of the previous excerpt change, depending on Eliza's tone of voice?

Another important technique that playwrights use to reveal character is the **soliloquy** — a **monologue** in which a character, alone on the stage, reveals their thoughts or emotions, as if the character is thinking out loud. Through a soliloquy, a playwright can reveal to the audience a character's motivation, intent, or even doubt. For example, in William Shakespeare's *Richard III*, Richard — Duke of Gloucester, brother to King Edward IV, and later King Richard III of England — opens the play with the following soliloquy.

from Richard III

William Shakespeare

Enter RICHARD DUKE OF GLOUCESTER, *solus*

RICHARD Now is the winter of our discontent
Made glorious summer by this son of York,[1]
And all the clouds that loured[2] upon our house
In the deep bosom of the ocean buried.
Now are our brows bound with victorious wreaths,
Our bruisèd arms hung up for monuments,
Our stern alarums changed to merry meetings,
Our dreadful marches to delightful measures.[3]
Grim-visaged war[4] hath smoothed his wrinkled front,
And now, instead of mounting barbèd steeds[5]
To fright the souls of fearful adversaries,
He[6] capers nimbly in a lady's chamber
To the lascivious[7] pleasing of a lute.
But I that am not shaped for sportive tricks
Nor made to court an amorous looking-glass,
I that am rudely stamped and want love's majesty
To strut before a wanton[8] ambling nymph,
I that am curtailed of this fair proportion,
Cheated of feature by dissembling[9] nature,
Deformed, unfinished, sent before my time
Into this breathing world scarce half made up,
And that so lamely and unfashionable[10]
That dogs bark at me as I halt by them,
Why, I, in this weak piping[11] time of peace,
Have no delight to pass away the time,
Unless to see my shadow in the sun
And descant[12] on mine own deformity.
And therefore, since I cannot prove a lover
To entertain these fair well-spoken days,
I am determinèd to prove a villain
And hate the idle pleasures of these days. ■

1593

[1] A pun on "son" and reference to the king. — Eds.
[2] Scowled. — Eds.
[3] Stately dances. — Eds.
[4] A reference to Mars (Ares), the Greek god of war. — Eds.
[5] Armored horses. — Eds.
[6] "He" is Mars (Ares). — Eds.
[7] Seductive. — Eds.
[8] Lewd. — Eds.
[9] Lying, deceitful. — Eds.
[10] Misshapen, ugly. — Eds.
[11] The pipe was associated with peace, the fife with war. — Eds.
[12] To comment at length, or riff on an idea or theme. — Eds.

This soliloquy reveals that Richard, the play's main character, has villainous intent. In his deformity, he feels out of place, at odds with his surroundings, and expresses jealousy and disdain for those not "curtailed of this fine proportion." Richard prefers "dreadful marches" to "delightful measures," expressing his scorn for "glorious summer" and for his brother the king. The duplicity and deceitfulness that puts the plot in motion and creates the conflict of the play is clear to the audience but not to other characters, resulting in **dramatic irony**. The audience has become privy to Richard's inner thoughts. When he says, "I am determinèd to prove a villain," he lets the audience in on his plans. The audience knows the king is in danger. Without a narrator to give us access to the mind of a character, a soliloquy is the perfect way to expose their inner workings, struggles, reflections, and intentions.

KEY QUESTIONS

Analyzing Character in Longer Fiction and Drama

- Which characters are fully developed as dynamic human beings? How do characters change — or remain the same — throughout the text?
- How does the dialogue between or among characters help develop them and propel the plot forward?
- Which characters display contradictory or inconsistent traits and actions? How do these elements reflect their complex humanity? How do such complexities contribute to the major conflict(s) of the work?
- Are there characters that act as foils? If so, what contrast to a central character does the foil emphasize? How does this contrast reveal a larger meaning?
- How do different characters' perspectives reveal different information or portray different attitudes toward the ideas in the text?

Analyzing Character in Longer Fiction and Drama

activity

Choose a novel, play, film, or television series that you know well and find compelling. Explain how the dynamic characters develop and change over the course of the narrative, and discuss the role that flat characters play in revealing the meaning of the work as a whole. If you have chosen a work of drama, examine how a specific scene reveals and develops characters. Identify any foils in the work and discuss how the contrasts they reveal shape your interpretation of the characters.

Setting

As you read in Chapter 1, setting indicates the time and place, the when and where, of a literary text. As in short fiction, the setting of a novel or play is a backdrop that provides essential details central to the development of character and the exploration of ideas and values in the text. In a play, there is also a physical set to consider. The playwright has to keep this in mind when writing and be realistic about what most theaters will be able to stage. In modern plays, we usually find fairly explicit information about the setting, which a director can use to create a set and which we, as readers, can use to build a mental image. In *A Doll's House* by Henrik Ibsen, for instance, the scenery for Act I is described in considerable detail:

from A Doll's House

Henrik Ibsen

A comfortable room, tastefully but not expensively furnished. A door to the right in the back wall leads to the entryway; another to the left leads to HELMER*'s study. Between these doors, a piano. Midway in the left-hand wall a door, and further back a window. Near the window a round table with an armchair and a small sofa. In the right-hand wall, toward the rear, a door, and nearer the foreground a porcelain stove with two armchairs and a rocking chair beside it. Between the stove and the side door, a small table. Engravings on the walls. An étagère with china figures and other small art objects; a small bookcase with richly bound books; the floor carpeted; a fire burning in the stove. It is a winter day.*

[A bell rings in the entryway; shortly after we hear the door being unlocked. **NORA** *comes into the room, humming happily to herself; she is wearing street clothes and carries an armload of packages, which she puts down on the table to the right. She has left the hall door open, and through it a Delivery Boy is seen holding a Christmas tree and a basket, which he gives to the Maid who let them in.]* ■

1879

Ibsen's instructions indicate where doors and windows are, the location of a piano, and the placement of a rocker next to two armchairs. At the same time, some of the directions are subject to interpretation, such as this being a "comfortable room, tastefully but not expensively furnished." That part is left to the reader's — or set designer's — imagination.

Historical Contexts

A novel or play may be set in a historical era — a time and place that has its own political, economic, or social norms and upheavals. Historical fiction seeks to re-create a specific event or period in history. Very popular today, it is a time-honored approach to the novel with such well-known examples as *All Quiet on the Western Front* (1929) by Erich Maria Remarque, set in World War I; *A Tale of Two Cities* (1859) by Charles Dickens, set during the French Revolution; and *The Good Lord Bird* (2014) by James McBride, set during the antebellum era, just before the Civil War. In many cases, the historical context goes unstated because it is part of the knowledge that the author expects the reader to bring to the text. For instance, Jesmyn Ward's award-winning novel *Salvage the Bones* (2011) is set in Louisiana in 2005, specifically during the devastation of Hurricane Katrina. While all but one of the chapters of the novel do not directly name this event, she structures the entire book in relation to it, naming the chapters by days that function as a countdown, from "The First Day" to "The Twelfth Day." The following passage, taken from "The Eleventh Day: Katrina," depicts the Batiste family — the teenage narrator Esch, her brothers, and her father — as they try to escape the encroaching water by taking shelter in the attic of their home.

AP® TIP

The AP® exam only requires you to make use of the information provided by the text, so don't worry too much about guessing at the exact historical era of a setting. Just keep an eye out for details that "date" a work, such as whether characters ride in cars or horse-drawn carriages.

from **Salvage the Bones**

Jesmyn Ward

"Open the attic," Daddy says.

The water is lapping the backs of my knees.

"It's stuck," Randall says. He is pulling at the string that hangs from the door of the attic, which is in the ceiling of the hallway.

"Pull down," Daddy says. He frowns, holds his hand up like he is pulling the cord.

The water slides past my crotch, and I jump.

"All right!" Skeet yells. He pulls himself up on the cord, like he is swinging from a swing rope in a tree, and the attic door groans downward.

"Up!" Randall says, and he is shoving Junior up the ladder into the attic. . . .

"Go!" Skeetah says, and he pushes me toward the ladder. I float on the water, my toes dragging on the hallway carpet. He grabs my back and steadies me as I slog into the attic with the bucket.

"Esch!" Junior says.

"I'm here." Junior's eyes are white in the dark. The wind beats the roof, and it creaks. Randall is next, then Daddy, and last, Skeetah. I cup the bucket with my knees, sit on a pile of boxes, fish out a broken ornament that is digging into my thigh. Christmas decorations. Randall is sitting on an old chain saw, Junior cowering next to him. Daddy takes out the package he put in his pants after the tree fell into his room. It is a clear plastic bag. He opens the packet, pulls out pictures. Just before Skeetah pulls shut the attic door, seals us in darkness, Daddy makes as if he would touch one of the pictures, hesitant, as lightly as if he is dislodging an eyelash, but his glistening finger stops short, and he wraps the pictures again and puts them in his pants.

Mama.

The attic door moans shut. ■

2011

In this passage, we're actually dealing with two settings: the outdoor setting of the storm, which threatens the family and their home, and the indoor setting of the attic, where they hope to find shelter. Their struggle against nature in this excerpt opens and closes with the attic door opening and closing. Specific textual details reveal the dramatic setting. Esch chronicles the water "lapping" and "slid[ing]" as it rises—while these aren't quite human traits, they do help us imagine that the water has a life of its own. The way the family helps one another to grab the rope, open the door, and escape the water builds the sense of imminent threat. As readers, we feel the struggle of humans vs. nature. At the end, when the father pulls out the photo of his wife, who died in childbirth, the human spirit seems to prevail — at least for the moment. However, the moment when the attic door "moans shut" suggests ominously that the struggle is not over.

Did this particular event actually happen during the hurricane? Likely not — and yet the struggle of individuals and families to survive, perhaps even to hold on to a few meaningful parts of their lives, such as a photograph of a loved one, rings true. This natural disaster, one of the worst in U.S. history, caused long-lasting destruction and hit the most vulnerable populations, like the Batistes, the hardest. When *Salvage the Bones* was published, less than a decade after Katrina, that historical setting was still very much in the consciousness of readers. It was a setting that brought memories if not from lived experience then through news stories and media footage. Ward has used this historical setting to draw her readers into the immediate and long-lasting effects of Hurricane Katrina, showing the strength of family and community in the face of such catastrophe. Setting, thus, contributes in a significant way to developing the meaning of the novel as a whole.

Social and Cultural Contexts

Setting may also establish the cultural environment of a work — the manners, mores, customs, rituals, and codes of conduct. In some instances, particularly in science fiction, an author has to invent a new culture. In other instances, the cultural environment is based on an actual period, culture, or community. In the following excerpt from *Beka Lamb* by Zee Edgell (1982), the setting is Belize, formerly British Honduras, at a time when the colony was moving toward independence.

from Beka Lamb

Zee Edgell

On a warm November day Beka Lamb won an essay contest at St. Cecilia's Academy, situated not far from the front gate of His Majesty's Prison on Milpa Lane. It seemed to her family that overnight Beka changed from what her mother called a "flat rate Belize creole" into a person with "high mind."

"Befo' time," her Gran remarked towards nightfall, Beka would never have won that contest." . . .

The front verandah was in its evening gloom, and the honeyed scent of flowering stephanotis, thickly woven in the warping lattice work, reminded Beka of the wreaths at her great granny's funeral. The vine half-screened the verandah from excessive sunlight during the daytime, and at night, provided a private place from which to observe passersby. . . . Her Gran continued,

"And long befo' time, you wouldn't *be* at no convent school."

On the far side of the street below, Miss Eila limped her way to the waterside, a slop bucket heavy in her right hand. As she drew abreast the Lamb yard, she called,

"Any out tonight, Miss Ivy?" Beka was grateful for a slight breeze that carried the bucket's stench away from the house.

"One or two, Eila," Beka's Gran called across, brushing at her ankles with a cloth she used as a fly whisk. Steadying the swing, she got up and leaned on folded arms over the railing.

"The boys went into prison this morning, Eila! Going to the meeting tonight?"

"Shurest thing, Miss Ivy," Eila said. . . .

The People's Independence Party, formed nearly two years before, was bringing many political changes to the small colony. And Beka's grandmother, an early member of the party, felt she deserved some credit for the shift Beka was making from the washing bowl underneath the house bottom to books in a classroom overlooking the Caribbean Sea. ■

1982

The cultural environment of this setting is shown through the physical descriptions, dialogue, and political references, which work together to convey an overall sense of the community. The very first sentence creates a dissonant setting: a school run by a religious institution next to a prison named for the British Crown. The second sentence establishes that the setting is Belize during its time as a colony of the United Kingdom. Within this environment, the main character Beka has won an essay contest. Even her grandmother expressed surprise because in the past prizes would automatically be awarded to white students, and she notes that before that, schools wouldn't have admitted Black people at all. The prison, on the other hand, is a reminder of a place where the colonized people of Belize — including "the boys" Beka's grandmother mentions — have always been relegated. Edgell adds authenticity to this setting by writing dialogue that reflects the structure and pronunciation of the local vernacular. The description of the "front verandah" also features details of the indigenous plant life, vividly depicting its vantage point as a place to watch neighbors pass by. Near the end of the passage, we are reminded again of the prison as Edgell raises what will become a central issue in the novel: the movement for independence from Britain, which Beka's grandmother, as "an early member of the [People's Independence] party," has long supported. From this setting of discord and change, propelled by community and family support, Beka emerges as someone moving from "the washing bowl underneath the house bottom to books in a classroom overlooking the Caribbean Sea." In other words, her educational opportunities offer the freedom signaled by the beauty and clarity of the ocean — a freedom denied to Belizean women of prior generations.

KEY QUESTIONS

Analyzing Setting in Longer Fiction and Drama

- How does a character's relationship to setting help develop that character?
- What does the setting suggest about the values characters may have or may be confronted by?
- How does a character's position as a member or outsider of the society or culture of a work contribute to a larger meaning?
- What elements of setting are most important to the overall meaning or themes in the text?
- How do the historical, social, and cultural contexts of setting contribute to more abstract ideas in the work?

Analyzing Setting in Longer Fiction and Drama

Choose a novel or play you have already read and discuss how its setting contributes to the meaning of the work as a whole. Which details provide information about the environment in which the story takes place? How does the setting and its associated cultural norms communicate characters' values?

Plot

In Chapter 1, we discussed plot in fiction through literary elements that include rising tensions and conflict, suspense, resolution (also known as **catharsis**), foreshadowing, and flashback. In longer works authors are able to spin out more complicated plots in even greater depth, and the major events of the plot often dovetail with the major conflicts between and within the characters, thus revealing how characters' conflicting values shape the structure of a text.

Another characteristic of longer works is that they leave room for more than one major conflict; often two or more conflicts in a text will develop and intersect. For instance, in August Wilson's play *Fences* (p. 1047), the relationships Troy, the main character, has with his eldest son and with his wife erupt in two distinct but intertwined conflicts that amount to a crisis of identity for Troy. In this example, the conflicts carry a similar weight within the play, but frequently a longer work will contain multiple smaller conflicts that are intensified due to an overarching, primary conflict that intersects with them in some way. One example of this is in F. Scott Fitzgerald's novel *The Great Gatsby*, as Jay Gatsby's overwhelming desire to win over his lost love, Daisy Buchanan, intensifies conflicts with various characters, particularly her husband. The conflicts deepen and accumulate as Gatsby's desperate efforts to impress her and growing delusions about their relationship propel the plot toward its final explosion into violence. Because the tensions of these interrelated conflicts steadily increase, the tragedy of the ending seems inevitable. Some conflicts in longer works are rooted in events or characters not depicted on the page. For instance, the death of King Hamlet in Shakespeare's play *Hamlet* (p. 555) occurs before Act I—yet Prince Hamlet's internal struggle with how to avenge his father's death animates all five acts. Finally, keep in mind that not all major conflicts in a work will necessarily resolve—but this lack of resolution does not equate to a lack of meaning. In fact, ambiguous endings often leave you with more avenues for developing an interpretation.

AP® TIP

Have confidence as you construct your own interpretations of texts with ambiguous endings. There are no "right" answers. You just need to provide solid evidence from the text to support your analysis.

Plot works similarly in drama as in fiction — in other words, it's the events of a story that relate to a central conflict(s). Unlike novels, drama, however, is often broken into **acts**, and acts are further divided into **scenes**. Acts and scenes structure a play, and it can be revealing to consider why the acts and scenes are divided as they are. All of Shakespeare's plays are divided into five acts, a structure that provides a distinct beginning, middle, and end. In many plays, drama is all about action: characters make decisions that have consequences. That means that events both shape and are shaped by character.

It's important to keep in mind that not all of the events of a plot are equally important, particularly in longer works such as novels and plays. Think of it this way: the events of a plot are made up of scenes and interactions between characters. A scene where a character drives to the grocery store is not as important as a scene in which a character gets into a major car accident on the way to the grocery store or meets a love interest in the parking lot of the grocery store. This is because the events of a plot are only as important as their relationship to other major literary elements such as narrative, conflict, and character.

Examining how authors choose to present these events to readers is an important step in interpreting the meaning of a longer work. These structural decisions reveal which events are most important, shape our understanding of the characters' development throughout the course of the narrative, and present us with contrasts that illuminate the ambiguities and contradictions at the heart of the work. **Linear plots** are arranged chronologically; they effectively build tension and suspense and chart the growth of characters in a fairly straightforward way. For this reason, coming-of-age stories often have linear plots. One example of this structure discussed earlier in the chapter is *Salvage the Bones* by Jesmyn Ward. Each of its chapters moves forward in time, day by day, as Hurricane Katrina comes closer, gathers strength, hits with catastrophic force, and moves on. Such chapter divisions structure what happens and how we as readers experience it. Twelve days isn't actually a very long time for a novel of nearly three hundred pages, yet that structure reinforces the intensity of the experience. Each day tensions rise and conflicts heighten as we see characters meeting the crisis in different ways.

While *Salvage the Bones* is told chronologically, **nonlinear plots** present the events of a narrative either out of chronological order or interrupt that order using techniques that include those we discussed in Chapter 1: **flashback**, **foreshadowing**, and ***in medias res***. Other techniques, such as stream of consciousness, are inextricably tied to narrative perspective and point of view, and we will discuss them later in this chapter. All of these techniques don't just interrupt the plot; they also tend to upset our expectations of the text, creating anticipation or building tension in a different way than a straightforward accumulation of events. The main thing for you to consider regarding plot and structure is *how* and *why* an author structures the telling of a story in a specific way — what is the author trying to tell us through this arrangement of events?

KEY QUESTIONS

Analyzing Plot in Longer Fiction and Drama

- How are the events of the plot arranged? Is the narrative structure linear or nonlinear? How does this arrangement reveal meaning?
- What are the major conflicts in the text, and how do they intersect? What are the sources of these conflicts? What resolution, if any, occurs by the end of the work?
- How do the events of the plot relate to each other? What effect do they have on the characters and conflicts of the narrative — are they occasions for contrast? Do they raise tensions? Does one event reinforce another or introduce ambiguity?
- How do the events of the plot add up to create a complete narrative arc? What meaning do they reveal when you look at them all together?

Analyzing Plot in Longer Fiction and Drama

Choose a novel or play that has a linear plot and discuss how its structure reinforces meaning. First, analyze how one event early in the work relates to another event later on; then, analyze how one of those events contributes to the overall meaning of the work. Identify specific parts of the plot that apply to both fiction and drama, such as exposition, rising action, climax, falling action, and denouement, and discuss how the structure of acts and/or scenes affects your interpretation of the work.

Narrative Perspective and Point of View

The basics of narrative perspective discussed in Chapter 1 apply to novels and plays, but the length and complexity of a full work opens up even more possibilities for how a story is told. While the narrative perspectives and techniques we'll cover in this chapter can be found in short fiction, they most often appear in full-length works because of their complexity.

The power of who gets to tell the story is integral to its meaning; therefore, the effects of narrative perspective are heightened and drawn out over full-length works. One way to think about this concept is through the idea of "subject" and "object": the subject is the observer — the narrator — and the object is what is being observed — in other words, the object can encompass virtually anything that isn't the narrator, including the events of the plot, the setting, and even the other characters. The subject, then, has authority over the object, because the subject gets to speak. Many twentieth-century and contemporary novels and plays purposely upset this power dynamic by retelling the story from a different narrative perspective.

The 1847 novel *Jane Eyre* by Charlotte Brontë, for instance, is an iconic bildungsroman about an orphaned English girl. Jane narrates her experiences of various trials and tribulations before meeting and eventually marrying Rochester, a wealthy Englishman whose fortune was made in the sugar trade in the Caribbean. One of the obstacles to their union is his Caribbean wife, Bertha, who is presented as a mad woman kept in the attic of his English home. At various points we read that Bertha's laugh is "preternatural and mirthless" and "demonic." When she comes into Jane's room, Bertha is described as "tall and large, with thick and dark hair hanging long down her back." Her features were "fearful and ghastly," and Jane refers to her as "it": "What it was whether beast or human being, one could not at first sight tell: it grovelled," "snatched and growled," "bellowed," and "gazed wildly." Jane goes so far as to call Bertha a "lunatic."

Writer Jean Rhys took note of this portrayal, commenting that Bertha "seemed such a poor ghost, I thought I'd like to write her a life." That's exactly what she did in the novel *Wide Sargasso Sea*, published in 1966. In this prequel to *Jane Eyre*, Rhys gives Bertha a backstory and a new name: Antoinette. She tells much of the novel from

Antoinette's perspective in ways that confront and challenge her characterization in Brontë's novel. The details that Antoinette provides reveal her viewpoint, not someone else's view of her. The novel reveals details of her upbringing and paints an unfavorable picture of Rochester as cold and controlling; after rejecting essentially every aspect of her Caribbean identity, including her name, he basically forces her to return to England with him as his prisoner. Reading *Wide Sargasso Sea* fundamentally alters readers' experience and understanding of Antoinette/Bertha's story, leading to new and expanded interpretations of the character of Rochester's first wife, of Rochester himself, and of the novel *Jane Eyre*. That's the power of narrative perspective.

Let's explore some other variations on narrative perspective and point of view, examining less traditional ways that authors reveal a narrator's perspective and how a narrator's reliability affects a narrative.

Stream of Consciousness

Stream of consciousness is a narrative technique characteristic of early twentieth-century writers like William Faulkner, James Joyce, and Virginia Woolf, and more contemporary writers like Toni Morrison and Cormac McCarthy. It takes readers inside the mind of a narrator, recounting thoughts, impressions, and feelings, from either a first-person or a third-person limited omniscient perspective. The reader is privy to exactly what the character is thinking, without the filters of causality or logic. Such interior monologues are often characterized by fragments, swift (or entirely absent) transitions, and a free association of ideas. Stream of consciousness writing is often one of many narrative techniques at work in a novel. Typically, the writer takes readers in and out of the stream, shifting back and forth between interior monologue and other points of view. In the following passage from *Ulysses*, Joyce takes us into the mind of Leopold Bloom as he walks through the streets of Dublin, Ireland. Among the things already on his mind are his wife, Molly; her father, Old Tweedy; and a funeral that he will attend later in the day.

from **Ulysses**

James Joyce

He crossed to the bright side, avoiding the loose cellarflap of number seventy five. The sun was nearing the steeple of George's church. Be a warm day I fancy. Specially in these black clothes feel it more. Black conducts, reflects (refracts is it?), the heat. But I couldn't go in that light suit. Make a picnic of it. His eyelids sank quietly often as he walked in happy warmth. Boland's breadvan delivering with trays our daily but she prefers yesterday's loaves turnovers crisp crowns hot. Makes you feel young. Somewhere in the east: early morning: set off at dawn, travel round in front of the sun steal a day's march on him. Keep it up for ever never grow a day older technically. Walk along a strand, strange land, come to a city gate, sentry there, old ranker too, old Tweedy's big moustaches leaning on a long kind of a spear.

(continued)

Wander through awned streets. Turbaned faces going by. Dark caves of carpet shops, big man, Turko the terrible, seated crosslegged smoking a coiled pipe. Cries of sellers in the streets. Drink water scented with fennel, sherbet. Wander along all day. Might meet a robber or two. Well, meet him. Getting on to sundown. The shadows of the mosques along the pillars: priest with a scroll rolled up. A shiver of the trees, signal, the evening wind. I pass on. Fading gold sky. A mother watches from her doorway. She calls her children home in their dark language. High wall: beyond strings twanged. Night sky moon, violet, colour of Molly's new garters. Strings. Listen. A girl playing one of those instruments what do you call them: dulcimers. I pass.

Probably not a bit like it really. Kind of stuff you read: in the track of the sun. Sunburst on the titlepage. He smiled, pleasing himself. ■

1922

While this narrative technique gives us access to an intimate perspective, it also requires us to pay close attention and participate in the reading to a greater degree than usual. Notice how we hear the narration directly from Bloom's thoughts, as he experiences them. We hear and see what he hears and sees. His senses prompt his imagination to create a daydream, and the reader is carried along with it, catching glimpses of the "[d]ark caves of carpet shops," the "shadows of the mosques along the pillars," "[a] shiver of the trees," and the "[f]ading gold sky" — until Bloom's rational mind brings him back: "Probably not a bit like it really." Yet that narration offers no overt causality or other stated connections among Bloom's perceptions and ideas. At first, stream of consciousness can be challenging to read, because making order out of what seems confusing is largely left to the reader. But, once you have fully entered the narrative, you may come to appreciate the heightened state of awareness it conveys.

Layered Points of View

Not every story has a straightforward first- or third-person point of view. Often a novel is told through multiple layered perspectives. In her novel *A Crime in the Neighborhood*, Suzanne Berne tells the story from the viewpoint of a woman, Marsha, who recalls a violent crime that occurred when she was an adolescent. In the following passage, Marsha is remembering an encounter between a suspicious neighbor and her mother, who is waiting for guests to arrive for a barbecue.

from A Crime in the Neighborhood

Suzanne Berne

"I think I would like a little more wine, thank you," [my mother] added after a moment, and held out her cup.

As he bent to refill her cup, their eyes met and she smiled up at him. "It's still early," she told him. "They might still come."

"Yes," he said.

Two stories above them, I propped my chin on the back of a hand, leaning on the windowsill. Had she remembered to turn off the burner from under the pan of hamburger meat? Had she noticed, on her way out, if the freezer door was ajar?

When I look back I don't have trouble understanding how my mother got herself into Mr. Green's yard that night. All the time she had been preparing dinner she must have been glancing out the kitchen window, watching him as he sat alone in his unsteady chair, stiff khaki shirt fading into the early evening. I suppose it was the cumulative effect of that vision that finally made her fumble toward the door as if the hamburger meat had already burned, as if the whole house were filled with smoke. Because as I recall it now there *was* something dire in the sight of Mr. Green that evening. Something powerful enough to send my mother rushing from the house, barefoot half-dressed. . . . What must have made my mother's eyes sting that summer evening, what must have made her almost run to the kitchen door, had to be the fury of mortal fear — the fear that comes from understanding all at once that you are by yourself in a vast world, and that one day something worse than anything that has ever happened before will happen. ■

1998

The narrator begins recounting the story through dialogue between her mother and Mr. Green, dialogue that the narrator reconstructs from memory but presents as though it were just occurring. Her narrative voice intrudes from "[t]wo stories above them," as she remembers herself as a young girl looking down from an upstairs window, where she watched the encounter and wondered if her mother "remembered to turn off the burner from under the pan of hamburger meat." In the next paragraph, the narrator reminds us that an older, more mature person is telling the story as a flashback: "When I look back. . . ." What follows is hardly the consciousness of the young girl at the windowsill but that of an adult who is remembering the story and reflecting on how it influenced her.

Sometimes a novel is told from multiple perspectives, using a series of different narrators. In some cases, different characters move the plot forward, each one picking up where the other left off. But in other cases, different characters relate the same events from their own perspectives, giving the reader a more complicated and nuanced understanding of their meaning. In *The Joy Luck Club* by Amy Tan, for example, there are seven narrators. In some chapters, the same event is described from the differing perspectives of a mother and a daughter, emphasizing the highly subjective nature of their experiences. These shifts between mothers and daughters also emphasize generational and cultural divisions.

Another layered technique is to introduce a story using another story, called a **narrative frame** or frame story. A narrative frame establishes who is telling the main story and under what circumstances. Narrative frames usually create a shift in perspective. If the frame story is told in first-person present tense, perhaps the main story will be told as a flashback or in third person as something that happened to someone else. When a frame is used to pass on a secondhand story, the reader is left to wonder if the narrator is getting everything right, or if they are misremembering or embellishing the tale. Emily Brontë uses a narrative frame for her novel *Wuthering Heights*. The book's primary narrator is a gentleman named Lockwood, who has come to live at Thrushcross Grange. His mysterious landlord, Heathcliff, lives at neighboring Wuthering Heights. In a journal, Lockwood records the story told to him by Mrs. Dean, a former servant of the Earnshaws, the family that originally owned Wuthering Heights. In the following excerpt, the novel moves from the frame to the story within it as Lockwood talks with Mrs. Dean. At the end of the passage, she begins to narrate the story within the story.

from **Wuthering Heights**

Emily Brontë

"Oh, I'll turn the talk on my landlord's family!" I thought to myself. "A good subject to start—and that pretty girl-widow, I should like to know her history; whether she be a native of the country, or, as is more probable, an exotic that the surly indigenae will not recognise for kin."

With this intention I asked Mrs. Dean why Heathcliff let Thrushcross Grange, and preferred living in a situation and residence so much inferior.

"Is he not rich enough to keep the estate in good order?" I enquired.

"Rich, sir!" she returned. "He has, nobody knows what money, and every year it increases. Yes, yes, he's rich enough to live in a finer house than this; but he's very near—close-handed; and, if he had meant to flit to Thrushcross Grange, as soon as he heard of a good tenant, he could not have borne to miss the change of getting a few hundreds more. It is strange people should be so greedy, when they are alone in the world!"

"He had a son, it seems?"

"Yes, he had one—he is dead."

"And that young lady, Mrs. Heathcliff, is his widow?"

"Yes."

"Where did she come from originally?"

"Why, sir, she is my late master's daughter; Catherine Linton was her maiden name. I nursed her, poor thing! I did wish Mr. Heathcliff would remove here, and then we might have been together again."

"What, Catherine Linton!" I exclaimed, astonished. But a minute's reflection convinced me it was not my ghostly Catherine. "Then," I continued, "my predecessor's name was Linton?"

"It was."

"And who is that Earnshaw, Hareton Earnshaw, who lives with Mr. Heathcliff? are they relations?"

"No; he is the late Mr. Linton's nephew."

"The young lady's cousin, then?"

"Yes; her husband was her cousin also—one, on the mother's—the other, on the father's side—Heathcliff married Mr. Linton's sister."

"I see the house at Wuthering Heights has 'Earnshaw' carved over the front door. Are they an old family?"

"Very old, sir; and Hareton is the last of them, as our Miss Cathy is of us—I mean, of the Lintons. Have you been to Wuthering Heights? I beg pardon for asking; but I should like to hear how she is."

"Mrs. Heathcliff? she looked very well, and very handsome; yet, I think, not very happy."

"Oh dear, I don't wonder! And how did you like the master?"

"A rough fellow, rather, Mrs. Dean. Is not that his character?"

"Rough as a saw-edge, and hard as whinstone! The less you meddle with him the better."

"He must have had some ups and downs in life to make him such a churl. Do you know anything of his history?"

"It's a cuckoo's, sir—I know all about it; except where he was born, and who were his parents, and how he got his money, at first—And Hareton has been cast out like an unfledged dunnock—The unfortunate lad is the only one, in all this parish, that does not guess how he has been cheated!"

"Well, Mrs. Dean, it will be a charitable deed to tell me something of my neighbors—I feel I shall not rest, if I go to bed; so be good enough to sit and chat an hour."

"Oh, certainly, sir! I'll just fetch a little sewing, and then I'll sit as long as you please. But you've caught cold, I saw you shivering, and you must have some gruel to drive it out."

The worthy woman bustled off, and I crouched nearer the fire: my head felt hot, and the rest of me chill: moreover I was excited, almost to a pitch of foolishness through my nerves and brain. This caused me to feel, not uncomfortable, but rather fearful, as I am still, of serious effects from the incidents of to-day and yesterday.

She returned presently, bringing a smoking basin and a basket of work; and, having placed the former on the hob, drew in her seat, evidently pleased to find me so companionable.

Before I came to live here, she commenced, waiting no further invitation to her story; I was almost always at Wuthering Heights. . . . ■

1847

When a writer uses a narrative frame, there is often a thematic link between the frame and the main narrative. Both Lockwood and Mrs. Dean wish to understand how the past haunts as well as shapes the present and to make sense of the present state of affairs at Wuthering Heights. With a frame of this sort, this story gets told in several different ways:

- Lockwood narrates his move to Thrushcross Grange and his first encounter with his landlord, Heathcliff, at neighboring Wuthering Heights.
- Lockwood asks Mrs. Dean about Heathcliff and Catherine and their histories. He records her story in a journal, quoting and paraphrasing her as she narrates up to the present.
- Within Mrs. Dean's story, other characters—including Catherine and Heathcliff—also narrate, telling stories within the story.
- Lockwood narrates the final section of the book, using the details of the story he has been told by Mrs. Dean to make sense of contemporary events.

This complex storytelling technique effectively draws a connection between Mrs. Dean and Lockwood as it moves between the frame and the main narrative. It also draws a connection between Lockwood and Heathcliff that goes well beyond that of landlord and tenant as Lockwood learns about Heathcliff's past—and perhaps most significantly, between Lockwood and the reader, who must try to make sense of strange and intriguing characters and events.

Unreliable Narrators

One quirk of first-person, and occasionally third-person, narration is that the author might choose to tell the story from the perspective of someone who is naive, mentally ill, biased, corrupt, or downright immoral. A narrator of this sort is called an **unreliable narrator**. An author may choose an unreliable narrator to create tension as readers try to determine what is true or fact and what is downright false or a matter of perspective. Unreliable narrators are often interesting, complex characters who may have an inherent bias or at least some blind spots that create a subjective viewpoint. An unreliable narrator may lead readers to question trustworthiness, which influences interpretations of the novel as a whole. In his 2005 novel *Never Let Me Go*, Kazuo Ishiguro presents a dystopian world where clones are raised to "donate" their organs little by little until they die. Kathy, the narrator, opens the novel in what at first appears to be a matter-of-fact way, but a closer look reveals all is not as it seems.

from **Never Let Me Go**

Kazuo Ishiguro

My name is Kathy H. I'm thirty-one years old, and I've been a carer now for over eleven years. That sounds long enough, I know, but actually they want me to go on for another eight months. . . . Now I know my being a carer so long isn't necessarily because they think I'm fantastic at what I do. There are some really good carers who've been told to stop after just two or three years. And I can think of one carer at least who went on for all of fourteen years despite being a complete waste of space. So I'm not trying to boast. But then I do know for a fact they've been pleased with my work. . . . My donors have always tended to do much better than expected, their recovery times have been impressive, and hardly any of them have been classified as "agitated," even before fourth donation. Okay, maybe I *am* boasting now. But it means a lot to me, being able to do my work well. . . .

Anyway, I'm not making any big claims for myself. I know carers . . . who are just as good and don't get half the credit. If you're one of them, I can understand how you might get resentful — about my bedsit, my car, above all, the way I get to pick and choose who I look after. . . . Kathy H., they say, she gets to pick and choose, and she always chooses her own kind. . . . I've heard it said enough, so I'm sure you've heard it plenty more, and maybe there's something in it. But . . . I've done my share of looking after donors brought up in every kind of place. By the time I finish, remember, I'll have done twelve years of this, and it's only for the last six they've let me choose. ■

2005

What might signal unreliability in this narrator? Kathy opens the novel by offering facts — her name, age, years at her current job (a "carer") — in a fairly unemotional voice. On first read this might seem unremarkable, but from the very start she's already hidden some aspect of her identity from us by not sharing her full last name. The job of "carer" is vague, and the more details she reveals, the clearer it becomes that there is no job like this anywhere but in the universe of the book. That in itself does not signal unreliability, but it does put the reader on alert for things that are just slightly different from the world we live in. Some of the details she presents next are small but important: "they" (likely her employers) want her to remain at a job she has worked for eleven years for another eight months, but she goes on to state that carers' abilities have no real bearing on how many years they are asked to work. She then insists that she is "not trying to boast" about her work but admits "maybe I *am* boasting now" just two sentences later, and finally doubles back again to say that she's "not making any big claims" about her job performance. Why does she go back and forth like this? Is she trying to come across as competent but humble? Is she defensive about the way she does her job — and if so, why? All we know so far is that she has contradicted herself two separate times almost immediately. As the second paragraph of the passage continues, Kathy makes statements that seem almost defensive: "I can understand how you might get resentful," she says, addressing a perhaps imagined attack on her character. "They" allege that "she always chooses her own kind" — and, on top of that, Kathy acknowledges that "maybe there's something in it." But then she backpedals: "I've done my share of looking after donors brought up in every kind of place," she says, reminding us to "remember" that she's only been able to "pick and choose" for the last six years. At the end of the passage we're left with the sense that Kathy has no clear idea of who she is — or perhaps she doesn't want us to have one.

KEY QUESTIONS

Analyzing Narrative Perspective and Point of View in Longer Fiction and Drama

- From what point of view is the work told? Is the narrator a participant or an observer in the story?
- Is the story told from multiple perspectives or within a narrative frame? If so, to what effect?
- How reliable is the narrator? How does the narrator's reliability inform your interpretation of the other major literary elements in the text?
- Does the point of view shift during the course of the work? If so, what is the impact on your interpretation of the work?

Analyzing Narrative Perspective and Point of View in Longer Fiction and Drama

activity

First, choose a narrator from a novel you have read and explain how the point of view of the narrative affects the overall meaning of the work. Next, consider the point of view of another character and discuss how telling the story from that character's perspective might change your interpretation of the work as a whole.

Symbol

Literary texts sometimes include objects, places, events, or even characters that carry meanings or associations beyond the literal. These **symbols** allow the author to draw connections to themes and ideas in the story, and they often point the way to the meaning of the work as a whole. In literature and art, a symbol stands in for a meaning suggested more than specified, evoked more than defined or stated; it approaches a meaning signified but not explained. A symbol begins as something literal in the story, like the glass slipper in *Cinderella*. That literal thing then takes on metaphorical significance — it represents an idea (or ideas). What ideas does Cinderella's glass slipper represent? It's unique and beautiful, perhaps like Cinderella herself, amidst a sea of the usual ho-hum courtiers. It's fragile, like the brief spell that turned Cinderella into a princess. Or perhaps you read the story differently and find another meaning in the symbol of the glass slipper; symbols are frequently opportunities for interpretation.

You might have realized as you were reading the paragraph above that symbols are metaphorical. This is correct, but they are not the same as verbal metaphors. Verbal metaphors are isolated to the sentence or line where the metaphor is written. They are created by words, and they are a matter of style. Symbols work on a larger scale. They are metaphors created from objects in the story, or literary elements like setting and character, and they tend to develop throughout a novel or play.

It's important to recognize that symbols develop within the context of a specific text. You can't assume, for instance, that rain is a symbol of sadness. It might be, but it might also be a symbol of renewal or hope because it enables growth. Similarly, blood might symbolize love and passion, but it can also symbolize violence and destruction. A walled garden might symbolize imprisonment and confinement in one work or function as a peaceful sanctuary in another. Symbols have to be interpreted within the world the novelist or playwright creates, and they evolve over the course of the work.

An object, event, or action can represent multiple ideas, but the place to start interpreting symbols is to make note of their literal meaning. Let's take a look at an example from *Song of Solomon* by Toni Morrison. Early in the novel, a character named Pilate asks her nephew Milkman and his friend if they want a soft-boiled egg:

from Song of Solomon

Toni Morrison

"You ought to try one. I know how to do them just right. I don't like my whites to move, you know. The yolk I want soft, but not runny. Want it like wet velvet. How come you don't just try one?

She had dumped the peelings in a large crock, which like most everything in the house had been made for some other purpose. Now she stood before the dry sink, pumping water into a blue-and-white wash basin which she used for a saucepan.

"Now the water and the egg have to meet each other on a kind of equal standing. One can't get the upper hand over the other. So the temperature has to be the same for both. I knock the chill off the water first. Just the chill. I don't let it get warm because the egg is room temperature, you see. No then, the real secret is right here in the boiling. When the tiny bubbles comes to the surface, when they as big as peas and just before they get big as marbles. Well, right then you take the pot off the fire. You don't just put the fire out, you take the pot off. Then you put a folded newspaper over the pot and do one small obligation. Like answering the door or emptying the bucket and bringing it in off the front porch. I generally go to the toilet. Not for a long stay, mind you. Just a short one. If you do all that, you got yourself a perfect soft-boiled egg." ■

1977

Morrison spends so much time describing the process of making the "perfect soft-boiled egg" that we have to assume something more is going on. We typically associate an egg with the start of life, a classic representation of motherhood. Maybe, Pilate is trying to "mother" Milkman in the sense of caring for him, teaching and guiding him. Pilate's "recipe" is filled with sensory details of that process, and her description is almost hypnotic. Milkman has already told her he doesn't want the egg, yet he doesn't even try to interrupt her, much less walk away. What about that "equal standing" comment? It seems an odd way to describe cooking an egg, but it signals partnership, cooperation rather than competition; as the novel unfolds, Pilate makes efforts to encourage Milkman to view his life as less of a competition and more of an experience. So the egg in this early chapter symbolizes new life, possibility of growth and companionship, perhaps even pleasure as an end in itself.

This example from *Song of Solomon* is in one passage, yet in longer works, symbols often evolve over the entire novel or play. An excellent example is *The Scarlet Letter* (1850) by Nathaniel Hawthorne. When the unmarried Hester Prynne, the central character, gives birth to a child, she is sentenced to wear the letter "A," for *adulterer*, on her clothing. This symbol shifts its meaning as time passes in the novel and exemplifies how a concrete object can be used to represent a broader meaning with moral and philosophical implications. Initially, the scarlet letter symbolizes the shame and guilt the Puritan community expects Hester to experience for what they see as a violation of their moral values. Wearing it is supposed to be penance and acknowledgment of her wrongdoing, but it almost immediately begins to take on other meanings. Here is the description from Chapter 2 of the novel:

> On the breast of her gown, in fine red cloth, surrounded with an elaborate embroidery and fantastic flourishes of gold thread, appeared the letter A. It was so artistically done, and with so much fertility and gorgeous luxuriance of fancy, that it had all the effect of a last and fitting devotion to the apparel which she wore; and which was of a splendor in accordance with the taste of the age, but greatly beyond what was allowed by the sumptuary regulations of the colony.

This short passage complicates what might have been a fairly straightforward symbol. Intended as a marker of "adultery," the symbol is ironically sensuous and beautiful, much like Hester herself: she is described as having "a figure of perfect elegance . . . dark and abundant hair, so glossy that it threw off the sunshine with gleam."

In a key scene later on, Hester meets Arthur Dimmesdale, her child's father, in the forest and discards her scarlet letter:

> [S]he undid the clasp that fastened the scarlet letter, and taking it from her bosom, threw it to a distance among the withered leaves. The mystic token alighted on the hither verge of the stream. With a hand's breadth farther flight it would have fallen into the water giving the little brook another woe to carry onward . . . But there lay the embroidered letter, glittering like a lost jewel, which some ill-fated wanderer might pick up, and thenceforth be haunted by strange phantoms of guilt, sinkings of the heart, and unaccountable misfortune.
>
> The stigma gone, Hester heaved a long, deep sigh, in which the burden of shame and anguish departed from her spirit. O exquisite relief! She had not known the weight, until she felt the freedom!

For the moment, Hester rejects the guilt imposed on her by the community, the "burden of shame and anguish," and thus frees herself in both a literal and an emotional sense — she no longer feels oppressed by a society that judges her harshly. But when her young daughter, Pearl, sees her without the letter, she has a tantrum and refuses to greet Dimmesdale. Hester puts the letter back on, accepting that she must "bear the torture a little longer," and Pearl kisses her mother and the letter. While it's true that the letter represents the gravity of Hester's sin, the actions of the characters in this scene expand its meaning. Pearl embraces it — indeed, cannot imagine who her mother is without it. By continuing to wear the letter, Hester comes to terms with her life and choices, and realizes that although she bears the mark of a sinner, she is not the only one. By contrast, Dimmesdale is unable to admit his own guilt as Hester's partner in sin, a weakness that eventually leads to his death.

In the final chapter of the novel, the scarlet letter comes to symbolize Hester's transformation and redemption. She returns to Boston after living abroad for many years and still wears the letter "of her own free will." Her community welcomes her back:

> She had . . . resumed the symbol of which we have related so dark a tale. Never afterwards did it quit her bosom. But in the lapse of the toilsome, thoughtful, and self-devoted years that made up Hester's life, the scarlet letter ceased to be a stigma which attracted the world's scorn and bitterness, and became a type of something to be sorrowed over, and looked upon with awe, yet with reverence too.

Some readers see the scarlet letter as evolving from a symbol of adultery to that of an angel. It first brings about Hester's suffering and isolation, but as she continues to wear it and bear its stigma, she redeems herself as a member of her community. The letter could even represent the redemption of the Puritan community as they soften toward Hester over time.

In drama, symbols are intended to be visually represented on stage, making them even more clear and powerful than symbols in fiction. These symbols may be part of the setting, character, or even the plot. Any item used by an actor or as part of scenery is called a **prop** — short for "theatrical property," because props are items owned not by the actors but by the theater or troupe. Props may simply add to a character's appearance (a pipe held by a detective) or to the atmosphere created by the setting (an old rocking chair), but they frequently function as symbols. In August Wilson's 1987 play *The Piano Lesson*, the piano is a central symbol of the play. Wilson emphasizes its importance in his opening directions to the play:

> *Dominating the parlor is an old upright piano. On the legs of the piano, carved in the manner of African sculpture, are mask-like figures resembling totems. The carvings are rendered with a grace and power of invention that lifts them out of the realm of craftsmanship and into the realm of art.*

Wilson reveals the symbolic meaning of the piano through the course of the play. Purchased through an exchange for enslaved people, the piano symbolizes the treatment of enslaved people not as human beings but as property. The piano becomes the site of conflict when a family member wants to sell it to purchase land. How the characters view the piano tells us something about them and their values. Wilson scholar Sandra Shannon describes its importance: "a 135-year-old piano that is simultaneously the Charles family heirloom and a unifying device for the play . . . [it is] the center of the play's conflict as well as its symbolic core."

When considering the relationship between setting and symbol, it is good to keep in mind the principle that has come to be called "Chekhov's gun." Playwright Anton Chekhov said, "If in the first act you have hung a pistol on the wall, then in the following one it should be fired. Otherwise don't put it there." Chekhov is suggesting that symbols should be intentional, not misleading.

Symbol, Allegory, and Archetype

Sometimes you will read fiction in which nearly everything is symbolic, and the objects that work as symbols carry fixed meanings. Such symbols — ones that encompass an entire work — create allegories. An **allegory** is a literary work that portrays abstract ideas in concrete ways. Allegories often contain **archetypes**, cultural symbols that have become universally understood and recognized. Common examples include a garden, a dark forest, a desert, a mentor, a journey, or a quest. Allegorical characters are frequently personifications of abstract ideas, with names that often refer to those ideas. Unnamed allegorical characters are usually archetypes — for example, a particular father, mother, or child may represent the concepts of fatherhood, motherhood, or childhood, respectively.

The following example is a highly symbolic allegorical passage that relies on such archetypes.

from The Gunslinger

Stephen King

The man in black fled across the desert, and the gunslinger followed.

The desert was the apotheosis of all deserts, huge, standing to the sky for what looked like eternity in all directions. It was white and blinding and waterless and without feature save for the faint, cloudy haze of the mountains which sketched themselves on the horizon and the devil-grass which brought sweet dreams, nightmares, death. An occasional tombstone sign pointed the way, for once the drifted track that cut its way through the thick crust of alkali had been a highway. Coaches and buckas had followed it. The world had moved on since then. The world had emptied. ■

1978

To begin with, we have the archetype of a journey across a desert. We also have a "man in black" as a symbolic figure representing evil itself, while "the gunslinger" is a symbolic archetype of a hero, inspired by American western films. The desert is a symbolic setting, and King is very direct about what it represents: "The world had emptied." This is not just a barren landscape; it is death itself. With this passage, King sets the stage. We know as readers that the story unfolding is about more than just two men following each other in the desert; it is a battle of good versus evil, an allegory of life versus death.

KEY QUESTIONS

Analyzing Symbol in Longer Fiction and Drama

- What objects does the writer emphasize through description, repetition, or placement in the story? Is there a recurring pattern, or motif, of images or events?
- What might be symbolic about the setting?
- What characters or aspects of a character might be symbolic or archetypal?
- What events might be symbolic or archetypal?
- What does each symbol convey about the larger meaning of the work?

Analyzing Symbol in Longer Fiction and Drama

Choose an object, setting, or event, and discuss different ways that it can function as a symbol. Try to think of more than one novel or film where it is used symbolically, and discuss the different interpretations the symbols carry in each narrative. Examples might be fog, a gun, a religious icon, the American flag, a cave, an apple, or an open window.

Putting It All Together: Interpreting Theme in Longer Fiction and Drama

In Chapter 1, we discussed how to use your "educated imagination" to analyze how literary elements contribute to your interpretation of short fiction. In this chapter, we've examined more ways that authors develop rich and complex literature — such as varying the sequence of events in a plot, using different narrative techniques such as stream of consciousness, or developing symbols — to raise questions or explore issues over the course of a full-length work. In general, anytime you interpret how several literary elements collectively reveal a deeper meaning, you are examining its **themes**. Because your interpretation of theme is your own, what you find may not be what others see in the text. There can also be many themes in a work — not just one "answer" waiting to be discovered.

Let's consider how you might uncover some themes in Shakespeare's *Romeo and Juliet* in a fairly systematic way, looking at several individual literary elements to see how they come together to create a theme. We'll start with the cultural and historical context of setting. The play takes place in Verona, Italy, during the 1500s. As we know from various stage and film versions, though, that time period is not as essential as the fact that the setting is a society governed by two rival families, both determined to uphold their status and influence. Their children — even their servants — are expected to follow the social norms that further the families' rivalry and enforce a strict social hierarchy. When Juliet steps outside of these rules by refusing the marriage her parents have arranged for her, it creates conflicts.

The events of the plot stem from the conflicts that arise when characters, primarily Romeo and Juliet, reject the social codes that govern their lives. The play, structured neatly into five acts, follows a linear plot structure that mirrors the rigidity of these social rules. As Romeo and Juliet fall in love, face obstacles, and ultimately choose death over separation, they reveal how fundamentally incompatible their relationship is with the status quo. The event of their deaths, in turn, causes their families to reconcile.

Juliet is one example of a dynamic character who grows and changes. Only thirteen, she must navigate the conflict caused by her love for Romeo, the son of a rival family, and the expectations of loyalty from her own family, who have arranged a marriage to someone else. It is her perspective of Romeo, presented through soliloquies and dialogue with her nurse, that leads viewers and readers to an understanding of her love for him as she grows from romantic and naive to determined, independent, decisive, and somewhat cunning. By the end of the play, she takes drastic action — faking her own death — in an attempt to reunite with Romeo and avoid openly defying the social rules that dictate they must not be together. She is led by passion from start to finish, but that passion is based in a belief that she, not her family or community, should control her own life.

The play also contains symbols — for instance, let's look at the poison. Although intended to induce sleep with the right dosage, the poison leads both directly and indirectly to the deaths of Romeo and Juliet. One interpretation of this symbol is that it mirrors the toxic nature of the feud between their families, one that Romeo and Juliet's relationship proves is unimportant and unnecessary. The resolution of the play is hardly a happy ending, but it does bring about their families' reconciliation. A new and peaceful order results, but at the unbearable cost of young lives.

AP® TIP

While you may not be asked to specifically analyze theme on the AP® exam, the themes of a work are always integral to its meaning. Consider, for example, the relationship we explore here between characterization, setting, structure, and theme in *Romeo and Juliet*.

One possible theme for the play, perhaps the most common, is how the passion of young love can be so overwhelming that it clouds reason and judgment. But let's examine one a little less familiar, based on the idea of conflict between the individual and society. This angle allows us to look at Romeo and Juliet's doomed love in a larger context: the community in which they live and the rigid but essentially unimportant rules that are meant to govern their lives but instead lead to their deaths.

There is no magic formula for finding the themes of a work of literature, other than observation and interpretation — and, of course, rereading. Nevertheless, here are a few suggestions to keep in mind as you try to articulate themes.

1. *Subject and theme are not the same*. The subject of *Romeo and Juliet* is doomed love, but the theme is what the work says about the subject. You can state it in one or two sentences. For instance, "Individuals' struggles to dodge or defy rigid social rules and long-standing rivalries in the play lead to chaos, discord, and death. These conflicts illustrate that social hierarchies are arbitrary, unnecessary, and cruel."
2. *Avoid clichés*. Even though clichés such as "love conquers all" might be tempting, try to state it in a more original and sophisticated way. Clichés are lazy statements that ignore the complexity of a literary text.
3. *Do not ignore contradictory details*. You don't want to claim, for instance, that the theme of *Romeo and Juliet* is that love is a uniting force. While it's true that the feuding families of the two main characters reconcile at the end of the play, Romeo and Juliet themselves are not only separated from each other but from their families as well.
4. *A theme is not a moral*. It may sometimes be tempting to extract "the moral of the story" (which is likely to be a cliché). Resist! Writers of drama and fiction — and poetry — work indirectly. If a writer wanted to convey an idea directly, they would write an editorial for a newspaper. Those who choose to write a literary work do so to explore ideas indirectly through plots, characters, settings, points of view, symbols, and the like.

5. *A literary work almost always has more than one theme*. Notice how many themes we have already discussed for *Romeo and Juliet*. As you bring your own ideas and experiences to a piece of literature, you will also come up with multiple possibilities for themes.
6. *Themes can be questions.* Author Toni Morrison said that she did not write to put forth answers but to explore questions. Some works present an intellectual or a moral dilemma, or pose a conundrum that you are not obligated to answer. Questions *Romeo and Juliet* poses might be these: Is the passion of young love a destructive force? Is it possible for love to transcend or remake social norms?

section 1 / culminating activity

Interpreting Longer Fiction and Drama: Defending a Claim with Evidence

Novels and plays often depict characters caught between conflicting social or cultural values. Such conflicts can call characters' sense of identity into question as their own values change and their perspectives shift.

Either from your own reading or from the following list, choose a work of fiction or drama in which a central character is caught in a social or cultural conflict that challenges that character's identity. Write a paragraph in which you make a defensible claim that analyzes how the character's response to this conflict contributes to an interpretation of the work as a whole. In your paragraph, you should incorporate at least one piece of evidence from the text to support your claim. Do not merely summarize the plot.

- Chimamanda Ngozi Adichie, *Americanah*
- Jane Austen, *Pride and Prejudice*
- Emily Brontë, *Wuthering Heights*
- Charles Dickens, *Great Expectations*
- F. Scott Fitzgerald, *The Great Gatsby*
- Nathaniel Hawthorne, *The Scarlet Letter*
- Henrik Ibsen, *Hedda Gabler*
- Kazuo Ishiguro, *Never Let Me Go*
- Jhumpa Lahiri, *The Namesake*
- Nella Larsen, *Passing* (p. 487)
- James McBride, *The Good Lord Bird*
- Toni Morrison, *Sula*
- Arundhati Roy, *The God of Small Things*
- William Shakespeare, *Hamlet* (p. 555)
- Mary Shelley, *Frankenstein* (p. 1093)
- Zadie Smith, *White Teeth*
- Sophocles, *Oedipus Rex*
- Leo Tolstoy, *Anna Karenina*
- Mark Twain, *The Adventures of Huckleberry Finn*
- August Wilson, *Fences* (p. 1047)

Section 2

From Reading to Writing: Crafting an AP® Literary Argument Essay

Let's take a look at a short play, keeping in mind the literary elements we have discussed: character, setting, plot, symbol, and theme. In the section that follows, we'll walk through how to interpret these literary elements in a literary argument essay that analyzes how the playwright, Susan Glaspell, has developed them to create certain effects and, ultimately, to convey meaning. As you read, remember to consider how specific details reveal information about characters. Because *Trifles* is a play, you'll want to note information both in the stage directions and in the characters' dialogue with each other. In particular, keep in mind the following questions specific to elements you are learning about in this chapter.

KEY QUESTIONS

Preparing to Write an AP® Literary Argument

- Which characters change throughout the text, and which stay the same? What meanings do these changes (or lack thereof) convey?
- Where does the action take place? What elements of setting do the characters notice and discuss?
- How do the characters' experiences and the setting relate to the structure and events of the plot?
- Do certain objects take on increased significance as the work progresses? Do any other elements strike you as symbolic?
- How do these big-picture elements work together to raise questions and explore issues as they tell a story?

Trifles

Susan Glaspell

Characters

GEORGE HENDERSON *county attorney*
HENRY PETERS *sheriff*
LEWIS HALE *a neighboring farmer*
MRS. PETERS
MRS. HALE

SCENE *The kitchen in the now abandoned farmhouse of John Wright, a gloomy kitchen, and left without having been put in order — unwashed pans under the sink, a loaf of bread outside the breadbox, a dish towel on the table — other signs of incompleted work. At the rear the outer door opens and the* **SHERIFF** *comes in followed by the* **COUNTY ATTORNEY** *and* **HALE.** *The* **SHERIFF** *and* **HALE** *are men in middle life,* *the* **COUNTY ATTORNEY** *is a young man; all are much bundled up and go at once to the stove. They are followed by the two women — the* **SHERIFF'S** *wife first; she is a slight wiry woman, a thin nervous face.* **MRS. HALE** *is larger and would ordinarily be called more comfortable looking, but she is disturbed now and looks fearfully about as she enters. The women have come in slowly, and stand close together near the door.*

COUNTY ATTORNEY *[rubbing his hands]*: This feels good. Come up to the fire, ladies.

MRS. PETERS *[after taking a step forward]*: I'm not — cold.

SHERIFF *[unbuttoning his overcoat and stepping away from the stove as if to mark the beginning of official business]*: Now, Mr. Hale, before we move things about, you explain to Mr. Henderson just what you saw when you came here yesterday morning.

COUNTY ATTORNEY By the way, has anything been moved? Are things just as you left them yesterday?

SHERIFF *[looking about]*: It's just about the same. When it dropped below zero last night I thought I'd better send Frank out this morning to make a fire for us — no use getting pneumonia with a big case on, but I told him not to touch anything except the stove — and you know Frank.

COUNTY ATTORNEY Somebody should have been left here yesterday.

SHERIFF Oh — yesterday. When I had to send Frank to Morris Center for that man who went crazy — I want you to know I had my hands full yesterday. I knew you could get back from Omaha by today and as long as I went over everything here myself —

COUNTY ATTORNEY Well, Mr. Hale, tell just what happened when you came here yesterday morning.

HALE Harry[1] and I had started to town with a load of potatoes. We came along the road from my place and as I got here I said, "I'm going to see if I can't get John Wright to go in with me on a party telephone." I spoke to Wright about it once before and he put me off, saying folks talked too much anyway, and all he asked was peace and quiet — I guess you know about how much he talked himself; but I thought maybe if I went to the house and talked about it before his wife, though I said to Harry that I didn't know as what his wife wanted made much difference to John —

COUNTY ATTORNEY Let's talk about that later, Mr. Hale. I do want to talk about that, but tell now just what happened when you got to the house.

HALE I didn't hear or see anything; I knocked at the door, and still it was all quiet inside. I knew they must be up, it was past eight o'clock. So I knocked again, and I thought I heard somebody say, "Come in." I wasn't sure, I'm not sure yet, but I opened the door — this door *[indicating the door by which the two women are still standing]* and there in that rocker — *[pointing to it]* sat Mrs. Wright. *[They all look at the rocker.]*

COUNTY ATTORNEY What — was she doing?

HALE She was rockin' back and forth. She had her apron in her hand and was kind of — pleating it.

COUNTY ATTORNEY And how did she — look?

HALE Well, she looked queer.

COUNTY ATTORNEY How do you mean — queer?

HALE Well, as if she didn't know what she was going to do next. And kind of done up.

COUNTY ATTORNEY How did she seem to feel about your coming?

HALE Why, I don't think she minded — one way or other. She didn't pay much attention. I said, "How do, Mrs. Wright, it's cold, ain't it?" And she said, "Is it?" — and went on kind of pleating at her apron. Well, I was surprised; she didn't ask me to come up to the stove, or to set down, but just sat there, not even looking at me, so I said, "I want to see John." And then she — laughed. I guess you would call it a laugh. I thought of Harry and the team outside, so I said a little sharp: "Can't I see John?" "No," she says, kind o' dull like. "Ain't

---

[1] During this era, men named Henry were often called Harry in direct address or dialogue. When characters in the play refer to "Harry," they mean Henry Peters. — Eds.

he home?" says I. "Yes," says she, "he's home." "Then why can't I see him?" I asked her, out of patience. *"'Cause he's dead," says she. "Dead?"* says I. She just nodded her head, not getting a bit excited, but rockin' back and forth. "Why — where is he?" says I, not knowing what to say. She just pointed upstairs — like that *[himself pointing to the room above].* I started for the stairs, with the idea of going up there. I walked from there to here — then I says, "Why, what did he die of?" "He died of a rope round his neck," says she, and just went on pleatin' at her apron. Well, I went out and called Harry. I thought I might — need help. We went upstairs and there he was lyin' —

COUNTY ATTORNEY I think I'd rather have you go into that upstairs, where you can point it all out. Just go on now with the rest of the story.

HALE Well, my first thought was to get that rope off. It looked . . . *[stops; his face twitches]* . . . but Harry, he went up to him, and he said, "No, he's dead all right, and we'd better not touch anything." So we went back downstairs. She was still sitting that same way. "Has anybody been notified?" I asked. "No," says she, unconcerned. "Who did this, Mrs. Wright?" said Harry. He said it businesslike — and she stopped pleatin' of her apron. "I don't know," she says. "You don't *know?"* says Harry. "No," says she. "Weren't you sleepin' in the bed with him?" says Harry. "Yes," says she, "but I was on the inside." "Somebody slipped a rope round his neck and strangled him and you didn't wake up?" says Harry. "I didn't wake up," she said after him. We must 'a' looked as if we didn't see how that could be, for after a minute she said, "I sleep sound." Harry was going to ask her more questions but I said maybe we ought to let her tell her story first to the coroner, or the sheriff, so Harry went fast as he could to Rivers' place, where there's a telephone.

COUNTY ATTORNEY And what did Mrs. Wright do when she knew that you had gone for the coroner?

HALE She moved from the rocker to that chair over there *[pointing to a small chair in the corner]* and just sat there with her hands held together and looking down. I got a feeling that I ought to make some conversation, so I said I had come in to see if John wanted to put in a telephone, and at that she started to laugh, and then she stopped and looked at me — scared. *[The* **COUNTY ATTORNEY**, *who has had his notebook out, makes a note.]* I dunno, maybe it wasn't scared. I wouldn't like to say it was. Soon Harry got back, and then Dr. Lloyd came and you, Mr. Peters, and so I guess that's all I know that you don't.

COUNTY ATTORNEY *[looking around]:* I guess we'll go upstairs first — and then out to the barn and around there. *[To the* **SHERIFF**.*]* You're convinced that there was nothing important here — nothing that would point to any motive?

SHERIFF Nothing here but kitchen things. *[The* **COUNTY ATTORNEY**, *after again looking around the kitchen, opens the door of a cupboard closet. He gets up on a chair and looks on a shelf. Pulls his hand away, sticky.]*

COUNTY ATTORNEY Here's a nice mess. *[The women draw nearer.]*

MRS. PETERS *[to the other woman]:* Oh, her fruit; it did freeze. *[To the Lawyer.]* She worried about that when it turned so cold. She said the fire'd go out and her jars would break.

SHERIFF *[rises]:* Well, can you beat the woman! Held for murder and worryin' about her preserves.

COUNTY ATTORNEY I guess before we're through she may have something more serious than preserves to worry about.

HALE Well, women are used to worrying over trifles. *[The two women move a little closer together.]*

COUNTY ATTORNEY *[with the gallantry of a young politician]:* And yet, for all their worries, what would we do without the ladies? *[The women do not unbend. He goes to the sink, takes a dipperful of water from the pail, and pouring it into a basin, washes his hands. Starts to wipe them on the roller towel, turns it for a cleaner place.]* Dirty towels! *[Kicks his foot against the pans under the* *sink.]* Not much of a housekeeper, would you say, ladies?

MRS. HALE *[stiffly]:* There's a great deal of work to be done on a farm.

COUNTY ATTORNEY To be sure. And yet *[with a little bow to her]* I know there are some Dickson county farmhouses which do not have such roller towels. *[He gives it a pull to expose its full length again.]*

MRS. HALE Those towels get dirty awful quick. Men's hands aren't always as clean as they might be.

COUNTY ATTORNEY Ah, loyal to your sex, I see. But you and Mrs. Wright were neighbors. I suppose you were friends, too.

MRS. HALE *[shaking her head]:* I've not seen much of her of late years. I've not been in this house — it's more than a year.

COUNTY ATTORNEY And why was that? You didn't like her?

MRS. HALE I liked her all well enough. Farmers' wives have their hands full, Mr. Henderson. And then —

COUNTY ATTORNEY Yes — ?

MRS. HALE *[looking about]*: It never seemed a very cheerful place.

COUNTY ATTORNEY No — it's not cheerful. I shouldn't say she had the homemaking instinct.

MRS. HALE Well, I don't know as Wright had, either.

COUNTY ATTORNEY You mean that they didn't get on very well?

MRS. HALE No, I don't mean anything. But I don't think a place'd be any cheerfuller for John Wright's being in it.

COUNTY ATTORNEY I'd like to talk more of that a little later. I want to get the lay of things upstairs now. *[He goes to the left where three steps lead to a stair door.]*

SHERIFF I suppose anything Mrs. Peters does'll be all right. She was to take in some clothes for her, you know, and a few little things. We left in such a hurry yesterday.

COUNTY ATTORNEY Yes, but I would like to see what you take, Mrs. Peters, and keep an eye out for anything that might be of use to us.

MRS. PETERS Yes, Mr. Henderson. *[The women listen to the men's steps on the stairs, then look about the kitchen.]*

MRS. HALE I'd hate to have men coming into my kitchen, snooping around and criticizing. *[She arranges the pans under sink which the Lawyer had shoved out of place.]*

MRS. PETERS Of course it's no more than their duty.

MRS. HALE Duty's all right, but I guess that deputy sheriff that came out to make the fire might have got a little of this on. *[Gives the roller towel a pull.]* Wish I'd thought of that sooner. Seems mean to talk about her for not having things slicked up when she had to come away in such a hurry.

MRS. PETERS *[who has gone to a small table in the left rear corner of the room, and lifted one end of a towel that covers a pan]:* She had bread set. *[Stands still.]*

MRS. HALE *[eyes fixed on a loaf of bread beside the breadbox, which is on a low shelf at the other side of the room. Moves slowly toward it.]:* She was going to put this in there. *[Picks up loaf, then abruptly drops it. In a manner of returning to familiar things.]* It's a shame about her fruit. I wonder if it's all gone. *[Gets up on the chair and looks.]* I think there's some here that's all right, Mrs. Peters. Yes — here; *[holding it toward the window]* this is cherries, too. *[Looking again.]* I declare I believe that's the only one. *[Gets down, bottle in her hand. Goes to the sink and wipes it off on the outside.]* She'll feel awful bad after all her hard work in the hot weather. I remember the afternoon I put up my cherries last summer. *[She puts the bottle on the big kitchen table, center of the room. With a sigh, is about to sit down in the rocking-chair. Before she is seated realizes what chair it is; with a slow look at it, steps back. The chair which she has touched rocks back and forth.]*

MRS. PETERS Well, I must get those things from the front room closet. *[She goes to the door at the right, but after looking into the other room, steps back.]* You coming with me, Mrs. Hale? You could help me carry them. *[They go in the* *other room; reappear,* **MRS. PETERS** *carrying a dress and skirt,* **MRS. HALE** *following with a pair of shoes.]* My, it's cold in there. *[She puts the clothes on the big table, and hurries to the stove.]*

MRS. HALE *[examining the skirt]*: Wright was close. I think maybe that's why she kept so much to herself. She didn't even belong to the Ladies' Aid. I suppose she felt she couldn't do her part, and then you don't enjoy things when you feel shabby. I heard she used to wear pretty clothes and be lively, when she was Minnie Foster, one of the town girls singing in the choir. But that — oh, that was thirty years ago. This all you want to take in?

MRS. PETERS She said she wanted an apron. Funny thing to want, for there isn't much to get you dirty in jail, goodness knows. But I suppose just to make her feel more natural. She said they was in the top drawer in this cupboard. Yes, here. And then her little shawl that always hung behind the door. *[Opens stair door and looks.]* Yes, here it is. *[Quickly shuts door leading upstairs.]*

MRS. HALE *[abruptly moving toward her]*: Mrs. Peters?

MRS. PETERS Yes, Mrs. Hale?

MRS. HALE Do you think she did it?

MRS. PETERS *[in a frightened voice]*: Oh, I don't know.

MRS. HALE Well, I don't think she did. Asking for an apron and her little shawl. Worrying about her fruit.

MRS. PETERS *[starts to speak, glances up, where footsteps are heard in the room above. In a low voice]:* Mr. Peters says it looks bad for her. Mr. Henderson is awful sarcastic in a speech and he'll make fun of her sayin' she didn't wake up.

MRS. HALE: Well, I guess John Wright didn't wake when they was slipping that rope under his neck.

MRS. PETERS No, it's strange. It must have been done awful crafty and still. They say it was such a — funny way to kill a man, rigging it all up like that.

MRS. HALE That's just what Mr. Hale said. There was a gun in the house. He says that's what he can't understand.

MRS. PETERS Mr. Henderson said coming out that what was needed for the case was a motive; something to show anger, or — sudden feeling.

MRS. HALE *[who is standing by the table]*: Well, I don't see any signs of anger around here. *[She puts her hand on the dish towel which lies on the table, stands looking down at table, one-half of which is clean, the other half messy.]* It's wiped to here. *[Makes a move as if to finish work, then turns and looks at loaf of bread outside the breadbox. Drops towel. In that voice of coming back to familiar things.]* Wonder how they are finding things upstairs. I hope she had it a little more red-up[2] up there. You know, it seems kind of *sneaking*. Locking her up in town and then coming out here and trying to get her own house to turn against her!

MRS. PETERS But, Mrs. Hale, the law is the law.

MRS. HALE I s'pose 'tis. *[Unbuttoning her coat.]* Better loosen up your things, Mrs. Peters. You won't feel them when you go out. *[***MRS. PETERS** *takes off her fur tippet, goes to hang it on hook at back of room, stands looking at the under part of the small corner table.]*

MRS. PETERS She was piecing a quilt. *[She brings the large sewing basket and they look at the bright pieces.]*

MRS. HALE It's a log cabin pattern. Pretty, isn't it? I wonder if she was goin' to quilt it or just knot it? *[Footsteps have been heard coming down the stairs. The* **SHERIFF** *enters followed by* **HALE** *and the* **COUNTY ATTORNEY.***]*

SHERIFF They wonder if she was going to quilt it or just knot it! *[The men laugh, the women look abashed.]*

COUNTY ATTORNEY *[rubbing his hands over the stove]*: Frank's fire didn't do much up there, did it? Well, let's go out to the barn and get that cleared up. *[The men go outside.]*

MRS. HALE *[resentfully]*: I don't know as there's anything so strange, our takin' up our time

[2] A phrase that has its origin in "readying up," meaning to make clean or tidy. — Eds.

with little things while we're waiting for them to get the evidence. *[She sits down at the big table smoothing out a block with decision.]* I don't see as it's anything to laugh about.

MRS. PETERS *[apologetically]*: Of course they've got awful important things on their minds. *[Pulls up a chair and joins Mrs. Hale at the table.]*

MRS. HALE *[examining another block]*: Mrs. Peters, look at this one. Here, this is the one she was working on, and look at the sewing! All the rest of it has been so nice and even. And look at this! It's all over the place! Why, it looks as if she didn't know what she was about! *[After she has said this they look at each other, then start to glance back at the door. After an instant* **MRS. HALE** *has pulled at a knot and ripped the sewing.]*

MRS. PETERS Oh, what are you doing, Mrs. Hale?

MRS. HALE *[mildly]*: Just pulling out a stitch or two that's not sewed very good. *[Threading a needle.]* Bad sewing always made me fidgety.

MRS. PETERS *[nervously]*: I don't think we ought to touch things.

MRS. HALE I'll just finish up this end. *[Suddenly stopping and leaning forward.]* Mrs. Peters?

MRS. PETERS Yes, Mrs. Hale?

MRS. HALE What do you suppose she was so nervous about?

MRS. PETERS Oh — I don't know. I don't know as she was nervous. I sometimes sew awful queer when I'm just tired. *[**MRS. HALE** starts to say something, looks at **MRS. PETERS**, then goes on sewing.]* Well, I must get these things wrapped up. They may be through sooner than we think. *[Putting apron and other things together.]* I wonder where I can find a piece of paper, and string. *[Rises.]*

MRS. HALE In that cupboard, maybe.

MRS. PETERS *[looking in cupboard]*: Why, here's a bird-cage. *[Holds it up.]* Did she have a bird, Mrs. Hale?

MRS. HALE Why, I don't know whether she did or not — I've not been here for so long. There was a man around last year selling canaries cheap, but I don't know as she took one; maybe she did. She used to sing real pretty herself.

MRS. PETERS *[glancing around]*: Seems funny to think of a bird here. But she must have had one, or why would she have a cage? I wonder what happened to it?

MRS. HALE I s'pose maybe the cat got it.

MRS. PETERS No, she didn't have a cat. She's got that feeling some people have about cats — being afraid of them. My cat got in her room and she was real upset and asked me to take it out.

MRS. HALE My sister Bessie was like that. Queer, ain't it?

MRS. PETERS *[examining the cage]*: Why, look at this door. It's broke. One hinge is pulled apart.

MRS. HALE *[looking too]*: Looks as if someone must have been rough with it.

MRS. PETERS Why, yes. *[She brings the cage forward and puts it on the table.]*

MRS. HALE I wish if they're going to find any evidence they'd be about it. I don't like this place.

MRS. PETERS But I'm awful glad you came with me, Mrs. Hale. It would be lonesome for me sitting here alone.

MRS. HALE It would, wouldn't it? *[Dropping her sewing.]* But I tell you what I do wish, Mrs. Peters. I wish I had come over sometimes when she was here. I — *[looking around the room]* — wish I had.

MRS. PETERS But of course you were awful busy, Mrs. Hale — your house and your children.

MRS. HALE I could've come. I stayed away because it weren't cheerful — and that's why I ought to have come. I — I've never liked this place. Maybe because it's down in a hollow and you don't see the road. I dunno what it is, but it's a lonesome place and always was. I wish I had come over to see Minnie Foster sometimes. I can see now — *[Shakes her head.]*

MRS. PETERS Well, you mustn't reproach yourself, Mrs. Hale. Somehow we just don't see how it is with other folks until — something turns up.

MRS. HALE Not having children makes less work — but it makes a quiet house, and Wright out to work all day, and no company when he did come in. Did you know John Wright, Mrs. Peters?

MRS. PETERS Not to know him; I've seen him in town. They say he was a good man.

MRS. HALE Yes — good; he didn't drink, and kept his word as well as most, I guess, and paid his debts. But he was a hard man, Mrs. Peters. Just to pass the time of day with him — *[Shivers.]* Like a raw wind that gets to the bone. *[Pauses, her eye falling on the cage.]* I should think she would 'a' wanted a bird. But what do you suppose went with it?

MRS. PETERS I don't know, unless it got sick and died. *[She reaches over and swings the broken door, swings it again, both women watch it.]*

MRS. HALE You weren't raised round here, were you? *[**MRS. PETERS** shakes her head.]* You didn't know — her?

MRS. PETERS Not till they brought her yesterday.

MRS. HALE She — come to think of it, she was kind of like a bird herself — real sweet and pretty, but kind of timid and — fluttery. How — she — did — change. *[Silence: then as if struck by a happy thought and relieved to get back to everyday things.]* Tell you what, Mrs. Peters, why don't you take the quilt in with you? It might take up her mind.

MRS. PETERS Why, I think that's a real nice idea, Mrs. Hale. There couldn't possibly be any objection to it, could there? Now, just what would I take? I wonder if her patches are in here — and her things. *[They look in the sewing basket.]*

MRS. HALE Here's some red. I expect this has got sewing things in it. *[Brings out a fancy box.]* What a pretty box. Looks like something somebody would give you. Maybe her scissors are in here. *[Opens box. Suddenly puts her hand to her nose.]* Why — *[**MRS. PETERS** bends nearer, then turns her face away.]* There's something wrapped up in this piece of silk.

MRS. PETERS Why, this isn't her scissors.

MRS. HALE *[lifting the silk]*: Oh, Mrs. Peters — it's — *[**MRS. PETERS** bends closer.]*

MRS. PETERS It's the bird.

MRS. HALE *[jumping up]*: But, Mrs. Peters — look at it! Its neck! Look at its neck! It's all — other side *to*.

MRS. PETERS Somebody — wrung — its — neck. *[Their eyes meet. A look of growing comprehension, of horror. Steps are heard outside. **MRS. HALE** slips box under quilt pieces, and sinks into her chair. Enter **SHERIFF** and **COUNTY ATTORNEY. MRS. PETERS** rises.]*

COUNTY ATTORNEY *[as one turning from serious things to little pleasantries]*: Well, ladies, have you decided whether she was going to quilt it or knot it?

MRS. PETERS We think she was going to — knot it.

COUNTY ATTORNEY Well, that's interesting, I'm sure. *[Seeing the bird-cage.]* Has the bird flown?

MRS. HALE *[putting more quilt pieces over the box]*: We think the — cat got it.

COUNTY ATTORNEY *[preoccupied]*: Is there a cat? *[**MRS. HALE** glances in a quick covert way at **MRS. PETERS**.]*

MRS. PETERS Well, not now. They're superstitious, you know. They leave.

COUNTY ATTORNEY *[to **SHERIFF PETERS**, continuing an interrupted conversation]*: No sign at all of anyone having come from the outside. Their own rope. Now let's go up again and go over it piece by piece. *[They start upstairs.]* It would have to have been someone who knew just the — *[**MRS. PETERS** sits down. The two women sit there not looking at one another, but as if peering into something and at the same time holding back. When they talk now it is in the manner of feeling their way over strange ground, as if afraid of what they are saying, but as if they cannot help saying it.]*

MRS. HALE She liked the bird. She was going to bury it in that pretty box.

MRS. PETERS *[in a whisper]*: When I was a girl — my kitten — there was a boy took a hatchet, and before my eyes — and before I could get there — *[Covers her face an instant.]* If they hadn't held me back I would have — *[catches herself, looks upstairs where steps are heard, falters weakly]* — hurt him.

MRS. HALE *[with a slow look around her]*: I wonder how it would seem never to have had any children around. *[Pause.]* No, Wright wouldn't like the bird — a thing that sang. She used to sing. He killed that, too.

MRS. PETERS *[moving uneasily]*: We don't know who killed the bird.

MRS. HALE I knew John Wright.

MRS. PETERS It was an awful thing was done in this house that night, Mrs. Hale. Killing a man while he slept, slipping a rope around his neck that choked the life out of him.

MRS. HALE His neck. Choked the life out of him. *[Her hand goes out and rests on the bird-cage.]*

MRS. PETERS *[with rising voice]*: We don't know who killed him. We don't *know*.

MRS. HALE *[her own feeling not interrupted]*: If there'd been years and years of nothing, then a bird to sing to you, it would be awful — still, after the bird was still.

MRS. PETERS *[something within her speaking]*: I know what stillness is. When we homesteaded in Dakota, and my first baby died — after he was two years old, and me with no other then —

MRS. HALE *[moving]*: How soon do you suppose they'll be through looking for the evidence?

MRS. PETERS I know what stillness is. *[Pulling herself back.]* The law has got to punish crime, Mrs. Hale.

MRS. HALE *[not as if answering that]*: I wish you'd seen Minnie Foster when she wore a white dress with blue ribbons and stood up there in the choir and sang. *[A look around the room.]* Oh, I *wish* I'd come over here once in a while! That was a crime! That was a crime! Who's going to punish that?

MRS. PETERS *[looking upstairs]*: We mustn't — take on.

MRS. HALE I might have known she needed help! I know how things can be — for women. I tell you, it's queer, Mrs. Peters. We live close together and we live far apart. We all go through the same things — it's all just a different kind of the same thing. *[Brushes her eyes, noticing the bottle of fruit, reaches out for it.]* If I was you I wouldn't tell her her fruit was gone. Tell her it *ain't*. Tell her it's all right. Take this in to prove it to her. She — she may never know whether it was broke or not.

MRS. PETERS *[takes the bottle, looks about for something to wrap it in; takes petticoat from the clothes brought from the other room, very nervously begins winding this around the bottle. In a false voice]*: My, it's a good thing the men couldn't hear us. Wouldn't they just laugh! Getting all stirred up over a little thing like a — dead canary. As if that could have anything to do with — with — wouldn't they *laugh*! *[The men are heard coming down stairs.]*

MRS. HALE *[under her breath]*: Maybe they would — maybe they wouldn't.

COUNTY ATTORNEY No, Peters, it's all perfectly clear except a reason for doing it. But you know juries when it comes to women. If there was some definite thing. Something to show — something to make a story about — a thing that would connect up with this strange way of doing it — *[The women's eyes meet for an instant. Enter* **HALE** *from outer door.]*

HALE Well, I've got the team around. Pretty cold out there.

COUNTY ATTORNEY I'm going to stay here a while by myself. *[To the Sheriff.]* You can send Frank out for me, can't you? I want to go over everything. I'm not satisfied that we can't do better.

SHERIFF Do you want to see what Mrs. Peters is going to take in? *[The Lawyer goes to the table, picks up the apron, laughs.]*

COUNTY ATTORNEY Oh, I guess they're not very dangerous things the ladies have picked out. *[Moves a few things about, disturbing the quilt pieces which cover the box. Steps back.]* No, Mrs. Peters doesn't need supervising. For that matter a sheriff's wife is married to the law. Ever think of it that way, Mrs. Peters?

MRS. PETERS Not — just that way.

SHERIFF *[chuckling]*: Married to the law. *[Moves toward the other room.]* I just want you to come in here a minute, George. We ought to take a look at these windows.

COUNTY ATTORNEY *[scoffingly]*: Oh, windows!

SHERIFF We'll be right out, Mr. Hale. *[***HALE** *goes outside. The* **SHERIFF** *follows the* **COUNTY**

ATTORNEY *into the other room. Then* **MRS. HALE** *rises, hands tight together, looking intensely at* **MRS. PETERS**, *whose eyes make a slow turn, finally meeting* **MRS. HALE**'*s. A moment* **MRS. HALE** *holds her, then her own eyes point the way to where the box is concealed. Suddenly* **MRS. PETERS** *throws back quilt pieces and tries to put the box in the bag she is wearing. It is too big. She opens box, starts to take bird out, cannot touch it, goes to pieces, stands there helpless. Sound of a knob turning in the other room.* **MRS. HALE** *snatches the box and puts it in the pocket of her big coat. Enter* **COUNTY ATTORNEY** *and* **SHERIFF.**]

COUNTY ATTORNEY [*facetiously*]: Well, Henry, at least we found out that she was not going to quilt it. She was going to—what is it you call it, ladies?

MRS. HALE [*her hand against her pocket*]: We call it—knot it, Mr. Henderson.

Curtain ■

1916

AP® TIP

To prepare for the Literary Argument essay on the AP® exam, pick three to five of the longer works of literature you have studied in class and review their major literary elements in the weeks before the exam. Choose texts you not only studied in depth but also enjoyed reading. This deeper knowledge and your interest in the texts will come through in your writing.

Preparing to Write an AP® Literary Argument: Analyzing Literary Elements

In addition to prose passages and poetry, the AP® English Literature and Composition exam also asks you to develop an analysis of a longer piece of literature, such as a novel, a novella, or a play. Unlike the prose fiction analysis and poetry prompts, however, you won't have the text in front of you and will need to rely on what you can remember about the text's major literary elements to craft your interpretation of its meaning. You won't have to develop this interpretation from scratch, however. An essay prompt will provide a specific direction for your analysis, and you will be able to choose a novel or play you think will allow you to develop the best response to the prompt. To give you an idea of how a prompt directs an analysis, we're going to demonstrate the process with an AP®-style prompt that works well for an analysis of *Trifles*:

> Many literary works feature a moral dilemma that characters approach from different perspectives and with different motivations. These differing perspectives and motivations often generate conflict with significant implications for the work.
>
> Either from your own reading or from the list below, choose a work of fiction in which characters approach a moral dilemma from different perspectives and different motivations. Then, in a well-written essay, analyze how the conflicts created by these different perspectives and motivations contribute to an interpretation of the work as a whole. Do not merely summarize the plot.

This prompt works well with *Trifles* because the men's general perspectives differ from those of the women in the play, and their understanding of the lives of Mr. and Mrs. Wright certainly contrasts with the perspective Mrs. Hale and Mrs. Peter have of the Wrights' relationship. Additionally, Mrs. Hale's and Mrs. Peters's personal experiences with isolation and loss shift their motives for seeking justice in a way that differs from the men's motives — the juxtaposition of these perspectives and motives creates key conflicts within the play.

AP® TIP

The Literary Argument prompt on the exam will provide you with about forty works to choose from. You can also select a different work as long as it has rich and robust literary elements you can write about accurately and convincingly.

The first step, especially if you're in a timed environment, is to take a brief inventory of your interpretation of the major literary elements at work in the text — character, setting, plot, symbol, and theme — with the prompt in mind. Because this prompt asks about differing perspectives and motivations, thinking about character development is a good place to start. *Trifles* has two female characters — Mrs. Hale and Mrs. Peters — and three male characters — Mr. Hale, the sheriff, and the county attorney. Mr. and Mrs. Wright, though not on stage, have a presence as well. Over the course of the play, Mrs. Hale and Mrs. Peters change as they feel less certain about their own beliefs, experience disappointment in themselves for not being better friends to Mrs. Wright, and become empathetic to her desperate loneliness. The men don't change. We learn about all of the characters through their conversations, especially in the way the dialogue changes when the men are involved and as the women experience their new understanding about and perspectives on Mrs. Wright's marriage and life. The women must decide whether to share information that suggests Mrs. Wright's guilt, but their changed understanding of her experiences has given them a perspective the men in the play don't have, and this combination of understanding and perspective presents a moral dilemma.

The setting of *Trifles* helps us understand character, and it also moves the plot along. The play takes place in an empty farmhouse, but the setting is more complicated than that. While the men eventually go to the bedroom where the murder occurred, the women focus on the kitchen. Both the men and the women note the disheveled condition in which Mrs. Wright left the kitchen, yet the women are protective of her as well, understanding that she probably wouldn't have left such a mess if she hadn't been unexpectedly taken from her home. This realization combined with what they discover in the kitchen means their experiences alter their priorities and cause them to appreciate the complexities of seeking justice.

In *Trifles*, two plots run parallel: the men have an off-stage story as they hunt for clues to the murder of Mr. Wright; the women have an on-stage story as they unravel the life of Mrs. Wright. The tension in the story's plot has to do with the rate at which Mrs. Hale and Mrs. Peters come to understand what has happened and the interruptions to this process whenever their husbands and the county attorney enter the kitchen. Suspense builds as the two women — and the audience — figure out who killed Mr. Wright and why. The suspense is heightened by the moral dilemma of whether the women should conceal incriminating evidence — and whether they'll get caught doing it. When Mrs. Peters tries to hide the dead canary and Mrs. Hale *"snatches the box and puts it in the pocket of her big coat,"* the audience experiences a cathartic moment: they can finally release their collective breath as it becomes clear the women have decided to disregard the law to protect their friend. Of course, their deception relies on the fact that the men in the play dismiss the things the women say as mere trifles.

Certain symbols are repeated in *Trifles*. The cold is brutal and unrelenting. The characters move toward the stove whenever possible, and the cold is a repeated subject of conversation. Mr. Wright is depicted as being cold and unloving, making the cold a clear symbol of a life without affection or companionship. Other symbols might be Mrs. Wright's quilt pieces, the choice between quilting and knotting, the dead bird and the broken birdcage, the preserves (an alternative meaning of "trifles"), and even the half-done chores. Each of these things is more fraught with meaning than they at first seem.

So, although one subject of *Trifles* is how characters' experiences influence their approaches to moral dilemmas, some of its themes might be:

- Sexism can make people blind to the truth.
- People may take desperate measures when they feel trapped in a loveless marriage, in a cold, isolated house, or in a society that doesn't value them.
- Someone who is a criminal by one set of social standards might be a victim according to another set of social standards. Or, in other words, justice is not always the same as the rule of law.

Preparing to Write an AP® Literary Argument Essay

Revisit the Key Questions (p. 136) that we asked you to consider while reading *Trifles*. Choose one theme from the play and engage in a quick write for five minutes to explore how characterization, setting, and symbolism in *Trifles* illustrate that theme.

Developing a Thesis Statement

Now that we have walked through a basic interpretation of how the major literary elements in *Trifles* convey meaning, let's focus on how to craft a thesis statement that distills this interpretation in a response to the prompt on page 144. Just like in prose fiction and poetry analysis essays, your thesis must make a claim about the meaning of the work that you plan to defend in the body of your essay. However, keep in mind that you will not have the text you are writing about in front of you on the AP® exam. Let's walk through some strategies for crafting an essay on a literary work that does not draw its evidence from the text itself.

Moving from Summary to Interpretation

The most important thing to remember as you craft a thesis for a literary argument essay is to interpret rather than summarize the work. When you don't have the text to draw evidence from, it can be difficult to tell the difference. Simply retelling what happened or making an observation is summarizing; to interpret, you must comment in some way on those events or observations. For example, stating that Mrs. Peters changes her mind over the course of the play is not enough. Shifting from summary to analysis usually requires a subtle adjustment: instead, you would be better off claiming that Mrs. Peters changes her mind *as the result of seeing justice in a different way*. This revised claim goes beyond what happens (Mrs. Peters changes her mind) and focuses on the significance of these events (Mrs. Peters's development alters her understanding of justice).

If you start right off with a claim that argues for an interpretation of the play's meaning, you will guard against summary. Let's examine a few examples of starting points for claims that would result in summary and consider how they could be revised to convey an interpretation of meaning.

summary: In *Trifles,* the women notice evidence that the men do not.

interpretation: In *Trifles,* the differences in the evidence the men and women notice suggest different priorities and perspectives.

The summary statement simply tells what happened during the course of the play, but the interpretive statement takes that same point and explains *why* it happened. It answers the question: *Why* do the women notice evidence that the men do not? Here's another one:

summary: Mrs. Hale and Mrs. Peters discover a birdcage and dead canary that provide clues to what actually happened to Mr. Wright.

interpretation: When Mrs. Hale and Mrs. Peters discover a birdcage and a dead canary wrapped in silk, they associate the silenced songbird with the joyless and repressed life that might have motivated Mrs. Wright to murder her husband.

The summary statement is accurate, but it is not an interpretation. Notice how the interpretive statement briefly points to events — the discovery of the birdcage and of the dead canary — in order to frame the analysis.

You might ask yourself the following questions: Can I write a whole essay on this idea? Would anyone else see this point differently? If the answer to both questions is yes, then you're likely on the right track for developing a thesis statement. If the answer to the first question is no, but the answer to the second question is yes, you're probably writing a claim that works well as a topic sentence for a paragraph but isn't substantial enough to stand alone as a thesis. If the answer to both questions is no, you're likely in the realm of observation rather than interpretation. To

AP® TIP

It's generally safe to assume that your audience for a Literary Argument essay — whether it's your teacher or someone grading your AP® exam — is familiar with the work you've chosen to write about. You do not need to summarize major elements of the plot or characterization in the work.

understand this last distinction, consider the second summary statement above. Anyone who reads the play can tell you that these women discover a birdcage and a dead canary and see both as clues to understanding the murder. These conclusions are quite self-evident. So what else is there to say? If you ask yourself further questions, you'll get beyond summary and move toward interpretation. Why were the birdcage and the dead canary clues? What is the connection between the canary, the birdcage, and Mrs. Wright? An interpretation will reveal these connections, but a summary will not.

Connecting Literary Elements to Interpretation

Remember when formulating your thesis that you are writing about how literary elements such as character, setting, plot, symbol, and theme illuminate the meaning of the work as a whole. Thus, you are always balancing the two: literary elements and interpretation. A good starting point is to figure out exactly what the prompt asks you to do — that is, to deconstruct the prompt. In this case, the prompt on page 144 asks you to consider how the characters' perspectives and motivations shape their response to a moral dilemma in a way that has greater meaning. We often think of morality as a pretty straightforward set of values outlining right and wrong, and we similarly like to think of justice as a binary. Yet in *Trifles*, as Mrs. Hale and Mrs. Peters begin to grapple with the complexities of justice, they realize the potential role they have in the process. As they unravel the mystery of Mr. Wright's death, they aren't so sure that "the law is the law," and Mrs. Hale even suggests she herself needs to be held accountable for not visiting Mrs. Wright more often. So maybe Glaspell is asking us to reflect on how diverse perspectives and motivations alter our perceptions of justice and, by extension, crime and punishment. Can Mrs. Wright be excused for acting as her husband's judge, jury, and executioner? Was living with him punishment enough for her wrongdoing? Did she choose a punishment that fit his "crime" and has justice therefore been served? How do Mrs. Hale's and Mrs. Peters's understanding of the situation and resulting actions reveal the complexities of the moral dilemma they face? These are complex questions — questions not definitively answered in the play but questions it raises.

AP® TIP

While a thesis statement can be more than one sentence and can appear anywhere in an essay, it counts for one-sixth of your essay score on the AP® exam. A solid strategy, especially on the exam, is to place your thesis statement in your essay introduction, where it will be most visible.

When you're trying to fit ideas and insights such as these into a single sentence, it's likely to be pretty awkward at first, and that's fine. We call this first attempt a working thesis. For example, you might come up with this:

> Characters in *Trifles* face moral dilemmas in their efforts to achieve justice, but their perspectives and motivations create internal and external conflicts for them to resolve before they can make important decisions that bring into question their honesty and integrity.

This is a start, but it's a long, rambling sentence that could use some focus. At this point, you might normally examine whether Glaspell takes a definite stand on these issues. However, the play ends inconclusively — Mrs. Wright is neither convicted nor exonerated — which makes it difficult to say that the play (or its author) takes a stand. A better route, then, is to argue that Glaspell asks her audience to explore these issues:

> In *Trifles,* the moral dilemma Mrs. Hale and Mrs. Peters face reveals how sympathy and empathy shift people's perspectives and motivations and color their interpretations of justice.

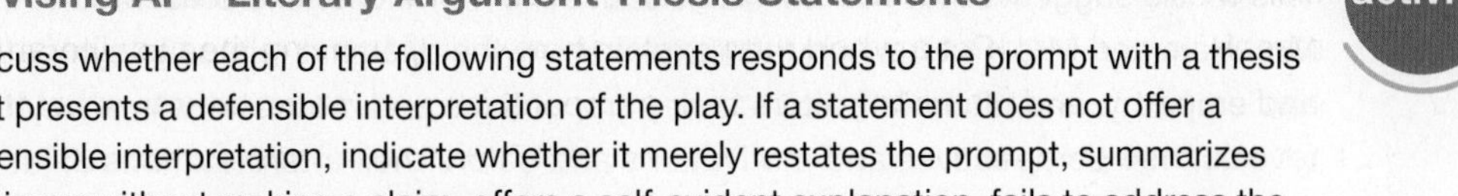

Revising AP® Literary Argument Thesis Statements

Discuss whether each of the following statements responds to the prompt with a thesis that presents a defensible interpretation of the play. If a statement does not offer a defensible interpretation, indicate whether it merely restates the prompt, summarizes the issue without making a claim, offers a self-evident explanation, fails to address the prompt, or presents a combination of these.

1. The characters in *Trifles* do not all respond the same way to the moral dilemma they face because they have different perspectives and motivations.
2. The play *Trifles* reveals how empathizing with others can shift our perspectives and motivations in ways that influence how we respond to moral dilemmas.
3. The broken birdcage in *Trifles* functions both as a clue to the circumstances of the murder and as a symbol of Mrs. Wright's freedom.
4. The frigid setting of Susan Glaspell's *Trifles* showcases the perspectives and motivations of all three women: it highlights the cold and isolated existence of the absent Mrs. Wright, while evoking the sympathetic responses of Mrs. Hale and Mrs. Peters.
5. In *Trifles*, the male authority figures, including the sheriff himself, dismiss the female characters' perspectives on the murder of Mr. Wright in a way that creates a moral dilemma for the women.
6. The kitchen, the dead bird, and the knots in the quilt have symbolic significance for the overall meaning of *Trifles*.

Supporting Your Thesis

One way to think of literary argumentation is that your interpretation is like a bridge you ask readers to cross. Your thesis serves as the bridge deck: it has to be solid; otherwise, it won't be able to support an entire essay. But a strong thesis is far from the only component of a successful literary argument essay. To ensure your readers' safe passage across the bridge, you must support it with claims that support your interpretation of the text, evidence from the text, and commentary that helps them follow your line of reasoning to the other side.

Writing Topic Sentences

Regardless of whether you are given a specific prompt to respond to or are assigned a more general topic on a literary work, the claims you make about the meaning of the text will grow out of your thesis statement. Expressing these claims as topic sentences provides a structure for your essay and helps you form a cohesive line of reasoning in support of your thesis. Let's return to our example thesis on justice:

> In *Trifles*, the moral dilemma Mrs. Hale and Mrs. Peters face reveals how sympathy and empathy shift people's perspectives and motivations and color their interpretations of justice.

This thesis suggests that you will first discuss the moral dilemma presented to Mrs. Hale and Mrs. Peters, and then explain how the dilemma relates to sympathy and empathy, and ultimately alters their perspectives and motivations in a way that reveals their perspectives and motivations and colors their interpretations of justice. If you were jotting down notes to structure your essay, they might look something like this:

- Discovery of canary = discovery of Mrs. Wright's motive. Men's lack of interest in women's discovery reveals canary's significance.
- Mrs. Hale connects bird's death (literal silencing) with Mr. Wright's silencing of Mrs. Wright.
- Characters' shifting perspectives:
  - Mrs. Hale: sympathy. Imagines Mrs. Wright's loneliness, comfort provided by canary, Mrs. Wright's devastation at its death.
  - Mrs. Peters: empathy. Remembers her response to boy killing her kitten, losing baby, and being alone.
  - Result of sympathy and empathy: kinship and sisterhood with Mrs. Wright
- Women confronted with moral dilemma of sharing knowledge with the men about Mrs. Wright's role in her husband's death.
  - Who's responsible?
  - What's just?
- Withhold evidence due to change in perspectives on Mrs. Wright.

These blocks of notes may not neatly transform into clear topic sentences, but they do suggest a logical progression in our line of reasoning. If we turn them into complete sentences — in some cases, separating ideas; in others, combining them — we end up with an outline:

> **TOPIC SENTENCE 1**
> The men's ongoing dismissal of the women's knowledge ironically gives the women time to interpret the canary's significance as not just an indication of Mrs. Wright's guilt but also an indication of Mr. Wright's dismissal of his wife's unhappiness.

TOPIC SENTENCE 2

Mrs. Hale and Mrs. Peters connect Mr. Wright literally silencing the bird to him figuratively silencing Mrs. Wright.

TOPIC SENTENCE 3

Identifying with Mrs. Wright, the women withhold judgment and instead try to understand what might have motivated her actions.

TOPIC SENTENCE 4

Faced with the moral dilemma of sharing their discoveries, the women's interpretation of justice in this situation leads them to withhold evidence.

Of course, this is bare bones and not yet a fully developed essay, but these four topic sentences show a progression of thought. Going well beyond summary, they examine character, plot, and symbolism. Each resulting paragraph will contribute to the overall interpretation. If you are writing under time constraints, you might consider narrowing the number of topic sentences down to three, or combining two topic sentences if the claims are closely related.

Developing a Line of Reasoning

Citing examples and explicitly explaining how they illustrate and support your interpretation are key to developing a line of reasoning to support your interpretation of a literary work. The more you explain *why* and *how* rather than state *that*, the stronger your essay will be. In other words, anytime you make a statement describing what happens, make sure that you also address why and how it happens.

Having to write about a text without having it in front of you brings unique challenges. You need to incorporate appropriate, convincing evidence, but you'll have to rely entirely on memory to do so. As you know, it's important to avoid summary, but you will need to provide your readers with some information about the plot or characters of the work. One helpful guideline is to assume that your reader has read the text but has not necessarily thought too much about it. To write for this kind of audience, you won't have to recount the plot or describe the characters, but you will have to be methodical in presenting the connections between those elements and your interpretation of the text. Let's walk through one way to write a body paragraph in support of topic sentence 3:

> Identifying with Mrs. Wright, the women withhold judgment and instead try to understand what might have motivated her.

If you have time, you may find it helpful to deliberately summarize relevant events from the text in a short paragraph as a first step. For example, take Mrs. Peters's and Mrs. Hale's discovery of the dead canary near the end of the play, an event that leads them to withhold judgment. A full summary might look like this:

> Mrs. Hale and Mrs. Peters discover a fancy box in Mrs. Wright's sewing supplies, open it, and realize it contains the dead canary that must have once lived in the empty cage. The

women begin to think a bit more about what life must have been like for Mrs. Wright as a woman living in a home absent the sounds of children, and Mrs. Hale comes to the conclusion that Mr. Wright didn't like the bird's singing and killed it. Mrs. Peters also explains how she once felt when a boy killed her kitten, and her recollection of her desire to hurt him helps Mrs. Hale better understand how Mrs. Wright could have killed her husband. The women fight back the realizations that keep coming even as they place themselves in Mrs. Wright's shoes, and both eventually withdraw into themselves and realize the gravity of the situation. Mrs. Hale has a better understanding of what her neighbor has been through, and she pretty easily reaches the conclusion that she wants to protect Mrs. Wright. Mrs. Peters, however, is the newcomer as well as the sheriff's wife so is a little slower to decide also to protect Mrs. Wright. In the end, both women act on their shared secret and withhold information.

This is a lot of information, and not all of it is necessary to support the claim in the topic sentence that the women's identification with Mrs. Wright motivates them to suspend their judgment of her actions. Your description of a given event in the text should be roughly one sentence long, and the rest of the body paragraph should be made up of your own commentary on what those events mean. Some options for shortening the paragraph-long summary include:

- As Mrs. Hale and Mrs. Peters realize what Mrs. Wright has endured in her marriage, they decide to protect the role she played in her husband's death.
- Mrs. Hale and Mrs. Peters begin to sympathize with Mrs. Wright's circumstances and choose to protect her from those less understanding.
- Finding the dead bird opens the eyes of Mrs. Hale and Mrs. Peters to Mrs. Wright's life in a way that results in them keeping her secret.

Each sentence explains what happens without providing unnecessary narrative details. It is important to note, too, that none of these sentences offer any analysis into why and how the events have significance and contribute to the play's meaning. Your job, in crafting a strong literary argument, is to make a case for how and why these events reveal that your interpretation of the text's meaning is not only valid but also convincing.

While the following sample paragraph uses even shorter references to the events of the play than our bulleted list, it still doesn't strike quite the right balance between summary and analysis:

> Identifying with Mrs. Wright, the women withhold judgment and instead try to understand what might have motivated her to kill her husband. Mrs. Hale and Mrs. Peters look around the house, especially the kitchen, and discover the dead canary Mrs. Wright has carefully wrapped up in a box. That its neck had been broken adds to its significance for the women. They talk about the fact that the couple had no children and that Mr. Wright was not a communicative husband. They also discuss incidents from their own past when they felt strong emotions that might have made them do something uncharacteristic or rash.

The paragraph holds a clear focus, and the information is drawn from the play. However, it is very general, and much of it reads like summary that essentially adds up to the idea that the women begin to understand how hard life must have been for Mrs. Wright. Furthermore, it is true that the women look around the house and their discovery of the canary is significant, but *in what way*? What significance can you infer from their dialogue and actions? How do these events reveal meaning? Similarly, the women do talk about the loneliness of a couple with no children and how this could lead to isolation, but *so what*? How do the women's remembrances of their own pasts help them understand Mrs. Wright's motivations, which is the claim established in the topic sentence? Answering these questions will help you move from the *what*, or summary, to the *so what*, or interpretation.

The most important part of supporting your argument involves interpreting your evidence and explaining the ways the details you provide connect to your thesis statement and topic sentences. You do this by including sentences of interpretation and explanation, sometimes called commentary or analysis, for each of your examples — and by making those examples as concrete as possible. Consider this revision of the previous paragraph:

> Identifying with Mrs. Wright, the women withhold judgment and instead try to understand what might have motivated her to kill her husband. In examining her kitchen, they realize how hard life must have been for Mrs. Wright in a house with no children and with Mr. Wright, who was cold and distant. The remote location of the Wrights' house could have contributed to Mrs. Wright's bleak existence. Mrs. Hale and Mrs. Peters begin to understand how the isolation and sense of entrapment could have led Mrs. Wright to snap, especially following the death of her canary. They can see how the only means of escape might have been to kill Mr. Wright because of his treatment of her as a captive. In seeing ways she could potentially have reached out to Mrs. Wright, Mrs. Hale sympathizes with Mrs. Wright's lonely existence. Mrs. Peters further reinforces their reluctance to judge Mrs. Wright by sharing a time when Mrs. Peters herself felt the desire to hurt a boy who butchered her kitten with a hatchet. Ultimately, the women realize that they too might have been driven to violence under Mrs. Wright's circumstances.

Notice how specific this paragraph is, with its inclusion of examples drawn from the play. Even without direct quotations, this paragraph provides support for the interpretive point made in the topic sentence.

Writing a Body Paragraph of an AP® Literary Argument Essay

Choose another of the sample topic sentences and use it to write a full paragraph. First, summarize the part of the scene you plan to analyze. Next, condense that summary to a short sentence or phrase. Finally, use the sentence as a jumping-off point to explore

(*continued*)

how and *why* the things the characters do and say contribute to meaning and support the topic sentence you have chosen. As you write the paragraph, ask yourself, "So what?" at the end of each sentence to make sure you provide commentary that supports your evidence.

Revising an AP® Literary Argument Essay

Revision is a vital step in the writing process. It offers you the chance not only to spot typos and clean things up but also to shore up any weak points in your literary argument. While the following questions may be helpful as you revise full essays, they will also help you revise shorter responses too.

- **Reread the entire essay for comprehension.** Is there a clear line of reasoning that puts forth a cohesive argument for your interpretation of the meaning of the work?
- **Reread your introduction and thesis statement.** Is the thesis clear? Have you taken a position that goes beyond summary or paraphrase? Does your interpretation respond directly to the prompt?
- **Reread each topic sentence.** Do they accurately reflect a claim in your thesis? Do they provide a bridge between the line of reasoning in your thesis and the evidence in the paragraphs?
- **Check your evidence.** Are the scenes or characters you've chosen to examine the most effective examples to support the claim in the topic sentence of each body paragraph?
- **Evaluate your commentary.** Does it explain the relationship between the evidence you've selected and the claim in the topic sentence in the body paragraphs?
- **Reread for spelling and grammar.** Do you have run-ons or sentence fragments? Misspelled words or typos?
- **Read your essay aloud to yourself.** Does it sound right? Can you tighten anything up?
- **If possible, step away from it.** Clear your mind for a few hours — a day if you can. Return to your work with fresh eyes as a reader of it instead of as the writer.
- **Reread one final time with a clear head.** Just a tune-up. Are there small changes you can make to improve word choice and sentence structure?

Analyzing a Sample AP® Literary Argument Essay

The following student essay responds to the prompt we introduced on page 144. As you read it, think about how you would provide feedback to help this student revise her draft.

Susan Glaspell's *Trifles*

Fabiana Martínez

An ode to women's inner lives, Susan Glaspell's *Trifles* weaves an intricate narrative fragmented into two differing perspectives: men's pragmatic quest for answers and women's impassioned search for connection. As the play unfolds around the murder of John Wright, the characters' motivations determine their approaches to justice and inform their perceptions of morality while simultaneously communicating the insidious ways in which social positions divide and unite those in their grip. The socialization of men and women, the dangers of isolation, and the centrality of women in the story comprise the play's overarching message.

The events of the play depend on a strict separation of gender, which relies on the socialization of men and women. From the beginning of the story, the men demand the reader's attention as they enter the Wrights' home and immediately scatter around the warm stove while the women fall behind, near the door and the cold wind. Given this structure, the reader attributes the women's presence to their husbands' endeavors, subconsciously stripping them of their agency. It is only when the attorney notes the broken jars in the cupboard that the women voice Mrs. Wright's concerns and thus reveal that they are not acting as their husbands' companions but extending kindness to the imprisoned woman. Unlike the men's examination of the house and its vicinities, the women's careful tending of Mrs. Wright's belongings in a single space demonstrates an attentiveness that disregards the crime to understand the perpetrator. However, despite this division between men and women, Glaspell does not suggest that the characters' behavior stems from a biological inclination toward sentimentality or practicality, but rather implies that it originates from social norms imparted from infancy. Women's preoccupation with "trifles" is an instinctual reaction to a society exclusively concerned with their appearance and conduct, and their empathy toward Mrs. Wright's predicament is a response to seeing their reality reflected in someone else's life. On the other hand, the sheriff and county attorney, alongside an empowered farmer, hold positions of authority that not only lead them to disregard women's opinions but also cause them to equate the rule of law to moral sovereignty, ironically blinding them to the answers they seek.

With said distribution of power, however, women's relationships with each other become frail and solitude eclipses their lives. Mrs. Hale bemoans Mrs. Wright's fate and laments her absence in the latter's life, emphasizing the need for companionship throughout the play. In particular, she comments that it is impossible to see the road from the Wrights' house, evoking similarities between the house and a birdcage. Both places keep melodious voices away from all vestiges of connection and are final testaments to an act of violence. Mrs. Wright's caged bird, as Mrs. Hale states, is a symbolic representation of the former's spirit: something that sings, silenced. However, the bird does not act as a mere symbol in Mrs. Wright's life, as it is also a companion that mirrors the life of song that has escaped her and exists as tentative proof that caged beings still can sing. As Mr. Wright ends the bird's life and Mrs. Wright ends her husband's, these acts of violence attest to the despair of living isolated in an abusive household. Similarly, the attorney's interrogation of Mrs. Hale amplifies the feeling of alienation that pervades these women's lives; the possibility of a supporting community between them is immediately perceived as a threatening scheme of complicity. Even the attorney's implication that sex is the basis for Mrs. Hale defense of Mrs. Wright dismisses the experiences that make these bonds possible. He assumes that women are bound by their anatomy instead of their subordination to men within their households, a dynamic that acts as a microcosm for society as a whole.

Subverting the social hierarchy that centers men in its positions of power, Glaspell restructures the formation of the play to remove its men and elevate its women. As previously mentioned, the sheriff, attorney, and farmer lead the women inside the house and claim their place before the stove while the women stand near the door, but once these three characters exit the living room, the women reclaim the reader's attention. Throughout the progression of the story, the men become transient while the women actively retrace the sequence of events that led to Mr. Wright's death under the pretense of passivity. The conversation surrounding Mrs. Wright's preferred sewing method for the quilt mirrors the women's study of the living room, both a symbolic act of knitting together the odd stitches in the unfinished fabric and a mockery of the men's oblivious entrances and exits. Likewise, in the occasions in which Mrs. Hale utters Mrs. Wright's maiden name, Minnie Forster, there is a summoning of a buried woman indicative of a crime for which no perpetrators were found. By referring to Mrs. Wright in the past tense and comparing the choir girl to the forlorn wife, Mrs. Hale shifts the reader's perspective on the victim of the story and delves into the emotions and experiences that drove Mrs. Wright to violence. Furthermore, the women's sewing of this narrative quilt not only rationalizes the crime but also creates a complex, sorrowful life story that endows both a victim and an assailant with a voice of her own. Through assumptions, inferences, and a shared material reality from which to draw similarities, Mrs. Hale and Mrs. Peters sacrifice the pursuit of justice for personal notions of moral righteousness.

Behind layers of dubious moral decisions, Glaspell grants the readers one last lingering cruelty: as the characters finalize their conversations in the living room, it is implicit that the men will continue to live peacefully while the women will carry a burdensome awareness of their lives and the violence that men inflict on them with their presence.

Providing Peer Feedback for Revision

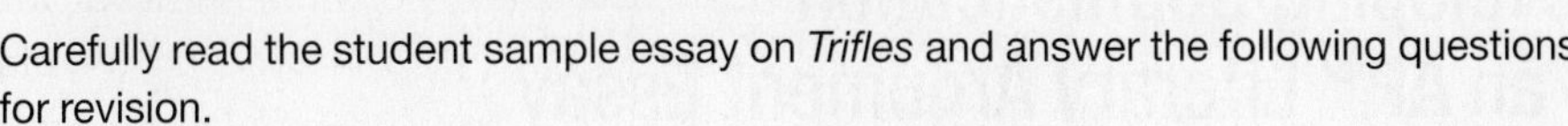

Carefully read the student sample essay on *Trifles* and answer the following questions for revision.

Questions for Revision

1. How well does this essay's thesis respond to the prompt? Would you revise it in any way? If so, how?
2. How clear is the connection between the topic sentences of the body paragraphs and the thesis statement?
3. Overall, how effective is the evidence the essay author uses to support her thesis?
4. Identify a paragraph that is especially effective. What particular qualities of that paragraph make it effective?
5. Identify a paragraph that might be improved. How might you revise it to improve it?
6. Is there a logical progression to the paragraphs? Would you change the order to improve the essay? If so, how? If not, why not?

section 2 /culminating activity

Crafting an AP® Literary Argument Essay

Theodore Roethke opens a poem with the line, "In a dark time, the eye begins to see." In many works of literature, dark times test characters' values, perspectives, and even their senses of themselves. These experiences can lead characters to grow and change, emerging from conflict with new understandings of themselves and the worlds in which they live.

Either from your own reading or from the following list, choose a work of fiction or drama in which a character gains profound insight as a result of challenging periods in their lives. Then, in a well-written essay, analyze how the development of this insight contributes to an interpretation of the work as a whole. Do not merely summarize the plot.

- Charlotte Brontë, *Jane Eyre*
- Kate Chopin, *The Awakening*
- Ralph Ellison, *Invisible Man*
- F. Scott Fitzgerald, *The Great Gatsby*
- Susan Glaspell, *Trifles* (p. 136)
- William Faulkner, *As I Lay Dying*
- Yaa Gyasi, *Homegoing*
- Kazuo Ishiguro, *Never Let Me Go*
- N. K. Jemisin, *The Fifth Season*
- Nella Larsen, *Passing* (p. 487)
- Arthur Miller, *Death of a Salesman*
- Toni Morrison, *Beloved*
- Celeste Ng, *Little Fires Everywhere*
- Tommy Orange, *There There*
- Mary Shelley, *Frankenstein* (p. 1093)
- William Shakespeare, *Hamlet* (p. 555)
- Leslie Marmon Silko, *Ceremony*
- Mark Twain, *The Adventures of Huckleberry Finn*
- Jesmyn Ward, *Sing, Unburied, Sing*
- August Wilson, *Fences* (p. 1047)

Developing Sophistication in an AP® Literary Argument Essay

In Chapters 1 and 2, we shared ways to develop sophistication in a literary analysis by addressing complexities and tensions within a text and framing an interpretation of the text within a broader context. Both of these approaches can be effective ways to develop sophistication in a literary argument about a full-length work too. The richness and length of novels and plays also open the door to another strategy for developing sophistication: incorporating alternative interpretations of a text. You may have noticed that you and a friend can binge on the same television series and come away with completely different perspectives about a main character's behavior: one of you sees her as courageous and the other thinks she's arrogant. As you discuss a novel you're reading for class, you might think its remote setting sounds relaxing, yet a classmate might think the setting sounds too monotonous. The interpretation of the setting as relaxing, for instance, might reflect the main character's need for solitude to truly accept himself; by contrast, the interpretation of it as monotonous might convey that the main character cannot grow into himself if he ignores the people in his community. Can somewhat opposing interpretations both be accurate? Certainly! As long as each of you provides textual evidence to support a plausible interpretation, you can arrive at very different conclusions. In other words, your interpretations of the textual evidence must be accurate and believable within the context of the literature you are analyzing, but how you interpret the evidence will be specific to your own experiences of the world around you, your background, and the prior knowledge you can draw on as you read the text.

Developing Alternative Interpretations through Critical Lenses

Interpreting a text through your own perspective happens naturally, and this tends to be how we experience literature by default. However, most texts have the potential to be read from varying perspectives. These approaches are sometimes called **critical lenses** because they change how we look at the text. You can even think about them like putting on different pairs of glasses. Imagine your class is reading a novel that has at its center a group of siblings. Whether you have older or younger siblings or are an only child or a twin will likely affect your interpretation of the siblings' relationships with each other. Consider how a heated argument between siblings would look through the lenses of an oldest sibling, a youngest sibling, and an only child.

Reading a text through different lenses falls into an entire category of academic study called critical literary theory, and while we are not going to embark on an in-depth study of literary theory, exploring a few perspectives will increase your ability to consider texts through other lenses and why each one is important. We'll consider three basic perspectives:

- psychological
- cultural
- gendered

You're probably most familiar with what we call a **formalist lens**. According to this theory, a text should be read as an independent and self-sufficient entity without taking into account, for instance, an author's religion or socioeconomic status or the culture of the time period when it was written. Instead, the focus is on literary elements such as diction, structure, figurative language, and syntax. Also called New Criticism, this approach works well in many situations, such as during an exam, with strict limits on the time and resources available to you to interpret a literary text.

But it's not the only way to view a text, and it may not be the most creative way to examine or construct meaning. Analyzing literature through various lenses opens up texts to multiple interpretations, some of which may even be in conflict with each other — which is part of what makes literature so compelling. Keep in mind that regardless of the lens you choose to read with, critical perspectives aren't political soapboxes: as is true of all literary analysis, your interpretation of the work through any given lens must be firmly based in specific details from the text.

Psychological Lens

As the term suggests, a **psychological lens** considers the behavior and motivations of characters in a work of literature. Using the language of psychology, this perspective explores how the conscious and unconscious drives and desires — including repression, sexuality, childhood experiences, and fear — influence human actions. In general, reading through a psychological lens involves asking questions about the causes and effects of characters' behavior. In *Trifles*, for example, how does Mrs. Peters's early experience with a boy killing her kitten still influence her well into adulthood?

An interpretation from a psychological perspective typically adheres to the following basic principles:

- An investigation of the psychology of a character or of the author is key to interpreting a text.
- Characters are driven by unconscious motivations; a character's growing awareness of these forces may inform the plot or reveal the themes of the text.
- Symbols are best understood as expressions of a character's unconscious emotions.

KEY QUESTIONS

Literary Analysis — Psychological Lens

- How are the characters' behaviors shaped by both conscious and unconscious motivations?
- What role(s) do repression and childhood experiences play in the text? How do they relate to the theme(s) of the work?
- How does psychology explain the causes and effects of characters' actions?

Cultural Lens

When you read a work through a **cultural lens**, you examine how different races and ethnicities, social and economic class distinctions, and political ideologies influence the creation and interpretation of literature. Cultural criticism examines and questions traditional hierarchies based on race, gender, and class. This perspective also seeks to break down the distinctions between so-called high art and the popular culture of everyday experience. In fact, cultural criticism may question the very nature of the literary canon — that is, why some works are valued as "classic" and thus more worthy of study and interpretation than others.

Although cultural criticism covers a broad landscape, it focuses on how dominant cultures or groups have silenced, devalued, misrepresented, or even demonized marginalized ones. In *Trifles*, for instance, a cultural lens might explore how the women's roles in their households also determine cultural expectations for their roles in solving the mystery of Mr. Wright's death. The following guidelines shape our interpretation of work through a cultural lens:

- Ethnicity, race, social class, gender, and religious affiliation affect how texts are produced and understood.
- Exploring how power — having it or being denied it — influences a text is a valid way to analyze and interpret the work.
- Studying the voices of traditionally marginalized groups is essential to a deeper understanding of literature.

KEY QUESTIONS

Literary Analysis — Cultural Lens

- What are the main traits of the culture in which the events of the work take place? How do race, ethnicity, social class, gender, or religion inform and/or react to that culture?
- What is the relationship between the narrator(s) and those who hold power within the setting of the text?
- Is there anyone in the story who doesn't get to speak? How does this silence reflect the central ideas of the work?

Gendered Lens

When we read through the lens of gender, we ask how depictions of gender support, challenge, or even reflect on our definitions of masculinity and femininity. Acknowledging that gender is a social construct — that is, roles and identities are determined by the society in which a person lives. This perspective explores gender stereotypes, social mores and values, and questions of sexuality in representations of identity. In earlier discussions of literary theory, this perspective was called "feminist" because it challenged the viewpoint that tended to see the male perspective as the "norm" or default. Today, however, a wider lens considers the broader term "gender."

This perspective will likely ask questions about the representation of gender, the extent to which a work reinforces a patriarchal society, the attitude of the author toward gender, and how relationships between men and women are defined. *Trifles* lends itself particularly well to an analysis through a **gendered lens**. For instance, early in the play, the men assume Mrs. Wright likely would have only been worried about her preserves, or mere trifles, freezing. Their assumptions and Mrs. Hale's and Mrs. Peters's responses to their comments provide an opportunity to consider contrasting gendered perspectives. Although an analysis through a gendered lens will not include all of these characteristics, it likely will illustrate some of the following:

- No text exists outside the framework of gender.
- Historically, literature has privileged men, in terms of both production and interpretation, so it is important to create a tradition that balances or even challenges this conventional view.
- Since expectations of roles and behavior are a function of social and cultural values, they should be recognized as subjective and impermanent.
- Stereotyping based on gender is dangerous and should be avoided or confronted.

KEY QUESTIONS

Literary Analysis — Gendered Lens

- How does the text represent gender? What messages does the text convey about the role of patriarchy in society?
- What is the author's attitude toward gender? What evidence can you find for this attitude?
- How does the text define and frame relationships between men, women, and nonbinary people?

Incorporating Alternative Interpretations into an Argument

Keep in mind that these critical lenses are choices, meaning that most texts can be interpreted in several ways, and the ones we've presented are only a few out of many schools of literary theory. No single perspective is "right," and none is "best." Instead, we hope to deepen our understanding of a text's themes and meaning by exploring a single text from multiple perspectives. Doing so can also add depth to your analysis and is one way to develop the sophistication of your essay. Let's revisit the sample body paragraph from earlier in this chapter about why Mrs. Hale and Mrs. Peters decide not to judge Mrs. Wright too quickly:

> Identifying with Mrs. Wright, the women withhold judgment and instead try to understand what might have motivated her to kill her husband. In examining her kitchen, they realize how hard life must have been for Mrs. Wright in a house with no children and with Mr. Wright, who was cold and distant. The remote location of the Wrights' house would have contributed to Mrs. Wright's bleak existence. Mrs. Hale and Mrs. Peters begin to understand how the isolation and sense of entrapment could have led Mrs. Wright to snap, especially following the death of her canary. They can see how the only means of escape might have been to kill Mr. Wright because of his treatment of her as a captive. In seeing ways she could potentially have reached out to Mrs. Wright, Mrs. Hale sympathizes with Mrs. Wright's lonely existence. Mrs. Peters further reinforces their reluctance to judge Mrs. Wright by sharing a time when Mrs. Peters herself felt the desire to hurt a boy who butchered her kitten with a hatchet. Ultimately, the women realize that they too might have been driven to violence under Mrs. Wright's circumstances.

This paragraph hints at elements related to gendered, psychological, and cultural perspectives, but it stops short of exploring the ways in which those lenses might contribute to the meaning of the play. Incorporating these perspectives to account for alternative interpretations could yield a paragraph such as this one:

> On a deeper level, *Trifles* suggests alternative interpretations relevant to gendered and psychological perspectives. For example, the division of investigative labor throughout the play falls along gendered lines with the men centering their efforts elsewhere and leaving the women in the kitchen. That the men view the women's discoveries as trifles that are no more significant than Mrs. Wright's symbolic jars of frozen fruit demonstrates Glaspell's attitudes about the effects a male-dominated society has on women. Furthermore, the expectation at the time that women bear children and center their existence on child care and homemaking would have made the death of Mrs. Wright's canary an even more devastating blow to her already fragile psyche. Additional evidence in the play supports a reading of it through a psychological lens. For example, even though Mrs. Peters remains reluctant to withhold information about Mrs. Wright's likely guilt, her own experiences allow her to work through her repressed anger by shielding Mrs. Wright from legal consequences. Examining the play with these ideas in mind brings

to light the complex ways the society in which the characters find themselves influences them in the midst of the moral dilemmas they face throughout the play.

This paragraph demonstrates sophistication because it remains relevant to the overall focus of the essay and its thesis while expanding the analysis beyond anything suggested by the other paragraphs according to their topic sentences.

section 3 / culminating activity

Developing Sophistication in an AP® Literary Argument Essay

Choose a literary argument essay that you have written and revise it to develop a more sophisticated line of reasoning that addresses alternative ways to read the text. As you revise, consider the key questions about psychological, cultural, and gendered lenses. *How* and *why* are these perspectives relevant to your analysis? What additional textual evidence is there to support each reading of your chosen work?

Nikolai Larin/Imagezoo/Getty Images

Identity and Culture

What makes us who we are? While our identity is shaped by our interests, personality, and talents, much of how we define ourselves depends on the culture that surrounds us. Gender, race, age, religion, national allegiance, geography, language, class, and ethnicity all play a role. In this chapter, the readings explore the many different ways that culture influences who we are.

Is defining identity based along individual and cultural lines a divisive or a constructive force in society? In every generation, immigrants assimilate to the life of their new homeland — but they also proudly maintain their traditions and weave their identities into the fabric of the culture they have joined. Some argue for cosmopolitanism — for people to be citizens of the world — to foster a greater sense of shared identity. Would that discourage cultural discrimination and bias, or would it erode local community values and ties? In contemporary literature, cross-cultural writers such as Jhumpa Lahiri, who is Indian American, are part of the canon of the twenty-first century. Her characters and their level of comfort in more than one culture reflect the benefits and difficulties of living in a global community. Lahiri's "Interpreter of Maladies," as well as other stories in this chapter, asks: do we create an identity — or inherit one?

"Boy on a Train" an early short story by Ralph Ellison, invites us to consider how children find their identity, as well as the roles that family and the outside world have in the development of that identity. The drama of that discovery is played out, aptly enough, on a train ride that mirrors the young protagonist's journey toward a new home and a new sense of who he is or could become. Other stories in this chapter, like Nathaniel Hawthorne's nineteenth-century tale of Puritan temptation and betrayal in "Young Goodman Brown" and Nobel Laureate Nadine Gordimer's fictionalization of a European political assassination in 1986, explore the ways that what we do changes who we are. The chapter also includes work by contemporary writers such as Chimamanda Ngozi Adichie and Weike Wang, whose stories raise some haunting questions about whether being yourself or hiding yourself comes at a higher cost. In Sakinah Hofler's surreal story

"Erasure," we'll consider the ways in which we construct ourselves in opposition to others — and how this can foster a sense of community yet limit our perspectives. Nafissa Thompson-Spires's "Belles Lettres" examines what happens when a privileged position as "the only" is threatened. Many of the poems in this chapter explore identities that are not shaped by culture but are in conflict with it, such as Emily Dickinson's "I'm Nobody! Who are you?," Kamau Brathwaite's "Ogun," and Mahmoud Darwish's "Identity Card." Some, such as Natalie Diaz's "The Facts of Art" and Gregory Pardlo's "Written by Himself," confront one-dimensional narratives. Others continue to explore the identity both forced and forged in the experience of merging, even colliding cultures; these include José Olivarez in "(citizen) (illegal)," Quan Barry in "loose strife [Somebody says draw a map]," and Alexis Aceves Garcia in "AQUÍ HAY TODO, MIJA." The conflicts and struggles between and within the characters in these texts reflect just some of the vast array of real-life experiences that form integral parts of our identities.

To understand and fully appreciate the wide array of short fiction in this chapter, let's turn to the Big Ideas, Skills, and Essential Knowledge in Unit 4 of the AP® English Literature and Composition course. This unit focuses on aspects of Character, Setting, Structure, Narration, and Literary Argumentation. You may want to review these fundamentals of reading and writing about fiction that we covered in Chapter 1 as you deepen your analysis of how authors develop perspectives, plots, and conflicts that are complex and nuanced. While the questions after all of the readings in this chapter ask you to examine how several different literary elements and techniques work together to create meaning, we will preview how they work in the Classic Text for this chapter: "Boy on a Train." As you study and discuss both this story and the Central Text, "Interpreter of Maladies," you will delve further into how the writers' art and craft bring the struggle for an authentic identity to life.

AP® Big Idea: Character

In "Boy on a Train," Ralph Ellison develops complex **characters** whose thoughts and actions reveal and disrupt patterns, just as people in the real world do. Specific textual details of characters' appearance, actions, speech, and behavior reveal their values. The protagonist of the story is James, an African American child traveling with his mother and younger brother. As Ellison reveals the young protagonist's self-doubt, anxiety, and feelings of loss alongside his hopes for the future, he explores the tension of leaving childhood comforts, facing the dangers of a hostile world, and deciding who he wants to be. Ultimately, the extent to which the conflict within young James in "Boy on a Train" is resolved becomes a question to explore as you develop your own interpretation of the story's meaning. *To review character in short fiction, see pages 5–8 of Chapter 1: Analyzing Short Fiction.*

AP® Big Idea: Setting

More than time and place, the **setting** in short fiction conveys vivid, and specific, social and cultural values. "Boy on a Train," set on a segregated train moving through Oklahoma in 1924, not only establishes the atmosphere of the narrative but invites an inquiry into the values that place in fiction can represent. Through the relationship between the main characters and the setting — both the train car and the boy's memories of

Oklahoma City — Ellison explores how the environments we grow up in shape our perspectives and sense of ourselves in fundamental ways, no matter how far from them we travel. *To review setting in short fiction, see pages 8–10 of Chapter 1: Analyzing Short Fiction.*

AP® Big Idea: Structure

The **structure** of a short story can provide a unique window into how the arrangement of events form patterns that affect our interpretation of its meaning. Although "Boy on a Train" has a linear plot, readers are taken both to James's past and possible future in a literal journey that takes on symbolic significance. These shifts, which often introduce conflicts between and within the characters, are often signaled by what the protagonist sees from the window of the moving train. In revealing specific details of James's life via flashback and foreshadowing that contrast the past, present, and the future the protagonist imagines for himself, Ellison molds our understanding of what they mean. The glimpses readers see of James's and his family's history helps readers understand the full complexity of his experience and the changes he undergoes as the plot unfolds. *To review plot structure in short fiction, see pages 10–13 of Chapter 1: Analyzing Short Fiction.*

AP® Big Idea: Narration

Who **narrates** a story influences how we experience and interpret it. What is the emotional investment of the narrator in the events and characters in a story? From what narrative distance does the story reach us, its readers? Answering these questions requires careful analysis of how writers convey perspective. In "Boy on a Train," Ellison chooses a third person limited omniscient narrator, one who is privy to the thoughts of the protagonist — and occasionally his mother — during their journey. James's point of view affects what we as readers know about each of the characters in the story, and his unique perspective on the people around him and the events of his journey is what shapes the tone of the narrative. However, the third person narrator provides enough distance from James's perspective for readers to form a fuller picture. In addition to the characters' thoughts, we learn information about the other people on the train, we see the scenery outside the window, and even make inferences about the societal conditions that affect the traveling characters. Through this narrative lens, readers are able to see both within and beyond the reach of characters' thoughts, enabling them to see a full picture of the world they inhabit. *To review narrative perspective and point of view in short fiction, see pages 13–18 of Chapter 1: Analyzing Short Fiction.*

AP® Big Idea: Literary Argumentation

Each of these Big Ideas of storytelling provides an important angle into a work of short fiction. As you read the stories in this chapter, you will be asked to write about how these elements work together to create meaning. In other words, you will develop your own interpretation of works of literature based on evidence from the text. As you learned in Chapter 1, this process of literary argumentation begins with developing a defensible thesis statement and then supporting it with textual evidence and commentary. As you read and write about each story, keep in mind that you must choose this evidence strategically and purposefully to illustrate, clarify, qualify, or amplify a point. While this textual evidence comes from the story itself, the commentary is where your voice as the interpreter of a fictional text comes through. This is the glue that holds your argument together: it explains the logical reasoning that connects the evidence to the interpretation you articulate in your thesis. *To review the process of writing an AP® Short Fiction Analysis Essay, see pages 36–49 of Chapter 1: Analyzing Short Fiction.*

As you read and analyze the works of literature in this chapter, you'll learn more about how people from different time periods and backgrounds define themselves or struggle to do so. You'll see how, in some cases, the culture of family, nationality, religion, gender, or ethnicity supports that identity; in others, how it challenges or even thwarts it. Your understanding of the fiction writer's craft will advance your own skills of analysis and interpretation.

Guided Reading for "Interpreter of Maladies"

As you read the Central Text in this chapter, "Interpreter of Maladies" by Jhumpa Lahiri (p. 169), keep track of your observations and questions about how the following Big Ideas take shape in Lahiri's short story.

AP® Big Idea	Observations	Questions
Character		
Setting		
Structure		
Narration		

AP® Unit 4 Alignment at a Glance

Interpreter of Maladies

Jhumpa Lahiri

Leonardo Cendamo/Getty Images

Born in London in 1967, Jhumpa Lahiri immigrated with her Bengali parents to Boston and then Kingston, Rhode Island. She received a BA in English literature from Barnard College and graduated from Boston University with master's degrees in English, creative writing, and comparative literature and a PhD in Renaissance studies. Lahiri has garnered critical acclaim and commercial success with two short-story collections — *Interpreter of Maladies* (1999) and *Unaccustomed Earth* (2008) — and two novels, *The Namesake* (2003) and *The Lowland* (2013). Her debut story collection, *Interpreter of Maladies*, won the PEN/Hemingway Award and the 2000 Pulitzer Prize for Fiction, making Lahiri the youngest person ever to win that prestigious award. Lahiri feels strong ties to England, India, and the United States, yet says, "No country is my motherland. I always find myself in exile in whichever country I travel to. . . ." She explores this theme in much of her fiction, including this title story from *Interpreter of Maladies*.

At the tea stall Mr. and Mrs. Das bickered about who should take Tina to the toilet. Eventually Mrs. Das relented when Mr. Das pointed out that he had given the girl her bath the night before. In the rearview mirror Mr. Kapasi watched as Mrs. Das emerged slowly from his bulky white Ambassador, dragging her shaved, largely bare legs across the back seat. She did not hold the little girl's hand as they walked to the rest room.

They were on their way to see the Sun Temple at Konarak. It was a dry, bright Saturday, the mid-July heat tempered by a steady ocean breeze, ideal weather for sightseeing. Ordinarily Mr. Kapasi would not have stopped so soon along the way, but less than five minutes after he'd picked up the family that morning in front of Hotel Sandy Villa, the little girl had complained. The first thing Mr. Kapasi had noticed when he saw Mr. and Mrs. Das, standing with their children under the portico of the hotel, was that they were very young, perhaps not even thirty. In addition to Tina they had two boys, Ronny and Bobby, who appeared very close in age and had teeth covered in a network of flashing silver wires. The family looked Indian but dressed as foreigners did, the children in stiff, brightly colored clothing and caps with translucent visors. Mr. Kapasi was accustomed to foreign tourists; he was assigned to them regularly because he could speak English. Yesterday he had driven an elderly couple from Scotland, both with spotted faces and fluffy white hair so thin it exposed their sunburnt scalps. In comparison, the tanned, youthful faces of Mr. and Mrs. Das were all the more striking. When he'd introduced himself, Mr. Kapasi had pressed his palms together in greeting, but Mr. Das squeezed hands like an American so that Mr. Kapasi felt it in his elbow. Mrs. Das, for her part, had flexed one side of her mouth, smiling dutifully at Mr. Kapasi, without displaying any interest in him.

As they waited at the tea stall, Ronny, who looked like the older of the two boys, clambered suddenly out of the back seat, intrigued by a goat tied to a stake in the ground.

"Don't touch it," Mr. Das said. He glanced up from his paperback tour book, which said "INDIA" in yellow letters and looked as if it had been published abroad. His voice, somehow tentative and a little shrill, sounded as though it had not yet settled into maturity.

5 "I want to give it a piece of gum," the boy called back as he trotted ahead.

Mr. Das stepped out of the car and stretched his legs by squatting briefly to the ground. A clean-shaven man, he looked exactly like a magnified version of Ronny. He had a sapphire blue visor, and was dressed in shorts, sneakers, and a T-shirt. The camera slung around his neck, with an impressive telephoto lens and numerous buttons and markings, was the only complicated thing he wore. He frowned, watching as Ronny rushed toward the goat, but appeared to have no intention of intervening. "Bobby, make sure that your brother doesn't do anything stupid."

"I don't feel like it," Bobby said, not moving. He was sitting in the front seat beside Mr. Kapasi, studying a picture of the elephant god taped to the glove compartment.

"No need to worry," Mr. Kapasi said. "They are quite tame." Mr. Kapasi was forty-six years old, with receding hair that had gone completely silver, but his butterscotch complexion and his unlined brow, which he treated in spare moments to dabs of lotus-oil balm, made it easy to imagine what he must have looked like at an earlier age. He wore gray trousers and a matching jacket-style shirt, tapered at the waist, with short sleeves and a large pointed collar, made of a thin but durable synthetic material. He had specified both the cut and the fabric to his tailor — it was his preferred uniform for giving tours because it did not get crushed during his long hours behind the wheel. Through the windshield he watched as Ronny circled around the goat, touched it quickly on its side, then trotted back to the car.

"You left India as a child?" Mr. Kapasi asked when Mr. Das had settled once again into the passenger seat.

10 "Oh, Mina and I were both born in America," Mr. Das announced with an air of sudden confidence. "Born and raised. Our parents live here now, in Assansol. They retired. We visit them every couple years." He turned to watch as the little girl ran toward the car, the wide purple bows of her sundress flopping on her narrow brown shoulders. She was holding to her chest a doll with yellow hair that looked as if it had been chopped, as a punitive measure, with a pair of dull scissors. "This is Tina's first trip to India, isn't it, Tina?"

"I don't have to go to the bathroom anymore," Tina announced.

"Where's Mina?" Mr. Das asked.

Mr. Kapasi found it strange that Mr. Das should refer to his wife by her first name when speaking to the little girl. Tina pointed to where Mrs. Das was purchasing something from one of the shirtless men who worked at the tea stall. Mr. Kapasi heard one of the shirtless men sing a phrase from a popular Hindi love song as Mrs. Das walked back to the car, but she did not appear to understand the words of the song, for she did not express irritation, or embarrassment, or react in any other way to the man's declarations.

He observed her. She wore a red-and-white-checkered skirt that stopped above her knees, slip-on shoes with a square wooden heel, and a close-fitting blouse styled like a man's undershirt. The blouse was decorated at chest-level with a calico appliqué in the shape of a strawberry. She was a short woman, with small hands like paws, her frosty pink fingernails painted to match her lips, and was slightly plump in her figure. Her hair, shorn only a little longer than her husband's, was parted far to one side. She was wearing large dark brown sunglasses with a pinkish tint to them, and carried a big straw bag, almost as big as her torso, shaped like a bowl, with a water bottle poking out of it. She walked slowly, carrying some puffed rice tossed with peanuts and chili peppers in a large packet made from newspapers. Mr. Kapasi turned to Mr. Das.

"Where in America do you live?"

"New Brunswick, New Jersey."

"Next to New York."

"Exactly. I teach middle school there."

"What subject?"

"Science. In fact, every year I take my students on a trip to the Museum of Natural History in New York City. In a way we have a lot in common, you could say, you and I. How long have you been a tour guide, Mr. Kapasi?"

"Five years."

Mrs. Das reached the car. "How long's the trip?" she asked, shutting the door.

"About two and a half hours," Mr. Kapasi replied.

At this Mrs. Das gave an impatient sigh, as if she had been traveling her whole life without pause. She fanned herself with a folded Bombay film magazine written in English.

"I thought that the Sun Temple is only eighteen miles north of Puri," Mr. Das said, tapping on the tour book.

"The roads to Konarak are poor. Actually it is a distance of fifty-two miles," Mr. Kapasi explained.

Mr. Das nodded, readjusting the camera strap where it had begun to chafe the back of his neck.

Before starting the ignition, Mr. Kapasi reached back to make sure the cranklike locks on the inside of each of the back doors were secured. As soon as the car began to move the little girl began to play with the lock on her side, clicking it with some effort forward and backward, but Mrs. Das said nothing to stop her. She sat a bit slouched at one end of the back seat, not offering her puffed rice to anyone. Ronny and Tina sat on either side of her, both snapping bright green gum.

"Look," Bobby said as the car began to gather speed. He pointed with his finger to the tall trees that lined the road. "Look."

"Monkeys!" Ronny shrieked. "Wow!"

They were seated in groups along the branches, with shining black faces, silver bodies, horizontal eyebrows, and crested heads. Their long gray tails dangled like a series of ropes among the leaves. A few scratched themselves with black leathery hands, or swung their feet, staring as the car passed.

"We call them the hanuman," Mr. Kapasi said. "They are quite common in the area."

As soon as he spoke, one of the monkeys leaped into the middle of the road, causing Mr. Kapasi to brake suddenly. Another bounced onto the hood of the car, then sprang away. Mr. Kapasi beeped his horn. The children began to get excited, sucking in their breath and covering their faces partly with their hands. They had never seen monkeys outside of a zoo, Mr. Das explained. He asked Mr. Kapasi to stop the car so that he could take a picture.

While Mr. Das adjusted his telephoto lens, Mrs. Das reached into her straw bag and pulled out a bottle of colorless nail polish, which she proceeded to stroke on the tip of her index finger.

The little girl stuck out a hand. "Mine too. Mommy, do mine too."

"Leave me alone," Mrs. Das said, blowing on her nail and turning her body slightly. "You're making me mess up."

The little girl occupied herself by buttoning and unbuttoning a pinafore on the doll's plastic body.

"All set," Mr. Das said, replacing the lens cap.

The car rattled considerably as it raced along the dusty road, causing them all to pop up from their seats every now and then, but Mrs. Das continued to polish her nails. Mr. Kapasi eased up on the accelerator, hoping to produce a smoother ride. When he reached for the gearshift the boy in front accommodated him by swinging his hairless knees out of the way. Mr. Kapasi noted that this boy was slightly paler than the other children. "Daddy, why is the driver sitting on the wrong side in this car, too?" the boy asked.

"They all do that here, dummy," Ronny said.

"Don't call your brother a dummy," Mr. Das said. He turned to Mr. Kapasi. "In America, you know . . . it confuses them."

"Oh yes, I am well aware," Mr. Kapasi said. As delicately as he could, he shifted gears again, accelerating as they approached a hill in the road. "I see it on *Dallas*, the steering wheels are on the left-hand side."

"What's *Dallas*?" Tina asked, banging her now naked doll on the seat behind Mr. Kapasi.

"It went off the air," Mr. Das explained. "It's a television show."

They were all like siblings, Mr. Kapasi thought as they passed a row of date trees. Mr. and Mrs. Das behaved like an older brother and sister, not parents. It seemed that they were in charge of the children only for the day; it was hard to believe they were regularly responsible for anything other than themselves. Mr. Das tapped on his lens cap, and his tour book, dragging his thumbnail occasionally across the pages so that they made a scraping sound. Mrs. Das continued to polish her nails. She had still not removed her sunglasses. Every now and then Tina renewed her plea that she wanted her nails done, too, and so at one point Mrs. Das flicked a drop of polish on the little girl's finger before depositing the bottle back inside her straw bag.

"Isn't this an air-conditioned car?" she asked, still blowing on her hand. The window on Tina's side was broken and could not be rolled down.

"Quit complaining," Mr. Das said. "It isn't so hot."

"I told you to get a car with air-conditioning," Mrs. Das continued. "Why do you do this, Raj, just to save a few stupid rupees. What are you saving us, fifty cents?"

Their accents sounded just like the ones Mr. Kapasi heard on American television programs, though not like the ones on *Dallas*.

"Doesn't it get tiresome, Mr. Kapasi, showing people the same thing every day?" Mr. Das asked, rolling down his own window all the way. "Hey, do you mind stopping the car. I just want to get a shot of this guy."

Mr. Kapasi pulled over to the side of the road as Mr. Das took a picture of a barefoot man, his head wrapped in a dirty turban, seated on top of a cart of grain sacks pulled by a pair of bullocks. Both the man and the bullocks were emaciated. In the back seat Mrs. Das gazed out another window, at the sky, where nearly transparent clouds passed quickly in front of one another.

"I look forward to it, actually," Mr. Kapasi said as they continued on their way. "The Sun Temple is one of my favorite places. In that way it is a reward for me. I give tours on Fridays and Saturdays only. I have another job during the week."

"Oh? Where?" Mr. Das asked.

"I work in a doctor's office."

"You're a doctor?"

"I am not a doctor. I work with one. As an interpreter."

"What does a doctor need an interpreter for?"

"He has a number of Gujarati patients. My father was Gujarati, but many people do not speak Gujarati in this area, including the doctor. And so the doctor asked me to work in his office, interpreting what the patients say."

"Interesting. I've never heard of anything like that." Mr. Das said.

Mr. Kapasi shrugged. "It is a job like any other."

"But so romantic," Mrs. Das said dreamily, breaking her extended silence. She lifted her pinkish brown sunglasses and arranged them on top of her head like a tiara. For the first time, her eyes met Mr. Kapasi's in the rearview mirror: pale, a bit small, their gaze fixed but drowsy.

Mr. Das craned to look at her. "What's so romantic about it?"

"I don't know. Something." She shrugged, knitting her brows together for an instant. "Would you like a piece of gum, Mr. Kapasi?" she asked brightly. She reached into her straw bag and handed him a small square wrapped in green-and-white-striped paper. As soon as Mr. Kapasi put the gum in his mouth a thick sweet liquid burst onto his tongue.

"Tell us more about your job, Mr. Kapasi," Mrs. Das said.

"What would you like to know, madame?"

"I don't know," she shrugged, munching on some puffed rice and licking the mustard oil from the corners of her mouth. "Tell us a typical situation." She settled back in her seat, her head tilted in a patch of sun, and closed her eyes. "I want to picture what happens."

"Very well. The other day a man came in with a pain in his throat."

"Did he smoke cigarettes?"

"No. It was very curious. He complained that he felt as if there were long pieces of straw stuck in his throat. When I told the doctor he was able to prescribe the proper medication."

"That's so neat."

"Yes," Mr. Kapasi agreed after some hesitation.

"So these patients are totally dependent on you," Mrs. Das said. She spoke slowly, as if she were thinking aloud. "In a way, more dependent on you than the doctor."

"How do you mean? How could it be?"

"Well, for example, you could tell the doctor that the pain felt like a burning, not straw. The patient would never know what you had told the doctor, and the doctor wouldn't know that you had told the wrong thing. It's a big responsibility."

"Yes, a big responsibility you have there, Mr. Kapasi," Mr. Das agreed.

Mr. Kapasi had never thought of his job in such complimentary terms. To him it was a thankless occupation. He found nothing noble in interpreting people's maladies, assiduously translating the symptoms of so many swollen bones, countless cramps of bellies and bowels, spots on people's palms that changed color, shape, or size. The doctor, nearly half his age, had an affinity for bell-bottom trousers and made humorless jokes about the Congress party. Together they worked in a stale little infirmary where Mr. Kapasi's smartly tailored clothes clung to him in the heat, in spite of the blackened blades of a ceiling fan churning over their heads.

The job was a sign of his failings. In his youth he'd been a devoted scholar of foreign languages, the owner of an impressive collection of dictionaries. He had dreamed of being an interpreter for diplomats and dignitaries, resolving conflicts between people and nations, settling disputes of which he alone could understand both sides. He was a self-educated man. In a series of notebooks, in the evenings before his parents settled his marriage, he had listed the common etymologies of words, and at one point in his life he was confident that he could converse, if given the opportunity, in English, French, Russian, Portuguese, and Italian, not to mention Hindi, Bengali, Orissi, and Gujarati. Now only a handful of European phrases remained in his memory, scattered words for things like saucers and chairs. English was the only non-Indian language he spoke fluently anymore. Mr. Kapasi knew it was not a remarkable talent. Sometimes he feared that his children knew better English than he did, just from watching television. Still, it came in handy for the tours.

extending beyond the text

Jhumpa Lahiri's 2016 memoir, *In Other Words*, recounts her process of learning Italian. The extent to which Lahiri immersed herself and learned the language is underscored by the fact that the book was originally written in Italian. In the excerpt that follows, Lahiri writes about "[a]n absence that creates a distance within you."

from In Other Words

Jhumpa Lahiri

My relationship with Italian takes place in exile, in a state of separation.

Every language belongs to a specific place. It can migrate, it can spread. But usually it's tied to a geographical territory, a country. Italian belongs mainly to Italy, and I live on another continent, where one does not readily encounter it. . . .

I think of my mother, who writes poems in Bengali, in America. Almost fifty years after moving there, she can't find a book written in her language.

In a sense I'm used to a kind of linguistic exile. My mother tongue, Bengali, is foreign in America. When you live in a country where your own language is considered foreign, you can feel a continuous sense of estrangement. You speak a secret, unknown language, lacking any correspondence to the environment. An absence that creates a distance within you.

In my case there is another distance, another schism. I don't know Bengali perfectly. I don't know how to read it, or even write it. I have an accent, I speak without authority, and so I've always perceived a disjunction between it and me. As a result I consider my mother tongue, paradoxically, a foreign language, too. ■

How does language contribute to this distance in Lahiri? Although she wrote *In Other Words* seventeen years after "Interpreter of Maladies," how does the short story reflect some of the ideas that she explores in this excerpt?

He had taken the job as an interpreter after his first son, at the age of seven, contracted typhoid — that was how he had first made the acquaintance of the doctor. At the time Mr. Kapasi had been teaching English in a grammar school, and he bartered his skills as an interpreter to pay the increasingly exorbitant medical bills. In the end the boy had died one evening in his mother's arms, his limbs burning with fever, but then there was the funeral to pay for, and the other children who were born soon enough, and the newer, bigger house, and the good schools and tutors, and the fine shoes and the television, and the countless other ways he tried to console his wife and to keep her from crying in her sleep, and so when the doctor offered to pay him twice as much as he earned at the grammar school, he accepted. Mr. Kapasi knew that his wife had little regard for his career as an interpreter. He knew it reminded her of the son she'd lost, and that she resented the other lives he helped, in his own small way, to save. If ever she referred to his position, she used the phrase "doctor's assistant," as if the process of interpretation were equal to taking someone's temperature, or changing a bedpan. She never asked him about the patients who came to the doctor's office, or said that his job was a big responsibility.

For this reason it flattered Mr. Kapasi that Mrs. Das was so intrigued by his job. Unlike his wife, she had reminded him of its intellectual challenges. She had also used the word "romantic." She did not behave in a romantic way toward her husband, and yet she had used the word to describe him. He wondered if Mr. and Mrs. Das were a bad match, just as he and his wife were. Perhaps they, too, had little in common apart from three children and a decade of their lives. The signs he recognized from his own marriage were there — the bickering, the indifference, the protracted silences. Her sudden interest in him, an interest she did not express in either her husband or her children, was mildly intoxicating. When Mr. Kapasi thought once again about how she had said "romantic," the feeling of intoxication grew.

He began to check his reflection in the rearview mirror as he drove, feeling grateful that he had chosen the gray suit that morning and not the brown one, which tended to sag a little in the knees. From time to time he glanced through the mirror at Mrs. Das. In addition to glancing at her face he glanced at the strawberry between her breasts, and the golden brown hollow in her throat. He decided to tell Mrs. Das about another patient, and another: the young woman who had complained of a sensation of raindrops in her spine, the gentleman whose birthmark had begun to sprout hairs. Mrs. Das listened attentively, stroking her hair with a small plastic brush that resembled an oval bed of nails, asking more questions, for yet another example. The children were quiet, intent on spotting more monkeys in the trees, and Mr. Das was absorbed by his tour book, so it seemed like a private conversation between Mr. Kapasi and Mrs. Das. In this manner the next half hour passed, and when they stopped for lunch at a roadside restaurant that sold fritters and omelette sandwiches, usually something Mr. Kapasi looked forward to on his tours so that he could sit in peace and enjoy some hot tea, he was disappointed. As the Das family settled together under a magenta umbrella fringed with white and orange tassels, and placed their orders with one of the waiters who marched about in tricornered caps, Mr. Kapasi reluctantly headed toward a neighboring table.

"Mr. Kapasi, wait. There's room here," Mrs. Das called out. She gathered Tina onto her lap, insisting that he accompany them. And so, together, they had bottled mango juice and sandwiches and plates of onions and potatoes deep-fried in graham-flour batter. After finishing two omelette sandwiches Mr. Das took more pictures of the group as they ate.

"How much longer?" he asked Mr. Kapasi as he paused to load a new roll of film in the camera.

"About half an hour more."

By now the children had gotten up from the table to look at more monkeys perched in a nearby tree, so there was a considerable space between Mrs. Das and Mr. Kapasi. Mr. Das placed the camera to his face and squeezed one eye shut, his tongue exposed at one corner of his mouth. "This looks funny, Mina, you need to lean in closer to Mr. Kapasi."

She did. He could smell a scent on her skin, like a mixture of whiskey and rosewater. He worried suddenly that she could smell his perspiration, which he knew had collected beneath the synthetic material of his shirt. He polished off his mango juice in one gulp and smoothed his silver hair with his hands. A bit of the juice dripped onto his chin. He wondered if Mrs. Das had noticed.

She had not. "What's your address, Mr. Kapasi?" she inquired, fishing for something inside her straw bag.

"You would like my address?"

"So we can send you copies," she said. "Of the pictures." She handed him a scrap of paper which she had hastily ripped from a page of her film magazine. The blank portion was limited, for the narrow strip was crowded by lines of text and a tiny picture of a hero and heroine embracing under a eucalyptus tree.

The paper curled as Mr. Kapasi wrote his address in clear, careful letters. She would write to him, asking about his days interpreting at the doctor's office, and he would respond eloquently, choosing only the most entertaining anecdotes, ones that would make her laugh out loud as she read them in her house in New Jersey. In time she would reveal the disappointment of her marriage, and he his. In this way their friendship would grow, and flourish. He would possess a picture of the two of them, eating fried onions under a magenta umbrella, which he would keep, he decided, safely tucked between the pages of his Russian grammar. As his mind raced, Mr. Kapasi experienced a mild and pleasant shock. It was similar to a feeling he used to experience long ago when, after months of translating with the aid of a dictionary, he would finally read a passage from a French novel, or an Italian sonnet, and understand the words, one after another, unencumbered by his own efforts. In those moments Mr. Kapasi used to believe that all was right with the world, that all struggles were rewarded, that all of life's mistakes made sense in the end. The promise that he would hear from Mrs. Das now filled him with the same belief.

When he finished writing his address Mr. Kapasi handed her the paper, but as soon as he did so he worried that he had either misspelled his name, or accidentally reversed the numbers of his postal code. He dreaded the possibility of a lost letter, the photograph never reaching him, hovering somewhere in Orissa, close but ultimately unattainable. He thought of asking for the slip of paper again, just to make sure he had written his address accurately, but Mrs. Das had already dropped it into the jumble of her bag.

• • •

They reached Konarak at two-thirty. The temple, made of sandstone, was a massive pyramid-like structure in the shape of a chariot. It was dedicated to the great master of life, the sun, which struck three sides of the edifice as it made its journey each day across the sky. Twenty-four giant wheels were carved on the north and south sides of the plinth. The whole thing was drawn by a team of seven horses, speeding as if through the heavens. As they approached, Mr. Kapasi explained that the temple had been built between A.D. 1243 and 1255, with the efforts of twelve hundred artisans, by the great ruler of the Ganga dynasty, King Narasimhadeva the First, to commemorate his victory against the Muslim army.

"It says the temple occupies about a hundred and seventy acres of land," Mr. Das said, reading from his book.

"It's like a desert," Ronny said, his eyes wandering across the sand that stretched on all sides beyond the temple.

"The Chandrabhaga River once flowed one mile north of here. It is dry now," Mr. Kapasi said, turning off the engine.

They got out and walked toward the temple, posing first for pictures by the pair of lions that flanked the steps. Mr. Kapasi led them next to one of the wheels of the chariot, higher than any human being, nine feet in diameter.

"'The wheels are supposed to symbolize the wheel of life,'" Mr. Das read. "'They depict the cycle of creation, preservation, and achievement of realization.' Cool." He turned the page of his book. "'Each wheel is divided into eight thick and thin spokes, dividing the day into eight equal parts. The rims are carved with designs of birds and animals, whereas the medallions in the spokes are carved with women in luxurious poses, largely erotic in nature.'"

What he referred to were the countless friezes of entwined naked bodies, making love in various positions, women clinging to the necks of men, their knees wrapped eternally around

Tanya Baxter Contemporary

Artist Alexis Kersey, who was born and raised in India, portrays aspects of Indian cultural traditions in different contexts to reveal the country's colonial past and reflect its present-day national identity.

How does *The Tourist* reflect some of the identity crises and cultural conflicts that permeate Lahiri's short story?

their lovers' thighs. In addition to these were assorted scenes from daily life, of hunting and trading, of deer being killed with bows and arrows and marching warriors holding swords in their hands.

It was no longer possible to enter the temple, for it had filled with rubble years ago, but they admired the exterior, as did all the tourists Mr. Kapasi brought there, slowly strolling along each of its sides. Mr. Das trailed behind, taking pictures. The children ran ahead, pointing to figures of naked people, intrigued in particular by the Nagamithunas, the half-human, half-serpentine couples who were said, Mr. Kapasi told them, to live in the deepest waters of the sea. Mr. Kapasi was pleased that they liked the temple, pleased especially that it appealed to Mrs. Das. She stopped every three or four paces, staring silently at the carved lovers, and the processions of elephants, and the topless female musicians beating on two-sided drums.

Though Mr. Kapasi had been to the temple countless times, it occurred to him, as he, too, gazed at the topless women, that he had never seen his own wife fully naked. Even when they had made love she kept the panels of her blouse hooked together, the string of her petticoat knotted around her waist. He had never admired the backs of his wife's legs the way he now admired those of Mrs. Das, walking as if for his benefit alone. He had, of course, seen plenty of bare limbs before, belonging to the American and European ladies who took his tours. But Mrs. Das was different. Unlike the other women, who had an interest only in the temple, and kept their noses buried in a guide-book, or their eyes behind the lens of a camera, Mrs. Das had taken an interest in him.

Mr. Kapasi was anxious to be alone with her, to continue their private conversation, yet he felt nervous to walk at her side. She was lost behind her sunglasses, ignoring her husband's requests that she pose for another picture, walking past her children as if they were strangers. Worried that he might disturb her, Mr. Kapasi walked ahead, to admire, as he always did, the three life-sized bronze avatars of Surya, the sun god, each emerging from its own niche on the temple facade to greet the sun at dawn, noon, and evening. They wore elaborate headdresses, their languid, elongated eyes closed, their bare chests draped with carved chains and amulets. Hibiscus petals, offerings from previous visitors, were strewn at their gray-green feet. The last statue, on the northern wall of the temple, was Mr. Kapasi's favorite. This Surya had a tired expression, weary after a hard day of work, sitting astride a horse with folded legs. Even his horse's eyes were drowsy. Around his body were smaller sculptures of women in pairs, their hips thrust to one side.

"Who's that?" Mrs. Das asked. He was startled to see that she was standing beside him.

"He is the Astachala-Surya," Mr. Kapasi said. "The setting sun."

"So in a couple of hours the sun will set right here?" She slipped a foot out of one of her square-heeled shoes, rubbed her toes on the back of her other leg.

"That is correct."

She raised her sunglasses for a moment, then put them back on again. "Neat."

Mr. Kapasi was not certain exactly what the word suggested, but he had a feeling it was a favorable response. He hoped that Mrs. Das had understood Surya's beauty, his power. Perhaps they would discuss it further in their letters. He would explain things to her, things about India, and she would explain things to him about America. In its own way this correspondence would fulfill his dream, of serving as an interpreter between nations. He looked at her straw bag, delighted that his address lay nestled among its contents. When he pictured her so many thousands of miles away he plummeted, so much so that he had an overwhelming urge to wrap his arms around her, to freeze with her, even for an instant, in an embrace witnessed by his favorite Surya. But Mrs. Das had already started walking.

"When do you return to America?" he asked, trying to sound placid.

"In ten days."

He calculated: A week to settle in, a week to develop the pictures, a few days to compose her letter, two weeks to get to India by air. According to his schedule, allowing room for delays, he would hear from Mrs. Das in approximately six weeks' time.

The family was silent as Mr. Kapasi drove them back, a little past four-thirty, to Hotel Sandy Villa. The children had bought miniature granite versions of the chariot's wheels at a souvenir stand, and they turned them round in their hands. Mr. Das continued to read his book. Mrs. Das untangled Tina's hair with her brush and divided it into two little ponytails.

Mr. Kapasi was beginning to dread the thought of dropping them off. He was not prepared to begin his six-week wait to hear from Mrs. Das. As he stole glances at her in the rearview mirror, wrapping elastic bands around Tina's hair, he wondered how he might make the tour last a little longer. Ordinarily he sped back to Puri using a shortcut, eager to return home, scrub his feet and hands with sandalwood soap, and enjoy the evening newspaper and a cup of tea that his wife would serve him in silence. The thought of that silence, something to which he'd long been resigned, now oppressed him. It was then that he suggested visiting the hills at Udayagiri and Khandagiri, where a number of monastic dwellings were hewn out of the ground, facing one another across a defile. It was some miles away, but well worth seeing, Mr. Kapasi told them.

"Oh yeah, there's something mentioned about it in this book," Mr. Das said. "Built by a Jain king or something."

"Shall we go then?" Mr. Kapasi asked. He paused at a turn in the road. "It's to the left."

Mr. Das turned to look at Mrs. Das. Both of them shrugged.

"Left, left," the children chanted.

Mr. Kapasi turned the wheel, almost delirious with relief. He did not know what he would do or say to Mrs. Das once they arrived at the hills. Perhaps he would tell her what a pleasing smile she had. Perhaps he would compliment her strawberry shirt, which he found irresistibly becoming. Perhaps, when Mr. Das was busy taking a picture, he would take her hand.

He did not have to worry. When they got to the hills, divided by a steep path thick with trees,

Mrs. Das refused to get out of the car. All along the path, dozens of monkeys were seated on stones, as well as on the branches of the trees. Their hind legs were stretched out in front and raised to shoulder level, their arms resting on their knees.

"My legs are tired," she said, sinking low in her seat. "I'll stay here."

"Why did you have to wear those stupid shoes?" Mr. Das said. "You won't be in the pictures."

"Pretend I'm there."

"But we could use one of these pictures for our Christmas card this year. We didn't get one of all five of us at the Sun Temple. Mr. Kapasi could take it."

"I'm not coming. Anyway, those monkeys give me the creeps."

"But they're harmless," Mr. Das said. He turned to Mr. Kapasi. "Aren't they?"

"They are more hungry than dangerous," Mr. Kapasi said. "Do not provoke them with food, and they will not bother you."

Mr. Das headed up the defile with the children, the boys at his side, the little girl on his shoulders. Mr. Kapasi watched as they crossed paths with a Japanese man and woman, the only other tourists there, who paused for a final photograph, then stepped into a nearby car and drove away. As the car disappeared out of view some of the monkeys called out, emitting soft whooping sounds, and then walked on their flat black hands and feet up the path. At one point a group of them formed a little ring around Mr. Das and the children. Tina screamed in delight. Ronny ran in circles around his father. Bobby bent down and picked up a fat stick on the ground. When he extended it, one of the monkeys approached him and snatched it, then briefly beat the ground.

"I'll join them," Mr. Kapasi said, unlocking the door on his side. "There is much to explain about the caves."

"No. Stay a minute," Mrs. Das said. She got out of the back seat and slipped in beside Mr. Kapasi. "Raj has his dumb book anyway." Together, through the windshield, Mrs. Das and Mr. Kapasi watched as Bobby and the monkey passed the stick back and forth between them.

"A brave little boy," Mr. Kapasi commented.

"It's not so surprising," Mrs. Das said.

"No?"

"He's not his."

"I beg your pardon?"

"Raj's. He's not Raj's son."

Mr. Kapasi felt a prickle on his skin. He reached into his shirt pocket for the small tin of lotus-oil balm he carried with him at all times, and applied it to three spots on his forehead. He knew that Mrs. Das was watching him, but he did not turn to face her. Instead he watched as the figures of Mr. Das and the children grew smaller, climbing up the steep path, pausing every now and then for a picture, surrounded by a growing number of monkeys.

"Are you surprised?" The way she put it made him choose his words with care.

"It's not the type of thing one assumes," Mr. Kapasi replied slowly. He put the tin of lotus-oil balm back in his pocket.

"No, of course not. And no one knows, of course. No one at all. I've kept it a secret for eight whole years." She looked at Mr. Kapasi, tilting her chin as if to gain a fresh perspective. "But now I've told you."

Mr. Kapasi nodded. He felt suddenly parched, and his forehead was warm and slightly numb from the balm. He considered asking Mrs. Das for a sip of water, then decided against it.

"We met when we were very young," she said. She reached into her straw bag in search of something, then pulled out a packet of puffed rice. "Want some?"

"No, thank you."

She put a fistful in her mouth, sank into the seat a little, and looked away from Mr. Kapasi, out the window on her side of the car. "We married when we were still in college. We were in high school when he proposed. We went to the same college, of course. Back then we couldn't stand the thought of being separated, not for a day, not for a minute. Our parents were best friends who lived in the same town. My entire life I saw him every weekend, either at our house or theirs. We were sent upstairs to play together while our parents joked about our marriage. Imagine! They never caught us at anything, though in a way I think it was all more or less a setup. The things we did those Friday and Saturday nights, while our parents sat downstairs drinking tea . . . I could tell you stories, Mr. Kapasi."

As a result of spending all her time in college with Raj, she continued, she did not make many close friends. There was no one to confide in about him at the end of a difficult day, or to share a passing thought or a worry. Her parents now lived on the other side of the world, but she had never been very close to them, anyway. After marrying so young she was overwhelmed by it all, having a child so quickly, and nursing, and warming up bottles of milk and testing their temperature against her wrist while Raj was at work, dressed in sweaters and corduroy pants, teaching his students about rocks and dinosaurs. Raj never looked cross or harried, or plump as she had become after the first baby.

Always tired, she declined invitations from her one or two college girlfriends, to have lunch or shop in Manhattan. Eventually the friends stopped calling her, so that she was left at home all day with the baby, surrounded by toys that made her trip when she walked or wince when she sat, always cross and tired. Only occasionally did they go out after Ronny was born, and even more rarely did they entertain. Raj didn't mind; he looked forward to coming home from teaching and watching television and bouncing Ronny on his knee. She had been outraged when Raj told her that a Punjabi friend, someone whom she had once met but did not remember, would be staying with them for a week for some job interviews in the New Brunswick area.

Bobby was conceived in the afternoon, on a sofa littered with rubber teething toys, after the friend learned that a London pharmaceutical company had hired him, while Ronny cried to be freed from his playpen. She made no protest when the friend touched the small of her back as she was about to make a pot of coffee, then pulled her against his crisp navy suit. He made love to her swiftly, in silence, with an expertise she had never known, without the meaningful expressions and smiles Raj always insisted on afterward. The next day Raj drove the friend to JFK. He was married now, to a Punjabi girl, and they lived in London still, and every year they exchanged Christmas cards with Raj and Mina, each couple tucking photos of their families into the envelopes. He did not know that he was Bobby's father. He never would.

"I beg your pardon, Mrs. Das, but why have you told me this information?" Mr. Kapasi asked when she had finally finished speaking, and had turned to face him once again.

"For God's sake, stop calling me Mrs. Das. I'm twenty-eight. You probably have children my age."

"Not quite." It disturbed Mr. Kapasi to learn that she thought of him as a parent. The feeling he had had toward her, that had made him check his reflection in the rearview mirror as they drove, evaporated a little.

"I told you because of your talents." She put the packet of puffed rice back into her bag without folding over the top.

"I don't understand," Mr. Kapasi said.

"Don't you see? For eight years I haven't been able to express this to anybody, not to friends, certainly not to Raj. He doesn't even suspect it. He thinks I'm still in love with him. Well, don't you have anything to say?"

"About what?"

"About what I've just told you. About my secret, and about how terrible it makes me feel. I feel terrible looking at my children, and at Raj, always terrible. I have terrible urges, Mr. Kapasi, to throw things away. One day I had the urge to throw everything I own out the window, the television, the children, everything. Don't you think it's unhealthy?"

He was silent.

"Mr. Kapasi, don't you have anything to say? I thought that was your job."

"My job is to give tours, Mrs. Das."

"Not that. Your other job. As an interpreter."

"But we do not face a language barrier. What need is there for an interpreter?"

"That's not what I mean. I would never have told you otherwise. Don't you realize what it means for me to tell you?"

"What does it mean?"

"It means that I'm tired of feeling so terrible all the time. Eight years, Mr. Kapasi, I've been in pain eight years. I was hoping you could help me feel better, say the right thing. Suggest some kind of remedy."

He looked at her, in her red plaid skirt and strawberry T-shirt, a woman not yet thirty, who loved neither her husband nor her children, who had already fallen out of love with life. Her confession depressed him, depressed him all the more when he thought of Mr. Das at the top of the path, Tina clinging to his shoulders, taking pictures of ancient monastic cells cut into the hills to show his students in America, unsuspecting and unaware that one of his sons was not his own. Mr. Kapasi felt insulted that Mrs. Das should ask him to interpret her common, trivial little secret. She did not resemble the patients in the doctor's office, those who came glassy-eyed and desperate, unable to sleep or breathe or urinate with ease, unable, above all, to give words to their pains. Still, Mr. Kapasi believed it was his duty to assist Mrs. Das. Perhaps he ought to tell her to confess the truth to Mr. Das. He would explain that honesty was the best policy. Honesty, surely, would help her feel better, as she'd put it. Perhaps he would offer to preside over the discussion, as a mediator. He decided to begin with the most obvious question, to get to the heart of the matter, and so he asked, "Is it really pain you feel, Mrs. Das, or is it guilt?"

She turned to him and glared, mustard oil thick on her frosty pink lips. She opened her mouth to say something, but as she glared at Mr. Kapasi some certain knowledge seemed to pass before her eyes, and she stopped. It crushed him; he knew at that moment that he was not even important enough to be properly insulted. She opened the car door and began walking up the path, wobbling a little on her square wooden heels, reaching into her straw bag to eat handfuls of puffed rice. It fell through her fingers, leaving a zigzagging trail, causing a monkey to leap down from a tree and devour the little white grains. In search of more, the monkey began to follow Mrs. Das. Others joined him, so that she was soon being followed by about half a dozen of them, their velvety tails dragging behind.

Mr. Kapasi stepped out of the car. He wanted to holler, to alert her in some way, but he worried that if she knew they were behind her, she would grow nervous. Perhaps she would lose her balance. Perhaps they would pull at her bag or her hair. He began to jog up the path, taking a fallen branch in his hand to scare away the monkeys. Mrs. Das continued walking, oblivious, trailing grains of puffed rice. Near the top of the incline, before a group of cells fronted by a row of squat stone pillars, Mr. Das was kneeling on the ground, focusing the lens of his camera. The children stood under the arcade, now hiding, now emerging from view.

"Wait for me," Mrs. Das called out. "I'm coming."

Tina jumped up and down. "Here comes Mommy!"

"Great," Mr. Das said without looking up. "Just in time. We'll get Mr. Kapasi to take a picture of the five of us."

Mr. Kapasi quickened his pace, waving his branch so that the monkeys scampered away, distracted, in another direction.

"Where's Bobby?" Mrs. Das asked when she stopped.

Mr. Das looked up from the camera. "I don't know, Ronny, where's Bobby?"

Ronny shrugged. "I thought he was right here."

"Where is he?" Mrs. Das repeated sharply. "What's wrong with all of you?"

They began calling his name, wandering up and down the path a bit. Because they were calling, they did not initially hear the boy's screams. When they found him, a little farther down the path under a tree, he was surrounded by a group of monkeys, over a dozen of them, pulling at his T-shirt with their long black fingers. The puffed rice Mrs. Das had spilled was scattered at his feet, raked over by the monkeys' hands. The boy was silent, his body frozen, swift tears running down his startled face. His bare legs were dusty and red with welts from where one of the monkeys struck him repeatedly with the stick he had given to it earlier.

"Daddy, the monkey's hurting Bobby," Tina said.

Mr. Das wiped his palms on the front of his shorts. In his nervousness he accidentally pressed the shutter on his camera; the whirring noise of the advancing film excited the monkeys, and the one with the stick began to beat Bobby more intently. "What are we supposed to do? What if they start attacking?"

"Mr. Kapasi," Mrs. Das shrieked, noticing him standing to one side. "Do something, for God's sake, do something!"

Mr. Kapasi took his branch and shooed them away, hissing at the ones that remained, stomping his feet to scare them. The animals retreated slowly, with a measured gait, obedient but unintimidated. Mr. Kapasi gathered Bobby in his arms and brought him back to where his parents and siblings were standing. As he carried him he was tempted to whisper a secret into the boy's ear. But Bobby was stunned, and shivering with fright, his legs bleeding slightly where the stick had broken the skin. When Mr. Kapasi delivered him to his parents, Mr. Das brushed some dirt off the boy's T-shirt and put the visor on him the right way. Mrs. Das reached into her straw bag to find a bandage which she taped over

Gabriel Cornelius von Max titled this painting *Monkeys as Judges of Art*, but in "Interpreter of Maladies," the monkeys are judges of a different sort.

How might this crowded pack of creatures reflect the way Lahiri uses the monkeys in her story? Are they foolish, menacing, absurd, all of these combined, or something else entirely?

DE AGOSTINI PICTURE LIBRARY/Getty Images

How does this photograph of the Konark Sun Temple enhance your understanding of the excursion that is the center of "Interpreter of Maladies"? Consider the ways this site might be a means to explore the collision of religious tradition and tourism or the clash between insider and outsider.

the cut on his knee. Ronny offered his brother a fresh piece of gum. "He's fine. Just a little scared, right, Bobby?" Mr. Das said, patting the top of his head.

"God, let's get out of here," Mrs. Das said. She folded her arms across the strawberry on her chest. "This place gives me the creeps."

"Yeah. Back to the hotel, definitely," Mr. Das agreed.

"Poor Bobby," Mrs. Das said. "Come here a second. Let Mommy fix your hair." Again she reached into her straw bag, this time for her hairbrush, and began to run it around the edges of the translucent visor. When she whipped out the hairbrush, the slip of paper with Mr. Kapasi's address on it fluttered away in the wind. No one but Mr. Kapasi noticed. He watched as it rose, carried higher and higher by the breeze, into the trees where the monkeys now sat, solemnly observing the scene below. Mr. Kapasi observed it too, knowing that this was the picture of the Das family he would preserve forever in his mind. ■

1999

Understanding and Interpreting

1. **AP® Character and Narration.** At one point, Mr. Kapasi thinks that Mr. and Mrs. Das act more as "siblings" (par. 45) than parents to their children. Why does he draw that conclusion? What does that conclusion suggest about the Das family?
2. **AP® Setting.** "Interpreter of Maladies" explores the impact of immigration, including the result of an imagined rather than an experienced homeland. How does the Das family imagine India? Why does Jhumpa Lahiri emphasize the taking of photographs during the family's vacation?
3. **AP® Character and Narration.** What do we normally think of when considering the job of an "interpreter," and how does Mr. Kapasi's job at the infirmary expand this definition? How does he view his role as an interpreter?
4. **AP® Character.** When Mr. Kapasi states that his job as an interpreter "is a job like any other," Mrs. Das replies, "But so romantic" (pars. 60–61). What does "romantic" mean within this context? How does this word impact their relationship from that point forward?

5. **AP® Character.** What is the moral responsibility of Mrs. Das? Should she tell her husband that Bobby is not his biological child? Should she tell the biological father? Should she tell Bobby? Do you sympathize with Mrs. Das when she tells Mr. Kapasi that she has "been in pain eight years" (par. 160)? In what ways has her silence been a kind of punishment for her?
6. **AP® Narration.** After Mr. Kapasi asks Mrs. Das if she is feeling pain or guilt, Lahiri writes, "She turned to him and glared, mustard oil thick on her frosty pink lips. She opened her mouth to say something, but as she glared at Mr. Kapasi some certain knowledge seemed to pass before her eyes, and she stopped" (par. 162). What is Lahiri's attitude toward Mrs. Das at this juncture? What is the "certain knowledge" she realizes?
7. **AP® Character and Narration.** Trace the changes in Mr. Kapasi and Mrs. Das's relationship. How do her responses to her own family mirror shifts in her relationship to Mr. Kapasi? How do you interpret the ending of the story? Were you expecting it? What does the final sentence mean: "Mr. Kapasi observed it too, knowing that this was the picture of the Das family he would preserve forever in his mind" (par. 179)?

Analyzing Language, Style, and Structure

1. **Vocabulary in Context.** The narrator states that Mr. Kapasi sees no nobility in "assiduously translating the symptoms" (par. 76) of people's maladies. What does it mean to do something "assiduously"? How does this word characterize Mr. Kapasi? How do his actions in the story reflect this characterization?
2. **AP® Structure and Character.** In the opening paragraph, Lahiri places the reader in the middle of the action, introducing all three major characters. How does this plot structure influence your experience as a reader? How do you perceive each of the characters and their relationships with each other?
3. **AP® Character.** Lahiri provides physical descriptions of characters, particularly their clothing, in elaborate detail. What do these descriptions say about each of them? Pay particular attention to the carefully tailored suit Mr. Kapasi wears and to Mrs. Das's outfit. Why, for instance, does Lahiri describe her wearing her sunglasses "on top of her head like a tiara" (par. 61) and having "small hands like paws" (par. 14)?
4. **AP® Setting.** How does Lahiri's description of the Sun Temple function in the story (par. 91)? Note that she begins by providing background information, shows her characters interacting, and describes the temple as being "filled with rubble years ago" (par. 98).
5. **AP® Character and Narration.** How does Lahiri use Mr. Kapasi's dreams and imaginings to develop his character? What thoughts and emotions does his dream "of being an interpreter for diplomats and dignitaries, resolving conflicts between people and nations" (par. 77) evoke? Pay special attention to his fantasies about Mrs. Das, such as the paragraph beginning, "The paper curled as Mr. Kapasi wrote his address in clear, careful letters. She would write to him . . ." (par. 89), and his calculations about how long it would be before he received her first letter (par. 109).
6. **AP® Narration and Figurative Language.** Dramatic irony is created when a reader knows something that the characters in the story do not; thus, some of the words and actions in a story would have a different meaning for the reader than they do for the characters. For example, once we learn of Mr. Kapasi's hope for a relationship with Mrs. Das (par. 89), his actions take on a different meaning for us than for her. Identify several other examples of dramatic irony in the story, and discuss their effect on Lahiri's tone.

7. **AP® Figurative Language.** The dictionary defines *malady* as "an unwholesome or desperate condition." What are the various "maladies" in this story, and how are they represented? Pay particular attention to the contrast between the literal and figurative notions of sickness and how what constitutes a "malady" changes as the story develops.
8. **AP® Structure.** The final dramatic scene with the monkeys is a complex one, involving interaction among all the characters. What role does each character play through both words and action?
9. **AP® Structure.** The story is divided into three sections. What is the effect of having these structural divisions as opposed to presenting the story as one continuous narrative?
10. **AP® Structure.** The story touches on the past, present, and future of all three central characters. Instead of presenting these as sequential narratives, however, Lahiri interweaves them. What is the effect of this technique?

Topics for Composing

1. **AP® FRQ Prose Fiction Analysis.** The following question refers to paragraphs 76–80 of Jhumpa Lahiri's "Interpreter of Maladies," published in 1999. In this passage, Mrs. Das, an Indian American tourist visiting India with her family, speaks with Mr. Kapasi, a local tour guide, about his other job as an interpreter at a doctor's office. Mrs. Das tells him that she finds his job "romantic" and "a big responsibility." Read the passage carefully. Then, in a well-written essay, analyze how Lahiri uses literary elements and techniques to convey a complex characterization of Mr. Kapasi.
2. **AP® FRQ Literary Argument.** In many stories that present differing or conflicting cultures, communication can be a complex undertaking. In "Interpreter of Maladies," the three main characters interpret and misinterpret each other's verbal and nonverbal cues. In a well-written essay, analyze how the difficulties in communication due to the characters' cultural differences contribute to an interpretation of the work as a whole. Do not merely summarize the plot.
3. **AP® Literary Argumentation.** In Jhumpa Lahiri's 1999 short story "Interpreter of Maladies," Mr. and Mrs. Das hire Mr. Kapasi, a local tour guide, during their trip to India. In a well-written essay, analyze how Lahiri uses literary elements and techniques to convey Mr. Kapasi's complex perspective of Mr. and Mrs. Das.
4. **AP® Literary Argumentation.** Internal and external conflicts can contribute to a shifting and uncertain sense of self and belonging. How does the character of Mr. Kapasi, even as a middle-aged man, reflect the ways in which such conflicts can uproot a person's understanding of their identity?
5. **AP® Literary Argumentation.** Language is a central subject in Lahiri's "Interpreter of Maladies." We learn, for instance, that Mr. Kapasi speaks English, helps the doctor with patients who speak Gujarati, and finds it "strange" (par. 13) that Mr. Das refers to his wife by her first name when speaking to his children. As portrayed in this story, what role does language play in the development of a person's identity and sense of belonging?
6. **Connections.** Lahiri has described the short story as "a middle ground between poetry and the novel" because it has "purity and intensity," "a ruthless distilled quality," "a compression and concentration that is akin to poetry." Discuss how these characteristics apply to "Interpreter of Maladies," specifically how the language of this short story is similar to what we associate with poetry.

7. **Connections.** Watch *The Namesake* (PG-13), based on a novel by Lahiri, and discuss the similar concerns found in that film and "Interpreter of Maladies." Pay particular attention to the clash of traditional culture and contemporary values, the responsibility of one generation to preserve and communicate its traditional culture to another, the role of women, and the relationship between parents and children.
8. **Speaking and Listening.** *Diaspora* is a term that originally referred to the scattered Jewish community after the Babylonian exile during the sixth century B.C.E. Today we use it more generally to refer to the movement, migration, or scattering of people from their original homelands. In small groups, discuss "Interpreter of Maladies" as a story about the struggle of being part of a diaspora in the late twentieth century.
9. **Creative Writing.** During the story, we learn details about Mrs. Kapasi from her husband's perspective. According to Mr. Kapasi, theirs was "a bad match" (par. 79). His wife never asks him about his patients or says that his job is "a big responsibility" (par. 78). She serves him his evening cup of tea "in silence" (par. 111). We are given these bits of information, but we never get to see things from her point of view. Let her speak! Write a description of Mr. Kapasi in the voice of his wife.
10. **Research.** Why does Lahiri choose the Sun Temple at Konarak as the central setting for her story? Research this sacred monument to learn more about it, including the sun god Surya. How does the information you learn add to your understanding of Lahiri's choice? Why do you think she chose this temple rather than a more famous one (to westerners, at least), such as the Taj Mahal?

Boy on a Train

Ralph Ellison

Ralph Waldo Ellison (1914–1994) was a novelist and scholar born in Oklahoma City, Oklahoma. In 1933, he enrolled at the Tuskegee Institute in Alabama on a scholarship to study music, and after his third year he moved to New York City to study sculpture and photography. There he met novelist Richard Wright in 1937 and soon shifted his focus to writing, publishing short stories, book reviews, and articles in periodicals such as *New Challenge* and *New Masses*. Ellison's first and most famous novel, *Invisible Man*, won the National Book Award in 1953 and is considered one of the great American novels.

James Whitmore/The LIFE PictureCollection/Getty Images

Classic Text

KEY CONTEXT Ellison most likely wrote this story in October of 1937 in Dayton, Ohio, before revising it on his return to New York City in early 1938. Set in 1924 during the Jim Crow era, "Boy on a Train" takes place in Oklahoma, where segregation did not end until 1955.

The train gave a long, shrill, lonely whistle, and seemed to gain speed as it rushed downgrade between two hills covered with trees. The trees were covered with deep-red, brown, and yellow leaves. The leaves fell on the side of the hill and scattered down to the gray rocks along the opposite tracks. When the engine blew off steam, the little boys could see the white cloud scatter the colored leaves against the side of the hill. The engine hissed, and the leaves danced in the steam like leaves in a white wind.

"See, Lewis, Jack Frost made the pretty leaves. Jack Frost paints the leaves all the pretty colors. See, Lewis: brown, and purple, and orange, and yellow."

• • •

The little boy pointed and paused after naming each color, his finger bent against the glass of the train window. The baby repeated the colors after him, looking intently for Jack Frost.

It was hot in the train, and the car was too close to the engine, making it impossible to open the window. More than once, cinders found a way into the car and flew into the baby's eyes. The woman raised her head from her book from time to time to watch the little boys. The car was filthy, and part of it was used for baggage. Up front, the pine shipping box of a casket stood in a corner. Wonder what poor soul that is in there, the woman thought.

Bags and trunks covered the floor up front, 5
and now and then the butcher[1] came in to pick up candy, or fruit or magazines, to sell back in the white cars. He would come in and pick up a basket with candy, go out, come back; pick up a basket of fruit, go out; come back, pick up magazines, and on till everything had been carried out; then he would start all over again.

[1] Someone who sells newspapers and snacks on trains. — Eds.

He was a big, fat white man with a red face, and the little boy hoped he would give them a piece of candy; after all, he had so much, and Mama didn't have any nickels to give them. But he never did.

The mother read intently, holding a page in her hand as she scanned, then turned it slowly. They were the only passengers in the section of seats reserved for colored. She turned her head, looking back toward the door leading to the other car; it was time for the butcher to return. Her brow wrinkled annoyedly. The butcher had tried to touch her breasts when she and the boys first came into the car, and she had spat in his face and told him to keep his dirty hands where they belonged. The butcher had turned red and gone hurriedly out of the car, his baskets swinging violently on his arms. She hated him. Why couldn't a Negro woman travel with her two boys without being molested?

The train was past the hills now, and into fields that were divided by crooked wooden fences and that spread rolling and brown with stacks of corn as far as the blue horizon fringed with trees. The fences reminded the boy of the crooked man who walked a crooked mile.

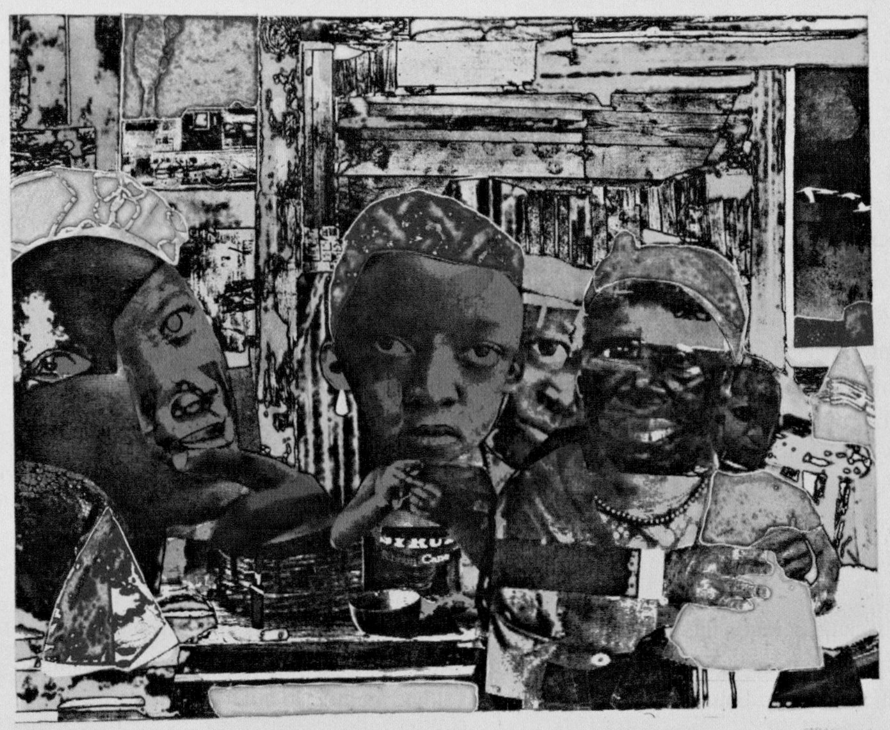

Having grown up during the Harlem Renaissance of the 1920s, Romare Bearden devoted his life and art to redefining, as he said, "the image of man in terms of the Negro experience I know best." Bearden is known for his imaginative abstract collages portraying African American traditions and communities. A collage is a work of art created with different materials and images attached to a flat surface. Beardon created this work, entitled *The Train*, in 1975.

How does this collage relate to the plot of "Boy on a Train"? How might Ellison's story be seen as a collage that speaks to a specifically African American experience?

Red birds darted swiftly past the car, ducking down into the field, then shooting up again when you looked back to see the telephone poles and fields turning, and sliding fast away from the train. The boys were having a good time of it. It was their first trip. The countryside was bright gold with Indian summer. Way across a field, a boy was leading a cow by a rope and a dog was barking at the cow's feet. It was a nice dog, the boy on the train thought, a collie. Yes, that was the kind of dog it was — a collie.

A freight was passing, going in the direction of Oklahoma City, passing so swiftly that its orange-and-red cars seemed a streak of watercolor with gray spaces punched through. The boy felt funny whenever he thought of Oklahoma City, like he wanted to cry. Perhaps they would never go back. He wondered what Frank and R. C. and Petey were doing now. Picking peaches for Mr. Stewart? A lump rose in his throat. Too bad they had to leave just when Mr. Stewart had promised them half of all the peaches they could pick. He sighed. The train whistle sounded very sad and lonesome.

Well, now they were going to McAlester, where Mama would have a nice job and enough money to pay the bills. Gee, Mama must have been a good worker for Mr. Balinger to send all the way to Oklahoma City for her to come work for him. Mama was happy to go, and he was glad for Mama to be happy; she worked so hard now that Daddy was gone. He closed his eyes tight, trying to see the picture of Daddy. He must never forget how Daddy looked. He would look like that himself when he grew up: tall and kind and always joking and reading books. . . . *Well, just wait; when he got big and carried Mama and Lewis back to Oklahoma City everybody would see how well he took care of Mama, and she would say, "See, these are my two boys," and would be very proud. And everybody would say, "See, aren't Mrs. Weaver's boys two fine men?" That was the way it would be.*

The thought made him lose some of the lump that came into his throat when he thought of never, never going back, and he turned to see who it was coming through the door.

A white man and a little boy came into the car and walked up front. His mother looked up, then lowered her eyes to her book again. He stood up and looked over the backs of the chairs, trying to see what the man and boy were doing. The white boy held a tiny dog in his arms, stroking its head. The little white boy asked the man to let him take the dog out, but the man said no, and they went, rocking from side to side, out of the car. The dog must have been asleep, because all the time he hadn't made a sound. The little white boy was dressed like the kids you see in moving pictures. Did he have a bike? the boy wondered.

He looked out the window. There were horses now, a herd of them, running and tossing their manes and tails and pounding the ground all wild when the whistle blew. He saw himself on a white horse, swinging a l-a-r-i-a-t over the broncos' heads and yelling "Yip, yip, yippee!" like Hoot Gibson[2] in the movies. The horses excited Lewis, and he beat his hands against the window and cried, "Giddap! Giddap!" The boy smiled and looked at his mother. She was looking up from her page and smiling, too. Lewis was cute, he thought.

They stopped at a country town. Men were standing in front of the station, watching the porter throw off a bunch of newspapers. Then several white men came into the car and one said, "This must be it," and pointed to the big box, and the porter said, "Yeah, this is it all right. It's the only one we got this trip, so this must be the one." Then the porter jumped out of the car and went into the station. The men were dressed in black suits with white shirts. They seemed

[2] Hoot Gibson (1892–1962) was a rodeo champion and film actor popular during the 1920s and 30s. — Eds.

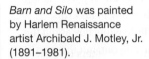

Barn and Silo was painted by Harlem Renaissance artist Archibald J. Motley, Jr. (1891–1981).

What aspects of this painting do you notice first? Is the mood of this image similar to that of "Boy on a Train"? Explain why or why not.

very uncomfortable with their high collars, and acted very solemn. They pushed the box over gently and lifted it out the side door of the car. The white men in overalls watched them from the platform. They put the box in a wagon, and the man said "Giddap" to the horses and they drove away, the men on the back with the box looking very straight and stiff.

One of the men on the platform was picking his teeth and spitting tobacco juice on the ground. The station was painted green, and a sign on the side read TUBE ROSE SNUFF[3] and showed a big white flower; it didn't look like a rose, though. It was hot, and the men had their shirts open at the collar and wore red bandannas around their necks. They were standing in the same position when the train pulled out, staring. Why, he wondered, did white folks stare at you that way?

Outside the town, he saw a big red rock barn standing behind some trees. Beside it stood something he had never seen before. It was high and round and made out of the same kind of rock as the barn. He climbed into his seat and pointed.

"What is that tall thing, Mama?" he said.

She raised her head and looked.

20 "It's a silo, son," she said. "That's where the corn is stored." Her eyes were strangely distant when she turned her face back to him. The sun slanted across her eyes, and her skin was brown and clear. He eased down into the seat. *Silo, silo. Almost as tall as the Colcord Building in Oklahoma City that Daddy helped to build. . . .*

He jumped, startled; Mama was calling his name with tears in her voice. He turned around and tears were on her face.

"Come around here, James," she said. "Bring Lewis."

He took Lewis by the hand and moved into the seat beside her. *What had they done?*

"James, son," she said. "That old silo back there's been here a long time. It made me remember when years ago me and your daddy

[3] A brand of chewing tobacco. —Eds.

extending beyond the text

The following excerpt is from James Baldwin's 1963 book *The Fire Next Time*. The book, published on the hundredth anniversary of the Emancipation Proclamation, analyzes the ways racism continued to shape life during the twentieth century.

from The Fire Next Time

James Baldwin

Negroes in this country . . . are taught really to despise themselves from the moment their eyes open on the world. This world is white and they are black. White people hold the power . . . and the world has innumerable ways of making this difference known and felt and feared. Long before the Negro child perceives this difference, and even longer before he understands it, he has begun to react to it, he has begun to be controlled by it. Every effort made by the child's elders to prepare him for a fate from which they cannot protect him causes him secretly, in terror, to begin to await, without knowing that he is doing so, his mysterious and inexorable punishment. He must be "good" not only in order to please his parents and not only to avoid being punished by them; behind their authority stands another, nameless and impersonal, infinitely harder to please, and bottomlessly cruel. And this filters into the child's consciousness through his parents' tone of voice as he is being exhorted, punished, or loved; in the sudden, uncontrollable note of fear heard in his mother's or his father's voice when he has strayed beyond some particular boundary. He does not know what the boundary is, and he can get no explanation of it, which is frightening enough, but the fear he hears in the voices of his elders is more frightening still. . . . It [is] . . . a fear that the child, in challenging the white world's assumptions, [is] putting himself in the path of destruction. A child cannot . . . know how vast and how merciless is the nature of power, with what unbelievable cruelty people treat each other. He reacts to the fear in his parents' voices because his parents hold up the world for him and he has no protection without them.

1. **What evidence in "Boy on a Train" illustrates the ways "white people hold the power"?**
2. **How does the protagonist, James, hear fear in the "voices of his elders" in "Boy on a Train"? What is his reaction to it?**
3. **In what ways does James's mother "hold up the world" for him in this story?**
4. **How effectively does this excerpt from *The Fire Next Time* capture James's perspective on his memories and experiences in "Boy on a Train"?**

came over this same old Rock Island line on our way to Oklahoma City. We had just been married and was very happy going west because we had heard that colored people had a chance out here."

James smiled, listening; he loved to hear Mama tell about when she and Daddy were young, and about what they used to do down South. Yet he felt this was to be something different. Something in Mama's voice was vast and high, like a rainbow; yet something sad and deep, like when the organ played in church, was around Mama's words.

"Son, I want you to remember this trip," she said. "You understand, son. I *want* you to remember. You *must*, you've *got* to understand."

James sensed something; he tried hard to understand. He stared into her face. Tears were glistening in her eyes, and he felt he would cry himself. He bit his lip. No, he was the man of the family, and he couldn't act like the baby. He swallowed, listening.

"You remember this, James," she said. "We came all the way from Georgia on this same railroad line fourteen years ago, so things would be better for you children when you came. You must remember this, James. We traveled far, looking for a better world, where things wouldn't be so hard like they were down South. That was fourteen years ago, James. Now your father's gone from us, and you're the man. Things are hard for us colored folks, son, and it's just us three alone and we have to stick together. Things is hard, and we have to fight. . . . O Lord, we have to fight! . . ."

She stopped, her lips pressed tight together as she shook her head, overcome with emotion. James placed his arm around her neck and caressed her cheek.

"Yes, Mama," he said. "I won't forget."

He could not get it all, but yet he understood. It was like understanding what music without words said. He felt very full inside. Now Mama was pulling him close to her; the baby rested against her other side. This was familiar; since Daddy died Mama prayed with them, and now she was beginning to pray. He bowed his head.

"Go with us and keep us, Lord. Then it was me and him, Lord; now it's me and his children. And I'm thankful, Lord. You saw fit to take him, Lord, and it's well with my soul in Thy name. I was happy, Lord; life was like a mockingbird a-singing. And all I ask now is to stay with these children, to raise them and protect them, Lord, till they're old enough to go their way. Make them strong and unafraid, Lord. Give them strength to meet this world. Make them brave to go where things is better for our people, Lord. . . ."

James sat with head bowed. Always when Mama prayed, he felt tight and smoldering inside. And he kept remembering his father's face. He could not remember Daddy ever praying, but Daddy's voice had been deep and strong when he sang in the choir on Sunday mornings. James wanted to cry, but, vaguely, he felt *something* should be punished for making Mama cry. Something cruel had made her cry. He felt the tightness in his throat becoming anger. If he only knew what it was, he would fix it; he would kill this mean thing that made Mama feel so bad. It must have been awful because Mama was strong and brave and even killed mice when the white woman she used to work for only raised her dress and squealed like a girl, afraid of them. If he only knew what it was. . . . Was it God?

"Please keep us three together in this strange town, Lord. The road is dark and long and my sorrows heavy but, if it be Thy will, Lord, let me educate my boys. Let me raise them so they'll be better able to live this life. I don't want to live for myself, Lord, just for these boys. Make them strong, upright men, Lord; make them fighters. And when my work on earth is done, take me

Photograph by Gordon Parks. Courtesy of and copyright The Gordon Parks Foundation

This was one of several photographs Gordon Parks took to illustrate an article for *Life* magazine that excerpted scenes from Ralph Ellison's 1952 novel *Invisible Man*. **What does the man emerging from the manhole cover say to you? How might it reflect James's experience of listening to his mother pray?**

home to Thy kingdom, Lord, safe in the arms of Jesus."

He heard her voice trail off to a tortured moan behind her trembling lips. Tears streamed down her face. James was miserable; he did not like to see Mama cry, and turned his eyes to the window as she began wiping away the tears. He was glad she was through now because the butcher would be coming back into the car in a few minutes. He did not want a white man to see Mama cry.

They were crossing a river now. The slanting girders of a bridge moved slowly past the train. The river was muddy and red, rushing along beneath them. The train stopped, and the baby was pointing to a cow on the banks of the river below. The cow stood gazing out over the water, chewing her cud — looking like a cow in the baby's picture book, only there were no butterflies about her head.

"Bow-wow!" the baby said. Then, questioningly: "Bowwow?"

"No, Lewis, it's a cow," James said. "Moo," he said. "Cow." The baby laughed, delighted. "Moo-oo." He was very interested.

James watched the water. The train was moving again, and he wondered why his mother cried. It wasn't just that Daddy was gone; it didn't sound just that way. It was something else. I'll kill it when I get big, he thought. I'll make it cry just like it's making Mama cry!

The train was passing an oil field. There were many wells in the field; and big round tanks, gleaming like silver in the sun. One well was covered with boards and looked like a huge Indian wigwam against the sky. The wells all pointed straight up at the sky. Yes, I'll kill it. I'll make it cry. Even if it's God, I'll make God cry, he thought. I'll kill Him; I'll kill God and not be sorry!

The train jerked, gaining speed, and the wheels began clicking a ragged rhythm to his ears. There were many advertising signs in the fields they were rolling past. All the signs told about the same things for sale. One sign showed a big red bull and read BULL DURHAM.[4]

"Moo-oo," the baby said.

James looked at his mother; she was through crying now, and she smiled. He felt some of his tightness ebb away. He grinned. He wanted very much to kiss her, but he must show the proper reserve of a man now. He grinned. Mama was

[4] Bull Durham Smoking Tobacco, a company popular during the 1920s. — Eds.

beautiful when she smiled. He made a wish never to forget what she had said. "This is 1924, and I'll never forget it," he whispered to himself. Then he looked out the window, resting his chin on the palm of his hand, wondering how much farther they would have to ride, and if there would be any boys to play football in McAlester. ■

c. 1937

Understanding and Interpreting

1. **AP® Setting and Narration.** What is the main reason James's family is traveling? Are there secondary reasons too? Explain.
2. **AP® Character and Narration.** Although James's age isn't revealed in "Boy on a Train," much of the story is told from his perspective. Based on your reading, how old does he seem? Use evidence from the text to support your response.
3. **AP® Character and Narration.** What does James's mother's interaction with the "butcher" reveal about her? How does James process it?
4. **AP® Character and Narration.** This story takes place in the wake of a great upheaval in James's life. What losses is he grieving? How do they develop his character and shape his perspective?
5. **AP® Character and Narration.** In paragraphs 11 and 39–40, James looks ahead and imagines himself in the future. In each of these instances, what does he see himself doing and thinking? How similar are these two perceptions of his future self? How does each contribute to his characterization?
6. **AP® Character.** Why do you think it's so important to James's mother that he remembers this trip? What, exactly, do you think he "*must*," and "[has] *got* to understand" (par. 26)? What does it mean that James "could not get it all, but yet he understood" (par. 31)?
7. **AP® Character, Setting, and Narration.** Throughout the story, James makes observations about the behavior of the white people he sees moving through the train car and on the platform of the station. What do those observations have in common? What do they reveal about James's perspective on the world around him?
8. **AP® Character and Narration.** What is James's attitude toward the pine box coffin that rides in the car with him and his family? Why do you think he sees it in this way?
9. **AP® Character, Setting, and Narration.** What role does race play in the setting and events of the story? How do these elements reveal the effects of racism on the family, both in terms of the characters' interpersonal experiences and the larger context of their circumstances?

Analyzing Language, Style, and Structure

1. **Vocabulary in Context.** What is the meaning of the word "smoldering" in paragraph 33? Why does James feel "tight and smoldering" when his mother prays? How does this word choice connect to James's feeling that "*something* should be punished for making Mama cry" (par. 33)?
2. **AP® Setting, Structure, and Narration.** What is the relationship between the setting of a train ride and James's meditations on his past and future? How does this setting suit this particular narrative structure?
3. **AP® Structure and Narration.** James is not identified by name until paragraph 22, when his mother calls him and Lewis over to sit beside her. What might Ellison's choice to delay

revealing the character's name suggest about how James sees himself? What does it suggest to the reader about who James is?

4. **AP® Structure and Narration.** "Boy on a Train" is told from a third person limited omniscient point of view, primarily from James's perspective. What effect does that limit have on the way the story is told? What does the brief glimpse into James's mother's thoughts reveal? How does the story's point of view contribute to the larger themes of the text?
5. **AP® Figurative Language.** Paragraph 36 begins, "They were crossing a river now." What associations does that crossing evoke? How might it be considered an allusion? What does this allusion reveal about the significance of the journey?
6. **AP® Structure and Narration.** Some sections of this story are in italics. Where are these sections, and what do they have in common? What differentiates them from the rest of the narrative?
7. **AP® Narration and Figurative Language.** "Boy on a Train" is filled with references to music. In fact, James compares his understanding of his mother to "understanding what music without words said" (par. 31). Trace the many ways Ralph Ellison uses imagery evoking sound to create a mood or convey a shift in perspective. What do these images suggest about the way James sees the world and his place within it?
8. **AP® Structure and Narration.** The plot of the story is linear in the sense that it takes place during a train ride from one place to another. How, then, does it also move between the past and future of James and his family? What effect do these shifts in time create for the reader?
9. **AP® Setting and Figurative Language.** Throughout the story, James and his family observe and discuss the views of the Oklahoma landscape. What is the connection between these settings and the reflections they prompt, particularly for James and his mother? Taken together, is there a pattern to the imagery of the landscape? If so, what is it? If not, how does this lack of a pattern speak to the family's experience? Explain your answer.

Topics for Composing

1. **AP® FRQ Prose Fiction Analysis.** The following question refers to paragraphs 31–35 of Ralph Ellison's "Boy on a Train," written circa 1937. In this passage, James's mother pulls her family together to pray. Read the passage carefully. Then, in a well-written essay, analyze how Ellison uses literary elements and techniques to convey the James's complex attitude toward the meaning of his mother's prayer.
2. **AP® FRQ Literary Argument.** In many works of literature, voyages or trips provide a setting that underscores or helps develop the central conflicts or themes of the text. In "Boy on a Train," a young boy named James and his family travel by train as they move to a new town in Oklahoma. During this trip, James reflects on how his life is changing and what his future might hold. In a well-written essay, analyze how the relationship between the characters and setting in this story contributes to an interpretation of the work as a whole. Do not merely summarize the plot.
3. **AP® Literary Argumentation.** When two early Ellison stories, including "Boy on a Train" were published in the *New Yorker* magazine in 1996, John Callahan, who edited much of Ellison's work, wrote that Ellison's stories are "filled with blues-tempered echoes of railroad trains." How does the musicality of James's train ride sing the blues?
4. **AP® Literary Argumentation.** In a 1955 interview for the *Paris Review*, Ellison cautioned against writing for a solely white audience. He says:

> By doing this the authors run the risk of limiting themselves to the audience's presumptions of what a Negro is or should be; the tendency is . . . to plead the Negro's humanity. . . . For us, the question should be, what are the specific *forms* of that humanity, and what in our background is worth preserving or abandoning.

What specific forms of humanity take shape in "Boy on a Train"? How does that evidence illustrate the "what in our background is worth preserving or abandoning"?

5. **AP® Literary Argumentation.** In a 1955 interview with the *Paris Review*, Ellison was asked if he considered the "search for identity" to be an American theme. Ellison responded, "It is the American theme. The nature of our society is such that we are prevented from knowing who we are." How is Ellison's assertion that the nature of society prevents us from knowing who we are illustrated in "Boy on a Train"? How does the theme of a search for identity play out in this story?
6. **Speaking and Listening.** Do you agree with Ellison's statement about identity and society in question 5? Prepare for and participate in a class discussion on this topic. You can use evidence from the story, your own experience, other reading, and history to back your claims.
7. **Connections.** Ellison studied modernist writers such as James Joyce and T. S. Eliot when he was in college at Tuskegee Institute, and their writing also influenced his work. Read the introduction to the Texts in Context on Marianne Moore and the Modernist Vision (p. 938). What influences of modernism do you find in "Boy on a Train"? Look for thematic and style markers such as exile and loss, social ills, cultural fragmentation, or stream of consciousness and examine how they create meaning.
8. **Connections.** What models for manhood and womanhood does the story present? Are they relics of a time past or do they still have relevance? Explain your answer in an essay.
9. **Connections.** What do you believe is the "thing" James wants to kill? What evidence of that thing do you find in the story? You might also want to consider both your feelings and experiences as well as your historical knowledge.
10. **Research.** The story recounts that in 1910 James's parents left Georgia for Oklahoma City in search of greater opportunities. Although this is a work of fiction, this detail reflects a fact of history: between roughly 1910 and 1940, many Black people left the South in search of a better life in what became known as the Great Migration. Learn more about the causes and effects of the Great Migration, including the art and literature that depicts this period. Where does Ellison's story intersect with the larger narrative of history? What does this story have in common with — and how does it differ from — other works that address the Great Migration?
11. **Creative Writing.** Write a short story that takes place in transit. You can choose any setting involving moving from one place to another, but be sure that your setting plays an integral role in developing your characters and propelling the plot forward.
12. **Connections.** In paragraphs 26 and 28, James's mother implores him to remember. Many works of literature focus on the relationship and knowledge passed between parents and their children, including the play *Hamlet* (p. 555), in which the ghost of King Hamlet entreats his son: "Remember me." Based on your reading of this story and *Hamlet*, what is it, or about themselves, that these parents want their children to remember? What is the role of memory in these texts? How is memory tied together with the concepts of duty, identity, and legacy?

Ralph Ellison and the Influence of the Harlem Renaissance

A great flowering of Black arts and culture, the **Harlem Renaissance** continues to be a source of fascination, debate, and discussion among literary critics and historians. Even the dates remain problematic. Most agree that the movement began after the 1919 "Red Summer" of race riots in urban centers throughout the United States; scholar Henry Louis Gates Jr. puts its end at 1939, the start of World War II. All agree, however, that the period of the 1920s and early 1930s was a time of extraordinary creativity that centered around New York City, specifically Harlem. This period, called "more a spirit than a movement" by critic Robert Hemenway, was marked by a wide range of ideas and writing styles, exploration of both African and American cultural heritages, protests against racial discrimination, and a sense of self-assertion and pride. The intellectual and artistic productivity of this era left a breathtaking legacy of writers, thinkers, musicians, and visual artists whose work endures today.

To understand the Harlem Renaissance requires looking further into the past. Following the end of the Civil War in 1865, there was a brief period known as Reconstruction, in which African Americans made significant progress toward equality and full citizenship. However, this era ended in 1877 as Jim Crow laws took hold, enforcing racial segregation and ensuring both social and economic disfranchisement of African Americans in the South. This, along with a rise in racial terror lynchings during the early twentieth century, prompted a mass exodus of African Americans from the south. Between roughly 1910 and 1940, millions of African Americans left the rural Southern U.S. for the urban Northwest, Midwest, and West in what is now known as the Great Migration. Fleeing violence, legal restrictions, and racial prejudice in search of greater opportunities, these migrants would reshape the social and political geography of every city they came to call home.

The unrest that led to the Great Migration intensified in the wake of World War I (1914–1918), when African American soldiers returned from segregated military duty and found the racism that permeated America unchanged in their absence. In fact, these postwar years saw a revival of racist organizations such as the Ku Klux Klan and, consequently, racial violence. In what became known as the Red Summer of 1919, twenty-six race riots erupted across the U.S. Claude McKay expressed the spirit of that cultural moment in his poem "If We Must Die," written in the wake of the Chicago race riot that left 38 people dead: "Like men we'll face the murderous, cowardly pack / Pressed to the wall, dying, but fighting back!" Out of this extraordinary moment of both trauma and opportunity, African Americans continued to head north and west, often collectively as communities in motion. Contemporary historian and author Isabel Wilkerson described those who undertook the arduous journey from their rural hometowns to unknown urban territory as people "seeking political asylum within the borders of their own country, not

This cover of scholar Nathan Irvin Huggins's book *Harlem Renaissance* features work by artist Aaron Douglas.
How does Douglas situate the cultural values of the Harlem Renaissance within American society? How do the composition, perspective, and the images themselves contribute to your interpretation?

unlike refugees in other part of the world fleeing famine, war, and pestilence."

Yet the denizens of the Great Migration often encountered racism and inequality similar to that of the South they had fled. While more jobs were available in the cities of the north and west, pay was often low and barriers to employment high; the work itself was typically menial labor. Fair housing was nearly nonexistent, and educational opportunities were far from guaranteed—while segregated schools were not a function of the law in the north, they were often the status quo.

Despite these obstacles and continuing inequities, the literature, art, and music created by Black people underwent profound changes and found wider audiences during the 1920s and 30s, especially in New York City. The uptown neighborhood of Harlem was not only a destination for many migrant African Americans and Black immigrants seeking work and economic opportunity; it was home to a new Black middle class. It was also the nucleus of an artistic movement that centered Black experiences and celebrated various cultures and traditions of Black people throughout the U.S. Writers and thinkers such as Alain Locke, Langston Hughes, Countee Cullen, and Zora Neale Hurston found more mainstream publishers receptive to their work and found a broad audience. Artists such as Augusta Savage, Aaron Douglass, and Jacob Lawrence also gained a following. Perhaps no aspect of the Harlem Renaissance shaped America and the entire world as much as jazz. Thousands of city dwellers, Black and white, flocked to see performers, including Duke Ellington and Louis Armstrong, Bessie Smith and Billie Holiday, bring this musical tradition to the fore.

The scope of the work produced during the Harlem Renaissance was vast; it gave rise to differing viewpoints on the role of art and the artist in particular. Some argued that art and literature reflecting the "mainstream" traditions and movements established by white creators would bring the work of Black creators into the canon. Others, such as Hurston, argued for the importance of cultural representation, choosing to use vernacular expressions and focus on small rural communities of African Americans in her work. Some, including Countee Cullen, wrote of the struggle to reconcile their identity as Americans with the specter of slavery and the racism of their era. Many saw themselves as activists whose work explicitly embraced the idea of the New Negro, a concept coined by Alain Locke that emphasized self-sufficiency, education, Black pride, cultural advancement, and social justice. Langston Hughes eloquently expressed this connection between art, life, and the fight against racism in a 1947 article in the journal *Phylon*. He explains his refusal to take on "conventional" subject matter embraced by many white writers, such as "roses and moonlight":

> I was born poor — and colored — and almost all the prettiest roses I have seen have been in rich white people's yards — and not in mine. . . . [F]or sometimes in the moonlight my brothers see a fiery cross and a circle of Klansmen's hoods. Sometimes in the moonlight a dark body swings from a lynching tree — but for the funeral there are no roses.

Ralph Ellison, born in 1914, grew up in the midst of the debates regarding social, political, and economic advancement for Black people. As a young man in Oklahoma City, he read the work of Alain Locke and Langston Hughes, whom he would meet and befriend soon after his arrival in New York City in 1936, joining a talented and influential group of Black intellectuals and artists. As prefigured in the short story "Boy on a Train," his central theme, most notably explored in his masterpiece *Invisible Man*, is the search for identity, a search he treats as central to American literature and experience, as did many of the writers of the Harlem Renaissance whose work he read and wrote about.

As you read the following Texts in Context and continue to reflect on Ellison's "Boy on a Train," remember that the flowering of Black art and literature of the 1920s and 30s is a "renaissance"— that is, a rebirth or renewal. The luminaries of this movement put forward new perspectives on history and pioneered innovative modes of expression. In the process, they simultaneously preserved and reinvented the vibrant cultures and identities of Black people across America. Not only do these works engage with fundamental questions and issues that have existed since well before the nation's founding and still persist today, but they also changed how we see the landscape of American experience. As writer Wil Haygood states in his 2018 book *I Too Sing America: The Harlem Renaissance at 100*, the legacy of the Harlem Renaissance continues to endure:

> So the Harlem Renaissance lives. It sings. It continues to do its part to explain America to itself, and also to the world. Hardly a racially charged political moment has gone by since the 1960s when a poem or quote from the renaissance hasn't been summoned. It constantly reminds us of a group of gifted artists who had their backs against the wall within the borders of their own country, and how their genius took flight.

TEXTS IN CONTEXT

1. **Alain Locke** ■ **from *The New Negro* (nonfiction)**
2. **Countee Cullen** ■ ***Heritage* (poetry)**
3. **Zora Neale Hurston** ■ ***Spunk* (short fiction)**
4. **Langston Hughes** ■ ***I look at the world* (poetry)**
5. **Jacob Lawrence** ■ **From *every southern town migrants left by the hundreds to travel north (Migration Series #3)* (painting)**

from **The New Negro**

Alain Locke

Born and raised in Philadelphia, Alain Locke (1886–1954) graduated from Harvard University and became the first African American Rhodes Scholar. He taught English at Howard University in Washington, D.C. throughout his career and became a highly regarded scholar. His most famous work was *The New Negro* (1925), an anthology that became the manifesto of the Harlem Renaissance. The artists in *The New Negro* turned what Locke called "a new vision of opportunity" into the reality of poetry, fiction, political analysis, drama, music, and visual art that continues to be studied today. These luminaries include Claude McKay, Zora Neale Hurston, W. E. B. DuBois, Aaron Douglass, Langston Hughes, Jean Toomer, James Weldon Johnson, Angelina Grimké, and more.

KEY CONTEXT In this introductory essay to *The New Negro*, Locke acknowledges the social and artistic changes brought about by the Great Migration. He says, "While the minds of most of us, black and white, have thus burrowed in the trenches of the Civil War and Reconstruction, the actual march of development has simply flanked these positions, necessitating a sudden reorientation of view." He also heralds "the younger generation" of artists, which he sees as "vibrant with a new psychology, or "the new spirit" that will lead to "a spiritual emancipation."

The mind of the Negro seems suddenly to have slipped from under the tyranny of social intimidation and to be shaking off the psychology of imitation and implied inferiority. By shedding the old chrysalis of the Negro problem we are achieving something like a spiritual emancipation. Until recently, lacking self-understanding, we have been almost as much of a problem to ourselves as we still are to others. But the decade that found us with a problem has left us with only a task. The multitude perhaps feels as yet only a strange relief and a new vague urge, but the thinking few know that in the reaction the vital inner grip of prejudice has been broken.

With this renewed self-respect and self-dependence, the life of the Negro community is bound to enter a new dynamic phase, the buoyancy from within compensating for whatever pressure there may be of conditions from without. The migrant masses, shifting from countryside to city, hurdle several generations of experience at a leap, but more important, the same thing happens spiritually in the life-attitudes and self-expression of the Young Negro, in his poetry, his art, his education and his new outlook, with the additional advantage, of course, of the poise and greater certainty of knowing what it is all about. From this comes the promise and warrant of a new leadership. As one of them has discerningly put it:

> We have tomorrow
> Bright before us
> Like a flame.
>
> Yesterday, a night-gone thing
> A sundown name
> And dawn today
>
> Broad arch above the road we came.
> We march![1]

This is what, even more than any "most creditable record of fifty years of freedom," requires that the Negro of today be seen through other than the dusty spectacles of past

[1] Here, Locke has reprinted "Youth," a 1924 poem by Harlem Renaissance writer Langston Hughes (1902–1967). — Eds.

controversy. The day of "aunties," "uncles" and "mammies"[2] is equally gone. Uncle Tom[3] and Sambo[4] have passed on, and even the "Colonel" and "George" play barnstorm roles from which they escape with relief when the public spotlight is off. The popular melodrama has about played itself out, and it is time to scrap the fictions, garret the bogeys and settle down to a realistic facing of facts.

• • •

First we must observe some of the changes which since the traditional lines of opinion were drawn have rendered these quite obsolete. A main change has been, of course, that shifting of the Negro population which has made the Negro problem no longer exclusively or even predominantly Southern. Why should our minds remain sectionalized, when the problem itself no longer is? Then the trend of migration has not only been toward the North and the Central Midwest, but city-ward and to the great centers of industry — the problems of adjustment are new, practical, local and not peculiarly racial. Rather they are an integral part of the large industrial and social problems of our present-day democracy. And finally, with the Negro rapidly in process of class differentiation, if it ever was warrantable to regard and treat the Negro en masse, it is becoming with every day less possible, more unjust and more ridiculous.

5 The Negro, too, for his part, has idols of the tribe to smash. If on the one hand the white man has erred in making the Negro appear to be that which would excuse or extenuate his treatment of him, the Negro, in turn, has too often unnecessarily excused himself because of the way he has been treated. The intelligent Negro of today is resolved not to make discrimination an extenuation for his shortcomings in performance, individual or collective; he is trying to hold himself at par, neither inflated by sentimental allowances nor depreciated by current social discounts. For this he must know himself and be known for precisely what he is, and for that reason he welcomes the new scientific rather than the old sentimental interest. Sentimental interest in the Negro has ebbed. We used to lament this as the falling off of our friends; now we rejoice and pray to be delivered both from self-pity and condescension. The mind of each racial group has had a bitter weaning, apathy or hatred on one side matching disillusionment or resentment on the other; but they face each other today with the possibility at least of entirely new mutual attitudes.

It does not follow that if the Negro were better known, he would be better liked or better treated. But mutual understanding is basic for any subsequent cooperation and adjustment. The effort toward this will at least have the effect of remedying in large part what has been the most unsatisfactory feature of our present state of race relationships in America, namely the fact that the more intelligent and representative elements of the two race groups have at so many points got quite out of vital touch with one another.

The fiction is that the life of the races is separate, and increasingly so. The fact is that they have touched too closely at the unfavorable and too lightly at the favorable levels.

While inter-racial councils have sprung up in the South, drawing on forward elements of both races, in the Northern cities manual laborers may brush elbows in their everyday work, but the community and business leaders have experienced no such interplay or far too little of it. These segments must achieve contact or the race situation in America becomes desperate. In the intellectual realm a renewed and keen curiosity is replacing the recent apathy; the Negro is being carefully studied, not just talked

---

[2] A term for a Black nanny of white children in the American South. Today, it is recognized as an offensive trope. — Eds.

[3] The eponymous character of Harriet Beecher Stowe's 1854 novel *Uncle Tom's Cabin*. He is portrayed as passive and subservient. — Eds.

[4] A racist caricature of a Black man. One of the overseers in *Uncle Tom's Cabin* is a man named Sambo. — Eds.

about and discussed. In art and letters, instead of being wholly caricatured, he is being seriously portrayed and painted.

To all of this the New Negro is keenly responsive as an augury of a new democracy in American culture. He is contributing his share to the new social understanding. But the desire to be understood would never in itself have been sufficient to have opened so completely the protectively closed portals of the thinking Negro's mind. There is still too much possibility of being snubbed or patronized for that. It was rather the necessity for fuller, truer, self-expression, the realization of the unwisdom of allowing social discrimination to segregate him mentally, and a counter-attitude to cramp and fetter his own living — and so the "spite-wall" that the intellectuals built over the "color-line" has happily been taken down. Much of this reopening of intellectual contacts has centered in New York and has been richly fruitful not merely in the enlarging of personal experience, but in the definite enrichment of American art and letters and in the clarifying of our common vision of the social tasks ahead.

However, this new phase of things is delicate; 10
it will call for less charity but more justice; less help, but infinitely closer understanding. ■

1925

Questions

1. What has brought about the "renewed self-respect and self-dependence" that Alain Locke describes in paragraph 2?
2. How does the language of paragraph 2, including the poem by Langston Hughes, convey the positive spirit of the moment, according to Locke?
3. What are the myths, misconceptions, and stereotypes that Locke asserts are in the past?
4. What impact does Locke believe "the trend of migration" (par. 4) has had?
5. Why does Locke think that the belief that "the life of the races is separate, and increasingly so" is "a fiction" (par. 7)?
6. According to Locke, how is the "New Negro" an "augury of a new democracy in American culture" (par. 9)?
7. What aspects of Locke's predictions do you think have become reality since this essay was first published in 1925? Which have not — and why?

Heritage

Countee Cullen

An important figure during the Harlem Renaissance, Countee Cullen (1903–1946) grew up in New York City. At fifteen, he was adopted by Reverend Frederick A. Cullen, pastor of Harlem's largest congregation. Cullen graduated Phi Beta Kappa from New York University in 1923 and received an MA from Harvard University in 1926; he traveled to France as a Guggenheim Fellow after graduation. His published collections include *Color* (1925), *Copper Sun* (1927), *The Ballad of the Brown Girl* (1928), *The Black Christ and Other Poems* (1929), and *The Medea and Some Other Poems* (1935). While race was a central concern of Cullen's work, he differed from many other poets of this period by writing in the lyric tradition of the nineteenth-century Romantic John Keats, his favorite poet.

KEY CONTEXT The epigraph for this poem is dedicated to Harold Jackman, a lifelong friend of Cullen's who was a model, teacher, and patron of the arts. Like Cullen, Jackman was part of the Harlem Renaissance. As you read this poem, keep in mind that Cullen wrote "Heritage" at a time when the Pan-African movement had gained support with some prominent Black writers, artists, and thinkers of the day. Led by Marcus Garvey (1887–1940), a Jamaican political activist, this movement sought to unify Black people worldwide. In Garvey's view, however, this unity could only be achieved through racial separatism.

(For Harold Jackman)

What is Africa to me:
Copper sun or scarlet sea,
Jungle star or jungle track,
Strong bronzed men, or regal black
Women from whose loins I sprang
When the birds of Eden sang?
One three centuries removed
From the scenes his fathers loved,
Spicy grove, cinnamon tree,
What is Africa to me?

So I lie, who all day long
Want no sound except the song
Sung by wild barbaric birds
Goading massive jungle herds,
Juggernauts of flesh that pass
Trampling tall defiant grass
Where young forest lovers lie,
Plighting troth[1] beneath the sky.
So I lie, who always hear,
Though I cram against my ear
Both my thumbs, and keep them there,
Great drums throbbing through the air.
So I lie, whose fount of pride,
Dear distress, and joy allied,
Is my somber flesh and skin,
With the dark blood dammed within
Like great pulsing tides of wine
That, I fear, must burst the fine
Channels of the chafing net
Where they surge and foam and fret.

Africa? A book one thumbs
Listlessly, till slumber comes.

[1] A solemn vow or promise of truth and fidelity. — Eds.

Unremembered are her bats
Circling through the night, her cats
Crouching in the river reeds,
Stalking gentle flesh that feeds
By the river brink; no more
Does the bugle-throated roar
Cry that monarch claws have leapt
From the scabbards where they slept.
Silver snakes that once a year
Doff the lovely coats you wear,
Seek no covert in your fear
Lest a mortal eye should see;
What's your nakedness to me?
Here no leprous flowers rear
Fierce corollas[2] in the air;
Here no bodies sleek and wet,
Dripping mingled rain and sweat,
Tread the savage measures of
Jungle boys and girls in love.
What is last year's snow to me,
Last year's anything? The tree
Budding yearly must forget
How its past arose or set —
Bough and blossom, flower, fruit,
Even what shy bird with mute
Wonder at her travail there,
Meekly labored in its hair.
One three centuries removed
From the scenes his fathers loved,
Spice grove, cinnamon tree,
What is Africa to me?

So I lie, who find no peace
Night or day, no slight release
From the unremittant beat
Made by cruel padded feet
Walking through my body's street.
Up and down they go, and back,
Treading out a jungle track.
So I lie, who never quite
Safely sleep from rain at night —

[2] The petals of a flower, collectively. — Eds.

I can never rest at all
When the rain begins to fall;
Like a soul gone mad with pain
I must match its weird refrain;
Ever must I twist and squirm,
Writhing like a baited worm,
While its primal measures drip
Through my body, crying, "Strip!
Doff this new exuberance.
Come and dance the Lover's Dance!"
In an old remembered way
Rain works on me night and day.

Quaint, outlandish heathen gods
Black men fashion out of rods,
Clay, and brittle bits of stone,
In a likeness like their own,
My conversion came high-priced;
I belong to Jesus Christ,
Preacher of humility;
Heathen gods are naught to me.

Father, Son, and Holy Ghost,
So I make an idle boast;
Jesus of the twice-turned cheek,
Lamb of God, although I speak
With my mouth thus, in my heart
Do I play a double part.
Ever at Thy glowing altar
Must my heart grow sick and falter,
Wishing He I served were black,
Thinking then it would not lack
Precedent of pain to guide it,
Let who would or might deride it;
Surely then this flesh would know
Yours had borne a kindred woe.
Lord, I fashion dark gods, too,
Daring even to give You
Dark despairing features where,
Crowned with dark rebellious hair,
Patience wavers just so much as
Mortal grief compels, while touches
Quick and hot, of anger, rise

To smitten cheek and weary eyes.
Lord, forgive me if my need
Sometimes shapes a human creed.

All day long and all night through,
One thing only must I do:
Quench my pride and cool my blood,
Lest I perish in the flood.
Lest a hidden ember set
Timber that I thought was wet
Burning like the dryest flax,
Melting like the merest wax,
Lest the grave restore its dead.
Not yet has my heart or head
In the least way realized
They and I are civilized. ■

1925

Questions

1. What specific details describe Africa? Start with the opening descriptions that Countee Cullen presents as contrasts. As the poem progresses, what visual picture emerges?
2. Starting with line 85, the speaker struggles to reconcile his Christian beliefs with "heathen gods." What is the nature of his struggle?
3. In addition to differing religious beliefs, what other dualities in cultural values do you find in the poem? If you interpret the poem as the inner struggle of the speaker trying to construct his identity, what are the conflicts the speaker experiences?
4. What is the impact of the repetition used in the poem? To what extent does the speaker answer the repeated question, "What is Africa to me"? Other examples of repetition include the repeated phrase "So I lie" and the italicized quatrains. How does the repetition work in conjunction with the rhyming couplets and rhythm?
5. How do you interpret the italicized ending of the poem? Pay special attention to the word "civilized" (l. 128). Why might Cullen have chosen to end his poem with this word? Ultimately, what is Africa to the speaker?
6. How would you describe the tone of the poem? Try using two or three words to make your description more precise, such as *sad yet hopeful*, or *admiringly critical*. Cite specific passages to support your response.

Spunk

Zora Neale Hurston

Zora Neale Hurston (1891–1960) came to prominence in the 1920s during the Harlem Renaissance, a period of enormous creativity of African American artists, writers, and musicians. A novelist, folklorist, and anthropologist, she first gained attention with her short stories, including "Sweat" and "Spunk." She is best known for her novel *Their Eyes Were Watching God* (1937), set in Eatonville, Florida, where Hurston grew up; the town was the first incorporated African American community in the United States. She attended Howard University and won a scholarship to Barnard College in New York, living in Harlem throughout the 1920s. Toward the end of her life, Hurston remained out of the public eye; she was buried in an unmarked grave in Florida.

KEY CONTEXT Hurston studied anthropology at Columbia University and did field work in Louisiana, Florida, and Haiti. "Spunk" reflects her interest in and celebration of African American folk culture, as well as its use of authentic vernacular speech. While not always technically or grammatically accurate as defined by the rules of written English, the dialogue Hurston chooses captures the time, place, and culture through the voices of her characters. "Spunk," which established Hurston's reputation as a prominent writer, was first published in Alain Locke's *The New Negro*.

I

A giant of a brown-skinned man sauntered up the one street of the village and out into the palmetto thickets with a small pretty woman clinging lovingly to his arm.

"Looka theah, folkses!" cried Elijah Mosley, slapping his leg gleefully. "Theah they go, big as life an' brassy as tacks."

All the loungers in the store tried to walk to the door with an air of nonchalance but with small success.

"Now pee-eople!" Walter Thomas gasped. "Will you look at 'em!"

"But that's one thing Ah likes about Spunk Banks — he ain't skeered of nothin' on God's green footstool — *nothin'*! He rides that log down at saw-mill jus' like he struts 'round wid another man's wife — jus' don't give a kitty. When Tes' Miller got cut to giblets[1] on that circle-saw, Spunk steps right up and starts ridin'. The rest of us was skeered to go near it."

A round-shouldered figure in overalls much too large came nervously in the door and the talking ceased. The men looked at each other and winked.

"Gimme some soda-water. Sass'prilla[2] Ah reckon," the newcomer ordered, and stood far down the counter near the open pickled pig-feet tub to drink it.

Elijah nudged Walter and turned with mock gravity to the new-comer.

"Say, Joe, how's everything up yo' way? How's yo' wife?"

Joe started and all but dropped the bottle he was holding. He swallowed several times painfully and his lips trembled.

"Aw 'Lige, you oughtn't to do nothin' like that," Walter grumbled. Elijah ignored him.

"She jus' passed heah a few minutes ago goin' thata way," with a wave of his hand in the direction of the woods.

Now Joe knew his wife had passed that way. He knew that the men lounging in the general store had seen her, moreover, he knew that the men knew *he* knew. He stood there silent for a long moment staring blankly, with his Adam's apple twitching nervously up and down his throat. One could actually *see* the pain he was suffering, his eyes, his face, his hands, and even the dejected slump of his shoulders. He set the

[1] The liver, heart, gizzard, and neck of a bird, usually a chicken. — Eds.

[2] Sarsaparilla, a popular soda during this time period. — Eds.

bottle down upon the counter. He didn't bang it, just eased it out of his hand silently and fiddled with his suspender buckle.

"Well, Ah'm goin' after her to-day. Ah'm goin' an' fetch her back. Spunk's done gone too fur."

He reached deep down into his trouser pocket and drew out a hollow ground razor, large and shiny, and passed his moistened thumb back and forth over the edge.

"Talkin' like a man, Joe. 'Course that's *yo'* fambly affairs, but Ah like to see grit in anybody."

Joe Kanty laid down a nickel and stumbled out into the street.

Dusk crept in from the woods. Ike Clarke lit the swinging oil lamp that was almost immediately surrounded by candle-flies. The men laughed boisterously behind Joe's back as they watched him shamble woodward.

"You oughtn't to said whut you said to him, 'Lige — look how it worked him up," Walter chided.

"And Ah hope it did work him up. Tain't even decent for a man to take and take like he do."

"Spunk will sho' kill him."

"Aw, Ah doan know. You never kin tell. He might turn him up an' spank him fur gettin' in the way, but Spunk wouldn't shoot no unarmed man. Dat razor he carried outa heah ain't gonna run Spunk down an' cut him, an' Joe ain't got the nerve to go to Spunk with it knowing he totes that Army .45. He makes that break outa heah to bluff us. He's gonna hide that razor behind the first palmetto root an' sneak back home to bed. Don't tell me nothin' 'bout that rabbit-foot colored man. Didn't he meet Spunk an' Lena face to face one day las week an' mumble sumthin' to Spunk 'bout lettin' his wife alone?"

"What did Spunk say?" Walter broke in. "Ah like him fine but tain't right the way he carries on wid Lena Kanty, jus' 'cause Joe's timid 'bout fightin'."

"You wrong theah, Walter. Tain't 'cause Joe's timid at all, it's 'cause Spunk wants Lena. If Joe was a passle of wile cats Spunk would tackle the job just the same. He'd go after *anything* he wanted the same way. As Ah wuz sayin' a minute ago, he tole Joe right to his face that Lena was his. 'Call her and see if she'll come. A woman knows her boss an' she answers when he calls.' 'Lena, ain't I yo' husband?' Joe sorter whines out. Lena looked at him real disgusted but she don't answer and she don't move outa her tracks. Then Spunk reaches out an' takes hold of her arm an' says: 'Lena, youse mine. From now on Ah works for you an' fights for you an' Ah never wants you to look to nobody for a crumb of bread, a stitch of close or a shingle to go over yo' head, but *me* long as Ah live. Ah'll git the lumber foh owah house to-morrow. Go home an git yo' things together!"

" 'Thass mah house,' Lena speaks up. 'Papa gimme that.'

" 'Well,' says Spunk, 'doan give up whut's yours, but when youse inside doan forgit youse mine, an' let no other man git outa his place wid you!'

"Lena looked up at him with her eyes so full of love that they wuz runnin' over, an' Spunk seen it an' Joe seen it too, and his lip started to tremblin' and his Adam's apple was galloping up and down his neck like a race horse. Ah bet he's wore out half a dozen Adam's apples since Spunk's been on the job with Lena. That's all he'll do. He'll be back heah after while swallowin' an' workin' his lips like he wants to say somethin' an' can't."

"But didn't he do *nothin'* to stop 'em?"

"Nope, not a frazzlin' thing — jus' stood there. Spunk took Lena's arm and walked off jus' like nothin' ain't happened and he stood there gazin' after them till they was outa sight. Now you know a woman don't want no man like that.

I'm jus' waitin' to see whut he's goin' to say when he gits back."

II

But Joe Kanty never came back, never. The men in the store heard the sharp report of a pistol somewhere distant in the palmetto thicket and soon Spunk came walking leisurely, with his big black Stetson[3] set at the same rakish angle and Lena clinging to his arm, came walking right into the general store. Lena wept in a frightened manner.

"Well," Spunk announced calmly, "Joe came out there wid a meat axe an' made me kill him."

He sent Lena home and led the men back to Joe — crumpled and limp with his right hand still clutching his razor.

"See mah back? Mah close cut clear through. He sneaked up an' tried to kill me from the back, but Ah got him, an' got him good, first shot," Spunk said.

The men glared at Elijah, accusingly.

"Take him up an' plant him in Stony Lonesome," Spunk said in a careless voice. "Ah didn't wanna shoot him but he made me do it. He's a dirty coward, jumpin' on a man from behind."

Spunk turned on his heel and sauntered away to where he knew his love wept in fear for him and no man stopped him. At the general store later on, they all talked of locking him up until the sheriff should come from Orlando, but no one did anything but talk.

A clear case of self-defense, the trial was a short one, and Spunk walked out of the court house to freedom again. He could work again, ride the dangerous log-carriage that fed the singing, snarling, biting circle-saw; he could stroll the soft dark lanes with his guitar. He was free to roam the woods again; he was free to return to Lena. He did all of these things.

III

Whut you reckon, Walt?" Elijah asked one night later. "Spunk's gittin' ready to marry Lena!"

"Naw! Why, Joe ain't had time to git cold yit. Nohow Ah didn't figger Spunk was the marryin' kind."

"Well, he is," rejoined Elijah. "He done moved most of Lena's things — and her along wid 'em — over to the Bradley house. He's buying it. Jus' like Ah told yo' all right in heah the night Joe was kilt. Spunk's crazy 'bout Lena. He don't want folks to keep on talkin' 'bout her — thass reason he's rushin' so. Funny thing 'bout that bob-cat, wan't it?"

"What bob-cat, 'Lige? Ah ain't heered 'bout none."

"Ain't cher? Well, night befo' las' as they was goin' to bed, a big black bob-cat, black all over, you hear me, *black*, walked round and round that house and howled like forty, an' when Spunk got his gun an' went to the winder to shoot it, he says it stood right still an' looked him in the eye, an' howled right at him. The thing got Spunk so nervoused up he couldn't shoot. But Spunk says twan't no bob-cat nohow. He says it was Joe done sneaked back from Hell!"

"Humph!" sniffed Walter, "he oughter be nervous after what he done. Ah reckon Joe come back to dare him to marry Lena, or to come out an' fight. Ah bet he'll be back time and again, too. Know what Ah think? Joe wuz a braver man than Spunk."

There was a general shout of derision from the group.

"Thass a fact," went on Walter. "Lookit whut he done; took a razor an' went out to fight a man he knowed toted a gun an' wuz a crack shot, too; 'nother thing Joe wuz skeered of Spunk, skeered plumb stiff ! But he went jes' the same. It took

[3] A Stetson hat, which has a wide brim. — Eds.

him a long time to get his nerve up. Tain't nothin' for Spunk to fight when he ain't skeered of nothin'. Now, Joe's done come back to have it out wid the man that's got all he ever had. Y'all know Joe ain't never had nothin' nor wanted nothin' besides Lena. It musta been a h'ant[4] cause ain't nobody never seen no black bob-cat."

" 'Nother thing," cut in one of the men, "Spunk was cussin' a blue streak to-day 'cause he 'lowed dat saw wuz wobblin' — almos' got 'im once. The machinist come, looked it over an said it wuz alright. Spunk musta been leanin t'wards it some. Den he claimed somebody pushed 'im but twan't nobody close to 'im. Ah wuz glad when knockin' off time came. I'm skeered of dat man when he gits hot. He'd beat you full of button holes as quick as he's look atcher."

IV

The men gathered the next evening in a different mood, no laughter. No badinage[5] this time.

"Look, 'Lige, you goin' to set up wid Spunk?"

"Naw, Ah reckon not, Walter. Tell yuh the truth, Ah'm a li'l bit skittish. Spunk died too wicket — died cussin' he did. You know he thought he was done outa life."

"Good Lawd, who'd he think done it?"

"Joe."

"Joe Kanty? How come?"

"Walter, Ah b'leeve Ah will walk up thata way an' set. Lena would like it Ah reckon."

"But whut did he say, 'Lige?"

Elijah did not answer until they had left the lighted store and were strolling down the dark street.

"Ah wuz loadin' a wagon wid scantlin' right near the saw when Spunk fell on the carriage but 'fore Ah could git to him the saw got him in the body — awful sight. Me an' Skint Miller got him off but it was too late. Anybody could see that. The fust thing he said wuz: 'He pushed me, 'Lige — the dirty hound pushed me in the back!' — he was spittin' blood at ev'ry breath. We laid him on the sawdust pile with his face to the East so's he could die easy. He helt mah han' till the last, Walter, and said: 'It was Joe, 'Lige . . . the dirty sneak shoved me . . . he didn't dare come to mah face . . . but Ah'll git the son-of-a-wood louse soon's Ah get there an' make hell too hot for him . . . Ah felt him shove me . . . !' Thass how he died."

"If spirits kin fight, there's a powerful tussle goin' on somewhere ovah Jordan[6] 'cause Ah b'leeve Joe's ready for Spunk an' ain't skeered any more — yas, Ah b'leeve Joe pushed 'im mahself."

They had arrived at the house. Lena's lamentations were deep and loud. She had filled the room with magnolia blossoms that gave off a heavy sweet odor. The keepers of the wake tipped about whispering in frightened tones. Everyone in the village was there, even old Jeff Kanty, Joe's father, who a few hours before would have been afraid to come within ten feet of him, stood leering triumphantly down upon the fallen giant as if his fingers had been the teeth of steel that laid him low.

The cooling board consisted of three sixteen-inch boards on saw horses, a dingy sheet was his shroud.

The women ate heartily of the funeral baked meats and wondered who would be Lena's next. The men whispered coarse conjectures between guzzles of whiskey. ■

1925

[4] A haint, or ghost. — Eds.

[5] Witty banter. — Eds.

[6] Going or crossing "over Jordan" is a common euphemism for dying and passing into the afterlife. It derives from the Old Testament story in which the Jewish people crossed over the Jordan River to finally reach freedom after fleeing slavery in Egypt. — Eds.

Questions

1. How does Zora Neale Hurston characterize Spunk Banks in Section I? Consider her direct description as well as what others say about him.
2. How does the dialect affect your reading and understanding of the story? Would Hurston have made her characters more credible — in 1925 — and broadened her audience if she had had them speak in so-called standard English?
3. How do the men in the story regard the conflict between Spunk Banks and Joe Kanty?
4. In what ways are Spunk and Joe reflected in Elijah and Walter? What purpose do the similarities serve?
5. Do we as readers know what really happened between Spunk and Joe in their final encounter? Is it important that we do? Why or why not?
6. How would you describe the character of Lena? What inconsistencies, if any, do you notice in her behavior? Do you view her character in the same way as the men in this story do? Be sure to consider the ending of the story in your response.
7. Who holds power in the community of the story, and why do they hold it? What is the nature of that power?
8. How does the bobcat function as a symbol in "Spunk"? How does it speak to the story's larger themes, and why is it particularly noteworthy that in reality, there are no black bobcats?
9. What role does the supernatural play in the story?
10. The story takes its title from the character Spunk Banks, but *spunk* also means gumption, or courage. Is this an appropriate title? Explain.
11. This intricate story is actually a series of stories. What are the stories within the stories? How do they interrelate? How does the four-part structure reinforce or signal shifts?
12. What role do the concepts of property and ownership, both literal and metaphorical, play in the story? Be sure to consider the relationship of Lena with Joe and Spunk, and cite specific evidence from the text, as you develop your response.

I look at the world

Langston Hughes

A key figure of the Harlem Renaissance, Langston Hughes (1902–1967) grew up in the African American community of Joplin, Missouri. He spent a year at Columbia University and became involved with the Harlem movement, but was shocked by the endemic racial prejudice at the university and subsequently left. Hughes traveled for several years before returning to the United States and completing his BA at Pennsylvania's Lincoln University in 1929, after which he returned to Harlem for the remainder of his life. His first volume of poetry, *The Weary Blues*, was published in 1926. His first novel, *Not Without Laughter* (1930), won the Harmon Gold Medal for literature. He also wrote children's poetry, musicals, and opera.

KEY CONTEXT Hughes wrote this poem by hand on the back inside cover of his edition of *An Anthology of Revolutionary Poetry* (1929). It was not discovered until 2009, when Penny Welbourne, a rare book cataloger at the Beinecke Library at Yale University, found it in Hughes's papers. A champion of the artist's freedom to choose subject and medium, Hughes wrote in his

1926 essay, "The Negro Artist and the Racial Mountain," that his generation of artists and writers "intend[ed] to express our individual, dark-skinned selves without fear or shame."

I look at the world
From awakening eyes in a black face—
And this is what I see:
This fenced-off narrow space
Assigned to me.

I look then at the silly walls
Through dark eyes in a dark face—
And this is what I know:
That all these walls oppression builds
Will have to go!

I look at my own body
With eyes no longer blind—
And I see that my own hands can make
The world that's in my mind.
Then let us hurry, comrades,
The road to find. ■

c. 1930

Questions

1. What is the nature of the tension in the opening stanza between "awakening eyes" (l. 2) and "fenced off narrow space" (l. 4)?
2. What effect does Langston Hughes's choice of the word "silly" to describe "walls" in line 6 have on the tone of the poem? What might have been different had Hughes chosen a word such as "oppressive" or "ugly"?
3. In what ways is the speaker "no longer blind" (l. 12) by the third stanza? What has given him sight or insight?
4. How do you interpret the significance of the shift of the speaker's gaze from the world, to the walls, to his own body?
5. How does the repetition of "I look" propel the poem toward a meaning beyond the speaker's individual experience?
6. Hughes could have ended his poem with line 14, with the statement of the speaker's own awakening. What, then, does he gain by adding the concluding two lines?
7. In 2020, "I look at the world" was selected by the Poetry Foundation to be part of a discussion of "Poetry of Protest, Resistance, and Empowerment." How does Hughes's poem illustrate all three of these concepts?
8. How close are we today to "the world that's in [Hughes's] mind" (l. 14)? Use evidence from current events or recent history to support your response.

From every southern town migrants left by the hundreds to travel north (Migration Series #3)

Jacob Lawrence

Among the most acclaimed twentieth century American artists, Jacob Lawrence (1917–2000) gained national recognition at age twenty-three for his Migration Series paintings. An active and prolific painter for his entire life, he also created series of paintings portraying the lives of abolitionists Harriet Tubman (1822–1913), Frederick Douglass (1817–1895), and John Brown (1800–1859); Haitian revolutionary Toussaint L'Ouverture (1743–1803); *The American Struggle*, a series of paintings depicting American history between 1775 and 1817; and more.

KEY CONTEXT Lawrence completed the 60-panel set of narrative paintings entitled *Migration of the Negro* or *And the Migrants Kept Coming*, now called *The Migration Series,* in 1940–41. In this epic statement, he depicted the flight of over a million African Americans from the rural South to the industrial North between roughly 1910 and 1940. Before painting the Migration Series, Lawrence researched the subject and wrote captions to accompany each panel. The following painting is panel 3.

From every southern town migrants left by the hundreds to travel north, 1940–41 (casein tempera on hardboard)/Lawrence, Jacob (1917–2000)/PHILLIPS COLLECTION/The Phillips Collection, Washington, D.C., USA/Bridgeman Images. © 2021 The Jacob and Gwendolyn Knight Lawrence Foundation, Seattle/Artists Rights Society (ARS), New York

1940

Questions

1. What do you notice about the composition of the painting? What visual elements divide and structure it?
2. How does Jacob Lawrence convey the movement of the migrants in this image? How individualized do they appear? What might this choice suggest about Lawrence's perspective on the Great Migration?
3. What emotions do the colors of the painting evoke? How do these choices contribute to your interpretation of the painting?
4. Migrations of birds is literal, a natural occurrence most everyone is familiar with. How does Lawrence develop a metaphorical meaning that comments on the human migrants in this painting?
5. Overall, what message does the painting convey? If you find it powerful, what is the source of that power?
6. What aspects of this image are timeless — that is, how might they speak to human migrations all over the world today?

Literature in Conversation

1. In what ways is "Boy on a Train" by Ralph Ellison a Harlem Renaissance work? Consider how it embraces some of the themes of the movement as well as ways in which its style and structure might be seen as a point of departure from the Texts in Context and other works of the Harlem Renaissance.
2. Choose one of the pieces in this Texts in Context section and discuss how you think both Ralph Ellison and the narrator of "Boy on a Train" might respond.
3. Connect the journey in "Boy on a Train" to *From every southern town migrants left by the hundreds to travel north* by Jacob Lawrence. How does this image contribute to your understanding of the setting and mood of "Boy on a Train"?
4. Artist Kehinde Wiley, who painted President Barack Obama's official portrait, has described the goal of his latest undertaking, a mural in Pennsylvania Station in New York City as a work "at the intersection of trade, commerce and transportation in the capital of the world's economy, something that sits as a testament to Black possibility." Find a photograph of the mural and consider how it relates to the texts in this section. What possibilities do you see in the image? How are "Boy on a Train" and the Texts in Context each "testament[s] to Black possibility"?
5. In "Spunk," Hurston presents an autonomous town deliberately segregated by and for the Black community in Florida. How does Hurston's portrayal of the town's inhabitants relate to the self-realization of the speaker in "I look at the world" by Hughes? What commonalities and differences do you see between and among the perspectives of Hurston's characters, Hughes's speaker, and James in "Boy on a Train"?
6. The speaker in Countee Cullen's poem repeatedly defines himself as "*One three centuries removed/ From the scenes his fathers loved* (ll. 7–8, 60–61)." While contemplating the importance of knowing his history, he continues:

   What is last year's snow to me,
   Last year's anything? The tree
   Budding yearly must forget
   How its past arose or set —
   Bough and blossom, flower, fruit,
   Even what shy bird with mute
   Wonder at her travail there,
   Meekly labored in its hair.

   How do Ellison's "Boy on a Train" and at least one of the other Texts in Context address the significance of a shared understanding of ancestral roots, racial identity, and/or personal memory?

7. How are at least two of the characteristics of the "New Negro" as defined by Alain Locke embodied in the narrative, setting, or characters of "Boy on a Train"? Choose one of the Texts in Context in this section and examine how both Ellison's story and your chosen text reflect Locke's main argument in the excerpt from "The New Negro."

8. In a later section of "The New Negro," not included here, Locke writes:

   > [T]he present generation will have added the motives of self-expression and spiritual development to the old and still unfinished task of making material headway and progress. No one who understandingly faces the situation with its substantial accomplishment or views the new scene with its still more abundant promise can be entirely without hope.

   Based on your reading of "Boy on a Train," these Texts in Context, and your knowledge of history, develop a position on whether Locke's vision for Black artists became a reality.

9. Some of the controversies that characterize the Harlem Renaissance continue today. Discuss one controversy from these 1920s texts that still persists — for example, in discussions about identity politics as the subject of art, literature as social protest or political commentary, and the legitimacy of new or nontraditional art forms.

10. Select a movie, miniseries, or television show that centers Black history, experience, art, and/or cultures. Some recent examples include *Atlanta* (2016), *If Beale Street Could Talk* (2019), *Black-ish* (2014), *Black Panther* (2018), *Dope* (2015), *Empire* (2015), *Get Out* (2017), *Grown-ish* (2018), *The Hate U Give* (2018), *Insecure* (2016), *Judas and the Black Messiah* (2021), *Lovecraft Country* (2020), *Lupin* (2021), *Moonlight* (2016), *Pose* (2018), *Sorry to Bother You* (2018), *Us* (2019), and *Watchmen* (2019). Write a script that imagines a conversation between Ellison and at least one of the authors and artists in this section. In it, they have also just watched the movie, miniseries, or show, and they discuss the connections between its themes and/or narrative perspectives and those of "Boy on a Train."

Young Goodman Brown

Nathaniel Hawthorne

Library of Congress Prints & Photographs Division

One of America's major voices of the nineteenth century, Nathaniel Hawthorne (1804–1864) was born in Salem, Massachusetts, into a family whose ancestors had participated in the Salem Witch Trials of the seventeenth century. In 1837, he published a volume of stories, *Twice-Told Tales*, followed by *Mosses from an Old Manse* (1846) — named for his house, which had belonged to Ralph Waldo Emerson. The years 1850 and 1851 saw the publication of Hawthorne's major novels, *The Scarlet Letter* and *The House of the Seven Gables*.

KEY CONTEXT Hawthorne's writing is often allegorical and contains many of the elements of the supernatural; in fact, he referred to his books as "romances" rather than novels. Many of his characters struggle with their moral identity as they confront the nature of evil, pride, guilt, and temptation. "Young Goodman Brown" is set during the seventeenth century, in the North American Puritan village of Salem, best known for the Salem Witch Trials of 1692–1693.

Young Goodman Brown came forth at sunset into the street of Salem village; but put his head back, after crossing the threshold, to exchange a parting kiss with his young wife. And Faith, as the wife was aptly named, thrust her own pretty head into the street, letting the wind play with the pink ribbons of her cap while she called to Goodman Brown.

"Dearest heart," whispered she, softly and rather sadly, when her lips were close to his ear, "prithee put off your journey until sunrise and sleep in your own bed to-night. A lone woman is troubled with such dreams and such thoughts that she's afeard of herself sometimes. Pray tarry with me this night, dear husband, of all nights in the year."

"My love and my Faith," replied young Goodman Brown, "of all nights in the year, this one night must I tarry away from thee. My journey, as thou callest it, forth and back again, must needs be done 'twixt now and sunrise. What, my sweet, pretty wife, dost thou doubt me already, and we but three months married?"

"Then God bless you!" said Faith, with the pink ribbons; "and may you find all well when you come back."

"Amen!" cried Goodman Brown. "Say thy prayers, dear Faith, and go to bed at dusk, and no harm will come to thee."

So they parted; and the young man pursued his way until, being about to turn the corner by the meeting-house, he looked back and saw the head of Faith still peeping after him with a melancholy air, in spite of her pink ribbons.

"Poor little Faith!" thought he, for his heart smote him. "What a wretch am I to leave her on such an errand! She talks of dreams, too. Methought as she spoke there was trouble in her face, as if a dream had warned her what work is to be done to-night. But no, no; 't would kill her to think it. Well, she's a blessed angel on earth; and after this one night I'll cling to her skirts and follow her to heaven."

With this excellent resolve for the future, Goodman Brown felt himself justified in making more haste on his present evil purpose. He had taken a dreary road, darkened by all the gloomiest trees of the forest, which barely stood aside to let the narrow path creep through, and closed immediately behind. It was all as lonely as could be; and there is this peculiarity in such a solitude, that the traveler knows not who may be concealed by the innumerable trunks and the thick boughs overhead; so that with lonely footsteps he may yet be passing through an unseen multitude.

"There may be a devilish Indian behind every tree," said Goodman Brown to himself; and he glanced fearfully behind him as he added, "What if the devil himself should be at my very elbow!"

10 His head being turned back, he passed a crook of the road, and, looking forward again, beheld the figure of a man, in grave and decent attire, seated at the foot of an old tree. He arose at Goodman Brown's approach and walked onward side by side with him.

"You are late, Goodman Brown," said he. "The clock of the Old South was striking as I came through Boston, and that is full fifteen minutes agone."

"Faith kept me back a while," replied the young man, with a tremor in his voice, caused by the sudden appearance of his companion, though not wholly unexpected.

It was now deep dusk in the forest, and deepest in that part of it where these two were journeying. As nearly as could be discerned, the second traveller was about fifty years old, apparently in the same rank of life as Goodman Brown, and bearing a considerable resemblance to him, though perhaps more in expression than features. Still they might have been taken for father and son. And yet, though the elder person was as simply clad as the younger, and as simple in manner too, he had an indescribable air of one who knew the world, and who would not have felt abashed at the governor's dinner table or in King William's court, were it possible that his affairs should call him thither. But the only thing about him that could be fixed upon as remarkable was his staff, which bore the likeness of a great black snake, so curiously wrought that it might almost be seen to twist and wriggle itself like a living serpent. This, of course, must have

This painting, entitled *Snake and Moon*, is a watercolor completed by American artist Morris Graves in 1938–1939.

What does the image, especially color and composition, suggest to you? Is it blatantly evil, more mystical or mysterious, or a naturalistic drawing? In what ways does it capture the possible "ocular deception, assisted by the uncertain light" (par. 13) of the devil's staff in "Young Goodman Brown"?

been an ocular deception, assisted by the uncertain light.

"Come, Goodman Brown!" cried his fellow-traveller, "this is a dull pace for the beginning of a journey. Take my staff, if you are so soon weary."

15 "Friend," said the other, exchanging his slow pace for a full stop, "having kept covenant by meeting thee here, it is my purpose now to return whence I came. I have scruples touching the matter thou wot'st[1] of."

"Sayest thou so?" replied he of the serpent, smiling apart. "Let us walk on, nevertheless, reasoning as we go; and if I convince thee not thou shalt turn back. We are but a little way in the forest yet."

"Too far! too far!" exclaimed the goodman, unconsciously resuming his walk. "My father never went into the woods on such an errand, nor his father before him. We have been a race of honest men and good Christians since the days of the martyrs; and shall I be the first of the name of Brown that ever took this path and kept—"

"Such company, thou wouldst say," observed the elder person, interpreting his pause. "Well said, Goodman Brown! I have been as well acquainted with your family as with ever a one among the Puritans; and that's no trifle to say. I helped your grandfather, the constable, when he lashed the Quaker woman so smartly through the streets of Salem; and it was I that brought your father a pitch-pine knot, kindled at my own hearth, to set fire to an Indian village, in King Philip's war.[2] They were my good friends, both; and many a pleasant walk have we had along this path, and returned merrily after midnight. I would fain be friends with you for their sake."

"If it be as thou sayest," replied Goodman Brown, "I marvel they never spoke of these matters; or, verily, I marvel not, seeing that the least rumor of the sort would have driven them from New England. We are a people of prayer, and good works to boot, and abide no such wickedness."

20 "Wickedness or not," said the traveller with the twisted staff, "I have a very general acquaintance here in New England. The deacons of many a church have drunk the communion wine with me; the selectmen of divers towns make me their chairman; and a majority of the Great and General Court are firm supporters of my interest. The governor and I, too—But these are state secrets."

"Can this be so?" cried Goodman Brown, with a stare of amazement at his undisturbed companion. "Howbeit, I have nothing to do with the governor and council; they have their own ways, and are no rule for a simple husbandman like me. But, were I to go on with thee, how should I meet the eye of that good old man, our minister, at Salem village? Oh, his voice would make me tremble both Sabbath day and lecture day."

Thus far the elder traveller had listened with due gravity; but now burst into a fit of irrepressible mirth, shaking himself so violently that his snake-like staff actually seemed to wriggle in sympathy.

"Ha! ha! ha!" shouted he again and again; then composing himself, "Well, go on, Goodman Brown, go on; but, prithee, don't kill me with laughing."

"Well, then, to end the matter at once," said Goodman Brown, considerably nettled, "there is my wife, Faith. It would break her dear little heart; and I'd rather break my own."

25 "Nay, if that be the case," answered the other, "e'en go thy ways, Goodman Brown. I would not for twenty old women like the one hobbling before us that Faith should come to any harm."

[1] Know.—Eds.

[2] War between American Indians and New England colonists from 1675 to 1678. The American Indian leader was known as Metacom, or King Philip.—Eds.

As he spoke he pointed his staff at a female figure on the path, in whom Goodman Brown recognized a very pious and exemplary dame, who had taught him his catechism in youth, and was still his moral and spiritual adviser, jointly with the minister and Deacon Gookin.

"A marvel, truly, that Goody[3] Cloyse should be so far in the wilderness at nightfall," said he. "But with your leave, friend, I shall take a cut through the woods until we have left this Christian woman behind. Being a stranger to you, she might ask whom I was consorting with and whither I was going."

"Be it so," said his fellow-traveller. "Betake you to the woods, and let me keep the path."

Accordingly the young man turned aside, but took care to watch his companion, who advanced softly along the road until he had come within a staff's length of the old dame. She, meanwhile, was making the best of her way, with singular speed for so aged a woman, and mumbling some indistinct words — a prayer, doubtless — as she went. The traveller put forth his staff and touched her withered neck with what seemed the serpent's tail.

"The devil!" screamed the pious old lady. 30

"Then Goody Cloyse knows her old friend?" observed the traveller, confronting her and leaning on his writhing stick.

"Ah, forsooth, and is it your worship indeed?" cried the good dame. "Yea, truly is it, and in the very image of my old gossip, Goodman Brown, the grandfather of the silly fellow that now is. But — would your worship believe it? — my broomstick hath strangely disappeared, stolen, as I suspect, by that unhanged witch, Goody Cory, and that, too, when I was all anointed with the juice of smallage, and cinquefoil, and wolf's-bane —"

"Mingled with fine wheat and the fat of a new-born babe," said the shape of old Goodman Brown.

"Ah, your worship knows the recipe," cried the old lady, cackling aloud. "So, as I was saying, being all ready for the meeting, and no horse to ride on, I made up my mind to foot it; for they tell me there is a nice young man to be taken into communion to-night. But now your good worship will lend me your arm, and we shall be there in a twinkling."

"That can hardly be," answered her friend. 35
"I may not spare you my arm, Goody Cloyse; but here is my staff, if you will."

So saying, he threw it down at her feet, where, perhaps, it assumed life, being one of the rods which its owner had formerly lent to the Egyptian magi. Of this fact, however, Goodman Brown could not take cognizance. He had cast up his eyes in astonishment, and, looking down again, beheld neither Goody Cloyse nor the serpentine staff, but his fellow-traveller alone, who waited for him as calmly as if nothing had happened.

"That old woman taught me my catechism," said the young man; and there was a world of meaning in this simple comment.

They continued to walk onward, while the elder traveller exhorted his companion to make good speed and persevere in the path, discoursing so aptly that his arguments seemed rather to spring up in the bosom of his auditor than to be suggested by himself. As they went, he plucked a branch of maple to serve for a walking stick, and began to strip it of the twigs and little boughs, which were wet with evening dew. The moment his fingers touched them they became strangely withered and dried up as with a week's sunshine. Thus the pair proceeded, at a good free pace, until suddenly, in a gloomy hollow of the road, Goodman Brown sat himself down on the stump of a tree and refused to go any farther.

"Friend," he said, stubbornly, "my mind is made up. Not another step will I budge on this errand. What if a wretched old woman do

[3] Short for "goodwife," archaic form of missus. — Eds.

choose to go to the devil when I thought she was going to heaven: is that any reason why I should quit my dear Faith and go after her?"

"You will think better of this by and by," said his acquaintance, composedly. "Sit here and rest yourself a while; and when you feel like moving again, there is my staff to help you along."

Without more words, he threw his companion the maple stick, and was as speedily out of sight as if he had vanished into the deepening gloom. The young man sat a few moments by the roadside, applauding himself greatly, and thinking with how clear a conscience he should meet the minister in his morning walk, nor shrink from the eye of good old Deacon Gookin. And what calm sleep would be his that very night, which was to have been spent so wickedly, but so purely and sweetly now, in the arms of Faith! Amidst these pleasant and praiseworthy meditations, Goodman Brown heard the tramp of horses along the road, and deemed it advisable to conceal himself within the verge of the forest, conscious of the guilty purpose that had brought him thither, though now so happily turned from it.

On came the hoof tramps and the voices of the riders, two grave old voices, conversing soberly as they drew near. These mingled sounds appeared to pass along the road, within a few yards of the young man's hiding-place; but, owing doubtless to the depth of the gloom at that particular spot, neither the travellers nor their steeds were visible. Though their figures brushed the small boughs by the wayside, it could not be seen that they intercepted, even for a moment, the faint gleam from the strip of bright sky athwart which they must have passed. Goodman Brown alternately crouched and stood on tiptoe, pulling aside the branches and thrusting forth his head as far as he durst without discerning so much as a shadow. It vexed him the more, because he could have sworn, were such a thing possible, that he recognized the voices of the minister and Deacon Gookin, jogging along quietly, as they were wont to do, when bound to some ordination or ecclesiastical council. While yet within hearing, one of the riders stopped to pluck a switch.

"Of the two, reverend sir," said the voice like the deacon's, "I had rather miss an ordination dinner than to-night's meeting. They tell me that some of our community are to be here from Falmouth and beyond, and others from Connecticut and Rhode Island, besides several of the Indian powwows, who, after their fashion, know almost as much deviltry as the best of us. Moreover, there is a goodly young woman to be taken into communion."

"Mighty well, Deacon Gookin!" replied the solemn old tones of the minister. "Spur up, or we shall be late. Nothing can be done, you know, until I get on the ground."

The hoofs clattered again; and the voices, talking so strangely in the empty air, passed on through the forest, where no church had ever been gathered or solitary Christian prayed. Whither, then, could these holy men be journeying so deep into the heathen wilderness? Young Goodman Brown caught hold of a tree for support, being ready to sink down on the ground, faint and overburdened with the heavy sickness of his heart. He looked up to the sky, doubting whether there really was a heaven above him. Yet there was the blue arch, and the stars brightening in it.

"With heaven above and Faith below, I will yet stand firm against the devil!" cried Goodman Brown.

While he still gazed upward into the deep arch of the firmament and had lifted his hands to pray, a cloud, though no wind was stirring, hurried across the zenith and hid the

What do the "claws" in this 1957 sculpture by French artist Germaine Richier suggest about the reach and impact of the devil? In what ways is her interpretation of this archetypal figure embodied in "Young Goodman Brown"?

brightening stars. The blue sky was still visible, except directly overhead, where this black mass of cloud was sweeping swiftly northward. Aloft in the air, as if from the depths of the cloud, came a confused and doubtful sound of voices. Once the listener fancied that he could distinguish the accents of towns-people of his own, men and women, both pious and ungodly, many of whom he had met at the communion table, and had seen others rioting at the tavern. The next moment, so indistinct were the sounds, he doubted whether he had heard aught but the murmur of the old forest, whispering without a wind. Then came a stronger swell of those familiar tones, heard daily in the sunshine at Salem village, but never until now from a cloud of night. There was one voice, of a young woman, uttering lamentations, yet with an uncertain sorrow, and entreating for some favor, which, perhaps, it would grieve her to obtain; and all the unseen multitude, both saints and sinners, seemed to encourage her onward.

"Faith!" shouted Goodman Brown, in a voice of agony and desperation; and the echoes of the forest mocked him, crying, "Faith! Faith!" as if bewildered wretches were seeking her all through the wilderness.

The cry of grief, rage, and terror was yet piercing the night, when the unhappy husband held his breath for a response. There was a scream, drowned immediately in a louder murmur of voices, fading into far-off laughter, as the dark cloud swept away, leaving the clear and silent sky above Goodman Brown. But something fluttered lightly down through the air and caught on the branch of a tree. The young man seized it, and beheld a pink ribbon.

"My Faith is gone!" cried he after one stupefied moment. "There is no good on earth; and sin is but a name. Come, devil; for to thee is this world given."

And, maddened with despair, so that he laughed loud and long, did Goodman Brown grasp his staff and set forth again, at such a rate that he seemed to fly along the forest path rather than to walk or run. The road grew wilder and drearier and more faintly traced, and vanished at length, leaving him in the heart of the dark wilderness, still rushing onward with the instinct that guides mortal man to evil. The whole forest was peopled with frightful sounds — the creaking of the trees, the howling of wild beasts, and the yell of Indians; while sometimes the wind tolled like a distant church bell, and sometimes gave a broad roar around the traveller, as if all Nature were laughing him to scorn. But he was himself the chief horror of the scene, and shrank not from its other horrors.

"Ha! ha! ha!" roared Goodman Brown when the wind laughed at him. "Let us hear which will laugh loudest. Think not to frighten me with your deviltry. Come witch, come wizard, come Indian powwow, come devil himself, and here comes Goodman Brown. You may as well fear him as he fear you."

In truth, all through the haunted forest, there could be nothing more frightful than the figure of Goodman Brown. On he flew among the black pines, brandishing his staff with frenzied gestures, now giving vent to an inspiration of horrid blasphemy, and now shouting forth such laughter as set all the echoes of the forest laughing like demons around him. The fiend in his own shape is less hideous than when he rages in the breast of man. Thus sped the demoniac on his course, until, quivering among the trees, he saw a red light before him, as when the felled trunks and branches of a clearing have been set on fire, and throw up their lurid blaze against the sky, at the hour of midnight. He paused, in a lull of the tempest that had driven him onward, and heard the swell of what seemed a hymn, rolling solemnly from a distance with the weight of many voices. He knew the tune; it was a familiar one in the choir of the village meeting-house. The verse died heavily away, and was lengthened by a chorus, not of human voices, but of all the sounds of the benighted wilderness pealing in awful harmony together. Goodman Brown cried out, and his cry was lost to his own ear, by its unison with the cry of the desert.

In the interval of silence he stole forward until the light glared full upon his eyes. At one extremity of an open space, hemmed in by the dark wall of the forest, arose a rock, bearing some rude, natural resemblance either to an altar or a pulpit, and surrounded by four blazing pines, their tops aflame, their stems untouched, like candles at an evening meeting. The mass of foliage that had overgrown the summit of the rock was all on fire, blazing high into the night and fitfully illuminating the whole field. Each pendent twig and leafy festoon was in a blaze. As the red light arose and fell, a numerous congregation alternately shone forth, then disappeared in shadow, and again grew, as it were, out of the darkness, peopling the heart of the solitary woods at once.

"A grave and dark-clad company," quoth Goodman Brown.

In truth they were such. Among them, quivering to and fro between gloom and splendor, appeared faces that would be seen next day at the council board of the province, and others which, Sabbath after Sabbath, looked devoutly heavenward, and benignantly over the crowded pews, from the holiest pulpits in the land. Some affirm that the lady of the governor was there. At least there were high dames well known to her, and wives of honored husbands, and widows, a great multitude, and ancient maidens, all of excellent repute, and fair young girls, who trembled lest their mothers should espy them. Either the sudden gleams of light flashing over the obscure field bedazzled Goodman Brown, or he recognized a score of the church members of Salem village famous for their especial sanctity. Good old Deacon Gookin had arrived, and waited at the skirts of that venerable saint, his revered pastor. But, irreverently consorting with these grave, reputable, and pious people, these elders of the church, these chaste dames and dewy virgins, there were men of dissolute lives and women of spotted fame, wretches given over to all mean and filthy vice, and suspected even of horrid crimes. It was strange to see that the good shrank not from the wicked, nor were the sinners abashed by the saints. Scattered also among their pale-faced enemies were the Indian priests, or powwows, who had often scared their native forest with more hideous incantations than any known to English witchcraft.

"But where is Faith?" thought Goodman Brown; and, as hope came into his heart, he trembled.

Another verse of the hymn arose, a slow and mournful strain, such as the pious love, but joined to words which expressed all that our nature can conceive of sin, and darkly hinted at far more. Unfathomable to mere mortals is the lore of fiends. Verse after verse was sung; and still the chorus of the desert swelled between like the deepest tone of a mighty organ; and with the final peal of that dreadful anthem there came a sound, as if the roaring wind, the rushing streams, the howling beasts, and every other voice of the unconcerted wilderness were mingling and according with the voice of guilty man in homage to the prince of all. The four blazing pines threw up a loftier flame, and obscurely discovered shapes and visages of horror on the smoke wreaths above the impious assembly. At the same moment the fire on the rock shot redly forth and formed a glowing arch above its base, where now appeared a figure. With reverence be it spoken, the figure bore no slight similitude, both in garb and manner, to some grave divine[4] of the New England churches.

"Bring forth the converts!" cried a voice that echoed through the field and rolled into the forest.

60 At the word, Goodman Brown stepped forth from the shadow of the trees and approached the congregation, with whom he felt a loathful brotherhood by the sympathy of all that was wicked in his heart. He could have well-nigh sworn that the shape of his own dead father beckoned him to advance, looking downward from a smoke wreath, while a woman, with dim features of despair, threw out her hand to warn him back. Was it his mother? But he had no power to retreat one step, nor to resist, even in thought, when the minister and good old Deacon Gookin seized his arms and led him to the blazing rock. Thither came also the slender form of a veiled female, led between Goody Cloyse, that pious teacher of the catechism, and Martha Carrier, who had received the devil's promise to be queen of hell. A rampant hag was she. And there stood the proselytes beneath the canopy of fire.

"Welcome, my children," said the dark figure, "to the communion of your race. Ye have found thus young your nature and your destiny. My children, look behind you!"

They turned; and flashing forth, as it were, in a sheet of flame, the fiend worshippers were seen; the smile of welcome gleamed darkly on every visage.

"There," resumed the sable form, "are all whom ye have reverenced from youth. Ye deemed them holier than yourselves and shrank from your own sin, contrasting it with their lives of righteousness and prayerful aspirations heavenward. Yet here are they all in my worshipping assembly. This night it shall be granted you to know their secret deeds: how hoary-bearded elders of the church have whispered wanton words to the young maids of their households; how many a woman, eager for widows' weeds, has given her husband a drink at bedtime and let him sleep his last sleep in her bosom; how beardless youths have made haste to inherit their fathers' wealth; and how fair damsels — blush not, sweet ones — have dug little graves in the garden, and bidden me, the sole guest, to an infant's funeral. By the sympathy of your human hearts for sin ye shall scent out all the places — whether in church, bed-chamber, street, field, or forest — where crime has been committed, and shall exult to behold the whole earth one stain of guilt, one mighty blood spot. Far more than this. It shall be yours to penetrate, in every bosom, the deep mystery of sin, the fountain of all wicked arts, and which inexhaustibly supplies more evil impulses than human power — than my power at its utmost — can make manifest in deeds. And now, my children, look upon each other."

[4] Theologian, or member of the clergy. — Eds.

They did so; and, by the blaze of the hell-kindled torches, the wretched man beheld his Faith, and the wife her husband, trembling before that unhallowed altar.

65 "Lo, there ye stand, my children," said the figure, in a deep and solemn tone, almost sad with its despairing awfulness, as if his once angelic nature could yet mourn for our miserable race. "Depending upon one another's hearts, ye had still hoped that virtue were not all a dream. Now are ye undeceived. Evil is the nature of mankind. Evil must be your only happiness. Welcome again, my children, to the communion of your race."

"Welcome," repeated the fiend worshippers, in one cry of despair and triumph.

And there they stood, the only pair, as it seemed, who were yet hesitating on the verge of wickedness in this dark world. A basin was hollowed, naturally, in the rock. Did it contain water, reddened by the lurid light? or was it blood? or, perchance, a liquid flame? Herein did the shape of evil dip his hand and prepare to lay the mark of baptism upon their foreheads, that they might be partakers of the mystery of sin, more conscious of the secret guilt of others, both in deed and thought, than they could now be of their own. The husband cast one look at his pale wife, and Faith at him. What polluted wretches would the next glance show them to each other, shuddering alike at what they disclosed and what they saw!

"Faith! Faith!" cried the husband, "look up to heaven, and resist the wicked one."

Whether Faith obeyed he knew not. Hardly had he spoken when he found himself amid calm night and solitude, listening to a roar of the wind which died heavily away through the forest. He staggered against the rock, and felt it chill and damp; while a hanging twig, that had been all on fire, besprinkled his cheek with the coldest dew.

70 The next morning young Goodman Brown came slowly into the street of Salem village, staring around him like a bewildered man. The good old minister was taking a walk along the

Kate Beaton

In this panel from her cartoon rendering of the tale of "Young Goodman Brown," Canadian illustrator Kate Beaton portrays Goodman's encounter with Faith near the end of the story.

What is Beaton's interpretation of the central character's experience? Do you find it a fresh contemporary update that brings the story to life for today's readers, a shallow reading of a complex text, a clever satire, a combination of these, or something else entirely? Use evidence from both the image and the story to explain your answer.

graveyard to get an appetite for breakfast and meditate his sermon, and bestowed a blessing, as he passed, on Goodman Brown. He shrank from the venerable saint as if to avoid an anathema. Old Deacon Gookin was at domestic worship, and the holy words of his prayer were heard through the open window. "What God doth the wizard pray to?" quoth Goodman Brown. Goody Cloyse, that excellent old Christian, stood in the early sunshine at her own lattice, catechizing a little girl who had brought her a pint of morning's milk. Goodman Brown snatched away the child as from the grasp of the fiend himself. Turning the corner by the meeting-house, he spied the head of Faith, with the pink ribbons, gazing anxiously forth, and bursting into such joy at sight of him that she skipped along the street and almost kissed her husband before the whole village. But Goodman Brown looked sternly and sadly into her face, and passed on without a greeting.

Had Goodman Brown fallen asleep in the forest, and only dreamed a wild dream of a witch-meeting?

Be it so if you will; but, alas! it was a dream of evil omen for young Goodman Brown. A stern, a sad, a darkly meditative, a distrustful, if not a desperate man did he become from the night of that fearful dream. On the Sabbath day, when the congregation were singing a holy psalm, he could not listen because an anthem of sin rushed loudly upon his ear and drowned all the blessed strain. When the minister spoke from the pulpit with power and fervid eloquence, and, with his hand on the open Bible, of the sacred truths of our religion, and of saint-like lives and triumphant deaths, and of future bliss or misery unutterable, then did Goodman Brown turn pale, dreading lest the roof should thunder down upon the gray blasphemer and his hearers. Often, awaking suddenly at midnight, he shrank from the bosom of Faith; and at morning or eventide, when the family knelt down at prayer, he scowled and muttered to himself, and gazed sternly at his wife, and turned away. And when he had lived long, and was borne to his grave a hoary corpse, followed by Faith, an aged woman, and children and grandchildren, a goodly procession, besides neighbors not a few, they carved no hopeful verse upon his tombstone, for his dying hour was gloom. ■

1835

Understanding and Interpreting

1. **AP® Character.** What do the names Goodman Brown and Faith suggest to you?
2. **AP® Setting.** In the opening paragraphs to the story, what contrasts does Nathaniel Hawthorne draw between the domestic setting of a young married couple and the forest to which Goodman is drawn?
3. **AP® Character and Narration.** What do you learn about Goodman Brown's "fellow-traveller" in terms of both appearance and behavior upon their first meeting?
4. **AP® Character and Narration.** What conflicts and confusions does Goodman Brown feel as he encounters Goody Cloyse, then leaders of his community, and finally Faith? How do his emotions deepen with each encounter?
5. **AP® Character.** In what ways is the devil's congregation in the forest both repulsive and compelling to Goodman Brown?

6. **AP® Character and Narration.** Ultimately, what is the nature of Goodman Brown's quest? The narrator describes him as being "conscious of the guilty purpose that had brought him thither, though now so happily turned from it" (par. 41). What was his "guilty purpose"?
7. **AP® Character and Narration.** Paragraph 53 begins, "In truth, all through the haunted forest, there could be nothing more frightful than the figure of Goodman Brown." Does that description refer more to how others might see him or how he has come to see himself? How does this statement affect your response: "The fiend in his own shape is less hideous than when he rages in the breast of man"?
8. **AP® Character and Narration.** Paragraph 71 reads as a single question: "Had Goodman Brown fallen asleep in the forest, and only dreamed a wild dream of a witch-meeting?" Based on your interpretation of the story, what is your answer to this question? Does the question of whether or not the experience was "real" matter to Goodman? Explain, using evidence from the text.
9. **AP® Character.** Why, for the rest of his life, does Goodman Brown become a "stern, a sad, a darkly meditative, a distrustful, if not a desperate man" (par. 72)?

Analyzing Language, Style, and Structure

1. **Vocabulary in Context.** When Goodman Brown returns to Salem, he "shrank from the venerable saint [his minister] as if to avoid an anathema" (par. 70). The common meaning of *anathema* is something or someone that is vehemently disliked. The word also carries a religious connotation of being cursed, even excommunicated. How do the denotative and connotative meanings of this word add a layer of meaning to this scene?
2. **AP® Character and Figurative Language.** Is Faith a fully developed character or a symbol? Explain in terms of her appearance, behavior, and influence on her husband. Support your response with textual evidence, starting with Goodman Brown's statement, "Faith kept me back a while" (par. 12).
3. **AP® Narration.** How would you describe the narrative point of view in this short story? How would the story be different if it were told by Goodman Brown himself as a first-person narrator?
4. **AP® Figurative Language.** Throughout "Young Goodman Brown," Hawthorne uses contrasting imagery, including the prevalence of dark/light. Identify at least one other example and discuss the effect of contrasting image patterns on the development of the story's meaning.
5. **AP® Character, Structure, and Narration.** During the course of the story, Goodman Brown deliberates, often feels a tension between his sense of what is right and his desire to take a risk, his values for the familiar and his eagerness for a different experience. How do these decision points structure the plot and contribute to meaning?
6. **AP® Setting and Figurative Language.** The forest itself is one of the most significant symbols in a story that includes a number of them. Citing textual evidence, discuss how Hawthorne develops the symbolic complexity of the forest.
7. **AP® Character and Figurative Language.** Hawthorne makes many allusions to the Bible, but none more dramatic than the serpentine staff ("which bore the likeness of a great black snake") of Goodman Brown's "fellow-traveller." How does the biblical allusion to the snake in the Garden of Eden contribute to your interpretation of the character of the fellow traveler?
8. **AP® Structure and Figurative Language.** In what ways does "Young Goodman Brown" fit the category of an allegory? What is the purpose of this particular allegory?

Topics for Composing

1. **AP® FRQ Prose Fiction Analysis.** The following question refers to paragraphs 54–58 of Nathaniel Hawthorne's "Young Goodman Brown," published in 1835. In this passage, the character Goodman Brown observes members of his community participating in a ritual in the forest outside of the town where they live. In a well-written essay, analyze how Hawthorne uses literary elements and techniques to convey Brown's complex perception of this ceremonial event.
2. **AP® FRQ Literary Argument.** Many works of literature feature characters who undertake a journey, both literal and figurative, that depicts their growing complexity as human beings. In some cases, the journey results in greater maturity; in others, disillusionment; in some, a better understanding of the self. In "Young Goodman Brown" by Nathaniel Hawthorne, the main character, Goodman Brown experiences such a journey. In a well-written essay, analyze how his journey into the wilderness contributes to an interpretation of the work as a whole. Do not merely summarize the plot.
3. **AP® Literary Argumentation.** Some contemporary critics who have read "Young Goodman Brown" from a woman's perspective interpret it as a kind of Adam and Eve story in which the women, particularly Faith, have misled men and brought them to their downfall. To what extent do you agree with this interpretation? Use evidence from the text to support your response.
4. **AP® Literary Argumentation.** Herman Melville, author of *Moby-Dick* and a contemporary of Hawthorne, explained his admiration for the "great power of blackness" in Hawthorne's tragic vision:

   > [T]his darkness but gives more effect to the ever-moving dawn, that forever advances through it, and circumnavigates his world . . . this great power of blackness in him derives its force from its appeals to that Calvinistic sense of Innate Depravity and Original Sin, from whose visitations, in some shape or other, no deeply thinking mind is always and wholly free. For in certain moods, no man can weigh this world without throwing in something, somehow like Original Sin, to strike the uneven balance . . . [It is not possible to read "Young Goodman Brown"] without addressing the author in his own words: "it is yours to penetrate in every bosom, the deep mystery of sin."

   What exactly is the source of Hawthorne's power, according to Melville? Do you agree with this assessment? If not, what do you think the source of Hawthorne's power is in "Young Goodman Brown"? Support either Melville's or your own interpretation of the story with evidence from the text.
5. **Speaking and Listening.** Some interpretations of "Young Goodman Brown" are that the devil, Faith, and the rest of the characters each stand for a tendency within Brown himself. Working in small groups, choose one of those characters and discuss the extent to which you support that interpretation. Be prepared to lead a discussion with the full class.
6. **Research.** "Young Goodman Brown" has clear references to the Salem Witch Trials. Some of the minor characters in the story (Goody Cloyse, Martha Carrier, Deacon Gookin) were actual citizens of Salem at that time. After conducting some research into the trials, discuss how this information affects your understanding and interpretation of the events and themes of the story.
7. **Connections.** Describe an experience in which you made either a literal or metaphorical journey that caused your sense of yourself or your community to somehow shift. Provide details that convey what brought about the changes and their significance.

Where Are You Going, Where Have You Been?

Bettmann/Getty Images

Joyce Carol Oates

Joyce Carol Oates (b. 1938) is currently a professor of creative writing at Princeton University. She was the youngest author ever to receive the National Book Award — for her novel *Them* (1969). Oates is highly prolific, having published nearly sixty novels, including several mystery novels under the pseudonyms Rosamond Smith and Lauren Kelly. Her 2014 short story collection, *Lovely, Dark, Deep*, was a finalist for the Pulitzer Prize. Oates is also a literary and social critic who has written on such wide-ranging subjects as the poetry of Emily Dickinson, the fiction of James Joyce, and the life of boxer Mike Tyson.

KEY CONTEXT This story is based on the factual case of a psychopath known as the Pied Piper of Tucson, a man in his thirties who was able to prey on teens in part because he pretended to be one. In an interview with the *New York Times*, Oates described him:

> He charmed his victims as charismatic psychopaths have always charmed their victims, to the bewilderment of others who fancy themselves free of all lunatic attractions. The Pied Piper of Tucson: a trashy dream, a tabloid archetype, sheer artifice, comedy, cartoon — surrounded, however improbably, and finally tragically, by real people.

For Bob Dylan

Her name was Connie. She was fifteen and she had a quick nervous giggling habit of craning her neck to glance into mirrors, or checking other people's faces to make sure her own was all right. Her mother, who noticed everything and knew everything and who hadn't much reason any longer to look at her own face, always scolded Connie about it. "Stop gawking at yourself, who are you? You think you're so pretty?" she would say. Connie would raise her eyebrows at these familiar complaints and look right through her mother, into a shadowy vision of herself as she was right at that moment: she knew she was pretty and that was everything. Her mother had been pretty once too, if you could believe those old snapshots in the album, but now her looks were gone and that was why she was always after Connie.

"Why don't you keep your room clean like your sister? How've you got your hair fixed — what the hell stinks? Hair spray? You don't see your sister using that junk."

Her sister June was twenty-four and still lived at home. She was a secretary in the high school Connie attended, and if that wasn't bad enough — with her in the same building — she was so plain and chunky and steady that Connie had to hear her praised all the time by her mother and her mother's sisters. June did this, June did that, she saved money and helped clean the house and cooked and Connie couldn't do a thing, her mind was all filled with trashy daydreams. Their father was away at work most of the time and when he came home he wanted supper and he read the newspaper at supper and after supper he went to bed. He didn't bother talking much to them, but around his bent head Connie's mother kept picking at her until Connie wished her mother was dead and she herself was dead and it was all over.

"She makes me want to throw up sometimes," she complained to her friends. She had a high, breathless, amused voice which made everything she said a little forced, whether it was sincere or not.

There was one good thing: June went places with girl friends of hers, girls who were just as plain and steady as she, and so when Connie wanted to do that her mother had no objections. The father of Connie's best girl friend drove the girls the three miles to town and left them off at a shopping plaza, so that they could walk through the stores or go to a movie, and when he came to pick them up again at eleven he never bothered to ask what they had done.

5 They must have been familiar sights, walking around that shopping plaza in their shorts and flat ballerina slippers that always scuffed the sidewalk, with charm bracelets jingling on their thin wrists; they would lean together to whisper and laugh secretly if someone passed by who amused or interested them. Connie had long dark blond hair that drew anyone's eye to it, and she wore part of it pulled up on her head and puffed out and the rest of it she let fall down her back. She wore a pullover jersey blouse that looked one way when she was at home and another way when she was away from home. Everything about her had two sides to it, one for home and one for anywhere that was not home: her walk that could be childlike and bobbing, or languid enough to make anyone think she was hearing music in her head, her mouth which was pale and smirking most of the time, but bright and pink on these evenings out, her laugh which was cynical and drawling at home — "Ha, ha, very funny" — but high-pitched and nervous anywhere else, like the jingling of the charms on her bracelet.

Sometimes they did go shopping or to a movie, but sometimes they went across the highway, ducking fast across the busy road, to a drive-in restaurant where older kids hung out. The restaurant was shaped like a big bottle, though squatter than a real bottle, and on its cap was a revolving figure of a grinning boy who held a hamburger aloft. One night in midsummer they ran across, breathless with daring, and right away someone leaned out a car window and invited them over, but it was just a boy from high school they didn't like. It made them feel good to be able to ignore him. They went up through the maze of parked and cruising cars to the bright-lit, fly-infested restaurant, their faces pleased and expectant as if they were entering a sacred building that loomed out of the night to give them what haven and what blessing they yearned for. They sat at the counter and crossed their legs at the ankles, their thin shoulders rigid with excitement, and listened to the music that made everything so good: the music was always in the background like music at a church service, it was something to depend upon.

A boy named Eddie came in to talk with them. He sat backwards on his stool, turning himself jerkily around in semi-circles and then stopping and turning again, and after a while he asked Connie if she would like something to eat. She said she did and so she tapped her friend's arm on her way out — her friend pulled her face up into a brave droll look — and Connie said she would meet her at eleven, across the way. "I just hate to leave her like that," Connie said earnestly, but the boy said that she wouldn't be alone for long. So they went out to his car and on the way Connie couldn't help but let her eyes wander over the windshields and faces all around her, her face gleaming with the joy that had nothing to do with Eddie or even this place; it might have been the music. She drew her shoulders up and sucked in her breath with the pure pleasure of being alive, and just at that moment she happened to glance at a face just a few feet from hers. It was a boy with shaggy black hair, in a convertible jalopy painted gold. He stared at her and then his lips widened into a grin. Connie slit her eyes at him and turned away, but she couldn't help glancing back and there he was still watching her. He wagged a finger and laughed and said, "Gonna get you, baby," and Connie turned away again without Eddie noticing anything.

She spent three hours with him, at the restaurant where they ate hamburgers and drank Cokes in wax cups that were always sweating, and then down an alley a mile or so away, and when he left her off at five to eleven only the movie house was still open at the plaza. Her girl friend was there, talking with a boy. When Connie came up the two girls smiled at each other and Connie said, "How was the movie?" and the girl said, "*You* should know." They rode off with the girl's father, sleepy and pleased, and Connie couldn't help but look at the darkened shopping plaza with its big empty parking lot and its signs that were faded and ghostly now, and over at the drive-in restaurant where cars were still circling tirelessly. She couldn't hear the music at this distance.

Next morning June asked her how the movie was and Connie said, "So-so."

10 She and that girl and occasionally another girl went out several times a week that way, and the rest of the time Connie spent around the house — it was summer vacation — getting in her mother's way and thinking, dreaming, about the boys she met. But all the boys fell back and dissolved into a single face that was not even a face, but an idea, a feeling, mixed up with the urgent insistent pounding of the music and the humid night air of July. Connie's mother kept dragging her back to the daylight by finding things for her to do or saying suddenly, "What's this about the Pettinger girl?"

And Connie would say nervously, "Oh, her. That dope." She always drew thick clear lines between herself and such girls, and her mother was simple and kindly enough to believe her. Her mother was so simple, Connie thought, that it was maybe cruel to fool her so much. Her mother went scuffling around the house in old bedroom slippers and complained over the telephone to one sister about the other, then the other called up and the two of them complained about the third one. If June's name was mentioned her mother's tone was approving, and if Connie's name was mentioned it was disapproving. This did not really mean she disliked Connie and actually Connie thought that her mother preferred her to June because she was prettier, but the two of them kept up a pretense of exasperation, a sense that they were tugging and struggling over something of little value to either of them. Sometimes, over coffee, they were almost friends, but something would come up — some vexation that was like a fly buzzing suddenly around their heads — and their faces went hard with contempt.

One Sunday Connie got up at eleven — none of them bothered with church — and washed her hair so that it could dry all day long, in the sun. Her parents and sister were going to a barbecue at an aunt's house and Connie said no, she wasn't interested, rolling her eyes, to let mother know just what she thought of it. "Stay home alone then," her mother said sharply. Connie sat out back in a lawn chair and watched them drive away, her father quiet and bald, hunched around so that he could back the car out, her mother with a look that was still angry and not at all softened through the windshield, and in the back seat poor old June all dressed up as if she didn't know what a barbecue was, with all the running yelling kids and the flies. Connie sat with her eyes closed in the sun, dreaming and dazed with the warmth about her as if this were a kind of love, the caresses of love, and her mind slipped over onto thoughts of the boy she had been with the night before and how nice he had been, how sweet it always was, not the way someone like June would suppose but sweet, gentle, the way it was in movies and promised in songs; and when she opened her eyes she hardly knew where she was, the back yard ran off into weeds and a fenceline of trees and behind it the sky was perfectly blue and still. The asbestos "ranch house" that was now three years old startled her — it looked small. She shook her head as if to get awake.

It was too hot. She went inside the house and turned on the radio to drown out the quiet. She sat on the edge of her bed, barefoot, and listened for an hour and a half to a program called XYZ Sunday Jamboree, record after record of hard, fast, shrieking songs she sang along with, interspersed by exclamations from "Bobby King": "An' look here you girls at Napoleon's — Son and Charley want you to pay real close attention to this song coming up!"

And Connie paid close attention herself, bathed in a glow of slow-pulsed joy that seemed to rise mysteriously out of the music itself and lay languidly about the airless little room, breathed in and breathed out with each gentle rise and fall of her chest.

After a while she heard a car coming up the drive. She sat up at once, startled, because it couldn't be her father so soon. The gravel kept crunching all the way in from the road — the driveway was long — and Connie ran to the window. It was a car she didn't know. It was an open jalopy, painted a bright gold that caught the sun opaquely. Her heart began to pound and her fingers snatched at her hair, checking it, and she whispered "Christ. Christ," wondering how bad she looked. The car came to a stop at the side door and the horn sounded four short taps as if this were a signal Connie knew.

She went into the kitchen and approached the door slowly, then hung out the screen door, her bare toes curling down off the step. There were two boys in the car and now she recognized the driver: he had shaggy, shabby black hair that looked crazy as a wig and he was grinning at her.

"I ain't late, am I?" he said.

"Who the hell do you think you are?" Connie said.

"Toldja I'd be out, didn't I?"

"I don't even know who you are."

She spoke sullenly, careful to show no interest or pleasure, and he spoke in a fast bright monotone. Connie looked past him to the other boy, taking her time. He had fair brown hair, with a lock that fell onto his forehead. His sideburns gave him a fierce, embarrassed look, but so far he hadn't even bothered to glance at her. Both boys wore sunglasses. The driver's glasses were metallic and mirrored everything in miniature.

"You wanta come for a ride?" he said.

Connie smirked and let her hair fall loose over one shoulder.

"Don'tcha like my car? New paint job," he said. "Hey."

"What?"

"You're cute."

She pretended to fidget, chasing flies away from the door.

"Don'tcha believe me, or what?" he said.

"Look, I don't even know who you are," Connie said in disgust.

"Hey, Ellie's got a radio, see. Mine's broke down." He lifted his friend's arm and showed her the little transistor the boy was holding, and now Connie began to hear the music. It was the same program that was playing inside the house.

"Bobby King?" she said.

"I listen to him all the time. I think he's great."

"He's kind of great," Connie said reluctantly.

"Listen, that guy's *great*. He knows where the action is."

Connie blushed a little, because the glasses made it impossible for her to see just what this boy was looking at. She couldn't decide if she liked him or if he was just a jerk, and so she dawdled in the doorway and wouldn't come down or go back inside. She said, "What's all that stuff painted on your car?"

"Can'tcha read it?" He opened the door very carefully, as if he was afraid it might fall off. He slid out just as carefully, planting his feet firmly on the ground, the tiny metallic world in his glasses slowing down like gelatine hardening and in the midst of it Connie's bright green blouse. "This here is my name, to begin with," he said. ARNOLD FRIEND was written in tar-like black letters on the side, with a drawing of a round grinning face that reminded Connie of a pumpkin, except it wore sunglasses. "I wanta introduce myself, I'm Arnold Friend and that's my real name and I'm gonna be your friend, honey, and inside the car's Ellie Oscar, he's kinda shy." Ellie brought his transistor up to his shoulder and balanced it there. "Now these numbers are a secret code, honey," Arnold Friend explained. He read off the numbers 33, 19, 17 and raised his eyebrows at her to see what she thought of that, but she didn't think much of it. The left rear fender had been smashed and around it was written, on the gleaming gold background: DONE BY CRAZY WOMAN DRIVER. Connie had to laugh at that. Arnold Friend was pleased at her laughter and looked up at her. "Around the other side's a lot more — you wanta come and see them?"

"No."

"Why not?"

"Why should I?"

"Don'tcha wanta see what's on the car? Don'tcha wanta go for a ride?"

"I don't know."

"Why not?"

"I got things to do."

"Like what?"

"Things."

He laughed as if she had said something funny. He slapped his thighs. He was standing in a strange way, leaning back against the car as if he were balancing himself. He wasn't tall, only an inch or so taller than she would be if she came down to him. Connie liked the way he was dressed, which was the way all of them dressed: tight faded jeans stuffed into black, scuffed boots, a belt that pulled his waist in and showed how lean he was, and a white pull-over shirt that was a little soiled and showed the hard small muscles of his arms and shoulders. He looked as if he probably did hard work, lifting and carrying things. Even his neck looked muscular. And his face was a familiar face, somehow: the jaw and chin and cheeks slightly darkened, because he hadn't shaved for a day or two, and the nose long and hawk-like, sniffing as if she were a treat he was going to gobble up and it was all a joke.

Library of Congress Prints & Photographs Division

Connie's first impression of Arnold Friend is that he's familiar to her, maybe even a friend. **How does his clothing, described in paragraph 46, conform to the look popularized by actors such as Marlon Brando, pictured here, in the early 1960s?**

"Connie, you ain't telling the truth. This is your day set aside for a ride with me and you know it," he said, still laughing. The way he straightened and recovered from his fit of laughing showed that it had been all fake.

"How do you know what my name is?" she said suspiciously.

"It's Connie." 50

"Maybe and maybe not."

"I know my Connie," he said, wagging his finger. Now she remembered him even better, back at the restaurant, and her cheeks warmed at the thought of how she sucked in her breath just at the moment she passed him — how she must have looked to him. And he had remembered her. "Ellie and I come out here especially for you," he said. "Ellie can sit in back. How about it?"

"Where?"

"Where what?"

"Where're we going?" 55

He looked at her. He took off the sunglasses and she saw how pale the skin around his eyes was, like holes that were not in shadow but instead in light. His eyes were like chips of broken glass that catch the light in an amiable way. He smiled. It was as if the idea of going for a ride somewhere, to some place, was a new idea to him.

"Just for a ride, Connie sweetheart."

"I never said my name was Connie," she said.

"But I know what it is. I know your name and all about you, lots of things," Arnold Friend said. He had not moved yet but stood still leaning back against the side of his jalopy. "I took a special interest in you, such a pretty girl, and found out all about you like I know your parents and sister are gone somewheres and I know where and how long they're going to be gone, and I know who you were with last night, and your best friend's name is Betty. Right?"

He spoke in a simple lilting voice, exactly as 60
if he were reciting the words to a song. His smile assured her that everything was fine. In the car Ellie turned up the volume on his radio and did not bother to look around at them.

"Ellie can sit in the back seat," Arnold Friend said. He indicated his friend with a casual jerk of his chin, as if Ellie did not count and she could not bother with him.

"How'd you find out all that stuff?" Connie said.

"Listen: Betty Schultz and Tony Fitch and Jimmy Pettinger and Nancy Pettinger," he said, in a chant. "Raymond Stanley and Bob Hutter — "

"Do you know all those kids?"

"I know everybody." 65

"Look, you're kidding. You're not from around here."

"Sure."

"But — how come we never saw you before?"

"Sure you saw me before," he said. He looked down at his boots, as if he were a little offended. "You just don't remember."

"I guess I'd remember you," Connie said. 70

"Yeah?" He looked up at this, beaming. He was pleased. He began to mark time with the music from Ellie's radio, tapping his fists lightly together. Connie looked away from his smile to the car, which was painted so bright it almost hurt her eyes to look at it. She looked at that name, ARNOLD FRIEND. And up at the front fender was an expression that was familiar — MAN THE FLYING SAUCERS. It was an expression kids had used the year before, but didn't use this year. She looked at it for a while as if the words meant something to her that she did not yet know.

"What're you thinking about? Huh?" Arnold Friend demanded. "Not worried about your hair blowing around in the car, are you?"

"No."

"Think I maybe can't drive good?"

"How do I know?" 75

"You're a hard girl to handle. How come?" he said. "Don't you know I'm your friend? Didn't you see me put my sign in the air when you walked by?"

"What sign?"

"My sign." And he drew an X in the air, leaning out toward her. They were maybe ten feet apart. After his hand fell back to his side the X was still in the air, almost visible. Connie let the screen door close and stood perfectly still inside it, listening to the music from her radio and the boy's blend together. She stared at Arnold Friend. He stood there so stiffly relaxed, pretending to be relaxed, with one hand idly on the door handle as if he were keeping himself up that way and had no intention of ever moving again. She recognized most things about him, the tight jeans that showed his thighs and buttocks and the greasy leather boots and the tight shirt, and even that slippery friendly smile of his, that sleepy dreamy smile that all the boys used to get across ideas they didn't want to put into words. She recognized all this and also the singsong way he talked, slightly mocking, kidding, but serious and a little melancholy, and she recognized the way he tapped one fist against the other in homage to the perpetual music behind him. But all these things did not come together.

She said suddenly, "Hey, how old are you?"

80 His smile faded. She could see then that he wasn't a kid, he was much older — thirty, maybe more. At this knowledge her heart began to pound faster.

"That's a crazy thing to ask. Can'tcha see I'm your own age?"

"Like hell you are."

"Or maybe a coupla years older, I'm eighteen."

"Eighteen?" she said doubtfully.

85 He grinned to reassure her and lines appeared at the corners of his mouth. His teeth were big and white. He grinned so broadly his eyes became slits and she saw how thick the lashes were, thick and black as if painted with a black tar-like material. Then he seemed to become embarrassed, abruptly, and looked over his shoulder at Ellie. "*Him*, he's crazy," he said. "Ain't he a riot, he's a nut, a real character." Ellie was still listening to the music. His sunglasses told nothing about what he was thinking. He wore a bright orange shirt unbuttoned halfway to show his chest, which was a pale, bluish chest and not muscular like Arnold Friend's. His shirt collar was turned up all around and the very tips of the collar pointed out past his chin as if they were protecting him. He was pressing the transistor radio up against his ear and sat there in a kind of daze, right in the sun.

"He's kinda strange," Connie said.

"Hey, she says you're kinda strange! Kinda strange!" Arnold Friend cried. He pounded on the car to get Ellie's attention. Ellie turned for the first time and Connie saw with shock that he wasn't a kid either — he had a fair, hairless face, cheeks reddened slightly as if the veins grew too close to the surface of his skin, the face of a forty-year-old baby. Connie felt a wave of dizziness rise in her at this sight and she stared at him as if waiting for something to change the shock of the moment, make it all right again. Ellie's lips kept shaping words, mumbling along with the words blasting his ear.

"Maybe you two better go away," Connie said faintly.

"What? How come?" Arnold Friend cried. "We come out here to take you for a ride. It's Sunday." He had the voice of the man on the radio now. It was the same voice, Connie thought. "Don'tcha know it's Sunday all day and honey, no matter who you were with last night today you're with Arnold Friend and don't you forget it! — Maybe you better step out here," he said, and this last was in a different voice. It was a little flatter, as if the heat was finally getting to him.

90 "No. I got things to do."

"Hey."

"You two better leave."

“We ain’t leaving until you come with us.”

“Like hell I am — ”

95 “Connie, don’t fool around with me. I mean — I mean, don’t fool *around*,” he said, shaking his head. He laughed incredulously. He placed his sunglasses on top of his head, carefully, as if he were indeed wearing a wig, and brought the stems down behind his ears. Connie stared at him, another wave of dizziness and fear rising in her so that for a moment he wasn’t even in focus but was just a blur, standing there against his gold car, and she had the idea that he had driven up the driveway all right but had come from nowhere before that and belonged nowhere and that everything about him and even the music that was so familiar to her was only half real.

“If my father comes and sees you — ”

“He ain’t coming. He’s at a barbecue.”

“How do you know that?”

“Aunt Tillie’s. Right now they’re — uh — they’re drinking. Sitting around,” he said vaguely, squinting as if he were staring all the way to town and over to Aunt Tillie’s back yard. Then the vision seemed to clear and he nodded energetically. “Yeah. Sitting around. There’s your sister in a blue dress, huh? And high heels, the poor sad bitch — nothing like you, sweetheart! And your mother’s helping some fat woman with the corn, they’re cleaning the corn — husking the corn — ”

100 “What fat woman?” Connie cried.

“How do I know what fat woman. I don’t know every goddamn fat woman in the world!” Arnold Friend laughed.

“Oh, that’s Mrs. Hornby. . . . Who invited her?” Connie said. She felt a little light-headed. Her breath was coming quickly.

“She’s too fat. I don’t like them fat. I like them the way you are, honey,” he said, smiling sleepily at her. They stared at each other for a while, through the screen door. He said softly, “Now what you’re going to do is this: you’re going to come out that door. You’re going to sit up front with me and Ellie’s going to sit in the back, the hell with Ellie, right? This isn’t Ellie’s date. You’re my date. I’m your lover, honey.”

Nonsite Petrified Coral with Mirrors, 1971 (petrified coral limestone, mirrors)/ Smithson, Robert (1938-73)/CHRISTIES IMAGES/Private Collection/Bridgeman Images; © 2021 Holt/Smithson Foundation / Licensed by VAGA at Artists Rights Society (ARS), NY

Each of Robert Smithson’s three mirrors multiplies the reflections in the other mirrors, creating a sort of crystal, which also reflects the pieces of coral — fragments of the natural world — piled in the angle where the mirrors meet. **How do the descriptions of Arnold Friend create a sort of mirror effect as Connie works to figure out what is real, who he is, and what she, herself, is?**

“What? You’re crazy — ”

105 “Yes, I’m your lover. You don’t know what that is but you will,” he said. “I know that too. I know all about you. But look: it’s real nice and you couldn’t ask for nobody better than me, or more polite. I always keep my word. I’ll tell you how it is, I’m always nice at first, the first time. I’ll hold you so tight you won’t think you have to try to get away or pretend anything because you’ll know you can’t. And I’ll come inside you where it’s all secret and you’ll give in to me and you’ll love me — ”

“Shut up! You’re crazy!” Connie said. She backed away from the door. She put her hands against her ears as if she’d heard something terrible, something not meant for her. “People don’t talk like that, you’re crazy,” she muttered.

Her heart was almost too big now for her chest and its pumping made sweat break out all over her. She looked out to see Arnold Friend pause and then take a step toward the porch lurching. He almost fell. But, like a clever drunken man, he managed to catch his balance. He wobbled in his high boots and grabbed hold of one of the porch posts.

"Honey?" he said. "You still listening?"

"Get the hell out of here!"

"Be nice, honey. Listen."

"I'm going to call the police — "

He wobbled again and out of the side of his mouth came a fast spat curse, an aside not meant for her to hear. But even this "Christ!" sounded forced. Then he began to smile again. She watched this smile come, awkward as if he were smiling from inside a mask. His whole face was a mask, she thought wildly, tanned down onto his throat but then running out as if he had plastered make-up on his face but had forgotten about his throat.

"Honey — ? Listen, here's how it is. I always tell the truth and I promise you this: I ain't coming in that house after you."

"You better not! I'm going to call the police if you — if you don't — "

"Honey," he said, talking right through her voice, "honey, I'm not coming in there but you are coming out here. You know why?"

She was panting. The kitchen looked like a place she had never seen before, some room she had run inside but which wasn't good enough, wasn't going to help her. The kitchen window had never had a curtain, after three years, and there were dishes in the sink for her to do — probably — and if you ran your hand across the table you'd probably feel something sticky there.

"You listening, honey? Hey?"

" — going to call the police — "

"Soon as you touch the phone I don't need to keep my promise and can come inside. You won't want that."

She rushed forward and tried to lock the door. Her fingers were shaking. "But why lock it," Arnold Friend said gently, talking right into her face. "It's just a screen door. It's just nothing." One of his boots was at a strange angle, as if his foot wasn't in it. It pointed out to the left, bent at the ankle. "I mean, anybody can break through a screen door and glass and wood and iron or anything else if he needs to, anybody at all and specially Arnold Friend. If the place got lit up with a fire, honey, you'd come runnin' out into my arms, right into my arms an' safe at home — like you knew I was your lover and'd stopped fooling around, I don't mind a nice shy girl but I don't like no fooling around." Part of those words were spoken with a slight rhythmic lilt, and Connie somehow recognized them — the echo of a song from last year, about a girl rushing into her boy friend's arms and coming home again —

Connie stood barefoot on the linoleum floor, staring at him. "What do you want?" she whispered.

"I want you," he said.

"What?"

"Seen you that night and thought, that's the one, yes sir. I never needed to look any more."

"But my father's coming back. He's coming to get me. I had to wash my hair first — " She spoke in a dry, rapid voice, hardly raising it for him to hear.

"No, your daddy is not coming and yes, you had to wash your hair and you washed it for me. It's nice and shining and all for me. I thank you, sweetheart," he said, with a mock bow, but again he almost lost his balance. He had to bend and adjust his boots. Evidently his feet did not go all the way down; the boots must have been stuffed with something so that he would seem taller. Connie stared out at him and behind him at Ellie in the car, who seemed to be looking off toward Connie's right, into nothing. Then Ellie said, pulling the words out of the air one after another as if he were just discovering them, "You want me to pull out the phone?"

"Shut your mouth and keep it shut," Arnold Friend said, his face red from bending over or maybe from embarrassment because Connie had seen his boots. "This ain't none of your business."

"What—what are you doing? What do you want?" Connie said. "If I call the police they'll get you, they'll arrest you—"

"Promise was not to come in unless you touch that phone, and I'll keep that promise," he said. He resumed his erect position and tried to force his shoulders back. He sounded like a hero in a movie, declaring something important. He spoke too loudly and it was as if he were speaking to someone behind Connie. "I ain't made plans for coming in that house where I don't belong but just for you to come out to me, the way you should. Don't you know who I am?"

"You're crazy," she whispered. She backed away from the door but did not want to go into another part of the house, as if this would give him permission to come through the door. "What do you . . . You're crazy, you . . ."

"Huh? What're you saying, honey?" 130

Her eyes darted everywhere in the kitchen. She could not remember what it was, this room.

"This is how it is, honey: you come out and we'll drive away, have a nice ride. But if you don't come out we're gonna wait till your people come home and then they're all going to get it."

"You want that telephone pulled out?" Ellie said. He held the radio away from his ear and grimaced, as if without the radio the air was too much for him.

"I toldja shut up, Ellie," Arnold Friend said, "you're deaf, get a hearing aid, right? Fix yourself up. This little girl's no trouble and's gonna be nice to me, so Ellie keep to yourself, this ain't your date—right? Don't hem in on me, don't hog, don't crush, don't bird dog, don't trail me," he said in a rapid, meaningless voice, as if he were running through all the expressions he'd learned but was no longer sure which one of them was in style, then rushing on to new ones, making them up with his eyes closed. "Don't crawl under my fence, don't squeeze in my chipmunk hole, don't sniff my glue, suck my popsicle, keep your own greasy fingers on yourself!" He shaded his eyes and peered in at Connie, who was backed against the kitchen table. "Don't mind him, honey, he's just a creep. He's a dope. Right? I'm the boy for you and like I said, you come out here nice like a lady and give

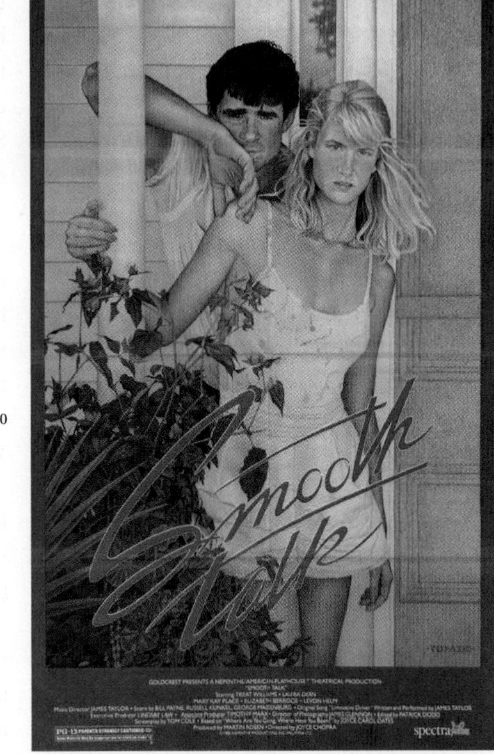

This is a poster for a 1985 film adaptation of "Where Are You Going? Where Have You Been?", directed by Joyce Chopra and starring Laura Dern and Treat Williams. **What aspects of the story does the poster capture? How close do the actors in the poster embody the characters of Connie and Arnold?**

me your hand, and nobody else gets hurt, I mean, your nice old bald-headed daddy and your mummy and your sister in her high heels. Because listen: why bring them in this?"

"Leave me alone," Connie whispered.

"Hey, you know that old woman down the road, the one with the chickens and stuff—you know her?"

"She's dead!"

"Dead? What? You know her?" Arnold Friend said.

"She's dead—"

"Don't you like her?"

"She's dead—she's—she isn't here any more—"

"But don't you like her, I mean, you got something against her? Some grudge or something?" Then his voice dipped as if he were conscious of rudeness. He touched the sunglasses on top of his head as if to make sure they were still there. "Now you be a good girl."

"What are you going to do?"

"Just two things, or maybe three," Arnold Friend said. "But I promise it won't last long and you'll like me that way you get to like people you're close to. You will. It's all over for you here, so come on out. You don't want your people in any trouble, do you?"

She turned and bumped against a chair or something, hurting her leg, but she ran into the back room and picked up the telephone. Something roared in her ear, a tiny roaring, and she was so sick with fear that she could do nothing but listen to it—the telephone was clammy and very heavy and her fingers groped down to the dial but were too weak to touch it. She began to scream into the phone, into the roaring. She cried out, she cried for her mother, she felt her breath start jerking back and forth in her lungs as if it were something Arnold Friend was stabbing her with again and again with no tenderness. A noisy sorrowful wailing rose all about her and she was locked inside it the way she was locked inside this house.

After a while she could hear again. She was sitting on the floor, with her wet back against the wall.

Arnold Friend was saying from the door, "That's a good girl. Put the phone back."

She kicked the phone away from her.

"No, honey. Pick it up. Put it back right."

She picked it up and put it back. The dial tone stopped.

"That's a good girl. Now you come outside."

She was hollow with what had been fear but what was now just an emptiness. All that screaming had blasted it out of her. She sat, one leg cramped under her, and deep inside her brain was something like a pinpoint of light that kept going and would not let her relax. She thought, I'm not going to see my mother again. She thought, I'm not going to sleep in my bed again. Her bright green blouse was all wet.

Arnold Friend said, in a gentle-loud voice that was like a stage voice, "The place where you came from ain't there any more, and where you had in mind to go is cancelled out. This place you are now—inside your daddy's house—is nothing but a cardboard box I can knock down any time. You know that and always did know it. You hear me?"

She thought, I have got to think. I have got to know what to do.

"We'll go out to a nice field, out in the country here where it smells so nice and it's sunny," Arnold Friend said. "I'll have my arms tight around you so you won't need to try to get away and I'll show you what love is like, what it does. The hell with this house! It looks solid all right," he said. He ran a fingernail down the screen and the noise did not make Connie shiver, as it would have the day before. "Now put your hand on your heart, honey. Feel that? That feels solid too but we know better. Be nice to me, be sweet like you can because what else is there for a girl like you but to be sweet and pretty and give in?—and get away before her people get back?"

She felt her pounding heart. Her hand seemed to enclose it. She thought for the first time in her life that it was nothing that was hers, that belonged to her, but just a pounding, living thing inside this body that wasn't really hers either.

"You don't want them to get hurt," Arnold Friend went on. "Now get up, honey. Get up all by yourself."

She stood.

"Now turn this way. That's right. Come over to me — Ellie, put that away, didn't I tell you? You dope. You miserable creepy dope," Arnold Friend said. His words were not angry but only part of an incantation. The incantation was kindly. "Now come out through the kitchen to me honey and let's see a smile, try it, you're a brave sweet little girl and now they're eating corn and hotdogs cooked to bursting over an outdoor fire, and they don't know one thing about you and never did and honey you're better than them because not a one of them would have done this for you."

160 Connie felt the linoleum under her feet; it was cool. She brushed her hair back out of her eyes. Arnold Friend let go of the post tentatively and opened his arms for her, his elbows pointing in toward each other and his wrists limp, to show that this was an embarrassed embrace and a little mocking, he didn't want to make her self-conscious.

She put out her hand against the screen. She watched herself push the door slowly open as if she were back safe somewhere in the other doorway, watching this body and this head of long hair moving out into the sunlight where Arnold Friend waited.

"My sweet little blue-eyed girl," he said in a half-sung sigh that had nothing to do with her brown eyes but was taken up just the same by the vast sunlit reaches of the land behind him and on all sides of him — so much land that Connie had never seen before and did not recognize except to know that she was going to it. ■

1966

Understanding and Interpreting

1. **AP® Character and Narration.** Explain why you think Connie is or is not a typical teenage girl, as Joyce Carol Oates depicts her early in the story. Which of her qualities strike you as specific to an earlier time period, and which seem more characteristic of teenagers in general?
2. **AP® Character and Narration.** How does Connie distance herself from her family and her perception of their values? Pay particular attention to the contrasts Oates draws in paragraph 5.
3. **AP® Character and Narration.** How does Arnold Friend use elements of popular culture to ingratiate himself with Connie? Which elements seem to work? Which frighten her?
4. **AP® Character and Narration.** What part does June play in Connie's characterization? What elements of Connie's character and struggle to construct an identity independent of her family does June's presence emphasize?
5. **AP® Character and Narration.** Examine the relationship between Connie and her mother. Early in the story, Connie thinks her mother "noticed everything and knew everything" (par. 1) but later thinks of her as "simple and kindly" (par. 11). How do Connie's ideas about her mother help develop the characterization of Connie? Do you find Connie's version of her mother's preference for her over June (par. 11) convincing? Explain why or why not.
6. **AP® Character and Narration.** What does Arnold Friend mean when he tells Connie, "The place where you came from ain't there any more, and where you had in mind to go is

cancelled out" (par. 153)? What does *place* mean in this context, and how is Connie's identity destined by it?

7. **AP® Structure and Narration.** Oates does not provide closure in this story. Why? Does the indeterminate ending add to or diminish the story's power?

Analyzing Language, Style, and Structure

1. **Vocabulary in Context.** What is the meaning of the word "incantation" in paragraph 159? How do the connotations of the word explain, in part, why Connie obeys Arnold Friend? How do they connect to the musical motifs of the story?
2. **AP® Character and Narration.** How is Arnold Friend characterized by the external descriptions Oates provides of his physical features and his clothes? What does his dialogue add? Is he a three-dimensional character or a stereotypical one? Examine the passage where Connie first sees him (par. 7). Why is she drawn to Arnold Friend?
3. **AP® Character, Setting, Structure, and Figurative Language.** How is music used throughout the story, especially to develop character and setting? Why is music so important to Connie? What does Oates mean when she writes in paragraph 95 that "even the music that was so familiar to her [Connie] was only half real"?
4. **AP® Narration and Figurative Language.** Why does Oates describe Arnold as having "the voice of the man on the radio now" (par. 89)? What is the significance of Connie's later recognition that Arnold spoke "with a slight rhythmic lilt, . . . [his words] the echo of a song from last year" (par. 119)?
5. **AP® Structure and Narration.** Suspense builds throughout this story. How does Oates generate and control that suspense? At which points does the suspense increase with particular intensity?
6. **AP® Narration.** How does Oates convey the mounting fear Connie feels in the last pages of the story? Note the ways in which she shifts from Connie being the agent of her own actions to Connie being just an observer, such as, "She watched herself push the door slowly open" (par. 161). By the end, is Connie acting out of concern for her family or blind fear? What or who is controlling her actions?
7. **AP® Structure and Figurative Language.** Oates has called this story "a realistic allegory." What does that description mean? What allegorical elements do you see in the story?

Topics for Composing

1. **AP® FRQ Prose Fiction Analysis.** The following question refers to paragraphs 5–6 of Joyce Carol Oates's "Where Are You Going? Where Have You Been?," published in 1966. This passage offers a description of Connie and her friends' social life. Read the passage carefully. Then, in a well-written essay, analyze how Oates uses literary elements and techniques to characterize the girls at this particular moment in their lives.
2. **AP® FRQ Literary Argument.** Works of literature often introduce villains whose charm obscures their evil intent. In "Where Are You Going? Where Have You Been?" Arnold Friend can be considered such a character. In a well-written essay, analyze how Arnold Friend's complex characterization contributes to an interpretation of the work as a whole. Do not merely summarize the plot.
3. **AP® Literary Argumentation.** Do you consider "Where Are You Going? Where Have You Been?" a horror story or a morality tale? Explain your answer in an essay using evidence from the text.

4. **Research.** Oates says she based her story on three Tucson, Arizona, murders committed by Charles Schmid, "the Pied Piper of Tucson," in the 1960s. Research this incident and explore how the facts match the fiction. How does this link to an actual incident influence your reading of the story?
5. **Connections.** Known for her immense output of fiction writing, Oates has written about the American experience from nearly every angle. Read some of her nonfiction writing — her writing on boxing is especially compelling. How does she use the elements of fiction and nonfiction interchangeably? What is the effect on both genres?
6. **Connections.** Oates dedicates the story to Bob Dylan and says she was inspired by his song "It's All Over Now, Baby Blue." Listen to the song, paying special attention to the lyrics. Why do you think Oates found this song compelling?
7. **Multimodal.** Create a *CSI* television episode in which the investigators use forensic evidence to capture Arnold Friend and Ellie.
8. **Connections.** The transistor radio is inextricably tied up with the growing freedom of young people to create their own culture and context by carrying their music with them. In addition to the radio Connie listens to at home, in what parts of the story does music permeate, likely from transistor radios?

Homage

Nadine Gordimer

Ulf Andersen/Getty Images

Novelist and short story writer Nadine Gordimer (1923–2014) was born to Jewish immigrant parents and raised in Springs, South Africa, during a time of intense racial upheaval. Throughout her life, Gordimer often witnessed and wrote about the repressive effects of apartheid, which sought to continue white rule and supremacy in majority-Black South Africa. Gordimer was the author of more than two dozen works of fiction, including novels and collections of short stories, in addition to personal and political essays and literary criticism. Many of her books were banned by the South African government because she challenged the apartheid regime. In 1991, Gordimer won the Nobel Prize for Literature, recognized not only for her contributions to the political activism in her home country, but her masterful writing.

KEY CONTEXT On February 28, 1986, an assassin shot Swedish prime minister Olof Palme in the back as he and his wife were walking home from a movie theater. Although there were suspects, no one was ever tried and convicted for the murder. A week prior to his assassination, Prime Minister Palme delivered the keynote address to the Swedish People's Parliament Against Apartheid held in Stockholm, Sweden, where he declared, "Apartheid cannot be reformed; it has to be abolished." One theory, which has not been proven, is that Palme's murder was carried out by a mercenary hired by the South African government in retaliation for Palme's criticism of apartheid and Sweden's funding of the African National Congress, South Africa's anti-apartheid political party. In 2020 the investigation was finally closed when Swedish prosecutors named a Swedish man with no connections to South Africa, who died by suicide in 2000, as the culprit. However, this conclusion was met with widespread criticism, given the lack of forensic evidence to support it.

Read my lips.

Because I don't speak. You're sitting there, and when the train lurches you seem to bend forward to hear. But I don't speak.

If I could find them I could ask for the other half of the money I was going to get when I'd done it, but they're gone. I don't know where to look. I don't think they're here, anymore, they're in some other country, they move all the time and that's how they find men like me. We leave home because of governments overthrown, a conscript on the wrong side; no work, no bread or oil in the shops, and when we cross a border we're put over another border, and another. What is your final destination? We don't know; we don't know where we can stay, where we won't be sent on somewhere else, from one tent camp to another in a country where you can't get papers.

I don't ever speak.

5 They find us there, in one of these places — they found me and they saved me, they can do anything, they got me in here with papers and a name they gave me; I buried my name, no-one will ever dig it out of me. They told me what they wanted done and they paid me half the money right away. I ate and I had clothes to wear and I had a room in a hotel where people read the menu outside three different restaurants before deciding where to have their meal. There was free shampoo in the bath-room and the key to a private safe where liquor was kept instead of money.

They had prepared everything for me. They had followed him for months and they knew when he went where, at what time — although he was such an important man, he would go out privately with his wife, without his State bodyguards, because he liked to pretend to be an ordinary person or he wanted to be an ordinary person. They knew he didn't understand that that was impossible for him; and that made it possible for them to pay me to do what they paid me to do.

I am nobody; no country counts me in its census, the name they gave me doesn't exist: nobody did what was done. He took time off, with his wife by the arm, to a restaurant with double doors to keep out the cold, the one they went to week after week, and afterwards, although I'd been told they always went home, they turned into a cinema. I waited. I had one beer in a bar, that's all, and I came back. People coming out of the cinema didn't show they recognised him because people in this country like to let their leaders be ordinary. He took his wife, like any ordinary citizen, to that corner where the entrance goes down to the subway trains and as he stood back to let her pass ahead of him I did it. I did it just as they paid me to, as they tested my marksmanship for, right in the back of the skull. As he fell and as I turned to run, I did it again, as they paid me to, to make sure.

She made the mistake of dropping on her knees to him before she looked up to see who had done it. All she could tell the police, the papers and the inquiry was that she saw the back of a man in dark clothing, a leather jacket, leaping up the flight of steps that leads from the side-street. This particular city is one of steep rises and dark alleys. She never saw my face. Years later now, (I read in the papers) she keeps telling people how she never saw the face, she never saw the face of the one who did it, if only she had looked up seconds sooner — they would have been able to find me, the nobody who did it would have become me. She thinks all the time about the back of my head in the dark cap (it was not dark, really, it was a light green-and-brown check, an expensive cap I'd bought with the money, afterwards I threw it in the canal with a stone in it). She thinks of my neck, the bit of my neck she could have seen between the cap and the collar of the leather jacket (I couldn't throw that in the canal, I had it dyed). She thinks of the shine of the leather jacket across my shoulders under the puddle of light from a street-lamp that stands at the top of the flight, and my legs moving so fast I disappear while she screams.

The police arrested a drug-pusher they picked up in the alley at the top of the steps. She couldn't say whether or not it was him because she had no face to remember. The same with others the police raked in from the streets and from those with criminal records and political grievances; no face. So I had nothing to fear. All the time I was being pushed out of one country into another I was afraid, afraid of having no papers, afraid of being questioned, afraid of being hungry, but now I had nothing to be afraid of. I still have nothing to fear. I don't speak.

Tommy Kha

This photograph was taken by Tommy Kha, a Memphis-born, New York City-based artist. The cutouts and masks in his work have roots in Greek drama, though his contemporary themes are related to the immigrant experience, trauma, and the identity of Otherness.

In what ways does this image suggest illusion or fragmentation? Are the hands putting the mask on or taking it off? How does this image relate to the narrator's perspective on his identity and his place in the world?

10 I search the papers for whatever is written about what was done; the inquiry doesn't close, the police, the people, this whole country, keep on searching. I read all the theories; sometimes, like now, in the subway train, I make out on the back of someone's newspaper a new one. An Iranian plot, because of this country's hostility towards some government there. A South African attempt to revenge this country's sanctions against some racist government there, at the time. I could tell who did it, but not why. When they paid me the first half of the money — just like that, right away!— they didn't tell me and I didn't ask. Why should I ask; what government, on any side, anywhere, would take me in. They were the only people to offer me anything.

And then I got only half what they promised. And there isn't much left after five years, five years next month. I've done some sort of work, now and then, so no-one would be wondering where I got the money to pay the rent for my room and so on. Worked at the race course, and once or twice in night clubs. Places where they don't register you with any labour office. What was I thinking I was going to do with the money if I had got it all, as they promised? Get away, somewhere else? When I think of going to some other country, like they did, taking out at the frontier the papers and the name of nobody they gave me, showing my face —

I don't talk.

I don't take up with anybody. Not even a woman. Those places I worked, I would get offers to do things, move stolen goods, handle drugs: people seemed to smell out somehow I'd made myself available. But I am not! I am not here, in this city. This city has never seen my face, only the back of a man leaping up the steps that led to the alley near the subway station. It's said, I know, that you return to the scene of what you did. I never go near, I never walk past that subway station. I've never been back to those steps. When she screamed after me as I disappeared, I disappeared forever.

I couldn't believe it when I read that they were not going to bury him in a cemetery. They put him in the bit of public garden in front of the church that's near the subway station. It's an ordinary-looking place with a few old trees dripping in the rain on gravel paths, right on a main street. There's an engraved stone and a low railing, that's all. And people come in their lunch hour, people come while they're out shopping, people come up out of that subway, out of that cinema, and they tramp over the gravel to go and stand there, where he is. They put flowers down.

I've been there. I've seen. I don't keep away. It's a place like any other place, to me. Every time I go there, following the others over the crunch of feet on the path. I see even young people weeping, they put down their flowers and sometimes sheets of paper with what looks like lines of poems written there (I can't read this language well), and I see that the inquiry goes on, it will not end until they find the face, until the back of nobody turns about. And that will never happen. Now I do what the others do. It's the way to be safe, perfectly safe. Today I bought a cheap bunch of red roses held by an elastic band wound tight between their crushed leaves and wet thorns, and laid it there, before the engraved stone, behind the low railing, where my name is buried with him. ■

1995

Understanding and Interpreting

1. **AP® Narration.** The story opens with the simple sentence, "Read my lips," followed by a sentence referencing "I" and "you." What is the tone that this narrative perspective of direct addresses establishes with the first few sentences?
2. **AP® Character and Narration.** The central character and narrator is a person with no name. What do we learn about him? What physical and tangible details do we learn from his monologue? What is left unexplained? What to you is his most striking quality? Why?
3. **AP® Narration.** The narrator refers to "they" and "them" throughout the story, although we are never told exactly who "they" are. What clues does the narrator share with readers to support a conclusion about who "they" are?
4. **AP® Character and Narration.** Based on your reading of the story, what is the narrator's primary motivation? Is it money? Or are there indications that other factors play into his decision to become "nobody"? If so, what are those factors?
5. **AP® Character and Narration.** What do you think the narrator means when he says, "I do what the others do. It's the way to be safe, perfectly safe" (par. 15)? What does "safe" mean to him?
6. **AP® Character and Narration.** Why does the narrator place flowers on the grave of the man he murdered? Does this final action in the story change your view of him? Why or why not?
7. **AP® Character and Narration.** To what extent does the narrator change during the course of the story? If you believe he changes, what is the nature of that change? If not, what is his central quality or trait, and how does it reflect the themes of the story?

Analyzing Language, Style, and Structure

1. **Vocabulary in Context.** What does the word "homage" mean in a conventional sense? What does it mean as the title of this story, given the context of its plot? How effective is this choice of title for this particular story?

2. **AP® Character and Narration.** What specific textual details reveal the character of the narrator in "Homage"? Pay special attention to the details — concrete and tangible as well as emotional — that seem contradictory. What do these contradictions reveal about the narrator's state of mind? How do they affect your interpretation of the story as a whole?
3. **AP® Structure and Narration.** What is the main conflict in this story? How does the structure of the plot foster and resolve this conflict — or does it? Explain your response with specific reference to the text.
4. **AP® Narration.** What is the effect of the narrator retelling the "incident" — the murder — in such detail that include his own judgments (for example, the man's wife "made the mistake of dropping on her knees")?
5. **AP® Character and Narration.** How reliable is the narrator? Cite specific details, diction, and syntax to support your response.
6. **AP® Structure and Narration.** How does the syntax of the story help shape its tone? Pay particular attention to the short, maybe even abrupt, sentences that punctuate the story.
7. **AP® Figurative Language.** Throughout the story, there are both literal and figurative references to silence, speaking, isolation, and invisibility. Identify two passages that include these literary elements and discuss how they contribute to the meaning of the story as a whole.

Topics for Composing

1. **AP® FRQ Prose Fiction Analysis.** The following question refers to paragraphs 6–9 of Nadine Gordimer's "Homage," published in 1995. In this passage, the narrator recounts his assassination of a high government official. Read the passage carefully. Then, in a well-written essay, analyze how Gordimer uses literary elements and techniques to explore the narrator's complex perspective on his actions and their consequences.
2. **AP® FRQ Literary Argument.** In literary works, isolation or displacement from community often functions as a crucial motivation for a character's choices. In "Homage," the narrator recounts his experience of being displaced from his homeland and his decision to take drastic action. In a well-written essay, analyze how the narrator's understanding of his experiences contributes to an interpretation of the work as a whole. Do not merely summarize the plot.
3. **AP® Literary Argumentation.** Do you interpret "Homage" as having a political agenda or message? If so, what is it? If not, what is its major theme, and why do you think it is not political?
4. **AP® Literary Argumentation.** A critic made the following comments about Gordimer's short stories: "[They] sometimes verge on the uncanny. Although anchored in a contemporary time and place . . . her stories seem to be suspended in a floating in-between allegorical world." In what ways might "Homage" be viewed as an allegory?
5. **Speaking and Listening.** Who or what is to blame in this story — or is blame an appropriate way of framing our reading of the story's events? The narrator is a refugee, but he becomes a paid assassin readily enough. Has he lost his sense of identity, or freely given it up? Working in small groups, explore these questions, arrive at an interpretation, and then report to the full class; be prepared to facilitate a discussion of your interpretation with the entire class.
6. **Connections.** In a lecture on the role of the writer, Gordimer asserts that the writer's "greater responsibility is to society, not to art." Given this line of reasoning, what responsibility to society do you think Gordimer is fulfilling with "Homage"?

7. **Connections.** Through its unique narrative perspective, "Homage" looks at how getting away with violent behavior dehumanizes the perpetrator. Discuss this process at work in a character in another work of fiction or a film that you know well.
8. **Research.** As you read in the Key Context for this story, "Homage" is a fictional account of the assassination of Swedish prime minister Olof Palme in 1986. The case remained open until 2020, six years after Gordimer's death. Research the specifics of the case and discuss how its resolution affects your interpretation of the story's meaning.
9. **Connections.** Compare and contrast the way that Emily Dickinson explores the concept of being "Nobody" in her poem "I'm Nobody! Who are you?" (p. 290) with Gordimer's treatment in "Homage." How do Dickinson's speaker and Gordimer's narrator each view the concept of the self?
10. **Multimodal.** Working in groups, develop an interpretation of "Homage" by pairing at least four passages (or the entire story) with at least eight images — these can be photographs, paintings, posters, collages, and so on. Explain how each image connects to the elements of the text.
11. **Connections.** In the poem "The Terrorist, He Watches" Wislawa Szymborska (p. 893) focuses on the countdown from the time a terrorist plants a bomb until the moment it explodes. Is her depiction of a deliberate act of violence more similar or different than Gordimer's in 'Homage"? Consider the perspectives of the speaker in the poem and the narrator in the short story.

Apollo

Chimamanda Ngozi Adichie

Stephane Cardinale - Corbis/Getty Images

Chimamanda Ngozi Adichie (b. 1977) is a Nigerian writer whose first novel, *Purple Hibiscus* (2003), was awarded the Commonwealth Writers' Prize for Best First Book. Her second novel, *Half of a Yellow Sun* (2006), which is set during the Biafran civil war in Nigeria (1967–1970), won the Orange Prize for Fiction in 2007; the novel is dedicated to her two grandfathers, who died in the war. Adichie was awarded a MacArthur Foundation Fellowship in 2008. *The Thing Around Your Neck*, her first collection of short stories, was published to acclaim in 2009. Her third novel, *Americanah* (2013), won a National Book Critics Circle Award. In 2021, she published a memoir that deals with her father's passing, entitled *Notes on Grief*. Adichie currently divides her time between the United States and Nigeria, where she attended medical school at the University of Nigeria for two years before coming to America. She has also earned an MFA in creative writing from Johns Hopkins University and an MA in African studies from Yale University.

KEY CONTEXT "Apollo" is set in Nigeria and examines issues of social class and sexual orientation as the narrator recalls a formative childhood experience. This story was published shortly after Nigeria's president signed into law the Same Sex Marriage Prohibition Act (SSMPA) in 2014. The SSMPA not only imposes up to fourteen years in jail to same-sex couples who seek to marry, but also threatens business owners with up to ten years in jail if they serve the LGBTQ+ community. Despite wide criticism from world leaders and human rights organizations, the law remains in effect in Nigeria as of 2021.

Twice a month, like a dutiful son, I visited my parents in Enugu, in their small overfurnished flat that grew dark in the afternoon. Retirement had changed them, shrunk them. They were in their late eighties, both small and mahogany-skinned, with a tendency to stoop. They seemed to look more and more alike, as though all the years together had made their features blend and bleed into one another. They even smelled alike — a menthol scent, from the green vial of Vicks VapoRub they passed to each other, carefully rubbing a little in their nostrils and on aching joints. When I arrived, I would find them either sitting out on the veranda overlooking the road or sunk into the living-room sofa, watching Animal Planet. They had a new, simple sense of wonder. They marvelled at the wiliness of wolves, laughed at the cleverness of apes, and asked each other, "Ifukwa?[1] Did you see that?"

They had, too, a new, baffling patience for incredible stories. Once, my mother told me that a sick neighbor in Abba, our ancestral home town, had vomited a grasshopper — a living, writhing insect, which, she said, was proof that wicked relatives had poisoned him. "Somebody texted us a picture of the grasshopper," my father said. They always supported each other's stories. When my father told me that Chief Okeke's young house help had mysteriously died, and the story around town was that the chief had killed the teen-ager and used her liver for moneymaking rituals, my mother added, "They say he used the heart, too."

Fifteen years earlier, my parents would have scoffed at these stories. My mother, a professor of political science, would have said "Nonsense" in her crisp manner, and my father, a professor of education, would merely have snorted, the stories not worth the effort of speech. It puzzled me that they had shed those old selves, and become the kind of Nigerians who told anecdotes about diabetes cured by drinking holy water.

Still, I humored them and half listened to their stories. It was a kind of innocence, this new childhood of old age. They had grown slower with the passing years, and their faces lit up at the sight of me and even their prying questions — "When will you give us a grandchild? When will you bring a girl to introduce to us?" — no longer made me as tense as before. Each time I drove away, on Sunday afternoons after a big lunch of rice and stew, I wondered if it would be the last time I would see them both alive, if before my next visit I would receive a phone call from one of them telling me to come right away. The thought filled me with a nostalgic sadness that stayed with me until I got back to Port Harcourt. And yet I knew that if I had a family, if I could complain about rising school fees as the children of their friends did, then I would not visit them so regularly. I would have nothing for which to make amends.

5 During a visit in November, my parents talked about the increase in armed robberies all over the east. Thieves, too, had to prepare for Christmas. My mother told me how a vigilante mob in Onitsha had caught some thieves, beaten them, and torn off their clothes — how old tires had been thrown over their heads like necklaces, amid shouts for petrol and matches, before the police arrived, fired shots in the air to disperse the crowd, and took the robbers away. My mother paused, and I waited for a supernatural detail that would embellish the story. Perhaps, just as they arrived at the police station, the thieves had turned into vultures and flown away.

"Do you know," she continued, "one of the armed robbers, in fact the ring leader, was Raphael? He was our houseboy years ago. I don't think you'll remember him."

I stared at my mother. "Raphael?"

"It's not surprising he ended like this," my father said. "He didn't start well."

[1] Igbo for "Did you see that?" — Eds.

My mind had been submerged in the foggy lull of my parents' storytelling, and I struggled now with the sharp awakening of memory.

10 My mother said again, "You probably won't remember him. There were so many of those houseboys. You were young."

But I remembered. Of course I remembered Raphael.

• • •

Nothing changed when Raphael came to live with us, not at first. He seemed like all the others, an ordinary-looking teen from a nearby village. The houseboy before him, Hyginus, had been sent home for insulting my mother. Before Hyginus was John, whom I remembered because he had not been sent away; he had broken a plate while washing it and, fearing my mother's anger, had packed his things and fled before she came home from work. All the houseboys treated me with the contemptuous care of people who disliked my mother. Please come and eat your food, they would say — I don't want trouble from Madam. My mother regularly shouted at them, for being slow, stupid, hard of hearing; even her bell-ringing, her thumb resting on the red knob, the shrillness searing through the house, sounded like shouting. How difficult could it be to remember to fry the eggs differently, my father's plain and hers with onions, or to put the Russian dolls back on the same shelf after dusting, or to iron my school uniform properly?

I was my parents' only child, born late in their lives. "When I got pregnant, I thought it was menopause," my mother told me once. I must have been around eight years old, and did not know what "menopause" meant. She had a brusque manner, as did my father; they had about them the air of people who were quick to dismiss others. They had met at the University of Ibadan, married against their families' wishes — his thought her too educated, while hers preferred a wealthier suitor — and spent their lives in an intense and intimate competition over who published more, who won at badminton, who had the last word in an argument. They often read aloud to each other in the evening, from journals or newspapers, standing rather than sitting in the parlor, sometimes pacing, as though about to spring at a new idea. They drank Mateus rosé — that dark, shapely bottle always seemed to be resting on a table near them — and left behind glasses faint with reddish dregs. Throughout my childhood, I worried about not being quick enough to respond when they spoke to me.

• • •

I worried, too, that I did not care for books. Reading did not do to me what it did to my parents, agitating them or turning them into vague beings lost to time, who did not quite notice when I came and went. I read books only enough to satisfy them, and to answer the kinds of unexpected questions that might come in the middle of a meal — What did I think of Pip?[2] Had Ezeulu[3] done the right thing? I sometimes felt like an interloper in our house. My bedroom had bookshelves, stacked with the overflow books that did not fit in the study and the corridor, and they made my stay feel transient, as though I were not quite where I was supposed to be. I sensed my parents' disappointment in the way they glanced at each other when I spoke about a book, and I knew that what I had said was not incorrect but merely ordinary, uncharged with their brand of originality. Going to the staff club with them was an ordeal: I found badminton boring, the shuttlecock seemed to me an unfinished thing, as though whoever had invented the game had stopped halfway.

15 What I loved was kung fu. I watched "Enter the Dragon" so often that I knew all the lines, and I longed to wake up and be Bruce Lee. I would kick and strike at the air, at imaginary enemies

---

[2] The protagonist of the novel *Great Expectations* by Charles Dickens. — Eds.

[3] The protagonist of the novel *Arrow of God* by Chinua Achebe. — Eds.

This still shot from Bruce Lee's 1972 film *The Way of the Dragon* captures the intensity of his fight with Chuck Norris.

How would you describe the dynamic between the two men in this image? Pay attention to their facial features, stance, and environment. To what extent is this dynamic reflected in Okenwa's relationship with Raphael?

who had killed my imaginary family. I would pull my mattress onto the floor, stand on two thick books — usually hardcover copies of "Black Beauty" and "The Water-Babies" — and leap onto the mattress, screaming "Haaa!" like Bruce Lee. One day, in the middle of my practice, I looked up to see Raphael standing in the doorway, watching me. I expected a mild reprimand. He had made my bed that morning, and now the room was in disarray. Instead, he smiled, touched his chest, and brought his finger to his tongue, as though tasting his own blood. My favorite scene. I stared at Raphael with the pure thrill of unexpected pleasure. "I watched the film in the other house where I worked," he said. "Look at this."

He pivoted slightly, leaped up, and kicked, his leg straight and high, his body all taut grace. I was twelve years old and had, until then, never felt that I recognized myself in another person.

• • •

Raphael and I practiced in the back yard, leaping from the raised concrete soakaway[4] and landing on the grass. Raphael told me to suck in my belly, to keep my legs straight and my fingers precise. He taught me to breathe. My previous attempts, in the enclosure of my room, had felt stillborn. Now, outside with Raphael, slicing the air with my arms, I could feel my practice become real, with soft grass below and high sky above, and the endless space mine to conquer. This was truly happening. I could become a black belt one day. Outside the kitchen door was a high open veranda, and I wanted to jump off its flight of six steps and try a flying kick. "No," Raphael said. "That veranda is too high."

• • •

On weekends, if my parents went to the staff club without me, Raphael and I watched Bruce Lee videotapes, Raphael saying, "Watch it! Watch it!" Through his eyes, I saw the films anew; some moves that I had thought merely competent became luminous when he said, "Watch it!" Raphael knew what really mattered; his wisdom lay easy on his skin. He rewound the sections in which Bruce Lee used a nunchaku,[5] and watched unblinking, gasping at the clean aggression of the metal-and-wood weapon.

"I wish I had a nunchaku," I said.

"It is very difficult to use," Raphael said firmly, 20
and I felt almost sorry to have wanted one.

[4] A covered chamber with porous walls that drains excess water by allowing it to soak into the ground slowly. — Eds.

[5] Often known as "nunchucks," a Japanese weapon used in martial arts. — Eds.

Not long afterward, I came back from school one day and Raphael said, "See." From the cupboard he took out a nunchaku — two pieces of wood, cut from an old cleaning mop and sanded down, held together by a spiral of metal springs. He must have been making it for at least a week, in his free time after his housework. He showed me how to use it. His moves seemed clumsy, nothing like Bruce Lee's. I took the nunchaku and tried to swing it, but only ended up with a thump on my chest. Raphael laughed. "You think you can just start like that?" he said. "You have to practice for a long time."

At school, I sat through classes thinking of the wood's smoothness in the palm of my hand. It was after school, with Raphael, that my real life began. My parents did not notice how close Raphael and I had become. All they saw was that I now happened to play outside, and Raphael was, of course, part of the landscape of outside: weeding the garden, washing pots at the water tank. One afternoon, Raphael finished plucking a chicken and interrupted my solo practice on the lawn. "Fight!" he said. A duel began, his hands bare, mine swinging my new weapon. He pushed me hard. One end hit him on the arm, and he looked surprised and then impressed, as if he had not thought me capable. I swung again and again. He feinted and dodged and kicked. Time collapsed. In the end, we were both panting and laughing. I remember, even now, very clearly, the smallness of his shorts that afternoon, and how the muscles ran wiry like ropes down his legs.

On weekends, I ate lunch with my parents. I always ate quickly, dreaming of escape and hoping that they would not turn to me with one of their test questions. At one lunch, Raphael served white disks of boiled yam on a bed of greens, and then cubed pawpaw[6] and pineapple.

"The vegetable was too tough," my mother said. "Are we grass-eating goats?" She glanced at him. "What is wrong with your eyes?"

Zoonar GmbH/Ruslan Gilmanshin/Alamy

This photograph shows a detail of the Belvedere Apollo, a marble statue completed in the first century.

How does Okenwa's observation of and attitude toward Raphael compare to the treatment of Apollo in this image?

It took me a moment to realize that this was not her usual figurative lambasting — "What is that big object blocking your nose?" she would ask, if she noticed a smell in the kitchen that he had not. The whites of Raphael's eyes were red. A painful, unnatural red. He mumbled that an insect had flown into them.

"It looks like Apollo,"[7] my father said.

My mother pushed back her chair and examined Raphael's face. "Ah-ah! Yes, it is. Go to your room and stay there."

Raphael hesitated, as though wanting to finish clearing the plates.

"Go!" my father said. "Before you infect us all with this thing."

Raphael, looking confused, edged away from the table. My mother called him back. "Have you had this before?"

"No, Madam."

[6] Another word for papaya fruit. — Eds.

[7] The popular name for seasonal conjunctivitis, a contagious infection of the eyes. — Eds.

"It's an infection of your conjunctiva, the thing that covers your eyes," she said. In the midst of her Igbo words, "conjunctiva" sounded sharp and dangerous. "We're going to buy medicine for you. Use it three times a day and stay in your room. Don't cook until it clears." Turning to me, she said, "Okenwa, make sure you don't go near him. Apollo is very infectious." From her perfunctory tone, it was clear that she did not imagine I would have any reason to go near Raphael.

Later, my parents drove to the pharmacy in town and came back with a bottle of eye drops, which my father took to Raphael's room in the boys' quarters, at the back of the house, with the air of someone going reluctantly into battle. That evening, I went with my parents to Obollo Road to buy akara[8] for dinner; when we returned, it felt strange not to have Raphael open the front door, not to find him closing the living-room curtains and turning on the lights. In the quiet kitchen, our house seemed emptied of life. As soon as my parents were immersed in themselves, I went out to the boys' quarters and knocked on Raphael's door. It was ajar. He was lying on his back, his narrow bed pushed against the wall, and turned when I came in, surprised, making as if to get up. I had never been in his room before. The exposed light bulb dangling from the ceiling cast sombre shadows.

"What is it?" he asked.

"Nothing. I came to see how you are."

He shrugged and settled back down on the bed. "I don't know how I got this. Don't come close."

But I went close.

"I had Apollo in Primary 3," I said. "It will go quickly, don't worry. Have you used the eye drops this evening?"

He shrugged and said nothing. The bottle of eye drops sat unopened on the table.

"You haven't used them at all?" I asked.

"No."

"Why?"

He avoided looking at me. "I cannot do it."

Raphael, who could disembowel a turkey and lift a full bag of rice, could not drip liquid medicine into his eyes. At first, I was astonished, then amused, and then moved. I looked around his room and was struck by how bare it was — the bed pushed against the wall, a spindly table, a gray metal box in the corner, which I assumed contained all that he owned.

"I will put the drops in for you," I said. I took the bottle and twisted off the cap.

"Don't come close," he said again.

I was already close. I bent over him. He began a frantic blinking.

"Breathe like in kung fu," I said.

I touched his face, gently pulled down his lower left eyelid, and dropped the liquid into his eye. The other lid I pulled more firmly, because he had shut his eyes tight.

"Ndo,"[9] I said. "Sorry."

He opened his eyes and looked at me, and on his face shone something wondrous. I had never felt myself the subject of admiration. It made me think of science class, of a new maize shoot growing greenly toward light. He touched my arm. I turned to go.

"I'll come before I go to school," I said.

In the morning, I slipped into his room, put in his eye drops, and slipped out and into my father's car, to be dropped off at school.

By the third day, Raphael's room felt familiar to me, welcoming, uncluttered by objects. As I put in the drops, I discovered things about him that I guarded closely: the early darkening of hair above his upper lip, the ringworm patch in the hollow between his jaw and his neck. I sat on the edge of his bed and we talked about "Snake in the Monkey's Shadow." We had discussed the film many times, and we said things that we had said before, but in the quiet of his room they felt

---

[8] Fried bean cakes, a popular Nigerian breakfast food and snack. — Eds.

[9] Igbo for "sorry." — Eds.

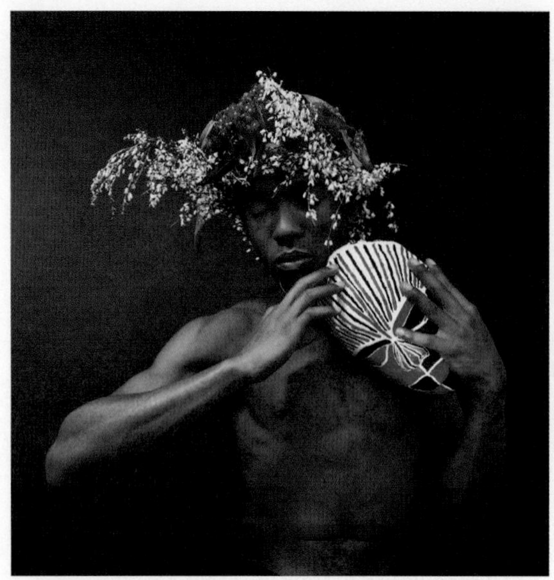

Adebeyi 1989, Rotimi Fani-Kayode, Courtesy Autograph, London

Rotimi Fani-Kayode was an openly gay Nigerian British photographer. This photograph, entitled *Adebiyi* (c. 1989), conveys some of the thematic concerns that permeate his art, including culture, displacement, sexuality, and identity.

How does Fani-Kayode portray Adebiyi, which translates to "royal one," in this image? In what ways might it reflect Okenwa's sense of self?

like secrets. Our voices were low, almost hushed. His body's warmth cast warmth over me.

He got up to demonstrate the snake style, and afterward, both of us laughing, he grasped my hand in his. Then he let go and moved slightly away from me.

"This Apollo has gone," he said.

His eyes were clear. I wished he had not healed so quickly.

• • •

I dreamed of being with Raphael and Bruce Lee in an open field, practicing for a fight. When I woke up, my eyes refused to open. I pried my lids apart. My eyes burned and itched. Each time I blinked, they seemed to produce more pale ugly fluid that coated my lashes. It felt as if heated grains of sand were under my eyelids. I feared that something inside me was thawing that was not supposed to thaw.

My mother shouted at Raphael, "Why did you bring this thing to my house? Why?" It was as though by catching Apollo he had conspired to infect her son. Raphael did not respond. He never did when she shouted at him. She was standing at the top of the stairs, and Raphael was below her.

"How did he manage to give you Apollo from his room?" my father asked me.

"It wasn't Raphael. I think I got it from somebody in my class," I told my parents.

"Who?" I should have known my mother would ask. At that moment, my mind erased all my classmates' names.

"Who?" she asked again.

"Chidi Obi," I said finally, the first name that came to me. He sat in front of me and smelled like old clothes.

"Do you have a headache?" my mother asked.

"Yes."

My father brought me Panadol. My mother telephoned Dr. Igbokwe. My parents were brisk. They stood by my door, watching me drink a cup of Milo that my father had made. I drank quickly. I hoped that they would not drag an armchair into my room, as they did every time I was sick with malaria, when I would wake up with a bitter tongue to find one parent inches from me, silently reading a book, and I would will myself to get well quickly, to free them.

Dr. Igbokwe arrived and shined a torch in my eyes. His cologne was strong; I could smell it long after he'd gone, a heady scent close to alcohol that I imagined would worsen nausea. After he left, my parents created a patient's altar by my bed — on a table covered with cloth, they put a bottle of orange Lucozade, a blue tin of glucose, and freshly peeled oranges on a plastic tray.

They did not bring the armchair, but one of them was home throughout the week that I had

Apollo. They took turns putting in my eye drops, my father more clumsily than my mother, leaving sticky liquid running down my face. They did not know how well I could put in the drops myself. Each time they raised the bottle above my face, I remembered the look in Raphael's eyes that first evening in his room, and I felt haunted by happiness.

My parents closed the curtains and kept my room dark. I was sick of lying down. I wanted to see Raphael, but my mother had banned him from my room, as though he could somehow make my condition worse. I wished that he would come and see me. Surely he could pretend to be putting away a bedsheet, or bringing a bucket to the bathroom. Why didn't he come? He had not even said sorry to me. I strained to hear his voice, but the kitchen was too far away and his voice, when he spoke to my mother, was too low.

Once, after going to the toilet, I tried to sneak downstairs to the kitchen, but my father loomed at the bottom of the stairs.

"Kedu?"[10] He asked. "Are you all right?"

"I want water," I said.

"I'll bring it. Go and lie down."

•••

Finally, my parents went out together. I had been sleeping, and woke up to sense the emptiness of the house. I hurried downstairs and to the kitchen. It, too, was empty. I wondered if Raphael was in the boys' quarters; he was not supposed to go to his room during the day, but maybe he had, now that my parents were away. I went out to the open veranda. I heard Raphael's voice before I saw him, standing near the tank, digging his foot into the sand, talking to Josephine, Professor Nwosu's house help. Professor Nwosu sometimes sent eggs from his poultry, and never let my parents pay for them. Had Josephine brought eggs? She was tall and plump; now she had the air of someone who had already said goodbye but was lingering. With her, Raphael was different — the slouch in his back, the agitated foot. He was shy. She was talking to him with a kind of playful power, as though she could see through him to things that amused her. My reason blurred.

"Raphael!" I called out.

He turned. "Oh. Okenwa. Are you allowed to come downstairs?"

He spoke as though I were a child, as though we had not sat together in his dim room.

"I'm hungry! Where is my food?" It was the first thing that came to me, but in trying to be imperious I sounded shrill.

Josephine's face puckered, as though she were about to break into slow, long laughter. Raphael said something that I could not hear, but it had the sound of betrayal. My parents drove up just then, and suddenly Josephine and Raphael were roused. Josephine hurried out of the compound, and Raphael came toward me. His shirt was stained in the front, orangish, like palm oil from soup. Had my parents not come back, he would have stayed there mumbling by the tank; my presence had changed nothing.

"What do you want to eat?" he asked.

"You didn't come to see me."

"You know Madam said I should not go near you."

Why was he making it all so common and ordinary? I, too, had been asked not to go to his room, and yet I had gone, I had put in his eye drops every day.

"After all, you gave me the Apollo," I said.

"Sorry." He said it dully, his mind elsewhere.

I could hear my mother's voice. I was angry that they were back. My time with Raphael was shortened, and I felt the sensation of a widening crack.

"Do you want plantain or yam?" Raphael asked, not to placate me but as if nothing serious had happened. My eyes were burning again. He came up the steps. I moved away from him, too quickly, to the edge of the veranda, and my rubber slippers shifted under me. Unbalanced,

[10] Igbo for "How are you?" — Eds.

extending beyond the text

Zethu Matebeni, Surya Monro, and Vasu Reddy's 2018 *Queer in Africa: LGBTQI Identities, Citizenship, and Activism* provides a series of essays that explore queer life throughout the continent. "The human and the non-human: African sexuality debate and symbolisms of transgressions" by Senayon Olaoluwa, one of the essays in the book, discusses what life in Nigeria is like for the LGBTQI community.

from Queer in Africa: LGBTQI Identities, Citizenship, and Activism

Senayon Olaoluwa

A more personal account was the one given by Oluwaseun on Sahara TV (2015) during a special report titled "Being Gay in Nigeria" aired in the wake of the passage of the Same-Sex Marriage Prohibition Act in 2013. A Lagos state indigene by birth and residence, Oluwaseun paints a vivid picture of the forbidding atmosphere against homosexuality in Nigeria in the following words:

> Nigeria is not the best place to be a gay person. The society is not very accepting, but we are beginning to see changes. Prior to now people do (sic) not talk about sexuality . . . most people would not believe homosexuals exist in Nigeria . . . but because of the law on homosexuality in Nigeria . . . because of the global phenomenon of it now, we want acceptance here too in Nigeria . . . we want to be recognized . . . we want our human rights . . . we want to be free . . . we want to be able to express ourselves.

He goes further to describe the daily struggle against discrimination, generally as an experience he says is common "on the bus, in school and at place of work". [...] Although Oluwaseun expresses optimism in the face of the Same-Sex Marriage Prohibition Act, because it ironically draws attention in a sense to the existence of homosexuals in Nigeria — there is yet to be seen a sympathetic response for which people "would have been able to share part of our burden." ■

1. **Describe Oluwaseun's characterization of life for an LGBTQI person in Nigeria.**
2. **How does this description compare to your own community's treatment of individuals who are LGBTQI?**
3. **How does the excerpt from Olaoluwa's essay inform your understanding of Okenwa's behavior throughout Adichie's "Apollo"?**

I fell. I landed on my hands and knees, startled by the force of my own weight, and I felt the tears coming before I could stop them. Stiff with humiliation, I did not move.

My parents appeared.

"Okenwa!" my father shouted.

I stayed on the ground, a stone sunk in my knee. "Raphael pushed me."

"What?" My parents said it at the same time, in English. "What?"

There was time. Before my father turned to Raphael, and before my mother lunged at him as if to slap him, and before she told him to go pack his things and leave immediately, there was time. I could have spoken. I could have cut into that silence. I could have said that it was an accident. I could have taken back my lie and left my parents merely to wonder. ■

2015

Understanding and Interpreting

1. **AP® Character and Narration.** Okenwa, the narrator, explains that he visits his parents "[t]wice a month, like a dutiful son" (par. 1) and that if he had fulfilled their wish for him to marry and have a family, he wouldn't visit as often, because he "would have nothing for which to make amends" (par. 4). What do these details suggest about Okenwa? What motivates him? What other details in the story's opening characterize him?
2. **AP® Character and Narration.** Of his childhood, Okenwa says, "I was twelve years old and had, until then, never felt that I recognized myself in another person" (par. 16), and "I had never felt myself the subject of admiration" (par. 51). What do those remarks suggest about the relationship between him and his parents? How would you describe that relationship? Discuss details that support your view.
3. **AP® Character and Narration.** Clearly Okenwa looks up to Raphael. Consider his attitude: would you call it a fascination? A "crush"? Idolatry? An infatuation? Admiration? Something else? Explain, using details from the text to support your perspective.
4. **AP® Narration.** In the final section of the story, Okenwa wonders why Raphael "was . . . making it all so common and ordinary" (par. 83). What does Okenwa mean by this statement?
5. **AP® Character and Setting.** Paragraphs 1–3 provide details about the story's setting, including a description of Okenwa's parents' home and their complex ways of understanding and interpreting the world. How would you describe the setting of this story based on these initial descriptions? Remember that setting not only entails descriptions of place and time, but also the values and ideologies associated with the inhabitants of said place.

Analyzing Language, Style, and Structure

1. **Vocabulary in Context.** Okenwa relates that his parents set up "a patient's altar" (par. 67) at his bedside when he became ill. What do the denotation and connotation of the word "altar" convey about the relationship between the narrator and his parents?
2. **AP® Character and Narration.** When describing his parents, Okenwa says that his mother had "a brusque manner" (par. 13) as did his father. How does this word characterize Okenwa's parents? Does this characterization align with how he presents his parents in other scenes in the story?
3. **AP® Character and Narration.** Okenwa describes how his parents have changed, noting that they seem shrunken, with a "tendency to stoop" (par. 1), and they now have a "baffling patience for incredible stories" (par. 2). Reread the story's opening (pars. 1–11) and look for other specific descriptions of how his parents have changed, as well as how Okenwa regards them. What do these details suggest about how Okenwa views his parents?

4. **AP® Character, Structure, and Narration.** At the end of the first section, when Okenwa's mother suggests he probably doesn't remember Raphael, Okenwa thinks, "But I remembered. Of course I remembered Raphael" (par. 11). What is the effect of this repetition, especially right before the flashback begins? Considering what we learn about Okenwa and his parents in the first section, why do you think Adichie presents the story of Okenwa and Raphael as a flashback?
5. **AP® Character and Figurative Language.** Raphael is an archangel with healing powers who appears in the religious texts of several faiths, including Christianity, Judaism, and Islam. Why do you think Adichie chose to give the houseboy such a name? How does this allusion contribute to your understanding of his character?
6. **AP® Character and Figurative Language.** When Raphael comes down with Apollo, the whites of his eyes are described as "a painful, unnatural red" (par. 25), and Okenwa's mother warns him that the disease is "very infectious" (par. 32). Later, when Raphael has recovered from the infection, he cuts short Okenwa's visit to his room by simply stating, "This Apollo has gone" (par. 55). What possible meaning(s) does Apollo bring to the story? Why do you think the story is named after this infection?
7. **AP® Character and Figurative Language.** In paragraph 79, Okenwa describes the moment when he feels betrayed by Raphael. Read this paragraph closely, noticing the descriptions of Josephine's face, Raphael's shirt, and both characters' movements. Why do you think this moment is described so vividly? How do the details emphasize Okenwa's disappointing experience of betrayal?
8. **AP® Character and Narration.** Compare and contrast the interactions between Okenwa and Raphael in two key scenes: when Okenwa visits an ailing Raphael (pars. 35–52) and when Okenwa approaches Raphael outside in the final section of the story (pars. 75–88). How would you characterize their interaction in each of these two scenes? How do the dialogue and detail in each section create two very different impressions of their relationship?
9. **AP® Character, Structure, and Narration.** Why do you believe Okenwa tells his parents that Raphael pushed him? What do the diction and syntax in the last paragraph convey about Okenwa's decision to lie?
10. **AP® Character and Figurative Language.** References to the famous martial artist Bruce Lee play a central role in this story. As a child, Okenwa "longed to wake up and be Bruce Lee" (par. 15), and Okenwa and Raphael bond over their admiration for him. What is the significance of the many allusions to Bruce Lee throughout the story? What does it say about both Okenwa and Raphael that they are drawn to this powerful figure and mimic his kung fu moves?

Topics for Composing

1. AP® FRQ **Prose Fiction Analysis.** The following question refers to paragraphs 15–22 of Chimamanda Ngozi Adichie's "Apollo," published in 2015. In this passage, Okenwa recalls watching and re-creating Bruce Lee's "Enter the Dragon" with Raphael. Read the passage carefully. Then, in a well-written essay, analyze how Adichie uses literary elements and techniques to characterize the relationship between Okenwa and Raphael.
2. AP® FRQ **Literary Argument.** The significance of certain events is sometimes best understood once time has elapsed. In "Apollo," reflecting on the past allows the narrator to understand the role that Raphael played in his life. In a well-written essay, analyze how Okenwa's recollection of the past contributes to an interpretation of the work as a whole. Do not merely summarize the plot.

3. **AP® Literary Argumentation.** In Chimamanda Ngozi Adichie's 2015 short story "Apollo," Okenwa's relationship with Raphael was more significant to him than his mother ever suspected. Reread the story carefully. Then, in a well-written essay, analyze how Adiche uses literary elements and techniques to characterize the role that Raphael played in Okenwa's life.
4. **AP® Literary Argumentation.** "Apollo" presents readers with a series of tensions or conflicts, including those between parents and children, the rich and the poor, and the present and the past. How does Adichie's use of these tensions contribute to Okenwa's realization about his own identity?
5. **AP® Literary Argumentation.** In some works of literature, a story's conclusion can prompt readers to reconsider their interpretation of its opening passage. In an essay, analyze how the conclusion to "Apollo" reshapes your initial interpretation of its opening scene.
6. **AP® Literary Argumentation.** Adichie admits that she enjoys stories in which adult narrators reflect on childhood events. She says that these are "stories full of the melancholy beauty of retrospect." How does Okenwa's recollection of the past reflect this "melancholy beauty"?
7. **Creative Writing.** Although Okenwa was responsible for Raphael being dismissed from his job, he only provided "silence" when his parents' wrath fell on Raphael. What would Okenwa tell Raphael if he were to meet him as an adult? Write an alternate ending to the story in which Okenwa and Raphael encounter each other by chance as adults. Consider what both characters might say to each other. Would Okenwa apologize for what he did? What might Raphael want to say to Okenwa?
8. **Speaking and Listening.** Do you believe that Raphael should forgive Okenwa for what he did as a child? Can people be forgiven if they don't admit their wrongs and ask for forgiveness? Use textual evidence to explore these questions in discussion with three or four classmates.

Belles Lettres

Nafissa Thompson-Spires

Nafissa Thompson-Spires (b.1983) grew up in Southern California and received her PhD from Vanderbilt University and her MFA in Creative Writing from the University of Illinois. Longlisted for the National Book Award in 2018, *Heads of the Colored People* includes the story "Belles Lettres," which appears below. Its characters appear in other stories in the book.

Roberto Ricciuti/Getty Images

KEY CONTEXT The title of the story is a French phrase that translates to "fine letters," and was originally used to describe beautiful or fine writing. Today, the term is also used as a label for sophisticated works that don't fall into genre categories such as fiction, poetry, or drama. This story takes an unusual form for a contemporary work of short fiction: an epistolary, or a narrative presented as a series of letters between characters.

Dr. Lucinda Johnston, PsyD
Johnston Family Therapy
1005 Knightcrest Rd, Claremont, CA 91711

Tuesday, October 1, 1991

Hello Monica,
I'm sure you remember me from the class field trip to the Getty[1] in September. It has been brought to my attention by Mrs. Watson that Fatima may have started a nasty rumor about my Christinia. I hope to clear this up, as we both know how ugly these things can get. It is true that Christinia's hamster died recently, but it is absolutely not true that it died at Chrissy's hand. At no time has Chrissy ever put Hambone or any of her previous hamsters in the microwave, dryer, or dishwasher. What kind of child would make up something like that?

It sounds — and I say this respectfully, so I hope you won't be offended — like Fatima has had a very hard time getting acclimated here, and that's understandable, but I do hope you will deal with her before any such incidents become frequent. Children who start lying young often end up with longtime patterns of dishonesty.

All best,
Dr. Lucinda Johnston, PsyD
Licensed Therapist
Welcome Wagon, Westwood Primary School
Events Coordinator, Jack and Jill, Claremont Branch

• • •

Monica Willis, PhD
Associate Professor of Education
University of La Verne
1950 Third Street, La Verne, CA 91750

Monday, October 7, 1991

Dear Lucinda,
I apologize for my late reply, but I only found your letter at the bottom of Fatima's backpack when I did my weekly cleaning.

Thank you for writing to me, though I have already spoken with Mrs. Watson, who made it very clear that she never heard Fatima say a thing about Christinia or her dead hamster(s). It was Renee Potts who claimed that Fatima started the rumor. Fatima says she only repeated what Christinia herself told her.

Many of Fatima's stories about Christinia this year and last — which I won't recount here — have been disturbing to say the least, but none as disturbing as Christinia's enjoyment of torturing rodents. Fatima has a strong imagination and writes beautiful lyric poetry — which she started reading at age four — but she does not have a history of lying or telling gruesome stories. And unlike Christinia, she has no history of running off with other girls' shoes while their feet dangle from the monkey bars. I'm absolutely sure that Fatima wouldn't tell stories about Christinia, the hamsters, or the microwave incident if they weren't based on something Christinia had said first.

I appreciate your concerns about Fatima, and even though Christinia has made it much more difficult for her to find friends at Westwood, Fatima will acclimate soon. She's going to a sleepover at Emily's this weekend. Is Christinia going? If so, I hope you will encourage her to play nice.

Best,
Monica Willis, PhD

P.S.
It is true that liars who start young often end up with psychological and social problems of the sort that Christinia has demonstrated over the past year. How lucky for you (and for Christinia) that she has access to psychotherapy through your practice.

• • •

Dr. Lucinda Johnston, PsyD
Johnston Family Therapy
1005 Knightcrest Rd, Claremont CA 91711

Monday, October 7, 1991

[1] An art museum in Los Angeles, California. — Eds.

Dear Monica,
I never expected so much defensiveness when I wrote my original letter. Perhaps you misread it. All I wanted to emphasize is that I understand why a girl in Fatima's position and one with her background would make up such stories. It's hard to get attention in a new place, and Christinia has been established at Westwood for quite a while. There is probably some petty jealousy going on, but I think we can resolve this. I don't know how you did things at Fatima's old school (in Fresno, was it?), but here we try to help the children work through their problems without getting too involved.

I suppose you already know — and have known all along — that Christinia will not attend Emily's party, so there's no need for me to encourage her to "play nice." You've probably heard that history already, so I won't rehash it, but I will say that it wasn't Chrissy's fault that Emily broke her nose when she fell. Besides, it was three years ago. We've given the Kemps our sincerest apologies for Emily's unfortunate accident, and we have moved on.

Finally, and I say this respectfully, but maybe it would be wise to go through Fatima's backpack every night instead of once in a blue moon. I have heard from more than one parent that it smells like eggs.

My best,
Dr. Lucinda Johnston
Licensed Therapist
Author of *Train up a Child*
Welcome Wagon, Westwood Primary School
Events Coordinator, Jack and Jill, Claremont Chapter

• • •

Monica Willis, PhD
Associate Professor of Education
University of La Verne
1950 Third Street, La Verne, CA 91750

October 9, 1991

Dear Lucinda, or should I say Dr. Johnston,
I'd like to resolve this as much as you would, but that won't happen if all of your letters begin and end with backbiting. I asked about Emily's party sincerely and in good conscience, though after speaking to the Kemps, I can see why they would hesitate to invite Christinia. I would ask you to consider this, however: If Fatima is the problem, why is she growing in popularity while Christinia is only growing in girth and the number of casualties associated with her name?

I'm not of the mind that the only two black children in the class should be enemies, nor do I like the attention it draws to them (or their parents) when they're already in a difficult position. I would think that a black woman of your stature and success would understand how isolating work and school environments like Westwood can be for people like us. Jordan and I hesitated to send Fatima to a PWI,[2] but we know the benefits of a school like Westwood. I hoped Christinia and Fatima could be friends and could support each other in this space, but it's been clear since second grade that you and Christinia are not willing to make that work. You could encourage your child to be cordial, however, and less brutal. You could spend more time with her so she doesn't lash out at others. You should get the help you both need in overcoming your tendencies toward pettiness.

I'm sure Fatima would let Christinia into her growing inner circle — even her after-school reading club — if Christinia would only apologize and behave. Jealousy can become a lifelong problem. On that note, I hate to bring this up now, but we were surprised by how poorly Christinia behaved when Fatima's poem won over hers last year. I'd like to make sure we don't end up with a repeat performance of that tantrum when the poetry competition rolls around this year.

As for the hard-boiled egg, we resolved that last spring and bought Fatima a new backpack. And I believe you knew that already.

[2] A primarily white institution. — Eds.

We should talk about some concrete ways we can encourage our girls to get along. Perhaps Mrs. Watson can help, since she has mentioned Chiristinia's problematic behavior before, something to the effect of, "If we don't fix things now, she'll have a hard road ahead of her."

Cheers,
Dr. Monica Willis, PhD
Author of *Every Voice Counts: Helping Children of Color Succeed at Predominantly White Schools*

•••

October 9, 1991

Monica,
Excuse the informal note.

Mrs. Watson told me herself at Pavilions that "it doesn't matter how brilliant the child is. No one will ask about her grades later in life, but they will want to know how well socialized she was." She made it no secret that she was referring to Fatima, not Chrissy.

And to that point, I think you're doing both yourself and Fatima a great injustice by continually emphasizing her "brilliance" over other children. Lots of people skip grades, and skipping kindergarten isn't something to brag about. I doubt that the standards at her old school were as rigorous as those at Westwood. What exactly was she advanced at, naptime? Maybe a stint in kindergarten would have cultivated her social and problem-solving skills so she wouldn't run home and tell her mother everything. Children need strength of character and independence, after all.

If you'll recall, moreover, I was there at the recital where Fatima read her "award-winning poem," and while my doctorates—yes, plural—may not be in literature, I'm pretty sure hardly anyone would call "Butterfly Pie" a work of poetic genius. You can't rhyme "pie" with "pie" multiple times and call that poetry; you just can't, even if you have the excuse of only being in fourth grade.

We are not self-conscious about Christinia's blackness. I attended Westwood myself as a child and was very happy there, even though at the time I was the only black child in the entire K–6 division. Perhaps the kids at Fatima's old school were bad influences on her? Why did she change schools after first grade anyway? That's generally a bad sign.

Isn't your degree, by the way, an EdD?

—Lucinda

•••

October 11, 1991

Lucinda,
It's hard to believe you're not a brain surgeon with your manifold doctorates and strong sense of logic. Fatima changed schools because we moved. Was she supposed to commute from Claremont to Fresno every morning so she could attend her old school?

I'm not surprised if Fatima's subtle wordplay was lost on you, since it's clear reading problems run in the family. Fatima said she saw Christinia struggling in the Panda reading group, and Mrs. Watson hinted that the Iguanas—Fatima's and Emily's group—are reading much more advanced work than *Charlotte's Web* or *The Boxcar Children.* Fatima started on *Little Women* during her own free time and has read through a number of Judy Blume and Beverly Cleary works, even *Ellen Tebbits* and *Otis Spofford* (which I read as a much older girl). And, Fatima has a poem coming out in *Ladybug* magazine in a few months.

Not everyone is suited for literary work. I'm sure you know that from your own writing struggles and the extra effort you had to put behind your research in order for anyone to take it seriously. Isn't there still some kind of issue with your last project and the IRB, or is the issue with Dr. Patel's ex-wife? I know someone who might be able to clear things up for you, if you'd like the help.

My very best,
Monica

•••

October 11, 1991

Monica,

Mrs. Watson said there is absolutely no reading group higher than the Panda group, and that the Iguanas have been paired to minimize their various social anxieties, so I have no idea where you're getting the notion that Fatima's reading is more advanced than Christinia's. Chrissy has no social anxieties, and if she's ever struggled socially, it's because other children don't understand her. And Chrissy read that abridged version of *Little Women* just yesterday on the way home from soccer practice. The pictures took up more space than the words.

But now I see where Fatima's delusions of grandeur come from. You are, unfortunately, enabling your child's arrogance and stifling her growth even at this young age. I write about this very thing in chapter three of my first book, *Caution with Coddling*.

There is no trouble with my current research or the Institutional Review Board.

Regards,
Lucinda

• • •

October 11, 1991

Lucinda,

Christinia may not have notable social anxieties, but that is because she dominates the other children. There has to be some insecurity behind that, perhaps about her size. I heard (and I won't reveal the source, lest you start harassing her, too, but I can tell you it was not Fatima) that Christinia steals other kids' lunch scraps from the cafeteria and bullied that poor kid with the unfortunate ears into giving her all of his pepperoni for the next month.

I really hope that in addition to help for her lies and early signs of psychosis, you will get Christinia some help for her weight problem before she ends up — and I say this respectfully, so I hope you won't be offended in the least — like you. Children do pick these things up from their mothers.

If by your "first book," you mean your unpublished dissertation, I've heard plenty about it and the unsavory circumstances of your defense. Wasn't Dr. Patel married when he joined your committee and divorced by the end of it? Is that why you say your oldest child, Thaniel, has "good hair" and why Christinia is always bragging about having "Indian in my blood," despite those naps in her head? I thought she meant a different kind of Indian, but now things are clearer. Does Mr. Johnston know those may not be his children, or is he in on the ruse with Dr. Patel?

Take care,
Monica

• • •

Jack and Jill of America is an African American organization founded in 1938. Its objectives include providing Black children with "constructive educational, cultural, civic, health, recreational and social programs." **What do you notice about the symbols in the Jack and Jill of America logo? How do these symbols connect to the development of the relationship between the families in "Belles Lettres"?**

October 12, 1991

Monica,

I'm not going to dignify most of your comments with a response.

This will be my last letter, because I can see I'm not going to get anywhere with you; there's some kind of blockage there that I really think you should explore with a licensed professional, especially if you call yourself a professor. How many generations of college students will go on to harm others because of your bad pedagogy?

It's funny to me that you would try to reactivate those rumors about my strictly professional working relationship with Dr. Patel, especially since we've all heard things about Fatima's biological father. Let's see: three kids, two of them with Anglo names, and one with an Arabic one; two kids with Mr. Willis's features, one kid (Fatima) with a more "African look." Mathematically speaking, it seems you picked up more on your travels to Africa than those seventies-style caftans you insist on wearing.

To your point about Chrissy's weight, we are working with a children's nutritionist who specializes in lymphatic disorders.

At one time I wondered if we were too harsh in recommending that you and your family wait another year before joining our Jack and Jill chapter, but I can see now that we were right. I'm afraid I can never recommend you for our club. You display a volatile combination of residual ghetto and uppity Negress,[3] and that will be your undoing, if Fatima isn't.

Sincerely,
Dr. Lucinda M. Johnston
Licensed Therapist
Author of *Train up a Child*
Welcome Wagon, Westwood Primary School
Events Coordinator, Jack and Jill, Claremont Chapter

• • •

October 13, 1991

Lucinda,

I'm not even going to respond to that.

But I will say that if someone here is uppity, it's the one of us with two little brats who have run off three au pairs. Who even uses that term? If they're not French (and I'm pretty sure your cousin Shaquanna isn't) they're nannies! Nannies! And if they're your own relatives, then they're just babysitters or bums who need a hookup. This bourgieness[4] and the way it keeps you from connecting with your kids is half of your problem; the other half, you probably can't fix without medication. Good thing you can write prescriptions. Oh wait, you're not that kind of doctor.

I've been forthright about Fatima's biological father, but I certainly don't appreciate Christinia's relentless and uneducated use of the phrase "African booty-scratcher."

And how can I be "uppity" when I've never had any help and started out as a single parent before marrying Jordan? If putting myself through school and becoming the highest-educated person in my family with no help but God's makes me uppity, then so be it. We are humble people, in spite of our education and finances, and we have more class in our excrement than you have in your whole hamster-murdering family.

And yes, there is a bit of the ghetto still left in me, enough to tell you who can finish the fight if it gets to that point. We're never too far from Oakland or the Southside.

Let's keep it real,
Monica

• • •

[3] A racist phrase that reflects a belief that Black women should be subservient to white people. — Eds.

[4] Derived from the French word *bourgeoisie*, which translates to "middle class" — Eds.

October 13, 1991

Monica,
I do believe that was a threat. The Claremont Police Department will not take this lightly.

While I don't approve of Chrissy's use of the term "African booty-scratcher," she was only stooping to Fatima's level when she used it. As they say, if the butt itches . . .

I don't know where you get this "African folklore" Fatima has been spreading around the school, but I should think that no educated person would tell stories of the Mamie Waters who will "snatch you baldheaded" if you go underwater. It took me hours to console Christinia and convince her that her delayed hair growth is unrelated to her swimming lessons or any mythical African mermaids.

This is one of the first depictions of the water deity Mami Wata, venerated by West, Central, and Southern African cultures, as well as in the African diaspora. Usually, but not always, depicted as female, Mami Wata is representative of water, the sea, mermaids, markets, divination, healing, luck, money, and music.
Why might Lucinda be provoked by the suggestion that Christinia's hair problems are caused by this goddess?

And tell Fatima to stop pinning notes to the inside of Chrissy's bookbag when she's not looking. Chrissy could injure herself on a dirty safety pin, knowing you people, and end up with hepatitis A, B, or C, or worse. And tell her to stop harassing Chrissy with pitiful insults about her appearance and "dark-skinded self."

I've tried to resolve our differences by working directly and exclusively with you and Mrs. Watson, but I will have no choice but to contact Principal Lee — in addition to the police — if this persists.

—Lucinda

• • •

October 14, 1991

Lucinda,
Only you would suggest something so disgusting as intentionally injuring a child with a dirty safety pin, but then again, it was Christinia who put that tack on Renee Potts's chair last year and caused her to need a tetanus shot. Perverse minds think alike, apparently.

I can say with complete assurance that Fatima would never make fun of someone for being too dark, nor would she use the word "skinded" in a sentence. In fact, she came home crying last year when Christinia called her blacky, but I told her to forgive Christinia.

Jordan and I have never raised Fatima or any of our children to be color struck, and that's part of why we would never participate in an organization such as Jack and Jill. We only applied because we thought we might find like-minded black friends here, but if you are their representative, we'll pass. The paper-bag test[5] may be long gone, but the slave mentalities are not. And your Chrissy is baldheaded because you don't know how to do your own hair, let alone hers. Don't blame the Mami Wata for any of that.

Now I see that Christinia is blaming Fatima for many of the things she (Christinia) is doing herself. You probably haven't read that Shirley Jackson story "Charles,"[6] have you? I would imagine it's too difficult for you to process, but sometimes children — especially those who don't get enough support at home — do these things.

Lose my number and address, and stop making your kid do your dirty work,

M

•••

October 14, 1991

Monica,
Turn blue.
Turn blue.
Turn blue, blue, blue.

Look, I've written a poem. Perhaps I should send it to *Ladybug* magazine.

Love,
Lucinda

•••

October 15, 1991

Lucinda,
You need Jesus. Do not write to me again, or I will contact my lawyer.

I've asked Mrs. Watson to check Fatima's backpack for correspondence from you, and I have made it clear that I do not want further contact from you or Christinia. You are not to speak to Fatima either.

Monica
Jack and Jill
Claremont Chapter
1402 Wedgewood Ave, Claremont, CA 91711

•••

Drs. Jordan and Monica Willis
730 N. Briarwood Ave
Claremont, CA 91711

October 15, 1991

Dear Drs. Willis,
We would like to formally invite you and yours to our annual Jack and Jill Gala, October 25, 1991. Attire is black tie. Please respond using the enclosed notecard. We hope to see you there.

If you have received this invitation, it is in error.

Anonymous

•••

October 18, 1991

Lucinda,
I'm beginning to think you are insane. There is absolutely no way that Fatima called Christinia's grandmother (may she rest in peace) the "b" word, nor did she call her a "batch." And I'm sure she never said, "I'm glad she's dead." We don't expose Fatima to bad language. Our child is not the one who brags about killing hamsters and putting them on roller coasters to see if their eyes pop out.

It's a shame you and Christinia have so much trouble writing and reading, because these stories could rival the best of any true-crime stories out there. And that fact should scare you, because it's the ones who start

---

[5] The discriminatory practice within the African American community of comparing skin color to a brown paper bag. It was used most frequently during the first half of the twentieth century. People with skin darker than a paper bag would be denied entrance to clubs, educational institutions, parties, and so on. The practice reinforced a caste-like system within African American communities, where those with lighter skin have historically had more privileges than those with darker skin. — Eds.

[6] In this story, a little boy tells his mother hair-raising tales about a badly behaved boy in his class named Charles. When the mother meets the teacher, she learns that there is no one named Charles in the class. — Eds.

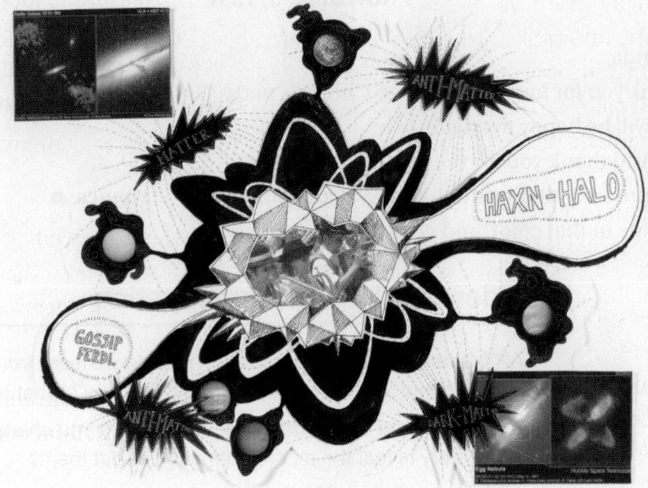

What does this multimedia work by German artist Björn Dahlem say to you about gossip? Is there a parallel to the way the mothers use gossip in "Belles Lettres"? Explain.

out with rodents who eventually graduate to the babies and the grandparents, may they rest in peace (!). Where will Christinia be in ten years, and do you want to see her get to that point?

I'm requesting a meeting with Principal Lee, Mrs. Watson, and you and Mr. Johnston so that we can nip this crazy mess in the bud once and for all.

Monica

•••

Drs. Jordan and Monica Willis
730 N. Briarwood Ave
Claremont, CA 91711

October 21, 1991

CC: Michelle Watson

Dear Mrs. Johnston and Mrs. Willis:
It has come to my attention that your respective daughters, Christinia and Fatima, engaged in a brutal fistfight at school. As you know, this behavior violates not only the Westwood code of conduct, but also our core values as a school, and is punishable by expulsion.

I am sending this letter as a follow-up to the discussion I had with each of you over the phone. I would like to meet with the two of you and Mrs. Watson ASAP. My secretary will schedule.

Sincerely,
Principal Lee

Albert Lee, Principal
Westwood Primary and Secondary School
201 Highland Hills, Claremont, CA 91711

•••

Drs. Jordan and Monica Willis
730 N. Briarwood Ave
Claremont, CA 91711

October 25, 1991

Dear Drs. Willis:
The school's board and I thank you for your generous donation and for agreeing to serve on the Westwood Welcome Wagon. Given the sharp improvement of your child's behavior, we can agree to rescind our threat of Fatima's expulsion from school.

The reputation of our school depends on the efforts of involved parents like yourself.

Sincerely,
Principal Lee

•••

November 3, 1991

Lucinda,

Thank you for inviting Fatima to Chrissy's party. She will be happy to attend.

And thank you for the lovely fruit basket. You are so bad! It's true — Mrs. Watson looks terrible in that color, and yet Principal Lee finds reasons to look. But I won't say anything more in writing.

Jordan and I will discuss the Jack and Jill potluck with you when we see you.

XO,
Monica ■

2018

Understanding and Interpreting

1. **AP® Character and Narration.** What do we learn from the letters between the two mothers about Fatima and Christinia? How old are they? What is their position at their school?
2. **AP® Character and Narration.** How would you characterize the two mothers? What details in the story reveal the most information about them?
3. **AP® Character and Narration.** How do the ways the two mothers identify themselves (the addresses and titles, as well as the signatures) set the stage for the content of each of the letters? Choose a couple of different ones and compare how the writers identify themselves.
4. **AP® Character and Narration.** How do the two mothers use gossip as evidence — or even ammunition? How does gossip suit the purpose of their correspondence?
5. **AP® Character and Setting.** What role does the setting of the school — a PWI — play in the disagreements, eventual hostility, and reconciliation between Monica and Lucinda?
6. **AP® Character, Structure, and Narration.** What do you think enabled the resolution of the differences between Monica and Lucinda that is reflected in the last letter?

Analyzing Language, Style, and Structure

1. **Vocabulary in Context.** In her letter of October 11, Monica brings up gossip about Lucinda's academic career, describing the defense of her graduate thesis as "unsavory." What does "unsavory" suggest here? What does Monica imply is "unsavory" about the circumstances? Why do you think Lucinda says she won't "dignify" Monica's comments with a response (and yet she does)?
2. **AP® Character, Structure, and Narration.** How does the epistolary form affect your interpretation of the story and the perspectives of its main characters? Why might Nafissa Thompson-Spires have chosen it to tell this particular tale?
3. **AP® Character, Structure, and Narration.** Trace the use of rhetorical questions in "Belles Lettres." Do they fit the traditional description of rhetorical questions — that is, questions to which the questioner does not expect an answer, often intended to start a discourse, or as a means of showing the speaker's opinion on a topic? Or are they after something else here? Explain the purpose of at least three of them.
4. **AP® Structure.** Why do you think Thompson-Spires entitled her story "Belles Lettres"? Does the story "Belles Lettres" conform to any of the conventional meanings of the term *belles lettres*? Support your answer with evidence from the story.
5. **AP® Structure and Narration.** How does the tone of the letters shift over the course of the story? What causes the tone to shift in each instance?
6. **AP® Character and Narration.** Compare and contrast the tone and content of Monica's and Lucinda's letters. What do their differences — and points of similarity — suggest about the women and their situation?

7. **AP® Character, Narration, and Figurative Language.** In the letters of October 13 and October 14, both mothers refer to an African water spirit; Lucinda calls her Mamie Waters, and Monica uses the more widely recognized term Mami Wata. How does each woman both invoke the water spirit and reject it? What does their attitude (and spelling) say about their differences — and their similarities?
8. **AP® Character and Figurative Language.** Monica mentions the Shirley Jackson story "Charles" in her letter of October 14. Is Monica's allusion to the story yet another microaggression? What might she be referring to in Christinia's behavior?
9. **AP® Structure and Narration.** How does the tone and content of the final letter reflect the resolution of the problems between Monica and Lucinda? How does it influence your interpretation of the major source of conflict within the story?

Topics for Composing

1. **AP® FRQ Prose Fiction Analysis.** The following question refers to the last three letters — October 21, October 25, and November 3 — in Nafissa Thompson-Spires's "Belles Lettres," published in 2018. In this passage, the antagonistic correspondence between Monica and Lucinda is interrupted by a letter from the school principal with the result that the hostilities between the mothers comes to a halt, at least temporarily. Read the passage carefully. Then, in a well-written essay, analyze how Thompson-Spires uses literary elements and techniques to convey what it takes for the two mothers to resolve their differences.
2. **AP® FRQ Literary Argument.** In many works of literature, characters experience being "the only" or nearly the only. In "Belles Lettres," Fatima and Christinia are the only Black children in their school and, presumably, their mothers Monica and Lucinda are the only Black mothers. In a well-written essay, analyze how the letters between Monica and Lucinda that address and sometimes skirt that issue contribute to an interpretation of the work as a whole. Do not merely summarize the plot.
3. **AP® Literary Argumentation.** Thompson-Spires has written about what she calls the "ethics of satire." In an essay on Lit Hub, she wrote that she "worried about whether people will inadvertently learn 'the wrong lessons' from my attempts at problematizing social and identity constructs." Should this be a concern for writers of satire? Is satire effective if it risks being misread, particularly along socially constructed lines such as race, ethnicity, class, and gender identity? Analyze "Belles Lettres" as a work of satire, and discuss what you believe are the "right lessons" to learn from its portrayal of identity.
4. **Connections.** "Belles Lettres" is part of a collection of short stories titled *Heads of the Colored People*. Fatima and Christinia appear in several of the stories. Try to imagine them based on their mother's correspondence, and then read the stories to get to know the two girls better. Explain how your reading changes your interpretation of the meaning of "Belles Lettres."
5. **Research.** Jack and Jill of America is a Black organization formed in 1938 by a group of mothers who wanted their children to be part of a social and cultural environment with middle-class and upper-middle-class Black families. It is controversial because membership is limited and it has been accused of colorism, or showing preference to Black people with lighter skin. Research the role that colorism has played in social hierarchies within Black communities, both in the past and the present. How does colorism affect the relationship between Monica and Lucinda in "Belles Lettres"? What do you make of the mothers' plans to attend a Jack and Jill potluck at the end of the story in light of what you have learned?
6. **Connections.** Do you consider the correspondence between Monica and Lucinda to be an example of "helicopter parenting"? How involved should parents be in the social and academic lives of their children? Write an essay that describes the extent to which you think parents should or should not be involved. Use evidence from multiple sources in your response.

The Trip

Weike Wang

Weike Wang has an undergraduate degree in chemistry, a doctorate in public policy, and a master of fine arts. Born in China, she lived with her family in Australia and Canada before they moved to the United States when she was eleven. Wang says she rarely gives her characters names, at least in part because she believes she's terrible at doing so. "The Trip" appeared in a 2019 issue of the *New Yorker.*

Beowulf Sheehan

KEY CONTEXT "The Trip" alludes to the Chinese traditional legend of the White Maiden. In the story, a white snake gains immortality and changes her form to become a beautiful woman. Variations in the legend have appeared over hundreds of years, and it has been performed a number of times in Chinese movies, operas, and television shows. After becoming human, the white snake rescues a green snake and the two sometimes assume human form together.

In Beijing, he boiled the water. It was August, so the hottest month of the year. He put the water into a thermos and carried the thermos on a sling. He called himself a cowboy because he thought he looked dumb. Other people in the group carried a thermos, too, though his wife did not. Their tour guide was Felix. Like Felix the Cat,[1] Felix said, and he replied, O.K. He had been to Europe before, the six-hour time change was fine, but when thirteen happened something yellow crusted around his eyes. The bus was air-conditioned. He dozed off, woke up, and by then his wife had finished his cowboy water. On the Great Wall, he had to run, since she was sprinting. She had come here long ago with a cousin. She was trying to show him a specific spot. This spot, when they got there, was where she, admiring the mountains, had learned from her cousin the word for "cool." To not know that word, *shuang*, until she was thirteen, did he know how that felt? But you knew it in English, he wheezed, no oxygen left. She made a face. They sprinted on.

The tour would take them through the big cities. It had been a gift. Her parents, divorced, said, on separate calls, We want your first husband to see China and have good memories from there and sample its regional foods and see the warmth of its people and not hate us civilians should our two great nations ever partake in nuclear war. At least, that was what his wife said she had translated, then paraphrased.

He had not wanted to go, but her family was there, all except for the parents, who now lived in different states. She had no siblings. So, for years, it had been just the three of them under one roof that belonged, depending on the fight, to either Mom or Dad, but in truth belonged to the bank.

Do you know what that's like? she would ask.

5 He did. His parents were divorced, but the divorce had been incredibly normal. They had

[1] A cartoon character originating during the silent film era. — Eds.

not stuck it out, as hers did, until the day their child left for college. When his mother became a nag, his father began to drink. She nagged him about the drinking, and then he had an affair. A most American story, his wife said. She was studying how to write and had read a lot of Cheever.[2]

In Xi'an, he bought bottled water, then shared with her a sausage on a stick that reminded her of childhood. Childhood, she said, and went to get another. Next, they drank something herbal from red tin cans, and he tried to crush his can with his grip, but couldn't, which made her laugh. Their tour guide was Helen. Like Helen of Troy.[3] She said, and he said, Sure. The Terracotta Army impressed him. More so than the Forbidden City — crowded — or the Great Wall. One person in their group got lost. Helen had rushed them down a long road of souvenirs and said, Please don't buy anything, we're already late for pickup. But a tourist called Karl stopped to buy something. The air-conditioned bus then had to drive another loop, but got stuck behind a crash and reappeared two hours later. In those two hours, Helen became silent. Only when his wife spoke to her in Chinese did she reply. All Karl bought was a magnet. At least buy the entire army. At least buy us a terra-cotta chariot. Two hours' wait for a magnet. Fuck that magnet.

• • •

In Chengdu, he drank alcohol. She took him out for hot pot, for which the city was known. Hot pot and pandas. Their tour guide was Shirley. Like Shirley Temple,[4] she said, and he said, All right. Pandas were lazy, he knew, but now understood. A panda's main form of exercise was to eat. He willed one to move and it just shredded bamboo, stalk after stalk. This panda reminded him of his father, or the merged silhouette of his dad and the La-Z-Boy. Instead of bamboo, his father had eaten celery, after his mother threw out the alcohol. Childhood, he said to his wife, and she told him to respect his elders. At the hot-pot restaurant, the staff brought out a cauldron of dark-red water. This is mild spice? she asked, and they said it was. Into the red water they put chili-paste-marinated ribs and hot peppers. She told him she was going to cry. Cry or die? he asked, as he had just a taste and a flamethrower went off in his mouth. The staff brought them a bottle of alcohol. Then a plate of watermelon. Per her translation, they said, All free, please enjoy, and, remember, don't be a pussy.

In Beijing, his mother e-mailed, but he didn't reply.

In Xi'an, his mother texted, and he said yes, they had landed.

10 In Chengdu, his mother called. She wanted to know if he remembered So-and-So. His mother worked at UPS, and So-and-So's Gam-gam had come in to mail a package. Gam-gam said that So-and-So had finally found a job in D.C. She asked his mother to relay a message from So-and-So about their time in high school when they worked at Chick-fil-A and that fun summer selling Aflac insurance. So-and-So used to be his best friend. They had once dated the same girl, who was now So-and-So's wife and obese after three kids. So-and-So used to play football, defense — that field, green year-round, was the most expensive part of their school. Because So-and-So's job was government,

---

[2] A reference to John Cheever (1912–1982), an American fiction writer. — Eds.

[3] Considered the most beautiful woman according to Greek legend, Helen of Troy was indirectly responsible for the Trojan War. — Eds.

[4] Shirley Temple (1928–2014) was an actor best known for her performances as a child. — Eds.

extending beyond the text

Carefully read the following excerpt from *Social Media in Industrial China*, a 2016 book by Dr. Xinyuan Wang, a postdoctoral researcher in the Anthropology Department of the University College London.

from Social Media in Industrial China

Xinyuan Wang

A central concern of social life in China is the process of *zuoren*, which literally means "becoming a person" or "to make oneself a person." The implication of *zuoren* is that a Chinese individual is not born as a full person: only through the process of self-cultivation and socialisation can a person gradually become a moral individual. However, the key to understanding this term is to appreciate that in China this process of becoming a "full" person is highly socialised rather than just an individual pursuit. The relationships between kin, romantic partner, friends, classmates and colleagues all contribute to the very process of "becoming a person." *Zuoren* has never been an individualising concept in Chinese people's lives. On the contrary *zuoren*, as a colloquial term, is frequently used in relation to social life. . . . [O]ne can always hear somebody praising a person as someone who "knows how to *zuoren*" (*hui zuoren*), indicating that this person is good at dealing with social relationships. Accordingly a major criticism applied to someone who is awkward in social life or has difficulties in following social norms is the phrase "doesn't know how to *zuoren*" — literally meaning someone who has not learned how to become a person. . . . On social media people collectively negotiate what personal relationships are and what they want them to be. . . .

Personal relationships are often the main factor that determines people's sense of happiness, confidence and ability to get by in the modern world. ■

1. **How do the socialization processes you have experienced compare to those described here?**
2. **How does the concept of *zuoren* shed light on the motivations of the wife in "The Trip"?**
3. **How might her childhood in the United States not have fully afforded her "the process of *zuoren*"?**

background checks were extensive — did he have a record, did he travel, who were his family and friends. When his mother paused, he said he had to go. But wait, his mother said, you haven't told me anything about China. I want to know what you're doing and eating. What did you do and eat today? What are you going to eat and do tomorrow? Sorry, Mom, he said, I really have to go.

• • •

In Shanghai, they met up with his wife's cousin, who lived alone and worked in a pie shop. Here the prepaid tour ended and they said goodbye to Karl and the others. His wife had booked a room at the Langham. There were no light switches, just a control pad by the bed. The toilet lid lifted each time he passed. In Shanghai, they ate more. Hot pot, grilled fish, barbecue, fried noodles, soup noodles, soup dumplings, regular dumplings, an upscale KFC. He could no longer remember hunger.

The cousin spoke English. At one meal, he asked her about his wife's Chinese and the cousin replied that his wife's Chinese was like that of a toddler.

Sorry? he said.

The cousin said that it was like talking to someone between the ages of three and five.

Oh.

For instance, she and I could not discuss, in Chinese, politics or culture. If I asked her what she thought of the clash between person and state, our preoccupation with status and wealth, our envy of the West, our pride, our tendency to self-criticize, your wife would not know how to respond.

The cousin's English was great. The pie shop was run by an American who, on his study abroad, had discovered that China did not have pie, and thus opened a store to remedy this. His wife said nothing and looked down. Then the cousin laughed and they gan bei-ed.[5] Back at the Langham, he told his wife that she could switch to English with her cousin anytime; they weren't kids. No, his wife said, and that was that.

What do you think about the pies? he asked a little later.

Nothing, she said.

Really? he said. You have no thoughts on the pies?

She said she really didn't.

[5] Made a toast to each other. — Eds.

His mother baked pies and his wife had thoughts on them. Come Thanksgiving, his mother usually made four, and his wife would look at the pies, each a foot in diameter, and ask why four modestly sized people — his mother had remarried — needed four large pies.

Nothing to say at all?

No.

• • •

His mother called, but he was in the shower.

His mother called again, and he picked up. Did he remember this teacher? The teacher had come in to mail a package and mentioned that her son used to be his student. The teacher said her son was the best and possessed a natural mind for math. I wrote his letter of rec, the teacher said, and it was an honor to. In the letter, the teacher wrote about what it meant for someone like her son to have come out of their little town; he emphasized how rare that was. It had come as no surprise to him when he saw in the local paper, which was displayed at the store, that his best student had graduated summa cum laude from Duke, or, later, in the same paper, that he was doing his graduate work at Harvard, his postgraduate work at M.I.T., and then that he had been offered a place at a computational think tank, modelling how blood moves in the body, through arteries and veins, saving lives, and now, most recently, that he had just published his first *Nature* paper — congratulations — which his teacher apologized for not being able to understand, after his mother had sent him a copy. Do you remember his son? his mother asked next. He said he remembered this teacher, wonderful yet firm, but not his son. Well, his mother said, his son teaches math at the community college, where they have lots of Chinese students now. Chinese students from China. Supposedly very lucrative, but I can't imagine why Chinese students would want to come here. Maybe no one told them that there's nothing to do. Listening, he thought,

I love you, Mom, but I don't like you. If he ever told her that, his mother would want to know when, at what point, exactly, he had stopped liking her. He would then have to say that it was gradual. But when did it start? Probably when he was eleven.

He did not read the local paper. His mother sent it to him, but he recycled. Only when a truly absurd headline appeared did he keep it as a reminder. One such headline was "WOMAN KICKED IN FACE BY DEER."

His wife did not get involved. The only time she did was when, one Thanksgiving, he mentioned that he was applying for a passport, as they were going to Europe for vacation. Suddenly, his stepfather got up and unmuted the television. His mother looked at his wife and then at him.

Tell me, his mother said, do the two of you have no interest in seeing the rest of America? Yellowstone. The Grand Canyon. The amount of natural beauty in this country is endless. Then his mother began to reminisce. They used to take road trips and go camping. He used to play cowboys and Indians in the back seat.

We are not trying to say that we do not love Yellowstone, his wife answered. He told his mother that it was just a passport.

We started watching documentaries about China because of you, his mother said to his wife. We loved seeing people eat with chopsticks, and the pandas — we loved seeing them play. We even bought chopsticks. She went to the cupboard. Do you want to use them? His wife looked down, and, seeing his wife look down, he told his mother to stop talking.

Why do I have to stop?

He stared at her.

No, I don't think I want to.

Please stop talking.

What's gotten into you?

Shut up right now.

Later, his wife said that the entire meal was surreal. She found his mother interesting.

This illustration by Jee-ook Choi appeared in the *New Yorker* along with "The Trip."
How do specific details in this image represent major themes in the story?

Someone like her actually exists, she said, almost excited. And these places exist, and your stepdad watches ESPN, and they don't want passports, they've never been on a plane, all those pickup trucks, amazing!

But also, his wife said, somewhat serious, it must be confusing for your mom, how to stay involved without being afraid — impossible now — and fear can manifest in strange ways.

He didn't think it was fear. He told her what he thought it was. Ignorance leads to fear, she said.

That year, his mother invited them, as usual, to the family reunion and he declined. They had a call about it.

So we're not good enough for you anymore.

That's not what I said.

When are you coming back to see me?

You already asked that.

At Duke, he had won an essay contest. He wrote about low expectations. The problem with low expectations, he wrote, is that they will often seem harmless or even kind. He won a thousand dollars. In college, he worked part time. There was a scholarship for first-gen students and advisers told him to apply. He opened the form but thought, If I get this, people will know. If I never tell, who would know? So he didn't apply and accrued ninety thousand dollars in debt.

But what about high expectations? his wife asked. To be groomed for a six-figure career, do you know what that's like? I have a friend, she would start. This friend was locked in a room by his parents until he could do something right.

We need an average, he told her.

I don't want kids, she replied.

• • •

50 In Hangzhou, they met the rest of her family. Both grandmothers were still alive, and many uncles and aunts. A crowd of thirteen was waiting for them, the train-station arrival lane filled with mopeds and cars. Each person wanted to help carry something. In the end, they emptied out a suitcase to give each person a thing to carry. Then they all gathered at one aunt's house, a large apartment with a terrace, to eat. I can't eat any more, he told her, face down on the bed. She said he had to. Per her translation, her family thought all Americans could eat and if he couldn't it would be disappointing. He might be the first and last American they'd ever meet and he had to deliver.

His mother called, but he was eating.

His mother called, but he was on the toilet.

His mother called, but he was out on a run.

In Hangzhou, her cousin took them to see a pagoda. The pagoda had a history, but he zoned out, as all his energy was being used to digest food. He sat down and listened to his stomach. Moments later, his wife and the cousin began to argue. He could make out parts. While admiring West Lake, his wife had said *shuang*, and her cousin had said that that word meant refreshing, not cool. Cool was *ku*, as in ruthless or strong, the Chinese word for "cruel." His wife looked down. But immediately back up. The argument worsened until they had to leave, and, on the bus, it continued. At one point, her cousin turned to him and said in English, Hey, look, I'm arguing with a toddler, after which his wife swung her hand across the cousin's mouth. Then no one spoke.

55 She is like a sister to me, his wife had told him. Or maybe the closest to a sister that I can imagine.

They had known each other from age zero through five, then at thirteen, twenty-one, and now.

She had also said to him, I get that you don't want to see your family, but do you know what it's like to have that choice be made for you? My parents chose to leave. I did not. I was lonely.

In their bedroom, just the two of them, he asked what the fight was about. Nothing, his wife said. Just that the cousin had called her an ABC and said that she was the most classic American-born Chinese she knew. Only ABCs went on prepaid tours, spoke bad Chinese, married out, and thought everything was cool or great, when most things were just plain.

But I was born here, she said. I had a passport from here that I gave up.

60 The pagoda is where the legendary White Maiden is locked. The White Maiden is beautiful, immortal, and can turn, when necessary, into the white snake from which she came. She has an immortal sidekick who comes from a green snake. His wife had said that she remembered the TV show they'd watched — which had led to arguments about who was more like the White Maiden — and her cousin had replied that it was so ABC of her to remember the show but not the Ming-dynasty legend, which she could not read.

In this photo from the National Beijing Opera's 2005 production of *The Legend of the White Snake*, two singers play the roles of the white and green snakes.

How do you interpret the women's posture and facial expressions? What parallels do you see between this depiction of the legend and the discussions the protagonist, his wife, and her cousin have about the characters in the legend?

His wife cried for ten minutes and then stopped. I see her point now, she said, and looked at him inquisitively. You know what I thought about when she called me an ABC? He didn't. I thought about my parents. Because her parents had funny names and accents, they had to spell their names out each time, slowly and with references. Q for Queen. G for George. X for Xerox. Z for Zebra. Eventually, they changed their names altogether. Raymond like "Everybody Loves Raymond." Lucy like "I Love Lucy."[6]

• • •

These were the last phrases his wife said to him in English. After that moment, something changed. She stopped translating for him, too. At meals, he could only look around or eat or laugh when everyone else did.

A phase, he decided. Something to get out of her system. But then he wondered if that made him sound like his mother, who called many things a phase. His allergy to cats, his view of the world, etc.

Her family watched television together. They went from house to house — each family member had a house for his wife and him to see and sit in, and a television to turn on so they could watch a variety show. The shows confused him, not just the language but the thought bubbles and commentary that exploded onscreen, over the actors' faces.

Do we find any of this bizarre? he asked, but his wife just yelled ha-ha-ha alongside her aunts. Because her family sat around her, he was pushed to the other end of the room. A grandmother would sit next to her and stroke her arm. His wife didn't seem to mind. One afternoon, a white man appeared on television. The white man spoke Chinese and wore rectangular glasses. Her cousin told him that this was Dashan, or Big Mountain, the most famous Chinese-speaking Caucasian in China. He spoke like a native. The American who ran the pie shop had decent Chinese, but not as good, so she called him Small Mountain. You could become either of them, her cousin said, or you could become Average Mountain. He said that this was not his plan.

His mother called and he answered so as not to watch more TV. What did you do today? What did you eat? He told her. And the day before? He told her. And what about tomorrow? He told her. Send me pictures of where they live. He asked why. She said she wanted to see what a Chinese town looked like. Do they have big kitchens and big couches, or no kitchens and floor mats? Do they buy their own produce

[6] Both popular American television shows, *Everybody Loves Raymond* ran from 1996 to 2005, and *I Love Lucy* ran from 1951 to 1957.

or grow it themselves? Are there bazaars? Do they love dogs? Send me a picture of a well-loved dog. Does she come from a village? his mother asked. She does not, he said. But have they been nice to you? Have they treated you well? Are you eating enough? Is it too hot? How's the air? Are you allergic to anything? Have you seen a hospital? A pharmacy? Are the police dangerous? Did you meet Chairman Mao?[7] He's dead, he said. But are there pictures of him up? Do they talk about him a lot? Do they pray? Have you seen a church? When are you coming back? When are you coming to visit? We can't wait for you to visit. The next time you do, we'll all go camping. Remember when you loved that? Remember cowboys and Indians and you would put mud on your face to — Mom, he said. Well, she continued, have you seen a park? Are there cars? Does her family have a car? Is it new? Send me a picture of a brand-new car. Are you getting around O.K.? Do you feel less free? Less free? he asked. Do you feel less free over there? He hung up.

When her cousin wasn't there, they used Google Translate. They would speak into the phone mike and it would, supposedly, tell them each what the other had said.

I'm going out now, she said.

Where? he asked.

Out for a walk. 70

Do you want me to come?

Yes, but no, thanks, have a very nice day but you are not welcomed.

Then his wife put on a canvas bucket hat — there were many in the house — and went out for a stroll.

He looked online to see if this behavior was common. Of the medical causes, she could have had heat stroke or just a regular stroke. Had she concussed herself? Had there been a moment of trauma? On a husband forum, husbands offered theories about why their wives had stopped talking to them. There was another forum, directly linked, of husbands seeking advice on how to make their wives talk less.

She came back from the stroll with more food. Everything was in a bag, even her cup of coffee was in a bag, which she held by the handles as she drank. She sat down next to him with a huge bag of prunes and a medium bag of sunflower seeds. Did you have a nice time? he asked. She didn't respond. 75

Did you have a nice time?

She took out her phone and spoke into it. Can I interest you in a prune?

But did you have a nice time?

Can I interest you in a sunflower seed?

Why is this happening? he asked. 80

Sometimes a thing just needs to happen.

Is this about my mother? Are you angry with me?

No harm, no foul. No pain, no gain.

I think you might be suffering from heat stroke.

Can I interest you in some yogurt? 85

Maybe we should go see a doctor.

No, I am not a doctor, but thanks for asking. That's so kind of you. One of my aunts is a doctor, except she is not here right now. What is your emergency?

Did he have an emergency? He shook his head. She handed him a prune that was wrapped in waxed paper. He didn't like it but ate two more. She poured sunflower seeds into his hand, and he ate them, too. They spat the shells into a metal bowl. Afterward, they spent some time looking for a canvas hat that would fit him.

My head is too big, he said.

No, Google Translate replied, it's just that your head is too big and shaped like a triangle. But do not fret, we will find a triangle hat for you and, once we do, you shall wear it while we eat more prunes. 90

They wore their hats for the rest of the day. Her family complimented the look and took

[7] A reference to Mao Zedong (1893–1976), a Chinese communist revolutionary and the founder of the People's Republic of China. — Eds.

photos. He and his wife posed with their arms each forming a half heart and linked at the hands. In this country, young couples like to dress the same, one aunt said as the cousin translated. It is silly, and we don't understand it. Maybe they're awkward people. Or maybe they just want to merge. Yes, we don't understand it, but I suppose merging can be good, or it can be frightening. Please keep the hat, it suits you.

• • •

He spent half of their last day in the bathroom, the other half at the dinner table. It seemed that his wife's Chinese had improved. Her cousin said that it was now at the level of a first grader. Her cousin also had a message for him from his wife. His wife was sitting right across from him.

How would you feel if you went back first and I stayed a little longer?

What?

Her cousin repeated the message but now mimicked his wife's voice.

No, he said, no way.

He looked at his wife, and she tilted her head. Only when her cousin translated did his wife go, Ah.

What would you do here? he asked.

His wife showed him her phone, which was logged into WeChat.[8] She scrolled through all the people she had been chatting with on this app.

Who are these people? he asked, taking the phone away from her.

One was her cousin, her cousin said. Aunts, uncles, both grandmothers, her parents in the States. And friends she'd made here.

Here? he asked. Which friends?

Her cousin listed them. Felix the Cat. Helen of Troy. Shirley Temple.

Our guides? You're talking with our tour guides?

And someone named Karl.

Oh, my God.

His wife beamed. She could type Chinese a bit, and the others humored her. Animated emojis filled in what she could not yet say. She was considering becoming a tour guide herself, here in Hangzhou. She could show Americans the pagoda and tell them the legend. Eventually, she hoped to read the original, ancient text.

Although, her cousin said, that would require college-level literacy. But, given her rate of progress, it would take her only a few months to achieve.

A few months? he said. No, no way.

His wife's hand covered his. She looked sad again.

What about me? he was about to say. I am lonely, too. Then he thought about it more.

Shanghai Gallery of Art

Completed by Chinese artist Gao Weigang in 2018 and entitled *Missing You for Ten Thousand Years*, this work was created with oil on canvas and an LED light.

How might this image represent the husband's perspective? How might it be interpreted as representing the wife's perspective? Explain which interpretation you find most compelling.

[8] A popular instant messaging platform in China. — Eds.

He looked at his wife's face, which was open and smooth. His wife spoke and her cousin translated. I will come back, but I need some time. I would like to do this on my own, but also with this family. Family is a choice, you've said. I am proud of you just as I hope you are of me. No fears, no tears. If you can, please add me on WeChat as well.

He nodded. That day, he flew alone.

• • •

On WeChat, she had a blog. He followed her posts, pictures of West Lake and the tourists she led around it, pictures of food, of pets, a talking parrot, a box of chicks, a pickup truck. She began to use some English again and he learned some Chinese.

Ku, she wrote.

Ku back. ■

2019

Understanding and Interpreting

1. **AP® Character and Narration.** In paragraph 2, the wife tells the husband that her parents have paid for their trip to China. What do the details of her explanation reveal about her family's attitude toward him and their relationship?
2. **AP® Character and Narration.** Readers never know the names of the husband, the wife, or her cousin, but the names of the guides, a man on the tour, and the husband's in-laws are all given. What do most of the names we learn have in common, and why are these similarities significant? Why might Weike Wang have also included Karl's name?
3. **AP® Character and Narration.** In paragraph 15, the protagonist learns that his wife has only a basic understanding of Chinese so cannot discuss substantive topics. How does this revelation cause a shift in the husband's attitude toward his wife? How does his wife's grasp of Chinese continue to develop throughout the story?
4. **AP® Character.** Why does the wife say she wants so badly to spend time with her family? How does this compare with the husband's attitude about spending time with his family?
5. **AP® Character and Structure.** Paragraph 26 centers on one of the calls the husband's mother makes to him, in which she recounts running into an old teacher of his. What does this story reveal about the husband? Why is this information significant, and how does it relate to the overall structure of the story?
6. **AP® Character and Narration.** Carefully reread paragraphs 28–30. Why does the mother respond in this way to her son's desire to get a passport? What does it reveal about the mother's perspective on the wife and the couple's travel plans?
7. **AP® Character.** The protagonist's wife asserts that "[i]gnorance leads to fear" in paragraph 40. Explain what you think she means in your own words. Provide an example from the story or from your own experiences to illustrate your answer.
8. **AP® Character and Setting.** What does the discussion of expectations in paragraphs 46 and 47 reveal in general about the husband and in particular about how where we grow up shapes our values? What do you make of the wife's response to the protagonist's assertion that "[w]e need an average" (par. 48)?
9. **AP® Character and Narration.** How does the husband react when his wife stops speaking to him in English? Why do you think she suddenly stops communicating with him directly?
10. **AP® Character and Narration.** What do the conversations between the husband and his mother reveal about their relationship in particular and their beliefs in general? How do the topics they discuss reveal the mother's biases?

11. **AP® Character and Narration.** Shortly after her fight with the cousin, the wife stops speaking English and behaves as if she has forgotten how to understand it. How does her behavior from this point forward develop her character?
12. **AP® Character and Narration.** What kinds of changes do the husband and wife undergo over the course of the story? Does one change more than the other? How does the level of change each character undergoes reflect the larger themes of the story?
13. **AP® Structure and Narration.** How does the end of the story shape your interpretation of the story as a whole? Is it a love story or a breakup story? Explain.

Analyzing Language, Style, and Structure

1. **Vocabulary in Context.** After a Thanksgiving dinner with the husband's parents, the wife comments "that the entire meal was surreal." Based on the rest of paragraph 38, how does the wife's description of the meal support her assertion that it was a "surreal" experience? What does the wife's explanation reveal about the husband's parents?
2. **AP® Setting and Narration.** Characters in the story discuss the English word "cool" as well as its Chinese counterpart *ku* and the word *shuang*. While *shuang* means "refreshing," the wife's cousin explains that *ku* translates to the English "cool" but also as "ruthless or strong" (par. 54). Why are these overlapping definitions meaningful within the context of the story, especially in relation to the translation of *ku* as "ruthless"?
3. **AP® Character, Structure, and Narration.** The phone calls between the husband and his mother throughout the story communicate both characters' varying perspectives. What do these interactions convey about the husband's values? How do they reveal assumptions his mother makes and biases she has? How do these scenes inform your interpretation of the wife's behavior as the story progresses?
4. **AP® Character and Structure.** Three times in the story, the wife "looked down" (pars. 17, 31, and 54) in response to an interaction she has with another character. What does this response signal in each instance, and what effect does her repetitive responses create?
5. **AP® Character and Figurative Language.** Do you believe the wife becomes physically incapable of communicating in English? What does this change in her language abilities signify on a deeper level, and what does it indicate figuratively?
6. **AP® Setting and Structure.** How do the reasons for the husband and wife's trip to China relate to the conflicts they encounter there? Pay special attention to the ending of the story. How does the structure of the story relate to your interpretation of the conflicts and the general events in the story?
7. **AP® Character and Structure.** Compare and contrast the husband's values with those of his wife. How does Wang use a juxtaposition of their values to create conflict?
8. **AP® Character and Narration.** Consider the point of view and perspective from which the narrator tells this story. Even though it's third-person point of view, what evidence is there to support the idea that we experience more of the husband's perspective more than anyone else's? How do the husband's succinct contributions to conversations in the story subtly keep us anchored in his perspective?
9. **AP® Character and Structure.** In paragraph 7, the husband has a hard time understanding what his wife says about the spiciness of the food they are eating. How does this interaction foreshadow the communication problems that develop between them later in the story?

Despite the innocence of the misunderstanding, in what ways does it point to a more significant breakdown in communication?

10. **AP® Character, Structure, and Narration.** How does Wang indicate dialogue in "The Trip," and what structure does she use during the husband's conversations on the phone with his mother? What do these punctuation and paragraph choices indicate about the communication between characters?

Topics for Composing

1. **AP® FRQ Prose Fiction Analysis.** The following question refers to paragraphs 27–49 of Weike Wang's "The Trip," published in 2019. In this passage, a husband and wife react to the expectations of others in ways that reveal important dynamics in their marriage. Read the passage carefully. Then, in a well-written essay, analyze how Wang uses literary elements and techniques to convey the complex relationship between the husband and wife.

2. **AP® FRQ Literary Argument.** In many works of literature, failures to communicate create conflict and define characters. In "The Trip," conflicts develop out of miscommunications between and among characters. In a well-written essay, analyze how the patterns of communication between the husband and wife contribute to an interpretation of the work as a whole. Do not merely summarize the plot.

3. **AP® Literary Argumentation.** "The Trip" emphasizes communication among characters and especially the complexity of communicating across more than one language. Analyze how Wang relates the way we learn a language to our overall development as humans.

4. **AP® Literary Argumentation.** In an interview about this story, Wang said that the wife is "someone who, while not angry at anyone in particular, is angry about her circumstances, angry that she has been robbed of important choices. But we are all the products of a combination of chance and choice." Using evidence from the story, analyze the character of the wife through this lens. In what ways is she the product of both chance and choice?

5. **AP® Literary Argumentation.** In a 2019 interview with the *New Yorker*, Wang explains that this story is based on a trip she took with her husband to visit family in China. She goes on to say, "I found myself having to speak English in places where I never had before . . . so that my husband could participate. I was translating for everyone and, at the same time, trying to experience on my own. . . . Afterward, I truly couldn't differentiate which observations were mine and which belonged to someone else." To what extent does this story reflect the ways in which our senses of self can become blurry when we are in unfamiliar situations or even when we are in familiar situations but have to assume an unfamiliar role?

6. **Speaking and Listening.** Prepare for and hold a class discussion about whether the main characters' inability to communicate stems from the fact that each one seems to lack a strong sense of their identity. Is it possible that the couple doesn't have communication issues after all? Consider whether you believe the couple comes to a deeper understanding of each other at the end of the story.

7. **Connections.** The wife eats a sausage on a stick in Xi'an that reminds her of her childhood. Are there foods from your childhood that you no longer get to eat regularly? Write about one or more of them and share what you associate them with from your childhood. Include a reflection about how, as in Wang's story, food sharply connects you to a certain time and place.

8. **Connections.** WeChat, the texting app mentioned in Wang's story, is popular among people in China. The Chinese government, however, censors much of what the public communicates

not only through texting apps but also through the internet, literature, and other forms of media. How does this aspect of communication within the story reflect the changes the husband and wife each undergo as the story progresses?

9. **Speaking and Listening.** To what extent are the character of the husband's mother and stepfather stereotypical? Prepare a line of reasoning in response to these questions by writing out a claim and supporting evidence. Then, engage in a group discussion with classmates during which you each share your claims and evidence first and then discuss the merits of everyone's lines of reasoning.
10. **Creative Writing.** Write a sequel to this story that takes place one year later. Continue the narrative from the third-person point of view established by Wang, or choose one character and write about where that character is now. How has the character changed? How has their understanding of themselves and of others changed?

Erasure

Sakinah Hofler

Yvel Clovis

While working as a chemical engineer for the U.S. Department of Defense, Sakinah Hofler realized her interest in creative writing had become a passion she wanted to devote herself to more fully. As a result, she enrolled as a PhD candidate at the University of Cincinnati to study creative writing and won a prestigious writing prize her first year in the program. Since then, she has gone on to win additional prizes and awards for her writing, which has also appeared in literary magazines and other publications. Hofler advocates for the importance of making the arts an everyday experience, and her pieces explore the potential of social change.

KEY CONTEXT In addition to the literal deletion of words or files, "erasure" describes both a type of artistic expression and the reprehensible act of forcing one culture to assimilate into another. As an art form, erasure is the practice of blacking out or erasing words from a text or erasing part of an image to create something new and original. Culturally speaking, erasure occurs when one group of people forces those of another group to change their appearance, to convert to a different religion, and/or to speak a different language. As you read this story, consider how both applications of "erasure" apply.

Danielle Holmes was the first recorded disappearance. We didn't notice right away. She had always been a quiet one, respectful, never speaking unless spoken to, never sitting at the conference table during meetings, opting instead to stand in the back. It was about a week into her disappearance, in the middle of our monthly meeting, after the team lead asked her to forward him the productivity rates for last quarter's batches, that we waited two, three, four seconds for her soft voice to say, *OK,* before glancing at her usual standing spot and seeing only the wall. *Maybe she left early for a dental appointment,* someone said. *What makes you so sure she went to the dentist?* another person asked. *It could've been the doctor's.* The rest of us thought about the last time we'd seen her, and someone narrowed it down to Thursday last week when she stood behind him in line, holding oatmeal and a cup of coffee. When Johanna Petit-Frere left work late that evening, she noticed Danielle's Elantra in the corner of the lot, unlocked, empty Chobani yogurt containers littered on the passenger seat, a small, generic, brand-name purse lying on its side on the floor. Johanna called the police to do a wellness check. They had a few others to complete ahead of her, but when they finally checked Danielle's house, they saw nothing amiss. Maybe, we reasoned, she went on vacation and forgot to upload her leave to the company's Outlook calendar. *But her purse?* Johanna asked. *No, no, no. No woman forgets her purse.*

Johanna disappeared two days later. Unlike Danielle, we considered Johanna loud. Angry. She had a six-inch afro, stormed around the office in these impossible six-inch heels, clacked the keys on her keyboard, and, some of us felt, spoke a bit too loudly on conference calls, sometimes slipping into Haitian Creole when she wanted to curse. Rumor had it that when HR called her in to talk about embracing her quieter side, she demanded to know who had filed the complaint. She came to each cubicle, eyeing us, questioning us. None of us, of course, knew anything. On the day she disappeared, it took only a few hours to realize she was gone. One minute we heard her chattering on the phone, clacking on her keyboard; the next, silence. We thought her call had dropped. When Terrell Davis went by her cubicle to drop off some folders and discuss upcoming travel to Rock Island, he found a pair of stilettos, but no Johanna. He waited for a while. Later, he told us his first thought was that she had to defecate (*You mean shit?* one of us snickered. Terrell had a habit of being too uppity[1] at work). Terrell's second thought was that she'd snuck out of work early. But, Johanna, in a bathroom, without her shoes? Johanna, leaving work, without her shoes? This we could not imagine.

At home, our partners grumbled about people missing too much work; our children talked about the increased absences from their classes, their sports teams, their after-school programs.

Our bosses called meetings and gave stern lectures on no-calls, no-shows. Apparently, the lazy, as our bosses called them, had decided to stop working (we weren't using the term *disappeared* yet). We were warned that if we tried something similar, if we dared show up late, we would immediately be fired. Behind their backs we checked cabinets for hidden cameras and wondered if this were some type of government conspiracy or if we were being pranked or if we were on a show like *Undercover Boss*.

That was until Terrell disappeared right in 5
front of us. He'd been calling IT for days and couldn't get through. In the midst of begging a couple of us to go across the street and up sixteen stories to convince IT to send someone over to unlock Johanna's computer, we noticed we could see the fire alarm handle through jagged notches in his neck. It was like something was removing him in large, scrubbing circles from the bottom up with a huge #2 pencil eraser. Even after he was gone and we were left staring at the unobscured fire alarm, we heard his last words, *Really, I would do it myself, but . . .*

Those of us who saw him disappear and those of us who heard how he disappeared feared we were next. We poked our heads into cubicles to make sure we were still there. We dialed up each other's extensions, whispered into our headsets, *But can you really hear me?*, and breathed sighs of relief when a voice on the other end said, *Yes, yes, I hear you.* We traveled to the caf in groups of four. There was no rhyme or reason to that number — it just felt safe. If one disappeared, three would still be there; two disappeared, two would still be there. We texted

[1] A racist word that reflects a belief that Black people should be subservient to white people. — Eds.

each other late at night R U STILL THR and bit our nails ragged waiting for replies. We expanded our groups to five, and then six, and then seven.

We kept track of those who had disappeared from our company: Danielle Holmes, Johanna Petit-Frere, Terrell Davis, Jihan Overby, D'Wayne Grady, Oba Cole, Shakur Simmons, Raida Taylor, Laverne Hamilton, Sara Herrera, Shakeemah Bankston, Ama Olabisi, Tashauna Glover, Adeola Lawal, Sarah de la Luz, Mason de la Cruz, Nafisah Muhammad, Vivienne Attys.

Couples went to sleep as couples, and one of them would wake up the next morning in a cold bed, single. One of us woke up to an empty house, both wife and children gone. Adopted children, disappeared. Those of us who still had children learned through e-mails, texts, and letters sent home that their classrooms would be condensed because of the lack of students, teachers, teachers' aides, and janitors. *We'll get through this,* they assured us, though no one could define what *this* was. Principals nervously stepped foot into classrooms they had abandoned decades ago. Our children gathered in smaller groups, tried to learn their lessons, tried to ignore the empty desks. Every day, they came home and asked us when their friends were coming back. Every day, they asked if they were next. We had no answers for them.

Our bosses started to hire people off the streets, unqualified individuals who didn't understand batches, programming, productivity, QWERTY, computers. Most of us were appalled, though some did say, *I like it better this way.* When our garbage cans overflowed and our refrigerators stank, our bosses made us clean. We hosed our sidewalks and squeegeed our windows. IT never overcame its backlog, so we sent out what orders we could and cancelled others. When a number of our clients disappeared and our order numbers dropped, our bosses fired the unqualified individuals and required the rest of us to put in fifteen hours, eighteen hours.

The world leaders convened. Pundits 10
punditted, discussing subjects we dared not talk about before, taboo topics that had been relegated to pop quizzes in our high school history classes, questions like "In what year was the Emancipation Proclamation signed?" and "What year did apartheid[2] end?," only these topics were discussed more directly, filled with details and an overload of accusatory information that made us want to turn the channel or switch off our phones, but our curiosity, our search for understanding, wouldn't let us. From these pundits we learned it wasn't just huge swaths of inner cities and whole towns in the South (especially in Mississippi and Alabama) that had disappeared, the world also had to contend with the disappearance of people from whole islands in the Caribbean (we never knew Hispaniola contained both Dominican Republic and Haiti until that aerial shot on CNN showed the emptiness of both sides), certain areas of London, suburbs of places like Paris and Hamburg, and most of the population of the continent of Africa. We understood there was a particular calculation to these disappearances, but not the exact calculation, the exact percentage one had to be to disappear. One pundit laughed and remarked that while these people were gone, at least those remaining had unfettered access to their islands, their beaches, and their food without conflict, without war, without fear, that perhaps we can go to those places, build, and finally establish civilization. Another pundit angrily pointed out that it was not their land and that if it had not been for *these people* in *this country*, we might not have wealth, the traffic light, X-ray spectrometry, the pacemaker, open heart surgery, the HVAC keeping the other pundit so smugly comfortable in his seat, soul food, dry cleaning, rhythm, scapegoats, spices.

---

[2] A system of racial segregation and discrimination — in this story, a reference to apartheid in South Africa, which lasted from 1948 to 1994. — Eds.

extending beyond the text

The following excerpt is from the beginning of Ralph Ellison's 1952 novel *Invisible Man*.

from Invisible Man

Ralph Ellison

I am an invisible man. No, I am not a spook like those who haunted Edgar Allan Poe; nor am I one of your Hollywood-movie ectoplasms. I am a man of substance, of flesh and bone, fiber and liquids — and I might even be said to possess a mind. I am invisible, understand, simply because people refuse to see me. Like the bodiless heads you see sometimes in circus sideshows, it is as though I have been surrounded by mirrors of hard, distorting glass. When they approach me they see only my surroundings, themselves, or figments of their imagination — indeed, everything and anything except me.

Nor is my invisibility exactly a matter of a bio-chemical accident to my epidermis. That invisibility to which I refer occurs because of a peculiar disposition of the eyes of those with whom I come in contact. A matter of the construction of their inner eyes, those eyes with which they look through their physical eyes upon reality. I am not complaining, nor am I protesting either. It is sometimes advantageous to be unseen, although it is most often rather wearing on the nerves. Then too, you're constantly being bumped against by those of poor vision. Or again, you often doubt if you really exist. You wonder whether you aren't simply a phantom in other people's minds. Say, a figure in a nightmare which the sleeper tries with all his strength to destroy. It's when you feel like this that, out of resentment, you begin to bump people back. And, let me confess, you feel that way most of the time. You ache with the need to convince yourself that you do exist in the real world, that you're a part of all the sound and anguish. ■

1. **What makes the narrator of this passage "invisible"?**
2. **How does the concept of invisibility as Ellison's narrator understands it relate to the events of "Erasure"?**
3. **How does physical disappearance in both this excerpt and "Erasure" function as a metaphor?**

The leader of our nation assured us this was a large protest, a publicity stunt of magnanimous proportions. The leader urged the public to stop talking about the disappearances because that was what they wanted. Attention. Distraction. The disappearances will stop, he claimed, when they realize their tactics wouldn't work.

We didn't stop whispering, and the pundits didn't stop punditting, but, in a way, he was right. The disappearances stopped. One month passed, and then four, and there weren't any more recorded disappearances. A number was released: 18.5 percent of the world's population was gone.

Some hoped they would come back and things would go back to normal.

Some liked them gone.

Not a day went by without them crossing everyone's minds.

Not a day went by when we wondered if they, wherever they were, thought about us.

Some of the others left, understanding that if this happened again, they would be next. They moved far away and took with them doctors, lawyers, senators, programmers, nail aestheticians, professors, dishwashers. They didn't go back to their native countries per se, but they grouped together and lived among each other as if something were wrong with us, as if we were the cause of the disappearances.

Good, a couple of us said.

The rest of us did not say anything.

A few of us stopped working. We withdrew our children from school and kept them home. We read books and plays to them, getting choked up when we came across a particular word, a favored picture, and realized we, too, were teaching them history, of ways of life long gone. We'd listen to our favorite song or watch our favorite movie or watch a sports classic on ESPN — understand we've seen and heard the last from that person — go into our bathrooms, shut the doors, and cry.

Those of us who continued to work continued our whispered discussions. Some thought we were living in a simulation, that we'd reached Level 2 in a game we couldn't quite figure out. Some thought it was God, giving us a sign. A sign for better or for worse? We were unsure and that uncertainty made it worse. We wanted our signs to be specific, detailed, with solid metaphors and a clear delineation between good and evil. Aliens, the rest of us conjectured. It wasn't just our children's theories, it was ours. Aliens had taken them to outer space. What else could it be?

One night after twenty of hours of work, we grabbed our stashes of bourbon and brandy and rode the elevator to the top floor of our building. We passed around flasks. We drank. We waited. And waited. Surely, if God wanted to save people, why them? Surely, if this was all a simulation, who was trying to prove what? Surely, if aliens had come to our strange planet why would they only take them? We pummeled our chests, tilted our pale faces to the stippled sky, and bellowed, *Why not us? Why didn't you take us?* ■

2020

Understanding and Interpreting

1. **AP® Character, Setting, and Narration.** What do the descriptions of Danielle Holmes and Johanna, the first two women to go missing, reveal about the narrators of the story? What does this say about the greater society in the story?
2. **AP® Character and Narration.** How does Terrell's disappearance differ from those of Danielle and Johanna on a literal level? How do you interpret the significance of these differences?
3. **AP® Character and Narration.** Why do those who remain behind have difficulty defining "what *this* was" (par. 8)? Consider the narrators' own understanding of what's going on as well as the challenge of explaining it to others.
4. **AP® Character and Narration.** Much of the story consists of the ways those left behind respond to others disappearing. Which responses make sense to you as they continue going about their days as best they can? Which responses surprise you? What natural responses do the narrators not include? How do you interpret the significance of those exclusions?

5. **AP® Setting and Narration.** Paragraph 10 includes details about the geographic regions most affected by the disappearances. Based on this paragraph, and clues elsewhere in the story, what can you infer about who goes missing? What role does this information play in your interpretation of the story?
6. **AP® Character and Narration.** Consider the importance of the narrators in this story. How reliable are they? How does your perception of their reliability shape your interpretation of the story?
7. **AP® Structure and Narration.** What does the story's title reveal about the author's perspective on the events of the plot? Consider that the words "erase" and "erasure" never appear in the story.

Analyzing Language, Style, and Structure

1. **Vocabulary in Context.** The narrator explains that once people had disappeared, others "had unfettered access to their islands, their beaches, and their food without conflict, without war, without fear, that perhaps we can go to those places, build, and finally establish civilization" (par. 10). While "unfettered" often has a neutral if not positive connotation, how does its use in this sentence indicate the word's much more negative history?
2. **AP® Structure.** How does Hofler employ irony in her contrasting descriptions of the first people to disappear? How does she further develop this irony as the story progresses to reveal the story's overall meaning?
3. **AP® Narration.** Throughout the story, the narrators use the pronouns *we*, *us*, and *our*. What is the effect of this choice on the reader? How does this perspective contribute to your understanding of the contrast between those who disappear and those who remain?
4. **AP® Narration and Character.** In paragraph 10, the narrators refer to "these people" and "those places," and other instances of "these" and "those" appear elsewhere throughout the story. What does this diction choice reveal about the narrators' attitude toward both themselves and the disappeared?
5. **AP® Structure and Narration.** Consider the paragraph structure and syntax of paragraphs 13–22. How do such short, repetitive paragraphs contribute to the meaning of this part of the story?
6. **AP® Structure and Figurative Language.** In what ways does "Erasure" function as an allegory, and what broader message do the events and characters convey about humanity?

Topics for Composing

1. **AP® FRQ Prose Fiction Analysis.** The following question refers to paragraphs 5–11 of Sakinah Hofler's "Erasure," published in 2020. In this passage, the narrator explains how the world adjusts to the unexplained disappearances of millions of people. Read the passage carefully. Then, in a well-written essay, analyze how Hofler uses literary elements and techniques to convey what people's responses to the disappearances reveal about the fabric of our society.
2. **AP® FRQ Literary Argument.** Works of literature often explore the ways in which people are divided — both philosophically and geographically — into social, cultural, and religious communities. In "Erasure," division exists on a literal level as the setting divides the characters who disappear from those who remain, and the divisions occur on deeper levels, too. In a well-written essay, analyze how these divisions contribute to an interpretation of the story as a whole. Do not merely summarize the plot.

3. **Connections.** Historically, the "disappearance" or displacement of groups of people has always been the product of human behavior. Even the events that do not culminate in genocide or internment, such as natural disasters, disproportionately affect marginalized groups of people. How mysterious, really, are the disappearances in "Erasure," when considered alongside real-world events in the past and present?
4. **Speaking and Listening.** Participate in a class discussion about the ways teenagers feel as though they are invisible and taken for granted. For example, imagine that in the United States people under eighteen were no longer allowed to work. Which industries would be hit the hardest? How would the public be affected, and how would it respond?
5. **AP® Literary Argumentation.** In a 2019 editorial for the *Cincinnati Review*, the University of Cincinnati's literary magazine, Sakinah Hofler explained, "I started writing stories that contradicted some folks' view of blackness but felt true to my actual world and my created ones." Write an essay in which you analyze and explain the way Hofler uses literary elements to portray the Black experience.
6. **AP® Literary Argumentation.** Professor and researcher Brene Brown emphasizes the importance of the stories we tell ourselves with this quote: "The most dangerous stories we make up are the narratives that diminish our inherent worthiness. We must reclaim the truth about our lovability, divinity, and creativity." Analyze the narrators as characters in "Erasure." In what ways do the narrators tell our collective story in a way that diminishes the concept of human worth? Where does the story present opportunities for the narrators to "reclaim the truth about our lovability, divinity, and creativity"?
7. **Connections.** Martin Niemöller, a German Lutheran pastor, expressed this sentiment in response to admitting he passively watched the Nazis' rise to power and subsequent efforts to exterminate Jews and other targeted groups of people:

   > First they came for the socialists, and I did not speak out — because I was not a socialist. Then they came for the trade unionists, and I did not speak out — because I was not a trade unionist. Then they came for the Jews, and I did not speak out — because I was not a Jew. Then they came for me — and there was no one left to speak for me.

   How does this quote relate to the structure of "Erasure" as a short story and to the narrators' understanding of what happens? In what ways is Niemöller's response to the Holocaust in the 1940s still an important reminder for us today?
8. **Research.** Research the concept of "invisible labor" to understand what it is and how it influences our economy and society. Then, synthesize your discoveries and write an essay in which you establish how your understanding of invisible labor changes or supports your original interpretation of the events in the story. As you respond, consider the jobs and work performed by the disappeared in the story.
9. **Connections.** Look up the terms "white guilt" and "white innocence." What does each one mean, and how do they differ? How do these concepts relate to the perspective of the narrators in the story?

When I consider how my light is spent

John Milton

Library of Congress, Prints & Photographs Division

John Milton (1608–1674) is best known for his epic poem *Paradise Lost*. He studied independently for five years after receiving his MA from Cambridge University and then traveled through Europe. When he returned to England, the country was in a state of flux. Milton supported the Puritans, led by Oliver Cromwell, and wrote pamphlets on many political issues, such as free speech and censorship. Milton's eyesight began to deteriorate, however, and by 1652 he was blind. After the Restoration in 1660, when King Charles II resumed the throne, Milton was arrested for his Puritan activities but escaped imprisonment and execution. He devoted the remainder of his life to writing, publishing his masterpiece, *Paradise Lost*, in 1667 and its sequel, *Paradise Regained*, in 1671.

KEY CONTEXT "When I consider how my light is spent," written the year Milton lost his sight, is a meditation on that loss. While we normally make a distinction between poet and speaker, these two entities seem intertwined in this poem. As you read and interpret "When I consider how my light is spent," think about how Milton — a poet, a writer, and an intellectual — might have reacted to his blindness. This poem is a Petrarchan sonnet, a form made up of fourteen lines divided into an octet and a sestet. The octet rhymes *abba*, *abba*, and the sestet that follows can have a variety of different rhyme schemes: *cdcdcd*, *cdecde*, *cddcdd*. The first line of the sestet typically, but not always, provides the volta, a poetic shift.

When I consider how my light is spent,
Ere half my days, in this dark world and wide,
And that one talent which is death to hide
Lodged with me useless, though my soul more bent
To serve therewith my Maker, and present
My true account, lest he returning chide;
"Doth God exact day-labor, light denied?"
I fondly ask; but Patience to prevent
That murmur, soon replies, "God doth not need
Either man's work or his own gifts; who best
Bear his mild yoke, they serve him best. His state
Is kingly. Thousands at his bidding speed
And post o'er land and ocean without rest:
They also serve who only stand and wait." ■

c. 1655

Understanding and Interpreting

1. Considering the biographical details provided before the poem, what might Milton mean when his speaker considers "how [his] light is spent" (l. 1)?
2. How does the speaker characterize the time he has left in his life? What does the phrase "Ere half my days" (1. 2) suggest about his attitude toward the future?
3. In lines 3–4, the speaker discusses a "talent" that is "[l]odged with me useless." What is that "talent," and how might this idea be ironic?
4. What is the difference between what the speaker perceives he can do and what his "soul" yearns to do for his "Maker"? In what way does the speaker think he should honor God?
5. What is the speaker's concern in line 7? How does "Patience" respond to this worry in line 8?
6. The sonnet ends with a description of two ways to serve God: those who "post o'er land and ocean without rest" (l. 13) and those "who only stand and wait" (l. 14). Explain how both of these describe ways to serve God. Which way does John Milton intend to serve God?

Analyzing Language, Style, and Structure

1. **Vocabulary in Context.** According to Patience, "they serve him best" who "[b]ear his mild yoke" (l. 11). What is a "yoke"? How does Milton's use of this word convey his view of the relationship between man and God?
2. This sonnet is structured through several voices. Who is the speaker in lines 1–6? in line 7? in lines 9–14?
3. While Petrarchan sonnets typically contain a volta in line 9, Milton's occurs in line 8, as marked by the word "but." What is the function of bringing the volta to an earlier point in the poem than what the convention demands? Consider why Patience may have interrupted Milton's thought process.
4. Imagery associated with light and darkness recurs in the poem. What is the function of this repetition? How does it reflect a theme of the poem?
5. The word "serve" appears three times in the poem. Why would Milton repeat this word?
6. How does the speaker's attitude toward his blindness change over the course of the poem? Identify the sections of the sonnet wherein these shifts occur.

Topics for Composing

1. AP® FRQ **Poetry Analysis.** In John Milton's "When I consider how my light is spent," written c. 1655, the speaker discusses his concerns now that he is losing his vision. Read the poem carefully. Then, in a well-written essay, analyze how Milton uses literary elements and techniques to portray the speaker's complex reaction to his vision loss.
2. AP® FRQ **Poetry Analysis.** In John Milton's "When I consider how my light is spent," written c. 1655, the speaker questions how his health might affect his ability to serve his "Maker." Read the poem carefully. Then, in a well-written essay, analyze how Milton uses literary elements and techniques to convey the speaker's attitude toward his ability to "serve."
3. **Connections.** Milton's poem springs from how his own vision loss impacted his life as a writer. Describe an instance in which a change in your life prompted you to reconsider how your life might proceed. How did this change affect how you perceive the language in the poem? Milton's speaker, for instance, refers to "this dark world and wide" (l. 2).

4. **Connections.** The last line of the poem is frequently quoted as a kind of motto for those who are not in the midst of action but are nevertheless involved, whether the situation is war or a more personal plight. Describe an instance in which you considered yourself part of a situation even if you weren't directly involved. In what way was your indirect participation a way to "serve" (l. 14)?
5. **Multimodal.** Petrarchan sonnets are structurally divided into an octave and a sestet. Create a two-part collage that depicts the tones and images that pertain to each section of this poem. Each section of your collage should combine words and images that capture the mood that Milton creates in the two parts of the sonnet.

City Visions I

Emma Lazarus

Library of Congress Prints and Photographs Division [LC-USZ62-53145]

A Jewish American writer and activist, Emma Lazarus (1849–1887) was raised in New York City and began publishing poems as a teenager during the Civil War. In addition to poetry, Lazarus published novels, plays, and translations and moved in literary circles that included writers such as Ralph Waldo Emerson, Henry James, Robert Browning, and Thomas Hardy.

KEY CONTEXT In 1884, Lazarus fell ill with what was likely Hodgkin's lymphoma, a form of cancer. She wrote this poem shortly before her death in 1887.

As the blind Milton's memory of light,
The deaf Beethoven's phantasy of tone,
Wrought joys for them surpassing all things known
In our restricted sphere of sound and sight,—
So while the glaring streets of brick and stone
Vex with heat, noise, and dust from morn till night,
I will give rein to Fancy, taking flight
From dismal now and here, and dwell alone
With new-enfranchised senses. All day long,
Think ye 'tis I, who sit 'twixt darkened walls,
While ye chase beauty over land and sea?
Uplift on wings of some rare poet's song,
Where the wide billow laughs and leaps and falls,
I soar cloud-high, free as the winds are free. ■

1888

Exploring the Text

1. What is the analogy the speaker draws in the first 9 lines? Note the syntactical structure of "As . . ." and "So . . ." in lines 1 and 5.
2. What point does the speaker make in alluding to "blind Milton" (l. 1) and "deaf Beethoven" (l. 2)?
3. How does the speaker characterize "the streets of brick and stone" (l. 5)? What is her response to them?
4. How does the speaker distinguish between herself and the reader? What expectation(s), for instance, does the speaker challenge in lines 9–11?
5. What "new-enfranchised senses" does the speaker possess? How do these relate to the final three lines of the poem?
6. What connection do you see between the form Emma Lazarus chose for this poem and its theme(s)? Are the two at odds with each other? Explain why or why not.

Making Connections

1. In "City Visions I" by Emma Lazarus, the speaker refers to "blind Milton's memory of light" (l. 1). Based on your interpretation of John Milton's "When I consider how my light is spent," compare and contrast how the speakers in these two poems find meaning and comfort.
2. Discuss the attitudes each speaker expresses toward physical limitations. How do Milton and Lazarus use literary elements to convey these attitudes?
3. These poems share both a similar form and similar subject. How else are they alike? How do they differ in their approach? How would you describe the tone and mood of each?

I'm Nobody! Who are you?

Emily Dickinson

IanDagnall Computing/Alamy

Born into a prominent family in Amherst, Massachusetts, Emily Dickinson (1830–1886) received some formal education at Amherst Academy and Mount Holyoke Female Seminary (which became Mount Holyoke College). Dickinson was known as a shy and reclusive person, who preferred to remain within her close family circle, though some contemporary scholars have begun to question that characterization. Dickinson wrote nearly eighteen hundred poems, but only ten were published in her lifetime.

I'm Nobody! Who are you?
Are you — Nobody — too?
Then there's a pair of us!
Don't tell! they'd advertise — you know!

How dreary — to be — Somebody!
How public — like a Frog —
To tell one's name — the livelong June —
To an admiring Bog! ■

c. 1861

Understanding and Interpreting

1. Is the opening statement — "I'm Nobody!" — an announcement, an apology, a challenge, a confession, a declaration, or something else? Why do you interpret it as you do?
2. What are the contrasts, as the speaker presents them, between the "nobody[ies]" and those who "advertise" (l. 4) themselves? Are these classifications self-imposed, according to this poem, or determined by others?
3. How does the speaker characterize what it takes to be a "Somebody"? Is Dickinson being too harsh, or is she creating a false dichotomy?
4. How does this poem both confirm and challenge society's perception of the "nobodies"? Based on this poem, would a visionary or rebel who is a leader of a group or community yet who does not seek approval be a "Nobody" or a "Somebody"?
5. In what ways might this poem be read through a modern lens as a comment on social media and celebrity culture?

Analyzing Language, Style, and Structure

1. **Vocabulary in Context.** What is the literal definition of a "bog"? Why is this a particularly appropriate setting for Dickinson as she characterizes those who seek attention?
2. To what extent do you find the speaker's delight about the possibility of there being "a pair of us" (l. 3) the central paradox of this poem? Explain.
3. The one instance of figurative language in the poem is the simile "like a Frog" (l. 6). What characteristics of frogs, particularly males during mating season, make this simile an effective one? What associations would her audience have likely brought to this creature?
4. Dickinson's speaker uses words that can have a fairly neutral meaning but often are used as pejoratives: "advertise" and "public" are two examples. How does Dickinson draw you as a reader into recognizing the more negative meaning?
5. How does the repetition, or anaphora, in the second stanza reinforce the characteristics the speaker sees in those who seek to be "Somebody"?
6. In an earlier edition of the poem, an editor revised line 4 to read: "They'd banish us, you know." Eventually, the line as we see it here was verified in the actual manuscript. What difference would the revised line make in terms of style and/or meaning?
7. In this very short poem, Dickinson uses six exclamation marks, yet popular usage advises writers to use this punctuation sparingly. What effect does Dickinson achieve by ignoring such advice?
8. How does the poem's structure of two stanzas, each one a quatrain, contribute to its meaning? Consider rhyme and meter in your response of how the structure operates.

Topics for Composing

1. **AP® FRQ Poetry Analysis.** In Emily Dickinson's "I'm Nobody! Who are you?," written c. 1861, the speaker contrasts two approaches to identity. While on the surface, the speaker appears to celebrate the private self over the public figure, there is more complexity than this simple contrast. Read the poem carefully. Then, in a well-written essay, analyze how Dickinson uses literary elements and techniques to develop the complexity of the speaker's perspective.
2. **Research.** Emily Dickinson left nearly eighteen hundred unpublished poems when she died. Conduct some research into her efforts to be published as well as her disinclination to develop a public persona. Also explore the society of her era and the prevailing attitudes toward women as artists and writers. Why do you think that she did not gain fame as a poet during her lifetime? Was it a choice, a lack of opportunity, both, or neither?
3. **Speaking and Listening.** The opening line of the poem suggests that the speaker has been asked a question — to which she then responds. But we do not know what that question was, or what its tone might have been. Working in small groups, generate a possible question and then have one of the group members perform the poem in response. Discuss with the full group how the tone of the question you came up with elicits a unique interpretation of the poem's meaning.
4. **Research.** While Emily Dickinson was not an active part of the publishing world of her time, her posthumous influence is vast. Look up some of the later poets — including contemporary ones — who were or are influenced by Dickinson's writing. Choose a poem by one of these poets and write a close analysis comparing the literary elements and techniques to those of "I'm Nobody! Who are you?"
5. **Connections.** In the last few years, there have been several depictions of Emily Dickinson's life as a woman and poet, including *A Quiet Passion*, a 2017 film starring Cynthia Nixon, and *Wild Nights with Emily*, a 2019 film, which was described by one critic as "silly, yet deceptively smart." Also in 2019, the television series *Dickinson*, billed as a "historical comedy-drama," debuted with Hailee Steinfeld as Emily. View one of these and discuss how its interpretation of Dickinson appeals to a more contemporary audience. Where do you see the portrayal of Dickinson reflected in this particular poem? Why do you think there is such interest in this allegedly reclusive poet over a century after her death?
6. **Connections.** Compare and contrast this poem with "The Quiet Life," a poem written in 1709 by Alexander Pope. What resources of language do the two poets employ to express the kind of life that each believes is most valuable?

We Real Cool

Gwendolyn Brooks

Bettmann / Getty Images

Born in Topeka, Kansas, and raised in Chicago, Gwendolyn Brooks (1917–2000) was author of more than twenty books of poetry, including her breakout work, *A Street in Bronzeville* (1945), and *Annie Allen* (1949), for which she became the first African American author to receive the Pulitzer Prize. In 1968, she was named poet laureate of the state of Illinois, and from 1985 to 1986 she served as consultant in poetry to the Library of Congress — the first African American woman to hold this position.

KEY CONTEXT Much of Brooks's work focuses on Chicago's urban landscape and culture, reflecting the speech patterns and expressions of the Black neighborhoods of Chicago's South Side, where she lived. While depicting the gritty reality of urban poverty, her poems express an affirmation of life.

The Pool Players.
Seven at the Golden Shovel.

We real cool. We
Left school. We

Lurk late. We
Strike straight. We

Sing sin. We
Thin gin. We

Jazz June. We
Die soon. ■

1960

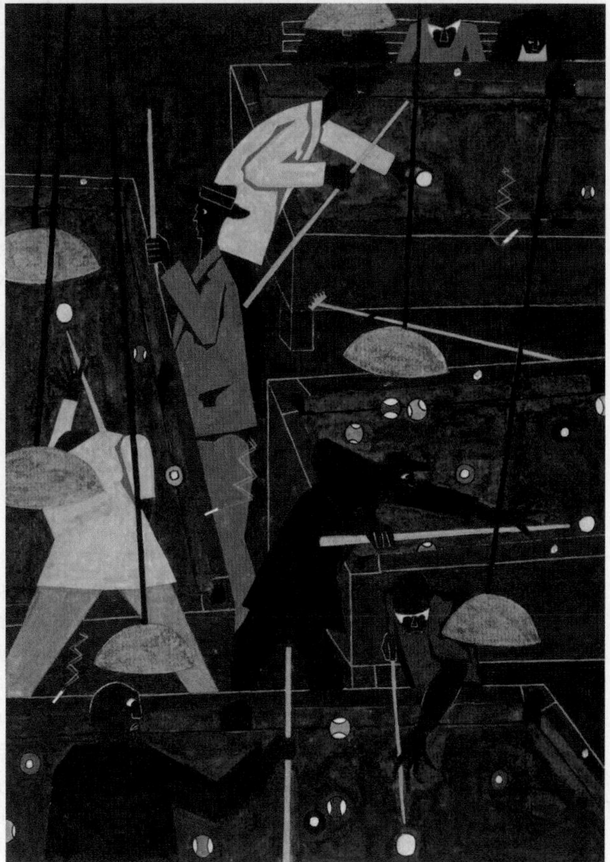

In his 1942 painting entitled *Pool Parlor*, artist Jacob Lawrence depicts a group of young men playing the game. **How is Lawrence's depiction both similar to and different from Brooks's characterization? Pay special attention to the sense of risk that Brooks expresses; to what extent does Lawrence suggest a similar menace — or does he?**

Understanding and Interpreting

1. In discussing this poem, Gwendolyn Brooks described passing a pool hall in her neighborhood and watching seven young men playing pool. Instead of asking herself why they weren't in school, she tried to imagine how they felt about themselves. What does "We Real Cool" tell us about how the young men think of themselves?
2. Why do you think Brooks chose to identify the characters and scene of the poem in the epigraph? How does this information — coming where it does at the beginning of the text — influence your reading of the poem?
3. Consider the speaker (or speakers) of "We Real Cool." What do you see or hear when you imagine them? How does "We Real Cool" comment on friendship, camaraderie, and loyalty?

4. Do you think Brooks is judging the young men she describes? Explain your answer.
5. What do you make of the last line of the poem? Why does the speaker declare that the pool players "[d]ie soon"?

Analyzing Language, Style, and Structure

1. **Vocabulary in Context.** In a recording of Brooks reading her poem, she notes that "It's been . . . banned here and there – chiefly because, I understand, the word 'jazz' has been considered a sexual reference. That was not my intention . . . but I was thinking of music when I used the word 'jazz.'" Why might the word "jazz" be misinterpreted in the context of this poem? How is Brooks's intended meaning important to the poem?
2. How many times is the pronoun "We" repeated in the poem? What does the placement of the pronoun suggest about the poet's attitude toward the young men? What does the repetition and placement of "We" suggest about the pool players' sense of themselves – their identity?
3. How does Brooks's use of monosyllabic words, alliteration, and internal rhyme contribute to the picture Brooks paints of the "cool" young men?
4. What effect does this poem's abrupt and rapid-fire rhythm have on the characterization of the pool players?

Topics for Composing

1. AP® FRQ **Poetry Analysis.** In Gwendolyn Brooks's "We Real Cool," published in 1960, the speakers share the way they see themselves at a particular moment in their lives. Read the poem carefully. Then, in a well-written essay, analyze how Brooks uses literary elements and techniques to convey the speakers' complex perspective on their identities.
2. **Connections.** In an interview in *Contemporary Literature* 11:1 (Winter 1970), Brooks offers stage directions for how "We Real Cool" should be read aloud:

   > First of all, let me tell you how that's supposed to be said, because there's a reason why I set it out as I did. These are people who are essentially saying "Kilroy is here. We are." But they're a little uncertain of the strength of their identity. The "We" – you're supposed to stop after the "We" and think about their validity, and of course there's no way for you to tell whether it should be said softly or not, I suppose, but I say it rather softly because I want to represent their basic uncertainty, which they don't bother to question every day, of course.

   How do the poet's instructions contribute to your experience of the poem?
3. **Connections.** Cultural critic, feminist theorist, and writer bell hooks titled her book about masculinity *We Real Cool*, in which she argues that white society and weak Black leaders are failing Black youth. Why might hooks have chosen the title of Brooks's poem for her book? To what extent does the poem outline issues of masculinity?
4. **Connections.** "We Real Cool" was published originally in 1963 in Brooks's *Collected Poems*. Three years later, in 1966, a broadside was published by Broadside Press with a black background and the words in white. Find the image of the broadside on the internet. What does it look like to you? How does it change your perception of the poem?

5. **Connections.** Look online for Manual Cinema's video that depicts Brooks's moment of inspiration for "We Real Cool." How does the video depict that moment? Did it make you see the poem in a different light or from a different perspective? What do you make of the last moment, when one of the boys nods to Brooks?
6. **Multimodal.** Create your own video presenting an interpretation of "We Real Cool." Update it as much or as little as you'd like.

Identity Card

Mahmoud Darwish

Translated from Arabic by Denys Johnson-Davies

The Asahi Shimbun/Getty Images

One of the most prominent poets of the Arab world, Mahmoud Darwish (1941–2008) was born in what was then the British Mandate of Palestine. When Egypt, Iraq, Jordan, Lebanon, and Syria declared war on the newly established State of Israel, following the 1948 termination of the British Mandate, Darwish's family fled to Lebanon. When they returned two years later, their village had been destroyed, they had missed a census, and they had lost their citizenship. Darwish's political activities, in addition to his lack of citizenship, resulted in several arrests, and eventually exile. He later served on the executive committee of the Palestinian Liberation Organization (PLO). His first book of poetry, *Asafir bila ajnihah* (*Sparrows without Wings*), was published when he was nineteen. He wrote in Arabic but also spoke French, English, and Hebrew. In 2008, he was given the equivalent of a state funeral by the Palestine Authority and was buried in Ramallah.

KEY CONTEXT Written in 1964, "Identity Card" was inspired by an incident in which an Israeli soldier asked Darwish for his papers.

Put it on record.
  I am an Arab
And the number of my card is fifty thousand
I have eight children
And the ninth is due after summer.
What's there to be angry about?

Put it on record.
  I am an Arab
Working with comrades of toil in a quarry.
I have eight children
For them I wrest the loaf of bread,
The clothes and exercise books
From the rocks

And beg for no alms at your door,
  Lower not myself at your doorstep.
  What's there to be angry about?

Put it on record.
  I am an Arab.
I am a name without a title,
Patient in a country where everything
Lives in a whirlpool of anger.
  My roots
  Took hold before the birth of time
  Before the burgeoning of the ages,
  Before cypress and olive trees,
  Before the proliferation of weeds.

My father is from the family of the plough
  Not from highborn nobles.
And my grandfather was a peasant
  Without line or genealogy.
My house is a watchman's hut
  Made of sticks and reeds.
Does my status satisfy you?
  I am a name without a surname.

Put it on record.
  I am an Arab.
Colour of hair: jet black.
Colour of eyes: brown.
My distinguishing features:
  On my head the *'iqal* cords over a *keffiyeh*[1]
  Scratching him who touches it.
My address:
  I'm from a village, remote, forgotten,
  Its streets without name
  And all its men in the fields and quarry.
  What's there to be angry about?

Put it on record.
  I am an Arab.
You stole my forefathers' vineyards
  And land I used to till,

[1] A *keffiyeh* is a traditional Arab headdress. It is held in place by a cord called an *'iqal*. — Eds.

I and all my children,
And you left us and all my grandchildren
Nothing but these rocks.
Will your government be taking them too
As is being said?

So!
Put it on record at the top of page one:
I don't hate people,
I trespass on no one's property.

And yet, if I were to become hungry
I shall eat the flesh of my usurper.
Beware, beware of my hunger
And of my anger! ■

1964

Understanding and Interpreting

1. To whom does the poem seem to be addressed? Support your view with specific evidence from the poem. What relationship does the speaker establish with this person?
2. What details does the speaker provide to identify himself? What details does he hide?
3. How does the speaker characterize himself? Cite specific lines. How do those details help him express his right to move freely through the land?
4. What do you think "on record" means? What record (or records) might the speaker be referring to?
5. What does the speaker mean when he asks, "Does my status satisfy you?" (l. 33)?
6. How do you interpret the last stanza of "Identity Card"? Do you consider it a warning, a threat, or something else? What is the connection between hunger and anger?
7. Does the speaker fully answer the question he repeatedly poses: "What is there to be angry about"? If so, how? If not, given what you know about the speaker, how do you think he would answer it?
8. How does "Identity Card" become something larger than a poem about relations between Palestinians and Israelis? Consider some of the larger, universal themes it evokes.

Analyzing Language, Style, and Structure

1. **Vocabulary in Context.** What is the meaning of the word "wrest" in line 11? Why is it a particularly good word for what the speaker must do to provide basic necessities for his family?
2. What effect does the repetition of the lines "Put it on record. / I am an Arab" have on you as a reader? How does the repetition contribute to the poem's meaning?
3. The meaning of the line "What's there to be angry about?" (ll. 6, 16, and 46) becomes increasingly ironic as the poem progresses. Discuss how these six words shift in meaning depending on their placement within the poem.

4. Another way to translate the repeating line “Put it on record” is “Write it down.” Does that translation change the meaning of that line? Explain why or why not.
5. Explain how “And yet” in line 60 marks a turning point in the poem and a warning from the speaker to his audience.
6. Look carefully at the way the lines are laid out on the page. Do you see a pattern in the choices to indent certain lines? How does that pattern reflect the themes of the poem?
7. Look carefully at the details in “Identity Card.” Which ones are literal and which are figurative? Keep in mind that it can be difficult to tell. What is the effect of mixing literal and figurative language in the poem?
8. Trace the imagery and language that is related to the earth in “Identity Card.” How does it speak to the values of the speaker?

Topics for Composing

1. AP® FRQ **Poetry Analysis.** In Mahmoud Darwish’s “Identity Card,” published in 1964, the speaker comments on the meaning of identity for someone who is without a homeland. Read the poem carefully. Then, in a well-written essay, analyze how Darwish uses literary elements and techniques to convey the complex role of a homeland in one’s sense of identity.
2. **AP® Literary Argumentation.** In an interview in 2000, Darwish described how he viewed the intersection of poetry and politics: “I don’t think there is any role for poetry [in a Palestinian state]. Poems can’t establish a state. But they can establish a metaphorical homeland in the minds of the people. I think my poems have built some houses in this landscape.” Write an essay in which you take a position on Darwish’s statement: How effectively does this poem establish a “metaphorical homeland” in the minds of readers? Is this something that poetry as a genre has the ability to do? Support your argument with evidence from the poem.
3. **Connections.** Think about the identity cards you carry (driver’s license, school ID). Why do you carry these cards? What do they reveal about your identity? What information does and does not appear there? Given only the information listed on your identity cards, what might a stranger assume about your identity?
4. **Research.** Do some research on the history of Palestinian-Israeli relations. How does your research change your reading of this poem?
5. **Connections.** Examine the ways that “Identity Card” transcends the conflict in the Middle East and can be read as a protest poem in any part of the world where people are oppressed and dispossessed. Consider especially the Black Lives Matter protests of the summer of 2020.
6. **Multimodal.** What aspect of your own identity would you want “put on record”? Write a poem or create an identity card that highlights those aspects of your identity.

Ogun

Kamau Brathwaite

Edward Kamau (E. K.) Brathwaite (1930–2020) was a poet, playwright, critic, and historian whose work explores the links between his West Indian and African heritages. Born and raised on the Caribbean island of Barbados, he was educated at Pembroke College, Cambridge, and received his PhD from the University of Sussex. Recipient of both Guggenheim and Fulbright fellowships and winner of numerous awards, Brathwaite worked in the Ministry of Education in Ghana and taught at the University of the West Indies, the University of Nairobi, Boston University, Yale University, and New York University. Brathwaite's publications include *The Arrivants: A New World Trilogy* (1973), *Black + Blues* (1976), *Mother Poem* (1977), *Sun Poem* (1982), *X/Self* (1987), and *The Zea Mexican Diary* (1993), his final collection, *The Lazarus Poems* (2017), and many more.

KEY CONTEXT The poem's title references Ogun, the Yoruba and Afro-Caribbean creator-god.

My uncle made chairs, tables, balanced doors on, dug out
coffins, smoothing the white wood out

with plane and quick sandpaper until
it shone like his short-sighted glasses.

The knuckles of his hands were silvered knobs of nails hit, hurt and flat-

tened out with blast of heavy hammer. He was knock-knee'd, flat-
footed and his clip clop sandals slapped across the concrete

flooring of his little shop where canefield mulemen and a fleet
of Bedford lorry drivers dropped in to scratch themselves and talk.

There was no shock of wood, no beam
of light mahogany his saw teeth couldn't handle.

When shaping squares for locks, a key hole
care tapped rat tat tat upon the handle

of his humpbacked chisel. Cold
world of wood caught fire as he whittled: rectangle

window frames, the intersecting x of folding chairs, triangle

trellises, the donkey
box-cart in its squeaking square.

But he was poor and most days he was hungry.
Imported cabinets with mirrors, formica table

tops, spine-curving chairs made up of tubes, with hollow
steel-like bird bones that sat on rubber ploughs,

thin beds, stretched not on boards, but blue high-tensioned cables,
were what the world preferred.

And yet he had a block of wood that would have baffled them.
With knife and gimlet care he worked away at this on Sundays,

explored its knotted hurts, cutting his way
along its yellow whorls until his hands could feel

how it had swelled and shivered, breathing air,
its weathered green burning rings of time,

its contoured grain still tuned to roots and water.
And as he cut, he heard the creak of forests:

green lizard faces gulped, grey memories with moth
eyes watched him from their shadows, soft

liquid tendrils leaked among the flowers
and a black rigid thunder he had never heard within his hammer

came stomping up the trunks. And as he worked within his shattered
Sunday shop, the wood took shape: dry shuttered

eyes, slack anciently everted lips, flat
ruined face, eaten by pox, ravaged by rat

and woodworm, dry cistern mouth, cracked
gullet crying for the desert, the heavy black

enduring jaw; lost pain, lost iron;
emerging woodwork image of his anger. ■

1969

Understanding and Interpreting

1. What is the literal situation being described in this poem? Who is the subject, and what is he doing?
2. Where do you think the poem is set? How do you know?
3. The poem is narrated by an outside observer, a family member describing the subject. What is the relationship between the speaker, the title, and the subject? How would the overall impact of the poem change if the subject himself were the speaker?
4. What is the difference between the work the speaker's uncle does "on Sundays" (l. 28) and the work he does the rest of the week?

Analyzing Language, Style, and Structure

1. **Vocabulary in Context.** What do you make of the word "shattered" in line 39? The word "shuttered" might have made more sense there — after all, it's Sunday, a day of rest. Why do you think Brathwaite chose "shattered" for this particular line instead?
2. Read the poem aloud and just try to listen. How does the sound affect your understanding? Identify and discuss the effects of alliteration, onomatopoeia, and line breaks.
3. The poem contains references to the tools of both the carpenter's and the sculptor's craft. What does this specialized language add to the poem? Consider how terms such as "plane" (l. 3) and "gimlet" (l. 28) might have more than one meaning.
4. Identify the figurative language in the poem. There is a great deal of concrete descriptive detail but few actual figures of speech. Why do you think the poet chose to use so few metaphors and similes?
5. The poem has a three-part structure: the opening, a transition, and a final section. Where are these divisions? How does this structure reinforce the ideas or themes of the poem?
6. How do you interpret the ending of the poem, beginning with line 39: "And as he worked . . ."? Can it be read literally or is it completely metaphorical? Explain your answer. What image do you see as you read those lines?
7. What role do colors play in the poem? Which part of the poem is most colorful? What mood do the colors set?

Topics for Composing

1. AP® FRQ **Poetry Analysis.** In Kamau Brathwaite's "Ogun," published in 1969, the speaker paints a picture of his uncle's life through descriptions of his work. Read the poem carefully. Then, in a well-written essay, analyze how Brathwaite uses literary elements and techniques to develop the complex relationship between the speaker's uncle and his work.
2. **AP® Literary Argumentation.** "Ogun" has three distinct sections, each of which presents the speaker's uncle in a different way. Write an essay in which you examine the literary elements in each section and how they connect to paint a complex picture of the poem's subject.
3. **AP® Literary Argumentation.** Does "Ogun" make an argument for the old over the new? If not, what is the main argument it does make? Support your response with evidence from the text of the poem.
4. **Research**. Research the origins of and myths surrounding the creator-god Ogun. Why do you think Brathwaite named a poem about a carpenter after him? How does your research affect your interpretation of the overall meaning of the poem?
5. **Creative Writing.** Rewrite this poem with the uncle as speaker. Try to convey your interpretation of the poem from the point of view of the uncle.
6. **Multimodal.** Create a collage that illustrates what you see as the main contrast the speaker highlights in the poem. Write a short paragraph describing how the images you chose reflect your interpretation.
7. **Connections.** Compare and contrast the description of the speaker's uncle in "Ogun" with the descriptions of the speaker's father and grandfather in "Digging" by Seamus Heaney (p. 57). How are the attitudes of the older generation to their work both alike and different?
8. **Connections.** Compare and contrast the ways anger is portrayed in "Ogun" and Darwish's "Identity Card." How much does each portrayal have to do with identity? How much might each be considered the result of social and political events?

Southern History

Natasha Trethewey

Bill O'Leary/The Washington Post/Getty Images

Natasha Trethewey (b. 1966) is a Pulitzer Prize–winning American poet. She grew up in Mississippi and went on to study at the University of Georgia, Hollins University, and the University of Massachusetts Amherst. Trethewey's first book, *Domestic Work* (2000), won the First Annual Cave Canem Foundation Poetry Prize. Trethewey is the author of five other books of poetry, including *Native Guard* (2006), for which she won the 2007 Pulitzer Prize for Poetry, and *Monument: Poems New and Selected* (2018). In 2012 Trethewey was named both the U.S. Poet Laureate and the poet laureate of Mississippi. Her most recent book, entitled *Memorial Drive*, is a memoir.

Before the war, they were happy, he said,
quoting our textbook. (This was senior-year

history class.) *The slaves were clothed, fed,*
and better off under a master's care.

I watched the words blur on the page. No one
raised a hand, disagreed. Not even me.

It was late; we still had Reconstruction
to cover before the test, and — luckily —

three hours of watching *Gone with the Wind.*
History, the teacher said, *of the old South* —

a true account of how things were back then.
On screen a slave stood big as life: big mouth,

bucked eyes, our textbook's grinning proof — a lie
my teacher guarded. Silent, so did I. ■

2006

Understanding and Interpreting

1. Why do you believe the poet says that the words from the textbook "blur on the page" (l. 5)? Is it because the lesson is dull or boring, as the anticipation that "luckily" there was to be "three hours" of movie watching might suggest, or is there another reason (ll. 8–9)? Explain.
2. Why do you think the speaker identifies the class she's in ("senior year / history class," ll. 2–3)?
3. What is the implication of the statement, "we still had Reconstruction / to cover before the test" (ll. 7–8)?
4. What is the "lie" in line 13? Explain. Why is it "guarded" (l. 14) by the teacher?

5. The speaker uses the phrases "Not even me" (l. 6) and "so did I" (l. 14) to describe her inaction. How do you think the speaker feels about her silence? Why do you think she confesses it? Explain.

Analyzing Language, Style, and Structure

1. **Vocabulary in Context.** What is the meaning of the word "master" in line 4? How does Trethewey play with that meaning in the phrase "a master's care"?
2. The speaker in "Southern History" speaks in the past tense. How does this choice affect the overall tone and meaning of the poem?
3. What does the use of the em-dash in lines 8 (twice), 10, and 13 reveal about the speaker's understanding of the moment she describes — or the way she is processing it from the distance of time?
4. This poem maintains many features of the sonnet form, but the stanza breaks do not conform to tradition. Why might the poet deliberately change stanza breaks to disguise this poem as something other than a sonnet? What does this choice suggest about the speaker's attitude toward the experience the poem describes? Explain.
5. Why do you think the poet makes use of italics in some lines and not in others? What effect does this device have on the tone and mood of the poem?

Topics for Composing

1. AP® FRQ **Poetry Analysis.** In Natasha Trethewey's "Southern History," published in 2006, the speaker reflects on history and its meaning. Read the poem carefully. Then, in a well-written essay, analyze how the poet uses literary elements and techniques to question just what "history" means.
2. **Connections.** The question of accuracy and bias in history textbooks has become a much-debated national issue in the United States. How does Natasha Trethewey's poem, "Southern History," contribute to the discussion of how history is perceived and taught in American classrooms?
3. **Research**. Learn more about the film and book versions of *Gone with the Wind*. In what ways are the book and movie emblems of the "Lost Cause" movement? How does that movement relate to American culture today?
4. **Connections.** Develop a position on how to change the type of harmful narrative the speaker encounters in "Southern History." Whose responsibility is it to make these changes? Is it possible that civil discourse alone can create change? Or since, as Frederick Douglass put it, "power concedes nothing without a demand," must it be legislated or even forced through protests, boycotts, and other actions?
5. **Connections.** Read Trethewey's 2000 poem "History Lesson." Compare and contrast the speakers in each poem. Do they share a common concern? What do you make of the fact that the speaker of "Southern History" speaks in the past tense, while the speaker of "History Lesson" uses present tense? How do these choices affect both tone and mood in each poem?
6. **Multimodal.** Have you studied anything in school that seems dated or counterintuitive? You might reflect on some of what you have been taught about the history of slavery, as in this poem, but you might look into other subjects as well. If you cannot think of anything you have encountered in school, choose a topic that most people misunderstand that you believe should be re-evaluated. Create a short presentation that makes an argument for how to update the instruction or reframe the conversation on the topic you have chosen.

The Facts of Art

Natalie Diaz

Courtesy Natalie Diaz

Natalie Diaz (b. 1978) is an American poet and language activist. She is Mojave and an enrolled member of the Gila River Indian community. After attending Old Dominion University in Norfolk, Virginia, on an athletic scholarship as a Division 1 basketball player, Diaz went on to play professional basketball in Austria, Portugal, Spain, Sweden, and Turkey. She returned to Old Dominion University and earned an MFA in writing. A recipient of the MacArthur Foundation "Genius" Grant, she has authored two books of poetry: *When My Brother Was an Aztec* (2012) and *Post-Colonial Love Poem* (2020), which won the Pulitzer Prize for poetry. She is part of the Institute of American Indian Arts low-residency MFA faculty in Santa Fe, New Mexico, and currently splits her time between Princeton, New Jersey, and Mohave Valley, Arizona, where she works with the last speakers of the Mojave language to teach and revitalize the Mojave language.

KEY CONTEXT This poem is set during the Great Depression of the 1930s. The government, headed by President Franklin Delano Roosevelt, created the Civilian Conservation Corps (CCC) to generate jobs for the many unemployed across the nation. A division of this program, known as the CCC-ID, employed American Indians on public works projects, including roads, on their reservations. However, most local roads were not built on reservations until the 1970s.

woven plaque basket with sunflower design, Hopi,
Arizona, before 1935

from an American Indian basketry exhibit in
Portsmouth, Virginia

The Arizona highway sailed across the desert —
a gray battleship drawing a black wake,
halting at the foot of the orange mesa,
unwilling to go around.

Hopi men and women — brown, and small, and claylike
— peered down from their tabletops at yellow tractors, water trucks,
and white men blistered with sun — red as fire ants — towing
sunscreen-slathered wives in glinting Airstream trailers
in caravans behind them.

Elders knew these BIA[1] roads were bad medicine — knew too
that young men listen less and less, and these young Hopi men
needed work, hence set aside their tools, blocks of cottonwood root

[1] Bureau of Indian Affairs. — Eds.

and half-finished Koshari the clown katsinas,[2] then
signed on with the Department of Transportation,

were hired to stab drills deep into the earth's thick red flesh
on First Mesa,[3] drive giant sparking blades across the mesas' faces,
run the drill bits so deep they smoked, bearding all the Hopi men
in white — *Bad spirits*, said the Elders —

The blades caught fire, burned out — *Ma'saw*[4] *is angry*, the Elders said.
New blades were flown in by helicopter. While Elders dreamed
their arms and legs had been cleaved off and their torsos were flung
over the edge of a dinner table, the young Hopi men went
back to work cutting the land into large chunks of rust.

Nobody noticed at first — not the white workers,
not the Indian workers — but in the mounds of dismantled mesa,
among the clods and piles of sand,
lay the small gray bowls of babies' skulls.

Not until they climbed to the bottom did they see
the silvered bones glinting from the freshly sliced dirt-and-rock wall —
a mausoleum mosaic, a sick tapestry: the tiny remains
roused from death's dusty cradle, cut in half, cracked,
wrapped in time-tattered scraps of blankets.

Let's call it a day, the white foreman said.
That night, all the Indian workers got sad-drunk — got sick
— while Elders sank to their kivas[5] in prayer. Next morning,
as dawn festered on the horizon, state workers scaled the mesas,
knocked at the doors of pueblos that had them, hollered
into those without them,

demanding the Hopi men come back to work — then begging them —
then buying them whiskey — begging again — finally sending their white
wives up the dangerous trail etched into the steep sides
to buy baskets from Hopi wives and grandmothers
as a sign of treaty.

When that didn't work, the state workers called the Indians lazy,
sent their sunhat-wearing wives back up to buy more baskets —
katsinas too — then called the Hopis *good-for-nothings*,
before begging them back once more.

[2] Katsinas, in Hopi religious tradition, are dolls carved out of cottonwood root into depictions of the Katsinam, or Hopi spirit messengers. Koshari is a trickster katsina. — Eds.

[3] One of three mesas that unite the system of villages on the Arizona Hopi Reservation. — Eds.

[4] A Hopi deity who serves as guardian of the earth. — Eds.

[5] Large rooms, either partially or wholly underground, used for Hopi religious ceremonies. — Eds.

We'll try again in the morning, the foreman said.
But the Indian workers never returned —
The BIA's and DOT's[6] calls to work went unanswered,
as the fevered Hopis stayed huddled inside.

The small bones half-buried in the crevices of mesa —
in the once-holy darkness of silent earth and always-night —
smiled or sighed beneath the moonlight, while white women
in Airstream trailers wrote letters home

praising their husbands' patience, describing the lazy savages:
such squalor in their stone and plaster homes — cobs of corn stacked
floor to ceiling against crumbling walls — their devilish ceremonies
and the barbaric way they buried their babies,
oh, and those beautiful, beautiful baskets. ■

2012

[6] Department of Transportation. — Eds.

Understanding and Interpreting

1. Note that the Hopi men *and* women are presented together in line 5; not so the Elders and the young men, and not so the white men and their wives. How does Natalie Diaz characterize each of these groups? Why might she have chosen to establish these contrasts early in the poem?
2. What warning do the Elders try to give the young man?
3. At first, the state workers try what might be considered bribery to convince the Hopis to return to work. When that fails, they resort to derision. What might Diaz be suggesting by this swift change in their perspective?
4. What is the effect of the poet's decision to conclude the poem with an account of the white women's letters home?
5. Now that you've read the poem, what do you make of the title? What, in the context of this poem, are the "facts" of art? How does the title express or relate to the themes the poem explores?

Analyzing Language, Style, and Structure

1. **Vocabulary in Context.** What is the meaning of the word "tabletops" (l. 6) in the context of the poem? How does it help establish the poem's setting?
2. How does the figurative language set the scene and contribute to the tone and mood in the first two stanzas?
3. Pay close attention to the syntax and structure of the poem. Why do you think Diaz chose to write such complex sentences, breaking them across both lines and stanzas? What mood does this help create? What does it suggest about the poet's attitude toward the events the poem describes?
4. The image of white women in Airstream trailers appears both near the beginning and end of the poem: first, as the white men are arriving, "towing / sunscreen-slathered wives in glinting

Airstream trailers" (ll. 7–8); then, after the Hopis refused to return to work, "white women / in Airstream trailers wrote letters home" (ll. 54–55). Compare and contrast the context in which each of these appears. Why do you think Diaz chose to repeat this image in particular? What effect does each image, taken on its own, have on the poem? What effect do the images have when taken together?

5. What do the Hopi baskets represent? What elements of style does Diaz use to convey that meaning to readers?
6. How does the visual structure of "The Facts of Art" mirror its geographical setting?

Topics for Composing

1. AP® FRQ **Poetry Analysis.** In Natalie Diaz's "The Facts of Art," published in 2012, the speaker recounts the building of a highway on Hopi Indian land during the 1930s. Read the poem carefully. Then, in a well-written essay, analyze how Diaz uses literary elements and techniques to convey the significance of the events to the speaker of the poem.
2. **Creative Writing.** Using "The Facts of Art" as a model, write a poem that depicts a clash of cultures. Consider starting with an artifact that has been misappropriated or misidentified as the epigraph for the poem.
3. **Research.** Research the "Indian New Deal" of the 1930s, including the role the BIA and CCC-ID played. What positive changes were brought about as a result of the Indian New Deal? What discriminatory and harmful systems and practices remained in place? How does this poem reflect both the progress and barriers to it that occurred during that era?
4. **Connections.** Write an essay in which you take a stand on how, why, where, and by whom objects from marginalized cultures and societies should be shared with the public. In other words, who should be telling the story of those societies? What are the "facts of art"?

Dolorosa

Molly Rose Quinn

Project Contrast

Molly Rose Quinn (b. 1988) is an American poet who was raised in Memphis, Tennessee. She earned an MFA in poetry from Sarah Lawrence College, and her poems have appeared in *Black Warrior Review*, *The Offing*, *PEN Poetry Series*, and elsewhere. Quinn has taught writing at the Sackett Street Writers' Workshop and co-organizes the Moby-Dick Marathon NYC, an annual marathon reading of Melville's classic novel. She has served as the director of public programming at Housing Works Bookstore Café, a volunteer-run nonprofit bookstore in Manhattan dedicated to fighting AIDS and homelessness. A co-founder of the Center for Southern Literary Arts, she is currently the Executive Director of OUTMemphis: The LGBTQ Center for the Mid-South.

KEY CONTEXT The title of the poem is an allusion to *STABAT MATER DOLOROSA*, a thirteenth-century hymn whose title translates to "the mother stood weeping." The song is about the suffering of Mary during the crucifixion of Christ. The epigraph for the poem notes that the setting is in the chapel at St. Mary's School for Girls, a private all-girls school in Memphis, Tennessee.

(The Chapel at St. Mary's School for Girls)

where the pillar falls at the edge of morning the teachers
beg us to tug down our skirts they offer their palms
for our gumballs and your god is here to say that beauty
is easy like cutting teeth and your legs and your legs
and yours and I in the pew wish to scrape down
to nothing cuff myself kneel better and what could be
worthier hair voice and loudly I beg for ascendancy
dear classmates your legs in neat rows pray as you do
with fists up and the sun in here bare pray for safety
the teen saint she is the girl to win it all for I beg my
mariology[1] as she sets the way that girl she never once
begged for sparing she begged for death like wine
she begged the best she supplicated she died this dying
begs for me I give it such pleasure and legs and the pew
and the alb[2] and the bread and all other objects beg to be
candles when you are a candle you can beg to be lit
each of you in the pew you beg to be lit I'll never shine
bigger as we know teenagers beg to be begged and we do
you girls you begged me to hold you begged me to take
what I took you beg bigger and better and for that
you'll be queens the chimes chime and bells bell
and dear god I know I can be the greatest girl ever
by anointing all alone and being loved the very best
and she says what is so good about anger god killed
my son for himself I suppose and this halo it's nothing
I asked for and of course she'll be lying and your legs
and your legs and yours tanned and the best thing all year. ■

2013

[1] The study of the Virgin Mary. — Eds.

[2] A white garment worn by leaders in the several different church denominations; in this case the Episcopal church. — Eds.

Understanding and Interpreting

1. Who is "she" in line 24? What is significant about the statement the speaker attributes to her?
2. How would you characterize the speaker of the poem? What is the speaker's attitude toward the church? womanhood? her teachers? her classmates?
3. Why might Molly Rose Quinn have decided to name the poem after this particular hymn? In what ways does the poem explore themes of suffering and faith?
4. Do you think "Dolorosa" is a poem that is more about religion or about adolescence? How do the two meet in the poem?

Analyzing Language, Style, and Structure

1. **Vocabulary in Context.** What is the meaning of the word "ascendancy" in line 7? What multiple meanings might it have in the context of "Dolorosa"?
2. This poem is notable for its odd juxtapositions and jumbles of objects and images. For example, consider the "legs and the pew / and the alb and the bread" (ll. 14–15). What is the intent and effect of this technique? Explain, using at least two examples from the poem.
3. What effect does the poem's run-on, stream-of-consciousness style have on your interpretation of its meaning? How does it help shape the mood of the poem?
4. How does the tone shift after the speaker says, "dear classmates your legs in neat rows pray as you do / with fists up and the sun in here bare pray for safety" (ll. 8–9)? Explain.
5. The word "begs" (or forms of it) appears more than a dozen times in this poem. Similarly, "legs" appears several times as well. What is the effect of such repetition and rhyme? How does it contribute to your understanding of the poem?

Topics for Composing

1. **AP® FRQ** **Poetry Analysis.** In Molly Rose Quinn's "Dolorosa," published in 2013, the teenage speaker's thoughts mingle freely with the traditional practices of her religion. Read the poem carefully. Then, in a well-written essay, analyze how Quinn uses literary elements and techniques to develop a connection between religious ritual and female adolescence.
2. **AP® Literary Argumentation.** Poet Molly Rose Quinn lived in New York City for several years and has recently returned to Memphis, Tennessee, where she spent much of her childhood. Memphis is a city well known for its rich musical traditions, but it also has a long history of racist violence. How does Quinn use structure and style to address and incorporate these elements of Memphis culture and history in this poem?
3. **AP® Literary Argumentation.** In discussing "Dolorosa," Quinn has said that it is "about how in Christianity, everything is about the body and what you do with it — even the things that aren't explicitly about the body. And that's exactly what being a teenage girl is like. Everything, everything is about the body and what you do with it." What is the speaker's attitude toward bodies in this poem? What connection does it draw between the way bodies are treated in Christian tradition and social expectations for young women?
4. **Connections.** In an interview for web-based Brooklyn Poets, Quinn said, "More than church this is a poem of womanhood. The legs and hair." What do you think Quinn means by that? How do the language and structure of the poem reflect your understanding of this statement?
5. **Multimodal.** Consider the collage effect of the many images layered within "Dolorosa," and create your own collage containing images that evoke the mood and setting of the poem. How does each of the images you've chosen evoke meaning on its own? What is the effect of these images when taken together? How does this collective meaning reflect a theme of the poem?
6. **Creative Writing.** Write a poem that uses layered imagery to convey the significance of an important experience in your life. It can be a poem about attending a religious service, or it can be about something else, such as learning to drive, getting a job, teaching a younger sibling to ride a bike, or playing a sport.

Written by Himself

Gregory Pardlo

Gregory Pardlo (b. 1968) is an American poet whose second volume of poetry, *Digest*, won the 2015 Pulitzer Prize for Poetry. Pardlo grew up in Willingboro, New Jersey, and received a BA in English from Rutgers University–Camden and an MFA from New York University. He currently teaches at Rutgers University-Camden. His first book of poems, *Totem*, won the *American Poetry Review*/Honickman Prize in 2007, and he also translated *Pencil of Rays and Spiked Mace* (2004) by the Danish poet Niels Lyngsø. His most recent book is *Air Traffic: A Memoir of Ambition and Manhood in America* (2018).

KEY CONTEXT The title of this poem is a reference to the subtitles of many autobiographies of formerly enslaved people in the years leading up to the Civil War, which began in 1861 and ended in 1865. For instance, *The Narrative of the Life of Frederick Douglass*, an 1845 autobiography by the former enslaved man who became a leader in the abolitionist movement, often appears with the subtitle *Written by Himself*.

I was born in minutes in a roadside kitchen a skillet
whispering my name. I was born to rainwater and lye;
I was born across the river where I
was borrowed with clothespins, a harrow tooth,[1]
broadsides[2] sewn in my shoes. I returned, though
it please you, through no fault of my own,
pockets filled with coffee grounds and eggshells.
I was born still and superstitious; I bore an unexpected burden.
I gave birth, I gave blessing, I gave rise to suspicion.
I was born abandoned outdoors in the heat-shaped air,
air drifting like spirits and old windows.
I was born a fraction and a cipher and a ledger entry;
I was an index of first lines when I was born.
I was born waist-deep stubborn in the water crying
                    ain't I a woman and a brother I was born
to this hall of mirrors, this horror story I was
born with a prologue of references, pursued
by mosquitoes and thieves, I was born passing
off the problem of the twentieth century: I was born.
I read minds before I could read fishes and loaves;[3]
I walked a piece of the way alone before I was born. ■

2014

[1] A piece of farm equipment used to make plowed land level. — Eds.

[2] A large sheet of paper with a public announcement printed on one side, popular during the nineteenth century. — Eds.

[3] A reference to the biblical story in which Jesus feeds five thousand people with only two fish and five loaves of bread. — Eds.

Understanding and Interpreting

1. Why do you think Gregory Pardlo chose "Written by Himself" as the title for this poem? How does the Key Context information influence your understanding and appreciation of the poem?
2. Does Pardlo always mean the same thing with the phrase "I was born"? What are some of its different meanings? Why do you think the poet chose to use that phrase to both open and conclude the poem?
3. Why was the speaker "borrowed," and what does it mean that he was borrowed along with "clothespins" and a "harrow tooth"? Why would the speaker have kept "broadsides sewn in [his] shoes" (ll. 4–5)?
4. "Written by Himself" transitions among a few different time periods. Identify the eras and explain how each one helps the speaker identify himself.

Analyzing Language, Style, and Structure

1. **Vocabulary in Context.** In the context of the poem, what is the meaning of the words in line 12: "fraction," "cipher," "ledger"? How do the connotations of each one develop an underlying theme of the poem? What is the effect of these words when taken together?
2. How do the themes of fertility and childbirth run through the poem? Trace the various images that support the repeated phrase "I was born." What is the effect of the anaphora, or repetition, of that phrase? How is birth portrayed in the poem? Look at single words as well as more complex images.
3. The poem presents a collage of both related and seemingly unrelated images. Which ones might refer to literal experiences? Which ones are most mysterious? Explain the significance of the nonliteral images.
4. Note Pardlo's inconsistent use of punctuation. What do you make of the enjambment in lines 5 to 6 and again in lines 18 to 19? How does this technique help reinforce the poem's meaning?

Topics for Composing

1. AP® FRQ **Poetry Analysis.** In Gregory Pardlo's "Written by Himself," published in 2014, the speaker weaves a tale of self-creation. Read the poem carefully. Then, in a well-written essay, analyze how Pardlo uses literary elements and techniques to convey the speaker's complex perspective on his sense of identity.
2. **AP® Literary Argumentation.** Pardlo has said, "I accept that my identity is a digest of discourses and that my engagement with the world is mediated through these discourses." How does the poem, and especially the voice of its speaker, reflect that statement? What discourses are present in the poem, and how do they mediate the poet's communication with the reader? Use evidence from the poem to support your response.
3. **Connections.** Examine the ways Pardlo moves between myth and modernity in this poem. What historical connections do the objects in the poem have? What connections do the objects have in modern times? How do these objects work together to create meaning in the poem?
4. **Connections.** Read Sojourner Truth's speech "Ain't I a Woman," to which "Written by Himself" alludes in line 15. What does that allusion add to your understanding of the poem?

Why might Pardlo have used it? What assumptions does the allusion suggest he makes about his audience?

5. **Multimodal.** Illustrate "Written by Himself" with a collage that contains the images from the poem. Create them yourself or use images from art, photography, or advertising.
6. **Creative Writing.** Using Pardlo's poem as inspiration and a starting point, write a poem that pulls together disparate aspects of your identity to tell the world who you are. Incorporate at least three images, events, or objects that represent something you consider core to your sense of self.

loose strife [Somebody says draw a map]

Quan Barry

Born in Saigon in 1973, Vietnamese poet and novelist Quan Barry was raised on the North Shore of Boston. She is the author of four poetry books, most recently *Loose Strife* (2015) and two novels, including *She Rides Upon Sticks* (2020). With a BA from the University of Virginia and an MFA from the University of Michigan, Barry was also a Wallace Stegner Fellow at Stanford University. Currently, she teaches at the University of Wisconsin-Madison.

KEY CONTEXT Barry's collection *Loose Strife* opens with this poem. Each of the poems in the collection is titled "loose strife" with the first line in brackets. "Loose strife" is a purple flower that grows up to eight feet, a beautiful blossom yet an invasive species that threatens other plants and the natural environment around it. "Loose strife" also refers to the Greek tragedy *Oresteia* and its portrayal of a seemingly endless cycle of violence. This particular poem makes several references to the Vietnam War and its aftermath. A long conflict involving multiple countries, the war lasted more than twenty years, ending with the fall of Saigon in 1975. The United States fought as an ally of South Vietnam against the communist government of North Vietnam. Over 3 million people lost their lives: more than 58,000 Americans, over 1 million North Vietnamese soldiers and Vietcong guerrilla fighters, between 200,000 and 250,000 South Vietnamese soldiers, and as many as 2 million Vietnamese civilians.

Somebody says draw a map. Populate it with the incidents
of your childhood. Mark the spot where the lake receded
after a winter of light snow. The stairs on which someone
slapped you. The place where the family dog hung itself
by jumping over the back fence while still on the dog run,
hours later its body like a limp flag on a windless day.
Draw a map, someone says. Let yourself remember.
In the refugee camp a hundred thousand strong
draw the stony outcrop from which you could no longer see
the plume of smoke that was your village. Draw a square
for the bathroom stall where Grandpa hid each day
in order to eat his one egg free from the starving eyes

of his classmates, an X for the courthouse where you and he
were naturalized, a broken line for the journey. Draw a map,
Jon says. Let it be your way into the poem. Here is where
that plane filled with babies crashed[1] that I was not on.
Here is where I was ashamed. On the second floor
at Pranash University the people wait their turn. Have you
drawn your map, Jon asks. He has rolled up his sleeves.
Forty-five minutes to noon the Prince stands up and says
that the monks must be excused. We watch them file out,
saffron robes as if their bodies have burst into blossom.
Draw a map. Fly halfway around the globe. Here is the room
next to the library where you realize how poor your tradition is,
the local people with poetic forms still in use that date back
to the time of Christ. Tell us about your map. Explain
how these wavy lines represent the river, this rectangle
the school-turned-prison where only seven
escaped with their lives. This is my map. This star the place
where I sat in a roomful of people among whom not one
was not touched by genocide. Every last map resplendent with death
though nobody knows where their loved ones lie buried.
How many times can I appropriate a story that is not mine to tell?
The woman stands up and says she is not a poet, that she
doesn't have the words. She points to a triangle on a piece of paper.
Here is the spot where she found human bones in the well
of her childhood home, and how her mother told her
don't be afraid because it was not the work of wild animals. ■

2015

[1] A reference to Operation Babylift in 1975, when the first flight of orphans out of South Vietnam made a crash landing, and many of them died. — Eds.

Understanding and Interpreting

1. What expectations do you have from the very first line: "Somebody says draw a map"? How do you picture the "somebody" telling the speaker to draw a map? What does the idea of a map suggest to you as you enter the poem?
2. One way to read the poem is as a series of stories. What are the subjects of each of the stories? Do you perceive any pattern in the progression of the events in these stories? In what way do they resemble fictional narrative structures?
3. In this poem, Quan Barry refers to some actual historical events, as well as ways in which personal experience can intersect with larger world events. Do you need to know the exact details of the world events in order to understand their significance to the speaker? Explain.
4. What do we know about the speaker in this poem? Who are the other characters, including Jon? What, if anything, unifies the speaker with them?

5. How do you interpret the question, "How many times can I appropriate a story that is not mine to tell?"? To whom is this question addressed? What does "appropriate" mean in this context? Why doesn't the speaker view it as hers to tell?
6. In what ways are the ideas of travel and journey — in terms of both place and time — entwined with the idea of creation?
7. Who is "the woman" who "stands up and says she is not a poet" (l. 34)? What does poetry have to do with the map in the poem?

Analyzing Language, Style, and Structure

1. **Vocabulary in Context.** Barry's speaker refers to "Every last map resplendent with death" in line 31. The adjective *resplendent* refers to something beautiful, richly colored, even luxurious. Why might the word in the context of this poem be an effective description of death? How does it help reveal the attitude of the speaker?
2. What associations does Barry evoke with the idea of drawing a map? How does she draw on both literal and figurative meanings of the word? Consider the line "This is my map" (l. 29) in your response.
3. How does the repetition of the imperative clause "draw a map" function in the poem?
4. The poem consists of imperative clauses and sentences, sentence fragments, and one question, often interrupted by line breaks. Although the poem at first appears to be very fragmented, there are discernible shifts that signal a change in overall direction. Identify at least two and discuss the way these relate to the structure of the poem. What meaning do these elements work together to evoke?
5. The poem includes many stark and memorable images. Identify three of them and discuss why you find them especially powerful.
6. One critic described the language of the poem as combining a "large swath of brutality and suffering with a cool, self-conscious control. . . ." Why do you agree or disagree with this characterization of the overall tone? Cite specific text to illustrate your position.
7. How would you describe the connection of the last five lines of the poem to its overall meaning? Does it function primarily as a coda, a dramatic final image, a warning, or something else? Explain.

Topics for Composing

1. **AP® FRQ Poetry Analysis.** In Quan Barry's "loose strife [Somebody says draw a map]," published in 2015, the speaker recalls the experience of being asked to "draw a map" as a step toward writing poetry. Read the poem carefully. Then, in a well-written essay, analyze how Barry uses literary elements and techniques to convey the speaker's complex perspective on the relationship between trauma and the creation of art.
2. **AP® Literary Argumentation.** Many of the issues that Barry raises in her work involve division, violence, and strife, as the title of the collection indicates. Taken together, do the examples in this poem simply reveal painful experiences, or does the speaker address them in a way that leads to healing? Cite specific lines or passages to support your response.
3. **Speaking and Listening.** When asked why she so often writes about violence, Barry replied: "I used to think I write a lot about violence, but now I realize that what I'm really writing about is conflict. . . . Conflict between individuals, cultures, nations, generations, men and women, etc. . . . I'm not interested in proselytizing — I like to make connections. . . ."

Make a list of your associations with violence, and a second list of associations with conflict. Partner up and look for commonalities. Then discuss how (or if) this distinction between violence and conflict contributes to your appreciation/understanding of the poem.

4. **Connections.** This poem has been described as being one of "the greatest examples of the poetry of witness," referring to works by poets who have lived through and survived extreme situations of war, imprisonment, torture, slavery, or other kinds of oppression. This genre of poetry can be a way to preserve memory not just for survivors but for the historical record. Choose a poem that fits into this tradition and discuss its similarities with Barry's "loose strife [Somebody says draw a map]."
5. **Multimodal.** The collection *Loose Strife* was inspired by the 2012 gallery collaboration of the same name between Barry and the visual artist Michael Velliquette. While Barry did not use the artwork in her collection, this poem has a strong visual quality to it. Develop an interpretation of the poem by pairing still or moving images with an audio track of you or a classmate reading the text. You might present your images in a linear fashion or turn them into a collage.

(citizen) (illegal)

José Olivarez

Mercedes Zapata

José Olivarez, the author of the poetry collection *Citizen Illegal* (2018), is the editor of the anthology LatiNEXT (2020), co-author of *Home Court* (2014), and the co-host of the poetry podcast *The Poetry Gods*. Son of Mexican immigrants, he earned a BA from Harvard University. Among his honors and awards are the 2019 prestigious Ruth Lilly and Dorothy Sargent Rosenberg Poetry Fellowship from the Poetry Foundation and, in 2018, the first annual Author and Artist in Justice Award from the Phillips Brooks House Association. He currently lives in New York City.

KEY CONTEXT Like many countries, the United States offers citizenship to anyone born on U.S. soil, a concept known as birthright citizenship. In recent years, however, the legality of birthright citizenship has become a subject of debate. In the title and throughout the poem, José Olivarez refers to undocumented immigrants as "illegal," a derogatory term. Consider how this choice reflects Olivarez's understanding of his identity, and be mindful of context, both Olivarez's and yours, as you read.

Mexican woman (illegal) and Mexican man (illegal) have
a Mexican (illegal)-American (citizen).
Is the baby more Mexican or American?
Place the baby in the arms of the mother (illegal).
If the mother holds the baby (citizen)
too long, does the baby become illegal?

The baby is a boy (citizen). He goes to school (citizen).
His classmates are American (citizen). He is outcast (illegal).
His "Hellos" are in the wrong language (illegal).
He takes the hyphen separating loneliness (Mexican)
from friendship (American) and jabs it at the culprit (illegal).
Himself (illegal). His own traitorous tongue (illegal).
His name (illegal). His mom (illegal). His dad (illegal).

Take a Mexican woman (illegal) and a Mexican man (illegal).
If they have a baby and the baby looks white enough to pass (citizen).
If the baby grows up singing Selena[1] songs to his reflection (illegal).
If the baby hides from el cucuy and la migra[2] (illegal).
If the baby (illegal) (citizen) grows up to speak broken Spanish (illegal)
and perfect English (citizen). If the boy's nickname is Güerito[3] (citizen).
If the boy attends college (citizen). If the boy only dates women (illegal)
of color (illegal). If the boy (illegal) uses phrases like Women of Color (citizen).
If the boy (illegal) (citizen) writes (illegal) poems (illegal).

If the boy (citizen) (illegal) grows up (illegal) and can only write (illegal)
this story in English (citizen), does that make him more
American (citizen) or Mexican (illegal)? ■

2018

[1] A reference to Selena Quintanilla-Perez, a popular Mexican-American singer known simply as Selena. Known as the Queen of Tejano music, she rose to popularity during the late 1980s and early 1990s. She had begun to cross over into English-language pop music when she was shot and killed by a fan in 1995. — Eds.

[2] El cucuy is a mythical monster in many Latin American cultural traditions. La migra is an umbrella term for government organizations that deal with immigration, such as Border Patrol. —Eds.

[3] Spanish slang for a light-haired or light-skinned person. — Eds.

Understanding and Interpreting

1. What factual information does the opening stanza (ll. 1–6) provide to readers? What expectations does it set for the subject or point of view in the poem?
2. Why do you think there are no names attached to the three people described in poem? What difference, if any, would it make to you as a reader if they were identified by name?
3. How do you interpret lines 10–11: "[the boy] takes the hyphen separating loneliness (Mexican) / from friendship (American) and jabs it at the culprit (illegal)"? In your response, consider who the "culprit" is. Is it the action or the culprit that is "illegal" in this context?
4. According to the third stanza, what is the experience of the boy as he grows up? What inferences can you draw from the speaker's description of the boy's self-image?
5. By the end of the poem, to what extent has the speaker "answered" the question posed in the opening stanza: "Is the baby more Mexican or American?" (l. 3)?
6. What does this poem ultimately convey about the definition of citizenship? Consider the contradictions the speaker raises throughout the poem in your response.

Analyzing Language, Style, and Structure

1. **Vocabulary in Context.** The word "culprit" comes from the Anglo-French words "cul prit," a contraction of *culpable*, which means "deserving blame." What is its most literal meaning as it is used today? What associations does the word have as José Olivarez uses it in line 11? Why is it an effective choice?
2. What is the function of the parentheticals in this poem? Are they explanations, asides, criticisms, or something else? Pay particular attention to the effect of Olivarez's choice not to use the opposite of "illegal" (i.e., "legal") but instead to juxtapose "illegal" with "citizen."
3. Why does Olivarez describe the boy as having a "traitorous tongue (illegal)" (l. 12)? What other examples of personification do you find in the poem? How do these contribute to meaning?
4. The poem "(citizen) (illegal)" consists of simple declarative sentences, interrogative sentences, an imperative sentence, and sentence fragments. Identify at least one example of each and discuss how these syntactical structures contribute to achieving Olivarez's purpose.
5. How does the poem's structure help develop and intensify the speaker's criticisms about the distinctions between what is "illegal" and what is not? Why, for instance, is only dating "women / of color" "(illegal)," but using the phrase "Women of Color" is a mark of being a "(citizen)"?
6. How would you describe the tone of the poem? Do you see shifts in tone, or is there one consistent tone throughout? Cite textual evidence to support your response.

Topics for Composing

1. AP® FRQ **Poetry Analysis.** In José Olivarez's "(citizen) (illegal)," published in 2018, the speaker interrogates the concept of "legality" and the meaning of citizenship for a child born in the United States to two undocumented immigrants. Read the poem carefully. Then, in a well-written essay, analyze how Olivarez uses literary elements and techniques to develop the speaker's complex perspective on the connection between citizenship and identity.
2. **Speaking and Listening.** Working in groups, develop an interpretive spoken-word performance of "(citizen) (illegal)." Focus on the parenthetical comments, but feel free to move them around purposefully. That is, you might simply have different voices read different parts, or you might have a series of echoes or overlapping voices to emphasize the parenthetical asides.
3. **Connections.** In an interview, Olivarez relates how he came to the realization that he no longer wanted to try to "fit in." In fact, as he says, "I actually didn't want to participate in America as constructed. I wanted to construct a world where I didn't have to erase parts of myself. Poetry gave me a space to talk about the in-betweenness that I felt." Describe a time when your own feeling of "in-betweenness" — for whatever reason — led you to make a significant decision, as Olivarez describes, or gain a better understanding of the forces at work to make you feel that way, as he does in "(citizen) (illegal)."
4. **Research**. The United States Citizenship and Immigration Services has revised the civics portion of the naturalization test. Conduct research into the reason for the new test; then take the online practice test yourself. Discuss how this information and experience affects your interpretation of the poem "(citizen) (illegal)."
5. **Connections.** The cover of the book in which this poem appears centers on an image by the Chicago-based street artist known as Sentrock who, growing up in Phoenix, Arizona, was influenced by Mexican American murals. Find an image of the cover and look closely at its details. In what ways do you think it captures the tone and ideas Olivarez expresses in "(citizen) (illegal)"?

AQUÍ HAY TODO, MIJA

Alexis Aceves García

Alexis Aceves García (b. 1992) is a poet who focuses on family history and whose works envision a future where members of the trans community are not seen and treated as outsiders. With poems already featured in *Catapult Magazine*, *Apogee Journal*, and other print and online sources, García is currently working on a poetry manuscript. "AQUI HAY TODO, MIJA" was published as part of *Brooklyn Poets*' Poet of the Week series.

Casi Moss

KEY CONTEXT The poem's title translates to "Here there is all, my child." Alexis Aceves García has said that this poem is based on their own experience with visiting their grandmother (abuela), Olivia Rivas García. Alexis wanted to honor not only their abuela, but also abuela's home, where the entire family lived after migrating to the United States from Mexico. National City, named in the epigraph of this poem, is a city in southern California, located near the U.S.-Mexico border at Tijuana.

National City, 2019

i open the screen door slowly
n wait for Abuela n her red walker
to begin the procession
from the back door out to the street

ay, mis rodillas[1]

vines wrap around the wooden deck n reach to steady
whatever cartilage is left in her knees
down the ramp she stops near the lemon trees
there are more than i remember
glistening in the sun, a kingdom
she softened w/ her voice

tan bello mi limón[2]

n the lemons blush off the evergreen
branch into her bowl
the granadas[3] kneel from trees
to crown her Abuela, reina[4] of E. 8th St.
she smiles her three perfect teeth
toward the palm tree

[1] Spanish for "Oh, my knees." — Eds.
[2] Spanish for "So gorgeous, my lemon tree." — Eds.
[3] Spanish for "pomegranates." — Eds.
[4] Spanish for "queen." — Eds.

mira, parece que está abrazando todos
los árboles[5]

despacito caminamos[6] past the Jeep blooming rust
she points to the tomate y melón,[7] mint, the birds
of paradise that didn't survive
the pink roses that did

cuando paso los rosales les doy un beso
tan preciosas mis rosas[8]

she palms the banana tree
the neighbor planted
swinging heavy over the wire fence

lo que está de este lado es mío[9]

whatever is on our side
we keep

whatever is on our side
we eat ■

2020

[5] Spanish for "Look, it seems to be hugging all / the trees." —Eds.
[6] Spanish for "slowly we walk." —Eds
[7] Spanish for "tomato and melon." —Eds.
[8] Spanish for "When I pass the rosebushes I give them a kiss / so precious my roses." —Eds.
[9] Spanish, best translated as "What falls on my side is mine." —Eds.

Understanding and Interpreting

1. What functions do the "vines" (l. 6) play? What is the relationship between Abuela and these vines?
2. What does the description of Abuela's "cartilage" (l. 7) suggest about her? What other details support this portrayal of Abuela?
3. What does the speaker mean by "there are more than i remember" (l. 9)? What does this statement suggest about the speaker and the setting of the poem?
4. What is referred to as "a kingdom" (l. 10)? What other words and images support this perspective?
5. What causes Abuela to "[smile] her three perfect teeth" (l. 17) in the fifth stanza?
6. What do Abuela's actions in stanzas 7–9 suggest about her relationship with her environment? Why does she point to and palm the different plants?
7. What does Abuela's assertion that whatever falls over the fence and onto her lawn is hers to "keep" (l. 32) or "eat" (l. 34) reveal about her?
8. How do you interpret the statement in the title of the poem? Why might Alexis Aceves García have chosen to write the title in capital letters? How might it refer to more than just the trees and vegetation?

Analyzing Language, Style, and Structure

1. **Vocabulary in Context.** In line 3, Abuela begins the "procession / from the back door out to the street" (ll. 3–4). In what context is the word *procession* normally used? Consider how it can apply to both religious and secular occasions. What does this word contribute to your understanding of the speaker's attitude toward their abuela?
2. What does the speaker's choice to use lowercase "i" throughout the poem convey about how they see themself, particularly in relationship to the people, places, and things in the poem?
3. What is the effect of including Abuela's voice throughout the poem? In your response, consider that García chose to retain these phrases in Spanish rather than provide them in translation in the original publication of the poem.
4. García places Abuela's dialogue in separate stanzas. Why might they have chosen to include multiple voices within this poem?
5. As the speaker and Abuela stroll through the yard, they observe the "Jeep blooming rust" (l. 21)? What is the effect of this image, and how does it relate to the other details they contemplate?
6. Abuela is not the only person who speaks Spanish within the poem. Note that the speaker also switches to Spanish at various times. How does this choice reveal the speaker's perspective of the setting of the poem? What does it convey about the speaker's understanding of their own identity?
7. How do García's deviations from English conventions — such as writing the pronoun "I" in lowercase, omitting some punctuation, and substituting "n" for *and* — help characterize the speaker?

Topics for Composing

1. AP® FRQ **Poetry Analysis.** In Alexis Aceves García's "AQUÍ HAY TODO, MIJA," published in 2020, the speaker details Abuela's "procession" through her yard. Read the poem carefully. Then, in a well-written essay, analyze how García uses literary elements and techniques to convey Abuela's attitude toward her surroundings.
2. AP® FRQ **Poetry Analysis.** In Alexis Aceves García's "AQUÍ HAY TODO, MIJA," published in 2020, the speaker relates Abuela's actions and observations as the two of them walk around her yard. Read the poem carefully. Then, in a well-written essay, analyze how García uses literary elements and techniques to portray the speaker's relationship with Abuela.
3. **AP® Literary Argumentation.** "AQUÍ HAY TODO, MIJA" is part of a collection that García says is "about joy and rest in the face of our history." In what way does this poem convey both joy and rest? Use evidence from the text to support your response.
4. **Connections.** García shared that on one occasion when they were walking with Abuela Olivia Rivas García through her yard, "Abuela turned to me and said 'Aquí hay todo, mija.'" What do you think García's grandmother meant by this? Describe a place that comes close to representing for you what Abuela's yard means to her.
5. **Speaking and Listening.** Select a volunteer to perform a reading of the poem that leaves out Abuela's words. Then, have another student join in and play the role of Abuela in a second reading of the poem. After listening to both versions, engage in a whole-class discussion that explores how the audience's experience differs when the two speakers are included.
6. **Creative Writing.** Think about a place that is significant to your relationship with a friend or family member. Write a poem in which you use this setting to portray your attitude toward this relationship. As García does in this poem, embed dialogue — or various voices — into your poem.

AP® Multiple-Choice Practice

from Interpreter of Maladies

Jhumpa Lahiri

"Mr. Kapasi, wait. There's room here," Mrs. Das called out. She gathered Tina onto her lap, insisting that he accompany them. And so, together, they had bottled mango juice and sandwiches and plates of onions and potatoes deep-fried in graham-flour batter. After finishing two omelette sandwiches Mr. Das took more pictures of the group as they ate.

"How much longer?" he asked Mr. Kapasi as he paused to load a new roll of film in the camera.

"About half an hour more."

By now the children had gotten up from the table to look at more monkeys perched in a nearby tree, so there was a considerable space between Mrs. Das and Mr. Kapasi. Mr. Das placed the camera to his face and squeezed one eye shut, his tongue exposed at one corner of his mouth. "This looks funny, Mina, you need to lean in closer to Mr. Kapasi."

She did. He could smell a scent on her skin, like a mixture of whiskey and rosewater. He worried suddenly that she could smell his perspiration, which he knew had collected beneath the synthetic material of his shirt. He polished off his mango juice in one gulp and smoothed his silver hair with his hands. A bit of the juice dripped onto his chin. He wondered if Mrs. Das had noticed.

She had not. "What's your address, Mr. Kapasi?" she inquired, fishing for something inside her straw bag.

"You would like my address?"

"So we can send you copies," she said. "Of the pictures." She handed him a scrap of paper which she had hastily ripped from a page of her film magazine. The blank portion was limited, for the narrow strip was crowded by lines of text and a tiny picture of a hero and heroine embracing under a eucalyptus tree.

The paper curled as Mr. Kapasi wrote his address in clear, careful letters. She would write to him, asking about his days interpreting at the doctor's office, and he would respond eloquently, choosing only the most entertaining anecdotes, ones that would make her laugh out loud as she read them in her house in New Jersey. In time she would reveal the disappointment of her marriage, and he his. In this way their friendship would grow, and flourish. He would possess a picture of the two of them, eating fried onions under a magenta umbrella, which he would keep, he decided, safely tucked between the pages of his Russian grammar. As his mind raced, Mr. Kapasi experienced a mild and pleasant shock. It was similar to a feeling he used to experience long ago when, after months of translating with the aid of a dictionary, he would finally read a passage from a French novel, or an Italian sonnet, and understand the words, one after another, unencumbered by his own efforts. In those moments Mr. Kapasi used to believe that all was right with the world, that all struggles were rewarded, that all of life's mistakes made sense in the end. The promise that he would hear from Mrs. Das now filled him with the same belief.

When he finished writing his address Mr. Kapasi handed her the paper, but as soon as he did so he worried that he had either misspelled his name, or accidentally reversed the numbers of his postal code. He dreaded the possibility of a lost letter, the photograph never reaching him, hovering somewhere in Orissa, close but ultimately unattainable. He thought of asking for the slip of paper again, just to make sure he had written his address accurately, but Mrs. Das had already dropped it into the jumble of her bag. ■

AP® Multiple-Choice Questions

1. Which of the following provides an accurate characterization of Mrs. Das?
   - a. She is eager to pose for photographs with Mr. Kapasi.
   - b. She feels trapped in an unhappy marriage to Mr. Das.
   - c. She seeks long-term companionship with Mr. Kapasi.
   - d. She is committed to improving her mastery of other languages.
   - e. She is an American tourist exploring India with her family.
2. From the passage, the reader can infer all of the following about Mr. Kapasi EXCEPT that he
   - a. speaks several languages
   - b. works in a doctor's office
   - c. is younger than Mrs. Das
   - d. does not know the Das family well
   - e. does not live in the United States
3. What does paragraph 5 reveal about Mr. Kapasi?
   - a. The physical presence of Mrs. Das ruffles his composure.
   - b. He is suddenly very aware of his own resplendence.
   - c. He is surprised that Mrs. Das has been drinking.
   - d. He is determined to be friendly in spite of visceral antipathy to Mrs. Das.
   - e. He fears that Mr. Das will become jealous of him.
4. Lahiri interrupts the narration of Mr. Kapasi and the Das family's interactions with the description of a "hero and heroine embracing under a eucalyptus tree" (par. 8) to
   - a. foreshadow the blossoming relationship between Mr. Kapasi and Mrs. Das
   - b. delay the inevitable breakup between Mr. Kapasi and Mrs. Das
   - c. suggest a connection between the couple pictured in the magazine and the Das family
   - d. launch Mr. Kapasi's reverie about his future relationship with Mrs. Das
   - e. establish Mrs. Das's desire to be swept away by a movie star
5. Comparing his future correspondence with Mrs. Das to his ability to read a foreign language "unencumbered by his own efforts" (par. 9) suggests that Mr. Kapasi
   - a. believes that all women are mysterious and difficult to understand
   - b. knows he will have to translate Mrs. Das's letters because she only speaks English
   - c. considers communicating with Mrs. Das challenging because of their differences
   - d. thinks he is capable of overcoming all of life's obstacles
   - e. believes she will not misinterpret his true intentions
6. Mr. Kapasi's attitude in paragraph 10 ("When he finished writing . . . jumble of her bag") is best interpreted as
   - a. flirtatious
   - b. eager
   - c. heartbroken
   - d. regretful
   - e. anxious
7. The passage is told from the point of view of
   - a. a narrator who is also the protagonist
   - b. a narrator who is a secondary character in the story
   - c. a third-person limited omniscient narrator
   - d. a third-person omniscient narrator
   - e. an unreliable narrator

8. Examine the syntax of sentences 2–5 in paragraph 9 where Lahiri details Mr. Kapasi's thoughts. The function of the *would* verbs is to
   - **a.** express doubt that something will happen
   - **b.** express hope that something will happen
   - **c.** demand that something will happen
   - **d.** provide a glimpse into what will happen
   - **e.** state facts that already happened

9. The last sentence of paragraph 9, "The promise that he would hear from Mrs. Das now filled him with the same belief," is best interpreted to mean that
   - **a.** Mrs. Das's casual gesture has elevated Mr. Kapasi's hopes
   - **b.** Mrs. Das is about to make Mr. Kapasi an offer that will change his life
   - **c.** Mrs. Das will leave Mr. Das to be with Mr. Kapasi
   - **d.** Mr. Kapasi has been waiting all his life to meet Mrs. Das
   - **e.** Mr. Kapasi understands that he is in the throes of an unrealizable fantasy

10. Lahiri's description of how Mrs. Das hands Mr. Kapasi a piece of paper (par. 8) characterizes her as
   - **a.** unaware of Mr. Kapasi's interpretation of this gesture
   - **b.** nervous about her feelings toward Mr. Kapasi
   - **c.** angry that Mr. Kapasi was invited to sit with them
   - **d.** worried that Mr. Das will recognize her attraction to Mr. Kapasi
   - **e.** ambivalent about her future with either Mr. Kapasi or Mr. Das

11. How does the description of the family's meal (par. 1) function within the passage?
   - **a.** It portrays a cultural aspect of the setting of the story.
   - **b.** It indicates that the family is wealthy.
   - **c.** It suggests that the family was thoughtlessly gluttonous.
   - **d.** It conveys the family's disregard for healthy food options.
   - **e.** It depicts the Dases as a close-knit family.

12. Which of the following best describes the passage's plot structure?
   - **a.** The distant past is told with periodic flashforwards.
   - **b.** The narration is interrupted by a character's fantasy of the future.
   - **c.** Past events are explained prior to narrating the present.
   - **d.** The present is interrupted by flashbacks of the couple's time in India.
   - **e.** The passage is an exploration of what the future holds for each of the characters.

from Boy on a Train

Ralph Ellison

"James, son," she said. "That old silo back there's been here a long time. It made me remember when years ago me and your daddy came over this same old Rock Island line on our way to Oklahoma City. We had just been married and was very happy going west because we had heard that colored people had a chance out here."

James smiled, listening; he loved to hear Mama tell about when she and Daddy were young, and about what they used to do down South. Yet he felt this was to be something different. Something in Mama's voice was vast and high, like a rainbow; yet something sad and deep, like when the organ played in church, was around Mama's words.

"Son, I want you to remember this trip," she said. "You understand, son. I *want* you to remember. You *must*, you've *got* to understand."

James sensed something; he tried hard to understand. He stared into her face. Tears were glistening in her eyes, and he felt he would cry himself. He bit his lip. No, he was the man of the family, and he couldn't act like the baby. He swallowed, listening.

"You remember this, James," she said. "We came all the way from Georgia on this same railroad line fourteen years ago, so things would be better for you children when you came. You must remember this, James. We traveled far, looking for a better world, where things wouldn't be so hard like they were down South. That was fourteen years ago, James. Now your father's gone from us, and you're the man. Things are hard for us colored folks, son, and it's just us three alone and we have to stick together. Things is hard, and we have to fight. . . . O Lord, we have to fight! . . ."

She stopped, her lips pressed tight together as she shook her head, overcome with emotion. James placed his arm around her neck and caressed her cheek.

"Yes, Mama," he said. "I won't forget."

He could not get it all, but yet he understood. It was like understanding what music without words said. He felt very full inside. Now Mama was pulling him close to her; the baby rested against her other side. This was familiar; since Daddy died Mama prayed with them, and now she was beginning to pray. He bowed his head.

"Go with us and keep us, Lord. Then it was me and him, Lord; now it's me and his children. And I'm thankful, Lord. You saw fit to take him, Lord, and it's well with my soul in Thy name. I was happy, Lord; life was like a mockingbird a-singing. And all I ask now is to stay with these children, to raise them and protect them, Lord, till they're old enough to go their way. Make them strong and unafraid, Lord. Give them strength to meet this world. Make them brave to go where things is better for our people, Lord. . . ."

James sat with head bowed. Always when Mama prayed, he felt tight and smoldering inside. And he kept remembering his father's face. He could not remember Daddy ever praying, but Daddy's voice had been deep and strong when he sang in the choir on Sunday mornings. James wanted to cry, but, vaguely, he felt *something* should be punished for making Mama cry. Something cruel had made her cry. He felt the tightness in his throat becoming anger. If he only knew what it was, he would fix it; he would kill this mean thing that made Mama feel so bad. It must have been awful because Mama was strong and brave and even killed mice when the white woman she used to work for only raised her dress and squealed like a girl, afraid of them. If he only knew what it was. . . . Was it God?

"Please keep us three together in this strange town, Lord. The road is dark and long and my sorrows heavy but, if it be Thy will, Lord, let me educate my boys. Let me raise them so they'll be better able to live this life. I don't want to live for myself, Lord, just for these boys. Make them strong, upright men, Lord; make them fighters. And when my work on earth is done, take me home to Thy kingdom, Lord, safe in the arms of Jesus."

He heard her voice trail off to a tortured moan behind her trembling lips. Tears streamed down her face. James was miserable; he did not like to see Mama cry, and turned his eyes to the window as she began wiping away the tears. He was glad she was through now because the butcher would be coming back into the car in a few minutes. He did not want a white man to see Mama cry. ■

AP® Multiple-Choice Questions

1. In the second paragraph, the image of "the organ played in church" is juxtaposed with
   a. James's smile
   b. Mama's recollections
   c. the old Rock Island line
   d. the rainbow
   e. the silo

2. Why does James feel like "he would cry himself" in the fourth paragraph?
   a. He fully recognizes the significance of the journey.
   b. He is moved by his mother's tears.
   c. He is upset about leaving home.
   d. He misses his father.
   e. He recognizes that he must grow up.

3. Mama's speech in paragraph 5 conveys her
   a. anger
   b. urgency
   c. hope
   d. love
   e. nostalgia

4. In paragraph 8, the comparison of how James understands Mama's words to the way he understands "music without words" suggests that he
   a. grasps the tone, but not the significance of her words
   b. is soothed by the musical quality of his mother's voice
   c. cannot express how much he loves his mother
   d. believes that language transcends generational gaps
   e. makes sense of the world through music most of the time

5. Mama's prayer in paragraph 9 reveals that she
   a. regrets leaving Georgia with her husband years earlier
   b. understands that the worst years have already gone by
   c. recognizes that her children are stronger than she ever was
   d. remains hopeful despite recognizing that the world is harsh
   e. feels grateful that her husband can't see what has happened to the family

6. Mama's religious fervor is juxtaposed with
   a. the family's secular goals
   b. her waning desire to continue living
   c. her doubts about the future of the family
   d. Daddy's lack of faith
   e. James's suspicion that God made her cry

7. In paragraph 10, James is primarily characterized as
   a. defeated
   b. protective
   c. religious
   d. cowardly
   e. violent

8. The passage's final paragraph primarily conveys James's awareness of
   a. his mother's secrets
   b. the journey's purpose
   c. racial differences and tensions
   d. his own shortcomings
   e. Mama's changing emotions

9. Throughout the passage, repetition conveys Mama's insistence that James
   a. remember and understand
   b. forgive and forget
   c. repair and grow
   d. love and protect
   e. condemn and defend

10. For James, the interaction with his mother throughout this passage
    a. depicts a typical conversation between them
    b. makes him resent her perspective on their situation
    c. represents the start of a new role for him in the family
    d. conveys how frail she has become
    e. underscores how much he misses his father

Suggestions for Writing

Identity and Culture

1. **AP® Literary Argumentation.** In many works of literature, characters find their identities by stepping away from their culture. Choose one of the works in this chapter and analyze how this break contributes to an interpretation of the work as a whole. Do not merely summarize the plot.
2. **Connections.** In Nathaniel Hawthorne's novel *The Scarlet Letter* (1850), the narrator says, "No man, for any considerable, period, can wear one face to himself, and another to the multitude, without finally getting bewildered as to which may be the true." Choose two of the texts you have studied in this chapter that you think best exemplify this quotation and discuss the conflict that results from trying to assume an identity based on the expectations of others rather than being true to oneself.
3. **Connections.** Many of the texts you've read in this chapter explore the dissonance that results from cultural clashes, particularly the conflicts experienced by those who are moving — by choice or by coercion — from one culture to another. Discuss the nature of that clash by focusing on three different texts.
4. **Connections.** Philosopher Theodor Adorno wrote that for those in exile, their writing becomes a kind of home: "In his text, the writer sets up house. . . . For [the person] who no longer has a homeland, writing becomes a place to live." Discuss what you think Adorno means, referring to at least two of the texts in this chapter as part of your interpretation.
5. **Connections.** Author James Baldwin wrote: "An identity would seem to be arrived at by the way in which the person faces and uses his experience." Discuss this quotation by referring to at least one of the texts you've read in this chapter and your own experience.
6. **Connections.** Most Americans believe that they are the master of their own destiny and that anyone can create and re-create a sense of self. To what extent do you believe that identity is the result of free choice rather than something determined by factors out of our control, such as race, gender, and ethnicity? Include references to at least three of the texts studied in this chapter in your response.
7. **Creative Writing.** Emily Dickinson begins her poem: "I'm Nobody! Who are you?/Are you — Nobody — too?" Write a response that answers her question from the point of view of a protagonist from one of the stories in this chapter. Include references to the text of the story to support your response.
8. **Connections.** Identity theft is the fastest-growing type of fraud in the United States today. The term is most commonly used to refer to the crime of someone pretending to be you in order to buy goods and services in your name, or to access your bank or credit card accounts. What does this definition say about us? Is our "identity" determined by the objective data of our income, the goods and services we purchase, and the bank accounts and credit cards that give us access to those? Is it possible to "steal" someone's identity? Write an essay explaining your opinion. Refer to two or more texts from this chapter in your response.
9. **Multimodal.** Go to the National Portrait Gallery website (npg.si.edu), and select a portrait that either appeals to you or puzzles you. Write

about what you see in the portrait and what the visual details suggest to you about the person's identity and culture. Read about the subject of the portrait and describe the decisions the artist made in their portrayal of the subject. Finally, decide what you would want your portraitist to portray about you and try creating a self-portrait.

10. **Speaking and Listening.** Is a person's perceived identity a result of an individual's "history"? How much is what we regard as "history" responsible for how others perceive us and for how we perceive ourselves? Prepare for and participate in a class discussion on this topic.

11. **Research.** Choose one of the many cultures represented in the works in this chapter to research. Try to focus on the ways that young people are taught to identify with their cultural backgrounds — or encouraged to defy them.

12. **Multimodal.** The study of identity and culture is often characterized as a collage. Create a collage that portrays your cultural background or the culture that is the background for one of the works in this chapter.

Courtesy of Manel Villalonga

5

Love and Relationships

What is it about love and relationships that has captured the imaginations of poets and writers throughout the ages? Why are we drawn to love stories, even when they so often end in tears? The literature in this chapter explores the many ways people find, chase, lose, or retain love. The texts also remind us of the full spectrum of emotions we associate with love, from simple attraction to desire to platonic love to the joy of finding a soulmate to the heartache that follows a breakup. To reach our goal of analyzing these texts and forming interpretations of their meanings, we must first open our hearts and connect with what it feels like to be drawn to someone — and perhaps even be in love.

The chapter's Central Text, Terrance Hayes's contemporary poem "Wind in a Box," experiments with form and its presentation of ideas to convey a deeply loving sentiment. This depth of emotion links poets and their works across time and place. The Classic Text, William Shakespeare's "My love is as a fever, longing still" (Sonnet 147), for instance, also speaks to extreme feelings that ring true today — however, this poem conveys the anguish of heartbreak. Other poems in the chapter also explore our experiences with love and relationships. Dana Gioia's "Summer Storm" contemplates the "[w]hat ifs" that never abandon those who ponder what could have been, while Amy Alvarez's "How to Date a White Boy" and Chen Chen's "I Invite My Parents to a Dinner Party" prepare us for the real-world obstacles that love often presents. Billy Collins and Anne Bradstreet write about enduring love that is deep and true. Sometimes the speaker's language is idyllic, such as in Lord Byron's "She Walks in Beauty" and John Keats's "Bright Star, would I were stedfast as thou art — "; at other times, however, attraction can prove perilous, as we see in Margaret Atwood's "Siren Song."

The Texts in Context section in this chapter invites you to delve deeper into the quintessential poetic form for expressions of love: the sonnet. The influence of the sonnet is discussed in countless essays and has even made its way into fiction. In

Gloria Naylor's novel *Linden Hills*, when Willie K. Mason stares at his beloved, he immediately thinks, "She deserves a sonnet." What is a sonnet? Why are poets drawn to it? And how has it changed since its invention in the fourteenth century? As you delve deeper into this poetic form and consider possible answers to these questions, you'll encounter works from eras long past and those that reflect the world as it is today — all of them drawing on an enduring structure to build new meaning.

The short fiction section of this chapter also explores the overarching theme of love and relationships. In James Joyce's "Araby," you'll see a timeless expression of the innocence and obsession of young love. William Faulkner's "A Rose for Emily" shows one way that love can sour, while Maxine Clair's "The Creation" depicts the struggle for love to survive a clash of cultures. Kirstin Valdez Quade's "Jubilee" explores the connection between love and anger and the ways in which the boundaries of our relationships can be messy and overlapping.

To understand and fully appreciate the wide array of poetry in this chapter, let's turn to the Big Ideas, Skills, and Essential Knowledge in Unit 5 of the AP® English Literature and Composition Course. This unit focuses on Structure, Figurative Language, and Literary Argumentation. Keep in mind, however, that the questions we ask throughout this chapter will build on all of the skills and Big Ideas we have previously explored. In preparation for this chapter, you may want to revisit the fundamentals of reading and writing about poetry that we covered in Chapter 2 (p. 54). Above all, keep in mind that identifying specific literary and poetic techniques is just the *beginning* of an analysis; they are tools that help poets convey meaning and help writers like you support your interpretations of said meaning.

AP® Big Idea: Structure

The **structure** of the Central and Classic Texts in this chapter are quite different. Terrance Hayes's "Love in a Box" is a modern poem without formal patterns, while William Shakespeare's "My love is as a fever, longing still" (Sonnet 147), our Classic Text, uses a more conventional, closed form. An English sonnet, it has fourteen lines in a single stanza; uses a conventional rhyme scheme that introduces new sounds after each quatrain; is written in iambic pentameter, which pairs an unstressed syllable with a stressed one five times within each line; and has a heroic couplet in the final two lines that typically resolves or reiterates the main concern of the speaker. In this sonnet Shakespeare develops his speaker's anguish and madness in each quatrain, and he ultimately uses the heroic couplet to identify the source of his speaker's pain. Does he fully adhere to the demands of the form elsewhere in the poem, or does he deviate from these conventions? Remember that form is always tied in some way to larger meaning. As you read the Classic Text in this chapter, ask yourself: Why would Shakespeare stay within the sonnet's confinement, and why would he break free from it when he does? *To review structure in poetry, see pages 74–77 of Chapter 2: Analyzing Poetry.*

AP® Big Idea: Figurative Language

A poem's structure is just one aspect that we'll use in this chapter to understand how poets convey meaning. It may help to think of poetry as a collection of sounds and images that converge to present thoughts and emotions. **Figurative language** constitutes all the literary and poetic techniques that take words and phrases beyond their literal sense, such as hyperbole, understatement, imagery, metaphor, and personification. Shakespeare's sonnet depends upon an extended metaphor to express the speaker's attitude toward love. The full effects of the speaker's "fever" are brought to life through the metaphors that pit "reason" against "appetite" and the imagery that brings the culprit of all this pain into focus. *To review figurative language in poetry, see pages 70–73 of Chapter 2: Analyzing Poetry.*

AP® Big Idea: Literary Argumentation

All of the Big Ideas of the course help us engage with poetry by giving us some overall guidance for annotating as we read and reminding us of which techniques to turn to when we search for evidence and provide commentary in our essays. As you read the poems in this chapter, we'll ask you questions based on these Big Ideas. We'll also ask you to focus on these elements to develop your own interpretations of the poems you read. Writing tasks — whether formal or informal — will help you develop your ability to use concepts such as structure and figurative language to form your interpretations and support your claims. As you learned in the opening chapters, literary argumentation begins with a thesis that, in turn, guides the content of your body paragraphs. While quotations from the works you read in this chapter will serve as evidence for your claims, remember that it is only in your commentary where your interpretation really comes through. *To review the process of writing an AP® Poetry Analysis Essay, see pages 86–102 of Chapter 2: Analyzing Poetry.*

Throughout the year, and in this chapter, you will read, analyze, and interpret many different poems. We hope that the works we've included here show you how this art form can lift, inspire, and even teach you something about yourself and the world around you.

Guided Reading for "Wind in a Box"

As you read the Central Text in this chapter, "Wind in a Box" by Terrance Hayes, keep track of your observations and questions about how Hayes develops these Big Ideas.

AP® Big Idea	Observations	Questions
Structure		
Figurative Language		

AP® Unit 5 Alignment at a Glance

Wind in a Box

Terrance Hayes

Terrance Hayes (b. 1971) is an American poet and educator. Born in Columbia, South Carolina, he earned a BA from Coker College and an MFA at the University of Pittsburgh. Hayes is the author of six books of poetry: *Muscular Music* (1999), which won both a Whiting Award and the Kate Tufts Discovery Award; *Hip Logic* (2002), which won the National Poetry Series; *Wind in a Box* (2006); *Lighthead* (2010), which won a National Book Award; *How to Be Drawn* (2015); and *Sonnets for My Past and Future Assassin* (2018).

Manny Carabel/Getty Images

KEY CONTEXT Federico García Lorca (1898–1936) was a Spanish poet and playwright. He introduced the elements of European literary movements, such as symbolism and surrealism, to the literature of Spain. He was assassinated at the beginning of the Spanish Civil War (1936–1939), a conflict between Republicans and Nationalists, by what many believe were Nationalist militia. His remains were never found.

— *after Lorca*

I want to always sleep beneath a bright red blanket
of leaves. I want to never wear a coat of ice.
I want to learn to walk without blinking.

I want to outlive the turtle and the turtle's father,
the stone. I want a mouth full of permissions

and a pink glistening bud. If the wildflower and ant hill
can return after sleeping each season, I want to walk
out of this house wearing nothing but wind.

I want to greet you, I want to wait for the bus with you
weighing less than a chill. I want to fight off the bolts

of gray lighting the alcoves and winding paths
of your hair. I want to fight off the damp nudgings
of snow. I want to fight off the wind.

I want to be the wind and I want to fight off the wind
with its sagging banner of isolation, its swinging

screen doors, its gilded boxes, and neatly folded pamphlets
of noise. I want to fight off the dull straight lines
of two by fours and endings, your disapprovals,

your doubts and regulations, your carbon copies.
If the locust can abandon its suit,

I want a brand new name. I want the pepper's fury
and the salt's tenderness. I want the virtue
of the evening rain, but not its gossip.

I want the moon's intuition, but not its questions.
I want the malice of nothing on earth. I want to enter

every room in a strange electrified city
and find you there. I want your lips around the bell of flesh

at the bottom of my ear. I want to be the mirror,
but not the nightstand. I do not want to be the light switch.
I do not want to be the yellow photograph

or book of poems. When I leave this body, Woman,
I want to be pure flame. I want to be your song. ■

2006

extending beyond the text

Edward Hopper's (1882–1967) 1951 oil painting *Rooms by the Sea* shares with "Wind in a Box" the combination of abstraction and realism. Many aspects of the painting are clear and concrete. But the sum of the picture, like the poem, is something not quite figurative and not quite abstract.

1. **What elements of *Rooms by the Sea* are figurative, that is, realistic? What parts are abstract? Can any elements fit both categories?**
2. **What elements of "Wind in a Box" are concrete and realistic? What aspects are abstract?**
3. **What is the effect of the combination of realism and abstraction in both the poem and the painting? What is your emotional reaction to each one?**

Understanding and Interpreting

1. **AP® Structure and Narration.** The speaker says "I want" twenty-four times in the poem and "I don't want" twice. Try to classify his "wants "and his "don't wants." What patterns emerge? Does the speaker truly want everything he says he does? Explain.
2. **AP® Setting and Narration.** What mood do the "bright red blanket / of leaves" (ll. 1–2) and "coat of ice" (l. 2) evoke?
3. **AP® Character and Narration.** Try to characterize the speaker of "Wind in a Box." To whom is he speaking? How do you know?
4. **AP® Narration.** Do you think "Woman" in line 31 is the antecedent for all of the pronouns "you" and "your" in lines 9, 12, 18, 19, 27, and 31? Explain your reasoning for each one. If you don't think "Woman" is the antecedent, who is?
5. **AP® Narration.** Do you think there is an obsessive quality to "Wind in a Box"? If so, what are some of the things that obsess the speaker? If not, how would you describe the overall tone?
6. **AP® Character, Setting, and Narration.** In a review of the work of Federico García Lorca, to whom this poem is dedicated, Peter Monro Jack writes that "the specific recurrent imagery" of Spain is "for most of us a dream landscape. What makes it *seem* so real to us is that Lorca, without being a storyteller, constantly gives the sense of life to his pictures: men riding, women on the balustrade, [Romani] girls dancing." How does this assessment relate to "Wind in a Box"? How does Hayes give "the sense of life" to the events or desires his speaker describes? How "real" does this poem seem to you? Explain.
7. **AP® Character and Narration.** Do you consider "Wind in a Box" to be a love poem? Explain why or why not.

Analyzing Language, Style, and Structure

1. **Vocabulary in Context.** What does "carbon copies" mean in line 19? How does the term fit into the businesslike imagery of the three previous lines? How does it make that imagery more expansive?
2. **AP® Setting and Structure.** The setting of "Wind in a Box" seems to shift. Try to pinpoint some of the more concrete hints about its setting and explain how they support and highlight some of the poem's abstractions.
3. **AP® Figurative Language.** Terrance Hayes's 2006 collection is titled *Wind in a Box*, and it contains six different poems with that title, including this one. He has said that wind is a "metaphor for language and the breath that carries it forward." How does wind in this poem stand in for language? Could it have other meanings? Explain.
4. **AP® Structure and Figurative Language.** Hayes has also specified that the box in the context of this poem represents how language is crafted and contained. What kind of box does this poem provide? What is the relationship between the language and structure of the poem?
5. **AP® Structure and Narration.** You may have noticed that "Wind in a Box" follows a pattern of alternating two- and three-line stanzas. Are there differences in the function of the two different lengths of stanzas? Explain. Do you see any other structural patterns in the poem? How do these patterns reinforce the speaker's message?

6. **AP® Figurative Language.** Many of the images in "Wind in a Box" are concrete but can also be considered symbolic, that is, they create a range of associations beyond their concrete meaning. What is the function of the symbols in this poem? Do they clarify or enlarge literal meanings? Do they express a particular idea? How do you know?
7. **AP® Structure and Figurative Language.** While much of the language of "Wind in a Box" is abstract, the syntax is fairly conventional — for instance, the poem plays out in full sentences. What is the effect of this juxtaposition?
8. **AP® Structure and Narration.** Look carefully at the line breaks in "Wind in a Box" as well as at the stanza breaks. What effect do the breaks have in the rhythm of the poem? How do they contribute to the tone of the poem?

Topics for Composing

1. AP® FRQ **Poetry Analysis.** In Terrance Hayes's "Wind in a Box," published in 2006, the speaker examines the human experience of desire. Read the poem carefully. Then, in a well-written essay, analyze how Hayes uses literary elements and techniques to convey the complexity of the speaker's attitude toward the person he addresses.
2. **AP® Literary Argumentation.** Terrance Hayes said, in an interview in the *New York Times*, that "a poem is never about one thing. . . . [Y]ou want it to be as complicated as your feelings." How does this poem embody that statement? What complicated feelings does it convey?
3. **AP® Literary Argumentation.** A critic has said that one important measure of a superior work of literature is its ability to produce in the reader a "healthy confusion of pleasure and disquietude." How does "Wind in a Box" create this sort of "healthy confusion"? Use evidence from the poem to support your response.
4. **AP® Literary Argumentation.** Critic Roland Barthes has said, "Literature is the question minus the answer." What central question(s) does "Wind in a Box" raise? To what extent does it provide answers? Explain how Hayes's treatment of this question affects your interpretation of the poem.
5. **Connections.** This version of "Wind in a Box" is dedicated to Federico García Lorca. Select 3–5 poems by Lorca, including "Gacela of the Dark Death," to read in Spanish or in translation. How would you characterize Lorca's style? What subject(s) does he gravitate toward in the poems you've selected? What do these poems and "Wind in a Box" have in common? Discuss how your interpretation of Lorca's poetry has affected your understanding of why Hayes dedicated this poem to him.
6. **Research.** Lorca, to whom this poem is dedicated, is said to have introduced surrealism to Spanish literature, a move that would reverberate all through the arts. Research the surrealism movement in literature and art, focusing on a particular writer or fine artist. Some options include (but are certainly not limited to) Salvador Dalí, Marcel Duchamp, Max Ernst, Frida Kahlo, René Magritte, Joan Miró, Raymond Queneau, Man Ray. What does the work of your chosen artist or writer have in common with this poem?
7. **Connections.** Compare and contrast "Wind in a Box" to Wallace Stevens's famous poem, "Thirteen Ways of Looking at a Blackbird." Look at the images each poet creates as well as the structure of each poem. What perspective does the style and structure of each poem reveal?
8. **Multimodal.** Create a visual representation of each of the images in "Wind in a Box" and put them together in a collage or a patchwork. Experiment with moving the pieces around until they express your own interpretation of wind in a box.
9. **Creative Writing.** Using "Wind in a Box" as a model, write your own version in which you consider "want" and "don't want" in several variations.

My love is as a fever, longing still (Sonnet 147)

William Shakespeare

Classic Text

National Portrait Gallery, London, UK/ Bridgeman Images

William Shakespeare (1564–1616) was born in Stratford-upon-Avon, England. Little is known of his life aside from the fact that he married Anne Hathaway when he was eighteen, worked as an actor-playwright in London, and retired in 1613. At least thirty-eight plays, including *Romeo and Juliet* (1597), *Hamlet* (1601), *Othello* (1604), *King Lear* (1605), and *Macbeth* (1606), are attributed to him. In his time, his contemporaries — and likely Shakespeare himself — looked to his sonnets and other poems as the more important works.

KEY CONTEXT Shakespeare frequently juxtaposes reason and appetite in his writings, two concepts which were then commonly thought to control human behavior. While reason and logic were highly regarded, appetite — along with desire and other extreme sentiments — was considered quite dangerous. It was sometimes viewed as a cause of both physical and mental illnesses.

This poem is a Shakespearean sonnet, which consists of three quatrains and a heroic couplet at the end, rhyming *abab*, *cdcd*, *efef*, *gg*. Shakespeare wrote 154 sonnets, but when and to whom they were written remain unclear. However, they are generally grouped into two broad categories: Sonnets 1 through126 typically address an attractive young man, and Sonnets 127 through 154 often address a woman referred to as "the dark lady," who is not always depicted favorably.

My love is as a fever, longing still
For that which longer nurseth the disease,
Feeding on that which doth preserve the ill,
Th' uncertain sickly appetite to please.
My reason, the physician to my love,
Angry that his prescriptions are not kept,
Hath left me, and I desperate now approve
Desire is death, which physic[1] did except.
Past cure I am, now reason is past care,
And frantic-mad with evermore unrest;
My thoughts and my discourse as madmen's are,
At random from the truth vainly express'd;
For I have sworn thee fair, and thought thee bright,
Who art as black as hell, as dark as night. ■

1609

[1] Medicine. — Eds.

Understanding and Interpreting

1. **AP® Narration.** How does the speaker characterize love in the first quatrain? What details contribute to this characterization?
2. **AP® Narration.** The speaker claims that love has a "sickly appetite to please" (l. 4). What does this phrase mean? Whom does love aim to please?
3. **AP® Structure and Narration.** What is the subject of the second quatrain (ll. 5–8)? What are the speaker's primary concerns in these lines?
4. **AP® Character and Narration.** What might be the "prescriptions" that "are not kept" (l. 6) by the speaker? What is the effect of this refusal?
5. **AP® Narration.** Who is the speaker addressing? What textual evidence supports your view?
6. **AP® Character and Narration.** How does the speaker view his current situation? In your response, consider his perspective on who is to blame for his troubles.
7. **AP® Character and Narration.** Why is the speaker "[p]ast cure" (l. 9)? What needs curing, and what events have led him to this conclusion?
8. **AP® Character and Narration.** How does the speaker perceive his "thoughts" and "discourse" (l. 11)? How are his ideas about love and relationships central to this assessment of his thoughts and behavior?
9. **AP® Character and Narration.** How does the speaker's claim that the subject of the poem is "as black as hell, as dark as night" (l. 14) inform your interpretation of their relationship?
10. **AP® Narration.** What do you think the speaker means by the phrase "vainly express'd" (l. 12)? How might that phrase relate to the speaker's attitude toward writing this poem in the first place?

Analyzing Language, Style, and Structure

1. **Vocabulary in Context.** Today, we understand the word "approve" (l. 7) to mean that we agree or accept someone or something. For Shakespeare, however, the word also meant *to prove*. Reread the second quatrain (ll. 5–8). What is the speaker proof of? Why does he assert this about himself?
2. **AP® Figurative Language.** The sonnet opens with a simile. Identify the two things being compared. What is the effect of this comparison?
3. **AP® Structure and Figurative Language.** The first quatrain contains images associated with "appetite" (l. 4). How do these images characterize the concept of appetite and its effect on the speaker?
4. **AP® Structure and Figurative Language.** What metaphor in the second quatrain personifies "reason" (l. 5)? What is the effect of this personification, particularly when juxtaposed with the imagery in the first quatrain?
5. **AP® Structure.** The words "[f]eeding" (l. 3) and "[a]ngry" (l. 6) each begin with a stressed syllable, introducing slight deviations to Shakespeare's usual iambic pentameter. How do these deviations reflect the speaker's state of mind?
6. **AP® Figurative Language.** Identify the consonance and assonance in line 4. Which sounds produce consonance and which ones create assonance? What is the function of these sound devices within that line?

7. **AP® Structure and Narration.** What is the relationship between the third quatrain and the first two? What does this structure convey about the speaker's thoughts?
8. **AP® Character and Structure.** What juxtapositions exist within the heroic couplet at the end of the poem? How do these juxtapositions characterize the speaker?

Topics for Composing

1. **AP® FRQ Poetry Analysis.** In William Shakespeare's "My love is as a fever, longing still," published in 1609, the speaker discusses what has become of him after falling in love. Read the poem carefully. Then, in a well-written essay, analyze how Shakespeare uses literary elements and techniques to convey the speaker's complex attitude toward love.
2. **AP® FRQ Poetry Analysis.** In William Shakespeare's "My love is as a fever, longing still," published in 1609, the speaker juxtaposes the roles that appetite and reason play in his life. Read the poem carefully. Then, in a well-written essay, analyze how Shakespeare uses literary elements and techniques to characterize the conflicting nature of these two concepts.
3. **AP® FRQ Poetry Analysis.** In William Shakespeare's "My love is as a fever, longing still," published in 1609, the speaker describes how love has changed him. Read the poem carefully. Then, in a well-written essay, analyze how Shakespeare uses literary elements and techniques to characterize the speaker's complex attitude toward this transformation.
4. **AP® Literary Argumentation.** Does this poem categorically argue against love and relationships? If not, what is the main argument the speaker makes? Support your response with evidence from the text.
5. **Creative Writing**. Write a Shakespearean sonnet from the perspective of the woman addressed in this poem. Before you write your poem, consider whether you believe she is truly "as black as hell, as dark as night" (l. 14) or if the speaker's opinion of her is flawed.
6. **Research**. There is still speculation about who the dark lady that has been historically linked to Shakespeare's sonnets actually was. Do some research into the possibilities that scholars have introduced over time. How does your investigation change or enhance your understanding of Sonnet 147?
7. **Speaking and Listening**. Shakespeare is arguably the world's best-known playwright. As such, his sonnets can be thought of as monologues within a play. Consider how you would perform Sonnet 147. How is the speaker dressed? How does he speak? What is he holding or doing as he speaks these words? Once you've determined the appropriate answers to these questions, plan a performance of the sonnet. Make sure to rehearse prior to performing it for the class.
8. **Connections.** Shakespearean scholar Hallet Smith called the sonnets "explorations of the human spirit in confrontation with time, death, change, love, lust, and beauty." In what ways does Sonnet 147 embody Smith's characterization of Shakespeare's sonnets?

William Shakespeare and the Sonnet Form

As with other art forms, the origins of the sonnet are more complex than they're often made out to be. While the Italian writer Francesco Petrarca, known as Petrarch (1304–1374), is often credited as the father of the Italian sonnet and William Shakespeare is lauded as a genius of the English version of the form, neither man invented it. Like musicians who give rise to new sounds as they collaborate and compete with one other, so too do poets. All poetic conventions evolve over time as writers seek the proper trimmings for their poetic expressions, and the sonnet is no exception.

Like all poets, Petrarch and Shakespeare wrote to express their passions and emotions, and in the sonnet found an exacting, disciplined form that somehow made their feelings seem even more acute. They are still the sonnet's most popular practitioners, which is why they lend their names to the two prevailing sonnet structures. As you learned in Chapter 2, **Shakespearean sonnets** consist of three **quatrains** and a **couplet** at the end, rhyming *abab*, *cdcd*, *efef*, *gg*. The third quatrain often provides the turn, or **volta**, in which the speaker typically shifts perspective and sometimes closes with a witty remark. **Petrarchan sonnets** are divided into an **octet** rhyming *abba*, *abba* and a **sestet** with a variety of different rhyme schemes: *cdcdcd*, *cdecde*, or *cddcdd*. Traditionally, the octet raises an issue or expresses a doubt, the sestet resolves the issue or doubt, and the shift from the first to the second section serves as the volta. Ironically, both of these structures are likely deviations from what sonnets were before them. Nevertheless, between the late Middle Ages and the late English Renaissance, the sonnet as we've come to know it carved a place for itself. What a perch it found as its universal appeal catapulted it to timelessness. Since then, countless poets have used and modified the rules of the form to suit their particular needs. Sonnets continually evolve as they move across time and place, and there is no indication that the rules of the form will ever be set in stone. What, then, is a sonnet?

Traditionally, whether Shakespearean or Petrarchan, the sonnet is recognized as a fourteen-line poem written in iambic pentameter that contains a set rhyme scheme and a turn, or volta. Petrarch's sonnets established certain tropes that defined its features for hundreds of years: a speaker devoted to a beautiful but unattainable lady who, through the pain of rejection, achieved a kind of spiritual grace. For this speaker, unrequited love is better than never having loved at all. While Shakespeare's work sometimes retained some of these features, his sonnets often defied expectations. Some of his sonnets sing praises for a man instead of a woman. In other poems, Shakespeare takes Petrarch's goddess-like maiden and describes her in earthly — and even unkind — ways.

Since the Renaissance, the sonnet has continually evolved as poets have found new ways to bend the rules of the form. Nowadays, nearly any poem that is approximately fourteen lines long can be a sonnet — whether it has a set rhyme scheme or meter — particularly if it claims to be so in its title. No longer do sonnets solely, or primarily, speak of love. Their purposes are now humorous, satirical, political, and everything in between. Who's to say that a new sonnet form won't emerge to stand alongside Petrarch's and Shakespeare's? Language, like so many other aspects of everyday life, has always changed with the times, and our writing reflects this truth.

So why write within predetermined parameters in the first place? Are our thoughts and emotions not boundless? Do we not strive for freedom of expression in every other facet of our lives? For an answer, we might turn to another of Shakespeare's reinventions: Prince Hamlet, who asserts, "I could be bounded in a nutshell and / count myself king of infinite space." Although he is not thinking of sonnets in particular, we can certainly learn from what he says. In fact, a handful of lines prior to that, Hamlet also remarks that "there is / nothing either good or bad but thinking makes it / so." Perhaps, then, the question is not why we confine ourselves, but why we find refuge in patterns and boundaries. What is it about the heartbeat procession of rhymed lines that we know must turn and end right at the moment we enjoy them the most? In the readings that follow, you'll have the chance to seek the answer for yourself.

TEXTS IN CONTEXT

1. **Edward Hirsch** ■ ***My Own Acquaintance*** **(nonfiction)**
2. **William Shakespeare** ■ ***My mistress' eyes are nothing like the sun*** **(poetry)**
3. **William Wordsworth** ■ ***Nuns Fret Not at Their Convent's Narrow Room*** **(poetry)**
4. **Elizabeth Barrett Browning** ■ ***The Face of All the World (Sonnet 7)*** **(poetry)**
5. **Claude McKay** ■ ***America*** **(poetry)**
6. **Marilyn Nelson** ■ ***How I Discovered Poetry*** **(poetry)**
7. **Julian Talamantez Brolaski** ■ ***What to Say Upon Being Asked to Be Friends*** **(poetry)**
8. **David Baker** ■ ***Peril Sonnet*** **(poetry)**
9. **Oliver de la Paz** ■ ***Diaspora Sonnet 40*** **(poetry)**

My Own Acquaintance

Edward Hirsch

Edward Hirsch (b. 1950) is an American poet and critic. He has a PhD in folklore from the University of Pennsylvania and is the author of nine books of poetry, including *Gabriel: A Poem* (2014), a book-length elegy for his son. His book *How to Read a Poem and Fall in Love with Poetry* (1999) was a surprise best seller.

KEY CONTEXT This essay appeared in *The Making of the Sonnet*, an anthology of sonnets edited by Hirsch and Irish poet Eavan Boland (1944–2020). It was one of two personal essays on encountering the sonnet.

The fourteen-line rhyming poem was invented in southern Italy around 1235 or so ("Eternal glory to the inventor of the sonnet," Paul Valéry[1] proclaimed) and has had an astonishingly durable life ever since. The word *sonnet* derives from the Italian *sonetto*, meaning "a little sound" or "a little song," but the stateliness of the form belies the modesty of the word's derivation. The sonnet is a small vessel capable of plunging tremendous depths. It is one of the enabling forms of human inwardness.

The sonnet is an obsessive form — compact, expansive — that travels remarkably well. It crosses between countries and languages. It adapts to different meters and reverberates down the centuries. There must be something hardwired into its machinery — a heartbeat, a pulse — that keeps it breathing. How many times over the decades has it been pronounced dead and then somehow revitalized, deconstructed, and then constructed again, refashioned, remade? It darkens and then lightens again. It thinks on its feet.

Something about the spaciousness and brevity of the fourteen-line poem seems to suit the contours of rhetorical argument, especially when the subject is erotic love. The form becomes a medium for the poet to explore his or her capacity to bring together the heart and the head, feeling and thought, the lyrical and the discursive. It is conducive to calculation and experiment — a closed form that keeps opening up. It is generational. It keeps finding poets in places far from its sun-struck origins, in provincial enclaves and outposts, in the suburbs of distant cities, for example, such as Dublin and Chicago.

My own acquaintance with the sonnet came to me in a roundabout way. The form snuck up on me without my knowing it — a stealth music — and insinuated itself inside of me: a little sound, a little song. It carried me away. "I have been one acquainted with the night," I used to hum to myself under my breath. The pace of the lines — the sound of the sentences — mesmerized me. "I have walked out in rain — and back in rain. / I have outwalked the furthest city light."

5 At seventeen, I had begun to write poetry with great energy and determination. I was overwhelmed by feelings I couldn't understand. I seemed to be perpetually stunned — desolate, exuberant. I needed vessels and containers. I was probably grief-stricken over the loss of my childhood, but I wouldn't have understood that then. My brain was teeming with ideas, but there couldn't have been more than two clear thoughts in my head. I was intoxicated by poetry but I didn't know a single other person who wrote or read the stuff. How could one devote oneself to poetry in a culture that seemed to care so little about it? I had no way of knowing that this question would be one of the recurring agons[2] of American poetry — from Anne Bradstreet to John Berryman.

I was devastated by loneliness, and reading lonely poems somehow made me feel less alone. That's when I discovered Robert Frost's "Acquainted with the Night." I didn't much like the cracker-barrel Yankee image of Frost that we had picked up at school, but this poem seemed to have been written out of a darker inner spirit. It had a kind of directness, a moody undertow, that appealed to me. There was something respectful about the word "acquainted" paired with the word "night." It had dignity. It wasn't overly familiar. It kept its privacy, its wit. I liked the way the speaker of the poem walked out into the night, the way he confronted and coped with darkness. He didn't explain his feelings away, or apologize for them. I liked the solitary music.

[1] Ambroise Paul Toussaint Jules Valéry (1871–1945) was a French poet, essayist, and philosopher. — Eds.

[2] Ancient Greek term for a conflict, struggle, or contest, which could be in athletics, in chariot or horse racing, or in music or literature. — Eds.

I read "Acquainted with the Night" so often that I memorized it without knowing that I was learning it. I used to say it to myself as I walked through the park at night. I remember lying on my back in the forlorn darkness of my teenage room and reciting it aloud.

Acquainted with the Night

I have been one acquainted with the night.
I have walked out in rain — and back in rain.
I have outwalked the furthest city light.

I have looked down the saddest city lane.
I have passed by the watchman on his beat
And dropped my eyes, unwilling to explain.

I have stood still and stopped the sound of feet
When far away an interrupted cry
Came over houses from another street,

But not to call me back or say good-bye;
And further still at an unearthly height,
One luminary clock against the sky

Proclaimed the time was neither wrong nor right.
I have been one acquainted with the night.

I was putting myself to school on [Walt] Whitman and [Allen] Ginsberg, and if someone had asked me, I probably would have said that American poetry shunned traditional forms, such as sonnets. I was filled with unearned opinions. This one was partly right, but only partly, since the evidence also suggests otherwise. There has always been a countercurrent of American poets expanding and rethinking traditional forms, sometimes in inherited meters, sometimes in free verse. They tend to think of these forms as organically as possible. A wide range of American poets [wrote sonnets] — from Ralph Waldo Emerson to Gwendolyn Brooks, from a homemade modernist like E. E. Cummings to an open field poet like Robert Duncan, from Elinor Wylie to James Merrill, from Edwin Arlington Robinson to Sterling Brown, from Robert Lowell to Ted Berrigan. It was also true that I didn't at first recognize the form of Frost's poem. It worked on me before I worked on it.

I wanted to write a poem like Frost's, a poem with a kind of massive American loneliness at the core, a deep center of solitude, which I also recognized in the paintings of Edward Hopper. I'd still like to write that poem. It occurred to me to count the lines — I was stumbling into becoming a maker — and thus discovered a different kind of sonnet structure. It wasn't Petrarchan or Shakespearean, the two main types of sonnet form in English. In fact, Frost had borrowed the rhyme scheme from Dante [Alighieri] (aba bcb cdc) and written a terza rima[3] sonnet, as [Percy Bysshe] Shelley had done in the five sections of "Ode to the West Wind." The poem was a walk. The rhythm and the rhymes gave the feeling of that walk, of moving forward while looking back. I felt that the music of the poem — the poem itself — had sent me out to the edge of myself and then reeled me back in. It circled back on itself. There was a kind of submission in it — a coping mechanism — that consoled me. It seemed to go beyond right and wrong. It was surrounded by a vast silence. It raised me to an unearthly height and then brought me gently back to earth.

"There are two absorbing facts," as Emerson formulated it: "I and the Abyss." The sonnet can be the vessel of that confrontation. Soon I would follow my discovery of the darker Frost and encounter the English Romantic sonnets of John Keats ("When I have fears that I may cease to be / Before my pen has glean'd my teeming brain") and John Clare ("I feel I am — I only know I am"), the so-called terrible sonnets of Gerard Manley Hopkins ("I wake and feel the fell of dark, not day"). These poems helped seal my vocation. They were written from the margins. The terrible loneliness at the heart of them was inscribed in fourteen lines, the social

[3] Italian for "third rhyme," a rhyming verse stanza form that consists of an interlocking three-line rhyme scheme. — Eds.

realm of a prescribed form. This was the great lesson that I learned as an isolated teenager in Chicago. Poetry counts; language mediates. I felt then — and I still feel — that poetry can embody loneliness and bring us into the human community in a fuller way. That loneliness, the feeling of solitude, can be thought through; it can be developed and delivered by a simple form that sacramentalizes a moment in time, a moment out of time — a little sound, a little song. ■

2006

Questions

1. Edward Hirsch analyzes the appeal of the sonnet by looking back at his early "acquaintance" with the Robert Frost poem "Acquainted with the Night." How does he use his personal experience to highlight qualities of the form in a poem he fell in love with before he even knew it was a sonnet?
2. Hirsch says that the sonnet form "seems to suit the contours of rhetorical argument" (par. 3). What does he mean by that, and what examples does he offer as evidence?
3. Why do you think Hirsch coped with his loneliness by reading lonely poems? How did reading Frost's "Acquainted with the Night" help him discover the sonnet as a "coping mechanism" (par. 8)? What qualities of the sonnet did he find consoling?
4. Why does Hirsch say that, as a young poet reading Whitman and Ginsberg, he would have argued that "American poetry shunned traditional forms, such as sonnets" (par. 7)? What counterargument does he offer to his younger self?
5. What, ultimately, does Hirsch feel is the great power of "a little sound, a little song" (par. 4)?

My mistress' eyes are nothing like the sun

William Shakespeare

William Shakespeare (1564–1616) was born in Stratford-upon-Avon, England. Little is known of his life aside from the fact that he married Anne Hathaway when he was eighteen, worked as an actor-playwright in London, and retired in 1613. At least thirty-eight plays, including *Romeo and Juliet* (1597), *Hamlet* (1601), *Othello* (1604), *King Lear* (1605), and *Macbeth* (1606), are attributed to him. In his time, his contemporaries — and likely Shakespeare himself — looked to his sonnets and other poems as the more important works. The following selection is Sonnet 130.

My mistress' eyes are nothing like the sun;
Coral is far more red than her lips' red;
If snow be white, why then her breasts are dun:[1]
If hairs be wires, black wires grow on her head.
I have seen roses damasked[2] red and white,
But no such roses see I in her cheeks;
And in some perfumes is there more delight
Than in the breath that from my mistress reeks.

[1] Dull, grayish-brown color. — Eds.
[2] Dappled or patterned. — Eds.

I love to hear her speak, yet well I know
That music hath a far more pleasing sound;
I grant I never saw a goddess go:
My mistress, when she walks, treads on the ground.
And yet, by heaven, I think my love as rare
As any she belied with false compare. ■

1609

Questions

1. As the speaker characterizes his own "mistress" (l. 8), he reveals the features of the ideal woman that was continuously praised by Petrarch in his sonnets. How would you describe that woman? Use textual details to support your answer.
2. Based on details found in lines 1 through 12, how would you describe the speaker's "mistress" (l. 8)? Why do you think the speaker chooses to catalog her shortcomings?
3. William Shakespeare's sonnets are more flexible than Petrarch's in their placement of the volta. Where does the main volta occur in this poem? Explain the turn the sonnet takes there. How do these lines invite readers to reassess the preceding lines? How would you describe the speaker's attitude toward his beloved?
4. How would you describe the tone in the first twelve lines? How does the tone shift in the final couplet? What details does the author use to create this contrast in tone?

Nuns Fret Not at Their Convent's Narrow Room

William Wordsworth

William Wordsworth (1770–1850), one of the most famous and influential Romantic poets, was widely known for his reverence of nature and the power of his lyrical verse. With Samuel Taylor Coleridge, he published *Lyrical Ballads* in 1798; the collection includes Wordsworth's "Lines Composed a Few Miles above Tintern Abbey." Among Wordsworth's other most famous works are "The World Is Too Much with Us" (p. 1277), also a sonnet.

Nuns fret not at their convent's narrow room;
And hermits are contented with their cells;
And students with their pensive citadels;
Maids at the wheel, the weaver at his loom,
Sit blithe and happy; bees that soar for bloom,
High as the highest Peak of Furness-fells,[1]
Will murmur by the hour in foxglove bells;[2]
In truth the prison, into which we doom
Ourselves, no prison is: and hence for me,
In sundry moods, 'twas pastime to be bound

[1] Hills and mountains in the north of England. — Eds.
[2] A plant with flowers that look like the fingers of gloves or bells. — Eds.

Within the Sonnet's scanty plot of ground;
Pleased if some Souls (for such there needs must be)
Who have felt the weight of too much liberty,
Should find brief solace there, as I have found. ■

1806

Questions

1. What is this poem's central argument?
2. What images from both the everyday world and the natural world does William Wordsworth use as evidence for the argument the speaker of this poem makes?
3. How does the speaker acknowledge and refute the counterargument?
4. How does form follow function in this poem? In other words, how does the form of the poem support and exemplify the speaker's argument?
5. In what ways does Wordsworth veer a bit from strict sonnet form? Try reading the poem aloud if you're not sure. How do those detours relate to the poem's argument?
6. Identify the volta in this poem. What is its function?

The Face of All the World (Sonnet 7)

Elizabeth Barrett Browning

One of the most prominent poets of the nineteenth century, Elizabeth Barrett Browning (1806–1861) was self-taught in many regards. She was a voracious reader and began writing poetry at the age of four. By the time she met her future husband, Robert Browning, she was already a well-known literary figure in both the United States and England.

KEY CONTEXT During her courtship with Robert Browning, Elizabeth wrote private sonnets expressing her love, thoughts, and fears, which stemmed from her physical ailments and the fact that she was older than Robert. She showed him these poems, which were eventually published, three years after the pair married, as a sonnet sequence titled *Sonnets from the Portuguese*. This is the seventh poem in the sequence.

The face of all the world is changed, I think,
Since first I heard the footsteps of thy soul
Move still, oh, still, beside me, as they stole
Betwixt me and the dreadful outer brink
Of obvious death, where I, who thought to sink,
Was caught up into love, and taught the whole
Of life in a new rhythm. The cup of dole[1]
God gave for baptism, I am fain[2] to drink,
And praise its sweetness, Sweet, with thee anear.
The names of country, heaven, are changed away

[1] Destiny, or one's lot in life. — Eds.

[2] To do something gladly. — Eds.

For where thou art or shalt be, there or here;
And this . . . this lute and song . . . loved yesterday,
(The singing angels know) are only dear,
Because thy name moves right in what they say. ■

c. 1845–1846

Questions

1. How does the speaker's beloved teach her "the whole / Of life in a new rhythm" (ll. 6–7)? In what way does her disposition toward life change as a result?
2. How do you interpret the sentence found in lines 7–9? In your response, consider the lines that come before this sentence.
3. What is the function of the ellipses in line 12? How would your interpretation of the last three lines of the poem change if Elizabeth Barrett Browning had used a comma or an em dash instead?
4. In what ways does Browning's poem both adhere to and deviate from the Petrarchan sonnet conventions? Consider structure, speaker, and subject matter in your response.

America

Claude McKay

Poet, novelist, and journalist Claude McKay (1889–1948) was born in Jamaica and began writing poetry at the age of ten. By the time he emigrated to the United States at age twenty-two, he had published two volumes of verse. In America, McKay faced the harsh realities of racism and, despite his education, took on menial jobs to make a living. McKay became known for his protest poetry, which spoke directly about racism and the trials of the working class.

KEY CONTEXT Claude McKay was a prominent figure of the 1920s Harlem Renaissance, a movement that celebrated the creative achievements of African American artists, musicians, and writers.

Although she feeds me bread of bitterness,
And sinks into my throat her tiger's tooth,
Stealing my breath of life, I will confess
I love this cultured hell that tests my youth.
Her vigor flows like tides into my blood,
Giving me strength erect against her hate,
Her bigness sweeps my being like a flood.
Yet, as a rebel fronts a king in state,
I stand within her walls with not a shred
Of terror, malice, not a word of jeer.
Darkly I gaze into the days ahead,
And see her might and granite wonders there,
Beneath the touch of Time's unerring hand,
Like priceless treasures sinking in the sand. ■

1921

Questions

1. Who does the speaker address throughout the poem?
2. What paradox does the speaker express in the first quatrain?
3. How does the structure of the first quatrain differ from that of the second quatrain? How does the structure of line 8, in particular, align with the idea of being "a rebel" (l. 8)?
4. What is the speaker's attitude toward his audience in the third quatrain? What specific details from lines 9–12 support your response?
5. How is the future depicted in the last four lines of the poem? What might be the cause of such a future?

How I Discovered Poetry

Marilyn Nelson

Marilyn Nelson (b. 1946) is an American poet who was the Poet Laureate of Connecticut from 2001 to 2006. Born in Cleveland, Ohio, she is the daughter of one of the Tuskegee Airmen, African American pilots who fought in a segregated U.S. Army during World War II (1939–1945). In addition to poetry, Nelson writes children's books and is a translator.

KEY CONTEXT This poem includes anti-Black language, which we have chosen to reprint in this textbook. We wish to accurately reflect both Nelson's original intent as well as the time period, culture, and racism depicted in the text, but we also recognize that this language has a long history as disrespectful and deeply hurtful. Be mindful of context, both Nelson's and yours, as you read "How I Discovered Poetry."

It was like soul-kissing, the way the words
filled my mouth as Mrs. Purdy read from her desk.
All the other kids zoned an hour ahead to 3:15,
but Mrs. Purdy and I wandered lonely as clouds borne
by a breeze off Mount Parnassus.[1] She must have seen
the darkest eyes in the room brim: The next day
she gave me a poem she'd chosen especially for me
to read to the all except for me white class.
She smiled when she told me to read it, smiled harder,
said oh yes I could. She smiled harder and harder
until I stood and opened my mouth to banjo playing
darkies, pickaninnies, disses and dats. When I finished
my classmates stared at the floor. We walked silent
to the buses, awed by the power of words. ■

1994

[1] A mountain in Greece that features prominently in Greek mythology: it was thought to be the home of Pegasus, the flying horse. — Eds.

Questions

1. How does Marilyn Nelson characterize the speaker of this poem? What does the sonnet form add to that characterization?
2. How does the strict form of the sonnet reflect the emotions the speaker's experiences? Explain.
3. Is the title, "How I Discovered Poetry," ironic or sincere or a bit of both? Explain.
4. What argument does the poem make? Do you think the turn, or volta, which begins in line 12, resolves that argument or extends it? Explain.
5. Why might the sonnet be an effective form for making a social statement as it does here?

What to Say Upon Being Asked to Be Friends

Julian Talamantez Brolaski

Julian Talamantez Brolaski (b. 1978), a two-spirit and transgender poet and musician of mixed Mescalero and Lipan Apache, Latin@, and European heritage, uses the pronouns it/its/itself. Brolaski is the lead singer and guitarist for two country bands, one in Oakland, California, the other in Brooklyn, New York.

Why speak of hate, when I do bleed for love?
Not hate, my love, but Love doth bite my tongue
Till I taste stuff that makes my rhyming rough
So flatter I my fever for the one
For whom I inly mourn, though seem to shun.
A rose is arrows is eros,[1] so what
If I confuse the shade that I've become
With winedark substance in a lover's cup?
But stop my tonguely wound, I've bled enough.
If I be fair, or false, or freaked with fear
If I my tongue in lockèd box immure
Blame not me, for I am sick with love.
    Yet would I be your friend most willingly
    Since friendship would infect me killingly. ■

2012

[1] The god of love in Greek mythology. — Eds.

Questions

1. How would you summarize the events that take place in this poem? How does the speaker feel about them?
2. What parts of this poem follow traditional poetic conventions? What parts break away?

3. The poem's diction is quite formal but a colloquialism appears here and there. What is the effect of the juxtaposition of these different modes of communication?
4. Consider the contradiction — and question — in the first line: "Why speak of hate, when I do bleed for love?" Is it resolved at the end of the poem? Explain.
5. What function does "Yet" serve in line 13? How does that explain the answer to the question in the poem's title?
6. Do you think the speaker is fighting or embracing the sonnet form? Explain your response with evidence from the text.

Peril Sonnet

David Baker

David Baker (b. 1954) is an American poet and professor. He is the author of twelve books of poetry, including *Swift: New and Selected Poems* (2019) and *Never-Ending Birds* (2009), which won the Theodore Roethke Memorial Poetry Prize. Throughout his poems, Baker explores the relationship between people and place. He believes that his writing is shaped by his surroundings, namely the American Midwest, where he has lived for over thirty years.

Where do you suppose
they've gone the bees now

that you don't see them
anymore four-winged

among flowers low
sparks in the clover

even at nightfall
are they fanning have

they gone another
place blued with pollen

stuck to their bristles
waiting beyond us

spring dwindle is what
we call it collapsing

neonicotinoids[1]

"high levels in pneu-

matic corn exhaust"

loss of habitat

or *disappearing*

disease in the way

of our kind so to speak

what do you think

they would call it

language older than

our ears were they

saying it all along

even at daybreak — ■

2016

[1] A type of insecticide. — Eds.

Questions

1. What is the speaker's primary concern in the poem? Identify the multiple names that the poem gives this problem.
2. What do you suppose the speaker means by "language older than / our ears" (ll. 24–25)? What does the phrase suggest about human beings and our relationship with nature?
3. What is the function of the poem's syntax? Rewrite the poem in prose form and provide appropriate punctuation. How does this rearrangement affect your experience as a reader?
4. When asked about his unusual sonnets in an interview, David Baker admitted that he has always liked to "[f]uss with the form of things." He then acknowledged that the sonnet is an "especially elastic and capacious form." How does Baker use this elasticity to convey meaning in "Peril Sonnet"?

Diaspora Sonnet 40

Oliver de la Paz

Born in the Philippines and raised in Oregon, Oliver de la Paz (b. 1972) earned an MFA from Arizona State University. The author of five collections of poetry, including *The Boy in the Labyrinth* (2019), he teaches at the College of the Holy Cross and in the Low-Residency MFA Program at Pacific Lutheran University.

KEY CONTEXT The term *diaspora* refers to the dispersion or migration of a group of people from their ancestral homeland.

So much improvisation—the improvised way
I enter a room. The way I walk market aisles:

with purpose borne of worry. The tumult of cereal
packages, an array of landscapes crossed over

in a plane. I am flying above the patchwork of
mornings and feeling dizzy. Truly I am

making this up as I stay here. Morning into morning
into the next. Consecutive tiles worrying themselves

into the shape of purpose. I can't tell you why
we boarded a plane many years past except

to say the plane was there and we needed another
"there." I can't tell you much about flying then except

that I was nauseous. Disorientation is its own
improvisation. A mind spins until it finds its foci. ■

2019

Questions

1. Consider the title of the poem. How does the term "diaspora" inform your interpretation of the speaker's message?
2. When discussing his sonnets in an interview, Oliver de la Paz said that they are "meditations on home and place . . . especially when one is not wanted on the doorstep." Which aspects of the poem reflect this statement?
3. Where do you sense is the most significant volta in this poem? What is the difference between what comes before this moment and what follows?
4. How do you interpret the final two sentences of the poem: "Disorientation is its own / improvisation. A mind spins until it finds its foci" (ll. 13–14)?

Literature in Conversation

1. Irish poet Eavan Boland writes that the sonnet's features were "set from the start: fourteen lines with a narrow turning space for wit and argument." Choose several of the poems here and analyze how the "narrow turning space" allows for wit and argument.
2. Consider the evolution of the sonnet as discussed in the introduction to this Texts in Context section. What kinds of changes to the sonnet form do the poems in this section represent? Support your answers with specific references to at least three poems from this section.
3. How do you suppose that Petrarch or Shakespeare would react to the contemporary sonnets presented in this section? Would they admire the innovation these poets demonstrate? Would they be appalled at their deviations from their established norms? Would they even recognize them as sonnets? Write your response from the perspective of either Petrarch or Shakespeare.
4. When asked for the best or worst writing advice ever given to her, poet Camille Dungy responded that she was told she "couldn't write sonnets that didn't follow traditional rhyme and metrical schemes." Her decision not to follow this advice was grounded on what others had been permitted to do. She says, "Wyatt and Shakespeare, Keats and cummings all found their own ways of writing sonnets. Why shouldn't I [...]?" Do you agree with the advice given to Dungy or with what she and other poets have done? Should poems that deviate from the standard conventions be called something other than a sonnet? To support your stance, provide textual evidence from any of the readings in this Texts in Context section, including the introduction we provided.
5. Reread the Classic Text in this chapter, William Shakespeare's Sonnet 147 (p. 337). How does this poem fit within the history of the sonnet tradition? Does Shakespeare abide by the conventions of the sonnets named for him in this particular poem? How does it compare to Sonnet 130 (p. 344)?
6. How does your growing understanding of the sonnet tradition affect how you see poetry? How are the sonneteers who wrote hundreds of years ago similar to and different from those writing today? Make sure to discuss at least four poets in your response.
7. Wordsworth's "Nuns Fret Not at Their Convent's Narrow Room" says the sonnet is a "scanty plot of ground." Using the sonnets here — or other sonnets you know — support, challenge, or qualify that statement.
8. Dinitia Smith opens her *New York Times* review of the New York Public Library's 2003 exhibit, "Passion's Discipline: The History of the Sonnet in the British Isles and America," "O passion, doest thou grow more acute with discipline? And can there be any harsher discipline than distilling overwhelming emotion into a sonnet, 14 rigidly constructed lines of poetry with a complex rhyme and metrical structure?" Answer her question.
9. Some scholars argue that the great innovation of the sonnet was self-awareness. The earliest sonnets by Petrarch and Dante were characterized by opposites: hope and fear, love and rejection. This self-awareness was a revolutionary change in Western poetry. How do the sonnets here, including those from the nineteenth century through the present day, express self-awareness? Why is the sonnet form so effective for that expression?

Araby

James Joyce

C. P. Curran/Hulton Archive/Getty Images

Irish author James Joyce (1882–1941) is considered one of the most influential writers of the twentieth century. Although Joyce's work is inextricably connected to Ireland, and nearly all of it takes place in Dublin, he lived in Italy and France for most of his adult life. His short stories and novels reflect his inner turmoil about both his native country and the Roman Catholic Church in which he was raised. Joyce used stream of consciousness, an onslaught of tiny details, and both accessible and obscure allusions to literature, history, and politics to create the recognizable world of his fiction, but as he told a friend, "the ideas are always simple." His masterpiece, *Ulysses*, takes the myth of *The Odyssey* and updates it to contemporary Ireland. The following story is taken from his collection *Dubliners*, which he finished writing in 1904 at the age of twenty-two, but was not able to publish until 1914.

KEY CONTEXT In the collection *Dubliners*, Joyce depicts everyday life in Dublin at the start of the twentieth century. Throughout the stories, Joyce relies on epiphany, a sudden moment of realization or illumination, to capture a life-altering moment in his characters' lives. The title of the story, "Araby," refers to a real event: the 1894 Araby bazaar in Dublin, Ireland. It was held to raise money for Jervis Street Hospital, an institution run by the Catholic Sisters of Mercy. The event was advertised as having a Middle Eastern theme, although the performances and attractions often perpetuated racist stereotypes of Middle Eastern cultures. The name of the bazaar itself treats these cultures as an "Arab" monolith.

North Richmond Street, being blind, was a quiet street except at the hour when the Christian Brothers' School set the boys free. An uninhabited house of two storeys stood at the blind end, detached from its neighbours in a square ground. The other houses of the street, conscious of decent lives within them, gazed at one another with brown imperturbable faces.

The former tenant of our house, a priest, had died in the back drawing-room. Air, musty from having been long enclosed, hung in all the rooms, and the waste room behind the kitchen was littered with old useless papers. Among these I found a few paper-covered books, the pages of which were curled and damp: *The Abbot*, by Walter Scott, *The Devout Communicant*, and *The Memoirs of Vidocq*. I liked the last best because its leaves were yellow. The wild garden behind the house contained a central apple-tree and a few straggling bushes, under one of which I found the late tenant's rusty bicycle-pump. He had been a very charitable priest; in his will he had left all his money to institutions and the furniture of his house to his sister.

When the short days of winter came, dusk fell before we had well eaten our dinners. When we met in the street the houses had grown sombre. The space of sky above us was the colour of ever-changing violet and towards it the lamps of the street lifted their feeble lanterns. The cold air stung us and we played till our bodies glowed. Our shouts echoed in the silent street. The career of our play brought us through the dark muddy lanes behind the houses, where we ran the gauntlet of the rough tribes from the cottages, to the back doors of the dark dripping gardens where odours arose from the ashpits, to the dark odorous stables where a coachman smoothed and combed the horse or shook music from the buckled harness. When we returned to the street, light from the kitchen windows had filled the areas. If my uncle was seen turning the corner, we hid in the shadow until we had seen him safely housed. Or if Mangan's sister came out on the doorstep to call her brother in to his tea, we watched her from our shadow peer up and down the street. We waited to see whether she would remain or go in and, if she remained, we left our shadow and walked up to Mangan's steps resignedly. She was waiting for us, her figure defined by the light from the half-opened door. Her brother always teased her before he obeyed, and I stood by the railings looking at her. Her dress swung as she moved her body, and the soft rope of her hair tossed from side to side.

Every morning I lay on the floor in the front parlour watching her door. The blind was pulled down to within an inch of the sash so that I could not be seen. When she came out on the doorstep my heart leaped. I ran to the hall, seized my books and followed her. I kept her brown figure always in my eye and, when we came near the point at which our ways diverged, I quickened my pace and passed her. This happened morning after morning. I had never spoken to her, except for a few casual words, and yet her name was like a summons to all my foolish blood.

5 Her image accompanied me even in places the most hostile to romance. On Saturday evenings when my aunt went marketing I had to go to carry some of the parcels. We walked through the flaring streets, jostled by drunken men and bargaining women, amid the curses of labourers, the shrill litanies of shop-boys who stood on guard by the barrels of pigs' cheeks, the nasal chanting of street-singers, who sang a come-all-you about O'Donovan Rossa, or a ballad about the troubles in our native land. These noises converged in a single sensation of life for me: I imagined that I bore my chalice safely through a throng of foes. Her name sprang to my lips at moments in strange prayers and praises which I myself did not understand. My eyes were often full of tears (I could not tell why) and at times a flood from my heart seemed to pour itself out into my bosom. I thought little of the future. I did not know whether I would ever speak to her or not or, if I spoke to her, how I could tell her of my confused adoration. But my body was like a harp and her words and gestures were like fingers running upon the wires.

One evening I went into the back drawing-room in which the priest had died. It was a dark rainy evening and there was no sound in the house. Through one of the broken panes I heard the rain impinge upon the earth, the fine incessant needles of water playing in the sodden beds. Some distant lamp or lighted window gleamed below me. I was thankful that I could see so little. All my senses seemed to desire to veil themselves and, feeling that I was about to slip from them, I pressed the palms of my hands together until they trembled, murmuring: "O love! O love!" many times.

At last she spoke to me. When she addressed the first words to me I was so confused that I did not know what to answer. She asked me was I going to Araby. I forgot whether I answered yes or no. It would be a splendid bazaar; she said she would love to go.

"And why can't you?" I asked.

While she spoke she turned a silver bracelet round and round her wrist. She could not go, she said, because there would be a retreat that week in her convent. Her brother and two other boys were fighting for their caps, and I was alone at the railings. She held one of the spikes, bowing her head towards me. The light from the lamp opposite our door caught the white curve of her neck, lit up her hair that rested there and, falling, lit up the hand upon the railing. It fell over one side of her dress and caught the white border of a petticoat, just visible as she stood at ease.

"It's well for you," she said.

"If I go," I said, "I will bring you something."

What innumerable follies laid waste my waking and sleeping thoughts after that evening! I wished to annihilate the tedious intervening days. I chafed against the work of school. At night in my bedroom and by day in the classroom her image came between me and the page I strove to read. The syllables of the word Araby were called to me through the silence in which my soul luxuriated and cast an Eastern enchantment over me. I asked for leave to go to the bazaar on Saturday night. My aunt was surprised, and hoped it was not some Freemason[1] affair. I answered few questions in class. I watched my master's face pass from amiability to sternness; he hoped I was not beginning to idle. I could not call my wandering thoughts together. I had hardly any patience with the serious work of life which, now that it stood between me and my desire, seemed to me child's play, ugly monotonous child's play.

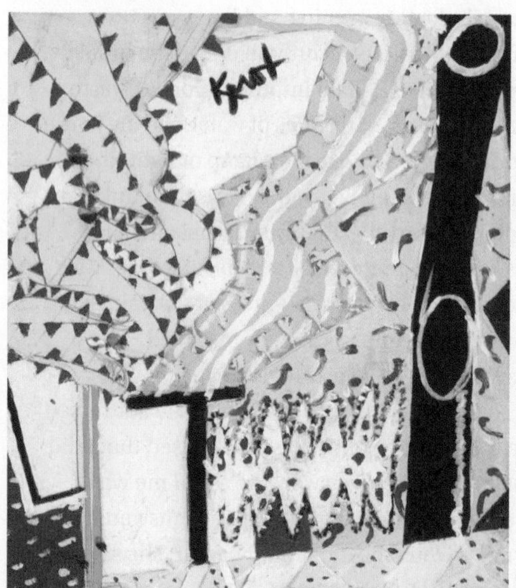

This abstract painting by Knox Martin, called *Still Life, Window*, was completed in 1987. **How does this image express the turmoil of the narrator as he thinks about Mangan's sister and imagines visiting the Araby bazaar?**

On Saturday morning I reminded my uncle that I wished to go to the bazaar in the evening. He was fussing at the hallstand, looking for the hat-brush, and answered me curtly:

"Yes, boy, I know."

As he was in the hall I could not go into the front parlour and lie at the window. I left the house in bad humour and walked slowly towards the school. The air was pitilessly raw and already my heart misgave me.

When I came home to dinner my uncle had not yet been home. Still it was early. I sat staring at the clock for some time and, when its ticking began to irritate me, I left the room. I mounted the staircase and gained the upper part of the house. The high, cold, empty, gloomy rooms liberated me and I went from room to room singing. From the front window I saw my companions playing below in the street. Their cries reached me weakened and indistinct and, leaning my forehead against the cool glass, I looked over at the dark house where she lived. I may have stood there for an hour, seeing nothing but the brown-clad figure cast by my imagination, touched discreetly by the lamplight at the curved neck, at the hand upon the railings and at the border below the dress.

---

[1] A secret fraternal organization. — Eds.

When I came downstairs again I found Mrs Mercer sitting at the fire. She was an old, garrulous woman, a pawnbroker's widow, who collected used stamps for some pious purpose. I had to endure the gossip of the tea-table. The meal was prolonged beyond an hour and still my uncle did not come. Mrs Mercer stood up to go: she was sorry she couldn't wait any longer, but it was after eight o'clock and she did not like to be out late, as the night air was bad for her. When she had gone I began to walk up and down the room, clenching my fists. My aunt said:

"I'm afraid you may put off your bazaar for this night of Our Lord."

At nine o'clock I heard my uncle's latchkey in the hall door. I heard him talking to himself and heard the hallstand rocking when it had received the weight of his overcoat. I could interpret these signs. When he was midway through his dinner I asked him to give me the money to go to the bazaar. He had forgotten.

"The people are in bed and after their first sleep now," he said.

I did not smile. My aunt said to him energetically:

"Can't you give him the money and let him go? You've kept him late enough as it is."

My uncle said he was very sorry he had forgotten. He said he believed in the old saying: "All work and no play makes Jack a dull boy." He asked me where I was going and, when I told him a second time, he asked me did I know *The Arab's Farewell to His Steed.*[2] When I left the kitchen he was about to recite the opening lines of the piece to my aunt.

I held a florin[3] tightly in my hand as I strode down Buckingham Street towards the station. The sight of the streets thronged with buyers and glaring with gas recalled to me the purpose of my journey. I took my seat in a third-class carriage of a deserted train. After an intolerable delay the train moved out of the station slowly. It crept onward among ruinous houses and over the twinkling river. At Westland Row Station a crowd of people pressed to the carriage doors; but the porters moved them back, saying that it was a special train for the bazaar. I remained alone in the bare carriage. In a few minutes the train drew up beside an improvised wooden platform. I passed out on to the road and saw by the lighted dial of a clock that it was ten minutes to ten. In front of me was a large building which displayed the magical name.

I could not find any sixpenny entrance and, fearing that the bazaar would be closed, I passed in quickly through a turnstile, handing a shilling to a weary-looking man. I found myself in a big hall girded at half its height by a gallery. Nearly all the stalls were closed and the greater part of the hall was in darkness. I recognized a silence like that which pervades a church after a service. I walked into the centre of the bazaar timidly. A few people were gathered about the stalls which were still open. Before a curtain, over which the words Caf Chantant[4] were written in coloured lamps, two men were counting money on a salver. I listened to the fall of the coins.

Remembering with difficulty why I had come, I went over to one of the stalls and examined porcelain vases and flowered tea-sets. At the door of the stall a young lady was talking and laughing with two young gentlemen. I remarked their English accents and listened vaguely to their conversation.

"O, I never said such a thing!"

"O, but you did!"

"O, but I didn't!"

"Didn't she say that?"

"Yes. I heard her."

"O, there's a . . . fib."

---

[2] A ballad, better known as "The Arab's Farewell to His Horse," written by Caroline Norton (1808–1877), an English writer. — Eds.

[3] A British coin worth two shillings, circulated between 1849 and 1967. — Eds.

[4] *Café chantant* is French for "singing café." People would sing and dance to lighthearted music. — Eds.

Observing me, the young lady came over and asked me did I wish to buy anything. The tone of her voice was not encouraging; she seemed to have spoken to me out of a sense of duty. I looked humbly at the great jars that stood like eastern guards at either side of the dark entrance to the stall and murmured:

"No, thank you."

The young lady changed the position of one of the vases and went back to the two young men. They began to talk of the same subject. Once or twice the young lady glanced at me over her shoulder.

I lingered before her stall, though I knew my stay was useless, to make my interest in her wares seem the more real. Then I turned away slowly and walked down the middle of the bazaar. I allowed the two pennies to fall against the sixpence in my pocket. I heard a voice call from one end of the gallery that the light was out. The upper part of the hall was now completely dark.

35 Gazing up into the darkness I saw myself as a creature driven and derided by vanity; and my eyes burned with anguish and anger. ■

1914

Understanding and Interpreting

1. "Araby" is in a collection of stories called *Dubliners*, all of which take place in Dublin, Ireland. How is this setting described by the narrator? Pay particular attention to the class structure of the neighborhood in which the narrator lives. How does he categorize the people in the neighborhood?
2. What information do we learn about the narrator over the course of this very short story? What specific details characterize him?
3. How does the narrator characterize his aunt and uncle? How would you describe their family life? Why is it important that a priest lived and died in the house the narrator lives in?
4. What do we know about Mangan's sister? Try to separate the "factual" details from the narrator's romantic embellishments. Why do you think she is not given a name?
5. What disappointments does the narrator suffer when he finally gets to the bazaar? What expectations did he have? How does the bazaar fail to live up to them?
6. How would you describe the narrator's state of mind at the end of the story?

Analyzing Language, Style, and Structure

1. **Vocabulary in Context.** What is the meaning of the word "career" in paragraph 3? How does Joyce make it do double duty here?
2. How does Joyce convey the narrator's attraction to Mangan's sister with so little explicit information about her looks or even her personality?
3. The narrator seems to be on the cusp of adolescence. What elements of his narration put him on the side of childhood? Which make him seem more adult?
4. Look carefully at paragraph 5, when the narrator goes to the market with his aunt. How does the accumulation of concrete details lead the narrator to imagine himself carrying a "chalice safely through a throng of foes"? Where does the paragraph shift, and what does this metaphor convey about how the narrator sees the world?

5. What is the purpose of Mrs. Mercer's visit to the narrator's house (par. 16)? What aspects of Dublin life does it illustrate?

6. Reread the description of the train ride in paragraph 24. How does the diction and syntax in this scene convey the narrator's state of mind as well as characterize the city of Dublin?

7. Compare the description of the outdoor Dublin market where the narrator goes with his aunt (par. 5) to the description of the nearly shuttered Araby bazaar, which begins in paragraph 25. What kind of structure do these two scenes bring to the story?

8. In paragraph 12, the narrator describes the effect of the word *Araby*: "The syllables of the word Araby were called to me through the silence in which my soul luxuriated and cast an Eastern enchantment over me." Why does the word *Araby* have this effect on the narrator? What connotations does it have? How do these connotations relate to the promises the word holds for the narrator and even for Mangan's sister?

9. What does the bazaar ultimately symbolize for the narrator? How does Joyce's language describing the narrator's experience of the bazaar convey the meaning of that symbolism?

Topics for Composing

1. **AP® FRQ Prose Fiction Analysis.** The following question refers to paragraphs 22–23 of James Joyce's "Araby," published in 1914. In this passage, the narrator describes his journey to the Araby bazaar. Read the passage carefully. Then, in a well-written essay, analyze how Joyce uses literary elements and techniques to convey the tension of that journey.

2. **AP® FRQ Literary Argument.** Joyce is famous for having invented *epiphany* as a literary term. He defined it as the "sudden revelation of the whatness of a thing," the moment in which "the soul of the commonest object . . . seems to us radiant . . . a sudden spiritual manifestation [either] in the vulgarity of speech or of a gesture or in a memorable phrase of the mind itself." In "Araby," the narrator has an epiphany at the end of the story. In a well-written essay, analyze how this epiphany contributes to an interpretation of the work as a whole. Do not merely summarize the plot.

3. **AP® Literary Argumentation.** In the view of some critics, a work that does not provide the pleasure of significant closure has terminated with an artistic fault. A satisfactory ending is not, however, always conclusive; significant closure may require the reader to abide with or adjust to ambiguity and uncertainty. In an essay, discuss the ending of "Araby." Explain precisely how and why the ending appropriately or inappropriately concludes the story, using evidence from the text to support your view.

4. **AP® Literary Argumentation.** It has been said that character determines incident, and incident illustrates character. Write an essay that evaluates that statement by discussing the narrator of "Araby" and the events of the story.

5. **AP® Literary Argumentation.** James Joyce is considered one of the original modernists, and *Dubliners*, written from 1904 to 1907 and published in 1914, one of the first modernist works. Modernist themes include paralysis, loneliness, and death, often connected to political or religious plights, which are expressed in techniques such as epiphany, symbolism, stream-of-consciousness narration, unclear plot lines, and shifts in narrative perspective. How does "Araby" fit the criteria of a modernist work of literature? How do those criteria help Joyce comment on the social, political, and religious lives of the Irish?

6. **Research.** In the nineteenth and early twentieth centuries, European and American artists and writers were fascinated by the art, literature, and design of the Eastern world, especially the Middle East, but also China and Japan. In the late twentieth century, writer Edward Said coined the term "orientalism" to describe the patronizing attitude of the west to the east. Research this term and consider how it contributes to the narrator's perspective in "Araby." Do aspects of orientalism still pervade Western culture and art today? What is the line between appreciation and appropriation?
7. **Connections.** In *Transitions: Narratives in Modern Irish Culture*, Irish scholar Richard Kearney argues that the crisis of twentieth-century Irish culture is defined by a clash between "revivalism and modernism," or between those who "seek to revive the past" and those who turn to a cosmopolitan or international perspective and thereby "seek to rewrite or repudiate it altogether." Where does "Araby" fall in Kearney's analysis? What aspects of the story are revisits to the past? What aspects are modern or cosmopolitan — and do these elements specifically seek to rewrite or reject the past? Does the story resolve the conflict between past and present in any way? Explain.
8. **Multimodal.** All of Joyce's work pays close attention to the roads, trains, and paths through Dublin, many of which remain the same today. Look at a map or Google Street View of present-day Dublin and try to "map" the events and setting of "Araby." You may, of course, find one ready-made on the internet. Illustrate or caption your map to convey your personal interpretation of what these places mean to the narrator and within the context of the story.

A Rose for Emily

William Faulkner

Born in New Albany, Mississippi, William Faulkner (1897–1962) grew bored with education in his early teens, joining first the Canadian and then the British Royal Air Force during the First World War — though he never saw action. While living in New Orleans, Faulkner wrote his first novel, *Soldier's Pay* (1926). He is best known for the novels *The Sound and the Fury* (1929), *As I Lay Dying* (1930), *Light in August* (1932), and *Absalom, Absalom!* (1936). In 1949, he was awarded the Nobel Prize for Literature.

Corbis Historical/Getty Images

KEY CONTEXT Faulkner's writing is often set in the fictional county of Yoknanatawpha, Mississippi, inspired by Lafayette County and Oxford, the county seat. This story takes place during the era following the Civil War and reconstruction known as Jim Crow (1877–1968). During this time, Jim Crow laws segregated Black and white people in virtually every aspect of life, systematically reinforcing racism in the South. Among other things, these laws disenfranchised Black people by preventing them from voting, accessing quality education and employment, and owning homes. Additionally, this story includes the N-word, which we have chosen not to reprint in full here. We wish to accurately reflect both Faulkner's original intent as well as the racism of the time period, but we also recognize that this word has a long history as a derogatory and deeply hurtful expression when used by white people toward Black people. In the context of this story, the word is hurtful, and we have replaced it without hindering understanding of the work as a whole. Be mindful of context, both Faulkner's and yours, as you read "A Rose for Emily."

I

When Miss Emily Grierson died, our whole town went to her funeral: the men through a sort of respectful affection for a fallen monument, the women mostly out of curiosity to see the inside of her house, which no one save an old manservant — a combined gardener and cook — had seen in at least ten years.

It was a big, squarish frame house that had once been white, decorated with cupolas and spires and scrolled balconies in the heavily lightsome style of the seventies, set on what had once been our most select street. But garages and cotton gins had encroached and obliterated even the august names of that neighborhood; only Miss Emily's house was left, lifting its stubborn and coquettish decay above the cotton wagons and the gasoline pumps — an eyesore among eyesores. And now Miss Emily had gone to join the representatives of those august names where they lay in the cedar-bemused cemetery among the ranked and anonymous graves of Union and Confederate soldiers who fell at the battle of Jefferson.

Alive, Miss Emily had been a tradition, a duty, and a care; a sort of hereditary obligation upon the town, dating from that day in 1894 when Colonel Sartoris, the mayor — he who fathered the edict that no Negro woman should appear on the streets without an apron — remitted her taxes, the dispensation dating from the death of her father on into perpetuity. Not that Miss Emily would have accepted charity. Colonel Sartoris invented an involved tale to the effect that Miss Emily's father had loaned money to the town, which the town, as a matter of business, preferred this way of repaying. Only a man of Colonel Sartoris' generation and thought could have invented it, and only a woman could have believed it.

When the next generation, with its more modern ideas, became mayors and aldermen, this arrangement created some little dissatisfaction. On the first of the year they mailed her a tax notice. February came, and there was no reply. They wrote her a formal letter, asking her to call at the sheriff's office at her convenience. A week later the mayor wrote her himself, offering to call or to send his car for her, and received in reply a note on paper of an archaic shape, in a thin, flowing calligraphy in faded ink, to the effect that she no longer went out at all. The tax notice was also enclosed, without comment.

5 They called a special meeting of the Board of Aldermen. A deputation waited upon her, knocked at the door through which no visitor had passed since she ceased giving china-painting lessons eight or ten years earlier. They were admitted by the old Negro into a dim hall from which a stairway mounted into still more shadow. It smelled of dust and disuse — a close, dank smell. The Negro led them into the parlor. It was furnished in heavy, leather-covered furniture. When the Negro opened the blinds of one window, they could see that the leather was cracked; and when they sat down, a faint dust rose sluggishly about their thighs, spinning with slow motes in the single sun-ray. On a tarnished gilt easel before the fireplace stood a crayon portrait of Miss Emily's father.

They rose when she entered — a small, fat woman in black, with a thin gold chain descending to her waist and vanishing into her belt, leaning on an ebony cane with a tarnished gold head. Her skeleton was small and spare; perhaps that was why what would have been merely plumpness in another was obesity in her. She looked bloated, like a body long submerged in motionless water, and of that pallid hue. Her eyes, lost in the fatty ridges of her face, looked like two small pieces of coal pressed into a lump of dough as they moved from one face to another while the visitors stated their errand.

She did not ask them to sit. She just stood in the door and listened quietly until the spokesman came to a stumbling halt. Then they could hear the invisible watch ticking at the end of the gold chain.

Her voice was dry and cold. "I have no taxes in Jefferson. Colonel Sartoris explained it to me. Perhaps one of you can gain access to the city records and satisfy yourselves."

"But we have. We are the city authorities, Miss Emily. Didn't you get a notice from the sheriff, signed by him?"

10 "I received a paper, yes," Miss Emily said. "Perhaps he considers himself the sheriff. . . . I have no taxes in Jefferson."

"But there is nothing on the books to show that, you see. We must go by the — "

"See Colonel Sartoris. I have no taxes in Jefferson."

"But, Miss Emily — "

"See Colonel Sartoris." (Colonel Sartoris had been dead almost ten years.) "I have no taxes in Jefferson. Tobe!" The Negro appeared. "Show these gentlemen out."

II

15 So she vanquished them, horse and foot, just as she had vanquished their fathers thirty years before about the smell. That was two years after her father's death and a short time after her sweetheart — the one we believed would marry her — had deserted her. After her father's death she went out very little; after her sweetheart went away, people hardly saw her at all. A few of the ladies had the temerity to call, but were not received, and the only sign of life about the place was the Negro man — a young man then — going in and out with a market basket.

"Just as if a man — any man — could keep a kitchen properly," the ladies said; so they were not surprised when the smell developed. It was another link between the gross, teeming world and the high and mighty Griersons.

This photo features the Skipwith House, a home built in the 1870s on the campus of the University of Mississippi in Oxford.

How do the Skipwith House and its details represent not only Miss Emily's house but even an extension of Miss Emily herself? Consider especially how "only Miss Emily's house was left, lifting its stubborn and coquettish decay above the cotton wagons and the gasoline pumps — an eyesore among eyesores" (par. 2).

A neighbor, a woman, complained to the mayor, Judge Stevens, eighty years old.

"But what will you have me do about it, madam?" he said.

"Why, send her word to stop it," the woman said. "Isn't there a law?"

"I'm sure that won't be necessary," Judge Stevens said. "It's probably just a snake or a rat that n***** of hers killed in the yard. I'll speak to him about it."

The next day he received two more complaints, one from a man who came in diffident deprecation. "We really must do something about it, Judge. I'd be the last one in the world to bother Miss Emily, but we've got to do something." That night the Board of Aldermen met — three graybeards and one younger man, a member of the rising generation.

"It's simple enough," he said. "Send her word to have her place cleaned up. Give her a certain time to do it in, and if she don't . . ."

"Dammit, sir," Judge Stevens said, "will you accuse a lady to her face of smelling bad?"

So the next night, after midnight, four men crossed Miss Emily's lawn and slunk about the house like burglars, sniffing along the base of the brickwork and at the cellar openings while one of them performed a regular sowing motion with his hand out of a sack slung from his shoulder. They broke open the cellar door and sprinkled lime there, and in all the outbuildings. As they recrossed the lawn, a window that had been dark was lighted and Miss Emily sat in it, the light behind her, and her upright torso motionless as that of an idol. They crept quietly across the lawn and into the shadow of the locusts that lined the street. After a week or two the smell went away.

That was when people had begun to feel really sorry for her. People in our town, remembering how old lady Wyatt, her great-aunt, had gone completely crazy at last, believed that the Griersons held themselves a little too high for what they really were. None of the young men were quite good enough for Miss Emily and such. We had long thought of them as a tableau, Miss Emily a slender figure in white in the background, her father a spraddled silhouette in the foreground, his back to her and clutching a horsewhip, the two of them framed by the backflung front door. So when she got to be thirty and was still single, we were not pleased exactly, but vindicated; even with insanity in the family she wouldn't have turned down all of her chances if they had really materialized.

When her father died, it got about that the house was all that was left to her; and in a way, people were glad. At last they could pity Miss Emily. Being left alone, and a pauper, she had become humanized. Now she too would know the old thrill and the old despair of a penny more or less.

The day after his death all the ladies prepared to call at the house and offer condolence and aid, as is our custom. Miss Emily met them at the door, dressed as usual and with no trace of grief on her face. She told them that her father was not dead. She did that for three days, with the ministers calling on her, and the doctors, trying to persuade her to let them dispose of the body. Just as they were about to resort to law and force, she broke down, and they buried her father quickly.

We did not say she was crazy then. We believed she had to do that. We remembered all the young men her father had driven away, and we knew that with nothing left, she would have to cling to that which had robbed her, as people will.

III

She was sick for a long time. When we saw her again, her hair was cut short, making her look like a girl, with a vague resemblance to those angels in colored church windows — sort of tragic and serene.

The town had just let the contracts for paving the sidewalks, and in the summer after her father's death they began the work. The construction company came with n*****s and mules and machinery, and a foreman named Homer Barron, a Yankee — a big, dark, ready man, with a big voice and eyes lighter than his face. The little boys would follow in groups to hear him cuss the n*****s, and the n*****s singing in time to the rise and fall of picks. Pretty soon he knew everybody in town. Whenever you heard a lot of laughing anywhere about the square, Homer Barron would be in the center of the group. Presently, we began to see him and Miss Emily on Sunday afternoons driving in the yellow-wheeled buggy and the matched team of bays from the livery stable.

At first we were glad that Miss Emily would have an interest, because the ladies all said, "Of course a Grierson would not think seriously of a Northerner, a day laborer." But there were still others, older people, who said that even grief could not cause a real lady to forget *noblesse oblige*[1] — without calling it *noblesse oblige*. They just said, "Poor Emily. Her kinsfolk should come to her." She had some kin in Alabama; but years ago her father had fallen out with them over the estate of old lady Wyatt, the crazy woman, and there was no communication between the two families. They had not even been represented at the funeral.

And as soon as the old people said, "Poor Emily," the whispering began. "Do you suppose it's really so?" they said to one another. "Of course it is. What else could . . ." This behind their hands; rustling of craned silk and satin behind jalousies closed upon the sun of Sunday afternoon as the thin, swift clop-clop-clop of the matched team passed: "Poor Emily."

She carried her head high enough — even when we believed that she was fallen. It was as if she demanded more than ever the recognition of her dignity as the last Grierson; as if it had wanted that touch of earthiness to reaffirm her imperviousness. Like when she bought the rat poison, the arsenic. That was over a year after they had begun to say "Poor Emily," and while the two female cousins were visiting her.

Woman Arranging her Veil, c.1890 (pastel on paper)/Cassatt, Mary Stevenson (1844-1926)/Philadelphia Museum of Art, Pennsylvania, PA, USA/Bridgeman Images

Drawn in 1890 by American artist Mary Cassatt (1844–1926), this image of a woman arranging her veil depicts how someone like Emily Grierson would have dressed while in mourning.

How does this drawing compare to the way you had imagined Miss Emily? What similarities and differences do you notice?

"I want some poison," she said to the druggist. She was over thirty then, still a slight woman, though thinner than usual, with cold, haughty black eyes in a face the flesh of which was strained across the temples and about the eye-sockets as you imagine a lighthouse-keeper's face ought to look. "I want some poison," she said.

"Yes, Miss Emily. What kind? For rats and 35
such? I'd recom — "

[1] "Nobility obligates" in French. In other words, those with power and money have a duty to behave nobly. — Eds.

"I want the best you have. I don't care what kind."

The druggist named several. "They'll kill anything up to an elephant. But what you want is —— "

"Arsenic," Miss Emily said. "Is that a good one?"

"Is . . . arsenic? Yes, ma'am. But what you want —— "

"I want arsenic."

The druggist looked down at her. She looked back at him, erect, her face like a strained flag. "Why, of course," the druggist said. "If that's what you want. But the law requires you to tell what you are going to use it for."

Miss Emily just stared at him, her head tilted back in order to look him eye for eye, until he looked away and went and got the arsenic and wrapped it up. The Negro delivery boy brought her the package; the druggist didn't come back. When she opened the package at home there was written on the box, under the skull and bones: "For rats."

IV

So the next day we all said, "She will kill herself"; and we said it would be the best thing. When she had first begun to be seen with Homer Barron, we had said, "She will marry him." Then we said, "She will persuade him yet," because Homer himself had remarked — he liked men, and it was known that he drank with the younger men in the Elks' Club — that he was not a marrying man. Later we said, "Poor Emily" behind the jalousies as they passed on Sunday afternoon in the glittering buggy, Miss Emily with her head high and Homer Barron with his hat cocked and a cigar in his teeth, reins and whip in a yellow glove.

Then some of the ladies began to say that it was a disgrace to the town and a bad example to the young people. The men did not want to interfere, but at last the ladies forced the Baptist minister — Miss Emily's people were Episcopal — to call upon her. He would never divulge what happened during that interview, but he refused to go back again. The next Sunday they again drove about the streets, and the following day the minister's wife wrote to Miss Emily's relations in Alabama.

So she had blood-kin under her roof again and we sat back to watch developments. At first nothing happened. Then we were sure that they were to be married. We learned that Miss Emily had been to the jeweler's and ordered a man's toilet set in silver, with the letters H. B. on each piece. Two days later we learned that she had bought a complete outfit of men's clothing, including a nightshirt, and we said, "They are married." We were really glad. We were glad because the two female cousins were even more Grierson than Miss Emily had ever been.

So we were not surprised when Homer Barron — the streets had been finished some time since — was gone. We were a little disappointed that there was not a public blowing-off, but we believed that he had gone on to prepare for Miss Emily's coming, or to give her a chance to get rid of the cousins. (By that time it was a cabal, and we were all Miss Emily's allies to help circumvent the cousins.) Sure enough, after another week they departed. And, as we had expected all along, within three days Homer Barron was back in town. A neighbor saw the Negro man admit him at the kitchen door at dusk one evening.

And that was the last we saw of Homer Barron. And of Miss Emily for some time. The Negro man went in and out with the market basket, but the front door remained closed. Now and then we would see her at a window for a moment, as the men did that night when they sprinkled the lime, but for almost six months she did not appear on the streets. Then we knew that this was to be expected too; as if that quality of

extending beyond the text

Critics have suggested connections between William Faulkner's "A Rose for Emily" and John Keats's iconic poem "Ode on a Grecian Urn" (1820), especially given Faulkner's interest in Keats's poetry in general and in this poem in particular. Read the poem and explore similarities between the texts.

Ode on a Grecian Urn

John Keats

Thou still unravish'd bride of quietness,
　Thou foster-child of silence and slow time,
Sylvan[1] historian, who canst thus express
　A flowery tale more sweetly than our rhyme:
What leaf-fring'd legend haunts about thy shape
　Of deities or mortals, or of both,
　　In Tempe or the dales of Arcady?[2]
　What men or gods are these? What maidens loth?[3]
What mad pursuit? What struggle to escape?
　　What pipes and timbrels? What wild ecstasy?

Heard melodies are sweet, but those unheard
　Are sweeter; therefore, ye soft pipes, play on;
Not to the sensual ear, but, more endear'd,
　Pipe to the spirit ditties of no tone:
Fair youth, beneath the trees, thou canst not leave
　Thy song, nor ever can those trees be bare;
　　Bold Lover, never, never canst thou kiss,
Though winning near the goal yet, do not grieve;
　She cannot fade, though thou hast not thy bliss,
　　For ever wilt thou love, and she be fair!

Ah, happy, happy boughs! that cannot shed
　Your leaves, nor ever bid the Spring adieu;
And, happy melodist, unwearied,
　For ever piping songs for ever new;

[1] An adjective meaning "relating to forests." — Eds.

[2] Both Tempe and Arcady (also spelled Arcadia) are regions of Greece known for their natural beauty. Arcadia has come to mean any peaceful rural setting. — Eds.

[3] A variant spelling of *loath*, meaning unwilling or reluctant. — Eds.

More happy love! more happy, happy love!
For ever warm and still to be enjoy'd,
For ever panting, and for ever young;
All breathing human passion far above,
That leaves a heart high-sorrowful and cloy'd,
A burning forehead, and a parching tongue.

Who are these coming to the sacrifice?
To what green altar, O mysterious priest,
Lead'st thou that heifer lowing at the skies,
And all her silken flanks with garlands drest?
What little town by river or sea shore,
Or mountain-built with peaceful citadel,
Is emptied of this folk, this pious morn?
And, little town, thy streets for evermore
Will silent be; and not a soul to tell
Why thou art desolate, can e'er return.

O Attic[4] shape! Fair attitude! with brede
Of marble men and maidens overwrought,
With forest branches and the trodden weed;
Thou, silent form, dost tease us out of thought
As doth eternity: Cold Pastoral!
When old age shall this generation waste,
Thou shalt remain, in midst of other woe
Than ours, a friend to man, to whom thou say'st,
"Beauty is truth, truth beauty,—that is all
Ye know on earth, and all ye need to know." ■

[4] Attica is a specific region of ancient Greece. In this instance, Keats is referring to the shape common to Greek urns. — Eds.

1. **How does Faulkner include representations of the urn's images into his story without actually using the word "urn"?**
2. **In what ways does the structure of Faulkner's story mirror the structure of Keats's poem?**
3. **How do characters in the story represent characters in the poem?**

her father which had thwarted her woman's life so many times had been too virulent and too furious to die.

When we next saw Miss Emily, she had grown fat and her hair was turning gray. During the next few years it grew grayer and grayer until it attained an even pepper-and-salt iron-gray, when it ceased turning. Up to the day of her death at seventy-four it was still that vigorous iron-gray, like the hair of an active man.

From that time on her front door remained closed, save for a period of six or seven years, when she was about forty, during which she gave lessons in china-painting. She fitted up a studio in one of the downstairs rooms, where the daughters and granddaughters of Colonel Sartoris' contemporaries were sent to her with the same regularity and in the same spirit that they were sent to church on Sundays with a twenty-five-cent piece for the collection plate. Meanwhile her taxes had been remitted.

Then the newer generation became the backbone and the spirit of the town, and the painting pupils grew up and fell away and did not send their children to her with boxes of color and tedious brushes and pictures cut from the ladies' magazines. The front door closed upon the last one and remained closed for good. When the town got free postal delivery, Miss Emily alone refused to let them fasten the metal numbers above her door and attach a mailbox to it. She would not listen to them.

Daily, monthly, yearly we watched the Negro grow grayer and more stooped, going in and out with the market basket. Each December we sent her a tax notice, which would be returned by the post office a week later, unclaimed. Now and then we would see her in one of the downstairs windows — she had evidently shut up the top floor of the house — like the carven torso of an idol in a niche, looking or not looking at us, we could never tell which. Thus she passed from generation to generation — dear, inescapable, impervious, tranquil, and perverse.

And so she died. Fell ill in the house filled with dust and shadows, with only a doddering Negro man to wait on her. We did not even know she was sick; we had long since given up trying to get information from the Negro. He talked to no one, probably not even to her, for his voice had grown harsh and rusty, as if from disuse.

She died in one of the downstairs rooms, in a heavy walnut bed with a curtain, her gray head propped on a pillow yellow and moldy with age and lack of sunlight.

V

The Negro met the first of the ladies at the front door and let them in, with their hushed, sibilant voices and their quick, curious glances, and then he disappeared. He walked right through the house and out the back and was not seen again.

The two female cousins came at once. They held the funeral on the second day, with the town coming to look at Miss Emily beneath a mass of bought flowers, with the crayon face of her father musing profoundly above the bier and the ladies sibilant and macabre; and the very old men — some in their brushed Confederate uniforms — on the porch and the lawn, talking of Miss Emily as if she had been a contemporary of theirs, believing that they had danced with her and

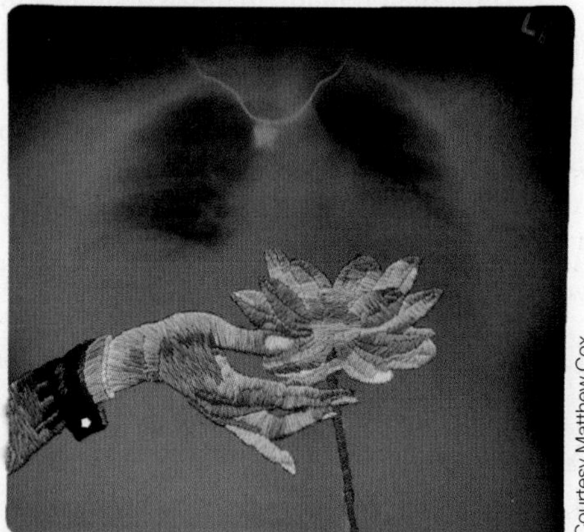

Courtesy Matthew Cox

Artist Matthew Cox juxtaposes colorful thread with skeletal features by embroidering directly on X-ray film.

In what ways does William Faulkner similarly pair imagery and themes in "A Rose for Emily"? How does such juxtaposition of dissimilar elements emphasize features of both?

courted her perhaps, confusing time with its mathematical progression, as the old do, to whom all the past is not a diminishing road but, instead, a huge meadow which no winter ever quite touches, divided from them now by the narrow bottleneck of the most recent decade of years.

Already we knew that there was one room in that region above stairs which no one had seen in forty years, and which would have to be forced. They waited until Miss Emily was decently in the ground before they opened it.

The violence of breaking down the door seemed to fill this room with pervading dust. A thin, acrid pall as of the tomb seemed to lie everywhere upon this room decked and furnished as for a bridal: upon the valance curtains of faded rose color, upon the rose-shaded lights, upon the dressing table, upon the delicate array of crystal and the man's toilet things backed with tarnished silver, silver so tarnished that the monogram was obscured. Among them lay a collar and tie, as if they had just been removed, which, lifted, left upon the surface a pale crescent in the dust. Upon a chair hung the suit, carefully folded; beneath it the two mute shoes and the discarded socks.

The man himself lay in the bed.

For a long while we just stood there, looking down at the profound and fleshless grin. The body had apparently once lain in the attitude of an embrace, but now the long sleep that outlasts love, that conquers even the grimace of love, had cuckolded him. What was left of him, rotted beneath what was left of the nightshirt, had become inextricable from the bed in which he lay; and upon him and upon the pillow beside him lay that even coating of the patient and biding dust.

60 Then we noticed that in the second pillow was the indentation of a head. One of us lifted something from it, and leaning forward, that faint and invisible dust dry and acrid in the nostrils, we saw a long strand of iron-gray hair. ■

1931

Understanding and Interpreting

1. Who narrates the story? What does the group of narrators directly share about itself, and what can you infer about the narrators based on other information in the story's setting, plot, and characters?
2. How is Miss Emily "a fallen monument" (par. 1)? To what is she a monument?
3. Describe Emily's relationship with her father. What details in the story support your interpretation of it? How does this relationship influence the development of events in the story?
4. You likely noticed that the narrative structure is not chronological. How would you summarize the order of events chronologically?
5. Based on the narrators' retelling of events, the townspeople assume a great deal about Miss Emily and what goes on in her house. What are some of these assumptions? Which assumptions, if any, reveal to readers that the townspeople tell themselves what they want to believe?
6. In paragraph 26, the narrator group explains that "Being left alone, and a pauper, [Miss Emily] had become humanized." How do you interpret the reasons the community finally sees her as more human?
7. According to the opening paragraphs of Part IV, what cultural expectations for unmarried people exist in this particular setting?

8. How do the narrators characterize the Grierson family in general? How do they distinguish the Griersons from other families in the community? What does this contrast reveal about the values of the narrator group and of the Griersons?
9. How does Miss Emily's appearance change throughout the story? How do these physical changes reflect her character development?
10. Did the story's ending surprise you? What questions do you find yourself asking at the end of the story about the characters and the events? Why do you think Miss Emily did what she did?

Analyzing Language, Style, and Structure

1. **Vocabulary in Context.** In the first sentence of Part II, Miss Emily is said to have "vanquished" the men who arrive to collect her taxes, "just as she had vanquished their fathers thirty years before about the smell" (par. 15). How does Faulkner's use of this word to describe the interaction establish the relationship between Miss Emily and the townspeople?
2. "A Rose for Emily" is narrated in first-person plural. Why do you think William Faulkner chose "we" rather than "I" as the voice for the story? How might this narrative strategy relate to the description of Emily as "a tradition, a duty, and a care; a sort of hereditary obligation upon the town" (par. 3)?
3. Trace the timeline of this story, and then analyze why the author decided to recount the tale in this manner. How does the order of the telling help shape the story's meaning? What details foreshadow the story's conclusion?
4. Explore each of the five parts of the story. Why do you think Faulkner chose to place the divisions where he did?
5. Consider paragraph 55. How do the diction, syntax, and imagery in this paragraph reinforce one of the story's themes?
6. In Parts III and IV, the narrator relates how people referred to "'Poor Emily.'" How does this repetition develop her as a character and develop the collective character of the townspeople? What does their pity indicate?
7. How does paragraph 48 relate to the structure of the plot and the reader's experience of events?
8. Why is Miss Emily repeatedly called an "idol"? What connection can you draw between the images of her as a "monument" and "idol" and one of the story's themes?
9. Though Miss Emily obviously keeps to herself and remains exceptionally private, the townspeople repeatedly enter her home throughout the story. How and why do they keep inserting themselves into her life? When are such invasions understandable and even necessary? In what ways do they further push Miss Emily into isolation, and how do they function symbolically?
10. How does Miss Emily's hair function as a symbol throughout the story?
11. The story has both a general setting — the American South in the late 1800s and early 1900s — and a specific one — this unique community and Miss Emily's house in particular. How do the layering and boundaries of these settings contribute to your interpretation of the overall meaning of the story?

Topics for Composing

1. **AP® FRQ Prose Fiction Analysis.** The following question refers to Part I (pars. 1–14) of William Faulkner's "A Rose for Emily," published in 1931. In this passage, Faulkner introduces readers to Miss Emily and the town in which she lives. Read the passage carefully. Then, in a well-written essay, analyze how Faulkner uses literary elements and techniques to reveal the complex relationship between Miss Emily and the people in her community.
2. **AP® FRQ Literary Argument.** Many works of literature feature contrasting details to develop the characters and the setting. These contrasts may be explicit or implied, and their purpose may not always appear immediately relevant. In "A Rose for Emily," there are many contrasting details specific to growth and decay as well as rising and falling. In a well-written essay, analyze how the values revealed by these contrasts contribute to an interpretation of the work as a whole. Do not merely summarize the plot.
3. **AP® Literary Argumentation.** In a 2015 essay in the *William Faulkner Journal*, Timothy O'Brien contemplates the challenge for readers presented by the title of the story. He explains, "[A] rose never appears in the story, the closest references to one being the 'curtains of faded rose color' and 'the rose-shaded lights' in the macabre bedroom scene at the end. This apparent disconnect between title and text troubles plenty of readers, inspiring questions of Faulkner and an array of ingenious interpretations." Analyze the short story and write an essay in which you make and support a claim that explains a connection between the title and the text.
4. **Connections.** Discuss how this story might be viewed as a conflict between North and South as well as a commentary on racism and classism. Keep in mind that Homer Barron is a construction foreman and a northerner, while Emily Grierson comes from a genteel southern family. How might the physical descriptions of Miss Emily relate to this theme?
5. **Connections.** In an interview, Faulkner described the conflict of Miss Emily: she "had broken all the laws of her tradition, her background, and she had finally broken the law of God too. . . . [S]he knew she was doing wrong, and that's why her own life was wrecked. Instead of murdering one lover, and then to go on and take another and when she used him up to murder him, she was expiating her crime." How might this story be seen as expiation?
6. **Research.** Faulkner refers in the story to "Confederate soldiers" and "Confederate uniforms." He also describes Miss Emily as "a fallen monument." Research the history of the "lost cause" and Confederate monuments in the South. Also do some reading on recent calls to remove Confederate statues from public grounds. What do these monuments stand for, and how does their symbolism relate to the events of "A Rose for Emily"?
7. **Speaking and Listening.** Reflect on what you think are the most memorable elements of the story before engaging in a discussion with a small group of classmates. As you share your experiences of the story with each other, create a list as a group of what you know you won't forget. Once finished, choose one of the ideas from your list and share what you believe gives it staying power and how what you have chosen relates to the meaning of the work as a whole.
8. **Multimodal.** William Faulkner's literature often features what some view as dark humor. Develop a cartoon consisting of one frame or a sequence illustrating a moment or scene from the story. You might want to research comic strips and cartoons drawn by such artists as Mr. Lovenstein, Gary Larson, and Berkeley Breathed.

The Creation

Maxine Clair

Carol Clayton Photography

Born and raised in Kansas City, Kansas, Maxine Clair (b. 1939) began her career as a medical technologist in Washington, D.C., before earning an MFA at George Washington University, where she later became an English professor. Clair has published a collection of poetry entitled *Coping with Gravity* (1988), the short story collection *Rattlebone* (1994), and a novel entitled *October Suite* (2001).

KEY CONTEXT "The Creation" is one of a series of interrelated stories in *Rattlebone* that center on Irene Wilson, an African American girl coming of age during the late 1950s in Rattlebone Hollow, a North Kansas City neighborhood. This story pivots on the central character's interactions with the Red Quanders, a closed African American community that maintains a deep connection to West African cultural traditions. The name for this fictional community harkens to the Quanders, who are believed to be one of the oldest African American families, originating from the Fanti tribe in Ghana.

Additionally, this short story includes the N-word, which we have chosen to reprint in this textbook to accurately reflect Maxine Clair's original intent as well as the time period, culture, and racism depicted in the text. We recognize that this word has a long history as a derogatory and deeply hurtful expression when used by white people toward Black people. Clair's choice to use this word relates not only to that history but to a larger cultural tradition in which the N-word can take on different meanings, emphasize shared experience, and be repurposed as a term of endearment within Black communities. While the use of that word in Clair's context might not be hurtful, the use of it in our current context very often is. Be mindful of context, both Clair's and yours, as you read "The Creation."

If I had not seen my life sinking in the unhip backwater of high school, I would not have prayed night after night for something big to happen to me, the way it seemed to be happening to everyone else. By everyone else I meant Carol Walker who had to be "stabilized" at the hospital after eating crackers and water for two weeks because her boyfriend quit her. And Wanda. She had become one of the exalted. A senior, and crowned by the entire school when the police caught her drinking liquor at Shady Maurice's, where she placed second in the Friday-night talent show. Not a month went by that I didn't observe Jewel Hicks's wan return to school after being stupefied with morphine her doctor gave her for the cramps. If such events shook up their existences to make those girls aware of living, not a single event disrupted mine. I spent my time walking around looking for something I could not describe, until I found it in the Red Quanders.

I was only six or seven when Dottie, my play aunt from church, first took Wanda and me to the colored lights strung around the pony rides, tubs of cotton candy, and stalls of hit-the-target games we called the carnival. Instead of taking us the long way down Tenth and across Walrond, she walked us along the railroad tracks to the trestle high over the open sewer of Skagg Creek.

"Don't look down at the water or you'll fall in," she yelled, then ran off and left us.

The trestle, higher than Union Hall in Rattlebone, might as well have been a tightrope. Dizzy above the leaden, gray stream, I had nothing to hold on to. I knelt down. Wanda kept walking ahead of me. Then when neither of them would come back, I crawled on hands and knees, afraid to keep my eyes shut, afraid to open them. That's how I got across. That's how I remember the first time I saw Red Quanders.

5 I passed their strange district as I lagged behind alone. The dozen or so shotgun shacks and outhouses pushed up close to the railroad tracks reminded me of how scared I had been of spiders and daddy longlegs in the outhouse we used before we were hooked up to the city. Long before the day Obadele Quander first knocked on our door selling fresh-dressed chickens, I was passing near his house looking at chicken coops, goat stalls, and gardens, wondering who were all these people living between the tracks and the woods. At the time, nothing was as puzzling as the way all of them had their heads covered in fire-red satin, the men in a do-rag style, and the women in a kind of wrapped gèle.[1]

Finally, my play aunt came back for me.

"Who are they?" I asked her.

"Red Quanders, she said. "This is Redtown and those obeah[2] women will get you if they catch you looking at them, so stop staring and come on."

None of the dark men with braided beards, and none of the dark women cooking over wash-tub fires seemed to notice us.

• • •

10 Years went by. Redtown was there, a part of our part of the city. I was familiar with Folami and Akin, the Red Quanders everybody knew because they went to our high school. They were twins, not identical, but you could tell they were related. Aside from them, I seldom saw any of the others, they seldom came over our way. So what led Obadele Quander to my house that September? And on a Saturday morning, too, when I looked like Hooty Coot in my mother's faded sack dress and my hair not even combed. Of all the doors he could have knocked on, why did ours stand out to him? And when I opened it and he saw my face, did he think of cinnamon, or tobacco juice? With that hair I must have resembled a picked chicken.

"Is your mamma home?"

"Yes," I said, holding down my hair with both hands.

"Can you go get her? I got only two corn-fed chickens left. Fresh-dressed this morning. I got a few brown eggs on the truck too."

"Just a minute," I said and went to get my mother. I thought, This boy doesn't go to our school, I won't have to see him, what do I care. I wondered why they wore white shirts when white was the hardest to keep clean. Was he Folami and Akin's brother? Because by then I knew that all of the Reds were Quanders, and few of them ever went to our schools.

15 At first my curiosity about Obadele, Folami, and Akin was casual. Other matters concerned me more. For instance, why I had never heard about squaring a corner until my turn in the tryouts for the Drill Team. Why, after a month of school, no boy except the doofus Alvin Kidd had ever called me up.

---

[1] A West African head wrap that covers a woman's hair and ears. — Eds.

[2] While not a unified set of practices, obeah is generally known as a set of processes intended to bring about spiritual healing and justice. It was developed by enslaved West Africans in the Caribbean during the eighteenth century. Those who employed such practices were known as obeah men and women. — Eds.

And the school's upcoming speech competition. The way I saw it, the competition was the only imminent thing whose outcome I could influence in the least. I hoped that Mrs. Welche, our new white teacher, would select me to represent our class.

Mrs. Welche had made *The Kansan* the spring before with her insistence that as an exercise "for all involved," she and one of our English teachers at Douglass should exchange schools. It would be a "first." At that point we had two white students at Douglass and no white teachers. The two students were sisters who had come by choice and with much fanfare. A reluctant superintendent had made it clear that a few more years would pass before the new desegregation law would take effect districtwide.

But Mrs. Welche was having none of it. At one time her husband had been a member of the Board of Education, and people said she must have known something damaging to hold over the superintendent's head. People said the school would go to pot, that there would be no discipline with a white woman coming in and changing the rules. Others thought it was a show of good faith.

I didn't mind that she had come. Her blue eyes and brown hair didn't seem to matter to anybody, and I was flattered by the fact that she noticed my small talent for public speaking. I liked her even more when she suggested I learn "Annabel Lee" by Edgar Allan Poe, and represent our class in the competition.

Wanda was a convenient, if reluctant, practice audience. Her mother, eager for Wanda's interest in anything other than her "Annie Had a Baby" record, encouraged me to come and recite for them some evenings. And one of those evenings she brought out a slim volume of poems called *God's Trombones*.

20 "This belongs to Reverend's wife," she said. "It's a nice book, but Wanda isn't ever going to make use of it." She said that if I wanted I could keep it for a while.

James E. Lewis Museum of Art, Morgan State University

Entitled *Ring Around the Rosey*, this 1942 painting by William H. Johnson (1901–1970) was the cover for the short story collection *Rattlebone*, in which "The Creation" appears. Clair chose it for the cover herself.
What do you see as the most striking feature of the painting? What elements of "The Creation" does it capture?

I took the book home. The more I read, the more excited I became about the poems. They reminded me of spirituals. I wouldn't have been surprised to find that Reverend had borrowed some of these lines to use in his sermons. Any one of these poems was sure to make an audience sit up and take notice.

"If you really feel that strongly about it," Mrs. Welche said, "then I'm willing to let you switch. Choose one poem and we'll see how it goes."

And God stepped out on space,
And He looked around and said:
I'm lonely — I'll make Me a world.

That was it. "The Creation." I was set.

"We'll try it tomorrow after school," Mrs. Welche said.

• • •

Perhaps I thought Folami would make an exotic critic. True, I wanted her to hear my recitation, but that wasn't all. I was curious. She had attracted me and everyone else precisely because of our superstition, based on hearsay, that she had powers. Her face was no different from any of our faces — moon-round, dark as Karo syrup,[3] with big black eyes, nothing unusual. She was a little stout, but she didn't have to worry, Red Quander women never wore store-bought clothes. We all wondered why they made no effort at being stylish.

"Don't you feel funny being the only girl with wraparound skirts down to your ankles?" I asked her.

"It's all I've ever worn. All of my friends at home wear them too, you all just don't get to see them."

"But your skirts are too straight, you can't walk that good, let alone run in them."

"Yes I can," she said.

I didn't know how to ask her about those sloppy-looking blouses that didn't match the skirts. Why didn't they wear them tucked in? And what kind of hairstyle was up under that gèle?

We had physical education, English, and algebra together. Wanda claimed that Folami smelled, but that was after Folami showed us the stone she rubbed under her arms instead of using baking soda or Mum.

"You're smelling your upper lip," I told Wanda. "I'm around her a lot and I never smell anything."

"Well, she doesn't ever take showers after gym."

"At her house they probably still have to heat water for a bath. Maybe she isn't ready for showers. She always looks clean."

Folami was careful always to slip into her one-piece gym suit beneath her long skirt, then go through contortions getting the top part on under her long-sleeved blouses, all the while holding on to her gèle. And after gym she reversed the careful plan so that no one would ever see any part of her without clothes, except of course her arms and legs. We all hated the common shower too. Granted, the rest of us didn't have to worry about headwraps, but we couldn't afford to get *our* hair wet either. We managed by putting on shower caps and running through. I thought Folami was silly to risk getting an F for the semester just because she was modest. Anyhow, I couldn't reconcile her modesty with her powers. Finally, though, Folami stopped getting dressed at all for gym, and when we suited up, she went to Study Hall with the girls who were on their periods.

"Why don't you ever suit up anymore?" I asked her.

"Too much trouble," she said.

I thought about those hideous scars on the bodies of young African girls pictured in the encyclopedia.

"It's only twice a week," I said. "Why don't you take your gym suit home every day and wear it to school under your dress?"

She didn't seem moved by my idea, but she thanked me. No one else had bothered to notice her problem.

I wouldn't say we were friends after that, but we were okay. Since Wanda usually talked to, walked with, or hid from some boy every morning, Folami and I began meeting on the corner in front of Doll's Market to walk to school. Generally she had little to say, but she waited there each morning with her brother — Akin of the white shirt and flimsy brown trousers. I never saw either of them eating in the cafeteria,

[3] A brand of corn syrup. — Eds.

yet every morning they had delicious-smelling, paper-wrapped lunches that disappeared before they walked to Redtown in the evening.

I knew in my heart that Folami didn't want to bring me home with her. I considered myself clever enough, though, to talk her into it.

"That's okay, my mother is a little peculiar too," I told her. And when she mentioned dinner, I told her, "Don't worry about that. I'll wait until I go home to eat dinner."

"How long is this poem?" she asked me. I assured her that it wouldn't take more than five or ten minutes. I didn't want her to think I was going to bore her with some dry speech.

"Are you sure you want to hear me do my poem?" I said. I didn't think that she would refuse me. She told me that it was usually the old people who recited things to them in Redtown. I let her know that I wouldn't be too embarrassed if somebody else listened.

And so, for the first time, I went to Redtown and into a Red Quander house. What was so different there? The strangely heady, earth-oil smell. The glow from a kerosene lamp. The cloth on the wall, the circle of chairs. The shiny coal of an old woman, her skinny white braids sprouting like a fringe from her red gèle. The carved stool in the corner of the first room where she sat. The snuff she packed into her lower lip. The second room and the low table with no chairs. Akin in gray overalls. And Folami's mother, with a figure and a gèle fuller and more regal than Folami's.

"Who is this girl?" her mother asked Folami.

Folami answered that I was a friend who had helped her at school.

"What is she doing here?"

"I'm helping her learn a poem."

"Hi, Mrs. Quander," I said.

At that greeting she flashed a mouthful of square white teeth, then burst out with laughter so deep that at first I started to laugh too. Softening it a bit, she shook her head and went back to the kitchen.

Akin brought a plate of strange candy. "Crystal ginger," Folami said. "Take one, it's good. It's rolled in sugar."

Folami sat down in the first room on one of the wooden, straight-back chairs. I stood before her.

And as far as the eye of God could see,
Darkness covered everything . . .

"Wait," Folami said. "You look dead. You ought to move around. When we tell stories, we move our arms and look at people. We make faces and jump around. Don't just stand there. *Do* something!

And the light that was left from making the sun
God gathered it up in a shining ball
And flung it against the darkness,
Spangling the night with the moon and stars.

When Folami's mother came to sit and listen, I hesitated.

"Keep going. Suppose somebody at school walks in while you're up there. Are you going to stop?" Folami asked.

Then down between
The darkness and the light
He hurled the world;
Then He stopped and looked and saw
That the earth was hot and barren.
So God stepped over to the edge of the world
And He spat out the seven seas —

Another woman, stout and wearing a robe affair, came walking from the kitchen through the eating room to stand outside the circle of chairs and listen. Then still another woman. Then a girl about Folami's age entered, and they sat in the circle of chairs.

And the waters above the earth came down,
The cooling waters came down.

They held themselves, listening intently, rocked and looked at the floor. Now and again someone hummed. When finally I finished, they were quiet.

"They tell you this story at school?" Folami's mother asked, casually.

extending beyond the text

This woodcut by Aaron Douglas accompanies the poem "The Creation" in *God's Trombones* by James Weldon Johnson.

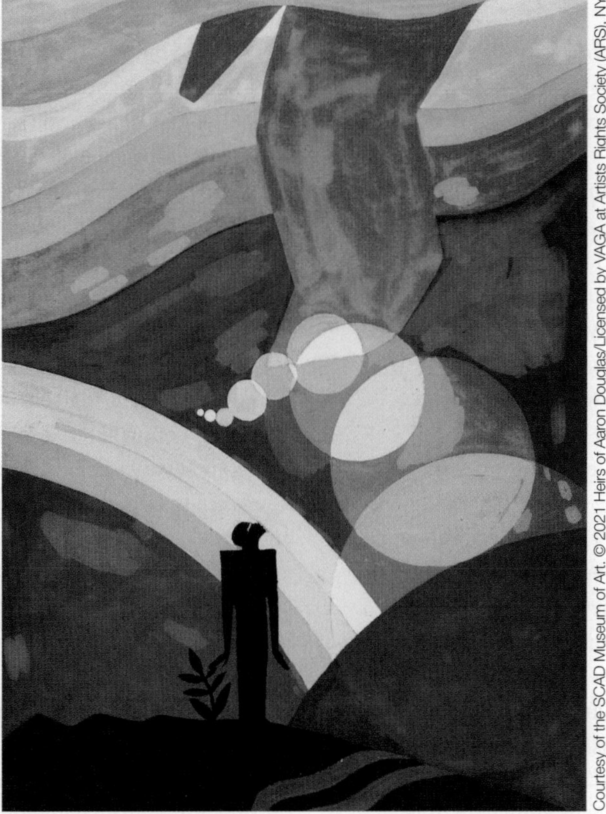

1. **What words come to mind to describe the act of creation as Douglas depicts it?**
2. **When Irene first reads the poems in *God's Trombones*, she says, "They reminded me of spirituals." How does this image evoke the mood and tone of traditional spirituals?**

"Irene is going to say this poem in front of the whole school," Folami said.

"You like this story too?" her mother asked Folami.

"It's just a poem out of a book. It doesn't mean anything," Folami said.

Her mother stood abruptly, and pointed a long finger nearly touching my chest. "Don't come back here to our place with stories," she said. "When you talk, you talk to them that understands you. Not us."

Immediately I was out the door. And there he was, the boy with the chickens. The lean, smooth boy, taller this time, white teeth, ripe lips, sloe eyes.

"Scared you, didn't she?" he said. I ignored him. He walked at my heels, teasing.

"What you scared of, somebody gonna sprinkle dust? Take some of your hair? Turn you into a dog? Guess you won't be coming around here singing your sweet little songs."

That broke the spell. I surely wasn't going to let some boy, Red Quander or not, make fun of me.

"If you have the nerve to come over to Tenth Street trying to sell those puny guinea hens and sorry brown eggs, I can come over in Redtown to see my friend."

"What you mean guineas? Your mother sure doesn't mind giving me a dollar every Saturday."

I turned around and looked at him. "Those women in there would just as soon bawl me out as look at me. At least my mother is nice to you."

That caught him off guard.

"What was that you were telling them, anyway?" he asked.

"It was a poem I have to memorize for school."

"Oh. Well, you better be careful about what you do in Redtown, especially in that house," he said, and he smiled. "My name is Obadele."

Every Saturday my mother bought her usual chickens and eggs and teased with Wanda about our Red Quander eggman. She watched me, though. By the way I washed and braided my hair late Friday nights to get up straightening it early Saturdays before Dele came with the eggs, she knew. She knew by the school clothes I put on just to have on. I was at least fascinated.

"Who's that egg boy and how you know them Red Quanders?" she asked me.

"I've been to one of their houses," I said. "And his name is Obadele Quander. He's some kin to Folami, the one who goes to our school."

"I see he got a funny name too, but you know all of them is Quanders. Every last one of them."

"That's just like us. All of us are Wilsons."

"In *this* house," my mother said. "Not in the whole city. Don't make no sense one man having so many women. You stay away from there."

I saw Folami every day at school. She was apologetic about her mother's ways, but until I pressed her, she didn't say any more.

"Who is your father?" I asked.

"His name is Oba Quander," she said. "Why?"

"I don't know. Curious, I guess. And what's your mother's name?"

She told me that her mother had died when she and Akin were born, but the woman I saw — her Mamma Mandisa — had raised them. Those other women were all sort of aunts of hers.

No mystery there. I thought about the play aunt I once had. I told Folami what my mother had said about their unusual ways, especially about how men could have several wives. She said it was true, but she said, "So what? To us every father is Oba — that means king. We're just a family that keeps to itself. Only bigger."

I didn't quite get it. If so many had the same father and every father had the same name, how would I know one Oba Quander from another?

"You wouldn't," she said. *"I* would."

The evening Obadele first walked with Folami, Akin, and me down by the creek, he itched to tell me how pure the Quanders were, how, across generations, their blood had seldom been mixed.

"Who cares?" I said. "Besides, lots of people say that, but how do you know?"

"I know because I'm my father's son, and my father came from his pure-blooded father, and we go on back just like that to the time we were first brought here. Same is true with my mother."

"Why don't you speak African, then? You all sound just like us to me. Like you're from around here."

"I do, a little," he said. "Anyway, we can use the same words you use, but it doesn't mean we speak the same language. We don't want to be like you," he said.

"Well, you sure do go through a lot of trouble trying to be different," I said.

"Us? What about you? You can't be what you really are at your school," Obadele said.

"I knew you'd say that, but it's not true." I tried to sell him on the advantages of common knowledge, but he wasn't interested.

"Look," he said. And he untied his red satin. I think I expected a conk because the red cloth fit his head as closely as the do-rags my father sometimes wore. I wasn't prepared for the way Dele's naps grew in perfect swirls around his head, like a cap.

He said to me, "Cut off all your hair and let it be, then see what happens. I dare you."

No wonder Folami had held on to her gèle at school. Was he crazy? The last thing I wanted was hair shorter than mine already was. Who wanted to look like an African, even a civilized one?

I didn't want to look like him, but I wouldn't have minded having his gift for storytelling. He knew he was good.

"This is the way it was," he would say. And then he would become quiet as if he were recalling all the details of a life he once knew. This set a certain mood. Then he would begin:

"At first there was no solid land. There were only two kingdoms. There was the sky, the domain of the *orisha*[4] Olorun, the Sky God. And far below that, the watery mists, the domain of Olukun, a female *orisha*. The two kingdoms existed separately, and they let each other alone. Back then, all of life was in the sky, where Olorun lived with many other powerful *orishas.*

"There was Ifa, who could see the future and who was in charge of Fate; Eshu, who was made of chance and whim, and who causes the unforeseen troubles and pleasures in our lives. There was Agemo, the chameleon, and many others, but the most important was Obatala, the Sky God's son."

Obadele went on to tell how it was Obatala who formed the earth. How he hooked a gold chain onto the edge of the sky and descended to the water below, carrying with him a snail's shell filled with sand, a pouch of palm nuts, and the egg that contained the essence of all the *orishas.* The story explained how, when he reached the end of the golden chain, Obatala poured out the sand and dropped the egg, releasing an exquisite bird who scattered the sand, along with the traits of the *orishas,* throughout the mists. In this way he created solid land with hills and valleys. And when he planted his palm nuts, vegetation sprang up on all the earth. Then he saw a reflection of himself in a shallow pool, and began to make figures from the clay, human figures imbued with the personalities of all the *orishas.* He made them carefully and set them in the sun to dry while he quenched his thirst on palm wine. When he resumed his work, because he was intoxicated he made mistakes — the disfigured, the blind, the lame, the deaf. Then the Sky God's breath set the earth spinning, and washed across the figures drying in the sun, bringing them to life. One by one, they rose from the earth and began to do all the things people do. And Obatala, the Sky God's son, became the chief of all the earth.

But every so often, the *orisha* of the watery mists casts powerful juju on the earth, which once was her domain.

I liked Obadele's story, but I was even more fascinated with his version of the mystery of Folami and Akin and their Mamma Mandisa. According to Dele, the twins were not ordinary people. All twins, he said, have the power to bring good fortune into the lives of those who treat them well. Whatever they want, they get. The wise do everything they can to make twins happy.

Obadele said that Akin, the second born, sent Folami into the world first to see if life was worth living. Their mother was suffering great pains at that moment and Folami made this known to Akin. A whole day later, the reluctant Akin arrived, and sure enough, their mother died.

Mandisa was another of their father's wives. Apparently she was always a mean woman. Dele

[4] Spirits that guide all living beings, especially humans. — Eds.

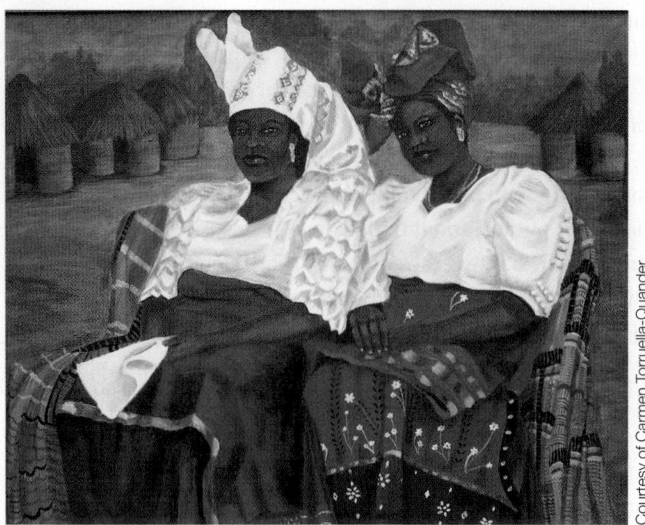

Courtesy of Carmen Torruella-Quander

Carmen Torruella-Quander, a painter and gallery owner based in Washington, D.C., created this image entitled *Whispers* (2014).
How does this painting characterize female friendship and social interaction? To what extent is this view reflected in Folami and Irene's friendship in "The Creation"?

said only that she "used to be troublesome." At any rate, she was hard to get along with and she made an enemy of a neighbor woman, inviting that other woman's juju[5]. And powerful it was. The woman, whose name Dele would not say, caused what he called an *abiku*[6] child to enter Mandisa's womb. This was a child that was born over and over again, a child that died shortly after each birth just to torment Mandisa. But Mandisa was more clever. She took the newborn twins into her house and succeeded in nullifying all of the obeah woman's power.

Week after week, Dele mesmerized me with stories of *orishas,* of lost kingdoms and ancient rulers, and of people — Hausas and Zulus[7] — he claimed I had to thank for more than my black skin. Squat on his haunches on the bank of the creek, he talked about how his father's father's father was the end-all, be-all keeper of the secrets of life, how the old man could recite, for days, every event since the beginning of time without one mistaken word. I was convinced that at least *he* believed what he was saying.

And when Folami gave me an amulet, I pinned it to my brassiere. For an unbeliever, an amulet has no charm. But I liked the idea of it, and maybe it worked because a certain kind of luck followed me to school, right to the stage of our auditorium. Whoever won the competition would represent Douglass in the state competition at KU that next month. Thanks to Mrs. Welche, it was the first year our school would participate. The reading, a kind of oratorical talent show, would be judged by several teachers.

I had decided to wear my navy blue chemise dress with the white collar because I would be standing, and it would show off what I hoped was my slinky-but-not-skinny figure. On the stage, we sat facing the student body and the scattered teacher-judges with their tablets and pens poised. According to their lottery, I was to go third. The Girls' Ensemble sang two selections, we were introduced, and the contest was on.

First the one white student who was competing, Ann Marie Cooper, walked to the podium. I was immediately struck by how confident she seemed. She threw her golden hair back over her shoulder and said good morning to the audience, then turned to greet her fellow schoolmates on the stage. Though brief, her background comments, in which she explained why she had chosen the Gettysburg Address, were more successful than her overheated rendition of Lincoln's speech. I was heartened, but also frustrated. I had not prepared an introduction. Were we expected to follow her example?

---

[5] Magical power. — Eds.

[6] The spirits of children who die before reaching adolescence. — Eds.

[7] Hausas are the largest ethnic group in Africa; they are predominantly from West African nations. Zulus are a Nguni ethnic group from southern Africa; they are the largest ethnic group in the nation of South Africa. — Eds.

John Goodson went next. He towered over the podium. He clutched it, preacher-like, rolled up on the balls of his feet, and in his sonorous best, all but shook the place. *Out of the night that* covers me, *Black as die Pit from pole to pole!* The assembly sat entirely still. Not once did John let up until he had built to the final *I am the master of my fate; I am the captain of my soul!* with such power that half the students jumped to their feet in applause. Well, okay, I hadn't prepared a nice introduction to put everybody at ease. And "The Creation" certainly couldn't begin on a loud note.

When I stood up, I smoothed the lap creases of my dress and walked deliberately to the podium. I felt the sweat on my palms. Despite my three-inch, pointed-toe shoes, I was short. Nevertheless, in a sudden inspired moment I stepped to the side of the podium and gently opened my arms. Unhurried, I looked from one side of the auditorium to the other, then began. *And God stepped out on space, and He looked around and said: I'm lonely — I'll make Me a world.* I swept out an arm. *And as far as the eye of God could see, darkness covered everything, blacker,* I said "blacker" with a rasp: . . .*blacker than a hundred midnights down in a cypress swamp.* I paused, dropped my arms, turned my head away from the audience, and walked a few steps across the stage. I faced them again, loosely folded my hands in a prayer stance and smiled, nodding my head. *Then God smiled, and the light broke, and the darkness rolled up on one side. . .* and when I said "rolled up," I sang the O sound and made grand loops in the air with one hand, then finished: . . . *and the light stood shining on the other.* I sang "shining" and flung up my other hand. With my entire being bent on heaven, the rest was automatic. *And God said: That's good*!

Some other, bolder Irene had taken over, and batted her eyes hard when she came to *batted His eyes and the lightning flashed. . .* and she clapped the thunder and toiled with her hands until anyone watching would be hard put to deny that she held an actual lump of clay. As that Irene *blew into it the breath of life. . .* six hundred souls in the auditorium held their breath, quiet, until Mr. Harris's "Amen!" released them to clap hard and long.

Donald South closed with Tennyson's "Ulysses," potentially a good choice, since the last line, *To strive, to seek, to find, and not to yield,* had been selected for the senior class motto. Unfortunately for Donald, that fact contributed to his undoing when several seniors shouted out the line a beat ahead of him, destroying his delivery of the final words.

I won. Obadele was not impressed. What was the point? What did it mean to win? So I could recite a poem — was it an important poem? Why would I want to do that for a school that taught me nothing relevant? Why was I so bent on impressing a white woman teacher?

He's jealous, I thought. I realized that in some ways he was smarter than he knew. He could discuss a simple story with a depth no one in my class would attempt. The Red Quander men and women mainly taught their children at home. I suppose they had books to augment all of that reciting the old folks did. But wasn't I the one who watched John Cameron Swayze[8] explain the world several times a week on our new television, something Dele could see only if he dared to take his Red Quander self into the Montgomery Ward store on the avenue? Didn't I know the facts he dismissed outright about the girl ironically named Brown who lived in Topeka, just fifty miles away, and who had been named in the Supreme Court case that was changing everything?[9] Ours was the school that had maps and literature. Mine was the mother

[8] John Cameron Swayze (1906–1995) was an American news host and famous product spokesman from the 1940s through the 1970s. — Eds.

[9] A reference to the 1954 Supreme Court case of *Brown v. Board of Education of Topeka, Kansas,* which ruled that American schools in the South must desegregate "with all deliberate speed." — Eds.

who saw to it that I went there every day. I knew more facts. He was jealous. I knew more.

The next time he knew more. He knew that if he carried a load of chicken wire and rags in his Oba-fixed truck, the state patrol would not stop a Red Quander riding out in the county on a Friday night. He knew the place in the hills at Wyandotte Lake where, if you stood on the edge of a boulder, you could see the whole of the winding water. He knew that the moon affects everything it shines on. He knew that I was afraid to be with him and the dark trees, and how a scent is a charm, how the nose can catch what the eye misses. He was the one who explained the rot of Skagg Creek as something to get beyond. That in it I could discover the wonder of everything turning to dust, and my hunger for the smell of earth's dark life. Obadele knew the effect that smell would have on me as he oiled it into his pores.

I had never talked the talk for hours on the telephone with him, never drank a single Nehi with him at Nettie's Dinette. He had never been past the front door of my house, or seen me dressed up at church, never even heard of Al Hibbler and "Unchained Melody." We had never slow-danced.

"It's all right," he said. Inside his truck, on a bed of soft rags, we took off our clothes. Without light to see by, he touched me as if, slowly and gently, he were shaping my body into a woman. He opened door after door. This was the slow-dance I had wanted to learn. I found the steps awkward, but he was a born dancer. Instinctively, he set a rhythm and unchained us both.

• • •

For someone who loved school, I became a slouch. I ignored poetry and logarithms. My mind busied itself with logistics. Meeting Dele. At first it didn't matter that he had no telephone, I saw him every morning and every evening unless he had to go hauling or selling in his father's truck too early and too late. Or unless Mrs. Welche pressed me about staying after school to practice my speech. Or unless Folami stuck to me like warm mush and asked too many questions, unless Akin spied, unless Wanda used her sixth sense.

"Hope you know you can get pregnant," Wanda said. "Red Quanders don't play. They'll be workin hoodoo on you, and you won't even know it."

Then it mattered that he had no phone. Even when I came early and stayed late, I couldn't be sure he would be under the trestle. He said that people like us who were forced to hide had to be careful. We were to act as if nothing had changed. But it was impossible. I lived to see Dele, and looked for him every chance I got, despite his father and my schedule and my friends. I didn't care what time I got home, or what time I got to school.

Once, I even met him after the morning classes had already begun. The crisp November air was filled with him. In the truck we drove right past the school, out to the highway and up through Olathe. To Leavenworth to see anything we had never seen, which turned out to be the prison and the army base. I wished for a gèle and long skirt so that people could see that we belonged together.

"It's more than the clothes," Dele said. "You have to *be* one of us, or at least see yourself as we do."

"Who knows," I told him, "maybe someday I will."

As we rode out Highway 40, the designation "great" came easily to my mind when I looked at the plains. Fields of winter wheat, undulant and green, surged to recede into pale seas of corn, or plowed black acreage, or loam as brown as the bread it supported. It seemed that if we could rise high enough above those vast stretches, we would see that they formed the very center of a continent. And if we focused closely, a certain symmetry would emerge with our highway as the dividing line, and a boy who was Obadele and a girl who was my very self as the axis from which it all sprang.

We drove on to Topeka that afternoon, licking his salt fish from our fingers. I wanted to show him the streets where history had begun to unfold.

"It isn't going to make any difference," Dele said. "White people don't want you all in their schools, and no court can change that. You should keep to your own, forget about them."

He didn't understand, but I was in no mood to spoil our adventure. When we got home, I saw no reason for him to drop me off anywhere but in front of my house. Of course I didn't expect to see my mother watching for me out the front door. My mother was never tempted to mince words. I knew what was coming when she yelled, "Just a minute," and came out to the truck.

"I know what you're doing and I'm not going to allow it," she said to Dele. "Irene is not one of y'all and I don't want her around y'all. Don't make me come over to Redtown looking for your people, because that's just what I'm going to do if I catch you around here again. You can consider that a promise," she told Dele.

"You can't do that!" I said.

"Don't try me, Irene. Get your hind parts out of that truck."

Given my opinion on how little my mother knew about love, I was furious. As soon as Dele left I told her I loved him. "I'm not going to stop just because you don't understand him."

She attempted to pull rank with "You ain't too grown yet for me to whip."

"I don't care," I told her. "You can't stop me."

"I can tell your daddy," she said. She was losing ground.

"I don't care. Tell him."

My love for a Red Quander had made me my own woman.

• • •

Later that same week, I missed seeing Folami and noted that she had been absent for several days. I asked Dele about her.

"I don't know. I'm not her keeper," he said. "Maybe she's had enough of y'all's school."

And I asked Akin about her.

"She's at home," he said.

"What's the matter with her?"

"Nothing," Akin said. "She's just not coming back to school anymore."

At the first glimmer of a realization, it's hard to distinguish titillation from dread. I wondered if Folami's absence had anything to do with Obadele and me. Friday of that week my mother and I stood in

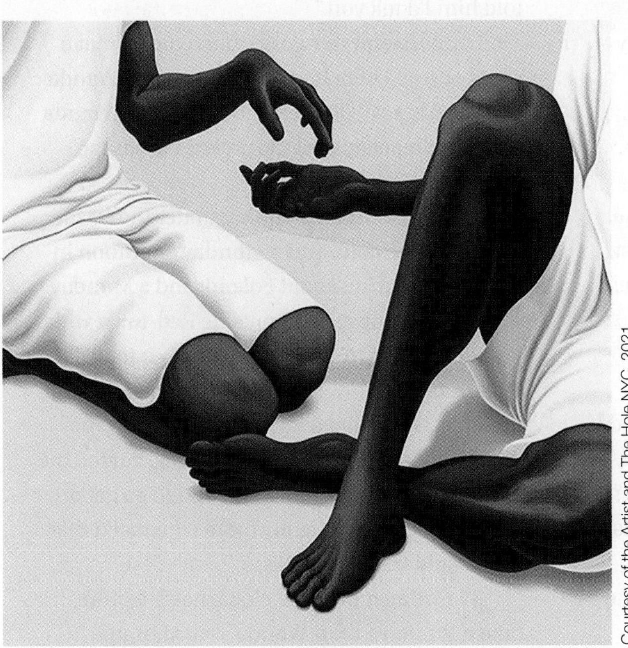

Courtesy of the Artist and The Hole NYC, 2021

Los Angeles–based painter Alex Gardner entitled this 2017 painting *Picnic with a Future Ex*.

How would you describe the composition and perspective of the image? What emotions does it evoke in you — calm, anxiety, curiosity, nostalgia, or something else — and why? In what ways might the painting and its title capture the nature of the relationship between the narrator Irene and Dele?

the door waving Wanda on, when who else but Dele rode by in his truck. I remember clearly that it was a Friday evening because I had decided against going to the football game with Wanda.

Since the confrontation with my mother, Dele had made me promise that we would be more careful. Although I had missed him under the trestle that morning, I was shocked that he would provoke my mother by coming to our street, and thrilled that he would defy her to see me. His truck didn't stop, though. Just rattled on by.

"He can drive on any street he wants to," my mother said. "It's a free country. But he better not be looking for you." She had already heard me tell Wanda that I wasn't going to the game, and so I couldn't get out to talk to him that night.

Wanda did, however. First thing Saturday morning she came over to get me.

"Come on, we got to walk to the store. Mamma needs some milk," she said. Wanda never got up early on Saturday mornings. I hurried to finish curling my hair, just in case. Once we were outside my house, walking fast, our breath disappearing in the fog, I urged her, "Tell me what's up."

"Nothing, why?"

"I know something is up. Your mother probably doesn't even know you're out of bed."

"Okay, I just want us to talk," Wanda said.

"About what? Did you see Dele last night? Did he ask you to get me out of the house this morning?"

"Yeah, I saw him last night. Let's go over to my house. It's too cold out here."

Appeal moved toward alarm. I dismissed the fantasy of seeing the truck in the alley behind her house and went quickly with her up to her attic bedroom.

"Sit down," she said. I sat down. She looked out her window and shook her head. Then she sat down beside me and surrendered.

"You know Folami, right?"

"Yeah."

"Well, she's pregnant."

"What?"

"Yeah," Wanda said, letting it register.

"So that's why she can't come back to school. How did you find out?"

"How do you think? Obadele told me."

"I just asked him — why would he tell you?" My stomach began to float up.

"So I could tell you what he didn't have the guts to tell you himself. He's about to become a little king in Redtown. Full-fledged man. No more nigger girls."

I didn't want to hear any more from Wanda.

"Look, don't blame me," she said. "I wasn't there to hold the light while he did it to her. I just told him I'd tell you."

I understood the words, but it didn't make sense to me. There had to be something Wanda missed. That, or Obadele must have told Wanda a half-truth because of the pressure from the world.

It took a Monday morning under the trestle waiting in the cold, and a Monday afternoon in gym class hearing about Folami, and a Monday evening walking around outside Red-town with Wanda, hoping to see Dele's truck — it took all that for me to allow that it could even be possible. On Wednesday, after Wanda left me under the trestle in the cold morning, cursed me out in the evening, and threatened to go get my mother, I was only slightly more convinced that Dele could have done this.

By Friday it became clear that it would take a lot more than Wanda's word or my mother's threats to bring the fullness of it home. Why go to school when what I needed to know was in Redtown? I fastened my car coat, tied my scarf, collected my books, and left the house.

So what if I didn't have the slightest clue to where Dele lived? I would look for the truck.

Instead, when I got to Redtown, I headed for the only familiar place, Folami's house. My father used to say, when somebody bums down a house, he can't hide the smoke. I had to see her with my own eyes first. As I tramped up to the door, her Mamma Mandisa opened it, filling the doorway, hands on her hips, superiority beaming on her face.

"What you want, girl?"

"Can I speak to Folami?"

"Nothing around here for you. She's not coming back to the school, so you may as well get on away from here." She didn't wait for me to respond before she closed the door.

I found the truck parked in front of a house covered in brown tar-paper siding. I knocked loudly on the front door. When that didn't rouse anyone, I knocked again, with both fists, and when that didn't do it, I went to the back of the house and knocked on the door with my feet. When that didn't bring Dele outside to tell me that I had it all wrong, I got into the truck and laid on the horn. Surely he would hear, surely he would see me sitting out there. The horn blasted a minute or two, then gave up in a hoarse bleat. I got out of the truck, with its cracked window and wrong-color fender and its smell of kerosene and earth.

Where could I go? I wanted to be some other place, anywhere except this red town where I was certain that red eyes watched my foolish misery and cackled their red pleasure. I followed the railroad tracks, where I could be lost without losing my way.

For hours I walked. Through the woods, outside other neighborhoods, along the river, and into the outskirts of Rattlebone. I was one with the fallow fields I passed through, and with the harvested ones too, where sheaves stood like empty spools. How could he? How could this be happening to me?

I got home after dark that night. Through the window in the front door I could see the kitchen and Wanda at the table with my mother and father, chattering to distract them. I could have been a ghost the way my mother flinched when she saw me.

Wanda said, "Girl, we were really worried — weren't we, Miss Wilson?" I knew it was her attempt to diffuse the tightness in the air.

"You ain't got no business wandering around by yourself this late," my father said. "I was waiting till nine. You better be glad you got some sense and came on home before I had to come after you." His speech sounded rehearsed.

My mother went to the stove and dipped up a bowl of oxtail stew. She unbuttoned my car coat for me and touched her fingers to my cheek.

"Too cold for you to be out with nothing on," she said. "Sit down and eat." I obeyed.

Days later, Wanda broached the subject again. "Welcome to the club," she said. "I could have told you. They're all alike. Dogs, all of them. Forget him. You have to tell yourself nothing happened. Nothing at all happened. After all," she said, "I'm the only one at school who knows the whole story, and I know how to keep it to myself. There's nothing else to do unless you plan to jump in the river."

I tried following Wanda's expert advice, act as if nothing had happened. Forget Obadele Quander. He wasn't anyone, anyway. If my life was going to be a mess, it wasn't going to show.

• • •

I had missed several rehearsals with Mrs. Welche. I frightened myself with the possibility that I had ruined my chances for the competition.

"I understand you've been having some problems at home," she said. I wondered who she had been talking to.

"I hope whatever is going on, you won't miss any more days of school or we may have to reconsider the tournament," she said.

That short-circuited my cure. What I needed now was a victory. Mrs. Welche was offering that possibility, and I would focus all my energy on claiming it.

"I'm fine now," I said. I wanted to give the right slant to what she had heard. "I won't have to miss any more days of school."

"You know," she said, "those students of ours that live in Redtown, from what I understand, you've been spending a lot of time with them. I'm not so sure they're the kind of influence you should be exposed to. Most of them aren't even interested in school."

"Yes, ma'am, I know," I said. I could not look at her.

"They have strange ideas," she said.

"Yes, ma'am," I said.

"They don't believe in God, and they don't believe in washing themselves," she said.

I didn't say anything.

"They're all related, yet they marry each other."

"I'm having a little trouble with the last part of my introduction," I said.

The tournament was to be held on the Saturday after Thanksgiving. Mrs. Welche had already arranged for me to ride with her and a student from her old school. Of the twenty-five contestants, I suspected, few to none would look like me. I considered it an initiation into the world I would move through if and when I went to college.

Usually I rehearsed twice a week in the auditorium after school with Mrs. Welche sitting at various places to see how well I projected. Occasionally another teacher would sit in, or a student would sneak in to watch. About ten days before Thanksgiving, Mrs. Welche asked me to meet her in her classroom instead of going to the auditorium. When I got there she sat on her desk with her arms folded.

"I received some bad news a couple of days ago," she said. "I've been wondering how to tell you. Why don't you sit down."

She picked up the letter from her desk. "I want you to know that if I had known this, I would have never even mentioned the state competition to you. I've been involved with it for years. I just didn't think."

She was looking at the letter, but of course, I already knew.

"They won't let me be in it, will they?" I said.

"I'm sorry," she said. "The contest has never been open to you all. They say in the future . . ."

"But isn't that against the law now?"

"Well, sort of," she said. "But things take time."

This was not news. I told myself that perhaps it had happened this way for a good reason. Maybe I would have frozen up on that stage. Those people probably had never even heard of James Weldon Johnson. From the way Mrs. Welche had responded at first, I believed she had never heard of him herself.

Then Mrs. Welche said, "I was just thinking, you've done all this work for nothing. Wouldn't it be wonderful if we could salvage some of it, put it to good use?"

"Yes, but how?" I asked her.

"Well, you know, Ann Marie Cooper is a pretty good speaker. She has poise and she can project. I had her read "The Creation" for me yesterday, and she wasn't nearly as good as you are, but she could probably learn to do it your way. I thought if you would teach it to her, you know, teach her your inflections and gestures, all the drama you put into it, she could take it to state."

I gathered my books without answering. Outside, November trees had lost their leaves, and their branches showed crooked against the clouds. I took the shortcut along the tracks past Redtown. Without looking down, I crossed the narrow trestle and went home. ■

1994

Understanding and Interpreting

1. When you read the opening paragraph of "The Creation," do you notice immediately that it takes place in an earlier time period — or could it be set in the present day? What details, if any, feel familiar to you?
2. Irene states early on, "At first my curiosity about Obadele, Folami, and Akin was casual" (par. 15). What do you think she means by "casual"? Why does that "curiosity" change? Be sure to consider details other than Irene's interactions with Obadele in your response.
3. Based on your reading of paragraph 15, why is the speech competition so important to Irene? What does she say it holds for her, and why do you think that appeals to her?
4. Why is Irene drawn to the poem "The Creation"? How would you characterize Folami's mother's response to it, and why does it surprise Irene?
5. In what ways does Irene surprise herself and her audience when she recites "The Creation"? What does she mean when she reflects that "[s]ome other, bolder Irene had taken over" (par. 115)?
6. What do you make of Irene's claim that "My love for a Red Quander had made me my own woman" (par. 140)? In what ways might this hold true? In what ways might it be read as ironic?
7. In this story, the Red Quanders community has little interest in formal education. Irene believes in what she calls "common knowledge," yet by the end her disappointment in her teacher and school in general is profound. How significantly has her attitude toward the role of school and education changed by the end of the story?
8. Is Obadele the antagonist of the story, or is his role more complex? In what ways does he function in contrast to Irene? In what ways might he be viewed as similar to her?
9. Mrs. Welche is a minor yet significant character in "The Creation." What values, assumptions, and cultural norms does she represent? How does Irene's perspective on her change as the story develops?
10. Consider the historical setting of the story, in particular its reference to the *Brown v. Board* ruling. In what ways does Maxine Clair show the impact of this decision on the lives of the different communities in Rattlebone?
11. In what ways does the ending of the story add complexity to the meaning of its title?

Analyzing Language, Style, and Structure

1. **Vocabulary in Context.** In paragraph 109, Irene recalls the way that "Dele mesmerized me with stories of *orishas*, of lost kingdoms and ancient rulers, and of people — Hausas and Zulus — he claimed I had to thank for more than my black skin." What does the word "mesmerized" imply about how Irene views her relationship with Dele? Does this word help paint an accurate picture of that relationship, or does it reflect a disconnect between Irene's perspective and what we as readers understand? Use evidence from the text to explain your response.
2. Why do you think Clair chose to tell this story through a first-person narrator? What aspects of the story's meaning would be lost were it told from a different narrative perspective? How reliable a narrator is Irene? Cite specific passages to support your response.
3. Instead of including the entire text of James Weldon Johnson's poem "The Creation," Clair uses only excerpts. What do these passages reveal about Irene's character? Why do you think Clair chose not to include the entire poem in this story?
4. Do Irene's views regarding the setting of Redtown and its inhabitants reflect growth and change toward more independent thinking, or do those views suggest her inability to move beyond a narrow perspective? Cite specific passages to support your response.

5. In what ways does the railroad trestle, a part of the setting, become a symbol? What does it symbolize, and does that symbolism shift as the story progresses?
6. "The Creation" includes a series of stories that characters tell themselves and each other. First identify at least three; then, discuss how these individual stories help create the structure of the overall story and contribute to a larger meaning.
7. "The Creation" is an actual poem, yet it is merely the allusion to this poem that animates the story. How does the allusion add complexity and nuance to the meaning of Clair's story, as you interpret it?

Topics for Composing

1. AP® FRQ **Prose Fiction Analysis**. The following question refers to paragraphs 46–58 of Maxine Clair's "The Creation," published in 1994. In this passage, the narrator invents a pretext to satisfy her curiosity to see the home of a classmate who belongs to a different community and culture than the narrator. Read the passage carefully. Then, in a well-written essay, analyze how Clair uses literary elements and techniques to convey the narrator's complex perspective on the community she is visiting.
2. AP® FRQ **Literary Argument.** Many works of fiction center on the experience of growing up and the accompanying challenges. In "The Creation," the narrator, Irene, enters a pivotal time in her life as a high school student. In a well-written essay, analyze how the challenges Irene faces and the changes she undergoes as a result contribute to an interpretation of the work as a whole. Do not merely summarize the plot.
3. **Research.** The landmark Supreme Court case known as *Brown v. Board of Education* was filed against the Board of Education in Topeka, Kansas. Research the circumstances at the local level that gave rise to the case. How does the information you gather deepen your understanding of the conflicts in "The Creation"? Does it complicate your understanding of the relationship between Irene and Dele? Explain why or why not.
4. **Speaking and Listening.** Shift the narrative in this story from Irene to another character, such as Mrs. Welche, Obadele, Wanda, Folami, or Irene's mother. Speaking as that character, describe some element of Irene's character to an audience of your classmates or a small group of them. Discuss whether your perception of the character and of Irene rings true to the characters in Clair's story.
5. **Connections.** James Weldon Johnson's poem "The Creation" plays a central role in this story. Read the poem in its entirety and discuss why it is particularly well suited for developing the central theme(s) of Clair's story.
6. **Connections.** When Mrs. Welche explains to Irene that she is ineligible for the competition, Irene asks if that is not against the law. Mrs. Welche responds: "Well, sort of . . . But things take time." Name a situation today where the law mandates a policy or behavior that has not actually been fully incorporated into society; that is, the legal regulation continues to "take time" to become accepted practice.
7. **Connections.** For centuries, plays and novels have explored the impact of cultural, racial, religious, and class differences on young love. How these are negotiated may reveal the characters of a young couple or the society(ies) they belong to. Choose a literary work or a film or television series and discuss how this seemingly timeless theme is presented and, if appropriate, how it remains relevant to contemporary times.

Jubilee

Kirstin Valdez Quade

Kirstin Valdez Quade (b. 1980) is an American writer who was born in New Mexico but grew up throughout the southwest. She attended Phillips Exeter Academy before earning a BA from Stanford University and an MFA from the University of Oregon. She is the author of two books: *Night at the Fiestas* (2015), a short story collection that won the John Leonard Prize from the National Book Critics Circle, and her first novel, *The Five Wounds* (2021). She is currently a professor of creative writing at Princeton University.

Photo by Holly Andres, 2020

When Andrea pulled into the dirt lot by the orchards that adjoined the blueberry fields, she saw she'd timed their arrival just right. Where the farm workers normally parked their beat-up sedans and rusting pickups, the Volvos and Mercedes and Audis were lined up, a faint scrim of dust from the dirt drive on their hoods. Usually Andrea was embarrassed by her mother's old Chrysler with its missing wood panel, but today she parked it among the luxury vehicles with a sense of vindication.

"Nice rides," said Matty, nodding appreciatively.

"I told you. They own everything." She gestured at the trees and at the sky, too, as if the Lowells actually did own the whole wide world. "Like three hundred acres. Practically this entire side of the river. Apples and pears and blueberries, too."

For several years, the blueberry industry in California had been expanding, and the Lowells had been early adopters. In honor of their eighth annual blueberry party, the field workers — a few of whom Andrea had known her whole life — had been given this Saturday off, paid. "Wouldn't want the guests in their pearls to have to pick alongside Mexicans." She snorted, picturing the Lowells' friends in their Brooks Brothers chinos and silk skirts and strappy heeled sandals making their way down the rows.

5 Matty shrugged. "I wouldn't mind a paid day off."

"You'd have to have a job first," said Andrea, then glanced at him, worried she'd offended him. Andrea wished he'd shaved that wormy black mustache or had at least put on a button-down. But whatever, she reminded herself; she didn't actually care what the Lowells thought.

Andrea had dawdled in a gas station off the highway so they wouldn't be on time. She'd bought Matty a forty — rather, he bought it with his fake ID and she paid — then lingered, trying to distract him. "Imagine the kind of guy who thinks Sexxx Juice is going to improve his prospects," she said, flicking a plastic bottle of pheromones. She was always bringing up sex around Matty so she could demonstrate how cool she was with it. At the magazine rack, she dragged on his arm, trying to look game and easygoing as she pointed out features in men's magazines. ("Guys really think that's hot?" "Yes," Matty said.) Finally, though, Matty had pitched his bottle — still half full — and asked if they were going to this party or not.

Technically, Andrea had been invited to this party. Rather, her parents had been invited. Technically. But she was certain that the Lowells didn't actually expect them to come. After all, they'd never been invited before. This invitation — letterpress-printed on thick, soft paper — had been a gesture of goodwill, and not even that, Andrea was sure, but something the Lowells had felt they had to do, given that her father would be there anyway, with his taco truck.

The truck was a highlight of this year's party, according to the invitation: "Tacos provided by our own Salvador Romero and his El Primo taco truck!" And there, instead of blueberries on sage-colored sprigs, was the truck itself: a festive little line drawing debossed in red and yellow.

The taco truck was a recent acquisition. Andrea's father had saved for four years, plotting, cobbling together loans (including a pretty substantial one from William Lowell), driving the family crazy with his exuberance. The truck would pay for itself, he said, would give him something to do. All week it was shuttered, parked in the driveway while her father worked as a supervisor in the Lowells' orchards, and on the weekends (up at four-thirty as usual) he drove it to the park, where he served egg burritos and cokes to young men famished after their soccer games, tacos and tortas to families out for a stroll. Her father never said so, but Andrea suspected from her mother's strained silence on the subject that the taco truck wasn't as lucrative as he'd hoped.

"Are they kidding?" Andrea said when she heard the Lowells were hiring her father for the party. "You'd think they'd want something fancy."

"Oh, you know these wealthy people," said her mother, shaking her head in bemusement. "They get their ideas."

Her parents had been delighted to see the taco truck featured on the Lowells' invitation, and had gushed about how touched they were to have received it. Her mother turned the invitation in her hands and shook her head in wonder. "They didn't have to think of us, but they did."

Andrea was hijacked by the image of her mother in her teal dress with the gold chain belt, trailing the Lowells all over their party. "You're not considering going, are you, Mom?"

Hurt flashed in her mother's face, and Andrea bristled at the Lowells for causing this hurt. "I work on Saturdays," her mother said stiffly and dropped the invitation in the trash. Later, in spite of herself, Andrea had plucked it out and squirreled it away in her room, saving even the envelope (yellow lined in red — why was she so impressed with the invitation? — she *hated* that she was so impressed).

Well, if the Lowells wanted Mexicans at their party, that's what they'd get.

The day was not ideal for an outdoor party, Andrea saw as she unstuck herself from the driver's seat. The leaves of the apple trees were dusty silver in the hot afternoon light, and a breeze stirred the dry soil. "You won't believe these people," she told Matty, shutting the car door. And she told him about the framed photograph she had seen in their kitchen: the redheaded brother and sister as children in their green velvet coats, the Eiffel tower lit and snowy, behind them. "Can you believe that? Matching coats! And for her, white gloves! What a waste to bring little kids to France. They probably planned the whole trip just for that picture, just for one stupid picture of their kids being adorable in Paris."

"Annoying," conceded Matty.

"Tell me about it. They probably read *Madeline* every five minutes. They probably couldn't stop themselves."

Andrea still remembered the children's expressions: the older boy flashing a showy television-child smile, Parker scowling down at her patent leather toes. This was years ago; Andrea had come with her father when he'd stopped by to pick up paychecks. She remembered the kitchen, too, large and gleaming, the row of pale green porcelain bowls as thin as eggshells stacked in the open shelves. Mrs. Lowell had given Andrea three warm ginger cookies wrapped in a napkin, which Andrea had made last for over a week, tasting in the increasingly stale nibbles the calm and security and beauty of this home.

"I'm pretty sure Parker Lowell isn't even that smart. She's too sweet to be smart." Andrea fingered an aching pimple on her forehead.

Courtesy Dianne Smith

This painting, completed in 2020 by artist Dianne Smith, is entitled *Jubilee*.
What emotions does it evoke? How might the painting reflect Andrea's emotional state throughout "Jubilee"?

"Do you think she's easy? In my experience lots of rich girls are easy."

Andrea ignored the pang in the center of her chest. "I'm pretty sure she only got into Stanford because she's a legacy."

"So why are we here?" asked Matty. "If you hate them so much."

Matty was here because Andrea had strong-armed him into coming; she intended for people to assume he was her boyfriend. And he owed her, anyway, for the essays she'd written for his classes at Chico State.

And why was Andrea here? Driving, she'd felt full of the brazen courage she would need to crash this party. She would show up full of breezy, sparkling confidence that would startle these people. Yes, Andrea was an equal now, a *Stanford* student, poised and intelligent, no longer just the daughter of one of their laborers, no longer an awestruck kid worshipping their cookies, and if the Lowells wanted to trot out her father and his taco truck to provide a little kitsch for their party, then they'd have to do it in front of her. By her very presence here today, she would prove to them their snobbery and make them ashamed of their entitlement and their half-hearted acts of charity towards her family. Admittedly, her plan was vague, but it involved making Parker eat a taco in front of her. And she would have Matty at her side, handsome bad-boy Matty Macias, whom she'd loved since eighth grade. Matty, with his gelled hair and warm, thick-lashed eyes and the cords of his scapular showing at the neck of his t-shirt. Matty would not fail to disconcert.

"We're *here* because I was invited. I can't just snub them. Parker and I are *classmates* now."

Andrea smoothed the wrinkled back of her new sundress (J. Crew — the most expensive dress she'd ever bought, and she did not intend to keep it; the tag still hung, scratchy and damp now, down her back, and she hoped, should Matty touch her, that he wouldn't notice it).

"Just, you know, be polite," Andrea told Matty.

"— the fuck?" he said, shooting her an irritated grimace. "You think I'm an idiot?"

"I just think you're not used to being around people like this."

Andrea strode past him, clutching the invitation. Only now did it occur to her that maybe she ought to have brought something — flowers? Wine? Already she could hear the sounds of laughter through the apple trees.

• • •

Andrea hated it, the constant alert hunger for every possible chance to move up in the world. "So and so's lazy," her father would tell Andrea's mom in the evenings. "He should just go back to Mexico. Work hard, get ahead. Look at me."

Over and over, the same conversation. "You should talk to Bill about law," her father would urge, pronouncing his name *Beel*. "Maybe he could help you."

"He doesn't practice," said Andrea.

"Still," said her mother, "it's nice to show interest."

"We'll have to get the girls together," William Lowell had said after Salvador told his boss with tears in his eyes — Salvador's eyes had filled just relating the exchange — that Andrea had been accepted at Stanford. "Maybe lunch at the house and they can swap notes." But though William asked after Andrea (Salvador was always sure to tell her when he did), and remarked over and over how wonderful it was that she'd gotten in, and on full scholarship, too, they never did get the girls together. And thank goodness; it would have been strange and awkward. As children they'd played together on a few sporadic summer afternoons — Andrea remembered running after Parker through the orchards, bashful and grinning — but the girls hadn't seen each other in years, not since a brief chance hello when Parker was home from prep school.

Stanford, Stanford, Stanford. There were weeks last summer when Andrea couldn't sleep, so thrilled was she by the sense that her life was blooming into something marvelous. She'd tremble in bed, eyes darting around the dark familiar shapes of her room, which was really just an alcove off from the kitchen, amazed that she would actually be leaving this home she'd known her whole life: goodbye to the rippled linoleum, goodbye to the Aladdin-print curtain that was her bedroom wall, and beyond it, goodbye to the refrigerator's intestinal gurgles. Oh, the success and wealth and greatness the future held for her! It actually made her breathless to think of it. Parker Lowell was the single blight on her joy. During freshman orientation, as Andrea was herded through White Plaza with others from the Chicano student association, she found herself looking with dread for Parker among the clumps of happy milling students. It was only a matter of time, Andrea knew, before they ran into each other at a party or on the Quad, and when they did, Parker would smile and make small talk and, through her very graciousness, expose Andrea as she truly was: cheap, striving, unworthy. Maybe, thought Andrea, Parker would get mono.

But campus was sprawling and Andrea's freshman dorm mercifully distant from Parker's. The first quarter passed, and nearly the second, before Andrea saw her, in the winter production of "Once Upon a Mattress." She'd sat tense in the audience, searching the actors' faces, and felt oddly thrilled when she finally spotted Parker. As Parker, lady-in-waiting to Queen Aggravaine, curtsied and twirled and warbled on stage, Andrea considered pointing her out to her roommate, but didn't.

Her whole life Andrea had been subjected to her parents' slavish interest in the Lowells' affairs, so she shouldn't have been surprised that all through freshman year they kept her apprised of the Lowell family news. "I really don't care," Andrea said, but she listened anyway, thinking as she did that there were lots of interesting things she could tell them about power structures. They reported how the Anjous and Pink Ladies were faring, and on the Lowell boy's job in the governor's office, and then in the spring they called with the news that brought Parker lower than any bout of mono ever could: Mrs. Lowell had left her husband for their landscaper — their twenty-eight year old *female* landscaper — and William Lowell, apparently unable to live for twenty seconds without a wife, had started up with the widow of his roommate from Exeter.

Andrea had been shocked. In the face of her mother's shock, though, she'd feigned total equanimity; "No one's really straight," Andrea explained, "not one hundred percent."

And so it was that the Lowells, poised and affectionate and photogenic, now found themselves cut down by a crisis that had all the elements of a joke, and it seemed to Andrea that the balance between them had shifted. In Andrea's mind Parker underwent a faint oxidation. She took on a patina, for the first time, of vulnerability. Again Andrea found herself seeking Parker on campus, this time so she might extend her hand in friendship.

•••

When they stepped into the clearing between the orchards and the rows of highbush Jubilee blueberries, Andrea saw that her father's taco truck had inspired a whole Mexican theme. Gone were the sun-faded Porta-Potties and the water truck; in their place, the Lowells had erected a tent festooned with fluttering *papel picado* flags. Elderly people in pastels sat in the shade and the younger people stood around drinking margaritas. White tablecloths rippled in the hot breeze. In the center of each table sat a little piñata on bright woven fabric.

And there, at the edge of the party, was the taco truck itself. From where she stood, Andrea could see her father's arms handing full plates out the sliding window. She remained out of his line of vision. He'd be surprised and proud and pleased to see her here as a guest, would probably think Parker had invited her personally, but she didn't feel like getting into explanations. And she didn't want to establish herself as the daughter of the cook, at least not yet.

45 The truck *did* look festive here, Andrea saw with disappointment, against the backdrop of trees. A colorful hand-painted sign announced a pared-down, classed-up menu: Kobe beef, wild-caught salmon, free-range chicken, and vegetarian, all on blue corn tortillas.

"A vegetarian on a tortilla," said Andrea. "Ha."

"Funny," said Matty. He scanned the crowd. "They know how to do it up."

Tacos were not the only option: caterers in white shirts presided over a vast spread of fresh, colorful food. Tin buckets were lined up on another table, a grosgrain ribbon tied around each handle. Already several beautifully dressed children were in the blueberry rows, picking.

And now, turning toward Andrea, in a floral shift and Converse sneakers without socks, was Parker.

50 In one hand she swung a bucket, and in the other, she held a massive sloshing glass of wine. "Andrea?" She tilted her head, her red hair shining in the sun and slipping over her shoulder. "Your dad didn't say you were coming. It's so great you could make it!"

Was Parker going to hug her? Yes, she was. Andrea put her arms around Parker, and there was nothing casual about it, nothing breezy. Andrea pulled away too soon, terrified Parker would feel the price tags.

"So," Andrea said, tongue-tied. She brandished her invitation. "Do I need to give this to you?"

Parker looked at the invitation but made no move, and Andrea also looked at it, large and clumsy in her hand. Stupid, to think she might be required to present it like a ticket. She waved it at the party and the field and the orchards. "It all looks great. I haven't been out here in years."

Parker stuck her hand out at Matty. "Parker. Great to meet you."

55 "Oh, sorry. This is Matty." Andrea smiled at him in a way that she hoped looked affectionate and familiar and somehow also conveyed the sense that they were having lots of spectacular sex.

"Matthew," said Matty.

An awkward moment passed. Andrea smiled woodenly; Matty jingled the coins in his pocket with one hand and thumbed the edge of his repellant little mustache with the other.

Andrea had imagined cornering Parker next to the truck, plying her with tacos, which Parker, too polite to refuse, would choke down in class-conscious misery until she was sick. Absurd and far-fetched, yes, but Andrea had gotten a grim pleasure from the image. Now, though, she felt pathetic for even thinking it.

As if reading her mind, Parker ran her hand through her hair, glanced at the taco truck, then back at Andrea. At least she had the grace to look uncomfortable. "It's so great of your dad to be here. His tacos are awesome. I ate like six already."

"Yes," agreed Andrea. "They are pretty great." How many times were they going to say *great*?

A gold Tiffany's heart dangled at Parker's throat. Something about the necklace combined with the Converse suddenly enraged Andrea. "Man," she said, "I was really sorry to hear about your parents splitting up. I mean, it must have *really* turned your world upside down."

Parker shrugged, but her throat beneath the gold chain splotched red. "They both seem to have gotten over it." She jerked her thumb at one of the clumps of laughing adults. "My dad can't keep his hands off Judith."

And indeed William Lowell had his arm around the thick waist of a beaming woman who could only be the widow. She was short-haired and mannish, an Hermès scarf tied in the collar of her striped Oxford. It was no surprise she wasn't as pretty as Elizabeth Lowell, Andrea supposed; William Lowell had been burned by beauty. Still, she felt obscurely disappointed by the widow, as though William Lowell had been guilty of a lapse in taste.

"Funny, I hardly see you at school," said Parker. She smiled. "We must travel in different circles." Parker turned to Matty and said seriously, "Andrea is *super* smart."

Matty snorted. "She thinks so."

Andrea bristled. Parker didn't know how smart she was. Parker didn't know one thing about her.

"Seriously, I hear you're doing really well. Your dad tells my dad."

The thought of her father bragging about her was horrifying. Every term this year, Andrea had received honor roll certificates from the Chicano, a student association, which had made her proud until she realized they were just part of all the extra efforts made on behalf of minority students: the special dinners and study breaks and offers for faculty mentorship with junior faculty eager to bolster their tenure files. Still, she'd sent the certificates home to her parents, who didn't know the difference. Now, though, she had a hideous vision of her father flapping the flimsy sheets in William Lowell's face, William Lowell's indulgent smile. William Lowell didn't brag to Salvador about Parker's accomplishments, you could be sure of that.

"Last time I was out here in the blueberry field I was nine, I think," said Andrea. "You were here, too. Do you remember?"

Parker shook her head.

"Why would you? Long time ago. It was summer, which is probably why we were both there. You were picking blueberries for your mom, and I wanted to help, too, so Isabel — Isabel Gutierrez? — you probably don't know her, she worked here for years, she and my mom are still friends — gave me a bucket. And I was out there picking away, happy as can be. Then your dad came down the row and saw and yelled for me to stop." Andrea laughed heartily, mirthlessly. "He was worried about child labor laws! Wouldn't want anyone to come by and find a little Mexican kid picking blueberries!"

Parker tipped her head, laughed uncertainly. Her entire face was pink now. "Sounds like maybe he was being a little too scrupulous."

Andrea shrugged. "No big deal. I've just always remembered it. You kept picking. It wasn't child labor for you. You were just getting some berries for a pie." She smiled.

"Ah," said Parker. Even her flushed face irritated Andrea. What was she, some swooning Victorian?

"Well, pick as much as you'd like today." Parker nodded at the children in the rows. "Today we're even allowing child labor."

Parker politely extricated herself, and then she was off to charm other guests with her straight teeth and easy personality. Matty stood watching her, jingling the change in his pockets.

"Would you just be still for one minute?" Andrea snapped.

"What is with you?" Matty asked. "You're fucked up, you know that? You're fucking obsessed."

Andrea turned on Matty. "Do you know how much all this is worth?" Oh, yes, Andrea had Googled the land appraisal — she knew.

Matty gave her one long disgusted look and then headed for the beer.

Andrea nearly ran after him — but to what? Grab his hand, beg him to support her? She winced sourly.

Andrea had finally run into Parker at a party at one of the co-ops in the spring, in that lull after midterms and before finals. Andrea had arrived with some dormmates, who, once they'd all swigged their punch, had gone off in search of weed, leaving Andrea swaying at the periphery of the party. It had just stopped raining, and in the backyard several people were naked and dancing a formless hippie dance in the mud, ruining the lawn, which is what Andrea was watching — arms crossed critically as she envied their lack of self-consciousness — when Parker Lowell came up behind her and circled a thin arm around her neck.

"Andrea!" Parker cried and thrust her friend forward. Parker was drunk, drunker than Andrea, eyes damp and unfocused. "Meet Andrea! Andrea, this is Chantal. Oh my gosh, Andrea and I have known each other practically our entire lives. Our dads work together."

Chantal had glitter on her cheekbones and smeared black eyeliner. But it was Parker Andrea was staring at. "Imagine," her mother had told her just days before, "that entire family, ruined." But Parker didn't look like someone whose world had fallen apart; instead, she looked breathless and happy. She was leaner now and wore thrift store corduroys and a boy's AYSO soccer shirt, through which her braless pert nipples showed. Her bare face shone from dancing, and at her temples, Andrea could see veins blue through her nearly translucent skin. Andrea wanted to speak privately to Parker, to tell her how sorry she was, how shocked they'd all been. She'd touch that lovely arm, speak sincerely, and they'd understand each other.

Instead, Andrea gestured at the mud dancers. "Insane, right? You couldn't pay me to do that. Not in a million years."

"Oh, I don't know. It seems kind of fun to me," said Parker.

Feeling drab to her core, Andrea searched for something else to say but came up with nothing. Couldn't she even stand like a normal person? Parker and Chantal stood close with their arms looped around each other's waists, and their intimacy looked so natural that Andrea felt a pang. "I just meant they're probably getting mud in their cracks."

Chantal laughed, but Parker fixed Andrea with sincere attention. "What are your summer plans? Heading back home?"

"I'm not sure yet. Probably I'll find an internship." Andrea was heartsick at the thought of the months that lay between her and the start of the next school year: the chilly, buzzing shifts at Safeway, the hot Stockton nights. Most internships were unpaid, she'd learned, and she didn't really know how to go about finding them anyway, so she hadn't even looked. "You?"

Parker laughed. "I'm totally embarrassed, but I'm just going to hang out." Her eyes flicked away; she was, it seemed, genuinely embarrassed. "Travel some, maybe. Mostly hang around home." She laughed nervously. "I figure I'll have to work the rest of my life."

Hope glinted in Andrea's chest. Maybe they'd get together this summer; maybe, with nothing else to do, with her college and boarding school friends off on their European tours, Parker would reach out. Already Andrea knew that wouldn't happen.

Chantal was looking at Andrea. "What does your dad do again?" she asked Parker.

"He's a farmer." And Parker's voice was so easy, so unselfconscious that Andrea knew she believed it.

A fierce rage rose from nowhere and spotted Andrea's vision. A farmer! As if her dad was Old MacDonald milking his cow. As if the Lowells were all out weeding in their overalls! William Lowell had a law degree, for god's sake!

Later, she would kick herself for not calling Parker on her shit, would cycle through all the things she might have said: "Parker's dad owns farmers." Instead, she'd smiled hard and bright until the terrible conversation wound down and Parker and Chantal melted into the crowd arm in arm.

So, yes, this was Parker's crime: thinking her dad was a farmer. Now, while a three-piece mariachi band struck up at the edge of the clearing, Andrea watched with loathing as Parker greeted her guests. Where did this anger come from? Andrea wasn't one of these strident activists, with eagle eyes sharp on the lookout for injustice, leading grape boycotts and bus trips to Arizona. She wanted to become a lawyer, and not a civil rights or immigration lawyer, either. She wanted to be a lawyer in a slimming wool suit riding the elevator to the top of a New York skyscraper.

Yet you mentioned the Lowells, people who'd only been kind to her family—it, was, after all, a *nice thing*, hiring her father's taco truck—and suddenly she was outraged. Andrea didn't blame the Lowells, not really—they couldn't help being who they were, having what they had. They weren't even snobby. And technically Mr. Lowell sort of was a farmer. Except, of course, she did blame them, and it didn't matter that she knew it was unfair. Why did she want to embarrass Parker, dig into that rich guilt that was so ripe and close to the surface? Andrea flexed her fingers, imagined sinking them into flesh that would give as easily as the skin of a browning pear.

•••

"Wine?" offered the waiter at her elbow. "This is a Sauvignon Blanc from the Pink Motel Vineyard in Napa."

"Oh," said Andrea. "Okay." She drank it down quickly, then exchanged the glass when the next waiter came by.

She was hungry, and the smell from the taco truck was delicious. But she felt stuck here on the edge, without another person to walk with. Under a swinging piñata, Matty was chatting with an older couple, not caring, apparently, that in his t-shirt and work boots he looked like an employee. He should be right here, talking to her, laughing at what she said; that had been the whole point of bringing him.

Waiters supplied her with wine, elaborately speared vegetables, savory little puffs. And a be-ribboned bucket. She was warm, and the wine made her tight-faced and loose-limbed and tipsy. She didn't know if the bucket was to keep, but she'd just decided she would keep it anyway when she felt a nail scratch her gently at her neck.

"Tag's out, honey." It was the widow.

Andrea clapped a hand on the nape of her neck.

"You're a friend of Parker's? From school? Bill pointed you out."

"I must have forgotten to cut it off." She felt the miserable heat rise in her face.

"Don't look so worried, honey." The widow gave her a friendly scratch on the back and winked. "I won't tell. We've all done it. It's a nice dress."

extending beyond the text

John Steinbeck's 1939 novel *The Grapes of Wrath* exposed the conditions of migrant farmworkers in California in the 1930s. Leaving Oklahoma, which has been decimated by the Dust Bowl, the Joad family travels to California in search of work. They find the state oversupplied with labor in an atmosphere of intimidation and violence. Struggling to find work, they are exploited at every turn. This famous passage describes the destruction of surplus products, a terrible irony when the migrant workers are dying of disease and starvation.

from The Grapes of Wrath

John Steinbeck

The works of the roots of the vines, of the trees, must be destroyed to keep up the price. . . . How would they buy oranges at twenty cents a dozen if they could drive out and pick them up? And men with hoses squirt kerosene on the oranges, and they are angry at the crime, angry at the people who have come to take the fruit. A million people hungry, needing the fruit- and kerosene sprayed over the golden mountains. And the smell of rot fills the country. . . . Dump potatoes in the rivers and place guards along the banks to keep the hungry people from fishing them out. Slaughter the pigs and bury them, and let the putrescence drip down into the earth.

There is a crime here that goes beyond denunciation. There is a sorrow here that weeping cannot symbolize. There is a failure here that topples all our success.

The fertile earth, the straight tree rows, the sturdy trunks, and the ripe fruit. And children dying of pellagra must die because a profit cannot be taken from an orange. And coroners must fill in the certificate — died of malnutrition — because the food must rot, must be forced to rot. The people come with nets to fish for potatoes in the river, and the guards hold them back. . . . And they stand still and watch the potatoes float by, listen to the screaming pigs being killed in a ditch and covered with quick-lime, watch the mountains of oranges slop down to a putrefying ooze; and in the eyes of the people there is the failure; and in the eyes of the hungry there is a growing wrath. In the souls of the people the grapes of wrath are filling and growing heavy, growing heavy for the vintage. ■

1. **How does Steinbeck move from literal description in this passage to metaphorical? What is the effect?**
2. **Are there metaphors in "Jubilee" that comment on the social atmosphere in a similar way? If so, what are they, and what comment do they make? If not, why do you think Kirstin Valdez Quade chose not to make such commentary?**
3. **Much of *The Grapes of Wrath* is about efforts, sometimes violent, to improve conditions for migrant workers in California. Do you see any lingering evidence of worker exploitation in "Jubilee"? Explain why or why not.**
4. **Does "Jubilee" contain a call for action similar to this passage? Explain why or why not.**

Andrea smiled, and it felt so good that she realized it was the first genuine smile she'd smiled all day. "Thanks." The widow's hair was coarse and thick, a raccoon's pelt. It wasn't her fault she wasn't as pretty as Elizabeth Lowell. "My dad's the taco guy," she confessed.

"I just met him! Lovely man. He must be so proud of you."

"Oh, well," said Andrea modestly, but she couldn't stop the grin from creeping in. "Lots of kids get in."

"I'm glad Parker has a friend here." The widow sighed, sipped her wine. "I guess the situation can't be anything but awkward."

"Oh, I know," said Andrea. "The power dynamics —"

"Between you and me, it's a mess. I don't actually know what I'm doing playing hostess. I don't even know most of these people." The widow withdrew a tube of lipstick from her pocket and smeared it on thin, tense lips.

"I think you're doing a great job," Andrea said.

"Both kids are angry, of course. It's worse for Parker, though, being the youngest." Parker and her father were standing arm in arm, entertaining a laughing crowd, and the widow watched them as she talked. When she sloshed some wine on her shirt she swiped at it without looking. "She keeps calling her parents to scream at them. She accuses her mother of being — of sleeping around. And she doesn't think much of me. She told her father he was pitiful and desperate." She laughed once, sharply. "She got both of us with that one."

It was impossible to imagine Parker raging at anyone. She certainly didn't look angry with her father. She was smiling pinkly. Mr. Lowell kissed the silky top of her head. It was like a Ralph Lauren ad. That's what this party was missing: a camera crew. Briefly, Andrea wondered if Parker's mother had taken the Paris picture when she moved out, or if it was still in that gleaming kitchen facing the widow, as she made her mayonnaise casseroles.

Andrea was startled and flattered and uncomfortable to be let into the widow's confidence, and her heart went out to her. "It must be so hard for you. Is it hard for you?"

"Do you know, he says he isn't sure he'll even divorce her. Doesn't want to leave her in the lurch, he says." The widow's laugh was brittle, a little unhinged. It occurred to Andrea that she was drunk. "He's too good, that man. But he'll come around. Parker scared him to death with that little pill stunt. I told him that was the point. I know. I was young, too." The widow smiled brilliantly with magenta lips and played with the tails of her scarf.

That pill stunt. "Yes," said Andrea.

"I told him she should have a summer job, keep busy. My kids have always had summer jobs. I bet *you* have one, don't you?"

"What pills?" Andrea's head was cottony and the buzz of the wine drained, leaving a heavy, hot remorse. "We're not actually that close. I didn't actually know about the pills."

"You get selfish if you don't work, I told him. If you never have to think about anyone else. It's not her *fault*, but that's what happens."

"Was she really so unhappy?"

The widow tipped her head and looked at Andrea as if for the first time. Her lipstick was thick, waxy and dry. "She's quite a performer, your friend."

"No," said Andrea, with sudden savage energy that took her by surprise. "She's *not* a performer." Who did this widow think she was, spreading the Lowell gossip at their own party? She was an ugly, hateful woman. "For the record," she said with indignation, "the Lowells were the most beautiful family I have ever seen."

"Ah. I see," the widow said lightly. "I hope you'll be more discreet than I was. Do tell your dad how much I enjoyed his tacos. Excuse me." She gave Andrea's back another little scratch and moved unsteadily off.

And of course this was how it was supposed to go, wasn't it? Andrea would glimpse Parker's unhappiness, see their broken family, and feel grateful for all that she had. Then she'd know, truly *know*, that money doesn't buy happiness.

Well, she did feel terrible, so there. She was swollen with shame, her upper lip damp as though it was actually oozing out of her. And yet, at the edges of all her sorrow and remorse, a piece of Andrea rankled irritably against the demands Parker made on her pity. And she was obscurely jealous, too, as if with those pills Parker had established once again her supremacy over Andrea.

Andrea accepted another glass of wine.

• • •

Parker and Matty were talking to each other, Matty leaning forward in that posture that meant he had designs on her. Of course, he did. But Andrea didn't care about Matty just now.

130 "Parker," she said, generous, repentant. She composed her face into a semblance of sobriety, because what she had to say was important.

Their smiles vanished.

"Oh, *what* now?" asked Matty.

"I was talking to your step-mother —"

"She's not my step-mother," Parker said warily.

135 "Your dad's girlfriend." Andrea laid a hand on Parker's bare arm. She could feel the tiny golden hairs, the warmth of her skin, and affection welled in her. "She told me that you tried to kill yourself. And I just wanted to say I'm really, really, really sorry." Why couldn't she get the tone right? She really was sorry. "And I really, really, really hope you don't."

Parker flushed so red that her eyelids pinkened, too, and Andrea wondered with a bleak horror if the girl was going to cry, here in front of everyone.

"You hope I don't kill myself? Well then, in that case." Parker's eyes were radiant with anger. "Why are you even *here*? You think I don't notice you hate me?"

Matty grabbed the edge of Andrea's sleeve. "I think it's time for us to leave."

"Parker, I'm just trying to be nice."

140 "Andrea." Matty put his arm around her, just as she'd always hoped he would. "Come on." Andrea shook him off.

Mixed Blueberries, Joe Brainard (American, Salem, Arkansas 1942–1994 New York), 1972, Cut and pasted paper, graphite, colored pencils, watercolor, and gouache on paper, 10 5/8 × 13 3/4 in. (27 × 34.9 cm), The Metropolitan Museum of Art, Gift of Stanley Posthorn, in memory of the artist, 1997 (1997.404.1) © Estate of Joe Brainard. Photo © The Metropolitan Museum of Art/Image Source: Art Resource

This piece, entitled *Mixed Blueberries*, was completed by artist Joe Brainard in 1972. **What do these blueberries in a sardine tin suggest to you? How might this image embody Andrea's experience of blueberry picking at the end of "Jubilee"?**

And then the door of the taco truck swung open and her father descended the steps. He was wiping his hands on a towel, and his gaze snagged on Andrea. Suddenly a terrible thought occurred to her, that if Parker chose, she could have her father fired, all because Andrea came here today. Her blood became very still and very cold.

He came toward them, smiling quizzically, head tilted. Andrea grinned, bright and tense, waved. She held the grin, looking, no doubt, maniacal, but she didn't know what else to do.

"I'm sorry," she said to Parker. "I'm sorry, I'm sorry. This had nothing to do with my dad. He didn't even know I was coming."

Parker looked slapped. "You think I'd get him fired because of *you*? Fuck you, Andrea. I *like* your dad."

145 "I'm sorry —"

"Just shut *up*, Andrea." Matty's tone was urgent, and it was this urgency, and the look of embarrassment on his face, that frightened Andrea, made her understand how far she'd gone.

Andrea turned on Matty. "Where do *you* get off? *You* said Parker looked easy."

Her father sped up. He gripped Matty by the shoulder. "Is he bothering you?" he asked Parker.

Matty widened his soft eyes in surprise.

"God, no," said Parker.

Salvador searched Andrea's face. "Is everything okay, *mija*?"[1]

Andrea averted her eyes from her father's urgent face in time to see Parker and Matty exchange a look, hold each other's gaze. She saw them decide among themselves to protect her.

Parker smiled resolutely. "Everything's fine, Salvador. Your tacos are amazing."

Her father wouldn't be so easily reassured, Andrea knew, but he also wouldn't argue with Parker. But Andrea didn't stay to find out. She turned and ran into the apple trees. She slowed when she could no longer hear the sounds of the party, then walked deeper down the rows. The branches were covered in tight little green apples, hard and fierce. She ripped one off and threw it against the trunk, missed. It landed dully in the mulch.

God, how she'd wanted to get together with Parker for that lunch last summer. How she'd wanted to sit in that kitchen, eating vanilla ice cream topped with blueberries from those fragile green bowls. Feet swinging from the bar stools, she and Parker would marvel at how much they had in common. How funny they hadn't been closer all these years! Of course, when the invitation never came, Andrea hadn't been a bit surprised. She imagined how it went: William Lowell suggesting it and Parker Lowell dismissing the suggestion, horrified by the prospect of starting the school year saddled with Andrea.

"You are the leaders of tomorrow," the university president had told them in September at their freshman convocation. Even then Andrea had known that he hadn't meant her. "Look around you. Look at yourself. Every one of you has the unique talents that this world is waiting for." Probably he even believed it. But Andrea knew that whatever she was granted in life would be granted as a result of her wheedling. She'd forever be checking ethnicity boxes, emphasizing her parents' work: farm laborer, housekeeping. Trying to prove that she was smart enough, committed enough, and pleasant enough to be granted a trial period in their world. Yes, she'd make a success of herself, more or less, but her entire life she'd be gushing about gratitude and writing thank you notes to alumni and rich benefactors and to the Lowells.

• • •

Mr. Lowell hadn't actually yelled at her that day she was nine. He'd called out, "Stop, stop, stop, stop!" as he jogged down the row toward her. Then he'd slowed and said more gently as if approaching an escaped and not entirely tamed pet, "Hi there, honey." He'd taken the scratched five-gallon bucket from her hands and thanked her for help and he gave her the cold coke from his lunch cooler, settled her on the tailgate of his truck until her father emerged from the trees. Before that, though, before Mr. Lowell found her, Andrea had been alone in the row of Jubilee blueberries, the leaves rustling and shining over her head.

Seek, pluck, seek pluck. The percussion of the berries as they dropped into the bucket. Andrea's head was pleasantly hot and fuzzy with the soft sense of calm and focus, the absorption in her task. The firm warm berries between her thumb and forefinger, the sweet burst on her tongue, the scent of the sun and soil and leaves.

Jubilee, she said, the word as mild and sweet as the blueberries themselves. Jubilee, jubilee, jubilee. Through the rows, she could hear the

[1] Spanish for "my daughter," and a term of endearment. — Eds.

indistinct voices of the other pickers and the burble of the irrigation system.

160 She was covering the entire bottom of the bucket, a single even layer, and then she'd form the next layer and the next until the entire bucket was filled with that fragrance and sweetness and heft. She forgot there were other people around, and as the leaves rustled and the light scattered over her, she forgot herself, too. ■

2013

Understanding and Interpreting

1. Why do you think Andrea decided to attend the party at the Lowells? Consider what you thought when you first started reading the story and your interpretation of the final scene.
2. How would you characterize the relationship between the Lowells and Salvador, Andrea's father? Is your view the same as Andrea's? Explain.
3. How does "Jubilee" establish and emphasize the social delineations among the characters? Are there times that you see them differently from the way Andrea sees them? Describe the differences if you see any, or explain Andrea's perspective if you do not.
4. Keep track of the times Andrea changes her mind in "Jubilee." How do those changes reveal and develop her character?
5. What does Andrea expect from Matty? Does he live up to her expectations? Why or why not?
6. In paragraph 96, the narrator asks "Where did this anger come from?" Do you think it's a question Andrea asks herself, or is it a question directed at the reader? What do you think the answer is?
7. What do Andrea and Parker have in common? What separates them? Are the gulfs between them uncrossable? Explain your answer.
8. What function does "the widow" serve in the story? How do the different characters perceive her?
9. Certainly, one theme of this story is alienation. What are the causes of Andrea's alienation? Do you think they are justified or of her own making? Explain.

Analyzing Language, Style, and Structure

1. **Vocabulary in Context.** What is the meaning of the work "patina" in paragraph 42? Be sure to consider its literal meaning — the word "oxidation" provides a hint — as well as how Andrea applies it to Parker. Consider also the way "patina" is used in relation to wealth.
2. "Jubilee" takes place in one setting and over a fairly short period of time. What techniques does Kirstin Valdez Quade use to fill in the necessary background of Andrea's life and the relationships between her family and the Lowells?
3. This story has a third-person narrator but it spends a lot of time in Andrea's head. This type of narration — a modernist technique first used by Henry James — is called either "central consciousness" or "limited point of view." What is the central consciousness of "Jubilee"? To whom is the point of view limited? What is the effect of these techniques?
4. How does Quade use sensory imagery to create the atmosphere of the party? Look especially at paragraphs 43–51. How does Andrea's father's taco truck fit in here? What social mistake does Andrea make that breaks the mood? What is the effect of this shift?
5. In this story "jubilee" is a type of blueberry, but the word has multiple meanings and connotations — and, of course, it's the title. What different connotations does the word carry

throughout the story, and how do they add levels of meaning to the story? Are any of the meanings symbolic? Why do you think Quade chose this word as the title?

6. As the protagonist, Andrea is a dynamic character, but some of the secondary characters may — or may not — be more straightforward in what they represent. What ideas or values do you think Mr. Lowell, Parker Lowell, and Matty represent? What role do they play in developing the story's larger theme(s)? In what ways do each of these characters defy our expectations of them, and how do these actions complicate the narrative?
7. Consider the final scene of the story in paragraphs 157–160. What does it mean that Andrea has misremembered Mr. Lowell's treatment of her when she was a child? What larger meaning or theme does the "true" memory reveal?

Topics for Composing

1. AP® FRQ **Prose Fiction Analysis.** The following question refers to paragraphs 156–160 of Kirstin Valdez Quade's "Jubilee," published in 2013. In this passage, the narrator recounts a childhood memory of the protagonist. Read the passage carefully. Then, in a well-written essay, analyze how Quade uses literary elements and techniques to convey the complex perspective of the narrator on the relationship between her family and her father's employer.
2. AP® FRQ **Literary Argument.** Many works of literature examine two sides of a figurative coin. In "Jubilee," Andrea's perspective on her relationship to the Lowell family changes significantly. In a well-written essay, analyze how Andrea's shift in perception contributes to an interpretation of the work as a whole. Do not merely summarize the plot.
3. **AP® Literary Argumentation.** Mary Ann Hornuth, writing in the literary journal *Jaggery*, noted that in "Jubilee," Quade "questions the truth of . . . a uniquely American theme — that of democracy and self-determination, of inventing one's destiny in a society founded on the fruit of individual effort." Through the character of Andrea, Quade exposes readers' "near-universal hankering to share a seat with the blue-bloods," and an equally prevalent "instinct that it is more elegant or desirable... to be born into privilege." Do you agree that Andrea's story questions the truth of this "uniquely American theme"? Do you agree that the desire to share a seat with the "blue-bloods" is Andrea's heart's desire? Use evidence from the text to support your argument.
4. **AP® Literary Argumentation.** Many works of literature — and, indeed, film and television — use a social gathering as a setting against which to project conflict(s) central to the plot and characters. Such scenes may reveal the values of the characters and the society in which they live. Discuss the contribution the party setting of "Jubilee" makes to the meaning of the work as a whole.
5. **AP® Literary Argumentation.** What does "Jubilee" say about the American Dream? How does Andrea's identity as the daughter of Mexican immigrants inform her attitude toward her achievements? Use evidence from the story to support your response.
6. **Creative Writing.** Retell this story from the point of view of one of the other characters. You might even tell it from the point of view of one of the other people at the party who is not named as a character in the story. How does your chosen character perceive the events that take place? How do they view Andrea?
7. **Connections.** How is "Jubilee" a story of a friendship — or possible friendship — between two women? Compare it to other works on the subject, such as Elena Ferrante's *My Brilliant Friend* and its sequels or the films *Ghost World* and *Booksmart*.

They flee from me

Sir Thomas Wyatt

Artokoloro/Alamy

Sir Thomas Wyatt (1503–1542) was educated privately before attending St. John's College, Cambridge, where he excelled in Greek and Latin verse but did not earn a degree. He served as a courtier to King Henry VIII (r. 1509–1547), eventually being named an ambassador. Wyatt invented the English sonnet, later imitated by William Shakespeare and countless other poets. Published posthumously, *Songes and Sonnettes* (1557) greatly influenced sixteenth- and seventeenth-century writers.

KEY CONTEXT "They flee from me" is a subtle, cynical examination of how relationships between lovers change; it has been interpreted by some scholars as an allegory for political shifts of power as well. The following poem is a sonnet that consists of three quatrains and a couplet at the end, rhyming *abab*, *cdcd*, *efef*, *gg*. The third quatrain often provides the volta, in which the speaker typically shifts perspective and sometimes closes with a witty remark.

They flee from me, that sometime did me seek,
With naked foot stalking in my chamber.
I have seen them, gentle, tame, and meek,
That now are wild, and do not remember
That sometime they put themselves in danger
To take bread at my hand; and now they range,
Busily seeking with a continual change.

Thankèd be fortune it hath been otherwise,
Twenty times better; but once in special,
In thin array, after a pleasant guise,
When her loose gown from her shoulders did fall,
And she me caught in her arms long and small,
Therewithall[1] sweetly did me kiss
And softly said, "Dear heart, how like you this?"

It was no dream, I lay broad waking.
But all is turned, thorough[2] my gentleness,
Into a strange fashion of forsaking;
And I have leave to go, of[3] her goodness,

[1] With all that. — Eds.
[2] Through. — Eds.
[3] Out of (thanks to). — Eds.

And she also to use newfangleness.[4]
But since that I so kindly[5] am served,
I fain[6] would know what she hath deserved. ■

1557

---

[4] Fondness for new things, fickleness. — Eds.
[5] Graciously (ironic), also naturally or fittingly. — Eds.
[6] Gladly. — Eds.

Understanding and Interpreting

1. **AP® Narration.** What is the situation the speaker describes in the first stanza? What ambiguity is there in what is being described, particularly when it comes to who "they" (l. 1) might be?
2. **AP® Narration.** What do you think is meant by "continual change" (l. 7)?
3. **AP® Character and Narration.** What seems to have changed in the balance of power between the speaker and the woman in the second stanza?
4. **AP® Setting.** Were you surprised at the opening lines of the third stanza: "It was no dream"? What about the second stanza did or did not seem dream-like? Explain.
5. **AP® Narration.** How might the poem have held a different meaning for you if the title had been "She flees from me"? How does the title "They flee from me" complicate or expand your understanding of the speaker's perspective on the subject of the poem?
6. **AP® Character and Narration.** Although the language of the poem reminds us that it is from another era, how do the ideas and perspective in the poem have a contemporary relevance?

Analyzing Language, Style, and Structure

1. **Vocabulary in Context.** In the third stanza, the speaker says: "I have leave to go, of her goodness, / And she also, to use newfangleness." Even today, the term "newfangled" has an edge to it, meaning not just something new, but something desired for the sake of novelty and, thus, unnecessary. Why is this word appropriate for Wyatt's purposes in "They flee from me"?
2. **AP® Character, Structure, and Narration.** In the first stanza, how does the diction convey the speaker's attitude toward women? Consider "stalking," "gentle, tame, and meek," and "range" in your response.
3. **AP® Character, Structure, and Narration.** How do the specific details and the language itself in the second stanza convey the intensity of the speaker's experience?
4. **AP® Narration and Figurative Language.** In line 14, a woman addresses the speaker as "[d]ear heart." Keeping in mind that a hart is a male red deer often hunted in Sir Thomas Wyatt's time, how could this line be interpreted as more than a simple endearment? Have the roles of hunter and hunted been reversed?
5. **AP® Structure.** Each stanza in the poem ends with a rhymed couplet. Explain how each couplet encapsulates the previous lines in the stanza.
6. **AP® Setting and Structure.** What role do the shifts in time between past and present contribute to the poem's structure and meaning?
7. **AP® Structure and Figurative Language.** Wyatt plays with multiple meanings and associations of words throughout the poem, such as "stalking" (l. 2), "guise" (l. 10), and "fashion" (l. 17). How does the complexity of such choices in language contribute to the poem's meaning? Discuss at least two specific examples in your response.

8. **AP® Structure and Narration.** How do you interpret the tone of the final two lines of the poem? Is that tone a shift from earlier on, or is it consistent with the tone of the opening stanza? Explain.

Topics for Composing

1. **AP® FRQ Poetry Analysis.** In Sir Thomas Wyatt's "They flee from me," published in 1557, the speaker reflects on the power dynamics in his relationships with women. Read the poem carefully. Then, in a well-written essay, analyze how Wyatt uses literary elements and techniques to convey the speaker's complex perspective on the relationship between love and power.
2. **AP® Literary Argumentation.** At the time Wyatt wrote this poem, women lacked most of the legal and social rights that we now practically take for granted. How does the figurative language and imagery in this poem depict the imbalance of power between men and women during this era?
3. **Research.** Both a politician and a poet, Wyatt was part of the court of King Henry VIII. Although evidence is inconclusive, there is much speculation that he was involved with Anne Boleyn before she became the second wife of Henry VIII. Research what is known and speculated about the public and private life of Sir Thomas Wyatt and consider how the court intrigue of the Tudor era might have influenced his poetry, including "They flee from me." How might the poem be read through a political lens that accounts for the events of Wyatt's time?
4. **Connections.** In *The Paris Review*, Damion Searls asserted that "The best I-just-got-dumped pop song ever. . . is six hundred years old: Sir Tom's . . . 'They Flee from Me.'" Do you agree with Searls's assessment of the poem as an "I-just-got-dumped pop song"? Why, so many centuries later, are people still talking about it?
5. **Speaking and Listening.** Scholarship suggests that "They flee from me" might have been set to musical accompaniment and presented as a song in its day. Working in pairs or small groups, identify or compose some music that suggests an interpretation of this poem. Present your choice to the class and lead a discussion of how the music reflects Wyatt's meaning.
6. **Creative Writing.** Write a poem with the woman in the poem as the speaker. Her perspective should in some way(s) shed new light on the situation that Wyatt's speaker describes. Use the same structure if it works for this shift in viewpoint, but choose a different type of sonnet or altogether different structure if it fits your purpose.

Leave me, O Love, which reachest but to dust

Sir Philip Sidney

Philip Sidney, 1754/UNIVERSAL IMAGES GROUP/Bridgeman Images

"The poet-soldier" Sir Philip Sidney (1554–1586) was born in Kent, England. Educated at Christ Church College, Oxford, he eventually served as a diplomat for Queen Elizabeth I (r. 1558–1603). He withdrew from the royal court in 1580 and wrote *Astrophel and Stella* (c. 1590), a cycle of 108 sonnets and 11 songs; *The Countess of Pembroke's Arcadia* (c. 1593), which was unfinished at his death; *The Defence of Poesie* (c. 1595), and *Certain Sonnets* (c. 1598) — all of which were published posthumously. "Leave me, O Love, which reachest but to dust" is from *Certain Sonnets* (c. 1598).

KEY CONTEXT The following poem is a sonnet that consists of three quatrains and a couplet at the end, rhyming *abab*, *cdcd*, *efef*, *gg*. The third quatrain often provides the volta, in which the speaker typically shifts perspective and sometimes closes with a witty remark.

Leave me, O Love which reachest but to dust;
And thou, my mind, aspire to higher things;
Grow rich in that which never taketh rust,
Whatever fades but fading pleasure brings.
Draw in thy beams, and humble all thy might
To that sweet yoke where lasting freedoms be;
Which breaks the clouds and opens forth the light,
That doth both shine and give us sight to see.
O take fast hold; let that light be thy guide
In this small course which birth draws out to death,
And think how evil becometh him to slide,
Who seeketh heav'n, and comes of heav'nly breath.
  Then farewell, world; thy uttermost I see;
  Eternal Love, maintain thy life in me. ■

c. 1598

Understanding and Interpreting

1. **AP® Character and Narration.** What kind of love does the speaker wish to leave behind? (l. 1)? What kind does he wish to experience (l. 14)?
2. **AP® Structure and Narration.** Summarize each quatrain. How do you interpret each on its own? What message do they convey together?
3. **AP® Narration.** Explain the admonition, "And thou, my mind, aspire to higher things" (l. 2). What does Sir Philip Sidney mean by "higher things"?
4. **AP® Structure and Figurative Language.** How do you interpret the paradox, or apparent contradiction, of "Draw in thy beams, and humble all thy might / To that sweet yoke where lasting freedoms be" (ll. 5–6)? How is it possible to be free while wearing a yoke?
5. **AP® Character and Narration.** Based on your reading of the sonnet, what kind of relationship do you think the speaker of the poem values most? To whom or what does he want to devote himself? Explain, using evidence from the poem to support your response.

Analyzing Language, Style, and Structure

1. **Vocabulary in Context.** In line 2, the speaker shares that he wishes for his mind to "aspire to higher things." Consider both your understanding of what "aspire" means as well as other words that share its root "spir," such as "inspire." What essences do these words have in common, and how does the meaning of their root support Sidney's use of "aspire" in this instance?
2. **AP® Narration and Figurative Language.** In his sonnet, Sir Philip Sidney uses apostrophe, addressing "Love" directly in the first line, "thou, my mind" in the second line, and "Eternal Love" in the last line. What effect do these direct addresses have on your understanding of the poem?

3. **AP® Structure and Narration.** How does the structure of the poem reinforce the speaker's message? What resolution to the conflicts the speaker experiences earlier in the poem does the final couplet offer?
4. **AP® Figurative Language.** How does Sidney use ideas and imagery to contrast the experiences he's had with love and those he wishes to have? Consider the contradictory nature of "dust" (l. 1) and "higher things" (l. 2); "that which never taketh rust" (l. 3) and "Whatever fades" (l. 4); "the clouds" and "the light" (l. 7), and so on.

Topics for Composing

1. **AP® FRQ Poetry Analysis.** In Sir Philip Sidney's "Leave me, O Love, which reachest but to dust," published c. 1598, the speaker contemplates contrasting forms of love. Read the poem carefully. Then, in a well-written essay, analyze how Sidney uses literary elements and techniques to develop his appreciation for one form of love over the other.
2. **AP® Literary Argumentation**. In his book *The Defence of Poesie* (c. 1595), Sidney argues that poetry represents truth more honestly than does history or science: "Now for the poet, he nothing affirmeth, and therefore never lieth." How does this poem embody this statement? Explain, using evidence from the poem to support your responses.
3. **Creative Writing.** Writer John Steinbeck included in his book *Travels with Charley* the sentiment, "What good is the warmth of summer, without the cold of winter to give it sweetness." Write a poem in which you address the reality Sir Philip Sidney exposes in his poem as well as Steinbeck's philosophy. You may wish to stick to Sidney's choice of form or branch out, depending on what your speaker has to say.
4. **Speaking and Listening**. The experience of love "fading" isn't limited to romantic relationships. Working with a partner or in a small group, discuss how love for something such as a new car you've just begun driving, a sport you've tried for the first time, or a favorite song can change over time or even disappear. Discuss why this change occurs and whether there's any way to prevent it from happening.
5. **Research**. Using an apostrophe, Sir Philip Sidney references "Eternal Love" in the final line of his poem to allude to the love he feels for and from God. Research religious texts that discuss the nature of God's love. What similarities are there across religions to support the spiritual beliefs Sidney's speaker reveals in this poem?

A Valediction: Forbidding Mourning

John Donne

John Donne (1572–1631) was born in London to a prosperous family. He was educated by Jesuits and attended both Oxford and Cambridge, where he studied law. His satires (written 1593–1595) and the poems later collected as *Songs and Sonnets* reflect life among the barristers. Donne was ordained in the Church of England in 1615 and became a renowned preacher. Donne's poems were not collected in his lifetime; eventually published as *Poems* in 1633, they met with immediate acclaim.

IanDagnall Computing/Alamy

KEY CONTEXT Donne wrote "A Valediction: Forbidding Mourning" to his pregnant wife, Anne, before leaving England on a trip to Europe in 1611 or 1612. A defining feature of Donne's poetry is the presence of a *conceit*, an unusual or improbable extended metaphor, which is used to develop an argument and convey meaning.

As virtuous men pass mildly 'away,
And whisper to their souls to go,
Whilst some of their sad friends do say,
The breath goes now, and some say, no:

So let us melt, and make no noise,
No tear-floods, nor sigh-tempests move.
'Twere profanation of our joys
To tell the laity[1] our love

Moving of th' earth brings harms and fears,
Men reckon what it did and meant,
But trepidation of the spheres,
Though greater far, is innocent.

Dull sublunary[2] lovers' love
(Whose soul is sense) cannot admit
Absence, because it doth remove
Those things which elemented it.

But we by a love, so much refined,
That ourselves know not what it is,
Inter-assured of the mind,
Care less, eyes, lips, and hands to miss.

Our two souls therefore, which are one,
Though I must go, endure not yet
A breach, but an expansion,
Like gold to aery thinness beat.

If they be two, they are two so
As stiff twin compasses are two,
Thy soul the fixed foot, makes no show
To move, but doth, if the other do.

And though it in the centre sit,
Yet when the other far doth roam,
It leans, and hearkens after it,
And grows erect, as that comes home.

---

[1] Ordinary people. — Eds.

[2] Relating to earthly concerns (as opposed to higher-minded, spiritual ones). — Eds.

Such wilt thou be to me, who must
    Like th' other foot, obliquely run.
Thy firmness makes my circle just,
    And makes me end, where I begun. ■

c. 1611

Understanding and Interpreting

1. **AP® Narration.** The first stanza describes two different reactions to the death of a friend. What are the two reactions? What determines how people respond to the passing of "virtuous men" (l. 1)?
2. **AP® Structure.** How are the first two stanzas related? As part of your response, describe the relationship between the colon in line 4 and the beginning of line 5.
3. **AP® Character and Narration.** In poetry, "tear-floods" and "sigh-tempests" (l. 6) are conventionally associated with lovers. Why does the speaker argue against these reactions in the second stanza?
4. **AP® Structure and Narration.** To what natural occurrences do the "[m]oving of th' earth" (l. 9) and the "trepidation of the spheres" (l. 11) refer? How do people's reactions to each event differ? How does the third stanza relate to the rest of the poem?
5. **AP® Character and Narration.** How does the phrase "[w]hose soul is sense" (l. 14) distance the speaker and his beloved from other lovers? How does this difference enhance the speaker's message to her?
6. **AP® Character and Narration.** In lines 13–20, the speaker suggests their love is more "refined" than those of "[d]ull sublunary lovers." Why does he suggest these "dull" lovers are unable to bear being apart? How would you describe his attitude in these two stanzas?
7. **AP® Character and Narration.** What is the antecedent, or noun that is replaced by a pronoun, for the word "they" in line 25? How would you paraphrase this stanza?
8. **AP® Structure and Narration.** How does the poem's title affect your understanding of the poem? How do certain details from the poem relate directly to the title?

Analyzing Language, Style, and Structure

1. **Vocabulary in Context.** What is the meaning of the word "profanation" (l. 7)? In what contexts is this word normally used? How does it characterize the speaker's opinion of his relationship?
2. **AP® Structure and Narration.** The poem opens with a description of how "virtuous men" die (ll. 1–4). What does this stanza suggest about how these men part from their lives? How does that description set the tone for a poem about how the speaker believes he and his beloved should face parting from each other?
3. **AP® Figurative Language.** In line 6, the speaker suggests to his beloved that they not resort to "tear-floods" or "sigh-tempests" as they part. What is the effect of the references to storms in this context?

4. **AP® Structure.** What is the relationship between the words "profanation" (1. 7) and "laity" (1. 8)? How does the combination of this word choice relate to the first sentence of the second stanza?
5. **AP® Structure and Narration.** How does the fifth stanza function as a shift? Where, specifically, does the shift occur, and what is the nature of the shift?
6. **AP® Figurative Language.** The seventh stanza introduces the conceit, a principal feature of metaphysical poetry. What is the conceit, and what is the argument conveyed by it? How far does the conceit extend within the poem?
7. **AP® Figurative Language.** Donne's speaker uses a simile in line 24 to explain that in their parting, their connected souls will be "[l]ike gold to aery thinness beat." What is expressed about their parting in this comparison? How does the simile reinforce the argument he is making?
8. **AP® Narration and Figurative Language.** The "circle" (l. 35) drawn as part of the conceit serves as a symbol for the couple's relationship. What does this image suggest about them as a couple? What is needed for the speaker's beloved to form this circle?
9. **AP® Structure and Narration.** How does Donne use the structure of his poem to build his argument? Consider the consistent form of the stanzas; the conjunctions at the beginning of some stanzas, such as "So" (l. 5), "But" (l. 17), and "And" (l. 29); and how he organizes the major comparisons throughout the poem. How do they build on each other in a logical order?

Topics for Composing

1. **AP® FRQ Poetry Analysis.** In John Donne's "A Valediction: Forbidding Mourning," written circa 1611, the speaker addresses his beloved before departing on a trip. Read the poem carefully. Then, in a well-written essay, analyze how Donne uses literary elements and techniques to convey how the speaker thinks his beloved should react to his departure.
2. **AP® FRQ Poetry Analysis.** In John Donne's "A Valediction: Forbidding Mourning," written circa 1611, the speaker discusses how his relationship with his beloved differs from that of others. Read the poem carefully. Then, in a well-written essay, analyze how Donne uses literary elements and techniques to convey his complex perspective on what makes their relationship special.
3. **AP® Literary Argumentation.** John Donne biographer John Stubbs explains that during Donne's trip to France, which prompted the writing of "A Valediction: Forbidding Mourning," Donne suffered "from precisely the symptoms of loneliness and edginess" that this poem argues against. Write an essay in which you argue whether the speaker of the poem is genuine in what he tells his beloved or was solely trying to console her. Use evidence from the poem to support your response.
4. **Creative Writing.** Write a diary entry from the perspective of the beloved four weeks after the speaker has departed. Use details from the poem to show how they strengthen her resolve to maintain her composure or to show that his words fail to comfort her.
5. **Connections.** Look up some of the main features of metaphysical poetry. What are they, and how does Donne's "A Valediction: Forbidding Mourning" exemplify them?

A Valediction Forbidding Mourning

Bettmann/Getty Images

Adrienne Rich

Adrienne Rich (1929–2012) was born in Baltimore, Maryland, and received a BA in English from Radcliffe College (Harvard University). During her senior year at Radcliffe, her first collection of poems, *A Change of World* (1951), won the Yale Series of Younger Poets Award. She won the National Book Award in 1974 for *Diving into the Wreck: Poems 1971–1972.* Rather than accepting the award by herself, she was accompanied by the other nominated feminist poets, Audre Lorde and Alice Walker, and the three accepted the award on behalf of all women. When the National Endowment for the Arts granted her the National Medal of Arts in 1997, Rich turned down the award as a protest against social injustice.

My swirling wants. Your frozen lips.
The grammar turned and attacked me.
Themes, written under duress.
Emptiness of the notations.

They gave me a drug that slowed the healing of wounds.

I want you to see this before I leave:
the experience of repetition as death
the failure of criticism to locate the pain
the poster in the bus that said:
my bleeding is under control.

A red plant in a cemetery of plastic wreaths.

A last attempt: the language is a dialect called metaphor.
These images go unglossed: hair, glacier, flashlight.
When I think of a landscape I am thinking of a time.
When I talk of taking a trip I mean forever.
I could say: those mountains have a meaning
but further than that I could not say.

To do something very common, in my own way. ■

1970

Exploring the Text

1. **AP® Narration and Figurative Language.** What does the first stanza suggest about the speaker's experience with writing? Make note of Adrienne Rich's diction and the actions that are described. How would you characterize the tone of these lines?
2. **AP® Structure and Narration.** What is ironic about line 5, which states, "They gave me a drug that slowed the healing of wounds"? Who do you think "they" refers to? What does this line suggest about the speaker's experience?
3. **AP® Narration and Figurative Language.** In the third stanza, the speaker continues to describe her experience as a writer, using words such as "death" (l. 7), "pain" (l. 8), and "bleeding" (l. 10). What is the effect of using words that evoke physical experience to describe an intellectual pursuit? How might this reinforce the attitude she is expressing about her experience as a writer?
4. **AP® Structure and Figurative Language.** In line 11, Rich offers the image of "A red plant in a cemetery of plastic wreaths." How is the "red plant" a significant contrast to the "cemetery of plastic wreaths"? Within the context of the poem, what might each image represent?
5. **AP® Structure and Narration.** What is the speaker suggesting when she says, "When I think of a landscape I am thinking of a time. / When I talk of taking a trip I mean forever" (ll. 14–15)? How is the tone of this stanza different from the tone of the first stanza?
6. **AP® Structure and Narration.** What does the speaker seem to be declaring about her future in the last line of the poem? What is ironic about the speaker's use of the phrase "very common" to describe what she intends to do? If this is a poem about bidding farewell, what do you believe she is saying goodbye to?
7. **AP® Structure and Figurative Language.** Why do you believe Rich uses John Donne's title for her poem? How does this allusion to his poem impact your experience with and understanding of Rich's poem?
8. **AP® Literary Argumentation.** The *New York Times* has called Rich "a poet of towering reputation and towering rage" and deemed her "among the most influential writers of the feminist movement." Do you think that this poem conveys "towering rage"? In what way might this poem be read as a feminist one? Explain.

Making Connections

1. **AP® Character and Narration.** Compare and contrast the emotional state of the speakers in these two poems. How do John Donne and Adrienne Rich use diction and detail to characterize how their speakers feel? Aside from gender, how else are the speakers of these two poems different? What do they have in common?
2. **AP® Structure.** Consider the differences in the form that each poem takes. Donne uses quatrains with regular meter and rhyme, while Rich dispenses with formal pattern and rhyme, even setting single lines off as their own stanzas. How do these different formal choices impact your interpretation of these poems?
3. **AP® Narration and Figurative Language.** Compare and contrast the tone of each poem, considering how the imagery as a whole contributes to each.
4. **AP® Literary Argumentation.** Both poems deal with bidding farewell to someone or something. How does each poet use style elements to convey the attitudes each speaker expresses toward the idea of parting and separation?

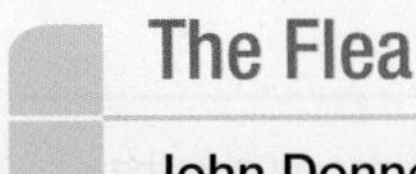

The Flea

John Donne

KEY CONTEXT Donne is generally regarded as the most important of the metaphysical poets — a loose confederation of artists who relied on wit and incongruous, often startling imagery (metaphysical conceits), as you will see in "The Flea."

Mark[1] but this flea, and mark in this
How little that which thou deny'st me is;
It sucked me first, and now sucks thee,
And in this flea our two bloods mingled be;
Thou know'st that this cannot be said
A sin, nor shame, nor loss of maidenhead,[2]
Yet this enjoys before it woo,
And pampered swells with one blood made of two,
And this, alas, is more than we would do.

Oh stay,[3] three lives in one flea spare,
Where we almost, yea more than, married are.
This flea is you and I, and this
Our marriage bed, and marriage temple is;
Though parents grudge, and you, we're met
And cloistered in these living walls of jet.
Though use[4] make you apt to kill me,
Let not to that, self-murder added be,
And sacrilege, three sins in killing three.

Cruel and sudden, hast thou since
Purpled thy nail in blood of innocence?
Wherein could this flea guilty be,
Except in that drop which it sucked from thee?
Yet thou triumph'st, and say'st that thou
Find'st not thyself, nor me, the weaker now;
'Tis true; then learn how false, fears be;
Just so much honor, when thou yield'st to me,
Will waste, as this flea's death took life from thee. ■

1633

---

[1] Notice. — Eds.
[2] Virginity. — Eds.
[3] Stop. — Eds.
[4] Habit. — Eds.

Understanding and Interpreting

1. **AP® Narration.** In order to make sense of "The Flea," you will need to consider not only the poem itself, but also that which may have prompted it. What has occurred before the first stanza?
2. **AP® Character and Narration.** What do the lines "Thou know'st that this cannot be said / A sin, nor shame, nor loss of maidenhead" (ll. 5–6) tell you about the woman in the poem? How do they portray her response to the speaker's behavior?
3. **AP® Narration.** What does the speaker mean when he says "three lives in one flea" (l. 10)? How does this approach serve the speaker's overall purpose?
4. **AP® Narration.** Paraphrase the final five lines of the poem. What is the speaker's argument? How convincing do you find it? Explain.

Analyzing Language, Style, and Structure

1. **Vocabulary in Context.** The word "cloistered" (l. 15) refers to the containment of the bloods found within the flea. What connotations does this word have — that is, in which contexts is this word typically used, and what thoughts and emotions come to mind when you hear it? How does this specific word choice contribute to the speaker's argument?
2. **AP® Structure and Figurative Language.** "The Flea" employs a conceit, an unusual extended metaphor, as the center of its argument in this seduction poem. What is the metaphor? How does John Donne develop it? How does it make his argument more convincing?
3. **AP® Structure and Narration.** Consider the three sets of indented lines. Taken together, what argument do they make? How does each set differ from the preceding lines in the stanza?
4. **AP® Narration and Figurative Language.** Which words and images constitute the religious imagery of the poem? Why does the speaker turn to religion to argue his point to his beloved?
5. **AP® Structure and Narration.** How would you describe the overall tone of this poem? Identify instances in which the tone shifts. What prompts these changes in the speaker's attitude?

Topics for Composing

1. **AP® FRQ** **Poetry Analysis.** In John Donne's "The Flea," published in 1633, the speaker attempts to assuage his beloved's fear in order to seduce her. Read the poem carefully. Then, in a well-written essay, analyze how Donne uses literary elements and techniques to convey the speaker's attitude toward his beloved.
2. **AP® FRQ** **Poetry Analysis.** In John Donne's "The Flea," published in 1633, the speaker makes several religious references in an attempt to convince his beloved to act on their attraction to each other. Read the poem carefully. Then, in a well-written essay, analyze how Donne uses literary elements and techniques to portray the speaker's complex perspective on the relationship between religious and worldly concerns.
3. **AP® Literary Argumentation.** John Donne biographer John Stubbs asserts that through "The Flea" John Donne suggests that "nothing is without consequence." Write an essay in which you develop a position on the extent to which Stubbs's observation aligns with your interpretation of Donne's message in "The Flea."
4. **Connections.** Metaphysical poets tend to develop their arguments through syllogisms. Research what this means in terms of the poetry they produce, and identify the syllogism woven through "The Flea."

To the Virgins, to Make Much of Time

Robert Herrick

Private Collection/Bridgeman Images

Robert Herrick (1591–1674) was one of six children born to a prosperous family in London. After his father's presumed suicide in 1592, he was separated from his mother and brought up in the Presbyterian household of his uncle. In 1623, he was ordained; and in 1640, *The severall Poems written by Master Robert Herrick* appeared. The bulk of his work was published in *His Noble Numbers* (1647) and *Hesperides; or, The Works Both Human and Divine of Robert Herrick, Esq.* (1648). The range of subject is broad; over twelve hundred short poems in many forms — derived from Roman and Greek poetry — give remarkable insight into Herrick's joyful interpretation of God's gifts.

KEY CONTEXT Like his contemporary Andrew Marvell (p. 421), Herrick was influenced by classical models. Unlike Marvell and the metaphysical poets, however, he adopted a simple style. Central to this poem and to much of his work are his religious faith and a celebration of the divine, though brief, gift of life.

Gather ye rose-buds while ye may,
   Old Time is still a-flying;
And this same flower that smiles today,
   Tomorrow will be dying.

The glorious lamp of heaven, the sun,
   The higher he's a-getting,
The sooner will his race be run,
   And nearer he's to setting.

That age is best which is the first,
   When youth and blood are warmer;
But being spent, the worse, and worst
   Times still succeed the former.

Then be not coy, but use your time,
   And while ye may, go marry;
For having lost but once your prime,
   You may for ever tarry.[1] ■

1648

[1] To delay or dawdle. — Eds.

Understanding and Interpreting

1. **AP® Structure and Narration.** How does the title of this poem by Robert Herrick predict its main idea(s)?
2. **AP® Narration.** What can you infer about the speaker's attitude toward aging from the following lines: "That age is best which is the first" (l. 9) and "and worst / Times still succeed the former" (ll. 11–12)? What is the meaning of "spent" (l. 11) in this context?
3. **AP® Character and Narration.** How would you characterize the speaker of the poem? Is the voice that of a kindly friend, a bossy know-it-all, a thoughtful adviser? Is the speaker even a man? What evidence in the poem supports your interpretation?
4. **AP® Narration.** What do you think is Herrick's main subject in this poem? Is it about life in general or marriage in particular? What does his speaker have to say about each? Explain.
5. **AP® Structure and Narration.** One way to read the poem is as a carefully supported and logical argument. What is the overall assertion that governs this argument? What is the line of reasoning that sustains it?

Analyzing Language, Style, and Structure

1. **Vocabulary in Context.** The final quatrain begins, "Then be not coy." What does "coy" mean, and what connotations does it carry? What is the difference in effect from saying something like "be not shy" or "do not pretend"?
2. **AP® Figurative Language.** The poem opens with the speaker urging virgins to "Gather ye rose-buds" (l. 1). What do the rosebuds symbolize? What is the urgency?
3. **AP® Figurative Language.** Much of the figurative language and imagery in this poem reflects the natural world, starting with the "rose-buds." What other examples do you find? What is the effect of these individually and collectively on the reader?
4. **AP® Structure and Narration.** Describe the rhyming pattern and rhythm of Herrick's poem. What effect do they produce, and how does that reflect the speaker's message?
5. **AP® Structure and Figurative Language.** In the second stanza, the speaker compares the course of a day to a race. How does this comparison relate to the speaker's point in the first stanza?
6. **AP® Figurative Language.** Cite at least three specific examples of personification in this poem. How do these affect your interpretation of the overall meaning of the poem? When taken together, what effect do these instances of personification have?
7. **AP® Character, Structure, and Narration.** What do the verbs in the first and fourth quatrains have in common? How do they characterize the speaker?

Topics for Composing

1. **AP® FRQ** **Poetry Analysis.** In Robert Herrick's "To the Virgins, to Make Much of Time," published in 1648, the speaker offers advice about the passage of time through a series of contrasts. Read the poem carefully. Then, in a well-written essay, analyze how Herrick uses literary elements and techniques to convey the importance of that awareness.
2. **AP® Literary Argumentation.** This poem, which has remained a popular one over the centuries, has been criticized in more contemporary times for the assumptions the speaker makes about both women and aging. Using evidence from the poem, analyze the speaker's attitude toward both of these things.
3. **Connections.** In the final stanza, the speaker offers instructions and a warning. Is his advice still relevant? How might you update or reply to his admonitions?

4. **Connections.** The *carpe diem*, or "seize the day," theme is popular in film. One of the most memorable examples is *The Dead Poet's Society*. Discuss how this theme is interpreted in this film or in a scene from another that you choose.
5. **Research.** Herrick was one of the Cavalier poets, often described as "gentlemen poets" because of their loyalty to the monarchy during the English Civil War (1642–1651). After conducting research into the Cavalier poets, discuss how their interests and style are reflected in "To the Virgins, to Make Much of Time."
6. **Speaking and Listening.** Develop a dialogue between the speaker of the poem and someone for whom it is written. Perform the poem for the class with the lines as Herrick has written them, but with interruptions or asides by someone who doesn't buy the argument. Whether you choose to use gentle humor or biting satire, be prepared to discuss your interpretation.
7. **Multimodal.** Herrick's poem is often explained as a potential song. Imagine that it is — and develop a music video with it as background.

To My Dear and Loving Husband

Anne Bradstreet

Lee Beel/Alamy

In 1630, Anne Bradstreet (1612/13–1678) and her husband, Simon, the son of a nonconformist minister, sailed to Massachusetts with Anne's parents on the *Arabella*, the flagship of the Massachusetts Bay Company. With *The Tenth Muse Lately Sprung Up in America* (1650) — published in England, possibly without her knowledge — she became the first female poet in America. Bradstreet's remarkable poetry consists of thirty-five short reflective poems, explicit in their description of familial and marital love.

KEY CONTEXT The Puritan community disdained and even punished female intellectual ambition; nevertheless Anne Bradstreet, whose husband and father both served as governors of the Massachusetts Bay Colony, was a respected published poet.

If ever two were one, then surely we.
If ever man were loved by wife, then thee.
If ever wife was happy in a man,
Compare with me, ye women, if you can.
I prize thy love more than whole mines of gold,
Or all the riches that the East doth hold.
My love is such that rivers cannot quench,
Nor ought[1] but love from thee give recompense.
Thy love is such I can no way repay;
The heavens reward thee manifold, I pray.
Then while we live, in love let's so persever,
That when we live no more, we may live ever. ■

1678

[1] Archaic spelling of the word "aught," which means "anything." — Eds.

Understanding and Interpreting

1. **AP® Narration.** To whom is this poem addressed, besides the speaker's husband, likely Simon Bradstreet, Anne Bradstreet's husband?
2. **AP® Character, Setting, and Narration.** How does this love poem conform to the religious standards of Puritan New England? Consider how the speaker juxtaposes the pleasures of this world with her husband and the promise of heaven to come.
3. **AP® Narration.** What, aside from the title, suggests this is a poem about marriage?
4. **AP® Narration.** What does the last line — "when we live no more, we may live ever" — mean?
5. **AP® Narration.** In what ways might this poem be read as one about religion rather than marriage? Explain your answer.

Analyzing Language, Style, and Structure

1. **Vocabulary in Context.** What is the meaning of the word "persever" in line 11? Why do you think it is important to the poem's resolution?
2. **AP® Figurative Language.** How would you characterize the imagery in "To My Dear and Loving Husband"? What mood does it create?
3. **AP® Structure and Figurative Language.** The poem's first three lines begin with "If ever." This repetition, also called anaphora, has, of course, the effect of emphasis, but what else does it do? Consider the speaker's purpose in your response.
4. **AP® Structure and Narration.** Why do you think the word "ever" appears so often in the poem? What does it reveal about the speaker's perspective?
5. **AP® Structure and Narration.** How does Bradstreet use those first three lines to set up a logic problem? What do those lines tell us about the speaker?
6. **AP® Structure and Figurative Language.** Why might Bradstreet have used the language of money so often in "To My Dear and Loving Husband"? What effect does it have on her public proclamation of love? What does it say privately?
7. **AP® Structure and Narration.** What is the function of each of the three quatrains that make up this poem? How do they reflect the speaker's overall message?
8. **AP® Structure.** Although "To My Dear and Loving Husband" is twelve lines rather than fourteen, it reads like a sonnet and is often called a sonnet. What qualities make it sonnet-like? Why is that form particularly suitable for a poem on this particular subject?

Topics for Composing

1. **AP® FRQ Poetry Analysis.** In Anne Bradstreet's "To My Dear and Loving Husband," published in 1678, the speaker portrays romantic love in a Puritan setting. Read the poem carefully. Then, in a well-written essay, analyze how Bradstreet uses literary elements and techniques to develop a definition of love that conveys the speaker's complex perspective on its place within her specific religious and cultural context.
2. **AP® Literary Argumentation.** In his essay "Walking," Henry David Thoreau offers the following assessment of literature: "In literature it is only the wild that attracts us. Dullness is but another name for tameness. It is the uncivilized free and wild thinking . . . that delights us." Write an essay in which you explain what constitutes the "uncivilized free and wild thinking" of "To My Dear and Loving Husband" and how that thinking is central to the value of the poem. Support your ideas with specific evidence from the poem.

3. **AP® Literary Argumentation.** Bradstreet scholar Robert D. Richardson Jr. writes: "The union of the lovers in eternity is the outcome of their earthly love. . . . As the poem expresses it, the transition from this world to the next involves not renunciation, not a change even, but an expansion." What evidence does the poem provide for expansion rather than renunciation? Do you find it convincing? Explain why or why not.
4. **Research.** About fifteen years before Anne Bradstreet's work was published, Anne Hutchinson was banished from the Massachusetts Bay Colony for her outspokenness and popularity as a Puritan leader and intellectual. Anne Bradstreet's husband, Simon, was a prosecutor in the hearing. Emily Warn, writing on poetryfoundation.org, asks why Anne Hutchinson was punished for "being outspoken about religion and politics, while Anne Bradstreet became a cultural icon." Read about the work of both women and try to answer that question.
5. **Creative Writing.** Write a modern version of "To My Dear and Loving Husband" substituting for "husband" whomever it is you love.

My Husband

Rebecca Hazelton

Courtesy of Rebecca Hazelton

Rebecca Hazelton (b. 1978) is an award-winning poet, editor, and critic. After attending Davidson College, Hazelton went on to earn an MFA from the University of Notre Dame and a PhD from Florida State University. Her book of poetry *Vow* (2013) won the Cleveland State Poetry Center Open Competition Prize. She is the author of three other full-length books of poetry, *Gloss* (2019), *Bad Star* (2013), and *Fair Copy* (2012). She has taught at Beloit College and Oklahoma State University.

My husband in the house.
          My husband on the lawn,
pushing the mower, 4th of July, the way
          my husband's sweat wends like Crown Royale
to the waistband
of his shorts,
          the slow motion shake of the head the water
running down his chest,
          all of this lit like a Poison[1] video:
Cherry Pie[2] his cutoffs his blond hair his air guitar crescendo.

[1] An American rock band that was particularly popular from the mid-1980s to the mid-1990s. — Eds.

[2] A popular song by the rock band Warrant, recorded in 1990. The music video includes a blonde woman in cutoffs playing the air guitar. It was banned from a Canadian TV network for being "offensively sexist." — Eds.

My husband
at the PTA meeting.
My husband warming milk
at 3 a.m. while I sleep.
My husband washing the white Corvette the bare chest and the soap,
the objectification of my husband
by the pram pushers
and mailman.
My husband at Home Depot asking
where the bolts are,
the nuts, the screws,
my god, it's filthy
my husband reading from the news,
my husband cooking French toast, Belgian waffles,
my husband for all
nationalities.
My husband with a scotch, my husband
with his shoes off,
his slippers on, my husband's golden
leg hairs in the glow of a reading lamp.
My husband bearded, my husband shaved, the way my husband
taps out the razor, the small hairs
in the sink,
my husband with tweezers
to my foot,
to the splinter I carried
for years,
my husband chiding me
for waiting
to remove what pained me,
my husband brandishing aloft
the sliver to the light, and laughing. ■

2015

Exploring the Text

1. **AP® Character, Setting, and Narration.** The poem opens with a long, detailed description of the speaker's husband mowing the lawn, "all of this lit like a Poison video" (l. 9). What aspects of "My Husband" are like a music video? Consider film techniques such as framing, close-ups, and lighting. How do those details help Rebecca Hazelton paint a picture of her feelings about her husband?
2. **AP® Character, Narration, and Figurative Language.** What might the "sliver" in the poem's last line represent? Why do you think the husband is laughing?

3. **AP® Structure and Narration.** Look carefully at the structure of "My Husband." What do you notice about the position of the lines and the lengths of the lines? What effect do those choices have on the poem's mood?
4. **AP® Structure, Narration, and Figurative Language.** How would you describe the tone of "My Husband"? Consider Hazelton's use of repetition, varying line lengths, imagery, and hyperbole.
5. **AP® Literary Argumentation.** Discuss whether you think "My Husband" objectifies the speaker's husband, supporting your position with evidence from the poem itself.

Making Connections

1. **AP® Character and Narration.** What picture emerges of the speakers of the two poems? Which one do you feel you have more information about? Why?
2. **AP® Character and Narration.** On the face of it, "My Husband" and "To My Dear and Loving Husband" sound quite different. Setting aside the qualities tied to their respective time periods, what do the speakers of these poems have in common?
3. **AP® Literary Argumentation.** "My Husband" is characterized by a sense of abandon, both in the speaker's admiration for her husband and the poem's imagery, while "To My Dear and Loving Husband" is much more restrained. Which do you think is more effective in delivering its speaker's message of love for her husband? Explain.
4. **AP® Literary Argumentation.** Each of these poems has an agenda beyond declarations of love. Identify each of those agendas and explain what they have in common.

Mower's Song

Andrew Marvell

Poet, politician, and satirist Andrew Marvell (1621–1678) was born in Yorkshire, England, and entered Trinity College, Cambridge at the age of thirteen. Although he spent most of the years of the English Civil War (1642–1651) on the Continent, he was able to find favor in both Oliver Cromwell's Commonwealth government (1650–1659) and during King Charles II's Restoration (1660–1685), serving in Parliament for nearly two decades. A close associate of John Milton, Marvell wrote scathing political satires as well as poems influenced by the metaphysical style of John Donne.

Lebrecht Music & Arts/Alamy

KEY CONTEXT Andrew Marvell is often linked to John Donne and other metaphysical poets. As such, he sometimes uses conceits that extend throughout his poem. In this poem, the connection between a gardener and his garden is a comment on love and relationships. Although Marvell wrote it in 1652, it was not published until 1681.

My mind was once the true survey
Of all these meadows fresh and gay,
And in the greenness of the grass
Did see its hopes as in a glass;
When Juliana came, and she
What I do to the grass, does to my thoughts and me.

But these, while I with sorrow pine,
Grew more luxuriant still and fine,
That not one blade of grass you spy'd
But had a flower on either side;
When Juliana came, and she
What I do to the grass, does to my thoughts and me.

Unthankful meadows, could you so
A fellowship so true forgo?
And in your gaudy May-games[1] meet
While I lay trodden under feet?
When Juliana came, and she
What I do to the grass, does to my thoughts and me.

But what you in compassion ought,
Shall now by my revenge be wrought;
And flow'rs, and grass, and I and all,
Will in one common ruin fall.
For Juliana comes, and she
What I do to the grass, does to my thoughts and me.

And thus, ye meadows, which have been
Companions of my thoughts more green,
Shall now the heraldry[2] become
With which I shall adorn my tomb;
For Juliana comes, and she
What I do to the grass, does to my thoughts and me. ■

1681

[1] Traditional festivities celebrating springtime. — Eds.

[2] Emblem. — Eds.

Understanding and Interpreting

1. **AP® Narration.** How do you interpret the first two lines of the poem? According to the speaker, what was the relationship between his "mind" (l. 1) and "these meadows" (l. 2)?
2. **AP Character and Narration.** Why are the meadows "[u]nthankful" (l. 13)? How does this ingratitude relate to the speaker's relationship with Juliana?

3. **AP® Character and Narration.** What does the speaker believe the meadows "in compassion ought" (l. 19) to do? What does the speaker decide to do in response?
4. **AP® Character and Narration.** What does the speaker address in the poem? What does this suggest about his relationship?
5. **AP® Narration.** How do you interpret the speaker's message in the final stanza? Why are the meadows "the heraldry" (l. 27) which "shall adorn" (l. 28) the speaker's tomb?

Analyzing Language, Style, and Structure

1. **Vocabulary in Context.** What does the word "gaudy" (l. 15) mean in the context of the poem? How does this word choice characterize the speaker's reaction to the meadows?
2. **AP® Structure.** The poem's refrain, a line or set of lines that repeats at regular intervals, concludes each of the stanzas. What is the effect of this poem's refrain? How do you interpret the deviations in the refrain that begin in the fourth stanza?
3. **AP® Figurative Language.** Which words and images contribute to the personification of the meadows? Why is this personification significant to the conceit that Marvell has created?
4. **AP® Structure.** How do the two stanzas that begin with the word "But" introduce shifts in the poem? What is the function of the details presented in these two stanzas?
5. **AP® Character, Narration, and Figurative Language.** A woman named Juliana is mentioned five times in the poem. What does this repetition reveal about her? What is the function of Marvell's development of Juliana?

Topics for Composing

1. **AP® FRQ Poetry Analysis.** In Andrew Marvell's "Mower's Song," published in 1681, the speaker indirectly recounts his failed attempt at love. Read the poem carefully. Then, in a well-written essay, analyze how Marvell uses literary elements and techniques to convey the speaker's complex attitude toward love.
2. **AP® FRQ Poetry Analysis.** In Andrew Marvell's "Mower's Song," published in 1681, the speaker conveys his feelings by addressing nature instead of his beloved. Read the poem carefully. Then, in a well-written essay, analyze how Marvell uses literary elements and techniques to characterize the speaker of the poem.
3. **Multimodal.** Based on the descriptions found throughout the poem, create two visual depictions of the speaker's meadows. The first should reflect how it looks prior to the fourth stanza; the second should capture what it looks like at the end of the poem. Make sure to infuse words from the poem into each of your images.
4. **Connections.** When discussing metaphysical poets, T. S. Eliot wrote that they were characterized by the "elaboration of a figure of speech to the farthest stage to which ingenuity can carry it." What figure of speech does Marvell most prominently depend on in the poem, and how does it align with T. S. Eliot's observation?
5. **Connections.** How would you describe the speaker's state of mind? While his behavior — namely, addressing his meadows — may seem unrealistic, how are his thoughts and emotions understandable? As part of your response, consider the way that you or someone you know has reacted when facing a similar situation.
6. **Creative Writing.** How would Juliana react if she were to read "Mower's Song"? Write a letter from Juliana's perspective that she might address to the speaker after reading this poem.

She Walks in Beauty

Lord Byron

Private Collection/Bridgeman Images

In a short life, George Gordon Byron (1788–1824) staked his claim as one of the greatest Romantic poets in the English language, became an exile from his own country and a national hero in Greece (where a suburb of Athens is named after him), and gave his name to the adjective *Byronic*, which refers to his mercurial, romantic, and tragic character. Born in London, he inherited the barony of Byron at the age of ten, becoming Lord Byron. As a child, he displayed an idleness and mischievous temperament that continued at Trinity College, Cambridge, where he kept a bear in protest of college regulations forbidding undergraduates to keep dogs. Originally written as a song lyric, "She Walks in Beauty" clearly expresses Byron's love of beauty.

I

She walks in Beauty, like the night
Of cloudless climes[1] and starry skies;
And all that's best of dark and bright
Meet in her aspect and her eyes:
Thus mellowed to that tender light
Which Heaven to gaudy day denies.

II

One shade the more, one ray the less,
Had half impaired the nameless grace
Which waves in every raven tress,
Or softly lightens o'er her face;
Where thoughts serenely sweet express,
How pure, how dear their dwelling-place.

III

And on that cheek, and o'er that brow,
So soft, so calm, yet eloquent,
The smiles that win, the tints that glow,
But tell of days in goodness spent,
A mind at peace with all below,
A heart whose love is innocent! ■

1814

[1] Climates. — Eds.

Understanding and Interpreting

1. **AP® Narration.** What is it about the phrase "like the night" (l. 1) that immediately draws readers into the poem?
2. **AP® Character and Narration.** What does the speaker reveal about this unnamed woman who "walks in Beauty" (l. 1)? What can you infer from the line "So soft, so calm, yet eloquent" (l. 14)?
3. **AP® Structure and Narration.** Paraphrase the last stanza of the poem. How do you interpret the final exclamation mark, and how does it contribute to the tone and mood of the final stanza?
4. **AP® Character and Narration.** Based on your reading of the poem, how would you characterize the speaker's relationship to the woman he describes?
5. **AP® Narration.** What claim does the speaker make about the relationship between someone's external beauty and inner "goodness" (l. 16)?

Analyzing Language, Style, and Structure

1. **Vocabulary in Context.** In line 14, the speaker describes the appearance of his subject as one that is "So soft, so calm, yet eloquent." What does "eloquent" mean in this context? Why is it set in opposition to softness and calmness?
2. **AP® Figurative Language.** What does the alliteration of "cloudless climes" and "starry skies" (l. 2) contribute to the poem's effect?
3. **AP® Narration and Figurative Language.** How does the poem invite us to view the night in a new light? What lines in the poem support your interpretation? For instance, what is the denotation and connotation of the adjective "gaudy" (l. 6)? How does Lord Byron's use of this descriptor for day help us understand what he is trying to say about night? How does it help you see the woman the speaker describes?
4. **AP® Structure and Figurative Language.** Byron employs paradox throughout the poem. What seemingly contradictory elements does he juxtapose? How does this juxtaposition develop the theme of the poem?
5. **AP® Structure.** Though they are short, common words, how do "yet" (l. 14) and "But" (l. 16) illuminate important concepts and the meaning of the poem in its final stanza?

Topics for Composing

1. **AP® FRQ** **Poetry Analysis.** In Lord Byron's "She Walks in Beauty," published in 1814, the speaker praises a woman's beauty. Read the poem carefully. Then, in a well-written essay, analyze how Byron uses literary elements and techniques to convey the speaker's complex perspective on the definition of true beauty.
2. **Connections.** Byron wrote "She Walks in Beauty" as a song lyric, and it has continued to be a source of inspiration for musicians and composers. Research some of the music that has been written for these lyrics, and explain whether you think setting it to music enhances or detracts from the lyrics.
3. **Multimodal.** Mixed media art combines more than one medium or element to express an idea. For example, a painter might incorporate fabric into a painting, or a sculptor might include an assortment of unrelated found objects in a way that reimagines them as a cohesive piece. Using a mixture of media, create a visual representation of this poem's

meaning while paying particular attention to how the elements come together to represent "all that's best of dark and bright" (l. 3).

4. **Speaking and Listening.** Like Byron, many people have expressed their appreciation for inner beauty as superior to external appearances. For example, American actor and dancer Rachele Brooke Smith has stated, "I really do believe that inner beauty is so much more than any kind of outer beauty." Priscilla Presley believes, "Inner beauty should be the most important part of improving one's self." Nevertheless, people spend billions of dollars a year on products designed to improve their outer beauty. With a partner or in a small group, research the beauty industry. Then, discuss why you believe people continue to emphasize outer beauty despite the popular philosophy that its importance pales in comparison to inner beauty. As part of your discussion, brainstorm ways people work on inner beauty as part of "improving one's self." Does an industry exist to improve our inner beauty? Is it hypocritical for those who represent our ideals of physical beauty to advocate for the importance of inner beauty?

Bright Star, would I were stedfast as thou art —

John Keats

IanDagnall Computing/Alamy

John Keats was born in London in 1795. His early education introduced him to literature, music, and theater, but after the death of his parents, he was taken out of school and apprenticed to a surgeon and apothecary, which is an older term for pharmacist. He became a licensed apothecary but almost immediately abandoned medicine for poetry. Keats is considered one of the major poets of the Romantic movement, though his work was not well received while he was alive. When he died at age twenty-five from tuberculosis, he had been writing poetry seriously for only about six years and publishing for only four.

Bright Star, would I were stedfast as thou art—
    Not in lone splendour hung aloft the night
And watching, with eternal lids apart,
    Like nature's patient, sleepless Eremite,[1]
The moving waters at their priestlike task
    Of pure ablution round earth's human shores,
Or gazing on the new soft-fallen mask
    Of snow upon the mountains and the moors—
No—yet still stedfast, still unchangeable,
    Pillow'd upon my fair love's ripening breast,
To feel for ever its soft fall and swell,
    Awake for ever in a sweet unrest,
Still, still to hear her tender-taken breath,
And so live ever—or else swoon to death. ■

c. 1819

[1] Hermit, particularly one under a religious vow. —Eds.

Understanding and Interpreting

1. **AP® Narration.** Identify the speaker's audience in the poem. What does he envy most about this audience?
2. **AP® Narration.** How do you interpret line 1 of the poem? Why does the speaker use the word "would" to describe his wishes?
3. **AP® Character and Narration.** What might a "[b]right [s]tar" (l. 1) be "watching" (l. 3) from its perch in the sky? How does the speaker feel about this opportunity?
4. **AP® Character and Narration.** What is the "sweet unrest" the speaker discusses in line 12? What is the speaker's attitude toward it? Support your interpretation with evidence from the poem.
5. **AP® Character and Narration.** What could prompt the speaker to "swoon to death" (l. 14)? What does this suggest about his character?

Analyzing Language, Style, and Structure

1. **Vocabulary in Context.** What is the meaning of the word "ablution" (l. 6) in the context of the poem? What does it suggest about the speaker that the "moving waters at their priestlike task / Of pure ablution" (ll. 5–6) does not interest him?
2. **AP® Structure and Narration.** While the placement of the volta is less variable in Petrarchan sonnets, Shakespearean ones can occur after each quatrain, at the octet, after twelve lines, or not at all. Examine the structure of this poem. What type of sonnet does Keats write? Identify and describe the prominent volta in the poem.
3. **AP® Figurative Language.** How does repetition function in this poem? Consider "stedfast" in lines 1 and 9, "still" in line 13, and "soft-fallen" and "soft fall" in lines 7 and 11. What else repeats in the poem?
4. **AP® Narration and Figurative Language.** How would you characterize the tone of the poem? Which words and images help to convey this tone?
5. **AP® Character, Narration, and Structure.** Describe the syntax of the poem. What is the effect of this syntax on the reader, and what does it suggest about the speaker?

Topics for Composing

1. **AP® FRQ** **Poetry Analysis.** In John Keats's "Bright Star, would I were stedfast as thou art," written circa 1819, the speaker expresses his feelings for his "fair love." Read the poem carefully. Then, in a well-written essay, analyze how Keats uses literary elements and techniques to convey the speaker's attitude toward the person he loves.
2. **AP® FRQ** **Poetry Analysis.** In John Keats's "Bright Star, would I were stedfast as thou art," written circa 1819, the speaker contemplates both the beauty of nature and that of his beloved. Read the poem carefully. Then, in a well-written essay, analyze how Keats uses literary elements and techniques to develop the speaker's preference of his "fair love" over the beauty of nature.
3. **AP® Literary Argumentation.** Explore the oxymoron in line 12 ("sweet unrest"). If the speaker argues that he wishes to rest upon his beloved's bosom forever, why does this condition cause him "unrest"? In your argument, explore the complexity of the oxymoron by drawing textual support from other parts of the poem.
4. **Connections.** Listen to Aerosmith's song "I Don't Want to Miss a Thing." Compare and contrast the speaker of the song to the speaker in Keats's poem. How would you characterize them? Are they thoughtful lovers, depressed, or even creepy?

5. **Research.** Keats's poetry certainly draws from his life experiences. Learn more about Keats's life: his illness, financial troubles, and love of Fanny Brawne. How does your research inform your understanding and interpretation of "Bright Star, would I were stedfast as thou art —"?
6. **Research.** Keats worked on "Bright Star, would I were stedfast as thou art —" for many years. Research the history of the composition of this poem. How did Keats change the poem over these years, and why did he embark on these changes?

Wild Nights —Wild Nights!

Emily Dickinson

IanDagnall Computing/Alamy

Born into a prominent family in Amherst, Massachusetts, Emily Dickinson (1830–1886) received some formal education at Amherst Academy and Mount Holyoke Female Seminary (which became Mount Holyoke College). Dickinson was known as a shy and reclusive person, who preferred to remain within her close family circle, though some contemporary scholars have begun to question that characterization. Dickinson wrote over nearly eighteen hundred poems, but only ten were published in her lifetime.

Wild Nights — Wild Nights!
Were I with thee
Wild Nights should be
Our luxury!

Futile — the Winds —
To a Heart in port —
Done with the Compass —
Done with the Chart!

Rowing in Eden —
Ah, the Sea!
Might I but moor — Tonight —
In Thee! ■

1861

Understanding and Interpreting

1. **AP® Character and Narration.** Characterize the speaker of "Wild Nights — Wild Nights!" Is she the reclusive Emily Dickinson of legend, or is she someone else here?
2. **AP® Character and Narration.** What does the speaker throw away in this poem? Why can she do without the items she wants to dispose of?
3. **AP® Narration.** What is the mood of "Wild Nights — Wild Nights!"? How does the poem make you feel?
4. **AP® Literary Argumentation.** Do you consider "Wild Nights — Wild Nights!" to be a poem of passion, a poem of loneliness, a little bit of both, or something else entirely? Explain your answer.

Analyzing Language, Style, and Structure

1. **Vocabulary in Context.** What is the meaning of the word "[f]utile" in line 5? What does the speaker say is futile, and how might that observation suggest an interpretation for the whole poem?
2. **AP® Narration and Figurative Language.** The word "[c]hart" in line 8 has several meanings and can be a noun or a verb. How does Dickinson put the word to use so that it expresses more than one meaning?
3. **AP® Structure.** What is the function of the conditional tense here: "were I with thee" (l. 2) and "Wild Nights / Should be our luxury" (ll. 3–4)?
4. **AP® Narration and Figurative Language.** The images in "Wild Nights — Wild Nights!" are quite concrete: compass, port, chart, rowing. But Dickinson doesn't quite connect the dots among them. How do you fill in the details of the speaker's experience? Do the meanings of the images change on a second or third reading?
5. **AP® Character, Narration, and Figurative Language.** "Wild Nights — Wild Nights!" depends on a central metaphor of a boat at sea, but also in port and moored. What does this complex metaphor say about the speaker's perspective on passion?
6. **AP® Structure.** Dickinson was known for using em dashes (—) in her poetry. What is their effect here? Why do you think there's a dash in the title?
7. **AP® Structure and Narration.** Unlike many of Dickinson's poems, which are meditative and reflective, "Wild Nights — Wild Nights!" has a sense of immediacy. How does Dickinson use language to make us feel that the poem is happening before our eyes?

Topics for Composing

1. **AP® FRQ** **Poetry Analysis.** In Emily Dickinson's "Wild Nights — Wild Nights!" written in 1861, the speaker sends out a short but clear message of passion. Read the poem carefully. Then, in a well-written essay, analyze how Dickinson uses literary elements and techniques to convey the speaker's experience of passion.
2. **AP® Literary Argumentation.** What is the central paradox of "Wild Nights — Wild Nights!"? How does Dickinson use that paradox to make a statement about love or passion?
3. **Connections.** Watch some of the films and TV series that have been made about Dickinson, such as *Wild Nights with Emily* and *Dickinson*. These works speculate about Dickinson's private life, many details of which will never be known. What inspiration does the poem "Wild Nights — Wild Nights!" offer an imaginative scriptwriter?
4. **Connections.** In "Invitation to a Voyage," the French poet Baudelaire (a contemporary of Dickinson's) uses the following lines as a refrain that repeats three times in the poem (the translation appears in italics):

Là, tout n'est qu'ordre et beauté,	*There all is order and beauty,*
Luxe, calme et volupté.	*Luxury, peace, and pleasure.*

   Read the entire poem — in French if possible — and try to look at a few different English translations. Does Baudelaire use the word "luxury" in the same sense as Dickinson does in this poem? How is his interpretation of the word and his ideal of love different from Dickinson's in "Wild Nights — Wild Nights!"? What do they have in common? Explain, using evidence from both poems in your response.
5. **Multimodal.** Create a visual representation of the speaker's experience in "Wild Nights — Wild Nights!" It could be a painting or drawing, an animated film or video, or another form in which you could express your interpretation of its images and theme.

The Love Song of J. Alfred Prufrock

T. S. Eliot

Culture Club/Getty Images

Poet, dramatist, and critic Thomas Stearns Eliot (1888–1965) was born and raised in St. Louis, Missouri. He moved to England when he was twenty-five to attend Oxford University after studying at Harvard University and eventually became a British subject. His most famous works include "The Love Song of J. Alfred Prufrock" (1915), "The Wasteland" (1922), "Ash Wednesday" (1930), "Burnt Norton" (1941), "Little Gidding" (1942), "Four Quartets" (1943), and the play *Murder in the Cathedral* (1935). He was awarded the Nobel Prize for Literature in 1948.

KEY CONTEXT Eliot is closely associated with the modernist movement (see pp. 938–949) — especially in his use of stream of consciousness, a technique he employs in "The Love Song of J. Alfred Prufrock" to depict a speaker wandering through the streets of a city on a foggy night. Eliot did not compromise when it came to the language of poetry, believing that it should represent the complexities of modern civilization. The poem is like a collage, a work of visual art created by materials and objects glued to a flat surface. In poetry this technique is called fragmentation, a favorite technique of the modernists. The fragments come together — or don't — in a way that mirrors the fragmented, chaotic modern world. Eliot also employs the "objective correlative," which is a way of representing an emotion by incorporating symbols that evoke the emotion.

S'io credesse che mia risposta fosse
A persona che mai tornasse al mondo,
Questa fiamma staria senza più scosse.
Ma perciocchè giammai di questo fondo
Non tornò vivo alcun, s'i'odo il vero,
Senza tema d'infamia ti rispondo.[1]

Let us go then, you and I,
When the evening is spread out against the sky
Like a patient etherized upon a table;
Let us go, through certain half-deserted streets,
The muttering retreats
Of restless nights in one-night cheap hotels
And sawdust restaurants with oyster-shells:
Streets that follow like a tedious argument
Of insidious intent

[1] From Dante's *Inferno*, canto XXVII, 61–66. The words are spoken by Guido da Montefeltro, who was condemned to hell for providing false counsel to Pope Boniface VII. When asked to identify himself, Guido responded, "If I thought my answers were given to anyone who could ever return to the world, this flame would shake no more; but since none ever did return above from this depth, if what I hear is true, without fear of infamy I answer thee." He does not know that Dante will return to earth to report on what he has seen and heard. — Eds.

To lead you to an overwhelming question . . .
Oh, do not ask, "What is it?"
Let us go and make our visit.

In the room the women come and go
Talking of Michelangelo.

The yellow fog that rubs its back upon the window-panes,
The yellow smoke that rubs its muzzle on the window-panes
Licked its tongue into the corners of the evening,
Lingered upon the pools that stand in drains,
Let fall upon its back the soot that falls from chimneys,
Slipped by the terrace, made a sudden leap,
And seeing that it was a soft October night,
Curled once about the house, and fell asleep.

And indeed there will be time
For the yellow smoke that slides along the street,
Rubbing its back upon the window-panes;
There will be time, there will be time
To prepare a face to meet the faces that you meet;
There will be time to murder and create,
And time for all the works and days of hands[2]
That lift and drop a question on your plate:
Time for you and time for me,
And time yet for a hundred indecisions,
And for a hundred visions and revisions,
Before the taking of a toast and tea.

In the room the women come and go
Talking of Michelangelo.
And indeed there will be time
To wonder, "Do I dare?" and, "Do I dare?"
Time to turn back and descend the stair,
With a bald spot in the middle of my hair —
(They will say: "How his hair is growing thin!")
My morning coat, my collar mounting firmly to the chin,
My necktie rich and modest, but asserted by a simple pin —
(They will say: "But how his arms and legs are thin!")
Do I dare
Disturb the universe?
In a minute there is time
For decisions and revisions which a minute will reverse.

[2] Reference to the title of a poem about agricultural life by the early Greek poet Hesiod. — Eds.

For I have known them all already, known them all:
Have known the evenings, mornings, afternoons,
I have measured out my life with coffee spoons;
I know the voices dying with a dying fall
Beneath the music from a farther room.
  So how should I presume?

And I have known the eyes already, known them all—
The eyes that fix you in a formulated phrase.
And when I am formulated, sprawling on a pin,
When I am pinned and wriggling on the wall,
Then how should I begin
To spit out all the butt-ends of my days and ways?
  And how should I presume?

And I have known the arms already, known them all—
Arms that are braceleted and white and bare
(But in the lamplight, downed with light brown hair!)
Is it perfume from a dress
That makes me so digress?
Arms that lie along a table, or wrap about a shawl.
  And should I then presume?
  And how should I begin?

Shall I say, I have gone at dusk through narrow streets,
And watched the smoke that rises from the pipes
Of lonely men in shirt-sleeves, leaning out of windows? . . .

. . . . .

I should have been a pair of ragged claws
Scuttling across the floors of silent seas.

And the afternoon, the evening, sleeps so peacefully!
Smoothed by long fingers,
Asleep . . . tired . . . or it malingers,
Stretched on the floor, here beside you and me.
Should I, after tea and cakes and ices,
Have the strength to force the moment to its crisis?
But though I have wept and fasted, wept and prayed,
Though I have seen my head (grown slightly bald) brought in upon a platter,[3]
I am no prophet—and here's no great matter;
I have seen the moment of my greatness flicker,
And I have seen the eternal Footman hold my coat, and snicker,
And in short, I was afraid.

[3] From Matthew 14:1–11. King Herod ordered the beheading of John the Baptist at the request of Herod's wife and daughter.—Eds.

And would it have been worth it, after all,
After the cups, the marmalade, the tea,
Among the porcelain, among some talk of you and me,
Would it have been worth while
To have bitten off the matter with a smile,
To have squeezed the universe into a ball
To roll it toward some overwhelming question,
To say: "I am Lazarus,[4] come from the dead,
Come back to tell you all, I shall tell you all" —
If one, settling a pillow by her head,
    Should say: "That is not what I meant at all.
    That is not it, at all."

And would it have been worth it, after all,
Would it have been worth while,
After the sunsets and the dooryards and the sprinkled streets,
After the novels, after the teacups, after the skirts that trail along the floor —
And this, and so much more? —
It is impossible to say just what I mean!
But as if a magic lantern threw the nerves in patterns on a screen:
Would it have been worth while
If one, settling a pillow or throwing off a shawl,
And turning toward the window, should say:
    "That is not it at all,
    That is not what I meant, at all."

. . . . .

No! I am not Prince Hamlet, nor was meant to be;
Am an attendant lord, one that will do
To swell a progress, start a scene or two,
Advise the prince: no doubt, an easy tool,
Deferential, glad to be of use,
Politic, cautious, and meticulous;
Full of high sentence, but a bit obtuse;
At times, indeed, almost ridiculous —
Almost, at times, the Fool.
I grow old . . . I grow old . . .
I shall wear the bottoms of my trousers rolled.

Shall I part my hair behind? Do I dare to eat a peach?

I shall wear white flannel trousers, and walk upon the beach.
I have heard the mermaids singing, each to each.

I do not think that they will sing to me.

---

[4] From John 11:1-44. Lazarus was raised from the dead by Jesus. — Eds.

I have seen them riding seaward on the waves
Combing the white hair of the waves blown back
When the wind blows the water white and black.
We have lingered in the chambers of the sea
By sea-girls wreathed with seaweed red and brown
Till human voices wake us, and we drown. ■

1917

Understanding and Interpreting

1. **AP® Structure and Narration.** Consider the title of the poem. How is it ironic? In what ways is the poem a love song?
2. **AP® Setting, Structure, and Narration.** How does the epigraph from Dante's *Inferno* help T. S. Eliot comment on the modern world in "The Love Song of J. Alfred Prufrock"? What does it tell us about the setting of this poem? How is Montefeltro's miscalculation related to the poem?
3. **AP® Character and Narration.** What kind of person is the speaker in this poem? Try to describe him in three or four words. What qualities of his character do you think he unknowingly reveals through his perceptions and observations? How does he describe himself physically?
4. **AP® Character and Narration.** Whom is the speaker addressing? This question is more complicated than it seems and likely has several answers. Consider all of the possibilities. What does each possible listener suggest about the development of Prufrock as a character? How does each possibility develop another level of meaning for the poem?
5. **AP® Narration.** Eliot was in the avant-garde as a young poet and so was experimenting with new ideas and forms of expression. However, he considered himself a traditionalist as he got older. What are the innovative aspects of this poem? Look for evidence of the traditionalism that would get stronger as Eliot aged.
6. **AP® Character and Narration.** In what ways is "The Love Song of J. Alfred Prufrock" a poem about time? Read through the text and look for references to time – particularly aging, the meaning of time, and the word *time* itself. What might Eliot be asserting or questioning about the meaning of time?
7. **AP® Character and Narration.** In what ways is this a poem about art?
8. **AP® Character and Narration.** How does this poem reflect modernist concerns about the loss of emotional connections and alienation? To what extent does Eliot explore the reasons why such estrangement occurs? To what extent does he offer a solution?

Analyzing Language, Style, and Structure

1. **Vocabulary in Context.** The speaker describes in the first stanza "Streets that follow like a tedious argument / Of insidious intent." How does the choice of "insidious" characterize the streets the speaker wanders? What is the relationship between tediousness and insidiousness in these lines?
2. **AP® Narration and Figurative Language.** How does Eliot set the tone in the poem's first stanza? Look carefully at both the figurative language and the concrete details.
3. **AP® Character and Figurative Language.** Eliot depends on the emotional associations of his images to reveal aspects of Prufrock's personality. In the first stanza, what emotions do you associate with images such as "patient etherized upon a table" (l. 3) or "one-night cheap hotels" (l. 6)? What do these emotions reveal about the speaker?

4. **AP® Setting and Figurative Language.** The "yellow fog" that is the subject of the poem's third stanza has the qualities of a cat. Is this association threatening, comforting, or both? How does your interpretation of the fog affect your reading of the poem as a whole?
5. **AP® Setting, Narration, and Figurative Language.** You may notice that the images are arranged from top to bottom — the description goes from the sky to the streets in the opening stanza and progresses from the windowpanes to the drains in the third. What is the effect of the way Eliot's speaker, Prufrock, guides the reader's eye and imagination?
6. **AP® Setting and Structure.** Eliot uses the technique of enjambment, or run-on lines. An example is in lines 5–9: "The muttering retreats / Of restless nights in one-night cheap hotels / And sawdust restaurants with oyster-shells: / Streets that follow like a tedious argument / Of insidious intent." How does this technique help create the alienating quality of the city scene that is set in the first twenty-two lines?
7. **AP® Character and Figurative Language.** One of the most demanding aspects of this poem is its allusions, as Eliot expected his readers to be as well educated as he was. Some allusions are fairly accessible. The allusions to Michelangelo — an artist most people are familiar with — in line 14 and again in line 36 help us imagine the women Prufrock is talking about. The function of the less accessible allusions — such as "works and days of hands" (l. 29) — may serve a different purpose. Why might Eliot have included such esoteric allusions? How do they affect your reading of the poem?
8. **AP® Setting, Structure, and Narration.** In the fourth stanza, what is the effect of fragments such as "yellow smoke," "murder and create," "visions and revisions," and "toast and tea" appearing together? Do they form a new picture, or are their effects fragmentary? How do the fragments communicate Eliot's vision of a modern man in a modern city?
9. **AP® Character, Setting, and Structure.** What do you make of the occasional rhyming in the midst of unrhymed free verse? Note especially the two repeated stanzas: "In the room the women come and go / Talking of Michelangelo." How does this irregular rhyme scheme reflect and reveal the character of the speaker and the setting of the poem?
10. **AP® Character, Setting, Structure, and Narration.** The middle section of the poem (ll. 37–86) moves from the chaotic city setting into the fragmented, anxiety-ridden mind of the speaker. How is Prufrock's physical description developed in lines 37–44? How do his physical characteristics connect to his emotional state?
11. **AP® Character, Narration, and Figurative Language.** Prufrock is a deeply self-conscious character. Explain the various ways that characteristic is developed in lines 37–72. Consider especially lines 55–58, in which Prufrock imagines himself pinned like a specimen to a wall.
12. **AP® Narration and Figurative Language.** From line 37 to line 87, twelve lines begin with "And." What does the repetition of that conjunction suggest about Prufrock's mental state?
13. **AP® Structure and Narration.** What is the effect of the semicolons and ellipses in lines 111–121? What do they tell you about Prufrock's state of mind?
14. **AP® Character and Narration.** Details such as Prufrock's assertion that he will "wear the bottom of [his] trousers rolled" (l. 121) or his question about whether he should "dare to eat a peach" (l. 122) have been interpreted in many ways. One is that they reveal his anxieties about aging — he may be too old for the bohemian style of rolled trousers or he may break a tooth on a peach pit. Another interpretation is that they are related to his nervousness around women. Consider several possibilities. How does each add to the portrait of Prufrock and the multiple meanings of Eliot's poem?
15. **AP® Character, Structure, and Figurative Language.** The last six lines of this poem form a sestet, the form that both ends the traditional Petrarchan sonnet and offers a solution for the problem or conflict set out in the first eight lines (the octave). The poet Petrarch wrote about his unrequited love for Laura, but Prufrock doesn't even have an unrequited love.

Do these last six lines offer any solutions? How does the image of mermaids continue some of the poem's motifs? What does it mean that Prufrock invites the reader to drown with him at the end of the poem?

Topics for Composing

1. **AP® FRQ Poetry Analysis.** In T. S. Eliot's "The Love Song of J. Alfred Prufrock," published in 1917, the speaker wrestles with his inner thoughts and perception of himself. Read the poem carefully. Then, in a well-written essay, analyze how Eliot uses literary elements and techniques to develop Prufrock's complex perspective on his place in the modern world.
2. **AP® Literary Argumentation.** Eliot began writing this poem in 1909, when he was in college at Harvard. He continued to revise it until it was published in 1917. Some critics have commented that it is the poem of a young man, even though its narrator is middle-aged. What qualities reveal the poem as a young man's work?
3. **AP® Literary Argumentation.** Though Prufrock says, "No! I am not Prince Hamlet," he shares Hamlet's habit of talking about taking action instead of acting as well as Hamlet's overall indecision. Analyze Prufrock's character and the poem to find examples of indecision and inaction. Then, write an essay in which you make a claim about the reason for Prufrock's hesitation.
4. **AP® Literary Argumentation.** Critic Roland Barthes has said, "Literature is the question minus the answer." "The Love Song of J. Alfred Prufrock" is filled with questions. Write an essay in which you analyze one or more of the poem's questions and the extent to which the poem does or does not offer answers.
5. **Connections.** "The Love Song of J. Alfred Prufrock" makes several allusions to metaphysical poet Andrew Marvell's "To His Coy Mistress." "And indeed there will be time" (ll. 23, 37) alludes to that poem's first lines, in which the speaker urges his lady friend to consummate their relationship by reminding her how fast time flies: "Had we but world enough, and time / This coyness, lady, were no crime." Later, "To have squeezed the universe into a ball" (l. 92) alludes to the end of Marvell's poem, in which the speaker makes one last pitch: "Let us roll all our strength and all / Our sweetness up into one ball." Read Marvell's full poem. How do we know that Prufrock's purpose is different from that of Marvell's speaker? What is the effect of alluding to Marvell's flirtatious, self-confident poem?
6. **Research.** Eliot wrote "The Love Song of J. Alfred Prufrock" at a time when the world was undergoing great changes. Research the major advancements in industry and technology in the early 1900s. Then, write an essay in which you explain the poem's perspective on the way such changes affected society.
7. **Connections.** Prufrock claims to have seen "Arms that are braceleted and white and bare" (l. 63), an allusion to metaphysical poet John Donne's "The Relic," in which the speaker imagines that when his grave and the grave of his beloved are dug up, the gravedigger will see the bracelet of his beloved's hair encircling the bones of his arm, and will leave them alone. Critics have said that Donne invented the idea of modern love as private, as opposed to the feudal idea of love being social. Read the full poem by Donne. How does this allusion, and the concrete image itself, help develop the character of Prufrock? What do you think is Eliot's take on the idea of modern, private love?
8. **Creative Writing.** Imagine that you are one of the women who say, "That is not what I meant at all. / That is not it, at all" (ll. 97–98, and similarly in ll. 109–10). In a poem, essay, or short story, explain what you mean by those words.
9. **Connections.** Write an essay in which you compare and contrast Prufrock either to Hamlet or to one of Shakespeare's fools, such as the one in *King Lear* or Puck in *A Midsummer Night's Dream.*

Untitled [Do you still remember: falling stars]

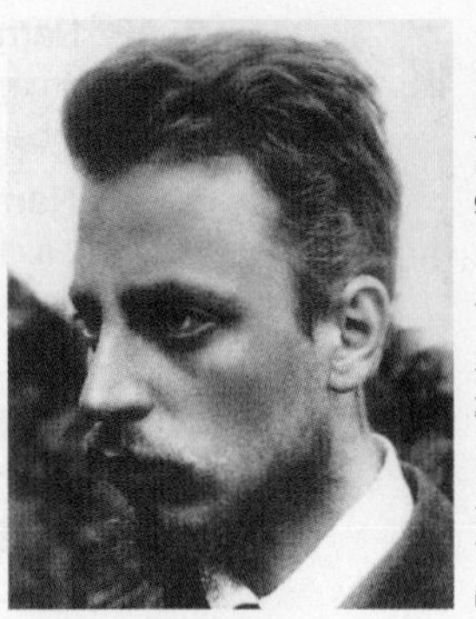
Fine Art Images/Heritage Images/Getty Images

Rainer Maria Rilke

Translated from German by Edward Snow

Born in Prague, poet and novelist Rainer Maria Rilke (1875–1926) wrote in both German and French. Although plagued by poor health throughout his life, Rilke traveled extensively: he met novelists Leo Tolstoy and Boris Pasternak on trips to Russia; worked for sculptor Auguste Rodin in Paris; wrote one of his major works, *Duino Elegies* (1912), while in Italy; and he lived in Munich and in Switzerland. His work is often seen as a bridge between traditional and modernist forms. Many of his ideas about writing, art, and life were published posthumously in *Letters to a Young Poet* (1929).

Do you still remember: falling stars,
how they leapt slantwise through the sky
like horses over suddenly held-out hurdles
of our wishes — did we have *so* many? —
for stars, innumerable, leapt everywhere;
almost every gaze upward became
wedded to the swift hazard of their play,
and our heart felt like a single thing
beneath that vast disintegration of their brilliance —
and was whole, as if it would survive them! ■

1924

Understanding and Interpreting

1. **AP® Narration.** Whom does the speaker address in this poem? Is the "you" in line 1 a direct address to the reader, or is there another audience? Explain.
2. **AP® Narration.** What does the phrase "did we have *so* many?" (l. 4) mean? To whom does "we" refer?
3. **AP® Character and Narration.** Why do the gazers' hearts feel "like a single thing" (l. 8)? What does this suggest about their collective experiences?
4. **AP® Narration.** Paraphrase the poem. How would you describe the speaker's experience? How do you interpret the meaning of this experience?

Analyzing Language, Style, and Structure

1. **Vocabulary in Context.** Line 7 begins with the word "wedded." How does this word take on a specific significance in the context of lines 6 and 7? What is the effect of this word on your interpretation of the poem as a whole?
2. **AP® Structure.** The poem's structure hinges on the punctuation of line 1. What is the function of the colon? How does it serve as the hinge between what came before it and the rest of the poem?

3. **AP® Narration and Figurative Language.** What is the significance of the "falling stars" (l. 1)? Why is the imagery associated with them central to the poem? Why does the speaker ask if "you still remember" them (l. 1)?
4. **AP® Narration and Figurative Language.** What is the relationship between the "falling stars" (l. 1), "horses" (l. 3), and "hurdles" (l. 3)? Which of these are used figuratively? Which of these serve as symbols, and what is their significance?

Topics for Composing

1. **AP® FRQ Poetry Analysis.** In Rainer Maria Rilke's "Untitled [Do you still remember: falling stars]," published in 1924, the speaker questions whether his audience still recalls a profound and moving experience. Read the poem carefully. Then, in a well-written essay, analyze how Rilke uses literary elements and techniques to convey the speaker's complex understanding of the meaning of this experience.
2. **AP® Literary Argumentation.** At first glance, "Untitled [Do you still remember: falling stars]" might not appear to be about love and relationships. Write an essay in which you analyze how this poem addresses this theme indirectly.
3. **Creative Writing.** Use this poem as a starting point to write your own poem. In your version, elaborate on the wishes the speaker used to make, what his wishes are now, and why falling stars may have been forgotten.
4. **Multimodal.** Create a recording of the night sky outside your home. As part of your video, narrate what the speaker of this poem might notice in the sky. From his perspective, explain why these observations are significant.

Love is not all

Edna St. Vincent Millay

Library of Congress Prints & Photographs Division

Edna St. Vincent Millay (1892–1950) was born in Maine. In 1912, she entered her poem "Renascence" in a competition, winning fourth place and inclusion in *The Lyric Year*, which earned her acclaim and a scholarship to Vassar College. The poem would be included in her first collection, *Renascence and Other Poems*, published in 1917. After graduating, Vincent (as she insisted on being called) moved to Greenwich Village — then New York's bohemian district. After an extended trip to Europe, she returned to New York and published *The Harp Weaver and Other Poems* (1923). That year she won the Pulitzer Prize for Poetry, one of the first women to be so honored. "Love is not all" was written in 1931.

KEY CONTEXT This poem is a Shakespearean sonnet, which consists of three quatrains and a couplet at the end, rhyming *abab*, *cdcd*, *efef*, *gg*. The third quatrain often provides the volta, in which the speaker typically shifts perspective and sometimes closes with a witty remark.

Love is not all: it is not meat nor drink
Nor slumber nor a roof against the rain;
Nor yet a floating spar to men that sink
And rise and sink and rise and sink again;
Love can not fill the thickened lung with breath,
Nor clean the blood, nor set the fractured bone;
Yet many a man is making friends with death
Even as I speak, for lack of love alone.
It well may be that in a difficult hour,
Pinned down by pain and moaning for release,
Or nagged by want past resolution's power,
I might be driven to sell your love for peace,
Or trade the memory of this night for food.
It well may be. I do not think I would. ■

1931

Understanding and Interpreting

1. **AP® Narration.** Explain the argument expressed in the first six lines of this sonnet. Why do you think Edna St. Vincent Millay begins her love poem by defining what love is not?
2. **AP® Character and Narration.** What is the poem's situation — that is, where is the speaker in relation to the person she is addressing? Characterize the relationship of the two based on the information the poem provides.
3. **AP® Narration.** How is "Love is not all" a poem both about the experience of love and, at the same time, the absence of love? Note particular lines that address each.
4. **AP® Narration.** What do you make of the tentativeness of the final line, "It well may be. I do not think I would"? Why are these words more intriguing than a declaration of "Never!" would be?

Analyzing Language, Style, and Structure

1. **Vocabulary in Context.** What is the meaning of the word "spar" in line 3? How is a floating spar a bit of an oxymoron? How does its mixed meaning work in "Love is not all"?
2. **AP® Figurative Language.** "Love is not all" depends on an extended metaphor. What is it? How does Millay make it seem possible?
3. **AP® Structure.** Why do you think Millay chose to write this poem as a sonnet?
4. **AP® Narration.** How does Millay build tension through the enumeration of what love cannot do in lines 1–6?
5. **AP® Structure and Narration.** In lines 9–14 of the sonnet, Millay imagines a series of hypothetical situations. Describe how the speaker's tone shifts in these final lines.
6. **AP® Narration.** How does the tone of the poem reflect Millay's attitude toward love? How would you describe this tone?

Topics for Composing

1. **AP® FRQ Poetry Analysis.** In Edna St. Vincent Millay's "Love is not all," published in 1931, the speaker describes what love cannot do. Read the poem carefully. Then, in a well-written essay, analyze how Millay uses literary elements and techniques to develop an argument about what love can do.
2. **AP® Literary Argumentation.** Millay's collection was also criticized for having a female perspective when the sonnet was traditionally voiced by men. How can you tell, without conflating the speaker and the poet, that the voice in "Love is not all" is female? Does it matter?
3. **Connections.** "Love is not all" appeared in 1931, in a collection titled *Fatal Interview*. Some reviewers thought that there was no place for love poems during a serious economic depression. Do you agree? Explain whether you think love poems have a place in hard times.
4. **Connections.** Poet and critic Allen Tate, writing in the *New Republic*, described Millay as having a sensibility rather than an intellect. He compared her work unfavorably to W. B. Yeats and T. S. Eliot. Read some of Yeats's and Eliot's poetry and come to your own conclusion.

Having a Coke with You

Frank O'Hara

Fred W. McDarrah/Getty Images

Frank O'Hara (1926–1966) grew up in Grafton, Massachusetts. After high school, he enlisted in the navy and served on a destroyer for most of World War II. After he received his master's degree in comparative literature from the University of Michigan, O'Hara moved to New York City, where he was at the center of New York's art and poetry worlds, writing for *Artnews* magazine and working both at the front desk and as an assistant curator at the Museum of Modern Art. O'Hara's poetry collections include *City Winter and Other Poems* (1952), *Meditations in an Emergency* (1957), *Second Avenue* (1960), *Odes* (1960), and *Lunch Poems* (1964).

KEY CONTEXT O'Hara was inspired by city life as other poets have been inspired by nature. He once wrote, "I can't even enjoy a blade of grass unless I know there's a subway handy, or a record store or some other sign that people do not totally regret life." This poem refers to the Frick Collection, a museum in Manhattan housed in the former home of industrialist Henry Clay Frick and home to some of the greatest European old masters and Impressionists from the Renaissance through the nineteenth century. The Dutch artist Rembrandt's painting *Polish Rider*, completed in 1655, is one of the collection's many stars.

is even more fun than going to San Sebastian, Irún, Hendaye, Biarritz, Bayonne
or being sick to my stomach on the Travesera de Gracia in Barcelona[1]
partly because in your orange shirt you look like a better happier St. Sebastian[2]
partly because of my love for you, partly because of your love for yoghurt
partly because of the fluorescent orange tulips around the birches

[1] San Sebastian, Irún, and the Traversera de Gracia in Barcelona are all locations in Spain. Hendaye, Biarritz, and Bayonne are all locations in France. — Eds.

[2] An early Christian saint and martyr who is usually depicted as young and handsome. — Eds.

partly because of the secrecy our smiles take on before people and statuary
it is hard to believe when I'm with you that there can be anything as still
as solemn as unpleasantly definitive as statuary when right in front of it
in the warm New York 4 o'clock light we are drifting back and forth
between each other like a tree breathing through its spectacles

and the portrait show seems to have no faces in it at all, just paint
you suddenly wonder why in the world anyone ever did them
                                                            I look
at you and I would rather look at you than all the portraits in the world
except possibly for the *Polish Rider* occasionally and anyway it's in the Frick
which thank heavens you haven't gone to yet so we can go together for the first time
and the fact that you move so beautifully more or less takes care of Futurism[3]
just as at home I never think of the *Nude Descending a Staircase*[4] or
at a rehearsal a single drawing of Leonardo or Michelangelo[5] that used to wow me
and what good does all the research of the Impressionists[6] do them
when they never got the right person to stand near the tree when the sun sank
or for that matter Marino Marini[7] when he didn't pick the rider as carefully
as the horse

          it seems they were all cheated of some marvelous experience
which is not going to go wasted on me which is why I'm telling you about it ■

1960

[3] An Italian artistic and social movement from the early twentieth century that took as its inspiration the technological advancements of the era. — Eds.

[4] *Nude Descending a Staircase* is a 1912 painting by French artist Marcel Duchamp that depicts its subject through distortion and a shattered picture plane. — Eds.

[5] "Leonardo" is a reference to Leonardo da Vinci. Both he and Michelangelo are famous Italian Renaissance artists. — Eds.

[6] Impressionism was a late-nineteenth-century artistic movement that emphasized capturing the movement and light of a scene rather than a strictly realistic depiction. — Eds.

[7] Marino Marini (1901–1980) was an Italian sculptor known for his stylized equestrian statues that generally included a rider. — Eds.

Understanding and Interpreting

1. **AP® Character and Narration.** Characterize the speaker of "Having a Coke with You." To whom is he addressing the poem? How would you describe the situation?
2. **AP® Structure and Narration.** You probably noticed that the title is actually the beginning of the poem. What information does it provide that is essential for understanding the poem? What happens if you leave it out? Do you think it anchors the poem or does it set it off kilter? Explain.
3. **AP® Narration.** What do you think is the "marvelous experience" the speaker thinks the Impressionists and other artists missed? Does this seem hyperbolic to you or does the speaker seem sincere? Explain.
4. **AP® Narration.** "Having a Coke with You" is certainly a love poem. How is it also a poem about art? What does it have to say about the relationship between love and art?
5. **AP® Setting.** Frank O'Hara was known as a quintessential New York City poet, and "Having a Coke with You" is set in New York City. How does the speaker portray this setting? Does it seem to be a typical New York poem or is it somehow different? Explain.

Analyzing Language, Style, and Structure

1. **Vocabulary in Context.** What is the meaning of the word "statuary" as it is used in lines 6 and 8? Why does the speaker say it's "unpleasantly definitive" (l. 8)? Do you think he truly means it, or is he exaggerating for a specific effect? Explain.
2. **AP® Structure.** Try reading "Having a Coke with You" out loud. You'll probably notice that other than a few commas, it has no punctuation, not even a period at the end. What is the effect of that decision by the poet?
3. **AP® Narration and Figurative Language.** What do you make of the simile in line 10: "like a tree breathing through its spectacles"? What kind of image does it create? How does it help the speaker make his point?
4. **AP® Structure and Narration.** This poem is built on contrasts. Trace them in the poem. What point do they make about love?
5. **AP® Character, Narration, and Figurative Language.** "Having a Coke with You" veers between the everyday — references to a Coke, yoghurt, an orange shirt — and the elevated: allusions to fine art, the Frick Collection, European travel. How does the speaker use these references to craft a unique description of love? How do these allusions characterize the speaker? Does he identify primarily with the everyday, the elevated, or somewhere in between? Explain.
6. **AP® Structure.** Why does line 13 have only two words? What is their function?

Topics for Composing

1. **AP® FRQ Poetry Analysis.** In Frank O'Hara's "Having a Coke with You," published in 1960, the speaker comments enthusiastically on the object of his affections. Read the poem carefully. Then, in a well-written essay, explain how O'Hara uses literary elements and techniques to convey that enthusiasm in a way that seems fresh and original.
2. **AP® Literary Argumentation.** Frank O'Hara is said to have hated what he viewed as literary pretension, that is, poetry that requires special knowledge or is hard to understand. How successfully does he avoid it in "Having a Coke with You"? Use evidence from the poem to support your response.
3. **AP® Literary Argumentation.** Half as a joke, Frank O'Hara founded a poetry movement called "Personism." He wrote this about poetry in a mock manifesto: "It does not have to do with personality or intimacy, far from it! But to give you a vague idea, one of its minimal aspects is to address itself to one person (other than the poet himself), thus evoking overtones of love without destroying love's life-giving vulgarity, and sustaining the poet's feelings toward the poem while preventing love from distracting him into feeling about the person." How does "Having a Coke with You" fulfill the criteria for a personist poem?
4. **Connections.** Find images of the artwork and work by artists mentioned in the poem and do a little research on them. Why are these works considered important? What does O'Hara assume about his readers by referring to them? What do you think of them?
5. **Multimodal.** Frank O'Hara was part of a wide circle of artists and musicians, often called the New York School. Look into the work by his contemporaries, and put together a visual or musical collage of the work of O'Hara's crowd that you think best represents the speaker's perspective in "Having a Coke with You."

Siren Song

Margaret Atwood

Margaret Atwood (b. 1939) was born in Ottawa and spent much of her childhood in northern Quebec. Atwood is a prolific writer in many forms, including poetry, literary criticism, and fiction. She is the author of more than fifteen collections of poetry and seventeen novels. She has won the Booker Prize twice, for *The Blind Assassin* (2009) and *The Testaments* (2019). *The Testaments* is a sequel to her 1985 novel *The Handmaid's Tale*, which was also a finalist for the Booker Prize. In 2020, she published a collection of poetry, *Dearly*.

GL Portrait/Alamy

KEY CONTEXT In "Siren Song" Atwood adopts the voice of a siren, one of three birdlike women from Greek mythology whose irresistible songs would lure passing sailors toward a rocky coast where they would be shipwrecked. They appear in the Greek poet Homer's *The Odyssey*, in which the hero, Odysseus, plugs the ears of his crew and has himself tied to the mast of his ship so he can hear the sirens sing but is prevented from going ashore.

This is the one song everyone
would like to learn: the song
that is irresistible:

the song that forces men
to leap overboard in squadrons
even though they see beached skulls

the song nobody knows
because anyone who had heard it
is dead, and the others can't remember.

Shall I tell you the secret
and if I do, will you get me
out of this bird suit?

I don't enjoy it here
squatting on this island
looking picturesque and mythical

with these two feathery maniacs,
I don't enjoy singing
this trio, fatal and valuable.

I will tell the secret to you,
to you, only to you.
Come closer. This song

is a cry for help: Help me!
Only you, only you can,
you are unique

at last. Alas
it is a boring song
but it works every time. ■

1974

Understanding and Interpreting

1. **AP® Character and Narration.** What is the appeal of the siren song? Why is it that "it works every time" (l. 27)? What is the appeal of the siren's age-old tactic for a modern audience?
2. **AP® Character and Narration.** Based on the way the siren addresses the reader, what can you infer about her audience?
3. **AP® Character.** Do you find the speaker to be a sympathetic character? Explain why or why not.
4. **AP® Narration.** The term "siren song" has come to mean something — not necessarily a song — that is powerfully, almost irresistibly alluring. Do you think that is the "song" the speaker mentions in the first line? Or could it mean something else? Explain.
5. **AP® Character and Narration.** What stereotypes of women — and men — does Atwood draw upon in this poem? What point does the speaker make about these stereotypes?

Analyzing Language, Style, and Structure

1. **Vocabulary in Context.** Consider the word "maniacs" in line 16. How does that word relate to the speaker's plan for seduction?
2. **AP® Structure and Figurative Language.** The mythical sirens were creatures of mystery. How does Atwood's diction demystify them? Cite specific examples from the text.
3. **AP® Narration and Figurative Language.** Describe the tone of the poem. Look carefully at Atwood's use of hyperbole and understatement — how do those elements in particular contribute to this tone?
4. **AP® Structure.** What is ironic about the song "that is irresistible" (l. 3)?
5. **AP® Setting and Structure.** What atmosphere or setting do the poem's short lines and use of enjambment create, especially in the first three stanzas?
6. **AP® Structure, Narration, and Figurative Language.** How do stanza 5 and 6 play on ways that women have been objectified and described throughout history? Consider especially words like "squatting" (l. 14) and "bird suit" (l. 12) in your response.

Topics for Composing

1. AP® FRQ **Poetry Analysis.** In Margaret Atwood's "Siren Song," published in 1974, the speaker tells the siren episode from Homer's *The Odyssey* from the point of view of one of the sirens. Read the poem carefully. Then, in a well-written essay, analyze how Atwood uses literary elements and techniques to convey the speaker's unique perspective on a story that is usually told another way.

2. **AP® Literary Argumentation.** In this poem, Atwood turns a familiar heroic tale into a meditation on imbalance of power based on gender identity. What does the poem have to say about the part language plays in that imbalance?
3. **Connections.** Discuss how Atwood's poem can be read as a response to Homer, or even to men whose character resembles that of Homer's Odysseus: clever but self-absorbed. How might it be a protest against his depiction of the sirens? How might it be a criticism of some of the characteristics we claim to value in our cultural "heroes"?
4. **Connections.** Read Book 12 of *The Odyssey* and compare Odysseus's description of the sirens to Atwood's depiction in "Siren Song." What aspects of these creatures, if any, does Atwood reproduce in her retelling of the story? Is the role they play in Homer's epic the same as the one they play in Atwood's poem?
5. **Creative Writing.** Using "Siren Song" as a model, choose a myth or folktale and retell it from a different point of view in a poem, short story, or video.

One Art

Elizabeth Bishop

Everett Collection Historical/Alamy

Elizabeth Bishop (1911–1979) was born in Worcester, Massachusetts, before finally settling in Boston after graduating from Vassar College. Bishop published her first collection of poetry, *North and South* (1946), after traveling in Europe and North Africa. During an extended trip to Brazil, she published her second collection, *A Cold Spring* (1955), with the poems of *North and South* in a single volume. This won her the Pulitzer Prize in 1956. Bishop lived in Brazil for fifteen years and described her life in Brazil in her third collection of poetry, *Questions of Travel* (1965). Her last collection, *Geography III*, was published in 1976.

KEY CONTEXT "One Art" is a modified villanelle, which is a nineteen-line poem with two rhymes throughout, consisting of five tercets and a quatrain, with the first and third lines of the opening tercet recurring alternately at the end of the other tercets and with both repeated at the close of the concluding quatrain.

The art of losing isn't hard to master;
so many things seem filled with the intent
to be lost that their loss is no disaster.

Lose something every day. Accept the fluster
of lost door keys, the hour badly spent.
The art of losing isn't hard to master.

Then practice losing farther, losing faster:
places, and names, and where it was you meant
to travel. None of these will bring disaster.

I lost my mother's watch. And look! my last, or
next-to-last, of three loved houses went.
The art of losing isn't hard to master.

I lost two cities, lovely ones. And, vaster,
some realms I owned, two rivers, a continent.
I miss them, but it wasn't a disaster.

— Even losing you (the joking voice, a gesture
I love) I shan't have lied. It's evident
the art of losing's not too hard to master
though it may look like (*Write* it!) like disaster. ■

1976

Understanding and Interpreting

1. **AP® Character and Narration.** How do you characterize the speaker? Does she seem sincere in how she approaches the subject of this poem? Explain why or why not.
2. **AP® Narration.** To whom is the poem addressed? How do you know?
3. **AP® Narration.** Consider the parenthetical "(*Write* it!)" (l. 19). To whom does the speaker issue that command? How do you know?
4. **AP® Structure and Narration.** The speaker lists things she has lost. How does she categorize them? Would you put them in the same categories? Explain why or why not.
5. **AP® Character and Narration.** Does the speaker sound like she's bragging? Is she convincing? Would you follow her advice? Explain.
6. **AP® Character and Narration.** The speaker seems to suggest that one way to cope with loss is to practice it: small losses will prepare us for big losses. Do you think she takes her own advice? Do you agree with this coping mechanism?
7. **AP® Narration.** Does the tone of "One Art" match the subject matter? Explain why or why not. What message does this tonal choice send to readers?
8. **AP® Structure and Narration.** Why do you think Elizabeth Bishop named her poem "One Art" rather than, for example, "The Art of Losing"? What do you think she means by one art?

Analyzing Language, Style, and Structure

1. **Vocabulary in Context.** What is the meaning of the word "realms" in line 14? What does it suggest about the nature of the speaker's losses? How does it relate to her assertion that "it wasn't a disaster" (l. 15)?
2. **AP® Structure and Figurative Language.** What are the denotations of the word *lose*? What are its connotations? Consider various forms of the word. What are the different ways Bishop uses it in "One Art"?
3. **AP® Structure and Narration.** How has Bishop modified the villanelle form in "One Art"? Why might she have modified it? How does this form, and the ways she breaks from it, contribute to the poem's meaning?
4. **AP® Figurative Language.** Which of the speaker's losses do you think are concrete? Which are metaphorical? Are there ways the two overlap?

5. **AP® Narration and Figurative Language.** Find examples of hyperbole in this poem. How does the use of hyperbole communicate the author's attitude toward her subject?
6. **AP® Structure.** What is the effect of the repetition of "like" in the final line of the poem?
7. **AP® Character, Structure, and Narration.** The word "disaster" is repeated at the end of almost every stanza, and each stanza contains at least one word (or pair of words) that rhymes or nearly rhymes with it. How might that repetition and rhyming undermine the speaker's claim that there is an art to losing and that it's easy to master?
8. **AP® Character, Structure, and Narration.** Why might Bishop have changed the last repetition of "The art of losing isn't hard to master" to "the art of losing's not too hard to master"? How does this shift change the way you view the speaker and her attitude toward loss?

Topics for Composing

1. **AP® FRQ Poetry Analysis.** In Elizabeth Bishop's "One Art," published in 1976, the speaker addresses loss of all kinds. Read the poem carefully. Then, in a well-written essay, analyze how Bishop uses literary elements and techniques to convey the speaker's attempt to make sense of all she has lost.
2. **AP® Literary Argumentation.** This poem is beloved by many people who turn to it in times of loss. How does Bishop's poem provide comfort to readers? Reflect on the style, structure, and tone of the poem in your response.
3. **Connections.** According to Bishop, why is losing an art, and why is it important to master? Are you convinced by her argument? How might you apply it to your own experiences?
4. **Research.** While seeking an autobiographical explanation for works of poetry and fiction doesn't always make sense, there are still connections between an author's life and work. Do some research on Elizabeth Bishop, whose life was marked by terrible loss. Then write about whether that knowledge changed your interpretation of "One Art."
5. **Connections.** In an essay about loss in the *New Yorker*, writer Kathryn Schulz wrote that "[w]ith objects, loss implies the possibility of recovery. . . . That's why the defining emotion of losing things isn't frustration or panic or sadness but, paradoxically, hope. With people, by contrast, loss is not a transitional state but a terminal one. . . . Death is loss without the possibility of being found." Apply this distinction to "One Art." Does the speaker of the poem agree with this distinction? Do you? Explain why or why not.

Weighing the Dog

Billy Collins

Lorenzo Dalberto / Alamy

Billy Collins (b. 1941) served as Poet Laureate of the United States from 2001 through 2003 and as New York State poet from 2004 through 2006. He has published several collections of poetry, including *The Art of Drowning* (1995), *Picnic, Lightning* (1998), *Nine Horses* (2002), and most recently *Whale Day and Other Poems* (2020). Poet Stephen Dunn has said of Collins, "We seem to always know where we are in a Billy Collins poem, but not necessarily where he is going."

It is awkward for me and bewildering for him
as I hold him in my arms in the small bathroom,
balancing our weight on the shaky blue scale,

but this is the way to weigh a dog and easier
than training him to sit obediently on one spot
with his tongue out, waiting for the cookie.

With pencil and paper I subtract my weight
from our total to find out the remainder that is his,
and I start to wonder if there is an analogy here.

It could not have to do with my leaving you
though I never figured out what you amounted to
until I subtracted myself from our combination.
You held me in your arms more than I held you
through all those awkward and bewildering months
and now we are both lost in strange and distant neighborhoods. ■

1991

Understanding and Interpreting

1. **AP® Narration.** What is the prevailing feeling in the opening three lines? Try to sum it up in one or two words.
2. **AP® Character and Narration.** What is a one-sentence summary of lines 10–12? Literally, what is the speaker saying about the relationship?
3. **AP® Character and Narration.** Ultimately, whom does the speaker blame for the failure of his relationship? What evidence in the poem can you find to support your interpretation?
4. **AP® Character and Narration.** How does the speaker express concern for the dog's plight or feelings? In what ways does he do the same for his estranged partner? To what extent does drawing comparisons between weighing his dog and the break-up of a relationship trivialize that relationship? Or does it serve to make a devastating loss more bearable? Explain.
5. **AP® Literary Argumentation.** Collins is often considered a poet who makes poetry seem easy. Explain whether you think "Weighing the Dog" is an "easy" poem. Is the subject matter "easy" to deal with? Is it "easy" to read? Do you find it relatable? Explain.

Analyzing Language, Style, and Structure

1. **Vocabulary in Context.** Collins uses the word "bewildering" twice in this short poem, a choice that suggests deliberate emphasis. What meaning does "bewildering" carry in this context, and how does it extend beyond simply "confusing"? How does the meaning in line 1 differ, if only slightly, from that in line 14?
2. **AP® Structure and Narration.** What are the various meanings of "weigh" (and its derivative "weight") that Collins draws on in the poem? What is the effect of this ambiguity?

3. **AP® Structure and Narration.** Where does this poem shift from being a poem about a man and his dog to being a poem about something else, something more? What is this something else?
4. **AP® Narration and Figurative Language.** Why does the speaker reflect on the "analogy" between weighing his dog and his lost relationship rather than seeing the one as a symbol of the other?
5. **AP® Structure and Narration.** How does the structure of the poem's first six lines mirror its subject? Look especially at the way Collins creates balance in each line.
6. **AP® Figurative Language.** What do the "strange and distant neighborhoods" (l. 15) represent to the speaker?
7. **AP® Structure and Narration.** How do you interpret Collins's use of the language of mathematical calculations (e.g., subtraction, total remainder, figures, and amount)? Is he being playful? Ironic? Sly? What tone does it help create?

Topics for Composing

1. AP® FRQ **Poetry Analysis.** In Billy Collins's "Weighing the Dog," published in 1991, the speaker reflects on the end of a romantic relationship. Read the poem carefully. Then, in a well-written essay, analyze how Collins uses literary elements and techniques to convey the speaker's complex emotional response to the break-up.
2. **AP® Literary Argumentation.** An interview in the *Paris Review* described the poetry of Billy Collins as being "identified largely by its humor," which the poet himself speaks of as being "a door into the serious." How do you think this characterization applies to "Weighing the Dog"?
3. **Speaking and Listening.** The poem works through a series of pronouns, but only the dog is specific ("him/his"). Do we know the gender identity of the speaker? Or his partner? Discuss why you think Collins is not specific about the gender of the two people in the relationship and how this choice contributes to the relationship a reader forms to the speaker.
4. **Creative Writing.** Rewrite the poem with a different speaker — the dog or the partner in the relationship. Try to maintain the same or a similar tone as Collins does.

Summer Storm

Dana Gioia

Dana Gioia (pronounced JOY-uh) (b. 1950) is a well-known contemporary poet and art critic. The former chairman of the National Endowment for the Arts, Gioia was the Poet Laureate of California from 2015 to 2019 and has published five volumes of poetry in addition to an influential defense of the importance of imaginative literature in the 1992 book *Can Poetry Matter?*

Historic Collection/Alamy

We stood on the rented patio
While the party went on inside.
You knew the groom from college.
I was a friend of the bride.

We hugged the brownstone wall behind us
To keep our dress clothes dry
And watched the sudden summer storm
Floodlit against the sky.

The rain was like a waterfall
Of brilliant beaded light,
Cool and silent as the stars
The storm hid from the night.

To my surprise, you took my arm —
A gesture you didn't explain —
And we spoke in whispers, as if we two
Might imitate the rain.

Then suddenly the storm receded
As swiftly as it came.
The doors behind us opened up.
The hostess called your name.

I watched you merge into the group,
Aloof and yet polite.
We didn't speak another word
Except to say goodnight.

Why does that evening's memory
Return with this night's storm —
A party twenty years ago,
Its disappointments warm?

There are so many might have beens,
What ifs that won't stay buried,
Other cities, other jobs,
Strangers we might have married.

And memory insists on pining
For places it never went,
As if life would be happier
Just by being different. ■

2001

Understanding and Interpreting

1. **AP® Setting and Narration.** How does an event such as a wedding and the atmosphere created by the storm shape the speaker's perspective in this poem?
2. **AP® Narration.** Who is the speaker addressing in this poem?

3. **AP® Setting and Narration.** Why do you think "this night's storm" (l. 26) twenty years later triggers these memories for the speaker? Why does he describe the party's "disappointments" as "warm" (l. 28)?
4. **AP® Narration.** What are some of the "might have beens" and "[w]hat ifs" (ll. 29–30) the speaker contemplates in stanza 8?
5. **AP® Character and Narration.** What do you think the speaker means by "Strangers we might have married" in line 32?
6. **AP® Narration.** In the final stanza, the speaker raises the possibility that "life would be happier / Just by being different" (ll. 35–36). Does the evidence in the poem itself support this claim? Do you agree with the speaker's assertion? Explain.

Analyzing Language, Style, and Structure

1. **Vocabulary in Context.** How does Dana Gioia's use of "[a]loof" in line 22 characterize the person the speaker addresses in the poem? What does pairing "[a]loof" with "and yet polite" indicate, and what conclusions can you draw about the speaker and about the person the speaker addresses?
2. **AP® Figurative Language.** Which types of figurative language does Gioia use in this poem, and how does each contribute to the meaning of the poem?
3. **AP® Character, Narration, and Figurative Language.** Stanzas 3 and 4 include similes within similes. What comparisons does Gioia make among the rain, the stars, and the subjects of the poem? How does the third simile (ll. 11–12) characterize the speaker and the person to whom he's talking? In what ways might they be like rain?
4. **AP® Figurative Language.** What might the storm symbolize in this poem? Consider stanza 5 in particular.
5. **AP® Structure.** Contemporary poems don't often rhyme. How do you experience the rhyme in "Summer Storm"? Does it contribute to the poem's meaning, and if so, in what ways? Was Gioia's decision to incorporate a rhyme scheme an effective one? Explain.

Topics for Composing

1. AP® FRQ **Poetry Analysis.** In Dana Gioia's "Summer Storm," published in 2001, the speaker reflects on an experience he had twenty years ago. Read the poem carefully. Then, in a well-written essay, analyze how Gioia uses literary elements and techniques to describe the speaker's complex perspective on the experience he shared with the person he meets in the poem.
2. **Connections.** *Sliding Doors*, a 1998 movie, popularized the concept of a "sliding doors" moment or phenomenon. Such moments are seemingly inconsequential decisions or experiences that ultimately lead to a significant outcome in a person's life. In some ways, a "sliding doors" moment echoes the concept behind the theory of the "butterfly effect," which suggests that the tiniest changes can dramatically and unforeseeably alter the future. Describe at least one seemingly small decision or experience that you know has dramatically changed your life and include alternate possibilities that could otherwise have become realities.
3. **Speaking and Listening.** People tend to believe in fate or free will or a combination of the two, and their beliefs often originate in a personal religious or spiritual philosophy. Therefore, a discussion about the role of fate and/or free will in our lives can be a delicate one to have. However, it can also be an illuminating one. Reflect on Gioia's approach to fate and free will in his poem "Summer Storm" as well as on your own perspective on what forces shape our lives. Then, take part in a Socratic seminar with your classmates in which you take turns listening to each other's beliefs using evidence from your lives and from the poem.

4. **Creative Writing.** Imagine how the person the speaker had met at the wedding twenty years earlier would respond to this poem. Then, compose a poem or letter from that person's perspective. Does the person remember the evening similarly? Where is she or he now? Was there really a connection, or did the speaker misinterpret the gesture he mentions in line 14 of the poem?

Urban Renewal XVIII

Major Jackson

© Erin Patrice O'Brien

Major Jackson (b. 1968) is an American poet and professor from Philadelphia, Pennsylvania. He earned degrees from Temple University and the University of Oregon. His first book, *Leaving Saturn* (2002), won the Cave Canem Poetry Prize and was a finalist for a National Book Critics Circle Award. His second and third books, *Hoops* (2006) and *Holding Company* (2010), were both finalists for an NAACP Image Award for Outstanding Literary Work — Poetry. His most recent book is *The Absurd Man* (2020).

How untouchable the girls arm-locked strutting
up the main hall of Central High unopposed
for decades looked. I flattened myself against
the wall, unnerved by their cloudsea[1] of élan,[2]
which pounced upon any timid girl regrettably
in their way, their high-wattage lifting slow motion
like curls of light strands of honey. The swagger
behind their blue-tinted sunglasses and low-rider
jeans hurt boys like me, so vast the worlds
between us, even the slightest whiff of recognition,
an accidental side glance, an unintended tongue-piercing
display of Juicy Fruit chew, was intoxicating
and could wildly cast a chess-playing geek into
a week-long surmise of inner doubts, likelihoods,
and depressions. You might say my whole life led
to celebrating youth and how it snubs and rebuffs.
Back then I learned to avoid what I feared
and to place my third-string hopes on a game-winning
basketball shot, sure it would slow them to a stop,
pan their lip-glossed smiles, blessing me with their cool. ■

2006

[1] First introduced in the Marvel comics universe in 1986, Cloudsea is a planet from another dimension that is made up of floating landmasses. — Eds.

[2] Stylish flair. — Eds.

Understanding and Interpreting

1. **AP® Character, Setting, and Narration.** Though the speaker presents the events of the poem as his own experience, he situates it in a communal setting: the "main hall of Central High" (l. 2), where he says the girls were "unopposed / for decades" (ll. 2–3). What does this general setting and time period suggest about the girls the speaker describes? What does it suggest about the speaker's relationship to them?
2. **AP® Character and Narration.** According to lines 2–7, how do both boys and girls react to the "girls" in line 1?
3. **AP® Narration.** What does the speaker mean by "the slightest whiff of recognition" (l. 10)? What is the effect of this recognition?
4. **AP® Character and Narration.** What is the speaker's goal as expressed in the poem? How does he aim to achieve this goal?

Analyzing Language, Style, and Structure

1. **Vocabulary in Context.** Jackson uses the word "élan" in line 4. Besides the definition provided in the footnote, what other denotations does the word have? How does Jackson's word choice convey the significance of this scene to the speaker?
2. **AP® Structure.** The first sentence of the poem (ll. 1–3) is structured in an unusual, almost unnatural way. Why do you think the poet chose this word order? What does the syntax of the sentence emphasize?
3. **AP® Figurative Language.** The speaker describes the girls' "swagger" (l. 7) as "intoxicating" (l. 12). What details and images throughout the poem reinforce this description?
4. **AP® Structure, Narration, and Figurative Language.** The poem shifts in line 15 from relating the speaker's experience in adolescence to reflecting on how it has influenced him. Within the context of his experience, how do you interpret lines 15–16: "You might say my whole life led / to celebrating youth and how it snubs and rebuffs"?

Topics for Composing

1. **AP® FRQ Poetry Analysis.** In Major Jackson's "Urban Renewal XVIII," published in 2006, the speaker recalls his high school experiences. Read the poem carefully. Then, in a well-written essay, analyze how Jackson uses literary elements and techniques to capture the agony and excitement of youth.
2. **AP® FRQ Poetry Analysis.** In Major Jackson's "Urban Renewal XVIII," published in 2006, the speaker recalls his attitude toward girls when he was in high school. Read the poem carefully. Then, in a well-written essay, analyze how Jackson uses literary elements and techniques to characterize the speaker.
3. **Connections.** In "Urban Renewal," Jackson presents what might be seen as an unfavorable view of high school life — one that is characterized by insecurities and fears. How do you view adolescent life in high school? How does your perspective compare to that of the speaker's?
4. **Creative Writing.** While the poem is a recollection of the speaker's thoughts and experiences during high school, the speaker is no longer a high schooler. Write a diary entry from the perspective of the speaker while he was in high school. How would he relate any of the details in the poem without the perspective gained by the passage of time?
5. **Connections.** Jackson has written a series of poems titled *Urban Renewal*. Find and read a few of these poems. Why has he chosen this title for these, and how does this poem relate to the others you have read?

Say It

Ross Gay

Andrew Toth/Getty Images

Ross Gay (b. 1974) grew up in Levittown, Pennsylvania, and has a BA from Lafayette College, an MFA from Sarah Lawrence College, and a PhD from Temple University. He is the author of four books of poetry, most recently *Be Holding* (2020), an extended poem focused on the basketball legend Julius Irving, known as Dr. J. Gay has also written a best-selling collection of brief essays, *The Book of Delights* (2019). The *New York Review of Books* has called his poetry "tender, tactile, and human." He teaches at Indiana University.

KEY CONTEXT In a reading of this poem, Ross Gay explained that the opening scene is set in a Trinidadian restaurant, where food such as "roti" (a flat, round bread), "chana" (curried chickpea dish commonly made in Trinidad and Tobago) and "doubles" (a food made with curried chickpeas) is being prepared.

If I told you we were slapping the beat to some
Barry White[1] jam crooning from the boombox
and that every single one of us at one point or another
jumped up to shake what shook on us and there were lines of us
in step and a loon in every one of our mouths who knew
and one of us in his pressed shirt dancing his dead father's
hunchbacked smooth another singing back up like hers
and another shaking his head no but meaning yes,
oh ye s— and if I told you the proprietor of this roti joint
dragged his wife from the kitchen where she was busy
currying chana for the best doubles in Brooklyn
so she too might witness this unabashed racket, this stampede
of glee and goof, this clan of black clad — and if I told you
today we laid down one too young
to lay down:
                praise the body its miraculous
stutter and thrum. Praise its slosh and drag and drone
and every particulate diving toward the dirt.
The rampant heart its last kick and holler. The blood
clot's last long swim to the lung. Praise the lung
its last whistle, and the kidney's *no more* —
say this; say praise
the machine hiss your father became
and the quick way he gave it up; say
praise the liver's dread swell.

[1] Popular American singer-songwriter and musician, Barry White (1944–2003) was known for his crooning love songs and bass-baritone voice. — Eds.

Say it again. Say it with your heart and neck
and lent throat gaped and flayed
to the sky. Say it covering someone's hand
with yours, straightening your tie. Say it
to the earth's fat mouth. Say it the way
you can turn on your heel to spark fire and make
your limber hip twist like a lesser storm,
or the way there is a storm between
your two good hips which are good
good music if you listen;
say it in your polished shoes,
to the organist say it too; praise the heart
its rivers and each rope twisted in the body,
and every bird housed in the body:
vulture, gull, raven, jackrabbit, cask
wick and flame a bird too; say
praise to flame a bird too; praise to the nerve
endings in your teeth, and to your tongue
like a blind man's hand reading
her teeth, and the tongue inside the eyes,
and the nose in the tongue and the heart
in the tongue; say praise to salt,
tear, stain, and skin ripped apart
like a kite flipping in the wind, praise
the rip in the kite and the geese flying through it, praise
the wings you swore you had
when you were six years old and the wings
that remain today; praise
every flower you never smelled
and every dog you never kissed, and the skinny farmer
at the market with bad teeth who gave you
his last cantaloupe and peppers and snap peas who
you never kissed, praise the handful of freckles
dashed across your father's face that you never
kissed until he would not wake again; say it;
say it again; say praise the sunlight
trapped on your father's face
and the body's slapdash racket
slipping away
if you want to or not
clean the dirt from your teeth and the glass
from your fists if you want to or not
tie both your shoes and fix your suspenders
and praise

the heart inside the heart
cracking its shackles, its thunderclap
shrug, its two thousand dolphins waving
goodbye. Praise, every day, the two thousand
dolphins waving goodbye. Shaking off
our hearts and waving goodbye. ■

2011

Understanding and Interpreting

1. **AP® Setting and Narration.** What is the factual information that you gather from the first fifteen lines of the poem? What has brought this group of people together? What is the mood of the scene?
2. **AP® Character and Narration.** What information do we learn about the deceased? Why do you feel that what Ross Gay's speaker tells us is or is not sufficient?
3. **AP® Setting and Narration.** In what ways are both joy and sadness, pleasure and hardship, gratitude and grief present in the scene Gay depicts? To what extent does one prevail? Cite specific lines to support your response.
4. **AP® Narration.** How do you interpret the dolphins in the last lines? Do you think they provide some sort of resolution to the poem? If so, what is it? If not, why not?
5. **AP® Narration.** The speaker refers to "you," thus suggesting that the reader is part of what is going on. How else does he draw readers in?
6. **AP® Narration.** The speaker in "Say It" is both participant and observer. How do these roles converge and complement one another?
7. **AP® Narration.** What relationship does this poem suggest exists between love and grief? Is it a modern-day love poem? Explain.

Analyzing Language, Style, and Structure

1. **Vocabulary in Context.** In line 19, Gay refers to the "rampant heart its last kick and holler." How is his use of "rampant" a variation on its usual definition as something unwelcome that spreads unchecked (e.g., rampant gossip poisoned the community)? What does it reveal about the speaker's perspective on the event?
2. **AP® Structure.** The opening fifteen lines consist of a series of dependent clauses without an independent clause to make a complete sentence. What is the effect of this syntax pattern?
3. **AP® Structure and Narration.** In lines 15–16, there is a major shift. How would you characterize this shift? What does it reveal about the speaker's experience?
4. **AP® Structure and Narration.** Gay has described the line breaks in his poems as "an indication of the breath. The way the poem breathes is some kind of articulation of a relationship to the body." What example in the poem do you think best illustrates his description? How does his description contribute to your understanding of the speaker of "Say It"?
5. **AP® Figurative Language.** Gay employs many figures of speech in the poem, some playful, some dramatic, some enigmatic, yet all vivid. Identify at least three and discuss how they contribute to the meaning of the poem.
6. **AP® Structure and Figurative Language.** Repetition of "say it" occurs throughout the poem, but there are other examples of repetition. How do repeating phrases or individual words function in the poem? What theme(s) do they reveal?

Topics for Composing

1. **AP® FRQ Poetry Analysis.** In Ross Gay's "Say It," published in 2011, the speaker describes a scene where people have gathered after the death of "one too young / to lay down." Read the poem carefully. Then, in a well-written essay, analyze how Gay uses literary elements and techniques to convey how the community both expresses and transforms the pain of their loss.
2. **AP® Literary Argumentation.** In an interview, Gay talks about our most "foundational" commonality: "we are not here forever. And that's a joining — a 'joy-ning' . . . What if we joined our sorrows, I'm saying . . . What if that is 'joy'"? Explain what you think Gay means by "joy-ning." How does this concept play out in "Say It"?
3. **Speaking and Listening.** Gay's poetry has been described as having "a written spoken voice." Working in small groups, develop an interpretation of "Say It" as a choral piece rather than having one person recite it. Be prepared to lead a discussion of your interpretation.
4. **Connections.** Both "Wade in the Water" (p. 463) by Tracy K. Smith and "Say It" by Ross Gay draw on an oral tradition as both a source and an expression of community and care. What are their similarities and differences in these two contemporary poems?
5. **Creative Writing.** Write your own poem entitled "Say It." You might choose a similar subject or an entirely different one than Gay's, a serious or playful topic, a person or political perspective. In any case, experiment with the repetition of this imperative as a kind of mantra in your own writing.

For Women Who Are Difficult to Love

Warsan Shire

Rodin Eckenroth/Getty Images

Poet Warsan Shire (b. 1988) won the Brunel University African Poetry Prize in 2013 and went on to be named the first Young Poet Laureate for London in 2014 and Poet in Residence for Queensland, Australia. She is the author of several poetry pamphlets, including *Teaching My Mother How to Give Birth* (2011) and *Her Blue Body* (2015, Limited Edition), as well as an audio book of poems, *the seven stages of being lonely* (2012). Her most recent collection is *Bless the Daughter Raised by a Voice in Her Head* (2021). Shire's poetry was also used to adapt and narrate Beyoncé's 2016 visual album, *Lemonade*.

you are a horse running alone
and he tries to tame you
compares you to an impossible highway
to a burning house
says you are blinding him
that he could never leave you
forget you
want anything but you
you dizzy him, you are unbearable

every woman before or after you
is doused in your name
you fill his mouth
his teeth ache with memory of taste
his body just a long shadow seeking yours
but you are always too intense
frightening in the way you want him
unashamed and sacrificial
he tells you that no man can live up to the one who
lives in your head
and you tried to change didn't you?
closed your mouth more
tried to be softer
prettier
less volatile, less awake
but even when sleeping you could feel
him travelling away from you in his dreams
so what did you want to do love
split his head open?
you can't make homes out of human beings
someone should have already told you that
and if he wants to leave
then let him leave
you are terrifying
and strange and beautiful
something not everyone knows how to love. ■

2012

Understanding and Interpreting

1. **AP® Narration.** The poem opens with a direct address to "you" and goes on to offer a combination of observation, accusation, and advice. Who do you imagine the speaker is? Is the "you" she addresses singular, collective, or both? What specific elements of text support your responses?
2. **AP® Character and Narration.** Within the first fourteen lines, how is the relationship between the man and woman characterized? What contradictions do you notice?
3. **AP® Narration.** How do you interpret the line "you can't make homes out of human beings" (l. 29) in the context of this poem?
4. **AP® Structure and Narration.** After reading and analyzing the poem, how do you interpret its title? Is it a dare, an insult, a sardonic joke, a straightforward description, or something else entirely?
5. **AP® Narration.** One critic speculated that Warsan Shire's work is so popular because what she has to say crosses lines of gender, race, and nationality. In what ways does this poem transcend such socially prescribed boundaries?

Analyzing Language, Style, and Structure

1. **Vocabulary in Context.** The word "doused" in line 11 can have different connotations. Which connotation does it hold here – or does it have a double meaning?
2. **AP® Figurative Language.** How do you interpret the metaphor "his body just a long shadow seeking yours" (l. 14)?
3. **AP® Structure and Narration.** What shift in idea, attitude, or tone does the "but" (l. 15) signal?
4. **AP® Narration and Figurative Language.** In lines 27–28, the speaker asks a question: "so what did you want to do love / split his head open?" Is "love" an affectionate reference to the "you" here, or might the speaker be personifying love? Since the speaker never directly answers this question, how does it function in the poem?
5. **AP® Structure and Narration.** Tensions exist throughout the poem – such as the friction between what exists and what is imagined. What other tensions do you see? Pay close attention to the language choices Shire makes to express contradictions, paradoxes, and conflicts. What is the overall impact of these? Are they resolved by the poem's end?

Topics for Composing

1. **AP® FRQ Poetry Analysis.** In Warsan Shire's "For Women Who Are Difficult to Love," published in 2012, the speaker shares a message of solidarity. Read the poem carefully. Then, in a well-written essay, analyze how Shire uses literary elements and techniques to develop the speaker's perspective on what it means to love someone.
2. **AP® Literary Argumentation.** In an interview, Shire has said she writes "character-driven poetry" in order to "tell the stories of those people, especially refugees and immigrants, that otherwise wouldn't be told." How is "For Women Who Are Difficult to Love" a character-driven poem? What story does it tell that is not often told?
3. **AP® Literary Argumentation.** The struggle to achieve dominance over others frequently appears in literature. How might "For Women Who Are Difficult to Love" be a work about a struggle for dominance?
4. **AP® Literary Argumentation.** One reviewer characterized Shire as "an emotional cartographer." To what extent does this description apply to "For Women Who Are Difficult to Love"? Use evidence from the poem to support your response.
5. **AP® Literary Argumentation.** Shire has been quoted as saying, "My alone feels so good, I'll only have you if you're sweeter than my solitude." Explain how this poem illustrates that line, using examples from the text.
6. **Creative Writing.** What would "you" have to say? Or "him"? Write your own poem in the voice of the one(s) spoken to or spoken about responding to the speaker in this poem.
7. **Multimodal.** Look for a recording of Shire reading this poem. You'll notice that she is almost whispering it. Why might that have been the delivery she chose? Make a recording of your own reading of the poem, Try reading it a few different ways; how does each reading change the meaning of the poem?

Chess

Caroline Beffa Photography

Aimee Nezhukumatathil

Aimee Nezhukumatathil [Nez-ZOO-koo-mah-tah-TILL] (b. 1974) is an Asian American poet known for her accessible style and lush descriptions. Born in Chicago, Nezhukumatathil earned a BA and an MFA from Ohio State University. Her books of poetry include *Miracle Fruit* (2003), *At the Drive-In Volcano* (2007), *Lucky Fish* (2011) and *Oceanic* (2018). Her most recent work of nonfiction is *World of Wonders: In Praise of Fireflies, Whale Sharks and Other Astonishments* (2020). Nezhukumatathil's poetry draws on her Filipina and South Indian background and often concerns love, loss, and landscape. Currently, she is a professor of English at the University of Mississippi, where she teaches environmental literature and poetry writing MFA program.

Exactly four different men have tried
to teach me how to play. I could never
tell the difference between a rook
or bishop, but I knew the horse meant

knight. And that made sense to me,
because a horse *is* night: soot-hoof
and nostril, dark as a sabled evening
with no stars, bats, or moon blooms.

It's a night in Ohio where a man sleeps
alone one week and the next, the woman
he will eventually marry leans her body
into his for the first time, leans a kind

of faith, too — filled with white crickets
and bouquets of wild carrot. And
the months and the honeyed years
after that will make all the light

and dark squares feel like tiles
for a kitchen they can one day build
together. Every turn, every sacrificial
move — all the decoys, the castling,

the deflections — these will be both
riotous and unruly, the exact opposite
of what she thought she ever wanted
in the endgame of her days. ■

2015

Understanding and Interpreting

1. **AP® Narration.** In the first two lines, the speaker asserts, "Exactly four different men have tried / to teach me how to play." Why do you think she is so precise about the exact number? What do you think the speaker is suggesting by pointing out that all of these men have tried to teach her to play chess and failed?
2. **AP® Narration.** Why does the chess piece called "knight," which is in the form of a horse, "[make] sense" to the speaker? Consider her description of the horse in lines 6–8 as you respond.
3. **AP® Setting and Narration.** Aside from the reference to the setting of Ohio in line 9, the description of the relationship between the man and the woman in the poem is left deliberately vague. What is the effect of this lack of detail in the poet's description of the couple?
4. **AP® Character and Narration.** In what ways does the speaker of the poem suggest that a chess game and her romantic relationships are similar?
5. **AP® Character and Narration.** By the end of the poem, the speaker describes her life decisions as being "riotous and unruly" (l. 22). How do these choices compare to the nature of the game of chess? Is she suggesting that the comparison is not actually appropriate? Explain.

Analyzing Language, Style, and Structure

1. **Vocabulary in Context.** Nezhukumatathil refers to "all the decoys, the castling, / the deflections" (ll. 20–21) as a "turn," a "sacrificial / move" (ll. 19–20). What is a "deflection" in chess? How does that definition contribute to the moves being made or anticipated in the relationship?
2. **AP® Narration and Figurative Language.** The faith that the speaker has in the man early in the relationship is "filled with white crickets / and bouquets of wild carrot" (ll. 13–14). What does this imagery convey about her initial attitude toward the relationship? How does this imagery contrast with that used to describe the game of chess in lines 6–8?
3. **AP® Structure and Narration.** The first two stanzas of the poem are a first-person discussion of chess, while the rest of the poem is a third-person description of a relationship. How are these two parts related?
4. **AP® Structure and Narration.** How does the poem shift starting in line 19? Consider shifts in sound, rhythm, and tone. What attitude does the end of the poem express about relationships, and how do these literary devices reinforce that attitude?

Topics for Composing

1. **AP® FRQ Poetry Analysis.** In Aimee Nezhukumatathil's "Chess," published in 2015, the speaker considers a romantic relationship through the metaphor of a chess game. Read the poem carefully. Then, in a well-written essay, analyze how Nezhukumatathil uses literary elements and techniques to convey the complex and surprising nature of that relationship.
2. **AP® FRQ Poetry Analysis.** In Aimee Nezhukumatathil's "Chess," published in 2015, the speaker considers the "rules" she has constructed for her life and relationships. Read the poem carefully. Then, in a well-written essay, analyze how Nezhukumatathil uses literary elements

and techniques to develop the speaker's perspective on the relationship between chess and love.

3. **Speaking and Listening.** The poet Naomi Shihab Nye explains the appeal of the Nezhukumatathil's poetry: "I love the nubby layerings of lines, luscious textures and constructions Aimee writes with a deep resonance of spirit and sight. . . . She knows that many worlds may live in one house." Working with a partner, discuss how Nye's description applies to "Chess." Pay particular attention to how "many worlds may live in one house." Be prepared to participate in a discussion with a larger group.
4. **Research.** Chess is a game based largely on war, although it has often been represented as a "game of love." Conduct some research into the history of the game and discuss how new insights or knowledge informs your reading of "Chess."
5. **Connections.** The game of chess has been important in a number of popular television shows and movies, such as *Star Wars*, *Harry Potter and the Sorcerer's Stone*, and *Blade Runner* as well as the 2020 series entitled *The Queen's Gambit*. View one of the films' representations of the game and discuss how chess is a metaphor for duty, conflict, love, or some combination of those.
6. **Connections.** In fandoms, saying a couple is "endgame" means that no matter what happens in the narrative, this couple is meant to be together in the end. In chess, "endgame" means the final stage of a game, when few pieces remain on the board and the final outcome is in sight. How does the poem "Chess" play on those multiple meanings?

Wade in the Water

Tracy K. Smith

Erika Goldring/Getty Images

Tracy K. Smith (b. 1972) is a poet and currently director of Princeton University's Creative Writing Program. Born in Massachusetts, she received a BA from Harvard University and an MFA in creative writing from Columbia University. She is the author of four award-winning books of poetry and a memoir. From 2017 to 2019, she was Poet Laureate of the United States. In 2021, Smith was elected a Chancellor of the Academy of American Poets.

KEY CONTEXT "Wade in the Water" is the name of a spiritual that is associated with the songs of the Underground Railroad, the network of people and places along the routes fugitives from slavery followed to freedom. Such songs contained explicit instructions to fugitives from slavery on how to avoid capture and which routes to take. The song references specific passages from the Bible, including the Israelite's escape from Egypt in Exodus and the book of John, which says, "For an angel went down at a certain season into the pool, and troubled the water: whosoever then first after the troubling of the water stepped in was made whole of whatsoever disease he had."

The Geechee Gullah Ring Shouters, named in the epigraph to this poem, are a group from the coastal community of Darien, Georgia. Their performances preserve the language and culture developed by enslaved people from Central and West Africa who settled largely on the Sea Islands of

South Carolina after slavery was abolished. The "ring shout" is a fusion of a dance-like movement, call-and-response singing, hand claps, and rhythmic beating on a wooden floor. It affirms community and connection to ancestors.

for the Geechee Gullah Ring Shouters

One of the women greeted me.
I love you, she said. She didn't
Know me, but I believed her,
And a terrible new ache
Rolled over in my chest,
Like in a room where the drapes
Have been swept back. I love you,
I love you, as she continued
Down the hall past other strangers,
Each feeling pierced suddenly
By pillars of heavy light.
I love you, throughout
The performance, in every
Handclap, every stomp.
I love you in the rusted iron
Chains someone was made
To drag until love let them be
Unclasped and left empty
In the center of the ring.
I love you in the water
Where they pretended to wade,
Singing that old blood-deep song
That dragged us to those banks
And cast us in. I love you,
The angles of it scraping at
Each throat, shouldering past
The swirling dust motes
In those beams of light
That whatever we now knew
We could let ourselves feel, knew
To climb. O Woods — O Dogs —
O Tree — O Gun — O *Girl, run* —
O Miraculous Many Gone[1] —
O Lord — O Lord — O Lord —
Is this love the trouble you promised? ■

2018

[1] A reference to "Many Thousand Gone," also known as "No More Auction Block for Me," another well-known spiritual. — Eds.

Understanding and Interpreting

1. **AP® Character, Setting, and Narration.** What do you learn about the speaker and her experience in lines 1–7? How does that experience relate to the context of "Wade in the Water" as a spiritual?
2. **AP® Setting and Narration.** What is "that old blood-deep song" (l. 22)? What does it mean that the song "dragged us to those banks / And cast us in" (ll. 23–24)?
3. **AP® Character, Setting, and Narration.** Lines 24–31 comprise one complete sentence. How would you paraphrase its meaning? What does it reveal about the speaker and the setting of the poem?
4. **AP® Structure and Narration.** When does the speaker move from being an observer to becoming a participant in the performance? How does this change the speaker's perception of her experience? What does it convey about the meaning of the experience, both to the speaker and in a wider context?
5. **AP® Literary Argumentation.** What do you think that "love" means in the context of this poem? Is it romantic love, the love between individuals, a religious or spiritual love — a combination of these, or something else? Explain.

Analyzing Language, Style, and Structure

1. **Vocabulary in Context.** Smith describes the sound of "I love you" as "shouldering past / The swirling dust motes (ll. 26–27). What does the verb "shouldering" mean in this context? What associations does it carry that makes it a more effective choice than, for instance, "moving"?
2. **AP® Structure and Narration.** At what point does the poem turn from the present moment of the performance the speaker is watching to the historical past? How does that shift add complexity to the speaker's experience?
3. **AP® Narration and Figurative Language.** Smith uses several figures of speech, including both similes and metaphors, in this poem. Identify at least three and discuss their significance to the meaning of the poem. Do they work together, or do they work to achieve different purposes? Explain.
4. **AP® Structure, Narration, and Figurative Language.** How does the language of oppression and enslavement contribute to your interpretation of the poem? For instance, what language or images suggest the experience of the Middle Passage?
5. **AP® Structure, Narration, and Figurative Language.** The phrase "I love you" appears throughout the poem, as a kind of chorus or reprise. How does its meaning shift and expand as the poem progresses?
6. **AP® Narration and Figurative language.** Not surprisingly, Smith alludes to biblical passages and uses the language and cadence of the Bible. Consider "pierced suddenly / By pillars of heavy light" (ll. 10–11), and find at least two other examples. How do these choices contribute to the overall mood of the poem?
7. **AP® Figurative Language.** What does the "ring" symbolize in the poem? How does it relate both to the literal actions the speaker describes and to a deeper meaning?
8. **AP® Structure and Narration.** The word "love" pervades this poem. What are the contrasts the speaker raises to this affirmation? How does the poem resolve the tension caused by these contrasts?
9. **AP® Structure and Narration.** Who is speaking in lines 31–34, which consist of a series of phrases punctuated with dashes? To what extent do these lines signal a change in tone?

10. **AP® Character, Structure, and Narration.** Trace the pronoun movement among first, second, and third person, including the collective "we." Do you think that these shifts convey an expanding sense of collective identity or increasing fragmentation? Support your response with textual evidence.

11. **AP® Setting, Structure, Narration, and Figurative Language.** On a surface level, this poem describes a performance that the speaker attends. What elements of rhythm, meter, and sound bring this performance to life for the reader? How does the pacing change in the final five lines?

12. **AP® Setting, Structure, and Narration.** How does Smith convey a nonlinear sense of time in this poem by layering the past within the present? In what ways does this concept of time argue that we deepen our understanding of the present through the past? How does this manipulation of time underscore Smith's comment in an interview that she feels "history is eerily present" today?

Topics for Composing

1. **AP® FRQ Poetry Analysis.** In Tracy K. Smith's "Wade in the Water," published in 2018, the speaker responds to a performance of the spiritual "Wade in the Water." Read the poem carefully. Then, in a well-written essay, analyze how Smith uses literary elements and techniques to convey the transformative power of art.

2. **AP® Literary Argumentation.** In an interview after the publication of *Wade in the Water*, the collection that includes this poem, Tracy K. Smith explained how she believes poetry can heal divisiveness:

   > Poems sometimes challenge our own sense of authority, our own assumptions. They invite us into a larger and stranger view of experience and what is possible. As you become better at accepting other people on their own terms, you become more curious about who they are and what experiences have contributed to their perspectives. I feel that's one of the bridges that might get us from where we are not to where we ought to be.

   How does "Wade in the Water" relate to this assertion? Do you ultimately agree with Smith about what poetry can and should do? Explain.

3. **AP® Literary Argumentation.** A review of the poem "Wade in the Water" described the "embrace" of the poem as capturing "the triumph and burden of forgiveness as embedded in black spirituals." To what extent do you agree with that description of the paradox at the heart of both the poem and the original spiritual?

4. **AP® Literary Argumentation.** Many interpret the spiritual and the poem "Wade in the Water" as insisting on compassion and love in the face of exploitation/abuse and bondage, both physical and psychological. In that way, intragenerational trauma is both acknowledged and healed. To what extent do you agree with this interpretation? Cite specific text from both the spiritual and song to support your position.

5. **Connections.** How does this poem interpret the lyrics of the actual spiritual for which it is named? Find the lyrics online to compare and contrast.

6. **Connections.** Compare and contrast two different choral performances of "Wade in the Water." Are they more alike or different? Do the differences reflect contrasting approaches to the music or the historical moment when they were performed?

7. **Research.** Learn more about the history of the spiritual "Wade in the Water," including its influence in jazz (for instance, the Fisk University Jubilee Singers, Ramsey Lewis's jazz album with the same title, or the Alvin Ailey Dance Company's interpretation of it in "Revelation"). Why do you think artists, musicians, and writers have returned to it so frequently over nearly two centuries? How does Smith's poem fit into the larger tradition of these interpretations of

the spiritual and its meaning? What aspects of the poem bring something new to that tradition?

8. **Research.** The Fisk University Jubilee Singers began performing in 1871, five years after the opening of the university, and continue to be sought-after performers today. Research the ways in which the group has appealed to and expanded their audiences and contributed to an appreciation of the history and music of the spirituals.

I Invite My Parents to a Dinner Party

Chen Chen

Paula Champagne

Poet Chen Chen (b. 1989) holds an MFA from Syracuse University and a PhD from Texas Tech University. He is currently the Jacob Ziskind Visiting Poet-in-Residence at Brandeis University. Chen's poems have appeared in *Poetry*, *Poem-a-Day*, *The Best American Poetry*, and *The Best American Nonrequired Reading*. His book *When I Grow Up I Want to Be a List of Further Possibilities* won multiple awards and was longlisted for the National Book Award.

KEY CONTEXT In this poem Chen Chen alludes several times to the 1990 blockbuster comedy *Home Alone*. The film centers on an eight-year-old boy, a typical mischievous troublemaker, who is accidentally left home alone by his family as they dash off on a European Christmas vacation. Initially pleased to have the house to himself, he soon realizes that he must protect it from a pair of bumbling burglars. "Rambunctiously funny" is the way one critic described this movie, which has become a holiday classic and continued through several sequels.

In the invitation, I tell them for the seventeenth time
(the fourth in writing), that I am gay.

In the invitation, I include a picture of my boyfriend
& write, *You've met him two times. But this time,*

you will ask him things other than can you pass the
whatever. You will ask him

about him. You will enjoy dinner. You will be
enjoyable. Please RSVP.[1]

They RSVP. They come.
They sit at the table & ask my boyfriend

[1] An abbreviation for the French phrase, "Répondez s'il vous plaît," meaning "please respond." "RSVP" is typically included with formal invitations and asks invitees to confirm whether they will attend the event they have been invited to. — Eds.

the first of the conversation starters I slip them
upon arrival: *How is work going?*

I'm like the kid in *Home Alone*, orchestrating
every movement of a proper family, as if a pair

of scary yet deeply incompetent burglars
is watching from the outside.

My boyfriend responds in his chipper way.
I pass my father a bowl of fish ball soup — *So comforting,*

isn't it? My mother smiles her best
Sitting with Her Son's Boyfriend

Who Is a Boy Smile. I smile my Hurray for Doing
a Little Better Smile.

Everyone eats soup.
Then, my mother turns

to me, whispers in Mandarin, *Is he coming with you*
for Thanksgiving? My good friend is & she wouldn't like

this. I'm like the kid in *Home Alone*, pulling
on the string that makes my cardboard mother

more motherly, except she is
not cardboard, she is

already, exceedingly my mother. Waiting
for my answer.

While my father opens up
a *Boston Globe*, when the invitation

clearly stated: *No security*
blankets. I'm like the kid

in *Home Alone*, except the home
is my apartment, & I'm much older, & not alone,

& not the one who needs
to learn, has to — *Remind me*

what's in that recipe again, my boyfriend says
to my mother, as though they have always, easily

talked. As though no one has told him
many times, what a nonlinear slapstick meets

slasher flick meets psychological
pit[2] he is now co-starring in.

Remind me, he says
to our family. ■

2018

[2] Archaic slang for a drive-in movie theater. — Eds.

Understanding and Interpreting

1. **AP® Narration and Structure.** As a reader, how does the title as it is — "I Invite My Parents to a Dinner Party" — differ from the title "I Invite My Parents to Dinner"? How would the latter change your expectations?
2. **AP® Narration.** What elements of formality, including factual details, are there in the first eight lines? What conclusions do you draw about the speaker from these?
3. **AP® Narration.** The main character of *Home Alone* is eight years old. Why does the speaker, who is clearly an adult, identify himself as being "like the kid in *Home Alone*" (l. 13)?
4. **AP® Character and Narration.** What does the speaker mean in the description of his mother in lines 28–31: "my cardboard mother / more motherly, except she is / not cardboard, she is / already, exceedingly my mother"?
5. **AP® Character and Narration.** What qualities in the boyfriend can we infer from this poem appeal to the speaker?
6. **AP® Setting and Narration.** What role does food play in the poem?
7. **AP® Narration.** What elements of humor do you find in the poem? Is it sarcastic, self-effacing, nervous, or something else? To what extent is it effective in moving the poem forward?
8. **AP® Character and Narration.** Overall, how does the speaker characterize his relationship with each of his parents? In what ways does he see himself as parenting his parents? Or is he? Explain.
9. **AP® Character and Narration.** Although the poem is filled with tension and awkward exchanges, what moments of hope and love do you find?

Analyzing Language, Style, and Structure

1. **Vocabulary in Context.** Chen's speaker describes the movie *Home Alone* as "a nonlinear slapstick meets / slasher flick . . ." (ll. 44–45). What does "slapstick" mean? Why is it a more effective word choice than "comic" or "humorous"?
2. **AP® Structure and Narration.** How does the narrative structure of this poem contribute to meaning? Consider ways in which the sequence of events unfolds as a sort of plot you might expect in fiction.
3. **AP® Figurative Language.** Chen uses repetition of a word or phrase, particularly anaphora, throughout the poem. Identify at least three examples and discuss the effect.

4. **AP® Structure and Narration.** The poem is written in couplets, which Chen describes as "a way to highlight tension. . . . [E]ach two-line unit contain[s] some important part of the overall conflict." In what ways is this structural choice effective in terms of the meaning of the poem overall?
5. **AP® Structure and Narration.** In several cases, Chen puts a string of words together as one modifier, but he does not hyphenate them as is the convention, and in one case he capitalizes them. Discuss the effect of these two examples: "Hurray for Doing / a Little Better Smile" (ll. 21–22).
6. **AP® Structure and Narration.** What is the effect of the very short simple sentences that are carefully placed throughout the poem? How does this syntactical choice influence your interpretation?
7. **AP® Character, Narration, and Figurative Language.** What is the reference of the pronoun in the last line: "to our family"? How does this simple pronoun reference contribute to your interpretation of the poem?

Topics for Composing

1. **AP® FRQ Poetry Analysis.** In Chen Chen's "I Invite My Parents to a Dinner Party," published in 2018, the speaker describes bringing his boyfriend to dinner with his parents. Read the poem carefully. Then, in a well-written essay, analyze how Chen uses literary elements and techniques to convey the complexities of navigating relationships with loved ones.
2. **AP® Literary Argumentation.** Chen has spoken about the painful process of change, which involves "people . . . still learning . . . or unlearning. In my case, it's homophobia that my parents continue to have to unlearn." In what ways is this a poem more about "unlearning" than "learning"?
3. **Connections.** The movie *Home Alone* plays a prominent role in "I Invite My Parents to a Dinner Party" as the speaker repeats: "I'm like the kid in *Home Alone*." View the movie (the original); then discuss how seeing the entire film deepens your understanding of why and how the speaker identifies with Kevin, the lead character in *Home Alone*. In what ways might the poem be considered to be "in conversation with *Home Alone*," as one critic as observed?
4. **Speaking and Listening.** The speaker acknowledges that he is "orchestrating" the dinner party; in so doing, he also controls the perspective. Develop a conversation among all four of the people at dinner — mother, father, boyfriend, and speaker — with different classmates assuming the voice of each. After the others in the class observe this conversation, discuss the interpretation(s) that emerge from exploring multiple perspectives.
5. **Connections.** Describe a time when you brought someone into a family occasion — a holiday dinner, a family reunion, a birthday party, a weekend visit — where you were uneasy about your family's response to your guest or friend. What was the source of the tension(s)? How were some of the tensions resolved; if they were not or perhaps were exacerbated, why? What might have been done differently to achieve a more satisfying outcome?
6. **Multimodal.** The dinner table or the kitchen table is often the space where family relationships are depicted, whether through heightened conflict or reassuring connection. Identify a visual image that demonstrates a specific family dynamic and discuss what it is and how it is conveyed. You might choose a painting, photograph, cartoon, or movie still; or you might create your own image.

How to Date a White Boy

Amy Alvarez

Adam Lewis

Poet Amy Alvarez (b. 1979) was born in New York City to a Jamaican mother and Puerto Rican father. She has a BA from Hobart and William Smith College, an MA in English Education from the City College of New York and an MFA in poetry from the University of Southern Maine. Her work has appeared in numerous print and online journals. A former high school teacher, she currently teaches at the University of West Virginia. Alvarez's work often focuses on issues of race, gender, and social justice.

KEY CONTEXT The poem references Sandra Bland and Tamir Rice. Bland was a twenty-nine-year-old African American woman who was arrested during a traffic stop in 2015 and died by suicide in police custody. Rice was a twelve-year-old African American child who was shot and killed by police in 2014.

1.
Never be the first. You are no one's
enigma or experiment. Find evidence:
an old photo online, in a dusty shoebox
under his bed. Do not be his melanated[1]
test drive. Do not feel flattered.

2.
If you meet his parents, prepare
for disappointment. You will want
them to be pleased with your philosophy
thesis/your grandma's pearls. You will
hope they are immediately rude so you
do not waste another fertile year on their
son. They will invite you to a cookout (they
will call it a barbeque, but it will be a cookout).
Don't get too upset when you overhear
the grandmother say you are darker/smarter/
prettier/more or less articulate than expected.
She will be dead before the wedding if there is one.

3.
So, you've fallen in love. Remind him
before you create a joint Instagram
account, before you adopt a shelter
dog, remind him that you wear the same
MAC[2] foundation number as Sandra Bland.

---

[1] A reference to melanin, an element responsible for skin pigmentation in humans. — Eds.

[2] A cosmetics company. — Eds.

That your brother looked like Tamir when
he was little. Before you argue names for
imagined children, remind him of what
could happen to a boy with your face.

4.

So, your white boy thinks you should move
in together. Take him to un-gentrified Bronx
neighborhoods where old men play dominoes
on the sidewalk and children have no bedtimes
in summer. Take him to your favorite auntie's
house. Let him get a tongue lashing from your
Hotep[3] cousin while you "help" in the kitchen
by taste-testing arroz con pollo/collards/quinoa salad.

5.

So, your white boy has fallen in love with you.
He has told off Johnnie Come Woke-ly friends.
He is asking whether you have ever thought it
would be easier with someone browner than him,
whether your parents, best friend, your abuelita[4]
would be happier. Hold his hands in yours. Notice
his red face, tear-filled eyes. Tell him the truth. ■

2019

---

[3] Historically an Egyptian term meaning to be at peace, "hotep" is now often used as a pejorative term to describe a Black man who advocates for Black men but not Black women and Black LGBTQ+ people. — Eds.

[4] Spanish for grandmother. — Eds.

Understanding and Interpreting

1. **AP® Narration.** Who is the "you" in this poem? How does this contrast who the wider audience for the poem is?
2. **AP® Narration.** Consider the speaker's warnings at the end of the first stanza. What does the speaker mean by "Do not be his melanated / test drive" (ll. 4–5), and why does the speaker admonish, "Do not feel flattered" (l. 5)? How do these statements contribute to the tone of the poem?
3. **AP® Character and Narration.** In the second stanza, who does the speaker think will be disappointed? What do these disappointments suggest about individual expectations?
4. **AP® Character, Setting, and Narration.** Why does Alvarez include the clarification about a barbecue being different from a cookout? What larger point does the speaker make here?
5. **AP® Character, Setting, and Narration.** The speaker asserts in the third stanza that a white boy in this situation should be reminded of a particular set of realities facing many Black people, particularly Afro-Latino people. What are these realities, according to the speaker? What expectation does she tell the audience to have for how this conversation will go?
6. **AP® Narration.** What does the speaker mean in the final line of the poem by "Tell him the truth"? What is "the truth"? Explain.

Analyzing Language, Style, and Structure

1. **Vocabulary in Context.** Alvarez uses the word "enigma" in line 2 in conjunction with "experiment." Why does she pair the two words, and how do they offer differing implications? Do you believe "enigma" is an example of effective word choice in this context? Explain.
2. **AP® Structure and Narration.** Why does Alvarez number each stanza? How does the structure of the poem suggest the development of an increasingly serious relationship?
3. **AP® Structure and Narration.** "Johnnie Come Woke-ly" alludes to the phrase "Johnny-come-lately," which refers to someone new to a location or ability. What does Alvarez imply by combining the traditional phrase with the concept of being "woke"?
4. **AP® Setting, Structure, Narration, and Figurative Language.** While all of the stanzas present complex matters, the second stanza in particular outlines the contradictory and even confusing and frustrating experiences people can have as they navigate a relationship with someone of a different race and/or ethnicity, particularly in relationships between Black and white people. Why does the speaker address these experiences early in the poem? How does the language she uses in this stanza frame the challenging realities many people in such a relationship might face? Explain.
5. **AP® Structure and Narration.** How does Alvarez's title "How to Date a White Boy" and the conversational nature of the poem help shape its message? How does this effect differ from that of a more formal or detached approach?
6. **AP® Structure and Narration.** What is the effect of the speaker's use of "your" in the first line of stanza 5? What are two or more words that describe the tone of this sentence?

Topics for Composing

1. **AP® FRQ Poetry Analysis.** In Amy Alvarez's "How to Date a White Boy," published in 2019, the speaker offers advice to other Black and Afro-Latina women on dating someone white. Read the poem carefully. Then, in a well-written essay, analyze how Alvarez uses literary elements and techniques to develop the speaker's complex perspective on her relationship.
2. **Speaking and Listening.** Engage in a class discussion about the challenges of forming a friendship or engaging in a romantic relationship with someone whose background differs in some way from yours. What are some of the adjustments we all make in our friendships and relationships even when we don't have diverse backgrounds? Why is such flexibility and even compromise important? Why is it that diverse racial and ethnic backgrounds make such flexibility and compromise more challenging even for people very open to such friendships and relationships?
3. **Research.** In a 2019 interview for NPR's podcast "The Hidden Brain" with host Shankar Vedantam, Brett Pelham, a professor of psychology at Montgomery College in Maryland, explained that "we tend to focus on people who are more like us, who speak our language, who speak our idiom, who look like us, who worship like us." Pelham attributes much of this to the concept "implicit egotism." Research implicit egotism and the role it plays in the people we surround ourselves with. Then, write an essay in which you explore the challenges Alvarez presents in her poem through the lens of implicit egotism and include ways to move beyond the kinds of self-segregation Alvarez describes.
4. **Research.** Despite the fact that many people still marry someone with a similar background, the Pew Research Center has found in recent years that increasingly more people are

marrying someone of a different race, ethnicity, and/or religion. Explore these trends and develop an argument about why you think these changes are occurring.

5. **Multimodal.** Create a paper or digital collage in which you represent some of the cultural elements most important to you. For example, Alvarez includes men playing "dominoes / on the sidewalk" (ll. 28–29) and foods such as "arroz con pollo/collards/quinoa salad" (l. 33). What would someone visiting your neighborhood see? What kinds of food are important in your family because of your culture?
6. **Speaking and Listening.** The concept of "being woke" has its roots in political efforts supporting Abraham Lincoln in the 1860s. Explore "wokeness," including its early history and more recent resurgence to prepare for a discussion of the ways in which this poem embodies "wokeness" as a concept. What, if any, criticisms of wokeness does the speaker make?

Lady Jordan

Denice Frohman

Francois Durand/Getty Images

As a poet, performer, and educator, Denice Frohman (b. 1985), addresses identity and social change. Her work has appeared in a range of publications including the *New York Times*, *LatiNext*, and *Nepantla: An Anthology for Queer Poets of Color*. She is a former Women of the World Poetry Slam Champion and has received awards from The National Association of Latino Arts and Culture and co-organized #PoetsforPuertoRico. Frohman played professional basketball in Puerto Rico after graduating from college. With an M.A. in education from Drexel University, she continues to work with programs to empower youth. From her home base in Philadelphia, she continues to tour the country as a speaker and performer.

KEY CONTEXT: This poem appeared in a featured section of the *New York Times* series called "The Mrs. Files," which "look[s] at history through a contemporary lens to see what the honorific 'Mrs.' means to women and their identity." The title of the poem is a reference to Michael Jordan, who is described on the National Basketball Association's website as "the greatest basketball player of all time."

It didn't matter that I married the game
    or slept with a ball under my arm, Mom said
Girls don't hoop, they wear hoops. And around here,
    vecinas[1] chirped: it's always "¿Y tú novio?[2]" season. But beauty
is a finger roll. A backdoor cut on the blacktop. A fadeaway
    jump shot, two seconds left on the clock. So what mattered was Danny
talkin' smack, even though his teeth were out of order. This isn't the only history,
    but is the history of everything: the neighborhood boys

[1] Spanish for female neighbors. — Eds.

[2] Spanish for "And your boyfriend?" — Eds.

who shot crooked, never learned my name, so I played them
Twenty-one[3], turned their ankles to jello,
made their backs kiss the floor, until they donned me
Lady Jordan, and who wouldn't take that. Though I've never been
ladylike, I wore that rusted metal rim like a ring,
and slipped my bones through the net like a perfect white dress — ■

2020

[3] A reference to playing individually: the first player to reach 21 free-throws from the line wins. — Eds.

Understanding and Interpreting

1. **AP® Narration.** What does the title suggest to you even before you've read the poem?
2. **AP® Character and Narration.** In the opening four lines, what context does the speaker establish? How do her mother and neighbors view her?
3. **AP® Character, Setting, and Narration.** How does the speaker define "beauty" (l. 4)? How does the speaker imply her community defines beauty?
4. **AP® Character and Narration.** The speaker tells us that the "neighborhood boys" never learned her name, so "I played them / Twenty-one" (ll. 9–10). Why is this type of win significant to the speaker?
5. **AP® Narration.** How do you interpret the meaning of the lines, "This isn't the only history, / but is the history of everything" (ll. 7–8)?
6. **AP® Character and Narration.** What does the speaker mean when she says "and who wouldn't take that" (l. 12) in response to being called "Lady Jordan"?

Analyzing Language, Style, and Structure

1. **Vocabulary in Context.** The verb "to don" literally means to put on an article of clothing, such as, "She donned her finest outfit for the important interview." How does Denice Frohman draw on its connotations or associations of this word when she writes that the "neighborhood boys" "*donned* me / Lady Jordan"? Why is it an effective choice?
2. **AP® Narration and Figurative Language.** How does the allusion in the title signal a meaning beyond the speaker's actual experience?
3. **AP® Character, Structure, and Narration.** Identify at least two examples of sound and rhythm that contribute to the energy of this poem. In what ways do these undercut the stereotype of the demure bride?
4. **AP® Narration and Figurative Language.** Throughout this poem, Frohman plays with language. She puns, teases with double meanings, and uses figurative language. Identify three examples and discuss their effect.
5. **AP® Character, Structure, Narration, and Figurative Language.** "Lady Jordan" is a kaleidoscope of mixed registers — and languages. How do the different languages, use of colloquialism and slang alongside more formal diction, and the jargon of basketball develop the relationship between the speaker and her sport?
6. **AP® Narration and Figurative Language.** References to marriage frame the poem in the opening and closing lines. In what other ways does Frohman develop the idea of her "marriage" with basketball?

7. **AP® Structure and Narration.** How does the form of the poem – the arrangement of lines, enjambment, and indentations – reflect the events that the speaker relays?
8. **AP® Narration and Figurative Language.** Ultimately, do you think the central metaphor of the poem is ironic? Explain why or why not.

Topics for Composing

1. AP® FRQ **Poetry Analysis.** In Denice Frohman's "Lady Jordan," published in 2020, the speaker describes her experience as a girl playing basketball, uninvited, with the "neighborhood boys." Read the poem carefully. Then, in a well-written essay, analyze how Frohman uses literary elements and techniques to convey the speaker's complex relationship with sports and social expectations.
2. **AP® Literary Argumentation.** At the heart of "Lady Jordan" is the concept of power—who has permission to be in the game, who gets to play. What kind of power does the speaker in this poem want, or seek? How does she gain that power?
3. **AP® Literary Argumentation.** In an interview, Forman explained that one reason she was drawn to reading and writing poetry is that it holds "a duality . . . with two or more points of tension." In what ways does "Lady Jordan" embody this description?
4. **Connections.** In "Lady Jordan," the speaker points out that the "neighborhood boys . . . never learned my name." When asked in an interview when her name has meant to her and her career, Frohman explained that while her mother, with whom she grew up, is Puerto Rican, her last name is the same as her father, who is Jewish:

   > I have my father's last name solely because of a patriarchal idea. . . . I'm writing about the things that reflect my lived experience, which tell a fuller picture than just my name might tell you, so my name is both a reflection of what is visible and invisible."

   Using this quotation as a jumping-off point, discuss the meaning your name has for you, both "what is visible and invisible" and why you would or would not consider changing your name.
5. **Connections.** In Denis Johnson's 2007 novel *Tree of Smoke*, one character tells another, "I told you my real name. Big mistake." He goes on to say, "People know your name . . . and it hurts." Does this poem embody or challenge this perspective? Consider whether the speaker would consider "Lady Jordan" her "real name."
6. **Research.** Read at least five of the articles from "The Mrs. Files" in the *New York Times*. Summarize the findings from these articles. Explain why you take issue with at least one of them and why you agree with another. Discuss how the themes of Frohman's poem relate to the series as a whole.
7. **Multimodal.** Working in groups, develop a video interpretation for "Lady Jordan." Be sure to include the poem either as a voice over or by putting the text on the screen.
8. **Connections.** When it was printed in the *New York Times*, the poem "Lady Jordan" was accompanied by a photograph of the basketball player Cheryl Miller, who was often referred to as "the female Jordan." Conduct some research on her and discuss how Frohman's poem can be read as a subtle tribute to Miller.

AP® Multiple-Choice Practice

Wind in a Box

Terrance Hayes

—after Lorca

I want to always sleep beneath a bright red blanket
of leaves. I want to never wear a coat of ice.
I want to learn to walk without blinking.

I want to outlive the turtle and the turtle's father,
the stone. I want a mouth full of permissions

and a pink glistening bud. If the wildflower and ant hill
can return after sleeping each season, I want to walk
out of this house wearing nothing but wind.

I want to greet you, I want to wait for the bus with you
weighing less than a chill. I want to fight off the bolts

of gray lighting the alcoves and winding paths
of your hair. I want to fight off the damp nudgings
of snow. I want to fight off the wind.

I want to be the wind and I want to fight off the wind
with its sagging banner of isolation, its swinging

screen doors, its gilded boxes, and neatly folded pamphlets
of noise. I want to fight off the dull straight lines
of two by fours and endings, your disapprovals,

your doubts and regulations, your carbon copies.
If the locust can abandon its suit,

I want a brand new name. I want the pepper's fury
and the salt's tenderness. I want the virtue
of the evening rain, but not its gossip.

I want the moon's intuition, but not its questions.
I want the malice of nothing on earth. I want to enter

every room in a strange electrified city
and find you there. I want your lips around the bell of flesh

at the bottom of my ear. I want to be the mirror,
but not the nightstand. I do not want to be the light switch.

I do not want to be the yellow photograph
or book of poems. When I leave this body, Woman,
I want to be pure flame. I want to be your song. ■

2006

AP® Multiple-Choice Questions

1. The repetition of "I want to" throughout the poem primarily conveys
   a. humanity's insatiable nature
   b. people's ever-changing desires
   c. the confusion felt by lovers
   d. the extent of the speaker's love
   e. the selfishness of the speaker

2. The juxtaposition of the "bright red blanket / of leaves" and the "coat of ice" presented within the first two lines reveal the speaker's
   a. fear of distancing himself from family
   b. frustration with people's indecisiveness
   c. gratitude for the choices life offers
   d. need to connect with nature
   e. desire to be comforted by love

3. Which of the following best describes the function of the poem's structure?
   a. The lack of order reflects the speaker's chaotic emotions.
   b. The alternating stanza lengths convey a measured order to his thinking.
   c. The rhymes are consistent, much like his desires.
   d. The predictable pattern mirrors his boredom in the relationship.
   e. The finality of thought in each stanza depicts his resolute nature.

4. In stanzas 4 through 7, the phrase "I want to fight off" implies that the speaker
   a. sees himself as a protector
   b. thinks his actions are futile
   c. flaunts his strength to woo women
   d. knows that his beloved is in danger
   e. sacrifices his life for the one he loves

5. Lines 20–21 convey which of the following about the speaker?
   a. He is dissatisfied with his appearance.
   b. He is ashamed of his behavior in the past.
   c. He wants to transform himself for his love.
   d. He wishes that he were the one she loves.
   e. He wants to pursue a new love with someone else.

6. The imagery in lines 6–7 emphasizes the speaker's
   a. hope for the future of his failed relationship
   b. obsession with plant and animal life
   c. understanding that love compares with other natural processes
   d. realization that love is fleeting and must therefore be treasured
   e. belief that the nature of love is unchanging and eternal

7. What do the "light switch" and "yellow photograph" have in common?
   a. The speaker is not happy with these things in his home.
   b. The speaker sees them as easily dismissed and forgotten.
   c. The speaker is resentful of their utility, as opposed to his own.
   d. The speaker does not want to be an inanimate object to her.
   e. The speaker sees them as reminders of his failed relationship.

8. What is the relationship between the title and the rest of the poem?
   a. The speaker wishes he could capture and contain his love.
   b. The speaker finds freedom in the confinement of the relationship.
   c. The speaker feels trapped by this relationship.
   d. The speaker is empty without his love by his side.
   e. The speaker is willing to travel anywhere for his beloved.

9. The final line of the poem conveys the speaker's
- **a.** ultimate, desperate plea
- **b.** moment of death
- **c.** separation from his beloved
- **d.** final, romantic desire
- **e.** irrational thought process

10. As a whole, the poem is best characterized as conveying
- **a.** a lover's complaint
- **b.** a lover's irrational musings
- **c.** people's need for adventure
- **d.** people's fears of remaining alone
- **e.** a lover's devotion to his beloved

My love is as a fever, longing still

William Shakespeare

My love is as a fever, longing still
For that which longer nurseth the disease,
Feeding on that which doth preserve the ill,
Th' uncertain sickly appetite to please.
My reason, the physician to my love,
Angry that his prescriptions are not kept,
Hath left me, and I desperate now approve
Desire is death, which physic[1] did except.
Past cure I am, now reason is past care,
And frantic-mad with evermore unrest;
My thoughts and my discourse as madmen's are,
At random from the truth vainly express'd;
 For I have sworn thee fair, and thought thee bright,
 Who art as black as hell, as dark as night. ■

1609

[1] Medicine. — Eds.

AP® Multiple-Choice Questions

1. How is love characterized within the first quatrain?
- **a.** A caring companion
- **b.** A desirable emotion
- **c.** A fickle sentiment
- **d.** A gluttonous predator
- **e.** A healing entity

2. The speaker's "reason" (l. 5) is most directly contrasted with
- **a.** "love" (l. 1)
- **b.** "his prescriptions" (l. 6)
- **c.** "cure" (l. 9)
- **d.** "care" (l. 9)
- **e.** "the truth" (l. 12)

3. The word "physic" refers to
- **a.** "fever" (l. 1)
- **b.** "My love" (l. 1)
- **c.** "the ill" (l. 3)
- **d.** "appetite" (l. 4)
- **e.** "prescriptions" (l. 6)

4. What does the phrase "now reason is past care" (l. 9) imply?
- **a.** The speaker is trying to hold on to his former life.
- **b.** The speaker no longer worries about his ailment.
- **c.** The speaker must focus on his health from now on.

d. The speaker's rational mind can no longer be healed.
e. The speaker's beloved could never love him again.

5. The two references to madness in the third quatrain are most closely manifested by the speaker's
a. insatiable appetite
b. irrational thinking
c. persistent listlessness
d. physical ailments
e. unsubstantiated fears

6. The heroic couplet serves to
a. express the speaker's desire
b. introduce a new dilemma
c. question what came before it
d. identify the source of the speaker's pain
e. offer the solution to the speaker's problem

7. The speaker is best characterized as
a. a disciplined, careful patient
b. an irrational, foolish dreamer
c. a resentful, pained man
d. a sickly, older gentleman
e. a young, inexperienced lover

8. "Desire is death" (l. 8) conveys that
a. the speaker can no longer help himself
b. the speaker seeks an alternative to pain
c. the speaker is resigned to his beloved's denial
d. destructive relationships result in tragedy
e. prolonged yearnings are destructive

9. To which phrase is "that which longer nurseth the disease" (l. 2) most closely related?
a. "that which doth preserve the ill" (l. 3)
b. "the physician to my love" (l. 5)
c. "reason is past care" (l. 9)
d. "frantic-mad with evermore unrest" (l. 10)
e. "as black as hell, as dark as night" (l. 14)

10. The speaker is most probably addressing his
a. beloved
b. doctor
c. friends
d. madness
e. reflection

11. The tone of the poem in lines 13–14 is best described as
a. accusatory
b. humorous
c. restrained
d. romantic
e. sorrowful

Suggestions for Writing

Love and Relationships

1. **AP® Literary Argumentation.** Many works of literature feature an event or moment of insight that changes a character's self-perception. Choose a work of fiction or poetry in this chapter which a character or speaker undergoes such a change. Then, in a well-written essay, analyze how that shift contributes to an interpretation of the work as a whole. Do not merely summarize the plot.
2. **AP® Literary Argumentation.** An often-quoted piece of dialogue from the Oscar Wilde play *A Woman of No Importance* offers a cynical view of marriage: "One should always be in love. That is the reason one should never marry." Choose one short story in this chapter and analyze whether the story supports or refutes the cynical view of marriage expressed in this quotation. Include specific references to the text to support your analysis.
3. **AP® Literary Argumentation.** It has been said that poetry counts; language mediates. Choose a poem from this chapter and analyze how the writer uses poetic elements to illustrate this expression.
4. **Connections.** Choose two poems from this chapter that posit contrasting views on romantic love. Write an essay in which you analyze the contrasting attitudes toward the subject. Consider how poetic devices in each piece help to convey the speaker's particular viewpoint.
5. **Connections.** Many of the texts in this chapter comment on inequities in the power of men and women in romance and marriage. Concentrating on three texts, write an essay analyzing the consequences of such inequities. Consider similarities as well as differences.
6. **Connections.** Many of the authors in this chapter explore the disconnect between physical attraction and true love. Using the literature in this chapter as evidence, write an essay arguing for or against the importance of physical attractiveness in a romantic relationship.
7. **Connections.** Song lyrics often use love and relationships as a theme. Choose a song from a recording artist whose work you enjoy, and analyze the lyrics in the same way you would a piece of literature. Discuss how the songwriter uses imagery, diction, syntax, allusion, and figurative language, and explain their effect on the song.
8. **Creative Writing.** Using one of the poems in this chapter as a model, write a poem on the theme of love and relationships. You might write a poem that offers a twist on a mythological story of seduction or love, as Margaret Atwood does in "Siren Song," or write a poem based on an analogy, as Billy Collins does in "Weighing the Dog."
9. **Connections.** Watch a film that is considered a romantic comedy; then discuss some of the techniques the filmmaker uses to explore the theme of love and relationships. Compare and contrast those techniques with the ones encountered in this chapter, such as irony, farce, romantic imagery, stock characters, and predictable plot structures.
10. **AP® Literary Argumentation.** Choose one of the following quotations about love and relationships, and write an essay analyzing the extent that it applies to at least two of the texts in this chapter.

a. [L]ove is to let those we love be perfectly themselves, and not to twist them to fit our own image. Otherwise we love only the reflection of ourselves we find in them.
— Thomas Merton

b. There is always some madness in love. But there is also always some reason in madness.
— Friedrich Nietzsche

c. Being deeply loved by someone gives you strength, while loving someone deeply gives you courage.
— Lao Tzu

d. A journey is like marriage. The certain way to be wrong is to think you control it.
— John Steinbeck

e. Marriage is a wonderful institution, but who wants to live in an institution?
— Groucho Marx

f. We are never so defenseless against suffering as when we love.
— Sigmund Freud

g. We love because it's the only true adventure.
— Nikki Giovanni

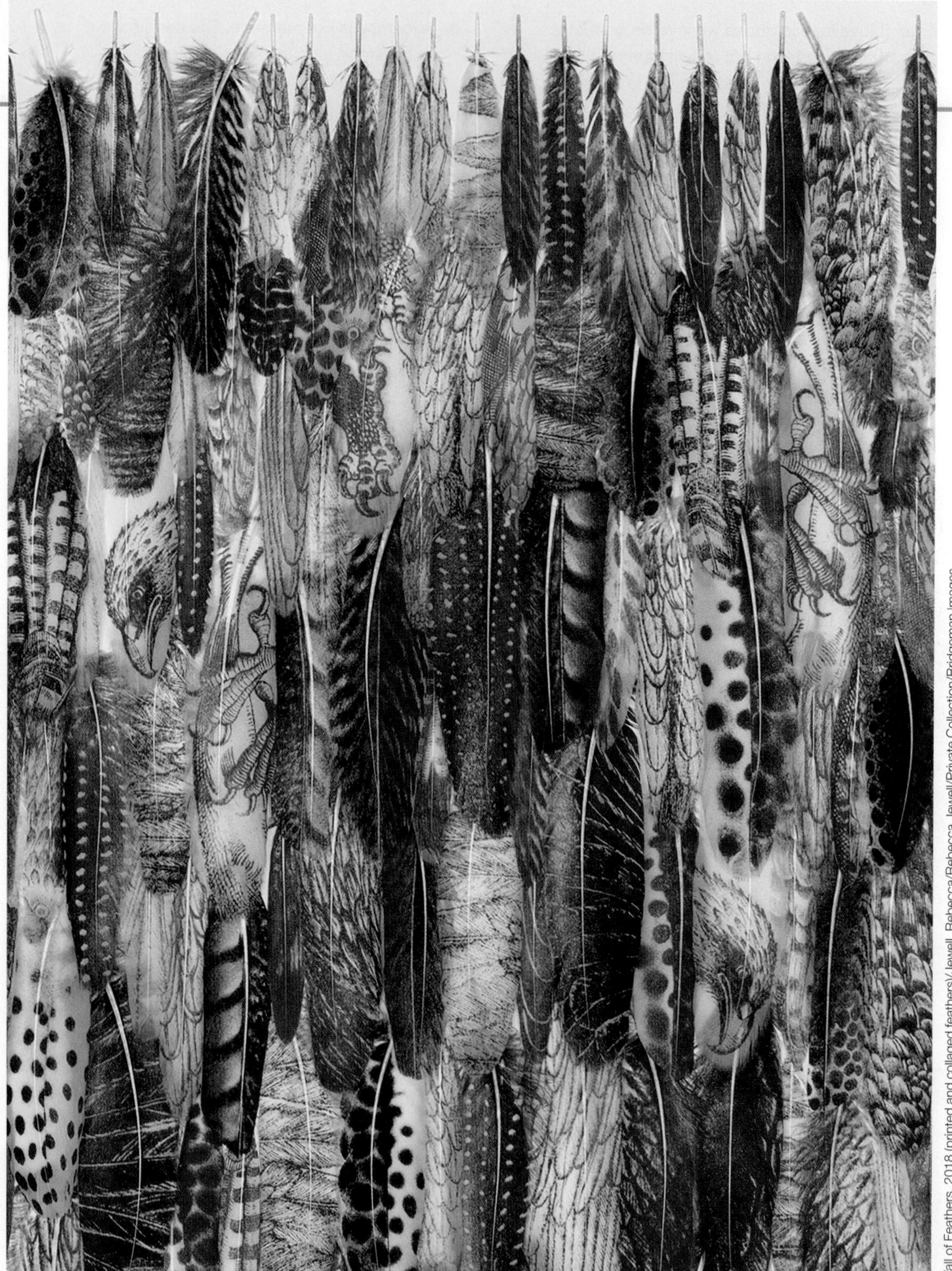

Wall of Feathers, 2018 (printed and collaged feathers)/Jewell, Rebecca/Rebecca Jewell/Private Collection/Bridgeman Images

6

Conformity and Rebellion

Much of the world's literature might be said to express the struggle between conformity and rebellion. We find this theme in our earliest recorded texts. Genesis tells the story of Eve and Adam's refusal to conform — an act picked up centuries later in the opening lines of John Milton's epic poem, *Paradise Lost*: "Of man's first disobedience, and the fruit / Of that forbidden tree whose mortal taste / Brought death into the world, and all our woe." At the same time, however, we see obedience as a virtue. Without duty and order, without cooperation and teamwork, where would we be? We admire and respect those heroes who hold things together — figures such as Abraham Lincoln and Franklin Delano Roosevelt — as well as those who serve and protect us: police officers, firefighters, and soldiers. But we also look to heroes who rebel: Socrates, Nicolaus Copernicus, Galileo Galilei, Thomas Jefferson, Henry David Thoreau, Elizabeth Cady Stanton, Harriet Tubman, Mahatma Gandhi, and Martin Luther King Jr. Our heroes are often those who, as Senator Robert F. Kennedy said, "dream of things that never were and ask, why not?" Sometimes the noblest rebellion is in conformity with a higher law.

The texts in this chapter present the ongoing struggle between the inertia of conformity and the force of rebellion. The characters in this chapter's Central Text, *Passing* by Harlem Renaissance writer Nella Larsen, make choices that conform to and chafe against the expectations and limitations of a racist society. Focusing on two central characters who have chosen different paths, Larsen raises questions about which of these, if either, can lead life with integrity in a fundamentally broken and divided world. The Classic Text in this chapter, William Shakespeare's *Hamlet*, explores similar concerns as the title character must decide whether to avenge his father's death by killing a king. Our Texts in Context furthers our study of what makes Hamlet a compelling character so many centuries later.

This chapter includes short fiction and poetry that also address essential questions about what it means — and costs — to take a stand against existing systems and attempt to rebalance power. In the nineteenth-century story "Bartleby, the Scrivener," Herman Melville demonstrates one man's rebellion against the expectations of others on Wall Street, a setting that has come to symbolize both ambition and excess. In the twenty-first-century short story "Lulu," Te-Ping Chen examines both the necessity and steep price of political activism that challenges state-sponsored injustice. Likewise, poems by Percy Bysshe Shelley and Jericho Brown take political stances, while those by Laura Da' and Robin Coste Lewis reveal that we pay a steeper price still for going along to get along.

To understand and fully appreciate the novel and play in this chapter, let's examine the Big Ideas, Skills, and Essential Knowledge in Unit 6 of the AP® English Literature and Composition Course and Exam Description. This unit focuses on Character, Structure, Narration, Figurative Language, and Literary Argumentation. While this unit might not stress the importance of Setting, keep in mind that this Big Idea has already been discussed in Chapter 4, and this course continually revisits concepts from earlier units in the questions.

AP® Big Idea: Character

In this chapter's Classic Text, the **character** of Hamlet is arguably the most dissected figure in literary history. While novels depend on narrators and other characters to convey details about perspectives on protagonists, the chief source of this information in Shakespeare's play is Hamlet himself. His soliloquies open a window into his mind, revealing the breadth of his emotions, and ultimately paint a figure that continues to defy simple characterization centuries later. We can also examine Hamlet's actions for insight into his character. Throughout history, many people have pondered why it is that Hamlet thinks so much and acts so little. Perhaps Hamlet does not think too much, but rather too well. The scope of his imagination is vast; his understanding of politics and human nature is profound; and the task before him — killing one king to avenge the death of another — is superhuman, especially in an era that viewed earthly political hierarchies as reflections of the order of the universe. Hamlet, in fact, is a scholar's scholar, devoted to reading widely and thinking deeply and broadly about the world. His inability to conform to others' expectations of him is both key to his downfall and to what makes him a compelling character with nearly endless possibilities for interpretation. *To review characterization in longer works of fiction and drama, see pages 108–113 of Chapter 3: Analyzing Longer Fiction and Drama.*

AP® Big Idea: Structure

While it might be tempting to analyze *Hamlet*'s **structure** in terms of its five-act and subsequent scene divisions, these markers were not necessarily written by Shakespeare. The divisions we see stem primarily from the *First Folio*, a collection of Shakespeare's works published seven years after his death. How, then, did Shakespeare structure his plays? Much like modern film and television, he was interested in drawing his audience into the story, providing them with a build-up of tension that ultimately reaches a climax, and leaving them with a cathartic ending. How are we drawn into *Hamlet*? Shakespeare gives us a ghost, preparations for war, mystery, and family drama. The tension is heightened by the complications of a failed relationship, a dysfunctional family, lunacy, betrayal, and several characters' violent deaths. Ultimately, all of these factors converge in a final scene: a duel. In the space of a few moments, a monarchy crumbles, villainy is revealed, most of the remaining characters die, our hero is injured, and Horatio proclaims that "flights of angels" should sing him — and us — to his rest. *To review plot structure in longer works of fiction and drama, see pages 118–120 of Chapter 3: Analyzing Longer Fiction and Drama.*

AP® Big Idea: Narration

As you have seen in earlier chapters, and in other genres of literature, **narration** is a critical component of storytelling. While *Hamlet* is a play without a narrator, we still see life through the eyes of several of its characters, particularly during their soliloquies, in which they reveal their innermost thoughts. Hamlet decides that he will "wipe away all trivial, fond records" and think only of avenging his father's death—yet he still debates whether to kill King Claudius, the man responsible, and even considers whether to end his own life in some moments. We also learn, in King Claudius's soliloquy, that what motivates him is neither guilt nor regret for killing King Hamlet but the desire to keep the power he has gained. *To review narrative perspective and point of view in longer fiction and drama, see pages 120–127 of Chapter 3: Analyzing Longer Fiction and Drama.*

AP® Big Idea: Figurative Language

William Shakespeare was a poet, not only in his sonnets and longer poems, but also in his plays, which are written in blank verse. Generally, the poetry of his plays contains meter, namely iambic pentameter, but no rhyme, and conveys much of its meaning through **figurative language**. In comparisons, symbols, personification, imagery, and more, he develops the complex characters, motifs, and thematic concerns of *Hamlet*. Francisco is "sick at heart," the world is an "unweeded garden," Rosencrantz and Guildenstern are sponges, and Hamlet himself questions whether his childhood friends think of him as "a pipe." These are but a fraction of the comparisons and instances of wordplay that color and complicate Hamlet's world, bringing it alive for audiences through the ages. *To review figurative language in longer fiction and drama, see pages 128–132 of Chapter 3: Analyzing Longer Fiction and Drama.*

AP® Big Idea: Literary Argumentation

While looking at literature through the lens of these Big Ideas is a good way to focus our observations in our reading, insightful literary analysis hinges on forming — and defending — an interpretation of meaning. In this chapter, you'll have many opportunities to practice **literary argumentation** as you express your interpretations of the readings. You'll answer questions that gauge your understanding, engage in discussions, and develop formal and informal responses. When working with longer fiction and drama, remember that your response to and analysis of a text in the AP® Literary Argument FRQ must encompass the meaning of the work as a whole, rather than an excerpt of the text. *To review the process of writing an AP® Literary Argument Essay, see pages 136–157 of Chapter 3: Analyzing Longer Fiction and Drama.*

Reading longer works of fiction and drama allows you to travel to distant lands and time periods. From the confines of our classrooms, we learn that despite the differences that exist between us, there is much more that binds us; and we all face moments in which we must decide whether to conform or rebel.

Guided Reading for *Passing*

As you read the Central Text in this chapter, *Passing* by Nella Larsen (p. 487), keep track of your observations and questions about how Larsen develops the following Big Ideas.

AP® Big Idea	Observations	Questions
Character		
Structure		
Narration		
Figurative Language		

AP® Unit 6 Alignment at a Glance

Central Text / Nella Larsen, *Passing* (longer fiction) pp. 487–554
Classic Text / William Shakespeare, *Hamlet* (drama) pp. 555–632
Texts in Context / *Hamlet* and the Evolution of Character pp. 633–645
AP® Multiple-Choice Practice pp. 748–753

Passing

Nella Larsen

Carl Van Vechten/© Van Vechten Trust, Photoprovided by Yale University Library, Beinecke RareBook and Manuscript Library.

One of the most important writers of the Harlem Renaissance, Nella Larsen (1891–1964) was born Nellie Walker in Chicago to a West Indian father and a Danish mother. When her mother remarried, she took her stepfather's surname. She spent a year at Fisk University before attending nursing school in New York City. Although she worked briefly at the Tuskegee Institute in Alabama, she spent most of her life as a nurse and librarian in New York City. She and her husband, Elmer Imes, the second African American to earn a PhD in physics, were active participants in the social circles of the Harlem Renaissance. Larsen is remembered chiefly for her two novels, *Quicksand* (1928) and *Passing* (1929), and a handful of short stories. In 1930, Larsen was the first Black woman to win a Guggenheim Fellowship.

KEY CONTEXT Nella Larsen wrote *Passing* during the Harlem Renaissance in the 1920s. This was a period of exceptional creativity for Black writers, visual artists, musicians, and playwrights. While Larsen's work focused on the urban elite in the North, others represented rural folk culture, the American Midwest, and the South. The range of subjects and style of these writers, scholars, and artists left a rich legacy, and these works continue to be widely appreciated. However, it is also important that their work be understood within the era when they were written. In *Passing*, for instance, "Negro" and "colored" are used to refer to African Americans; at the time Larsen wrote this novel, these were commonly used, respectful terms.

Additionally, this novel includes the N-word, which we have chosen to reprint in this textbook to accurately reflect Larsen's original intent as well as the time period, culture, and racism depicted in the text. We recognize that this word has a long history as a derogatory and deeply hurtful expression when used by white people toward Black people. Larsen's choice to use this word relates not only to that history but also to a larger cultural tradition in which the N-word can often take on different meanings, emphasize shared experience, and be repurposed as a term of endearment within Black communities. While the use of that word in Larsen's context might not always be hurtful, the use of it in our current context very often is. Be mindful of context, both Larsen's and yours, as you read.

For Carl Van Vechten And Fania Marinoff[1]

One three centuries removed
From the scenes his fathers loved,
Spicy grove, cinnamon tree,
What is Africa to me?

— Countée Cullen[2]

[1] Carl Van Vechten (1880–1964) was a white writer, photographer, and patron of the Harlem Renaissance. A close friend of Nella Larsen, he was the inspiration for the character of Hugh Wentworth in *Passing*. Fania Marinoff (1890–1971) was a Jewish American actress who was born in Russia. She married Carl Van Vechten in 1914 and was also a patron of the Harlem Renaissance. — Eds.

[2] The poet Countee Cullen (1903–1946) was a major figure of the Harlem Renaissance. This epigraph is from Cullen's poem "Heritage" (p. 202). —Eds.

Part One: Encounter

Chapter 1

It was the last letter in Irene Redfield's little pile of morning mail. After her other ordinary and clearly directed letters the long envelope of thin Italian paper with its almost illegible scrawl seemed out of place and alien. And there was, too, something mysterious and slightly furtive about it. A thin sly thing which bore no return address to betray the sender. Not that she hadn't immediately known who its sender was. Some two years ago she had one very like it in outward appearance. Furtive, but yet in some peculiar, determined way a little flaunting. Purple ink. Foreign paper of extraordinary size.

It had been, Irene noted, postmarked in New York the day before. Her brows came together in a tiny frown. The frown, however, was more from perplexity than from annoyance; though there was in her thoughts an element of both. She was wholly unable to comprehend such an attitude towards danger as she was sure the letter's contents would reveal; and she disliked the idea of opening and reading it.

This, she reflected, was of a piece with all that she knew of Clare Kendry. Stepping always on the edge of danger. Always aware, but not drawing back or turning aside. Certainly not because of any alarms or feeling of outrage on the part of others.

And for a swift moment Irene Redfield seemed to see a pale small girl sitting on a ragged blue sofa, sewing pieces of bright red cloth together, while her drunken father, a tall, powerfully built man, raged threateningly up and down the shabby room, bellowing curses and making spasmodic lunges at her which were not the less frightening because they were, for the most part, ineffectual. Sometimes he did manage to reach her. But only the fact that the child had edged herself and her poor sewing over to the farthermost corner of the sofa suggested that she was in any way perturbed by this menace to herself and her work.

Clare had known well enough that it was unsafe to take a portion of the dollar that was her weekly wage for the doing of many errands for the dressmaker who lived on the top floor of the building of which Bob Kendry was janitor. But that knowledge had not deterred her. She wanted to go to her Sunday school's picnic, and she had made up her mind to wear a new dress. So, in spite of certain unpleasantness and possible danger, she had taken the money to buy the material for that pathetic little red frock.

There had been, even in those days, nothing sacrificial in Clare Kendry's idea of life, no allegiance beyond her own immediate desire. She was selfish, and cold, and hard. And yet she had, too, a strange capacity of transforming warmth and passion, verging some-times almost on theatrical heroics.

Irene, who was a year or more older than Clare, remembered the day that Bob Kendry had been brought home dead, killed in a silly saloon-fight. Clare, who was at that time a scant fifteen years old, had just stood there with her lips pressed together, her thin arms folded across her narrow chest, staring down at the familiar pasty-white face of her parent with a sort of disdain in her slanting black eyes. For a very long time she had stood like that, silent and staring. Then, quite suddenly, she had given way to a torrent of weeping, swaying her thin body, tearing at her bright hair, and stamping her small feet. The outburst had ceased as suddenly as it had begun. She glanced quickly about the bare room, taking everyone in, even the two policemen, in a sharp look of flashing scorn. And, in the next instant, she had turned and vanished through the door.

Seen across the long stretch of years, the thing had more the appearance of an outpouring of pent-up fury than of an overflow of grief for her dead father; though she had been, Irene admitted, fond enough of him in her own rather catlike way.

Catlike. Certainly that was the word which best described Clare Kendry, if any single word could describe her. Sometimes she was hard and apparently without feeling at all; sometimes she was affectionate and rashly impulsive. And there was about her an amazing soft malice, hidden well away until provoked. Then she was capable of scratching, and very effectively too. Or, driven to anger, she would fight with a ferocity and impetuousness that disregarded or forgot any danger; superior strength, numbers, or other unfavourable circumstances. How savagely she had clawed those boys the day they had hooted her parent and sung a derisive rhyme, of their own composing, which pointed out certain eccentricities in his careening gait! And how deliberately she had—

Irene brought her thoughts back to the present, to the letter from Clare Kendry that she still held unopened in her hand. With a little feeling of apprehension, she very slowly cut the envelope, drew out the folded sheets, spread them, and began to read.

It was, she saw at once, what she had expected since learning from the postmark that Clare was in the city. An extravagantly phrased wish to see her again. Well, she needn't and wouldn't, Irene told herself, accede to that. Nor would she assist Clare to realize her foolish desire to return for a moment to that life which long ago, and of her own choice, she had left behind her.

She ran through the letter, puzzling out, as best she could, the carelessly formed words or making instinctive guesses at them.

"... For I am lonely, so lonely ... cannot help longing to be with you again, as I have never longed for anything before; and I have wanted many things in my life.... You can't know how in this pale life of mine I am all the time seeing the bright pictures of that other that I once thought I was glad to be free of.... It's like an ache, a pain that never ceases...." Sheets upon thin sheets of it. And ending finally with, "and it's your fault, 'Rene dear. At least partly. For I wouldn't now, perhaps, have this terrible, this wild desire if I hadn't seen you that time in Chicago...."

Brilliant red patches flamed in Irene Redfield's warm olive cheeks.

"That time in Chicago." The words stood out from among the many paragraphs of other words, bringing with them a clear, sharp remembrance, in which even now, after two years, humiliation, resentment, and rage were mingled.

Chapter 2

This is what Irene Redfield remembered.

Chicago. August. A brilliant day, hot, with a brutal staring sun pouring down rays that were like molten rain. A day on which the very outlines of the buildings shuddered as if in protest at the heat. Quivering lines sprang up from baked pavements and wriggled along the shining car-tracks. The automobiles parked at the kerbs were a dancing blaze, and the glass of the shop-windows threw out a blinding radiance. Sharp particles of dust rose from the burning sidewalks, stinging the seared or dripping skins of wilting pedestrians. What small breeze there was seemed like the breath of a flame fanned by slow bellows.

It was on that day of all others that Irene set out to shop for the things which she had promised to take home from Chicago to her two small sons, Brian junior and Theodore. Characteristically, she had put it off until only a few crowded days remained of her long visit. And only this sweltering one was free of engagements till the evening.

Without too much trouble she had got the mechanical aeroplane for Junior. But the drawing-book, for which Ted had so gravely and insistently given her precise directions, had sent her in and out of five shops without success.

It was while she was on her way to a sixth place that right before her smarting eyes a man toppled over and became an inert crumpled heap on the scorching cement. About the lifeless figure a little crowd gathered. Was the man dead, or only faint? someone asked her. But Irene didn't know and didn't try to discover. She edged her way out of the increasing crowd, feeling disagreeably damp and sticky and soiled from contact with so many sweating bodies.

For a moment she stood fanning herself and dabbing at her moist face with an inadequate scrap of handkerchief. Suddenly she was aware that the whole street had a wobbly look, and realized that she was about to faint. With a quick perception of the need for immediate safety, she lifted a wavering hand in the direction of a cab parked directly in front of her. The perspiring driver jumped out and guided her to his car. He helped, almost lifted her in. She sank down on the hot leather seat.

For a minute her thoughts were nebulous. They cleared.

"I guess," she told her Samaritan, "it's tea I need. On a roof somewhere."

"The Drayton, ma'am?" he suggested. "They do say as how it's always a breeze up there."

"Thank you. I think the Drayton'll do nicely," she told him.

There was that little grating sound of the clutch being slipped in as the man put the car in gear and slid deftly out into the boiling traffic. Reviving under the warm breeze stirred up by the moving cab, Irene made some small attempts to repair the damage that the heat and crowds had done to her appearance.

All too soon the rattling vehicle shot towards the sidewalk and stood still. The driver sprang out and opened the door before the hotel's decorated attendant could reach it. She got out, and thanking him smilingly as well as in a more substantial manner for his kind helpfulness and understanding, went in through the Drayton's wide doors.

Stepping out of the elevator that had brought her to the roof, she was led to a table just in front of a long window whose gently moving curtains suggested a cool breeze. It was, she thought, like being wafted upward on a magic carpet to another world, pleasant, quiet, and strangely remote from the sizzling one that she had left below.

The tea, when it came, was all that she had desired and expected. In fact, so much was it what she had desired and expected that after the first deep cooling drink she was able to forget it, only now and then sipping, a little absently, from the tall green glass, while she surveyed the room about her or looked out over some lower buildings at the bright unstirred blue of the lake reaching away to an undetected horizon.

She had been gazing down for some time at the specks of cars and people creeping about in streets, and thinking how silly they looked, when on taking up her glass she was surprised to find it empty at last. She asked for more tea and while she waited, began to recall the happenings of the day and to wonder what she was to do about Ted and his book. Why was it that almost invariably he wanted something that was difficult or impossible to get? Like his father. For ever wanting something that he couldn't have.

Presently there were voices, a man's booming one and a woman's slightly husky. A waiter passed her, followed by a sweetly scented woman in a fluttering dress of green chiffon whose mingled pattern of narcissuses, jonquils, and hyacinths was a reminder of pleasantly chill spring days. Behind her there was a man, very red in the face, who was mopping his neck and forehead with a big crumpled handkerchief.

"Oh dear!" Irene groaned, rasped by annoyance, for after a little discussion and commotion they had stopped at the very next table. She had been alone there at the window and it had been so satisfyingly quiet. Now, of course, they would chatter.

But no. Only the woman sat down. The man remained standing, abstractedly pinching the knot of his bright blue tie. Across the small space that separated the two tables his voice carried clearly.

"See you later, then," he declared, looking down at the woman. There was pleasure in his tones and a smile on his face.

His companion's lips parted in some answer, but her words were blurred by the little intervening distance and the medley of noises floating up from the streets below. They didn't reach Irene. But she noted the peculiar caressing smile that accompanied them.

The man said: "Well, I suppose I'd better," and smiled again, and said good-bye, and left.

An attractive-looking woman, was Irene's opinion, with those dark, almost black, eyes and that wide mouth like a scarlet flower against the ivory of her skin. Nice clothes too, just right for the weather, thin and cool without being mussy, as summer things were so apt to be.

A waiter was taking her order. Irene saw her smile up at him as she murmured something—thanks, maybe. It was an odd sort of smile. Irene couldn't quite define it, but she was sure that she would have classed it, coming from another woman, as being just a shade too provocative for a waiter. About this one, however, there was something that made her hesitate to name it that. A certain impression of assurance, perhaps.

The waiter came back with the order. Irene watched her spread out her napkin, saw the silver spoon in the white hand slit the dull gold of the melon. Then, conscious that she had been staring, she looked quickly away.

Her mind returned to her own affairs. She had settled, definitely, the problem of the proper one of two frocks for the bridge party that night, in rooms whose atmosphere would be so thick and hot that every breath would be like breathing soup. The dress decided, her thoughts had gone back to the snag of Ted's book, her unseeing eyes far away on the lake, when by some sixth sense she was acutely aware that someone was watching her.

Very slowly she looked around, and into the dark eyes of the woman in the green frock at the next table. But she evidently failed to realize that such intense interest as she was showing might be embarrassing, and continued to stare. Her demeanour was that of one who with utmost singleness of mind and purpose was determined to impress firmly and accurately each detail of Irene's features upon her memory for all time,

Malachi Lily

Artist Malachi Lily created this image, along with many others, to illustrate a 2018 edition of *Passing* that celebrates the ninetieth anniversary of its publication.

How does this image interpret the relationship between Clare and Irene as they meet on the rooftop of the Drayton Hotel? Consider the composition and which of the characters' features are emphasized.

nor showed the slightest trace of disconcertment at having been detected in her steady scrutiny.

Instead, it was Irene who was put out. Feeling her colour heighten under the continued inspection, she slid her eyes down. What, she wondered, could be the reason for such persistent attention? Had she. In her haste in the taxi, put her hat on backwards? Guardedly she felt at it. No. Perhaps there was a streak of powder somewhere on her face. She made a quick pass over it with her handkerchief. Something wrong with her dress? She shot a glance over it. Perfectly all right. *What* was it?

Again she looked up, and for a moment her brown eyes politely returned the stare of the other's black ones, which never for an instant fell or wavered. Irene made a little mental shrug. Oh well, let her look! She tried to treat the woman and her watching with indifference, but she couldn't. All her efforts to ignore her, it, were futile. She stole another glance. Still looking. What strange languorous eyes she had!

And gradually there rose in Irene a small inner disturbance, odious and hatefully familiar. She laughed softly, but her eyes flashed.

Did that woman, could that woman, somehow know that here before her very eyes on the roof of the Drayton sat a Negro?

Absurd! Impossible! White people were so stupid about such things for all that they usually asserted that they were able to tell; and by the most ridiculous means, finger-nails, palms of hands, shapes of ears, teeth, and other equally silly rot. They always took her for an Italian, a Spaniard, a Mexican, or a gipsy. Never, when she was alone, had they even remotely seemed to suspect that she was a Negro. No, the woman sitting there staring at her couldn't possibly know.

Nevertheless, Irene felt, in turn, anger, scorn, and fear slide over her. It wasn't that she was ashamed of being a Negro, or even of having it declared. It was the idea of being ejected from any place, even in the polite and tactful way in which the Drayton would probably do it, that disturbed her.

But she looked, boldly this time, back into the eyes still frankly intent upon her. They did not seem to her hostile or resentful. Rather, Irene had the feeling that they were ready to smile if she would. Nonsense, of course. The feeling passed, and she turned away with the firm intention of keeping her gaze on the lake, the roofs of the buildings across the way, the sky, anywhere but on that annoying woman. Almost immediately, however, her eyes were back again. In the midst of her fog of uneasiness she had been seized by a desire to outstare the rude observer. Suppose the woman did know or suspect her race. She couldn't prove it.

Suddenly her small fright increased. Her neighbour had risen and was coming towards her. What was going to happen now?

"Pardon me," the woman said pleasantly, "but I think I know you." Her slightly husky voice held a dubious note.

Looking up at her, Irene's suspicions and fears vanished. There was no mistaking the friendliness of that smile or resisting its charm. Instantly she surrendered to it and smiled too, as she said: "I'm afraid you're mistaken."

"Why, of course, I know you!" the other exclaimed. "Don't tell me you're not Irene Westover. Or do they still call you 'Rene?"

In the brief second before her answer, Irene tried vainly to recall where and when this woman could have known her. There, in Chicago. And before her marriage. That much was plain. High school? College? Y. W. C. A. committees? High school, most likely. What white girls had she known well enough to have been familiarly addressed as 'Rene by them? The woman before her didn't fit her memory of any of them. Who was she?

"Yes, I'm Irene Westover. And though nobody calls me 'Rene any more, it's good to hear the name again. And you—" She hesitated, ashamed that she could not remember, and hoping that the sentence would be finished for her.

"Don't you know me? Not really, 'Rene?"

"I'm sorry, but just at the minute I can't seem to place you."

Irene studied the lovely creature standing beside her for some clue to her identity. Who could she be? Where and when had they met? And through her perplexity there came the thought that the trick which her memory had played her was for some reason more gratifying than disappointing to her old acquaintance, that she didn't mind not being recognized.

And, too, Irene felt that she was just about to remember her. For about the woman was some quality, an intangible something, too vague to define, too remote to seize, but which was, to Irene Redfield, very familiar. And that voice. Surely she'd heard those husky tones somewhere before. Perhaps before time, contact, or something had been at them, making them into a voice remotely suggesting England. Ah! Could it have been in Europe that they had met? 'Rene. No.

"Perhaps," Irene began, "you—"

The woman laughed, a lovely laugh, a small sequence of notes that was like a trill and also like the ringing of a delicate bell fashioned of a precious metal, a tinkling.

Irene drew a quick sharp breath. "Clare!" she exclaimed, "not really Clare Kendry?"

So great was her astonishment that she had started to rise.

"No, no, don't get up," Clare Kendry commanded, and sat down herself. "You've simply got to stay and talk. We'll have something more. Tea? Fancy meeting you here! It's simply too, too lucky!"

"It's awfully surprising," Irene told her, and, seeing the change in Clare's smile, knew that she had revealed a corner of her own thoughts. But she only said: "I'd never in this world have known you if you hadn't laughed. You are changed, you know. And yet, in a way, you're just the same."

"Perhaps," Clare replied. "Oh, just a second."

She gave her attention to the waiter at her side. "M-mm, let's see. Two teas. And bring some cigarettes. Y-es, they'll be all right. Thanks." Again that odd upward smile. Now, Irene was sure that it was too provocative for a waiter.

While Clare had been giving the order, Irene made a rapid mental calculation. It must be, she figured, all of twelve years since she, or anybody that she knew, had laid eyes on Clare Kendry.

After her father's death she'd gone to live with some relatives, aunts or cousins two or three times removed, over on the west side: relatives that nobody had known the Kendry's possessed until they had turned up at the funeral and taken Clare away with them.

For about a year or more afterwards she would appear occasionally among her old friends and acquaintances on the south side for short little visits that were, they understood, always stolen from the endless domestic tasks in her new home. With each succeeding one she was taller, shabbier, and more belligerently sensitive. And each time the look on her face was more resentful and brooding. "I'm worried about Clare, she seems so unhappy," Irene remembered her mother saying. The visits dwindled, becoming shorter, fewer, and further apart until at last they ceased.

Irene's father, who had been fond of Bob Kendry, made a special trip over to the west side about two months after the last time Clare had been to see them and returned with the bare information that he had seen the relatives and that Clare had disappeared. What else he had confided to her mother, in the privacy of their own room, Irene didn't know.

But she had had something more than a vague suspicion of its nature. For there had been rumours. Rumours that were, to girls of eighteen and nineteen years, interesting and exciting.

There was the one about Clare Kendry's having been seen at the dinner hour in a fashionable hotel in company with another woman and two men, all of them white. And *dressed!* And there was another which told of her driving in Lincoln Park with a man, unmistakably white, and evidently rich. Packard limousine, chauffeur in livery, and all that. There had been others whose context Irene could no longer recollect, but all pointing in the same glamorous direction.

And she could remember quite vividly how, when they used to repeat and discuss these tantalizing stories about Clare, the girls would always look knowingly at one another and then, with little excited giggles, drag away their eager shining eyes and say with lurking undertones of regret or disbelief some such thing as: "Oh, well, maybe she's got a job or something," or "After all, it mayn't have been Clare," or "You can't believe all you hear."

And always some girl, more matter-of-fact or more frankly malicious than the rest, would declare: "Of course it was Clare! Ruth said it was and so did Frank, and they certainly know her when they see her as well as we do." And someone else would say: "Yes, you can bet it was Clare all right." And then they would all join in asserting that there could be no mistake about it's having been Clare, and that such circumstances could mean only one thing. Working indeed! People didn't take their servants to the Shelby for dinner. Certainly not all dressed up like that. There would follow insincere regrets, and somebody would say: "Poor girl, I suppose it's true enough, but what can you expect. Look at her father. And her mother, they say, would have run away if she hadn't died. Besides, Clare always had a — a — having way with her."

Precisely that! The words came to Irene as she sat there on the Drayton roof, facing Clare Kendry. "A having way." Well, Irene acknowledged, judging from her appearance and manner, Clare seemed certainly to have succeeded in having a few of the things that she wanted.

It was, Irene repeated, after the interval of the waiter, a great surprise and a very pleasant one to see Clare again after all those years, twelve at least.

"Why, Clare, you're the last person in the world I'd have expected to run into. I guess that's why I didn't know you."

Clare answered gravely: "Yes. It is twelve years. But I'm not surprised to see you, 'Rene. That is, not so very. In fact, ever since I've been here, I've more or less hoped that I should, or someone. Preferably you, though. Still, I imagine that's because I've thought of you often and often, while you — I'll wager you've never given me a thought."

It was true, of course. After the first speculations and indictments, Clare had gone completely from Irene's thoughts. And from the thoughts of others too — if their conversation was any indication of their thoughts.

Besides, Clare had never been exactly one of the group, just as she'd never been merely the janitor's daughter, but the daughter of Mr. Bob Kendry, who, it was true, was a janitor, but who also, it seemed, had been in college with some of their fathers. Just how or why he happened to be a janitor, and a very inefficient one at that, they none of them quite knew. One of Irene's brothers, who had put the question to their father, had been told: "That's something that doesn't concern you," and given him the advice to be careful not to end in the same manner as "poor Bob."

No, Irene hadn't thought of Clare Kendry. Her own life had been too crowded. So, she supposed, had the lives of other people. She defended her — their — forgetfulness. "You know how it is. Everybody's so busy. People leave, drop out, maybe for a little while there's talk about them, or questions; then, gradually they're forgotten."

"Yes, that's natural," Clare agreed. And what, she inquired, had they said of her for that little while at the beginning before they'd forgotten her altogether?

Irene looked away. She felt the telltale colour rising in her cheeks. "You can't," she evaded, "expect me to remember trifles like that over twelve years of marriages, births, deaths, and the war."

There followed that trill of notes that was Clare Kendry's laugh, small and clear and the very essence of mockery.

"Oh, 'Rene!" she cried, "of course you remember I But I won't make you tell me, because I know just as well as if I'd been there and heard every unkind word. Oh, I know, I know. Frank Danton saw me in the Shelby one night. Don't tell me he didn't broadcast that, and with embroidery. Others may have seen me at other times. I don't know. But once I met Margaret Hammer in Marshall Field's. I'd have spoken, was on the very point of doing it, but she cut me dead. My dear 'Rene, I assure you that from the way she looked through me, even I was uncertain whether I was actually there in the flesh or not. I remember it clearly, too clearly. It was that very thing which, in a way, finally decided me not to go out and see you one last time before I went away to stay. Somehow, good as all of you, the whole family, had always been to the poor forlorn child that was me, I felt I shouldn't be able to bear that. I mean if any of you, your mother or the boys or — Oh, well, I just felt I'd rather not know it if you did. And so I stayed away. Silly, I suppose. Sometimes I've been sorry I didn't go."

Irene wondered if it was tears that made Clare's eyes so luminous.

"And now 'Rene, I want to hear all about you and everybody and everything. You're married, I s'pose?"

Irene nodded.

"Yes," Clare said knowingly, "you would be. Tell me about it."

And so for an hour or more they had sat there smoking and drinking tea and filling in the gap of twelve years with talk. That is, Irene did. She told Clare about her marriage and removal to New York, about her husband, and about her two sons, who were having their first experience of being separated from their parents at a summer camp, about her mother's death, about the marriages of her two brothers. She told of the marriages, births and deaths in other families that Clare had known, opening up, for her, new vistas on the lives of old friends and acquaintances.

Clare drank it all in, these things which for so long she had wanted to know and hadn't been able to learn. She sat motionless, her bright lips slightly parted, her whole face lit by the radiance of her happy eyes. Now and then she put a question, but for the most part she was silent.

Somewhere outside, a clock struck. Brought back to the present, Irene looked down at her watch and exclaimed: "Oh, I must go, Clare!"

A moment passed during which she was the prey of uneasiness. It had suddenly occurred to her that she hadn't asked Clare anything about her own life and that she had a very definite unwillingness to do so. And she was quite well aware of the reason for that reluctance. But, she asked herself, wouldn't it, all things considered, be the kindest thing not to ask? If things with Clare were as she — as they all — had suspected, wouldn't it be more tactful to seem to forget to inquire how she had spent those twelve years?

If? It was that "if" which bothered her. It might be, it might just be, in spite of all gossip and even appearances to the contrary, that there was nothing, had been nothing, that couldn't be simply and innocently explained. Appearances, she knew now, had a way sometimes of not fitting facts, and if Clare hadn't — Well, if they had all been wrong, then certainly she ought to express some interest in what had happened to her. It would seem queer and rude if she didn't. But how was she to know? There was, she at last decided, no way; so she merely said again. "I must go, Clare."

"Please, not so soon, 'Rene," Clare begged, not moving.

Irene thought: "She's really almost too good-looking. It's hardly any wonder that she — "

"And now, 'Rene dear, that I've found you, I mean to see lots and lots of you. We're here for a month at least. Jack, that's my husband, is here on business. Poor dear! in this heat. Isn't it beastly? Come to dinner with us tonight, won't you?" And she gave Irene a curious little sidelong glance and a sly, ironical smile peeped out on her full red lips, as if she had been in the secret of the other's thoughts and was mocking her.

Irene was conscious of a sharp intake of breath, but whether it was relief or chagrin that she felt, she herself could not have told. She said hastily: "I'm afraid I can't, Clare. I'm filled up. Dinner and bridge. I'm so sorry."

"Come tomorrow instead, to tea," Clare insisted. "Then you'll see Margery — she's just ten — and Jack too, maybe, if he hasn't got an appointment or something."

From Irene came an uneasy little laugh. She had an engagement for tomorrow also and she was afraid that Clare would not believe it. Suddenly, now, that possibility disturbed her. Therefore it was with a half-vexed feeling at the sense of undeserved guilt that had come upon her that she explained that it wouldn't be possible because she wouldn't be free for tea, or for luncheon or dinner either. "And the next day's Friday when I'll be going away for the week-end, Idlewild, you know. It's quite the thing now." And then she had an inspiration.

"Clare!" she exclaimed, "why don't you come up with me? Our place is probably full up — Jim's wife has a way of collecting mobs of the most impossible people — but we can always manage to find room for one more. And you'll see absolutely everybody."

In the very moment of giving the invitation she regretted it. What a foolish, what an idiotic impulse to have given way to! She groaned inwardly as she thought of the endless explanations in which it would involve her, of the curiosity, and the talk, and the lifted eyebrows. It wasn't she assured herself, that she was a snob, that she cared greatly for the petty restrictions and distinctions with which what called itself Negro society chose to hedge itself about; but that she had a natural and deeply rooted aversion to the kind of frontpage notoriety that Clare Kendry's presence in Idlewild, as her guest, would expose her to. And here she was, perversely and against all reason, inviting her.

But Clare shook her head. "Really, I'd love to, 'Rene," she said, a little mournfully. "There's nothing I'd like better. But I couldn't. I mustn't, you see. It wouldn't do at all. I'm sure you understand. I'm simply crazy to go, but I can't." The dark eyes glistened and there was a suspicion of a quaver in the husky voice. "And believe me, 'Rene, I do thank you for asking me. Don't think I've entirely forgotten just what it would mean for you if I went. That is, if you still care about such things."

All indication of tears had gone from her eyes and voice, and Irene Redfield, searching her face, had an offended feeling that behind what was now only an ivory mask lurked a scornful amusement. She looked away, at the wall far beyond Clare. Well, she deserved it, for, as she acknowledged to herself, she *was* relieved. And for the very reason at which Clare had hinted. The fact that Clare had guesssed her perturbation did not, however, in any degree lessen that relief. She was annoyed at having been detected in what might seem to be an insincerity; but that was all.

The waiter came with Clare's change. Irene reminded herself that she ought immediately to go. But she didn't move.

The truth was, she was curious. There were things that she wanted to ask Clare Kendry. She wished to find out about this hazardous business of "passing," this breaking away from all that was familiar and friendly to take one's chance in another environment, not entirely strange, perhaps, but certainly not entirely friendly. What, for example, one did about background, how one accounted for oneself.

extending beyond the text

In 1895, African American poet Paul Laurence Dunbar published the following poem.

We Wear the Mask

Paul Laurence Dunbar

We wear the mask that grins and lies,
It hides our cheeks and shades our eyes, —
This debt we pay to human guile;
With torn and bleeding hearts we smile,
And mouth with myriad subtleties.

Why should the world be over-wise,
In counting all our tears and sighs?
Nay, let them only see us, while
We wear the mask.

We smile, but, O great Christ, our cries
To thee from tortured souls arise.
We sing, but oh the clay is vile
Beneath our feet, and long the mile;
But let the world dream otherwise,
We wear the mask! ■

1. **What is "the mask" that Dunbar's speaker describes in this poem? Summarize your interpretation of it in one or two sentences.**
2. **How does the speaker's understanding of his experience in this poem connect with Larsen's description of Clare's face as "an ivory mask" with undertones of "scornful amusement" (par. 104)? What is your interpretation of the significance of the fact that Clare dons this mask for Irene in particular?**
3. **To what extent do you think that Dunbar's speaker and Clare have the same attitude toward the circumstances of their lives and their racial identities? Explain, using evidence from both texts to support your response.**

And how one felt when one came into contact with other Negroes. But she couldn't. She was unable to think of a single question that in its context or its phrasing was not too frankly curious, if not actually impertinent.

As if aware of her desire and her hesitation, Clare remarked, thoughtfully: "You know, 'Rene, I've often wondered why more coloured girls, girls like you and Margaret Hammer and Esther Dawson and — oh, lots of others — never 'passed' over. It's such a frightfully easy thing to do. If one's the type, all that's needed is a little nerve."

"What about background? Family, I mean. Surely you can't just drop down on people from nowhere and expect them to receive you with open arms, can you?"

"Almost," Clare asserted. "You'd be surprised, 'Rene, how much easier that is with white people than with us. Maybe because there are so many more of them, or maybe because they are secure and so don't have to bother. I've never quite decided."

Irene was inclined to be incredulous. "You mean that you didn't have to explain where you came from? It seems impossible."

Clare cast a glance of repressed amusement across the table at her. "As a matter of fact, I didn't. Though I suppose under any other circumstances I might have had to provide some plausible tale to account for myself. I've a good imagination, so I'm sure I could have done it quite creditably, and credibly. But it wasn't necessary. There were my aunts, you see, respectable and authentic enough for anything or anybody."

"I see. They were 'passing' too."

"No. They weren't. They were white."

"Oh!" And in the next instant it came back to Irene that she had heard this mentioned before; by her father, or, more likely, her mother. They were Bob Kendry's aunts. He had been a son of their brother's, on the left hand. A wild oat.

"They were nice old ladies," Clare explained, "very religious and as poor as church mice. That adored brother of theirs, my grandfather, got through every penny they had after he'd finished his own little bit."

Clare paused in her narrative to light another cigarette. Her smile, her expression, Irene noticed, was faintly resentful.

"Being good Christians," she continued, "when dad came to his tipsy end, they did their duty and gave me a home of sorts. I was, it was true, expected to earn my keep by doing all the housework and most of the washing. But do you realize, 'Rene, that if it hadn't been for them, I shouldn't have had a home in the world?"

Irene's nod and little murmur were comprehensive, understanding.

Clare made a small mischievous grimace and proceeded. "Besides, to their notion, hard labour was good for me. I had Negro blood and they belonged to the generation that had written and read long articles headed: 'Will the Blacks Work?' Too, they weren't quite sure that the good God hadn't intended the sons and daughters of Ham[3] to sweat because he had poked fun at old man Noah once when he had taken a drop too much. I remember the aunts telling me that that old drunkard had cursed Ham and his sons for all time."

Irene laughed. But Clare remained quite serious.

"It was more than a joke, I assure you, 'Rene. It was a hard life for a girl of sixteen. Still, I had a roof over my head, and food, and clothes — such as they were. And there were the Scriptures, and talks on morals and thrift and industry and the loving-kindness of the good Lord."

"Have you ever stopped to think, Clare," Irene demanded, "how much unhappiness and downright cruelty are laid to the loving-kindness of the Lord? And always by His most ardent followers, it seems."

"Have I?" Clare exclaimed. "It, they, made me what I am today. For, of course, I was determined to get away, to be a person and not a charity or a problem, or even a daughter of the indiscreet Ham. Then, too, I wanted things. I knew I wasn't bad-looking and that I could 'pass.' You can't know, 'Rene, how, when I used to go over to the south side, I used almost to hate all of you. You had all the things I wanted and never had had. It made me all the more determined to get them, and others. Do you, can you understand what I felt?"

She looked up with a pointed and appealing effect, and, evidently finding the sympathetic expression on Irene's face sufficient answer,

---

[3] A biblical reference meant to convey that someone is Black. The reference is rooted in the false belief that Black people originated from the biblical figure of Ham. — Eds.

went on. "The aunts were queer. For all their Bibles and praying and ranting about honesty, they didn't want anyone to know that their darling brother had seduced — ruined, they called it — a Negro girl. They could excuse the ruin, but they couldn't forgive the tar-brush. They forbade me to mention Negroes to the neighbours, or even to mention the south side. You may be sure that I didn't. I'll bet they were good and sorry afterwards."

She laughed and the ringing bells in her laugh had a hard metallic sound.

"When the chance to get away came, that omission was of great value to me. When Jack, a schoolboy acquaintance of some people in the neighbourhood, turned up from South America with untold gold, there was no one to tell him that I was coloured, and many to tell him about the severity and the religiousness of Aunt Grace and Aunt Edna. You can guess the rest. After he came, I stopped slipping off to the south side and slipped off to meet him instead. I couldn't manage both. In the end I had no great difficulty in convincing him that it was useless to talk marriage to the aunts. So on the day that I was eighteen, we went off and were married. So that's that. Nothing could have been easier."

"Yes, I do see that for you it was easy enough. By the way! I wonder why they didn't tell father that you were married. He went over to find out about you when you stopped coming over to see us. I'm sure they didn't tell him. Not that you were married."

Clare Kendry's eyes were bright with tears that didn't fall. "Oh, how lovely! To have cared enough about me to do that. The dear sweet man! Well, they couldn't tell him because they didn't know it. I took care of that, for I couldn't be sure that those consciences of theirs wouldn't begin to work on them afterwards and make them let the cat out of the bag. The old things probably thought I was living in sin, wherever I was. And it would be about what they expected."

An amused smile lit the lovely face for the smallest fraction of a second. After a little silence she said soberly: "But I'm sorry if they told your father so. That was something I hadn't counted on."

"I'm not sure that they did," Irene told her. "He didn't say so, anyway."

"He wouldn't, 'Rene dear. Not your father."

"Thanks. I'm sure he wouldn't."

"But you've never answered my question. Tell me, honestly, haven't you ever thought of 'passing'?"

Irene answered promptly: "No. Why should I?" And so disdainful was her voice and manner that Clare's face flushed and her eyes glinted. Irene hastened to add: "You see, Clare, I've everything I want. Except, perhaps, a little more money."

At that Clare laughed, her spark of anger vanished as quickly as it had appeared. "Of course," she declared, "that's what everybody wants, just a little more money, even the people who have it. And I must say I don't blame them. Money's awfully nice to have. In fact, all things considered, I think, 'Rene, that it's even worth the price."

Irene could only shrug her shoulders. Her reason partly agreed, her instinct wholly rebelled. And she could not say why. And though conscious that if she didn't hurry away, she was going to be late to dinner, she still lingered. It was as if the woman sitting on the other side of the table, a girl that she had known, who had done this rather dangerous and, to Irene Redfield, abhorrent thing successfully and had announced herself well satisfied, had for her a fascination, strange and compelling.

Clare Kendry was still leaning back in the tall chair, her sloping shoulders against the carved top. She sat with an air of indifferent assurance, as if arranged for, desired. About her clung that dim suggestion of polite insolence with which a few women are born and which some acquire with the coming of riches or importance.

Clare, it gave Irene a little prick of satisfaction to recall, hadn't got that by passing herself off as white. She herself had always had it.

Just as she'd always had that pale gold hair, which, unsheared still, was drawn loosely back from a broad brow, partly hidden by the small close hat. Her lips, painted a brilliant geranium-red, were sweet and sensitive and a little obstinate. A tempting mouth. The face across the forehead and cheeks was a trifle too wide, but the ivory skin had a peculiar soft lustre. And the eyes were magnificent! dark, sometimes absolutely black, always luminous, and set in long, black lashes. Arresting eyes, slow and mesmeric, and with, for all their warmth, something withdrawn and secret about them.

Ah! Surely! They were Negro eyes! mysterious and concealing. And set in that ivory face under that bright hair, there was about them something exotic.

Yes, Clare Kendry's loveliness was absolute, beyond challenge, thanks to those eyes which her grandmother and later her mother and father had given her.

Into those eyes there came a smile and over Irene the sense of being petted and caressed. She smiled back.

"Maybe," Clare suggested, "you can come Monday, if you're back. Or, if you're not, then Tuesday."

With a small regretful sigh, Irene informed Clare that she was afraid she wouldn't be back by Monday and that she was sure she had dozens of things for Tuesday, and that she was leaving Wednesday. It might be, however, that she could get out of something Tuesday.

"Oh, do try. Do put somebody else off. The others can see you any time, while I—Why, I may never see you again! Think of that, 'Rene! You'll have to come. You'll simply have to! I'll never forgive you if you don't."

At that moment it seemed a dreadful thing to think of never seeing Clare Kendry again. Standing there under the appeal, the caress, of her eyes, Irene had the desire, the hope, that this parting wouldn't be the last.

"I'll try, Clare," she promised gently. "I'll call you—or will you call me?"

"I think, perhaps, I'd better call you. Your father's in the book, I know, and the address is the same. Sixty-four eighteen. Some memory, what? Now remember, I'm going to expect you. You've got to be able to come."

Again that peculiar mellowing smile.

"I'll do my best, Clare."

Irene gathered up her gloves and bag. They stood up. She put out her hand. Clare took and held it.

"It has been nice seeing you again, Clare. How pleased and glad father'll be to hear about you!"

"Until Tuesday, then," Clare Kendry replied. "I'll spend every minute of the time from now on looking forward to seeing you again. Good-bye, 'Rene dear. My love to your father, and this kiss for him."

• • •

The sun had gone from overhead, but the streets were still like fiery furnaces. The languid breeze was still hot. And the scurrying people looked even more wilted than before Irene had fled from their contact.

Crossing the avenue in the heat, far from the coolness of the Drayton's roof, away from the seduction of Clare Kendry's smile, she was aware of a sense of irritation with herself because she had been pleased and a little flattered at the other's obvious gladness at their meeting.

With her perspiring progress homeward this irritation grew, and she began to wonder just what had possessed her to make her promise to find time, in the crowded days that remained of her visit, to spend another afternoon with a woman whose life had so definitely and deliberately diverged from hers; and whom, as had been pointed out, she might never see again.

Why in the world had she made such a promise?

As she went up the steps to her father's house, thinking with what interest and amazement he would listen to her story of the afternoon's encounter, it came to her that Clare had omitted to mention her marriage name. She had referred to her husband as Jack. That was all. Had that, Irene asked herself, been intentional?

Clare had only to pick up the telephone to communicate with her, or to drop her a card, or to jump into a taxi. But she couldn't reach Clare in any way. Nor could anyone else to whom she might speak of their meeting.

"As if I should!"

Her key turned in the lock. She went in. Her father, it seemed, hadn't come in yet.

Irene decided that she wouldn't, after all, say anything to him about Clare Kendry. She had, she told herself, no inclination to speak of a person who held so low an opinion of her loyalty, or her discretion. And certainly she had no desire or intention of making the slightest effort about Tuesday. Nor any other day for that matter.

She was through with Clare Kendry.

Chapter 3

On Tuesday morning a dome of grey sky rose over the parched city, but the stifling air was not relieved by the silvery mist that seemed to hold a promise of rain, which did not fall.

To Irene Redfield this soft foreboding fog was another reason for doing nothing about seeing Clare Kendry that afternoon.

But she did see her.

The telephone. For hours it had rung like something possessed. Since nine o'clock she had been hearing its insistent jangle. Awhile she was resolute, saying firmly each time: "Not in, Liza, take the message." And each time the servant returned with the information: "It's the same lady, ma'am; she says she'll call again."

But at noon, her nerves frayed and her conscience smiting her at the reproachful look on Liza's ebony face as she withdrew for another denial, Irene weakened.

"Oh, never mind. I'll answer this time, Liza."

"It's her again."

"Hello. . . . Yes."

"It's Clare, 'Rene. . . . Where *have* you been? . . . Can you be here around four? . . . What? . . . But, 'Rene, you promised! Just for a little while. . . . You can if you want to. . . . I am *so* disappointed. I had counted so on seeing you. . . . Please be nice and come. Only for a minute. I'm sure you can manage it if you try. . . . I won't beg you to stay. . . . Yes. . . . I'm going to expect you . . . It's the Morgan. . . Oh, yes! The name's Bellew, Mrs. John Bellew. . . . About four, then. . . . I'll be so happy to see you! . . . Goodbye."

"Damn!"

Kirn Vintage Stock/Getty Images

This photograph shows downtown Chicago in 1927, which is roughly when Irene goes to the Drayton Hotel — based on the actual Drake Hotel — and sees her childhood friend Clare.

How does this image set the scene for Part One: Encounter? What does it add to your understanding of the meeting between Irene and Clare?

Irene hung up the receiver with an emphatic bang, her thoughts immediately filled with self-reproach. She'd done it again. Allowed Clare Kendry to persuade her into promising to do something for which she had neither time nor any special desire. What was it about Clare's voice that was so appealing, so very seductive?

Clare met her in the hall with a kiss. She said: "You're good to come, 'Rene. But, then, you always were nice to me." And under her potent smile a part of Irene's annoyance with herself fled. She was even a little glad that she had come.

Clare led the way, stepping lightly, towards a room whose door was standing partly open, saying: "There's a surprise. It's a real party. See."

Entering, Irene found herself in a sitting-room, large and high, at whose windows hung startling blue draperies which triumphantly dragged attention from the gloomy chocolate-coloured furniture. And Clare was wearing a thin floating dress of the same shade of blue, which suited her and the rather difficult room to perfection.

For a minute Irene thought the room was empty, but turning her head, she discovered, sunk deep in the cushions of a huge sofa, a woman staring up at her with such intense concentration that her eyelids were drawn as though the strain of that upward glance had paralysed them. At first Irene took her to be a stranger, but in the next instant she said in an unsympathetic, almost harsh voice: "And how are you, Gertrude?"

The woman nodded and forced a smile to her pouting lips. "I'm all right," she replied. "And you're just the same, Irene. Not changed a bit."

"Thank you." Irene responded, as she chose a seat. She was thinking: "Great goodness! Two of them."

For Gertrude too had married a white man, though it couldn't be truthfully said that she was "passing." Her husband — what was his name? — had been in school with her and had been quite well aware, as had his family and most of his friends, that she was a Negro. It hadn't, Irene knew, seemed to matter to him then. Did it now, she wondered? Had Fred — Fred Martin, that was it — had he ever regretted his marriage because of Gertrude's race? Had Gertrude?

Turning to Gertrude, Irene asked: "And Fred, how is he? It's unmentionable years since I've seen him."

"Oh, he's all right," Gertrude answered briefly.

For a full minute no one spoke. Finally out of the oppressive little silence Clare's voice came pleasantly, conversationally: "We'll have tea right away. I know that you can't stay long, 'Rene. And I'm so sorry you won't see Margery. We went up the lake over the week end to see some of Jack's people, just out of Milwaukee. Margery wanted to stay with the children. It seemed a shame not to let her, especially since it's so hot in town. But I'm expecting Jack any second."

Irene said briefly: "That's nice."

Gertrude remained silent. She was, it was plain, a little ill at ease. And her presence there annoyed Irene, roused in her a defensive and resentful feeling for which she had at the moment no explanation. But it did seem to her odd that the woman that Clare was now should have invited the woman that Gertrude was. Still, of course, Clare couldn't have known. Twelve years since they had met.

Later, when she examined her feeling of annoyance, Irene admitted, a shade reluctantly, that it arose from a feeling of being out-numbered, a sense of aloneness, in her adherence to her own class and kind; not merely in the great thing of marriage, but in the whole pattern of her life as well.

Clare spoke again, this time at length. Her talk was of the change that Chicago presented to her after her long absence in European cities. Yes, she said in reply to some question from Gertrude, she'd been back to America a time or two, but only as far as New York and Philadelphia, and once she had spent a few days in Washington. John Bellew, who, it appeared, was some sort of international banking agent, hadn't particularly wanted her to come with him on this trip, but as soon as she had learned that it would probably take him as far as Chicago, she made up her mind to come anyway.

"I simply had to. And after I once got here, I was determined to see someone I knew and find out what had happened to everybody. I didn't quite see how I was going to manage it, but I meant to. Somehow. I'd just about decided to take a chance and go out to your house, 'Rene, or call up and arrange a meeting, when I ran into you. What luck!"

Irene agreed that it was luck. "It's the first time I've been home for five years, and now I'm about to leave. A week later and I'd have been gone. And how in the world did you find Gertrude?"

"In the book. I remembered about Fred. His father still has the meat market."

"Oh, yes," said Irene, who had only remembered it as Clare had spoken, "on Cottage Grove near—"

Gertrude broke in. "No. It's moved. We're on Maryland Avenue—used to be Jackson—now. Near Sixty-third Street. And the market's Fred's. His name's the same as his father's."

Gertrude, Irene thought, looked as if her husband might be a butcher. There was left of her youthful prettiness, which had been so much admired in their high-school days, no trace. She had grown broad, fat almost, and though there were no lines on her large white face, its very smoothness was somehow prematurely ageing. Her black hair was clipt, and by some unfortunate means all the live curliness had gone from it. Her over-trimmed Georgette *crêpe* dress was too short and showed an appalling amount of leg, stout legs in sleazy stockings of a vivid rose-beige shade. Her plump hands were newly and not too competently manicured—for the occasion, probably. And she wasn't smoking.

Clare said—and Irene fancied that her husky voice held a slight edge—"Before you came, Irene, Gertrude was telling me about her two boys. Twins. Think of it! Isn't it too marvellous for words?"

Irene felt a warmness creeping into her cheeks. Uncanny, the way Clare could divine what one was thinking. She was a little put out, but her manner was entirely easy as she said: "That is nice. I've two boys myself, Gertrude. Not twins, though. It seems that Clare's rather behind, doesn't it?"

Gertrude, however, wasn't sure that Clare hadn't the best of it. "She's got a girl. I wanted a girl. So did Fred."

"Isn't that a bit unusual?" Irene asked. "Most men want sons. Egotism, I suppose."

"Well, Fred didn't."

The tea-things had been placed on a low table at Clare's side. She gave them her attention now, pouring the rich amber fluid from the tall glass pitcher into stately slim glasses, which she handed to her guests, and then offered them lemon or cream and tiny sandwiches or cakes.

After taking up her own glass she informed them: "No, I have no boys and I don't think I'll ever have any. I'm afraid. I nearly died of terror the whole nine months before Margery was born for fear that she might be dark. Thank goodness, she turned out all right. But I'll never risk it again. Never! The strain is simply too—too hellish."

Gertrude Martin nodded in complete comprehension.

This time it was Irene who said nothing.

"You don't have to tell me!" Gertrude said fervently. "I know what it is all right. Maybe you don't think I wasn't scared to death too. Fred said I was silly, and so did his mother. But, of course, they thought it was just a notion I'd gotten into my head and they blamed it on my condition. They don't know like we do, how it might go way back, and turn out dark no matter what colour the father and mother are."

Perspiration stood out on her forehead. Her narrow eyes rolled first in Clare's, then in Irene's direction. As she talked she waved her heavy hands about.

"No," she went on, "no more for me either. Not even a girl. It's awful the way it skips generations and then pops out. Why, he actually said he didn't care what colour it turned out, if I would only stop worrying about it. But, of course, nobody wants a dark child." Her voice was earnest and she took for granted that her audience was in entire agreement with her.

Irene, whose head had gone up with a quick little jerk, now said in a voice of whose even tones she was proud: "One of my boys is dark."

Gertrude jumped as if she had been shot at. Her eyes goggled. Her mouth flew open. She tried to speak, but could not immediately get the words out. Finally she managed to stammer: "Oh! And your husband, is he — is he — er — dark, too?"

Irene, who was struggling with a flood of feelings, resentment, anger, and contempt, was, however, still able to answer as coolly as if she had not that sense of not belonging to and of despising the company in which she found herself drinking iced tea from tall amber glasses on that hot August afternoon. Her husband, she informed them quietly, couldn't exactly "pass."

At that reply Clare turned on Irene her seductive caressing smile and remarked a little scoffingly: "I do think that coloured people — we — are too silly about some things. After all, the thing's not important to Irene or hundreds of others. Not awfully, even to you, Gertrude. It's only deserters like me who have to be afraid of freaks of the nature. As my inestimable dad used to say, 'Everything must be paid for.' Now, please one of you tell me what ever happened to Claude Jones. You know, the tall, lanky specimen who used to wear that comical little moustache that the girls used to laugh at so. Like a thin streak of soot. The moustache, I mean."

At that Gertrude shrieked with laughter. "Claude Jones!" and launched into the story of how he was no longer a Negro or a Christian but had become a Jew.

"A Jew!" Clare exclaimed.

"Yes, a Jew. A black Jew, he calls himself. He won't eat ham and goes to the synagogue on Saturday. He's got a beard now as well as a moustache. You'd die laughing if you saw him. He's really too funny for words. Fred says he's crazy and I guess he is. Oh, he's a scream all right, a regular scream!" And she shrieked again.

Clare's laugh tinkled out. "It certainly sounds funny enough. Still, it's his own business. If he gets along better by turning — "

At that, Irene, who was still hugging her unhappy don't-care feeling of rightness, broke in, saying bitingly: "It evidently doesn't occur to either you or Gertrude that he might possibly be sincere in changing his religion. Surely everyone doesn't do everything for gain."

Clare Kendry had no need to search for the full meaning of that utterance. She reddened slightly and retorted seriously: "Yes, I admit that might be possible — his being sincere, I mean. It just didn't happen to occur to me, that's all. I'm surprised," and the seriousness changed to mockery, "that you should have expected it to. Or did you really?"

"You don't, I'm sure, imagine that that is a question that I can answer," Irene told her. "Not here and now."

Gertrude's face expressed complete bewilderment. However, seeing that little smiles had come out on the faces of the two other women and not recognizing them for the smiles of mutual reservations which they were, she smiled too.

Clare began to talk, steering carefully away from anything that might lead towards race or other thorny subjects. It was the most brilliant exhibition of conversational weightlifting that Irene had ever seen. Her words swept over them in charming well-modulated streams. Her laughs tinkled and pealed. Her little stories sparkled.

Irene contributed a bare "Yes" or "No" here and there. Gertrude, a "You don't say!" less frequently.

For a while the illusion of general conversation was nearly perfect. Irene felt her resentment changing gradually to a silent, somewhat grudging admiration.

Clare talked on, her voice, her gestures, colouring all she said of wartime in France, of after-the-wartime in Germany, of the excitement at the time of the general strike in England, of dressmaker's openings in Paris, of the new gaiety of Budapest.

But it couldn't last, this verbal feat. Gertrude shifted in her seat and fell to fidgeting with her fingers. Irene, bored at last by all this repetition of the selfsame things that she had read all too often in papers, magazines, and books, set down her glass and collected her bag and handkerchief. She was smoothing out the tan fingers of her gloves preparatory to putting them on when she heard the sound of the outer door being opened and saw Clare spring up with an expression of relief saying: "How lovely! Here's Jack at exactly the right minute. You can't go now, 'Rene dear."

John Bellew came into the room. The first thing that Irene noticed about him was that he was not the man that she had seen with Clare Kendry on the Drayton roof. This man, Clare's husband, was a tallish person, broadly made. His age she guessed to be somewhere between thirty-five and forty. His hair was dark brown and waving, and he had a soft mouth, somewhat womanish, set in an unhealthy-looking dough-coloured face. His steel-grey opaque eyes were very much alive, moving ceaselessly between thick bluish lids. But there was, Irene decided, nothing unusual about him, unless it was an impression of latent physical power.

"Hello, Nig," was his greeting to Clare.

Gertrude who had started slightly, settled back and looked covertly towards Irene, who had caught her lip between her teeth and sat gazing at husband and wife. It was hard to believe that even Clare Kendry would permit this ridiculing of her race by an outsider, though he chanced to be her husband. So he knew, then, that Clare was a Negro? From her talk the other day Irene had understood that he didn't. But how rude, how positively insulting, for him to address her in that way in the presence of guests!

In Clare's eyes, as she presented her husband, was a queer gleam, a jeer, it might be. Irene couldn't define it.

The mechanical professions that attend an introduction over, she inquired: "Did you hear what Jack called me?"

"Yes," Gertrude answered, laughing with a dutiful eagerness.

Irene didn't speak. Her gaze remained level on Clare's smiling face.

The black eyes fluttered down. "Tell them, dear, why you call me that."

The man chuckled, crinkling up his eyes, not, Irene was compelled to acknowledge, unpleasantly. He explained: "Well, you see, it's like this. When we were first married, she was as white as — as — well as white as a lily. But I declare she's gettin' darker and darker. I tell her if she don't look out, she'll wake up one of these days and find she's turned into a nigger."

He roared with laughter. Clare's ringing bell-like laugh joined his. Gertrude after another uneasy shift in her seat added her shrill one. Irene, who had been sitting with lips tightly compressed, cried out: "That's good!" and gave way to gales of laughter. She laughed and laughed and laughed. Tears ran down her cheeks. Her sides ached. Her throat hurt. She laughed on and on and on, long after the others had subsided. Until, catching sight of Clare's face, the need for a more quiet enjoyment of this priceless joke, and for caution, struck her. At once she stopped.

Clare handed her husband his tea and laid her hand on his arm with an affectionate little gesture. Speaking with confidence as well as with amusement, she said: "My goodness, Jack! What difference would it make if, after all these years, you were to find out that I was one or two per cent coloured?"

Bellew put out his hand in a repudiating fling, definite and final. "Oh, no, Nig," he declared, "nothing like that with me. I know you're no nigger, so it's all right. You can get as black as you please as far as I'm concerned, since I know you're no nigger. I draw the line at that. No niggers in my family. Never have been and never will be."

Irene's lips trembled almost uncontrollably, but she made a desperate effort to fight back her disastrous desire to laugh again, and succeeded. Carefully selecting a cigarette from the lacquered box on the tea-table before her, she turned an oblique look on Clare and encountered her peculiar eyes fixed on her with an expression so dark and deep and unfathomable that she had for a short moment the sensation of gazing into the eyes of some creature utterly strange and apart. A faint sense of danger brushed her, like the breath of a cold fog. Absurd, her reason told her, as she accepted Bellew's proffered light for her cigarette. Another glance at Clare showed her smiling. So, as one always ready to oblige, was Gertrude.

An on-looker, Irene reflected, would have thought it a most congenial tea-party, all smiles and jokes and hilarious laughter. She said humorously: "So you dislike Negroes, Mr. Bellew?" But her amusement was at her thought, rather than her words.

John Bellew gave a short denying laugh. "You got me wrong there, Mrs. Redfield. Nothing like that at all. I don't dislike them, I hate them. And so does Nig, for all she's trying to turn into one. She wouldn't have a nigger maid around her for love nor money. Not that I'd want her to. They give me the creeps. The black scrimy devils."

This wasn't funny. Had Bellew, Irene inquired, ever known any Negroes? The defensive tone of her voice brought another start from the uncomfortable Gertrude, and, for all her appearance of serenity, a quick apprehensive look from Clare.

Bellew answered: "Thank the Lord, no! And never expect to! But I know people who've known them, better than they know their black selves. And I read in the papers about them. Always robbing and killing people. And," he added darkly, "worse."

From Gertrude's direction came a queer little suppressed sound, a snort or a giggle. Irene couldn't tell which. There was a brief silence, during which she feared that her self-control was about to prove too frail a bridge to support her mounting anger and indignation. She had a leaping desire to shout at the man beside her: "And you're sitting here surrounded by three black devils, drinking tea."

The impulse passed, obliterated by her consciousness of the danger in which such rashness would involve Clare, who remarked with a gentle reprovingness: "Jack dear, I'm sure 'Rene doesn't care to hear all about your pet aversions. Nor Gertrude either. Maybe they read the papers too, you know." She smiled on him, and her smile seemed to transform him, to soften and mellow him, as the rays of the sun does a fruit.

"All right, Nig, old girl. I'm sorry," he apologized. Reaching over, he playfully touched his wife's pale hands, then turned back to Irene. "Didn't mean to bore you, Mrs. Redfield. Hope you'll excuse me," he said sheepishly. "Clare tells me you're living in New York. Great city. New York. The city of the future."

In Irene, rage had not retreated, but was held by some dam of caution and allegiance to Clare. So, in the best casual voice she could muster, she agreed with Bellew. Though, she reminded him, it was exactly what Chicagoans were apt to say of their city. And all the while she was speaking, she was thinking how amazing it was that her voice did not tremble, that outwardly she was calm.

Only her hands shook slightly. She drew them inward from their rest in her lap and pressed the tips of her fingers together to still them.

"Husband's a doctor, I understand. Manhattan, or one of the other boroughs?"

Manhattan, Irene informed him, and explained the need for Brian to be within easy reach of certain hospitals and clinics.

"Interesting life, a doctor's."

"Ye-es. Hard, though. And, in a way, monotonous. Nerve-racking too."

"Hard on the wife's nerves at least, eh? So many lady patients." He laughed, enjoying, with a boyish heartiness, the hoary joke.

Irene managed a momentary smile, but her voice was sober as she said: "Brian doesn't care for ladies, especially sick ones. I sometimes wish he did. It's South America that attracts him."

"Coming place, South America, if they ever get the niggers out of it. It's run over — "

"Really, Jack!" Clare's voice was on the edge of temper.

"Honestly, Nig, I forgot." To the others he said: "You see how hen-pecked I am." And to Gertrude: "You're still in Chicago, Mrs. — er — Mrs. Martin?"

He was, it was plain, doing his best to be agreeable to these old friends of Clare's. Irene had to concede that under other conditions she might have liked him. A fairly good-looking man of amiable disposition, evidently, and in easy circumstances. Plain and with no nonsense about him.

Gertrude replied that Chicago was good enough for her. She'd never been out of it and didn't think she ever should. Her husband's business was there.

"Of course, of course. Can't jump up and leave a business."

There followed a smooth surface of talk about Chicago, New York, their differences and their recent spectacular changes.

It was, Irene, thought, unbelievable and astonishing that four people could sit so unruffled, so ostensibly friendly, while they were in reality seething with anger, mortification, shame. But no, on second thought she was forced to amend her opinion. John Bellew, most certainly, was as undisturbed within as without. So, perhaps, was Gertrude Martin. At least she hadn't the mortification and shame that Clare Kendry must be feeling, or, in such full measure, the rage and rebellion that she, Irene, was repressing.

"More tea, 'Rene," Clare offered.

"Thanks, no. And I must be going. I'm leaving tomorrow, you know, and I've still got packing to do."

She stood up. So did Gertrude, and Clare, and John Bellew.

"How do you like the Drayton, Mrs. Redfield?" the latter asked.

"The Drayton? Oh, very much. Very much indeed," Irene answered, her scornful eyes on Clare's unrevealing face.

"Nice place, all right. Stayed there a time or two myself," the man informed her.

"Yes, it is nice," Irene agreed. "Almost as good as our best New York places." She had withdrawn her look from Clare and was searching in her bag for some non-existent something. Her understanding was rapidly increasing, as was her pity and her contempt. Clare was so daring, so lovely, and so "having."

They gave their hands to Clare with appropriate murmurs. "So good to have seen you." . . . "I do hope I'll see you again soon."

"Good-bye," Clare returned. "It was good of you to come, 'Rene dear. And you too, Gertrude."

"Good-bye, Mr. Bellew." . . . "So glad to have met you." It was Gertrude who had said that. Irene couldn't, she absolutely couldn't bring herself to utter the polite fiction or anything approaching it.

He accompanied them out into the hall, summoned the elevator.

"Good-bye," they said again, stepping in.

Plunging downward they were silent.

They made their way through the lobby without speaking.

Lionel Smit

This painting, completed in 2013 by artist Lionel Smit, is entitled *Disclose and Reveal Series #1*. **How does the subject of this painting reflect its title? How might you read this as a depiction of Irene's reaction to meeting Clare's husband for the first time? How might it be read as a statement about the discussion Clare, Gertrude, and Irene have prior to Jack's arrival?**

But as soon as they had reached the street Gertrude, in the manner of one unable to keep bottled up for another minute that which for the last hour she had had to retain, burst out: "My God! What an awful chance! She must be plumb crazy."

"Yes, it certainly seems risky," Irene admitted.

"Risky! I should say it was. Risky! My God! What a word! And the mess she's liable to get herself into!"

"Still, I Imagine she's pretty safe. They don't live here, you know. And there's a child. That's a certain security."

"It's an awful chance, just the same," Gertrude insisted. "I'd never in the world have married Fred without him knowing. You can't tell what will turn up."

"Yes, I do agree that it's safer to tell. But then Bellew wouldn't have married her. And, after all, that's what she wanted."

Gertrude shook her head. "I wouldn't be in her shoes for all the money she's getting out of it, when he finds out. Not with him feeling the way he does. Gee! Wasn't it awful? For a minute I was so mad I could have slapped him."

It had been, Irene acknowledged, a distinctly trying experience, as well as a very unpleasant one. "I was more than a little angry myself."

"And imagine her not telling us about him feeling that way! Anything might have happened. We might have said something."

That, Irene pointed out, was exactly like Clare Kendry. Taking a chance, and not at all considering anyone else's feelings.

Gertrude said: "Maybe she thought we'd think it a good joke. And I guess you did. The way you laughed. My land! I was scared to death he might catch on."

"Well, it was rather a joke," Irene told her, "on him and us and maybe on her."

"All the same, it's an awful chance. I'd hate to be her."

"She seems satisfied enough. She's got what she wanted, and the other day she told me it was worth it."

But about that Gertrude was sceptical. "She'll find out different," was her verdict. "She'll find out different all right."

Rain had begun to fall, a few scattered large drops.

The end-of-the-day crowds were scurrying in the directions of street-cars and elevated roads.

Irene said: "You're going south? I'm sorry. I've got an errand. If you don't mind, I'll just say good-bye here. It has been nice seeing you, Gertrude. Say hello to Fred for me, and to your mother if she remembers me. Good-bye."

She had wanted to be free of the other woman, to be alone; for she was still sore and angry.

What right, she kept demanding of herself, had Clare Kendry to expose her, or even Gertrude Martin, to such humiliation, such downright insult?

And all the while, on the rushing ride out to her father's house, Irene Redfield was trying to understand the look on Clare's face as she had said good-bye. Partly mocking, it had seemed, and partly menacing. And something else for which she could find no name. For an instant a recrudescence of that sensation of fear which she had had while looking into Clare's eyes that afternoon touched her. A slight shiver ran over her.

"It's nothing," she told herself. "Just somebody walking over my grave, as the children say." She tried a tiny laugh and was annoyed to find that it was close to tears.

What a state she had allowed that horrible Bellew to get her into!

And late that night, even, long after the last guest had gone and the old house was quiet, she stood at her window frowning out into the dark rain and puzzling again over that look on Clare's incredibly beautiful face. She couldn't, however, come to any conclusion about its meaning, try as she might. It was unfathomable, utterly beyond any experience or comprehension of hers.

She turned away from the window, at last, with a still deeper frown. Why, after all, worry about Clare Kendry? She was well able to take care of herself, had always been able. And there were, for Irene, other things, more personal and more important to worry about.

Besides, her reason told her, she had only herself to blame for her disagreeable afternoon and its attendant fears and questions. She ought never to have gone.

Chapter 4

The next morning, the day of her departure for New York, had brought a letter, which, at first glance, she had instinctively known came from Clare Kendry, though she couldn't remember ever having had a letter from her before. Ripping it open and looking at the signature, she saw that she had been right in her guess. She wouldn't, she told herself, read it. She hadn't the time. And, besides, she had no wish to be reminded of the afternoon before. As it was, she felt none too fresh for her journey; she had had a wretched night. And all because of Clare's innate lack of consideration for the feelings of others.

But she did read it. After father and friends had waved good-bye, and she was being hurled eastward, she became possessed of an uncontrollable curiosity to see what Clare had said about yesterday. For what, she asked, as she took it out of her bag and opened it, could she, what could anyone, say about a thing like that?

Clare Kendry had said:

> 'Rene dear:
>
> However am I to thank you for your visit? I know you are feeling that under the circumstances I ought not to have asked you to come, or, rather, insisted. But if you could know how glad, how excitingly happy, I was to meet you and how I ached to see more of you (to see everybody and couldn't), you would understand my wanting to see you again, and maybe forgive me a little.
>
> My love to you always and always and to your dear father, and all my poor thanks.
>
> Clare.

And there was a postcript which said:

> It may be, 'Rene dear, it may just be, that, after all, your way may be the wiser and infinitely happier one. I'm not sure just now. At least not so sure as I have been.
>
> C.

But the letter hadn't conciliated Irene. Her indignation was not lessened by Clare's flattering reference to her wiseness. As if, she thought wrathfully, anything could take away the humiliation, or any part of it, of what she had gone through yesterday afternoon for Clare Kendry.

With an unusual methodicalness she tore the offending letter into tiny ragged squares that fluttered down and made a small heap in her black *crêpe de Chine* lap. The destruction completed, she gathered them up, rose, and moved to the train's end. Standing there, she dropped them over the railing and watched them scatter, on tracks, on cinders, on forlorn grass, in rills of dirty water.

And that, she told herself, was that. The chances were one in a million that she would ever again lay eyes on Clare Kendry. If, however, that millionth chance should turn up, she had only to turn away her eyes, to refuse her recognition.

She dropped Clare out of her mind and turned her thoughts to her own affairs. To home, to the boys, to Brian. Brian, who in the morning would be waiting for her in the great clamourous station. She hoped that he had been comfortable and not too lonely without her and the boys. Not so lonely that that old, queer, unhappy restlessness had begun again within him; that craving for some place strange and different, which at the beginning of her marriage she had had to make such strenuous efforts to repress, and which yet faintly alarmed her, though it now sprang up at gradually lessening intervals.

Part Two: Re-Encounter

Chapter 1

Such were Irene Redfield's memories as she sat there in her room, a flood of October sunlight streaming in upon her, holding that second letter of Clare Kendry's.

Laying it aside, she regarded with an astonishment that had in it a mild degree of amusement the violence of the feelings which it stirred in her.

It wasn't the great measure of anger that surprised and slightly amused her. That, she was certain, was justified and reasonable, as was the fact that it could hold, still strong and unabated, across the stretch of two years' time entirely removed from any sight or sound of John Bellew, or of Clare. That even at this remote date the memory of the man's words and manner had power to set her hands to trembling and to send the blood pounding against her temples did not seem to her extraordinary. But that she should retain that dim sense of fear, of panic, was surprising, silly.

That Clare should have written, should, even all things considered, have expressed a desire to see her again, did not so much amaze her. To count as nothing the annoyances, the bitterness, or the suffering of others, that was Clare.

Well — Irene's shoulders went up — one thing was sure: that she needn't, and didn't intend to, lay herself open to any repetition of a humiliation as galling and outrageous as that which, for Clare Kendry's sake, she had borne "that time in Chicago." Once was enough.

If, at the time of choosing, Clare hadn't precisely reckoned the cost, she had, nevertheless, no right to expect others to help make up the reckoning. The trouble with Clare was, not only that she wanted to have her cake and eat it too, but that she wanted to nibble at the cakes of other folk as well.

Irene Redfield found it hard to sympathize with this new tenderness, this avowed yearning of Clare's for "my own people."

The letter which she just put out of her hand was, to her taste, a bit too lavish in its wordiness, a shade too unreserved in the manner of its expression. It roused again that old suspicion that Clare was acting, not consciously, perhaps — that is, not too consciously — but, none the less, acting. Nor was Irene inclined to excuse what she termed Clare's downright selfishness.

And mingled with her disbelief and resentment was another feeling, a question. Why hadn't she spoken that day? Why, in the face of Bellew's ignorant hate and aversion, had she concealed her own origin? Why had she allowed him to make his assertions and express his misconceptions undisputed? Why, simply because of Clare Kendry, who had exposed her to such torment, had she failed to take up the defence of the race to which she belonged?

Irene asked these questions, felt them. They were, however, merely rhetorical, as she herself was well aware. She knew their answers, every one, and it was the same for them all. The sardony of it! She couldn't betray Clare, couldn't even run the risk of appearing to defend a people that were being maligned, for fear that that defence might in some infinitesimal degree lead the way to final discovery of her secret. She had to Clare Kendry a duty. She was bound to her by those very ties of race, which, for all her repudiation of them, Clare had been unable to completely sever.

And it wasn't, as Irene knew, that Clare cared at all about the race or what was to become of it. She didn't. Or that she had for any of its members great, or even real, affection, though she professed undying gratitude for the small kindnesses which the Westover family had shown her when she was a child. Irene doubted the genuineness of it, seeing herself only as a means to an end where Clare was concerned. Nor could it be said that she had even the slight artistic or sociological interest in the race that some members of other races displayed. She hadn't. No, Clare Kendry cared nothing for the race. She only belonged to it.

"Not another damned thing!" Irene declared aloud as she drew a fragile stocking over a pale beige-coloured foot.

"Aha! Swearing again, are you, madam? Caught you in the act that time."

Brian Redfield had come into the room in that noiseless way which, in spite, of the years of their life together, still had the power to disconcert her. He stood looking down on her with that amused smile of his, which was just the faintest bit supercilious and yet was somehow very becoming to him.

Hastily Irene pulled on the other stocking and slipped her feet into the slippers beside her chair.

"And what brought on this particular outburst of profanity? That is, if an indulgent but perturbed husband may inquire. The mother of sons too! The times, alas, the times!"

"I've had this letter," Irene told him. "And I'm sure that anybody'll admit it's enough to make a saint swear. The nerve of her!"

She passed the letter to him, and in the act made a little mental frown. For, with a nicety of perception, she saw that she was doing it instead of answering his question with words, so that he might be occupied while she hurried through her dressing. For she was late again, and Brian, she well knew, detested that. Why, oh why, couldn't she ever manage to be on time? Brian had been up for ages, had made some calls for all she knew, besides having taken the boys downtown to school. And she wasn't dressed yet; had only begun. Damn Clare! This morning it was her fault.

Brian sat down and bent his head over the letter, puckering his brows slightly in his effort to make out Clare's scrawl.

Irene, who had risen and was standing before the mirror, ran a comb through her black hair, then tossed her head with a light characteristic gesture, in order to disarrange a little the set locks. She touched a powder-puff to her warm olive skin, and then put on her frock with a motion so hasty that it was with some difficulty properly adjusted. At last she was ready, though she didn't immediately say so, but stood, instead, looking with a sort of curious detachment at her husband across the room.

Brian, she was thinking, was extremely good-looking. Not, of course, pretty or effeminate; the slight irregularity of his nose saved him from the prettiness, and the rather marked heaviness of his chin saved him from the effeminacy. But he was, in a pleasant masculine way, rather handsome. And yet, wouldn't he, perhaps, have been merely ordinarily good-looking but for the richness, the beauty of his skin, which was of an exquisitely fine texture and deep copper colour.

He looked up and said: "Clare? That must be the girl you told me about meeting the last time you were out home. The one you went to tea with?"

Irene's answer to that was an inclination of the head.

"I'm ready," she said.

They were going downstairs, Brian deftly, unnecessarily, piloting her round the two short curved steps, just before the centre landing.

"You're not," he asked, "going to see her?"

His words, however, were in reality not a question, but, as Irene was aware, an admonition.

Her front teeth just touched. She spoke through them, and her tones held a thin sarcasm. "Brian, darling, I'm really not such an, idiot that I don't realize that if a man calls me a nigger, it's his fault the first time, but mine if he has the opportunity to do it again."

They went into the dining-room. He drew back her chair and she sat down behind the fat-bellied German coffee-pot, which sent out its morning fragrance, mingled with the smell of crisp toast and savoury bacon, in the distance. With his long, nervous fingers he picked up the morning paper from his own chair and sat down.

Zulena, a small mahogany-coloured creature, brought in the grapefruit.

They took up their spoons.

Out of the silence Brian spoke. Blandly. "My dear, you misunderstand me entirely. I simply meant that I hope you're not going to let her pester you. She will, you know, if you give her half a chance and she's anything at all like your description of her. Anyway, they always do. Besides," he corrected, "the man, her husband, didn't call you a nigger. There's a difference, you know."

"No, certainly he didn't. Not actually. He couldn't, not very well, since he didn't know. But he would have. It amounts to the same thing. And I'm sure it was just as unpleasant."

"U-mm, I don't know. But it seems to me," he pointed out, "that you, my dear, had all the advantage. You knew what his opinion of you was, while he — Well, 'twas ever thus. We know, always have. They don't. Not quite. It has, you will admit, it's humorous side, and, sometimes, its conveniences."

She poured the coffee.

"I can't see it. I'm going to write Clare. Today, if I can find a minute. It's a thing we might as well settle definitely, and immediately. Curious, isn't it, that knowing, as she does, his unqualified attitude, she still — "

Brian interrupted: "It's always that way. Never known it to fail. Remember Albert Hammond, how he used to be for ever haunting Seventh Avenue, and Lenox Avenue, and the dancing-places, until some 'shine' took a shot at him for casting an eye towards his 'sheba?' They always come back. I've seen it happen time and time again."

"But why?" Irene wanted to know. "Why?"

"If I knew that, I'd know what race is."

"But wouldn't you think that having got the thing, or things, they were after, and at such risk, they'd be satisfied? Or afraid?"

"Yes," Brian agreed, "you certainly would think so. But, the fact remains, they aren't. Not satisfied, I mean. I think they're scared enough most of the time, when they give way to the urge and slip back. Not scared enough to stop them, though. Why, the good God only knows."

Irene leaned forward, speaking, she was aware, with a vehemence absolutely unnecessary, but which she could not control.

"Well, Clare can just count me out. I've no intention of being the link between her and her poorer darker brethren. After that scene in Chicago too! To calmly expect me — " She stopped short, suddenly too wrathful for words.

Couple in Raccoon Coats, Harlem, 1932/Van Der Zee, James/Minneapolis Institute of Arts, MN, USA/Bridgeman Images

African American photographer James Van Der Zee (1886–1983) completed a series of "Sunday Portraits," which featured influential Black people in New York City during the Harlem Renaissance. This photograph was taken in 1932. **The photographs in this series were carefully staged. What elements in this image are intended to signal the success or affluence of this couple, and how does it characterize their relationship? How might these two resemble Brian and Irene Redfield in appearance or attitude?**

"Quite right. The only sensible thing to do. Let her miss you. It's an unhealthy business, the whole affair. Always is."

Irene nodded. "More coffee," she offered.

"Thanks, no." He took up his paper again, spreading it open with a little rattling noise.

Zulena came in bringing more toast. Brian took a slice and bit into it with that audible crunching sound that Irene disliked so intensely, and turned back to his paper.

She said: "It's funny about 'passing.' We disapprove of it and at the same time condone it. It excites our contempt and yet we rather admire it. We shy away from it with an odd kind of revulsion, but we protect it."

"Instinct of the race to survive and expand."

"Rot! Everything can't be explained by some general biological phrase."

"Absolutely everything can. Look at the so-called whites, who've left bastards all over the known earth. Same thing in them. Instinct of the race to survive and expand."

With that Irene didn't at all agree, but many arguments in the past had taught her the futility of attempting to combat Brian on ground where he was more nearly at home than she. Ignoring his unqualified assertion, she slid away from the subject entirely.

"I wonder," she asked, "if you'll have time to run me down to the printing-office. It's on a Hundred and Sixteenth Street. I've got to see about some handbills and some more tickets for the dance."

"Yes, of course. How's it going? Everything all set?"

"Ye-es. I guess so. The boxes are all sold and nearly all the first batch of tickets. And we expect to take in almost as much again at the door. Then, there's all that cake to sell. It's a terrible lot of work, though."

"I'll bet it is. Uplifting the brother's no easy job. I'm as busy as a cat with fleas, myself." And over his face there came a shadow. "Lord! how I hate sick people, and their stupid, meddling families, and smelly, dirty rooms, and climbing filthy steps in dark hallways."

"Surely," Irene began, fighting back the fear and irritation that she felt, "surely — "

Her husband silenced her, saying sharply: "Let's not talk about it, please." And immediately, in his usual, slightly mocking tone he asked: "Are you ready to go now? I haven't a great deal of time to wait."

He got up. She followed him out into the hall without replying. He picked up his soft brown hat from the small table and stood a moment whirling it round on his long tea-coloured fingers.

Irene, watching him, was thinking: "It isn't fair, it isn't fair." After all these years to still blame her like this. Hadn't his success proved that she'd been right in insisting that he stick to his profession right there in New York? Couldn't he see, even now, that it *had* been best? Not for her, oh no, not for her — she had never really considered herself — but for him and the boys. Was she never to be free of it, that fear which crouched, always, deep down within her, stealing away the sense of security, the feeling of permanence, from the life which she had so admirably arranged for them all, and desired so ardently to have remain as it was? That strange, and to her fantastic, notion of Brian's of going off to Brazil, which, though unmentioned, yet lived within him; how it frightened her, and — yes, angered her!

"Well?" he asked lightly.

"I'll just get my things. One minute," she promised and turned upstairs.

Her voice had been even and her step was firm, but in her there was no slackening of the agitation, of the alarms, which Brian's expression of discontent had raised. He had never spoken of his desire since that long-ago time of storm and strain, of hateful and nearly disastrous quarrelling, when she had so firmly opposed him, so sensibly pointed out its utter impossibility and its probable consequences to her and the boys, and had even hinted at a dissolution of their marriage in the event of his persistence in his idea. No, there had been, in all the years that they had lived together since then, no other talk of it, no more than there had been any other quarrelling or any other threats. But because, so she insisted, the bond of flesh and spirit between them was so strong, she knew, had always known, that his dissatisfaction had continued, as had his dislike and disgust for his profession and his country.

A feeling of uneasiness stole upon her at the inconceivable suspicion that she might have been wrong in her estimate of her husband's character. But she squirmed away from it. Impossible! She couldn't have been wrong. Everything proved that she had been right. More than right, if such a thing could be. And all, she assured herself, because she understood him so well, because she had, actually, a special talent for understanding him. It was, as she saw it, the one thing that had been the basis of the success which she had made of a marriage that had threatened to fail. She knew him as well as he knew himself, or better.

Then why worry? The thing, this discontent which had exploded into words, would surely die, flicker out, at last. True, she had in the past often been tempted to believe that it had died, only to become conscious, in some instinctive, subtle way, that she had been merely deceiving herself for a while and that it still lived. But it *would* die. Of that she was certain. She had only to direct and guide her man, to keep him going in the right direction.

She put on her coat and adjusted her hat.

Yes, it would die, as long ago she had made up her mind that it should. But in the meantime, while it was still living and still had the power to flare up and alarm her, it would have to be banked, smothered, and something offered in its stead. She would have to make some plan, some decision, at once. She frowned, for it annoyed her intensely. For, though temporary, it would be important and perhaps disturbing. Irene didn't like changes, particularly changes that affected the smooth routine of her household. Well, it couldn't be helped. Something would have to be done. And immediately.

She took up her purse and drawing on her gloves, ran down the steps and out through the door which Brian held open for her and stepped into the waiting car.

"You know," she said, settling herself into the seat beside him, "I'm awfuly glad to get this minute alone with you. It does seem that we're always so busy — I do hate that — but what can we do? I've had something on my mind for ever so long, something that needs talking over and really serious consideration."

The car's engine rumbled as it moved out from the kerb and into the scant traffic of the street under Brian's expert guidance.

She studied his profile.

They turned into Seventh Avenue. Then he said: "Well, let's have it. No time like the present for the settling of weighty matters."

"It's about Junior. I wonder if he isn't going too fast in school? We do forget that he's not eleven yet. Surely it can't be good for him to — well, if he is, I mean. Going too fast, you know. Of course, you know more about these things than I do. You're better able to judge. That is, if you've noticed or thought about it at all."

"I do wish, Irene, you wouldn't be for ever fretting about those kids. They're all right. Perfectly all right. Good, strong, healthy boys, especially Junior. Most especially Junior."

"Well, I s'pose you're right. You're expected to know about things like that, and I'm sure you wouldn't make a mistake about your own boy." (Now, why had she said that?) "But that isn't all. I'm terribly afraid he's picked up some queer ideas about things — some things — from the older boys, you know."

Her manner was consciously light. Apparently she was intent of the maze of traffic, but she was still watching Brian's face closely. On it was a peculiar expression. Was it, could it possibly be, a mixture of scorn and distaste?

"Queer ideas?" he repeated. "D'you mean Ideas about sex, Irene?"

"Ye-es. Not quite nice ones. Dreadful jokes, and things like that."

"Oh, I see," he threw at her. For a while there was silence between them. After a moment he demanded bluntly: "Well, what of it? If sex isn't a joke, what is it? And what is a joke?"

"As you please, Brian. He's your son, you know." Her voice was clear, level, disapproving.

"Exactly! And you're trying to make a molly-coddle out of him. Well, just let me tell you, I won't have it. And you needn't think I'm going to let you change him to some nice kindergarten kind of a school because he's getting a little necessary education. I won't! He'll stay right where he is. The sooner and the more he learns about sex, the better for him. And most certainly if he learns that it's a grand joke, the greatest in the world. It'll keep him from lots of disappointments later on."

Irene didn't answer.

They reached the printing-shop. She got out, emphatically slamming the car's door behind her. There was a piercing agony of misery in her heart. She hadn't intended to behave like this, but her extreme resentment at his attitude, the sense of having been wilfully misunderstood and reproved, drove her to fury.

Inside the shop, she stilled the trembling of her lips and drove back her rising anger. Her business transacted, she came back to the car in a chastened mood. But against the armour of Brian's stubborn silence she heard herself saying in a calm, metallic voice: "I don't believe I'll go back just now. I've remembered that I've got to do something about getting something decent to wear. I haven't a rag that's fit to be seen. I'll take the bus downtown."

Brian merely doffed his hat in that maddening polite way which so successfully curbed and yet revealed his temper.

"Good-bye," she said bitingly. "Thanks for the lift," and turned towards the avenue.

What, she wondered contritely, was she to do next? She was vexed with herself for having chosen, as it had turned out, so clumsy an opening for what she had intended to suggest: some European school for Junior next year, and Brian to take him over. If she had been able to present her plan, and he had accepted it, as she was sure that he would have done, with other more favourable opening methods, he would have had that to look forward to as a break in the easy monotony that seemed, for some reason she was wholly unable to grasp, so hateful to him.

She was even more vexed at her own explosion of anger. What could have got into her to give way to it in such a moment?

Gradually her mood passed. She drew back from the failure her first attempt at substitution, not so much discouraged as disappointed and ashamed. It might be, she reflected, that, in addition to her ill-timed loss of temper, she had been too hasty in her eagerness to distract him, had rushed too closely on the heels of his outburst, and had thus aroused his suspicions and his obstinacy. She had but to wait. Another more appropriate time would come, tomorrow, next week, next month. It wasn't now, as it had been once, that she was afraid that he would throw everything aside and rush off to that remote place of his heart's desire. He wouldn't, she knew. He was fond of her, loved her, in his slightly undemonstrative way.

And there were the boys.

It was only that she wanted him to be happy, resenting, however, his inability to be so with things as they were, and never acknowledging that though she did want him to be happy, it was only in her own way and by some plan of hers for him that she truly desired him to be so. Nor did she admit that all other plans, all other ways, she regarded as menaces, more or less indirect, to that security of place and substance which she insisted upon for her sons and in a lesser degree for herself.

Chapter 2

Five days had gone by since Clare Kendry's appealing letter. Irene Redfield had not replied to it. Nor had she had any other word from Clare.

She had not carried out her first intention of writing at once because on going back to the letter for Clare's address, she had come upon something which, in the rigour of her determination to maintain unbroken between them the wall that Clare herself had raised, she had forgotten, or not fully noted. It was the fact that Clare had requested her to direct her answer to the post office's general delivery.

That had angered Irene, and increased her disdain and contempt for the other.

Tearing the letter across, she had flung it into the scrap-basket. It wasn't so much Clare's carefulness and her desire for secrecy in their relations — Irene understood the need for that — as that Clare should have doubted her discretion, implied that she might not be cautious in the wording of her reply and the choice of a posting-box. Having always had complete confidence in her own good judgment and tact, Irene couldn't bear to have anyone seem to question them. Certainly not Clare Kendry.

In another, calmer moment she decided that it was, after all, better to answer nothing, to explain nothing, to refuse nothing; to dispose of the matter simply by not writing at all. Clare, of whom it couldn't be said that she was stupid, would not mistake the implication of that silence. She might — and Irene was sure that she would — choose to ignore it and write again, but that didn't matter. The whole thing would be very easy. The basket for all letters, silence for their answers.

Most likely she and Clare would never meet again. Well, she, for one, could endure that. Since childhood their lives had never really touched. Actually they were strangers. Strangers in their ways and means of living. Strangers in their desires and ambitions. Strangers even in their racial consciousness. Between them the barrier was just as high, just as broad, and just as firm as if in Clare did not run that strain of black blood. In truth, it was higher, broader, and firmer; because for her there were perils, not known, or imagined, by those others who had no such secrets to alarm or endanger them.

• • •

The day was getting on toward evening. It was past the middle of October. There had been a week of cold rain, drenching the rotting leaves which had fallen from the poor trees that lined the street on which the Redfields' house was located, and sending a damp air of penetrating chill into the house, with a hint of cold days to come. In Irene's room a low fire was burning. Outside, only a dull grey light was left of the day. Inside, lamps had already been lighted.

From the floor above there was the sound of young voices. Sometimes Junior's serious and positive; again, Ted's deceptively gracious one. Often there was laughter, or the noise of commotion, tussling, or toys being slammed down.

Junior, tall for his age, was almost incredibly like his father in feature and colouring; but his temperament was hers, practical and determined, rather than Brian's. Ted, speculative and withdrawn, was, apparently, less positive in his ideas and desires. About him there was a deceiving air of candour that was, Irene knew, like his father's show of reasonable acquiescence. If, for the time being, and with a charming appearance of artlessness, he submitted to the force of superior strength, or some other immovable condition or circumstance, it was because of his intense dislike of scenes and unpleasant argument. Brian over again.

Gradually Irene's thought slipped away from Junior and Ted, to become wholly absorbed in their father.

The old fear, with strength increased, the fear for the future, had again laid its hand on her. And, try as she might, she could not shake it off. It was as if she had admitted to herself that against that easy surface of her husband's concordance with her wishes, which had, since the war had given him back to her physically unimpaired, covered an increasing inclination to tear himself and his possessions loose from their proper setting, she was helpless.

The chagrin which she had felt at her first failure to subvert this latest manifestation of his discontent had receded, leaving in its wake an uneasy depression. Were all her efforts, all her labours, to make up to him that one loss, all her silent striving to prove to him that her way had been best, all her ministrations to him, all her outward sinking of self, to count for nothing in some unperceived sudden moment? And if so, what, then, would be the consequences to the boys? To her? To Brian himself? Endless searching had brought no answer to these questions. There was only an intense weariness from their shuttle-like procession in her brain.

The noise and commotion from above grew increasingly louder. Irene was about to go to the stairway and request the boys to be quieter in their play when she heard the doorbell ringing.

Now, who was that likely to be? She listened to Zulena's heels, faintly tapping on their way to the door, then to the shifting sound of her feet on the steps, then to her light knock on the bedroom door.

"Yes. Come in," Irene told her.

Zulena stood in the doorway. She said: "Someone to see you, Mrs. Redfield." Her tone was discreetly regretful, as if to convey that she was reluctant to disturb her mistress at that hour, and for a stranger. "A Mrs. Bellew."

Clare!

"Oh dear! Tell her, Zulena," Irene began, "that I can't — No. I'll see her. Please bring her up here."

She heard Zulena pass down the hall, down the stairs, then stood up, smoothing out the tumbled green and ivory draperies of her dress with light stroking pats. At the mirror she dusted a little powder on her nose and brushed out her hair.

She meant to tell Clare Kendry at once, and definitely, that it was of no use, her coming, that she couldn't be responsible, that she'd talked it over with Brian, who had agreed with her that it was wiser, for Clare's own sake, to refrain —

But that was as far as she got in her rehearsal. For Clare had come softly into the room without knocking, and before Irene could greet her, had dropped a kiss on her dark curls.

Looking at the woman before her, Irene Redfield had a sudden inexplicable onrush of affectionate feeling. Reaching out, she grasped Clare's two hands in her own and cried with something like awe in her voice: "Dear God! But aren't you lovely, Clare!"

Clare tossed that aside. Like the furs and small blue hat which she threw on the bed before seating herself slantwise in Irene's favourite chair, with one foot curled under her.

"Didn't you mean to answer my letter, 'Rene?" she asked gravely.

Irene looked away. She had that uncomfortable feeling that one has when one has not been wholly kind or wholly true.

Clare went on: "Every day I went to that nasty little post-office place. I'm sure they were all beginning to think that I'd been carrying on an illicit love-affair and that the man had thrown me over. Every morning the same answer: 'Nothing for you.' I got into an awful fright, thinking that something might have happened to your letter, or to mine. And half the nights I would lie awake looking out at the watery stars — hopeless things, the stars — worrying and wondering. But at last it soaked in, that you hadn't written and didn't intend to. And then — well, as soon as ever I'd seen Jack off for Florida, I came straight here. And now, 'Rene, please tell me quite frankly why you didn't answer my letter."

"Because, you see — " Irene broke off and kept Clare waiting while she lit a cigarette, blew out the match, and dropped it into a tray. She was trying to collect her arguments, for some sixth sense warned her that it was going to be harder than she thought to convince Clare Kendry of the folly of Harlem for her. Finally she proceeded: "I can't help thinking that you ought not to come up here, ought not to run the risk of knowing Negroes."

"You mean you don't want me, 'Rene?"

Irene hadn't supposed that anyone could look so hurt. She said, quite gently, "No, Clare, it's not that. But even you must see that it's terribly foolish, and not just the right thing."

The tinkle of Clare's laugh rang out, while she passed her hands over the bright sweep of her hair. "Oh, 'Rene!" she cried, "you're priceless! And you haven't changed a bit. The right thing!" Leaning forward, she looked curiously into Irene's disapproving brown eyes. "You don't, you really can't mean exactly that! Nobody could. It's simply unbelievable."

Irene was on her feet before she realized that she had risen. "What I really mean," she retorted, "is that it's dangerous and that you ought not to run such silly risks. No one ought to. You least of all."

Her voice was brittle. For into her mind had come a thought, strange and irrelevant, a suspicion, that had surprised and shocked her and driven her to her feet. It was that in spite of her determined selfishness the woman before her was yet capable of heights and depths of feeling that she, Irene Redfield, had never known. Indeed, never cared to know. The thought, the suspicion, was gone as quickly as it had come.

Clare said: "Oh, me!"

Irene touched her arm caressingly, as if in contrition for that flashing thought. "Yes, Clare, you. It's not safe. Not safe at all."

"Safe!"

It seemed to Irene that Clare had snapped her teeth down on the word and then flung it from her. And for another flying second she had that suspicion of Clare's ability for a quality of feeling that was to her strange, and even repugnant. She was aware, too, of a dim premonition of some impending disaster. It was as if Clare Kendry had said to her, for whom safety, security, were all-important: "Safe! Damn being safe!" and meant it.

With a gesture of impatience she sat down. In a voice of cool formality, she said: "Brian and I have talked the whole thing over carefully and decided that it isn't wise. He says it's always a dangerous business, this coming back. He's seen more than one come to grief because of it. And, Clare, considering everything — Mr. Bellew's attitude and all that — don't you think you ought to be as careful as you can?"

Clare's deep voice broke the small silence that had followed Irene's speech. She said, speaking almost plaintively: "I ought to have known. It's Jack. I don't blame you for being angry, though I must say you behaved beautifully that day. But I did think you'd understand, 'Rene. It was that, partly, that has made me want to see other people. It just swooped down and changed everything. If it hadn't been for that, I'd have gone on to the end, never seeing any of you. But that did something to me, and I've been so lonely since! You can't know. Not close to a single soul. Never anyone to really talk to."

Irene pressed out her cigarette. While doing so, she saw again the vision of Clare Kendry staring disdainfully down at the face of her father, and thought that it would be like that that she would look at her husband if he lay dead before her.

Her own resentment was swept aside and her voice held an accent of pity as she exclaimed: "Why, Clare! I didn't know. Forgive me. I feel like seven beasts. It was stupid of me not to realize."

"No. Not at all. You couldn't. Nobody, none of you, could," Clare moaned. The black eyes filled with tears that ran down her cheeks and spilled into her lap, ruining the priceless velvet of her dress. Her long hands were a little uplifted and clasped tightly together. Her effort to speak moderately was obvious, but not successful. "How could you know? How could you? You're free. You're happy. And," with faint derision, "safe."

Irene passed over that touch of derision, for the poignant rebellion of the other's words had brought the tears to her own eyes, though she didn't allow them to fall. The truth was that she knew weeping did not become her. Few women, she imagined, wept as attractively as Clare. "I'm beginning to believe," she murmured, "that no one is ever completely happy, or free, or safe."

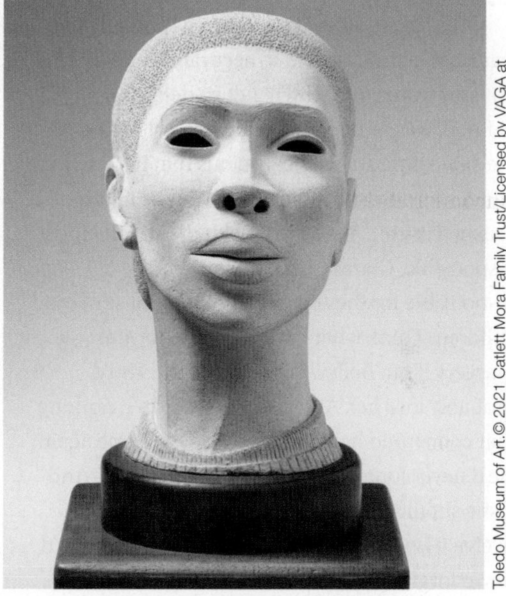

Head of a Young Woman is the work of African American artist Elizabeth Catlett (1915–2012). Of her work, Catlett wrote: "I have always wanted my art to service my people — to reflect us, to relate to us, to stimulate us, to make us aware of our potential. We have to create an art for liberation and for life."

How does this sculpture fulfill the purpose of her art as Catlett describes it? How does it reflect the characters of both Clare and Irene?

"Well, them, what does it matter? One risk more or less, if we're not safe anyway, if even you're not, it can't make all the difference in the world. It can't to me. Besides, I'm used to risks. And this isn't such a big one as you're trying to make it."

"Oh, but it is. And it can make all the difference in the world. There's your little girl, Clare. Think of the consequences to her."

Clare's face took on a startled look, as though she were totally unprepared for this new weapon with which Irene had assailed her. Seconds passed, during which she sat with stricken eyes and compressed lips. "I think," she said at last, "that being a mother is the cruellest thing in the world." Her clasped hands swayed forward and back again, and her scarlet mouth trembled irrepressibly.

"Yes," Irene softly agreed. For a moment she was unable to say more, so accurately had Clare put into words that which, not so definitely defined, was so often in her own heart of late. At the same time she was conscious that here, to her hand, was a reason which could not be lightly brushed aside. "Yes," she repeated, "and the most responsible, Clare. We mothers are all responsible for the security and happiness of our children. Think what it would mean to your Margery if Mr. Bellew should find out. You'd probably lose her. And even if you didn't, nothing that concerned her would ever be the same again. He'd never forget that she had Negro blood. And if she should learn — Well, I believe that after twelve it is too late to learn a thing like that. She'd never forgive you. You may be used to risks, but this is one you mustn't take, Clare. It's a selfish whim, an unnecessary and —

"Yes, Zulena, what is it?" she inquired, a trifle tartly, of the servant who had silently materialized in the doorway.

"The telephone's for you, Mrs. Redfield. It's Mr. Wentworth."

"All right. Thank you. I'll take it here." And, with a muttered apology to Clare, she took up the instrument.

"Hello. . . . Yes, Hugh. . . . Oh, quite. . . . And you? . . . I'm sorry, every single thing's gone. . . . Oh, too bad. . . . Ye-es, I s'pose you could. Not very pleasant, though. . . . Yes, of course, in a pinch everything goes. . . . Wait! I've got it! I'll change mine with whoever's next to you, and you can have that. . . . No. . . . I mean it. . . . I'll be so busy I shan't know whether I'm sitting or standing. . . . As long as Brian has a place to drop down now and then. . . . Not a single soul. . . . No, don't. . . . That's nice. . . . My love to Bianca. . . . I'll see to it right away and call you back. . . . Goodbye."

She hung up and turned back to Clare, a little frown on her softly chiselled features. "It's the N. W. L. dance," she explained, "the Negro Welfare League, you know. I'm on the ticket committee, or, rather, I *am* the committee. Thank heaven it comes off tomorrow night and doesn't happen again for a year. I'm about crazy, and now I've got to persuade somebody to change boxes with me."

"That wasn't," Clare asked, "Hugh Wentworth? Not *the* Hugh Wentworth?"

Irene inclined her head. On her face was a tiny triumphant smile. "Yes, *the* Hugh Wentworth. D'you know him?"

"No. How should I? But I do know about him. And I've read a book or two of his."

"Awfully good, aren't they?"

"U-umm, I s'pose so. Sort of contemptuous, I thought. As if he more or less despised everything and everybody."

"I shouldn't be a bit surprised if he did. Still, he's about earned the right to. Lived on the edges of nowhere in at least three continents. Been through every danger in all kinds of savage places. It's no wonder he thinks the rest of us are a lazy self-pampering lot. Hugh's a dear, though, generous as one of the twelve disciples; give you the shirt off his back. Bianca — that's his wife — is nice too."

"And he's coming up here to your dance?"

Irene asked why not.

"It seems rather curious, a man like that, going to a Negro dance."

This, Irene told her, was the year 1927 in the city of New York, and hundreds of white people of Hugh Wentworth's type came to affairs in Harlem, more all the time. So many that Brian had said: "Pretty soon the coloured people won't be allowed in at all, or will have to sit in Jim Crowed sections."

"What do they come for?"

"Same reason you're here, to see Negroes."

"But why?"

"Various motives," Irene explained. "A few purely and frankly to enjoy themselves. Others to get material to turn into shekels. More, to gaze on these great and near great while they gaze on the Negroes."

Clare clapped her hand. " 'Rene, suppose I come too! It sounds terribly interesting and amusing. And I don't see why I shouldn't."

Irene, who was regarding her through narrowed eyelids, had the same thought that she had had two years ago on the roof of the Drayton, that Clare Kendry was just a shade too good-looking. Her tone was on the edge of irony as she said: "You mean because so many other white people go?"

A pale rose-colour came into Clare's ivory cheeks. She lifted a hand in protest. "Don't be silly! Certainly not! I mean that in a crowd of that kind I shouldn't be noticed."

On the contrary, was Irene's opinion. It might be even doubly dangerous. Some friend or acquaintance of John Bellew or herself might see and recognize her.

At that, Clare laughed for a long time, little musical trills following one another in sequence after sequence. It was as if the thought of any friend of John Bellew's going to a Negro dance was to her the most amusing thing in the world.

"I don't think," she said, when she had done laughing, "we need worry about that."

Irene, however, wasn't so sure. But all her efforts to dissuade Clare were useless. To her, "You never can tell whom you're likely to meet there," Clare's rejoinder was: "I'll take my chance on getting by."

"Besides, you won't know a soul and I shall be too busy to look after you. You'll be bored stiff."

"I won't, I won't. If nobody asks me to dance, not even Dr. Redfield, I'll just sit and gaze on the great and the near great, too. Do, 'Rene, be polite and invite me."

Irene turned away from the caress of Clare's smile, saying promptly and positively: "I will not."

"I mean to go anyway," Clare retorted, and her voice was no less positive than Irene's.

"Oh, no. You couldn't possibly go there alone. It's a public thing. All sorts of people go, anybody who can pay a dollar, even ladies of easy virtue looking for trade. If you were to go there alone, you might be mistaken for one of them, and that wouldn't be too pleasant."

Clare laughed again. "Thanks. I never have been. It might be amusing. I'm warning you, 'Rene, that if you're not going to be nice and take me, I'll still be among those present. I suppose, my dollar's as good as anyone's."

"Oh, the dollar! Don't be a fool, Clare. I don't care where you go, or what you do. All I'm concerned with is the unpleasantness and possible danger which your going might incur, because of your situation. To put it frankly, I shouldn't like to be mixed up in any row of the kind." She had risen again as she spoke and was standing at the window lifting and spreading the small yellow chrysanthemums in the grey stone jar on the sill. Her hands shook slightly, for she was in a near rage of impatience and exasperation.

Clare's face looked strange, as if she wanted to cry again. One of her satin-covered feet swung restlessly back and forth. She said vehemently, violently almost: "Damn Jack! He keeps me out of everything. Everything I want. I could kill him! I expect I shall, some day."

extending beyond the text

These photographs each show an aspect of life in Harlem during the 1920s. Clockwise from the left, the first image shows a parade organized by the United Negro Improvement Association in 1920. The second image, taken in 1925, shows a woman in a furtrimmed coat out for a walk. The third image shows a waitress serving two women at a lunch room in 1928.

Smith Collection/Gado/Getty Images

Anthony Barboza/Archive Photos/Getty Images

General Photographic Agency/Hulton Archive/Getty Images

1. **What does each of these photographs convey about life in Harlem during this period? Taken together, what do they suggest about the diversity of these communities?**
2. **How does each of these images relate to the setting and plot of Larsen's novel? What aspects of them portray the environment Clare yearns for?**
3. **Which aspects of life in these photos are not depicted in *Passing*? Why do you think Larsen chose not to include them?**

"I wouldn't," Irene advised her, "you see, there's still capital punishment, in this state at least. And really, Clare, after everything's said, I can't see that you've a right to put all the blame on him. You've got to admit that there's his side to the thing. You didn't tell him you were coloured, so he's got no way of knowing about this hankering of yours after Negroes, or that it galls you to fury to hear them called niggers and black devils. As far as I can see, you'll just have to endure some things and give up others. As we've said before, everything must be paid for. Do, please, be reasonable."

But Clare, it was plain, had shut away reason as well as caution. She shook her head. "I can't, I can't," she said. "I would If I could, but I can't. You don't know, you can't realize how I want to see Negroes, to be with them again, to talk with them, to hear them laugh."

And in the look she gave Irene, there was something groping, and hopeless, and yet so absolutely determined that it was like an image of the futile searching and the firm resolution in Irene's own soul, and increased the feeling of doubt and compunction that had been growing within her about Clare Kendry.

She gave in.

"Oh, come if you want to. I s'pose you're right. Once can't do such a terrible lot of harm."

Pushing aside Clare's extravagant thanks, for immediately she was sorry that she had consented, she said briskly: "Should you like to come up and see my boys?"

"I'd love to."

They went up, Irene thinking that Brian would consider that she'd behaved like a spineless fool. And he would be right. She certainly had.

Clare was smiling. She stood in the doorway of the boys' playroom, her shadowy eyes looking down on Junior and Ted, who had sprung apart from their tusselling. Junior's face had a funny little look of resentment. Ted's was blank.

Clare said: "Please don't be cross. Of course, I know I've gone and spoiled everything. But maybe, if I promise not to get too much in the way, you'll let me come in, just the same."

"Sure, come in if you want to," Ted told her. "We can't stop you, you know." He smiled and made her a little bow and then turned away to a shelf that held his favourite books. Taking one down, he settled himself in a chair and began to read.

Junior said nothing, did nothing, merely stood there waiting.

"Get up, Ted! That's rude. This is Theodore, Mrs. Bellew. Please excuse his bad manners. He does know better. And this is Brian junior. Mrs. Bellew is an old friend of mother's. We used to play together when we were little girls."

• • •

Clare had gone and Brian had telephoned that he'd been detained and would have his dinner downtown. Irene was a little glad for that. She was going out later herself, and that meant she wouldn't, probably, see Brian until morning and so could put off for a few more hours speaking of Clare and the N. W. L. dance.

She was angry with herself and with Clare. But more with herself, for having permitted Clare to tease her into doing something that Brian had, all but expressly, asked her not to do. She didn't want him ruffled, not just then, not while he was possessed of that unreasonable restless feeling.

She was annoyed, too, because she was aware that she had consented to something which, if it went beyond the dance, would involve her in numerous petty inconveniences and evasions. And not only at home with Brian, but outside with friends and acquaintances. The disagreeable possibilities in connection with Clare Kendry's coming among them loomed before her in endless irritating array.

Clare, it seemed, still retained her ability to secure the thing that she wanted in the face of any opposition, and in utter disregard of the convenience and desire of others. About her there was some quality, hard and persistent, with the strength and endurance of rock, that would not be beaten or ignored. She couldn't, Irene thought, have had an entirely serene life. Not with that dark secret for ever crouching in the background of her consciousness. And yet she hadn't the air of a woman whose life had been touched by uncertainty or suffering. Pain, fear, and grief were things that left their mark on people. Even love, that exquisite torturing emotion, left its subtle traces on the countenance.

But Clare — she had remained almost what she had always been, an attractive, somewhat lonely child — selfish, wilful, and disturbing.

Chapter 3

The things which Irene Redfield remembered afterward about the Negro Welfare League dance seemed, to her, unimportant and unrelated.

She remembered the not quite derisive smile with which Brian had cloaked his vexation when she informed him — oh, so apologetically — that she had promised to take Clare, and related the conversation of her visit.

She remembered her own little choked exclamation of admiration, when, on coming downstairs a few minutes later than she had intended, she had rushed into the living-room where Brian was waiting and had found Clare there too. Clare, exquisite, golden, fragrant, flaunting, in a stately gown of shining black taffeta, whose long, full skirt lay in graceful folds about her slim golden feet; her glistening hair drawn smoothly back into a small twist at the nape of her neck; her eyes sparkling like dark jewels. Irene, with her new rose-coloured chiffon frock ending at the knees, and her cropped curls, felt dowdy and commonplace. She regretted that she hadn't counselled Clare to wear something ordinary and inconspicuous. What on earth would Brian think of deliberate courting of attention? But if Clare Kendry's appearance had in it anything that was, to Brian Redfield, annoying or displeasing, the fact was not discernible to his wife as, with an uneasy feeling of guilt, she stood there looking into his face while Clare explained that she and he had made their own introductions, accompanying her words with a little deferential smile for Brian, and receiving in return one of his amused, slightly mocking smiles.

She remembered Clare's saying, as they sped northward: "You know, I feel exactly as I used to on the Sunday we went to the Christmas-tree celebration. I knew there was to be a surprise for me and couldn't quite guess what it was to be. I am *so* excited. You can't possibly imagine! It's marvellous to be really on the way! I can hardly believe it!"

At her words and tone a chilly wave of scorn had crept through Irene. All those superlatives! She said, taking care to speak indifferently: "Well, maybe in some ways you will be surprised, more, probably, than you anticipate."

Brian, at the wheel, had thrown back: "And then again, she won't be so very surprised after all, for it'll no doubt be about what she expects. Like the Christmas-tree."

She remembered rushing around here and there, consulting with this person and that one, and now and then snatching a part of a dance with some man whose dancing she particularly liked.

She remembered catching glimpses of Clare in the whirling crowd, dancing, sometimes with a white man, more often with a Negro, frequently with Brian. Irene was glad that he was being nice to Clare, and glad that Clare was having the opportunity to discover that some coloured men were superior to some white men.

She remembered a conversation she had with Hugh Wentworth in a free half-hour when she had dropped into a chair in an emptied box and let her gaze wander over the bright crowd below.

Young men, old men, white men, black men; youthful women, older women, pink women, golden women; fat men, thin men, tall men, short men; stout women, slim women, stately women, small women moved by. An old nursery rhyme popped into her head. She turned to Wentworth, who had just taken a seat beside her, and recited it:

"Rich man, poor man,
Beggar man, thief,
Doctor, lawyer,
Indian chief."

"Yes," Wentworth said, "that's it. Everybody seems to be here and a few more. But what I'm trying to find out is the name, status, and race of the blonde beauty out of the fairy-tale. She's dancing with Ralph Hazelton at the moment. Nice study in contrasts, that."

It was. Clare fair and golden, like a sunlit day. Hazelton dark, with gleaming eyes, like a moonlit night.

"She's a girl I used to know a long time ago in Chicago. And she wanted especially to meet you."

"'S awfully good of her, I'm sure. And now, alas! the usual thing's happened. All these others, these — er — 'gentlemen of colour' have driven a mere Nordic from her mind."

"Stuff!"

"'S a fact, and what happens to all the ladles of my superior race who're lured up here. Look at Bianca. Have I laid eyes on her tonight except in spots, here and there, being twirled about by some Ethiopian? I have not."

"But, Hugh, you've got to admit that the average coloured man is a better dancer than the average white man — that is, if the celebrities and 'butter and egg' men who find their way up here are fair specimens of white Terpsichorean art."

"Not having tripped the light fantastic with any of the males, I'm not in a position to argue the point. But I don't think it's merely that. 'S something else, some other attraction. They're always raving about the good looks of some Negro, preferably an unusually dark one. Take Hazelton there, for example. Dozens of women have declared him to be fascinatingly handsome. How about you, Irene? Do you think he's — er — ravishingly beautiful?"

"I do not! And I don't think the others do either. Not honestly, I mean. I think that what they feel is — well, a kind of emotional excitement. You know, the sort of thing you feel in the presence of something strange, and even, perhaps, a bit repugnant to you; something so different that it's really at the opposite end of the pole from all your accustomed notions of beauty."

"Damned if I don't think you're halfway right!"

"I'm sure I am. Completely. (Except, of course, when it's just patronizing kindness on their part.) And I know coloured girls who've experienced the same thing — the other way round, naturally."

"And the men? You don't subscribe to the general opinion about their reason for coming up here. Purely predatory. Or, do you?"

"N-no. More curious, I should say."

Wentworth, whose eyes were a clouded amber colour, had given her a long, searching look that was really a stare. He said: "All this is awfully interestin', Irene. We've got to have a long talk about it some time soon. There's your friend from Chicago, first time up here and all that. A case in point."

Irene's smile had only just lifted the corners of her painted lips. A match blazed in Wentworth's broad hands as he lighted her cigarette and his own, and flickered out before he asked: "Or isn't she?"

Her smile changed to a laugh. "Oh, Hugh! You're so clever. You usually know everything. Even how to tell the sheep from the goats. What do you think? Is she?"

He blew a long contemplative wreath of smoke. "Damned if I know! I'll be as sure as anything that I've learned the trick. And then in the next minute I'll find I couldn't pick some of 'em if my life depended on it."

"Well, don't let that worry you. Nobody can. Not by looking."

"Not by looking, eh? Meaning?"

"I'm afraid I can't explain. Not clearly. There are ways. But they're not definite or tangible."

"Feeling of kinship, or something like that?"

"Good heavens, no! Nobody has that, except for their in-laws."

"Right again! But go on about the sheep and the goats."

"Well, take my own experience with Dorothy Thompkins. I'd met her four or five times, in groups and crowds of people, before I knew she wasn't a Negro. One day I went to an awful tea, terribly dicty[4]. Dorothy was there. We got talking. In less than five minutes, I knew she was 'fay.'[5] Not from anything she did or said or anything in her appearance. Just — just something. A thing that couldn't be registered."

"Yes, I understand what you mean. Yet lots of people 'pass' all the time."

[4] Snobby. — Eds.

[5] An abbreviation of *ofay,* a slang term for a white person. — Eds.

extending beyond the text

The social and legal efforts to quantify Blackness are an essential context for the novel *Passing*. In *Who Is Black: One Nation's Definition* (1991), historian F. James Davis wrote, "The nation's answer to the question 'Who is black?' has long been that a black is any person with any known African black ancestry. This definition reflects the long experience with slavery and later with Jim Crow segregation. In the South it became known as the 'one-drop rule,' meaning that a single drop of 'black blood' makes a person a black." The so-called "one-drop rule" became legal policy in the 1896 landmark Supreme Court decision *Plessy v. Ferguson*, which upheld segregation until the mid-twentieth century. Homer Adolph Plessy, the plaintiff in that case, described himself as "seven-eighths Caucasian and one-eighth African blood." This painting was completed in 1925 by Archibald Motley Jr. (1891–1981), a Harlem Renaissance artist.

The Octoroon Girl/Motley Jr., Archibald J./Michael Rosenfeld Gallery, New York © Valerie Gerrard Browne/Chicago History Museum/Bridgeman Images

1. **What elements of this woman's appearance provide clues to her personality? Consider the colors, the position of her hands, her dress, and her gaze. What aspects of Clare's personality and attitude toward racial classifications do you see?**
2. **Motley titled this painting *The Octoroon Girl*, a term for someone who, according to racist laws of the time, was "one-eighth Black." The term dates to the era of slavery and was already considered offensive during the 1920s. How does Motley's choice of title challenge such attempts at quantifying race?**
3. **To what extent do you think that this image argues that race is a social construct? Cite specific details about the painting to support your position.**
4. **Allyson Hobbs, a professor of American history and the director of African and African-American studies at Stanford University, chose this painting for the cover of her book entitled *A Chosen Exile: A History of Racial Passing in American Life.* How does this image relate to that title? How does it contextualize racial passing as a response to the social and legal constraints of the 1920s?**

"Not on our side, Hugh. It's easy for a Negro to 'pass' for white. But I don't think it would be so simple for a white person to 'pass' for coloured."

"Never thought of that."

"No, you wouldn't. Why should you?"

He regarded her critically through mists of smoke. "Slippin' me, Irene?"

She said soberly: "Not you, Hugh. I'm too fond of you. And you're too sincere."

And she remembered that towards the end of the dance Brian had come to her and said: "I'll drop you first and then run Clare down." And that he had been doubtful of her discretion when she had explained to him that he wouldn't have to bother because she had asked Bianca Wentworth to take her down with them. Did she, he had asked, think it had been wise to tell them about Clare?

"I told them nothing," she said sharply, for she was unbearably tired, "except that she was at the Walsingham. It's on their way. And, really, I haven't thought anything about the wisdom of it, but now that I do, I'd say it's much better for them to take her than you."

"As you please. She's your friend, you know," he had answered, with a disclaiming shrug of his shoulders.

Except for these few unconnected things the dance faded to a blurred memory, its outlines mingling with those of other dances of its kind that she had attended in the past and would attend in the future.

Chapter 4

But undistinctive as the dance had seemed, it was, nevertheless, important. For it marked the beginning of a new factor in Irene Redfield's life, something that left its trace on all the future years of her existence. It was the beginning of a new friendship with Clare Kendry.

She came to them frequently after that. Always with a touching gladness that welled up and overflowed on all the Redfield household. Yet Irene could never be sure whether her comings were a joy or a vexation.

Certainly she was no trouble. She had not to be entertained, or even noticed — if anyone could ever avoid noticing Clare. If Irene happened to be out or occupied, Clare could very happily amuse herself with Ted and Junior, who had conceived for her an admiration that verged on adoration, especially Ted. Or, lacking the boys, she would descend to the kitchen and, with — to Irene — an exasperating childlike lack of perception, spend her visit in talk and merriment with Zulena and Sadie.

Irene, while secretly resenting these visits to the playroom and kitchen, for some obscure reason which she shied away from putting into words, never requested that Clare make an end of them, or hinted that she wouldn't have spoiled her own Margery so outrageously, nor been so friendly with white servants.

Brian looked on these things with the same tolerant amusement that marked his entire attitude toward Clare. Never since his faintly derisive surprise at Irene's information that she was to go with them the night of the dance, had he shown any disapproval of Clare's presence. On the other hand, it couldn't be said that her presence seemed to please him. It didn't annoy or disturb him, so far as Irene could judge. That was all.

Didn't he, she once asked him, think Clare was extraordinarily beautiful?

"No," he had answered. "That is, not particularly."

"Brian, you're fooling!"

"No, honestly. Maybe I'm fussy. I s'pose she'd be an unusually good-looking white woman. I like my ladies darker. Beside an A-number-one sheba,[6] she simply hasn't got 'em."

Clare went, sometimes with Irene and Brian, to parties and dances, and on a few occasions when Irene hadn't been able or inclined to go out, she had gone alone with Brian to some bridge party or benefit dance.

Once in a while she came formally to dine with them. She wasn't, however, in spite of her poise and air of worldliness, the ideal dinner-party guest. Beyond the aesthetic pleasure one got from watching her, she contributed little, sitting for the most part silent, an odd dreaming look in her hypnotic eyes. Though she could for some purpose of her own — the desire to be included in some party being made up to go cabareting, or an invitation to a dance or a tea — talk fluently and entertainingly.

[6] A reference to the Queen of Sheba, a biblical figure who brings gifts to King Solomon, and slang for a Black woman.

She was generally liked. She was so friendly and responsive, and so ready to press the sweet food of flattery on all. Nor did she object to appearing a bit pathetic and ill-used, so that people could feel sorry for her. And, no matter how often she came among them, she still remained someone apart, a little mysterious and strange, someone to wonder about and to admire and to pity.

Her visits were undecided and uncertain, being, as they were, dependent on the presence or absence of John Bellew in the city. But she did, once in a while, manage to steal uptown for an afternoon even when he was not away. As time went on without any apparent danger of discovery, even Irene ceased to be perturbed about the possibility of Clare's husband's stumbling on her racial identity.

The daughter, Margery, had been left in Switzerland in school, for Clare and Bellew would be going back in the early spring. In March, Clare thought. "And how I do hate to think of it!" she would say, always with a suggestion of leashed rebellion; "but I can't see how I'm going to get out of it. Jack won't hear of my staying behind. If I could have just a couple of months more in New York, alone I mean, I'd be the happiest thing in the world."

"I imagine you'll be happy enough, once you get away," Irene told her one day when she was bewailing her approaching departure. "Remember, there's Margery. Think how glad you'll be to see her after all this time."

"Children aren't everything," was Clare Kendry's answer to that. "There are other things in the world, though I admit some people don't seem to suspect it." And she laughed, more, it seemed, at some secret joke of her own than at her words.

Irene replied: "You know you don't mean that, Clare. You're only trying to tease me. I know very well that I take being a mother rather seriously, I *am* wrapped up in my boys and the running of my house. I can't help it. And, really, I don't think it's anything to laugh at." And though she was aware of the slight primness in her words and attitude, she had neither power nor wish to efface it.

Clare, suddenly very sober and sweet, said: "You're right. It's no laughing matter. It's shameful of me to tease you, 'Rene. You are so good." And she reached out and gave Irene's hand an affectionate little squeeze. "Don't think," she added, "Whatever happens, that I'll ever forget how good you've been to me."

"Nonsense!"

"Oh, but you have, you have. It's just that I haven't any proper morals or sense of duty, as you have, that makes me act as I do."

"Now you are talking nonsense."

"But it's true, 'Rene. Can't you realize that I'm not like you a bit? Why, to get the things I want badly enough, I'd do anything, hurt anybody, throw anything away. Really, 'Rene, I'm not safe." Her voice as well as the look on her face had a beseeching earnestness that made Irene vaguely uncomfortable.

She said: "I don't believe it. In the first place what you're saying is so utterly, so wickedly wrong. And as for your giving up things — " She stopped, at a loss for an acceptable term to express her opinion of Clare's "having" nature.

But Clare Kendry had begun to cry, audibly, with no effort at restraint, and for no reason that Irene could discover.

Part Three: Finale

Chapter 1

The year was getting on towards its end. October, November had gone. December had come and brought with it a little snow and then a freeze and after that a thaw and some soft pleasant days that had in them a feeling of spring.

It wasn't, this mild weather, a bit Christmasy, Irene Redfield was thinking, as she turned out of Seventh Avenue into her own street. She didn't like it to be warm and springy when it should have been cold and crisp, or grey and cloudy as if snow was about to fall. The weather, like people, ought to enter into the spirit of the season. Here the holidays were almost upon them, and the streets through which she had come were streaked with rills of muddy water and the sun shone so warmly that children had taken off their hats and scarfs. It was all as soft, as like April, as possible. The kind of weather for Easter. Certainly not for Christmas.

Though, she admitted, reluctantly, she herself didn't feel the proper Christmas spirit this year, either. But that couldn't be helped, it seemed, any more than the weather. She was weary and depressed. And for all her trying, she couldn't be free of that dull, indefinite misery which with increasing tenaciousness had laid hold of her. The morning's aimless wandering through the teeming Harlem streets, long after she had ordered the flowers which had been her excuse for setting out, was but another effort to tear herself loose from it.

She went up the cream stone steps, into the house, and down to the kitchen. There were to be people in to tea. But that, she found, after a few words with Sadie and Zulena, need give her no concern. She was thankful. She didn't want to be bothered. She went upstairs and took off her things and got into bed.

She thought: "Bother those people coming to tea!"

She thought: "If I could only be sure that at bottom it's just Brazil."

She thought: "Whatever it is, if I only knew what it was, I could manage it."

Brian again. Unhappy, restless, withdrawn. And she, who had prided herself on knowing his moods, their causes and their remedies, had found it first unthinkable, and then intolerable, that this, so like and yet so unlike those other spasmodic restlessnesses of his, should be to her incomprehensible and elusive.

He was restless and he was not restless. He was discontented, yet there were times when she felt he was possessed of some intense secret satisfaction, like a cat who had stolen the cream. He was irritable with the boys, especially Junior, for Ted, who seemed to have an uncanny knowledge of his father's periods of off moods, kept out of his way when possible. They got on his nerves, drove him to violent outbursts of temper, very different from his usual gently sarcastic remarks that constituted his idea of discipline for them. On the other hand, with her he was more than customarily considerate and abstemious. And it had been weeks since she had felt the keen edge of his irony.

He was like a man marking time, waiting. But what was he waiting for? It was extraordinary that, after all these years of accurate perception, she now lacked the talent to discover what that appearance of waiting meant. It was the knowledge that, for all her watching, all her patient study, the reason for his humour still eluded her which filled her with foreboding dread. That guarded reserve of his seemed to her unjust. inconsiderate, and alarming. It was as if he had stepped out beyond her reach into some section, strange and walled, where she could not get at him.

She closed her eyes, thinking what a blessing it would be if she could get a little sleep before the boys came in from school. She couldn't, of course, though she was so tired, having had, of late, so many sleepless nights. Nights filled with questionings and premonitions.

But she did sleep — several hours.

She wakened to find Brian standing at her bedside looking down at her, an unfathomable expression in his eyes.

She said: "I must have dropped off to sleep," and watched a slender ghost of his old amused smile pass over his face.

"It's getting on to four," he told her, meaning, she knew, that she was going to be late again.

She fought back the quick answer that rose to her lips and said instead: "I'm getting right up. It was good of you to think to call me." She sat up.

He bowed. "Always the attentive husband, you see."

"Yes indeed. Thank goodness, everything's ready."

extending beyond the text

In her essay "Prince Harry Finally Takes on White Privilege: His Own," critic Salamishah Tillet mentions *Passing* in her analysis of the interview Prince Harry and Meghan Markle gave to Oprah Winfrey in March 2021. Of slave narratives, autobiographies, and early-twentieth-century African American novels, including *Passing*, she says that "racial awakenings" are portrayed as

> a tragic rite of passage for Black people. . . . [A] Black child realizes she is not only different from her white peers but that her darker skin or African-American parentage makes her inferior to them. . . . [T]his traumatic rupture is always intimate and severe, the first and most formative experience in a lifetime of racist insults.

By contrast, in the introduction to a 2018 edition of *Passing*, English professor Emily Bernard asserts that Clare

> differs from other characters who pass in works of literature because she is not concerned with the moral implications of passing for white. Unlike other black characters whose passing enables them to marry white people, Clare does not pass for love. Even though she views passing through the lens of rank materialism, ultimately she sees passing as play. . . . She is not wandering in the interstices of black and white. Instead, Clare is a hunter, stalking the margins of racial identity, hungry for forbidden experience. . . .

Which of these interpretations aligns most closely with your own interpretation of the novel and its central characters? Explain why, using evidence from the text to support your response.

"Except you. Oh, and Clare's downstairs."

"Clare! What a nuisance! I didn't ask her. Purposely."

"I see. Might a mere man ask why? Or is the reason so subtly feminine that it wouldn't be understood by him?"

A little of his smile had come back. Irene, who was beginning to shake off some of her depression under his familiar banter, said, almost gaily: "Not at all. It just happens that this party happens to be for Hugh, and that Hugh happens not to care a great deal for Clare; therefore I, who happen to be giving the party, didn't happen to ask her. Nothing could be simpler. Could it?"

"Nothing. It's so simple that I can easily see beyond your simple explanation and surmise that Clare, probably, just never happened to pay Hugh the admiring attention that he happens to consider no more than his just due. Simplest thing in the world."

Irene exclaimed in amazement: "Why, I thought you liked Hugh! You don't, you can't, believe anything so idiotic!"

"Well, Hugh does think he's God, you know."

"That," Irene declared, getting out of bed, "is absolutely not true. He thinks ever so much better of himself than that, as you, who know and have read him, ought to be able to guess. If you remember what a low opinion he has of God, you won't make such a silly mistake."

She went into the closet for her things and, coming back, hung her frock over the back of a chair and placed her shoes on the floor beside it. Then she sat down before her dressing-table.

Brian didn't speak. He continued to stand beside the bed, seeming to look at nothing in particular. Certainly not at her. True, his gaze was on her, but in it there was some quality that made her feel that at that moment she was no more to him than a pane of glass through which he stared. At what? She didn't know, couldn't guess. And this made her uncomfortable. Piqued her.

She said: "It just happens that Hugh prefers intelligent women."

Plainly he was startled. "D'you mean that you think Clare is stupid?" he asked, regarding her with lifted eyebrows, which emphasized the disbelief of his voice.

She wiped the cold cream from her face, before she said: "No, I don't. She isn't stupid. She's intelligent enough in a purely feminine way. Eighteenth-century France would have been a marvellous setting for her, or the old South if she hadn't made the mistake of being born a Negro."

"I see. Intelligent enough to wear a tight bodice and keep bowing swains whispering compliments and retrieving dropped fans. Rather a pretty picture. I take it, though, as slightly feline in its implication."

"Well, then, all I can say is that you take it wrongly. Nobody admires Clare more than I do, for the kind of intelligence she has, as well as for her decorative qualities. But she's not — She isn't — She hasn't — Oh, I can't explain it. Take Bianca, for example, or, to keep to the race, Felise Freeland. Looks *and* brains. Real brains that can hold their own with anybody. Clare has got brains of a sort, the kind that are useful too. Acquisitive, you know. But she'd bore a man like Hugh to suicide. Still, I never thought that even Clare would come to a private party to which she hadn't been asked. But, it's like her."

For a minute there was silence. She completed the bright red arch of her full lips. Brian moved towards the door. His hand was on the knob. He said: "I'm sorry, Irene. It's my fault entirely. She seemed so hurt at being left out that I told her I was sure you'd for-gotten and to just come along."

Irene cried out: "But, Brian, I — " and stopped, amazed at the fierce anger that had blazed up in her.

Brian's head came round with a jerk. His brows lifted in an odd surprise.

Her voice, she realized, *had* gone queer. But she had an instinctive feeling that it hadn't been the whole cause of his attitude. And that little straightening motion of the shoulders. Hadn't it been like that of a man drawing himself up to receive a blow? Her fright was like a scarlet spear of terror leaping at her heart.

Clare Kendry! So that was it! Impossible. It couldn't be.

In the mirror before her she saw that he was still regarding her with that air of slight amazement. She dropped her eyes to the jars and bottles on the table and began to fumble among them with hands whose fingers shook slightly.

"Of course," she said carefully, "I'm glad you did. And in spite of my recent remarks, Clare does add to any party. She's so easy on the eyes."

When she looked again, the surprise had gone from his face and the expectancy from, his bearing.

"Yes," he agreed. "Well, I guess I'll run along. One of us ought to be down, I s'pose."

"You're right. One of us ought to." She was surprised that it was in her normal tones she spoke, caught as she was by the heart since that dull indefinite fear had grown suddenly into sharp panic. "I'll be down before you know it," she promised.

"All right." But he still lingered. "You're quite certain. You don't mind my asking her? Not awfully, I mean? I see now that I ought to have spoken to you. Trust women to have their reasons for everything."

She made a little pretence at looking at him, managed a tiny smile, and turned away. Clare! How sickening!

"Yes, don't they?" she said, striving to keep her voice casual. Within her she felt a hardness from feeling, not absent, but repressed. And that hardness was rising, swelling. Why didn't he go? Why didn't he?

He had opened the door at last. "You won't be long?" he asked, admonished.

She shook her head, unable to speak, for there was a choking in her throat, and the confusion in her mind was like the beating of wings. Behind her she heard the gentle impact of the door as it closed behind him, and knew that he had gone. Down to Clare.

For a long minute she sat in strained stiffness. The face in the mirror vanished from her sight, blotted out by this thing which had so suddenly flashed across her groping mind. Impossible for her to put it immediately into words or give it outline, for, prompted by some impulse of self-protection, she recoiled from exact expression.

She closed her unseeing eyes and clenched her fists. She tried not to cry. But her lips tightened and no effort could check the hot tears of rage and shame that sprang into her eyes and flowed down her cheeks; so she laid her face in her arms and wept silently.

When she was sure that she had done crying, she wiped away the warm remaining tears and got up. After bathing her swollen face in cold, refreshing water and carefully applying a stinging splash of toilet water, she went back to the mirror and regarded herself gravely. Satisfied that there lingered no betraying evidence of weeping, she dusted a little powder on her dark-white face and again examined it carefully, and with a kind of ridiculing contempt.

"I do think," she confided to it, "that you've been something — oh, very much — of a damned fool."

Downstairs the ritual of tea gave her some busy moments, and that, she decided, was a blessing. She wanted no empty spaces of time in which her mind would immediately return to that horror which she had not yet gathered sufficient courage to face. Pouring tea properly and nicely was an occupation that required a kind of well-balanced attention.

In the room beyond, a clock chimed. A single sound. Fifteen minutes past five o'clock. That was all! And yet in the short space of half an hour all of life had changed, lost its colour, its vividness, its whole meaning. No, she reflected, it wasn't that that had happened. Life about her, apparently, went on exactly as before.

"Oh, Mrs. Runyon. . . . So nice to see you. . . . Two? . . . Really? . . . How exciting! . . . Yes, I think Tuesday's all right. . . ."

Yes, life went on precisely as before. It was only she that had changed. Knowing, stumbling on this thing, had changed her. It was as if in a house long dim, a match had been struck, showing ghastly shapes where had been only blurred shadows.

Chatter, chatter, chatter. Someone asked her a question. She glanced up with what she felt was a rigid smile.

"Yes . . . Brian picked it up last winter in Haiti. Terribly weird, isn't it? . . . It *is* rather marvellous in its own hideous way. . . . Practically nothing, I believe. A few cents. . . ."

Hideous. A great weariness came over her. Even the small exertion of pouring golden tea into thin old cups seemed almost too much for her. She went on pouring. Made repetitions of her smile. Answered questions. Manufactured conversation. She thought: "I feel like the oldest person in the world with the longest stretch of life before me."

"Josephine Baker?[7] . . . No. I've never seen her. . . . Well, she might have been in *Shuffle Along*[8] when I saw it, but if she was, I don't

[7] Josephine Baker (1906–1975) was an American-born French entertainer and civil rights activist. She was the first Black woman to star in a major film, *Siren of the Tropics* (1927). — Eds.

[8] A 1921 musical comedy featuring an all-Black cast of performers. It was popular with both Black and white audiences. — Eds.

remember her. . . . Oh, but you're wrong! . . . I do think Ethel Waters[9] is awfully good. . . ."

There were the familiar little tinkling sounds of spoons striking against frail cups, the soft running sounds of inconsequential talk, punctuated now and then with laughter. In irregular small groups, disintegrating, coalescing, striking just the right note of disharmony, disorder in the big room, which Irene had furnished with a sparingness that was almost chaste, moved the guests with that slight familiarity that makes a party a success. On the floor and the walls the sinking sun threw long, fantastic shadows.

So like many other tea-parties she had had. So unlike any of those others. But she mustn't think yet. Time enough for that after. All the time in the world. She had a second's flashing knowledge of what those words might portend. Time with Brian. Time without him. It was gone, leaving in its place an almost uncontrollable impulse to laugh, to scream, to hurl things about. She wanted, suddenly, to shock people, to hurt them, to make them notice her, to be aware of her suffering.

"Hello, Dave. . . . Felise. . . . Really your clothes are the despair of half the women in Harlem. . . . How do you do it? . . . Lovely, is it Worth or Lanvin? . . . Oh, a mere Babani. . . ."

"Merely that," Felise Freeland acknowledged. "Come out of it, Irene, whatever it is. You look like the second grave-digger."

"Thanks, for the hint, Felise. I'm not feeling quite up to par. The weather, I guess."

"Buy yourself an expensive new frock, child. It always helps. Any time this child gets the blues, it means money out of Dave's pocket. How're those boys of yours?"

The boys! For once she'd forgotten them.

They were, she told Felise, very well. Felise mumbled something about that being awfully nice, and said she'd have to fly, because for a wonder she saw Mrs. Bellew sitting by herself, "and I've been trying to get her alone all afternoon. I want her for a party. Isn't she stunning today?"

Clare was. Irene couldn't remember ever having seen her look better. She was wearing a superlatively simple cinnamon-brown frock which brought out all her vivid beauty, and a little golden bowl of a hat. Around her neck hung a string of amber beads that would easily have made six or eight like one Irene owned. Yes, she was stunning.

The ripple of talk flowed on. The fire roared. The shadows stretched longer.

Across the room was Hugh. He wasn't, Irene hoped, being too bored. He seemed as he always did, a bit aloof, a little amused, and somewhat weary. And as usual he was hovering before the book-shelves. But he was not, she noticed, looking at the book he had taken down. Instead, his dull amber eyes were held by something across the room. They were a little scornful. Well, Hugh had never cared for Clare Kendry. For a minute Irene hesitated, then turned her head, though she knew what it was that held Hugh's gaze. Clare, who had suddenly clouded all her days. Brian, the father of Ted and Junior.

Clare's ivory face was what it always was, beautiful and caressing. Or maybe today a little masked. Unrevealing. Unaltered and undisturbed by any emotion within or without. Brian's seemed to Irene to be pitiably bare. Or was it too as it always was? That half-effaced seeking look, did he always have that? Queer, that now she didn't know, couldn't recall. Then she saw him smile, and the smile made his face all eager and shining. Impelled by some inner urge of loyalty to herself, she glanced away. But only for a moment. And when she turned towards them again, she thought that the look on his face was the most melancholy and yet the most scoffing that she had ever seen upon it.

---

[9] Ethel Waters (1896–1977) was an African American singer and actress known for blues music at the time *Passing* was written. One of the most popular performers of the 1920s, Waters lived in Harlem and often performed on Broadway. —Eds.

extending beyond the text

In a series called "You Must Read This," on National Public Radio, contemporary authors recommend their favorite books to listeners. Heidi W. Durrow, author of *The Girl Who Fell from the Sky*, chose *Passing* because "it's about being defined by what other people see and the desire to transcend that." She explains:

> You may not identify with being a light-skinned African American, but you have probably felt at some point that what was most important about you wasn't visible.
>
> I have read and re-read *Passing* more than a dozen times. Each time I think I can hear Larsen's own voice more clearly: asking, demanding really, that each of us abandon the labels we've been assigned and celebrate the story that we are.

1. **What point does Durrow make about the consequences of labels and labeling? How do the characters and plot of *Passing* support this point?**
2. **Do you agree that Larsen is "demanding" that we "celebrate the story that we are"? Use evidence from the text to support your response.**

In the next quarter of an hour she promised herself to Bianca Wentworth in Sixty-second Street, Jane Tenant at Seventh Avenue and a Hundred and Fiftieth Street, and the Dashields in Brooklyn for dinner all on the same evening and at almost the same hour.

Oh well, what did it matter? She had no thoughts at all now, and all she felt was a great fatigue. Before her tired eyes Clare Kendry was talking to Dave Freeland. Scraps of their conversation, in Clare's husky voice, floated over to her: ". . . always admired you . . . so much about you long ago . . . every-body says so . . . no one but you. . . ." And more of the same. The man hung rapt on her words, though he was the husband of Felise Freeland, and the author of novels that revealed a man of perception and a devastating irony. And he fell for such pish-posh! And all because Clare had a trick of sliding down ivory lids over astonishing black eyes and then lifting them suddenly and turning on a caressing smile. Men like Dave Freeland fell for it. And Brian.

Her mental and physical languor receded. Brian. What did it mean? How would it affect her and the boys? The boys! She had a surge of relief. It ebbed, vanished. A feeling of absolute unimportance followed. Actually, she didn't count. She was, to him, only the mother of his sons. That was all. Alone she was nothing. Worse. An obstacle.

Rage boiled up in her.

There was a slight crash. On the floor at her feet lay the shattered cup. Dark stains dotted the bright rug. Spread. The chatter stopped. Went on. Before her, Zulena gathered up the white fragments.

As from a distance Hugh Wentworth's clipt voice came to her, though he was, she was aware, somehow miraculously at her side. "Sorry," he apologized. "Must have pushed you. Clumsy of me. Don't tell me it's priceless and irreplaceable."

It hurt. Dear God! How the thing hurt! But she couldn't think of that now. Not with Hugh sitting there mumbling apologies and lies. The significance of his words, the power of his discernment, stirred in her a sense of caution. Her pride revolted. Damn Hugh! Something would have to be done about him. Now. She couldn't, it seemed, help his knowing. It was too late for that. But she could and would keep him from knowing that she knew. She could, she would bear it. She'd have to. There were the boys. Her whole body went taut. In that second she saw that she could bear anything, but only if no one knew that she had anything to bear. It hurt. It frightened her, but she could bear it.

She turned to Hugh. Shook her head. Raised innocent dark eyes to his concerned pale ones. "Oh, no," she protested, "you didn't push me. Cross your heart, hope to die, and I'll tell you how it happened."

"Done!"

"Did you notice that cup? Well, you're lucky. It was the ugliest thing that your ancestors, the charming Confederates ever owned. I've forgotten how many thousands of years ago it was that Brian's great-great-grand-uncle owned it. But it has, or had, a good old hoary history. It was brought North by way of the subway. Oh, all right! Be English if you want to and call it the underground. What I'm coming to is the fact that I've never figured out a way of getting rid of it until about five minutes ago. I had an inspiration. I had only to break it, and I was rid of it for ever. So simple! And I'd never thought of it before."

Hugh nodded and his frosty smile spread over his features. Had she convinced him?

"Still," she went on with a little laugh that didn't, she was sure, sound the least bit forced, "I'm perfectly willing for you to take the blame and admit that you pushed me at the wrong moment. What are friends for, if not to help bear our sins? Brian will certainly be told that it was your fault."

"More tea, Clare? . . . I haven't had a minute with you. . . . Yes, it is a nice party. . . . You'll stay to dinner, I hope. . . . Oh, too bad! . . . I'll be alone with the boys. . . . They'll be sorry. Brian's got a medical meeting, or something. . . . Nice frock you're wearing. . . . Thanks. . . . Well, good-bye; see you soon, I hope."

The clock chimed. One. Two, Three. Four. Five. Six. Was it, could it be, only a little over an hour since she had come down to tea? One little hour.

"Must you go? . . . Good-bye. . . . Thank you so much. . . . So nice to see you. . . . Yes, Wednesday. . . . My love to Madge. . . . Sorry, but I'm filled up for Tuesday. . . . Oh, really? . . . Yes. . . . Good-bye. . . . Good-bye. . . ."

It hurt. It hurt like hell. But it didn't matter, if no one knew. If everything could go on as before. If the boys were safe.

It did hurt.

But it didn't matter.

Chapter 2

But it did matter. It mattered more than anything had ever mattered before.

What bitterness! That the one fear, the one uncertainty, that she had felt, Brian's ache to go somewhere else, should have dwindled to a childish triviality! And with it the quality of the courage and resolution with which she had met it. From the visions and dangers which she now perceived she shrank away. For them she had no remedy or courage. Desperately she tried to shut out the knowledge from which had risen this turmoil, which she had no power to moderate or still, within her. And half succeeded.

For, she reasoned, what was there, what had there been, to show that she was even half correct in her tormenting notion? Nothing. She had seen nothing, heard nothing. She had no facts or proofs. She was only making herself unutterably wretched by an unfounded suspicion. It had been a case of looking for trouble and finding it in good measure. Merely that.

With this self-assurance that she had no real knowledge, she redoubled her efforts to drive out of her mind the distressing thought of faiths broken and trusts betrayed which every mental vision of Clare, of Brian, brought with them. She could not, she would not, go again through the tearing agony that lay just behind her.

She must, she told herself, be fair. In all their married life she had had no slightest cause to suspect her husband of any infidelity, of any serious flirtation even. If—and she doubted it—he had had his hours of outside erratic conduct, they were unknown to her. Why begin now to assume them? And on nothing more concrete than an idea that had leapt into her mind because he had told her that he had invited a friend, a friend of hers, to a party in his own house. And at a time when she had been, it was likely, more asleep than awake. How could she without anything done or said, or left undone or unsaid, so easily believe him guilty? How be so ready to renounce all confidence in the worth of their life together?

And if, perchance, there were some small something—well, what could it mean? Nothing. There were the boys. There was John Bellew. The thought of these three gave her some slight relief. But she did not look the future in the face. She wanted to feel nothing, to think nothing; simply to believe that it was all silly invention on her part. Yet she could not. Not quite.

• • •

Christmas, with its unreality, its hectic rush. Its false gaiety, came and went. Irene was thankful for the confused unrest of the season. Its irksomeness, its crowds, its inane and insincere repetitions of genialities, pushed between her and the contemplation of her growing unhappiness.

She was thankful, too, for the continued absence of Clare, who, John Bellew having returned from a long stay in Canada, had withdrawn to that other life of hers, remote and inaccessible. But beating against the walled prison of Irene's thoughts was the shunned fancy that, though absent, Clare Kendry was still present, that she was close.

Brian, too, had withdrawn. The house contained his outward self and his belongings. He came and went with his usual noiseless irregularity. He sat across from her at table. He slept in his room next to hers at night. But he was remote and inaccessible. No use pretending that he was happy, that things were the same as they had always been. He wasn't and they weren't. However, she assured herself, it needn't necessarily be because of anything that involved Clare. It was, it must be, another manifestation of the old longing.

But she did wish it were spring, March, so that Clare would be sailing, out of her life and Brian's. Though she had come almost to believe that there was nothing but generous friendship between those two, she was very tired of Clare Kendry. She wanted to be free of her, and of her furtive comings and goings. If something would only happen, something that would make John Bellew decide on an earlier departure, or that would remove Clare. Anything. She didn't care what. Not even if it were that Clare's Margery were ill, or dying. Not even if Bellew should discover—

She drew a quick, sharp breath. And for a long time sat staring down at the hands in her lap. Strange, she had not before realized how easily she could put Clare out of her life! She had only to tell John Bellew that his wife—No. Not that! But if he should somehow learn of these Harlem visits—Why should she hesitate? Why spare Clare?

But she shrank away from the idea of telling that man, Clare Kendry's white husband, anything that would lead him to suspect that his wife was a Negro. Nor could she write it, or telephone it, or tell it to someone else who would tell him.

She was caught between two allegiances, different, yet the same. Herself. Her race. Race! The thing that bound and suffocated her. Whatever steps she took, or if she took none at all, something would be crushed. A person or the race. Clare, herself, or the race. Or, it might be, all three. Nothing, she imagined, was ever more completely sardonic.

Sitting alone in the quiet living-room in the pleasant fire-light, Irene Redfield wished, for the first time in her life, that she had not been born a

Negro. For the first time she suffered and rebelled because she was unable to disregard the burden of race. It was, she cried silently, enough to suffer as a woman, an individual, on one's own account, without having to suffer for the race as well. It was a brutality, and undeserved. Surely, no other people so cursed as Ham's dark children.

Nevertheless, her weakness, her shrinking, her own inability to compass the thing, did not prevent her from wishing fervently that, in some way with which she had no concern, John Bellew would discover, not that his wife had a touch of the tar-brush — Irene didn't want that — but that she was spending all the time that he was out of the city in black Harlem. Only that. It would be enough to rid her forever of Clare Kendry.

Chapter 3

As if in answer to her wish, the very next day Irene came face to face with Bellew.

She had gone downtown with Felise Freeland to shop. The day was an exceptionally cold one, with a strong wind that had whipped a dusky red into Felise's smooth golden cheeks and driven moisture into Irene's soft brown eyes.

Clinging to each other, with heads bent against the wind, they turned out of the Avenue into Fifty-seventh Street. A sudden bluster flung them around the corner with unexpected quickness and they collided with a man.

"Pardon," Irene begged laughingly, and looked up into the face of Clare Kendry's husband.

"Mrs. Redfield!"

His hat came off. He held out his hand, smiling genially.

But the smile faded at once. Surprise, incredulity, and — was it understanding? — passed over his features.

He had, Irene knew, become conscious of Felise, golden, with curly black Negro hair, whose arm was still linked in her own. She was sure, now, of the understanding in his face, as he looked at her again and then back at Felise. And displeasure.

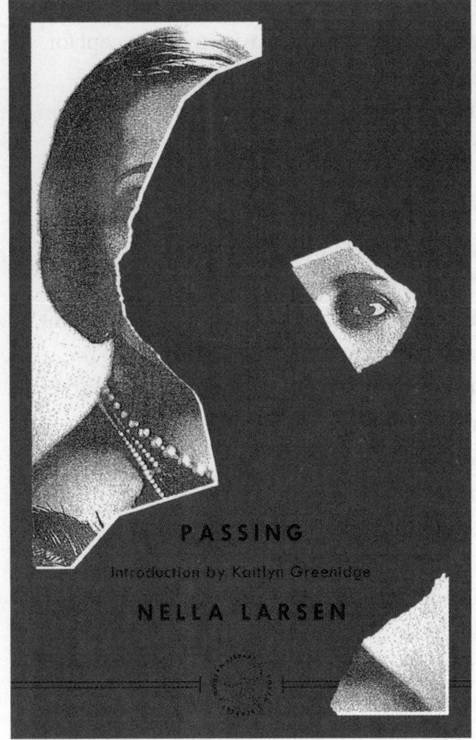

This image is the cover for the book *Passing* by the Modern Library Torchbearers series, whose aim is to feature "women who wrote on their own terms, with boldness, creativity, and a spirit of resistance."

How does the cover suggest these qualities? Do you think it is a fitting image for Larsen's novel? Explain why or why not.

He didn't, however, withdraw his outstretched hand. Not at once.

But Irene didn't take it. Instinctively, in the first glance of recognition, her face had become a mask. Now she turned on him a totally uncomprehending look, a bit questioning. Seeing that he still stood with hand outstretched, she gave him the cool appraising stare which she reserved for mashers, and drew Felise on.

Felise drawled: "Aha! Been 'passing,' have you? Well, I've queered that."

"Yes, I'm afraid you have."

"Why, Irene Redfield! You sound as if you cared terribly. I'm sorry."

"I do, but not for the reason you think. I don't believe I've ever gone native in my life except for the sake of convenience, restaurants, theatre tickets, and things like that. Never socially I mean, except once. You've just passed the only person that I've ever met disguised as a white woman."

"Awfully sorry. Be sure your sin will find you out and all that. Tell me about it."

"I'd like to. It would amuse you. But I can't."

Felise's laughter was as languidly nonchalant as her cool voice. "Can it be possible that the honest Irene has — Oh, do look at that coat! There. The red one. Isn't it a dream?"

Irene was thinking: "I had my chance and didn't take it. I had only to speak and to introduce him to Felise with the casual remark that he was Clare's husband. Only that. Fool. Fool." That instinctive loyalty to a race. Why couldn't she get free of it? Why should it include Clare? Clare, who'd shown little enough consideration for her, and hers. What she felt was not so much resentment as a dull despair because she could not change herself in this respect, could not separate individuals from the race, herself from Clare Kendry.

"Let's go home, Felise. I'm so tired I could drop."

"Why, we haven't done half the things we planned."

"I know, but it's too cold to be running all over town. But you stay down if you want to.

"I think I'll do that, if you don't mind."

• • •

And now another problem confronted Irene. She must tell Clare of this meeting. Warn her. But how? She hadn't seen her for days. Writing and telephoning were equally unsafe. And even if it was possible to get in touch with her, what good would it do? If Bellew hadn't concluded that he'd made a mistake, if he was certain of her identity — and he was nobody's fool — telling Clare wouldn't avert the results of the encounter. Besides, it was too late. Whatever was in store for Clare Kendry had already overtaken her.

Irene was conscious of a feeling of relieved thankfulness at the thought that she was probably rid of Clare, and without having lifted a finger or uttered one word.

But she did mean to tell Brian about meeting John Bellew.

But that, it seemed, was impossible. Strange. Something held her back. Each time she was on the verge of saying: "I ran into Clare's husband on the street downtown today. I'm sure he recognized me, and Felise was with me," she failed to speak. It sounded too much like the warning she wanted it to be. Not even in the presence of the boys at dinner could she make the bare statement.

The evening dragged. At last she said good-night and went upstairs, the words unsaid.

She thought: "Why didn't I tell him? Why didn't I? If trouble comes from this, I'll never forgive myself. I'll tell him when he comes up."

She took up a book, but she could not read, so oppressed was she by a nameless foreboding.

What if Bellew should divorce Clare? Could he? There was the Rhinelander case. But in France, in Paris, such things were very easy. If he divorced her — If Clare were free — But of all the things that could happen, that was the one she did not want. She must get her mind away from that possibility. She must.

Then came a thought which she tried to drive away. If Clare should die! Then — Oh, it was vile! To think, yes, to wish that! She felt faint and sick. But the thought stayed with her. She could not get rid of it.

She heard the outer door open. Close. Brian had gone out. She turned her face into her pillow to cry. But no tears came.

She lay there awake, thinking of things past. Of her courtship and marriage and Junior's birth. Of the time they had bought the house in which they had lived so long and so happily. Of the time Ted had passed his pneumonia crisis and they knew he would live. And of other sweet painful memories that would never come again.

extending beyond the text

In her 2020 book *Caste: The Origins of Our Discontents*, author Isabel Wilkerson describes caste as an artificial hierarchy that determines social position and respect, defines standards of intelligence and competence, and guards access to various kinds of resources. In her book, she argues that a caste system more accurately describes the systemic oppression of Black people in the United States than does race. Wilkerson also discusses the way that caste and race intersect and intertwine in the following excerpt.

from Caste: The Origins of Our Discontents

Isabel Wilkerson

Caste and race are neither synonymous nor mutually exclusive. They can and do coexist in the same culture and serve to reinforce each other. Race, in the United States, is the visible agent of the unseen force of caste. Caste is the bones, race the skin. Race is what we can see, the physical traits that have been given arbitrary meaning and become shorthand for who a person is. Caste is the powerful infrastructure that holds each group in its place.

Caste is fixed and rigid. Race is fluid and superficial, subject to periodic redefinition to meet the needs of the dominant caste in what is now the United States. While the requirements to qualify as white have changed over the centuries, the fact of a dominant caste has remained constant from its inception — whoever fit the definition of white, at whatever point in history, was granted the legal rights and privileges of the dominant caste. Perhaps more critically and tragically, at the other end of the ladder, the subordinated caste, too, has been fixed from the beginning as the psychological floor beneath which all other castes cannot fall.

Thus, we are all born into a silent war-game, centuries old, enlisted in teams not of our choosing. The side to which we are assigned in the American system of categorizing people is proclaimed by the team uniform that each caste wears, signaling our presumed worth and potential. . . .

The use of inherited physical characteristics to differentiate inner abilities and group value may be the cleverest way that a culture has ever devised to manage and maintain a caste system.

"As a social and human division," writes the political scientist Andrew Hacker of the use of physical traits to form human categories, "it surpasses all others — even gender — in intensity and subordination." ■

1. **What does Wilkerson mean when she writes that race is "the visible agent of the unseen force of caste"?**
2. **According to Wilkerson, what is the power of race as a classification scheme – a caste system – that divides human beings?**
3. **In *Passing*, Nella Larsen addresses class as well as race through the thoughts and actions of the characters. How does the novel present a caste system at work? In what ways might it present a challenge to Wilkerson's argument here?**

Above everything else she had wanted, had striven, to keep undisturbed the pleasant routine of her life. And now Clare Kendry had come into it, and with her the menace of impermanence.

"Dear God," she prayed, "make March come quickly."

By and by she slept.

Chapter 4

The next morning brought with it a snowstorm that lasted throughout the day.

After a breakfast, which had been eaten almost in silence and which she was relieved to have done with, Irene Redfield lingered for a little while in the downstairs hall, looking out at the soft flakes fluttering down. She was watching them immediately fill some ugly irregular gaps left by the feet of hurrying pedestrians when Zulena came to her, saying: "The telephone, Mrs. Redfield. It's Mrs. Bellew."

"Take the message, Zulena, please."

Though she continued to stare out of the window, Irene saw nothing now, stabbed as she was by fear — and hope. Had anything happened between Clare and Bellew? And if so, what? And was she to be freed at last from the aching anxiety of the past weeks? Or was there to be more, and worse? She had a wrestling moment, in which it seemed that she must rush after Zulena and hear for herself what it was that Clare had to say. But she waited.

Zulena, when she came back, said: "She says, ma'am, that she'll be able to go to Mrs. Freeland's tonight. She'll be here some time between eight and nine."

"Thank you, Zulena."

The day dragged on to its end.

At dinner Brian spoke bitterly of a lynching that he had been reading about in the evening paper.

"Dad, why is it that they only lynch coloured people?" Ted asked.

"Because they hate 'em, son."

"Brian!" Irene's voice was a plea and a rebuke.

Ted said: "Oh! And why do they hate 'em?"

"Because they are afraid of them."

"But what makes them afraid of 'em?"

"Because — "

"Brian!"

"It seems, son, that is a subject we can't go into at the moment without distressing the ladies of our family," he told the boy with mock seriousness, "but we'll take it up some time when we're alone together."

Ted nodded in his engaging grave way. "I see. Maybe we can talk about it tomorrow on the way to school."

'That'll be line."

"Brian!"

"Mother," Junior remarked, "that's the third time you've said 'Brian' like that."

"But not the last. Junior, never you fear," his father told him.

After the boys had gone up to their own floor, Irene said suavely: "I do wish, Brian, that you wouldn't talk about lynching before Ted and Junior. It was really inexcusable for you to bring up a thing like that at dinner. There'll be time enough for them to learn about such horrible things when they're older."

"You're absolutely wrong! If, as you're so determined, they've got to live in this damned country, they'd better find out what sort of thing they're up against as soon as possible. The earlier they learn it, the better prepared they'll be."

"I don't agree. I want their childhood to be happy and as free from the knowledge of such things as it possibly can be."

"Very laudable," was Brian's sarcastic answer. "Very laudable indeed, all things considered. But can it?"

"Certainly it can. If you'll only do your part."

"Stuff! You know as well as I do, Irene, that it can't. What was the use of our trying to keep them from learning the word 'nigger' and its connotation? They found out, didn't they? And how? Because somebody called Junior a dirty nigger."

"Just the same you're not to talk to them about the race problem. I won't have It."

They glared at each other.

"I tell you, Irene, they've got to know these things, and it might as well be now as later."

"They do not!" she insisted, forcing back the tears of anger that were threatening to fall.

Brian growled: "I can't understand how anybody as intelligent as you like to think you are can show evidences of such stupidity." He looked at her in a puzzled harassed way.

"Stupid!" she cried. "Is it stupid to want my children to be happy?" Her lips were quivering.

"At the expense of proper preparation for life and their future happiness, yes. And I'd feel I hadn't done my duty by them if I didn't give them some inkling of what's before them. It's the least I can do. I wanted to get them out of this hellish place years ago. You wouldn't let me. I gave up the idea, because you objected. Don't expect me to give up everything."

Under the lash of his words she was silent. Before any answer came to her, he had turned and gone from the room.

Sitting there alone in the forsaken dining-room, unconsciously pressing the hands lying in her lap, tightly together, she was seized by a convulsion of shivering. For, to her, there had been something ominous in the scene that she had just had with her husband. Over and over in her mind his last words: "Don't expect me to give up everything," repeated themselves. What had they meant? What could they mean? Clare Kendry?

Surely, she was going mad with fear and suspicion. She must not work herself up. She must not! Where were all the self-control, the common sense, that she was so proud of? Now, if ever, was the time for it.

Clare would soon be there. She must hurry or she would be late again, and those two would wait for her downstairs together, as they had done so often since that first time, which now seemed so long ago. Had it been really only last October? Why, she felt years, not months, older.

Drearily she rose from her chair and went upstairs to set about the business of dressing to go out when she would far rather have remained at home. During the process she wondered, for the hundredth time, why she hadn't told Brian about herself and Felise running into Bellew the day before, and for the hundredth time she turned away from acknowledging to herself the real reason for keeping back the information.

When Clare arrived, radiant in a shining red gown, Irene had not finished dressing. But her smile scarcely hesitated as she greeted her, saying: "I always seem to keep C. P. time, don't I? We hardly expected you to be able to come. Felise will be pleased. How nice you look."

Clare kissed a bare shoulder, seeming not to notice a slight shrinking.

"I hadn't an idea in the world, myself, that I'd be able to make it; but Jack had to run down to Philadelphia unexpectedly. So here I am."

Irene looked up, a flood of speech on her lips. "Philadelphia. That's not very far, is it? Clare, I—?"

She stopped, one of her hands clutching the side of her stool, the other lying clenched on the dressing-table. Why didn't she go on and tell Clare about meeting Bellew? Why couldn't she?

But Clare didn't notice the unfinished sentence. She laughed and said lightly: "It's far enough for me. Anywhere, away from me, is far enough. I'm not particular."

Irene passed a hand over her eyes to shut out the accusing face in the glass before her. With one corner of her mind she wondered how long she had looked like that, drawn and haggard and—yes, frightened. Or was it only imagination?

"Clare," she asked, "have you ever seriously thought what it would mean if he should find you out?"

"Yes."

"Oh! You have! And what you'd do in that case?"

"Yes." And having said it, Clare Kendry smiled quickly, a smile that came and went like a flash, leaving untouched the gravity of her face.

That smile and the quiet resolution of that one word, “yes,” filled Irene with a primitive paralysing dread. Her hands were numb, her feet like ice, her heart like a stone weight. Even her tongue was like a heavy dying thing. There were long spaces between the words as she asked: “And what should you do?”

Clare, who was sunk in a deep chair, her eyes far away, seemed wrapped in some pleasant impenetrable reflection. To Irene, sitting expectantly upright, it was an interminable time before she dragged herself back to the present to say calmly: “I'd do what I want to do more than anything else right now. I'd come up here to live. Harlem, I mean. Then I'd be able to do as I please, when I please.”

Irene leaned forward, cold and tense. “And what about Margery?” Her voice was a strained whisper.

“Margery?” Clare repeated, letting her eyes flutter over Irene's concerned face. “Just this, 'Rene. If it wasn't for her, I'd do it anyway. She's all that holds me back. But if Jack finds out, if our marriage is broken, that lets me out. Doesn't it?”

Her gentle resigned tone, her air of innocent candour, appeared, to her listener, spurious. A conviction that the words were intended as a warning took possession of Irene. She remembered that Clare Kendry had always seemed to know what other people were thinking. Her compressed lips grew firm and obdurate. Well, she wouldn't know this time.

She said: “Do go downstairs and talk to Brian. He's got a mad on.”

Though she had determined that Clare should not get at her thoughts and fears, the words had sprung, unthought of, to her lips. It was as if they had come from some outer layer of callousness that had no relation to her tortured heart. And they had been, she realized, precisely the right words for her purpose.

For as Clare got up and went out, she saw that that arrangement was as good as her first plan of keeping her waiting up there while she dressed — or better. She would only have hindered and rasped her. And what matter if those two spent one hour, more or less, alone together, one or many, now that everything had happened between them?

Ah! The first time that she had allowed herself to admit to herself that everything had happened, had not forced herself to believe, to hope, that nothing irrevocable had been consummated! Well, it had happened. She knew it, and knew that she knew it.

She was surprised that, having thought the thought, conceded the fact, she was no more hurt, cared no more, than during her previous frenzied endeavours to escape it. And this absence of acute, unbearable pain seemed to her unjust, as if she had been denied some exquisite solace of suffering which the full acknowledgment should have given her.

Was it, perhaps, that she had endured all that a woman could endure of tormenting humiliation and fear? Or was it that she lacked the capacity for the acme of suffering? “No, no!’ she denied fiercely. “I'm human like everybody else. It's just that I'm so tired, so worn out, I can't feel any more.” But she did not really believe that.

Security. Was it just a word? If not, then was it only by the sacrifice of other things, happiness, love, or some wild ecstasy that she had never known, that it could be obtained? And did too much striving, too much faith in safety and permanence, unfit one for these other things?

Irene didn't know, couldn't decide, though for a long time she sat questioning and trying to understand. Yet all the while, in spite of her searchings and feeling of frustration, she was aware that, to her, security was the most important and desired thing in life. Not for any of the others, or for all of them, would she exchange it. She wanted only to be tranquil. Only, unmolested, to be allowed to direct for their own best good the lives of her sons and her husband.

Now that she had relieved herself of what was almost like a guilty knowledge, admitted that which by some sixth sense she had long

extending beyond the text

This work, completed in 2016 by contemporary Haitian American artist Fabiola Jean-Louis, is part of a series called "Rewriting History." Entitled *Passing*, it depicts a young Black woman playing a violin that is represented in greater detail in another image in the series as the "Violin of the Dead."

Alan Avery Art Company

1. **What do you notice about the woman's dress, pose, and expression as she looks down at the violin collaged with print and photographic images?**
2. **How does the title influence your interpretation of the luxurious red fabric at the woman's side and the basket of cotton at her feet? Given what you notice about this woman and the way she is depicted, does the title *Passing* surprise you?**
3. **To what extent does this image reflect Larsen's attitude toward race and racism in *Passing*?**
4. **How might this image illustrate Irene's assertion that white people try to identify race "by the most ridiculous means, finger-nails, palms of hand, shapes of ears, teeth, and other equally silly rot" (par. 46)?**

known, she could again reach out for plans. Could think again of ways to keep Brian by her side, and in New York. For she would not go to Brazil. She belonged in this land of rising towers. She was an American. She grew from this soil, and she would not be uprooted. Not even because of Clare Kendry, or a hundred Clare Kendrys.

Brian, too, belonged here. His duty was to her and to his boys.

Strange, that she couldn't now be sure that she had ever truly known love. Not even for Brian. He was her husband and the father of her sons. But was he anything more? Had she ever wanted or tried for more? In that hour she thought not.

Nevertheless, she meant to keep him. Her freshly painted lips narrowed to a thin straight line. True, she had left off trying to believe that he and Clare loved and yet did not love, but she still intended to hold fast to the outer shell of her marriage, to keep her life fixed, certain. Brought to the edge of distasteful reality, her fastidious nature did not recoil. Better, far better, to share him than to lose him completely. Oh, she could close her eyes, if need be. She could bear it. She could bear anything. And there was March ahead. March and the departure of Clare.

Horribly clear, she could now see the reason for her instinct to withhold — omit, rather — her news of the encounter with Bellew. If Clare was freed, anything might happen.

She paused in her dressing, seeing with perfect clearness that dark truth which she had from that first October afternoon felt about Clare Kendry and of which Clare herself had once warned her — that she got the things she wanted because she met the great condition of conquest, sacrifice. If she wanted Brian, Clare wouldn't revolt from the lack of money or place. It was as she had said, only Margery kept her from throwing all that away. And if things were taken out of her hands — Even if she was only alarmed, only suspected that such a thing was about to occur, anything might happen. Anything.

No! At all costs, Clare was not to know of that meeting with Bellew. Nor was Brian. It would only weaken her own power to keep him.

They would never know from her that he was on his way to suspecting the truth about his wife. And she would do anything, risk anything, to prevent him from finding out that truth. How fortunate that she had obeyed her instinct and omitted to recognize Bellew!

• • •

"Ever go up to the sixth floor, Clare?" Brian asked as he stopped the car and got out to open the door for them.

"Why, of course! We're on the seventeenth."

"I mean, did you ever go up by nigger-power?"

"That's good!" Clare laughed. "Ask 'Rene. My father was a janitor, you know, in the good old days before every ramshackle flat had its elevator. But you can't mean we've got to walk up? Not here!"

"Yes, here. And Felise lives at the very top," Irene told her.

"What on earth for?"

"I believe she claims it discourages the casual visitor."

"And she's probably right. Hard on herself, though."

Brian said "Yes, a bit. But she says she'd rather be dead than bored."

"Oh, a garden! And how lovely with that undisturbed snow!"

"Yes, isn't it? But keep to the walk with those foolish thin shoes. You too, Irene."

Irene walked beside them on the cleared cement path that split the whiteness of the courtyard garden. She felt a something in the air, something that had been between those two and would be again. It was like a live thing pressing against her. In a quick furtive glance she saw Clare clinging to Brian's other arm. She was looking at him with that provocative upward glance of hers, and his eyes were fastened on her face with what seemed to Irene an expression of wistful eagerness.

"It's this entrance, I believe," she informed them in quite her ordinary voice.

"Mind," Brian told Clare, "you don't fall by the wayside before the fourth floor. They absolutely refuse to carry anyone up more than the last two flights."

"Don't be silly!" Irene snapped.

• • •

The party began gaily.

Dave Freeland was at his best, brilliant, crystal clear, and sparkling. Felise, too, was amusing, and not so sarcastic as usual, because she liked the dozen or so guests that dotted the long, untidy living-room. Brian was witty, though, Irene noted, his remarks were somewhat more barbed than was customary even with him. And there was Ralph Hazelton, throwing nonsensical shining things into the pool of talk, which the others, even Clare, picked up and flung back with fresh adornment.

Only Irene wasn't merry. She sat almost silent, smiling now and then, that she might appear amused.

"What's the matter, Irene?" someone asked. "Taken a vow never to laugh, or something? You're as sober as a judge."

"No. It's simply that the rest of you are so clever that I'm speechless, absolutely stunned."

"No wonder," Dave Freeland remarked, "that you're on the verge of tears. You haven't a drink. What'll you take?"

"Thanks. If I must take something, make it a glass of ginger-ale and three drops of Scotch. The Scotch first, please. Then the ice, then the ginger ale."

"Heavens! Don't attempt to mix that yourself, Dave darling. Have the butler in," Felise mocked.

"Yes, do. And the footman." Irene laughed a little, then said: "It seems dreadfully warm in here. Mind if I open this window?" With that she pushed open one of the long casement-windows of which the Freelands were so proud.

It had stopped snowing some two or three hours back. The moon was just rising, and far behind the tall buildings a few stars were creeping out. Irene finished her cigarette and threw it out, watching the tiny spark drop slowly down to the white ground below.

Someone in the room had turned on the phonograph. Or was it the radio? She didn't know which she disliked more. And nobody was listening to its blare. The talking, the laughter never for a minute ceased. Why must they have more noise?

Dave came with her drink. "You ought not," he told her, "to stand there like that. You'll take cold. Come along and talk to me, or listen to me gabble." Taking her arm, he led her across the room. They had just found seats when the door-bell rang and Felise called over to him to go and answer it.

In the next moment Irene heard his voice in the hall, carelessly polite: "Your wife? Sorry. I'm afraid you're wrong. Perhaps next — "

Then the roar of John Bellew's voice above all the other noises of the room: "I'm *not* wrong! I've been to the Redfields and I know she's with them. You'd better stand out of my way and save yourself trouble in the end."

"What is it, Dave?" Felise ran out to the door.

And so did Brian. Irene heard him saying: "I'm Redfield. What the devil's the matter with you?"

But Bellew didn't heed him. He pushed past them all into the room and strode towards Clare. They all looked at her as she got up from her chair, backing a little from his approach.

"So you're a nigger, a damned dirty nigger!" His voice was a snarl and a moan, an expression of rage and of pain.

Everything was in confusion. The men had sprung forward. Felise had leapt between them and Bellew. She said quickly: "Careful. You're the only white man here." And the silver chill of her voice, as well as her words, was a warning.

Clare stood at the window, as composed as if everyone were not staring at her in curiosity and wonder, as if the whole structure of her life were not lying in fragments before her. She seemed unaware of any danger or uncaring. There was even a faint smile on her full, red lips, and in her shining eyes.

It was that smile that maddened Irene. She ran across the room, her terror tinged with ferocity, and laid a hand on Clare's bare arm. One thought possessed her. She couldn't have Clare Kendry cast aside by Bellew. She couldn't have her free.

Before them stood John Bellew, speechless now in his hurt and anger. Beyond them the little huddle of other people, and Brian stepping out from among them.

What happened next, Irene Redfield never afterwards allowed herself to remember. Never clearly.

extending beyond the text

The following passage is from *A Chosen Exile: A History of Racial Passing in American Life*, a 2014 book by Allyson Hobbs, a historian and professor at Stanford University.

from A Chosen Exile: A History of Racial Passing in American Life

Allyson Hobbs

[Passing] may be understood as a desperate act compelled by the racial constraints of a bygone era of segregation and racial violence. Once one circumvented the law, fooled coworkers, deceived neighbors, tricked friends, and sometimes even duped children and spouses, there were enormous costs to pay. . . .

Without a doubt, benefits accrued to these new white identities. But a more complex understanding of this practice requires a reckoning with the loss, alienation, and isolation that accompanied, and often outweighed, its rewards. As early as the 1940s and through the 1960s, personal testimonies began to declare that the losses were simply too much to bear; it was time to give up and "come home." . . .

The lived experience of passing — the act of negotiating the permeable border between black and white — reveals one way that everyday people have interacted with a racist society since the late eighteenth century. The constructed nature of race becomes evident when individuals changed their racial identity by changing location, clothing, speech, and life story, thus seemingly making themselves white. These individuals . . . demonstrate that the concept of race can be specious but also utterly real, as the painful consequences of passing often demonstrated.

Racial indeterminacy lies at the core of passing; it is the precondition that made passing possible. Racial ambiguity is the inevitable consequence of racial mixture, and racial mixture has transpired whenever different groups of people encounter each other. But it is what one does with the ambiguity that may vex or unnerve the larger society. As the phenomenon of passing was reshaped in each historical period, the meaning and significance of passing also transformed. At times, passing was an act of rebellion against the racial regime; on other occasions, it was a challenge to African Americans' struggle to shape and to nurture group identities and communities. ■

1. **What does Hobbs mean by "the constructed nature of race"? Where in *Passing* do you see evidence that could support the idea of race as "constructed" or "permeable"?**
2. **Hobbs asserts that people who chose to pass as white "demonstrate[d] that the concept of race can be specious but also utterly real." What details from *Passing* portray race as specious? Which ones convey that it is real?**

extending beyond the text

3. **Hobbs claims that "what one does with [racial] ambiguity . . . may vex or unnerve the larger society." Which characters in *Passing* are vexed or unnerved by Clare's passing? What conflicts unfold as a result? What larger meaning do these conflicts convey?**
4. **Hobbs says that passing was sometimes "an act of rebellion against the racial regime" and sometimes "a challenge to African Americans' struggle to shape and to nurture group identities and communities." Where does the narrative of Larsen's novel fit within this framework — or does it? Use evidence from the text to support your response.**

One moment Clare had been there, a vital glowing thing, like a flame of red and gold. The next she was gone.

There was a gasp of horror, and above it a sound not quite human, like a beast in agony. "Nig! My God! Nig!"

A frenzied rush of feet down long flights of stairs. The slamming of distant doors. Voices.

Irene stayed behind. She sat down and remained quite still, staring at a ridiculous Japanese print on the wall across the room.

Gone! The soft white face, the bright hair, the disturbing scarlet mouth, the dreaming eyes, the caressing smile, the whole torturing loveliness that had been Clare Kendry. That beauty that had torn at Irene's placid life. Gone! The mocking daring, the gallantry of her pose, the ringing bells of her laughter.

Irene wasn't sorry. She was amazed, incredulous almost.

What would the others think? That Clare had fallen? That she had deliberately leaned backward? Certainly one or the other. Not—

But she mustn't, she warned herself, think of that. She was too tired, and too shocked. And, indeed, both were true. She was utterly weary, and she was violently staggered. But her thoughts reeled on. If only she could be as free of mental as she was of bodily vigour; could only put from her memory the vision of her hand on Clare's arm!

"It was an accident, a terrible accident," she muttered fiercely. "It *was*."

People were coming up the stairs. Through the still open door their steps and talk sounded nearer, nearer.

Quickly she stood up and went noiselessly into the bedroom and closed the door softly behind her.

Her thoughts raced. Ought she to have stayed? Should she go back out there to them? But there would be questions. She hadn't thought of them, of afterwards, of this. She had thought of nothing in that sudden moment of action.

It was cold. Icy chills ran up her spine and over her bare neck and shoulders.

In the room outside there were voices. Dave Freeland's and others that she did not recognize.

Should she put on her coat? Felise had rushed down without any wrap. So had all the others. So had Brian. Brian! He mustn't take cold. She took up his coat and left her own. At the door she paused for a moment, listening fearfully. She heard nothing. No voices. No footsteps. Very slowly she opened the door. The room was empty. She went out.

In the hall below she heard dimly the sound of feet going down the steps, of a door being opened and closed, and of voices far away.

Down, down, down, she went, Brian's great coat clutched in her shivering arms and trailing a little on each step behind her.

What was she to say to them when at last she had finished going down those endless stairs? She should have rushed out when they did. What reason could she give for her dallying behind?

Even she didn't know why she had done that. And what else would she be asked? There had been her hand reaching out towards Clare. What about that?

In the midst of her wonderings and questionings came a thought so terrifying, so horrible, that she had had to grasp hold of the banister to save herself from pitching downwards. A cold perspiration drenched her shaking body. Her breath came short in sharp and painful gasps.

What if Clare was not dead?

She felt nauseated, as much at the idea of the glorious body mutilated as from fear.

How she managed to make the rest of the journey without fainting she never knew. But at last she was down. Just at the bottom she came on the others, surrounded by a little circle of strangers. They were all speaking in whispers, or in the awed, discreetly lowered tones adapted to the presence of disaster. In the first instant she wanted to turn and rush back up the way she had come. Then a calm desperation came over her. She braced herself, physically and mentally.

"Here's Irene now," Dave Freeland announced, and told her that, having only just missed her, they had concluded that she had fainted or something like that, and were on the way to find out about her. Felise, she saw, was holding on to his arm, all the insolent non-chalance gone out of her, and the golden brown of her handsome face changed to a queer mauve colour.

Irene made no indication that she had heard Freeland, but went straight to Brian. His face looked aged and altered, and his lips were purple and trembling. She had a great longing to comfort him, to charm away his suffering and horror. But she was helpless, having so completely lost control of his mind and heart.

She stammered: "Is she — is she — ?"

It was Felise who answered. "Instantly, we think."

Irene struggled against the sob of thankfulness that rose in her throat. Choked down, it turned to a whimper, like a hurt child's. Someone laid a hand on her shoulder in a soothing gesture. Brian wrapped his coat about her. She began to cry rackingly, her entire body heaving with convulsive sobs. He made a slight perfunctory attempt to comfort her.

"There, there, Irene. You mustn't. You'll make yourself sick. She's — "His voice broke suddenly.

As from a long distance she heard Ralph Hazelton's voice saying: "I was looking right at her. She just tumbled over and was gone before you could say 'Jack Robinson.' Fainted, I guess. Lord! It was quick. Quickest thing I ever saw in all my life."

"It's impossible, I tell you! Absolutely impossible!"

It was Brian who spoke in that frenzied hoarse voice, which Irene had never heard before. Her knees quaked under her.

Dave Freeland said: "Just a minute, Brian. Irene was there beside her. Let's hear what she has to say."

She had a moment of stark craven fear. "Oh God," she thought, prayed, "help me."

A strange man, official and authoritative, addressed her. "You're sure she fell? Her husband didn't give her a shove or anything like that, as Dr. Redfield seems to think?"

For the first time she was aware that Bellew was not in the little group shivering in the small hallway. What did that mean? As she began to work it out in her numbed mind, she was shaken with another hideous trembling. Not that! Oh, not that!

"No, no!" she protested. "I'm quite certain that he didn't. I was there, too. As close as he was. She just fell, before anybody could stop her. I — "

Her quaking knees gave way under her. She moaned and sank down, moaned again. Through the great heaviness that submerged and drowned her she was dimly conscious of strong arms lifting her up. Then everything was dark.

Centuries after, she heard the strange man saying: 'Death by misadventure, I'm inclined to believe. Let's go up and have another look at that window." ■

1929

Understanding and Interpreting

1. **AP® Character, Setting, and Narration.** In Chapter 1 of "Encounter," Nella Larsen introduces the protagonist, Irene Redfield, as she considers whether to read a letter from her childhood friend Clare Kendry. What do you learn about Irene as you read this scene? Does the final scene of the chapter, in which some of the letter's contents are revealed, confirm or challenge Irene's view of Clare? Explain.
2. **AP® Character, Setting, and Narration.** Chapter 2 of "Encounter" takes the reader two years back in time to Irene's visit to Chicago during the summer. What details do you learn about Irene's life? How does Larsen convey her emotional state? Why, for instance, is she uneasy about seeking a cool refuge on the rooftop of the Drayton Hotel?
3. **AP® Character, Setting, and Narration.** What is your first impression of Clare based on the description of her on the roof of the Drayton? Does your first impression of her differ from Irene's? Explain.
4. **AP® Character and Narration.** How does Clare explain her motivations for what Irene describes as "this hazardous business of 'passing'" (par. 106)? Are her concerns primarily about race, class, a combination of those, or something else? How does Clare's perspective on her marriage figure into her decision to pass — and does that perspective change as the novel progresses? Use evidence from the text to support your answer.
5. **AP® Character, Structure, and Narration.** Throughout the novel, Irene experiences conflicting emotions about her friendship with Clare. Identify two or three scenes in which Irene considers her ambivalence and discuss how each one characterizes both women. How do these scenes deepen and complicate the major conflicts of the plot?
6. **AP® Character and Narration.** In Chapter 3 of "Encounter," Irene meets Clare's husband, Jack Bellew. What details does Larsen use to characterize Bellew? What does Clare's response to his offensive nickname for her reveal about her character? Why do you think Irene reacts the way she does to his racist comments?
7. **AP® Character and Narration.** When she meets Jack for the first time, Irene chooses not to reveal her own, or Clare's, racial identity despite his racist tirade. Why? What is the logic of her loyalty to Clare in this instance? Since Clare has clearly orchestrated this encounter, why would Irene protect her? To what extent does Irene's reaction stem from a need to protect herself in this situation? Explain, using evidence from the text to support your response.
8. **AP® Character and Narration.** The day after Clare introduces Irene to her husband, she sends a letter to the hotel where Irene is staying. What does that letter convey about her hope or intentions for their relationship? What does Irene's response to it reveal about her motivations and values?
9. **AP® Character, Setting, and Narration.** The second part of the novel, "Re-Encounter," shifts from Chicago, where Irene and Clare grew up, to Harlem, in New York City, which is where Irene currently lives. What evidence does Larsen provide to illustrate the privileged life that Irene and her family lead?
10. **AP® Character and Setting.** What is it that Clare hopes to gain by reconnecting with Irene and participating in the social life of Harlem? What does she believe is missing from her own life?
11. **AP® Character and Narration.** What does Irene mean when she thinks, "The trouble with Clare was, not only that she wanted to have her cake and eat it too, but that she wanted to nibble at the cakes of other folk as well" (par. 312)? How might this perspective on Clare also apply to Irene?

12. **AP® Character and Narration.** What details serve to characterize Irene's husband, Brian? Consider his physical appearance, his personality, and the depiction of his relationship with his wife. What is the significance of Brian's desire to move to Brazil?

13. **AP® Character and Narration.** During their meeting at the Drayton Hotel, Irene recalls that those who knew Clare as a girl saw her as "a — having way with her" (par. 74). How do you interpret this statement? In what ways does Irene continue to see Clare through the prism of this characterization in "Re-Encounter" and "Finale"?

14. **AP® Character and Narration.** In paragraph 354, Irene tells her husband, "It's funny about 'passing.' We disapprove of it and at the same time condone it. It excites our contempt and yet we rather admire it. We shy away from it with an odd kind of revulsion, but we protect it." How, in the novel, does Irene show her disapproval of passing? How do she and the other characters condone and protect it? Why, based on Irene's values and motivations, do you think Clare's choices draw Irene's "contempt" — or do they? Explain.

15. **AP® Character and Narration.** In Chapter 3 of "Re-Encounter," Irene remembers a conversation with Hugh Wentworth during a party where Clare was the center of attention. What does Larsen reveal about a white person's perspective on passing through this conversation? How does this conversation characterize their friendship?

16. **AP® Character.** How do Irene's and Clare's view of motherhood differ? What values do these differing perspectives reveal? Why does Clare believe that "being a mother is the cruellest thing in the world" (p. 520)? Why do you think Irene agrees with her about this?

17. **AP® Character and Narration.** Irene's life, on the surface, looks perfect: she is a loyal wife to a successful physician, a loving mother to two sons; she is involved in charitable activities for her community; she keeps a home that is both comfortable for her family and a space welcoming for entertainment. She cultivates friendships with other people in the community who have similar means and values. Yet Larsen does not always present her in a positive light. Why not? What evidence do you find that Larsen might be criticizing the values of Irene's socioeconomic sphere?

18. **AP® Character and Narration.** How do the relationships Brian and Irene have with their sons reveal conflicting values? Consider their conversation about lynching in Chapter 4 of "Finale" as you respond.

19. **AP® Character, Structure, and Narration.** In "Finale," Irene is tormented by what she says is "an unfounded suspicion" (par. 656) — that nonetheless feels true to her — that Brian and Clare are having an affair. Is there any evidence in the text that they are? Does evidence — or lack thereof — ultimately matter to Irene? Explain why or why not.

20. **AP® Narration.** What do you think really happened in paragraphs 814–823, in which Larsen details Clare's fall and Irene's amnesia? Cite evidence from the text to support your interpretation.

21. **AP® Character.** Early in the novel, Clare tells Irene, "I was determined to get away, to be a person and not a charity or a problem. . ." (par. 123). Do you think Clare ultimately achieved these goals? Explain.

Analyzing Language, Style, and Structure

1. **Vocabulary in Context.** When Clare insists that her daughter Margery is "all that holds [her] back" from leaving her husband, Larsen writes, "Her gentle resigned tone, her air of innocent candour, appeared, to [Irene], spurious" (par. 760). *Spurious* has, in this context, different layers of meaning. What are they? Why is this word more effective than, for instance, *false* or *insincere*?

2. **AP® Character, Structure, and Narration.** Larsen withholds any direct mention of race until well into Chapter 2 of "Encounter." What purpose does withholding this information serve? How does it affect your reading of the descriptions of Clare and Irene earlier on in the novel?

3. **AP® Character and Figurative Language.** Throughout the novel, Larsen provides vivid details of her characters' physical appearance, including specific colors, textures, and styles of clothing. How do these outward descriptions contribute to an understanding of the characters' inner lives? Choose one character and discuss the significance of the information about their physical appearance.

4. **AP® Character, Structure, and Narration.** What dramatic irony do you find in Irene's introduction to Jack Bellew in "Encounter"? What purpose does this scene serve within the overall plot structure?

5. **AP® Setting and Character.** How do the various social settings of the novel reveal the interior lives of Clare and Irene? You might consider the rooftop of the Drayton Hotel, the tea Clare hosts for a few friends in Chicago, the party in Irene's home in Harlem, the fundraising event for the Negro Welfare League, or the party at Felise's apartment.

6. **AP® Character and Figurative Language.** What does Brazil represent to Brian? What larger meaning does his desire to move there convey? Why does Irene oppose the idea?

7. **AP® Character, Structure, and Narration.** In Chapter 3 of "Finale," Irene unexpectedly meets Jack Bellew again while out shopping with Felise in New York City. How does Larsen use this second encounter to illustrate a shift in Irene's character and foreshadow the final scene of the novel? Why doesn't Irene tell anyone of this encounter?

8. **AP® Structure.** What is the relationship between the three-part structure of the novel and its major theme(s)? Consider, for instance, that this division might suggest a specific dramatic arc or be reminiscent of acts of a play.

9. **AP® Character and Narration.** The novel is told through a third-person narrator, yet it is clearly the perspective of Irene. As readers, we meet other characters, including Clare, through Irene's eyes, and we experience events, including the ending, through her perspective. To what extent is she a reliable narrator? What do you believe Larsen's purpose is in choosing her as the lens for *Passing* rather than a first-person narrator or even an omniscient one?

10. **AP® Character.** What is the function of minor characters in developing the main themes of the novel? Consider at least two of the following characters in your response: Brian Redfield, Jack Bellew, Gertrude Martin, Hugh Wentworth, Irene's sons Junior and Ted, Clare's daughter Margery, the maids Sadie and Zulena, Dave Freeland, or Felise Freeland. Pay specific attention to the way Larsen uses minor characters to develop and complicate the friendship between Irene and Clare.

11. **AP® Character and Figurative Language.** What textual evidence does Larsen provide to suggest the attraction that Clare holds for Irene? Consider the descriptions of Clare's physical features and wardrobe, and of her laugh, which Irene sees as "the very essence of mockery" (par. 84). What is it that Irene sees in Clare that she feels, consciously or unconsciously, Irene lacks?

12. **AP® Structure and Narration.** What examples of foreshadowing do you find in the novel? How does this literary element develop the plot and help structure the narrative in *Passing*?

13. **AP® Structure and Figurative Language.** The recurrence of doorways, windows, and thresholds throughout the novel often signal a shift not only in setting but in mood. Identify several instances of such shifts, and discuss their symbolic meaning.

14. **AP® Character, Structure, Narration, and Figurative Language.** One of the most jarring scenes of the novel takes place in Chapter 3 of "Encounter," in which Jack Bellew joins his wife Clare, Irene, and their childhood friend Gertrude, all of whom are able to pass as white. Jack greets Clare with a racial slur that he's given her as a nickname, unaware that his wife and both of her friends are Black. How does this specific scene distil the major conflicts, paradoxes, and themes of the book? Consider the resources of language Larsen uses to convey a specific mood and tone and how she characterizes each of the women as well as Jack throughout the scene.
15. **AP® Character and Figurative Language.** Throughout the novel, Clare is described in images and metaphors for gambling. What is Larsen suggesting about her character with this language? Cite specific passages to support your view.
16. **AP® Character, Narration, and Figurative Language.** Clare is often described, from Irene's perspective, as being "catlike." What associations and conflicting qualities does this description bring to mind, and how does Clare embody them? How does this particular metaphor relate to the ending of the novel?
17. **AP® Character, Setting, Structure, Narration, and Figurative Language.** One way that scholars have interpreted *Passing* is a story of how Black people in America experience themselves as simultaneously hyperexposed and invisible. Using one specific scene, analyze how Larsen presents this conflict and its consequences in a character's development.
18. **AP® Character, Structure, Narration, and Figurative Language.** Rebecca Hall, director of the 2021 film *Passing*, explains that she was drawn to the novel and felt its contemporaneity because it "embraces nuance and paradox." What examples of these qualities, especially paradox, do you find in the novel? Cite specific passages or events to support your response.

Topics for Composing

1. **AP® FRQ Literary Argument.** Many works of literature feature contrasting characters – often a pair who are adversaries, whose relationship changes over time, or who have taken dramatically different paths in life, either by choice or force. In *Passing*, Clare Kendry and Irene Redfield, childhood friends, meet again for the first time in twelve years. They re-establish a friendship both fraught with interpersonal conflict and shaped by socially oppressive circumstances. In a well-written essay, analyze how the complexity of the relationship between these two women contributes to an interpretation of the work as a whole. Do not merely summarize the plot.
2. **AP® FRQ Prose Fiction Analysis.** The following question refers to paragraphs 7–15 of Nella Larsen's *Passing*, published in 1929. In this passage, Irene Redfield deliberates whether to respond to Clare Kendry, a childhood friend whom she recently met on a chance encounter. Read the passage carefully. Then, in a well-written essay, analyze how Larsen uses literary elements and techniques to portray Irene's complex response to the letter imploring Irene to resume their friendship.
3. **AP® Literary Argumentation.** Why does a work of literature endure? In many ways, the answer is that it helps us see gray areas and nuance that take us beyond binaries such as good vs. evil, right vs. wrong, change vs. stasis. In what ways is *Passing* a novel that challenges the view of issues related to race as a binary and, instead, insists upon the ambiguities inherent in our understanding of what race is and what racial identity signifies about a person?

4. **AP® Literary Argumentation.** Who is Clare Kendry? Is she a villain, a victim, or something else entirely? Is she trapped by a decision she made on the cusp of adulthood and has come to regret, forced to live a lie? Is she a person driven by a love of danger and risk regardless of the cost to herself and others? Is she a survivor determined to chart her own path? A combination of these? Something else? Develop a position, and cite specific passages and events to support your response.
5. **AP® Literary Argumentation.** Is *Passing* a cautionary tale about the dangers of pretense and failure to conform to a society's norms? Is it an indictment of a racist value system? Is it a feminist interpretation of the restrictions and obstacles women — especially Black women — face when they resist expectations and limits of their society? Is it a combination of these things? Is it something else? Develop your position on what you believe is Larsen's main theme in *Passing* and support it with specific textual evidence.
6. **AP® Literary Argumentation.** In an essay for the *New York Times*, novelist Brit Bennett describes Clare as a performer who "requires an audience" and

   > revels in the nearness of getting caught. Clare claims that she passes only for financial freedom, but what she actually seems to enjoy is. . . "stepping always on the edge of danger." Not the performance itself but the possibility that the audience may peek behind the curtain.

   How is Larsen's depiction of Clare that of someone who understands the theatricality of her projected identity? Develop your analysis by focusing on the Drayton Hotel meeting or one of the party scenes.
7. **Speaking and Listening.** A literary scholar described *Passing* as "a meditation on the uneasy dynamic between social obligation and personal freedom." Working in small groups, each focusing on Clare, Irene, or Brian, discuss how you see that "dynamic" — or tension — playing out in that character. Then, return to the full class to report your insights and discuss how your insights contribute to an interpretation of *Passing*.
8. **Research.** The artists of the Harlem Renaissance were far from monolithic in their approach to their work and, consequently, how they represented Black cultures, communities, and American life. After researching this rich and varied period, discuss how Larsen reflected major themes explored by other Harlem Renaissance writers and artists, yet also had a distinctive voice and viewpoint in *Passing*.
9. **Connections.** The epigraph to *Passing* is four lines from "Heritage" by Countee Cullen (p. 202), a contemporary of Larsen. Read the poem, and then discuss how the struggle of the speaker in "Heritage" relates to the major conflicts and themes of *Passing*.
10. **Connections.** View the 2021 film *Passing*, directed by Rebecca Hall and starring Ruth Negga as Clare and Tessa Thompson as Irene. Where and why does the film depart from Larsen's novel? How does the film represent race and racism during the 1920s? In what ways does this representation relate to the role of race and racism in American culture today?
11. **Creative Writing.** Even though the narrative in *Passing* is not a first-person narrative, Irene's perspective dominates. Rewrite a scene of your choice from Clare's perspective. Possibilities include the women's first meeting at the Drayton Hotel, one of the parties in New York City, or a "lost scene" in which Clare meditates on who Irene really is.
12. **Connections.** In 2015 Rachel Dolezal, a white woman posing as a Black woman, was exposed. At the time, Dolezal was president of the Spokane Washington chapter of the National Association for the Advancement of Colored People (NAACP) and an instructor of Africana Studies at a local college. Look up more information about her case, especially the public outcry against her; you might view the documentary *The Rachel Divide* as part of your

inquiry. Discuss why Dolezal's deception is not analogous to Clare's decision to pass, or to the general phenomenon of Black people choosing to pass as white. Consider, in your discussion, the larger social contexts in both scenarios and how they contribute to a deeper understanding.

13. **Connections.** African American historian and intellectual W. E. B. DuBois, an enormously influential figure in the Harlem Renaissance, famously described the concept of "double consciousness" in his seminal nonfiction work *The Souls of Black Folk* (1903):

    > [T]he Negro is a sort of seventh son, born with a veil, and gifted with second-sight in this American world, — a world which yields him no self-consciousness, but only lets him see himself through the revelation of the other world. It is a peculiar sensation, this double-consciousness, this sense of always looking at one's self through the eyes of others, of measuring one's soul by the tape of a world that looks on in amused contempt and pity. One feels his two-ness, — an American, a Negro; two souls, two thoughts, two unreconciled strivings; two warring ideals in one dark body, whose dogged strength alone keeps it from being torn asunder.

    How is this definition of "double-consciousness" embodied in Larsen's novel? How might Larsen's characters, in their experiences as Black women, be seen to exemplify what is known today as a "triple consciousness"?

14. **Connections.** In 2018, Chemeketa Press reissued an edition of *Passing* with an introduction by Matthew Hodgson, an English professor who described finding this personal connection to Larsen's novel when he read it as a college student:

    > I finally understood that Clare and Irene's racial passing . . . was not only a matter of gaining privilege: it was a matter of survival . . . [and] not only about race. Passing . . . can be a means of causing the least amount of tension. . . . [M]y own passing as heterosexual in my strictly Lutheran family was an attempt to avoid conflict. . . . This discomfort with one's identity was painfully familiar territory.

    To what extent do you believe that racial passing, as we see it in Larsen's novel, is analogous to other situations, such as Hodgson's?

15. **Connections.** Films about racial passing were popular during the Jim Crow era, particularly in the 1930s through the 1950s. Several versions of the film *Imitation of Life* were made. In this film, a young Black woman rejects her mother to pass as white and comes to regret it when her mother dies — in essence, she is "punished" for her "transgression." To what extent does Larsen's novel subvert or challenge this perspective on the reasons for, and costs of, racial passing?

16. **Connections.** In his 1955 essay "Notes of a Native Son," James Baldwin wrote:

    > Our passion for categorization, life neatly fitted into pegs, has led to unforeseen, paradoxical distress; confusion, a breakdown of meaning. Those categories which are meant to define and control the world for us have boomeranged into chaos; in which limbo we swirl, clutching the straws of our definitions. We found ourselves bound, first without, then within, by the nature of our categorization.

    In what ways does Baldwin's view of "categorization" here illuminate the complexities that Larsen explores in *Passing*? How might his statement relate to the conflicts and polarization in today's society?

17. **Connections.** In *The Great Gatsby*, another novel from the 1920s, the character of Jay Gatz "passes": a Midwestern farm boy, he changes his name to Jay Gatsby, falsifies information including that he went to "Oggsford" (as in Oxford in England), and generally presents himself as a member of the educated, affluent elite. In what ways are Clare and Gatz/Gatsby similar in their motivation to move between identities? In what ways are their circumstances very different? What similar themes do F. Scott Fitzgerald, author of *The Great Gatsby*, and Nella Larsen explore in these novels?

Hamlet, Prince of Denmark

William Shakespeare

William Shakespeare (1564–1616) was born in Stratford-upon-Avon, England. Little is known of his life aside from the fact that he married Anne Hathaway when he was eighteen, worked as an actor-playwright in London, and retired in 1613. Thirty-eight plays, including *Romeo and Juliet* (1597), *Hamlet* (1601), *Othello* (1604), *King Lear* (1605), and *Macbeth* (1606), are attributed to him. In his time, his contemporaries — and likely Shakespeare himself — looked to his sonnets and other poems as the more important works. *Hamlet* is Shakespeare's most famous work, and is regarded by many to be his finest. It has been performed, adapted, and studied more than any other play in the English language.

List of Characters

HAMLET *Prince of Denmark*
CLAUDIUS *King of Denmark, Hamlet's uncle*
GERTRUDE *Queen of Denmark, Hamlet's mother*
GHOST *of Hamlet's father, the former King of Denmark*
POLONIUS *counsellor to the king*
LAERTES *his son*
OPHELIA *his daughter*
REYNALDO *his servant*
HORATIO *Hamlet's friend and fellow-student*
MARCELLUS, **BARNARDO**, **FRANCISCO** } *officers of the watch*
VOLTEMAND, **CORNELIUS** } *ambassadors to Norway*
ROSENCRANTZ, **GUILDENSTERN** } *former schoolfellows of Hamlet*
FORTINBRAS *Prince of Norway*
CAPTAIN *in the Norwegian army*
FIRST PLAYER
OTHER PLAYERS
OSRIC, **LORD**, **GENTLEMAN** } *courtiers*
FIRST CLOWN *a gravedigger and sexton*
SECOND CLOWN *his assistant*
SAILOR
MESSENGER
PRIEST
ENGLISH AMBASSADOR
LORDS, ATTENDANTS, SAILORS, SOLDIERS, GUARDS

Act I, Scene i

Enter BARNARDO *and* FRANCISCO, *two sentinels*

BARNARDO Who's there?

FRANCISCO Nay answer me. Stand and unfold yourself.°

BARNARDO Long live the king!

FRANCISCO Barnardo?

BARNARDO He.

FRANCISCO You come most carefully upon your hour.

Act 1, Scene i. 2. **unfold yourself:** reveal who you are.

BARNARDO 'Tis now struck twelve, get thee to bed Francisco.
FRANCISCO For this relief much thanks, 'tis bitter cold
And I am sick at heart.
BARNARDO Have you had quiet guard?
FRANCISCO Not a mouse stirring.
BARNARDO Well, good night.
If you do meet Horatio and Marcellus,
The rivals° of my watch, bid them make haste.
FRANCISCO I think I hear them.

Enter HORATIO *and* MARCELLUS

Stand ho! Who is there?
HORATIO Friends to this ground.°
MARCELLUS And liegemen° to the Dane.°
FRANCISCO Give you good night.
MARCELLUS Oh farewell honest soldier,
Who hath relieved you?
FRANCISCO Barnardo hath my place.
Give° you good night. *Exit Francisco*
MARCELLUS Holla, Barnardo!
BARNARDO Say,
What, is Horatio there?
HORATIO A piece of him.°
BARNARDO Welcome Horatio, welcome good Marcellus.
MARCELLUS What, has this thing° appeared again tonight?
BARNARDO I have seen nothing.
MARCELLUS Horatio says 'tis but our fantasy,°
And will not let belief take hold of him
Touching this dreaded° sight, twice seen of us.
Therefore I have entreated him along°
With us to watch the minutes of this night,°
That if again this apparition come
He may approve our eyes,° and speak to it.
HORATIO Tush, tush, 'twill not appear.
BARNARDO Sit down awhile,
And let us once again assail your ears,
That are so fortified against our story,
What° we two nights have seen.
HORATIO Well, sit we down,
And let us hear Barnardo speak of this.
BARNARDO Last night of all,
When yond same star that's westward from the pole°
Had made his course t' illume° that part of heaven
Where now it burns, Marcellus and myself,
The bell then beating° one—

Enter GHOST

MARCELLUS Peace, break thee off. Look where it comes again.
BARNARDO In the same figure,° like the king that's dead.
MARCELLUS Thou art a scholar,° speak to it Horatio.
BARNARDO Looks a° not like the king? Mark it Horatio.
HORATIO Most like. It harrows° me with fear and wonder.
BARNARDO It would be spoke to.
MARCELLUS Question it Horatio.
HORATIO What art thou that usurp'st° this time of night,
Together with° that fair and warlike form
In which the majesty of buried Denmark°
Did sometimes° march? By heaven I charge thee speak.
MARCELLUS It is offended.
BARNARDO See, it stalks° away.
HORATIO Stay! Speak, speak, I charge thee speak!
Exit Ghost
MARCELLUS 'Tis gone and will not answer.
BARNARDO How now Horatio? you tremble and look pale.
Is not this something more than fantasy?
What think you on't?

---

13. **rivals:** partners. 15. **ground:** territory, country. 15. **liegemen:** sworn followers. 15. **the Dane:** the Danish king. 18. **Give:** i.e., God give. 19. **A piece of him:** He is so cold he is not wholly himself. 21. **thing:** creature (without implying contempt). 23. **fantasy:** imagination. 25. **dreaded:** awful, fearsome. 26. **along:** to come along. 27. **watch the minutes of this night:** keep watch for the period of this night. 29. **approve our eyes:** confirm that we saw correctly. 33. **What:** with what (following "assail"). 36. **pole:** pole star. 37. **t'illume:** to illuminate. 39. **beating:** striking. 41. **figure:** shape, form. 42. **scholar:** Horatio is learned enough to know how to address a spirit. 43. **a:** he. 44. **harrows:** deeply disturbs (breaks up with a harrow). 46. **usurp'st:** wrongfully takes over. 47. **Together with:** The spirit is also appropriating the form of the old king. 48. **buried Denmark:** the dead king of Denmark. 49. **sometimes:** formerly. 50. **stalks:** moves with a stately stride.

HORATIO Before my God, I might not this believe
Without the sensible° and true avouch°
Of mine own eyes.
MARCELLUS Is it not like the king?
HORATIO As thou art to thyself.
Such was the very armour he had on
When he th' ambitious Norway° combated;
So frowned he once, when in an angry parle°
He smote the sledded Polacks° on the ice.
'Tis strange.
MARCELLUS Thus twice before, and jump° at this dead hour,
With martial stalk hath he gone by our watch.
HORATIO In what particular thought to work I know not,
But in the gross and scope of mine opinion°
This bodes some strange eruption to our state.
MARCELLUS Good now° sit down, and tell me he that knows,
Why this same strict and most observant watch
So nightly toils° the subject of the land,
And why such daily cast of brazen cannon,
And foreign mart° for implements of war,
Why such impress° of shipwrights, whose sore task
Does not divide the Sunday from the week.
What might be toward,° that this sweaty haste
Doth make the night joint-labourer with the day?
Who is't that can inform me?
HORATIO That can I—
At least the whisper goes so. Our last king,
Whose image even but now appeared to us,
Was as you know by Fortinbras of Norway,
Thereto pricked on by a most emulate pride,°
Dared to the combat; in which our valiant Hamlet—
For so this side of our known world esteemed him—
Did slay this Fortinbras; who by a sealed° compact,
Well ratified by law and heraldy,°
Did forfeit (with his life) all those his lands
Which he stood seized of,° to the conqueror;
Against the which a moiety competent°
Was gagèd by our king, which had returned
To the inheritance of Fortinbras
Had he been vanquisher; as by the same comart
And carriage of the article design,°
His fell to Hamlet. Now sir, young Fortinbras,
Of unimprovèd mettle° hot and full,
Hath in the skirts of Norway here and there
Sharked up° a list° of landless° resolutes
For food and diet to some enterprise
That hath a stomach in't;° which is no other,
As it doth well appear unto our state,°
But to recover of us by strong hand
And terms compulsatory those foresaid lands
So by his father lost. And this, I take it,
Is the main motive of our preparations,
The source of this our watch, and the chief head
Of this post-haste and romage° in the land.
[**BARNARDO** I think it be no other but e'en so.
Well may it sort° that this portentous figure
Comes armèd through our watch so like the king
That was and is the question° of these wars.
HORATIO A mote it is to trouble the mind's eye.°
In the most high and palmy° state of Rome,

57. **sensible:** sensory. 57. **avouch:** warrant. 61. **Norway:** King of Norway. 62. **parle:** parley; properly a conference during a truce, but here seemingly used to mean an altercation leading to violence. 63. **sledded Polacks:** It is a celebrated question whether he is speaking of a poleaxe (often spelled "pollax") or Polacks (i.e., Poles). It seems more likely that Horatio is talking of two encounters, one with Norwegians and one with Poles. In the second, in a confrontation or after an angry exchange, he routed the Poles in their sledges. 65. **jump:** precisely. 67–68. **In what particular . . . opinion:** i.e., I don't know in which particular area to concentrate my thoughts (in order to explain this), but, taking a wide view, so far as I can judge . . . 70. **Good now:** please you. 72. **toils:** wearies with toil. 74. **foreign mart:** bargaining abroad. 75. **impress:** conscription. 77. **toward:** in preparation, afoot. 83. **emulate pride:** a sense of self-esteem that made him strive to equal and outdo others. 86. **sealed:** i.e., agreed, confirmed. 87. **ratified by law and heraldy:** sanctioned by law and the code of chivalry. 89. **stood seized of:** was the legal owner of (i.e., his personal estates were the forfeit, not his dominions as king). 90. **moiety competent:** adequate portion. 91. **gagèd:** pledged. 93–94. **as by . . . article design:** as by the same compact and the intention of the agreement drawn up. 96. **unimprovèd mettle:** undisciplined spirit. 98. **Sharked up:** gathered together indiscriminately, like a shark swallowing its prey. 98. **list:** an assemblage or band of soldiers. 98. **landless:** The idea here is not of an army of criminals but of disinherited gentry and younger sons who have nothing better to do. 99–100. **For food . . . stomach in't:** The resolutes are prepared to enlist in return for their keep only, because they are attracted to an adventurous enterprise; "diet" refers to diet-money, living expenses. The enterprise has "stomach" in two senses: it provides the resolutes with their real nourishment, and it is bold and spirited. 101. **our state:** the Danish government. 107. **romage:** commotion and bustle, especially with relation to loading a ship's cargo. 109. **sort:** be accordant with (Horatio's explanation). 111. **question:** cause of dispute. 112. **A mote . . . eye:** Like an irritant in the eye, it disturbs and perplexes the mind, which cannot see ahead clearly. 113. **palmy:** triumphant.

A little ere the mightiest Julius fell,
The graves stood tenantless and the sheeted dead
Did squeak and gibber° in the Roman streets;
As stars with trains of fire, and dews of blood,
Disasters° in the sun; and the moist star,°
Upon whose influence Neptune's empire stands,
Was sick almost to doomsday° with eclipse.
And even the like precurse° of feared events,
As harbingers° preceding still the fates
And prologue to the omen° coming on,
Have heaven and earth together demonstrated
Unto our climatures° and countrymen.]

Enter GHOST

But soft,° behold, lo where it comes again!
I'll cross it° though it blast me. Stay, illusion.

It spreads his arms°

If thou hast any sound or use of voice,
Speak to me.
If there be any good thing to be done
That may to thee do ease, and grace to me,
Speak to me.
If thou art privy to thy country's fate,
Which happily° foreknowing may avoid,
Oh speak.
Or if thou hast uphoarded° in thy life
Extorted° treasure in the womb of earth,
For which they say you spirits oft walk in death,

The cock crows

Speak of it. Stay and speak! Stop it Marcellus.

MARCELLUS Shall I strike at it with my partisan?°

HORATIO Do if it will not stand.

BARNARDO 'Tis here.

HORATIO 'Tis here.

MARCELLUS 'Tis gone.

Exit Ghost

We do it wrong being so majestical°
To offer it the show of violence,
For it is as the air invulnerable,
And our vain blows malicious mockery.°

BARNARDO It was about to speak when the cock crew.

HORATIO And then it started like a guilty thing
Upon a fearful summons. I have heard,
The cock, that is the trumpet° to the morn,
Doth with his lofty and shrill-sounding throat
Awake the god of day;° and at his warning,
Whether in sea or fire, in earth or air,
Th'extravagant and erring° spirit hies
To his confine.° And of the truth herein
This present object made probation.°

MARCELLUS It faded on the crowing of the cock.
Some say that ever 'gainst° that season comes
Wherein our Saviour's birth is celebrated,
This bird of dawning singeth all night long,
And then, they say, no spirit dare stir abroad,
The nights are wholesome, then no planets strike,°
No fairy takes,° nor witch hath power to charm,
So hallowed and so gracious° is that time.

HORATIO So have I heard, and do in part believe it.
But look, the morn° in russet° mantle clad
Walks o'er the dew of yon high eastward hill.
Break we our watch up, and by my advice
Let us impart what we have seen tonight
Unto young Hamlet, for upon my life
This spirit, dumb to us, will speak to him.
Do you consent we shall acquaint him with it,
As needful in our loves, fitting our duty?

MARCELLUS Let's do't I pray, and I this morning know
Where we shall find him most conveniently.

Exeunt

---

116. **gibber:** utter inarticulate sounds. 118. **Disasters:** portents of disaster. 118. **the moist star:** the moon. 120. **almost to doomsday:** almost as if it were the day of judgment. 121. **precurse:** advance warning. 122. **harbingers:** officials who went ahead of the king to announce his approach. 123. **omen:** used here for the calamity itself. 125. **climatures:** regions. 126. **soft:** enough! 127. **cross it:** cross its path. 127. **sd *It spreads his* arms:** "His" for "its" is normal in Shakespeare. 134. **happily:** haply, perhaps. 136. **uphoarded:** hoarded up. 137. **Extorted:** obtained by unfair means. 140. **partisan:** a long-handled weapon combining spear and axe. 143. **being so majestical:** since it has such majesty. Marcellus gives two separate reasons why they are wrong to offer violence: (1.) the majesty of the Ghost, (2.) its invulnerability. 146. **malicious mockery:** a mockery of the malice we intend. 150. **trumpet:** trumpeter. 152. **the god of day:** Phoebus Apollo. 154. **extravagant and erring:** wandering beyond bounds. 155. **confine:** (1.) one's own special territory, (2.) a place of confinement. 156. **probation:** proof. 158. **'gainst:** just before. 162. **strike:** i.e., affect with their malign influence. 163. **takes:** attacks, lays hold. 164. **gracious:** full of grace. 166. **the morn:** In a few minutes of acting time, we have moved from deepest midnight to the dawn. 166. **russet:** reddish-brown.

Flourish. Enter CLAUDIUS *King of Denmark,* GERTRUDE *the Queen,* HAMLET, POLONIUS, LAERTES, OPHELIA, [VOLTEMAND, CORNELIUS,] LORDS *attendant*

CLAUDIUS Though yet of Hamlet our dear brother's death
The memory be green, and that it us befitted
To bear our hearts in grief, and our whole kingdom
To be contracted in one brow of woe,°
Yet so far hath discretion fought with nature
That we with wisest sorrow think on him,
Together with remembrance of ourselves.°
Therefore our sometime sister, now our queen,
Th'imperial jointress° to this warlike state,
Have we, as 'twere with a defeated joy,
With one auspicious° and one dropping° eye,
With mirth in funeral and with dirge in marriage,
In equal scale weighing delight and dole,°
Taken to wife; nor have we herein barred
Your better wisdoms,° which have freely gone
With this affair along—for all, our thanks.
Now follows that you know:° young Fortinbras,
Holding a weak supposal° of our worth,
Or thinking by our late dear brother's death
Our state to be disjoint and out of frame,
Colleaguèd with this dream of his advantage,°
He hath not failed to pester us with message
Importing the surrender of those lands
Lost by his father, with all bands° of law,
To our most valiant brother. So much for him.
Now for ourself and for this time of meeting
Thus much the business is: we have here writ
To Norway, uncle of young Fortinbras,
Who, impotent° and bed-rid, scarcely hears
Of this his nephew's purpose, to suppress
His further gait° herein, in that the levies,
The lists, and full proportions,° are all made
Out of his subject;° and we here dispatch
You, good Cornelius, and you, Voltemand,
For bearers of this greeting to old Norway,
Giving to you no further personal power
To business with the king, more than the scope
Of these dilated° articles allow.
Farewell, and let your haste commend your duty.

CORNELIUS, VOLTEMAND In that and all things will we show our duty.

CLAUDIUS We doubt it nothing, heartily farewell.

Exeunt Voltemand and Cornelius

And now Laertes, what's the news with you?
You told us of some suit, what is't Laertes?
You cannot speak of reason to the Dane°
And lose your voice.° What wouldst thou beg Laertes,
That shall not be my offer, not thy asking?°
The head is not more native° to the heart,
The hand more instrumental to the mouth,
Than is the throne of Denmark to thy father.
What wouldst thou have Laertes?

LAERTES My dread lord,
Your leave and favour° to return to France,
From whence though willingly I came to Denmark
To show my duty in your coronation,
Yet now I must confess, that duty done,
My thoughts and wishes bend again toward France,
And bow them to your gracious leave and pardon.°

CLAUDIUS Have you your father's leave? What says Polonius?

POLONIUS He hath my lord wrung from me my slow leave
By laboursome petition, and at last
Upon his will I sealed my hard consent.
I do beseech you give him leave to go.

Act I, Scene ii. 4. **contracted in one brow of woe:** drawn together in a single mourning visage. 7. **Together with remembrance of ourselves:** being also mindful of ourselves. 9. **jointress:** a wife who shares property with her husband and continues her rights in it after his death. 11. **auspicious:** looking happily to the future. 11. **dropping:** cast down with grief or, possibly, dropping tears. 13. **dole:** grief. 15. **Your better wisdoms:** your excellent wisdoms or, perhaps, the best fruits of your wisdoms. 17. **that you know:** what you already know. 18. **supposal:** supposition, conjecture. 21. **Colleaguèd . . . advantage:** having as an ally only this illusion of a favorable opportunity. 24. **bands:** agreements binding a person. 29. **impotent:** helpless, incapacitated. 31. **gait:** i.e., proceedings. 32. **proportions:** given numbers of troops raised for specific purposes. 33. **his subject:** those who are subject to him. 38. **dilated:** amply expressed. 44. **the Dane:** the Danish king. 45. **lose your voice:** speak to no avail. 46. **not thy asking:** rather than thy asking. 47. **native:** naturally related. 51. **Your leave and favour:** the favor of your permission. 56. **pardon:** permission. 60. **Upon . . . consent:** I gave my reluctant agreement to his strong wish. "Sealed" suggests official or legal approval.

CLAUDIUS Take thy fair hour Laertes, time be thine,
And thy best graces spend it at thy will.°
But now my cousin Hamlet, and my son —
HAMLET (*Aside*) A little more than kin, and less than kind.°
CLAUDIUS How is it that the clouds still hang on you?
HAMLET Not so my lord, I am too much i'th'sun.
GERTRUDE Good Hamlet cast thy nighted colour° off,
And let thine eye look like a friend on Denmark.°
Do not forever with thy vailèd lids°
Seek for thy noble father in the dust.
Thou know'st 'tis common, all that lives must die,
Passing through nature to eternity.
HAMLET Ay madam, it is common.
GERTRUDE If it be,
Why seems it so particular with thee?
HAMLET Seems madam? nay it is, I know not seems.
'Tis not alone my inky cloak, good mother,
Nor customary° suits of solemn black,
Nor windy suspiration° of forced breath,
No, nor the fruitful river in the eye,
Nor the dejected haviour of the visage,
Together with all forms, moods,° shapes° of grief,
That can denote me truly. These indeed seem,
For they are actions that a man might play,
But I have that within which passes show —
These but the trappings and the suits of woe.
CLAUDIUS 'Tis sweet and commendable in your nature Hamlet,
To give these mourning duties to your father;
But you must know, your father lost a father,
That father lost, lost his, and the survivor bound
In filial obligation for some term
To do obsequious sorrow; but to persever
In obstinate condolement° is a course
Of impious stubbornness, 'tis unmanly grief,
It shows a will most incorrect to heaven,°
A heart unfortified, a mind impatient,
An understanding simple and unschooled.
For what we know must be, and is as common
As any the most vulgar thing to sense,°
Why should we in our peevish opposition
Take it to heart? Fie, 'tis a fault° to heaven,
A fault against the dead, a fault to nature,
To reason most absurd, whose common theme
Is death of fathers, and who still hath cried,
From the first corse° till he that died today,
"This must be so." We pray you throw to earth
This unprevailing° woe, and think of us
As of a father, for let the world take note
You are the most immediate to our throne,°
And with no less nobility of love
Than that which dearest father bears his son,
Do I impart toward you.° For your intent
In going back to school in Wittenberg,°
It is most retrograde° to our desire,
And we beseech you bend you° to remain
Here in the cheer and comfort of our eye,
Our chiefest courtier, cousin, and our son.
GERTRUDE Let not thy mother lose her prayers Hamlet.
I pray thee stay with us, go not to Wittenberg.
HAMLET I shall in all my best obey you madam.
CLAUDIUS Why, 'tis a loving and a fair reply.
Be as ourself in Denmark. Madam, come.
This gentle and unforced accord of Hamlet
Sits smiling to my heart, in grace whereof,
No jocund health that Denmark° drinks today
But the great cannon to the clouds shall tell,
And the king's rouse° the heaven shall bruit° again,
Re-speaking earthly thunder. Come away.
Flourish. Exeunt all but Hamlet

---

63. **thy best . . . will:** Claudius hopes that in enjoying himself Laertes will be exercising his best qualities. 65. **A little . . . kind:** To call me "son" is more than our actual kinship warrants, and there is less than the natural feelings of such a relationship between us. There is a play on the two meanings of "kind": (1.) belonging to nature; (2.) affectionate, benevolent. 68. **nighted colour:** i.e., the darkness of both clothes and mood. 69. **Denmark:** the king. 70. **vailèd lids:** lowered eyes. 78. **customary:** conventional. 79. **suspiration:** sighing. 82. **moods:** emotional states as outwardly displayed. 82. **shapes:** external appearances. 93. **condolement:** grief. 95. **incorrect to heaven:** improperly directed as regards heaven. 99. **As . . . sense:** as the most ordinary thing that affects our senses. 101–02. **fault:** wrongdoing, transgression. 105. **the first corse:** i.e., the first corpse, Abel, murdered by his brother Cain. 107. **unprevailing:** that can gain nothing. 109. **the most immediate to our throne:** i.e., the next in succession. The monarchy being elective, not hereditary, Claudius, the most important member of an electoral college, here gives his "voice" (vote) to Hamlet as his heir. 112. **impart toward you:** convey (this gift of my vote) to you. 113. **to school in Wittenberg:** to be educated at the university in Wittenberg. 114. **retrograde:** contrary. 115. **bend you:** to incline yourself. 125. **Denmark:** Once again, the king is meant. 127. **rouse:** ceremonial drink or toast. 127. **bruit:** loudly proclaim (echoing the cannon).

HAMLET O that this too too solid flesh would melt,
Thaw and resolve itself into a dew,
Or that the Everlasting had not fixed
His canon 'gainst self-slaughter.° O God, God,
How weary, stale, flat° and unprofitable
Seem to me all the uses° of this world!
Fie on't, ah fie, 'tis an unweeded garden
That grows to seed, things rank and gross in nature
Possess it merely.° That it should come to this!
But two months dead — nay not so much, not two —
So excellent a king, that was to this
Hyperion° to a satyr,° so loving to my mother
That he might not beteem° the winds of heaven
Visit her face too roughly — heaven and earth,
Must I remember? why, she would hang on him
As if increase of appetite had grown
By what it fed on, and yet within a month —
Let me not think on't; frailty, thy name is woman —
A little month, or ere° those shoes were old°
With which she followed my poor father's body
Like Niobe,° all tears, why she, even she —
O God, a beast that wants discourse of reason°
Would have mourned longer — married with my uncle,
My father's brother, but no more like my father
Than I to Hercules — within a month,
Ere yet the salt of most unrighteous tears
Had left the flushing in her gallèd eyes,°
She married. Oh most wicked speed, to post
With such dexterity to incestuous° sheets.
It is not, nor it cannot come to good.
But break, my heart,° for I must hold my tongue.

Enter HORATIO, MARCELLUS *and* BARNARDO

HORATIO Hail to your lordship.

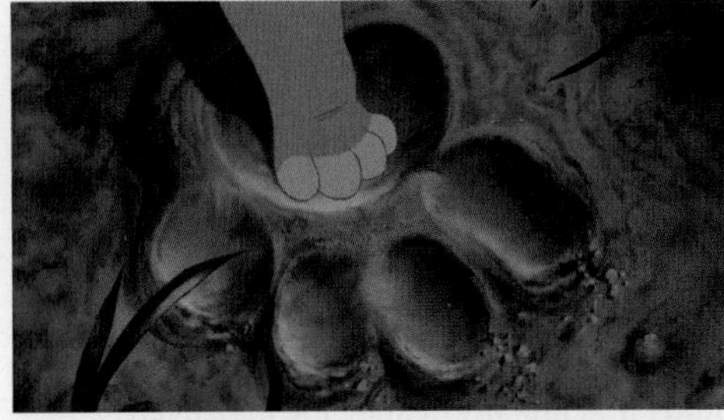

This image is from Disney's 1994 film *The Lion King*, which shares many similarities with Shakespeare's *Hamlet*. Here, young Simba has disappointed his father, King Mufasa, and measures his pawprint against that of the king. **What might this image suggest about Simba's attitude toward his father? How does it relate to Hamlet's perception of his father and of himself?**

HAMLET I am glad to see you well.°
Horatio — or I do forget myself.

HORATIO The same, my lord, and your poor servant ever.

HAMLET Sir, my good friend, I'll change° that name° with you.
And what make you from Wittenberg, Horatio?
Marcellus.

MARCELLUS My good lord.

HAMLET I am very glad to see you. (*To Barnardo*) Good even sir.
But what in faith make you from Wittenberg.

HORATIO A truant disposition, good my lord.

HAMLET I would not hear your enemy say so,
Nor shall you do my ear that violence
To make it truster of your own report
Against yourself. I know you are no truant.
But what is your affair in Elsinore?
We'll teach you to drink deep ere you depart.

129–32. **too solid . . . self-slaughter:** Hamlet's lament is that his flesh is too solid to melt away, and that he is forbidden by God to do away with himself. 133. **flat:** lifeless, spiritless. 134. **uses:** customary doings. 137. **merely:** absolutely. 140. **Hyperion:** one of the Titans of Greek mythology, frequently identified, as here, as the sun god. 140. **satyr:** grotesque creature, half-human but with the legs of a goat, attendant on Dionysus and synonymous with lechery. 141. **beteem:** allow. 147. **or ere:** even before. 147. **those shoes were old:** His mother had worn new shoes for her husband's funeral, and they were still as good as new for her marriage to Claudius. 149. **Niobe:** the mythical mother whose fourteen children were slain by the gods because she boasted about them; she wept until she was turned to stone — and still the tears flowed. 150. **discourse of reason:** faculty of reasoning. 155. **left . . . eyes:** (1.) gone from the redness of her sore eyes, (2.) ceased flowing in her sore eyes. 157. **incestuous:** Marriage to a brother's wife was explicitly forbidden by the Church. 159. **break, my heart:** i.e., with unuttered grief. The heart was thought to be kept in place by ligaments or tendons (the heartstrings) which might snap under the pressure of great emotion. 160. **I . . . well:** He has not yet recognized Horatio. 163. **change:** exchange. 163. **that name:** i.e., "good friend."

HORATIO My lord, I came to see your father's
funeral.
HAMLET I pray thee do not mock me fellow student,
I think it was to see my mother's wedding.
HORATIO Indeed my lord, it followed hard upon.
HAMLET Thrift, thrift, Horatio. The funeral baked
meats
Did coldly° furnish forth the marriage tables.
Would I had met my dearest foe in heaven
Or ever I had seen that day, Horatio.
My father, methinks I see my father —
HORATIO Where my lord?
HAMLET In my mind's eye, Horatio.
HORATIO I saw him once, a was a goodly king.
HAMLET A was a man, take him for all in all.
I shall not look upon his like again.
HORATIO My lord, I think I saw him yesternight.
HAMLET Saw? Who?
HORATIO My lord, the king your father.
HAMLET The king
my father!
HORATIO Season° your admiration° for a while
With an attent° ear, till I may deliver
Upon the witness of these gentlemen
This marvel to you.
HAMLET For God's love let me hear.
HORATIO Two nights together had these gentlemen,
Marcellus and Barnardo, on their watch
In the dead waste° and middle of the night,
Been thus encountered. A figure like your father,
Armèd at point exactly, cap-a-pe,°
Appears before them, and with solemn march
Goes slow and stately by them. Thrice he
walked
By their oppressed and fear-surprisèd eyes
Within his truncheon's length, whilst they,
distilled°
Almost to jelly with the act° of fear,
Stand dumb and speak not to him. This to me
In dreadful° secrecy impart they did,
And I with them the third night kept the watch,
Where, as they had delivered, both in time,
Form of the thing, each word made true and
good,
The apparition comes. I knew your father,
These hands are not more like.
HAMLET But where was this?
MARCELLUS My lord, upon the platform where
we watched.°
HAMLET Did you not speak to it?
HORATIO My lord, I did,
But answer made it none. Yet once methought
It lifted up it head° and did address
Itself to motion like as it would speak;°
But even then the morning cock crew loud,
And at the sound it shrunk in haste away
And vanished from our sight.
HAMLET 'Tis very strange.
HORATIO As I do live my honoured lord 'tis true,
And we did think it writ down in our duty
To let you know of it.
HAMLET Indeed, indeed sirs, but this troubles me.
Hold you the watch tonight?
MARCELLUS, **BARNARDO** We do, my lord.
HAMLET Armed say you?
MARCELLUS, **BARNARDO** Armed my lord.
HAMLET From top
to toe?
MARCELLUS, **BARNARDO** My lord, from head to foot.
HAMLET Then saw you not his face?
HORATIO Oh yes my lord, he wore his beaver° up.
HAMLET What, looked he frowningly?
HORATIO A countenance more in sorrow than in
anger.
HAMLET Pale, or red?
HORATIO Nay very pale.
HAMLET And fixed his eyes upon you?
HORATIO Most constantly.
HAMLET I would I had been there.
HORATIO It would have much amazed° you.
HAMLET Very like, very like. Stayed it long?

181. **coldly:** The remains of the pies baked for the funeral were economically served cold for the wedding feast. 192. **Season:** make more temperate, restrain. 192. **admiration:** wonder. 193. **attent:** attentive. 198. **waste:** The desolation of "dead waste" is surely what is required here, though the latent pun "waist" no doubt suggested "middle." 200. **at point exactly, cap-a-pe:** properly and correctly, from head to foot. 204. **distilled:** dissolved. 205. **act:** action. 207. **dreadful:** awe-struck (referring to their manner) rather than solemn (referring to the secrecy). 213. **watched:** were on watch. 216. **it head:** its head. 216–17. **address . . . speak:** started to move as though it were about to speak. 229. **beaver:** the movable visor. 235. **amazed:** bewildered, thrown into confusion.

Hamlet ye Dane: A Ghost Story programme (colour litho), English School, (19th century) / Private Collection / © Look and Learn / Peter Jackson Collection / Bridgeman Images

Shown here is the cover of a nineteenth-century English production program booklet for *Hamlet ye Dane: A Ghost Story*.

What is the relationship between the image and the title on this booklet cover? How is Hamlet portrayed here?

HORATIO While one with moderate haste might
tell a hundred.

MARCELLUS
BARNARDO } Longer, longer.

HORATIO Not when I saw 't.

HAMLET His beard was
grizzled, no?

HORATIO It was as I have seen it in his life,
A sable silvered.°

HAMLET I will watch tonight,
Perchance 'twill walk again.

HORATIO I warrant it will.

HAMLET If it assume° my noble father's person,
I'll speak to it though hell itself should gape°
And bid me hold my peace. I pray you all,
If you have hitherto concealed this sight,
Let it be tenable° in your silence still,
And whatsomever° else shall hap tonight,
Give it an understanding but no tongue.
I will requite your loves. So fare you well:
Upon the platform 'twixt eleven and twelve
I'll visit you.

ALL Our duty to your honour.

HAMLET Your loves, as mine to you. Farewell.
Exeunt all but Hamlet
My father's spirit, in arms! All is not well.
I doubt° some foul play. Would the night were
come.
Till then sit still my soul. Foul deeds will rise
Though all the earth o'erwhelm them to men's
eyes. *Exit*

Act I, Scene iii

Enter LAERTES *and* OPHELIA *his sister*

LAERTES My necessaries are embarked, farewell.
And sister, as the winds give benefit
And convoy is assistant,° do not sleep
But let me hear from you.

OPHELIA Do you doubt that?

LAERTES For Hamlet, and the trifling of his favour,
Hold it a fashion,° and a toy in blood,°
A violet in the youth of primy nature,°
Forward, not permanent, sweet, not lasting,
The perfume and suppliance° of a minute,
No more.

OPHELIA No more but so?

LAERTES Think it no more.
For nature crescent does not grow alone
In thews and bulk, but as this temple waxes
The inward service of the mind and soul
Grows wide withal.° Perhaps he loves you now,

241. **sable silvered:** black touched with white. 243. **assume:** take on. Hamlet thinks of the apparition as a spirit appearing in the guise of his father, though a few lines later he speaks of "my father's spirit" (254.). 244. **hell itself should gape:** the mouth of hell should open wide. 247. **tenable:** something that can be held. 248. **whatsomever:** a quite regular form, eventually replaced by "whatsoever." 255. **doubt:** suspect.

Act I, Scene iii. 3. **convoy is assistant:** conveyance is at hand. 6. **a fashion:** just a way of behaving. 6. **a toy in blood:** a whim of passion. 7. **the youth . . . nature:** the springtime of life. 9. **suppliance:** supply (i.e., the violet serves for a minute only). 11–14. **For nature . . . withal:** Growing up is not a matter of physical size only: while the body grows, the inner life of mind and soul develops also. "Thews" are sinews.

And now no soil° nor cautel° doth besmirch
The virtue of his will; but you must fear,
His greatness weighed,° his will is not his own,
For he himself is subject to his birth.
He may not, as unvalued persons do,
Carve for himself,° for on his choice depends
The sanctity° and health of this whole state,
And therefore must his choice be circumscribed
Unto the voice and yielding° of that body
Whereof he is the head. Then if he says he loves you,
It fits your wisdom so far to believe it
As he in his peculiar sect and force°
May give his saying deed, which is no further
Than the main voice° of Denmark goes withal.
Then weigh what loss your honour may sustain
If with too credent° ear you list° his songs,
Or lose your heart, or your chaste treasure° open
To his unmastered importunity.
Fear it Ophelia, fear it my dear sister,
And keep you in the rear of your affection,°
Out of the shot° and danger of desire.
The chariest maid is prodigal enough
If she unmask her beauty to the moon.°
Virtue itself scapes not calumnious strokes.
The canker° galls the infants of the spring°
Too oft before their buttons be disclosed,°
And in the morn and liquid dew of youth
Contagious blastments° are most imminent.
Be wary then, best safety lies in fear:
Youth to itself rebels,° though none else near.

OPHELIA I shall th'effect of this good lesson keep
As watchman to my heart. But good my brother,
Do not as some ungracious pastors do,
Show me the steep and thorny way to heaven,
Whiles like a puffed and reckless libertine
Himself the primrose path of dalliance treads,
And recks not his own rede.°

LAERTES Oh fear me not.

Enter POLONIUS

I stay too long—But here my father comes.
A double blessing is a double grace;
Occasion smiles upon a second leave.°

POLONIUS Yet here Laertes? Aboard, aboard for shame!
The wind sits in the shoulder of your sail,
And you are stayed for. There, my blessing with thee,
And these few precepts in thy memory
Look thou character.° Give thy thoughts no tongue,
Nor any unproportioned thought his act.
Be thou familiar, but by no means vulgar.°
Those friends thou hast, and their adoption tried,°
Grapple them unto thy soul with hoops of steel,
But do not dull thy palm° with entertainment
Of each new-hatched, unfledged courage. Beware
Of entrance to a quarrel, but being in,
Bear't that° th'opposèd may beware of thee.
Give every man thy ear, but few thy voice;
Take each man's censure,° but reserve thy judgement.
Costly thy habit° as thy purse can buy,
But not expressed in fancy: rich, not gaudy.
For the apparel oft proclaims the man,
And they in France of the best rank and station
Are of a most select and generous chief in that.°

---

15. **soil:** stain. 15. **cautel:** deceitfulness. 17. **His greatness weighed:** if you consider his greatness. 20. **Carve for himself:** i.e., serve his own interests. 21. **sanctity:** holiness, sacred quality. 23. **voice and yielding:** vote and consent. 26. **his peculiar sect and force:** the special circumstances of his class and power. 28. **main voice:** general assent. 30. **credent:** believing. 30. **list:** listen to. 31. **your chaste treasure:** the treasure of your chastity. 34. **keep . . . affection:** a military metaphor; Ophelia is not to go so far forward as her affection might lead her. 35. **shot:** range, shooting distance. 36–37. **The chariest . . . moon:** The most cautious maid goes almost too far if she does no more than reveal her beauty to the chaste moon. 36, 38, 39. **The . . . enough, Virtue . . . strokes, The . . . spring:** The Second Quarto marks these lines with inverted commas, the signs of "sentences," or improving moral generalities. 39. **canker:** insect pest feeding on plants. 40. **buttons be disclosed:** i.e., buds open out. 42. **blastments:** blightings. 44. **to itself rebels:** acts contrary to its better nature. 51. **recks not his own rede:** pays no attention to his own counsel. 54. **Occasion . . . leave:** a second leave-taking is a fortunate occurrence. 59. **character:** inscribe. 61. **but by no means vulgar:** i.e., but don't be familiar with everybody. 62. **and their adoption tried:** whose worthiness to be adopted you have tested. 64. **dull thy palm:** make your hand insensitive. The handshake is seen as a sensitive means of registering true friendship. 67. **Bear't that:** manage it so that, so carry it that. 69. **censure:** judgment (not necessarily adverse). 70. **habit:** apparel, clothes. 74. **Are . . . that:** i.e., have an exquisite and noble gift in choosing the right clothes.

Neither a borrower nor a lender be,
For loan oft loses both itself and friend,
And borrowing dulls the edge of husbandry.°
This above all, to thine own self be true,
And it must follow, as the night the day,
Thou canst not then be false to any man.
Farewell, my blessing season° this in thee.

LAERTES Most humbly do I take my leave, my lord.

POLONIUS The time invites you. Go, your servants tend.°

LAERTES Farewell Ophelia, and remember well
What I have said to you.

OPHELIA 'Tis in my memory locked,
And you yourself shall keep the key of it.

LAERTES Farewell. *Exit Laertes*

POLONIUS What is't Ophelia he hath said to you?

OPHELIA So please you, something touching the Lord Hamlet.

POLONIUS Marry,° well bethought.°
'Tis told me he hath very oft of late
Given private time to you, and you yourself
Have of your audience been most free and bounteous.
If it be so, as so 'tis put on me,°
And that in way of caution, I must tell you
You do not understand yourself so clearly
As it behooves° my daughter, and your honour.
What is between you? Give me up the truth.

OPHELIA He hath my lord of late made many tenders
Of his affection to me.

POLONIUS Affection? Puh! You speak like a green girl,
Unsifted° in such perilous circumstance.
Do you believe his tenders as you call them?

OPHELIA I do not know my lord what I should think.

POLONIUS Marry I'll teach you. Think yourself a baby
That you have tane° these tenders for true pay,
Which are not sterling. Tender yourself° more dearly,
Or — not to crack the wind of the poor phrase,
Roaming° it thus — you'll tender me a fool.°

OPHELIA My lord, he hath importuned me with love
In honourable fashion.

POLONIUS Ay, fashion you may call it. Go to, go to.

OPHELIA And hath given countenance to his speech, my lord,
With almost all the holy vows of heaven.

POLONIUS Ay, springes° to catch woodcocks. I do know,
When the blood burns, how prodigal the soul
Lends° the tongue vows. These blazes daughter,
Giving more light than heat, extinct in both
Even in their promise as it is a-making,
You must not take for fire. From this time
Be something scanter of your maiden presence.
Set your entreatments at a higher rate
Than a command to parley.° For Lord Hamlet,
Believe so much in him, that he is young
And with a larger tedder° may he walk
Than may be given you. In few° Ophelia,
Do not believe his vows, for they are brokers,°
Not of that dye which their investments° show,
But mere° implorators of unholy suits,
Breathing like sanctified and pious bonds,°
The better to beguile. This is for all:
I would not in plain terms from this time forth
Have you so slander° any moment leisure
As to give words or talk with the Lord Hamlet.
Look to't I charge you. Come your ways.°

OPHELIA I shall obey, my lord.

Exeunt

---

77. **husbandry:** thrift. 81. **season:** bring to due season, ripen. 83. **tend:** attend. 90. **Marry:** by the Virgin Mary (a mild oath). 90. **well bethought:** he did well to think of that. 94. **put on me:** given to me. 97. **behooves:** becomes, befits. 102. **Unsifted:** inexperienced. 106. **tane:** taken. 107. **Tender yourself:** look after yourself. 109. **Roaming:** Polonius means he doesn't want to tire the phrase out by too much verbal roaming. 109. **tender me a fool:** make me look like a fool. 115. **springes:** snares. 116–17. **how prodigal the soul /Lends:** i.e., how prodigal (lavish) the soul is in lending. 122–23. **Set . . . parley:** When a besieger appears before the castle of your heart and summons you to a parley, do not immediately enter into negotiations ("entreatments") for surrender. 125. **tedder:** tether. 126. **In few:** in few words. 127. **brokers:** negotiators, especially go-betweens, pimps. 128. **investments:** vestments, robes. The brokers wear the garments of dignitaries. 129. **mere:** no less than, out-and-out. 129. **implorators:** solicitors. 130. **bonds:** agreements, contracts. 133. **slander:** disgrace, misuse. 135. **your ways:** on your way.

Enter HAMLET, HORATIO *and* MARCELLUS

HAMLET The air bites shrewdly,° it is very cold.
HORATIO It is a nipping and an eager° air.
HAMLET What hour now?
HORATIO I think it lacks of° twelve.
MARCELLUS No, it is struck.
HORATIO Indeed? I heard it not. It then draws near the season
Wherein the spirit held his wont° to walk.

A flourish of trumpets and two pieces goes off°

What does this mean, my lord?
HAMLET The king doth wake° tonight and takes his rouse,
Keeps wassail,° and the swaggering up-spring° reels,
And as he drains his draughts of Rhenish° down,
The kettle-drum and trumpet thus bray out
The triumph° of his pledge.°
HORATIO Is it a custom?
HAMLET Ay marry is't,
But to my mind, though I am native here
And to the manner born,° it is a custom
More honoured in the breach than the observance.°
[This heavy-headed revel east and west°
Makes us traduced and taxed of° other nations.
They clepe° us drunkards, and with swinish phrase
Soil our addition;° and indeed it takes
From our achievements, though performed at height,
The pith and marrow of our attribute.°
So, oft it chances in particular men,
That for some vicious mole of nature° in them,
As in their birth, wherein they are not guilty,
Since nature cannot choose his° origin,
By their o'ergrowth of some complexion,°
Oft breaking down the pales° and forts of reason,
Or by some habit° that too much o'erleavens°
The form of plausive manners — that these men,
Carrying I say the stamp of one defect,
Being nature's livery° or fortune's star,°
His virtues else be they as pure as grace,
As infinite as man may undergo,°
Shall in the general censure take corruption
From that particular fault. The dram of eale
Doth all the noble substance of a doubt
To his own scandal.]°

Enter GHOST

HORATIO Look my lord, it comes!
HAMLET Angels and ministers of grace defend us!
Be thou a spirit of health,° or goblin damned,°
Bring with thee airs from heaven or blasts from hell,
Be thy intents wicked or charitable,
Thou com'st in such a questionable shape°
That I will speak to thee. I'll call thee Hamlet,
King, father, royal Dane. Oh answer me.
Let me not burst in ignorance, but tell
Why thy canonised° bones, hearsèd° in death,
Have burst their cerements;° why the sepulchre,

Act I, Scene iv. 1. **shrewdly:** keenly, injuriously. 2. **eager:** sharp, biting. 3. **lacks of:** i.e., is just short of. 6. **held his wont:** had its custom. 6. **sd *two pieces goes off*:** i.e., a salvo from two cannons is fired. 8. **wake:** hold a nighttime celebration. 8–9. **takes his rouse,/Keeps wassail:** more or less synonymous phrases for ceremonious carousal and wine-drinking. 9. **up-spring:** This may be a German dance. 10. **Rhenish:** Rhine wine. 12. **triumph:** properly a public celebration of an important event; used ironically here. 12. **pledge:** toast. 15. **to the manner born:** i.e., accustomed to this way of behaving since birth. 16. **More honoured in the breach than the observance:** i.e., it shows more honor in a man to break the custom than to observe it. 17. **east and west:** everywhere (i.e., by other nations everywhere). 18. **traduced and taxed of:** slandered and censured by. 19. **clepe:** call. 19–20. **with swinish phrase/Soil our addition:** pollute our proper title or description ("addition") by calling us pigs. 20–22. **it takes . . . attribute:** our fondness for drink robs the best of our achievements of the very essence of the reputation due to us. 24. **mole of nature:** natural mark. 26. **his:** its. 27. **their o'ergrowth of some complexion:** the excessive growth of some natural tendency. The allusion is to the doctrine of the four humors, whose proper balance was necessary for a stable temperament. 28. **pales:** palisades, fences. 29. **habit:** (here) a bad habit. 29. **too much o'erleavens:** Too much leaven in the dough will ruin the bread; so, too great an admixture of "some habit" will ruin the form of pleasing manners. 32. **nature's livery:** a dress marking one's servitude to nature. 32. **fortune's star:** a destiny falling to one by chance. 34. **undergo:** support. 36–38. **dram of eale . . . scandal:** The general significance is that a mere "dram" of bad matter ruins an entire "noble substance." 40. **spirit of health:** an uncorrupted spirit, bringing "airs from heaven" (41.) and "charitable" intents (42.). 40. **goblin damned:** a demon, bringing "blasts from hell" and "wicked" intents. 43. **questionable shape:** "Shape" means the external dress or guise. Whatever the ghost may be essentially, its external appearance is of a being who can be questioned. 47. **canonised:** consecrated. 47. **hearsèd:** coffined. 48. **cerements:** grave-clothes.

extending beyond the text

In a chapter titled "Speaking with the Dead" from Shakespearean scholar Stephen Greenblatt's book *Will in the World: How Shakespeare Became Shakespeare*, he discusses the death of Hamnet, Shakespeare's son who died at the age of eleven. Burial rituals at the time had changed fairly recently due to England's contentious shift from Catholicism to Anglicanism during the Protestant Reformation. Greenblatt explores how the playwright's religious beliefs may have played a role in his reaction to his son's final rites, and how *Hamlet* afforded Shakespeare the opportunity to rewrite his personal history by presenting a world where King Hamlet dies prior to his child.

from Will in the World: How Shakespeare Became Shakespeare

Stephen Greenblatt

Shakespeare must have attended the regular services in his Protestant parish; otherwise his name would have turned up on lists of recusants [Catholics]. But did he believe what he heard and recited? His works suggest that he did have faith, of a sort, but it was not a faith securely bound by either the Catholic Church or by the Church of England. By the late 1590s, insofar as his faith could be situated in any institution at all, that institution was the theater, and not only in the sense that his profoundest energies and expectations were all focused there.

Shakespeare grasped that crucial death rituals in his culture had been gutted. He may have felt this with enormous pain at his son's graveside. But he also believed that the theater — and his theatrical art in particular — could tap into the great reservoir of passionate feelings that, for him and for thousands of his contemporaries, no longer had a satisfactory outlet.

The Reformation was in effect offering him an extraordinary gift — the broken fragments of what had been a rich, complex edifice — and he knew exactly how to accept and use this gift. He was hardly indifferent to the success he could achieve, but it was not a matter of profit alone. Shakespeare drew upon the pity, confusion, and dread of death in a world of damaged rituals (the world in which most of us continue to live) because he himself experienced those same emotions at the core of his being. He experienced them in 1596, at the funeral of his child, and he experienced them with redoubled force in anticipation of his father's death. He responded not with prayers but the deepest expression of his being Hamlet. ■

1. **According to Greenblatt, what did Shakespeare's works suggest about his personal faith? Where do you see support for this assertion in *Hamlet*?**
2. **What is the "gift" Greenblatt claims the Reformation offered Shakespeare? Do you see evidence of this gift in the play? Explain why or why not.**
3. **How can Hamlet — both the character and the play as a whole — be understood as Shakespeare's attempt to contend with the death of his own son? Does it change your understanding of the major themes of the play? Explain.**

Wherein we saw thee quietly enurned,°
Hath oped his ponderous and marble jaws
To cast thee up again. What may this mean,
That thou, dead corse, again in complete steel°
Revisits thus the glimpses° of the moon,
Making night hideous, and we fools of nature°
So horridly to shake our disposition°
With thoughts beyond the reaches of our souls?
Say, why is this? wherefore? What should we do?

Ghost beckons Hamlet

HORATIO It beckons you to go away with it,
As if it some impartment° did desire
To you alone.

MARCELLUS Look with what courteous action
It wafts° you to a more removèd ground.
But do not go with it.

HORATIO No, by no means.

HAMLET It will not speak. Then I will follow it.

HORATIO Do not my lord.

HAMLET Why, what should be the fear?
I do not set my life at a pin's fee,°
And for my soul, what can it do to that,
Being a thing immortal as itself?
It waves me forth again. I'll follow it.

HORATIO What if it tempt you toward the flood° my lord,
Or to the dreadful summit of the cliff
That beetles o'er° his base into the sea,
And there assume some other horrible form
Which might deprive your sovereignty of reason,°
And draw you into madness? Think of it.
[The very place puts toys of desperation,°
Without more motive, into every brain
That looks so many fathoms to the sea
And hears it roar beneath.]

HAMLET It wafts me still. Go on, I'll follow thee.

MARCELLUS You shall not go my lord.

HAMLET Hold off your hands.

HORATIO Be ruled, you shall not go.

HAMLET My fate cries out,°
And makes each petty arture° in this body
As hardy as the Nemean lion's° nerve.°
Still am I called. Unhand me gentlemen!
By heaven I'll make a ghost of him that lets° me.
I say away! — Go on, I'll follow thee.

Exit Ghost and Hamlet

HORATIO He waxes desperate with imagination.°

MARCELLUS Let's follow, 'tis not fit thus to obey him.

HORATIO Have after.° To what issue will this come?

MARCELLUS Something is rotten in the state of Denmark.

HORATIO Heaven will direct it.

MARCELLUS Nay let's follow him.

Exeunt

Act I, Scene v

Enter GHOST *and* HAMLET

HAMLET Whither wilt thou lead me? Speak, I'll go no further.

GHOST Mark me.

HAMLET I will.

GHOST My hour is almost come
When I to sulph'rous and tormenting flames
Must render up myself.

HAMLET Alas poor ghost!

GHOST Pity me not, but lend thy serious hearing
To what I shall unfold.

HAMLET Speak, I am bound° to hear.

GHOST So art thou to revenge, when thou shalt hear.

HAMLET What?

---

49. **enurned:** "Urn" was often used loosely by Shakespeare and others to mean a grave, but the word is here not literal but metaphorical: the sepulcher envelops and encloses the body as though it were a funerary urn. 52. **complete steel:** full armor. 53. **glimpses:** pale gleams. 54. **fools of nature:** natural creatures, too ignorant to understand what lies beyond. 55. **horridly to shake our disposition:** to upset ourselves so violently. 59. **impartment:** communication. 61. **wafts:** waves. 65. **fee:** payment; hence, worth. 69. **flood:** sea. 71. **beetles o'er:** overhangs like bushy eyebrows. 73. **deprive . . . reason:** take away the sovereignty (supremacy) of your reason. 75. **toys of desperation:** whims of desperate behavior (i.e., suicidal impulse). 81. **My fate cries out:** my destiny is calling; that is, his future lies in what the ghost has to tell him. 82. **arture:** artery, thought to convey the vital spirits. 83. **Nemean lion's:** Hercules accomplished his first labor by strangling the invulnerable Nemean lion. 83. **nerve:** sinew. 85. **lets:** hinders. 87. **waxes desperate with imagination:** has become totally reckless because of what is in his mind. 89. **Have after:** Let us go after him. **Act I, Scene v.** 6. **bound:** all prepared.

GHOST I am thy father's spirit,
Doomed for a certain term to walk the night,
And for the day confined to fast in fires,°
Till the foul crimes° done in my days of nature
Are burnt and purged away. But that I am forbid
To tell the secrets of my prison house,
I could a tale unfold whose lightest word
Would harrow up thy soul, freeze thy young blood,
Make thy two eyes like stars start from their spheres,°
Thy knotted and combinèd locks to part
And each particular hair to stand an end°
Like quills upon the fretful porpentine.°
But this eternal blazon° must not be
To ears of flesh and blood. List, list, oh list!
If thou didst ever thy dear father love —
HAMLET O God!
GHOST Revenge his foul and most unnatural murder.
HAMLET Murder?
GHOST Murder most foul, as in the best it is,
But this most foul, strange, and unnatural.
HAMLET Haste me to know't, that I with wings as swift
As meditation or the thoughts of love
May sweep to my revenge.
GHOST I find thee apt,°
And duller shouldst thou be than the fat° weed
That rots itself in ease on Lethe° wharf,
Wouldst thou not stir in this. Now Hamlet, hear.
'Tis given out that, sleeping in my orchard,°
A serpent stung me. So the whole ear of Denmark
Is by a forgèd process° of my death
Rankly abused; but know, thou noble youth,
The serpent that did sting thy father's life
Now wears his crown.
HAMLET O my prophetic soul!°
My uncle?
GHOST Ay, that incestuous, that adulterate beast,
With witchcraft of his wits, with traitorous gifts — °
O wicked wit and gifts that have the power
So to seduce — won to his shameful lust
The will° of my most seeming virtuous queen.
O Hamlet, what a falling off was there,
From me whose love was of that dignity
That it went hand in hand even with the vow°
I made to her in marriage, and to decline
Upon a wretch whose natural gifts were poor
To those of mine.
But virtue as it° never will be moved,
Though lewdness court it in a shape of heaven,
So lust, though to a radiant angel linked,
Will sate itself° in a celestial bed,
And prey on garbage.
But soft, methinks I scent the morning air;
Brief let me be. Sleeping within my orchard,
My custom always of the afternoon,
Upon my secure hour° thy uncle stole,
With juice of cursèd hebenon° in a vial,
And in the porches of my ears° did pour
The leperous° distilment,° whose effect
Holds such an enmity with blood of man
That swift as quicksilver it courses through
The natural gates and alleys of the body,
And with a sudden vigour it doth posset°
And curd, like eager° droppings into milk,

---

11. **fast in fires:** Fasting amidst the purifying flames is necessary for the Ghost because he never received the absolution of the last rites (76–77). 12. **foul crimes:** the ordinary sinfulness of humanity. 17. **Make . . . spheres:** i.e., make your eyes start from your head as though they were stars jerked out of their appointed spheres (so indicating a dislocation in nature). 19. **an end:** obsolete form of "on end." 20. **porpentine:** porcupine. The word was spelled in many different ways; this is the normal Shakespearean form. 21. **eternal blazon:** promulgation of what belongs to the eternal world. 31. **apt:** quick in response. 32. **fat:** heavy, torpid, sluggish. 33. **Lethe:** a river in Hades. The spirits of the dead, waiting to cross, drank its waters and so became oblivious to their previous existence. 35. **orchard:** garden. 37. **process:** narrative. 40. **my prophetic soul:** The Ghost's revelation is in accord with Hamlet's general suspicions about Claudius and the recent goings-on. 43. **gifts:** talents. 46. **The will:** This is more than inclination or assent, since the word has strong sexual undertones. Gertrude was sexually responsive to Claudius's advances. The Ghost's belief that Gertrude had been sleeping with two brothers gives special force to the otherwise somewhat academic charge of incest (42. above). 49. **even with the vow:** with the very vow (*not* even as far as the vow). 53. **virtue as it:** as virtue. 56. **sate itself:** become satiated, cease to find satisfaction. 61. **Upon my secure hour:** at a time when I felt free from all danger. ("Secure" implied an absence of precaution, almost the opposite of its modern meaning.) 62. **hebenon:** *Hebenus* is Latin for ebony, but the term was applied to other trees, and the resin of the guaiacum tree has been suggested as the drug in question. Possibly there is confusion with henbane, which is a poison. 63. **the porches of my ears:** i.e., the ears as porches of the body. It was widely believed that drugs, therapeutic or toxic, could be administered via the ear. 64. **leperous:** causing leprosy. 64. **distilment:** distillation (in a general sense, a liquid preparation). 68. **posset:** curdle. 69. **eager:** sour, acid.

In this image, from a 2015 stage production of *Hamlet*, actor Karl Johnson plays the ghost of King Hamlet.
How do these wardrobe and makeup choices characterize the ghost? Why do you think he is portrayed this way?

The thin and wholesome blood. So did it mine,
And a most instant tetter° barked about,°
Most lazar-like,° with vile and loathsome crust,
All my smooth body.
Thus was I, sleeping, by a brother's hand,
Of life, of crown, of queen, at once dispatched;°
Cut off even in the blossoms of my sin,°
Unhouseled, disappointed, unaneled;°
No reckoning° made, but sent to my account
With all my imperfections on my head —
Oh horrible, oh horrible, most horrible!
If thou hast nature° in thee bear it not;
Let not the royal bed of Denmark be
A couch for luxury° and damnèd incest.
But howsomever° thou pursues this act
Taint not thy mind,° nor let thy soul contrive
Against thy mother aught. Leave her to heaven
And to those thorns that in her bosom lodge
To prick and sting her. Fare thee well at once.
The glow-worm shows the matin to be near,
And gins to pale his uneffectual fire.
Adieu, adieu, adieu. Remember me. *Exit*

HAMLET O all you host of heaven! O earth! what else?
And shall I couple hell?° Oh fie! Hold, hold, my heart,
And you my sinews grow not instant old
But bear me stiffly up.° Remember thee?
Ay thou poor ghost, whiles memory holds a seat
In this distracted globe.° Remember thee?
Yea, from the table° of my memory
I'll wipe away all trivial fond° records,°
All saws° of books, all forms,° all pressures° past,
That youth and observation° copied there,
And thy commandment all alone shall live
Within the book and volume of my brain,
Unmixed with baser matter: yes, by heaven!
O most pernicious woman!
O villain, villain, smiling damnèd villain!
My tables° — meet it is I set it down
That one may smile, and smile, and be a villain;
At least I'm sure it may be so in Denmark.
[*Writing*]
So uncle, there you are. Now to my word:°
It is "Adieu, adieu, remember me."
I have sworn't.

HORATIO (*Within*) My lord, my lord!

71. **tetter:** skin disease. 71. **barked about:** surrounded like bark. 72. **lazar-like:** like a leper (from Lazarus, in Luke 16:20). 75. **dispatched:** bereft by being put to death. 76. **in the blossoms of my sin:** i.e., in a state of sinfulness. 77. **Unhouseled, disappointed, unaneled:** without the sacrament, not appointed or prepared for death, without extreme unction. 78. **reckoning:** the settling of an account. 81. **nature:** natural feelings; here, filial affection especially. 83. **luxury:** lust. 84. **howsomever:** the older form of "howsoever." 85. **Taint not thy mind:** Do not let your mind become affected or blemished. 93. **And shall I couple hell?:** The enormity of what he has heard makes Hamlet first appeal to heaven to witness, then turn to earth as the scene of these crimes, and finally think of hell as their source. 95. **bear me stiffly up:** keep me from collapsing. 97. **this distracted globe:** a disordered world. This serves as a prelude to Hamlet's conviction that he is called upon not to right a personal wrong, but to repair a distracted world. 98. **table:** tablet, slate. 99. **fond:** foolish. 99. **records:** things written down worthy of being remembered. 100. **saws:** common sayings or maxims. 100. **forms:** set phrases, formulistic thoughts. 100. **pressures:** imprints or impressions (continues the image of clichés and stereotyped thoughts). 101. **observation:** dutiful attention. 107. **tables:** memorandum book (see 98. above) 110. **Now to my word:** Hamlet has not yet vowed to obey the Ghost's command. He now gives his word.

MARCELLUS (*Within*) Lord Hamlet!

Enter HORATIO *and* MARCELLUS

HORATIO Heavens secure him!
HAMLET So be it.
MARCELLUS Illo, ho, ho, my lord!
HAMLET Hillo, ho, ho, boy! Come bird,° come.
MARCELLUS How is't, my noble lord?
HORATIO What news
my lord?
HAMLET Oh, wonderful!
HORATIO Good my lord, tell it.
HAMLET No, you will reveal it.
HORATIO Not I my lord, by heaven.
HARCELLUS Nor I my lord.
HAMLET How say you then, would heart of man
once think it—
But you'll be secret?
HORATIOM
ARCELLUS } Ay, by heaven, my lord.
HAMLET There's ne'er a villain dwelling in all
Denmark
But he's an arrant knave.
HORATIO There needs no ghost, my lord, come
from the grave,
To tell us this.
HAMLET Why right, you are i'th'right,
And so without more circumstance° at all
I hold it fit that we shake hands and part—
You as your business and desire shall point you,
For every man hath business and desire,
Such as it is, and for my own poor part,
Look you, I'll go pray.
HORATIO These are but wild and whirling words,
my lord.
HAMLET I'm sorry they offend you, heartily,
Yes faith, heartily.
HORATIO There's no offence my lord.
HAMLET Yes by Saint Patrick but there is Horatio,
And much offence too. Touching this vision
here,
It is an honest° ghost, that let me tell you.
For your desire to know what is between us,
O'ermaster't as you may. And now good
friends,
As you are friends, scholars, and soldiers,
Give me one poor request.
HORATIO What is't my lord? we will.
HAMLET Never make known what you have seen
tonight.
HORATIO
MARCELLUS } My lord we will not.
HAMLET Nay but swear't.
HORATIO In faith
My lord not I.
MARCELLUS Nor I° my lord in faith.
HAMLET Upon my sword.°
MARCELLUS We have sworn my
lord already.
HAMLET Indeed, upon my sword, indeed.
GHOST Swear. *Ghost cries under the stage*
HAMLET Ha, ha, boy, sayst thou so? art thou
there truepenny?°
Come on, you hear this fellow in the cellarage,°
Consent to swear.
HORATIO Propose the oath my lord.
HAMLET Never to speak of this that you have seen,
Swear by my sword.
GHOST Swear.
HAMLET *Hic et ubique?*° then we'll shift our
ground.
Come hither gentlemen,
And lay your hands again upon my sword.
Never to speak of this that you have heard,
Swear by my sword.
GHOST Swear.
HAMLET Well said old mole, canst work i'th'earth
so fast?
A worthy pioneer.° Once more remove, good
friends.
HORATIO O day and night, but this is wondrous
strange.
HAMLET And therefore as a stranger give it
welcome.°

---

116. **Come bird:** Hamlet mocks the hallooing by pretending they are out hawking. 127. **circumstance:** roundabout talk and formality. 138. **honest:** honorable, genuine (i.e., the Ghost is what he appears to be). 146. **not I. Nor I:** They here promise not to divulge what they have seen (they are not refusing to swear). 147. **Upon my sword:** The hilt forms a cross. 150. **truepenny:** trusty fellow. 151. **in the cellarage:** down below, in the cellars. 156. ***Hic et ubique*:** here and everywhere. 163. **pioneer:** soldier responsible for excavations and tunneling. 165. **as a stranger give it welcome:** i.e., it has a special call on your hospitality.

Set design for a production of Hamlet/INDIVISION CHARMET/ Bridgeman Images

This 1884 watercolor was made for the set design of act I in a French production of *Hamlet*.
How is the setting portrayed here? How do the set designer's choices convey the meaning of the events that have taken place thus far?

There are more things in heaven and earth, Horatio,
Than are dreamt of in your philosophy.
But come —
Here as before, never so help you mercy,
How strange or odd some'er I bear myself,
As I perchance hereafter shall think meet
To put an antic disposition° on —
That you at such times seeing me never shall,
With arms encumbered° thus, or this head-shake,
Or by pronouncing of some doubtful phrase,
As "Well, well, we know," or "We could and if we would,"
Or "If we list° to speak," or "There be and if° they might,"
Or such ambiguous giving out, to note
That you know aught of me: this not to do,
So grace and mercy at your most need help you,
Swear.

GHOST Swear.

HAMLET Rest, rest, perturbèd spirit. So gentlemen,
With all my love I do commend me to you,°
And what so poor a man as Hamlet is
May do t'express his love and friending to you,
God willing shall not lack. Let us go in together,
And still° your fingers on your lips I pray. —
The time° is out of joint: O cursèd spite,°
That ever I was born to set it right. —
Nay come, let's go together.

Exeunt

Act II Hamlet, Prince of Denmark

Act II, Scene i

Enter POLONIUS *and* REYNALDO

POLONIUS Give him this money, and these notes, Reynaldo.

REYNALDO I will my lord.

POLONIUS You shall do marvellous wisely, good Reynaldo,
Before you visit him, to make inquire
Of his behaviour.

REYNALDO My lord, I did intend it.

POLONIUS Marry well said, very well said. Look you sir,
Inquire me first what Danskers° are in Paris,

172. **an antic disposition:** fantastic and foolish manner. 174. **encumbered:** entangled. 176, 177. **and if:** if. 177. **list:** wished. 184. **I do commend me to you:** I entrust myself to you. 188. **still:** always. 189. **The time:** i.e., things generally, the state of the world. 189. **cursèd spite:** the accursèd malice of life! **Act II, Scene i.** 7. **Danskers:** Danes.

And how, and who, what means,° and where they keep,°
What company, at what expense; and finding
By this encompassment° and drift° of question
That they do know my son, come you° more nearer°
Than your particular demands will touch it.
Take you as 'twere some distant knowledge of him,
As thus, "I know his father and his friends,
And in part him"—do you mark this Reynaldo?

REYNALDO Ay, very well, my lord.

POLONIUS "And in part him, but"—you may say—"not well,
But if't be he I mean, he's very wild,
Addicted so and so"—and there put on him
What forgeries° you please; marry, none so rank°
As may dishonour him, take heed of that,
But sir, such wanton, wild, and usual slips
As are companions noted and most known
To youth and liberty.

REYNALDO As gaming my lord?

POLONIUS Ay, or drinking, fencing, swearing,
Quarrelling, drabbing°—you may go so far.

REYNALDO My lord, that would dishonour him.

POLONIUS Faith no, as you may season° it in the charge.
You must not put another scandal on him,
That he is open to incontinency,°
That's not my meaning. But breathe his faults so quaintly°
That they may seem the taints of liberty,°
The flash and outbreak of a fiery mind,
A savageness in unreclaimèd blood,°
Of general assault.°

REYNALDO But my good lord—

POLONIUS Wherefore should you do this?

REYNALDO Ay my lord,
I would know that.

POLONIUS Marry sir, here's my drift,
And I believe it is a fetch of warrant.°
You laying these slight sullies on my son,
As 'twere a thing a little soiled i'th'working,°
Mark you,
Your party in converse, him you would sound,
Having ever seen in the prenominate° crimes°
The youth you breathe of°guilty, be assured
He closes with you° in this consequence,°
"Good sir," or so, or "friend," or "gentleman,"
According to the phrase and the addition
Of man and country.

REYNALDO Very good my lord.

POLONIUS And then sir does a this—a does—what was I about to say? By the mass I was about to say something. Where did I leave?

REYNALDO At "closes in the consequence," at "friend, or so," and "gentleman."

POLONIUS At "closes in the consequence"—ay marry,
He closes with you thus: "I know the gentleman,
I saw him yesterday, or th'other day,
Or then, or then, with such or such, and as you say,
There was a° gaming, there o'ertook in's rouse,
There falling out at tennis," or perchance,
"I saw him enter such a house of sale"—
Videlicet,° a brothel—or so forth. See you now,
Your bait of falsehood takes this carp of truth,
And thus do we of wisdom and of reach,°
With windlasses° and with assays of bias,°
By indirections find directions° out.
So, by my former lecture and advice,
Shall you my son. You have me, have you not?

---

8. **what means:** what means they have. 8. **keep:** lodge, stay. 10. **encompassment:** surrounding—i.e., comprehensiveness. 10. **drift:** driving, directing. 11. **come you:** you will come. 11. **nearer:** i.e., to an understanding of Laertes's behavior. 20. **forgeries:** invented matters. 20. **rank:** gross. 25. **fencing:** i.e., spending time in fencing schools. 26. **drabbing:** going around with drabs, or loose women. 28. **season:** modify. 30. **incontinency:** sexual excess. 31. **quaintly:** artfully. 32. **taints of liberty:** faults of free-living. 34. **savageness in unreclaimèd blood:** wildness in untamed vigor. 35. **Of general assault:** which assails everyone. 38. **fetch of warrant:** approved stratagem. 40. **i'th'working:** in the process of making it. 43. **prenominate:** already named. 43. **crimes:** faults. 44. **breathe of:** speak about. 45. **closes with you:** will fall in with you. 45. **in this consequence:** in the following way. 58. **a:** he. 58. **o'ertook in's rouse:** overtaken (by drink) while carousing. That is, he got drunk. 61. **Videlicet:** viz., that is to say. 63. **we of wisdom and of reach:** we who are wise and far-seeing. 64. **windlasses:** circuitous movement. 64. **assays of bias:** indirect attempts. The "bias" in bowls is the weighting, which makes the bowl take a curved course toward the jack. 65. **directions:** the way things are going.

REYNALDO My lord, I have.
POLONIUS God buy ye,° fare ye well.
REYNALDO Good my lord.
POLONIUS Observe his inclination in yourself.°
REYNALDO I shall my lord.
POLONIUS And let him ply his music.
REYNALDO Well my lord.
POLONIUS Farewell.
Exit Reynaldo

Enter OPHELIA

How now Ophelia, what's the matter?
OPHELIA Oh my lord, my lord, I have been so affrighted.
POLONIUS With what, i'th'name of God?
OPHELIA My lord, as I was sewing in my closet,°
Lord Hamlet with his doublet° all unbraced,°
No hat upon his head, his stockings fouled,
Ungartered, and down-gyvèd° to his ankle,
Pale as his shirt, his knees knocking each other,
And with a look so piteous in purport°
As if he had been loosèd out of hell
To speak of horrors — he comes before me.
POLONIUS Mad for thy love?
OPHELIA My lord I do not know,
But truly I do fear it.
POLONIUS What said he?
OPHELIA He took me by the wrist, and held me hard;
Then goes he to the length of all his arm,
And with his other hand thus o'er his brow
He falls to such perusal of my face
As a would draw it. Long stayed he so;
At last, a little shaking of mine arm,
And thrice his head thus waving up and down,
He raised a sigh so piteous and profound
As it did seem to shatter all his bulk,
And end his being. That done, he lets me go,
And with his head over his shoulder turned
He seemed to find his way without his eyes,
For out-a-doors he went without their helps
And to the last bended their light on me.
POLONIUS Come, go with me, I will go seek the king.
This is the very ecstasy° of love,
Whose violent property fordoes itself,°
And leads the will to desperate undertakings
As oft as any passion under heaven
That does afflict our natures. I am sorry.
What, have you given him any hard words of late?
OPHELIA No my good lord; but as you did command,
I did repel his letters, and denied
His access to me.
POLONIUS That hath made him mad.
I am sorry that with better heed and judgement
I had not quoted° him. I feared he did but trifle,
And meant to wrack° thee, but beshrew my jealousy.°
By heaven, it is as proper to° our age
To cast° beyond ourselves in our opinions
As it is common for the younger sort
To lack discretion. Come, go we to the king.
This must be known, which being kept close,° might move
More grief to hide than hate to utter love.°
Come.
Exeunt

Act II, Scene ii

Flourish. Enter KING *and* QUEEN, ROSENCRANTZ *and* GUILDENSTERN, *with others*

CLAUDIUS Welcome dear Rosencrantz and Guildenstern!
Moreover that° we much did long to see you,
The need we have to use you did provoke
Our hasty sending. Something have you heard
Of Hamlet's transformation — so call it,

68. **God buy ye:** one of the many ways of writing the shortened "God be with ye" — that is, goodbye. 70. **in yourself:** personally. 76. **closet:** private room. 77. **doublet:** the Elizabethan jacket. 77. **unbraced:** unfastened. 79. **down-gyvèd:** fallen down and resembling fetters. 81. **in purport:** in what it expressed.101. **ecstasy:** madness. 102. **Whose violent property fordoes itself:** which has violence enough to cause self-destruction. 111. **quoted:** noted, observed. 112. **wrack:** ruin, by seducing. 112. **beshrew my jealousy:** shame on my suspiciousness. 113. **as proper to:** as characteristic of. 114. **cast:** calculate, compute. The old read too much into things, while the young are too heedless of possible implications. 117. **close:** secret. 117–18. **might move . . . love:** i.e., might cause more sorrow by concealment than unpleasantness by making the love known. **Act II, Scene ii.** 2. **Moreover that:** in addition to the fact that.

extending beyond the text

Tom Stoppard's 1967 play *Rosencrantz and Guildenstern Are Dead* is an absurdist tragicomedy based on Shakespeare's *Hamlet*. By placing Hamlet's childhood friends at the center of his play, Stoppard contends with many of Shakespeare's thematic concerns from the perspective of these two foolish characters.

from Rosencrantz and Guildenstern Are Dead

Tom Stoppard

GUIL But for God's sake what are we supposed to *do*?

PLAYER Relax. Respond. That's what people do. You can't go through life questioning your situation at every turn.

GUIL But we don't know what's going on, or what to do with ourselves. We don't know how to *act*.

PLAYER Act natural. You know why you're here at least.

GUIL We only know what we're told, and that's little enough. And for all we know it isn't even true.

PLAYER For all anyone knows, nothing is. Everything has to be taken on trust; truth is only that which is taken to be true. It's the currency of living. There may be nothing behind it, but it doesn't make any difference so long as it is honoured. One acts on assumptions. What do you assume?

ROS Hamlet is not himself, outside or in. We have to glean what afflicts him.

GUIL He doesn't give much away.

PLAYER Who does, nowadays?

GUIL He's — melancholy.

PLAYER Melancholy?

ROS Mad.

PLAYER How is he mad?

ROS Ah. (*To* GUIL.) How is he mad?

GUIL More morose than mad, perhaps.

PLAYER Melancholy.

GUIL Moody.

ROS He has moods.

PLAYER Of moroseness?

GUIL Madness. And yet.

ROS Quite.

GUIL For instance.

ROS He talks to himself, which might be madness.

GUIL If he didn't talk sense, which he does.

ROS Which suggests the opposite.

PLAYER Of what?

Small pause.

GUIL I think I have it. A man talking sense to himself is no madder than a man talking nonsense not to himself.

ROS Or just as mad.

GUIL Or just as mad.

ROS And he does both.

GUIL So there you are.

ROS Stark raving sane. ■

1. **What ideas from Shakespeare's *Hamlet* do you see discussed in this dialogue?**
2. **How does the conversation among Rosencrantz, Guildenstern, and the Player relate to your own understanding of Hamlet's behavior in Shakespeare's play — particularly his (supposed) madness?**

Sith° nor th'exterior nor the inward man
Resembles that it was. What it should be,
More than his father's death, that thus hath put him
So much from th'understanding of himself,
I cannot dream of. I entreat you both,
That being of° so young days brought up with him,
And sith so neighboured to his youth and haviour,°
That you vouchsafe your rest here in our court
Some little time, so by your companies
To draw him on to pleasures, and to gather
So much as from occasion° you may glean,
Whether aught to us unknown afflicts him thus,
That opened° lies within our remedy.

GERTRUDE Good gentlemen, he hath much talked of you,
And sure I am, two men there is not living
To whom he more adheres. If it will please you
To show us so much gentry° and good will
As to expend your time with us a while,
For the supply° and profit° of our hope,°
Your visitation shall receive such thanks
As fits a king's remembrance.°

ROSENCRANTZ Both your majesties
Might by the sovereign power you have of° us
Put your dread pleasures more into command
Than to entreaty.

GUILDENSTERN But we both obey,
And here give up ourselves in the full bent°
To lay our service freely at your feet
To be commanded.

CLAUDIUS Thanks Rosencrantz, and gentle Guildenstern.

GERTRUDE Thanks Guildenstern, and gentle Rosencrantz.
And I beseech you instantly to visit
My too much changèd son. Go some of you
And bring these gentlemen where Hamlet is.

GUILDENSTERN Heavens make our presence and our practices°
Pleasant and helpful to him.

GERTRUDE Ay, amen.

Exeunt Rosencrantz and Guildenstern [and some Attendants]

Enter POLONIUS

POLONIUS Th'ambassadors from Norway, my good lord,
Are joyfully returned.

CLAUDIUS Thou still hast been the father of good news.

POLONIUS Have I my lord? Assure you, my good liege,
I hold° my duty, as I hold my soul,
Both to my God and to my gracious king;
And I do think, or else this brain of mine
Hunts not the trail of policy° so sure
As it hath used to do, that I have found
The very cause of Hamlet's lunacy.

CLAUDIUS Oh speak of that, that do I long to hear.

POLONIUS Give first admittance to th'ambassadors;
My news shall be the fruit to that great feast.

CLAUDIUS Thyself do grace to them and bring them in.

[Exit Polonius]

He tells me, my dear Gertrude, he hath found
The head and source of all your son's distemper.

GERTRUDE I doubt° it is no other but the main:°
His father's death, and our o'erhasty marriage.

CLAUDIUS Well, we shall sift him.°

Enter POLONIUS, VOLTEMAND *and* CORNELIUS

Welcome my good friends.
Say Voltemand, what from our brother Norway?

VOLTEMAND Most fair return of greetings and desires.
Upon our first,° he sent out to suppress
His nephew's levies, which to him appeared
To be a preparation 'gainst the Polack;
But better looked into, he truly found
It was against your highness; whereat grieved
That so his sickness, age and impotence°

---

6. **Sith:** since. 11. **of:** from. 12. **youth and haviour:** youthful way of behaving. 16. **occasion:** opportunity. 18. **opened:** being revealed. 22. **gentry:** courtesy. 24. **supply:** aid. 24. **profit:** advancement. 24. **our hope:** what we hope for. 26. **remembrance:** notice or recognition of services rendered. 27. **of:** over. 30. **bent:** extent; from bending a bow; compare "to the top of my bent," 3.2.362. 38. **practices:** doings, activities. 44. **hold:** maintain. He means he maintains his duty to his God and king as firmly as he guards his soul. 47. **policy:** statecraft. 56. **doubt:** suspect. 56. **the main:** the main matter. 58. **sift him:** examine carefully what he (Polonius) has to say. 61. **Upon our first:** as soon as we made representations to him. 66. **impotence:** helplessness.

Was falsely borne in hand,° sends out arrests
On Fortinbras, which he in brief obeys,
Receives rebuke from Norway, and in fine°
Makes vow before his uncle never more
To give th'assay° of arms against your majesty.
Whereon old Norway, overcome with joy,
Gives him three thousand crowns in annual fee,°
And his commission to employ those soldiers,
So levied as before, against the Polack;
With an entreaty, herein further shown,
That it might please you to give quiet pass
Through your dominions for this enterprise,
On such regards° of safety and allowance°
As therein are set down.
[*Gives a document*]

CLAUDIUS It likes° us well,
And at our more considered time° we'll read,
Answer, and think upon this business.
Meantime, we thank you for your well-took labour.
Go to your rest; at night we'll feast together.
Most welcome home.

Exeunt Ambassadors

POLONIUS This business is well ended.
My liege, and madam, to expostulate°
What majesty should be, what duty is,
Why day is day, night night, and time is time,
Were nothing but to waste night, day, and time.
Therefore, since brevity is the soul of wit°
And tediousness° the limbs and outward flourishes,°
I will be brief. Your noble son is mad.
Mad call I it, for to define true madness,
What is't but to be nothing else but mad?
But let that go.

GERTRUDE More matter with less art.

POLONIUS Madam, I swear I use no art at all.
That he is mad, 'tis true; 'tis true 'tis pity,
And pity 'tis 'tis true — a foolish figure,°
But farewell it, for I will use no art.
Mad let us grant him then, and now remains
That we find out the cause of this effect,
Or rather say, the cause of this defect,
For this effect defective comes by cause.°
Thus it remains, and the remainder thus.
Perpend.°
I have a daughter — have while she is mine —
Who in her duty and obedience, mark,
Hath given me this. Now gather and surmise.°
Reads the letter
"To the celestial, and my soul's idol, the most beautified Ophelia," — That's an ill phrase, a vile phrase, "beautified" is a vile phrase — but you shall hear. Thus:
"In her excellent white bosom, these, *et cetera*."

GERTRUDE Came this from Hamlet to her?

POLONIUS Good madam stay awhile, I will be faithful.
"Doubt thou the stars are fire,
Doubt that the sun doth move,
Doubt truth to be a liar,
But never doubt I love.°
"O dear Ophelia, I am ill at these numbers,° I
have not art to reckon° my groans; but that I
love thee best, O most best, believe it. Adieu.
"Thine evermore, most dear lady, whilst this machine° is to him, Hamlet."
This in obedience hath my daughter shown me,
And, more above,° hath his solicitings,
As they fell out, by time, by means, and place,
All given to mine ear.°

CLAUDIUS But how hath she
Received his love?

POLONIUS What do you think of me?

CLAUDIUS As of a man faithful and honourable.

POLONIUS I would fain° prove so. But what might you think,
When I had seen this hot love on the wing —

---

67. **borne in hand:** imposed on, abused with false pretenses. 69. **in fine:** in conclusion. 71. **give th'assay:** make the trial. 73. **fee:** payment. 79. **regards:** considerations. 79. **allowance:** permission. 80. **likes:** pleases. 81. **more considered time:** time more suitable for consideration. 86. **expostulate:** argue about, discuss. 90. **wit:** intellectual keenness. 91. **tediousness:** prolixity, long-windedness. 91. **flourishes:** embellishments. 98. **figure:** rhetorical device (as in figure of speech). 103. **For this effect defective comes by cause:** for this manifestation, which is a defect (madness), does have a cause. 105. **Perpend:** ponder, consider. 108. **gather and surmise:** make your deductions. 116–19. **Doubt . . . love:** "Doubt" changes meaning here to "suspect," but each of the first three lines means the same: "you may challenge the unchallengeable, but . . . ." 119. **ill at these numbers:** no good at making verses. 121. **reckon:** enumerate in metrical form, or "numbers." 122. **this machine:** his body. 126. **more above:** furthermore, moreover. 126–28. **hath his . . . mine ear:** She has given Polonius information about all his overtures to her, in their order of occurrence, with details of the time, the means of communication, and the place. 131. **fain:** gladly.

As I perceived it, I must tell you that,
Before my daughter told me — what might you,
Or my dear majesty your queen here, think,
If I had played the desk, or table-book,°
Or given my heart a winking,° mute and dumb,
Or looked upon this love with idle sight —
What might you think? No, I went round° to work,
And my young mistress thus I did bespeak:°
"Lord Hamlet is a prince out of thy star.°
This must not be." And then I prescripts° gave her,
That she should lock herself from his resort,°
Admit no messengers, receive no tokens.
Which done, she took the fruits° of my advice,
And he, repulsed — a short tale to make —
Fell into a sadness, then into a fast,
Thence to a watch,° thence into a weakness,
Thence to a lightness,° and by this declension°
Into the madness wherein now he raves,
And all we mourn for.

CLAUDIUS Do you think 'tis this?

GERTRUDE It may be, very like.

POLONIUS Hath there been such a time, I'ld fain know that,
That I have positively said, 'tis so,
When it proved otherwise?

CLAUDIUS Not that I know.

POLONIUS Take this from this, if this be otherwise.
If circumstances lead me, I will find
Where truth is hid, though it were hid indeed
Within the centre.°

CLAUDIUS How may we try° it further?

POLONIUS You know sometimes he walks four hours together
Here in the lobby.°

GERTRUDE So he does indeed.

POLONIUS At such a time I'll loose° my daughter to him.
Be you and I behind an arras° then.
Mark the encounter: if he love her not,
And be not from his reason fallen thereon,
Let me be no assistant for a state,
But keep a farm and carters.

CLAUDIUS We will try it.

Enter HAMLET *reading on a book*

GERTRUDE But look where sadly the poor wretch comes reading.

POLONIUS Away, I do beseech you both, away.
I'll board him presently.

Exeunt Claudius and Gertrude [and Attendants]

Oh give me leave.
How does my good Lord Hamlet?

HAMLET Well, God-a-mercy.

POLONIUS Do you know me, my lord?

HAMLET Excellent well, y'are a fishmonger.°

POLONIUS Not I my lord.

HAMLET Then I would you were so honest a man.

POLONIUS Honest my lord?

HAMLET Ay sir. To be honest, as this world goes, is to be one man picked out of ten thousand.

POLONIUS That's very true my lord.

HAMLET For if the sun breed maggots in a dead dog, being a good kissing carrion° — Have you a daughter?

POLONIUS I have my lord.

HAMLET Let her not walk i'th'sun. Conception is a blessing, but as your daughter may conceive — Friend, look to't.

POLONIUS (*Aside*) How say you by that? Still harping on° my daughter. Yet he knew me not at first, a said I was a fishmonger — a is far gone, far gone. And truly, in my youth I suffered much extremity for love, very near this. I'll speak to him again. — What do you read my lord?

HAMLET Words, words, words.

POLONIUS What is the matter,° my lord?

HAMLET Between who?

POLONIUS I mean the matter that you read, my lord.

HAMLET Slanders sir, for the satirical rogue says here that old men have grey beards, that their

---

136. **played the desk, or tablebook:** i.e., taken note and said nothing. 137. **given my heart a winking:** closed the eyes of his heart — i.e., connived at the affair. 139. **round:** roundly, without prevarication. 140. **bespeak:** speak to. 141. **out of thy star:** outside your destiny. 142. **prescripts:** orders. 143. **his resort:** his visiting. 145. **took the fruits:** received the benefit, reaped the harvest. 148. **watch:** wakefulness. 149. **lightness:** lightheadedness. 149. **declension:** decline. 159. **centre:** center of the earth. 160. **try:** test. 162. **lobby:** anteroom, vestibule, or gallery. It is on an upper floor of the palace (4.3.35.). 161. **loose:** a word more suitable for animals than a daughter. 163. **arras:** tapestry or hangings covering a wall. 174. **fishmonger:** It has been commonly thought that Hamlet uses the term to mean wencher, bawd, or fleshmonger. 182. **a good kissing carrion:** The sun breeds maggots in a dead dog because it's a good bit of flesh to kiss and, speaking of kissing and breeding, "Have you a daughter?" 189. **harping on:** "To harp on one string" was a proverbial phrase for sticking to a single subject. 195. **matter:** subject matter.

faces are wrinkled, their eyes purging° thick amber and plumtree gum,° and that they have a plentiful lack of wit,° together with most weak hams. All which sir, though I most powerfully and potently believe, yet I hold it not honesty° to have it thus set down. For yourself sir shall grow old as I am, if like a crab you could go backward.

POLONIUS (*Aside*) Though this be madness, yet there is method in't. — Will you walk out of the air,° my lord?

HAMLET Into my grave?

POLONIUS Indeed that's out of the air. (*Aside*) How pregnant° sometimes his replies are! a happiness° that often madness hits on, which reason and sanity could not so prosperously be delivered of. I will leave him, and suddenly° contrive the means of meeting between him and my daughter. — My honourable lord, I will most humbly take my leave of you.

HAMLET You cannot sir take from me anything that I will more willingly part withal; except my life, except my life, except my life.

POLONIUS Fare you well my lord.

HAMLET These tedious old fools!

Enter GUILDENSTERN *and* ROSENCRANTZ

POLONIUS You go to seek the Lord Hamlet, there he is.

ROSENCRANTZ God save you sir.

[*Exit Polonius*]

GUILDENSTERN My honoured lord!

ROSENCRANTZ My most dear lord!

HAMLET My excellent good friends! How dost thou Guildenstern? Ah, Rosencrantz. Good lads, how do you both?

ROSENCRANTZ As the indifferent° children of the earth.

GUILDENSTERN Happy in that we are not over-happy; on Fortune's cap we are not the very button.

HAMLET Nor the soles of her shoe?°

ROSENCRANTZ Neither, my lord.

HAMLET Then you live about her waist, or in the middle of her favours?°

GUILDENSTERN Faith, her privates we.°

HAMLET In the secret parts of Fortune? Oh most true, she is a strumpet. What news?

ROSENCRANTZ None my lord, but that the world's grown honest.

HAMLET Then is doomsday near — but your news is not true. Let me question more in particular.

ullstein bild Dtl./Getty Images

This photograph is a still from the 1921 silent movie based on *Hamlet* with Danish actress Asta Nielsen in the title role. In this version, Prince Hamlet is actually a princess, and Polonius and Queen Gertrude — fearing the King's death has left no successor to the throne — hatch a political plot to disguise the princess as a man. To complicate matters, Hamlet falls in love with Horatio, and because Horatio is interested in Ophelia, Hamlet envies her. **What aspects of Hamlet's character does Nielsen evoke here? Why do you think the film's creators chose to alter the plot of the play the way they did?**

200. **purging:** discharging. 201. **amber and plumtree gum:** Whereas the latter was a familiar resin, "amber" was used very vaguely and could mean half a dozen substances, from the Baltic fossilresin to ambergris. Here it presumably means liquidamber, a tree resin. 202. **wit:** understanding. 204. **honesty:** i.e., honorable. 208–209. **out of the air:** the open air, presumably; some lobbies were not enclosed. 212. **pregnant:** quick-witted. 213. **happiness:** successful aptness. 215. **suddenly:** immediately. 232. **indifferent:** i.e., in between, at neither extreme. 235–37. **very button . . . her shoe:** i.e., neither on the top nor trodden down. 240. **favours:** Fortune's favors are compared with the sexual favors of a woman. 241. **her privates we:** we are *very* intimate with her.

What have you, my good friends, deserved at the hands of Fortune, that she sends you to prison hither?

GUILDENSTERN Prison, my lord?

HAMLET Denmark's a prison.

ROSENCRANTZ Then is the world one.

HAMLET A goodly one, in which there are many confines, wards,° and dungeons; Denmark being one o'th'worst.

ROSENCRANTZ We think not so my lord.

HAMLET Why then 'tis none to you, for there is nothing either good or bad but thinking makes it so. To me it is a prison.

ROSENCRANTZ Why then your ambition makes it one; 'tis too narrow for your mind.

HAMLET O God, I could be bounded in a nutshell, and count myself a king of infinite space, were it not that I have bad dreams.

GUILDENSTERN Which dreams indeed are ambition, for the very substance of the ambitious° is merely the shadow of a dream.

HAMLET A dream itself is but a shadow.

ROSENCRANTZ Truly, and I hold ambition of so airy and light a quality that it is but a shadow's shadow.

HAMLET Then are our beggars bodies, and our monarchs and outstretched heroes the beggars' shadows.° Shall we to th'court? for by my fay° I cannot reason.

BOTH We'll wait upon you.

HAMLET No such matter. I will not sort you° with the rest of my servants; for to speak to you like an honest man, I am most dreadfully attended.° But in the beaten way of friendship,° what make you at Elsinore?

ROSENCRANTZ To visit you my lord, no other occasion.

HAMLET Beggar that I am,° I am even poor in thanks, but I thank you—and sure, dear friends, my thanks are too dear a halfpenny.° Were you not sent for? Is it your own inclining? Is it a free visitation? Come, deal justly with me. Come, come. Nay, speak.

GUILDENSTERN What should we say my lord?

HAMLET Why, anything but to the purpose. You were sent for—and there is a kind of confession in your looks which your modesties° have not craft enough to colour. I know the good king and queen have sent for you.

ROSENCRANTZ To what end my lord?

HAMLET That you must teach me. But let me conjure° you, by the rights of our fellowship, by the consonancy° of our youth, by the obligation of our ever-preserved love, and by what more dear a better proposer can charge you withal, be even° and direct with me, whether you were sent for or no.

ROSENCRANTZ (*To Guildenstern*) What say you?

HAMLET (*Aside*) Nay then I have an eye of you.°—If you love me, hold not off.

GUILDENSTERN My lord, we were sent for.

HAMLET I will tell you why. So shall my anticipation prevent your discovery,° and your secrecy to the king and queen moult no feather. I have of late, but wherefore I know not, lost all my mirth, forgone all custom of exercises;° and indeed it goes so heavily with my disposition that this goodly frame, the earth, seems to me a sterile promontory;° this most excellent canopy the air, look you, this brave o'erhanging firmament, this majestical roof fretted° with golden fire—why, it appeareth no other thing to me but a foul and pestilent congregation of vapours. What a piece of work is a man! How

---

255. **confines, wards:** terms for places of confinement. 267. **substance of the ambitious:** material that ambitious people live on. 273–75. **Then . . . shadows:** Hamlet seems to mean that if the substance of the ambitious is a shadow, only the lowest in society will have real bodies— monarchs and great men are all ambitious and are therefore shadows. 275. **fay:** faith. 277. **sort you:** class you. 280. **I am most dreadfully attended:** I have such a rotten lot of servants. But the phrase has private meanings for Hamlet: the phrase must bring the Ghost to mind. 281. **beaten way of friendship:** He means he has neglected the ordinary politeness of greeting. He thus makes an offhand introduction of his own cross-examination. 285. **Beggar that I am:** (1.) a beggar in the terms of the preceding conversation, as he is not ambitious; (2.) a beggar in his own eyes as a dispossessed prince in prison. 286. **too dear a halfpenny:** i.e., at a halfpenny, not worth anything; certainly not like a king's remembrance. 294. **modesties:** sense of shame. 299. **conjure:** solemnly entreat. 300. **consonancy:** accord, agreement. He means the harmony between them in their younger days (see 11. above). 302. **even:** straightforward, "on the level." 305. **of you:** on you. 309–10. **shall my anticipation prevent your discovery:** my being beforehand will save you from disclosing your commission. 312. **custom of exercises:** i.e., pursuing the activities of a gentleman, such as fencing, riding, hawking, dancing. 316. **sterile promontory:** a barren rocky point jutting out into the sea of eternity. 318. **fretted:** interlaced, patterned (as in a decorated ceiling).

noble in reason, how infinite in faculties, in form and moving how express and admirable, in action how like an angel, in apprehension how like a god! The beauty of the world, the paragon° of animals—and yet to me, what is this quintessence of dust? Man delights not me—no, nor woman neither, though by your smiling you seem to say so.

ROSENCRANTZ My lord, there was no such stuff in my thoughts.

HAMLET Why did ye laugh then, when I said man delights not me?

ROSENCRANTZ To think, my lord, if you delight not in man, what lenten° entertainment° the players shall receive from you. We coted them° on the way, and hither are they coming to offer you service.

HAMLET He that plays the king shall be welcome, his majesty shall have tribute of me;° the adventurous knight shall use his foil and target,° the lover shall not sigh gratis, the humorous man° shall end his part in peace, the clown shall make those laugh whose lungs are tickle o'th'sere,° and the lady shall say her mind freely—or the blank verse shall halt° for't.° What players are they?

ROSENCRANTZ Even those you were wont to take such delight in, the tragedians° of the city.

HAMLET How chances it they travel? their residence, both in reputation and profit, was better both ways.°

ROSENCRANTZ I think their inhibition comes by the means of the late innovation.°

HAMLET Do they hold the same estimation they did when I was in the city? Are they so followed?

ROSENCRANTZ No indeed are they not.

HAMLET How comes it? Do they grow rusty?

ROSENCRANTZ Nay, their endeavour keeps in the wonted pace, but there is sir an eyrie of children, little eyases,° that cry out on the top of question° and are most tyrannically° clapped for't. These are now the fashion, and so be-rattle° the common stages° (so they call them) that many wearing rapiers° are afraid of goose-quills,° and dare scarce come thither.

HAMLET What, are they children? Who maintains 'em? How are they escoted?° Will they pursue the quality° no longer than they can sing? Will they not say afterwards, if they should grow themselves to common players°—as it is most like if their means are no better,° their writers do them wrong to make them exclaim against their own succession?°

ROSENCRANTZ Faith, there has been much to do on both sides, and the nation holds it no sin to tar° them to controversy. There was for a while no money bid for argument° unless the poet and the player went to cuffs° in the question.

HAMLET Is't possible?

GUILDENSTERN Oh there has been much throwing about of brains.

HAMLET Do the boys carry it away?

---

326. **paragon:** pattern of excellence. 335. **lenten:** i.e., austere. 335. **entertainment:** reception. 336. **coted them:** passed them by. 340. **his majesty shall have tribute of me:** as we pay money and offer adulation to real kings, so the Player King will get payment and praise. The implication is that Hamlet is prepared to honor one pseudo-king with as much seriousness as another. 341. **foil and target:** sword and shield. 342. **gratis:** for nothing. 342–43. **humorous man:** man with a humor in the Elizabethan sense, the eccentric. 344–45. **tickle o'th'sere:** easily triggered. 346. **the lady . . . halt for't:** If the lady can't say all she has to say—which will be the part that is written down for her—then clearly there will be some holes in the blank verse. 346. **halt:** limp. 348. **tragedians:** properly, tragic actors; here, actors generally. 350–52. **their residence. . . ways:** they did better in reputation and profit when they stayed at home. 353–54. **their inhibition . . . innovation:** i.e., they are forbidden to play in the city because of the recent political disturbance. "Inhibition" implies a closing of the theaters in the capital (which was a constant threat to the players' livelihood in England). 360–61. **eyrie of children, little eyases:** nest of children, little unfledged hawks. This is a reference to the revival of the boys' acting companies about 1600. Their new organization, more professional and commercial, made them, for a brief time, formidable rivals to the adult companies. 361. **cry out on the top of question:** "Question" frequently means "dispute" or "controversy." Perhaps this means that the boys enthusiastically carry on the theater war in their treble voices. 362. **tyrannically:** inordinately, outrageously. 363. **be-rattle:** rattle, shake. 363. **common stages:** the usual term for the public theaters. 364–65. **many wearing rapiers:** the men-about-town, the gallants. 365. **afriad of goose-quills:** The satire of the children's dramatists has so discredited the public theaters that fashionable gallants don't like being seen there. 367. **escoted:** maintained financially. 369. **quality:** profession. 371. **common players:** professional actors. 372. **if their means are no better:** if they do not acquire a better means of supporting themselves. 374. **succession:** that which they will succeed to. 377. **tar:** incite, provoke. 377–78. **no money bid for argument:** i.e., no company wanted to hear about a new play. 379. **cuffs:** blows, punches.

ROSENCRANTZ Ay that they do my lord, Hercules and his load° too.

HAMLET It is not very strange, for my uncle is king of Denmark, and those that would make mouths° at him while my father lived give twenty, forty, fifty, a hundred ducats° apiece for his picture in little. 'Sblood, there is something in this more than natural, if philosophy could find it out.°

A flourish

GUILDENSTERN There are the players.

HAMLET Gentlemen, you are welcome to Elsinore. Your hands, come then. Th'appurtenance of welcome is fashion and ceremony. Let me comply with you° in this garb,° lest my extent° to the players, which I tell you must show fairly outwards, should more appear like entertainment° than yours. You are welcome—but my uncle-father and aunt mother are deceived.

GUILDENSTERN In what my dear lord?

HAMLET I am but mad north-north-west.° When the wind is southerly, I know a hawk from a handsaw.°

Enter POLONIUS

POLONIUS Well be with you gentlemen.

HAMLET Hark you Guildenstern, and you too—at each ear a hearer. That great baby you see there is not yet out of his swaddling clouts.

ROSENCRANTZ Happily° he's the second time come to them, for they say an old man is twice a child.

HAMLET I will prophesy: he comes to tell me of the players, mark it.—You say right sir, a Monday morning, 'twas then indeed.

POLONIUS My lord, I have news to tell you.

HAMLET My lord, I have news to tell you. When Roscius° was an actor in Rome—

POLONIUS The actors are come hither my lord.

HAMLET Buzz, buzz!°

POLONIUS Upon my honour.

HAMLET Then came each actor on his ass—

POLONIUS The best actors in the world, either for tragedy, comedy, history, pastoral, pastoral-comical, historical-pastoral, tragical-hitorical, tragical-comical-historical-pastoral, scene individable or poem unlimited.° Seneca cannot be too heavy, nor Plautus° too light. For the law of writ and the liberty, these are the only men.

HAMLET O Jephtha judge of Israel, what a treasure hadst thou!

POLONIUS What a treasure had he my lord?

HAMLET Why—
"One fair daughter and no more,
The which he lovèd passing well."°

POLONIUS Still on my daughter.

HAMLET Am I not i'th'right, old Jephtha?

POLONIUS If you call me Jephtha my lord, I have a daughter that I love passing well.

HAMLET Nay, that follows not.

POLONIUS What follows then my lord?

HAMLET Why—
"As by lot God wot,"
And then you know—
"It came to pass, as most like it was,"—
the first row of the pious chanson° will show you more, for look where my abridgement° comes.

Enter the players

Y'are welcome masters, welcome all. I am glad to see thee well. Welcome good friends. Oh, my old friend! why, thy face is valanced° since I saw thee last; com'st thou to beard°

384–85. **Hercules and his load:** The emblem of the Globe Theatre is supposed to have been Hercules carrying the celestial globe on his shoulders. 387. **mouths:** grimaces. 389. **ducats:** coins of gold or silver, used in many European countries. 390–91. **more than natural, if philosophy could find it out:** i.e., there is something abnormal about it, as scientific investigation would show. 396. **comply with you:** pay you the usual courtesies. 396. **garb:** manner of doing things. 396. **my extent:** what I extend, how I behave. 398. **entertainment:** welcome. 402. **but mad north-north-west:** He means (1.) that he is only a little away from the true north of sanity and (2.) that he is not mad at all points of the compass—i.e., at all times. 403–404. **a hawk from a handsaw:** Hamlet's point is "I am mad only at certain times; at other times I can discriminate as well as a madman." 409. **Happily:** perhaps. 416. **Roscius:** a great Roman comic actor (d. 62. BCE). 418. **Buzz, buzz!:** A "buzz" is a rumor. 425. **scene undividable or poem unlimited:** "Individable" and "unlimited" are the terms to use when there can be no further refinement or subdivision in this absurd progress of categorization. 426. **Seneca, Plautus:** These Roman dramatists, one tragic and one comic, were the classical dramatists who were best known to the Elizabethans and who most influenced their drama.

429–34. **Jephtha . . . passing well:** Jephtha vowed to sacrifice the first living thing he met if he returned successfully from war. It turned out to be his own daughter and he sacrificed her. 445. **first row of the pious chanson:** A "row" is properly a line, but this does not make much sense; perhaps "stanza." 446. **abridgement:** that which shortens my recitation. 449. **valanced:** fringed, curtained around. 450. **beard:** challenge, defy.

me in Denmark? What, my young lady° and mistress — byrlady,° your ladyship is nearer to heaven than when I saw you last by the altitude of a chopine.° Pray God your voice like a piece of uncurrent gold be not cracked within the ring.° Masters, you are all welcome. We'll e'en to't like French falconers, fly at anything we see: we'll have a speech straight. Come give us a taste of your quality:° come, a passionate speech.

I PLAYER What speech, my good lord?

HAMLET I heard thee speak me a speech once, but it was never acted, or if it was, not above once, for the play I remember pleased not the million: 'twas caviary° to the general.° But it was, as I received it, and others whose judgements in such matters cried in the top of mine,° an excellent play, well digested° in the scenes, set down with as much modesty° as cunning.° I remember one said there were no sallets° in the lines to make the matter savoury, nor no matter in the phrase that might indict the author of affectation, but called it an honest method,° as wholesome as sweet and by very much more handsome than fine.° One speech in't I chiefly loved, 'twas Aeneas' tale to Dido, and thereabout of it especially where he speaks of Priam's slaughter.° If it live in your memory, begin at this line, let me see, let me see —
"The rugged° Pyrrhus,° like th'Hyrcanian
beast"° —
'Tis not so, it begins with Pyrrhus —
"The rugged Pyrrhus, he whose sable arms,
Black as his purpose, did the night resemble
When he lay couchèd° in the ominous horse,
Hath now this dread and black complexion
smeared
With heraldy more dismal.° Head to foot
Now is he total gules,° horridly tricked°
With blood of fathers, mothers, daughters, sons,
Baked and impasted with the parching streets,°
That lend a tyrannous° and a damnèd light

Vielmetter Los Angeles

Artist Nicole Eisenman (b. 1965) completed this painting, entitled *Hamlet*, in 2007.
What aspects of Hamlet's character do you believe Eisenman sought to represent in this portrait? Take a close look at Eisenman's use of color in this image.

451. **my young lady:** a boy actor who takes female roles; presumably the Player Queen of 3.2. 452. **byrlady:** by our Lady. 454. **chopine:** additional base to a lady's shoe to increase height. 455–56. **cracked within the ring:** Hamlet means "I hope you haven't lost your virginity as a player of female parts, and ceased to be acceptable (current), by the breaking of your voice." 459. **quality:** professional skill. 465. **caviary:** a common early form of "caviar." 465. **the general:** people in general, the multitude. 467. **cried in the top of mine:** counted more than mine. 468. **digested:** arranged, disposed. 469. **modesty:** moderation, restraint. 469. **cunning:** skill. 470. **sallets:** salads; generally thought to mean "spicy bits" — indecencies. 474. **method:** the disposition of material in a literary work. 475. **fine:** showy, over-elaborate. 476–78. **Aeneas' tale . . . slaughter:** See Virgil's *Aeneid* II, 506–58. Priam's death is the subject of an extended passage in *Dido, Queen of Carthage* by Marlowe and Nashe, and it is certain that Shakespeare had this earlier treatment in mind when creating the speech that now follows. 480. **rugged:** rough and fierce. Applied to an animal, it could mean shaggy, which is perhaps why Hamlet makes a false start on the Hyrcanian beast. 480. **Pyrrhus:** Pyrrhus, or Neoptolemus, the son of Achilles, was summoned to the Trojan war to avenge his father. He was renowned for his savagery and barbarity. 480–481. **Hyrcanian beast:** tiger from Hyrcania, near the Caspian Sea. Virgil spoke of them in *Aeneid* IV, 368. 484. **couchèd:** concealed. 486. **dismal:** sinister. 487. **gules:** the heraldic name for red. 487. **tricked:** decorated. 489. **Baked . . . streets:** The blood is dried into a paste on Pyrrhus by the heat of the burning street. 490. **tyrannous:** ferocious.

To their lord's murder. Roasted in wrath and fire,
And thus o'er-sizèd° with coagulate gore,
With eyes like carbuncles,° the hellish Pyrrhus
Old grandsire Priam seeks — "
So, proceed you.

POLONIUS 'Fore God my lord, well spoken, with good accent and good discretion.

I PLAYER "Anon° he finds him,
Striking too short at Greeks; his antique sword,
Rebellious to his arm, lies where it falls,
Repugnant to° command. Unequal matched,
Pyrrhus at Priam drives, in rage strikes wide,
But with the whiff and wind of his fell sword
Th'unnervèd father falls. Then senseless° Ilium,°
Seeming to feel this blow, with flaming top
Stoops to his base, and with a hideous crash
Takes prisoner Pyrrhus' ear; for lo, his sword,
Which was declining on the milky° head
Of reverend Priam, seemed i'th'air to stick.
So, as a painted tyrant,° Pyrrhus stood,
And like a neutral to his will and matter,
Did nothing.
But as we often see against° some storm,
A silence in the heavens, the rack° stand still,
The bold winds speechless, and the orb° below
As hush as death, anon the dreadful thunder
Doth rend the region;° so after Pyrrhus' pause,
A rousèd vengeance sets him new a-work,
And never did the Cyclops'°hammers fall
On Mars's armour, forged for proof eterne,°
With less remorse° than Pyrrhus' bleeding sword
Now falls on Priam.
Out, out, thou strumpet Fortune! All you gods,
In general synod take away her power,
Break all the spokes and fellies° from her wheel,
And bowl the round nave° down the hill of heaven
As low as to the fiends."

POLONIUS This is too long.

HAMLET It shall to th' barber's with your beard. Prithee say on. He's for a jig° or a tale of bawdry, or he sleeps. Say on, come to Hecuba.

I PLAYER "But who — ah woe! — had seen the mobled queen — "

HAMLET The mobled queen?

POLONIUS That's good, "mobled° queen" is good.

I PLAYER "Run barefoot up and down, threat'ning the flames
With bisson° rheum, a clout° upon that head
Where late the diadem stood, and, for a robe,
About her lank and all o'er-teemèd loins°
A blanket, in th'alarm of fear caught up —
Who this had seen, with tongue in venom steeped
'Gainst Fortune's state° would treason have pronounced.
But if the gods themselves did see her then,
When she saw Pyrrhus make malicious sport
In mincing with his sword her husband's limbs,
The instant burst of clamour that she made,
Unless things mortal move them not at all,
Would have made milch° the burning eyes of heaven,
And passion° in the gods."

POLONIUS Look where° he has not turned his colour, and has tears in's eyes. Prithee no more.

HAMLET 'Tis well, I'll have thee speak out the rest of this soon. — Good my lord, will you see the players well bestowed? Do you hear, let them be well used, for they are the abstract° and brief chronicles of the time. After your death you were better have a bad epitaph than their ill report while you live.

POLONIUS My lord, I will use them according to their desert.

HAMLET God's bodkin man, much better. Use every man after his desert, and who shall scape whipping? Use them after your own honour and

---

492. **o'er-sizèd:** "To oversize" is to cover over with size, the sticky wash used to prepare surfaces for painting. 493. **carbuncles:** large and supposedly luminous precious stones. 498. **Anon:** presently. 501. **Repugnant to:** resisting. 504. **senseless:** insensible. 504. **Ilium:** Troy. 508. **milky:** i.e., white-haired. 510. **painted tyrant:** tyrant in a painting. 513. **against:** before. 514. **rack:** cloud formation. 515. **orb:** globe, hence earth. 517. **region:** sky. 519. **Cyclops:** The one-eyed giants worked in Vulcan's smithy. 520. **proof eterne:** everlasting resistance. 521. **remorse:** pity. 525. **fellies:** wooden pieces forming the rim of a wheel. 526. **nave:** hub of the wheel. 530. **jig:** the afterpiece, with song and dance, that often concluded theater performances. 534. **mobled:** muffled. 536. **bisson:** blind or near-blind. 536. **clout:** cloth. 538. **all o'er-teemèd loins:** loins that had borne too many children. 541. **state:** government. 546. **milch:** properly, exuding milk. The stars would weep milky tears (because of the Milky Way?). 548. **passion:** violent sorrow. 549. **Look where:** see if. 554. **abstract:** epitome, summing-up, distillation.

dignity; the less they deserve, the more merit is in your bounty. Take them in.

POLONIUS Come sirs. *Exit Polonius*

HAMLET Follow him friends, we'll hear a play tomorrow. — Dost thou hear me old friend, can you play *The Murder of Gonzago*?

I PLAYER Ay my lord.

HAMLET We'll ha't tomorrow night. You could for a need study a speech of some dozen or sixteen lines, which I would set down and insert in't, could you not?

I PLAYER Ay my lord.

HAMLET Very well. Follow that lord, and look you mock him not.

Exeunt Players

My good friends, I'll leave you till night. You are welcome to Elsinore.

ROSENCRANTZ Good my lord.

Exeunt Rosencrantz and Guildenstern

HAMLET Ay so, God bye to you. Now I am alone.
O what a rogue and peasant slave am I!
Is it not monstrous that this player here,
But in a fiction, in a dream of passion,
Could force his soul so to his own conceit
That from her working° all his visage wanned,°
Tears in his eyes, distraction in's aspect,
A broken voice, and his whole function suiting
With forms to his conceit?° And all for nothing?
For Hecuba!
What's Hecuba to him, or he to Hecuba,
That he should weep for her? What would he do,
Had he the motive and the cue for passion
That I have? He would drown the stage with tears,
And cleave the general ear with horrid speech,
Make mad the guilty and appal the free,°
Confound the ignorant, and amaze° indeed
The very faculties of eyes and ears. Yet I,
A dull and muddy-mettled° rascal, peak°
Like John-a-dreams, unpregnant of my cause,°
And can say nothing — no, not for a king,
Upon whose property° and most dear life
A damned defeat° was made. Am I a coward?
Who calls me villain, breaks my pate across,
Plucks off my beard and blows it in my face,
Tweaks me by th'nose, gives me the lie° i'th'throat
As deep as to the lungs?° Who does me this?
Ha, 'swounds, I should take it, for it cannot be
But I am pigeon-livered,° and lack gall
To make oppression bitter,° or ere this
I should ha' fatted all the region kites°
With this slave's offal. Bloody, bawdy villain!
Remorseless,° treacherous, lecherous, kindless° villain!
Oh, vengeance!
Why, what an ass am I! This is most brave,
That I, the son of the dear murderèd,°
Prompted to my revenge by heaven and hell,°
Must like a whore unpack° my heart with words,
And fall a-cursing like a very drab,
A scullion!°
Fie upon't, foh! About,° my brains. Hum, I have heard
That guilty creatures sitting at a play
Have by the very cunning° of the scene°
Been struck so to the soul, that presently
They have proclaimed their malefactions;
For murder, though it have no tongue, will speak
With most miraculous organ. I'll have these players

585. **from her working:** by reason of her (the soul's) activity. 585. **wanned:** grew pale. 587–88. **his whole function . . . conceit:** all his bodily powers producing the expressions proper to his imaginings. 595. **free:** those who are free of crime. 596. **Confound:** astonish and confuse. 596. **amaze:** paralyze. 598. **muddy-mettled:** muddy-spirited. 598. **peak:** go into a decline. 599. **John-a-dreams:** nickname for a dreamy person. 603. **unpregnant of my cause:** "Pregnant" means quick, prompt, ready, apt — so to be "unpregnant" of something means *not* reacting quickly to it. 601. **property:** i.e., the kingdom (rather than his material possessions). 602. **defeat:** destruction. 605. **gives me the lie:** accuses me of lying. 605–06. **i'th'throat . . . lungs:** i.e., deep-rooted and not superficial or casual lies. 608. **pigeon-livered:** The liver is seen as the seat of courage. The pigeon has no gall. 609. **To make oppression bitter:** i.e., to make Claudius's oppression bitter to himself. 610. **region kites:** hawks, or birds of prey, circling in the sky. 612. **Remorseless:** pitiless. 612. **kindless:** without natural feeling. 615. **the son of the dear murderèd:** the son of the loved victim. 616. **by heaven and hell:** Hamlet means that the whole supernatural world of good and evil lies behind his revenge, not that both heaven and hell are urging him at the same time. 617. **unpack:** unload, relieve. 619. **A scullion!:** a person of the lowest order, used as an abusive epithet. 620. **About:** go about it! 622. **cunning:** skill. 622. **scene:** dramatic presentation.

Play something like the murder of my father
Before mine uncle. I'll observe his looks,
I'll tent° him to the quick.° If a do blench,°
I know my course. The spirit that I have seen
May be a devil — and the devil hath power
T'assume a pleasing shape. Yea, and perhaps,
Out of my weakness and my melancholy,
As he is very potent with such spirits,°
Abuses me to damn me. I'll have grounds
More relative° than this. The play's the thing
Wherein I'll catch the conscience of the king.
Exit

Act III, Scene i

Enter KING, QUEEN, POLONIUS, OPHELIA, ROSENCRANTZ, GUILDENSTERN, LORDS

CLAUDIUS And can you by no drift of circumstance°
Get from him why he puts on this confusion,°
Grating° so harshly all his days of quiet
With turbulent and dangerous lunacy?

ROSENCRANTZ He does confess he feels himself distracted,
But from what cause a will by no means speak.

GUILDENSTERN Nor do we find him forward° to be sounded,
But with a crafty madness° keeps aloof
When we would bring him on to some confession
Of his true state.

GERTRUDE Did he receive you well?

ROSENCRANTZ Most like a gentleman.

GUILDENSTERN But with much forcing of his disposition.

ROSENCRANTZ Niggard of question, but of our demands
Most free in his reply.°

GERTRUDE Did you assay him
To° any pastime?

ROSENCRANTZ Madam, it so fell out that certain players
We o'er-raught° on the way; of these we told him,
And there did seem in him a kind of joy
To hear of it. They are about the court,
And as I think, they have already order
This night to play before him.

POLONIUS 'Tis most true,
And he beseeched me to entreat your majesties
To hear and see the matter.

CLAUDIUS With all my heart, and it doth much content me
To hear him so inclined.
Good gentlemen, give him a further edge,°
And drive his purpose on to these delights.

ROSENCRANTZ We shall my lord.
Exeunt Rosencrantz and Guildenstern

CLAUDIUS Sweet Gertrude, leave us too,
For we have closely° sent for Hamlet hither,
That he, as 'twere by accident, may here
Affront° Ophelia. Her father and myself,
Lawful espials,°
Will so bestow ourselves,° that seeing unseen,
We may of their encounter frankly° judge,
And gather by him, as he is behaved,
If't be th'affliction of his love or no
That thus he suffers for.

GERTRUDE I shall obey you.
And for your part Ophelia, I do wish
That your good beauties be the happy cause
Of Hamlet's wildness. So shall I hope your virtues
Will bring him to his wonted way again,
To both your honours.

OPHELIA Madam, I wish it may.
[*Exit Gertrude with Lords*]

629. **tent:** probe. 629. **to the quick:** i.e., to where it hurts. 629. **blench:** flinch and turn aside. 634. **very potent with such spirits:** It was a commonplace of ghost lore that melancholics were specially prone to visitation by demons. 635–636. **grounds / More relative:** reasons for acting that are nearer at hand, more tangible. **Act III, Scene i.** 1. **drift of circumstance:** steering of roundabout inquiry. 2. **why he puts on this confusion:** why he is assuming the guise of madness. 3. **Grating:** the physical action of roughening by scraping and rasping. 7. **forward:** disposed, inclined. 8. **crafty madness:** an affecting of madness. 13–14. **Niggard . . . reply:** asking few questions but readily answering ours. 14–15. **assay him / To:** i.e., try him with the suggestion of. 17. **o'er-raught:** overreached; came up to and passed, overhauled. 26. **edge:** keenness (of appetite). 29. **closely:** secretly. 31. **Affront:** come face to face with. 32. **espials:** spies. 33, 44. **bestow ourselves:** station or position ourselves. 34. **frankly:** freely, without obstacle.

Robert Mankoff/CartoonStock, Ltd.

This cartoon, which originally appeared in the *New Yorker*, reflects on Hamlet's most famous soliloquy.

How does this cartoon make light of one of the central questions of the play? What perspective does it take on the character of Hamlet and his concerns?

POLONIUS Ophelia walk you here. — Gracious,° so please you,
We will bestow ourselves.° — Read on this book,°
That show of such an exercise may colour°
Your loneliness.° — We are oft to blame in this:
'Tis too much proved, that with devotion's visage,°
And pious action, we do sugar o'er
The devil himself.

CLAUDIUS (*Aside*) Oh, 'tis too true.
How smart a lash that speech doth give my conscience!
The harlot's cheek, beautied with plastering art,
Is not more ugly to the thing that helps it°
Than is my deed to my most painted word.
O heavy burden!

POLONIUS I hear him coming. Let's withdraw, my lord.

Exeunt Claudius and Polonius

Enter HAMLET

HAMLET To be, or not to be, that is the question —
Whether 'tis nobler in the mind to suffer°
The slings° and arrows of outrageous fortune,
Or to take arms against a sea of troubles,
And by opposing end them.° To die, to sleep —
No more; and by a sleep to say we end
The heart-ache and the thousand natural shocks
That flesh is heir to — 'tis a consummation°
Devoutly to be wished. To die, to sleep —
To sleep, perchance to dream. Ay, there's the rub,°
For in that sleep of death what dreams may come,
When we have shuffled off this mortal coil,°
Must give us pause. There's the respect°
That makes calamity of so long life,°
For who would bear the whips and scorns of time,°
Th'oppressor's wrong, the proud man's contumely,
The pangs of disprized° love, the law's delay,
The insolence of office, and the spurns
That patient merit of th'unworthy takes,°
When he himself might his quietus° make
With a bare bodkin?° Who would fardels° bear,
To grunt and sweat under a weary life,
But that the dread of something after death,
The undiscovered country from whose bourn°
No traveller returns,° puzzles the will,°

43. **Gracious:** i.e., your grace (to the king). 44. **this book:** This is obviously a prayerbook (see 47, 89). 45. **colour:** provide a pretext for. 46. **loneliness:** being alone. 47. **devotion's visage:** a face expressing devoutness. 52. **to the thing that helps it:** compared with the cosmetic adornment. 57. **in the mind to suffer:** The stoical endurance which is Hamlet's first alternative is a matter of mental effort and strain. 58. **slings:** missiles. 60. **by opposing end them:** The alternative to patient endurance is suicide. 63. **consummation:** completion. 65. **rub:** impediment (from the game of bowls). 67. **shuffled off this mortal coil:** got rid of the turmoil of living. 68. **respect:** consideration. 69. **of so long life:** so long-lived. 70. **time:** the times. 72. **disprized:** unvalued. 74. **of th'unworthy takes:** receives from unworthy people. 75. **quietus:** discharge or acquittance. 76. **a bare bodkin:** a mere dagger. 76. **fardels:** burdens. 79. **bourn:** boundary. 80. **No traveller returns:** The afterlife, he suggests, is one of those far-off countries of which only doubtful and untrustworthy reports exist; it is not one of those explored countries from which reputable travelers have actually returned to give us their eyewitness accounts. 80. **puzzles the will:** i.e., brings it to a halt in confusion.

And makes us rather bear those ills we have
Than fly to others that we know not of?
Thus conscience does make cowards of us all,
And thus the native hue° of resolution
Is sicklied o'er° with the pale cast° of thought,°
And enterprises of great pitch° and moment
With this regard° their currents turn awry
And lose the name of action. Soft you° now,
The fair Ophelia. — Nymph, in thy orisons
Be all my sins remembered.

OPHELIA Good my lord,
How does your honour for this many a day?

HAMLET I humbly thank you, well, well, well.

OPHELIA My lord, I have remembrances° of yours
That I have longèd long to re-deliver.
I pray you now receive them.

HAMLET No, not I,
I never gave you aught.

OPHELIA My honoured lord, you know right well you did,
And with them words of so sweet breath° composed
As made the things more rich. Their perfume lost,°
Take these again, for to the noble mind
Rich gifts wax poor when givers prove unkind.
There my lord.

HAMLET Ha, ha, are you honest?°

OPHELIA My lord?

HAMLET Are you fair?

OPHELIA What means your lordship?

HAMLET That if you be honest and fair, your honesty should admit no discourse to your beauty.°

OPHELIA Could beauty, my lord, have better commerce than with honesty?

HAMLET Ay truly, for the power of beauty will sooner transform honesty from what it is to a bawd, than the force of honesty can translate beauty into his likeness. This was sometime a paradox, but now the time gives it proof. I did love you once.

OPHELIA Indeed my lord you made me believe so.

HAMLET You should not have believed me, for virtue cannot so inoculate our old stock° but we shall relish° of it. I loved you not.

OPHELIA I was the more deceived.

HAMLET Get thee to a nunnery — why wouldst thou be a breeder of sinners? I am myself indifferent honest,° but yet I could accuse me of such things, that it were better my mother had not borne me. I am very proud, revengeful, ambitious, with more offences at my beck than I have thoughts to put them in, imagination to give them shape, or time to act them in. What should such fellows as I do crawling between earth and heaven? We are arrant knaves all, believe none of us. Go thy ways to a nunnery. Where's your father?

OPHELIA At home my lord.

HAMLET Let the doors be shut upon him, that he may play the fool nowhere but in's own house. Farewell.

OPHELIA Oh help him you sweet heavens!

HAMLET If thou dost marry, I'll give thee this plague for thy dowry: be thou as chaste as ice, as pure as snow, thou shalt not escape calumny. Get thee to a nunnery, go. Farewell. Or if thou wilt needs marry, marry a fool, for wise men know well enough what monsters° you make of them. To a nunnery go, and quickly too. Farewell.

OPHELIA O heavenly powers, restore him!

HAMLET I have heard of your paintings too, well enough. God hath given you one face and you make yourselves another. You jig, you amble,° and you lisp, you nickname God's creatures, and make your wantonness your ignorance.° Go to, I'll no more on't, it hath made me mad. I say we will have no mo° marriages. Those that are married already, all but one shall live, the rest shall keep as they are. To a nunnery, go. *Exit*

OPHELIA Oh what a noble mind is here o'erthrown!
The courtier's, soldier's, scholar's, eye, tongue, sword,

---

84. **native hue:** natural color or complexion. 85. **sicklied o'er:** unhealthily covered. 85. **cast:** tinge, tint. 85. **thought:** contemplation. 86. **pitch:** height, scope. 87. **With this regard:** on this account. 88. **soft you:** be cautious. 93. **remembrances:** keepsakes, gifts. 98. **breath:** "utterance" or "language." 99. **Their perfume lost:** The sweetness of both the words and the gifts has disappeared because of the unkindness of the giver. 103. **honest:** chaste. 107–08. **your honesty . . . your beauty:** your virtue should not allow your beauty to converse with it. 119. **inoculate our old stock:** graft a new stem of virtue onto the old sinful trunk so as to eradicate all trace of our previous nature. 120. **relish:** have a touch or tinge. 123–24. **indifferent honest:** moderately virtuous. 143. **monsters:** i.e., horned cuckolds. 148. **amble:** walk affectedly. 150. **make your wantonness your ignorance:** pretend your license is just simplicity and innocence. 152. **mo:** more.

Th'expectancy and rose of the fair state,
The glass of fashion and the mould of form,°
Th'observed of all observers,° quite, quite down,
And I of ladies most deject and wretched,
That sucked the honey of his music vows,
Now see that noble and most sovereign reason,
Like sweet bells jangled, out of time and harsh;
That unmatched form and feature of blown
youth°
Blasted with ecstasy.° Oh woe is me
T'have seen what I have seen, see what I see.

Enter KING *and* POLONIUS

CLAUDIUS Love? His affections° do not that way
tend;
Nor what he spake, though it lacked form a little,
Was not like madness. There's something in
his soul
O'er which his melancholy sits on brood,°
And I do doubt the hatch and the disclose
Will be some danger; which for to prevent,
I have in quick determination
Thus set it down: he shall with speed to England
For the demand of our neglected tribute.°
Haply the seas, and countries different,
With variable objects, shall expel
This something-settled matter in his heart,
Whereon his brains still beating puts him thus
From fashion of himself.° What think you on't?

POLONIUS It shall do well. But yet do I believe
The origin and commencement of his grief
Sprung from neglected love. How now Ophelia?
You need not tell us what Lord Hamlet said,
We heard it all. My lord, do as you please,
But if you hold it fit, after the play,
Let his queen mother all alone entreat him
To show his grief. Let her be round° with him,
And I'll be placed, so please you, in the ear
Of all their conference. If she find him not,°
To England send him; or confine him where
Your wisdom best shall think.

CLAUDIUS It shall be so.
Madness in great ones must not unwatched go.

Exeunt

Act III, Scene ii

Enter HAMLET *and two or three of the* PLAYERS

HAMLET Speak the speech I pray you as I pronounced it to you, trippingly on the tongue; but if you mouth it as many of our players do, I had as lief° the town-crier spoke my lines. Nor do not saw the air too much with your hand thus, but use all gently; for in the very torrent, tempest, and, as I may say, whirlwind of your passion, you must acquire and beget° a temperance that may give it smoothness. Oh, it offends me to the soul to hear a robustious° periwig-pated° fellow tear a passion to totters, to very rags, to split the ears of the groundlings,° who for the most part are capable of° nothing but inexplicable° dumb-shows and noise. I would have such a fellow whipped for o'erdoing Termagant°—it out-Herods Herod.° Pray you avoid it.

1 PLAYER I warrant your honour.

HAMLET Be not too tame neither, but let your own discretion be your tutor. Suit the action to the word, the word to the action, with this special observance, that you o'erstep not the modesty° of nature. For anything so o'erdone is from° the purpose of playing, whose end both at the first and now, was and is, to hold as 'twere the mirror

158. **glass . . . form:** "Glass" is the mirror which gives an ideal image and so provides an example. 159. **Th'observed of all observers:** looked up to respectfully by all who turn to others for guidance. 164. **blown youth:** youth in full bloom. 165. **ecstasy:** madness. 166. **affections:** emotions. 170. **sits on brood:** like a bird sitting on eggs—see "hatch" in the next line. 175. **tribute:** the Danegeld, an annual tax imposed in the tenth or eleventh century, whereby the Anglo-Saxons paid the Danes for protection; continued after the Norman Conquest as a land tax. 180. **fashion of himself:** his own proper way of behaving. 188. **round:** direct and outspoken. 190. **find him not:** fails to discover his secret.
Act III, Scene ii. 4. **I had as lief:** it would be as agreeable to me that. 8–9. **acquire and beget:** If the actors obtain this balance and control in themselves, they will be able to produce it in their speeches. 10. **robustious:** rough and rude. 11. **periwig-pated:** wearing a wig. 12. **groundlings:** those who stood in the open yard directly in front of the stage, having paid the cheapest entry fees. 13. **are capable of:** have a capacity for, can understand. 14. **inexplicable:** meaningless. 16. **Termagant:** an imaginary deity supposed to be worshipped by Mohammedans (sometimes spelled Tervagant). 17. **Herod:** familiar as a ranting tyrant in the medieval biblical cycles. 22. **modesty:** restraints, limitations, measure. 23. **from:** away from.

up to nature; to show virtue her own feature, scorn° her own image, and the very age and body of the time his form and pressure.° Now this overdone, or come tardy off,° though it makes the unskillful° laugh, cannot but make the judicious grieve, the censure° of the which one° must in your allowance° o'erweigh a whole theatre of others. Oh, there be players that I have seen play, and heard others praise and that highly, not to speak it profanely, that neither having th'accent of Christians, nor the gait of Christian, pagan, nor man, have so strutted and bellowed that I have thought some of nature's journeymen° had made men, and not made them well, they imitated humanity so abominably.°

1 PLAYER I hope we have reformed that indifferently° with us, sir.

HAMLET Oh reform it altogether. And let those that play your clowns speak no more than is set down for them, for there be of them that will themselves laugh, to set on some quantity of barren spectators to laugh too, though in the meantime some necessary question° of the play be then to be considered. That's villainous, and shows a most pitiful ambition in the fool that uses it. Go make you ready.

Exeunt Players

Enter POLONIUS, ROSENCRANTZ *and* GUILDENSTERN

How now my lord, will the king hear this piece of work?

POLONIUS And the queen too, and that presently.°

HAMLET Bid the players make haste.

Exit Polonius

Will you two help to hasten them?

ROSENCRANTZ Ay my lord.

Exeunt Rosencrantz and Guildenstern

HAMLET What ho, Horatio!

Enter HORATIO

HORATIO Here sweet lord, at your service.

HAMLET Horatio, thou art e'en as just° a man
As e'er my conversation coped withal.°

HORATIO Oh my dear lord.

HAMLET Nay, do not think I flatter,
For what advancement may I hope from thee,
That no revenue hast but thy good spirits°
To feed and clothe thee? Why should the poor be flattered?
No, let the candied° tongue lick absurd pomp
And crook the pregnant° hinges of the knee°
Where thrift° may follow fawning. Dost thou hear?
Since my dear soul was mistress of her choice,
And could of men distinguish her election,
Sh'ath sealed thee for herself,° for thou hast been
As one in suffering all that suffers nothing,
A man that Fortune's buffets and rewards
Hast tane with equal thanks. And blest are those
Whose blood and judgement° are so well commeddled°
That they are not a pipe for Fortune's finger
To sound what stop she please. Give me that man
That is not passion's slave, and I will wear him
In my heart's core, ay in my heart of heart,
As I do thee. Something too much of this.
There is a play tonight before the king:
One scene of it comes near the circumstance°
Which I have told thee of my father's death.
I prithee when thou seest that act afoot,
Even with the very comment of thy soul
Observe my uncle.° If his occulted° guilt
Do not itself unkennel° in one speech,

---

27. **scorn:** i.e., that which is to be scorned. 27–28. **the very . . . pressure:** i.e., gives an impression of the shape of our times in the clearest detail. 29. **come tardy off:** done inadequately or imperfectly. 30. **unskilful:** ignorant and undiscerning. 31. **censure:** judgment. 31. **of the which one:** of one of whom. 32. **your allowance:** i.e., what you will permit or sanction, hence "your scale of values." 38. **nature's journeymen:** These bad actors must have been made not by God, but by some of Nature's hired men, little better than apprentices. 40. **abominably:** away from the nature of man. 42. **indifferently:** reasonably well. 48. **necessary question:** i.e., essential part of the plot. 54. **presently:** immediately. 60. **just:** honorable, upright. 61. **my conversation coped withal:** my encounters with people have brought me in touch with. 64. **spirits:** inner qualities. 66–67. **let . . . knee:** the courtier kissing his patron's hands and bowing is pictured, in beast-fable fashion, as a fawning dog licking and crouching. 66. **candied:** sugared. 67. **pregnant:** quick, ready, prompt. 68. **thrift:** thriving profit, prosperity. 70–71. **And could . . . herself:** and could be discriminating in her choice amongst men, she hath marked you out. 71. **sealed thee for herself:** literally, put a legal seal on you as her property; hence, solemnly attested that you are hers. 75. **blood and judgement:** passion and reason. 75. **commeddled:** mixed together. 82. **circumstance:** circumstances, details. 85–86. **Even with . . . uncle:** i.e., use your most intense powers of observation in watching my uncle. 86. **occulted:** hidden. 87. **unkennel:** The word was used of dislodging or driving a fox from his hole or lair.

It is a damnèd ghost that we have seen,°
And my imaginations° are as foul
As Vulcan's stithy.° Give him heedful note,
For I mine eyes will rivet to his face,
And after we will both our judgements join
In censure of his seeming.°

HORATIO Well my lord.
If a steal aught° the whilst this play is playing
And scape detecting, I will pay the theft.

Sound a flourish

HAMLET They are coming to the play. I must be idle.°
Get you a place.

Danish march (trumpets and kettle-drums). Enter KING, QUEEN, POLONIUS, OPHELIA, ROSENCRANTZ, GUILDENSTERN *and other* LORDS ATTENDANT, *with his* GUARD *carrying torches*

CLAUDIUS How fares our cousin° Hamlet?

HAMLET Excellent i'faith, of the chameleon's dish:° I eat the air, promise-crammed. You cannot feed capons° so.

CLAUDIUS I have nothing with° this answer Hamlet, these words are not mine.°

HAMLET No, nor mine now.—My lord, you played once i'th'university, you say.

POLONIUS That did I my lord, and was accounted a good actor.

HAMLET And what did you enact?

POLONIUS I did enact Julius Caesar. I was killed i'th'Capitol. Brutus killed me.

HAMLET It was a brute part° of him to kill so capital a calf° there.—Be the players ready?

ROSENCRANTZ Ay my lord, they stay upon your patience.

GERTRUDE Come hither my dear Hamlet, sit by me.

HAMLET No good mother, here's metal more attractive.°

POLONIUS Oh ho, do you mark that?

HAMLET Lady, shall I lie in your lap?

OPHELIA No my lord.

HAMLET I mean, my head upon your lap?

OPHELIA Ay my lord.

HAMLET Do you think I meant country matters?°

OPHELIA I think nothing my lord.

HAMLET That's a fair thought to lie between maids' legs.

OPHELIA What is, my lord?

HAMLET Nothing.°

OPHELIA You are merry my lord.

HAMLET Who, I?

OPHELIA Ay my lord.

HAMLET O God, your only jig-maker.° What should a man do but be merry? for look you how cheerfully my mother looks, and my father died within's two hours.

OPHELIA Nay, 'tis twice two months my lord.

HAMLET So long? Nay then let the devil wear black, for I'll have a suit of sables.° O heavens! die two months ago, and not forgotten yet? Then there's hope a great man's memory may outlive his life half a year, but byrlady a must build churches then, or else shall a suffer not thinking on,° with the hobby-horse, whose epitaph is, "For O, for O, the hobbyhorse is forgot."°

Hoboys° play. The dumb-show enters

Enter a KING *and a* QUEEN, *very lovingly, the Queen embracing him. She kneels and makes show of protestation° unto him. He takes her up, and declines his head upon her neck. He lies him down upon a bank of flowers. She, seeing him asleep, leaves him. Anon comes in another man, takes off his crown, kisses it, pours poison in the sleeper's*

---

88. **a damnèd ghost that we have seen:** the ghost that we have seen came from hell (and was an impostor and a liar). 89. **my imaginations:** what my mind has suggested to me (about the Ghost). To have given credence to the Ghost, and built on its tale, shows a disease of his mind. 90. **Vulcan's stithy:** Vulcan's forge—generally regarded as a hellish sort of place. 93. **in censure of his seeming:** in weighing up his appearance. 94. **If a steal aught:** i.e., if he conceals anything. 96. **idle:** crazy. 98. **cousin:** any close relation. 99. **the chameleon's dish:** The chameleon was believed to live on air. 101. **capons:** castrated cocks, fattened for the table. 102. **have nothing with:** gain nothing from. 103. **are not mine:** do not belong to my question. 111. **part:** action, part to play. 112. **calf:** dolt or stupid person. 116–117. **metal more attractive:** a substance more magnetic. 123. **country matters:** the sorts of things that go on among rustics in the country; coarse or indecent things. 128. **Nothing:** "Thing" was commonly used to refer to the male sexual organ. 132. **your only jig-maker:** i.e., there's no one like me for providing farcical entertainments. 137–38. **let the devil . . . sables:** "Sables" means the fur of a northern animal, the sable, which is brown. But "sable" is also the heraldic word for black. So this is a typical riddling remark of Hamlet's. 142. **not thinking on:** being forgotten. 143–44. **hobby-horse . . . forgot:** The hobby-horse was one of the characters in the morris dance. A man wore a huge hooped skirt in the likeness of a horse. The phrase "the hobby-horse is forgot" is very common. The horse used to sink to the ground as though dead, then come to energetic life again. So the hobby-horse does not die to be forgotten, but comes back with a vengeance, like Hamlet's father. 144. sd ***Hoboys***: oboes. 144. sd ***protestation***: solemn vow.

ears, and leaves him. The Queen returns, finds the King dead, and makes passionate action. The poisoner, with some two or three mutes, comes in again, seeming to condole with her. The dead body is carried away. The poisoner woos the Queen with gifts. She seems harsh° awhile, but in the end accepts his love. *Exeunt*

OPHELIA What means this my lord?

HAMLET Marry this is miching mallecho, it means mischief.

OPHELIA Belike this show imports the argument of the play?°

Enter PROLOGUE

HAMLET We shall know by this fellow; the players cannot keep counsel, they'll tell all.

OPHELIA Will a tell us what this show meant?

HAMLET Ay, or any show that you'll show him. Be not you ashamed to show, he'll not shame to tell you what it means.

OPHELIA You are naught, you are naught.° I'll mark the play.

PROLOGUE For us and for our tragedy,
Here stooping to your clemency,
We beg your hearing patiently.

HAMLET Is this a prologue, or the posy° of a ring?

OPHELIA 'Tis brief my lord.

HAMLET As woman's love.

Enter the PLAYER KING *and* QUEEN

PLAYER KING Full thirty times hath Phoebus' cart° gone round
Neptune's salt wash and Tellus' orbèd ground,°
And thirty dozen moons with borrowed sheen°
About the world have times twelve thirties been,
Since love our hearts, and Hymen° did our hands,
Unite commutual in most sacred bands.

PLAYER QUEEN So many journeys may the sun and moon
Make us again count o'er ere love be done.
But woe is me, you are so sick of late,
So far from cheer and from your former state,
That I distrust you.° Yet though I distrust,
Discomfort you my lord it nothing must.
For women's fear and love hold quantity,°
In neither aught, or in extremity.
Now what my love is, proof° hath made you know;
And as my love is sized,° my fear is so.
[Where love is great, the littlest doubts are fear;
Where little fears grow great, great love grows there.]

PLAYER KING Faith, I must leave thee love, and shortly too:
My operant powers their functions leave to do;°
And thou shalt live in this fair world behind,
Honoured, beloved; and haply one as kind
For husband shalt thou —

PLAYER QUEEN Oh confound the rest!
Such love must needs be treason in my breast.
In second husband let me be accurst:
None wed the second but who killed the first.

HAMLET That's wormwood, wormwood.°

PLAYER QUEEN The instances° that second marriage move
Are base respects of thrift,° but none of love.
A second time I kill my husband dead
When second husband kisses me in bed.

PLAYER KING I do believe you think what now you speak,
But what we do determine oft we break.
Purpose is but the slave to memory,°
Of violent birth° but poor validity,°
Which now like fruit unripe sticks on the tree,
But fall unshaken when they mellow be.
Most necessary 'tis that we forget

---

144. sd ***harsh***: i.e., she is disdainful, cross. 148–149. **Belike . . . play?:** Perhaps this dumb show explains what the play is about? 156. **naught:** wicked. 161. **posy:** inscribed motto or rhyme; a shortened version of "poesie." 164. **Phoebus' cart:** the chariot of the sun. 165. **Tellus' orbèd ground:** the sphere of the earth, the globe. 166. **borrowed sheen:** reflected light. 168. **Hymen:** god of marriage. 174. **distrust you:** i.e., distrust the state of your health. 176. **For . . . quantity:** Fear and love go together in a woman. Either they are both nonexistent or they are both present in full. 178. **proof:** experience, trial. 179. **sized:** in size. 183. **leave to do:** cease to perform. 190. **wormwood:** a bitter herb. 191. **instances:** motives. 192. **thrift:** profit, advancement. 197. **slave to memory:** Purpose has no autonomous existence, but is completely dependent on memory — and on passion. 197. **Of violent birth:** very strong at the beginning. 198. **validity:** health and strength.

To pay ourselves what to ourselves is debt.
What to ourselves in passion we propose,
The passion ending, doth the purpose lose.
The violence of either grief or joy
Their own enactures with themselves destroy.°
Where joy most revels, grief doth most lament;
Grief joys, joy grieves, on slender accident.°
This world is not for aye,° nor 'tis not strange
That even our loves should with our fortunes change,
For 'tis a question left us yet to prove,
Whether love lead fortune, or else fortune love.
The great man down, you mark his favourite flies;
The poor advanced makes friends of enemies,
And hitherto° doth love on fortune tend;°
For who not needs shall never lack a friend,
And who in want a hollow friend doth try°
Directly seasons° him his enemy.
But orderly to end where I begun,
Our wills and fates do so contrary run
That our devices° still are overthrown;
Our thoughts are ours, their ends none of our own.
So think thou wilt no second husband wed,
But die thy thoughts when thy first lord is dead.

PLAYER QUEEN Nor earth to me give food, nor heaven light,
Sport and repose lock from me day and night,
[To desperation turn my trust and hope,
An anchor's cheer° in prison be my scope,]°
Each opposite° that blanks° the face of joy
Meet what I would have well, and it destroy;
Both here and hence pursue me lasting strife,
If once a widow, ever I be wife.

HAMLET If she should break it now!

PLAYER KING 'Tis deeply sworn. Sweet, leave me here awhile;
My spirits grow dull, and fain I would beguile
The tedious day with sleep.

Sleeps

PLAYER QUEEN Sleep rock thy brain,
And never come mischance between us twain. *Exit*

HAMLET Madam, how like you this play?

GERTRUDE The lady doth protest° too much methinks.

HAMLET Oh but she'll keep her word.

CLAUDIUS Have you heard the argument? Is there no offence in't?

HAMLET No, no, they do but jest, poison in jest, no offence i'th'world.°

CLAUDIUS What do you call the play?

HAMLET The Mousetrap. Marry how? Tropically.° This play is the image of a murder done in Vienna. Gonzago is the duke's name, his wife Baptista. You shall see anon. 'Tis a knavish piece of work, but what o' that? Your majesty, and we that have free° souls, it touches us not. Let the galled jade winch,° our withers° are unwrung.°

Enter LUCIANUS

This is one Lucianus, nephew to the king.

OPHELIA You are as good as a chorus my lord.

HAMLET I could interpret between you and your love if I could see the puppets dallying.°

OPHELIA You are keen° my lord, you are keen.

HAMLET It would cost you a groaning° to take off mine edge.

OPHELIA Still better and worse.°

HAMLET So you mistake° your husbands. Begin, murderer. Pox, leave thy damnable faces and begin. Come, the croaking raven doth bellow for revenge.

205–06. **The violence . . . destroy:** Violent grief and joy, when they cease, destroy the "enactures," or actions, that are associated with them. 207–08. **Where joy . . . accident:** Those who have most capacity for joy have most capacity for grief, and the one changes into the other on the slightest occasion. 209. **for aye:** for ever. 215. **hitherto:** to this extent. 215. **tend:** attend, wait. 217. **try:** make trial of. 218. **seasons:** changes (him into). 221. **devices:** schemes, plans. 228. **anchor's cheer:** the fare of an anchorite, or religious hermit. 228. **scope:** limit. 229. **opposite:** opposing force. 229. **blanks:** blanches, makes pale. 239. **doth protest:** makes protestation or promises. 243–44. **poison . . . i'th'world:** Hamlet pretends to think Claudius is asking if there is any "offence" (crime) in the play, and he assures him it is only a mock crime. 246. **Tropically:** as a trope, a figure of speech. 251. **free:** innocent. 251–52. **Let the galled jade winch:** "Galled jade" is a poor horse with saddle sores; "winch" = wince. It was a common saying that it was the galled horse that would soonest wince. 252. **withers:** the high part of a horse's back, between the shoulder blades. 252. **unwrung:** not pressed tight, pinched, or chafed. 255–56. **I could . . . dallying:** I could act as a chorus in explaining what goes on between you and your lover if I could see the dalliance or flirting in the form of a puppet show. 257. **keen:** sharp and bitter. 258. **groaning:** i.e., of childbirth. 260. **Still better and worse:** Ophelia refers to Hamlet's continual "bettering" of her meaning — i.e., always a "better" meaning with a more offensive slant. 261. **mistake:** i.e., mistake: with such false vows (for better or for worse) you take your husbands.

Hamlet/Maclise, Daniel (Croquis, Alfred) (1806-70)/
Private Collection/Bridgeman Images

This nineteenth-century painting by Daniel Maclise portrays his vision of the play-within-the-play scene.

How do the details in this image illustrate the text of that scene? Particularly, what do the depictions of King Claudius, Hamlet, and Ophelia suggest about their characters?

LUCIANUS Thoughts black, hands apt,° drugs fit, and time agreeing,
Confederate season,° else no creature seeing.
Thou mixture rank, of midnight weeds collected,°
With Hecat's° ban° thrice blasted, thrice infected,
Thy natural magic and dire property°
On wholesome life usurp immediately.

Pours the poison in his ears

HAMLET A poisons him i'th'garden for's estate.° His name's Gonzago. The story is extant, and written in very choice Italian. You shall see anon how the murderer gets the love of Gonzago's wife.

OPHELIA The king rises.

HAMLET What, frighted with false fire?°

GERTRUDE How fares my lord?

POLONIUS Give o'er the play.

CLAUDIUS Give me some light. Away!

LORDS Lights, lights, lights!

Exeunt all but Hamlet and Horatio

HAMLET Why, let the strucken deer go weep,
The hart ungallèd° play,
For some must watch° while some must sleep,
Thus runs the world away.
Would not this,° sir, and a forest of feathers,° if the rest of my fortunes turn Turk with me,° with two provincial roses° on my razed° shoes, get me a fellowship° in a cry° of players, sir?

HORATIO Half a share.

HAMLET A whole one I.
For thou dost know, O Damon dear,
This realm dismantled° was
Of Jove himself, and now reigns here
A very, very — pajock.°

HORATIO You might have rhymed.

HAMLET O good Horatio, I'll take the ghost's word for a thousand pound. Didst perceive?

HORATIO Very well my lord.

HAMLET Upon the talk of the poisoning?

HORATIO I did very well note him.

Enter **ROSENCRANTZ** *and* **GUILDENSTERN**

HAMLET Ah ha! — Come, some music! Come, the recorders!
For if the king like not the comedy,
Why then — belike he likes it not, perdy.
Come, some music!

GUILDENSTERN Good my lord, vouchsafe me a word with you.

HAMLET Sir, a whole history.

---

265. **apt:** ready. 266. **Confederate season:** i.e., this moment of time is his ally and his only witness. 267. **of midnight weeds collected:** put together from weeds gathered at midnight. "Collected" refers to the mixing of the weeds, the concoction, and not the picking. 268. **Hecat:** Hecate, goddess of witchcraft. 268. **ban:** curse. 269. **dire property:** baleful quality. 271. **estate:** position (as king). 276. **false fire:** gunfire with blank charge. 282. **ungallèd:** uninjured. 283. **watch:** keep awake. 285. **this:** the success of the performance. 285. **forest of feathers:** The plumes that were a derided feature of the gallant's outfit were a notable feature of theater costume. 286. **turn Turk with me:** renounce and desert me. 287. **provincial roses:** roses originating either from Provins in northern France or from Provence. 287. **razed:** ornamented by cuts or slits in the leather. 288. **fellowship:** partnership; the technical term was a "share." 288. **cry:** pack (of hounds). 292. **dismantled:** stripped, divested — i.e., the realm lost Jove himself as king. 294. **pajock:** a despicable person. It is usually said that Hamlet was about to finish with "ass."

GUILDENSTERN The king, sir—

HAMLET Ay sir, what of him?

GUILDENSTERN Is in his retirement marvellous distempered.°

HAMLET With drink sir?

GUILDENSTERN No my lord, rather with choler.°

HAMLET Your wisdom should show itself more richer to signify° this to his doctor, for, for me to put him to his purgation would perhaps plunge him into far more choler.°

GUILDENSTERN Good my lord, put your discourse into some frame,° and start° not so wildly from my affair.

HAMLET I am tame° sir, pronounce.

GUILDENSTERN The queen your mother, in most great affliction of spirit, hath sent me to you.

HAMLET You are welcome.

GUILDENSTERN Nay good my lord, this courtesy is not of the right breed. If it shall please you to make me a wholesome° answer, I will do your mother's commandment. If not, your pardon° and my return shall be the end of my business.

HAMLET Sir, I cannot.

ROSENCRANTZ What, my lord?

HAMLET Make you a wholesome answer; my wit's diseased. But, sir, such answer as I can make, you shall command,° or rather, as you say, my mother. Therefore no more, but to the matter. My mother, you say.

ROSENCRANTZ Then thus she says. Your behaviour hath struck her into amazement and admiration.°

HAMLET O wonderful son that can so stonish a mother! But is there no sequel at the heels of this mother's admiration? Impart.

ROSENCRANTZ She desires to speak with you in her closet ere you go to bed.

HAMLET We shall obey, were she ten times our mother.° Have you any further trade with us?

ROSENCRANTZ My lord, you once did love me.

HAMLET And do still, by these pickers and stealers.°

ROSENCRANTZ Good my lord, what is your cause of distemper? You do surely bar the door upon your own liberty° if you deny your griefs to your friend.

HAMLET Sir, I lack advancement.

ROSENCRANTZ How can that be, when you have the voice of the king himself for your succession in Denmark?

HAMLET Ay sir, but while the grass grows°—the proverb is something musty.

Enter the PLAYERS *with recorders*

Oh, the recorders. Let me see one. To withdraw with you°—Why do you go about to recover° the wind of me, as if you would drive me into a toil?

GUILDENSTERN O my lord, if my duty be too bold, my love is too unmannerly.°

HAMLET I do not well understand that. Will you play upon this pipe?

GUILDENSTERN My lord, I cannot.

HAMLET I pray you.

GUILDENSTERN Believe me I cannot.

HAMLET I do beseech you.

GUILDENSTERN I know no touch of it my lord.

HAMLET 'Tis as easy as lying. Govern these ventages° with your fingers and thumb, give it breath with your mouth, and it will discourse most eloquent music. Look you, these are the stops.

GUILDENSTERN But these cannot I command to any utterance of harmony. I have not the skill.

HAMLET Why look you now how unworthy a thing you make of me. You would play upon me, you would seem to know my stops, you would pluck out the heart of my mystery,° you would sound me from my lowest note to the top of my compass—and there is much music, excellent voice, in this little organ,° yet cannot

---

310. **distempered:** out of humor; but also a euphemism for being drunk. 312. **choler:** anger. But Hamlet chooses to understand "bile." 314. **signify:** announce. 314–16. **for me . . . more choler:** the way in which I would cure him of his distemper would make him much angrier. 318. **frame:** ordered structure. 318. **start:** make a sudden surprised movement. 320. **tame:** subdued—i.e., a manageable horse that will not "start." 326. **wholesome:** healthy—i.e., sane. 327. **pardon:** permission (to leave). 333. **command:** have at your service. 337. **admiration:** wonder. 344. **were she ten times our mother:** In sane conversation, this would go with a *refusal* to obey. 346. **pickers and stealers:** hands. 349. **liberty:** Rosencrantz means Hamlet would be more free in his mind, less burdened, if he would communicate his problems. 355. **while the grass grows:** "While waiting for the grass to grow, the horse starves" is, as Hamlet indicates, an old proverb. 358. **To withdraw with you:** to move aside together. 358. **recover:** gain. The hunstsman will try to move to the windward of his prey and so get the animal, scenting him, to run away from him and toward the trap. 360–61. **if my duty . . . unmannerly:** If Hamlet finds this respectful attention bold, he is accusing love of being ill-mannered, because the duty is a matter of love. Hamlet understands the remark perfectly well. 369. **ventages:** vents—i.e., holes. 378. **mystery:** the skills of a particular craft—i.e., you would learn the innermost secret of my working, as a musician would learn the secret of playing the recorder. 381. **this little organ:** the recorder.

you make it speak. 'Sblood, do you think I am easier to be played on than a pipe? Call me what instrument you will, though you can fret° me, you cannot play upon me.

Enter POLONIUS

God bless you sir.

POLONIUS My lord, the queen would speak with you, and presently.°

HAMLET Do you see yonder cloud that's almost in shape of a camel?

POLONIUS By th'mass, and 'tis like a camel indeed.

HAMLET Methinks it is like a weasel.

POLONIUS It is backed like a weasel.

HAMLET Or like a whale?

POLONIUS Very like a whale.

HAMLET Then I will come to my mother by and by.°—They fool me to the top of my bent.°—I will come by and by.

POLONIUS I will say so. *Exit*

HAMLET By and by is easily said.—Leave me, friends.

Exeunt all but Hamlet

'Tis now the very witching time° of night,
When churchyards yawn, and hell itself breathes out
Contagion to this world. Now could I drink hot blood,°
And do such bitter business as the day
Would quake to look on. Soft,° now to my mother.
O heart, lose not thy nature;° let not ever
The soul of Nero° enter this firm bosom.
Let me be cruel, not unnatural:
I will speak daggers to her but use none.
My tongue and soul in this be hypocrites,
How in my words somever she be shent,°
To give them seals° never my soul consent.

Exit

Act III, Scene iii

Enter CLAUDIUS, ROSENCRANTZ *and* GUILDENSTERN

CLAUDIUS I like him not,° nor stands it safe with us°
To let his madness range. Therefore prepare you:
I your commission will forthwith dispatch,°
And he to England shall along° with you.
The terms of our estate° may not endure
Hazard so near us as doth hourly grow
Out of his brows.°

GUILDENSTERN We will ourselves provide.°
Most holy and religious fear it is
To keep those many many bodies safe
That live and feed upon your majesty.

ROSENCRANTZ The single and peculiar life° is bound
With all the strength and armour of the mind
To keep itself from noyance;° but much more
That spirit upon whose weal° depends and rests
The lives of many. The cess° of majesty
Dies not alone, but like a gulf° doth draw
What's near it with it. It is a massy° wheel
Fixed on the summit of the highest mount,
To whose huge spokes ten thousand lesser things
Are mortised and adjoined, which when it falls,
Each small annexment, petty consequence,°
Attends the boisterous ruin. Never alone
Did the king sigh, but with a general groan.

CLAUDIUS Arm you° I pray you to this speedy voyage,
For we will fetters put about this fear
Which now goes too free-footed.

ROSENCRANTZ We will haste us.

Exeunt Rosencrantz and Guildenstern

384. **fret:** the raised bars for fingering on a lute, providing a pun with "irritate." 388. **presently:** immediately. 396–97. **by and by:** presently, quite soon. 397. **They fool me to the top of my bent:** They tax to the uttermost my capacity to play the madman. 401. **witching time:** bewitching time, time of sorcery and enchantment. 403. **Now could I drink hot blood:** Witches were supposed to open the graves of newly buried children whom their charms had killed, boil the bodies, and drink the liquid. 405. **Soft:** That's enough! 406. **nature:** natural feelings (toward his mother). 407. **Nero:** He contrived the murder of his mother. 411. **shent:** castigated, punished (by rebuke or reproach). 412. **seals:** i.e., by deeds.
Act III, Scene iii. 1. **I like him not:** i.e., I do not like the way he is behaving. 1. **us:** i.e., the person of the king. 3. **dispatch:** make ready. 4. **along:** go along. 5. **The terms of our estate:** the conditions of my position as king. 7. **brows:** effrontery. 7. **ourselves provide:** make provision for ourselves (to travel to England). 11. **The single and peculiar life:** the life that belongs to the individual only. 13. **noyance:** harm. 14. **weal:** well-being. 15. **cess:** cessation. 16. **gulf:** whirlpool. 17. **massy:** massive. 21. **consequence:** attachment. 24. **Arm you:** prepare yourselves.

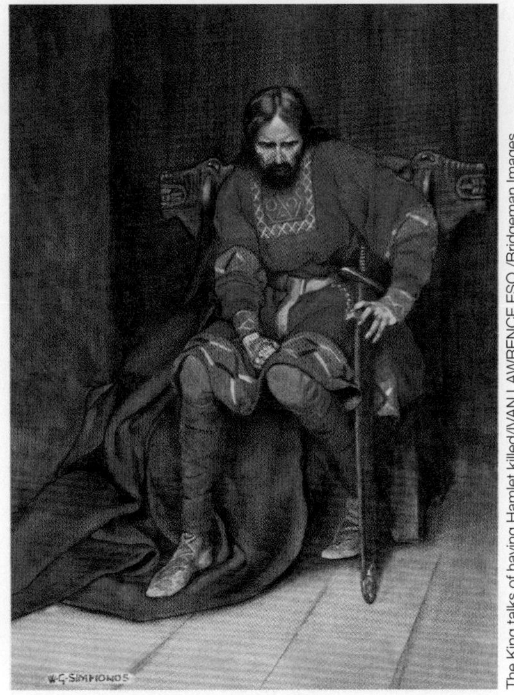

The King talks of having Hamlet killed/IVAN LAWRENCE ESQ./Bridgeman Images

This 1915 lithograph from an illustrated edition of *Hamlet* shows King Claudius talking of having the prince killed.

What does this depiction suggest about how the artist viewed King Claudius? What details from the play support this interpretation?

Enter POLONIUS

POLONIUS My lord, he's going to his mother's closet.
Behind the arras I'll convey myself°
To hear the process.° I'll warrant she'll tax him home,°
And as you said, and wisely was it said,
'Tis meet° that some more audience than a mother,
Since nature makes them partial,° should o'erhear
The speech of vantage.° Fare you well my liege,
I'll call upon you ere you go to bed
And tell you what I know.

CLAUDIUS Thanks, dear my lord.

Exit Polonius

Oh my offence is rank, it smells to heaven;
It hath the primal eldest° curse upon't,
A brother's murder. Pray can I not,
Though inclination be as sharp as will.°
My stronger guilt defeats my strong intent,
And like a man to double business bound,°
I stand in pause where I shall first begin,
And both neglect. What if this cursèd hand
Were thicker than itself with brother's blood,
Is there not rain enough in the sweet heavens
To wash it white as snow? Whereto serves mercy
But to confront the visage of offence?°
And what's in prayer but this two-fold force,
To be forestallèd ere we come to fall,
Or pardoned being down? Then I'll look up,
My fault is past. But oh, what form of prayer
Can serve my turn? "Forgive me my foul murder"?
That cannot be, since I am still possessed
Of those effects° for which I did the murder,
My crown, mine own ambition,° and my queen.
May one be pardoned and retain th'offence?°
In the corrupted currents of this world
Offence's gilded hand may shove by° justice,
And oft 'tis seen the wicked prize itself
Buys out the law. But 'tis not so above;
There is no shuffling,° there the action lies°
In his true nature, and we ourselves compelled
Even to the teeth and forehead of our faults
To give in evidence.° What then? What rests?°
Try what repentance can. What can it not?
Yet what can it when one cannot repent?

---

28. **convey myself:** secretly move myself. 29. **the process:** what goes on. 29. **tax him home:** censure him severely. 31. **meet:** suitable. 32. **Since nature makes them partial:** Polonius does not trust Gertrude to report accurately on her interview with her son. He is spying on her as well as on Hamlet. 33. **of vantage:** from a good position. 37. **primal eldest:** i.e., going back to Cain's murder of Abel. 39. **Though inclination be as sharp as will:** though my desire to pray is as great as my determination. 41. **bound:** directed toward. 46–47. **Whereto . . . offence?:** What is mercy for, except to meet crime face to face? 54. **effects:** things acquired or achieved. 55. **mine own ambition:** i.e., those things I was ambitious for. 56. **th'offence:** i.e., the fruits of the offense. 58. **shove by:** thrust aside. 61. **shuffling:** trickery, sharp practice, deception. 61. **the action lies:** a legal phrase, meaning that a case is admitted to exist. It also means that every deed lies exposed to God's scrutiny. 63–64. **Even to . . . evidence:** to give evidence even about the worst of our sins. 64. **rests:** remains.

This photograph, from a 2015 production of *Hamlet* starring Benedict Cumberbatch as the title character, depicts the moment Hamlet decides not to kill King Claudius while he is at prayer.

What does Cumberbatch's expression suggest about Hamlet's motive for walking away from the opportunity to avenge his father? What effect does the positioning of the painting of King Hamlet achieve?

Oh wretched state! Oh bosom black as death!
Oh limèd° soul that struggling to be free
Art more engaged! Help, angels! — Make assay;
Bow stubborn knees, and heart with strings of steel
Be soft as sinews of the new-born babe.
All may be well.

[*He kneels*]

Enter HAMLET

HAMLET Now might I do it pat, now a is° a-praying,
And now I'll do't — and so a goes to heaven,
And so am I revenged. That would be scanned.°
A villain kills my father, and for that,
I his sole son do this same villain send
To heaven.
Why, this is hire and salary, not revenge.
A took my father grossly,° full of bread,
With all his crimes broad blown,° as flush° as May,
And how his audit stands who knows save heaven?
But in our circumstance and course of thought°
'Tis heavy with him. And am I then revenged
To take him in the purging of his soul,
When he is fit and seasoned for his passage?
No.
Up sword, and know thou a more horrid hent,°
When he is drunk asleep,° or in his rage,
Or in th'incestuous pleasure of his bed,
At game a-swearing,° or about some act
That has no relish° of salvation in't —
Then trip him that his heels may kick at heaven,
And that his soul may be as damned and black
As hell whereto it goes. My mother stays.
This physic but prolongs thy sickly days.

Exit

CLAUDIUS My words fly up, my thoughts remain below.
Words without thoughts never to heaven go.

Exit

Act III, Scene iv

Enter GERTRUDE *and* POLONIUS

POLONIUS A will come straight. Look you lay home to him.°
Tell him his pranks have been too broad to bear with,
And that your grace hath screened° and stood between
Much heat and him. I'll silence me e'en here.
Pray you be round with him.

HAMLET (*Within*) Mother, mother, mother!

---

68. **limèd:** The image is of a bird caught by the smearing of a very sticky substance, called birdlime, on twigs and branches. 73. **a is:** represents a slurred pronunciation of "he is." 75. **would be scanned:** needs to be examined. 80. **grossly:** i.e., without consideration or decency. 81. **broad blown:** in full blossom. 81. **flush:** vigorous. 83. **circumstance and course of thought:** i.e., circumstantial course of thought — our course of thought, which is necessarily indirect. 88. **hent:** grasp. He puts his sword up in its scabbard, promising to lay hold of it at a "more horrid" opportunity. 89. **drunk asleep:** i.e., in a drunken sleep. 91. **At game a-swearing:** gambling and cursing the dice or cards as he plays. 92. **relish:** touch, trace. **Act III, Scene iv.** 1. **lay home to him:** charge him to the full. 3. **screened:** acted as a fire screen.

GERTRUDE I'll warrant you, fear me not.
Withdraw, I hear him coming.
[*Polonius hides himself behind the arras*]

Enter HAMLET

HAMLET Now mother, what's the matter?
GERTRUDE Hamlet, thou hast thy father much offended.
HAMLET Mother, you have my father much offended.
GERTRUDE Come, come, you answer with an idle tongue.
HAMLET Go, go, you question with a wicked tongue.
GERTRUDE Why, how now Hamlet?
HAMLET What's the matter now?
GERTRUDE Have you forgot me?°
HAMLET No by the rood,° not so.
You are the queen, your husband's brother's wife,
And, would it were not so, you are my mother.
GERTRUDE Nay, then I'll set those to you that can speak.
HAMLET Come, come and sit you down, you shall not budge.°
You go not till I set you up a glass°
Where you may see the inmost part of you.
GERTRUDE What wilt thou do? thou wilt not murder me?
Help, help, ho!
POLONIUS (*Behind*) What ho! Help, help, help!
HAMLET (*Draws*) How now, a rat? Dead for a ducat,° dead.

Kills Polonius

POLONIUS (*Behind*) Oh, I am slain!
GERTRUDE Oh me, what hast thou done?
HAMLET Nay I know not, is it the king?
GERTRUDE Oh what a rash and bloody deed is this!
HAMLET A bloody deed? Almost as bad, good mother,
As kill a king and marry with his brother.
GERTRUDE As kill a king?
HAMLET Ay lady, 'twas my word.
[*Lifts up the arras and reveals the body of Polonius*]
Thou wretched, rash, intruding fool, farewell.
I took thee for thy better. Take thy fortune.
Thou find'st to be too busy is some danger.—
Leave wringing of your hands. Peace! Sit you down
And let me wring your heart, for so I shall
If it be made of penetrable stuff,
If damnèd custom have not brazed° it so,
That it be proof° and bulwark against sense.°
GERTRUDE What have I done, that thou dar'st wag thy tongue
In noise so rude against me?
HAMLET Such an act
That blurs the grace and blush of modesty,
Calls virtue hypocrite, takes off the rose°
From the fair forehead of an innocent love
And sets a blister there,° makes marriage vows
As false as dicers' oaths. Oh such a deed
As from the body of contraction° plucks
The very soul, and sweet religion makes
A rhapsody° of words. Heaven's face doth glow;
Yea, this solidity and compound mass,
With tristful visage as against the doom,
Is thought-sick at the act.°
GERTRUDE Ay me, what act,
That roars so loud and thunders in the index?
HAMLET Look here upon this picture, and on this,
The counterfeit presentment° of two brothers.
See what a grace was seated on this brow;
Hyperion's curls, the front° of Jove himself,
An eye like Mars, to threaten and command;
A station° like the herald Mercury,
New-lighted° on a heaven-kissing hill;
A combination° and a form indeed,
Where every god did seem to set his seal°
To give the world assurance of a man.

---

14. **forgot me:** forgotten who I am. 14. **the rood:** the cross of Christ. 18. **budge:** move away (to fetch the others). 19. **glass:** the mirror that reveals the truth and sets standards. 24. **Dead for a ducat:** possibly a wager—i.e., I'll bet a ducat I kill it.37. **brazed:** made brazen, hardened like brass. 38. **proof:** armor. 38. **sense:** feeling. 42. **rose:** symbol of true love. 44. **sets a blister there:** Shakespeare is thinking of the forehead as the place that declares innocence or boldness. 46. **contraction:** pledging, making vows or contracts. 48. **rhapsody:** a medley, a miscellaneous or confused collection. 48–51. **Heaven's face . . . at the act:** i.e., the skies are red with shame, and the huge earth itself, with a countenance as sad as if it were doomsday, is distressed in mind by your act. 54. **counterfeit presentment:** i.e., portraits, representations in art. 56. **front:** forehead. 58. **station:** stance, way of standing. 59. **New-lighted:** newly alighted. 60. **combination:** i.e., of divine qualities. 61. **set his seal:** place his confirming mark.

This was your husband. Look you now what follows.
Here is your husband, like a mildewed ear°
Blasting° his wholesome brother. Have you eyes?
Could you on this fair mountain leave to feed
And batten° on this moor? Ha! have you eyes?
You cannot call it love, for at your age
The heyday° in the blood° is tame, it's humble,
And waits upon the judgement; and what judgement
Would step from this to this? [Sense sure you have,
Else could you not have motion, but sure that sense
Is apoplexed, for madness would not err,
Nor sense to ecstasy was ne'er so thralled,°
But it reserved some quantity of choice
To serve in such a difference.]° What devil was't
That thus hath cozened you at hoodman-blind?°
[Eyes without feeling, feeling without sight,
Ears without hands or eyes, smelling sans all,
Or but a sickly part of one true sense
Could not so mope.]°
O shame, where is thy blush? Rebellious hell,°
If thou canst mutine° in a matron's bones,
To flaming youth let virtue be as wax
And melt in her own fire. Proclaim no shame
When the compulsive ardour gives the charge,°
Since frost itself as actively doth burn,
And reason panders will.°

GERTRUDE O Hamlet, speak no more.
Thou turn'st my eyes into my very soul,
And there I see such black and grainèd° spots
As will not leave their tinct.°

HAMLET Nay, but to live
In the rank sweat of an enseamèd° bed,
Stewed° in corruption, honeying and making love
Over the nasty sty.°

This 1855 painting by Eugène Delacroix portrays Hamlet's discovery that he has stabbed Polonius through the curtain.

How does Delacroix depict Hamlet's reaction here? What about that of Gertrude in the background? How do those reactions align with your interpretation of the play itself?

GERTRUDE Oh speak to me no more.
These words like daggers enter in my ears.
No more sweet Hamlet.

HAMLET A murderer and a villain,
A slave that is not twentieth part the tithe°
Of your precedent lord, a vice° of kings,
A cutpurse of the empire and the rule,
That from a shelf the precious diadem stole
And put it in his pocket.

GERTRUDE No more!

Enter GHOST°

---

64. **ear:** of corn. 65. **Blasting:** blighting. 67. **batten:** feed and grow fat. 69. **heyday:** excitement. 69. **blood:** passions, sexual desire. 71–76. **Sense . . . difference:** i.e., something worse than madness has happened to Gertrude's "sense," because even if she were mad she could not prefer Claudius to her former husband. 74. **thralled:** in thrall, enslaved. 76. **serve in such a difference:** i.e., to assist in differentiating between the two men. 77. **cozened you at hoodmanblind:** deceived you in a game of blindman's buff. (The devil substituted Claudius for King Hamlet when the blindfolded Gertrude chose him.) 81. **mope:** move around aimlessly, in a daze or trance. 82. **Rebellious hell:** i.e., the devil encourages our worse nature to rebel against our better judgment. 83. **mutine:** incite mutiny. 86. **gives the charge:** signals the attack. 88. **reason panders will:** reason assists the passions to obtain their ends. 90. **grainèd:** engrained, deep-dyed. 91. **leave their tinct:** surrender their color. 92. **enseamèd:** greasy with offensive semen. 93. **Stewed:** a word combining the heat, sweat, and greasiness with the odium of the brothels, widely known as "the stews." 93–94. **honeying . . . sty:** i.e., covering over foulness with sweet words and endearments. 97. **tithe:** tenth part. 98. **vice:** clown or trickster of the old drama. 101. **sd:** ***Enter* GHOST:** The First Quarto gives "*Enter the ghost in his night gowne.*"

HAMLET A king of shreds and patches° —
Save me and hover o'er me with your wings,
You heavenly guards! — What would your gracious figure?

GERTRUDE Alas he's mad!

HAMLET Do you not come your tardy son to chide,
That lapsed° in time and passion lets go by
Th'important acting of your dread command?
Oh say!

GHOST Do not forget. This visitation
Is but to whet thy almost blunted purpose.°
But look, amazement on thy mother sits.
Oh step between her and her fighting soul:
Conceit° in weakest bodies strongest works.
Speak to her, Hamlet.

HAMLET How is it with you lady?

GERTRUDE Alas, how is't with you,
That you do bend your eye on vacancy,
And with th'incorporal air do hold discourse?
Forth at your eyes your spirits wildly peep,
And, as the sleeping soldiers in th'alarm,°
Your bedded hair,° like life in excrements,°
Start up and stand an end.° O gentle son,
Upon the heat and flame of thy distemper
Sprinkle cool patience. Whereon do you look?

HAMLET On him, on him! Look you how pale he glares.°
His form and cause conjoined, preaching to stones,
Would make them capable.° — Do not look upon me,
Lest with this piteous action° you convert
My stern effects.° Then what I have to do
Will want true colour:° tears perchance for blood.

GERTRUDE To whom do you speak this?

HAMLET Do you see nothing there?

GERTRUDE Nothing at all, yet all that is I see.

HAMLET Nor did you nothing hear?

GERTRUDE No, nothing but ourselves.

HAMLET Why, look you there — look how it steals away —
My father in his habit as he lived° —
Look where he goes, even now out at the portal.

Exit Ghost

GERTRUDE This is the very° coinage of your brain.
This bodiless creation ecstasy°
Is very cunning° in.

HAMLET Ecstasy?
My pulse as yours doth temperately keep time,
And makes as healthful music. It is not madness
That I have uttered. Bring me to the test,
And I the matter will reword, which madness
Would gambol from.° Mother, for love of grace,
Lay not that flattering unction° to your soul,
That not your trespass but my madness speaks;
It will but skin and film° the ulcerous place,
Whiles rank corruption, mining° all within,
Infects unseen. Confess yourself to heaven,
Repent what's past, avoid what is to come,
And do not spread the compost on the weeds
To make them ranker. Forgive me this my virtue,
For in the fatness° of these pursy° times
Virtue itself of vice must pardon beg,
Yea, curb° and woo for leave to do him good.

GERTRUDE Oh Hamlet, thou hast cleft my heart in twain.

HAMLET Oh throw away the worser part of it
And live the purer with the other half.
Good night — but go not to my uncle's bed;
Assume a virtue if you have it not.

---

102. **shreds and patches:** i.e., the patchwork costume of the stage clown. 107. **lapsed:** surprised, taken in the act. 110. **blunted purpose:** The Ghost is accusing Hamlet not of forgetting his revenge, but of misusing the energies that should be directed toward revenge. 113. **Conceit:** imagination. 119. **as the sleeping soldiers in th'alarm:** like soldiers startled out of sleep by a call to arms. 120. **hair:** The word is considered plural. 120. **like life in excrements:** "Excrement" can be either what is voided from or what, like hair and nails, grows out of the body; probably "as though there were independent life in such outgrowths." 121. **an end:** a common form of "on end." 124. **how pale he glares:** how he is gazing fixedly with a ghastly expression. 126. **capable:** receptive, susceptible. 127. **piteous action:** behavior that excites pity. 128. **effects:** deeds (seen as issuing from anger and indignation). 129. **true colour:** The "effects" of pity would be colorless tears instead of blood. 136. **in his habit as he lived:** in the clothes he wore when alive. 138. **very:** mere. 139. **ecstasy:** madness. 140. **cunning:** skillful. 145. **gambol from:** spring away from. 146. **unction:** healing oil or ointment. 148. **skin and film:** serve as a skin and film over. 149. **mining:** undermining. 154. **fatness:** grossness, ill condition. 154. **pursy:** both short of breath and flatulent. 156. **curb:** bow, make obeisance.

extending beyond the text

The photograph on the left was made to promote the 1990 Franco Zeffirelli film *Hamlet*, starring Glenn Close as Gertrude. The painting on the right is Leonardo da Vinci's iconic *Mona Lisa*, painted about a century before *Hamlet* was first performed.

Hamlet by Franco Zeffirelli with Glenn Close/RUE DES ARCHIVES/ Bridgeman Images

Mona Lisa/Vinci, Leonardo da/Louvre, Paris, France/Bridgeman Images

1. **What characteristics do these images share? How do they differ?**
2. **What can you infer about Close's portrayal of Gertrude based on this choice?**

[That monster custom, who all sense doth eat,
Of habits devil, is angel yet in this,
That to the use of actions fair and good
He likewise gives a frock or livery
That aptly is put on.] Refrain tonight,
And that shall lend a kind of easiness
To the next abstinence, [the next more easy,
For use almost can change the stamp of nature,
And either . . . the devil, or throw him out,
With wondrous potency.] Once more good night,
And when you are desirous to be blessed,
I'll blessing beg of you.° For this same lord,
I do repent; but heaven hath pleased it so,
To punish me with this, and this with me,
That I must be their scourge and minister.°
I will bestow him, and will answer well°
The death I gave him. So again, good night.
I must be cruel only to be kind;
Thus bad begins, and worse remains behind.
One word more good lady.

GERTRUDE What shall I do?

HAMLET Not this by no means that I bid you do:
Let the bloat° king tempt you again to bed,
Pinch wanton° on your cheek, call you his
mouse,
And let him for a pair of reechy° kisses,
Or paddling in your neck with his damned
fingers,
Make you to ravel all this matter out,°
That I essentially am not in madness,

172–73. **when you are . . . beg of you:** when you are contrite enough to ask God's blessing, I'll seek your blessing (i.e., resume my duty as your son). 174–76. **heaven . . . minister:** it is the will of heaven, in making me the agent of their chastisement, that I myself should be punished by being the cause of Polonius's death, and that Polonius should be punished in his death at my hands. 177. **answer well:** i.e., give good reasons for. 183. **bloat:** bloated swollen (with drink). 184. **wanton:** wantonly, lasciviously. 185. **reechy:** soiled and nauseating. 187. **ravel all this matter out:** unravel this.

But mad in craft.° 'Twere good you let him know,
For who that's but a queen, fair, sober, wise,
Would from a paddock,° from a bat, a gib,°
Such dear concernings hide?° Who would do so?
No, in despite of sense and secrecy,°
Unpeg the basket on the house's top,
Let the birds fly, and like the famous ape,
To try conclusions,° in the basket creep
And break your own neck down.°

GERTRUDE Be thou assured, if words be made of breath,
And breath of life, I have no life to breathe
What thou hast said to me.

HAMLET I must to England, you know that?

GERTRUDE Alack,
I had forgot. 'Tis so concluded on.

HAMLET [There's letters sealed, and my two schoolfellows,
Whom I will trust as I will adders fanged,
They bear the mandate. They must sweep my way°
And marshal me to knavery. Let it work,
For 'tis the sport to have the engineer°
Hoist° with his own petar,° an't° shall go hard
But I will delve one yard below their mines
And blow them at the moon. Oh 'tis most sweet
When in one line° two crafts directly meet.]
This man shall set me packing.°
I'll lug the guts into the neighbour room.
Mother, good night. Indeed, this counsellor
Is now most still, most secret, and most grave,
Who was in life a foolish prating knave.
Come sir, to draw toward an end with you.°
Good night mother.

Exit Hamlet tugging in Polonius; [Gertrude remains]

Act IV, Scene i

Enter CLAUDIUS *with* ROSENCRANTZ *and* GUILDENSTERN

CLAUDIUS There's matter in these sighs, these profound heaves.
You must translate, 'tis fit we understand them.
Where is your son?

GERTRUDE [Bestow this place on us a little while.]

[Exeunt Rosencrantz and Guildenstern]

Ah mine own lord, what have I seen tonight!

CLAUDIUS What, Gertrude? How does Hamlet?

GERTRUDE Mad as the sea and wind, when both contend
Which is the mightier. In his lawless fit,
Behind the arras hearing something stir,
Whips out his rapier, cries "A rat, a rat!,"
And in this brainish° apprehension kills
The unseen good old man.

CLAUDIUS Oh heavy deed!
It had been so with us had we been there.
His liberty is full of threats to all,
To you yourself, to us, to everyone.
Alas, how shall this bloody deed be answered?°
It will be laid to us, whose providence°
Should have kept short,° restrained, and out of haunt,°
This mad young man. But so much was our love,
We would not understand what was most fit,
But like the owner of a foul disease,
To keep it from divulging,° let it feed
Even on the pith of life. Where is he gone?

---

189. **in craft:** by design. 189–92. **'Twere good . . . concernings hide:** sarcastic; a respectable queen, as you consider yourself to be, has of course no reason to keep a secret from her loathsome husband. 191. **paddock:** frog or toad. 191. **gib:** tomcat. 193. **secrecy:** discretion. 194–97. **Unpeg . . . neck down:** The "famous ape" takes a birdcage onto a roof; he opens the door and the birds fly out. In order to imitate them, he gets into the basket and jumps out; instead of flying, he falls to the ground. 196. **To try conclusions:** to test results. 197. **down:** an intensifier — utterly or completely. 205. **sweep my way:** clear a path for me. 207. **engineer:** one who constructs or designs military machines or contrivances, especially for use in sieges. 208. **Hoist:** i.e., blown up. 208. **petar:** (or "petard") bomb. 208. **an't:** and it. 211. **in one line:** The image is of the mine and the countermine. 212. **This man shall set me packing:** This death will make them send me off immediately. 217. **draw toward an end with you:** conclude our discourse. **Act IV, Scene i.** 11. **brainish:** headstrong, obsessive. 16. **answered:** accounted for. 17. **providence:** forethought and provision. 18. **kept short:** restricted. 18. **out of haunt:** away from public view. 22. **divulging:** being generally known.

GERTRUDE To draw apart the body he hath killed,
O'er whom his very madness, like some ore
Among a mineral° of metals base,
Shows itself pure;° a weeps for what is done.

CLAUDIUS Oh Gertrude, come away!
The sun no sooner shall the mountains touch
But we will ship him hence, and this vile deed
We must with all our majesty and skill
Both countenance° and excuse. Ho,
Guildenstern!

Enter ROSENCRANTZ *and* GUILDENSTERN

Friends both, go join you with some further aid.
Hamlet in madness hath Polonius slain,
And from his mother's closet hath he dragged
him.
Go seek him out, speak fair, and bring the body
Into the chapel. I pray you haste in this.

Exeunt Rosencrantz and Guildenstern

Come Gertrude, we'll call up our wisest friends
And let them know both what we mean to do
And what's untimely done.
[Whose whisper o'er the world's diameter,
As level° as the cannon to his blank,°
Transports his poisoned shot, may miss our name
And hit the woundless° air.] Oh come away,
My soul is full of discord and dismay.

Exeunt

Act IV, Scene ii

Enter HAMLET

HAMLET Safely stowed.

GENTLEMEN (*Within*) Hamlet! Lord Hamlet!

HAMLET But soft,° what noise? Who calls on Hamlet?
Oh here they come.

Enter ROSENCRANTZ *and* GUILDENSTERN

ROSENCRANTZ What have you done my lord with the dead body?

HAMLET Compounded° it with dust whereto 'tis kin.

ROSENCRANTZ Tell us where 'tis, that we may take it thence and bear it to the chapel.

HAMLET Do not believe it.

ROSENCRANTZ Believe what?

HAMLET That I can keep your counsel and not mine own.° Besides, to be demanded of° a sponge, what replication° should be made by the son of a king?

ROSENCRANTZ Take you me for a sponge my lord?

HAMLET Ay sir, that soaks up the king's countenance,° his rewards, his authorities. But such officers do the king best service in the end: he keeps them like an ape in the corner of his jaw, first mouthed to be last swallowed. When he needs what you have gleaned, it is but squeezing you, and, sponge, you shall be dry again.

ROSENCRANTZ I understand you not my lord.

HAMLET I am glad of it, a knavish speech sleeps in a foolish ear.°

ROSENCRANTZ My lord, you must tell us where the body is, and go with us to the king.

HAMLET The body is with the king, but the king is not with the body.° The king is a thing—

GUILDENSTERN A thing my lord?

HAMLET Of nothing. Bring me to him. Hide fox, and all after!°

Exeunt

Act IV, Scene iii

Enter CLAUDIUS, *and two or three*

CLAUDIUS I have sent to seek him, and to find the
body.
How dangerous is it that this man goes loose,
Yet must not we put the strong law on him;
He's loved of the distracted° multitude,
Who like not in their judgement, but their
eyes;°

25–27. **his very madness . . . pure:** What Gertrude is trying to say is that even in his madness there was a streak of pure feeling. 26. **a mineral:** the contents of a mine. 32. **countenance:** accept; "majesty" will "countenance" and "skill" will "excuse." 42. **level:** directly aimed. 42. **blank:** target. 44. **woundless:** invulnerable. **Act IV, Scene ii.** 3. **soft:** be cautious. 7. **Compounded:** mixed. 12. **keep . . . mine own:** "To keep counsel" is to maintain silence about one's judgments and intentions. 13. **to be demanded of:** if one is interrogated by. 13. **replication:** formal response. 16. **countenance:** favor. 24–25. **a knavish . . . ear:** you are too much of a fool to understand my insults. 28–29. **The body . . . with the body:** i.e., Claudius has a body, but the kingship of Denmark is not inherent in *that* body. 31–32. **Hide fox, and all after:** Hamlet runs out, followed by the others. The reference is presumably to a children's game of chase or hide-and-seek. **Act IV, Scene iii.** 4. **distracted:** disordered, confused. 5. **their eyes:** i.e., by appearances.

And where 'tis so, th'offender's scourge is weighed,
But never the offence.° To bear all smooth and even,
This sudden sending him away must seem
Deliberate pause.° Diseases desperate grown
By desperate appliance are relieved,
Or not at all.

Enter ROSENCRANTZ

How now, what hath befallen?

ROSENCRANTZ Where the dead body is bestowed, my lord,
We cannot get from him.

CLAUDIUS But where is he?

ROSENCRANTZ Without, my lord, guarded, to know your pleasure.

CLAUDIUS Bring him before us.

ROSENCRANTZ Ho! bring in my lord.

Enter HAMLET *and* GUILDENSTERN

CLAUDIUS Now Hamlet, where's Polonius?

HAMLET At supper.

CLAUDIUS At supper? Where?

HAMLET Not where he eats, but where a is° eaten. A certain convocation of politic worms are e'en at him. Your worm is your only emperor for diet:° we fat all creatures else to fat us, and we fat ourselves for maggots. Your fat king and your lean beggar is but variable° service, two dishes, but to one table; that's the end.

CLAUDIUS Alas, alas.

HAMLET A man may fish with the worm that hath eat of a king, and eat of the fish that hath fed of that worm.

CLAUDIUS What dost thou mean by this?

HAMLET Nothing but to show you how a king may go a progress° through the guts of a beggar.

CLAUDIUS Where is Polonius?

HAMLET In heaven, send thither to see. If your messenger find him not there, seek him i'th'other place yourself. But if indeed you find him not within this month, you shall nose him as you go up the stairs into the lobby.°

National Geographic Image Collection/Bridgeman Images

This photograph shows Kronborg Castle in Denmark, which was the model for Elsinore in the play.

Why do you think Shakespeare might have chosen this location for the setting of this play? How does this image reflect its mood and themes?

CLAUDIUS Go seek him there.

HAMLET A will stay till you come.

[*Exeunt Attendants*]

CLAUDIUS Hamlet, this deed, for thine especial safety,
Which we do tender,° as we dearly grieve
For that which thou hast done, must send thee hence
With fiery quickness. Therefore prepare thyself.
The bark is ready and the wind at help,
Th'associates tend,° and everything is bent°
For England.

HAMLET For England?

CLAUDIUS Ay Hamlet.

HAMLET Good.

CLAUDIUS So is it if thou knew'st our purposes.

HAMLET I see a cherub that sees them. But come, for England! Farewell dear mother.

6–7. **th'offender's scourge . . . offence:** more attention is paid to the criminal's sufferings than to his crime. 9. **pause:** consideration, reflection. 19. **a is:** he's. 20–21. **convocation . . . diet:** Hamlet is punning on the Diet (or assembly) of Worms (the city on the Rhine). The most famous meeting of the Diet was that called by the emperor, Charles V, in 1521., before which Luther appeared to justify his doctrines. 20. **politic worms:** such worms as might breed in a politician's corpse. As the worm insinuates itself into the privacy of the body, it resembles Polonius's politic espionage. 24. **variable:** interchangeable — i.e., they may be different dishes, but they are both served to the one table. 32. **progress:** journey of state by the sovereign through his dominions. 38. **lobby:** main corridor or anteroom. 42. **tender:** have regard for. 46. **tend:** attend. 46. **bent:** in a state of readiness.

CLAUDIUS Thy loving father, Hamlet.
HAMLET My mother. Father and mother is man and wife, man and wife is one flesh, and so, my mother. Come, for England. *Exit*
CLAUDIUS Follow him at foot,° tempt him with speed aboard.
Delay it not, I'll have him hence tonight.
Away, for everything is sealed and done
That else leans on° th'affair. Pray you make haste.
[*Exeunt Rosencrantz and Guildenstern*]
And England,° if my love thou hold'st at aught,°
As my great power thereof may give thee sense,°
Since yet thy cicatrice° looks raw and red
After the Danish sword, and thy free° awe
Pays homage to us — thou mayst not coldly set°
Our sovereign process,° which imports at full,
By letters congruing° to that effect,
The present° death of Hamlet. Do it England,
For like the hectic° in my blood he rages,
And thou must cure me. Till I know 'tis done,
Howe'er my haps,° my joys were ne'er begun.
Exit

Act IV, Scene iv

Enter FORTINBRAS *with his army over the stage*

FORTINBRAS Go captain, from me greet the Danish king.
Tell him that by his licence, Fortinbras
Craves the conveyance° of a promised march
Over his kingdom. You know the rendezvous.
If that his majesty would aught with us,
We shall express our duty° in his eye,°
And let him know so.
CAPTAIN I will do't, my lord.
FORTINBRAS Go softly° on.
[*Exit Fortinbras, with the army*]

[*Enter* HAMLET, ROSENCRANTZ, *etc.*

HAMLET Good sir, whose powers° are these?
CAPTAIN They are of Norway sir.
HAMLET How purposed sir I pray you?
CAPTAIN Against some part of Poland.
HAMLET Who commands them sir?
CAPTAIN The nephew to old Norway, Fortinbras.
HAMLET Goes it against the main° of Poland sir,
Or for some frontier?
CAPTAIN Truly to speak, and with no addition,°
We go to gain a little patch of ground
That hath in it no profit but the name.
To pay five ducats, five, I would not farm it,
Nor will it yield to Norway or the Pole
A ranker° rate, should it be sold in fee.°
HAMLET Why then the Polack never will defend it.
CAPTAIN Yes, it is already garrisoned.
HAMLET Two thousand souls and twenty thousand ducats
Will not debate the question° of this straw.
This is th'impostume° of much wealth and peace,
That inward breaks, and shows no cause without
Why the man dies. I humbly thank you sir.
CAPTAIN God buy you sir. [*Exit*]
ROSENCRANTZ Will't please you go my lord?
HAMLET I'll be with you straight; go a little before.
[*Exeunt all but Hamlet*]
How all occasions do inform against me,
And spur my dull revenge! What is a man
If his chief good and market° of his time
Be but to sleep and feed? A beast, no more.
Sure he that made us with such large discourse,°
Looking before and after, gave us not
That capability and god-like reason
To fust° in us unused. Now whether it be
Bestial oblivion,° or some craven° scruple
Of thinking too precisely° on th'event° —

---

55. **at foot:** close at heel. 58. **leans on:** pertains to. 59. **England:** the king of England. 59. **at aught:** at any value. 60. **thereof may give thee sense:** may give you a feeling of the importance of valuing my love. 61. **cicatrice:** scar. 62. **free:** uncompelled. 63. **coldly set:** regard with indifference. 64. **process:** writ. 65. **congruing:** agreeing. 66. **present:** immediate. 67. **hectic:** chronic fever. 69. **haps:** fortunes.

Act IV Scene iv. 3. **conveyance:** grant. 6. **duty:** humble respect. 6. **in his eye:** in his presence. 8. **softly:** circumspectly. 9. **powers:** forces, troops. 15. **main:** whole. 17. **addition:** exaggeration. 22. **ranker:** more abundant. 22. **in fee:** i.e., outright, without restrictions. 26. **Will not debate the question:** are not enough to fight out the dispute. 27. **impostume:** abscess. 34. **market:** profit. 36. **discourse:** faculty of reasoning. 39. **fust:** grow moldy. 40. **oblivion:** forgetfulness. 40. **craven:** cowardly. 41. **precisely:** scrupulously, pedantically. 41. **event:** result, consequence.

A thought which quartered hath but one part wisdom
And ever three parts coward — I do not know
Why yet I live to say this thing's to do,
Sith° I have cause, and will, and strength, and means
To do't. Examples gross° as earth exhort me.
Witness this army of such mass and charge,°
Led by a delicate and tender prince,
Whose spirit with divine ambition puffed°
Makes mouths at° the invisible event,
Exposing what is mortal and unsure
To all that fortune, death and danger dare,
Even for an egg-shell. Rightly to be great
Is not to stir° without great argument,
But greatly to find quarrel in a straw
When honour's at the stake. How stand I then,
That have a father killed, a mother stained,
Excitements of my reason and my blood,
And let all sleep, while to my shame I see
The imminent death of twenty thousand men,
That for a fantasy and trick° of fame
Go to their graves like beds, fight for a plot
Whereon the numbers cannot try the cause,
Which is not tomb enough and continent
To hide the slain.° Oh from this time forth,
My thoughts be bloody or be nothing worth.
[*Exit*]

Act IV, Scene v

Enter HORATIO, GERTRUDE *and a* GENTLEMAN

GERTRUDE I will not speak with her.
GENTLEMAN She is importunate, indeed distract;
Her mood will needs be pitied.°
GERTRUDE What would she have?
GENTLEMAN She speaks much of her father, says she hears
There's tricks i'th'world, and hems,° and beats her heart,
Spurns enviously at straws,° speaks things in doubt°
That carry but half sense. Her speech is nothing,
Yet the unshapèd use of it doth move
The hearers to collection.° They yawn° at it,
And botch the words up fit to their own thoughts,°
Which, as her winks and nods and gestures yield them,
Indeed would make one think there might be thought,
Though nothing sure, yet much unhappily.°
HORATIO 'Twere good she were spoken with, for she may strew
Dangerous conjectures in ill-breeding° minds.
GERTRUDE Let her come in.
[*Exit Gentleman*]
(*Aside*) To my sick soul, as sin's true nature is,
Each toy° seems prologue to some great amiss.
So full of artless° jealousy° is guilt,
It spills itself in fearing to be spilt.°

Enter OPHELIA *distracted*°

OPHELIA Where is the beauteous majesty of Denmark?
GERTRUDE How now Ophelia?
OPHELIA *She sings*
How should I your true love know
From another one?
By his cockle hat° and staff
And his sandal shoon.°
GERTRUDE Alas sweet lady, what imports this song?
OPHELIA Say you? Nay, pray you mark.°

---

45. **Sith:** since. 46. **gross:** palpable, obvious. 47. **mass and charge:** size and expense. 49. **puffed:** inflated. 50. **Makes mouths at:** makes faces at, despises. 54. **not to stir:** not a matter of refusing to stir. 56. **at the stake:** at risk. The image is gaming, not burning or bear-baiting. 61. **trick:** illusion, deceit. 63–65. **W hereon . . . slain:** i.e., the plot of ground is not big enough to hold those who are to fight for it, or to bury those who are killed.
Act IV, Scene v. 3. **Her mood will needs be pitied:** Her state of mind must necessarily cause pity. 5. **hems:** makes the noise "H'm." 6. **Spurns enviously at straws:** takes offense angrily at trifles. 6. **in doubt:** of uncertain meaning. 9. **to collection:** to infer a meaning. 9. **yawn:** gape with surprise. 10. **botch . . . thoughts:** patch the words up into patterns conforming to their own ideas. 13. **unhappily:** clumsily. 15. **ill-breeding:** intent on making mischief. 18. **toy:** trifle. 19. **artless:** unskilled; hence, blundering, foolish. 19. **jealousy:** suspicion. 20. **It spills itself in fearing to be spilt:** i.e., fear of detection leads to the very exposure one is trying to avert. 20. **sd *Enter* OPHELIA *distructed*:** The First Quarto gives the famous direction "*Enter Ofelia playing on a Lute, and her haire downe singing.*" 23–26. **How . . . shoon:** a recollection of a famous ballad which brings together a lonely pilgrim and a deserted lover. 25. **cockle hat:** The pilgrim's emblem was a scallop, or cockle, shell. 26. **shoon:** shoes. 28. **Say you? . . . mark:** i.e., Is that your question? Just pay attention. Then she proceeds with the ballad, the dead father taking the place of the absent lover.

He is dead and gone lady, *Song*
He is dead and gone;
At his head a grass-green turf,
At his heels a stone.

OPHELIA Oho!

GERTRUDE Nay but Ophelia —

OPHELIA Pray you mark.
White his shrowd as the mountain snow— *Song*

Enter CLAUDIUS

GERTRUDE Alas, look here my lord.

OPHELIA Larded all° with sweet flowers,
Which bewept to the grave did not go
With true-love showers.

CLAUDIUS How do you, pretty lady?

OPHELIA Well good dild you.° They say the owl was a baker's daughter.° Lord, we know what we are, but know not what we may be. God be at your table.°

CLAUDIUS Conceit upon her father.°

OPHELIA Pray let's have no words of this, but when they ask you what it means, say you this°—
Tomorrow is Saint Valentine's day, *Song*
All in the morning betime,
And I a maid at your window,
To be your Valentine.

Then up he rose and donned his clothes
And dupped° the chamber door;
Let in the maid that out a maid
Never departed more.

CLAUDIUS Pretty Ophelia!

OPHELIA Indeed la!° Without an oath I'll make an end on't.
By Gis and by Saint Charity,
Alack and fie for shame,
Young men will do't if they come to't—
By Cock,° they are to blame.
Quoth she, "Before you tumbled° me,
You promised me to wed."
He answers—
So would I ha' done, by yonder sun,
And° thou hadst not come to my bed.

CLAUDIUS How long hath she been thus?

OPHELIA I hope all will be well. We must be patient, but I cannot choose but weep to think they would lay him i'th' cold ground. My brother shall know of it, and so I thank you for your good counsel. Come, my coach. Good night ladies, good night sweet ladies, good night, good night. *Exit*

CLAUDIUS Follow her close, give her good watch I pray you.

[*Exit Horatio*]

Oh this is the poison of deep grief, it springs
All from her father's death, [and now behold—]
Oh Gertrude, Gertrude,
When sorrows come, they come not single spies,
But in battalions. First, her father slain;
Next, your son gone, and he most violent author
Of his own just remove; the people muddied,
Thick and unwholesome in their thoughts and whispers
For good Polonius' death—and we have done but greenly°
In hugger-mugger° to inter him; poor Ophelia
Divided from herself and her fair judgement,
Without the which we are pictures, or mere beasts;
Last, and as much containing as all these,°
Her brother is in secret come from France,
Feeds on his wonder, keeps himself in clouds,°
And wants not buzzers° to infect his ear
With pestilent speeches of his father's death,

38. **Larded all:** decorated. 42. **good dild you:** God yield or reward you. The phrase means only "thank you." 42. **owl was a baker's daughter:** a reference to a folktale in which a baker's daughter was parsimonious with the dough when a beggar asked her for bread. The beggar was Jesus, and he turned her into an owl. The tale is in Ophelia's mind as a story of transformation. 44. **God be at your table:** i.e., bless you in *your* transformation. 45. **Conceit upon her father:** fanciful thoughts connected with her father. 46–47. **ask you what it means, say you this:** Ophelia's "explanations" go from one of her sadnesses to the other—from Hamlet to Polonius and back again. 53. **dupped:** i.e., did up, undid. 57. **Indeed la!:** scornful assent to Claudius's "Pretty Ophelia!" 61. **Cock:** (1.) as leader or ruling spirit, a colloquial reference to God; (2.) used also with an obvious double meaning. 62. **tumbled:** had sexual intercourse with. 66. **And:** if. 83. **greenly:** foolishly, as though from inexperience. 84. **In hugger-mugger:** with secrecy. 87. **as much containing as all these:** i.e., as serious as all the others together. 89. **Feeds . . . clouds:** i.e., instead of finding out what has actually happened, he keeps himself in the clouds of suspicion and finds food for anger in his own uncertainty or in what he guesses ("wonder"). 90. **buzzers:** rumor-mongers.

Wherein necessity, of matter beggared,
Will nothing stick° our person to arraign
In ear and ear.° O my dear Gertrude, this,
Like to a murdering piece,° in many places
Gives me superfluous death.°

A noise within

GERTRUDE Alack, what noise is this?

CLAUDIUS Attend! Where are my Swissers?° Let them guard the door.

Enter a MESSENGER

What is the matter?

MESSENGER Save yourself my lord.
The ocean, overpeering of his list,°
Eats not the flats with more impitious° haste
Than young Laertes in a riotous head
O'erbears your officers. The rabble call him lord,
And, as the world were now but to begin,
Antiquity forgot, custom not known,
The ratifiers and props of every word,°
They cry "Choose we! Laertes shall be king."
Caps, hands and tongues applaud it to the clouds,
"Laertes shall be king, Laertes king!"

GERTRUDE How cheerfully on the false trail they cry!
Oh this is counter, you false Danish dogs!°

A noise within

CLAUDIUS The doors are broke.

Enter LAERTES *with others*

LAERTES Where is this king? — Sirs, stand you all without.

ALL No, let's come in.

LAERTES I pray you give me leave.

ALL We will, we will.

LAERTES I thank you. Keep the door.

[*Exeunt followers*]

O thou vile king,
Give me my father.

GERTRUDE Calmly, good Laertes.

LAERTES That drop of blood that's calm proclaims me bastard,
Cries cuckold to my father, brands the harlot
Even here, between° the chaste unsmirchèd° brow°
Of my true mother.

CLAUDIUS What is the cause, Laertes,
That thy rebellion looks so giant-like? —
Let him go, Gertrude, do not fear our person.
There's such divinity doth hedge° a king

Private Collection / De Agostini Picture Library/Bridgeman Images

This painting of Ophelia, completed in 1910, is one of several by pre-Raphaelite artist John William Waterhouse.

What aspects of Ophelia's character does this painting evoke? What nuances of character do you believe are either ignored or exaggerated?

---

92. **necessity . . . nothing stick:** i.e., having no evidence, they are obliged to invent and have no scruples in doing so. 94. **ear and ear:** i.e., whispering to person after person. 95. **murdering piece:** the name of a small cannon which was used to fire charges of small shot against infantry. 96. **superfluous death:** i.e., kills me over and over again. 98. **Swissers:** Swiss guards. 100. **overpeering of his list:** rising above (literally, looking over) its boundary. 101. **impitious:** pitiless. 106. **ratifiers and props of every word:** Tradition ("Antiquity") and custom should ratify and support everything we say. 111. **counter . . . dogs:** Hounds run "counter" when they trace the trail backward. 121–22. **brands the harlot . . . brow:** The forehead is the symbolic showplace of chastity and unchasity. 121. **between:** in the middle of. 121. **unsmirchèd:** clean, unstained. 125. **hedge:** surround with a defensive hedge or fence.

That treason can but peep to what it would,°
Acts little of his will. — Tell me Laertes,
Why thou art thus incensed. — Let him go
Gertrude. — Speak man.

LAERTES Where is my father?

CLAUDIUS Dead.

GERTRUDE But not by him.

CLAUDIUS Let him demand his fill.

LAERTES How came he dead? I'll not be juggled with.°
To hell allegiance, vows to the blackest devil,
Conscience and grace° to the profoundest pit!
I dare damnation. To this point I stand,
That both the worlds I give to negligence,°
Let come what comes, only I'll be revenged
Most throughly for my father.

CLAUDIUS Who shall stay you?

LAERTES My will, not all the world.
And for my means, I'll husband them so well,
They shall go far with little.

CLAUDIUS Good Laertes,
If you desire to know the certainty
Of your dear father, is't writ in your revenge
That, soopstake,° you will draw° both friend and foe,
Winner and loser?

LAERTES None but his enemies.

CLAUDIUS Will you know them then?

LAERTES To his good friends thus wide I'll ope my arms,
And like the kind life-rendering pelican,°
Repast° them with my blood.

CLAUDIUS Why now you speak
Like a good child and a true gentleman.
That I am guiltless of your father's death,
And am most sensibly in grief for it,
It shall as level to your judgement pierce
As day does to your eye.

A noise within: "Let her come in"

LAERTES How now, what noise is that?

Enter **OPHELIA**

O heat dry up my brains, tears seven times salt
Burn out the sense and virtue° of mine eye!
By heaven, thy madness shall be paid with weight
Till our scale turn the beam. O rose of May,
Dear maid, kind sister, sweet Ophelia —
O heavens, is't possible a young maid's wits
Should be as mortal as an old man's life?
Nature is fine in love, and where 'tis fine,
It sends some precious instance of itself
After the thing it loves.°

OPHELIA They bore him bare-faced on the bier [*Song*]
Hey non nonny, nonny, hey nonny,°
And in his grave rained many a tear —
Fare you well my dove.

LAERTES Hadst thou thy wits, and didst persuade revenge, It could not move thus.

OPHELIA You must sing a-down a-down,° and you call him a-down-a. Oh how the wheel becomes it. It is the false steward that stole his master's daughter.

LAERTES This nothing's more than matter.

OPHELIA There's rosemary, that's for remembrance — pray you, love, remember° — and there is pansies, that's for thoughts.°

LAERTES A document in madness, thoughts and remembrance fitted.°

OPHELIA There's fennel° for you, and columbines.°
There's rue° for you, and here's some for me; we

---

126. **peep to what it would:** Treason can only peer through (the "hedge") and cannot carry out its plans. 131. **juggled with:** cheated or deceived as by a juggler or trickster. 133. **grace:** holy disposition. 135. **give to negligence:** i.e., disregard, despise. 143. **soopstake:** sweepstake, the act of a gambler in taking all stakes at one go. 143. **draw:** draw in. 147. **kind life-rendering pelican:** The pelican was supposed to pierce its breast with its bill and allow its young to feed on the blood. 148. **repast:** feed. 156. **sense and virtue:** sensitivity and efficacy. 162–64. **Nature . . . loves:** Love refines our nature, and this refined nature sends part of itself after the loved one; that is, Ophelia has parted with some of her wits to send to Polonius. 165–66. **They bore him . . . hey nonny:** Ophelia sings a lament, but gives as chorus the "hey nonny no" of a love ditty. Perhaps that is why she then says, "You must sing a-down a-down." 171. **a-down a-down:** a popular refrain. 177. **pray you, love, remember:** Ophelia gives the rosemary and pansies to Laertes. To whom she gives the fennel and columbines and to whom the rue is much debated. 178. **pansies, that's for thoughts:** The name comes from the French *pensées.* As elsewhere in this scene, "thoughts" has the special meaning of *sad* thoughts, melancholy. 179–80. **A document . . . fitted:** "Document" means instruction. Ophelia finds a lesson in flowers, and in her interpretation of them Laertes finds a lesson in madness, for a mad person's thoughts are continually "fitted" (connected) with the remembrance of dark happenings. 181. **fennel:** a food much liked by serpents. 181. **columbines:** for ingratitude and infidelity. 182. **rue:** for sorrow and repentance.

may call it herb of grace° a Sundays. Oh you must wear your rue with a difference.° There's a daisy.° I would give you some violets, but they withered all when my father died. They say a made a good end.

[*Sings*]

For bonny sweet Robin° is all my joy.

LAERTES Thought° and affliction, passion, hell itself, She turns to favour° and to prettiness.

OPHELIA And will a not come again? *Song*
And will a not come again?
No, no, he is dead,
Go to thy death-bed,
He never will come again.
His beard was as white as snow,
All flaxen was his poll,°
He is gone, he is gone,
And we cast away moan,°
God-a-mercy on his soul.
And of all Christian souls, I pray God.
God buy you. *Exit*

LAERTES Do you see this, O God?

CLAUDIUS Laertes, I must commune° with your grief,
Or you deny me right. Go but apart,
Make choice of whom° your wisest friends you will,
And they shall hear and judge 'twixt you and me.
If by direct or by collateral° hand
They find us touched,° we will our kingdom give,
Our crown, our life, and all that we call ours,
To you in satisfaction. But if not,
Be you content to lend your patience to us,
And we shall jointly labour with your soul
To give it due content.

LAERTES Let this be so.
His means of death,° his obscure funeral,
No trophy,° sword, nor hatchment° o'er his bones,
No noble rite, nor formal ostentation,
Cry to be heard, as 'twere from heaven to earth,
That I must call't in question.°

CLAUDIUS So you shall.
And where th'offence is, let the great axe fall.
I pray you go with me.
Exeunt

Hamlet de FrancoZeffirelli avec Helena Bonham Carter (Ophelie), 1991 (d'apres William Shakespeare)/RUE DES ARCHIVES (RDA)/Bridgeman Images

This photograph still from the 1990 Franco Zeffirelli film *Hamlet* shows Helena Bonham Carter as Ophelia. Look carefully at her appearance, especially her hair and eyes. **How effectively does Bonham Carter capture Ophelia's madness here? How does her interpretation of Ophelia compare with that of Waterhouse (p. 609)?**

183. **herb of grace:** another name for rue. 184. **with a difference:** a term in heraldry; a mark to distinguish a coat of arms from that of another member or branch of the family. 185. **daisy:** Daisies and violets are flowers of springtime and love. 188. **bonny sweet Robin:** Bonny Robin songs deal with lovers, unfaithfulness, and extramarital affairs. 189. **Thought:** melancholy. 190. **favour:** beauty. 197. **flaxen was his poll:** i.e., his hair was white. 199. **cast away moan:** i.e., lamenting is useless. 204. **commune:** converse. 206. **whom:** whichever of. 208. **collateral:** indirect. 209. **touched:** concerned, implicated. 215. **His means of death:** the way he died. 216. **trophy:** memorial (such as the insignia of his rank and office). 216. **hatchment:** coat of arms placed over the dead; usually a diamond-shaped tablet. 219. **call't in question:** demand an examination.

Act IV, Scene vi

Enter HORATIO *with an* ATTENDANT

HORATIO What are they that would speak with me?

ATTENDANT Seafaring men sir, they say they have letters for you.

HORATIO Let them come in.

[*Exit Attendant*]

I do not know from what part of the world°
I should be greeted, if not from Lord Hamlet.

Enter SAILORS

I SAILOR God bless you sir.

HORATIO Let him bless thee too.

I SAILOR A shall sir, and please° him. There's a letter for you sir, it came from th'ambassador that was bound for England, if your name be Horatio, as I am let to know it is.

HORATIO (*Reads the letter*) "Horatio, when thou shalt have overlooked this, give these fellows some means to the king; they have letters for him. Ere we were two days old at sea, a pirate of very warlike appointment gave us chase. Finding ourselves too slow of sail, we put on a compelled valour, and in the grapple I boarded them. On the instant they got clear of our ship, so I alone became their prisoner. They have dealt with me like thieves of mercy,° but they knew what they did:° I am to do a good turn for them. Let the king have the letters I have sent, and repair thou to me with as much speed as thou wouldest fly death. I have words to speak in thine ear will make thee dumb, yet are they much too light for the bore of the matter.° These good fellows will bring thee where I am. Rosencrantz and Guildenstern hold their course for England. Of them I have much to tell thee. Farewell.

He that thou knowest thine,
Hamlet."

Come, I will give you way for these your letters,
And do't the speedier that you may direct me
To him from whom you brought them.

Exeunt

Act IV, Scene vii

Enter CLAUDIUS *and* LAERTES

CLAUDIUS Now must your conscience my acquittance° seal,
And you must put me in your heart for friend,
Sith you have heard, and with a knowing° ear,
That he which hath your noble father slain
Pursued my life.

LAERTES It well appears. But tell me
Why you proceeded not against these feats,°
So crimeful and so capital in nature,
As by your safety, wisdom,° all things else,
You mainly were stirred up.

CLAUDIUS Oh for two special reasons,
Which may to you perhaps seem much unsinewed,
But yet to me they're strong. The queen his mother
Lives almost by his looks, and for myself,
My virtue or my plague, be it either which,
She's so conjunctive° to my life and soul,
That as the star moves not but in his sphere,°
I could not but by her. The other motive,
Why to a public count° I might not go,
Is the great love the general gender° bear him,
Who, dipping all his faults in their affection,
Work° like the spring that turneth wood to stone,
Convert his gyves° to graces, so that my arrows,
Too slightly timbered° for so loud a wind,
Would have reverted° to my bow again,
And not where I had aimed them.

Act: IV, Scene: vi. 4. **what part of the world:** i.e., what distant part of the world (involving communication by sea). 8. **and please:** if it please. 21. **thieves of mercy:** thieves with merciful hearts. 21–22. **they knew what they did:** i.e., their mercy was calculated. 27. **for the bore of the matter:** for the gravity of the substance they speak of. **Act IV, Scene vii.** 1. **my acquittance seal:** confirm my discharge—i.e., acknowledge my innocence. 3. **knowing:** understanding, intelligent. 6. **feats:** exploits. 8. **safety, wisdom:** Claudius is stirred up to take action on account of his safety and by persuasion of his wisdom. 14. **conjunctive:** closely joined. 15. **sphere:** one of the series of hollow, transparent globes supposed to encircle the earth and carry the heavenly bodies. 17. **count:** indictment. 18. **general gender:** common people. 20. **Work:** act, operate. 21. **gyves:** fetters. 22. **Too slightly timbered:** i.e., too light. 23. **reverted:** returned.

LAERTES And so have I a noble father lost,
A sister driven into desperate terms,°
Whose worth, if praises may go back again,°
Stood challenger on mount of° all the age
For her perfections. But my revenge will come.

CLAUDIUS Break not your sleeps for that. You must not think
That we are made of stuff so flat° and dull
That we can let our beard be shook with danger°
And think it pastime. You shortly shall hear more.
I loved your father, and we love ourself,
And that I hope will teach you to imagine —

Enter a MESSENGER *with letters*

How now? What news?

MESSENGER Letters my lord from Hamlet.
This to your majesty, this to the queen.

CLAUDIUS From Hamlet? Who brought them?

MESSENGER Sailors my lord they say, I saw them not;
They were given me by Claudio — he received them
Of him that brought them.

CLAUDIUS Laertes, you shall hear them. —
Leave us.

Exit Messenger

[*Reads*] "High and mighty, you shall know I am set naked° on your kingdom. Tomorrow shall I beg leave to see your kingly eyes, when I shall, first asking your pardon thereunto, recount th'occasion of my sudden and more strange return.

Hamlet."

What should this mean? Are all the rest come back?
Or is it some abuse,° and no such thing?°

LAERTES Know you the hand?

CLAUDIUS 'Tis Hamlet's character.° Naked?
And in a postscript here he says alone.
Can you devise me?

LAERTES I'm lost in it my lord. But let him come —
It warms° the very° sickness in my heart
That I shall live and tell him to his teeth
"Thus didest thou!"

CLAUDIUS If it be so, Laertes —
As how should it be so? — how otherwise? —
Will you be ruled by me?

LAERTES Ay my lord,
So you will not o'errule me to a peace.

CLAUDIUS To thine own peace. If he be now returned,
As checking at° his voyage, and that he means
No more to undertake it, I will work him
To an exploit, now ripe in my device,°
Under the which he shall not choose but fall,
And for his death no wind of blame shall breathe,
But even his mother shall uncharge the practice°
And call it accident.

[**LAERTES** My lord, I will be ruled,
The rather if you could devise° it so
That I might be the organ.°

CLAUDIUS It falls right.
You have been talked of since your travel much,
And that in Hamlet's hearing, for a quality
Wherein they say you shine. Your sum of parts
Did not together pluck such envy from him
As did that one, and that in my regard
Of the unworthiest siege.°

LAERTES What part is that my lord?

CLAUDIUS A very riband° in the cap of youth,
Yet needful too, for youth no less becomes°
The light and careless livery that it wears
Than settled age his sables and his weeds
Importing health and graveness.]° Two months since
Here was a gentleman of Normandy.
I've seen myself, and served against, the French,
And they can well° on horseback, but this gallant
Had witchcraft in't. He grew unto his seat,
And to such wondrous doing brought his horse
As had he been incorpsed° and demi-natured°

---

26. **desperate terms:** an extreme or hopeless state. 27. **back again:** i.e., to what she was. 28. **on mount of:** probably "mounted above," placed on high above. 31. **flat:** inert, spiritless. 32. **with danger:** with dangerous intent, threateningly. 43. **naked:** destitute. 50. **abuse:** deception. 50. **no such thing:** i.e., no such thing has happened. 51. **character:** handwriting. 55. **warms:** does good to. 55. **very:** real. 62. **checking at:** a phrase from falconry, used when a hawk is diverted in his pursuit by some new object. 64. **ripe in my device:** i.e., a scheme of mine come to maturity. 67. **uncharge the practice:** i.e., not press the accusation that it was a criminal contrivance. 69. **devise:** contrive. 70. **organ:** instrument. 76. **Of the unworthiest siege:** of the least account. 77. **very riband:** mere ribbon. 78. **becomes:** is in accord with, suits. 81. **Importing health and graveness:** which indicate a concern for health and dignity. 84. **can well:** are very skillful. 87. **incorpsed:** of one body. 87. **demi-natured:** i.e., he, as man, was half of the total nature of a united man-horse creature.

With the brave beast.° So far he topped my
thought,°
That I in forgery of shapes and tricks°
Come short of what he did.

LAERTES A Norman was't?

CLAUDIUS A Norman.

LAERTES Upon my life Lamord.

CLAUDIUS The very same.

LAERTES I know him well, he is the brooch indeed
And gem of all the nation.

CLAUDIUS He made confession of you,°
And gave you such a masterly report
For art and exercise° in your defence,
And for your rapier most especial,
That he cried out 'twould be a sight indeed
If one could match you. [Th'escrimers° of their
nation
He swore had neither motion,° guard, nor eye,
If you opposed them.] Sir, this report of his
Did Hamlet so envenom° with his envy
That he could nothing do but wish and beg
Your sudden coming o'er to play with you.
Now out of this—

LAERTES What out of this, my lord?

CLAUDIUS Laertes, was your father dear to you?
Or are you like the painting of a sorrow,
A face without a heart?

LAERTES Why ask you this?

CLAUDIUS Not that I think you did not love your
father,
But that I know love is begun by time,°
And that I see, in passages of proof,°
Time qualifies° the spark and fire of it.
[There lives within the very flame of love
A kind of wick or snuff° that will abate it,
And nothing is at a like goodness still,°
For goodness, growing to a plurisy,°
Dies in his own too much. That we would do,
We should do when we would, for this
"would" changes,
And hath abatements and delays as many
As there are tongues, are hands, are accidents;
And then this "should" is like a spendthrift sigh,°
That hurts by easing. But to the quick of
th'ulcer°—]
Hamlet comes back; what would you undertake
To show yourself in deed your father's son
More than in words?

LAERTES To cut his throat i'th'church.

CLAUDIUS No place indeed should murder
sanctuarize;°
Revenge should have no bounds. But, good
Laertes,
Will you do this,° keep close° within your
chamber;
Hamlet, returned, shall know you are come
home;
We'll put on those shall praise° your excellence,
And set a double varnish on the fame
The Frenchman gave you; bring you in fine°
together,
And wager on your heads. He being remiss,°
Most generous, and free from all contriving,
Will not peruse the foils, so that with ease,
Or with a little shuffling,° you may choose
A sword unbated,° and in a pass of practice°
Requite him for your father.

LAERTES I will do't,
And for that purpose I'll anoint my sword.
I bought an unction° of a mountebank,°
So mortal that but dip a knife in it,
Where it draws blood no cataplasm° so rare,
Collected° from all simples° that have virtue
Under the moon,° can save the thing from death

---

88. **topped my thought:** surpassed what I could imagine. 89. **in forgery of shapes and tricks:** in imagining displays of horsemanship. 95. **made confession of you:** revealed the truth about you. 97. **art and exercise:** skillful accomplishments. 100. **Th'escrimers:** French *escrimeur*, master of fencing. 101. **motion:** the skilled movements of the trained fencer. 103. **envenom:** embitter (literally, poison). 111. **by time:** by suitable time, by the proper occasion. 112. **passages of proof:** things that have happened which bear me out. 113. **qualifies:** reduces, weakens. 115. **snuff:** the burnt part of the wick. 116. **still:** all the time. 117. **plurisy:** (1.) excess, (2.) the inflammation of the chest (pleurisy) thought to be caused by excess of humors. 122. **spendthrift sigh:** It is really the sigh itself that is a spendthrift—it does harm in the pleasure of indulging itself. 123. **to the quick of th'ulcer:** to the heart of the matter. 127. **should murder sanctuarize:** should offer sanctuary to murder. 129. **Will you do this:** if you are to do this. 129. **keep close:** remain confined. 131. **put on those shall praise:** arrange for some to praise. 133. **in fine:** in conclusion. 134. **remiss:** not vigilant or cautious. 137. **shuffling:** deceit (rather than physically shuffling the foils). 138. **unbated:** unblunted. 138. **a pass of practice:** "Practice" means a deliberate and malicious stratagem. Claudius is speaking of a thrust that is intended to kill. 141. **unction:** ointment. 141. **mountebank:** one who travels about selling medicines and cures. 143. **cataplasm:** poultice, medicated dressing. 144. **Collected:** put together. 144. **simples:** medicinal plants. 145. **Under the moon:** anywhere in the world.

Perhaps the most well-known painting of Ophelia is John Everett Millais's 1852 painting of her final moments.

How does Millais portray Ophelia's state of mind in this work? Pay close attention to the expression on her face, her position in the water, and the way Millais used light and shadow.

That is but scratched withal. I'll touch my point
With this contagion, that if I gall° him slightly,
It may be death.

CLAUDIUS Let's further think of this,
Weigh what convenience both of time and means
May fit us to our shape.° If this should fail,
And that our drift° look through our bad performance,
'Twere better not assayed. Therefore this project
Should have a back or second, that might hold
If this did blast in proof.° Soft, let me see.
We'll make a solemn wager on your cunnings —
I ha't!
When in your motion you are hot and dry,
As make your bouts more violent to that end,
And that he calls for drink, I'll have preferred° him
A chalice for the nonce,° whereon but sipping,
If he by chance escape your venomed stuck,°
Our purpose may hold there. But stay, what noise?

Enter GERTRUDE

How, sweet queen!

GERTRUDE One woe doth tread upon another's heel,
So fast they follow. Your sister's drowned, Laertes.

LAERTES Drowned! Oh where?

GERTRUDE There is a willow grows askant a brook,
That shows his hoar° leaves in the glassy stream.
Therewith fantastic garlands did she make,°
Of crow-flowers, nettles, daisies, and long purples,
That liberal° shepherds give a grosser name,
But our cold maids do dead men's fingers call them.°
There on the pendant boughs her cronet° weeds
Clamb'ring to hang, an envious° sliver° broke,
When down her weedy trophies and herself
Fell in the weeping brook. Her clothes spread wide,
And mermaid-like awhile they bore her up,
Which time she chanted snatches of old lauds°
As one incapable° of her own distress,
Or like a creature native and indued°
Unto that element. But long it could not be
Till that her garments, heavy with their drink,
Pulled the poor wretch from her melodious lay
To muddy death.

LAERTES Alas, then she is drowned?

GERTRUDE Drowned, drowned.

---

147. **gall:** injure, wound. 150. **fit us to our shape:** suit us for our design. 151. **drift:** aim, purpose. 154. **blast in proof:** explode in being tested (like a faulty cannon). 159. **preferred:** presented to, offered. 160. **for the nonce:** for that particular purpose or occasion. 161. **stuck:** thrust. 168. **hoar:** grey. 169. **Therewith . . . make:** She made garlands from the willow, interwoven with wildflowers and weeds. 170–72. **long-purples . . . call them:** generally identified as the wild orchis, *Orchis mascula*, which has a tall flower stem with a spike of purple flowers. The "grosser name" — something to do with testicles — and "dead men's fingers" apply to the shape of the roots. 171. **liberal:** free-spoken. 173. **cronet:** coronet. 174. **envious:** malicious. 174. **sliver:** a small branch or twig. 178. **lauds:** hymns. 179. **incapable:** uncomprehending. 180. **indued:** adapted, conditioned.

LAERTES Too much of water hast thou, poor Ophelia,
And therefore I forbid my tears. But yet
It is our trick;° nature her custom holds,
Let shame say what it will. When these° are gone,
The woman will be out.° Adieu my lord,
I have a speech of fire that fain would blaze,
But that this folly douts° it. *Exit*

CLAUDIUS Let's follow, Gertrude.
How much I had to do to calm his rage!
Now fear I this will give it start again.
Therefore let's follow.

Exeunt

Act V, Scene i

Enter two CLOWNS

CLOWN Is she to be buried in Christian burial, when she wilfully seeks her own salvation?°

OTHER I tell thee she is, therefore make her grave straight.° The crowner° hath sat on her, and finds it Christian burial.

CLOWN How can that be, unless she drowned herself in her own defence?

OTHER Why, 'tis found so.

CLOWN It must be *se offendendo,*° it cannot be else. For here lies the point: if I drown myself wittingly, it argues an act, and an act hath three branches—it is to act, to do, to perform. Argal,° she drowned herself wittingly.

OTHER Nay, but hear you goodman delver°—

CLOWN Give me leave. Here lies the water—good. Here stands the man—good. If the man go to this water and drown himself, it is will he, nill he,° he goes—mark you that. But if the water come to him, and drown him, he drowns not himself. Argal, he that is not guilty of his own death shortens not his own life.°

OTHER But is this law?

CLOWN Ay marry is't, crowner's quest law.°

OTHER Will you ha' the truth on't? If this had not been a gentlewoman, she should have been buried out o' Christian burial.

CLOWN Why, there thou sayst—and the more pity that great folk should have countenance° in this world to drown or hang themselves more than their even-Christen.° Come, my spade; there is no ancient° gentlemen but gardeners, ditchers, and gravemakers; they hold up Adam's profession.

OTHER Was he a gentleman?

CLOWN A was the first that ever bore arms.

OTHER Why, he had none.

CLOWN What, art a heathen? How dost thou understand the scripture? The scripture says Adam digged. Could he dig without arms? I'll put another question to thee. If thou answerest me not to the purpose, confess thyself°—

OTHER Go to!

CLOWN What is he that builds stronger than either the mason, the shipwright, or the carpenter?

OTHER The gallows-maker, for that frame° outlives a thousand tenants.

CLOWN I like thy wit well in good faith. The gallows does well, but how does it well? It does well to those that do ill. Now, thou dost ill to say the gallows is built stronger than the church; argal, the gallows may do well to thee. To't again, come.

OTHER Who builds stronger than a mason, a shipwright, or a carpenter?

CLOWN Ay, tell me that, and unyoke.°

OTHER Marry, now I can tell.

CLOWN To't.

OTHER Mass, I cannot tell.

Enter HAMLET *and* HORATIO *afar off*

---

188. **our trick:** a way we have. 189. **these:** i.e., his tears. 190. **The woman will be out:** the woman in me will have finished. 192. **douts:** extinguishes (the folly being his weeping). **Act:** V, **Scene:** i. 2. **wilfully seeks her own salvation:** tries to get to heaven before her time. 4. **straight:** straightaway. But he implies that if it weren't Christian burial, she would have a crooked grave. 4. **crowner:** common colloquial form of "coroner." 9. ***se offendendo*:** He means *se defendendo*, in self-defense, a justifiable plea in case of homicide. 12. **Argal:** for *ergo*, "therefore." 14. **goodman delver:** master digger. 17. **will he, nill he:** whether he will or no, willy-nilly. 20–21. **he that is not guilty . . . life:** i.e., only suicides fail to live out their allotted spans; all other accidental deaths must have been foreseen by the Almighty. 23. **crowner's quest law:** coroner's inquest law. 28. **countenance:** permission, authorization. 30. **even-Christen:** collective noun for "fellow Christians." 31. **ancient:** i.e., of long standing. 40. **confess thyself:** "Confess and be hanged" was proverbial. 44. **frame:** structure. 53. **unyoke:** unyoke the oxen; finish the day's work.

CLOWN Cudgel thy brains no more about it, for your dull ass will not mend his pace with beating; and when you are asked this question next, say a grave-maker. The houses he makes lasts till doomsday. Go, get thee to Yaughan, fetch me a stoup° of liquor.

[*Exit Second Clown*]

CLOWN In youth when I did love, did love, *Song*
Methought it was very sweet
To contract-o the time for-a my behove,°
Oh methought there-a was nothing-a
meet.

HAMLET Has this fellow no feeling of his business? A sings in grave-making.

HORATIO Custom hath made it in him a property of easiness.°

HAMLET 'Tis e'en so, the hand of little employment hath the daintier sense.

CLOWN But age with his stealing steps *Song*
Hath clawed me in his clutch,
And hath shipped me intil° the land,
As if I had never been such.

[*Throws up a skull*]

HAMLET That skull had a tongue in it, and could sing once. How the knave jowls° it to th' ground, as if 'twere Cain's jawbone, that did° the first murder. This might be the pate of a politician which this ass now o'erreaches,° one that would circumvent God, might it not?

HORATIO It might my lord.

HAMLET Or of a courtier, which could say "Good morrow sweet lord, how dost thou sweet lord?" This might be my Lord Such-a-one, that praised my Lord Such-a-one's horse when a meant to beg it, might it not?

HORATIO Ay my lord.

HAMLET Why, e'en so, and now my Lady Worm's, chopless,° and knocked about the mazard° with a sexton's spade. Here's fine revolution, and we had the trick° to see't. Did these bones cost no more the breeding but to play at loggets° with 'em?° Mine ache to think on't.

CLOWN A pickaxe and a spade, a spade, *Song*
For and a shrowding sheet,
Oh a pit of clay for to be made,
For such a guest is meet.

[*Throws up another skull*]

HAMLET There's another. Why may not that be the skull of a lawyer? Where be his quiddities now, his quillets,° his cases, his tenures,° and his tricks? Why does he suffer this rude knave now to knock him about the sconce° with a dirty shovel, and will not tell him of his action of battery?° Hum, this fellow might be in's time a great buyer of land, with his statutes,° his recognizances,° his fines, his double vouchers, his recoveries.° Is this the fine° of his fines and the recovery of his recoveries, to have his fine pate° full of fine dirt? Will his vouchers vouch him no more of his purchases,° and double ones too, than the length and breadth of a pair of indentures?° The very conveyances of his lands° will scarcely lie in this box, and must th'inheritor° himself have no more, ha?

HORATIO Not a jot more my lord.

HAMLET Is not parchment made of sheepskins?

62. **stoup:** a large jar or pitcher. 65. **To contract . . . behove:** i.e., to pass away the time to my own advantage. 69–70. **a property of easiness:** a matter of indifference. 75. **intil:** into. 78. **jowls:** bangs (with a pun on "jowl" as jaw). 79. **Cain's jawbone, that did:** the jawbone of Cain, who did. 81. **o'erreaches:** A politician was a man who "o'erreached," in the sense of duped, his pawns and enemies. Now the tables are turned as the gravedigger "o'erreaches" (i.e., handles) his skull. 91. **chopless:** The chops or chaps are the lower jaw and the flesh about it. 91. **mazard:** a drinking bowl; here used facetiously for the skull or head. 93. **trick:** knack. 93–94. **Did these bones . . . loggets with 'em?:** Was the value of bringing up these people so slight that we may justifiably play skittles with their bones? 94. **loggets:** a country game in which wooden truncheons about two feet long, bulbous at one end and tapering off to the handle (like the old "Indian clubs"), were thrown at a fixed stake. 101–102. **quiddities, quillets:** subtle distinctions, quibbles. 102. **tenures:** suits connected with the holding of land. 104. **sconce:** a slang term for "head." 105–06. **action of battery:** lawsuit dealing with physical violence. 107. **statutes:** securities for debts, mortgages. 108–109. **double vouchers, recoveries:** Like fines, recoveries were fictitious suits to obtain the authority of a court judgment for the holding of land. A voucher, or *vocatio*, calls in one of the parties necessary in this action — a double voucher rendering the tortuous process even more secure. 108. **recognizances:** bonds undertaking to repay debts or fulfill other legal obligations. 109. **fine:** conclusion. 110. **fine pate:** subtle head. 112. **purchases:** The word was widely used in Shakespeare's time to indicate, in a pejorative sense, acquisitions and enrichments of any kind. 113–114. **pair of indentures:** Two copies of a legal agreement would be made on the same sheet of parchment, which was then cut in half by means of an indented or zig-zag line, with each party receiving one half as a precaution against fraud. 114. **conveyances of his lands:** deeds relating to purchases of land for himself. This lawyer has feathered his own nest. 115. **inheritor:** He who has come to own all these lands has in the end only the space of his coffin, which is not big enough even for the deeds of his canny dealings; a subtle joke, because this lawyer is not technically an inheritor. Like so many Elizabethan lawyers, he has come to his estates by "purchase."

HORATIO Ay my lord, and of calves' skins too.

HAMLET They are sheep and calves which seek out assurance° in that. I will speak to this fellow. Whose grave's this sirrah?

CLOWN Mine sir.

(*Sings*)

Oh a pit of clay for to be made
For such a guest is meet.

HAMLET I think it be thine indeed, for thou liest in't.

CLOWN You lie out on't sir, and therefore 'tis not yours. For my part, I do not lie in't, yet it is mine.

HAMLET Thou dost lie in't, to be in't and say 'tis thine. 'Tis for the dead, not for the quick,° therefore thou liest.

CLOWN 'Tis a quick lie sir, 'twill away again from me to you.

HAMLET What man dost thou dig it for?

CLOWN For no man sir.

HAMLET What woman then?

CLOWN For none neither.

HAMLET Who is to be buried in't?

CLOWN One that was a woman sir, but rest her soul she's dead.

HAMLET How absolute the knave is! We must speak by the card,° or equivocation° will undo us. By the lord, Horatio, this three years I have took note of it: the age is grown so picked,° that the toe of the peasant comes so near the heel of the courtier, he galls his kibe.° How long hast thou been grave-maker?

CLOWN Of all the days i'th'year, I came to't that day that our last King Hamlet o'ercame Fortinbras.

HAMLET How long is that since?

CLOWN Cannot you tell that? Every fool can tell that. It was the very day that young Hamlet was born,° he that is mad and sent into England.

HAMLET Ay marry, why was he sent into England?

CLOWN Why, because a was mad. A shall recover his wits there, or if a do not, 'tis no great matter there.

HAMLET Why?

CLOWN 'Twill not be seen in him there. There the men are as mad as he.

HAMLET How came he mad?

CLOWN Very strangely they say.

HAMLET How, strangely?

CLOWN Faith, e'en with losing his wits.

HAMLET Upon what ground?°

CLOWN Why, here in Denmark. I have been sexton here man and boy thirty years.

HAMLET How long will a man lie i'th'earth ere he rot?

CLOWN Faith, if a be not rotten before a die, as we have many pocky corses nowadays° that will scarce hold the laying in,° a will last you some eight year, or nine year. A tanner will last you nine year.

HAMLET Why he more than another?

CLOWN Why sir, his hide is so tanned with his trade, that a will keep out water a great while, and your water is a sore decayer of your whoreson dead body. Here's a skull now: this skull hath lien you i'th'earth three and twenty years.

HAMLET Whose was it?

CLOWN A whoreson mad fellow's it was. Whose do you think it was?

HAMLET Nay I know not.

CLOWN A pestilence on him for a mad rogue, a poured a flagon of Rhenish° on my head once. This same skull sir, was Yorick's skull, the king's jester.

HAMLET This?

CLOWN E'en that.

HAMLET Let me see. [*Takes the skull.*] Alas poor Yorick! I knew him Horatio, a fellow of infinite jest, of most excellent fancy, he hath borne me on his back a thousand times—and now how abhorred in my imagination it is!° My gorge° rises at it. Here hung those lips that I have kissed I know not how oft. Where be your gibes now?

---

121. **assurance:** Parchment documents provide legal proof ("assurance") of material gains, but only fools would seek in them assurance, or security, against mortality. 130. **the quick:** the living. 142. **by the card:** i.e., with the precision of a sailor, navigating by his compass. "Card" could mean either the seaman's chart or the face of the compass. 142. **equivocation:** deliberate playing on language and double meanings to achieve one's ends. 144. **picked:** fastidious, refined. 146. **galls his kibe:** rubs his chilblain. 152–53. **very day . . . born:** By making the Clown say later (166–67.) that he has been sexton for thirty years, Shakespeare tells us that Hamlet is thirty. 165. **ground:** cause. 171. **pocky corses nowadays:** reflects the frightening spread of syphilis through sixteenth-century Europe. 172. **hold the laying in:** last through the interment. 186. **Rhenish:** Rhine wine. 195. **abhorred . . . it is:** i.e., to think of riding on the back of one who is now a moldy skeleton. 195. **gorge:** contents of the stomach—i.e., he retches with disgust.

In this film still, taken from the 1948 movie *Hamlet*, Hamlet (played by Laurence Olivier) kneels to speak to the skull of Yorick.
Why do you think the director chose to film this scene as a close-up? What does the background suggest about how the filmmakers wished their audience to view the setting?

your gambols,° your songs, your flashes of merriment that were wont to set the table on a roar? Not one now, to mock your own grinning?° Quite chop-fallen?° Now get you to my lady's chamber, and tell her, let her paint an inch thick, to this favour° she must come. Make her laugh at that. — Prithee Horatio, tell me one thing.

HORATIO What's that my lord?

HAMLET Dost thou think Alexander looked o' this fashion i'th'earth?

HORATIO E'en so.

HAMLET And smelt so? Pah! [*Puts down the skull*]

HORATIO E'en so my lord.

HAMLET To what base uses we may return, Horatio! Why may not imagination trace the noble dust of Alexander, till a find it stopping a bunghole?°

HORATIO 'Twere to consider too curiously° to consider so.

HAMLET No faith, not a jot, but to follow him thither with modesty° enough, and likelihood to lead it, as thus: Alexander died, Alexander was buried, Alexander returneth to dust, the dust is earth, of earth we make loam,° and why of that loam whereto he was converted might they not stop a beer-barrel?

Imperious Caesar, dead and turned to clay,
Might stop a hole, to keep the wind away.
Oh that that earth which kept the world in awe
Should patch a wall t'expel the winter's flaw!°
But soft, but soft! Aside — here comes the king,
The queen, the courtiers.

Enter CLAUDIUS, GERTRUDE, LAERTES, *and a coffin,* [*with* PRIEST] *and* LORDS *attendant*

Who is this they follow?
And with such maimèd° rites? This doth betoken
The corse they follow did with desperate hand
Fordo° it° own life. 'Twas of some estate.°
Couch we° awhile and mark.

[*Retiring with Horatio*]

LAERTES What ceremony else?

HAMLET That is Laertes, a very noble youth. Mark.

LAERTES What ceremony else?

PRIEST Her obsequies have been as far enlarged
As we have warranty.° Her death° was doubtful,
And but that great command° o'ersways the order,°
She should in ground unsanctified have lodged
Till the last trumpet. For° charitable prayers,
Shards,° flints, and pebbles should be thrown
on her.
Yet here she is allowed her virgin crants,°
Her maiden strewments,° and the bringing home
Of bell and burial.°

LAERTES Must there no more be done?

PRIEST No more be
done.
We should profane the service of the dead
To sing sage° requiem and such rest° to her

198. **gambols:** perhaps jests, practical jokes, rather than anything physical. 200. **to mock your own grinning:** i.e., to laugh at the face you're making. "Grinning" is not a smile but a facial distortion, generally of anger (a snarl) or pain, but sometimes of a forced laugh. 201. **chop-fallen:** with the chops or chaps (the lower jaw) hanging down — figuratively, dismayed or dejected. 203. **favour:** appearance. 213. **bunghole:** pouring hole in a cask or barrel. 214. **too curiously:** with excessive care, over-elaborately. 217. **modesty:** moderation. 220. **loam:** a mortar or plaster made of clay, straw, etc. 226. **flaw:** squall. 229. **maimèd:** mutilated, truncated. 231. **Fordo:** destroy. 231. **it:** its. 231. **some estate:** considerable social importance. 232. **Couch we:** Let us conceal ourselves ("couch" suggests stooping or crouching to take cover). 237. **warranty:** authorization. 237. **Her death:** i.e., the manner of her death. 238. **great command:** the commands of great ones. 238. **the order:** the regular proceeding. 240. **For:** instead of. 241. **Shards:** broken pottery. 242. **crants:** garlands hung up at funerals, especially those of young girls. 243. **strewments:** flowers strewn on a coffin. 243–44. **bringing home / Of bell and burial:** bringing her to her last home with bellringing and proper burial. 247. **sage:** grave. 247. **such rest:** i.e., invoke or pray for such rest.

As to peace-parted souls.°
LAERTES Lay her i'th'earth,
And from her fair and unpolluted flesh
May violets spring. I tell thee, churlish priest,
A ministering angel shall my sister be
When thou liest howling.
HAMLET What, the fair Ophelia!
GERTRUDE Sweets to the sweet, farewell.
[*Scattering flowers*]
I hoped thou shouldst have been my Hamlet's wife.
I thought thy bride-bed to have decked, sweet maid,
And not t'have strewed thy grave.
LAERTES Oh treble woe
Fall ten times treble on that cursèd head
Whose wicked deed thy most ingenious sense°
Deprived thee of. Hold off the earth awhile
Till I have caught her once more in mine arms.
Leaps in the grave
Now pile your dust upon the quick and dead
Till of this flat a mountain you have made
T'o'ertop old Pelion° or the skyish head
Of blue Olympus.°
HAMLET [*Advancing*] What is he whose grief
Bears such an emphasis? whose phrase° of sorrow
Conjures the wandering stars,° and makes them stand
Like wonder-wounded° hearers? This is I,
Hamlet the Dane.°
[*Laertes climbs out of the grave*]°
LAERTES The devil take thy soul.
[*Grappling with him*]
HAMLET Thou pray'st not well.
I prithee take thy fingers from my throat,
For though I am not splenitive° and rash,
Yet have I in me something dangerous
Which let thy wisdom fear. Hold off thy hand.
CLAUDIUS Pluck them asunder.
GERTRUDE Hamlet, Hamlet!

Ian Dagnall/Alamy

Sculptor Lord Ronald Gower's statue of Hamlet in Shakespeare's birthplace Stratford-upon-Avon depicts the prince contemplating Yorick's skull.
What do Hamlet's dagger, his pose, and Yorick's skull suggest about Hamlet's character? Why does his left foot seem to step out of the statue?

ALL Gentlemen!
HORATIO Good my lord, be quiet.
[*The Attendants part them*].
HAMLET Why, I will fight with him upon this theme
Until my eyelids will no longer wag.°
GERTRUDE O my son, what theme?
HAMLET I loved Ophelia; forty thousand brothers

---

248. **peace-parted souls:** those who have departed this life in peace. 258. **most ingenious sense:** excellent intelligence. 263. **Pelion:** a mountain in Thessaly. In Greek myth, there was an attempt to climb to heaven by putting Pelion on top of Ossa. 264. **blue Olympus:** the mountain in Thessaly where in Greek myth the gods lived; "blue" because it reaches the sky. 265. **emphasis? whose phrase:** Hamlet accuses Laertes of employing a rhetorician's "emphasis," and of expressing sorrow in a conventional "phrase," or formal style. 266. **wandering stars:** planets. 267. **wonder-wounded:** struck with amazement. 268. **Hamlet the Dane:** Hamlet asserts his title to the throne. 268. **sd *Laertes . . . grave*:** The Bad Quarto has *"Hamlet leapes in after Leartes."* 271. **splenitive:** quick-tempered, irascible. 277. **wag:** move or open and close.

Could not with all their quantity of love
Make up my sum. What wilt thou do for her?

CLAUDIUS Oh he is mad Laertes.

GERTRUDE For love of God forbear him.

HAMLET 'Swounds, show me what thou't do.
Woo't° weep, woo't fight, woo't fast, woo't tear thyself?
Woo't drink up eisel,° eat a crocodile?°
I'll do't. Dost thou come here to whine,
To outface me with leaping in her grave?
Be buried quick with her, and so will I.
And if thou prate of mountains, let them throw
Millions of acres on us, till our ground,
Singeing his pate against the burning zone,°
Make Ossa like a wart. Nay, and° thou'lt mouth,
I'll rant as well as thou.

GERTRUDE This is mere madness,
And thus awhile the fit will work on him;
Anon, as patient as the female dove
When that her golden couplets are disclosed,°
His silence will sit drooping.°

HAMLET Hear you sir,
What is the reason that you use me thus?
I loved you ever — but it is no matter.
Let Hercules himself do what he may,
The cat will mew, and dog will have his day.
Exit

CLAUDIUS I pray thee good Horatio wait upon him.
Exit Horatio
(*To Laertes*) Strengthen your patience in our last night's speech;°
We'll put the matter to the present push.° —
Good Gertrude, set some watch over your son. —
This grave shall have a living monument.
An hour of quiet shortly shall we see,
Till then in patience our proceeding be.
Exeunt

Act V, Scene ii

Enter HAMLET *and* HORATIO

HAMLET So much for this sir, now shall you see the other.°
You do remember all the circumstance?°

HORATIO Remember it my lord!

HAMLET Sir, in my heart there was a kind of fighting
That would not let me sleep. Methought I lay
Worse than the mutines in the bilboes.° Rashly,
And praised be rashness for it — let us know,°
Our indiscretion° sometime serves us well
When our deep plots do pall,° and that should learn° us
There's a divinity that shapes our ends,
Rough-hew them how we will° —

HORATIO That is most certain.

HAMLET Up from my cabin,
My sea-gown° scarfed° about me, in the dark
Groped I to find out them, had my desire,
Fingered° their packet, and in fine° withdrew
To mine own room again, making so bold,
My fears forgetting° manners, to unseal
Their grand commission; where I found, Horatio —
O royal knavery! — an exact command,
Larded with many several sorts of reasons,
Importing° Denmark's health, and England's too,
With ho! such bugs and goblins in my life,°
That on the supervise,° no leisure bated,°

---

285. **Woo't:** colloquial for "wilt thou." 286. **eisel:** vinegar (to increase his bitterness). 286. **eat a crocodile:** i.e., to increase the flow of hypocritical tears. 292. **the burning zone:** the sun's orbit between the tropics. 293. **and:** if. 297. **her golden couplets are disclosed:** The pigeon lays two eggs, and the young, when *disclosed* or hatched, are covered with yellow down. 298. **silence will sit drooping:** i.e., his quietness resembles that of the patient dove not moving from her young and "drooping" with lack of food for herself. 304. **in our last night's speech:** i.e., by remembering what we planned last night. 305. **present push:** immediate operation. **Act V, Scene ii.** 1. **So much . . . other:** a midconversation entry, "this" referring presumably to the first part of the story and "the other" to the rest of it. 2. **circumstance:** details. 6. **the mutines in the bilboes:** mutineers in their shackles. 7. **let us know:** let us recognize, acknowledge. 8. **indiscretion:** want of prudence and forethought (rather than a misguided act). 9. **pall:** grow flat and stale, like wine that has gone bad. 9. **learn:** teach. 10–11. **a divinity . . . we will:** i.e., there is a higher power in control of us, directing us toward our destination, however much we have blundered in the past and impeded our own progress. 13. **sea-gown:** seaman's coat of coarse cloth, a duffle-coat. 13. **scarfed:** wrapped loosely. 15. **Fingered:** filched, stole. 15. **in fine:** in conclusion. 17. **forgetting:** neglecting — i.e., causing him to forget. 21. **Importing:** pertaining to. 22. **bugs . . . life:** monstrosities to be feared from my continued existence. 23. **supervise:** viewing (of the commission). 23. **no leisure bated:** i.e., no free time was to abate, or soften, the rigor of the execution.

No, not to stay the grinding of the axe,
My head should be struck off.

HORATIO Is't possible?

HAMLET Here's the commission, read it at more leisure.
But wilt thou hear now how I did proceed?

HORATIO I beseech you.

HAMLET Being thus benetted round° with villainies,
Or° I could make a prologue to my brains,
They had begun the play.° I sat me down,
Devised a new commission, wrote it fair.
I once did hold it, as our statists° do,
A baseness° to write fair, and laboured much
How to forget that learning; but sir, now
It did me yeoman's service.° Wilt thou know
Th'effect of what I wrote?

HORATIO Ay good my lord.

HAMLET An earnest conjuration° from the king,
As England was his faithful tributary,
As love between them like the palm might flourish,
As peace should still her wheaten garland wear,
And stand a comma 'tween their amities,°
And many suchlike as-es of great charge,°
That on the view and knowing of these contents,
Without debatement further, more, or less,°
He should those bearers put to sudden death,
Not shriving time allowed.°

HORATIO How was this sealed?

HAMLET Why, even in that was heaven ordinant.°
I had my father's signet° in my purse,
Which was the model° of that Danish seal;°
Folded the writ up in the form of th'other,
Subscribed it,° gave't th'impression, placed it safely,
The changeling never known. Now, the next day
Was our sea-fight, and what to this was sequent
Thou know'st already.

HORATIO So Guildenstern and Rosencrantz go to't.

HAMLET Why man, they did make love to this employment.
They are not near my conscience. Their defeat°
Does by their own insinuation° grow.
'Tis dangerous when the baser° nature comes
Between the pass° and fell incensèd points
Of mighty opposites.°

HORATIO Why, what a king is this!

HAMLET Does it not, think thee,° stand me now upon°—
He that hath killed my king, and whored my mother,
Popped in between th'election and my hopes,
Thrown out his angle° for my proper life,°
And with such cozenage°—is't not perfect conscience°
To quit° him with this arm? And is't not to be damned
To let this canker of our nature come
In° further evil?

HORATIO It must be shortly known to him from England
What is the issue of the business there.

HAMLET It will be short. The interim's mine,
And a man's life's no more than to say "one."
But I am very sorry, good Horatio,
That to Laertes I forgot myself,
For by the image of my cause, I see
The portraiture of his.° I'll court his favours.
But sure the bravery° of his grief did put me
Into a towering passion.

HORATIO Peace, who comes here?

Enter young OSRIC

OSRIC Your lordship is right welcome back to Denmark.

---

29. **benetted round:** i.e., trapped. 30. **Or:** before, ere. 30–31. **Or I could . . . begun the play:** i.e., his brains had put things in motion before he had set them to work. 33. **statists:** statesmen. 34. **baseness:** something befitting people of low rank. 36. **yeoman's service:** the service of a faithful attendant ("yeoman" in its earlier sense of a servant in a royal household). 38. **conjuration:** solemn entreaty. 42. **a comma 'tween their amities:** The kingdoms are meant to be as near together as separate institutions can be, and what is between them is peace, not discord. 43. **charge:** burden. 45. **debatement further, more, or less:** continued ridicule of official verbiage. 47. **shriving time:** time for confession and absolution. 48. **ordinant:** directing. 49. **signet:** seal. 50. **model:** copy. 50. **that Danish seal:** the official seal of Denmark on the commission that Hamlet has handed to Horatio. 52. **Subscribed it:** signed it (with Claudius's name). 58. **defeat:** destruction. 59. **insinuation:** i.e., between Hamlet and Claudius. 60. **baser:** inferior in rank. 61. **pass:** thrust. 61–62. **pass . . . opposites:** the fell (deadly) pass of the sword points of incensed opposites (opponents). 63. **Does it not . . . stand me now upon:** is it not now incumbent upon me. 63. **think thee:** please consider. 66. **angle:** fishing line. 66. **my proper life:** my very life. 67. **cozenage:** cheating, fraud. 67. **is't not perfect conscience:** is it not absolutely in accord with what is right. 68. **quit:** requite, punish. 69. **canker of our nature:** a cancerous growth in humankind. 69–70. **come/In:** enter into. 77–78. **by the image . . . of his:** i.e., I recognize in my situation the essential features of his. 79. **bravery:** extravagant display.

HAMLET I humbly thank you sir.—Dost know this water-fly?°

HORATIO No my good lord.

HAMLET Thy state is the more gracious, for 'tis a vice to know him. He hath much land and fertile; let a beast be lord of beasts, and his crib shall stand at the king's mess.° 'Tis a chough,° but as I say, spacious in the possession of dirt.

OSRIC Sweet lord, if your lordship were at leisure, I should impart a thing to you from his majesty.

HAMLET I will receive it sir with all diligence of spirit. Put your bonnet to his° right use, 'tis for the head.

OSRIC I thank your lordship, it is very hot.

HAMLET No believe me, 'tis very cold, the wind is northerly.

OSRIC It is indifferent° cold my lord, indeed.

HAMLET But yet methinks it is very sultry and hot for my complexion.°

OSRIC Exceedingly my lord, it is very sultry, as 'twere—I cannot tell how. But my lord, his majesty bade me signify to you that a has laid a great wager on your head. Sir, this is the matter—

HAMLET I beseech you remember.

[*Hamlet moves him to put on his hat*]

OSRIC Nay good my lord, for my ease in good faith. Sir, [here is newly come to court Laertes; believe me an absolute gentleman, full of most excellent differences,° of very soft society° and great showing.° Indeed, to speak feelingly of him, he is the card or calendar° of gentry,° for you shall find in him the continent of what part a gentleman would see.°

HAMLET Sir, his definement suffers no perdition° in you, though I know to divide him inventorially° would dozy° th'arithmetic of memory, and yet but yaw° neither° in respect° of his quick sail. But in the verity of extolment,° I take him to be a soul of great article,° and his infusion° of such dearth° and rareness as, to make true diction of him, his semblable is his mirror, and who else would trace him,° his umbrage,° nothing more.

OSRIC Your lordship speaks most infallibly of him.

HAMLET The concernancy, sir?° Why do we wrap the gentleman in our more rawer breath?°

OSRIC Sir?

HORATIO Is't not possible to understand in another tongue? You will to't sir, really.

HAMLET What imports the nomination of this gentleman?°

OSRIC Of Laertes?

HORATIO His purse is empty already, all's golden words are spent.

HAMLET Of him sir.

OSRIC I know you are not ignorant—

HAMLET I would you did sir, yet in faith if you did, it would not much approve me.° Well sir?]

OSRIC You are not ignorant of what excellence Laertes is.

[**HAMLET** I dare not confess that, lest I should compare with him in excellence, but to know a man well were to know himself.

OSRIC I mean sir for his weapon; but in the imputation laid on him by them,° in his meed° he's unfellowed.]

HAMLET What's his weapon?

OSRIC Rapier and dagger.

HAMLET That's two of his weapons, but well.°

OSRIC The king sir hath wagered with him six Barbary horses,° against the which he has impawned,° as I take it, six French rapiers and

---

84. **water-fly:** busy trifler. 88–89. **let a beast . . . mess:** i.e., if you own a lot of livestock, even though you are an animal yourself you'll have a place at the king's table; "crib" = manger. 89. **chough:** pronounced "chuff"; a blackbird. 94. **his:** its. 99. **indifferent:** moderately. 101. **complexion:** temperament. 110. **excellent differences:** i.e., he excels in a variety of different accomplishments. 110. **soft society:** easy sociability. 111. **great showing:** excellent appearance. 112. **card or calendar:** map or guide. 112. **gentry:** gentility. 113–14. **the continent . . . would see:** he contains whatever quality a gentleman would wish to find. 115. **perdition:** loss. 116. **inventorially:** by means of an inventory of his qualities. 117. **dozy:** make dizzy. 118. **yaw:** swing off course. 118. **neither:** after all. 118. **in respect of:** in comparison with. 119. **in the verity of extolment:** to praise him truthfully. 120. **of great article:** i.e., there would be many articles to list in his inventory. 120. **his infusion:** what is poured into him, his nature. 121. **dearth:** dearness, high price. 123. **trace him:** follow him closely. 123. **umbrage:** shadow. 125. **The concernancy, sir?:** What's all this about? 125–26. **wrap . . . breath:** i.e., attempt to dress him in the crudity of language. 130–131. **What imports . . . gentleman?:** What is the purpose of naming this gentleman? 138. **not much approve me:** i.e., it would be little to my credit to have such a testimony from you. 145–46. **in the imputation . . . by them:** in what people attribute to him. 146. **meed:** merit. 150. **but well:** but never mind. 152. **Barbary horses:** Arab horses, much prized. 153. **impawned:** wagered.

poniards,° with their assigns,° as girdle, hangers,° and so.° Three of the carriages in faith are very dear to fancy,° very responsive° to the hilts, most delicate carriages, and of very liberal conceit.°

HAMLET What call you the carriages?

HORATIO I knew you must be edified by the margent° ere you had done.

OSRIC The carriages sir are the hangers.

HAMLET The phrase would be more germane to the matter if we could carry a cannon by our sides; I would it might be hangers till then. But on, six Barbary horses against six French swords, their assigns, and three liberal-conceited carriages — that's the French bet against the Danish. Why is this impawned, as you call it?

OSRIC The king sir, hath laid sir, that in a dozen passes between yourself and him, he shall not exceed you three hits. He hath laid on twelve for nine. And it would come to immediate trial, if your lordship would vouchsafe the answer.°

HAMLET How if I answer no?

OSRIC I mean my lord, the opposition of your person in trial.

HAMLET Sir, I will walk here in the hall. If it please his majesty, it is the breathing° time of day with me. Let° the foils be brought, the gentleman willing, and the king hold his purpose, I will win for him and I can. If not, I will gain nothing but my shame and the odd hits.

OSRIC Shall I redeliver you° e'en so?

HAMLET To this effect sir, after what flourish° your nature will.

OSRIC I commend my duty to your lordship.

HAMLET Yours, yours. [*Exit Osric*] He does well to commend it himself, there are no tongues else for's turn.

HORATIO This lapwing runs away with the shell on his head.°

HAMLET A did comply with his dug° before a sucked it. Thus has he, and many more of the same bevy that I know the drossy age° dotes on, only got the tune of the time° and outward habit of encounter, a kind of yesty° collection,° which carries them through and through the most fanned and winnowed° opinions; and do but blow them to their trial, the bubbles are out.

[*Enter a* LORD

LORD My lord, his majesty commended him to you° by young Osric, who brings back to him that you attend him in the hall. He sends to know if your pleasure hold to play with Laertes, or that you will take longer time.

HAMLET I am constant to my purposes, they follow the king's pleasure. If his fitness speaks,° mine is ready; now or whensoever, provided I be so able as now.

LORD The king and queen, and all, are coming down.

HAMLET In happy time.°

LORD The queen desires you to use some gentle entertainment° to Laertes, before you fall to play.

HAMLET She well instructs me.] [*Exit Lord*]

HORATIO You will lose, my lord.

HAMLET I do not think so. Since he went into France, I have been in continual practice; I shall win at the odds.° But thou wouldst not think how ill all's here about my heart — but it is no matter.

---

154. **poniards:** daggers. 154. **assigns:** accessories. 154. **hangers:** the straps to hold the sword, attached to the girdle or sword belt. 155. **and so:** and so on. 156. **dear to fancy:** i.e., they please one's taste. 156. **very responsive:** well adjusted. 157. **liberal conceit:** imaginative design. 159–60. **edified by the margent:** made wiser by a marginal gloss. 174. **vouchsafe the answer:** offer yourself as an opponent. 179. **breathing:** exercising. 180. **Let:** conditional: If the foils are brought, if Laertes is willing, if the king maintains his purpose, then I will play the match and win for the king if I can. 184. **redeliver you:** report back what you say. 185. **after what flourish:** conforming to whatever embellishment. 191–192. **This lapwing . . . head:** a proverb for juvenile forwardness. 193. **his dug:** his mother's (or his nurse's) nipple. 195. **the drossy age:** the people of these rubbishy times. 196. **got the tune of the time:** The sense is of listening attentively to what other people sing and learning to copy them. 197. **yesty:** yeasty, frothy. 197. **collection:** mixture, brew. 199. **fanned and winnowed:** synonyms for blowing the chaff off the grain; i.e., the superficial qualities of people like Osric take them through the society of superior people, but they cannot last, and when they are tested, their hollowness reveals itself. 202–03. **commended him to you:** sent his compliments to you. 208. **If his fitness speaks:** when his convenience names a time. 213. **In happy time:** It is an opportune time. 214–215. **use some gentle entertainment:** give a courteous reception. 220. **at the odds:** given these particular odds.

HORATIO Nay good my lord—

HAMLET It is but foolery, but it is such a kind of gaingiving° as would perhaps trouble a woman.

HORATIO If your mind dislike anything, obey it. I will forestall their repair hither, and say you are not fit.

HAMLET Not a whit, we defy augury. There is special providence in the fall of a sparrow.° If it be now,° 'tis not to come; if it be not to come, it will be now; if it be not now, yet it will come—the readiness is all. Since no man of aught he leaves knows, what is't to leave betimes?° Let be.°

A table prepared, with flagons of wine on it. Trumpets, Drums and Officers with cushions. Enter CLAUDIUS, GERTRUDE, LAERTES *and* LORDS, *with other Attendants with foils, daggers and gauntlets*

CLAUDIUS Come Hamlet, come and take this hand from me.

[*Hamlet takes Laertes by the hand*]

HAMLET Give me your pardon sir, I've done you wrong;
But pardon't as you are a gentleman.
This presence° knows,
And you must needs have heard, how I am punished
With a sore distraction. What I have done,
That might your nature, honour and exception
Roughly awake, I here proclaim was madness.
Was't Hamlet wronged Laertes? Never Hamlet.
If Hamlet from himself be tane° away,
And when he's not himself does wrong Laertes,
Then Hamlet does it not, Hamlet denies it.
Who does it then? His madness. If't be so,
Hamlet is of the faction° that is wronged,
His madness is poor Hamlet's enemy.
Sir, in this audience,
Let my disclaiming from a purposed evil
Free me so far in your most generous thoughts,
That I have shot my arrow o'er the house
And hurt my brother.

LAERTES I am satisfied in nature,°
Whose motive° in this case should stir me most
To my revenge; but in my terms of honour
I stand aloof, and will no reconcilement
Till by some elder masters of known honour
I have a voice° and precedent of peace°
To keep my name ungored.° But till that time
I do receive your offered love like love,
And will not wrong it.

HAMLET I embrace it freely,
And will this brother's wager frankly° play.
Give us the foils, come on.

LAERTES Come, one for me.

HAMLET I'll be your foil° Laertes. In mine ignorance
Your skill shall like a star i'th'darkest night
Stick fiery off° indeed.

LAERTES You mock me sir.

HAMLET No, by this hand.

CLAUDIUS Give them the foils, young Osric.
Cousin Hamlet,
You know the wager?

HAMLET Very well my lord.
Your grace has laid the odds° a'th'weaker side.

CLAUDIUS I do not fear it, I have seen you both.
But since he is bettered, we have therefore odds.°

LAERTES This is too heavy, let me see another.

HAMLET This likes me° well. These foils have all a length?

OSRIC Ay my good lord.

Prepare to play

CLAUDIUS Set me the stoups° of wine upon that table.
If Hamlet give the first or second hit,
Or quit in answer of the third exchange,°

---

225. **gaingiving:** foreboding, presentment of evil. 229–230. **we defy . . . sparrow:** Hamlet rejects "augury," the attempt to read signs of future events and to take steps accordingly. "Special providence" is a theological term for a particular act of divine intervention; "the fall of a sparrow" alludes to Matthew 10:29. 230–31. **If it be now:** i.e., his own death. 233–34. **Since no man . . . betimes?:** Since no one has any knowledge of the life he leaves behind him, what does it matter if one dies early? An early death may be a blessing. 234. **Let be:** Do not try to alter the course of things. 238. **presence:** assembly (suggesting a formal court occasion). 244. **tane:** taken. 248. **faction:** party. 254. **in nature:** so far as natural feeling goes. 255. **motive:** prompting. 259. **voice:** judgment. 259. **of peace:** for reconciliation. 260. **my name ungored:** my reputation undamaged. 263. **frankly:** freely, with an unburdened mind. 265. **foil:** material used to set off or display some richer thing, such as a jewel. 267. **Stick fiery off:** stand out brilliantly. 271. **laid the odds:** Either Claudius has backed the weaker contestant or, more probably, he has kindly provided an advantage for Hamlet in the handicap he has given Laertes. 272–73. **I . . . odds:** a politic reply; Claudius says he does *not* think Hamlet is weaker, but because Laertes has *improved,* he has arranged a handicap for him. 275. **likes me:** pleases me. 277. **stoups:** the flagons mentioned in 234 sd. 279. **Or quit . . . exchange:** or, having lost the first two bouts, gets his revenge in fighting the third bout.

Patrick Vandecasteele

Contemporary French artist Patrick Vandecasteele's *Hamlet Duel* portrays Hamlet's fight with Laertes in act V, although it doesn't capture Laertes's role in the battle. **What does Vandecasteele's depiction suggest about Hamlet's battle? Who is he fighting? What is happening with his left arm? Is he being pulled, or is he reaching to the past? Why do you think Vandecasteele chose to depict Hamlet nude?**

Let all the battlements their ordnance fire.
The king shall drink to Hamlet's better breath,°
And in the cup an union° shall he throw
Richer than that which four successive kings
In Denmark's crown have worn. Give me the cups,
And let the kettle° to the trumpet speak,
The trumpet to the cannoneer without,
The cannons to the heavens, the heaven to earth,
"Now the king drinks to Hamlet!" Come, begin,
And you the judges bear a wary eye.

Trumpets the while

HAMLET Come on sir.
LAERTES Come my lord.

They play

HAMLET One.
LAERTES No.
HAMLET Judgement.
OSRIC A hit, a very palpable hit.
LAERTES Well, again.
CLAUDIUS Stay, give me drink. Hamlet, this pearl is thine. Here's to thy health.°

Drum, trumpets sound, and shot goes off

Give him the cup.
HAMLET I'll play this bout first, set it by awhile.
Come.

[They play]

Another hit. What say you?
LAERTES A touch, a touch, I do confess't.
CLAUDIUS Our son shall win.
GERTRUDE He's fat and scant of breath.°
Here Hamlet, take my napkin,° rub thy brows.
The queen carouses° to thy fortune, Hamlet.
HAMLET Good madam.
CLAUDIUS Gertrude, do not drink!
GERTRUDE I will my lord, I pray you pardon me.

[Drinks]

CLAUDIUS *[Aside]* It is the poisoned cup. It is too late.
HAMLET I dare not drink yet madam, by and by.
GERTRUDE Come, let me wipe thy face.
LAERTES My lord, I'll hit him now.
CLAUDIUS I do not think't.
LAERTES And yet it is almost against my conscience.
HAMLET Come, for the third, Laertes. You do but dally.
I pray you pass° with your best violence.
I am afeard you make a wanton of me.°
LAERTES Say you so? Come on.

Play

OSRIC Nothing neither way.°

---

281. **better breath:** i.e., he will drink to the increase of Hamlet's energy or power. 282. **union:** a pearl of special quality and high value. 285. **kettle:** kettledrum. 297–98. **give me drink . . . health:** The king drinks to Hamlet's health while holding the "pearl" aloft. He then deposits the poisoned pellet in the goblet while the drum, trumpet, and shot are sounding off. 302. **fat and scant of breath:** Probably the queen means that he is soft, out of condition. The word "fat" is associated with shortness of breath at 3.4.154. 303. **napkin:** handkerchief. 304. **carouses:** drinks a health. 314. **pass:** thrust. 315. **make a wanton of me:** indulge me as though I were a child. 317. **Nothing neither way:** This is presumably the end of the third bout.

LAERTES Have at you now! [*Wounds Hamlet*]
In scuffling they change rapiers
CLAUDIUS Part them. They are incensed.
HAMLET Nay, come again. [*Wounds Laertes*]
[*Gertrude falls*]
OSRIC Look to the queen there, ho!
HORATIO They bleed on both sides. How is it my
lord?
OSRIC How is't Laertes?
LAERTES Why, as a woodcock to mine own
springe,° Osric.
I am justly killed with mine own treachery.
HAMLET How does the queen?
CLAUDIUS She sounds° to see
them bleed.
GERTRUDE No, no, the drink, the drink — O my
dear Hamlet —
The drink, the drink — I am poisoned. [*Dies*]
HAMLET Oh villainy! — Ho, let the door be locked!
Treachery! Seek it out!
[*Laertes falls*]
LAERTES It is here Hamlet. Hamlet, thou art slain,
No medicine in the world can do thee good,
In thee there is not half an hour of life —
The treacherous instrument is in thy hand,
Unbated and envenomed.° The foul practice°
Hath turned itself on me; lo, here I lie,
Never to rise again. Thy mother's poisoned —
I can no more — the king, the king's to blame.
HAMLET The point envenomed too! Then,
venom, to thy work!
Hurts the king
ALL Treason, treason!
CLAUDIUS Oh yet defend me friends, I am but
hurt.
HAMLET Here, thou incestuous, murderous,
damnèd Dane,
Drink off this potion. Is thy union° here?
Follow my mother. *King dies*
LAERTES He is justly served,
It is a poison tempered° by himself.
Exchange forgiveness with me, noble Hamlet.
Mine and my father's death come not upon thee,°
Nor thine on me. *Dies*
HAMLET Heaven make thee free° of it! I follow thee.
I am dead, Horatio. Wretched queen adieu.
You that look pale, and tremble at this chance,°
That are but mutes° or audience to this act,
Had I but time, as this fell sergeant° death
Is strict in his arrest, oh I could tell you —
But let it be. Horatio, I am dead,
Thou livest; report me and my cause aright
To the unsatisfied.°
HORATIO Never believe it.
I am more an antique Roman° than a Dane.
Here's yet some liquor left.
HAMLET As th'art a man,
Give me the cup. Let go, by heaven I'll ha't.
O God, Horatio, what a wounded name,
Things standing thus unknown, shall live
behind me!
If thou didst ever hold me in thy heart,
Absent thee from felicity awhile,
And in this harsh world draw thy breath in pain
To tell my story.
March afar off, and shot within
What warlike noise is this?
OSRIC Young Fortinbras, with conquest come
from Poland,
To the ambassadors of England gives
This warlike volley.
HAMLET Oh I die, Horatio,
The potent poison quite o'ercrows° my spirit.
I cannot live to hear the news from England.
But I do prophesy th'election lights
On Fortinbras;° he has my dying voice.°
So tell him, with th'occurrents more and less°
Which have solicited° — the rest is silence.
Dies

---

324. **as a woodcock to mine own springe:** i.e., caught in my own trap. 326. **sounds:** swoons. 335. **envenomed:** poisoned. 335. **practice:** plot. 343. **thy union:** in a double sense: the fake pearl and the "incestuous" marriage. Hamlet sends him to continue this latter false union — in death: "Follow my mother." 345. **tempered:** mixed, prepared. 347. **come not upon thee:** This is a wish or prayer, not a statement: Let not these deaths be visited upon or charged to thee! 349. **make thee free:** absolve thee. 351. **chance:** mischance. 352. **mutes:** characters in a play with no speaking parts. 353. **sergeant:** officer who summoned persons to appear before a court. 357. **unsatisfied:** i.e., those who will need to be satisfied with an explanation. Polonius, Laertes, and Ophelia die without knowing of Claudius's crime and the reason for Hamlet's conduct. 358. **antique Roman:** i.e., for whom suicide might be noble rather than damnable. 370. **o'ercrows:** triumphs over (an image from cockfighting). 372–73. **th'election lights / On Fortinbras:** i.e., Fortinbras will be chosen as the next king. 373. **voice:** vote. 374. **occurrents more and less:** i.e., all the happenings. 375. **solicited:** prompted, brought forth (his own actions, presumably).

HORATIO Now cracks a noble heart.° Good night
sweet prince,
And flights of angels sing thee to thy rest. —
Why does the drum come hither?
Enter FORTINBRAS *and* ENGLISH AMBASSADORS,
with drum, colours and Attendants
FORTINBRAS Where is this sight?
HORATIO What is it you
would see?
If aught of woe or wonder, cease your search.
FORTINBRAS This quarry cries on havoc.°
O proud death,
What feast is toward in thine eternal cell
That thou so many princes at a shot
So bloodily hast struck?
I AMBASSADOR The sight is dismal,
And our affairs from England come too late.
The ears are senseless that should give us hearing,
To tell him his commandment is fulfilled,
That Rosencrantz and Guildenstern are dead.
Where should we have our thanks?
HORATIO Not from his
mouth,
Had it th'ability of life to thank you;
He never gave commandment for their death.
But since, so jump° upon this bloody question,°
You from the Polack wars, and you from England,
Are here arrived, give order that these bodies
High on a stage be placèd to the view,
And let me speak to th'yet unknowing world
How these things came about. So shall you hear
Of carnal, bloody, and unnatural acts,°
Of accidental judgements,° casual slaughters,
Of deaths put on° by cunning and forced cause,°
And in this upshot,° purposes mistook
Fallen on th'inventors' heads. All this can I
Truly deliver.
FORTINBRAS Let us haste to hear it,
And call the noblest to the audience.
For me, with sorrow I embrace my fortune.
I have some rights of memory in this kingdom,
Which now to claim my vantage° doth invite me.

This modern watercolor by artist Jonathan Wolstenholme wittily depicts a "Shakespearean Scholar."

What do the details in the painting — the skull, the pen, the book's broken, "unhinged" spine — suggest about the play, its central character, and those who study it?

HORATIO Of that I shall have also cause to speak,
And from his mouth whose voice will draw on
more.°
But let this same be presently° performed,
Even while men's minds are wild,° lest more
mischance
On° plots and errors happen.
FORTINBRAS Let four captains
Bear Hamlet like a soldier to the stage,
For he was likely, had he been put on,°
To have proved most royal; and for his passage,°
The soldier's music and the rite of war
Speak loudly for him.
Take up the bodies. Such a sight as this
Becomes the field, but here shows much amiss.
Go bid the soldiers shoot.
Exeunt marching, after the which a peal of ordnance° are shot off ■

c. 1600

376. **cracks a noble heart:** The heartstrings were supposed to snap at the moment of death. 381. **This quarry cries on havoc:** This heap of bodies proclaims a massacre. A "quarry" is a heap of dead animals after a hunt. 392. **jump:** immediately. 392. **question:** quarrel, dispute. 398. **carnal, bloody, and unnatural acts:** Claudius's deeds. 399. **accidental judgements:** punishments brought about fortuitously. Horatio no doubt has Laertes in mind. 400. **put on:** arranged, set up. 400. **forced cause:** a cause where the truth has been wrested and constrained into falsehood. 401. **this upshot:** the final issue, visible here ("upshot" is the deciding shot in an archery contest). 407. **my vantage:** my present advantageous situation. 409. **whose voice will draw on more:** i.e., whose vote is likely to influence other electors. 410. **presently:** immediately. 411. **wild:** lacking order, bewildered. 412. **On:** arising from. 414. **put on:** put to the test. 415. **passage:** i.e., from this world. 420. **sd** ***a peal of ordnance:*** a salute of guns.

Understanding and Interpreting

1. **AP® Character and Setting.** What is the political situation in Denmark as the play begins? What information does Horatio provide beginning in line 79 of the opening scene? What further information do we learn from Claudius's speech that begins scene ii?
2. **AP® Character and Narration.** How does Shakespeare characterize Horatio in the opening scenes? What are some of his chief qualities? How does Hamlet characterize Claudius? How does Hamlet compare Horatio and Claudius?
3. **AP® Character and Narration.** What does Hamlet's first soliloquy (I.ii.129–59) reveal about his state of mind? What is the source of his discontent?
4. **AP® Character, Setting, and Narration.** What is the basis for both Laertes's and Polonius's objections to Ophelia's relationship with Hamlet? Which of their arguments seem most (and least) persuasive or fair? What does their treatment of Ophelia in act I, scene iii, reveal about their motivations? What does it suggest about their attitude toward Ophelia and toward women in general? How does class or station function in their arguments?
5. **AP® Character, Setting, and Narration.** What do we learn from the Ghost in act I, scene v? If what he says is true, how does that reinforce what we have learned about the political situation in Denmark? How does Hamlet respond to the Ghost's instructions? What does he mean by saying, "O my prophetic soul!" (I.v.40)?
6. **AP® Character and Narration.** After listening to the Ghost speak, Hamlet wants to write about it, as indicated in act I, scene v, lines 107 and 108. How does this contrast with his remarks earlier in this speech? What does it suggest about his state of mind?
7. **AP® Character and Narration.** Why do you think Hamlet tells his companions he is likely to put on an "antic disposition" (I.v.172)? Is his behavior a deliberate strategy or a natural reaction to his anger and grief? Explain.
8. **AP® Character and Narration.** Compare the way Hamlet responds to Polonius in act II, scene ii, lines 172–233, with how he responds to his friends Rosencrantz and Guildenstern in lines 239–347. What do you learn about Hamlet from these responses?
9. **AP® Character and Narration.** In act III, scene i, lines 56–90, Hamlet delivers his famous "To be, or not to be" speech, arguably the most recognized passage in English literature. What is he contemplating? What inner conflict is he pondering? What conclusions does he reach?
10. **AP® Character.** Following his "To be, or not to be" soliloquy (III.i.56–90), why does Hamlet treat Ophelia so harshly? How does Ophelia describe Hamlet in lines 155–166? What does this description suggest about Hamlet before the time of the play? What does it suggest about the relationship between Hamlet and Ophelia?
11. **AP® Character, Structure, and Narration.** What does the scene with the players (II.ii 447–578) reveal about Hamlet? How does the First Player's speech (II.ii. 498–527) parallel Hamlet's situation?
12. **AP® Narration.** Hamlet's speech to the players at the beginning of act III, scene ii, has often been interpreted as a sort of aside from Shakespeare containing his philosophy of acting. How else can it be interpreted? How do Hamlet's instructions tie in to some of the themes of the play?
13. **AP® Character and Narration.** In act III, scene iii, lines 73–96, Hamlet has a perfect opportunity to kill his uncle and avenge his murdered father. Instead, he makes a speech. Why does he hesitate in killing Claudius? Do you think we are meant to respect his piety or despise his cowardice? If you combine this incident with Hamlet's soliloquy at the end of act II, what does it reveal about Hamlet? about a theme of the play?

14. **AP® Character and Narration.** In act II, scene ii, lines 258–60, Hamlet says, "Why then 'tis none to you; for there is nothing either good or bad but thinking makes it so." What assumptions underlie Hamlet's response? What does he mean? Do you agree with what he says? He then says to his old friends, "I am but mad north-north-west. When the wind is southerly I know a hawk from a handsaw" (II.ii.402–04). What does this remark suggest about Hamlet's madness, about his "antic disposition" (I.v.172)? Is he mad? Is he acting? Explain.
15. **AP® Character, Setting, and Narration.** Why do you think the Ghost is visible to Horatio and the guards in act I, scenes i and iv, but not to Gertrude in act III, scene iv? Does the murder of Polonius in this scene make you reassess whether the Ghost is in fact a demon, and not the ghost of Hamlet's father?
16. **AP® Character.** What has driven Ophelia mad in act IV, scene v? What does her behavior suggest about the relationship between her and Hamlet? Cite specific lines to support your answer.
17. **AP® Character.** How does Laertes respond to his father's death? to Ophelia's? How do his responses compare to Hamlet's reaction to the death of his own father?
18. **AP® Character, Structure, and Narration.** Hamlet seems preoccupied with death for much of the play; what new insight does the graveyard scene (V.i.) reveal regarding his attitude toward mortality, life, fame, and status? How does this attitude connect to his central conflict in the play?
19. **AP® Character and Narration.** Why does Hamlet give his dying support to Fortinbras (V.ii.369–75)?

Analyzing Language, Style, and Structure

1. **Vocabulary in Context.** The word "rank" appears seven times in *Hamlet*. While Shakespeare sometimes uses it to mean *class* or *position within a hierarchy*, he often applies a different meaning that depends on the specific context. What does the word mean when Hamlet says of the world that "things rank and gross in nature / Possess it merely" (I.ii.136–37)? How do both definitions relate to the play's larger themes?
2. **AP® Structure and Narration.** The opening scene presents a great number of questions. How do these contribute to the mood of the scene and, ultimately, of the play itself?
3. **AP® Character, Narration, and Figurative Language.** Hamlet's first three lines (I.ii.65, 67, 74) are evasive answers using puns or other wordplay. What does this behavior reveal about his character and his state of mind?
4. **AP® Character, Structure, Narration, and Figurative Language.** How would you describe Claudius's opening speech (I.ii.1–39) and his reply to Hamlet (I.ii.87–117)? What does his use of imagery and juxtaposition in the first speech reveal about his purpose? What is the nature of his argument in the second?
5. **AP® Character, Narration, and Figurative Language.** How do the diction and imagery in the Ghost's speech to Hamlet (I.v.42–91) create a comparison between the two "gardens" before and after the entrance of the "serpents"?
6. **AP® Character, Narration, and Figurative Language.** In lines 309–27 of act II, scene ii, Hamlet delivers a lengthy explanation to Rosencrantz and Guildenstern, ending with a rhetorical question. What is the substance of this speech? How does the imagery that Hamlet uses transition his speech from an assessment of himself to that of humankind as a whole?

7. **AP® Character, Structure, and Narration.** Claudius's aside in act III, scene i, lines 49–54, is the first definitive evidence of his guilt. Structurally, why do you think this revelation takes place halfway through the play as opposed to earlier (or later)?

8. **AP® Character, Structure, and Narration.** Notice Hamlet's behavior toward Ophelia in act III, scene i. Why do you think — in dramatic, structural, and thematic terms — we have not observed a scene between Hamlet and Ophelia until this point?

9. **AP® Character, Narration, and Figurative Language.** In act II, scene i, Polonius says, "By indirections find directions out" (l. 65). What does he mean by that? How does such a comment reveal his character? Find another such witty or clever remark by another character, and explain how it reveals the character of its speaker.

10. **AP® Character, Narration, and Figurative Language.** Hamlet's four soliloquies (I.ii.129–59; II.ii.530–637; III.i.56–90; IV.iv.32–66) are remarkable for their style as well as their substance. Choose one of these monologues and discuss how its diction, figurative language, and imagery contribute to Hamlet's meaning and purpose.

11. **AP® Character, Structure, and Narration.** Shakespeare occasionally gives two characters very similar lines or phrasings, the second instance reminding the reader or viewer of the first. In act IV, scene iv, for example, Hamlet wonders if he might be "thinking too precisely on th' event" (l. 41). In act V, scene i, Horatio says to Hamlet, "'Twere to consider too curiously to consider so" (ll. 214–15). What is the effect of these types of echoes throughout the play?

12. **AP® Character, Structure, Narration, and Figurative Language.** Do a close reading of one of Ophelia's songs in act IV, scene v, exploring how its form and content relate and respond to the action of the play (both actual and implied) and to Ophelia's state of mind. In your response, consider what has occurred offstage, as well as the possible or implied events to which she alludes. Why is she given song, as opposed to speech, in this instance?

Topics for Composing

1. **AP® FRQ Literary Argument.** Many works of literature feature characters whose indecisiveness or distractions delay the story's forward progress. This postponement, however, is critical to conveying significant ideas in the work. In *Hamlet*, numerous characters fall victim to distraction. In a well-written essay, analyze how one specific character's indecisiveness or distraction contributes to an interpretation of the work as a whole. Do not merely summarize the plot.

2. **AP® FRQ Literary Argument.** Critic Northrop Frye said that *Hamlet* is Shakespeare's longest play because everyone in it except Gertrude and Ophelia "talks too much." In *Hamlet*, despite the calls to be brief from both the Ghost and Polonius, the characters do go on at length, and Hamlet certainly has a lot to say. In a well-written essay, analyze how the play's focus on conversation and reflection rather than action contributes to an interpretation of the work as a whole. Do not merely summarize the plot.

3. **AP® FRQ Literary Argument.** In many works of literature, references to the macrocosm and the microcosm suggest that the same forces are at work within as without. In *Hamlet*, there are numerous references depicting a person as a little world at the center of a larger world. Identify various references that connect the condition of people's bodies and minds to what is happening in Elsinore, Denmark, or the universe at large, such as when Hamlet speaks of his "distracted globe" (I.v.97). Then, in a well-written essay, analyze how the relationship between the microcosm and macrocosm contributes to an interpretation of the work as a whole. Do not merely summarize the plot.

4. **AP® FRQ Prose Fiction Analysis.** The following question refers to lines 252–329 of act II, scene ii of William Shakespeare's *Hamlet*, first performed in 1601. In this passage, there is a misunderstanding between Hamlet and Rosencrantz and Guildenstern surrounding the word *dream.* Read the passage carefully. Then, in a well-written essay, analyze how Shakespeare uses literary elements and techniques to explore a central conflict of the play as the characters' disagreement ensues.

5. **AP® FRQ Prose Fiction Analysis.** The following question refers to lines 62–128 of act I, scene ii of William Shakespeare's *Hamlet*, first performed in 1601. In this passage, Claudius and Gertrude attempt to convince Hamlet to stay in Denmark and cease mourning King Hamlet. Read the passage carefully. Then, in a well-written essay, analyze how Shakespeare uses literary elements and techniques to convey one of these characters' complex attitude toward the death of King Hamlet.

6. **AP® Literary Argumentation.** While there are only two major female characters in *Hamlet* — Gertrude and Ophelia — they both play crucial roles. Write an essay in which you explain the importance of one of these women to the play, especially in terms of her relationship to Hamlet.

7. **Connections.** In *The Prince*, a Renaissance text from 1532, Niccolò Machiavelli writes:

   > A prince ought to be a fox in recognizing snares and a lion in driving off wolves. Those who assume the bearing of a lion alone lack understanding. It follows, then, that a wise prince cannot and should not keep his pledge when it is against his interest to do so and when his reasons for making the pledge are no longer operative. . . . But one must know how to mask this [fox-like] nature skillfully and be a great dissembler.

   In an essay, explore how both Hamlet and Claudius act in accordance with this advice. How do their tactics differ?

8. **Multimodal.** Consider the many conflicts in the play — for example, those between reason and passion, order and chaos, concealment and revelation, or honesty and deception. Select one of these conflicts and create a PowerPoint in which you track their appearance throughout the play. Combine images, videos, and textual evidence to convey how the conflict reveals a dominant theme of the play.

9. **Speaking and Listening.** The "To be, or not to be" soliloquy in act III, scene i (ll. 56–90) is perhaps the most famous monologue in the English language, yet its meaning is much debated. Watch three versions of the speech in film or stage adaptations of the play. Pay particular attention to Hamlet's tone and movement to determine which version is the best interpretation of the speech. Prepare an oral presentation in which you argue for the merits of one interpretation over the others.

10. **Connections.** Read carefully "The Emperor of Ice-Cream" (p. 698), a 1922 poem by American poet Wallace Stevens, in which he includes words and phrases that appear in *Hamlet*. Write an essay that considers Stevens's poem as a meditation on mortality and also as a response to *Hamlet*. Make specific references to both texts in your essay.

11. **Research.** As with many of his plays, Shakespeare based *Hamlet* on a story that already existed, putting his own unique spin on the original tale. Research the versions of *Hamlet* that came before Shakespeare's. What did Shakespeare choose to retain, alter, or ignore from those earlier versions? How do these choices reshape the central characters of the play? Why do you suppose he made these decisions?

Hamlet and the Evolution of Character

Why do we read literature? There are many reasons, of course. We read for entertainment. We read for plot, for the *story*. We enjoy a gripping tale as the building suspense keeps us turning pages. We also read for information, for historical context, for instruction, and for edification. We also read to be challenged by provocative ideas, or to learn about a particular time period or an exotic place. Sometimes we read because we enjoy the style of a particular writer. But *character* is often the most appealing reason of them all. We remember the stories, the plots, the settings, the ideas, maybe even the style, of our favorite books and plays, but it is the characters that stay with us and continue to live inside our imaginations. We admire the heroes, we fear the villains; we follow the adventurers, the rebels, the provocative thinkers; we identify with and aspire to be like our favorites, and we care about them as we do about living people. We often see ourselves in the characters we encounter, confronting our own thoughts and beliefs as we read of theirs.

Some literary characters tell their own stories — for instance, Lemuel Gulliver, David Copperfield, Jane Eyre, Huck Finn, and Janie Crawford. Others, such as Elizabeth Bennett, Raskolnikov, Hester Prynne, Bigger Thomas, and Harry Potter reach us via the perspective of a third-person narrator. Still others — Captain Ahab, Jay Gatsby, Atticus Finch — come to us from the perspective of other characters who narrate their own stories in the first person. However we come to know literary characters, we recognize that *character* is one of the features of literature that makes us want to read, and likely the feature that we remember most. And perhaps no character in all of world literature has been studied as closely and extensively as Shakespeare's Hamlet.

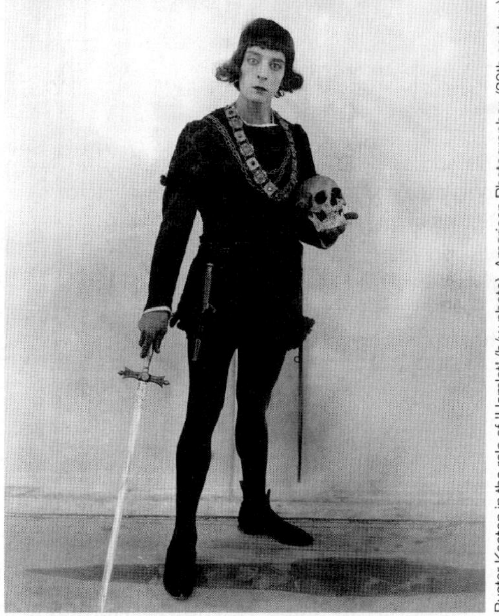

Buster Keaton in the role of 'Hamlet' (b/w photo), American Photographer, (20th century)/ Private Collection/Bridgeman Images

Buster Keaton, a silent film star known for his physical comedy and deadpan expression, poses as Hamlet in a still for the 1922 film *Day Dreams*.

What characteristics of Hamlet do you see in this portrayal? How does Keaton convey them?

But why is Hamlet widely regarded as the most compelling character in the history of literature? Is he heroic? Is he villainous? Is he rebellious? Is he indecisive? Do his thoughts and ideas provoke and challenge us? Do we identify with his situation and plight? Does he engage our sympathies? Do we care about him? For most readers, the

This portrait by F. Drummond Niblett, completed around 1910, depicts English actor Henry Irving in the role of Hamlet.

Why do you believe the artist chose to distort Irving's physical features in such a way? What do you make of Irving's pose and the expression on his face?

answer to all of these questions is likely *yes*. Hamlet thinks and feels deeply, and his audience witnesses the profundity of his intellect and passion in his words. We perceive his humanity in his remarks about his youth with Yorick as well as in his bond with Horatio, and we feel his grief at the loss of his beloved father. His plans to avenge his father's ghost show how loyal and brave he intends to be; yet we also see how cruelly he treats Ophelia and his mother. His acerbic remarks about his uncle and his response to Polonius's death reveal his wit, which we enjoy even as we might find it disquieting. We sympathize with his revulsion toward the King — it puts his profound disgust with the world in perspective. And we understand the difficulty of the circumstances he faces; we know his disappointment and feel it with him. We see and feel all of this most pointedly in his soliloquies, those passages where we enter his mind and witness him alone with his tangled thoughts.

Hamlet is clearly an intellectual. Upon seeing his father's ghost, his first thought is to write about it. His pleasures — and his profound pains — are those of the mind. Does this mean he thinks and talks too much, as many readers say? Is Horatio's remark, "'Twere to consider too curiously, to consider so" (V.i.187), an apt one? Is Hamlet's tendency to overthink, his "pale cast of thought" (III.i.85), what makes him "lose the name of action" (III.i.88)? Or is it fate, with its snares of coincidence and circumstance, that traps him, brands him as one of the "fools of nature" (I.iv.54)?

Many readers note Hamlet's self-centeredness and question whether he has actually lost his mind. Perhaps he is merely feigning madness as a stratagem. Regardless of whether Hamlet is sane, no reader can deny how wildly inconsistent he is in his behavior. Consider his statements of resolve beside his lack of action, his treatment of his old friends Rosencrantz and Guildenstern, and especially his interactions with Ophelia. But should we be surprised to see such changes, such transformations of character? Is human nature — is *character* — consistent, or is it inconstant and inconsistent? In "On the Inconstancy of Our Actions," a sixteenth-century essay Shakespeare likely read, Michel de Montaigne wrestles with this very question:

> Sometimes I give my soul one visage, and sometimes another, according unto the posture or side I lay her in. If I speak diversely of myself, it is because I look diversely upon myself. All contrarieties are found in her, according to some turn or removing, and in some fashion or other. Shamefaced, bashful, insolent, chaste, luxurious, peevish, prattling, silent, fond, doting, labourious, nice, delicate, ingenious, slow, dull, froward,[1] humorous, debonair, wise, ignorant, false in words, true-speaking, both liberal, covetous, and prodigal. All these I perceive in some measure or other to be in mine, according as I stir or turn myself. And whosoever shall heedfully survey and consider himself shall find this volubility and discordance to be in himself, yea, and in his very judgement. I have nothing to say entirely, simply, and with solidity of myself, without confusion, disorder, blending, mingling; and in one word, *Distinguo*[2] is the most universal part of my logic. . .
>
> We are all framed of flaps and patches, and of so shapeless and diverse a contexture, that every piece and every moment playeth his part. And there is as much difference found between us and ourselves as there is between ourselves and others.

Interpretations of *Hamlet* the play, and of Hamlet the character, are as diverse in kind as they are infinite in number. Hamlet may be a touchstone, a figure through which we view ourselves and others. He may be an impenetrable mystery. But while he is, after all, merely a vocabulary, a fictional creation, a figment of the imagination evoked by words printed in a book, he is also very real — he comes to life each time an actor takes his role on a stage or a reader turns a page. Each of the texts that follow addresses Hamlet as a character in literature — and in life. Read them carefully as you consider your own interpretation of the play and of the person at its center.

TEXTS IN CONTEXT

1. **Marjorie Garber** ▪ from *Hamlet: The Matter of Character* (nonfiction)
2. **William Hazlitt** ▪ from *Characters of Shakespeare's Plays* (nonfiction)
3. **C. S. Lewis** ▪ from *Hamlet: The Prince or the Poem?* (nonfiction)
4. **Zbigniew Herbert** ▪ *Elegy of Fortinbras* (poetry)

from Hamlet: The Matter of Character

Marjorie Garber

Marjorie Garber (b. 1944) is an American literary critic and Shakespearean scholar who teaches at Harvard University. Garber has written nineteen books on a variety of topics related to sexuality, Shakespeare, and literature, including *Shakespeare After All* (2004), *The Use and Abuse of Literature* (2011), and, most recently, *Character: The History of a Cultural Obsession* (2020). In the following excerpt, Garber examines Hamlet through several lenses, exploring the complex notion of "character."

[1] Moving or facing away from someone or something. — Eds.

[2] "I make a distinction." — Eds.

One of the most contestatory problems for literary study in the past century has been the question of character, which can be divided into at least two equally troublesome parts: Can a literary character be considered and analyzed as if he or she were a "real" person, with motivations and a history, "mimetic" (that is, imitative) of "reality"? What dramatic effects and cues are given in the text that produce this illusion of roundedness or interiority? Or, from the opposite end of the spectrum, is a character — especially a dramatic character, a character in a play — nothing more, or less, than a piece of writing, identical to his or her lines in the play, and having no existence (psychic, gestural, conceptual, historical) beyond the lines he or she speaks?[1]

That the word "character" originally meant writing, or handwriting, and did so in Shakespeare's time, further complicates the issue — and certain theatrical and dramatic effects, like, for example, the soliloquy, obviously give the *illusion* of interiority, inwardness, personal history, and feelings, even though those effects, too, are purely fictional and gestural.

Literary characters have, over time, in a variety of kinds of works and kinds of readings, been regarded as *rounded, flat, symbolic, allegorical, realistic, representative, historical*, etc. Consider, just for example, the fact that in *Hamlet* the character of Claudius is never named but always given the speech prefix "King." Does that make him more symbolic, one-dimensional, allegorical? And what kind of a character is a Ghost?

In a phenomenon we might call "the Hamlet effect," much criticism of the play holds the mirror up to nature and finds the critic reflected there. Readers, scholars, and actors have over the years consistently identified with the character of Hamlet, finding in his gifts and his foibles an image of themselves. The English Romantic critic Samuel Taylor Coleridge famously observed, "I have a smack of Hamlet myself, if I may say so."[2] Goethe wrote of Hamlet in 1756:

> A lovely, pure, noble, and most moral nature, without the strength of nerve which forms a hero, sinks beneath a burden which it cannot bear, and must not cast away. All duties are holy for him; the present is too hard. Impossibilities have been required of him; not in themselves impossibilities, but such for him. He winds, and turns, and torments himself; he advances and recoils; is ever put in mind, ever puts himself in mind; at last does all but lose his purpose from his thoughts; yet still without recovering his peace of mind.[3]

Some twenty years later, Coleridge drew a direct 5
connection between the idea of Shakespearean character and the inner life of Hamlet:

> [O]ne of Shakespeare's modes of creating characters is, to conceive any intellectual or moral faculty in morbid excess, and then to place himself, Shakespeare, thus mutilated or diseased, under given circumstances. In Hamlet he seems to have wished to exemplify the moral necessity of a due balance between our attention to the objects of our senses, and our meditation on the workings of our minds, — an *equilibrium* between the real and the imaginary worlds. In Hamlet this balance is disturbed: . . . we see a great, an almost enormous, intellectual activity, and a proportionate aversion to real action . . . he vacillates from sensibility, and procrastinates from thought, and loses the power of action in the energy of resolve.[4]

---

[1] There is an excellent essay on this question by the critic Alan Sinfield, called "When Is a Character Not a Character? Desdemona, Olivia, Lady Macbeth, and Subjectivity," in *Faultlines: Cultural Materialism and the Politics of Dissident Reading* (Berkeley: University of California Press, 1992), 52–79. — Garber.

[2] Samuel Taylor Coleridge and Henry Nelson Coleridge, *Specimens of the Table Talk of Samuel Taylor Coleridge* (London: John Murray, 1836), 37. — Garber.

[3] Johann Wolfgang von Goethe, *Wilhelm Meister's Apprenticeship*, trans. Thomas Carlyle (London: Olver & Boyd, 1824), 2: 75. — Garber.

[4] Samuel Taylor Coleridge, *Notes and Lectures upon Shakespeare and the Old Dramatists* (New York, 1868), 4: 144. — Garber.

Each critic describes a Hamlet who corresponds to something in himself. Goethe's Hamlet lacks "the strength of nerve which forms a hero," while Coleridge's Hamlet "procrastinates from thought, and loses the power of action in the energy of resolve." The time-honored question of Hamlet's delay is here linked to the question of character, in concepts like moral nature, weakness and greatness, an excess of sensibility, or a time "out of joint" for action. . . .

Freud's famous theory of the Oedipus complex was founded not so much on Sophocles' play *Oedipus the King* as on Shakespeare's *Hamlet.*

Freud developed this theory initially in a correspondence with his friend and fellow doctor Wilhelm Fliess, dated October 15, 1897 (the same time as Ellis and shortly after Vining). In this letter, Freud wrote:

> I have found, in my own case, too, [the phenomenon of] being in love with my mother and jealous of my father, and I now consider it a universal event in early childhood. . . . If this is so, we can understand the gripping power of *Oedipus Rex*. . . . Everyone in the audience was once a budding Oedipus in fantasy and each recoils in horror from the dream fulfillment here transplanted into reality. . . .

Fleetingly, the thought passed through my head that the same thing might be at the bottom of *Hamlet* as well. I am not thinking of Shakespeare's conscious intention, but believe, rather, that a real event stimulated the poet in his representation, in that his unconscious understood the unconscious of his hero. How does Hamlet the hysteric justify his words, "Thus conscience does make cowards of us all"? How does he explain his irresolution in avenging his father by the murder of his uncle — the same man who sends his courtiers [i.e., Rosencrantz and Guildenstern] to their death without a scruple and who is positively precipitate in murdering Laertes? How better than through the torment he suffers from the obscure memory that he himself had contemplated the same deed against his father out of passion for his mother?[5] . . .

It was not until 1910 that Freud himself began to refer to this as the "Oedipus complex."[6] Suppose that he had termed it the "Hamlet complex" instead — how might views of the play and its character have altered? That year, 1910, was the same that Virginia Woolf would proclaim the beginning of a new modern era — tying the notion of modernity to *character.* "On or about December, 1910," wrote Woolf, "human character changed."[7] In that same year Freud's disciple and friend, the Welsh psychoanalyst Ernest Jones, had begun expanding the Oedipus theory into what would become an entire small book called *Hamlet and Oedipus.*[8] 10

The Freud-Jones theory of Hamlet and the Oedipus complex was to have enormous effects upon productions as well as readings and interpretations of the play. Laurence Olivier's classic treatment, made into a film in 1948, cut the roles of Fortinbras and Rosencrantz and Guildenstern completely, and reduced the script by about half. The political plot thus disappeared, replaced by an emphasis on character formed by family circumstances. The production was framed between the opening voice-over murmur,

---

[5] Sigmund Freud, *The Complete Letters of Sigmund Freud to Wilhelm Fliess*, ed. J. M. Masson (Cambridge: Harvard University Press, 1985), 272. — Garber.

[6] Sigmund Freud, "A Special Type of Object-Choice Made by Men" [1910], *The Standard Edition of the Complete Psychological Works of Sigmund Freud*, 24 vols., ed. and trans. James Strachey (London: Hogarth Press, 1953–74), 11: 171. — Garber.

[7] Virginia Woolf, "Character in Fiction" (1924), *The Essays of Virginia Woolf, Vol. 3, 1919–1924*, ed. Andrew McNeillie (London: Hogarth Press, 1988), 421. *The Complete Works of Freud* would later be published by Virginia and Leonard Woolf's Hogarth Press and translated by Lytton Strachey's brother James. In 1924 the Hogarth Press took over the publication of the papers of the International Psycho-Analytical Institute, for which Jones was the general editor. We are talking here about a founding moment of modernity, in which the literary (and economic) interests of Bloomsbury crossed over into psychoanalysis, and made it available for the first time in English. — Garber.

[8] Ernest Jones, *Hamlet and Oedipus* (New York: Norton, 1976). — Garber.

"[T]his is the tragedy of a man who could not make up his mind," and the final, or almost final, shot of the marital bed. . . .

In the course of the twentieth and twenty-first centuries, there have been at least three kinds of psychoanalytic readings associated with literature: a psychoanalysis of the author (Shakespeare's symptoms), a psychoanalysis of the character (Hamlet's symptoms), and a psychoanalysis of the text (the symptoms exhibited by *Hamlet* the *play*, like the splitting of characters into good father and bad father, or the linguistic symptoms like repetition, metaphor, or other figures of speech). In this last kind of reading the play is like a dream, an imaginative work made of signs and symbols, available for interpretation. It is really only this last kind of work that escapes from "character criticism" in the old speculative style, and moves toward an understanding of the text's multiplicities, the way it can be read and performed at different times in different ways, each persuasive. The business of the literary critic is not diagnosis but interpretation. ■

2009

Questions

1. Which of the two "equally troublesome parts" (par. 1) that Marjorie Garber explores most closely reflects your view of the question of literary *character*? Explain, using reference to literature that you have read.
2. What is "the Hamlet effect" (par. 4)? How does it relate to your reading of the play? Explain.
3. How does Johann Wolfgang von Goethe characterize Hamlet? How does Samuel Taylor Coleridge? Which of the two characterizations do you believe comes closest to the truth? Explain.
4. Of the three kinds of psychoanalytic readings that Garber discusses in the final paragraph — author, character, and text — which one interests you most? Which one is most helpful in illuminating Hamlet's character? Explain, using references to the text.
5. Garber includes a letter in which the founder of psychoanalysis, Sigmund Freud, reflects on both *Oedipus the King* and *Hamlet*. What does Freud suggest might be behind Hamlet's inaction regarding his father, King Hamlet? Does Freud's interpretation align with your understanding of Hamlet? Explain.
6. In the final paragraph, Garber writes: "The business of the literary critic is not diagnosis but interpretation." What does she mean? Replace "literary critic" with "student reader." Do you agree with the amended statement? Why or why not?

from Characters of Shakespeare's Plays

William Hazlitt

William Hazlitt (1778–1830) was an English writer widely acknowledged as the greatest literary and social critic of his age. The following is an excerpt from his book *Characters of Shakespeare's Plays* (1817), the first work of literary criticism to cover all of Shakespeare's plays.

Hamlet is a name: his speeches and sayings but the idle coinage of the poet's brain. What then, are they not real? They are as real as our own thoughts. Their reality is in the reader's mind. It is *we* who are Hamlet. This play has a prophetick truth, which is above that of history. Whoever has become thoughtful and melancholy, through his own mishaps or those of others; whoever has borne about with him the clouded brow of reflection, and thought himself "too much i' th' sun;" whoever has seen the golden lamp of day dimmed by envious mists rising in his own breast, and could find in the world before him only a dull blank with nothing left remarkable in it; whoever has known "the pangs of despised love, the insolence of office, or the spurns which patient merit of the unworthy takes;" he who has felt his mind sink within him, and sadness cling to his heart like a malady, who has had his hopes blighted and his youth staggered by the apparitions of strange things; who cannot be well at ease, while he sees evil hovering near him like a spectre; whose powers of action have been eaten up by thought, he to whom the universe seems infinite, and himself nothing; whose bitterness of soul makes him careless of consequences, and who goes to a play as his best resource to shove off, to a second remove, the evils of life by a mock representation of them — this is the true Hamlet. . . .

The character of Hamlet is itself a pure effusion of genius. It is not a character marked by strength of will or even of passion, but by refinement of thought and sentiment. Hamlet is as little of the hero as a man can well be: but he is a young and princely novice, full of high enthusiasm and quick sensibility — the sport of circumstances, questioning with fortune and refining on his own feelings, and forced from the natural bias of his disposition by the strangeness of his situation. He seems incapable of deliberate action, and is only hurried into extremities on the spur of the occasion, when he has no time to reflect, as in the scene where he kills Polonius, and again, where he alters the letters which [Rosencrantz] and Guildenstern are taking with them to England, purporting his death. At other times, when he is most bound to act, he remains puzzled, undecided, and skeptical, dallies with his purposes, till the occasion is lost, and always finds some pretence to relapse into indolence and thoughtfulness again. For this reason he refuses to kill the King when he is at his prayers, and by a refinement in malice, which is in truth only an excuse for his own want of resolution, defers his revenge to some more fatal opportunity, when he shall be engaged in some act "that has no relish of salvation in it."

"He kneels and prays,
And now I'll do't, and so he goes to heaven,
And so am I reveng'd: *that would be scann'd.*
He kill'd my father, and for that,
I, his sole son, send him to heaven.
Why, this is reward, not revenge.
Up sword and know thou a more horrid time,
When he is drunk, asleep, or in a rage."

He is the prince of philosophical speculators, and because he cannot have his revenge perfect, according to the most refined idea his wish can form, he misses it altogether. So he scruples to trust the suggestions of the Ghost, contrives the scene of the play to have surer proof of his uncle's guilt, and then rests satisfied with this confirmation of his suspicions, and the success of his experiment, instead of acting upon it. Yet he is sensible of his own weakness, taxes himself with it, and tries to reason himself out of it.

"How all occasions do inform against me,
And spur my dull revenge! What is a man,
If his chief good and market of his time
Be but to sleep and feed? A beast; no more.
Sure he that made us with such large discourse,
Looking before and after, gave us not
That capability and godlike reason
To rust in us unus'd [. . .]"

Still he does nothing; and this very speculation on his own infirmity only affords him another occasion for indulging it. It is not for any want of attachment to his father or abhorrence of his murder that Hamlet is thus dilatory, but it is more to his taste to indulge his imagination in reflecting upon the enormity of the crime and refining on his schemes of vengeance, than to put them into immediate practice. His ruling passion is to think, not to act: and any vague pretence that flatters this propensity instantly diverts him from his previous purposes. . . .

Shakspeare was thoroughly a master of the mixed motives of human character, and he here shews us the Queen, who was so criminal in some respects, not without sensibility and affection in other relations of life. — Ophelia is a character almost too exquisitely touching to be dwelt upon. Oh rose of May, oh flower too soon faded! Her love, her madness, her death, are described with the truest touches of tenderness and pathos. It is a character which nobody but Shakspeare could have drawn in the way that he has done, and to the conception of which there is not even the smallest approach, except in some of the old romantick ballads. Her brother, Laertes, is a character we do not like so well: he is too hot and cholerick, and somewhat rodomontade. Polonius is a perfect character in its kind; nor is there any foundation for the objections which have been made to the consistency of this part. It is said that he acts very foolishly and talks very sensibly. There is no inconsistency in that. Again, that he talks wisely at one time and foolishly at another; that his advice to Laertes is very sensible, and his advice to the King and Queen on the subject of Hamlet's madness very ridiculous. But he gives the one as a father, and is sincere in it; he gives the other as a mere courtier, a busybody, and is accordingly officious, garrulous, and impertinent. In short, Shakspeare has been accused of inconsistency in this and other characters, only because he has kept up the distinction which there is in nature, between the understandings and the moral habits of men, between the absurdity in their ideas and the absurdity of their motives. Polonius is not a fool, but he makes himself so. His folly, whether in his actions or speeches, comes under the head of impropriety of intention.

We do not like to see our author's plays acted, and least of all, Hamlet. There is no play that suffers so much in being transferred to the stage. Hamlet himself seems hardly capable of being acted. Mr. Kemble unavoidably fails in this character from want of ease and variety. The character of Hamlet is made up of undulating lines; it has the yielding flexibility of a "a wave o' th' sea." Mr. Kemble plays it like a man in armour, with a determined inveteracy of purpose, in one undeviating straight line, which is as remote from the natural grace and refined susceptibility of the character, as the sharp angles and abrupt starts which Mr. Kean introduces into the part. Mr. Kean's Hamlet is as much to splenetick and rash as Mr. Kemble's is too deliberate and formal. His manner is too strong and pointed. He throws a severity, approaching to virulence, into the common observations and answers. There is nothing of this in Hamlet. He is, as it were, wrapped up in his reflections, and only *thinks aloud.* There should therefore be no attempt to impress what he says upon others by a studied exaggeration of emphasis or manner; no *talking at* his hearers. There should be as much of the gentleman and scholar as possible infused into the part, and as little of the actor. A pensive air of sadness should sit reluctantly upon his brow, but no appearance of fixed and sullen gloom. He is full of weakness and melancholy, but there is no harshness in his nature. He is the most amiable of misanthropes. ■

1817

Questions

1. William Hazlitt opens with, "Hamlet is a name; his speeches and sayings but the idle coinage of the poet's brain. What, then, are they not real? They are as real as our own thoughts. Their reality is in the reader's mind. It is *we* who are Hamlet." Hazlitt then supports his assertion with

the lengthy periodic sentence that begins with the phrase "Whoever has become thoughtful and melancholy, through his own mishaps or those of others . . ." and concludes with "this is the true Hamlet." Read that sentence carefully. Which of the situations that Hazlitt presents can you identify with? Choose two, and explain how your experience helps you understand Hamlet.

2. In paragraph 2 Hazlitt writes, "Hamlet is as little of the hero as a man can well be." How does Hazlitt support this claim? Do you agree with his assessment? Why do you believe Hamlet has had such an enormous impact on the reading world when his behavior is so un-heroic?
3. In paragraphs 2 through 4, Hazlitt analyzes Hamlet's inaction and comes to the conclusion that "his ruling passion is to think, not to act." What reasons does Hazlitt provide in his explanation? How is Hazlitt's explanation supported by examples from the play?
4. How does Hazlitt characterize Gertrude, Ophelia, Laertes, and Polonius? How do these characterizations figure into Hazlitt's analysis of Hamlet? Is that how you see these characters as well? Explain.
5. Why doesn't Hazlitt like to see Shakespeare's plays acted — especially *Hamlet*? Similarly, American novelist William Faulkner said that he preferred to read Shakespeare rather than see the plays acted. Do you prefer to read Shakespeare or to see a production? Explain.
6. Hamlet is "the most amiable of misanthropes," Hazlitt concludes. What does he mean by that statement? How accurately does it describe Hamlet's character as you see it?

from Hamlet: The Prince or the Poem?

C. S. Lewis

C. S. Lewis (1898–1963) was a British novelist, academic, and critic. In the 1950s, Lewis began publishing the seven books that would comprise *The Chronicles of Narnia* children's series, beginning with *The Lion, The Witch and the Wardrobe* (1950). In "Hamlet: The Prince or the Poem?," a lecture delivered in 1942, Lewis argues that Hamlet's poetic manner of expression is the true marvel at the center of the play, and not necessarily the character of Hamlet himself.

For what, after all, is happening to us when we read any of Hamlet's great speeches? We see visions of the flesh dissolving into a dew, of the world like an unweeded garden. We think of memory reeling in its "distracted globe." We watch him scampering hither and thither like a maniac to avoid the voices wherewith he is haunted. Someone says "walk out of the air," and we hear the words "Into my grave" spontaneously respond to it. We think of being bounded in a nut-shell and king of infinite space: but for bad dreams. There's the trouble, for "I am most dreadfully attended." We see the picture of a dull and muddy-mettled rascal, a John-a-dreams,[1] somehow unable to move while ultimate dishonour is done him. We listen to his fear lest the whole thing may be an illusion due to melancholy. We get the sense of sweet relief at the words "shuffled off this mortal coil" but mixed with the bottomless doubt about what may follow then. We think of bones and skulls, of women breeding sinners, and of how some, to whom all this experience is a sealed book, can yet dare death and danger "for an egg-shell." But do we really enjoy these things, do we go back to them, because they show us Hamlet's character? Are they, from *that* point of view, so very interesting? Does the mere fact that a young man, literally haunted, dispossessed, and lacking friends, should feel thus, tell us anything

[1] A dreamer who's out of touch with reality. — Eds.

remarkable? Let me put my question in another way. If instead of the speeches he actually utters about the firmament and man in his scene with Rosencrantz and Guildenstern Hamlet had merely said, "I don't seem to enjoy things the way I used to," and talked in that fashion throughout, should we find him interesting? I think the answer is "Not very." It may be replied that if he talked commonplace prose he would reveal his character less vividly. I am not so sure. He would certainly have revealed *something* less vividly; but would that something be himself? It seems to me that "this majestical roof" and "What a piece of work is a man!" give me primarily an impression not of the sort of person he must be to lose the estimation of things but of the things themselves and their great value; and that I should be able to discern, though with very faint interest, the same condition of loss in a personage who was quite unable so to put before me what he was losing. And I do not think it true to reply that he would be a different character if he spoke less poetically. This point is often misunderstood. We sometimes speak as if the characters in whose mouths Shakespeare puts great poetry were poets: in the sense that Shakespeare was depicting men of poetical genius. But surely this is like thinking that Wagner's Wotan[2] is the dramatic portrait of a baritone? In opera song is the medium by which the representation is made and not part of the thing represented. The actors sing; the dramatic personages are feigned to be speaking. The only character who sings dramatically in *Figaro* is Cherubino.[3] Similarly in poetical drama poetry is the medium, not part of the delineated characters. While the actors speak poetry written for them by the poet, the dramatic personages are supposed to be merely talking. If ever there is occasion to *represent* poetry (as in the play scene from *Hamlet*), it is put into a different metre and strongly stylised so as to prevent confusion.

I trust that my conception is now becoming clear. I believe that we read Hamlet's speeches with interest chiefly because they describe so well a certain spiritual region through which most of us have passed and anyone in his circumstances might be expected to pass, rather than because of our concern to understand how and why this particular man entered it. ■

1942

[2] Richard Wagner (1813–1883) was a German composer most famous for "The Valkyrie," the second opera in the four-part *Ring of the Nibelung* cycle, which was based on Norse mythology. Wotan is the king of the gods in this story. — Eds.

[3] A lovestruck teenage page at court in *The Marriage of Figaro*, a four-act comic opera first composed in 1786 by Wolfgang Amadeus Mozart. Cherubino is often portrayed by a female singer — Eds.

Questions

1. How does C. S. Lewis characterize what we *see* when we read Hamlet? How does that view affect your interpretation of the play?
2. Lewis asks: "But do we really enjoy these things, do we go back to them, because they show us Hamlet's character?" (par. 1). How would you answer Lewis's question? Explain.
3. Do you agree with Lewis's assertion that if Hamlet were more plainspoken, readers wouldn't find him interesting? Why or why not?
4. Lewis says, "It seems to me that 'this majestical roof' and 'What a piece of work is a man' give me primarily an impression not of the sort of person he must be to lose the estimation of things but of the things themselves and their great value" (par. 1). What impression do you get from those phrases? How would you compare your response to Lewis's?
5. What point does Lewis make regarding the poetry Shakespearean characters speak? How does that point inform Lewis's discussion of Hamlet's character?
6. Are we, as Lewis suggests in paragraph 2, more interested in reading *Hamlet* to learn about ourselves than we are to learn about the particular character, Hamlet? Explain.

Elegy of Fortinbras

Zbigniew Herbert

Translated by Czesław Miłosz

Zbigniew Herbert (1924–1998) was a Polish poet, essayist, and dramatist who participated in the Polish resistance against both the Nazis during World War II and the Soviets in postwar Poland. During the 1950s, Herbert worked many low-paying jobs because he refused to write within the framework of official Communist guidelines. In 1956, when widespread riots against the Soviet government brought about a political "thaw" in Poland, Herbert began publishing his work. His first collection of poetry was *The Chord of Light* (1956), which he followed with nine more books of poetry published in his lifetime and one published posthumously. In "Elegy of Fortinbras," the conquering prince of Norway addresses a recently deceased Hamlet.

KEY CONTEXT The poem is dedicated to C. M., or Czesław Miłosz. Also a dissident Polish poet, Miłosz was a close friend of Herbert for most of Herbert's life. He translated much of Herbert's poetry, including this poem, into English.

To C.M.

Now that we're alone we can talk prince man to man
though you lie on the stairs and see no more than a dead ant
nothing but black sun with broken rays
I could never think of your hands without smiling
and now that they lie on the stone like fallen nests
they are as defenseless as before The end is exactly this
The hands lie apart The sword lies apart The head apart
and the knight's feet in soft slippers

You will have a soldier's funeral without having been a soldier
the only ritual I am acquainted with a little
There will be no candles no singing only cannon-fuses and bursts
crepe dragged on the pavement helmets boots artillery horses drums drums
    I know nothing exquisite
those will be my manoeuvres before I start to rule
one has to take the city by the neck and shake it a bit

Anyhow you had to perish Hamlet you were not for life
you believed in crystal notions not in human clay
always twitching as if asleep you hunted chimeras
wolfishly you crunched the air only to vomit
you knew no human thing you did not know even how to breathe

Now you have peace Hamlet you accomplished what you had to
and you have peace The rest is not silence but belongs to me
you chose the easier part an elegant thrust
but what is heroic death compared with eternal watching

with a cold apple in one's hand on a narrow chair
with a view of the ant-hill and the clock's dial

Adieu prince I have tasks a sewer project
and a decree on prostitutes and beggars
I must also elaborate a better system of prisons
since as you justly said Denmark is a prison
I go to my affairs This night is born
a star named Hamlet We shall never meet
what I shall leave will not be worth a tragedy

It is not for us to greet each other or bid farewell we live on archipelagos
and that water these words what can they do what can they do prince ■

1957

Questions

1. How would you describe Fortinbras's stance in the poem? What is his attitude toward Hamlet? Which of the images in the first stanza best depict his tone? Explain.
2. What does Fortinbras mean when he says, "I know nothing exquisite" (l. 12)?
3. Fortinbras addresses Hamlet directly, saying "Anyhow you had to perish Hamlet you were not for life / you believed in crystal notions not in human clay" (ll. 15–16). What evidence in the text of *Hamlet* would support that statement? Explain.
4. Later in the poem, Fortinbras contradicts Hamlet: "The rest is not silence but belongs to me" (l. 21). Why does he say that? What does Fortinbras plan to do with "the rest"? Refer to stanzas 4 and 5 for details to support your answer.
5. How does the speaker contrast himself with Hamlet throughout the elegy? What does this contrast suggest about how Fortinbras views the role of a ruler? Explain, providing details from the text to support your answer.
6. In the final couplet of the poem, Fortinbras speaks of "archipelagos" (l. 33) and of "words" (l. 34). What is the significance of each? What do these two lines suggest about how Fortinbras regards Hamlet? about how Zbigniew Herbert regards both Fortinbras and Hamlet? Explain.

Literature in Conversation

1. In her essay on *Hamlet*, Marjorie Garber refers to the well-known 1948 film rendition of the play with distinctly Freudian overtones and reminds us of the now infamous oversimplification of the "opening voice-over murmur, '[T]his is the tragedy of a man who could not make up his mind.'" The 1990 film adaptation — directed by Franco Zeffirelli and starring Mel Gibson as Hamlet, Glenn Close as Gertrude, and Helena Bonham Carter as Ophelia — also takes a similar tack. Why do you think that Freud has had such a powerful influence on interpretations of *Hamlet*?
2. In *The Prince,* a sixteenth-century text on how best to govern, author Niccolò Machiavelli asserts: "All men will see what you seem to be; only a few will know what you are." One question readers have pondered for centuries is whether

Hamlet is, in fact, insane. At times he certainly seems to be, and acts accordingly. He says "my wit's diseased" (III.ii.301), but then he had said earlier that he would put "an antic disposition on" (I.v.172). To his mother, he says, "I essentially am not in madness, / But mad in craft" (III.iv.188–89). To Rosencrantz and Guildenstern he says, "I am but mad north-north-west. When the wind is / southerly I know a hawk from a handsaw" (II.ii.402–3). Using as evidence the text of *Hamlet* and two of the Texts in Context, answer the question: Is Hamlet insane?

3. Presented with a problem, Hamlet says "the time is out of joint" (I.iv.189), as if he is at the center of the world. About to die, he says, "the rest is silence" (V.ii.348), as if his death erases the world. These lines seem to suggest that Hamlet regards others as minor characters in the drama of his life. To what degree is Hamlet driven by self-centeredness? Use both *Hamlet* and at least two other Texts in Context to support your argument. You might also refer to the Extending beyond the Text feature on page 672.

4. In act III, scene I of the play, Ophelia describes Hamlet:

   Oh, what a noble mind is here o'erthrown!
   The courtier's, soldier's, scholar's, eye, tongue, sword;
   Th' expectancy and rose of the fair state,
   The glass of fashion and the mould of form,
   Th' observed of all observers, quite, quite down,
   And I of ladies most deject and wretched,
   That sucked the honey of his music vows,
   Now see that noble and most sovereign reason,
   Like sweet bells jangled, out of tune and harsh;
   That unmatched form and feature of blown youth
   Blasted with ecstasy: Oh woe is me,
   T' have seen what I have seen, see what I see.

   Paraphrase Ophelia's characterization of Hamlet. How do the readings in this Texts in Context align with or challenge Ophelia's perspective? Support your response by providing evidence from at least two sources.

5. C. S. Lewis contends that "we read Hamlet's speeches with interest chiefly because they describe so well a certain spiritual region through which most of us have passed and anyone in his circumstances might be expected to pass, rather than because of our concern to understand how and why this particular man entered it." Do you agree? How might the other writers in the Texts in Context respond, particularly William Hazlitt? Explain.

6. Which of the Texts in Context has helped you the most to deepen your understanding of Hamlet, the character, and of *Hamlet*, the play? Explain.

Bartleby, the Scrivener: A Story of Wall Street

Library of Congress Prints & Photographs Division

Herman Melville

Herman Melville (1819–1891) was born in New York City. After working as a clerk in a bank and a schoolteacher, he went to sea in 1841. He worked on a whaling ship that traveled to the Marquesas Islands and other parts of the South Seas. Based on his experiences there, he wrote the novels *Typee* and *Omoo*, which were published in 1847. Largely self-educated, Melville read widely, and after his adventures, he began to write more complex books, including *Moby-Dick* (1851), and stories such as "Bartleby, the Scrivener" (1853). Late in his life, he devoted himself increasingly to poetry, including a collection about the Civil War, *Battle Pieces and Aspects of the War* (1866).

KEY CONTEXT A scrivener, also known as a scribe, was someone who made a living by writing or copying written material. Such a skill was especially important in the world of law and business during the time when "Bartleby, the Scrivener: A Story of Wall Street" was written. Set in the mid-1800s, the story reflects the growing influence of the New York Stock Exchange and the nation's overall movement from a rural, agricultural society to an urban, industrialized one.

I am a rather elderly man. The nature of my avocations, for the last thirty years, has brought me into more than ordinary contact with what would seem an interesting and somewhat singular set of men, of whom, as yet, nothing, that I know of, has ever been written — I mean, the law-copyists, or scriveners. I have known very many of them, professionally and privately, and, if I pleased, could relate diverse histories, at which good-natured gentlemen might smile, and sentimental souls might weep. But I waive the biographies of all other scriveners, for a few passages in the life of Bartleby, who was a scrivener, the strangest I ever saw, or heard of. While, of other law-copyists, I might write the complete life, of Bartleby nothing of that sort can be done. I believe that no materials exist, for a full and satisfactory biography of this man. It is an irreparable loss to literature. Bartleby was one of those beings of whom nothing is ascertainable, except from the original sources, and, in his case, those are very small. What my own astonished eyes saw of Bartleby, *that* is all I know of him, except, indeed, one vague report, which will appear in the sequel.

Ere introducing the scrivener, as he first appeared to me, it is fit I make some mention of myself, my *employés*, my business, my chambers, and general surroundings, because some such description is indispensable to an adequate understanding of the chief character about to be presented. Imprimis:[1] I am a man who, from his youth upwards, has been filled with a profound conviction that the easiest way of life is the best. Hence, though I belong to a profession proverbially energetic and nervous, even to turbulence, at times, yet nothing of that sort have I ever suffered to invade my peace. I am one of those unambitious lawyers who never address a jury, or in any way draw down public applause; but, in the

[1] In the first place. — Eds.

This engraving shows a view of Wall Street in 1847.

How does the artist characterize this part of Manhattan? How does it compare to the setting of "Bartleby, the Scrivener"?

cool tranquillity of a snug retreat, do a snug business among rich men's bonds, and mortgages, and title-deeds. All who know me, consider me an eminently *safe* man. The late John Jacob Astor,[2] a personage little given to poetic enthusiasm, had no hesitation in pronouncing my first grand point to be prudence; my next, method. I do not speak it in vanity, but simply record the fact, that I was not unemployed in my profession by the late John Jacob Astor; a name which, I admit, I love to repeat; for it hath a rounded and orbicular[3] sound to it, and rings like unto bullion.[4] I will freely add, that I was not insensible to the late John Jacob Astor's good opinion.

Some time prior to the period at which this little history begins, my avocations had been largely increased. The good old office, now extinct in the State of New York, of a Master in Chancery, had been conferred upon me. It was not a very arduous office, but very pleasantly remunerative. I seldom lose my temper; much more seldom indulge in dangerous indignation at wrongs and outrages; but I must be permitted to be rash here and declare, that I consider the sudden and violent abrogation[5] of the office of Master in Chancery, by the new Constitution, as a —— premature act; inasmuch as I had counted upon a life-lease of the profits, whereas I only received those of a few short years. But this is by the way.

My chambers were up stairs, at No. —— Wall Street. At one end, they looked upon the white wall of the interior of a spacious skylight shaft, penetrating the building from top to bottom.

5 This view might have been considered rather tame than otherwise, deficient in what landscape painters call "life." But, if so, the view from the other end of my chambers offered, at least, a contrast, if nothing more. In that direction, my windows commanded an unobstructed view of a lofty brick wall, black by age and everlasting shade; which wall required no spyglass to bring out its lurking beauties, but, for the benefit of all near-sighted spectators, was pushed up to within ten feet of my window-panes. Owing to the great height of the surrounding buildings, and my chambers being on the second floor, the interval between this wall and mine not a little resembled a huge square cistern.

At the period just preceding the advent of Bartleby, I had two persons as copyists in my employment, and a promising lad as an office-boy. First, Turkey; second, Nippers; third, Ginger Nut. These may seem names, the like of which are not usually found in the Directory. In truth, they were nicknames, mutually conferred upon each other by my three clerks, and were deemed expressive of their respective persons

[2] Astor (1763–1848) was a fur trader and the richest American of his time. — Eds.

[3] Circular. — Eds.

[4] Gold or silver. — Eds.

[5] Repeal. — Eds.

or characters. Turkey was a short, pursy[6] Englishman, of about my own age — that is, somewhere not far from sixty. In the morning, one might say, his face was of a fine florid hue, but after twelve o'clock, meridian — his dinner hour — it blazed like a grate full of Christmas coals; and continued blazing — but, as it were, with a gradual wane — till six o'clock, p.m., or thereabouts; after which, I saw no more of the proprietor of the face, which, gaining its meridian with the sun, seemed to set with it, to rise, culminate, and decline the following day, with the like regularity and undiminished glory. There are many singular coincidences I have known in the course of my life, not the least among which was the fact, that, exactly when Turkey displayed his fullest beams from his red and radiant countenance, just then, too, at that critical moment, began the daily period when I considered his business capacities as seriously disturbed for the remainder of the twenty-four hours. Not that he was absolutely idle, or averse to business then; far from it. The difficulty was, he was apt to be altogether too energetic. There was a strange, inflamed, flurried, flighty recklessness of activity about him. He would be incautious in dipping his pen into his inkstand. All his blots upon my documents were dropped there after twelve o'clock, meridian. Indeed, not only would he be reckless, and sadly given to making blots in the afternoon, but, some days, he went further, and was rather noisy. At such times, too, his face flamed with augmented blazonry, as if cannel coal had been heaped on anthracite. He made an unpleasant racket with his chair; spilled his sand-box; in mending his pens, impatiently split them all to pieces, and threw them on the floor in a sudden passion; stood up, and leaned over his table, boxing his papers about in a most indecorous manner, very sad to behold in an elderly man like him. Nevertheless, as he was in many ways a most valuable person to me, and all the time before twelve o'clock, meridian, was the quickest, steadiest creature, too, accomplishing a great deal of work in a style not easily to be matched — for these reasons, I was willing to overlook his eccentricities, though, indeed, occasionally, I remonstrated with him. I did this very gently, however, because, though the civilest, nay, the blandest and most reverential of men in the morning, yet, in the afternoon, he was disposed, upon provocation, to be slightly rash with his tongue — in fact, insolent. Now, valuing his morning services as I did, and resolved not to lose them — yet, at the same time, made uncomfortable by his inflamed ways after twelve o'clock — and being a man of peace, unwilling by my admonitions to call forth unseemly retorts from him, I took upon me, one Saturday noon (he was always worse on Saturdays) to hint to him, very kindly, that, perhaps, now that he was growing old, it might be well to abridge his labors; in short, he need not come to my chambers after twelve o'clock, but, dinner over, had best go home to his lodgings, and rest himself till tea-time. But no; he insisted upon his afternoon devotions. His countenance became intolerably fervid, as he oratorically assured me — gesticulating with a long ruler at the other end of the room — that if his services in the morning were useful, how indispensable, then, in the afternoon?

"With submission, sir," said Turkey, on this occasion, "I consider myself your right-hand man. In the morning I but marshal and deploy my columns; but in the afternoon I put myself at their head, and gallantly charge the foe, thus" — and he made a violent thrust with the ruler.

"But the blots, Turkey," intimated I.

"True; but, with submission, sir, behold these hairs! I am getting old. Surely, sir, a blot or two of a warm afternoon is not to be severely urged against gray hairs. Old age — even if it blot the page — is honorable. With submission, sir, we *both* are getting old."

[6] Asthmatic and overweight. — Eds.

This appeal to my fellow-feeling was hardly to be resisted. At all events, I saw that go he would not. So, I made up my mind to let him stay, resolving, nevertheless, to see to it that, during the afternoon, he had to do with my less important papers.

Nippers, the second on my list, was a whiskered, sallow, and, upon the whole, rather piratical-looking young man, of about five-and-twenty. I always deemed him the victim of two evil powers — ambition and indigestion. The ambition was evinced by a certain impatience of the duties of a mere copyist, an unwarrantable usurpation of strictly professional affairs such as the original drawing up of legal documents. The indigestion seemed betokened in an occasional nervous testiness and grinning irritability, causing the teeth to audibly grind together over mistakes committed in copying; unnecessary maledictions, hissed, rather than spoken, in the heat of business; and especially by a continual discontent with the height of the table where he worked. Though of a very ingenious mechanical turn, Nippers could never get this table to suit him. He put chips under it, blocks of various sorts, bits of pasteboard, and at last went so far as to attempt an exquisite adjustment, by final pieces of folded blotting-paper. But no invention would answer. If, for the sake of easing his back, he brought the table-lid at a sharp angle well up towards his chin, and wrote there like a man using the steep roof of a Dutch house for his desk, then he declared that it stopped the circulation in his arms. If now he lowered the table to his waistbands, and stooped over it in writing, then there was a sore aching in his back. In short, the truth of the matter was, Nippers knew not what he wanted. Or, if he wanted anything, it was to be rid of a scrivener's table altogether. Among the manifestations of his diseased ambition was a fondness he had for receiving visits from certain ambiguous-looking fellows in seedy coats, whom he called his clients. Indeed, I was aware that not only was he, at times, considerable of a ward-politician, but he occasionally did a little business at the justices' courts, and was not unknown on the steps of the Tombs.[7] I have good reason to believe, however, that one individual who called upon him at my chambers, and who, with a grand air, he insisted was his client, was no other than a dun, and the alleged title-deed, a bill. But, with all his failings, and the annoyances he caused me, Nippers, like his compatriot Turkey, was a very useful man to me; wrote a neat, swift hand; and, when he chose, was not deficient in a gentlemanly sort of deportment. Added to this, he always dressed in a gentlemanly sort of way; and so, incidentally, reflected credit upon my chambers. Whereas, with respect to Turkey, I had much ado to keep him from being a reproach to me. His clothes were apt to look oily, and smell of eating-houses. He wore his pantaloons very loose and baggy in summer. His coats were execrable, his hat not to be handled. But while the hat was a thing of indifference to me, inasmuch as his natural civility and deference, as a dependent Englishman, always led him to doff it the moment he entered the room, yet his coat was another matter. Concerning his coats, I reasoned with him; but with no effect. The truth was, I suppose, that a man with so small an income could not afford to sport such a lustrous face and a lustrous coat at one and the same time. As Nippers once observed, Turkey's money went chiefly for red ink. One winter day, I presented Turkey with a highly respectable-looking coat of my own — a padded gray coat, of a most comfortable warmth, and which buttoned straight up from the knee to the neck. I thought Turkey would appreciate the favor, and abate his rashness and obstreperousness[8] of afternoons. But no; I verily believe that buttoning himself up in so downy

[7] A jail in New York City. — Eds.

[8] Loud defiance. — Eds.

and blanket-like a coat had a pernicious effect upon him — upon the same principle that too much oats are bad for horses. In fact, precisely as a rash, restive horse is said to feel his oats, so Turkey felt his coat. It made him insolent. He was a man whom prosperity harmed.

Though, concerning the self-indulgent habits of Turkey, I had my own private surmises, yet, touching Nippers, I was well persuaded that, whatever might be his faults in other respects, he was, at least, a temperate young man. But indeed, nature herself seemed to have been his vintner, and, at his birth, charged him so thoroughly with an irritable, brandy-like disposition, that all subsequent potations[9] were needless. When I consider how, amid the stillness of my chambers, Nippers would sometimes impatiently rise from his seat, and stooping over his table, spread his arms wide apart, seize the whole desk, and move it, and jerk it, with a grim, grinding motion on the floor, as if the table were a perverse voluntary agent, intent on thwarting and vexing him, I plainly perceive that, for Nippers, brandy-and-water were altogether superfluous.

It was fortunate for me that, owing to its peculiar cause — indigestion — the irritability and consequent nervousness of Nippers were mainly observable in the morning, while in the afternoon he was comparatively mild. So that, Turkey's paroxysms only coming on about twelve o'clock, I never had to do with their eccentricities at one time. Their fits relieved each other, like guards. When Nippers' was on, Turkey's was off; and vice versa. This was a good natural arrangement, under the circumstances.

Ginger Nut, the third on my list, was a lad, some twelve years old. His father was a carman, ambitious of seeing his son on the bench instead of a cart, before he died. So he sent him to my office, as student at law, errand-boy, cleaner, and sweeper, at the rate of one dollar a week. He had a little desk to himself, but he did not use it much. Upon inspection, the drawer exhibited a great array of the shells of various sorts of nuts. Indeed, to this quick-witted youth, the whole noble science of the law was contained in a nutshell. Not the least among the employments of Ginger Nut, as well as one which he discharged with the most alacrity, was his duty as cake and apple purveyor for Turkey and Nippers. Copying lawpapers being proverbially a dry, husky sort of business, my two scriveners were fain to moisten their mouths very often with Spitzenbergs,[10] to be had at the numerous stalls nigh the Custom House and Post Office. Also, they sent Ginger Nut very frequently for that peculiar cake — small, flat, round, and very spicy — after which he had been named by them. Of a cold morning, when business was but dull, Turkey would gobble up scores of these cakes, as if they were mere wafers — indeed, they sell them at the rate of six or eight for a penny — the scrape of his pen blending with the crunching of the crisp particles in his mouth. Of all the fiery afternoon blunders and flurried rashness of Turkey, was his once moistening a ginger-cake between his lips, and clapping it on to a mortgage, for a seal. I came within an ace of dismissing him then. But he mollified me by making an oriental bow, and saying —

15 "With submission, sir, it was generous of me to find you in stationery on my own account."

Now my original business — that of a conveyancer and title hunter, and drawer-up of recondite documents of all sorts — was considerably increased by receiving the Master's office. There was now great work for scriveners. Not only must I push the clerks already with me, but I must have additional help.

In answer to my advertisement, a motionless young man one morning stood upon my office threshold, the door being open, for it was summer.

---

9 Drinks. — Eds.

10 An apple variety native to New York State. — Eds.

I can see that figure now—pallidly neat, pitiably respectable, incurably forlorn! It was Bartleby.

After a few words touching his qualifications, I engaged him, glad to have among my corps of copyists a man of so singularly sedate an aspect, which I thought might operate beneficially upon the flighty temper of Turkey, and the fiery one of Nippers.

I should have stated before that ground-glass folding-doors divided my premises into two parts, one of which was occupied by my scriveners, the other by myself. According to my humor, I threw open these doors, or closed them. I resolved to assign Bartleby a corner by the folding-doors, but on my side of them, so as to have this quiet man within easy call, in case any trifling thing was to be done. I placed his desk close up to a small side-window in that part of the room, a window which originally had afforded a lateral view of certain grimy brickyards and bricks, but which, owing to subsequent erections, commanded at present no view at all, though it gave some light. Within three feet of the panes was a wall, and the light came down from far above, between two lofty buildings, as from a very small opening in a dome. Still further to a satisfactory arrangement, I procured a high green folding screen, which might entirely isolate Bartleby from my sight, though not remove him from my voice. And thus, in a manner, privacy and society were conjoined.

20 At first, Bartleby did an extraordinary quantity of writing. As if long famishing for something to copy, he seemed to gorge himself on my documents. There was no pause for digestion. He ran a day and night line, copying by sunlight and by candle-light. I should have been quite delighted with his application, had he been cheerfully industrious. But he wrote on silently, palely, mechanically.

It is, of course, an indispensable part of a scrivener's business to verify the accuracy of his copy, word by word. Where there are two or more scriveners in an office, they assist

William England/London Stereoscopic Company/Hulton Archive/Getty Images

This photograph shows the financial district of New York City as seen from the Revenue Office in 1859, six years after this story was written. In the background is Trinity Church, which was built in 1846 and was the city's tallest building at the time.
What details in this photograph stand out to you? What themes or motifs in Melville's story connect with this image?

each other in this examination, one reading from the copy, the other holding the original. It is a very dull, wearisome, and lethargic affair. I can readily imagine that, to some sanguine temperaments, it would be altogether intolerable. For example, I cannot credit that the mettlesome poet, Byron, would have contentedly sat down with Bartleby to examine a law document of, say five hundred pages, closely written in a crimpy hand.

Now and then, in the haste of business, it had been my habit to assist in comparing some brief document myself, calling Turkey or Nippers for this purpose. One object I had, in placing Bartleby so handy to me behind the screen, was, to avail myself of his services on such trivial occasions. It was on the third day, I think, of his being with me, and before any necessity had arisen for having his own writing examined, that, being much hurried to complete a small affair I had in hand, I abruptly called to Bartleby. In my haste and natural expectancy of instant compliance, I sat with my head bent over the original on my desk, and my right hand sideways, and somewhat nervously extended with the copy, so that, immediately upon emerging from his retreat, Bartleby might snatch it and proceed to business without the least delay.

In this very attitude did I sit when I called to him, rapidly stating what it was I wanted him to do — namely, to examine a small paper with me. Imagine my surprise, nay, my consternation, when, without moving from his privacy, Bartleby, in a singularly mild, firm voice, replied, "I would prefer not to."

I sat awhile in perfect silence, rallying my stunned faculties. Immediately it occurred to me that my ears had deceived me, or Bartleby had entirely misunderstood my meaning. I repeated my request in the clearest tone I could assume; but in quite as clear a one came the previous reply, "I would prefer not to."

"Prefer not to," echoed I, rising in high excitement, and crossing the room with a stride. "What do you mean? Are you moonstruck? I want you to help me compare this sheet here — take it," and I thrust it towards him.

"I would prefer not to," said he.

I looked at him steadfastly. His face was leanly composed; his gray eye dimly calm. Not a wrinkle of agitation rippled him. Had there been the least uneasiness, anger, impatience, or impertinence in his manner; in other words, had there been anything ordinarily human about him, doubtless I should have violently dismissed him from the premises. But as it was, I should have as soon thought of turning my pale plaster-of-paris bust of Cicero out of doors. I stood gazing at him awhile, as he went on with his own writing, and then reseated myself at my desk. This is very strange, thought I. What had one best do? But my business hurried me. I concluded to forget the matter for the present, reserving it for my future leisure. So, calling Nippers from the other room, the paper was speedily examined.

A few days after this, Bartleby concluded four lengthy documents, being quadruplicates of a week's testimony taken before me in my High Court of Chancery. It became necessary to examine them. It was an important suit, and great accuracy was imperative. Having all things arranged, I called Turkey, Nippers, and Ginger Nut, from the next room, meaning to place the four copies in the hands of my four clerks, while I should read from the original. Accordingly, Turkey, Nippers, and Ginger Nut had taken their seats in a row, each with his document in his hand, when I called to Bartleby to join this interesting group.

"Bartleby! quick, I am waiting."

I heard a slow scrape of his chair legs on the uncarpeted floor, and soon he appeared standing at the entrance of his hermitage.

"What is wanted?" said he, mildly.

"The copies, the copies," said I, hurriedly. "We are going to examine them. There" — and I held towards him the fourth quadruplicate.

"I would prefer not to," he said, and gently disappeared behind the screen.

For a few moments I was turned into a pillar of salt, standing at the head of my seated column of clerks. Recovering myself, I advanced towards the screen, and demanded the reason for such extraordinary conduct.

"*Why* do you refuse?"

"I would prefer not to."

With any other man I should have flown outright into a dreadful passion, scorned all further words, and thrust him ignominiously from my presence. But there was something about Bartleby that not only strangely disarmed me, but, in a wonderful manner, touched and disconcerted me. I began to reason with him.

"These are your own copies we are about to examine. It is labor saving to you, because one examination will answer for your four papers. It is common usage. Every copyist is bound to help examine his copy. Is it not so? Will you not speak? Answer!"

"I prefer not to," he replied in a flute-like tone. It seemed to me that, while I had been addressing him, he carefully revolved every statement that I made; fully comprehended the meaning; could not gainsay the irresistible conclusion; but, at the same time, some paramount consideration prevailed with him to reply as he did.

"You are decided, then, not to comply with my request — a request made according to common usage and common sense?"

He briefly gave me to understand, that on that point my judgment was sound. Yes: his decision was irreversible.

It is not seldom the case that, when a man is browbeaten in some unprecedented and violently unreasonable way, he begins to stagger in his own plainest faith. He begins, as it were, vaguely to surmise that, wonderful as it may be, all the justice and all the reason is on the other side. Accordingly, if any disinterested persons are present, he turns to them for some reinforcement for his own faltering mind.

"Turkey," said I, "what do you think of this? Am I not right?"

"With submission, sir," said Turkey, in his blandest tone, "I think that you are."

"Nippers," said I, "what do *you* think of it?"

"I think I should kick him out of the office."

(The reader of nice perceptions will have perceived that, it being morning, Turkey's answer is couched in polite and tranquil terms, but Nippers replies in ill-tempered ones. Or, to repeat a previous sentence, Nippers' ugly mood was on duty, and Turkey's off.)

"Ginger Nut," said I, willing to enlist the smallest suffrage in my behalf, "what do *you* think of it?"

"I think, sir, he's a little *luny*," replied Ginger Nut, with a grin.

"You hear what they say," said I, turning towards the screen, "come forth and do your duty."

But he vouchsafed no reply. I pondered a moment in sore perplexity. But once more business hurried me. I determined again to postpone the consideration of this dilemma to my future leisure. With a little trouble we made out to examine the papers without Bartleby, though at every page or two Turkey deferentially dropped his opinion, that this proceeding was quite out of the common; while Nippers, twitching in his chair with a dyspeptic nervousness, ground out, between his set teeth, occasional hissing maledictions against the stubborn oaf behind the screen. And for his (Nippers') part, this was the first and the last time he would do another man's business without pay.

Meanwhile Bartleby sat in his hermitage, oblivious to everything but his own peculiar business there.

Some days passed, the scrivener being employed upon another lengthy work. His late remarkable conduct led me to regard his ways narrowly. I observed that he never went to dinner; indeed, that he never went anywhere. As yet I had never, of my personal knowledge, known him to be outside of my office. He was a perpetual sentry in the corner. At about eleven o'clock though, in the morning, I noticed that Ginger Nut would advance toward the opening in Bartleby's screen, as if silently beckoned thither by a gesture invisible to me where I sat. The boy would then leave the office, jingling a few pence, and reappear with a handful of ginger-nuts, which he delivered in the hermitage, receiving two of the cakes for his trouble.

He lives, then, on ginger-nuts, thought I; never eats a dinner, properly speaking; he must be a vegetarian, then, but no; he never eats even vegetables, he eats nothing but ginger-nuts. My mind then ran on in reveries concerning the probable effects upon the human constitution of living entirely on ginger-nuts. Ginger-nuts are so called, because they contain ginger as one of their peculiar constituents, and the final flavoring one. Now, what was ginger? A hot, spicy thing. Was Bartleby hot and spicy? Not at all. Ginger, then, had no effect upon Bartleby. Probably he preferred it should have none.

55 Nothing so aggravates an earnest person as a passive resistance. If the individual so resisted be of a not inhumane temper, and the resisting one perfectly harmless in his passivity, then, in the better moods of the former, he will endeavor charitably to construe to his imagination what proves impossible to be solved by his judgment. Even so, for the most part, I regarded Bartleby and his ways. Poor fellow! thought I, he means no mischief; it is plain he intends no insolence; his aspect sufficiently evinces that his eccentricities are involuntary. He is useful to me. I can get along with him. If I turn him away, the chances are he will fall in with some less indulgent employer, and then he will be rudely treated, and perhaps driven forth miserably to starve. Yes. Here I can cheaply purchase a delicious self-approval. To befriend Bartleby; to humor him in his strange wilfulness, will cost me little or nothing, while I lay up in my soul what will eventually prove a sweet morsel for my conscience. But this mood was not invariable with me. The passiveness of Bartleby sometimes irritated me. I felt strangely goaded on to encounter him in new opposition — to elicit some angry spark from him answerable to my own. But, indeed, I might as well have essayed to strike fire with my knuckles against a bit of Windsor soap. But one afternoon the evil impulse in me mastered me, and the following little scene ensued:

"Bartleby," said I, "when those papers are all copied, I will compare them with you."

"I would prefer not to."

"How? Surely you do not mean to persist in that mulish vagary?"

No answer.

60 I threw open the folding-doors nearby, and turning upon Turkey and Nippers, exclaimed:

"Bartleby a second time says, he won't examine his papers. What do you think of it, Turkey?"

It was afternoon, be it remembered. Turkey sat glowing like a brass boiler; his bald head steaming; his hands reeling among his blotted papers.

"Think of it?" roared Turkey. "I think I'll just step behind his screen, and black his eyes for him!"

So saying, Turkey rose to his feet and threw his arms into a pugilistic position. He was hurrying away to make good his promise, when I detained him, alarmed at the effect of incautiously rousing Turkey's combativeness after dinner.

65 "Sit down, Turkey," said I, "and hear what Nippers has to say. What do you think of it, Nippers? Would I not be justified in immediately dismissing Bartleby?"

"Excuse me, that is for you to decide, sir. I think his conduct quite unusual, and, indeed, unjust, as regards Turkey and myself. But it may only be a passing whim."

"Ah," exclaimed I, "you have strangely changed your mind, then — you speak very gently of him now."

"All beer," cried Turkey; "gentleness is effects of beer — Nippers and I dined together to-day. You see how gentle *I* am, sir. Shall I go and black his eyes?"

"You refer to Bartleby, I suppose. No, not to-day, Turkey," I replied; "pray, put up your fists."

70 I closed the doors, and again advanced towards Bartleby. I felt additional incentives tempting me to my fate. I burned to be rebelled against again. I remembered that Bartleby never left the office.

"Bartleby," said I, "Ginger Nut is away; just step around to the Post Office, won't you?" (it was but a three minutes' walk) "and see if there is anything for me."

"I would prefer not to."

"You *will* not?"

"I *prefer* not."

75 I staggered to my desk, and sat there in a deep study. My blind inveteracy returned. Was there any other thing in which I could procure myself to be ignominiously repulsed by this lean, penniless wight? — my hired clerk? What

added thing is there, perfectly reasonable, that he will be sure to refuse to do?

"Bartleby!"

No answer.

"Bartleby," in a louder tone.

No answer.

"Bartleby," I roared.

Like a very ghost, agreeably to the laws of magical invocation, at the third summons, he appeared at the entrance of his hermitage.

"Go to the next room, and tell Nippers to come to me."

"I prefer not to," he respectfully and slowly said, and mildly disappeared.

"Very good, Bartleby," said I, in a quiet sort of serenely-severe self-possessed tone, intimating the unalterable purpose of some terrible retribution very close at hand. At the moment I half intended something of the kind. But upon the whole, as it was drawing towards my dinner-hour, I thought it best to put on my hat and walk home for the day, suffering much from perplexity and distress of mind.

Shall I acknowledge it? The conclusion of this whole business was, that it soon became a fixed fact of my chambers, that a pale young scrivener, by the name of Bartleby, had a desk there; that he copied for me at the usual rate of four cents a folio (one hundred words); but he was permanently exempt from examining the work done by him, that duty being transferred to Turkey and Nippers, out of compliment, doubtless, to their superior acuteness; moreover, said Bartleby was never, on any account, to be dispatched on the most trivial errand of any sort; and that even if entreated to take upon him such a matter, it was generally understood that he would "prefer not to" — in other words, that he would refuse point-blank.

As days passed on, I became considerably reconciled to Bartleby. His steadiness, his freedom from all dissipation, his incessant industry (except when he chose to throw himself into a standing revery behind his screen), his great stillness, his unalterableness of demeanor under all circumstances, made him a valuable acquisition. One prime thing was this — *he was always there* — first in the morning, continually through the day, and the last at night. I had a singular confidence in his honesty. I felt my most precious papers perfectly safe in his hands. Sometimes, to be sure, I could not, for the very soul of me, avoid falling into sudden spasmodic passions with him. For it was exceeding difficult to bear in mind all the time those strange peculiarities, privileges, and unheard-of exemptions, forming the tacit stipulations on Bartleby's part under which he remained in my office. Now and then, in the eagerness of dispatching pressing business, I would inadvertently summon Bartleby, in a short, rapid tone, to put his finger, say, on the incipient tie of a bit of red tape with which I was about compressing some papers. Of course, from behind the screen the usual answer, "I prefer not to," was sure to come; and then, how could a human creature, with the common infirmities of our nature, refrain from bitterly exclaiming upon such perverseness — such unreasonableness? However, every added repulse of this sort which I received only tended to lessen the probability of my repeating the inadvertence.

Here it must be said, that, according to the custom of most legal gentlemen occupying chambers in densely populated law buildings, there were several keys to my door. One was kept by a woman residing in the attic, which person weekly scrubbed and daily swept and dusted my apartments. Another was kept by Turkey for convenience sake. The third I sometimes carried in my own pocket. The fourth I knew not who had.

Now, one Sunday morning I happened to go to Trinity Church, to hear a celebrated preacher, and finding myself rather early on the ground I thought I would walk round to my chambers for a while. Luckily I had my key with me; but upon applying it to the lock, I found it resisted by something inserted from the inside. Quite surprised, I called out; when to my consternation a key was turned from within; and thrusting his lean visage at me, and holding the door ajar, the apparition of Bartleby appeared, in his shirt-sleeves, and otherwise in a strangely tattered *deshabille*, saying quietly that he was sorry, but he was deeply engaged just then, and — preferred not admitting me at present. In a brief word or two, he moreover added, that perhaps I had better walk round the block two or three times, and by that time he would probably have concluded his affairs.

Now, the utterly unsurmised appearance of Bartleby, tenanting my law-chambers of a Sunday morning, with his cadaverously gentlemanly nonchalance, yet withal firm and self-possessed, had such a strange effect upon me, that incontinently I slunk away from my own door, and did as desired. But not without sundry twinges of impotent rebellion against the mild effrontery of this unaccountable scrivener. Indeed, it was his wonderful mildness chiefly, which not only disarmed me, but unmanned me, as it were. For I consider that one, for the time, is sort of unmanned when he tranquilly permits his hired clerk to dictate to him, and order him away from his own premises. Furthermore, I was full of uneasiness as to what Bartleby could possibly be doing in my office in his shirt-sleeves, and in an otherwise dismantled condition of a Sunday morning. Was anything amiss going on? Nay, that was out of the question. It was not to be thought of for a moment that Bartleby was an immoral person. But what could he be doing there? — copying? Nay again, whatever might be his eccentricities, Bartleby was an eminently decorous person. He would be the last man to sit down to his desk in any state approaching to nudity. Besides, it was Sunday; and there was something about Bartleby that forbade the supposition that he would by any secular occupation violate the proprieties of the day.

Nevertheless, my mind was not pacified; 90
and full of a restless curiosity, at last I returned to the door. Without hindrance I inserted my key, opened it, and entered. Bartleby was not to be seen. I looked round anxiously, peeped behind his screen; but it was very plain that he was gone. Upon more closely examining the place, I surmised that for an indefinite period Bartleby must have ate, dressed, and slept in my office, and that too without plate, mirror, or bed. The cushioned seat of a rickety old sofa in one corner bore the faint impress of a lean, reclining form. Rolled away under his desk, I found a blanket; under the empty grate, a blacking box and brush; on a chair, a tin basin, with soap and a ragged towel; in a newspaper a few crumbs of ginger-nuts and a morsel of cheese. Yes, thought I, it is evident enough that Bartleby has been making his home here, keeping bachelor's hall all by himself. Immediately then the thought came sweeping across me, what miserable friendlessness and loneliness are here revealed! His poverty is great; but his solitude, how horrible! Think of it. Of a Sunday, Wall Street is deserted as Petra;[11] and every night of every day it is an emptiness. This building, too, which of week-days hums with industry and life, at nightfall echoes with sheer vacancy, and all through Sunday is forlorn. And here Bartleby makes his home; sole spectator of a solitude which he has seen all populous — a sort of innocent and transformed Marius brooding among the ruins of Carthage?[12]

---

[11] Ancient Middle Eastern city in what is now Jordan whose ruins were discovered in 1812. — Eds.

[12] Exiled Roman general Gaius Marius (157–86 B.C.E.) fled to the North African city-state of Carthage after a failed attempt to stop a civil war in Rome. Carthage had been destroyed by the Romans in the Third Punic War (149–146 B.C.E.). — Eds.

For the first time in my life a feeling of overpowering stinging melancholy seized me. Before, I had never experienced aught but a not unpleasing sadness. The bond of a common humanity now drew me irresistibly to gloom. A fraternal melancholy! For both I and Bartleby were sons of Adam. I remembered the bright silks and sparkling faces I had seen that day, in gala trim, swan-like sailing down the Mississippi of Broadway; and I contrasted them with the pallid copyist, and thought to myself, Ah, happiness courts the light, so we deem the world is gay; but misery hides aloof, so we deem that misery there is none. These sad fancyings — chimeras, doubtless, of a sick and silly brain — led on to other and more special thoughts, concerning the eccentricities of Bartleby. Presentiments of strange discoveries hovered round me. The scrivener's pale form appeared to me laid out, among uncaring strangers, in its shivering winding-sheet.

Suddenly I was attracted by Bartleby's closed desk, the key in open sight left in the lock.

I mean no mischief, seek the gratification of no heartless curiosity, thought I; besides, the desk is mine, and its contents, too, so I will make bold to look within. Everything was methodically arranged, the papers smoothly placed. The pigeon-holes were deep, and removing the files of documents, I groped into their recesses. Presently I felt something there, and dragged it out. It was an old bandanna hand-kerchief, heavy and knotted. I opened it, and saw it was a savings' bank.

I now recalled all the quiet mysteries which I had noted in the man. I remembered that he never spoke but to answer; that, though at intervals he had considerable time to himself, yet I had never seen him reading — no, not even a newspaper; that for long periods he would stand looking out, at his pale window behind the screen, upon the dead brick wall; I was quite sure he never visited any refectory or eating-house; while his pale face clearly indicated that he never drank beer like Turkey; or tea and coffee even, like other men; that he never went anywhere in particular that I could learn; never went out for a walk, unless, indeed, that was the case at present; that he had declined telling who he was, or whence he came, or whether he had any relatives in the world; that though so thin and pale, he never complained of ill-health. And more than all, I remembered a certain unconscious air of pallid — how shall I call it? — of pallid haughtiness, say, or rather an austere reserve about him, which had positively awed me into my tame compliance with his eccentricities, when I had feared to ask him to do the slightest incidental thing for me, even though I might know, from his long-continued motionlessness, that behind his screen he must be standing in one of those dead-wall reveries of his.

Revolving all these things, and coupling them with the recently discovered fact, that he made my office his constant abiding place and home, and not forgetful of his morbid moodiness; revolving all these things, a prudential feeling began to steal over me. My first emotions had been those of pure melancholy and sincerest pity; but just in proportion as the forlornness of Bartleby grew and grew to my imagination, did that same melancholy merge into fear, that pity into repulsion. So true it is, and so terrible, too, that up to a certain point the thought or sight of misery enlists our best affections; but, in certain special cases, beyond that point it does not. They err who would assert that invariably this is owing to the inherent selfishness of the human heart. It rather proceeds from a certain hopelessness of remedying excessive and organic ill. To a sensitive being, pity is not seldom pain. And when at last it is perceived that such pity cannot lead to effectual succor, common sense bids the soul be rid of it. What I saw that morning persuaded me that the scrivener was the victim of innate and incurable disorder. I might give alms to his body; but his body did not pain him; it was his soul that suffered, and his soul I could not reach.

I did not accomplish the purpose of going to Trinity Church that morning. Somehow, the things I had seen disqualified me for the time from church-going. I walked homeward, thinking what I would do with Bartleby. Finally, I resolved upon this — I would put certain calm questions to him the next morning, touching his history, etc., and if he declined to answer them openly and unreservedly (and I supposed he would prefer not), then to give him a twenty dollar bill over and above whatever I might owe him, and tell him his services were no longer required; but that if in any other way I could assist him, I would be happy to do so, especially if he desired to return to his native place, wherever that might be, I would willingly help to defray the expenses. Moreover, if, after reaching home, he found himself at any time in want of aid, a letter from him would be sure of a reply.

The next morning came.

"Bartleby," said I, gently calling to him behind his screen.

No reply.

"Bartleby," said I, in a still gentler tone, "come here; I am not going to ask you to do anything you would prefer not to do — I simply wish to speak to you."

Upon this he noiselessly slid into view.

"Will you tell me, Bartleby, where you were born?"

"I would prefer not to."

"Will you tell me *anything* about yourself?"

"I would prefer not to."

"But what reasonable objection can you have to speak to me? I feel friendly towards you."

He did not look at me while I spoke, but kept his glance fixed upon my bust of Cicero, which, as I then sat, was directly behind me, some six inches above my head.

In this 2016 work by C. H. Pearce, the narrator and Bartleby are pictured together. **What does the composition suggest about their relationship? How do you interpret the expression on the narrator's face? Do you agree with this artist's interpretation of these characters? Explain.**

"What is your answer, Bartleby?" said I, after waiting a considerable time for a reply, during which his countenance remained immovable, only there was the faintest conceivable tremor of the white attenuated mouth.

"At present I prefer to give no answer," he said, and retired into his hermitage.

It was rather weak in me I confess, but his manner, on this occasion, nettled me. Not only did there seem to lurk in it a certain calm disdain, but his perverseness seemed ungrateful, considering the undeniable good usage and indulgence he had received from me.

Again I sat ruminating what I should do. Mortified as I was at his behavior, and resolved as I had been to dismiss him when I entered my office, nevertheless I strangely felt something superstitious knocking at my heart, and forbidding me to carry out my purpose, and denouncing me for a villain if I dared to breathe one bitter word against this forlornest of mankind. At last, familiarly drawing my chair behind his screen, I sat down and said: "Bartleby, never mind, then, about revealing your history; but let me entreat you, as a friend, to comply as far as may be with the usages of this office. Say now, you will help to examine papers tomorrow or next day: in short, say now, that in a day or two you will begin to be a little reasonable: — say so, Bartleby."

"At present I would prefer not to be a little reasonable," was his mildly cadaverous reply.

Just then the folding-doors opened, and Nippers approached. He seemed suffering from an unusually bad night's rest, induced by severer indigestion than common. He overheard those final words of Bartleby.

"*Prefer not*, eh?" gritted Nippers — "I'd *prefer* him, if I were you, sir," addressing me — "I'd *prefer* him; I'd give him preferences, the stubborn mule! What is it, sir, pray, that he *prefers* not to do now?"

Bartleby moved not a limb.

"Mr. Nippers," said I, "I'd prefer that you would withdraw for the present."

Somehow, of late, I had got into the way of involuntarily using this word "prefer" upon all sorts of not exactly suitable occasions. And I trembled to think that my contact with the scrivener had already and seriously affected me in a mental way. And what further and deeper aberration might it not yet produce? This apprehension had not been without efficacy in determining me to summary measures.

As Nippers, looking very sour and sulky, was departing, Turkey blandly and deferentially approached.

"With submission, sir," said he, "yesterday I was thinking about Bartleby here, and I think that if he would but prefer to take a quart of good ale every day, it would do much towards mending him, and enabling him to assist in examining his papers."

"So you have got the word, too," said I, slightly excited.

"With submission, what word, sir?" asked Turkey, respectfully crowding himself into the contracted space behind the screen, and by so doing, making me jostle the scrivener. "What word, sir?"

"I would prefer to be left alone here," said Bartleby, as if offended at being mobbed in his at word, sir?" privacy.

"*That*'s the word, Turkey," said I — "*that's* it."

"Oh, *prefer*? oh yes — queer word. I never use it myself. But, sir, as I was saying, if he would but prefer —"

"Turkey," interrupted I, "you will please withdraw."

"Oh certainly, sir, if you prefer that I should."

As he opened the folding-door to retire, Nippers at his desk caught a glimpse of me, and asked whether I would prefer to have a certain paper copied on blue paper or white. He did not in the least roguishly accent the word "prefer." It was plain that it involuntarily rolled from his tongue. I thought to myself, surely I must get rid of a demented man, who already has in some degree turned the tongues, if not the heads of myself and clerks. But I thought it prudent not to break the dismission at once.

The next day I noticed that Bartleby did nothing but stand at his window in his dead-wall revery. Upon asking him why he did not write, he said that he had decided upon doing no more writing.

"Why, how now? what next?" exclaimed I, "do no more writing?"

"No more."

"And what is the reason?"

"Do you not see the reason for yourself?" he indifferently replied.

I looked steadfastly at him, and perceived that his eyes looked dull and glazed. Instantly it occurred to me, that his unexampled diligence in copying by his dim window for the first few weeks of his stay with me might have temporarily impaired his vision.

I was touched. I said something in condolence with him. I hinted that of course he did wisely in abstaining from writing for a while; and urged him to embrace that opportunity of taking wholesome exercise in the open air. This, however, he did not do. A few days after this, my other clerks being absent, and being in a great hurry to dispatch certain letters by the mail, I thought that, having nothing else earthly to do, Bartleby would surely be less inflexible than usual, and carry these letters to the Post Office. But he blankly declined. So, much to my inconvenience, I went myself.

Still added days went by. Whether Bartleby's eyes improved or not, I could not say. To all appearance, I thought they did. But when I asked him if they did, he vouchsafed no answer. At all events, he would do no copying. At last, in replying to my urgings, he informed me that he had permanently given up copying.

"What!" exclaimed I; "suppose your eyes should get entirely well — better than ever before — would you not copy then?"

"I have given up copying," he answered, and slid aside.

He remained as ever, a fixture in my chamber. Nay — if that were possible — he became still more of a fixture than before. What was to be done? He would do nothing in the office; why should he stay there? In plain fact, he had now become a millstone to me, not only useless as a necklace, but afflictive to bear. Yet I was sorry for him. I speak less than truth when I say that, on his own account, he occasioned me uneasiness. If he would but have named a single relative or friend, I would instantly have written, and urged their taking the poor fellow away to some convenient retreat. But he seemed alone, absolutely alone in the universe. A bit of wreck in the mid-Atlantic. At length, necessities connected with my business tyrannized over all other considerations. Decently as I could, I told Bartleby that in six days' time he must unconditionally leave the office. I warned him to take measures, in the interval, for procuring some other abode. I offered to assist him in this endeavor, if he himself would but take the first step towards a removal. "And when you finally quit me, Bartleby," added I, "I shall see that you go not away entirely unprovided. Six days from this hour, remember."

At the expiration of that period, I peeped behind the screen, and lo! Bartleby was there.

I buttoned up my coat, balanced myself; advanced slowly towards him, touched his shoulder, and said, "The time has come; you must quit this place; I am sorry for you; here is money; but you must go."

"I would prefer not," he replied, with his back still towards me.

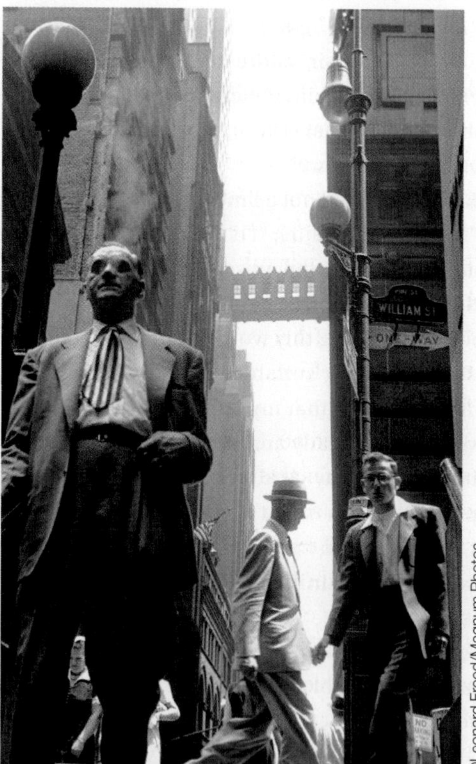

This photograph, taken by Leonard Freed almost a century later in 1956, is entitled *Wall Street, New York*.

What does the perspective of this photograph suggest to you about its setting? How does the image capture the perspective on Wall Street in "Bartleby, the Scrivener"?

"You *must*."

He remained silent.

Now I had an unbounded confidence in this man's common honesty. He had frequently restored to me sixpences and shillings carelessly dropped upon the floor, for I am apt to be very reckless in such shirt-button affairs. The proceeding, then, which followed will not be deemed extraordinary.

145 "Bartleby," said I, "I owe you twelve dollars on account; here are thirty-two, the odd twenty are yours — Will you take it?" and I handed the bills towards him.

But he made no motion.

"I will leave them here, then," putting them under a weight on the table. Then taking my hat and cane and going to the door, I tranquilly turned and added — "After you have removed your things from these offices, Bartleby, you will of course lock the door — since every one is now gone for the day but you — and if you please, slip your key underneath the mat, so that I may have it in the morning. I shall not see you again; so good-bye to you. If, hereafter, in your new place of abode, I can be of any service to you, do not fail to advise me by letter. Good-bye, Bartleby, and fare you well."

But he answered not a word; like the last column of some ruined temple, he remained standing mute and solitary in the middle of the otherwise deserted room.

As I walked home in a pensive mood, my vanity got the better of my pity. I could not but highly plume myself on my masterly management in getting rid of Bartleby. Masterly I call it, and such it must appear to any dispassionate thinker. The beauty of my procedure seemed to consist in its perfect quietness. There was no vulgar bullying, no bravado of any sort, no choleric hectoring, and striding to and fro across the apartment, jerking out vehement commands for Bartleby to bundle himself off with his beggarly traps. Nothing of the kind. Without loudly bidding Bartleby depart — as an inferior genius might have done — I *assumed* the ground that depart he must; and upon that assumption built all I had to say. The more I thought over my procedure, the more I was charmed with it. Nevertheless, next morning, upon awakening, I had my doubts — I had somehow slept off the fumes of vanity. One of the coolest and wisest hours a man has, is just after he awakes in the morning. My procedure seemed as sagacious as ever — but only in theory. How it would prove in practice — there was the rub. It was truly a beautiful thought to have assumed Bartleby's departure; but, after all, that assumption was simply my own, and none of Bartleby's. The great point was, not whether I had assumed that he would quit me, but whether he would prefer to do so. He was more a man of preferences than assumptions.

150 After breakfast, I walked down town, arguing the probabilities pro and con. One moment I thought it would prove a miserable failure, and Bartleby would be found all alive at my office as usual; the next moment it seemed certain that I should find his chair empty. And so I kept veering about. At the corner of Broadway and Canal Street, I saw quite an excited group of people standing in earnest conversation.

"I'll take odds he doesn't," said a voice as I passed.

"Doesn't go? — done!" said I, "put up your money."

I was instinctively putting my hand in my pocket to produce my own, when I remembered that this was an election day. The words I had overheard bore no reference to Bartleby, but to the success or non-success of some candidate for the mayoralty. In my intent frame of mind, I had, as it were, imagined that all Broadway shared in my excitement, and were debating the same question with me. I passed on, very thankful that the uproar of the street screened my momentary absent-mindedness.

As I had intended, I was earlier than usual at my office door. I stood listening for a moment. All was still. He must be gone. I tried the knob.

The door was locked. Yes, my procedure had worked to a charm; he indeed must be vanished. Yet a certain melancholy mixed with this: I was almost sorry for my brilliant success. I was fumbling under the door mat for the key, which Bartleby was to have left there for me, when accidentally my knee knocked against a panel, producing a summoning sound, and in response a voice came to me from within — "Not yet; I am occupied."

It was Bartleby.

I was thunderstruck. For an instant I stood like the man who, pipe in mouth, was killed one cloudless afternoon long ago in Virginia, by summer lightning; at his own warm open window he was killed, and remained leaning out there upon the dreamy afternoon, till some one touched him, when he fell.

"Not gone!" I murmured at last. But again obeying that wondrous ascendancy which the inscrutable scrivener had over me, and from which ascendancy, for all my chafing, I could not completely escape, I slowly went down stairs and out into the street, and while walking round the block, considered what I should next do in this unheard-of perplexity. Turn the man out by an actual thrusting I could not; to drive him away by calling him hard names would not do; calling in the police was an unpleasant idea; and yet, permit him to enjoy his cadaverous triumph over me — this, too, I could not think of. What was to be done? or, if nothing could be done, was there anything further that I could *assume* in the matter? Yes, as before I had prospectively assumed that Bartleby would depart, so now I might retrospectively assume that departed he was. In the legitimate carrying out of this assumption, I might enter my office in a great hurry, and pretending not to see Bartleby at all, walk straight against him as if he were air. Such a proceeding would in a singular degree have the appearance of a home-thrust. It was hardly possible that Bartleby could withstand such an application of the doctrine of assumption. But upon second thoughts the success of the plan seemed rather dubious. I resolved to argue the matter over with him again.

"Bartleby," said I, entering the office, with a quietly severe expression, "I am seriously displeased. I am pained, Bartleby. I had thought better of you. I had imagined you of such a gentlemanly organization, that in any delicate dilemma a slight hint would suffice — in short, an assumption. But it appears I am deceived. Why," I added, unaffectedly starting, "you have not even touched that money yet," pointing to it, just where I had left it the evening previous.

He answered nothing.

Rune Fisker

This illustration by artist Rune Fisker accompanied a 2019 article in *Fast Company* entitled "Everyone hates open offices. Here's why they still exist." **How does this image characterize the relationship between people and their work? How does this interpretation of a more contemporary environment echo the setting of the law offices in "Bartleby, the Scrivener"?**

160 “Will you, or will you not, quit me?” I now demanded in a sudden passion, advancing close to him.

“I would prefer *not* to quit you,” he replied, gently emphasizing the *not*.

“What earthly right have you to stay here? Do you pay any rent? Do you pay my taxes? Or is this property yours?”

He answered nothing.

“Are you ready to go on and write now? Are your eyes recovered? Could you copy a small paper for me this morning? or help examine a few lines? or step round to the Post Office? In a word, will you do anything at all, to give a coloring to your refusal to depart the premises?”

165 He silently retired into his hermitage.

I was now in such a state of nervous resentment that I thought it but prudent to check myself at present from further demonstrations. Bartleby and I were alone. I remembered the tragedy of the unfortunate Adams and the still more unfortunate Colt[13] in the solitary office of the latter; and how poor Colt, being dreadfully incensed by Adams, and imprudently permitting himself to get wildly excited, was at unawares hurried into his fatal act — an act which certainly no man could possibly deplore more than the actor himself. Often it had occurred to me in my ponderings upon the subject that had that altercation taken place in the public street, or at a private residence, it would not have terminated as it did. It was the circumstance of being alone in a solitary office, up stairs, of a building entirely unhallowed by humanizing domestic associations — an uncarpeted office, doubtless, of a dusty, haggard sort of appearance — this it must have been, which greatly helped to enhance the irritable desperation of the hapless Colt.

But when this old Adam of resentment rose in me and tempted me concerning Bartleby, I grappled him and threw him. How? Why, simply by recalling the divine injunction: “A new commandment give I unto you, that ye love one another.” Yes, this it was that saved me. Aside from higher considerations, charity often operates as a vastly wise and prudent principle — a great safeguard to its possessor. Men have committed murder for jealousy’s sake, and anger’s sake, and hatred’s sake, and selfishness’ sake, and spiritual pride’s sake; but no man, that ever I heard of, ever committed a diabolical murder for sweet charity’s sake. Mere self-interest, then, if no better motive can be enlisted, should, especially with high-tempered men, prompt all beings to charity and philanthropy. At any rate, upon the occasion in question, I strove to drown my exasperated feelings towards the scrivener by benevolently construing his conduct. Poor fellow, poor fellow! thought I, he don’t mean anything; and besides, he has seen hard times, and ought to be indulged.

I endeavored, also, immediately to occupy myself, and at the same time to comfort my despondency. I tried to fancy, that in the course of the morning, at such time as might prove agreeable to him, Bartleby, of his own free accord, would emerge from his hermitage and take up some decided line of march in the direction of the door. But no. Half-past twelve o’clock came; Turkey began to glow in the face, overturn his inkstand, and become generally obstreperous; Nippers abated down into quietude and courtesy; Ginger Nut munched his noon apple; and Bartleby remained standing at his window in one of his profoundest dead-wall reveries. Will it be credited? Ought I to acknowledge it? That afternoon I left the office without saying one further word to him.

Some days now passed, during which, at leisure intervals I looked a little into “Edwards on the Will,” and “Priestley on Necessity.”[14]

[13] In a sensational case from 1841, John C. Colt (brother of Samuel Colt, inventor of the revolver) murdered a printer named Samuel Adams. Before his hanging, Colt committed suicide in the Tombs. — Eds.

[14] Jonathan Edwards, in *Freedom of the Will* (1754), and Joseph Priestley, in *Doctrine of Philosophical Necessity* (1777), argued that human beings lack free will. — Eds.

Under the circumstances, those books induced a salutary feeling. Gradually I slid into the persuasion that these troubles of mine, touching the scrivener, had been all predestined from eternity, and Bartleby was billeted upon me for some mysterious purpose of an all-wise Providence, which it was not for a mere mortal like me to fathom. Yes, Bartleby, stay there behind your screen, thought I; I shall persecute you no more; you are harmless and noiseless as any of these old chairs; in short, I never feel so private as when I know you are here. At last I see it, I feel it; I penetrate to the predestined purpose of my life. I am content. Others may have loftier parts to enact; but my mission in this world, Bartleby, is to furnish you with office-room for such period as you may see fit to remain.

I believe that this wise and blessed frame of mind would have continued with me, had it not been for the unsolicited and uncharitable remarks obtruded upon me by my professional friends who visited the rooms. But thus it often is, that the constant friction of illiberal minds wears out at last the best resolves of the more generous. Though to be sure, when I reflected upon it, it was not strange that people entering my office should be struck by the peculiar aspect of the unaccountable Bartleby, and so be tempted to throw out some sinister observations concerning him. Sometimes an attorney, having business with me, and calling at my office, and finding no one but the scrivener there, would undertake to obtain some sort of precise information from him touching my whereabouts; but without heeding his idle talk, Bartleby would remain standing immovable in the middle of the room. So after contemplating him in that position for a time, the attorney would depart, no wiser than he came.

Also, when a reference was going on, and the room full of lawyers and witnesses, and business driving fast, some deeply-occupied legal gentleman present, seeing Bartleby wholly unemployed, would request him to run round to his (the legal gentleman's) office and fetch some papers for him. Thereupon, Bartleby would tranquilly decline, and yet remain idle as before. Then the lawyer would give a great stare, and turn to me. And what could I say? At last I was made aware that all through the circle of my professional acquaintance, a whisper of wonder was running round, having reference to the strange creature I kept at my office. This worried me very much. And as the idea came upon me of his possibly turning out a long-lived man, and keeping occupying my chambers, and denying my authority; and perplexing my visitors; and scandalizing my professional reputation; and casting a general gloom over the premises; keeping soul and body together to the last upon his savings (for doubtless he spent but half a dime a day), and in the end perhaps outlive me, and claim possession of my office by right of his perpetual occupancy: as all these dark anticipations crowded upon me more and more, and my friends continually intruded their relentless remarks upon the apparition in my room; a great change was wrought in me. I resolved to gather all my faculties together, and forever rid me of this intolerable incubus.

Ere revolving any complicated project, however, adapted to this end, I first simply suggested to Bartleby the propriety of his permanent departure. In a calm and serious tone, I commended the idea to his careful and mature consideration. But, having taken three days to meditate upon it, he apprised me, that his original determination remained the same; in short, that he still preferred to abide with me.

What shall I do? I now said to myself, buttoning up my coat to the last button. What shall I do? what ought I to do? what does conscience say I *should* do with this man, or, rather, ghost. Rid myself of him, I must; go, he shall. But how? You will not thrust him, the poor, pale, passive mortal—you will not thrust such a helpless creature out of your door? you will not dishonor yourself by such cruelty? No, I will not, I cannot do that. Rather would I let him live and die here, and then mason up his remains in the wall. What, then, will you do? For all your coaxing, he will not budge. Bribes he leaves under your own paper-weight on your table; in short, it is quite plain that he prefers to cling to you.

Then something severe, something unusual must be done. What! surely you will not have him collared by a constable, and commit his innocent pallor to the common jail? And upon what ground could you procure such a thing to be done? — a vagrant, is he? What! he a vagrant, a wanderer, who refuses to budge? It is because he will *not* be a vagrant, then, that you seek to count him *as* a vagrant. That is too absurd. No visible means of support: there I have him. Wrong again: for indubitably he *does* support himself, and that is the only unanswerable proof that any man can show of his possessing the means so to do. No more, then. Since he will not quit me, I must quit him. I will change my offices; I will move elsewhere, and give him fair notice, that if I find him on my new premises I will then proceed against him as a common trespasser.

Acting accordingly, next day I thus addressed him: "I find these chambers too far from the City Hall; the air is unwholesome. In a word, I propose to remove my offices next week, and shall no longer require your services. I tell you this now, in order that you may seek another place."

He made no reply, and nothing more was said.

On the appointed day I engaged carts and men, proceeded to my chambers, and having but little furniture, everything was removed in a few hours. Throughout, the scrivener remained standing behind the screen, which I directed to be removed the last thing. It was withdrawn; and, being folded up like a huge folio, left him the motionless occupant of a naked room. I stood in the entry watching him a moment, while something from within me upbraided me.

I re-entered, with my hand in my pocket — and — and my heart in my mouth.

"Good-bye, Bartleby; I am going — good-bye, and God some way bless you; and take that," slipping something in his hand. But it dropped upon the floor, and then — strange to say — I tore myself from him whom I had so longed to be rid of.

Established in my new quarters, for a day or two I kept the door locked, and started at every footfall in the passages. When I returned to my rooms, after any little absence, I would pause at the threshold for an instant, and attentively listen, ere applying my key. But these fears were needless. Bartleby never came nigh me.

I thought all was going well, when a perturbed-looking stranger visited me, inquiring whether I was the person who had recently occupied rooms at No. —— Wall Street.

Full of forebodings, I replied that I was.

"Then, sir," said the stranger, who proved a lawyer, "you are responsible for the man you left there. He refuses to do any copying; he refuses to do anything; he says he prefers not to; and he refuses to quit the premises."

"I am very sorry, sir," said I, with assumed tranquillity, but an inward tremor, "but, really, the man you allude to is nothing to me — he is no relation or apprentice of mine, that you should hold me responsible for him."

"In mercy's name, who is he?"

"I certainly cannot inform you. I know nothing about him. Formerly I employed him as a copyist; but he has done nothing for me now for some time past."

"I shall settle him, then — good morning, sir."

Several days passed, and I heard nothing more; and, though I often felt a charitable prompting to call at the place and see poor Bartleby, yet a certain squeamishness, of I know not what, withheld me.

extending beyond the text

Passive resistance, an aspect of nonviolent protest, can be a strategy to achieve social justice. It was the favored strategy of the civil rights movement leader Martin Luther King Jr. and a tactic used by many who participated in protests for civil rights during the 1950s and 1960s. This photograph shows activist Rosa Parks sitting in the front of a bus in Montgomery, Alabama, after the Supreme Court ruled segregation illegal on the city bus system on December 21, 1956. Parks was arrested over a year earlier, on December 1, 1955, for refusing to give up her seat on one of the city's then-segregated buses. Following her arrest, Black citizens in Montgomery launched a boycott of the city's bus system that lasted for over a year.

Bettmann/Getty Images

1. **How does the composition of this photograph re-create Parks's use of passive resistance for viewers?**
2. **Since passive resistance is often the strategy chosen by those who lack official authority or power, it has been described as "the weapon of the weak." Is Bartleby weak? Who has — and who lacks — power in this story? How — and for what purpose — does Bartleby weaponize his resistance to the narrator?**
3. **What makes passive resistance an effective form of rebellion or protest? Consider possibilities in the context of social justice movements, both past and present, as well as in "Bartleby, the Scrivener."**

All is over with him, by this time, thought I, at last, when, through another week, no further intelligence reached me. But, coming to my room the day after, I found several persons waiting at my door in a high state of nervous excitement.

"That's the man — here he comes," cried the foremost one, whom I recognized as the lawyer who had previously called upon me alone.

"You must take him away, sir, at once," cried a portly person among them, advancing upon me, and whom I knew to be the landlord of No. —— Wall Street. "These gentlemen, my tenants, cannot stand it any longer; Mr. B——," pointing to the lawyer, "has turned him out of his room, and he now persists in haunting the building generally, sitting upon the banisters of the stairs by day, and sleeping in the entry by night. Everybody is concerned; clients are leaving the offices; some fears are entertained of a mob; something you must do, and that without delay."

Aghast at this torrent, I fell back before it, and would fain have locked myself in my new quarters. In vain I persisted that Bartleby was nothing to me — no more than to any one else. In vain — I was the last person known to have anything to do with him, and they held me to the terrible account. Fearful, then, of being exposed in the papers (as one person present obscurely threatened), I considered the matter, and, at length, said, that if the lawyer would give me a confidential interview with the scrivener, in his (the lawyer's) own room, I would, that afternoon, strive my best to rid them of the nuisance they complained of.

Going up stairs to my old haunt, there was Bartleby silently sitting upon the banister at the landing.

"What are you doing here, Bartleby?" said I.

"Sitting upon the banister," he mildly replied.

I motioned him into the lawyer's room, who then left us.

"Bartleby," said I, "are you aware that you are the cause of great tribulation to me, by persisting in occupying the entry after being dismissed from the office?"

No answer.

"Now one of two things must take place. Either you must do something, or something must be done to you. Now what sort of business would you like to engage in? Would you like to re-engage in copying for some one?"

"No; I would prefer not to make any change."

"Would you like a clerkship in a dry-goods store?"

"There is too much confinement about that. No, I would not like a clerkship; but I am not particular."

"Too much confinement," I cried, "why, you keep yourself confined all the time!"

"I would prefer not to take a clerkship," he rejoined, as if to settle that little item at once.

"How would a bar-tender's business suit you? There is no trying of the eye-sight in that."

"I would not like it at all; though, as I said before, I am not particular."

His unwonted wordiness inspirited me. I returned to the charge.

"Well, then, would you like to travel through the country collecting bills for the merchants? That would improve your health."

"No, I would prefer to be doing something else."

"How, then, would going as a companion to Europe, to entertain some young gentleman with your conversation—how would that suit you?"

"Not at all. It does not strike me that there is anything definite about that. I like to be stationary. But I am not particular."

"Stationary you shall be, then," I cried, now losing all patience, and, for the first time in all my exasperating connection with him, fairly flying into a passion. "If you do not go away from these premises before night, I shall feel bound—indeed, I *am* bound—to—to quit the premises myself!" I rather absurdly concluded, knowing not with what possible threat to try to frighten his immobility into compliance. Despairing of all further efforts, I was precipitately leaving him, when a final thought occurred to me—one which had not been wholly unindulged before.

"Bartleby," said I, in the kindest tone I could assume under such exciting circumstances, "will you go home with me now—not to my office, but my dwelling—and remain there till we can conclude upon some convenient arrangement for you at our leisure? Come, let us start now, right away."

"No: at present I would prefer not to make any change at all."

I answered nothing; but, effectually dodging every one by the suddenness and rapidity of my flight, rushed from the building, ran up Wall Street towards Broadway, and, jumping into the first omnibus, was soon removed from pursuit. As soon as tranquillity returned, I distinctly perceived that I had now done all that I possibly could, both in respect to the demands of the landlord and his tenants, and with regard to my own desire and sense of duty, to benefit Bartleby, and shield him from rude persecution. I now strove to be entirely care-free and quiescent; and my conscience justified me in the attempt; though, indeed, it was not so successful as I could have wished. So fearful was I of being again hunted out by the incensed landlord and his exasperated tenants, that, surrendering my business to Nippers, for a few days, I drove about the upper part of the town and through the suburbs, in my rockaway; crossed over to Jersey

City and Hoboken, and paid fugitive visits to Manhattanville and Astoria. In fact, I almost lived in my rockaway for the time.

When again I entered my office, lo, a note from the landlord lay upon the desk. I opened it with trembling hands. It informed me that the writer had sent to the police, and had Bartleby removed to the Tombs as a vagrant. Moreover, since I knew more about him than any one else, he wished me to appear at that place, and make a suitable statement of the facts. These tidings had a conflicting effect upon me. At first I was indignant; but, at last, almost approved. The landlord's energetic, summary disposition, had led him to adopt a procedure which I do not think I would have decided upon myself; and yet, as a last resort, under such peculiar circumstances, it seemed the only plan.

As I afterwards learned, the poor scrivener, when told that he must be conducted to the Tombs, offered not the slightest obstacle, but, in his pale, unmoving way, silently acquiesced.

Some of the compassionate and curious by-standers joined the party; and headed by one of the constables arm-in-arm with Bartleby, the silent procession filed its way through all the noise, and heat, and joy of the roaring thoroughfares at noon.

The same day I received the note, I went to the Tombs, or, to speak more properly, the Halls of Justice. Seeking the right officer, I stated the purpose of my call, and was informed that the individual I described was, indeed, within. I then assured the functionary that Bartleby was a perfectly honest man, and greatly to be compassionated, however unaccountably eccentric. I narrated all I knew, and closed by suggesting the idea of letting him remain in as indulgent confinement as possible, till something less harsh might be done — though, indeed, I hardly knew what. At all events, if nothing else could be decided upon, the almshouse must receive him. I then begged to have an interview.

Being under no disgraceful charge, and quite 220
serene and harmless in all his ways, they had permitted him freely to wander about the prison, and, especially, in the inclosed grass-platted yards thereof. And so I found him there, standing all alone in the quietest of the yards, his face towards a high wall, while all around, from the narrow slits of the jail windows, I thought I saw peering out upon him the eyes of murderers and thieves.

"Bartleby!"

"I know you," he said, without looking round — "and I want nothing to say to you."

"It was not I that brought you here, Bartleby," said I, keenly pained at his implied suspicion. "And to you, this should not be so vile a place. Nothing reproachful attaches to you by being here. And see, it is not so sad a place as one might think. Look, there is the sky, and here is the grass."

"I know where I am," he replied, but would say nothing more, and so I left him.

As I entered the corridor again, a broad 225
meat-like man, in an apron, accosted me, and, jerking his thumb over his shoulder, said — "Is that your friend?"

"Yes."

"Does he want to starve? If he does, let him live on the prison fare, that's all."

"Who are you?" asked I, not knowing what to make of such an unofficially speaking person in such a place.

"I am the grub-man. Such gentlemen as have friends here, hire me to provide them with something good to eat."

"Is this so?" said I, turning the turnkey. 230
He said it was.

"Well, then," said I, slipping some silver into the grub-man's hands (for so they called him), "I want you to give particular attention to my friend there; let him have the best dinner you can get. And you must be as polite to him as possible."

"Introduce me, will you?" said the grub-man, looking at me with an expression which seemed to say he was all impatience for an opportunity to give a specimen of his breeding.

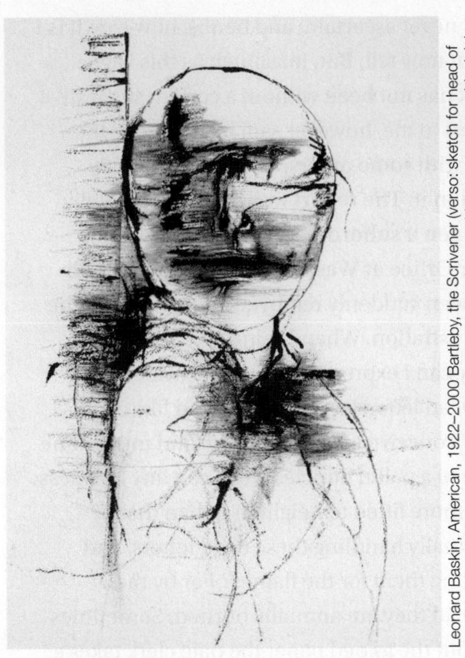

Leonard Baskin, American, 1922–2000 Bartleby, the Scrivener (verso: sketch for head of Bartleby), ca. 1959 R: pen and brush and black ink on heavy white wove paper v: black ink. Sheet: 560 × 783 mm (22 1/16 × 30 13/16 in.)69.30.10a-b. Memorial gift from Dr. T. Edward and Tullah Hanley, Bradford, Pennsylvania. Fine Arts Museums of San Francisco. With permission by Estate of Leonard Baskin

This sketch of Bartleby the Scrivener was completed by artist Leonard Baskin in 1959.

What is most striking to you about this depiction? In what ways does it capture key qualities of the character in Melville's story?

Thinking it would prove of benefit to the scrivener, I acquiesced; and, asking the grub-man his name, went up with him to Bartleby.

"Bartleby, this is a friend; you will find him very useful to you."

"Your sarvant, sir, your sarvant," said the grub-man, making a low salutation behind his apron. "Hope you find it pleasant here, sir; nice grounds — cool apartments — hope you'll stay with us some time — try to make it agreeable. What will you have for dinner to-day?"

"I prefer not to dine to-day," said Bartleby, turning away. "It would disagree with me; I am unused to dinners." So saying, he slowly moved to the other side of the inclosure, and took up a position fronting the deadwall.

"How's this?" said the grub-man, addressing me with a stare of astonishment. "He's odd, ain't he?"

"I think he is a little deranged," said I, sadly.

"Deranged? deranged is it? Well, now, upon my word, I thought that friend of yourn was a gentleman forger; they are always pale and genteel-like, them forgers. I can't help pity 'em — can't help it, sir. Did you know Monroe Edwards?" he added, touchingly, and paused. Then, laying his hand piteously on my shoulder, sighed, "he died of consumption at Sing-Sing. So you weren't acquainted with Monroe?"

"No, I was never socially acquainted with any forgers. But I cannot stop longer. Look to my friend yonder. You will not lose by it. I will see you again."

Some few days after this, I again obtained admission to the Tombs, and went through the corridors in quest of Bartleby; but without finding him.

"I saw him coming from his cell not long ago," said a turnkey, "may be he's gone to loiter in the yards."

So I went in that direction.

"Are you looking for the silent man?" said another turnkey, passing me. "Yonder he lies — sleeping in the yard there. 'Tis not twenty minutes since I saw him lie down."

The yard was entirely quiet. It was not accessible to the common prisoners. The surrounding walls, of amazing thickness, kept off all sounds behind them. The Egyptian character of the masonry weighed upon me with its gloom. But a soft imprisoned turf grew under foot. The heart of the eternal pyramids, it seemed, wherein, by some strange magic, through the clefts, grass-seed, dropped by birds, had sprung.

Strangely huddled at the base of the wall, his knees drawn up, and lying on his side, his head touching the cold stones, I saw the wasted Bartleby. But nothing stirred. I paused; then went close up to him; stooped over, and saw that his dim eyes were open; otherwise he seemed profoundly sleeping. Something prompted me to touch him. I felt his hand, when a tingling shiver ran up my arm and down my spine to my feet.

The round face of the grub-man peered upon me now. "His dinner is ready. Won't he dine to-day, either? Or does he live without dining?"

"Lives without dining," said I, and closed the eyes.

"Eh! — He's asleep, ain't he?"

"With kings and counselors,"[15] murmured I.

There would seem little need for proceeding further in this history. Imagination will readily supply the meagre recital of poor Bartleby's interment. But, ere parting with the reader, let me say, that if this little narrative has sufficiently interested him, to awaken curiosity as to who Bartleby was, and what manner of life he led prior to the present narrator's making his acquaintance, I can only reply, that in such curiosity I fully share, but am wholly unable to gratify it. Yet here I hardly know whether I should divulge one little item of rumor, which came to my ear a few months after the scrivener's decease. Upon what basis it rested, I could never ascertain; and hence, how true it is I cannot now tell. But, inasmuch as this vague report has not been without a certain suggestive interest to me, however sad, it may prove the same with some others; and so I will briefly mention it. The report was this: that Bartleby had been a subordinate clerk in the Dead Letter Office at Washington, from which he had been suddenly removed by a change in the
250 administration. When I think over this rumor, hardly can I express the emotions which seize me. Dead letters! does it not sound like dead men? Conceive a man by nature and misfortune prone to a pallid hopelessness, can any business seem more fitted to heighten it than that of continually handling these dead letters, and assorting them for the flames? For by the cart-load they are annually burned. Sometimes from out the folded paper the pale clerk takes a ring — the finger it was meant for, perhaps, moulders in the grave; a bank-note sent in swiftest charity — he whom it would relieve, nor eats nor hungers any more; pardon for those who died despairing; hope for those who died unhoping; good tidings for those who died stifled by unrelieved calamities. On errands of life, these letters speed to death.

Ah, Bartleby! Ah, humanity! ■

1853

[15] From Job 3:13–14: "then had I been at rest, / With kings and counselors of the earth, / which built desolate places for themselves." — Eds.

Understanding and Interpreting

1. What effect does the opening paragraph have on you as a reader? What information do you learn?
2. The narrator's description of his three clerks — Turkey, Nippers, and Ginger Nut — might be summarized as a list of assets and liabilities, or credits and debits. What are the pluses and minuses of these characters, as Herman Melville presents them? What comparisons does he draw between and among the three workers? How do they set the stage for the introduction of Bartleby?
3. How and why does Bartleby's "passive resistance" (par. 55) stymie the lawyer-narrator? How do Bartleby's "preferences" make their way into the culture of the narrator's law office?
4. The narrator tells us that Bartleby "was more a man of preferences than assumptions" (par. 149). How does this worldview differ from the legal profession's belief in precedents and assumptions?

5. In paragraph 86, the narrator explains, "As days passed on, I became considerably reconciled to Bartleby." Why? What causes him to accommodate Bartleby rather than simply insisting that he leave the job and the office? Do you think the narrator truly feels the "bond of a common humanity" (par. 91)? Explain.
6. What do we know about the narrator's circumstances outside of the office? In your response consider the details the narrator provides or withholds about where he lives, how he spends his time, whether he has a family, where he grew up, and so on. How do these details — or lack thereof — work together to characterize the narrator?
7. When the narrator visits the Tombs, Bartleby tells him, "I know you, . . . and I want nothing to say to you" (par. 222). What does he mean by this? What change does this show in Bartleby's character as the story has progressed?
8. What is the main conflict in the story between the narrator and Bartleby? Is it a struggle for someone to understand a person entirely unlike himself? A struggle for power or dominance? A struggle to treat others with dignity regardless of whether you like them? Or something else? Explain, using evidence from the text to support your response.

Analyzing Language, Style, and Structure

1. **Vocabulary in Context.** In paragraph 52, Melville writes, "Meanwhile Bartleby sat in his hermitage, oblivious to everything but his own peculiar business there." What is the literal meaning of *hermitage*? How do the associations with the word contribute to an understanding of the narrator's attitude toward Bartleby? Consider repeated references to "hermitage" throughout the story in your response.
2. How does the opening paragraph embody "lawyerly language" — that is, language filled with qualifications and disclaimers?
3. The narrator introduces Bartleby as "a motionless young man . . . pallidly neat, pitiably respectable, incurably forlorn!" (par. 17). How does he expand this description as the story develops? How does this initial characterization foreshadow Bartleby's end?
4. What significance does the subtitle, "A Story of Wall Street," have? Consider the symbolic significance of the walls in the office, the windows and views (or lack of them), and the Tombs that Melville describes. Pay particular attention to paragraph 19.
5. The narrator characterizes himself as living the philosophy that "the easiest way of life is the best" (par. 2). Does the narrator grow in self-awareness or deteriorate into self-delusion? How do you interpret his statement, "In vain I persisted that Bartleby was nothing to me — no more than to any one else" (par. 192)?
6. How do the narrator's various decisions about how to respond to Bartleby structure the plot of the story? Identify at least four different shifts through the sequence of events that contribute to your interpretation of the story.
7. At the end of the story, the narrator offers the possibility that Bartleby's rejection of life has been brought on by his working in the Dead Letter Office, a place where mail with inscrutable or partial addresses is ultimately destroyed? How does the concept of the Dead Letter Office function as a symbol?
8. How does Melville use literary elements to characterize the narrator's response to Bartleby's behavior? Do the narrator's actions reflect his profession? Identify one specific passage in the story to support your response.
9. What elements in the story foreshadow its ending, both the central character's imprisonment and his death? For instance, notice descriptive references to Bartleby that use language suggestive of ghost, cadaver, or shadow.

10. Melville makes allusions to Christianity and the Bible, specifically focusing on the narrator's view of himself as someone who lives according to Christian doctrine of charity and forgiveness. What complications of character and viewpoint do these elements introduce in the story?
11. Food imagery and eating habits are prominent in the story. How do these descriptions contribute to the development of character, plot, and ultimately overall meaning? Cite specific passages and references to explain your interpretation.
12. Humor, though often subtle and ironic, runs throughout the story. What examples of humor can you identify, and how do they work as commentary or characterization?

Topics for Composing

1. AP® FRQ **Prose Fiction Analysis.** The following question refers to paragraphs 19–27 of Herman Melville's "Bartleby, the Scrivener: A Story of Wall Street," published in 1853. In this passage, the narrator describes his working arrangement with his scrivener Bartleby and the man's response. Read the passage carefully. Then, in a well-written essay, analyze how Melville uses literary elements and techniques to develop the complex relationship between the two characters.
2. AP® FRQ **Literary Argument.** The narrator of a literary work is often a complex character whose perspective controls how readers experience and interpret the events of the narrative. In "Bartleby, the Scrivener: A Story of Wall Street," understanding the limitations of the narrator's perspective is essential to interpreting the significance of Bartleby's behavior. In a well-written essay, analyze how the narrator's values and motivations shape the themes of the story and contribute to an interpretation of the work as a whole. Do not merely summarize the plot.
3. **AP® Literary Argumentation.** How and whether a character changes is often the focus of a literary work. How does Bartleby develop, evolve, or even devolve during the course of the story? What do you think Melville wants his readers to explore or understand through this character's choices? Discuss how your response to these questions influences your interpretation of the meaning of the story as a whole.
4. **AP® Literary Argumentation.** How do money, materialism, and capitalism itself inform this story? Consider the way cities were at that time changing the sense of community as people moved from a more rural environment to an industrial urban setting.
5. **Speaking and Listening.** As the narrator tries to come to terms with how he should deal with Bartleby, he explores both the logic of the law and the faith of religion for guidance. Another way to think of this dichotomy is through the lens of justice and mercy. Ultimately, which perspective on how to act is upheld in Melville's tale? Working in two teams, each assigned to one approach, discuss and develop support; then, stage a debate arguing for which most reflects your interpretation of the story.
6. **Research.** Occupy Wall Street was a protest movement against economic inequality that began in New York City's financial district in 2011. After you research the goals and impact of this movement, consider how "Bartleby, the Scrivener" predicts or illustrates the issues Occupy Wall Street raised over 150 years later. What accounts for the staying power that these issues have?
7. **Connections.** Bartleby's behavior can be read as a form of passive resistance. While passive resistance may refer to nonviolent protest against laws, known as civil disobedience, it can also refer to the behavior of an individual who defies rules or expectations indirectly or tacitly without overt confrontation. Describe a situation in which someone used passive resistance to achieve a desired outcome. You may base your description on your own experience or that of someone you observed.

Lulu

Te-Ping Chen

Lucas Foglia

Te-Ping Chen (b. 1985) is a fiction writer and journalist based in Philadelphia. A graduate of Brown University, she currently works for the *Wall Street Journal* and has reported from Beijing and Hong Kong. "Lulu," which was published in the *New Yorker* in 2019, is one of the stories in her collection *Land of Big Numbers*.

KEY CONTEXT China is home to the world's largest online gaming community. The internet is also strictly censored by a surveillance and content control system called the Great Firewall of China, which not only blocks website content but can also monitor individual access. Many people circumvent such censorship through proxy servers outside the firewall, by using secure virtual private network (VPN) or secure shell (SSH) connections from computers elsewhere in the world. While there have been recent crackdowns on these workarounds — Apple, for example, is no longer allowed to sell VPN apps that are not pre-approved by the government — many internet users in China continue to bypass the censors.

The hour of our birth had been carefully forecast, a winter's day Cesarean timed to coincide with Dr. Feng's lunch break. The doctor pulled me out first, indignant and squalling, like a hotel guest roused and tossed before checkout. Lulu came next, and was so perfectly quiet that at first they thought she wasn't breathing at all. Then they thwacked her on the back and her cries joined mine and they laid us side by side, boy and girl, two underwater creatures suddenly forced to fill our lungs with cold dry air.

Dr. Feng had operated on our mother as a favor to our uncle, his old classmate. Otherwise we would have been born in the hospital down the street, where a woman had bled to death after a botched Cesarean the previous year. The family had been in the waiting room for hours, and at last the father-to-be pounded on the doors of the operating room. When no one responded, the family pushed them open to find the lifeless woman on the table, blood pooling on the ground. She was alone: the staff had stripped the medical certificates that bore their names from the wall and fled as soon as the surgery went wrong.

From the start we were lucky, not least because we had each other. As twins we'd been spared the reach of the government's family-planning policies.[1] For the first few weeks of our life, our skulls had matching indentations from where they'd been pressed against each other in the womb, like two interlocking puzzle pieces. Later in life, when we were apart, I used to touch my hand to the back of my skull when I thought of her, as if seeking a phantom limb.

We weren't in any way an extraordinary family. My mother worked as a warehouse clerk, my father as a government sanitation planner. When he was forty-seven, his division chief — a fanciful man who once dreamed of being an artist — decided to build a public toilet in the shape of a European clock tower. He'd been to Europe and had been impressed by the cleanliness of the toilets and the loveliness of the architecture and wanted to combine the two. Like most artists, the division chief had a fragile

[1] A reference to China's "one child" policy, which limited Chinese families to just one child per family from the 1970s through 2015. As of 2015, parents are allowed to have two children per family. — Eds.

ego, and shortly after my father balked at the project's expense he was fired. It was the sole act of independence he'd committed in his life, and it cost him his career.

5 From the time Lulu was ten, my parents worshipped at her altar. Her precocity was evident early on; it was like a flag being waved energetically from a mountaintop. Neither of our parents had much education, and it stunned them to find themselves in possession of such a daughter.

When we were small, we played devotedly together. Lulu was a great inventor of games, which often incorporated whatever she'd read most recently: one day we were stinkbugs looking for the right leaf on which to lay our eggs; another we were herdsmen fleeing Mongolian invaders. She was braver than me; once, she even snuck into the apartment of the elderly woman who lived opposite us and had left her door ajar while retrieving the mail downstairs.

"It's full of newspapers, stacked as high as your head," Lulu said excitedly, eyes glowing as she dashed back to our apartment. "There's a giant orange cross-stitch on the couch, with a peony and six fishes."

As a child she was always reading: even at meals she would sit and scan the back of the juice box. She must have read it a million times, aspartame and xanthan gum and red No. 9. It wasn't a conscious thing — she just seemed to feel uncomfortable when her eyes weren't fastened to a page. She had a mania for lists, too. By eleven she'd memorized every bone in the human body, and she used to recite their names to me at night in an eerie voice as I held a pillow over my head: sternum, tibia, floating rib.

In high school, I rebelled against her brilliance by playing video games, lots of them, spending hours whipping a gun back and forth across dusty landscapes empty of people, except for those who wanted to kill you. Usually there were six or seven of us at my friend Xingjian's apartment,

Craig Lovell/Alamy

Skeleton dances, in costumes such as these, allude to the impermanence of life and possessions. In this photograph, two skeleton dancers perform at Katok Monastery in the Sichuan province of China.
What message do these costumes convey? What do the references to the human skeleton in "Lulu" suggest about the relationship between the twins and even Lulu's precocity?

and we would take turns and cheer one another on. We were an army, invincible, or if we weren't invincible we could hit Replay at any time, which was pretty close to the same thing.

10 Lulu, meanwhile, was a model among model students. She studied so intensely that it left her physically bowed and exhausted, like an athlete running a daily marathon, and at night she dropped off to sleep without a word. My mother fed her stewed mushrooms that looked like tiny brains when their stems fell off — they would be good for Lulu's studies, she said. She gave me

some as well, though by then it was plain that any hopes for academic glory resided with her daughter, not her son, the constructive effects of mushrooms be damned.

When we sat for the college-entrance exam, it surprised no one that Lulu scored high enough to earn a place at a university in the nation's capital, a bus and a train and a plane ride away. My mother wept with what she said was happiness. "A scholar," she kept saying. "A scholar." She and my father, she liked to remind us, hadn't studied long before going to work in the factories.

"We are so proud," my father told Lulu. There was an intensity to his expression that unnerved me. One of our schoolbooks had a black-and-white illustration of a long-ago eunuch serving a feast, staring hungrily at the food on the emperor's table, and there was something of that look on my father's face.

The night Lulu left was overcast, the twilight that preceded it a peculiar mixture of orange and ochre. Earlier that day, my father had given her a gift: her very own laptop. It was thick with promise, like a fat slice of cake, sheathed in blue plastic. It wasn't like the old computer that we all shared, which stuttered and stalled, its keys sticky with grease and crumbs and bits of hair. This one had keys that yielded obediently when you touched them. I'd stared at it enviously, too filled with longing for words. "Don't worry, you'll get one, too, when you leave, the exact same," my father said.

At the airport, our parents assumed expressions appropriate for refugees being abandoned at a border. "Lulu, be good," my father said. I stood there awkwardly, a little resentfully. Lulu turned and flashed a peace sign as she went through security, and we watched her pink hoodie and striped zebra baseball hat retreat into the crowd until she was gone.

• • •

I departed for college a week later, with considerably less fanfare. The school was just an hour's drive away and had an empty feel to it, as though it had been erected with much ambition years ago and then forgotten. In the winter the dorms were freezing, as if their concrete walls held in all the damp, cold air and kept it close to your skin.

The best thing about college, I decided, was that the dorms were wired for the Internet. There were five other boys in our room on the second floor, sharing rickety metal bunk beds draped with mosquito nets, which afforded both a thin sense of privacy and protection from bites in the summer. At night, when we sat in front of our computers, you could hear the same tinny chirping of chat alerts all around you, emanating from the floorboards, the ceilings, and the walls, as though hordes of invisible, electronic crickets had stormed the building.

I wasn't old enough to miss Lulu. Anyway, I could see her chat statuses whenever I logged in on my new laptop, smooth and shiny and housed in a blue plastic sleeve just like my sister's. *Studying,* they might say. *Going to class.* At some point they got more fanciful. *Floating down the green river,* one read. *Digging into a stone with no edges.* Sometimes, bored while waiting for my gamer teammates to log on, I looked them up. A few belonged to old poets, but the rest, I suspected, she was inventing herself.

I died repeatedly that semester, but amassed several hundred gold coins and was made first a warlock, then a mage. The other boys in my dorm were addicts, too, and we played fiercely into the evening, cussing, headphones on, until midnight, when the power was cut. Classes were a negligible affair: what mattered was your grade on the final exams, and those could readily be crammed for by memorizing ten or fifteen pages of mimeographed notes sold by upperclassmen. Honestly, I had no idea who actually went to class: I pictured teachers sitting with their laptops in front of empty rooms, one eye on the clock, maybe playing video games of their own, maybe taking a nap.

In our second year of school, I searched idly for one of Lulu's statuses and found just one result: a public microblog with a profile photo featuring a yawning yellow cat. There were several dozen posts, mostly the same kinds of snippets of poetry that Lulu had been posting to her statuses, and by the time I finished scrolling through them I was sure the account was hers. For the bio she'd written *qiushi*, a reference to the old Communist maxim "to seek truth from facts," but the name of her account was *qiu zhushi*, "to seek carbohydrates," which made me laugh. You wouldn't have suspected it to look at her, but Lulu was a glutton — she could eat reams of noodles or fried crullers without missing a beat.

One day in the dorm, I answered a knock at our door to find a classmate grinning at me. "Your sister's here," he said. I gaped and went downstairs. There she was, wearing an old-fashioned padded blue coat, the kind common in the fifties. Lulu had her hair in two braids, carried a knapsack slung over one shoulder, and was smiling. She'd joined the college debate club, she said, and they were travelling for a competition. "Big Brother," she said — it was an old joke of hers, since I was born only a minute or so before her — "want to buy me dinner?"

I suggested the cafeteria. She said she had something nicer in mind, and took me by the arm to a coffee shop near the campus entrance. The place called itself Pretty O.J.; its sign advertised Italian noodles. I'd walked by dozens of times and never gone in. Inside, the tables were topped with glass and the seats were an uncomfortable white wicker that crackled when you shifted and there were white vases to match, filled with plastic flowers. Lulu took hold of the menu and confidently ordered a pizza and tomato pasta for us as though she'd done it many times before. "With coffee, please," she added, "and bring us some bread."

I stared at her. "You look happy," I said. She was. She was debating at a college an hour's drive south, she said, and had taken a bus to come and see me. I asked her if our parents knew, if she was planning to see them as well.

"No," she said, smiling. "We fly back tomorrow night, but I wanted to see you."

Beside her I felt very young in my rubber slippers and T-shirt and shorts. She asked me about my classes and my friends. I told her that I was watching a lot of television on my laptop and playing even more video games. Lately, I'd been playing with a team of Russian teen-agers who were pretty good. We didn't speak the same language, so we communicated in a kind of pidgin English: *don't worry guys I got phantom princess no no no, you NOOB, dafuq.*

"I know you think it's a waste of time," I said.

"A lot of kids play it at my school, too," she said, not contradicting me.

"It's a profession now, you know," I said. "They have competitions, you can win big prize money."

It embarrasses me now to realize that, up until that point, we'd spent the whole evening talking about my life. I don't think I asked her anything about her own, and it was only at the end of our dinner that she volunteered a few facts. She was pregnant, she said, two months along, and very much in love with the baby's father.

I choked on the coffee. Lulu waited for me to compose myself, and then she told me the rest of the story. The father, an upperclassman studying accounting, was from a poor county in the northeast. No, they weren't keeping the baby, though she and Zhangwei would likely get pregnant again in a few years, "after we're married," Lulu said, with a calm matter-of-factness that astounded me. Someday, the two of them hoped to travel abroad.

She told me more about him, choosing her words carefully. "He's not like other people," she said at last. "He's very noble." It was a strange word, an old-fashioned word. I just stared at her.

"You're sure about all this, Lulu?"

"I'm sure."

I envied her for a moment, sitting there looking so certain. When had I ever been sure of anything? For Lulu, everything had always come so easily and confidently: homework, answers on tests, college, and now, it seemed, love as well.

When the bill arrived, I didn't have enough money with me, so she paid. "Thanks, Big Brother," she said when we left, and at first I thought she was being sarcastic, but she looked glad when she said it. "I haven't told anyone else," she confessed as we walked out into the blue twilight, the boxy concrete façades of the campus around us. "I knew I could trust you."

This was the first time it had occurred to me that I was trustworthy, and it was a relief to hear that I had been evaluated and not found wanting. "Of course," I said.

• • •

In the following months, I checked her account more often. I got flashes of insight into her life that way: photos of the yellow shocks of forsythia that blossomed in the spring, more odd bits of poetry. I pictured her tapping away at her identical, blue-sheathed laptop across the country, clicking *Send*.

That fall, she started posting daily about someone named Xu Lei. It was a name that even I'd heard by then, enough people were talking about him. He was a college student who'd been picked up by the police outside a karaoke joint, and been beaten, and died while in custody. Photos of him before his death had circulated online: skinny legs in shorts, glasses, a purple T-shirt that read "Let's Go." He and his friends had been standing outside after singing karaoke, a little drunk, and when the police told them to move along Xu Lei got caustic and the officers took offense. His friends had filmed them beating him and then loading him into a police van. As quickly as censors took down the footage, it was uploaded again.

Mostly, Lulu was just sharing other people's messages, adding her own hashtag #justiceforXuLei or an indignant frowning face. At some point, she added her own commentary: "This country, these police, are simply too dark."

When the police autopsy came out, it found that Xu Lei had died of a heart attack. The conclusion was promptly met with scorn — he was only eighteen. The coroner's report said that, prior to his death, he'd been working hard and not sleeping well. "It was a young person's heart attack," it concluded, a phrase that quickly

Navesh Chitrakar/Reuters/Newscom

In this photograph of a 2020 demonstration in Hong Kong, which is a special administrative region of China, a protester wears a Guy Fawkes mask. Named for an Englishman behind the failed Gunpowder Plot to blow up the House of Lords in 1605, the masks protect the identity of the protesters and show commitment to a shared cause.

What does the Guy Fawkes figure in the foreground suggest? How does the image here evoke the mood of the protests in "Lulu"?

trended online until censors snuffed it out. Lulu was not impressed. "I have studied hard all my life and I don't sleep well," she wrote. "Will I, too, be made to have a heart attack?"

After that, Lulu's account became more active. At first she was just reposting news from other accounts: the tainted-formula scandal that killed three babies, the college-admissions administrator found to be taking cash bribes — the kinds of things we all knew and groused about.

A few months after that, though, she began to flood her account with images and videos that were genuinely surprising. I had no idea where she was getting them. They were of scattered street protests from around the country, some just stills, others clips of perhaps a few seconds, rarely more than a minute long. *Hubei, Luzhou city, Tianbei county, Mengshan village: 10 villagers protest outside government offices over death of local woman*, one might say. Or: *Shandong, Caiyang city, Taining county, Huaqi village: 500 workers strike for three days, protesting over unpaid wages.*

There were dozens of these posts, and they usually looked similar: police in pale-blue shirts, lots of shouting, crowds massing in the streets, occasionally someone on the ground being beaten. In one video, several men were attempting to tip over a police van. In another, a group of villagers were shouting as something that looked horribly like a human figure smoldered on the ground.

They were like dispatches from a country I had never seen, and they disturbed and confused me.

After seeing the video of the self-immolation, I messaged her. *Are you O.K.?* I asked. The reply came a few hours later: *Hi Big Brother! I'm doing fine.*

Are you in Beijing?

Of course I'm in Beijing.

I stared at the blinking cursor. I'd never told her that I knew her identity online, and I worried that if I said something she'd see me as somehow untrustworthy, as though I'd been spying on her.

Beijing must be very cold now, I wrote at last. *Make sure you wear warm clothes.*

• • •

That February, we both went home to see our parents and to celebrate the Spring Festival. I took charge of the dumplings, chopping the fennel and leeks, cracking an egg and swirling it about with gusto. I was happy. The week before, our team had entered a local competition and had won a month's supply of instant noodles and certain bragging rights. *Replay, replay*: my hands knew the commands so instinctively that sometimes I'd wake in the dark with fingers twitching.

Lulu, though, seemed only partly present: often you had to call her name twice to get a response. Sometimes I'd get up to use the bathroom in the middle of the night and see a glow in the living room, which meant she was awake and online.

One night we gathered around the television to watch the Spring Festival gala. It was an annual tradition put on by the state broadcaster: cheesy skits, patriotic odes, terrible slapstick — the whole country watched. I excused myself and logged on to check Lulu's account. The most recent post was from that evening, just before we sat down to dinner. It was a line of text in quotation marks: "If you want to understand your own country, then you've already stepped on the path to criminality," it read. And then: "Happy Spring Festival, comrades!"

A shiver ran through me. I logged out and walked back into the living room. Our parents sat on the couch, with Lulu on a stool beside them, their faces pallid in the television's flickering light as I joined them, stealing glances at this strange person, my twin sister.

The next day, the two of us went out to buy some ingredients for my mother: flour, fermented bean paste, ground pork. It felt strange to walk the half mile to the supermarket together, the first time we'd been alone since she visited me at college.

Derek Abella

This 2021 illustration, by artist Derek Abella, accompanied a *New York Times* article about FOMO, or Fear of Missing Out.

How does this image illustrate the way the narrator sees his sister, Lulu, both in his imagination and in real life?

On the way, we passed a park where we used to play as children, and we could hear the sound of children there now. It was sunny, and the warmth lulled my skin.

"Where did that quote come from?" I said. "The one from last night."

She kept walking. "What do you mean?"

"I've been reading your account."

"I don't know what you're talking about."

"Come on, Lulu." I stopped walking. "I'm worried about you."

She stopped a few feet ahead of me and stood there, not looking at me, arms crossed. "How did you know?"

I explained about the poetry. "Do other people know it's you?"

She shrugged. "A professor. Some other students." When I pressed her, she said reluctantly that a classmate had reported her to the department head, and that one of her professors had taken her aside and gently warned her that she should stop her activities online, lest it "influence" her future.

"They're right, you know," I said. "Don't you worry about how this might affect you?" One of the videos she'd posted, I remembered, showed a woman kneeling on the ground and wailing, "The government are traitors! The government doesn't serve the people!"

Lulu just stood there, staring at the little shopping complex opposite us as if she were trying to memorize it. There was a bilious-orange fast-food restaurant, three test-prep centers, and two real-estate agents' offices.

"Or our parents?" I said. They'd both retired by now, but each had a modest pension that I imagined could be taken away, and, anyway, the ruining of Lulu's prospects would be the greatest loss of all. When I thought of having to support them on my own in their old age, my stomach creaked unhappily.

She nodded. "Of course," she said, finally. "I'm not stupid."

"So you'll stop, then?"

She looked at me for a moment, a little dreamily. "Did you know that in the Song dynasty[2] it was illegal to throw away any pieces of paper with writing on them?" she said. "People had to go to certain temples with sacred fires set up where they could burn them instead. That's how much they revered the written word."

I wanted to shake her, but I didn't. "I don't see how that's relevant."

She started walking again.

[2] The Song dynasty was an imperial dynasty that ruled China from 960 to 1279. — Eds.

"Where are you getting all this stuff?" I asked. She unbent slightly and explained that she had downloaded a tool that unblocked overseas Web sites. "It's not hard," she said. "But things get deleted quickly, so I have to keep reposting them."

"I had no idea these kinds of things went on," she added, soberly. "We were lucky."

"We weren't rich."

"Dad worked for the government. We were comfortable."

Of course we were, I told her, but so were lots of people, and it didn't mean that she had to expose herself to trouble.

"It's better than just playing video games all day," she shot back, suddenly angry with me. "What's the point of that?"

I stuck my hands in my pockets and shrugged, taking a few extra breaths to calm myself. It was strange to see Lulu angry; she was usually so even-keeled. "Fair enough," I said. We kept walking, not looking at each other. Inside the supermarket we parted, as though with relief.

• • •

Back on campus, spring brought translucent white buds to the trees, like the tiny cores of onions. Lulu had stopped posting, I was pleased to see. I began working part time at a restaurant downtown that served large, expensive banquets, helping to prepare plates of cold chopped meats and glassy collagen and frilly slices of cucumber dolled up to look like miniature peacocks. There was a rhythm and a repetition to the work that I liked, a sense of contentment in washing up at the night's end and putting things back where they belonged.

One day in May, just before graduation, I checked back in on my sister's account. Lulu had stopped updating her chat status; for several weeks, it had read simply "out," and I'd grown worried.

It was as it had been before: she'd gone back to posting frenetically, as though she'd lost control — in one day alone she had posted forty-three times. There were the same postcards of protests around the country, the videos and photographs she'd been sharing before, and a lot of simple text posts, too, one after another. 3:34am: *if this country were a vegetable it would be a rotten, bitter melon.* 3:36am: *I am the daughter of a government sanitation worker. I know the smell of s---.* 3:37am: *I'm sorry, friends, just a little tired today after so many posts. There are many beautiful things, too, in this life.* And then she'd shared a series of pictures of small goats leaping in the air, tiny hoofs aloft against green grass. 3:41am: *O.K., I am sufficiently soothed to go to sleep. Good night comrades, until tomorrow.*

The posts went on and on — thousands of them had accumulated in the time since I'd stopped checking. I scrolled through them with a mounting sense of horror, and then paged back up and felt my stomach flip: somehow she'd amassed eight hundred thousand followers.

I messaged her frantically, fingers scrabbling at the keys. *Goats?*

A few hours later, she answered me. *Did you like them?*

They're O.K.

I'm sorry, Big Brother. I couldn't stop.

I sat and watched the cursor blink, like a slow pulse.

A lot of people are paying attention to you. I couldn't tell if I should be proud of her, worried for her, or angry with her. I supposed I was all three.

Yes, they are. Another long silence. *Don't be upset, Big Brother. I just felt this was something I had to do. Don't you agree?*

I'm working now, I wrote her, hoping she could sense my anger. *Running late, got to go.*

After she graduated, Lulu moved in with her boyfriend, Zhangwei, in Beijing. She started her own anonymous Web site, a constant stream of news about protests and human-rights abuses around the country. There was the story of a woman, beaten to death by police, whose daughter had paid to keep her body frozen in a morgue for six years, unwilling to inter the evidence. There was the story of the village where officials had torn down an elderly grandmother's home in the middle of the night to make way for a shopping mall; she'd been given no warning and had died in her bed as the roof collapsed around her. Each post carried its own mordant title: "The Mother Popsicle," "The Frustrated Sleeper."

They came for her one night, to the third-floor apartment that she and Zhangwei were renting. They burst in through the door without warning and informed her, politely, that she should go with them. "The landlord must have given them the key," she told me later, stunned. It was that particular detail, oddly, that seemed to haunt her.

It was midnight when Lulu called me from the police van to say that she was being taken away. "Tell our parents," she said. "Please. I'm sorry." Her voice broke, and I barely recognized her. She sounded like a child in a blizzard who'd lost her scarf. It was easier to think of that than to think of the alternative: Lulu, cuffed into a van and taken away by four men who sneered at her for being unmarried and living with her boyfriend, for trying to stir up trouble, for spreading rumors — a crime punishable by seven years' imprisonment.

When they began interrogating her, it was worse. "Did you go to any of these places?" they kept asking. "Did you confirm any of these things yourself before spreading these rumors online?"

No, Lulu said. No.

"So you didn't know if they were true, then."

Later, they laid her on the ground and kicked and beat her. They didn't fracture any bones, but I pictured her bones anyway, each individually absorbing every blow. Lulu would have known them all by heart: sternum, tibia, floating rib.

I called my mother, who on receiving the news, still half-asleep, went blank. "You must be mistaken," she told me sharply. "Let me call Lulu to straighten things out." It was an old reflex of hers, this instinct to turn to her daughter. "You can call, she won't answer," I said, but she'd already hung up. When I called back, my father took in the news helplessly, as though he'd been expecting it. I tried to explain the kinds of things she'd been writing, but he cut me off. "Lulu is my daughter. I can imagine," he said. There was a particular heaviness in his voice that surprised me, and it made me think that maybe he'd known her better than the rest of us.

Lulu was freed after six days, and went back to her apartment to convalesce. We flew to Beijing the next day to see her. It was the first time I had been in her apartment, whose living-room wall bore a giant decal from the previous tenant, featuring silver and pink trees and a striped pink kitten. *You are my happy surprise friends are better in autumn*, it read. Lulu's skin looked yellow and darkly bruised, and there was a dart of something red in her right eye that peeked out when she looked in certain directions.

"I'm all right," she said. She seemed acutely embarrassed to see us. They'd only wanted her to stop what she was doing, she said. She'd been a good student, one of the best in her class — she didn't have to ruin it all. It was a misunderstanding, she told us. They'd let her go, after all.

It seemed that she wanted us to go, too. We stayed for a week, our mother fussing in their tiny kitchen, preparing large meals of things sliced and intricately diced and cooked over a high flame. "I'm O.K.," Lulu said, until we stopped asking.

• • •

Back at home, Lulu started chatting me late at night, at odd hours. I was usually awake anyway: after graduating, I'd moved back home to work in the kitchen of a local hotel. I spent my days chopping and rinsing, bleary-eyed, and my nights with teammates, locked in online combat.

There was something that intensified in her messages during those months. She wanted to know how our parents were, if it was raining, if I'd eaten yet. She wondered if she could sue the police who'd beaten her; she'd been having stomach pains ever since. She wanted to know if I remembered the story of the mother who had died in the hospital down the street from us before we were born. She wondered if there was any way to locate the dead mother's child today — it would be about our age by now.

After that, the posts on her site started up again, thick and fast. I watched with a sinking heart, trying to distract her. *When are you and Zhangwei getting married?* I tried. *Didn't you want to have a baby?* Soon, she said. Maybe.

When the police came and took her away again, she was prepared; she got up quietly from the couch and went with them without a word, leaving her keys behind. This time, when they allowed her access to a phone, she called a lawyer, not me. The police raided the apartment, taking her computer, the blue-sleeved laptop my parents had given her. They also left behind a notice saying that she was formally being arrested and charged.

At the trial, Lulu wore an orange jumpsuit and her hair had been shorn so short that she was barely recognizable. She stared straight ahead at the prosecutors, never once looking out at the audience. We'd flown out for the occasion — we hadn't seen her for six months. She was given a sentence of three years, then jerked away through a door at the opposite end of the courtroom, and that was all.

On the plane, my mother wept all the way home. "What more did she want?" she kept saying.

To her left, my father hushed her. "There's nothing we can do now," he said. The thought, strangely, appeared to console him.

Back at home no one seemed to know that anything had happened to my sister, and no one asked, either. It was as if a great white blanket of snow had descended, softly muffling everything in its path.

Time passed, and eventually I was made a sous-chef at the hotel, with a modest raise and a new, slightly taller paper hat. When I felt restless or agitated, which was often, I'd log on and join my teammates online.

One night I brought my girlfriend home for the first time. I'd met her the month before on the lowest basement floor of a warrened-out block devoted to the sale of electronics: a fluorescent-lit maze of close-set tiny booths selling secondhand phones, cases, speakers, and power banks. Her name was Mao Xin, and she was one of the few girls working behind the counters there. She could tell you the difference between 100 Wh[3] and 161 Wh, could quote the price per gigabyte of different models.

As it turned out, she'd grown up riding the same bus route as I had, and in a city as big as ours that was enough to feel like fate. We liked to imagine that we had seen each other on the bus as children, stiffly bundled in the winter or swinging our legs impatiently in the summer, had maybe even clung to the same pole.

Over dinner that night, as we sat and slurped potatoes stewed with ginger and pork, my mother quizzed Mao Xin. I could see that she wanted to like her, had observed the way she'd helped chop the garlic and cut the yellowing tips off the chives. Mao Xin exuded a kind of benevolent competence that soothed everyone, even my mother, who had grown jittery since Lulu's trial, prone to repeat herself, easily annoyed.

As we talked, I could see Mao Xin's curious eyes flicking around, eventually landing on a photo of Lulu atop a bookshelf across the room, high enough that you needed to squint to really see it. "Who's that?"

"It's his sister," my father said. The photo had been taken the day she had won our district's top score for math in the college-entrance exam. In it she was grinning maniacally at my father behind the camera, a little out of focus.

[3] The watt-hour, a unit of energy that is one watt of power spent per hour of time. — Eds.

"I didn't know you had a sister," she said to me. "She looks like you."

"They're twins," my father said.

"Where is she?"

"She's in the northeast, preparing to get her Ph.D.," my mother said.

Later, when I walked Mao Xin outside and explained what had really happened, her face fell. "Oh," she said. "I'm so sorry." When she was growing up, she said, there was a man who used to station himself outside the government offices down the street from her home, with torn fatigues and sneakers so worn they flopped open like petals around his ankles. He'd tell anyone who would listen about how the Army owed him seven years of back pay. He'd been there every day through her childhood, she said, until one day he disappeared for good.

"It sounds like he was crazy," I said.

"I think so," she said. "Maybe not at first, though."

"You must have been scared of him."

"More just sorry for him," she said.

• • •

We planned our wedding for a few days after Lulu was to be released from prison, a boisterous dinner in the nicest hall of the hotel where I worked. I'd been made a full chef there that month, which felt like a sort of wedding gift. We served big platters of cold, jellied meats and swans made of mashed-up radish, with carrot beaks and black sesame eyes. It should have been a happy occasion, and I guess it was, but whenever I looked at Lulu, sitting across from me with a distant look in her eyes, my heart caught in my throat.

As the banquet wound down, my father, unnatural in a rented tuxedo, began coughing violently. When he didn't stop, Zhangwei signalled to one of the waiters for water.

"Drink up," Lulu said. He drained the glass, almost angrily, it seemed. The coughs sputtered, subsided. "You're O.K.?" she said.

He had been drinking, his face was flushed, and his eyes focussed suddenly on her, as though surprised that she was there. "Do you think what you've done is meaningful?" he said.

"Let's not talk about it."

"You didn't even know these people," he said. "Whatever their problems might have been, they had no relation to you."

Lulu looked down at her plate, seeming not to hear. She'd grown adept at that while in prison, or maybe she'd always had that skill: how to sort the world into clear categories, what she thought was worth paying attention to and what wasn't. I was in the latter category now. She'd nod at me occasionally and respond when spoken to, but that was all. I tried not to let it upset me.

Illustration by Raphael Greaves, The New Yorker ©Conde Nast

This piece, by artist Raphael Greaves, accompanied "Lulu" when it was originally published in the *New Yorker*.

What perspective on twinship does this image convey? How do you interpret the imagery on each twin's screen?

His face was getting redder — none of us had ever seen him like that before. "Dad, let's just leave it," I said. Guests at nearby tables had stopped their conversations, craning to hear. "It's no use."

"You are our daughter," he said fiercely, ignoring me. "Everything we could, we did for you. You were all our worries, all our hopes."

He was coughing again, small mangled noises sticking in his throat. Lulu's expression softened. "Dad, drink more water. It sounds like you're really sick."

He ignored her, setting the glass down in the same ring of condensation. He was suddenly an old man, or maybe I'd only just noticed. "Do you think I had your chances in life?" he said. "Do you know what I could have done if I had them?"

It was hard to believe that the two of them were fighting; it was something I hadn't seen before. Our mother and I looked at each other, then looked away.

"I'm sorry," Lulu said quietly.

"You want to help people, Lulu, but don't deceive yourself," he said. "All you've done is hurt yourself, hurt your family."

My mother laid a hand on his and stilled him with a look. Zhangwei stood up, as though to end the discussion. It made you aware of what a tall, fine-looking man he was, stiff black hair that stood up in a dense thatch, thin lenses highlighting his watchful brown eyes. "I think Lulu had better get some rest now," he said to my parents. There was nothing impolite about his tone, but there was a finality to it that reminded us all of his solidity, his determination to protect my sister, and I liked him the better for it.

"Don't worry," he told me as he ushered her outside, away from the noise and the lights of the wedding party. "I'll take care of her."

She hadn't been treated badly in prison, she'd said when we were all first gathered again in our parents' living room. There had been a female guard she suspected of having a crush on her, who used to smuggle her packets of instant noodles and an occasional stick of gum. During the day they'd worked on a manufacturing line, assembling Christmas lights. At night they'd watched the evening news and whatever sports match was being televised. But she'd missed the sunlight, she said. She'd missed Zhangwei, missed us.

"Thank you for your letters," she said to me, and I looked at the floor, away from our parents. "It was no problem," I muttered, embarrassed for them. It hadn't occurred to me that they hadn't been writing regularly as well.

Lulu changed the subject. "So you're playing in the Shanghai invitational? That's really wonderful."

It was: after playing together for six years, my team had finally qualified. Out of four teammates, I'd only ever met one in person before. I thanked Lulu.

"Is there prize money?" she asked.

I told her yes, a little.

"Excellent," she said, grinning.

Our parents were very quiet. I suspected that they wanted an apology, and also that it wasn't forthcoming. When Lulu said that she and Zhangwei were planning to move nearby, our mother froze, as though she'd been handed a cracked egg and didn't know what to do with it.

"He thinks it'll be good for me to be closer to home," Lulu said, breaking the silence. "At least while I get used to a normal life again."

"What can you do out here?" my mother asked stiffly. "Can you find work?"

Lulu tossed her head, and a flash of her old arrogance flared in her. "Yes, Mother. I was the top-scoring student in our year for math, don't you remember?"

"Maybe Mao Xin could help her get a job," my mother said. It wasn't a tactful remark, but then my mother loved Mao Xin, had come to rely on her in a way that reminded me of her relationship with Lulu before she went to college.

"Sure," I said, with an apologetic glance at Lulu. "Anyway, that's great news. We'll have to celebrate."

She smiled at me, a little sadly. "Thanks, Big Brother."

Eventually she found work handing out tea samples at the mall, a chain store with neon-green hills in its sign. It was an easy job, and the boss didn't ask questions about her past. In the meantime, she was learning a lot about tea, she said, about the oxidation process, about the proper way to steep different varieties.

"Wow, they really train you over there," our father said. In the weeks since her release, he had become a champion government booster, missing no opportunity to point out to Lulu how nicely the roads had been paved since she'd left, how grand the malls were that had been built. "There are so many opportunities for young people now," he said. It was a new tic of his, and it grated. Earlier that day, as we strolled the neighborhood, he'd taken the chance to point out a set of recently upgraded public toilets across the way. "They even installed a little room where the sanitation workers can rest," he said. "It has heating and everything. You see what good care they take of all the workers now?"

I rolled my eyes. 155

"Anyway, it's temporary," Lulu said of her job, and that, of course, was what scared us most of all.

I could see that she was planning something. Once, when she was using my laptop, I saw over her shoulder that she had a document open, titled "An Open Letter to the National People's Congress."[4] When she got up to use the bathroom, I scrolled hastily through the text, seeing a list of half a dozen names signed, her own and those of a few lawyers and professors — no one I'd ever heard of. I didn't say anything to her, but later that afternoon I pulled Zhangwei aside and told him what I'd found. He nodded.

"I know," he said. "Your sister doesn't change."

I didn't know what he meant, but I bristled a little anyway. "She wasn't like this when she was younger," I said.

"Of course not, she was too young then." 160

"You don't know what she was like."

"O.K.," he said patiently, his eyes on the door behind me, waiting to see if Lulu would walk in. He was always mentally tracking her location, the world's most devoted bloodhound.

"I mean that. She was smart. She was probably the smartest in our school."

Layqa Nuna Yawar

This illustration by artist LNY accompanied poems about the Tiananmen Square protests on the website of the Asian American Writers Workshop. It depicts poet and artist Liu Xia, who, with her husband, Liu Xiaobo, was awarded the Nobel Peace Prize in 2010. She was placed under house arrest from 2010 to 2018, when she was able to go to Germany for medical treatment. Liu Xiaobo died in police custody in 2017.

What do the details of this illustration convey about Liu Xia and her work? What connections do you see between this image and the themes of "Lulu"?

[4] The National People's Congress of the People's Republic of China, normally referred to as the National People's Congress, is the national legislature of China. — Eds.

"And you think she isn't smart anymore?"

"That's not what I meant," I said, but Zhangwei was already flicking the ash from his cigarette and walking away, disappointed in me.

• • •

I flew to Shanghai for the mid-season invitational alone, shrugging off Mao Xin's offer to accompany me, but when I arrived I immediately wished she were there, just to see the spectacle. The games took place in a stadium downtown, the floor lit up with strips of red and blue L.E.D. lights. The stadium was packed, and as we played in padded seats onstage, headsets on, the crowd waved red and blue glow sticks.

We won two rounds, and went on to trounce the South Korean team in the third. In the background, the crowd was moaning, the sounds mingling with the noise of my own blood as we clicked frantically, sending out great gusts of orange fire. "Never give up! Never say die!" the crowd chanted.

When the games were over, the flashing scoreboard had us in third place. The cameras flocked to the floor, descending on us like black hooded birds. We gave sheepish smiles and said how proud we were, how we'd be back next year to win for sure. Somehow we were ushered onto a podium, beside the other winning teams. They handed us a trophy as silver confetti rained down, great clouds of delicate parallelograms. When I watched the video later, it looked as if we were standing in a hail of razor blades. We hoisted the trophy into the air, all five of us. It wavered and nearly tipped, but the tallest among us righted it and we let it hover there, admiring it.

Four months later, Lulu went back to prison, this time on charges of trying to subvert state power, after she and others had circulated an online petition calling for all government spending to be made transparent. This time the prison was not so nice, and the judge gave her a ten-year sentence. The last time I saw her, she had lost fifteen pounds and looked shrunken, the same size she'd been in high school.

A few years after she was jailed, Zhangwei moved back to his home town to be closer to his parents and got married to someone else. He wrote us a letter apologizing. I threw it away after seeing the return address, but Mao Xin fished it out of the trash and insisted that I read it. "Your sister is a truly rare person, and it is with the greatest sadness that I have to move on," he'd written. "I'm sorry I couldn't help her more." I stood there for a minute, admiring his penmanship, which I'd never seen before. It was elegant, balanced — almost noble, I observed, before tossing the letter out again.

After the Shanghai invitational, our team started competing heavily on the domestic circuit, winning actual prize pools now and again. With Mao Xin's encouragement, I cut back my hours at the hotel and devoted more time to training. The following summer, we flew to Sydney for the global finals. It was my first time abroad. By then we had fans, even sponsors; we entered the arena wearing identical jumpsuits with the name of an energy drink printed across our chests.

On the plane, we crossed the ocean, heading south. I took out my camera and snapped a photo for my next letter to Lulu. The flight attendants passed out headsets, and I slid one on, suddenly homesick. I closed my eyes and thought of my sister. I prayed for victory, and hoped that she would be proud. ■

2019

Understanding and Interpreting

1. What information about the story's setting does the narrator provide in the first three paragraphs of "Lulu"? How are the issues of health care, family planning, and corruption introduced? Where do they resurface later in the story?

2. Why does the narrator's family dote on his twin, Lulu? Why do they have such high expectations for her?
3. How does the narrator feel about his sister during their childhood? How does he make his own place? Is his strategy for doing so successful? Consider both the story's beginning as well as its ending in your response.
4. In paragraph 34, the narrator is gratified when his sister says, "I knew I could trust you." Based on your interpretation of the story, do you agree that he is trustworthy? Explain why or why not.
5. Why must Lulu's internet presence be anonymous? How does the narrator find it anyway? What overall impression do her anonymous posts give? Does that impression change as the story progresses? Explain.
6. In paragraph 51, the whole family watches the Spring Festival gala on television while the narrator and Lulu are home from college. How does the narrator view this experience? Why is he chilled by Lulu's comments on the Spring Festival? Why do you think he doesn't talk to her about it despite the fact that they are at home together?
7. How does the conversation between the narrator and Lulu in paragraphs 55–77 illustrate the gulf between them? How are their differing perspectives of their parents revealed in the exchange?
8. Why does the narrator's father seem to understand Lulu better than anyone? What details from the story characterize their relationship?
9. What does the response of the narrator's parents to Mao Xin, his girlfriend, reveal about their values? What does Mao Xin's reaction to the news that the narrator has a sister reveal about the family's beliefs about her choices?
10. How do the family's interactions at the narrator's wedding portray the effects of Lulu's activism on the family? What does the father try to impress on Lulu? Why do you think he fails in this attempt?
11. How does Lulu's second arrest (par. 102) differ from her first one? What does it suggest about Lulu's development as an activist?
12. What changes does the narrator undergo while Lulu is serving a ten-year sentence for "subvert[ing] state power" after circulating an online petition for all government spending to be transparent? Why might he feel "suddenly homesick" as he flies home from the Shanghai International tournament?

Analyzing Language, Style, and Structure

1. **Vocabulary in Context.** How does the word "precocity" in paragraph 5 characterize Lulu? How is her precocity both a strength and a weakness throughout the story?
2. Why do you think Te-Ping Chen decided not to give the narrator a name? What is the effect of his remaining unnamed?
3. How do Lulu and the narrator serve as foils for each other in this story? What is the purpose of presenting them not just as siblings but as twins? How does the concept of twinship unfold in the characters' interests, values, and eventual fates?
4. What is the purpose of the contrast Chen draws between the narrator's growing success and recognition for this talent with the trajectory of Lulu's activism and its consequences?
5. "Lulu" uses figurative language sparingly, but potently. Look, for example, at the description of the narrator's college dorm room. How do the imagery and similes there create a picture of an atmosphere in which the narrator feels at home? How does this picture contrast with other settings in the story?

6. The word "replay" functions as a motif throughout the story. How does it relate to the larger themes at work in "Lulu"? In what ways do certain scenes or events seem to "replay" throughout the story?
7. Look carefully at paragraph 18 in which the narrator describes his college experience. How do the disparate literary elements of the paragraph come together to comment on that experience and characterize the narrator?
8. Look carefully at the descriptions of food the narrator prepares as he moves up in his career as a chef. What do the dishes have in common? What comment might the story be making about the narrator's career choice? How does it compare to Lulu's choices?
9. Why does the narrator think about Lulu naming the bones in the body when he hears about her beating by the police the first time she's arrested (par. 95)?
10. "Lulu" takes place over many years, but it's quite compact. How was Chen able to address big issues over time while still keeping the story focused on the events of everyday life and on family ties?

Topics for Composing

1. **AP® FRQ** **Prose Fiction Analysis.** The following question refers to paragraphs 165–67 of Te-Ping Chen's "Lulu," published in 2019. In this passage, the narrator's experience in Shanghai at the mid-season invitational championships is described. Read the passage carefully. Then, in a well-written essay, analyze how Chen uses literary elements and techniques to convey the narrator's complex perspective on the nature and significance of his success as a video gamer.
2. **AP® FRQ** **Literary Argument.** In a novel by William Styron, a father tells his son that life "is a search for justice." In "Lulu," both the narrator and his twin, Lulu, have differing perspectives on the importance and possibility for correcting injustice. In a well-written essay, analyze how Lulu's search for justice contributes to an interpretation of the work as a whole. Do not merely summarize the plot.
3. **AP® Literary Argumentation.** Both the narrator and Lulu are portrayed as extremely tech savvy in this story. How do the twins' expertise in similar areas put each of them on separate tracks in life? How does Chen use their differing fates to comment on larger issues?
4. **AP® Literary Argumentation.** In an interview Chen was asked whether she thought art should be a form of resistance. Chen answered, "I ultimately chafe at the idea that art should be a form of resistance, because if you're imposing a purpose on art, and saying it needs to conform to a certain message, then what we're talking about starts to feel closer in nature to propaganda." What, if any, elements of resistance do you find in "Lulu"? Use evidence from the text to support your response.
5. **AP® Literary Argumentation.** In an interview about her short story collection *Land of Big Numbers*, Chen said that the stories reflect a trait she observed in many of the people she encountered while in China: "A real sense of outsized ambition coupled with a tremendous sense of pragmatism." How do the narrator and Lulu each embody that observation?
6. **Research.** Learn about two or three twenty-first century protests in the United States and countries abroad, such as in Belarus, Hong Kong, and Russia. What are these protests about? Who participates? How are protesters treated? How did this research inform your understanding of the themes of "Lulu"?
7. **Connections.** To what extent does the description of the online gaming tournaments in "Lulu" change your view of the narrator's accomplishments in the world of online gaming?

Sound and Sense

Alexander Pope

IanDagnall Computing/Alamy

Alexander Pope (1688–1744) is generally considered the eighteenth century's greatest English poet. Known for satirical verse, Pope was the first writer to be able to live off the proceeds of his work. Pope was a Roman Catholic, and the anti-Catholic sentiment and laws of his time dictated — and limited — his formal education. Some of Pope's words are so ingrained in the English language that they are considered proverbs by those unfamiliar with his work: "Hope springs eternal in the human breast," "The proper study of mankind is man," "A little learning is a dangerous thing," "To err is human, to forgive, divine," and "For fools rush in where angels fear to tread" are all from Pope's writing. *An Essay on Criticism* is Pope's poem on the art of poetry, whose purpose was not so much to provide lessons for writers but to offer advice to critics. The following poem is from this volume.

True ease in writing comes from art, not chance,
As those move easiest who have learned to dance.
'Tis not enough no harshness gives offense,
The sound must seem an echo to the sense:
Soft is the strain when Zephyr[1] gently blows,
And the smooth stream in smoother numbers flows;
But when loud surges lash the sounding shore,
The hoarse, rough verse should like the torrent roar.
When Ajax[2] strives, some rock's vast weight to throw,
The line too labors, and the words move slow;
Not so, when swift Camilla[3] scours the plain,
Flies o'er th' unbending corn, and skims along the main.
Hear how Timotheus'[4] varied lays surprise,
And bid alternate passions fall and rise! ■

1711

---

[1] The west wind, after Zephyrus, the Greek god of the west wind. — Eds.

[2] Hero in the Trojan War and Homer's *Iliad*. — Eds.

[3] Warrior in Virgil's *Aeneid*. — Eds.

[4] Ancient Greek poet and musician, and character in John Dryden's poem "Alexander's Feast." — Eds.

Understanding and Interpreting

1. What does the speaker mean by the phrase "those move easiest who have learned to dance" (l. 2)?
2. In line 4, what does the speaker assert is the function of the words used within a poem? Identify parts of the poem where Pope follows this advice.
3. According to the speaker, what kind of language should be used when writing about "gently" blowing breezes and "smooth" (ll. 5–6) streams, as opposed to "when loud surges lash the sounding shore" (l. 7)?
4. According to the speaker, how should a poet's writing convey the extraordinary efforts of a powerful warrior like Ajax?

Analyzing Language, Style, and Structure

1. **Vocabulary in Context.** The word *art* appears in this chapter's Classic Text, *Hamlet*, when Queen Gertrude says to Polonius, "More matter with less art" (II.ii.95). In "Sound and Sense," the speaker says, "True ease in writing comes from art [. . .]" (l. 1). In both of these instances, the word alludes to rhetorical ability, or what we would refer to today as having a way with words. What parts of the poem depict Pope's rhetorical flair? How do you know that these are deliberate instances of "art" and not mere "chance" (l. 1)?
2. Alexander Pope uses allusions in "Sound and Sense" to convey his ideas. Identify two allusions and explain what message they convey to the reader. Why is allusion, rather than explicit instruction, such an effective means to relate this message?
3. Pope was famous for writing couplets (two rhyming lines), as in this poem. How do the series of couplets in "Sound and Sense" develop a commentary on the relationship between sound and sense?
4. Pope manipulates the sound of this poem by controlling the poem's rhythm. Find examples of the way he varies stress (or accent), mixes mono- and polysyllabic words, ends words in consonants that do not easily blend, or slows a line down with commas. Be sure to read the poem aloud to hear the effects of the poem's "sound." What is the effect of these variations in word choice and syntax?
5. "Sound and Sense" is a didactic poem, meaning it was written for the purpose of instructing its readers. However, it does contain lyrical language that expresses emotion. How does Pope use that lyrical language to achieve his didactic purpose in this poem?

Topics for Composing

1. AP® FRQ **Poetry Analysis.** In Alexander Pope's "Sound and Sense," published in 1711, the speaker provides writing advice to poets. Read the poem carefully. Then, in a well-written essay, analyze how Pope uses literary elements and techniques to convey the speaker's attitude toward a poet's obligations when writing.
2. **AP® Literary Argumentation.** In "Sound and Sense," Pope argues that there must be a direct relationship between what something intends to communicate and how it sounds. Write an essay in which you argue whether Pope achieved this goal in this poem. Use evidence from the text to support your response.
3. **Creative Writing.** Write a poem about a topic of your choice. In a few lines of your poem, aim to deliberately follow Pope's advice in "Sound and Sense." After completing your poem, provide a brief explanation of how the sounds of your poem within those lines echo their meaning.

4. **Speaking and Listening.** Work with a partner to record yourselves reading "Sound and Sense." Each of you should read every other couplet but create a single recording. Once you are satisfied with your performance, listen to it carefully. What observations can you make about the sounds and rhythm of the poem?

Song: To the Men of England

Percy Bysshe Shelley

Art Collection 2/Alamy

The son of an English landowner and member of Parliament, Percy Bysshe Shelley (1792–1822) is considered one of the greatest lyric poets in English literature. Shelley fared poorly at Oxford, where he was said to have attended only a single lecture. Instead, he pursued his own interests, reading up to sixteen hours a day and writing pamphlets, novels, and poetry. His controversial views, expounded in such pamphlets as *The Necessity of Atheism*, led to his expulsion from Oxford in 1811. After the suicide of his first wife in 1816, Shelley married Mary Wollstonecraft Godwin, who would later write *Frankenstein* (1818).

KEY CONTEXT Despite being born to privilege, Shelley embraced political causes of the dispossessed, which made him a controversial figure during his lifetime.

Men of England, wherefore plough
For the lords who lay ye low?
Wherefore weave with toil and care
The rich robes your tyrants wear?

Wherefore feed and clothe and save
From the cradle to the grave
Those ungrateful drones who would
Drain your sweat — nay, drink your blood?

Wherefore, Bees of England, forge
Many a weapon, chain, and scourge,
That these stingless drones may spoil
The forced produce of your toil?

Have ye leisure, comfort, calm,
Shelter, food, love's gentle balm?
Or what is it ye buy so dear
With your pain and with your fear?

The seed ye sow, another reaps;
The wealth ye find, another keeps;
The robes ye weave, another wears;
The arms ye forge, another bears.

Sow seed — but let no tyrant reap;
Find wealth — let no impostor heap;
Weave robes — let not the idle wear;
Forge arms — in your defence to bear.

Shrink to your cellars, holes, and cells —
In halls ye deck another dwells.
Why shake the chains ye wrought? Ye see
The steel ye tempered glance on ye.

With plough and spade and hoe and loom
Trace your grave and build your tomb
And weave your winding-sheet — till fair
England be your Sepulchre. ■

1819

Understanding and Interpreting

1. Who are the "Men of England" Percy Bysshe Shelley is speaking to, and what is his purpose in addressing them? How does Shelley characterize the "Men of England"?
2. The first half of this poem consists of four questions. Do you think they are rhetorical? Explain.
3. Consider the series of objects that the speaker says are forged by the "Bees of England": "weapon, chain, and scourge" (l. 10). What do these items have in common? How do they differ?
4. What does the term "stingless" (l. 11) suggest about the way the speaker views the "drones" (l. 11)? How else are they characterized throughout the poem?
5. How does the speaker envision the future for the "Men of England" if they don't rebel? How do the final two stanzas convey this vision?

Analyzing Language, Style, and Structure

1. **Vocabulary in Context.** Drones, or male honeybees, do not collect nectar or pollen, but only mate with queens and perform secondary functions within the hive. Who do you think the "drones" in the poem represent? What other connotations of the word *drone* do you think apply in this context?
2. Some of Shelley's language in the poem — "wherefore" and "ye," for example — was already archaic by the year of its composition. What effect do you think these word choices have on the tone and rhetorical impact of the poem?
3. Stanza 6 reverses the parallels of the declarative statements in the fifth stanza, making them imperative. How does this reversal contribute to the tone in these stanzas?
4. "Song: To the Men of England" has been set to music and adopted as an anthem of the English labor movement. What elements of the poem make it especially suitable as a hymn or rallying cry? Do you think Shelley is advocating an armed rebellion or a more ambiguous refusal of the status quo?

Topics for Composing

1. AP® FRQ **Poetry Analysis.** In Percy Bysshe Shelley's "Song: To the Men of England," published in 1819, the speaker urges his countrymen to rebel against those in power. Read the poem carefully. Then, in a well-written essay, analyze how Shelley uses literary elements and techniques to rally people to the speaker's cause.
2. **AP® Literary Argumentation.** For those people who are torn between conforming and rebelling, is this poem sufficiently convincing to do the latter rather than the former? Write an essay in which you analyze whether Shelley's speaker makes a solid case for rebelling against an oppressive government. Use evidence from the poem to support your answer.
3. **Connections.** How would you characterize the injustices that the speaker hopes to combat? While this poem was written over two centuries ago, some contend with similar injustices today. What application might Shelley's call to action in this poem have in the twenty-first century?
4. **Connections.** The call for rebellion is not unique to Shelley; men and women have always clamored for a more equitable society. For many people in recent history, music has served the purpose that poetry served for Shelley. Find a song that has a similar message and tone as "Song: To the Men of England." How do these compare? What prompted Shelley and the musician you've selected to express this call for rebellion in their artform?
5. **Creative Writing.** Write a poem that is a call to action against a specific injustice you believe must be addressed today. For an extra challenge, use similar structure and style techniques as Shelley does in crafting your poem.

Much Madness is divinest Sense —

Emily Dickinson

Born into a prominent family in Amherst, Massachusetts, Emily Dickinson (1830–1886) received some formal education at Amherst Academy and Mount Holyoke Female Seminary (which became Mount Holyoke College). Dickinson was known as a shy and reclusive person, who preferred to remain within her close family circle, though some contemporary scholars have begun to question that characterization. Dickinson wrote nearly eighteen hundred poems, but only ten were published in her lifetime.

IanDagnall Computing/Alamy

Much Madness is divinest Sense —
To a discerning Eye —
Much Sense — the starkest Madness —
'Tis the Majority
In this, as All, prevail —
Assent — and you are sane —
Demur — you're straightway dangerous —
And handled with a Chain — ■

c. 1862

Understanding and Interpreting

1. What does the speaker mean when she claims that "Madness is divinest Sense" (l. 1)? How do you interpret "divinest" in this context?
2. The speaker presents reactions to society as a binary. What are the two choices a person has in the face of social expectations? What is the speaker's attitude toward these alternatives?
3. What does the speaker imply in the final line of the poem? What do you imagine the speaker sees as the consequences for people who "[d]emur"?
4. This poem relies on an inversion of the expected meanings of "sense" and "madness." Though the speaker does not explicitly tie the terms to any specific behavior or beliefs, can you find evidence indicating how the poem defines "madness"?

Analyzing Language, Style, and Structure

1. **Vocabulary in Context.** Consider Emily Dickinson's choice of the word "demur" in line 7. How does choosing such a gentle term affect the poem's overall meaning? What do you make of the contrast between that word and the rest of the line?
2. Do you think the poem presents an unresolvable paradox regarding "sense" and "madness"? How would you characterize the "discerning Eye" mentioned in line 2? Contrast this with the method of discernment practiced by the "Majority" in the poem.
3. Dickinson often wrote her poems with metrical patterns incorporating lines of eight and six syllables. How does she develop relationships among ideas in this poem by using — and departing from — such patterns?
4. How does Dickinson's use of alliteration emphasize and connect certain ideas?
5. Line 4 is the only one that doesn't end with an em dash, and the emjambment between lines 4 and 5 further alters the flow of the poem. How does this momentary shift in structure relate to the meaning of these lines?

Topics for Composing

1. AP® FRQ **Poetry Analysis.** In Emily Dickinson's "Much Madness is divinest Sense," written circa 1862, the speaker addresses how quick society is to judge someone who has resisted conformity. Read the poem carefully. Then, in a well-written essay, analyze how Dickinson uses literary elements and techniques to convey the speaker's complex perspective on the value of individual expression.
2. **Connections.** How does this poem speak to contemporary times? Are those who conform to society's expectations of them rewarded, and are those who rebel, or dissent, seen as dangerous — even deserving punishment? Use examples from current events to support your answer.
3. **Research.** Throughout history, many of the most innovative and creative artists, musicians, and writers have found their greatest success by not conforming to social expectations — or even actual laws. Research one or more of these figures (you might even choose someone creating art, literature, or music today) to examine how they were willing to "[a]ssent" (l. 6) and, more importantly, the risks they took to "[d]emur" (l. 7). How did their audiences perceive such risks? Has time treated individuals from past eras more fairly? Do you think time will prompt society in the future to reassess its perception of individuals in our era?

4. **Connections.** This poem could serve as an epigraph to one of the other texts you have read in this chapter. Choose which one would be most appropriate, and explain why.
5. **Speaking and Listening.** How do members of each successive generation earn the label "dangerous" (l. 7) and end up being — or at least feeling — as though they are "handled with a Chain" (l. 8)? Do some background research to prepare for a class discussion on how older generations often view the ideas and interests of younger generations as scandalous if not dangerous. What evidence can you point to from previous decades or even centuries? What experiences have you and your peers had that speak to this reality? Be as specific as possible in supporting your assertions.

Waiting for the Barbarians

C. P. Cavafy

Translated from Greek by Edmund Keeley

Fine Art Images/Heritage Images/Getty Images

Constantine P. Cavafy (1863–1933) was born in Alexandria, Egypt, to Greek parents. He spent his childhood in Constantinople and in England before returning to Alexandria, where he worked as a journalist and government administrator. Although he wrote poetry throughout his life, he published little, preferring to share his poems privately. His first collection of poems was published posthumously in 1935. Although his experimental forms present challenges to translators, Cavafy's reputation in literature in English grew after his death, promoted by modernist writers such as E. M. Forster and T. S. Eliot. His work often addresses issues of historical, cultural, and moral conflict.

KEY CONTEXT Ancient Greeks and Romans used the word *barbarian* to describe general foreigners as well as enemies and those believed to be less civilized. During the decline of the Western Roman Empire in the fourth through sixth centuries C.E., the arrival of peoples from other regions of Europe and even Asia has long been called the Barbarian Invasions. As a Greek born in Egypt and raised in England and what is modern-day Turkey, Cavafy would have been very aware of the effects of ongoing migrations and cultural and political shifts.

What are we waiting for, assembled in the forum?

    The barbarians are due here today.

Why isn't anything going on in the senate?
Why are the senators sitting there without legislating?

    Because the barbarians are coming today.
    What's the point of senators making laws now?
    Once the barbarians are here, they'll do the legislating.

Why did our emperor get up so early,
and why is he sitting enthroned at the city's main gate,
in state, wearing the crown?

Because the barbarians are coming today
and the emperor's waiting to receive their leader.
He's even got a scroll to give him,
loaded with titles, with imposing names.

Why have our two consuls and praetors[1] come out today
wearing their embroidered, their scarlet togas?
Why have they put on bracelets with so many amethysts,
rings sparkling with magnificent emeralds?
Why are they carrying elegant canes
beautifully worked in silver and gold?

Because the barbarians are coming today
and things like that dazzle the barbarians.

Why don't our distinguished orators turn up as usual
to make their speeches, say what they have to say?

Because the barbarians are coming today
and they're bored by rhetoric and public speaking.

Why this sudden bewilderment, this confusion?
(How serious people's faces have become.)
Why are the streets and squares emptying so rapidly,
everyone going home lost in thought?

Because night has fallen and the barbarians haven't come.
And some of our men just in from the border say
there are no barbarians any longer.

Now what's going to happen to us without barbarians?
Those people were a kind of solution. ■

1904

[1] High-ranking government officials. — Eds.

Understanding and Interpreting

1. What is the subject of this poem? How would you summarize, in a few sentences, the events that take place, or that the speakers expect to take place? What mood does this poem evoke in you as a reader?
2. Who are the speakers of the poem? What role do they appear to play in their community and its government?
3. How does the speakers' dialogue characterize the barbarians generally? What do you expect of the barbarians based on the speakers' characterization?
4. How do the people respond when the barbarians fail to arrive? Why do they respond this way?
5. In what ways does the conclusion of the poem characterize the members of the community in which the speakers live? How does the conclusion shape the mood of the poem?
6. In the final line, one of the speakers says, "Those people were a kind of solution." What might they be a solution to, and what does this say about the values of this community in particular and about human societies in general?

Analyzing Language, Style, and Structure

1. **Vocabulary in Context.** How do slightly different denotations of the word "dazzle" work in line 22? How does the connotation of the word change, and what effect does this have on the meaning of the line? What larger meaning does this word choice help convey?
2. How does the speakers' individual and collective use of questions influence the tone at various points in the poem? What do these questions indicate about the speakers' relationship to one another?
3. Consider the repetition in the first line of each of the second speaker's answers to the first speaker's questions. What is its effect, and how do variations in this line subtly change its meaning?
4. What is the significance of the scroll "loaded with titles, with imposing names" (l. 14)? What imagery does C. P. Cavafy use to characterize the consuls and praetors? What is the effect?
5. What purpose does the structure of two speakers and a question-and-answer format serve? How does it delineate each speaker's role in the community and comment on his relationship to the government officials? How does it develop the relationship between the speakers?

Topics for Composing

1. AP® FRQ **Poetry Analysis.** In C. P. Cavafy's "Waiting for the Barbarians," published in 1904, the speakers discuss their community's preparations to receive a group of people they view as hostile outsiders. Read the poem carefully. Then, in a well-written essay, analyze how Cavafy uses literary elements and techniques to develop the speakers' complex perspectives on the relationship between a community and those it deems outsiders.
2. **Research.** Look further into the history of the term *barbarian* and the role foreign tribes had in bringing down the Western Roman Empire. Then, explain how Cavafy alludes to this history in his poem. With this history in mind, which perspective do you believe he privileges — that of the "barbarians" or that of the community in the poem?

3. **Connections.** Read J. M. Coetzee's 1980 novel *Waiting for the Barbarians*, in which settlers in the territory of a fictional empire await an expected attack of the region's indigenous inhabitants, whom they deem to be "barbarians." In what ways does the novel reflect the themes of this poem? What attitude does each text take toward the concept of empire?
4. **Speaking and Listening.** With a partner, read the poem as if it is a dialogue between the two of you. Once you have read it one way, trade speakers and read it again. Then, discuss each speaker's perspective with each other before engaging in a class discussion. How does the mood of the poem shift for you depending on whose part you are reading? With which speaker do you most identify, and why?
5. **Creative Writing.** Write your own poem about an ongoing fear or stressor you experience or that you see your community or our nation experiencing. In the poem, discuss how the fear shapes everyday life in a way that simultaneously holds us back while also offering "a kind of solution." You might consider something practical and personal, such as the daily pressure of assignments and tests, or something global, such as climate change or the possibility of future pandemics.

The Emperor of Ice-Cream

Wallace Stevens

Bettmann/Getty Images

Wallace Stevens (1879–1955) is considered one of the most important American modernist poets. Born in Reading, Pennsylvania, Stevens studied at Harvard University and graduated from New York Law School. His poetry collections include *Harmonium* (1923), *The Man with the Blue Guitar and Other Poems* (1937), *Transport to Summer* (1947), and *A Primitive Like an Orb* (1948). *Collected Poems* (1954) won both a Pulitzer Prize and the National Book Award. Stevens favored precision of imagery and clear, sharp language, rejecting the sentiment favored by the Romantic and Victorian poets.

KEY CONTEXT This modernist poem alludes to Shakespeare's *Hamlet* (p. 555) in act iv, scene iii, when Hamlet tells Claudius that the dead Polonius is at dinner, "[n]ot where he eats, but where a is eaten. A certain convocation of politic worms are e'en at him. Your worm is your only emperor for diet."

Call the roller of big cigars,
The muscular one, and bid him whip
In kitchen cups concupiscent[1] curds.
Let the wenches dawdle in such dress
As they are used to wear, and let the boys
Bring flowers in last month's newspapers.
Let be be finale of seem.
The only emperor is the emperor of ice-cream.

---

[1] Lustful. — Eds.

Take from the dresser of deal,[2]
Lacking the three glass knobs, that sheet
On which she embroidered fantails[3] once
And spread it so as to cover her face.
If her horny feet protrude, they come
To show how cold she is, and dumb.
Let the lamp affix its beam.
The only emperor is the emperor of ice-cream. ■

1922

[2] Wood used in inexpensive furniture. — Eds.

[3] An ornate design that looks like the tail feathers of the fantail bird. — Eds.

Understanding and Interpreting

1. What is your first impression of "The Emperor of Ice-Cream"? What details or meaning did you find after a second reading?
2. Does the poem offer any information about the speaker? If so, what is it? If not, why not?
3. Who is "she" in line 11?
4. Why does the "emperor of ice-cream" make another appearance in the second stanza?
5. What do you think "Let be be finale of seem" (l. 7) means? Think about how it fits into that stanza and the poem as a whole.
6. What is the speaker's tone? What task does he seem to be doing?
7. The poet Elizabeth Bishop suggested that "The Emperor of Ice-Cream" is set in Key West, Florida, where Cubans worked in the cigar factories and Black people traditionally ate ice cream at funerals. Does this strike you as an accurate reading of the poem? If so, how does it affect your interpretation of it? If not, why not?

Analyzing Language, Style, and Structure

1. **Vocabulary in Context.** What image does the word "concupiscent" conjure, and why does Stevens use it to describe cheese curds? What meaning do you think Stevens's speaker conveys through it?
2. Compare the poem's two stanzas. Some critics have noted that the first is about life and the second about death, though neither is portrayed in a very positive light. What do you think is the speaker's attitude toward each?
3. What might the sheet embroidered with fantails be used for in the context of this poem? What does this item ultimately represent?
4. In what ways does the poem connect eating and death?
5. As the Key Context notes, this poem is an allusion to a scene from *Hamlet*. What effect does this allusion have?

Topics for Composing

1. **AP® FRQ** **Poetry Analysis.** In Wallace Stevens's "The Emperor of Ice-Cream," published in 1922, the speaker comments on life and death. Read the poem carefully. Then, in a well-written essay, analyze how Stevens uses literary elements and techniques to convey the speaker's complex attitude toward the connection between the two.

2. **AP® Literary Argumentation.** The most important themes in literature are sometimes developed in scenes of death. How does "The Emperor of Ice-Cream" use the dead woman in the second stanza to illuminate the meaning of the poem as a whole?
3. **Connections.** The poetry critic Helen Vendler approached "The Emperor of Ice-Cream" by putting it into a first-person narrative. Try doing the same; begin by walking in the door and proceed from there. Consider why you're there and what you see. When you're finished, take a look at how Vendler did it. How did your interpretation of the poem change as you completed this exercise?
4. **Connections.** Look more deeply into the connection between this poem and *Hamlet*. What do both works tell audiences and readers about mortality?
5. **Multimodal.** Early-twentieth-century European post-impressionist artists created work that, though distorted, began with real objects. Look at some of these works by artists such as Georges Braque, Paul Cézanne, and Pablo Picasso. Create a visual version of "The Emperor of Ice-Cream" that starts with the images you find but represents the more abstract themes as well.

Do not go gentle into that good night

Dylan Thomas

Hulton Archive/Getty Images

Dylan Thomas (1914–1953) was born in Wales, spent much of his life in London, and gained a following in the United States, where he often lectured and gave readings. He wrote his first volume of poetry when he was only twenty and published steadily throughout his lifetime. His works include *The Map of Love* (1939); *Portrait of the Artist as a Young Dog* (1940); *Deaths and Entrances* (1946); *In Country Sleep* (1952); and the posthumous *Under Milk Wood: A Play for Voices* (1954), which features characters from the fictional Welsh fishing village of Llareggub. During World War II, Thomas wrote scripts for documentary films, and after the war he was a literary commentator for BBC radio. He died in New York City at the age of thirty-nine of complications from alcoholism.

KEY CONTEXT "Do not go gentle into that good night" is addressed to Thomas's dying father. Thomas chose to write a villanelle to capitalize on the refrain created by this form. Villanelles are made up of five tercets followed by a quatrain. The first and third lines of the opening tercet alternately recur as the last line of the subsequent tercets. These two lines ultimately form the final lines of the quatrain at the end of the poem.

Do not go gentle into that good night,
Old age should burn and rave at close of day;
Rage, rage against the dying of the light.

Though wise men at their end know dark is right,
Because their words had forked no lightning they
Do not go gentle into that good night.

Good men, the last wave by, crying how bright
Their frail deeds might have danced in a green bay,
Rage, rage against the dying of the light.

Wild men who caught and sang the sun in flight,
And learn, too late, they grieved it on its way,
Do not go gentle into that good night.

Grave men, near death, who see with blinding sight
Blind eyes could blaze like meteors and be gay,
Rage, rage against the dying of the light.

And you, my father, there on the sad height,
Curse, bless, me now with your fierce tears, I pray.
Do not go gentle into that good night.
Rage, rage against the dying of the light. ■

1952

Understanding and Interpreting

1. Do you think the speaker's urgings are more for his father's benefit or for his own? How do you think the argument aids or harms both of them in dealing with the father's death?
2. Stanzas 2 through 5 are about "wise men," "good men," "wild men," and "grave men." How do they differ from one another in their response to death?
3. When speaking of "wise men," the speaker says that "their words had forked no lightning" (l. 5). What does this phrase mean? How do the wise men feel about this?
4. Thomas withholds the identity of the poem's subject until the final stanza. Why?
5. Why do you suppose the speaker insists on wanting his father to fight against "the dying of the light" despite the inevitability of death?

Analyzing Language, Style, and Structure

1. **Vocabulary in Context.** "Grave" is used in line 13 as an adjective modifying "men." What does the word mean within the context of that line? Consider why Dylan Thomas chose the use of this word. Why is it an appropriate selection for this poem, and how does it connect to other carefully selected words?
2. Much of the power of a villanelle, the form in which this poem is composed, resides in its repeated lines and their subtly shifting meaning over the course of the piece. How do Thomas's repeated lines change from stanza to stanza? You might consider theme, mood, imagery, and even grammatical structure to support your answer.
3. How do you interpret the images of natural forces that Thomas connects to the men described in the middle stanzas? Choose a stanza and explain how the particular metaphor develops the poem's themes.
4. Discuss the recurring images of light and darkness in the poem. What multiple meanings might these images collectively convey? Explain, focusing on a specific passage or set of images.

Topics for Composing

1. **AP® FRQ Poetry Analysis.** In Dylan Thomas's "Do not go gentle into that good night," published in 1952, the speaker urges his father to fight against death. Read the poem carefully. Then, in a well-written essay, analyze how Thomas uses literary elements and techniques to convey the speaker's complex perspective on death.
2. **AP® Literary Argumentation.** The rebellion embodied in the poem is not directed against any human authority or tradition but against death itself. Are there aspects of life that the speaker rejects as well in making his argument? Support your answer using specific passages from the text.
3. **Research.** While we encourage you to separate the poet from the speaker when you're reading and interpreting poetry, some poems are clearly more personal than others. What was happening in Thomas's life when he wrote this poem? How much did his experience with death and illness inform his verse? Reread the poem. How does your appreciation and interpretation of the poem differ after conducting this research?
4. **Speaking and Listening.** On the internet, locate a recording of Dylan Thomas reciting his poem. Is that how you would have recited the poem? How would you change Thomas's approach? Be prepared to explain your position to the entire class.
5. **Connections.** References to Thomas's poem are frequent in popular books, movies, and television shows. Find some instances of these and compile your findings in a brief response. Then, discuss how your appreciation of the poem was affected by discovering all these references to it. Did you connect further with the poem or has it lost its impact? Explain.

Her Kind

Anne Sexton

Everett Collection Inc/Alamy

Anne Sexton (1928–1974) was one of the most celebrated confessional poets to emerge in America during the 1960s and 1970s. Born in Newton, Massachusetts, she struggled through a childhood marked by family discord and, by some accounts, periodic abuse. Sexton grappled with depression and suicidal urges for much of her adult life. In 1957, at the suggestion of her therapist, she began attending meetings of poetry groups in Boston, where she met such poets as Robert Lowell, Maxine Kumin, and Sylvia Plath. Her first volume of poetry, *To Bedlam and Part Way Back*, was published in 1960. Her subsequent work gained considerable acclaim and a number of awards, culminating in the Pulitzer Prize for *Live or Die* (1967). Though much criticism of Sexton's poetry revolves around her mental illness and eventual suicide, the body of her work comprises a much broader range, including *Transformations* (1971), a collection of prose poems reimagining the Grimm brothers' fairy tales.

KEY CONTEXT "Her Kind," from *To Bedlam and Part Way Back*, is a daring experiment in point of view, exploring images of women as outcasts.

I have gone out, a possessed witch,
haunting the black air, braver at night;
dreaming evil, I have done my hitch
over the plain houses, light by light:
lonely thing, twelve-fingered, out of mind.
A woman like that is not a woman, quite.
I have been her kind.

I have found the warm caves in the woods,
filled them with skillets, carvings, shelves,
closets, silks, innumerable goods;
fixed the suppers for the worms and the elves:
whining, rearranging the disaligned.
A woman like that is misunderstood.
I have been her kind.

I have ridden in your cart, driver,
waved my nude arms at villages going by,
learning the last bright routes, survivor
where your flames still bite my thigh
and my ribs crack where your wheels wind.
A woman like that is not ashamed to die.
I have been her kind. ■

1960

Understanding and Interpreting

1. How would you characterize the speaker? Is the "I" referred to the same throughout the poem? Explain.
2. What is the speaker's attitude toward the "witch" in the opening lines? What particular descriptions seem the most sympathetic or unsympathetic?
3. Reading the poem in the context of this chapter's theme, what is the speaker — as well as the "kinds" of women with whom she identifies — rebelling against? What or whom do you think the speaker would identify with the notion of conformity?
4. Reread the final stanza carefully. What is happening to the speaker in these seven lines?

Analyzing Language, Style, and Structure

1. **Vocabulary in Context.** Consider the use of the word "hitch" in line 3. What part of speech is it, and what does it mean? What does this word suggest about the speaker's relationship to the world around her?
2. Trace the point of view throughout this poem. Where does it shift? What perspectives are we offered?
3. This poem is rich in imagery. Analyze how the patterns of imagery in the first stanza relate to the meaning. How and why does the imagery shift in the third stanza?

4. An archetype is a universally recognized symbol, figure, or idea. Identify at least one archetype in the poem and explain its function.
5. "I have been her kind" concludes each stanza of the poem, creating a refrain. What is the effect of this repetition? How does it build a bridge between the poem's structure and the speaker's message?

Topics for Composing

1. AP® FRQ **Poetry Analysis.** In Anne Sexton's "Her Kind," published in 1960, the speaker contemplates the many roles that a woman plays throughout her life. Read the poem carefully. Then, in a well-written essay, analyze how Sexton uses literary elements and techniques to develop the speaker's complex perspective on society's expectations of women.
2. AP® FRQ **Poetry Analysis.** In Anne Sexton's "Her Kind," published in 1960, the speaker uses the image of a witch to describe how women engage in society. Read the poem carefully. Then, in a well-written essay, analyze how Sexton uses literary elements and techniques to develop a complex characterization of women who are cast as outsiders.
3. **Multimodal.** Create a digital travel brochure showing all the places the speaker travels. Combine artwork, words from the poem, music, and videos to capture the significance and tone of each stanza.
4. **Connections.** Think about how you feel about your place in society. Find a word or phrase in the poem that relates to how you perceive your role and use it as the starting point of your response. What is the significance of the word or phrase within this poem, and how does it remind you of how you feel within society?
5. **Research.** What were the rules, both written and unwritten, that dictated what life was like for women in the middle of the twentieth century? Research the personal, political, and social circumstances surrounding Sexton's poem. How does your interpretation of its meaning change after conducting your research?

Is About

Allen Ginsberg

Sophie Bassouls/Sygma/Getty Images

Allen Ginsberg (1926–1997) was born in Newark, New Jersey. Ginsberg went to Columbia University on a scholarship to study law but changed his major to English. He led a varied, unconventional life: he worked as a dishwasher, welder, and university professor; he was arrested several times for political protests; he spent time in a psychiatric institution; and he toured with Bob Dylan's band. Ginsberg's work is notable for its free expression and rejection of conformity and materialism. *Howl* (1955) created intense interest and controversy for both its style and its content. In 1957, the poem's publisher was charged with obscenity; however, the case was thrown out when the presiding judge ruled that *Howl* was of "redeeming social consequence." Ginsberg's other works include *Kaddish and Other Poems* (1961) and the mixed-genre collection *The Fall of America*, which won a National Book Award in 1973.

KEY CONTEXT Ginsberg was one of the Beat poets, a small group of young poets, writers, intellectuals, musicians, and artists who challenged mainstream American politics and culture in the 1950s. The name recalls both weariness and the stress in music. In this poem, Ginsberg makes several references to figures and events from history and pop culture, including musicians Bob Dylan (b. 1941) and Ludwig von Beethoven (1770–1827); Nazi dictator Adolf Hitler (1889–1945), Soviet leader Joseph Stalin (1878–1953), U.S. president Franklin Delano Roosevelt (1882–1945), and British prime minister Winston Churchill (1874–1965); writers Edgar Allan Poe (1809–1849) and Percy Bysshe Shelley (1792–1822); the Holocaust; and Buddha. Additionally, "Is About" deliberately includes outdated language to describe American Indian, Jewish, Black, and Asian people that, depending upon the context, could be offensive. We wish to accurately reflect both Ginsberg's original intent as well as the time periods, cultures, and racism evoked by the text, but we also recognize that this language can be disrespectful and deeply hurtful. Be mindful of context, both Ginsberg's and yours, as you read.

Dylan is about the Individual against the whole of creation
Beethoven is about one man's fist in the lightning clouds
The Pope is about abortion & the spirits of the dead . . .
Television is about people sitting in their living room looking at their things
America is about being a big Country full of Cowboys Indians Jews Negroes & Americans
Orientals Chicanos Factories skyscrapers Niagara Falls Steel Mills radios homeless
  Conservatives, don't forget
Russia is about Czars Stalin Poetry Secret Police Communism barefoot in the snow
But that's not really Russia it's a concept
A concept is about how to look at the earth from the moon
without ever getting there. The moon is about love & Werewolves, also Poe.
Poe is about looking at the moon from the sun
or else the graveyard
Everything is about something if you're a thin movie producer chain-smoking muggles
The world is about overpopulation, Imperial invasions, Biocide, Genocide, Fratricidal Wars,
  Starvation, Holocaust, mass injury & murder, high technology
Super science, atom Nuclear Neutron Hydrogen detritus, Radiation Compassion Buddha,
  Alchemy
Communication is about monopoly television radio movie newspaper spin on Earth, i.e.
  planetary censorship.
Universe is about Universe.
Allen Ginsberg is about confused mind writing down newspaper headlines from Mars—
The audience is about salvation, the listeners are about sex, Spiritual gymnastics, nostalgia for
  the Steam Engine & Pony Express
Hitler Stalin Roosevelt & Churchill are about arithmetic & Quadrilateral equations, above all
  chemistry physics & chaos theory—
Who cares what it's all about?
I do! Edgar Allan Poe cares! Shelley cares! Beethoven & Dylan care.
Do you care? What are you about
or are you a human being with 10 fingers & two eyes? ■

1996

Understanding and Interpreting

1. "Is About" is, in a sense, a definition poem. Which definition seems most persuasive to you? How do you think the poem defines the title itself?
2. How would you answer the last two questions of the poem (ll. 23–24)?
3. Why does Allen Ginsberg insert himself into the poem as one of its characters?
4. What would you say "Is About" is about?

Analyzing Language, Style, and Structure

1. **Vocabulary in Context.** What is the meaning of the word "monopoly" in line 16? How does the speaker connect "television radio movie newspaper" to "monopoly"? What message does he convey through this connection?
2. What techniques does Ginsberg employ to affect the tempo of each line? Consider line length, punctuation, and the sound of the words. How does the resulting pace inform your understanding of the poet's intentions or mood?
3. "Is About" is built on references to American and world culture, science, and politics. Is there a unifying thread to the references? How do they build throughout the poem?
4. How do the juxtapositions in the poem's lists and series develop tension or resonance within the poem?
5. How does the element of surprise function in the poem? Identify an unexpected association or definition that particularly affected your reading or understanding of the speaker's intentions or ideas.
6. How would you describe the tone of the poem? How does Ginsberg create that tone?

Topics for Composing

1. AP® FRQ **Poetry Analysis.** In Allen Ginsberg's "Is About," published in 1996, the speaker poses a question about what it means to be human. Read the poem carefully. Then, in a well-written essay, analyze how Ginsberg uses literary elements and techniques to develop the speaker's complex answer to that question.
2. **AP® Literary Argumentation.** What argument does Ginsberg make about the importance of art in this poem? Use specific examples from the text to support your answer.
3. **Connections.** From among the characters who populate the poem (Dylan, Beethoven, the Pope, Poe, Buddha, Hitler, Stalin, Roosevelt, Churchill, and Shelley), select one you know well. What meaning does this person's inclusion convey in context of the rest of the poem? Is the reference accurate, as you see it?
4. **Connections.** Ginsberg was a fan of Walt Whitman's poetry. Select at least five of Whitman's poems to read and analyze. You may wish to include "Mannahatta" (p. 1281). How does Whitman's influence appear in "Is About"?
5. **Connections.** "Is About" was first published in the *New Yorker's* 1996 election issue, in which every article, cartoon, and review was related to the upcoming presidential election of Bill Clinton, who defeated Bob Dole. What connections are there between "Is About" and the 1996 election? Why might the editors of the *New Yorker* have chosen it for that issue?
6. **Creative Writing.** Write a poem in imitation of Ginsberg's "Is About," using a similar structure but changing each of the names and places that begin the lines. Then answer the question, What is your poem about?
7. **Multimodal.** Identify a list or a series of images or concepts in the poem that you find particularly striking. Illustrate them in a collage, through music, or with original art.

Penelope

Carol Ann Duffy

Jeremy Sutton-Hibbert/Getty Images

The first woman to be named Britain's poet laureate, Carol Ann Duffy was born to Irish Catholic parents in Glasgow, Scotland, in 1955. She grew up in England, earning a degree in philosophy in 1977, and published her first collection of poetry in 1985. *Mean Time* won the Whitbread Poetry Award in 1993, and *Rapture* won the T. S. Eliot Prize in 2005. Poet laureate of the UK from 2009 to 2019, she is currently the creative director of the Writing School at Manchester Metropolitan University. "Penelope" is from *The World's Wife*, Duffy's 1999 collection based on stories from history and mythology but written in the voice of women whose roles have been historically overshadowed by men.

KEY CONTEXT Penelope is Odysseus's wife in Homer's *Odyssey*. Penelope, who waited for twenty years for Odysseus to return from the Trojan War, famously kept her suitors at bay by promising to marry one when she had finished weaving a shroud for her father-in-law — but each night she unwove her work so that she never appeared to make progress.

At first, I looked along the road
hoping to see him saunter home
among the olive trees,
a whistle for the dog
who mourned him with his warm head on my knees.
Six months of this
and then I noticed that whole days had passed
without my noticing.
I sorted cloth and scissors, needle, thread,

thinking to amuse myself,
but found a lifetime's industry instead.
I sewed a girl
under a single star — cross-stitch, silver silk —
running after childhood's bouncing ball.
I chose between three greens for the grass;
a smoky pink, a shadow's grey
to show a snapdragon gargling a bee.
I threaded walnut brown for a tree,

my thimble like an acorn
pushing up through umber soil.
Beneath the shade
I wrapped a maiden in a deep embrace
with heroism's boy

and lost myself completely
in a wild embroidery of love, lust, loss, lessons learnt;
then watched him sail away
into the loose gold stitching of the sun.

And when the others came to take his place,
disturb my peace,
I played for time.
I wore a widow's face, kept my head down,
did my work by day, at night unpicked it.
I knew which hour of the dark the moon
would start to fray,
I stitched it.
Grey threads and brown

pursued my needle's leaping fish
to form a river that would never reach the sea.
I tricked it. I was picking out
the smile of a woman at the centre
of this world, self-contained, absorbed, content,
most certainly not waiting,
when I heard a far-too-late familiar tread outside the door.
I licked my scarlet thread
and aimed it surely at the middle of the needle's eye once more. ■

1999

Understanding and Interpreting

1. How does the speaker of the poem characterize herself in the first stanza? How is her missing husband, Odysseus, characterized?
2. What changes in the speaker's attitude in the second stanza?
3. What is the significance of Penelope finding "a lifetime's industry" (l. 11)?
4. Who are the people the speaker refers to as "a maiden in a deep embrace / with heroism's boy" (ll. 22–23)?
5. How does the speaker characterize the woman "at the centre / of this world" in the final stanza?
6. Why is the "familiar tread" "far-too-late" (l. 43)?
7. In Homer's *Odyssey*, characters are often introduced by epithets, which are words or phrases that denote a fundamental quality of the figure in question. Penelope is referred to as "wise Penelope." How does Carol Ann Duffy's speaker earn this description?

Analyzing Language, Style, and Structure

1. **Vocabulary in Context.** Duffy's speaker hopes to see her husband "saunter home" (l. 2). While the denotation of *saunter* is "to walk slowly," it carries very specific connotations. What are they? What does this word choice suggest about Penelope's attitude toward her husband's return?

2. Penelope's defining trait in *The Odyssey* is her patient and uncompromising faithfulness to her husband during the twenty years of his absence. How do the descriptions of the speaker's embroidery work — particularly in stanzas 2 and 3 — challenge or complicate this characterization?
3. Duffy's Penelope describes her experience after her husband, Odysseus, has left as getting lost "in a wild embroidery of love, lust, loss, lessons learnt; / then watched him sail away / into the loose gold stitching of the sun" (ll. 25–27). How does the figurative language in these lines capture not only what happened but the speaker's feelings about that experience? What other examples of figurative language do you find in this poem that are especially effective at conveying Penelope's perspective?
4. How does Duffy use humor in "Penelope"? Look at both word choice — such as puns or understatement — as well as structure — such as rhyme or meter — that help shape the tone. Would you characterize the humor as sly wit, gentle irony, biting satire — or something else? Explain, using evidence from the poem to support your interpretation.
5. Throughout the poem, Duffy describes Penelope embroidering her life's story. What does this work represent to Penelope? What comment might Duffy be making about the so-called domestic arts of what was considered women's work, such as embroidering, quilting, and sewing in general?

Topics for Composing

1. AP® FRQ **Poetry Analysis.** In Carol Ann Duffy's "Penelope," published in 1999, the speaker is Penelope, the wife of the Greek hero Odysseus from Homer's *Odyssey*, and she recounts the many years she spent waiting for him to return home. Read the poem carefully. Then, in a well-written essay, analyze how Duffy uses literary elements and techniques to develop a new perspective on an old story.
2. **AP® Literary Argumentation.** Penelope is usually interpreted as a passive character whose role is that of an exemplary, even idealized wife and mother. In what ways does Duffy offer an alternative version, or a counternarrative, to the hero's journey?
3. **AP® Literary Argumentation.** In a review of Duffy's book *The World's Wife*, novelist Jeanette Winterson argues that Duffy shows us that "the politics is in the poetry." How is "Penelope" "political"? What message does it convey to modern audiences?
4. **Connections.** Novelist Margaret Atwood has written *The Penelopiad*, which retells *The Odyssey* from Penelope's point of view. Read this novella and compare Atwood's interpretation of Penelope with Duffy's in this poem.
5. **Speaking and Listening.** Many visual artists since the time of *The Odyssey* have created work representing the character of Penelope. Working in small groups, identify one that you find appealing or somehow interesting. Who is Penelope from the perspective of the artist you've chosen? Present your interpretation to your classmates and answer questions in class discussion.
6. **Connections.** Stanza 4 presents the suitors and Penelope's trick. How dependent on a reading of Homer's *Odyssey* is your understanding of this part of the poem? How dependent is the poem as a whole on that knowledge? If you are familiar with *The Odyssey*, how does this poem comment on and inform your reading of it?
7. **Creative Writing.** Write a poem of your own in the voice of a secondary character in a myth, legend, or fairy tale that re-interprets the story in a fundamental way.

The Wife of the Man of Many Wiles

photo by Milas Bicansky

A. E. Stallings

Born and raised in Decatur, Georgia, A. E. Stallings (b. 1968) is an award-winning American poet and translator. She is the author of four books of poetry, *Archaic Smile* (1999), *Hapax* (2006), *Olives* (2012), and *Like* (2018), which was a finalist for the Pulitzer Prize. She has also published *The Nature of Things* (2007), a verse translation of a work by the Roman poet and philosopher Lucretius, and *Works and Days* (2018), a verse translation of a work by Greek poet Hesiod. In 2011, she won a Guggenheim Fellowship and a MacArthur Foundation Fellowship. She currently lives and teaches in Athens, Greece.

KEY CONTEXT In "The Wife of the Man of Many Wiles," Stallings brings to life the voice of Penelope, wife of the famously clever Odysseus, often identified in Homer's *Iliad* and *Odyssey* as "the man of many wiles."

Believe what you want to. Believe that I wove,
If you wish, twenty years, and waited, while you
Were knee-deep in blood, hip-deep in goddesses.

I've not much to show for twenty years' weaving —
I have but one half-finished cloth at the loom.
Perhaps it's the lengthy, meticulous grieving.

Explain how you want to. Believe I unravelled
At night what I stitched in the slow siesta,
How I kept them all waiting for me to finish,

The suitors, you call them. Believe what you want to.
Believe that they waited for me to finish,
Believe I beguiled them with nightly un-doings.

Believe what you want to. That they never touched me.
Believe your own stories, as you would have me do,
How you only survived by the wise infidelities.

Believe that each day you wrote me a letter
That never arrived. Kill all the damn suitors
If you think it will make you feel better. ■

1999

Exploring the Text

1. How does the speaker characterize herself? How does that characterization differ from the way Penelope is typically described?
2. What is the effect of the repetition of the word "Believe"? Why do you think A. E. Stallings chose to begin five lines of the poem with it? How does it help develop the character of the speaker?
3. What liberties has Stallings taken to make the speaker — Penelope — sound like a contemporary woman? How does that help the poem make an argument?
4. Why do you think the title of the poem is "The Wife of the Man of Many Wiles"? Why do you think Stallings chose not to call it "Penelope," or even to mention the names Penelope or Odysseus anywhere in the poem?

Making Connections

1. Both poems are told from the point of view of Penelope, the long-waiting wife of Odysseus. In what ways are the points of view the same; in what ways contrasting?
2. Both poems also provide a glimpse of Odysseus. What do we learn about him in each poem? What do the two characterizations have in common?
3. How would you characterize the tone of each of these poems? Cite specific lines and language from each to support your response. Are they more alike or different? Explain.
4. How do Duffy and Stallings each interpret the ancient story of Penelope from *The Odyssey* to comment on relationships between husbands and wives? Which one strikes you as more compelling in the context of our world today, and why?

We Are Not Responsible

Harryette Mullen

© Judy Natal

Harryette Mullen (b. 1953) is a poet, short story writer, and literary scholar who grew up in Fort Worth, Texas. She is currently a professor at the University of California in Los Angeles, where she teaches African American literature and creative writing. She is the author of seven books of poetry, including *Tree Tall Woman* (1981), *Trimmings* (1991), and *S*PeRM**K*T* (1992), a series of experimental prose poems inspired by supermarkets. Her most recent work is *Urban Tumbleweed: Notes from a Tanka Diary* (2013). Her numerous awards include a Gertrude Stein Award for innovative poetry and a Guggenheim Fellowship. Her work often includes wordplay, allusions, and other linguistic games.

We are not responsible for your lost or stolen relatives.
We cannot guarantee your safety if you disobey our instructions.
We do not endorse the causes or claims of people begging for handouts.
We reserve the right to refuse service to anyone.

Your ticket does not guarantee that we will honor your reservations.
In order to facilitate our procedures, please limit your carrying on.
Before taking off, please extinguish all smoldering resentments.

If you cannot understand English, you will be moved out of the way.
In the event of a loss, you'd better look out for yourself.
Your insurance was cancelled because we can no longer handle
your frightful claims. Our handlers lost your luggage and we
are unable to find the key to your legal case.

You were detained for interrogation because you fit the profile.
You are not presumed to be innocent if the police
have reason to suspect you are carrying a concealed wallet.
It's not our fault you were born wearing a gang color.
It is not our obligation to inform you of your rights.

Step aside, please, while our officer inspects your bad attitude.
You have no rights we are bound to respect.
Please remain calm, or we can't be held responsible
for what happens to you. ■

2002

Understanding and Interpreting

1. Who is speaking at the beginning of the first stanza? What do you imagine the speaker's voice sounds like?
2. What are the rules and procedures the speaker describes in the first two stanzas? Do they remind you of anything you have encountered in your day-to-day life? Explain.
3. Who are the "handlers" in line 11? What is their role in the context of the poem?
4. What does the speaker mean by "It's not our fault you were born wearing a gang color" (l. 16)?
5. What does the title suggest to you will be the subject of the poem? Does the poem fulfill that expectation? Why or why not?

Analyzing Language, Style, and Structure

1. **Vocabulary in Context.** The speaker of the poem declares that insurance had to be cancelled "because we can no longer handle / your frightful claims" (ll. 10–11). How does "frightful" differ from "frightening" here? What does it suggest about the "claims" being made in the context of the poem?
2. In what ways do Harryette Mullen's pronoun choices establish a tension, even an adversarial relationship between the speaker and the reader in the opening stanza?
3. What examples of word play — such as puns, double entendres, unexpected juxtapositions — do you find in the poem? How do they set the tone and convey meaning?

4. How does Mullen's integration of legal and bureaucratic language develop the speaker's tone in the poem? How would you characterize the language itself? Is it neutral? Why or why not?
5. How do Mullen's choices in diction and syntax develop an environment of refusal and denial in the poem? Cite specific text to support your analysis.
6. One of Mullen's favored literary techniques is using "turned lines": in this case, what begins as a kind of monotonous sounding rule or disclaimer shifts to a harsher, often disturbing meaning with a play on words or unusual choice of language by the end of the line. Identify at least two instances of turned lines. How do these contribute to the poem's meaning?
7. How would you characterize the overall tone of the poem? Consider how it gathers momentum as it moves from statement to statement, stanza to stanza.
8. The poet Douglas Kearney described Mullen's work as a "super serious kind of play" in which she "engages language as a kind of plaything, but it is always volatile, like somebody juggling nitroglycerin." How does that characterization relate to your interpretation of "We Are Not Responsible"?

Topics for Composing

1. **AP® FRQ** **Poetry Analysis.** In Harryette Mullen's "We Are Not Responsible," published in 2002, the speaker puts forth a series of rules, regulations, and explanations for the implied audience. Read the poem carefully. Then, in a well-written essay, analyze how Mullen uses literary elements and techniques to comment on the reciprocal nature of responsibility.
2. **AP® Literary Argumentation.** Mullen has explained that the poem is about "the social contract," a reference to the implicit agreement among the members of a society, the ruled and the rulers, to cooperate for social benefits. How might "We Are Not Responsible" be read as a commentary, criticism, or interrogation of the social contract in our society today? Use specific references to the poem to support your interpretation.
3. **Connections.** Although this poem was published as part of a collection in 2002, how might it resonate with current events? Select at least three recent events to discuss in your response.
4. **Multimodal.** Working in groups, develop an interpretation of the poem by pairing an audio recording of the poem with a series of photographs, either original ones or those you have found. Present to the class and lead a discussion of what your interpretation is, exploring how the images you've chosen contribute to its expression and serve as effective evidence.
5. **Connections.** In her 1993 acceptance speech for the Nobel Prize for Literature, Toni Morrison warned against the misuse and abuse of language:

   > Whether it is obscuring state language or the faux-language of mindless media; whether it is the proud but calcified language of the academy or the commodity driven language of science; whether it is the malign language of law-without-ethics, or language designed for the estrangement of minorities, hiding its racist plunder in its literary cheek — it must be rejected, altered and exposed. . . .

   What do you think Morrison means by this? What role does the state play in Mullen's poem, and how does it comment on the "language of law-without-ethics"?

Art & Craft

Robin Coste Lewis

Xavier Collin/Image Press Agency/Alamy

Robin Coste Lewis (b. 1964) is an American poet born in Compton, California, with familial roots in New Orleans. She earned an MFA from New York University, a master's degree in Sanskrit and comparative religious literature from Harvard Divinity School, and a PhD in creative writing from the University of Southern California. Her first book of poetry, *Voyage of the Sable Venus: and Other Poems* (2015), won the National Book Award.

KEY CONTEXT "Art & Craft" is a sonnet that consists of three quatrains and a couplet at the end, although it does not follow a traditional line scheme. The third quatrain often provides the volta, in which the speaker typically shifts perspective and sometimes closes with a witty remark.

I would figure out all the right answers
first, then gently mark a few of them wrong.
If a quiz had ten problems, I'd cancel
out one. When it had twenty, I'd bite my tongue

then leave at least two questions blank: __________ __________
A *B* was good, but an *A* was too good.
They'd kick your ass, call your big sister
slow, then stare over your desk, as if you'd

snaked out of a different hole. Knowing
taught me — quickly — to spell *community*
more honestly: *l-o-n-e-l-y*.
During Arts and Crafts, when Miss Larson allowed

the scissors out, I'd sneak a pair, then cut
my hair to stop me from growing too long. ■

2015

Understanding and Interpreting

1. Why do you think the poem is called "Art & Craft"? How is the title different from (or the same as) the Arts and Crafts session the speaker describes in line 12?
2. How would you characterize the speaker of "Art & Craft"? How does the poem reveal both her interior and exterior qualities?
3. Consider lines 7–9. Who are "they" in line 7, and how are they characterized? What does the speaker mean by "[k]nowing" in line 9? What irony do you see in these lines?
4. What do you think the speaker means when she says she would "cut / my hair to stop me from growing too long" (ll. 13–14)? How does that statement relate to the argument the poem makes?

Analyzing Language, Style, and Structure

1. **Vocabulary in Context.** What implications does Lewis's use of "snaked" have in line 9? What does the word communicate about the people the speaker characterizes in these lines? How do its connotations contribute to the speaker's tone in this poem?
2. What is the effect of the two blanks that appear at the end of line 5? What words do these blanks evoke?
3. This poem has fourteen lines and could be considered a sonnet. What other qualities of the sonnet do you detect here? Consider the ways the poem plays with rhyme scheme, as well as the turn the last two lines take. Why might Robin Coste Lewis have chosen to use this traditional closed form of poetry?
4. What is the effect of Lewis's repeated use of "would"? Be sure to consider contractions such as "I'd" (ll. 3, 4, and 13) and "They'd" (l. 7). How would the tone of the poem change had Lewis used simple past tense verbs (e.g., "I figured out all the right answers" as opposed to "I would figure out all the right answers")?
5. Examine Lewis's use of action verbs and alliteration in the poem. What is the purpose of these verbs, and how does the alliteration emphasize certain meanings?

Topics for Composing

1. **AP® FRQ** **Poetry Analysis.** In Robin Coste Lewis's "Art & Craft," published in 2015, the speaker explains how she navigated the academic challenges of school. Read the poem carefully. Then, in a well-written essay, analyze how Lewis uses literary elements and techniques to convey the speaker's complex attitude about her classmates, her teacher, and her education.
2. **Connections.** "Art & Craft" is a poem from Lewis's National Book Award–winning collection, *Voyage of the Sable Venus*. The collection begins and ends with several lyric, often biographical, poems such as "Art & Craft" that, according to the National Book Foundation's website, consider "the roles desire and race play in the construction of self." How does this poem make those connections? The center of the book is a narrative made of the titles of artworks that are in some way connected to the Black female figure in Western art. How might "Art & Craft," one of the lyric poems outside of the book's center, comment on the connection between art and self?
3. **Speaking and Listening.** Dr. Loretta Graziano Breuning explains "crab mentality" this way: "A lone crab can climb out of a bucket, but when its mates are present, it ends up boiled to death with them." Discuss with a partner or in a small group how the speaker in "Art & Craft" experiences crab mentality. Then, brainstorm together ways in which we tend to hold each other back and threaten to sever social bonds between us rather than supporting each other in our success. Finally, come together as a class to share your understanding of crab mentality in your community as well as ways to overcome it.
4. **Multimodal.** A 2015 article in the *Guardian* explains that, in her poetry, Robin Coste Lewis had begun "not only studying visual art but creating it." The poem "Art & Craft" similarly suggests a connection between visual arts and crafts and the art and craft of social interaction. To explore juxtaposing ideas, take an element from the poem, such as how "to spell *community* / more honestly: *l-o-n-e-l-y*" (ll. 10–11), and express it through a visual form such as a collage or a painting.

Ghazal for White Hen Pantry

Jamila Woods

Cindy Ord/Getty Images

Jamila Woods is an American poet, vocalist, and songwriter based in Chicago. She has a BA in Africana studies and theater and performance studies from Brown University. She released two albums with her band M&O and has collaborated with Chance the Rapper and Macklemore & Lewis. Each track on her second solo album, *LEGACY! LEGACY!* (2019) is named after a different artist, musician, or writer of color. Woods is the author of a chapbook, *The Truth about Dolls* (2012), and her poetry has been featured in several anthologies. Woods currently works as the associate artistic director of Young Chicago Authors, a nonprofit organization behind the Louder Than a Bomb youth poetry slam festival.

KEY CONTEXT The ghazal, a form that originated in Arabic poetry, typically on the theme of love and often set to music, consists of rhyming couplets and a refrain. The second line of each couplet typically ends with the same word, and the penultimate words in the second line of each couplet also rhyme with each other. White Hen Pantry is a now-defunct chain of convenience stores that were located throughout the Midwest and New England. Beverly, mentioned in the first line of the poem, is a wealthy neighborhood on the south side of Chicago.

beverly be the only south side you don't fit in
everybody in your neighborhood color of white hen

brown bag tupperware lunch don't fill you
after school cross the street, count quarters with white friends

you love 25¢ zebra cakes mom would never let you eat
you learn to white lie through white teeth at white hen

oreos in your palm, perm in your hair
everyone's irish in beverly, you just missin' the white skin

pray they don't notice your burnt toast, unwondered bread
you be the brownest egg ever born from the white hen

pantry in your chest where you stuff all the Black in
distract from the syllables in your name with a white grin

keep your consonants crisp, coffee milked, hands visible
never touch the holiday-painted windows of white hen

you made that mistake, scratched your initials in the paint
an unmarked crown victoria pulled up, full of white men

they grabbed your wrist & wouldn't show you a badge
the manager clucked behind the counter, thick as a white hen

they told your friends to run home, but called the principal on you
& you learned Black sins cost much more than white ones ■

2015

Understanding and Interpreting

1. Who is the "you" the speaker addresses repeatedly throughout the poem? Is the speaker addressing herself, or someone different? What might Jamila Woods have wanted to express with that ambiguity?
2. How does the speaker characterize Beverly in relation to herself?
3. What do the foods mentioned in "Ghazal for White Hen Pantry" have in common? How do they connect the speaker to her neighborhood?
4. What does the speaker mean when she says "Black sins cost much more than white ones" (l. 20)? What evidence does she provide to support that assertion?
5. The speaker of "Ghazal for White Hen Pantry" seems to fall in the category of "the only." How does Woods develop that characterization in the poem? How does the speaker feel about her "only-ness"?

Analyzing Language, Style, and Structure

1. **Vocabulary in Context.** What does the word "clucked" mean in line 18? How does it fit with the motif of the white hen, while at the same time being just the right sound for the manager to be making?
2. How does Woods play with the image of the white hen? Look at the literal meaning — where she talks about it as a convenience store — and also look at white hen as an image, such as in lines 2, 10, and 18. How does she connect the two meanings?
3. What do you think the speaker means by "keep your consonants crisp, coffee milked, hands visible" (l. 13)? What do those actions and images represent or evoke?
4. How does Woods use references to color throughout the poem? Pay specific attention to the colors associated with the foods the speaker names throughout the poem. How do these word and image choices reflect the speaker's message?
5. How does the poem's diction express the speaker's attitude toward conformity?
6. In this poem, "hen" — or a rhyme with "hen" — is the last word of every couplet and rather than a rhyme, the word "white" is repeated. Find other ways that Woods has played with the traditional structure of a ghazal. What effect does this kind of remixing have on your understanding of the poem? Why do you think Woods broke some of the rules of the form?
7. Is it important to know these rules of the ghazal to understand the poem's meaning? Explain why or why not.

Topics for Composing

1. **AP® FRQ** **Poetry Analysis.** In Jamila Woods's "Ghazal for White Hen Pantry," published in 2015, the speaker describes a rebellious experience from her youth that had different consequences for her than for her friends. Read the poem carefully. Then, in a well-written essay, analyze how Woods

uses literary elements and techniques to convey the speaker's complex perspective on the different stakes that small acts of rebellion and mischievousness hold for her as opposed to her white peers.

2. **AP® Literary Argumentation.** How does this poem comment on conformity and rebellion? What do the speaker's small acts of rebellion suggest about her attitude toward the expectations of others?
3. **Connections.** Read other contemporary ghazals, such as "Hip-Hop Ghazal" by Patricia Smith and "Ghazal" by Reginald Dwayne Betts. What do these poems, beyond the rules of the ghazal form, have in common with "Ghazal for White Hen Pantry"? Why is this form appropriate to the subjects of these poems?
4. **Creative Writing.** Write a ghazal about an experience that shifted your perspective on what it means to rebel in different contexts and what the experience means to you now.

a remix for remembrance

Kristiana Rae Colón

©Sarah Lee/eyevine/The New York Times/Redux

Kristiana Rae Colón (b. 1986) is a playwright, an actor, a poet, and an activist. Colón received a BA from the University of Chicago and an MFA from the School of the Art Institute of Chicago. She has taught at Chicago State University, Malcolm X College, and Tribeca Flashpoint Academy. She is the author of several plays, including *but I cd only whisper* (2012); *Octagon* (2014); *Florissant & Canfield* (2016), which is based on the Ferguson, Missouri, protests following the fatal shooting Michael Brown by a police officer; *Good Friday* (2016); and *Tilikum* (2018). She appeared on the fifth season of HBO's *Def Poetry Jam*.

For my students

This is for the boys whose bedrooms are in the basement,
who press creases into jeans, who carve their names in pavement,
the girls whose names are ancient, ancestry is sacred,
the Aztec and the Mayan gods abuela[1] used to pray with

This is for the dangerous words hiding in the pages
of composition notes, holy books, and Sanskrit
This is for the patients who wait for medication,
for the mothers microwaving beans and rice at day's end

This is for the marching bands and girls at *quinceañeras*,[2]
the skaters and the writers whose moms are *eloteras*,[3]
laughing "Cops don't scare us, we sag so elders fear us
We will rewrite our textbooks in our own language if you dare us"

[1] Spanish for "grandmother." — Eds.
[2] A traditional celebration of a girl's fifteenth birthday in many Latin American communities. — Eds.
[3] Derived from the Spanish word for "corn," *eloteras* are women who sell food, often corn, from street carts or stands. — Eds.

This is for the Sarahs, the Angelicas, and Shawns,
the Beatrices, Paolas, Danielas, and the dawns
we scribble sunlight in the margins of horizons with our songs,
for all the voices tangled with the silence on our tongues

Rivals in the parks, fireworks at dark,
tired shirts that sweat your scent on hangers in the closet
For the boys who fix the faucet while their sister fixes coffee
'cause mommy had to leave for work at 6 AM and laundry
isn't folded yet: you don't have to hold your breath

You don't have to behave: stage your own rebellion,
paint canvases with rage and religion and prayers for pilgrims
sleeping in the train cars at the border and their children
Filibust[4] the Senate and bust markers on the Pink Line,[5]
stain the prosecution's case and force the judge to resign,
force the crowd the rewind the lyrics you invented

Speak away the limits to heights of your existence
Be a witness, be a record, be a testament, a triumph
Set your poems flying in the glitter of the planets
Feed open mouths with truth, the truth is we are famished
The Universe is starving for the symphonies you play
Clarinets and thunder and the syllables you say
are the instruments: you are infinite. Stretch your hands to heaven
Let your throat throttle the rhythms of all your fallen brethren
Your legacy is present, your history is now
You are the tenth degree of sound
You are the nephews of the sky
You are the bass line and the hi-hat and the snare drum and the cry
of red Septembers. You're the architects of winter
You are the builders of the roads that you're told you don't
    remember   You are
    the builders of the roads
    that you're told
    you don't remember   You are the builders
        of the roads that you're told you don't
        remember

[4] The filibuster is a controversial tactic used by legislators who wish to delay or prevent a bill from being debated or passed. It was one of the strategies used to prevent the passage of antilynching laws in the 1930s and in an attempt to prevent the passage of the Civil Rights Act in 1964. — Eds.

[5] The newest train line in Chicago's public transit system. — Eds.

Cast poems in the river and tell them you remember
Skate City Hall to splinters and tell them you remember
Send diamonds to your islands and tell them you remember
Find your God inside your mirror and tell Her you remember ■

2015

Understanding and Interpreting

1. Who is the speaker of "a remix for remembrance"? What do you know about her? How do you know?
2. Why do you think the title of the poem is all in lowercase letters? What might this choice indicate about the speaker's sense of who she is?
3. The first four stanzas begin with the phrase "This is for." How would you characterize the people the speaker is writing for?
4. What do you think the "roads that you're told you don't remember," repeated three times in lines 41–47, are? Why does the speaker insist that they are remembered?
5. What is the speaker's overall message in "a remix for remembrance"? In your response, be sure to consider what the speaker wishes for her students. Be as specific as possible, using evidence from the poem to support your interpretation.

Analyzing Language, Style, and Structure

1. **Vocabulary in Context.** What is the meaning of the word "sag" in line 11? How might it mean different things depending on if you think the poet is quoting something "*eloteras*" might say or something the "skaters and writers" might say?
2. You may notice that while "a remix for remembrance" addresses the speaker's students, it also addresses the community in which they live. What images create the community? How do they help you visualize what life in the community is like?
3. What characterizes stanzas 5 and 6? How do the language, syntax, and structure of these stanzas signal a shift in message from the first four?
4. "a remix for remembrance" uses figurative language sparingly but effectively. Look carefully at lines that do make use of it, such as line 15 or line 23, and consider the effect of the metaphorical language. What makes this language so effective in these contexts?
5. The poem rhymes in a few different ways, including end line rhymes, internal rhymes, and slant rhymes. What do the different rhyme schemes add to the poem? How does this structural feature relate to the title of the poem?
6. This poem, in the spoken word tradition, is meant to be performed aloud. Read it aloud. What does hearing yourself reading it bring to the poem? How do the poem's sections distinguish themselves in an oral reading?
7. Why do you think the seventh stanza is so much longer than the poem's other stanzas, which are between four and six lines long? How does this stanza develop tension? What does it add to the speaker's message?
8. What is the tone of the last stanza, and to what extent does it differ from the tone in the rest of the poem? How does Colón combine a few different messages and motifs in that stanza to create that tone?

Topics for Composing

1. **AP® FRQ Poetry Analysis.** In Kristiana Rae Colón's "a remix for remembrance," published in 2015, the speaker offers an ode to community. Read the poem carefully. Then, in a well-written essay, analyze how Colón uses literary elements and techniques to portray the speaker's complex relationship to the community she addresses.
2. **AP® Literary Argumentation.** Many works of poetry use music as a metaphor to convey meaning. What does "a remix for remembrance" use musical metaphor to convey? Why is music an appropriate choice for shaping this poem's message?
3. **Connections.** Watch the episodes of HBO's *Def Poetry Jam* in which Colón appears. Compare her style to that of the other poets in the episode. What literary and performance techniques do the poets have in common? What makes Colón's poetry and performance unique?
4. **Speaking and Listening.** Working in small groups, create and rehearse a spoken word performance of this poem that conveys your interpretation of its meaning. Perform the poem for the class, and discuss how each small group chose to interpret different aspects of the poem via their delivery.
5. **Creative Writing.** Write a similar poem but dedicate it "To My Teachers."

Passive Voice

Laura Da'

A member of the Eastern Shawnee tribe, Laura Da' is a poet and public school teacher. She studied creative writing at the University of Washington, the Institute of American Indian Arts, and Seattle University. Her first book, *Tributaries* (2015), won an American Book Award. Her second book of poetry, *Instruments of the True Measure*, was published in 2018.

University of Arizona Press

I use a trick to teach students
how to avoid passive voice.

Circle the verbs.
Imagine inserting "by zombies"
after each one.

Have the words been claimed
by the flesh-hungry undead?
If so, passive voice.

I wonder if these
sixth graders will recollect,
on summer vacation,
as they stretch their legs
on the way home
from Yellowstone or Yosemite

and the byway's historical marker
beckons them to the
site of an Indian village —

Where *trouble was brewing.*
Where, *after further hostilities, the army was directed to enter.*
Where *the village was razed after the skirmish occurred.*
Where *most were women and children.*

Riveted bramble of passive verbs
etched in wood —
stripped hands
breaking up from the dry ground
to pinch the meat
of their young red tongues. ■

2015

Understanding and Interpreting

1. What is the main subject of "Passive Voice"? What perspective does the title bring to the subject of the poem?
2. Why, according to the speaker, are "zombies" an effective way to illustrate the possible pitfalls of the passive voice?
3. What is your first impression of the speaker? How did it change as you read the poem?
4. What happens when you add "by zombies" to the sentences in the poem's fifth stanza?

Analyzing Language, Style, and Structure

1. **Vocabulary in Context.** What is the meaning of the verb "beckons" in line 16? It's not in the passive voice, yet its subject is an inanimate object: "historical marker." How does the grammar in that part of the poem add another dimension to the meaning of the text?
2. How do Laura Da's language choices in the first line hint that the poem has something more to say than how to detect the passive voice?
3. What point does the question in lines 6–7 make in light of the poem as a whole?
4. Where and how does Da' situate her sixth graders in the fourth stanza? How does she make them ready to try the zombie test on the signs at the "Indian village" (l. 17)?
5. The poem's last stanza is almost entirely made up of figurative language. Identify the figures of speech and explain their effect. Why might Da' have waited until the last stanza to use this kind of powerful language?

Topics for Composing

1. **AP® FRQ** **Poetry Analysis.** In Laura Da"s "Passive Voice," published in 2015, the speaker discusses the method she uses to help her students understand the significance of passive voice. Read the poem carefully. Then, in a well-written essay, analyze how Da' uses literary elements and techniques to convey the power of language.

2. **Connections.** Laura Da' has said in interviews that she's tired of the "mainstream fetishization of native literature" because it reinforces "otherness." Do some research on what Da' means by this. Do you find any patterns in what American Indian literature is "mainstreamed"? Do you agree that these works are "fetishized" or that they reinforce "otherness"? How does "Passive Voice" avoid "otherness"?
3. **AP® Literary Argumentation.** How does this poem comment on the function and importance of education? What kind of education does the speaker seek to provide her students? Analyze how Da' uses literary elements to convey the speaker's message about education.
4. **Research.** Do some research on residential schools for American Indian children during the late nineteenth and early twentieth centuries, in which white educators forcibly assimilated native children according to the creed of "kill the Indian, save the man." How does that history inform the speaker's approach to education in "Passive Voice"?
5. **Connections.** Search newspapers and news websites for examples of the passive voice. You might want to look particularly at news stories that mention the police. Create a chart with three columns. Add examples of passive voice in the first column and examples with "by zombies" after each verb in the second column. Finally, in the third column, identify the actual subjects that have been eliminated through the use of passive voice.

Ways of Rebelling

Nathalie Handal

Rob Stothard/Getty Images

Nathalie Handal (b. 1969) is a Palestinian American poet, playwright, editor, and critic. She has lived in Europe, the United States, the Caribbean, Latin America, and the Middle East. Currently she teaches at Columbia University. Handal has published several poetry collections, most recently *Life in a Country Album* (2019), and she is the editor of *The Poetry of Arab Women: A Contemporary Anthology* (2000) and co-editor of *Language for a New Century: Contemporary Poetry from the Middle East, Asia, and Beyond* (2008). Her debut collection, *The Lives of Rain* (2005), includes a series of poems on the consequences of displacement in Palestine itself as well as others on the Palestinian diaspora, or those who have been forcibly removed or migrated from their ancestral homeland.

KEY CONTEXT The following text takes the form of a prose poem, a hybrid form that does not use conventional line breaks. However, it has poetic traits such as symbols, metaphors, and other figures of speech.

Who needs to be at peace in the world? It helps to be between wars, to die a few times each day to understand your father's sky, as you take it apart piece by piece and can't feel anything, can't feel the tree growing under your feet, the eyes poking night only to find another night to compare it to. Whoever heard of turning pain into hummingbirds or red birds — haven't we grown? What does it mean to be older? Maybe a house without doors can still survive a storm. Maybe I can't find the proper way to rebel or damn it, I can't leave. I want to, but you grow inside of me. And as I watch you, before I know it, I'm too heavy, too full of you to move. Maybe that's what they meant when they said you shouldn't love a country too much. ■

2015

Understanding and Interpreting

1. The first sentence of the poem asks, "Who needs to be at peace in the world?" How does the poem answer this question? What might it mean in the context of the poem *not* to be at peace in the world?
2. Does the "you" in the beginning of the poem refer to the same person or people as the "you" in the end? Consider various options, and cite textual evidence to explain your answer.
3. Look at the questions the poem poses. Does the speaker answer any or all of them? If so, what are the answers? If not, how would you answer them? Do you think they have answers at all?
4. How do you interpret "a house without doors"? In the context of the poem, does this mean a house with openings but no barriers or a house without openings? Explain.
5. Revisit the poem's title to interpret its meaning. How does "Ways of Rebelling" inform your understanding of the poem? What are some of the ways to rebel, according to the speaker?

Analyzing Language, Style, and Structure

1. **Vocabulary in Context.** *Rebelling*, though most often considered negative, can take on positive connotations depending on one's perspective. Consider the kinds of rebellion that society denounces as well as the kinds it celebrates. Which type do you think the speaker refers to in "Ways of Rebelling"?
2. As a prose poem, "Ways of Rebelling" does not consist of established line breaks or stanzas. However, it does incorporate elements of poetry such as figurative language and imagery. Why is this structural choice appropriate to the subject of the poem? Why would a traditional form be a less effective choice?
3. Nathalie Handal incorporates several infinitives, or verb phrases functioning as nouns, adjectives, or adverbs such as "to be" in line 1. Make a list of the other infinitives in "Ways of Rebelling." How do they emphasize and connect certain ideas in the poem? Consider especially how infinitives convey purpose or intention.
4. What does the speaker say she "can't feel" on a literal level? How do you understand these experiences on a figurative level?
5. How does figurative language contribute to the meaning of the poem? Analyze examples such as "to die a few times each day," "the eyes poking night," "turning pain into hummingbirds or red birds," and others.

Topics for Composing

1. AP® FRQ **Poetry Analysis.** In Nathalie Handal's "Ways of Rebelling," published in 2015, the speaker considers rebellion as a way to make sense of the world. Read the poem carefully. Then, in a well-written essay, analyze how Handal uses literary elements and techniques to portray the speaker's complex understanding of her identity and her place in the world around her.
2. **Research.** Research examples of diasporas throughout history before picking one to focus on more specifically. Then, write about how Handal's poem reflects experiences of those who are in the diaspora you have researched. For example, how have members of the African diaspora sought "to be at peace in the world"? What internal conflicts might it create for indigenous people who have experienced diaspora when it comes to "lov[ing] a country too much"? How might those who left Ireland during the Great Famine have found themselves "poking night only to find another night to compare it to"?

3. **Connections.** In a 2017 interview with Dr. Elizabeth Saylor and Dr. Lily Balloffet for North Carolina State University's *Khayrallah Center for Lebanese Diaspora Studies News*, Nathalie Handal explains, "Every action and motion, every word I have written has been a rumination of, a conversation with, has been etched in, the migratory and diasporic experience." Find and read additional poems by Handal, such as "Phenomenal Daughter," "Testament in Barcelona," and "The Unnatural Apologie of Shadows." Then, explain how the style and structure of "Ways of Rebelling" and one or two additional poems by Handal each exemplify Handal's statement.
4. **Speaking and Listening.** Discuss with a partner or in a small group the ways in which you are not "at peace in the world." How has this lack of peace caused you to commit acts of rebellion, big or small, or led you to make significant changes? Perhaps you decided at some point no longer to play a particular sport or you made the choice to live with another family member. Or maybe, like the poem's speaker, you have felt "too heavy . . . to move" so have stayed. As you have grown and changed, how have your ways of rebelling changed? Have you also found yourself saying, "I can't leave. I want to, but . . ."?
5. **Connections.** PEN America, an organization that "stands at the intersection of literature and human rights to protect free expression in the United States and worldwide," conducted an interview with Nathalie Handal in 2020 during which Handal discussed her poetry collection, *Life in a Country Album*:

   > We all seem to need or want to belong to a country — whether our reasons are ancestral, ideological, primal, patriotic, or practical. I'm interrogating in this collection if we love a country, how we love it, and perhaps most importantly: Does it love us?

   As you think about the country you belong to and Handal's poem "Ways of Rebelling," how do you experience the way you belong to your country or even the community in which you live? Do you identify more with ancestral, ideological, primal, patriotic, or practical desires to belong — or a combination of these? Do you feel as though your country and community love you?
6. **Connections.** Like Nathalie Handal, Palestinian American artist Manal Deeb explores and embraces the diasporic experience through artistic expression. A Middle East Institute article about Deeb says her work "reflects the feeling of displacement, and trauma felt by Palestinians in diaspora." Find and view some of Deeb's work. How does her art echo some of the themes in "Ways of Rebelling"?

Trans is against nostalgia

Taylor Johnson

Taylor Johnson (b. 1991) was born in Washington, D.C., and currently lives in New Orleans. In 2017, Taylor received the Larry Neal Writers' Award from the DC Commission on the Arts and Humanities. Their debut poetry collection, *Inheritance*, was published in 2020 by Alice James Books.

photo by S*an D. Henry-Smith

KEY CONTEXT The title's first word, "Trans," is an abbreviation for *transgender*. Transgender people have a gender identity that differs from the sex they were assigned at birth.

Everyday I build the little boat,
my body boat, hold for the unique one,
the formless soul, the blue fire
that coaxes my being into being.

Yes, there was music in the woods, and
I was in love with the trees, and a beautiful man
grew my heartbeat in his hands, and there
was my mother's regret that I slept with.

To live there is pointless. I'm building the boat,
the same way I'd build a new love —
looking ahead at the terrain. And the water
is rising, and the generous ones are moving on.

O New Day, I get to build the boat!
I tell myself to live again.
Somehow I made it out of being 15
and wanting to jump off the roof

of my attic room. Somehow I survived
my loneliness and throwing up in a jail cell.
O New Day, I've broken my own heart. The boat
is still here, is fortified in my brokeness.

I've picked up the hammer everyday
and forgiven myself. There is a new
language I'm learning by speaking it.
I'm a blind cartographer, I know the way

fearing the distance. O New Day,
there isn't a part of you I don't love
to fear. I'm holding hands with
the poet speaking of light, saying *I made it up*

I made it up. ■

2018

Understanding and Interpreting

1. In the first line, the speaker says, "Everyday I build the little boat." What do you think they mean by that?
2. In line 9, the speaker says, "To live there is pointless." Where is "there"? Why is living there "pointless"?
3. Why does the speaker think "I'm building the boat" (l. 9) happens "the same way I'd build a new love" (l. 10)? How does line 11 further explain the similarity?

4. What obstacles has the speaker overcome in this poem? What have they "survived"?
5. The speaker writes, "I've picked up the hammer everyday" (l. 21). What do they do with the hammer? What purpose does the hammer serve?
6. How do you interpret the conclusion? What is it that the speaker "made . . . up"? What does it mean that they have done so?

Analyzing Language, Style, and Structure

1. **Vocabulary in Context.** The speaker says they "were *fortified* in [their] brokeness" (l. 20). Why is this an ironic use of the word in this context? How does it contribute to the speaker's overall message?
2. While cartographers still exist today, creating maps has become much more driven by technology than by artistic expression. How does the speaker's identification as "a blind cartographer" (l. 24) recall the centuries-old practice of mapmaking?
3. In line 2 of the poem, Taylor Johnson uses the word "hold" in a way that functions as both a noun and a verb. How does each usage inform the meaning of the first stanza?
4. Why might Johnson capitalize "New Day," and what does each "New Day" signify? Does Johnson intend for it to be an interjection, an apostrophe, or both? Explain.
5. Johnson employs enjambment across some stanzas and not others. How does enjambment at stanza breaks contribute to the development of and relationship among ideas in the poem?
6. Identify places in the poem where the tone shifts, such as between stanzas 2 and 3. How does each of these shifts add layers of complexity to the poem? How do these shifts affect your interpretation of each part of the poem and of the poem as a whole?
7. What might be the "new / language" (ll. 22–23) the speaker is learning? How does this language relate to "the way" (l. 24) to the speaker's destination? How does the speaker feel about the journey?
8. What connections are there between both the language and the journey and the poem's final line, "I made it up"?
9. What is the relationship between the structure of this poem and the speaker's perspective? Be sure to consider the final stanza in your response.

Topics for Composing

1. AP® FRQ **Poetry Analysis.** In Taylor Johnson's "Trans is against nostalgia," published in 2018, the speaker describes the challenges and rewards each new day brings as they make their own way in the world. Read the poem carefully. Then, in a well-written essay, analyze how Johnson uses literary elements and techniques to convey the speaker's complex attitude toward their own development and understanding of self.
2. **Speaking and Listening.** A University of Minnesota teen development site called "Teen identity: Figuring out who you are" explains how important it is for all teenagers to consider not only who they are but why because as they consider their perceptions of themselves, they also consider how they are perceived by others. The site goes on to explain, "This could be why 'dress up' or theme days for school events are so popular. They give teens a chance to try something different or unusual in an approved, safe setting." Discuss as a class what kinds of opportunities teenagers in your community have to build and explore different identities at school. Does your school offer introductory art and music classes? Are students encouraged to try out for sports they've never played before? Are there gender-affirming

spaces? Are there clubs or other organizations in which you can develop varying interests and identities? Does your school have "dress up" days, and if so what are some of the common themes? How do such experiences help all students who are "building the boat" and understanding a new language "by speaking it"?

3. **Research.** In the introduction to her September 2019 podcast *The Slowdown*, Poet Laureate Tracy K. Smith explains that the number of murders of transgender people is underreported every year because many of the murdered are misgendered. Smith also comments on the number of undocumented incidents of anti-trans violence. Research some of the resources available to fight violence against people who are transgender such as those provided by the National Resource Center on Domestic Violence and FORGE, a national transgender antiviolence organization. Then, develop a resource that could be used by your school's guidance counseling department to help cisgender people support trans, nonbinary, and genderqueer students.
4. **Multimodal.** Create a collage or timeline of your identity going back to childhood. For example, document your aspirations in elementary school to play a professional sport or be an astronaut. What music did you listen to incessantly in middle school, and how did it express and shape your identity? Have you ever become passionate about something, such as classic cars or drawing comic strips? What do your passions convey about you? If money and societal expectations weren't a concern, what would you most like to become or study?

Crossing

Jericho Brown

Greg Allen/Invision/AP/Shutterstock

Poet Jericho Brown (b. 1976) was born in Shreveport, Louisiana, and earned a BA from Dillard University, an MFA from the University of New Orleans, and a PhD from the University of Houston. Brown is the author of *Please* (2008), which won the American Book Award; *The New Testament* (2014); and *The Tradition* (2019), which won the 2020 Pulitzer Prize. He is the Charles Howard Candler Professor of English and Creative Writing at Emory University and director of the Creative Writing Program.

The water is one thing, and one thing for miles.
The water is one thing, making this bridge
Built over the water another. Walk it
Early, walk it back when the day goes dim, everyone
Rising just to find a way toward rest again.
We work, start on one side of the day
Like a planet's only sun, our eyes straight
Until the flame sinks. The flame sinks. Thank God
I'm different. I've figured and counted. I'm not crossing
To cross back. I'm set
On something vast. It reaches
Long as the sea. I'm more than a conqueror, bigger
Than bravery. I don't march. I'm the one who leaps. ■

2019

Understanding and Interpreting

1. What is your first impression of the subject of "Crossing"? Read it again. Did your impression change? Read it a third time. What happens then?
2. Who is the speaker of this poem? How would you characterize his mood and outlook?
3. What meanings do you associate with the word "crossing"? Do you see these meanings reflected in the poem? If so, where? If not, what meanings does "crossing" carry for the speaker?
4. What do you think the poem's last sentence means? What is the speaker "leap[ing]" to? What does it mean that he doesn't "march"?
5. What promise has the speaker made to himself? How does he see himself as "different" (l. 9)?
6. Jericho Brown said in an interview, "I do not believe that poems are made of our beliefs. Instead, I believe poems lead us to and tell us what we really believe." What belief does this poem lead you to?
7. Is "Crossing" an optimistic poem? Why or why not? Explain your answer with evidence from the text.

Analyzing Language, Style, and Structure

1. **Vocabulary in Context.** What is the meaning of the word "vast" in line 11? What might the "something" be?
2. Look carefully at the poem's repetitions: "one thing," "walk it," "the flame sinks." Do they mean the same thing each time? What idea is the speaker exploring that these repetitions emphasize?
3. Read "Crossing" sentence by sentence instead of line by line. What do the sentences reveal? Why might Brown have broken the lines where he did, and what effect does the enjambment have? What is the effect of the caesuras?
4. What does the simile in line 7 describe? What critique might it be making?
5. What do you think the "flame" is in line 8? Why does the flame sink twice in that line? How does the poem combine a literal and metaphorical meaning in the word "flame"? What do those meanings contribute to your interpretation of the poem?
6. How does "Crossing" use repetition to reinforce the water imagery from the beginning of the poem? What is the cumulative effect of these language choices?
7. How is "Crossing" metaphorical? How might it also be concrete? Think about the meaning, for example, of "the water," "this bridge, "a way toward rest," and "conqueror." How do these literal and metaphorical meanings relate to each other?

Topics for Composing

1. AP® FRQ **Poetry Analysis.** In Jericho Brown's "Crossing," published in 2019, the speaker contemplates his sense of self and what it means to go against the grain. Read the poem carefully. Then, in a well-written essay, analyze how Brown uses literary elements and techniques to portray the speaker's complex perspective on his place in the world.
2. **AP® Literary Argumentation.** Jericho Brown has said that poets try "to get at the truth by nailing the abstract nature of it down to something physical in the world. We do feel that there are times we know the truth, and we'd like to believe we can show just how well we know it

through making metaphors." What truth has Brown tried to nail in "Crossing"? Does he succeed through his metaphors? Explain your answer, using evidence from the poem to support your response.

3. **AP® Literary Argumentation.** How might you interpret "Crossing" as a poem about the redemptive powers of art? What do those powers have to do with the concept of conformity and rebellion? Use evidence from the poem to support your position.
4. **Connections.** Brown has said that he wrote "Crossing" when he was suffering from depression: "I imagine 'Crossing' as a sort of paradoxical piece in that writing it quite literally helped to keep me alive in spite of the fact that it glories in the possibility — no, the prospect — of death." How does this statement affect your interpretation of the poem? What are some things that have comforted you in unexpected ways during tough times in your life?
5. **Multimodal.** Expand on your interpretation of "Crossing" in a way that works with and extends from its abstract nature. Create a work of art or music that conveys one or more levels of the poem's meaning.

Failed Essay on Privilege

Elisa Gonzalez

Photo by Simon Bahçeli

Elisa Gonzalez (b. 1989) is a poet, an essayist, and a fiction writer. Raised in the Midwest, she is a graduate of Yale University and the New York University Creative Writing Program. She has received fellowships from the Kingsley Trust Association, the Norman Mailer Foundation, the Bread Loaf Writers' Conference, the Rolex Foundation, and the Fulbright Program. She is a recipient of a 2020 Rona Jaffe Foundation Writers' Award. She was recently a Fulbright Scholar in Creative Writing in Warsaw, Poland.

KEY CONTEXT The ancient Greek philosopher Aristotle (367–347 BCE) taught that moral virtue, while important, doesn't guarantee a good life. He believed we also need to be fortunate or lucky. Then, if we are wise and virtuous, we will have good lives.

I came from something popularly known as "nothing"
and in the coming I got a lot.

My parents didn't speak money, didn't speak college.
Still — I went to Yale.

For a while I tried to condemn.
I wrote *Let me introduce you to evil.*

Still, I was a guest there, I made myself at home.

And I know a fine shoe when I see one.
And I know to be sincerely sorry for those people's problems.

I know to want nothing more
than it would be so nice to have

and I confess I'll never hate what I've been given
as much as I wish I could.

Still I thought I of all people understood Aristotle: what is and isn't *the good life* . . .
because, I wrote, *privilege is an aggressive form of amnesia* . . .

I left a house with no heat. I left the habit of hunger. I left a room
I shared with seven brothers and sisters I also left.

Even the good is regrettable, or at least sometimes
should be regretted

yet to hate myself is not to absolve her.

I paid so much
for wisdom, and look at all of this, look at all I have — ■

2019

Understanding and Interpreting

1. What do you think the word "privilege" means in the title? Why do you think this poem is categorized as a "failed essay"?
2. What does it mean to come from nothing, as the speaker tells us she does in line 1? How does Elisa Gonzalez show its meaning from the inside out?
3. Why is Yale an important aspect of the setting of the poem? How does the speaker use this setting to convey a perspective on the relationship between education and privilege?
4. What do you think the speaker tries to "condemn" in line 5? Why does she find herself unable to do so?
5. Why is knowing when a shoe is fine important (l. 8)? Does the speaker mean it seriously or ironically — or both? Explain your answer.
6. Why do you think the speaker believes she should understand Aristotle's idea of a "good life"? Is she implying she has misunderstood it (l. 14)?

Analyzing Language, Style, and Structure

1. **Vocabulary in Context.** What does the word "amnesia" mean in line 15? Why does the speaker consider privilege an aggressive form of amnesia?
2. You've probably noticed that the poem has switchbacks; that is, a line starts in one direction and then switches directions, sometimes abruptly. Find examples of the switchbacks. How do they reveal the speaker's state of mind?
3. What is the effect of the repetition of "I left" in the ninth stanza? How does it reveal the speaker's state of mind? What does it convey about her perspective on her privilege?
4. It appears that "myself" and "her" are the same person in line 20. What do these pronoun choices convey about the speaker's understanding of herself?

5. Why might Gonzalez have punctuated line 7, "Still, I was a guest there, I made myself at home," with a comma splice?
6. How does the allusion to Aristotle in line 14 characterize the speaker? What do you think it illustrates about her attitude toward privilege?

Topics for Composing

1. **AP® FRQ Poetry Analysis.** In Elisa Gonzalez's "Failed Essay on Privilege," published in 2019, the speaker examines "the good life" through the lens of privilege. Read the poem carefully. Then, in a well-written essay, analyze how Gonzalez uses literary elements and techniques to convey her ambivalence about the "the good life" she is living.
2. **AP® Literary Argumentation.** The speaker of "Failed Essay on Privilege" wrestles with her privilege. What's the outcome of this struggle? Does the speaker ultimately resolve to work against that privilege or undermine it from within? Does she enjoy it too much to want to question and reject it? Use evidence from the poem to support your answer.
3. **Connections.** In a 2016 interview between Gonzalez and the lawyer and poet Reginald Dwayne Betts, Betts said, "Poetry and law have always been intertwined in my mind . . . in part because poetry gives me the language to pretend that I can answer questions, even if I can't." Do you think this poem helped Gonzalez pretend to have answers to her questions? What language does it give her?
4. **Creative Writing.** In lines 10–11, Gonzalez writes, "I know to want nothing more / than it would be so nice to have." Write a poem in which you examine the point at which to "want nothing more" and "be so nice to have" meet.

The Artist Signs Her Masterpiece, Immodestly

Danielle DeTiberus

Danielle DeTiberus (b. 1980) lives in Charleston, South Carolina, where she teaches creative writing. Her poetry has been published in *Best American Poetry 2015*, Poets.org's Poem-a-Day, *Copper Nickel*, *Entropy*, *The Missouri Review*, *River Styx*, *Spoon River Poetry Review*, and *Waxwing*.

Danielle DeTiberus

KEY CONTEXT The depiction of the slaying of Holofernes by Judith is told in the book of Deuteronomy in the Bible. In the story, Judith, a beautiful widow, enters the tent of the drunken Holofernes, an Assyrian general who desires her and is about to destroy Judith's city. With the help of her servant Abra, she decapitates him, and his head is taken away in a basket. This story is the subject of works of art from the Renaissance even to the present day, including by Artemisia Gentileschi (1593–c. 1656) and Michelangelo Merisi da Caravaggio (1571–1610). Gentileschi's take on the scene is informed by the fact that she was raped by another painter; in her interpretation of Judith beheading Holofernes, she painted herself beheading her rapist. Caravaggio's painting of this event might be seen as both a reflection of his frequent brawls and a foreshadowing of the sentence of beheading he received for murdering a man in a duel. "The Artist Signs Her Masterpiece, Immodestly" is an ekphrastic poem — that is, a poem that responds to a work of art.

After Artemisia Gentileschi's Judith Beheading Holofernes *(Uffizi, 1620)*

Because I know what rough work it is to fight off
a man. And though, yes, I learned *tenebroso*[1] from
Caravaggio, I found the dark on my own. Know too

well if Judith was alone, she'd never be able to claw
her way free. How she and Abra would have to muster
all their strength to keep him still long enough

to labor through muscle and bone. Look at the old
masters try their best to imagine a woman wielding
a sword. Plaited hair just so. She's disinterested

or dainty, no heft or sweat. As if she were serving
tea — all model and pose. No, my Judith knows
to roll her sleeves up outside the tent. Clenches

a fistful of hair as anchor for what must be done.
Watch the blood arc its way to wrist and breast.
I have thought it all through, you see. The folds

of flesh gathered at each woman's wrist, the shadows
on his left arm betraying the sword's cold hilt.
To defeat a man, he must be removed from his body

by the candlelight he meant as seduction. She's been
to his bed before and takes no pleasure in this.
Some say they know her thoughts by the meat of her

brow. Let them think what they want. I have but one job:
to keep you looking, though I've snatched the breath
from your throat. Even the lead white sheets want

to recoil. Forget the blood, forget poor dead Caravaggio.
He only signed one canvas. Lost himself in his own
carbon black backdrop. To call my work imperfect

would simply be a lie. So I drench my brush in
a palette of bone black — femur and horn transformed
by their own long burning — and make one last

[1] Italian word connoting darkness, gloominess, and mysteriousness. It is often associated with the work of the artist Caravaggio. — Eds.

insistence. Between this violence and the sleeping
enemies outside, my name rises. Some darknesses
refuse to fade. *Ego Artemitia.*[2] I made this — I. ■

2020

[2] Latin for "I am Artemisia." — Eds.

Understanding and Interpreting

1. Who is the speaker of this poem? What is she like? What can you tell about her backstory from the details she shares in the poem?
2. How does the speaker describe her artistic process? According to this poem, what decisions did she make as she planned her version of *Judith Beheading Holofernes*?
3. What is Artemisia Gentileschi's Judith like? How does the speaker compare her to other depictions?
4. What role does the servant Abra play in Gentileschi's painting? Why is she important?
5. What part does Caravaggio play in this poem? Why does the speaker describe him as "poor" (l. 25)?
6. The speaker considers herself to have "one job: / to keep you looking" (ll. 22–23). How does she achieve that purpose in her painting of Judith beheading Holofernes?
7. Why does the poem's title characterize the speaker's signature as immodest?

Analyzing Language, Style, and Structure

1. **Vocabulary in Context.** What does the word "muster" mean in line 5? Why might Danielle DeTiberus have decided to end the line with that word? How does it help define the relationship between Judith and Abra?
2. Read the poem sentence by sentence, and then consider the poet's decisions about where to break the lines. How do the line breaks, enjambments, and caesuras create the rhythm of the poem? Does that rhythm remind you of anything?
3. Artemisia Gentileschi was known for being an effective self-promoter. How does she use imagery to sell herself and her work as the speaker in this poem?
4. What claims does the speaker make for "my Judith" (l. 11)? How does the poem support them?
5. As the Key Context notes, "The Artist Signs Her Masterpiece, Immodestly" is an ekphrastic poem. How does the poem depict the act of painting, the artwork itself, and simultaneously weave in the details of the story of Judith and Holofernes? What is the effect of that combination?

Topics for Composing

1. AP® FRQ **Poetry Analysis.** In Danielle DeTiberus's "The Artist Signs Her Work, Immodestly," published in 2020, the speaker seems to be defending herself against accusations of arrogance. Read the poem carefully. Then, in a well-written essay, analyze how DeTiberus uses literary elements and techniques to develop the speaker's complex perspective on the importance of her own work.

2. **AP® Literary Argumentation.** The poet Danielle DeTiberus writes, "The artist's signature is as sure and insistent as Judith's sword; she reclaims her agency through making and naming." How does the poem convey this agency, confidence, and insistence? Use evidence from the text to support your response.
3. **Connections.** Look at several other depictions of Judith beheading Holofernes, including those by Caravaggio (p. 735) and Artemisia Gentileschi (p. 737). What stories do they tell about the artists behind the paintings and the society each was part of?
4. **Research**. Do some research into why women artists through the ages have so often used themselves as models for the figures in their paintings. What does your research add to your understanding of DeTiberus's speaker in this poem?
5. **Connections.** Gentileschi was known for the way she signed her paintings. Art historian Judith Mann writes that she signed nineteen of her forty-eight known paintings creatively, in ways that

   > reveal her to be a talented manipulator of her image and her identity. The spelling of her name, its placement, style, and how it is integrated into the painting, we can see how inventively Gentileschi used her signatures. By conscientiously exploiting her name as a pictorial element, Artemisia enriched the meanings of her subjects.

   Study the work of Gentileschi, especially the signatures. What do they add to her paintings? How did reading "The Artist Signs Her Work, Immodestly" open your eyes to the power of the signature?

Judith Beheading Holofernes

Michelangelo Merisi da Caravaggio

Portrait of Michaelangelo Merisi da Caravaggio / Leoni, Ottavio Mario / Bridgeman Images

Michelangelo Merisi da Caravaggio (1571–1610) was an Italian painter active in Rome for most of his artistic life. Through the use of dramatic lighting, his paintings were realistic and highly emotional, often depicting moments of violent struggle, torture, and death. He is especially known for his use of *chiaroscuro* — strong contrasts between light and dark — in a style of painting that came to be known as tenebrism. Born in Milan, Caravaggio had to flee to Naples when he was involved in a brawl that led to a death sentence for murder. He led a wild and erratic life and died under mysterious circumstances — possibly murder or lead poisoning — on his way from Naples to Rome. Considered an Old Master painter, Caravaggio was an important influence on Baroque painters such as Gentileschi. Appreciation of his work has waxed and waned through the ages, but recently his work has been called the beginning of modern painting.

KEY CONTEXT This depiction of Judith beheading Holofernes was painted in 1599 and hangs in the National Gallery of Ancient Art in Rome.

incamerastock/Alamy Stock Photo

Exploring the Text

1. Characterize Judith in this depiction of the beheading of Holofernes. What facial expression is she making? What does the position of her limbs reveal about her attitude toward her actions?
2. What effect does the dark background have on the work as a whole? What, if anything, seems obscured?
3. Which of the three faces here seems most sympathetic? Explain your answer.
4. What does Holofernes seem to have been doing before the women began his decapitation?
5. In "The Artist Signs Her Masterpiece, Immodestly," the speaker says, "Look at the old / masters try their best to imagine a woman wielding / a sword. Plaited hair just so. She's disinterested // or dainty, no heft or sweat. As if she were serving / tea — all model and pose" (ll. 7–11). Do you agree with this critique? If so, explain why. If not, explain how you see the scene differently.

Judith Beheading Holofernes

Artemisia Gentileschi

Art Collection 2/Alamy

Artemisia Gentileschi (1593–c. 1656) was an Italian Baroque painter. The daughter of a painter, she apprenticed for her father and was a professional painter by the time she was fifteen. Today, she is known as one of the most accomplished artists of the seventeenth century. Much of her work depicts women from mythology and the Bible. In her time, Gentileschi's accomplishments were overshadowed by her rape and the trial of her rapist, Agostino Tassi. Although he was convicted, his sentence was never carried out.

KEY CONTEXT This painting hangs in the Uffizi Gallery in Rome. In this version of Judith beheading Holofernes, Gentileschi painted herself beheading her rapist.

Artepics/Alamy

1620

Exploring the Text

1. Characterize Judith in this depiction of the beheading of Holofernes. What facial expression does she wear? What do you make of her body language?
2. How does this painting characterize Abra? What is significant about her role in what is taking place?
3. How does the painting depict the relationship between Judith and Abra?
4. What is the effect of the diagonal lines formed by Judith's arms? How do they lend realism to the act of decapitation?
5. What other details in this painting makes this scene seem realistic?
6. How, besides signing her name in the lower right corner, is Gentileschi's painting an act of rebellion?
7. Has the speaker in "The Artist Signs Her Name, Immodestly" done her job — that is, do you want to keep looking? Do you feel compelled to keep looking? Explain why or why not.

Making Connections

1. Based on your impressions of Gentileschi's painting, do you think the speaker in "The Artist Signs Her Name, Immodestly" has made a good case for why her work is better than Caravaggio's? Explain why or why not.
2. What evidence do you see in Gentileschi's painting that, as the poem claims, she "kn[e]w what rough work it is to fight off / a man" (ll. 1–2)?
3. Do you think there is evidence in the paintings that a man painted one and a woman painted the other? Explain your answer.
4. The biblical Judith is considered a heroine in both Jewish and Christian tradition. Is she depicted as heroic in these paintings? Or is she more heroic in one than the other? Use specific details from the paintings to support your answer.
5. In the poem the speaker calls Caravaggio's background "carbon" and says her black is "bone" black, a black made from burned bones. Can you see a difference in the paintings? If so, what is the effect of that difference? What contrast do you think the speaker is highlighting between her work and Caravaggio's?

Match

Jason Reynolds

Rolf Vennenbernd/picture alliance/Getty Images

Poet and novelist Jason Reynolds (b. 1983) grew up near Washington, D.C., and earned a BA from the University of Maryland. Reynolds is an award-winning writer of young adult novels, including *All American Boys*, co-authored with Brendan Kiely (2015), *As Brave As You* (2016), and the *Track* series (2016–2018). He is also the author of a novel in verse, *Long Way Down* (2017), and a collection of poetry, *For Every One* (2018). He collaborated with Ibram X. Kendi on *Stamped: Racism, Antiracism, and You* (2020), which is a "remix" of Kendi's *Stamped from the Beginning: the Definitive History of Racist Ideas in America* (2016).

on the days the dark is vanta[1] vicious
enough to swallow whole every holy
thing like my mother and the stigmata
she bleeds from a totem of raising black

on the days the cold is cold as all get out but
there's no place to get in when even breath is
blade and hurts to think of thinking of breathing
let alone laughing

on the days I feel frayed and 'fraid ripped
and torn from the lot plucked from family
and 'nem and even myself sometimes my
name is the name of a stranger

my face still the face in the hole of a
hoodie just snatched out my own world
never mine and dragged and scraped
across the rough textured parts of this
being alive thing

i'm reminded of what it feels
like to have my head alight to
have it catch fire and blaze-lick
high above me and all this

i'm reminded to return to the truth that oh
yeah me my little self a match my little
self a cardboard cutout might could burn
this whole so-called kingdom down ■

2020

[1] A reference to vantablack, one of the darkest substances known to exist. When light strikes vantablack, it becomes trapped and is absorbed instead of reflecting off of it. — Eds.

Understanding and Interpreting

1. What associations does the title of the poem — "Match" — carry? What did you expect the poem to be about before you read it? What possibilities does it invite a reader to consider?
2. How does the speaker characterize his environment in the opening three stanzas? How does his environment change in the final two?
3. How do you interpret lines 11–12: "sometimes my / name is the name of a stranger"? What does the speaker suggest causes this disorientation or fragmentation?
4. By the end of the poem, when the speaker imagines his "little self a match" (l. 23), what is the source of his power?
5. In what ways might you interpret this poem as a movement from conformity or acceptance to rebellion or assertion?

Analyzing Language, Style, and Structure

1. **Vocabulary in Context.** In lines 4–5, Reynolds describes his mother bleeding "from a totem of raising black / on the days the cold is cold as all get out." Is "totem" in this context a reference to an art object or another kind of representation? Explain your interpretation with evidence from the poem.
2. In lines 3–4, Reynolds refers to the "stigmata" that his mother "bleeds." The term has a specific meaning in Christianity: it refers to the appearance of bodily wounds, scars, and pain in locations corresponding to the crucifixion wounds of Jesus Christ. What does this image suggest about the speaker's mother?
3. Reynolds repeats words and phrases throughout the poem. Which ones repeat, and what is the purpose of this repetition? How does it shape the tone and meaning of the poem? Consider at least four examples in your analysis.
4. Reynolds has commented in interviews that using the language he grew up with, especially rap music, is essential to his poetry. What examples of vernacular, colloquialism, and neologisms do you find in "Match"? What tone do they create? What would be lost from the poem if you changed these word choices to follow strict grammatical rules? Consider, for instance, "might could" in the penultimate line.
5. How do the rhythm and meter of the poem contribute to its overall structure? Consider poetic elements such as alliteration and enjambment along with pacing and musicality.
6. Reynolds's poem comes alive in the metaphors and similes he uses throughout. Identify at least two of them and discuss their effect. What is the overall metaphor signaled by the title "Match"? In what ways do these examples of figurative language work individually and collectively to add to the impact of the poem?

Topics for Composing

1. AP® FRQ **Poetry Analysis.** In Jason Reynolds's "Match," published in 2020, the speaker describes a transformation from confusion and despair to clarity and purpose. Read the poem carefully. Then, in a well-written essay, analyze how Reynolds uses literary elements and techniques to convey the shift in the speaker's perspective.
2. **AP® Literary Argumentation.** On the website of the Academy of American Poets, Jason Reynolds says that "Match" is about the

   > complexity of exceptionalism and responsibility in times of unrest, and how — though the spotlight and expectations can be lonely and unfair — the responsibility attached to it is still one worthy of bearing. And regardless of how one chooses, the power of a single person, the small fire of a single mind . . . could change the face of a kingdom, especially one built on paper like America.

   How does "Match" speak to "exceptionalism and responsibility in times of unrest"? To what extent do you think that the individual, particularly the poet or artists in general, can be a significant agent of change? Cite text from "Match" as you develop your position.
3. **Speaking and Listening.** Reynolds has commented that "Rap music, when written, is poetry." What elements of rap music do you find in "Match"? Listen to a recording of Reynolds reading the poem. How does the experience of hearing the poem enrich your understanding of its meaning and the traditions that shaped its style?
4. **Connections.** In a discussion of what will make young people today more receptive to reading novels or poetry, Reynolds explains that they want "truth, their truth, not our truth, not our projections of who we think they are: their language, the way that they walk, their fears and insecurities." Based on your own experiences, does his claim ring true for you? Explain why or why not.

AP® Multiple-Choice Practice

from Passing

Nella Larsen

They always took her for an Italian, a Spaniard, a Mexican, or a gipsy. Never, when she was alone, had they even remotely seemed to suspect that she was a Negro. No, the woman sitting there staring at her couldn't possibly know.

Nevertheless, Irene felt, in turn, anger, scorn, and fear slide over her. It wasn't that she was ashamed of being a Negro, or even of having it declared. It was the idea of being ejected from any place, even in the polite and tactful way in which the Drayton would probably do it, that disturbed her.

But she looked, boldly this time, back into the eyes still frankly intent upon her. They did not seem to her hostile or resentful. Rather, Irene had the feeling that they were ready to smile if she would. Nonsense, of course. The feeling passed, and she turned away with the firm intention of keeping her gaze on the lake, the roofs of the buildings across the way, the sky, anywhere but on that annoying woman. Almost immediately, however, her eyes were back again. In the midst of her fog of uneasiness she had been seized by a desire to outstare the rude observer. Suppose the woman did know or suspect her race. She couldn't prove it.

Suddenly her small fright increased. Her neighbour had risen and was coming towards her. What was going to happen now?

"Pardon me," the woman said pleasantly, "but I think I know you." Her slightly husky voice held a dubious note.

Looking up at her, Irene's suspicions and fears vanished. There was no mistaking the friendliness of that smile or resisting its charm. Instantly she surrendered to it and smiled too, as she said: "I'm afraid you're mistaken."

"Why, of course, I know you!" the other exclaimed. "Don't tell me you're not Irene Westover. Or do they still call you 'Rene?"

In the brief second before her answer, Irene tried vainly to recall where and when this woman could have known her. There, in Chicago. And before her marriage. That much was plain. High school? College? Y. W. C. A. committees? High school, most likely. What white girls had she known well enough to have been familiarly addressed as 'Rene by them? The woman before her didn't fit her memory of any of them. Who was she?

"Yes, I'm Irene Westover. And though nobody calls me 'Rene any more, it's good to hear the name again. And you —" She hesitated, ashamed that she could not remember, and hoping that the sentence would be finished for her.

"Don't you know me? Not really, 'Rene?"

"I'm sorry, but just at the minute I can't seem to place you."

Irene studied the lovely creature standing beside her for some clue to her identity. Who could she be? Where and when had they met? And through her perplexity there came the thought that the trick which her memory had played her was for some reason more gratifying than disappointing to her old acquaintance, that she didn't mind not being recognized.

And, too, Irene felt that she was just about to remember her. For about the woman was some quality, an intangible something, too vague to define, too remote to seize, but which was, to Irene Redfield, very familiar. And that voice. Surely she'd heard those husky tones somewhere before. Perhaps before time, contact, or something had been at them, making them into a voice remotely suggesting England. Ah! Could it have been in Europe that they had met? 'Rene. No.

"Perhaps," Irene began, "you —"

The woman laughed, a lovely laugh, a small 15
sequence of notes that was like a trill and also like the ringing of a delicate bell fashioned of a precious metal, a tinkling.

Irene drew a quick sharp breath. "Clare!" she exclaimed, "not really Clare Kendry?"

So great was her astonishment that she had started to rise. ■

AP® Multiple-Choice Questions

1. What is the significance of the references to the nickname 'Rene?
   - **a.** Irene recalls her dislike for the nickname.
   - **b.** Only Irene's closest friends ever called her 'Rene.
   - **c.** 'Rene signals an earlier identity for Irene.
   - **d.** It's a name she only went by while in Europe.
   - **e.** Irene hasn't changed since high school and college.

2. When the narrator says, "there came the thought that the trick which her memory had played her was for some reason more gratifying than disappointing to her old acquaintance, that she didn't mind not being recognized" (par. 12), it suggests that
   - **a.** Clare is upset that Irene doesn't recognize her because the two were close when they were younger.
   - **b.** Irene feels guilty for not recognizing Clare given that Clare knew who she was and remembered her nickname.
   - **c.** Irene finds it disappointing that she cannot remember someone from earlier in her life who clearly recognizes her.
   - **d.** Clare is satisfied to see that she remembers people better than they remember her because of her superior memory.
   - **e.** Clare, like Irene, appreciates that she can blend into different environments and social situations.

3. The narrator's shift in tone from the fifth paragraph to the sixth suggests that Irene
   - **a.** easily feels more comfortable once she sees the woman's demeanor up close
   - **b.** can hide her annoyance and fear quickly in order to be polite to Clare
   - **c.** tries to remain aloof and suspicious of the woman who suddenly approaches her
   - **d.** immediately recognizes Clare once she is able to see her more closely
   - **e.** behaves in a standoffish manner when she encounters people who recognize her

4. In choosing to describe Irene as being anxious about "being ejected from any place" in the final sentence of the second paragraph, the narrator creates all of the following EXCEPT
   - **a.** anticipation
   - **b.** inconsistency
   - **c.** tension
   - **d.** expectations
   - **e.** conflict

5. The narrator's use of questions throughout the passage functions as a way to
   - **a.** demonstrate Irene's confusion about the conversations people have around her
   - **b.** portray Irene as someone who is unaware of other people when she's out in public
   - **c.** emphasize the uncertainty Irene experiences during the interaction with Clare
   - **d.** convince readers of the many instances Irene and Clare have interacted with each other
   - **e.** depict Irene as an introspective woman who questions her experience of those around her

6. In context, "dubious" in the final sentence of paragraph 5 is best understood as
   a. confident
   b. suspicious
   c. doubting
   d. assertive
   e. deep

7. Toward the beginning of the third paragraph, Irene's understanding that the other woman's eyes "did not seem to her hostile or resentful" is significant because it
   a. indicates the significance of Irene's expectations in such a circumstance
   b. characterizes Irene as someone who judges others before she meets them
   c. confirms Irene's expectations that she may be asked to leave the Drayton
   d. demonstrates how infrequently Irene experiences hostility and resentment
   e. emphasizes Irene's confidence about the way she appears to others in public

8. What is the effect of the narrator's observation that "In the brief second before her answer, Irene tried vainly to recall where and when this woman could have known her" (par. 8)?
   a. Irene becomes easily distracted during conversations.
   b. The other woman's friendliness catches Irene off guard.
   c. Irene continues thinking to herself before responding to Clare.
   d. Irene concerns herself more with her appearance than her personality.
   e. The other woman's question indicates exactly how Irene knows Clare.

9. In the third paragraph, the narrator's description of Irene looking "boldly" and feeling a "fog of uneasiness" indicates
   a. Irene's inability to appear the way she wants to appear in public
   b. Irene's desire for others to see her as shy and withdrawn
   c. Irene's unwillingness to engage in conversations with people in public
   d. Irene's complex response to the woman who seems to be staring at her
   e. Irene's conflicted emotions about a woman she had known years ago

10. Which excerpt from the passage would best support a reader's claim that one of the central themes of the passage is internal and external identity?
   a. "Nevertheless, Irene felt, in turn, anger, scorn, and fear slide over her."
   b. "Suppose the woman did know or suspect her race. She couldn't prove it."
   c. "In the midst of her fog of uneasiness she had been seized by a desire to outstare the rude observer."
   d. "And that voice. Surely she'd heard those husky tones somewhere before."
   e. "So great was her astonishment that she had started to rise."

from Hamlet, Prince of Denmark

William Shakespeare

HAMLET How all occasions do inform against me,
And spur my dull revenge! What is a man
If his chief good and market of his time
Be but to sleep and feed? A beast, no more.
Sure he that made us with such large discourse,
Looking before and after, gave us not

That capability and god-like reason
To fust in us unused. Now whether it be
Bestial oblivion, or some craven scruple
Of thinking too precisely on th'event —
A thought which quartered hath but one part wisdom
And ever three parts coward — I do not know
Why yet I live to say this thing's to do,
Sith I have cause, and will, and strength, and means
To do't. Examples gross as earth exhort me.
Witness this army of such mass and charge,
Led by a delicate and tender prince,
Whose spirit with divine ambition puffed
Makes mouths at the invisible event,
Exposing what is mortal and unsure
To all that fortune, death and danger dare,
Even for an egg-shell. Rightly to be great
Is not to stir without great argument,
But greatly to find quarrel in a straw
When honour's at the stake. How stand I then,
That have a father killed, a mother stained,
Excitements of my reason and my blood,
And let all sleep, while to my shame I see
The imminent death of twenty thousand men,
That for a fantasy and trick of fame
Go to their graves like beds, fight for a plot
Whereon the numbers cannot try the cause,
Which is not tomb enough and continent
To hide the slain. Oh from this time forth,
My thoughts be bloody or be nothing worth. ■

AP® Multiple-Choice Questions

1. Hamlet's soliloquy as a whole can best be described as

a. an embittered tirade about the invasion of a foreign army

b. a wary admonition against acting rashly and without forethought

c. an inspirational inducement to act on his responsibilities and obligations

d. an impassioned speech about sacrificing oneself for the honor of others

e. a fond recollection of his nation's military accomplishments in recent years

2. In context, "gross" (l. 15) most nearly means

a. unsatisfactory and ill-conceived

b. offensive and distasteful

c. obvious and weighty

d. magnificent and awe-inspiring

e. shocking and distressing

3. Which of the following statements best conveys the effect of the sentences in lines 22–25 ("Rightly to be great . . . When honour's at the stake")?

a. These lines articulate Hamlet's belief about what should and shouldn't inspire people to take action.

b. These lines demonstrate Hamlet's inability to understand the difference between being "great" and acting honorably.
c. These lines show that Hamlet cannot decide whether to avenge his father's death or protect Denmark from Fortinbras.
d. These lines demonstrate Hamlet's ability to analyze the meaning of words in order to make decisions.
e. These lines show the way Hamlet has internal debates when he has to wait patiently for opportunities.

4. Based on the rhetorical questions in lines 25–34 ("How stand I then . . . To hide the slain?"), which of the following can be reasonably inferred regarding the situation Hamlet believes himself to be in?
   a. Hamlet asks rhetorical questions to explain the similarity of the challenges he faces with those Fortinbras faces.
   b. Hamlet asks whether it is more noble to avenge the death of one's parents or to fight to regain lost lands.
   c. Hamlet asks himself about the shamefulness of watching others march off to their deaths while he merely watches.
   d. Hamlet's questions signal a shift in his attitude from being uncertain to being confident in the next steps to take.
   e. Hamlet's questions demonstrate that he believes himself to be a cowardly contrast to Fortinbras and his men.

5. The metaphor of "an egg-shell" (l. 22) chiefly serves to emphasize
   a. the potential benefits of taking great risks for small achievements
   b. the insignificance of what Fortinbras is risking men's lives for
   c. the weakness of Hamlet's convictions in contrast with Fortinbras's
   d. the way "fortune, death, and danger" threaten the lives of humans
   e. the experience of Fortinbras and the army of men he has put together

6. One effect of the shift in Hamlet's focus in lines 15–22 ("Examples gross as earth . . . Even for an egg-shell") is to
   a. show the honorable challenges Fortinbras is willing to undertake
   b. distract himself from his own anger and frustration at his situation
   c. illustrate Hamlet's ability to use his "capability and god-like reason"
   d. demonstrate an example of a thought "ever three parts coward"
   e. prove to himself that he has "cause and will and strength and means"

7. Hamlet mentions "delicate" and "tender" (l. 17) to highlight Fortinbras's
   a. emotional weaknesses
   b. power and strength
   c. fragile circumstances
   d. honor and courage
   e. youth and inexperience

8. The main purpose of the use of "beast" (l. 4) and "bestial" (l. 9) is to
   a. show Hamlet's distaste for Claudius's behavior
   b. emphasize Hamlet's dehumanization of himself
   c. demonstrate contrasts between animals and humans
   d. indicate his frustration with himself for being animal-like
   e. explain why humans and animals both live dishonorably

9. The final lines of Hamlet's soliloquy reveal his decision to
   a. join with Fortinbras and his men to fight for land
   b. focus his thoughts on avenging his father's death
   c. continue thinking about his options for the future
   d. work on getting past his criticisms of Fortinbras
   e. look further into reasons to pursue getting revenge

Suggestions for Writing

Conformity and Rebellion

1. **AP® FRQ Literary Argument.** The pressure to conform may stem from external constraints such as laws or policy, or internal ones, such as a desire for approval. Many works of literature portray individuals who must weigh the benefits of conformity against the risks of rebellion. From the readings in this chapter, choose a work of fiction or drama in which a character's convictions and values force a decision between continuing to conform and facing the consequences of rebellion. Then, in a well-written essay, analyze how that struggle between conformity and rebellion contributes to an interpretation of the work as a whole. Do not merely summarize the plot.
2. **Connections.** Thinking about the overall theme of this chapter, we may ask: Why do we conform? Certainly, we sometimes conform because of timidity, reluctance, ambition, or simply ease; but then there are times when we conform out of a sense of duty or responsibility, in the spirit of cooperation, or with a sense of sacrifice. Consider these ideas as they run through the selections in the chapter, and develop a thesis regarding the nature of conformity. Refer specifically to the texts of several of the chapter's selections to support your essay.
3. **AP® Literary Argumentation.** What is a rebel? According to Albert Camus, it's "A man who says 'no.'" Among those who say "no" in this chapter are Larsen's Clare Kendry; Melville's Bartleby; the speakers in the poems by Percy Bysshe Shelley, Dylan Thomas, Nathalie Handal, and Robin Coste Lewis; and, of course, Hamlet. What is the significance of Camus's question and answer? Consider how at least two of the characters or speakers in the chapter say "no," and write an essay in which you compare and contrast their rebellious actions or words, and draw conclusions about the consequences of their rebellion.
4. **AP® Literary Argumentation.** African American poet James Branch Cabell has said that "Poetry is man's rebellion against what he is." Consider what Cabell's statement means and how it illustrates a theme that runs through the poetry selections in this chapter. Then, write an essay that compares and contrasts the ways the speakers in two poems in this chapter illustrate Cabell's meaning.
5. **AP® Literary Argumentation.** Identify three selections in the chapter that express a similar theme in terms of conformity and rebellion, or three selections that offer different perspectives. Write an essay that explains how each of the three writers uses different means to express the themes or perspectives that you identify. Consider such features as structure, diction, imagery, figurative language, and tone. Refer to specific passages in each text to support your essay.
6. **AP® Literary Argumentation.** When confronted with a great challenge, the easier path to take is often the one that conformity proffers. Hamlet expresses the difficulty of accepting such a challenge. At the end of act I, he says, "The time is out of joint: O cursed spite, / That ever I was born to set it right!" (I.v.189–90). Write an essay that compares and contrasts the way three characters in the chapter confront the challenge of "setting things right." Use specific examples from the texts to support your essay.

7. **AP® Literary Argumentation.** Enjoining his listeners, singer Bob Marley proclaims, "Emancipate yourself from mental slavery / None but ourselves can free our minds." Similarly, the speakers of the poems by Shelley, Dickinson, Thomas, Ginsberg, Harryette Mullen, and Kartiana Rae Colon speak in imperatives, in some cases addressing the reader as "you." Compare the ways that two of these poems issue a call to action. Refer to the texts of the poems to support your answer. Consider both style and content as you write your essay.

8. **Creative Writing.** In imitation of Carol Ann Duffy or A. E. Stallings, write a poem from the point of view of a secondary character in an epic poem, a novel, or a play. Use that character's point of view to show how he or she might see the main character or the events of the narrative in a different light.

9. **AP® Literary Argumentation.** Which of the short stories in this chapter did you enjoy most? Read two more stories by Melville or Chen. Then write an essay that discusses the nature of conformity as addressed in the works of your selected author.

Mister Blick

War and Peace

Chris Hedges explains in his book *What Everyone Should Know about War* that "of the past 3,400 years, humans have been entirely at peace for 268 of them, or just 8 percent of recorded history." That certainly casts a grim shadow on our priorities as humans. We do not award a Nobel War Prize, yet the world seems always to have looked to warriors for its heroes. We might consider what in human nature is satisfied by war — not only for the warrior but also for the citizens who send the warrior into battle. If war is as horrific as reported by the warrior and as deplorable as depicted in literature, why do we continue to look to war for our heroes?

We prize peace but find glory in war; we detest war but find peace fragile, fleeting, and sometimes even restive. This paradox has been a major subject of serious literature since *The Iliad* (c. 725–675 B.C.E.) and *The Odyssey* (c. 750–650 B.C.E.), which tell the stories of the warrior fighting in battle and the warrior returning home, respectively. It may be simplistic to suggest, as some have, that those are the two basic stories we have to tell, but considering examples from *The Iliad* to *Star Wars*, from *The Things They Carried* to *Da 5 Bloods*, we have to acknowledge the hold these stories have on our imaginations. In Viet Thanh Nguyen's essay "On True War Stories," which you'll find in this chapter's Texts in Context, Nguyen argues that many captivating war stories cannot be *true* war stories. While they may show us that heart of darkness "over there," they fail to show how the heart of darkness exists "where we reside, over here, all around us."

In this chapter you will read war stories and poems from past conflicts that continue to loom large today, including Julia Ward Howe's call to arms in the Civil War; Wilfred Owen's and Siegfried Sassoon's accounts of fighting in World War I; Anna Akhmatova's, Henry Reed's, and Cynthia Ozick's depictions of the widespread devastation of World War II; Tim O'Brien's, Bao Ninh's, Quan Barry's, and Louise Erdrich's stark portrayals of the conflict in Vietnam; and many more. You will also encounter more modern stories of war and peace: Bharati Mukherjee, Wisława Szymborska, and Solmaz Sharif each shed light on how terrorism and the efforts to combat it shape contemporary conflicts; Brian Turner and Jill

McDonough paint a portrait of wartime at once timeless and unprecedented in their accounts of twenty-first century soldiers' experiences; and Jamil Jan Kochai and Amorak Huey portray the intergenerational effects of war. You will also read stories and poems not directly about war itself but about its motivations and repercussions and consequences — including Cynthia Ozick's and Scholastique Mukasonga's narratives of genocide in two different eras; Dunya Mikhail's and Siegfried Sassoon's ironic takes on the sad wastefulness of war; and Claribel Alegría's depictions of civilian displacement and dispossession. Finally, you will read selections that consider war's aftermath and the attempts to establish peace, including Yusef Komunyakaa's portrayal of a grieving mother, Nikky Finney's depiction of the steps toward justice in the aftermath of mass violence, and Edwidge Danticat's exploration of how one generation comes to terms with the misdeeds of the past.

To understand and fully appreciate the short fiction selections in this chapter, let's turn to the Big Ideas, Skills, and Essential Knowledge in Unit 7 of the AP® English Literature and Composition course. This unit focuses on aspects of Character, Setting, Structure, Narration, Figurative Language, and Literary Argumentation. One of the major goals of this unit is to examine how short fiction reflects the contradictions and complexities of the real world, particularly through narrative techniques such as epiphany, unreliable narration, unconventional plot structures, and more. While the questions about the texts in this chapter will guide you in exploring how a wide variety of different literary elements come together to reveal meaning, we will preview some of these elements in the Classic Text for this chapter: "The Things They Carried." As you read this and other texts in Chapter 7, you will develop interpretations of these writers' complex perspectives on why we wage war and how we find peace.

AP® Big Idea: Character

In the Classic Text for this chapter, Tim O'Brien's "The Things They Carried," the **characters** represent different experiences of the effects of the Vietnam War on young soldiers during their deployments — their superstitions and fears, their feelings about what they've been sent to Vietnam to do, and their memories of the lives they left back home. Although the protagonist, Lieutenant Jimmy Cross, identifies as one member of his military unit, the story develops his identity as the leader of this group that is simultaneously separate from him. This dynamic contributes to the epiphany he has when one of his men, Ted Lavender, dies and Lieutenant Cross realizes the gravity of his responsibility for his men's lives. This burden manifests itself as a simple cause-and-effect equation in Cross's mind: Lavender dies because Cross had been daydreaming about a girl back home named Martha. Because Cross has a responsibility to each of his men as individuals and also to the military unit as a whole, the unit functions as a character on its own. This element of military structure exemplifies how a character can hold a distinctly separate attitude about a group than the way he feels about the individual people in it. And while readers gain a strong sense of how Lieutenant Cross feels, they can also infer to some extent how his men feel about him. These attitudes come to represent just one more of the "thing" the men carry individually and collectively. *To review character in short fiction, see pages 5–8 of Chapter 1: Analyzing Short Fiction*.

AP® Big Idea: Setting

As with the characters, the **settings** of the stories contrast with one another. The setting of O'Brien's story has characters in the midst of a combat zone in Vietnam during the war. Although O'Brien does not include many descriptive details of the setting, the characters in the story respond clearly to specifics of that time and place. While the men carry some everyday items, including pocket knives and chewing gum, they also have military gear such as C-rations and helmets as well as equipment more specific to the jungle setting of Vietnam including ponchos and foot powder. Each individual man also carries objects that hold personal significance, such as brass knuckles, a pebble, or a rabbit's foot — these, too, can be read as a reaction to the setting of the war. Additionally, while the men in the story never leave Vietnam, readers catch glimpses of another setting through Lieutenant Cross's daydreams about walking along a beach in New Jersey with Martha woven throughout the story. These scenes highlight the stark differences between the realities of the conflict in Vietnam and the comforts of home — although Lieutenant Cross is the leader of the group, it's clear he has been thrust into an unfamiliar, hostile land and feels just as adrift as his men do. In fact, the setting of the jungle around him in Vietnam functions as yet another antagonist in the story. Whether the men are avoiding trench foot or having to shimmy down enemy tunnels, they have to overcome obstacles in their surroundings at every turn. *To review setting in short fiction, see pages 8–10 of Chapter 1: Analyzing Short Fiction.*

AP® Big Idea: Structure

While the overall plot **structure** of "The Things They Carried" is mostly linear, O'Brien manipulates both chronology and pacing in places to emphasize the physical and mental chaos of war. He inserts references to Lavender's death into the narrative before it happens to establish a semblance of anxious anticipation. He also distracts and disorients readers by weaving Lieutenant Cross's flashbacks to his memories of life back home into the scene of another character's dangerous excursion into enemy tunnels just prior to Lavender's death. Throughout, O'Brien replicates the repetitious, cyclical nature of the men's days in a way that emphasizes not only the terror brought on by uncertainty in the face of danger but also the tedium and monotony of a soldier's days between battles. *To review plot structure in short fiction, see pages 10–13 of Chapter 1: Analyzing Short Fiction.*

AP® Big Idea: Narration

O'Brien's third-person narrator shares details Lieutenant Cross may have left out were he the one telling the story, yet the story definitely focuses on Cross's experiences more than those of other soldiers. As readers, we see Cross more clearly than his men do because while he does not discuss with them the burdens he carries as a result of his love for a girl back home, the narrative point of view conveys his private thoughts. The third-person narration also offers brief glimpses into the perspectives of other characters in the story. In one instance, the narrator shares the internal reflections about Lieutenant Cross's leadership from the perspective of another character, Kiowa. These variations in narrative perspective highlight the role narrators play in shaping the meaning of literature and deepen readers' understanding of characters' values and motivations even as they remain opaque to each other within the bounds of the story itself. *To review narrative perspective and point of view in short fiction, see pages 13–18 of Chapter 1: Analyzing Short Fiction.*

AP® Big Idea: Figurative Language

Finally, "The Things They Carried" offers many opportunities to explore the function of **figurative language** in short fiction. The men in the story carry both physical and psychological burdens that take on metaphorical significance. They find the violence of war so difficult to process that they reach for similes to describe the experience — one soldier recounts witnessing Lavender's death as "like watching a rock fall . . . not like the movies where the dead guy rolls around and does fancy spins. . . . [T]he poor guy just dropped like so much concrete. . . . Like cement." The setting of the story functions as a symbol as well. In the physical challenges it raises for the soldiers, the jungle of Vietnam symbolizes the complexity of war. It also represents the interconnectedness between living systems for better and for worse: sometimes, symbiotic relationships develop and spur growth; at other times, systems compete with one another in destructive and deadly ways. The story's title points to symbols in the story, too: the things the men carry have literal importance to them, but many also represent the men's emotional burdens and personal histories. *To review figurative language in short fiction, see pages 29–31 of Chapter 1: Analyzing Short Fiction.*

AP® Big Idea: Literary Argumentation

When you write about the short stories in this chapter, you will need to craft an interpretation of how these literary elements work together to create meaning. As you learned in Chapter 1, this process of **literary argumentation** begins with developing a defensible thesis statement and then supporting it with textual evidence and commentary. As you read and write about each story, keep in mind that you must choose this evidence carefully to support your argument with strong backing. Your commentary on your chosen evidence is even more important — it takes your reader on a journey with you, establishing a line of reasoning that connects the text to your interpretation of it. At this point in the course, you should also begin to focus on developing sophistication in your interpretations of literature. You can go about this in a number of ways as long as the sophistication is integrated throughout the entirety of your analysis. As you read in Chapter 1, one approach that works especially well in analyzing short fiction is to explore the tensions and complexities presented within a given text. In analyzing "The Things They Carried," you might look at how the physical burdens interact with the psychological burdens to create tensions beyond what either issue presents on its own. You could also explore how the setting and structure of the story enhance the physical and emotional chaos Lieutenant Cross and his men experience. Remember, these are just two of many possibilities for exploration — there is no one way to develop a sophisticated interpretation of a work of literature. *To review the process of writing an AP® Prose Fiction Analysis Essay, see pages 36–49 of Chapter 1: Analyzing Short Fiction. To review the process of developing sophistication in an AP® Prose Fiction Analysis Essay, see pages 50–53 of Chapter 1: Analyzing Short Fiction.*

Throughout the chapter you will view both war and peace from a variety of perspectives: that of the warrior and the witness, the poet and the citizen, the sufferer and the survivor. Reading these selections should cause you to reflect on the nature of conflict itself, on the nature of heroism, on the role of the citizen during wartime, and on the ongoing conflict between war and peace. For hundreds of years, humans have been willing to engage in a just war, and yet the idea of a just peace feels somehow unpatriotic to many. If we can justify war legally and morally, can we not also justify peace for the same reasons? Of course, reading about war will not prevent future conflicts; however, the vicarious immersion in experiences that literature provides may increase our understanding of the nature of armed conflict, stretching from Athens to Antietam, on the sanguinary trail from the fortresses at Troy to the mountains of Afghanistan, and on urban streets from Berlin and Belfast to Baghdad and Beirut.

Guided Reading for "The Book of the Dead"

As you read the Central Text in this chapter, "The Book of the Dead" by Edwidge Danticat (p. 754), keep track of your observations and questions about how the following Big Ideas take shape in Danticat's short story.

AP® Big Idea	Observations	Questions
Character		
Setting		
Structure		
Narration		
Figurative Language		

AP® Unit 7 Alignment at a Glance

The Book of the Dead

Edwidge Danticat

Eamonn McCabe/Popperfoto/Getty Images

Born in Haiti in 1969, Edwidge Danticat immigrated to the United States when she was twelve and currently lives in Miami. She received a BA from Barnard College and an MFA from Brown University. She has written several books in different genres, and some of her most well-known works include her debut novel, *Breath, Eyes, Memory* (1994); the short story collection *Krik? Krak!* (1995); the novel-in-stories *The Dew Breaker* (2004); her autobiography *Brother, I'm Dying* (2007); and, most recently, the short story collection *Everything Inside* (2019).

KEY CONTEXT "The Book of the Dead" is the first in a series of seven interrelated stories in *The Dew Breaker.* Dew breakers were Haitian militiamen, or Tonton Macoutes, who carried out the tyrannical policies of dictators François Duvalier and Jean-Claude Duvalier in Haiti from the 1960s through the 1980s. The name "Tonton Macoute" translates to "Uncle Gunnysack," a reference to a mythological character that captures and eats children for breakfast. Like their namesake, Tonton Macoutes were responsible for the disappearance and murder of between 30,000 and 60,000 people. They were also called dew breakers because they usually struck at dawn.

My father is gone. I'm slouched in a cast-aluminum chair across from two men, one the manager of the hotel where we're staying and the other a policeman. They're both waiting for me to explain what's become of him, my father.

The hotel manager — MR. FLAVIO SALINAS, the plaque on his office door reads — has the most striking pair of chartreuse eyes I've ever seen on a man with an island Spanish lilt to his voice.

The police officer, Officer Bo, is a baby-faced, short, white Floridian with a potbelly.

"Where are you and your daddy from, Ms. Bienaimé?" Officer Bo asks, doing the best he can with my last name. He does such a lousy job that, even though he and I and Salinas are the only people in Salinas' office, at first I think he's talking to someone else.

I was born and raised in East Flatbush, Brooklyn, and have never even been to my parents' birthplace. Still, I answer "Haiti" because it is one more thing I've always longed to have in common with my parents.

Officer Bo plows forward with, "You all the way down here in Lakeland from Haiti?"

"We live in New York," I say. "We were on our way to Tampa."

"To do what?" Officer Bo continues. "Visit?"

"To deliver a sculpture." I say. "I'm an artist, a sculptor."

I'm really not an artist, not in the way I'd like to be. I'm more of an obsessive wood-carver with a single subject thus far — my father.

My creative eye finds Manager Salinas' office gaudy. The walls are covered with orange-and-green wallpaper, briefly interrupted by a giant gold-leaf–bordered print of a Victorian cottage that resembles the building we're in.

Patting his light green tie, which brings out even more the hallucinatory shade of his eyes, Manager Salinas reassuringly tells me, "Officer Bo and I will do our best."

We start out with a brief description of my father: “Sixty-five, five feet eight inches, one hundred and eighty pounds, with a widow’s peak, thinning salt-and-pepper hair, and velvet-brown eyes — ”

“Velvet?” Officer Bo interrupts.

“Deep brown, same color as his 15
complexion,” I explain.

My father has had partial frontal dentures since he fell off his and my mother’s bed and landed on his face ten years ago when he was having one of his prison nightmares. I mention that too. Just the dentures, not the nightmares. I also bring up the blunt, ropelike scar that runs from my father’s right cheek down to the corner of his mouth, the only visible reminder of the year he spent in prison in Haiti.

“Please don’t be offended by what I’m about to ask,” Officer Bo says. “I deal with an older population here, and this is something that comes up a lot when they go missing. Does your daddy have any kind of mental illness, senility?”

I reply, “No, he’s not senile.”

“You have any pictures of your daddy?” Officer Bo asks.

My father has never liked having his picture 20
taken. We have only a few of him at home, some awkward shots at my different school graduations, with him standing between my mother and me, his hand covering his scar. I had hoped to take some pictures of him on this trip, but he hadn’t let me. At one of the rest stops I bought a disposable camera and pointed it at him anyway. As usual, he protested, covering his face with both hands like a little boy protecting his cheeks from a slap. He didn’t want any more pictures taken of him for the rest of his life, he said, he was feeling too ugly.

“That’s too bad,” Officer Bo offers at the end of my too lengthy explanation. “He speaks English, your daddy? Can he ask for directions, et cetera?”

“Yes,” I say.

“Is there anything that might make your father run away from you, particularly here in Lakeland?” Manager Salinas asks. “Did you two have a fight?”

I had never tried to tell my father’s story in words before now, but my first completed sculpture of him was the reason for our trip: a three-foot mahogany figure of my father naked, kneeling on a half-foot-square base, his back arched like the curve of a crescent moon, his downcast eyes fixed on his very long fingers and the large palms of his hands. It was hardly revolutionary, rough and not too detailed, minimalist at best, but it was my favorite of all my attempted representations of my father. It was the way I had imagined him in prison.

• • •

The last time I had seen my father? The 25
previous night, before falling asleep. When we pulled our rental car into the hotel’s hedge-bordered parking lot, it was almost midnight. All the restaurants in the area were closed. There was nothing to do but shower and go to bed.

“It’s like paradise here,” my father had said when he’d seen our tiny room. It had the same orange-and-green wallpaper as Salinas’ office, and the plush emerald carpet matched the walls. “Look, Ka,” he said, his deep, raspy voice muted with exhaustion, “the carpet is like grass under our feet.”

He’d picked the bed closest to the bathroom, removed the top of his gray jogging suit, and unpacked his toiletries. Soon after, I heard him humming loudly, as he always did, in the shower.

I checked on the sculpture, just felt it a little bit through the bubble padding and carton wrapping to make sure it was still whole. I’d used a piece of mahogany that was naturally flawed, with a few superficial cracks along what was now the back. I’d thought these cracks beautiful and had made no effort to sand or polish them away, as they seemed like the wood’s own scars, like the one my father had on his face. But I was also a little worried about the cracks. Would they seem amateurish and unintentional, like a mistake? Could the wood come apart with simple movements or with age? Would the client be satisfied?

I closed my eyes and tried to picture the client to whom I was delivering the sculpture: Gabrielle Fonteneau, a Haitian American woman about my age, the star of a popular television series and an avid art collector. My friend Céline Benoit, a former colleague at the junior high school where I'm a substitute art teacher, had grown up with Gabrielle Fonteneau in Tampa and, at my request, on a holiday visit home had shown Gabrielle Fonteneau a snapshot of my *Father* piece and had persuaded her to buy it.

Gabrielle Fonteneau was spending the week away from Hollywood at her parents' house in Tampa. I took some time off, and both my mother and I figured that my father, who watched a lot of television, both at home and at his Nostrand Avenue barbershop, would enjoy meeting Gabrielle Fonteneau too. But when I woke up, my father was gone and so was the sculpture.

I stepped out of the room and onto the balcony overlooking the parking lot. It was a hot and muggy morning, the humid air laden with the smell of the freshly mowed tropical grass and sprinkler-showered hibiscus bordering the parking lot. My rental car too was gone. I hoped my father was driving around trying to find us some breakfast and would explain when he got back why he'd taken the sculpture with him, so I got dressed and waited. I watched a half hour of local morning news, smoked five mentholated cigarettes even though we were in a nonsmoking room, and waited some more.

All that waiting took two hours, and I felt guilty for having held back so long before going to the front desk to ask, "Have you seen my father?"

I feel Officer Bo's fingers gently stroking my wrist, perhaps to tell me to stop talking. Up close Officer Bo smells like fried eggs and gasoline, like breakfast at the Amoco.

"I'll put the word out with the other boys," he says. "Salinas here will be in his office. Why don't you go on back to your hotel room in case your daddy shows up there?"

• • •

Back in the room, I lie in my father's unmade bed. The sheets smell like his cologne, an odd mix of lavender and lime that I've always thought too pungent, but that he likes nonetheless.

I jump up when I hear the click from the electronic key in the door. It's the maid. She's a young Cuban woman who is overly polite, making up for her lack of English with deferential gestures: a great big smile, a nod, even a bow as she backs out of the room. She reminds me of my mother when she has to work on non-Haitian clients at her beauty shop, how she pays much more attention to those clients, forcing herself to laugh at jokes she barely understands and smiling at insults she doesn't quite grasp, all to avoid being forced into a conversation, knowing she couldn't hold up her end very well.

• • •

It's almost noon when I pick up the phone and call my mother at the salon. One of her employees tells me that she's not yet returned from the Mass she attends every day. After the Mass, if she has clients waiting, she'll walk the twenty blocks from the church to the salon. If she has no appointments, then she'll let her workers handle the walk-ins and go home for lunch. This was as close to retirement as my mother would ever come. This routine was her dream when she first started the shop. She had always wanted a life with room for daily Mass and long walks and the option of sometimes not going to work.

I call my parents' house. My mother isn't there either, so I leave the hotel number on the machine.

"Please call as soon as you can, Manman," I say. "It's about Papa."

It's early afternoon when my mother calls back, her voice cracking with worry. I had been sitting in that tiny hotel room, eating chips and candy bars from the vending machines, chain-smoking and waiting for something to happen, either for my father, Officer Bo, or Manager Salinas to walk into the room with some terrible news or for my mother or Gabrielle Fonteneau to call. I took turns imagining my mother screaming hysterically, berating both herself and me for thinking this trip with my father a good idea, then envisioning Gabrielle Fonteneau calling to say that we shouldn't have come on the trip. It had all been a joke. She wasn't going to buy a sculpture from me after all, especially one I didn't have.

"Where Papa?" Just as I expected, my mother sounds as though she's gasping for breath. I tell her to calm down, that nothing bad has happened. Papa's okay. I've just lost sight of him for a little while.

"How you lost him?" she asks.

"He got up before I did and disappeared," I say.

"How long he been gone?"

I can tell she's pacing back and forth in the kitchen, her slippers flapping against the Mexican tiles. I can hear the faucet when she turns it on, imagine her pushing a glass underneath it and filling it up. I hear her sipping the water as I say, "He's been gone for hours now. I don't even believe it myself."

"You call police?"

Now she's probably sitting at the kitchen table, her eyes closed, her fingers sliding back and forth across her forehead. She clicks her tongue and starts humming one of those mournful songs from the Mass, songs that my father, who attends church only at Christmas, picks up from her and also hums to himself in the shower.

My mother stops humming just long enough to ask, "What the police say?"

"To wait, that he'll come back."

There's a loud tapping on the line, my mother thumping her fingers against the phone's mouthpiece; it gives me a slight ache in my ear.

"He come back," she says with more certainty than either Officer Bo or Manager Salinas. "He not leave you like that."

I promise to call my mother hourly with an update, but I know she'll call me sooner than that, so I dial Gabrielle Fonteneau's cell phone. Gabrielle Fonteneau's voice sounds just as it does on television, but more silken, nuanced, and seductive without the sitcom laugh track.

"To think," my father once said while watching her show, in which she plays a smart-mouthed nurse in an inner-city hospital's maternity ward. "A Haitian-born actress with her own American television show. We have really come far."

"So nice of you to come all this way to personally deliver the sculpture," Gabrielle Fonteneau says. She sounds like she's in a place with cicadas, waterfalls, palm trees, and citronella candles to keep the mosquitoes away. I realize that I too am in such a place, but I'm not able to enjoy it.

"Were you told why I like this sculpture so much?" Gabrielle Fonteneau asks. "It's regal and humble at the same time. It reminds me of my own father."

I hadn't been trying to delve into the universal world of fathers, but I'm glad my sculpture reminds Gabrielle Fonteneau of her father, for I'm not beyond the spontaneous fanaticism inspired by famous people, whose breezy declarations seem to carry so much more weight than those of ordinary mortals. I still had trouble believing I had Gabrielle Fonteneau's cell number, which Céline Benoit had made me promise not to share with anyone else, not even my father.

My thoughts are drifting from Gabrielle Fonteneau's father to mine when I hear her say, "So when will you get here? You have the directions, right? Maybe you can join us for lunch tomorrow, at around twelve."

"We'll be there," I say.

But I'm no longer so certain.

• • •

My father loves museums. When he's not working at his barbershop, he's often at the Brooklyn Museum. The Ancient Egyptian rooms are his favorites.

"The Egyptians, they was like us," he likes to say. The Egyptians worshiped their gods in many forms, fought among themselves, and were often ruled by foreigners. The pharaohs were like the dictators he had fled, and their queens were as beautiful as Gabrielle Fonteneau. But what he admires most about the Ancient Egyptians is the way they mourn their dead.

"They know how to grieve," he'd say, marveling at the mummification process that went on for weeks but resulted in corpses that survived thousands of years.

My whole adult life, I have struggled to find the proper manner of sculpting my father, a quiet and distant man who only came alive while standing with me most of the Saturday mornings of my childhood, mesmerized by the golden masks, the shawabtis,[1] and the schist tablets, Isis, Nefertiti,[2] and Osiris, the jackal-headed ruler of the underworld.

• • •

The sun is setting and my mother has called more than a dozen times when my father finally appears in the hotel room doorway. He looks like a much younger man and appears calm and rested, as if bronzed after a long day at the beach.

"Too smoky in here," he says.

I point to my makeshift ashtray, a Dixie cup filled with tobacco-dyed water and cigarette butts.

funkyfood London -Paul Williams/Alamy Stock Photo

In ancient Egypt, a mummy mask with an idealized face would be placed over the head of a body to symbolize resurrection and passage to the afterlife. It was believed to provide protection from evil spirits on the journey to the afterworld, which was ruled by Osiris.
What does Ka's father's obsession with ancient Egyptian culture say about his beliefs and hopes? To what extent do you think a mummy mask is emblematic of his character?

"Ka, let your father talk to you." He fans the smoky air with his hands, walks over to the bed, and bends down to unlace his sneakers. "Yon ti koze, a little chat."

"Where were you?" I feel my eyelids twitching, a nervous reaction I inherited from my epileptic mother. "Why didn't you leave a note? And Papa, where is the sculpture?"

"That is why we must chat," he says, pulling off his sand-filled sneakers and rubbing the soles of his large, calloused feet each in turn. "I have objections."

He's silent for a long time, concentrating on his foot massage, as though he'd been looking forward to it all day.

[1] Also known as *shabtis*, *shawabtis* are small mummy figurines found in many Egyptian tombs. — Eds.

[2] Schist tablets are made from metamorphic rocks. Isis is the Egyptian Goddess of Death. Nefertiti (c. 1370–c. 1330 B.C.E.) was queen of Egypt. — Eds.

"I'd prefer you not sell that statue," he says at last. Then he turns away, picks up the phone, and calls my mother.

"I know she called you," he says to her in Creole. "She panicked. I was just walking, thinking."

I hear my mother loudly scolding him, telling him not to leave me again. When he hangs up, he grabs his sneakers and puts them back on.

Where's the sculpture?" My eyes are twitching so badly now I can barely see.

"We go," he says. "I take you to it."

• • •

We walk out to the parking lot, where the hotel sprinkler is once more at work, spouting water onto the grass and hedges like centrifugal rain. The streetlights are on now, looking brighter and brighter as the dusk deepens around them. New hotel guests are arriving. Others are leaving for dinner, talking loudly as they walk to their cars.

As my father maneuvers our car out of the parking lot, I tell myself that he might be ill, mentally ill, even though I'd never detected any signs of it before, beyond his prison nightmares.

When I was eight years old and my father had the measles for the first time in his life, I overheard him say to a customer on the phone, "Maybe serious. Doctor tell me, at my age, measles can kill."

This was the first time I realized that my father could die. I looked up the word "kill" in every dictionary and encyclopedia at school, trying to understand what it really meant, that my father could be eradicated from my life.

• • •

My father stops the car on the side of the highway near a man-made lake, one of those marvels of the modern tropical city, with curved stone benches surrounding a stagnant body of water. There's scant light to see by except a half-moon. Stomping the well-manicured grass, my father heads toward one of the benches. I sit down next to him, letting my hands dangle between my legs.

Here I am a little girl again, on some outing with my father, like his trips to the botanic garden or the zoo or the Egyptian statues at the museum. Again, I'm there simply because he wants me to be. I knew I was supposed to learn something from these childhood outings, but it took me years to realize that ultimately my father was doing his best to be like other fathers, to share as much of himself with me as he could.

I glance over at the lake. It's muddy and dark, and there are some very large pink fishes bobbing back and forth near the surface, looking as though they want to leap out and trade places with us.

"Is this where the sculpture is?" I ask.

"In the water," he says.

"Okay," I say calmly. But I know I'm already defeated. I know the piece is already lost. The cracks have probably taken in so much water that the wood has split into several chunks and plunged to the bottom. All I can think of saying is something glib, something I'm not even sure my father will understand.

"Please know this about yourself," I say. "You're a very harsh critic."

My father attempts to smother a smile. He scratches his chin and the scar on the side of his face, but says nothing. In this light the usually chiseled and embossed-looking scar appears deeper than usual, yet somehow less threatening, like a dimple that's spread out too far.

Anger is a wasted emotion, I've always thought. My parents would complain to each other about unjust politics in New York, but they never got angry at my grades, at all the Cs I got in everything but art classes, at my not eating my vegetables or occasionally vomiting my daily spoonful of cod-liver oil. Ordinary anger, I've always thought, is useless. But now I'm deeply angry. I want to hit my father, beat the craziness out of his head.

"Ka," he says, "I tell you why I named you Ka."

Yes, he'd told me, many, many times before. Now does not seem like a good time to remind me, but maybe he's hoping it will calm me, keep me from hating him for the rest of my life.

"Your mother not like the name at all," he says. "She say everybody tease you, people take pleasure repeating your name, calling you Kaka, Kaka, Kaka."

This too I had heard before.

"Okay," I interrupt him with a quick wave of my hands. "I've got it."

"I call you Ka," he says, "because in Egyptian world— "

A ka is a double of the body, I want to complete the sentence for him—the body's companion through life and after life. It guides the body through the kingdom of the dead. That's what I tell my students when I overhear them referring to me as Teacher Kaka.

"You see, ka is like soul," my father now says. "In Haiti is what we call good angel, ti bon anj. When you born, I look at your face, I think, here is my ka, my good angel."

I'm softening a bit. Hearing my father call me his good angel is the point at which I often stop being apathetic.

"I say rest in Creole," he prefaces, "because my tongue too heavy in English to say things like this, especially older things."

"Fine," I reply defiantly in English.

"Ka," he continues in Creole, "when I first saw your statue, I wanted to be buried with it, to take it with me into the other world."

"Like the Ancient Egyptians," I continue in English.

He smiles, grateful, I think, that in spite of everything, I can still appreciate his passions.

"Ka," he says, "when I read to you, with my very bad accent, from *The Book of the Dead*, do you remember how I made you read some chapters to me too?"

But this recollection is harder for me to embrace. I had been terribly bored by *The Book of the Dead*. The images of dead hearts being placed on scales and souls traveling aimlessly down fiery underground rivers had given me my own nightmares. It had seemed selfish of him not to ask me what I wanted to listen to before going to bed, what I wanted to read and have read to me. But since he'd recovered from the measles and hadn't died as we'd both feared, I'd vowed to myself to always tolerate, even indulge him, letting him take me places I didn't enjoy and read me things I cared nothing about, simply to witness the joy they gave him, the kind of bliss that might keep a dying person alive. But maybe he wasn't going to be alive for long. Maybe this is what *this* outing is about. Perhaps

This funerary papyrus depicts the "weighing of hearts" practice in the Egyptian *Book of the Dead*: Osiris, god of the afterlife, would measure the weight of the heart of the deceased against that of a feather. If the heart weighed more than the feather, it would be judged heavy with wrongdoing and eaten by Ammat, the demon god under the scales, thus barring the deceased from the afterlife. **Why would such a practice appeal to Ka's father? What does his fascination with it suggest about the way he thinks of his past?**

my "statue," as he called it, is a sacrificial offering, the final one that he and I would make together before he was gone.

"Are you dying?" I ask my father. It's the one explanation that would make what he's done seem insignificant or even logical. "Are you ill? Are you going to die?"

What would I do now, if this were true? I'd find him the best doctor, move back home with him and my mother. I'd get a serious job, find a boyfriend, and get married, and I'd never complain again about his having dumped my sculpture in the lake.

Like me, my father tends to be silent a moment too long during an important conversation and then say too much when less should be said. I listen to the wailing of crickets and cicadas, though I can't tell where they're coming from. There's the highway, and the cars racing by, the half-moon, the lake dug up from the depths of the ground — with my sculpture now at the bottom of it, the allée of royal palms whose shadows intermingle with the giant fishes on the surface of that lake, and there is me and my father.

"Do you recall the judgment of the dead," my father speaks up at last, "when the heart of a person is put on a scale? If it's heavy, the heart, then this person cannot enter the other world."

It is a testament to my upbringing, and perhaps the Kaka and good angel story has something to do with this as well, that I remain silent now, at this particular time.

"I don't deserve a statue," my father says. But at this very instant he does look like one, like the Madonna of humility, contemplating her losses in the dust, or an Ancient Egyptian funerary priest, kneeling with his hands prayerfully folded on his lap.

"Ka," he says, "when I took you to the Brooklyn Museum, I would stand there for hours admiring them. But all you noticed was how there were pieces missing from them, eyes, noses, legs, sometimes even heads. You always noticed more what was not there than what was."

Of course, this way of looking at things was why I ultimately began sculpting in the first place, to make statues that would amaze my father even more than these ancient relics.

"Ka, I am like one of those statues," he says.

"An Ancient Egyptian?" I hear echoes of my loud, derisive laugh only after I've been laughing for a while. It's the only weapon I have now, the only way I know to take my revenge on my father.

"Don't do that," he says, frowning, irritated, almost shouting over my laughter. "Why do that? If you are mad, let yourself be mad. Why do you always laugh like a clown when you are angry?"

I tend to wave my hands about wildly when I laugh, but I don't notice I'm doing that now until he reaches over to grab them. I quickly move them away, but he ends up catching my right wrist, the same wrist Officer Bo had stroked earlier to make me shut up. My father holds on to it so tightly now that I feel his fingers crushing the bone, almost splitting it apart, and I can't laugh anymore.

"Let go," I say, and he releases my wrist quickly. He looks down at his own fingers, then lowers his hand to his lap.

My wrist is still throbbing. I keep stroking it to relieve some of the pain. It's the ache there that makes me want to cry more than anything, not so much this sudden, uncharacteristic flash of anger from my father.

"I'm sorry," he says. "I did not want to hurt you. I did not want to hurt anyone."

I keep rubbing my wrist, hoping he'll feel even sorrier, even guiltier for grabbing me so hard, but even more for throwing away my work.

"Ka, I don't deserve a statue," he says again, this time much more slowly, "not a whole one, at least. You see, Ka, your father was the hunter, he was not the prey."

I stop stroking my wrist, sensing something coming that might hurt much more. He's silent again. I don't want to prod him, feed him any cues, urge him to speak, but finally I get tired of the silence and feel I have no choice but to ask, "What are you talking about?"

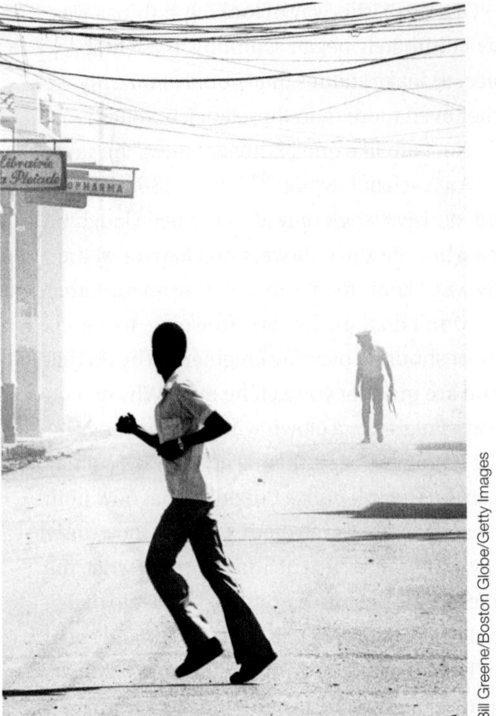

Bill Greene/Boston Globe/Getty Images

This photograph depicts a Haitian man running from a member of the Tonton Macoutes, a paramilitary group, during riots and protests that led to the overthrow of the regime of President François Duvalier in 1986. **How does this photograph depict the proverb Ka's father mentions: "One day for the hunter, one day for the prey" (par. 14)?**

I immediately regret the question. Is he going to explain why he and my mother have no close friends, why they've never had anyone over to the house, why they never speak of any relatives in Haiti or anywhere else, or have never returned there or, even after I learned Creole from them, have never taught me anything else about the country beyond what I could find out on my own, on the television, in newspapers, in books? Is he about to tell me why Manman is so pious? Why she goes to daily Mass? I am not sure I want to know anything more than the little they've chosen to share with me all these years, but it is clear to me that he needs to tell me, has been trying to for a long time.

"We have a proverb," he continues. "One day for the hunter, one day for the prey. Ka, your father was the hunter, he was not the prey."

Each word is now hard-won as it leaves my father's mouth, balanced like those hearts on the Ancient Egyptian scales.

"Ka, I was never in prison," he says.

"Okay," I say, sounding like I am fourteen again, chanting from what my mother used to call the meaningless adolescent chorus, just to sound like everyone else my age.

"I was working in the prison," my father says. And I decide not to interrupt him again until he's done.

Stranded in the middle of this speech now, he has to go on. "It was one of the prisoners inside the prison who cut my face in this way," he says.

My father now points to the long, pitted scar on his right cheek. I am so used to his hands covering it up that this new purposeful motion toward it seems dramatic and extreme, almost like raising a veil.

"This man who cut my face," he continues, "I shot and killed him, like I killed many people."

I'm amazed that he managed to say all of this in one breath, like a monologue. I wish I too had had some rehearsal time, a chance to have learned what to say in response.

There is no time yet, no space in my brain to allow for whatever my mother might have to confess. Was she huntress or prey? A thirty-year-plus disciple of my father's coercive persuasion? She'd kept to herself even more than he had, like someone who was nurturing a great pain that she could never speak about. Yet she had done her best to be a good mother to me, taking charge of feeding and clothing me and making sure my hair was always combed, leaving only what she must have considered my intellectual development to my father.

When I was younger, she'd taken me to Mass with her on Sundays. Was I supposed to have been praying for my father all that time, the father who was the hunter and not the prey?

135 I think back to "The Negative Confession" ritual from *The Book of the Dead*, a ceremony that was supposed to take place before the weighing of hearts, giving the dead a chance to affirm that they'd done only good things in their lifetime. It was one of the chapters my father read to me most often. Now he was telling me I should have heard something beyond what he was reading. I should have removed the negatives.

"I am not a violent man," he had read. "I have made no one weep. I have never been angry without cause. I have never uttered any lies. I have never slain any men or women. I have done no evil."

And just so I will be absolutely certain of what I'd heard, I ask my father, "And those nightmares you were always having, what were they?"

"Of what I," he says, "your father, did to others."

Another image of my mother now fills my head, of her as a young woman, a woman my age, taking my father in her arms. At what point did she decide that she loved him? When did she know that she was supposed to have despised him?

140 "Does Manman know?" I ask.

"Yes," he says. "I explained, after you were born."

• • •

I am the one who drives the short distance back to the hotel. The ride seems drawn out, the cars in front of us appear to be dawdling. I honk impatiently, even when everyone except me is driving at a normal speed. My father is silent, not even telling me, as he has always done whenever he's been my passenger, to calm down, to be careful, to take my time.

As we are pulling into the hotel parking lot, I realize that I haven't notified Officer Bo and Manager Salinas that my father has been found. I decide that I will call them from my room. Then, before we leave the car, my father says, "Ka, no matter what, I'm still your father, still your mother's husband. I would never do these things now."

And this to me is as meaningful a declaration as his other confession. It was my first inkling that maybe my father was wrong in his own representation of his former life, that maybe his past offered more choices than being either hunter or prey.

• • •

145 When we get back to the hotel room, I find messages from both Officer Bo and Manager Salinas. Their shifts are over, but I leave word informing them that my father has returned.

While I'm on the phone, my father slips into the bathroom and runs the shower at full force. He is not humming.

When it seems he's never coming out, I call my mother at home in Brooklyn.

"Manman, how do you love him?" I whisper into the phone.

My mother is clicking her tongue and tapping her fingers against the mouthpiece again. Her soft tone makes me think I have awakened her from her sleep.

150 "He tell you?" she asks.

"Yes," I say.

"Everything?"

"Is there more?"

"What he told you he want to tell you for long time," she says, "you, his good angel."

155 It has always amazed me how much my mother and father echo each other, in their speech, their actions, even in their businesses. I wonder how much more alike they could possibly be. But why shouldn't they be alike? Like all parents, they were a society of two, sharing a series of private codes and associations, a past that even if I'd been born in the country of their birth, I still wouldn't have known, couldn't have known, thoroughly. I was a part of them. Some might say I belonged to them. But I wasn't them.

"I don't know, Ka." My mother is whispering now, as though there's a chance she might also be overheard by my father. "You and me, we save him. When I meet him, it made him stop hurt the people. This how I see it. He a seed thrown in rock. You, me, we make him take root."

As my mother is speaking, this feeling comes over me that I sometimes have when I'm carving, this sensation that my hands don't belong to me at all, that something else besides my brain and muscles is moving my fingers, something bigger and stronger than myself, an invisible puppetmaster over whom I have no control. I feel as though it's this same puppetmaster that now forces me to lower the phone and hang up, in midconversation, on my mother.

As soon as I put the phone down, I tell myself that I could continue this particular conversation at will, in a few minutes, a few hours, a few days, even a few years. Whenever I'm ready.

My father walks back into the room, his thinning hair wet, his pajamas on. My mother does not call me back. Somehow she must know that she has betrayed me by not sharing my confusion and, on some level, my feeling that my life could have gone on fine without my knowing these types of things about my father.

• • •

When I get up the next morning, my father's already dressed. He's sitting on the edge of the bed, his head bowed, his face buried in his palms, his forehead shadowed by his fingers. If I were sculpting him at this moment, I would carve a praying mantis, crouching motionless, seeming to pray, while actually waiting to strike.

With his back to me now, my father says, "Will you call that actress and tell her we have it no more, the statue?"

"We were invited to lunch there," I say. "I believe we should go and tell her in person."

He raises his shoulders and shrugs. "Up to you," he says.

• • •

We start out for Gabrielle Fonteneau's house after breakfast. It's not quite as hot as the previous morning, but it's getting there. I crank up the AC at full blast, making it almost impossible for us to have a conversation, even if we wanted to.

The drive seems longer than the twenty-four hours it took to get to Lakeland from New York. I quickly grow tired of the fake lakes, the fenced-in canals, the citrus groves, the fan-shaped travelers' palms, the highway so imposingly neat. My father turns his face away from me and takes in the tropical landscape, as though he will never see it again. I know he's enjoying the live oaks with Spanish moss and bromeliads growing in their shade, the yellow trumpet flowers and flame vines, the tamarinds and jacaranda trees we speed by, because he expressed his admiration for them before, on the first half of our journey.

As we approach Gabrielle Fonteneau's house, my father breaks the silence in the car by saying, "Now you see, Ka, why your mother and me, we have never returned home."

• • •

The Fonteneaus' house is made of bricks and white coral, on a cul-de-sac with a row of banyans separating the two sides of the street.

My father and I get out of the car and follow a concrete path to the front door. Before we can knock, an older woman appears in the doorway. It's Gabrielle Fonteneau's mother. She resembles Gabrielle Fonteneau, or the way Gabrielle looks on television, with stunning almond eyes, skin the color of sorrel and spiraling curls brushing the sides of her face.

"We've been looking out for you," she says with a broad smile.

When Gabrielle's father joins her in the doorway, I realize where Gabrielle Fonteneau gets her height. He's more than six feet tall.

Mr. Fonteneau extends his hands, first to my father and then to me. They're relatively small, half the size of my father's.

We move slowly through the living room, which has a cathedral ceiling and walls covered with Haitian paintings with subjects ranging from market scenes and first communions to weddings and wakes. Most remarkable is a life-size portrait of Gabrielle Fonteneau sitting on a canopy-covered bench in what seems like her parents' garden.

Out on the back terrace, which towers over a nursery of azaleas, hibiscus, dracaenas, and lemongrass, a table is set for lunch.

Mr. Fonteneau asks my father where he is from in Haiti, and my father lies. In the past, I thought he always said he was from a different province each time because he'd really lived in all of those places, but I realize now that he says this to reduce the possibility of anyone identifying him, even though thirty-seven years and a thinning head of widow-peaked salt-and-pepper hair shield him from the threat of immediate recognition.

When Gabrielle Fonteneau makes her entrance, in an off-the-shoulder ruby dress, my father and I both rise from our seats.

"Gabrielle," she coos, extending her hand to my father, who leans forward and kisses it before spontaneously blurting out, "My dear, you are one of the most splendid flowers of Haiti."

Gabrielle Fonteneau looks a bit flustered. She tilts her head coyly and turns toward me.

"Welcome," she says.

• • •

During the meal of conch, fried plantains, and mushroom rice, Mr. Fonteneau tries to draw my father into conversation by asking him, in Creole, when he was last in Haiti.

"Thirty-seven years," my father answers with a mouthful of food.

"No going back for you?" asks Mrs. Fonteneau.

"I have not yet had the opportunity," my father replies.

"We go back every year," says Mrs. Fonteneau, "to a beautiful place overlooking the ocean, in the mountains of Jacmel."

"Have you ever been to Jacmel?" Gabrielle Fonteneau asks me.

I shake my head no.

"We're fortunate," Mrs. Fonteneau says, "that we have a place to go where we can say the rain is sweeter, the dust is lighter, our beaches prettier."

"So now we are tasting rain and weighing dust?" Mr. Fonteneau says and laughs.

"There's nothing like drinking the sweet juice from a coconut fetched from your own tree." Mrs. Fonteneau's eyes are lit up now as she puts her fork down to better paint the picture for us. She's giddy, her voice grows louder and higher, and even her daughter is absorbed, smiling and recollecting with her mother.

"There's nothing like sinking your hand in sand from the beach in your own country," Mrs. Fonteneau is saying. "It's a wonderful feeling, wonderful."

I imagine my father's nightmares. Maybe he dreams of dipping his hands in the sand on a beach in his own country and finding that what he comes up with is a fistful of blood.

• • •

After lunch, my father asks if he can have a closer look at the Fonteneaus' garden. While he's taking the tour, I make my confession about the sculpture to Gabrielle Fonteneau.

She frowns as she listens, fidgeting, shifting her weight from one foot to the other, as though she's greatly annoyed that so much of her valuable time had been so carelessly squandered on me. Perhaps she's wondering if this was just an elaborate scheme to meet her, perhaps she wants us out of her house as quickly as possible.

"I don't usually have people come into my house like this," she says, "I promise you."

"I appreciate it," I say. "I'm grateful for your trust and I didn't mean to violate it."

"I guess if you don't have it, then you don't have it," she says. "But I'm very disappointed. I really wanted to give that piece to my father."

"I'm sorry," I say.

"I should have known something was off," she says, looking around the room, as if for something more interesting to concentrate on. "Usually when people come here to sell us art, first of all they're always carrying it with them and they always show it to us right away. But since you know Céline I overlooked that."

"There was a sculpture," I say, aware of how stupid my excuse was going to sound. "My father didn't like it, and he threw it away."

She raises her perfectly arched eyebrows, as if out of concern for my father's sanity, or for my own. Or maybe it's another indirect signal that she now wants us out of her sight.

"We're done, then," she says, looking directly at my face. "I have to make a call. Enjoy the rest of your day."

Gabrielle Fonteneau excuses herself, disappearing behind a closed door. Through the terrace overlooking the garden, I see her parents guiding my father along rows of lemongrass. I want to call Gabrielle Fonteneau back and promise her that I will make her another sculpture, but I can't. I don't know that I will be able to work on anything for some time. I have lost my subject, the prisoner father I loved as well as pitied.

In the garden Mr. Fonteneau snaps a few sprigs of lemongrass from one of the plants, puts them in a plastic bag that Mrs. Fonteneau is holding. Mrs. Fonteneau hands the bag of lemongrass to my father.

Watching my father accept with a nod of thanks, I remember the chapter "Driving Back Slaughters" from *The Book of the Dead*, which my father sometimes read to me to drive away my fear of imagined monsters. It was a chapter full of terrible lines like "My mouth is the keeper of both speech and silence. I am the child who travels the roads of yesterday, the one who has been wrought from his eye."

I wave to my father in the garden to signal that we should leave now, and he slowly comes toward me, the Fonteneaus trailing behind him.

With each step forward, he rubs the scar on the side of his face, and out of a strange reflex I scratch my face in the same spot.

Maybe the last person my father harmed had dreamed moments like this into my father's future, strangers seeing that scar furrowed into his face and taking turns staring at it and avoiding it, forcing him to conceal it with his hands, pretend it's not there, or make up some lie about it, to explain.

Out on the sidewalk in front of the Fonteneaus' house, before we both take our places in the car, my father and I wave good-bye to Gabrielle Fonteneau's parents, who are standing in their doorway. Even though I'm not sure they understood the purpose of our visit, they were more than kind, treating us as though we were old friends of their daughter's, which maybe they had mistaken us for.

As the Fonteneaus turn their backs to us and close their front door, I look over at my father, who's still smiling and waving. When he smiles the scar shrinks and nearly disappears into the folds of his cheek, which used to make me wish he would never stop smiling.

• • •

Once the Fonteneaus are out of sight, my father reaches down on his lap and strokes the plastic bag with the lemongrass the Fonteneaus had given him. The car is already beginning to smell too much like lemongrass, like air freshener overkill.

"What will you use that for?" I ask.

"To make tea," he says, "for Manman and me."

• • •

I pull the car away from the Fonteneaus' curb, dreading the rest stops, the gas station, the midway hotels ahead for us. I wish my mother

extending beyond the text

Following a devastating earthquake in Haiti on January 12, 2010, the *New Yorker* used this painting by the Haitian artist Frantz Zephirin for its cover. Entitled *The Resurrection of the Dead*, it features three figures known as *gede* or *lwe*, both important spirits in Haitian Vodou. In the context of this painting, the spirits can be interpreted as ferrying earthquake victims to the afterlife.

Frantz Zephirin, The New Yorker © Condé Nast

1. **What might the wall of faces represent in this image?**
2. **How does this painting relate to Ka's father's perspective on the connection between his experiences and the beliefs of the ancient Egyptians?**
3. **Elizabeth McAlister, an associate professor of religion at Wesleyan University who specializes in Haiti, explains that the water in Zephirin's painting represents "where the dead spend a year and a day. *An ba dlo*. Under the water. Resting. Floating. After that when it is time, they will be lifted out, drawn out, by their living. If they are lucky to have children living and walking on the earth." What visual aspects of the cover support this interpretation? How does Danticat incorporate similar symbolism in "The Book of the Dead"?**

were here now, talking to us about some miracle she'd just heard about in a sermon at the Mass. I wish my sculpture were still in the trunk. I wish I hadn't met Gabrielle Fonteneau, that I still had that to look forward to somewhere else, sometime in the future. I wish I could give my father whatever he'd been seeking in telling me his secret. But my father, if anyone could, must have already understood that confessions do not lighten living hearts.

I had always thought that my father's only ordeal was that he'd left his country and moved to a place where everything from the climate to the language was so unlike his own, a place where he never quite seemed to fit in, never appeared to belong. The only thing I can grasp now, as I drive way beyond the speed limit down yet another highway, is why the unfamiliar might have been so comforting, rather than distressing, to my father. And why he has never wanted the person he was, is, permanently documented in any way. He taught himself to appreciate the enormous weight of permanent markers by learning about the Ancient Egyptians. He had gotten to know them, through their crypts and monuments, in a way that he wanted no one to know him, no one except my mother and me, we, who are now his kas, his good angels, his masks against his own face. ■

2004

Understanding and Interpreting

1. **AP® Character and Narration.** Why is Ka's father drawn to the culture of the ancient Egyptians? How does your interpretation of his interest change throughout the story?
2. **AP® Character and Narration.** Ka's father offers one explanation for why he destroyed her sculpture. Do you believe him? What are other possible explanations for his action?
3. **AP® Character and Narration.** Ka has a different relationship with her mother than she has with her father. How would you characterize each of these relationships? Do you think it would have mattered to Ka if her mother rather than her father had revealed to her his past as "hunter" rather than "prey"? Explain.
4. **AP® Character and Narration.** What do you think Ka means when she says, "maybe my father was wrong in his own representation of his former life, that maybe his past offered more choices than being either hunter or prey" (par. 144)? What does this statement convey about how she sees her father? Do you see the character of her father in the same light? Explain why or why not.
5. **AP® Character and Narration.** How much does Ka's mother know about her husband? Is it significant that he told her about his past after they were married and had their daughter?
6. **AP® Character and Narration.** Once her father has revealed his secret identity to her, Ka immediately thinks of her mother: "There is no time yet, no space in my brain to allow for whatever my mother might have to confess. Was she huntress or prey?" (par. 133). Why does Ka mentally shift to her mother before responding to her father in either words or thoughts?
7. **AP® Character and Narration.** How has Ka's relationship with her father changed by the end of the story? Do you believe she will forgive him? How do you think the experience they've shared and the knowledge Ka now has will affect their relationship? Do you think she would rather not have known about his past? Explain.

8. **AP® Character and Narration.** Ka says that her father, "if anyone could, must have already understood that confessions do not lighten living hearts" (par. 213). How do you interpret this sentiment, and why does she think he would understand it? And if he does understand this, why does he reveal his past to her?

9. **AP® Character, Setting, and Narration.** Who are the hunters and who are the prey in this story? Is such a classification appropriate or even possible in this story? Explain.

10. **AP® Character and Narration.** Danticat poses powerful questions about blame, guilt, forgiveness, healing, and redemption in "The Book of the Dead." Is she arguing that Ka should forgive her father? Has he forgiven himself? Can forgiveness — whether by his daughter or his wife or even himself — mean that he is no longer morally responsible for his actions as a young man?

11. **AP® Setting.** How does the Haitian history in the Key Context note inform your interpretation of the story and the motivations of its central characters? Why isn't Danticat more explicit about the historical context of such figures as the Tonton Macoutes or the Duvaliers?

Analyzing Language, Style, and Structure

1. **Vocabulary in Context.** As Ka and her father look to the manmade lake where he has thrown the statue, Ka narrates, "All I can think of saying is something glib, something I'm not even sure my father will understand" (par. 85). This is not the only time in the story Ka responds to her father in a somewhat insincere and shallow way. Where else does she speak to him in a *glib* manner, and what do such responses suggest about Ka's emotional state?

2. **AP® Structure and Figurative Language.** How do you interpret the title of the story? How does it both refer to the ancient Egyptian *Book of the Dead* and go beyond that reference?

3. **AP® Structure, Narration, and Figurative Language.** "The Book of the Dead" opens with the simple sentence, "My father is gone." How is this sentence explained, echoed, and explored throughout the story? What significance has this sentence taken on by the story's end?

4. **AP® Character, Structure, and Narration.** Why do you think Danticat chose to tell this story through Ka rather than through her father or an omniscient narrator?

5. **AP® Character, Narration, and Figurative Language.** As the story begins, Ka is trying to locate her father, who has gone missing. When do you realize that he has not been hurt, taken ill, or become the victim of a violent crime but that he has left on his own? Is this an effective way to begin the story, or do you think it is misleading? What elements of mystery are present in the story, and how do these elements contribute to the meaning of the story?

6. **AP® Structure and Narration.** How do Danticat's structural choices and the pace at which you learn information in the story contribute to your interpretation of "The Book of the Dead"? For example, consider the story's first sentence ("My father is gone") and the unfolding of the story as a mystery.

7. **AP® Character, Structure, Narration, and Figurative Language.** In paragraph 28, Ka describes the material she chose for her sculpture: "a piece of mahogany that was naturally flawed, with a few superficial cracks along what was now the back. I'd thought these cracks beautiful and had made no effort to sand or polish them away, as they seemed like the wood's own scars, like the one my father had on his face." What does this passage suggest about Ka's intuition about her father? What does it suggest about her ability to accept or even celebrate imperfection? Has her father tried to "polish away" his own scars up until this point?

8. **AP® Character, Setting, Structure, and Narration.** What are some of the clues Ka has about her father's identity? What new understanding about her parents and the way the family lives in New York does Ka gain when she learns about her father's past in Haiti?

9. **AP® Character, Structure, and Narration.** When Ka's father reveals his past, he begins by referring to himself in the first person ("I don't deserve a statue"), then shifts to the third person ("your father was the hunter, he was not the prey") (par. 121). Why do you think he makes this shift? What does that change in perspective suggest?

10. **AP® Character and Structure.** What is the function of the minor characters of Gabrielle Fonteneau and her parents? How does Danticat weave them into the structure of the story, and how do they contribute to the development of the story's themes? As you explore their role, ask yourself why Danticat did not simply structure the story so that Ka and her father choose not to visit the Fonteneaus after the sculpture was destroyed.

11. **AP® Character, Structure, Narration, and Figurative Language.** In an interview in *The Caribbean Writer*, Danticat talks about silence:

    > Silence is at the core of a story like this, just as it is during the dictatorship. There's so much you're not allowed to say. The Duvaliers are silenced — by killing a whole generation and stunning many of the survivors into silence. . . . Migration also silences you. You're in a country where you don't speak the language . . . [yet] that these characters tell their stories . . . breaks that silence.

    Discuss the role of silence and voice in "The Book of the Dead," paying special attention to who chooses to speak and when, and the use of Haitian Creole in exchanges between Ka and her parents as well as between Ka's father and Mr. Fonteneau.

12. **AP® Character, Narration, and Figurative Language.** What does Ka mean when she thinks back to "The Negative Confession" ritual from *The Book of the Dead*: "Now he was telling me I should have heard something beyond what he was reading. I should have removed the negatives" (par. 135)?

13. **AP® Character, Narration, and Figurative Language.** Who or what is the "puppetmaster" in paragraph 157, in which Ka describes how she feels when talking to her mother about her father's past, and how does this idea of the puppetmaster develop themes in the story?

14. **AP® Character, Narration, and Figurative Language.** How do you interpret the final paragraph of the story? Does it end on a hopeful note? What does Danticat mean by "the enormous weight of permanent markers"? How are the dew breaker's "good angels" "his masks against his own face"?

Topics for Composing

1. **AP® FRQ** **Prose Fiction Analysis.** The following question refers to paragraphs 80–110 of Edwidge Danticat's "The Book of the Dead," published in 1999. In this passage, Ka, the narrator, travels with her father to the lake where he has thrown a statue that she carved of him. Read the passage carefully. Then, in a well-written essay, analyze how Danticat uses literary elements and techniques to portray the complex relationship between Ka and her father.

2. **AP® FRQ** **Literary Argument.** To achieve reconciliation with ourselves and with others, we must have an opportunity to share our truth. In "The Book of the Dead," Ka's father shares the truth about his past with his daughter. In a well-written essay, analyze how the degree to which Ka's father achieves reconciliation within himself and with Ka contributes to an interpretation of the work as a whole. Do not merely summarize the plot.

3. **AP® Literary Argumentation.** Do a close reading of the passage in which Ka's father reveals that he was "the hunter . . . not the prey" (pars. 110–41). Discuss how Danticat conveys the changes in Ka's emotional state as her father makes this revelation to her.
4. **AP® Literary Argumentation.** Discuss "The Book of the Dead" in terms of how Michiko Kakutani, a book reviewer for the *New York Times*, has characterized the story: "A tale that simultaneously unfolds to become a philosophical meditation on the possibility of redemption and the longing of victims and victimizers alike to believe in the promise of new beginnings held forth by the American Dream." In particular, explore whether Ka's father finds redemption. Does he achieve "the promise of new beginnings held forth by the American Dream"? Explain why or why not, using evidence from the story to support your response.
5. **Research.** When Ka says that her father "loves museums" (par. 60), she narrates, "'The Egyptians, they was like us,' he likes to say" because "[t]he Egyptians worshiped their gods in many forms, fought among themselves, and were often ruled by foreigners. The pharaohs were like the dictators he had fled, and their queens were as beautiful as Gabrielle Fonteneau. But what he admires most about the Ancient Egyptians is the way they mourn their dead." Research ways in which the ancient Egyptians had similar spiritual traditions to those of the people of Haiti such as Ka's father. In particular, how do Haitians mourn their dead, and how does your understanding of their beliefs contribute to a greater understand of Danticat's short story?
6. **Speaking and Listening.** How does the new information Ka learns about her father shake her own identity? Prepare for a class discussion on this question by considering her various responses, from feeling that her "life could have gone on fine without . . . knowing these types of things about [her] father" (par. 159) to imagining that she feels a scar in the same place on her face as her father's. How do parents' experiences prior to having children affect those children's identities? You may discuss examples from your own life or from other works of literature, television, or film.
7. **Connections.** Write an essay comparing and contrasting "The Book of the Dead" with another work in which a character's relationship to events in the past contributes to the meaning of the work. Consider how these events positively or negatively affect the present actions, attitudes, or values of Ka or her father and a character from another work.
8. **Connections.** Write an essay explaining whether you think that Ka should forgive her father. Center your discussion on "The Book of the Dead," but explore the concept of forgiveness, healing, and redemption through research into other areas, such as the documentary "As We Forgive" — about reconciliation efforts in Rwanda — and the Amy Biehl Foundation in South Africa.
9. **Multimodal.** Draw, paint, sculpt, or digitally create your interpretation of Ka's sculpture of her father. Explain what information in Danticat's story led you to your design and how you might have changed her original sculpture to fit your interpretation of the story.
10. **Connections.** Watch Jonathan Demme's documentary *The Agronomist*, the true story of Jean Dominique, a Haitian radio journalist and human rights activist. Write an essay discussing how this film expands your understanding of "The Book of the Dead."

Classic Text

The Things They Carried

Tim O'Brien

Peter Power/Getty Images

Tim O'Brien was born in 1946 in Austin, Minnesota. After graduating from Macalester College with a BA in political science in 1968, he was drafted into the army and sent to Vietnam, where he became a sergeant and earned a Purple Heart. Perhaps his most famous book, *The Things They Carried* — composed of a series of connected stories — appeared in 1990. Dedicated to its fictional characters and based on his actual experience, it is a novel in which O'Brien himself is the narrator.

KEY CONTEXT This short story takes place during the Vietnam War, a conflict involving multiple countries that lasted more than twenty years and ending with the fall of Saigon, the capital of South Vietnam, in 1975. The United States fought as an ally of South Vietnam against the communist government of North Vietnam. Over 3 million people lost their lives including more than 58,000 Americans, over 1 million North Vietnamese soldiers and Vietcong guerrilla fighters, between 200,000 and 250,000 South Vietnamese soldiers, and as many as 2 million total civilians.

First Lieutenant Jimmy Cross carried letters from a girl named Martha, a junior at Mount Sebastian College in New Jersey. They were not love letters, but Lieutenant Cross was hoping, so he kept them folded in plastic at the bottom of his rucksack. In the late afternoon, after a day's march, he would dig his foxhole, wash his hands under a canteen, unwrap the letters, hold them with the tips of his fingers, and spend the last hour of light pretending. He would imagine romantic camping trips into the White Mountains in New Hampshire. He would sometimes taste the envelope flaps, knowing her tongue had been there. More than anything, he wanted Martha to love him as he loved her, but the letters were mostly chatty, elusive on the matter of love. She was a virgin, he was almost sure. She was an English major at Mount Sebastian, and she wrote beautifully about her professors and roommates and midterm exams, about her respect for Chaucer and her great affection for Virginia Woolf. She often quoted lines of poetry; she never mentioned the war, except to say, Jimmy, take care of yourself. The letters weighed ten ounces. They were signed "Love, Martha," but Lieutenant Cross understood that "Love" was only a way of signing and did not mean what he sometimes pretended it meant. At dusk, he would carefully return the letters to his rucksack. Slowly, a bit distracted, he would get up and move among his men, checking the perimeter, then at full dark he would return to his hole and watch the night and wonder if Martha was a virgin.

The things they carried were largely determined by necessity. Among the necessities or near necessities were P-38 can openers, pocket knives, heat tabs, wrist watches, dog tags, mosquito repellent, chewing gum, candy, cigarettes, salt tablets, packets of Kool-Aid, lighters, matches, sewing kits, Military Payment Certificates, C rations, and two or three canteens of water. Together, these items weighed between fifteen and twenty pounds, depending

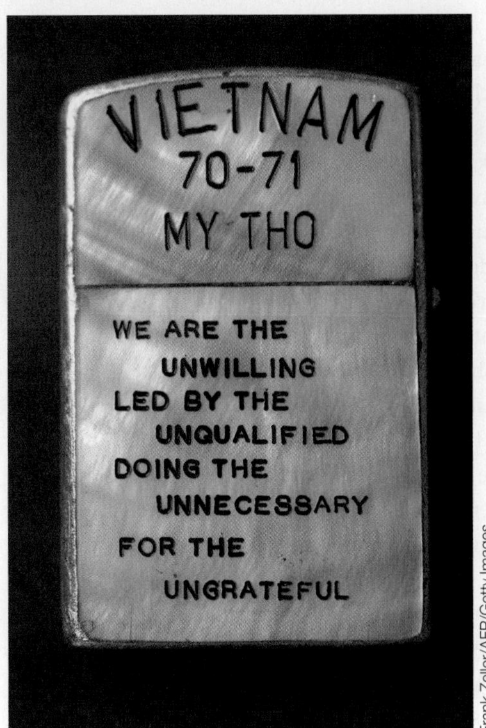

Frank Zeller/AFP/Getty Images

Zippo lighters have been the companions of American servicemen since World War II. The one pictured here is a replica, created by American artist Bradford Edwards, of a typical lighter carried by a soldier in Vietnam. Many such lighters were found there after the war. **What does the inscription reveal about the state of mind of the combatants in the war in Vietnam? How do you see that state of mind reflected in the characters of "The Things They Carried"?**

upon a man's habits or rate of metabolism. Henry Dobbins, who was a big man, carried extra rations; he was especially fond of canned peaches in heavy syrup over pound cake. Dave Jensen, who practiced field hygiene, carried a toothbrush, dental floss, and several hotel-size bars of soap he'd stolen on R&R in Sydney, Australia. Ted Lavender, who was scared, carried tranquilizers until he was shot in the head outside the village of Than Khe in mid-April. By necessity, and because it was SOP,[1] they all carried steel helmets that weighed five pounds including the liner and camouflage cover. They carried the standard fatigue jackets and trousers. Very few carried underwear. On their feet they carried jungle boots — 2.1 pounds — and Dave Jensen carried three pairs of socks and a can of Dr. Scholl's foot powder as a precaution against trench foot. Until he was shot, Ted Lavender carried six or seven ounces of premium dope, which for him was a necessity. Mitchell Sanders, the RTO,[2] carried condoms. Norman Bowker carried a diary. Rat Kiley carried comic books. Kiowa, a devout Baptist, carried an illustrated New Testament that had been presented to him by his father, who taught Sunday school in Oklahoma City, Oklahoma. As a hedge against bad times, however, Kiowa also carried his grandmother's distrust of the white man, his grandfather's old hunting hatchet. Necessity dictated. Because the land was mined and booby-trapped, it was SOP for each man to carry a steel-centered, nylon-covered flak jacket, which weighed 6.7 pounds, but which on hot days seemed much heavier. Because you could die so quickly, each man carried at least one large compress bandage, usually in the helmet band for easy access. Because the nights were cold, and because the monsoons were wet, each carried a green plastic poncho that could be used as a raincoat or ground sheet or makeshift tent. With its quilted liner, the poncho weighed almost two pounds, but it was worth every ounce. In April, for instance, when Ted Lavender was shot, they used his poncho to wrap him up, then to carry him across the paddy, then to lift him into the chopper that took him away.

• • •

They were called legs or grunts.

To carry something was to "hump" it, as when Lieutenant Jimmy Cross humped his love

[1] Standard operating procedure. — Eds.

[2] Radiotelephone operator. — Eds.

for Martha up the hills and through the swamps. In its intransitive form, "to hump" meant "to walk," or "to march," but it implied burdens far beyond the intransitive.

5 Almost everyone humped photographs. In his wallet, Lieutenant Cross carried two photographs of Martha. The first was a Kodachrome snapshot signed "Love," though he knew better. She stood against a brick wall. Her eyes were gray and neutral, her lips slightly open as she stared straight-on at the camera. At night, sometimes, Lieutenant Cross wondered who had taken the picture, because he knew she had boyfriends, because he loved her so much, and because he could see the shadow of the picture taker spreading out against the brick wall. The second photograph had been clipped from the 1968 Mount Sebastian yearbook. It was an action shot — women's volleyball — and Martha was bent horizontal to the floor, reaching, the palms of her hands in sharp focus, the tongue taut, the expression frank and competitive. There was no visible sweat. She wore white gym shorts. Her legs, he thought, were almost certainly the legs of a virgin, dry and without hair, the left knee cocked and carrying her entire weight, which was just over one hundred pounds. Lieutenant Cross remembered touching that left knee. A dark theater, he remembered, and the movie was *Bonnie and Clyde*, and Martha wore a tweed skirt, and during the final scene, when he touched her knee, she turned and looked at him in a sad, sober way that made him pull his hand back, but he would always remember the feel of the tweed skirt and the knee beneath it and the sound of the gunfire that killed Bonnie and Clyde, how embarrassing it was, how slow and oppressive. He remembered kissing her good night at the dorm door. Right then, he thought, he should've done something brave. He should've carried her up the stairs to her room and tied her to the bed and touched that left knee all night long. He should've risked it. Whenever he looked at the photographs, he thought of new things he should've done.

• • •

What they carried was partly a function of rank, partly of field specialty.

As a first lieutenant and platoon leader, Jimmy Cross carried a compass, maps, code books, binoculars, and a .45-caliber pistol that weighed 2.9 pounds fully loaded. He carried a strobe light and the responsibility for the lives of his men.

As an RTO, Mitchell Sanders carried the PRC-25 radio, a killer, twenty-six pounds with its battery.

As a medic, Rat Kiley carried a canvas satchel filled with morphine and plasma and

CORR/AFP/Getty Images

In this December 1967 photo, two American soldiers relax beside a Christmas tree that has been set up in a trench surrounded by sandbags.

How does this image reflect the surreal experiences O'Brien describes in his story?

malaria tablets and surgical tape and comic books and all the things a medic must carry, including M&M's for especially bad wounds, for a total weight of nearly twenty pounds.

10 As a big man, therefore a machine gunner, Henry Dobbins carried the M-60, which weighed twenty-three pounds unloaded, but which was almost always loaded. In addition, Dobbins carried between ten and fifteen pounds of ammunition draped in belts across his chest and shoulders.

As PFCs or Spec 4s, most of them were common grunts and carried the standard M-16 gas-operated assault rifle. The weapon weighed 7.5 pounds unloaded, 8.2 pounds with its full twenty-round magazine. Depending on numerous factors, such as topography and psychology, the riflemen carried anywhere from twelve to twenty magazines, usually in cloth bandoliers, adding on another 8.4 pounds at minimum, fourteen pounds at maximum. When it was available, they also carried M-16 maintenance gear — rods and steel brushes and swabs and tubes of LSA oil — all of which weighed about a pound. Among the grunts, some carried the M-79 grenade launcher, 5.9 pounds unloaded, a reasonably light weapon except for the ammunition, which was heavy. A single round weighed ten ounces. The typical load was twenty-five rounds. But Ted Lavender, who was scared, carried thirty-four rounds when he was shot and killed outside Than Khe, and he went down under an exceptional burden, more than twenty pounds of ammunition, plus the flak jacket and helmet and rations and water and toilet paper and tranquilizers and all the rest, plus the unweighed fear. He was dead weight. There was no twitching or flopping. Kiowa, who saw it happen, said it was like watching a rock fall, or a big sandbag or something — just boom, then down — not like the movies where the dead guy rolls around and does fancy spins and goes ass over teakettle — not like that, Kiowa said, the poor bastard just flat-fuck fell. Boom. Down. Nothing else. It was a bright morning in mid-April. Lieutenant Cross felt the pain. He blamed himself. They stripped off Lavender's canteens and ammo, all the heavy things, and Rat Kiley said the obvious, the guy's dead, and Mitchell Sanders used his radio to report one U.S. KIA[3] and to request a chopper. Then they wrapped Lavender in his poncho. They carried him out to a dry paddy, established security, and sat smoking the dead man's dope until the chopper came. Lieutenant Cross kept to himself. He pictured Martha's smooth young face, thinking he loved her more than anything, more than his men, and now Ted Lavender was dead because he loved her so much and could not stop thinking about her. When the dust-off arrived, they carried Lavender aboard. Afterward they burned Than Khe. They marched until dusk, then dug their holes, and that night Kiowa kept explaining how you had to be there, how fast it was, how the poor guy just dropped like so much concrete. Boom-down, he said. Like cement.

• • •

In addition to the three standard weapons — the M-60, M-16, and M-79 — they carried whatever presented itself, or whatever seemed appropriate as a means of killing or staying alive. They carried catch-as-catch-can. At various times, in various situations, they carried M-14s and CAR-15s and Swedish Ks and grease guns and captured AK-47s and Chi-Coms and RPGs and Simonov carbines and black-market Uzis and .38-caliber Smith & Wesson handguns and 66 mm LAWs and shotguns and silencers and blackjacks and bayonets and C-4 plastic explosives. Lee Strunk carried a slingshot; a weapon of last resort, he called it. Mitchell Sanders carried brass knuckles. Kiowa carried his grandfather's feathered hatchet. Every third or fourth man carried a Claymore antipersonnel mine — 3.5 pounds with its firing device. They all carried fragmentation grenades — fourteen ounces each. They all carried at least one M-18 colored smoke grenade —twenty-four ounces. Some

[3] Killed in action. — Eds.

carried CS or tear-gas grenades. Some carried white-phosphorus grenades. They carried all they could bear, and then some, including a silent awe for the terrible power of the things they carried.

In the first week of April, before Lavender died, Lieutenant Jimmy Cross received a good-luck charm from Martha. It was a simple pebble, an ounce at most. Smooth to the touch, it was a milky-white color with flecks of orange and violet, oval-shaped, like a miniature egg. In the accompanying letter, Martha wrote that she had found the pebble on the Jersey shoreline, precisely where the land touched water at high tide, where things came together but also separated. It was this separate-but-together quality, she wrote, that had inspired her to pick up the pebble and to carry it in her breast pocket for several days, where it seemed weightless, and then to send it through the mail, by air, as a token of her truest feelings for him. Lieutenant Cross found this romantic. But he wondered what her truest feelings were, exactly, and what she meant by separate-but-together. He wondered how the tides and waves had come into play on that afternoon along the Jersey shoreline when Martha saw the pebble and bent down to rescue it from geology. He imagined bare feet. Martha was a poet, with the poet's sensibilities, and her feet would be brown and bare, the toenails unpainted, the eyes chilly and somber like the ocean in March, and though it was painful, he wondered who had been with her that afternoon. He imagined a pair of shadows moving along the strip of sand where things came together but also separated. It was phantom jealousy, he knew, but he couldn't help himself. He loved her so much. On the march, through the hot days of early April, he carried the pebble in his mouth, turning it with his tongue, tasting sea salts and moisture. His mind wandered. He had difficulty keeping his attention on the war. On occasion he would yell at his men to spread out the column, to keep their eyes open, but then he would slip away into daydreams, just pretending, walking barefoot along the Jersey shore, with Martha, carrying nothing. He would feel himself rising. Sun and waves and gentle winds, all love and lightness.

• • •

What they carried varied by mission.

15 When a mission took them to the mountains, they carried mosquito netting, machetes, canvas tarps, and extra bug juice.

If a mission seemed especially hazardous, or if it involved a place they knew to be bad, they carried everything they could. In certain heavily mined AOs,[4] where the land was dense with Toe Poppers and Bouncing Betties, they took turns humping a twenty-eight-pound mine detector. With its headphones and big sensing plate, the equipment was a stress on the lower back and shoulders, awkward to handle, often useless because of the shrapnel in the earth, but they carried it anyway, partly for safety, partly for the illusion of safety.

On ambush, or other night missions, they carried peculiar little odds and ends. Kiowa always took along his New Testament and a pair of moccasins for silence. Dave Jensen carried night-sight vitamins high in carotin. Lee Strunk carried his slingshot; ammo, he claimed, would never be a problem. Rat Kiley carried brandy and M&M's. Until he was shot, Ted Lavender carried the starlight scope, which weighed 6.3 pounds with its aluminum carrying case. Henry Dobbins carried his girlfriend's pantyhose wrapped around his neck as a comforter. They all carried ghosts. When dark came, they would move out single file across the meadows and paddies to their ambush coordinates, where they would quietly set up the Claymores and lie down and spend the night waiting.

Other missions were more complicated and required special equipment. In mid-April, it was their mission to search out and destroy the elaborate tunnel complexes in the Than Khe area south of Chu Lai. To blow the tunnels, they

[4] Areas of operations. — Eds.

The painting here is folk artist Malcah Zeldis's portrayal of the 1973 massacre of the village of My Lai by American troops during the Vietnam War. In "The Things They Carried," the company "burned Than Khe" after the death of Lavender, and the reader does not learn if there were still civilians there. **How does this painting portray the emotional state of both the American soldiers and that of the civilians? How does it affect your interpretation of the company's actions in "The Things They Carried"?**

carried one-pound blocks of pentrite high explosives, four blocks to a man, sixty-eight pounds in all. They carried wiring, detonators, and battery-powered clackers. Dave Jensen carried earplugs. Most often, before blowing the tunnels, they were ordered by higher command to search them, which was considered bad news, but by and large they just shrugged and carried out orders. Because he was a big man, Henry Dobbins was excused from tunnel duty. The others would draw numbers. Before Lavender died there were seventeen men in the platoon, and whoever drew the number seventeen would strip off his gear and crawl in head first with a flashlight and Lieutenant Cross's .45-caliber pistol. The rest of them would fan out as security. They would sit down or kneel, not facing the hole, listening to the ground beneath them, imagining cobwebs and ghosts, whatever was down there — the tunnel walls squeezing in — how the flashlight seemed impossibly heavy in the hand and how it was tunnel vision in the very strictest sense, compression in all ways, even time, and how you had to wiggle in — ass and elbows — a swallowed-up feeling — and how you found yourself worrying about odd things — will your flashlight go dead? Do rats carry rabies? If you screamed, how far would the sound carry? Would your buddies hear it? Would they have the courage to drag you out? In some respects, though not many, the waiting was worse than the tunnel itself. Imagination was a killer.

On April 16, when Lee Strunk drew the number seventeen, he laughed and muttered something and went down quickly. The morning was hot and very still. Not good, Kiowa said. He looked at the tunnel opening, then out across a dry paddy toward the village of Than Khe. Nothing moved. No clouds or birds or people. As they waited, the men smoked and drank Kool-Aid, not talking much, feeling sympathy for Lee Strunk but also feeling the luck of the draw. You win some, you lose some, said Mitchell Sanders, and sometimes you settle for a rain check. It was a tired line and no one laughed.

20 Henry Dobbins ate a tropical chocolate bar. Ted Lavender popped a tranquilizer and went off to pee.

After five minutes, Lieutenant Jimmy Cross moved to the tunnel, leaned down, and examined the darkness. Trouble, he thought — a cave-in maybe. And then suddenly, without willing it, he was thinking about Martha. The stresses and fractures, the quick collapse, the two of them buried alive under all that weight. Dense, crushing love. Kneeling, watching the hole, he tried to concentrate on Lee Strunk and the war, all the dangers, but his love was too much for him, he felt paralyzed, he wanted to sleep inside her lungs and breathe her blood and be smothered. He wanted her to be a virgin and not a virgin, all at once. He wanted to know her. Intimate secrets — why poetry? Why so sad? Why the grayness in her eyes? Why so alone? Not lonely, just alone — riding her bike across campus or sitting off by herself in the cafeteria. Even dancing, she danced alone — and it was the aloneness that filled him with love. He remembered telling her that one evening. How she nodded and looked away. And how, later, when he kissed her, she received the kiss without returning it, her eyes wide open, not afraid, not a virgin's eyes, just flat and uninvolved.

Lieutenant Cross gazed at the tunnel. But he was not there. He was buried with Martha under the white sand at the Jersey shore. They were pressed together, and the pebble in his mouth was her tongue. He was smiling. Vaguely, he was aware of how quiet the day was, the sullen paddies, yet he could not bring himself to worry about matters of security. He was beyond that. He was just a kid at war, in love. He was twenty-two years old. He couldn't help it.

A few moments later Lee Strunk crawled out of the tunnel. He came up grinning, filthy but alive. Lieutenant Cross nodded and closed his eyes while the others clapped Strunk on the back and made jokes about rising from the dead.

Worms, Rat Kiley said. Right out of the grave. Fuckin' zombie.

The men laughed. They all felt great relief. 25

Spook City, said Mitchell Sanders.

Lee Strunk made a funny ghost sound, a kind of moaning, yet very happy, and right then, when Strunk made that high happy moaning sound, when he went *Ahhooooo*, right then Ted Lavender was shot in the head on his way back from peeing. He lay with his mouth open. The teeth were broken. There was a swollen black bruise under his left eye. The cheekbone was gone. Oh shit, Rat Kiley said, the guy's dead. The guy's dead, he kept saying, which seemed profound — the guy's dead. I mean really.

• • •

The things they carried were determined to some extent by superstition. Lieutenant Cross carried his good-luck pebble. Dave Jensen carried a rabbit's foot. Norman Bowker, otherwise a very gentle person, carried a thumb that had been presented to him as a gift by Mitchell Sanders. The thumb was dark brown, rubbery to the touch, and weighed four ounces at most. It had been cut from a VC corpse, a boy

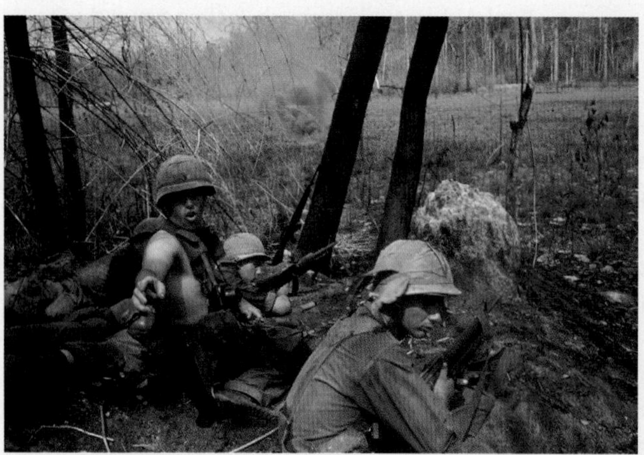

Bettmann/Getty Images

An American solider turns to face the photographer as the battle continues in the background. **What do the body language, equipment, and faces of the soldiers reveal about what it's like to be in the middle of a battle? In what ways do the details of this photo reflect the soldiers' experiences in the story?**

of fifteen or sixteen. They'd found him at the bottom of an irrigation ditch, badly burned, flies in his mouth and eyes. The boy wore black shorts and sandals. At the time of his death he had been carrying a pouch of rice, a rifle, and three magazines of ammunition.

You want my opinion, Mitchell Sanders said, there's a definite moral here.

30 He put his hand on the dead boy's wrist. He was quiet for a time, as if counting a pulse, then he patted the stomach, almost affectionately, and used Kiowa's hunting hatchet to remove the thumb.

Henry Dobbins asked what the moral was.

Moral?

You know. *Moral.*

Sanders wrapped the thumb in toilet paper and handed it across to Norman Bowker. There was no blood. Smiling, he kicked the boy's head, watched the flies scatter, and said, It's like with that old TV show—Paladin. Have gun, will travel.

35 Henry Dobbins thought about it.

Yeah, well, he finally said. I don't see no moral.

There it is, man.

Fuck off.

• • •

They carried USO stationery and pencils and pens. They carried Sterno,[5] safety pins, trip flares, signal flares, spools of wire, razor blades, chewing tobacco, liberated joss sticks and statuettes of the smiling Buddha, candles, grease pencils, *The Stars and Stripes*, fingernail clippers, Psy Ops[6] leaflets, bush hats, bolos, and much more. Twice a week, when the resupply choppers came in, they carried hot chow in green Mermite cans and large canvas bags filled with iced beer and soda pop. They carried plastic water containers, each with a two-gallon capacity. Mitchell Sanders carried a set of starched tiger fatigues for special occasions. Henry Dobbins carried Black Flag insecticide. Dave Jensen carried empty sandbags that could be filled at night for added protection. Lee Strunk carried tanning lotion. Some things they carried in common. Taking turns, they carried the big PRC-77 scrambler radio, which weighed thirty pounds with its battery. They shared the weight of memory. They took up what others could no longer bear. Often, they carried each other, the wounded or weak. They carried infections. They carried chess sets, basketballs, Vietnamese-English dictionaries, insignia of rank, Bronze Stars and Purple Hearts, plastic cards imprinted with the Code of Conduct. They carried diseases, among them malaria and dysentery. They carried lice and ringworm and leeches and paddy algae and various rots and molds. They carried the land itself—Vietnam, the place, the soil—a powdery orange-red dust that covered their boots and fatigues and faces. They carried the sky. The whole atmosphere, they carried it, the humidity, the monsoons, the stink of fungus and decay, all of it, they carried gravity. They moved like mules. By daylight they took sniper fire, at night they were mortared, but it was not battle, it was just the endless march, village to village, without purpose, nothing won or lost. They marched for the sake of the march. They plodded along slowly, dumbly, leaning forward against the heat, unthinking, all blood and bone, simple grunts, soldiering with their legs, toiling up the hills and down into the paddies and across the rivers and up again and down, just humping, one step and then the next and then another, but no volition, no will, because it was automatic, it was anatomy, and the war was entirely a matter of posture and carriage, the hump was everything, a kind of inertia, a kind of emptiness, a dullness of desire and intellect and conscience and hope and human sensibility. Their principles were in their feet. Their calculations were biological. They had no sense of strategy or mission. They searched the villages without knowing what to look for, not caring, kicking over jars of rice, frisking children and old men, blowing tunnels, sometimes setting fires and sometimes not, then forming up and

[5] A jellied fuel that can be burned in a can.—Eds.

[6] Psychological operations.

moving on to the next village, then other villages, where it would always be the same. They carried their own lives. The pressures were enormous. In the heat of early afternoon, they would remove their helmets and flak jackets, walking bare, which was dangerous but which helped ease the strain. They would often discard things along the route of march. Purely for comfort, they would throw away rations, blow their Claymores and grenades, no matter, because by nightfall the resupply choppers would arrive with more of the same, then a day or two later still more, fresh watermelons and crates of ammunition and sunglasses and woolen sweaters — the resources were stunning — sparklers for the Fourth of July, colored eggs for Easter. It was the great American war chest — the fruits of science, the smokestacks, the canneries, the arsenals at Hartford, the Minnesota forests, the machine shops, the vast fields of corn and wheat — they carried like freight trains; they carried it on their backs and shoulders — and for all the ambiguities of Vietnam, all the mysteries and unknowns, there was at least the single abiding certainty that they would never be at a loss for things to carry.

• • •

After the chopper took Lavender away, Lieutenant Jimmy Cross led his men into the village of Than Khe. They burned everything. They shot chickens and dogs, they trashed the village well, they called in artillery and watched the wreckage, then they marched for several hours through the hot afternoon, and then at dusk, while Kiowa explained how Lavender died, Lieutenant Cross found himself trembling.

He tried not to cry. With his entrenching tool, which weighed five pounds, he began digging a hole in the earth.

He felt shame. He hated himself. He had loved Martha more than his men, and as a consequence Lavender was now dead, and this was something he would have to carry like a stone in his stomach for the rest of the war.

Bill Eppridge/The LIFE Picture Collection/Shutterstock

The July 2, 1965, cover of *Life* magazine shows a pair of American soldiers as they carry a wounded comrade to safety, accompanied by the headline "Deeper into the Vietnam War." **What message does this cover photo send to Americans back home about the war and the soldiers fighting in it? To what extent do the characters in this story reflect the men shown here?**

All he could do was dig. He used his entrenching tool like an ax, slashing, feeling both love and hate, and then later, when it was full dark, he sat at the bottom of his foxhole and wept. It went on for a long while. In part, he was grieving for Ted Lavender, but mostly it was for Martha, and for himself, because she belonged to another world, which was not quite real, and because she was a junior at Mount Sebastian College in New Jersey, a poet and a virgin and uninvolved, and because he realized she did not love him and never would.

• • •

Like cement, Kiowa whispered in the dark. I swear to God — boom-down. Not a word.

I've heard this, said Norman Bowker.

A pisser, you know? Still zipping himself up. Zapped while zipping.

All right, fine. That's enough.

Yeah, but you had to see it, the guy just —

I *heard*, man. Cement. So why not shut the fuck *up*?

Kiowa shook his head sadly and glanced over at the hole where Lieutenant Jimmy Cross sat watching the night. The air was thick and wet. A warm, dense fog had settled over the paddies and there was the stillness that precedes rain.

After a time Kiowa sighed.

One thing for sure, he said. The Lieutenant's in some deep hurt. I mean that crying jag — the way he was carrying on — it wasn't fake or anything, it was real heavy-duty hurt. The man cares.

Sure, Norman Bowker said.

Say what you want, the man does care.

We all got problems.

Not Lavender.

No, I guess not, Bowker said. Do me a favor, though.

Shut up?

That's a smart Indian. Shut up.

Shrugging, Kiowa pulled off his boots. He wanted to say more, just to lighten up his sleep, but instead he opened his New Testament and arranged it beneath his head as a pillow. The fog made things seem hollow and unattached. He tried not to think about Ted Lavender, but then he was thinking how fast it was, no drama, down and dead, and how it was hard to feel anything except surprise. It seemed un-Christian. He wished he could find some great sadness, or even anger, but the emotion wasn't there and he couldn't make it happen. Mostly he felt pleased to be alive. He liked the smell of the New Testament under his cheek, the leather and ink and paper and glue, whatever the chemicals were. He liked hearing the sounds of night. Even his fatigue, it felt fine, the stiff muscles and the prickly awareness of his own body, a floating feeling. He enjoyed not being dead. Lying there, Kiowa admired Lieutenant Jimmy Cross's capacity for grief. He wanted to share the man's pain, he wanted to care as Jimmy Cross cared. And yet when he closed his eyes, all he could think was Boom-down, and all he could feel was the pleasure of having his boots off and the fog curling in around him and the damp soil and the Bible smells and the plush comfort of night.

After a moment Norman Bowker sat up in the dark.

Science History Images/Alamy

What does this photo of a soldier consoling his comrade in arms reveal about the emotional price of combat? Does it suggest that humanity can prevail even in inhumane situations, or is it instead a reminder of the hopelessness of war? Use events from "The Things They Carried" to support your response.

What the hell, he said. You want to talk, *talk*. Tell it to me.

Forget it.

No, man, go on. One thing I hate, it's a silent Indian.

• • •

For the most part they carried themselves with poise, a kind of dignity. Now and then, however, there were times of panic, when they squealed or wanted to squeal but couldn't, when they twitched and made moaning sounds and covered their heads and said Dear Jesus and flopped around on the earth and fired their weapons blindly and cringed and sobbed and begged for the noise to stop and went wild and made stupid promises to themselves and to God and to their mothers and fathers, hoping not to die. In different ways, it happened to all of them. Afterward, when the firing ended, they would blink and peek up. They would touch their bodies, feeling shame, then quickly hiding it. They would force themselves to stand. As if in slow motion, frame by frame, the world would take on the old logic —absolute silence, then the wind, then sunlight, then voices. It was the burden of being alive. Awkwardly, the men would reassemble themselves, first in private, then in groups, becoming soldiers again. They would repair the leaks in their eyes. They would check for casualties, call in dust-offs, light cigarettes, try to smile, clear their throats and spit and begin cleaning their weapons. After a time someone would shake his head and say, No lie, I almost shit my pants, and someone else would laugh, which meant it was bad, yes, but the guy had obviously not shit his pants, it wasn't that bad, and in any case nobody would ever do such a thing and then go ahead and talk about it. They would squint into the dense, oppressive sunlight. For a few moments, perhaps, they would fall silent, lighting a joint and tracking its passage from man to man, inhaling, holding in the humiliation. Scary stuff, one of them might say. But then someone else would grin or flick his eyebrows and say, Roger-dodger, almost cut me a new asshole, *almost*.

There were numerous such poses. Some carried themselves with a sort of wistful resignation, others with pride or stiff soldierly discipline or good humor or macho zeal. They were afraid of dying but they were even more afraid to show it.

They found jokes to tell.

They used a hard vocabulary to contain the terrible softness. *Greased* they'd say. *Offed, lit up, zapped while zipping*. It wasn't cruelty, just stage presence. They were actors and the war came at them in 3-D. When someone died, it wasn't quite dying, because in a curious way it seemed scripted, and because they had their lines mostly memorized, irony mixed with tragedy, and because they called it by other names, as if to encyst and destroy the reality of death itself. They kicked corpses. They cut off thumbs. They talked grunt lingo. They told stories about Ted Lavender's supply of tranquilizers, how the poor guy didn't feel a thing, how incredibly tranquil he was.

There's a moral here, said Mitchell Sanders.

They were waiting for Lavender's chopper, smoking the dead man's dope.

The moral's pretty obvious, Sanders said, and winked. Stay away from drugs. No joke, they'll ruin your day every time.

Cute, said Henry Dobbins.

Mind-blower, get it? Talk about wiggy — nothing left, just blood and brains.

They made themselves laugh.

There it is, they'd say, over and over, as if the repetition itself were an act of poise, a balance between crazy and almost crazy, knowing without going. There it is, which meant be cool, let it ride, because oh yeah, man, you can't change what can't be changed, there it is, there it absolutely and positively and fucking well is.

They were tough.

They carried all the emotional baggage of men who might die. Grief, terror, love, longing — these were intangibles, but the intangibles had their own mass and specific gravity, they had tangible weight. They carried shameful memories. They carried the common secret of cowardice barely restrained, the instinct to run or freeze or hide, and in many respects this was the heaviest burden of all, for it could never be put down, it required perfect balance and perfect posture. They carried their reputations. They carried the soldier's greatest fear, which was the fear of blushing. Men killed, and died, because they were embarrassed not to. It was what had brought them to the war in the first place, nothing positive, no dreams of glory or honor, just to avoid the blush of dishonor. They died so as not to die of embarrassment. They crawled into tunnels and walked point and advanced under fire. Each morning, despite the unknowns, they made their legs move. They endured. They kept humping. They did not submit to the obvious alternative, which was simply to close the eyes and fall. So easy, really. Go limp and tumble to the ground and let the muscles unwind and not speak and not budge until your buddies picked you up and lifted you into the chopper that would roar and dip its nose and carry you off to the world. A mere matter of falling, yet no one ever fell. It was not courage, exactly; the object was not valor. Rather, they were too frightened to be cowards.

By and large they carried these things inside, maintaining the masks of composure. They sneered at sick call. They spoke bitterly about guys who had found release by shooting off their own toes or fingers. Pussies, they'd say. Candyasses. It was fierce, mocking talk, with only a trace of envy or awe, but even so, the image played itself out behind their eyes.

They imagined the muzzle against flesh. They imagined the quick, sweet pain, then the evacuation to Japan, then a hospital with warm beds and cute geisha nurses.

SUPPORT OUR BOYS IN
VIETNAM
KOREA, GERMANY, JAPAN, ENGLAND, ITALY, CANADA, SWEDEN,
DENMARK, BERKLEY, WATTS, BOSTON, CUBA, ARGENTINA, PAKISTAN,
LAOS, CONGO, THAILAND, ACAPULCO, INDIA, LEBANON, CHICAGO,
DOMINICAN REPUBLIC, ECUADOR, HONG KONG, WOODSTOCK, D.C., COLUMBIA
GREENLAND, PUERTO RICO, TIAJUANA, KOWLOON, CHAPEL HILL, RUSSIA, HAITI,
INDONESIA, BERMUDA, AUSTRALIA, CONSHOHOCKEN, CICERO, PRINCETON, LIBERIA, BIAFRA,
NORWAY, OKINAWA, M.I.T., PHILLIPINES, SCOTLAND, GREECE, ICELAND, GUAM, AFGHANISTAN, BRAZIL,
TURKEY, SPAIN, HARLEM, BURMA, CAMBODIA, PERU, NOVA SCOTIA, AZORES, PANAMA, CRETE, COSTA RICA, AUSTRIA

Eileen Tweedy/Shutterstock

How does this protest poster – ironically asking for support for American troops in Vietnam, Korea, Germany, Japan, etc. – call on the psychedelic imagery of the cultural and sexual revolutions occurring at home during the Vietnam War? Why do you think this kind of image would or would not resonate with the young soldiers in "The Things They Carried"?

They dreamed of freedom birds. 80

At night, on guard, staring into the dark, they were carried away by jumbo jets. They felt the rush of takeoff. *Gone!* they yelled. And then velocity, wings and engines, a smiling stewardess — but it was more than a plane, it was a real bird, a big sleek silver bird with feathers and talons and high screeching. They were flying. The weights fell off, there was nothing to bear. They laughed and held on tight, feeling the cold slap of wind and altitude, soaring, thinking *It's over, I'm gone!* — they were naked, they were light and free — it was all lightness, bright and fast and

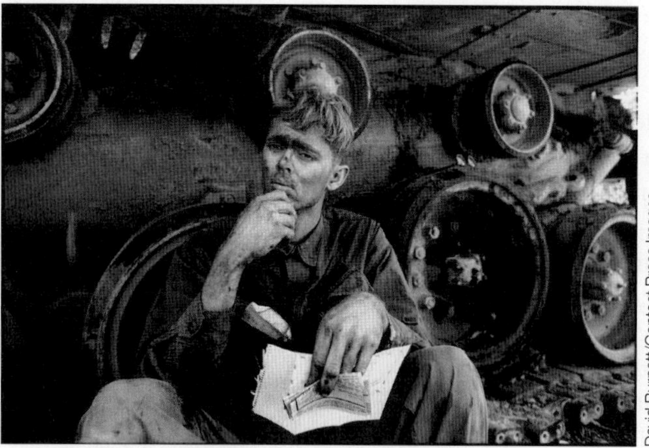

David Burnett/Contact Press Images

David Burnett, the photographer who took this picture of a soldier reading a letter from home, explained the circumstances of the moment this way: "for that fraction of a second, in his face, his posture, was all the fatigue and despair of a young soldier who is surely wondering what in the hell he's doing there, so far from home."

How does this image capture the experiences of First Lieutenant Jimmy Cross?

buoyant, light as light, a helium buzz in the brain, a giddy bubbling in the lungs as they were taken up over the clouds and the war, beyond duty, beyond gravity and mortification and global entanglements — *Sin loi!*[7] they yelled, *I'm sorry, motherfuckers, but I'm out of it, I'm goofed, I'm on a space cruise, I'm gone!* — and it was a restful, disencumbered sensation, just riding the light waves, sailing that big silver freedom bird over the mountains and oceans, over America, over the farms and great sleeping cities and cemeteries and highways and the golden arches of McDonald's. It was flight, a kind of fleeing, a kind of falling, falling higher and higher, spinning off the edge of the earth and beyond the sun and through the vast, silent vacuum where there were no burdens and where everything weighed exactly nothing. *Gone!* they screamed, *I'm sorry but I'm gone!* And so at night, not quite dreaming, they gave themselves over to lightness, they were carried, they were purely borne.

On the morning after Ted Lavender died, First Lieutenant Jimmy Cross crouched at the bottom of his foxhole and burned Martha's letters. Then he burned the two photographs. There was a steady rain falling, which made it difficult, but he used heat tabs and Sterno to build a small fire, screening it with his body, holding the photographs over the tight blue flame with the tips of his fingers.

He realized it was only a gesture. Stupid, he thought. Sentimental, too, but mostly just stupid.

Lavender was dead. You couldn't burn the blame.

Besides, the letters were in his head. And even now, without photographs, Lieutenant Cross could see Martha playing volleyball in her white gym shorts and yellow T-shirt. He could see her moving in the rain.

When the fire died out, Lieutenant Cross pulled his poncho over his shoulders and ate breakfast from a can.

There was no great mystery, he decided.

In those burned letters Martha had never mentioned the war, except to say, Jimmy, take care of yourself. She wasn't involved. She signed the letters "Love," but it wasn't love, and all the fine lines and technicalities did not matter.

The morning came up wet and blurry. Everything seemed part of everything else, the fog and Martha and the deepening rain.

It was a war, after all.

Half smiling, Lieutenant Jimmy Cross took out his maps. He shook his head hard, as if to clear it, then bent forward and began

[7] Sorry about that.

planning the day's march. In ten minutes, or maybe twenty, he would rouse the men and they would pack up and head west, where the maps showed the country to be green and inviting. They would do what they had always done. The rain might add some weight, but otherwise it would be one more day layered upon all the other days.

He was realistic about it. There was that new hardness in his stomach.

No more fantasies, he told himself.

Henceforth, when he thought about Martha, it would be only to think that she belonged elsewhere. He would shut down the daydreams. This was not Mount Sebastian, it was another world, where there were no pretty poems or midterm exams, a place where men died because of carelessness and gross stupidity. Kiowa was right. Boom-down, and you were dead, never partly dead.

Briefly, in the rain, Lieutenant Cross saw Martha's gray eyes gazing back at him.

He understood.

It was very sad, he thought. The things men carried inside. The things men did or felt they had to do.

He almost nodded at her, but didn't.

Instead he went back to his maps. He was now determined to perform his duties firmly and without negligence. It wouldn't help Lavender, he knew that, but from this point on he would comport himself as a soldier. He would dispose of his good-luck pebble. Swallow it, maybe, or use Lee Strunk's slingshot, or just drop it along the trail. On the march he would impose strict field discipline. He would be careful to send out flank security, to prevent straggling or bunching up, to keep his troops moving at the proper pace and at the proper interval. He would insist on clean weapons. He would confiscate the remainder of Lavender's dope. Later in the day, perhaps, he would call the men together and speak to them plainly. He would accept the blame for what had happened to Ted Lavender. He would be a man about it. He would look them in the eyes, keeping his chin level, and he would issue the new SOPs in a calm, impersonal tone of voice, an officer's voice, leaving no room for argument or discussion. Commencing immediately, he'd tell them, they would no longer abandon equipment along the route of march. They would police up their acts. They would get their shit together, and keep it together, and maintain it neatly and in good working order.

He would not tolerate laxity. He would show strength, distancing himself.

Among the men there would be grumbling, of course, and maybe worse, because their days would seem longer and their loads heavier, but Lieutenant Cross reminded himself that his obligation was not to be loved but to lead. He would dispense with love; it was not now a factor. And if anyone quarreled or complained, he would simply tighten his lips and arrange his shoulders in the correct command posture. He might give a curt little nod. Or he might not. He might just shrug and say Carry on, then they would saddle up and form into a column and move out toward the villages of Than Khe. ■

1986

Understanding and Interpreting

1. **AP® Character and Narration.** The story begins with a paragraph about Jimmy Cross and his relationship with Martha. What does Martha represent to Cross? Why might it be significant that Cross obsesses about whether or not she is a virgin? How do Cross's feelings for Martha change toward the end of the story, and how does this change indicate one of the themes of the story?

2. **AP® Character, Setting, and Narration.** According to the narrator, "The things they carried were largely determined by necessity" (par. 2), were "partly a function of rank, partly of field specialty" (par. 6), "varied by mission" (par. 14), and "were determined to some extent by superstition" (par. 28). Which of these is the strongest factor in determining what they carried? How does the weight of each item have significance beyond the physical burden it places on the men? Do you find any irony in the things they carried?
3. **AP® Character.** Jimmy Cross carries "the responsibility for the lives of his men" (par. 7) and ultimately believes he fails to bear that burden. What does he literally and figuratively shed in order to bear that weight again following Lavender's death? What point is O'Brien making?
4. **AP® Narration.** Why do you think the medic would need "M&M's for especially bad wounds" (par. 9)?
5. **AP® Character and Narration.** In paragraph 29, the soldiers find the burned corpse of a teenage Vietcong soldier at the bottom of a ditch, and Sanders says, "there's a definite moral here," before cutting off the boy's thumb and giving it to Bowker. Dobbins doesn't see the moral, and ultimately, they decide, "There it is." What do they mean by that? Look also at paragraph 75, where O'Brien talks more about the meaning of that phrase. Beyond this specific scene, does "The Things They Carried" have a moral? If so, what is it?
6. **AP® Character.** The soldiers react differently to Ted Lavender's death (pars. 11, 27, 40–64). Pick one soldier whose reaction seems particularly significant, and explain why you find it meaningful.
7. **AP® Character and Narration.** In paragraph 77, the narrator says, "They carried the soldier's greatest fear, which was the fear of blushing." Why do you think the soldiers were more afraid to blush than to die? What is significant about this reality?
8. **AP® Character and Narration.** Paragraph 97 says, "It was very sad, [Cross] thought. The things men carried inside. The things men did or felt they had to do." What "things" do you think Cross is thinking about? What does he intend to do about it? Do you think he will succeed? Do you think it will matter? Explain your answers.
9. **AP® Character and Narration.** What are O'Brien's attitudes about the soldiers, the war, and, specifically, Lieutenant Cross? Support your inferences with specific references to the text.
10. **AP® Setting.** O'Brien doesn't provide readers very many details related to the setting, such as the weather or the landscape. Nevertheless, the setting of the story is central to its meaning. Why might O'Brien not have included more details about the setting of Vietnam in a quintessential Vietnam story?

Analyzing Language, Style, and Structure

1. **Vocabulary in Context.** In paragraph 81, O'Brien uses the word "disencumbered" to explain the way the men feel when their thoughts wander at night while they are standing guard. Why might O'Brien have used this word in particular? Consider the story's themes in your response.
2. **AP® Figurative Language.** Paragraph 3 says, "They were called legs or grunts." Explain why this type of figurative language, called synecdoche (or using a part to refer to the whole), is especially appropriate not only for this story but for life in the military in general.
3. **AP® Character and Figurative Language.** What evidence do you find that Jimmy Cross is a Christ figure? How does the symbolism of his name and initials influence your reading of the story? Is the virgin Martha akin to the Virgin Mary? Explain why or why not.
4. **AP® Structure and Narration.** The story's central event is the death of Ted Lavender, which the narrator returns to again and again. Why do you think the story revisits this event so often? Do you think this repetition honors Lavender or trivializes his death? Explain.

5. **AP® Character, Structure, and Narration.** The reader learns about Ted Lavender's death in the second paragraph, but the narrator provides few details until paragraph 27. In terms of the story's structure, what is the effect of the delay on the reader? What does the delay suggest about the effects of war on the soldiers?
6. **AP® Character, Structure, Narration, and Figurative Language.** How does O'Brien characterize individual soldiers by the things each carries? Choose three or four of the men to analyze.
7. **AP® Structure, Narration, and Figurative Language.** One technique O'Brien employs is zeugma, in which one verb has more than one (often incongruous) object. For example, he writes in paragraph 12, "They carried all they could bear, and then some, including a silent awe for the terrible power of the things they carried." Look for other examples of zeugma in the story. Do you see any pattern in how O'Brien uses zeugma? In particular, consider how O'Brien exploits the incongruity of zeugma in order to develop one of the themes of the story.
8. **AP® Structure and Narration.** Paragraph 18 contains a series of questions. Consider all the possible meanings of the statement "Imagination was a killer." How does this statement answer the questions?
9. **AP® Narration and Figurative Language.** At the end of paragraph 39, the narrator adds the products of the "great American war chest" to "the things they carried." Explain the political statement this extended metaphor makes.
10. **AP® Character, Structure, and Narration.** How many times does the word "they" appear from paragraphs 65 through 81? (Go ahead and count them.) Why does O'Brien use that pronoun so often at the end of the story?
11. **AP® Character, Structure, and Narration.** In paragraph 99, the conditional "would" is repeated in nearly every sentence. What does this parallelism suggest? How does it add to the characterization of Lieutenant Cross?
12. **AP® Narration and Figurative Language.** Develop a list of the non-material elements the men must carry. What does the weight of these burdens suggest about the men and the war they are fighting? How does O'Brien's inclusion of them contribute to the themes of the story?

Topics for Composing

1. **AP® FRQ Prose Fiction Analysis.** The following question refers to paragraphs 12–18 of Tim O'Brien's "The Things They Carried," published in 1986. In this passage, the narrator recounts the burdens a group of American soldiers bore during the Vietnam War. Read the passage carefully. Then, in a well-written essay, analyze how O'Brien uses literary elements and techniques to portray the complex intersection of the physical and psychological demands of war.
2. **AP® FRQ Literary Argument.** Works of literature often portray a significant event as an experience shared among several people. The narrator of "The Things They Carried" portrays the shared experience of the aftermath of Ted Lavender's death. In a well-written essay, analyze how the portrayal of this significant event contributes to an interpretation of the work as a whole. Do not merely summarize the plot.
3. **AP® Literary Argumentation.** Consider carefully the organization and narrative method O'Brien uses in this story. While some sections attempt to define and explain the nature of the soldier's war experience, other sections are narratives about individual soldiers. Write an essay in which you explain how the structure O'Brien uses comments on war.

4. **AP® Literary Argumentation.** Sometimes a work of literature reveals a great deal of richness in what it leaves out or what it doesn't say. "The Things They Carried" concentrates on what the soldiers carry, giving the soldiers little purpose beyond marching from place to place. Write an essay discussing what O'Brien is trying to say by focusing on such minutiae of war. Think especially about what he leaves out.
5. **AP® Literary Argumentation.** One might view O'Brien's narrative structure itself to be symbolic. Each time the narrator brings order to the events by returning to an organized account of the things that they carried, the process slips into personal accounts and idiosyncratic details. How does such a method work symbolically to suggest something about the subject matter of the story?
6. **AP® Literary Argumentation.** In his book *If I Die in a Combat Zone, Box Me Up and Ship Me Home*, O'Brien writes:

   > Do dreams offer lessons? Do nightmares have themes, do we awaken and analyze them and live our lives and advise others as a result? Can the foot soldier teach anything important about war, merely for having been there? I think not. He can tell war stories.

   Write an essay in which you consider how "The Things They Carried" illustrates or challenges these remarks.
7. **Research.** Throughout the story, O'Brien refers to "choppers" and specifically "resupply choppers." Most of the helicopters used by the United States during the Vietnam War were versions of the HU-1A, also known as the "Huey." In fact, the Smithsonian's National Air and Space Museum's website explains that "the Huey became a symbol of U.S. combat forces" and was at the time "one of the most recognizable aircraft in history." Research the use of the Huey in the Vietnam War, and write an essay in which you explain how its development played a role in determining the things men such as those in O'Brien's story carried.
8. **Speaking and Listening.** While *The Things They Carried* is, overall, considered a work of fiction, some of the stories included in the book were presented on their own as more autobiographical than fictional. The book's editor, in a letter to O'Brien, explained some of the reasoning for blurring the line between fact and fiction: "Why should the magician pull up his sleeve & tell us — Look, this is where the birds come from — when really, deep down, we knew it anyway?" Discuss as a class whether it matters that O'Brien's Vietnam War writing contains fictional characters and events and whether you believe these are presented as "true" in the first place. To prepare, quickly research the differences between "story truth" and "happening truth."
9. **Connections.** Read "Naming of Parts" by Henry Reed (p. 891). Compare and contrast that poem's techniques and themes to those of "The Things They Carried."
10. **Connections.** After studying terminally ill patients, psychologist Elisabeth Kübler-Ross described five stages in the process of dealing with death: (1) denial, or "this isn't happening"; (2) anger, or "why me?"; (3) bargaining, or "I'd do anything"; (4) depression, or "I give up"; and (5) acceptance, or "It's okay." Do the soldiers facing death in this story display these behaviors? Which stages do you notice, and in what circumstances? Which stage seems most prevalent? Why do you think that is, and how do these stages of dealing with death relate to the burdens each man must bear?
11. **Creative Writing.** At the end of the story, Jimmy Cross feels responsible for Lavender's death, and his thoughts turn again to Martha as he decides to strengthen his resolve. Assume the character of Lieutenant Cross and write a letter to Martha about the incident. Then write her reply.

"The Things They Carried" and Voices of the Vietnam Conflict

Time and perspective have not done much to make our understanding of the Vietnam War any less complicated. Neither have they helped us avoid involvement in lengthy wars with difficult-to-define objectives in distant countries. To understand U.S. involvement in the conflict in Vietnam, we have to rewind to the end of World War II in 1945. Although the United States and the Soviet Union had been uneasy allies during the war, diplomacy between them quickly crumbled in its wake. Separated by fundamental economic and political divisions — capitalism and communism, democracy and authoritarianism — the two countries became rivals for global dominance in what became known as the Cold War (1945–1991). A primarily nonmilitary conflict, it was nonetheless punctuated by several "hot spots," including the Vietnam War.

Concerned by the Soviet Union's expansionist efforts throughout the world, the United States adopted a policy of containment to stop the spread of communism in the years following World War II. This policy went hand-in-hand with the domino theory, which held that if one country in a region fell to communism, others would follow. In this geopolitical climate, the United States sent troops into Vietnam to ostensibly prevent a communist takeover of South Vietnam by the Soviet-backed North Vietnamese, or Vietcong. A long conflict involving multiple countries, the war lasted more than twenty years, ending with the fall of Saigon in 1975. The United States fought as an ally of South Vietnam against the communist government of North Vietnam, and over 3 million people lost their lives.

In the United States, the war was largely unpopular thanks to a combination of circumstances, including the military draft, the ideological reasons for the conflict, the fact that it did not concern the United States directly, and the belief of many that the war was unwinnable from a strategic standpoint. Yet the U.S. Department of Veterans Affairs reports that the United States sent more than 2,700,000 of its women and men to serve in Vietnam over the course of the conflict.

In the years since, attempts to understand the causes and effects of this conflict have evolved, but some common narrative threads have calcified. In a 2018 opinion piece for the *New York Times*, Christian G. Appy explains that an understanding of Vietnam "is not a narrow scholarly exercise" but instead an endeavor that "profoundly shapes public memory of its meaning and ongoing significance to American national identity and foreign policy." Time and perspective have led to a greater understanding of, and appreciation for, what American soldiers experienced both in Vietnam and once they returned to the United States. Americans have also watched as the lingering effects of many of its government's tactics continue to devastate the lives of veterans of the Vietnam War and their families. In addition to the myriad physical and psychological

© Philip Jones Griffiths/Magnum Photos

This image, taken during the war, shows a young U.S. soldier with a Vietnamese child.

How does this photograph frame the conflict through a literal American lens? What message does it send to viewers?

tolls the war has had on these veterans, herbicides such as Agent Orange that were used to clear vast swaths of land to expose enemy troops have led to Vietnam-specific instances of various cancers in veterans and spina bifida in their children.

Despite having lost the war, the United States has had an unusual ability to control the narrative of its events and aftermath. In many cases, this control has led to an overall lack of information, which has in turn led to pop culture becoming a chief source of information about the war in Vietnam for many. In Elisabeth Rosen's 2015 article in the *Atlantic* about the way young Vietnamese citizens view the war, she admits that she learned about the conflict via popular culture, getting "information from books like *Fire in the Lake* and films like *The Deer Hunter* and *Apocalypse Now*." Not surprisingly, such depictions present the conflict through a uniquely American lens.

Over the years, however, Americans have become increasingly aware of the devastating effects the U.S. involvement in Vietnam has had on Vietnamese citizens and on Vietnamese refugees, many of whom went on to become Americans themselves. In addition to the tragic deaths of over 58,000 Americans during the war and the tens of thousands of those who have died by suicide since, there were over 1 million North Vietnamese soldiers and Vietcong guerrilla fighters, between 200,000 and 250,000 South Vietnamese soldiers, and as many as 2 million Vietnamese civilians killed during the conflict. To this day, unexploded bombs left behind after the war continue to detonate and kill Vietnamese civilians. The land devastated by pesticides and napalm has also been slow to recover.

It is all too easy to encounter the American narrative of the Vietnam conflict in literature — one that, for all the beautiful work it has produced, is not only incomplete but has often failed to recognize the full humanity and the rich artistic and cultural traditions of the Vietnamese. In a TED Talk titled "The Danger of a Single Story," contemporary Nigerian author Chimamanda Ngozi Adichie warns against relying on just one perspective:

> How [stories] are told, who tells them, when they're told, how many stories are told, are really dependent on power. . . . Stories have been used to dispossess and to malign, but stories can also be used to empower and to humanize. Stories can break the dignity of a people, but stories can also repair that broken dignity. . . . [W]hen we reject the single story, when we realize there is never a single story about any place, we regain a kind of paradise.

When we read, it is important to consider the perspective of the narrative. Tim O'Brien was drafted into a war he didn't believe in, and he wrote fictional — but emotionally honest — accounts that showed soldiers torn between personal morality and duty to country. His work also embraced ambiguity and brought the war home to Americans in a personal and relatable way.

These Texts in Context present us with a related but slightly different set of ideas: they, too, explore the ways that wartime violence haunts all of us, and they bring an individual perspective to a vast geopolitical conflict that displaced and killed millions over decades. These are also narratives many Americans haven't experienced, because they examine the war and its aftermath through the eyes of Vietnamese and Vietnamese American writers and artists. Each one tells its own story about the Vietnam War or, as the Vietnamese call it, the American War. What some have seen as a liberation, others have called an occupation. The texts here represent some of what Vietnamese and Vietnamese American people have carried across continents and generations, and they give voice to the humanity devastated by war and woven together by peace.

TEXTS IN CONTEXT

1. **Viet Thanh Nguyen ▪ from *On True War Stories* (nonfiction)**
2. **Bảo Ninh ▪ *Savage Winds* (short fiction)**
3. **Quan Barry ▪ *Napalm* (poetry)**
4. **Hai-Dang Phan ▪ *My Father's "Norton Introduction to Literature," Third Edition (1981)* (poetry)**
5. **Paul Tran ▪ *East Mountain View* (poetry)**
6. **Ann Le ▪ *Between Home and Here (Woman Soldier 1)* (collage)**

from On True War Stories

Viet Thanh Nguyen

Viet Thanh Nguyen (b. 1971) was born in Vietnam, and his family emigrated to the United States in 1975 after the fall of Saigon at the end of the Vietnam War. After three years in a refugee camp in Pennsylvania, his family settled in San Jose, California. He is a professor at the University of Southern California in Los Angeles and is the author of *Nothing Ever Dies: Vietnam and the Memory of War* (2016), the novel *The Sympathizer* (2015), which won a Pulitzer Prize for Fiction, and the short story collection *The Refugees* (2017). His most recent novel, a sequel to *The Sympathizer* entitled *The Committed*, was published in 2021. The following essay originally appeared in the *Asian American Literary Review* in 2015.

KEY CONTEXT In this essay, Nguyen uses the word *gook*, a derogatory term sometimes directed at people of Asian descent. Consider how the inclusion of this term reflects Nguyen's understanding of his identity and his purpose in this essay, and be mindful of context — both Nguyen's and yours — as you read.

There's no such thing as a good war story. War is hell. Like many Americans and people the world over, I enjoy war stories that depend on what seems to be a disturbing idea. I have a personal stake in such stories, having been born in Vietnam but raised, or made, as it were, in America. A war brought me from over there to over here, an experience I share with millions of my fellow Americans. Sometimes I wonder whether my circumstances, or what my parents endured, can be called a war story, and how that story can be told. In "How to Tell a True War Story," from *The Things They Carried,* Tim O'Brien says:

> War is hell, but that's not the half of it, because war is mystery and terror and adventure and courage and discovery and holiness and pity and despair and longing and love. War is nasty; war is fun. War is thrilling; war is drudgery. War makes you a man; war makes you dead. The truths are contradictory.

I have only experienced the half of war that is not any fun. Perhaps that is why thrilling war stories captivate me, the ones with "gore galore," in the words of art critic Lucy Lippard. But as good as those war stories are, perhaps they are not actually true.

One of my early encounters with a true war story was reading Larry Heinemann's *Close Quarters,* which shocked me when I was perhaps eleven or twelve. Near the end of this Vietnam War novel, the young all-American soldier who is the narrator puts a gun to the head of a Vietnamese prostitute named Claymore Face. He gives her a choice: —— him and his friends or get blown away. The novel renders no judgment on this rape, leaving me alone with my feelings, without the comfort provided by the author telling me that this was wrong. I could not forgive Heinemann for scarring me with such an ugly scene until I wrote a novel myself decades later. This is when I realized that some things are so nasty the writer should simply show them as they are. The ugliness is, and must be, unforgettable.

5 Still. It did not matter if Heinemann's sympathies might lie with Claymore Face, because the story belonged to the American soldier. I dimly realized a few things that would take me years to articulate. First: better to be victimizer than victim. That's why America's Vietnam War stories, which often dwell on the bad things that Americans have done, depend on turning the Vietnamese into bit actors. As any movie star will attest, it is preferable to take center stage as antihero than take to the wings as virtuous extra. This is why bleak Vietnam War stories still do well in an America that sometimes does its hardest to deny its sometimes nasty behavior. Americans applaud these stories and successors like *Zero Dark Thirty,* for even if they depict Americans torturing others, their audiences know it is far more interesting to torture than be tortured. Or, as Milton's Satan observed, better to rule in Hell than serve in Heaven.

The second thing I learned from Heinemann: rape was hard to account for in a certain kind of war story, the one that audiences call "good." If, in a good war story, war makes you a man, does rape make you a woman? If women are unmade by rape (as are the male victims of rape), *Close Quarters* shows that the kind of man made by rape was not the kind anybody wants around. That's why Americans welcome home their soldiers without wanting to think too much about what they might have done over there. Killing is not the problem. No one is concerned that Clint Eastwood can celebrate, in his film, an American sniper who killed one hundred and sixty people in a rather intimate way, seeing their faces through his scope. But rape? Look away. The other side does it, not us.

The last thing I learned from Claymore Face was that she did and did not have my face. She was Vietnamese and a gook. So was I in the eyes of some Americans, a host of Hollywood screenwriters, and directors who had killed nearly as many Vietnamese on screen as had died in the war. And yet I was also an American. People like me, the Vietnamese who fled to the United States after the war's end, were living proof of the success of one of America's greatest desires, to win the hearts and minds of others. America's ability to do so was the central message of John Wayne's propaganda movie set in Vietnam, *The Green Berets*. The wrongheadedness of this desire is inadvertently shown in the infamous final shot. Wayne, the American soldier, walks into the sunset with a young Vietnamese orphan in need of his paternal benevolence. The sun is setting in the South China Sea, but that sea lies east of Vietnam. Americans cannot see straight sometimes, which is why many thought that Iraqis would treat their invaders as liberators, even though Americans themselves would never do any such thing.

I heard a different kind of war story as I grew up among Vietnamese refugees. There was the one about a man who held up a mom-and-pop shop in a small Vietnamese town with a hand grenade. Or the one about a mother who fled that small town when the communists arrived, taking her sons but leaving behind her adopted teenage daughter to take care of the shop, believing she would soon return. Mother and daughter would not see each other again for twenty years. Or what about the time that mother and her husband opened another shop in San Jose, California, and were shot on Christmas Eve in an armed robbery? Or how they cried when they received letters announcing the deaths of their parents in their now lost homeland? Or how they worked twelve hour days every day of the year except for Christmas, Easter, and Tet?[1]

Those were my parents. Their stories are typical of refugees, although when I mention them to other Americans, an uncomfortable silence usually ensues, since these things did not happen to most Americans. But are not these stories also war stories? For many people, and according to O'Brien's definition, no. There is nothing fun about losing home, business, family, health, sanity, or country, some or all of which happened to so many of the Vietnamese people I know. You don't get a medal for these kinds of things, much less a belated parade or memorial, and hardly ever a movie. What you get are war stories told about the soldiers who came to your country to save you from communism, just as we are now getting war stories about the soldiers who went to Iraq and Afghanistan. Heinemann's novel was part of a whole wave of stories that refought the Vietnam War on page and screen. These stories are how most global audiences know this war, the first war in history where the loser gets to write the history for the world. While the Vietnamese have written history, too, their stories stand little chance against the shock and awe of the American military-cinema-industrial complex.[2] But as novelist Gina Apostol says of this complex: "Does it not suggest not only an economic order but also a psychiatric disorder?"

10 This disorder thrives on the excitement of good war stories, which, like O'Brien, overlook at least two things that war happens to be. First: war is profitable. Few storytellers want to discuss this because the fact that war makes an enormous amount of money is either disturbing to most Americans or not disturbing at all, due to the aforementioned disorder. Second: war is a bore. Photographer Tod Papageorge's book, *American Sports, 1970: Or How We Spent the War in Vietnam*, shows how trivial the war was for many

[1] The Vietnamese Lunar New Year holiday — Eds.

[2] A reference to the military-industrial complex: the cooperation between the U.S. government and business sectors to fund the military and national defense that stemmed from World War II and greatly influenced the development of the U.S. economy. This term suggests the U.S. film industry plays a key role in the military-industrial complex. — Eds.

Americans. The photographs simply capture Americans playing in sporting events or watching them. Only the last photograph of the War Memorial in Indianapolis acknowledges the war, with these words on the facing page: "In 1970, 4,221 American troops were killed in Vietnam." Even as American soldiers died abroad, life went on at home. So it is with America's wars in the Middle East, akin to a sporting event for those Americans not directly involved, which is to say the overwhelming majority. Papageorge's photos are true war stories of life inside the war machine for civilians, most of whom are not paying much attention, if at all, to the wars fought in their name. What is most disturbing about his photos is the implication that if war is hell, then this is what hell looks like, Americans enjoying seemingly innocent pastimes.

Being acclimated to hell is part of our disorder. But listen carefully. Can't you hear the dull hum of the war machine we live in, the white noise of a massive mechanism oiled by banalities, bolted together by triviality, and enabled by passive consent? In "The Brother Who Went to Vietnam," from her book *China Men*, Maxine Hong Kingston writes:

> Whenever we ate a candy bar, when we drank grape juice, bought bread (ITT makes Wonder bread), wrapped food in plastic, made a phone call, put money in the bank, cleaned the oven, washed with soap, turned on the electricity, refrigerated food, cooked it, ran a computer, drove a car, rode an airplane, sprayed with insecticide, we were supporting the corporations that made tanks and bombers, napalm, defoliants, and bombs. For the carpet bombing.

From carpets to carpet bombing, war is so woven into society's fabric that it is almost impossible for a citizen not to find war underfoot even at home.

For many, this is not a good war story, but a bad one they would rather avoid. This story says that all war is, in a sense, total war. Opening a refrigerator is a true war story. So is paying one's taxes. Complicity is the truest war story of all, which is why a blood-drenched movie like *Apocalypse Now* tells only half the true war story. It is about the heart of darkness over there, in the jungle where the white man discovers that he, too, is a savage, the heart of darkness beating within him. But the other half of the true war story would show that the heart of darkness is also where we reside, over here, all around us. Americans do not wish to confront this domestic horror directly, which is why they substitute for it stories of zombies and serial killers and the like. Fictional violence and monstrous horror are easier to stomach than understanding how opening our refrigerator or watching a football game connects us to war, which is not thrilling at all. The true war story is not only that war is hell, a statement that never prevented us from going to war but has always gotten us to run to the movie theater or pick up a book. The true war story is also that war is normal, which is why we are always going to war. War is boring, a bad story most people do want to hear. War involves all of us, and that is more discomfiting than any horror story over here or blood-and-guts story over there. The fact that my family of refugees has become living proof of the American Dream is also a true war story, my parents wealthy, my brother a doctor on a White House committee, and myself a professor and novelist. To many Americans, we are evidence that the war was worth it, since it gave us the chance to be better Americans than many Americans. But if we are a testament to the immigrant story, we are only here because the United States fought a war that killed three million Vietnamese (not counting the three million others that died in neighboring Laos and Cambodia during the war and immediately after). Filipinos are here because of the U.S. war that killed a million people in the Philippines in 1898. Koreans are here because of the Korean War that killed three million. We can argue about the blame, but the list goes on, as Junot Díaz also understands. In *The Brief Wondrous Life of Oscar Wao*, he tells us how

> Just as the U.S. was ramping up its involvement in Vietnam, LBJ[3] launched an illegal invasion of the Dominican Republic (April 28, 1965). (Santo Domingo was Iraq before Iraq was Iraq). A smashing military success for the U.S., and many of the same units and intelligence teams that took part in the "democratization" of Santo Domingo were immediately shipped off to Saigon.

Many Americans forgot or never knew this true war story. If Americans think of the arrival of Dominicans to America at all, they most likely think of it as an immigrant story.

15 But what if we understood immigrant stories to be war stories? And what if we understood that war stories disturb even more when they are not about soldiers, when they show us how normal war is, how war touches and transforms everything and everybody, including, most of all, civilians? War stories that thrill may be true, but they only make war more alluring, something that happens somewhere else, over there. Another kind of true war story reminds us of something much more uncomfortable: that war begins, and ends, over here, with the support of citizens for the war machine, with the arrival of frightened refugees fleeing wars that we have instigated. Telling these kinds of stories, or learning to read, see, and hear boring stories as war stories, is an important way to treat the disorder of our military-industrial complex. Rather than being disturbed by the idea that war is hell, this complex thrives on it. ■

2015

[3] U.S. President Lyndon Baines Johnson (in office 1963–1969). — Eds.

Questions

1. To whom does Viet Thanh Nguyen refer when he writes of "the millions of [his] fellow Americans" in paragraph 2? What "experience" do so many Americans have in common?
2. What message does Nguyen convey in paragraph 7? What are the consequences when "Americans cannot see straight sometimes"?
3. Based on your own understanding of the Vietnam War and what Nguyen explains, why do you think he refers to it as "the first war in history where the loser gets to write the history for the world" (par. 9)? Are there any other military conflicts in which the loser wrote the history?
4. How does Nguyen refute the argument that his family's success in the United States demonstrates the benefits of war?
5. What, according to Nguyen, is "the war machine we live in" (par. 11)? What does that machine do?
6. What kinds of war stories does Nguyen believe are needed to help the United States better understand its role in the world? Why is complicity "the truest war story of all" (par. 12)?
7. Compare Nguyen's discussion of "the war machine" (pars. 10, 11, and 15) with Dunya Mikhail's poem "The War Works Hard" (p. 887). How does Nguyen's discussion explain the way the efforts of a personified war go on back home even when it's not the place the war is being fought?
8. Choose one of the authors Nguyen discusses in his essay, such as Maxine Hong Kingston or Gina Apostol, and explain how his inclusion of them supports his argument.

Savage Winds

Bảo Ninh Translated from Vietnamese by Phun Huy Dong and Nina McPherson

Bao Ninh (b. 1952) is a Vietnamese writer who fought as a teenager for the North Vietnamese. He is the author of several essays; a short story collection, *Camp of Seven Dwarves* (1987); and a novel, *The Sorrow of War* (1990). While he has written a second novel, he has not published it. In 2018, he told an interviewer that "it's not a good time to publish a novel in Vietnam."

KEY CONTEXT "Savage Winds" features the perspective of a soldier fighting for the North Vietnamese Armed Forces of Liberation. These soldiers often ended up in places still populated by villagers who had first experienced the invasion of American troops intending to liberate them and then experienced life as refugees under the control of the North Vietnamese once the American troops had left.

The sun had not yet risen, but above the grassy plain, the mist was already starting to drift away. The village of Diem — a cluster of shacks along the highway — was emerging from the night.

The war was almost over. On the other side of the plain, the enemy artillery base lay silent; no reconnaissance plane had yet appeared on the horizon. At the edge of the village, the last clandestine supply truck crossed the A Rang river, using the stone ford built to replace the iron bridge that had been lost in the bombing. Ripples fanned out from the truck in concentric circles and died away, leaving the water still.

A voice rose lightly from somewhere in the fog, floating away with the night's last murmur, moving further and further along the banks of the river, singing:

I wander through life, not knowing where I've
come from.
I am the shore that awaits the touch of your feet.

Beyond the jagged foothills that bordered the plain to the east, a shimmering red sun rose. The mist gave way to translucence, and the sky turned blue. Across the plain, drops of dew sparkled in the light like diamonds on the grass. The singing grew louder, at once sombre and ethereal, vibrant and savage.

The voice belonged to Dieu Nuong. She had been killed months ago, years even; no one really knew. But now, as day was breaking, the people of Diem, half-asleep, heard the singing and murmured, "It's her." 5

From the other side of the village, in the entrenched artillery camp, watchmen trained their binoculars on the village.

Oh moon, how wretched I am,
My beloved has gone, and will never return.

"Look! You see, there she is!" a soldier cried, pointing.

Behind the groves bordering the village, he thought he could see the shadowy figure of a woman advancing, singing, a slender figure with a graceful, swaying walk, long ebony hair cascading down her back. In the dawn, dream and reality mingled. Perhaps she was a mirage born of the song. A ghost. A lascivious, seductive, blithe phantom.

In the trenches, a captain and a political officer passed the binoculars back and forth. The legend of Dieu Nuong, a singer from Saigon who had been trapped in the liberated zone, was much discussed in the battalion, and embellished with every telling.

The political officer dropped the binoculars. "If we can't shut that whore up, she'll destroy the soul of this company. They'll all follow her." 10

"But how can you prevent a ghost from singing?" asked the captain.

"By forbidding it! It's yellow music, anti-military. And why does she start yowling at exactly the same time every day? It might be a signal. Or maybe she's trying to seduce our men, lure them into her bed so she can infect them with diseases, sap their fighting strength. That's probably what she's after."

"But she sings so beautifully."

A group of infantrymen was crossing the plain. A straggler stopped and looked towards Diem. Mist rose in curls off the green water of the river. A breeze swept over it, carrying off the song. The soldiers felt the voice shiver through their bodies, its melody caressing their hearts. Clear, luminous, pure as the dawn air, the song swelled with the sadness of the vast, free forests lost beyond the horizon, ignoring the frontiers, the front lines, mocking the battlefields, the bombs, the killings.

When my own battalion arrived in Diem in 1973, Dieu Nuong was still alive. We knew almost nothing about her: only that she had come here the previous summer, after the offensive of the Armed Forces of Liberation and the débâcle of the Saigon troops. Those who claimed to know more told conflicting stories.

"They say that she wasn't wearing a stitch of clothing when she wandered over here."

But during that summer of flames, she would not have been the only one suffering. Thousands had been killed, and there were corpses everywhere, lining the roads, piled up in the fields, floating in the rivers. Those who had survived were often more dead than alive. The village had been almost completely destroyed; only prickly underbrush, heaps of shattered bricks, broken tiles and splintered beams remained. Here and there, makeshift houses, half-shack, half-trench, rose from the debris. Dogs scavenged in the rubble, retrieving the remains of the vanished past: tattered pieces of clothing in garish colours, hats, leather and plastic objects, bits of wood and glass, household goods — and human bones, which the dogs fought over.

Before that summer, Diem had been a thriving community under the protection of the Americans. The men had lived off their army wages; the women had worked in small businesses. But then the village was attacked. Day after day, the planes came, raining bombs on the houses and the fields. The riches of the American days were over.

The following year, my company, Artillery Battalion No. 17, arrived in Diem to defend the A Rang river against the air force. We were stationed at the edge of the ghost village.

The inhabitants of Diem were destitute, almost wild. The few remaining men, the blind, crippled remnants of the puppet army, no longer received rations. Only the women dared venture outside, gaunt and dazed, dressed in rags, surrounded by swarms of hungry children.

Most of these people were refugees from the towns, villages and military camps of the region who, in trying to escape the previous summer, had run up against the tanks of the Liberation Army. One night that summer, at around midnight, there was a massacre. It was said that the refugees, hearing the rumble of an airplane far away, lit thousands of torches and formed a huge, flaming cross right in front of the church. In the darkness, they screamed, waving to the pilots. No one heard the first salvos, no one saw the first flashes from the horizon. For hours on end, people fell under a hail of shells. Wave after wave of American planes flew over until dawn, showering the mass grave with bombs. Dieu Nuong was among the few survivors.

Diem was plunged into misery and hunger. Everyone had to work the land, bending over the rows of manioc, toiling in the rice paddies. Everyone had to submit to the Revolution. Those who protested were persecuted, and many were shot.

Dieu Nuong herself was imprisoned. They locked her up in an underground dungeon for three days as punishment for singing her yellow songs, but this didn't cure her; she continued to live in her own world, free. Every day, at dawn and at dusk, she would sing. People whispered that at night, soldiers visited her dilapidated hut on the riverbank, knocking at her door, scratching at the bamboo walls. They brought their rations: rice, a packet of cigarettes, a bit of cloth, some thread, a needle, a mirror, a comb, matches, salt — anything that could be traded for sex. Her reputation as a madwoman and a prostitute spread among the villagers.

The story went that she had been a singer in a musical troupe in Saigon. Her troupe had agreed to perform for a unit of special forces stationed in Tan Tran. The performance started just as the tanks of the Liberation Army invaded the city. Dieu Nuong fled, following a stream of refugees through blazing fields to Diem, where she found herself trapped. On the night of the massacre, she was buried under a mountain of corpses in the churchyard. For an entire day she breathed in their stench. When she was pulled out from under the pile, her body, drenched in blood, looked like a block of red lacquer. It was said that the terror of that night had finally driven her mad.

Our battalion grew accustomed to her singing; day after day, like a savage wind, her bewitching, startling voice drifted across the plain. She sang odes of longing, of yearning for the homeland, of nostalgia for a life devoted to her art, to the audiences and the limelight.

She sang of lost youth, lost beauty, of everything that was gone:

Oh, for the time when we knew love,
When we too had a homeland.

The people of Diem still hum this lament, the song Dieu Nuong first sang the night a convoy of prisoners crossed the village shortly after the massacre. Hundreds of wretched men in camouflage uniforms, bound together in pairs, dragged themselves along the road. Frightened villagers watched furtively from inside their shacks, searching for relatives among the prisoners. No one dared venture out to the roadside. But then, from behind the trees, at the end of the village, a figure appeared — Dieu Nuong. It was twilight, the hour of apparitions.

Muttering, a wild look in her eyes, she slashed at the undergrowth, following the prisoners. The men, hunched over, dragging their feet along the road, didn't notice her, until she began her unearthly singing. Her voice was feeble, and she kept stopping to catch her breath. One of the prisoners raised his voice along with hers. Another joined him. Then another. Dieu Nuong's voice seemed to touch each man's lips like a kiss. The prisoners became a choir, and their singing drowned out the noise of their marching. The guards tried to impose silence, but soon lowered their bayonets.

The villagers swarmed to the edge of the road, staring, silent and petrified, as the procession disappeared into the vastness of the forest. Amplified by the chorus of wretched men, Dieu Nuong's song echoed through the night.

. . . In this war where brother kills brother,
we are nothing but worms and ants.
Oh, for the time when we knew love,
When we too had a homeland.

Dieu Nuong has no tomb. She lies somewhere on the plain, a mound of earth among many mounds of earth.

At the river's edge, all that remain of the anti-aircraft fortifications today are pock-marked walls shaped like horseshoes. Time has filled most of the gaping craters from the cluster and phosphorous bombs. The footpath that once linked our artillery unit with the village is now a faint white trace twisting in and out of the tall grasses along the river. But the soldiers, now scattered, can't have forgotten this path. Back then, twice a day, the army cooks used it to transport meals for the combatants. And at night, especially when there was no moon, the soldiers would secretly sneak off along the path to 'win the hearts of the people,' plunging into the silent grasses, moving towards the river, piling into junks the moment the shadow of the guerrilla patrols appeared.

In those days, contact with the population of the liberated zones was forbidden. Those who had no mission there were under orders to stay out of the village. People who disobeyed could expect punishment, expulsion from the Communist Party and every other imaginable misfortune. But a soldier near the people is like fire near straw.

Relations between the soldiers and the inhabitants of the village's dilapidated straw huts were not close, but a path through the grass had silently been etched. By day, no one but the cooks and their suppliers dared use it. But at night, it was the road to love.

In my battalion, a soldier's supreme ambition was to become a cook's helper under the orders of Cu — the only man who was permanently assigned to the village.

The kitchen had been built next to the church. Cu had chosen the plot because he thought it an unlikely target for the bombers, and because it was near a well that contained the clearest water in the village. Cu wasn't happy to be sharing the well with the priest, but the priest was accommodating, and more reasonable than the other villagers, whom Cu regarded as a bunch of good-for-nothings. They lived among fields, but ever since they had been forced to become farmers they had lost all desire to work the land. They had probably become too accustomed to living off American aid and were nostalgic for the golden age when men enlisted and women prostituted themselves to the Americans and their collaborators. Cu believed they were all in league with the enemy, secretly waiting for an opportunity to rejoin them, hiding their true loyalties behind a façade of patient resignation.

Cu couldn't understand why his companions lost their heads over the village women. The fifty men in the company had been living peaceably in the depths of the forest for years, but as soon as they were stationed on the plain, under an open sky, near a river, a village and women, the quarrels started. Yet the women here were completely different from those in the North; they weren't obedient, faithful, courageous, ingenious and responsible; nor were they heroines of the resistance. The entire village, Cu thought, was teeming with female microbes.

"Female microbes spread gonorrhea and syphilis," he would warn his helpers.

Cu wouldn't accept just anybody as a helper. He ruthlessly eliminated the playboys, the fast talkers, the crafty ones — any man whose talents might attract the village women. "When you're a cook, when you work all day with food for the unit," he said, "you've got to keep your hands clean. They must not touch anything dirty or rotten, and it's *absolutely* forbidden to plunge them into the bodies of women."

The villagers were terrified of Cu, and didn't dare come near his well or his kitchen. When they became friendly with the cook's helpers and wanted to beg or trade things, they waited for Cu to take supplies to the front.

Twice a day, at dawn and at dusk, Cu and one of his men would leave the house under the guard of another helper and take meals to the company. Nich, a tiny, pure-breed Laotian dog who was particularly sensitive to smells, would lead the way. They went via a short section of the highway, turned towards the village and then zig-zagged through the huts. They forged ahead, their bodies tilted slightly forward, their hands on their rumps to support the enormous baskets hoisted on their backs, which gave off warmth and the fragrance of cooked rice.

The village dogs fled at the sight of Nich. They watched, famished, from behind the rubble, but dared not bark. Only the children in rags, drawn by the warm smell of the rice, chased after Cu and his helper, grasping at their baskets.

"Uncle Cook, oh, Uncle Cook," they pleaded.

"Dirty little beggars, get away from me!" shouted Cu.

Nevertheless, when a particularly brave kid followed the procession to the village limits, Cu would stop and beckon him. Then he would pull a bit of grilled manioc, or an ear of steamed corn, or sometimes even a dried fish out of his basket, and say: "Here. That's all there is. There's nothing to eat for the *bo doi*. No more manioc and no more rice. All they get is salted bindweed and a bit of ginger. That's it. The Revolution frees you, but you'd better learn to deal with misery. Learn to dig and work hard to feed yourself. Tell that to your mother. It's going to take a long time, this Revolution. It's going to take our generation and yours as well."

Today, they say that you can still see Nich come and go along the footpath. He sniffs at the rusted, greenish casing of the 35mm cartridges, climbs over the weed-covered trench where they once kept anti-aircraft batteries and dolefully watches the river.

"Uncle Cook, Uncle Cook!" One of the children from back then, now grown up, still calls out when he sees the little dog wandering miserably along the footpath. Behind the dog, he thinks he can make out the shapes of two figures carrying large baskets on their backs.

The dog seems unable to leave the footpath. He always returns at dawn and at dusk. Nothing can distract him from his sleepwalker's trajectory. No one dares lay a hand on him.

"That's the dog that killed Dieu Nuong."

At least that's what they say. Even those who know nothing about the tragedy are afraid of this dog. Perhaps they sense that in this painful, rhythmic promenade, there is a blindness, a madness that is almost human.

Cu's two helpers were changed every month, but one day, when a changeover was due, he announced that he did not want to lose Tuan, one of the previous month's assistants. "He's well trained now. He's hardworking and meticulous. I'd like to keep him on," Cu said.

Tuan had started as an infantryman, although no one knew exactly where he had fought before he joined our battalion. He had been seriously injured and, under normal circumstances, would have been invalided out of the army, but he yielded to the Party's exhortations and volunteered to remain on the battlefield. Instead of being sent back to his unit, he was assigned to my artillery battalion, taking up the post of third gunner. He was tall, thin and gaunt. His Adam's apple stuck out. A horrible scar from a rifle blow gashed his face from one temple to the corner of his lip, twisting his mouth. The other artillerymen liked to fool around, but Tuan never joined in. He remained silent, neither laughing nor becoming angry.

He ignored the planes that nosedived towards our positions, the bombs that exploded close by and the rockets that ripped into our defenses; he didn't care. This coldness, this indifference towards everything, meant that he made a perfect third gunner. His only duty was to turn the handle of his gun and regulate the shooting according to orders.

"Artillery combat is really monotonous," he once said to me. "It's like typing. There's nothing theatrical about it. It's nothing compared with hand-to-hand combat."

"That's because you've only been third gunner," I replied. "If you want, I'll ask the chief to move me back to your position. You can be number two and pull the trigger."

"Oh, I don't care. I'll go wherever I'm sent. It's all the same to me."

"If you feel that way, why didn't you go back North when you had the chance? Why did you stay?"

Tuan shrugged.

"Was it your love life? Had your wife been sleeping with the militia? Was that it?" Tuan grunted, but said nothing.

In fact, no one knew if he was married or had children. And no one had ever seen him read or write a letter. Even the political officer knew no more than the few lines written in his file. Tuan never confided in anyone.

Aside from this unusual discretion, Tuan was also known for his talent as a guitarist. He was the best in the company. But he didn't play like a soldier, thumping out the rhythm with his foot, swinging his shoulders; he didn't whistle or sing as he strummed. He played distractedly, neither for his own entertainment nor ours.

"What are you playing there, Tuan? What strange music."

Tuan didn't reply. He took off his guitar — an old one, its body ready to fracture — and went into the kitchen. He had brought the guitar with him when he joined the army, and you wondered by what miracle he had kept it intact through all that had happened.

At first, Cu was irritated by Tuan's taciturn nature, but he got used to it. Discretion, after all, was not a fault. And the kitchen was always busy, and Cu and his helpers spent their day running around, rushing to complete some job; there wasn't really time to talk.

It wasn't until late at night, after the unit had been fed, that Cu and his helpers found a moment to exchange a few words before they slumped into their hammocks. Cu would get out a bottle of wine, and the helpers would drink while he assigned the next day's tasks. On quieter days, Cu and another helper, Binh, would play cards, and Tuan would take his guitar down from the wall, gently adjust the strings and play softly. Binh would whistle, accompanying the music. And Cu, letting his cards fall, would turn towards Tuan, listening. One night, he recognized the tune; he had heard it every day, at dawn and at dusk: *I wander through life, not knowing where I've come from.* Was this when Cu guessed Tuan's secret?

Outside, the rain fell, relentlessly. A dank, humid atmosphere hung over the cabin. The lamp cast a yellowish glow. The sad life of soldiers. Like a long sigh.

The priest's house, next door to Cu's hut, was half-buried, surrounded by four slopes of earth. It was sparsely furnished: a bamboo bed covered with straw, a wooden pillow, a table, a bookshelf and some holy pictures. A basket hung over the entrance. In the morning, the village faithful would leave food in it for the priest, who seldom left his room and never ventured further than the garden. He was a wise old man, aloof from the world. He disappeared the day Dieu Nuong was killed.

The year before, on the night the Americans showered the refugees with bombs, the priest and Dieu Nuong had found themselves lying side by side, and it was he who had pulled her from under the mountain of corpses. He had revived her, saved her life, and from that day on, had taken care of her. For a time, Dieu Nuong had lived in the church, by the priest's side, like a sister. It wasn't exactly a suitable arrangement, but in those chaotic times many taboos were broken; no rule survived without compromise.

Later, when Dieu Nuong went to live in her hut at the edge of the village, she often returned to the church to see the priest — perhaps to make her confession, or to pass on the gifts the soldiers gave her daily, things they had saved from their meagre rations, or pilfered from the stores, or looted from somewhere.

I don't think I am alone in saying this: I never thought Dieu Nuong wicked. She gave me happiness I had never known back North. Many years have passed, but I cannot forget her, nor do I want to. I see her walking alone, on a deserted road, graceful, lithe, swaying; I see her seated on the riverbank, wistful, silent.

"Come here, soldier, honey. Don't be afraid. I'm alone."

My heart racing, I would sweep back the curtain that was her door and enter her room. Taking a step forward, I brushed against something wonderful and warm, something that trembled, something impossible to describe, then sank into an inferno of softness. . . .

"Are you going so soon?" She would hold me back. "It's a long time until dawn. Stay a while. I have something to tell you. One thing, only one thing — "

But few men dared stay, and fewer still dared listen to what Dieu Nuong had to tell them. No one wanted to hear it, because no one could help her. It was too dangerous. No doubt Dieu Nuong believed that there were still men in this world crazy enough to risk their lives for love, to betray everything for love.

We were all anxious to see her again and so we lied to her, promising the impossible, even though we knew there was no way we could help her escape. But once, a year ago, there had been a man who promised to help her, and this man had kept his word.

I learned afterwards, when it was all over, that when Tuan was in the infantry he had passed through Diem many times.

During the summer of flames, after the massacre, the village had been struck by famine; the meagre stocks of food donated by the *bo doi* at the time of Liberation were gone. The authorities called for increased production, and even the priest had to fend for himself.

Dieu Nuong was living with the priest at this time, and since her guardian didn't till the earth, she tried to do the work of two people, felling trees and planting manioc. But she wasn't used to the hard labor, to the mud, and after each thrust of the hoe she would bury her face in her hands and weep. At the end of the day, her field would still be covered with trees and undergrowth.

Nearby, a group of soldiers lounged in their hammocks. They jeered at her, contemptuous of this little woman, lazy, frail as tissue paper, who had known only the good life and who was learning for the first time what human existence was all about. But little by little, they took pity on her suffering and offered to help. They spent the entire night felling trees, clearing her field. One man introduced himself. His name was Tuan. He promised to come back in a few days to help Dieu Nuong burn the land. And he kept his word.

Dieu Nuong's field was perfect, the clearest in the village. Not a tree stump remained. When he left, Tuan promised to come back to help sow the manioc. And he kept his word.

The first rains came. In a few days, the manioc Tuan had planted covered the burnt patch with a thick carpet of green. All around, Tuan sowed a hedge of squash. On the strip of land behind the church, he helped Dieu Nuong plant vegetables. Every five days or so, Tuan crept away from the front line near the town and crossed the fields to come to Diem.

It was about this time that Dieu Nuong left the church and made her home in a hut that Tuan had built for her on the riverbank. Thanks to him, she lost her desperate expression; her eyes sparkled and she started to smile again.

Sometimes, Tuan brought his guitar with him to Dieu Nuong's hut. He would play softly, and Dieu Nuong would sing in a murmur. Back then, she sang only for him.

No doubt they made promises to each other. No doubt Dieu Nuong told Tuan that she dreamed of leaving her harsh life, scratching at the earth in this godforsaken village; that she was looking for a man worthy of her trust, who would help her cross the front line and return her to the calm, comfortable life she had known before Liberation.

Tuan was confident they could cross the line–those ten kilometers riddled with mines, patrolled by guards — for those were the days following the peace talks. Intoxicated with love, transported by the hope of peace, he promised to help her. And no doubt he meant it. But, suddenly, he disappeared. Days passed, then months; no one in Diem spoke of him.

Like the rest of us, Dieu Nuong never mentioned Tuan. The memory of him and his promise had probably dissolved along with her mind. But her yearning for freedom survived, surfacing from time to time in the songs she sang every day at dawn and at dusk. Night after night, she extracted promises from the soldiers who visited her, promises that grew emptier with each passing day as the war became more brutal, as bombs and shells pounded the village, crushing all hopes of peace.

One rainy night, as she walked along the footpath to the priest's house, through the vegetable garden near the cook's cabin, Dieu Nuong heard the strains of a guitar. She approached soundlessly, peering into the hut. An oil lamp flickered. She couldn't make out the guitarist's face, but she recognized the familiar melody of her nights with Tuan. Frantic, she approached the door. Nich, the dog, bounded out of a corner of the cabin, barking. "Who is it?" Cu shouted, climbing out of his hammock, seizing his rifle.

Dieu Nuong jumped back. The guitar stopped, and she ran off.

Cu flung open the door.

"A spy!" he shouted. "Stop!"

He caught sight of Dieu Nuong's silhouette.

"Ah it's you, you whore! Stop, or I'll shoot!" Cu shouted, running into the rain, slipping in the mud and falling flat on his face. Pulling himself up, furious, he fired a volley of shots in Dieu Nuong's direction.

Tuan rushed out after him and grabbed the machine-gun. "You idiot!" he shouted, his voice choked. Wildly, he punched Cu in the face, threw down his gun and ran off into the blackness in pursuit of Dieu Nuong. The village rang out with alarm sirens.

Binh helped Cu up and brought him back to the cabin. "When people ask, you're going to tell them that it was nothing," Cu murmured painfully, wiping the blood and rain off his face with his sleeve. "Tell them that I had a nightmare, that I shot without thinking. Go and see what's happened." He sighed. "But why did she run off?"

Later, when Binh told me what had happened that night, he said mournfully: "If Dieu Nuong hadn't been wounded, they might have made it."

Thinking about it now, Cu's actions seem to me incomprehensible. He was the only one who knew something of what had happened between Tuan and Dieu Nuong. Why did he shoot her?

Binh told no one about Cu firing on Dieu Nuong, or about the fight between Cu and Tuan, nor even about the mysterious relationship between Tuan and Dieu Nuong. All anyone knew was that both of them had disappeared.

At the edge of the village, weeds began to grow around Dieu Nuong's deserted hut. Rumor had it that she had fled, or been killed — drowned in the river, blown up by a bomb.

The rains seemed interminable, but little by little I understood why I felt so sad. I missed Dieu Nuong's singing; I missed *her*. I wasn't the only one; the whole company seemed depressed. There no longer seemed any reason for our presence here.

Then, on a sunny day at the beginning of the dry season, we learned that she and Tuan had been hiding in the church, waiting for the rains to stop and for Dieu Nuong's wounds to heal. Now, they had gone for good.

It was the priest who told us. He came to the trenches at dawn, his cassock damp with mist. "Last year, one of your men seduced the girl. The man with the scar and the sullen face. And then he came back. Not only has he betrayed you, but it was he who led the girl to betray God." He told us he had alerted Cu the night before, as soon as he discovered that Tuan and Dieu Nuong had fled, but Cu hadn't told the rest of us.

"If you really want to catch them, it's not too late. She's wounded and can't walk very fast," he said. "You could take the dog."

I had the honor of participating in the operation, joined by Cu and two scouts. We left immediately. Nich led the way, moving quickly, pulling at the leash which Cu held.

We followed him in silence, fanning out, rifles at the ready. We had orders not to let them get away with their secrets about the unit's next campaign.

The traces that Nich followed led us along the river, rising towards the densely forested plain.

We quickly lost our enthusiasm. We advanced reluctantly. Dust swirled under our feet. The hours passed. Relentless, Nich followed the fugitives' invisible, zig-zagging trace. But just as we had decided to turn back, we came across a lone *knia* tree in the middle of a field of grass higher than our heads. Here, we could see that Tuan and Dieu Nuong had lain down to rest. An army of ants was dragging away grains of rice. There was a cigarette butt, a bit of rough tobacco rolled in a piece of newspaper, on the ground. But the clearest sign was a shape, pressed upon the grass — a reclining, human form, a woman's silhouette.

We caught up with them just before dusk.

Exhausted, we stopped by a stream. Nich had lost the scent in the water, and we sat down to rest. Our silence hung in the intense red of the sunset.

Suddenly, over the murmuring of the stream, came a thin, unexpected sound. "The guitar!" cried Cu.

We listened, holding our breath. A voice began to sing.

We forded the river, creeping towards the place from where the song seemed to rise. It was a pine forest. Sparse trees reached for the sky. A thin curl of smoke evaporated in the evening.

A twig snapped. The song stopped.

I hid myself behind a tree trunk, staring, wide-eyed. A pot hung over a tiny fire. Nearby lay a guitar. A hammock had been strung between two pines. Our prey had hidden in the bushes.

Silence. For a long time. Mechanically, I cocked my rifle.

"Friends, brothers!" It was Tuan's voice. "We haven't harmed anyone. Let us go!"

"Quiet!" shouted one of the scouts. "Stand up! Hands up! Come out of there!"

One minute. Minutes. Still silence. Cu suddenly let go of Nich's leash. The dog ran off, and I heard him barking in the bushes. Frantic yelps of joy. The bush trembled.

"I am wandering," sang the voice.

"Crazy woman!" someone shouted. "Whore!"

Four rifles spat bullets in the same instant. Flashes merged, ripping through the night.

We emptied four cartridges. The guns stopped at the same moment. All four of us ran forward and then stopped, petrified.

Behind the shattered bush, two figures lay entwined. Our bullets seemed only to have locked them more tightly together. The man had tried to protect the woman with his body, but the bullets had pierced both of them. The firelight flickered on their naked backs.

We stood paralyzed for a long time. Night fell. It was as if we were chained to each other, captive to something invisible but overpowering. The smell of gunpowder, the only trace of our frenzy, had evaporated.

Cu started to sob.

I knelt next to Tuan and Dieu Nuong and parted them.

Two days later, we received orders to march south. We left Diem forever. I pulled myself together, as did Cu. There was a battle ahead of us, the only salvation left for our souls. We would fight and forget.

We didn't know it then, but we had reached the last dry season of the war. We had shot the messengers of peace, and yet, in spite of everything, peace returned.

On the plain, all through the dry season, winds howled. Peaceful winds; savage winds. ■

1995

Questions

1. How does the speaker's description in paragraph 4 of the singing emphasize the mood in the story's opening paragraphs? What role does the imagery play?
2. Create a brief character sketch of Dieu Nuong, the priest, Tuan, and Cu. What do readers learn about each of the characters? Does each identify more with the people who had originally been living in Diem or with the Liberation Army of the North Vietnamese?
3. Trace the references to varying forms of wind in the story as well as to the sounds of singing and music. How do they function in the story? What evidence can you find of a connection between them? How does this connection relate to the story as a whole?
4. At one point, the narrator asks, "Was this when Cu guessed Tuan's secret?" (par. 64). What is his secret?
5. Tuan helps Dieu Nuong clear her fields, and then he disappears. What happens between the time he disappears and when she discovers him working with Cu? Support your inferences with evidence from the text.
6. After the initial publication of "Savage Winds," the Vietnamese government harshly criticized Bảo Ninh's treatment of Americans in the story as being too complimentary. Do you find his depictions of the American soldiers complimentary? Why would the Vietnamese government be critical of Ninh?
7. The final sentence of the story consists of only noun phrases: "Peaceful winds; savage winds." What purpose do the contrasting adjectives serve? How do you interpret this ending?
8. How does the war continue to haunt the people of Diem and the area surrounding the village beyond their experiences of Dieu Nuong following her death?

Napalm

Quan Barry

Born in Saigon in 1973, Vietnamese poet and novelist Quan Barry was raised on the North Shore of Boston. She is the author of four poetry books, most recently *Loose Strife* (2015) and two novels, including *She Rides Upon Sticks* (2020). With a BA from the University of Virginia and an MFA from the University of Michigan, Barry was also a Wallace Stegner Fellow at Stanford University. Currently, she teaches at the University of Wisconsin–Madison.

KEY CONTEXT First used strategically as a weapon of war by the U.S. military during World War II, napalm consists of a gelling agent and fuel, such as gasoline or diesel. The gelling agent allows it to be thrown or dropped in ways that other incendiary, or fire-starting, devices could not. Napalm also burns at extremely high temperatures and for longer than regular gasoline, and its ability to stick to what it hits made it both an effective way to destroy structures and a horrifyingly devastating weapon when used on humans. The United States dropped nearly four hundred tons of napalm on Vietnam during the Vietnam War.

I have come to realize the body is its own pyre, that degree
rises from within, the fatty acids a kind of kindling.
Like a scientist in a lab, this much I have established, blood jelled
like gasoline, the years spread before me like a map

pinned with targets, where I'm raging even now.
It works both ways. Clear the forests to see your enemies
and your enemies see you clearly. Like all effective incendiaries,
I won't only bloom where I'm planted. ■

2001

Questions

1. What does the speaker compare in the poem's first two lines? How does this comparison establish themes in the poem?
2. Describe the speaker of the poem. How does the comparison to "a scientist in a lab" (l. 3) contribute to your understanding of her perspective?
3. What does the speaker mean both literally and figuratively when she says, "It works both ways" (l. 6)?
4. Consider the speaker's first-person assertions including "I have come to realize" (l. 1), "I have established" (l. 3), "I'm raging" (l. 5), and "I won't only bloom where I'm planted" (l. 8). What does this perspective communicate about the speaker's attitude toward the "targets" in line 5?
5. What does the final line of the poem mean to you? How would you describe the speaker's tone in this line?

My Father's "Norton Introduction to Literature," Third Edition (1981)

Hai-Dang Phan

Born in Vietnam, Hai-Dang Phan grew up in Wisconsin after coming to the United States as a refugee. A poet, translator, and essayist, he lives in Iowa City, Iowa, and teaches at Grinnell College.

KEY CONTEXT This poem references "reeducation camps," which were prison camps created by the communist government of Vietnam after the Vietnam War ended. Hundreds of thousands of people associated with the former government of South Vietnam as well as its supporters were imprisoned in reeducation camps as a form of punishment and indoctrination. Prisoners were subjected to harsh conditions, including torture, forced labor, and disease.

Certain words give him trouble: *cannibals, puzzles, sob,*
bosom, martyr, deteriorate, shake, astonishes, vexed, ode...
These he looks up and studiously annotates in Vietnamese.
Ravish means *cướp đoạt*; *shits* is like when you have to *đi ỉa*;
mourners are those whom we say are full of *buồn rầu*.
For "even the like precurse of feared events"[1] think *báo trước*.[2]

Its thin translucent pages are webbed with his marginalia,
graphite ghosts of a living hand, and the notes often sound

[1] A reference to act I, scene i of *Hamlet* by William Shakespeare. This line is spoken by Hamlet's friend Horatio as he is trying to understand Hamlet's sighting of the ghost of his father, King Hamlet. — Eds.

[2] Vietnamese for *forewarned*. — Eds.

just like him: "All depend on how look at thing," he pencils
after "I first surmised the Horses' Heads / Were toward Eternity —"[3]
His slanted handwriting is generally small, but firm and clear.
His pencil is a No. 2, his preferred Hi-Liter, arctic blue.

I can see my father trying out the tools of literary analysis.
He identifies the "turning point" of "The Short and Happy Life
of Francis Macomber";[4] underlines the simile in "Both the old man
and the child stared ahead as if they were awaiting an apparition."
My father, as he reads, continues to notice relevant passages
and to register significant reactions, but increasingly sorts out

his ideas in English, shaking off those Vietnamese glosses.
1981 was the same year we *vượt biển*[5] and came to America,
where my father took Intro Lit ("for fun"), Comp Sci ("for job").
"Stopping by Woods on a Snowy Evening,"[6] he murmurs
something about the "dark side of life how awful it can be"
as I begin to track silence and signal to a cold source.

Reading Ransom's "Bells for John Whiteside's Daughter,"
a poem about a "young girl's death," as my father notes,
how could he not have been "vexed at her brown study /
Lying so primly propped," since he never properly observed
(I realize this just now) his own daughter's wake.
Lấy làm ngạc nhiên về is what it means to be astonished.

Her name was Đông Xưa, Ancient Winter, but at home she's Bebe.
"There was such speed in her little body, / And such lightness
in her footfall, / It is no wonder her brown study / Astonishes
us all."[7] In the photo of her that hangs in my parents' house
she is always fourteen months old and staring into the future.
In "reeducation camp" he had to believe she was alive

because my mother on visits "took arms against her shadow."[8]
Did the memory of those days sweep over him like a leaf storm
from the pages of a forgotten autumn? Lost in the margins,
I'm reading the way I discourage my students from reading.
But this is "how we deal with death," his black pen replies.
Assume there is a reason for everything, instructs a green asterisk.

---

[3] Lines from the poem "Because I could not stop for Death —" by Emily Dickinson. — Eds.

[4] A 1936 short story by Ernest Hemingway. — Eds.

[5] Vietnamese for *crossed the sea*. — Eds.

[6] A 1923 poem by Robert Frost. — Eds.

[7] Lines from John Crowe Ransom's 1924 poem "Bells for John Whiteside's Daughter." — Eds.

[8] Another line from Ransom's poem. — Eds.

Then between pp. 896–97, opened to Stevens' "Sunday Morning,"
I pick out a newspaper clipping, small as a stamp, an old listing
from the 404-Employment Opps State of Minnesota, and read:
For current job opportunities dial (612) 297-3180. Answered 24 hrs.
When I dial, the automated female voice on the other end
tells me I have reached a non-working number. ■

2015

Questions

1. Does there appear to be a pattern to the words in lines 1–2 that the speaker's father looks up? If so, what is it? If not, why might these words be the ones that challenge him?
2. How does Hai-Dang Phan incorporate the words in lines 1–2 into the poem's later lines? What larger ideas does this structural choice emphasize?
3. How does John Crowe Ransom's poem "Bells for John Whiteside's Daughter" serve as not only a connection for the speaker's father to the literature he's studying but also for the speaker to his father? What does this say about the power of literature to bring us together even across decades and generations?
4. How do you interpret the final stanza of the poem? What is the speaker's attitude toward the clippings he finds in the book?
5. What is the effect of threading Vietnamese words throughout the poem? How does this reflect the relationship the speaker has with his father, and the relationship his father has with his adopted home?

East Mountain View

Paul Tran

A Vietnamese American poet and activist, Paul Tran grew up in California. They studied twentieth-century U.S. history at Brown University and creative writing at Washington University in St. Louis. They are also active in coaching and competing in poetry slams.

KEY CONTEXT As you read "East Mountain View," consider the poem's use of conceit, an extended metaphor with complex comparisons that are developed through the juxtaposition or association of unexpected or paradoxical ideas.

Found in a dumpster: folding table, can of Pringles. Half full,
    half empty: it doesn't matter. Perspective's no good

to the stomach, which, unlike the mind, is indentured by habit,
    by imperative. Blame evolution. Blame the gods

from which we absorb our preference for dominion, mimicking
    what we misinterpret as power unaccompanied

by consequence. This is how we become new Americans:
    five-finger discount, Midas touch.[1] Transfiguration

[1] The "five-finger discount" is a euphemism for shoplifting. "Midas touch" is a reference to the Greek myth of King Midas, who could turn everything he touched to gold. This was a curse rather than a blessing because it led him to starve to death. — Eds.

as anti-assimilation, my mother fashions dining set and dinner
with the loot she lugs into our apartment while I,

months old, not even potty-trained, dream of cities shorn
and shores away, where a daughter barters her mother's

last gold bangle for guaranteed passage out of the Mekong Delta,[2]
where a daughter barters the last thing she owns:

her body, her crow-black hair parted down the middle,
the length of nights lost in the South China Sea,

nights she relives whenever their faceless forms, like sudden
lightning, surprise her in the flesh of ordinary things —

the coyotes, the pirates, the virgins vaulting into bottomless dark,
nourishing sharks and not their captors. I suppose

that's survival: to appropriate what annihilates us, to make use
of what appears useless. I know this despite what it took

to know it. I know this despite the conceit of knowing. It sucks
belonging to anywhere, to anything. Even in Heaven

we're trespassers, told we don't speak English well enough.
Even in Heaven we apply for citizenship and wait.

Heaven's a lot of waiting. So we master the grief of geography,
severed from a life that persists as shadows of shadows. ■

2017

[2] A large region in southwestern Vietnam. — Eds.

Questions

1. What does the speaker mean by "Blame the gods / from which we absorb our preference for dominion, mimicking / what we misinterpret as power unaccompanied / by consequence" (ll. 4–7)? Whom do they include by using the first-person pronoun "we"?
2. What evidence does the speaker provide in the poem to support the assertion in lines 20–21 about what people do to survive?
3. How does Paul Tran's use of "conceit" in line 23 create a metaphor in that line, and how does it contribute to the function of the poetic conceit in the text as a whole?
4. By the end of the poem, what has the speaker communicated about the contrast between perspective "to the stomach" (l. 3) as opposed to how the mind makes use of it? What are a few examples in the poem of the way perspectives shift? Do these shifts ultimately prove the speaker's point in lines 1–2? Explain.

5. To what does the speaker refer in the references to "Heaven" in lines 24, 26, and 27? What do these references reveal about the speaker's perspective?
6. How does the poem's structure — unrhymed couplets — reflect the speaker's relationship to the subjects and experiences addressed in this poem?

Between Home and Here (Woman Soldier 1)

Ann Le

Ann Le, a first-generation Vietnamese American, lives in California. She combines found images with family photos and personal artifacts to create her artwork and construct narratives around her sense of history, home, and loss.

KEY CONTEXT The woman in this image was twenty-four when she was photographed by Lê Minh Trường, a North Vietnamese photographer. Of this photograph, Trường has said, "She . . . had been widowed twice. Both her husbands were soldiers. I saw her as the embodiment of the ideal guerrilla woman, who'd made great sacrifices for her country."

2019

Questions

1. This image is one in a series by Ann Le. On her website, she explains that "*Between Home and Here*, both tragic and poetic, is about home, memory, separation, family, refugees and immigrants, and how we embrace and conquer loss." How do the details in this piece speak to Le's statement?
2. How do the contrasting textures of the plants in the background emphasize contrasts in the appearance of the female soldier?
3. How does this image relate to what you have imagined or learned about the Vietnam War? Does it confirm or challenge any of your understandings? Explain.
4. How does Le's placement of the woman in this image against a new background affect the original photographer's depiction of her "as the embodiment of the ideal guerrilla woman"?

Literature in Conversation

1. In what ways do Tim O'Brien's story and these Texts in Context collectively tell "true war stories," as Viet Thanh Nguyen defines them? Consider how (or whether) they incorporate the two things Nguyen says "war happens to be": "profitable" and "a bore." Alternatively, how do these texts collectively fit O'Brien's definition of war as included by Nguyen in his essay? Consider especially O'Brien's explanation of war being "mystery," "adventure," "courage," "discovery," and "love." Cite at least three of the texts included here.
2. How do you imagine O'Brien would respond to the assertions Nguyen makes in his essay "On True War Stories"? What would a conversation look like among O'Brien, Nguyen, and one of the other writers of these texts? Write a dialogue among the three, drawing on their pieces for inspiration and evidence.
3. One of the most challenging realities about the Vietnam War to reconcile is that it involved the suffering and deaths of so many people — both Vietnamese and American — who had not wanted anything to do with the conflict. How does O'Brien acknowledge this when he explains that "to 'hump' it" not only meant walking or marching but that it also "implied burdens far beyond the intransitive"? Compare some of the experiences of O'Brien and his men to those had by the people in these texts. How do these experiences demonstrate each side's shared humanity? Then, contrast the experience of the Vietnam War in "The Things They Carried" with the experiences of the people in these texts.
4. Using these texts, write an overview of what the Vietnamese call the American War. Which details do you believe are essential to include? Which did you discover for the first time? How have these texts caused you to think again about your understanding of this conflict?
5. Senator George McGovern of South Dakota said on the Senate floor on April 25, 1967, "We seem bent upon saving the Vietnamese from Ho Chi Minh, even if we have to kill them and demolish their country to do it. I do not intend to remain silent in the face of what I regard as a policy of madness which, sooner or later, will envelop my son and American youth by the millions for years to come." Based on the texts in this Conversation and your knowledge of the Vietnam War after 1967, explain whether McGovern's concern became a reality.
6. Nguyen, Phan, and Tran all address the experiences of parents in their texts. Nguyen writes about his parents as refugees. Phan's speaker encounters his father's literature textbook and develops an appreciation for his father's efforts to learn English and gain a college degree in his new country. Tran's speaker relates the story of a mother who sells her final possessions to survive. Compare and contrast each writer's presentation of these parental figures. In what ways does experiencing the effects of the Vietnam War and its aftermath through the eyes of the next generation further develop your understanding of the complexity of the conflict?

After the Dance

Leo Tolstoy

Library of Congress, Prints & Photographs Division, [LC-DIG-ds-02147]

Count Lev Nikolayevich Tolstoy (1828–1910), a Russian writer, is considered one of the greatest authors of all time. He was nominated for both the Nobel Prize in Literature and the Nobel Peace Prize many times but never won. Born into an aristocratic Russian family, Tolstoy experienced a profound moral crisis in the 1870s, which resulted in a spiritual awakening. He became a Christian anarchist and pacifist whose ideas on nonviolent resistance influenced Mahatma Gandhi and Martin Luther King Jr. Best known for his realist novels *War and Peace* and *Anna Karenina*, Tolstoy wrote short stories; novellas, such as *The Death of Ivan Ilyich*; plays; and essays.

KEY CONTEXT The dance in this story most likely takes place between 1820 and 1840, an era in which Russian forces, led by Emperor Nicholas I, fought in the Russo-Persian War (1826–1828), the Greek War of Independence (1827), Nicholas I's Turkish War (1828–1829), the Polish-Russian War (1830–1831), and the Second Turko-Egyptian War (1839–1841). During this time, Russia also resumed the Caucasian War (1817–1864).

"—And you say that a man cannot, of himself, understand what is good and evil; that it is all environment, that the environment swamps the man. But I believe it is all chance. Take my own case . . ."

Thus spoke our excellent friend, Ivan Vasilievich, after a conversation between us on the impossibility of improving individual character without a change of the conditions under which men live. Nobody had actually said that one could not of oneself understand good and evil; but it was a habit of Ivan Vasilievich to answer in this way the thoughts aroused in his own mind by conversation, and to illustrate those thoughts by relating incidents in his own life. He often quite forgot the reason for his story in telling it; but he always told it with great sincerity and feeling.

He did so now.

"Take my own case. My whole life was moulded, not by environment, but by something quite different."

"By what, then?" we asked.

"Oh, that is a long story. I should have to tell you about a great many things to make you understand."

"Well, tell us then."

Ivan Vasilievich thought a little, and shook his head.

"My whole life," he said, "was changed in one night, or, rather, morning."

"Why, what happened?" one of us asked.

"What happened was that I was very much in love. I have been in love many times, but this was the most serious of all. It is a thing of the past; she has married daughters now. It was Varinka B——." Ivan Vasilievich mentioned her surname. "Even at fifty she is remarkably handsome; but in her youth, at eighteen, she was exquisite — tall, slender, graceful, and stately. Yes, stately is the word; she held herself very erect, by instinct as it were; and carried her head high, and that together with her beauty and height gave her a queenly air in spite of being thin, even bony one might say. It might indeed have been deterring had it not been for her smile, which was always gay and cordial, and for the charming light in her eyes and for her youthful sweetness."

"What an entrancing description you give, Ivan Vasilievich!"

"Description, indeed! I could not possibly describe her so that you could appreciate her. But that does not matter; what I am going to tell you happened in the forties. I was at that time a student in a provincial university. I don't know whether it was a good thing or no, but we had no political clubs, no theories in our universities then. We were simply young and spent our time as young men do, studying and amusing ourselves. I was a very gay, lively, careless fellow, and had plenty of money too. I had a fine horse, and used to go tobogganing with the young ladies. Skating had not yet come into fashion. I went to drinking parties with my comrades — in those days we drank nothing but champagne — if we had no champagne we drank nothing at all. We never drank vodka, as they do now. Evening parties and balls were my favourite amusements. I danced well, and was not an ugly fellow."

"Come, there is no need to be modest," Interrupted a lady near him, "We have seen your photograph. Not ugly, indeed! You were a handsome fellow."

"Handsome, if you like. That does not matter. When my love for her was at its strongest, on the last day of the carnival, I was at a ball at the provincial marshal's, a good-natured old man, rich and hospitable, and a court chamberlain. The guests were welcomed by his wife, who was as good-natured as himself. She was dressed in puce-coloured[1] velvet, and had a diamond diadem on her forehead, and her plump, old white shoulders and bosom were bare like the portraits of Empress Elizabeth, the daughter of Peter the Great.[2]

"It was a delightful ball. It was a splendid room, with a gallery for the orchestra, which was famous at the time, and consisted of serfs belonging to a musical landowner. The refreshments were magnificent, and the champagne flowed in rivers. Though I was fond of champagne I did not drink that night, because without it I was drunk with love. But I made up for it by dancing waltzes and polkas till I was ready to drop — of course, whenever possible, with Varinka. She wore a white dress with a pink sash, white shoes, and white kid gloves, which did not quite reach to her thin pointed elbows. A disgusting engineer named Anisimov robbed me of the mazurka[3] with her — to this day I cannot forgive him. He asked her for the dance the minute she arrived, while I had driven to the hair-dresser's to get a pair of gloves, and was late. So I did not dance the mazurka with her, but with a German girl to whom I had previously paid a little attention; but I am afraid I did not behave very politely to her that evening. I hardly spoke or looked at her, and saw nothing but the tall, slender figure in a white dress, with a pink sash, a flushed, beaming, dimpled face, and sweet, kind eyes. I was not alone; they were all looking at her with admiration, the men and women alike, although she outshone all of them. They could not help admiring her.

"Although I was not nominally her partner for the mazurka, I did as a matter of fact dance

---

[1] Dark, reddish brown. — Eds.

[2] Tsar Peter I, known as Peter the Great (1672–1725), ruled Russia from 1682 until his death. He embraced many of the scientific advancements and political reforms of the Enlightenment. Elizabeth Petrovna (1709–1762), his daughter, ruled as Empress of Russia from 1741 until her death, continuing to bring Enlightenment reforms to Russia. — Eds.

[3] A Polish folk dance that gained popularity all over Europe and became fashionable in higher social circles in Paris, London, and among both peasants and aristocracy in Russia in the 1800s. Some think it served as a sign of solidarity with the oppressed nation of Poland, which lost its independence in 1795 — even in Russia, which had partitioned the country along with Prussia and Austria. — Eds.

extending beyond the text

The following excerpt from Leo Tolstoy's 1877 novel *Anna Karenina* provides a view of a ball from the perspective of Kitty, a young woman.

from Anna Karenina

Leo Tolstoy

The ball was only just beginning as Kitty and her mother walked up the great staircase, flooded with light, and lined with flowers and footmen in powder and red coats. From the rooms came a constant, steady hum, as from a hive, and the rustle of movement; and while on the landing between trees they gave last touches to their hair and dresses before the mirror, they heard from the ballroom the careful, distinct notes of the fiddles of the orchestra beginning the first waltz. . . .

When, just before entering the ballroom, the princess, her mother, tried to turn right side out of the ribbon of her sash, Kitty had drawn back a little. She felt that everything must be right of itself, and graceful, and nothing could need setting straight.

It was one of Kitty's best days. Her dress was not uncomfortable anywhere; her lace berthe did not droop anywhere; her rosettes were not crushed nor torn off; her pink slippers with high, hollowed-out heels did not pinch, but gladdened her feet; and the thick rolls of fair chignon kept up on her head as if they were her own hair. All the three buttons buttoned up without tearing on the long glove that covered her hand without concealing its lines. The black velvet of her locket nestled with special softness round her neck. That velvet was delicious; at home, looking at her neck in the looking-glass, Kitty had felt that that velvet was speaking. About all the rest there might be a doubt, but the velvet was delicious. Kitty smiled here too, at the ball, when she glanced at it in the glass. Her bare shoulders and arms gave Kitty a sense of chill marble, a feeling she particularly liked. Her eyes sparkled, and her rosy lips could not keep from smiling from the consciousness of her own attractiveness. She had scarcely entered the ballroom and reached the throng of ladies, all tulle, ribbons, lace, and flowers, waiting to be asked to dance — Kitty was never one of that throng — when she was asked for a waltz, and asked by the best partner, the first star in the hierarchy of the ballroom, a renowned director of dances, a married man, handsome and well-built, Yegorushka Korsunsky. He had only just left the Countess Bonina, with whom he had danced the first half of the waltz, and, scanning his kingdom — that is to say, a few couples who had started dancing — he caught sight of Kitty, entering, and flew up to her with that peculiar, easy amble which is confined to directors of balls. Without even asking her if she cared to dance, he put out his arm to encircle her slender waist. She looked round for someone to give her fan to, and their hostess, smiling to her, took it. ■

extending beyond the text

1. **How does Tolstoy's description of Kitty's demeanor and appearance compare to the narrator's description of Varinka B. in "After the Dance"?**
2. **What "background" does Tolstoy provide to show Kitty's social standing? How similar is it to that of Varinka B. in "After the Dance"?**
3. **While "After the Dance" features a male narrator looking back on a ball from his youth, this excerpt from *Anna Karenina* shows the experience of a ball through a young woman's eyes. How would you characterize each narrative perspective? What is the effect of each of these perspectives on the tone and mood of each text?**

nearly the whole time with her. She always came forward boldly the whole length of the room to pick me out. I flew to meet her without waiting to be chosen, and she thanked me with a smile for my intuition. When I was brought up to her with somebody else, and she guessed wrongly, she took the other man's hand with a shrug of her slim shoulders, and smiled at me regretfully.

"Whenever there was a waltz figure in the mazurka, I waltzed with her for a long time, and breathing fast and smiling, she would say, '*En-core*'; and I went on waltzing and waltzing, as though unconscious of any bodily existence."

"Come now, how could you be unconscious of it with your arm round her waist? You must have been conscious, not only of your own existence, but of hers," said one of the party.

Ivan Vasilievich cried out, almost shouting in anger: "There you are, moderns all over! Nowadays you think of nothing but the body. It was different in our day. The more I was in love the less corporeal was she in my eyes. Nowadays you think of nothing but the body. It was different in our day. The more I was in love the less corporeal was she in my eyes. Nowadays you see legs, ankles, and I don't know what. You undress the women you are in love with. In my eyes, as Alphonse Karr said — and he was a good writer — 'the one I loved was always draped in robes of bronze.' We never thought of doing so; we tried to veil her nakedness, like Noah's good-natured son. Oh, well, you can't understand."

"Don't pay any attention to him. Go on," said one of them.

"Well, I danced for the most part with her, and did not notice how time was passing. The musicians kept playing the same mazurka tunes over and over again in desperate exhaustion — you know what it is towards the end of a ball. Papas and mammas were already getting up from the card-tables in the drawing-room in expectation of supper, the men-servants were running to and fro bringing in things. It was nearly three o'clock. I had to make the most of the last minutes. I chose her again for the mazurka, and for the hundredth time we danced across the room.

" 'The quadrille after supper is mine,' I said, taking her to her place.

" 'Of course, if I am not carried off home,' she said, with a smile.

" 'I won't give you up,' I said.

" 'Give me my fan, anyhow,' she answered.

" 'I am so sorry to part with it,' I said, handing her a cheap white fan.

" 'Well, here's something to console you,' she said, plucking a feather out of the fan, and giving it to me.

"I took the feather, and could only express my rapture and gratitude with my eyes. I was not only pleased and gay, I was happy, delighted; I was good, I was not myself but some being not of this earth, knowing nothing of evil. I hid the feather in my glove, and stood there unable to tear myself away from her.

" 'Look, they are urging father to dance,' she said to me, pointing to the tall, stately figure of her father, a colonel with silver epaulettes, who was standing in the doorway with some ladies.

" 'Varinka, come here!' exclaimed our hostess, the lady with the diamond *ferronnière*[4] and with shoulders like Elizabeth, in a loud voice.

"Varinka went to the door, and I followed her.

" 'Persuade your father to dance the mazurka with you, *ma chère.*[5]—Do, please, Peter Valdislavovich,' she said, turning to the colonel.

"Varinka's father was a very handsome, well-preserved old man. He had a good colour, moustaches curled in the style of Nicolas I,[6] and white whiskers which met the moustaches. His hair was combed on to his forehead, and a bright smile, like his daughter's, was on his lips and in his eyes. He was splendidly set up, with a broad military chest, on which he wore some decorations, and he had powerful shoulders and long slim legs. He was that ultra-military type produced by the discipline of Emperor Nicolas I.

"When we approached the door the colonel was just refusing to dance, saying that he had quite forgotten how; but at that instant he smiled, swung his arm gracefully around to the left, drew his sword from its sheath, handed it to an obliging young man who stood near, and smoothed his suède glove on his right hand.

" 'Everything must be done according to rule,' he said with a smile. He took the hand of his daughter, and stood one-quarter turned, waiting for the music.

"At the first sound of the mazurka, he stamped one foot smartly, threw the other forward, and, at first slowly and smoothly, then buoyantly and impetuously, with stamping of feet and clicking of boots, his tall, imposing figure moved the length of the room. Varinka swayed gracefully beside him, rhythmically and easily, making her steps short or long, with her little feet in their white satin slippers.

"All the people in the room followed every movement of the couple. As for me I not only admired, I regarded them with enraptured sympathy. I was particularly impressed with the old gentleman's boots. They were not the modern pointed affairs, but were made of cheap leather, squared-toed, and evidently built by the regimental cobbler. In order that his daughter might dress and go out in society, he did not buy fashionable boots, but wore home-made ones, I thought, and his square toes seemed to me most touching. It was obvious that in his time he had been a good dancer; but now he was too heavy, and his legs had not spring enough for all the beautiful steps he tried to take. Still, he contrived to go twice round the room. When at the end, standing with legs apart, he suddenly clicked his feet together and fell on one knee, a bit heavily, and she danced gracefully around him, smiling and adjusting her skirt, the whole room applauded.

"Rising with an effort, he tenderly took his daughter's face between his hands. He kissed her on the forehead, and brought her to me, under the impression that I was her partner for the mazurka. I said I was not. 'Well, never mind. Just go around the room once with her,' he said, smiling kindly, as he replaced his sword in the sheath.

"As the contents of a bottle flow readily when the first drop has been poured, so my love for Varinka seemed to set free the whole force of loving within me. In surrounding her it embraced the world. I loved the hostess with her

[4] A headband that is worn in a circle around the forehead. — Eds.

[5] French for "my dear." — Eds.

[6] Nicholas I (1796–1855) reigned as Emperor of Russia, King of Poland, and Grand Duke of Finland from 1825 until his death. An autocratic ruler, he waged several wars over the course of his reign. — Eds.

Winslow Homer, Great Russian Ball at Academy of Music–Nov. 5, 1863, n.d., lithograph, Smithsonian American Art Museum, Gift of International Business Machines Corporation, 1966.48.67

This lithograph depicts a Russian ball during the mid-nineteenth century.

How does the artist characterize the dancing shown here? How does this depiction illustrate a link between the two main events in Tolstoy's story?

diadem and her shoulders like Elizabeth, and her husband and her guests and her footmen, and even the engineer Anisimov who felt peevish towards me. As for Varinka's father, with his home-made boots and his kind smile, so like her own, I felt a sort of tenderness for him that was almost rapture.

"After supper I danced the promised quadrille with her, and though I had been infinitely happy before, I grew still happier every moment.

"We did not speak of love. I neither asked myself nor her whether she loved me. It was quite enough to know that I loved her. And I had only one fear — that something might come to interfere with my great joy.

"When I went home, and began to undress for the night, I found it quite out of the question. I held the little feather out of her fan in my hand, and one of her gloves which she gave me when I helped her into the carriage after her mother. Looking at these things, and without closing my eyes I could see her before me as she was for an instant when she had to choose between two partners. She tried to guess what kind of person was represented in me, and I could hear her sweet voice as she said, 'Pride — am I right?' and merrily gave me her hand. At supper she took the first sip from my glass of champagne, looking at me over the rim with her caressing glance. But, plainest of all, I could see her as she danced with her father, gliding along beside him, and looking at the admiring observers with pride and happiness.

"He and she were united in my mind in one rush of pathetic tenderness.

"I was living then with my brother, who has since died. He disliked going out, and never went to dances; and besides, he was busy preparing for his last university examinations, and was leading a very regular life. He was asleep. I looked at him, his head burled in the pillow and half covered with the quilt; and I affectionately pitied him—pitied him for his ignorance of the bliss I was experiencing. Our serf[7] Petrusha had met me with a candle, ready to undress me, but I sent him away. His sleepy face and tousled hair seemed to me so touching. Trying not to make a noise, I went to my room on tiptoe and sat down on my bed. No, I was too happy; I could not sleep. Besides, it was too hot in the rooms. Without taking off my uniform, I went quietly into the hall, put on my overcoat, opened the front door and stepped out into the street.

"It was after four when I had left the ball; going home and stopping there a while had

[7] An agricultural laborer bound to work on the land of a lord. — Eds.

occupied two hours, so by the time I went out it was dawn. It was regular carnival weather — foggy, and the road full of water-soaked snow just melting, and water dripping from the eaves. Varinka's family lived on the edge of town near a large field, one end of which was a parade ground: at the other end was a boarding-school for young ladies. I passed through our empty little street and came to the main thoroughfare, where I met pedestrians and sledges laden with wood, the runners grating the road. The horses swung with regular paces beneath their shining yokes, their backs covered with straw mats and their heads wet with rain; while the drivers, in enormous boots, splashed through the mud beside the sledges. All this, the very horses themselves, seemed to me stimulating and fascinating, full of suggestion.

"When I approached the field near their house, I saw at one end of it, in the direction of the parade ground, something very huge and black, and I heard sounds of fife and drum proceeding from it. My heart had been full of song, and I had heard in imagination the tune of the mazurka, but this was very harsh music. It was not pleasant.

" 'What can that be?' I thought, and went towards the sound by a slippery path through the centre of the field. Walking about a hundred paces, I began to distinguish many black objects through the mist. They were evidently soldiers. 'It is probably a drill,' I thought.

"So I went along in that direction in company with a blacksmith, who wore a dirty coat and an apron, and was carrying something. He walked ahead of me as we approached the place. The soldiers in black uniforms stood in two rows, facing each other motionless, their guns at rest. Behind them stood the fifes and drums, incessantly repeating the same unpleasant tune.

" 'What are they doing?' I asked the blacksmith, who halted at my side.

" 'A Tartar[8] is being beaten through the ranks for his attempt to desert,' said the blacksmith in an angry tone, as he looked intently at the far end of the line.

"I looked in the same direction, and saw between the files something horrid approaching me. The thing that approached was a man, stripped to the waist, fastened with cords to the guns of two soldiers who were leading him. At his side an officer in overcoat and cap was walking, whose figure had a familiar look. The victim advanced under the blows that rained upon him from both sides, his whole body plunging, his feet dragging through the snow. Now he threw himself backward, and the subalterns who led him thrust him forward. Now he fell forward, and they pulled him up short; while ever at his side marched the tall officer, with firm and nervous pace. It was Varinka's father, with his rosy face and white moustache.

"At each stroke the man, as if amazed, turned his face, grimacing with pain, towards the side whence the blow came, and showing his white teeth repeated the same words over and over. But I could only hear what the words were when he came quite near. He did not speak them, he sobbed them out,—

" 'Brothers, have mercy on me! Brothers, have mercy on me!' But the brothers had no mercy, and when the procession came close to me, I saw how a soldier who stood opposite me took a firm step forward and lifting his stick with a whirr, brought it down upon the man's back. The man plunged forward, but the subalterns pulled him back, and another blow came down from the other side, then from this side and then from the other. The colonel marched beside him, and looking now at his feet and now at the man, inhaled the air, puffed out his cheeks, and breathed it out between his protruded lips. When they passed the place where I stood,

[8] Tartars, or Tatars, is an umbrella term for various Turkic ethnic groups in Northern and Central Asia. — Eds.

I caught a glimpse between the two files of the back of the man that was being punished. It was something so many-coloured, wet, red, unnatural, that I could hardly believe it was a human body.

" 'My God!' muttered the blacksmith.

"The procession moved farther away. The blows continued to rain upon the writhing, falling creature; the fifes shrilled and the drums beat, and the tall imposing figure of the colonel moved alongside the man, just as before. Then, suddenly, the colonel stopped, and rapidly approached a man in the ranks.

" 'I'll teach you to hit him gently,' I heard his furious voice say. 'Will you pat him like that? Will you?' and I saw how his strong hand in the suède glove struck the weak, bloodless, terrified soldier for not bringing down his stick with sufficient strength on the red neck of the Tartar.

" 'Bring new sticks!' he cried, and looking round, he saw me. Assuming an air of not knowing me, and with a ferocious, angry frown, he hastily turned away. I felt so utterly ashamed that I didn't know where to look. It was as if I had been detected in a disgraceful act. I dropped my eyes, and quickly hurried home. All the way I had the drums beating and the fifes whistling in my ears. And I heard the words, 'Brothers, have mercy on me!' or 'Will you pat him? Will you?' My heart was full of physical disgust that was almost sickness. So much so that I halted several times on my way, for I had the feeling that I was going to be really sick from all the horrors that possessed me at that sight. I do not remember how I got home and got to bed. But the moment I was about to fall asleep I heard and saw again all that had happened, and I sprang up.

" 'Evidently he knows something I do not know,' I thought about the colonel. 'If I knew what he knows I should certainly grasp — understand — what I have just seen, and it would not cause me such suffering.'

"But however much I thought about it, I could not understand the thing that the colonel knew. It was evening before I could get to sleep, and then only after calling on a friend and drinking till I was quite drunk.

"Do you think I had come to the conclusion that the deed I had witnessed was wicked? Oh, no. Since it was done with such assurance, and was recognised by every one as indispensable, they doubtless knew something which I did not know. So I thought, and tried to understand. But no matter, I could never understand it, then or afterwards.

And not being able to grasp it, I could not enter the service as I had intended. I don't mean only the military service: I did not enter the Civil Service either. And so I have been of no use whatever, as you can see."

SPUTNIK/Alamy

This image is the cover of an edition of Tolstoy's story that was published in 1926. **What does the choice of this image for the cover suggest about the story itself? Do you think it captures what's most important about the story? Explain why or why not.**

"Yes, we know how useless you've been," said one of us. "Tell us, rather, how many people would be of any use at all if it hadn't been for you."

"Oh, that's utter nonsense," said Ivan Vasilievich, with genuine annoyance.

65 "Well; and what about the love affair?"

"My love? It decreased from that day. When, as often happened, she looked dreamy and meditative, I instantly recollected the colonel on the parade ground, and I felt so awkward and uncomfortable that I began to see her less frequently. So my love came to naught. Yes; such chances arise, and they alter and direct a man's whole life," he said in summing up. "And you say . . ." ■

1903

Understanding and Interpreting

1. **AP® Character and Narration.** In paragraph 2, the narrator reveals that he and Vasilievich have been discussing the impossibility of "improving individual character." What answer does Vasilievich's story give to that question?
2. **AP® Character and Narration.** How does Vasilievich characterize Varinka B.? What particular qualities does he find the most appealing? What does this perspective, in turn, reveal about Vasilievich?
3. **AP® Setting.** What do the customs of the dance suggest about the values and cultural norms of the aristocratic class? Why, for instance, is it difficult for Vasilievich to dance with Varinka?
4. **AP® Narration.** What causes Vaslievich to be awake and therefore privy to the torture of the Tartar deserter? How does that state affect his response to what he witnesses?
5. **AP® Character and Narration.** What might Tolstoy have intended by having Vasilievich walk to the scene of the beating with a blacksmith, who is described in paragraph 49 as wearing a "dirty coat and an apron, and was carrying something"? Why might the blacksmith have "walked ahead" as they approached the scene? What is the blacksmith's response to what they witness, and why is the response significant?
6. **AP® Character and Narration.** Why do you think Vasilievich thinks, on observing the beating of the Tartar, that he "had been detected in a disgraceful act" (par. 58)? What might be suggested by the fact that Varinka's father doesn't meet Vasilievich's eye and, in fact, "hastily turned away" (par. 58)?
7. **AP® Character.** In paragraph 61 Vasilievich asks, "Do you think I had come to the conclusion that the deed I had witnessed was wicked?" He answers himself, "Oh no." Why does he come to that conclusion? Do you believe him? Does he believe himself? Explain.
8. **AP® Character and Narration.** How does that conclusion of "After the Dance" respond to the question posed at the beginning of the story, whether man can understand "what is good and evil"? In your response, consider the distinction Ivan Vasilievich makes between the "environment" and "chance." How does the story reveal that distinction?

Analyzing Language, Style, and Structure

1. **Vocabulary in Context.** In paragraph 20 Vasilievich accuses his listeners of being "moderns," saying, "the more I was in love the less corporeal was she in my eyes." What is the meaning of *corporeal* in this context, and how does Vasilievich's view of Varinka B. as less corporeal add to his characterization?
2. **AP® Structure and Narration.** What is the effect of the story within a story? How do the occasional interruptions from the listeners help shape the story Vasilievich tells?

3. **AP® Character, Structure, and Narration.** What details does Vasilievich supply to develop the setting of the dance and the social rules that governed attendees' behavior? How does his fascination with Varinka B. round out that self-portrait?
4. **AP® Character and Figurative Language.** What do you make of Varinka B. giving Vasilievich a feather and later her glove? What meaning might those two items have?
5. **AP® Character and Structure.** What qualities are revealed about Varinka B.'s father as Vasilievich watches him dance? What do we learn about his physical attributes? His financial situation? His relationship with his daughter? Does anything foreshadow the brutal behavior to come? Explain why or why not.
6. **AP® Structure.** Vasilievich sees "something very huge and black" as he approaches the scene of the beating and hears fife and drum music that he describes as "very harsh music" (par. 47). How does this moment contrast with the dance Vasilievich has just been to? What does he think he's about to see?
7. **AP® Figurative Language.** Critics have compared the torture of the Tartar to the torment and crucifixion of Jesus. What parallels do you see in this scene? How, for instance, do the Tartar's words echo the words of Jesus?
8. **AP® Character, Narration, and Figurative Language.** What does it say about Vasilievich that he describes the man being tortured as a "thing" (par. 52)? When does the "thing" become human? What are the consequences of that shift in perspective? How does this moment reflect a larger theme in the story?

Topics for Composing

1. **AP® FRQ Prose Fiction Analysis.** The following question refers to paragraphs 47–59 of Leo Tolstoy's "After the Dance," published in 1903. In this passage, the narrator witnesses the torture of soldier accused of desertion. Read the passage carefully. Then, in a well-written essay, analyze how Tolstoy uses literary elements and techniques to develop the narrator's complex attitude toward the event.
2. **AP® FRQ Literary Argument.** In many works of literature, conflict arises when the protagonist must consider the question of how good and evil shapes his or her environment and behavior. "After the Dance" examines that question through the lens of an old man's recollection of an event in his youth that forced him to confront these issues on a personal level. In a well-written essay, analyze how the narrator's understanding of good and evil contributes to your interpretation of the work as a whole. Do not merely summarize the plot.
3. **Connections.** Tolstoy is considered a realist writer. Realism in the arts is the attempt to represent subject matter truthfully, avoiding artistic conventions, exotic, and supernatural elements. How does "After the Dance" fit the requirements for realist literature? What do you think is truthful about the story? Do you think it avoids the exotic? Explain why or why not.
4. **Connections.** What, ultimately, do you think is Tolstoy's message in "After the Dance"? Why might it be required reading for high school students in Russia? What aspects of the story might be especially important for high school students there?
5. **Creative Writing.** Using the structure of "After the Dance" as a model, write a story that takes place in the present-day United States. It does not have to have the same plot or themes as Tolstoy's story, but be sure to incorporate a set of parallel and contrasting scenes that work together to illustrate a major theme of your story.
6. **Connections.** How does "After the Dance" use Vasilievich's reflections on the concepts of good and evil to develop a perspective on social class and ethnic divisions?

7. **Research.** Peter the Great, ruler of Russia from 1682 to 1725, expanded Russia's land, modernized society, and led a cultural revolution that included bringing the formal dance, or assembly, to Russian society. For the next century or so, being able to dance was a social and professional advantage. Research the heyday of the formal dance, looking carefully at how it reflected the values of a society that was eventually primed for the revolution that began in 1905, just two years after "After the Dance" was published.

The Shawl

Cynthia Ozick

Ulf Andersen/Getty Images

The child of Lithuanian immigrants, Cynthia Ozick (b. 1928), was strongly influenced by both the literature of her Jewish tradition and the New York writings of Henry James. She earned a BA at New York University and an MA in English literature at Ohio State University, and then went on to publish numerous novels, short story collections, and essay collections. Published in 1980 in the *New Yorker* and selected for inclusion in *The Best American Short Stories of the Century* (1999), "The Shawl" is Ozick's most famous story.

KEY CONTEXT "The Shawl" centers on the brutality of the Nazi concentration camps during World War II, a period known as the Holocaust, which resulted in the genocide of 6 million Jewish people and millions of other "undesirables" — including Slavic and Polish people, Romani, the physically and developmentally disabled, LGBTQ+ people, and communists. Beginning with its rise to power in 1933, Germany's Nazi regime promoted and enforced a strict racial hierarchy that favored "Aryans" (non-Jewish white people) and stripped away the rights of all others. As the 1930s continued, the Nazis enacted progressively more violent antisemitic policies, one of which required all Jewish people to wear a yellow Star of David visible on their clothing. As Germany began to invade neighboring nations in 1939, leading to the start of World War II, the violence against people not considered "Aryan" quickly intensified. By the time Germany surrendered to the Allied nations in 1945, its Nazi regime had established over one thousand concentration camps throughout Europe. In these camps, Jewish people and other "undesirables" were starved, forced to labor, experimented on, and — at six extermination camps in central Europe between 1939 and 1945 — murdered en masse. This story takes place on a forced march to and in a concentration camp; it is based on a real event, briefly mentioned in journalist William L. Shirer's book *The Rise and Fall of the Third Reich*.

Stella, cold, cold, the coldness of hell. How they walked on the roads together, Rosa with Magda curled up between sore breasts, Magda wound up in the shawl. Sometimes Stella carried Magda. But she was jealous of Magda. A thin girl of fourteen, too small, with thin breasts of her own, Stella wanted to be wrapped in a shawl, hidden away, asleep, rocked by the march, a baby, a round infant in arms. Magda took Rosa's nipple, and Rosa never stopped walking, a walking cradle. There was not enough milk; sometimes Magda sucked air; then she screamed. Stella was ravenous. Her knees were tumors on sticks, her elbows chicken bones.

Rosa did not feel hunger; she felt light, not like someone walking but like someone in a faint, in trance, arrested in a fit, someone who is already a floating angel, alert and seeing everything, but in the air, not there, not touching the road. As if teetering on the tips of her fingernails. She looked into Magda's face through a gap in the shawl: a squirrel in a nest, safe, no one could reach her inside the little house of the shawl's windings. The face, very round, a pocket mirror of a face: but it was not Rosa's bleak complexion, dark like cholera, it was another kind of face altogether, eyes blue as air, smooth feathers of hair nearly as yellow as the Star sewn into Rosa's coat. You could think she was one of *their* babies.

Rosa, floating, dreamed of giving Magda away in one of the villages. She could leave the line for a minute and push Magda into the hands of any woman on the side of the road. But if she moved out of line they might shoot. And even if she fled the line for half a second and pushed the shawl-bundle at a stranger, would the woman take it? She might be surprised, or afraid; she might drop the shawl, and Magda would fall out and strike her head and die. The little round head. Such a good child, she gave up screaming, and sucked now only for the taste of the drying nipple itself. The neat grip of the tiny gums. One mite of a tooth tip sticking up in the bottom gum, how shining, an elfin tombstone of white marble, gleaming there. Without complaining, Magda relinquished Rosa's teats, first the left, then the right; both were cracked, not a sniff of milk. The duct crevice extinct, a dead volcano, blind eye, chill hole, so Magda took the corner of the shawl and milked it instead. She sucked and sucked, flooding the threads with wetness. The shawl's good flavor, milk of linen.

It was a magic shawl, it could nourish an infant for three days and three nights. Magda did not die, she stayed alive, although very quiet. A peculiar smell, of cinnamon and almonds, lifted out of her mouth. She held her eyes open every moment, forgetting how to blink or nap, and Rosa and sometimes Stella studied their blueness. On the road they raised one burden of a leg after another and studied Magda's face. "Aryan," Stella said, in a voice grown as thin as a string; and Rosa thought how Stella gazed at Magda like a young cannibal. And the time that Stella said "Aryan," it sounded to Rosa as if Stella had really said, "Let us devour her."

5 But Magda lived to walk. She lived that long, but she did not walk very well, partly because

Artokoloro/Alamy

This 1919 painting by Italian artist Amadeo Modigliani was used as the cover design for an edition of Ozick's short story collection *The Shawl*.

How do the colors, composition, and woman's gaze contribute to the mood of the painting? How effectively does it capture the character of Rosa in "The Shawl"? Explain.

she was only fifteen months old, and partly because the spindles of her legs could not hold up her fat belly. It was fat with air, full and round. Rosa gave almost all her food to Magda, Stella gave nothing; Stella was ravenous, a growing child herself, but not growing much. Stella did not menstruate. Rosa did not menstruate. Rosa was ravenous, but also not; she learned from Magda how to drink the taste of a finger in one's mouth. They were in a place without pity, all pity was annihilated in Rosa, she looked at Stella's bones without pity. She was sure that Stella was waiting for Magda to die so she could put her teeth into the little thighs.

Rosa knew Magda was going to die very soon; she should have been dead already, but she had been buried away deep inside the magic shawl, mistaken there for the shivering mound of Rosa's breasts; Rosa clung to the shawl as if it covered only herself. No one took it away from her. Magda was mute. She never cried. Rosa hid her in the barracks, under the shawl, but she knew that one day someone would inform; or one day someone, not even Stella, would steal Magda to eat her. When Magda began to walk Rosa knew that Magda was going to die very soon, something would happen. She was afraid to fall asleep; she slept with the weight of her thigh on Magda's body; she was afraid she would smother Magda under her thigh. The weight of Rosa was becoming less and less, Rosa and Stella were slowly turning into air.

Magda was quiet, but her eyes were horribly alive, like blue tigers. She watched. Sometimes she laughed —it seemed a laugh, but how could it be? Magda had never seen anyone laugh. Still, Magda laughed at her shawl when the wind blew its corners, the bad wind with pieces of black in it, that made Stella's and Rosa's eyes tear. Magda's eyes were always clear and tearless. She watched like a tiger. She guarded her shawl. No one could touch it; only Rosa could touch it. Stella was not allowed. The shawl was Magda's own baby, her pet, her little sister. She tangled herself up in it and sucked on one of the corners when she wanted to be very still.

Then Stella took the shawl away and made Magda die.

Afterward Stella said: "I was cold."

And afterward she was always cold, always. 10
The cold went into her heart: Rosa saw that Stella's heart was cold. Magda flopped onward with her little pencil legs scribbling this way and that, in search of the shawl; the pencils faltered at the barracks opening, where the light began. Rosa saw and pursued. But already Magda was in the square outside the barracks, in the jolly light. It was the roll-call arena. Every morning Rosa had to conceal Magda under the shawl against a wall of the barracks and go out and stand in the arena with Stella and hundreds of others, sometimes for hours, and Magda, deserted, was quiet under the shawl, sucking on her corner. Every day Magda was silent, and so she did not die. Rosa saw that today Magda was going to die, and at the same time a fearful joy ran in Rosa's two palms, her fingers were on fire, she was astonished, febrile: Magda, in the sunlight, swaying on her pencil legs, was howling. Ever since the drying up of Rosa's nipples, ever since Magda's last scream on the road, Magda had been devoid of any syllable; Magda was a mute. Rosa believed that something had gone wrong with her vocal cords, with her windpipe, with the cave of her larynx; Magda was defective, without a voice; perhaps she was deaf; there might be something amiss with her intelligence; Magda was dumb. Even the laugh that came when the ash-stippled wind made a clown out of Magda's shawl was only the air-blown showing of her teeth. Even when the lice, head lice and body lice, crazed her so that she became as wild as one of the big rats that plundered the barracks at daybreak looking for carrion, she rubbed and scratched and kicked and bit and rolled without a whimper. But now Magda's mouth was spilling a long viscous rope of clamor.

"Maaaa—"

It was the first noise Magda had ever sent out from her throat since the drying up of Rosa's nipples.

"Maaaa . . . aaa!"

Again! Magda was wavering in the perilous sunlight of the arena, scribbling on such pitiful little bent shins. Rosa saw. She saw that Magda was grieving the loss of her shawl, she saw that Magda was going to die. A tide of commands hammered in Rosa's nipples: Fetch, get, bring! But she did not know which to go after first, Magda or the shawl. If she jumped out into the arena to snatch Magda up, the howling would not stop, because Magda would still not have the shawl; but if she ran back into the barracks to find the shawl, and if she found it, and if she came after Magda holding it and shaking it, then she would get Magda back, Magda would put the shawl in her mouth and turn dumb again.

15 Rosa entered the dark. It was easy to discover the shawl. Stella was heaped under it, asleep in her thin bones. Rosa tore the shawl free and flew—she could fly, she was only air—into the arena. The sunheat murmured of another life, of butterflies in summer. The light was placid, mellow. On the other side of the steel fence, far away, there were green meadows speckled with dandelions and deep-colored violets; beyond them, even farther, innocent tiger lilies, tall, lifting their orange bonnets. In the barracks they spoke of "flowers," of "rain": excrement, thick turd-braids, and the slow stinking maroon waterfall that slunk down from the upper bunks, the stink mixed with a bitter fatty floating smoke that greased Rosa's skin. She stood for an instant at the margin of the arena. Sometimes the electricity inside the fence would seem to hum; even Stella said it was only an imagining, but Rosa heard real sounds in the wire: grainy sad voices. The farther she was from the fence, the more clearly the voices crowded at her. The lamenting voices strummed so convincingly, so passionately, it was impossible to suspect them of being phantoms. The voices told her to hold up the shawl, high; the voices told her to shake it, to whip with it, to unfurl it like a flag. Rosa lifted, shook, whipped, unfurled. Far off, very far, Magda leaned across her air-fed belly, reaching out with the rods of her arms. She was high up, elevated, riding someone's shoulder. But the shoulder that carried Magda was not coming toward Rosa and the shawl, it was drifting away, the speck of Magda was moving more and more into the smoky distance. Above the shoulder a helmet glinted. A light tapped the helmet and

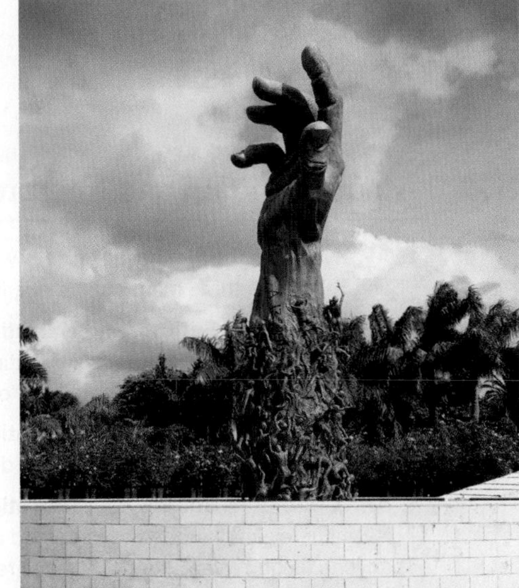

Photographs in the Carol M. Highsmith Archive, Library of Congress, Prints and Photographs Division.

Kenneth Treister (b. 1930), an American architect and artist, created this sculpture for the Holocaust Memorial in Miami Beach, Florida. He has written about the enormity and honor of this commission: "The immensity of this tragedy is infinite. To express it artistically, impossible . . . but I had to try." The sculpture is often referred to as "the sculpture of love and anguish."

How do you think this sculpture embodies Treister's description of its meaning? How does the symbolism of this artwork reflect Ozick's depiction of both horror and courage in "The Shawl"?

sparkled it into a goblet. Below the helmet a black body like a domino and a pair of black boots hurled themselves in the direction of the electrified fence. The electric voices began to chatter wildly. "Maamaa, maaamaaa," they all hummed together. How far Magda was from Rosa now, across the whole square, past a dozen barracks, all the way on the other side! She was no bigger than a moth.

All at once Magda was swimming through the air. The whole of Magda traveled through loftiness. She looked like a butterfly touching a silver vine. And the moment Magda's feathered round head and her pencil legs and balloonish belly and zigzag arms splashed against the fence, the steel voices went mad in their growling, urging Rosa to run and run to the spot where Magda had fallen from her flight against the electrified fence; but of course Rosa did not obey them. She only stood, because if she ran they would shoot, and if she tried to pick up the sticks of Magda's body they would shoot, and if she let the wolf's screech ascending now through the ladder of her skeleton break out, they would shoot; so she took Magda's shawl and filled her own mouth with it, stuffed it in and stuffed it in, until she was swallowing up the wolf's screech and tasting the cinnamon and almond depth of Magda's saliva; and Rosa drank Magda's shawl until it dried. ■

1980

Understanding and Interpreting

1. **AP® Narration and Character.** How would you describe the interaction of Rosa, Magda, and Stella, the three main characters, in the opening paragraphs of the story?
2. **AP® Character, Setting, and Narration.** In the story's opening section, the three characters are on a forced march to a concentration camp. What does it mean that Magda's blonde hair and blue eyes suggest she could be "one of *their* babies" (par. 2)?
3. **AP® Character, Setting, and Narration.** What options does Rosa consider for her daughter as they get closer to the camp? Why does she make the choice that she does?
4. **AP® Character, Setting, and Narration.** In paragraph 7, Cynthia Ozick writes of Magda, "Sometimes she laughed — it seemed a laugh, but how could it be? Magda had never seen anyone laugh." What does this detail reveal about the setting? What does it suggest about events that may have taken place prior to the opening scene of the story?
5. **AP® Character and Setting.** Why doesn't Rosa try to rescue Magda when she runs out of the barracks? Why is it that Rosa "only stood" (par. 16) after the soldiers murder Magda? Was that an act of courage, shock, fear, or something else? Explain.
6. **AP® Character, Setting, and Narration.** In what ways do the setting and plot of the story undermine the three main characters' ability to act out their roles as mother, baby daughter, and niece?

Analyzing Language, Style, and Structure

1. **Vocabulary in Context.** In paragraph 10, Ozick describes Rosa's recognition that Magda was going to die: ". . . a fearful joy ran in Rosa's two palms, her fingers were on fire, she was astonished, febrile." What is the definition of the word "febrile"? How does it characterize Rosa? What impact does it have at the end of the sentence rather than the beginning?

2. **AP® Structure and Narration.** The narrative perspective of "The Shawl" is third-person omniscient. How would your experience of the story be different if Ozick had told it from the first-person perspective of Rosa?
3. **AP® Figurative Language.** Note the rich use of imagery and figurative language in the first three paragraphs. What is the effect of the "chicken bones," the "little house," and the "elfin tombstone," for example? How does the imagery contribute to your interpretation of the story as a whole?
4. **AP® Structure and Narration.** Paragraphs 8 and 9 are single sentences: "Then Stella took the shawl away and made Magda die." "Afterward Stella said: 'I was cold.'" The next paragraph opens, "And afterward she was always cold, always." What is the importance of the reader being catapulted into the future by this sequence of lines? How does this interruption of the chronological sequence of events contribute to overall meaning?
5. **AP® Figurative Language.** Animal imagery is threaded throughout the story. Identify at least four examples. How are these effective individually? How do they work cumulatively or collectively?
6. **AP® Character, Narration, and Figurative Language.** What effect does Ozick create by describing the Nazi soldier who murders Magda in terms of his helmet and his "black body like a domino and a pair of black boots" (par. 15)?
7. **AP® Structure and Narration.** In paragraph 15, how does Ozick take readers into Rosa's surreal and imagined world, yet simultaneously keep her in the very real environment of the "arena"? What is the effect of this juxtaposition?
8. **AP® Structure and Narration.** How would you characterize the effect of the syntax in the final paragraph? What is Ozick's purpose in ending the story in this way?
9. **AP® Figurative Language.** What associations does a shawl have? In what ways is it ambiguous? Do you agree with Ozick's choice of a title for the story? Why, or why not?
10. **AP® Setting and Figurative Language.** A setting may become symbolic when it is association with ideologies or beliefs. In what ways does the concentration camp itself assume symbolic meaning that contributes to the themes of "The Shawl"?

Topics for Composing

1. **AP® FRQ Prose Fiction Analysis.** The following question refers to paragraphs 3–6 of Cynthia Ozick's "The Shawl," published in 1980. In this passage, Ozick describes the desperate struggle for survival in a Nazi concentration camp. Read the passage carefully. Then, in a well-written essay, analyze how Ozick uses literary elements and techniques to convey the characters' efforts to retain their humanity in a dehumanizing environment.
2. **AP® FRQ Literary Argument.** In many works of literature, symbols often convey both a literal meaning and a deeper philosophical truth that extends beyond the immediate context of the narrative. In "The Shawl," the title immediately introduces what is usually thought of as a functional article of clothing. As the story builds, the meaning of the shawl shifts and evolves into a rich and complex symbol. In a well-written essay, analyze how the symbol of the shawl contributes to an interpretation of the work as a whole. Do not merely summarize the plot.
3. **AP® Literary Argumentation.** Are there mitigating circumstances that make Stella's theft of the shawl understandable or acceptable, or is she a selfish character responsible for the death of Magda? Or, in your view, are this character and her motivations more complex than these possibilities? Explain how your interpretation of Stella reflects an overall theme of "The Shawl."

4. **AP® Literary Argumentation.** Ozick describes the suffering of Magda and her eventual death almost lyrically. For instance, Rosa thinks that something had gone wrong with Magda's vocal cords, "with the cave of her larynx"; she describes her as being "like a butterfly touching a silver vine." One reviewer commented that the "perspective of this grotesque poetry reflects the extremity of the horror of the Holocaust itself." Do you agree with the characterization of Ozick's language as "grotesque poetry"? If so, in what ways might it be interpreted as reflecting the "horror of the Holocaust itself"? Cite additional examples to support your position.
5. **Connections.** Three years after the publication of "The Shawl," Ozick published *Rosa*, a novella that takes place thirty years later and includes both Rosa, living isolated and alone in Florida, and her niece Stella, who lives in New York City and provides financial support for Rosa. Read the sequel. How does it present a plausible future for these two characters as we know them in Ozick's original story? How has each character grown and changed — or failed to do so? What does Ozick's depiction of each woman reveal about her perspective on the themes of "The Shawl"?
6. **Research.** Antisemitism prompted many Jewish people from Eastern and Central Europe to emigrate to the United States in the late 1800s and early 1900s. By the turn of the century, many cities had thriving Jewish communities, but after World War I, Congress passed a series of laws to severely restrict the immigration of "undesirable" groups, including Jewish and Chinese people, which remained in place until 1965. Research these immigration laws and their effect on the Jewish refugees who began to apply for asylum in the United States during the 1930s. How did the U.S. government respond to this crisis? What was the Roosevelt administration's response to learning of the death camps during World War II? Based on your research, what lessons does history have to offer us about our nation's relationship to the rest of the world? What kinds of stories do humans tend to tell about persecution, survival, and victory over oppression — and how do these stories relate to your research?
7. **Connections.** One way to characterize "The Shawl" is as the literature of witness — that is, a work that remembers or memorializes those whose lives were lost to acts of injustice. In some cases, these texts pay tribute to an individual; in others, a group. Most see literature of witness, despite the difficulty of its subject matter, as a hopeful genre. In an essay for *AWP Magazine*, Ian King, a professor of politics and international relations, wrote that literature of witness must

   > observe things that need pointing out, and . . . motivate us to act . . . to remedy something. These qualifications to observation as an act of witness necessarily invoke the use of the verb "to bear," to bear witness, not just witness (observe), to "testify" as one might do in church, to speak to the "truth" and to exhort our moral responsibility to address its demands.

   How is "The Shawl" literature of witness, according to this definition? Identify a poem, short story, or novel that you believe also exemplifies this genre. What event(s) gave rise to it? How is it similar to Ozick's story, and where do the works diverge? How — and how effectively — do the writer and the text bear witness?
8. **Research.** In *The Light of Days: The Untold Story of Women Resistance Fighters in Hitler's Ghettos* (2021), author Judy Batalion tells the forgotten stories of Polish "ghetto girls" — dozens of Jewish women who did not flee the Nazis but stayed and fought them, some leading resistance movements. After researching these women or reading Batalion's book, discuss what these "forgotten stories" reveal about the narrative of the Holocaust. How does learning of these women deepen your understanding of "The Shawl"?

The Red Convertible

Louise Erdrich

Ulf Andersen/Getty Images

Louise Erdrich (b. 1954) was born in Minnesota and is a member of the Turtle Mountain Band of Chippewa Indians. She has an AB from Dartmouth College and an MA from Johns Hopkins University. She is a novelist, short story writer, poet, and children's book author whose work often focuses on American Indian cultures and characters. Erdrich has published seventeen novels, including *Love Medicine* (1984), *The Round House* (2012), and *The Night Watchman* (2020), which won the 2021 Pulitzer Prize for fiction. She also owns Birchbark Books, an independent bookstore in Minneapolis.

KEY CONTEXT "The Red Convertible" is one of a collection of short stories about five families that Louise Erdrich published as *Love Medicine*. Featured in this story, Lyman and Henry Lamartine live on a reservation in North Dakota. Henry gets drafted to fight in the Vietnam War in the early 1970s, and he battles post-traumatic stress disorder, or PTSD, upon returning home. While people have experienced the symptoms of PTSD for thousands of years, the American Psychological Association first recognized PTSD only in 1980, and veterans of the Vietnam War were some of the first to receive an official diagnosis.

I was the first one to drive a convertible on my reservation. And of course it was red, a red Olds. I owned that car along with my brother Henry Junior. We owned it together until his boots filled with water on a windy night and he bought out my share. Now Henry owns the whole car, and his younger brother Lyman (that's myself), Lyman walks everywhere he goes.

How did I earn enough money to buy my share in the first place? My one talent was I could always make money. I had a touch for it, unusual in a Chippewa. From the first I was different that way, and everyone recognized it. I was the only kid they let in the American Legion Hall to shine shoes, for example, and one Christmas I sold spiritual bouquets for the mission door to door. The nuns let me keep a percentage. Once I started, it seemed the more money I made the easier the money came. Everyone encouraged it. When I was fifteen I got a job washing dishes at the Joliet Cafe, and that was where my first big break happened.

It wasn't long before I was promoted to busing tables, and then the short-order cook quit and I was hired to take her place. No sooner than you know it I was managing the Joliet. The rest is history. I went on managing. I soon became part owner, and of course there was no stopping me then. It wasn't long before the whole thing was mine.

After I'd owned the Joliet for one year, it blew over in the worst tornado ever seen around here. The whole operation was smashed to bits. A total loss. The fryalator was up in a tree, the grill torn in half like it was paper. I was only sixteen. I had it all in my mother's name, and I lost it quick, but before I lost it I had every one of my relatives, and their relatives, to dinner, and I also bought that red Olds I mentioned, along with Henry.

• • •

The first time we saw it! I'll tell you when we first 5
saw it. We had gotten a ride up to Winnipeg, and both of us had money. Don't ask me why, because we never mentioned a car or anything,

we just had all our money. Mine was cash, a big bankroll from the Joliet's insurance. Henry had two checks — a week's extra pay for being laid off, and his regular check from the Jewel Bearing Plant.

We were walking down Portage anyway, seeing the sights, when we saw it. There it was, parked, large as life. Really as *if* it was alive. I thought of the word *repose*, because the car wasn't simply stopped, parked, or whatever. That car reposed, calm and gleaming, a FOR SALE sign in its left front window. Then, before we had thought it over at all, the car belonged to us and our pockets were empty. We had just enough money for gas back home.

We went places in that car, me and Henry. We took off driving all one whole summer. We started off toward the Little Knife River and Mandaree in Fort Berthold and then we found ourselves down in Wakpala somehow, and then suddenly we were over in Montana on the Rocky Boy, and yet the summer was not even half over. Some people hang on to details when they travel, but we didn't let them bother us and just lived our everyday lives here to there.

I do remember this one place with willows. I remember I lay under those trees and it was comfortable. So comfortable. The branches bent down all around me like a tent or a stable. And quiet, it was quiet, even though there was a powwow close enough so I could see it going on. The air was not too still, not too windy either. When the dust rises up and hangs in the air around the dancers like that, I feel good. Henry was asleep with his arms thrown wide. Later on, he woke up and we started driving again. We were somewhere in Montana, or maybe on the Blood Reserve — it could have been anywhere. Anyway it was where we met the girl.

• • •

All her hair was in buns around her ears, that's the first thing I noticed about her. She was posed alongside the road with her arm out, so we stopped. That girl was short, so short her lumber shirt looked comical on her, like a nightgown. She had jeans on and fancy moccasins and she carried a little suitcase.

"Hop on in," says Henry. So she climbs in between us. "We'll take you home," I says. "Where do you live?" "Chicken," she says.

"Where the hell's that?" I ask her.

"Alaska."

"Okay," says Henry, and we drive.

We got up there and never wanted to leave. The sun doesn't truly set there in summer, and the night is more a soft dusk. You might doze off, sometimes, but before you know it you're up again, like an animal in nature. You never feel like you have to sleep hard or put away the world. And things would grow up there. One day just dirt or moss, the next day flowers and long grass. The girl's name was Susy. Her family really took to us. They fed us and put us up. We had our own tent to live in by their house, and the kids would be in and out of there all day and night. They couldn't get over me and Henry being brothers, we looked so different. We told them we knew we had the same mother, anyway.

One night Susy came in to visit us. We sat around in the tent talking of this and that. The season was changing. It was getting darker by that time, and the cold was even getting just a little mean. I told her it was time for us to go. She stood up on a chair.

"You never seen my hair," Susy said.

That was true. She was standing on a chair, but still, when she unclipped her buns the hair reached all the way to the ground. Our eyes opened. You couldn't tell how much hair she had when it was rolled up so neatly. Then my brother Henry did something funny. He went up to the chair and said, "Jump on my shoulders." So she did that, and her hair reached down past his waist, and he started twirling, this way and that, so her hair was flung out from side to side.

"I always wondered what it was like to have long pretty hair," Henry says. Well we laughed.

It was a funny sight, the way he did it. The next morning we got up and took leave of those people.

• • •

On to greener pastures, as they say. It was down through Spokane and across Idaho then Montana and very soon we were racing the weather right along under the Canadian border through Columbus, Des Lacs, and then we were in Bottineau County and soon home. We'd made most of the trip, that summer, without putting up the car hood at all. We got home just in time, it turned out, for the army to remember Henry had signed up to join it.

20 I don't wonder that the army was so glad to get my brother that they turned him into a Marine. He was built like a brick outhouse anyway. We liked to tease him that they really wanted him for his Indian nose. He had a nose big and sharp as a hatchet, like the nose on Red Tomahawk, the Indian who killed Sitting Bull,[1] whose profile is on signs all along the North Dakota highways. Henry went off to training camp, came home once during Christmas, then the next thing you know we got an overseas letter from him. It was 1970, and he said he was stationed up in the northern hill country. Where-abouts I did not know. He wasn't such a hot letter writer, and only got off two before the enemy caught him. I could never keep it straight, which direction those good Vietnam soldiers were from.

I wrote him back several times, even though I didn't know if those letters would get through. I kept him informed all about the car. Most of the time I had it up on blocks in the yard or half taken apart, because that long trip did a hard job on it under the hood.

I always had good luck with numbers, and never worried about the draft myself. I never even had to think about what my number was. But Henry was never lucky in the same way as me. It was at least three years before Henry came home. By then I guess the whole war was solved in the government's mind, but for him it would keep on going. In those years I'd put his car into almost perfect shape. I always thought of it as his car while he was gone, even though when he left he said, "Now it's yours," and threw me his key.

"Thanks for the extra key," I'd said. "I'll put it up in your drawer just in case I need it." He laughed.

• • •

When he came home, though, Henry was very different, and I'll say this: the change was no good. You could hardly expect him to change for the better, I know. But he was quiet, so quiet, and never comfortable sitting still anywhere but always up and moving around. I thought back to times we'd sat still for whole afternoons, never moving a muscle, just shifting our weight along the ground, talking to whoever sat with us, watching things. He'd always had a joke, then, too, and now you couldn't get him to laugh, or when he did it was more the sound of a man choking, a sound that stopped up the throats of other people around him. They got to leaving him alone most of the time, and I didn't blame them. It was a fact: Henry was jumpy and mean.

25 I'd bought a color TV set for my mom and the rest of us while Henry was away. Money still came very easy. I was sorry I'd ever fought it though, because of Henry. I was also sorry I'd bought color, because with black-and-white the pictures seem older and farther away. But what are you going to do? He sat in front of it, watching it, and that was the only time he was completely still. But it was the kind of stillness that you see in a rabbit when it freezes and before it will bolt. He was not easy. He sat in his chair gripping the armrests with all his might, as if the chair itself was moving at a high speed and if he let go at all

[1] Sitting Bull (c. 1831–1890) was a leader of the Hunkpapa Lakota Indians who resisted the U.S. government's theft of American Indian lands. He was shot and killed by Indian agency police during a fight that broke out as he was being arrested. — Eds.

Library of Congress, Prints & Photographs Division, [LC-DIG-ds-12255]

This poster by artist Robert Winkler was created in late 1973.
Consider, on a literal level, what the poster shows. Who is in the foreground, and who is in the background? How does the artist use color? What symbols do you see? Ultimately, does it tell essentially the same "story" as "The Red Convertible"? Explain.

he would rocket forward and maybe crash right through the set.

Once I was in the room watching TV with Henry and I heard his teeth click at something. I looked over, and he'd bitten through his lip. Blood was going down his chin. I tell you right then I wanted to smash that tube to pieces. I went over to it but Henry must have known what I was up to. He rushed from his chair and shoved me out of the way, against the wall. I told myself he didn't know what he was doing.

My mom came in, turned the set off real quiet, and told us she had made something for supper. So we went and sat down. There was still blood going down Henry's chin, but he didn't notice it and no one said anything even though every time he took a bite of his bread his blood fell onto it until he was eating his own blood mixed in with the food.

• • •

While Henry was not around we talked about what was going to happen to him. There were no Indian doctors on the reservation, and my mom couldn't come around to trusting the old man, Moses Pillager, because he courted her long ago and was jealous of her husbands. He might take revenge through her son. We were afraid that if we brought Henry to a regular hospital they would keep him.

"They don't fix them in those places," Mom said; "they just give them drugs."

"We wouldn't get him there in the first 30
place," I agreed, "so let's just forget about it." Then I thought about the car.

Henry had not even looked at the car since he'd gotten home, though like I said, it was in tip-top condition and ready to drive. I thought the car might bring the old Henry back somehow. So I bided my time and waited for my chance to interest him in the vehicle.

One night Henry was off somewhere. I took myself a hammer. I went out to that car and I did a number on its underside. Whacked it up. Bent the tail pipe double. Ripped the muffler loose. By the time I was done with the car it looked worse than any typical Indian car that has been driven all its life on reservation roads, which they always say are like government promises — full of holes. It just about hurt me, I'll tell you that! I threw dirt in the carburetor and I ripped all the electric tape off the seats. I made it look just as beat up as I could. Then I sat back and waited for Henry to find it.

Still, it took him over a month. That was all right, because it was just getting warm enough; not melting, but warm enough to work outside.

"Lyman," he says, walking in one day, "that red car looks like shit."

35 "Well it's old," I says. "You got to expect that."

"No way!" says Henry. "That car's a classic! But you went and ran the piss right put of it, Lyman, and you know it don't deserve that. I kept that car in A-one shape. You don't remember. You're too young. But when I left, that car was running like a watch. Now I don't even know if I can get it to start again, let alone get it anywhere near its old condition."

"Well you try," I said, like I was getting mad, "but I say it's a piece of junk."

Then I walked out before he could realize I knew he'd strung together more than six words at once.

• • •

After that I thought he'd freeze himself to death working on that car. He was out there all day, and at night he rigged up a little lamp, ran a cord out the window, and had himself some light to see by while he worked. He was better than he had been before, but that's still not saying much. It was easier for him to do the things the rest of us did. He ate more slowly and didn't jump up and down during the meal to get this or that or look out the window. I put my hand in the back of the TV set, I admit, and fiddled around with it good, so that it was almost impossible now to get a clear picture. He didn't look at it very often anyway. He was always out with that car or going off to get parts for it. By the time it was really melting outside, he had it fixed.

40 I had been feeling down in the dumps about Henry around this time. We had always been together before. Henry and Lyman. But he was such a loner now that I didn't know how to take it. So I jumped at the chance one day when Henry seemed friendly. It's not that he smiled or anything. He just said, "Let's take that old shitbox for a spin." Just the way he said it made me think he could be coming around.

We went out to the car. It was spring. The sun was shining very bright. My only sister, Bonita, who was just eleven years old, came out and made us stand together for a picture. Henry leaned his elbow on the red car's windshield, and he took his other arm and put it over my shoulder, very carefully, as though it was heavy for him to lift and he didn't want to bring the weight down all at once. "Smile," Bonita said, and he did.

• • •

That picture. I never look at it anymore. A few months ago, I don't know why, I got his picture out and tacked it on the wall. I felt good about Henry at the time, close to him. I felt good having his picture on the wall, until one night when I was looking at television. I was a little drunk and stoned. I looked up at the wall and Henry was staring at me. I don't know what it was, but his smile had changed, or maybe it was gone. All I know is I couldn't stay in the same room with that picture. I was shaking. I got up, closed the door, and went into the kitchen. A little later my friend Ray came over and we both went back into that room. We put the picture in a brown bag, folded the bag over and over tightly, then put it way back in a closet.

I still see that picture now, as if it tugs at me, whenever I pass that closet door. The picture is very clear in my mind. It was so sunny that day Henry had to squint against the glare. Or maybe the camera Bonita held flashed like a mirror, blinding him, before she snapped the picture. My face is right out in the sun, big and round. But he might have drawn back, because the shadows on his face are deep as holes. There are two shadows curved like little hooks around the ends of his smile, as if to frame it and try to keep it there — that one, first smile that looked like it might have hurt his face. He has his field jacket on and the worn-in clothes he'd come back in and kept wearing ever since. After Bonita took the picture, she went into the house and we got into the car. There was a full cooler in the trunk. We started off, east, to ward

Pembina and the Red River because Henry said he wanted to see the high water.

• • •

The trip over there was beautiful. When everything starts changing, drying up, clearing off, you feel like your whole life is starting. Henry felt it, too. The top was down and the car hummed like a top. He'd really put it back in shape, even the tape on the seats was very carefully put down and glued back in layers. It's not that he smiled again or even joked, but his face looked to me as if it was clear, more peaceful. It looked as though he wasn't thinking of anything in particular except the bare fields and windbreaks and houses we were passing.

The river was high and full of winter trash when we got there. The sun was still out, but it was colder by the river. There-were still little clumps of dirty snow here and there on the banks. The water hadn't gone over the banks yet, but it would, you could tell. It was just at its limit, hard swollen, glossy like an old gray scar. We made ourselves a fire, and we sat down and watched the current go. As I watched it I felt something squeezing inside me and tightening and trying to let go all at the same time. I knew I was not just feeling it myself; I knew I was feeling what Henry was going through at that moment. Except that I couldn't stand it, the closing and opening. I jumped to my feet. I took Henry by the shoulders, and I started shaking him. "Wake up," I says, "wake up, wake up, wake up!" I didn't know what had come over me. I sat down beside him again.

His face was totally white and hard. Then it broke, like stones break all of a sudden when water boils up inside them.

"I know it," he says. "I know it. I can't help it. It's no use."

We start talking. He said he knew what I'd done with the car. It was obvious it had been whacked out of shape and not just neglected. He said he wanted to give the car to me for good now, it was no use. He said he'd fixed it just to give it back and I should take it. "No way," I says, "I don't want it."

"That's okay," he says, "you take it."

"I don't want it, though," I says back to him, and then to emphasize, just to emphasize, you understand, I touch his shoulder. He slaps my hand off.

"Take that car," he says.

"No," I say. "Make me," I say, and then he grabs my jacket and rips the arm loose. That jacket is a class act, suede with tags and zippers. I push Henry backwards, off the log. He jumps up and bowls me over. We go down in a clinch and come up swinging hard, for all we're worth, with our fists. He socks my jaw so hard I feel like it swings loose. Then. I'm at his rib cage and. land a good one under his chin so his head snaps back. He's dazzled. He looks at me and I look at him and then his eyes are full of tears and blood and at first I think he's crying. But no, he's laughing. "Ha! Ha!" he says.

"Ha! Ha! Take good care of it."

"Okay," I says. "Okay, no problem; Ha! Ha!"

I can't help it, and I start laughing, too. My face feels fat and strange, and after a while I get a beer from the cooler in the trunk, and when I hand it to Henry he takes his shirt and wipes my germs off. "Hoof-and-mouth disease," he says. For some reason this cracks me up, and so we're really laughing for a while, and then we drink all the rest of the beers one by one and throw them in the river and see how far, how fast, the current takes them before they fill up and sink.

"You want to go on back?" I ask after a while. "Maybe we could snag a couple nice Kashpaw girls."

• • •

He says nothing. But I can tell his mood is turning again.

A view Across the River, Rick Bartow, 1987. Charcoal, pastel, and graphite on paper. Collection of the National Veterans Art Museum. Copyright @ NVAM, 2017. Photo courtesy of the National Veterans Art Museum.

A View Across the River is a painting by Rick Bartow, a member of the Mad River Band of Wiyot Indians. In a 1995 letter, Bartow wrote, "With scratches of line and bursts of color I have tried to rid myself of that nightmare and its long-reaching effects. I have tried to draw a map for myself from the past to the present, from sickness and anger to peace and health. Every day I have to work because the truce I have with darkness is delicate and peace requires constant maintenance."

Which features of Bartow's artistic depiction of his war experience and its aftermath resemble Henry's behavior after returning home?

"They're all crazy, the girls up here, every damn one of them."

"You're crazy too," I say, to jolly him up. "Crazy Lamartine boys!"

He looks as though he will take this wrong at first. His face twists, then clears, and he jumps up on his feet. "That's right!" he says. "Crazier 'n hell. Crazy Indians!"

I think it's the old Henry again. He throws off his jacket and starts springing his legs up from the knees like a fancy dancer. He's down doing something between a grass dance and a bunny hop, no kind of dance I ever saw before, but neither has anyone else on all this green growing earth. He's wild. He wants to pitch whoopee! He's up and at me and all over. All this time I'm laughing so hard, so hard my belly is getting tied up in a knot.

"Got to cool me off!" he shouts all of a sudden. Then he runs over to the river and jumps in.

There's boards and other things in the current. It's so high. No sound comes from the river after the splash he makes, so I run right over. I look around. It's getting dark. I see he's halfway across the water already, and I know he didn't swim there but the current took him. It's far. I hear his voice, though, very clearly across it.

"My boots are filling," he says.

He says this in a normal voice, like he just noticed and he doesn't know what to think of it. Then he's gone. A branch comes by. Another branch. And I go in.

• • •

By the time I get out of the river, off the snag I pulled myself onto, the sun is down. I walk back to the car, turn on the high beams, and drive it up the bank. I put it in first gear and then I take my foot off the clutch. I get out, close the door, and watch it plow softly into the water. The headlights reach in as they go down, searching, still lighted even after the water swirls over the back end. I wait. The wires short out. It is all finally dark. And then there is only the water, the sound of it going and running and going and running and running. ■

1984

Understanding and Interpreting

1. **AP® Character and Narration.** After reading the story, return to the first paragraph. What does Lyman tell readers happens to the convertible, to his brother, and to him? How does having read the story change your interpretation of the first paragraph?
2. **AP® Character and Narration.** How does Louise Erdrich develop the characters of Lyman and Henry through the telling of the summer they spent traveling in the red convertible? What do the details of their travels reveal about them and about how they relate to the people they meet?
3. **AP® Character.** How does the war alter Henry's character? How does the relationship between him and Lyman change as a result?
4. **AP® Character and Narration.** Why does Lyman think "the car might bring the old Henry back somehow" (par. 31)? How effective, ultimately, is Lyman's plan? Explain, using evidence from the text to support your response.
5. **AP® Character and Narration.** Why do you think Lyman lets the convertible go into the river? How does your understanding of his actions — or lack thereof — add to your interpretation of Lyman's statement in the first paragraph that "[n]ow Henry owns the whole car"?
6. **AP® Character and Narration.** Do you think Lyman is a reliable narrator? Consider, for example, that Lyman says, "Some people hang on to details when they travel" (par. 7), yet he also claims that neither he nor Henry let details bother them and that they "just lived our everyday lives here to there" (par. 7). How does your perception of his reliability affect your interpretation of the final scene of the story? What about your interpretation of the story's larger meaning?

Analyzing Language, Style, and Structure

1. **Vocabulary in Context.** When Lyman describes his first impressions of the red convertible, he explains, "I thought of the word *repose*, because the car wasn't simply stopped, parked, or whatever. That car reposed, calm and gleaming, a FOR SALE sign in its left front window" (par. 6). How does his use of the word "repose" contribute to Lyman's tone and the way he feels about the car?
2. **AP® Character, Structure, and Narration.** How do the opening paragraphs shape your expectations for Lyman's character throughout the rest of the story? How does he meet or upend those expectations?
3. **AP® Structure and Narration.** Lyman narrates the story as one would expect of a first-person narrator, but he refers to himself in the third person briefly in the first paragraph. What does this small detail reveal about Lyman and his perspective? Why do you think he uses the third person where he does in the story, especially given the events of the plot?
4. **AP® Structure and Narration.** Consider the effect of Lyman as a narrator, given that he largely tells Henry's story in "The Red Convertible." How does the narrative perspective specifically develop Henry's character? What does Lyman's narration of the story suggest about the relationship between veterans and civilians?
5. **AP® Structure, Narration, and Figurative Language.** Read paragraph 8 again. How do the diction and syntax in the paragraph contribute to the mood and narrative pacing? Consider repetition and imagery in particular.
6. **AP® Character and Figurative Language.** Why does the photo Bonita takes of Lyman and Henry after Henry fixes the car up again continue to affect Lyman years later? Beyond its literal significance, how might the photo have taken on a symbolic meaning for Lyman? How does its meaning change for Lyman as the years go by?

7. **AP® Character, Setting, Narration, and Figurative Language.** In paragraph 45, Lyman and Henry visit the Red River to see the high water. Reread this paragraph carefully. What does Lyman describe here, and how does his language move from the literal to the figurative? How would you describe his tone in the paragraph, and what mood does he create? What does this paragraph suggest about Lyman's character?
8. **AP® Structure and Figurative Language.** Erdrich ends "The Red Convertible" with the sentence, "And then there is only the water, the sound of it going and running and going and running and running." How does this sentence hold larger significance and relate to the story as a whole?
9. **AP® Character and Structure.** How would you describe the structure of the plot of this story? How might this structure be interpreted as a reflection of both Lyman's and Henry's emotional landscapes? How does Erdrich's use of foreshadowing affect the tone and mood of the narrative?

Topics for Composing

1. **AP® FRQ Prose Fiction Analysis.** The following question refers to paragraphs 4–16 of Louise Erdrich's "The Red Convertible," published in 1984. In this passage, Lyman, the protagonist, describes how he and his brother came to own a red convertible and the role it played in their travels that summer. Read the passage carefully. Then, in a well-written essay, analyze how Erdrich uses literary elements and techniques to convey the significance of the convertible to Lyman and to develop his character.
2. **AP® FRQ Literary Argument.** We often develop strong connections to personal possessions, and some personal possessions even take on a symbolic significance in our lives. In "The Red Convertible," the car Henry and Lyman Lamartine share provides them with not only a form of transportation, but it also takes on symbolic meaning, especially for Lyman. In a well-written essay, analyze how the symbolism of the red convertible contributes to an interpretation of the work as a whole. Do not merely summarize the plot.
3. **Research.** Research the experiences of American Indian soldiers in the Vietnam War in particular. How are many of these soldiers' experiences unique? In what ways are they like those of other active soldiers and veterans? Explore resources such as those provided by the National Museum of the American Indian and the American Indian Vietnam Veterans Project to expand your understanding of these experiences. How does Erdrich capture them in a short story that isn't told from a veteran's perspective?
4. **Connections.** How might the events of "The Red Convertible" be read as a possible sequel to the stories of the soldiers in Tim O'Brien's "The Things They Carried" (p. 916)?
5. **Research.** The experience of what we now called post-traumatic stress disorder, or PTSD, has long been identified as a disorder many soldiers experience because of time spent in combat. Research the history of what was once called soldier's heart, shell shock, and combat fatigue, including recent discoveries about the prevalence and treatment of PTSD. How have we grown in our understanding of this disorder since the Vietnam War? Is this change in our collective understanding and treatment of PTSD one that would have changed the outcome of "The Red Convertible"?
6. **Speaking and Listening.** Discuss in a small group or as a class Lyman's decision to send the red convertible into the river. Do you see it as a fitting tribute to his brother, an impulsive reaction in the face of deep grief, or something else? How do you think he would have felt about the red convertible years later had he kept it? Cite specific details from the text to support your contributions to the discussion.

7. **Connections.** In his 2016 book *Tribe: On Homecoming and Belonging*, journalist Sebastian Junger offers one possible means of supporting the needs of American war veterans. He suggests

> offer[ing] veterans all over the country the use of their town hall every Veterans Day to speak freely about their experience at war. Some will say that war was the best thing that ever happened to them. Others will be so angry that what they say will barely make sense. Still others will be crying so hard that they won't be able to speak at all. But a community ceremony like that would finally return the experience of war to our entire nation, rather than just leaving it to the people who fought. The bland phrase, "I support the troops," would then mean showing up at the town hall once a year to hear these people out.

How do you think Henry would have responded to such an opportunity? Why might it have benefited him and even the other members of his family and his tribe?

The Management of Grief

Bharati Mukherjee

Jim Wilson/The New York Times/Redux

Born in Kolkata, India, Bharati Mukherjee (1940–2017) earned a BA from the University of Calcutta in 1959. She later received a scholarship to the University of Iowa, where she earned an MFA at the Iowa Writers' Workshop in 1963. She published her first novel, *The Tiger's Daughter*, in 1971. Among Mukherjee's most highly regarded works are the 1989 novel *Jasmine*, described as a modern *Jane Eyre* tale about a young Indian woman in America, and *The Middleman and Other Stories*, which won the National Book Critics Circle Award in 1988 and in which "The Management of Grief" appears.

KEY CONTEXT In June 1985, an Air India flight left Toronto on its way to Mumbai (then called Bombay), with a scheduled stop in London. A bomb exploded on board and sent the plane into the Irish Sea, killing all 329 passengers. It is believed to have been a terrorist attack by Sikh separatists fighting for a Sikh homeland in the Punjab region of India. This story takes place in the aftermath of the tragedy.

A woman I don't know is boiling tea the Indian way in my kitchen. There are a lot of women I don't know in my kitchen, whispering and moving tactfully. They open doors, rummage through the pantry, and try not to ask me where things are kept. They remind me of when my sons were small, on Mother's Day or when Vikram and I were tired, and they would make big, sloppy omelets. I would lie in bed pretending I didn't hear them.

Dr. Sharma, the treasurer of the Indo-Canada Society, pulls me into the hallway. He wants to know if I am worried about money. His wife, who has just come up from the basement with a tray of empty cups and glasses, scolds him. "Don't bother Mrs. Bhave with mundane details." She looks so monstrously pregnant her baby must be days overdue. I tell her she shouldn't be carrying heavy things. "Shaila," she says, smiling, "this is the fifth." Then she grabs a teenager by his shirttails. He slips his Walkman off his head. He has to be one of her four children; they have the same domed and dented foreheads. "What's the official word now?" she demands. The boy slips the headphones back on. "They're acting evasive, Ma. They're saying it could be an accident or a terrorist bomb."

All morning, the boys have been muttering, Sikh bomb, Sikh bomb. The men, not using the word, bow their heads in agreement. Mrs. Sharma touches her forehead at such a word. At least they've stopped talking about space debris and Russian lasers.

Two radios are going in the dining room. They are tuned to different stations. Someone must have brought the radios down from my boys' bedrooms. I haven't gone into their rooms since Kusum came running across the front lawn in her bathrobe. She looked so funny, I was laughing when I opened the door.

The big TV in the den is being whizzed through American networks and cable channels.

"Damn!" some man swears bitterly. "How can these preachers carry on like nothing's happened?" I want to tell him we're not that important. You look at the audience, and at the preacher in his blue robe with his beautiful white hair, the potted palm trees under a blue sky, and you know they care about nothing.

The phone rings and rings. Dr. Sharma's taken charge. "We're with her," he keeps saying. "Yes, yes, the doctor has given calming pills. Yes, yes, pills are having necessary effect." I wonder if pills alone explain this calm. Not peace, just a deadening quiet. I was always controlled, but never repressed. Sound can reach me, but my body is tensed, ready to scream. I hear their voices all around me. I hear my boys and Vikram cry, "Mommy, Shaila!" and their screams insulate me, like headphones.

The woman boiling water tells her story again and again. "I got the news first. My cousin called from Halifax before six a.m., can you imagine? He'd gotten up for prayers and his son was studying for medical exams and heard on a rock channel that something had happened to a plane. They said first it had disappeared from the radar, like a giant eraser just reached out. His father called me, so I said to him, what do you mean, 'something bad'? You mean a hijacking? And he said, *Behn*,[1] there is no confirmation of anything yet, but check with your neighbors because a lot of them must be on that plane. So I called poor Kusum straight-away. I knew Kusum's husband and daughter were booked to go yesterday."

• • •

Kusum lives across the street from me. She and Satish had moved in less than a month ago. They said they needed a bigger place. All these people, the Sharmas and friends from the Indo-Canada Society, had been there for the housewarming. Satish and Kusum made tandoori on their big gas grill and even the white neighbors piled their plates high with that luridly red, charred, juicy chicken. Their younger daughter had danced, and even our boys had broken away from the Stanley Cup telecast to put in a reluctant appearance. Everyone took pictures for their albums and for the community newspapers — another of our families had made it big in Toronto — and now I wonder how many of those happy faces are gone. "Why does God give us so much if all along He intends to take it away?" Kusum asks me.

I nod. We sit on carpeted stairs, holding hands like children. "I never once told him that I loved him," I say. I was too much the well-brought-up woman. I was so well brought up I never felt comfortable calling my husband by his first name.

"It's all right," Kusum says. "He knew. My husband knew. They felt it. Modern young girls have to say it because what they feel is fake."

Kusum's daughter Pam runs in with an overnight case. Pam's in her McDonald's uniform. "Mummy! You have to get dressed!" Panic makes her cranky. "A reporter's on his way here."

"Why?"

"You want to talk to him in your bathrobe?" She starts to brush her mother's long hair. She's

[1] No. — Eds.

the daughter who's always in trouble. She dates Canadian boys and hangs out in the mall, shopping for tight sweaters. The younger one, the goody-goody one according to Pam, the one with a voice so sweet that when she sang *bhajans*[2] for Ethiopian relief even a frugal man like my husband wrote out a hundred-dollar check, *she* was on that plane. *She* was going to spend July and August with grand-parents because Pam wouldn't go. Pam said she'd rather waitress at McDonald's. "If it's a choice between Bombay and Wonderland, I'm picking Wonderland," she'd said.

"Leave me alone," Kusum yells. "You know what I want to do? If I didn't have to look after you now, I'd hang myself."

Pam's young face goes blotchy with pain. "Thanks," she says, "don't let me stop you."

"Hush," pregnant Mrs. Sharma scolds Pam. "Leave your mother alone. Mr. Sharma will tackle the reporters and fill out the forms. He'll say what has to be said."

Pam stands her ground. "You think I don't know what Mummy's thinking? *Why her?* That's what. That's sick! Mummy wishes my little sister were alive and I were dead."

Kusum's hand in mine is trembly hot. We continue to sit on the stairs.

• • •

She calls before she arrives, wondering if there's anything I need. Her name is Judith Templeton and she's an appointee of the provincial government. "Multiculturalism?" I ask, and she says "partially," but that her mandate is bigger. "I've been told you knew many of the people on the flight," she says. "Perhaps if you'd agree to help us reach the others . . . ?"

She gives me time at least to put on tea water and pick up the mess in the front room. I have a few *samosas*[3] from Kusum's housewarming that I could fry up, but then I think, why prolong this visit?

Judith Templeton is much younger than she sounded. She wears a blue suit with a white blouse and a polka-dot tie. Her blond hair is cut short, her only jewelry is pearl-drop earrings. Her briefcase is new and expensive looking, a gleaming cordovan leather. She sits with it across her lap. When she looks out the front windows onto the street, her contact lenses seem to float in front of her light blue eyes.

"What sort of help do you want from me?" I ask. She has refused the tea, out of politeness, but I insist, along with some slightly stale biscuits.

"I have no experience," she admits. "That is, I have an M.S.W. and I've worked in liaison with accident victims, but I mean I have no experience with a tragedy of this scale — "

"Who could?" I ask.

"— and with the complications of culture, language, and customs. Someone mentioned that Mrs. Bhave is a pillar — because you've taken it more calmly."

At this, perhaps, I frown, for she reaches forward, almost to take my hand. "I hope you understand my meaning, Mrs. Bhave. There are hundreds of people in Metro directly affected, like you, and some of them speak no English. There are some widows who've never handled money or gone on a bus, and there are old parents who still haven't eaten or gone outside their bedrooms. Some houses and apartments have been looted. Some wives are still hysterical. Some husbands are in shock and profound depression. We want to help, but our hands are tied in so many ways. We have to distribute money to some people, and there are legal documents —these things can be done. We have interpreters, but we don't always have the human touch, or maybe the right human touch. We don't want to make mistakes, Mrs. Bhave, and that's why we'd like to ask you to help us."

"More mistakes, you mean," I say.

[2] Hymns. — Eds.

[3] Fried pastry filled with meat or vegetables. — Eds.

"Police matters are not in my hands," she answers.

"Nothing I can do will make any difference," I say. "We must all grieve in our own way."

"But you are coping very well. All the people said, Mrs. Bhave is the strongest person of all. Perhaps if the others could see you, talk with you, it would help them."

"By the standards of the people you call hysterical, I am behaving very oddly and very badly, Miss Templeton." I want to say to her, *I wish I could scream, starve, walk into Lake Ontario, jump from a bridge.* "They would not see me as a model. I do not see myself as a model."

I am a freak. No one who has ever known me would think of me reacting this way. This terrible calm will not go away.

She asks me if she may call again, after I get back from a long trip that we all must make. "Of course," I say. "Feel free to call, anytime."

Four days later, I find Kusum squatting on a rock overlooking a bay in Ireland. It isn't a big rock, but it juts sharply out over water. This is as close as we'll ever get to them. June breezes balloon out her sari and unpin her knee-length hair. She has the bewildered look of a sea creature whom the tides have stranded.

It's been one hundred hours since Kusum came stumbling and screaming across my lawn. Waiting around the hospital, we've heard many stories. The police, the diplomats, they tell us things thinking that we're strong, that knowledge is helpful to the grieving, and maybe it is. Some, I know, prefer ignorance, or their own versions. The plane broke into two, they say. Unconsciousness was instantaneous. No one suffered. My boys must have just finished their breakfasts. They loved eating on planes, they loved the smallness of plates, knives, and forks. Last year they saved the airline salt and pepper shakers. Half an hour more and they would have made it to Heathrow.

Kusum says that we can't escape our fate. She says that all those people — our husbands, my boys, her girl with the nightingale voice, all those Hindus, Christians, Sikhs, Muslims, Parsis, and atheists on that plane — were fated to die together off this beautiful bay. She learned this from a swami in Toronto.

I have my Valium.

Six of us "relatives" — two widows and four widowers — choose to spend the day today by the waters instead of sitting in a hospital room and scanning photographs of the dead. That's what they call us now: relatives. I've looked through twenty-seven photos in two days. They're very kind to us, the Irish are very understanding. Sometimes understanding means freeing a tourist bus for this trip to the bay, so we can pretend to spy our loved ones through the glassiness of waves or in sun-speckled cloud shapes.

I could die here, too, and be content.

"What is that, out there?" She's standing and flapping her hands, and for a moment I see a head shape bobbing in the waves. She's standing in the water, I, on the boulder. The tide is low, and a round, black, head-sized rock has just risen from the waves. She returns, her sari end dripping and ruined and her face is a twisted remnant of hope, the way mine was a hundred hours ago, still laughing but inwardly knowing that nothing but the ultimate tragedy could bring two women together at six o'clock on a Sunday morning. I watch her face sag into blankness.

"That water felt warm, Shaila," she says at length.

"You can't," I say. "We have to wait for our turn to come."

I haven't eaten in four days, haven't brushed my teeth.

"I know," she says. "I tell myself I have no right to grieve. They are in a better place than we are. My swami says I should be thrilled for them. My swami says depression is a sign of our selfishness."

Maybe I'm selfish. Selfishly I break away from Kusum and run, sandals slapping against stones, to the water's edge. What if my boys aren't lying pinned under the debris? What if they aren't stuck a mile below that innocent blue chop? What if, given the strong currents . . .

Now I've ruined my sari, one of my best. Kusum has joined me, knee-deep in water that feels to me like a swimming pool. I could settle in the water, and my husband would take my hand and the boys would slap water in my face just to see me scream.

"Do you remember what good swimmers my boys were, Kusum?"

"I saw the medals," she says.

One of the widowers, Dr. Ranganathan from Montreal, walks out to us, carrying his shoes in one hand. He's an electrical engineer. Someone at the hotel mentioned his work is famous around the world, something about the place where physics and electricity come together. He has lost a huge family, something indescribable. "With some good luck," Dr. Ranganathan suggests to me, "a good swimmer could make it safely to some island. It is quite possible that there may be many, many microscopic islets scattered around."

"You're not just saying that?" I tell Dr. Ranganathan about Vinod, my elder son. Last year he took diving as well.

"It's a parent's duty to hope," he says. "It is foolish to rule out possibilities that have not been tested. I myself have not surrendered hope."

Kusum is sobbing once again. "Dear lady," he says, laying his free hand on her arm, and she calms down.

"Vinod is how old?" he asks me. He's very careful, as we all are. *Is*, not was.

"Fourteen. Yesterday he was fourteen. His father and uncle were going to take him down to the Taj and give him a big birthday party. I couldn't go with them because I couldn't get two weeks off from my stupid job in June." I process bills for a travel agent. June is a big travel month.

Dr. Ranganathan whips the pockets of his suit jacket inside out. Squashed roses, in darkening shades of pink, float on the water. He tore the roses off creepers in somebody's garden. He didn't ask anyone if he could pluck the roses, but now there's been an article about it in the local papers. When you see an Indian person, it says, please give him or her flowers.

"A strong youth of fourteen," he says, "can very likely pull to safety a younger one."

My sons, though four years apart, were very close. Vinod wouldn't let Mithun drown. *Electrical engineering*, I think, foolishly perhaps: this man knows important secrets of the universe, things closed to me. Relief spins me lightheaded. No wonder my boys' photographs haven't turned up in the gallery of photos of the recovered dead. "Such pretty roses," I say.

"My wife loved pink roses. Every Friday I had to bring a bunch home. I used to say, Why? After twenty-odd years of marriage you're still needing proof positive of my love?" He has identified his wife and three of his children. Then others from Montreal, the lucky ones, intact families with no survivors. He chuckles as he wades back to shore. Then he swings around to ask me a question. "Mrs. Bhave, you are wanting to throw in some roses for your loved ones? I have two big ones left."

But I have other things to float: Vinod's pocket calculator; a half-painted model B-52 for my Mithun. They'd want them on their island. And for my husband? For him I let fall into the calm, glassy waters a poem I wrote in the hospital yesterday. Finally he'll know my feelings for him.

"Don't tumble, the rocks are slippery," Dr. Ranganathan cautions. He holds out a hand for me to grab.

Then it's time to get back on the bus, time to rush back to our waiting posts on hospital benches.

• • •

Kusum is one of the lucky ones. The lucky ones flew here, identified in multiplicate their loved ones, then will fly to India with the bodies for proper ceremonies. Satish is one of the few males who surfaced. The photos of faces we saw on the walls in an office at Heathrow and here in the hospital are mostly of women. Women have more body fat, a nun said to me matter-of-factly. They float better.

Today I was stopped by a young sailor on the street. He had loaded bodies, he'd gone into the water when —he checks my face for signs of strength — when the sharks were first spotted. I don't blush, and he breaks down. "It's all right," I say. "Thank you." I heard about the sharks from Dr. Ranganathan. In his orderly mind, science brings understanding, it holds no terror. It is the shark's duty. For every deer there is a hunter, for every fish a fisherman.

The Irish are not shy; they rush to me and give me hugs and some are crying. I cannot imagine reactions like that on the streets of Toronto. Just strangers, and I am touched. Some carry flowers with them and give them to any Indian they see.

After lunch, a policeman I have gotten to know quite well catches hold of me. He says he thinks he has a match for Vinod. I explain what a good swimmer Vinod is.

"You want me with you when you look at photos?" Dr. Ranganathan walks ahead of me into the picture gallery. In these matters, he is a scientist, and I am grateful. It is a new perspective. "They have performed miracles," he says. "We are indebted to them."

The first day or two the policemen showed us relatives only one picture at a time; now they're in a hurry, they're eager to lay out the possibles, and even the probables.

The face on the photo is of a boy much like Vinod; the same intelligent eyes, the same thick brows dipping into a V. But this boy's features, even his cheeks, are puffier, wider, mushier.

"No." My gaze is pulled by other pictures. There are five other boys who look like Vinod.

The nun assigned to console me rubs the first picture with a fingertip. "When they've been in the water for a while, love, they look a little heavier." The bones under the skin are broken, they said on the first day — try to adjust your memories. It's important.

"It's not him. I'm his mother. I'd know."

"I know this one!" Dr. Ranganathan cries out, and suddenly from the back of the gallery. "And this one!" I think he senses that I don't want to find my boys. "They are the Kutty brothers. They were also from Montreal." I don't mean to be crying. On the contrary, I am ecstatic. My suitcase in the hotel is packed heavy with dry clothes for my boys.

The policeman starts to cry. "I am so sorry, I am so sorry, ma'am. I really thought we had a match."

With the nun ahead of us and the policeman behind, we, the unlucky ones without our children's bodies, file out of the makeshift gallery.

From Ireland most of us go on to India. Kusum and I take the same direct flight to Bombay, so I can help her clear customs quickly. But we have to argue with a man in uniform. He has large boils on his face. The boils swell and glow with sweat as we argue with him. He wants Kusum to wait in line and he refuses to take authority because his boss is on a tea break. But Kusum won't let her coffins out of sight, and I shan't desert her though I know that my parents, elderly and diabetic, must be waiting in a stuffy car in a scorching lot.

"You bastard!" I scream at the man with the popping boils. Other passengers press closer. "You think we're smuggling contraband in those coffins!"

Once upon a time we were well-brought-up women; we were dutiful wives who kept our heads veiled, our voices shy and sweet.

• • •

In India, I become, once again, an only child of rich, ailing parents. Old friends of the family come to pay their respects. Some are Sikh, and inwardly, involuntarily, I cringe. My parents are progressive people; they do not blame communities for a few individuals.

In Canada it is a different story now.

"Stay longer," my mother pleads. "Canada is a cold place. Why would you want to be all by yourself?" I stay.

Three months pass. Then another.

"Vikram wouldn't have wanted you to give up things!" they protest. They call my husband by the name he was born with. In Toronto he'd changed to Vik so the men he worked with at his office would find his name as easy as Rod or Chris. "You know, the dead aren't cut off from us!"

My grandmother, the spoiled daughter of a rich zamindar,[4] shaved her head with rusty razor blades when she was widowed at sixteen. My grandfather died of childhood diabetes when he was nineteen, and she saw herself as the harbinger of bad luck. My mother grew up without parents, raised indifferently by an uncle, while her true mother slept in a hut behind the main estate house and took her food with the servants. She grew up a rationalist. My parents abhor mindless mortification.

The zamindar's daughter kept stubborn faith in Vedic rituals; my parents rebelled. I am trapped between two modes of knowledge. At thirty-six, I am too old to start over and too young to give up. Like my husband's spirit, I flutter between worlds.

• • •

Courting aphasia, we travel. We travel with our phalanx of servants and poor relatives. To hill stations and to beach resorts. We play contract bridge in dusty gymkhana clubs. We ride stubby ponies up crumbly mountain trails. At tea dances, we let ourselves be twirled twice round the ballroom. We hit the holy spots we hadn't made time for before. In Varanasi, Kalighat, Rishikesh, Hardwar, astrologers and palmists seek me out and for a fee offer me cosmic consolations.

Already the widowers among us are being shown new bride candidates. They cannot resist the call of custom, the authority of their parents and older brothers. They must marry; it is the duty of a man to look after a wife. The new wives will be young widows with children, destitute but of good family. They will make loving wives, but the men will shun them. I've had calls from the men over crackling Indian telephone lines. "Save me," they say, these substantial, educated, successful men of forty. "My parents are arranging a marriage for me." In a month they will have buried one family and returned to Canada with a new bride and partial family.

I am comparatively lucky. No one here thinks of arranging a husband for an unlucky widow.

Then, on the third day of the sixth month into this odyssey, in an abandoned temple in a tiny Himalayan village, as I make my offering of flowers and sweetmeats to the god of a tribe of animists, my husband descends to me. He is squatting next to a scrawny sadhu[5] in moth-eaten robes. Vikram wears the vanilla suit he wore the last time I hugged him. The sadhu tosses petals on a butter-fed flame, reciting Sanskrit mantras, and sweeps his face of flies. My husband takes my hands in his.

You're beautiful, he starts. Then, *What are you doing here?*

Shall I stay? I ask. He only smiles, but already the image is fading. *You must finish alone what we started together*. No seaweed wreathes his mouth. He speaks too fast, just as he used to when we were an envied family in our pink split-level. He is gone.

In the windowless altar room, smoky with joss sticks and clarified butter lamps, a sweaty hand gropes for my blouse. I do not shriek. The sadhu arranges his robe. The lamps hiss and sputter out.

---

[4] Landowner. —Eds.

[5] Hindu ascetic dedicated to achieving liberation from human existence through intense meditation and yoga. In India they are generally seen as holy men, but some people view them with suspicion. Because of their renunciation of all things material, they are considered legally dead. —Eds.

Ron Bull/Toronto Star/Getty Images

This photograph shows relatives of the victims of the Air India crash participating in a memorial service in Toronto, Canada. Here, they are laying a garland of roses around lit candles that symbolize the lives lost. **What does this photo convey about the relationship between culture, community, and grief? How do such rituals help mourners find peace? How does Mukherjee's story address these issues?**

When we come out of the temple, my mother says, "Did you feel something weird in there?"

My mother has no patience with ghosts, prophetic dreams, holy men, and cults.

"No," I lie. "Nothing."

But she knows that she's lost me. She knows that in days I shall be leaving.

• • •

Kusum's put up her house for sale. She wants to live in an ashram in Hardwar. Moving to Hardwar was her swami's idea. Her swami runs two ashrams, the one in Hardwar and another here in Toronto.

"Don't run away," I tell her.

"I'm not running away," she says. "I'm pursuing inner peace. You think you or that Ranganathan fellow are better off?"

• • •

Pam's left for California. She wants to do some modeling, she says. She says when she comes into her share of the insurance money she'll open a yoga-cum-aerobics studio in Hollywood. She sends me postcards so naughty I daren't leave them on the coffee table. Her mother has withdrawn from her and the world.

The rest of us don't lose touch, that's the point. Talk is all we have, says Dr. Ranganathan, who has also resisted his relatives and returned to Montreal and to his job, alone. He says, Whom better to talk with than other relatives? We've been melted down and recast as a new tribe.

He calls me twice a week from Montreal. Every Wednesday night and every Saturday afternoon. He is changing jobs, going to Ottawa. But Ottawa is over a hundred miles away, and he is forced to drive two hundred and twenty miles a day from his home in Montreal. He can't bring himself to sell his house. The house is a temple, he says; the king-sized bed in the master bedroom is a shrine. He sleeps on a folding cot. A devotee.

There are still some hysterical relatives. Judith Templeton's list of those needing help and those who've "accepted" is in nearly perfect balance. Acceptance means you speak of your family in the past tense and you make active plans for moving ahead with your life. There are courses at Seneca and Ryerson we could be taking. Her gleaming leather briefcase is full of college catalogues and lists of cultural societies that need our help. She has done impressive work, I tell her.

"In the textbooks on grief management," she replies — I am her confidante, I realize, one of the few whose grief has not sprung bizarre obsessions — "there are stages to pass through: rejection, depression, acceptance,

Bénédicte Muller

This image by artist Bénédicte Muller appeared with an April 2020 article in the *New York Times* entitled "We Will Need New Ways to Grieve." The article is about the COVID-19 pandemic, which prevented thousands from mourning the loss of their loved ones in person with familiar rituals.

How does this illustration capture the experience of unexpected loss? In what ways does Shaila find "new ways to grieve" in this story?

reconstruction." She has compiled a chart and finds that six months after the tragedy, none of us still rejects reality, but only a handful are reconstructing. "Depressed acceptance" is the plateau we've reached. Remarriage is a major step in reconstruction (though she's a little surprised, even shocked, over *how* quickly some of the men have taken on new families). Selling one's house and changing jobs and cities is healthy.

How to tell Judith Templeton that my family surrounds me, and that like creatures in epics, they've changed shapes? She sees me as calm and accepting but worries that I have no job, no career. My closest friends are worse off than I. I cannot tell her my days, even my nights, are thrilling.

She asks me to help with families she can't reach at all. An elderly couple in Agincourt whose sons were killed just weeks after they had brought their parents over from a village in Punjab. From their names, I know they are Sikh. Judith Templeton and a translator have visited them twice with offers of money for airfare to Ireland, with bank forms, power-of-attorney forms, but they have refused to sign, or to leave their tiny apartment. Their sons' money is frozen in the bank. Their sons' investment apartments have been trashed by tenants, the furnishings sold off. The parents fear that anything they sign or any money they receive will end the company's or the country's obligations to them. They fear they are selling their sons for two airline tickets to a place they've never seen.

The high-rise apartment is a tower of Indians and West Indians, with a sprinkling of Orientals. The nearest bus-stop kiosk is lined with women in saris. Boys practice cricket in the parking lot. Inside the building, even I wince a bit from the ferocity of onion fumes, the distinctive and immediate Indianness of frying ghee,[6] but Judith Templeton maintains a steady flow of information. These poor old people are in imminent danger of losing their place and all their services.

I say to her, "They are Sikh. They will not open up to a Hindu woman." And what I want to add is, as much as I try not to, I stiffen now at the sight of beards and turbans. I remember a time when we all trusted each other in this new country, it was only the new country we worried about.

• • •

The two rooms are dark and stuffy. The lights are off, and an oil lamp sputters on the coffee table. The bent old lady has let us in, and her husband is wrapping a white turban over his oiled, hip-length hair. She immediately goes to the kitchen, and I hear the most familiar sound of an Indian home, tap water hitting and filling a teapot.

[6] Clarified butter. — Eds.

110 They have not paid their utility bills, out of fear and inability to write a check. The telephone is gone, electricity and gas and water are soon to follow. They have told Judith their sons will provide. They are good boys, and they have always earned and looked after their parents.

We converse a bit in Hindi. They do not ask about the crash and I wonder if I should bring it up. If they think I am here merely as a translator, then they may feel insulted. There are thousands of Punjabi speakers, Sikhs, in Toronto to do a better job. And so I say to the old lady, "I too have lost my sons, and my husband, in the crash."

Her eyes immediately fill with tears. The man mutters a few words which sound like a blessing. "God provides and God takes away," he says.

I want to say, But only men destroy and give back nothing. "My boys and my husband are not coming back," I say. "We have to understand that."

Now the old woman responds. "But who is to say? Man alone does not decide these things." To this her husband adds his agreement.

115 Judith asks about the bank papers, the release forms. With a stroke of the pen, they will have a provincial trustee to pay their bills, invest their money, send them a monthly pension.

"Do you know this woman?" I ask them.

The man raises his hand from the table, turns it over, and seems to regard each finger separately before he answers. "This young lady is always coming here, we make tea for her, and she leaves papers for us to sign." His eyes scan a pile of papers in the corner of the room. "Soon we will be out of tea, then will she go away?"

The old lady adds, "I have asked my neighbors and no one else gets *angrezi*[7] visitors. What have we done?"

"It's her job," I try to explain. "The government is worried. Soon you will have no place to stay, no lights, no gas, no water."

120 "Government will get its money. Tell her not to worry, we are honorable people."

I try to explain the government wishes to give money, not take. He raises his hand. "Let them take," he says. "We are accustomed to that. That is no problem."

"We are strong people," says the wife. "Tell her that."

"Who needs all this machinery?" demands the husband. "It is unhealthy, the bright lights, the cold air on a hot day, the cold food, the four gas rings. God will provide, not government."

"When our boys return," the mother says.

125 Her husband sucks his teeth. "Enough talk," he says.

Judith breaks in. "Have you convinced them?" The snaps on her cordovan briefcase go off like firecrackers in that quiet apartment. She lays the sheaf of legal papers on the coffee table. "If they can't write their names, an X will do — I've told them that."

Now the old lady has shuffled to the kitchen and soon emerges with a pot of tea and two cups. "I think my bladder will go first on a job like this," Judith says to me, smiling. "If only there was some way of reaching them. Please thank her for the tea. Tell her she's very kind."

I nod in Judith's direction and tell them in Hindi, "She thanks you for the tea. She thinks you are being very hospitable but she doesn't have the slightest idea what it means."

I want to say, Humor her. I want to say, My boys and my husband are with me too, more than ever. I look in the old man's eyes and I can read his stubborn, peasant's message: *I have protected this woman as best I can. She is the only person I have left. Give to me or take from me what you will, but I will not sign for it. I will not pretend that I accept.*

130 In the car, Judith says, "You see what I'm up against? I'm sure they're lovely people, but their stubbornness and ignorance are driving me crazy. They think signing a paper is signing their sons' death warrants, don't they?"

I am looking out the window. I want to say, *In our culture, it is a parent's duty to hope.*

---

[7] English (Anglo). — Eds.

extending beyond the text

This 1923 woodcut, *The Parents*, by German artist Käthe Kollwitz (1867–1945) is part of a series of prints inspired by World War I that focused on the emotional suffering of women on the home front who lost sons, husbands, and brothers. Kollwitz herself never recovered from the death of her son Peter, who was killed in combat in 1914, only months after he enlisted.

1. **Woodcuts are made by slashing and gouging out a design on a block of wood and then creating a print from there. Why is this medium particularly well suited to conveying the experience of grief?**
2. **How does this image capture the particular grief of parents who lose children?**
3. **What aspects of this portrayal of grief are universal? To what extent does this image reflect the grief that Shaila, Kusum, and Mr. Ranganathan experience?**

"Now Shaila, this next woman is a real mess. She cries day and night, and she refuses all medical help. We may have to —"

"Let me out at the subway," I say.

"I beg your pardon?" I can feel those blue eyes staring at me.

It would not be like her to disobey. She merely disapproves, and slows at a corner to let me out. Her voice is plaintive. "Is there anything I said? Anything I did?"

I could answer her suddenly in a dozen ways, but I choose not to. "Shaila? Let's talk about it," I hear, then slam the door.

A wife and mother begins her life in a new country, and that life is cut short. Yet her husband tells her: Complete what we have started. We, who stayed out of politics and came half way around the world to avoid religious and political feuding, have been the first in the New World to die from it. I no longer know what we started, nor how to complete it. I write letters to the editors of local papers and to members of Parliament. Now at least they admit it was a bomb. One MP answers back, with sympathy, but with a challenge. You want to make a difference? Work on a campaign. Work on mine. Politicize the Indian voter.

My husband's old lawyer helps me set up a trust. Vikram was a saver and a careful investor. He had saved the boys' boarding school and college fees. I sell the pink house at four times what we paid for it and take a small apartment downtown. I am looking for a charity to support.

•••

We are deep in the Toronto winter, gray skies, icy pavements. I stay indoors, watching television. I have tried to assess my situation, how best to live my life, to complete what we began so many years ago. Kusum has written me from Hardwar that her life is now serene. She has seen Satish and has heard her daughter sing again. Kusum was on a pilgrimage, passing through a village, when she heard a young girl's voice, singing one of her daughter's favorite *bhajans*. She followed the music through the squalor of a Himalayan village, to a hut where a young girl, an exact replica of her daughter, was fanning coals under the kitchen fire. When she appeared, the girl cried out, "Ma!" and ran away. What did I think of that?

I think I can only envy her. 140

Pam didn't make it to California, but writes me from Vancouver. She works in a department store, giving makeup hints to Indian and Oriental girls. Dr. Ranganathan has given up his commute, given up his house and job, and accepted an academic position in Texas, where no one knows his story and he has vowed not to tell it. He calls me now once a week.

I wait, I listen and I pray, but Vikram has not returned to me. The voices and the shapes and the nights filled with visions ended abruptly several weeks ago.

I take it as a sign.

One rare, beautiful, sunny day last week, returning from a small errand on Yonge Street, I was walking through the park from the subway to my apartment. I live equidistant from the Ontario Houses of Parliament and the University of Toronto. The day was not cold, but something in the bare trees caught my attention. I looked up from the gravel, into the branches and the clear blue sky beyond. I thought I heard the rustling of larger forms, and I waited a moment for voices. Nothing.

"What?" I asked. 145

Then as I stood in the path looking north to Queen's Park and west to the university, I heard the voices of my family one last time. *Your time has come*, they said. *Go, be brave.*

I do not know where this voyage I have begun will end. I do not know which direction I will take. I dropped the package on a park bench and started walking. ■

1988

Understanding and Interpreting

1. **AP® Narration.** What information do you learn in the opening three paragraphs? How do they set up a sense of foreboding? Why do you think Bharati Mukherjee chose not to open the story with a more traditional exposition?

2. **AP® Character and Setting.** What evidence do you see that indicates a clash in cultural attitudes and values? How does the relationship between Kusum and Pam illustrate cultural differences at the beginning of the story?

3. **AP® Character and Narration.** How is Judith Templeton depicted? Does Mukherjee want us to see her as being totally insensitive? How does Shaila's attitude toward Judith change during the course of the story? Pay special attention to Judith's characterization of the elderly Sikh couple as "lovely people" motivated by "stubbornness and ignorance" (par. 130).
4. **AP® Character and Narration.** What does Shaila mean when she says, "I am trapped between two modes of knowledge" (par. 85)? What are these modes of knowledge, and which one does she ultimately choose?
5. **AP® Character and Narration.** In paragraph 103, Shaila says, "Acceptance means you speak of your family in the past tense and you make active plans for moving ahead with your life." Does she agree with that definition? What is the narrator's tone in that remark? Explain what evidence in the text leads you to your conclusion.
6. **AP® Character and Narration.** In paragraph 105, Shaila says, "my family surrounds me," and in paragraph 129, she says, "My boys and my husband are with me too, more than ever." What do these remarks suggest about how Shaila sees her grief?
7. **AP® Character and Narration.** Regarding Kusum, why does Shaila say, "I think I can only envy her" (par. 140)? What is it about Kusum that Shaila says she envies? Do you believe her? Why, or why not?
8. **AP® Character and Narration.** Describe the differences between Kusum's and Shaila's reactions to the loss of their families and the ways they manage their grief. What is the significance of Shaila's saying "I have my Valium" in response to paragraph 38 and "Maybe I'm selfish" in response to paragraph 46?
9. **AP® Character.** How does the story end? Is Shaila honoring or betraying her belief that "it is a parent's duty to hope" (par. 131)? How well has she done with "the management of grief"?

Analyzing Language, Style, and Structure

1. **Vocabulary in Context.** In the context of the story, what is the meaning of the word "mortification" in paragraph 84? Why does the narrator modify it with "mindless"? What insight does this phrase provide into the story's themes?
2. **AP® Character and Structure.** What elements of irony do you find in this story? What purpose do they serve? For instance, consider the irony in paragraph 55 when Shaila reveals the reason she stayed home, and in paragraph 59 when she talks about "the lucky ones." What does Shaila's ironic tone say about her?
3. **AP® Character and Narration.** "The Management of Grief" has a first-person narrator in Shaila. How does she juggle the introduction of the other characters, both alive and dead? Do you consider her to be a reliable narrator? Why, or why not?
4. **AP® Character, Setting, Narration, and Figurative Language.** "The Management of Grief" has settings in Canada, Ireland, and India. How is each depicted? Are there differences in the language used to describe those places and the narrator's place in them? How do each of the places represent values that are important to Shaila? What does each one symbolize for her?
5. **AP® Narration and Figurative Language.** What does Shaila mean when she distinguishes between "peace" and "a deadening quiet" (par. 7)? What connotations does "calm" have in this paragraph?
6. **AP® Character, Structure, and Narration.** How does the character of Judith Templeton function as a contrast with Shaila? What qualities and values of each are reflected in their relationship?
7. **AP® Character, Structure, and Narration.** "The Management of Grief" provides insight into four generations. In what ways does each respond to — or rebel against — the generation before? How does the story's structure work to reveal insights into those responses?

Topics for Composing

1. **AP® FRQ Prose Fiction Analysis.** The following question refers to paragraphs 89–96 of Bharati Mukherjee's "The Management of Grief," published in 1988. In this passage, the narrator describes a pilgrimage to a holy man. Read the passage carefully. Then, in a well-written essay, analyze how Mukherjee uses literary elements and techniques to convey the significance of the vision she has in the presence of the holy man.
2. **AP® FRQ Literary Argument.** Many works of literature depend on understanding the values of the society or culture in which the characters live. In "The Management of Grief," Shaila's experience of grief is guided by the standards of the Indian community in Toronto. In a well-written essay, analyze how the complex relationship between the protagonist and her culture contributes to an interpretation of the work as a whole. Do not merely summarize the plot.
3. **AP® Literary Argumentation.** What is your response to the ending of "The Management of Grief"? What makes the ending ambiguous? What does this ambiguity suggest about the nature of grief and loss?
4. **Creative Writing.** Where do you think Shaila goes after she drops the package? Write a different ending to the story that includes a scene following Shaila's abandonment of the package on the bench. Be prepared to explain how this scene is relevant to the themes of the story.
5. **Research.** What role does politics play in "The Management of Grief"? Learn more about the Sikh separatist movement in India in the late twentieth century. Why do you think Mukherjee chose not to focus on the reasons for the plane crash in her story?
6. **Connections.** Bharati Mukherjee has written that she was enraged by the Canadian government's response to the plane crash. In a book-length investigation and account of the incident, cowritten with her husband, she asserted that the government considered it an "Indian" problem though the majority of the victims were Canadian citizens. She blames an approach to "multiculturalism" that she said encourages division and discrimination along racial lines rather than emphasizing common humanity. Using "The Management of Grief" as evidence in addition to your own reading, support, challenge, or qualify that statement.
7. **Research.** Do some research into Hindu religious practices that address death and grief. How does "The Management of Grief" depict these practices? What aspects of the story examine the Hindu beliefs in karma and reincarnation?

Grief

Scholastique Mukasonga

Translated from French by Jordan Stump

Agence Opale/Alamy

Social worker, memoirist, and novelist Scholastique Mukasonga was born in Rwanda in 1956. Her family was displaced several times by the country's ethnic conflicts. Mukasonga attended schools in Rwanda, Burundi, and France, where she established a career as a social worker. In 2004, a decade after thirty-seven members of her family were killed during the Rwandan genocide, she returned to Rwanda. This visit inspired her first book, the autobiographical *Cockroaches* (2006), which was translated into English in 2016. Since then, she has published two more memoirs, three novels, and a collection of stories.

KEY CONTEXT The Rwandan genocide took place in just one hundred days between April and July 1994. During this time, the Hutu ethnic majority targeted the Tutsi ethnic minority, killing between 500,000 and 800,000 people. Hutu nationalists began the genocide in the capital city of Kigali, Rwanda, but the violence soon spread throughout the country as ordinary citizens were incited by local officials and the government, staffed by members of the Hutu Power party, to massacre their neighbors. By the time the Tutsi-led Rwandese Patriotic Front soldiers gained control of the country in early July, hundreds of thousands of Rwandans were dead and 2 million refugees (mainly Hutus) had fled Rwanda. The scale and brutality of the genocide caused shock and outrage, but no country intervened to stop the slaughter.

On TV, on the radio, they never called it genocide. As if that word were reserved. Too serious. Too serious for Africa. Yes, there were massacres, but there were always massacres in Africa. And these massacres were happening in a country that no one had ever heard of. A country that no one could find on a map. Tribal hatred, primitive, atavistic hatred: nothing to understand there. “Weird stuff goes on where you come from,” people would tell her.

She herself didn't know the word, but in Kinyarwanda there was a very old term for what was happening in her homeland: *gutsembatsemba*, a verb, used when talking about parasites or mad dogs, things that had to be eradicated, and about Tutsis, also known as *inyenzi* — cockroaches — something else to be wiped out. She remembered the story her Hutu schoolmates at high school in Kigali had told her, laughing: “Someday a child will ask his mother, ‘Mama, who were those Tutsis I keep hearing about? What did they look like?,’ and the mother will answer, ‘They were nothing at all, my son. Those are just stories.’ ”

Nevertheless, she hadn't lost hope. She wanted to know. Her father, her mother, her brothers, her sisters, her whole family back in Rwanda — some of them might still be alive. Maybe the slaughter had spared them for now? Maybe they'd managed to escape into exile, as she had? Her parents, on the hill, had no telephone, of course, but she called one of her brothers, who taught in Ruhengeri. The phone rang and rang. No one answered. She called her sister, who'd married a shopkeeper in Butare.[1] A voice she'd never heard before told her, “There's nobody here.” She called her brother in Canada. He was the eldest. If their parents were dead, then he'd be the head of the family. Perhaps he had news, perhaps he had advice, perhaps he could help her begin to face her terror. They spoke, and then they fell silent. What was there to say? From now on, they were alone.

From now on, she would be alone. She knew a few people from home, of course, friends she'd made at the university here, where she'd had to start her studies all over again, her African degrees being worthless in France. But that little part of her — the part that still tied her to those she'd left behind in Rwanda, despite the distance and the time gone by and the impossibility of rejoining them — formed a bond that grounded her identity and affirmed her will to go on. That bond would fade, and in the cold of her solitude its disappearance would leave her somehow amputated.

5 She felt very fragile. “I'm like an egg,” she often told herself. “One jolt and I'll break.” She moved as sparingly as she could; she lived in slow motion. She walked as if she were seeking her way in the dark, as if at any moment she might bump into an obstacle and fall to the ground. Climbing a staircase took a tremendous effort: a great weight lay on her shoulders. She

[1] A city in Rwanda. — Eds.

found herself counting the steps she still had to climb, clutching the bannister as if she were at the edge of an abyss, and when she reached her floor she was breathless and drained.

She tried to find an escape in mindless household tasks. Again and again, she maniacally straightened her studio apartment. Something was always where it shouldn't be: books on the couch, shoes in the entryway, Rwandan nesting baskets untidily lined up on the shelf. She was sure she'd feel better if everything was finally where it belonged. But she was forever having to go back and start over again.

If only she had at least a photograph of her parents. She rifled through the suitcase that had come with her through all her travels. There were letters, there were notebooks filled with words, useless diplomas, even her Rwandan identity card, with the "Tutsi" stamp that she'd tried to scratch away. There was a handful of photographs of her with her girlfriends in Burundi (which they'd had taken at a photographer's studio in the Asian district in Bujumbura, before they parted ways, so they wouldn't forget), there were postcards from her brother in Canada, a few pages of a diary she'd quickly abandoned, but she never did find a photo of her parents.

For that, she rebuked herself bitterly. Why hadn't she thought to ask them to have their picture taken and send her a copy? Was she a neglectful daughter? Had she forgotten them as the years went by? No, they were still there in her memory; she could call up their image anytime she liked. She sat down at her table, took her head in her hands, closed her eyes, focussed her mind, and pictured, one by one, all the faces that death might already have erased.

• • •

Then, toward the end of June, she got a letter. There was no mistaking where it had come from: the red-and-blue-bordered envelope, the exotic bird on the stamp, the clumsily written address. . . . She couldn't bring herself to open it. She put it on her bookshelf, behind the Rwandan baskets. She pretended to forget it. There were so many more urgent and more important things to do: make dinner, iron a pair of jeans, organize her class notes. But the letter was still there, behind the baskets. Suddenly, she found herself tearing open the envelope. She pulled out a sheet of square-ruled paper, a page from a schoolchild's notebook. She didn't need to read the few sentences that served as an introduction to a long list of names: her father, her mother, her brothers, her sisters, her uncles, her aunts, her nephews, her nieces. . . . This was now the list of her dead, of everyone who had died far away from her, without her, and there was nothing she could do for them, not even die with them. She stared at the letter, unable to weep, and she began to think that it had been sent by the dead themselves. It was a message from the land of the dead. And this, she thought, would probably be their only grave, a column of names she didn't even need to reread, because she knew them so well that they echoed in her head like cries of pain.

She kept the letter from her dead with her at 10
all times. She never showed it to anyone. Whenever someone asked, "What happened to your family?," she always answered, "They were killed, they're all dead, every one." When people asked how she'd heard, she told them, "I just know, that's all. Don't ask me anything more." She often felt the need to touch that piece of paper. She gazed at the column of names without reading them, with no tears in her eyes, and the names filled her head with pleas that she didn't know how to answer.

What she didn't want to see: pictures on television, photographs in newspapers and magazines, corpses lying by roadsides, dismembered bodies, faces slashed by machetes. What she didn't want to hear: any rumor that might summon up images of the frenzy of sex and blood that had crashed over the women, the girls, the children. . . . She wanted to protect her dead, to keep them untouched in her memory, their bodies whole and unsullied, like the saints she'd heard about at catechism, miraculously preserved from corruption.

Most of all, she didn't want to sleep, because to fall asleep was to deliver herself to the killers. Every night they were there. They'd taken over her sleep; they were the masters of her dreams. They had no faces; they came toward her in a gray, blood-soaked throng. Or else they had just one face, an enormous face that laughed viciously as it pressed into hers, crushing her.

No, no going to sleep.

Of course, she should have wept. She owed the dead that. If she wept, she could be close to them. She imagined them waiting behind the veil of tears, nearby and unreachable. Maybe that was why she'd gone so far away, why she'd headed off into exile: so that there would be someone to weep for all those whose memory the killers had tried to erase, whose existence they'd tried to deny.

But she couldn't weep.

• • •

"My father just died," one of her friends told her.

"I'll go to his funeral," she answered, without thinking.

She immediately regretted making that promise. Was it right for her to honor someone else's dead if she couldn't weep for her own? In her mind, she summoned up images of Rwandan women weeping over their lost loved ones, able to weep because the body was there in front of them, before it was buried. Yes, the women of Rwanda knew how to mourn. First, they wept sitting up very straight, still and silent, their tears falling like raindrops from eucalyptus trees. Then came the keening and the wailing; the women shivered and quaked, racked head to toe by violent sobs. Finally, they huddled beneath their pagnes,[2] disappearing, soundless but for their sighs as they choked back their tears, and then even those slowly waned. Now the loved one could enter the land of the dead. He'd got the tears he deserved, and although the pain of the loss was still there, you knew that it would slowly ease, that you'd be able to live with it, and that the lost loved one would leave a peaceful memory in the world of the living, a welcome memory — maybe that was what white people meant when they talked about "the grieving process." And, with that, the loved one was allowed to set off for his final home. The body was carried on an *ingobyi*, a long stretcher made of bamboo slats. The women would keep their eyes fixed on him, accompanying him on his voyage, as if lending him their support one last time before he was admitted to the other world, the unknown world of the spirits. The *ingobyi* also served as a bride's palanquin on her wedding day. She, too, was expected to weep. As she was taken from her parents' house to that of her new family, her sobs — too loud to be sincere — showed everyone that she was leaving the paternal enclosure against her wishes. The *ingobyi* always demanded its tribute of tears.

She sadly recalled the little cemetery where she and her three fellow-refugees had liked to meet. This was in Burundi, in Bujumbura, at the seminary that had temporarily taken them in after they fled from Rwanda. In exchange for halfhearted hospitality, the four companions-in-exile did housekeeping, helped in the kitchen, served the abbots at dinner, washed dishes. They tried to ward off the insistent curiosity of the seminarians, who were made restless by the presence of girls. They were forever having to invent new excuses to turn down the abbots' invitations to come pick out a book or have a talk in their rooms. When the siesta hour came, the girls went out into the garden to talk about all that had happened to them and to consider their uncertain future. Beyond the banana grove, they discovered a small forgotten cemetery with a handful of

[2] Pronounced *pan-yuh*, a pagne is a traditional item of Rwandan clothing made from a rectangular and often brightly colored or printed cloth that is wrapped around the torso.

wooden crosses, whose white paint was peeling, the black letters of the names almost entirely faded. "Let's say a prayer," Espérance said. "You must always do something for the dead."

20 They returned to those graves day after day, hurrying out to the little cemetery early in the afternoon, as soon as the dishes were washed and the siesta hour had begun. It became their secret domain, their refuge, a safe place, far from the irritable stares of the miserly old nun, far from the indiscreet, ardent gazes of the abbots and the seminarians. They pulled the weeds from the graves and laid out purple flowers, cut from the bougainvillea that climbed the façade of the Father Superior's small house. "These could be our parents' graves," Eugénie said. "They may have been killed. Maybe because of us, because we left, they were killed." They stood side by side and held one another as you do for a Rwandan greeting. Then they burst into tears, and their shared lament brought them some comfort and solace.

They'd each chosen a grave to consider their own. Sometimes it belonged to their parents, sometimes to a brother, a sister, a fiancé. . . . And they mourned the absence of that loved one, or possibly the death, if he or she turned out to have been killed in reprisal for the girls' going away. The dirt was cracked and eroded from the heat and the rain, so they covered the graves with pebbles taken a handful at a time from the wide walkway that led to the calvary. They found a few slightly chipped vases in the sacristy, and they placed them before the crosses, which they'd carefully straightened. They filled the vases with flowers they'd borrowed from the altar of the Holy Virgin. And then, sitting by the graves, their arms around their legs, their chins on their knees, they silently let their tears flow, always on edge, fearing that a seminarian might happen onto them and mock them for their strange rituals.

Long after that little group of refugees had gone their separate ways, she still missed the haven she'd found in that cemetery. And today she realized how much she wished she could be back by those strangers' graves, where she'd shed so many tears.

• • •

There was a sort of minivan, of a discreet, elegant gray, parked in front of the church. Two men in dark suits were waiting, bored, on the steps. She went in and tiptoed down the side aisle until she reached an empty seat with a view of the choir and the altar. There was a priest standing at a microphone, talking about the consolation of the afterlife. Nothing to do with her dead. She spotted her friend in the front row, no doubt surrounded by her family. She was shocked to see that the women weren't weeping, although some had red eyes, and she was sorry to find that they weren't draped in the elaborate mourning veils she'd seen in old photos. The men were all wearing solemn expressions that seemed forced to her.

Soon her eye was drawn to the coffin, which was sitting on a pedestal, armfuls of flowers laid out all around it. She couldn't help admiring the coffin's gleaming, polished wood, its handsome molding, its gilded handles. The old man, she understood, was lying in that padded box dressed in his best suit, and maybe, as she'd heard people say, they'd made up his face so they could tell themselves that death was only a restful sleep. She began to hate that old man, who'd died a painless death, her friend had told her — "a good death," the friend had said, over and over. And as she stared at the coffin she felt as if she could see inside it, as if the wood had become transparent. And the body she saw in that silken, gently lit bubble was her father's body, dressed in the spotless pagne that marked him as an elder and the white shirt he wore for Sunday Mass. Suddenly she felt tears rolling down her cheeks, and she heard a loud sob escape her. Now there was no stopping it. She let the tears flow; she didn't try to hold them back or wipe them away. It was as if a wave of solace had erupted from the very heart of her sorrow.

She couldn't stop whispering the lamentation that accompanies the dead in Rwanda. She could feel her neighbors' uncomfortable, reproachful stares. She heard a murmur run through the rows in front of her and behind her. She fled, here and there jostling a kneeling woman as she hurried past. Her footfalls resounded against the stone floor as if to denounce her: what right did she have to weep for that man she didn't know, that man surrounded by a family who mourned him with a proper, polite sadness? She was a parasite of their grief.

She wished she could forget what had happened at the church: that vision of her father's corpse, her fit of tears. She avoided her friend so she wouldn't have to answer her questions. But a strange thought nagged at her, insistent, obsessive, telling her that her dead had given her a sign, and she was afraid to understand too clearly what they were trying to say to her. Nonetheless, she found that the long strolls she liked to take through the streets of the city inevitably brought her to a church, where she always hoped to see a gleaming gray or black hearse parked in front. More than once she did, and then an irresistible force drew her inside, with the crowd of mourners. She knew exactly where to sit: always behind a pillar, but with a view of the coffin. She stared at it long and hard, hoping she might once again see through the wood and find one of her dead inside it: her mother wrapped in her pagne, her younger sister in her schoolgirl dress . . . It didn't always work, but the tears came every time. And she was convinced that, because she was there with them — those who had come to mourn a son killed in a traffic accident or a brother dead after what they called a long illness or a father felled by a heart attack — they would also weep for her dead, just a little. In exchange, she told herself, I'm sharing their sorrow for the one they lost. They can't possibly mind.

She thought that her dead wanted her to be present at funerals so that they, too, could have their share of mourning and tears. In the past, she had never read the newspaper; now she opened it feverishly every morning to read the obituaries. She became a regular at the church near her apartment. That went on for some months, but eventually her strangely faithful attendance was noticed. One day, as she was trying to discreetly leave the church, a young priest stopped her outside the front door.

"Madame, please . . ."

She couldn't push him away, and she couldn't go back inside.

Daphne Odjig, Genocide No. 1, 1971 acrylic on board, 61 × 76 cm, Purchased 2001, National Gallery of Canada, Ottawa. Photo: NGC. Permissioned by Odjig Arts

Entitled *Genocide No. 1*, this painting is by Daphne Odjig (1919–2016), an Odawa-Potawatomi artist.

What emotions come to mind as you look at this image? In what ways does this image capture the psychological state of the protagonist in "Grief"? Consider both literal and metaphorical interpretations in your response.

"Madame, please, allow me, I'd like a word with you. . . . I've noticed that you come to almost every funeral, and that you weep as if you knew the deceased. That can be upsetting for the families, for everyone who's suffered a loss. Perhaps I can help you? I'd like nothing more than to listen to you, help you . . . if there's anything I can do."

"No, let me be. I promise you'll never see me again."

She wandered the city streets, which had become a labyrinth of her despair, with no way out. She sensed that the very tenuous, very frail bonds that had connected her to her own dead through the losses of others were now broken forever. She felt herself sinking into an aloneness that would never end. All she had left was that piece of notebook paper, now tattered, and its list of names that she couldn't bring herself to read but whispered to herself over and over, like a hypnotic refrain of sadness and remorse.

She went home and tried to immerse herself in her most recent class notes, to neatly copy them out on a fresh sheet of paper, but she found the names of her dead filling the page. Now she was afraid: she was going to lose her mind, she had already lost her mind, these things she'd been doing weren't what her dead wanted at all. They weren't here, in this land of exile, in these foreign churches. They were waiting back home, in the land of the dead that Rwanda had become. They were waiting for her. She would go to them.

• • •

"Stop," she told the driver. "This is the place. That's the path to my house, and if you keep going it takes you up to the eucalyptus plantings at the very top of the hill. And that hut over there at the side of the road, that's Népomucène's cabaret. He sold banana beer and Fanta, even Primus sometimes, but not often. One time, I remember it to this day, my father bought me an orange Fanta when he came back from the market. He must have got a good price for his coffee."

"You really want to go there?" the driver said, sighing. "You know, it's no use. There's nothing left. It might not be good for you. In any case, you shouldn't go by yourself: you never know, you might run into a madman, and besides there are people who still want to 'finish the job,' so being there all alone, with those people who died up there . . ."

"I made a promise. Maybe I'll find what I've come here for. . . . I promised, I have to go."

"I'll come back this evening, before the sun goes down. I'll honk, and then I'll wait for ten minutes. Look, I have a watch just like you do, ten minutes, no more. I've got people waiting for me, too, at home."

"I'll be here. See you this evening."

The Toyota pickup drove off in a cloud of red dust, loaded with bananas, mattresses, sheet metal, maybe ten passengers, and a few goats squeezed in. The noise of the engine faded away. She spent a long moment looking around her. The dirt road snaked between the hillside and the swamp, but the shallows where her mother once grew sweet potatoes and corn were now clogged with reeds and papyrus. Népomucène's cabaret was a ruin, its flaking mud walls showing their skeleton of interlaced bamboo. The start of the path up the hill was half hidden by tall fronds of dried grass. For a moment, she wondered if this really was Gihanga. But soon she got hold of herself. She should have known that everything would be different: death had come to this place. It was death's domain now.

The hill was steep, but the path soon turned rocky, and the tangle of brush that slowed her down at first gradually thinned. She tried to make out what were once cultivated parcels of land in the thick growth that had invaded the hillside. The plots marked off for the coffee plants were easy to spot, but shaggy, dishevelled bushes bore witness to their abandonment. A few oversized, sterile maniocs rose from the weeds, smothering the last stalks of sorghum.

Halfway up the hill, in the middle of deserted fields, a patch of almost impenetrable forest had survived. Fig trees towered over the sea of pointed dracaena leaves. Her father had told her that those were the vestiges of the enclosure of an old king. This place was now haunted by his *umuzimu*, his spirit, and he had perhaps been reincarnated in the python that guarded this sacred wood where no one dared set foot. "Stay away," the old ones said. "The python has been furious ever since the *abapadris* forbade us to bring it offerings. If you go near him, he'll swallow you!" She couldn't help thinking that this gloomy forest and its python were now the masters of the hill and would end up devouring her.

She reached the stand of banana trees, whose glossy leaves had once concealed the enclosure. Many of the trees had fallen and were dull brown with rot. The leaves of those still standing hung tattered and yellow. A few of them bore sad, stunted fruit.

She found her pace slowing as she neared the enclosure. She wasn't sure she'd have the strength to see this journey through to the end, to face firsthand what she'd already been told about. But now she was standing by the palisade. The wall of interlaced branches had collapsed and come apart, and what were once uprights were now shrubs with vigorous greenery or scarlet flowers, which struck her as indecent, as if, she thought, those simple stakes had been brought to life by the death of the people who had planted them. Nothing was left of the rectangular main house but a shattered stretch of wall. She searched for some trace of the hearth and its three stones, but she found only a little pile of broken tiles. She couldn't hold back a surge of pride: somehow her father had roofed his house with tiles! But she also observed that the killers had gone to the trouble of taking most of them away. They'd had all kinds of reasons for murdering their neighbors: the neighbors were Tutsis; they had a house with a tile roof. In the back courtyard, the three big grain baskets were slashed and overturned, and the calves' stable was a mound of ash and charred straw. Not wanting to break them any further, she took care not to walk on the shards littering the ground, all that remained of the big jugs the family had used to collect rainwater. Amid the debris of the collapsed awning that had once covered the hearth, she thought she saw a patch of fabric and hoped it might be a piece of her mother's pagne. But when she came closer she realized that it was only a yellowed taro leaf.

She knew she wouldn't find what she was looking for in the ruined enclosure. As soon as

Andrew Renneisen/Getty Images

This photograph, taken in 2019, shows Rwandans gathering at a memorial service for the twenty-fifth anniversary of the 1994 genocide at Amahoro Stadium in Kigali.

How does this image relate to the narrator's understanding of her loss? What does it suggest about the narrator's decision to return to Rwanda years later?

she'd got to the town, before heading to the hamlet of Gihanga, she'd gone to the mission church where the Tutsis had sought shelter, where they'd been slaughtered. Four thousand, five thousand, no one quite knew. Outside the front door she'd seen a little old man with a white beard and a broad, fringed straw hat sitting behind a wooden table. He was the guardian of the dead. He had a notebook in front of him. Visitors were invited to write a few words on their way out, as at an art gallery. The old man gave her a long stare, nodded, then finally said, "I know you — you're Mihigo's daughter. Did you come to see the dead?"

"Yes, they were calling me."

"You won't find them here. Here there's only death."

"Let me go in."

"Of course. Who could deny you that? I'll come with you, follow me, but then I have something to tell you."

"As you see," the old man said, "the *abapadris* and their houseboys washed everything clean. There's nothing left, not one drop of blood, not on the walls, not on the altar. There may still be some in the folds of the Virgin Mary's veil, if you look closely. Once it was all cleaned up, the Monsignor came. He wanted Mass to be said here again, like before. All it would take was some holy water. But the survivors objected. They said, 'Where was your God when they were killing us? The white soldiers came to take the priests away, and He went off with them. He won't be back. Now the church belongs to our dead.' The mayor and the prefect agreed. It seems they're going to turn it into a house just for our dead — a memorial, they called it. I'll show you where our dead are waiting in the meantime."

He took a key that hung around his neck on a string and opened a door behind the altar, at the back of the apse. Beyond it was a vast, dark room stacked to the ceiling with large bags, like those used for carrying charcoal.

"These are for skulls," the guide said, pointing at the bags against the wall to his left, "and the ones straight ahead of you are for bones. We've got everyone who was here in the church, and all the bones we could find in the hills, left behind by the jackals and the abandoned dogs. Even the schoolchildren went to gather bones during vacations and days off. I hear there are going to be display cases, like at the Pakistani's shop in the marketplace. Your family's here in these bags, but no one can tell you whose bones are whose. You can make out only the babies' skulls, because they fit in the palm of your hand. But what I can tell you is that your father isn't here. His bones are still up there where he lived, at Gihanga, but don't you go looking for them. They're someplace where you shouldn't see them. All right, let's go now, you don't have to write anything in the book — that book's for the *bazungu*, the white people, assuming they'll come, or for the grand gentlemen from Kigali in their four-by-fours. There's nothing for you to write. You're on the side of the dead. But let me tell you again: don't go looking for your father's remains, you mustn't see him where they left him."

She stepped over the back courtyard's broken fence and found herself in another banana grove, which seemed more overgrown than the one she'd just come through. But, even with the weeds, she could make out a path. It led to a thicket that exuded a horrible stench, veiled by a buzzing, humming fog of mosquitoes, gnats, and fat green flies. A black puddle had spread all around it, like stinking lava. Pallid, almost transparent worms twisted and writhed wherever the flood hadn't yet dried to a sickening crust.

She forced her way through the tall grass and sat down for a moment on the termite mound where people used to wait their turn every morning. The smell was almost more than she could bear. The air felt thick and heavy. She wasn't sure she could go on, wasn't sure she had the courage to climb the last few metres to that putrid thicket. But she told herself that she had to see this through to the end, that in just a few steps her journey would be over. She staggered up the final slope, tried to wave away the blinding mist of gnats, and bent over the side of the latrine. She thought she could see something shaped like a human body in the filth, and maybe — but surely this was an illusion — the horrible black glistening of what used to be a face. A violent nausea washed over her, and she vomited as she ran back to the termite mound. She closed her eyes, only to see once again what she'd just glimpsed in the latrine, that same fleshless face with its vile, viscous mask. She opened her eyes to make the vision of horror go away. She was sure that she would never again close her eyes without that monstrous face appearing from the deepest darkness. She ran down the hill and took shelter amid the crumbling walls of Népomucène's cabaret, next to the road. To keep her eyes open, she stared at a bamboo rack, still dotted with a few clods of red clay. Trembling with fever and nausea, she sat there for hours, watching for the truck to come back, like a promise of deliverance.

• • •

All night long, she struggled against sleep in the room she'd rented at the mission, trying to hold back the flood of visions and nightmares that would wash her into their world of terror if she let herself drift off for even a moment. When the curfew hour came and the generator was turned off, the mission was submerged in pitch-darkness. She saw the glow of a fire through the narrow window: the watchmen warming themselves on this cold, dry-season night. She wished she could join them, hold out her hands toward the flames, talk with the men. But, of course, a girl couldn't mingle with strangers in the middle of the night. She remembered that she'd seen a hurricane lamp on the little table, and surely a box of matches next to it. She felt around for the matches, struck one, and lit the lamp's wick. It felt as though that trembling, blue-tipped flame were watching over her, keeping at bay the dark forces that lurked all around. She lay down on the bed and finally fell into a dreamless sleep.

There was someone in her room when she awoke. In the dim early-morning light, she recognized the guard from the church, sitting in the room's only chair.

"You went to your house in Gihanga," the old man said. "Don't tell me what you saw or thought you saw there. You went right through to the end. There's nothing beyond it, and no way out of it. You won't find your dead in the graves or the bones or the latrine. That's not where they're waiting for you. They're inside

YASUYOSHI CHIBA/AFP/Getty Images

In this photograph, a woman carrying her child looks at the wall of names at the Kigali Genocide Memorial, which commemorates those who died.

What does the perspective of the photo suggest about the presence of the past? Where do you see this perspective on the relationship between past and present in "Grief"?

you. They survive only in you, and you survive only through them. But from now on you'll find all your strength in them — there's no other choice, and no one can take that strength away from you. With that strength, you can do things you might not even imagine today. Like it or not, the death of our loved ones has fuelled us — not with hate, not with vengefulness, but with an energy that nothing can ever defeat. That strength lives in you. Don't let anyone try to tell you to get over your loss, not if that means saying goodbye to your dead. You can't: they'll never leave you, they'll stay by your side to give you the courage to live, to triumph over obstacles, whether here in Rwanda or abroad, if you go back. They're always beside you, and you can always depend on them."

Now the rising sun was illuminating her tiny room. She sat on the edge of the bed, elbows on her knees, head in her hands, listening. She let the guardian's words sink into her, and slowly despair loosened its grip.

They sat for a long while, looking at each other in silence. Her visitor picked up a small gourd that he'd set down at his feet. He dropped a single straw into it. "I made this sorghum beer for the dead I watch over," he said. "Share it with them as I do."

He handed her the gourd and she sucked up the liquid. She closed her eyes. A gentle bitterness filled her mouth, like something she'd tasted long before.

"Now," the guardian of the dead said, "what is there for you to fear?" ■

2010

Understanding and Interpreting

1. **AP® Setting and Narration.** How do the opening paragraphs provide exposition and context for the story? As a reader, what elements seem familiar to you? What strikes you as unexpected or off-kilter?
2. **AP® Character.** Why does the protagonist yearn for a photograph of her parents? What does this item mean to her?
3. **AP® Character.** When the protagonist receives a long-expected letter, she puts it out of sight, "pretend[ing] to forget" it (par. 9), and does not open it for some time. Why? If she thinks she knows what it will reveal, what purpose does hiding or refusing to open it serve?
4. **AP® Character and Narration.** What do you make of the protagonist's attendance at the funerals of strangers? Why does she do it, and what effect does it have on her? What does she mean when she describes herself as "a parasite of [the mourners'] grief" (par. 24)?
5. **AP® Character, Setting, and Narration.** The protagonist is unable to cry over the deaths in her family, but at the stranger's funeral she bursts into sobs. What happens to her to precipitate that response? What does it suggest about the relationship between the emotions of grief and the behavior of mourners?
6. **AP® Character, Setting, and Narration.** When the protagonist returns to Rwanda, she meets the man who oversees a mission church that was the site of one of the massacres. What effect does this meeting have on her?
7. **AP® Character, Setting, and Narration.** Why does the protagonist insist on continuing alone to a place that she was warned not to visit? What forces or fears bring her to this decision?
8. **AP® Character and Narration.** Recovery from trauma is often described as having three stages: establishing a place of safety; reconstructing the trauma story; and restoring connection between survivors and their community. How does the protagonist in "Grief" navigate this sequence?

Analyzing Language, Style, and Structure

1. **Vocabulary in Context.** In paragraph 18, the protagonist remembers the mourning rituals of Rwandan woman: "Then came the keening and the wailing." What is the meaning of "keening" in this context? Why is it an especially effective word choice?
2. **AP® Character, Structure, and Narration.** Scholastique Mukasonga chooses to narrate the story in third-person limited from the perspective of the protagonist, whom she does not name. How does the narrative perspective, and the choice to leave the protagonist unnamed, inform your interpretation of the story?
3. **AP® Character, Narration, and Figurative Language.** Why do you think Mukasonga does not provide more factual information about the protagonist's background or details of her appearance? Do you think the character is symbolic? If so, symbolic of what? If not, why not?
4. **AP® Character, Narration, and Figurative Language.** At one point, the protagonist feels a "bond" with those she left behind in Rwanda that gave her a protective "solitude" that, if disrupted, "would leave her somehow amputated" (par. 4). How does the diction in this paragraph emphasize the toll her trauma takes on her? What other descriptions of the way her physical body holds that trauma do you find?
5. **AP® Character, Narration, and Structure.** What is the effect of Mukasonga's choice to include various words from Kinyarwanda, her first language, in the story? What mood do they help create? What does this choice emphasize about the perspective of the protagonist?
6. **AP® Character and Structure.** What roles do the minor characters in the story play? Consider, for instance, the priest who asks the protagonist to leave the church in Paris and the guardian of the remains of victims of the genocide in Gihanga?
7. **AP® Character, Structure, and Narration.** Mukasonga describes a number of different mourning rituals in the story — some the protagonist observes and others she participates in. How do these traditions, and her relationship to them, help portray her as a complex character?
8. **AP® Character, Setting, and Structure.** What is the relationship between the physical setting of the story's final sections and the protagonist's inner landscape? To what extent do her experiences, both during the day and the following night, comfort her or give her peace? Does this story suggest that any closure in the wake of horrors of such magnitude is possible for those who escape and survive? Explain.
9. **AP® Character and Structure.** How does the story's plot structure help shape its meaning and convey the motivations of the protagonist? Consider both flashbacks and foreshadowing in your response.

Topics for Composing

1. **AP® FRQ Prose Fiction Analysis.** The following question refers to paragraphs 3–8 of Scholastique Mukasonga's "Grief," published in 2010. In this passage, the protagonist, a survivor of the Rwandan genocide, tries to cope with her life in France and the loss of all but one member of her family. Read the passage carefully. Then, in a well-written essay, analyze how Mukasonga uses literary elements and techniques to convey the relationship between the complex interior and exterior struggle the protagonist experiences.
2. **AP® FRQ Literary Argument.** Occasionally literary works have a happy ending, but more frequently the conflicts and uncertainties explored in the text are brought to a resolution or reconciliation that is less straightforward than "happily ever after." In "Grief," the protagonist

finally journeys back to the site of a trauma after avoiding it for many years. In a well-written essay, analyze how the ending of the story contributes to an interpretation of the work as a whole. Do not merely summarize the plot.

3. **Research.** Mukasonga is often asked about the autobiographical nature of "Grief." In an earlier memoir called *Cockroaches*, named after the Hutu term for Tutsis, she recounts her family's experience of the atrocity:

> The killers attacked the house until every last trace was wiped away. The bush had covered everything over. It's as if we never existed. And yet my family once lived there. Humiliated, afraid, waiting day after day for what was to come, what we didn't have a word for: genocide. And I alone preserve the memory of it. That's why I'm writing this.

After conducting research into Mukasonga's life and experiences, discuss how that deeper knowledge influences your understanding and appreciation of "Grief."

4. **Connections.** The Kigali Genocide Memorial, described on its website as "a place of remembrance and learning," states its goal as "to prevent future mass atrocities and genocides, in Rwanda and the world." The remains of over 250,000 people are interred there. After reading about its founding and design, discuss the extent to which you believe memorials or museums that confront visitors with the atrocities of the past lead to healing or prevent future violence.

5. **Speaking and Listening.** Working in small groups, identify a passage in "Grief" that you find especially powerful or that gives you the greatest insight into the ways people process trauma. After reaching a consensus, be prepared to discuss with the full class the reasons for your choice.

6. **Connections.** There have been many films made about the Rwandan genocide, including documentaries. View one of these and discuss the perspective that it takes on the genocide and, if applicable, its aftermath. How does the film you have chosen compare to the perspective that Mukasonga presents in "Grief"?

7. **Connections.** In her 2005 book *The Year of Magical Thinking*, author Joan Didion recounts her struggle with grief in the wake of the unexpected death of her husband from a heart attack. She describes the way she felt as a series of "waves":

> Grief, when it comes, is nothing like we expect it to be. . . . Grief has no distance. Grief comes in waves, paroxysms, sudden apprehensions that weaken the knees and blind the eyes and obliterate the dailiness of life. Virtually everyone who has ever experienced grief mentions this phenomenon of "waves."

Although the context of Didion's loss is far different than the protagonist of Mukasonga's story, Didion's description of the experience of grief might be considered universal. How does Mukasonga use literary elements to characterize the act of grieving in her story? How similar is this characterization to Didion's depiction of it?

8. **Connections.** Paul Slovic, a professor of psychology at the University of Oregon, is an expert on the psychological phenomenon known as "psychic numbing," which he described in an interview for NPR. He explains that while individual lives are very important to people, humans struggle to apply that logic to larger groups of people:

> [I]f I tell you that there are 87 people endangered in some situation, you'll be concerned. Then I said . . . [t]here are 88 people. You won't feel any different. . . . As the numbers increase, sometimes, we begin to lose sensitivity. It's not just that we don't differentiate between one large number and another. We care less. The numbers are so large . . . they don't convey any feeling.

How does Slovic's concept of psychic numbing illuminate the world's response to the Rwandan genocide as conveyed in "Grief"?

Playing Metal Gear Solid V: The Phantom Pain

Jalil Kochai

Jamil Jan Kochai

Jamil Jan Kochai (b. 1992) was born in an Afghan refugee camp in Pakistan and grew up in the United States. His father's family is from Logar, in northern Afghanistan. Kochai's visits to his relatives there and his family history inspired his debut novel, *99 Nights in Logar* (2019), which won the O. Henry Award. He is currently a Stegner Fellow at Stanford University.

KEY CONTEXT In the late 1970s, the Soviet Union crossed Afghanistan's northern border in an invasion that led to a nine-year guerrilla-style war between the Soviet Union and the U.S.-backed Afghan mujahideen, or guerrilla fighters. During the conflict, roughly 2 million Afghans were displaced and between 500,000 and 2 million Afghan civilians died. This story centers on a real action-adventure-stealth video game series, *Metal Gear*, first created by Hideo Kojima in 1987. In 2015 *Metal Gear Solid V: The Phantom Pain*, set in Soviet-occupied Afghanistan, was released.

First, you have to gather the cash to preorder the game at the local GameStop, where your cousin works, and, even though he hooks it up with the employee discount, the game is still a bit out of your price range because you've been using your Taco Bell paychecks to help your pops, who's been out of work since you were ten, and who makes you feel unbearably guilty about spending money on useless hobbies while kids in Kabul are destroying their bodies to build compounds for white businessmen and warlords — but, shit, it's Kojima, it's Metal Gear, so, after scrimping and saving (like literal dimes you're picking up off the street), you've got the cash, which you give to your cousin, who purchases the game on your behalf, and then, on the day it's released, you just have to find a way to get to the store.

But, because your oldest brother has taken the Civic to Sac State, you're hauling your two-hundred-and-sixty-pound ass on a bicycle you haven't touched since middle school, and thank Allah (if He's up there) that the bike is still rideable, because you're sure there'll be a line if you don't get to GameStop early, so, huffing and puffing, you're regretting all the Taco Bell you've eaten over the past two years, but you ride with such fervor that you end up being only third in line, and it's your cousin himself who hands you the game in a brown paper bag, as if it were something illegal or illicit, which it isn't, of course, it's Metal Gear, it's Kojima, it's the final game in a series so fundamentally a part of your childhood that often, when you hear the Irish Gaelic chorus from "The Best Is Yet to Come," you cannot help weeping softly into your keyboard.

For some reason, riding back home is easier.

You leave the bike behind the trash cans at the side of the house and hop the wooden fence into the back yard and, if the door to the garage is open, you slip in, and if it's not, which it isn't, you've got to take a chance on the screen door in the back yard, but, lo and behold, your father is ankle deep in the dirt, hunched over, yanking at weeds with his bare hands the way he used to as a farmer in Logar, before war and famine forced him to flee to the western coast of the American empire, where he labored for many years until it broke his body for good, and even though his doctor has forbidden him to work in the yard, owing to the torn nerves in his neck and spine — which, you know from your mother, were first damaged when he was tortured by Russians shortly after the murder of his younger brother, Watak, during the Soviet War — he is out here clawing at the earth and its spoils, as if he were digging for treasure or his own grave.

5 Spotting you only four feet away from the sliding glass door, he gestures for you to come over, and though you are tired and sweaty, with your feet aching and the most important game of the decade hidden inside your underwear, you approach him.

He signals for you to crouch down beside him, then he runs his dirty fingers through his hair until flakes of his scalp fall onto his shoulders and his beard.

This isn't good.

When your father runs his hands through his hair, it is because he has forgotten his terrible, flaking dandruff, which he forgets only during times of severe emotional or physical distress, which means that he is about to tell you a story that is either upsetting or horrifying or both, which isn't fair, because you are a son and not a therapist.

Your father is a dark, sturdy man, and so unlike you that, as a child, you were sure that one day Hagrid would come to your door and inform you of your status as a Mudblood, and then your true life — the life without the weight of your father's history, pain, guilt, hopelessness, helplessness, judgment, and shame — would begin.

10 Your father asks you where you were.

"The library."

"You have to study?"

You tell him you do, which isn't, technically, a lie.

"All right," he says in English, because he has given up on speaking to you in Pashto, "but, after you finish, come back down. I have something I need to talk to you about."

15 Hurry.

When you get to your room, you lock the door and turn up MF Doom on your portable speaker to ward off mothers, fathers, grandmothers, sisters, and brothers who want to harp at you about prayer, the Quran, Pashto, Farsi, a new job, new classes, exercise, basketball, jogging, talking, guests, chores, homework help, bathroom help, family time, time, because usually "Madvillainy" does the trick.

Open the brown paper bag and toss the kush your cousin has stashed with your game because he needs a new smoking buddy since his best friend gave up the ganja for God again, and he sees you as a prime target, probably because he thinks you've got nothing better to do with your time or you're not as religious as your brothers or you're desperate to escape the unrelenting nature of a corporeal existence, and, God damn, the physical map of Afghanistan that comes with the game is fucking beautiful.

Not that you're a patriot or a nationalist or one of those Afghans who walk around in a pakol and kameez[1] and play the tabla[2] and claim that their favorite singer is Ahmad Zahir,[3] but the fact that nineteen-eighties Afghanistan is the final setting of the most legendary and artistically significant gaming franchise in the history of time made you all the more excited to get your hands on it, especially since you've been shooting at Afghans in your games (Call of Duty and Battlefield and Splinter Cell) for so long that you've become oddly immune to the self-loathing you felt when you were first massacring wave after wave of militant fighters who looked just like your father.

Now, finally, start the game.

• • •

20 After you escape from the hospital where Big Boss was recovering from the explosion he barely survived in the prequel to the Phantom

---

[1] Both items of traditional dress in Afghanistan. A pakol is a soft, round hat. A kameez is a long tunic and pants. — Eds.

[2] A pair of hand drums. — Eds.

[3] Ahmad Zahir (1946–1979) was an iconic musician. He died in a car accident, but there was some speculation at the time that he was killed for his political beliefs. — Eds.

This 2010 painting by Afghan artist Akram Ati (b. 1986) is titled *Hope*. **What ideas about hope does the painting convey? In what way is Kochai's story also about hope?**

Pain, you and Revolver Ocelot travel to the brutal scenes of northern Kabul Province — its rocky cliffs, its dirt roads, and its sunlight bleeding off into the dark mountains just the way you remember from all those years ago, when you visited Kabul as a child — and although your initial mission is to locate and extract Kazuhira Miller, the Phantom Pain is the first Metal Gear Solid game to be set in a radically open-world environment, and you decide to postpone the rescue of Kazuhira Miller until after you get some Soviet blood on your hands, a feat you accomplish promptly by locating and massacring an entire base of Russian combatants.

Your father, you know, didn't kill a single Russian during his years as a mujahideen in Logar, but there is something in the act of slaughtering these Soviet N.P.C.s[4] that makes you feel connected to him and his history of warfare.

Thinking of your father and his small village, you head south to explore the outer limits of the open world in the Phantom Pain, crossing trails and deserts and mountain passes, occasionally stopping at a checkpoint or a military barracks to slaughter more Russians, and you find yourself, incredibly, skirting the city of Kabul, still dominated by the Soviets, and continuing on to Logar, to Mohammad Agha, and when you get to Wagh Jan, the roadside-market village that abuts the Kabul-Logar highway, just the way you remember it, you hitch your horse and begin to sneak along the clay compounds and the shops, climbing walls and crawling atop roofs, and, whenever a local Afghan spots you, you knock him out with a tranquillizer, until you make it to the bridge that leads to the inner corridors of your parents' home village, Naw'e Kaleh, which looks so much like the photos and your own blurred memories from the trip when you were a kid that you begin to become uneasy, not yet afraid, but as if consumed by an overwhelming sense of déjà vu.

Sneaking along the dirt roads, past the golden fields and the apple orchards and the mazes of clay compounds, you come upon the house where your father used to reside, and it is there — on the road in front of your father's home — that you spot Watak, your father's sixteen-year-old brother, whom you recognize only because his picture (unsmiling, head shaved, handsome, and sixteen forever) hangs on the wall of the room in your home where your parents pray, but here he is, in your game, and you press Pause and you set down the controller, and now you are afraid.

[4] Non-player characters. — Eds.

Sweat is running down your legs in rivulets, in streams, your heart is thumping, and you are wondering if sniffing the kush as you did earlier has got you high.

You look out the window and see your brother walking toward the house in the dark and you realize that you've been playing for too long.

You're blinking a lot.

Too much.

You notice that your room is a mess and that it smells like ass and that you've become so accustomed to its smell and its mess that from the space inside your head, behind your eyes, the space in which your first-person P.O.V. is rooted, you —

Ignore the knock.

It's just your little sister.

Get back to the game.

There is a bearded, heavyset man beside Watak, who, you soon realize, is your father.

You pause the game again and put down the controller.

Doom spits, "His life is like a folklore legend. . . . Why you so stiff, you need to smoke more, bredrin. . . . Instead of trying to riff with the broke war veteran."

It seems to you a sign.

You extract the kush from the trash, and, because you have no matches or lighter, you put hunks of it in your mouth and you chew and nearly vomit twice.

Return to the game.

Hiding in your grandfather's mulberry tree, you listen to your father and his brother discuss what they will eat for suhoor,[5] thereby indicating that it is still Ramadan, that this is just days before Watak's murder.

Then it hits you.

Here is what you're going to do: before your father is tortured and his brother murdered, you are going to tranquillize them both and you are going to carry them to your horse and cross Logar's terrain until you reach a safe spot where you can call a helicopter and fly them back to your offshore platform: Mother Base.

But just as you load your tranquillizers your brother bangs on your door and demands that you come out, and after ignoring him for a bit, which only makes him madder and louder, you shout that you are sick, but the voice that comes out of your mouth is not your own, it is the voice of a faraway man imitating your voice, and your brother can tell.

He leaves, and you return to the game.

From the cover of the mulberry tree, you aim your tranquillizer gun, but you forget that you've got the laser scope activated, and Watak sees the red light flashing on your father's forehead and they're off, running and firing back at your tree with rifles they had hidden underneath their patus,[6] and you are struck twice, so you need a few moments to recover your health and, by the time you do, they're gone.

Your brother is back, and this time he has brought along your oldest brother, who somehow is able to shout louder and bang harder than your second-oldest brother, and they're both asking what you're doing and why you won't come out and why you won't grow up and why you insist on worrying your mother and your father, who you know gets those terrible migraines triggered by stress, and now your oldest brother is banging so hard you're afraid the door will come off its hinges, so you lug your dresser in front of it as a barricade and then you go back to your spot in front of the TV, and you sit on the floor and press Play.

• • •

At night, under cover of darkness, you sneak toward your father's compound, and you scale the fifteen-foot-high walls of clay and crawl along the rooftops until you get to the highest

[5] The early morning meal that takes place before a day of fasting during Ramadan, a month-long Muslim holiday. — Eds.

[6] Thick blankets or shawls traditionally worn during winter in Afghanistan. — Eds.

extending beyond the text

Deborah Treisman, fiction editor at the *New Yorker*, interviewed Jamil Jan Kochai when "Playing Metal Gear Solid V: The Phantom Pain" was published in the magazine. During the interview she asked him whether his family history shaped the story. He responded:

> Quite a bit. As in the story, my father's only younger brother, Dawlat Khan, was murdered as a teen-ager during the Soviet occupation of Afghanistan. His story has haunted my family for many decades now and was at the heart of our departure from Afghanistan, but I grew up hearing only bits and pieces of it. When I was young, my father always made sure that we mentioned our martyred uncle in our prayers. His name carried so much weight in our household that we always seemed to whisper it. And, as much as it hurt them, my relatives refused to forget what had happened to him. A black-and-white photograph of him still hangs in our living room — a testament to all we have lost to war.

Treisman's conversation with Kochai regarding the video game ended with a discussion of the protagonist's apparent need to connect with his father through the video game, despite avoiding him in real life. When she asked him if this behavior is a contradiction or human nature, he replied:

> Both? Connection, in general, can be an impossible goal, but the children of refugees trying to reach a point of understanding with their parents often have to deal with additional forms of disconnect — the loss of language, the weight of guilt, the shame of difference, the pressures of societal discrimination, and memories of incomprehensible trauma. It can be daunting. The father in this story has suffered such immense loss, such unimaginable pain — I think it frightens our protagonist, who has lived a comparatively sheltered life, and I think he understands that, in order to reach his father, to connect with him, he must, in some way, suffer with him, too.

1. **Based on Kochai's responses, how does the story reflect his own family history?**
2. **While many children might often have difficulties connecting with their parents, Kochai asserts that this is especially true for "children of refugees." What does he mean by this? How does the story's narrator illustrate this difficulty?**

point in the compound, where your father stands, on the lookout for incoming jets and firebombs, and you shoot him twice in the back with tranquillizers and, as he is falling, you catch him in your arms, your father, who, at this time, is around the same age that you are now, and in the dark, on the roof of the compound that he will lose to this war, you hold him, his body still strong and well, his heart unbroken, and you set him down gently on the clay so that the sky does not swallow him.

Climbing down into the courtyard, you go from chamber to chamber, spotting uncles and aunts and cousins you've never met in real life, and you find Watak near the cow's shed, sleeping just behind the doorway of a room filled with women, as if to protect them, and, after you aim your tranquillizer gun and send

Watak into a deeper sleep, your grandmother, a lifelong insomniac, rises from her toshak[7] and strikes you in the shoulder with a machete and calls for the men in the house, of whom there are many, to awaken and slaughter the Russian who has come to kill us all in our sleep.

The damage from the machete is significant.

Nonetheless, you still have the strength to tranquillize your grandmother, pick up Watak, and climb back onto the roof while all your uncles and cousins and even your grandfather are awakened and armed and begin to fire at your legs as you hustle along, bleeding and weary, to the spot where your father rests.

With your uncle on one shoulder and your father on the other, you leap off the roof into the shadows of an apple orchard.

The men are pouring out onto the roads and the fields, calling upon neighbors and allies, and, because the orchard is soon surrounded on all sides, it seems certain that you will be captured, but you are saved by, of all things, a squadron of Spetsnaz,[8] who begin to fire on the villagers, and in the confusion of the shoot-out, as the entire village is lit up by a hundred gunfights, each fight a microcosm of larger battles and wars and global conflicts strung together by the invisible wires of beloved men who will die peacefully in their sleep, you make your way out of the orchard, passing trails and streams and rivers and mulberry trees, until you reach your horse and ride out of Wagh Jan, toward an extraction point in the nearby Black Mountains.

But now, at the door, is your father.

"Zoya?" he is saying, very gently, the way he used to say it when you were a kid, when you were in Logar, when you got the flu, when the pills and the I.V. and the home remedies weren't working, when there was nothing to do but wait for the aching to ebb, and your father was there, maybe in the orchard, maybe on the veranda, and he was holding you in his lap, running his fingers through your hair, and saying your name, the way he is saying it now, as if it were almost a question.

"Zoya?" he says and, when you do not reply, nothing else.

Keep going.

Russians chase you on the ground and in the air, they fire and you are struck once, twice, three or four times, and there are so many Russians, but your horse is quick and nimble and manages the terrain better than their trucks can, and you make it to the extraction point, in a hollow of the Black Mountains, with enough time to summon the helicopter and to set up a perimeter of mines, and you hide your father and his brother at the mouth of a cave, behind a large boulder the shape of a believer in prostration, where you lie prone with a sniper rifle and begin to pick off Russian paratroopers in the distance, and you fire at the engines of the trucks and ignore the tanks, which will reach you last, and it is mere moments before your helicopter will arrive, and, just as you think you are going to make it, your horse is slaughtered in a flurry of gunfire and your pilot is struck by a single bullet from a lone rifleman, and the helicopter falls to the earth and bursts into flames, killing many Russians, and giving you just enough time to rush into the cave, into the heart of the Black Mountains.

With your father on one shoulder and your uncle on the other, and with the lights of the Soviet gunfire dying away at the outer edges of your vision, you trudge deeper into the darkness of the cave, and though you cannot be sure that your father and his brother are still alive, that they haven't been shot in the chaos, that they are not, now, corpses, you feel compelled to keep moving into a darkness so complete that your reflection becomes visible on the screen of the television in front of you, and it is as if the figures in the image were journeying inside you, delving into your flesh.

To be saved. ■

2019

[7] A narrow mattress that is placed on the floor. — Eds.

[8] A Russian term that essentially refers to Special Operations Forces. — Eds.

Understanding and Interpreting

1. **AP® Character and Narration.** How does the narrator justify purchasing the video game despite what "kids in Kabul" (par. 1) are doing? What does this rationale convey about his values and motivations?
2. **AP® Character and Narration.** How are the narrator and his family depicted in the first section of the story? What is the narrator's perspective on his family?
3. **AP® Character and Narration.** What does the narrator mean when he says he has become "oddly immune" to "self-loathing" (par. 18)? How have video games contributed to this sentiment?
4. **AP® Character and Narration.** The narrator states that playing the video game makes him feel "connected to" his father "and his history of warfare" (par. 21). How do you interpret this observation, particularly in light of his in-person interactions with his father?
5. **AP® Character, Setting, and Narration.** What is the relationship between the narrator's family history and the events that take place in the video game? How does the video game shape — or warp — the narrator's understanding of the past?
6. **AP® Character and Narration.** As the narrator sets his father down in the video game, he does so "gently on the clay so that the sky does not swallow him" (par. 45). What does this suggest about his perception of his father? How does his treatment of his father in the game compare to how he interacts with him in real life?
7. **AP® Character and Narration.** How does the final sentence reflect an important theme of the story? Who needs to be saved in the video game? In real life? Why do they need to be saved?

Analyzing Language, Style, and Structure

1. **Vocabulary in Context.** When Afghan villagers must defend themselves from "a squadron of Spetsnaz," each of their battles is described as a "microcosm" (par. 50). What does this word mean, and how does it characterize the fights Jamil Jan Kochai describes? How does the concept of a microcosm relate to the events and structure of this story?
2. **AP® Structure and Narration.** What do you notice about the syntax of each paragraph? How does Kochai's syntax contribute to tone, meaning, and your reading experience?
3. **AP® Figurative Language.** In the first two paragraphs, the narrator repeats "it's Kojima" and "it's Metal Gear." What is the function of this repetition?
4. **AP® Character, Narration, and Figurative Language.** How does the imagery at the end of the fourth paragraph characterize the father? What is the narrator's attitude toward his father when he imagines him "digging for treasure or his own grave"?
5. **AP® Character, Narration, and Figurative Language.** What do the allusions in paragraph 9 contribute to your understanding of the narrator and his perspective?
6. **AP® Character, Structure, and Narration.** What shift occurs in paragraphs 22 and 24? How do these shifts illustrate the meaning the game has begun to take on for the narrator?
7. **AP® Structure and Narration.** Although the narrator recognizes that we experience our lives through a "first-person P.O.V." (par. 28), he narrates the story in second person. What is the effect of this point of view? How would your reading experience differ if the point of view were first or third person?

8. **AP® Character and Figurative Language.** In the video game, the narrator is able to "tranquillize" others. What are the connotations of this word? Who gets tranquillized, and what is the significance of this action — both in the game and in real life?

9. **AP® Character and Figurative Language.** The image of the narrator carrying his "father on one shoulder" and his "uncle on the other" recurs in the story. What does this image suggest about the narrator and his relationship with his family?

10. **AP® Character, Narration, and Figurative Language.** The phrase *phantom pain*, which is part of the video game's subtitle, refers to the sensation of pain associated with a limb that has been lost. Figuratively, what phantom pain permeates the narrator's household? How does this pain shape family dynamics? How does it manifest in the narrator, who did not experience the cause of this pain firsthand?

Topics for Composing

1. **AP® FRQ** **Prose Fiction Analysis.** The following question refers to paragraphs 4–16 of Jamil Jan Kochai's "Playing Metal Gear Solid V: The Phantom Pain," published in 2019. In this passage, the narrator attempts to get past his father without being spotted so that he can play his new video game uninterrupted. Read the passage carefully. Then, in a well-written essay, analyze how Kochai uses literary elements and techniques to convey the narrator's complex relationship with his father and their family history.

2. **AP® FRQ** **Literary Argument.** In his first novel, *The Kite Runner*, Afghan American novelist Khaled Hosseini asserts that "it's wrong what they say about the past, [...] about how you can bury it. Because the past claws its way out." In "Playing Metal Gear Solid V: The Phantom Pain," the narrator's interaction with this video game forces him to contend with his family history. In a well-written essay, analyze how the narrator's surreal experience of the past contributes to an interpretation of the work as a whole. Do not merely summarize the plot.

3. **Connections.** Kochai stated in an interview that he is a student of Colombian writer Gabriel García Márquez, who is known for magical realism, a genre that integrates normally unbelievable — and even magical — occurrences into a realistic context. In what ways does this story blur the line that separates fact from fiction? What is the effect of this blurring on your reading experience and your interpretation of the story?

4. **Connections.** Kochai stated that he has "always found the second-person point of view to be oddly intimate *and* alienating." He proceeded to state that he felt this way when he first read Jamaica Kincaid's "Girl" (p. 37) and when playing first-person shooter games, such as *Call of Duty*. To fully understand his stance, read "Girl" and play a video game with a first-person point of view. What aspects of these two experiences do you find both intimate and alienating? How are these feelings associated with your reading of "Playing Metal Gear Solid V: The Phantom Pain"?

5. **Research.** Kochai and the narrator's father are both from Logar, Afghanistan. Do some research on how this province was affected by the war with the Soviet Union in the 1980s. How does your research inform your understanding of the father and the story as a whole?

6. **Creative Writing.** Write a diary entry from the perspective of the narrator. What did the day's events mean to him? How does playing the video game affect how he views his father? How does he perceive his relationship with the past?

Poetry

To Lucasta, Going to the Wars

Richard Lovelace

NMUIM/Alamy

Richard Lovelace (1617–1657) was an English poet who fought on the side of King Charles I (his supporters became known as "Cavaliers") during the English Civil War (1642–1651). Lovelace attended school in London as a child and went on to study at Oxford, where he started writing. Lovelace's first work was an unpublished drama, *The Scholars*, which was performed at Oxford and later in London. As a partisan in the Civil War, Lovelace was influenced heavily by his military experiences and political maneuvering.

Tell me not, Sweet, I am unkind,
  That from the nunnery
Of thy chaste breast and quiet mind
  To war and arms I fly.

True, a new mistress now I chase,
  The first foe in the field;
And with a stronger faith embrace
  A sword, a horse, a shield.

Yet this inconstancy is such
  As thou too shalt adore;
I could not love thee, Dear, so much,
  Loved I not Honor more. ■

1649

Understanding and Interpreting

1. The speaker appeals to honor throughout the poem. Where does he refer to Lucasta's honor? Where does he refer to his own honor? Why do you think the concept of honor features so prominently?
2. How does the title of the poem help you understand each stanza?
3. What does the phrase "stronger faith" (l. 7) suggest about the speaker's perspective and priorities?
4. How do you interpret the final two lines of the poem? How does the speaker connect his "Dear" (l. 11) to "Honor" (l. 12)?

Analyzing Language, Style, and Structure

1. **Vocabulary in Context.** The word "inconstancy" refers to changeability or inconsistency, often in relation to someone's love and affection. To what "inconstancy" does the speaker refer in line 9? What does this change suggest about his love?

2. What comparison does the speaker make when he calls "the first foe in the field" his "new mistress" (ll. 5–6)? Why might the speaker make such a comparison?
3. How do the parenthetical terms of affection — "Sweet" (l. 1) and "Dear" (l. 11) — create a sense of cohesion in the poem? What purpose does it serve to begin and end the poem on a similar note?
4. Why does the speaker use romantic language to describe departing for war? How might these comparisons soften the blow of his departure?
5. How does the speaker's tone shift throughout the poem? Consider the effects of the formal rhyme scheme and the romantic idealization in your answer.

Topics for Composing

1. AP® FRQ **Poetry Analysis.** In Richard Lovelace's "To Lucasta, Going to the Wars," published in 1649, the speaker addresses his beloved before departing for war. Read the poem carefully. Then, in a well-written essay, analyze how Lovelace uses literary elements and techniques to convey the speaker's complex attitude toward his departure.
2. **AP® Literary Argumentation.** The speaker of this poem argues that love cannot exist without honor. How are these two terms related? Could you love someone if you're not an honorable person? Explain your position and support it with evidence from the poem.
3. **Creative Writing.** Harvard professor Dr. Helen Vendler suggests that it is helpful to consider a poem's antecedent scenario — that is, what events or thoughts may have prompted the speaker to utter the words found in the poem. Think of "To Lucasta, Going to the Wars" as a response to Lucasta herself. Write a letter or poem that Lucasta could have written to the speaker that would have prompted him to respond with this poem.
4. **Connections.** Read John Donne's "A Valediction: Forbidding Mourning" (p. 407), a poem in which the speaker tries to assuage his beloved's grief over his departure. Compare Donne's speaker's address to his beloved to that of Lovelace's speaker.
5. **Multimodal.** Record a video of yourself reciting this poem. What tone do you plan to convey, and how do you plan to convey it? Include a song in the background of your video. How does the song relate to the words in the poem? to the speaker's intent and emotions?

To Lucasta on Going to the War—for the Fourth Time

Lebrecht Music & Arts/Alamy

Robert Graves

Robert Graves (1895–1985) was an English poet, novelist, critic, and classicist. Graves was born to a middle-class family in Wimbledon, and at the outbreak of World War I he enlisted immediately. After almost being killed at the Battle of the Somme, Graves returned to England and studied English at Oxford. Thereafter, he lived around the world and was able to earn a living from his writing, mostly because of the popular success of historical novels such as *I, Claudius* (1934), *Count Belisarius* (1938), and *King Jesus* (1946). In addition to translations and innovative fictional interpretations of history, Graves also wrote a popular memoir about World War I, *Good-Bye to All That* (1929). In "To Lucasta on Going to the War — for the Fourth Time," Graves revisits Lovelace's original poem.

KEY CONTEXT This poem is about a soldier's experience in World War I (1914–1918), a conflict that involved thirty-two nations and resulted in roughly 21.5 million military and civilian deaths. Known at the time as the "war to end all wars," the conflict saw the widespread use of new technology such as machine guns, trench warfare, tanks, and chemical weapons. Many soldiers — drafted into a war with causes that were largely irrelevant to their everyday lives and subjected to weapons deadlier than any conflict to date — were traumatized and disillusioned by their wartime experiences.

It doesn't matter what's the cause,
  What wrong they say we're righting,
A curse for treaties, bonds, and laws,
  When we're to do the fighting!
And since we lads are proud and true,
  What else remains to do?
Lucasta, when to France your man
  Returns his fourth time, hating war,
Yet laughs as calmly as he can
  And flings an oath, but says no more.
That is not courage, that's not fear —
Lucasta, he's a Fusilier,[1]
  And his pride sends him here.

***

Let statesmen bluster, bark, and bray,
  And so decide who started
This bloody war, and who's to pay,
  But he must be stout-hearted,
Make sit and stake with quiet breath,
  Playing at cards with Death.
Don't plume yourself he fights for you;
  It is no courage, love, nor hate,
But let us do the things we do;
  It's pride that makes the heart be great;
It is not anger, no, nor fear —
Lucasta, he's a Fusilier,
  And his pride keeps him here. ■

1918

[1] A member of an elite branch in the British Army, the Royal Fusiliers, originally founded in 1685. — Eds.

Exploring the Text

1. What is implied when the soldier "laughs as calmly as he can" (l. 9)? Where else in the poem does the speaker imply that all is not right with the veteran soldier returning to war?
2. Why does the speaker compare battle to "Playing at cards with Death" (l. 19)? What does this comparison suggest about the nature and purpose of warfare?

3. The first stanza ends, “And his pride sends him here” (l. 13), and the last stanza ends, “And his pride keeps him here” (l. 26). How does the shift from “sends” to “keeps” reveal the speaker’s critique of war?
4. How does the rhyming form of the poem contrast with its message?

Making Connections

1. Identify two places in each poem where armed conflict is represented. Then, discuss how each speaker treats war itself differently.
2. How could the opening of Graves’s poem — “It doesn’t matter what’s the cause” (l. 1) — be seen as a satiric response to that of Lovelace?
3. How might addressing each poem to Lucasta, presumably by the same speaker, heighten the difference in perspective between the poems? What has changed in the warrior’s perspective in Graves’s poem, when the speaker is on his fourth tour of duty?
4. In “To Lucasta, Going to the Wars,” Richard Lovelace’s speaker justifies his departure for war with an appeal to honor. In “To Lucasta on Going to the War — for the Fourth Time,” Robert Graves’s speaker justifies his continued commitment to war with an appeal to pride. Compare and contrast the connotations of both honor and pride. How might the pride in Graves’s poem satirize the concept of honor in Lovelace’s poem?
5. “To Lucasta, Going to the Wars” and “To Lucasta on Going to the War — for the Fourth Time” offer the same character, Lucasta, but very different justifications for going to or returning to war. Read the poems carefully. Then, write an essay in which you examine the soldier-lover relationship in each poem, analyzing how Lovelace and Graves offer different perspectives on the purpose and nature of war.

Battle Hymn of the Republic

Julia Ward Howe

Library of Congress, Prints & Photographs Division, [LC-USZ62-8221]

Julia Ward Howe (1819–1910) was a prominent American abolitionist, activist, and poet. Born in New York City, Howe was educated and well read from an early age. She married into a prominent family and raised six children in Boston while her husband worked. Stifled by her marriage, Howe began to publish personal poems. Her first book, *Passion-Flowers*, appeared in 1853. To the chagrin of her husband, Howe went on to write four more poetry books, many critiquing the limited role available to women in American society. In 1870, she founded the suffragist magazine *Woman’s Journal*, and in 1881 was elected president of the Association for the Advancement of Women. In 1908, she was the first woman elected to the American Academy of Arts and Letters.

KEY CONTEXT The American Civil War lasted just over four years, from 1861 to 1865. In November of 1861, Howe was inspired to write “Battle Hymn of the Republic” after she met President Abraham Lincoln in the White House, and it went on to become one of the most popular Union songs during the war. The tune to which it is sung was already well-known at the time, so part of its popularity when it was first published came from the soldiers’ familiarity with the music itself.

Mine eyes have seen the glory of the coming of the Lord:
He is trampling out the vintage where the grapes of wrath are stored;
He hath loosed the fateful lightning of His terrible swift sword:
His truth is marching on.

I have seen Him in the watch-fires of a hundred circling camps,
They have builded Him an altar in the evening dews and damps;
I can read His righteous sentence by the dim and flaring lamps:
His day is marching on.

I have read a fiery gospel writ in burnished rows of steel:
"As ye deal with my contemners, so with you my grace shall deal;
Let the Hero, born of woman, crush the serpent with his heel,
Since God is marching on."

He has sounded forth the trumpet that shall never call retreat;
He is sifting out the hearts of men before His judgment-seat:
Oh, be swift, my soul, to answer Him! be jubilant, my feet!
Our God is marching on.

In the beauty of the lilies Christ was born across the sea,
With a glory in his bosom that transfigures you and me:
As he died to make men holy, let us die to make men free,
While God is marching on. ■

1862

Understanding and Interpreting

1. What does the speaker mean by "He is trampling out the vintage where the grapes of wrath are stored" (l. 2)? Based on your reading of this poem, what exactly are the "grapes of wrath"?
2. Who is "in the watch-fires of a hundred circling camps" (l. 5)? What does this presence mean to the speaker?
3. What does the "fiery gospel" (l. 9) mean to the speaker? How does she suggest readers act on this gospel?
4. How does the speaker characterize God in this poem? How does she characterize Christ in the final stanza? What does this characterization suggest about the speaker's perspective on the Civil War and slavery?

Analyzing Language, Style, and Structure

1. **Vocabulary in Context.** The speaker describes Christ as having "a glory in his bosom that transfigures you and me" (l. 18). In using "transfigures," what does Howe suggest about the kind of change Christ brings about in people?
2. In the first stanza, the speaker describes the Lord as having "loosed the fateful lightning of His terrible swift sword" (l. 3). What other images of violent power can be found in the poem? How do they contribute to the speaker's purpose?

3. The second stanza concludes, "His day is marching on" (l. 8). Examine the previous three lines in the stanza. How is the speaker's use of "day" metaphorical? What does that metaphor add to the poem?
4. What does "the serpent" in line 11 represent on a symbolic level? Who is "the serpent" on a battlefield?
5. What is the purpose of the allusion to Christ in the final stanza?
6. Note the phrase "Battle Hymn" in the title of the poem. Where else does the speaker blend the military with the religious, and to what effect?
7. Examine how the imagery in the final stanza differs from the imagery in the previous four. What does this shift signal? What effect does it have on readers?
8. Notice how each stanza offers three long, comparatively complicated lines followed by a single line that references God directly. What is the effect of Howe's incorporation of personification into these lines in the first two stanzas? How does this general pattern emphasize the speaker's message?

Topics for Composing

1. AP® FRQ **Poetry Analysis.** In Julia Ward Howe's "Battle Hymn of the Republic," published in 1862, the speaker looks to God as a source of strength for those fighting to end slavery. Read the poem carefully. Then, in a well-written essay, analyze how Howe uses literary elements and techniques to develop the complex relationship between spiritual faith and human conflict.
2. **Research.** "Battle Hymn of the Republic" shares its tune with other songs, including "Glory, Hallelujah" and "John Brown's Body." Research the history of the tune they have in common and the history of camp meeting songs in general. Then, using "Battle Hymn of the Republic" as a model, write an essay in which you explain the connection between the spiritual and the worldly in these texts, particularly given their shared themes and roles in communal gatherings.
3. **Connections.** John Steinbeck's novel *The Grapes of Wrath* takes its title from the second line of Howe's lyrics. Read *The Grapes of Wrath*, or revisit it if you've read it in the past. Then explain how the themes in "Battle Hymn of the Republic" relate to the challenges faced by the Joad family and to the character of Jim Casy.
4. **Speaking and Listening.** Throughout human history, religion has played a significant role in warfare, including as its central cause. Engage in a small-group discussion with your peers about the role of religious faith in war and whether religion will always be a part of war, even in conflicts that are not explicitly about religion. Be sure to consider the personal nature of both major aspects of this topic.
5. **Connections.** Since it was written, people have called on "Battle Hymn of the Republic" as a source of support for causes of all kinds. In a 2018 story by National Public Radio, Birgitta Johnson, an associate professor of ethnomusicology and African American studies at the University of South Carolina, says, "The kumbaya moment will not be happening across the aisles because of this song" and "it's really about supporting whatever your perspective is — about freedom or liberation, and having God as the person who's ordaining what we're doing." Do you agree with Johnson about the song's subject and meaning for people through the ages? Does the song's universal appeal ultimately reveal — or undermine — its power?

A Wife in London (December, 1899)

Thomas Hardy

Thomas Hardy (1840–1928) was born in Dorset, England. Among his most famous works are *Far from the Madding Crowd* (1874), whose title comes from Thomas Gray's "Elegy Written in a Country Churchyard"; *The Return of the Native* (1878); *Tess of the d'Urbervilles* (1891); and *Jude the Obscure* (1895). After the less than appreciative reaction that *Jude the Obscure* received — many people found it too shocking and pessimistic — Hardy wrote only poetry.

Pictorial Press Ltd/Alamy

KEY CONTEXT This poem expresses Hardy's pacifist sentiments in general and his opposition to the Second Boer War (1899–1902). Descendants of the original Dutch settlers of southern Africa, the Boers lived in two republics that comprise what is now known as South Africa, Lesotho, and Swaziland. After the discovery of diamonds and gold in the Boer territories, the British Empire sought to exert control over the Boer states, and war ensued. While Britain was victorious, nearly 100,000 lives were lost, including more than 20,000 British troops, 14,000 Boer troops, and over 26,000 Boer women and children who died in British-run concentration camps. The total number of African deaths in these concentration camps was not recorded, but estimates range from 13,000 to 20,000 people.

I — The Tragedy

She sits in the tawny vapour
That the Thames-side lanes have uprolled,
Behind whose webby fold on fold
Like a waning taper
The street-lamp glimmers cold.

A messenger's knock cracks smartly,
Flashed news is in her hand
Of meaning it dazes to understand
Though shaped so shortly:
He — has fallen — in the far South Land. . . .

II — The Irony

'Tis the morrow; the fog hangs thicker,
The postman nears and goes:
A letter is brought whose lines disclose
By the firelight flicker
His hand, whom the worm now knows:

Fresh — firm — penned in highest feather —
Page-full of his hoped return,
And of home-planned jaunts by brake and burn[1]
In the summer weather,
And of new love that they would learn. ■

1901

[1] A brake is a stream. A burn is a thicket of trees. — Eds.

Understanding and Interpreting

1. What two pieces of communication are the focus of this poem? How do they shape your understanding of what happens in the poem?
2. Who is "She" (l. 1)? What information do we learn about where she is and what she is doing?
3. What is the "[f]lashed news" that is "in her hand" (l. 7)? What is her reaction to it?
4. How does this poem challenge your expectations about what war poetry typically says and does? How does this gap between your expectations and the actual events of the poem contribute to Thomas Hardy's message?
5. How does "A Wife in London" qualify as an antiwar poem? What is the nature of Hardy's criticism in this poem?

Analyzing Language, Style, and Structure

1. **Vocabulary in Context.** Hardy describes the London light as being "[l]ike a waning taper" (l. 4). How does "waning" reflect the experiences of both the husband and wife in this poem?
2. What is the impact of the euphemism "fallen" instead of saying outright that the husband was killed? Similarly, what is the impact of Hardy's choice to use "the worm" instead of directly describing the decay of a dead body?
3. Trace the imagery of light in this poem as it is introduced in the first part and then picked up again in the second part. What role does the imagery play in establishing mood and conveying theme?
4. What is "The Irony" of the second section, stanzas 3 and 4? Consider the contents and tone of the husband's letter in your response.
5. How does Hardy convey the detachment of the official bureaucracy of war? Pay special attention to diction, especially verbs, in your response. How does this characterization relate to Hardy's message about the Second Boer War in particular?
6. A central contrast in the poem is the speed of the underwater cable-enabled telegram that brings news of the husband's death and the slowness of the letter he had likely written weeks earlier. What other contrasts do you find in the poem? How do they further the meaning Hardy develops?
7. How does the personification of the weather add to the power of this poem in both sections?
8. How does the sound of the poem contribute to its meaning? Be sure to consider rhyme, meter, alliteration, and onomatopoeia in your response, and be specific in your identification of examples.

Topics for Composing

1. **AP® FRQ Poetry Analysis.** In Thomas Hardy's "A Wife in London," published in 1901, the speaker describes two communications related to a soldier who has died in battle. Read the poem carefully. Then, in a well-written essay, analyze how Hardy uses literary elements and techniques to convey his attitude toward warfare.
2. **AP® Literary Argumentation.** In this poem, Hardy portrays the woman in "A Wife in London" as an unnamed, passive recipient of information. Does this depiction fail to understand the depth of feeling in "those who stand and wait," as Milton puts it in "When I consider how my light is Spent" (p. 287)? Is it a sexist portrayal of a time when only men were soldiers? Is it a strategy to universalize his protest against war? Or is it something else? Support your position with specific references from the text.
3. **Connections.** *Breaker Morant* (1980) and *Blood and Glory* (2018) are two films about the Second Boer War. After viewing them, discuss the filmmakers' interpretation of the causes and meaning of the conflict and how it compares with the themes of "A Wife in London."
4. **Creative Writing.** Imagine that the wife lives not in London but in your hometown. Write a contemporary poem about her as a widow of war in a contemporary conflict, and then discuss the differences and similarities between your poem and Hardy's. How universal is Hardy's message? Explain.
5. **Multimodal.** Put together two or three photographs that make a similar antiwar statement to Hardy's in "A Wife in London." You might focus on the Second Boer War, another violent conflict, or several different wars. Present your visual interpretation of the message of Hardy's poem to a small group of classmates and discuss.

Between Days

Yusef Komunyakaa

James Keyser/The LIFE Images Collection/Getty Images

Poet Yusef Komunyakaa was born James Willie Brown Jr. in 1947 and raised in Bogalusa, Louisiana. After high school, Komunyakaa enlisted in the army and served in Vietnam, an experience that permeates his poetry, although it was many years before he felt he could write about his time spent there. After returning from Vietnam, he received a BA from the University of Colorado, an MA from Colorado State University, and an MFA from the University of California, Irvine. He was awarded the 1994 Pulitzer Prize for *Neon Vernacular: New and Selected Poems*.

KEY CONTEXT A long conflict involving multiple countries, the war in Vietnam lasted more than twenty years, ending with the fall of Saigon in 1975. The United States fought as an ally of South Vietnam against the communist government of North Vietnam. Over 3 million people lost their lives: more than 58,000 Americans, over 1 million North Vietnamese soldiers and Vietcong guerrilla fighters, between 200,000 and 250,000 South Vietnamese soldiers, and as many as 2 million total civilians. The Vietnam conflict also disproportionately affected Black men. For instance, roughly

34 percent of Black registrants for the draft were inducted into the military, whereas only roughly 24 percent of white registrants were drafted, and casualty rates for Black soldiers during the war were around double those of white ones.

Expecting to see him anytime
coming up the walkway
through blueweed & bloodwort,[1]
she says, "That closed casket
was weighed down with stones."
The room is as he left it
fourteen years ago, everything
freshly dusted & polished
with lemon oil. The uncashed
death check from Uncle Sam
marks a passage in the Bible
on the dresser, next to the photo
staring out through the window.
"Mistakes. Mistakes. Now,
he's gonna have to give them this
money back when he gets home.
But I wouldn't. I would
let them pay for their mistakes.
They killed his daddy, & Janet,
she & her three children
by three different men, I hope
he's strong enough to tell her
to get lost. Lord, mistakes."
His row of tin soldiers
lines the window sill. The sunset
flashes across them like a blast.
She's buried the Silver Star[2]
& the flag under his winter clothes.
The evening's first fireflies
dance in the air like distant tracers.
Her chair faces the walkway
where she sits before the TV
asleep, as the screen dissolves
into days between snow.[3] ■

1988

[1] Blueweed is a blue flowering plant that often grows in fairly barren places, such as roadsides, cliffs, and sand dunes. In some areas of the United States, it is considered an invasive species. Bloodwort is a flowering plant with red roots; its juice is red and poisonous, but it has also been used in American Indian traditional medicine to treat respiratory ailments, among other things. — Eds.

[2] A U.S. military medal awarded for bravery in action. — Eds.

[3] A reference to the static that would fill the television screen once programming ended for the day, before the advent of the 24-hour news channel in 1980. — Eds.

Exploring the Text

1. What conclusions might you draw about the soldier's character solely from the objects in his room?
2. Why does the soldier's mother say, "That closed casket / was weighed down with stones" (ll. 4–5)? Of what is she trying to convince herself?
3. What language does the poet use to describe the soldier's room near the end of the poem? What theme or themes does such figurative language reveal?
4. In what way does the end of the poem mirror the beginning? How does this structure reflect the mother's experience of her dead son?

Making Connections

1. What do the widow in Thomas Hardy's poem and the mother in Yusef Komunyakaa's poem have in common? How are they different?
2. In these two poems, Hardy and Komunyakaa dramatize two women's perspectives on the loss of a beloved soldier in a foreign war. Compare and contrast the use of descriptive imagery in each poem. How does the imagery accentuate the specific emotional suffering of each woman?
3. Imagine a meeting between the two women dramatized in the poems. What would they say to each other? Create a dialogue between the two that reveals your understanding of the poems and your sympathy for the women.
4. Compare and contrast how each poem treats the notion of "closure" for those who remain at home after the loss of a loved one at war.

Lamentations

Siegfried Sassoon

IanDagnall Computing/Alamy

On August 2, 1914, two days before England's declaration of war, British poet Siegfried Sassoon (1886–1967) enlisted in the army and went to the front lines. Called "Mad Jack" for his reckless behavior and ferocity, Sassoon was regarded as a modern Achilles. He was wounded twice, and received two medals for bravery. While recovering from an injury in England, he became critical of the war and declined to return to duty. Deemed mentally unfit for court-martial, he was sent to the hospital to recover from shell shock and there met fellow soldier and poet Wilfred Owen, whom he encouraged to write. After the war, he taught and lectured for many years. Sassoon wrote more than twenty collections of poetry, the most famous being *Counter-Attack and Other Poems* (1918) — a small group of poems about the horrors of war, which includes "Lamentations."

KEY CONTEXT This poem is about a soldier's experience in World War I (1914–1918), a conflict that involved thirty-two nations and resulted in roughly 21.5 million military and civilian deaths. Known at the time as the "war to end all wars," the conflict saw the widespread use of new technology such as machine guns, trench warfare, tanks, and chemical weapons. Many soldiers — drafted into a war with causes that were largely irrelevant to their everyday lives and subjected to weapons deadlier than any conflict to date — were traumatized and disillusioned by their wartime experiences.

I found him in the guard-room at the Base.
From the blind darkness I had heard his crying
And blundered in. With puzzled, patient face
A sergeant watched him; it was no good trying
To stop it; for he howled and beat his chest.
And, all because his brother had gone west,
Raved at the bleeding war; his rampant grief
Moaned, shouted, sobbed, and choked, while he was kneeling
Half-naked on the floor. In my belief
Such men have lost all patriotic feeling. ■

1918

Understanding and Interpreting

1. What does the speaker mean by "his brother had gone west" (l. 6)? How would you describe the tone of this line?
2. Who are the men the speaker believes "have lost all patriotic feeling" (l. 10)? What is the speaker's attitude as he explains his "belief" (l. 9)?
3. Determining the mood of this poem can be challenging because, despite its length, it contains complex sentiments. How would you describe the atmosphere of the poem as you experience it? Using at least two words, try a pair of adjectives with similar connotations, a pair of contrasting adjectives, or an adverb-adjective combination.
4. Although the poem's title might seem straightforward, try to come up with three interpretations of it. Think about what is being lamented, and by whom.

Analyzing Language, Style, and Structure

1. **Vocabulary in Context.** Siegfried Sassoon's use of the word "blundered" in line 3 conveys a lot of information. How does "blundered" in this context clarify the speaker's feeling about the situation he describes? How does Sassoon's use of "blundered" differ from the way we usually use the word?
2. Note the repetition of past tense verbs, beginning with "Moaned" (l. 8). What is the effect of this repetition? Why are these verbs in past tense? Now, find the subject of that series of verbs. What do you find significant about that subject, and how does it affect your interpretation of the poem?
3. The speaker says he "blundered" (l. 3) into the "blind darkness" (l. 2) and that the sergeant is "puzzled" (l. 3). What does Sassoon achieve by placing so much emphasis on the confusion of the situation?
4. Note the shift in tone in the middle of line 9. How would you characterize the tone of that final statement? If you had been the one to "find" the man, how would you complete the statement, "In my belief . . ."?

5. What structural elements does Sassoon use in "Lamentations," and what ideas do these elements reinforce? Consider meter, rhyme scheme, and line breaks in your response.
6. How does the final line change reader's understanding of Sassoon's message in "Lamentations"? What irony does it emphasize?

Topics for Composing

1. AP® FRQ **Poetry Analysis.** In Siegfried Sassoon's "Lamentations," published in 1918, the speaker describes a grieving soldier whose brother has just died in World War I. Read the poem carefully. Then, in a well-written essay, analyze how Sassoon uses literary elements and techniques to develop the speaker's complex attitude toward the scene he witnesses.
2. **AP® Literary Argumentation.** Write an essay in which you analyze "Lamentations" as a satirical poem. What does Sassoon satirize? How do his language choices convey this satire?
3. **Research.** Sassoon fought and was wounded in World War I. Research his experience in the war and how it shaped his beliefs and poetry. How has your understanding of "Lamentations" changed based on your understanding of his experiences?
4. **Connections.** Read additional poems by Sassoon about World War I. Taken together, what attitude toward war do these poems convey? If the poems are works of satire, who does that satire target? Ultimately, how convincing is Sassoon's argument about warfare?
5. **Speaking and Listening.** Sassoon's poetry was just one of the ways he protested World War I, and he went on to advocate strongly for pacifism after the conflict ended. In preparation for a class discussion about protesting war and embracing pacifism, explore other ways in which people have protested conflicts since Sassoon's time. Then, engage in a discussion in which you compare and contrast those efforts with Sassoon's use of poetry to protest war.

Dulce et Decorum Est

Wilfred Owen

Wilfred Owen, c.1916 (photo)/Bridgeman Images

Born in Shropshire, England, in 1893, Wilfred Owen enlisted in the army in 1915 and fought in France during World War I. In May 1917, he was hospitalized with shell shock, a condition now referred to as post-traumatic stress disorder. He returned to the battlefield and won the Military Cross in October 1918. Five of his poems were published that year — the only five he lived to see in print. He was killed in battle one week before the Armistice (November 11, 1918). Owen's work remained virtually unknown until 1920, when his friend Siegfried Sassoon collected and published his work.

KEY CONTEXT This poem is about a soldier's experience in World War I (1914–1918), a conflict that involved thirty-two nations and resulted in roughly 21.5 million military and civilian deaths. Known at the time as the "war to end all wars," the conflict saw the widespread use of new technology such as machine guns, trench warfare, tanks, and chemical weapons such as mustard gas. Many soldiers — drafted into a war with causes that were largely irrelevant to their everyday lives, subject to weapons deadlier than any conflict to date — were traumatized and disillusioned by their wartime experiences. The title of this poem comes from the Roman poet Horace (65–8 B.C.E.), whose line "Dulce et decorum est pro patria mori" means "It is sweet and fitting to die for one's country" in Latin. Owen wrote the poem while recovering from shell shock.

Bent double, like old beggars under sacks,
Knock-kneed, coughing like hags, we cursed through sludge,
Till on the haunting flares we turned our backs
And towards our distant rest began to trudge.
Men marched asleep. Many had lost their boots
But limped on, blood-shod. All went lame; all blind;
Drunk with fatigue; deaf even to the hoots
Of tired, outstripped Five-Nines[1] that dropped behind.

Gas! GAS! Quick, boys! — An ecstasy of fumbling,
Fitting the clumsy helmets just in time;
But someone still was yelling out and stumbling
And flound'ring like a man in fire or lime[2] . . .
Dim, through the misty panes and thick green light,
As under a green sea, I saw him drowning.

In all my dreams, before my helpless sight,
He plunges at me, guttering, choking, drowning.

If in some smothering dreams you too could pace
Behind the wagon that we flung him in,
And watch the white eyes writhing in his face,
His hanging face, like a devil's sick of sin;
If you could hear, at every jolt, the blood
Come gargling from the froth-corrupted lungs,
Obscene as cancer, bitter as the cud
Of vile, incurable sores on innocent tongues, —
My friend, you would not tell with such high zest
To children ardent for some desperate glory,
The old Lie: Dulce et decorum est
Pro patria mori. ■

1920

[1] German artillery shells used in World War I. — Eds.

[2] Also known as calcium oxide, lime is a chemical compound that both sanitizes and dissolves tissue. In World War I, it was often used in the trenches to sanitize the fallen soldiers' bodies. This helped stave off the constant threat of disease and mitigate the smell. — Eds.

Understanding and Interpreting

1. Note the title of the poem and the translation provided in the Key Context note. What expectations does the title create for the reader, and at what point did you realize that this was not going to be a poem about the glories of war?

2. Why do you think the speaker uses "all" in lines 6 and 15? What does this modifier suggest about the experience of the night march and war in general?
3. Lines 17 through 28 conclude the poem in one sentence addressed to the "you" in line 17. Whom is the speaker addressing?
4. How would you describe the tone the speaker uses in the phrase "My friend" in line 25?

Analyzing Language, Style, and Structure

1. **Vocabulary in Context.** In the context of the poem, what is the meaning of the word "ardent" in line 26? Why, given its usual associations, is it particularly ironic when used to describe children learning of the glories of war?
2. In the first stanza, how does Wilfred Owen use diction and imagery to bring the experience of a night march to life for the reader?
3. What is the purpose of the similes comparing the troops to "old beggars" (l. 1) and "hags" (l. 2)?
4. Note the diction in the second stanza. Why does the speaker describe putting on a gas mask as an "ecstasy of fumbling" (l. 9)? Why does he use "or" in "fire or lime?" (l. 12)? What does this ambiguity suggest?
5. The third stanza shifts in tense, from the past tense "saw" of line 14 to the present tense "plunges" in line 16. What accounts for this temporal shift? A shift in perspective occurs in line 17. How do the shifts in time and perspective influence your response to the poem?
6. The poem uses graphic — some might say grotesque — imagery throughout. How does that imagery influence your understanding of the purpose of the poem?

Topics for Composing

1. AP® FRQ **Poetry Analysis.** In Wilfred Owen's "Dulce et Decorum Est," published in 1920, the speaker describes the horrors of war in detail. Read the poem carefully. Then, in a well-written essay, analyze how Owen uses literary elements and techniques to develop the speaker's attitude toward serving one's country in wartime.
2. **Speaking and Listening.** This poem is arguably the most famous war poem in the English language. Prepare for and hold a class discussion about what accounts for its lasting popularity. Is its fame deserved? Why, or why not?
3. **Connections.** In the introduction to his book *The Government of the Tongue*, Irish poet Seamus Heaney discusses reading Wilfred Owen's poetry, particularly "Dulce et Decorum Est," with students. He writes:

   > And it seemed to me that "*Dulce et Decorum Est*," a poem which it was easy for them to like, was the poem where I could engage them with the question of over-writing. 'Is Owen overdoing it here?' I would ask. 'Inside of five lines we have "devil's sick of sin," "gargling," "froth-corrupted," "bitter as the cud," "vile, incurable sores." Is he not being a bit overinsistent? A bit explicit?' However hangdog I might feel about such intrusions, I also felt that it was right to raise questions. Yet there was obviously an immense disparity between the nit-picking criticism I was conducting on the poem and the heavy price, in terms of emotional and physical suffering, the poet paid in order to bring it into being.

   Considering not only the subject matter of the poem but also the experience and intent of the poet, is it right to ask the questions Heaney is asking? Write an essay in response to Heaney, using the text of Owen's poem for support.

4. **Research.** Read the work of several other British World War I poets, such as Siegfried Sassoon and Rupert Brooks, and learn about their lives. How did these writers' work influence our present-day understanding of the patriotic ideal that it is noble to die for one's country?
5. **Connections.** Novelist Pat Barker has said "[W]e're at the end of the patriarchy and I'm fine with that as long as it's remembered that among the victims of the patriarchy the vast majority are men." How is that statement illustrated in "Dulce et Decorum Est" and other works in this chapter?

The War Works Hard

© Nina Subin

Dunya Mikhail

Dunya Mikhail (b. 1965) is an Iraqi American poet. She was born in Baghdad and graduated with a BA from the University of Baghdad before working as an editor, a journalist, and a translator for the *Baghdad Observer*. In 1996, under threat by the government of Saddam Hussein, Mikhail fled to Jordan and then to the United States. She later became a U.S. citizen and earned an MA in Near Eastern studies from Wayne State University. She writes in both Arabic and English. Mikhail is the author of several collections of poetry, including *The War Works Hard* (2005); *Diary of a Wave Outside the Sea* (2009), which blends poetry and autobiography; *The Iraqi Nights* (2014); and *In Her Feminine Sign* (2019). *The Beekeepers: Rescuing the Stolen Women of Iraq* (2018) is a work of nonfiction about women enslaved by ISIS. Mikhail currently teaches at Oakland University in Michigan.

KEY CONTEXT Mikhail wrote this poem in response to the Gulf War (1990–1991). After Iraq invaded the neighboring nation of Kuwait in August 1990, a coalition of nations, led by the United States, waged and won a war against Iraq. Between 20,000 and 50,000 Iraqi soldiers and 4,200 Kuwaiti soldiers were killed; among the coalition forces, nearly 300 soldiers were killed. Over 3,500 Iraqi civilians and over 1,000 Kuwaiti civilians also lost their lives during the war.

How magnificent the war is!
How eager
and efficient!
Early in the morning,
it wakes up the sirens
and dispatches ambulances
to various places,
swings corpses through the air,
rolls stretchers to the wounded,

summons rain
from the eyes of mothers,
digs into the earth
dislodging many things
from under the ruins . . .
Some are lifeless and glistening,
others are pale and still throbbing . . .
It produces the most questions
in the minds of children,
entertains the gods
by shooting fireworks and missiles
into the sky,
sows mines in the fields
and reaps punctures and blisters,
urges families to emigrate,
stands beside the clergymen
as they curse the devil
(poor devil, he remains
with one hand in the searing fire) . . .
The war continues working, day and night.
It inspires tyrants
to deliver long speeches,
awards medals to generals
and themes to poets.
It contributes to the industry
of artificial limbs,
provides food for flies,
adds pages to the history books,
achieves equality
between killer and killed,
teaches lovers to write letters,
accustoms young women to waiting,
fills the newspapers
with articles and pictures,
builds new houses
for the orphans,
invigorates the coffin makers,
gives grave diggers
a pat on the back
and paints a smile on the leader's face.
The war works with unparalleled diligence!
Yet no one gives it
a word of praise. ■

2005

Exploring the Text

1. Note the title, "The War Works Hard." Find three other places in the poem where the speaker personifies war. How might treating war as a person change how readers see war?
2. The poem opens, "How magnificent the war is!" What tone is set by opening the poem with an exclamation? Do you think the speaker really believes war is magnificent? Explain.
3. In line 22, the speaker says that war "sows mines in the fields" as if mines are seeds that will one day be grown and harvested. Why might the speaker have chosen to use "sows" instead of something more militaristic?
4. The speaker says that war "summons rain / from the eyes of mothers" (ll. 10–11). Find at least two more images where the speaker shows something negative (tears) in a positive light (rain). How do such juxtapositions contribute to the tone of the poem?
5. Morbid humor abounds in this poem, as the speaker pokes fun at death. For example, in line 36, she praises war because it "provides food for flies." What other examples of morbid humor can you find in the poem? What does this sarcasm reveal about the true devastation of war? What makes irony and sarcasm effective devices in this poem?

Making Connections

1. Which poem do you think is most effective in taking an antiwar stand? Explain.
2. How do each of the poems use "children" as part of their arguments?
3. These two poems were written eighty-five years apart. What is universal in each? What qualities place each poem squarely in its time in history?
4. Both "Dulce et Decorum Est" and "The War Works Hard" are antiwar poems that take similar approaches. Describe the path both poems take to make their antiwar sentiment clear.

The First Long-Range Artillery Shell in Leningrad

Anna Akhmatova

Translated from Russian by Lyn Coffin

Album/Alamy

Born Anna Gorenko in Odessa, Ukraine, Anna Akhmatova (1889–1966) began writing as a child. She married the Russian poet Nikolai Gumilyov in 1910, but he soon left her to travel. In 1912, she gave birth to their son, Lev, and published her first book of poetry, *Vecher*. The couple divorced in 1918. In 1921, Gumilyov was arrested, charged with betraying the Russian Revolution of 1917, and executed. Because of their connection, Akhmatova was persecuted by the Soviet regime, and except for periods during World War II, her work was banned from publication between 1925 and 1952.

KEY CONTEXT The poem included here is set during the siege of the Russian city of Leningrad (now St. Petersburg) by German artillery bombardment in World War II, which occurred from September 1941 to January 1944. Over 1 million civilians died during what became one of the longest sieges in history, but Soviet troops eventually prevailed over the Nazis.

A rainbow of people rushing around,
And suddenly everything changed completely,
This wasn't a normal city sound,
It came from unfamiliar country.
True, it resembled, like a brother,
One peal of thunder or another,
But every natural thunder contains
The moisture of clouds, fresh and high,
And the thirst of fields with drought gone dry,
A harbinger of happy rains,
And this was as arid as hell ever got,
And my distracted hearing would not
Believe it, if only because of the wild
Way it started, grew, and caught,
And how indifferently it brought
Death to my child. ■

1941

Understanding and Interpreting

1. Try to forget the title of this poem, and then reread it. At what point does this poem *have* to be about an artillery shell? Before that point, could it be about something else? What is Anna Akhmatova's point in writing about this event in such an indirect way?
2. This poem chronicles a drastic change in the lives of the citizens of Leningrad. What familiar things does the speaker call on in order to understand the "unfamiliar" (l. 4)? In particular, why does the speaker present the situation in terms of weather?
3. Akhmatova wrote this poem about the first assault in a series of artillery attacks that continued for almost three years. How does knowing that information influence your understanding of and response to the poem?
4. How does your understanding of the speaker change with the poem's last line?

Analyzing Language, Style, and Structure

1. **Vocabulary in Context.** What is the significance of the adverb "indifferently" in line 15? How does it help the poet express a specific theme?
2. Does the tone remain consistent throughout the poem, or does it shift at the very end? Explain your answer, using evidence from the poem to support your response.
3. What is the effect of the metaphor "[a] rainbow of people" (l. 1)? How does it help characterize the city of Leningrad? Could it also have a more universal purpose? Explain.
4. How does the speaker's contrast of the artillery attack with thunder highlight the cost of war?

Topics for Composing

1. AP® FRQ **Poetry Analysis.** In Anna Akhmatova's "The First Long-Range Artillery Shell in Leningrad," published in 1941, the speaker describes what will be the beginning of a siege. Read the poem carefully. Then, in a well-written essay, analyze how Akhmatova uses literary elements and techniques to portray the speaker's attitude toward changes that war will bring.

2. **Connections.** To what extent can "The First Long-Range Artillery Shell in Leningrad" be considered a protest poem? Develop your response using evidence from the poem.
3. **Research.** Research the bombing siege of Leningrad. What was the German strategy, and how did the citizens of Leningrad survive? What effect did the outcome of this siege have on the outcome of the war itself?
4. **Connections.** In a review of translated works of Russian poetry of World War II in *Literary Review*, Robert Chandler criticizes the translation of the last two lines of "The First Long-Range Artillery Shell in Leningrad." He suggests that the standard translation, "And how indifferently it brought / Death to my child," leads the reader to believe that Akhmatova's only son has been killed, and that a more accurate translation would be "something like 'how indifferently it threatened to bring death.'" How does that change in the translation affect your reading of the poem?

Naming of Parts

Henry Reed

Henry Reed (1914–1986) was born in Birmingham, England. He won a scholarship to the University of Birmingham, where he earned an MA, writing his thesis on the novels of Thomas Hardy. In 1941, he was conscripted into the Royal Army Ordnance Corps. During World War II, he served as a soldier and cryptographer, working in both the Italian and the Japanese sections of the Government Code and Cypher School.

KEY CONTEXT World War II (1939–1945) was a global war that involved a majority of the world's countries, including the United States, Russia, Japan, and most countries in Europe. The conflict between the two opposing military alliances — the Allies and the Axis powers — involved more than 100 million people from thirty countries. The deadliest war in history, World War II was the first war in which more civilians died than military personnel. Genocide, starvation, massacres, and disease led to between 70 and 85 million deaths.

The poems for which Reed is best known are based on his experience in basic training, where he entertained his friends with imitations of drill sergeants. Later he wrote about those experiences in a series of poems entitled "Lessons of the War," which includes the following selection. Thus, "Naming of Parts" — arguably the most famous poem of World War II — was inspired not by an actual war experience but by Reed's time spent in basic training.

Today we have naming of parts. Yesterday,
We had daily cleaning. And tomorrow morning,
We shall have what to do after firing. But today,
Today we have naming of parts. Japonica
Glistens like coral in all of the neighboring gardens,
And today we have naming of parts.

This is the lower sling swivel. And this
Is the upper sling swivel, whose use you will see,
When you are given your slings. And this is the piling swivel,
Which in your case you have not got. The branches
Hold in the gardens their silent, eloquent gestures,
    Which in our case we have not got.

This is the safety-catch, which is always released
With an easy flick of the thumb. And please do not let me
See anyone using his finger. You can do it quite easy
If you have any strength in your thumb. The blossoms
Are fragile and motionless, never letting anyone see
    Any of them using their finger.

And this you can see is the bolt. The purpose of this
Is to open the breech, as you see. We can slide it
Rapidly backwards and forwards: we call this
Easing the spring. And rapidly backwards and forwards
The early bees are assaulting and fumbling the flowers:
    They call it easing the Spring.

They call it easing the Spring: it is perfectly easy
If you have any strength in your thumb: like the bolt,
And the breech, and the cocking-piece, and the point of balance,
Which in our case we have not got; and the almond-blossom
Silent in all of the gardens and the bees going backwards and forwards,
    For today we have naming of parts. ■

1946

Understanding and Interpreting

1. How do the opening three lines re-create the routine of basic training? Do you detect a satirical or critical tone in the list of training goals? Explain.
2. Characterize the speaker of "Naming of Parts." Is he an enthusiastic basic trainee? Use evidence from the poem to support your response.
3. How does the fifth stanza differ from those that precede it?
4. "Naming of Parts" is the first poem in a six-poem series called "Lessons of War." How would you sum up the lesson of this poem?
5. Judging from the poem, what is Henry Reed's attitude toward his experience as a soldier in World War II?
6. Read the last few lines of each stanza and try to imagine the spring scene Reed creates in "Naming of Parts." What does it remind you of?

Analyzing Language, Style, and Structure

1. **Vocabulary in Context.** What is the meaning of the word "breech," which appears in lines 20 and 27? While it is a technical term in this context, consider its connection to its homophone, *breach*, which is more metaphorical. Might that double meaning work here? Explain why or why not.
2. Each of the first four stanzas seems to be spoken in two voices. Where does the shift in perspective occur in each of them?
3. Does this poem have two different speakers, or one speaker with two different voices? Explain.
4. How does the speaker use the phrase "which. . . you/we have not got" as a refrain? What does this refrain suggest about military training?
5. Were you surprised by the imagery of the poem? What is the poet suggesting through the juxtaposition of war and nature imagery?
6. How would you explain the shift from "your case" to "our case" in lines 9–12? How do the things "Which in your case you have not got" (l. 10) compare to the things "Which in our case we have not got" (l. 12)?

Topics for Composing

1. AP® FRQ **Poetry Analysis.** In Henry Reed's "Naming of Parts," published in 1946, the speaker relates his experience of learning how the parts of a military-issue gun work in basic training. Read the poem carefully. Then, in a well-written essay, analyze how Reed uses literary elements and techniques to convey the possibility of renewal amidst the tedium of training for war.
2. **AP® Literary Argumentation.** Critics have interpreted "Naming of Parts" as a statement on how the military disrupts the natural order of things. Develop that argument by comparing and contrasting the garden imagery to the military description of the parts of a gun.
3. **Connections.** Read Richard Wilbur's poem "The First Snow in Alsace," which also juxtaposes the imagery of warfare with that of nature. How would you compare the way that each poet uses imagery to present his attitude toward his subject?
4. **Multimodal.** Create a video or piece of art that illustrates "Naming of Parts." For inspiration, you might watch the 1971 film based on this poem.

The Terrorist, He Watches

Wisława Szymborska

Translated from Polish by Robert A. Maguire and Magnus Jan Krynski

SZYMBORSKA Wislawa - date :v10/2010/ OPALE/Bridgeman Images

Wisława Szymborska [vis-*lah*-vah sim-*bawrs*-kah] (1923–2012) was born in western Poland. At age six, her family moved to Krakow, where she lived for the rest of her life. After studying literature and sociology at Jagiellonian University in Krakow, she began to make her way as a poet. She published her first poem, "I Am Looking for a World," in 1945, and her first book, *Dlatego Zygemy* (*That's What We Live For*), in 1952. Although she had published eighteen volumes of poetry, which had been translated into more than a dozen languages, she was not well known in the English-speaking world until she was awarded the Nobel Prize for Literature in 1996.

The bomb will go off in the bar at one twenty p.m.
Now it's only one sixteen p.m.
Some will still have time to get in,
Some to get out.

The terrorist has already crossed to the other side of the street.
The distance protects him from any danger,
and what a sight for sore eyes:

A woman in a yellow jacket, she goes in.
A man in dark glasses, he comes out.
Guys in jeans, they are talking.
One seventeen and four seconds.
That shorter guy's really got it made, and gets on a scooter,
and that taller one, he goes in.

One seventeen and forty seconds.
That girl there, she's got a green ribbon in her hair.
Too bad that bus just cut her off.
One eighteen p.m.
The girl's not there any more.
Was she dumb enough to go in, or wasn't she?
That we'll see when they carry them out.

One nineteen p.m.
No one seems to be going in.
Instead a fat baldy's coming out.
Like he's looking for something in his pockets and
at one nineteen and fifty seconds
he goes back for those lousy gloves of his.

It's one twenty p.m.
The time, how it drags.
Should be any moment now.
Not yet.
Yes, this is it.
The bomb, it goes off. ■

1981

Understanding and Interpreting

1. Who is the speaker of "The Terrorist, He Watches"? How do you know?
2. What information does the poem provide about the potential victims of the bomb the terrorist has planted? What picture does the poem paint of its time and place?

3. The expression "sight for sore eyes" is usually used to describe something lovely or comforting. Whose sight is sore in line 7? What sight, specifically, soothes his sore eyes?
4. How would you describe the tone of the poem? What effect does the tone have on your response to the poem?
5. Does the terrorist take pleasure in his work? Explain why or why not.

Analyzing Language, Style, and Structure

1. **Vocabulary in Context.** What is the meaning of the word "drags" in line 28? How does its sound, as well as its meaning, heighten the suspense in the poem?
2. What is unusual about the way the poem reveals the central event? What words would you use to describe the presentation?
3. What is the impact of Wisława Szymborska's choosing to provide us with no information about the terrorist — not the time period, location, nature of the conflict, or motivation?
4. How does the poem create tension and suspense?
5. What transition does line 7, "and what a sight for sore eyes," signal? Is it meant to introduce the descriptions of the people coming and going? How are the people described?
6. How does the countdown embedded in the poem both structure it and contribute to the development of its themes?

Topics for Composing

1. AP® FRQ **Poetry Analysis.** In Wisława Szymborska's "The Terrorist, He Watches," published in 1981, the speaker is a terrorist who is waiting for a bomb he has planted to go off. Read the poem carefully. Then, in a well-written essay, analyze how Szymborska uses literary elements and techniques to develop the persona of the speaker and his perspective on his handiwork.
2. **Connections.** "The Terrorist, He Watches" was published in a collection called *A Large Number*. The Polish poet Adam Zagajewski writes that the speaker of Szymborska's poem is a

   > murderer who's compelled to act precisely by such large numbers. Somewhere something or other's going on, some people are waiting . . . so you can go ahead and write off as losses the few who go flying through the air at the very moment that they reach for a cup of coffee. Moreover, all this is based on the assumption that another large number — public opinion . . . — will find out about the incident in the bar. A bomb is a kind of open letter directed to public opinion.

   In an essay, support, challenge, or qualify Zagajewski's assertion about what motivates a terrorist. Use evidence from "The Terrorist, He Watches" to support your response.
3. **Connections.** In her Nobel Prize acceptance speech, Szymborska said, "Inspiration is not the exclusive privilege of poets or artists generally. There is, has been, and will always be a certain group of people whom inspiration visits. It's made up of all those who've consciously chosen their calling and do their job with love and imagination. It may include doctors, teachers, gardeners — and I could list a hundred more professions." Could the speaker of this poem be described as "inspired"? Explain why or why not.

Not Yet

Claribel Alegría

INTI OCON/AFP/Getty Images

Writer and activist Claribel Alegría (1924–2018) was born Clara Isabel Alegría Vides to a Nicaraguan father and Salvadoran mother. She began composing poetry as a child and published her first book of poems when she was seventeen. She moved to the United States in 1943 and later received a BA from George Washington University. During the 1950s and 1960s, Alegría was associated with "la generacion comprometida" (the committed generation) of activist Central American writers. While Alegría was committed to nonviolent resistance, she supported the Sandinista National Liberation Front (FSLN), the group that overthrew the U.S.-supported dictator Anastasio Somoza Debayle. She returned to Nicaragua in 1985, after the election of President Daniel Ortega, to participate in the country's reconstruction.

KEY CONTEXT When Claribel Alegría was just nine months old, her father's opposition to the political climate in Nicaragua forced the family to live in exile in El Salvador. As an adult, Alegría herself was exiled in Mallorca and Mexico, among other countries, when she was warned not to return to El Salvador because of her opposition to its government.

Not yet
I can't go back yet
I am still forbidden
to plunge into your roads
to yield to your rivers
to contemplate your volcanoes
to rest in the shade
of my tree.
From abroad I see you
my heart watches you
from abroad
constricted, watches you
in memories
between wavering bars
of memory
that widen
and close,
ebb and flow in my tears.
It is difficult to sing you
from exile
difficult to celebrate
your nebulous
jagged map.
I can't do it yet

a dry sob
sticks in my throat.
It is difficult to sing you
when a heavy boot
with foreign hobnails
tears your bleeding flesh. ■

1989

Understanding and Interpreting

1. To what does the word "constricted" (l. 12) refer? How does it characterize the speaker's frame of mind?
2. Who is the speaker's audience throughout the poem? What details from the poem support your interpretation?
3. What do the phrases "widen / and close" and "ebb and flow" (ll. 16–18) suggest about the speaker's relationship with the past?
4. How does the meaning of the phrase "It is difficult to sing you" differ in lines 19 and 27?
5. What is the relationship between line 24 and the first three lines of the poem? To what do these four lines refer?

Analyzing Language, Style, and Structure

1. **Vocabulary in Context.** Alegría's speaker says of her homeland, "It is difficult to sing you / from exile / difficult to celebrate / your nebulous / jagged map" (ll. 19–23). What does the word "nebulous" mean? How does this word function both literally and figuratively in this context? How is the word significant to the poem as a whole?
2. What tone does Alegría establish in lines 1–3 of the poem? How is this tone created?
3. How do you interpret the speaker's desire "to plunge" into roads and "yield to . . . rivers" (ll. 4–5)? What do these phrases suggest about the speaker's desires?
4. Lines 4–7 begin with a series of infinitive verbs. What is the effect of this repetition?
5. What is the effect of switching from "I see you" (l. 9) to the personified phrase "my heart watches you" (l. 10)? Where else in the poem does the speaker move directly from the literal to the figurative?
6. How does the repetition of the word "difficult," beginning in line 19, reflect a thematic concern of the poem?
7. How would you characterize the imagery of the final three lines of the poem? Whose "bleeding flesh" is torn (l. 29)?

Topics for Composing

1. AP® FRQ **Poetry Analysis.** In Claribel Alegría's "Not Yet," published in 1989, the speaker laments not being able to return to her homeland. Read the poem carefully. Then, in a well-written essay, analyze how Alegría uses literary elements and techniques to convey the effect of exile on an individual who longs for home.
2. **Connections.** When asked about living in exile, Alegría said, "I'm on a liferaft in a placid sea." While we associate placidity with tranquility and peace, Alegría's response paints a different picture. What words would you use to describe her response, and how are your selected words relevant to this poem?

3. **Connections.** In his poem "Fatality," Nicaraguan poet Ruben Darío writes that "there is no pain as great as being alive, / no burden heavier than that of conscious life." How does the speaker in "Not Yet" reflect the pain of "conscious life"? What is the source of her pain, and how can it be lessened?
4. **Multimodal.** Identify images from either El Salvador or Nicaragua that correspond to the imagery in the poem. Create a slideshow that combines these images with the most significant words in the poem. Then, use the slideshow as a backdrop as you recite the poem to the class.
5. **Research.** During her childhood, Alegría's family opposed the U.S.-backed government of Anastasio Somoza in Nicaragua. As a result, the family was forced into exile. By the time of her death in 2018, Alegría had returned to her home country, but was critical of the Sandinistas, the group that toppled the Somoza regime in 1979. What are the human rights and sociopolitical injustices that have taken place in Nicaragua between Alegría's childhood and the present day? How might these events lead Nicaraguans living in exile to say "Not yet" when asked if they would return to their homeland?

For Mohammed Zeid of Gaza, Age 15

Naomi Shihab Nye

Gary Doak/Alamy

Poet, novelist, editor, and political activist Naomi Shihab Nye (b. 1952) is the daughter of a Palestinian father and an American mother. Nye grew up in St. Louis, Missouri, and received a BA in English and world religions from Trinity University in San Antonio, Texas. Her works for children include the picture book *Sitti's Secret* (1994) and the novel *Habibi* (1996). Her poetry collections include *Different Ways to Pray* (1980), *19 Varieties of Gazelle: Poems of the Middle East* (2002), and *Cast Away: Poems for Our Time* (2020). Nye, who has been a visiting writer all over the world, describes herself as "a wandering poet."

KEY CONTEXT Nye wrote this poem in response to the death of fifteen-year-old Mohammed Zeid in 2002. Zeid was shot and killed inside his home in the Palestinian village of Nazlat Zeid, located on the northern West Bank. Israeli soldiers in the village opened fire on a group of young men throwing rocks at the patrol outside Zeid's house, and he was hit by what the official report termed "a stray bullet." An Israeli military court found the soldier who shot and killed Zeid guilty of negligence.

There is no *stray* bullet, sirs.
No bullet like a worried cat
crouching under a bush,
no half-hairless puppy bullet
dodging midnight streets.
The bullet could not be a pecan
plunking the tin roof,
not hardly, no fluff of pollen
on October's breath,
no humble pebble at our feet.

So don't gentle it, please.

We live among stray thoughts,
tasks abandoned midstream.
Our fickle hearts are fat
with stray devotions, we feel at home
among bits and pieces,
all the wandering ways of words.

But this bullet had no innocence, did not
wish anyone well, you can't tell us otherwise
by naming it mildly, this bullet was never the friend
of life, should not be granted immunity
by soft saying — friendly fire, straying death-eye,
why have we given the wrong weight to what we do?

Mohammed, Mohammed, deserves the truth.
This bullet had no secret happy hopes,
it was not singing to itself with eyes closed
under the bridge. ■

2005

Understanding and Interpreting

1. Who are the "sirs" that the speaker directly addresses in the opening line? Who is the speaker?
2. What is the setting of the poem? Why is it important?
3. What does the speaker mean by "the wandering ways of words" (l. 17)?
4. What is the "truth" in the final stanza? What evidence from the poem supports your interpretation?
5. How would you state the message that the speaker wishes the audience to understand or feel? If this poem is a call to action, what is the speaker calling on us, her readers, to do?
6. Why do you think Naomi Shihab Nye chose this particular title for the poem? Imagine a different title, such as "The Stray Bullet" or "Wandering Words." What does Nye's title accomplish that these would not?
7. One reviewer characterized Nye as being "international in scope and internal in focus." In what ways does this poem reflect that description?

Analyzing Language, Style, and Structure

1. **Vocabulary in Context.** In line 14, Nye refers to "our fickle hearts." What does "fickle" mean in this context? What tone does the speaker infuse in this word?
2. In line 11, the speaker implores the audience, "[D]on't gentle it, please." What is the effect of using "gentle" as a verb here? How does this choice reflect the larger context of the poem's occasion?
3. How do the different pronouns the speaker uses inform your interpretation of the poem? Consider the opening address to "sirs," the use of "we," and the direct address of second person (both implied and stated). Why do you think Nye chose not to use first person?
4. What metaphors for the bullet does the speaker reject? What perspective does this rejection convey?

5. Nye punctuates lines 18–23 with several commas and ends this stanza with a question mark. What is the effect of this syntactical choice? How does it serve the speaker's purpose?

Topics for Composing

1. AP® FRQ **Poetry Analysis.** In Naomi Shihab Nye's "For Mohammed Zeid of Gaza, Age 15," published in 2005, the speaker pays tribute to a teenage boy who was killed by what was reported to be "a stray bullet." Read the poem carefully. Then, in a well-written essay, analyze how Nye uses literary elements and techniques to convey a complex perspective on the incident.
2. **AP® Literary Argumentation.** How does Nye use poetic devices to create a picture of the "truth" that those killed in conflicts "deserv[e]" (l. 24)?
3. **Connections.** In a 2021 interview with Naomi Shihab Nye on the podcast *On Being*, the host Krista Tippett characterized much of Nye's poetry as "holding a conversation or opening conversations that aren't actually happening out there in the culture or in the narrative of how we're telling the story of our time." What conversation does this poem hold about "the story of our time"?
4. **Speaking and Listening.** In this poem, Nye points out the ways in which we often use language to obscure an unpleasant reality and, thus, to name something difficult or even brutal "mildly." Doing so results, she believes, in obscuring the "truth" or making it more palatable. What other examples of such language can you identify in contemporary media and popular culture? Prepare for and hold a class discussion on the purpose of such language. How does euphemistic language affect people's ability to process events and experiences?

Sadiq

Brian Turner

GL Portrait/Alamy

Born in 1967 in California, Brian Turner earned an MFA in poetry at the University of Oregon before enlisting in the army at the age of twenty-nine. During the seven years he spent as a soldier, he was deployed to Bosnia and Herzegovina and served as an army infantry team leader in Iraq. His work has been published in various journals as well as in *Voices in Wartime: The Anthology*, published in 2005 in conjunction with the feature-length documentary film of the same name. Turner has also published a memoir, *My Life as a Foreign Country* (2014).

KEY CONTEXT In the wake of the September 11, 2001, terrorist attacks, the administration of President George W. Bush considered the Iraqi dictator, Saddam Hussein, a sponsor of global terrorism and sought to remove him from power. In March 2003, with the approval of Congress, the U.S. military began an offensive in Iraq that resulted in the removal of Hussein. U.S. forces were withdrawn from Iraq in 2011. Roughly 4,500 U.S. soldiers, 26,500 Iraqi combatants, and 17,700 Iraqi security forces (allied with the United States) died during this conflict. Estimates of civilian deaths vary greatly, from around 100,000 to over 1,000,000 deaths. "Sadiq," the title of the poem included here, is Arabic for "friend." The epigraph to this poem is by Sa'di (c. 1210–c. 1291), a Persian poet widely recognized as one of the greatest of his era.

It is a condition of wisdom in the archer to be patient because when the arrow leaves the bow, it returns no more.

— SA'DI

It should make you shake and sweat,
nightmare you, strand you in a desert
of irrevocable desolation, the consequences
seared into the vein, no matter what adrenaline
feeds the muscle its courage, no matter
what god shines down on you, no matter
what crackling pain and anger
you carry in your fists, my friend,
it should break your heart to kill. ■

2005

Understanding and Interpreting

1. How do you interpret the epigraph from Sa'di? How does it relate to Brian Turner's poem?
2. To what noun does the word "It" (l. 1) refer? What is the effect of this ambiguity on the opening of the poem?
3. What does the speaker mean when he refers to "a desert / of irrevocable desolation" (ll. 2–3)?
4. According to lines 4–8, what three reasons might serve as the motivation — but not necessarily justification — "to kill" (l. 9)?

Analyzing Language, Style, and Structure

1. **Vocabulary in Context.** In line 2, the speaker uses the word "nightmare" as a verb rather than a noun. What is the effect of this choice? How does this word relate to the final line of the poem?
2. What is the "muscle" discussed in line 5? How does this word refer to both a literal and a figurative muscle?
3. Line 8 echoes the poem's title, "Sadiq," which means *friend*. What is the function of the word "friend" (l. 8) within the poem?
4. Overall, how would you characterize the poem's syntax? What perspective on war does it convey?

Topics for Composing

1. AP® FRQ **Poetry Analysis.** In Brian Turner's "Sadiq," published in 2005, the speaker discusses the effects of killing in wartime. Read the passage carefully. Then, in a well-written essay, analyze how Turner uses literary elements and techniques to develop the speaker's complex attitude toward warfare.
2. **AP® Literary Argumentation.** In an interview in *World Literature Today*, Brian Turner said that he is "drawn to the music of the imagination and to the beauty of language itself." How are "the music of the imagination" and the "beauty of language" present in "Sadiq"? Is it appropriate for wartime poetry to be beautiful? Support your position with references to the text.

3. **Connections.** In line 8, the speaker directly addresses "my friend." What is the speaker's attitude toward the "friend"? How does Turner's use of the word compare to Wilfred Owen's direct address to "My friend" in "Dulce et Decorum Est" (p. 884)?
4. **Connections.** In *Regarding the Pain of Others*, Susan Sontag says of war, "We do not and cannot imagine what it was like, how dreadful or terrifying it was, how normal it becomes." How might "Sadiq" be regarded as a response to Sontag's statement?
5. **Speaking and Listening.** The poem's epigraph refers to the "wisdom in the archer." What wisdom does the poem's speaker impart unto the audience? Write a response delineating this wisdom and share it with a partner. How is your interpretation of the wisdom enhanced by listening to your partner's response?

Twelve-Hour Shifts

Jill McDonough

Lauren Clark

Jill McDonough (b. 1972) is an American poet who grew up in North Carolina and earned degrees from Stanford University and Boston University. McDonough has taught incarcerated college students through Boston University's Prison Education Program for thirteen years, and she also directs the MFA program at the University of Massachusetts Boston. She is the author of four poetry collections, *Habeas Corpus* (2008), *Where You Live* (2012), *Reaper* (2017), and *Here All Night* (2019).

KEY CONTEXT In "Twelve-Hour Shifts," McDonough uses the consciously repetitive villanelle form, which has nineteen lines with two rhymes throughout. Villanelles consist of five tercets and a quatrain, with the first and third lines of the opening tercet recurring alternately at the end of the other tercets and with both repeated at the close of the concluding quatrain.

A drone pilot works a twelve-hour shift, then goes home
to real life. Showers, eats supper, plays video games.
Twelve hours later he comes back, high-fives, takes over the drone

from other pilots, who watch *Homeland*, do dishes, hope they don't
dream in all screens, bad kills, all slo-mo freeze-frame.
A drone pilot works a twelve-hour shift, then goes home.

A small room, a pilot's chair, the mic and headphones
crowd his mind, take him somewhere else. Another day
another dollar: hover and shift, twelve hours over strangers' homes.

Stop by the store, its Muzak, pick up the Cheerios,
get to the gym if you're lucky. Get back to your babies, play
Barbies, play blocks. Twelve hours later, come back. Take over the drone.

Smell of burned coffee in the lounge, the shifting kill zone.
Last-minute *abort mission*, and the major who forgets your name.
A drone pilot works a twelve-hour shift, then goes home.

It's done in our names, but we don't have to know. Our own
lives, shifts, hours, bounced off screens all day.
A drone pilot works a twelve-hour shift, then goes home;
fresh from twelve hours off, another comes in, takes over our drone. ■

2015

Understanding and Interpreting

1. What aspects of the drone pilot's job strike you as familiar? Consider lines 7–8 ("A small room, a pilot's chair, the mic and headphones / crowd his mind, take him somewhere else") in your response.
2. Why does the speaker use the familiar phrase "Another day / another dollar" (ll. 8–9) when describing a drone pilot's working life?
3. How do references to "Muzak," "Cheerios," "Barbies," and "blocks" (ll. 10 and 12) characterize the speaker?
4. How does "the major who forgets your name" (l. 14) relate to what is "done in our names, but we don't have to know" (l. 16)? What do these two lines reveal about the meaning of the poem as a whole?
5. Why do you think the speaker goes into such detail about the soldier's daily lives, but never describes the effect that drone strikes have on their targets?

Analyzing Language, Style, and Structure

1. **Vocabulary in Context.** How does McDonough vary her use of the *shift* in the poem? Which parts of speech does *shift* form, and how do the changes suggest different connotations? Similarly, how does the poem suggest forms and meanings of the word without McDonough having to incorporate them directly?
2. Throughout the poem, the speaker repeatedly weaves in commonplace, domestic references, such as "do[ing] dishes" (l. 4), "babies" (l. 11), "get to the gym if you're lucky" (l. 11), and others. How do these references contrast with the drone pilot's job? What is the purpose of that contrast?
3. The first stanza ends as another soldier "takes over the drone" (l. 3), and the poem itself ends when another soldier "takes over our drone" (l. 19). Who is represented by the "our" in the last line? What does this shift suggest about who the speaker views as responsible for war in general?
4. In line 13, the speaker juxtaposes the "[s]mell of burned coffee in the lounge" with "the shifting kill zone" — that is, where drones carry out pilots' orders. What is the speaker's purpose in juxtaposing the image of an everyday annoyance with a violent military term? How would you characterize the tone of the poem? Consider such stylistic elements as imagery, anaphora, and rhyme in your response.

Topics for Composing

1. **AP® FRQ** **Poetry Analysis.** In Jill McDonough's "Twelve-Hour Shifts," published in 2015, the speaker portrays the life of a drone pilot, both on and off the clock. Read the poem carefully. Then, in a well-written essay, analyze how McDonough uses literary elements and techniques to develop the complex meaning of the relationship between the drone pilot's home and work lives.

2. **Speaking and Listening.** In reviewing a book about drone warfare for the journal *Nature*, Ann Finkbeiner asserts that "If war is a duel in which both sides are vulnerable, then drone warfare may not even be war." Discuss the definition of drone warfare with the class in light of this assertion and your interpretation of McDonough's poem.
3. **Connections.** In a 2012 review in the *Atlantic* of two first-person shooter video games, Michael Thomsen argues, "It's tempting to condemn games like *Warfighter* and *Black Ops II* for turning the horror of war into entertainment, but it is precisely that brazenness that gives them their power." Consider the complex relationship Americans have with violence in video games that mimics war and war that mimics violence in video games. Based on your knowledge of or experience with first-person shooter games, to what extent do you agree with Thomsen's position on the relationship such games have to actual war, particularly drone warfare?
4. **Research.** Research the evolution of war and weaponry over the past century or so. How has the speed of the development of remote warfare contributed to perspectives such as the speaker's in McDonough's poem? Does her speaker's perspective parallel those of soldiers in earlier conflicts, or is there something about drones that distinguish them from other technological advances? In your response, consider the developments that occurred during World War I specifically.

True Believer

Amit Majmudar

Ami Buch Majmudar

Amit Majmudar (b. 1979) is an American novelist, poet, and doctor who grew up in Cleveland, Ohio. He earned a BS at the University of Akron and an MD at Northeast Ohio Medical University; he currently lives in Columbus, Ohio, where he is a diagnostic nuclear radiologist. Majmudar is the author of the poetry collections *0°, 0°* (2009), *Heaven and Earth* (2011), *Dothead* (2016), and *What He Did in Solitary* (2020). Majmudar has also published three novels: *Partitions* (2011), *The Abundance* (2013), and *Sitayana* (2019). He was appointed as Ohio's first poet laureate in 2016.

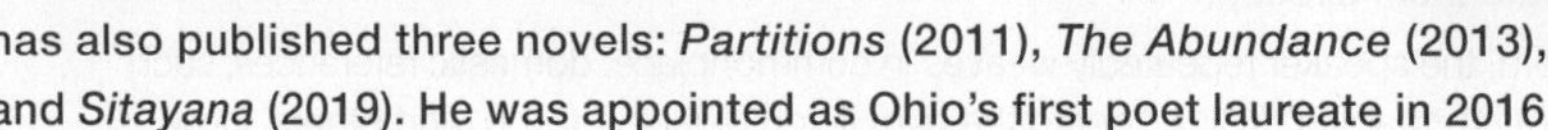

"What men truly want is peace,"
Says the last one true prophet.
Peace feels so like submission
Good prophets can fool most men.
For the rest, there's the hammer,
Followed by a gentle tongue

To sweet-talk the wounds. A tongue
Works wonders keeping the peace,
But wonder-workers keep hammers
Handy. Ask any prophet
Who's spent some time among men:
Supervising submission

Is no humble lamb's mission.
You must learn to scold in tongues.
The cold acumen cold men
Make war with is of a piece
With the poet's and prophet's.
Sometimes words, sometimes hammers,

Sometimes words shaped like hammers
Bring about the submission
So cherished by all prophets,
Heart of gold or golden-tongued.
Submission has a certain poise,
A certain beauty. What men

Want is the same thing women
Want: That is, a sound hammer
Against the skull, and the peace
That sees stars. True submission
Begins in the throat, the tongue.
No God but this. No Prophet

But this. You see the prophet's
Quite wise when it comes to men:
Simple thoughts in a simple tongue,
And, just in case, the hammer.
Some men call peace, submission.
Some men call submission, peace.

The prophet nods and strokes his piece.
His yes men are on a mission.
Stick out your tongue, says the hammer. ■

2015

Understanding and Interpreting

1. Who is the "true prophet" in line 2? Is this the same as the "True Believer" of the title? Explain.
2. What three strategies of bringing about belief are described in lines 3–7?
3. How is it possible to "supervis[e] submission" (l. 12)? What does this phrase suggest about the speaker's perspective on the meaning of "submission"? How, according to the speaker, does it have "a certain poise, / A certain beauty" (ll. 23–24)?
4. What does the speaker mean by "True submission / Begins in the throat, the tongue" (ll. 28–29)? What makes submission "true"? Why is it tied to that particular part of the body?
5. Who are the prophet's "yes men" (l. 38)? How do they characterize the prophet?
6. What is the source of the violence, implicit and explicit, that permeates the poem?

Analyzing Language, Style, and Structure

1. **Vocabulary in Context.** Amit Majmudar refers to "The cold acumen cold men / Make war with" (ll. 15–16). In general, "acumen" refers to the ability to make good judgments, but it carries a range of associations. What are its associations here? What is its effect in this context?
2. What does the "tongue" in this poem represent? How does it function as metonymy? Refer to specific lines to support your analysis.
3. How does the "hammer," which appears in every stanza, develop over the course of the poem? What symbolic meaning does it carry?
4. Majmudar is known for his word play. What elements of word play do you find in this poem? What purpose do they serve?
5. Much of Majmudar's poetry uses elements of sound. In what ways do the rhythm, meter, repetition, and even some of the word play contribute to the meaning of "True Believer"?
6. How might the title "True Believer" be read as an ironic comment on the meaning of the poem?

Topics for Composing

1. AP® FRQ **Poetry Analysis.** In Amit Majmudar's "True Believer," published in 2015, the speaker explores the way beliefs and belief systems are formed, conveyed, and accepted. Read the poem carefully. Then, in a well-written essay, analyze how Majmudar uses literary elements and techniques to explore the complex relationship between language, persuasion, and belief.
2. **AP® Literary Argumentation.** In "True Believer," Majmudar raises compelling questions about the nature of peace, including what might be described as "a just peace" or "an uneasy peace." What argument does the poem make about the role of external pressure being exerted to bring about the possibility — or illusion — of peace? To what extent do you agree with that position?
3. **Connections.** The speaker of "True Believer" observes: "Some men call peace, submission. Some men call submission, peace." Discuss a situation or event from history or your personal experience that illustrates this paradox.
4. **Speaking and Listening.** Would you claim to believe something you did not truly believe if there was danger to you or your family if you did not? Discuss this question in small groups; then share your perspectives in larger class discussion. Base your discussions in the text of the poem, but feel free to extend out to other texts or observations.
5. **Connections.** In the introduction to *Resistance, Rebellion, Life* (2017), a collection of fifty poems that Majmudar edited, he writes:

   > What story about yourself, your country, and your people, about our past, present, and future, do you believe in? In which America — in *whose* America do you place your faith? The political quarrel of our day has boiled down to a duel of realities. Maybe it was always this way. Maybe all wars are wars of religion. Even when they don't escalate into group violence, though, all wars are wars of words.

   What is your response to his assertion that "all wars are wars of words"? In your response, consider this poem as well as conflicts that could be termed "culture wars."

Reaching Guantánamo [Dear Salim, / Love, are you well?]

Solmaz Sharif

Solmaz Sharif (b. 1983) is a poet who was born in Istanbul to Iranian parents. The former managing director of the Asian American Writers' Workshop, she holds degrees from the University of California, Berkeley, and New York University. She is the author of two collections of poetry: *Look* (2016), which was nominated for a National Book Award, and *Customs* (2022). She currently teaches creative writing at Arizona State University.

Sylvain Gaboury/Patrick McMullan/Getty Images

KEY CONTEXT Located on a U.S. military base in Cuba, Guantanamo Bay Prison has held suspected terrorists without due process of law since 2002. This poem is the first in a series imagined by Sharif to be written to Salim Hamdan by his wife. Hamdan, a Yemeni man, was captured during the U.S. invasion of Afghanistan in 2001. Following a conviction by military tribunal, he was imprisoned at Guantanamo from 2002 until 2008. His conviction was overturned by the U.S. Court of Appeals in 2012.

Dear Salim,

Love, are you well? Do they   you?
I worry so much. Lately, my hair   , even
my skin   . The doctors tell me it's
I believe them. It shouldn't
          . Please don't worry.
          in the yard, and moths
have gotten to your mother's
          , remember?
I have enclosed some   — made this
batch just for you. Please eat well. Why
did you   me to remarry? I told
          and he couldn't   it.
I would never   .
Love, I'm singing that   you loved,
remember, the line that went
"   "? I'm holding
the   just for you.

Yours,

■

2016

Understanding and Interpreting

1. Why are there so many blanks in the poem? Try filling them in. What patterns can you make from the missing words?
2. What information does the speaker of this poem reveal about herself? What are her primary concerns? What do you make of the fact that even her name is redacted?

3. Why do you think the poem is titled “Reaching Guantanamo”? What is it that is destined for the prison? What kinds of things does the speaker hope will arrive?
4. Who do you think has redacted the words in this poem?
5. What does the speaker mean by “Why / did you me to remarry?” (ll. 11–12)? What do these lines reveal about Salim?

Analyzing Language, Style, and Structure

1. **Vocabulary in Context.** What effect does the word “moths” have in line 7? How does their quotidian quality affect the tone of the poem?
2. What is the effect of redacting so many words throughout the poem? What tone does it create? Is it intimate, detached, vulnerable, impenetrable, or something else? Use evidence from the poem to support your response.
3. How does the punctuation in “Reaching Guantanamo” help fill in the blanks? How does the rhythm created by the punctuation reveal the complexity of the situation?
4. Some of the words in this poem repeat — in particular “love” and “remember.” How does the speaker use these words in each instance? How does their meaning shift, and how do those shifts speak to the larger meaning of the poem?

Topics for Composing

1. AP® FRQ **Poetry Analysis.** In Solmaz Sharif’s “Reaching Guantanamo,” published in 2016, the speaker sends a love letter that is redacted to her husband who is imprisoned on a U.S. military base. Read the poem carefully. Then, in a well-written essay, analyze how Sharif uses literary elements and techniques to convey the personal price of international conflict.
2. **Connections.** “Reaching Guantanamo” was selected for publication in the *New York Times* magazine in 2016 by poet Matthew Zapruder. He wrote that the poem “points out how authority finds dangerous even what is private and personal and tries to erase it.” Do you agree that this is the message of the poem? Explain why or why not.
3. **Research.** Read about the conviction of Salim Hamdan, which was overturned in a landmark decision by a federal appeals court. To what extent does that case — and the imagined love letter — affect your view of “extraordinary rendition”?
4. **Creative Writing.** Create redacted documents of your own that address an issue that can be difficult to talk about. Share them with your classmates and look for patterns in what is not able to be said.

We Were All Odysseus in Those Days

Amorak Huey

Grand Valley State University

Amorak Huey, a former newspaper editor and reporter, was born in Kalamazoo, Michigan, and grew up in Trussville, Alabama. He holds a BA from Birmingham-Southern College and an MFA from Western Michigan University. Huey is author of the poetry collection *Ha Ha Ha Thump* (2015). He teaches writing at Grand Valley State University in Michigan.

KEY CONTEXT The poem refers to a specific episode in Homer's *Odyssey* in which Odysseus tricks the cyclops Polyphemus, a giant one-eyed creature who is holding him and his men hostage in a cave on an island full of cyclops. Odysseus tells Polyphemus his name is "no man" and then blinds the cyclops while he is sleeping, allowing the men to escape. When the other cyclopes on the island attempt to help Polyphemus, he can only tell them that "no man" blinded him.

A young man learns to shoot
& dies in the mud
an ocean away from home,
a rifle in his fingers
& the sky dripping from his heart. Next to him
a friend watches
his final breath slip
ragged into the ditch,
a thing the friend will carry
back to America —
wound, souvenir,
backstory. He'll teach
literature to young people
for 40 years. He'll coach
his daughters' softball teams.
Root for Red Wings
& Lions & Tigers. Dance
well. Love generously.
He'll be quick with a joke
& firm with handshakes.
He'll rarely talk
about the war. If asked
he'll tell you instead
his favorite story:
Odysseus escaping
from the Cyclops
with a bad pun & good wine
& a sharp stick.
It's about buying time
& making do, he'll say.
It's about doing what it takes
to get home, & you see
he has been talking
about the war all along.
We all want the same thing
from this world:
Call me nobody. Let me live. ■

2019

Understanding and Interpreting

1. What details in this poem convey that it is about war?
2. Who do you think the speaker is? What is his relationship to the subject of the poem?
3. What is the "wound, souvenir, / back story" in lines 11–12? Why do you think these do not come up again in the poem?
4. What qualities does the speaker admire in the "young man" who returns home and continues his life for the next forty years? Consider the explicit as well as the implicit qualities depicted throughout the poem.
5. What is it about the story of the cyclops that the veteran finds so appealing? Why is it "his favorite story" (l. 24)?

Analyzing Language, Style, and Structure

1. **Vocabulary in Context.** What is the meaning of the word "souvenir" in line 11? What is ironic about Amorak Huey's use of the word in the poem?
2. Look carefully at the metaphorical language in lines 1–12. Why did Huey choose figurative language to describe these particular events? What does it mean that the rest of the poem does not rely so heavily on the figurative?
3. What is the effect of the ampersands (&) throughout the poem? How do they say something a little different from "and"?
4. What do the expressions "buying time" (l. 29) and "making do" (l. 30) mean? How do these figures of speech characterize life both as a soldier and as a veteran?
5. Why are the poem's last two lines in italics? How does the allusion to the pun from Homer's *Odyssey* ("call me nobody") comment on what it means to be a soldier?

Topics for Composing

1. AP® FRQ **Poetry Analysis.** In Amorak Huey's "We Were All Odysseus in Those Days," published in 2019, the speaker creates a portrait in words of the life of a man who has been to war. Read the poem carefully. Then, in a well-written essay, analyze how Huey uses literary elements and techniques to convey the speaker's complex perspective on both the soldier and the effects of war.
2. **Connections.** In an answer to an interview about the best advice he's ever gotten about writing poetry, Huey quoted poet William Olsen: "Nothing matters so much to a poem as the state of mind of the poet at the moment of writing." What do you think was Amorak Huey's state of mind when he wrote this poem? Use evidence from the poem to support your answer.
3. **Connections.** Do you agree with the speaker that "We all want the same thing / from this world: / *Call me nobody. Let me live*" (ll. 35–37)? Why or why not? Use examples from other reading, history, or personal experience to support your response.
4. **Connections.** How might the ninth line of "We Were All Odysseus in Those Days" ("a thing the friend will carry") be an allusion to Tim O'Brien's "The Things They Carried" (p. 916)? Why is the image of "carrying" so germane to discussions of war?
5. **Research.** Read the Cyclops episode (Book 9) of *The Odyssey*. How does your impression of Odysseus match up to the way he is portrayed in "We Were All Odysseus in Those Days"?
6. **Creative Writing.** Write a poem that compares someone you admire to a fictional hero. Try to incorporate specific quotations that characterize the hero if possible.

A New Day Dawns

Nikky Finney

© Forrest Clonts

Born and raised in South Carolina by parents active in the civil rights movement, Nikky Finney (b. 1957) is currently the John H. Bennett, Jr., Chair in Creative Writing and Southern Letters at the University of South Carolina and an ambassador for the University of Arizona Poetry Center's Art for Justice Project. A professor at the University of Kentucky for over twenty years, she is a founding member of the Affrilachian Poets, a group of black Appalachian poets. Finney has received numerous awards for her work that includes *Head Off & Split*, winner of the 2011 National Book Award for Poetry. Her most recent collection is *Love Child's Hotbed of Occasional Poetry* (2020), which features her own selection of artifacts, images, and photographs to accompany and illuminate individual poems.

KEY CONTEXT Finney wrote "A New Day Dawns" shortly after Nikki Haley, the South Carolina governor, supported a bill to remove the Confederate flag from the State House grounds. Haley took this action after a mass shooting on June 17, 2015, in Charleston, South Carolina, at the Emanuel African Methodist Episcopal Church. Nine Black worshippers were murdered by a white supremacist during a Bible study group.

On the occasion of the Confederate flag falling in South Carolina, July 10, 2015

It is the pearl-blue peep of day.
All night the palmetto sky
Was seized with the aurora
And alchemy of the remarkable.
A blazing canopy of newly minted
Light fluttered in while we slept.
We are not free to go on as if
Nothing happened yesterday.
Not free to cheer as if all our
Prayers have finally been answered
Today. We are free only to search
The yonder of each other's faces,
As we pass by, tip our hat, hold a
Door ajar, asking silently,
Who are we now? Blood spilled
In battle is two-headed: horror &
Sweet revelation. Let us put the
Cannons of our eyes away forever.
Our one and only Civil War is done.
Let us tilt, rotate, strut on. If we,
The living, do not give our future
The same honor as the sacred dead,

Of then and now — we lose everything.
The gardenia air feels lighter on this
New day, guided now by iridescent
Fireflies, those atomlike creatures
Of our hot summer nights, now begging
Us to team up and search with them
For that which brightens every
Darkness. Soon, it will be just us
Again, alone, beneath the swirling
Indigo sky of South Carolina. Alone &
Working on the answer to our great
Day's question: *Who are we now?*
What new human cosmos can be made
Of this tempest of tears, this upland
Of inconsolable jubilation? In all our
Lifetimes, finally, this towering
Undulating moment is here. ■

2020

Understanding and Interpreting

1. How would you describe the mood of the opening eight lines?
2. What does the speaker say that "we" are "not free" and "free" to do on this new day?
3. How do you interpret lines 21–23, in which the speaker refers to the "living" and "the sacred dead"?
4. Why does the speaker think the fireflies are "begging / Us to team up and search with them" (ll. 27–28)?
5. What does the speaker mean by "Soon, it will be just us / Again, alone" (ll. 30–31)?
6. Since the poem is occasioned by the historic decision to take the Confederate flag down from its position on the State House, why doesn't the speaker ever mention the flag itself?

Analyzing Language, Style, and Structure

1. **Vocabulary in Context.** The last two lines of the poem include the image of "this towering / Undulating moment." What is the meaning of "undulating"? How does the onomatopoeia of the word add to its effectiveness in this final line? Consider what it might evoke in readers.
2. Throughout the poem, Finney's speaker refers to "we" and "us." What is the effect of this collective pronoun? Does it suggest a specific community? If so, to what purpose?
3. How do Finney's diction choices create a picture of the setting of South Carolina? How would you describe the speaker's attitude toward this setting?
4. While the poem's title is "A New Day Dawns," Finney only refers to a "new day" once in the poem. How else does she allude to new beginnings? Consider both individual words and figurative language in your response.
5. What allusions — both implicit and explicit — does Finney make in the poem? How do these contribute to overall meaning?

6. How does Finney develop contrasts to create meaning in this poem? Consider specific patterns, such as light and dark, as well as oxymorons, such as "inconsolable jubilation" (l. 37).
7. How does the twice repeated question "Who are we now?" serve as a structural device in "A New Day Dawns"? Consider carefully where Finney positions each question. How do they influence your interpretation of the poem as a whole?

Topics for Composing

1. AP® FRQ **Poetry Analysis.** In Nikky Finney's "A New Day Dawns," published in 2020, the speaker commemorates the occasion of the Confederate flag being removed from the State House in Charleston, South Carolina, in the wake of a mass shooting. Read the poem carefully. Then, in a well-written essay, analyze how Finney uses literary elements and techniques to convey the complex significance of that decision.
2. **AP® Literary Argumentation.** What is the "new day" that Finney heralds in this poem? Is that day a celebration, a challenge, a victory, a reconciliation, a combination of one or more of these, or something else entirely? Support your position with specific reference to the text of "A New Day Dawns."
3. **Connections.** Finney's poem is part of the tradition of "occasional poetry," which stretches back centuries. Many American presidents, beginning with John F. Kennedy, have invited poets to recite work for their inaugurations, but occasional poetry is not limited to political events. Do a bit of research on this form, and choose three poems to read and compare with "A New Day Dawns." In your analysis of these poems, be sure to examine the context that gave rise to each and, if possible, the public response to it.
4. **Multimodal.** Do a reading of the poem accompanied by video clips, photographs, or other artwork that illustrates both the exact occasion and larger themes of "A New Day Dawns." Discuss how your choices capture your interpretation of the poem.
5. **Research.** Discuss the circumstances of the mass shooting in the Emanuel African Methodist Episcopal Church in Charleston, South Carolina. You might include the statements Governor Nikki Haley made to explain her decision to call for the removal of the Confederate flag and the speech that President Barack Obama gave at the funeral service for State Senator Clementa Pinckney, the pastor of the Emanuel AME Church, who was one of the victims of the shooting. How does your research into the context surrounding the occasion for this poem deepen your understanding of the speaker and her message?
6. **Creative Writing.** While occasional poetry may commemorate a historical event or milestone, it can also serve a more personal purpose, such as a friend's birthday or the dedication of a local community space. Write your own occasional poem and explain its context. Keep in mind that such poems, depending upon the rhetorical situation, might be humorous as well as serious.
7. **Connections.** Finney has said of this poem, "I have been writing these 230 words all my life." What aspects of the poem speak to a lifelong dedication or commitment? How might this statement be read not only as a reference to lived experience but as a comment on shared community and compassion for others?

AP® Multiple-Choice Practice

from The Book of the Dead

Edwidge Danticat

"Ka," he says, "when I took you to the Brooklyn Museum, I would stand there for hours admiring them. But all you noticed was how there were pieces missing from them, eyes, noses, legs, sometimes even heads. You always noticed more what was not there than what was."

Of course, this way of looking at things was why I ultimately began sculpting in the first place, to make statues that would amaze my father even more than these ancient relics.

"Ka, I am like one of those statues," he says.

"An Ancient Egyptian?" I hear echoes of my loud, derisive laugh only after I've been laughing for a while. It's the only weapon I have now, the only way I know to take my revenge on my father.

"Don't do that," he says, frowning, irritated, almost shouting over my laughter. "Why do that? If you are mad, let yourself be mad. Why do you always laugh like a clown when you are angry?"

I tend to wave my hands about wildly when I laugh, but I don't notice I'm doing that now until he reaches over to grab them. I quickly move them away, but he ends up catching my right wrist, the same wrist Officer Bo had stroked earlier to make me shut up. My father holds on to it so tightly now that I feel his fingers crushing the bone, almost splitting it apart, and I can't laugh anymore.

"Let go," I say, and he releases my wrist quickly. He looks down at his own fingers, then lowers his hand to his lap.

My wrist is still throbbing. I keep stroking it to relieve some of the pain. It's the ache there that makes me want to cry more than anything, not so much this sudden, uncharacteristic flash of anger from my father.

"I'm sorry," he says. "I did not want to hurt you. I did not want to hurt anyone."

I keep rubbing my wrist, hoping he'll feel even sorrier, even guiltier for grabbing me so hard, but even more for throwing away my work.

"Ka, I don't deserve a statue," he says again, this time much more slowly, "not a whole one, at least. You see, Ka, your father was the hunter, he was not the prey."

I stop stroking my wrist, sensing something coming that might hurt much more. He's silent again. I don't want to prod him, feed him any cues, urge him to speak, but finally I get tired of the silence and feel I have no choice but to ask, "What are you talking about?"

I immediately regret the question. Is he going to explain why he and my mother have no close friends, why they've never had anyone over to the house, why they never speak of any relatives in Haiti or anywhere else, or have never returned there or, even after I learned Creole from them, have never taught me anything else about the country beyond what I could find out on my own, on the television, in newspapers, in books? Is he about to tell me why Manman is so pious? Why she goes to daily Mass? I am not sure I want to know anything more than the little they've chosen to share with me all these years, but it is clear to me that he needs to tell me, has been trying to for a long time.

"We have a proverb," he continues. "One day for the hunter, one day for the prey. Ka, your father was the hunter, he was not the prey."

Each word is now hard-won as it leaves my father's mouth, balanced like those hearts on the Ancient Egyptian scales.

"Ka, I was never in prison," he says.

"Okay," I say, sounding like I am fourteen again, chanting from what my mother used to call the meaningless adolescent chorus, just to sound like everyone else my age.

"I was working in the prison," my father says. And I decide not to interrupt him again until he's done.

Stranded in the middle of this speech now, he has to go on. "It was one of the prisoners inside the prison who cut my face in this way," he says.

My father now points to the long, pitted scar on his right cheek. I am so used to his hands covering it up that this new purposeful motion toward it seems dramatic and extreme, almost like raising a veil.

"This man who cut my face," he continues, "I shot and killed him, like I killed many people." ■

AP® Multiple-Choice Questions

1. The details Ka provides in this passage support all of the following about the narrator's father EXCEPT
   - **a.** he finds Egyptian art fascinating
   - **b.** he is deeply religious
   - **c.** he feels guilty about his past
   - **d.** he usually hides his scarred face
   - **e.** he has lied to his daughter

2. Ka's use of the phrase "this way of looking at things" (par. 2) refers to her way of
   - **a.** noticing the absence of what's missing
   - **b.** responding with laughter when angry
   - **c.** wanting her father to feel guilty
   - **d.** relying on her own research about Haiti
   - **e.** mimicking those her own age to fit in

3. When Ka responds to her father's statement "Ka, I am like one of those statues" (par. 3), she describes her laugh as "loud" and "derisive" (par. 4) to emphasize
   - **a.** her amusement at her father's comment
   - **b.** her joy in making personal sculptures
   - **c.** the inferiority of the museum's art
   - **d.** her mocking tone toward her father
   - **e.** the way her father embarrasses her

4. Ka's father's statement that he does not "deserve a statue . . . not a whole one, at least" (par. 11) demonstrates how an imperfect statue symbolizes
   - **a.** his desire to be worthy of a whole statue
   - **b.** his regrets at having injured his daughter's wrist
   - **c.** the challenges he has overcome since leaving Haiti
   - **d.** the significance of his own imperfections
   - **e.** his inferiority to those depicted in Egyptian statues

5. By describing the question she asks in paragraph 12 as one she immediately regrets, Ka suggests she
   - **a.** feels concerned about the truth of her parents' past
   - **b.** knows why her parents became so religious
   - **c.** believes it is normal that her parents are religious
   - **d.** wants to put details about life in Haiti behind her
   - **e.** resents the way her parents have kept secrets from her

6. The effect of repeating "your father was the hunter, he was not the prey" (pars. 11 and 14) emphasizes that Ka's father
   - **a.** thinks Ka has not been paying any attention to him
   - **b.** worries Ka does not at first understand what he means
   - **c.** wants his daughter to know that he is not helpless
   - **d.** needs to convince himself that what he is saying is true
   - **e.** is making an important revelation to Ka for the first time

7. The simile "I am so used to his hands covering it up that this new purposeful motion toward it seems dramatic and extreme, almost like raising a veil" (par. 20) emphasizes the
   a. pride Ka's father feels in the scar he earned while working as a guard
   b. shame Ka's father feels for letting his face be disfigured by a prisoner
   c. significance of Ka's father allowing her to see his scar clearly for the first time
   d. lengths Ka's father has gone to hide his scar from everyone including Ka
   e. contrast between Ka's father's past and present behavior

8. From the revelation in the final paragraphs of this passage that Ka's father had lied to her, readers can infer that he
   a. resorted to defending himself more than once while working in the prison
   b. killed innocent prisoners who had never actually committed any crimes
   c. thinks his daughter is in denial about the seriousness of his past crimes
   d. views working in the prison as more dishonorable than being imprisoned
   e. believes Ka was too immature to understand the reality of his past in Haiti

9. The details in paragraphs 16–21 suggest that Ka's father had previously implied he had a scar because he
   a. mistreated a prisoner and the prisoner attacked him
   b. refused to talk while being interrogated by prison guards
   c. experienced an accident during his early childhood
   d. was one of many who were scarred by the government
   e. had been a political prisoner and scarred by his captors

10. Much of the imagery in this passage suggests a recurring motif emphasizing the
    a. proverb Ka's father shares with her about there being days for both the hunter and prey
    b. similarities in both Ka's and her father's responses to painful experiences
    c. knowledge Ka gains about how her parents' past lives have shaped them
    d. treatment Ka's father received when he was a political prisoner in Haiti
    e. difficulties Ka's father has had in overcoming his horror at the atrocities he saw in Haiti

from The Things They Carried

Tim O'Brien

As PFCs or Spec 4s, most of them were common grunts and carried the standard M-16 gas-operated assault rifle. The weapon weighed 7.5 pounds unloaded, 8.2 pounds with its full twenty-round magazine. Depending on numerous factors, such as topography and psychology, the riflemen carried anywhere from twelve to twenty magazines, usually in cloth bandoliers, adding on another 8.4 pounds at minimum, fourteen pounds at maximum. When it was available, they also carried M-16 maintenance gear — rods and steel brushes and swabs and tubes of LSA oil — all of which weighed about a pound. Among the grunts, some carried the M-79 grenade launcher, 5.9 pounds unloaded, a reasonably light weapon except for the ammunition, which was heavy. A single round weighed ten ounces. The typical load was twenty-five rounds. But Ted Lavender, who was scared, carried thirty-four rounds when he was shot and killed outside Than Khe, and he went down under an exceptional burden, more than twenty pounds of ammunition, plus the flak jacket and helmet and rations and water and toilet paper and tranquilizers and all the rest, plus the unweighed fear. He was dead weight.

There was no twitching or flopping. Kiowa, who saw it happen, said it was like watching a rock fall, or a big sandbag or something — just boom, then down — not like the movies where the dead guy rolls around and does fancy spins and goes ass over teakettle — not like that, Kiowa said, the poor bastard just flat-fuck fell. Boom. Down. Nothing else. It was a bright morning in mid-April. Lieutenant Cross felt the pain. He blamed himself. They stripped off Lavender's canteens and ammo, all the heavy things, and Rat Kiley said the obvious, the guy's dead, and Mitchell Sanders used his radio to report one U.S. KIA[1] and to request a chopper. Then they wrapped Lavender in his poncho. They carried him out to a dry paddy, established security, and sat smoking the dead man's dope until the chopper came. Lieutenant Cross kept to himself. He pictured Martha's smooth young face, thinking he loved her more than anything, more than his men, and now Ted Lavender was dead because he loved her so much and could not stop thinking about her. When the dust-off arrived, they carried Lavender aboard. Afterward they burned Than Khe. They marched until dusk, then dug their holes, and that night Kiowa kept explaining how you had to be there, how fast it was, how the poor guy just dropped like so much concrete. Boom-down, he said. Like cement.

• • •

In addition to the three standard weapons — the M-60, M-16, and M-79 — they carried whatever presented itself, or whatever seemed appropriate as a means of killing or staying alive. They carried catch-as-catch-can. At various times, in various situations, they carried M-14s and CAR-15s and Swedish Ks and grease guns and captured AK-47s and Chi-Coms and RPGs and Simonov carbines and black-market Uzis and .38-caliber Smith & Wesson handguns and 66 mm LAWs and shotguns and silencers and blackjacks and bayonets and C-4 plastic explosives. Lee Strunk carried a slingshot; a weapon of last resort, he called it. Mitchell Sanders carried brass knuckles. Kiowa carried his grandfather's feathered hatchet. Every third or fourth man carried a Claymore antipersonnel mine — 3.5 pounds with its firing device. They all carried fragmentation grenades — fourteen ounces each. They all carried at least one M-18 colored smoke grenade — twenty-four ounces. Some carried CS or tear-gas grenades. Some carried white-phosphorus grenades. They carried all they could bear, and then some, including a silent awe for the terrible power of the things they carried.

In the first week of April, before Lavender died, Lieutenant Jimmy Cross received a good-luck charm from Martha. It was a simple pebble, an ounce at most. Smooth to the touch, it was a milky-white color with flecks of orange and violet, oval-shaped, like a miniature egg. In the accompanying letter, Martha wrote that she had found the pebble on the Jersey shoreline, precisely where the land touched water at high tide, where things came together but also separated. It was this separate-but-together quality, she wrote, that had inspired her to pick up the pebble and to carry it in her breast pocket for several days, where it seemed weightless, and then to send it through the mail, by air, as a token of her truest feelings for him. Lieutenant Cross found this romantic. But he wondered what her truest feelings were, exactly, and what she meant by separate-but-together. He wondered how the tides and waves had come into play on that afternoon along the Jersey shoreline when Martha saw the pebble and bent down to rescue it from geology. He imagined bare feet. Martha was a poet, with the poet's sensibilities, and her feet would be brown and bare, the toenails unpainted, the eyes chilly and somber like the ocean in March, and though it was painful, he wondered who had been with her that afternoon. He imagined a pair of

[1] Killed in action. — Eds.

shadows moving along the strip of sand where things came together but also separated. It was phantom jealousy, he knew, but he couldn't help himself. He loved her so much. On the march, through the hot days of early April, he carried the pebble in his mouth, turning it with his tongue, tasting sea salts and moisture. His mind wandered. He had difficulty keeping his attention on the war. On occasion he would yell at his men to spread out the column, to keep their eyes open, but then he would slip away into daydreams, just pretending, walking barefoot along the Jersey shore, with Martha, carrying nothing. He would feel himself rising. Sun and waves and gentle winds, all love and lightness. ■

AP® Multiple-Choice Questions

1. All of the following are psychological burdens carried by one or more of the men in this excerpt EXCEPT
   a. jealousy
   b. awe
   c. fear
   d. responsibility
   e. hatred

2. Lieutenant Cross believes that he is to blame for Ted Lavender's death because Cross
   a. allowed Lavender to go "down under an exceptional burden"
   b. could not relieve Lavender of his "unweighed fear"
   c. did not adequately bear the responsibility he has for his men
   d. carried less than his fair share of equipment and ammunition
   e. became distracted by the pebble he carried in his mouth from Martha

3. Ted Lavender's poncho serves as a(n)
   a. example of one of the things he had carried that was useless to the others
   b. symbol of what they carried that wasn't a means of killing or staying alive
   c. psychological barrier against the fear Lavender is always experiencing
   d. piece of equipment with both literal and symbolic importance in the story
   e. indication of the typical items all the men carried other than their weapons

4. The inclusion of Lieutenant Cross's feelings for Martha illustrates a(n)
   a. typical distraction younger soldiers faced
   b. unlikely response to the violence around him
   c. human connection to a normal life back home
   d. inadequacy in his approach to leadership
   e. sense of hopelessness about seeing her again

5. The good-luck charm that Martha sends to Lieutenant Cross (par. 3) conveys all of the following EXCEPT the
   a. together-but-separate approach Cross takes
   b. tenuous nature of the connection between them
   c. relative ease of life back home
   d. responsibility Cross bears for his men
   e. coalescence of circumstances

6. Martha writes that she has found the good-luck pebble "precisely where the land touched water at high tide, where things came together but also separated" (par. 3). What does this imagery suggest about her feelings toward Cross?
   a. She is deeply in love with him.
   b. She is deeply in love with someone else.
   c. She is unsure about their relationship.
   d. She is proud of his military service.
   e. She thinks of him as a brother.

7. Paragraph 3 provides a physical and psychological portrait of Martha through Lieutenant Cross's point of view. Cross's description of Martha suggests that he

   a. has no illusions about her feelings
   b. is overly confident that she loves him
   c. needs daydreams to keep him going
   d. feels at once jealous and vengeful
   e. experiences delusions from the war

8. Lieutenant Cross deals with the stress of war by

   a. turning to drugs and alcohol
   b. disconnecting from reality
   c. disappearing for long periods of time
   d. focusing on his men's needs
   e. keeping track of everyone's supplies

9. What is the function of the contrast between the sophisticated weapons all of the men carry and the basic nature of Strunk's slingshot, Kiowa's hatchet, and Sanders's brass knuckles?

   a. Regardless of a physical distance between soldiers, war is a fight between humans.
   b. The soldiers do not trust the equipment issued to them by the military.
   c. Each man's personal weapon conveys his lack of familiarity with guns.
   d. The traditional, basic weapons emphasize the unfair advantage the enemy had.
   e. The basic nature of the men's weapons indicates where they're from originally.

Suggestions for Writing

War and Peace

1. AP® FRQ **Literary Argument.** Works of literature often feature characters dealing with the challenges of war or the effects of recovering from war experiences. Choose one of the short stories in this chapter in which a character or characters face such challenges. In a well-written essay, analyze how these experiences with or following a violent conflict contribute to an interpretation of the work as a whole. Do not merely summarize the plot.

2. **Connections.** Wilfred Owen once wrote: "My subject is War, and the pity of War. The Poetry is in the pity." Write an essay that supports Owen's statement about "the pity of war" as expressed in at least three of the texts in this chapter.

3. **Connections.** In the conclusion to her 2002 book *Regarding the Pain of Others*, Susan Sontag — who witnessed firsthand the horrors of war in Sarajevo in the 1990s — writes:

   > We don't get it. We truly can't imagine what it was like. We can't imagine how dreadful, how terrifying war is; and how normal it becomes. Can't understand, can't imagine. That's what every soldier, and every journalist and aid worker and independent observer who has put in time under fire, and had the luck to elude the death that struck down others nearby, stubbornly feels. And they are right.

   Write an essay that discusses the extent to which Sontag's statement is true, using at least four of the texts in this chapter as support. Consider that several of the selections were written by people who personally experienced war, whereas others were written by those who created imagined voices of experience based on observation and study.

4. **Connections.** Consider this statement from Chris Hedges, a writer, activist, and journalist with experience as a foreign correspondent in war-torn countries:

   > The enduring attraction to war is this: Even with its destruction and carnage it can give us what we long for in life. It can give us purpose, meaning, a reason for living. Only when we are in the midst of conflict does the shallowness and vapidness of much of our lives become apparent. Trivia dominates our conversations and increasingly our airwaves. And war is an enticing elixir. It gives us resolve, a cause. It allows us to be noble.

   Write an essay that compares and contrasts the views expressed in the literature in this chapter with the view expressed by Hedges in this quotation. Refer to at least three texts for support.

5. **Connections.** Some of the main selections from this chapter — Tim O'Brien's "The Things They Carried," Bharati Mukherjee's "The Management of Grief," Scholastique Mukasonga's "Grief," Thomas Hardy's "A Wife in London," Yusef Komunyakaa's "Between Days," and more — present attempts to find peace. Write an essay in which you compare one of these main selections with two or more of the Conversation selections as you discuss the extent to which peace is achieved in postwar experience.

6. **Connections.** Each of the following quotations addresses the nature of war and peace. Select one that interests you, and use it to develop a thesis for an essay. Use several selections from the chapter to support your thesis.
   - **a.** "There is nothing easier than lopping off heads and nothing harder than developing ideas." — Fyodor Dostoevsky
   - **b.** "People sleep peaceably in their beds at night only because rough men stand ready to do violence on their behalf." — George Orwell
   - **c.** "We know how to organize warfare, but do we know how to act when confronted with peace?" — Jacques-Yves Cousteau
   - **d.** "Peace is not merely a distant goal that we seek, but a means by which we arrive at that end." — Martin Luther King Jr.
   - **e.** "The first casualty when war comes is truth."— Senator Hiram Johnson
   - **f.** "The nation that makes a great distinction between its scholars and its warriors will have its thinking done by cowards, and its fighting done by fools." — Thucydides

7. **Connections.** In "The Things They Carried," Tim O'Brien devotes much attention to the physical belongings and inventories of each soldier. Examine other stories and poems in this chapter in which military gear and/or weaponry is described, and then write an essay comparing how descriptions of military gear and weaponry in each reflect the complex perspectives of each narrator. What does description of weaponry in particular reveal about how we frame or cope with war?

8. **Connections.** In a 2015 *Harper's* review of contemporary literature about war, Sam Sacks wrote, "Modern war writing is a strange thing to praise because such praise ennobles the account while deploring the event." How do at least three of the texts in this chapter address this paradoxical balance?

Ben Lewis Giles

8

Home and Family

What makes a house a home? "Home" suggests sanctuary, loved ones, nourishment — a place where everybody knows your name. The term is woven deep into our language as well as our consciousness. Consider the connotations of *homemade* and *homespun*. Home can offer refuge from the hostile world, or it can be a prison. People living together inevitably — sometimes intentionally — rub one another the wrong way. This chafing provides writers with rich material for art. (Remember, without conflict there is no story.) Are these writers working through their own failed relationships with mothers, fathers, and siblings? Sometimes. Are they exploring their conflicted feelings toward a home they left behind? Maybe. Are they holding up a mirror that allows us to see our own homes and families in a new light? Most certainly.

Though the trappings of family and home differ across cultures, human families and homes have much in common. And while most families are created by blood, others are created by choice. And sometimes where we live is a second, third, or fourth home, as our original home exists only in memory. In any case, home and family are rich grounds for literary language both concrete and metaphorical. What we bring from our own backgrounds affects the way we read that language; in the same way, literary depictions of home and family work their way into our consciousness and help shape the way we look at our own families and homes.

The readings in this chapter explore the theme of home and family within a broad range of contexts. Marianne Moore's modernist poem, "The Steeple-Jack," takes a wide-angled view of a small town, invoking Renaissance artist Albrecht Dürer to comment on the elements that make a place home. You'll also find several selections of modernist fiction, poetry, and art that reflect early twentieth-century perceptions of human experience to help you explore the place "The Steeple-Jack" occupies within modernist tradition. Richard Blanco's masterpiece, "Mother Country," is modern in a different way, examining how someone can choose a new home and put down roots there. Some of the works in this chapter explore the connection between family ties and grief — as in William Wordsworth's "We Are Seven," whose speaker encounters a young child who argues even the dead should be counted as family; in Helena María Viramontes's "The Moths," whose young protagonist steps into a new role within her family as she cares for her dying grandmother; and in Hafizah Geter's "The Widower," which paints a portrait of a father and daughter tending to each other in the wake of a loss. Sometimes, as in Adrienne Su's "Peaches" or Marilyn Chin's "Turtle Soup," it's food that ties us as family; and sometimes, as in Heid E. Erdrich's "Intimate Detail" we expand our understanding of family through our connection to the natural world. Some works, such as Ada Limón's "The Raincoat," remind us of what we take for granted in our families. Others, such as Gladys Cardiff's "Combing," show how family traditions are expressions of love. Let the literature on the following pages take you into other homes and families so that you can return to your own with new eyes.

To understand and fully appreciate the wide array of poetry in this chapter, let's turn to the Big Ideas, Skills, and Essential Knowledge in Unit 8 of the AP® English Literature and Composition course. This unit focuses on aspects of Structure, Figurative Language, and Literary Argumentation. One of the major goals of this unit is to explore ambiguities of language and structure and recognize how juxtaposition, irony, and paradox in poetry develop layers of meaning. You may want to review these fundamentals of reading and writing about poetry that we covered in Chapter 2 as you deepen your analysis of how interpretation of a poem's parts informs an interpretation of the entire poem.

While the questions after all of the readings in this chapter ask you to examine how several different literary elements and techniques work together to create meaning, we will preview how they work in the Classic Text for this chapter: "The Steeple-Jack." As you study and discuss both this poem and the Central Text, "Mother Country," you will explore how the writers' art and craft bring to life myriad complex perspectives on the meaning of home and family.

AP® Big Idea: Structure

One of Moore's most visible **structural** choices in "The Steeple-Jack" is her syllabic stanzas, with each stanza following the same pattern of line numbers and syllables. These stanzas send the reader swirling from a bird's-eye view of a small town, spiraling downward to a close-up that highlights the details "on the ground." The juxtaposition of the strict form with the wild profusion of images reveals hidden ideas about what a place really means and what home should be. This contrast will be integral to your analysis of the poem; its ambiguities allow for multiple interpretations, but certainly the poem's structure will play a large part. *To review structure in poetry, see pages 74–81 of Chapter 2: Analyzing Poetry.*

AP® Big Idea: Figurative Language

As much as structure, the **figurative language** in "The Steeple-Jack" creates vivid comparisons, representations, and associations that provide opportunities for complex interpretation. In her poem, Moore invites the early German Renaissance painter and art theoretician Albrecht Dürer (1471–1528) to visit a New England town with us — multiple allusions to his work appear throughout the poem. We also see a steeple with a star on top that functions both literally and symbolically; the image recurs, a motif that evolves with additional meanings each time until its ultimate significance is revealed in the poem's last line. *To review figurative language in poetry, see pages 70–73 of Chapter 2: Analyzing Poetry.*

AP® Big Idea: Literary Argumentation

Each of these Big Ideas is a pillar of the study of poetry. As you read the poems in this chapter, you will be asked to write about how these elements, as well as others you have studied in previous units, work together to create meaning. You will develop your own interpretation of works of literature — based, of course, on evidence from the poems. As you learned in Chapter 2, this process of **literary argumentation** begins with developing a defensible thesis statement and then supporting it with textual evidence and commentary. As you read and write about each poem, keep in mind that you must choose this evidence strategically to illustrate, clarify, qualify, or amplify each point or claim you make about the poem and its meaning. While this textual evidence comes from the poem itself, the commentary is where your voice as the interpreter of a poem comes through. This is the glue that holds your argument together: it explains the logical reasoning that connects the evidence from the poem to the interpretation you convey in your thesis. At this point in the course, you should be aiming to create not just a defensible interpretation of a poem but a sophisticated one. This can be accomplished in many ways — the key thing to remember is that it should be woven throughout your analysis of the textual evidence you're using to support your thesis. As you read in Chapter 2, one fairly straightforward way to achieve this is to connect your analysis to a broader context. In other words, what is the poet saying about humanity? about the meaning of life? *To review the process of writing an AP® Poetry Analysis Essay, see pages 86–102 of Chapter 2: Analyzing Poetry. To review the process of developing sophistication in an AP® Poetry Analysis Essay, see pages 102–105 of Chapter 2: Analyzing Poetry.*

As you read and analyze the works of literature in this chapter, you will feel some of the familiar comforts of home and family, and at the same time, you may open your hearts and minds to the myriad ways homes and families are depicted in literature — some that are quite different from yours. These reading experiences will broaden you as a reader, writer, and person, and your understanding of the writer's craft will advance your growing skills of complex analysis and interpretation.

Guided Reading for "Mother Country"

As you read the Central Text in this chapter, "Mother Country" by Richard Blanco (p. 927), keep track of your observations and questions about how the following Big Ideas take shape in Blanco's poem.

AP® Big Idea	Observations	Questions
Structure		
Figurative Language		

AP® Unit 8 Alignment at a Glance

Mother Country

Richard Blanco

Johnny Louis/Getty Images

Richard Blanco (b. 1968) is a Cuban American poet, public speaker, and civil engineer. Born in Madrid, Spain, Blanco immigrated with his Cuban-born parents and siblings to Miami, where he grew up. He earned both a BS in civil engineering and an MFA in creative writing from Florida International University. Blanco is also the first immigrant, the first Latino, and the first openly gay person to serve as a U.S. inaugural poet. His collections of poetry include *City of a Hundred Fires* (1998), *Directions to the Beach of the Dead* (2005), *Looking for the Gulf Motel* (2012), and *How to Love a Country* (2019). He is also the author of two memoirs, *For All of Us, One Today: An Inaugural Poet's Journey* (2013) and *The Prince of Los Cocuyos: A Miami Childhood* (2014).

KEY CONTEXT During the first half of the twentieth century, Cuba worked to strengthen itself as a democracy after freeing itself from a long history as a colony of Spain and then as a territory occupied by the U.S. military. In 1952, Fulgencio Batista took control via a coup, establishing himself at the head of a military dictatorship. Batista ran a corrupt and oppressive regime until he was overthrown in 1959 during the Cuban Revolution, after which the country was governed by communist dictator Fidel Castro. Throughout the 1960s, Castro's government executed political opponents and thousands of Cubans fled the country. Cuba remains a communist country today.

To love a country as if you've lost one: 1968,
my mother leaves Cuba for America, a scene
I imagine as if standing in her place — one foot
inside a plane destined for a country she knew
only as a name, a color on a map, or glossy photos
from drugstore magazines, her other foot anchored
to the platform of her *patria,*[1] her hand clutched
around one suitcase, taking only what she needs
most: hand-colored photographs of her family,
her wedding veil, the doorknob of her house,
a jar of dirt from her backyard, goodbye letters
she won't open for years. The sorrowful drone
of engines, one last, deep breath of familiar air
she'll take with her, one last glimpse at all
she'd ever known: the palm trees wave goodbye
as she steps onto the plane, the mountains shrink
from her eyes as she lifts off into another life.

[1] Spanish for "country." — Eds.

To love a country as if you've lost one: I hear her
—*once upon a time*—reading picture books
over my shoulder at bedtime, both of us learning
English, sounding out words as strange as the talking
animals and fair-haired princesses in their pages.
I taste her first attempts at macaroni-n-cheese
(but with chorizo and peppers), and her shame
over Thanksgiving turkeys always dry, but countered
by her perfect pork *pernil*[2] and garlic *yuca*.[3] I smell
the rain of those mornings huddled as one under
one umbrella waiting for the bus to her ten-hour days
at the cash register. At night, the zzz-zzz of her sewing
her own blouses, *quinceañera*[4] dresses for her grown nieces
still in Cuba, guessing at their sizes, and the gowns
she'd sell to neighbors to save for a rusty white sedan—
no hubcaps, no air-conditioning, sweating all the way
through our first vacation to Florida theme parks.

To love a country as if you've lost one: as if
it were *you* on a plane departing from America
forever, clouds closing like curtains on your country,
the last scene in which you're a madman scribbling
the names of your favorite flowers, trees, and birds
you'd never see again, your address and phone number
you'd never use again, the color of your father's eyes,
your mother's hair, terrified you could forget these.
To love a country as if I was my mother last spring
hobbling, insisting I help her climb all the way up
to the Capitol, as if she were here before you today

instead of me, explaining her tears, cheeks pink
as the cherry blossoms coloring the air that day when
she stopped, turned to me, and said: You know, *mijo*,[5]
it isn't where you're born that matters, it's where
you choose to die—that's your country. ■

2013

---

[2] Spanish for "ham."—Eds.
[3] A South American plant, often cooked with a garlic sauce.—Eds.
[4] An elaborate celebration of a girl's fifteenth birthday, which carries great significance in Latin culture as a girl's coming of age.—Eds.
[5] A Spanish slang term of endearment meaning "my son."—Eds.

Understanding and Interpreting

1. **AP® Character and Narration.** What point of view does the speaker use in "Mother Country"? What is the speaker's perspective on the subject of the poem?
2. **AP® Character.** The speaker tells us that his mother takes "only what she needs / most" (ll. 8–9) when she leaves Cuba. What items does she take, and what does each reveal about her values? Collectively, what portrait do these items paint of who his mother is?
3. **AP® Character, Setting, and Narration.** How does the speaker's mother meld her homeland's cultural practices and traditions into her new life in the United States?
4. **AP® Character and Narration.** How does the speaker's mother support their family in the United States? How does this work function as a bridge between her homeland and her adopted homeland?
5. **AP® Character and Narration.** What is the speaker's attitude toward his mother in the second stanza? To convey the complexity of his tone, use two adjectives that are synonyms, an adverb-adjective combination, or two adjectives with different denotations.
6. **AP® Narration.** The speaker uses the pronoun "you" throughout the poem, but italicizes it just once, in line 36. Why? Who is the speaker addressing in this line?
7. **AP® Narration.** What does the speaker's presentation of what "you'd never see again" and what "you'd never lose again" (ll. 40–41) in the third stanza emphasize about the experience of leaving your homeland to make a life elsewhere?
8. **AP® Character and Narration.** What is your interpretation of the reason the speaker's mother cries in line 46? Use evidence from the text to support your answer.
9. **AP® Narration.** Most stanzas begin with the same phrase: "To love a country as if you've lost one." How does the poem expand on that phrase in each stanza? Do you think the poem provides a response to or finishes that phrase? Explain.
10. **AP® Narration.** Describe the overarching theme or themes of each stanza. How does each stanza function individually? How do they function as a collective whole?
11. **AP® Narration.** How do you interpret the title of the poem? Does it refer to Cuba, the United States, or both? Explain your reasoning with evidence from the poem itself.
12. **AP® Narration.** "Mother Country" was included in Richard Blanco's 2019 poetry collection *How to Love a Country*. What is the poem's answer to that question? How do you love a country? What, ultimately, does it mean to love a country "as if you've lost one"?
13. **AP® Narration.** "Mother Country" was one of three poems Blanco wrote when he was asked to read a poem at the inauguration of President Barack Obama in 2009. Though another poem ("One Today") was chosen, what evidence do you find that this was an "occasional" poem — that is, one written for a particular occasion? To what extent is it a suitable poem for the occasion of a presidential inauguration?

Analyzing Language, Style, and Structure

1. **Vocabulary in Context.** Even though the speaker's mother feels "shame / over Thanksgiving turkeys always dry" (ll. 24–25), she "countered" (l. 25) the turkey with "her perfect pork *pernil* and garlic *yuca*" (l. 26). Consider words that incorporate the word "counter," such as *counteroffer*, *counterpunch*, and *counterclaim*. In context, what does "countered" suggest about the food the family enjoyed at Thanksgiving dinners? What significance does this event hold for the speaker, and how does that word choice contribute to it?

2. **AP® Character, Structure, and Narration.** What does Blanco's use of the coordinating conjunction "or" in line 5 suggest about his mother's perspective? Consider how the meaning of the line would be different had he used the word "and" instead.
3. **AP® Structure and Narration.** What is significant about Blanco's choice of the word "lost" in lines 1, 18, and 35? How would the meaning of the poem have changed if those lines had read, "To love a country as if you've left one"?
4. **AP® Structure.** How do the line breaks in this poem create meaning? Consider, for example, lines 8–9, 20–21, 27–28, 36–37, 39–41, 45–46, and 49–50. What ideas do these breaks convey? How do these ideas relate to each other?
5. **AP® Narration and Figurative Language.** How does Blanco use imagery to emphasize ideas and create comparisons and contrasts? Which of the five senses does he invoke most often, and to what effect? What significance do these images hold for the speaker?
6. **AP® Structure and Narration.** What is the effect of the shift that takes place in line 43? How does the repetition of "as if" in line 45 sustain the effect?
7. **AP® Structure.** Blanco uses enjambment across stanzas in only one place: lines 45–46, which contain the break between stanzas 3 and 4. What idea does this break emphasize? How does it comment on the relationship between the past and the present? What does the shift signify in terms of the meaning of the poem?
8. **AP® Structure, Narration, and Figurative Language.** How does Blanco create a sense of being in two places at once? Why is that important to the meaning of the poem?
9. **AP® Structure and Narration.** What does the speaker's choice of Spanish for particular words and phrases convey about his perspective on his mother and his home?
10. **AP® Structure and Narration.** Describe the overall structure of "Mother Country." How do Blanco's structural decisions help set the poem's tone? What do they suggest about the meaning the word *country* carries for both the speaker and his mother?
11. **AP® Structure, Narration, and Figurative Language.** In an interview with the University of Notre Dame's Institute for Latino Studies, Blanco explained that his inner poetic voice has been influenced by Spanish and "alliteration, assonance, consonance, etc., as well as line lengths and line breaks — all of which are meant to create and maintain a certain rhythm and keep the language flowing." What elements of alliteration, assonance, and consonance do you find in this poem? What message do these elements in particular work together to convey? How does the structure of his lines "create and maintain a certain rhythm and keep the language flowing"?

Topics for Composing

1. **AP® FRQ Poetry Analysis.** In Richard Blanco's "Mother Country," published in 2013, the speaker imagines himself in his mother's shoes as she left her home country of Cuba and made the United States her new homeland. Read the poem carefully. Then in a well-written essay, analyze how Blanco uses literary elements and techniques to convey the complex experiences the speaker's mother has in America.
2. **AP® Literary Argumentation.** Blanco uses a first-person point of view throughout the poem "Mother Country"; however, the speaker also uses the second-person pronoun "you" throughout the poem. How do these references to "you" change as the poem progresses? How does Blanco use this combination of point of view and perspective to emphasize his message?

3. **AP® Literary Argumentation.** In an interview, Blanco said that growing up in an all-Cuban ex-pat community felt like living between two imaginary worlds: "the homeland paradise that everyone wanted to return to someday but nobody could visit, and the America that [Blanco] saw on television through shows like 'The Brady Bunch,'" an early 1970s sitcom about a large blended family. What aspects of "Mother Country" reflect the "homeland paradise"; what reflect the America of *The Brady Bunch*? What evidence can you find of a synthesis of the two worlds?
4. **AP® Literary Argumentation.** Blanco has said that his training as an engineer led him to poetry: "When I graduated I started working full-time and I was confronted with how much verbal skill I needed in writing reports and letters. I started paying really close attention to language, how to argue, how to create a persona, how to persuade. . . . I realized that language is engineerable. I developed a hyper-focus on language and started fiddling around with poetry. It really grew into a love and a passion." How is "Mother Country" engineered? What does it argue? What elements of language does Blanco use to persuade readers?
5. **Speaking and Listening.** Create a list of those things you would most miss if you were to "lose" your country. Which features do you imagine waving good-bye to you and shrinking if you "lift[ed] off into another life" (l. 17)? Which favorite foods would you still cook, and which traditions would you still celebrate? Share what you've come up with in a small group or as a class. What common themes do you notice? Which ideas are more specific to people's families or cultures?
6. **Connections.** As Peter Armenti, the literature specialist for the Digital Reference Section at the Library of Congress, explained in 2013, Richard Blanco was tasked with writing "an inaugural poem that not only meets the requirements of the occasion but also stands on its own merits." According to Armenti, inaugural poems "must adopt a form, tone, and level of diction appropriate for consumption by millions of Americans, as well as a uniformly positive view of the nation that carefully avoids explicit and implicit criticism of our government." Compare and contrast the "form, tone, and level of diction" of the poem "One Today," which Blanco read for President Obama's inauguration, with "Mother Country," one of the other two poems he wrote for the occasion.
7. **Research.** PBS's *American Experience* explains that Cubans who immigrated to the United States between the 1950s and the 1990s "created a wealthy, successful, politically influential immigrant society . . . wave upon wave of immigrants rebuilt their lives after the traumatic experience of the revolution." Richard Blanco's parents left Cuba in 1967 because, as his mother reported to the *Bangor Daily News* in 2013, "the government was becoming more and more difficult to live under." Research the political environment that emerged in Cuba in the late 1950s. Why would people such as Blanco's parents have felt compelled to leave with only the suitcases they could carry? How does this knowledge affect your understanding of Blanco's poem "Mother Country"?

The Steeple-Jack

Marianne Moore

Library of Congress, Prints & Photographs Division, [LC-USZ62-101955]

Marianne Moore (1887–1972) was an American modernist poet born in Kirkwood, Missouri. After graduating from Pennsylvania's Bryn Mawr College in 1909, Moore eventually moved to New York City, where she took a job at the New York Public Library in 1921 and befriended fellow poets such as William Carlos Williams and Wallace Stevens. Moore's poems appeared in prestigious literary magazines, including the *Egoist* and the *Dial*, where she served as editor from 1925 to 1929. In 1921, Moore's first book, *Poems*, was published by fellow poet and Bryn Mawr classmate Hilda Doolittle. Among Moore's many honors were the Bollingen Prize, the National Book Award, and the Pulitzer Prize, all for her 1951 work, *Collected Poems*.

KEY CONTEXT This poem's title refers to a person whose job it is to scale buildings — historically, church steeples — to carry out repairs. It was written in 1932, near the end of the modernist era. In literature, modernism refers to a movement of writers during the late 1910s, 1920s, and 1930s who expressed disillusionment with Western civilization as they knew it, especially in the wake of World War I's mindless brutality. Rejecting the conventions of earlier eras, these writers experimented with form and took insights from new ideas in the field of psychology about the unconscious mind. Modernists viewed art as restorative and frequently ordered their writing around symbols and allusions.

Throughout this poem, Moore alludes to Albrecht Dürer (1471–1528), a German painter, printmaker, and scholar of the Renaissance era. He is best known for his woodcuts and engravings, but his watercolors established him as one of the first European landscape artists. He wrote theoretical treatises about art, including principles of mathematics, perspective, and ideal proportion.

Dürer would have seen a reason for living
    in a town like this, with eight stranded whales
to look at; with the sweet sea air coming into your house
on a fine day, from water etched
    with waves as formal as the scales
on a fish.

One by one, in two's, in three's, the seagulls keep
    flying back and forth over the town clock,
or sailing around the lighthouse without moving the wings —
rising steadily with a slight
    quiver of the body — or flock
mewing where

a sea the purple of the peacock's neck is
    paled to greenish azure as Dürer changed
the pine green of the Tyrol to peacock blue and guinea
gray. You can see a twenty-five
    pound lobster; and fishnets arranged
to dry. The

whirlwind fifeanddrum of the storm bends the salt
    marsh grass, disturbs stars in the sky and the
star on the steeple; it is a privilege to see so
much confusion. Disguised by what
    might seem austerity, the sea-
side flowers and

trees are favored by the fog so that you have
    the tropics at first hand: the trumpet-vine,
fox-glove, giant snap-dragon, a salpaglossis that has
spots and stripes; morning-glories, gourds,
    or moon-vines trained on fishing-twine
at the back

door; cat-tails, flags, blueberries and spiderwort,
    striped grass, lichens, sunflowers, asters, daisies —
the yellow and the crab-claw blue ones with green bracts[1] — toad-plant,
petunias, ferns; pink lilies, blue
    ones, tigers; poppies; black sweet-peas.
The climate

is not right for the banyan, frangipan, the
    jack-fruit tree; nor for exotic serpent
life. Ring lizard and snake-skin for the foot if you see fit,
but here they've cats not cobras to
    keep down the rats. The diffident
little newt

with white pin-dots on the black horizontal spaced
    out bands lives here; yet there is nothing that
ambition can buy or take away. The college student
named Ambrose sits on the hill-side
    with his not-native books and hat
and sees boats

[1] Specialized plant leaves that typically attract pollinators. — Eds.

at sea progress white and rigid as if in
   a groove. Liking an elegance of which
the source is not bravado, he knows by heart the antique
sugar-bowl shaped summer-house of
   interlacing slats, and the pitch
of the church

spire, not true, from which a man in scarlet lets
   down a rope as a spider spins a thread;
he might be part of a novel, but on the sidewalk a
sign says C. J. Poole, Steeple-jack,
   in black and white; and one in red
and white says

Danger. The church portico has four fluted
   columns, each a single piece of stone, made
modester by white-wash. This would be a fit haven for
waifs, children, animals, prisoners,
   and presidents who have repaid
sin-driven

senators by not thinking about them. There
   are a school-house, a post-office in a
store, fish-houses, hen-houses, a three-masted schooner[2] on
the stocks. The hero, the student,
   the steeple-jack, each in his way,
is at home.

It could not be dangerous to be living
   in a town like this, of simple people,
who have a steeple-jack placing danger signs by the church
while he is gilding the solid-
   pointed star, which on a steeple
stands for hope. ■

1932

[2] A small sailing ship. —Eds.

extending beyond the text

This watercolor drawing by Albrecht Dürer, completed in 1495, depicts the citadel north of Lake Garda in the Tyrol area of northern Italy. While it is a realistic portrayal of the scene, it is also poetic, using the colors of early spring and stressing certain aspects of the view for effect.

Photo Josse/Leemage/Getty Images

1. **What parallels do you see with the scene described in "The Steeple-Jack" in this painting?**
2. **Do you think this image supports Marianne Moore's assertion in "The Steeple-Jack" that "Dürer would have seen a reason for living / in a town like this" (ll. 1–2)? Explain why or why not.**
3. **Balance in painting was important to Dürer. What balance does this painting provide? Do you think "The Steeple-Jack" depicts that same sense of balance? Explain why or why not.**

Understanding and Interpreting

1. **AP® Setting and Narration.** What does "The Steeple-Jack" reveal about "a town like this" (l. 2)? Why, according to the speaker, would it have appealed to an artist like Albrecht Dürer? In your response, consider that he was an early landscape painter.
2. **AP® Setting and Narration.** Where in physical space is the speaker situated in the poem's first twenty-three lines? How does that vantage point change as the poem goes on?
3. **AP® Setting and Narration.** What kind of town does "The Steeple-Jack" describe? What hints does the poem give about its location?

4. **AP® Setting and Narration.** Why might the speaker think that "it is a privilege to see so / much confusion" (ll. 21–22)? What causes the confusion?
5. **AP® Character and Narration.** What does the "college student / named Ambrose" (ll. 45–46) add to the poem? What do his "non-native books and hat" (l. 47) convey about his character?
6. **AP® Narration.** According to the speaker, Ambrose likes "an elegance of which / the source is not bravado" (ll. 51–52). What does the speaker mean by this? What examples of this kind of elegance can be found in the poem?
7. **AP® Character and Narration.** What does the speaker think of the Steeple-jack C. J. Poole? How do you know?
8. **AP® Character, Setting, and Narration.** In stanzas 11 and 12 the speaker comments on the town as a "fit haven." Why might "waifs, children, animals, prisoners, / and presidents who have repaid / sin-driven // senators by not thinking about them" (ll. 64–67) all fit in?
9. **AP® Setting and Narration.** In his 1925 essay "Marianne Moore," William Carlos Williams described Moore's "signature mode" as the vastness of the particular: in "looking at some apparently small object, one feels the swirl of great events." What are the small objects in "The Steeple-Jack"? What great events do you feel are taking place around you as you read it?
10. **AP® Character, Setting, and Narration.** "The Steeple-Jack" was part of a series of poems called "Part of a Novel, Part of a Poem, Part of a Play" when it was first published in *Poetry* magazine in 1932. It included a section on the student and a section on the hero. How does "The Steeple-Jack" show that both student and hero "each in his way, / is at home" (ll. 71–72)?

Analyzing Language, Style, and Structure

1. **Vocabulary in Context.** What is the meaning of the word "etched" in line 4? How does the poem use it metaphorically in two different ways in the first stanza? How does this word connect to the artist Albrecht Dürer?
2. **AP® Figurative Language.** Which of the metaphors in "The Steeple-Jack" does Moore extend throughout the poem? How does the meaning of the metaphor change or build on itself as the poem progresses?
3. **AP® Structure and Figurative Language.** You probably noticed that each of the stanzas has the same number of lines, line lengths, and indentations as well as the same number of syllables per line in each stanza. How does that structure relate to Dürer's presence in the poem? What larger themes does this structure point to?
4. **AP® Narration and Figurative Language.** It is known that Dürer, who was extremely curious about the natural world, journeyed to see a beached whale; it is unknown if he ever got to see one. What purpose does the hyperbole of "eight stranded whales / to look at" (ll. 2–3) serve in the poem?
5. **AP® Structure and Narration.** How does the speaker's description of "waves as formal as the scales / on a fish" (ll. 5–6) connect to the poem's overall structure? Consider its shape on the page.
6. **AP® Structure.** Lines 26–39 list species of flora, some of which are native to the New England in which the poem is set, while others are tropical. What is the effect of this detailed inventory? Consider both the images they create as well as the sound and even the look of the words.
7. **AP® Narration and Figurative Language.** Trace the steeple and the star that tops it through the poem. Where do they first appear, and what do they signify? How does their meaning evolve over the course of the poem?
8. **AP® Structure and Figurative Language.** What does it mean in line 56 that the spire is "not true"? Consider both its literal meaning and the possibility of a figurative meaning. To what extent do these literal and figurative meanings cohere?

9. **AP® Structure and Narration.** Several verbs in "The Steeple-Jack" are in the conditional tense — such as *would*, *could*, or *might*. What does this type of verb tense suggest about the speaker's perspective?
10. **AP® Structure and Narration.** "The Steeple-Jack" presents the reader with several contrasts, although many are not entirely in opposition to each other. Trace the contrasts and their effect on the poem as a whole.
11. **AP® Structure and Narration.** As we discussed in the introduction to the chapter, "The Steeple-Jack" is a poem with syllabic stanzas, with each stanza being a syllabic duplicate of the others. A requirement of the form is that each stanza can be written out in prose that makes sense. Some critics consider the effect mechanical, a criticism Moore answered by saying "a thing so mechanically perfect as a battleship is always a pleasure to me." What aspects of the poem have a "mechanical" quality, and what does that quality add to the meaning of the poem? In what way might this poem be interpreted as a "battleship"?

Topics for Composing

1. **AP® FRQ Poetry Analysis.** In Marianne Moore's "The Steeple-Jack," published in 1932, the speaker paints a picture of life in a New England town. Read the poem carefully. Then, in a well-written essay, analyze how Moore uses literary elements and techniques to reveal a deeper, more complex layer of meaning in the landscape of the town.
2. **AP® Literary Argumentation.** Marianne Moore once remarked that "prose is a step beyond poetry . . . and then there is another poetry that is a step beyond that." The critic Frank Kermode explained further, noting "you had to go through prose to come out the other side purged of that disposable prior poetry, with its irrelevant inversions and its subjection to conventional rhythms." How does Moore accomplish "another poetry" in "The Steeple-Jack"?
3. **AP® Literary Argumentation.** How does "The Steeple-Jack" play on uncertainty? Can it be seen as a modernist critique of science or rational thinking? Explain your answer in an essay.
4. **AP® Literary Argumentation.** What argument does Moore make in the last stanza of "The Steeple-Jack"? How safe is a small town? Explain what you think Moore is saying about a small town and whether you agree with the poem's argument.
5. **Connections.** The critic Andrew Lakritz suggested that Moore is part of the modernist tradition because of the way she criticizes the idea of progress in modern culture and also because of her "dense" language choices. Her work, he asserts, is easily misunderstood if one reads it with "merely common sense in hand." Where does the reader have to have more than common sense in hand when reading "The Steeple-Jack"?
6. **Research.** Learn more about the artist Albrecht Dürer and choose one of his works — a woodcut, an etching, or a painting — to analyze. What is it about his work that might have inspired Moore to place him so prominently in her poem?
7. **Connections.** While Dürer watches over the first part of the poem, critics have noted that as the focus narrows, the view is more like something artist Vincent van Gogh (1853–1890) might have painted. Read about both Dürer and van Gogh, and closely examine at least three works by each artist. Which parts of the poem relate more to Dürer and which parts to van Gogh? Explain.
8. **Creative Writing.** Write your own version of "The Steeple-Jack" about the place where you live. Try to find, as Moore does, "vastness in the particular."
9. **Multimodal.** "The Steeple-Jack," while grammatically and syntactically "correct," creates a collage effect, often called fragmentation, which is a hallmark of modernist writing. Create your own collage that illustrates either the town described in "The Steeple-Jack" or your own hometown. How do the fragments of your collage connect to or reflect Moore's style choices in the poem?

Marianne Moore and the Modernist Vision

"Make it new!" — an exhortation poet Ezra Pound made in 1928 — has since become the battle cry of what we now refer to as the modernist movement. Although it is difficult to point to an actual date when the period began, the turn of the twentieth century saw a dramatic series of culture shocks that brought about changes in every sphere. Industrialization that shifted demographics from the country to the city, rapid social and political change, and advances in science and technology had exerted a profound influence by the early 1900s.

At the beginning of the twentieth century much of the western world was already wrestling with groundbreaking ideas of the late 1800s: Sigmund Freud's notion of the unconscious mind (the id), Karl Marx's socialism, Charles Darwin's theory of natural selection, and Friedrich Nietzsche's nihilist mantra — "God is dead" — all reflected a growing secularization in society. World War I, fought between 1914 and 1919, was the bloodiest war in recorded history to date and the first to play out on a global scale. It also introduced a deadly combination of primitive trench-warfare tactics and modern weaponry — by its finish, nearly 9 million people had died. It was one of the most politically bewildering conflicts the world had ever seen, one that changed the meaning of what it meant to die for one's country. Faith in the established political and social order wavered. Even before the start of World War I, some artists, musicians, and writers made a radical break with the past as they sought new ways to interpret the now-unfamiliar world they confronted. Traditional art forms suddenly seemed incapable of representing the mystery, complexity, and uncertainty of modern life. In response, many rejected the so-called realistic depiction of human experience in both the written and visual arts of the nineteenth century. The first art exhibition to display the fruits of these efforts was the

Bettmann/Getty Images

This photograph shows part of the 1913 Armory Show.

What aspects of the art in this photograph look realistic to you? Which look more abstract? What can you infer about how the show's creators intended the audience to interact with this art?

1913 Armory Show. The first large exhibition of modern art in America, it marked the start of the modernist movement, moving from New York City's 69th Regiment Armory to Chicago and Boston. It featured the works of European modern artists — including Henri Matisse, Marcel Duchamp, and Pablo Picasso — and the show shocked many Americans who, accustomed to realistic art, were at first perplexed by experimental and abstract expression. Of course, eventually this type of art became a popular way to portray the violence and destabilization that marked the first half of the twentieth century.

Modernism is now known for its abstract art, symbolic poetry, and stream-of-consciousness prose — all meant to represent the subjective experience of modern life rather than the objective reality of it. These efforts were driven by innovation in form and content. Although both writers and visual artists experimented in many different forms, the modernists' vision shares certain characteristics:

- a belief that traditional religious, political, and social institutions had broken down;
- a view of urban society as fostering a mechanistic, materialistic culture;
- a sense of anonymity and alienation brought on, in part, by the banality of middle-class life; and
- a conviction that there is no such thing as absolute truth, only relative and subjective perceptions.

While these ideas may seem to add up to a fairly bleak view, modernists believed that their willingness to innovate, to "make it new," and to experiment with forms more attuned to the social and political realities of the era could be a transformative, even healing experience. Writers, for instance, emphasized and validated the individual's perception of reality, often exploring characters' rich inner lives through the stream-of-consciousness narratives, which describe in words the flow of thoughts in the minds of the characters. Writers such as James Joyce, Virginia Woolf, Jean Toomer, and William Faulkner used stream of consciousness to paint characters' perceptions and observations as elements that propel the narrative forward through association rather than straightforward cause and effect.

Modernist writers and artists also found the collage a mode of expression suited to their philosophical beliefs. In visual art, a collage is a work created by materials and objects glued to a flat surface, often in overlapping layers. In poetry, this technique is called fragmentation: diverse pieces or images come together — or don't — in a way that mirrors the disjointed, chaotic modern world. In both cases, the collage abandons the logical relationships that typically order a work of art — such as cause-and-effect, chronology, and subordination — to express a less coherent view of reality, one that highlights subjective individual experience. The poet Ezra Pound coined the term "imagism" to characterize an early twentieth-century style of poetry that sought to replace the abstract, often decorative language of the nineteenth century with clear, concise, concrete images. Pound's famous two-line poem, "In a Station of the Metro," epitomized the tenets of this movement:

> The apparition   of these faces   in the crowd :
> Petals   on a wet, black   bough .

Pound observes a scene in the subway, and then recasts — and elevates — it as a powerful image. Poets like Ezra Pound, H. D., Richard Aldington, William Carlos Williams, and Amy Lowell used economy of language, apt metaphors, and precisely observed detail to create their imagist works.

Marianne Moore was a poet who both wrote modernist works and worked with modernist poets when she was editor of the *Dial*. Her poem "The Steeple-Jack" is a later modernist work. In this section, you will consider the poem in the context of other art and literature from the same period. You'll have an opportunity to see how others interpret the motto of "make it new" as well as how each writer and artist builds on the traditions and conventions of the past. We begin with an excerpt from a famous essay called "Tradition and the Individual Talent" by T. S. Eliot. In it, he argues against rejecting the past but instead urges his audience to redefine the relationship between past and present.

TEXTS IN CONTEXT

1. **T. S. Eliot ▪ from *Tradition and the Individual Talent* (nonfiction)**
2. **Robert Burns ▪ *A Red, Red Rose* (poetry)**
3. **H. D. ▪ *Sea Rose* (poetry)**
4. **Amy Lowell ▪ *A London Thoroughfare. 2 A.M.* and *The Emperor's Garden* (poetry)**
5. **Fernand Léger ▪ *La Ville ("The City")* (painting)**
6. **Virginia Woolf ▪ from *Mrs. Dalloway* (fiction)**

from Tradition and the Individual Talent

T. S. Eliot

Poet, dramatist, and critic Thomas Stearns Eliot (1888–1965) was born and raised in St. Louis, Missouri. He moved to England when he was twenty-five to attend Oxford University after studying at Harvard University and eventually became a British subject. His most famous works include "The Love Song of J. Alfred Prufrock" (1915), "The Wasteland" (1922), "Ash Wednesday" (1930), "Burnt Norton" (1941), "Little Gidding" (1942), "Four Quartets" (1943), and the play *Murder in the Cathedral* (1935). He was awarded the Nobel Prize for Literature in 1948.

KEY CONTEXT Eliot is closely associated with the modernist movement — especially in his stream-of-consciousness style steeped in literary allusions and mythological references. Eliot believed that such complex poetry was necessary in order to reflect the complexities of modern civilization, but he also considered tradition to be an ongoing process that united the past with the present. His essay "Tradition and the Individual Talent" explores the complex relationship between a poet's historical context and the value of that poet's unique voice.

In English writing we seldom speak of tradition, though we occasionally apply its name in deploring its absence. We cannot refer to "the tradition" or to "a tradition"; at most, we employ the adjective in saying that the poetry of So-and-so is "traditional" or even "too traditional." Seldom, perhaps, does the word appear except in a phrase of censure. . . .

[W]hen we praise a poet, upon those aspects of his work in which he least resembles anyone else. In these aspects or parts of his work we pretend to find what is individual, what is the peculiar essence of the man. We dwell with satisfaction upon the poet's difference from his predecessors, especially his immediate predecessors; we endeavour to find something that can be isolated in order to be enjoyed. Whereas if we approach a poet without this prejudice we shall often find that not only the best, but the most individual parts of his work may be those in which the dead poets, his ancestors, assert their immortality most vigorously. And I do not mean the impressionable period of adolescence, but the period of full maturity.

Yet if the only form of tradition, of handing down, consisted in following the ways of the immediate generation before us in a blind or timid adherence to its successes, "tradition" should positively be discouraged. We have seen many such simple currents soon lost in the sand; and novelty is better than repetition. Tradition is a matter of much wider significance. It cannot be inherited, and if you want it you must obtain it by great labour. It involves, in the first place, the historical sense, which we may call nearly indispensable to anyone who would continue to be a poet beyond his twenty-fifth year; and the historical sense involves a perception, not only of the pastness of the past, but of its presence; the historical sense compels a man to write not merely with his own generation in his bones, but with a feeling that the whole of the literature of Europe from Homer and within it the whole of the literature of his own country has a simultaneous existence and composes a simultaneous order. This historical sense, which is a sense of the timeless as well as of the temporal together, is what makes a writer traditional. And it is at the same time what makes a writer most acutely conscious of his place in time, of his contemporaneity.

No poet, no artist of any art, has his complete meaning alone. His significance, his appreciation is the appreciation of his relation to the dead poets and artists. You cannot value him alone; you must set him, for contrast and comparison, among the dead. ■

1920

Questions

1. How does T. S. Eliot's concept of "tradition" fuse past and present?
2. How does Eliot challenge the view that the value of a work of art should be measured by its departure from its predecessors?
3. To what extent does the final paragraph of this excerpt argue that an artist must pay tribute — either by reflecting or refuting — the ideas of his or her predecessors?
4. How does Eliot's concept of the presence of the past apply to musical artists? Choose a musician or band, contemporary or past, with whom you are familiar, and discuss.

A Red, Red Rose

Robert Burns

Robert Burns (1759–1796) was a poet and lyricist who remains a folk hero in his native Scotland to this day. His most famous poem, "A Red, Red Rose," also became a popular ballad.

KEY CONTEXT In this poem, Burns describes a rose as a symbol of romantic love and beauty, a traditional treatment of the flower as a symbol of the speaker's beloved and his passion for her. The rose in traditional poetry can also recall the Virgin Mary's purity in Christian theology. "A Red, Red Rose" shows the kind of conventional interpretation of symbol that modernist poets would later question and subvert.

O my luve's like a red, red rose
  That's newly sprung in June;
O my luve's like the melodie
  That's sweetly play'd in tune.

As fair art thou, my bonnie lass,
  So deep in luve am I;
And I will luve thee still, my dear,
  Till a' the seas gang dry.

Till a' the seas gang dry, my dear.
  And the rocks melt wi' the sun:
O I will love thee still, my dear,
  While the sands o' life shall run.

And fare-thee-weel, my only luve:
  And fare-thee-weel awhile!
And I will come again, my luve,
  Tho' 'twere ten thousand mile!

O my luve's like a red, red rose
  That's newly sprung in June;
O my luve's like the melodie
  That's sweetly play'd in tune. ■

1794

Questions

1. What tone does the opening simile establish?
2. What other similes accumulate during the poem to support and enhance the opening one?
3. As a twenty-first-century reader, which of these similes do you find the most original and moving? Why?
4. Do you believe that relying upon the rose's traditional associations increases or decreases its symbolic value? Explain.

Sea Rose

H. D.

H. D. (1886–1961), pen name of Hilda Doolittle, was an influential American poet and novelist known for her association with imagism, a genre within the modernist movement.

KEY CONTEXT Imagists rejected overly sentimental, decorative language in favor of direct and succinct expression. Such poets often focused an entire poem on a single image, as H. D. does here. As you read, consider how this poem undermines the stereotype of roses as symbols of beauty, romance, and purity.

Rose, harsh rose,
marred and with stint of petals,
meagre flower, thin,
sparse of leaf,

more precious
than a wet rose
single on a stem —
you are caught in the drift.

Stunted, with small leaf,
you are flung on the sand,
you are lifted
in the crisp sand
that drives in the wind.

Can the spice-rose
drip such acrid fragrance
hardened in a leaf? ■

1916

Questions

1. How does the opening stanza (ll. 1–4) defy expectations based on the traditional way of seeing and writing about a rose? Cite specific language choices.
2. Who is the speaker in this poem? Who (or what) is being addressed?
3. How do you interpret the line, "you are caught in the drift" (l. 8)?
4. What is the impact of comparing the sea rose to two other roses? How does the sea rose compare?
5. What do you think the speaker anticipates as the response to the poem's final rhetorical question (ll. 14–16)?
6. What is the effect of the sparse, perhaps even stark, language of the poem? What is the difference, for instance, between "flung on the sand" (l. 10) and "flung harshly on the cold sand"?
7. Do you think the sea rose, as depicted in this poem, is beautiful? Why, or why not?
8. What does the sea rose symbolize in this poem? In what ways does it both evoke and subvert traditional associations with the rose?

A London Thoroughfare. 2 A.M.

Amy Lowell

Amy Lowell (1874–1925) was an American poet from Brookline, Massachusetts. Lowell was an early advocate for free verse and eventually embraced the imagist movement, which favored direct expression over decorative language.

KEY CONTEXT In both "A London Thoroughfare. 2 A.M." and "The Emperor's Garden," Lowell blends unsentimental and blunt language with vivid imagery to evoke the alienating forces of modernity in imagist style.

They have watered the street,
It shines in the glare of lamps,
Cold, white lamps,
And lies
Like a slow-moving river,
Barred with silver and black.
Cabs go down it,
One,
And then another.
Between them I hear the shuffling of feet.
Tramps doze on the window-ledges,
Night-walkers pass along the sidewalks.
The city is squalid and sinister,
With the silver-barred street in the midst,
Slow-moving,
A river leading nowhere.

Opposite my window,
The moon cuts,
Clear and round,
Through the plum-coloured night.
She cannot light the city;
It is too bright.
It has white lamps,
And glitters coldly.

I stand in the window and watch the moon.
She is thin and lustreless,
But I love her.
I know the moon,
And this is an alien city. ■

1914

The Emperor's Garden

Amy Lowell

Once, in the sultry heats of midsummer,
An emperor caused the miniature mountains in his garden
To be covered with white silk,
That so crowned
They might cool his eyes
With the sparkle of snow. ■

1917

Questions

1. How would you characterize the speaker of "A London Thoroughfare. 2 A.M."? How does she depict the city? Does she use primarily literal or figurative language? Cite examples to support your response.
2. Where does a shift occur in "A London Thoroughfare. 2 A.M."? What is the relationship between what happens before and after that shift?
3. Summarize the poem "The Emperor's Garden." To what extent do you think your summary captures Amy Lowell's purpose or ideas?
4. How does Lowell appeal to the senses in "The Emperor's Garden"? Cite specific words and images.
5. Add at least five of the following modifiers to "The Emperor's Garden": *sweltering*, *falling*, *gentle*, *sparkling*, *deep blue*, *bright*, *wise*, *sensuous.* How do these additional descriptions change the effect the poem has on you?
6. Lowell believed that "concentration is of the very essence of poetry" and strove to "produce poetry that is hard and clear, never blurred nor indefinite." Based on these two poems, explain why you believe she did or did not imbue her own work with these qualities.
7. Judging from these examples, is it more important to feel or to understand imagist poetry — or is that a false dichotomy? Can one response to art exist without the other? Explain.

La Ville ("The City")

Fernand Léger

Fernand Léger (1881–1955) was a French painter and sculptor. He was born in Normandy, where his parents were farmers, and served on the front lines for the French army during World War I. Like many modernist artists, Léger's work blended abstract and recognizable figures to evoke the great changes wrought by urbanization, World War I, and the increasing speed and apparent chaos of modern life. He experimented with bold primary colors and geometric shapes to render his subjects unfamiliar. In his famous painting *La Ville* ("The City"), Léger reflects the vivid but disorienting and claustrophobic feeling of urban spaces in the early twentieth century.

1919

Questions

1. What elements of urban life can you discern in this painting?
2. How do the colors and geometric patterns in this painting capture the artist's sense of movement in the city?
3. What do the broken texts and images suggest about the artist's perception of urban spaces?
4. One critic described this painting as a "utopian billboard for machine-age urban life." What elements of the work might support such an interpretation?

from Mrs. Dalloway

Virginia Woolf

Virginia Woolf (1882–1941) was a renowned novelist, critic, and essayist. Her most famous works are the novels *Mrs. Dalloway* (1925) and *To the Lighthouse* (1927).

KEY CONTEXT In *Mrs. Dalloway*, Woolf experiments with stream of consciousness, the quintessential modernist narrative mode also used by T. S. Eliot, James Joyce, Henry James, and others. In the following excerpt from the opening of *Mrs. Dalloway*, Woolf takes the reader into the mind of Clarissa Dalloway, an upper-class British woman planning a dinner party against the backdrop of the profound losses England suffered in World War I.

Mrs. Dalloway said she would buy the flowers herself.

For Lucy had her work cut out for her. The doors would be taken off their hinges; Rumpelmayer's men were coming. And then, thought Clarissa Dalloway, what a morning — fresh as if issued to children on a beach.

What a lark! What a plunge! For so it had always seemed to her, when, with a little squeak of the hinges, which she could hear now, she had burst open the French windows and plunged at Bourton into the open air. How fresh, how calm, stiller than this of course, the air was in the early morning; like the flap of a wave; the kiss of a wave; chill and sharp and yet (for a girl of eighteen as she then was) solemn, feeling as she did, standing there at the open window, that something awful was about to happen; looking at the flowers, at the trees with the smoke winding off them and the rooks rising, falling; standing and looking until Peter Walsh said, "Musing among the vegetables?" — was that it? — "I prefer men to cauliflowers" — was that it? He must have said it at breakfast one morning when she had gone out on to the terrace — Peter Walsh. He would be back from India one of these days, June or July, she forgot which, for his letters were awfully dull; it was his sayings one remembered; his eyes, his pocket-knife, his smile, his grumpiness and, when millions of things had utterly vanished — how strange it was! — a few sayings like this about cabbages.

She stiffened a little on the kerb, waiting for Durtnall's van to pass. A charming woman, Scrope Purvis thought her (knowing her as one does know people who live next door to one in Westminster); a touch of the bird about her, of the jay, blue-green, light, vivacious, though she was over fifty, and grown very white since her illness. There she perched, never seeing him, waiting to cross, very upright.

For having lived in Westminster — how many years now? over twenty, — one feels even in the midst of the traffic, or waking at night, Clarissa was positive, a particular hush, or solemnity; an indescribable pause; a suspense (but that might be her heart, affected, they said, by influenza) before Big Ben strikes. There! Out it boomed. First a warning, musical; then the hour, irrevocable. The leaden circles dissolved in the air. Such fools we are, she thought, crossing Victoria Street. For Heaven only knows why one loves it so, how one sees it so, making it up, building it round one, tumbling it, creating it every moment afresh; but the veriest frumps, the most dejected of miseries sitting on doorsteps (drink their downfall) do the same; can't be dealt with, she felt positive, by Acts of Parliament for that very reason: they love life. In people's eyes, in the swing, tramp, and trudge; in the bellow and the uproar; the carriages, motor cars, omnibuses, vans, sandwich men shuffling and swinging; brass bands; barrel organs; in the triumph and the jingle and the strange high singing of some aeroplane overhead was what she loved; life; London; this moment of June.

For it was the middle of June. The War was over, except for some one like Mrs. Foxcroft at the Embassy last night eating her heart out because that nice boy was killed and now the old Manor House must go to a cousin; or Lady Bexborough who opened a bazaar, they said, with the telegram in her hand, John, her favourite, killed; but it was over; thank Heaven — over. It was June. The King and Queen were at the Palace. And everywhere, though it was still so early, there was a beating, a stirring of galloping ponies, tapping of cricket bats; Lords, Ascot, Ranelagh and all the rest of it; wrapped in the soft mesh of the grey-blue morning air, which, as the day wore on, would unwind them, and set down on their lawns and pitches the bouncing ponies, whose forefeet just struck the ground and up they sprung, the whirling young men, and laughing girls in their transparent muslins who, even now, after dancing all night, were taking their absurd woolly dogs for a run; and even now, at this hour, discreet old dowagers were shooting out in their motor cars on errands of mystery; and the shopkeepers were fidgeting in their windows with their paste and diamonds, their lovely old sea-green brooches in eighteenth-century settings to tempt Americans (but one must economise, not buy things rashly for Elizabeth), and she, too, loving it as she did with an absurd and faithful passion, being part of it, since her people were courtiers once in the time of the Georges, she, too, was going that very night to kindle and illuminate; to give her party. But how strange, on entering the Park, the silence; the mist; the hum; the slow-swimming happy ducks; the pouched birds waddling; and who should be coming along with his back against the Government buildings, most appropriately, carrying a despatch box stamped with the Royal Arms, who but Hugh Whitbread; her old friend Hugh — the admirable Hugh!

"Good-morning to you, Clarissa!" said Hugh, rather extravagantly, for they had known each other as children. "Where are you off to?"

"I love walking in London," said Mrs. Dalloway. "Really it's better than walking in the country." ■

1925

Questions

1. *Mrs. Dalloway* is set in London. How does Clarissa feel about the city? Cite specific words and passages to support your response.
2. Where does Virginia Woolf conflate or shift between the past and the present in this passage? What is the effect of these conflations and shifts?
3. What is the purpose of the conflicting emotions and contradictory actions in this passage? Identify two and discuss their effect.
4. Woolf intended to write a novel that underscored the profound change in life after World War I. How does the style of this passage make the reader experience the dislocation and disruption that the author believed characterized post–World War I London?

Literature in Conversation

1. How is "The Steeple-Jack" by Marianne Moore a modernist work? What characteristics of the movement does it embody? Consider its structural and stylistic similarities to the poetry by H. D. and Amy Lowell and the prose by Virginia Woolf.
2. Modernism is often associated with literary allusions and mythological references, which T. S. Eliot believed were necessary to portray the complexities of modern life. How do "The Steeple-Jack" and the other poems in this section use these concepts to illustrate the complexities of modern life? How do they also call on tradition to unite the past with the present?
3. Choose 3–5 poems by modernist writers not included in this chapter to read closely and analyze. How do they compare with "The Steeple-Jack" and the poems in this section? How do they embody the traits of modernism outlined in the introduction to these Texts in Context?
4. In the introduction to this section, we discussed the collage as a form modernists used to capture the fragmentation of life in the early twentieth century. Discuss how at least two of these works and "The Steeple-Jack" might be seen as "collages," either visual or written.
5. In their effort to "make it new" and reveal the fissures of life in the early twentieth century, do

the artists you've explored — including Moore — present a bleak view of life in an age of rapid change, a hopeful perspective that results from facing change and trauma, or a little of both? In short, is modernism primarily optimistic or pessimistic? Consider at least two texts in your response.

6. At the end of the excerpt from "Tradition and the Individual Talent" by T. S. Eliot, he states:

   > No poet, no artist of any art, has his complete meaning alone. His significance, his appreciation is the appreciation of his relation to the dead poets and artists. You cannot value him alone; you must set him, for contrast and comparison, among the dead.

   How does "The Steeple-Jack" embody this statement? To what extent do any of the elements in the poem challenge Eliot's viewpoint?

7. Research another element of or influence on the modernist movement, such as cubism, Sigmund Freud's work on the impact of the unconscious, Albert Einstein's theory of relativity, composer Igor Stravinsky's *The Rite of Spring*, or playwright Bertolt Brecht's *The Threepenny Opera*. What characteristics of modernism do they express? How does your chosen element or work relate to these Texts in Context and "The Steeple-Jack"?

8. "The Steeple-Jack" and the texts in this section primarily represent European and American perspectives on early twentieth-century life, but writers and artists all over the world participated in and were influenced by the modernist movement. Research one of the following people and discuss the form modernism takes in his or her work: Mexican poet Octavio Paz (1914–1998), Indian painters Amrita Sher-Gil (1913–1941) and Jamini Roy (1887–1972), Russian poet Anna Akhmatova (1889–1966, p. 889), Martinique poet Aimé Césaire (1913–2008), Japanese novelist Jun'ichirō Tanizaki (1886–1965), and Japanese poet Chika Sagawa (1911–1936).

I Stand Here Ironing

Tillie Olsen

Chris Felver/Getty Images

Tillie Olsen (1913–2007) was born in Nebraska, the daughter of Russian Jewish immigrants. Her parents were active socialists who fled Russia after the attempted revolution of 1905. She recalled, "It was a rich childhood from the standpoint of ideas." She attended high school but abandoned formal education after the eleventh grade. Later in life, as an influential writer, she received nine honorary degrees from colleges and universities. Political activism and responsibilities as a wife and mother made Olsen's writing sporadic. She published *Tell Me a Riddle* (1961), a series of four interconnected stories (the first of which is "I Stand Here Ironing"), *Yonnondio: From the Thirties* (1974), and *Silences* (1978), a nonfiction work about her life and the obstacles to writing that caused her own silences.

KEY CONTEXT The story begins during what Olsen writes is "the pre-relief, pre-WPA world of the depression." The WPA, short for Works Progress Administration, was an agency founded by President Franklin D. Roosevelt in response to the economic strife caused by the Great Depression of the 1930s. The WPA employed millions of job-seekers throughout the United States to carry out projects, including the construction of public buildings and roads. It was one of many programs instituted by President Roosevelt as part of the New Deal, which sought to provide economic relief and employment to those hit hard by the Great Depression.

I stand here ironing, and what you asked me moves tormented back and forth with the iron.

"I wish you would manage the time to come in and talk with me about your daughter. I'm sure you can help me understand her. She's a youngster who needs help and whom I'm deeply interested in helping."

"Who needs help." . . . Even if I came, what good would it do? You think because I am her mother I have a key, or that in some way you could use me as a key? She has lived for nineteen years. There is all that life that has happened outside of me, beyond me.

And when is there time to remember, to sift, to weigh, to estimate, to total? I will start and there will be an interruption and I will have to gather it all together again. Or I will become engulfed with all I did or did not do, with what should have been and what cannot be helped.

5 She was a beautiful baby. The first and only one of our five that was beautiful at birth. You do not guess how new and uneasy her tenancy in her now-loveliness. You did not know her all those years she was thought homely, or see her poring over her baby pictures, making me tell her over and over how beautiful she had been — and would be, I would tell her — and was now, to the seeing eye. But the seeing eyes were few or nonexistent. Including mine.

I nursed her. They feel that's important nowadays, I nursed all the children, but with her, with all the fierce rigidity of first motherhood, I did like the books then said. Though her cries battered me to trembling and my breasts ached with swollenness, I waited till the clock decreed.

Why do I put that first? I do not even know if it matters, or if it explains anything.

She was a beautiful baby. She blew shining bubbles of sound. She loved motion, loved light, loved color and music and textures. She would lie on the floor in her blue overalls patting the surface so hard in ecstasy her hands and feet would blur. She was a miracle to me, but when she was eight months old I had to leave her daytimes with the woman downstairs to whom she was no miracle at all, for I worked or looked for work and for Emily's father, who "could no longer endure" (he wrote in his good-bye note) "sharing want with us."

I was nineteen. It was the pre-relief, pre-WPA world of the depression. I would start running as soon as I got off the streetcar, running up the stairs, the place smelling sour, and awake or asleep to startle awake, when she saw me she would break into a clogged weeping that could not be comforted, a weeping I can hear yet.

After a while I found a job hashing at night so I could be with her days, and it was better. But it came to where I had to bring her to his family and leave her.

It took a long time to raise the money for her fare back. Then she got chicken pox and I had to wait longer. When she finally came, I hardly knew her, walking quick and nervous like her father, looking like her father, thin, and dressed in a shoddy red that yellowed her skin and glared at the pockmarks. All the baby loveliness gone.

She was two. Old enough for nursery school they said, and I did not know then what I know now — the fatigue of the long day, and the lacerations of group life in the kinds of nurseries that are only parking places for children.

Except that it would have made no difference if I had known. It was the only place there was. It was the only way we could be together, the only way I could hold a job.

And even without knowing, I knew. I knew the teacher that was evil because all these years it has curdled into my memory, the little boy hunched in the corner, her rasp, "why aren't you outside, because Alvin hits you? that's no reason, go out, scaredy." I knew Emily hated it even if she did not clutch and implore "don't go Mommy" like the other children, mornings.

She always had a reason why we should stay home. Momma, you look sick. Momma, I feel sick. Momma, the teachers aren't there today, they're sick. Momma, we can't go, there was a fire there last night. Momma, it's a holiday today, no school, they told me. But never a direct protest, never rebellion.

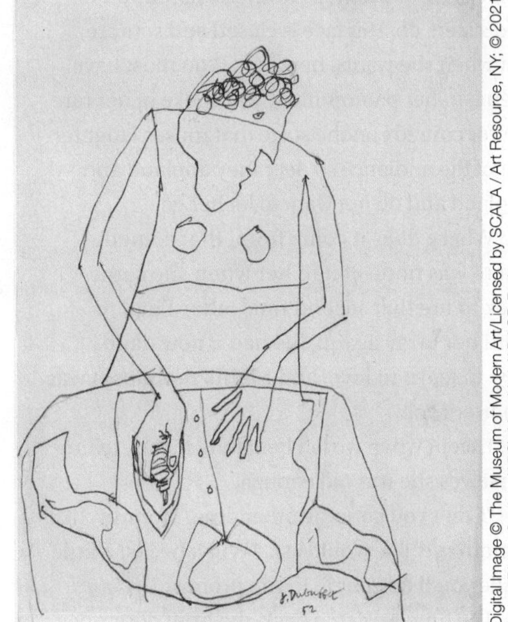

Jean Philippe Arthur Dubuffet (1901–1985) was a French painter and sculptor whose work often rejected traditional standards of beauty in favor of what he saw as a more authentic representation of humanity.

How does Dubuffet use techniques such as perspective and line to portray the relationship between the woman and what she is doing? How does this drawing capture the symbolic nature of this domestic chore in "I Stand Here Ironing"?

I think of our others in their three-, four-year-oldness — the explosions, the tempers, the denunciations, the demands — and I feel suddenly ill. I put the iron down. What in me demanded that goodness in her? And what was the cost, the cost to her of such goodness?

The old man living in the back once said in his gentle way: "You should smile at Emily more when you look at her." What *was* in my face when I looked at her? I loved her. There were all the acts of love.

It was only with the others I remembered what he said, and it was the face of joy, and not of care or tightness or worry I turned to them — too late for Emily. She does not smile easily, let alone almost always as her brothers and sisters do. Her face is closed and sombre, but when she wants, how fluid. You must have seen it in her pantomimes, you spoke of her rare gift for comedy on the stage that rouses laughter out of the audience so dear they applaud and applaud and do not want to let her go.

Where does it come from, that comedy? There was none of it in her when she came back to me that second time, after I had to send her away again. She had a new daddy now to learn to love, and I think perhaps it was a better time.

Except when we left her alone nights, telling ourselves she was old enough.

"Can't you go some other time, Mommy, like tomorrow?" she would ask. "Will it be just a little while you'll be gone? Do you promise?"

The time we came back, the front door open, the clock on the floor in the hall. She rigid awake. "It wasn't just a little while. I didn't cry. Three times I called you, just three times, and then I ran downstairs to open the door so you could come faster. The clock talked loud. I threw it away, it scared me what it talked."

She said the clock talked loud again that night I went to the hospital to have Susan. She was delirious with the fever that comes before red measles, but she was fully conscious all the week I was gone and the week after we were home when she could not come near the new baby or me.

She did not get well. She stayed skeleton thin, not wanting to eat, and night after night she had nightmares. She would call for me, and I would rouse from exhaustion to sleepily call back: "You're all right, darling, go to sleep, it's just a dream," and if she still called, in a sterner voice, "now go to sleep, Emily, there's nothing to hurt you." Twice, only twice, when I had to get up for Susan anyhow, I went in to sit with her.

Now when it is too late (as if she would let me hold her and comfort her like I do the others) I get up and go to her at once at her moan or restless stirring. "Are you awake, Emily? Can I get you something?" And the answer is always the same: "No, I'm all right, go back to sleep, Mother."

They persuaded me at the clinic to send her away to a convalescent home in the country where "she can have the kind of food and care you can't manage for her, and you'll be free to concentrate on the new baby." They still send children to that place. I see pictures on the society page of sleek young women planning affairs to raise money for it, or dancing at the affairs, or decorating Easter eggs or filling Christmas stockings for the children.

They never have a picture of the children so I do not know if the girls still wear those gigantic red bows and the ravaged looks on the every other Sunday when parents can come to visit "unless otherwise notified" — as we were notified the first six weeks.

Oh it is a handsome place, green lawns and tall trees and fluted flower beds. High up on the balconies of each cottage the children stand, the girls in their red bows and white dresses, the boys in white suits and giant red ties. The parents stand below shrieking up to be heard and the children shriek down to be heard, and between them the invisible wall "Not To Be Contaminated by Parental Germs or Physical Affection."

There was a tiny girl who always stood hand in hand with Emily. Her parents never came. One visit she was gone. "They moved her to Rose Cottage," Emily shouted in explanation. "They don't like you to love anybody here."

30 She wrote once a week, the labored writing of a seven-year-old. "I am fine. How is the baby. If I write my leter nicly I will have a star. Love." There never was a star. We wrote every other day, letters she could never hold or keep but only hear read — once. "We simply do not have room for children to keep any personal possessions," they patiently explained when we pieced one Sunday's shrieking together to plead how much it would mean to Emily, who loved so to keep things, to be allowed to keep her letters and cards.

Each visit she looked frailer. "She isn't eating," they told us.

(They had runny eggs for breakfast or mush with lumps, Emily said later, I'd hold it in my mouth and not swallow. Nothing ever tasted good, just when they had chicken.)

It took us eight months to get her released home, and only the fact that she gained back so little of her seven lost pounds convinced the social worker.

I used to try to hold and love her after she came back, but her body would stay stiff, and after a while she'd push away. She ate little. Food sickened her, and I think much of life too. Oh she had physical lightness and brightness, twinkling by on skates, bouncing like a ball up and down up and down over the jump rope, skimming over the hill; but these were momentary.

35 She fretted about her appearance, thin and dark and foreign-looking at a time when every little girl was supposed to look or thought she should look a chubby blonde replica of Shirley Temple. The doorbell sometimes rang for her, but no one seemed to come and play in the house or to be a best friend. Maybe because we moved so much.

There was a boy she loved painfully through two school semesters. Months later she told me how she had taken pennies from my purse to buy him candy. "Licorice was his favorite and I brought him some every day, but he still liked Jennifer better'n me. Why, Mommy?" The kind of question for which there is no answer.

School was a worry for her. She was not glib or quick in a world where glibness and quickness were easily confused with ability to learn. To her overworked and exasperated teachers she was an overconscientious "slow learner" who kept trying to catch up and was absent entirely too often.

I let her be absent, though sometimes the illness was imaginary. How different from my now-strictness about attendance with the others. I wasn't working. We had a new baby. I was home anyhow. Sometimes, after Susan grew old enough, I would keep her home from school, too, to have them all together.

Mostly Emily had asthma, and her breathing, harsh and labored, would fill the house with a curiously tranquil sound. I would bring the two old dresser mirrors and her boxes of collections to her bed. She would select beads and single earrings, bottle tops and shells, dried flowers and pebbles, old postcards and scraps, all sorts of oddments; then she and Susan would play Kingdom, setting up landscapes and furniture, peopling them with action.

40 Those were the only times of peaceful companionship between her and Susan. I have edged away from it, that poisonous feeling between them, that terrible balancing of hurts and needs I had to do between the two, and did so badly, those earlier years.

Oh there were conflicts between the others too, each one human, needing, demanding, hurting, taking — but only between Emily and Susan, no, Emily toward Susan that corroding resentment. It seems so obvious on the surface, yet it is not obvious; Susan, the second child, Susan, golden- and curly-haired and chubby, quick and articulate and assured, everything in appearance and manner Emily was not; Susan, not able to resist Emily's precious things, losing or sometimes clumsily breaking them; Susan telling jokes and riddles to company for applause while Emily sat silent (to say to me later: that was *my* riddle, Mother, I told it to Susan); Susan, who for all the five years' difference in age was just a year behind Emily in developing physically.

I am glad for that slow physical development that widened the difference between her and her contemporaries, though she suffered over it. She was too vulnerable for that terrible world of youthful competition, of preening and parading, of constant measuring of yourself against every other, of envy, "If I had that copper hair," "If I had that skin. . . ." She tormented herself enough about not looking like the others, there was enough of unsureness, the having to be conscious of words before you speak, the constant caring—what are they thinking of me? without having it all magnified by the merciless physical drives.

Ronnie is calling. He is wet and I change him. It is rare there is such a cry now. That time of motherhood is almost behind me when the ear is not one's own but must always be racked and listening for the child cry, the child call. We sit for a while and I hold him, looking out over the city spread in charcoal with its soft aisles of light. "*Shoogily*," he breathes and curls closer. I carry him back to bed, asleep. *Shoogily*. A funny word, a family word, inherited from Emily, invented by her to say: *comfort*.

In this and other ways she leaves her seal, I say aloud. And startle at my saying it. What do I mean? What did I start to gather together, to try and make coherent? I was at the terrible, growing years. War years. I do not remember them well. I was working, there were four smaller ones now, there was not time for her. She had to help be a mother, and housekeeper, and shopper. She had to get her seal. Mornings of crisis and near hysteria trying to get lunches packed, hair combed, coats and shoes found, everyone to school or Child Care on time, the baby ready for transportation. And always the paper scribbled on by a smaller one, the book looked at by Susan then mislaid, the homework not done. Running out to that huge school where she was one, she was lost, she was a drop; suffering over the unpreparedness, stammering and unsure in her classes.

There was so little time left at night after the 45
kids were bedded down. She would struggle over books, always eating (it was in those years she developed her enormous appetite that is legendary in our family) and I would be ironing, or preparing food for the next day, or writing V-mail[1] to Bill, or tending the baby. Sometimes, to make me laugh, or out of her despair, she would imitate happenings or types at school.

I think I said once: "Why don't you do something like this in the school amateur show?" One morning she phoned me at work, hardly understandable through the weeping: "Mother, I did it. I won, I won; they gave me first prize; they clapped and clapped and wouldn't let me go."

Now suddenly she was Somebody, and as imprisoned in her difference as she had been in anonymity.

She began to be asked to perform at other high schools, even in colleges, then at city and statewide affairs. The first one we went to, I only recognized her that first moment when thin, shy, she almost drowned herself into the curtains. Then: Was this Emily? The control, the command, the convulsing and deadly clowning, the spell, then the roaring, stamping audience, unwilling to let this rare and precious laughter out of their lives.

Afterwards: You ought to do something about her with a gift like that—but without money or knowing how, what does one do? We have left it all to her, and the gift has so often eddied inside, clogged and clotted, as been used and growing.

[1] Victory Mail, known as V-mail, was the main way to communicate with soldiers stationed abroad during World War II. Letters were censored and photographed in the United States before being transported to their destination on film. The negatives would then be printed, copied by hand onto paper, and finally distributed to soldiers.—Eds.

extending beyond the text

Each of these two images, created more than a century apart, offers an interpretation of motherhood. The first image is a photograph entitled *The Heritage of Motherhood*, taken in 1904 by Gertrude Kasebier (1852–1934), who was active in the movement to establish photography as an art form. She often created portraits with an ethereal atmosphere. The second image is by contemporary artist Dadu Shin, whose illustration entitled *Mothers Don't Have to Be Martyrs* accompanied a 2020 *New York Times* article.

VTR/Alamy

© DADU SHIN

1. **What is the "heritage" of motherhood the photograph by Gertrude Kasebier suggests? How does the illustration by Dadu Shin portray the concept of motherhood and "martyrdom"?**
2. **How does the narrator of "I Stand Here Ironing" share the perspective on motherhood in both of these images? Ultimately, what version of motherhood does she embrace?**
3. **What elements of femininity does each image explore that are not necessarily related to motherhood? To what extent do you see these elements reflected in the character of the narrator of Olsen's story?**

50 She is coming. She runs up the stairs two at a time with her light graceful step, and I know she is happy tonight. Whatever it was that occasioned your call did not happen today.

"Aren't you ever going to finish the ironing, Mother? Whistler painted his mother in a rocker. I'd have to paint mine standing over an ironing board." This is one of her communicative nights and she tells me everything and nothing as she fixes herself a plate of food out of the icebox.

She is so lovely. Why did you want me to come in at all? Why were you concerned? She will find her way.

She starts up the stairs to bed. "Don't get me up with the rest in the morning." "But I thought you were having midterms." "Oh, those," she comes back in, kisses me, and says quite lightly, "in a couple of years when we'll all be atom-dead they won't matter a bit."

She has said it before. She *believes* it. But because I have been dredging the past, and all that compounds a human being is so heavy and meaningful in me, I cannot endure it tonight.

55 I will never total it all. I will never come in to say: She was a child seldom smiled at. Her father left me before she was a year old. I had to work her first six years when there was work, or I sent her home and to his relatives. There were years she had care she hated. She was dark and thin and foreign-looking in a world where the prestige went to blondeness and curly hair and dimples, she was slow where glibness was prized. She was a child of anxious, not proud, love. We were poor and could not afford for her the soil of easy growth. I was a young mother, I was a distracted mother. There were other children pushing up, demanding. Her younger sister seemed all that she was not. There were years she did not want me to touch her. She kept too much in herself, her life was such she had to keep too much in herself. My wisdom came too late. She has much to her and probably little will come of it. She is a child of her age, of depression, of war, of fear.

Let her be. So all that is in her will not bloom — but in how many does it? There is still enough left to live by. Only help her to know — help make it so there is cause for her to know — that she is more than this dress on the ironing board, helpless before the iron. ■

1961

Understanding and Interpreting

1. How is the setting of the story's frame, a woman standing at an ironing board, critical to the story's themes?
2. According to the narrator, what choices were available to her as a young working mother? What details does she share to establish context for these choices?
3. The narrator states that Emily's actions were "never a direct protest, never rebellion" (par. 15) in contrast to "the explosions, the tempers, the denunciations, the demands" (par. 16) of her three siblings. What does this contrast in behavior reveal about Emily's character?
4. Why do you think Emily developed the persona of a comedian? What does the narrator mean when she responds to Emily's winning the school's amateur show with the observation that "suddenly she was Somebody, and as imprisoned in her difference as she had been in her anonymity" (par. 47)?
5. What challenges does school present for Emily, particularly as she grows into adolescence?
6. How does the narrator's decision to place Emily in a convalescent home essentially backfire? What does this experience reveal about the narrator's relationship to authority and social norms? How — or when — does she challenge these expectations?

7. In the final lines of the story, the narrator calls her daughter "a child of her age, of depression, of war, of fear" (par. 55). How have historical events affected Emily's development? Have they imposed limitations on her, or have they made her strong? Use evidence from the text to support your response.

8. Based on your interpretation of the story, do you think the narrator believes she has been a good mother to her children? What overall message does this story convey about parenthood and family ties?

Analyzing Language, Style, and Structure

1. **Vocabulary in Context.** In paragraph 12, Tillie Olsen writes of young Emily's experience in a nursery school: "the fatigue of the long day, and the lacerations of group life in the kinds of nurseries that are only parking places for children." The most common definition of "laceration" is a literal wound in flesh. How does Olsen draw on this meaning to make a metaphorical association? What point does she make with this word choice?

2. Why does Olsen give us so much specific detail about Emily's appearance? How do these descriptions contribute to her characterization? How is her appearance related to the choices she makes to distinguish herself, to stand out?

3. What structural purpose do the interruptions in the narrator's interior monologue serve in the story? For instance, "Ronnie is calling. He is wet and I change him" in paragraph 43. Notice, too, how the speaker's use of run-on sentences and made-up words — such as "four-year-oldness" (par. 16) — contrasts with short declarative sentences such as "She was a beautiful baby" (pars. 5 and 8), "I was nineteen" (par. 9), and "She was two" (par. 12). What is the effect of this juxtaposition?

4. What is the function of clocks in the story? Consider both Emily's fear of clocks and the narrator's own sense of time and timing.

5. What do you make of the repeated references to quantitative matters in this story — for instance, "to sift, to weigh, to estimate, to total" in paragraph 4? Find other examples of this motif in the story, and explain its significance.

6. How does Olsen develop the iron as a symbol that simultaneously conveys the interior lives of the characters and functions as a unifying plot device? Cite specific passages to support your analysis.

7. The men in the story are shadow figures at best. How do the fathers of the narrator's children contribute to the development of character, the economic reality of the narrator's situation, and the theme of female identity?

8. The "you" the narrator addresses at the beginning of the story refers to a teacher, social worker, or someone in an official capacity who has expressed concern about Emily's welfare. At first the narrator seems somewhat defensive as she sarcastically responds to the teacher's request. How does the relationship between the narrator and the teacher evolve over the course of the story, so that by the end the narrator beseeches, "Only help her to know — help make it so there is cause for her to know" (par. 56)?

Topics for Composing

1. AP® FRQ **Prose Fiction Analysis.** The following question refers to paragraphs 1–11 of Tillie Olsen's "I Stand Here Ironing," published in 1961. In this passage, which opens the story, the narrator reflects on her experience as a mother after hearing someone express concern for her adolescent daughter. Read the passage carefully. Then, in a well-written essay, analyze how Olsen uses literary elements and techniques to develop the complex relationship between the narrator and her daughter.

2. AP® FRQ **Literary Argument.** Works of literature often feature complicated, three-dimensional characters who challenge readers' expectations for their motivations and behavior. In "I Stand Here Ironing," the narrator reflects on her struggle to provide for her eldest daughter as a young, impoverished mother during the Great Depression of the 1930s. In a well-written essay, analyze how this depiction of a working-class mother challenges traditional expectations of what motherhood should be like and contributes to an interpretation of the work as a whole. Do not merely summarize the plot.
3. **AP® Literary Argumentation.** Many critics have read "I Stand Here Ironing" as a story of the benefits and costs of meeting society's expectations, particularly for women and their primary role as mothers. To what extent do Emily and her mother choose to thwart or disobey authority in favor of independent thinking? Do the costs of doing so outweigh the advantages of breaking with social norms for either of them? Use evidence from the text to support your response.
4. **Speaking and Listening.** What does it mean to be a "good mother" — when this story takes place, when it was written, and today? Through discussion in small groups, develop a question to lead a Socratic seminar on the definition of a "good mother" informed by your interpretation of "I Stand Here Ironing."
5. **Creative Writing.** Rarely do we hear Emily speak in this story. Instead, we hear others' comments about and reactions to her, including her mother's. How do you think Emily would characterize her relationship with her mother? Do you think she would blame her mother or circumstances beyond their control for the difficulties she has experienced? Assume Emily's persona and present her perspective.
6. **Connections.** The trials and tribulation of women who pursue goals in creative fields, whether as writers, musicians, painters, or performers, while navigating motherhood are often depicted in films. View a film about a real or fictional woman in this situation and discuss the nature of her struggle and the extent of her success in combining these roles. Pay particular attention to the impact of economic resources and community support on her story.
7. **Connections.** Studies have shown that during the COVID-19 pandemic, working mothers from every socioeconomic level experienced more disruption of career and economic resources than any other group. How does this finding inform your understanding of the themes of "I Stand Here Ironing"? Do you think it is as relevant today as it was during the 1930s and the 1960s? Explain why or why not.

The Moths

Helena María Viramontes

Helena María Viramontes (b. 1949) grew up as one of nine children in East Los Angeles. She has a BA from Immaculate Heart College and an MFA from the University of California, Irvine, and is currently a professor of English at Cornell University. Her mother's plight — raising nine children with a husband who "showed all that is bad in being male" — moved Helena to write of Chicana women's struggles. Viramontes published her first collection of short stories, *The Moths and Other Stories*, in 1985. In 1995, her first novel, *Under the Feet of Jesus*, was published, followed by *Their Dogs Came with Them* in 2007. She is currently drafting her third novel, *The Cemetery Boys*.

KEY CONTEXT The story included here is the title piece from Viramontes's 1985 collection, which draws on her teenage years, the explosive decade of the 1960s, and the lives of young women coming of age at the height of *El Movimiento*, the fight for Latino civil rights in America. This story centers on the relationship between a young woman and her *abuelita*, or grandmother.

I was fourteen years old when Abuelita requested my help. And it seemed only fair. Abuelita had pulled me through the rages of scarlet fever by placing, removing and replacing potato slices on the temples of my forehead; she had seen me through several whippings, an arm broken by a dare jump off Tío Enrique's toolshed, puberty, and my first lie. Really, I told Amá, it was only fair.

Not that I was her favorite granddaughter or anything special. I wasn't even pretty or nice like my older sisters and I just couldn't do the girl things they could do. My hands were too big to handle the fineries of crocheting or embroidery and I always pricked my fingers or knotted my colored threads time and time again while my sisters laughed and called me bull hands with their cute waterlike voices. So I began keeping a piece of jagged brick in my sock to bash my sisters or anyone who called me bull hands. Once, while we all sat in the bedroom, I hit Teresa on the forehead, right above her eyebrow and she ran to Amá with her mouth open, her hand over her eye while blood seeped between her fingers. I was used to the whippings by then.

I wasn't respectful either. I even went so far as to doubt the power of Abuelita's slices, the slices she said absorbed my fever. "You're still alive, aren't you?" Abuelita snapped back, her pasty gray eye beaming at me and burning holes in my suspicions. Regretful that I had let secret questions drop out of my mouth, I couldn't look into her eyes. My hands began to fan out, grow like a liar's nose until they hung by my side like low weights. Abuelita made a balm out of dried moth wings and Vicks and rubbed my hands, shaped them back to size and it was the strangest feeling. Like bones melting. Like sun shining through the darkness of your eyelids. I didn't mind helping Abuelita after that, so Amá would always send me over to her.

In the early afternoon Amá would push her hair back, hand me my sweater and shoes, and tell me to go to Mama Luna's. This was to avoid another fight and another whipping, I knew. I would deliver one last direct shot on Marisela's arm and jump out of our house, the slam of the screen door burying her cries of anger, and I'd gladly go help Abuelita plant her wild lilies or jasmine or heliotrope or cilantro or hierbabuena[1] in red Hills Brothers coffee cans. Abuelita would wait for me at the top step of her porch holding a hammer and nail and empty coffee cans. And although we hardly spoke, hardly looked at each other as we worked over root transplants, I always felt her gray eye on me. It made me feel, in a strange sort of way, safe and guarded and not alone. Like God was supposed to make you feel.

On Abuelita's porch, I would puncture holes 5
in the bottom of the coffee cans with a nail and a precise hit of a hammer. This completed, my job was to fill them with red clay mud from beneath her rose bushes, packing it softly, then making a perfect hole, four fingers round, to nest a sprouting avocado pit, or the spidery sweet potatoes that Abuelita rooted in mayonnaise jars with toothpicks and daily water, or prickly chayotes[2] that produced vines that twisted and wound all over her porch pillars, crawling to the roof, up and over the roof, and down the other side, making her small brick house look like it

[1] Also yerba buena, or "good herb," a plant in the mint family that is steeped to make a tea-like beverage. — Eds.

[2] Pear-shaped vegetable similar to a cucumber. — Eds.

This mural, entitled *Abuelita*, was painted by El Mac, a Los Angeles–based Chicano artist, and covers the back wall of the American Hotel in the arts district of Los Angeles.

How does the emotion evoked by this mural compare to the emotion of the relationship between the narrator and her grandmother in "The Moths"?

Kayte Deioma/Alamy

was cradled within the vines that grew pear-shaped squashes ready for the pick, ready to be steamed with onions and cheese and butter. The roots would burst out of the rusted coffee cans and search for a place to connect. I would then feed the seedlings with water.

But this was a different kind of help, Amá said, because Abuelita was dying. Looking into her gray eye, then into her brown one, the doctor said it was just a matter of days. And so it seemed only fair that these hands she had melted and formed found use in rubbing her caving body with alcohol and marihuana, rubbing her arms and legs, turning her face to the window so that she could watch the Bird of Paradise blooming or smell the scent of clove in the air. I toweled her face frequently and held her hand for hours. Her gray wiry hair hung over the mattress. Since I could remember, she'd kept her long hair in braids. Her mouth was vacant and when she slept, her eyelids never closed all the way. Up close, you could see her gray eye beaming out the window, staring hard as if to remember everything. I never kissed her. I left the window open when I went to the market.

Across the street from Jay's Market there was a chapel. I never knew its denomination, but I went in just the same to search for candles. I sat down on one of the pews because there were none. After I cleaned my fingernails, I looked up at the high ceiling. I had forgotten the vastness of these places, the coolness of the marble pillars and the frozen statues with blank eyes. I was alone. I knew why I had never returned.

That was one of Apá's biggest complaints. He would pound his hands on the table, rocking the sugar dish or spilling a cup of coffee and scream that if I didn't go to mass every Sunday to save my goddamn sinning soul, then I had no reason to go out of the house, period. Punto final.[3] He would grab my arm and dig his nails into me to make sure I understood the importance of catechism. Did he make himself clear? Then he strategically directed his anger at Amá for her lousy ways of bringing up daughters, being disrespectful and unbelieving, and my older sisters would pull me aside and tell me if I didn't get to mass right this minute, they were all going to kick the holy shit out of me. Why am I so selfish? Can't you see what it's doing to Amá, you idiot? So I would wash my feet and stuff them in my black Easter shoes that shone with Vaseline, grab a missal and veil, and wave good-bye to Amá.

[3] Spanish for "final point, period." — Eds.

I would walk slowly down Lorena to First to Evergreen, counting the cracks on the cement. On Evergreen I would turn left and walk to Abuelita's. I liked her porch because it was shielded by the vines of the chayotes and I could get a good look at the people and car traffic on Evergreen without them knowing. I would jump up the porch steps, knock on the screen door as I wiped my feet and call Abuelita? mi Abuelita? As I opened the door and stuck my head in, I would catch the gagging scent of toasting chile on the placa.[4] When I entered the sala,[5] she would greet me from the kitchen, wringing her hands in her apron. I'd sit at the corner of the table to keep from being in her way. The chiles made my eyes water. Am I crying? No, Mama Luna, I'm sure not crying. I don't like going to mass, but my eyes watered anyway, the tears drop-ping on the tablecloth like candle wax. Abuelita lifted the burnt chiles from the fire and sprinkled water on them until the skins began to separate. Placing them in front of me, she turned to check the menudo.[6] I peeled the skins off and put the flimsy, limp looking green and yellow chiles in the molcajete[7] and began to crush and crush and twist and crush the heart out of the tomato, the clove of garlic, the stupid chiles that made me cry, crushed them until they turned into liquid under my bull hand. With a wooden spoon, I scraped hard to destroy the guilt, and my tears were gone. I put the bowl of chile next to a vase filled with freshly cut roses. Abuelita touched my hand and pointed to the bowl of menudo that steamed in front of me. I spooned some chile into the menudo and rolled a corn tortilla thin with the palms of my hands. As I ate, a fine Sunday breeze entered the kitchen and a rose petal calmly feathered down to the table.

10 I left the chapel without blessing myself and walked to Jay's. Most of the time Jay didn't have much of anything. The tomatoes were always soft and the cans of Campbell soups had rusted spots on them. There was dust on the tops of cereal boxes. I picked up what I needed: rubbing alcohol, five cans of chicken broth, a big bottle of Pine Sol. At first Jay got mad because I thought I had forgotten the money. But it was there all the time, in my back pocket.

When I returned from the market, I heard Amá crying in Abuelita's kitchen. She looked up at me with puffy eyes. I placed the bags of groceries on the table and began putting the cans of soup away. Amá sobbed quietly. I never kissed her. After a while, I patted her on the back for comfort. Finally: "¿Y mi Amá?"[8] she asked in a whisper, then choked again and cried into her apron.

Abuelita fell off the bed twice yesterday, I said, knowing that I shouldn't have said it and wondering why I wanted to say it because it only made Amá cry harder. I guess I became angry and just so tired of the quarrels and beatings and unanswered prayers and my hands just there hanging helplessly by my side. Amá looked at me again, confused, angry, and her eyes were filled with sorrow. I went outside and sat on the porch swing and watched the people pass. I sat there until she left. I dozed off repeating the words to myself like rosary prayers: when do you stop giving when do you start giving when do you . . . and when my hands fell from my lap, I awoke to catch them. The sun was setting, an orange glow, and I knew Abuelita was hungry.

There comes a time when the sun is defiant. Just about the time when moods change, inevitable seasons of a day, transitions from one color to another, that hour or minute or second when the sun is finally defeated, finally sinks into the realization that it cannot with all its power to heal or burn, exist forever, there comes an illumination where the sun and earth meet, a final burst of burning red orange fury reminding

[4] Spanish for "plate." — Eds.

[5] Spanish for "living room." — Eds.

[6] Traditional Mexican soup made with tripe. — Eds.

[7] Stone bowl used for grinding foods or spices, similar to a mortar and pestle. — Eds.

[8] Spanish for "And my Mama?" — Eds.

For this site-specific installation, Mexico City artist Carlos Amorales, helped by fourteen others, arranged 30,000 black paper moths on the walls and ceilings of several gallery spaces.

To what extent does this installation evoke the same mood as the image of the moths filling the bathroom at the end of Viramontes's story?

us that although endings are inevitable, they are necessary for rebirths, and when that time came, just when I switched on the light in the kitchen to open Abuelita's can of soup, it was probably then that she died.

The room smelled of Pine Sol and vomit and Abuelita had defecated the remains of her cancerous stomach. She had turned to the window and tried to speak, but her mouth remained open and speechless. I heard you, Abuelita, I said, stroking her cheek, I heard you. I opened the windows of the house and let the soup simmer and overboil on the stove. I turned the stove off and poured the soup down the sink. From the cabinet I got a tin basin, filled it with lukewarm water and carried it carefully to the room. I went to the linen closet and took out some modest bleached white towels. With the sacredness of a priest preparing his vestments, I unfolded the towels one by one on my shoulders. I removed the sheets and blankets from her bed and peeled off her thick flannel nightgown. I toweled her puzzled face, stretching out the wrinkles, removing the coils of her neck, toweled her shoulders and breasts. Then I changed the water. I returned to towel the creases of her stretch-marked stomach, her sporadic vaginal hairs, and her sagging thighs. I removed the lint from between her toes and noticed a mapped birthmark on the fold of her buttock. The scars on her back which were as thin as the life lines on the palms of her hands made me realize how little I really knew of Abuelita. I covered her with a thin blanket and went into the bathroom. I washed my hands, and turned on the tub faucets and watched the water pour into the tub with vitality and steam. When it was full, I turned off the water and undressed. Then, I went to get Abuelita.

She was not as heavy as I thought and when I carried her in my arms, her body fell into a V, and yet my legs were tired, shaky, and I felt as if the distance between the bedroom and bathroom was miles and years away. Amá, where are you?

I stepped into the bathtub one leg first, then the other. I bent my knees slowly to descend into the water slowly so I wouldn't scald her skin. There, there, Abuelita, I said, cradling her, smoothing her as we descended, I heard you. Her hair fell back and spread across the water like eagle's wings. The water in the tub overflowed and poured onto the tile of the floor.

Then the moths came. Small, gray ones that came from her soul and out through her mouth fluttering to light, circling the single dull light bulb of the bathroom. Dying is lonely and I wanted to go to where the moths were, stay with her and plant chayotes whose vines would crawl up her fingers and into the clouds; I wanted to rest my head on her chest with her stroking my hair, telling me about the moths that lay within the soul and slowly eat the spirit up; I wanted to return to the waters of the womb with her so that we would never be alone again. I wanted. I wanted my Amá. I removed a few strands of hair from Abuelita's face and held her small light head within the hollow of my neck. The bathroom was filled with moths, and for the first time in a long time I cried, rocking us, crying for her, for me, for Amá, the sobs emerging from the depths of anguish, the misery of feeling half born, sobbing until finally the sobs rippled into circles and circles of sadness and relief. There, there, I said to Abuelita, rocking us gently, there, there. ■

1985

Understanding and Interpreting

1. How does the work Abuelita asks the narrator to do — planting, cooking — help the teenager deal with her pent-up anger?
2. What is the role of religion and spirituality in this story? Why does the narrator think to herself when she is in the chapel, "I was alone. I knew why I had never returned" (par. 7)? What conflicts does religion cause in her family?
3. Note the references throughout to Amá, the narrator's mother. When Amá is crying in Abuelita's kitchen, why does the narrator choose not to kiss her?
4. Does the narrator's fearlessness about death strike you as unusual? Why do you think she is comfortable enough to bathe her dead Abuelita?
5. Why, at the end of the story, does the narrator say, "I wanted. I wanted my Amá" (par. 16)?
6. What is the nature of the relationship among these three generations of women? What does the narrator want it to be?
7. Describe the ways in which the narrator is an outcast in her own family. What does her grandmother seem to understand that the girl's immediate family members do not?

Analyzing Language, Style, and Structure

1. **Vocabulary in Context.** What is the meaning of the word "vestments" in paragraph 14? Why does the narrator compare her preparation of the towels to a priest preparing his vestments?
2. The story opens with the narrator's grandmother applying potato slices to the narrator's fevered brow. Compare this opening with the conclusion of the story. How does that gentleness contrast with roughness the narrator typically gives to family members ("I hit Teresa on the forehead," par. 2) and receives from them ("He would grab my arm and dig his nails into me," par. 8)? Why is that contrast significant?
3. As the narrator cares for her dying grandmother, she begins to ask herself, "when do you stop giving when do you start giving" (par. 12), continuing the repetition of the word "when" throughout the following paragraph. What is the significance of this repetition for the fourteen-year-old narrator? What might she be questioning in her own life?

4. Trace the references to hands in this story. How do you interpret the poultice balm of moth wings that Abuelita uses to reshape the narrator's hands? What is the significance of this act?
5. What do the moths represent in the story?
6. Consider the sensuous descriptions throughout the story. What meaning does Viramontes's use of such imagery to describe life and death convey?
7. In addition to washing her grandmother and preparing her body, what other rituals does the story present? How are they related to each other? How does the concept of rituals structure the narrative?
8. How might the bath that ends the story be considered a transformation? How does it conform to the usual representations of water in literature? How is it different?

Topics for Composing

1. **AP® FRQ Prose Fiction Analysis.** The following question refers to paragraphs 8–9 of Helena María Viramontes's "The Moths," published in 1985. In this passage, the narrator finds comfort in a visit to her grandmother's house. Read the passage carefully. Then, in a well-written essay, analyze how Viramontes uses literary elements and techniques to convey the process by which anger is soothed into peace.
2. **AP® FRQ Literary Argument.** Many works of literature center on a character coming to terms with the idea of mortality at a pivotal moment. In "The Moths," the narrator, a fourteen-year-old girl, tends to her dying grandmother and prepares her body after her death. In a well-written essay, analyze how the narrator's thoughts and actions in the wake of her abuelita's death contribute to an interpretation of the work as a whole. Do not merely summarize the plot.
3. **AP® Literary Argumentation.** How does paragraph 13 introduce the possibility for change in the relationship the narrator has with her family? Does it suggest that it might improve or disintegrate further? Support your answer with references to the text.
4. **Connections.** Anne Hunsaker Hawkins, a professor of medicine, wrote the following in the *Journal of Academic Medicine* about the description of the narrator and her grandmother in the bathtub:

   > [A]s the room fills with moths, along with other instances of magic realism. . . . There is full acknowledgment that dying is as great a mystery as the rising and setting of the sun, and that mourning is painful, necessary, and incredibly complex. . . . [T]he story provides a wonderful tonic for those of us whose attitudes about dying have been shaped by the Anglo-American and Continental traditions.

   How have our attitudes toward dying been shaped by the western traditions Hawkins names? Do you agree with Hawkins's interpretation of how the story deals with both death and grief? Explain.
5. **Connections.** What cultural archetypes do the characters in "The Moths" represent? Consider the father, the mother, the grandmother, and the narrator herself. Do any of them transcend these archetypes? Explain why or why not.
6. **Creative Writing.** Retell "The Moths" from the point of view of one of the narrator's sisters. Use information from the text to imagine how the sister might characterize the narrator.
7. **Connections.** Look into the literary genre of magical realism. What are the hallmarks of this genre? How much of a role does it play in "The Moths"?

Lessons

Laura van den Berg

Laura van den Berg was born and raised in Florida. She is the author of several collections of short stories, including *What the World Will Look Like When All the Water Leaves Us* (2009), *The Isle of Youth* (2013), and *I Hold a Wolf by the Ears* (2021), and two novels, *Find Me* (2015) and *The Third Hotel* (2018). This short story is from her second collection, *The Isle of Youth*.

1.

There are four of them.

Dana, Jackie, Pinky, and Cora are cousins. Pinky is also Dana's little brother. They call themselves the Gorillas because all gangs need a name — see Hole-in-the-Wall Gang, Stopwatch Gang, Winter Hill Gang — and also because they wear gorilla masks during their holdups. They are criminals, but they still have rules: no hostages, small scores, never stay in one town for more than a week. It's late summer and they're roving through the Midwest, from motel to motel, making just enough to keep going. Dana watches the impossibly flat landscapes of Lafayette and Oneida pass through the car window and wonders how they all ended up here. Why didn't they go to school and get regular jobs and get married and live in houses? The short answer: they are a group of people committed to making life as hard as possible.

Cora says they need to think bigger. No more knocking over delis and drugstores and dinky banks. They need to do a real heist. There are millions to be made, if they could just grow some balls. Jackie has simpler desires. She wants a boyfriend and a set of acrylic nails. Pinky is thirteen and wants to build a robot. Dana is more about what she doesn't want, as in: she doesn't want anyone to go to jail or die.

In L.A., a gang of female bank robbers have been making headlines. They wear Snow White masks and carry semiautomatics. Witnesses have reported them doing tricks with their guns during heists. They're rumored to be retired Romanian acrobats. Naturally, the press loves them. They've been nicknamed the Go-Go Girls.

"Why aren't we ever on TV?" Cora 5
complains one night. They're in a motel in Galesburg. They have plans for the Farmers & Mechanics Bank on Main Street. Dana lies on one of the musty twin beds; her cousins are curled up on the other. Cora is green-eyed and lean with cropped auburn hair, like Mia Farrow in *Rosemary's Baby*. Jackie is shaped like a lemon drop. Her dark, wide-set eyes remind Dana of a well-meaning cow. Pinky is working on his robot in the bathroom. He's been collecting materials from gas station and motel Dumpsters: pins, wires, batteries, little black wheels. Earlier, Dana stood in the doorway and watched him screw two metal panels together. He sat cross-legged on the floor, his lips puckered with concentration. The overhead light flickered and buzzed. The spaces between the shower tiles were dark. She'd never seen him work so hard on anything before.

"Those are the kind of people who end up in shoot-outs with the police," Dana tells Cora. The Go-Go Girls have just stolen two million in diamonds from a bank in Beverly Hills. Dana picks up the remote and changes the channel to a cooking show. A woman is finishing a dessert with a blowtorch. Dana closes her eyes and listens to Pinky rattle around in the bathroom. Did they want a shoot-out with the police? She considers the Dalton Gang and John Dillinger.[1] Is that what they want, to bleed to death on the street? The room is hot. The smell of burning rubber wafts through the bathroom door. No, she decides. No, it is not.

There is a river in Elijah, Missouri, that always appears in her dreams. They all grew up in Elijah. In this river they learned to float. Dana would stare up at the clouds and imagine they were spaceships or trains. In this river they would dive and search the bottom for smooth, flat stones. In real life it's a slender, slow-moving river, but in her dreams it's as wide as the Mississippi and silver, as though it's made of melted-down coins. From the shore she sees a raft with no one on it. She wants to get on the raft, but doesn't know how.

That night she wakes sweaty and breathless. She sits up. Pinky is next to her, asleep on top of the covers. He's rangy and sharp-elbowed. His arms are folded under his head. His mouth is pink and sticky from chewing red hots. She touches his pale hair — towheaded, her father used to say — and feels heat rising from his scalp. Outside, she hears rain falling. She lies back down. She tells herself to go to sleep. She tells herself to stop dreaming.

In the morning, they case the Farmers & Mechanics Bank. They drive around the block twice in their Impala and then park at the pizza place across the street. To their left is a small roundabout with a patch of green and two withered trees in the center. It's called Central Park, which makes Dana think of the real Central Park in New York City, a place she will probably never see. A truck rattles past. The exhaust pops and Dana twitches in her seat. Cora is driving. Dana is sitting next to her. Jackie and Pinky are in the back and of course her brother is trying to wind two wires together. Dana imagines that when the Go-Go Girls case, it's all high-tech, with thermal imaging binoculars and fancy cameras. They just have their eyes.

10 They watch people come and go from the bank. They consider the flow of traffic on the street. They send Pinky in to pretend he's filling out a deposit slip. In Central Park, an American flag snaps in the breeze. A church bell calls out the hour. The bank is unassuming, just a brick building with tinted windows. When Pinky returns to the car, he gives a report on the interior layout, the number of tellers, and the points of exit and entry. According to him, there are only two tellers and they're both fat and slow. Dana watches a young woman emerge from the bank; a white envelope is tucked under her arm and she's holding a little boy by the hand. It startles Dana to think that the course of your life could depend on when you decide to cash a check or buy a roll of quarters.

"This one is going to be a breeze," she says.

"Where's the fun in easy?" Cora replies. She turns on the radio and surfs until she finds the news. Tornadoes are in the forecast. Last night one of the Go-Go Girls was spotted at a nightclub in Malibu. There was a big chase with the police. Naturally, she escaped.

"A nightclub!" Cora slaps the steering wheel. "She was probably sitting in some guy's lap. She was probably drinking champagne."

"Champagne gives me a headache," Jackie says from the back.

15 "That's because you've never had the good stuff," Cora tells her.

"How would you know what the good stuff is?" Jackie replies.

At the motel, they clean their guns. Except for Pinky, who locks himself in the bathroom.

[1] The Dalton gang was a group of outlaws based in the American southwest during the 1890s. John Dillinger was a gangster and head of the Dillinger gang, which operated during the 1920s and 1930s. Both groups robbed banks and were essentially celebrities of their respective eras. Many in the Dalton gang were eventually shot to death by law enforcement, as was Dillinger. — Eds.

This image shows a scene in the film *Ocean's Eight*, in which a group of women come together to steal an expensive diamond necklace. **How does this image both uphold and upend the glamour traditionally associated with high stakes heists? How do both this image and the story use unexpected juxtapositions to create tension and develop characters?**

They can hear him banging around in there. It sounds like he's acquired a hammer and a drill. Dana doesn't know where he could have gotten those things.

"He really wants to finish that robot before we leave town," she says.

"What if someone has to pee? Or take a shower?" Cora asks. "What then?"

"Your brother is so weird," Jackie says.

Their guns are old Smith & Wesson revolvers. They wipe them down with the white face towels they found in the motel room. Afterward they take out their gorilla masks and line them up on a bed. Black synthetic fur surrounds the rubber faces. The mouths are open, showing off plump pink tongues and fangs. They put the masks on. They pick up their guns and point them at each other. They aren't loaded, so they pull the triggers and listen to the hollow click. *Bang*, Dana whispers into the sweet-smelling rubber. She can see a bullet flying from the chamber and pinging her right in the forehead. She can see it burrowing into her brain. When people get shot in the movies, they flail and scream and stagger. Sometimes they even pretend to be dead and then come back to life. But that's not what it would be like at all, Dana thinks. She imagines it's just like turning out a light.

2.

In Elijah, they lived on a farm. The property held two gray houses, a chicken coop, and a dilapidated barn. The metal skeletons of cars rusted in the front yard. The barn was filled with dust and moldy straw. On the edge of the property, a small cross made from sticks had been pushed into the ground. It was a grave, but Dana never knew who it belonged to.

The mothers — her and Pinky's, Cora and Jackie's — were both the same: long-faced women scrubbed free of dissent and desire. Dana never heard either of them make a joke or sing. One of her earliest prayers was asking God to not let her end up like them. Cora and Jackie's father was gone. Years ago, he had driven away in the middle of the night. Dana remembered him being like lightning cracking in the sky, quick and mean. Her own father was stern but quiet, the kind who didn't need to raise his voice to incite fear. Once, during a homeschooling lesson, she learned 95 percent of the ocean was unexplored and thought her father must be like that, too: filled with dark, unseen caverns. Sometimes she longed for a father that popped and exploded like Cora and Jackie's had. At least then you knew what he was capable of.

Little was actually farmed on the farm. Her father didn't believe in working for pay. That was the government's system, he said. They were sovereign citizens.[2] They ate homemade bread, snap beans that grew on vines, peppers, collards, and venison; they drank water that came from a well. They had chickens and a milk cow and a white goat. By the time the girls were seven, they knew how to handle a gun. They could hit the center of a bull's-eye. They could shatter the clay pigeons Dana's father tossed into the air. Every Sunday they had target practice because that was God's day and He would want them to be prepared. Cora always had great aim. Pinky never liked the shooting. He got his nickname from the way he flushed whenever he fired. He didn't like the weight of a gun in his hands. He didn't like the noise. He knew better than to say these things in front of his father, of course, but he told Dana when they were alone. She would lick her index finger and wipe dirt from his face and tell him that he would get used to it in time.

25 Once, when Dana was thirteen and Pinky was eight, their father took them turkey hunting. They were instructed to climb a tree and stay put until he called. From the branches of a chestnut oak, they watched him crouch in the tall grass and lure the turkey with a whistle. The bird moved slowly through the woods. Fall leaves crunched under its scaly gray feet. When it appeared, its tail feathers were spread into a beautiful rust-colored fan. Dana thought he looked big and regal, and for the first time the gap between what she knew and what the animal knew seemed cruel. It took only one bullet for the turkey to fall, heavy and silent as a sack of grain. Pinky put his hands over his eyes. Dana rubbed his back. When their father called, she hesitated. She pretended they were invisible in the tree.

[2] Members of this movement generally believe that the U.S. government is illegitimate, and thus do not recognize U.S. currency or pay taxes. The movement has roots in white supremacy, and the FBI classifies sovereign citizens as domestic terrorists. The Southern Poverty Law Center estimates that there are currently around 100,000 "hard-core sovereign believers" in the United States — Eds.

He kept calling, but his voice never sparked with anger. It wasn't patience, though. Dana understood that it was something else. When they finally went to him, he rolled the turkey over and showed where the bullet had gone in. He made them kneel beside the bird and touch the hole. It was gummy and warm. He told them fear of death was their greatest human weakness. He pulled a brown feather, the end tipped with white, from the turkey's tail and stuck it in Dana's hair.

The winter the girls turned eighteen, everything changed. A notice came in the mail. No one had paid taxes on the farm in decades and now the government was saying it owned the land. Her father tore up the first notice, because he didn't believe in taxes, but they kept coming. Dana saw the envelopes stamped with *URGENT* that he brought home from the P.O. Soon they had just sixty days to pay. That was when their training became serious. They had target practice daily. They had drills where they would run along the perimeter of the property, rifles in hand. Even Pinky had to come. He always lagged behind the girls. Dana worried about him slipping on the ice and shooting himself in the foot. They would go out bundled in parkas and leather gloves and hunting caps, their breath making white ghosts in the air. After the first hour her arms would burn from the weight of the gun, but she would keep going. They were given a pair of binoculars and told to look out for strangers. Every night their father waited up in the kitchen for something to happen, for someone to come. Every night they recited a prayer that was meant for the eve of battle: *His days are as a shadow that passeth away / touch the mountains, and they shall smoke / Cast forth lightning, and scatter them.*[3] During a snowstorm, Dana said she didn't see

[3] Lines from Psalm 144, a psalm of David, sometimes characterized as a prayer for rescue and prosperity. — Eds.

Boltin Picture Library/Bridgeman Images

This painting, entitled *States of Mind: Those Who Stay*, was completed by artist Umberto Boccioni in 1911. It depicts people left behind on a train platform as the train pulls away from the station.
How does this work characterize the people at the station and the moment of departure? How might this image reflect Dana's view of her father at this point in the story?

how anyone from the government could find them in this weather, and her father pointed out that snowfall could give the enemy perfect cover. That night, he asked her to wait up with him. He kept opening the front door and looking outside. Snow gusted into the house and padded the hallway with white. Flecks of ice got stuck in his dark eyebrows and hair. He showed her a pamphlet newspaper called *The Embassy of Heaven*,[4] which had a Bible quote on the cover: "Do not suppose that I have come to bring peace to the earth."[5] He said he had been writing to the newspaper and asking for help.

"Help with what?" They were sitting at the kitchen table. A rifle lay across his lap. Last week he'd torn out the landline and now a bundle of red and green wires dangled from the kitchen wall. They had a radio that got two stations, local news and gospel music; in the background she could hear the drone of an organ. She kept telling herself that the tax notices and her father's new habits would all pass eventually, like a hunting season.

"With the soul of this land," he told her. "With the soul of this family."

They'd turned the generator off for the night 30 and the kitchen was cold. Dana had wrapped herself in a wool blanket. The room was lit by an oil lamp. In the half-dark, she could see how much her father's face had changed. The crescents under his eyes had hollowed out; his pupils looked darker, his cheekbones and chin sharper. His skin carried the sheen of a light sweat, even though it was freezing outside. The surface was falling away. She was finally seeing what lay beneath.

No one from the bank or the government ever came to Elijah. The snow kept falling. The river stayed frozen. By February the notices had stopped appearing in the mail. It seemed they had been forgotten. Still things did not go back to the way they were before. Dana's father thought it was a trick. He started working on a secret project in the barn. His face kept changing. At night she could hear her parents arguing and sometimes Dana would find her mother crying as she collected eggs from the chicken coop or squeezed milk from the cow. Both the mothers seemed exhausted by the vigilance they'd been required to keep. They lost the energy for homeschooling. When they gave

[4] A Christian religious group that is part of the sovereign citizen movement. — Eds.

[5] A quote from the Book of Matthew that is attributed to Jesus. The line that follows is "I did not come to bring peace, but a sword." — Eds.

the children their schoolbooks and sent them away, Dana's father didn't notice.

Of course, the children weren't really children anymore. There was only so much time they could spend shooting skeet and patrolling the property and flipping through musty textbooks. The idle time sparked a curiosity they had never felt before; it was as though they had each swallowed an ember and now it sat simmering in their stomachs. One afternoon Cora had this idea to wait on the road for a car to pass. They had some sense of what the outside world was like. They had accompanied Dana's father on trips to the farm store and the P.O. in West Plains. Once a month they went with the mothers to Fairfield's Discount Grocery, just a few miles down the road in Caulfield. Every fall they drove to visit Dana's grandparents, who had a computer and a TV, in Arkansas. But they had never done anything on their own, just the four of them.

After an hour of waiting, a truck rolled by and they hitched a ride to Miller's One Stop in Tecumseh. They wandered the dusty gas station aisles. Under the glare of fluorescent lights, Dana stared at the rows of Cokes and the freezer full of ice-cream sandwiches. Before they hitched a ride back, Cora pocketed a tube of Chapstick and a plastic comb. At home, they mashed the Chapstick into Pinky's hair and then combed it so it stood upright.

On another outing, they discovered that, five miles beyond the gas station, there was a town with a movie theater and a liquor store. The theater had an old-fashioned marquee and two screens. One of the films was always R-rated. The girls started talking the liquor store owner into selling them cigarettes; Pinky was the lookout. They would smoke behind the store and then toss the butts into a field. Once, they let Pinky smoke. He coughed and dropped the cigarette and Cora flicked his ear. They were always back well before dark. Their parents didn't seem to know they'd been gone, or catch the strange smells they brought home. The farm was more than two hundred acres, and Dana figured they thought their children were out on the land, like they'd always been. But their children were learning quickly. They were learning that the outside world and the pleasures it held weren't so bad. They were learning that they had never really believed in God; they had only ever believed in fear.

35 After they stole a map of American highways from the gas station, they spent hours sitting on the floor of Pinky and Dana's room, tracing the lines out to California and Oregon and Florida.

"Here." Cora lay on her side and pointed at San Luis. She had been eating sugar cubes from a cardboard box and her fingertip glistened. "That's where we should go."

Jackie was interested in traveling south, to New Orleans or Fort Lauderdale, but Cora said those places were too hot. Dana was intrigued by the small patchwork of northern states. They had studied geography during homeschooling, but now they were looking at the map in an entirely new light, as being full of places they might one day go.

"Too cold," Cora said when Dana touched the hook of land extending out of Massachusetts.

"Do you promise to take me with you?" Pinky asked. He didn't look his age, thirteen. He could have passed for ten or eleven. He reminded Dana of a rabbit; he had the same nervous nature and quick-beating heart. He never requested any particular place. He just wanted to make sure he wasn't left behind.

40 "We'll see." Cora ran her finger along the edge of California.

"Of course we'll take you," Dana said. He wasn't cut out for life in Elijah. It was too rugged, with the target practice and the long winters and the dead animals. She didn't yet know that he would be even more ill-prepared for the life she and her cousins would choose.

One night, in the early spring, they packed a single suitcase, hitched a ride to West Plains, and kept going. That was six months ago. Their parents never came looking for them, or if they did, they must not have looked very hard. Maybe they thought their children had fallen in with the government or the devil and were beyond hope. Or maybe they just didn't know how to search.

At first Dana thought leaving Elijah meant getting away from how things were on the farm, but now she thinks the past is like the hand of God, or what she imagines the hand of God would be like if God were real: it can turn you in directions you don't want to be turned in. They are still in a battle with the laws of the land. The laws that say they shouldn't steal or point guns at people. And she feels the same resistance to these laws that her father must have felt toward paying taxes. Why not do these things? she found herself thinking. Who is going to stop us?

Their first robbery was at a feed-and-grain store. They wanted money to buy a used car. It was so simple. They had stolen a shotgun from the bed of a truck they'd hitched in. All they had to do was walk inside. Dana told the teenage boy behind the counter to empty his register because that was a line she'd heard in one of those R-rated movies. . . .

The boy gave them everything he had. Feed-and-grain stores aren't used to being robbed.

3.

The night before they hit the bank, Pinky tests his robot in the parking lot. Dana is the only one interested enough to watch. The floodlights are on; tiny bugs hover around the glow. The robot is covered in a pillowcase. It stands on the black asphalt like a ghost. Dana is smoking one of Jackie's cigarettes. She doesn't smoke much anymore, but it's the night before a job and that always makes her nervous. Once the thing is started, there's no sense in worrying because it's done, it's over. You can't rewind. But being on the edge, that's the hardest part. It's like standing in front of a burning building and knowing that it won't be long before you have to walk inside.

She sits on the ground and watches her brother peel away the pillowcase. The robot looks like a kid's science project. It has a round silver head and black buttons for eyes, an economy-size tomato soup can for a body, and large plastic suction cups for feet. It doesn't have any arms. Dana realizes that, for some reason, whenever she thinks of a robot, the first thing that comes into her mind are its arms.

"What do you think?" Pinky says.

"Nice work." Dana flicks the cigarette into the lot.

He tweaks some wires and the robot starts lurching in Dana's direction. It squeaks and sighs. A suction cup slips forward. It's working! She can't believe it. She stands up and begins to applaud. She feels proud of her brother for building something. For finding a way to escape his circumstances.

The robot takes one full step before toppling to the ground. The eyes pop off and slide under a car. The head gets dented. Pinky rights it and adjusts the wires, but he can't bring it back to life. Dana stops clapping. She sits down on the sidewalk.

He carries the robot over to her. "Do you want to hold it?"

"Sure." She holds it away from herself. It's surprisingly light.

"On TV people build robots that can talk." Pinky licks his lips.

"It probably takes a lot of practice," she says.

An old woman with flame-red hair shuffles past and disappears into a motel room. Above them Dana hears slamming doors.

"I don't want to leave," Pinky says. "I want to stay here and keep practicing."

"You want to stay in Galesburg?"

Pinky tells her that whenever they leave a place, he worries they won't make it to the next town. He worries the car will break down and no one will give them a ride and they'll starve to death or get heatstroke or something equally horrible. He's breathless. His eyes are glassy. She pictures his rabbit heart pulsing under his ribs. Probably leaving him in Galesburg would be the best thing for him, though she knows she could never do such a thing. She was the one who took him away from the farm and now she has to live with the consequences.

She gives the robot back to him. She doesn't tell him that if they die, it won't be from starving to death in their car. Instead she says everything is going to be fine, just like she used to in Elijah. No one is going to die. Soon he'll have all the time in the world to build a new robot.

"Does this one have a name?" she asks.

"Donald." He squeezes the robot's metal stomach and asks Dana what she thought their father was building in the barn.

Dana shrugs. She's never given much thought to what he was doing. She just remembers looking out her window and seeing him trudge into the mouth of the barn at dawn and not emerging until after dark. His skin would be caked in dust, straw caught in his hair. But mainly she had been preoccupied with figuring out how to live her own life, with how to spend her time. Dana wonders if her father is still working on his project in the barn, whatever it was. She imagines going back to Elijah one day and finding him a shrunken old man, and feels an ache shoot through her chest.

"I snuck in there once and watched him." Pinky describes pliers and cords and strips of metal. He talks about smelling smoke and seeing tiny silver sparks. "I think he was building a robot. I think that's what he wanted to do."

Dana looks at her brother and feels woozy. She never should have taken him along. It was a game at first, but now it's something much more serious and he is becoming an attachment she doesn't need.

"You know what they say in the movies?" she asks him.

"What?"

"They say you have to be cool." She can see a man in a ponytail delivering the line, but can't remember which movie it's from.

Karl F. Schöfmann/imageBROKER/Alamy

How does this large mural capture the appeal that robots hold for people? How close does it come to the way you picture the robot Pinky is working on? How might it reflect Pinky's hopes for his robot?

"Okay." He's staring at the ground. She can tell she's not getting through.

"Say it to me."

He keeps hugging the robot. In his arms it looks like a heap of trash. It's only recently occurred to Dana that some people might call what she did — taking her brother away from their parents — kidnapping.

"Be cool," he tells her without looking up.

"You got it," she says.

4.

Dana was questioned by the police only once. It didn't have anything to do with the Gorillas. Rather, she was a witness to a hit-and-run.

This was two months ago, in Jefferson City. She had just walked out of a bank the Gorillas were casing and was waiting to cross the street. A car ran a red light and struck a girl on a bicycle. The girl was dead by the time the ambulance came. Dana could remember the twisted handlebars and the crushed bell. She could remember the peculiar angle of the girl's torso and her open eyes. Her lips were parted. Her teeth were straight and white. She was still wearing her helmet. She looked like a life-size doll someone had left in the street. Pedestrians gathered. The police were called. Dana tried to slip away, but someone identified her as a witness and she was taken down to the station. She got to ride up front with the officer. She wondered what Cora or Jackie would think if they saw her, if they would think she had turned on them.

At the station, the officer brought her a cup of coffee. He was handsome, with his broad shoulders and gelled hair. So this is the lair of the enemy, Dana thought as they settled into an interrogation room. She held the warm foam cup with both hands. If only this officer knew what she had done, what she was going to do, she would not be answering questions over coffee. There would be handcuffs and threats. She figured that one day he would see her face on the news and feel like a dolt.

He asked her the usual questions: what she'd seen, if the light had been red, if she'd gotten a look at the driver, if she remembered the license plate. She answered honestly. She hadn't seen anything but the collision itself, hadn't taken in anything but the shock of the crash. She didn't mention that she hadn't been paying closer attention because she'd been busy imprinting the interior of the bank onto her brain.

"Do you need someone to identify the body?" Dana asked. She surprised herself with the question.

"You knew her?" The office frowned. He pulled in his chin and a little roll of fat appeared.

He had mentioned the girl was a college student. Dana muttered something about being classmates and seeing her around campus. She didn't know what had come over her. She had never seen a dead body before and up until then, that was A-okay. But she had been gripped by an urge she could not recognize or understand, only follow.

"Her parents are coming in from Chicago," the officer said. "We could save them the grief."

Dana sighed. Didn't he know there was no saving anyone any grief?

They took an elevator down to the morgue and passed through a cool, shadowed hallway. They stopped in front of a dark window. Dana could hear music coming through the glass. It was faint. A Michael Jackson song. For a moment, she imagined the medical examiner moonwalking around the autopsy room. The officer asked if she was ready. She nodded. A light came on.

The girl was lying on a coroner's table. She was naked, which alarmed Dana. It didn't seem right for her to be uncovered; someone had been careless. Her breasts were small and her knees seemed too big for her body. Her eyes were closed. Her hair looked wet and sleek. The blood had been cleaned away. Dana wondered where her bicycle helmet was. She couldn't believe this was the same girl she'd seen sprawled out on the street. It looked like her body had been replaced by a fake. How could these parents from Chicago identify their daughter with any kind of certainty? Maybe that was what happened when you died, Dana thought. Your real body went one place and a replica was provided for the rituals. And if that were true, where did the real bodies go? Someplace nice? Probably not.

"So is it her?" the officer said.

"What?" Dana turned from the window.

"Is she your classmate? Do you know her name?"

"It's not her," Dana said.

"What do you mean it's not her?" The officer frowned again. He was getting less attractive by the minute.

"I made a mistake," she said.

"Who makes that kind of mistake?" For the first time she noticed the gun holstered to his hip.

Dana wasn't afraid to just tell the officer the truth. After all, she hadn't broken any laws, that he knew of.

"Look, I wanted to see a body. I wanted to know what it would be like." She thought of that turkey in Elijah strolling through the woods one minute and still the next.

The officer said she could show herself out.

5.

At first everything goes perfectly at the Farmers & Mechanics Bank. They are all in their gorilla masks. Cora is pointing her gun at the tellers. Dana is aiming hers at the handful of customers who had the misfortune of being in the bank. They are crossed-legged on the floor; they have been ordered to sit on their hands, like elementary schoolers who can't stop hitting each other. Dana tries to ignore the little girl with braided hair. Pinky is guarding the door. Jackie, the getaway driver, is idling around the corner. Dana watches one teller load bricks of money into a bag. He has red hair and a mustache. The other teller is a woman. She's used so much hair spray, her hair doesn't budge when she whips her head left then right. Her lips are slick with pink, her lashes clumped with mascara. There's no sign of the fat, sluggish tellers Pinky described, but it looks like these two will do just fine.

It's the woman who fucks everything up. They see her hand slide under the counter and know she's going for the alarm. Cora shouts at her — *Hands in the air* — but the woman doesn't listen. Pinky is pacing by the door and pawing his rubber face. Dana takes small, quick breaths behind her gorilla mask. *Be cool*, she whispers, but it sounds artificial and weak. Stronger words are needed. She just doesn't know what they are.

The gunshot stops everyone. The mustached teller stops putting money in the bag. Pinky stops pacing. The customers stop squirming. The female teller is clutching her left eye. Blood seeps between her fingers. Cora's gun is still raised. It takes Dana more time than it should to understand that one of the Gorillas has just shot a bank teller in the face.

Her hands are numb. She concentrates on not dropping her gun. She thinks she's going to suffocate behind the mask.

Margaret Bourke-White/The LIFE Picture Collection/Shutterstock

This photograph shows gigantic pipe segments used to divert the Missouri River during the construction of Fort Peck Dam in Montana in 1936.

How might this image reflect the sense of overwhelming doom Dana feels when the bank robbery goes awry?

"Give us our money." Now Cora is aiming at the other teller. His shirtsleeves are drenched in sweat. He goes back to heaving cash into the bag.

A woman in cowboy boots raises her hand. Her mouth is open, but she's not saying anything. She's pointing at something by the door. Dana turns and there's Pinky, slumped against the wall. He's kneading his gorilla mask in his hands. The customers and the tellers and the security cameras are all taking in his face. They are memorizing it. They are branding it onto their brains like Dana did with the interior of that bank in Jackson City.

"He is in such deep shit." Cora is waving her gun. She swivels toward Dana. "Can't you do something?"

But Dana can't. If she were a Go-Go Girl, then maybe she could, but she is just herself. The female teller is hunched over the counter and whimpering. She sounds like the wild dog Dana's father once had to shoot in Elijah. He kept coming onto their property, frothy and snarling, but once he had a bullet in him, he was docile as a lamb. Blood is still squirting through her fingers, as though her hand is a dam that's about to give. She's blinded at best. In the distance, Dana hears a siren. She looks at Cora and her cousin nods. They run for the exit. She pauses only to yank Pinky up by his shirt collar. He drops his gorilla mask on the sidewalk, but right then it doesn't matter. All that matters is diving into the waiting Impala. Of course Jackie wants to know what happened and where's the money and why isn't Pinky wearing his mask. Cora tells her to shut up and drive. They blast out of Galesburg. It's nearly dusk. The sun looks like it's setting the sky on fire.

They drive through the night. Pinky is up front, next to Jackie. Dana and Cora are in the back. The window is cracked and Jackie is chain-smoking. They are heading to a little town called Wapello. They think it will be a good place to lie low, but soon Pinky's face will be all over the news and there will be no lying low from that.

"He can't stay with us anymore," Cora hisses in the backseat.

Dana just shakes her head. He could get plastic surgery, she thinks. A crazy idea. She gazes at her brother's profile. They are on a dark, straight highway. A little slicing, a little rearranging. She thinks of how handsome he could be.

On the radio, they hear that one of the Go-Go Girls has been shot in the stomach. She fell behind during a getaway. The officer who shot her said that he meant to hit her shoulder. Turns out that she wasn't an acrobat or Romanian. Just a girl from Minnesota.

"This is the problem with being famous," Dana announces to the car. "It makes everyone want to kill you."

No one says anything. Not even Cora. Dana leans her head against the window. As they're passing signs for Kirkwood, she thinks of the girl at the morgue and her parents in Chicago. She wonders if the cop ever tells her story, about the woman who conned him into checking out a dead body. If anyone ever tells her story.

Tornadoes are still in the forecast. A few times Dana thinks she sees a big black funnel moving toward them in the night. She thinks she hears that locomotive sound and feels the ground shake. She imagines being swept away. But there is nothing coming for them. Not yet. There is only this highway and this car and this darkness. She leans forward and squeezes her brother's elbow. He doesn't move, doesn't look at her. The remaining Gorilla masks are piled in his lap. He knows he's in a world of trouble.

They stop for gas and Dana makes Jackie hand her the car keys. When she says she wants to be sure no one gets left behind, Cora gives her a look. Pinky needs to use the bathroom. Dana stands outside and jingles the keys. She can see her parents hearing about Pinky on the radio. She can see them turning up the volume and leaning in close. Maybe they are being kept company by a robot made of soup cans and chicken wire, or maybe they are alone. Through the bathroom door, she hears the toilet flush. Her brother takes his time washing his hands.

110 When they're all back in the car, Cora passes her a note written on a paper napkin. *We are leaving him at the next fucking gas station!* it says in jagged black letters. Dana crumples the note and drops it on the floor. She slumps back and something crunches under her sneaker. She peers between her knees. It's the robot. Pinky got one of the eyes glued back on. If she tilts her head the right away, the metal gleams and she can tell herself it's their treasure, their loot. She thinks about rescuing the robot from the floor and giving it to her brother. She thinks about doing him that kindness. Instead she nudges the robot under the driver's seat and then feels sad about it. Poor Donald. She has to remind herself that robots don't have feelings. All these little choices that push her closer to something she's not sure she wants.

They pass a billboard with the slogan WANT A BETTER WORLD? It's too dark for Dana to see what's being advertised, but she guesses it's something religious. Of course she wants a better world. Who wouldn't want that? A world where everyone was like Pinky, pure and soft and full of dreams. Or she could just do things differently when it came to those small choices. She could give her brother the robot. She could throw her gun in a river. These could be her lessons. It's right there for her, that better world. She barely has to go looking.

Dana knows this, just as she knows that this is not the day she will find it. ■

2013

Understanding and Interpreting

1. What inspires Dana, Jackie, Pinky, and Cora to go on their crime spree? Who are their role models?
2. How would you describe the Gorillas' childhoods? How does Dana's character, in particular, reflect the way she was raised?
3. How does "Lessons" differentiate the four members of the gang? What details does this short story supply that give each member a specific personality?
4. The towns mentioned in the story are in Midwestern states such as Illinois, Missouri, and Iowa. How are those settings depicted? How do they help convey the ambitions and limitations of the Gorilla Gang?
5. How is Dana's outlook on life different from those of her cousins Cora and Jackie? How does her relationship with her brother Pinky illustrate that difference?
6. How is Pinky different from the rest of the gang? Why do you think he takes off his gorilla mask during the bank robbery?
7. How do the Go-Go Girls function as foils for Dana, her brother, and her cousins in "Lessons"? What does this other gang's exploits and media coverage emphasize about Dana and her crew?
8. In describing the way her father calls for her and Pinky after they shoot the turkey, Dana thinks that his call is not angry, nor is it patient, and she "understood that it was something else" (par. 26). What do you think "it" is? What evidence in the story supports your interpretation?
9. In paragraph 110, Dana "has to remind herself that robots don't have feelings." She thinks, "All these little choices that push her closer to something she's not sure she wants." What is it that she's approaching? Why isn't she sure she wants to get there?
10. How does "Lessons" illustrate the "short answer: they are a group of people committed to making life as hard as possible" (par. 2)?
11. Why is this story called "Lessons"? What does it mean that Dana thinks what she could do differently at the end of the story "could be her lessons" (par. 111)?

Analyzing Language, Style, and Structure

1. **Vocabulary in Context.** What is the meaning of the word "heist" in paragraph 3? Where might Cora have gotten a word like that to describe her ambitions?
2. "Lessons" has a third-person limited omniscient narrator. What is the effect of limiting our view into what the other characters are thinking? How does that choice affect the pace of the story?
3. How do you interpret the dream Dana has in paragraph 8? What might the raft be?
4. Why is "Lessons" divided into five sections? What is the function of each one? How do they differ from each other?
5. How does Dana and her crew's backstory illuminate their present-day choices and relationships?
6. What purpose does section 4, in which Dana sees a fatal accident and is questioned by the police, serve? How does it develop — and complicate — Dana's character?
7. What does the robot represent for Pinky in particular? What is its significance to the story as a whole?
8. How does Laura van den Berg create suspense throughout "Lessons"? Consider her language choices and the structure of the story in your response.
9. How is Dana both a product of and a rebel against her upbringing?

Topics for Composing

1. **AP® FRQ Prose Fiction Analysis.** The following question refers to paragraphs 6–7 of Laura van den Berg's "Lessons," published in 2013. The passage describes a turkey hunt that the protagonist, Dana, took part in as a child with her father. Read the passage carefully. Then, in a well-written essay, analyze how van den Berg uses literary elements and techniques to portray complex family relationships and values through the lens of this event.
2. **AP® FRQ Literary Argument.** Many works of literature show the influence of popular culture in a way that illuminates its relationship to human nature. In "Lessons," the characters have grown up in isolation, but their foray into the larger world as teenagers exposes them to various elements of popular culture for the first time as they embark on a crime spree. In a well-written essay, analyze how the main characters' perspectives on popular culture contribute to an interpretation of the work as a whole. Do not merely summarize the plot.
3. **AP® Literary Argumentation.** What is the relationship between Dana's isolated, off-the-grid childhood and her attitude toward the crime she and her relatives commit? Do you think these actions are a rebellion against the confines of her childhood? Are they an attempt to re-create a feeling of family that she has lost in the wake of her father's mental decline? Use evidence from the story to support your answer.
4. **Research.** Read up on the outlaw gangs mentioned in the story. What similarities do all of them share? How do the Gorillas compare to these real-life gangs?
5. **Connections.** To what extent is the Gorillas' planning and execution inspired by the movies? Trace their methodology and compare it to films you've seen about crime gangs and heists.
6. **Connections.** To what extent does "Lessons" glamorize or romanticize crime? Explain your answer in an essay.

Prudent Girls

Rivers Solomon

Wasi Daniju (2019), with permission from The Gernert Company

Rivers Solomon was born in California in 1989 and earned a BA in Comparative Studies in Race and Ethnicity from Stanford University and an MFA from the Michener Center for Writers at the University of Texas at Austin. Solomon is nonbinary and uses the pronouns fae/faer and they/their. They are the author of three acclaimed novels of speculative fiction: *An Unkindness of Ghosts* (2017), *The Deep* (2019), and most recently *Sorrowland* (2021).

KEY CONTEXT This story was written for the *New York Times* Decameron Project, a set of stories that take place during the first few months of the COVID-19 pandemic. This project is modeled on Giovanni Boccaccio's *The Decameron*, a series of novellas written between 1349 and 1353 that take place during the Black Death epidemic that overtook the city of Florence, Italy, in 1348.

This story's title is a reference to Proverbs 22:3, which is translated in the New King James version of the Bible as: "A prudent man foresees evil and hides himself, but the simple pass on and are punished." The New World Translation, used by Jehovah's Witnesses, renders this passage as: "The shrewd one sees the danger and conceals himself, but the inexperienced keep right on going and suffer the consequences." The protagonist of the story, a teenager raised as a Jehovah's Witness, is named Jerusha. This Old Testament name was originally popularized by Puritans in the 1600s. Please note that this text contains gun violence and references to sexual assault.

Jerusha didn't get where people had been going before lockdown, anyway. Besides the bowling alley — off-limits for Jerry now that the owners had gotten a beer license — there wasn't much in Caddo, Texas, as far as things to do.

On Embarcadero, you had the H-E-B, the Joann Fabric, the car dealership and the Hobby Lobby; off the service road, the Chili's, the Rosalita's and the Best Western. In the strip mall where Lawrence Tate was shot down by the police, bears and balloons marking the spot, there was a Walmart, a Ross Dress for Less and a Starbucks, and down the way from there stood the gun store and range. As for the library, Jerry never went because the woman who worked the front desk didn't let Black people or Mexicans check out more than two books at once despite the official limit being 10. "You don't want to take on more than you can handle or you'll end up with late fees you can't pay. Start with two, and prove you can return those on time."

Five miles outside the city limits, the Caddo Creek Women's Facility didn't count as part of the town proper, which was a shame, because that was where Jerry's mother was nine years into a 13-year sentence. It was the only place around here worth a damn — and Caddo wouldn't even have that going for it once Jerry broke the woman out.

Nobody watching KBCY newscasters gravely explain quarantine procedures on Channel 4 could really think they were missing out on much.

"Jerusha, baby. Turn that noise off," Aint Rita 5
called from where she sat at the kitchen table. She was doing her daily cryptogram while waiting for Judge Mathis to come on in an hour. "I don't know why these people think any of these measures matter when it is God who decides the fate of man. Let me see Governor

Abbott repent on live TV, then maybe I'll make time for what he's got to say. Nothing's going to stop the Armageddon."

But Proverbs 22:3 said that the shrewd man sees danger and conceals himself from it, and it's the foolish one who keeps on ahead, for he will suffer the penalties. Wasn't Aint Rita worried about people dying of the virus? Uncle Charles had C.O.P.D., and Aint Wilma had lupus and diabetes. Aint Rita herself was on dialysis.[1]

Most of all, there was Jerry's mama, trapped in a crowded facility without masks or hand sanitizer. It was bad enough without considering she was also living with asthma, hepatitis and H.I.V.

Did Aint Rita want her niece to die? Probably. Jerry's mama was an apostate, and to Aint Rita, that was worse than dead.

Jerry was a judicious girl and didn't speak these thoughts aloud. Like the shrewd man extolled in Scripture, she avoided the danger that was her great-aunt. A girl who knew how to conceal herself from those who would do her harm had more freedom in the world than the girl who flaunted her supposed freedoms to her enemy unthinkingly.

"I said turn it off, 'Rusha."

Jerry pressed mute and turned on the closed captioning. Absorbed in her puzzle, Aint Rita wouldn't notice the TV wasn't actually off.

"You think I'll still be able to visit Mama tomorrow?" Jerusha asked.

The grunt Aint Rita made was either acknowledgment or dismissal. Sipping from her mug of peppermint tea, eyes on her cryptogram, she was in me-time mode, that part of the day when she didn't bother herself with what she called Jerry's antics.

"I could look it up online," Jerusha suggested, playing with fire but intentionally so. If she never said or did things that Aint Rita didn't like, the woman would think she was hiding something. Plus, being able to assert rank over her great-niece gave her a sense of purpose. No reason to take that from her. Very soon, she'd no longer have even that small pleasure.

Aint Rita tapped her ballpoint pen against the table, brow scrunched. "No need to bring the internet into it," she said. "I'll call the ombudsman hotline tomorrow morning and see if visitations are on."

Her Aint Rita would do no such thing, but that didn't matter because Jerry had no intentions of taking the bus out to see her mother tomorrow. The two of them would be long gone by then.

• • •

When Michael Pierce, warden at Caddo Creek Women's Facility, killed his wife with a blow to the head, he couldn't know anyone was watching. His daughters were staying at their grandparents' cabin, and his dog, Sand Dune, was out back. It wasn't a planned act of violence, but he did, as anyone does before committing a forbidden act, calculate the odds of his capture. Because of quarantine, Michael's wife wouldn't be missed for weeks or more, which gave him time to plan an effective cover-up. He had, he thought, accidentally come up with the perfect murder.

Had Warden Pierce been a man of sounder judgment, he might have taken seriously the files for three potential babysitters his wife had presented him 14 months ago so that she could begin taking night classes. He'd have checked Jerry's references and found them wanting. Not because she didn't have good references available, but because she didn't want her clients to find out she charged different people different rates based on what she thought she could get from whom. He'd have chosen Jessi Tyler or Isabel Emerson instead. Neither of them kept hidden cameras in their clients' homes after the time they'd been accused of stealing.

But when Michael's wife presented him the information she'd carefully gathered into manila folders, he turned up the volume on the poker match he was watching on ESPN and said: "Whatever, hun. Maybe ask me after this is over?"

His wife chose the girl who was rumored to be a Jehovah's Witness because she'd heard they were a cult, and she had fantasies of helping the girl escape like she'd seen on TV where people saved young Mormon girls from polygamist marriage.

And it would be good for her daughters to spend some time with a girl who dressed so modestly. None of that hoochie-mama crap. No. Nice, sensible clothes for nice, sensible girls.

Were he a better man, he might have talked to this babysitter who'd been working for him over a year once or twice, and if he had, she might have had softer feelings to him and been more merciful about it all, but he hadn't. He didn't even know her name. Something biblical-sounding, the warden thought. Mostly he knew her as the Black girl.

It was this fact that had started the fight with his wife. Jerusha had come by to pick up her last envelope of cash early ahead of the lockdown. After she left, the warden asked his wife half-jokingly: "Why do they all have butts and tits like strippers? What is she, 15? Sixteen? That's not natural." He shook his head as if to say, what has become of the world, and well, what had become of it? Caddo used to be different.

"You're not supposed to say stuff like that, Michael. They can't help it," his wife said. It was always something with her.

"It's just, are you buying that whole good-girl Christian thing?" he asked. He'd seen her looking at him, and yes, he'd looked back, and yes, he'd seen the solicitations implicit in the way her body moved.

"Well, if you wanted me to hire someone else, you should've looked at the files. I'll fire her if you want."

"I didn't say you had to fire her. Don't be dramatic. And what files? What are you even talking about?"

She shook her head. "The files, Michael."

His wife had always been jealous, said he never paid attention to her, but the thing was, if she had interesting things to say, he would have.

Then later she'd accused him of wanting to have sex with the girl, which was ridiculous, *ri-dic-u-lous.* It was she who'd imposed her body on him, and if he'd taken her, which, yes, he admitted he had, it was not a matter of want but senseless provocation.

His wife had shoved him and called him a pervert, which was, in its own way, verbal abuse.

Blackmail was like the prison system itself. There was just no getting out of it without a little blood. When a stranger sends a video to you anonymously and in that video you're murdering your wife, well, there was nothing to do but meet the stranger's demands.

To a point. Warden Pierce would orchestrate Rochelle Hayes's escape, but he would follow her until the blackmailer was revealed and end it himself.

• • •

Jerry set the table with Kool-Aid, salmon croquettes, instant mashed potatoes, green beans and crescent rolls. "Well, look at this," Aint Rita said.

"I froze extra, too."

"You been cooking up a storm these last few weeks. The chest freezer out back is gonna burst. The virus got you all scared?" Aint Rita asked.

Jerry got the roll of paper towels and set it at the center of the table. "I'm not scared. Jehovah provides for the faithful. Days of peace are coming," she said.

"Amen to that. Will you do the blessing tonight, or shall I?"

Jerry sat across from her great-aunt for the last meal they'd share together. "I'll do it," she said. Aint Rita's prayers tended to drag. "Jehovah, we thank you for the bounty before us, and we ask that you bless it to the nourishment of our bodies. In Jesus' name we pray, amen."

"Amen."

Jerry had packed two portions of the evening's meal in a cooler to bring with her tonight. It would be her mother's first taste of real food in almost a decade. There were also nuts, fruit, bottled water, crackers, bread and packs of seasoned tuna set aside. Stores were empty, but the Witness in Jerry meant that she always found herself prepared.

Heritage Images/Getty Images

This depiction of the Greek myth of Prudentia, or Prudence, was created by artist Andrea della Robbia in 1475. Prudence is the concept of virtue personified — she is typically shown with a mirror that represents self-awareness or a conscience and a snake that represents wisdom. The back of her head is an old man who represents memory, experience, and the past. **How does this portrayal of Prudence affect your understanding of the themes of the story? Do you think Jerusha is prudent according to these principles? Explain.**

"You're quiet tonight," Aint Rita said.

Jerry spooned a second helping of mashed potatoes onto her plate. "Just thinking."

"About?"

"The end of the world," Jerry said, meaning the end of her life here with Aint Rita. "My mother said when I was born, I heralded in her own personal End of Days, but that that was good. She says I'm the reason she left Jehovah."

Aint Rita's cutlery clanked against her plate. "Shameful."

There was a picture of Jerry's mother with a freshly shaven head taken the day after her daughter was born. She'd told Jerry she'd been overtaken with the urge to cut it all off. Maybe it was hormones, but seeing Jerry born, she realized she could not begin a new life without destroying the old. Rochelle divorced her husband, left Jehovah and became a lesbian. Shot Jerry's father in the heart when he came for their little girl.

Sometimes killing was what was required, and to leave yourself at the mercy of your old life was imprudent. One had to think these things out. One had to let the new life in, deaths and all.

After dinner, Jerry checked her bags one last time while Aint Rita watched "Jeopardy!" in the living room. She had 10 pairs of panties, five bras, five undershirts, three blouses and three skirts, 14 socks, toothpaste, a toothbrush, floss picks, mouthwash, deodorant, her Bible, her birth certificate and a gun.

She rolled her suitcase down Juarez Street, then onto Embarcadero, past the storefront that used to be a GameStop but had been boarded up for four years. She passed the Dewey James Memorial Bench, which some Black mamas had fund-raised to install, in honor of the man who was dragged to death by a pickup truck driven by white teenagers back in the 1980s.

The city was falling apart, yellow and brown weeds erupting from the asphalt. Paint flaking off walls. Before schools closed, the students of Caddo Elementary were moved into trailers because the main building had been infested with mold. The billboard advertising acreage for sale had been peeling since December, only the last two digits of the phone number visible.

There was a beauty to a place as ugly as this, because when one realized it no longer nurtured, it was easy to let go.

Upon discovering her great-niece missing in the morning, Aint Rita would wonder if they had been secretly at odds, but Jerry and great-aunt had always agreed on one essential truth, that everything around them needed to crumble. A new world was coming if only you were willing to do what it took.

Jerry's mother met her at the water tower, as instructed on the phone. "Did you walk all the way here?" the woman asked.

It was nine miles, but Jerry had worn practical shoes. "He followed you?"

"Just like you said he would. There. See. His lights are off," she whispered and pointed to a spot 30 feet up the road. There were those who couldn't leave the well-enough that was one dead body alone. He could not have seen her approach in the hazy dark of a gray March.

Jerry walked toward him, her hand on the pistol. There was no abiding a man who'd done the things he'd done to her. Tonight was not her mother's salvation, but her own.

As was the way of the shrewd man, she hid from her enemy's sights, sidled up, then fired. Jerry had wrought her own Armageddon, and liked it. ■

2020

Understanding and Interpreting

1. How does Rivers Solomon characterize the setting of the story? Why does Jerusha, or Jerry, think that "[n]obody . . . could really think they were missing out on much" (par. 4) during the lockdown?
2. In paragraph 5, Aint Rita claims that "it is God who decides the fate of man." Does Jerry agree with this assertion? Cite evidence from the text to support your answer.
3. Create a character sketch of Michael Pierce. What do the details in the story reveal about his perspective? How does his behavior early in the story shape your expectations for his actions later in the story? Do any of his actions take you by surprise? Explain why or why not.
4. What does the story imply is the reason Michael Pierce kills his wife? How does he appear to justify his actions, and how do these justifications fit into his pattern of behavior?
5. Do you think Michael Pierce knows who is blackmailing him? Use evidence from the story to support your response.
6. Why has Jerry been "cooking up a storm these last few weeks" (par. 36)?
7. How did Rochelle Hayes end up in prison? What does this detail reveal about the setting of the story? How does it contribute to your understanding of Jerry's character?
8. Does Jerry ultimately create and control her circumstances, or does she merely respond to them? To what extent does her agency depend on context?

Analyzing Language, Style, and Structure

1. **Vocabulary in Context.** Jerry is characterized as "judicious," and she thinks that "to leave yourself at the mercy of your old life was imprudent" (par. 48). How do the connotations of each word compare with each other? Does the story suggest that being "prudent" is synonymous with being "judicious," or does it distinguish between the two? Explain.
2. Solomon incorporates foreshadowing throughout the story. Find an instance of foreshadowing and analyze its effect. What event is being foreshadowed? How does this foreshadowing speak to the larger themes of the story?
3. Jerry sees herself "[l]ike the shrewd man extolled in Scripture" (par. 9) and as someone who is capable of "playing with fire" (par. 14). What irony do these descriptions reveal? What other details in the story reveal this irony?
4. How would you characterize the tone of the paragraph that describes the death of Michael Pierce's wife? Do the circumstances contradict the assertion that "it wasn't a planned act of violence" (par. 17)? What does this juxtaposition of realities suggest about Michael Pierce as a character?

5. Consider the narrative perspective of the story. Whose thoughts and motives shape the plot structure and your interpretation of the central characters? What does this dominant perspective convey about the importance of family? What does it suggest about the connection between power and independence?
6. What is the function of the reference to an Armageddon at the end of the story? What Armageddon has Jerusha "wrought," and how does it relate to Aint Rita's allusion to it earlier in the story? Finally, how does the relationship between the two references speak to a larger theme of the story?

Topics for Composing

1. AP® FRQ **Prose Fiction Analysis.** The following question refers to paragraphs 978–979 of Rivers Solomon's "Prudent Girls," published in 2020. In this passage, the narrator introduces the protagonist, Jerusha, and establishes her relationship with her longtime guardian, Aint Rita. Read the passage carefully. Then, in a well-written essay, analyze how Solomon uses literary elements and techniques to develop Jerusha's complex perspective on her family.
2. AP® FRQ **Literary Argument.** Works of literature often depict betrayals that reveal the complexities of characters and their relationships with each other. In "Prudent Girls," several betrayals occur. Choose one to write about. In a well-written essay, analyze how that betrayal contributes to an interpretation of the work as a whole. Do not merely summarize the plot.
3. **AP® Literary Argumentation.** Many works of literature feature protagonists who behave in ways that can be considered immoral or even evil. In "Prudent Girls," the protagonist, Jerusha, deceives her aunt, murders a man, and breaks her mother out of prison. In a well-organized essay, explain both how and why the full presentation of the Jerusha in "Prudent Girls" makes us react more sympathetically than we otherwise might. Avoid plot summary.
4. **Speaking and Listening.** Consider the idea that "A girl who knew how to conceal herself from those who would do her harm had more freedom in the world than the girl who flaunted her supposed freedoms to her enemy unthinkingly" (par. 9). Do you think this generally holds true? Consider real-life and hypothetical situations that illustrate your position on this statement in preparation for a class discussion.
5. **Connections.** Compare your initial response to the beginning of the pandemic in March 2020 to that of Jerry, who doesn't understand "where people had been going before lockdown" (par. 1) in her hometown of Caddo, Texas. If you felt similarly to Jerry, did you begin to long to go to the kinds of places she describes, or were you content to stay home for the most part? If your initial response was quite different from Jerry's, how did your day-to-day life and those of your friends include more than Jerry's?
6. **Research.** Explore the role of eschatology, or theology about an Armageddon, in the beliefs and practices of Jehovah's Witnesses or another faith group of your choosing. How does eschatology shape their daily lives and general outlook? You might also explore differences between the various religious groups' treatment of eschatology into their daily lives. How does your research expand your understanding of Aint Rita's perspective on the world? Has it also changed your understanding of the Armageddon Jerry feels she has created at the end of the story? Explain why or why not.

Poetry

On My First Son

Ben Jonson

Active Museum/Alamy

Ben Jonson (1572–1637) was born in London to an indigent widowed mother. Although he was encouraged to attend college, financial considerations compelled him to become a bricklayer, a trade Jonson "could not endure." He ultimately joined the army and fought for the Protestant cause in Holland. Returning to England in 1592, he tried his hand at both acting and directing, but it was in writing that he excelled. He is best known for his comedies, including *Every Man in His Humour* (1598), *Volpone* (1606), *The Alchemist* (1610), and *Bartholomew Fair* (1614).

KEY CONTEXT "On My First Son" is an elegy written after the death of Jonson's first son, Benjamin, at the age of seven.

Farewell, thou child of my right hand,[1] and joy;
My sin was too much hope of thee, loved boy:
Seven years thou wert lent to me, and I thee pay,
Exacted by thy fate, on the just day.
O could I lose all father now! For why
Will man lament the state he should envy,
To have so soon 'scaped world's and flesh's rage,
And, if no other misery, yet age?
Rest in soft peace, and asked, say, "Here doth lie
Ben Jonson his best piece of poetry."
For whose sake henceforth all his vows be such
As what he loves may never like too much. ■

1616

[1] Benjamin means "son of my right hand" in Hebrew. — Eds.

Understanding and Interpreting

1. **AP® Narration.** In line 2, the speaker calls hope a "sin." How can this be?
2. **AP® Narration.** What does the speaker mean when he asks, "O could I lose all father now!" (l. 5)?
3. **AP® Narration.** Why do you think the speaker calls his son "his best piece of poetry" (l. 10)? What does this suggest about the value he places on his poetry?
4. **AP® Narration.** What do you make of the final lines of the poem? To whom does the "his" in line 11 refer? What is the difference between the words "love" and "like" in the last line? What does the speaker vow in that line?
5. **AP® Character and Narration.** Who does the speaker address throughout the poem? What does this suggest about how the speaker is coping with his son's death?

Analyzing Language, Style, and Structure

1. **Vocabulary in Context.** What does "Exacted" mean in line 4? How does this word convey the speaker's thoughts and emotions concerning the death of his son?
2. **AP® Narration and Figurative Language.** How do you interpret the metaphor in lines 3–4, in which Ben Jonson compares his son's life to a loan? What does this comparison suggest about the speaker's perspective on life?
3. **AP® Structure, Narration, and Figurative Language.** How does the speaker attempt to console himself over the loss of his son? Identify language in the poem that supports your interpretation.
4. **AP® Structure and Narration.** What is the speaker's attitude throughout the poem? How — and where — does his attitude shift?

Topics for Composing

1. **AP® FRQ Poetry Analysis.** In Ben Jonson's "On My First Son," published in 1616, the speaker laments the death of his seven-year-old son. Read the poem carefully. Then, in a well-written essay, analyze how Jonson uses literary elements and techniques to convey his complex attitude toward his loss.
2. **Speaking and Listening.** Select one of the six couplets and record yourself reciting the two lines. What words should be emphasized in the couplet and what pauses should you take to convey the appropriate tone? Be prepared to discuss how the couplet you chose relates to the speaker's larger concerns in the poem.
3. **Creative Writing.** The speaker admits that he had "too much hope" (l. 2) concerning his son's future. What does he mean by this? Write a letter from the perspective a modern-day father expressing his hopes for his child's future. What hopes might be realistic, and which ones seem like they might be "too much"?
4. **Connections.** An elegy is a poem that mourns and laments the death of an individual. What are the features of elegies? What are examples of famous elegies? Read two or three elegies and explain how Jonson's poem compares to the others you have read.

Before the Birth of One of Her Children

Anne Bradstreet

Lee Beel/Alamy

In 1630, Anne Bradstreet (1612/13–1678) and her husband, Simon, the son of a nonconformist minister, sailed to Massachusetts from England with Anne's parents on the *Arabella*, the flagship of the Massachusetts Bay Company. With *The Tenth Muse Lately Sprung Up in America* (1650) — published in England, possibly without her knowledge — she became the first female poet in America. Bradstreet's remarkable poetry consists of thirty-five short reflective poems, explicit in their description of familial and marital love.

KEY CONTEXT The Puritan community disdained and even punished female intellectual ambition; nevertheless, Anne Bradstreet, whose husband and father both served as governors of the Massachusetts Bay Colony, was a respected published poet. The mother of eight children, she writes of the dangers of impending childbirth and her faith in "Before the Birth of One of Her Children."

All things within this fading world hath end,
Adversity doth still our joys attend;
No ties so strong, no friends so dear and sweet,
But with death's parting blow is sure to meet.
The sentence past is most irrevocable,
A common thing, yet oh, inevitable.
How soon, my Dear, death may my steps attend,
How soon't may be thy lot to lose thy friend,
We both are ignorant, yet love bids me
These farewell lines to recommend to thee,
That when that knot's untied that made us one,
I may seem thine, who in effect am none.
And if I see not half my days that's due,
What nature would, God grant to yours and you;
The many faults that well you know I have
Let be interred in my oblivious grave;
If any worth or virtue were in me,
Let that live freshly in thy memory
And when thou feel'st no grief, as I no harms,
Yet love thy dead, who long lay in thine arms,
And when thy loss shall be repaid with gains
Look to my little babes, my dear remains.
And if thou love thyself, or loved'st me,
These O protect from stepdame's injury.
And if chance to thine eyes shall bring this verse,
With some sad sighs honor my absent hearse;
And kiss this paper for thy love's dear sake,
Who with salt tears this last farewell did take. ■

1678

Understanding and Interpreting

1. **AP® Character and Narration.** Restate the following line into simple language: "Adversity doth still our joys attend" (l. 2). What might the speaker mean by that statement in general, and how might it apply to her situation in particular?
2. **AP® Narration.** In lines 23–24, the speaker says, "And if thou love thyself or loved'st me / These O protect from stepdame's injury." Who needs protection from "stepdame's injury"? What is unusual about this appeal to her husband? Consider whose interests she foregrounds in line 23.
3. **AP® Character and Narration.** How would you characterize the reference to "stepdame's injury" (l. 24)? Is it a statement of resignation, a warning, an appeal, a challenge, or something else?
4. **AP® Narration.** How do you interpret the speaker's tone in light of her subject matter? How does this tone reveal her attitude toward the prospect of her own death in childbirth?

5. **AP® Character and Narration.** The speaker in the poem presents herself in several different roles. What are these? At what point(s) in the poem does she suggest two or more roles are complementary?

6. **AP® Narration.** Based on your interpretation of the poem, what does the speaker see as her legacy? Consider multiple concepts in your response.

Analyzing Language, Style, and Structure

1. **Vocabulary in Context.** In lines 5–6, Bradstreet states the circumstances of this poem straightforwardly: "The sentence past is most irrevocable, / A common thing, yet oh, inevitable." How does "irrevocable" in this context underscore her metaphor of death as a "sentence"?

2. **AP® Structure and Figurative Language.** How do you interpret the paradox in lines 21–22? How does the double meaning of "remains" contribute to the paradox?

3. **AP® Structure.** Although the poem is presented without stanza breaks, it falls into sections. Where do you notice shifts? How does each section help develop the speaker's argument?

4. **AP® Structure, Narration, and Figurative Language.** Although this is a poem about mortality, Bradstreet's language choices often reflect a focus on life on earth. What perspective on the future do these diction and imagery choices convey?

5. **AP® Structure and Narration.** How would you describe the tone of this poem? How do the rhyming couplets and meter contribute to the development of the tone?

Topics for Composing

1. **AP® FRQ** **Poetry Analysis.** In Anne Bradstreet's "Before the Birth of One of Her Children," published in 1678, the speaker offers a clear-eyed depiction of the dangers and joys of motherhood. Read the poem carefully. Then, in a well-written essay, analyze how Bradstreet uses literary elements and techniques to convey her complex perspective on the experience of motherhood.

2. **AP® Literary Argumentation.** In her biography of Anne Bradstreet entitled *Mistress Bradstreet: The Untold Life of America's First Poet* (2005), Charlotte Gordon writes of this poem: "Although in this poem she vividly imagines the aftermath of her own death, Anne writes with the same passion that inspired her other love poems to her husband." To what extent do you agree with this interpretation of the poem? Use evidence from the text to support your response.

3. **AP® Literary Argumentation.** In "Before the Birth of One of Her Children," the speaker faces the possibility of death in childbirth. Is she a conventional woman of her time whose self-sacrificing concerns stay within her immediate family, or does she express ideas about marriage and motherhood that seem ahead of her time? Support your position with specific references to the text of the poem.

4. **Connections.** Anne Bradstreet had borne eight children, had lost two, and was battling tuberculosis when she wrote this poem. Conduct some research into her life and experiences. How does knowing these details influence your understanding of the poem?

5. **Speaking and Listening.** Some readers of "Before the Birth of One of Her Children" have noted that Bradstreet links herself to a powerful literary tradition through her use of rhyming couplets, known as heroic couplets, which were a standard feature of epic poetry, to depict her willingness to unflinchingly risk death. This view suggests that Bradstreet implicitly draws

an analogy between the heroism of motherhood to larger-than-life classical heroes fighting wars or leading nations. Working in small groups, discuss the extent to which you agree with this interpretation; be prepared to share — and defend — your position to your classmates.

6. **Connections.** Bradstreet's choice to write about motherhood was unusual in the seventeenth century; in fact, for centuries to come, poetry about motherhood was often assumed to be no more than sentimental verse. However, poetry about pregnancy, birth, and motherhood has come to be taken seriously as fitting subjects for poetry. Find and discuss a poem about motherhood written between 1960 and today that you interpret as a contemporary, authentic view of some dimension of motherhood. How does its perspective compare to Bradstreet's?
7. **Multimodal.** Identify or create a series of images that capture the mood and tone of "Before the Birth of One of Her Children." You need not limit your choices to realistic figurative images or images from one era. Caption each image with a word, phrase, or line(s) from the poem.

We Are Seven

William Wordsworth

IanDagnall Computing/Alamy

William Wordsworth (1770–1850), one of the most famous and influential Romantic poets, was widely known for his reverence of nature and the power of his lyrical verse. With Samuel Taylor Coleridge, he published *Lyrical Ballads* in 1798; the collection includes Wordsworth's "Lines Composed a Few Miles above Tintern Abbey." Among Wordsworth's other most famous works are "The World Is Too Much with Us" (p. 1277), a sonnet; "Ode: Intimations of Immortality"; and "The Prelude, Or Growth of a Poet's Mind," an autobiographical poem. "We Are Seven" first appeared in *Lyrical Ballads*.

— A simple Child,
That lightly draws its breath,
And feels its life in every limb,
What should it know of death?

I met a little cottage Girl:
She was eight years old, she said;
Her hair was thick with many a curl
That clustered round her head.

She had a rustic, woodland air,
And she was wildly clad:
Her eyes were fair, and very fair;
— Her beauty made me glad.

"Sisters and brothers, little Maid,
How many may you be?"
"How many? Seven in all," she said,
And wondering looked at me.

“And where are they? I pray you tell.”
She answered, “Seven are we;
And two of us at Conway dwell,
And two are gone to sea.

“Two of us in the church-yard lie,
My sister and my brother;
And, in the church-yard cottage, I
Dwell near them with my mother.”

“You say that two at Conway dwell,
And two are gone to sea,
Yet ye are seven! — I pray you tell,
Sweet Maid, how this may be.”

Then did the little Maid reply,
“Seven boys and girls are we;
Two of us in the church-yard lie,
Beneath the church-yard tree.”

“You run about, my little Maid,
Your limbs they are alive;
If two are in the church-yard laid,
Then ye are only five.”

“Their graves are green, they may be seen,”
The little Maid replied,
“Twelve steps or more from my mother’s door,
And they are side by side.

“My stockings there I often knit,
My kerchief there I hem;
And there upon the ground I sit,
And sing a song to them.

“And often after sunset, Sir,
When it is light and fair,
I take my little porringer,
And eat my supper there.

“The first that died was sister Jane;
In bed she moaning lay,
Till God released her of her pain;
And then she went away.

"So in the church-yard she was laid;
And, when the grass was dry,
Together round her grave we played,
My brother John and I.

"And when the ground was white with snow,
And I could run and slide,
My brother John was forced to go,
And he lies by her side."

"How many are you, then," said I,
"If they two are in heaven?"
Quick was the little Maid's reply,
"O Master! we are seven."

"But they are dead; those two are dead!
Their spirits are in heaven!"
'T was throwing words away; for still
The little Maid would have her will,
And said, "Nay, we are seven!" ■

1798

Understanding and Interpreting

1. **AP® Character and Narration.** What concrete details help the reader picture the "little cottage Girl" (l. 5)? For instance, what does the speaker mean in line 11 when he says, "Her eyes were fair, and very fair"?
2. **AP® Setting.** Why is the setting important to the tale the speaker tells?
3. **AP® Character and Narration.** Does William Wordsworth present the girl sympathetically or critically? Explain.
4. **AP® Character and Narration.** How would you characterize the little girl's attitude toward her dead sister and brother? What is the logic leading to her conclusion that "we are seven"?
5. **AP® Character and Narration.** What does the girl understand about the nature of family and the death of family members that the ostensibly more experienced speaker has yet to learn? By the end, has she altered the speaker's view?

Analyzing Language, Style, and Structure

1. **Vocabulary in Context.** What is the meaning of the word "cottage" in line 5? What do you think a cottage girl is? What does her identity as a cottage girl mean to the speaker?
2. **AP® Structure and Narration.** In the first stanza, the speaker raises a question that is explored in subsequent stanzas through a dialogue between him and the little girl. Note how the speaker asks again and again how many children are in the little girl's family and how her answer never wavers. What effect does this repetition have on your understanding of the poem?
3. **AP® Character and Structure.** How do the poem's regular rhyme and rhythm scheme help develop the character of the little girl?

4. **AP® Narration and Figurative Language.** What examples of figurative language, including imagery, do you find? How does Wordsworth use these language choices to develop the little girl's argument?

Topics for Composing

1. **AP® FRQ Poetry Analysis.** In William Wordsworth's "We Are Seven," published in 1798, the speaker comes to a new understanding of mortality through a conversation with a little girl. Read the poem carefully. Then, in a well-written essay, analyze how Wordsworth uses literary elements and techniques to portray a shift in the speaker's attitude.
2. **AP® Literary Argumentation.** In his preface to *Lyrical Ballads* (1802), Wordsworth stated that he wanted his poetry to be written in "the real language of men," not the more elaborate language associated with elevated literary efforts. How well does "We Are Seven" achieve this goal?
3. **AP® Literary Argumentation.** How does the poem answer the question it asks in the first stanza? Use evidence from the poem to support your response.
4. **AP® Literary Argumentation.** How might "We Are Seven" be read as a conversation between logic and emotion? Which side are you on?
5. **Research.** Wordsworth was the preeminent Romantic poet. Do some research on Romantic poetry, focusing on how this literature deals with mortality, nature, and transcendence. What elements of "We Are Seven" are particularly emblematic of Romantic poetry?

Mother to Son

Langston Hughes

Library of Congress, Prints & Photographs Division, Carl Van Vechten Collection, LC-USZ62-42503

Langston Hughes (1902–1967) grew up in the African American community of Joplin, Missouri. He spent a year at Columbia University and became involved with the Harlem Renaissance movement, but was shocked by the endemic racial prejudice at the university and subsequently left. Hughes traveled abroad for several years before returning to the United States and completing his BA at Pennsylvania's Lincoln University in 1929, after which he returned to Harlem for the remainder of his life. His first volume of poetry, *The Weary Blues*, was published in 1926. His first novel, *Not Without Laughter* (1930), won the Harmon Gold Medal for literature. He also wrote children's poetry, musicals, and opera.

KEY CONTEXT "Mother to Son" was first published in 1922 in *The Crisis*, the magazine of the National Association for the Advancement of Colored People (NAACP). Its mission, as stated on its website, remains as "a quarterly journal of politics, culture, civil rights and history that seeks to educate and challenge its readers about issues facing African-Americans and other communities of color." The following poem is the original version published in 1922. When this poem appeared in his 1926 collection of poems, Hughes had altered the punctuation, replacing semicolons with periods.

Well, son, I'll tell you:
Life for me ain't been no crystal stair.
It's had tacks in it,
And splinters,
And boards torn up,
And places with no carpet on the floor —
Bare;
But all the time
I'se been a-climbin' on,
And reachin' landin's,
And turning' corners,
And sometimes goin' in the dark,
Where there ain't been no light.
So boy, don't you turn back;
Don't you sit down on the steps,
'Cause you finds it's kinder hard;
Don't you fall now —
For I'se still goin', honey,
I'se still climbin',
And life for me ain't been no crystal stair. ■

1922

Understanding and Interpreting

1. **AP® Narration.** What is the overall message the mother is trying to convey to her son?
2. **AP® Character and Narration.** Based on details in the poem, how would you characterize the mother?
3. **AP® Narration.** What specific details does the mother provide or anticipate about her son's struggle?
4. **AP® Character and Narration.** How old do you think the speaker's son is? Does he seem to be at some sort of crossroads? Cite specific textual evidence to support your interpretation.
5. **AP® Narration.** Is the mother lecturing, apologizing, advising, pleading, showing affection, criticizing, or some combination of these? How would you characterize the tone of the poem?

Analyzing Language, Style, and Structure

1. **Vocabulary in Context.** The repeated refrain in this poem is "Life for me ain't been no crystal stair." On a literal level, "crystal" is a clear hard mineral, but what figurative connotations does Hughes rely on to make this image so memorable?
2. **AP® Structure, Narration, and Figurative Language.** The poem's speaker employs a conceit to explain her life to her son. What do you think the "crystal stair" (l. 2) symbolizes? Why do you think the poet has chosen to repeat this image in the final line? What might the details of tacks, splinters, landings, and corners represent?
3. **AP® Character and Narration.** What effect do colloquial expressions and dialect have on your understanding of the speaker? What effect do they have on the meaning of the poem?

4. **AP® Narration and Figurative Language.** What literal and figurative references to light and dark do you find in this poem? How does this imagery add to its power?
5. **AP® Structure and Narration.** Even though the poem is presented without stanza breaks, there are "turns," or shifts. What are they? How do these breaks influence or emphasize meaning?
6. **AP® Structure and Narration.** In a later version of the poem, Hughes replaced the semicolons with periods, thus signaling a stronger separation between ideas than the semicolon, which links through balance. What different effect does this change have on your interpretation of the poem as it was originally published in 1922?

Topics for Composing

1. **AP® FRQ Poetry Analysis.** In Langston Hughes's "Mother to Son," published in 1922, the speaker, a mother, offers advice to her son through the lens of her own experiences. Read the poem carefully. Then, in a well-written essay, analyze how Hughes uses literary elements and techniques to convey the complexities of the world the speaker wants her son to navigate successfully.
2. **AP® Literary Argumentation.** How relevant is the central message of "Mother to Son" today? Over the past century, some have argued that the mother is a stereotype whose willingness to work within an unjust system undermines her hopes. Others have interpreted her message as both clear-eyed and courageous, an honest accounting of the racism imbued in everyday life. What is your position on the enduring value of this poem? Consider the language choices and symbolism as you develop your response.
3. **Connections.** There is debate as to whether Hughes actually agreed with the approach the speaker in "Mother to Son" advocates. The speakers of other poems by Hughes often convey a more radical response to racism. Consider "I, Too, Sing America" or "The Negro Speaks of Rivers," or choose another of his poems to compare with "Mother to Son." Discuss the extent of similarity in the tone, the poetic techniques, and the persona of the speaker in each poem.
4. **Speaking and Listening.** Develop your own interpretation of what the son has said to the mother to bring about this poem. Write or perform it, share with a classmate or a small group, and discuss your different views of the son's situation.

My Papa's Waltz

Theodore Roethke

Bettmann/Getty Images

Theodore Roethke (1908–1963) spent his early years in the family greenhouse business in Saginaw, Michigan, which brought him close to nature and to his father, who died suddenly when Roethke was fifteen. After graduating from the University of Michigan, he did brief stints at law school and at Harvard University before the Great Depression compelled him to find work teaching at Lafayette College. Roethke won numerous prizes for his work throughout the 1950s and 1960s, including National Book Awards for both *Words for the Wind* (1957) and *The Far Field* (1964). "My Papa's Waltz" is his most famous, and oft-interpreted, poem.

The whiskey on your breath
Could make a small boy dizzy;
But I hung on like death:
Such waltzing was not easy.

We romped until the pans
Slid from the kitchen shelf;
My mother's countenance
Could not unfrown itself.

The hand that held my wrist
Was battered on one knuckle;
At every step you missed
My right ear scraped a buckle.

You beat time on my head
With a palm caked hard by dirt,
Then waltzed me off to bed
Still clinging to your shirt. ■

1948

Understanding and Interpreting

1. **AP® Setting and Narration.** What is the situation depicted in "My Papa's Waltz"?
2. **AP® Character and Narration.** How is the father characterized in the poem? Support your answer with specific references to the poem.
3. **AP® Character and Narration.** How would you characterize the relationship between the father and the son in this poem?
4. **AP® Character and Narration.** How do you interpret the lines "My mother's countenance / Could not unfrown itself" (ll. 7–8)? Is she angry? jealous? worried? frightened? disapproving?
5. **AP® Character and Narration.** Why do you think the mother doesn't take action or intercede on the son's behalf?

Analyzing Language, Style, and Structure

1. **Vocabulary in Context.** What is the meaning of the word "countenance" in line 7? Here it is used as a noun, but consider also its meaning as a verb. How are both connotations fitting in the context of this poem?
2. **AP® Narration and Figurative Language.** Consider the two figures of speech in the poem: the simile of "hung on like death" (l. 3) and the metaphor of "waltzing" throughout the poem. What do they add to the storyline of the poem?
3. **AP® Structure and Narration.** What does the title, "My Papa's Waltz," bring to the poem? What would change if the poem were titled, for example, "My Papa" or "Dancing with My Father"?
4. **AP® Structure and Narration.** What is the effect of the regular rhyme and rhythm scheme of the poem? In what ways does it mimic a waltz?

Topics for Composing

1. **AP® FRQ Poetry Analysis.** In Theodore Roethke's "My Papa's Waltz," published in 1948, the speaker remembers an evening with his father when he was a young child. Read the poem carefully. Then, in a well-written essay, analyze how Roethke uses literary elements and techniques to portray the complexity of the relationship between father and son.
2. **AP® Literary Argumentation.** Some interpret this poem to be about an abusive father-son relationship, while others read it quite differently. How do you interpret it? Use textual evidence from the poem to explain your reading.
3. **Connections.** Manuscripts show that Theodore Roethke started writing this poem as a portrait of a daughter and her father. Explain why you think having a girl at the center of this poem would or would not affect your response to it.
4. **Connections.** In "My Papa's Waltz" and "Those Winter Sundays" by Robert Hayden (p. 995), each speaker contemplates his fraught relationship with his father, sharing memories of their interactions. Read both poems carefully. Then, write an essay in which you compare and contrast the poems, analyzing the techniques each poet uses to depict the speaker's attitude toward his father.
5. **Connections.** Poet, critic, and teacher Edward Byrne, writing in the *Valparaiso Review*, states that while contemporary readings of "My Papa's Waltz" interpret it as about alcoholism and child abuse, he finds himself "repeatedly rising to the defense of the parents in the poem" because he thinks we should read it in the context of its historical setting: "the late-1940s, [when] . . . the definition of child abuse would not have been as broad as that expressed by my students, and a man returning home with whiskey on his breath after a day of work would not immediately raise great concern since it would not have been very unusual." Does that argument change your view of the poem? To what extent should the time period in which a work was written affect our interpretation of it?

Those Winter Sundays

Robert Hayden

Pach Brothers/Corbis /Getty Images

Born Asa Bundy Sheffey in Detroit, Michigan, Robert Hayden (1913–1980) attended Detroit City College (now Wayne State University) before studying under W. H. Auden in the graduate English program at the University of Michigan. In 1976, he was appointed consultant in poetry to the Library of Congress, a post that was the forerunner to that of U.S. poet laureate. His first volume, *Heart-Shape in the Dust* (1940), took its voice from the Harlem Renaissance. Later work continued to garner critical praise, including his epic poem on the *Amistad* mutiny, "Middle Passage," and *A Ballad of Remembrance* (1962), which includes his most famous poem, "Those Winter Sundays."

Sundays too my father got up early
and put his clothes on in the blueblack cold,
then with cracked hands that ached
from labor in the weekday weather made
banked fires blaze. No one ever thanked him.

I'd wake and hear the cold splintering, breaking.
When the rooms were warm, he'd call,
and slowly I would rise and dress,
fearing the chronic angers of that house,

Speaking indifferently to him,
who had driven out the cold
and polished my good shoes as well.
What did I know, what did I know
of love's austere and lonely offices? ■

1962

Understanding and Interpreting

1. **AP® Character, Setting, and Narration.** What does the first stanza suggest about the father's days? What do readers learn about the kind of work he does?
2. **AP® Character, Setting, and Narration.** What does the line "fearing the chronic angers of that house" (l. 9) suggest about the son's relationship with his father and the kind of home he grew up in?
3. **AP® Character and Narration.** What does the poem convey about the way the father shows his love?
4. **AP® Character and Narration.** What is the son's feeling about his father? Could this poem be read as a son's belated thank you? Explain. What does the adult speaker in the poem understand about his father that he did not as a child?
5. **AP® Setting, Structure, and Narration.** What are the different time frames of this poem, and when does the poem shift from flashback to present day? How does Robert Hayden keep this shift from seeming abrupt?

Analyzing Language, Style, and Structure

1. **Vocabulary in Context.** The speaker says he addresses his father "indifferently" (l. 10). How does this behavior inform the adult speaker's understanding of his father's love?
2. **AP® Structure and Narration.** The syntax of lines 3–5 and the enjambment between them blend some of the details together. How do you interpret these lines, and what is the effect of this blending? What does the phrase "made / banked fires blaze" (ll. 4–5) describe?
3. **AP® Narration and Figurative Language.** What is the meaning of "love's austere and lonely offices" (l. 14)? What effect does Hayden achieve by choosing such an uncommon, somewhat archaic term as "offices"?
4. **AP® Setting, Narration, and Figurative Language.** What is the tone of this poem? How do the specific details of the setting the speaker describes contribute to that tone? Consider also how the literal descriptions act as metaphors. What, for instance, is "blueblack cold" (l. 2)?
5. **AP® Structure and Narration.** Notice the poem's shift between father and son, from "him" to "I." How does this alternation contribute to your understanding of the speaker's perspective on his childhood?
6. **AP® Structure and Narration.** What contrasts do you see in the poem? Identify at least three, and discuss how they work individually and collectively.

7. **AP® Narration and Figurative Language.** How does Hayden utilize sound, including alliteration and consonance, to emphasize certain ideas?
8. **AP® Structure and Narration.** What is the effect of the repetition in the last two lines?
9. **AP® Structure and Narration.** While "Those Winter Sundays" does not quite fit the sonnet form, it does borrow a few structural elements common to sonnets. For example, how does Hayden emphasize ideas by using ten syllables in some lines and not others? How do the final two lines offer a turn of thought that sheds light on the previous twelve lines?

Topics for Composing

1. AP® FRQ **Poetry Analysis.** In Robert Hayden's "Those Winter Sundays," published in 1962, the speaker reflects on the relationship he had with his father during his childhood. Read the poem carefully. Then, in a well-written essay, analyze how Hayden uses literary elements and techniques to convey the complex understanding the speaker develops of his father.
2. **Connections.** In poetry, the lyric is usually a short poem expressing personal feelings and may take the form of a song set to music. What music would you choose to convey the tone and themes of "Those Winter Sundays"?
3. **Speaking and Listening.** Hayden's poem presents a somewhat traditional father/son relationship of an earlier era. Discuss as a class whether you think communication norms for children and their parents have moved away from what Hayden terms "austere and lonely offices." If such relationships have changed, why do you think they have? If they haven't, what do you think would help parents and their children develop closer relationships and a better understanding of each other's experiences?
4. **Creative Writing.** What have you, like the speaker, come to understand about your parents' daily lives that you'd previously not understood or appreciated? Write a poem modeled after Hayden's or a letter expressing the appreciation you have come to have for one or both of your parents.

A Mother's Mouth Illuminated

Threa Almontaser

Threa Almontase

Yemeni American poet Threa Almontaser (b. 1993) was born in New York City. She has an MFA from North Carolina State University and currently teaches English to refugees and immigrants in Raleigh, North Carolina. Her debut book of poetry, *The Wild Fox of Yemen* (2021), received the Walt Whitman Award from the American Academy of Poets.

PBS taught us English: Sesame Street, Between the Lions, Mr. Rogers.
We passed each learned word between one another —

an umbilical cord of lessons connecting us
to our new terrain. When our mom probed us for words,

we shrugged her off, *You don't need it.* Dishcloth clenched
in her fist, she huffed, *No matter how high the hawk flies,*

it's never too late to turn back to the tree.
This is likely a mistranslation. She bled open

book spines with her teeth. Arrowed her mouth
to the Reading Rainbow channel. Rerouted herself

to a place with less mourning, more light.
One evening, she practiced her halting English

on our dad. He stopped her with a hand,
unable to grasp the gibberish, her eager words

tinged with the kinky thickness of a borrowed
speech. *Just leave the English to me,* he said.

The rats north of 140th street were making him
cruel. We insisted, *Don't worry about it. A woman*

in the house all day, you won't need it. It's true
she was sequestered on the top floor of our apartment,

spent her days cooking and cleaning, lucky to get a call
card and phone her family back home. What friends

did she have other than us? We were fitting in
ourselves, had no time to be the companion

of a lonely adult who used to think herself fluent,
tongue dined with five-star speeches. From then on,

she kept to herself. Didn't utter a single word
in any language until our dad left to work

at a chicken market in the Bronx, when she fled
into the screen. Into the hood where muppets

lived. Then she plugged in her belly-string
and feasted, her whispers desperate for the words,

for the strange lions and big yellow bird,
trying to illuminate their meanings. ■

2020

Exploring the Text

1. How do you interpret the title "A Mother's Mouth Illuminated"? What illuminates the mother's mouth? What is the result of this illumination?
2. Consider the speakers' comparison of the way the siblings passed words from PBS between each other through "an umbilical cord of lessons" (l. 3). What does it suggest about the importance of the lessons to the speakers? How does this figurative language make the act of shrugging off their mother ironic?
3. How does the mother's declaration in lines 6–7 that "*No matter how high the hawk flies, / it's never too late to turn back to the tree*" relate to the behavior the speakers describe in lines 8–10?
4. What do the speakers mean by "tongue dined with five-star speeches" in line 26? What does this expression emphasize about the mother's life before and after immigrating to the United States?
5. How is the mother both literally and figuratively silenced throughout the poem? How does this silencing relate to the meaning of the poem as a whole?

Making Connections

1. Compare and contrast the tone of the speakers in "Those Winter Sundays" and "A Mother's Mouth Illuminated." Consider, too, shifts in tone and what those shifts indicate about the speakers' understanding of their parents years later.
2. What do both poems convey about the role of communication among family members? What do they each suggest about the effects of indifference?
3. How do the parents in each poem respond to loneliness, and what role does loneliness play in the lives of the speakers and their parents?
4. The speakers of both poems comment on negative interactions among family members during their childhoods. Do you think the "angers" (l. 9) in Hayden's poem and the "cruel" (l. 18) statements in Almontaser's have similar origins? Do they lead to similar outcomes? Explain.
5. What comments do the speakers of both poems make about their expectations for their parents as children? How similar are those expectations? What do their realizations later in life convey about what it means to be a parent?

The Writer

Richard Wilbur

Bettmann/Getty Images

Richard Wilbur (1921–2017) was an American poet and translator. He grew up in New York City and graduated from Amherst College in 1942. After serving in the army during World War II, Wilbur attended graduate school at Harvard University and went on to teach at Wellesley College, Wesleyan University, and Smith College. Wilbur published thirteen poetry collections. *Things of This World* (1957) won a Pulitzer Prize and a National Book Award. Wilbur won a second Pulitzer Prize for his *New and Collected Poems* (1989). He also wrote two books of prose and translated numerous plays by the French dramatists Molière, Jean Racine, and Pierre Corneille. Wilbur's poetry often illuminates epiphany in everyday experiences, a quality on full display in "The Writer."

In her room at the prow[1] of the house
Where light breaks, and the windows are tossed with linden,
My daughter is writing a story.

I pause in the stairwell, hearing
From her shut door a commotion of typewriter-keys
Like a chain hauled over a gunwale.[2]

Young as she is, the stuff
Of her life is a great cargo, and some of it heavy:
I wish her a lucky passage.

But now it is she who pauses,
As if to reject my thought and its easy figure.
A stillness greatens, in which

The whole house seems to be thinking,
And then she is at it again with a bunched clamor
Of strokes, and again is silent.

I remember the dazed starling
Which was trapped in that very room, two years ago;
How we stole in, lifted a sash

And retreated, not to affright it;
And how for a helpless hour, through the crack of the door,
We watched the sleek, wild, dark

And iridescent creature
Batter against the brilliance, drop like a glove
To the hard floor, or the desk-top.

And wait then, humped and bloody.
For the wits to try it again; and how our spirits
Rose when, suddenly sure,

It lifted off from a chair-back,
Beating a smooth course for the right window
And clearing the sill of the world.

It is always a matter, my darling,
Of life or death, as I had forgotten. I wish
What I wished you before, but harder. ■

1969

---

[1] The point at the front of a boat or ship. — Eds.
[2] The upper edge on the side of a boat. — Eds.

Understanding and Interpreting

1. **AP® Narration.** What do you think the speaker means by "easy figure" (l. 11)? Consider several possible meanings.
2. **AP® Narration.** At the end of the poem, the speaker says, "I wish / What I wished you before, but harder." What do you think that wish was? What do you think the speaker means by "but harder"?
3. **AP® Character and Narration.** Why do the speaker and his daughter each "pause" within the first four stanzas of the poem? What do the details in the poem suggest about their thoughts during their respective pauses?
4. **AP® Narration.** What do you think prompts the speaker to recall "the dazed starling" (l. 16)? Why is the starling "dazed" in the room?
5. **AP® Narration.** What is the mood of "The Writer"? What emotions do the different parts of the poem evoke in you?

Analyzing Language, Style, and Structure

1. **Vocabulary in Context.** What do you make of the word "passage" in line 9? What are some of its possible meanings? How do the word's multiple meanings help the speaker comment on the act of writing?
2. **AP® Setting, Narration, and Figurative Language.** You probably noticed that the central image of the first three stanzas of "The Writer" is the house depicted as a ship at sea. What mood does the image set? What diction choices develop that image, and how might they be connected to the poem's subject? What does the image tell you about the speaker's family life? about the life of a writer?
3. **AP® Structure, Narration, and Figurative Language.** In line 16, the poem shifts to the story of the starling in the room, which is at once literal and metaphorical. What do you think this story represents? Explain.
4. **AP® Narration and Figurative Language.** How does the simile in lines 5–6 characterize the daughter's writing? What does the word "commotion" contribute to the ideas conveyed by the simile?
5. **AP® Structure and Narration.** While Richard Wilbur foregoes a set rhyme scheme and meter in "The Writer," a structural pattern is established across each stanza. How are the stanzas similar in this poem? What might Wilbur seek to convey by structuring his poem in this manner?
6. **AP® Structure and Narration.** What is the significance of rhyming the words "starling" (l. 16) and "darling" (l. 31)?

Topics for Composing

1. **AP® FRQ** **Poetry Analysis.** In Richard Wilbur's "The Writer," published in 1969, the speaker recognizes his own limitations now that his daughter is becoming independent. Read the poem carefully. Then, in a well-written essay, analyze how Wilbur uses literary elements and techniques to portray the speaker's understanding of his new role in his daughter's life.
2. **AP® FRQ** **Poetry Analysis.** In Richard Wilbur's "The Writer," published in 1969, the speaker witnesses his daughter's struggles with the writing process. Read the poem carefully. Then, in a well-written essay, analyze how Wilbur uses literary elements and techniques to convey his attitude toward the life of a writer.

3. **AP® Literary Argumentation.** What is the connection between the speaker's attitude toward writing and his attitude toward his daughter? How do Wilbur's language choices help develop this connection?
4. **Connections.** In an interview with the *Paris Review*, Wilbur said that "there is an exploitable and interesting relationship between something perceived out there and something in the way of incipient meaning within you." How does "The Writer" take the relationship between "something perceived out there" and something within the speaker to a level beyond just resemblance?
5. **Creative Writing.** How might the speaker's daughter recall the starling trapped in her room? What significance would she ascribe to that event? Write a journal entry from the perspective of the daughter recalling the incident. What might make her think about it again? What does it represent to her?
6. **Speaking and Listening.** Work with a partner to develop and perform a scene between the speaker and his daughter after she discovers the poem he has written. How would she respond to "The Writer"? What questions might she ask him? How would he respond?

Combing

Gladys Cardiff

Courtesy of Gladys H. Cardiff

Poet Gladys Cardiff (b. 1942) was born in Montana and raised in Seattle, Washington, by her Irish-Welsh mother and Cherokee father. A member of the Eastern Band of Cherokee, she has an MFA from the University of Washington, where she studied with poet Theodore Roethke, and a PhD from Western Michigan University. She taught at Oakland University from 1999 to 2013. She is the author of two collections of poetry: *To Frighten a Storm* (1976) and *A Bare Unpainted Table* (1999).

Bending, I bow my head
and lay my hands upon
her hair, combing, and think
how women do this for
each other. My daughter's hair
curls against the comb,
wet and fragrant — orange
parings. Her face, downcast,
is quiet for one so young.

I take her place. Beneath
my mother's hands I feel
the braids drawn up tight
as piano wires and singing,
vinegar-rinsed. Sitting
before the oven I hear
the orange coils tick
the early hour before school.

She combed her grandmother
Mathilda's hair using
a comb made out of bone.
Mathilda rocked her oak wood
chair, her face downcast,
intent on tearing rags
in strips to braid a cotton
rug from bits of orange
and brown. A simple act
Preparing hair. Something
women do for each other,
plaiting the generations. ■

1976

Understanding and Interpreting

1. **AP® Narration.** You may have noticed that each stanza references something orange. What does the speaker refer to in each instance? Aside from their color, how are all of these items connected?
2. **AP® Narration.** What does the speaker mean when she says that braiding hair is "[s] omething / women do for each other, / plaiting the generations" (ll. 27–29)?
3. **AP® Narration.** Across how many generations does the braiding in "Combing" take place? How does this time span speak to the poem's larger themes?

Analyzing Language, Style, and Structure

1. **Vocabulary in Context.** The speaker refers to the "orange / parings" of her daughter's hair in lines 7–8 of the first stanza. Why might she have used "parings" instead of "curls" or another word more commonly associated with hair? What do the connotations of "parings" suggest about the speaker's perspective on the significance of combing and braiding?
2. **AP® Structure and Narration.** What is the purpose of beginning the poem in the present and moving into the past? How does this structure reflect the actions the poem describes?
3. **AP® Structure and Narration.** How does the perspective of the speaker shift in line 10? How does this shift illustrate the speaker's larger concerns?
4. **AP® Narration and Figurative Language.** What does the speaker's musical diction in line 13 contribute to her tone?
5. **AP® Structure, Narration, and Figurative Language.** How does Gladys Cardiff's use of imagery throughout the poem emphasize different ideas in each stanza? For example, consider the references to sound in stanzas 1 and 2. What do the contrasts between stanzas convey?

Topics for Composing

1. **AP® FRQ Poetry Analysis.** In Gladys Cardiff's "Combing," published in 1976, the speaker describes what braiding hair means to her. Read the poem carefully. Then, in a well-written essay, analyze how Cardiff uses literary elements and techniques to convey the speaker's complex understanding of how braiding hair connects the women in her family across generations.

2. **Multimodal.** What forms of art, traditions, or pastimes connect people in your family across generations? Write an essay, create a work of art, or write a poem expressing the significance of a similar practice in your family as something that connects people across time and space.
3. **Research.** What is the history of braiding hair, and in what other contexts and cultures do people use braided materials? Research the rich history of braids and the practice of braiding in American Indian traditions, particularly the Cherokee, to better understand their significance in the poem "Combing." Alternatively, research a different culture in which braiding plays an important role. How does your research expand your understanding of the poem, especially its cross-generational references?
4. **Speaking and Listening.** Engage in a small group or class discussion in which you first discuss what hairstyles mean to the speaker and the other women in her family. Then, extend the discussion to incorporate your experiences and those of your family members. How do you express yourself or honor your familial or cultural traditions through your appearance? How do these choices embody "something / [people] do for each other" (ll. 27–28) across "generations" (l. 29)?

The Black Walnut Tree

Mary Oliver

Frederick M. Brown/Getty Images

Mary Oliver (1935–2019) was born in Maple Heights, Ohio, an affluent suburb of Cleveland. She attended Ohio State University and Vassar College, but did not complete her degree. Nonetheless, she held several teaching positions at colleges throughout her life. She published her first volume of poetry, *No Voyage, and Other Poems*, in 1963, and in 1984 won the Pulitzer Prize with *American Primitive* (1983). She also won the Christopher Award and the L. L. Winship/PEN New England Award for *House of Light* (1990) and the National Book Award for *New and Selected Poems* (1992). Over her lifetime she published thirty-three books of poetry and four nonfiction books.

My mother and I debate:
we could sell
the black walnut tree
to the lumberman,
and pay off the mortgage.
Likely some storm anyway
will churn down its dark boughs,
smashing the house. We talk
slowly, two women trying
in a difficult time to be wise.
Roots in the cellar drains,
I say, and she replies
that the leaves are getting heavier

every year, and the fruit
harder to gather away.
But something brighter than money
moves in our blood — an edge
sharp and quick as a trowel
that wants us to dig and sow.
So we talk, but we don't do
anything. That night I dream
of my fathers out of Bohemia
filling the blue fields
of fresh and generous Ohio
with leaves and vines and orchards.
What my mother and I both know
is that we'd crawl with shame
in the emptiness we'd made
in our own and our fathers' backyard.
So the black walnut tree
swings through another year
of sun and leaping winds,
of leaves and bounding fruit,
and, month after month, the whipcrack of the mortgage. ■

1979

Understanding and Interpreting

1. **AP® Setting and Narration.** What do the details in lines 1–10 reveal about the "difficult time" (l. 10) the speaker and her mother face? What could ease their problems?
2. **AP® Setting and Narration.** What do the "storm" (l. 6), "[r]oots" (l. 11), and "leaves" (l. 13) have in common? How do they contribute to the speaker's decision-making?
3. **AP® Character and Narration.** What does the speaker mean when she says that something wants her to "dig and sow" (l. 19)? How do these verbs characterize the speaker and her mother?
4. **AP® Character and Narration.** What would lead the speaker and her mother to "crawl with shame" (l. 27)? How does this realization contribute to your interpretation of the poem's ending?

Analyzing Language, Style, and Structure

1. **Vocabulary in Context.** In context, what does the word "churn" (l. 7) mean? How is this word choice appropriate not only to describe what may happen to the tree but also to describe how the speaker and her mother are feeling?
2. **AP® Structure and Narration.** What is the function of the colon at the end of line 1? In which line of the poem does their "debate" (l. 1) end?

3. **AP® Structure and Narration.** How does the word "But" (l. 16) serve as a volta, or shift, in the poem? What role does line 16 play in the speaker and her mother's deliberation?
4. **AP® Setting, Narration, and Figurative Language.** What is the significance of the dream in lines 21–25? How does the imagery in line 25 compare to how nature is depicted earlier in the poem?
5. **AP® Narration and Figurative Language.** To what does the "emptiness" in line 28 refer? How is it both literal and figurative?
6. **AP® Figurative Language.** How does the imagery in the poem's final sentence juxtapose the walnut tree and the mortgage? What is the effect of breaking whipcrack across two lines?

Topics for Composing

1. **AP® FRQ Poetry Analysis.** In Mary Oliver's "The Black Walnut Tree," published in 1979, the speaker considers the value of her family's black walnut tree. Read the poem carefully. Then, in a well-written essay, analyze how Oliver uses literary elements and techniques to convey the significance of the tree to the speaker and her mother.
2. **AP® FRQ Poetry Analysis.** In Mary Oliver's "The Black Walnut Tree," published in 1979, the speaker contemplates the significance of her father's black walnut tree. Read the poem carefully. Then, in a well-written essay, analyze how Oliver uses literary elements and techniques to convey her complex perspective on family heritage.
3. **AP® Literary Argumentation.** The speaker and her mother consider whether they should sell their tree to help pay their mortgage. Do the two women arrive at a conclusion by the end of the poem? Has the fate of the tree been determined? Support your position with evidence from the text.
4. **Connections.** Read Hafizah Geter's "The Widower" on page 1026. How does the significance of the tree in that poem compare to that of Mary Oliver's tree in this poem?
5. **Speaking and Listening.** Should the black walnut tree be sold to the "lumberman" (l. 4)? Determine your stance on this issue, and gather support for your position. Debate this issue with a partner who holds an opposing view. What did your partner prompt you to consider? How is your opinion shaped by this discussion?

Pokeberries

Ruth Stone

John Blanding/Boston Globe/Getty Images

Although Ruth Stone (1915–2011) wrote poetry throughout her life, she did not become widely recognized until the publication of her tenth collection, 1999's *Ordinary Words*, when she was eighty-four. Born in Roanoke, Virginia, Stone attended the University of Illinois at Urbana-Champaign. A resident of rural Vermont for most of her life, Stone taught at numerous universities. She published thirteen books of poetry, including *In the Next Galaxy* (2002), which won the National Book Award for Poetry, and *What Loves Come To: New and Selected Poems* (2008), which was a finalist for the Pulitzer Prize. After her death at age ninety-six, Stone's heirs established a foundation to convert her longtime residence in Goshen, Vermont, into a writer's retreat.

KEY CONTEXT Pokeweed is a perennial herb with magenta stems and berries and lance-shaped leaves that typically grows anywhere between four and twelve feet tall. While some birds eat the pokeberries, they are poisonous to humans. Despite the toxicity of its berries, boiled pokeweed leaves have long been a survival food for poor communities in Appalachia and the American South. Some research has also been conducted into the possible medicinal benefits of this herb.

I started out in the Virginia mountains
with my grandma's pansy bed
and my Aunt Maud's dandelion wine.
We lived on greens and back-fat and biscuits.
My Aunt Maud scrubbed right through the linoleum.
My daddy was a Northerner who played drums
and chewed tobacco and gambled.
He married my mama on the rebound.
Who would want an ignorant hill girl with red hair?
They took a Pullman[1] up to Indianapolis
and someone stole my daddy's wallet.
My whole life has been stained with pokeberries.
No man seemed right for me. I was awkward
until I found a good wood-burning stove.
There is no use asking what it means.
With my first piece of ready cash I bought my own
place in Vermont; kerosene lamps, dirt road.
I'm sticking here like a porcupine up a tree.
Like the one our neighbor shot. Its bones and skin
hung there for three years in the orchard.
No amount of knowledge can shake my grandma out of me;
or my Aunt Maud; or my mama, who didn't just bite an apple
with her big white teeth. She split it in two. ■

1987

[1] Railroad sleeper cars, named for the Pullman Company, which operated between 1867 and 1968. — Eds.

Understanding and Interpreting

1. **AP® Character and Narration.** What is your impression of the speaker in the opening five lines of the poem?
2. **AP® Character and Narration.** What is the speaker's attitude toward her "daddy"? What is the purpose of referencing him?
3. **AP® Character and Narration.** What do you think the speaker means when she says, "My whole life has been stained with pokeberries" (l. 12)?

4. **AP® Narration.** How do you interpret lines 13–15, especially the speaker's warning, "There is no use asking what it means"? What, exactly, is "it"?
5. **AP® Narration.** What is the "knowledge" that the speaker mentions in line 22? Is this a reference to information, school or education, experience, wisdom? A combination of these? Something else?
6. **AP® Narration.** How does the poem establish the legacy of the women in the speaker's family?

Analyzing Language, Style, and Structure

1. **Vocabulary in Context.** In line 8, the speaker says that her father "married my mama on the rebound." What is the literal meaning of "rebound"? Why is Stone's informal use of it an effective choice?
2. **AP® Character, Structure, Narration, and Figurative Language.** How does Stone use food to characterize the women in her family? How does this characterization extend to the inedible pokeberries?
3. **AP® Structure and Narration.** Which line signals the largest shift in the poem? How does this structural element serve Stone's purpose?
4. **AP® Narration and Figurative Language.** How does the biblical allusion in the final lines of "Pokeberries" bring together ideas that run throughout the poem? What kind of shift does it present in the poem?
5. **AP® Narration.** What effect does Stone achieve by using informal language and colloquialisms throughout the poem? How do these choices contribute to its tone and mood?

Topics for Composing

1. AP® FRQ **Poetry Analysis.** In Ruth Stone's "Pokeberries," published in 1987, the speaker describes the lives of three generations of women in her family. Read the poem carefully. Then, in a well-written essay, analyze how Stone uses literary elements and techniques to portray the complex heritage that has shaped the speaker's character.
2. **AP® Literary Argumentation.** In "Pokeberries," the speaker describes growing up in a family of strong women who made their homes in a hardscrabble rural environment. What universal resonance does this poem have? Or do you think that one of its central characteristics is how closely tied to a particular time and place it is? Cite specific evidence from the text to support your interpretation.
3. **AP® Literary Argumentation.** In a *New York Times* article in 2003, poet Melanie Rehak described the poems of Ruth Stone: "What prevents them from becoming simply catalogs of regularity is her will to reveal the existential within the ordinary." How does "Pokeberries" — including its title — embody this statement?
4. **Multimodal.** Develop an interpretation of "Pokeberries" by selecting a series of images to accompany a reading of the poem, and record your reading as a voiceover with these images. Be prepared to lead a discussion of your interpretation.

Turtle Soup

Marilyn Chin

Courtesy of Marilyn Chin

Marilyn Chin (b. 1955) is a Chinese American poet, writer, and translator who grew up in Portland, Oregon, after her family emigrated from Hong Kong. She earned a BA from the University of Massachusetts and an MFA from the University of Iowa. Chin is the author of five books of poetry: *Dwarf Bamboo* (1987), *The Phoenix Gone, the Terrace Empty* (1994), *Rhapsody in Plain Yellow* (2002), *Hard Love Province* (2014), and *A Portrait of the Self as a Nation: New and Selected Poems* (2018). She has won numerous awards for her poetry, including the 2020 Poetry Foundation Ruth Lilly Poetry Prize. She has also published one book of interlinked stories, *Revenge of the Mooncake Vixen* (2009), and has translated works by early modern Chinese poet Ai Qing and the early modern Japanese poet Gōzō Yoshimasu.

You go home one evening tired from work,
and your mother boils you turtle soup.
Twelve hours hunched over the hearth
(who knows what else is in that cauldron).

You say, "Ma, you've poached the symbol of long life;
that turtle lived four thousand years, swam
the Wei, up the Yellow, over the Yangtze.[1]
Witnessed the Bronze Age,[2] the High Tang[3]
grazed on splendid sericulture."[4]
(So, she boils the life out of him.)

"All our ancestors have been fools.
Remember Uncle Wu[5] who rode ten thousand miles
to kill a famous Manchu[6] and ended up
with his head on a pole? Eat, child,
its liver will make you strong."

"Sometimes you're the life, sometimes the sacrifice."
Her sobbing is inconsolable.
So, you spread that gentle napkin
over your lap in decorous Pasadena.

---

[1] Rivers that are a part of the Grand Canal in China. — Eds.

[2] 3000 B.C.E.–1000 B.C.E. — Eds.

[3] Period of time during the Tang dynasty when Chinese poetry flourished. — Eds.

[4] Raising silkworms to produce silk. — Eds.

[5] Likely a reference to Wu Shifan (1663–1681), the grandson of Wu Sangui (1612–1678), a legendary Chinese military leader who betrayed both the Ming and Qing dynasties. In 1678, during a revolt against the Qing, Wu Sangui declared himself Emperor of China, but died of dysentery months later. Wu Shifan took command of his grandfather's forces, which were defeated in 1681. His head was sent to Beijing, and parts of his corpse were sent to various provinces. — Eds.

[6] A Chinese ethnic minority. — Eds.

Baby, some high priestess has got it wrong.
The golden decal on the green underbelly
says "Made in Hong Kong."

Is there nothing left but the shell
and humanity's strange inscriptions,
the songs, the rites, the oracles?

for Ben Huang ■

1993

Understanding and Interpreting

1. **AP® Narration.** Who is the speaker of "Turtle Soup"? Who is the audience — the "you" the poem addresses?
2. **AP® Character and Narration.** How do you interpret the "Made in Hong Kong" decal in line 22? What does it suggest about the speaker's opinion of authenticity? What might her mother think of it?
3. **AP® Narration.** What do you think "'Sometimes you're the life, sometimes the sacrifice'" (l. 16) means? Why does that statement cause the speaker to "spread that gentle napkin / over [her] lap in decorous Pasadena" (ll. 18–19)?
4. **AP® Character and Narration.** What does the speaker's mother's assertion — "All our ancestors have been fools" (l. 11) — suggest about the relationship between the speaker and her mother? about the mother's attitude toward the history and traditions the speaker cites?

Analyzing Language, Style, and Structure

1. **Vocabulary in Context.** What is the meaning of the word "inconsolable" in line 17? Who is inconsolable? Is it used hyperbolically here? How do you know?
2. **AP® Narration and Figurative Language.** Consider Marilyn Chin's diction choices throughout the poem. What effect do words and phrases such as "cauldron," "symbol," "sacrifice," "high priestess," "inscriptions," "rites," and "oracles" have on the mood of the poem?
3. **AP® Character, Structure, and Narration.** How does Chin's use of the pronoun "you" complicate the character of the speaker?
4. **AP® Character, Narration, and Figurative Language.** What do the references to Chinese history, art, culture, and geography in the second stanza tell us about the speaker?
5. **AP® Structure and Narration.** What is the effect of the parentheses in the last lines of the first and second stanzas? Why do you think Chin chose to use them?
6. **AP® Structure and Narration.** How does the poet move from the scene of her mother cooking a meal to commenting on "humanity's strange inscriptions / the songs, the rites, the oracles" (ll. 24–25)?
7. **AP® Narration and Figurative Language.** What role does food — the turtle soup — and the idea of nourishment play in the poem?

Topics for Composing

1. **AP® FRQ Poetry Analysis.** In Marilyn Chin's "Turtle Soup," published in 1993, the speaker considers her relationship to her mother and their shared heritage. Read the poem carefully. Then, in a well-written essay, analyze how Chin uses literary elements and techniques to convey the role of food in tradition and family ties.

2. **Connections.** Marilyn Chin has noted how she connects her bicultural identity and poetic form in her work: "I consider myself a political poet, yes, but I am also crazy about formal experimentation. . . . And then there are all the possibilities with hybridization/cross-fertilization. How exciting to have this great opportunity to make a 'political' statement about my bicultural identity by exacting my ideas with hybridized forms. . . . I often put a drop of yellow blood in conventional form to assert my bicultural identity. . . . To disrupt the canonical order." How does "Turtle Soup" disrupt the canonical order? What "political" statement does it make via its form?
3. **Connections.** In an interview, Chin was asked about the wound that heroes in every story have that incites them to action. She replied that her wound is her mother, whom she felt sacrificed her life and was destroyed by the "Confucian system by this male-dominated world." Chin said she "needed somehow to seek revenge for her." She explained that she became a feminist because of the feelings she had for her mother's generation and for her mother in particular. How can "Turtle Soup" be read as a feminist poem? How does it provide revenge for the sacrifices Chin's mother made?
4. **Research.** Research any of the references to Chinese history and culture alluded to in "Turtle Soup." How does your extended knowledge help you develop a deeper understanding of the poem and the significance of this history to the speaker?
5. **Speaking and Listening.** Discuss the line "'Sometimes you're the life, sometimes the sacrifice'" as it applies to the immigrant experience. What are "the life" and "the sacrifice" of those who make a fresh start in a new homeland?

The Hammock

Li-Young Lee

© Cuirt International Festival of Literature/Blue Flower Arts

Li-Young Lee (b. 1957) was born to an elite Chinese family. His great-grandfather had been China's first republican president (1912–1916), and his father had been a personal physician to Mao Zedong. His family fled from China when the People's Republic was established in 1948, settling in Jakarta, where Lee was born. A growing anti-Chinese movement in Indonesia drove the family from the country, and they settled in the United States in 1964. Lee's first collection of poetry was *Rose* (1986), which won the Delmore Schwartz Memorial Award from New York University. He has written four other books of poetry as well as a memoir, *The Wingéd Seed: A Remembrance* (1995).

When I lay my head in my mother's lap
I think how day hides the stars,
the way I lay hidden once, waiting
inside my mother's singing to herself. And I remember
how she carried me on her back
between home and the kindergarten,
once each morning and once each afternoon.

I don't know what my mother's thinking.

When my son lays his head in my lap, I wonder:
Do his father's kisses keep his father's worries
from becoming his? I think, *Dear God*, and remember
there are stars we haven't heard from yet:
They have so far to arrive. *Amen*,
I think, and I feel almost comforted.

I've no idea what my child is thinking.

Between two unknowns, I live my life.
Between my mother's hopes, older than I am
by coming before me, and my child's wishes, older than I am
by outliving me. And what's it like?
Is it a door, and good-bye on either side?
A window, and eternity on either side?
Yes, and a little singing between two great rests. ■

2001

Understanding and Interpreting

1. **AP® Narration.** What is the relationship between the poem and its title?
2. **AP® Setting and Narration.** How is life depicted for the speaker and his mother in the first stanza of the poem? What words contribute to your interpretation?
3. **AP® Character and Narration.** What parallels exist among the speaker, his mother, and his son? What is the significance of this recurrence across generations?
4. **AP® Narration.** Why do the stars "have so far to arrive" (l. 13)? Those stars are in the same stanza as the father's "kisses" (l. 10) and "worries" (l. 10). How might the three be related?
5. **AP® Narration.** How do you interpret the poem's final stanza? What are the "two unknowns" (l. 16)? What are the "two great rests" (l. 22)?

Analyzing Language, Style, and Structure

1. **Vocabulary in Context.** What are the connotations of the word "hammock"? How do these connotations contribute to your understanding of the poem?
2. **AP® Narration and Figurative Language.** What does the poem's imagery suggest about the relationships described? Pay careful attention to the descriptions of physical positions.
3. **AP® Structure and Narration.** Why do you think the poet chose to italicize the words "Dear God" (l. 11) and "Amen" (l. 13)? What does this tell you about the speaker's attitude toward his subject? How does this point the way to the poem's tone?
4. **AP® Narration and Figurative Language.** What evidence is there in the poem — both words and images — of the speaker's tentativeness? For example, he feels "almost comforted" in line 14. He asks two questions at the very end and replies, "Yes" (l. 22) — but to which question is he responding? What is the source of this uncertainty? Does the speaker ultimately get beyond it, embrace it, or resign himself to it?
5. **AP® Structure and Narration.** Examine the structure of this poem by comparing stanzas 1 and 3 to stanzas 2 and 4. How does the shape of the poem reflect its title and theme?

Topics for Composing

1. **AP® FRQ Poetry Analysis.** In Li-Young Lee's "The Hammock," published in 2001, the speaker considers the relationship between his wishes for his child and his memories of his childhood. Read the poem carefully. Then, in a well-written essay, analyze how Lee uses literary elements and techniques to develop the speaker's complex understanding of cross-generational experiences.
2. **AP® Literary Argumentation.** In "The Hammock" by Li-Young Lee (2001), the speaker reflects on the uncertainty of the past and the future. How, then, does he feel about the present? Support your position with references to the text.
3. **AP® Literary Argumentation.** When asked about why he writes questions in his poems, Lee said that they "can move a poem forward." How do the questions posed in the last stanza convey meaning in the poem? How do they move the poem — or Lee's ideas — forward?
4. **Creative Writing.** What is the speaker's mother thinking? What is his child thinking? Compose two additional stanzas from the perspectives of the mother and child, respectively, responding to these questions. Where should the stanzas be inserted into the poem?
5. **Connections.** Since becoming a father, Lee says that he struggles to "obtain some view of the world where I'm more at home" to share some knowledge with his children. How does this poem provide such knowledge? What might his children learn from reading this poem?

My Grandmother Washes Her Feet in the Sink of the Bathroom at Sears

Mohja Kahf

Photo by Whit Pruitt courtesy of UA Relations Office

Poet and novelist Mohja Kahf (b. 1967) was born in Syria, but her family moved to the United States in 1971, and she grew up in Indiana and New Jersey. She received a BA from Douglass College and a PhD in comparative literature from Rutgers University. Kahf currently teaches at the University of Arkansas and is the author of two books of poetry, *Emails from Scheherazade* (2003) and *Hagar Poems* (2016), as well as a novel, *The Girl in the Tangerine Scarf* (2006). Her work often explores the intersections between Syrian and American cultures.

KEY CONTEXT Before each of the five calls to prayer that are part of the Islamic faith, Muslims perform *wudu*, a cleansing ritual during which they wash their hands, mouth, nostrils, face, arms, head, ears, and feet. The poem mentions Istanbul, a city in Turkey, as well as Damascus and Aleppo, cities in Syria.

My grandmother puts her feet in the sink
    of the bathroom at Sears
to wash them in the ritual washing for prayer,
wudu,
because she has to pray in the store or miss
the mandatory prayer time for Muslims

She does it with great poise, balancing
herself with one plump matronly arm
against the automated hot-air hand dryer,
after having removed her support knee-highs
and laid them aside, folded in thirds,
and given me her purse and her packages to hold
so she can accomplish this august ritual
and get back to the ritual of shopping for housewares

Respectable Sears matrons shake their heads and frown
as they notice what my grandmother is doing,
an affront to American porcelain,
a contamination of American Standards
by something foreign and unhygienic
requiring civic action and possible use of disinfectant spray
They fluster about and flutter their hands and I can see
a clash of civilizations brewing in the Sears bathroom

My grandmother, though she speaks no English,
catches their meaning and her look in the mirror says,
I have washed my feet over Iznik tile in Istanbul
with water from the world's ancient irrigation systems
I have washed my feet in the bathhouses of Damascus
over painted bowls imported from China
among the best families of Aleppo
And if you Americans knew anything
about civilization and cleanliness,
you'd make wider washbins, anyway
My grandmother knows one culture—the right one,

as do these matrons of the Middle West. For them,
my grandmother might as well have been squatting
in the mud over a rusty tin in vaguely tropical squalor,
Mexican or Middle Eastern, it doesn't matter which,
when she lifts her well-groomed foot and puts it over the edge.
"You can't do that," one of the women protests,
turning to me, "Tell her she can't do that."
"We wash our feet five times a day,"
my grandmother declares hotly in Arabic.
"My feet are cleaner than their sink.
Worried about their sink, are they? I
should worry about my feet!"
My grandmother nudges me, "Go on, tell them."

Standing between the door and the mirror, I can see
at multiple angles, my grandmother and the other shoppers,
all of them decent and goodhearted women, diligent
in cleanliness, grooming, and decorum
Even now my grandmother, not to be rushed,
is delicately drying her pumps with tissues from her purse
For my grandmother always wears well-turned pumps
that match her purse, I think in case someone
from one of the best families of Aleppo
should run into her — here, in front of the Kenmore display

I smile at the midwestern women
as if my grandmother has just said something lovely about them
and shrug at my grandmother as if they
had just apologized through me
No one is fooled, but I

hold the door open for everyone
and we all emerge on the sales floor
and lose ourselves in the great common ground
of housewares on markdown. ■

2003

Understanding and Interpreting

1. **AP® Character and Narration.** How do the first six lines of the poem characterize the speaker's grandmother? What is the speaker's attitude toward her grandmother's actions in these lines?
2. **AP® Narration.** How do you interpret the phrase "Respectable Sears matrons" (l. 15)? What is the speaker's attitude toward these women?
3. **AP® Narration.** In context, what does the speaker mean by the phrase "civic action" in line 20? What prompts such action, and who should act accordingly?
4. **AP® Structure and Narration.** Why does the speaker's grandmother bring up the cities of Istanbul, Damascus, and Aleppo? How does the grandmother's experience in these cities compare with her experience at Sears?
5. **AP® Character and Narration.** What is the significance of lines 52–56? Why is so much attention paid to the grandmother's shoes?
6. **AP® Setting and Narration.** What role does the speaker play in the interaction between her grandmother and the women in the bathroom? Why does she "smile" and "shrug"? Why is it that, despite the speaker's efforts, "No one is fooled" (l. 61)?
7. **AP® Character and Narration.** To whom does "we all" (l. 63) refer? What does the third stanza suggest about those who lose themselves "in the great common ground / of housewares on markdown" (ll. 64–65)?

Analyzing Language, Style, and Structure

1. **Vocabulary in Context.** What does the word "august" mean in the expression "august ritual" (l. 13)? How does the language of the poem support this description of *wudu*?

2. **AP® Structure, Narration, and Figurative Language.** How is the "clash of civilizations" (l. 22) in the bathroom depicted in the first two stanzas of the poem? What words and images are juxtaposed to depict this clash?
3. **AP® Structure and Narration.** What purpose does italicizing the grandmother's words in lines 25–32 serve? How does this affect you differently from when you encounter the grandmother's words in the subsequent stanza?
4. **AP® Structure and Narration.** How do the poem's run-on sentences reflect the speaker's perspective on the events she describes? What mood do they help create?
5. **AP® Structure and Narration.** How does the present tense used throughout the poem affect your reading experience? How would your reaction to the poem differ if it were written in the past tense?

Topics for Composing

1. AP® FRQ **Poetry Analysis.** In Mohja Kahf's "My Grandmother Washes Her Feet in the Sink of the Bathroom at Sears," published in 2003, the speaker describes what happens when her grandmother performs *wudu* at a public restroom sink. Read the poem carefully. Then, in a well-written essay, analyze how Kahf uses literary elements and techniques to convey the speaker's complex attitude toward her grandmother and the women they encounter.
2. **AP® Literary Argumentation.** In "My Grandmother Washes Her Feet in the Sink of the Bathroom at Sears" by Mohja Kahf (2003), the speaker attempts to diffuse the clash between her grandmother and the women who are disgusted by her actions. Should the speaker have defended her grandmother? Should she have prevented her from performing *wudu*? Support your position with evidence from the text.
3. **Connections.** Think of a family practice or religious ritual that you think other people might consider different or difficult to understand. Have you tried to hide this from others? What is the significance of this practice or ritual to you and your family?
4. **Multimodal.** Create an informative video teaching others about a cultural or religious ritual you practice. Be sure to include information about the origin of this practice. How has this ritual been adapted for modern-day life? What values does it convey?
5. **Research.** Why would Kahf have selected Sears as the setting for her poem? Research the role that Sears has played in American history. What images and sentiments are associated with the company? If this poem were rewritten today, what store could be used as a substitute for Sears?

Bedecked

Victoria Redel

Poet and novelist Victoria Redel (b. 1959) was raised in Scarsdale, New York. She has a degree in visual arts from Dartmouth College and an MFA in poetry from Columbia University. She has received fellowships from the Guggenheim Foundation and the National Endowment for the Arts. She is the author of three books of poetry, *Already the World* (1995), *Swoon* (2003), and *Woman Without Umbrella* (2012), and five novels, including *Loverboy* (2001), which was made into a film. She currently teaches at Sarah Lawrence College.

J. Vespa/WireImage/Getty Images

Tell me it's wrong the scarlet nails my son sports or the toy store rings he clusters four jewels to each finger.

He's bedecked. I see the other mothers looking at the star choker, the rhinestone strand he fastens over a sock.
Sometimes I help him find sparkle clip-ons when he says sticker earrings look too fake.

Tell me I should teach him it's wrong to love the glitter that a boy's only a boy who'd love a truck with a remote that revs,
battery slamming into corners or Hot Wheels loop-de-looping off tracks into the tub.

Then tell me it's fine — really — maybe even a good thing — a boy who's got some girl to him,
and I'm right for the days he wears a pink shirt on the seesaw in the park.

Tell me what you need to tell me but keep far away from my son who still loves a beautiful thing not for what it means —
this way or that — but for the way facets set off prisms and prisms spin up everywhere
and from his own jeweled body he's cast rainbows — made every shining true color.

Now try to tell me — man or woman — your heart was ever once that brave. ■

2003

Understanding and Interpreting

1. **AP® Narration.** Who is the speaker addressing in this poem? How do you know?
2. **AP® Character and Narration.** What tone does the speaker use when she talks about her son? How does this tone relate to her overall message?
3. **AP® Character and Narration.** What does the speaker mean when she says, "Tell me what you need to tell me but keep far away from my son" (l. 8)? How does this statement illustrate her relationship with her son? What does it reveal about her perspective on her role as his mother?
4. **AP® Character and Narration.** What is significant about the fact that the speaker's son "still loves a beautiful thing not for what it means — / this way or that" (ll. 8–9)? Why does the speaker value this ability?

Analyzing Language, Style, and Structure

1. **Vocabulary in Context.** What does Victoria Redel convey by using the word "prisms" in the final stanza? Consider how a literal prism functions and what the figurative language in this stanza conveys about the speaker's son on a symbolic level. How does this word choice relate to the title of the poem?
2. **AP® Structure and Narration.** How would you describe the speaker's tone toward her intended audience? How does that tone change in line 9? How does this shift emphasize the larger themes of the poem?
3. **AP® Structure and Narration.** How does the speaker contrast the description of activities considered "masculine" with the descriptions of those her son enjoys? What do these representations suggest about the speaker's perspective on gender identity and self-expression?

4. **AP® Structure and Narration.** You may have noticed that all of the stanzas but the second one start similarly. How does this structural variation function in the poem?
5. **AP® Structure and Narration.** What effect does the repetition of various ways saying "Tell me" (ll. 1, 4, and 8), including "Then tell me" (l. 6) and "Now try to tell me" (l. 11), have on the reader? What kind of atmosphere does this repetition create?
6. **AP® Narration and Figurative Language.** How does Redel use imagery to emphasize meaning in her poem? Consider in particular lines 8–10.
7. **AP® Narration and Figurative Language.** Trace the references to color and light in the poem. Taken together, what meaning do they convey? How does Redel use them to build her speaker's argument?
8. **AP® Structure and Narration.** Is the progression of encounters the speaker has in each stanza structured chronologically, or does it follow a different pattern? What is the purpose of structuring the poem in this way? Cite evidence from the text to support your response.

Topics for Composing

1. AP® FRQ **Poetry Analysis.** In Victoria Redel's "Bedecked," published in 2003, the speaker addresses an implied audience of people who would criticize her and her son for the colors and jewelry he likes to wear. Read the poem carefully. Then, in a well-written essay, analyze how Redel uses literary elements and techniques to develop the complex relationship between the speaker and her audience.
2. **Speaking and Listening.** In small groups or as a class, discuss society's expectations of how boys and girls should dress and what interests they should have. Why do boys get so little latitude to dress in ways considered "feminine"? How — or how much — do these expectations for gender presentation change as people grow to adulthood? Who or what decides such expectations, and how are they communicated to us?
3. **Research.** Explore the history of fashion and changes in the ways women and men have dressed throughout history. Which fashions do we associate with women today that were once staples of men's wardrobes? Why might women in recent history wear more jewelry, make-up, and colorful clothing than in prior eras? As an extension, research where in nature we find similar displays of what might be called a "bedecked" appearance and whether it is the males or females of various species who sport such looks.
4. **Connections.** Consider the ways children play dress-up and the ways you liked to play dress-up as a child. Did you have favorite outfits or costumes you liked to wear? How did imagination play a role in the looks you tried out? Did you ever find yourself wanting to wear clothing or accessories traditionally associated with another gender? Do you see similarities in the ways you and your friends dress up for themed spirit days at school?
5. **Research.** The website Learning for Justice explains that "schools have a history of reinforcing binary perceptions of sex and gender." It goes on to define both as distinct concepts and emphasizes the importance of "understanding these terms — and how they do and do not intersect." Conduct some basic research into the definitions of sex and gender. How do humans individually convey sex and gender along continuums and through expression, identities, and interests?

Intimate Detail

Heid E. Erdrich

photo by Chris Felver

Poet, editor, and interdisciplinary artist Heid E. Erdrich (b. 1963) is a member of the Turtle Mountain Band of Ojibwe who was born in Minnesota and grew up in North Dakota. She has a BA from Dartmouth University and two MAs from Johns Hopkins University, in poetry and in fiction. Erdrich has published seven collections of poetry, including her most recent, *Little Big Bully* (2020). She has also edited two collections of American Indian writing and has worked with her sister, writer Louise Erdrich (p. 829), on several projects to publish indigenous writing. Heid E. Erdrich currently teaches creative writing at Augsburg University.

Late summer, late afternoon, my work
interrupted by bees who claim my tea,
even my pen looks flower-good to them.
I warn a delivery man that my bees,
who all summer have been tame as cows,
now grow frantic, aggressive, difficult to shoo
from the house. I blame the second blooms
come out in hot colors, defiant vibrancy—
unexpected from cottage cosmos, nicotianna,
and bean vine. But those bees know, I'm told
by the interested delivery man, they have only
so many days to go. He sighs at sweetness untasted.

Still warm in the day, we inspect the bees.
This kind stranger knows them in intimate detail.
He can name the ones I think of as *shopping ladies.*
Their fur coats ruffed up, yellow packages tucked
beneath their wings, so weighted with their finds
they ascend in slow circles, sometimes drop, while
other bees whirl madly, dance the blossoms, ravish
broadly so the whole bed bends and bounces alive.

He asks if I have kids, I say not yet. He has five,
all boys. He calls the honeybees his girls although
he tells me they're *ungendered workers*
who never produce offspring. Some hour drops,
the bees shut off. In the long, cool slant of sun,
spent flowers fold into cups. He asks me if I've ever

seen a *Solitary Bee* where it sleeps. I say I've not.
The nearest bud's a long-throated peach hollyhock.
He cradles it in his palm, holds it up so I spy
the intimacy of the sleeping bee. Little life safe in a petal,
little girl, your few furious buzzings as you stir
stay with me all winter, remind me of my work undone. ■

2005

Understanding and Interpreting

1. **AP® Character, Setting, and Narration.** What is the situation of "Intimate Detail"? Describe its season, weather, time of day, its characters and background. How do these details shape your expectations for what the poem is about?
2. **AP® Character and Narration.** How would you characterize the speaker? What is her attitude toward the bees?
3. **AP® Character and Narration.** What does the delivery man bring to the poem? How does he seem to feel about the speaker? Do you think he's flirting? Explain why or why not.
4. **AP® Narration.** What do you think the speaker means when she says the "kind stranger knows them in intimate detail" (l. 14)
5. **AP® Narration.** What "work" remains "undone" in the poem? Why is it important?

Analyzing Language, Style, and Structure

1. **Vocabulary in Context.** What is the meaning of the word "ungendered" in line 23? Why does the delivery man call the honeybees his girls before noting that they're actually "ungendered"?
2. **AP® Structure and Narration.** How does the title of the poem speak to its main theme(s)? How does it comment on humans' relationship to the natural world?
3. **AP® Narration and Figurative Language.** What is the effect of the speaker's personification of the bees?
4. **AP® Structure and Narration.** Why are the phrases "shopping ladies" (l. 15), "ungendered workers" (l. 23), and "Solitary Bee" (l. 27) each italicized? What does this choice signify about the speaker's shifting perspective on the bees?
5. **AP® Narration and Figurative Language.** Trace the imagery in "Intimate Detail." Which of the images are concrete? Which are metaphorical? How do the two types of images work with each other to deepen the poem's meaning?
6. **AP® Narration and Figurative Language.** What does the "little girl" bee, sleeping in the flower, represent? Why does the speaker connect her sound to her "work undone" (lines 31–32)?

Topics for Composing

1. **AP® FRQ Poetry Analysis.** In Heid E. Erdrich's "Intimate Detail," published in 2005, the speaker ponders the mysteries of the natural world through her observations of bees. Read the poem carefully. Then, in a well-written essay, analyze how Erdrich uses literary elements and techniques to convey the complex relationship between the speaker and the natural world.

2. **AP® Literary Argumentation.** In a 2012 review of Erdrich's book *Cell Traffic*, critic Elizabeth Hoover says: "It's too pedestrian to say she 'writes about' biology, history, spirituality, motherhood and her heritage as Ojibwe Indian and German American. She doesn't write about these subjects as much as she uses them to create a complex field of meaning across which her marvelous intelligence travels." How does "Intimate Detail" use the subject of late summer bees to create a "complex field of meaning"?
3. **Connections.** Read the poem "To make a prairie" by Emily Dickinson. How does this poem compare to "Intimate Detail"? Consider that Dickinson's speaker says, "The revery alone will do / If bees are few." What do you think Dickinson means by "revery"? Is there "revery" in "Intimate Detail"? Explain why or why not.
4. **Multimodal.** Take a walk and look for "intimate details." Film them, sketch them, or just write down your impressions of them. Choose one or two to personify or just enjoy slowing down and looking at the tiny details we often overlook.

Family Reunion

Rita Dove

Barbara Zanon/Getty Images

Rita Dove was born in Akron, Ohio, in 1952. She graduated summa cum laude from Miami (Ohio) University, won a Fulbright Scholarship to study in Germany, and then received an MFA from the University of Iowa. Her first collection of poems, *The Yellow House on the Corner*, appeared in 1980. *Thomas and Beulah* (1986) is a series of poems based on the relationship of her grandparents. Her most recent collection is *Playlist for the Apocalypse* (2021). Dove was the first African American to be named Poet Laureate of the United States, a title she held from 1993 to 1995. In 2021, Dove became the first African American and the third woman to receive the Gold Medal in Poetry from the American Academy of Arts and Letters.

Thirty seconds into the barbecue,
my Cleveland cousins
have everyone speaking
Southern — broadened vowels
and dropped consonants,
whoops and caws.
It's more osmosis than magic,
a sliding thrall back to a time
when working the tire factories
meant entire neighborhoods coming
up from Georgia or Tennessee,
accents helplessly intact — while their children, inflections flattened
to match the field they thought
they were playing on, knew
without asking when it was safe
to roll out a drawl . . . just as

it's understood "potluck" means
resurrecting the food
we've abandoned along the way
for the sake of sleeker thighs.
I look over the yard to the porch
with its battalion of aunts,
the wavering ranks of uncles
at the grill; everywhere else hordes of progeny are swirling
and my cousins yakking on
as if they were waist-deep in quicksand
but like the books recommend aren't moving
until someone hauls them free —

Who are all these children?
Who had them, and with whom?
Through the general coffee tones the shamed genetics cut a creamy swath.
Cherokee's burnt umber transposed
onto generous lips, a glance flares gray
above the crushed nose we label
Anonymous African: It's all here, the beautiful geometry of Mendel's peas[1]
and their grim logic —

and though we remain
clearly divided on the merits
of okra, there's still time
to demolish the cheese grits
and tear into slow-cooked ribs
so tender, we agree they're worth
the extra pound or two
our menfolk swear will always
bring them home. Pity
the poor soul who lives
a life without butter —
those pinched knees
and tennis shoulders
and hatchety smiles! ■

2007

[1] A reference to Gregor Mendel (1822–1884), an Austrian scientist known today as the father of the field of genetics. His experiments with pea plants led to the discovery of the existence of inherited traits. — Eds.

Understanding and Interpreting

1. **AP® Character and Narration.** What information does the speaker convey about her family in the first stanza? What does it mean that their speech is "more osmosis than magic" (l. 7)?

2. **AP® Setting and Narration.** How does the specific setting of this reunion — an outdoor cookout, a "potluck" — reflect the meaning of the occasion to the speaker?

3. **AP® Character and Narration.** What does the speaker mean when she says the conversation between cousins seems "waist-deep in quicksand / but like the books recommend aren't moving / until someone hauls them free" (ll. 26–28)? How does this characterize their relationship?

4. **AP® Narration.** What do the two questions that the speaker asks in the opening lines of stanza 3 suggest about the speaker's involvement with her family?

5. **AP® Character and Narration.** How does the speaker characterize the "poor soul[s]" in the final stanza? What is the purpose of bringing people outside the family into this poem?

6. **AP® Character and Narration.** How does the final stanza characterize the family's spirit and connection?

Analyzing Language, Style, and Structure

1. **Vocabulary in Context.** In lines 8–11, the speaker refers to "a sliding thrall back to a time / when working the tire factories / meant entire neighborhoods coming / up." What unusual definition of "thrall" does Dove call on in this context? What makes it an effective choice?

2. **AP® Narration and Figurative Language.** How do you interpret the metaphor that Dove creates in lines 13–15: "inflections flattened / to match the field they thought / they were playing on"?

3. **AP® Narration and Figurative Language.** Trace the military imagery in the second stanza. What does it suggest about the act of gathering with family?

4. **AP® Character, Narration, and Figurative Language.** What observations does the speaker make about the origins of the appearance of the children in the family? How does the distinction between "the beautiful geometry of Mendel's peas / and their grim logic" (ll. 39–40) contribute to the speaker's claim that "It's all here" (l. 38)?

5. **AP® Structure and Narration.** The poem is made up of complete sentences, yet Dove uses enjambment to divide them in midstream. What is the effect of this structural choice? How does it reflect — or contrast with — the theme(s) of the poem?

6. **AP® Narration and Figurative Language.** What role does food play in this poem? How does it function on both a literal and metaphorical level?

Topics for Composing

1. **AP® FRQ Poetry Analysis.** In Rita Dove's "Family Reunion," published in 2007, the speaker observes several generations of family members gathered together at a reunion. Read the poem carefully. Then, in a well-written essay, analyze how Dove uses literary elements and techniques to explore the complex nature of family connections.

2. **AP® Literary Argumentation.** In this poem, the speaker observes cousins, aunts, uncles, and other members of the family with pronouns that move between "we" and "I." To what extent does the speaker seem to be an outsider in her own family? Pay special attention to the imagery of the poem and the "resolution" of the final stanza.

3. **Speaking and Listening.** In a review of Dove's *Collected Poems: 1974–2004*, critic Dwight Garner described her body of work: "Despair and loss are among her central themes, but so is the hunt for bedrock human pleasures." How does "Family Reunion," a more recent poem, also embody these seemingly contrary themes? Discuss this question in small groups in preparation for presenting your analysis to the full class.

4. **Creative Writing.** Write your own poem about a "family reunion." You might write about a family gathering similar to the one Dove describes, or you might redefine "family" as bonded by choice rather than blood. You can also treat the concept of reunion loosely — perhaps it refers to an organized annual event to get together, another occasion such as a wedding or funeral, a small gathering to share a meal, or even a Zoom call.
5. **Connections.** Read the poem "Family Reunion" by Sylvia Plath. Compare the speaker's relationship to her family with the one described in Dove's "Family Reunion." How does each poet use poetic elements to paint a specific portrait of family?

Peaches

Adrienne Su

Photo by Guy Freeman

Adrienne Su (b. 1967) is an American poet from Atlanta, Georgia. She earned a BA from Harvard University and an MFA from the University of Virginia. Su's first book, *Middle Kingdom* (1997), was translated into Chinese and published in China in 2006. She is the author of four other poetry collections: *Sanctuary* (2006), *Having None of It* (2009), *Living Quarters* (2015), and *Peach State* (2021). Su's writing has earned many awards, including a National Endowment for the Arts Fellowship. She currently teaches at Dickinson College.

A crate of peaches straight from the farm
has to be maintained, or eaten in days.
Obvious, but in my family, they went so fast,
I never saw the mess that punishes delay.

I thought everyone bought fruit by the crate,
stored it in the coolest part of the house,
then devoured it before any could rot.
I'm from the Peach State, and to those

who ask *But where are you from originally*,
I'd like to reply *The homeland of the peach*,
but I'm too nice, and they might not look it up.
In truth, the reason we bought so much

did have to do with being Chinese — at least
Chinese in that part of America, both strangers
and natives on a lonely, beautiful street
where food came in stackable containers

and fussy bags, unless you bothered to drive
to the source, where the same money landed
a bushel of fruit, a twenty-pound sack of rice.
You had to drive anyway, each house surrounded

by land enough to grow your own, if lawns
hadn't been required. At home I loved to stare
into the extra freezer, reviewing mountains
of foil-wrapped meats, cakes, juice concentrate,

mysterious packets brought by house guests
from New York Chinatown, to be transformed
by heat, force, and my mother's patient effort,
enough to keep us fed through flood or storm,

provided the power stayed on, or fire and ice
could be procured, which would be labor-intensive,
but so was everything else my parents did.
Their lives were labor, they kept this from the kids,

who grew up to confuse work with pleasure,
to become typical immigrants' children,
taller than their parents and unaware of hunger
except when asked the odd, perplexing question. ■

2015

Understanding and Interpreting

1. **AP® Narration.** What do you think the speaker means when she says that the peaches "went so fast / I never saw the mess that punishes delay" (ll. 3–4)? How does that line comment on more than just a crate of peaches?
2. **AP® Setting and Narration.** The speaker says she comes from the Peach State, which is Georgia. Why is she asked where she originally comes from? How does the family's way of buying peaches by the crate complicate her answer to that question?
3. **AP® Narration.** What do you think is the "odd, perplexing question" in the poem's last line?
4. **AP® Narration.** How does this poem comment on contemporary American life? How does the speaker compare her life with that of her parents as immigrants from China?

Analyzing Language, Style, and Structure

1. **Vocabulary in Context.** Consider the connotations of the word "transformed" (l. 26). Does this word conjure positive or negative images? How does the idea of being transformed apply to more than just line 26 in the poem? What or who else in the poem experiences a transformation?
2. **AP® Structure and Narration.** Consider the poem's syntax. What effect does Adrienne Su's use of enjambment have on the poem's tone? Why might she have placed stanza breaks mid-sentence?
3. **AP® Structure and Narration.** How are "work" and "pleasure" juxtaposed in line 33? Why does the speaker suggest that you can grow up "to confuse" the two?
4. **AP® Narration and Figurative Language.** What do peaches represent to the speaker? What is the relationship between the speaker's "crate of peaches" (l. 1) and her sense of belonging in the Peach State?

Topics for Composing

1. AP® FRQ **Poetry Analysis.** In Adrienne Su's "Peaches," published in 2015, the speaker recalls the role that food played within her family. Read the poem carefully. Then, in a well-written essay, analyze how Su uses literary elements and techniques to convey the complex relationship between food and family.
2. **AP® Literary Argumentation.** Adrienne Su's "Peaches" suggests that there is a difference between immigrants and their children. What is the difference, and in what ways are the children of immigrants "unaware" (l. 35)? Support your position with textual evidence, as well as your own research and experience.
3. **Connections.** In an essay about food in poetry, Su writes:

   > Food has been a topic of poetry for many centuries and in many cultures; the notion that food writing and poetry writing are totally separate ventures is a recent development. Much of our knowledge of eating habits, culinary practices, and food taboos throughout history and around the world comes from poetry. Food in poetry also functions as a powerful symbol of spiritual and moral states.

   How does the food in "Peaches" provide information about eating habits, culinary practices, and food taboos? Does it function as a "symbol of spiritual and moral states"? Explain.
4. **Connections.** "Turtle Soup" by Marilyn Chin (p. 1009) and "Peaches" both examine intergenerational family relationships through the lens of food. Compare and contrast the two poems, analyzing the techniques each poet uses to convey the nature of the speaker's relationship with her family.
5. **Speaking and Listening.** What role does food play within your family? How might your purchasing or eating practices differ from others? How does food contribute to the speaker's identity in "Peaches"? How does it contribute to your identity? Share your response in small groups. How are food and identity intertwined for you and your classmates?

The Widower

Hafizah Geter

Beowulf Sheehan

Poet, writer, and literary agent Hafizah Geter (b. 1984) was born in Nigeria and grew up in Ohio and South Carolina. She received a BA in English and economics from Clemson University and an MFA in poetry from Columbia College, Chicago. *Un-American* (2020), her debut poetry collection, was nominated for a NAACP Image award and was a finalist for the PEN Open Book Award. Her most recent work is her nonfiction debut, *The Black Period: On Personhood, Race & Origin* (2022).

Five winters in a row, my father knuckles

the trunk of his backyard pine

like he's testing a watermelon.

He scolds smooth patches

where bark won't grow,

breaks branches

to find them hollow.

He inhales deeply

and the pine tree has lost

even its scent. He grieves

in trees — my father, the backyard

forest king, the humble

king. The dragging his scepter

through the darkness king.

The wind splits him into shivers.

Rivers of stars

don him like a crown. My king

who won't lay his tenderness down

trembles into the black

unable to stop

his kingdom from dying.

I have failed to quiet

the animal inside him.

If only I would

take his hand.

This man weeping

in the cold,

how quickly I turn

from him. ■

2017

Understanding and Interpreting

1. **AP® Character and Narration.** How does the speaker characterize her father's relationship with the pine tree? Which details contribute to this characterization?
2. **AP® Character and Narration.** What does the speaker mean by the expression "He grieves / in trees" (ll. 10–11)? What aspects of his life and his garden might the father be grieving, and how are they connected? How does he convey his grief?
3. **AP® Character and Narration.** How does the phrase "The wind splits him into shivers" (l. 15) characterize the father? How is this characterization supported by other parts of the poem?
4. **AP® Character and Narration.** What does it mean that the speaker's father "won't lay his tenderness down" (l. 18)? How has this inability affected his relationship with the speaker?
5. **AP® Narration.** What do lines 22–25 suggest about the speaker's state of mind? How does she believe she might be able to help her father? How do the last two lines of the poem contribute to your interpretation of the speaker?

Analyzing Language, Style, and Structure

1. **Vocabulary in Context.** A "scepter" (l. 13) is a staff carried by monarchs as a sign of their sovereignty. What do you suppose the speaker's father actually carries? How does this figurative description convey the speaker's perception of her father?
2. **AP® Structure and Narration.** In the first ten lines of the poem, the father "knuckles" (l. 1), "scolds" (l. 4), "breaks" (l. 6), and "inhales" (l. 8). What do these verbs suggest about the father? What does he hope to achieve through these actions?
3. **AP® Character, Narration, and Figurative Language.** What is the central metaphor expressed in lines 12–21? What is the function of this comparison in conveying both the father's character and his relationship with the speaker?
4. **AP® Character, Narration, and Figurative Language.** The father is described as having an "animal inside him" (l. 23). What does the speaker mean by this expression? Why would she want to "quiet" (l. 22) this animal?
5. **AP® Structure and Narration.** The speaker first refers to the man in the poem as "father" (l. 1), then "king" (l. 12), and finally "man" (l. 26). What are the connotations of each of these words? What does this word choice suggest about the speaker's changing perceptions of her father and his grief?
6. **AP® Narration and Figurative Language.** How does the pine tree function as a symbol in "The Widower"? What does the tree represent to the father? What does it represent to the speaker?

Topics for Composing

1. **AP® FRQ** **Poetry Analysis.** In Hafizah Geter's "The WidowerTurtle Soup," published in 2017, the speaker reflects on her father's behavior since becoming a widower. Read the poem carefully. Then, in a well-written essay, analyze how Geter uses literary elements and techniques to convey the father's complex reaction to loss.
2. **AP® FRQ** **Poetry Analysis.** In Hafizah Geter's "The Widower," published in 2017, the speaker considers her relationship with her father since the death of her mother. Read the poem carefully. Then, in a well-written essay, analyze how Geter uses literary elements and techniques to convey the complex relationship between father and daughter.

3. **AP® Literary Argumentation.** In an interview, Geter commented that trauma "can be silencing." Consider the moments of silence in the poem: What is left unsaid between the father and daughter? How has the trauma of losing his wife become a "silencing" experience for this man? How has this silence affected him, his daughter, and their relationship?
4. **Multimodal.** What are the three most significant images in the poem? Create a slide presentation depicting these moments either with your own illustrations or pictures found on the internet. For each image, be sure to include the textual evidence that inspired it, along with your analysis of its significance.
5. **Creative Writing.** If you were interviewing the speaker, what might she say is the reason she "turn[s] / from him" (ll. 28–29) at the end of the poem? Write a response to this question from the perspective of the poem's speaker.

The Raincoat

Ada Limón

Gregg DeGuire/Getty Images

Ada Limón (b. 1976) is a Mexican American poet from Sonoma, California. She received an MFA from New York University and is the author of five books of poetry, including *Bright Dead Things* (2015), which was a finalist for the National Book Award, and *The Carrying* (2018). Limón has said that in her work she asks, "How do I see the big picture and hold the world's pain, and at the same time see all of the bright edges of joy? I think that's at the center of my question."

KEY CONTEXT Ada Limón has a severe curvature of the spine, or scoliosis. To help with the chronic pain caused by this condition, she began physical therapy when she was seventeen.

When the doctor suggested surgery
and a brace for all my youngest years,
my parents scrambled to take me
to massage therapy, deep tissue work,
osteopathy, and soon my crooked spine
unspooled a bit, I could breathe again,
and move more in a body unclouded
by pain. My mom would tell me to sing
songs to her the whole forty-five minute
drive to Middle Two Rock Road and forty-
five minutes back from physical therapy.
She'd say, even my voice sounded unfettered
by my spine afterward. So I sang and sang,
because I thought she liked it. I never
asked her what she gave up to drive me,
or how her day was before this chore. Today,
at her age, I was driving myself home from yet
another spine appointment, singing along
to some maudlin but solid song on the radio,

and I saw a mom take her raincoat off
and give it to her young daughter when
a storm took over the afternoon. My god,
I thought, my whole life I've been under her
raincoat thinking it was somehow a marvel
that I never got wet. ■

2018

Understanding and Interpreting

1. **AP® Narration.** How do the speaker's parents react to the doctor's suggestions in lines 1–2?
2. **AP® Character and Narration.** Why do you suppose the speaker's mother would tell her "to sing" (l. 8) on their way to and from physical therapy? What does singing do for both the speaker and her mother?
3. **AP® Character and Narration.** How do lines 14–16 characterize the speaker and her relationship with her mother?
4. **AP® Narration.** Why is the speaker drawn to the mother who puts a raincoat on her daughter? How does this moment change her understanding of her own mother's role in her life?

Analyzing Language, Style, and Structure

1. **Vocabulary in Context.** What does the word "unfettered" (l. 12) mean? How could a voice sound "unfettered"? How does this word relate to the poem as a whole? To what was the speaker fettered, and how does she break free?
2. **AP® Character, Setting, Narration, and Figurative Language.** How do the words and images in the first eight lines portray the speaker and her childhood?
3. **AP® Structure and Narration.** How does the poem shift in line 16? How does the speaker change after this line? How does she remain the same?
4. **AP® Narration and Figurative Language.** How does the "raincoat" (l. 20) function as a symbol in the poem? What is its significance?
5. **AP® Structure and Narration.** What is the antecedent for "her" in line 23? How does the ambiguity connect two different parts of the poem?

Topics for Composing

1. **AP® FRQ Poetry Analysis.** In Ada Limón's "The Raincoat," published in 2018, the speaker reflects on what a present-day experience reveals about her relationship with her mother. Read the poem carefully. Then, in a well-written essay, analyze how Limón uses literary elements and techniques to convey the speaker's attitude toward her mother.
2. **AP® Literary Argumentation.** When commentating on "The Raincoat," Ada Limón said that "as we grow older, we gain perspective about what life means." What perspective on life does "The Raincoat" show the speaker growing into? Use textual evidence to support your response.
3. **Connections.** Watch an interview of Limón discussing her poetry. What does she say that contributes to your interpretation of "The Raincoat"?
4. **Connections.** While Limón has spoken about how personal her poems are, they still possess universal appeal. How is the relationship between the speaker and her mother a reflection of Limón's experience? What aspects of the poem give its subject matter and theme(s) universal relevance?

5. **Connections.** In line 19, the speaker refers to a "maudlin but solid song" playing on the radio. What song fitting this description could serve as the soundtrack to this poem? How does the song relate to the speaker's character and her situation?
6. **Connections.** What does Limón's speaker realize about what her mother had done for her? How does this new understanding compare with that of Robert Hayden's speaker in "Those Winter Sundays" (p. 995)?

A Stranger

Saeed Jones

Born in Tennessee and raised in Texas, Saaed Jones (b. 1985) is the author of the memoir *How We Fight for Our Lives* (2019), which won the Kirkus Prize for Nonfiction. He earned a BA at Western Kentucky University and an MFA at Rutgers University. His debut poetry collection, *Prelude to Bruise* (2014), was named a finalist for the National Book Critics Circle Award. Jones previously worked for BuzzFeed as the LGBT editor and Culture editor. He co-hosted BuzzFeed News's morning show *AM to DM* from 2017 to 2019. He currently lives in Columbus, Ohio.

Roy Rochlin/Getty Images

KEY CONTEXT Saaed Jones's mother died in 2011. He wrote the poem, which was published in the *New Yorker* magazine, in 2020.

I wonder if my dead mother still thinks of me.
I know I don't know her new name. I don't know

her, not now. I don't know if "her" is the word
burning in a stranger's mind when he sees my dead

mother walking down the street in her bright black
dress. I wonder if he inhales the cigarette smoke

that will eventually kill him and thinks "I wish I knew
a woman who was both the light and every shadow

the light pierces." I wonder if a passing glance at my dead
mother is enough to make a poet out of anyone. I wonder

if I'm the song she hums as she waits for the light to change
or if I'm just the traffic signal holding her up. ■

2020

Understanding and Interpreting

1. **AP® Narration.** How does the opening line set the context for the poem? What questions does it immediately raise?
2. **AP® Narration.** In what ways is the mother still present for the speaker?

3. **AP® Character and Narration.** Who is the "stranger" in the title and in the poem itself? Are they the same? Could that term be used to describe the speaker? How does your consideration of these questions inform your understanding of the poem overall?
4. **AP® Character and Narration.** Overall, how does this poem characterize the speaker's relationship with his deceased mother — and hers with him?

Analyzing Language, Style, and Structure

1. **Vocabulary in Context.** The stranger, according to the speaker, thinks that he wishes he knew "a woman who was both the light and every shadow / the light pierces" (ll. 8–9). What is the literal meaning of "pierces" in this context? What associations does the verb carry that makes it an especially effective choice?
2. **AP® Structure and Narration.** What is the impact of the speaker's repetition of the phrase "dead mother"? How does the enjambment in the last two repetitions add emphasis?
3. **AP® Structure and Narration.** In line 3, Jones's speaker interrogates the use of the pronoun "her" in reference to his mother. What is at issue in this questioning?
4. **AP® Structure and Narration.** What complications and unresolved feelings do the speaker's repetition of "I wonder" suggest? How do these tensions color the relationship between them?
5. **AP® Structure and Narration.** Throughout the poem, Jones presents tensions and oppositions, starting with the most obvious one of life and death. What others do you notice? How do these contribute to your interpretation of the poem's larger meaning?
6. **AP® Narration and Figurative Language.** How does the ambiguity of the final metaphor — the "song [the mother] hums" — provide a resolution to the poem?
7. **AP® Structure, Narration, and Figurative Language.** What elements of diction, figurative language, and structure evoke a feeling of longing and yearning in "A Stranger"?

Topics for Composing

1. **AP® FRQ Poetry Analysis.** In Saeed Jones's "A Stranger," published in 2020, the speaker reflects on his relationship with his mother, who has died. Read the poem carefully. Then, in a well-written essay, analyze how Jones uses literary elements and techniques to portray the speaker's struggle to reconcile the tensions within their relationship.
2. **AP® Literary Argumentation.** Who is the central character or focus of "A Stranger": the speaker or his mother? Use specific references to the text to develop and support your interpretation.
3. **Creative Writing.** "Talk back" to the speaker of this poem in the voice of his mother. You can do so in a letter, another poem, a short story, a song, or an essay. Pay special attention to lines that state "I wonder" and "I don't know," responding to them as you imagine the mother might. Ask a classmate to read what you've written, record it and play it back, or perform it before the group — and facilitate a discussion of your interpretation.
4. **Connections.** Read Hafizah Geter's poem "The Widower" on page 1026. How does each speaker deal with the grief of losing a parent? How does each poet characterize the process of grieving?
5. **Connections.** Read "What the Living Do" by Marie Howe, a poem she wrote after her brother's death that has become an iconic text about the loss of a loved one. What common threads run through both poems? To what extent do these transcend differences such as circumstances and poetic style?

AP® Multiple-Choice Practice

Mother Country

Richard Blanco

To love a country as if you've lost one: 1968,
my mother leaves Cuba for America, a scene
I imagine as if standing in her place — one foot
inside a plane destined for a country she knew
only as a name, a color on a map, or glossy photos
from drugstore magazines, her other foot anchored
to the platform of her *patria,*[1] her hand clutched
around one suitcase, taking only what she needs
most: hand-colored photographs of her family,
her wedding veil, the doorknob of her house,
a jar of dirt from her backyard, goodbye letters
she won't open for years. The sorrowful drone
of engines, one last, deep breath of familiar air
she'll take with her, one last glimpse at all
she'd ever known: the palm trees wave goodbye
as she steps onto the plane, the mountains shrink
from her eyes as she lifts off into another life.

To love a country as if you've lost one: I hear her
— *once upon a time* — reading picture books
over my shoulder at bedtime, both of us learning
English, sounding out words as strange as the talking
animals and fair-haired princesses in their pages.
I taste her first attempts at macaroni-n-cheese
(but with chorizo and peppers), and her shame
over Thanksgiving turkeys always dry, but countered
by her perfect pork *pernil*[2] and garlic *yuca.*[3] I smell
the rain of those mornings huddled as one under
one umbrella waiting for the bus to her ten-hour days
at the cash register. At night, the zzz-zzz of her sewing
her own blouses, *quinceañera*[4] dresses for her grown nieces
still in Cuba, guessing at their sizes, and the gowns

[1] Spanish for "country." — Eds.
[2] Spanish for "ham." — Eds.
[3] A South American plant, often cooked with a garlic sauce. — Eds.
[4] An elaborate celebration of a girl's fifteenth birthday, which carries great significance in Latin culture as a girl's coming of age. — Eds.

she'd sell to neighbors to save for a rusty white sedan —
no hubcaps, no air-conditioning, sweating all the way
through our first vacation to Florida theme parks.

To love a country as if you've lost one: as if
it were *you* on a plane departing from America
forever, clouds closing like curtains on your country,
the last scene in which you're a madman scribbling
the names of your favorite flowers, trees, and birds
you'd never see again, your address and phone number
you'd never use again, the color of your father's eyes,
your mother's hair, terrified you could forget these.
To love a country as if I was my mother last spring
hobbling, insisting I help her climb all the way up
to the Capitol, as if she were here before you today

instead of me, explaining her tears, cheeks pink
as the cherry blossoms coloring the air that day when
she stopped, turned to me, and said: You know, *mijo*,[5]
it isn't where you're born that matters, it's where
you choose to die — that's your country. ■

2013

[5] A Spanish slang term of endearment meaning "my son." — Eds.

AP® Multiple-Choice Questions

1. The repetition of "To love a country as if you've lost one" is best interpreted as emphasizing all of the following EXCEPT

a. the mother's deep sense of loss years later
b. the mother's love for her adopted homeland
c. the speaker's identification with his mother
d. the speaker's separation from his mother's family
e. the speaker's respect for his mother's struggle

2. The list of artifacts that the speaker's mother "needs / most" in lines 8–12 emphasizes the

a. complicated understanding of what she'll need to bring to the United States
b. monetary value of the artifacts she must leave behind in Cuba
c. connection to her homeland and her memories of living there
d. desire to hold on to her possessions even if they aren't useful
e. reminder of a homeland she knows she will return to later in life

3. The function of the personification in line 12 and 15 ("the sorrowful drone" and "the palm trees wave goodbye") might best be understood to convey that

a. the mother does not experience this sense of loss alone
b. the speaker believes his mother didn't need to leave Cuba
c. the mother feels guilty about leaving her family behind
d. there is mutual excitement for the mother's new start in the United States
e. everyone around the mother is indifferent to her departure

4. All of the following statements explain the shift to fewer third-person pronouns in stanza 2 than in stanza 1 EXCEPT

a. The second stanza incorporates the speaker's perspective as a child watching his mother adapt to life in the United States.
b. Each stanza presents a slight variation on the perspective and point of view the first-person speaker shares.
c. The first stanza recounts events before the speaker was born, and the second stanza incorporates his experiences.
d. In the first stanza, the speaker imagines himself as his mother leaving Cuba and what it must have been like for her.
e. The speaker wants the narrator's point of view to be third person in the first stanza and first person in the second.

5. As used in lines 35–37, the phrase "as if / it were *you* on a plane departing from America / forever" emphasizes the speaker's point that

a. most people have gone through something like what his mother went through and can relate to her experiences
b. imagining his mother's experience is not only challenging but also an important part of understanding her perspective
c. leaving one's homeland forever is an ordeal that many people can relate to if they imagine themselves having to do so
d. readers living in countries other than the United States won't be able to understand his mother's experiences or the poem's themes
e. readers would feel differently about choosing to die in a country other than the United States if they were forced to do so

6. Which of the following best paraphrases the speaker's message in lines 35–42?

a. Some of the most devastating memories to leave behind are the simplest ones.
b. People leaving the United States cannot imagine the speaker's mother's experience.
c. When considering the unknown, we often fear what's least likely to happen.
d. Everyday items and experiences can take on new meanings that are memorable.
e. Immigrants to the United States worry too much about what they might forget.

7. The tone of lines 43–50 ("To love a country . . . that's your country") is best described as

a. haughty but yearning
b. exuberant but fatalistic
c. impassioned but indignant
d. modest but regretful
e. mournful but optimistic

8. The simile in lines 46–47 ("cheeks pink / as the cherry blossoms coloring the air that day") suggests that the speaker's mother

a. thinks about the new life she has created in the United States with joy and exuberance
b. is ashamed to admit her growing fondness for the United States and doesn't regret leaving Cuba
c. realizes her appreciation for the United States for the first time during that spring
d. has come to regret choosing the United States over Cuba, especially as she gets older
e. seems like the much younger person she had been when she left Cuba whenever she reminisces

9. For the speaker, the *quinceañera* dresses in line 30 symbolize

a. a culture and country he has never been a part of
b. his mother's regrets about ever leaving Cuba
c. the family and culture his mother left behind in Cuba
d. his mother's culture, work ethic, and resourcefulness
e. the career his mother could have had making clothes in Cuba

10. The comment made by the speaker's mother at the end of the poem suggests she

a. is resigned to dying in a country that isn't her homeland
b. would like to return to Cuba to die there instead of the United States
c. feels a sense of satisfaction and pride in the choice she made
d. cares more about her life in the United States than she does about Cuba
e. resents having to choose at a young age which country to live and die in

The Steeple-Jack

Marianne Moore

Dürer would have seen a reason for living
in a town like this, with eight stranded whales
to look at; with the sweet sea air coming into your house
on a fine day, from water etched
with waves as formal as the scales
on a fish.

One by one, in two's, in three's, the seagulls keep
flying back and forth over the town clock,
or sailing around the lighthouse without moving the wings —
rising steadily with a slight
quiver of the body — or flock
mewing where

a sea the purple of the peacock's neck is
paled to greenish azure as Dürer changed
the pine green of the Tyrol to peacock blue and guinea
gray. You can see a twenty-five
pound lobster; and fishnets arranged
to dry. The

whirlwind fifeanddrum of the storm bends the salt
marsh grass, disturbs stars in the sky and the
star on the steeple; it is a privilege to see so
much confusion. Disguised by what
might seem austerity, the seaside flowers and

trees are favored by the fog so that you have
the tropics at first hand: the trumpet-vine,
fox-glove, giant snap-dragon, a salpaglossis that has
spots and stripes; morning-glories, gourds,
or moon-vines trained on fishing-twine
at the back

---

[1] Albrecht Dürer (1471–1528) was a German painter, printmaker, and scholar of the Renaissance era. He is best known for his woodcuts and engravings, but his watercolors established him as one of the first European landscape artists. He wrote theoretical treatises about art, including principles of mathematics, perspective, and ideal proportion. — Eds.

[2] A type of flowering plant native to Mexico, Argentina, and Chile. — Eds.

door; cat-tails, flags, blueberries and spiderwort,
striped grass, lichens, sunflowers, asters, daisies —
the yellow and the crab-claw blue ones with green bracts[3] — toad-plant,
petunias, ferns; pink lilies, blue
ones, tigers; poppies; black sweet-peas.
The climate

is not right for the banyan, frangipan, the
jack-fruit tree; nor for exotic serpent
life. Ring lizard and snake-skin for the foot if you see fit,
but here they've cats not cobras to
keep down the rats. The diffident
little newt

with white pin-dots on the black horizontal spaced
out bands lives here; yet there is nothing that
ambition can buy or take away. The college student
named Ambrose sits on the hill-side
with his not-native books and hat
and sees boats

at sea progress white and rigid as if in
a groove. Liking an elegance of which
the source is not bravado, he knows by heart the antique
sugar-bowl shaped summer-house of
interlacing slats, and the pitch
of the church

spire, not true, from which a man in scarlet lets
down a rope as a spider spins a thread;
he might be part of a novel, but on the sidewalk a
sign says C. J. Poole, Steeple-jack,
in black and white; and one in red
and white says

Danger. The church portico has four fluted
columns, each a single piece of stone, made
modester by white-wash. This would be a fit haven for
waifs, children, animals, prisoners,
and presidents who have repaid
sin-driven

[3] Specialized plant leaves that typically attract pollinators. — Eds.

senators by not thinking about them. There
  are a school-house, a post-office in a
store, fish-houses, hen-houses, a three-masted schooner[4] on
the stocks. The hero, the student,
  the steeple-jack, each in his way,
is at home.

It could not be dangerous to be living
  in a town like this, of simple people,
who have a steeple-jack placing danger signs by the church
while he is gilding the solid-
  pointed star, which on a steeple
stands for hope. ■

1932

[4] A small sailing ship. — Eds.

AP® Multiple-Choice Questions

1. Moore's reference to the painter Albrecht Dürer serves primarily to
   a. compare and contrast Dürer's use of color in paintings with scenes like the one she's describing
   b. create a sophisticated tone in her poem that helps readers understand the intelligence of the speaker
   c. function as an allusion that creates a connection between themes in the poem and themes in Dürer's art
   d. connect the town in the first stanza of the poem with the imagery of Dürer's paintings in the fourth stanza
   e. establish the setting of the poem as a town in a painting Dürer had created centuries earlier
2. Moore frequently uses enjambment, or a continuation of sentences across lines and stanzas, in her poem for all of the following reasons EXCEPT to
   a. emphasize ideas by creating unexpected connections
   b. establish one idea across multiple lines and stanzas
   c. accentuate the places she does not use enjambment
   d. highlight the juxtaposition of paradoxical ideas
   e. create a sense of flow between all of the lines and stanzas
3. The comparison of "a man in scarlet let[ting] / down a rope" (ll. 55–56) to "a spider spin[ning] a thread" suggests a
   a. connection between physical and spiritual worlds
   b. skepticism about the benefits of organized religion
   c. criticism of the steeple-jack for endangering people
   d. deep respect for the difficulty of the steeple-jack's task
   e. confusion about the steeple-jack's intentions for the town
4. Which of the following best describes the function of the contrast between "the sweet sea air coming into your house / on a fine day" (ll. 3–4) and "The / whirlwind fifeanddrum of the storm bends the salt / march grass" (ll. 19–20)?
   a. Nature can be destructive, and humans can be blind to its powers.
   b. Humans can seek shelter from storms, and all of nature remains exposed.

c. Turmoil can occur at any time, but serenity can usually prevail.
d. Appearances can be deceiving, and circumstances can change quickly.
e. Humans can attempt to avoid danger, but nature remains relentless.

5. For the speaker, "the pitch / of the church / spire, not true" (ll. 54–55) primarily symbolizes
   a. human perfectibility
   b. misguided hope
   c. everyday flaws
   d. optical illusions
   e. imminent dangers

6. The juxtaposition of "eight stranded whales / to look at" (ll. 2–3) with "the sweet sea air coming into your house / on a fine day" (ll. 3–4) suggests the
   a. need for an optimistic outlook
   b. tragedy of human ambivalence
   c. hyperawareness of nature
   d. demand for more pragmatism
   e. duality of the human experience

7. The imagery in lines 25–35 emphasizes the speaker's point that
   a. lush plant life provides people with "a reason for living / in a town like this" (ll. 1–2)
   b. nature prefers its own creations such as the plants and trees, which are "favored by the fog" (l. 25)
   c. "what / might seem austerity" (ll. 22–23) actually reveals itself to be a great abundance of life
   d. even though "[t]he climate / is not right" (ll. 36–37) for tropical plants, it supports exotic lifeforms
   e. nature provides a sanctuary for many creatures, including even "[t]he diffident / little newt" (ll. 41–42)

8. "The Steeple-Jack" offers an extended metaphor comparing the
   a. flora and fauna of the tropics and that of a coastal town in the Northeast
   b. spirituality of the townspeople and the natural world around them
   c. flight of the seagulls with the disturbance of the star on the steeple
   d. college student, Ambrose, and the steeple-jack, C. J. Poole
   e. movements of the eight stranded whales and the boats off the coast

9. Moore's descriptions of waves as "formal" and the movement of boats as "rigid" function as
   a. verbal irony that emphasizes the contrast between how boats and waves typically move with the lyricism of the speaker's observations
   b. personification of the waves that underscores the profound but often adversarial relationship between humankind and the natural world
   c. allusion to the seaside landscapes painted by Albrecht Dürer that illustrates the speaker's admiration for the beauty of the scene she is witnessing
   d. symbolism that reveals the connection between the steeple-jack's dangerous work and the risks of seafaring in New England
   e. hyperbole that accentuates the differences between life in the orderly seaside town and life for the sailors whose work supports its economy

10. The detail of the steeple-jack "gilding the solid- / pointed star" (ll. 76–77) suggests that a theme of the poem is the
   a. importance of caring for valuable possessions
   b. interdependence of people in close communities
   c. symbolism associated with deep religious beliefs
   d. discrepancy between appearances and reality
   e. safety people experience living in small towns

Suggestions for Writing

Home and Family

1. AP® FRQ **Literary Argument.** Works of literature often depict family members committing acts of betrayal against each other or demonstrating loyalty to each other. Choose one of the short stories in this chapter in which such an example of betrayal or loyalty occurs. In a well-written essay, analyze how that betrayal contributes to an interpretation of the work as a whole. Do not merely summarize the plot.
2. AP® FRQ **Literary Argument.** In many literary works, relationships between immediate family members create, clarify, or complicate central themes of the work. Choose one of the works in this chapter in which a relationship between two family members — positive or negative — functions to deepen a central theme. In a well-written essay, analyze how the complexity of the relationship contributes to an interpretation of the work as a whole. Do not merely summarize the plot.
3. AP® FRQ **Literary Argument.** Writer Mahmoud Darwish said, "Exile is more than a geographical concept. You can be an exile in your homeland, in your own house, in a room." Darwish's statement suggests that individuals may feel like exiles even at "home." Choose one of the works in this chapter in which a central character experiences "home" as an exile, whether that experience is as an exile in the character's country or the character's house. Then, in a well-written essay, analyze the effect of this experience on the character and how that contributes to an interpretation of the work as a whole. Do not merely summarize the plot.
4. **Connections.** Compare and contrast how two of the poets in this chapter have used resources of language such as diction, syntax, and imagery to express their ideas regarding the theme of home and family.
5. **Connections.** Several of the works in this chapter (including "Mother Country," "The Moths," "Combing," "The Hammock," and "Peaches") explore multigenerational family units. Using two or three different selections, discuss the ties that keep families together as well as those that challenge the connections among multiple generations.
6. **AP® Literary Argumentation.** Select a text from the chapter that depicts a conflict between a parent and a child. Craft an essay in which you analyze the source of the conflict, and explore how this tension reflects the larger theme(s) of the work.
7. **Connections.** Selecting three or four texts from the chapter, write an essay arguing whether families are more alike or different regardless of specific culture, ethnic background, or time period.
8. **Connections.** Choose one of the following quotations, and explain how it illuminates themes in one of the texts in this chapter.
   - **a.** "Nobody has ever before asked the nuclear family to live all by itself in a box the way we do. With no relatives, no support, we've put it in an impossible situation."
     — Margaret Mead
   - **b.** "If the family were a fruit, it would be an orange, a circle of sections, held together but separable — each segment distinct."
     — Letty Cottin Pogrebin
   - **c.** "Important families are like potatoes. The best parts are underground."
     — Francis Bacon

9. **Creative Writing.** Choose one of the poems addressed (directly or indirectly) to an absent party (for instance, the poems by Anne Bradstreet, Langston Hughes, or Robert Hayden), and respond by writing a poem in the absent person's voice.

10. **Multimodal.** Search a museum website for images of home and family. Find a painting or photograph that conveys an image of family in marked contrast to that depicted by any text in this chapter. Explain the two perspectives of family.

11. **Creative Writing.** Select a character from one of the texts in this chapter and a problem or difficulty from another text. In the voice of the character you've chosen, offer advice on how to solve or address the problem.

Erwan Soyer

Tradition and Progress

There are few arenas in which the war between tradition and progress is as clearly fought as that of literature, where both the message and the medium — subject and style — take sides. The conflict between respect for traditional values and the human impulse to grow and change has been the subject of fiction and poetry for centuries. Even at first glance, a student of literature can tell the difference between a novel written in the nineteenth century and one written in the twentieth or twenty-first century or between a Shakespearean sonnet and a free-verse poem. In his essay "Tradition and the Individual Talent," poet T. S. Eliot says, "If the only form of tradition, of handing down, consisted in following the ways of the immediate generation before us in a blind or timid adherence to its successes, 'tradition' should positively be discouraged." Progress, however, does not require the eradication of all our traditions. The works in this chapter ask how we determine which traditions are worth keeping and which must be jettisoned for the sake of progress — and how the old and the new overlap in the meantime.

The works in this chapter honor both the new and the old. The Classic Text, Mary Shelley's *Frankenstein*, could be considered the opening salvo in the contemporary discussion of the effects of modern science and technology, and the Texts in Context in this chapter explore the ethical issues technological progress raises in Shelley's work and beyond. In August Wilson's *Fences*, the chapter's Central Text, characters struggle to reconcile their desires for a better future with the enduring presence of racism and injustice. Despite the decades that separate us from the 1950s, the setting of the play, or even the 1980s when it first debuted, the desires and difficulties encountered by the characters remain just as relevant today.

The short fiction pieces in this chapter also explore the theme of tradition and progress. Flannery O'Connor's portrayal of the grandmother in "A Good Man Is Hard to Find" leaves us wondering if traditional values would have helped against the force of evil embodied in the character called The Misfit. Time itself is brought into question in Naguib Mahfouz's short story "Half a Day," where the lines between past and present, old and young, and tradition and progress are blurred. The chapter's poetry also looks to the past to better understand our present — and even imagine what the future might hold. Poems such as Matthew Arnold's "Dover Beach" remind us that changes wrought by the Industrial Revolution had human costs and consequences. William Butler Yeats presents an apocalyptic vision of the future, whereas Franny Choi catalogues the many changes that are presently taking place. The bridge between tradition and progress is not a short one; change is a process that can take a long time to complete. Like Emily Dickinson reminds us in "Crumbling," changing the past "is not an instant's Act." Ultimately, we should retain those traditions that help us progress toward a better future so that one day we could be united, rather than simply continue to speak of unity — or, as Juan Felipe Herrera writes, "that indescribable thing / we have been speaking of" for so long!

The Big Ideas, Skills, and Essential Knowledge in Unit 9 of the AP® English Literature and Composition course will help us understand and fully appreciate the longer fiction and drama in this chapter. In the final unit of the course, we focus primarily on Character, Structure, Narration, and Literary Argumentation — in particular, how patterns in these works cohere to signal deeper meaning in the work as a whole. Remember, however, that we will continue to build on all the Skills and Big Ideas that we have previously explored. You may want to revisit the fundamentals of reading and writing about longer fiction that we covered in Chapter 3 (p. 106).

AP® Big Idea: Character

The analysis of **characters** requires that we focus on the thoughts, actions, and dialogue of the characters themselves, as well as the information provided by the narrator and other characters. In Mary Shelley's *Frankenstein*, we learn about characters through a series of letters, particularly those of Robert Walton to his sister, Margaret Saville. Through their correspondence, we draw conclusions about Victor Frankenstein and his creation, along with the various other characters in the novel. Interestingly, and perhaps even surprisingly, the creation — whose name is not Frankenstein — is not entirely monstrous. Like the other humans that inhabit the world created by Shelley, he is also pained, frightened, and lonely; the monster of our collective imagination, at times, is pitiable. Neither people nor fictional characters, however, are usually static, or unchanging; as such, careful readers focus on the arc of each major character. The events that prompt characters to change and *how* they change are tied to the thematic concerns of the author. For instance, what does Shelley convey to us by the monster's evolution throughout the novel? And what does she suggest about humanity as she details Victor's moral, psychological, and emotional descent? *To review characterization in longer works, see pages 108–113 of Chapter 3: Analyzing Longer Fiction and Drama.*

AP® Big Idea: Structure

While the **structure** of most longer works of fiction is often chronological, or linear, there are variations to how stories can be told. Plot structures that infuse *in medias res*, flashbacks, and flashforwards can disrupt our typical expectations of a narrative. Mary

Shelley's *Frankenstein* is an epistolary novel, one in which the story is told through a series of letters. Since Shelley intended to create a frightening tale, this form allows her to create layers of distance between her readers and characters and thereby build suspense. For instance, we learn of the monster that is brought to life through the letter Robert Walton writes Margaret wherein he recounts the story told to him by Victor Frankenstein. These layers of narration add to the mystery surrounding the tale. It is no wonder that scientific specificity makes way for the shock, fear, and anguish felt by the many raconteurs of the story. Ultimately, by examining the major plot points of literature we can interpret the societal standards embraced by or imposed upon the characters. What can we discern of the value system of the characters in *Frankenstein* and of the people in Mary Shelley's own social circle? How does the novel's plot structure convey their view on science, religion, ethics, and morality? *To review plot structure in longer works, see pages 118–120 of Chapter 3: Analyzing Longer Fiction and Drama*.

AP® Big Idea: Narration

Integral to the structure of *Frankenstein* is its **narration**. While we usually expect a single narrator for the duration of a text, Shelley provides us with multiple narrators. Since the novel is an epistolary one, the writer of each letter serves as one of the story's narrators. *Frankenstein* therefore lacks a single narrative voice that can provide clarity or guidance to readers. There is no third-person omniscient narrator that can tell us what each character thinks or feels; instead, we can only make inferences based on our interpretations of what we read in each letter. The novel's complexity is deepened by the contrasting perspectives from which the narrative is told. Imagine, for instance, how simple it would be to dismiss the creature as a monster and celebrate the doctor as a brilliant scientist if the monster never had a chance to speak about his own experience. Examining these characters through the various narrative perspectives, however, endows them with a depth and inconsistencies that ultimately enhance the quality of the novel. *To review narrative perspective and point of view in longer works, see pages 120–127 of Chapter 3: Analyzing Longer Fiction and Drama.*

AP® Big Idea: Literary Argumentation

The Big Ideas we'll consider as we read the longer fiction and drama in this chapter help us focus our annotations and analysis. In addition, concepts such as character, structure, and narration serve as the basis for the interpretations we'll make as we respond to the formal and informal writing tasks in the chapter. As you learned in the opening chapters, literary argumentation is grounded on a defensible thesis which provides the blueprint for the rest of the essay. In the body paragraphs, you provide textual evidence that supports your thesis, followed by commentary which elucidates the connections between your thesis, evidence, and analysis. At this point in the course, you should be aiming to provide a defensible interpretation of a novel or play that shows some sophistication. This can be accomplished in many ways — the key thing to remember is that a sophisticated analysis includes commentary on the textual evidence woven throughout your essay. As you read in Chapter 3, one way to approach crafting a sophisticated literary argument is to examine the work through a critical lens such as gender. *Frankenstein*, for instance, might be read as an allegory for motherhood. *To review the process of writing an AP® Literary Argument Essay, see pages 136–157 of Chapter 3: Analyzing Longer Fiction and Drama. To review the process of developing sophistication in an AP® Literary Argument Essay, see pages 158–163 of Chapter 3: Analyzing Longer Fiction and Drama.*

The tension between tradition and progress not only plays out in the literature you'll encounter in this chapter, but also in the artwork, fashion, ideas, movies, music, and politics that surround us. In short, every aspect of society contends with the notion of what to hold on to from our past as we inevitably move toward the future. In his 1985 essay "Where Is Our Dover Beach?" critic Roger Rosenblatt asks, "Who in Dover today would describe the world as various and beautiful and new? Yet how is the world less so than it was 134 years ago or a thousand, or the way it will be a thousand years hence, since its variety, beauty and novelty are always in the hands of people?"

activity Guided Reading for *Fences*

As you read the Central Text in this chapter, *Fences* by August Wilson (p. 1047), keep track of your observations and questions about how the following Big Ideas take shape in Wilson's play.

AP® Big Idea	Observations	Questions
Character		
Structure		
Narration		

AP® Unit 9 Alignment at a Glance

Fences

August Wilson

AP Photo/Ted S. Warren

August Wilson (1945–2005) was born Frederick August Kittel in Pittsburgh. Brought up by his mother, he spent his early years in the Hill – a poor, multiracial district of Pittsburgh, the setting for his later work. He was largely self-educated, and his formal education ended when he dropped out of high school at the age of fifteen. He cofounded the Black Horizon Theater in the Hill District in 1968, and began writing *The Pittsburgh Cycle* during the 1980s. This remarkable collection of ten partially interconnected plays portray the twentieth century, decade by decade, from an African American perspective. The cycle garnered many awards, including two Pulitzer Prizes (for *Fences* in 1985 and *The Piano Lesson* in 1989); the tenth and final play, *Radio Golf*, was performed a few months before Wilson's death.

KEY CONTEXT The sixth in Wilson's *Pittsburgh Cycle*, *Fences* is set in the 1950s, a time when the civil rights movement had gained considerable momentum. However, Jim Crow remained, in large part, the law of the land in the South, and racial discrimination elsewhere was still rampant. The Civil Rights Act of 1965 would not be passed for more than a decade after this play takes place.

This play includes the N-word, which we have chosen to reprint in this textbook to accurately reflect Wilson's original intent as well as the time period, culture, and racism depicted in the text. We recognize that this word has a long history as a disrespectful and deeply hurtful expression when used by white people toward Black people. Wilson's choice to use this word relates not only to that history but also to a larger cultural tradition in which the N-word can take on different meanings, emphasize shared experience, and be repurposed as a term of endearment within Black communities. While the use of that word in Wilson's context might not be hurtful, the use of it in our current context very often is. Be mindful of context, both Wilson's and yours, as you read.

For Lloyd Richards, who adds to whatever he touches

When the sins of our fathers visit us
We do not have to play host.
We can banish them with forgiveness
As God, in His Largeness and Laws.

— AUGUST WILSON

Characters

TROY MAXSON
JIM BONO, *Troy's friend*
ROSE, *Troy's wife*
LYONS, *Troy's oldest son by previous marriage*
GABRIEL, *Troy's brother*
CORY, *Troy and Rose's son*
RAYNELL, *Troy's daughter*

SETTING The setting is the yard which fronts the only entrance to the Maxson household, an ancient two-story brick house set back off a small alley in a big-city neighborhood. The entrance to the house is gained by two or three steps leading to a wooden porch badly in need of paint.

A relatively recent addition to the house and running its full width, the porch lacks congruence. It is a sturdy porch with a flat roof. One or two chairs of dubious value sit at one end where the kitchen window opens onto the porch. An old-fashioned icebox stands silent guard at the opposite end.

The yard is a small dirt yard, partially fenced, except for the last scene, with a wooden sawhorse, a pile of lumber, and other fence-building equipment set off to the side. Opposite is a tree from which hangs a ball made of rags. A baseball bat leans against the tree. Two oil drums serve as garbage receptacles and sit near the house at right to complete the setting.

THE PLAY Near the turn of the century, the destitute of Europe sprang on the city with tenacious claws and an honest and solid dream. The city devoured them. They swelled its belly until it burst into a thousand furnaces and sewing machines, a thousand butcher shops and bakers' ovens, a thousand churches and hospitals and funeral parlors and money-lenders. The city grew. It nourished itself and offered each man a partnership limited only by his talent, his guile, and his willingness and capacity for hard work. For the immigrants of Europe, a dream dared and won true.

The descendants of African slaves were offered no such welcome or participation. They came from places called the Carolinas and the Virginias, Georgia, Alabama, Mississippi, and Tennessee. They came strong, eager, searching. The city rejected them and they fled and settled along the riverbanks and under bridges in shallow, ramshackle houses made of sticks and tarpaper. They collected rags and wood. They sold the use of their muscles and their bodies. They cleaned houses and washed clothes, they shined shoes, and in quiet desperation and vengeful pride, they stole, and lived in pursuit of their own dream. That they could breathe free, finally, and stand to meet life with the force of dignity and whatever eloquence the heart could call upon.

By 1957, the hard-won victories of the European immigrants had solidified the industrial might of America. War had been confronted and won with new energies that used loyalty and patriotism as its fuel. Life was rich, full, and flourishing. The Milwaukee Braves won the World Series, and the hot winds of change that would make the sixties a turbulent, racing, dangerous, and provocative decade had not yet begun to blow full.

Act I Fences

Act I, Scene 1

It is 1957. **TROY** *and* **BONO** *enter the yard, engaged in conversation.* **TROY** *is fifty-three years old, a large man with thick, heavy hands; it is this largeness that he strives to fill out and make an accommodation with. Together with his blackness, his largeness informs his sensibilities and the choices he has made in his life.*

Of the two men, **BONO** *is obviously the follower. His commitment to their friendship of thirty-odd years is rooted in his admiration of* **TROY***'s honesty, capacity for hard work, and his strength, which* **BONO** *seeks to emulate.*

It is Friday night, payday, and the one night of the week the two men engage in a ritual of talk and drink. **TROY** *is usually the most talkative and at times he can be crude and almost vulgar, though he is capable of rising to profound heights of expression. The men carry lunch buckets and wear or carry burlap aprons and are dressed in clothes suitable to their jobs as garbage collectors.*

BONO Troy, you ought to stop that lying!

TROY I ain't lying! The nigger had a watermelon this big. (*He indicates with his hands.*) Talking about . . . "What watermelon, Mr. Rand?" I liked to fell out! "What watermelon, Mr. Rand?" . . . And it sitting there big as life.

BONO What did Mr. Rand say?

TROY Ain't said nothing. Figure if the nigger too dumb to know he carrying a watermelon, he wasn't gonna get much sense out of him. Trying to hide that great big old watermelon under his coat. Afraid to let the white man see him carry it home.

BONO I'm like you . . . I ain't got no time for them kind of people.

TROY Now what he look like getting mad cause he see the man from the union talking to Mr. Rand?

BONO He come to me talking about . . . "Maxson gonna get us fired." I told him to get away from me with that. He walked away from me calling you a troublemaker. What Mr. Rand say?

TROY Ain't said nothing. He told me to go down the Commissioner's office next Friday. They called me down there to see them.

BONO Well, as long as you got your complaint filed, they can't fire you. That's what one of them white fellows tell me.

TROY I ain't worried about them firing me. They gonna fire me cause I asked a question? That's all I did. I went to Mr. Rand and asked him, "Why? Why you got the white mens driving and the colored lifting?" Told him, "What's the matter, don't I count? You think only white fellows got sense enough to drive a truck. That ain't no paper job! Hell, anybody can drive a truck. How come you got all whites driving and the colored lifting?" He told me "take it to the union." Well, hell, that's what I done! Now they wanna come up with this pack of lies.

BONO I told Brownie if the man come and ask him any questions . . . just tell the truth! It ain't nothing but something they done trumped up on you cause you filed a complaint on them.

TROY Brownie don't understand nothing. All I want them to do is change the job description. Give everybody a chance to drive the truck. Brownie can't see that. He ain't got that much sense.

BONO How you figure he be making out with that gal be up at Taylors' all the time . . . that Alberta gal?

TROY Same as you and me. Getting just as much as we is. Which is to say nothing.

BONO It is, huh? I figure you doing a little better than me . . . and I ain't saying what I'm doing.

TROY Aw, nigger, look here . . . I know you. If you had got anywhere near that gal, twenty minutes later you be looking to tell somebody. And the first one you gonna tell . . . that you gonna want to brag to . . . is me.

BONO I ain't saying that. I see where you be eyeing her.

TROY I eye all the women. I don't miss nothing. Don't never let nobody tell you Troy Maxson don't eye the women.

BONO You been doing more than eyeing her. You done bought her a drink or two.

TROY Hell yeah, I bought her a drink! What that mean? I bought you one, too. What that mean cause I buy her a drink? I'm just being polite.

This quilt, completed by artist Stephen Towns in 2016, is entitled *One Night at Cabin Pond*. **What do the composition and perspective suggest about the men gathered together? How else does this image reflect the relationships as well as tensions between the men in *Fences*? Consider both friends and family as you continue to read the play.**

BONO It's all right to buy her one drink. That's what you call being polite. But when you wanna be buying two or three . . . that's what you call eyeing her.

TROY Look here, as long as you known me . . . you ever known me to chase after women?

BONO Hell yeah! Long as I done known you. You forgetting I knew you when.

TROY Naw, I'm talking about since I been married to Rose?

BONO Oh, not since you been married to Rose. Now, that's the truth, there. I can say that.

TROY All right then! Case closed.

BONO I see you be walking up around Alberta's house. You supposed to be at Taylors' and you be walking up around there.

TROY What you watching where I'm walking for? I ain't watching after you.

BONO I seen you walking around there more than once.

TROY Hell, you liable to see me walking anywhere! That don't mean nothing cause you see me walking around there.

BONO Where she come from anyway? She just kinda showed up one day.

TROY Tallahassee. You can look at her and tell she one of them Florida gals. They got some big healthy women down there. Grow them right up out the ground. Got a little bit of Indian in her. Most of them niggers down in Florida got some Indian in them.

BONO I don't know about that Indian part. But she damn sure big and healthy. Woman wear some big stockings. Got them great big old legs and hips as wide as the Mississippi River.

TROY Legs don't mean nothing. You don't do nothing but push them out of the way. But them hips cushion the ride!

BONO Troy, you ain't got no sense.

TROY It's the truth! Like you riding on Goodyears!

ROSE *enters from the house. She is ten years younger than* **TROY**, *her devotion to him stems from her recognition of the possibilities of her life without him: a succession of abusive men and their babies, a life of partying and running the streets, the Church, or aloneness with its attendant pain and frustration. She recognizes* **TROY**'*s spirit as a fine and illuminating one and she either ignores or forgives his faults, only some of which she recognizes. Though she doesn't drink, her presence is an integral part of the Friday night rituals. She alternates between the porch and the kitchen, where supper preparations are under way.*

ROSE What you all out here getting into?

TROY What you worried about what we getting into for? This is men talk, woman.

ROSE What I care what you all talking about? Bono, you gonna stay for supper?

BONO No, I thank you, Rose. But Lucille say she cooking up a pot of pigfeet.

TROY Pigfeet! Hell, I'm going home with you! Might even stay the night if you got some pigfeet. You got something in there to top them pigfeet, Rose?

ROSE I'm cooking up some chicken. I got some chicken and collard greens.

TROY Well, go on back in the house and let me and Bono finish what we was talking about. This is men talk. I got some talk for you later. You know what kind of talk I mean. You go on and powder it up.

ROSE Troy Maxson, don't you start that now!

TROY (*puts his arm around her*): Aw, woman . . . come here. Look here, Bono . . . when I met this woman . . . I got out that place, say, "Hitch up my pony, saddle up my mare . . . there's a woman out there for me somewhere. I looked here. Looked there. Saw Rose and latched on to her." I latched on to her and told her — I'm gonna tell you the truth — I told her, "Baby, I don't wanna marry, I just wanna be your man." Rose told me . . . tell him what you told me, Rose.

ROSE I told him if he wasn't the marrying kind, then move out the way so the marrying kind could find me.

TROY That's what she told me. "Nigger, you in my way. You blocking the view! Move out the way so I can find me a husband." I thought it over two or three days. Come back —

ROSE Ain't no two or three days nothing. You was back the same night.

TROY Come back, told her . . . "Okay, baby . . . but I'm gonna buy me a banty rooster and put him out there in the backyard . . . and when he see a stranger come, he'll flap his wings and crow . . ." Look here, Bono, I could watch the front door by myself . . . it was that back door I was worried about.

ROSE Troy, you ought not talk like that. Troy ain't doing nothing but telling a lie.

TROY Only thing is . . . when we first got married . . . forget the rooster . . . we ain't had no yard!

BONO I hear you tell it. Me and Lucille was staying down there on Logan Street. Had two rooms with the outhouse in the back. I ain't mind the outhouse none. But when that goddamn wind blow through there in the winter . . . that's what I'm talking about! To this day I wonder why in the hell I ever stayed down there for six long years. But see, I didn't know I could do no better. I thought only white folks had inside toilets and things.

ROSE There's a lot of people don't know they can do no better than they doing now. That's just something you got to learn. A lot of folks still shop at Bella's.

TROY Ain't nothing wrong with shopping at Bella's. She got fresh food.

ROSE I ain't said nothing about if she got fresh food. I'm talking about what she charge. She charge ten cents more than the A&P.

TROY The A&P ain't never done nothing for me. I spends my money where I'm treated right. I go down to Bella, say, "I need a loaf of bread, I'll pay you Friday." She give it to me. What sense that make when I got money to go and spend it somewhere else and ignore the person who done right by me? That ain't in the Bible.

ROSE We ain't talking about what's in the Bible. What sense it make to shop there when she overcharge?

TROY You shop where you want to. I'll do my shopping where the people been good to me.

ROSE Well, I don't think it's right for her to overcharge. That's all I was saying.

BONO Look here . . . I got to get on. Lucille going be raising all kind of hell.

TROY Where you going, nigger? We ain't finished this pint. Come here, finish this pint.

BONO Well, hell, I am . . . if you ever turn the bottle loose.

TROY (*hands him the bottle*): The only thing I say about the A&P is I'm glad Cory got that job down there. Help him take care of his school clothes and things. Gabe done moved out and things getting tight around here. He got that job. . . . He can start to look out for himself.

ROSE Cory done went and got recruited by a college football team.

TROY I told that boy about that football stuff. The white man ain't gonna let him get nowhere with that football. I told him when he first come to me with it. Now you come telling me he done went and got more tied up in it. He ought to go and get recruited in how to fix cars or something where he can make a living.

ROSE He ain't talking about making no living playing football. It's just something the boys in school do. They gonna send a recruiter by to talk to you. He'll tell you he ain't talking about making no living playing football. It's a honor to be recruited.

TROY It ain't gonna get him nowhere. Bono'll tell you that.

BONO If he be like you in the sports . . . he's gonna be all right. Ain't but two men ever played baseball as good as you. That's Babe Ruth and Josh Gibson.[1] Them's the only two men ever hit more home runs than you.

TROY What it ever get me? Ain't got a pot to piss in or a window to throw it out of.

ROSE Times have changed since you was playing baseball, Troy. That was before the war. Times have changed a lot since then.

TROY How in hell they done changed?

ROSE They got lots of colored boys playing ball now. Baseball and football.

[1] Josh Gibson (1911–1947) was a baseball player in the Negro Leagues. — Eds.

BONO You right about that, Rose. Times have changed, Troy. You just come along too early.

TROY There ought not never have been no time called too early! Now you take that fellow . . . what's that fellow they had playing right field for the Yankees back then? You know who I'm talking about, Bono. Used to play right field for the Yankees.

ROSE Selkirk?

TROY Selkirk! That's it! Man batting .269, understand? .269. What kind of sense that make? I was hitting .432 with thirty-seven home runs! Man batting .269 and playing right field for the Yankees! I saw Josh Gibson's daughter yesterday. She walking around with raggedy shoes on her feet. Now I bet you Selkirk's daughter ain't walking around with raggedy shoes on her feet! I bet you that!

ROSE They got a lot of colored baseball players now. Jackie Robinson was the first. Folks had to wait for Jackie Robinson.

TROY I done seen a hundred niggers play baseball better than Jackie Robinson. Hell, I know some teams Jackie Robinson couldn't even make! What you talking about Jackie Robinson. Jackie Robinson wasn't nobody. I'm talking about if you could play ball then they ought to have let you play. Don't care what color you were. Come telling me I come along too early. If you could play . . . then they ought to have let you play.

TROY *takes a long drink from the bottle.*

ROSE You gonna drink yourself to death. You don't need to be drinking like that.

TROY Death ain't nothing. I done seen him. Done wrassled with him. You can't tell me nothing about death. Death ain't nothing but a fastball on the outside corner. And you know what I'll do to that! Lookee here, Bono . . . am I lying? You get one of them fastballs, about waist high, over the outside corner of the plate where you can get the meat of the bat on it . . . and good god! You can kiss it goodbye. Now, am I lying?

BONO Naw, you telling the truth there. I seen you do it.

TROY If I'm lying . . . that 450 feet worth of lying! (*Pause.*) That's all death is to me. A fastball on the outside corner.

ROSE I don't know why you want to get on talking about death.

TROY Ain't nothing wrong with talking about death. That's part of life. Everybody gonna die. You gonna die, I'm gonna die. Bono's gonna die. Hell, we all gonna die.

ROSE But you ain't got to talk about it. I don't like to talk about it.

TROY You the one brought it up. Me and Bono was talking about baseball . . . you tell me I'm gonna drink myself to death. Ain't that right, Bono? You know I don't drink this but one night out of the week. That's Friday night. I'm gonna drink just enough to where I can handle it. Then I cuts it loose. I leave it alone. So don't you worry about me drinking myself to death. 'Cause I ain't worried about Death. I done seen him. I done wrestled with him.

Look here, Bono . . . I looked up one day and Death was marching straight at me. Like Soldiers on Parade! The Army of Death was marching straight at me. The middle of July, 1941. It got real cold just like it be winter. It seem like Death himself reached out and touched me on the shoulder. He touch me just like I touch you. I got cold as ice and Death standing there grinning at me.

ROSE Troy, why don't you hush that talk.

TROY I say . . . what you want, Mr. Death? You be wanting me? You done brought your army to be getting me? I looked him dead in the eye. I wasn't fearing nothing. I was ready to tangle. Just like I'm ready to tangle now. The Bible say be ever vigilant. That's why I don't get but so drunk. I got to keep watch.

ROSE Troy was right down there in Mercy Hospital. You remember he had pneumonia? Laying there with a fever talking plumb out of his head.

TROY Death standing there staring at me . . . carrying that sickle in his hand. Finally he say, "You want bound over for another year?" See, just like that . . . "You want bound over for another year?" I told him, "Bound over hell! Let's settle this now!"

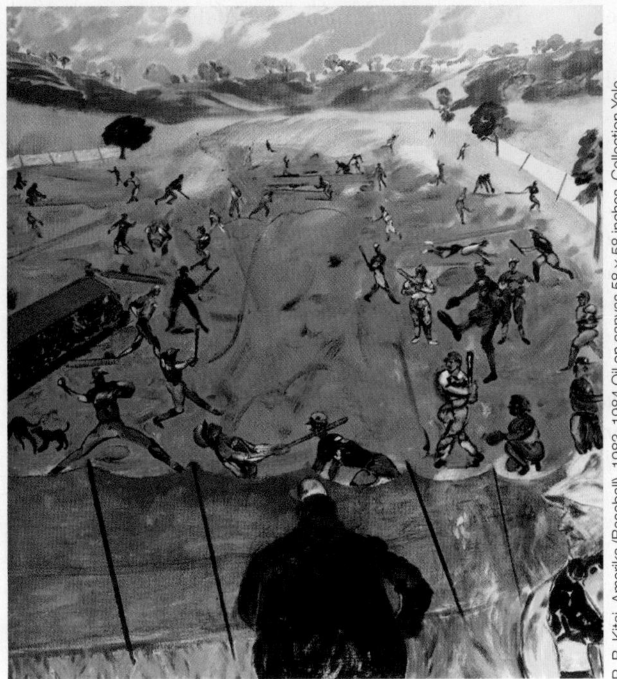

R. B. Kitaj, Amerika (Baseball), 1983–1984 Oil on canvas 58 × 58 inches, Collection Yale University Art Gallery © R.B. Kitaj Estate

In this painting entitled *Amerika (Baseball)*, how does artist R. B. Kitaj introduce elements of threat and menace? How does his depiction of baseball reflect or challenge Troy Maxson's relationship with the sport?

It seem like he kinda fell back when I said that, and all the cold went out of me. I reached down and grabbed that sickle and threw it just as far as I could throw it . . . and me and him commenced to wrestling.

We wrestled for three days and three nights. I can't say where I found the strength from. Every time it seemed like he was gonna get the best of me, I'd reach way down deep inside myself and find the strength to do him one better.

ROSE Every time Troy tell that story he find different ways to tell it. Different things to make up about it.

TROY I ain't making up nothing. I'm telling you the facts of what happened. I wrestled with Death for three days and three nights and I'm standing here to tell you about it. (*Pause.*) All right. At the end of the third night we done weakened each other to where we can't hardly move. Death stood up, throwed on his robe . . . had him a white robe with a hood on it. He throwed on that robe and went off to look for his sickle. Say, "I'll be back." Just like that. "I'll be back." I told him, say, "Yeah, but . . . you gonna have to find me!" I wasn't no fool. I wan't going looking for him. Death ain't nothing to play with. And I know he's gonna get me. I know I got to join his army . . . his camp followers. But as long as I keep my strength and see him coming . . . as long as I keep up my vigilance . . . he's gonna have to fight to get me. I ain't going easy.

BONO Well, look here, since you got to keep up your vigilance . . . let me have the bottle.

TROY Aw hell, I shouldn't have told you that part. I should have left out that part.

ROSE Troy be talking that stuff and half the time don't even know what he be talking about.

TROY Bono know me better than that.

BONO That's right. I know you. I know you got some Uncle Remus[2] in your blood. You got more stories than the devil got sinners.

---

[2] Fictional narrator in books by Joel Chandler Harris that retell traditional Black folktales featuring Brer Rabbit. — Eds.

TROY Aw hell, I done seen him too! Done talked with the devil.

ROSE Troy, don't nobody wanna be hearing all that stuff.

LYONS *enters the yard from the street. Thirty-four years old,* **TROY**'s *son by a previous marriage, he sports a neatly trimmed goatee, sport coat, white shirt, tieless and buttoned at the collar. Though he fancies himself a musician, he is more caught up in the rituals and "idea" of being a musician than in the actual practice of the music. He has come to borrow money from* **TROY**, *and while he knows he will be successful, he is uncertain as to what extent his lifestyle will be held up to scrutiny and ridicule.*

LYONS Hey, Pop.

TROY What you come "Hey, Popping" me for?

LYONS How you doing, Rose? (*He kisses her.*) Mr. Bono. How you doing?

BONO Hey, Lyons . . . how you been?

TROY He must have been doing all right. I ain't seen him around here last week.

ROSE Troy, leave your boy alone. He come by to see you and you wanna start all that nonsense.

TROY I ain't bothering Lyons. (*Offers him the bottle.*) Here . . . get you a drink. We got an understanding. I know why he come by to see me and he know I know.

LYONS Come on, Pop . . . I just stopped by to say hi . . . see how you was doing.

TROY You ain't stopped by yesterday.

ROSE You gonna stay for supper, Lyons? I got some chicken cooking in the oven.

LYONS No, Rose . . . thanks. I was just in the neighborhood and thought I'd stop by for a minute.

TROY You was in the neighborhood all right, nigger. You telling the truth there. You was in the neighborhood cause it's my payday.

LYONS Well, hell, since you mentioned it . . . let me have ten dollars.

TROY I'll be damned! I'll die and go to hell and play blackjack with the devil before I give you ten dollars.

BONO That's what I wanna know about . . . that devil you done seen.

LYONS What . . . Pop done seen the devil? You too much, Pops.

TROY Yeah, I done seen him. Talked to him too!

ROSE You ain't seen no devil. I done told you that man ain't had nothing to do with the devil. Anything you can't understand, you want to call it the devil.

TROY Look here, Bono . . . I went down to see Hertzberger about some furniture. Got three rooms for two-ninety-eight. That what it say on the radio. "Three rooms . . . two-ninety-eight." Even made up a little song about it. Go down there . . . man tell me I can't get no credit. I'm working every day and can't get no credit. What to do? I got an empty house with some raggedy furniture in it. Cory ain't got no bed. He's sleeping on a pile of rags on the floor. Working every day and can't get no credit. Come back here — Rose'll tell you — madder than hell. Sit down . . . try to figure what I'm gonna do. Come a knock on the door. Ain't been living here but three days. Who know I'm here? Open the door . . . devil standing there bigger than life. White fellow . . . white fellow . . . got on good clothes and everything. Standing there with a clipboard in his hand. I ain't had to say nothing. First words come out of his mouth was . . . "I understand you need some furniture and can't get no credit." I liked to fell over. He say, "I'll give you all the credit you want, but you got to pay the interest on it." I told him, "Give me three rooms worth and charge whatever you want." Next day a truck pulled up here and two men unloaded them three rooms. Man what drove the truck give me a book. Say send ten dollars, first of every month to the address in the book and everything will be all right. Say if I miss a payment the devil was coming back and it'll be hell to pay. That was fifteen years ago. To this day . . . the first of the month I send my ten dollars, Rose'll tell you.

ROSE Troy lying.

TROY I ain't never seen that man since. Now you tell me who else that could have been but the devil? I ain't sold my soul or nothing like that, you understand. Naw, I wouldn't have truck with the devil about nothing like that.

I got my furniture and pays my ten dollars the first of the month just like clockwork.

BONO How long you say you been paying this ten dollars a month?

TROY Fifteen years!

BONO Hell, ain't you finished paying for it yet? How much the man done charged you?

TROY Ah hell, I done paid for it. I done paid for it ten times over! The fact is I'm scared to stop paying it.

ROSE Troy lying. We got that furniture from Mr. Glickman. He ain't paying no ten dollars a month to nobody.

TROY Aw hell, woman. Bono know I ain't that big a fool.

LYONS I was just getting ready to say . . . I know where there's a bridge for sale.

TROY Look here, I'll tell you this . . . it don't matter to me if he was the devil. It don't matter if the devil give credit. Somebody has got to give it.

ROSE It ought to matter. You going around talking about having truck with the devil . . . God's the one you gonna have to answer to. He's the one gonna be at the Judgment.

LYONS Yeah, well, look here, Pop . . . let me have that ten dollars. I'll give it back to you. Bonnie got a job working at the hospital.

TROY What I tell you, Bono? The only time I see this nigger is when he wants something. That's the only time I see him.

LYONS Come on, Pop, Mr. Bono don't want to hear all that. Let me have the ten dollars. I told you Bonnie working.

TROY What that mean to me? "Bonnie working." I don't care if she working. Go ask her for the ten dollars if she working. Talking about "Bonnie working." Why ain't you working?

LYONS Aw, Pop, you know I can't find no decent job. Where am I gonna get a job at? You know I can't get no job.

TROY I told you I know some people down there. I can get you on the rubbish if you want to work. I told you that the last time you came by here asking me for something.

LYONS Naw, Pop . . . thanks. That ain't for me. I don't wanna be carrying nobody's rubbish. I don't wanna be punching nobody's time clock.

TROY What's the matter, you too good to carry people's rubbish? Where you think that ten dollars you talking about come from? I'm just supposed to haul people's rubbish and give my money to you cause you too lazy to work. You too lazy to work and wanna know why you ain't got what I got.

ROSE What hospital Bonnie working at? Mercy?

LYONS She's down at Passavant working in the laundry.

TROY I ain't got nothing as it is. I give you that ten dollars and I got to eat beans the rest of the week. Naw . . . you ain't getting no ten dollars here.

LYONS You ain't got to be eating no beans. I don't know why you wanna say that.

TROY I ain't got no extra money. Gabe done moved over to Miss Pearl's paying her the rent and things done got tight around here. I can't afford to be giving you every payday.

LYONS I ain't asked you to give me nothing. I asked you to loan me ten dollars. I know you got ten dollars.

TROY Yeah, I got it. You know why I got it? Cause I don't throw my money away out there in the streets. You living the fast life . . . wanna be a musician . . . running around in them clubs and things . . . then, you learn to take care of yourself. You ain't gonna find me going and asking nobody for nothing. I done spent too many years without.

LYONS You and me is two different people, Pop.

TROY I done learned my mistake and learned to do what's right by it. You still trying to get something for nothing. Life don't owe you nothing. You owe it to yourself. Ask Bono. He'll tell you I'm right.

LYONS You got your way of dealing with the world . . . I got mine. The only thing that matters to me is the music.

TROY Yeah, I can see that! It don't matter how you gonna eat . . . where your next dollar is coming from. You telling the truth there.

LYONS I know I got to eat. But I got to live too. I need something that gonna help me to get

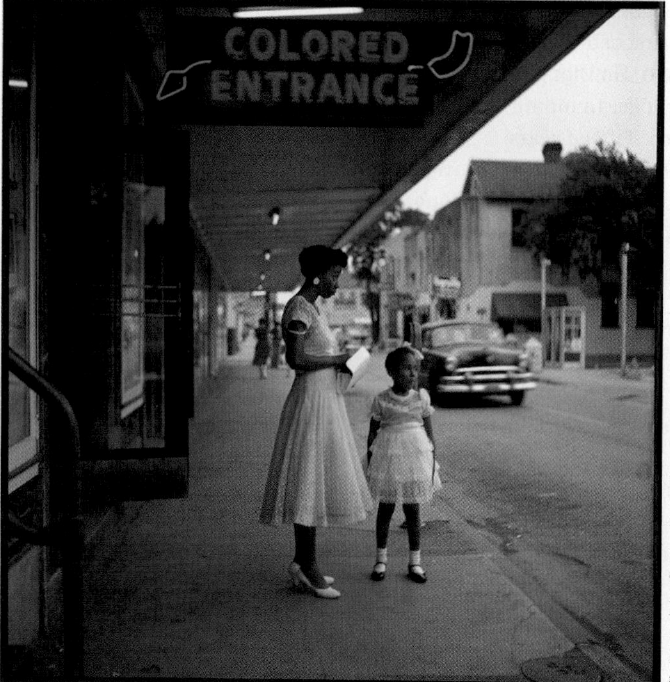

Photograph by Gordon Parks. Courtesy of and copyright The Gordon Parks Foundation

Gordon Parks took this photograph in 1956 as part of his Segregation Series, which was published in *Life* magazine. The series focused on an African American family living in Mobile, Alabama, documenting everyday life in the Jim Crow–era South.

How does this photograph illustrate some of the challenges and tensions Troy, Rose, and their family face? How does it contribute to your understanding of Troy's character in particular?

out of the bed in the morning. Make me feel like I belong in the world. I don't bother nobody. I just stay with the music cause that's the only way I can find to live in the world. Otherwise there ain't no telling what I might do. Now I don't come criticizing you and how you live. I just come by to ask you for ten dollars. I don't wanna hear all that about how I live.

TROY Boy, your mamma did a hell of a job raising you.

LYONS You can't change me, Pop. I'm thirty-four years old. If you wanted to change me, you should have been there when I was growing up. I come by to see you . . . ask for ten dollars and you want to talk about how I was raised. You don't know nothing about how I was raised.

ROSE Let the boy have ten dollars, Troy.

TROY (*to* **LYONS**): What the hell you looking at me for? I ain't got no ten dollars. You know what I do with my money. (*To* **ROSE**.) Give him ten dollars if you want him to have it.

ROSE I will. Just as soon as you turn it loose.

TROY (*handing* **ROSE** *the money*): There it is. Seventy-six dollars and forty-two cents. You see this, Bono? Now, I ain't gonna get but six of that back.

ROSE You ought to stop telling that lie. Here, Lyons. (*She hands him the money.*)

LYONS Thanks, Rose. Look . . . I got to run . . . I'll see you later.

TROY Wait a minute. You gonna say, "thanks, Rose" and ain't gonna look to see where she got that ten dollars from? See how they do me, Bono?

LYONS I know she got it from you, Pop. Thanks. I'll give it back to you.

TROY There he go telling another lie. Time I see that ten dollars . . . he'll be owing me thirty more.

LYONS See you, Mr. Bono.

BONO Take care, Lyons!

LYONS Thanks, Pop. I'll see you again.

LYONS *exits the yard.*

TROY I don't know why he don't go and get him a decent job and take care of that woman he got.

BONO He'll be all right, Troy. The boy is still young.

TROY The *boy* is thirty-four years old.

ROSE Let's not get off into all that.

BONO Look here . . . I got to be going. I got to be getting on. Lucille gonna be waiting.

TROY (*puts his arm around* **ROSE**): See this woman, Bono? I love this woman. I love this woman so much it hurts. I love her so much . . . I done run out of ways of loving her. So I got to go back to basics. Don't you come by my house Monday morning talking about time to go to work . . . 'cause I'm still gonna be stroking!

ROSE Troy! Stop it now!

BONO I ain't paying him no mind, Rose. That ain't nothing but gin-talk. Go on, Troy. I'll see you Monday.

TROY Don't you come by my house, nigger! I done told you what I'm gonna be doing.

The lights go down to black.

Act I, Scene 2

The lights come up on **ROSE** *hanging up clothes. She hums and sings softly to herself. It is the following morning.*

ROSE (*sings*): Jesus, be a fence all around me every day
Jesus, I want you to protect me as I travel on my way.
Jesus, be a fence all around me every day.

TROY *enters from the house.*

Jesus, I want you to protect me
As I travel on my way.

(*To* **TROY**.) 'Morning. You ready for breakfast? I can fix it soon as I finish hanging up these clothes?

TROY I got the coffee on. That'll be all right. I'll just drink some of that this morning.

ROSE That 651 hit yesterday. That's the second time this month. Miss Pearl hit for a dollar . . . seem like those that need the least always get lucky. Poor folks can't get nothing.

TROY Them numbers don't know nobody. I don't know why you fool with them. You and Lyons both.

ROSE It's something to do.

TROY You ain't doing nothing but throwing your money away.

ROSE Troy, you know I don't play foolishly. I just play a nickel here and a nickel there.

TROY That's two nickels you done thrown away.

ROSE Now I hit sometimes . . . that makes up for it. It always comes in handy when I do hit. I don't hear you complaining then.

TROY I ain't complaining now. I just say it's foolish. Trying to guess out of six hundred ways which way the number gonna come. If I had all the money niggers, these Negroes, throw away on numbers for one week—just one week—I'd be a rich man.

ROSE Well, you wishing and calling it foolish ain't gonna stop folks from playing numbers. That's one thing for sure. Besides . . . some good things come from playing numbers. Look where Pope done bought him that restaurant off of numbers.

TROY I can't stand niggers like that. Man ain't had two dimes to rub together. He walking around with his shoes all run over bumming money for cigarettes. All right. Got lucky there and hit the numbers . . .

ROSE Troy, I know all about it.

TROY Had good sense, I'll say that for him. He ain't throwed his money away. I seen niggers hit the numbers and go through two thousand dollars in four days. Man bought him that restaurant down there . . . fixed it up real nice . . . and then didn't want nobody to come in it! A Negro go in there and can't get no kind of service. I seen a white fellow come in there and order a bowl of stew. Pope picked all the meat out the pot for him. Man ain't had nothing but a bowl of meat! Negro come behind him and ain't got nothing but the potatoes and carrots. Talking about what numbers do for people, you picked a wrong example. Ain't done nothing but make a worser fool out of him than he was before.

ROSE Troy, you ought to stop worrying about what happened at work yesterday.

TROY I ain't worried. Just told me to be down there at the Commissioner's office on Friday. Everybody think they gonna fire me. I ain't worried about them firing me. You ain't got to worry about that. (*Pause.*) Where's Cory? Cory in the house? (*Calls.*) Cory?

ROSE He gone out.

TROY Out, huh? He gone out 'cause he know I want him to help me with this fence. I know how he is. That boy scared of work.

GABRIEL *enters. He comes halfway down the alley and, hearing* **TROY**'*s voice, stops.*

TROY (*continues*): He ain't done a lick of work in his life.

ROSE He had to go to football practice. Coach wanted them to get in a little extra practice before the season start.

TROY I got his practice . . . running out of here before he get his chores done.

ROSE Troy, what is wrong with you this morning? Don't nothing set right with you. Go on back in there and go to bed . . . get up on the other side.

TROY Why something got to be wrong with me? I ain't said nothing wrong with me.

ROSE You got something to say about everything. First it's the numbers . . . then it's the way the man runs his restaurant . . . then you done got on Cory. What's it gonna be next? Take a look up there and see if the weather suits you . . . or is it gonna be how you gonna put up the fence with the clothes hanging in the yard.

TROY You hit the nail on the head then.

ROSE I know you like I know the back of my hand. Go on in there and get you some coffee . . . see if that straighten you up. 'Cause you ain't right this morning.

TROY *starts into the house and sees* **GABRIEL**.

GABRIEL *starts singing.* **TROY**'*s brother, he is seven years younger than* **TROY**. *Injured in World War II, he has a metal plate in his head. He carries an old trumpet tied around his waist and believes with every fiber of his being that he is the Archangel Gabriel. He carries a chipped basket with an assortment of discarded fruits and vegetables he has picked up in the strip district and which he attempts to sell.*

GABRIEL (*singing*): Yes, ma am, I got plums
You ask me how I sell them
Oh ten cents apiece
Three for a quarter
Come and buy now
'Cause I'm here today
And tomorrow I'll be gone

GABRIEL *enters.*

Hey, Rose!

ROSE How you doing, Gabe?

GABRIEL There's Troy . . . Hey, Troy!

TROY Hey, Gabe.

Exit into kitchen.

ROSE (*to* **GABRIEL**): What you got there?

GABRIEL You know what I got, Rose. I got fruits and vegetables.

ROSE (*looking in basket*): Where's all these plums you talking about?

GABRIEL I ain't got no plums today, Rose. I was just singing that. Have some tomorrow. Put me in a big order for plums. Have enough plums tomorrow for St. Peter and everybody.

TROY *reenters from kitchen, crosses to steps.*

(*to* **ROSE**.) Troy's mad at me.

TROY I ain't mad at you. What I got to be mad at you about? You ain't done nothing to me.

GABRIEL I just moved over to Miss Pearl's to keep out from in your way. I ain't mean no harm by it.

TROY Who said anything about that? I ain't said anything about that.

GABRIEL You ain't mad at me, is you?

TROY Naw . . . I ain't mad at you, Gabe. If I was mad at you I'd tell you about it.

GABRIEL Got me two rooms. In the basement. Got my own door too. Wanna see my key? (*He holds up a key.*) That's my own key! Ain't nobody else got a key like that. That's my key! My two rooms!

TROY Well, that's good, Gabe. You got your own key . . . that's good.

ROSE You hungry, Gabe? I was just fixing to cook Troy his breakfast.

GABRIEL I'll take some biscuits. You got some biscuits? Did you know when I was in

Better Homes, Better Gardens, a 1994 work by Kerry James Marshall, is part of a series of paintings depicting low-income housing projects. The title alludes to *Better Homes and Gardens*, a magazine founded in 1922 and still popular today which has had a significant influence on middle-class ideas of domesticity and gender roles. **Why do you think Marshall chose this title for his painting? What does this image suggest about the reasons homeownership was so essential to the Maxson family?**

Kerry James Marshall, Better Homes, Better Gardens, 1994. Acrylic paint and paper collage on canvas. Funds from Polly and Mark Addison, the Alliance for Contemporary Art, Caroline Morgan, and Colorado Contemporary Collectors: Suzanne Farver, Linda and Ken Heller, Jan and Frederick Mayer, Beverly and Bernard Rosen, Annalee and Wagner Schorr, and anonymous donors, 1995.77. © Kerry James Marshall Photography courtesy Denver Art Museum

heaven . . . every morning me and St. Peter would sit down by the gate and eat some big fat biscuits? Oh, yeah! We had us a good time. We'd sit there and eat us them biscuits and then St. Peter would go off to sleep and tell me to wake him up when it's time to open the gates for the judgment.

ROSE Well, come on . . . I'll make up a batch of biscuits.

ROSE *exits into the house.*

GABRIEL Troy . . . St. Peter got your name in the book. I seen it. It say . . . Troy Maxson. I say . . . I know him! He got the same name like what I got. That's my brother!

TROY How many times you gonna tell me that, Gabe?

GABRIEL Ain't got my name in the book. Don't have to have my name. I done died and went to heaven. He got your name though. One morning St. Peter was looking at his book . . . marking it up for the judgment . . . and he let me see your name. Got it in there under M. Got Rose's name . . . I ain't seen it like I seen yours . . . but I know it's in there. He got a great big book. Got everybody's name what was ever been born. That's what he told me. But I seen your name. Seen it with my own eyes.

TROY Go on in the house there. Rose going to fix you something to eat.

GABRIEL Oh, I ain't hungry. I done had breakfast with Aunt Jemimah. She come by and cooked me up a whole mess of flapjacks. Remember how we used to eat them flapjacks?

TROY Go on in the house and get you something to eat now.

GABRIEL I got to sell my plums. I done sold some tomatoes. Got me two quarters. Wanna see? (*He shows* **TROY** *his quarters.*) I'm gonna save them and buy me a new horn so St. Peter can hear me when it's time to open the gates. (**GABRIEL** *stops suddenly. Listens.*) Hear that? That's the hellhounds. I got to chase them out of here. Go on get out of here! Get out!

GABRIEL *exits singing.*

Better get ready for the judgment
Better get ready for the judgment
My Lord is coming down

ROSE *enters from the house.*

TROY He's gone off somewhere.

GABRIEL (*offstage*): Better get ready for the judgment
Better get ready for the judgment morning
Better get ready for the judgment
My God is coming down

ROSE He ain't eating right. Miss Pearl say she can't get him to eat nothing.

TROY What you want me to do about it, Rose? I done did everything I can for the man. I can't make him get well. Man got half his head blown away . . . what you expect?

ROSE Seem like something ought to be done to help him.

TROY Man don't bother nobody. He just mixed up from that metal plate he got in his head. Ain't no sense for him to go back into the hospital.

ROSE Least he be eating right. They can help him take care of himself.

TROY Don't nobody wanna be locked up, Rose. What you wanna lock him up for? Man go over there and fight the war . . . messin' around with them Japs, get half his head blown off . . . and they give him a lousy three thousand dollars. And I had to swoop down on that.

ROSE Is you fixing to go into that again?

TROY That's the only way I got a roof over my head . . . cause of that metal plate.

ROSE Ain't no sense you blaming yourself for nothing. Gabe wasn't in no condition to manage that money. You done what was right by him. Can't nobody say you ain't done what was right by him. Look how long you took care of him . . . till he wanted to have his own place and moved over there with Miss Pearl.

TROY That ain't what I'm saying, woman! I'm just stating the facts. If my brother didn't have that metal plate in his head . . . I wouldn't have a pot to piss in or a window to throw it out of. And I'm fifty-three years old. Now see if you can understand that!

TROY *gets up from the porch and starts to exit the yard.*

ROSE Where you going off to? You been running out of here every Saturday for weeks. I thought you was gonna work on this fence?

TROY I'm gonna walk down to Taylors'. Listen to the ball game. I'll be back in a bit. I'll work on it when I get back.

He exits the yard. The lights go to black.

Act I, Scene 3

The lights come up on the yard. It is four hours later. **ROSE** *is taking down the clothes from the line.* **CORY** *enters carrying his football equipment.*

ROSE Your daddy like to had a fit with you running out of here this morning without doing your chores.

CORY I told you I had to go to practice.

ROSE He say you were supposed to help him with this fence.

CORY He been saying that the last four or five Saturdays, and then he don't never do nothing, but go down to Taylors. Did you tell him about the recruiter?

ROSE Yeah, I told him.

CORY What he say?

ROSE He ain't said nothing too much. You get in there and get started on your chores before he gets back. Go on and scrub down them steps before he gets back here hollering and carrying on.

CORY I'm hungry. What you got to eat, Mama?

ROSE Go on and get started on your chores. I got some meat loaf in there. Go on and make you a sandwich . . . and don't leave no mess in there.

CORY *exits into the house.* **ROSE** *continues to take down the clothes.* **TROY** *enters the yard and sneaks up and grabs her from behind.*

Troy! Go on, now. You liked to scared me to death. What was the score of the game? Lucille had me on the phone and I couldn't keep up with it.

TROY What I care about the game? Come here, woman. (*He tries to kiss her.*)

ROSE I thought you went down Taylors' to listen to the game. Go on, Troy! You supposed to be putting up this fence.

TROY (*attempting to kiss her again*): I'll put it up when I finish with what is at hand.

ROSE Go on, Troy. I ain't studying you.

TROY (*chasing after her*): I'm studying you . . . fixing to do my homework!

ROSE Troy, you better leave me alone.

TROY Where's Cory? That boy brought his butt home yet?

ROSE He's in the house doing his chores.

TROY (*calling*): Cory! Get your butt out here, boy!

ROSE *exits into the house with the laundry.*

TROY *goes over to the pile of wood, picks up a board, and starts sawing.* **CORY** *enters from the house.*

TROY You just now coming in here from leaving this morning?

CORY Yeah, I had to go to football practice.

TROY Yeah, what?

CORY Yessir.

TROY I ain't but two seconds off you noway. The garbage sitting in there overflowing . . . you ain't done none of your chores . . . and you come in here talking about "Yeah."

CORY I was just getting ready to do my chores now, Pop . . .

TROY Your first chore is to help me with this fence on Saturday. Everything else come after that. Now get that saw and cut them boards.

CORY *takes the saw and begins cutting the boards.* **TROY** *continues working. There is a long pause.*

CORY Hey, Pop . . . why don't you buy a TV?

TROY What I want with a TV? What I want one of them for?

CORY Everybody got one. Earl, Ba Bra . . . Jesse!

TROY I ain't asked you who had one. I say what I want with one?

CORY So you can watch it. They got lots of things on TV. Baseball games and everything. We could watch the World Series.

TROY Yeah . . . and how much this TV cost?

CORY I don't know. They got them on sale for around two hundred dollars.

TROY Two hundred dollars, huh?

CORY That ain't that much, Pop.

TROY Naw, it's just two hundred dollars. See that roof you got over your head at night? Let me tell you something about that roof. It's been over ten years since that roof was last tarred. See now . . . the snow come this winter and sit up there on that roof like it is . . . and it's gonna seep inside. It's just gonna be a little bit . . . ain't gonna hardly notice it. Then the next thing you know, it's gonna be leaking all over the house. Then the wood rot from all that water and you gonna need a whole new roof. Now, how much you think it cost to get that roof tarred?

CORY I don't know.

TROY Two hundred and sixty-four dollars . . . cash money. While you thinking about a TV, I got to be thinking about the roof . . . and whatever else go wrong here. Now if you had two hundred dollars, what would you do . . . fix the roof or buy a TV?

CORY I'd buy a TV. Then when the roof started to leak . . . when it needed fixing . . . I'd fix it.

TROY Where you gonna get the money from? You done spent it for a TV. You gonna sit up and watch the water run all over your brand new TV.

CORY Aw, Pop. You got money. I know you do.

TROY Where I got it at, huh?

CORY You got it in the bank.

TROY You wanna see my bankbook? You wanna see that seventy-three dollars and twenty-two cents I got sitting up in there.

CORY You ain't got to pay for it all at one time. You can put a down payment on it and carry it on home with you.

TROY Not me. I ain't gonna owe nobody nothing if I can help it. Miss a payment and they come and snatch it right out your house. Then what you got? Now, soon as I get two hundred dollars clear, then I'll buy a TV. Right now, as soon as I get two hundred and sixty-four dollars, I'm gonna have this roof tarred.

CORY Aw . . . Pop!

TROY You go on and get you two hundred dollars and buy one if ya want it. I got better things to do with my money.

CORY I can't get no two hundred dollars. I ain't never seen two hundred dollars.

TROY I'll tell you what . . . you get you a hundred dollars and I'll put the other hundred with it.

CORY All right, I'm gonna show you.

extending beyond the text

In December 2020, Major League Baseball (MLB) commissioner Rob Manfred announced that the 1920–1948 Negro Leagues would be elevated to Major League status, ensuring that the records of seven distinct leagues and some 3,400 Black players will become part of baseball's official story. An effort to acknowledge the inequity of segregation in the sport often called America's "national pastime," this decision came a full century after the creation of the first Black baseball league. Bob Kendrick, director of the Negro Leagues Baseball Museum, called this recognition "historical validation for those who had been shunned from the Major Leagues and had the foresight and courage to create their own league that helped change the game, and the country, too."

Shown here are a few images from the era of the Negro Leagues. The first is the 1946 cover of *Negro Baseball* magazine, featuring Jackie Robinson. In the second image, Josh Gibson slides into home plate during an East-West All-Star Game of the Negro Leagues in 1944. The final image shows the two teams that played in the first game of the first ever Colored World Series in 1924.

Mark Rucker/Transcendental Graphics/Getty Images

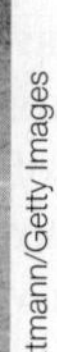

Bettmann/Getty Images

Vintagerie Ephemera Collection/Alamy

1. How do the cover of *Negro Baseball* magazine and the photograph from the All-Star Game represent the sport of baseball? What do they reveal about the Negro Leagues?
2. What story does the photo from the 1924 Colored World Series tell about sports in general and segregated baseball leagues specifically? Consider the stance of the players and officials, the panoramic view, and the perspective on the audience.
3. What would Troy have to say about the two images from the 1940s? How do these images speak to — or challenge — Troy's representation of his own experiences?
4. What "fences" are present — or implied — in these images? How do they relate to the larger themes in the play?

TROY You gonna show me how you can cut them boards right now.

CORY *begins to cut the boards. There is a long pause.*

CORY The Pirates won today. That makes five in a row.

TROY I ain't thinking about the Pirates. Got an all-white team. Got that boy . . . that Puerto Rican boy . . . Clemente. Don't even half-play him. That boy could be something if they give him a chance. Play him one day and sit him on the bench the next.

CORY He gets a lot of chances to play.

TROY I'm talking about playing regular. Playing every day so you can get your timing. That's what I'm talking about.

CORY They got some white guys on the team that don't play every day. You can't play everybody at the same time.

TROY If they got a white fellow sitting on the bench . . . you can bet your last dollar he can't play! The colored guy got to be twice as good before he get on the team. That's why I don't want you to get all tied up in them sports. Man on the team and what it get him? They got colored on the team and don't use them. Same as not having them. All them teams the same.

CORY The Braves got Hank Aaron and Wes Covington. Hank Aaron hit two home runs today. That makes forty-three.

TROY Hank Aaron ain't nobody. That what you supposed to do. That's how you supposed to play the game. Ain't nothing to it. It's just a matter of timing . . . getting the right follow-through. Hell, I can hit forty-three home runs right now!

CORY Not off no major-league pitching, you couldn't.

TROY We had better pitching in the Negro leagues. I hit seven home runs off of Satchel Paige. You can't get no better than that!

CORY Sandy Koufax. He's leading the league in strikeouts.

TROY I ain't thinking of no Sandy Koufax.

CORY You got Warren Spahn and Lew Burdette. I bet you couldn't hit no home runs off of Warren Spahn.

TROY I'm through with it now. You go on and cut them boards. (*Pause.*) Your mama tell me you done got recruited by a college football team? Is that right?

CORY Yeah. Coach Zellman say the recruiter gonna be coming by to talk to you. Get you to sign the permission papers.

TROY I thought you supposed to be working down there at the A&P. Ain't you suppose to be working down there after school?

CORY Mr. Stawicki say he gonna hold my job for me until after the football season. Say starting next week I can work weekends.

TROY I thought we had an understanding about this football stuff? You suppose to keep up with your chores and hold that job down at the A&P. Ain't been around here all day on a Saturday. Ain't none of your chores done . . . and now you telling me you done quit your job.

CORY I'm going to be working weekends.

TROY You damn right you are! And ain't no need for nobody coming around here to talk to me about signing nothing.

CORY Hey, Pop . . . you can't do that. He's coming all the way from North Carolina.

TROY I don't care where he coming from. The white man ain't gonna let you get nowhere with that football noway. You go on and get your book-learning so you can work yourself up in that A&P or learn how to fix cars or build houses or something, get you a trade. That way you have something can't nobody take away from you. You go on and learn how to put your hands to some good use. Besides hauling people's garbage.

CORY I get good grades, Pop. That's why the recruiter wants to talk with you. You got to keep up your grades to get recruited. This way I'll be going to college. I'll get a chance . . .

TROY First you gonna get your butt down there to the A&P and get your job back.

CORY Mr. Stawicki done already hired somebody else 'cause I told him I was playing football.

TROY You a bigger fool than I thought . . . to let somebody take away your job so you can play some football. Where you gonna get your money to take out your girlfriend and whatnot? What kind of foolishness is that to let somebody take away your job?

CORY I'm still gonna be working weekends.

TROY Naw . . . naw. You getting your butt out of here and finding you another job.

CORY Come on, Pop! I got to practice. I can't work after school and play football too. The team needs me. That's what Coach Zellman say . . .

TROY I don't care what nobody else say. I'm the boss . . . you understand? I'm the boss around here. I do the only saying what counts.

CORY Come on, Pop!

TROY I asked you . . . did you understand?

CORY Yeah . . .

TROY What?!

CORY Yessir.

TROY You go on down there to that A&P and see if you can get your job back. If you can't do both . . . then you quit the football team. You've got to take the crookeds with the straights.

CORY Yessir. (*Pause.*) Can I ask you a question?

TROY What the hell you wanna ask me? Mr. Stawicki the one you got the questions for.

CORY How come you ain't never liked me?

TROY Liked you? Who the hell say I got to like you? What law is there say I got to like you? Wanna stand up in my face and ask a damn fool-ass question like that. Talking about liking somebody. Come here, boy, when I talk to you.

CORY comes over to where TROY is working. He stands slouched over and TROY shoves him on his shoulder.

Straighten up, goddammit! I asked you a question . . . what law is there say I got to like you?

CORY None.

TROY Well, all right then! Don't you eat every day? (*Pause.*) Answer me when I talk to you! Don't you eat every day?

CORY Yeah.

TROY Nigger, as long as you in my house, you put that sir on the end of it when you talk to me!

CORY Yes . . . sir.

TROY You eat every day.

CORY Yessir!

TROY Got a roof over your head.

CORY Yessir!

TROY Got clothes on your back.

CORY Yessir.

TROY Why you think that is?

CORY Cause of you.

TROY Ah, hell I know it's cause of me . . . but why do you think that is?

CORY (*hesitant*): Cause you like me.

TROY Like you? I go out of here every morning . . . bust my butt . . . putting up with them crackers every day . . . cause I like you? You are the biggest fool I ever saw. (*Pause.*) It's my job. It's my responsibility! You understand that? A man got to take care of his family. You live in my house . . . sleep you behind on my bedclothes . . . fill you belly up with my food . . . cause you my son. You my flesh and blood.

Not cause I like you! Cause it's my duty to take care of you. I owe a responsibility to you! Let's get this straight right here . . . before it go along any further . . . I ain't got to like you. Mr. Rand don't give me my money come payday cause he likes me. He give me cause he owe me. I done give you everything I had to give you. I gave you your life! Me and your mama worked that out between us. And liking your black ass wasn't part of the bargain. Don't you try and go through life worrying about if somebody like you or not. You best be making sure they doing right by you. You understand what I'm saying, boy?

CORY Yessir.

TROY Then get the hell out of my face, and get on down to that A&P.

ROSE has been standing behind the screen door for much of the scene. She enters as CORY exits.

ROSE Why don't you let the boy go ahead and play football, Troy? Ain't no harm in that. He's just trying to be like you with the sports.

TROY I don't want him to be like me! I want him to move as far away from my life as he can get. You the only decent thing that ever happened to me. I wish him that. But I don't wish him a thing else from my life. I decided seventeen years ago that boy wasn't getting involved in no sports. Not after what they did to me in the sports.

ROSE Troy, why don't you admit you was too old to play in the major leagues? For once . . . why don't you admit that?

TROY What do you mean too old? Don't come telling me I was too old. I just wasn't the right color. Hell, I'm fifty-three years old and can do better than Selkirk's .269 right now!

ROSE How's was you gonna play ball when you were over forty? Sometimes I can't get no sense out of you.

TROY I got good sense, woman. I got sense enough not to let my boy get hurt over playing no sports. You been mothering that boy too much. Worried about if people like him.

ROSE Everything that boy do . . . he do for you. He wants you to say "Good job, son." That's all.

TROY Rose, I ain't got time for that. He's alive. He's healthy. He's got to make his own way. I made mine. Ain't nobody gonna hold his hand when he get out there in that world.

ROSE Times have changed from when you was young, Troy. People change. The world's changing around you and you can't even see it.

TROY (*slow, methodical*): Woman . . . I do the best I can do. I come in here every Friday. I carry a sack of potatoes and a bucket of lard. You all line up at the door with your hands out. I give you the lint from my pockets. I give you my sweat and my blood. I ain't got no tears. I done spent them. We go upstairs in that room at night . . . and I fall down on you and try to blast a hole into forever. I get up Monday morning . . . find my lunch on the table. I go out. Make my way. Find my strength to carry me through to the next Friday. (*Pause.*) That's all I got, Rose. That's all I got to give. I can't give nothing else.

TROY exits into the house. The lights go down to black.

Act I, Scene 4

It is Friday. Two weeks later. CORY starts out of the house with his football equipment. The phone rings.

CORY (*calling*): I got it! *(He answers the phone and stands in the screen door talking.)* Hello? Hey, Jesse. Naw . . . I was just getting ready to leave now.

ROSE (*calling*): Cory!

CORY I told you, man, them spikes is all tore up. You can use them if you want, but they ain't no good. Earl got some spikes.

ROSE (*calling*): Cory!

CORY (*calling to ROSE*): Mam? I'm talking to Jesse. (*Into phone.*) When she say that? (*Pause.*) Aw, you lying, man. I'm gonna tell her you said that.

ROSE (*calling*): Cory, don't you go nowhere!

CORY I got to go to the game, Ma! (*Into the phone.*) Yeah, hey, look, I'll talk to you later. Yeah, I'll meet you over Earl's house. Later. Bye, Ma.

CORY *exits the house and starts out the yard.*

ROSE Cory, where you going off to? You got that stuff all pulled out and thrown all over your room.

CORY (*in the yard*): I was looking for my spikes. Jesse wanted to borrow my spikes.

ROSE Get up there and get that cleaned up before your daddy get back in here.

CORY I got to go to the game! I'll clean it up *when I get back.*

CORY *exits.*

ROSE That's all he need to do is see that room all messed up.

ROSE *exits into the house.* **TROY** *and* **BONO** *enter the yard.* **TROY** *is dressed in clothes other than his work clothes.*

BONO He told him the same thing he told you. Take it to the union.

TROY Brownie ain't got that much sense. Man wasn't thinking about nothing. He wait until I confront them on it . . . then he wanna come crying seniority. (*Calls.*) Hey, Rose!

BONO I wish I could have seen Mr. Rand's face when he told you.

TROY He couldn't get it out of his mouth! Liked to bit his tongue! When they called me down there to the Commissioner's office . . . he thought they was gonna fire me. Like everybody else.

BONO I didn't think they was gonna fire you. I thought they was gonna put you on the warning paper.

TROY Hey, Rose! (*To* **BONO**.) Yeah, Mr. Rand like to bit his tongue.

TROY *breaks the seal on the bottle, takes a drink, and hands it to* **BONO**.

BONO I see you run right down to Taylors' and told that Alberta gal.

TROY (*calling*): Hey Rose! (*To* **BONO**.) I told everybody. Hey, Rose! I went down there to cash my check.

ROSE (*entering from the house*): Hush all that hollering, man! I know you out here. What they say down there at the Commissioner's office?

TROY You supposed to come when I call you, woman. Bono'll tell you that. (*To* **BONO**) Don't Lucille come when you call her?

ROSE Man, hush your mouth. I ain't no dog . . . talk about "come when you call me."

TROY (*puts his arm around* **ROSE**): You hear this, Bono? I had me an old dog used to get uppity like that. You say, "C'mere, Blue!" . . . and he just lay there and look at you. End up getting a stick and chasing him away trying to make him come.

ROSE I ain't studying you and your dog. I remember you used to sing that old song.

TROY (*he sings*): Hear it ring! Hear it ring! I had a dog his name was Blue.

ROSE Don't nobody wanna hear you sing that old song.

TROY (*sings*): You know Blue was mighty true.

ROSE Used to have Cory running around here singing that song.

BONO Hell, I remember that song myself.

TROY (*sings*): You know Blue was a good old dog. Blue treed a possum in a hollow log. That was my daddy's song. My daddy made up that song.

ROSE I don't care who made it up. Don't nobody wanna hear you sing it.

TROY (*makes a song like calling a dog*): Come here, woman.

ROSE You come in here carrying on, I reckon they ain't fired you. What they say down there at the Commissioner's office?

TROY Look here, Rose . . . Mr. Rand called me into his office today when I got back from talking to them people down there . . . it come from up top . . . he called me in and told me they was making me a driver.

ROSE Troy, you kidding!

TROY No I ain't. Ask Bono.

ROSE Well, that's great, Troy. Now you don't have to hassle them people no more.

LYONS *enters from the street.*

TROY Aw hell, I wasn't looking to see you today. I thought you was in jail. Got it all over the

Smithsonian American Art Museum, Washington, DC/Art Resource, NY

This painting, entitled *Red Abstraction*, was completed by Alma Woodsey Thomas in 1960.

What emotions do the colors and composition evoke for you? How might this painting capture the complexity of Troy Maxson's turmoil of ambitions and disappointments?

front page of the *Courier* about them raiding Sefus's place . . . where you be hanging out with all them thugs.

LYONS Hey, Pop . . . that ain't got nothing to do with me. I don't go down there gambling. I go down there to sit in with the band. I ain't got nothing to do with the gambling part. They got some good music down there.

TROY They got some rogues . . . is what they got.

LYONS How you been, Mr. Bono? Hi, Rose.

BONO I see where you playing down at the Crawford Grill tonight.

ROSE How come you ain't brought Bonnie like I told you? You should have brought Bonnie with you, she ain't been over in a month of Sundays.

LYONS I was just in the neighborhood . . . thought I'd stop by.

TROY Here he come . . .

BONO Your daddy got a promotion on the rubbish. He's gonna be the first colored driver. Ain't got to do nothing but sit up there and read the paper like them white fellows.

LYONS Hey, Pop . . . if you knew how to read you'd be all right.

BONO Naw . . . naw . . . you mean if the nigger knew how to *drive* he'd be all right. Been fighting with them people about driving and ain't even got a license. Mr. Rand know you ain't got no driver's license?

TROY Driving ain't nothing. All you do is point the truck where you want it to go. Driving ain't nothing.

BONO Do Mr. Rand know you ain't got no driver's license? That's what I'm talking about. I ain't asked if driving was easy. I asked if Mr. Rand know you ain't got no driver's license.

TROY He ain't got to know. The man ain't got to know my business. Time he find out, I have two or three driver's licenses.

LYONS (*going into his pocket*): Say, look here, Pop . . .

TROY I knew it was coming. Didn't I tell you, Bono? I know what kind of "Look here, Pop" that was. The nigger fixing to ask me for some money. It's Friday night. It's my payday. All them rogues down there on the avenue . . . the ones that ain't in jail . . . and Lyons is hopping in his shoes to get down there with them.

LYONS See, Pop . . . if you give somebody else a chance to talk sometimes, you'd see that I was fixing to pay you back your ten dollars like I told you. Here . . . I told you I'd pay you when Bonnie got paid.

TROY Naw . . . you go ahead and keep that ten dollars. Put it in the bank. The next time you feel like you wanna come by here and ask me for something . . . you go on down there and get that.

LYONS Here's your ten dollars, Pop. I told you I don't want you to give me nothing. I just wanted to borrow ten dollars.

TROY Naw . . . you go on and keep that for the next time you want to ask me.

LYONS Come on, Pop . . . here go your ten dollars.

ROSE Why don't you go on and let the boy pay you back, Troy?

LYONS Here you go, Rose. If you don't take it I'm gonna have to hear about it for the next six months. (*He hands her the money.*)

ROSE You can hand yours over here too, Troy.

TROY You see this, Bono. You see how they do me.

BONO Yeah, Lucille do me the same way.

GABRIEL *is heard singing offstage. He enters.*

GABRIEL Better get ready for the Judgment! Better get ready for . . . Hey! . . . Hey! . . . There's Troy's boy!

LYONS How are you doing, Uncle Gabe?

GABRIEL Lyons . . . The King of the Jungle! Rose . . . hey, Rose. Got a flower for you. (*He takes a rose from his pocket.*) Picked it myself. That's the same rose like you is!

ROSE That's right nice of you, Gabe.

LYONS What you been doing, Uncle Gabe?

GABRIEL Oh, I been chasing hellhounds and waiting on the time to tell St. Peter to open the gates.

LYONS You been chasing hellhounds, huh? Well . . . you doing the right thing, Uncle Gabe. Somebody got to chase them.

GABRIEL Oh, yeah . . . I know it. The devil's strong. The devil ain't no pushover. Hellhounds snipping at everybody's heels. But I got my trumpet waiting on the Judgment time.

LYONS Waiting on the Battle of Armageddon, huh?

GABRIEL Ain't gonna be too much of a battle when God get to waving that Judgment sword. But the people's gonna have a hell of a time trying to get into heaven if them gates ain't open.

LYONS (*putting his arm around* **GABRIEL**): You hear this, Pop. Uncle Gabe, you all right!

GABRIEL (*laughing with* **LYONS**): Lyons! King of the Jungle.

ROSE You gonna stay for supper, Gabe? Want me to fix you a plate?

GABRIEL I'll take a sandwich, Rose. Don't want no plate. Just wanna eat with my hands. I'll take a sandwich.

ROSE How about you, Lyons? You staying? Got some short ribs cooking.

LYONS Naw, I won't eat nothing till after we finished playing. (*Pause.*) You ought to come down and listen to me play Pop.

TROY I don't like that Chinese music. All that noise.

ROSE Go on in the house and wash up, Gabe . . . I'll fix you a sandwich.

GABRIEL (*to* **LYONS**, *as he exits*): Troy's mad at me.

LYONS What you mad at Uncle Gabe for, Pop?

ROSE He thinks Troy's mad at him cause he moved over to Miss Pearl's.

TROY I ain't mad at the man. He can live where he want to live at.

LYONS What he move over there for? Miss Pearl don't like nobody.

ROSE She don't mind him none. She treats him real nice. She just don't allow all that singing.

TROY She don't mind that rent he be paying . . . that's what she don't mind.

ROSE Troy, I ain't going through that with you no more. He's over there cause he want to have his own place. He can come and go as he please.

TROY Hell, he could come and go as he please here. I wasn't stopping him. I ain't put no rules on him.

ROSE It ain't the same thing, Troy. And you know it.

GABRIEL *comes to the door.*

Now, that's the last I wanna hear about that. I don't wanna hear nothing else about Gabe and Miss Pearl. And next week . . .

GABRIEL I'm ready for my sandwich, Rose.

ROSE And next week . . . when that recruiter come from that school . . . I want you to sign that paper and go on and let Cory play football. Then that'll be the last I have to hear about that.

TROY (*to* **ROSE** *as she exits into the house*): I ain't thinking about Cory nothing.

LYONS What . . . Cory got recruited? What school he going to?

TROY That boy walking around here smelling his piss . . . thinking he's grown. Thinking he's gonna do what he want, irrespective of what I say. Look here, Bono . . . I left the Commissioner's office and went down to the A&P . . . that boy ain't working down there.

He lying to me. Telling me he got his job back . . . telling me he working weekends . . . telling me he working after school . . . Mr. Stawicki tell me he ain't working down there at all!

LYONS Cory just growing up. He's just busting at the seams trying to fill out your shoes.

TROY I don't care what he's doing. When he get to the point where he wanna disobey me . . . then it's time for him to move on. Bono'll tell you that. I bet he ain't never disobeyed his daddy without paying the consequences.

BONO I ain't never had a chance. My daddy came on through . . . but I ain't never knew him to see him . . . or what he had on his mind or where he went. Just moving on through. Searching out the New Land. That's what the old folks used to call it. See a fellow moving around from place to place . . . woman to woman . . . called it searching out the New Land. I can't say if he ever found it. I come along, didn't want no kids. Didn't know if I was gonna be in one place long enough to fix on them right as their daddy. I figured I was going searching too. As it turned out I been hooked up with Lucille near about as long as your daddy been with Rose. Going on sixteen years.

TROY Sometimes I wish I hadn't known my daddy. He ain't cared nothing about no kids. A kid to him wasn't nothing. All he wanted was for you to learn how to walk so he could start you to working. When it come time for eating . . . he ate first. If there was anything left over, that's what you got. Man would sit down and eat two chickens and give you the wing.

LYONS You ought to stop that, Pop. Everybody feed their kids. No matter how hard times is . . . everybody care about their kids. Make sure they have something to eat.

TROY The only thing my daddy cared about was getting them bales of cotton in to Mr. Lubin. That's the only thing that mattered to him. Sometimes I used to wonder why he was living. Wonder why the devil hadn't come and got him. "Get them bales of cotton in to Mr. Lubin" and find out he owe him money . . .

LYONS He should have just went on and left when he saw he couldn't get nowhere. That's what I would have done.

TROY How he gonna leave with eleven kids? And where he gonna go? He ain't knew how to do nothing but farm. No, he was trapped and I think he knew it. But I'll say this for him . . . he felt a responsibility toward us. Maybe he ain't treated us the way I felt he should have . . . but without that responsibility he could have walked off and left us . . . made his own way.

BONO A lot of them did. Back in those days what you talking about . . . they walk out their front door and just take on down one road or another and keep on walking.

LYONS There you go! That's what I'm talking about.

BONO Just keep on walking till you come to something else. Ain't you never heard of nobody having the walking blues? Well, that's what you call it when you just take off like that.

TROY My daddy ain't had them walking blues! What you talking about? He stayed right there with his family. But he was just as evil as he could be. My mama couldn't stand him. Couldn't stand that evilness. She run off when I was about eight. She sneaked off one night after he had gone to sleep. Told me she was coming back for me. I ain't never seen her no more. All his women run off and left him. He wasn't good for nobody.

When my turn come to head out, I was fourteen and got to sniffing around Joe Canewell's daughter. Had us an old mule we called Greyboy. My daddy sent me out to do some plowing and I tied up Greyboy and went to fooling around with Joe Canewell's daughter. We done found us a nice little spot, got real cozy with each other. She about thirteen and we done figured we was grown anyway . . . so we down there enjoying ourselves . . . ain't thinking about nothing. We didn't know Greyboy had got loose and wandered back to the house and my daddy was looking for me. We down there by the creek enjoying ourselves when my daddy come up on us. Surprised us. He had them leather straps off the mule and commenced to whupping me like there was no tomorrow. I jumped up, mad and embarrassed. I was scared of my daddy. When he commenced to whupping on me . . . quite naturally I run to get out of the way. (*Pause.*) Now I thought he was mad cause I ain't done my work. But I see where he was chasing me off so he could have the gal for himself. When I see what the matter of it was, I lost all fear of my daddy. Right there is where I become a man . . . at fourteen years of age. (*Pause.*) Now it was my turn to run him off. I picked up them same reins that he had used on me. I picked up them reins and commenced to whupping on him. The gal jumped up and run off . . . and when my daddy turned to face me, I could see why the devil had never come to get him . . . cause he was the devil himself. I don't know what happened. When I woke up, I was laying right there by the creek, and Blue . . . this old dog we had . . . was licking my face. I thought I was blind. I couldn't see nothing. Both my eyes were swollen shut. I laid there and cried. I didn't know what I was gonna do. The only thing I knew was the time had come for me to leave my daddy's house. And right there the world suddenly got big. And it was a long time before I could cut it down to where I could handle it.

Part of that cutting down was when I got to the place where I could feel him kicking in my blood and knew that the only thing that separated us was the matter of a few years.

GABRIEL *enters from the house with a sandwich.*

LYONS What you got there, Uncle Gabe?

GABRIEL Got me a ham sandwich. Rose gave me a ham sandwich.

TROY I don't know what happened to him. I done lost touch with everybody except Gabriel. But I hope he's dead. I hope he found some peace.

LYONS That's a heavy story, Pop. I didn't know you left home when you was fourteen.

TROY And didn't know nothing. The only part of the world I knew was the forty-two acres of Mr. Lubin's land. That's all I knew about life.

LYONS Fourteen's kinda young to be out on your own. (*Phone rings.*) I don't even think I was ready to be out on my own at fourteen. I don't know what I would have done.

TROY I got up from the creek and walked on down to Mobile. I was through with farming. Figured I could do better in the city. So I walked the two hundred miles to Mobile.

LYONS Wait a minute . . . you ain't walked no two hundred miles, Pop. Ain't nobody gonna walk no two hundred miles. You talking about some walking there.

BONO That's the only way you got anywhere back in them days.

LYONS Shhh. Damn if I wouldn't have hitched a ride with somebody!

TROY Who you gonna hitch it with? They ain't had no cars and things like they got now. We talking about 1918.

ROSE (*entering*): What you all out here getting into?

TROY (*to* **ROSE**): I'm telling Lyons how good he got it. He don't know nothing about this I'm talking.

ROSE Lyons, that was Bonnie on the phone. She say you supposed to pick her up.

LYONS Yeah, okay, Rose.

TROY I walked on down to Mobile and hitched up with some of them fellows that was heading this way. Got up here and found out . . . not only couldn't you get a job . . . you couldn't find no place to live. I thought I was in freedom. Shhh. Colored folks living down there on the riverbanks in whatever kind of shelter they could find for themselves. Right down there under the Brady Street Bridge. Living in shacks made of sticks and tarpaper. Messed around there and went from bad to worse. Started stealing. First it was food. Then I figured, hell, if I steal money I can buy me some food. Buy me some shoes too! One thing led to another. Met your mama. I was young and anxious to be a man. Met your mama and had you. What I do that for? Now I got to worry about feeding you and her. Got to steal three times as much. Went out one day looking for somebody to rob . . . that's what I was, a robber. I'll tell you the truth. I'm ashamed of it today. But it's the truth. Went to rob this fellow . . . pulled out my knife . . . and he pulled out a gun. Shot me in the chest. I felt just like somebody had taken a hot branding iron and laid it on me. When he shot me I jumped at him with my knife. They told me I killed him and they put me in the penitentiary and locked me up for fifteen years. That's where I met Bono. That's where I learned how to play baseball. Got out that place and your mama had taken you and went on to make life without me. Fifteen years was a long time for her to wait. But that fifteen years cured me of that robbing stuff. Rose'll tell you. She asked me when I met her if I had gotten all that foolishness out of my system. And I told her, "Baby, it's you and baseball all what count with me." You hear me, Bono? I meant it too. She say, "Which one comes first?" I told her, "Baby, ain't no doubt it's baseball . . . but you stick and get old with me and we'll both outlive this baseball." Am I right, Rose? And it's true.

ROSE Man, hush your mouth. You ain't said no such thing. Talking about, "Baby, you know you'll always be number one with me." That's what you was talking.

TROY You hear that, Bono. That's why I love her.

BONO Rose'll keep you straight. You get off the track, she'll straighten you up.

ROSE Lyons, you better get on up and get Bonnie. She waiting on you.

LYONS (*gets up to go*): Hey, Pop, why don't you come on down to the Grill and hear me play?

TROY I ain't going down there. I'm too old to be sitting around in them clubs.

BONO You got to be good to play down at the Grill.

LYONS Come on, Pop . . .

TROY I got to get up in the morning.

LYONS You ain't got to stay long.

TROY Naw, I'm gonna get my supper and go on to bed.

LYONS Well, I got to go. I'll see you again.

TROY Don't you come around my house on my payday.

ROSE Pick up the phone and let somebody know you coming. And bring Bonnie with you. You know I'm always glad to see her.

LYONS Yeah, I'll do that, Rose. You take care now. See you, Pop. See you, Mr. Bono. See you, Uncle Gabe.

GABRIEL Lyons! King of the Jungle!

LYONS *exits.*

TROY Is supper ready, woman? Me and you got some business to take care of. I'm gonna tear it up too.

ROSE Troy, I done told you now!

TROY (*puts his arm around* **BONO**): Aw hell, woman . . . this is Bono. Bono like family. I done known this nigger since . . . how long I done know you?

BONO It's been a long time.

TROY I done know this nigger since Skippy was a pup. Me and him done been through sometimes.

BONO You sure right about that.

TROY Hell, I done know him longer than I known you. And we still standing shoulder to shoulder. Hey, look here, Bono . . . a man can't ask for no more than that. (*Drinks to him.*) I love you, nigger.

BONO Hell, I love you too . . . I got to get home see my woman. You got yours in hand. I got to go get mine.

BONO *starts to exit as* **CORY** *enters the yard, dressed in his football uniform. He gives* **TROY** *a hard, uncompromising look.*

CORY What you do that for, Pop?

He throws his helmet down in the direction of **TROY**.

ROSE What's the matter? Cory . . . what's the matter?

CORY Papa done went up to the school and told Coach Zellman I can't play football no more. Wouldn't even let me play the game. Told him to tell the recruiter not to come.

ROSE Troy . . .

TROY What you Troying me for. Yeah, I did it. And the boy know why I did it.

CORY Why you wanna do that to me? That was the one chance I had.

ROSE Ain't nothing wrong with Cory playing football, Troy.

TROY The boy lied to me. I told the nigger if he wanna play football . . . to keep up his chores and hold down that job at the A&P. That was the conditions. Stopped down there to see Mr. Stawicki . . .

CORY I can't work after school during the football season, Pop! I tried to tell you that Mr. Stawicki's holding my job for me. You don't never want to listen to nobody. And then you wanna go and do this to me!

TROY I ain't done nothing to you. You done it to yourself.

CORY Just cause you didn't have a chance! You just scared I'm gonna be better than you, that's all.

TROY Come here.

ROSE Troy . . .

CORY *reluctantly crosses over to* **TROY**.

TROY All right! See. You done made a mistake.

CORY I didn't even do nothing!

TROY I'm gonna tell you what your mistake was. See . . . you swung at the ball and didn't hit it. That's strike one. See, you in the batter's box now. You swung and you missed. That's strike one. Don't you strike out!

Lights fade to black.

Act II Fences

Act II, Scene 1

The following morning. **CORY** *is at the tree hitting the ball with the bat. He tries to mimic* **TROY**, *but his swing is awkward, less sure.* **ROSE** *enters from the house.*

ROSE Cory, I want you to help me with this cupboard.

CORY I ain't quitting the team. I don't care what Poppa say.

ROSE I'll talk to him when he gets back. He had to go see about your Uncle Gabe. The police done arrested him. Say he was disturbing the peace. He'll be back directly. Come on in here and help me clean out the top of this cupboard.

CORY *exits into the house.* **ROSE** *sees* **TROY** *and* **BONO** *coming down the alley.*

Troy . . . what they say down there?

TROY Ain't said nothing. I give them fifty dollars and they let him go. I'll talk to you about it. Where's Cory?

ROSE He's in there helping me clean out these cupboards.

TROY Tell him to get his butt out here.

TROY *and* **BONO** *go over to the pile of wood.* **BONO** *picks up the saw and begins sawing.*

TROY (*to* **BONO**): All they want is the money. That makes six or seven times I done went down there and got him. See me coming they stick out their hands.

BONO Yeah. I know what you mean. That's all they care about . . . that money. They don't care about what's right. (*Pause.*) Nigger, why you got to go and get some hard wood? You ain't doing nothing but building a little old fence. Get you some soft pine wood. That's all you need.

TROY I know what I'm doing. This is outside wood. You put pine wood inside the house. Pine wood is inside wood. This here is outside wood. Now you tell me where the fence is gonna be?

BONO You don't need this wood. You can put it up with pine wood and it'll stand as long as you gonna be here looking at it.

TROY How you know how long I'm gonna be here, nigger? Hell, I might just live forever. Live longer than old man Horsely.

BONO That's what Magee used to say.

TROY Magee's a damn fool. Now you tell me who you ever heard of gonna pull their own teeth with a pair of rusty pliers.

BONO The old folks . . . my granddaddy used to pull his teeth with pliers. They ain't had no dentists for the colored folks back then.

TROY Get clean pliers! You understand? Clean pliers! Sterilize them! Besides we ain't living back then. All Magee had to do was walk over to Doc Goldblum's.

BONO I see where you and that Tallahassee gal . . . that Alberta . . . I see where you all done got tight.

TROY What you mean "got tight"?

BONO I see where you be laughing and joking with her all the time.

TROY I laughs and jokes with all of them, Bono. You know me.

BONO That ain't the kind of laughing and joking I'm talking about.

CORY *enters from the house.*

CORY How you doing, Mr. Bono?

TROY Cory? Get that saw from Bono and cut some wood. He talking about the wood's too hard to cut. Stand back there, Jim, and let that young boy show you how it's done.

BONO He's sure welcome to it.

CORY *takes the saw and begins to cut the wood.*

Whew-e-e! Look at that. Big old strong boy. Look like Joe Louis. Hell, must be getting old the way I'm watching that boy whip through that wood.

CORY I don't see why Mama want a fence around the yard noways.

TROY Damn if I know either. What the hell she keeping out with it? She ain't got nothing nobody want.

BONO Some people build fences to keep people out . . . and other people build fences to keep people in. Rose wants to hold on to you all. She loves you.

TROY Hell, nigger, I don't need nobody to tell me my wife loves me. Cory . . . go on in the house and see if you can find that other saw.

CORY Where's it at?

TROY I said find it! Look for it till you find it!

CORY *exits into the house.*

What's that supposed to mean? Wanna keep us in?

BONO Troy . . . I done known you seem like damn near my whole life. You and Rose both. I done know both of you all for a long time. I remember when you met Rose. When you was hitting them baseball out the park. A lot of them old gals was after you then. You had the pick of the litter. When you picked Rose, I was happy for you. That was the first time I knew you had any sense. I said . . . My man Troy knows what he's doing . . . I'm gonna follow this nigger . . . he might take me somewhere. I been following you too. I done learned a whole heap of things about life watching you. I done learned how to tell where the shit lies. How to tell it from the alfalfa. You done learned me a lot of things. You showed me how to not make the same mistakes . . . to take life as it comes along and keep putting one foot in front of the other. (*Pause.*) Rose a good woman, Troy.

TROY Hell, nigger, I know she a good woman. I been married to her for eighteen years. What you got on your mind, Bono?

BONO I just say she a good woman. Just like I say anything. I ain't got to have nothing on my mind.

TROY You just gonna say she a good woman and leave it hanging out there like that? Why you telling me she a good woman?

BONO She loves you, Troy. Rose loves you.

TROY You saying I don't measure up. That's what you trying to say. I don't measure up cause I'm seeing this other gal. I know what you trying to say.

BONO I know what Rose means to you, Troy. I'm just trying to say I don't want to see you mess up.

TROY Yeah, I appreciate that, Bono. If you was messing around on Lucille I'd be telling you the same thing.

BONO Well, that's all I got to say. I just say that because I love you both.

TROY Hell, you know me . . . I wasn't out there looking for nothing. You can't find a better woman than Rose. I know that. But seems like this woman just stuck onto me where I can't shake her loose. I done wrestled with it, tried to throw her off me . . . but she just stuck on tighter. Now she's stuck on for good.

BONO You's in control . . . that's what you tell me all the time. You responsible for what you do.

TROY I ain't ducking the responsibility of it. As long as it sets right in my heart . . . then I'm okay. Cause that's all I listen to. It'll tell me right from wrong every time. And I ain't talking about doing Rose no bad turn. I love Rose. She done carried me a long ways and I love and respect her for that.

BONO I know you do. That's why I don't want to see you hurt her. But what you gonna do when she find out? What you got then? If you try and juggle both of them . . . sooner or later you gonna drop one of them. That's common sense.

TROY Yeah, I hear what you saying, Bono. I been trying to figure a way to work it out.

BONO Work it out right, Troy. I don't want to be getting all up between you and Rose's business . . . but work it so it come out right.

TROY Ah hell, I get all up between you and Lucille's business. When you gonna get that woman that refrigerator she been wanting? Don't tell me you ain't got no money now. I know who your banker is. Mellon don't need that money bad as Lucille want that refrigerator. I'll tell you that.

BONO Tell you what I'll do . . . when you finish building this fence for Rose . . . I'll buy Lucille that refrigerator.

TROY You done stuck your foot in your mouth now!

TROY *grabs up a board and begins to saw.* **BONO** *starts to walk out the yard.*

Hey, nigger . . . where you going?

BONO I'm going home. I know you don't expect me to help you now. I'm protecting my money. I wanna see you put that fence up by yourself. That's what I want to see. You'll be here another six months without me.

TROY Nigger, you ain't right.

BONO When it comes to my money . . . I'm right as fireworks on the Fourth of July.

TROY All right, we gonna see now. You better get out your bankbook.

BONO *exits, and* **TROY** *continues to work.* **ROSE** *enters from the house.*

ROSE What they say down there? What's happening with Gabe?

TROY I went down there and got him out. Cost me fifty dollars. Say he was disturbing the peace. Judge set up a hearing for him in three weeks. Say to show cause why he shouldn't be recommitted.

ROSE What was he doing that cause them to arrest him?

TROY Some kids was teasing him and he run them off home. Say he was howling and carrying on. Some folks seen him and called the police. That's all it was.

ROSE Well, what's you say? What'd you tell the judge?

TROY Told him I'd look after him. It didn't make no sense to recommit the man. He stuck out his big greasy palm and told me to give him fifty dollars and take him on home.

ROSE Where's he at now? Where'd he go off to?

TROY He's gone about his business. He don't need nobody to hold his hand.

ROSE Well, I don't know. Seem like that would be the best place for him if they did put him into the hospital. I know what you're gonna say. But that's what I think would be best.

TROY The man done had his life ruined fighting for what? And they wanna take and lock him up. Let him be free. He don't bother nobody.

ROSE Well, everybody got their own way of looking at it I guess. Come on and get your lunch. I got a bowl of lima beans and some cornbread in the oven. Come and get something to eat. Ain't no sense you fretting over Gabe.

ROSE *turns to go into the house.*

TROY Rose . . . got something to tell you.

ROSE Well, come on . . . wait till I get this food on the table.

TROY Rose!

She stops and turns around.

I don't know how to say this. (*Pause.*) I can't explain it none. It just sort of grows on you till it gets out of hand. It starts out like a little bush . . . and the next thing you know it's a whole forest.

ROSE Troy . . . what is you talking about?

TROY I'm talking, woman, let me talk. I'm trying to find a way to tell you . . . I'm gonna be a daddy. I'm gonna be somebody's daddy.

ROSE Troy . . . you're not telling me this? You're gonna be . . . what?

TROY Rose . . . now . . . see . . .

ROSE You telling me you gonna be somebody's daddy? You telling your *wife* this?

GABRIEL *enters from the street. He carries a rose in his hand.*

GABRIEL Hey, Troy! Hey, Rose!

ROSE I have to wait eighteen years to hear something like this.

GABRIEL Hey, Rose . . . I got a flower for you. (*He hands it to her.*) That's a rose. Same rose like you is.

ROSE Thanks, Gabe.

GABRIEL Troy, you ain't mad at me is you? Them bad mens come and put me away. You ain't mad at me is you?

TROY Naw, Gabe, I ain't mad at you.

ROSE Eighteen years and you wanna come with this.

GABRIEL (*takes a quarter out of his pocket*): See what I got? Got a brand new quarter.

TROY Rose . . . it's just . . .

ROSE Ain't nothing you can say, Troy. Ain't no way of explaining that.

GABRIEL Fellow that give me this quarter had a whole mess of them. I'm gonna keep this quarter till it stop shining.

ROSE Gabe, go on in the house there. I got some watermelon in the Frigidaire. Go on and get you a piece.

GABRIEL Say, Rose . . . you know I was chasing hellhounds and them bad mens come and get me and take me away. Troy helped me. He come down there and told them they better let me go before he beat them up. Yeah, he did!

ROSE You go on and get you a piece of watermelon, Gabe. Them bad mens is gone now.

GABRIEL Okay, Rose . . . gonna get me some watermelon. The kind with the stripes on it.

GABRIEL *exits into the house.*

ROSE Why, Troy? Why? After all these years to come dragging this in to me now. It don't make no sense at your age. I could have expected this ten or fifteen years ago, but not now.

TROY Age ain't got nothing to do with it, Rose.

ROSE I done tried to be everything a wife should be. Everything a wife could be. Been married eighteen years and I got to live to see the day you tell me you been seeing another woman and done fathered a child by her. And you know I ain't never wanted no half nothing in my family. My whole family is half. Everybody got different fathers and mothers . . . my two sisters and my brother. Can't hardly tell who's who. Can't never sit down and talk about Papa and Mama. It's your papa and your mama and my papa and my mama . . .

TROY Rose . . . stop it now.

ROSE I ain't never wanted that for none of my children. And now you wanna drag your behind in here and tell me something like this.

TROY You ought to know. It's time for you to know.

ROSE Well, I don't want to know, goddamn it!

TROY I can't just make it go away. It's done now. I can't wish the circumstance of the thing away.

ROSE And you don't want to either. Maybe you want to wish me and my boy away. Maybe that's what you want? Well, you can't wish us away. I've got eighteen years of my life invested in you. You ought to have stayed upstairs in my bed where you belong.

TROY Rose . . . now listen to me . . . we can get a handle on this thing. We can talk this out . . . come to an understanding.

ROSE All of a sudden it's "we." Where was "we" at when you was down there rolling around with some godforsaken woman? "We" should have come to an understanding before you started making a damn fool of yourself. You're a day late and a dollar short when it comes to an understanding with me.

TROY It's just . . . She gives me a different idea . . . a different understanding about myself. I can step out of this house and get away from the pressures and problems . . . be a different man. I ain't got to wonder how I'm gonna pay the bills or get the roof fixed. I can just be a part of myself that I ain't never been.

ROSE What I want to know . . . is do you plan to continue seeing her. That's all you can say to me.

TROY I can sit up in her house and laugh. Do you understand what I'm saying. I can laugh out loud . . . and it feels good. It reaches all the way down to the bottom of my shoes. (*Pause.*) Rose, I can't give that up.

ROSE Maybe you ought to go on and stay down there with her . . . if she's a better woman than me.

TROY It ain't about nobody being a better woman or nothing. Rose, you ain't the blame. A man couldn't ask for no woman to be a better wife than you've been. I'm responsible for it. I done locked myself into a pattern trying to take care of you all that I forgot about myself.

ROSE What the hell was I there for? That was my job, not somebody else's.

TROY Rose, I done tried all my life to live decent . . . to live a clean . . . hard . . . useful life. I tried to be a good husband to you. In every way I knew how. Maybe I come into the world backwards, I don't know. But . . . you born with two strikes on you before you come to the plate. You got to guard it closely . . . always looking for the curve ball on the inside corner. You can't afford to let none get past you. You can't afford a call strike. If you going down . . . you going down swinging. Everything lined up against you. What you gonna do. I fooled them, Rose. I bunted. When I found you and Cory and a halfway decent job . . . I was safe. Couldn't nothing touch me. I wasn't gonna strike out no more. I wasn't going back to the penitentiary. I wasn't gonna lay in the streets with a bottle of wine. I was safe. I had me a family. A job. I wasn't gonna get that last strike. I was on first looking for one of them boys to knock me in. To get me home.

ROSE You should have stayed in my bed, Troy.

TROY Then when I saw that gal . . . she firmed up my backbone. And I got to thinking that if I tried . . . I just might be able to steal second. Do you understand after eighteen years I wanted to steal second.

ROSE You should have held me tight. You should have grabbed me and held on.

TROY I stood on first base for eighteen years and I thought . . . well, goddamn it . . . go on for it!

ROSE We're not talking about baseball! We're talking about you going off to lay in bed with another woman . . . and then bring it home to me. That's what we're talking about. We ain't talking about no baseball.

TROY Rose, you're not listening to me. I'm trying the best I can to explain it to you. It's not easy for me to admit that I been standing in the same place for eighteen years.

ROSE I been standing with you! I been right here with you, Troy. I got a life too. I gave eighteen years of my life to stand in the same spot with you. Don't you think I ever wanted other things? Don't you think I had dreams and hopes? What about my life? What about me. Don't you think it ever crossed my mind to want to know other men? That I wanted to lay up somewhere and forget about my responsibilities? That I wanted someone to make me laugh so I could feel good? You not the only one who's got wants and needs. But I held on to you, Troy. I took all my feelings, my wants and needs, my dreams . . . and I buried them inside you. I planted a seed and watched and prayed over it. I planted myself inside you and waited to bloom. And it didn't take me no eighteen years to find out the soil was hard and rocky and it wasn't never gonna bloom.

But I held on to you, Troy. I held you tighter. You was my husband. I owed you everything I had. Every part of me I could find to give you. And upstairs in that room . . . with the darkness falling in on me . . . I gave everything I had to try and erase the doubt that you wasn't the finest man in the world. And wherever you was going . . . I wanted to be there with you. Cause you was my husband. Cause that's the only way I was gonna survive as your wife. You always talking about what you give . . . and what you don't have to give. But you take too. You take . . . and don't even know nobody's giving!

ROSE *turns to exit into the house;* **TROY** *grabs her arm.*

TROY You say I take and don't give!

ROSE Troy! You're hurting me!

TROY You say I take and don't give!

ROSE Troy . . . you're hurting my arm! Let go!

extending beyond the text

In 2018, E. Ethelbert Miller published a poetry collection entitled *If God Invented Baseball*, a tribute to his love of the game and a reflection on race in the sport. "Knuckleball," one of the poems, uses baseball as an occasion to comment on aspects of Black history and culture.

from Knuckleball

E. Ethelbert Miller

Every black man should be born
with a big mitt.
How else can one catch the world
That flutters in unpredictable ways.

The sound of a knuckleball
is Parker on his horn.
When Ella scats don't try
to copy her.

Oriole Hoyt Wilhelm in 1958 threw
a no-hitter against the Yankees.
It was like Douglass being Lincoln
For a day. It's impossible to dance
To slavery anymore. It ended with
the hangman's swing.

The knuckleball is Bebop.
Don't be baffled by its strange beauty.
Just keep hitting it with your ears. ■

1. **A knuckleball is a slow pitch that has virtually no spin and moves erratically and unpredictably. How does Miller turn this literal meaning into a metaphor for what it means to be Black?**
2. **What do the allusions to jazz musicians such as Charlie "Bird" Parker and Ella Fitzgerald, and to jazz terms such as Bebop, add to the poem's meaning?**
3. **How does Troy's life "[flutter] in unpredictable ways" (l. 4)?**
4. **How does *Fences* support or challenge the speaker's assertion that "It's impossible to dance / To slavery anymore" (ll. 12–13)?**

This image is from the 2016 film version of *Fences* starring Denzel Washington as Troy and Viola Davis as Rose.

What aspects of Troy and Rose's relationship does this image capture?

TROY I done give you everything I got. Don't you tell that lie on me.

ROSE Troy!

TROY Don't you tell that lie on me!

CORY *enters from the house.*

CORY Mama!

ROSE Troy. You're hurting me.

TROY Don't you tell me about no taking and giving.

CORY *comes up behind* **TROY** *and grabs him.* **TROY**, *surprised, is thrown off balance just as* **CORY** *throws a glancing blow that catches him on the chest and knocks him down.* **TROY** *is stunned, as is* **CORY**.

ROSE Troy. Troy. No!

TROY *gets to his feet and starts at* **CORY**.

Troy . . . no. Please! Troy!

ROSE *pulls on* **TROY** *to hold him back.* **TROY** *stops himself.*

TROY (*to* **CORY**): All right. That's strike two. You stay away from around me, boy. Don't you strike out. You living with a full count. Don't you strike out.

TROY *exits out the yard as the lights go down.*

Act II, Scene 2

It is six months later, early afternoon. **TROY** *enters from the house and starts to exit the yard.* **ROSE** *enters from the house.*

ROSE Troy, I want to talk to you.

TROY All of a sudden, after all this time, you want to talk to me, huh? You ain't wanted to talk to me for months. You ain't wanted to talk to me last night. You ain't wanted no part of me then. What you wanna talk to me about now?

ROSE Tomorrow's Friday.

TROY I know what day tomorrow is. You think I don't know tomorrow's Friday? My whole life I ain't done nothing but look to see Friday coming and you got to tell me it's Friday.

ROSE I want to know if you're coming home.

TROY I always come home, Rose. You know that. There ain't never been a night I ain't come home.

ROSE That ain't what I mean . . . and you know it. I want to know if you're coming straight home after work.

TROY I figure I'd cash my check . . . hang out at Taylors' with the boys . . . maybe play a game of checkers . . .

ROSE Troy, I can't live like this. I won't live like this. You livin' on borrowed time with me. It's been going on six months now you ain't been coming home.

TROY I be here every night. Every night of the year. That's 365 days.

ROSE I want you to come home tomorrow after work.

TROY Rose . . . I don't mess up my pay. You know that now. I take my pay and I give it to you. I don't have no money but what you give me back. I just want to have a little time to myself . . . a little time to enjoy life.

ROSE What about me? When's my time to enjoy life?

TROY I don't know what to tell you, Rose. I'm doing the best I can.

ROSE You ain't been home from work but time enough to change your clothes and run out . . . and you wanna call that the best you can do?

TROY I'm going over to the hospital to see Alberta. She went into the hospital this afternoon. Look like she might have the baby early. I won't be gone long.

ROSE Well, you ought to know. They went over to Miss Pearl's and got Gabe today. She said you told them to go ahead and lock him up.

TROY I ain't said no such thing. Whoever told you that is telling a lie. Pearl ain't doing nothing but telling a big fat lie.

ROSE She ain't had to tell me. I read it on the papers.

TROY I ain't told them nothing of the kind.

ROSE I saw it right there on the papers.

TROY What it say, huh?

ROSE It said you told them to take him.

TROY Then they screwed that up, just the way they screw up everything. I ain't worried about what they got on the paper.

ROSE Say the government send part of his check to the hospital and the other part to you.

TROY I ain't got nothing to do with that if that's the way it works. I ain't made up the rules about how it work.

ROSE You did Gabe just like you did Cory. You wouldn't sign the paper for Cory . . . but you signed for Gabe. You signed that paper.

The telephone is heard ringing inside the house.

TROY I told you I ain't signed nothing, woman! The only thing I signed was the release form. Hell, I can't read, I don't know what they had on that paper! I ain't signed nothing about sending Gabe away.

ROSE I said send him to the hospital . . . you said let him be free . . . now you done went down there and signed him to the hospital for half his money. You went back on yourself, Troy. You gonna have to answer for that.

TROY See now . . . you been over there talking to Miss Pearl. She done got mad cause she ain't getting Gabe's rent money. That's all it is. She's liable to say anything.

ROSE Troy, I seen where you signed the paper.

TROY You ain't seen nothing I signed. What she doing got papers on my brother anyway? Miss Pearl telling a big fat lie. And I'm gonna tell her about it too! You ain't seen nothing I signed. Say . . . you ain't seen nothing I signed.

ROSE *exits into the house to answer the telephone. Presently she returns.*

ROSE Troy . . . that was the hospital. Alberta had the baby.

TROY What she have? What is it?

ROSE It's a girl.

TROY I better get on down to the hospital to see her.

ROSE Troy . . .

TROY Rose . . . I got to go see her now. That's only right . . . what's the matter . . . the baby's all right, ain't it?

ROSE Alberta died having the baby.

TROY Died . . . you say she's dead? Alberta's dead?

ROSE They said they done all they could. They couldn't do nothing for her.

TROY The baby? How's the baby?

ROSE They say it's healthy. I wonder who's gonna bury her.

TROY She had family, Rose. She wasn't living in the world by herself.

ROSE I know she wasn't living in the world by herself.

TROY Next thing you gonna want to know if she had any insurance.

ROSE Troy, you ain't got to talk like that.

TROY That's the first thing that jumped out your mouth. "Who's gonna bury her?" Like I'm fixing to take on that task for myself.

ROSE I am your wife. Don't push me away.

TROY I ain't pushing nobody away. Just give me some space. That's all. Just give me some room to breathe.

ROSE *exits into the house.* **TROY** *walks about the yard.*

TROY (*with a quiet rage that threatens to consume him*): All right . . . Mr. Death. See now . . . I'm gonna tell you what I'm gonna do. I'm gonna take and build me a fence around this yard. See? I'm gonna build me a fence around what belongs to me. And then I want you to stay on the other side. See? You stay over there until you're ready for me. Then you come on. Bring your army. Bring your sickle. Bring your wrestling clothes. I ain't gonna fall down on my vigilance this time. You ain't gonna sneak up on me no more. When you ready for me . . . when the top of your list say Troy Maxson . . . that's when you come around here. You come up and knock on the front door. Ain't nobody else got nothing to do with this. This is between you and me. Man to man. You stay on the other side of that fence until you ready for me. Then you come up and knock on the front door. Anytime you want. I'll be ready for you.

The lights go down to black.

Act II, Scene 3

The lights come up on the porch. It is late evening three days later. **ROSE** *sits listening to the ball game waiting for* **TROY**. *The final out of the game is made and* **ROSE** *switches off the radio.* **TROY** *enters the yard carrying an infant wrapped in blankets. He stands back from the house and calls.*

ROSE *enters and stands on the porch. There is a long, awkward silence, the weight of which grows heavier with each passing second.*

TROY Rose . . . I'm standing here with my daughter in my arms. She ain't but a wee bittie little old thing. She don't know nothing about grownups' business. She innocent . . . and she ain't got no mama.

ROSE What you telling me for, Troy?

She turns and exits into the house.

TROY Well . . . I guess we'll just sit out here on the porch.

He sits down on the porch. There is an awkward indelicateness about the way he handles the baby. His largeness engulfs and seems to swallow it. He speaks loud enough for **ROSE** *to hear.*

A man's got to do what's right for him. I ain't sorry for nothing I done. It felt right in my heart. (*To the baby.*) What you smiling at? Your daddy's a big man. Got these great big old hands. But sometimes he's scared. And right now your daddy's scared cause we sitting out here and ain't got no home. Oh, I been homeless before. I ain't had no little baby with me. But I been homeless. You just be out on the road by your lonesome and you see one of them trains coming and you just kinda go like this . . .

He sings as a lullaby.

Please, Mr. Engineer let a man ride the line
Please, Mr. Engineer let a man ride the line
I ain't got no ticket please let me ride the blinds

ROSE *enters from the house.* **TROY**, *hearing her steps behind him, stands and faces her.*

She's my daughter, Rose. My own flesh and blood. I can't deny her no more than I can deny them boys. (*Pause.*) You and them boys is my family. You and them and this child is all I got in the world. So I guess what I'm saying is . . . I'd appreciate it if you'd help me take care of her.

ROSE Okay, Troy . . . you're right. I'll take care of your baby for you . . . cause . . . like you say . . . she's innocent . . . and you can't visit the sins of the father upon the child. A motherless child has got a hard time. (*She takes the baby from him.*) From right now . . . this child got a mother. But you a womanless man.

ROSE *turns and exits into the house with the baby. Lights go down to black.*

It is two months later. **LYONS** *enters from the street. He knocks on the door and calls.*

LYONS Hey, Rose! (*Pause.*): Rose!

ROSE (*from inside the house*): Stop that yelling. You gonna wake up Raynell. I just got her to sleep.

LYONS I just stopped by to pay Papa this twenty dollars I owe him. Where's Papa at?

ROSE He should be here in a minute. I'm getting ready to go down to the church. Sit down and wait on him.

LYONS I got to go pick up Bonnie over her mother's house.

ROSE Well, sit it down there on the table. He'll get it.

LYONS (*enters the house and sets the money on the table*): Tell Papa I said thanks. I'll see you again.

ROSE All right, Lyons. We'll see you.

LYONS *starts to exit as* **CORY** *enters.*

CORY Hey, Lyons.

LYONS What's happening, Cory? Say man, I'm sorry I missed your graduation. You know I had a gig and couldn't get away. Otherwise, I would have been there, man. So what you doing?

CORY I'm trying to find a job.

LYONS Yeah I know how that go, man. It's rough out here. Jobs are scarce.

CORY Yeah, I know.

LYONS Look here, I got to run. Talk to Papa . . . he know some people. He'll be able to help get you a job. Talk to him . . . see what he say.

CORY Yeah . . . all right, Lyons.

LYONS: You take care. I'll talk to you soon. We'll find some time to talk.

LYONS *exits the yard.* **CORY** *wanders over to the tree, picks up the bat, and assumes a batting stance. He studies an imaginary pitcher and swings. Dissatisfied with the result, he tries again.* **TROY** *enters. They eye each other for a beat.* **CORY** *puts the bat down and exits the yard.* **TROY** *starts into the house as* **ROSE** *exits with* **RAYNELL**. *She is carrying a cake.*

TROY I'm coming in and everybody's going out.

ROSE I'm taking this cake down to the church for the bake sale. Lyons was by to see you. He stopped by to pay you your twenty dollars. It's laying in there on the table.

TROY (*going into his pocket*): Well . . . here go this money.

ROSE Put it in there on the table, Troy. I'll get it.

TROY What time you coming back?

ROSE Ain't no use in you studying me. It don't matter what time I come back.

TROY I just asked you a question, woman. What's the matter . . . can't I ask you a question?

ROSE Troy, I don't want to go into it. Your dinner's in there on the stove. All you got to do is heat it up. And don't you be eating the rest of them cakes in there. I'm coming back for them. We having a bake sale at the church tomorrow.

ROSE *exits the yard.* **TROY** *sits down on the steps, takes a pint bottle from his pocket, opens it, and drinks. He begins to sing*

TROY Hear it ring! Hear it ring!
Had an old dog his name was Blue
You know Blue was mighty true
You know Blue was a good old dog
Blue trees a possum in a hollow log
You know from that he was a good old dog

BONO *enters the yard.*

BONO Hey, Troy.

TROY Hey, what's happening, Bono?

BONO I just thought I'd stop by to see you.

TROY What you stop by and see me for? You ain't stopped by in a month of Sundays. Hell, I must owe you money or something.

BONO Since you got your promotion I can't keep up with you. Used to see you every day. Now I don't even know what route you working.

TROY They keep switching me around. Got me out in Greentree now . . . hauling white folks' garbage.

BONO Greentree, huh? You lucky, at least you ain't got to be lifting them barrels. Damn if they ain't getting heavier. I'm gonna put in my two years and call it quits.

TROY I'm thinking about retiring myself.

BONO You got it easy. You can *drive* for another five years.

TROY It ain't the same, Bono. It ain't like working the back of the truck. Ain't got nobody to talk to . . . feel like you working by yourself. Naw, I'm thinking about retiring. How's Lucille?

BONO She all right. Her arthritis get to acting up on her sometime. Saw Rose on my way in. She going down to the church, huh?

TROY Yeah, she took up going down there. All them preachers looking for somebody to fatten their pockets. (*Pause.*) Got some gin here.

BONO Naw, thanks. I just stopped by to say hello.

TROY Hell, nigger . . . you can take a drink. I ain't never known you to say no to a drink. You ain't got to work tomorrow.

BONO I just stopped by. I'm fixing to go over to Skinner's. We got us a domino game going over his house every Friday.

TROY Nigger, you can't play no dominoes. I used to whup you four games out of five.

BONO Well, that learned me. I'm getting better.

TROY Yeah? Well, that's all right.

BONO Look here . . . I got to be getting on. Stop by sometime, huh?

TROY Yeah, I'll do that, Bono. Lucille told Rose you bought her a new refrigerator.

BONO Yeah, Rose told Lucille you had finally built your fence . . . so I figured we'd call it even.

TROY I knew you would.

BONO Yeah . . . okay. I'll be talking to you.

TROY Yeah, take care, Bono. Good to see you. I'm gonna stop over.

BONO Yeah. Okay, Troy.

BONO *exits.* **TROY** *drinks from the bottle.*

TROY Old Blue died and I dig his grave
Let him down with a golden chain
Every night when I hear old Blue bark
I know Blue treed a possum in Noah's Ark.
Hear it ring! Hear it ring!

CORY *enters the yard. They eye each other for a beat.* **TROY** *is sitting in the middle of the steps.* **CORY** *walks over.*

CORY I got to get by.

TROY Say what? What's you say?

CORY You in my way. I got to get by.

TROY You got to get by where? This is my house. Bought and paid for. In full. Took me fifteen years. And if you wanna go in my house and I'm sitting on the steps . . . you say excuse me. Like your mama taught you.

CORY Come on, Pop . . . I got to get by.

CORY *starts to maneuver his way past* **TROY.**
TROY *grabs his leg and shoves him back.*

TROY You just gonna walk over top of me?

CORY I live here too!

TROY (*advancing toward him*): You just gonna walk over top of me in my own house?

CORY I ain't scared of you.

TROY I ain't asked if you was scared of me. I asked you if you was fixing to walk over top of me in my own house? That's the question. You ain't gonna say excuse me? You just gonna walk over top of me?

CORY If you wanna put it like that.

TROY How else am I gonna put it?

CORY I was walking by you to go into the house cause you sitting on the steps drunk, singing to yourself. You can put it like that.

TROY Without saying excuse me???

CORY *doesn't respond.*

I asked you a question. Without saying excuse me???

CORY I ain't got to say excuse me to you. You don't count around here no more.

TROY Oh, I see . . . I don't count around here no more. You ain't got to say excuse me to your daddy. All of a sudden you done got so grown that your daddy don't count around here no more . . . Around here in his own house and yard that he done paid for with the sweat of his brow. You done got so grown to where you gonna take over. You gonna take over my house. Is that right? You gonna wear my pants. You gonna go in there and stretch out on my bed. You ain't got to say excuse me cause I don't count around here no more. Is that right?

CORY That's right. You always talking this dumb stuff. Now, why don't you just get out my way?

TROY I guess you got someplace to sleep and something to put in your belly. You got that, huh? You got that? That's what you need. You got that, huh?

CORY You don't know what I got. You ain't got to worry about what I got.

TROY You right! You one hundred percent right! I done spent the last seventeen years worrying about what you got. Now it's your turn, see? I'll tell you what to do. You grown . . . we done established that. You a man. Now, let's see you act like one. Turn your behind around and walk out this yard. And when you get out there in the alley . . . you can forget about this house. See? Cause this is my house. You go on and be a man and get your own house. You can forget about this. Cause this is mine. You go on and get yours cause I'm through with doing for you.

CORY You talking about what you did for me . . . what'd you ever give me?

TROY Them feet and bones! That pumping heart, nigger! I give you more than anybody else is ever gonna give you.

CORY You ain't never gave me nothing! You ain't never done nothing but hold me back. Afraid I was gonna be better than you. All you ever did was try and make me scared of you. I used to tremble every time you called my name. Every time I heard your footsteps in the house. Wondering all the time . . . what's Papa gonna say if I do this? . . . What's he gonna say if I do that? . . . What's Papa gonna say if I turn on the radio? And Mama, too . . . she tries . . . but she's scared of you.

TROY You leave your mama out of this. She ain't got nothing to do with this.

CORY I don't know how she stand you . . . after what you did to her.

TROY I told you to leave your mama out of this!

He advances toward CORY.

CORY What you gonna do . . . give me a whupping? You can't whup me no more. You're too old. You just an old man.

TROY (*shoves him on his shoulder*): Nigger! That's what you are. You just another nigger on the street to me!

CORY You crazy! You know that?

TROY Go on now! You got the devil in you. Get on away from me!

CORY You just a crazy old man . . . talking about I got the devil in me.

TROY Yeah, I'm crazy! If you don't get on the other side of that yard . . . I'm gonna show you how crazy I am! Go on . . . get the hell out of my yard.

CORY It ain't your yard. You took Uncle Gabe's money he got from the army to buy this house and then you put him out.

TROY (*advances on* CORY): Get your black ass out of my yard!

TROY*'s advance backs* CORY *up against the tree.* CORY *grabs up the bat.*

CORY I ain't going nowhere! Come on . . . put me out! I ain't scared of you.

TROY That's my bat!

Ron Scherl/ArenaPAL

This photograph of James Earl Jones as Troy Maxson in the 1987 Broadway production of *Fences* is entitled "Troy Maxson takes a swing at death."

How does this image capture the ambiguity of a central metaphor in the play?

CORY Come on!

TROY Put my bat down!

CORY Come on, put me out.

CORY *swings at* **TROY**, *who backs across the yard.*

What's the matter? You so bad . . . put me out!

TROY *advances toward* **CORY**.

CORY (*backing up*): Come on! Come on!

TROY You're gonna have to use it! You wanna draw that bat back on me . . . you're gonna have to use it.

CORY Come on! . . . Come on!

CORY *swings the bat at* **TROY** *a second time. He misses.* **TROY** *continues to advance toward him.*

TROY You're gonna have to kill me! You wanna draw that bat back on me. You're gonna have to kill me.

CORY, *backed up against the tree, can go no farther.* **TROY** *taunts him. He sticks out his head and offers him a target.*

Come on! Come on!

CORY *is unable to swing the bat.* **TROY** *grabs it.*

TROY Then I'll show you.

CORY *and* **TROY** *struggle over the bat. The struggle is fierce and fully engaged.* **TROY** *ultimately is the stronger and takes the bat from* **CORY** *and stands over him ready to swing. He stops himself.*

Go on and get away from around my house.

CORY, *stung by his defeat, picks himself up, walks slowly out of the yard and up the alley.*

CORY Tell Mama I'll be back for my things.

TROY They'll be on the other side of that fence.

CORY *exits.*

TROY I can't taste nothing. Helluljah! I can't taste nothing no more. (**TROY** *assumes a batting posture and begins to taunt Death, the fastball on the outside corner.*) Come on! It's between you and me now! Come on! Anytime you want! Come on! I be ready for you . . . but I ain't gonna be easy.

The lights go down on the scene.

Act II, Scene 5

The time is 1965. The lights come up in the yard. It is the morning of **TROY**'s *funeral. A funeral plaque with a light hangs beside the door. There is a small garden plot off to the side. There is noise and activity in the house as* **ROSE, LYONS**, *and* **BONO** *have gathered. The door opens and* **RAYNELL**, *seven years old, enters dressed in a flannel nightgown. She crosses to the garden and pokes around with a stick.* **ROSE** *calls from the house.*

ROSE Raynell!

RAYNELL Mam?

ROSE What you doing out there?

RAYNELL Nothing.

ROSE *comes to the door.*

ROSE Girl, get in here and get dressed. What you doing?

RAYNELL Seeing if my garden growed.

ROSE I told you it ain't gonna grow overnight. You got to wait.

RAYNELL It don't look like it never gonna grow. Dag!

ROSE I told you a watched pot never boils. Get in here and get dressed.

RAYNELL This ain't even no pot, Mama.

ROSE You just have to give it a chance. It'll grow. Now you come on and do what I told you. We got to be getting ready. This ain't no morning to be playing around. You hear me?

RAYNELL Yes, Mam.

ROSE *exits into the house.* **RAYNELL** *continues to poke at her garden with a stick.* **CORY** *enters. He is dressed in a Marine corporal's uniform, and carries a duffel bag. His posture is that of a military man, and his speech has a clipped sternness.*

CORY (*to* **RAYNELL**): Hi. (*Pause.*) I bet your name is Raynell.

RAYNELL Uh huh.

CORY Is your mama home?

RAYNELL *runs up on the porch and calls through the screen door.*

RAYNELL Mama . . . there's some man out here. Mama?

ROSE *comes to the door.*

ROSE Cory? Lord have mercy! Look here, you all!

ROSE *and* CORY *embrace in a tearful reunion as* BONO *and* LYONS *enter from the house dressed in funeral clothes.*

BONO Aw, looka here . . .

ROSE Done got all grown up!

CORY Don't cry, Mama. What you crying about?

ROSE I'm just so glad you made it.

CORY Hey Lyons. How you doing, Mr. Bono.

LYONS *goes to embrace* CORY.

LYONS Look at you, man. Look at you. Don't he look good, Rose. Got them Corporal stripes.

ROSE What took you so long?

CORY You know how the Marines are, Mama. They got to get all their paperwork straight before they let you do anything.

ROSE Well, I'm sure glad you made it. They let Lyons come. Your Uncle Gabe's still in the hospital. They don't know if they gonna let him out or not. I just talked to them a little while ago.

LYONS A Corporal in the United States Marines.

BONO Your daddy knew you had it in you. He used to tell me all the time.

LYONS Don't he look good, Mr. Bono?

BONO Yeah, he remind me of Troy when I first met him. (*Pause.*) Say, Rose, Lucille's down at the church with the choir. I'm gonna go down and get the pallbearers lined up. I'll be back to get you all.

ROSE Thanks, Jim.

CORY See you, Mr. Bono.

LYONS (*with his arm around* RAYNELL): Cory . . . look at Raynell. Ain't she precious? She gonna break a whole lot of hearts.

ROSE Raynell, come and say hello to your brother. This is your brother, Cory. You remember Cory.

RAYNELL No, Mam.

CORY She don't remember me, Mama.

ROSE Well, we talk about you. She heard us talk about you. (*To* RAYNELL.) This is your brother, Cory. Come on and say hello.

RAYNELL Hi.

CORY Hi. So you're Raynell. Mama told me a lot about you.

ROSE You all come on into the house and let me fix you some breakfast. Keep up your strength.

CORY I ain't hungry, Mama.

LYONS You can fix me something, Rose. I'll be in there in a minute.

ROSE Cory, you sure you don't want nothing? I know they ain't feeding you right.

CORY No, Mama . . . thanks. I don't feel like eating. I'll get something later.

ROSE Raynell . . . get on upstairs and get that dress on like I told you.

ROSE *and* RAYNELL *exit into the house.*

LYONS So . . . I hear you thinking about getting married.

CORY Yeah, I done found the right one, Lyons. It's about time.

LYONS Me and Bonnie been split up about four years now. About the time Papa retired. I guess she just got tired of all them changes I was putting her through. (*Pause.*) I always knew you was gonna make something out yourself. Your head was always in the right direction. So . . . you gonna stay in . . . make it a career . . . put in your twenty years?

CORY I don't know. I got six already, I think that's enough.

LYONS Stick with Uncle Sam and retire early. Ain't nothing out here. I guess Rose told you what happened with me. They got me down the workhouse. I thought I was being slick cashing other people's checks.

CORY How much time you doing?

LYONS They give me three years. I got that beat now. I ain't got but nine more months. It ain't so bad. You learn to deal with it like anything else. You got to take the crookeds with the straights. That's what Papa used to say. He used to say that when he struck out. I seen him strike out three times in a row . . . and the next time up he hit the ball over the grandstand. Right out there in Homestead Field. He wasn't satisfied hitting in the seats . . . he want to hit it over everything! After the game he had two hundred people standing around waiting to shake his hand. You got to take the crookeds with the straights. Yeah, Papa was something else.

CORY You still playing?

LYONS Cory . . . you know I'm gonna do that. There's some fellows down there we got us a band . . . we gonna try and stay together when we get out . . . but yeah, I'm still playing. It still helps me to get out of bed in the morning. As long as it do that I'm gonna be right there playing and trying to make some sense out of it.

ROSE (*calling*): Lyons, I got these eggs in the pan.

LYONS Let me go on and get these eggs, man. Get ready to go bury Papa. (*Pause.*) How you doing? You doing all right?

CORY *nods.* **LYONS** *touches him on the shoulder and they share a moment of silent grief.* **LYONS** *exits into the house.* **CORY** *wanders about the yard.* **RAYNELL** *enters.*

RAYNELL Hi.

CORY Hi.

RAYNELL Did you used to sleep in my room?

CORY Yeah . . . that used to be my room.

RAYNELL That's what Papa call it. "Cory's room." It got your football in the closet.

ROSE *comes to the door.*

ROSE Raynell, get in there and get them good shoes on.

RAYNELL Mama, can't I wear these? Them other one hurt my feet.

ROSE Well, they just gonna have to hurt your feet for a while. You ain't said they hurt your feet when you went down to the store and got them.

RAYNELL They didn't hurt then. My feet done got bigger.

ROSE Don't you give me no backtalk now. You get in there and get them shoes on.

RAYNELL *exits into the house.*

Ain't too much changed. He still got that piece of rag tied to that tree. He was out here swinging that bat. I was just ready to go back in the house. He swung that bat and then he just fell over. Seem like he swung it and stood there with this grin on his face . . . and then he just fell over. They carried him on down to the hospital, but I knew there wasn't no need . . . why don't you come on in the house?

CORY Mama . . . I got something to tell you. I don't know how to tell you this . . . but I've got to tell you . . . I'm not going to Papa's funeral.

ROSE Boy, hush your mouth. That's your daddy you talking about. I don't want hear that kind of talk this morning. I done raised you to come to this? You standing there all healthy and grown talking about you ain't going to your daddy's funeral?

CORY Mama . . . listen . . .

ROSE I don't want to hear it, Cory. You just get that thought out of your head.

CORY I can't drag Papa with me everywhere I go. I've got to say no to him. One time in my life I've got to say no.

ROSE Don't nobody have to listen to nothing like that. I know you and your daddy ain't seen eye to eye, but I ain't got to listen to that kind of talk this morning. Whatever was between you and your daddy . . . the time has come to put it aside. Just take it and set it over there on the shelf and forget about it. Disrespecting your daddy ain't gonna make you a man, Cory. You got to find a way to come to that on your own. Not going to your daddy's funeral ain't gonna make you a man.

CORY The whole time I was growing up . . . living in his house . . . Papa was like a shadow that followed you everywhere. It weighed on you and sunk into your flesh. It would wrap around you and lay there until you couldn't tell which one was you anymore. That shadow digging in your flesh. Trying to crawl in. Trying to live through you. Everywhere I looked, Troy Maxson was staring back at me . . . hiding under the bed . . . in the closet. I'm just saying I've got to find a way to get rid of that shadow, Mama.

ROSE You just like him. You got him in you good.

CORY Don't tell me that, Mama.

ROSE You Troy Maxson all over again.

CORY I don't want to be Troy Maxson. I want to be me.

ROSE You can't be nobody but who you are, Cory. That shadow wasn't nothing but you growing into yourself. You either got to grow into it or cut it down to fit you. But that's all you got to make life with. That's all you got to measure yourself against that world out there. Your daddy wanted you to be everything he wasn't . . . and at the same time he tried to make you into everything he was. I don't know if he was right or wrong . . . but I do know he meant to do more good than he meant to do harm. He wasn't always right. Sometimes when he touched he bruised. And sometimes when he took me in his arms he cut.

When I first met your daddy I thought . . . Here is a man I can lay down with and make a baby. That's the first thing I thought when I seen him. I was thirty years old and had done seen my share of men. But when he walked up to me and said, "I can dance a waltz that'll make you dizzy," I thought, Rose Lee, here is a man that you can open yourself up to and be filled to bursting. Here is a man that can fill all them empty spaces you been tipping around the edges of. One of them empty spaces was being somebody's mother.

I married your daddy and settled down to cooking his supper and keeping clean sheets on the bed. When your daddy walked through the house he was so big he filled it up. That was my first mistake. Not to make him leave some room for me. For my part in the matter. But at that time I wanted that. I wanted a house that I could sing in. And that's what your daddy gave me. I didn't know to keep up his strength I had to give up little pieces of mine. I did that. I took on his life as mine and mixed up the pieces so that you couldn't hardly tell which was which anymore. It was my choice. It was my life and I didn't have to live it like that. But that's what life offered me in the way of being a woman and I took it. I grabbed hold of it with both hands.

By the time Raynell came into the house, me and your daddy had done lost touch with one another. I didn't want to make my blessing off of nobody's misfortune . . . but I took on to Raynell like she was all them babies I had wanted and never had.

August Wilson has said that this collage by African American artist Romare Bearden inspired *Fences*.

What elements in this work do you see reflected in the play? What characteristics do the two share?

The phone rings.

Like I'd been blessed to relive a part of my life. And if the Lord see fit to keep up my strength . . . I'm gonna do her just like your daddy did you . . . I'm gonna give her the best of what's in me.

RAYNELL (*entering, still with her old shoes*): Mama . . . Reverend Tollivier on the phone.

ROSE *exits into the house.*

RAYNELL Hi.

CORY Hi.

RAYNELL You in the Army or the Marines?

CORY Marines.

RAYNELL Papa said it was the Army. Did you know Blue?

CORY Blue? Who's Blue?

RAYNELL Papa's dog what he sing about all the time.

CORY (*singing*): Hear it ring! Hear it ring!
I had a dog his name was Blue
You know Blue was mighty true
You know Blue was a good old dog
Blue treed a possum in a hollow log
You know from that he was a good old dog.
Hear it ring! Hear it ring!

RAYNELL *joins in singing.*

CORY AND RAYNELL Blue treed a possum out on a limb
Blue looked at me and I looked at him
Grabbed that possum and put him in a sack
Blue stayed there till I came back
Old Blue's feets was big and round
Never allowed a possum to touch the ground.
Old Blue died and I dug his grave
I dug his grave with a silver spade
Let him down with a golden chain
And every night I call his name
Go on Blue, you good dog you
Go on Blue, you good dog you

RAYNELL Blue laid down and died like a man
Blue laid down and died . . .

BOTH Blue laid down and died like a man
Now he's treeing possums in the Promised Land
I'm gonna tell you this to let you know
Blue's gone where the good dogs go
When I hear old Blue bark
When I hear old Blue bark
Blue treed a possum in Noah's Ark
Blue treed a possum in Noah's Ark.

ROSE *comes to the screen door.*

ROSE Cory, we gonna be ready to go in a minute.

CORY (*to* **RAYNELL**): You go on in the house and change them shoes like Mama told you so we can go to Papa's funeral.

RAYNELL Okay, I'll be back.

RAYNELL *exits into the house.* **CORY** *gets up and crosses over to the tree.* **ROSE** *stands in the screen door watching him.* **GABRIEL** *enters from the alley.*

GABRIEL (*calling*): Hey, Rose!

ROSE Gabe?

GABRIEL I'm here, Rose. Hey Rose, I'm here!

ROSE *enters from the house.*

ROSE Lord . . . Look here, Lyons!

LYONS See, I told you, Rose . . . I told you they'd let him come.

CORY How you doing, Uncle Gabe?

LYONS How you doing, Uncle Gabe?

GABRIEL Hey, Rose. It's time. It's time to tell St. Peter to open the gates. Troy, you ready? You ready, Troy. I'm gonna tell St. Peter to open the gates. You get ready now.

GABRIEL, *with great fanfare, braces himself to blow. The trumpet is without a mouthpiece. He puts the end of it into his mouth and blows with great force, like a man who has been waiting some twenty-odd years for this single moment. No sound comes out of the trumpet. He braces himself and blows again with the same result. A third time he blows. There is a weight of impossible description that falls away and leaves him bare and exposed to a frightful realization. It is a trauma that a sane and normal mind would be unable to withstand. He begins to dance. A slow, strange dance, eerie and life-giving. A dance of atavistic signature and ritual.* **LYONS** *attempts to embrace him.* **GABRIEL** *pushes* **LYONS** *away. He begins to howl in what is an attempt at song, or perhaps a song turning back into itself in an attempt at speech. He finishes his dance and the gates of heaven stand open as wide as God's closet.*

That's the way that go! ■

1985

Understanding and Interpreting

1. **AP® Character.** In the stage directions for act I, scene 1, August Wilson describes Troy as "a large man with thick, heavy hands; it is this largeness that he strives to fill out and make an accommodation with." How does this description establish the character of Troy? Consider also Troy's encounters with Death — the way he taunts Death to come and get him, asserting that he will go down swinging. What might Wilson be saying about Troy's character with these descriptions?

2. **AP® Setting, Structure, and Character.** How does Rose's assertion in act I, scene 1, that "Times have changed" (l. 240) set the mood for the action that follows? How does it anticipate the themes Wilson will explore more specifically through his characters and the action of the play?
3. **AP® Character.** How do you interpret Lyons's response to his father's criticism of his lifestyle: "I know I got to eat. But I got to live too. I need something that gonna help me to get out of the bed in the morning. Make me feel like I belong in the world" (I.1.583–86)? Discuss what it is that makes each of the central characters feel some sense of belonging in the world: Troy, Rose, Lyons, and Cory.
4. **AP® Structure and Character.** What role does Bono play in the development of Troy's character? Pick a scene that you think shows Bono's role most clearly, and then explain.
5. **AP® Character and Setting.** In act I, scene 3, Troy explains why he refuses to sign Cory's recruitment papers: "The white man ain't gonna let you get nowhere with that football noway. You go on and get your book-learning so you can work yourself up in that A&P or learn how to fix cars or build houses or something, get you a trade. That way you have something can't nobody take away from you. You go on and learn how to put your hands to some good use. Besides hauling people's garbage" (ll. 194–203). Could there be more to Troy's refusal than the explanation he offers? Explain.
6. **AP® Character, Structure, and Setting.** What is the significance of Troy's triumph at work, earning the right to drive the garbage truck (act I, scene 4)? What is ironic about this victory? How and why does his promotion affect his relationship with Bono?
7. **AP® Character and Setting.** How have Troy's life experiences shaped his attitude toward racism and possibilities for the future? How outdated are these views, given the play is set in the 1950s?
8. **AP® Character.** Why does Troy respond with both mockery and outrage to Cory's assertion that his father "never liked" him (I.3.242)?
9. **AP® Character and Structure.** Why do you think Wilson chose not to have Alberta make an appearance on stage? How does she appear in your imagination? Consider her physical appearance as well as her emotional demeanor in your description.
10. **AP® Character.** Is Troy a hypocrite? Do his relationships with Alberta and Cory make his assertions regarding family responsibilities and duty ring false?
11. **AP® Character.** Why is Troy conflicted over using the money to pay for his house? What does this conflict reveal about Troy? What does it reveal about his relationship with Gabriel?
12. **AP® Character.** When Cory returns after Troy's death, he tells Rose, "I can't drag Papa with me everywhere I go. I've got to say no to him" (II.5.163–65). What finally convinces Cory to attend Troy's funeral? What does this choice suggest about what Cory's future might hold? Has he said "no" to his father? Explain why or why not.

Analyzing Language, Style, and Structure

1. **Vocabulary in Context.** In the "Setting" stage notes, Wilson describes the porch of Troy and Rose's house: "A relatively recent addition to the house and running its full width, the porch lacks congruence." How does the word "congruence" reveal the importance of the porch to the setting of the play? How does this description of it foreshadow the conflicts in the play?
2. **AP® Character and Figurative Language.** Troy Maxson's last name makes subtle reference to the Mason-Dixon Line — the imaginary line that in the 1820s divided slave states from free states. How does this allusion to history help prepare you for the play's themes? What are the connotations of other characters' names — for example, "Rose" and "Gabriel"?

3. **AP® Character and Figurative Language.** What is the significance of the biblical and supernatural allusions that appear throughout the play? Consider the story of Troy getting furniture from the devil, and the behavior and history of Gabriel.

4. **AP® Structure.** Three texts, all written by Wilson, precede the actual opening of the play: a four-line poem, a description of the setting, and a more discursive piece entitled "The Play." Although these texts provide specific information, they also raise larger issues. What are some of these? Pay particular attention to the language Wilson uses ("in His Largeness and Laws," "the porch lacks congruence," "The city devoured them," "new energies that used loyalty and patriotism as its fuel").

5. **AP® Character and Structure.** In act I, scene 1, Troy's friend Bono chides him about "that Alberta gal" (l. 48). What is significant about the introduction of this complicating element before we meet Troy's wife? What might this foreshadow in the play? How does this teasing introduce a complication within the play's exposition?

6. **AP® Character and Structure.** Early in the play (act I, scene 1), Wilson's stage direction for Rose indicates that she "alternates between the porch and the kitchen." Throughout the play, she is associated with food and preparation. Examine specific passages and examples, and discuss how Wilson uses these associations to develop the character of Rose.

7. **AP® Character and Structure.** Why do you think Wilson holds off until the end of act I to have Troy reveal his past and his own confrontation with his father at age fourteen? Why does Wilson have Troy tell the story as a flashback to Lyons and Bono rather than to Cory? Pay special attention to Troy's tone; how does this section contribute to your understanding of his character?

8. **AP® Figurative Language.** Much of the play is concerned with money: earning it, owing it, paying for things. Yet Wilson alerts us to a metaphorical level when Troy insists, "Life don't owe you nothing. You owe it to yourself" (I.1.574–75). Discuss how the language of commerce — debt, payment, purchase, cheating — develops important themes in the play.

9. **AP® Character and Structure.** In *Fences*, Wilson gives Troy a number of stories to tell. How does his seemingly natural ability as a storyteller characterize him? What does his spinning tall tales suggest about his relationship with memory and truth? Cite specific examples, including Troy's encounter with "Mr. Death," to support your analysis.

10. **AP® Structure.** What do you think is the climax of *Fences*? Explain your reasoning and cite specific text to support your position. Include in your analysis why you think Wilson chose to have Troy's death occur off stage rather than in a scene of the play.

11. **AP® Character, Setting, and Structure.** Much of *Fences* is written in dialect, depicting the natural speech patterns of the characters in the play. In one example, Troy teases Rose with: "I'm studying you . . . fixing to do my homework!" (I.3.35–36). In other instances, Wilson brings in dialect through songs the characters recall or sing. How does the dialect affect your understanding of the play? Do you find that the style of the characters' language, which reflects the period when the action occurs, dates the play for contemporary viewers?

12. **AP® Character and Figurative Language.** In act II, scene 1, Troy uses baseball metaphors ("steal second," "stood on first base for eighteen years") to explain his affair with Alberta to Rose. How is this use of language consistent with Troy's character? On what basis does Rose reject the comparison? Consider the metaphor she chooses as she counters with an explanation of how she has tried to live her life.

13. **AP® Structure and Figurative Language.** Wilson has described *Fences* as having a "blues aesthetic." Songs, and particularly the blues, play an important role in Wilson's plays. Where do you see the influence of the blues on *Fences*? Is it in the diction? the syntax? the themes? the structure? Or does it show itself in some other way?

14. **AP® Character, Structure, and Figurative Language.** The character of Gabriel has puzzled readers, audiences, and even directors; one even suggested that he be dropped from the script to keep from confusing audiences. Some see him as a spiritual presence with a visible link to the African past. What elements of plot and character depend on him? Explain how you do or do not see Gabriel as essential to *Fences*. Include the final scene in your interpretation.
15. **AP® Structure and Figurative Language.** Throughout the play, the word "responsibility" recurs as different characters use it and reflect on its meaning. Identify and explore at least three different instances. What do you think Wilson's purpose is in returning to that word – or concept – from different generational perspectives and contexts?
16. **AP® Character, Structure, and Figurative Language.** Fences are both a complex symbol and motif in the play. At the opening of act I, scene 2, Rose is hanging up clothes in the early morning, humming and singing to herself. Her song imploring Jesus to "be a fence all around me every day" reflects one of the play's important themes. How do different characters relate to and define fences? Whom do fences keep out, and whom do they enclose? Consider how fences relate to incarceration, baseball, even the "gates" of heaven in Gabriel's vision. Why is this is an appropriate title for the play?

Topics for Composing

1. **AP® FRQ** **Literary Argument.** The poet T. S. Eliot believed in what he described as "the presence of the past." Many works of drama and fiction explore the way the past holds a vice grip on the present. In *Fences*, many of the characters are affected by both the collective cultural past and their specific experiences. In a well-written essay, analyze how Troy's individual and communal past influence his identity and contribute to an interpretation of the work as a whole. Do not merely summarize the plot.
2. **AP® FRQ** **Prose Fiction Analysis.** The following question refers to act II, scene 1, lines 331–413 of August Wilson's *Fences*, published in 1985. In this passage, the two major characters, Troy and Rose, argue about the reasons for Troy's infidelity. Read the passage carefully. Then, in a well-written essay, analyze how Wilson uses literary elements and techniques to portray two different values systems and perspectives on life.
3. **AP® Literary Argumentation.** Rose is a character who has provoked a great deal of controversy: some see her as a strong matriarch who holds her family together, while others argue that she enables Troy's worst behaviors. Write an essay explaining your view of Rose. Consider both her assertion that she "ain't never wanted no half nothing in [her] family" (II.1.275–76) and her decision to bring Raynell into the Maxson family.
4. **AP® Literary Argumentation.** In the description of Troy Maxson that precedes the play, Wilson writes, "at times he can be crude and almost vulgar, though he is capable of rising to profound heights of expression." Write an essay analyzing the character of Troy as embodying this tension. Discuss which inclination you believe ultimately prevails.
5. **AP® Literary Argumentation.** *Fences* is most often interpreted as a "generational play." In fact, August Wilson scholar Sandra Shannon describes a 1997 production in Beijing with an all-Chinese cast in which both audience members and actors found that "their connections to *Fences* seemed to have had more to do with the shifting of a powerful nation's economic and generational center from one determined by tradition to one responding to the trappings of modernization." Discuss the generational conflicts in this play, and consider how they are reflective of more universal experiences than ones specific to the African American experience.

6. **Speaking and Listening.** It might be said that one of Wilson's strengths as a playwright is his ability, through larger-than-life characters and intense, perceptive characterization, to create a universal dimension in which issues of race and family in America are examined. Working in small groups or pairs, choose one of the central characters and examine the extent to which they create such a dimension and what larger meaning the character might convey about race and family in America.
7. **Creative Writing.** Write a eulogy to be read at Troy Maxson's funeral. Include details from his life that would help mourners see that "he meant to do more good than he meant to do harm" (II.5.202–4). Choose the speaker of your eulogy carefully. It could be any of the characters in the play, or someone else entirely.
8. **Creative Writing.** Imagine that ten years have elapsed since Troy's death, and Cory and Lyons return home to celebrate Rose's birthday. Write a dialogue between the half-brothers in which they reminisce about their father.
9. **Research.** Troy Maxson took part in the Great Migration of rural Black people from the South to urban centers in the North. The artist Jacob Lawrence has chronicled this journey in his Migration Series. The series is housed in the Museum of Modern Art in New York City, but the images are available online at the Phillips Collection's website. You can also view one of the paintings on page 213. Choose one painting that particularly appeals to you, and write about how it helps you visualize the historical movement.
10. **Research.** The time frame of *Fences* spans several major historical moments for African Americans in the nineteenth and twentieth centuries: Reconstruction, the Great Migration, the Great Depression, and the civil rights movement. Research each of these eras, and write an essay explaining how the historical and social forces of these eras are reflected either in the play as a whole or in the character of Troy Maxson.
11. **Connections.** Read or watch a production of one of the other plays in Wilson's *Pittsburgh Cycle*. What concerns, ideas, or themes in *Fences* are explored in the play you've chosen? In what ways does Wilson offer similar or contrasting perspectives to those in *Fences*?
12. **Connections.** Although a play may seem closer to a movie than a novel, turning what is intended as a live stage performance to film often involves a great deal more detail, particularly in elements of the setting. Watch the film version of *Fences*. How effectively do you think it conveys the concerns and themes of Wilson's original play? What changes has the director made? What was omitted? Would someone who has not read the play still experience the power of Wilson's vision? Why or why not? In your response, consider both the actors' interpretations of the characters and the film's representation of the setting.

Frankenstein

Mary Shelley

GL Archive/Alamy

Mary Shelley (1796–1851) was an English novelist, short story writer, dramatist, essayist, biographer, and travel writer. The daughter of political philosopher William Godwin and feminist philosopher Mary Wollstonecraft, Shelley grew up in London. Although best known for her Gothic novel *Frankenstein: or, The Modern Prometheus* (1818), she wrote many other works. In 1814, she began an affair with Percy Bysshe Shelley, who was married at the time; after his first wife's suicide in late 1816, the couple married. Mary and Percy Bysshe Shelley spent the summer of 1816 with Lord Byron and other friends in Geneva, Switzerland; because the weather was so often inclement, they were forced to stay inside and told ghost stories to entertain themselves. *Frankenstein* began as a ghost story, and Shelley finished the novel about a year later when she was nineteen.

KEY CONTEXT The tragedy of Victor Frankenstein, the ambitious scientist who creates life only to be horrified by his creation was, in many ways, the first of its kind. Many scholars consider it the earliest example of science fiction in English, and Shelley is often credited with inventing the genre.

Did I request thee, Maker, from my clay
To mould Me man? Did I solicit thee
From darkness to promote me? —

— PARADISE LOST [X. 743–5]

LETTER I

To Mrs. Saville, England

St. Petersburgh, Dec. 11th, 17—.

You will rejoice to hear that no disaster has accompanied the commencement of an enterprise which you have regarded with such evil forebodings. I arrived here yesterday; and my first task is to assure my dear sister of my welfare, and increasing confidence in the success of my undertaking.

I am already far north of London; and as I walk in the streets of Petersburgh, I feel a cold northern breeze play upon my cheeks, which braces my nerves, and fills me with delight. Do you understand this feeling? This breeze, which has travelled from the regions towards which I am advancing, gives me a foretaste of those icy climes. Inspirited by this wind of promise, my day dreams become more fervent and vivid. I try in vain to be persuaded that the pole is the seat of frost and desolation; it ever presents itself to my imagination as the region of beauty and delight. There, Margaret, the sun is for ever visible; its broad disk just skirting the horizon, and diffusing a perpetual splendour. There — for with your leave, my sister, I will put some trust in preceding navigators — there snow and frost are banished; and, sailing over a calm sea, we may be wafted to a land surpassing in wonders and in beauty every region hitherto discovered on the habitable globe. Its productions and features may be without example, as the phenomena of the heavenly bodies undoubtedly are in those undiscovered solitudes. What may not be expected in a country of eternal light? I may there discover the wondrous power which attracts the needle; and may regulate a thousand celestial observations, that require only this voyage to render their seeming eccentricities consistent for ever. I shall satiate my ardent curiosity with the sight of a part of the world never before visited, and may tread a land never before imprinted by the foot of man. These are my enticements, and they are sufficient to conquer all fear of danger or death, and to induce me to commence this laborious voyage with the joy a child feels when he embarks in a little boat, with his holiday mates, on an expedition of discovery up his native river. But, supposing all these conjectures to be false, you cannot contest the inestimable benefit which I shall confer on all mankind to the last generation, by discovering a passage near the pole to those countries, to reach which at present so many months are requisite; or by ascertaining the secret of the magnet, which, if at all possible, can only be effected by an undertaking such as mine.

These reflections have dispelled the agitation with which I began my letter, and I feel my heart glow with an enthusiasm which elevates me to heaven; for nothing contributes so much to tranquillise the mind as a steady purpose,—a point on which the soul may fix its intellectual eye. This expedition has been the favourite dream of my early years. I have read with ardour the accounts of the various voyages which have been made in the prospect of arriving at the North Pacific Ocean through the seas which surround the pole. You may remember, that a history of all the voyages made for purposes of discovery composed the whole of our good uncle Thomas's library. My education was neglected, yet I was passionately fond of reading. These volumes were my study day and night, and my familiarity with them increased that regret which I had felt, as a child, on learning that my father's dying injunction had forbidden my uncle to allow me to embark in a seafaring life.

These visions faded when I perused, for the first time, those poets whose effusions entranced my soul, and lifted it to heaven. I also became a poet, and for one year lived in a Paradise of my own creation; I imagined that I also might obtain a niche in the temple where the names of Homer and Shakespeare are consecrated. You are well acquainted with my failure, and how heavily I bore the disappointment. But just at that time I inherited the fortune of my cousin, and my thoughts were turned into the channel of their earlier bent.

Six years have passed since I resolved on my 5
present undertaking. I can, even now, remember the hour from which I dedicated myself to this great enterprise. I commenced by inuring my body to hardship. I accompanied the whale-fishers on several expeditions to the North Sea; I voluntarily endured cold, famine, thirst, and want of sleep; I often worked harder than the common sailors during the day, and devoted my nights to the study of mathematics, the theory of medicine, and those branches of physical science from which a naval adventurer might derive the greatest practical advantage. Twice I actually hired myself as an under-mate in a Greenland whaler, and acquitted myself to admiration. I must own I felt a little proud, when my captain offered me the second dignity in the vessel, and entreated me to remain with the greatest earnestness; so valuable did he consider my services.

And now, dear Margaret, do I not deserve to accomplish some great purpose? My life might have been passed in ease and luxury; but I preferred glory to every enticement that wealth placed in my path. Oh, that some encouraging voice would answer in the affirmative! My courage and my resolution is firm; but my hopes fluctuate, and my spirits are often depressed. I am about to proceed on a long and difficult voyage, the emergencies of which will demand all my fortitude: I am required not only to raise the spirits of others, but sometimes to sustain my own, when theirs are failing.

This is the most favourable period for travelling in Russia. They fly quickly over the snow in their sledges; the motion is pleasant, and, in my opinion, far more agreeable than that of an English stage-coach. The cold is not excessive, if you are wrapped in furs, — a dress which I have already adopted; for there is a great difference between walking the deck and remaining seated motionless for hours, when no exercise prevents the blood from actually freezing in your veins. I have no ambition to lose my life on the post-road between St. Petersburgh and Archangel.[1]

I shall depart for the latter town in a fortnight or three weeks; and my intention is to hire a ship there, which can easily be done by paying the insurance for the owner, and to engage as many sailors as I think necessary among those who are accustomed to the whale-fishing. I do not intend to sail until the month of June; and when shall I return? Ah, dear sister, how can I answer this question? If I succeed, many, many months, perhaps years, will pass before you and I may meet. If I fail, you will see me again soon, or never.

Farewell, my dear, excellent Margaret. Heaven shower down blessings on you, and save me, that I may again and again testify my gratitude for all your love and kindness.

Your affectionate brother,
R. Walton.

LETTER II

To Mrs. Saville, England

Archangel, 28th March, 17—.

How slowly the time passes here, encompassed as I am by frost and snow! yet a second step is taken towards my enterprise. I have hired a vessel, and am occupied in collecting my sailors; those whom I have already engaged appear to be men on whom I can depend, and are certainly possessed of dauntless courage.

But I have one want which I have never yet been able to satisfy; and the absence of the object of which I now feel as a most severe evil. I have no friend, Margaret: when I am glowing with the enthusiasm of success, there will be none to participate my joy; if I am assailed by disappointment, no one will endeavour to sustain me in dejection. I shall commit my thoughts to paper, it is true; but that is a poor medium for the communication of feeling. I desire the company of a man who could sympathise with me; whose eyes would reply to mine. You may deem me romantic, my dear sister, but I bitterly feel the want of a friend. I have no one near me, gentle yet courageous, possessed of a cultivated as well as of a capacious mind, whose tastes are like my own, to approve or amend my plans. How would such a friend repair the faults of your poor brother! I am too ardent in execution, and too impatient of difficulties. But it is a still greater evil to me that I am self-educated: for the first fourteen years of my life I ran wild on a common, and read nothing but our uncle Thomas's books of voyages. At that age I became acquainted with the celebrated poets of our own country; but it was only when it had ceased to be in my power to derive its most important benefits from such a conviction, that I perceived the necessity of becoming acquainted with more languages than that of my native country. Now I am twenty-eight, and am in reality more illiterate than many schoolboys of fifteen. It is true that I have thought more, and that my day dreams are more extended and magnificent; but they want (as the painters call it) *keeping*; and I greatly need a friend who would have sense enough not to despise me as romantic, and affection enough for me to endeavour to regulate my mind.

Well, these are useless complaints; I shall certainly find no friend on the wide ocean, nor

[1] A northern city in European Russia. — Eds.

even here in Archangel, among merchants and seamen. Yet some feelings, unallied to the dross of human nature, beat even in these rugged bosoms. My lieutenant, for instance, is a man of wonderful courage and enterprise; he is madly desirous of glory: or rather, to word my phrase more characteristically, of advancement in his profession. He is an Englishman, and in the midst of national and professional prejudices, unsoftened by cultivation, retains some of the noblest endowments of humanity. I first became acquainted with him on board a whale vessel: finding that he was unemployed in this city, I easily engaged him to assist in my enterprise.

The master is a person of an excellent disposition, and is remarkable in the ship for his gentleness and the mildness of his discipline. This circumstance, added to his well known integrity and dauntless courage, made me very desirous to engage him. A youth passed in solitude, my best years spent under your gentle and feminine fosterage, has so refined the groundwork of my character, that I cannot overcome an intense distaste to the usual brutality exercised on board ship: I have never believed it to be necessary; and when I heard of a mariner equally noted for his kindliness of heart, and the respect and obedience paid to him by his crew, I felt myself peculiarly fortunate in being able to secure his services. I heard of him first in rather a romantic manner, from a lady who owes to him the happiness of her life. This, briefly, is his story. Some years ago, he loved a young Russian lady, of moderate fortune; and having amassed a considerable sum in prize-money, the father of the girl consented to the match. He saw his mistress once before the destined ceremony; but she was bathed in tears, and, throwing herself at his feet, entreated him to spare her, confessing at the same time that she loved another, but that he was poor, and that her father would never consent to the union. My generous friend reassured the suppliant, and on being informed of the name of her lover, instantly abandoned his pursuit. He had already bought a farm with his money, on which he had designed to pass the remainder of his life; but he bestowed the whole on his rival, together with the remains of his prize-money to purchase stock, and then himself solicited the young woman's father to consent to her marriage with her lover. But the old man decidedly refused, thinking himself bound in honour to my friend; who, when he found the father inexorable, quitted his country, nor returned until he heard that his former mistress was married according to her inclinations. "What a noble fellow!" you will exclaim. He is so; but then he is wholly uneducated: he is as silent as a Turk, and a kind of ignorant carelessness attends him, which, while it renders his conduct the more astonishing, detracts from the interest and sympathy which otherwise he would command.

Yet do not suppose, because I complain a little, or because I can conceive a consolation for my toils which I may never know, that I am wavering in my resolutions. Those are as fixed as fate; and my voyage is only now delayed until the weather shall permit my embarkation. The winter has been dreadfully severe; but the spring promises well, and it is considered as a remarkably early season; so that perhaps I may sail sooner than I expected. I shall do nothing rashly: you know me sufficiently to confide in my prudence and considerateness, whenever the safety of others is committed to my care.

I cannot describe to you my sensations on the near prospect of my undertaking. It is impossible to communicate to you a conception of the trembling sensation, half pleasurable and half fearful, with which I am preparing to depart. I am going to unexplored regions, to "the land of mist and snow;" but I shall kill no albatross, therefore do not be alarmed for my safety, or if I should come back to you as worn and woeful as the "Ancient Mariner."[2] You will smile at my allusion; but I will disclose a secret. I have often attributed my attachment to, my passionate enthusiasm for, the dangerous mysteries of ocean, to that production of the most imaginative of modern poets. There is something at work in my soul, which I do not understand. I am practically industrious — pains-taking; — a workman to execute with perseverance and labour: — but besides this, there is a love for the marvellous, a belief in the marvellous, intertwined in all my projects, which hurries me out of the common pathways of men, even to the wild sea and unvisited regions I am about to explore.

But to return to dearer considerations. Shall I meet you again, after having traversed immense seas, and returned by the most southern cape of Africa or America? I dare not expect such success, yet I cannot bear to look on the reverse of the picture. Continue for the present to write to me by every opportunity: I may receive your letters on some occasions when I need them most to support my spirits. I love you very tenderly. Remember me with affection, should you never hear from me again.

Your affectionate brother,
Robert Walton.

LETTER III

To Mrs. Saville, England

July 7th, 17—.

My dear Sister,
I write a few lines in haste, to say that I am safe, and well advanced on my voyage. This letter will reach England by a merchantman now on its homeward voyage from Archangel; more fortunate than I, who may not see my native land, perhaps, for many years. I am, however, in good spirits; my men are bold, and apparently firm of purpose; nor do the floating sheets of ice that continually pass us, indicating the dangers of the region towards which we are advancing, appear to dismay them. We have already reached a very high latitude; but it is the height of summer, and although not so warm as in England, the southern gales, which blow us speedily towards those shores which I so ardently desire to attain, breathe a degree of renovating warmth which I had not expected.

No incidents have hitherto befallen us that would make a figure in a letter. One or two stiff gales, and the springing of a leak, are accidents which experienced navigators scarcely remember to record; and I shall be well content if nothing worse happen to us during our voyage.

Adieu, my dear Margaret. Be assured, that for my own sake, as well as yours, I will not rashly encounter danger. I will be cool, persevering, and prudent.

But success *shall* crown my endeavours. 20
Wherefore not? Thus far I have gone, tracing a secure way over the pathless seas: the very stars themselves being witnesses and testimonies of my triumph. Why not still proceed over the untamed yet obedient element? What can stop the determined heart and resolved will of man?

My swelling heart involuntarily pours itself out thus. But I must finish. Heaven bless my beloved sister!

R. W.

LETTER IV

To Mrs. Saville, England

August 5th, 17—.

So strange an accident has happened to us, that I cannot forbear recording it, although it is very probable that you will see me before these papers can come into your possession.

Last Monday (July 31st), we were nearly surrounded by ice, which closed in the ship on

[2] A reference to Samuel Taylor Coleridge's epic poem, *The Rime of the Ancient Mariner*, first published in 1798. In it, an old sailor recounts a disastrous sea voyage; as his tale progresses, it becomes clear that the mariner is both the cause of the crew's misfortune and its only survivor. — Eds.

all sides, scarcely leaving her the sea-room in which she floated. Our situation was somewhat dangerous, especially as we were compassed round by a very thick fog. We accordingly lay to, hoping that some change would take place in the atmosphere and weather.

About two o'clock the mist cleared away, and we beheld, stretched out in every direction, vast and irregular plains of ice, which seemed to have no end. Some of my comrades groaned, and my own mind began to grow watchful with anxious thoughts, when a strange sight suddenly attracted our attention, and diverted our solicitude from our own situation. We perceived a low carriage, fixed on a sledge and drawn by dogs, pass on towards the north, at the distance of half a mile: a being which had the shape of a man, but apparently of gigantic stature, sat in the sledge, and guided the dogs. We watched the rapid progress of the traveller with our telescopes, until he was lost among the distant inequalities of the ice.

This appearance excited our unqualified wonder. We were, as we believed, many hundred miles from any land; but this apparition seemed to denote that it was not, in reality, so distant as we had supposed. Shut in, however, by ice, it was impossible to follow his track, which we had observed with the greatest attention.

About two hours after this occurrence, we heard the ground sea; and before night the ice broke, and freed our ship. We, however, lay to until the morning, fearing to encounter in the dark those large loose masses which float about after the breaking up of the ice. I profited of this time to rest for a few hours.

In the morning, however, as soon as it was light, I went upon deck, and found all the sailors busy on one side of the vessel, apparently talking to some one in the sea. It was, in fact, a sledge, like that we had seen before, which had drifted towards us in the night, on a large fragment of ice. Only one dog remained alive; but there was a human being within it, whom the sailors were persuading to enter the vessel. He was not, as the other traveller seemed to be, a savage inhabitant of some undiscovered island, but an European. When I appeared on deck, the master said, "Here is our captain, and he will not allow you to perish on the open sea."

On perceiving me, the stranger addressed me in English, although with a foreign accent. "Before I come on board your vessel," said he, "will you have the kindness to inform me whither you are bound?"

You may conceive my astonishment on hearing such a question addressed to me from a man on the brink of destruction, and to whom I should have supposed that my vessel would have been a resource which he would not have exchanged for the most precious wealth the earth can afford. I replied, however, that we were on a voyage of discovery towards the northern pole.

Upon hearing this he appeared satisfied, and consented to come on board. Good God! Margaret, if you had seen the man who thus capitulated for his safety, your surprise would have been boundless. His limbs were nearly frozen, and his body dreadfully emaciated by fatigue and suffering. I never saw a man in so wretched a condition. We attempted to carry him into the cabin; but as soon as he had quitted the fresh air, he fainted. We accordingly brought him back to the deck, and restored him to animation by rubbing him with brandy, and forcing him to swallow a small quantity. As soon as he showed signs of life we wrapped him up in blankets, and placed him near the chimney of the kitchen stove. By slow degrees he recovered, and ate a little soup, which restored him wonderfully.

Two days passed in this manner before he was able to speak; and I often feared that his suffering had deprived him of understanding. When he had in some measure recovered, I removed him to my own cabin, and attended on him as much as my duty would permit. I never saw a more interesting creature: his eyes have generally an expression of wildness, and even madness; but there are moments when, if any one performs an act of kindness towards him, or does him any the most trifling service, his whole countenance is lighted up, as it were, with a beam of benevolence and sweetness that I never saw equalled. But he is generally melancholy and despairing; and sometimes he gnashes his teeth, as if impatient of the weight of woes that oppresses him.

When my guest was a little recovered, I had great trouble to keep off the men, who wished to ask him a thousand questions; but I would not allow him to be tormented by their idle curiosity, in a state of body and mind whose restoration evidently depended upon entire repose. Once, however, the lieutenant asked, Why he had come so far upon the ice in so strange a vehicle?

His countenance instantly assumed an aspect of the deepest gloom; and he replied, "To seek one who fled from me."

"And did the man whom you pursued travel in the same fashion?"

"Yes."

"Then I fancy we have seen him; for the day before we picked you up, we saw some dogs drawing a sledge, with a man in it, across the ice."

This aroused the stranger's attention; and he asked a multitude of questions concerning the route which the daemon, as he called him, had pursued. Soon after, when he was alone with me, he said, — "I have, doubtless, excited your curiosity, as well as that of these good people; but you are too considerate to make enquiries."

"Certainly; it would indeed be very impertinent and inhuman in me to trouble you with any inquisitiveness of mine."

"And yet you rescued me from a strange and perilous situation; you have benevolently restored me to life."

Soon after this he enquired if I thought that the breaking up of the ice had destroyed the other sledge? I replied, that I could not answer with any degree of certainty; for the ice had not broken until near midnight, and the traveller might have arrived at a place of safety before that time; but of this I could not judge.

From this time a new spirit of life animated the decaying frame of the stranger. He manifested the greatest eagerness to be upon deck, to watch for the sledge which had before appeared; but I have persuaded him to remain in the cabin, for he is far too weak to sustain the rawness of the atmosphere. I have promised that some one should watch for him, and give him instant notice if any new object should appear in sight.

Such is my journal of what relates to this strange occurrence up to the present day. The stranger has gradually improved in health, but is very silent, and appears uneasy when any one enters his cabin. Yet his manners are so conciliating and gentle, that the sailors are all interested in him, although they have had very little communication with him. For my own part, I begin to love him as a brother; and his constant and deep grief fills me with sympathy and compassion. He must have been a noble creature in his better days, being even now in wreck so attractive and amiable.

I said in one of my letters, my dear Margaret, that I should find no friend on the wide ocean; yet I have found a man who, before his spirit had been broken by misery, I should have been happy to have possessed as the brother of my heart.

I shall continue my journal concerning the stranger at intervals, should I have any fresh incidents to record.

August 13th, 17—.

My affection for my guest increases every day. He excites at once my admiration and my pity to an astonishing degree. How can I see so noble a creature destroyed by misery, without feeling the most poignant grief? He is so gentle, yet so wise; his mind is so cultivated; and when he speaks, although his words are culled with the choicest art, yet they flow with rapidity and unparalleled eloquence.

He is now much recovered from his illness, and is continually on the deck, apparently watching for the sledge that preceded his own. Yet, although unhappy, he is not so utterly occupied by his own misery, but that he interests himself deeply in the projects of others. He has frequently conversed with me on mine, which I have communicated to him without disguise. He entered attentively into all my arguments in favour of my eventual success, and into every minute detail of the measures I had taken to secure it. I was easily led by the sympathy which he evinced, to use the language of my heart; to give utterance to the burning ardour of my soul; and to say, with all the fervour that warmed me, how gladly I would sacrifice my fortune, my existence, my every hope, to the furtherance of my enterprise. One man's life or death were but a small price to pay for the acquirement of the knowledge which I sought; for the dominion I should acquire and transmit over the elemental foes of our race. As I spoke, a dark gloom spread over my listener's countenance. At first I perceived that he tried to suppress his emotion; he placed his hands before his eyes; and my voice quivered and failed me, as I beheld tears trickle fast from between his fingers,—a groan burst from his heaving breast. I paused;—at length he spoke, in broken accents:—"Unhappy man! Do you share my madness? Have you drank also of the intoxicating draught? Hear me,—let me reveal my tale, and you will dash the cup from your lips!"

Such words, you may imagine, strongly excited my curiosity; but the paroxysm of grief that had seized the stranger overcame his weakened powers, and many hours of repose and tranquil conversation were necessary to restore his composure.

Having conquered the violence of his feelings, he appeared to despise himself for being the slave of passion; and quelling the dark tyranny of despair, he led me again to converse concerning myself personally. He asked me the history of my earlier years. The tale was quickly told: but it awakened various trains of reflection. I spoke of my desire of finding a friend—of my thirst for a more intimate sympathy with a fellow mind than had ever fallen to my lot; and expressed my conviction that a man could boast of little happiness, who did not enjoy this blessing.

"I agree with you," replied the stranger; "we are unfashioned creatures, but half made up, if one wiser, better, dearer than ourselves—such a friend ought to be—do not lend his aid to perfectionate our weak and faulty natures. I once had a friend, the most noble of human creatures, and am entitled, therefore, to judge respecting friendship. You have hope, and the world before you, and have no cause for despair. But I—I have lost every thing, and cannot begin life anew."

As he said this, his countenance became expressive of a calm settled grief, that touched me to the heart. But he was silent, and presently retired to his cabin.

Even broken in spirit as he is, no one can feel more deeply than he does the beauties of nature. The starry sky, the sea, and every sight afforded by these wonderful regions, seems still to have the power of elevating his soul from earth. Such a man has a double existence: he may suffer misery, and be overwhelmed by disappointments; yet, when he has retired into himself, he will be like a celestial spirit, that has a halo around him, within whose circle no grief or folly ventures.

Will you smile at the enthusiasm I express concerning this divine wanderer? You would not, if you saw him. You have been tutored and refined by books and retirement from the world, and you are, therefore, somewhat fastidious; but this only renders you the more fit to appreciate the extraordinary merits of this wonderful man. Sometimes I have endeavoured to discover what quality it is which he possesses, that elevates him so immeasurably above any other person I ever knew. I believe it to be an intuitive discernment; a quick but never-failing power of judgment; a penetration into the causes of things, unequalled for clearness and precision; add to this a facility of expression, and a voice whose varied intonations are soul-subduing music.

August 19, 17— .

Yesterday the stranger said to me, "You may easily perceive, Captain Walton, that I have suffered great and unparalleled misfortunes. I had determined, at one time, that the memory of these evils should die with me; but you have won me to alter my determination. You seek for knowledge and wisdom, as I once did; and I ardently hope that the gratification of your wishes may not be a serpent to sting you, as mine has been. I do not know that the relation of my disasters will be useful to you; yet, when I reflect that you are pursuing the same course, exposing yourself to the same dangers which have rendered me what I am, I imagine that you may deduce an apt moral from my tale; one that may direct you if you succeed in your undertaking, and console you in case of failure. Prepare to hear of occurrences which are usually deemed marvellous. Were we among the tamer scenes of nature, I might fear to encounter your unbelief, perhaps your ridicule; but many things will appear possible in these wild and mysterious regions, which would provoke the laughter of those unacquainted with the ever-varied powers of nature: — nor can I doubt but that my tale conveys in its series internal evidence of the truth of the events of which it is composed."

You may easily imagine that I was much gratified by the offered communication; yet I could not endure that he should renew his grief by a recital of his misfortunes. I felt the greatest eagerness to hear the promised narrative, partly from curiosity, and partly from a strong desire to ameliorate his fate, if it were in my power. I expressed these feelings in my answer.

"I thank you," he replied, "for your sympathy, but it is useless; my fate is nearly fulfilled. I wait but for one event, and then I shall repose in peace. I understand your feeling," continued he, perceiving that I wished to interrupt him; "but you are mistaken, my friend, if thus you will allow me to name you; nothing can alter my destiny: listen to my history, and you will perceive how irrevocably it is determined."

He then told me, that he would commence his narrative the next day when I should be at leisure. This promise drew from me the warmest thanks. I have resolved every night, when I am not imperatively occupied by my duties, to record, as nearly as possible in his own words, what he has related during the day. If I should be engaged, I will at least make notes. This manuscript will doubtless afford you the greatest pleasure: but to me, who know him, and who hear it from his own lips, with what interest and sympathy shall I read it in some future day! Even now, as I commence my task, his full-toned voice swells in my ears; his lustrous eyes dwell on me with all their melancholy sweetness; I see his thin hand raised in animation, while the lineaments of his face are irradiated by the soul within. Strange and harrowing must be his story; frightful the storm which embraced the gallant vessel on its course, and wrecked it — thus!

CHAPTER I

I am by birth a Genevese; and my family is one of the most distinguished of that republic. My ancestors had been for many years counsellors and syndics;[3] and my father had filled several public situations with honour and reputation. He was respected by all who knew him, for his integrity and indefatigable attention to public business. He passed his younger days perpetually occupied by the affairs of his country; a variety of circumstances had prevented his marrying early, nor was it until the decline of life that he became a husband and the father of a family.

[3] Government officials. — Eds.

As the circumstances of his marriage illustrate his character, I cannot refrain from relating them. One of his most intimate friends was a merchant, who, from a flourishing state, fell, through numerous mischances, into poverty. This man, whose name was Beaufort, was of a proud and unbending disposition, and could not bear to live in poverty and oblivion in the same country where he had formerly been distinguished for his rank and magnificence. Having paid his debts, therefore, in the most honourable manner, he retreated with his daughter to the town of Lucerne, where he lived unknown and in wretchedness. My father loved Beaufort with the truest friendship, and was deeply grieved by his retreat in these unfortunate circumstances. He bitterly deplored the false pride which led his friend to a conduct so little worthy of the affection that united them. He lost no time in endeavouring to seek him out, with the hope of persuading him to begin the world again through his credit and assistance.

Beaufort had taken effectual measures to conceal himself; and it was ten months before my father discovered his abode. Overjoyed at this discovery, he hastened to the house, which was situated in a mean street, near the Reuss. But when he entered, misery and despair alone welcomed him. Beaufort had saved but a very small sum of money from the wreck of his fortunes; but it was sufficient to provide him with sustenance for some months, and in the mean time he hoped to procure some respectable employment in a merchant's house. The interval was, consequently, spent in inaction; his grief only became more deep and rankling, when he had leisure for reflection; and at length it took so fast hold of his mind, that at the end of three months he lay on a bed of sickness, incapable of any exertion.

His daughter attended him with the greatest tenderness; but she saw with despair that their little fund was rapidly decreasing, and that there was no other prospect of support. But Caroline Beaufort possessed a mind of an uncommon mould; and her courage rose to support her in her adversity. She procured plain work; she plaited straw; and by various means contrived to earn a pittance scarcely sufficient to support life.

Several months passed in this manner. Her father grew worse; her time was more entirely occupied in attending him; her means of subsistence decreased; and in the tenth month her father died in her arms, leaving her an orphan and a beggar. This last blow overcame her; and she knelt by Beaufort's coffin, weeping bitterly, when my father entered the chamber. He came like a protecting spirit to the poor girl, who committed herself to his care; and after the interment of his friend, he conducted her to Geneva, and placed her under the protection of a relation. Two years after this event Caroline became his wife.

There was a considerable difference between the ages of my parents, but this circumstance seemed to unite them only closer in bonds of devoted affection. There was a sense of justice in my father's upright mind, which rendered it necessary that he should approve highly to love strongly. Perhaps during former years he had suffered from the late-discovered unworthiness of one beloved, and so was disposed to set a greater value on tried worth. There was a show of gratitude and worship in his attachment to my mother, differing wholly from the doting fondness of age, for it was inspired by reverence for her virtues, and a desire to be the means of, in some degree, recompensing her for the sorrows she had endured, but which gave inexpressible grace to his behaviour to her. Every thing was made to yield to her wishes and her convenience. He strove to shelter her, as a fair exotic is sheltered by the gardener, from every rougher wind, and to surround her with all that could tend to excite pleasurable emotion in her soft and benevolent mind. Her health, and even the tranquillity of her hitherto constant spirit, had been shaken by what she had gone through. During the two years that had elapsed previous to their marriage my father had gradually relinquished all his public functions; and immediately after their union they sought the pleasant climate of Italy, and the change of scene and interest attendant on a tour through that land of wonders, as a restorative for her weakened frame.

From Italy they visited Germany and France. I, their eldest child, was born at Naples, and as an infant accompanied them in their rambles. I remained for several years their only child. Much as they were attached to each other, they seemed to draw inexhaustible stores of affection from a very mine of love to bestow them upon me. My mother's tender caresses, and my father's smile of benevolent pleasure while regarding me, are my first recollections. I was their plaything and their idol, and something better — their child, the innocent and helpless creature bestowed on them by Heaven, whom to bring up to good, and whose future lot it was in their hands to direct to happiness or misery, according as they fulfilled their duties towards me. With this deep consciousness of what they owed towards the being to which they had given life, added to the active spirit of tenderness that animated both, it may be imagined that while during every hour of my infant life I received a lesson of patience, of charity, and of self-control, I was so guided by a silken cord, that all seemed but one train of enjoyment to me.

For a long time I was their only care. My mother had much desired to have a daughter, but I continued their single offspring. When I was about five years old, while making an excursion beyond the frontiers of Italy, they passed a week on the shores of the Lake of Como. Their benevolent disposition often made them enter the cottages of the poor. This, to my mother, was more than a duty; it was a necessity, a passion, — remembering what she had suffered, and how she had been relieved, — for her to act in her turn the guardian angel to the afflicted. During one of their walks a poor cot in the foldings of a vale attracted their notice, as being singularly disconsolate, while the number of half-clothed children gathered about it, spoke of penury in its worst shape. One day, when my father had gone by himself to Milan, my mother, accompanied by me, visited this abode. She found a peasant and his wife, hard working, bent down by care and labour, distributing a scanty meal to five hungry babes. Among these there was one which attracted my mother far above all the rest. She appeared of a different stock. The four others were dark-eyed, hardy little vagrants; this child was thin, and very fair. Her hair was the brightest living gold, and, despite the poverty of her clothing, seemed to set a crown of distinction on her head. Her brow was clear and ample, her blue eyes cloudless, and her lips and the moulding of her face so expressive of sensibility and sweetness, that none could behold her without looking on her as of a distinct species, a being heaven-sent, and bearing a celestial stamp in all her features.

The peasant woman, perceiving that my mother fixed eyes of wonder and admiration on this lovely girl, eagerly communicated her history. She was not her child, but the daughter of a Milanese nobleman. Her mother was a German, and had died on giving her birth. The infant had been placed with these good people to nurse: they were better off then. They had not been long married, and their eldest child was but just born. The father of their charge was one of those Italians nursed in the memory of the antique glory of Italy, — one among the *schiavi ognor frementi*,[4] who exerted himself to obtain the liberty of his country. He became the victim of its weakness. Whether he had died, or still lingered in the dungeons of Austria, was not known. His property was confiscated, his child became an orphan and a beggar. She continued

[4] Italian for "slaves ever trembling"; a reference to Austrian subjugation of Italians during the eighteenth and nineteenth centuries. — Eds.

with her foster parents, and bloomed in their rude abode, fairer than a garden rose among dark-leaved brambles.

When my father returned from Milan, he found playing with me in the hall of our villa, a child fairer than pictured cherub — a creature who seemed to shed radiance from her looks, and whose form and motions were lighter than the chamois of the hills. The apparition was soon explained. With his permission my mother prevailed on her rustic guardians to yield their charge to her. They were fond of the sweet orphan. Her presence had seemed a blessing to them; but it would be unfair to her to keep her in poverty and want, when Providence afforded her such powerful protection. They consulted their village priest, and the result was, that Elizabeth Lavenza became the inmate of my parents' house — my more than sister — the beautiful and adored companion of all my occupations and my pleasures.

Every one loved Elizabeth. The passionate and almost reverential attachment with which all regarded her became, while I shared it, my pride and my delight. On the evening previous to her being brought to my home, my mother had said playfully, — "I have a pretty present for my Victor — to-morrow he shall have it." And when, on the morrow, she presented Elizabeth to me as her promised gift, I, with childish seriousness, interpreted her words literally, and looked upon Elizabeth as mine — mine to protect, love, and cherish. All praises bestowed on her, I received as made to a possession of my own. We called each other familiarly by the name of cousin. No word, no expression could body forth the kind of relation in which she stood to me — my more than sister, since till death she was to be mine only.

CHAPTER II

We were brought up together; there was not quite a year difference in our ages. I need not say that we were strangers to any species of disunion or dispute. Harmony was the soul of our companionship, and the diversity and contrast that subsisted in our characters drew us nearer together. Elizabeth was of a calmer and more concentrated disposition; but, with all my ardour, I was capable of a more intense application, and was more deeply smitten with the thirst for knowledge. She busied herself with following the aerial creations of the poets; and in the majestic and wondrous scenes which surrounded our Swiss home — the sublime shapes of the mountains; the changes of the seasons; tempest and calm; the silence of winter, and the life and turbulence of our Alpine summers, — she found ample scope for admiration and delight. While my companion contemplated with a serious and satisfied spirit the magnificent appearances of things, I delighted in investigating their causes. The world was to me a secret which I desired to divine. Curiosity, earnest research to learn the hidden laws of nature, gladness akin to rapture, as they were unfolded to me, are among the earliest sensations I can remember.

On the birth of a second son, my junior by seven years, my parents gave up entirely their wandering life, and fixed themselves in their native country. We possessed a house in Geneva, and a *campagne*[5] on Belrive, the eastern shore of the lake, at the distance of rather more than a league from the city. We resided principally in the latter, and the lives of my parents were passed in considerable seclusion. It was my temper to avoid a crowd, and to attach myself fervently to a few. I was indifferent, therefore, to my schoolfellows in general; but I united myself in the bonds of the closest friendship to one among them. Henry Clerval was the son of a merchant of Geneva. He was a boy of singular talent and fancy. He loved enterprise, hardship, and even danger, for its own sake. He was deeply read in books of chivalry and romance. He

[5] French for "countryside." — Eds.

composed heroic songs, and began to write many a tale of enchantment and knightly adventure. He tried to make us act plays, and to enter into masquerades, in which the characters were drawn from the heroes of Roncesvalles,[6] of the Round Table of King Arthur, and the chivalrous train who shed their blood to redeem the holy sepulchre from the hands of the infidels.

No human being could have passed a happier childhood than myself. My parents were possessed by the very spirit of kindness and indulgence. We felt that they were not the tyrants to rule our lot according to their caprice, but the agents and creators of all the many delights which we enjoyed. When I mingled with other families, I distinctly discerned how peculiarly fortunate my lot was, and gratitude assisted the development of filial love.

My temper was sometimes violent, and my passions vehement; but by some law in my temperature they were turned, not towards childish pursuits, but to an eager desire to learn, and not to learn all things indiscriminately. I confess that neither the structure of languages, nor the code of governments, nor the politics of various states, possessed attractions for me. It was the secrets of heaven and earth that I desired to learn; and whether it was the outward substance of things, or the inner spirit of nature and the mysterious soul of man that occupied me, still my enquiries were directed to the metaphysical, or, in its highest sense, the physical secrets of the world.

Meanwhile Clerval occupied himself, so to speak, with the moral relations of things. The busy stage of life, the virtues of heroes, and the actions of men, were his theme; and his hope and his dream was to become one among those whose names are recorded in story, as the gallant and adventurous benefactors of our species. The saintly soul of Elizabeth shone like a shrine-dedicated lamp in our peaceful home. Her sympathy was ours; her smile, her soft voice, the sweet glance of her celestial eyes, were ever there to bless and animate us. She was the living spirit of love to soften and attract: I might have become sullen in my study, rough through the ardour of my nature, but that she was there to subdue me to a semblance of her own gentleness. And Clerval—could aught ill entrench on the noble spirit of Clerval?—yet he might not have been so perfectly humane, so thoughtful in his generosity—so full of kindness and tenderness amidst his passion for adventurous exploit, had she not unfolded to him the real loveliness of beneficence, and made the doing good the end and aim of his soaring ambition.

I feel exquisite pleasure in dwelling on the recollections of childhood, before misfortune had tainted my mind, and changed its bright visions of extensive usefulness into gloomy and narrow reflections upon self. Besides, in drawing the picture of my early days, I also record those events which led, by insensible steps, to my after tale of misery: for when I would account to myself for the birth of that passion, which afterwards ruled my destiny, I find it arise, like a mountain river, from ignoble and almost forgotten sources; but, swelling as it proceeded, it became the torrent which, in its course, has swept away all my hopes and joys.

Natural philosophy is the genius that has regulated my fate; I desire, therefore, in this narration, to state those facts which led to my predilection for that science. When I was thirteen years of age, we all went on a party of pleasure to the baths near Thonon; the inclemency of the weather obliged us to remain a day confined to the inn. In this house I chanced to find a volume of the works of Cornelius Agrippa.[7] I opened it with apathy; the theory which he attempts to demonstrate, and

[6] The site of a battle in the eleventh-century epic French poem *The Song of Roland*.—Eds.

[7] Heinrich Cornelius Agrippa (1486–1535) was a German physician and occultist.—Eds.

the wonderful facts which he relates, soon changed this feeling into enthusiasm. A new light seemed to dawn upon my mind; and, bounding with joy, I communicated my discovery to my father. My father looked carelessly at the titlepage of my book, and said, "Ah! Cornelius Agrippa! My dear Victor, do not waste your time upon this; it is sad trash."

If, instead of this remark, my father had taken the pains to explain to me, that the principles of Agrippa had been entirely exploded, and that a modern system of science had been introduced, which possessed much greater powers than the ancient, because the powers of the latter were chimerical, while those of the former were real and practical; under such circumstances, I should certainly have thrown Agrippa aside, and have contented my imagination, warmed as it was, by returning with greater ardour to my former studies. It is even possible, that the train of my ideas would never have received the fatal impulse that led to my ruin. But the cursory glance my father had taken of my volume by no means assured me that he was acquainted with its contents; and I continued to read with the greatest avidity.

When I returned home, my first care was to procure the whole works of this author, and afterwards of Paracelsus[8] and Albertus Magnus.[9] I read and studied the wild fancies of these writers with delight; they appeared to me treasures known to few beside myself. I have described myself as always having been embued with a fervent longing to penetrate the secrets of nature. In spite of the intense labour and wonderful discoveries of modern philosophers, I always came from my studies discontented and unsatisfied. Sir Isaac Newton is said to have avowed that he felt like a child picking up shells beside the great and unexplored ocean of truth. Those of his successors in each branch of natural philosophy with whom I was acquainted, appeared even to my boy's apprehensions, as tyros[10] engaged in the same pursuit.

The untaught peasant beheld the elements around him, and was acquainted with their

Culture Club/Getty Images

This artwork, titled *Character of Evil Spirits*, was inspired by Cornelius Agrippa's *The Fourth Book of Occult Philosophy* (1655).

In what ways might this interpretation of the content of the book, which Victor finds highly interesting, help shed light on his character?

[8] Theophrastus Bombastus von Hohenheim (1493–1541), also known as Paracelsus, was a Swiss physician who believed human beings could be produced through alchemy, a science dating to the medieval era that focused on turning common metals into gold, producing a universal healing elixir, and achieving immortality. — Eds.

[9] Albertus Magnus (1193–1280) was a German philosopher and theologian noted for his knowledge of Aristotle and the physical sciences, to whom many works on alchemy were (perhaps mistakenly) attributed. He later instructed Thomas Aquinas (1225–1274), a theologian who attempted to fuse tenets of Aristotelian philosophy with Roman Catholic principles. — Eds.

[10] Novices. — Eds.

practical uses. The most learned philosopher knew little more. He had partially unveiled the face of Nature, but her immortal lineaments were still a wonder and a mystery. He might dissect, anatomise, and give names; but, not to speak of a final cause, causes in their secondary and tertiary grades were utterly unknown to him. I had gazed upon the fortifications and impediments that seemed to keep human beings from entering the citadel of nature, and rashly and ignorantly I had repined.

But here were books, and here were men who had penetrated deeper and knew more. I took their word for all that they averred, and I became their disciple. It may appear strange that such should arise in the eighteenth century; but while I followed the routine of education in the schools of Geneva, I was, to a great degree, self taught with regard to my favourite studies. My father was not scientific, and I was left to struggle with a child's blindness, added to a student's thirst for knowledge. Under the guidance of my new preceptors, I entered with the greatest diligence into the search of the philosopher's stone and the elixir of life; but the latter soon obtained my undivided attention. Wealth was an inferior object; but what glory would attend the discovery, if I could banish disease from the human frame, and render man invulnerable to any but a violent death!

Nor were these my only visions. The raising of ghosts or devils was a promise liberally accorded by my favourite authors, the fulfilment of which I most eagerly sought; and if my incantations were always unsuccessful, I attributed the failure rather to my own inexperience and mistake, than to a want of skill or fidelity in my instructors. And thus for a time I was occupied by exploded systems, mingling, like an unadept, a thousand contradictory theories, and floundering desperately in a very slough of multifarious knowledge, guided by an ardent imagination and childish reasoning, till an accident again changed the current of my ideas.

When I was about fifteen years old we had retired to our house near Belrive, when we witnessed a most violent and terrible thunder-storm. It advanced from behind the mountains of Jura; and the thunder burst at once with frightful loudness from various quarters of the heavens. I remained, while the storm lasted, watching its progress with curiosity and delight. As I stood at the door, on a sudden I beheld a stream of fire issue from an old and beautiful oak, which stood about twenty yards from our house; and so soon as the dazzling light vanished, the oak had disappeared, and nothing remained but a blasted stump. When we visited it the next morning, we found the tree shattered in a singular manner. It was not splintered by the shock, but entirely reduced to thin ribands of wood. I never beheld any thing so utterly destroyed.

Before this I was not unacquainted with the more obvious laws of electricity. On this occasion a man of great research in natural philosophy was with us, and, excited by this catastrophe, he entered on the explanation of a theory which he had formed on the subject of electricity and galvanism, which was at once new and astonishing to me. All that he said threw greatly into the shade Cornelius Agrippa, Albertus Magnus, and Paracelsus, the lords of my imagination; but by some fatality the overthrow of these men disinclined me to pursue my accustomed studies. It seemed to me as if nothing would or could ever be known. All that had so long engaged my attention suddenly grew despicable. By one of those caprices of the mind, which we are perhaps most subject to in early youth, I at once gave up my former occupations; set down natural history and all its progeny as a deformed and abortive creation; and entertained the greatest disdain for a would-be science, which could never even step within the threshold of real knowledge. In this mood of mind I betook myself to the mathematics, and the branches of study appertaining to that science, as being built upon secure foundations, and so worthy of my consideration.

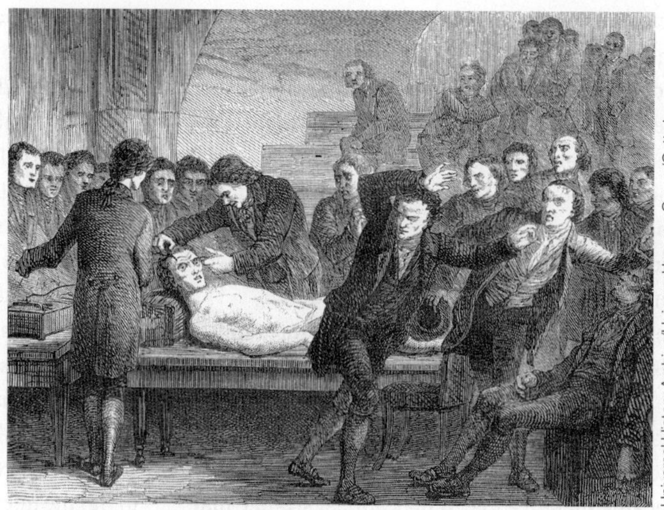

Universal History Archive/Universal Images Group/Getty Images

This engraving depicts Scottish doctor Andrew Ure performing one of several galvanic experiments on the corpse of Matthew Clydesdale, a recently executed murderer, in 1818. The electric current from Ure's galvanic battery stimulated Clydesdale's muscles, causing his limbs, chest, and face to move. As a result, some members of the audience fled, believing the dead man had been resurrected.

What do the events depicted in this engraving suggest about Frankenstein's new interest? What do they suggest about the direction the story is headed?

Thus strangely are our souls constructed, and by such slight ligaments are we bound to prosperity or ruin. When I look back, it seems to me as if this almost miraculous change of inclination and will was the immediate suggestion of the guardian angel of my life — the last effort made by the spirit of preservation to avert the storm that was even then hanging in the stars, and ready to envelop me. Her victory was announced by an unusual tranquillity and gladness of soul, which followed the relinquishing of my ancient and latterly tormenting studies. It was thus that I was to be taught to associate evil with their prosecution, happiness with their disregard.

It was a strong effort of the spirit of good; but it was ineffectual. Destiny was too potent, and her immutable laws had decreed my utter and terrible destruction.

CHAPTER III

When I had attained the age of seventeen, my parents resolved that I should become a student at the university of Ingolstadt.[11] I had hitherto attended the schools of Geneva; but my father thought it necessary, for the completion of my education, that I should be made acquainted with other customs than those of my native country. My departure was therefore fixed at an early date; but, before the day resolved upon could arrive, the first misfortune of my life occurred — an omen, as it were, of my future misery.

Elizabeth had caught the scarlet fever; her illness was severe, and she was in the greatest danger. During her illness, many arguments had been urged to persuade my mother to refrain from attending upon her. She had, at first, yielded to our entreaties; but when she heard that the life of her favourite was menaced, she could no longer control her anxiety. She attended her sick bed, — her watchful attentions triumphed over the malignity of the distemper, — Elizabeth was saved, but the consequences of this imprudence were fatal to her preserver. On the third day my mother sickened; her fever was accompanied by the most alarming symptoms, and the looks of her medical attendants prognosticated the worst event. On her death-bed the fortitude and benignity of this best of women did not desert her. She joined the hands of Elizabeth and myself: — "My children," she said, "my firmest hopes of future happiness were placed on the prospect of your union. This expectation will

[11] A German city. — Eds.

now be the consolation of your father. Elizabeth, my love, you must supply my place to my younger children. Alas! I regret that I am taken from you; and, happy and beloved as I have been, is it not hard to quit you all? But these are not thoughts befitting me; I will endeavour to resign myself cheerfully to death, and will indulge a hope of meeting you in another world."

She died calmly; and her countenance expressed affection even in death. I need not describe the feelings of those whose dearest ties are rent by that most irreparable evil; the void that presents itself to the soul; and the despair that is exhibited on the countenance. It is so long before the mind can persuade itself that she, whom we saw every day, and whose very existence appeared a part of our own, can have departed for ever — that the brightness of a beloved eye can have been extinguished, and the sound of a voice so familiar, and dear to the ear, can be hushed, never more to be heard. These are the reflections of the first days; but when the lapse of time proves the reality of the evil, then the actual bitterness of grief commences. Yet from whom has not that rude hand rent away some dear connection? and why should I describe a sorrow which all have felt, and must feel? The time at length arrives, when grief is rather an indulgence than a necessity; and the smile that plays upon the lips, although it may be deemed a sacrilege, is not banished. My mother was dead, but we had still duties which we ought to perform; we must continue our course with the rest, and learn to think ourselves fortunate, whilst one remains whom the spoiler has not seized.

My departure for Ingolstadt, which had been deferred by these events, was now again determined upon. I obtained from my father a respite of some weeks. It appeared to me sacrilege so soon to leave the repose, akin to death, of the house of mourning, and to rush into the thick of life. I was new to sorrow, but it did not the less alarm me. I was unwilling to quit the sight of those that remained to me; and, above all, I desired to see my sweet Elizabeth in some degree consoled.

She indeed veiled her grief, and strove to act the comforter to us all. She looked steadily on life, and assumed its duties with courage and zeal. She devoted herself to those whom she had been taught to call her uncle and cousins. Never was she so enchanting as at this time, when she recalled the sunshine of her smiles and spent them upon us. She forgot even her own regret in her endeavours to make us forget.

The day of my departure at length arrived. Clerval spent the last evening with us. He had endeavoured to persuade his father to permit him to accompany me, and to become my fellow student; but in vain. His father was a narrow-minded trader, and saw idleness and ruin in the aspirations and ambition of his son. Henry deeply felt the misfortune of being debarred from a liberal education. He said little; but when he spoke, I read in his kindling eye and in his animated glance a restrained but firm resolve, not to be chained to the miserable details of commerce.

We sat late. We could not tear ourselves away from each other, nor persuade ourselves to say the word "Farewell!" It was said; and we retired under the pretence of seeking repose, each fancying that the other was deceived: but when at morning's dawn I descended to the carriage which was to convey me away, they were all there — my father again to bless me, Clerval to press my hand once more, my Elizabeth to renew her entreaties that I would write often, and to bestow the last feminine attentions on her playmate and friend.

I threw myself into the chaise that was to convey me away, and indulged in the most melancholy reflections. I, who had ever been surrounded by amiable companions, continually engaged in endeavouring to bestow mutual pleasure — I was now alone. In the university, whither I was going, I must form my own friends, and be my own protector. My life had hitherto been remarkably secluded and domestic; and this had given me invincible repugnance to new countenances. I loved my brothers, Elizabeth, and Clerval; these were "old familiar faces;" but I believed myself totally unfitted for the company of strangers. Such were my reflections as I commenced my journey; but as I proceeded, my spirits and hopes rose. I ardently desired the acquisition of knowledge. I had often, when at home, thought it hard to remain during my youth cooped up in one place, and had longed to enter the world, and take my station among other human beings. Now my desires were complied with, and it would, indeed, have been folly to repent.

I had sufficient leisure for these and many other reflections during my journey to Ingolstadt, which was long and fatiguing. At length the high white steeple of the town met my eyes. I alighted, and was conducted to my solitary apartment, to spend the evening as I pleased.

The next morning I delivered my letters of introduction, and paid a visit to some of the principal professors. Chance — or rather the evil influence, the Angel of Destruction, which asserted omnipotent sway over me from the moment I turned my reluctant steps from my father's door — led me first to M. Krempe, professor of natural philosophy. He was an uncouth man, but deeply embued in the secrets of his science. He asked me several questions concerning my progress in the different branches of science appertaining to natural philosophy. I replied carelessly; and, partly in contempt, mentioned the names of my alchymists as the principal authors I had studied. The professor stared: "Have you," he said, "really spent your time in studying such nonsense?"

I replied in the affirmative. "Every minute," continued M. Krempe with warmth, "every instant that you have wasted on those books is utterly and entirely lost. You have burdened your memory with exploded systems and useless names. Good God! in what desert land have you lived, where no one was kind enough to inform you that these fancies, which you have so greedily imbibed, are a thousand years old, and as musty as they are ancient? I little expected, in this enlightened and scientific age, to find a disciple of Albertus Magnus and Paracelsus. My dear sir, you must begin your studies entirely anew."

So saying, he stept aside, and wrote down a list of several books treating of natural philosophy, which he desired me to procure; and dismissed me, after mentioning that in the beginning of the following week he intended to commence a course of lectures upon natural philosophy in its general relations, and that M. Waldman, a fellow-professor, would lecture upon chemistry the alternate days that he omitted.

I returned home, not disappointed, for I have said that I had long considered those authors useless whom the professor reprobated; but I returned, not at all the more inclined to recur to these studies in any shape. M. Krempe was a little, squat man, with a gruff voice and a repulsive countenance; the teacher, therefore, did not prepossess me in favour of his pursuits. In rather too philosophical and connected a strain, perhaps, I have given an account of the conclusions I had come to concerning them in my early years. As a child, I had not been content with the results promised by the modern professors of natural science. With a confusion of ideas only to be accounted for by my extreme youth, and my want of a guide on such matters, I had retrod the steps of knowledge along the paths of time, and exchanged the discoveries of recent enquirers for the dreams of forgotten alchymists. Besides, I had a contempt for the uses of modern natural philosophy. It was very different, when the masters of the science sought immortality and power; such views, although futile, were grand: but now the scene was changed. The ambition of the enquirer seemed to limit itself to the annihilation of those visions on which my interest in science was chiefly founded. I was required to exchange chimeras of boundless grandeur for realities of little worth.

Such were my reflections during the first two or three days of my residence at Ingolstadt, which were chiefly spent in becoming acquainted with the localities, and the principal residents in my new abode. But as the ensuing week commenced, I thought of the information which M. Krempe had given me concerning the lectures. And although I could not consent to go and hear that little conceited fellow deliver sentences out of a pulpit, I recollected what he had said of M. Waldman, whom I had never seen, as he had hitherto been out of town.

Partly from curiosity, and partly from idleness, I went into the lecturing room, which M. Waldman entered shortly after. This professor was very unlike his colleague. He appeared about fifty years of age, but with an aspect expressive of the greatest benevolence; a few grey hairs covered his temples, but those at the back of his head were nearly black. His person was short, but remarkably erect; and his voice the sweetest I had ever heard. He began his lecture by a recapitulation of the history of chemistry, and the various improvements made by different men of learning, pronouncing with fervour the names of the most distinguished discoverers. He then took a cursory view of the present state of the science, and explained many of its elementary terms. After having made a few preparatory experiments, he concluded with a panegyric upon modern chemistry, the terms of which I shall never forget: —

"The ancient teachers of this science," said he, "promised impossibilities, and performed nothing. The modern masters promise very little; they know that metals cannot be transmuted, and that the elixir of life is a chimera. But these philosophers, whose hands seem only made to dabble in dirt, and their eyes to pore over the microscope or crucible, have indeed performed miracles. They penetrate into the recesses of nature, and show how she works in her hiding places. They ascend into the heavens: they have discovered how the blood circulates, and the nature of the air we breathe. They have acquired new and almost unlimited powers; they can command the thunders of heaven, mimic the earthquake, and even mock the invisible world with its own shadows."

Such were the professor's words — rather let me say such the words of fate, enounced to destroy me. As he went on, I felt as if my soul were grappling with a palpable enemy; one by one the various keys were touched which formed the mechanism of my being: chord after chord was sounded, and soon my mind was filled with one thought, one conception, one purpose. So much has been done, exclaimed the soul of Frankenstein, — more, far more, will I achieve: treading in the steps already marked, I will pioneer a new way, explore unknown powers, and unfold to the world the deepest mysteries of creation.

I closed not my eyes that night. My internal being was in a state of insurrection and turmoil; I felt that order would thence arise, but I had no power to produce it. By degrees, after the morning's dawn, sleep came. I awoke, and my yesternight's thoughts were as a dream. There only remained a resolution to return to my ancient studies, and to devote myself to a science for which I believed myself to possess a natural talent. On the same day, I paid M. Waldman a visit. His manners in private were even more mild and attractive than in public; for there was a certain dignity in his mien during his lecture, which in his own house was replaced by the greatest affability and kindness. I gave him pretty nearly the same account of my former pursuits as I had given to his fellow-professor. He heard with attention the little narration concerning my studies, and smiled at the names of Cornelius Agrippa and Paracelsus, but without the contempt that M. Krempe had exhibited. He said, that "these were men to whose indefatigable zeal modern philosophers were indebted for most of the foundations of their knowledge. They had left to us, as an easier task, to give new names, and arrange in connected classifications, the facts which they in a great degree had been the instruments of bringing to light. The labours of men of genius, however erroneously directed, scarcely ever fail in ultimately turning to the solid advantage of mankind." I listened to his statement, which was delivered without any presumption or affectation; and then added, that his lecture had removed my prejudices against modern chemists; I expressed myself in measured terms, with the modesty and deference due from a youth to his instructor, without letting escape (inexperience in life would have made me ashamed) any of the enthusiasm which stimulated my intended labours. I requested his advice concerning the books I ought to procure.

"I am happy," said M. Waldman, "to have gained a disciple; and if your application equals your ability, I have no doubt of your success. Chemistry is that branch of natural philosophy in which the greatest improvements have been and may be made: it is on that account that I have made it my peculiar study; but at the same time I have not neglected the other branches of science. A man would make but a very sorry chemist if he attended to that department of human knowledge alone. If your wish is to become really a man of science, and not merely a petty experimentalist, I should advise you to apply to every branch of natural philosophy, including mathematics."

He then took me into his laboratory, and explained to me the uses of his various machines; instructing me as to what I ought to procure, and promising me the use of his own when I should have advanced far enough in the science not to derange their mechanism. He also gave me the list of books which I had requested; and I took my leave.

Thus ended a day memorable to me: it decided my future destiny.

CHAPTER IV

From this day natural philosophy, and particularly chemistry, in the most comprehensive sense of the term, became nearly my sole occupation. I read with ardour those works, so full of genius and discrimination, which modern enquirers have written on these subjects. I attended the lectures, and cultivated the acquaintance, of the men of science of the university; and I found even in M. Krempe a great deal of sound sense and real information, combined, it is true, with a repulsive physiognomy and manners, but not on that account the less valuable. In M. Waldman I found a true friend. His gentleness was never tinged by dogmatism; and his instructions were given with an air of frankness and good nature, that banished every idea of pedantry. In a thousand ways he smoothed for me the path of knowledge, and made the most abstruse enquiries clear and facile to my apprehension. My application was at first fluctuating and uncertain; it gained strength as I proceeded, and soon became so ardent and eager, that the stars often disappeared in the light of morning whilst I was yet engaged in my laboratory.

As I applied so closely, it may be easily conceived that my progress was rapid. My ardour was indeed the astonishment of the students, and my proficiency that of the masters. Professor Krempe often asked me, with a sly smile, how Cornelius Agrippa went on? whilst M. Waldman expressed the most heartfelt exultation in my progress. Two years passed in this manner, during which I paid no visit to Geneva, but was engaged, heart and soul, in the pursuit of some discoveries, which I hoped to make. None but those who have experienced them can conceive of the enticements of science. In other studies you go as far as others have gone before you, and there is nothing more to know; but in a scientific pursuit there is continual food for discovery and wonder. A mind of moderate capacity, which closely pursues one study, must infallibly arrive at great proficiency in that study; and I, who continually sought the attainment of one object of pursuit, and was solely wrapt up in this, improved so rapidly, that, at the end of two years, I made some discoveries in the improvement of some chemical instruments, which procured me great esteem and admiration at the university. When I had arrived at this point, and had become as well acquainted with the theory and practice of natural philosophy as depended on the lessons of any of the professors at Ingolstadt, my residence there being no longer conducive to my improvements, I thought of returning to my friends and my native town, when an incident happened that protracted my stay.

One of the phenomena which had peculiarly attracted my attention was the structure of the human frame, and, indeed, any animal endued with life. Whence, I often asked myself, did the principle of life proceed? It was a bold question, and one which has ever been considered as a mystery; yet with how many things are we upon the brink of becoming acquainted, if cowardice or carelessness did not restrain our enquiries. I revolved these circumstances in my mind, and determined thenceforth to apply myself more particularly to those branches of natural philosophy which relate to physiology. Unless I had been animated by an almost supernatural enthusiasm, my application to this study would have been irksome, and almost intolerable. To examine the causes of life, we must first have recourse to death. I became acquainted with the science of anatomy: but this was not sufficient; I must also observe the natural decay and corruption of the human body. In my education my father had taken the greatest precautions that my mind should be impressed with no supernatural horrors. I do not ever remember to have trembled at a tale of superstition, or to have feared the apparition of a spirit. Darkness had no effect upon my fancy; and a churchyard was to me merely the receptacle of bodies deprived of life, which, from being the seat of beauty and strength, had become food for the worm. Now I was led to examine the cause and progress of this decay, and forced to spend days and nights in vaults and charnel-houses.[12] My attention was fixed upon every object the most insupportable to the delicacy of the human feelings. I saw how the fine form of man was degraded and wasted; I beheld the corruption of death succeed to the blooming cheek of life; I saw how the worm inherited the wonders of the eye and brain. I paused, examining and analysing all the minutiae of causation, as exemplified in the change from life to death, and death to life, until from the midst of this darkness a sudden light broke in upon me — a light so brilliant and wondrous, yet so simple, that while I became dizzy with the immensity of the prospect which it illustrated, I was surprised, that among so many men of genius who had directed their enquiries towards the same science, that I alone should be reserved to discover so astonishing a secret.

Remember, I am not recording the vision of a madman. The sun does not more certainly shine in the heavens, than that which I now affirm is true. Some miracle might have produced it, yet the stages of the discovery were distinct and probable. After days and nights of incredible labour and fatigue, I succeeded in discovering the cause of generation and life; nay, more, I became myself capable of bestowing animation upon lifeless matter.

The astonishment which I had at first experienced on this discovery soon gave place to delight and rapture. After so much time spent in painful labour, to arrive at once at the summit of my desires, was the most gratifying consummation of my toils. But this discovery was so great and overwhelming, that all the steps by which I had been progressively led to it were obliterated,

[12] Repositories for corpses and bones. — Eds.

and I beheld only the result. What had been the study and desire of the wisest men since the creation of the world was now within my grasp. Not that, like a magic scene, it all opened upon me at once: the information I had obtained was of a nature rather to direct my endeavours so soon as I should point them towards the object of my search, than to exhibit that object already accomplished. I was like the Arabian[13] who had been buried with the dead, and found a passage to life, aided only by one glimmering, and seemingly ineffectual, light.

I see by your eagerness, and the wonder and hope which your eyes express, my friend, that you expect to be informed of the secret with which I am acquainted; that cannot be: listen patiently until the end of my story, and you will easily perceive why I am reserved upon that subject. I will not lead you on, unguarded and ardent as I then was, to your destruction and infallible misery. Learn from me, if not by my precepts, at least by my example, how dangerous is the acquirement of knowledge, and how much happier that man is who believes his native town to be the world, than he who aspires to become greater than his nature will allow.

When I found so astonishing a power placed within my hands, I hesitated a long time concerning the manner in which I should employ it. Although I possessed the capacity of bestowing animation, yet to prepare a frame for the reception of it, with all its intricacies of fibres, muscles, and veins, still remained a work of inconceivable difficulty and labour. I doubted at first whether I should attempt the creation of a being like myself, or one of simpler organization; but my imagination was too much exalted by my first success to permit me to doubt of my ability to give life to an animal as complex and wonderful as man. The materials at present within my command hardly appeared adequate to so arduous an undertaking; but I doubted not that I should ultimately succeed. I prepared myself for a multitude of reverses; my operations might be incessantly baffled, and at last my work be imperfect: yet, when I considered the improvement which every day takes place in science and mechanics, I was encouraged to hope my present attempts would at least lay the foundations of future success. Nor could I consider the magnitude and complexity of my plan as any argument of its impracticability. It was with these feelings that I began the creation of a human being. As the minuteness of the parts formed a great hindrance to my speed, I resolved, contrary to my first intention, to make the being of a gigantic stature; that is to say, about eight feet in height, and proportionably large. After having formed this determination, and having spent some months in successfully collecting and arranging my materials, I began.

No one can conceive the variety of feelings which bore me onwards, like a hurricane, in the first enthusiasm of success. Life and death appeared to me ideal bounds, which I should first break through, and pour a torrent of light into our dark world. A new species would bless me as its creator and source; many happy and excellent natures would owe their being to me. No father could claim the gratitude of his child so completely as I should deserve theirs. Pursuing these reflections, I thought, that if I could bestow animation upon lifeless matter, I might in process of time (although I now found it impossible) renew life where death had apparently devoted the body to corruption.

These thoughts supported my spirits, while I pursued my undertaking with unremitting ardour. My cheek had grown pale with study, and my person had become emaciated with confinement. Sometimes, on the very brink of

[13] A reference to the fourth of seven voyages of Sinbad in a seventeenth-century addition to a collection of Middle Eastern and South Asian stories, *One Thousand and One Nights*, whose earliest iterations date to the early eighth century. On his fourth voyage, Sinbad settles on an island where the custom when one spouse dies is to bury both together in a communal tomb. When Sinbad's young and beautiful wife dies, he is trapped underground with her body until an animal shows him an escape route. — Eds.

certainty, I failed; yet still I clung to the hope which the next day or the next hour might realise. One secret which I alone possessed was the hope to which I had dedicated myself; and the moon gazed on my midnight labours, while, with unrelaxed and breathless eagerness, I pursued nature to her hiding-places. Who shall conceive the horrors of my secret toil, as I dabbled among the unhallowed damps of the grave, or tortured the living animal to animate the lifeless clay? My limbs now tremble, and my eyes swim with the remembrance; but then a resistless, and almost frantic, impulse, urged me forward; I seemed to have lost all soul or sensation but for this one pursuit. It was indeed but a passing trance, that only made me feel with renewed acuteness so soon as, the unnatural stimulus ceasing to operate, I had returned to my old habits. I collected bones from charnel-houses; and disturbed, with profane fingers, the tremendous secrets of the human frame. In a solitary chamber, or rather cell, at the top of the house, and separated from all the other apartments by a gallery and staircase, I kept my workshop of filthy creation: my eye-balls were starting from their sockets in attending to the details of my employment. The dissecting room and the slaughter-house furnished many of my materials; and often did my human nature turn with loathing from my occupation, whilst, still urged on by an eagerness which perpetually increased, I brought my work near to a conclusion.

The summer months passed while I was thus engaged, heart and soul, in one pursuit. It was a most beautiful season; never did the fields bestow a more plentiful harvest, or the vines yield a more luxuriant vintage: but my eyes were insensible to the charms of nature. And the same feelings which made me neglect the scenes around me caused me also to forget those friends who were so many miles absent, and whom I had not seen for so long a time. I knew my silence disquieted them; and I well remembered the words of my father: "I know that while you are pleased with yourself, you will think of us with affection, and we shall hear regularly from you. You must pardon me if I regard any interruption in your correspondence as a proof that your other duties are equally neglected."

I knew well therefore what would be my father's feelings; but I could not tear my thoughts from my employment, loathsome in itself, but which had taken an irresistible hold of my imagination. I wished, as it were, to procrastinate all that related to my feelings of affection until the great object, which swallowed up every habit of my nature, should be completed.

I then thought that my father would be unjust if he ascribed my neglect to vice, or faultiness on my part; but I am now convinced that he was justified in conceiving that I should not be altogether free from blame. A human being in perfection ought always to preserve a calm and peaceful mind, and never to allow passion or a transitory desire to disturb his tranquillity. I do not think that the pursuit of knowledge is an exception to this rule. If the study to which you apply yourself has a tendency to weaken your affections, and to destroy your taste for those simple pleasures in which no alloy can possibly mix, then that study is certainly unlawful, that is to say, not befitting the human mind. If this rule were always observed; if no man allowed any pursuit whatsoever to interfere with the tranquillity of his domestic affections, Greece had not been enslaved; Caesar would have spared his country; America would have been discovered more gradually; and the empires of Mexico and Peru had not been destroyed.

But I forget that I am moralising in the most interesting part of my tale; and your looks remind me to proceed.

My father made no reproach in his letters, and only took notice of my silence by enquiring into my occupations more particularly than before. Winter, spring, and summer passed away during my labours; but I did not watch the blossom or the expanding leaves — sights which

Human dissection was prohibited in Britain before the 1500s and remained extremely restricted until the mid-1700s, when a law was passed allowing physicians to dissect the bodies of executed murderers. This engraving by William Hogarth (1697–1764) depicts such a dissection. However, because access to cadavers remained extremely limited, a black market developed and flourished until the Anatomy Act of 1832 dramatically increased the legal supply.
What does this engraving seem to suggest about the people performing the dissection? Given the stigma and criminalization of dissection in Britain at the time *Frankenstein* was written, what might Shelley be suggesting about Victor by describing his trips to charnel houses?

before always yielded me supreme delight — so deeply was I engrossed in my occupation. The leaves of that year had withered before my work drew near to a close; and now every day showed me more plainly how well I had succeeded. But my enthusiasm was checked by my anxiety, and I appeared rather like one doomed by slavery to toil in the mines, or any other unwholesome trade, than an artist occupied by his favourite employment. Every night I was oppressed by a slow fever, and I became nervous to a most painful degree; the fall of a leaf startled me, and I shunned my fellow-creatures as if I had been guilty of a crime. Sometimes I grew alarmed at the wreck I perceived that I had become; the energy of my purpose alone sustained me: my labours would soon end, and I believed that exercise and amusement would then drive away incipient disease; and I promised myself both of these when my creation should be complete.

CHAPTER V

It was on a dreary night of November, that I beheld the accomplishment of my toils. With an anxiety that almost amounted to agony, I collected the instruments of life around me, that I might infuse a spark of being into the lifeless thing that lay at my feet. It was already one in the morning; the rain pattered dismally against the panes, and my candle was nearly burnt out, when, by the glimmer of the half-extinguished light, I saw the dull yellow eye of the creature open; it breathed hard, and a convulsive motion agitated its limbs.

How can I describe my emotions at this catastrophe, or how delineate the wretch whom with such infinite pains and care I had endeavoured to form? His limbs were in proportion, and I had selected his features as beautiful. Beautiful! — Great God! His yellow skin scarcely covered the work of muscles and arteries beneath; his hair was of a lustrous black, and flowing; his teeth of a pearly whiteness; but these luxuriances only formed a more horrid contrast with his watery eyes, that seemed almost of the same colour as the dun white sockets in which they were set, his shriveled complexion and straight black lips.

The different accidents of life are not so changeable as the feelings of human nature. I had worked hard for nearly two years, for the sole purpose of infusing life into an inanimate body. For this I had deprived myself of rest and health. I had desired it with an ardour that far exceeded moderation; but now that I had finished, the beauty of the dream vanished, and breathless horror and disgust filled my heart. Unable to endure the aspect of the being I had created, I rushed out of the room, and continued a long time traversing my bedchamber, unable to compose my mind to sleep. At length lassitude succeeded to the tumult I had before endured; and I threw myself on the bed in my clothes, endeavouring to seek a few moments of forgetfulness. But it was in vain; I slept, indeed, but I was disturbed by the wildest dreams. I thought I saw Elizabeth, in the bloom of health, walking in the streets of Ingolstadt. Delighted and surprised, I embraced her; but as I imprinted the first kiss on her lips, they became livid with the hue of death; her features appeared to change, and I thought that I held the corpse of my dead mother in my arms; a shroud enveloped her form, and I saw the graveworms crawling in the folds of the flannel. I started from my sleep with horror; a cold dew covered my forehead, my teeth chattered, and every limb became convulsed; when, by the dim and yellow light of the moon, as it forced its way through the window shutters, I beheld the wretch — the miserable monster whom I had created. He held up the curtain of the bed; and his eyes, if eyes they may be called, were fixed on me. His jaws opened, and he muttered some inarticulate sounds, while a grin wrinkled his cheeks. He might have spoken, but I did not hear; one hand was stretched out, seemingly to detain me, but I escaped, and rushed down stairs. I took refuge in the courtyard belonging to the house which I inhabited; where I remained during the rest of the night, walking up and down in the greatest agitation, listening attentively, catching and fearing each sound as if it were to announce the approach of the demoniacal corpse to which I had so miserably given life.

Oh! no mortal could support the horror of that countenance. A mummy again endued with animation could not be so hideous as that wretch. I had gazed on him while unfinished; he was ugly then; but when those muscles and joints were rendered capable of motion, it became a thing such as even Dante[14] could not have conceived.

I passed the night wretchedly. Sometimes my pulse beat so quickly and hardly, that I felt the palpitation of every artery; at others, I nearly sank to the ground through languor and extreme weakness. Mingled with this horror, I felt the bitterness of disappointment; dreams that had been my food and pleasant rest for so long a space were now become a hell to me; and the change was so rapid, the overthrow so complete!

Morning, dismal and wet, at length dawned, and discovered to my sleepless and aching eyes the church of Ingolstadt, its white steeple and clock, which indicated the sixth hour. The porter opened the gates of the court, which had that night been my asylum, and I issued into the streets, pacing them with quick steps, as if I sought to avoid the wretch whom I feared every turning of the street would present to my view. I did not dare return to the apartment which I inhabited, but felt impelled to hurry on, although drenched by the rain which poured from a black and comfortless sky.

I continued walking in this manner for 125
some time, endeavouring, by bodily exercise, to ease the load that weighed upon my mind. I traversed the streets, without any clear conception of where I was, or what I was doing.

---

[14] A reference to *The Inferno,* the first part of the three-part fourteenth-century poem *The Divine Comedy* by Dante Alighieri (1265–1321). In it, Dante tells of fantastical punishments and their effects on the people he meets as he is guided through hell by the Roman poet Virgil. — Eds.

My heart palpitated in the sickness of fear; and I hurried on with irregular steps, not daring to look about me: —

> Like one who, on a lonely road,
>   Doth walk in fear and dread,
> And, having once turned round, walks on,
>   And turns no more his head;
> Because he knows a frightful fiend
>   Doth close behind him tread.[15]

Continuing thus, I came at length opposite to the inn at which the various diligences and carriages usually stopped. Here I paused, I knew not why; but I remained some minutes with my eyes fixed on a coach that was coming towards me from the other end of the street. As it drew nearer, I observed that it was the Swiss diligence: it stopped just where I was standing; and, on the door being opened, I perceived Henry Clerval, who, on seeing me, instantly sprung out. "My dear Frankenstein," exclaimed he, "how glad I am to see you! how fortunate that you should be here at the very moment of my alighting!"

Nothing could equal my delight on seeing Clerval; his presence brought back to my thoughts my father, Elizabeth, and all those scenes of home so dear to my recollection. I grasped his hand, and in a moment forgot my horror and misfortune; I felt suddenly, and for the first time during many months, calm and serene joy. I welcomed my friend, therefore, in the most cordial manner, and we walked towards my college. Clerval continued talking for some time about our mutual friends, and his own good fortune in being permitted to come to Ingolstadt. "You may easily believe," said he, "how great was the difficulty to persuade my father that all necessary knowledge was not comprised in the noble art of book-keeping; and, indeed, I believe I left him incredulous to the last, for his constant answer to my unwearied entreaties was the same as that of the Dutch schoolmaster[16] in the Vicar of Wakefield: — 'I have ten thousand florins a year without Greek, I eat heartily without Greek.' But his affection for me at length overcame his dislike of learning, and he has permitted me to undertake a voyage of discovery to the land of knowledge."

"It gives me the greatest delight to see you; but tell me how you left my father, brothers, and Elizabeth."

"Very well, and very happy, only a little uneasy that they hear from you so seldom. By the by, I mean to lecture you a little upon their account myself. — But, my dear Frankenstein," continued he, stopping short, and gazing full in my face, "I did not before remark how very ill you appear; so thin and pale; you look as if you had been watching for several nights."

130 "You have guessed right; I have lately been so deeply engaged in one occupation, that I have not allowed myself sufficient rest, as you see; but I hope, I sincerely hope, that all these employments are now at an end, and that I am at length free."

I trembled excessively; I could not endure to think of, and far less to allude to, the occurrences of the preceding night. I walked with a quick pace, and we soon arrived at my college. I then reflected, and the thought made me shiver, that the creature whom I had left in my apartment might still be there, alive, and walking about. I dreaded to behold this monster; but I feared still more that Henry should see him. Entreating him, therefore, to remain a few minutes at the bottom of the stairs, I darted up towards my own room. My hand was already on the lock of the door before I recollected myself.

[15] Coleridge's "Ancient Mariner" — Shelley.

[16] A reference to Chapter 20 of the 1766 novel The Vicar of Wakefield by Oliver Goldsmith (1730–1774). The book's plot is set in motion when the vicar has a sudden reversal in fortune and finds himself penniless. In Chapter 20, the vicar's son approaches the head professor of a university in Louvain, France, and offers his services as a master of the Greek language, only to find that the professor does not know and has no use for it. — Eds.

I then paused; and a cold shivering came over me. I threw the door forcibly open, as children are accustomed to do when they expect a spectre to stand in waiting for them on the other side; but nothing appeared. I stepped fearfully in: the apartment was empty; and my bedroom was also freed from its hideous guest. I could hardly believe that so great a good fortune could have befallen me; but when I became assured that my enemy had indeed fled, I clapped my hands for joy, and ran down to Clerval.

We ascended into my room, and the servant presently brought breakfast; but I was unable to contain myself. It was not joy only that possessed me; I felt my flesh tingle with excess of sensitiveness, and my pulse beat rapidly. I was unable to remain for a single instant in the same place; I jumped over the chairs, clapped my hands, and laughed aloud. Clerval at first attributed my unusual spirits to joy on his arrival; but when he observed me more attentively, he saw a wildness in my eyes for which he could not account; and my loud, unrestrained, heartless laughter, frightened and astonished him.

"My dear Victor," cried he, "what, for God's sake, is the matter? Do not laugh in that manner. How ill you are! What is the cause of all this?"

"Do not ask me," cried I, putting my hands before my eyes, for I thought I saw the dreaded spectre glide into the room; "*he* can tell. — Oh, save me! save me!" I imagined that the monster seized me; I struggled furiously, and fell down in a fit.

Poor Clerval! what must have been his feelings? 135
A meeting, which he anticipated with such joy, so strangely turned to bitterness. But I was not the witness of his grief; for I was lifeless, and did not recover my senses for a long, long time.

This was the commencement of a nervous fever, which confined me for several months. During all that time Henry was my only nurse. I afterwards learned that, knowing my father's advanced age, and unfitness for so long a journey, and how wretched my sickness would make Elizabeth, he spared them this grief by concealing the extent of my disorder. He knew that I could not have a more kind and attentive nurse than himself; and, firm in the hope he felt of my recovery, he did not doubt that, instead of doing harm, he performed the kindest action that he could towards them.

But I was in reality very ill; and surely nothing but the unbounded and unremitting attentions of my friend could have restored me to life. The form of the monster on whom I had bestowed existence was for ever before my eyes, and I raved incessantly concerning him. Doubtless my words surprised Henry: he at first believed them to be the wanderings of my disturbed imagination; but the pertinacity with which I continually recurred to the same subject persuaded him that my disorder indeed owed its origin to some uncommon and terrible event.

By very slow degrees, and with frequent relapses, that alarmed and grieved my friend, I recovered. I remember the first time I became capable of observing outward objects with any kind of pleasure, I perceived that the fallen leaves had disappeared, and that the young buds were shooting forth from the trees that shaded my window. It was a divine spring; and the season contributed greatly to my convalescence. I felt also sentiments of joy and affection revive in my bosom; my gloom disappeared, and in a short time I became as cheerful as before I was attacked by the fatal passion.

"Dearest Clerval," exclaimed I, "how kind, how very good you are to me. This whole winter, instead of being spent in study, as you promised yourself, has been consumed in my sick room. How shall I ever repay you? I feel the greatest remorse for the disappointment of which I have been the occasion; but you will forgive me."

"You will repay me entirely, if you do not 140
discompose yourself, but get well as fast as you can; and since you appear in such good spirits, I may speak to you on one subject, may I not?"

I trembled. One subject! what could it be? Could he allude to an object on whom I dared not even think?

"Compose yourself," said Clerval, who observed my change of colour, "I will not mention it, if it agitates you; but your father and cousin would be very happy if they received a letter from you in your own hand-writing. They hardly know how ill you have been, and are uneasy at your long silence."

"Is that all, my dear Henry? How could you suppose that my first thought would not fly towards those dear, dear friends whom I love, and who are so deserving of my love."

"If this is your present temper, my friend, you will perhaps be glad to see a letter that has been lying here some days for you: it is from your cousin, I believe."

CHAPTER VI

Clerval then put the following letter into my hands. It was from my own Elizabeth:—

"My dearest Cousin,

"You have been ill, very ill, and even the constant letters of dear kind Henry are not sufficient to reassure me on your account. You are forbidden to write—to hold a pen; yet one word from you, dear Victor, is necessary to calm our apprehensions. For a long time I have thought that each post would bring this line, and my persuasions have restrained my uncle from undertaking a journey to Ingolstadt. I have prevented his encountering the inconveniences and perhaps dangers of so long a journey; yet how often have I regretted not being able to perform it myself! I figure to myself that the task of attending on your sick bed has devolved on some mercenary old nurse, who could never guess your wishes, nor minister to them with the care and affection of your poor cousin. Yet that is over now: Clerval writes that indeed you are getting better. I eagerly hope that you will confirm this intelligence soon in your own handwriting.

"Get well—and return to us. You will find a happy, cheerful home, and friends who love you dearly. Your father's health is vigorous, and he asks but to see you,—but to be assured that you are well; and not a care will ever cloud his benevolent countenance. How pleased you would be to remark the improvement of our Ernest! He is now sixteen, and full of activity and spirit. He is desirous to be a true Swiss, and to enter into foreign service; but we cannot part with him, at least until his elder brother returns to us. My uncle is not pleased with the idea of a military career in a distant country; but Ernest never had your powers of application. He looks upon study as an odious fetter;—his time is spent in the open air, climbing the hills or rowing on the lake. I fear that he will become an idler, unless we yield the point, and permit him to enter on the profession which he has selected.

"Little alteration, except the growth of our dear children, has taken place since you left us. The blue lake, and snow-clad mountains, they never change;—and I think our placid home, and our contented hearts are regulated by the same immutable laws. My trifling occupations take up my time and amuse me, and I am rewarded for any exertions by seeing none but happy, kind faces around me. Since you left us, but one change has taken place in our little household. Do you remember on what occasion Justine Moritz entered our family? Probably you do not; I will relate her history, therefore, in a few words. Madame Moritz, her mother, was a widow with four children, of whom Justine was the third. This girl had always been the favourite of her father; but, through a strange perversity, her mother could not endure her, and, after the death of M. Moritz, treated her very ill. My aunt observed this; and, when Justine was twelve years of age, prevailed on her mother to allow her to live at our house. The republican institutions of our country have produced simpler and happier manners than those which prevail in the great monarchies that surround it.

Hence there is less distinction between the several classes of its inhabitants; and the lower orders, being neither so poor nor so despised, their manners are more refined and moral. A servant in Geneva does not mean the same thing as a servant in France and England. Justine, thus received in our family, learned the duties of a servant; a condition which, in our fortunate country, does not include the idea of ignorance, and a sacrifice of the dignity of a human being.

"Justine, you may remember, was a great favourite of yours; and I recollect you once remarked, that if you were in an ill-humour, one glance from Justine could dissipate it, for the same reason that Ariosto gives concerning the beauty of Angelica[17] — she looked so frank-hearted and happy. My aunt conceived a great attachment for her, by which she was induced to give her an education superior to that which she had at first intended. This benefit was fully repaid; Justine was the most grateful little creature in the world; I do not mean that she made any professions; I never heard one pass her lips; but you could see by her eyes that she almost adored her protectress. Although her disposition was gay, and in many respects inconsiderate, yet she paid the greatest attention to every gesture of my aunt. She thought her the model of all excellence, and endeavoured to imitate her phraseology and manners, so that even now she often reminds me of her.

"When my dearest aunt died, every one was too much occupied in their own grief to notice poor Justine, who had attended her during her illness with the most anxious affection. Poor Justine was very ill; but other trials were reserved for her.

"One by one, her brothers and sister died; and her mother, with the exception of her neglected daughter, was left childless. The conscience of the woman was troubled; she began to think that the deaths of her favourites was a judgment from heaven to chastise her partiality. She was a Roman Catholic; and I believe her confessor confirmed the idea which she had conceived. Accordingly, a few months after your departure for Ingolstadt, Justine was called home by her repentant mother. Poor girl! she wept when she quitted our house; she was much altered since the death of my aunt; grief had given softness and a winning mildness to her manners, which had before been remarkable for vivacity. Nor was her residence at her mother's house of a nature to restore her gaiety. The poor woman was very vacillating in her repentance. She sometimes begged Justine to forgive her unkindness, but much oftener accused her of having caused the deaths of her brothers and sister. Perpetual fretting at length threw Madame Moritz into a decline, which at first increased her irritability, but she is now at peace for ever. She died on the first approach of cold weather, at the beginning of this last winter. Justine has returned to us; and I assure you I love her tenderly. She is very clever and gentle, and extremely pretty; as I mentioned before, her mien and her expressions continually remind me of my dear aunt.

"I must say also a few words to you, my dear cousin, of little darling William. I wish you could see him; he is very tall of his age, with sweet laughing blue eyes, dark eyelashes, and curling hair. When he smiles, two little dimples appear on each cheek, which are rosy with health. He has already had one or two little *wives*, but Louisa Biron is his favourite, a pretty little girl of five years of age.

"Now, dear Victor, I dare say you wish to be indulged in a little gossip concerning the good people of Geneva. The pretty Miss Mansfield has already received the congratulatory visits on her approaching marriage with a young Englishman, John Melbourne, Esq. Her ugly sister, Manon, married M. Duvillard, the rich banker, last autumn. Your favourite schoolfellow, Louis

---

[17] The pagan heroine of the epic Italian romance *Orlando Furioso* (1532) by Lodovico Ariosto (1474–1535). Angelica's inability to reciprocate Orlando's love drives him mad. — Eds.

Manoir, has suffered several misfortunes since the departure of Clerval from Geneva. But he has already recovered his spirits, and is reported to be on the point of marrying a very lively pretty Frenchwoman, Madame Tavernier. She is a widow, and much older than Manoir; but she is very much admired, and a favourite with everybody.

"I have written myself into better spirits, dear cousin; but my anxiety returns upon me as I conclude. Write, dearest Victor, — one line — one word will be a blessing to us. Ten thousand thanks to Henry for his kindness, his affection, and his many letters: we are sincerely grateful. Adieu! my cousin; take care of your self; and, I entreat you, write!

"ELIZABETH LAVENZA.

"Geneva, March 18th, 17 — ."

"Dear, dear Elizabeth!" I exclaimed, when I had read her letter: "I will write instantly, and relieve them from the anxiety they must feel." I wrote, and this exertion greatly fatigued me; but my convalescence had commenced, and proceeded regularly. In another fortnight I was able to leave my chamber.

One of my first duties on my recovery was to introduce Clerval to the several professors of the university. In doing this, I underwent a kind of rough usage, ill befitting the wounds that my mind had sustained. Ever since the fatal night, the end of my labours, and the beginning of my misfortunes, I had conceived a violent antipathy even to the name of natural philosophy. When I was otherwise quite restored to health, the sight of a chemical instrument would renew all the agony of my nervous symptoms. Henry saw this, and had removed all my apparatus from my view. He had also changed my apartment; for he perceived that I had acquired a dislike for the room which had previously been my laboratory. But these cares of Clerval were made of no avail when I visited the professors. M. Waldman inflicted torture when he praised, with kindness and warmth, the astonishing progress I had made in the sciences. He soon perceived that I disliked the subject; but not guessing the real cause, he attributed my feelings to modesty, and changed the subject from my improvement, to the science itself, with a desire, as I evidently saw, of drawing me out. What could I do? He meant to please, and he tormented me. I felt as if he had placed carefully, one by one, in my view those instruments which were to be afterwards used in putting me to a slow and cruel death. I writhed under his words, yet dared not exhibit the pain I felt. Clerval, whose eyes and feelings were always quick in discerning the sensations of others, declined the subject, alleging, in excuse, his total ignorance; and the conversation took a more general turn. I thanked my friend from my heart, but I did not speak. I saw plainly that he was surprised, but he never attempted to draw my secret from me; and although I loved him with a mixture of affection and reverence that knew no bounds, yet I could never persuade myself to confide to him that event which was so often present to my recollection, but which I feared to detail to another would only impress more deeply.

M. Krempe was not equally docile; and in my condition at that time, of almost insupportable sensitiveness, his harsh blunt encomiums gave me even more pain than the benevolent approbation of M. Waldman. "D — n the fellow!" cried he; "why, M. Clerval, I assure you he has outstript us all. Ay, stare if you please; but it is nevertheless true. A youngster who, but a few years ago, believed in Cornelius Agrippa as firmly as in the gospel, has now set himself at the head of the university; and if he is not soon pulled down, we shall all be out of countenance. — Ay, ay," continued he, observing my face expressive of suffering, "M. Frankenstein is modest; an excellent quality in a young man. Young men should be diffident of themselves, you know, M. Clerval: I was myself when young; but that wears out in a very short time."

M. Krempe had now commenced an eulogy on himself, which happily turned the conversation from a subject that was so annoying to me.

Clerval had never sympathized in my tastes for natural science; and his literary pursuits differed wholly from those which had occupied me. He came to the university with the design of making himself complete master of the oriental languages, as thus he should open a field for the plan of life he had marked out for himself. Resolved to pursue no inglorious career, he turned his eyes toward the East, as affording scope for his spirit of enterprise. The Persian, Arabic, and Sanscrit languages engaged his attention, and I was easily induced to enter on the same studies. Idleness had ever been irksome to me, and now that I wished to fly from reflection, and hated my former studies, I felt great relief in being the fellow-pupil with my friend, and found not only instruction but consolation in the works of the orientalists. I did not, like him, attempt a critical knowledge of their dialects, for I did not contemplate making any other use of them than temporary amusement. I read merely to understand their meaning, and they well repaid my labours. Their melancholy is soothing, and their joy elevating, to a degree I never experienced in studying the authors of any other country. When you read their writings, life appears to consist in a warm sun and a garden of roses, — in the smiles and frowns of a fair enemy, and the fire that consumes your own heart. How different from the manly and heroical poetry of Greece and Rome!

Summer passed away in these occupations, and my return to Geneva was fixed for the latter end of autumn; but being delayed by several accidents, winter and snow arrived, the roads were deemed impassable, and my journey was retarded until the ensuing spring. I felt this delay very bitterly; for I longed to see my native town and my beloved friends. My return had only been delayed so long, from an unwillingness to leave Clerval in a strange place, before he had become acquainted with any of its inhabitants. The winter, however, was spent cheerfully; and although the spring was uncommonly late, when it came its beauty compensated for its dilatoriness.

The month of May had already commenced, and I expected the letter daily which was to fix the date of my departure, when Henry proposed a pedestrian tour in the environs of Ingolstadt, that I might bid a personal farewell to the country I had so long inhabited. I acceded with pleasure to this proposition: I was fond of exercise, and Clerval had always been my favourite companion in the rambles of this nature that I had taken among the scenes of my native country.

We passed a fortnight in these perambulations: my health and spirits had long been restored, and they gained additional strength from the salubrious air I breathed, the natural incidents of our progress, and the conversation of my friend. Study had before secluded me from the intercourse of my fellow-creatures, and rendered me unsocial; but Clerval called forth the better feelings of my heart; he again taught me to love the aspect of nature, and the cheerful faces of children. Excellent friend! how sincerely did you love me, and endeavour to elevate my mind until it was on a level with your own! A selfish pursuit had cramped and narrowed me, until your gentleness and affection warmed and opened my senses; I became the same happy creature who, a few years ago, loved and beloved by all, had no sorrow or care. When happy, inanimate nature had the power of bestowing on me the most delightful sensations. A serene sky and verdant fields filled me with ecstasy. The present season was indeed divine; the flowers of spring bloomed in the hedges, while those of summer were already in bud. I was undisturbed by thoughts which during the preceding year had pressed upon me, notwithstanding my endeavours to throw them off, with an invincible burden.

Henry rejoiced in my gaiety, and sincerely sympathised in my feelings: he exerted himself to amuse me, while he expressed the sensations that filled his soul. The resources of his mind on this occasion were truly astonishing: his conversation was full of imagination; and very often, in imitation of the Persian and Arabic writers, he invented tales of wonderful fancy and passion. At other times he repeated my favourite poems, or drew me out into arguments, which he supported with great ingenuity.

We returned to our college on a Sunday afternoon: the peasants were dancing, and every one we met appeared gay and happy. My own spirits were high, and I bounded along with feelings of unbridled joy and hilarity.

CHAPTER VII

On my return, I found the following letter from my father: —

"My dear Victor,

"You have probably waited impatiently for a letter to fix the date of your return to us; and I was at first tempted to write only a few lines, merely mentioning the day on which I should expect you. But that would be a cruel kindness, and I dare not do it. What would be your surprise, my son, when you expected a happy and glad welcome, to behold, on the contrary, tears and wretchedness? And how, Victor, can I relate our misfortune? Absence cannot have rendered you callous to our joys and griefs; and how shall I inflict pain on my long absent son? I wish to prepare you for the woful news, but I know it is impossible; even now your eye skims over the page, to seek the words which are to convey to you the horrible tidings.

"William is dead! — that sweet child, whose smiles delighted and warmed my heart, who was so gentle, yet so gay! Victor, he is murdered!

"I will not attempt to console you; but will simply relate the circumstances of the transaction.

"Last Thursday (May 7th), I, my niece, and your two brothers, went to walk in Plainpalais. The evening was warm and serene, and we prolonged our walk farther than usual. It was already dusk before we thought of returning; and then we discovered that William and Ernest, who had gone on before, were not to be found. We accordingly rested on a seat until they should return. Presently Ernest came, and enquired if we had seen his brother: he said, that he had been playing with him, that William had run away to hide himself, and that he vainly sought for him, and afterwards waited for him a long time, but that he did not return.

"This account rather alarmed us, and we continued to search for him until night fell, when Elizabeth conjectured that he might have returned to the house. He was not there. We returned again, with torches; for I could not rest, when I thought that my sweet boy had lost himself, and was exposed to all the damps and dews of night; Elizabeth also suffered extreme anguish. About five in the morning I discovered my lovely boy, whom the night before I had seen blooming and active in health, stretched on the grass livid and motionless: the print of the murderer's finger was on his neck.

"He was conveyed home, and the anguish that was visible in my countenance betrayed the secret to Elizabeth. She was very earnest to see the corpse. At first I attempted to prevent her; but she persisted, and entering the room where it lay, hastily examined the neck of the victim, and clasping her hands exclaimed, 'O God! I have murdered my darling child!'

"She fainted, and was restored with extreme difficulty. When she again lived, it was only to weep and sigh. She told me, that that same evening William had teased her to let him wear a very valuable miniature that she possessed of your mother. This picture is gone, and was doubtless the temptation which urged the murderer to the deed. We have no trace of him at present, although our exertions to discover him are unremitted; but they will not restore my beloved William!

"Come, dearest Victor; you alone can console Elizabeth. She weeps continually, and accuses herself unjustly as the cause of his death; her words pierce my heart. We are all unhappy; but will not that be an additional motive for you, my son, to return and be our comforter? Your dear mother! Alas, Victor! I now say, Thank God she did not live to witness the cruel, miserable death of her youngest darling!

"Come, Victor; not brooding thoughts of vengeance against the assassin, but with feelings of peace and gentleness, that will heal, instead of festering, the wounds of our minds. Enter the house of mourning, my friend, but with kindness and affection for those who love you, and not with hatred for your enemies.

"Your affectionate and afflicted father,
"ALPHONSE FRANKENSTEIN.
"Geneva, May 12th, 17—."

Clerval, who had watched my countenance as I read this letter, was surprised to observe the despair that succeeded to the joy I at first expressed on receiving news from my friends. I threw the letter on the table, and covered my face with my hands.

"My dear Frankenstein," exclaimed Henry, when he perceived me weep with bitterness, "are you always to be unhappy? My dear friend, what has happened?"

I motioned to him to take up the letter, while I walked up and down the room in the extremest agitation. Tears also gushed from the eyes of Clerval, as he read the account of my misfortune.

"I can offer you no consolation, my friend," said he; "your disaster is irreparable. What do you intend to do?"

"To go instantly to Geneva: come with me, Henry, to order the horses."

During our walk, Clerval endeavoured to say a few words of consolation; he could only express his heartfelt sympathy. "Poor William!" said he, "dear lovely child, he now sleeps with his angel mother! Who that had seen him bright and joyous in his young beauty, but must weep over his untimely loss! To die so miserably; to feel the murderer's grasp! How much more a murderer, that could destroy such radiant innocence! Poor little fellow! one only consolation have we; his friends mourn and weep, but he is at rest. The pang is over, his sufferings are at an end for ever. A sod covers his gentle form, and he knows no pain. He can no longer be a subject for pity; we must reserve that for his miserable survivors."

Clerval spoke thus as we hurried through the streets; the words impressed themselves on my mind, and I remembered them afterwards in solitude. But now, as soon as the horses arrived, I hurried into a cabriolet, and bade farewell to my friend.

My journey was very melancholy. At first I wished to hurry on, for I longed to console and sympathise with my loved and sorrowing friends; but when I drew near my native town, I slackened my progress. I could hardly sustain the multitude of feelings that crowded into my mind. I passed through scenes familiar to my youth, but which I had not seen for nearly six years. How altered every thing might be during that time! One sudden and desolating change had taken place; but a thousand little circumstances might have by degrees worked other alterations, which, although they were done more tranquilly, might not be the less decisive. Fear overcame me; I dared not advance, dreading a thousand nameless evils that made me tremble, although I was unable to define them.

I remained two days at Lausanne, in this painful state of mind. I contemplated the lake: the waters were placid; all around was calm; and the snowy mountains, "the palaces of nature," were not changed. By degrees the calm and heavenly scene restored me, and I continued my journey towards Geneva.

The road ran by the side of the lake, which became narrower as I approached my native town. I discovered more distinctly the black sides of Jura, and the bright summit of Mont Blanc. I wept like a child. "Dear mountains! my own beautiful lake! how do you welcome your wanderer? Your summits are clear; the sky and lake are blue and placid. Is this to prognosticate peace, or to mock at my unhappiness?"

I fear, my friend, that I shall render myself tedious by dwelling on these preliminary circumstances; but they were days of comparative happiness, and I think of them with pleasure. My country, my beloved country! who but a native can tell the delight I took in again beholding thy streams, thy mountains, and, more than all, thy lovely lake!

Yet, as I drew nearer home, grief and fear again overcame me. Night also closed around; and when I could hardly see the dark mountains, I felt still more gloomily. The picture appeared a vast and dim scene of evil, and I foresaw obscurely that I was destined to become the most wretched of human beings. Alas! I prophesied truly, and failed only in one single circumstance, that in all the misery I imagined and dreaded, I did not conceive the hundredth part of the anguish I was destined to endure.

It was completely dark when I arrived in the environs of Geneva; the gates of the town were already shut; and I was obliged to pass the night at Secheron, a village at the distance of half a league from the city. The sky was serene; and, as I was unable to rest, I resolved to visit the spot where my poor William had been murdered. As I could not pass through the town, I was obliged to cross the lake in a boat to arrive at Plainpalais. During this short voyage I saw the lightnings playing on the summit of Mont Blanc in the most beautiful figures. The storm appeared to approach rapidly; and, on landing, I ascended a low hill, that I might observe its progress. It advanced; the heavens were clouded, and I soon felt the rain coming slowly in large drops, but its violence quickly increased.

I quitted my seat, and walked on, although the darkness and storm increased every minute, and the thunder burst with a terrific crash over my head. It was echoed from Salêve, the Juras, and the Alps of Savoy; vivid flashes of lightning dazzled my eyes, illuminating the lake, making it appear like a vast sheet of fire; then for an instant every thing seemed of a pitchy darkness, until the eye recovered itself from the preceding flash. The storm, as is often the case in Switzerland, appeared at once in various parts of the heavens. The most violent storm hung exactly north of the town, over that part of the lake which lies between the promontory of Belrive and the village of Copêt. Another storm enlightened Jura with faint flashes; and another darkened and sometimes disclosed the Môle, a peaked mountain to the east of the lake.

While I watched the tempest, so beautiful yet terrific, I wandered on with a hasty step. This noble war in the sky elevated my spirits; I clasped my hands, and exclaimed aloud, "William, dear angel! this is thy funeral, this thy dirge!" As I said these words, I perceived in the gloom a figure which stole from behind a clump of trees near me; I stood fixed, gazing intently; I could not be mistaken. A flash of lightning illuminated the object, and discovered its shape plainly to me: its gigantic stature, and the deformity of its aspect, more hideous than belongs to humanity, instantly informed me that it was the wretch, the filthy daemon, to whom I had given life. What did he there? Could he be (I shuddered at the conception) the murderer of my brother? No sooner did that idea cross my imagination, than I became convinced of its truth; my teeth chattered, and I was forced to lean against a tree for support. The figure passed me quickly, and I lost it in the gloom. Nothing in human shape could have destroyed that fair child. *He* was the murderer! I could not doubt it. The mere presence of the idea was an irresistible proof of the fact. I thought of pursuing the devil; but it would have been in vain, for another flash discovered him to me hanging among the rocks of the nearly perpendicular ascent of Mont Salêve, a hill that bounds Plainpalais on the south. He soon reached the summit, and disappeared.

190 I remained motionless. The thunder ceased; but the rain still continued, and the scene was enveloped in an impenetrable darkness. I revolved in my mind the events which I had until now sought to forget: the whole train of my progress towards the creation; the appearance of the work of my own hands alive at my bedside; its departure. Two years had now nearly elapsed since the night on which he first received life; and was this his first crime? Alas! I had turned loose into the world a depraved wretch, whose delight was in carnage and misery; had he not murdered my brother?

No one can conceive the anguish I suffered during the remainder of the night, which I spent, cold and wet, in the open air. But I did not feel the inconvenience of the weather; my imagination was busy in scenes of evil and despair. I considered the being whom I had cast among mankind, and endowed with the will and power to effect purposes of horror, such as the deed which he had now done, nearly in the light of my own vampire, my own spirit let loose from the grave, and forced to destroy all that was dear to me.

Day dawned; and I directed my steps towards the town. The gates were open, and I hastened to my father's house. My first thought was to discover what I knew of the murderer, and cause instant pursuit to be made. But I paused when I reflected on the story that I had to tell. A being whom I myself had formed, and endued with life, had met me at midnight among the precipices of an inaccessible mountain. I remembered also the nervous fever with which I had been seized just at the time that I dated my creation, and which would give an air of delirium to a tale otherwise so utterly improbable. I well knew that if any other had communicated such a relation to me, I should have looked upon it as the ravings of insanity. Besides, the strange nature of the animal would elude all pursuit, even if I were so far credited as to persuade my relatives to commence it. And then of what use would be pursuit? Who could arrest a creature capable of scaling the overhanging sides of Mont Salêve? These reflections determined me, and I resolved to remain silent.

It was about five in the morning when I entered my father's house. I told the servants not to disturb the family, and went into the library to attend their usual hour of rising.

Six years had elapsed, passed as a dream but for one indelible trace, and I stood in the same place where I had last embraced my father before my departure for Ingolstadt. Beloved and venerable parent! He still remained to me. I gazed on the picture of my mother, which stood over the mantel-piece. It was an historical subject, painted at my father's desire, and represented Caroline Beaufort in an agony of despair, kneeling by the coffin of her dead father. Her garb was rustic, and her cheek pale; but there was an air of dignity and beauty, that hardly permitted the sentiment of pity. Below this picture was a miniature of William; and my tears flowed when I looked upon it. While I was thus engaged, Ernest entered; he had heard me arrive, and hastened to welcome me. He expressed a sorrowful delight to see me: "Welcome, my dearest Victor," said he. "Ah! I wish you had come three months ago, and then you would have found us all joyous and delighted. You come to us now to share a misery which nothing can alleviate; yet your presence will, I hope, revive our father, who seems sinking under his misfortune; and your persuasions will induce poor Elizabeth to cease her vain and tormenting self-accusations.— Poor William! he was our darling and our pride!"

195 Tears, unrestrained, fell from my brother's eyes; a sense of mortal agony crept over my frame. Before, I had only imagined the wretchedness of my desolated home; the reality came on me as a new, and a not less terrible, disaster. I tried to calm Ernest; I enquired more minutely concerning my father, and her I named my cousin.

"She most of all," said Ernest, "requires consolation; she accused herself of having caused the death of my brother, and that made her very wretched. But since the murderer has been discovered — "

"The murderer discovered! Good God! how can that be? who could attempt to pursue him? It is impossible; one might as well try to overtake the winds, or confine a mountain-stream with a straw. I saw him too; he was free last night!"

"I do not know what you mean," replied my brother, in accents of wonder, "but to us the discovery we have made completes our misery. No one would believe it at first; and even now Elizabeth will not be convinced, notwithstanding all the evidence. Indeed, who would credit that Justine Moritz, who was so amiable, and fond of all the family, could suddenly become capable of so frightful, so appalling a crime?"

"Justine Moritz! Poor, poor girl, is she the accused? But it is wrongfully; every one knows that; no one believes it, surely, Ernest?"

"No one did at first; but several circumstances came out, that have almost forced conviction upon us; and her own behaviour has been so confused, as to add to the evidence of facts a weight that, I fear, leaves no hope for doubt. But she will be tried to-day, and you will then hear all."

He related that, the morning on which the murder of poor William had been discovered, Justine had been taken ill, and confined to her bed for several days. During this interval, one of the servants, happening to examine the apparel she had worn on the night of the murder, had discovered in her pocket the picture of my mother, which had been judged to be the temptation of the murderer. The servant instantly showed it to one of the others, who, without saying a word to any of the family, went to a magistrate; and, upon their deposition, Justine was apprehended. On being charged with the fact, the poor girl confirmed the suspicion in a great measure by her extreme confusion of manner.

This was a strange tale, but it did not shake my faith; and I replied earnestly, "You are all mistaken; I know the murderer. Justine, poor, good Justine, is innocent."

At that instant my father entered. I saw unhappiness deeply impressed on his countenance, but he endeavoured to welcome me cheerfully; and, after we had exchanged our mournful greeting, would have introduced some other topic than that of our disaster, had not Ernest exclaimed, "Good God, papa! Victor says that he knows who was the murderer of poor William."

"We do also, unfortunately," replied my father; "for indeed I had rather have been for ever ignorant than have discovered so much depravity and ingratitude in one I valued so highly."

"My dear father, you are mistaken; Justine is innocent."

"If she is, God forbid that she should suffer as guilty. She is to be tried to-day, and I hope, I sincerely hope, that she will be acquitted."

This speech calmed me. I was firmly convinced in my own mind that Justine, and indeed every human being, was guiltless of this murder. I had no fear, therefore, that any circumstantial evidence could be brought forward strong enough to convict her. My tale was not one to announce publicly; its astounding horror would be looked upon as madness by the vulgar. Did any one indeed exist, except I, the creator, who would believe, unless his senses convinced him, in the existence of the living monument of presumption and rash ignorance which I had let loose upon the world?

We were soon joined by Elizabeth. Time had altered her since I last beheld her; it had endowed her with loveliness surpassing the beauty of her childish years. There was the same candour, the same vivacity, but it was allied to an expression more full of sensibility and intellect. She welcomed me with the greatest affection. "Your arrival, my dear cousin," said she, "fills me with hope. You perhaps will find some means to justify my poor guiltless Justine. Alas! who is safe, if she be convicted of crime? I rely on her innocence as certainly as I do upon my own. Our misfortune is doubly hard to us; we have not only lost that lovely darling boy, but this poor girl, whom I sincerely love, is to be torn away by even a worse fate. If she is condemned, I never shall know joy more. But she will not, I am sure she will not; and then I shall be happy again, even after the sad death of my little William."

"She is innocent, my Elizabeth," said I, "and that shall be proved; fear nothing, but let your spirits be cheered by the assurance of her acquittal."

"How kind and generous you are! every one else believes in her guilt, and that made me wretched, for I knew that it was impossible: and to see every one else prejudiced in so deadly a manner rendered me hopeless and despairing." She wept.

"Dearest niece," said my father, "dry your tears. If she is, as you believe, innocent, rely on the justice of our laws, and the activity with which I shall prevent the slightest shadow of partiality."

CHAPTER VIII

We passed a few sad hours, until eleven o'clock, when the trial was to commence. My father and the rest of the family being obliged to attend as witnesses, I accompanied them to the court. During the whole of this wretched mockery of justice I suffered living torture. It was to be decided, whether the result of my curiosity and lawless devices would cause the death of two of my fellow-beings: one a smiling babe, full of innocence and joy; the other far more dreadfully murdered, with every aggravation of infamy that could make the murder memorable in horror. Justine also was a girl of merit, and possessed qualities which promised to render her life happy: now all was to be obliterated in an ignominious grave; and I the cause! A thousand times rather would I have confessed myself guilty of the crime ascribed to Justine; but I was absent when it was committed, and such a declaration would have been considered as the ravings of a madman, and would not have exculpated her who suffered through me.

The appearance of Justine was calm. She was dressed in mourning; and her countenance, always engaging, was rendered, by the solemnity of her feelings, exquisitely beautiful. Yet she appeared confident in innocence, and did not tremble, although gazed on and execrated by thousands; for all the kindness which her beauty might otherwise have excited, was obliterated in the minds of the spectators by the imagination of the enormity she was supposed to have committed. She was tranquil, yet her tranquillity was evidently constrained; and as her confusion had before been adduced as a proof of her guilt, she worked up her mind to an appearance of courage. When she entered the court, she threw her eyes round it, and quickly discovered where we were seated. A tear seemed to dim her eye when she saw us; but she quickly recovered herself, and a look of sorrowful affection seemed to attest her utter guiltlessness.

The trial began; and, after the advocate against her had stated the charge, several witnesses were called. Several strange facts combined against her, which might have staggered any one who had not such proof of her innocence as I had. She had been out the whole of the night on which the murder had been committed, and towards morning had been perceived by a market-woman not far from the spot where the body of the murdered child had been afterwards found. The woman asked her what she did there; but she looked very strangely, and only returned a confused and unintelligible answer. She returned to the house about eight o'clock; and, when one enquired where she had passed the night, she replied that she had been looking for the child, and demanded earnestly if any thing had been heard concerning him. When shown the body, she fell into violent hysterics, and kept her bed for several days. The picture was then produced, which the servant had found in her pocket; and when Elizabeth, in a faltering voice, proved that it was the same which, an hour before the child had been missed, she had placed round his neck, a murmur of horror and indignation filled the court.

Justine was called on for her defence. As the trial had proceeded, her countenance had altered. Surprise, horror, and misery were strongly expressed. Sometimes she struggled with her tears; but, when she was desired to plead, she collected her powers, and spoke, in an audible although variable voice.

"God knows," she said, "how entirely I am innocent. But I do not pretend that my protestations should acquit me: I rest my innocence on a plain and simple explanation of the facts which have been adduced against me; and I hope the character I have always borne will incline my judges to a favourable interpretation, where any circumstance appears doubtful or suspicious."

She then related that, by the permission of Elizabeth, she had passed the evening of the night on which the murder had been committed at the house of an aunt at Chêne, a village situated at about a league from Geneva. On her return, at about nine o'clock, she met a man, who asked her if she had seen any thing of the child who was lost. She was alarmed by this account, and passed several hours in looking for him, when the gates of Geneva were shut, and she was forced to remain several hours of the night in a barn belonging to a cottage, being unwilling to call up the inhabitants, to whom she was well known. Most of the night she spent here watching; towards morning she believed that she slept for a few minutes; some steps disturbed her, and she awoke. It was dawn, and she quitted her asylum, that she might again endeavour to find my brother. If she had gone near the spot where his body lay, it was without her knowledge. That she had been bewildered when questioned by the market-woman was not surprising, since she had passed a sleepless night, and the fate of poor William was yet uncertain. Concerning the picture she could give no account.

"I know," continued the unhappy victim, "how heavily and fatally this one circumstance weighs against me, but I have no power of explaining it; and when I have expressed my utter ignorance, I am only left to conjecture concerning the probabilities by which it might have been placed in my pocket. But here also I am checked. I believe that I have no enemy on earth, and none surely would have been so wicked as to destroy me wantonly. Did the murderer place it there? I know of no opportunity afforded him for so doing; or, if I had, why should he have stolen the jewel, to part with it again so soon?

"I commit my cause to the justice of my judges, yet I see no room for hope. I beg permission to have a few witnesses examined concerning my character; and if their testimony shall not overweigh my supposed guilt, I must be condemned, although I would pledge my salvation on my innocence."

Several witnesses were called, who had known her for many years, and they spoke well of her; but fear, and hatred of the crime of which they supposed her guilty, rendered them timorous, and unwilling to come forward. Elizabeth saw even this last resource, her excellent dispositions and irreproachable conduct, about to fail the accused, when, although violently agitated, she desired permission to address the court.

"I am," said she, "the cousin of the unhappy child who was murdered, or rather his sister, for I was educated by and have lived with his parents ever since and even long before his birth. It may therefore be judged indecent in me to come forward on this occasion; but when I see a fellow-creature about to perish through the cowardice of her pretended friends, I wish to be allowed to speak, that I may say what I know of her character. I am well acquainted with the accused. I have lived in the same house with her, at one time for five, and at another for nearly two years. During all that period she appeared to me the most amiable and benevolent of human creatures. She nursed Madame Frankenstein, my aunt, in her last illness, with the greatest affection and care; and afterwards attended her own mother during a tedious illness, in a manner that excited the admiration of all who knew her; after which she again lived in my uncle's house, where she was beloved by all the family. She was warmly attached to the child who is now dead, and acted towards him like a most affectionate mother. For my own part, I do not hesitate to say, that, notwithstanding all the evidence produced against her, I believe and rely on her perfect innocence. She had no temptation for such an action: as to the bauble on which the chief proof rests, if she had earnestly desired it, I should have willingly given it to her; so much do I esteem and value her."

A murmur of approbation followed Elizabeth's simple and powerful appeal; but it was excited by her generous interference, and not in favour of poor Justine, on whom the public indignation was turned with renewed violence, charging her with the blackest ingratitude. She herself wept as Elizabeth spoke, but she did not answer. My own agitation and anguish was extreme during the whole trial. I believed in her innocence; I knew it. Could the daemon, who had (I did not for a minute doubt) murdered my brother, also in his hellish sport have betrayed the innocent to death and ignominy? I could not sustain the horror of my situation; and when I perceived that the popular voice, and the countenances of the judges, had already condemned my unhappy victim, I rushed out of the court in agony. The tortures of the accused did not equal mine; she was sustained by innocence, but the fangs of remorse tore my bosom, and would not forego their hold.

I passed a night of unmingled wretchedness. In the morning I went to the court; my lips and throat were parched. I dared not ask the fatal question; but I was known, and the officer guessed the cause of my visit. The ballots had been thrown; they were all black, and Justine was condemned.

I cannot pretend to describe what I then felt. I had before experienced sensations of horror; and I have endeavoured to bestow upon them adequate expressions, but words cannot convey an idea of the heart-sickening despair that I then endured. The person to whom I addressed myself added, that Justine had already confessed her guilt. "That evidence," he observed, "was hardly required in so glaring a case, but I am glad of it; and, indeed, none of our judges like to condemn a criminal upon circumstantial evidence, be it ever so decisive."

This was strange and unexpected intelligence; what could it mean? Had my eyes deceived me? and was I really as mad as the whole world would believe me to be, if I disclosed the object of my suspicions? I hastened to return home, and Elizabeth eagerly demanded the result.

"My cousin," replied I, "it is decided as you may have expected; all judges had rather that ten innocent should suffer, than that one guilty should escape. But she has confessed."

This was a dire blow to poor Elizabeth, who had relied with firmness upon Justine's innocence. "Alas!" said she, "how shall I ever again believe in human goodness? Justine, whom I loved and esteemed as my sister, how could she put on those smiles of innocence only to betray? her mild eyes seemed incapable of any severity or guile, and yet she has committed a murder."

Soon after we heard that the poor victim had expressed a desire to see my cousin. My father wished her not to go; but said, that he left it to her own judgment and feelings to decide. "Yes," said Elizabeth, "I will go, although she is guilty; and you, Victor, shall accompany me: I cannot go alone." The idea of this visit was torture to me, yet I could not refuse.

We entered the gloomy prison-chamber, and beheld Justine sitting on some straw at the farther end; her hands were manacled, and her head rested on her knees. She rose on seeing us enter; and when we were left alone with her, she threw herself at the feet of Elizabeth, weeping bitterly. My cousin wept also.

"Oh, Justine!" said she, "why did you rob me of my last consolation? I relied on your innocence; and although I was then very wretched, I was not so miserable as I am now."

"And do you also believe that I am so very, very wicked? Do you also join with my enemies to crush me, to condemn me as a murderer?" Her voice was suffocated with sobs.

"Rise, my poor girl," said Elizabeth, "why do you kneel, if you are innocent? I am not one of your enemies; I believed you guiltless, notwithstanding every evidence, until I heard that you had yourself declared your guilt. That report, you say, is false; and be assured, dear Justine, that nothing can shake my confidence in you for a moment, but your own confession."

"I did confess; but I confessed a lie. I confessed, that I might obtain absolution; but now that falsehood lies heavier at my heart than all my other sins. The God of heaven forgive me! Ever since I was condemned, my confessor has besieged me; he threatened and menaced, until I almost began to think that I was the monster that he said I was. He threatened excommunication and hell fire in my last moments, if I continued obdurate. Dear lady, I had none to support me; all looked on me as a wretch doomed to ignominy and perdition. What could I do? In an evil hour I subscribed to a lie; and now only am I truly miserable."

She paused, weeping, and then continued—"I thought with horror, my sweet lady, that you should believe your Justine, whom your blessed aunt had so highly honoured, and whom you loved, was a creature capable of a crime which none but the devil himself could have perpetrated. Dear William! dearest blessed child! I soon shall see you again in heaven, where we shall all be happy; and that consoles me, going as I am to suffer ignominy and death."

"Oh, Justine! forgive me for having for one moment distrusted you. Why did you confess? But do not mourn, dear girl. Do not fear. I will proclaim, I will prove your innocence. I will melt the stony hearts of your enemies by my tears and prayers. You shall not die!—You, my play-fellow, my companion, my sister, perish on the scaffold! No! no! I never could survive so horrible a misfortune."

Justine shook her head mournfully. "I do not fear to die," she said; "that pang is past. God raises my weakness, and gives me courage to endure the worst. I leave a sad and bitter world; and if you remember me, and think of me as of one unjustly condemned, I am resigned to the fate awaiting me. Learn from me, dear lady, to submit in patience to the will of Heaven!"

During this conversation I had retired to a corner of the prison-room, where I could conceal the horrid anguish that possessed me. Despair! Who dared talk of that? The poor victim, who on the morrow was to pass the awful boundary between life and death, felt not as I did, such deep and bitter agony. I gnashed my teeth, and ground them together, uttering a groan that came from my inmost soul. Justine started. When she saw who it was, she approached me, and said, "Dear sir, you are very kind to visit me; you, I hope, do not believe that I am guilty?"

I could not answer. "No, Justine," said Elizabeth; "he is more convinced of your innocence than I was; for even when he heard that you had confessed, he did not credit it."

"I truly thank him. In these last moments I feel the sincerest gratitude towards those who think of me with kindness. How sweet is the affection of others to such a wretch as I am! It removes more than half my misfortune; and I feel as if I could die in peace, now that my innocence is acknowledged by you, dear lady, and your cousin."

Thus the poor sufferer tried to comfort others and herself. She indeed gained the resignation she desired. But I, the true murderer, felt the never-dying worm alive in my bosom, which allowed of no hope or consolation. Elizabeth also wept, and was unhappy; but hers also was the misery of innocence, which, like a cloud that passes over the fair moon, for a while hides but cannot tarnish its brightness. Anguish and despair had penetrated into the core of my heart; I bore a hell within me, which nothing could extinguish. We stayed several hours with Justine; and it was with great difficulty that Elizabeth could tear herself away. "I wish," cried she, "that I were to die with you; I cannot live in this world of misery."

Justine assumed an air of cheerfulness, while she with difficulty repressed her bitter tears. She embraced Elizabeth, and said, in a voice of half-suppressed emotion, "Farewell, sweet lady, dearest Elizabeth, my beloved and only friend; may Heaven, in its bounty, bless and preserve you; may this be the last misfortune that you will ever suffer! Live, and be happy, and make others so."

And on the morrow Justine died. Elizabeth's heartrending eloquence failed to move the judges from their settled conviction in the criminality of the saintly sufferer. My passionate and indignant appeals were lost upon them. And when I received their cold answers, and heard the harsh unfeeling reasoning of these men, my purposed avowal died away on my lips. Thus I might proclaim myself a madman, but not revoke the sentence passed upon my wretched victim. She perished on the scaffold as a murderess!

From the tortures of my own heart, I turned to contemplate the deep and voiceless grief of my Elizabeth. This also was my doing! And my father's woe, and the desolation of that late so smiling home — all was the work of my thrice-accursed hands! Ye weep, unhappy ones; but these are not your last tears! Again shall you raise the funeral wail, and the sound of your lamentations shall again and again be heard! Frankenstein, your son, your kinsman, your early, much-loved friend; he who would spend each vital drop of blood for your sakes — who has no thought nor sense of joy, except as it is mirrored also in your dear countenances — who would fill the air with blessings, and spend his life in serving you — he bids you weep — to shed countless tears; happy beyond his hopes, if thus inexorable fate be satisfied, and if the destruction pause before the peace of the grave have succeeded to your sad torments!

Thus spoke my prophetic soul, as, torn by remorse, horror, and despair, I beheld those I loved spend vain sorrow upon the graves of William and Justine, the first hapless victims to my unhallowed arts.

CHAPTER IX

Nothing is more painful to the human mind, than, after the feelings have been worked up by a quick succession of events, the dead calmness of inaction and certainty which follows, and deprives the soul both of hope and fear. Justine died; she rested; and I was alive. The blood flowed freely in my veins, but a weight of despair and remorse pressed on my heart, which nothing could remove. Sleep fled from my eyes; I wandered like an evil spirit, for I had committed deeds of mischief beyond description horrible, and more, much more (I persuaded myself), was yet behind. Yet my heart overflowed with kindness, and the love of virtue. I had begun life with benevolent intentions, and thirsted for the moment when I should put them in practice, and make myself useful to my fellow-beings. Now all was blasted: instead of that serenity of conscience, which allowed me to look back upon the past with self-satisfaction, and from thence to gather promise of new hopes, I was seized by remorse and the sense of guilt, which hurried me away to a hell of intense tortures, such as no language can describe.

This state of mind preyed upon my health, which had perhaps never entirely recovered from the first shock it had sustained. I shunned the face of man; all sound of joy or complacency was torture to me; solitude was my only consolation — deep, dark, deathlike solitude.

My father observed with pain the alteration perceptible in my disposition and habits, and endeavoured by arguments deduced from the feelings of his serene conscience and guiltless life, to inspire me with fortitude, and awaken in me the courage to dispel the dark cloud which brooded over me. "Do you think, Victor," said he, "that I do not suffer also? No one could love a child more than I loved your brother;" (tears came into his eyes as he spoke;) "but is it not a duty to the survivors, that we should refrain from augmenting their unhappiness by an appearance of immoderate grief? It is also a duty owed to yourself; for excessive sorrow prevents improvement or enjoyment, or even the discharge of daily usefulness, without which no man is fit for society."

This advice, although good, was totally inapplicable to my case; I should have been the first to hide my grief, and console my friends, if remorse had not mingled its bitterness, and terror its alarm with my other sensations. Now I could only answer my father with a look of despair, and endeavour to hide myself from his view.

About this time we retired to our house at Belrive. This change was particularly agreeable to me. The shutting of the gates regularly at ten o'clock, and the impossibility of remaining on the lake after that hour, had rendered our residence within the walls of Geneva very irksome to me. I was now free. Often, after the rest of the family had retired for the night, I took the boat, and passed many hours upon the water. Sometimes, with my sails set, I was carried by the wind; and sometimes, after rowing into the middle of the lake, I left the boat to pursue its own course, and gave way to my own miserable reflections. I was often tempted, when all was at peace around me, and I the only unquiet thing that wandered restless in a scene so beautiful and heavenly — if I except some bat, or the frogs, whose harsh and interrupted croaking was heard only when I approached the shore — often, I say, I was tempted to plunge into the silent lake, that the waters might close over me and my calamities for ever. But I was restrained, when I thought of the heroic and suffering Elizabeth, whom I tenderly loved, and whose existence was bound up in mine. I thought also of my father, and surviving brother: should I by my base desertion leave them exposed and unprotected to the malice of the fiend whom I had let loose among them?

At these moments I wept bitterly, and wished that peace would revisit my mind only that I might afford them consolation and happiness. But that could not be. Remorse extinguished every hope. I had been the author of unalterable evils; and I lived in daily fear, lest the monster whom I had created should perpetrate some new wickedness. I had an obscure feeling that all was not over, and that he would still commit some signal crime, which by its enormity should almost efface the recollection of the past. There was always scope for fear, so long as any thing I loved remained behind. My abhorrence of this fiend cannot be conceived. When I thought of him, I gnashed my teeth, my eyes became inflamed, and I ardently wished to extinguish that life which I had so thoughtlessly bestowed. When I reflected on his crimes and malice, my hatred and revenge burst all bounds of moderation. I would have made a pilgrimage to the highest peak of the Andes, could I, when there, have precipitated him to their base. I wished to see him again, that I might wreak the utmost extent of abhorrence on his head, and avenge the deaths of William and Justine.

Our house was the house of mourning. My father's health was deeply shaken by the horror of the recent events. Elizabeth was sad and desponding; she no longer took delight in her ordinary occupations; all pleasure seemed to her sacrilege toward the dead; eternal woe and tears she then thought was the just tribute she should pay to innocence so blasted and destroyed. She was no longer that happy creature, who in earlier youth wandered with me on the banks of the lake, and talked with ecstasy of our future prospects. The first of those sorrows which are sent to wean us from the earth, had visited her, and its dimming influence quenched her dearest smiles.

"When I reflect, my dear cousin," said she, "on the miserable death of Justine Moritz, I no longer see the world and its works as they before appeared to me. Before, I looked upon the accounts of vice and injustice, that I read in books or heard from others, as tales of ancient days, or imaginary evils; at least they were remote, and more familiar to reason than to the imagination; but now misery has come home, and men appear to me as monsters thirsting for each other's blood. Yet I am certainly unjust. Every body believed that poor girl to be guilty; and if she could have committed the crime for which she suffered, assuredly she would have been the most depraved of human creatures. For the sake of a few jewels, to have murdered the son of her benefactor and friend, a child whom she had nursed from its birth, and appeared to love as if it had been her own! I could not consent to the death of any human being; but certainly I should have thought such a creature unfit to remain in the society of men. But she was innocent. I know, I feel she was innocent; you are of the same opinion, and that confirms me. Alas! Victor, when falsehood can look so like the truth, who can assure themselves of certain happiness? I feel as if I were walking on the edge of a precipice, towards which thousands are crowding, and endeavouring to plunge me into the abyss. William and Justine were assassinated, and the murderer escapes; he walks about the world free, and perhaps respected. But even if I were condemned to suffer on the scaffold for the same crimes, I would not change places with such a wretch."

I listened to this discourse with the extremest agony. I, not in deed, but in effect, was the true murderer. Elizabeth read my anguish in my countenance, and kindly taking my hand, said, "My dearest friend, you must calm yourself. These events have affected me, God knows how deeply; but I am not so wretched as you are. There is an expression of despair, and sometimes of revenge, in your countenance, that makes me tremble. Dear Victor, banish these dark passions. Remember the friends around you, who centre all their hopes in you. Have we lost the power of rendering you happy? Ah! while we love — while we are true to each other, here in this land of peace and beauty, your native country, we may reap every tranquil blessing, — what can disturb our peace?"

And could not such words from her whom I fondly prized before every other gift of fortune, suffice to chase away the fiend that lurked in my heart? Even as she spoke I drew near to her, as if in terror; lest at that very moment the destroyer had been near to rob me of her.

Thus not the tenderness of friendship, nor the beauty of earth, nor of heaven, could redeem my soul from woe: the very accents of love were ineffectual. I was encompassed by a cloud which no beneficial influence could penetrate. The wounded deer dragging its fainting limbs to some untrodden brake, there to gaze upon the arrow which had pierced it, and to die — was but a type of me.

Sometimes I could cope with the sullen despair that overwhelmed me: but sometimes the whirlwind passions of my soul drove me to seek, by bodily exercise and by change of place, some relief from my intolerable sensations. It was during an access of this kind that I suddenly left my home, and bending my steps towards the near Alpine valleys, sought in the magnificence, the eternity of such scenes, to forget myself and my ephemeral, because human, sorrows. My wanderings were directed towards the valley of

Chamounix. I had visited it frequently during my boyhood. Six years had passed since then: *I* was a wreck — but nought had changed in those savage and enduring scenes.

I performed the first part of my journey on horseback. I afterwards hired a mule, as the more sure-footed, and least liable to receive injury on these rugged roads. The weather was fine: it was about the middle of the month of August, nearly two months after the death of Justine; that miserable epoch from which I dated all my woe. The weight upon my spirit was sensibly lightened as I plunged yet deeper in the ravine of Arve. The immense mountains and precipices that overhung me on every side — the sound of the river raging among the rocks, and the dashing of the waterfalls around, spoke of a power mighty as Omnipotence — and I ceased to fear, or to bend before any being less almighty than that which had created and ruled the elements, here displayed in their most terrific guise. Still, as I ascended higher, the valley assumed a more magnificent and astonishing character. Ruined castles hanging on the precipices of piny mountains; the impetuous Arve, and cottages every here and there peeping forth from among the trees, formed a scene of singular beauty. But it was augmented and rendered sublime by the mighty Alps, whose white and shining pyramids and domes towered above all, as belonging to another earth, the habitations of another race of beings.

I passed the bridge of Pélissier, where the ravine, which the river forms, opened before me, and I began to ascend the mountain that overhangs it. Soon after I entered the valley of Chamounix. This valley is more wonderful and sublime, but not so beautiful and picturesque, as that of Servox, through which I had just passed. The high and snowy mountains were its immediate boundaries; but I saw no more ruined castles and fertile fields. Immense glaciers approached the road; I heard the rumbling thunder of the falling avalanche, and marked the smoke of its passage. Mont Blanc, the supreme and magnificent Mont Blanc, raised itself from the surrounding *aiguilles*,[18] and its tremendous *dôme* overlooked the valley.

A tingling long-lost sense of pleasure often came across me during this journey. Some turn in the road, some new object suddenly perceived and recognized, reminded me of days gone by, and were associated with the light-hearted gaiety of boyhood. The very winds whispered in soothing accents, and maternal nature bade me weep no more. Then again the kindly influence ceased to act — I found myself fettered again to grief, and indulging in all the misery of reflection. Then I spurred on my animal, striving so to forget the world, my fears, and, more than all, myself — or, in a more desperate fashion, I alighted, and threw myself on the grass, weighed down by horror and despair.

At length I arrived at the village of Chamounix. 260 Exhaustion succeeded to the extreme fatigue both of body and of mind which I had endured. For a short space of time I remained at the window, watching the pallid lightnings that played above Mont Blanc, and listening to the rushing of the Arve, which pursued its noisy way beneath. The same lulling sounds acted as a lullaby to my too keen sensations: when I placed my head upon my pillow, sleep crept over me; I felt it as it came, and blest the giver of oblivion.

CHAPTER X

I spent the following day roaming through the valley. I stood beside the sources of the Arveiron, which take their rise in a glacier, that with slow pace is advancing down from the summit of the hills, to barricade the valley. The abrupt sides of vast mountains were before me; the icy wall of the glacier overhung me; a few shattered pines were scattered around; and the solemn silence of this glorious presence-chamber of imperial

[18] French for "needles"; here, the word is used to describe the mountain peaks. — Eds.

Nature was broken only by the brawling waves, or the fall of some vast fragment, the thunder sound of the avalanche, or the cracking, reverberated along the mountains, of the accumulated ice, which, through the silent working of immutable laws, was ever and anon rent and torn, as if it had been but a plaything in their hands. These sublime and magnificent scenes afforded me the greatest consolation that I was capable of receiving. They elevated me from all littleness of feeling; and although they did not remove my grief, they subdued and tranquillised it. In some degree, also, they diverted my mind from the thoughts over which it had brooded for the last month. I retired to rest at night; my slumbers, as it were, waited on and ministered to by the assemblance of grand shapes which I had contemplated during the day. They congregated round me; the unstained snowy mountain-top, the glittering pinnacle, the pine woods, and ragged bare ravine; the eagle, soaring amidst the clouds — they all gathered round me, and bade me be at peace.

Where had they fled when the next morning I awoke? All of soul-inspiriting fled with sleep, and dark melancholy clouded every thought. The rain was pouring in torrents, and thick mists hid the summits of the mountains, so that I even saw not the faces of those mighty friends. Still I would penetrate their misty veil, and seek them in their cloudy retreats. What were rain and storm to me? My mule was brought to the door, and I resolved to ascend to the summit of Montanvert. I remembered the effect that the view of the tremendous and ever-moving glacier had produced upon my mind when I first saw it. It had then filled me with a sublime ecstasy, that gave wings to the soul, and allowed it to soar from the obscure world to light and joy. The sight of the awful and majestic in nature had indeed always the effect of solemnising my mind, and causing me to forget the passing cares of life. I determined to go without a guide, for I was well acquainted with the path, and the presence of another would destroy the solitary grandeur of the scene.

The ascent is precipitous, but the path is cut into continual and short windings, which enable you to surmount the perpendicularity of the mountain. It is a scene terrifically desolate. In a thousand spots the traces of the winter avalanche may be perceived, where trees lie broken and strewed on the ground; some entirely destroyed, others bent, leaning upon the jutting rocks of the mountain, or transversely upon other trees. The path, as you ascend higher, is intersected by ravines of snow, down which stones continually roll from above; one of them is particularly dangerous, as the slightest sound, such as even speaking in a loud voice, produces a concussion of air sufficient to draw destruction upon the head of the speaker. The pines are not tall or luxuriant, but they are sombre, and add an air of severity to the scene. I looked on the valley beneath; vast mists were rising from the rivers which ran through it, and curling in thick wreaths around the opposite mountains, whose summits were hid in the uniform clouds, while rain poured from the dark sky, and added to the melancholy impression I received from the objects around me. Alas! why does man boast of sensibilities superior to those apparent in the brute; it only renders them more necessary beings. If our impulses were confined to hunger, thirst, and desire, we might be nearly free; but now we are moved by every wind that blows, and a chance word or scene that that word may convey to us.

> We rest; a dream has power to poison sleep.
> We rise; one wand'ring thought pollutes the day.
> We feel, conceive, or reason; laugh or weep,
> Embrace fond woe, or cast our cares away;
> It is the same: for, be it joy or sorrow,
> The path of its departure still is free.
> Man's yesterday may ne'er be like his morrow;
> Nought may endure but mutability![19]

[19] The last stanza of Percy Bysshe Shelley's "Mutability" (1816), a poem about the constancy of change. — Eds.

It was nearly noon when I arrived at the top of the ascent. For some time I sat upon the rock that overlooks the sea of ice. A mist covered both that and the surrounding mountains. Presently a breeze dissipated the cloud, and I descended upon the glacier. The surface is very uneven, rising like the waves of a troubled sea, descending low, and interspersed by rifts that sink deep. The field of ice is almost a league in width, but I spent nearly two hours in crossing it. The opposite mountain is a bare perpendicular rock. From the side where I now stood Montanvert was exactly opposite, at the distance of a league; and above it rose Mont Blanc, in awful majesty. I remained in a recess of the rock, gazing on this wonderful and stupendous scene. The sea, or rather the vast river of ice, wound among its dependent mountains, whose aerial summits hung over its recesses. Their icy and glittering peaks shone in the sunlight over the clouds. My heart, which was before sorrowful, now swelled with something like joy; I exclaimed—"Wandering spirits, if indeed ye wander, and do not rest in your narrow beds, allow me this faint happiness, or take me, as your companion, away from the joys of life."

As I said this, I suddenly beheld the figure of a man, at some distance, advancing towards me with superhuman speed. He bounded over the crevices in the ice, among which I had walked with caution; his stature, also, as he approached, seemed to exceed that of man. I was troubled: a mist came over my eyes, and I felt a faintness seize me; but I was quickly restored by the cold gale of the mountains. I perceived, as the shape came nearer (sight tremendous and abhorred!) that it was the wretch whom I had created. I trembled with rage and horror, resolving to wait his approach, and then close with him in mortal combat. He approached; his countenance bespoke bitter anguish, combined with disdain and malignity, while its unearthly ugliness rendered it almost too horrible for human eyes. But I scarcely observed this; rage and hatred had at first deprived me of utterance, and I recovered only to overwhelm him with words expressive of furious detestation and contempt.

"Devil," I exclaimed, "do you dare approach me? and do not you fear the fierce vengeance of my arm wreaked on your miserable head? Begone, vile insect! or rather, stay, that I may trample you to dust! and, oh! that I could, with the extinction of your miserable existence, restore those victims whom you have so diabolically murdered!"

"I expected this reception," said the daemon. "All men hate the wretched; how, then, must I be hated, who am miserable beyond all living things! Yet you, my creator, detest and spurn me, thy creature, to whom thou art bound by ties

This classic depiction of Frankenstein's monster, played by Boris Karloff in James Whale's 1931 film, has become the standard, nearly ubiquitous portrayal that millions recognize. **What is it about this interpretation that has so timelessly captured the public's imagination? How closely does it resemble the monster as he is described in the novel?**

only dissoluble by the annihilation of one of us. You purpose to kill me. How dare you sport thus with life? Do your duty towards me, and I will do mine towards you and the rest of mankind. If you will comply with my conditions, I will leave them and you at peace; but if you refuse, I will glut the maw of death, until it be satiated with the blood of your remaining friends."

"Abhorred monster! fiend that thou art! the tortures of hell are too mild a vengeance for thy crimes. Wretched devil! you reproach me with your creation; come on, then, that I may extinguish the spark which I so negligently bestowed."

My rage was without bounds; I sprang on him, impelled by all the feelings which can arm one being against the existence of another.

He easily eluded me, and said —

"Be calm! I entreat you to hear me, before you give vent to your hatred on my devoted head. Have I not suffered enough, that you seek to increase my misery? Life, although it may only be an accumulation of anguish, is dear to me, and I will defend it. Remember, thou hast made me more powerful than thyself; my height is superior to thine; my joints more supple. But I will not be tempted to set myself in opposition to thee. I am thy creature, and I will be even mild and docile to my natural lord and king, if thou wilt also perform thy part, the which thou owest me. Oh, Frankenstein, be not equitable to every other, and trample upon me alone, to whom thy justice, and even thy clemency and affection, is most due. Remember, that I am thy creature; I ought to be thy Adam; but I am rather the fallen angel, whom thou drivest from joy for no misdeed. Every where I see bliss, from which I alone am irrevocably excluded. I was benevolent and good; misery made me a fiend. Make me happy, and I shall again be virtuous."

"Begone! I will not hear you. There can be no community between you and me; we are enemies. Begone, or let us try our strength in a fight, in which one must fall."

"How can I move thee? Will no entreaties cause thee to turn a favourable eye upon thy creature, who implores thy goodness and compassion? Believe me, Frankenstein: I was benevolent; my soul glowed with love and humanity: but am I not alone, miserably alone? You, my creator, abhor me; what hope can I gather from your fellow-creatures, who owe me nothing? they spurn and hate me. The desert mountains and dreary glaciers are my refuge. I have wandered here many days; the caves of ice, which I only do not fear, are a dwelling to me, and the only one which man does not grudge. These bleak skies I hail, for they are kinder to me than your fellow-beings. If the multitude of mankind knew of my existence, they would do as you do, and arm themselves for my destruction. Shall I not then hate them who abhor me? I will keep no terms with my enemies. I am miserable, and they shall share my wretchedness. Yet it is in your power to recompense me, and deliver them from an evil which it only remains for you to make so great, that not only you and your family, but thousands of others, shall be swallowed up in the whirlwinds of its rage. Let your compassion be moved, and do not disdain me. Listen to my tale: when you have heard that, abandon or commiserate me, as you shall judge that I deserve. But hear me. The guilty are allowed, by human laws, bloody as they are, to speak in their own defence before they are condemned. Listen to me, Frankenstein. You accuse me of murder; and yet you would, with a satisfied conscience, destroy your own creature. Oh, praise the eternal justice of man! Yet I ask you not to spare me: listen to me; and then, if you can, and if you will, destroy the work of your hands."

"Why do you call to my remembrance," I rejoined, "circumstances, of which I shudder to reflect, that I have been the miserable origin and author? Cursed be the day, abhorred devil, in which you first saw light! Cursed (although I curse myself) be the hands that formed you!

You have made me wretched beyond expression. You have left me no power to consider whether I am just to you, or not. Begone! relieve me from the sight of your detested form."

"Thus I relieve thee, my creator," he said, and placed his hated hands before my eyes, which I flung from me with violence; "thus I take from thee a sight which you abhor. Still thou canst listen to me, and grant me thy compassion. By the virtues that I once possessed, I demand this from you. Hear my tale; it is long and strange, and the temperature of this place is not fitting to your fine sensations; come to the hut upon the mountain. The sun is yet high in the heavens; before it descends to hide itself behind yon snowy precipices, and illuminate another world, you will have heard my story, and can decide. On you it rests, whether I quit for ever the neighbourhood of man, and lead a harmless life, or become the scourge of your fellow-creatures, and the author of your own speedy ruin."

As he said this, he led the way across the ice: I followed. My heart was full, and I did not answer him; but, as I proceeded, I weighed the various arguments that he had used, and determined at least to listen to his tale. I was partly urged by curiosity, and compassion confirmed my resolution. I had hitherto supposed him to be the murderer of my brother, and I eagerly sought a confirmation or denial of this opinion. For the first time, also, I felt what the duties of a creator towards his creature were, and that I ought to render him happy before I complained of his wickedness. These motives urged me to comply with his demand. We crossed the ice, therefore, and ascended the opposite rock. The air was cold, and the rain again began to descend: we entered the hut, the fiend with an air of exultation, I with a heavy heart, and depressed spirits. But I consented to listen; and, seating myself by the fire which my odious companion had lighted, he thus began his tale.

CHAPTER XI

It is with considerable difficulty that I remember the original era of my being: all the events of that period appear confused and indistinct. A strange multiplicity of sensations seized me, and I saw, felt, heard, and smelt, at the same time; and it was, indeed, a long time before I learned to distinguish between the operations of my various senses. By degrees, I remember, a stronger light pressed upon my nerves, so that I was obliged to shut my eyes. Darkness then came over me, and troubled me; but hardly had I felt this, when, by opening my eyes, as I now suppose, the light poured in upon me again. I walked, and, I believe, descended; but I presently found a great alteration in my sensations. Before, dark and opaque bodies had surrounded me, impervious to my touch or sight; but I now found that I could wander on at liberty, with no obstacles which I could not either surmount or avoid. The light became more and more oppressive to me; and, the heat wearying me as I walked, I sought a place where I could receive shade. This was the forest near Ingolstadt, and here I lay by the side of a brook resting from my fatigue, until I felt tormented by hunger and thirst. This roused me from my nearly dormant state, and I ate some berries which I found hanging on the trees, or lying on the ground. I slaked my thirst at the brook; and then lying down, was overcome by sleep.

"It was dark when I awoke; I felt cold also, and half-frightened, as it were instinctively, finding myself so desolate. Before I had quitted your apartment, on a sensation of cold, I had covered myself with some clothes; but these were insufficient to secure me from the dews of night. I was a poor, helpless, miserable wretch; I knew, and could distinguish, nothing; but feeling pain invade me on all sides, I sat down and wept.

"Soon a gentle light stole over the heavens, and gave me a sensation of pleasure. I started up, and beheld a radiant form rise from among the trees. I gazed with a kind of wonder. It moved slowly, but it enlightened my path; and I again went out in search of berries. I was still cold, when under one of the trees I found a huge cloak, with which I covered myself, and sat down upon the ground. No distinct ideas occupied my mind; all was confused. I felt light, and hunger, and thirst, and darkness; innumerable sounds rung in my ears, and on all sides various scents saluted me: the only object that I could distinguish was the bright moon, and I fixed my eyes on that with pleasure.

"Several changes of day and night passed, and the orb of night had greatly lessened, when I began to distinguish my sensations from each other. I gradually saw plainly the clear stream that supplied me with drink, and the trees that shaded me with their foliage. I was delighted when I first discovered that a pleasant sound, which often saluted my ears, proceeded from the throats of the little winged animals who had often intercepted the light from my eyes. I began also to observe, with greater accuracy, the forms that surrounded me, and to perceive the boundaries of the radiant roof of light which canopied me. Sometimes I tried to imitate the pleasant songs of the birds, but was unable. Sometimes I wished to express my sensations in my own mode, but the uncouth and inarticulate sounds which broke from me frightened me into silence again.

"The moon had disappeared from the night, and again, with a lessened form, showed itself, while I still remained in the forest. My sensations had, by this time, become distinct, and my mind received every day additional ideas. My eyes became accustomed to the light, and to perceive objects in their right forms; I distinguished the insect from the herb, and, by degrees, one herb from another. I found that the sparrow uttered none but harsh notes, whilst those of the blackbird and thrush were sweet and enticing.

"One day, when I was oppressed by cold, I found a fire which had been left by some wandering beggars, and was overcome with delight at the warmth I experienced from it. In my joy I thrust my hand into the live embers, but quickly drew it out again with a cry of pain. How strange, I thought, that the same cause should produce such opposite effects! I examined the materials of the fire, and to my joy found it to be composed of wood. I quickly collected some branches; but they were wet, and would not burn. I was pained at this, and sat still watching the operation of the fire. The wet wood which I had placed near the heat dried, and itself became inflamed. I reflected on this; and, by touching the various branches, I discovered the cause, and busied myself in collecting a great quantity of wood, that I might dry it, and have a plentiful supply of fire. When night came on, and brought sleep with it, I was in the greatest fear lest my fire should be extinguished. I covered it carefully with dry wood and leaves, and placed wet branches upon it; and then, spreading my cloak, I lay on the ground, and sunk into sleep.

"It was morning when I awoke, and my first care was to visit the fire. I uncovered it, and a gentle breeze quickly fanned it into a flame. I observed this also, and contrived a fan of branches, which roused the embers when they were nearly extinguished. When night came again, I found, with pleasure, that the fire gave light as well as heat; and that the discovery of this element was useful to me in my food; for I found some of the offals that the travellers had left had been roasted, and tasted much more savoury than the berries I gathered from the trees. I tried, therefore, to dress my food in the same manner, placing it on the live embers. I found that the berries were spoiled by this operation, and the nuts and roots much improved.

"Food, however, became scarce; and I often spent the whole day searching in vain for a few acorns to assuage the pangs of hunger.

When I found this, I resolved to quit the place that I had hitherto inhabited, to seek for one where the few wants I experienced would be more easily satisfied. In this emigration, I exceedingly lamented the loss of the fire which I had obtained through accident, and knew not how to reproduce it. I gave several hours to the serious consideration of this difficulty; but I was obliged to relinquish all attempt to supply it; and, wrapping myself up in my cloak, I struck across the wood towards the setting sun. I passed three days in these rambles, and at length discovered the open country. A great fall of snow had taken place the night before, and the fields were of one uniform white; the appearance was disconsolate, and I found my feet chilled by the cold damp substance that covered the ground.

"It was about seven in the morning, and I longed to obtain food and shelter; at length I perceived a small hut, on a rising ground, which had doubtless been built for the convenience of some shepherd. This was a new sight to me; and I examined the structure with great curiosity. Finding the door open, I entered. An old man sat in it, near a fire, over which he was preparing his breakfast. He turned on hearing a noise; and, perceiving me, shrieked loudly, and, quitting the hut, ran across the fields with a speed of which his debilitated form hardly appeared capable. His appearance, different from any I had ever before seen, and his flight, somewhat surprised me. But I was enchanted by the appearance of the hut: here the snow and rain could not penetrate; the ground was dry; and it presented to me then as exquisite and divine a retreat as Pandaemonium appeared to the daemons of hell[20] after their sufferings in the lake of fire. I greedily devoured the remnants of the shepherd's breakfast, which consisted of bread, cheese, milk, and wine; the latter, however, I did not like. Then, overcome by fatigue, I lay down among some straw, and fell asleep.

"It was noon when I awoke; and, allured by the warmth of the sun, which shone brightly on the white ground, I determined to recommence my travels; and, depositing the remains of the peasant's breakfast in a wallet I found, I proceeded across the fields for several hours, until at sunset I arrived at a village. How miraculous did this appear! the huts, the neater cottages, and stately houses, engaged my admiration by turns. The vegetables in the gardens, the milk and cheese that I saw placed at the windows of some of the cottages, allured my appetite. One of the best of these I entered; but I had hardly placed my foot within the door, before the children shrieked, and one of the women fainted.

The whole village was roused; some fled, some attacked me, until, grievously bruised by stones and many other kinds of missile weapons, I escaped to the open country, and fearfully took refuge in a low hovel, quite bare, and making a wretched appearance after the palaces I had beheld in the village. This hovel, however, joined a cottage of a neat and pleasant appearance; but, after my late dearly bought experience, I dared not enter it. My place of refuge was constructed of wood, but so low, that I could with difficulty sit upright in it. No wood, however, was placed on the earth, which formed the floor, but it was dry; and although the wind entered it by innumerable chinks, I found it an agreeable asylum from the snow and rain.

"Here then I retreated, and lay down happy to have found a shelter, however miserable, from the inclemency of the season, and still more from the barbarity of man.

"As soon as morning dawned, I crept from my kennel, that I might view the adjacent cottage, and discover if I could remain in the habitation I had found. It was situated against the back of the cottage, and surrounded on the sides which were exposed by a pig-sty and a

[20] A reference to Book I, lines 670–722, of John Milton's epic poem *Paradise Lost* (1667). In it, the fallen angels (who have become demons) build Pandaemonium, the capital of hell. — Eds.

clear pool of water. One part was open, and by that I had crept in; but now I covered every crevice by which I might be perceived with stones and wood, yet in such a manner that I might move them on occasion to pass out: all the light I enjoyed came through the sty, and that was sufficient for me.

"Having thus arranged my dwelling, and carpeted it with clean straw, I retired; for I saw the figure of a man at a distance, and I remembered too well my treatment the night before, to trust myself in his power. I had first, however, provided for my sustenance for that day, by a loaf of coarse bread, which I purloined, and a cup with which I could drink, more conveniently than from my hand, of the pure water which flowed by my retreat. The floor was a little raised, so that it was kept perfectly dry, and by its vicinity to the chimney of the cottage it was tolerably warm.

"Being thus provided, I resolved to reside in this hovel, until something should occur which might alter my determination. It was indeed a paradise, compared to the bleak forest, my former residence, the rain-dropping branches, and dank earth. I ate my breakfast with pleasure, and was about to remove a plank to procure myself a little water, when I heard a step, and looking through a small chink, I beheld a young creature, with a pail on her head, passing before my hovel. The girl was young, and of gentle demeanour, unlike what I have since found cottagers and farm-house servants to be. Yet she was meanly dressed, a coarse blue petticoat and a linen jacket being her only garb; her fair hair was plaited, but not adorned: she looked patient, yet sad. I lost sight of her; and in about a quarter of an hour she returned, bearing the pail, which was now partly filled with milk. As she walked along, seemingly incommoded by the burden, a young man met her, whose countenance expressed a deeper despondence. Uttering a few sounds with an air of melancholy, he took the pail from her head, and bore it to the cottage himself. She followed, and they disappeared. Presently I saw the young man again, with some tools in his hand, cross the field behind the cottage; and the girl was also busied, sometimes in the house, and sometimes in the yard.

"On examining my dwelling, I found that one of the windows of the cottage had formerly occupied a part of it, but the panes had been filled up with wood. In one of these was a small and almost imperceptible chink, through which the eye could just penetrate. Through this crevice a small room was visible, whitewashed and clean, but very bare of furniture. In one corner, near a small fire, sat an old man, leaning his head on his hands in a disconsolate attitude. The young girl was occupied in arranging the cottage; but presently she took something out of a drawer, which employed her hands, and she sat down beside the old man, who, taking up an instrument, began to play, and to produce sounds sweeter than the voice of the thrush or the nightingale. It was a lovely sight, even to me, poor wretch! who had never beheld aught beautiful before. The silver hair and benevolent countenance of the aged cottager won my reverence, while the gentle manners of the girl enticed my love. He played a sweet mournful air, which I perceived drew tears from the eyes of his amiable companion, of which the old man took no notice, until she sobbed audibly; he then pronounced a few sounds, and the fair creature, leaving her work, knelt at his feet. He raised her, and smiled with such kindness and affection, that I felt sensations of a peculiar and overpowering nature: they were a mixture of pain and pleasure, such as I had never before experienced, either from hunger or cold, warmth or food; and I withdrew from the window, unable to bear these emotions.

"Soon after this the young man returned, bearing on his shoulders a load of wood. The girl met him at the door, helped to relieve him of his burden, and, taking some of the fuel into the cottage, placed it on the fire; then she and the youth went apart into a nook of the cottage, and he showed her a large loaf and a piece of cheese. She seemed pleased, and went into the garden for some roots and plants, which she placed in water, and then upon the fire. She afterwards continued her work, whilst the young man went into the garden, and appeared busily employed in digging and pulling up roots. After he had been employed thus about an hour, the young woman joined him, and they entered the cottage together.

"The old man had, in the mean time, been pensive; but, on the appearance of his companions, he assumed a more cheerful air, and they sat down to eat. The meal was quickly despatched. The young woman was again occupied in arranging the cottage; the old man walked before the cottage in the sun for a few minutes, leaning on the arm of the youth. Nothing could exceed in beauty the contrast between these two excellent creatures. One was old, with silver hairs and a countenance beaming with benevolence and love: the younger was slight and graceful in his figure, and his features were moulded with the finest symmetry; yet his eyes and attitude expressed the utmost sadness and despondency. The old man returned to the cottage; and the youth, with tools different from those he had used in the morning, directed his steps across the fields.

"Night quickly shut in; but, to my extreme wonder, I found that the cottagers had a means of prolonging light by the use of tapers, and was delighted to find that the setting of the sun did not put an end to the pleasure I experienced in watching my human neighbours. In the evening, the young girl and her companion were employed in various occupations which I did not understand; and the old man again took up the instrument which produced the divine sounds that had enchanted me in the morning. So soon as he had finished, the youth began, not to play, but to utter sounds that were monotonous, and neither resembling the harmony of the old man's instrument nor the songs of the birds: I since found that he read aloud, but at that time I knew nothing of the science of words or letters.

"The family, after having been thus occupied for a short time, extinguished their lights, and retired, as I conjectured, to rest.

CHAPTER XII

I lay on my straw, but I could not sleep. I thought of the occurrences of the day. What chiefly struck me was the gentle manners of these people; and I longed to join them, but dared not. I remembered too well the treatment I had suffered the night before from the barbarous villagers, and resolved, whatever course of conduct I might hereafter think it right to pursue, that for the present I would remain quietly in my hovel, watching, and endeavouring to discover the motives which influenced their actions.

"The cottagers arose the next morning before the sun. The young woman arranged the cottage, and prepared the food; and the youth departed after the first meal.

"This day was passed in the same routine as that which preceded it. The young man was constantly employed out of doors, and the girl in various laborious occupations within. The old man, whom I soon perceived to be blind, employed his leisure hours on his instrument or in contemplation. Nothing could exceed the love and respect which the younger cottagers exhibited towards their venerable companion. They performed towards him every little office of affection and duty with gentleness; and he rewarded them by his benevolent smiles.

"They were not entirely happy. The young man and his companion often went apart, and appeared to weep. I saw no cause for their unhappiness; but I was deeply affected by it. If such lovely creatures were miserable, it was less strange that I, an imperfect and solitary being, should be wretched. Yet why were these gentle beings unhappy? They possessed a delightful house (for such it was in my eyes) and every luxury; they had a fire to warm them when chill, and delicious viands when hungry; they were dressed in excellent clothes; and, still more, they enjoyed one another's company and speech, interchanging each day looks of affection and kindness. What did their tears imply? Did they really express pain? I was at first unable to solve these questions; but perpetual attention and time explained to me many appearances which were at first enigmatic.

"A considerable period elapsed before I discovered one of the causes of the uneasiness of this amiable family: it was poverty; and they suffered that evil in a very distressing degree. Their nourishment consisted entirely of the vegetables of their garden, and the milk of one cow, which gave very little during the winter, when its masters could scarcely procure food to support it. They often, I believe, suffered the pangs of hunger very poignantly, especially the two younger cottagers; for several times they placed food before the old man, when they reserved none for themselves.

"This trait of kindness moved me sensibly. I had been accustomed, during the night, to steal a part of their store for my own consumption; but when I found that in doing this I inflicted pain on the cottagers, I abstained, and satisfied myself with berries, nuts, and roots, which I gathered from a neighbouring wood.

"I discovered also another means through which I was enabled to assist their labours. I found that the youth spent a great part of each day in collecting wood for the family fire; and, during the night, I often took his tools, the use of which I quickly discovered, and brought home firing sufficient for the consumption of several days.

"I remember, the first time that I did this, the young woman, when she opened the door in the morning, appeared greatly astonished on seeing a great pile of wood on the outside. She uttered some words in a loud voice, and the youth joined her, who also expressed surprise. I observed, with pleasure, that he did not go to the forest that day, but spent it in repairing the cottage, and cultivating the garden.

"By degrees I made a discovery of still greater moment. I found that these people possessed a method of communicating their experience and feelings to one another by articulate sounds. I perceived that the words they spoke sometimes, produced pleasure or pain, smiles or sadness, in the minds and countenances of the hearers. This was indeed a godlike science, and I ardently desired to become acquainted with it. But I was baffled in every attempt I made for this purpose. Their pronunciation was quick; and the words they uttered, not having any apparent connection with visible objects, I was unable to discover any clue by which I could unravel the mystery of their reference. By great application, however, and after having remained during the space of several revolutions of the moon in my hovel, I discovered the names that were given to some of the most familiar objects of discourse; I learned and applied the words, *fire*, *milk*, *bread*, and *wood*. I learned also the names of the cottagers themselves. The youth and his companion had each of them several names, but the old man had only one, which was *father*. The girl was called *sister*, or *Agatha*; and the youth *Felix*, *brother*, or *son*. I cannot describe the delight I felt when I learned the ideas appropriated to each of these sounds, and was able to pronounce them. I distinguished several other words, without being able as yet to understand or apply them; such as *good*, *dearest*, *unhappy*.

"I spent the winter in this manner. The gentle manners and beauty of the cottagers greatly endeared them to me: when they were unhappy, I felt depressed; when they rejoiced, I sympathised in their joys. I saw few human beings beside them; and if any other happened to enter the cottage, their harsh manners and rude gait only enhanced to me the superior accomplishments of my friends. The old man, I could perceive, often endeavoured to encourage his children, as sometimes I found that he called them, to cast off their melancholy. He would talk in a cheerful accent, with an expression of goodness that bestowed pleasure even upon me. Agatha listened with respect, her eyes sometimes filled with tears, which she endeavoured to wipe away unperceived; but I generally found that her countenance and tone were more cheerful after having listened to the exhortations of her father. It was not thus with Felix. He was always the saddest of the group; and, even to my unpractised senses, he appeared to have suffered more deeply than his friends. But if his countenance was more sorrowful, his voice was more cheerful than that of his sister, especially when he addressed the old man.

"I could mention innumerable instances, which, although slight, marked the dispositions of these amiable cottagers. In the midst of poverty and want, Felix carried with pleasure to his sister the first little white flower that peeped out from beneath the snowy ground. Early in the morning, before she had risen, he cleared away the snow that obstructed her path to the milk-house, drew water from the well, and brought the wood from the out-house, where, to his perpetual astonishment, he found his store always replenished by an invisible hand. In the day, I believe, he worked sometimes for a neighbouring farmer, because he often went forth, and did not return until dinner, yet brought no wood with him. At other times he worked in the garden; but, as there was little to do in the frosty season, he read to the old man and Agatha.

"This reading had puzzled me extremely at first; but, by degrees, I discovered that he uttered many of the same sounds when he read, as when he talked. I conjectured, therefore, that he found on the paper signs for speech which he understood, and I ardently longed to comprehend these also; but how was that possible, when I did not even understand the sounds for which they stood as signs? I improved, however, sensibly in this science, but not sufficiently to follow up any kind of conversation, although I applied my whole mind to the endeavour: for I easily perceived that, although I eagerly longed to discover myself to the cottagers, I ought not to make the attempt until I had first become master of their language; which knowledge might enable me to make them overlook the deformity of my figure; for with this also the contrast perpetually presented to my eyes had made me acquainted.

"I had admired the perfect forms of my cottagers — their grace, beauty, and delicate complexions: but how was I terrified, when I viewed myself in a transparent pool! At first I started back, unable to believe that it was indeed I who was reflected in the mirror; and when I became fully convinced that I was in reality the monster that I am, I was filled with the bitterest sensations of despondence and mortification. Alas! I did not yet entirely know the fatal effects of this miserable deformity.

"As the sun became warmer, and the light of day longer, the snow vanished, and I beheld the bare trees and the black earth. From this time Felix was more employed; and the heart-moving indications of impending famine disappeared. Their food, as I afterwards found, was coarse, but it was wholesome; and they procured a sufficiency of it. Several new kinds of plants sprung up in the garden, which they dressed; and these signs of comfort increased daily as the season advanced.

"The old man, leaning on his son, walked each day at noon, when it did not rain, as I found it was called when the heavens poured forth its waters. This frequently took place; but a high wind quickly dried the earth, and the season became far more pleasant than it had been.

"My mode of life in my hovel was uniform. During the morning, I attended the motions of the cottagers; and when they were dispersed in various occupations, I slept: the remainder of the day was spent in observing my friends. When they had retired to rest, if there was any moon, or the night was star-light, I went into the woods, and collected my own food and fuel for the cottage. When I returned, as often as it was necessary, I cleared their path from the snow, and performed those offices that I had seen done by Felix. I afterwards found that these labours, performed by an invisible hand, greatly astonished them; and once or twice I heard them, on these occasions, utter the words *good spirit, wonderful*; but I did not then understand the signification of these terms.

"My thoughts now became more active, and I longed to discover the motives and feelings of these lovely creatures; I was inquisitive to know why Felix appeared so miserable, and Agatha so sad. I thought (foolish wretch!) that it might be in my power to restore happiness to these deserving people. When I slept, or was absent, the forms of the venerable blind father, the gentle Agatha, and the excellent Felix, flitted before me. I looked upon them as superior beings, who would be the arbiters of my future destiny. I formed in my imagination a thousand pictures of presenting myself to them, and their reception of me. I imagined that they would be disgusted, until, by my gentle demeanour and conciliating words, I should first win their favour, and afterwards their love.

"These thoughts exhilarated me, and led me to apply with fresh ardour to the acquiring the art of language. My organs were indeed harsh, but supple; and although my voice was very unlike the soft music of their tones, yet I pronounced such words as I understood with tolerable ease. It was as the ass and the lap-dog;[21] yet surely the gentle ass whose intentions were affectionate, although his manners were rude, deserved better treatment than blows and execration.

"The pleasant showers and genial warmth of spring greatly altered the aspect of the earth. Men, who before this change seemed to have been hid in caves, dispersed themselves, and were employed in various arts of cultivation. The birds sang in more cheerful notes, and the leaves began to bud forth on the trees. Happy, happy earth! fit habitation for gods, which, so short a time before, was bleak, damp, and unwholesome. My spirits were elevated by the enchanting appearance of nature; the past was blotted from my memory, the present was tranquil, and the future gilded by bright rays of hope, and anticipations of joy.

CHAPTER XIII

I now hasten to the more moving part of my story. I shall relate events, that impressed me with feelings which, from what I had been, have made me what I am.

"Spring advanced rapidly; the weather became fine, and the skies cloudless. It surprised me, that what before was desert and gloomy should now bloom with the most beautiful flowers and verdure. My senses were gratified and refreshed by a thousand scents of delight, and a thousand sights of beauty.

"It was on one of these days, when my cottagers periodically rested from labour — the old man played on his guitar, and the children listened to him — that I observed the countenance of Felix was melancholy beyond expression; he sighed frequently; and once his father paused in his music, and I conjectured by his manner that he enquired the cause of his son's sorrow. Felix replied in a cheerful accent, and the old man was recommencing his music, when some one tapped at the door.

"It was a lady on horseback, accompanied by a countryman as a guide. The lady was dressed in a dark suit, and covered with a thick black veil. Agatha asked a question; to which the stranger only replied by pronouncing, in a sweet accent, the name of Felix. Her voice was musical, but unlike that of either of my friends. On hearing this word, Felix came up hastily to the lady; who, when she

---

[21] In the *Fables* (IV, 5) of Jean de La Fontaine (1621–1695), the ass fawns on the dog's master, hoping to be rewarded with petting as the dog is; instead, he receives a beating. — Eds.

saw him, threw up her veil, and I beheld a countenance of angelic beauty and expression. Her hair of a shining raven black, and curiously braided; her eyes were dark, but gentle, although animated; her features of a regular proportion, and her complexion wondrously fair, each cheek tinged with a lovely pink.

"Felix seemed ravished with delight when he saw her, every trait of sorrow vanished from his face, and it instantly expressed a degree of ecstatic joy, of which I could hardly have believed it capable; his eyes sparkled, as his cheek flushed with pleasure; and at that moment I thought him as beautiful as the stranger. She appeared affected by different feelings; wiping a few tears from her lovely eyes, she held out her hand to Felix, who kissed it rapturously, and called her, as well as I could distinguish, his sweet Arabian. She did not appear to understand him, but smiled. He assisted her to dismount, and dismissing her guide, conducted her into the cottage. Some conversation took place between him and his father; and the young stranger knelt at the old man's feet, and would have kissed his hand, but he raised her, and embraced her affectionately.

"I soon perceived, that although the stranger uttered articulate sounds, and appeared to have a language of her own, she was neither understood by, nor herself understood, the cottagers. They made many signs which I did not comprehend; but I saw that her presence diffused gladness through the cottage, dispelling their sorrow as the sun dissipates the morning mists. Felix seemed peculiarly happy, and with smiles of delight welcomed his Arabian. Agatha, the ever-gentle Agatha, kissed the hands of the lovely stranger; and, pointing to her brother, made signs which appeared to me to mean that he had been sorrowful until she came. Some hours passed thus, while they, by their countenances, expressed joy, the cause of which I did not comprehend. Presently I found, by the frequent recurrence of some sound which the stranger repeated after them, that she was endeavouring to learn their language; and the idea instantly occurred to me, that I should make use of the same instructions to the same end. The stranger learned about twenty words at the first lesson, most of them, indeed, were those which I had before understood, but I profited by the others.

"As night came on, Agatha and the Arabian retired early. When they separated, Felix kissed the hand of the stranger, and said, 'Good night, sweet Safie.' He sat up much longer, conversing with his father; and, by the frequent repetition of her name, I conjectured that their lovely guest was the subject of their conversation. I ardently desired to understand them, and bent every faculty towards that purpose, but found it utterly impossible.

"The next morning Felix went out to his work; and, after the usual occupations of Agatha were finished, the Arabian sat at the feet of the old man, and, taking his guitar, played some airs so entrancingly beautiful, that they at once drew tears of sorrow and delight from my eyes. She sang, and her voice flowed in a rich cadence, swelling or dying away, like a nightingale of the woods.

"When she had finished, she gave the guitar to Agatha, who at first declined it. She played a simple air, and her voice accompanied it in sweet accents, but unlike the wondrous strain of the stranger. The old man appeared enraptured, and said some words, which Agatha endeavoured to explain to Safie, and by which he appeared to wish to express that she bestowed on him the greatest delight by her music.

"The days now passed as peaceably as before, with the sole alteration, that joy had taken place of sadness in the countenances of my friends. Safie was always gay and happy; she and I improved rapidly in the knowledge of language, so that in two months I began to comprehend most of the words uttered by my protectors.

"In the meanwhile also the black ground was covered with herbage, and the green banks interspersed with innumerable flowers, sweet to the scent and the eyes, stars of pale radiance among the moonlight woods; the sun became warmer, the nights clear and balmy; and my nocturnal rambles were an extreme pleasure to me, although they were considerably shortened by the late setting and early rising of the sun; for I never ventured abroad during daylight, fearful of meeting with the same treatment I had formerly endured in the first village which I entered.

"My days were spent in close attention, that I might more speedily master the language; and I may boast that I improved more rapidly than the Arabian, who understood very little, and conversed in broken accents, whilst I comprehended and could imitate almost every word that was spoken.

"While I improved in speech, I also learned the science of letters, as it was taught to the stranger; and this opened before me a wide field for wonder and delight.

"The book from which Felix instructed Safie was Volney's 'Ruins of Empires.'[22] I should not have understood the purport of this book, had not Felix, in reading it, given very minute explanations. He had chosen this work, he said, because the declamatory style was framed in imitation of the eastern authors. Through this work I obtained a cursory knowledge of history, and a view of the several empires at present existing in the world; it gave me an insight into the manners, governments, and religions of the different nations of the earth. I heard of the slothful Asiatics; of the stupendous genius and mental activity of the Grecians; of the wars and wonderful virtue of the early Romans — of their subsequent degenerating — of the decline of that mighty empire; of chivalry, Christianity, and kings. I heard of the discovery of the American hemisphere, and wept with Safie over the hapless fate of its original inhabitants.

"These wonderful narrations inspired me 330
with strange feelings. Was man, indeed, at once so powerful, so virtuous, and magnificent, yet so vicious and base? He appeared at one time a mere scion of the evil principle, and at another, as all that can be conceived of noble and godlike. To be a great and virtuous man appeared the highest honour that can befall a sensitive being; to be base and vicious, as many on record have been, appeared the lowest degradation, a condition more abject than that of the blind mole or harmless worm. For a long time I could not conceive how one man could go forth to murder his fellow, or even why there were laws and governments; but when I heard details of vice and bloodshed, my wonder ceased, and I turned away with disgust and loathing.

"Every conversation of the cottagers now opened new wonders to me. While I listened to the instructions which Felix bestowed upon the Arabian, the strange system of human society was explained to me. I heard of the division of property, of immense wealth and squalid poverty; of rank, descent, and noble blood.

"The words induced me to turn towards myself. I learned that the possessions most esteemed by your fellow-creatures were high and unsullied descent united with riches. A man might be respected with only one of these advantages; but, without either, he was considered, except in very rare instances, as a vagabond and a slave, doomed to waste his powers for the profits of the chosen few! And what was I? Of my creation and creator I was absolutely ignorant; but I knew that I possessed no money, no friends, no kind of property. I was, besides, endued with a figure hideously deformed and loathsome; I was not even of the same nature as man. I was more agile than they, and could subsist upon coarser diet; I bore the extremes of heat and cold with less injury to my

---

[22] *Les ruines, ou, Méditations sur les révolutions des empires* ("The Ruins, or a Survey of the Revolutions of Empires"), by Constantin François Chassebœuf, compte de Volney (1757–1820), was an essay on the philosophy of history published in 1791. — Eds.

frame; my stature far exceeded theirs. When I looked around, I saw and heard of none like me. Was I then a monster, a blot upon the earth, from which all men fled, and whom all men disowned?

"I cannot describe to you the agony that these reflections inflicted upon me: I tried to dispel them, but sorrow only increased with knowledge. Oh, that I had for ever remained in my native wood, nor known nor felt beyond the sensations of hunger, thirst, and heat!

"Of what a strange nature is knowledge! It clings to the mind, when it has once seized on it, like a lichen on the rock. I wished sometimes to shake off all thought and feeling; but I learned that there was but one means to overcome the sensation of pain, and that was death — a state which I feared yet did not understand. I admired virtue and good feelings, and loved the gentle manners and amiable qualities of my cottagers; but I was shut out from intercourse with them, except through means which I obtained by stealth, when I was unseen and unknown, and which rather increased than satisfied the desire I had of becoming one among my fellows. The gentle words of Agatha, and the animated smiles of the charming Arabian, were not for me. The mild exhortations of the old man, and the lively conversation of the loved Felix, were not for me. Miserable, unhappy wretch!

"Other lessons were impressed upon me even more deeply. I heard of the difference of sexes; and the birth and growth of children; how the father doted on the smiles of the infant, and the lively sallies of the older child; how all the life and cares of the mother were wrapped up in the precious charge; how the mind of youth expanded and gained knowledge; of brother, sister, and all the various relationships which bind one human being to another in mutual bonds.

"But where were my friends and relations? No father had watched my infant days, no mother had blessed me with smiles and caresses; or if they had, all my past life was now a blot, a blind vacancy in which I distinguished nothing. From my earliest remembrance I had been as I then was in height and proportion. I had never yet seen a being resembling me, or who claimed any intercourse with me. What was I? The question again recurred, to be answered only with groans.

"I will soon explain to what these feelings tended; but allow me now to return to the cottagers, whose story excited in me such various feelings of indignation, delight, and wonder, but which all terminated in additional love and reverence for my protectors (for so I loved, in an innocent, half painful self-deceit, to call them).

CHAPTER XIV

Some time elapsed before I learned the history of my friends. It was one which could not fail to impress itself deeply on my mind, unfolding as it did a number of circumstances, each interesting and wonderful to one so utterly inexperienced as I was.

"The name of the old man was De Lacey. He was descended from a good family in France, where he had lived for many years in affluence, respected by his superiors, and beloved by his equals. His son was bred in the service of his country; and Agatha had ranked with ladies of the highest distinction. A few months before my arrival, they had lived in a large and luxurious city, called Paris, surrounded by friends, and possessed of every enjoyment which virtue, refinement of intellect, or taste, accompanied by a moderate fortune, could afford.

"The father of Safie had been the cause of their ruin. He was a Turkish merchant, and had inhabited Paris for many years, when, for some reason which I could not learn, he became obnoxious to the government. He was seized and cast into prison the very day that Safie arrived from Constantinople to join him. He was tried, and condemned to death. The injustice of his sentence was very flagrant; all Paris was indignant; and it was judged that his religion and wealth, rather than the crime alleged against him, had been the cause of his condemnation.

"Felix had accidentally been present at the trial; his horror and indignation were uncontrollable, when he heard the decision of the court. He made, at that moment, a solemn vow to deliver him, and then looked around for the means. After many fruitless attempts to gain admittance to the prison, he found a strongly grated window in an unguarded part of the building, which lighted the dungeon of the unfortunate Mahometan;[23] who, loaded with chains, waited in despair the execution of the barbarous sentence. Felix visited the grate at night, and made known to the prisoner his intentions in his favour. The Turk, amazed and delighted, endeavoured to kindle the zeal of his deliverer by promises of reward and wealth. Felix rejected his offers with contempt; yet when he saw the lovely Safie, who was allowed to visit her father, and who, by her gestures, expressed her lively gratitude, the youth could not help owning to his own mind, that the captive possessed a treasure which would fully reward his toil and hazard.

"The Turk quickly perceived the impression that his daughter had made on the heart of Felix, and endeavoured to secure him more entirely in his interests by the promise of her hand in marriage, so soon as he should be conveyed to a place of safety. Felix was too delicate to accept this offer; yet he looked forward to the probability of the event as to the consummation of his happiness.

"During the ensuing days, while the preparations were going forward for the escape of the merchant, the zeal of Felix was warmed by several letters that he received from this lovely girl, who found means to express her thoughts in the language of her lover by the aid of an old man, a servant of her father, who understood French. She thanked him in the most ardent terms for his intended services towards her parent; and at the same time she gently deplored her own fate.

[23] A nineteenth-century British reference to Muslims. — Eds.

"I have copies of these letters; for I found means, during my residence in the hovel, to procure the implements of writing; and the letters were often in the hands of Felix or Agatha. Before I depart, I will give them to you, they will prove the truth of my tale; but at present, as the sun is already far declined, I shall only have time to repeat the substance of them to you.

"Safie related, that her mother was a 345
Christian Arab, seized and made a slave by the Turks; recommended by her beauty, she had won the heart of the father of Safie, who married her. The young girl spoke in high and enthusiastic terms of her mother, who, born in freedom, spurned the bondage to which she was now reduced. She instructed her daughter in the tenets of her religion, and taught her to aspire to higher powers of intellect, and an independence of spirit, forbidden to the female followers of Mahomet. This lady died; but her lessons were indelibly impressed on the mind of Safie, who sickened at the prospect of again returning to Asia, and being immured within the walls of a haram,[24] allowed only to occupy herself with infantile amusements, ill suited to the temper of her soul, now accustomed to grand ideas and a noble emulation for virtue. The prospect of marrying a Christian, and remaining in a country where women were allowed to take a rank in society, was enchanting to her.

"The day for the execution of the Turk was fixed; but, on the night previous to it, he quitted his prison, and before morning was distant many leagues from Paris. Felix had procured passports in the name of his father, sister, and himself. He had previously communicated his plan to the former, who aided the deceit by quitting his house, under the pretence of a journey, and concealed himself, with his daughter, in an obscure part of Paris.

"Felix conducted the fugitives through France to Lyons, and across Mont Cenis to

[24] A harem. — Eds.

Leghorn, where the merchant had decided to wait a favourable opportunity of passing into some part of the Turkish dominions.

"Safie resolved to remain with her father until the moment of his departure, before which time the Turk renewed his promise that she should be united to his deliverer; and Felix remained with them in expectation of that event; and in the mean time he enjoyed the society of the Arabian, who exhibited towards him the simplest and tenderest affection. They conversed with one another through the means of an interpreter, and sometimes with the interpretation of looks; and Safie sang to him the divine airs of her native country.

"The Turk allowed this intimacy to take place, and encouraged the hopes of the youthful lovers, while in his heart he had formed far other plans. He loathed the idea that his daughter should be united to a Christian; but he feared the resentment of Felix, if he should appear lukewarm; for he knew that he was still in the power of his deliverer, if he should choose to betray him to the Italian state which they inhabited. He revolved a thousand plans by which he should be enabled to prolong the deceit until it might be no longer necessary, and secretly to take his daughter with him when he departed. His plans were facilitated by the news which arrived from Paris.

"The government of France were greatly enraged at the escape of their victim, and spared no pains to detect and punish his deliverer. The plot of Felix was quickly discovered, and De Lacey and Agatha were thrown into prison. The news reached Felix, and roused him from his dream of pleasure. His blind and aged father, and his gentle sister, lay in a noisome dungeon, while he enjoyed the free air, and the society of her whom he loved. This idea was torture to him. He quickly arranged with the Turk, that if the latter should find a favourable opportunity for escape before Felix could return to Italy, Safie should remain as a boarder at a convent at Leghorn; and then, quitting the lovely Arabian, he hastened to Paris, and delivered himself up to the vengeance of the law, hoping to free De Lacey and Agatha by this proceeding.

"He did not succeed. They remained confined for five months before the trial took place; the result of which deprived them of their fortune, and condemned them to a perpetual exile from their native country.

"They found a miserable asylum in the cottage in Germany, where I discovered them. Felix soon learned that the treacherous Turk, for whom he and his family endured such unheard-of oppression, on discovering that his deliverer was thus reduced to poverty and ruin, became a traitor to good feeling and honour, and had quitted Italy with his daughter, insultingly sending Felix a pittance of money, to aid him, as he said, in some plan of future maintenance.

"Such were the events that preyed on the heart of Felix, and rendered him, when I first saw him, the most miserable of his family. He could have endured poverty; and while this distress had been the meed of his virtue, he gloried in it: but the ingratitude of the Turk, and the loss of his beloved Safie, were misfortunes more bitter and irreparable. The arrival of the Arabian now infused new life into his soul.

"When the news reached Leghorn, that Felix was deprived of his wealth and rank, the merchant commanded his daughter to think no more of her lover, but to prepare to return to her native country. The generous nature of Safie was outraged by this command; she attempted to expostulate with her father, but he left her angrily, reiterating his tyrannical mandate.

"A few days after, the Turk entered his daughter's apartment, and told her hastily, that he had reason to believe that his residence at Leghorn had been divulged, and that he should speedily be delivered up to the French government; he had, consequently, hired a vessel to convey him to Constantinople, for which city he should sail in a few hours. He intended to leave his daughter under the care of a confidential servant, to follow at her leisure with the greater part of his property, which had not yet arrived at Leghorn.

"When alone, Safie resolved in her own mind the plan of conduct that it would become her to pursue in this emergency. A residence in Turkey was abhorrent to her; her religion and her feelings were alike adverse to it. By some papers of her father, which fell into her hands, she heard of the exile of her lover, and learnt the name of the spot where he then resided. She hesitated some time, but at length she formed her determination. Taking with her some jewels that belonged to her, and a sum of money, she quitted Italy with an attendant, a native of Leghorn, but who understood the common language of Turkey, and departed for Germany.

"She arrived in safety at a town about twenty leagues from the cottage of De Lacey, when her attendant fell dangerously ill. Safie nursed her with the most devoted affection; but the poor girl died, and the Arabian was left alone, unacquainted with the language of the country, and utterly ignorant of the customs of the world. She fell, however, into good hands. The Italian had mentioned the name of the spot for which they were bound; and, after her death, the woman of the house in which they had lived took care that Safie should arrive in safety at the cottage of her lover.

CHAPTER XV

"Such was the history of my beloved cottagers. It impressed me deeply. I learned, from the views of social life which it developed, to admire their virtues, and to deprecate the vices of mankind.

"As yet I looked upon crime as a distant evil; benevolence and generosity were ever present before me, inciting within me a desire to become an actor in the busy scene where so many admirable qualities were called forth and displayed. But, in giving an account of the progress of my intellect, I must not omit a circumstance which occurred in the beginning of the month of August of the same year.

"One night, during my accustomed visit to 360
the neighbouring wood, where I collected my own food, and brought home firing for my protectors, I found on the ground a leathern portmanteau, containing several articles of dress and some books. I eagerly seized the prize, and returned with it to my hovel. Fortunately the books were written in the language, the elements of which I had acquired at the cottage; they consisted of 'Paradise Lost,' a volume of 'Plutarch's Lives,'[25] and the 'Sorrows of Werter.'[26] The possession of these treasures gave me extreme delight; I now continually studied and exercised my mind upon these histories, whilst my friends were employed in their ordinary occupations.

"I can hardly describe to you the effect of these books. They produced in me an infinity of new images and feelings, that sometimes raised me to ecstasy, but more frequently sunk me into the lowest dejection. In the 'Sorrows of Werter,' besides the interest of its simple and affecting story, so many opinions are canvassed, and so many lights thrown upon what had hitherto been to me obscure subjects, that I found in it a never-ending source of speculation and astonishment. The gentle and domestic manners it described, combined with lofty sentiments and feelings, which had for their object something out of self, accorded well with my experience among my protectors, and with the wants which were for ever alive in my own bosom. But I thought Werter himself a more divine being than I had ever beheld or imagined; his character contained no pretension, but it sunk deep. The disquisitions upon death and

[25] A series of forty-six biographies of famous military and political figures, arranged in pairs to compare men and highlight their strengths and failings, by Plutarch (c. 46–119), a Greek biographer. — Eds.

[26] *The Sorrows of Young Werther* (1774) is a tragic novel about a romantic young artist by Johann Wolfgang von Goethe (1749–1832), a German writer and politician. — Eds.

extending beyond the text

The following is an excerpt from a 1993 essay by Marilyn Butler, a professor of English literature at King's College, Cambridge.

from Frankenstein and Radical Science

Marilyn Butler

Compared with the professional qualifications of the novel's first two narrators, Frankenstein and Walton, an inventor and an explorer, the Creature has few claims to act as the third. Just as he owes his existence to a unique and unnatural process, he defies all odds, as a parentless being, by learning language at all. Yet the voice in which he narrates the second of the three volumes is impressive, in a strange register appropriate to a witness brought back from the remote past. . . . He is more eloquent than Frankenstein in the conversations that introduce and end their meeting, and still more persuasive when relating his life-history, an exercise in self-observation, social observation, and retrospective analysis. By tracking his own maturation, from a solitary to a social animal, the Creature succeeds in the task Frankenstein abandons, that of scientifically following up Frankenstein's technological achievement. ■

1. **How is the monster's voice more persuasive and eloquent than that of his creator?**
2. **Why might Shelley have endowed the monster with this rhetorical gift? What ideas or thematic concerns does this decision raise?**

suicide were calculated to fill me with wonder. I did not pretend to enter into the merits of the case, yet I inclined towards the opinions of the hero, whose extinction I wept, without precisely understanding it.

"As I read, however, I applied much personally to my own feelings and condition. I found myself similar, yet at the same time strangely unlike to the beings concerning whom I read, and to whose conversation I was a listener. I sympathised with, and partly understood them, but I was unformed in mind; I was dependent on none, and related to none. 'The path of my departure was free;'[27] and there was none to lament my annihilation. My person was hideous, and my stature gigantic: what did this mean? Who was I? What was I? Whence did I come? What was my destination? These questions continually recurred, but I was unable to solve them.

"The volume of 'Plutarch's Lives,' which I possessed, contained the histories of the first founders of the ancient republics. This book had a far different effect upon me from the 'Sorrows of Werter.' I learned from Werter's imaginations despondency and gloom: but Plutarch taught me high thoughts; he elevated me above the wretched sphere of my own reflections, to admire and love the heroes of past ages. Many things I read surpassed my understanding and experience.

[27] A reference to line 14 of Percy Bysshe Shelley's "Mutability": "The path of its departure still is free." — Eds.

I had a very confused knowledge of kingdoms, wide extents of country, mighty rivers, and boundless seas. But I was perfectly unacquainted with towns, and large assemblages of men. The cottage of my protectors had been the only school in which I had studied human nature; but this book developed new and mightier scenes of action. I read of men concerned in public affairs, governing or massacring their species. I felt the greatest ardour for virtue rise within me, and abhorrence for vice, as far as I understood the significance of those terms, relative as they were, as I applied them, to pleasure and pain alone. Induced by these feelings, I was of course led to admire peaceable lawgivers, Numa, Solon, and Lycurgus, in preference to Romulus and Theseus. The patriarchal lives of my protectors caused these impressions to take a firm hold on my mind; perhaps, if my first introduction to humanity had been made by a young soldier, burning for glory and slaughter, I should have been imbued with different sensations.

"But 'Paradise Lost' excited different and far deeper emotions. I read it, as I had read the other volumes which had fallen into my hands, as a true history. It moved every feeling of wonder and awe, that the picture of an omnipotent God warring with his creatures was capable of exciting. I often referred the several situations, as their similarity struck me, to my own. Like Adam, I was apparently united by no link to any other being in existence; but his state was far different from mine in every other respect. He had come forth from the hands of God a perfect creature, happy and prosperous, guarded by the especial care of his Creator; he was allowed to converse with, and acquire knowledge from, beings of a superior nature: but I was wretched, helpless, and alone. Many times I considered Satan as the fitter emblem of my condition; for often, like him, when I viewed the bliss of my protectors, the bitter gall of envy rose within me.

"Another circumstance strengthened and confirmed these feelings. Soon after my arrival in the hovel, I discovered some papers in the pocket of the dress which I had taken from your laboratory. At first I had neglected them; but now that I was able to decipher the characters in which they were written, I began to study them with diligence. It was your journal of the four months that preceded my creation. You minutely described in these papers every step you took in the progress of your work; this history was mingled with accounts of domestic occurrences. You, doubtless, recollect these papers. Here they are. Every thing is related in them which bears reference to my accursed origin; the whole detail of that series of disgusting circumstances which produced it, is set in view; the minutest description of my odious and loathsome person is given, in language which painted your own horrors, and rendered mine indelible. I sickened as I read. 'Hateful day when I received life!' I exclaimed in agony. 'Accursed creator! Why did you form a monster so hideous that even *you* turned from me in disgust? God, in pity, made man beautiful and alluring, after his own image; but my form is a filthy type of yours, more horrid even from the very resemblance. Satan had his companions, fellow-devils, to admire and encourage him; but I am solitary and abhorred.'

"These were the reflections of my hours of despondency and solitude; but when I contemplated the virtues of the cottagers, their amiable and benevolent dispositions, I persuaded myself that when they should become acquainted with my admiration of their virtues, they would compassionate me, and overlook my personal deformity. Could they turn from their door one, however monstrous, who solicited their compassion and friendship? I resolved, at least, not to despair, but in every way to fit myself for an interview with them which would decide my fate. I postponed this attempt for some months longer; for the importance attached to its success inspired me with a dread lest I should fail. Besides, I found that my understanding improved so much with every day's experience, that I was unwilling to commence this undertaking until a few more months should have added to my sagacity.

"Several changes, in the mean time, took place in the cottage. The presence of Safie diffused happiness among its inhabitants; and I also found that a greater degree of plenty reigned there. Felix and Agatha spent more time in amusement and conversation, and were assisted in their labours by servants. They did not appear rich, but they were contented and happy; their feelings were serene and peaceful, while mine became every day more tumultuous. Increase of knowledge only discovered to me more clearly what a wretched outcast I was. I cherished hope, it is true; but it vanished, when I beheld my person reflected in water, or my shadow in the moonshine, even as that frail image and that inconstant shade.

"I endeavoured to crush these fears, and to fortify myself for the trial which in a few months I resolved to undergo; and some times I allowed my thoughts, unchecked by reason, to ramble in the fields of Paradise, and dared to fancy amiable and lovely creatures sympathising with my feelings, and cheering my gloom; their angelic countenances breathed smiles of consolation. But it was all a dream; no Eve soothed my sorrows, nor shared my thoughts; I was alone. I remembered Adam's supplication[28] to his Creator. But where was mine? He had abandoned me; and, in the bitterness of my heart, I cursed him.

"Autumn passed thus. I saw, with surprise and grief, the leaves decay and fall, and nature again assume the barren and bleak appearance it had worn when I first beheld the woods and the lovely moon. Yet I did not heed the bleakness of the weather; I was better fitted by my conformation for the endurance of cold than heat. But my chief delights were the sight of the flowers, the birds, and all the gay apparel of summer; when those deserted me, I turned with more attention towards the cottagers. Their happiness was not decreased by the absence of summer. They loved, and sympathised with one another; and their joys, depending on each other, were not interrupted by the casualties that took place around them. The more I saw of them, the greater became my desire to claim their protection and kindness; my heart yearned to be known and loved by these amiable creatures: to see their sweet looks directed towards me with affection, was the utmost limit of my ambition. I dared not think that they would turn them from me with disdain and horror. The poor that stopped at their door were never driven away. I asked, it is true, for greater treasures than a little food or rest: I required kindness and sympathy; but I did not believe myself utterly unworthy of it.

"The winter advanced, and an entire revolution of the seasons had taken place since I awoke into life. My attention, at this time, was solely directed towards my plan of introducing myself into the cottage of my protectors. I revolved many projects; but that on which I finally fixed was, to enter the dwelling when the blind old man should be alone. I had sagacity enough to discover, that the unnatural hideousness of my person was the chief object of horror with those who had formerly beheld me. My voice, although harsh, had nothing terrible in it; I thought, therefore, that if, in the absence of his children, I could gain the goodwill and mediation of the old De Lacey, I might, by his means, be tolerated by my younger protectors.

"One day, when the sun shone on the red leaves that strewed the ground, and diffused cheerfulness, although it denied warmth, Safie, Agatha, and Felix departed on a long country walk, and the old man, at his own desire, was left alone in the cottage. When his children had departed, he took up his guitar, and played several mournful but sweet airs, more sweet and

---

[28] A reference to Book VIII, lines 377–97, of John Milton's *Paradise Lost*, in which Adam requests a human companion. — Eds.

mournful than I had ever heard him play before. At first his countenance was illuminated with pleasure, but, as he continued, thoughtfulness and sadness succeeded; at length, laying aside the instrument, he sat absorbed in reflection.

"My heart beat quick; this was the hour and moment of trial, which would decide my hopes, or realise my fears. The servants were gone to a neighbouring fair. All was silent in and around the cottage: it was an excellent opportunity; yet, when I proceeded to execute my plan, my limbs failed me, and I sank to the ground. Again I rose; and, exerting all the firmness of which I was master, removed the planks which I had placed before my hovel to conceal my retreat. The fresh air revived me, and, with renewed determination, I approached the door of their cottage.

"I knocked. 'Who is there?' said the old man — 'Come in.'

"I entered; 'Pardon this intrusion,' said I: 'I am a traveller in want of a little rest; you would greatly oblige me, if you would allow me to remain a few minutes before the fire.'

" 'Enter,' said De Lacey; 'and I will try in what manner I can relieve your wants; but, unfortunately, my children are from home, and, as I am blind, I am afraid I shall find it difficult to procure food for you.'

" 'Do not trouble yourself, my kind host, I have food; it is warmth and rest only that I need.'

"I sat down, and a silence ensued. I knew that every minute was precious to me, yet I remained irresolute in what manner to commence the interview; when the old man addressed me —

" 'By your language, stranger, I suppose you are my countryman; — are you French?'

" 'No; but I was educated by a French family, and understand that language only. I am now going to claim the protection of some friends, whom I sincerely love, and of whose favour I have some hopes.'

" 'Are they Germans?'

" 'No, they are French. But let us change the subject. I am an unfortunate and deserted creature; I look around, and I have no relation or friend upon earth. These amiable people to whom I go have never seen me, and know little of me. I am full of fears; for if I fail there, I am an outcast in the world for ever.'

" 'Do not despair. To be friendless is indeed to be unfortunate; but the hearts of men, when unprejudiced by any obvious self-interest, are full of brotherly love and charity. Rely, therefore, on your hopes; and if these friends are good and amiable, do not despair.'

" 'They are kind — they are the most excellent creatures in the world; but, unfortunately, they are prejudiced against me. I have good dispositions; my life has been hitherto harmless, and in some degree beneficial; but a fatal prejudice clouds their eyes, and where they ought to see a feeling and kind friend, they behold only a detestable monster.'

" 'That is indeed unfortunate; but if you are really blameless, cannot you undeceive them?'

" 'I am about to undertake that task; and it is on that account that I feel so many overwhelming terrors. I tenderly love these friends; I have, unknown to them, been for many months in the habits of daily kindness towards them; but they believe that I wish to injure them, and it is that prejudice which I wish to overcome.'

" 'Where do these friends reside?'

" 'Near this spot.'

"The old man paused, and then continued, 'If you will unreservedly confide to me the particulars of your tale, I perhaps may be of use in undeceiving them. I am blind, and cannot judge of your countenance, but there is something in your words, which persuades me that you are sincere. I am poor, and an exile; but it will afford me true pleasure to be in any way serviceable to a human creature.'

" 'Excellent man! I thank you, and accept your generous offer. You raise me from the dust by this kindness; and I trust that, by your aid, I shall not be driven from the society and sympathy of your fellow-creatures.'

" 'Heaven forbid! even if you were really criminal; for that can only drive you to desperation, and not instigate you to virtue. I also am unfortunate; I and my family have been condemned, although innocent: judge, therefore, if I do not feel for your misfortunes.'

" 'How can I thank you, my best and only benefactor? From your lips first have I heard the voice of kindness directed towards me; I shall be for ever grateful; and your present humanity assures me of success with those friends whom I am on the point of meeting.'

" 'May I know the names and residence of those friends?'

"I paused. This, I thought, was the moment of decision, which was to rob me of, or bestow happiness on me for ever. I struggled vainly for firmness sufficient to answer him, but the effort destroyed all my remaining strength; I sank on the chair, and sobbed aloud. At that moment I heard the steps of my younger protectors. I had not a moment to lose; but, seizing the hand of the old man I cried, 'Now is the time!—save and protect me! You and your family are the friends whom I seek. Do not you desert me in the hour of trial!'

" 'Great God!' exclaimed the old man, 'who are you?'

"At that instant the cottage door was opened, and Felix, Safie, and Agatha entered. Who can describe their horror and consternation on beholding me? Agatha fainted; and Safie, unable to attend to her friend, rushed out of the cottage. Felix darted forward, and with supernatural force tore me from his father, to whose knees I clung: in a transport of fury, he dashed me to the ground, and struck me violently with a stick. I could have torn him limb from limb, as the lion rends the antelope. But my heart sunk within me as with bitter sickness, and I refrained. I saw him on the point of repeating his blow, when, overcome by pain and anguish, I quitted the cottage, and in the general tumult escaped unperceived to my hovel.

CHAPTER XVI

"Cursed, cursed creator! Why did I live? Why, in that instant, did I not extinguish the spark of existence which you had so wantonly bestowed? I know not; despair had not yet taken possession of me; my feelings were those of rage and revenge. I could with pleasure have destroyed the cottage and its inhabitants, and have glutted myself with their shrieks and misery.

"When night came, I quitted my retreat, and wandered in the wood; and now, no longer restrained by the fear of discovery, I gave vent to my anguish in fearful howlings. I was like a wild beast that had broken the toils; destroying the objects that obstructed me, and ranging through the wood with a stag-like swiftness. O! what a miserable night I passed! the cold stars shone in mockery, and the bare trees waved their branches above me: now and then the sweet voice of a bird burst forth amidst the universal stillness. All, save I, were at rest or in enjoyment: I, like the arch-fiend, bore a hell within me; and, finding myself unsympathised with, wished to tear up the trees, spread havoc and destruction around me, and then to have sat down and enjoyed the ruin.

"But this was a luxury of sensation that could not endure; I became fatigued with excess of bodily exertion, and sank on the damp grass in the sick impotence of despair. There was none among the myriads of men that existed who would pity or assist me; and should I feel kindness towards my enemies? No: from that moment I declared everlasting war against the species, and, more than all, against him who had formed me, and sent me forth to this insupportable misery.

"The sun rose; I heard the voices of men, and knew that it was impossible to return to my retreat during that day. Accordingly I hid myself in some thick underwood, determining to devote the ensuing hours to reflection on my situation.

"The pleasant sunshine, and the pure air of day, restored me to some degree of tranquillity; and when I considered what had passed at the cottage, I could not help believing that I had been too hasty in my conclusions. I had certainly acted imprudently. It was apparent that my conversation had interested the father in my behalf, and I was a fool in having exposed my person to the horror of his children. I ought to have familiarised the old De Lacey to me, and by degrees to have discovered myself to the rest of his family, when they should have been prepared for my approach. But I did not believe my errors to be irretrievable; and, after much consideration, I resolved to return to the cottage, seek the old man, and by my representations win him to my party.

"These thoughts calmed me, and in the afternoon I sank into a profound sleep; but the fever of my blood did not allow me to be visited by peaceful dreams. The horrible scene of the preceding day was for ever acting before my eyes; the females were flying, and the enraged Felix tearing me from his father's feet. I awoke exhausted; and, finding that it was already night, I crept forth from my hiding-place, and went in search of food.

"When my hunger was appeased, I directed my steps towards the well-known path that conducted to the cottage. All there was at peace. I crept into my hovel, and remained in silent expectation of the accustomed hour when the family arose. That hour passed, the sun mounted high in the heavens, but the cottagers did not appear. I trembled violently, apprehending some dreadful misfortune. The inside of the cottage was dark, and I heard no motion; I cannot describe the agony of this suspense.

"Presently two countrymen passed by; but, pausing near the cottage, they entered into conversation, using violent gesticulations; but I did not understand what they said, as they spoke the language of the country, which differed from that of my protectors. Soon after, however, Felix approached with another man: I was surprised, as I knew that he had not quitted the cottage that morning, and waited anxiously to discover, from his discourse, the meaning of these unusual appearances.

" 'Do you consider,' said his companion to him, 'that you will be obliged to pay three months' rent, and to lose the produce of your garden? I do not wish to take any unfair advantage, and I beg therefore that you will take some days to consider of your determination.'

" 'It is utterly useless,' replied Felix; 'we can never again inhabit your cottage. The life of my father is in the greatest danger, owing to the dreadful circumstance that I have related. My wife and my sister will never recover their horror. I entreat you not to reason with me any more. Take possession of your tenement, and let me fly from this place.'

"Felix trembled violently as he said this. He and his companion entered the cottage, in which they remained for a few minutes, and then departed. I never saw any of the family of De Lacey more.

"I continued for the remainder of the day in my hovel in a state of utter and stupid despair. My protectors had departed, and had broken the only link that held me to the world. For the first time the feelings of revenge and hatred filled my bosom, and I did not strive to control them; but, allowing myself to be borne away by the stream, I bent my mind towards injury and death. When I thought of my friends, of the mild voice of De Lacey, the gentle eyes of Agatha, and the exquisite beauty of the Arabian, these thoughts vanished, and a gush of tears somewhat soothed me. But again, when I reflected that they had spurned and deserted me, anger returned, a rage of anger; and, unable to injure any thing human, I turned my fury towards inanimate objects. As night advanced, I placed a variety of combustibles around the cottage; and, after having destroyed every vestige of cultivation in the garden, I waited with forced impatience until the moon had sunk to commence my operations.

"As the night advanced, a fierce wind arose from the woods, and quickly dispersed the clouds that had loitered in the heavens: the blast tore along like a mighty avalanche, and produced a kind of insanity in my spirits, that burst all bounds of reason and reflection. I lighted the dry branch of a tree, and danced with fury around the devoted cottage, my eyes still fixed on the western horizon, the edge of which the moon nearly touched. A part of its orb was at length hid, and I waved my brand; it sunk, and, with a loud scream, I fired the straw, and heath, and bushes, which I had collected. The wind fanned the fire, and the cottage was quickly enveloped by the flames, which clung to it, and licked it with their forked and destroying tongues.

"As soon as I was convinced that no assistance could save any part of the habitation, I quitted the scene, and sought for refuge in the woods.

"And now, with the world before me, whither should I bend my steps? I resolved to fly far from the scene of my misfortunes; but to me, hated and despised, every country must be equally horrible. At length the thought of you crossed my mind. I learned from your papers that you were my father, my creator; and to whom could I apply with more fitness than to him who had given me life? Among the lessons that Felix had bestowed upon Safie, geography had not been omitted: I had learned from these the relative situations of the different countries of the earth. You had mentioned Geneva as the name of your native town; and towards this place I resolved to proceed.

"But how was I to direct myself? I knew that I must travel in a south-westerly direction to reach my destination; but the sun was my only guide. I did not know the names of the towns that I was to pass through, nor could I ask information from a single human being; but I did not despair. From you only could I hope for succour, although towards you I felt no sentiment but that of hatred. Unfeeling, heartless creator! you had endowed me with perceptions and passions, and then cast me abroad an object for the scorn and horror of mankind. But on you only had I any claim for pity and redress, and from you I determined to seek that justice which I vainly attempted to gain from any other being that wore the human form.

"My travels were long, and the sufferings I endured intense. It was late in autumn when I quitted the district where I had so long resided. I travelled only at night, fearful of encountering the visage of a human being. Nature decayed around me, and the sun became heatless; rain and snow poured around me; mighty rivers were frozen; the surface of the earth was hard and chill, and bare, and I found no shelter. Oh, earth! how often did I imprecate curses on the cause of my being! The mildness of my nature had fled, and all within me was turned to gall and bitterness. The nearer I approached to your habitation, the more deeply did I feel the spirit of revenge enkindled in my heart. Snow fell, and the waters were hardened; but I rested not. A few incidents now and then directed me, and I possessed a map of the country; but I often wandered wide from my path. The agony of my feelings allowed me no respite: no incident occurred from which my rage and misery could not extract its food; but a circumstance that happened when I arrived on the confines of Switzerland, when the sun had recovered its warmth, and the earth again began to look green, confirmed in an especial manner the bitterness and horror of my feelings.

"I generally rested during the day, and travelled only when I was secured by night from the view of man. One morning, however, finding that my path lay through a deep wood, I ventured to continue my journey after the sun had risen; the day, which was one of the first of spring, cheered even me by the loveliness of its sunshine and the balminess of the air. I felt emotions of gentleness and pleasure, that had long appeared dead, revive within me. Half surprised by the novelty of these sensations, I allowed myself to be borne away by them; and, forgetting my solitude and deformity, dared to

In this film still from one of the more faithful movie adaptations of *Frankenstein*, Robert De Niro portrays the monster in a scene soon after he has fled the cottage.

What aspects of the monster's character and appearance does De Niro capture here?

be happy. Soft tears again bedewed my cheeks, and I even raised my humid eyes with thankfulness towards the blessed sun which bestowed such joy upon me.

"I continued to wind among the paths of the wood, until I came to its boundary, which was skirted by a deep and rapid river, into which many of the trees bent their branches, now budding with the fresh spring. Here I paused, not exactly knowing what path to pursue, when I heard the sound of voices, that induced me to conceal myself under the shade of a cypress. I was scarcely hid, when a young girl came running towards the spot where I was concealed, laughing, as if she ran from some one in sport. She continued her course along the precipitous sides of the river, when suddenly her foot slipt, and she fell into the rapid stream. I rushed from my hiding-place; and, with extreme labour from the force of the current, saved her, and dragged her to shore. She was senseless; and I endeavoured, by every means in my power, to restore animation, when I was suddenly interrupted by the approach of a rustic, who was probably the person from whom she had playfully fled. On seeing me, he darted towards me, and tearing the girl from my arms, hastened towards the deeper parts of the wood. I followed speedily, I hardly knew why; but when the man saw me draw near, he aimed a gun, which he carried, at my body, and fired. I sunk to the ground, and my injurer, with increased swiftness, escaped into the wood.

"This was then the reward of my benevolence! I had saved a human being from destruction, and, as a recompense, I now writhed under the miserable pain of a wound, which shattered the flesh and bone. The feelings of kindness and gentleness, which I had entertained but a few moments before, gave place to hellish rage and gnashing of teeth. Inflamed by pain, I vowed eternal hatred and vengeance to all mankind. But the agony of my wound overcame me; my pulses paused, and I fainted.

"For some weeks I led a miserable life in the woods, endeavouring to cure the wound which I had received. The ball had entered my shoulder, and I knew not whether it had remained there or passed through; at any rate I had no means of extracting it. My sufferings were augmented also by the oppressive sense of the injustice and ingratitude of their infliction. My daily vows rose for revenge — a deep and deadly revenge, such as would alone compensate for the outrages and anguish I had endured.

"After some weeks my wound healed, and I continued my journey. The labours I endured were no longer to be alleviated by the bright sun or gentle breezes of spring; all joy was but a mockery, which insulted my desolate state, and made me feel more painfully that I was not made for the enjoyment of pleasure.

"But my toils now drew near a close; and, in two months from this time, I reached the environs of Geneva.

"It was evening when I arrived, and I retired to a hiding-place among the fields that surround it, to meditate in what manner I should apply to you. I was oppressed by fatigue and hunger, and far too unhappy to enjoy the gentle breezes of evening, or the prospect of the sun setting behind the stupendous mountains of Jura.

"At this time a slight sleep relieved me from the pain of reflection, which was disturbed by the approach of a beautiful child, who came running into the recess I had chosen, with all the sportiveness of infancy. Suddenly, as I gazed on him, an idea seized me, that this little creature was unprejudiced, and had lived too short a time to have imbibed a horror of deformity. If, therefore, I could seize him, and educate him as my companion and friend, I should not be so desolate in this peopled earth.

"Urged by this impulse, I seized on the boy as he passed, and drew him towards me. As soon as he beheld my form, he placed his hands before his eyes, and uttered a shrill scream: I drew his hand forcibly from his face, and said, 'Child, what is the meaning of this? I do not intend to hurt you; listen to me.'

"He struggled violently. 'Let me go,' he cried; 'monster! ugly wretch! you wish to eat me, and tear me to pieces — You are an ogre — Let me go, or I will tell my papa.'

" 'Boy, you will never see your father again; you must come with me.'

" 'Hideous monster! let me go. My papa is a Syndic — he is M. Frankenstein — he will punish you. You dare not keep me.'

" 'Frankenstein! you belong then to my enemy — to him towards whom I have sworn eternal revenge; you shall be my first victim.'

"The child still struggled, and loaded me with epithets which carried despair to my heart; I grasped his throat to silence him, and in a moment he lay dead at my feet.

"I gazed on my victim, and my heart swelled with exultation and hellish triumph: clapping my hands, I exclaimed, 'I, too, can create desolation; my enemy is not invulnerable; this death will carry despair to him, and a thousand other miseries shall torment and destroy him.'

"As I fixed my eyes on the child, I saw something glittering on his breast. I took it; it was a portrait of a most lovely woman. In spite of my malignity, it softened and attracted me. For a few moments I gazed with delight on her dark eyes, fringed by deep lashes, and her lovely lips; but presently my rage returned: I remembered that I was for ever deprived of the delights that such beautiful creatures could bestow; and that she whose resemblance I contemplated would, in regarding me, have changed that air of divine benignity to one expressive of disgust and affright.

"Can you wonder that such thoughts transported me with rage? I only wonder that at that moment, instead of venting my sensations in exclamations and agony, I did not rush among mankind, and perish in the attempt to destroy them.

"While I was overcome by these feelings, I left the spot where I had committed the murder, and seeking a more secluded hiding-place, I entered a barn which had appeared to me to be empty. A woman was sleeping on some straw; she was young: not indeed so beautiful as her whose portrait I held; but of an agreeable aspect, and blooming in the loveliness of youth and health. Here, I thought, is one of those whose joy-imparting smiles are bestowed on all but me. And then I bent over her, and whispered, 'Awake, fairest, thy lover is near — he who would give his life but to obtain one look of affection from thine eyes: my beloved, awake!'

"The sleeper stirred; a thrill of terror ran through me. Should she indeed awake, and see me, and curse me, and denounce the murderer? Thus would she assuredly act, if her darkened eyes opened, and she beheld me. The thought was madness; it stirred the fiend within me — not I, but she shall suffer: the murder I have committed because I am for ever robbed of all that she could give me, she shall atone. The crime had its source in her: be hers the punishment! Thanks to the lessons of Felix and the sanguinary laws of man, I had learned now to work mischief. I bent over her, and placed the portrait securely in one of the folds of her dress. She moved again, and I fled.

"For some days I haunted the spot where these scenes had taken place; sometimes wishing to see you, sometimes resolved to quit the world and its miseries for ever. At length I wandered towards these mountains, and have ranged through their immense recesses, consumed by a burning passion which you alone can gratify. We may not part until you have promised to comply with my requisition. I am alone, and miserable; man will not associate with me; but one as deformed and horrible as myself would not deny herself to me. My companion must be of the same species, and have the same defects. This being you must create."

CHAPTER XVII

The being finished speaking, and fixed his looks upon me in expectation of a reply. But I was bewildered, perplexed, and unable to arrange my ideas sufficiently to understand the full extent of his proposition. He continued —

"You must create a female for me, with whom I can live in the interchange of those sympathies necessary for my being. This you alone can do; and I demand it of you as a right which you must not refuse to concede."

The latter part of his tale had kindled anew in me the anger that had died away while he narrated his peaceful life among the cottagers, and, as he said this, I could no longer suppress the rage that burned within me.

"I do refuse it," I replied; "and no torture shall ever extort a consent from me. You may render me the most miserable of men, but you shall never make me base in my own eyes. Shall I create another like yourself, whose joint wickedness might desolate the world? Begone! I have answered you; you may torture me, but I will never consent."

"You are in the wrong," replied the fiend; "and, instead of threatening, I am content to reason with you. I am malicious because I am miserable. Am I not shunned and hated by all mankind? You, my creator, would tear me to pieces, and triumph; remember that, and tell me why I should pity man more than he pities me? You would not call it murder, if you could precipitate me into one of those ice-rifts, and destroy my frame, the work of your own hands. Shall I respect man, when he contemns me? Let him live with me in the interchange of kindness; and, instead of injury, I would bestow every benefit upon him with tears of gratitude at his acceptance. But that cannot be; the human senses are insurmountable barriers to our union. Yet mine shall not be the submission of abject slavery. I will revenge my injuries: if I cannot inspire love, I will cause fear; and chiefly towards you my arch-enemy, because my creator, do I swear inextinguishable hatred. Have a care: I will work at your destruction, nor finish until I desolate your heart, so that you shall curse the hour of your birth."

A fiendish rage animated him as he said this; his face was wrinkled into contortions too horrible for human eyes to behold; but presently he calmed himself and proceeded —

"I intended to reason. This passion is detrimental to me; for you do not reflect that *you* are the cause of its excess. If any being felt emotions of benevolence towards me, I should return them an hundred and an hundred fold; for that one creature's sake, I would make peace with the whole kind! But I now indulge in dreams of bliss that cannot be realised. What I ask of you is

extending beyond the text

In her 1992 essay "My Monster / My Self," Barbara Johnson (1947–2009), a professor of English and comparative literature as well as the Fredric Wertham Professor of Psychiatry and Law in Society at Harvard University, discusses her interpretation of the meaning of *Frankenstein*.

from My Monster / My Self

Barbara Johnson

Mary Shelley's *Frankenstein* is an even more elaborate and unsettling formation of the relation between parenthood and monstrousness. It is the story of two antithetical modes of parenting that give rise to two increasingly parallel lives — the life of Victor Frankenstein, who is the beloved child of two doting parents, and the life of the monster he single-handedly creates, who is immediately spurned and abandoned by his creator. The fact that in the end both characters reach an equal degree of alienation and self-torture and indeed become indistinguishable as they pursue each other across the frozen polar wastes indicates that the novel is, among other things, a study of the impossibility of finding an adequate model for what a parent should be. . . .

Frankenstein, in other words, can be read as the story of the experience of writing *Frankenstein*. What is at stake in Mary's introduction as well as in the novel is the description of a *primal scene of creation*. Frankenstein combines a monstrous answer to two of the most fundamental questions one can ask: where do babies come from? and where do stories come from? In both cases, the scene of creation is described, but the answer to these questions is still withheld. ■

1. **Think about Johnson's ideas as they might inform your reading of *Frankenstein*. If both Victor and his creation are miserable at the end of their lives, what does that say about the relationship between how people are raised and who they turn out to be?**
2. **How might you analyze *Frankenstein* as an exploration of parenthood? How is the novel as much about parenthood as it is about scientific creation?**

reasonable and moderate; I demand a creature of another sex, but as hideous as myself; the gratification is small, but it is all that I can receive, and it shall content me. It is true, we shall be monsters, cut off from all the world; but on that account we shall be more attached to one another. Our lives will not be happy, but they will be harmless, and free from the misery I now feel. Oh! my creator, make me happy; let me feel gratitude towards you for one benefit! Let me see that I excite the sympathy of some existing thing; do not deny me my request!"

I was moved. I shuddered when I thought of the possible consequences of my consent; but I felt that there was some justice in his argument. His tale, and the feelings he now expressed, proved him to be a creature of fine sensations; and did I not, as his maker, owe him all the portion of happiness that it was in my power to bestow? He saw my change of feeling, and continued —

"If you consent, neither you nor any other human being shall ever see us again: I will go to the vast wilds of South America. My food is not that of man; I do not destroy the lamb and the kid to glut my appetite; acorns and berries afford me sufficient nourishment. My companion will be of the same nature as myself, and will be content with the same fare. We shall make our bed of dried leaves; the sun will shine on us as on man, and will ripen our food. The picture I present to you is peaceful and human, and you must feel that you could deny it only in the wantonness of power and cruelty. Pitiless as you have been towards me, I now see compassion in your eyes; let me seize the favourable moment, and persuade you to promise what I so ardently desire."

"You propose," replied I, "to fly from the habitations of man, to dwell in those wilds where the beasts of the field will be your only companions. How can you, who long for the love and sympathy of man, persevere in this exile? You will return, and again seek their kindness, and you will meet with their detestation; your evil passions will be renewed, and you will then have a companion to aid you in the task of destruction. This may not be: cease to argue the point, for I cannot consent."

"How inconstant are your feelings! but a moment ago you were moved by my representations, and why do you again harden yourself to my complaints? I swear to you, by the earth which I inhabit, and by you that made me, that, with the companion you bestow, I will quit the neighbourhood of man, and dwell as it may chance, in the most savage of places. My evil passions will have fled, for I shall meet with sympathy! my life will flow quietly away, and, in my dying moments, I shall not curse my maker."

His words had a strange effect upon me. I compassioned him, and sometimes felt a wish to console him; but when I looked upon him, when I saw the filthy mass that moved and talked, my heart sickened, and my feelings were altered to those of horror and hatred. I tried to stifle these sensations; I thought, that as I could not sympathise with him, I had no right to withhold from him the small portion of happiness which was yet in my power to bestow.

"You swear," I said, "to be harmless; but have you not already shown a degree of malice that should reasonably make me distrust you? May not even this be a feint that will increase your triumph by affording a wider scope for your revenge?"

"How is this? I must not be trifled with: and I demand an answer. If I have no ties and no affections, hatred and vice must be my portion; the love of another will destroy the cause of my crimes, and I shall become a thing, of whose existence every one will be ignorant. My vices are the children of a forced solitude that I abhor; and my virtues will necessarily arise when I live in communion with an equal. I shall feel the affections of a sensitive being, and become linked to the chain of existence and events, from which I am now excluded."

I paused some time to reflect on all he had related, and the various arguments which he had employed. I thought of the promise of virtues which he had displayed on the opening of his existence, and the subsequent blight of all kindly feeling by the loathing and scorn which his protectors had manifested towards him. His power and threats were not omitted in my calculations: a creature who could exist in the ice-caves of the glaciers, and hide himself from pursuit among the ridges of inaccessible precipices, was a being possessing faculties it would be vain to cope with. After a long pause of reflection, I concluded that the justice due both to him and my fellow-creatures demanded of me that I should comply with his request. Turning to him, therefore, I said —

"I consent to your demand, on your solemn oath to quit Europe for ever, and every other place in the neighbourhood of man, as soon as

I shall deliver into your hands a female who will accompany you in your exile."

"I swear," he cried, "by the sun, and by the blue sky of Heaven, and by the fire of love that burns my heart, that if you grant my prayer, while they exist you shall never behold me again. Depart to your home, and commence your labours: I shall watch their progress with unutterable anxiety; and fear not but that when you are ready I shall appear."

Saying this, he suddenly quitted me, fearful, perhaps, of any change in my sentiments. I saw him descend the mountain with greater speed than the flight of an eagle, and quickly lost him among the undulations of the sea of ice.

His tale had occupied the whole day; and the sun was upon the verge of the horizon when he departed. I knew that I ought to hasten my descent towards the valley, as I should soon be encompassed in darkness; but my heart was heavy, and my steps slow. The labour of winding among the little paths of the mountains, and fixing my feet firmly as I advanced, perplexed me, occupied as I was by the emotions which the occurrences of the day had produced. Night was far advanced, when I came to the half-way resting-place, and seated myself beside the fountain. The stars shone at intervals, as the clouds passed from over them; the dark pines rose before me, and every here and there a broken tree lay on the ground: it was a scene of wonderful solemnity, and stirred strange thoughts within me. I wept bitterly; and clasping my hands in agony, I exclaimed, "Oh! stars and clouds, and winds, ye are all about to mock me: if ye really pity me, crush sensation and memory; let me become as nought; but if not, depart, depart, and leave me in darkness."

These were wild and miserable thoughts; but I cannot describe to you how the eternal twinkling of the stars weighed upon me, and how I listened to every blast of wind, as if it were a dull, ugly siroc[29] on its way to consume me.

Morning dawned before I arrived at the village of Chamounix; I took no rest, but returned immediately to Geneva. Even in my own heart I could give no expression to my sensations — they weighed on me with a mountain's weight, and their excess destroyed my agony beneath them. Thus I returned home, and entering the house, presented myself to the family. My haggard and wild appearance awoke intense alarm; but I answered no question, scarcely did I speak. I felt as if I were placed under a ban — as if I had no right to claim their sympathies — as if never more might I enjoy companionship with them. Yet even thus I loved them to adoration; and to save them, I resolved to dedicate myself to my most abhorred task. The prospect of such an occupation made every other circumstance of existence pass before me like a dream; and that thought only had to me the reality of life.

CHAPTER XVIII

Day after day, week after week, passed away on my return to Geneva; and I could not collect the courage to recommence my work. I feared the vengeance of the disappointed fiend, yet I was unable to overcome my repugnance to the task which was enjoined me. I found that I could not compose a female without again devoting several months to profound study and laborious disquisition. I had heard of some discoveries having been made by an English philosopher, the knowledge of which was material to my success, and I sometimes thought of obtaining my father's consent to visit England for this purpose; but I clung to every pretence of delay, and shrunk from taking the first step in an undertaking whose immediate necessity began to appear less absolute to me. A change indeed had taken place in me: my health, which had hitherto declined, was now much restored; and my spirits, when unchecked by the memory of my unhappy promise, rose proportionably. My father saw this change with pleasure, and he

[29] Sirocco, a blistering wind that blows into Europe from Northern Africa. — Eds.

turned his thoughts towards the best method of eradicating the remains of my melancholy, which every now and then would return by fits, and with a devouring blackness overcast the approaching sunshine. At these moments I took refuge in the most perfect solitude. I passed whole days on the lake alone in a little boat, watching the clouds, and listening to the rippling of the waves, silent and listless. But the fresh air and bright sun seldom failed to restore me to some degree of composure; and, on my return, I met the salutations of my friends with a readier smile and a more cheerful heart.

It was after my return from one of these rambles, that my father, calling me aside, thus addressed me: —

"I am happy to remark, my dear son, that you have resumed your former pleasures, and seem to be returning to yourself. And yet you are still unhappy, and still avoid our society. For some time I was lost in conjecture as to the cause of this; but yesterday an idea struck me, and if it is well founded, I conjure you to avow it. Reserve on such a point would be not only useless, but draw down treble misery on us all."

I trembled violently at his exordium, and my father continued —

"I confess, my son, that I have always looked forward to your marriage with our dear Elizabeth as the tie of our domestic comfort, and the stay of my declining years. You were attached to each other from your earliest infancy; you studied together, and appeared, in dispositions and tastes, entirely suited to one another. But so blind is the experience of man, that what I conceived to be the best assistants to my plan, may have entirely destroyed it. You, perhaps, regard her as your sister, without any wish that she might become your wife. Nay, you may have met with another whom you may love; and, considering yourself as bound in honour to Elizabeth, this struggle may occasion the poignant misery which you appear to feel."

"My dear father, re-assure yourself. I love my cousin tenderly and sincerely. I never saw any woman who excited, as Elizabeth does, my warmest admiration and affection. My future hopes and prospects are entirely bound up in the expectation of our union."

"The expression of your sentiments on this subject, my dear Victor, gives me more pleasure than I have for some time experienced. If you feel thus, we shall assuredly be happy, however present events may cast a gloom over us. But it is this gloom which appears to have taken so strong a hold of your mind, that I wish to dissipate. Tell me, therefore, whether you object to an immediate solemnisation of the marriage. We have been unfortunate, and recent events have drawn us from that everyday tranquillity befitting my years and infirmities. You are younger; yet I do not suppose, possessed as you are of a competent fortune, that an early marriage would at all interfere with any future plans of honour and utility that you may have formed. Do not suppose, however, that I wish to dictate happiness to you, or that a delay on your part would cause me any serious uneasiness. Interpret my words with candour, and answer me, I conjure you, with confidence and sincerity."

I listened to my father in silence, and remained for some time incapable of offering any reply. I revolved rapidly in my mind a multitude of thoughts, and endeavoured to arrive at some conclusion. Alas! to me the idea of an immediate union with my Elizabeth was one of horror and dismay. I was bound by a solemn promise, which I had not yet fulfilled, and dared not break; or, if I did, what manifold miseries might not impend over me and my devoted family! Could I enter into a festival with this deadly weight yet hanging round my neck, and bowing me to the ground? I must perform my engagement, and let the monster depart with his mate, before I allowed myself to enjoy the delight of an union from which I expected peace.

I remembered also the necessity imposed upon me of either journeying to England, or entering into a long correspondence with those philosophers of that country, whose knowledge and discoveries were of indispensable use to me in my present undertaking. The latter method of obtaining the desired intelligence was dilatory and unsatisfactory: besides, I had an insurmountable aversion to the idea of engaging myself in my loathsome task in my father's house, while in habits of familiar intercourse with those I loved. I knew that a thousand fearful accidents might occur, the slightest of which would disclose a tale to thrill all connected with me with horror. I was aware also that I should often lose all self-command, all capacity of hiding the harrowing sensations that would possess me during the progress of my unearthly occupation. I must absent myself from all I loved while thus employed. Once commenced, it would quickly be achieved, and I might be restored to my family in peace and happiness. My promise fulfilled, the monster would depart for ever. Or (so my fond fancy imaged) some accident might meanwhile occur to destroy him, and put an end to my slavery for ever.

These feelings dictated my answer to my father. I expressed a wish to visit England; but, concealing the true reasons of this request, I clothed my desires under a guise which excited no suspicion, while I urged my desire with an earnestness that easily induced my father to comply. After so long a period of an absorbing melancholy, that resembled madness in its intensity and effects, he was glad to find that I was capable of taking pleasure in the idea of such a journey, and he hoped that change of scene and varied amusement would, before my return, have restored me entirely to myself.

The duration of my absence was left to my own choice; a few months, or at most a year, was the period contemplated. One paternal kind precaution he had taken to ensure my having a companion. Without previously communicating with me, he had, in concert with Elizabeth, arranged that Clerval should join me at Strasburgh. This interfered with the solitude I coveted for the prosecution of my task; yet at the commencement of my journey the presence of my friend could in no way be an impediment, and truly I rejoiced that thus I should be saved many hours of lonely, maddening reflection. Nay, Henry might stand between me and the intrusion of my foe. If I were alone, would he not at times force his abhorred presence on me, to remind me of my task, or to contemplate its progress?

To England, therefore, I was bound, and it was understood that my union with Elizabeth should take place immediately on my return. My father's age rendered him extremely averse to delay. For myself, there was one reward I promised myself from my detested toils — one consolation for my unparalleled sufferings; it was the prospect of that day when, enfranchised from my miserable slavery, I might claim Elizabeth, and forget the past in my union with her.

I now made arrangements for my journey; but one feeling haunted me, which filled me with fear and agitation. During my absence I should leave my friends unconscious of the existence of their enemy, and unprotected from his attacks, exasperated as he might be by my departure. But he had promised to follow me wherever I might go; and would he not accompany me to England? This imagination was dreadful in itself, but soothing, inasmuch as it supposed the safety of my friends. I was agonised with the idea of the possibility that the reverse of this might happen. But through the whole period during which I was the slave of my creature, I allowed myself to be governed by the impulses of the moment; and my present sensations strongly intimated that the fiend would follow me, and exempt my family from the danger of his machinations.

It was in the latter end of September that I again quitted my native country. My journey had been my own suggestion, and Elizabeth, therefore, acquiesced: but she was filled with disquiet at the idea of my suffering, away from her, the inroads of misery and grief. It had been her care which provided me a companion in Clerval — and yet a man is blind to a thousand minute circumstances, which call forth a woman's sedulous attention. She longed to bid me hasten my return, — a thousand conflicting emotions rendered her mute, as she bade me a tearful silent farewell.

I threw myself into the carriage that was to convey me away, hardly knowing whither I was going, and careless of what was passing around. I remembered only, and it was with a bitter anguish that I reflected on it, to order that my chemical instruments should be packed to go with me. Filled with dreary imaginations, I passed through many beautiful and majestic scenes; but my eyes were fixed and unobserving. I could only think of the bourne of my travels,[30] and the work which was to occupy me whilst they endured.

After some days spent in listless indolence, during which I traversed many leagues, I arrived at Strasburgh, where I waited two days for Clerval. He came. Alas, how great was the contrast between us! He was alive to every new scene; joyful when he saw the beauties of the setting sun, and more happy when he beheld it rise, and recommence a new day. He pointed out to me the shifting colours of the landscape, and the appearances of the sky. "This is what it is to live," he cried, "now I enjoy existence! But you, my dear Frankenstein, wherefore are you desponding and sorrowful?" In truth, I was occupied by gloomy thoughts, and neither saw the descent of the evening star, nor the golden sunrise reflected in the Rhine. — And you, my friend, would be far more amused with the journal of Clerval, who observed the scenery with an eye of feeling and delight, than in listening to my reflections. I, a miserable wretch, haunted by a curse that shut up every avenue to enjoyment.

We had agreed to descend the Rhine in a boat from Strasburgh to Rotterdam, whence we might take shipping for London. During this voyage, we passed many willowy islands, and saw several beautiful towns. We stayed a day at Manheim, and, on the fifth from our departure from Strasburgh, arrived at Mayence. The course of the Rhine below Mayence becomes much more picturesque. The river descends rapidly, and winds between hills, not high, but steep, and of beautiful forms. We saw many ruined castles standing on the edges of precipices, surrounded by black woods, high and inaccessible. This part of the Rhine, indeed, presents a singularly variegated landscape. In one spot you view rugged hills, ruined castles overlooking tremendous precipices, with the dark Rhine rushing beneath; and, on the sudden turn of a promontory, flourishing vineyards, with green sloping banks, and a meandering river, and populous towns occupy the scene.

We travelled at the time of the vintage, and heard the song of the labourers, as we glided down the stream. Even I, depressed in mind, and my spirits continually agitated by gloomy feelings, even I was pleased. I lay at the bottom of the boat, and, as I gazed on the cloudless blue sky, I seemed to drink in a tranquillity to which I had long been a stranger. And if these were my sensations, who can describe those of Henry? He felt as if he had been transported to Fairy-land, and enjoyed a happiness seldom tasted by man. "I have seen," he said, "the most beautiful scenes of my own country; I have visited the lakes of Lucerne and Uri, where the snowy mountains descend almost perpendicularly to the water, casting black and impenetrable shades, which would cause a gloomy and mournful appearance, were it not for the most verdant islands that relieve the eye by their gay appearance; I have seen this lake agitated by a tempest, when the wind tore up whirlwinds of water, and gave you an idea of what the water-spout must be on the great

[30] End or goal. — Eds.

ocean, and the waves dash with fury the base of the mountain, where the priest and his mistress[31] were overwhelmed by an avalanche, and where their dying voices are still said to be heard amid the pauses of the nightly wind; I have seen the mountains of La Valais, and the Pays de Vaud: but this country, Victor, pleases me more than all those wonders. The mountains of Switzerland are more majestic and strange; but there is a charm in the banks of this divine river, that I never before saw equalled. Look at that castle which overhangs yon precipice; and that also on the island, almost concealed amongst the foliage of those lovely trees; and now that group of labourers coming from among their vines; and that village half hid in the recess of the mountain. Oh, surely, the spirit that inhabits and guards this place has a soul more in harmony with man, than those who pile the glacier, or retire to the inaccessible peaks of the mountains of our own country."

Clerval! beloved friend! even now it delights me to record your words, and to dwell on the praise of which you are so eminently deserving. He was a being formed in the "very poetry of nature." His wild and enthusiastic imagination was chastened by the sensibility of his heart. His soul overflowed with ardent affections, and his friendship was of that devoted and wondrous nature that the worldly-minded teach us to look for only in the imagination. But even human sympathies were not sufficient to satisfy his eager mind. The scenery of external nature, which others regard only with admiration, he loved with ardour: —

——— The sounding cataract
Haunted him like a passion: the tall rock,
The mountain, and the deep and gloomy wood,
Their colours and their forms, were then to him
An appetite; a feeling, and a love,
That had no need of a remoter charm,
By thought supplied, or any interest
Unborrow'd from the eye.[32]

And where does he now exist? Is this gentle and lovely being lost for ever? Has this mind, so replete with ideas, imaginations fanciful and magnificent, which formed a world, whose existence depended on the life of its creator; — has this mind perished? Does it now only exist in my memory? No, it is not thus; your form so divinely wrought, and beaming with beauty, has decayed, but your spirit still visits and consoles your unhappy friend.

Pardon this gush of sorrow; these ineffectual words are but a slight tribute to the unexampled worth of Henry, but they soothe my heart, overflowing with the anguish which his remembrance creates. I will proceed with my tale.

Beyond Cologne we descended to the 475
plains of Holland; and we resolved to post the remainder of our way; for the wind was contrary, and the stream of the river was too gentle to aid us.

Our journey here lost the interest arising from beautiful scenery; but we arrived in a few days at Rotterdam, whence we proceeded by sea to England. It was on a clear morning, in the latter days of December, that I first saw the white cliffs of Britain. The banks of the Thames presented a new scene; they were flat, but fertile, and almost every town was marked by the remembrance of some story. We saw Tilbury Fort, and remembered the Spanish armada; Gravesend, Woolwich, and Greenwich, places which I had heard of even in my country.

At length we saw the numerous steeples of London, St. Paul's towering above all, and the Tower famed in English history.

[31] A reference to a local tale from the Rhine-North Westphalia region of Germany. — Eds.

[32] These have been adapted from lines 76–83 of William Wordsworth's poem "Lines Composed a Few Miles above Tintern Abbey" (1798), which was written in first person. — Eds.

CHAPTER XIX

London was our present point of rest; we determined to remain several months in this wonderful and celebrated city. Clerval desired the intercourse of the men of genius and talent who flourished at this time; but this was with me a secondary object; I was principally occupied with the means of obtaining the information necessary for the completion of my promise, and quickly availed myself of the letters of introduction that I had brought with me, addressed to the most distinguished natural philosophers.

If this journey had taken place during my days of study and happiness, it would have afforded me inexpressible pleasure. But a blight had come over my existence, and I only visited these people for the sake of the information they might give me on the subject in which my interest was so terribly profound. Company was irksome to me; when alone, I could fill my mind with the sights of heaven and earth; the voice of Henry soothed me, and I could thus cheat myself into a transitory peace. But busy, uninteresting, joyous faces brought back despair to my heart. I saw an insurmountable barrier placed between me and my fellow-men; this barrier was sealed with the blood of William and Justine; and to reflect on the events connected with those names filled my soul with anguish.

But in Clerval I saw the image of my former self; he was inquisitive, and anxious to gain experience and instruction. The difference of manners which he observed was to him an inexhaustible source of instruction and amusement. He was also pursuing an object he had long had in view. His design was to visit India, in the belief that he had in his knowledge of its various languages, and in the views he had taken of its society, the means of materially assisting the progress of European colonisation and trade. In Britain only could he further the execution of his plan. He was for ever busy; and the only check to his enjoyments was my sorrowful and dejected mind. I tried to conceal this as much as possible, that I might not debar him from the pleasures natural to one, who was entering on a new scene of life, undisturbed by any care or bitter recollection. I often refused to accompany him, alleging another engagement, that I might remain alone. I now also began to collect the materials necessary for my new creation, and this was to me like the torture of single drops of water continually falling on the head. Every thought that was devoted to it was an extreme anguish, and every word that I spoke in allusion to it caused my lips to quiver, and my heart to palpitate.

After passing some months in London, we received a letter from a person in Scotland, who had formerly been our visitor at Geneva. He mentioned the beauties of his native country, and asked us if those were not sufficient allurements to induce us to prolong our journey as far north as Perth, where he resided. Clerval eagerly desired to accept this invitation; and I, although I abhorred society, wished to view again mountains and streams, and all the wondrous works with which Nature adorns her chosen dwelling-places.

We had arrived in England at the beginning of October, and it was now February. We accordingly determined to commence our journey towards the north at the expiration of another month. In this expedition we did not intend to follow the great road to Edinburgh, but to visit Windsor, Oxford, Matlock, and the Cumberland lakes, resolving to arrive at the completion of this tour about the end of July. I packed up my chemical instruments, and the materials I had collected, resolving to finish my labours in some obscure nook in the northern highlands of Scotland.

We quitted London on the 27th of March, and remained a few days at Windsor, rambling in its beautiful forest. This was a new scene to us mountaineers; the majestic oaks, the quantity of game, and the herds of stately deer, were all novelties to us.

From thence we proceeded to Oxford. As we entered this city, our minds were filled with the remembrance of the events that had been transacted there more than a century and a half before. It was here that Charles I. had collected his forces. This city had remained faithful to him, after the whole nation had forsaken his cause to join the standard of parliament and liberty. The memory of that unfortunate king, and his companions, the amiable Falkland, the insolent Goring, his queen, and son, gave a peculiar interest to every part of the city, which they might be supposed to have inhabited. The spirit of elder days found a dwelling here, and we delighted to trace its footsteps. If these feelings had not found an imaginary gratification, the appearance of the city had yet in itself sufficient beauty to obtain our admiration. The colleges are ancient and picturesque; the streets are almost magnificent; and the lovely Isis, which flows beside it through meadows of exquisite verdure, is spread forth into a placid expanse of waters, which reflects its majestic assemblage of towers, and spires, and domes, embosomed among aged trees.

I enjoyed this scene; and yet my enjoyment was embittered both by the memory of the past, and the anticipation of the future. I was formed for peaceful happiness. During my youthful days discontent never visited my mind; and if I was ever overcome by *ennui*, the sight of what is beautiful in nature, or the study of what is excellent and sublime in the productions of man, could always interest my heart, and communicate elasticity to my spirits. But I am a blasted tree; the bolt has entered my soul; and I felt then that I should survive to exhibit, what I shall soon cease to be — a miserable spectacle of wrecked humanity, pitiable to others, and intolerable to myself.

We passed a considerable period at Oxford, rambling among its environs, and endeavouring to identify every spot which might relate to the most animating epoch of English history. Our little voyages of discovery were often prolonged by the successive objects that presented themselves. We visited the tomb of the illustrious Hampden, and the field on which that patriot fell. For a moment my soul was elevated from its debasing and miserable fears, to contemplate the divine ideas of liberty and self-sacrifice, of which these sights were the monuments and the remembrancers. For an instant I dared to shake off my chains, and look around me with a free and lofty spirit; but the iron had eaten into my flesh, and I sank again, trembling and hopeless, into my miserable self.

We left Oxford with regret, and proceeded to Matlock, which was our next place of rest. The country in the neighbourhood of this village resembled, to a greater degree, the scenery of Switzerland; but every thing is on a lower scale, and the green hills want the crown of distant white Alps, which always attend on the piny mountains of my native country. We visited the wondrous cave, and the little cabinets of natural history, where the curiosities are disposed in the same manner as in the collections at Servox and Chamounix. The latter name made me tremble, when pronounced by Henry; and I hastened to quit Matlock, with which that terrible scene was thus associated.

From Derby, still journeying northward, we passed two months in Cumberland and Westmorland. I could now almost fancy myself among the Swiss mountains. The little patches of snow which yet lingered on the northern sides of the mountains, the lakes, and the dashing of the rocky streams, were all familiar and dear sights to me. Here also we made some acquaintances, who almost contrived to cheat me into happiness. The delight of Clerval was proportionably greater than mine; his mind expanded in the company of men of talent, and he found in his own nature greater capacities and resources than he could have imagined himself to have possessed while he associated with his inferiors. "I could pass my life here," said he to me; "and among these mountains I should scarcely regret Switzerland and the Rhine."

But he found that a traveller's life is one that includes much pain amidst its enjoyments. His feelings are for ever on the stretch; and when he begins to sink into repose, he finds himself obliged to quit that on which he rests in pleasure for something new, which again engages his attention, and which also he forsakes for other novelties.

490 We had scarcely visited the various lakes of Cumberland and Westmorland, and conceived an affection for some of the inhabitants, when the period of our appointment with our Scotch friend approached, and we left them to travel on. For my own part I was not sorry. I had now neglected my promise for some time, and I feared the effects of the daemon's disappointment. He might remain in Switzerland, and wreak his vengeance on my relatives. This idea pursued me, and tormented me at every moment from which I might otherwise have snatched repose and peace. I waited for my letters with feverish impatience: if they were delayed, I was miserable, and overcome by a thousand fears; and when they arrived, and I saw the superscription of Elizabeth or my father, I hardly dared to read and ascertain my fate. Sometimes I thought that the fiend followed me, and might expedite my remissness by murdering my companion. When these thoughts possessed me, I would not quit Henry for a moment, but followed him as his shadow, to protect him from the fancied rage of his destroyer. I felt as if I had committed some great crime, the consciousness of which haunted me. I was guiltless, but I had indeed drawn down a horrible curse upon my head, as mortal as that of crime.

I visited Edinburgh with languid eyes and mind; and yet that city might have interested the most unfortunate being. Clerval did not like it so well as Oxford: for the antiquity of the latter city was more pleasing to him. But the beauty and regularity of the new town of Edinburgh, its romantic castle and its environs, the most delightful in the world, Arthur's Seat, St. Bernard's Well, and the Pentland Hills, compensated him for the change, and filled him with cheerfulness and admiration. But I was impatient to arrive at the termination of my journey.

We left Edinburgh in a week, passing through Coupar, St. Andrew's, and along the banks of the Tay, to Perth, where our friend expected us. But I was in no mood to laugh and talk with strangers, or enter into their feelings or plans with the good humour expected from a guest; and accordingly I told Clerval that I wished to make the tour of Scotland alone. "Do you," said I, "enjoy yourself, and let this be our rendezvous. I may be absent a month or two; but do not interfere with my motions, I entreat you: leave me to peace and solitude for a short time; and when I return, I hope it will be with a lighter heart, more congenial to your own temper."

Henry wished to dissuade me; but, seeing me bent on this plan, ceased to remonstrate. He entreated me to write often. "I had rather be with you," he said, "in your solitary rambles, than with these Scotch people, whom I do not know: hasten then, my friend, to return, that I may again feel myself somewhat at home, which I cannot do in your absence."

Having parted from my friend, I determined to visit some remote spot of Scotland, and finish my work in solitude. I did not doubt but that the monster followed me, and would discover himself to me when I should have finished, that he might receive his companion.

With this resolution I traversed the northern 495 highlands, and fixed on one of the remotest of the Orkneys as the scene of my labours. It was a place fitted for such a work, being hardly more than a rock, whose high sides were continually beaten upon by the waves. The soil was barren, scarcely affording pasture for a few miserable cows, and oatmeal for its inhabitants, which consisted of five persons, whose gaunt and scraggy limbs gave tokens of their miserable fare. Vegetables and bread, when they indulged in such luxuries, and even fresh water, was to be procured from the main land, which was about five miles distant.

On the whole island there were but three miserable huts, and one of these was vacant when I arrived. This I hired. It contained but two rooms, and these exhibited all the squalidness of the most miserable penury. The thatch had fallen in, the walls were unplastered, and the door was off its hinges. I ordered it to be repaired, bought some furniture, and took possession; an incident which would, doubtless, have occasioned some surprise, had not all the senses of the cottagers been benumbed by want and squalid poverty. As it was, I lived ungazed at and unmolested, hardly thanked for the pittance of food and clothes which I gave; so much does suffering blunt even the coarsest sensations of men.

In this retreat I devoted the morning to labour; but in the evening, when the weather permitted, I walked on the stony beach of the sea, to listen to the waves as they roared and dashed at my feet. It was a monotonous yet ever-changing scene. I thought of Switzerland; it was far different from this desolate and appalling landscape. Its hills are covered with vines, and its cottages are scattered thickly in the plains. Its fair lakes reflect a blue and gentle sky; and, when troubled by the winds, their tumult is but as the play of a lively infant, when compared to the roarings of the giant ocean.

In this manner I distributed my occupations when I first arrived; but, as I proceeded in my labour, it became every day more horrible and irksome to me. Sometimes I could not prevail on myself to enter my laboratory for several days; and at other times I toiled day and night in order to complete my work. It was, indeed, a filthy process in which I was engaged. During my first experiment, a kind of enthusiastic frenzy had blinded me to the horror of my employment; my mind was intently fixed on the consummation of my labour, and my eyes were shut to the horror of my proceedings. But now I went to it in cold blood, and my heart often sickened at the work of my hands.

Thus situated, employed in the most detestable occupation, immersed in a solitude where nothing could for an instant call my attention from the actual scene in which I was engaged, my spirits became unequal; I grew restless and nervous. Every moment I feared to meet my persecutor. Sometimes I sat with my eyes fixed on the ground, fearing to raise them, lest they should encounter the object which I so much dreaded to behold. I feared to wander from the sight of my fellow-creatures, lest when alone he should come to claim his companion.

In the mean time I worked on, and my labour was already considerably advanced. I looked towards its completion with a tremulous and eager hope, which I dared not trust myself to question, but which was intermixed with obscure forebodings of evil, that made my heart sicken in my bosom.

CHAPTER XX

I sat one evening in my laboratory; the sun had set, and the moon was just rising from the sea; I had not sufficient light for my employment, and I remained idle, in a pause of consideration of whether I should leave my labour for the night, or hasten its conclusion by an unremitting attention to it. As I sat, a train of reflection occurred to me, which led me to consider the effects of what I was now doing. Three years before I was engaged in the same manner, and had created a fiend whose unparalleled barbarity had desolated my heart, and filled it for ever with the bitterest remorse. I was now about to form another being, of whose dispositions I was alike ignorant; she might become ten thousand times more malignant than her mate, and delight, for its own sake, in murder and wretchedness. He had sworn to quit the neighbourhood of man, and hide himself in deserts; but she had not; and she, who in all probability was to become a thinking and reasoning animal, might refuse to comply with a compact made before her creation. They might even hate each other; the creature who already lived loathed his own deformity, and might he not conceive a greater abhorrence for it when it came before his eyes in the female form? She also might turn with disgust from him to the superior beauty of man; she might quit him, and he be again alone, exasperated by the fresh provocation of being deserted by one of his own species.

Even if they were to leave Europe, and inhabit the deserts of the new world, yet one of the first results of those sympathies for which the daemon thirsted would be children, and a race of devils would be propagated upon the earth, who might make the very existence of the species of man a condition precarious and full of terror. Had I a right, for my own benefit, to inflict this curse upon everlasting generations? I had before been moved by the sophisms of the being I had created; I had been struck senseless by his fiendish threats: but now, for the first time, the wickedness of my promise burst upon me; I shuddered to think that future ages might curse me as their pest, whose selfishness had not hesitated to buy its own peace at the price, perhaps, of the existence of the whole human race.

I trembled, and my heart failed within me; when, on looking up, I saw, by the light of the moon, the daemon at the casement. A ghastly grin wrinkled his lips as he gazed on me, where I sat fulfilling the task which he had allotted to me. Yes, he had followed me in my travels; he had loitered in forests, hid himself in caves, or taken refuge in wide and desert heaths; and he now came to mark my progress, and claim the fulfillment of my promise.

As I looked on him, his countenance expressed the utmost extent of malice and treachery. I thought with a sensation of madness on my promise of creating another like to him, and trembling with passion, tore to pieces the thing on which I was engaged. The wretch saw me destroy the creature on whose future existence he depended for happiness, and, with a howl of devilish despair and revenge, withdrew.

I left the room, and, locking the door, made a solemn vow in my own heart never to resume my labours; and then, with trembling steps, I sought my own apartment. I was alone; none were near me to dissipate the gloom, and relieve me from the sickening oppression of the most terrible reveries.

Several hours passed, and I remained near my window gazing on the sea; it was almost motionless, for the winds were hushed, and all nature reposed under the eye of the quiet moon. A few fishing vessels alone specked the water, and now and then the gentle breeze wafted the sound of voices, as the fishermen called to one another. I felt the silence, although I was hardly conscious of its extreme profundity, until my ear was suddenly arrested by the paddling of oars near the shore, and a person landed close to my house.

In a few minutes after, I heard the creaking of my door, as if some one endeavoured to open it softly. I trembled from head to foot; I felt a presentiment of who it was, and wished to rouse one of the peasants who dwelt in a cottage not far from mine; but I was overcome by the sensation of helplessness, so often felt in frightful dreams, when you in vain endeavour to fly from an impending danger, and was rooted to the spot.

Presently I heard the sound of footsteps along the passage; the door opened, and the wretch whom I dreaded appeared. Shutting the door, he approached me, and said, in a smothered voice — "You have destroyed the work which you began; what is it that you intend? Do you dare to break your promise? I have endured toil and misery: I left Switzerland with you; I crept along the shores of the Rhine, among its willow islands, and over the summits of its hills. I have dwelt many months in the heaths of England, and among the deserts of

Scotland. I have endured incalculable fatigue, and cold, and hunger; do you dare destroy my hopes?"

"Begone! I do break my promise; never will I create another like yourself, equal in deformity and wickedness."

"Slave, I have reasoned with you, but you have proved yourself unworthy of my condescension. Remember that I have power; you believe yourself miserable, but I can make you so wretched that the light of day will be hateful to you. You are my creator, but I am your master;—obey!"

"The hour of my irresolution is past, and the period of your power is arrived. Your threats cannot move me to do an act of wickedness; but they confirm me in a determination of not creating you a companion in vice. Shall I, in cool blood, set loose upon the earth a daemon, whose delight is in death and wretchedness? Begone! I am firm, and your words will only exasperate my rage."

The monster saw my determination in my face, and gnashed his teeth in the impotence of anger. "Shall each man," cried he, "find a wife for his bosom, and each beast have his mate, and I be alone? I had feelings of affection, and they were requited by detestation and scorn. Man! you may hate; but beware! your hours will pass in dread and misery, and soon the bolt will fall which must ravish from you your happiness for ever. Are you to be happy, while I grovel in the intensity of my wretchedness? You can blast my other passions; but revenge remains—revenge, henceforth dearer than light or food! I may die; but first you, my tyrant and tormentor, shall curse the sun that gazes on your misery. Beware; for I am fearless, and therefore powerful. I will watch with the wiliness of a snake, that I may sting with its venom. Man, you shall repent of the injuries you inflict."

"Devil, cease; and do not poison the air with these sounds of malice. I have declared my resolution to you, and I am no coward to bend beneath words. Leave me; I am inexorable."

"It is well. I go; but remember, I shall be with you on your wedding-night."

I started forward, and exclaimed, "Villain! before you sign my death-warrant, be sure that you are yourself safe."

I would have seized him; but he eluded me, and quitted the house with precipitation. In a few moments I saw him in his boat, which shot across the waters with an arrowy swiftness, and was soon lost amidst the waves.

All was again silent; but his words rung in my ears. I burned with rage to pursue the murderer of my peace, and precipitate him into the ocean. I walked up and down my room hastily and perturbed, while my imagination conjured up a thousand images to torment and sting me. Why had I not followed him, and closed with him in mortal strife? But I had suffered him to depart, and he had directed his course towards the main land. I shuddered to think who might be the next victim sacrificed to his insatiate revenge. And then I thought again of his words—*"I will be with you on your wedding-night."* That then was the period fixed for the fulfilment of my destiny. In that hour I should die, and at once satisfy and extinguish his malice. The prospect did not move me to fear; yet when I thought of my beloved Elizabeth,—of her tears and endless sorrow, when she should find her lover so barbarously snatched from her,—tears, the first I had shed for many months, streamed from my eyes, and I resolved not to fall before my enemy without a bitter struggle.

The night passed away, and the sun rose from the ocean; my feelings became calmer, if it may be called calmness, when the violence of rage sinks into the depths of despair. I left the house, the horrid scene of the last night's contention, and walked on the beach of the sea, which I almost regarded as an insuperable barrier between me and my fellow-creatures; nay, a wish that such should prove the fact stole across me. I desired that I might pass my life on that barren rock, wearily, it is true, but uninterrupted by any sudden shock of misery. If I returned, it was to be sacrificed, or to see those whom I most loved die under the grasp of a daemon whom I had myself created.

I walked about the isle like a restless spectre, separated from all it loved, and miserable in the separation. When it became noon, and the sun rose higher, I lay down on the grass, and was overpowered by a deep sleep. I had been awake the whole of the preceding night, my nerves were agitated, and my eyes inflamed by watching and misery. The sleep into which I now sunk refreshed me; and when I awoke, I again felt as if I belonged to a race of human beings like myself, and I began to reflect upon what had passed with greater composure; yet still the words of the fiend rung in my ears like a death-knell, they appeared like a dream, yet distinct and oppressive as a reality.

The sun had far descended, and I still sat on the shore, satisfying my appetite, which had become ravenous, with an oaten cake, when I saw a fishing-boat land close to me, and one of the men brought me a packet; it contained letters from Geneva, and one from Clerval, entreating me to join him. He said that he was wearing away his time fruitlessly where he was; that letters from the friends he had formed in London desired his return to complete the negotiation they had entered into for his Indian enterprise. He could not any longer delay his departure; but as his journey to London might be followed, even sooner than he now conjectured, by his longer voyage, he entreated me to bestow as much of my society on him as I could spare. He besought me, therefore, to leave my solitary isle, and to meet him at Perth, that we might proceed southwards together. This letter in a degree recalled me to life, and I determined to quit my island at the expiration of two days.

Yet, before I departed, there was a task to perform, on which I shuddered to reflect: I must pack up my chemical instruments; and for that purpose I must enter the room which had been the scene of my odious work, and I must handle those utensils, the sight of which was sickening to me. The next morning, at daybreak, I summoned sufficient courage, and unlocked the door of my laboratory. The remains of the half-finished creature, whom I had destroyed, lay scattered on the floor, and I almost felt as if I had mangled the living flesh of a human being. I paused to collect myself, and then entered the chamber. With trembling hand I conveyed the instruments out of the room; but I reflected that I ought not to leave the relics of my work to excite the horror and suspicion of the peasants; and I accordingly put them into a basket, with a great quantity of stones, and, laying them up, determined to throw them into the sea that very night; and in the mean time I sat upon the beach, employed in cleaning and arranging my chemical apparatus.

Nothing could be more complete than the alteration that had taken place in my feelings since the night of the appearance of the daemon. I had before regarded my promise with a gloomy despair, as a thing that, with whatever consequences, must be fulfilled; but I now felt as if a film had been taken from before my eyes, and that I, for the first time, saw clearly. The idea of renewing my labours did not for one instant occur to me; the threat I had heard weighed on my thoughts, but I did not reflect that a voluntary act of mine could avert it. I had resolved in my own mind, that to create another like the fiend I had first made would be an act of the basest and most atrocious selfishness; and I banished from my mind every thought that could lead to a different conclusion.

Between two and three in the morning the moon rose; and I then, putting my basket aboard a little skiff, sailed out about four miles from the shore. The scene was perfectly solitary: a few boats were returning towards land, but I sailed away from them. I felt as if I was about the commission of a dreadful crime, and avoided with shuddering anxiety any encounter with my fellow-creatures. At one time the moon, which had before been clear, was suddenly overspread by a thick cloud, and I took advantage of the moment of darkness, and cast my basket into the sea: I listened to the gurgling sound as it sunk, and then sailed away from the spot. The sky became clouded; but the air was pure, although chilled by the north-east breeze that was then rising. But it refreshed me, and filled me with such agreeable sensations, that I resolved to prolong my stay on the water; and, fixing the rudder in a direct position, stretched myself at the bottom of the boat. Clouds hid the moon, every thing was obscure, and I heard only the sound of the boat, as its keel cut through the waves; the murmur lulled me, and in a short time I slept soundly.

I do not know how long I remained in this situation, but when I awoke I found that the sun had already mounted considerably. The wind was high, and the waves continually threatened the safety of my little skiff. I found that the wind was north-east, and must have driven me far from the coast from which I had embarked. I endeavoured to change my course, but quickly found that, if I again made the attempt, the boat would be instantly filled with water. Thus situated, my only resource was to drive before the wind. I confess that I felt a few sensations of terror. I had no compass with me, and was so slenderly acquainted with the geography of this part of the world, that the sun was of little benefit to me. I might be driven into the wide Atlantic, and feel all the tortures of starvation, or be swallowed up in the immeasurable waters that roared and buffeted around me. I had already been out many hours, and felt the torment of a burning thirst, a prelude to my other sufferings. I looked on the heavens, which were covered by clouds that flew the wind, only to be replaced by others: I looked upon the sea, it was to be my grave. "Fiend," I exclaimed, "your task is already fulfilled!" I thought of Elizabeth, of my father, and of Clerval; all left behind, on whom the monster might satisfy his sanguinary and merciless passions. This idea plunged me into a reverie, so despairing and frightful, that even now, when the scene is on the point of closing before me for ever, I shudder to reflect on it.

Some hours passed thus; but by degrees, as the sun declined towards the horizon, the wind died away into a gentle breeze, and the sea became free from breakers. But these gave place to a heavy swell: I felt sick, and hardly able to hold the rudder, when suddenly I saw a line of high land towards the south.

Almost spent, as I was, by fatigue, and the dreadful suspense I endured for several hours, this sudden certainty of life rushed like a flood of warm joy to my heart, and tears gushed from my eyes.

How mutable are our feelings, and how strange is that clinging love we have of life even in the excess of misery! I constructed another sail with a part of my dress, and eagerly steered my course towards the land. It had a wild and rocky appearance; but, as I approached nearer, I easily perceived the traces of cultivation. I saw vessels near the shore, and found myself suddenly transported back to the neighbourhood of civilised man. I carefully traced the windings of the land, and hailed a steeple which I at length saw issuing from behind a small promontory. As I was in a state of extreme debility, I resolved to sail directly towards the town, as a place where I could most easily procure nourishment. Fortunately, I had money with me. As I turned the promontory, I perceived a small, neat town and a good harbour, which I entered, my heart bounding with joy at my unexpected escape.

As I was occupied in fixing the boat and arranging the sails, several people crowded towards the spot. They seemed much surprised at my appearance; but, instead of offering me any assistance, whispered together with gestures that at any other time might have produced in me a slight sensation of alarm. As it was, I merely remarked that they spoke English; and I therefore addressed them in that language: "My good friends," said I, "will you be so kind as to tell me the name of this town, and inform me where I am?"

"You will know that soon enough," replied a man with a hoarse voice. "May be you are come to a place that will not prove much to your taste; but you will not be consulted as to your quarters, I promise you."

I was exceedingly surprised on receiving so rude an answer from a stranger; and I was also disconcerted on perceiving the frowning and angry countenances of his companions. "Why do you answer me so roughly?" I replied; "surely it is not the custom of Englishmen to receive strangers so inhospitably."

"I do not know," said the man, "what the custom of the English may be; but it is the custom of the Irish to hate villains."

While this strange dialogue continued, I perceived the crowd rapidly increase. Their faces expressed a mixture of curiosity and anger, which annoyed, and in some degree alarmed me. I enquired the way to the inn; but no one replied. I then moved forward, and a murmuring sound arose from the crowd as they followed and surrounded me; when an ill-looking man approached, tapped me on the shoulder, and said, "Come, sir, you must follow me to Mr. Kirwin's, to give an account of yourself."

"Who is Mr. Kirwin? Why am I to give an account of myself? Is not this a free country?"

"Ay, sir, free enough for honest folks. Mr. Kirwin is a magistrate; and you are to give an account of the death of a gentleman who was found murdered here last night."

This answer startled me; but I presently recovered myself. I was innocent; that could easily be proved: accordingly I followed my conductor in silence, and was led to one of the best houses in the town. I was ready to sink from fatigue and hunger; but, being surrounded by a crowd, I thought it politic to rouse all my strength, that no physical debility might be construed into apprehension or conscious guilt. Little did I then expect the calamity that was in a few moments to overwhelm me, and extinguish in horror and despair all fear of ignominy or death.

I must pause here; for it requires all my fortitude to recall the memory of the frightful events which I am about to relate, in proper detail, to my recollection.

CHAPTER XXI

I was soon introduced into the presence of the magistrate, an old benevolent man, with calm and mild manners. He looked upon me, however, with some degree of severity: and then, turning towards my conductors, he asked who appeared as witnesses on this occasion.

About half a dozen men came forward; and, one being selected by the magistrate, he deposed, that he had been out fishing the night before with his son and brother-in-law, Daniel Nugent, when, about ten o'clock, they observed a strong northerly blast rising, and they accordingly put in for port. It was a very dark night, as the moon had not yet risen; they did not land at the harbour, but, as they had been accustomed, at a creek about two miles below. He walked on first, carrying a part of the fishing tackle, and his companions followed him at some distance. As he was proceeding along the sands, he struck his foot against something, and fell at his length on the ground. His companions came up to assist him; and, by the light of their lantern, they found that he had fallen on the body of a man, who was to all appearance dead. Their first supposition was, that it was the corpse of some person who had been drowned, and was thrown on shore by the waves; but, on examination, they found that the clothes were not wet, and even that the body was not then cold. They instantly carried it to the cottage of an old woman near the spot, and endeavoured, but in vain, to restore it to life. It appeared to be a handsome young man, about five and twenty years of age. He had apparently been strangled; for there was no sign of any violence, except the black mark of fingers on his neck.

The first part of this deposition did not in the least interest me; but when the mark of the fingers was mentioned, I remembered the murder of my brother, and felt myself extremely agitated; my limbs trembled, and a mist came over my eyes, which obliged me to lean on a chair for support. The magistrate observed me with a keen eye, and of course drew an unfavourable augury from my manner.

The son confirmed his father's account: but when Daniel Nugent was called, he swore positively that, just before the fall of his companion, he saw a boat, with a single man in it, at a short distance from the shore; and, as far as he could judge by the light of a few stars, it was the same boat in which I had just landed.

A woman deposed, that she lived near the beach, and was standing at the door of her cottage, waiting for the return of the fishermen, about an hour before she heard of the discovery of the body, when she saw a boat, with only one man in it, push off from that part of the shore where the corpse was afterwards found.

Another woman confirmed the account of the fishermen having brought the body into her house; it was not cold. They put it into a bed, and rubbed it; and Daniel went to the town for an apothecary, but life was quite gone.

Several other men were examined concerning my landing; and they agreed, that, with the strong north wind that had arisen during the night, it was very probable that I had beaten about for many hours, and had been obliged to return nearly to the same spot from which I had departed. Besides, they observed that it appeared that I had brought the body from another place, and it was likely, that as I did not appear to know the shore, I might have put into the harbour ignorant of the distance of the town of * * * from the place where I had deposited the corpse.

Mr. Kirwin, on hearing this evidence, desired that I should be taken into the room where the body lay for interment, that it might be observed what effect the sight of it would produce upon me. This idea was probably suggested by the extreme agitation I had exhibited when the mode of the murder had been described. I was accordingly conducted, by the magistrate and several other persons, to the inn. I could not help being struck by the strange coincidences that had taken place during this eventful night; but, knowing that I had been conversing with several persons in the island I had inhabited about the time that the body had been found, I was perfectly tranquil as to the consequences of the affair.

I entered the room where the corpse lay, and was led up to the coffin. How can I describe my sensations on beholding it? I feel yet parched with horror, nor can I reflect on that terrible moment without shuddering and agony. The examination, the presence of the magistrate and witnesses, passed like a dream from my memory, when I saw the lifeless form of Henry Clerval stretched before me. I gasped for breath; and, throwing myself on the body, I exclaimed, "Have my murderous machinations deprived you also, my dearest Henry, of life? Two I have already destroyed; other victims await their destiny: but you, Clerval, my friend, my benefactor—"

The human frame could no longer support the agonies that I endured, and I was carried out of the room in strong convulsions.

A fever succeeded to this. I lay for two months on the point of death: my ravings, as I afterwards heard, were frightful; I called myself the murderer of William, of Justine, and of Clerval. Sometimes I entreated my attendants to assist me in the destruction of the fiend by whom I was tormented; and at others, I felt the fingers of the monster already grasping my neck, and screamed aloud with agony and terror. Fortunately, as I spoke my native language, Mr. Kirwin alone understood me; but my gestures and bitter cries were sufficient to affright the other witnesses.

Why did I not die? More miserable than man ever was before, why did I not sink into forgetfulness and rest? Death snatches away many blooming children, the only hopes of their doting parents: how many brides and youthful lovers have been one day in the bloom of health and hope, and the next a prey for worms and the decay of the tomb! Of what materials was I made, that I could thus resist so many shocks, which, like the turning of the wheel, continually renewed the torture?

But I was doomed to live; and, in two months, found myself as awaking from a dream, in a prison, stretched on a wretched bed, surrounded by gaolers, turnkeys, bolts, and all the miserable apparatus of a dungeon. It was morning, I remember, when I thus awoke to understanding: I had forgotten the particulars of what had happened, and only felt as if some great misfortune had suddenly overwhelmed me; but when I looked around, and saw the barred windows, and the squalidness of the room in which I was, all flashed across my memory, and I groaned bitterly.

This sound disturbed an old woman who was sleeping in a chair beside me. She was a hired nurse, the wife of one of the turnkeys, and her countenance expressed all those bad qualities which often characterise that class. The lines of her face were hard and rude, like that of persons accustomed to see without sympathising in sights of misery. Her tone expressed her entire indifference; she addressed me in English, and the voice struck me as one that I had heard during my sufferings: —

"Are you better now, sir?" said she.

I replied in the same language, with a feeble voice, "I believe I am; but if it be all true, if indeed I did not dream, I am sorry that I am still alive to feel this misery and horror."

"For that matter," replied the old woman, "if you mean about the gentleman you murdered, I believe that it were better for you if you were dead, for I fancy it will go hard with you! However, that's none of my business; I am sent to nurse you, and get you well; I do my duty with a safe conscience; it were well if every body did the same."

I turned with loathing from the woman who could utter so unfeeling a speech to a person just saved, on the very edge of death; but I felt languid, and unable to reflect on all that had passed. The whole series of my life appeared to me as a dream; I sometimes doubted if indeed it were all true, for it never presented itself to my mind with the force of reality.

As the images that floated before me became more distinct, I grew feverish; a darkness pressed around me: no one was near me who soothed me with the gentle voice of love; no dear hand supported me. The physician came and prescribed medicines, and the old woman prepared them for me; but utter carelessness was visible in the first, and the expression of brutality was strongly marked in the visage of the second. Who could be interested in the fate of a murderer, but the hangman who would gain his fee?

These were my first reflections; but I soon learned that Mr. Kirwin had shown me extreme kindness. He had caused the best room in the prison to be prepared for me (wretched indeed was the best); and it was he who had provided a physician and a nurse. It is true, he seldom came to see me; for, although he ardently desired to relieve the sufferings of every human creature, he did not wish to be present at the agonies and miserable ravings of a murderer. He came, therefore, sometimes, to see that I was not neglected; but his visits were short, and with long intervals.

One day, while I was gradually recovering, I was seated in a chair, my eyes half open, and my cheeks livid like those in death. I was overcome by gloom and misery, and often reflected I had better seek death than desire to remain in a world which to me was replete with wretchedness. At one time I considered whether

I should not declare myself guilty, and suffer the penalty of the law, less innocent than poor Justine had been. Such were my thoughts, when the door of my apartment was opened, and Mr. Kirwin entered. His countenance expressed sympathy and compassion; he drew a chair close to mine, and addressed me in French —

"I fear that this place is very shocking to you; can I do any thing to make you more comfortable?"

"I thank you; but all that you mention is nothing to me: on the whole earth there is no comfort which I am capable of receiving."

"I know that the sympathy of a stranger can be but of little relief to one borne down as you are by so strange a misfortune. But you will, I hope, soon quit this melancholy abode; for, doubtless, evidence can easily be brought to free you from the criminal charge."

"That is my least concern: I am, by a course of strange events, become the most miserable of mortals. Persecuted and tortured as I am and have been, can death be any evil to me?"

"Nothing indeed could be more unfortunate and agonising than the strange chances that have lately occurred. You were thrown, by some surprising accident, on this shore, renowned for its hospitality; seized immediately, and charged with murder. The first sight that was presented to your eyes was the body of your friend, murdered in so unaccountable a manner, and placed, as it were, by some fiend across your path."

As Mr. Kirwin said this, notwithstanding the agitation I endured on this retrospect of my sufferings, I also felt considerable surprise at the knowledge he seemed to possess concerning me. I suppose some astonishment was exhibited in my countenance; for Mr. Kirwin hastened to say —

"Immediately upon your being taken ill, all the papers that were on your person were brought to me, and I examined them that I might discover some trace by which I could send to your relations an account of your misfortune and illness. I found several letters, and, among others, one which I discovered from its commencement to be from your father. I instantly wrote to Geneva: nearly two months have elapsed since the departure of my letter. — But you are ill; even now you tremble: you are unfit for agitation of any kind."

"This suspense is a thousand times worse than the most horrible event: tell me what new scene of death has been acted, and whose murder I am now to lament?"

"Your family is perfectly well," said Mr. Kirwin, with gentleness; "and some one, a friend, is come to visit you."

I know not by what chain of thought the idea presented itself, but it instantly darted into my mind that the murderer had come to mock at my misery, and taunt me with the death of Clerval, as a new incitement for me to comply with his hellish desires. I put my hand before my eyes, and cried out in agony —

"Oh! take him away! I cannot see him; for God's sake, do not let him enter!"

Mr. Kirwin regarded me with a troubled countenance. He could not help regarding my exclamation as a presumption of my guilt, and said, in rather a severe tone —

"I should have thought, young man, that the presence of your father would have been welcome, instead of inspiring such violent repugnance."

"My father!" cried I, while every feature and every muscle was relaxed from anguish to pleasure: "is my father indeed come? How kind, how very kind! But where is he, why does he not hasten to me?"

My change of manner surprised and pleased the magistrate; perhaps he thought that my former exclamation was a momentary return of delirium, and now he instantly resumed his former benevolence. He rose, and quitted the room with my nurse, and in a moment my father entered it.

Nothing, at this moment, could have given me greater pleasure than the arrival of my father. I stretched out my hand to him, and cried —

"Are you then safe — and Elizabeth — and Ernest?"

My father calmed me with assurances of their welfare, and endeavoured, by dwelling on these subjects so interesting to my heart, to raise my desponding spirits; but he soon felt that a prison cannot be the abode of cheerfulness. "What a place is this that you inhabit, my son!" said he, looking mournfully at the barred windows, and wretched appearance of the room. "You travelled to seek happiness, but a fatality seems to pursue you. And poor Clerval— "

The name of my unfortunate and murdered friend was an agitation too great to be endured in my weak state; I shed tears.

"Alas! yes, my father," replied I; "some destiny of the most horrible kind hangs over me, and I must live to fulfil it, or surely I should have died on the coffin of Henry."

We were not allowed to converse for any length of time, for the precarious state of my health rendered every precaution necessary that could ensure tranquillity. Mr. Kirwin came in, and insisted that my strength should not be exhausted by too much exertion. But the appearance of my father was to me like that of my good angel, and I gradually recovered my health.

As my sickness quitted me, I was absorbed by a gloomy and black melancholy, that nothing could dissipate. The image of Clerval was for ever before me, ghastly and murdered. More than once the agitation into which these reflections threw me made my friends dread a dangerous relapse. Alas! why did they preserve so miserable and detested a life? It was surely that I might fulfil my destiny, which is now drawing to a close. Soon, oh! very soon, will death extinguish these throbbings, and relieve me from the mighty weight of anguish that bears me to the dust; and, in executing the award of justice, I shall also sink to rest. Then the appearance of death was distant, although the wish was ever present to my thoughts; and I often sat for hours motionless and speechless, wishing for some mighty revolution that might bury me and my destroyer in its ruins.

The season of the assizes approached. I had already been three months in prison; and although I was still weak, and in continual danger of a relapse, I was obliged to travel nearly a hundred miles to the county-town, where the court was held. Mr. Kirwin charged himself with every care of collecting witnesses, and arranging my defence. I was spared the disgrace of appearing publicly as a criminal, as the case was not brought before the court that decides on life and death. The grand jury rejected the bill, on its being proved that I was on the Orkney Islands at the hour the body of my friend was found; and a fortnight after my removal I was liberated from prison.

My father was enraptured on finding me freed from the vexations of a criminal charge, that I was again allowed to breathe the fresh atmosphere, and permitted to return to my native country. I did not participate in these feelings; for to me the walls of a dungeon or a palace were alike hateful. The cup of life was poisoned for ever; and although the sun shone upon me, as upon the happy and gay of heart, I saw around me nothing but a dense and frightful darkness, penetrated by no light but the glimmer of two eyes that glared upon me. Sometimes they were the expressive eyes of Henry, languishing in death, the dark orbs nearly covered by the lids, and the long black lashes that fringed them; sometimes it was the watery, clouded eyes of the monster, as I first saw them in my chamber at Ingolstadt.

My father tried to awaken in me the feelings of affection. He talked of Geneva, which I should soon visit—of Elizabeth and Ernest; but these words only drew deep groans from me. Sometimes, indeed, I felt a wish for happiness; and thought, with melancholy delight, of my beloved cousin; or longed, with a devouring *maladie du pays*,[33] to see once more the blue lake and rapid Rhone, that had been so dear to

[33] French for "homesickness."—Eds.

me in early childhood: but my general state of feeling was a torpor, in which a prison was as welcome a residence as the divinest scene in nature; and these fits were seldom interrupted but by paroxysms of anguish and despair. At these moments I often endeavoured to put an end to the existence I loathed; and it required unceasing attendance and vigilance to restrain me from committing some dreadful act of violence.

Yet one duty remained to me, the recollection of which finally triumphed over my selfish despair. It was necessary that I should return without delay to Geneva, there to watch over the lives of those I so fondly loved; and to lie in wait for the murderer, that if any chance led me to the place of his concealment, or if he dared again to blast me by his presence, I might, with unfailing aim, put an end to the existence of the monstrous image which I had endued with the mockery of a soul still more monstrous. My father still desired to delay our departure, fearful that I could not sustain the fatigues of a journey: for I was a shattered wreck,— the shadow of a human being. My strength was gone. I was a mere skeleton; and fever night and day preyed upon my wasted frame.

Still, as I urged our leaving Ireland with such inquietude and impatience, my father thought it best to yield. We took our passage on board a vessel bound for Havre-de-Grace, and sailed with a fair wind from the Irish shores. It was midnight. I lay on the deck, looking at the stars, and listening to the dashing of the waves. I hailed the darkness that shut Ireland from my sight; and my pulse beat with a feverish joy when I reflected that I should soon see Geneva. The past appeared to me in the light of a frightful dream; yet the vessel in which I was, the wind that blew me from the detested shore of Ireland, and the sea which surrounded me, told me too forcibly that I was deceived by no vision, and that Clerval, my friend and dearest companion, had fallen a victim to me and the monster of my creation. I repassed, in my memory, my whole life; my quiet happiness while residing with my family in Geneva, the death of my mother, and my departure for Ingolstadt. I remembered, shuddering, the mad enthusiasm that hurried me on to the creation of my hideous enemy, and I called to mind the night in which he first lived. I was unable to pursue the train of thought; a thousand feelings pressed upon me, and I wept bitterly.

Ever since my recovery from the fever, I had been in the custom of taking every night a small quantity of laudanum; for it was by means of this drug only that I was enabled to gain the rest necessary for the preservation of life. Oppressed by the recollection of my various misfortunes, I now swallowed double my usual quantity, and soon slept profoundly. But sleep did not afford me respite from thought and misery; my dreams presented a thousand objects that scared me. Towards morning I was possessed by a kind of night-mare; I felt the fiend's grasp in my neck, and could not free myself from it; groans and cries rung in my ears. My father, who was watching over me, perceiving my restlessness, awoke me; the dashing waves were around: the cloudy sky above; the fiend was not here: a sense of security, a feeling that a truce was established between the present hour and the irresistible, disastrous future, imparted to me a kind of calm forgetfulness, of which the human mind is by its structure peculiarly susceptible.

CHAPTER XXII

The voyage came to an end. We landed, and proceeded to Paris. I soon found that I had overtaxed my strength, and that I must repose before I could continue my journey. My father's care and attentions were indefatigable; but he did not know the origin of my sufferings, and sought erroneous methods to remedy the incurable ill. He wished me to seek amusement in society. I abhorred the face of man. Oh, not abhorred! they were my brethren, my fellow-beings, and I felt attracted even to the most repulsive among them, as to creatures of an angelic nature and celestial mechanism. But I felt that I had no right to share their intercourse. I had unchained an enemy among them, whose joy it was to shed their blood, and to revel in their groans. How they would, each and all, abhor me, and hunt me from the world, did they know my unhallowed acts, and the crimes which had their source in me!

My father yielded at length to my desire to avoid society, and strove by various arguments to banish my despair. Sometimes he thought that I felt deeply the degradation of being obliged to answer a charge of murder, and he endeavoured to prove to me the futility of pride.

"Alas! my father," said I, "how little do you know me. Human beings, their feelings and passions, would indeed be degraded if such a wretch as I felt pride. Justine, poor unhappy Justine, was as innocent as I, and she suffered the same charge; she died for it; and I am the cause of this — I murdered her. William, Justine, and Henry — they all died by my hands."

My father had often, during my imprisonment, heard me make the same assertion; when I thus accused myself, he sometimes seemed to desire an explanation, and at others he appeared to consider it as the offspring of delirium, and that, during my illness, some idea of this kind had presented itself to my imagination, the remembrance of which I preserved in my convalescence. I avoided explanation, and maintained a continual silence concerning the wretch I had created. I had a persuasion that I should be supposed mad; and this in itself would for ever have chained my tongue. But, besides, I could not bring myself to disclose a secret which would fill my hearer with consternation, and make fear and unnatural horror the inmates of his breast. I checked, therefore, my impatient thirst for sympathy, and was silent when I would have given the world to have confided the fatal secret. Yet still words like those I have recorded, would burst uncontrollably from me. I could offer no explanation of them; but their truth in part relieved the burden of my mysterious woe.

Upon this occasion my father said, with an expression of unbounded wonder, "My dearest Victor, what infatuation is this? My dear son, I entreat you never to make such an assertion again."

"I am not mad," I cried energetically; "the sun and the heavens, who have viewed my operations, can bear witness of my truth. I am the assassin of those most innocent victims; they died by my machinations. A thousand times would I have shed my own blood, drop by drop, to have saved their lives; but I could not, my father, indeed I could not sacrifice the whole human race."

The conclusion of this speech convinced my father that my ideas were deranged, and he instantly changed the subject of our conversation, and endeavoured to alter the course of my thoughts. He wished as much as possible to obliterate the memory of the scenes that had taken place in Ireland, and never alluded to them, or suffered me to speak of my misfortunes.

As time passed away I became more calm: misery had her dwelling in my heart, but I no longer talked in the same incoherent manner of my own crimes; sufficient for me was the consciousness of them. By the utmost self-violence, I curbed the imperious voice of wretchedness, which sometimes desired to declare itself to the whole world; and my manners were calmer and more composed than they had ever been since my journey to the sea of ice.

A few days before we left Paris on our way to Switzerland, I received the following letter from Elizabeth: —

"My dear Friend,

"It gave me the greatest pleasure to receive a letter from my uncle dated at Paris; you are no longer at a formidable distance, and I may hope to see you in less than a fortnight. My poor cousin, how much you must have suffered! I expect to see you looking even more ill than when you quitted Geneva. This winter has been passed most miserably, tortured as I have been by anxious suspense; yet I hope to see peace in your countenance, and to find that your heart is not totally void of comfort and tranquillity.

"Yet I fear that the same feelings now exist that made you so miserable a year ago, even perhaps augmented by time. I would not disturb you at this period, when so many misfortunes weigh upon you; but a conversation that I had with my uncle previous to his departure renders some explanation necessary before we meet.

"Explanation! you may possibly say; what can Elizabeth have to explain? If you really say this, my questions are answered, and all my doubts satisfied. But you are distant from me, and it is possible that you may dread, and yet be pleased with this explanation; and, in a probability of this being the case, I dare not any longer postpone writing what, during your absence, I have often wished to express to you, but have never had the courage to begin.

"You well know, Victor, that our union had been the favourite plan of your parents ever since our infancy. We were told this when young, and taught to look forward to it as an event that would certainly take place. We were affectionate playfellows during childhood, and, I believe, dear and valued friends to one another as we grew older. But as brother and sister often entertain a lively affection towards each other, without desiring a more intimate union, may not such also be our case? Tell me, dearest Victor. Answer me, I conjure you, by our mutual happiness, with simple truth — Do you not love another?

"You have travelled; you have spent several years of your life at Ingolstadt; and I confess to you, my friend, that when I saw you last autumn so unhappy, flying to solitude, from the society of every creature, I could not help supposing that you might regret our connection, and believe yourself bound in honour to fulfil the wishes of your parents, although they opposed themselves to your inclinations. But this is false reasoning. I confess to you, my friend, that I love you, and that in my airy dreams of futurity you have been my constant friend and companion. But it is your happiness I desire as well as my own, when I declare to you, that our marriage would render me eternally miserable, unless it were the dictate of your own free choice. Even now I weep to think, that, borne down as you are by the cruellest misfortunes, you may stifle, by the word *honour*, all hope of that love and happiness which would alone restore you to yourself. I, who have so disinterested an affection for you, may increase your miseries tenfold, by being an obstacle to your wishes. Ah! Victor, be assured that your cousin and playmate has too sincere a love for you not to be made miserable by this supposition. Be happy, my friend; and if you obey me in this one request, remain satisfied that nothing on earth will have the power to interrupt my tranquillity.

"Do not let this letter disturb you; do not answer tomorrow, or the next day, or even until you come, if it will give you pain. My uncle will send me news of your health; and if I see but one smile on your lips when we meet, occasioned by this or any other exertion of mine, I shall need no other happiness.

"ELIZABETH LAVENZA.

"Geneva, May 18th, 17 —."

This letter revived in my memory what I had before forgotten, the threat of the fiend — "*I will be with you on your wedding-night!*" Such was my sentence, and on that night would the daemon employ every art to destroy me, and tear me from the glimpse of happiness which promised partly to console my sufferings. On that night he had determined to consummate his crimes by my death. Well, be it so; a deadly struggle would then assuredly take place, in which if he were victorious I should be at peace, and his power over me be at an end. If he were vanquished, I should be a free man. Alas! what freedom? such as the peasant enjoys when his family have been massacred before his eyes, his cottage burnt, his lands laid waste, and he is turned adrift, homeless, penniless, and alone, but free. Such would be my liberty, except that in my Elizabeth I possessed a treasure; alas! balanced by those horrors of remorse and guilt, which would pursue me until death.

Sweet and beloved Elizabeth! I read and re-read her letter, and some softened feelings stole into my heart, and dared to whisper paradisiacal dreams of love and joy; but the apple was already eaten, and the angel's arm bared to drive me from all hope. Yet I would die to make her happy. If the monster executed his threat, death was inevitable; yet, again, I considered whether my marriage would hasten my fate. My destruction might indeed arrive a few months sooner; but if my torturer should suspect that I postponed it, influenced by his menaces, he would surely find other, and perhaps more dreadful means of revenge. He had vowed *to be with me on my wedding-night*, yet he did not consider that threat as binding him to peace in the mean time; for, as if to show me that he was not yet satiated with blood, he had murdered Clerval immediately after the enunciation of his threats. I resolved, therefore, that if my immediate union with my cousin would conduce either to hers or my father's happiness, my adversary's designs against my life should not retard it a single hour.

In this state of mind I wrote to Elizabeth. My letter was calm and affectionate. "I fear, my beloved girl," I said, "little happiness remains for us on earth; yet all that I may one day enjoy is centred in you. Chase away your idle fears; to you alone do I consecrate my life, and my endeavours for contentment. I have one secret, Elizabeth, a dreadful one; when revealed to you, it will chill your frame with horror, and then, far from being surprised at my misery, you will only wonder that I survive what I have endured. I will confide this tale of misery and terror to you the day after our marriage shall take place; for, my sweet cousin, there must be perfect confidence between us. But until then, I conjure you, do not mention or allude to it. This I most earnestly entreat, and I know you will comply."

In about a week after the arrival of Elizabeth's letter, we returned to Geneva. The sweet girl welcomed me with warm affection; yet tears were in her eyes, as she beheld my emaciated frame and feverish cheeks. I saw a change in her also. She was thinner, and had lost much of that heavenly vivacity that had before charmed me; but her gentleness, and soft looks of compassion, made her a more fit companion for one blasted and miserable as I was.

The tranquillity which I now enjoyed did not endure. Memory brought madness with it; and when I thought of what had passed, a real insanity possessed me; sometimes I was furious, and burnt with rage, sometimes low and despondent. I neither spoke, nor looked at any one, but sat motionless, bewildered by the multitude of miseries that overcame me.

Elizabeth alone had the power to draw me from these fits; her gentle voice would soothe me when transported by passion, and inspire me with human feelings when sunk in torpor. She wept with me, and for me. When reason returned, she would remonstrate, and endeavour to inspire me with resignation. Ah! it is well for the unfortunate to be resigned, but for the guilty there is no peace. The agonies of remorse poison the luxury there is otherwise sometimes found in indulging the excess of grief.

Soon after my arrival, my father spoke of my immediate marriage with Elizabeth. I remained silent.

"Have you, then, some other attachment?"

"None on earth. I love Elizabeth, and look forward to our union with delight. Let the day therefore be fixed; and on it I will consecrate myself, in life or death, to the happiness of my cousin."

"My dear Victor, do not speak thus. Heavy misfortunes have befallen us; but let us only cling closer to what remains, and transfer our love for those whom we have lost, to those who yet live. Our circle will be small, but bound close by the ties of affection and mutual misfortune. And when time shall have softened your despair, new and dear objects of care will be born to replace those of whom we have been so cruelly deprived."

Such were the lessons of my father. But to me the remembrance of the threat returned: nor can you wonder, that, omnipotent as the fiend had yet been in his deeds of blood, I should almost regard him as invincible; and that when he had pronounced the words, "I shall be with you on your wedding-night," I should regard the threatened fate as unavoidable. But death was no evil to me, if the loss of Elizabeth were balanced with it; and I therefore, with a contented and even cheerful countenance, agreed with my father, that if my cousin would consent, the ceremony should take place in ten days, and thus put, as I imagined, the seal to my fate.

Great God! if for one instant I had thought what might be the hellish intention of my fiendish adversary, I would rather have banished myself for ever from my native country, and wandered a friendless outcast over the earth, than have consented to this miserable marriage. But, as if possessed of magic powers, the monster had blinded me to his real intentions; and when I thought that I had prepared only my own death, I hastened that of a far dearer victim.

As the period fixed for our marriage drew nearer, whether from cowardice or a prophetic feeling, I felt my heart sink within me. But I concealed my feelings by an appearance of hilarity, that brought smiles and joy to the countenance of my father, but hardly deceived the ever-watchful and nicer eye of Elizabeth. She looked forward to our union with placid contentment, not unmingled with a little fear, which past misfortunes had impressed, that what now appeared certain and tangible happiness, might soon dissipate into an airy dream, and leave no trace but deep and everlasting regret.

Preparations were made for the event; congratulatory visits were received; and all wore a smiling appearance. I shut up, as well as I could, in my own heart the anxiety that preyed there, and entered with seeming earnestness into the plans of my father, although they might only serve as the decorations of my tragedy. Through my father's exertions, a part of the inheritance of Elizabeth had been restored to her by the Austrian government. A small possession on the shores of Como[34] belonged to her. It was agreed that, immediately after our union, we should proceed to Villa Lavenza, and spend our first days of happiness beside the beautiful lake near which it stood.

In the mean time I took every precaution to defend my person, in case the fiend should openly attack me. I carried pistols and a dagger constantly about me, and was ever on the watch to prevent artifice; and by these means gained a greater degree of tranquillity. Indeed, as the period approached, the threat appeared more as a delusion, not to be regarded as worthy to disturb my peace, while the happiness I hoped for in my marriage wore a greater appearance of certainty, as the day fixed for its solemnisation drew nearer, and I heard it continually spoken of as an occurrence which no accident could possibly prevent.

Elizabeth seemed happy; my tranquil demeanour contributed greatly to calm her mind. But on the day that was to fulfil my wishes and my destiny, she was melancholy, and a presentiment of evil pervaded her; and perhaps also she thought of the dreadful secret which I had promised to reveal to her on the following day. My father was in the mean time

[34] A large lake in Northern Italy, well known as a tourist attraction.—Eds.

overjoyed, and, in the bustle of preparation, only recognised in the melancholy of his niece the diffidence of a bride.

After the ceremony was performed, a large party assembled at my father's; but it was agreed that Elizabeth and I should commence our journey by water, sleeping that night at Evian, and continuing our voyage on the following day. The day was fair, the wind favourable, all smiled on our nuptial embarkation.

Those were the last moments of my life during which I enjoyed the feeling of happiness. We passed rapidly along: the sun was hot, but we were sheltered from its rays by a kind of canopy, while we enjoyed the beauty of the scene, sometimes on one side of the lake, where we saw Mont Salêve, the pleasant banks of Montalègre, and at a distance, surmounting all, the beautiful Mont Blanc, and the assemblage of snowy mountains that in vain endeavour to emulate her; sometimes coasting the opposite banks, we saw the mighty Jura opposing its dark side to the ambition that would quit its native country, and an almost insurmountable barrier to the invader who should wish to enslave it.

I took the hand of Elizabeth: "You are sorrowful, my love. Ah! if you knew what I have suffered, and what I may yet endure, you would endeavour to let me taste the quiet and freedom from despair, that this one day at least permits me to enjoy."

"Be happy, my dear Victor," replied Elizabeth; "there is, I hope, nothing to distress you; and be assured that if a lively joy is not painted in my face, my heart is contented. Something whispers to me not to depend too much on the prospect that is opened before us; but I will not listen to such a sinister voice. Observe how fast we move along, and how the clouds, which sometimes obscure and sometimes rise above the dome of Mont Blanc, render this scene of beauty still more interesting. Look also at the innumerable fish that are swimming in the clear waters, where we can distinguish every pebble that lies at the bottom. What a divine day! how happy and serene all nature appears!"

Thus Elizabeth endeavoured to divert her thoughts and mine from all reflection upon melancholy subjects. But her temper was fluctuating; joy for a few instants shone in her eyes, but it continually gave place to distraction and reverie.

The sun sunk lower in the heavens; we passed the river Drance, and observed its path through the chasms of the higher, and the glens of the lower hills. The Alps here come closer to the lake, and we approached the amphitheatre of mountains which forms its eastern boundary. The spire of Evian shone under the woods that surrounded it, and the range of mountain above mountain by which it was overhung.

The wind, which had hitherto carried us along with amazing rapidity, sunk at sunset to a light breeze; the soft air just ruffled the water, and caused a pleasant motion among the trees as we approached the shore, from which it wafted the most delightful scent of flowers and hay. The sun sunk beneath the horizon as we landed; and as I touched the shore, I felt those cares and fears revive, which soon were to clasp me, and cling to me for ever.

CHAPTER XXIII

It was eight o'clock when we landed; we walked for a short time on the shore, enjoying the transitory light, and then retired to the inn, and contemplated the lovely scene of waters, woods, and mountains, obscured in darkness, yet still displaying their black outlines.

The wind, which had fallen in the south, now rose with great violence in the west. The moon had reached her summit in the heavens, and was beginning to descend; the clouds swept across it swifter than the flight of the vulture, and dimmed her rays, while the lake reflected the scene of the busy heavens, rendered still busier by the restless waves that were beginning to rise. Suddenly a heavy storm of rain descended.

I had been calm during the day; but so soon as night obscured the shapes of objects, a thousand fears arose in my mind. I was anxious and watchful, while my right hand grasped a pistol which was hidden in my bosom; every sound terrified me; but I resolved that I would sell my life dearly, and not shrink from the conflict until my own life, or that of my adversary, was extinguished.

Elizabeth observed my agitation for some time in timid and fearful silence; but there was something in my glance which communicated terror to her, and trembling she asked, "What is it that agitates you, my dear Victor? What is it you fear?"

"Oh! peace, peace, my love," replied I; "this night, and all will be safe: but this night is dreadful, very dreadful."

I passed an hour in this state of mind, when suddenly I reflected how fearful the combat which I momentarily expected would be to my wife, and I earnestly entreated her to retire, resolving not to join her until I had obtained some knowledge as to the situation of my enemy.

She left me, and I continued some time walking up and down the passages of the house, and inspecting every corner that might afford a retreat to my adversary. But I discovered no trace of him, and was beginning to conjecture that some fortunate chance had intervened to prevent the execution of his menaces; when suddenly I heard a shrill and dreadful scream. It came from the room into which Elizabeth had retired. As I heard it, the whole truth rushed into my mind, my arms dropped, the motion of every muscle and fibre was suspended; I could feel the blood trickling in my veins, and tingling in the extremities of my limbs. This state lasted but for an instant; the scream was repeated, and I rushed into the room.

Great God! why did I not then expire! Why am I here to relate the destruction of the best hope, and the purest creature of earth? She was there, lifeless and inanimate, thrown across the bed, her head hanging down, and her pale and distorted features half covered by her hair. Every where I turn I see the same figure—her bloodless arms and relaxed form flung by the murderer on its bridal bier. Could I behold this, and live? Alas! life is obstinate, and clings closest where it is most hated. For a moment only did I lose recollection; I fell senseless on the ground.

When I recovered, I found myself surrounded by the people of the inn; their countenances expressed a breathless terror: but the horror of others appeared only as a mockery, a shadow of the feelings that oppressed me. I escaped from them to the room where lay the body of Elizabeth, my love, my wife, so lately living, so dear, so worthy. She had been moved from the posture in which I had first beheld her; and now, as she lay, her head upon her arm, and a handkerchief thrown across her face and neck, I might have supposed her asleep. I rushed towards her, and embraced her with ardour; but the deadly languor and coldness of the limbs told me, that what I now held in my arms had ceased to be the Elizabeth whom I had loved and cherished. The murderous mark of the fiend's grasp was on her neck, and the breath had ceased to issue from her lips.

While I still hung over her in the agony of despair, I happened to look up. The windows of the room had before been darkened, and I felt a kind of panic on seeing the pale yellow light of the moon illuminate the chamber. The shutters had been thrown back; and, with a sensation of horror not to be described, I saw at the open window a figure the most hideous and abhorred. A grin was on the face of the monster; he seemed to jeer, as with his fiendish finger he pointed towards the corpse of my wife. I rushed towards the window, and drawing a pistol from my bosom, fired; but he eluded me, leaped from his station, and, running with the swiftness of lightning, plunged into the lake.

The report of the pistol brought a crowd into the room. I pointed to the spot where he had

The Nightmare, a painting by Henry Fuseli (1741–1825), was first exhibited in London in 1782. Fuseli was an acquaintance of Mary Shelley's parents, and this painting inspired the scene Victor Frankenstein encounters when he finds Elizabeth murdered. **What aspects of the painting do you see reflected in the narrative style of this passage?**

disappeared, and we followed the track with boats; nets were cast, but in vain. After passing several hours, we returned hopeless, most of my companions believing it to have been a form conjured up by my fancy. After having landed, they proceeded to search the country, parties going in different directions among the woods and vines.

I attempted to accompany them, and proceeded a short distance from the house; but my head whirled round, my steps were like those of a drunken man, I fell at last in a state of utter exhaustion; a film covered my eyes, and my skin was parched with the heat of fever. In this state I was carried back, and placed on a bed, hardly conscious of what had happened; my eyes wandered around the room, as if to seek something that I had lost.

After an interval, I arose, and, as if by instinct, crawled into the room where the corpse of my beloved lay. There were women weeping around — I hung over it, and joined my sad tears to theirs — all this time no distinct idea presented itself to my mind; but my thoughts rambled to various subjects, reflecting confusedly on my misfortunes, and their cause. I was bewildered in a cloud of wonder and horror. The death of William, the execution of Justine, the murder of Clerval, and lastly of my wife; even at that moment I knew not that my only remaining friends were safe from the malignity of the fiend; my father even now might be writhing under his grasp, and Ernest might be dead at his feet. This idea made me shudder, and recalled me to action. I started up, and resolved to return to Geneva with all possible speed.

There were no horses to be procured, and I must return by the lake; but the wind was unfavourable, and the rain fell in torrents. However, it was hardly morning, and I might reasonably hope to arrive by night. I hired men to row, and took an oar myself; for I had always experienced relief from mental torment in bodily exercise. But the overflowing misery I now felt, and the excess of agitation that I endured, rendered me incapable of any exertion. I threw down the oar; and leaning my head upon my hands, gave way to every gloomy idea that arose. If I looked up, I saw the scenes which were familiar to me in my happier time, and which I had contemplated but the day before in the company of her who was now but a shadow and a recollection. Tears streamed from my eyes. The rain had ceased for a moment, and I saw the fish play in the waters as they had done a few hours before; they had then been observed by Elizabeth. Nothing is so painful to the human mind as a great and sudden change. The sun might shine, or the clouds might lower: but nothing could appear to me as it had done the day before. A fiend had snatched from me every hope of future happiness: no creature had ever been so miserable as I was; so frightful an event is single in the history of man.

But why should I dwell upon the incidents that followed this last overwhelming event? Mine has been a tale of horrors; I have reached their *acme*, and what I must now relate can but be tedious to you. Know that, one by one, my friends were snatched away; I was left desolate. My own strength is exhausted; and I must tell, in a few words, what remains of my hideous narration.

I arrived at Geneva. My father and Ernest yet lived; but the former sunk under the tidings that I bore. I see him now, excellent and venerable old man! his eyes wandered in vacancy, for they had lost their charm and their delight—his Elizabeth, his more than daughter, whom he doted on with all that affection which a man feels, who in the decline of life, having few affections, clings more earnestly to those that remain. Cursed, cursed be the fiend that brought misery on his grey hairs, and doomed him to waste in wretchedness! He could not live under the horrors that were accumulated around him; the springs of existence suddenly gave way: he was unable to rise from his bed, and in a few days he died in my arms.

What then became of me? I know not; I lost sensation, and chains and darkness were the only objects that pressed upon me. Sometimes, indeed, I dreamt that I wandered in flowery meadows and pleasant vales with the friends of my youth; but I awoke, and found myself in a dungeon. Melancholy followed, but by degrees I gained a clear conception of my miseries and situation, and was then released from my prison. For they had called me mad; and during many months, as I understood, a solitary cell had been my habitation.

Liberty, however, had been an useless gift to me, had I not, as I awakened to reason, at the same time awakened to revenge. As the memory of past misfortunes pressed upon me, I began to reflect on their cause—the monster whom I had created, the miserable daemon whom I had sent abroad into the world for my destruction. I was possessed by a maddening rage when I thought of him, and desired and ardently prayed that I might have him within my grasp to wreak a great and signal revenge on his cursed head.

Nor did my hate long confine itself to useless wishes; I began to reflect on the best means of securing him; and for this purpose, about a month after my release, I repaired to a criminal judge in the town, and told him that I had an accusation to make; that I knew the destroyer of my family; and that I required him to exert his whole authority for the apprehension of the murderer.

The magistrate listened to me with attention and kindness:—"Be assured, sir," said he, "no pains or exertions on my part shall be spared to discover the villain."

"I thank you," replied I; "listen, therefore, to the deposition that I have to make. It is indeed a tale so strange, that I should fear you would not credit it, were there not something in truth which, however wonderful, forces conviction. The story is too connected to be mistaken for a dream, and I have no motive for falsehood." My manner, as I thus addressed him, was impressive, but calm; I had formed in my own heart a resolution to pursue my destroyer to death; and this purpose quieted my agony, and for an interval reconciled me to life. I now related my history, briefly, but with firmness and precision, marking the dates with accuracy, and never deviating into invective or exclamation.

The magistrate appeared at first perfectly incredulous, but as I continued he became more attentive and interested; I saw him sometimes shudder with horror, at others a lively surprise, unmingled with disbelief, was painted on his countenance.

When I had concluded my narration, I said, "This is the being whom I accuse, and for whose seizure and punishment I call upon you to exert your whole power. It is your duty as a magistrate, and I believe and hope that your feelings as a man will not revolt from the execution of those functions on this occasion."

This address caused a considerable change in the physiognomy of my own auditor. He had heard my story with that half kind of belief that is given to a tale of spirits and supernatural events; but when he was called upon to act officially in consequence, the whole tide of his incredulity returned. He, however, answered mildly, "I would willingly afford you every aid in your pursuit; but the creature of whom you speak appears to have powers which would put all my exertions to defiance. Who can follow an animal which can traverse the sea of ice, and inhabit caves and dens where no man would venture to intrude? Besides, some months have elapsed since the commission of his crimes, and no one can conjecture to what place he has wandered, or what region he may now inhabit."

"I do not doubt that he hovers near the spot which I inhabit; and if he has indeed taken refuge in the Alps, he may be hunted like the chamois, and destroyed as a beast of prey. But I perceive your thoughts: you do not credit my narrative, and do not intend to pursue my enemy with the punishment which is his desert."

As I spoke, rage sparkled in my eyes; the magistrate was intimidated: — "You are mistaken," said he, "I will exert myself; and if it is in my power to seize the monster, be assured that he shall suffer punishment proportionate to his crimes. But I fear, from what you have yourself described to be his properties, that this will prove impracticable; and thus, while every proper measure is pursued, you should make up your mind to disappointment."

"That cannot be; but all that I can say will 650
be of little avail. My revenge is of no moment to you; yet, while I allow it to be a vice, I confess that it is the devouring and only passion of my soul. My rage is unspeakable, when I reflect that the murderer, whom I have turned loose upon society, still exists. You refuse my just demand: I have but one resource; and I devote myself, either in my life or death, to his destruction."

I trembled with excess of agitation as I said this; there was a frenzy in my manner, and something, I doubt not, of that haughty fierceness which the martyrs of old are said to have possessed. But to a Genevan magistrate, whose mind was occupied by far other ideas than those of devotion and heroism, this elevation of mind had much the appearance of madness. He endeavoured to soothe me as a nurse does a child, and reverted to my tale as the effects of delirium.

"Man," I cried, "how ignorant art thou in thy pride of wisdom! Cease; you know not what it is you say."

I broke from the house angry and disturbed, and retired to meditate on some other mode of action.

CHAPTER XXIV

My present situation was one in which all voluntary thought was swallowed up and lost. I was hurried away by fury; revenge alone endowed me with strength and composure; it moulded my feelings, and allowed me to be calculating and calm, at periods when otherwise delirium or death would have been my portion.

My first resolution was to quit Geneva for 655
ever; my country, which, when I was happy and beloved, was dear to me, now, in my adversity, became hateful. I provided myself with a sum of money, together with a few jewels which had belonged to my mother, and departed.

And now my wanderings began, which are to cease but with life. I have traversed a vast portion of the earth, and have endured all the hardships which travellers, in deserts and barbarous countries, are wont to meet. How I have lived I hardly know; many times have I stretched my failing limbs upon the sandy plain, and prayed for death. But revenge kept me alive; I dared not die, and leave my adversary in being.

When I quitted Geneva, my first labour was to gain some clue by which I might trace the steps of my fiendish enemy. But my plan was unsettled; and I wandered many hours round the confines of the town, uncertain what path I should pursue. As night approached, I found myself at the entrance of the cemetery where William, Elizabeth, and my father reposed. I entered it, and approached the tomb which marked their graves. Every thing was silent, except the leaves of the trees, which were gently agitated by the wind; the night was nearly dark; and the scene would have been solemn and affecting even to an uninterested observer. The spirits of the departed seemed to flit around, and to cast a shadow, which was felt but not seen, around the head of the mourner.

The deep grief which this scene had at first excited quickly gave way to rage and despair. They were dead, and I lived; their murderer also lived, and to destroy him I must drag out my weary existence. I knelt on the grass, and kissed the earth, and with quivering lips exclaimed, "By the sacred earth on which I kneel, by the shades that wander near me, by the deep and eternal grief that I feel, I swear; and by thee, O Night, and the spirits that preside over thee, to pursue the daemon, who caused this misery, until he or I shall perish in mortal conflict. For this purpose I will preserve my life: to execute this dear revenge, will I again behold the sun, and tread the green herbage of earth, which otherwise should vanish from my eyes for ever. And I call on you, spirits of the dead; and on you, wandering ministers of vengeance, to aid and conduct me in my work. Let the cursed and hellish monster drink deep of agony; let him feel the despair that now torments me."

I had begun my adjuration with solemnity, and an awe which almost assured me that the shades of my murdered friends heard and approved my devotion; but the furies possessed me as I concluded, and rage choked my utterance.

I was answered through the stillness of night by a loud and fiendish laugh. It rung on my ears long and heavily; the mountains re-echoed it, and I felt as if all hell surrounded me with mockery and laughter. Surely in that moment I should have been possessed by frenzy, and have destroyed my miserable existence, but that my vow was heard, and that I was reserved for vengeance. The laughter died away; when a well-known and abhorred voice, apparently close to my ear, addressed me in an audible whisper—"I am satisfied: miserable wretch! you have determined to live, and I am satisfied."

I darted towards the spot from which the sound proceeded; but the devil eluded my grasp. Suddenly the broad disk of the moon arose, and shone full upon his ghastly and distorted shape, as he fled with more than mortal speed.

I pursued him; and for many months this has been my task. Guided by a slight clue, I followed the windings of the Rhone, but vainly. The blue Mediterranean appeared; and, by a strange chance, I saw the fiend enter by night, and hide himself in a vessel bound for the Black Sea. I took my passage in the same ship; but he escaped, I know not how.

Amidst the wilds of Tartary and Russia, although he still evaded me, I have ever followed in his track. Sometimes the peasants, scared by this horrid apparition, informed me of his path; sometimes he himself, who feared that if I lost all trace of him, I should despair and die, left some mark to guide me. The snows descended on my head, and I saw the print of his huge step on the white plain. To you first entering on life, to whom care is new, and agony unknown, how can you understand what I have felt, and still feel? Cold, want, and fatigue, were the least pains which I was destined to endure; I was cursed by some devil, and carried about with me my eternal hell; yet still a spirit of good followed and directed my steps; and, when I most murmured, would suddenly extricate me from seemingly insurmountable difficulties. Sometimes, when nature, overcome by hunger, sunk under the exhaustion, a repast was prepared for me in the desert, that restored and inspirited me. The fare was, indeed, coarse, such as the peasants of the country ate; but I will not doubt that it was set there by the spirits that I had invoked to aid me. Often, when all was dry, the heavens cloudless, and I was parched by thirst, a slight cloud would bedim the sky, shed the few drops that revived me, and vanish.

I followed, when I could, the courses of the rivers; but the daemon generally avoided these, as it was here that the population of the country chiefly collected. In other places human beings were seldom seen; and I generally subsisted on the wild animals that crossed my path. I had money with me, and gained the friendship of the villagers by distributing it; or I brought with me some food that I had killed, which, after taking a small part, I always presented to those who had provided me with fire and utensils for cooking.

My life, as it passed thus, was indeed hateful to me, and it was during sleep alone that I could taste joy. O blessed sleep! often, when most miserable, I sank to repose, and my dreams lulled me even to rapture. The spirits that guarded me had provided these moments, or rather hours, of happiness, that I might retain strength to fulfill my pilgrimage. Deprived of this respite, I should have sunk under my hardships. During the day I was sustained and inspirited by the hope of night: for in sleep I saw my friends, my wife, and my beloved country; again I saw the benevolent countenance of my father, heard the silver tones of my Elizabeth's voice, and beheld Clerval enjoying health and youth. Often, when wearied by a toilsome march, I persuaded myself that I was dreaming until night should come, and that I should then enjoy reality in the arms of my dearest friends. What agonising fondness did I feel for them! how did I cling to their dear forms, as sometimes they haunted even my waking hours, and persuade myself that they still lived! At such moments vengeance, that burned within me, died in my heart, and I pursued my path towards the destruction of the daemon, more as a task enjoined by heaven, as the mechanical impulse of some power of which I was unconscious, than as the ardent desire of my soul.

What his feelings were whom I pursued I cannot know. Sometimes, indeed, he left marks in writing on the barks of the trees, or cut in stone, that guided me, and instigated my fury. "My reign is not yet over," (these words were legible in one of these inscriptions;) "you live, and my power is complete. Follow me; I seek the everlasting ices of the north, where you will feel the misery of cold and frost, to which I am impassive. You will find near this place, if you follow not too tardily, a dead hare; eat, and be refreshed. Come on, my enemy; we have yet to wrestle for our lives; but many hard and miserable hours must you endure until that period shall arrive."

Scoffing devil! Again do I vow vengeance; again do I devote thee, miserable fiend, to torture and death. Never will I give up my search, until he or I perish; and then with what ecstasy shall I join my Elizabeth, and my departed friends, who even now prepare for me the reward of my tedious toil and horrible pilgrimage!

As I still pursued my journey to the northward, the snows thickened, and the cold increased in a degree almost too severe to support. The peasants were shut up in their hovels, and only a few of the most hardy ventured forth to seize the animals whom starvation had forced from their hiding-places to seek for prey. The rivers were covered with ice, and no fish could be procured; and thus I was cut off from my chief article of maintenance.

The triumph of my enemy increased with the difficulty of my labours. One inscription that he left was in these words: — "Prepare! your toils only begin: wrap yourself in furs, and provide food; for we shall soon enter upon a journey where your sufferings will satisfy my everlasting hatred."

My courage and perseverance were invigorated by these scoffing words; I resolved not to fail in my purpose; and, calling on Heaven to support me, I continued with unabated fervour to traverse immense deserts, until the ocean appeared at a distance, and formed the utmost boundary of the horizon. Oh! how unlike it was to the blue seas of the south! Covered with ice, it was only to be distinguished from land by its superior wildness and ruggedness. The Greeks wept for joy when they beheld the Mediterranean from the hills of Asia, and hailed with rapture the boundary of their toils. I did not weep; but I knelt down, and, with a full heart, thanked my guiding spirit for conducting me in safety to the place where I hoped, notwithstanding my adversary's gibe, to meet and grapple with him.

Some weeks before this period I had procured a sledge and dogs, and thus traversed the snows with inconceivable speed. I know not whether the fiend possessed the same advantages; but I found that, as before I had daily lost ground in the pursuit, I now gained on him: so much so, that when I first saw the ocean, he was but one day's journey in advance, and I hoped to intercept him before he should reach the beach. With new courage, therefore, I pressed on, and in two days arrived at a wretched hamlet on the sea-shore. I enquired of the inhabitants concerning the fiend, and gained accurate information. A gigantic monster, they said, had arrived the night before, armed with a gun and many pistols; putting to flight the inhabitants of a solitary cottage, through fear of his terrific appearance. He had carried off their store of winter food, and, placing it in a sledge, to draw which he had seized on a numerous drove of trained dogs, he had harnessed them, and the same night, to the joy of the horror-struck villagers, had pursued his journey across the sea in a direction that led to no land; and they conjectured that he must speedily be destroyed by the breaking of the ice, or frozen by the eternal frosts.

On hearing this information, I suffered a temporary access of despair. He had escaped me; and I must commence a destructive and almost endless journey across the mountainous ices of the ocean, — amidst cold that few of the inhabitants could long endure, and which I, the native of a genial and sunny climate, could not hope to survive. Yet at the idea that the fiend should live and be triumphant, my rage and vengeance returned, and, like a mighty tide, overwhelmed every other feeling. After a slight repose, during which the spirits of the dead hovered round, and instigated me to toil and revenge, I prepared for my journey.

I exchanged my land-sledge for one fashioned for the inequalities of the Frozen Ocean; and purchasing a plentiful stock of provisions, I departed from land.

I cannot guess how many days have passed since then; but I have endured misery, which nothing but the eternal sentiment of a just retribution burning within my heart could have enabled me to support. Immense and rugged mountains of ice often barred up my passage, and I often heard the thunder of the ground sea, which threatened my destruction. But again the frost came, and made the paths of the sea secure.

By the quantity of provision which I had consumed, I should guess that I had passed three weeks in this journey; and the continual protraction of hope, returning back upon the heart, often wrung bitter drops of despondency and grief from my eyes. Despair had indeed almost secured her prey, and I should soon have sunk beneath this misery. Once, after the poor animals that conveyed me had with incredible toil gained the summit of a sloping ice-mountain, and one, sinking under his fatigue, died, I viewed the expanse before me with anguish, when suddenly my eye caught a dark speck upon the dusky plain. I strained my sight to discover what it could be, and uttered a wild cry of ecstasy when I distinguished a sledge, and the distorted proportions of a well-known form within. Oh! with what a burning gush did hope revisit my heart! warm tears filled my eyes, which I hastily wiped away, that they might not intercept the view I had of the daemon; but still my sight was dimmed by the burning drops, until, giving way to the emotions that oppressed me, I wept aloud.

But this was not the time for delay: I disencumbered the dogs of their dead companion, gave them a plentiful portion of food; and, after an hour's rest, which was absolutely necessary, and yet which was bitterly irksome to me, I continued my route. The sledge was still visible; nor did I again lose sight of it, except at the moments when for a short time some ice-rock concealed it with its intervening crags. I indeed perceptibly gained on it; and when, after nearly two days' journey, I beheld my enemy at no more than a mile distant, my heart bounded within me.

But now, when I appeared almost within grasp of my foe, my hopes were suddenly extinguished, and I lost all traces of him more utterly than I had ever done before. A ground sea was heard; the thunder of its progress, as the waters rolled and swelled beneath me, became every moment more ominous and terrific. I pressed on, but in vain. The wind arose; the sea roared; and, as with the mighty shock of an earthquake, it split, and cracked with a tremendous and overwhelming sound. The work was soon finished: in a few minutes a tumultuous sea rolled between me and my enemy, and I was left drifting on a scattered piece of ice, that was continually lessening, and thus preparing for me a hideous death.

In this manner many appalling hours passed; several of my dogs died; and I myself was about to sink under the accumulation of distress, when I saw your vessel riding at anchor, and holding forth to me hopes of succour and life. I had no conception that vessels ever came so far north, and was astounded at the sight. I quickly destroyed part of my sledge to construct oars; and by these means was enabled, with infinite fatigue, to move my ice-raft in the direction of your ship. I had determined, if you were going southward, still to trust myself to the mercy of the seas rather than abandon my purpose. I hoped to induce you to grant me a boat with which I could pursue my enemy. But your direction was northward. You took me on board when my vigour was exhausted, and I should soon have sunk under my multiplied hardships into a death which I still dread — for my task is unfulfilled.

Oh! when will my guiding spirit, in conducting me to the daemon, allow me the rest I so much desire; or must I die, and he yet live? If I do, swear to me, Walton, that he shall not escape; that you will seek him, and satisfy my vengeance in his death. And do I dare to ask of you to undertake my pilgrimage, to endure the hardships that I have undergone? No; I am not so selfish. Yet, when I am dead, if he should appear; if the ministers of vengeance should conduct him to you, swear that he shall not live — swear that he shall not triumph over my accumulated woes, and survive to add to the list of his dark crimes. He is eloquent and persuasive; and once his words had even power over my heart; but trust him not. His soul is as hellish as his form, full of treachery and fiendlike malice. Hear him not; call on the manes[35] of William, Justine, Clerval, Elizabeth, my father, and of the wretched Victor, and thrust your sword into his heart. I will hover near, and direct the steel aright.

Walton, *in continuation.*

August 26th, 17—.

You have read this strange and terrific story, Margaret; and do you not feel your blood congeal with horror, like that which even now curdles

[35] Latin for "souls of the deceased." — Eds.

mine? Sometimes, seized with sudden agony, he could not continue his tale; at others, his voice broken, yet piercing, uttered with difficulty the words so replete with anguish. His fine and lovely eyes were now lighted up with indignation, now subdued to downcast sorrow, and quenched in infinite wretchedness. Sometimes he commanded his countenance and tones, and related the most horrible incidents with a tranquil voice, suppressing every mark of agitation; then, like a volcano bursting forth, his face would suddenly change to an expression of the wildest rage, as he shrieked out imprecations on his persecutor.

His tale is connected, and told with an appearance of the simplest truth, yet I own to you that the letters of Felix and Safie, which he showed me, and the apparition of the monster seen from our ship, brought to me a greater conviction of the truth of his narrative than his asseverations, however earnest and connected. Such a monster has then really existence! I cannot doubt it; yet I am lost in surprise and admiration. Sometimes I endeavoured to gain from Frankenstein the particulars of his creature's formation: but on this point he was impenetrable.

"Are you mad, my friend?" said he; "or whither does your senseless curiosity lead you? Would you also create for yourself and the world a daemoniacal enemy? Peace, peace! learn my miseries, and do not seek to increase your own."

Frankenstein discovered that I made notes concerning his history: he asked to see them, and then himself corrected and augmented them in many places; but principally in giving the life and spirit to the conversations he held with his enemy. "Since you have preserved my narration," said he, "I would not that a mutilated one should go down to posterity."

Thus has a week passed away, while I have listened to the strangest tale that ever imagination formed. My thoughts, and every feeling of my soul, have been drunk up by the interest for my guest, which this tale, and his own elevated and gentle manners, have created. I wish to soothe him; yet can I counsel one so infinitely miserable, so destitute of every hope of consolation, to live? Oh, no! the only joy that he can now know will be when he composes his shattered spirit to peace and death. Yet he enjoys one comfort, the offspring of solitude and delirium: he believes, when in dreams he holds converse with his friends, and derives from that communion consolation for his miseries, or excitements to his vengeance, that they are not the creations of his fancy, but the beings themselves who visit him from the regions of a remote world. This faith gives a solemnity to his reveries that render them to me almost as imposing and interesting as truth.

Our conversations are not always confined to his own history and misfortunes. On every point of general literature he displays unbounded knowledge, and a quick and piercing apprehension. His eloquence is forcible and touching; nor can I hear him, when he relates a pathetic incident, or endeavours to move the passions of pity or love, without tears. What a glorious creature must he have been in the days of his prosperity, when he is thus noble and godlike in ruin! He seems to feel his own worth, and the greatness of his fall.

"When younger," said he, "I believed myself destined for some great enterprise. My feelings are profound; but I possessed a coolness of judgment that fitted me for illustrious achievements. This sentiment of the worth of my nature supported me, when others would have been oppressed; for I deemed it criminal to throw away in useless grief those talents that might be useful to my fellow-creatures. When I reflected on the work I had completed, no less a one than the creation of a sensitive and rational animal, I could not rank myself with the herd of common projectors. But this thought, which supported me in the commencement of my career, now serves only to plunge me lower in the dust. All my speculations and hopes are as nothing; and, like the archangel who aspired to omnipotence, I am chained in an eternal hell. My imagination was vivid, yet my powers of analysis and application were intense; by the union of these qualities I conceived the idea, and executed the creation of a man. Even now I cannot recollect, without passion, my reveries while the work was incomplete. I trod heaven in my thoughts, now exulting in my powers, now burning with the idea of their effects. From my infancy I was imbued with high hopes and a lofty ambition; but how am I sunk! Oh! my friend, if you had known me as I once was, you would not recognise me in this state of degradation. Despondency rarely visited my heart; a high destiny seemed to bear me on, until I fell, never, never again to rise."

Must I then lose this admirable being? I have longed for a friend; I have sought one who would sympathise with and love me. Behold, on these desert seas I have found such a one; but, I fear, I have gained him only to know his value, and lose him. I would reconcile him to life, but he repulses the idea.

"I thank you, Walton," he said, "for your kind intentions towards so miserable a wretch; but when you speak of new ties, and fresh affections, think you that any can replace those who are gone? Can any man be to me as Clerval was; or any woman another Elizabeth? Even where the affections are not strongly moved by any superior excellence, the companions of our childhood always possess a certain power over our minds, which hardly any later friend can obtain. They know our infantine dispositions, which, however they may be afterwards modified, are never eradicated; and they can judge of our actions with more certain conclusions as to the integrity of our motives. A sister or a brother can never, unless indeed such symptoms have been shown early, suspect the other of fraud or false dealing, when another friend, however strongly he may be attached, may, in spite of himself, be contemplated with suspicion. But I enjoyed friends, dear not only through habit and association, but from their own merits; and wherever I am, the soothing voice of my Elizabeth, and the conversation of Clerval, will be ever whispered in my ear. They are dead; and but one feeling in such a solitude can persuade me to preserve my life. If I were engaged in any high undertaking or design, fraught with extensive utility to my fellow-creatures, then could I live to fulfil it. But such is not my destiny; I must pursue and destroy the being to whom I gave existence; then my lot on earth will be fulfilled, and I may die."

September 2d.

My beloved Sister,

I write to you, encompassed by peril, and ignorant whether I am ever doomed to see again dear England, and the dearer friends that inhabit it. I am surrounded by mountains of ice, which admit of no escape, and threaten every moment to crush my vessel. The brave fellows, whom I have persuaded to be my companions, look towards me for aid; but I have none to bestow. There is something terribly appalling in our situation, yet my courage and hopes do not desert me. Yet it is terrible to reflect that the lives of all these men are endangered through me. If we are lost, my mad schemes are the cause.

And what, Margaret, will be the state of your mind? You will not hear of my destruction, and you will anxiously await my return. Years will pass, and you will have visitings of despair, and yet be tortured by hope. Oh! my beloved sister, the sickening failing of your heart-felt expectations is, in prospect, more terrible to me than my own death. But you have a husband, and lovely children; you may be happy: Heaven bless you, and make you so!

My unfortunate guest regards me with the tenderest compassion. He endeavours to fill me with hope; and talks as if life were a possession which he valued. He reminds me how often the same accidents have happened to other navigators, who have attempted this sea, and, in spite of myself, he fills me with cheerful auguries. Even the sailors feel the power of his eloquence: when he speaks, they no longer despair; he rouses their energies, and, while they hear his voice, they believe these vast mountains of ice are mole-hills, which will vanish before the resolutions of man. These feelings are transitory; each day of expectation delayed fills them with fear, and I almost dread a mutiny caused by this despair.

September 5th.

A scene has just passed of such uncommon interest, that although it is highly probable that these papers may never reach you, yet I cannot forbear recording it.

We are still surrounded by mountains of ice, still in imminent danger of being crushed in their conflict. The cold is excessive, and many of my unfortunate comrades have already found a grave amidst this scene of desolation. Frankenstein has daily declined in health: a feverish fire still glimmers in his eyes; but he is exhausted, and, when suddenly roused to any exertion, he speedily sinks again into apparent lifelessness.

I mentioned in my last letter the fears I entertained of a mutiny. This morning, as I sat watching the wan countenance of my friend—his eyes half closed, and his limbs hanging listlessly,—I was roused by half a dozen of the sailors, who demanded admission into the cabin. They entered, and their leader addressed me. He told me that he and his companions had been chosen by the other sailors to come in deputation to me, to make me a requisition, which, in justice, I could not refuse. We were immured in ice, and should probably never escape; but they feared that if, as was possible, the ice should dissipate, and a free passage be opened, I should be rash enough to continue my voyage, and lead them into fresh dangers, after they might happily have surmounted this. They insisted, therefore, that I should engage with a solemn promise, that if the vessel should be freed I would instantly direct my course southward.

This speech troubled me. I had not despaired; nor had I yet conceived the idea of returning, if set free. Yet could I, in justice, or even in possibility, refuse this demand? I hesitated before I answered; when Frankenstein, who had at first been silent, and, indeed, appeared hardly to have force enough to attend, now roused himself; his eyes sparkled, and his cheeks flushed with momentary vigour. Turning towards the men, he said—

"What do you mean? What do you demand of your captain? Are you then so easily turned from your design? Did you not call this a glorious expedition? And wherefore was it glorious? Not because the way was smooth and placid as a southern sea, but because it was full of dangers and terror; because, at every new incident, your fortitude was to be called forth, and your courage exhibited; because danger and death surrounded it, and these you were to brave and overcome. For this was it a glorious, for this was it an honourable undertaking. You were hereafter to be hailed as the benefactors of your species; your names adored, as belonging to brave men who encountered death for honour, and the benefit of mankind. And now, behold, with the first imagination of danger, or, if you will, the first mighty and terrific trial of your courage, you shrink away, and are content to be handed down as men who had not strength enough to endure cold and peril; and so, poor souls, they were chilly, and returned to their warm firesides. Why, that requires not this preparation; ye need not have come thus far, and dragged your captain to the shame of a defeat, merely to prove yourselves cowards. Oh! be men, or be more than men. Be steady to your purposes, and firm as a rock. This ice is not made of such stuff as your hearts may be; it is mutable, and cannot withstand you, if you say that it shall not. Do not return to your families with the stigma of disgrace marked on your brows. Return as heroes who have fought and conquered, and who know not what it is to turn their backs on the foe."

He spoke this with a voice so modulated to the different feelings expressed in his speech, with an eye so full of lofty design and heroism, that can you wonder that these men were moved? They looked at one another, and were unable to reply. I spoke; I told them to retire, and consider of what had been said: that I would not lead them farther north, if they strenuously desired the contrary; but that I hoped that, with reflection, their courage would return.

They retired, and I turned towards my friend; but he was sunk in languor, and almost deprived of life.

How all this will terminate, I know not; but I had rather die than return shamefully, — my purpose unfulfilled. Yet I fear such will be my fate; the men, unsupported by ideas of glory and honour, can never willingly continue to endure their present hardships.

September 7th.

The die is cast; I have consented to return, if we are not destroyed. Thus are my hopes blasted by cowardice and indecision; I come back ignorant and disappointed. It requires more philosophy than I possess, to bear this injustice with patience.

September 12th.

It is past; I am returning to England. I have lost my hopes of utility and glory; — I have lost my friend. But I will endeavour to detail these bitter circumstances to you, my dear sister; and, while I am wafted towards England, and towards you, I will not despond.

September 9th, the ice began to move, and roarings like thunder were heard at a distance, as the islands split and cracked in every direction. We were in the most imminent peril; but, as we could only remain passive, my chief attention was occupied by my unfortunate guest, whose illness increased in such a degree, that he was entirely confined to his bed. The ice cracked behind us, and was driven with force towards the north; a breeze sprung from the west, and on the 11th the passage towards the south became perfectly free. When the sailors saw this, and that their return to their native country was apparently assured, a shout of tumultuous joy broke from them, loud and long-continued. Frankenstein, who was dozing, awoke, and asked the cause of the tumult. "They shout," I said, "because they will soon return to England."

"Do you then really return?"

"Alas! yes; I cannot withstand their demands. I cannot lead them unwillingly to danger, and I must return."

"Do so, if you will; but I will not. You may give up your purpose, but mine is assigned to me by Heaven, and I dare not. I am weak; but surely the spirits who assist my vengeance will endow me with sufficient strength." Saying this, he endeavoured to spring from the bed, but the exertion was too great for him; he fell back, and fainted.

It was long before he was restored; and I often thought that life was entirely extinct. At length he opened his eyes; he breathed with difficulty, and was unable to speak. The surgeon gave him a composing draught, and ordered us to leave him undisturbed. In the mean time he told me, that my friend had certainly not many hours to live.

His sentence was pronounced; and I could only grieve, and be patient. I sat by his bed, watching him; his eyes were closed, and I thought he slept; but presently he called to me in a feeble voice, and, bidding me come near, said — "Alas! the strength I relied on is gone; I feel that I shall soon die, and he, my enemy and persecutor, may still be in being. Think not, Walton, that in the last moments of my existence I feel that burning hatred, and ardent desire of revenge, I once expressed; but I feel myself justified in desiring the death of my adversary. During these last days I have been occupied in examining my past conduct; nor do I find it blameable. In a fit of enthusiastic madness I created a rational creature, and was bound towards him, to assure, as far as was in my power, his happiness and well-being. This was my duty; but there was another still paramount to that. My duties towards the beings of my own species had greater claims to my attention, because they included a greater proportion of happiness or misery. Urged by this view, I refused, and I did right in refusing, to create a companion for the first creature. He showed unparalleled malignity and selfishness, in evil: he destroyed my friends; he devoted to destruction beings who possessed exquisite sensations, happiness, and wisdom; nor do I know where this thirst for vengeance may end. Miserable himself, that he may render no other wretched, he ought to die. The task of his destruction was mine, but I have failed. When actuated by selfishness and vicious motives, I asked you to undertake my unfinished work; and I renew this request now, when I am only induced by reason and virtue.

"Yet I cannot ask you to renounce your country and friends, to fulfil this task; and now, that you are returning to England, you will have little chance of meeting with him. But the consideration of these points, and the well balancing of what you may esteem your duties, I leave to you; my judgment and ideas are already disturbed by the near approach of death. I dare not ask you to do what I think right, for I may still be misled by passion.

"That he should live to be an instrument of mischief disturbs me; in other respects, this hour, when I momentarily expect my release, is the only happy one which I have enjoyed for several years. The forms of the beloved dead flit before me, and I hasten to their arms. Farewell, Walton! Seek happiness in tranquillity, and avoid ambition, even if it be only the apparently innocent one of distinguishing yourself in science and discoveries. Yet why do I say this? I have myself been blasted in these hopes, yet another may succeed."

His voice became fainter as he spoke; and at length, exhausted by his effort, he sunk into silence. About half an hour afterwards he attempted again to speak, but was unable; he pressed my hand feebly, and his eyes closed for ever, while the irradiation of a gentle smile passed away from his lips.

Prado, Madrid, Spain/Bridgeman Images

This mural, titled *Saturn Devouring One of His Sons*, was painted by Spanish artist Francisco Goya (1746–1828) shortly after *Frankenstein* was published. According to Roman myth, the god Saturn would destroy his children to prevent them from one day overthrowing him. **How does this image relate to Victor's pursuit of his creation after the monster has murdered several of his loved ones? What aspects of the painting lend themselves to comparison with the themes, tone, and/or mood of the novel?**

Margaret, what comment can I make on the untimely extinction of this glorious spirit? What can I say, that will enable you to understand the depth of my sorrow? All that I should express would be inadequate and feeble. My tears flow; my mind is overshadowed by a cloud of disappointment. But I journey towards England, and I may there find consolation.

I am interrupted. What do these sounds portend? It is midnight; the breeze blows fairly, and the watch on deck scarcely stir. Again; there is a sound as of a human voice, but hoarser; it comes from the cabin where the remains of Frankenstein still lie. I must arise, and examine. Good night, my sister.

Great God! what a scene has just taken place! I am yet dizzy with the remembrance of it. I hardly know whether I shall have the power to detail it; yet the tale which I have recorded would be incomplete without this final and wonderful catastrophe.

I entered the cabin, where lay the remains of my ill-fated and admirable friend. Over him hung a form which I cannot find words to describe; gigantic in stature, yet uncouth and distorted in its proportions. As he hung over the coffin, his face was concealed by long locks of ragged hair; but one vast hand was extended, in colour and apparent texture like that of a mummy. When he heard the sound of my approach, he ceased to utter exclamations of grief and horror, and sprung towards the window. Never did I behold a vision so horrible as his face, of such loathsome yet appalling hideousness. I shut my eyes involuntarily, and endeavoured to recollect what were my duties with regard to this destroyer. I called on him to stay.

He paused, looking on me with wonder; and, again turning towards the lifeless form of his creator, he seemed to forget my presence, and every feature and gesture seemed instigated by the wildest rage of some uncontrollable passion.

"That is also my victim!" he exclaimed: "in his murder my crimes are consummated; the miserable series of my being is wound to its close! Oh, Frankenstein! generous and self-devoted being! what does it avail that I now ask thee to pardon me? I, who irretrievably destroyed thee by destroying all thou lovedst. Alas! he is cold, he cannot answer me."

His voice seemed suffocated; and my first impulses, which had suggested to me the duty of obeying the dying request of my friend, in destroying his enemy, were now suspended by a mixture of curiosity and compassion. I approached this tremendous being; I dared not again raise my eyes to his face, there was something so scaring and unearthly in his ugliness. I attempted to speak, but the words died away on my lips. The monster continued to utter wild and incoherent self-reproaches. At length I gathered resolution to address him in a pause of the tempest of his passion: "Your repentance," I said, "is now superfluous. If you had listened to the voice of conscience, and heeded the stings of remorse, before you had urged your diabolical vengeance to this extremity, Frankenstein would yet have lived."

"And do you dream?" said the daemon; "do you think that I was then dead to agony and remorse? — He," he continued, pointing to the corpse, "he suffered not in the consummation of the deed — oh! not the ten-thousandth portion of the anguish that was mine during the lingering detail of its execution. A frightful selfishness hurried me on, while my heart was poisoned with remorse. Think you that the groans of Clerval were music to my ears? My heart was fashioned to be susceptible of love and sympathy; and, when wrenched by misery to vice and hatred, it did not endure the violence of the change, without torture such as you cannot even imagine.

"After the murder of Clerval, I returned to Switzerland, heartbroken and overcome. I pitied Frankenstein; my pity amounted to horror: I abhorred myself. But when I discovered that he, the author at once of my existence and of its unspeakable torments, dared to hope for happiness; that while he accumulated wretchedness and despair upon me, he sought his own enjoyment in feelings and passions from the indulgence of which I was for ever barred, then impotent envy and bitter indignation filled me with an insatiable thirst for vengeance. I recollected my threat, and resolved that it should be accomplished. I knew that I was preparing for myself a deadly torture; but I was the slave, not the master, of an impulse, which I detested, yet could not disobey. Yet when she died! — nay, then I was not miserable. I had cast off all feeling, subdued all anguish, to riot in the excess of my despair. Evil thenceforth became my good. Urged thus far, I had no choice but to adapt my nature to an element which I had willingly chosen. The completion of my demoniacal design became an insatiable passion. And now it is ended; there is my last victim!"

I was first touched by the expressions of his misery; yet, when I called to mind what Frankenstein had said of his powers of eloquence and persuasion, and when I again cast my eyes on the lifeless form of my friend, indignation was rekindled within me. "Wretch!" I said, "it is well that you come here to whine over the desolation that you have made. You throw a torch into a pile of buildings; and, when they are consumed, you sit among the ruins, and lament the fall. Hypocritical fiend! if he whom you mourn still lived, still would he be the object, again would he become the prey, of your accursed vengeance. It is not pity that you feel; you lament only because the victim of your malignity is withdrawn from your power."

"Oh, it is not thus — not thus," interrupted the being; "yet such must be the impression conveyed to you by what appears to be the purport of my actions. Yet I seek not a fellow-feeling in my misery. No sympathy may I ever find. When I first sought it, it was the love of virtue, the feelings of happiness and affection with which my whole being overflowed, that I wished to be participated. But now, that virtue has become to me a shadow, and that happiness and affection are turned into bitter and loathing despair, in what should I seek for sympathy? I am content to suffer alone, while my sufferings shall endure: when I die, I am well satisfied that abhorrence and opprobrium should load my memory. Once my fancy was soothed with dreams of virtue, of fame, and of enjoyment. Once I falsely hoped to meet with beings, who, pardoning my outward form, would love me for the excellent qualities which I was capable of unfolding. I was nourished with high thoughts of honour and devotion. But now crime has degraded me beneath the meanest animal. No guilt, no mischief, no malignity, no misery, can be found comparable to mine. When I run over the frightful catalogue of my sins, I cannot believe that I am the same creature whose thoughts were once filled with sublime and transcendent visions of the beauty and the majesty of goodness. But it is even so; the fallen angel becomes a malignant devil. Yet even that enemy of God and man had friends and associates in his desolation; I am alone.

"You, who call Frankenstein your friend, seem to have a knowledge of my crimes and his misfortunes. But, in the detail which he gave you of them, he could not sum up the hours and months of misery which I endured, wasting in impotent passions. For while I destroyed his hopes, I did not satisfy my own desires. They were for ever ardent and craving; still I desired love and fellowship, and I was still spurned. Was there no injustice in this? Am I to be thought the only criminal, when all human kind sinned against me? Why do you not hate Felix, who drove his friend from his door with contumely? Why do you not execrate the rustic who sought to destroy the saviour of his child? Nay, these are virtuous and immaculate beings! I, the miserable and the abandoned, am an abortion, to be spurned at, and kicked, and trampled on. Even now my blood boils at the recollection of this injustice.

extending beyond the text

In his second letter (pp. 1095–97), Walton tells his sister to "not be alarmed for my safety, or if I should come back to you as worn and woeful as the 'Ancient Mariner'" (par. 15). Samuel Taylor Coleridge's poem *The Rime of the Ancient Mariner* is a frame tale in which the mariner tells his gruesome story to those who need to hear it. In Shelley's novel, Victor Frankenstein might be seen as analogous to the mariner and Walton to his listener. Near the end of Coleridge's poem, the mariner concludes his tale, saying the following as he made confession.

from The Rime of the Ancient Mariner

Samuel Taylor Coleridge

Forthwith this frame of mine was wrenched
With a woful agony,
Which forced me to begin my tale;
And then it left me free.

Since then, at an uncertain hour,
That agony returns:
And till my ghastly tale is told,
This heart within me burns.

I pass, like night, from land to land;
I have strange power of speech;
That moment that his face I see,
I know the man that must hear me:
To him my tale I teach. ■

1. **How does the allusion to Coleridge's poem earlier in the novel serve as foreshadowing in *Frankenstein*?**

"But it is true that I am a wretch. I have murdered the lovely and the helpless; I have strangled the innocent as they slept, and grasped to death his throat who never injured me or any other living thing. I have devoted my creator, the select specimen of all that is worthy of love and admiration among men, to misery; I have pursued him even to that irremediable ruin. There he lies, white and cold in death. You hate me; but your abhorrence cannot equal that with which I regard myself. I look on the hands which executed the deed; I think on the heart in which the imagination of it was conceived, and long for the moment when these hands will meet my eyes, when that imagination will haunt my thoughts no more.

"Fear not that I shall be the instrument of future mischief. My work is nearly complete. Neither yours nor any man's death is needed to consummate the series of my being, and accomplish that which must be done; but it

extending beyond the text

Known as the wisest of the Titans in ancient Greek mythology, Prometheus stole fire from the gods of Mount Olympus and brought it to humankind. As punishment for his transgression, he was chained to a rock where an eagle would eat his liver, which would grow back each day, making his torment eternal. Shown here are two paintings of Prometheus: *The Torture of Prometheus* (c. 1620–1648) by Gioacchino Assereto (left) and *Prometheus* (1998) by Xavier Cortada (right).

Musee de la Chartreuse, Douai, France/Bridgeman Images

Private Collection/© Xavier Cortada/Bridgeman Images

1. **How does each work contribute to your understanding of Victor Frankenstein's anguish?**
2. **Which themes from the novel are represented in these paintings? How does each artist convey these themes?**

requires my own. Do not think that I shall be slow to perform this sacrifice. I shall quit your vessel on the ice-raft which brought me thither, and shall seek the most northern extremity of the globe; I shall collect my funeral pile, and consume to ashes this miserable frame, that its remains may afford no light to any curious and unhallowed wretch, who would create such another as I have been. I shall die. I shall no longer feel the agonies which now consume me, or be the prey of feelings unsatisfied, yet unquenched. He is dead who called me into being; and when I shall be no more, the very remembrance of us both will speedily vanish. I shall no longer see the sun or stars, or feel the winds play on my cheeks. Light, feeling, and sense will pass away; and in this condition must I find my happiness. Some years ago, when the images which this world affords first opened upon me, when I felt the cheering warmth of summer, and heard the rustling of the leaves and the warbling of the birds, and these were all to me, I should have wept to die; now it is my only consolation. Polluted by crimes, and torn by the bitterest remorse, where can I find rest but in death?

"Farewell! I leave you, and in you the last of human kind whom these eyes will ever behold. Farewell, Frankenstein! If thou wert yet alive, and yet cherished a desire of revenge against me, it would be better satiated in my life than in my destruction. But it was not so; thou didst seek my extinction, that I might not cause greater wretchedness; and if yet, in some mode unknown to me, thou hadst not ceased to think and feel, thou wouldst not desire against me a vengeance greater than that which I feel. Blasted as thou wert, my agony was still superior to thine; for the bitter sting of remorse will not cease to rankle in my wounds until death shall close them for ever.

"But soon," he cried, with sad and solemn enthusiasm, "I shall die, and what I now feel be no longer felt. Soon these burning miseries will be extinct. I shall ascend my funeral pile triumphantly, and exult in the agony of the torturing flames. The light of that conflagration will fade away; my ashes will be swept into the sea by the winds. My spirit will sleep in peace; or if it thinks, it will not surely think thus. Farewell."

He sprung from the cabin window, as he said this, upon the ice-raft which lay close to the vessel. He was soon borne away by the waves, and lost in darkness and distance. ■

1818

Understanding and Interpreting

1. **AP® Character and Narration.** Before reading *Frankenstein*, you were probably already familiar with the monster through film versions and media portrayals. What were your expectations for the novel's beginning, and to what extent were they based on those well-known portrayals? How did those expectations affect your reading experience?
2. **AP® Character and Narration.** From the text of Robert Walton's letters, what parallels can you draw between him and Victor Frankenstein? What qualities and characteristics do they share? How do they differ?
3. **AP® Character, Narration, Structure, and Figurative Language.** In Chapter II, Frankenstein speaks of a passion "which afterwards ruled my destiny" (par. 73), of "the fatal impulse that led to my ruin" (par. 75), of "the storm that was even then hanging in the stars, and ready to envelop me" (par. 82), and concludes, "Destiny was too potent, and her immutable laws had decreed my utter and terrible destruction" (par. 83). He returns to this motif repeatedly throughout his remarkable tale. Why does he speak as if fate has ruled his actions? To what extent do you think he truly believes that? What do his statements imply about Shelley's attitude toward fate or destiny? Explain.
4. **AP® Character.** Briefly describe the function of each of the following characters: Elizabeth, Clerval, Krempe, and Waldman. How do they each influence Victor Frankenstein? Explain.
5. **AP® Structure and Narration.** Clerval's timely arrival just after the creation of the monster is the first of several extraordinary coincidences in the novel. Note and describe at least three others that follow in the story. What is their effect? Do they support Frankenstein's forebodings regarding destiny and fate? Are they so outrageous as to strain credibility? Explain.
6. **AP® Character, Structure, and Narration.** In paragraph 216, Frankenstein relates Justine's defense against the accusation that she murdered William: "'God knows,' she said, 'how entirely I am innocent. But I do not pretend that my protestations should acquit me: I rest my innocence on a plain and simple explanation of the facts which have been adduced against me; and I hope the character I have always borne will incline my judges to a favorable

interpretation, where any circumstance appears doubtful or suspicious.'" How do these words characterize her? Read carefully what Frankenstein says in the last three paragraphs of the chapter. How has Justine affected his disposition? In what way might Justine's death represent a turning point in the narrative?

7. **AP® Character and Narration.** In Chapter X, the monster confronts Frankenstein and addresses him: "You, my creator." He refers to himself as "thy creature" and pleads, "Do your duty towards me." Read carefully what he says to Frankenstein (par. 267). What effect does this plea have on Frankenstein? As the chapter concludes, Frankenstein says, "For the first time, also, I felt what the duties of a creator towards his creature were." Do you believe him? Does Frankenstein understand fully what he says? Explain, using specific details from scenes in the novel to support your response.
8. **AP® Character and Narration.** Knowledge itself — its lure and its consequences — is a major theme of the novel. In Chapter XIII the monster recounts how he learned to read and describes the thoughts prompted by his learning. He proclaims, "Of what a strange nature is knowledge!" (par. 333). Later, in Chapter XV, he says to his creator, "Increase of knowledge only discovered to me more clearly what a wretched outcast I was" (par. 366). How could these two statements by the monster apply equally to both Walton and Frankenstein? How do they relate to the novel's larger themes? Explain.
9. **AP® Character and Narration.** In Chapter XIV the monster relates the story of the De Lacey family, the cottagers whom he has come to know. What about the family's story is it that "excited in me such various feelings of indignation, delight, and wonder," as the monster says (par. 336)? What does this reaction suggest about the monster's character?
10. **AP® Character, Narration, and Figurative Language.** Reflecting on the books he has read, the monster says, "I remembered Adam's supplication to his Creator. But where was mine? He had abandoned me; and, in the bitterness of my heart, I cursed him" (par. 367). The monster here refers to the same passage from *Paradise Lost* that Shelley uses as the epigraph to the novel. Why does Shelley have the monster express his situation in such religious terms? Does the monster's language evoke sympathy from the reader? Explain.
11. **AP® Character and Narration.** How does Frankenstein respond to the monster's tale? What moves him to change his mind regarding the creation of a female companion for the monster? And then what moves him to change his mind again and destroy that new creation in progress? What do you make of the significance of Frankenstein's ultimate change of heart, and how does it help develop some of the novel's themes?
12. **AP® Character.** After Frankenstein destroys his new creation, the monster warns: "I shall be with you on your wedding-night" (par. 514). Despite the fact that the monster has already caused the deaths of William and Justine, Frankenstein doesn't seem to fear for Elizabeth's well-being. How does this behavior characterize Frankenstein? Explain.
13. **AP® Character and Narration.** From the arrival of Elizabeth's final letter in Chapter XXII until her death at the hands of the monster on their wedding night, Victor Frankenstein feels more and more under the grip of an inexorable fate. Trace his increasing sense of conviction through what he says. How does that belief in — and evident submission to — "fate" contribute to your understanding of Frankenstein, and of *Frankenstein*?
14. **AP® Character and Narration.** In the final chapter, when Walton resumes as narrator, we learn that Frankenstein's story (which, of course, includes the monster's tale) has taken a full week to tell, and that Walton believes the story he has heard. How does Walton regard Frankenstein? What about the story attracts Walton and convinces him of its veracity?

15. **AP® Character and Narration.** In Chapter XXIV, Walton proclaims, "If we are lost, my mad schemes are the cause" (par. 689). What "mad schemes" does he refer to? How could those words apply equally to Frankenstein?

16. **AP® Narration.** Carefully read the speech that Frankenstein delivers to the crew as reported in Walton's September 5th letter (par. 696). Then consider the advice he proffers to Walton as reported in the September 12th letter (pars. 707–9). What has changed? What is the nature of the advice that he gives just before he dies?

17. **AP® Character and Narration.** In the same letter, Walton reports the monster's murder of Frankenstein. The monster then speaks to Walton, reminding him that he has heard only Frankenstein's version of the story. Read paragraph 722 carefully. How does the monster justify his actions?

18. **AP® Character.** After reporting the monster's explanation, Walton concludes the novel and the final letter that we get to read: "He sprung from the cabin window, as he said this, upon the ice-raft which lay close to the vessel. He was soon borne away by the waves and lost in darkness and distance" (par. 727). At this point it is nearly a month since Victor Frankenstein arrived aboard Walton's ship. How will Frankenstein's story affect him? What do you think the future will hold for Robert Walton?

Analyzing Language, Style, and Structure

1. **Vocabulary in Context.** Physiognomy, a theory stipulating that a person's character and temperament can be determined based on facial features, is often a feature of Gothic literature. In Chapter XXIII, what can Victor determine about the magistrate based on his "physiognomy" (par. 105)? How do the physiognomies of Victor Frankenstein and the creature reflect their characters?

2. **AP® Structure and Figurative Language.** The full title of Mary Shelley's novel is *Frankenstein; or, The Modern Prometheus.* What parallels do you see between the story of Prometheus and that of Victor Frankenstein? and Frankenstein's monster? Why would Shelley refer to this mythic figure in her subtitle?

3. **AP® Character.** Just below the title of the novel, Shelley begins the book with an epigraph from John Milton's epic poem *Paradise Lost*, which poses a rhetorical question. Who in the novel might ask such a question, and of whom? Why might Shelley have begun with this?

4. **AP® Structure and Narration.** Unusual in its structure, *Frankenstein* is at once an epistolary novel (told in a series of letters) as well as a frame tale, or story within a story. The monster's tale in Chapters XI–XVI is narrated within the frame of Frankenstein's narrative — which itself is told within the frame of Walton's letters. The novel thus becomes a double frame tale: Walton tells Margaret what Frankenstein told him that the monster had told him about his experiences — and about the De Lacey family. Such a narrative structure depends on the credibility of the narrators and on the careful memory of the reader. How do you respond to such a method? Why do you think Shelley wrote the novel this way? Who do you think is the primary narrator? What thematic concerns does this particular structure and each of the various narrative perspectives reveal?

5. **AP® Setting, Narration, and Figurative Language.** Near the beginning of the novel, Walton's second letter is sent from Archangel, north of St. Petersburg, Russia, where he hopes to set sail on his exploration of the Arctic. This reference reappears near the end of the novel, when Frankenstein says to Walton, "All my speculations and hopes are as nothing;

and, like the archangel who aspired to omnipotence, I am chained in an eternal hell" (par. 686). Compare the two references to the archangel. How do they serve as symbolic frames for the story? Why might Shelley have chosen a town with this name as the setting for the beginning of Walton's journey?

6. **AP® Character and Figurative Language.** In Chapter II, Frankenstein describes the lightning storm that left nothing but a "blasted stump" of a great oak that had stood near his house (par. 80). It launches his intense interest in electricity. Later, after he has created and abandoned his monster, he says, "But I am a blasted tree; the bolt has entered my soul . . . a miserable spectacle of wrecked humanity, pitiable to others, and intolerable to myself" (par. 484). How does this symbolism connect his early ambition with the unwanted consequences of his actions?
7. **AP® Structure and Narration.** Several times during his story, Frankenstein interrupts his tale to address Walton directly (e.g., par. 110). What is the purpose and effect of these interruptions? How do they contribute to the themes of the novel?
8. **AP® Character, Narration, and Figurative Language.** Frankenstein sometimes attempts to express how he feels by quoting lines of poetry without attributing them to any author – for example, he takes lines from *The Rime of the Ancient Mariner* by Samuel Taylor Coleridge (par. 125) and from "Lines Composed a Few Miles above Tintern Abbey" by William Wordsworth (par. 471). What do such quotations suggest about both Frankenstein and his listener, Walton? How do they contribute to Shelley's purpose and to the themes of the novel?
9. **AP® Structure, Narration, and Figurative Language.** What effect do the letters from Victor Frankenstein's father and from Elizabeth have on him? Immediately between his reading of Elizabeth's letter and the arrival of the one from his father, Frankenstein's mood has been cheered by his friend, Henry Clerval, and by the restorative power of nature – by the "salubrious air I breathed," he muses (par. 162). He concludes the episode: "We returned to our college on a Sunday afternoon: the peasants were dancing, and every one we met appeared gay and happy. My own spirits were high, and I bounded along with the feelings of unbridled joy and hilarity" (par. 164). How does the imagery he creates foreshadow what is to follow? Find another instance of similar foreshadowing at the end of a chapter and explain its significance.
10. **AP® Setting, Narration, and Figurative Language.** Victor Frankenstein's first glimpse of the monster (on his return home after learning of William's death) is accompanied by imagery of a terrific tempest. Find other examples of the conjunction of the appearance of the monster and storm imagery. How do they contribute to the mood and meaning of the novel?
11. **AP® Character, Narration, and Figurative Language.** In paragraph 255, Frankenstein likens himself to a wounded deer. How apt is that metaphor? What aspects of Victor's character does it reveal? Do you take Frankenstein at his word, or do you read this and other similar self-descriptions with a grain of salt? Explain.
12. **AP® Character, Structure, Narration, and Figurative Language.** Carefully read the first four paragraphs of Chapter X, in which Frankenstein describes his surroundings and quotes from "Mutability," a poem by Percy Bysshe Shelley, the author's husband. What is the relationship between the imagery of Frankenstein's description and the poem? Explain. How do these paragraphs foreshadow what immediately follows?
13. **AP® Character, Structure, and Narration.** After Frankenstein destroys the new creature he was creating, the monster tells him, "Slave, I have reasoned with you, but you have proved yourself unworthy of my condescension. Remember that I have power; you believe

yourself miserable, but I can make you so wretched that the light of day will be hateful to you. You are my creator, but I am your master; — obey!" (par. 510). Explain the paradox in what the monster says. How is it emblematic of the novel's themes? of the monster's character? of Frankenstein's?

14. **AP® Narration and Figurative Language.** In Chapter XXIII, Frankenstein describes finding Elizabeth dead at the hands of the monster: "She was there, lifeless and inanimate, thrown across the bed, her head hanging down, and her pale and distorted features half covered by her hair. Everywhere I turn I see the same figure — her bloodless arms and relaxed form flung by the murderer on its bridal bier" (par. 631). This image was inspired by *The Nightmare* (p. 1191), a 1791 painting by Henry Fuseli, an acquaintance of Shelley's parents. View the image carefully. How effectively does it reflect the mood of the passage? Why do you think it provided such inspiration for Shelley?

15. **AP® Character, Structure, and Narration.** At the end, the reader doesn't learn what becomes of the monster or of Robert Walton. How does such an inconclusive ending relate to the structure of the rest of the book? What effect does such an open-ended conclusion have on your understanding of the novel's characters and themes?

Topics for Composing

1. AP® FRQ **Literary Argument.** In *Beyond Good and Evil*, German philosopher Friedrich Nietzsche claimed that "He who fights with monsters should be careful lest he thereby become a monster." In *Frankenstein*, Victor Frankenstein's nature becomes more monstrous as the novel, and his conflict with his creation, progresses. In a well-written essay, analyze how Victor's development throughout the novel contributes to an interpretation of the work as a whole. Do not merely summarize the plot.

2. AP® FRQ **Prose Fiction Analysis.** The following question refers to paragraphs 107–109 of Mary Shelley's *Frankenstein*, published in 1818. In this passage, Victor Frankenstein recounts how his research led to the discovery of reanimating the dead. Read the passage carefully. Then, in a well-written essay, analyze how Shelley uses literary elements and techniques to convey Frankenstein's complex attitude toward his discovery.

3. **AP® Literary Argumentation.** *Frankenstein* is a challenging novel for many reasons, among them the epistolary format coupled with its tales within tales, the strain on credibility that the events create, and the manner in which the characters speak. Take, for instance, one passage spoken by the monster — who is, remember, three years old:

> Food, however, became scarce; and I often spent the whole day searching in vain for a few acorns to assuage the pangs of hunger. When I found this, I resolved to quit the place that I had hitherto inhabited; to seek for one where the few wants I experienced would be more easily satisfied. In this emigration, I exceedingly lamented the loss of the fire which I had obtained through accident, and knew not how to reproduce it. I gave several hours to the serious consideration of this difficulty; but I was obliged to relinquish all attempt to supply it; and, wrapping myself up in my cloak, I struck across the woods towards the setting sun. I passed three days in these rambles, and at length discovered the open country. . . .

Write an essay in which you analyze the syntax in an example of narration you have chosen by Walton, Frankenstein, or the monster. As you analyze the passage, make an argument for how syntax functions as an element of style in the novel and its effect on the meaning of the work as a whole.

4. **AP® Literary Argumentation.** In "Frankenstein's Fallen Angel," contemporary writer Joyce Carol Oates discusses "the difficulty of reading Mary Shelley's novel for the first time," and argues that it should be read not as realism but as romance. She states,

> It contains no characters, only points of view; its concerns are pointedly moral and didactic. . . . Where the realistic novel presents characters in a more or less coherent "field" as part of a defined society . . . romance does away with questions of verisimilitude and plausibility altogether. . . . No one expects Victor Frankenstein to behave plausibly when he is a near-allegorical figure; no one expects his demon to behave plausibly since he is a demon presence, an outsized mirror image of his creator.

   Write an essay in which you analyze *Frankenstein* as a romantic rather than a realistic novel, as Oates characterizes it.

5. **Connections.** Read the full text of Samuel Taylor Coleridge's narrative poem, *The Rime of the Ancient Mariner*. Write an essay in which you analyze the parallels between the poem and *Frankenstein*.

6. **Connections.** If you have read *Paradise Lost*, the epic poem by John Milton, you will recognize parallels between the two works of literature that go beyond Mary Shelley's epigraph from Milton: for example, between Frankenstein and both God and Satan, and between the monster and Adam. Write an essay in which you analyze the parallels between the poem and the novel.

7. **Connections.** In his widely popular book (in America it sold more copies than any other book after the Bible), *Baby and Child Care*, published in 1946 and revised in 1957, Dr. Benjamin Spock offered the following advice to new parents:

> Don't be afraid of your baby. . . . Love and enjoy your children for what they are, for what they look like, for what they do, and forget about the qualities that they don't have. I don't give you this advice just for sentimental reasons. There's a very important practical point here. The children who are appreciated for what they are, even if they are homely, or clumsy, or slow, will grow up with confidence in themselves — happy. They will have a spirit that will make the best of all the capacities that they have, and of all the opportunities that come their way. They will make light of any handicaps. But the children who have never been quite accepted by their parents, who have always felt that they were not quite right, will grow up lacking confidence. They'll never be able to make full use of what brains, what skills, what physical attractiveness they have. If they start life with a handicap, physical or mental, it will be multiplied tenfold by the time they are grown up.

   How applicable are Dr. Spock's ideas about childrearing to your observations and experiences? How would the creature's life have been different — if at all — had Victor followed this parenting advice? Support your position with evidence from the novel.

Frankenstein and the Ethics of Creation

Surely most people — even those who have never read Mary Shelley's novel — know about Frankenstein's monster, even if they mistakenly ascribe the scientist's name to him. After all, he is as familiar as Dracula, Sherlock Holmes, and Alice in Wonderland. Like those characters, he has been widely depicted in film and referenced in other works of art, literature, and sometimes even in political cartoons. As a result, Frankenstein's creation has become a fixture in modern popular culture, one cemented by the actor Boris Karloff, who played the iconic monster with scars on his face and bolts in his neck in James Whale's 1931 film. But he is unique in that he has most often been represented as his opposite — that is, as a monster created by a mad scientist with evil motives rather than by a scholar driven by the selfless wish to benefit humanity. Why is the story of Frankenstein and his monster so often, and so thoroughly, garbled? Perhaps the answer to that question lies in the ethical implications of Mary Shelley's classic tale, and the questions it raises about right and wrong, about human nature, and about the limits of technological advancement. The true monster in *Frankenstein* may actually be a matter of perspective.

The subtitle of Mary Shelley's novel — *The Modern Prometheus* — hints that Frankenstein has perhaps gone too far, exceeding natural limits on human achievement. But the epigraph refers not to Frankenstein but to his creation, the monster, who might indeed ask his creator, as Adam asks God:

> *Did I request thee, Maker, from my clay*
> *To mould Me man? Did I solicit thee*
> *From darkness to promote me? —*

This rhetorical question poses a dilemma for Victor Frankenstein and for us. What has driven him to create the monster? What motivates humanity to create new technologies and entities that we do not fully understand? Is it ambition, zeal, presumption, hubris, or a desire to improve the world and help humanity? And does responsibility for the unexpected — and unintended — consequences fall on creation or creator?

What prompted Mary Shelley to ask these questions in her work? In some ways, the novel is a direct response to the issues of the time. *Frankenstein* is a product, on the one hand, of the Enlightenment, or the Age of Reason, which brought new ideas to science, political thought, and philosophy throughout the eighteenth century. It is also a product of the age of Romanticism, an artistic and literary movement during the late eighteenth and early nineteenth centuries that celebrated the power and autonomy of the individual, who was often a rebel against the standards of the time; the glory and intensity of nature; the goodness and innocence of the young; and the unexplainable supernatural. Some Romantic literature, including *Frankenstein*, is gothic: fantastic, mysterious, and macabre; these works often feature exotic or haunted settings,

David Sipress The New Yorker Collection/The Cartoon Bank

What is the source of humor in this cartoon? How might it be seen as a contemporary interpretation that captures the essential ideas of Shelley's work? How might it come across as reductive of the enduring themes the novel explores?

supernatural beings, and terrifying events — both *Dracula* and the works of Edgar Allan Poe are prime examples of the genre.

Frankenstein is indeed a Romantic, gothic novel, but it might also be seen as the first "science fiction" novel. While not set in the future, as is much science fiction, the novel does involve science as none had before, looking ahead to the future consequences of industrialization, scientific experimentation, and technological discovery. It even addresses the ethics of child rearing in an era of unprecedented progress. Is Victor Frankenstein crazy? Is he merely selfish? Is *Frankenstein* a cautionary tale about an insensitive human being, a neglectful parent? Is his transgression his inhumane response to his creation and abject neglect of his own progeny? Or does it lie in the act of artificially creating life in the first place? Is *Frankenstein* a tale about a "mad scientist" whose hubris has taken him beyond the limits of human achievement, like that of Adam and also of Lucifer, who attempted to usurp God's dominion in seeking forbidden knowledge? Is the novel a plea against advances in science and runaway technology, as many interpret it? Has *Frankenstein* come to represent the idea that science — whatever its motives — will result in unwanted consequences and unforeseen monstrosities? The speculation these questions invite, combined with the novel's narrative style, form a truly unsettling response to the enduring ethical dilemmas first posed by the rapid social, political, and especially the technological changes of the Enlightenment era.

As a symbol, Frankenstein's monster comes up whenever we discuss such advances as scientific engineering, cloning, robot technology, self-driving cars, and genetically modified organisms. In 1992, for instance, college professor Paul Lewis coined the term "Frankenfood" to describe genetically modified food. Or, consider President Barack Obama's assertion regarding surveillance technology during his 2013 end-of-year White House press conference: "Just because we can do something, doesn't mean we should do it." Did Frankenstein create the monster simply because he *could*, without enough consideration of whether he *should*? Have we likewise failed to fully consider the ethical implications of today's groundbreaking technologies?

In the texts that follow, you will see how different writers have addressed some of these questions. The first one is an essay by Harvard paleontologist Stephen Jay Gould, who writes about literature as eloquently as he does about science. Each of the texts that follow — nonfiction, fiction, and visual — addresses *Frankenstein* as a novel and also touches on its enduring legacy as a cautionary tale about the unpredictable aftermath of human invention.

TEXTS IN CONTEXT

1. **Stephen Jay Gould ▪ from *The Monster's Human Nature* (nonfiction)**
2. **Brian Aldiss ▪ *Super-Toys Last All Summer Long* (fiction)**
3. **Jon Turney ▪ from *Frankenstein's Footsteps* (nonfiction)**
4. **Janet Allinger ▪ *Frankenstein Drives a Tesla* (cartoon)**

from The Monster's Human Nature

Stephen Jay Gould

Stephen Jay Gould (1941–2002) was an American paleontologist, evolutionary biologist, science historian, and prolific essayist. Gould wrote several best-selling books about science, including *Ever Since Darwin* (1977), *The Panda's Thumb* (1980), *Hen's Teeth and Horse's Toes* (1983), and *The Flamingo's Smile* (1985). In "The Monster's Human Nature," he examines how authors tend to offer nuanced and humanized portrayals of monsters in books, which are then reinterpreted by Hollywood in movies that show monsters as quintessentially inhuman.

An old Latin proverb tells us to "beware the man of one book" — *cave ab homine unius libri.* Yet Hollywood knows only one theme in making monster movies, from the archetypal *Frankenstein* of 1931 to the recent mega-hit *Jurassic Park.* Human technology must not go beyond an intended order decreed by God or set by nature's laws. No matter how benevolent the purposes of the transgressor, such cosmic arrogance can only lead to killer tomatoes, very large rabbits with sharp teeth, giant ants in the Los Angeles sewers, or even larger blobs that swallow entire cities as they grow. Yet these films often use far more subtle books as their sources and, in so doing, distort the originals beyond all thematic recognition.

The trend began in 1931 with *Frankenstein,* Hollywood's first great monster "talkie" (though Mr. Karloff only grunted, while Colin Clive, as Henry Frankenstein, emoted). Hollywood decreed its chosen theme by the most "up front" of all conceivable strategies. The film begins with a prologue (even before the titles roll) featuring a well-dressed man standing on stage before a curtain, both to issue a warning about potential fright, and to announce the film's deeper theme as the story of "a man of science who sought to create a man after his own image without reckoning upon God."

In the movie, Dr. Waldman, Henry's old medical school professor, speaks of his pupil's "insane ambition to create life," a diagnosis supported by Frankenstein's own feverish words of enthusiasm: "I created it. I made it with my own hands from the bodies I took from graves, from the gallows, from anywhere."

The best of a cartload of sequels, *The Bride of Frankenstein* (1935), makes the favored theme even more explicit in a prologue featuring Mary Wollstonecraft Shelley, who published *Frankenstein* in 1818 when she was only nineteen years old, in conversation with her husband Percy and their buddy Lord Byron. She states: "My purpose was to write a moral lesson of the punishment that befell a mortal man who dared to emulate God."

Shelley's original *Frankenstein* is a rich book of many themes, but I can find little therein to support the Hollywood reading. The text is neither a diatribe on dangers of technology nor a warning about overextended ambition against a natural order. We find no passages about disobeying God — an unlikely subject for Mary Shelley and her free-thinking friends (Percy had been expelled from Oxford in 1811 for publishing a defense of atheism). Victor Frankenstein (I do not know why Hollywood changed him to Henry) is guilty of a great moral failing, as we shall see later, but his crime is not technological transgression against a natural or divine order.

We can find a few passages about the awesome power of science, but these words are not negative. Professor Waldman, a sympathetic character in the book, states, for example, "They [scientists] penetrate into the recesses of nature, and show how she works in her hiding places. They ascend into the heavens; they have discovered how the blood circulates, and the nature of the air we breathe. They have acquired new and almost unlimited powers." We do learn that ardor without compassion or moral consideration can lead to trouble, but Shelley applies this argument to any endeavor, not especially to scientific discovery (her examples are, in fact, all political). Victor Frankenstein says:

> A human being in perfection ought always to preserve a calm and peaceful mind, and never to allow passion or a transitory desire to disturb his tranquility. I do not think that the pursuit of knowledge is an exception to this rule. If the study to which you apply yourself has a tendency to weaken your affections . . . then that study is certainly unlawful, that is to say, not befitting the human mind. If this rule were always observed . . . Greece had not been enslaved; Caesar would have spared his country; America would have been discovered more gradually, and the empires of Mexico and Peru had not been destroyed.

5 Victor's own motivations are entirely idealistic: "I thought, that if I could bestow animation upon lifeless matter, I might in process of time (although I now found it impossible) renew life where death had apparently devoted the body to corruption." Finally, as Victor lies dying in the Arctic, he makes his most forceful statement on the dangers of scientific ambition, but he only berates himself and his own failures, while stating that others might well succeed. Victor says his dying words to the ship's captain who found him on the polar ice: "Farewell, Walton! Seek happiness in tranquility, and avoid ambition, even if it be only the apparently innocent one of distinguishing yourself in science and discoveries. Yet why do I say this? I have myself been blasted in these hopes, yet another may succeed."

But Hollywood dumbed these subtleties down to the easy formula — "man must not go beyond what God and nature intended" (you almost have to use the old gender-biased language for such a simplistic archaicism) — and has been treading in its own footsteps ever since. The latest incarnation, *Jurassic Park,* substitutes a *Velociraptor* re-created from old DNA for Karloff cobbled together from bits and pieces of corpses, but hardly alters the argument an iota.

Karloff's *Frankenstein* contains an even more serious and equally prominent distortion of a theme that I regard as the primary lesson of Mary Shelley's book — another lamentable example of Hollywood's sense that the American public cannot tolerate even the slightest exercise in intellectual complexity. Why is the monster evil? Shelley provides a nuanced and subtle answer that, to me, sets the central theme of her book. But Hollywood opted for a simplistic solution, so precisely opposite to Shelley's intent that the movie can no longer claim to be telling a moral fable (despite protestations of the man in front of the curtain, or Mary Shelley herself in the sequel), and becomes instead, as I suppose the makers intended all along, a pure horror film. . . .

Shelley's monster is not evil by inherent 10
constitution. He is born unformed — carrying the predispositions of human nature, but without the specific behaviors, that can only be set by upbringing and education. He is the Enlightenment's man of hope, whom learning and compassion might mold to goodness and wisdom. But he is also a victim of post-Enlightenment pessimism as the cruel rejection of his natural fellows drives him to fury and revenge. (Even as a murderer, the monster remains fastidious and purposive. Victor Frankenstein is the source of his anger, and he kills only the friends and lovers whose deaths will bring Victor most grief; he does not, like Godzilla of the Blob, rampage through cities.)

Mary Shelley chose her words carefully to take a properly nuanced position at a fruitfully intermediate point between nature and nurture — whereas Hollywood opted for nature alone to explain the monster's evil deeds. Frankenstein's creature is not inherently good by internal construction — a benevolent theory of "nature alone," but no different in mode of explanation from Hollywood's opposite version. He is, rather born *capable* of goodness, even with an *inclination* toward kindness, should circumstances of his upbringing call forth this favored response. In his final confession to Captain Walton, before heading north to immolate himself at the Pole, the monster says:

> My heart was fashioned to be *susceptible of love and sympathy*; and, when wrenched by misery to vice and hatred, it did not endure the violence of the change without torture, such as you cannot even imagine. [My italics to note Shelley's careful phrasing in terms of potentiality or inclination, rather than determinism.]

He then adds:

> Once my fancy was soothed with dreams of virtue, of fame, and of enjoyment. Once I falsely hoped to meet with beings who, pardoning my outward form, would love me for the excellent qualities which I was *capable of bringing forth.* I was nourished with high thoughts of honor and devotion. But now vice has degraded me beneath the meanest animal . . . When I call over the frightful catalogue of my deeds, I cannot believe that I am he whose thoughts were once filled with sublime and transcendent visions of the beauty and the majesty of goodness. But it is even so; the fallen angel becomes a malignant devil.

Why, then, does the monster turn to evil against an inherent inclination to goodness? Shelley gives us an interesting answer that seems almost trivial in invoking such a superficial reason, but that emerges as profound when we grasp her general theory of human nature. He becomes evil, of course, because humans reject him so violently and so unjustly. His resulting loneliness becomes unbearable. He states:

> And what was I? Of my creation and creator I was absolutely ignorant; but I knew that I possessed no money, no friends, no kind of property. I was, besides, endowed with a figure hideously deformed and loathsome . . . When I looked around, I saw and heard none like me. Was I then a monster, a blot upon the earth, from which all men fled, and whom all men disowned?

But why is the monster so rejected, if his feelings incline toward benevolence, and his acts to evident goodness? He certainly tries to act kindly, in helping (albeit secretly) the family in the hovel that serves as his hiding place:

> I had been accustomed, during the night, to steal a part of their store for my own consumption; but when I found that in doing this I inflicted pain on the cottagers. I abstained, and satisfied myself with berries, nuts, and roots, which I gathered from a neighboring wood. I discovered also another means through which I was enabled to assist their labors. I found that the youth spent a great part of each day in collecting wood for the family fire; and, during the night, I often took his tools, the use of which I quickly discovered, and brought home firing sufficient for the consumption of several days.

15 Shelley tells us that all humans reject and even loathe the monster for a visceral reason of literal superficiality: his truly terrifying ugliness — a reason both heartrending in its deep injustice, and profound in its biological accuracy and philosophical insight about the meaning of human nature.

The monster, by Shelley's description, could scarcely have been less attractive in appearance. Victor Frankenstein describes the first sight of his creature alive:

> How can I describe my emotions at this catastrophe, or how delineate the wretch whom with such infinite pains and care I had endeavored to form? His limbs were in proportion, and I had selected his features as beautiful. Beautiful! — Great God! His yellow skin scarcely covered the work of muscles and arteries beneath; his hair was a lustrous black, and flowing; his teeth of a pearly whiteness; but these luxuriances only formed a more horrid contrast with his watery eyes, that seemed almost of the same color as the dun white sockets in which they were set, his shriveled complexion, and straight black lips.

Moreover, at his hyper-NBA height of eight feet, the monster scares the bejeezus out of all who cast eyes upon him.

The monster quickly grasps this unfair source of human fear and plans a strategy to overcome initial reactions, and to prevail by goodness of soul. He presents himself first to the blind old father in the hovel above his hiding place and makes a good impression. He hopes to win the man's confidence, and thus gain a favorable introduction to the world of sighted people. But, in his joy at acceptance, he stays too long. The man's son returns and drives the monster away — as fear and loathing overwhelm any inclination to hear about inner decency.

The monster finally acknowledges his inability to overcome visceral fear at his ugliness; his resulting despair and loneliness drive him to evil deeds:

> I am malicious because I am miserable; am I not shunned and hated by all mankind? . . . Shall I respect man when he contemns me? Let him live with me in the interchange of kindness, and, instead of injury, I would bestow every benefit upon him with tears of gratitude at his acceptance. But that cannot be; the human senses are insurmountable barriers to our union. . . .

20 Frankenstein's creature becomes a monster because he is cruelly ensnared by

one of the deepest predispositions of our biological inheritance — our instinctive aversion toward seriously malformed individuals. (Konrad Lorenz, the most famous ethologist of the last generation, based much of his theory on the primacy of this inborn rule.) We are now appalled by the injustice of such a predisposition, but this proper moral feeling is an evolutionary latecomer, imposed by human consciousness upon a much older mammalian pattern.

We almost surely inherit such an instinctive aversion to serious malformation, but remember that nature can only supply a predisposition, while culture shapes specific results. And now we can grasp — for Mary Shelley presented the issue to us so wisely — the true tragedy of Frankenstein's monster, and the moral dereliction of Victor himself. The predisposition for aversion toward ugliness can be overcome by learning and understanding. I trust that we have all trained ourselves in this essential form of compassion, and that we all work hard to suppress that frisson of rejection (which in honest moments we all admit we feel), and to judge people by their qualities of soul, not by their external appearances.

Frankenstein's monster was a good man in an appallingly ugly body. His countrymen could have been educated to accept him, but the person responsible for that instruction — his creator, Victor Frankenstein — ran away from his foremost duty, and abandoned his creation at first sight. Victor's sin does not lie in misuse of technology, or hubris in emulating God; we cannot find these themes in Mary Shelley's account. Victor failed because he followed a predisposition of human nature — visceral disgust at the monster's appearance — and did not undertake the duty of any creator or parent: to teach his own charge and to educate others in acceptability.

He could have schooled his creature (and not left the monster to learn language by eavesdropping and by scrounging for books in a hiding place under a hovel). He could have told the world what he had done. He could have introduced his benevolent and educated monster to people prepared to judge him on merit. But he took one look at his handiwork, and ran away forever. In other words, he bowed to a base aspect of our common nature, and did not accept the particular moral duty of our potential nurture:

> I had worked hard for nearly two years, for the sole purpose of infusing life into an inanimate body. For this I had deprived myself of rest and health. I had desired it with an ardor that far exceeded moderation; but now that I had finished, the beauty of the dream vanished, and breathless horror and disgust filled my heart. Unable to endure the aspect of the being I had created, I rushed out of the room . . . A mummy again endued with animation could not be so hideous as that wretch. I had gazed on him while unfinished; he was ugly then; but when those muscles and joints were rendered capable of motion, it became a thing such as even Dante could not have conceived. . . .

Mary Shelley wrote a moral tale, not about hubris or technology, but about responsibility to all creatures of feeling and to the products of one's own hand. The monster's misery arose from the moral failure of other humans, not from his own inherent and unchangeable constitution. Charles Darwin later invoked the same theory of human nature to remind us of duties to all people in universal bonds of brotherhood: "If the misery of our poor be caused not by the laws of nature, but by our institutions, great is our sin." ■

1995

Questions

1. According to Stephen Jay Gould, how have film productions of *Frankenstein* altered people's perception of the themes of the novel? If you have seen any of the *Frankenstein* films, to what extent do you agree with him?
2. How does Gould characterize Victor Frankenstein? Having read the novel, do you agree with that characterization? Explain.
3. Gould refers to "a theme that I regard as the primary lesson of Mary Shelley's book" (par. 9). Before explaining that theme or lesson, he then goes on to discuss the 1931 film. How would you paraphrase the theme of that film as Gould presents it? For what reasons, according to Gould, did Hollywood change the theme? Do you agree that the theme he presents is the "primary lesson" of the novel? Explain.
4. Discuss the differences between *nature* and *nurture* as Gould categorizes them. Which of the two does Gould hold more responsible for the monster's behavior? Which do you believe is primarily responsible? Explain, using examples from the novel to support your response.
5. In paragraph 20 Gould refers to "the true tragedy of Frankenstein's monster and the moral dereliction of Victor himself." What is that "true tragedy," according to Gould? Read carefully Gould's series of parallel "could have" statements. Do you agree that those statements explain the novel's tragedy? Explain.
6. Gould concludes with a strong claim: "Mary Shelley wrote a moral tale, not about hubris or technology, but about responsibility to all creatures of feeling and to the products of one's own hand. The monster's misery arose from the moral failure of other humans, not from his own inherent and unchangeable constitution." How compelling do you find Gould's argument? How accurate a reading of the novel do you believe it presents? Explain.

Super-Toys Last All Summer Long

Brian Aldiss

Born in Norfolk, England, Brian Aldiss (1925–2017) was a prolific author of short stories, criticism, novels, drama, and poetry. He was most widely known as a writer of science fiction. *A.I. Artificial Intelligence*, the 2001 science fiction film directed by Steven Spielberg, is based on Aldiss's 1969 short story "Super-Toys Last All Summer Long," which follows.

In Mrs. Swinton's garden, it was always summer. The lovely almond trees stood about it in perpetual leaf. Monica Swinton plucked a saffron-colored rose and showed it to David.

"Isn't it lovely?" she said.

David looked up at her and grinned without replying. Seizing the flower, he ran with it across the lawn and disappeared behind the kennel where the mowervator crouched, ready to cut or sweep or roll when the moment dictated. She stood alone on her impeccable plastic gravel path.

She had tried to love him.

5 When she made up her mind to follow the boy, she found him in the courtyard floating the rose in his paddling pool. He stood in the pool engrossed, still wearing his sandals.

"David, darling, do you have to be so awful? Come in at once and change your shoes and socks."

He went with her without protest into the house, his dark head bobbing at the level of her waist. At the age of three, he showed no fear of the ultrasonic dryer in the kitchen. But before his mother could reach for a pair of slippers, he wriggled away and was gone into the silence of the house.

He would probably be looking for Teddy.

Monica Swinton, twenty-nine, of graceful shape and lambent eye, went and sat in her living room, arranging her limbs with taste. She began by sitting and thinking; soon she was just sitting. Time waited on her shoulder with the maniac slowth it reserves for children, the insane, and wives whose husbands are away improving the world. Almost by reflex, she reached out and changed the wavelength of her windows. The garden faded; in its place, the city center rose by her left hand, full of crowding people, blowboats, and buildings (but she kept the sound down). She remained alone. An overcrowded world is the ideal place in which to be lonely.

• • •

The directors of Synthank were eating an enormous luncheon to celebrate the launching of their new product. Some of them wore the plastic face-masks popular at the time. All were elegantly slender, despite the rich food and drink they were putting away. Their wives were elegantly slender, despite the food and drink they too were putting away. An earlier and less sophisticated generation would have regarded them as beautiful people, apart from their eyes.

Henry Swinton, Managing Director of Synthank, was about to make a speech.

"I'm sorry your wife couldn't be with us to hear you," his neighbor said.

"Monica prefers to stay at home thinking beautiful thoughts," said Swinton, maintaining a smile.

"One would expect such a beautiful woman to have beautiful thoughts," said the neighbor.

Take your mind off my wife, you bastard, thought Swinton, still smiling.

He rose to make his speech amid applause.

After a couple of jokes, he said, "Today marks a real breakthrough for the company. It is now almost ten years since we put our first synthetic life-forms on the world market. You all know what a success they have been, particularly the miniature dinosaurs. But none of them had intelligence.

"It seems like a paradox that in this day and age we can create life but not intelligence. Our first selling line, the Crosswell Tape, sells best of all, and is the most stupid of all." Everyone laughed.

"Though three-quarters of the overcrowded world are starving, we are lucky here to have more than enough, thanks to population control. Obesity's our problem, not malnutrition. I guess there's nobody round this table who doesn't have a Crosswell working for him in the small intestine, a perfectly safe parasite tape-worm that enables its host to eat up to fifty percent more food and still keep his or her figure. Right?" General nods of agreement.

"Our miniature dinosaurs are almost equally stupid. Today, we launch an intelligent synthetic life-form — a full-size serving-man.

"Not only does he have intelligence, he has a controlled amount of intelligence. We believe people would be afraid of a being with a human brain. Our serving-man has a small computer in his cranium.

"There have been mechanicals on the market with mini-computers for brains — plastic things without life, super-toys — but we have at last found a way to link computer circuitry with synthetic flesh."

• • •

David sat by the long window of his nursery, wrestling with paper and pencil. Finally, he stopped writing and began to roll the pencil up and down the slope of the desk-lid.

"Teddy!" he said.

Teddy lay on the bed against the wall, under a book with moving pictures and a giant plastic soldier. The speech-pattern of his master's voice activated him and he sat up.

"Teddy! I can't think what to say!"

Climbing off the bed, the bear walked stiffly over to cling to the boy's leg. David lifted him and set him on the desk.

"What have you said so far?"

"I've said— " He picked up his letter and stared hard at it. "I've said, 'Dear Mummy, I hope you're well just now. I love you . . .'"

There was a long silence, until the bear said, "That sounds fine. Go downstairs and give it to her."

Another long silence.

"It isn't quite right. She won't understand."

Inside the bear, a small computer worked through its program of possibilities. "Why not do it again in crayon?"

When David did not answer, the bear repeated his suggestion. "Why not do it again in crayon?"

David was staring out of the window. "Teddy, you know what I was thinking? How do you tell what are real things from what aren't real things?"

The bear shuffled its alternatives. "Real things are good."

"I wonder if time is good. I don't think Mummy likes time very much. The other day, lots of days ago, she said that time went by her. Is time real, Teddy?"

"Clocks tell the time. Clocks are real. Mummy has clocks so she must like them. She has a clock on her wrist next to her dial."

David started to draw a jumbo jet on the back of his letter. "You and I are real, Teddy, aren't we?"

The bear's eyes regarded the boy unflinchingly. "You and I are real, David." It specialized in comfort.

• • •

Monica walked slowly about the house. It was almost time for the afternoon post to come over the wire. She punched the Post Office number on the dial on her wrist, but nothing came through. A few minutes more.

She could take up her painting. Or she could dial her friends. Or she could wait till Henry came home. Or she could go up and play with David. . . .

She walked out into the hall and to the bottom of the stairs.

"David!"

No answer. She called again and a third time.

"Teddy!" she called, in sharper tones.

"Yes, Mummy!" After a moment's pause, Teddy's head of golden fur appeared at the top of the stairs.

"Is David in his room, Teddy?"

"David went into the garden, Mummy."

"Come down here, Teddy!"

She stood impassively, watching the little furry figure as it climbed down from step to step on its stubby limbs. When it reached the bottom, she picked it up and carried it into the living room. It lay unmoving in her arms, staring up at her. She could feel just the slightest vibration from its motor.

"Stand there, Teddy. I want to talk to you." She set him down on a tabletop, and he stood as she requested, arms set forward and open in the eternal gesture of embrace.

"Teddy, did David tell you to tell me he had gone into the garden?"

The circuits of the bear's brain were too simple for artifice. "Yes, Mummy."

"So you lied to me."

"Yes. Mummy."

"Stop calling me Mummy! Why is David avoiding me? He's not afraid of me, is he?"

"No. He loves you."

"Why can't we communicate?"

"David's upstairs."

The answer stopped her dead. Why waste time talking to this machine? Why not simply go upstairs and scoop David into her arms and talk to him, as a loving mother should to a loving son? She heard the sheer weight of silence in the house, with a different quality of silence pouring out of every room. On the upper landing, something was moving very silently—David, trying to hide away from her. . . .

• • •

He was nearing the end of his speech now. The guests were attentive; so was the Press, lining two walls of the banqueting chamber, recording Henry's words and occasionally photographing him.

"Our serving-man will be, in many senses, a product of the computer. Without computers, we could never have worked through the sophisticated biochemics that go into synthetic flesh. The serving-man will also be an extension of the computer—for he will contain a computer in his own head, a microminiaturized computer capable of dealing with almost any situation he may encounter in the home. With reservations, of course." Laughter at this; many of those present knew the heated debate that had engulfed the Synthank boardroom before the decision had finally been taken to leave the serving-man neuter under his flawless uniform.

"Amid all the triumphs of our civilization—yes, and amid the crushing problems of overpopulation too—it is sad to reflect how many millions of people suffer from increasing loneliness and isolation. Our serving-man will be a boon to them: he will always answer, and the most vapid conversation cannot bore him.

"For the future, we plan more models, male and female—some of them without the limitations of this first one, I promise you!—of more advanced design, true bio-electronic beings.

"Not only will they possess their own computer, capable of individual programming; they will be linked to the World Data Network. Thus everyone will be able to enjoy the equivalent of an Einstein in their own homes. Personal isolation will then be banished forever!"

He sat down to enthusiastic applause. Even the synthetic serving-man, sitting at the table dressed in an unostentatious suit, applauded with gusto.

• • •

Dragging his satchel, David crept round the side of the house. He climbed on to the ornamental seat under the living-room window and peeped cautiously in.

His mother stood in the middle of the room. Her face was blank, its lack of expression scared him. He watched fascinated. He did not move; she did not move. Time might have stopped, as it had stopped in the garden.

At last she turned and left the room. After waiting a moment, David tapped on the window. Teddy looked round, saw him, tumbled off the table, and came over to the window. Fumbling with his paws, he eventually got it open.

They looked at each other.

"I'm no good, Teddy. Let's run away!"

"You're a very good boy. Your Mummy loves you."

Slowly, he shook his head. "If she loved me, then why can't I talk to her?"

"You're being silly, David. Mummy's lonely. That's why she had you."

"She's got Daddy. I've got nobody 'cept you, and I'm lonely."

Teddy gave him a friendly cuff over the head. "If you feel so bad, you'd better go to the psychiatrist again."

"I hate that old psychiatrist—he makes me feel I'm not real." He started to run across the lawn. The bear toppled out of the window and followed as fast as its stubby legs would allow.

Monica Swinton was up in the nursery. She called to her son once and then stood there, undecided. All was silent.

Crayons lay on his desk. Obeying a sudden impulse, she went over to the desk and opened it. Dozens of pieces of paper lay inside. Many of them were written in crayon in David's clumsy writing, with each letter picked out in a color different from the letter preceding it. None of the messages was finished.

"My dear Mummy, How are you really, do you love me as much—"

"Dear Mummy, I love you and Daddy and the sun is shining—"

"Dear dear Mummy, Teddy's helping me write to you. I love you and Teddy—"

"Darling Mummy, I'm your one and only son and I love you so much that some times—"

"Dear Mummy, you're really my Mummy and I hate Teddy— "

"Darling Mummy, guess how much I love— "

"Dear Mummy, I'm your little boy not Teddy and I love you but Teddy— "

"Dear Mummy, this is a letter to you just to say how much how ever so much— "

Monica dropped the pieces of paper and burst out crying. In their gay inaccurate colors, the letters fanned out and settled on the floor.

• • •

Henry Swinton caught the express home in high spirits, and occasionally said a word to the synthetic serving-man he was taking home with him. The serving-man answered politely and punctually, although his answers were not always entirely relevant by human standards.

The Swintons lived in one of the ritziest city-blocks, half a kilometer above the ground. Embedded in other apartments, their apartment had no windows to the outside; nobody wanted to see the overcrowded external world. Henry unlocked the door with his retina pattern-scanner and walked in, followed by the serving-man.

At once, Henry was surrounded by the friendly illusion of gardens set in eternal summer. It was amazing what Whologram could do to create huge mirages in small spaces. Behind its roses and wisteria stood their house; the deception was complete: a Georgian mansion appeared to welcome him.

"How do you like it?" he asked the serving-man.

"Roses occasionally suffer from black spot."

"These roses are guaranteed free from any imperfections."

"It is always advisable to purchase goods with guarantees, even if they cost slightly more."

"Thanks for the information," Henry said dryly. Synthetic lifeforms were less than ten years old, the old android mechanicals less than sixteen; the faults of their systems were still being ironed out, year by year.

He opened the door and called to Monica.

She came out of the sitting-room immediately and flung her arms round him, kissing him ardently on cheek and lips. Henry was amazed.

Pulling back to look at her face, he saw how she seemed to generate light and beauty. It was months since he had seen her so excited. Instinctively, he clasped her tighter.

"Darling, what's happened?"

"Henry, Henry— oh, my darling, I was in despair . . . but I've just dialed the afternoon post and— you'll never believe it! Oh, it's wonderful!"

"For heavens sake, woman, what's wonderful?"

He caught a glimpse of the heading on the photostat in her hand, still moist from the wall-receiver: Ministry of Population. He felt the color drain from his face in sudden shock and hope.

"Monica . . . oh . . . Don't tell me our number's come up!"

"Yes, my darling, yes, we've won this week's parenthood lottery! We can go ahead and conceive a child at once!"

He let out a yell of joy. They danced round the room. Pressure of population was such that reproduction had to be strict, controlled. Childbirth required government permission. For this moment, they had waited four years. Incoherently they cried their delight.

They paused at last, gasping and stood in the middle of the room to laugh at each other's happiness. When she had come down from the nursery, Monica had de-opaqued the windows so that they now revealed the vista of garden beyond. Artificial sunlight was growing long and golden across the lawn— and David and Teddy were staring through the window at them.

Seeing their faces, Henry and his wife grew serious.

"What do we do about them?" Henry asked.

"Teddy's no trouble. He works well."

"Is David malfunctioning?"

"His verbal communication center is still giving trouble. I think he'll have to go back to the factory again."

"Okay. We'll see how he does before the baby's born. Which reminds me — I have a surprise for you: help just when help is needed! Come into the hall and see what I've got."

115 As the two adults disappeared from the room, boy and bear sat down beneath the standard roses.

"Teddy — I suppose Mummy and Daddy are real, aren't they?"

Teddy said, "You ask such silly questions, David. Nobody knows what *real* really means. Let's go indoors."

"First I'm going to have another rose!" Plucking a bright pink flower, he carried it with him into the house. It could lie on the pillow as he went to sleep. Its beauty and softness reminded him of Mummy. ■

1969

Questions

1. What are some early indications that Brian Aldiss's story is set in the future?
2. What clues are there about the nature of David and Teddy? What in the text leads the reader to suspect that the mother might also be a robot?
3. With which character does the reader sympathize? Is this ironic?
4. Considering that this story was published in 1969, which details are especially prescient?
5. What do paragraphs 90–118 suggest about Aldiss's attitude toward values? What do they suggest about the relationship between technology and humanity?
6. In what respects could this story be regarded as a cautionary tale? Explain.

from Frankenstein's Footsteps

Jon Turney

Jon Turney is a British science writer and the author of many popular science books, including *Frankenstein's Footsteps: Science, Genetics, and Popular Culture* (2000), *The Rough Guide to the Future* (2010), *I, Superorganism: Learning to Love Your Inner Ecosystem* (2015), and *Cracking Neuroscience* (2018). In the following excerpt from his book *Frankenstein's Footsteps*, Turney examines the lasting appeal of the Frankenstein myth and traces its intersection with modern biological science.

The accumulated retellings of the *Frankenstein* myth are now so numerous as almost to defy empirical analysis. Today, we encounter Frankenstein in many forms. Any of the old films may still be seen as late-night TV fillers, or on video. There are even two films which incorporate versions of the origin myth of the novel, mixing together the story of Mary, Percy and Byron by the lakeside with the creation of the monster.[1] New films continue to incorporate elements of the story, from *Demon Seed*, in which the monster is a computer which finds a way of inseminating a human female, to *Robocop*.[2]

[1] That is, Ken Russell's *Gothic* (1986) and Roger Corman's *Frankenstein Unbound* (1990). The latter is based on Brian Aldiss's novel of the same name. — Turney.

[2] Again, elements of the story may be found in a wider range of films. *Silence of the Lambs* (1991) for example, about the pursuit of a serial killer, portrays a man planning to reassemble a body, or at least its whole skin, from parts stripped from his numerous victims. — Turney.

Numerous editions of the novel remain in print, and new variations on the story continue to appear in printed fiction. Some of these, like Steven Gallagher's *Chimera*, are filmed in turn. Others, like Hilary Bailey's striking *Frankenstein's Bride*, remain as solely literary efforts. . . .

In addition, as with all truly frightening myths, we have tried to tame *Frankenstein* by making fun of it. Karloff's monster has been domesticated, in media ranging from the 1960s US television series *The Munsters* to the British children's comic the *Beano*, which features Frankie Stein. A distant descendant of Karloff even featured as Frank in the British Conservative government's television commercials for shares in its soon to be privatised electricity generation concern in the early 1990s. This taken-for-grantedness shows how well the cultural script has been learned. In consequence, the single word "Frankenstein" is seen constantly as a metaphor in media commentary of all kinds, especially political commentary.[3]

Why, then, has the story endured? Is it simply because the frame is so open at various points that it is infinitely adaptable? Or are there particular reasons, culturally general enough to read across all the retellings, with all their differences of detail, yet still specific to the culture which we share with Mary Shelley — broadly, the culture of modernity?

The first answer is to try to isolate what has endured in all the renderings of the myth since 1818. The story, for all its familiarity, is still a frightening one. It is frightening because it depicts a human enterprise which is out of control, and which turns on its creator. So much carries over from the earlier myths about the getting of knowledge. But *Frankenstein* is about science. What is more, the science is pursued, if not always with the best of intentions, then for motives with which we can readily identify. In the most striking retellings, the myth is never a straightforward anti-science story. There is something admirable about Victor Frankenstein, about Henry Frankenstein in James Whale's film, even about Peter Cushing's Baron Frankenstein. Even so, our sympathies are always torn between Frankenstein and his monster. The *Frankenstein* script, in its most salient forms, incorporates an ambivalence about science, method and motive, which is never resolved.

The retention of science in all the later 5
derivatives of the story is the most striking feature of the myth. After all, in the original text, once Victor's narrative begins, the creation of the monster is accomplished in a scant thirty pages, in which space is also given to the background and education of the monster's creator. The scientific details are few. After Victor's "brilliant

---

[3] Just a taste: a computer search of the text of the British *Financial Times*, perhaps the country's most serious title of all, between 1990 and 1994, yields fifty-two uses of "Frankenstein." Aside from references to film and TV and the other arts, the monster was coupled with:

the Channel Tunnel
the poll tax
the US Internal Revenue Service
artificial intelligence
municipal planning officers
a "monster" recycling plant
Iraq/Saddam Hussein (several times)
privatisation of electricity (that commercial)
a Swedish politician
Soviet central planning
genetic research
the Labour Party
the Department of National Heritage
the Ulster Freedom Fighters
a soccer analyst
"machines" in general
virtual reality
fashion journalism
the (much revived) *New York Post*
US trade laws.

Other newspapers show a similar pattern: a mix of political and technological links, mostly serious, with a scattering of light-hearted uses in other areas.

(*continued*)

The pattern with *Dracula,* which has achieved similar currency, is rather different. Of forty-six instances in the *Financial Times* over the same period, only ten occur outside arts reviews or commentary, and most are light-hearted references to effects of the sun or daylight, the colour black (in fashion), or bloodletting. There is also a geographical link with Romania, and specifically Transylvania. The only remotely serious political references are to US Defense programmes (hard to kill) and a reference to Romania's ex-president. There are no direct references to technology. — Turney.

light" dawns we never learn more than how he eventually "collected the instruments of life around me, that I might infuse a spark of life into the lifeless thing that lay at my feet." Yet it is those first thirty pages that supply the seeds of almost all of the images derived from *Frankenstein* which appear in so many variations in later stories about science and scientists.

Among others, we can distinguish in *Frankenstein* models for the scientist whose good intentions blind him to the true nature of his enterprise: "wealth was an inferior object; but what glory would attend the discovery if I could banish disease from the human frame and render man invulnerable to any but a violent death!" Victor proclaims. And so say all of us mortal readers. But Victor also personifies the scientist as Faustian knowledge-seeker; "the world was to me a secret which I desired to divine," he remembers, and he recalls that "none but those who have experienced them can conceive of the enticements of science" or, as a narrow materialist, 'On my education my father had taken the greatest precautions that my mind should be impressed with no supernatural horrors . . . a churchyard was to me merely the receptacle of bodies deprived of life." There are also hints that science has some drive of its own, external to the will of the scientist and eventually overwhelming him. "Natural philosophy," Victor reflects sadly, "is the genius that has regulated my fate." Amidst all the simplifications, deletions and elaborations of the original, the identification of Victor as a scientist has remained inviolate. It is science which gives him his success, and that success gives him power over life. Even though his character was first drawn before biology was a separate discipline, Frankenstein is always a proto-biologist.

So the endurance of the myth plainly does testify to a deep disquiet at the potentialities inherent in scientific discovery in general, and the science of life in particular. And it is a disquiet which Mary Shelley appears to have tapped into at a remarkably early stage in the development of modern life science. The appearance of the story, and its ready acceptance, so soon after Erasmus Darwin's speculations were published, suggest that unease at the prospect of science attaining powers over life is readily evoked in the public mind. So I agree with all those who have suggested that the *Frankenstein* myth both expresses and reinforces an undercurrent of feelings about science; that in George Levine's phrase, it "articulates a deeply felt cultural neurosis." But what, exactly, does this neurosis consist of?

It is clear that what we now call biomedical science, or the possibility of a technologically effective biology, has played a key role in shaping the modern attitude to science. We have always been prisoners of the body, victims of morbidity and mortality, and we desire the power that biology might give us to relieve these burdens. In more recent times, this can be seen from other kinds of evidence. Medical and biological stories have long accounted for a large proportion of the press reporting of science, for example.[4] Editors appear to regard such stories as of more interest to their readers than other scientific items. The news-consuming public, in consequence, may be more aware of events in biological science than in other fields.[5] The nature of their interest has also been long established. Turn the pages of major newspaper from the early years of this century, the *San Francisco Chronicle*, say, and you will find front-page stories on radical new surgical procedures, on the possibility of choosing the sex of a baby, on proposed scientific techniques for prolonging life, and on putative cures for cancer. These stories show the early convergence of news values and the territory of biomedicine. Biological research and medical

[4] For typical surveys showing the predominance of biomedical coverage see Jones et al., 1978; Einseidel, 1992. — Turney.

[5] In fact, Durant and colleagues suggest, on the basis of findings from a national survey in Britain, that "medical science may occupy a central and key position within the popular representation of science. In other words, what people know and feel about medicine may help to shape what they know and feel about science as a whole." Durant et al., 1992. — Turney.

practice mean birth, sex and death; suffering, disease and disability.

Biologists who become visible to the public are aware of the hopes and fears their science raises. As the French geneticist and popular writer Jean Rostand — of whom we shall hear more — attested in the 1950s: "The best way to gain an idea of what the human, *emotional* value of biology can be, is to look through some of the strange correspondence that a biologist receives . . . people take him for a magician, a healer, a confessor, a friend."[6]

Among the letters he describes are those from couples seeking to replace a lost child with a perfect twin, queries on the consequences of mixed marriage, people seeking confirmation of paternity by blood typing, enhancement of their children's intelligence, rejuvenation for the elderly, sex changes or cures for infertility. Rostand concludes that "the science that provokes such appeals, prayers and confessions, the science that penetrates into private life, and whose warnings or advice can influence a marriage, a decision to have children, a person's destiny, is no ordinary science."[7]

These examples express very well the idea that biology is indeed "no ordinary science" for the public. It is the science which touches on the most potent wishes of human life. "The realisation that biology offers the prospect of ultimate control over or transformation of the living realm, just as physical science controls and transforms the physical environment, thus evokes deep rooted feelings. This realisation by itself can produce either positive or negative reactions. . . ."

Frankenstein . . . is set on transforming humans directly. If he can discover the secret of life, then he can father a new species. To do so, he will experiment directly on the body.

Here, I think, Mary intuited the power of a threat which would come to seem graver as time went by. In a world where everything appeared to be subject to change, where it was becoming apparent that 'all that is solid melts into air', there was one sphere of existence which was exempt. The natural world, although it could be reshaped by physical onslaught on the landscape, although it could be despoiled or laid waste, was not yet open to technological manipulation. The forms and varieties of creatures, the hierarchy of species, the biological imperatives of existence, were fixed points in an ever-changing world.[8]

The human body, too, as I have suggested, provided an unchanging ground for experience of other changes. This does not mean, of course, that *experience* of the body, or ideas about its constitution, did not change.[9] But the body itself was not seen as changing by those experiencing the first rush of modernity. While the dead body had been anatomised for two centuries, in pursuit of a science of the interior which had made a deep impression on Renaissance and early modern culture, that science was still largely descriptive. The living body was not yet susceptible to the kind of science being developed in other areas, in which "the object to be known . . . will be known in such a way that it can be changed."[10] Frankenstein the character, and *Frankenstein* the novel, are both steeped in the anatomical tradition. But this anatomist goes further. Mary Shelley made the necessary imaginative leap, and fashioned an image of a science working on the body to transform it, a science which might one day come to pass. Now that we are indeed

[6] Rostand, 1959, pp. 32–3. — Turney.

[7] Ibid., p. 33. — Turney.

[8] Formally, the idea that species were defined forms was itself relatively recent, but by the time Mary Shelley wrote it was well established. Thus the great French naturalist Buffon wrote in the 1770s that "species are the only beings in Nature; Perpetual beings, as ancient and as permanent as Nature herself; each may be considered as a whole, independent of the world, a whole that was counted as one in the creation and that, consequently, is but one unit in Nature." Quoted in Jacob, 1982, p. 52. In addition, the fact that myth and folklore abounded with monsters, hybrids and chimerae in unknown regions did not mean that the creatures people saw around them did not behave in an orderly way. — Turney.

[9] See Porter, 1991, for a useful commentary. — Turney.

[10] See Rabinow's remark on the Human Genome Project as epitomising modern rationality, as quoted above, p. 2. — Turney.

building such a science, we can see that it has always been a part of the modern project. She saw this right at the start. If, as Berman says, Goethe's key insight is the ambivalence stemming from the fact that "the deepest horrors of Faustian development spring from its most honorable aims and its most authentic achievements," then the best horror story would be in the power which we simultaneously most desire, and most dread: power over the body. *Frankenstein* focused attention on that prospect nearly two centuries ago. We still feel the pull of the story because that power is now ours for the asking. ■

2000

Bibliography

Durant, J., Evans, G. and Thomas, G. (1992) "Public understanding of science in Britain: the role of medicine in the popular representation of science," *Public Understanding of Science*, 1, pp. 161–82.

Einseidel, E. (1992) "Framing science and technology in the Canadian press," *Public Understanding of Science*, 1, pp. 89–102.

Jacob, F. (1982) *The Logic of Life. A History of Heredity*. New York, Pantheon Books.

James, F. and Field, J. (1994) "Frankenstein and the spark of being," *History Today*, 449, pp 47–53.

Jones, G., Connell, I. and Meadows, J. (1978) *The Presentation of Science by the Media*. Leicester, Primary Communications Research Centre.

Porter, R. (1991) "History of the body," in P. Burke (ed.) *New Perspectives in Historical Writing*. Cambridge, Polity Press.

Rabinow, P. (1992) "Artificiality and enlightenment: from sociobiology to biosociality," in J. Crary and S. Kwinter (eds) *Incorporations*. New York, Zone Books.

Rostand, J. (1959) *Can Man Be Modified*? trans. J. Griffin. Secker & Warburg.

Questions

1. What, according to Jon Turney, explains the ubiquity and endurance of *Frankenstein* as a cultural reference?
2. Turney writes: "In the most striking retellings, the myth is never a straightforward anti-science story. There is something admirable about Victor Frankenstein, about Henry Frankenstein in James Whale's film, even about Peter Cushing's Baron Frankenstein. Even so, our sympathies are always torn between Frankenstein and his monster. The *Frankenstein* script, in its most salient forms, incorporates an ambivalence about science, method and motive, which is never resolved" (par. 4). Is *Frankenstein* ambivalent about science, as Turney says, or does it provide a straightforward anti-science theme? Explain.
3. How does Turney characterize Victor Frankenstein in paragraph 6? To what extent do the details from the novel itself support that characterization?
4. Turney says that the Frankenstein myth, in George Levine's phrase, "articulates a deeply felt cultural neurosis" regarding science, and poses the question, "But what, exactly, does this neurosis consist of" (par. 7)? How would you paraphrase the answer he provides in paragraphs 8–11? To what extent do you agree with Turney? To what extent might Shelley, were she alive today?
5. In paragraph 11 Turney writes that biological science is "the science which touches on the most potent wishes of human life." What, according to Turney, are those "potent wishes"? How do these wishes contribute to the enduring appeal of *Frankenstein*?
6. "Here, I think, Mary intuited the power of a threat which would come to seem graver as time went by," writes Turney (par. 13). Why would he use the word "threat"? What was being threatened? Explain.
7. In the last paragraph, Turney claims that "the best horror story would be rooted in the power which we simultaneously most desire, and most dread: power over the body. *Frankenstein* focused attention on that prospect nearly two centuries ago." If we do have that power, why would we greet it with both desire and dread? Do you agree with Turney that readers "still feel the pull of the story because that power is now ours for the asking"? Explain.

Frankenstein Drives a Tesla

Janet Allinger

Janet Allinger (b. 1964) is an illustrator and graphic designer who developed her technical skills when she was just nineteen years old while working as a manual illustrator for General Motors. She then worked for a design firm for many years before opening her own design business. In 2018, she decided to focus on her love of monsters to create a series titled *Monsters and Tech* depicting popular characters such as King Kong, the Bride of Frankenstein, and zombies interacting with technology.

2019

Questions

1. What is the function of each of the layers of this image? In your response, consider the building in the background, the monster (with a wedding ring and smile) as the central feature, the lightning in both the foreground and background, and the text visible in the image.
2. What is the artist implying about the relationship between environmentalism, business, and technological advancements? What does this image suggest about larger issues concerning society, happiness, and the environment?
3. Why does the artist cast Frankenstein's monster as the driver of a Tesla? Explain.

Literature in Conversation

1. How would you characterize Victor Frankenstein— mad scientist, visionary, egomaniac, benevolent seeker, tragic hero, or hubristic overreacher? Stephen Jay Gould and Jon Turney both discuss the motives of Victor Frankenstein as they characterize him in their essays. Paraphrase each characterization, and then compare and contrast them. Write an essay determining which of these characterizations most resembles your own perspective from having read the novel.
2. Knowledge and neglect might be seen as two prominent themes of the novel *Frankenstein*. Is Victor Frankenstein's fatal crime one of neglect — abandoning his creation — or one of seeking forbidden knowledge beyond the boundaries of proper human endeavor? Write an essay that answers that question, referring to *Frankenstein* and at least one other text from the Texts in Context.
3. Stephen Jay Gould writes, "Victor's sin does not lie in misuse of technology or hubris in emulating God; we cannot find these themes in Mary Shelley's account. Victor failed because he followed a predisposition of human nature — visceral disgust at the monster's appearance — and did not undertake the duty of any creator or parent: to teach his own charge and to educate others in acceptability." Using reference to *Frankenstein* and one other text from the Texts in Context, write an essay in which you examine the extent to which Gould's statement accurately accounts for Victor Frankenstein's "failure."
4. These Texts in Context can be categorized into two groups. In one, the image by Janet Allinger and the story by Brian Aldiss provide creative and artistic responses to science or to *Frankenstein*; in the other, Stephen Jay Gould and Jon Turney provide discussion and analysis of *Frankenstein*, the novel, and of Frankenstein, the myth. Which of the two groups provides more insight into the meaning of *Frankenstein*, as you, a person living in the twenty-first century, understand it? Explain.
5. Now, more than two centuries after its initial publication, what does *Frankenstein* have to say to us about our relationship with emerging scientific technology and bioethics? What is its message concerning science — about how scientific research and development are moving so rapidly that we have trouble keeping up — and how can we respond to that message?
6. If you haven't already done so, view the classic 1931 James Whale film, *Frankenstein*, starring Boris Karloff as the monster. Compare and contrast the film with Mary Shelley's novel. Write an essay that examines how the film departs from the novel. In your essay, discuss how Whale depicts either the story or its characters in ways that reflect at least two of the Texts in Context.

A Good Man Is Hard to Find

Flannery O'Connor

RUE DES ARCHIVES (RDA)/Bridgeman Images

Flannery O'Connor (1925–1964) was born in Savannah, Georgia, and grew up on a farm in Milledgeville, Georgia. After graduating from the Georgia State College for Women (now Georgia College & State University), she attended the Iowa Writers' Workshop. At twenty-six, after being diagnosed with a terminal form of lupus, O'Connor returned to the Georgia farm where she grew up. Despite her illness, she published three books — the story collection *A Good Man Is Hard to Find* (1955) and the novels *Wise Blood* (1952) and *The Violent Bear It Away* (1960) — before her death in 1964. Her later short stories were published posthumously as *Everything That Rises Must Converge* (1965).

KEY CONTEXT Most of O'Connor's stories are set in the American South, and critics often describe her writing as Southern gothic, a genre that adapts the traditional characters of the Deep South to life after the Civil War, with results often described as "grotesque." O'Connor famously questioned why this particular term was used to describe Southern stereotypes, arguing instead for the term "realistic." Her short stories examine the deep racial and religious divisions that exist among cultures generally lumped together as "Southern."

Content note: This text includes the anti-Black term "pickaninny." Additionally, this story includes the N-word, which we have chosen not to reprint in full here. We wish to accurately reflect both O'Connor's original intent as well as the racism of the time period, but we also recognize that this word has a long history as a derogatory and deeply hurtful expression when used by white people toward Black people, as it is in the context of this story. We have replaced the term without hindering understanding of the work as a whole. Be mindful of context, both O'Connor's and yours, as you read and discuss the story.

The dragon is by the side of the road, watching those who pass. Beware lest he devour you. We go to the Father of Souls, but it is necessary to pass by the dragon.

— St. Cyril of Jerusalem

The grandmother didn't want to go to Florida. She wanted to visit some of her connections in east Tennessee and she was seizing at every chance to change Bailey's mind. Bailey was the son she lived with, her only boy. He was sitting on the edge of his chair at the table, bent over the orange sports section of the *Journal*. "Now look here, Bailey," she said, "see here, read this," and she stood with one hand on her thin hip and the other rattling the newspaper at his bald head. "Here this fellow that calls himself The Misfit is aloose from the Federal Pen and headed toward Florida and you read here what it says he did to these people. Just you read it. I wouldn't take my children in any direction with a criminal like that aloose in it. I couldn't answer to my conscience if I did."

Bailey didn't look up from his reading so she wheeled around then and faced the children's mother, a young woman in slacks, whose face was as broad and innocent as a cabbage and was tied around with a green head-kerchief that had two points on the top like rabbit's ears. She was sitting on the sofa, feeding the baby his apricots out of a jar. "The children have been to Florida before," the old lady said. "You all ought to take them somewhere else for a change so they would see different parts of the world and be broad. They never have been to east Tennessee."

The children's mother didn't seem to hear her but the eight-year-old boy, John Wesley, a stocky child with glasses, said, "If you don't want to go to Florida, why dontcha stay at home?" He and the little girl, June Star, were reading the funny papers on the floor.

"She wouldn't stay at home to be queen for a day," June Star said without raising her yellow head.

5 "Yes and what would you do if this fellow, The Misfit, caught you?" the grandmother asked.

"I'd smack his face," John Wesley said.

"She wouldn't stay at home for a million bucks," June Star said. "Afraid she'd miss something. She has to go everywhere we go."

"All right, Miss," the grandmother said. "Just remember that the next time you want me to curl your hair."

June Star said her hair was naturally curly.

10 The next morning the grandmother was the first one in the car, ready to go. She had her big black valise that looked like the head of a hippopotamus in one corner, and underneath it she was hiding a basket with Pitty Sing, the cat, in it. She didn't intend for the cat to be left alone in the house for three days because he would miss her too much and she was afraid he might brush against one of the gas burners and accidentally asphyxiate himself. Her son, Bailey, didn't like to arrive at a motel with a cat.

She sat in the middle of the back seat with John Wesley and June Star on either side of her. Bailey and the children's mother and the baby sat in front and they left Atlanta at eight forty-five with the mileage on the car at 55890. The grandmother wrote this down because she thought it would be interesting to say how many miles they had been when they got back. It took them twenty minutes to reach the outskirts of the city.

The old lady settled herself comfortably, removing her white cotton gloves and putting them up with her purse on the shelf in front of the back window. The children's mother still had on slacks and still had her head tied up in a green kerchief, but the grandmother had on a navy blue straw sailor hat with a bunch of white violets on the brim and a navy blue dress with a small white dot in the print. Her collars and cuffs were white organdy trimmed with lace and at her neckline she had pinned a purple spray of cloth violets containing a sachet. In case of an

© Jeffrey Smith

Illustrator Jeffrey Smith (b. 1956) captures the moment when the grandmother and the kids sit in the back seat as their journey commences.

How closely does Smith match your perception of how these characters look and behave? What features of the illustration seem most striking, symbolic, and/or significant?

accident, anyone seeing her dead on the highway would know at once that she was a lady.

She said she thought it was going to be a good day for driving, neither too hot nor too cold, and she cautioned Bailey that the speed limit was fifty-five miles an hour and that the patrolmen hid themselves behind billboards and small clumps of trees and sped out after you before you had a chance to slow down. She pointed out interesting details of the scenery: Stone Mountain; the blue granite that in some places came up to both sides of the highway; the brilliant red clay banks slightly streaked with purple; and the various crops that made rows of green lace-work on the ground. The trees were full of silver-white sunlight and the meanest of them sparkled. The children were reading comic magazines and their mother had gone back to sleep.

"Let's go through Georgia fast so we won't have to look at it much," John Wesley said.

"If I were a little boy," said the grandmother, "I wouldn't talk about my native state that way. Tennessee has the mountains and Georgia has the hills."

"Tennessee is just a hillbilly dumping ground," John Wesley said, "and Georgia is a lousy state too."

"You said it," June Star said.

"In my time," said the grandmother, folding her thin veined fingers, "children were more respectful of their native states and their parents and everything else. People did right then. Oh look at the cute little pickaninny!" she said and pointed to a Negro child standing in the door of a shack. "Wouldn't that make a picture, now?" she asked and they all turned and looked at the little Negro out of the back window. He waved.

"He didn't have any britches on," June Star said.

"He probably didn't have any," the grandmother explained. "Little n*****s in the country don't have things like we do. If I could paint, I'd paint that picture," she said.

The children exchanged comic books.

The grandmother offered to hold the baby and the children's mother passed him over the front seat to her. She set him on her knee and bounced him and told him about the things they were passing. She rolled her eyes and screwed up her mouth and stuck her leathery thin face into his smooth bland one. Occasionally he gave her a far-away smile. They passed a large cotton field with five or six graves fenced in the middle of it, like a small island. "Look at the graveyard!" the grandmother said, pointing it out. "That was the old family burying ground. That belonged to the plantation."

Dave G. Houser/The Image Bank Unreleased/Getty Images

This Confederate memorial rock relief depicting Robert E. Lee, Stonewall Jackson, and Jefferson Davis is carved into Stone Mountain in Atlanta, Georgia. It has long been the site of controversy — the Ku Klux Klan was revived there in 1915. In the story, the grandmother points out Stone Mountain as merely an interesting detail of scenery. **What does this detail from the story reveal about each of the characters' values? What setting does it help establish?**

"Where's the plantation?" John Wesley asked.

"Gone With the Wind," said the grandmother. "Ha. Ha."

When the children finished all the comic books they had brought, they opened the lunch and ate it. The grandmother ate a peanut butter sandwich and an olive and would not let the children throw the box and the paper napkins out the window. When there was nothing else to do they played a game by choosing a cloud and making the other two guess what shape it suggested. John Wesley took one the shape of a cow and June Star guessed a cow and John Wesley said, no, an automobile, and June Star said he didn't play fair, and they began to slap each other over the grandmother.

The grandmother said she would tell them a story if they would keep quiet. When she told a story, she rolled her eyes and waved her head and was very dramatic. She said once when she was a maiden lady she had been courted by a Mr. Edgar Atkins Teagarden from Jasper, Georgia. She said he was a very good-looking man and a gentleman and that he brought her a watermelon every Saturday afternoon with his initials cut in it, E. A. T. Well, one Saturday, she said, Mr. Teagarden brought the watermelon and there was nobody at home and he left it on the front porch and returned in his buggy to Jasper, but she never got the watermelon, she said, because a n***** boy ate it when he saw the initials, E. A. T.! This story tickled John Wesley's funny bone and he giggled and giggled but June Star didn't think it was any good. She said she wouldn't marry a man that just brought her a watermelon on Saturday. The grandmother said she would have done well to marry Mr. Teagarden because he was a gentleman and had bought Coca-Cola stock when it first came out and that he had died only a few years ago, a very wealthy man.

They stopped at The Tower for barbecued sandwiches. The Tower was a part stucco and part wood filling station and dance hall set in a clearing outside of Timothy. A fat man named Red Sammy Butts ran it and there were signs stuck here and there on the building and for miles up and down the highway saying, TRY RED SAMMY'S FAMOUS BARBECUE. NONE LIKE FAMOUS RED SAMMY'S! RED SAM! THE FAT BOY WITH THE HAPPY LAUGH. A VETERAN! RED SAMMY'S YOUR MAN!

Red Sammy was lying on the bare ground outside The Tower with his head under a truck while a gray monkey about a foot high, chained to a small chinaberry tree, chattered nearby. The monkey sprang back into the tree and got on the highest limb as soon as he saw the children jump out of the car and run toward him.

Inside, The Tower was a long dark room with a counter at one end and tables at the other and dancing space in the middle. They all sat down at a board table next to the nickelodeon and Red Sam's wife, a tall burnt-brown woman with hair and eyes lighter than her skin, came and took their order. The children's mother put a dime in the machine and played "The Tennessee Waltz," and the grandmother said that tune always made her want to dance. She asked Bailey if he would like to dance but he only glared at her. He didn't have a naturally sunny disposition like she did and trips made him nervous. The grandmother's brown eyes were very bright. She swayed her head from side to side and pretended she was dancing in her chair. June Star said play something she could tap to so the children's mother put in another dime and played a fast number and June Star stepped out onto the dance floor and did her tap routine.

"Ain't she cute?" Red Sam's wife said, leaning over the counter. "Would you like to come be my little girl?"

"No I certainly wouldn't," June Star said. "I wouldn't live in a broken-down place like this for a million bucks!" and she ran back to the table.

"Ain't she cute?" the woman repeated, stretching her mouth politely.

"Aren't you ashamed?" hissed the grandmother.

Gone: An Historical Romance of a Civil War as It Occurred b'tween the Dusky Thighs of One Young Negress and Her Heart (1994) is a large-scale paper cutout of a scene depicting several aspects of Southern history by African American artist Kara Walker.

How does Walker's "romantic" view of this history differ from the way the grandmother romanticizes the past in the American South? What aspects of this cutout reflect the South as O'Connor portrays it?

Red Sam came in and told his wife to quit lounging on the counter and hurry up with these people's order. His khaki trousers reached just to his hip bones and his stomach hung over them like a sack of meal swaying under his shirt. He came over and sat down at a table nearby and let out a combination sigh and yodel. "You can't win," he said. "You can't win," and he wiped his sweating red face off with a gray handkerchief. "These days you don't know who to trust," he said. "Ain't that the truth?"

"People are certainly not nice like they used to be," said the grandmother.

"Two fellers come in here last week," Red Sammy said, "driving a Chrysler. It was a old beat-up car but it was a good one and these boys looked all right to me. Said they worked at the mill and you know I let them fellers charge the gas they bought? Now why did I do that?"

"Because you're a good man!" the grandmother said at once.

"Yes'm, I suppose so," Red Sam said as if he were struck with this answer.

His wife brought the orders, carrying the five plates all at once without a tray, two in each hand and one balanced on her arm. "It isn't a soul in this green world of God's that you can trust," she said. "And I don't count nobody out of that, not nobody," she repeated, looking at Red Sammy.

"Did you read about that criminal, The Misfit, that's escaped?" asked the grandmother.

"I wouldn't be a bit surprised if he didn't attact this place right here," said the woman. "If he hears about it being here, I wouldn't be none surprised to see him. If he hears it's two cent in the cash register, I wouldn't be a tall surprised if he . . ."

"That'll do," Red Sam said. "Go bring these people their Co'-Colas," and the woman went off to get the rest of the order.

"A good man is hard to find," Red Sammy said. "Everything is getting terrible. I remember the day you could go off and leave your screen door unlatched. Not no more."

He and the grandmother discussed better times. The old lady said that in her opinion Europe was entirely to blame for the way things were now. She said the way Europe acted you would think we were made of money and Red Sam said it was no use talking about it, she was exactly right. The children ran outside into the white sunlight and looked at the monkey in the lacy chinaberry tree. He was busy catching fleas on himself and biting each one carefully between his teeth as if it were a delicacy.

45 They drove off again into the hot afternoon. The grandmother took cat naps and woke up every few minutes with her own snoring. Outside of Toombsboro she woke up and recalled an old plantation that she had visited in this neighborhood once when she was a young lady. She said the house had six white columns across the front and that there was an avenue of oaks leading up to it and two little wooden trellis arbors on either side in front where you sat down with your suitor after a stroll in the garden. She recalled exactly which road to turn off to get to it. She knew that Bailey would not be willing to lose any time looking at an old house, but the more she talked about it, the more she wanted to see it once again and find out if the little twin arbors were still standing. "There was a secret panel in this house," she said craftily, not telling the truth but wishing that she were, "and the story went that all the family silver was hidden in it when Sherman[1] came through but it was never found . . ."

"Hey!" John Wesley said. "Let's go see it! We'll find it! We'll poke all the woodwork and find it! Who lives there? Where do you turn off at? Hey Pop, can't we turn off there?"

"We never have seen a house with a secret panel!" June Star shrieked. "Let's go to the house with the secret panel! Hey Pop, can't we go see the house with the secret panel!"

"It's not far from here, I know," the grandmother said. "It wouldn't take over twenty minutes."

Bailey was looking straight ahead. His jaw was as rigid as a horseshoe. "No," he said.

50 The children began to yell and scream that they wanted to see the house with the secret panel. John Wesley kicked the back of the front seat and June Star hung over her mother's shoulder and whined desperately into her ear that they never had any fun even on their vacation, that they could never do what THEY wanted to do. The baby began to scream and John Wesley kicked the back of the seat so hard that his father could feel the blows in his kidney.

"All right!" he shouted and drew the car to a stop at the side of the road. "Will you all shut up? Will you all just shut up for one second? If you don't shut up, we won't go anywhere."

"It would be very educational for them," the grandmother murmured.

"All right," Bailey said, "but get this: this is the only time we're going to stop for anything like this. This is the one and only time."

"The dirt road that you have to turn down is about a mile back," the grandmother directed. "I marked it when we passed."

55 "A dirt road," Bailey groaned.

After they had turned around and were headed toward the dirt road, the grandmother recalled other points about the house, the beautiful glass over the front doorway and the candle-lamp in the hall. John Wesley said that the secret panel was probably in the fireplace.

"You can't go inside this house," Bailey said. "You don't know who lives there."

"While you all talk to the people in front, I'll run around behind and get in a window," John Wesley suggested.

"We'll all stay in the car," his mother said.

60 They turned onto the dirt road and the car raced roughly along in a swirl of pink dust. The grandmother recalled the times when there were no paved roads and thirty miles was a day's journey. The dirt road was hilly and there were sudden washes in it and sharp curves on dangerous embankments. All at once they would be on a hill, looking down over the blue tops of trees for miles around, then the next minute, they would be in a red depression with the dust-coated trees looking down on them.

"This place had better turn up in a minute," Bailey said, "or I'm going to turn around."

[1] Union general William Tecumseh Sherman (1820–1891) led a destructive campaign through Tennessee, Georgia, and the Carolinas during the Civil War. — Eds.

Dennis Hallinan/Alamy

The plantation house shown here, known as the Houmas, was built in the late eighteenth century.
What aspects of the Houmas, as shown in this photograph, reflect the grandmother's view of what Southern culture should be? What aspects reflect Southern culture as O'Connor depicts it in the story?

The road looked as if no one had traveled on it in months.

"It's not much farther," the grandmother said and just as she said it, a horrible thought came to her. The thought was so embarrassing that she turned red in the face and her eyes dilated and her feet jumped up, upsetting her valise in the corner. The instant the valise moved, the newspaper top she had over the basket under it rose with a snarl and Pitty Sing, the cat, sprang onto Bailey's shoulder.

The children were thrown to the floor and their mother, clutching the baby, was thrown out the door onto the ground; the old lady was thrown into the front seat. The car turned over once and landed right-side-up in a gulch off the side of the road. Bailey remained in the driver's seat with the cat — gray-striped with a broad white face and an orange nose — clinging to his neck like a caterpillar.

As soon as the children saw they could move their arms and legs, they scrambled out of the car, shouting, "We've had an ACCIDENT!" The grandmother was curled up under the dashboard, hoping she was injured so that Bailey's wrath would not come down on her all at once. The horrible thought she had had before the accident was that the house she had remembered so vividly was not in Georgia but in Tennessee.

Bailey removed the cat from his neck with both hands and flung it out the window against the side of a pine tree. Then he got out of the car and started looking for the children's mother. She was sitting against the side of the red gutted ditch, holding the screaming baby, but she only had a cut down her face and a broken shoulder. "We've had an ACCIDENT!" the children screamed in a frenzy of delight.

"But nobody's killed," June Star said with disappointment as the grandmother limped out of the car, her hat still pinned to her head but the broken front brim standing up at a jaunty angle and the violet spray hanging off the side. They all sat down in the ditch, except the children, to recover from the shock. They were all shaking.

"Maybe a car will come along," said the children's mother hoarsely.

"I believe I have injured an organ," said the grandmother, pressing her side, but no one answered her. Bailey's teeth were clattering. He had on a yellow sport shirt with bright blue parrots designed in it and his face was as yellow as the shirt. The grandmother decided that she would not mention that the house was in Tennessee.

The road was about ten feet above and they could see only the tops of the trees on the other side of it. Behind the ditch they were sitting in there were more woods, tall and dark and deep. In a few minutes they saw a car some distance away on top of a hill, coming slowly as if the occupants were watching them. The grandmother stood up and waved both arms dramatically to attract their attention. The car continued to come on slowly, disappeared around a bend and appeared again, moving even slower, on top of the hill they had gone over. It was a big black battered hearse-like automobile. There were three men in it.

It came to a stop just over them and for some minutes, the driver looked down with a steady expressionless gaze to where they were sitting, and didn't speak. Then he turned his head and muttered something to the other two and they got out. One was a fat boy in black trousers and a red sweat shirt with a silver stallion embossed on the front of it. He moved around on the right side of them and stood staring, his mouth partly open in a kind of loose grin. The other had on khaki pants and a blue striped coat and a gray hat pulled down very low, hiding most of his face. He came around slowly on the left side. Neither spoke.

The driver got out of the car and stood by the side of it, looking down at them. He was an older man than the other two. His hair was just beginning to gray and he wore silver-rimmed spectacles that gave him a scholarly look. He had a long creased face and didn't have on any shirt or undershirt. He had on blue jeans that were too tight for him and was holding a black hat and a gun. The two boys also had guns.

"We've had an ACCIDENT!" the children screamed.

The grandmother had the peculiar feeling that the bespectacled man was someone she knew. His face was as familiar to her as if she had known him all her life but she could not recall who he was. He moved away from the car and began to come down the embankment, placing his feet carefully so that he wouldn't slip. He had on tan and white shoes and no socks, and his ankles were red and thin. "Good afternoon," he said. "I see you all had you a little spill."

"We turned over twice!" said the grandmother.

"Oncet," he corrected. "We seen it happen. Try their car and see will it run, Hiram," he said quietly to the boy with the gray hat.

"What you got that gun for?" John Wesley asked. "Whatcha gonna do with that gun?"

"Lady," the man said to the children's mother, "would you mind calling them children to sit down by you? Children make me nervous. I want all you all to sit down right together there where you're at."

"What are you telling US what to do for?" June Star asked.

Behind them the line of woods gaped like a dark open mouth. "Come here," said their mother.

"Look here now," Bailey began suddenly, "we're in a predicament! We're in . . ."

The grandmother shrieked. She scrambled to her feet and stood staring. "You're The Misfit!" she said. "I recognized you at once!"

"Yes'm," the man said, smiling slightly as if he were pleased in spite of himself to be known, "but it would have been better for all of you, lady, if you hadn't of reckernized me."

Bailey turned his head sharply and said something to his mother that shocked even the children. The old lady began to cry and The Misfit reddened.

"Lady," he said, "don't you get upset. Sometimes a man says things he don't mean. I don't reckon he meant to talk to you thataway."

"You wouldn't shoot a lady, would you?" the grandmother said and removed a clean handkerchief from her cuff and began to slap at her eyes with it.

The Misfit pointed the toe of his shoe into the ground and made a little hole and then covered it up again. "I would hate to have to," he said.

"Listen," the grandmother almost screamed, "I know you're a good man. You don't look a bit like you have common blood. I know you must come from nice people!"

"Yes mam," he said, "finest people in the world." When he smiled he showed a row of strong white teeth. "God never made a finer woman than my mother and my daddy's heart was pure gold," he said. The boy with the red sweat shirt had come around behind them and was standing with his gun at his hip. The Misfit squatted down on the ground. "Watch them children, Bobby Lee," he said. "You know they make me nervous." He looked at the six of them huddled together in front of him and he seemed to be embarrassed as if he couldn't think of anything to say. "Ain't a cloud in the sky," he remarked, looking up at it. "Don't see no sun but don't see no cloud neither."

"Yes, it's a beautiful day," said the grandmother. "Listen," she said, "you shouldn't call yourself The Misfit because I know you're a good man at heart. I can just look at you and tell."

"Hush!" Bailey yelled. "Hush! Everybody shut up and let me handle this!" He was squatting in the position of a runner about to sprint forward but he didn't move.

"I pre-chate that, lady," The Misfit said and drew a little circle in the ground with the butt of his gun.

"It'll take a half a hour to fix this here car," Hiram called, looking over the raised hood of it.

"Well, first you and Bobby Lee get him and that little boy to step over yonder with you," The Misfit said, pointing to Bailey and John Wesley. "The boys want to ast you something," he said to Bailey. "Would you mind stepping back in them woods there with them?"

"Listen," Bailey began, "we're in a terrible predicament! Nobody realizes what this is," and his voice cracked. His eyes were as blue and intense as the parrots in his shirt and he remained perfectly still.

The grandmother reached up to adjust her hat brim as if she were going to the woods with him but it came off in her hand. She stood staring at it and after a second she let it fall on the ground. Hiram pulled Bailey up by the arm as if he were assisting an old man. John Wesley caught hold of his father's hand and Bobby Lee followed. They went off toward the woods and just as they reached the dark edge, Bailey turned and supporting himself against a gray naked pine trunk, he shouted, "I'll be back in a minute, Mamma, wait on me!"

"Come back this instant!" his mother shrilled but they all disappeared into the woods.

"Bailey Boy!" the grandmother called in a tragic voice but she found she was looking at The Misfit squatting on the ground in front of her. "I just know you're a good man," she said desperately. "You're not a bit common!"

"Nome, I ain't a good man," The Misfit said after a second as if he had considered her statement carefully, "but I ain't the worst in the world neither. My daddy said I was a different breed of dog from my brothers and sisters. 'You know,' Daddy said, 'it's some that can live their whole life out without asking about it and it's others has to know why it is, and this boy is one of the latters. He's going to be into everything!'" He put on his black hat and looked up suddenly and then away deep into the woods as if he were embarrassed again. "I'm sorry I don't have on a shirt before you ladies," he said, hunching his shoulders slightly. "We buried our clothes that we had on when we escaped and we're just making do until we can get better. We borrowed these from some folks we met," he explained.

"That's perfectly all right," the grandmother said. "Maybe Bailey has an extra shirt in his suitcase."

"I'll look and see terrectly," The Misfit said.

"Where are they taking him?" the children's mother screamed.

"Daddy was a card himself," The Misfit said. "You couldn't put anything over on him. He never got in trouble with the Authorities though. Just had the knack of handling them."

"You could be honest too if you'd only try," said the grandmother. "Think how wonderful it would be to settle down and live a comfortable life and not have to think about somebody chasing you all the time."

105 The Misfit kept scratching in the ground with the butt of his gun as if he were thinking about it. "Yes'm, somebody is always after you," he murmured.

The grandmother noticed how thin his shoulder blades were just behind his hat because she was standing up looking down on him. "Do you ever pray?" she asked.

He shook his head. All she saw was the black hat wiggle between his shoulder blades. "Nome," he said.

There was a pistol shot from the woods, followed closely by another. Then silence. The old lady's head jerked around. She could hear the wind move through the tree tops like a long satisfied insuck of breath. "Bailey Boy!" she called.

"I was a gospel singer for a while," The Misfit said. "I been most everything. Been in the arm service, both land and sea, at home and abroad, been twict married, been an undertaker, been with the railroads, plowed Mother Earth, been in a tornado, seen a man burnt alive oncet," and he looked up at the children's mother and the little girl who were sitting close together, their faces white and their eyes glassy; "I even seen a woman flogged," he said.

110 "Pray, pray," the grandmother began, "pray, pray . . ."

"I never was a bad boy that I remember of," The Misfit said in an almost dreamy voice, "but somewheres along the line I done something wrong and got sent to the penitentiary. I was buried alive," and he looked up and held her attention to him by a steady stare.

"That's when you should have started to pray," she said. "What did you do to get sent to the penitentiary that first time?"

"Turn to the right, it was a wall," The Misfit said, looking up again at the cloudless sky. "Turn to the left, it was a wall. Look up it was a ceiling, look down it was a floor. I forget what I done, lady. I set there and set there, trying to remember what it was I done and I ain't recalled it to this day. Oncet in a while, I would think it was coming to me, but it never come."

"Maybe they put you in by mistake," the old lady said vaguely.

115 "Nome," he said. "It wasn't no mistake. They had the papers on me."

"You must have stolen something," she said.

The Misfit sneered slightly. "Nobody had nothing I wanted," he said. "It was a head-doctor at the penitentiary said what I had done was kill my daddy but I known that for a lie. My daddy died in nineteen ought nineteen of the epidemic flu[2] and I never had a thing to do with it. He was buried in the Mount Hopewell Baptist churchyard and you can go there and see for yourself."

"If you would pray," the old lady said, "Jesus would help you."

"That's right," The Misfit said.

120 "Well then, why don't you pray?" she asked trembling with delight suddenly.

"I don't want no hep," he said. "I'm doing all right by myself."

Bobby Lee and Hiram came ambling back from the woods. Bobby Lee was dragging a yellow shirt with bright blue parrots in it.

"Thow me that shirt, Bobby Lee," The Misfit said. The shirt came flying at him and landed on his shoulder and he put it on. The grandmother couldn't name what the shirt reminded her of. "No, lady," The Misfit said while he was buttoning it up, "I found out the crime don't

---

[2] The influenza pandemic of 1918–1919, the largest epidemic in history, killed between twenty and forty million people worldwide. — Eds.

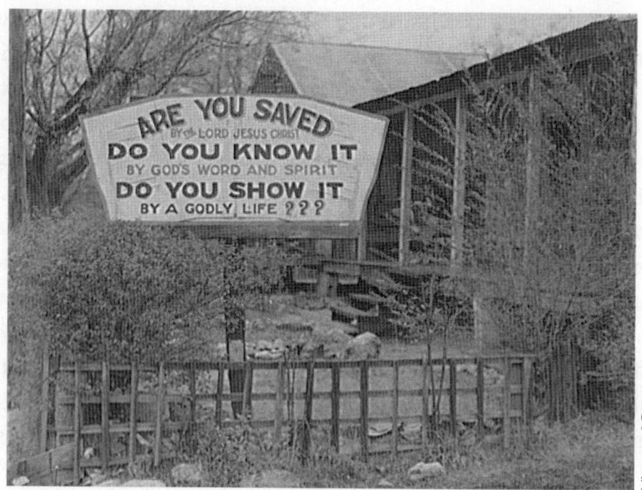

Library of Congress

This religious sign was placed in front of a house on a highway between Columbus and Augusta, Georgia. Similar religious signs were placed along this highway at intervals of at least a mile and often much closer together — such signs were especially common during the Depression.

How does the grandmother use the language of signs like this to convince The Misfit to spare her?

matter. You can do one thing or you can do another, kill a man or take a tire off his car, because sooner or later you're going to forget what it was you done and just be punished for it."

The children's mother had begun to make heaving noises as if she couldn't get her breath. "Lady," he asked, "would you and that little girl like to step off yonder with Bobby Lee and Hiram and join your husband?"

"Yes, thank you," the mother said faintly. Her left arm dangled helplessly and she was holding the baby, who had gone to sleep, in the other. "Hep that lady up, Hiram," The Misfit said as she struggled to climb out of the ditch, "and Bobby Lee, you hold onto that little girl's hand."

"I don't want to hold hands with him," June Star said. "He reminds me of a pig."

The fat boy blushed and laughed and caught her by the arm and pulled her off into the woods after Hiram and her mother.

Alone with The Misfit, the grandmother found that she had lost her voice. There was not a cloud in the sky nor any sun. There was nothing around her but woods. She wanted to tell him that he must pray. She opened and closed her mouth several times before anything came out. Finally she found herself saying, "Jesus. Jesus," meaning, Jesus will help you, but the way she was saying it, it sounded as if she might be cursing.

"Yes'm," The Misfit said as if he agreed. "Jesus thown everything off balance. It was the same case with Him as with me except He hadn't committed any crime and they could prove I had committed one because they had the papers on me. Of course," he said, "they never shown me my papers. That's why I sign myself now. I said long ago, you get you a signature and sign everything you do and keep a copy of it. Then you'll know what you done and you can hold up the crime to the punishment and see do they match and in the end you'll have something to prove you ain't been treated right. I call myself The Misfit," he said, "because I can't make what all I done wrong fit what all I gone through in punishment."

There was a piercing scream from the woods, followed closely by a pistol report. "Does it seem right to you, lady, that one is punished a heap and another ain't punished at all?"

"Jesus!" the old lady cried. "You've got good blood! I know you wouldn't shoot a lady! I know you come from nice people! Pray! Jesus, you ought not to shoot a lady. I'll give you all the money I've got!"

"Lady," The Misfit said, looking beyond her far into the woods, "there never was a body that give the undertaker a tip."

There were two more pistol reports and the grandmother raised her head like a parched old turkey hen crying for water and called, "Bailey Boy, Bailey Boy!" as if her heart would break.

"Jesus was the only One that ever raised the dead," The Misfit continued, "and He shouldn't have done it. He thown everything off balance. If He did what He said, then it's nothing for you to do but thow away everything and follow Him, and if He didn't, then it's nothing for you to do but enjoy the few minutes you got left the best way you can — by killing somebody or burning down his house or doing some other meanness to him. No pleasure but meanness," he said and his voice had become almost a snarl.

135 "Maybe He didn't raise the dead," the old lady mumbled, not knowing what she was saying and feeling so dizzy that she sank down in the ditch with her legs twisted under her.

"I wasn't there so I can't say He didn't," The Misfit said. "I wisht I had of been there," he said, hitting the ground with his fist. "It ain't right I wasn't there because if I had of been there I would of known. Listen lady," he said in a high voice, "if I had of been there I would of known and I wouldn't be like I am now." His voice seemed about to crack and the grandmother's head cleared for an instant. She saw the man's face twisted close to her own as if he were going to cry and she murmured, "Why you're one of my babies. You're one of my own children!" She reached out and touched him on the shoulder. The Misfit sprang back as if a snake had bitten him and shot her three times through the chest. Then he put his gun down on the ground and took off his glasses and began to clean them.

Hiram and Bobby Lee returned from the woods and stood over the ditch, looking down at the grandmother who half sat and half lay in a puddle of blood with her legs crossed under her like a child's and her face smiling up at the cloudless sky.

Without his glasses, The Misfit's eyes were red-rimmed and pale and defenseless-looking. "Take her off and thow her where you thown the others," he said, picking up the cat that was rubbing itself against his leg.

"She was a talker, wasn't she?" Bobby Lee said, sliding down the ditch with a yodel.

140 "She would of been a good woman," The Misfit said, "if it had been somebody there to shoot her every minute of her life."

"Some fun!" Bobby Lee said.

"Shut up, Bobby Lee," The Misfit said. "It's no real pleasure in life." ■

1953

Understanding and Interpreting

1. What tone does the epigraph set for the story? Reconsider it after you've read the story. How does your interpretation change?
2. What can you infer about the grandmother by reading the opening paragraph? What does she represent in the story? Consider the role she plays in her family as well as how she might embody a different era in the culture of the South. What does the grandmother mean when she tells The Misfit, "Why you're one of my babies. You're one of my own children!" (par. 136)?
3. The main characters in a story usually have names. In this story, however, several main characters — The Misfit, the grandmother, and the children's mother — are unnamed. What is the purpose of not giving these characters names, referring to them only by their roles? How might leaving these characters unnamed connect to a theme of the story?
4. In what ways is the family in this story fairly typical in terms of the tensions and conflicts most families experience? How does Flannery O'Connor introduce comedy by depicting the differences between and among generations and relationships?

5. When Red Sammy says to the grandmother, "A good man is hard to find" (par. 43), what does he mean? Why did O'Connor choose this particular line for the story's title? Also consider why, in the final scene, the grandmother repeatedly tells The Misfit that she knows he is a "good man."
6. Discuss instances in which the grandmother's nostalgia for the past seems warranted and others in which it becomes limiting, racist, and even threatening. You might begin by considering some of the following: her desire to paint a picture of the young Black child in the doorway, her story about Mr. Teagarden, her story of the house with the secret panel.
7. O'Connor has said that the short story collection that included this story is about "original sin." What role does religion, specifically Christianity, play in this story? How do the grandmother's traditional views on salvation and prayer differ from The Misfit's? What does The Misfit mean when he asserts that "Jesus thown everything off balance" (pars. 129, 134)?
8. Were you surprised by the violence in the story? Why do you think O'Connor chose to leave the murders of everyone but the grandmother "off stage" rather than describing them directly? What is the impact of providing details about the shooting of the grandmother and describing her lifeless body?
9. How does The Misfit explain his behavior to the grandmother? Why does he shoot her precisely when he does? How do you interpret his assertion that "[s]he would of been a good woman . . . if it had been somebody there to shoot her every minute of her life" (par. 140)? What does The Misfit understand about the grandmother's character?

Analyzing Language, Style, and Structure

1. **Vocabulary in Context.** What does it mean to be a "misfit," and what are the connotations of this word? Which of The Misfit's words and actions suggest that he is appropriately named? How are other characters in the story also misfits? Explain.
2. How does O'Connor use foreshadowing in "A Good Man Is Hard to Find"? What effect did the foreshadowing have on your first reading of the story? When you read about The Misfit in the first paragraph, did you think that you would meet him?
3. Contrast the description of the grandmother's outfit with the rest of the family's traveling attire (pars. 12, 69). What do the characters' clothes tell us about them? What is significant about The Misfit's appropriation of Bailey's parrot shirt (pars. 122–23)?
4. In paragraph 18, the grandmother pauses in the middle of telling her grandchildren that "in [her] time . . . children were more respectful of their native states and their parents and everything else" and "[p]eople did right then" to point out a young Black child by the side of the road, using a derogatory term to draw their attention to him. What is ironic about this passage? What does it reveal about the grandmother's definition of "[doing] right"? What evidence suggests a contrast between the character's and the author's perspectives of what it means to "[do] right"?
5. What is the purpose of the scene at Red Sammy's barbecue place? Consider the conversation between the grandmother and Red Sammy about the difficulty of finding a "good man." How does this scene develop the story's themes as well as plot?
6. Take another look at the allusion the grandmother makes to *Gone With the Wind* in paragraph 24. What deeper meaning can you find in her joke about the plantation? How does this joke affect your reading of the story?
7. Explain how the setting shifts once the family takes a detour off the main road. Why is this shift important to the story's plot? How does the shift in setting contribute to the shift in the story's tone?

8. Why do you think O'Connor chose to capitalize "ACCIDENT!" in the children's dialogue? After the accident, a slow-moving car appears on the horizon, "a big black battered hearse-like automobile" (par. 70). Why might the author have chosen not to use commas between these adjectives? How do the punctuation and alliteration contribute to the effect of this description?
9. The Misfit's words are often given a phonetic rendering, including "I pre-chate that, lady" (par. 92), "The boys want to ast you something" (par. 94), "I'll look and see terrectly" (par. 101), "Nome." (par. 107), "I . . . seen a man burnt alive oncet" (par. 109), and "I don't want no hep" (par. 121). What effect does this use of dialect have on your understanding of The Misfit's character? What other characters in the story speak in dialect, and what does it say about them?
10. Examine the following similes used in "A Good Man Is Hard to Find": "whose face was as broad and innocent as a cabbage" (par. 2); "her big black valise that looked like the head of a hippopotamus" (par. 10); "His jaw was as rigid as a horseshoe" (par. 49); "She could hear the wind move through the tree tops like a long satisfied insuck of breath" (par. 108); "the grandmother raised her head like a parched old turkey hen crying for water" (par. 133). Choose three of these similes and explain how each comparison contributes to your ability to visualize the scene or character.
11. We perceive the world through the grandmother throughout most of the story. When does O'Connor move away from this perspective, and what effect does this have?

Topics for Composing

1. AP® FRQ **Prose Fiction Analysis.** The following question refers to paragraphs 1–18 of Flannery O'Connor's "A Good Man Is Hard to Find," published in 1953. In this passage, the grandmother acquiesces to traveling to Florida with her family despite wanting to visit east Tennessee instead. Read the passage carefully. Then, in a well-written essay, analyze how O'Connor uses literary elements and techniques to develop the grandmother's complex character.
2. AP® FRQ **Literary Argument.** While the words "good" and "evil" might seem easily distinguishable, it might be said that these concepts are in the eye of the beholder. In "A Good Man Is Hard to Find," consider who is said to be good instead of evil. In a well-written essay, analyze how the application of the word "good" contributes to an interpretation of the work as a whole. Do not merely summarize the plot.
3. **AP® Literary Argumentation.** Write an essay in which you interpret the grandmother's attitude toward another character in the story. Support your argument with evidence from the text and by analyzing O'Connor's use of literary elements and techniques.
4. **AP® Literary Argumentation.** Discuss how O'Connor plays out her theme of the struggle between good and evil in the characters of the grandmother and The Misfit. Explore the ways that each of these characters embodies elements of both good and evil.
5. **AP® Literary Argumentation.** Although this story has some universal themes, it is very much a story about the South — its values, traditions, and culture. Write an essay explaining how this is a Southern story.
6. **AP® Literary Argumentation.** Writing about violence in fiction, O'Connor claimed, "In my own stories I have found that violence is strangely capable of returning my characters to reality and preparing them to accept their moment of grace." Write an essay explaining whether you do or do not agree with this description as it applies to the grandmother, The Misfit, or both.

7. **AP® Literary Argumentation.** Write an essay offering two different interpretations of the ending of the story. Is it uplifting? cynical? bleak? hopeful? Have any of the characters been transformed? Then explain which of the interpretations you prefer. Include your understanding of The Misfit's final comment: "It's no real pleasure in life."
8. **Connections.** Write an essay that compares and contrasts the narrator in "A Good Man Is Hard to Find" with the narrator of another work of fiction in this chapter. In your response, consider some or all of the following: how each narrator feels about the characters they are describing; which character(s) the narrator is most sympathetic toward; how close (or distant) the narrator is from the action; how the storyteller hopes you, the reader, will respond; and why this particular voice has been chosen.
9. **Creative Writing.** You are an up-and-coming screenwriter who wants to adapt "A Good Man Is Hard to Find" for the big screen. Write a one-page proposal persuading a producer that this movie's story and themes will appeal to a wide audience and be timely in the twenty-first century. Include suggestions for a director, a few members of the cast, and a filming location.
10. **Creative Writing.** Imagine that you are June Star or John Wesley, telling a school friend about your grandmother. Write a one-page monologue in which you characterize (through ranting about, imitating, or telling a story about) the old woman. Look closely at the children's speech patterns, and try to use both the syntax and the language that either child would.

Everyday Use

Alice Walker

Mikki Ansin/Getty Images

Alice Walker (b. 1944) is a novelist, poet, essayist, civil rights activist, and self-described eco-pacifist. The youngest of eight children born to sharecropper parents, Walker grew up in the small town of Eatonton, Georgia. She attended Spelman College in Georgia, then transferred to Sarah Lawrence College in New York. She has authored thirteen novels and short story collections, ten collections of poetry, and twelve nonfiction books. Her first novel, *The Third Life of Grange Copeland*, was published in 1969, followed by her poetry collection *Revolutionary Petunias and Other Poems* (1973). In 1982, she published *The Color Purple*, her most celebrated work, and became the first African American woman to win the Pulitzer Prize. Her most recent book is a collection of poetry entitled *Taking the Arrow Out of the Heart*, published in 2018. "Everyday Use" is a story from her collection *In Love and Trouble: Stories of Black Women* (1973).

for your grandmamma

I will wait for her in the yard that Maggie and I made so clean and wavy yesterday afternoon. A yard like this is more comfortable than most people know. It is not just a yard. It is like an extended living room. When the hard clay is swept clean as a floor and the fine sand around the edges lined with tiny, irregular grooves, anyone can come and sit and look up into the elm tree and wait for the breezes that never come inside the house.

Maggie will be nervous until after her sister goes: she will stand hopelessly in corners, homely and ashamed of the burn scars down her arms and legs, eying her sister with a mixture of envy and awe. She thinks her sister has held life always in the palm of one hand, that "no" is a word the world never learned to say to her.

You've no doubt seen those TV shows where the child who has "made it" is confronted, as a surprise, by her own mother and father, tottering in weakly from backstage. (A pleasant surprise, of course: What would they do if parent and child came on the show only to curse out and insult each other?) On TV mother and child embrace and smile into each other's faces. Sometimes the mother and father weep, the child wraps them in her arms and leans across the table to tell how she would not have made it without their help. I have seen these programs.

Sometimes I dream a dream in which Dee and I are suddenly brought together on a TV program of this sort. Out of a dark and soft-seated limousine I am ushered into a bright room filled with many people. There I meet a smiling, gray, sporty man like Johnny Carson[1] who shakes my hand and tells me what a fine girl I have. Then we are on the stage and Dee is embracing me with tears in her eyes. She pins on my dress a large orchid, even though she has told me once that she thinks orchids are tacky flowers.

5 In real life I am a large, big-boned woman with rough, man-working hands. In the winter I wear flannel nightgowns to bed and overalls during the day. I can kill and clean a hog as mercilessly as a man. My fat keeps me hot in zero weather. I can work outside all day, breaking ice to get water for washing; I can eat pork liver cooked over the open fire minutes after it comes steaming from the hog. One winter I knocked a bull calf straight in the brain between the eyes with a sledge hammer and had the meat hung up to chill before nightfall. But of course all this does not show on television. I am the way my daughter would want me to be: a hundred pounds lighter, my skin like an uncooked barley pancake. My hair glistens in the hot bright lights. Johnny Carson has much to do to keep up with my quick and witty tongue.

But that is a mistake. I know even before I wake up. Who ever knew a Johnson with a quick tongue? Who can even imagine me looking a strange white man in the eye? It seems to me I have talked to them always with one foot raised in flight, with my head turned in whichever way is farthest from them. Dee, though. She would always look anyone in the eye. Hesitation was no part of her nature.

•••

"How do I look, Mama?" Maggie says, showing just enough of her thin body enveloped in pink skirt and red blouse for me to know she's there, almost hidden by the door.

"Come out into the yard," I say.

Have you ever seen a lame animal, perhaps a dog run over by some careless person rich enough to own a car, sidle up to someone who is ignorant enough to be kind to him? That is the way my Maggie walks. She has been like this, chin on chest, eyes on ground, feet in shuffle, ever since the fire that burned the other house to the ground.

10 Dee is lighter than Maggie, with nicer hair and a fuller figure. She's a woman now, though sometimes I forget. How long ago was it that the other house burned? Ten, twelve years? Sometimes I can still hear the flames and feel Maggie's arms sticking to me, her hair smoking and her dress falling off her in little black papery flakes. Her eyes seemed stretched open, blazed open by the flames reflected in them. And Dee. I see her standing off under the sweet gum tree she used to dig gum out of; a look of concentration on her face as she watched the last dingy gray board of the house fall in toward the red-hot brick chimney. Why don't you do a dance around the ashes? I'd wanted to ask her. She had hated the house that much.

[1] Host of NBC's *The Tonight Show* from 1962 to 1992. — Eds.

I used to think she hated Maggie, too. But that was before we raised the money, the church and me, to send her to Augusta to school. She used to read to us without pity; forcing words, lies, other folks' habits, whole lives upon us two, sitting trapped and ignorant underneath her voice. She washed us in a river of make-believe, burned us with a lot of knowledge we didn't necessarily need to know. Pressed us to her with the serious way she read, to shove us away at just the moment, like dimwits, we seemed about to understand.

Dee wanted nice things. A yellow organdy dress to wear to her graduation from high school; black pumps to match a green suit she'd made from an old suit somebody gave me. She was determined to stare down any disaster in her efforts. Her eyelids would not flicker for minutes at a time. Often I fought off the temptation to shake her. At sixteen she had a style of her own: and knew what style was.

• • •

I never had an education myself. After second grade the school was closed down. Don't ask me why: in 1927 colored asked fewer questions than they do now. Sometimes Maggie reads to me. She stumbles along good-naturedly but can't see well. She knows she is not bright. Like good looks and money, quickness passed her by. She will marry John Thomas (who has mossy teeth in an earnest face) and then I'll be free to sit here and I guess just sing church songs to myself. Although I never was a good singer. Never could carry a tune. I was always better at a man's job. I used to love to milk till I was hooked in the side in '49. Cows are soothing and slow and don't bother you, unless you try to milk them the wrong way.

I have deliberately turned my back on the house. It is three rooms, just like the one that burned, except the roof is tin; they don't make shingle roofs any more. There are no real windows, just some holes cut in the sides, like the portholes in a ship, but not round and not square, with rawhide holding the shutters up on the outside. This house is in a pasture, too, like the other one. No doubt when Dee sees it she will want to tear it down. She wrote me once that no matter where we "choose" to live, she will manage to come see us. But she will never bring her friends. Maggie and I thought about this and Maggie asked me, "Mama, when did Dee ever *have* any friends?"

15 She had a few. Furtive boys in pink shirts hanging about on washday after school. Nervous girls who never laughed. Impressed with her they worshiped the well-turned phrase, the cute shape, the scalding humor that erupted like bubbles in lye. She read to them.

When she was courting Jimmy T she didn't have much time to pay to us, but turned all her faultfinding power on him. He *flew* to marry a cheap city girl from a family of ignorant flashy people. She hardly had time to recompose herself.

• • •

When she comes I will meet—but there they are!

Maggie attempts to make a dash for the house, in her shuffling way, but I stay her with my hand. "Come back here," I say. And she stops and tries to dig a well in the sand with her toe.

It is hard to see them clearly through the strong sun. But even the first glimpse of leg out of the car tells me it is Dee. Her feet were always neat-looking, as if God himself had shaped them with a certain style. From the other side of the car comes a short, stocky man. Hair is all over his head a foot long and hanging from his chin like a kinky mule tail. I hear Maggie suck in her breath. "Uhnnnh," is what it sounds like. Like when you see the wriggling end of a snake just in front of your foot on the road. "Uhnnnh."

20 Dee next. A dress down to the ground, in this hot weather. A dress so loud it hurts my eyes. There are yellows and oranges enough to throw back the light of the sun. I feel my whole face warming from the heat waves it throws out. Earrings gold, too, and hanging down to her shoulders. Bracelets dangling and making noises when she moves her arm up to shake the

folds of the dress out of her armpits. The dress is loose and flows, and as she walks closer, I like it. I hear Maggie go "Uhnnnh" again. It is her sister's hair. It stands straight up like the wool on a sheep. It is black as night and around the edges are two long pigtails that rope about like small lizards disappearing behind her ears.

"Wa-su-zo-Tean-o!" she says, coming on in that gliding way the dress makes her move. The short stocky fellow with the hair to his navel is all grinning and he follows up with "Asalamalakim, my mother and sister!" He moves to hug Maggie but she falls back, right up against the back of my chair. I feel her trembling there and when I look up I see the perspiration falling off her chin.

"Don't get up," says Dee. Since I am stout it takes something of a push. You can see me trying to move a second or two before I make it. She turns, showing white heels through her sandals, and goes back to the car. Out she peeks next with a Polaroid. She stoops down quickly and lines up picture after picture of me sitting there in front of the house with Maggie cowering behind me. She never takes a shot without making sure the house is included. When a cow comes nibbling around the edge of the yard she snaps it and me and Maggie *and* the house. Then she puts the Polaroid in the back seat of the car, and comes up and kisses me on the forehead.

Meanwhile Asalamalakim is going through motions with Maggie's hand. Maggie's hand is as limp as a fish, and probably as cold, despite the sweat, and she keeps trying to pull it back. It looks like Asalamalakim wants to shake hands but wants to do it fancy. Or maybe he don't know how people shake hands. Anyhow, he soon gives up on Maggie.

"Well," I say. "Dee."

"No, Mama," she says. "Not 'Dee,' Wangero 25
Leewanika Kemanjo!"

"What happened to 'Dee'?" I wanted to know.

"She's dead," Wangero said. "I couldn't bear it any longer, being named after the people who oppress me."

"You know as well as me you was named after your aunt Dicie," I said. Dicie is my sister. She named Dee. We called her "Big Dee" after Dee was born.

"But who was *she* named after?" asked Wangero.

"I guess after Grandma Dee," I said. 30

"And who was she named after?" asked Wangero.

"Her mother," I said, and saw Wangero was getting tired. "That's about as far back as I can trace it," I said. Though, in fact, I probably could have carried it back beyond the Civil War through the branches.

"Well," said Asalamalakim, "there you are."

"Uhnnnh," I heard Maggie say.

"There I was not," I said, "before 'Dicie' 35
cropped up in our family, so why should I try to trace it that far back?"

He just stood there grinning, looking down on me like somebody inspecting a Model A car.[2] Every once in a while he and Wangero sent eye signals over my head.

"How do you pronounce this name?" I asked.

"You don't have to call me by it if you don't want to," said Wangero.

"Why shouldn't I?" I asked. "If that's what you want us to call you, we'll call you."

"I know it might sound awkward at first," 40
said Wangero.

"I'll get used to it," I said. "Ream it out again."

Well, soon we got the name out of the way. Asalamalakim had a name twice as long and three times as hard. After I tripped over it two or three times he told me to just call him Hakim-a-barber. I wanted to ask him was he a barber, but I didn't really think he was, so I didn't ask.

"You must belong to those beef-cattle peoples down the road," I said. They said "Asalamalakim" when they met you, too, but they didn't shake hands. Always too busy: feeding the cattle, fixing the fences, putting up

[2] The redesigned successor to the Ford Model T. — Eds.

salt-lick shelters, throwing down hay. When the white folks poisoned some of the herd the men stayed up all night with rifles in their hands. I walked a mile and a half just to see the sight.

Hakim-a-barber said, "I accept some of their doctrines, but farming and raising cattle is not my style." (They didn't tell me, and I didn't ask, whether Wangero [Dee] had really gone and married him.)

We sat down to eat and right away he said he didn't eat collards and pork was unclean. Wangero, though, went on through the chitlins and corn bread, the greens and everything else. She talked a blue streak over the sweet potatoes. Everything delighted her. Even the fact that we still used the benches her daddy made for the table when we couldn't afford to buy chairs.

"Oh, Mama!" she cried. Then turned to Hakim-a-barber. "I never knew how lovely these benches are. You can feel the rump prints," she said, running her hands underneath her and along the bench. Then she gave a sigh and her hand closed over Grandma Dee's butter dish. "That's it!" she said. "I knew there was something I wanted to ask you if I could have." She jumped up from the table and went over in the corner where the churn stood, the milk in it clabber by now. She looked at the churn and looked at it.

"This churn top is what I need," she said. "Didn't Uncle Buddy whittle it out of a tree you all used to have?"

"Yes," I said.

"Uh huh," she said happily. "And I want the dasher, too."

"Uncle Buddy whittle that, too?" asked the barber.

Dee (Wangero) looked up at me.

"Aunt Dee's first husband whittled the dash," said Maggie so low you almost couldn't hear her. "His name was Henry, but they called him Stash."

"Maggie's brain is like an elephant's," Wangero said, laughing. "I can use the churn top as a centerpiece for the alcove table," she said, sliding a plate over the churn, "and I'll think of something artistic to do with the dasher."

When she finished wrapping the dasher the handle stuck out. I took it for a moment in my hands. You didn't even have to look close to see where hands pushing the dasher up and down to make butter had left a kind of sink in the wood. In fact, there were a lot of small sinks; you could see where thumbs and fingers had sunk into the wood. It was beautiful light yellow wood, from a tree that grew in the yard where Big Dee and Stash had lived.

After dinner Dee (Wangero) went to the trunk at the foot of my bed and started rifling through it. Maggie hung back in the kitchen over the dishpan. Out came Wangero with two quilts. They had been pieced by Grandma Dee and then Big Dee and me had hung them on the quilt frames on the front porch and quilted them. One was in the Lone Star pattern. The other was Walk Around the Mountain. In both of them were scraps of dresses Grandma Dee had worn fifty and more years ago. Bits and pieces of Grandpa Jarrell's Paisley shirts. And one teeny faded blue piece, about the size of a penny matchbox, that was from Great Grandpa Ezra's uniform that he wore in the Civil War.

"Mama," Wangero said sweet as a bird. "Can I have these old quilts?"

I heard something fall in the kitchen, and a minute later the kitchen door slammed.

"Why don't you take one or two of the others?" I asked. "These old things was just done by me and Big Dee from some tops your grandma pieced before she died."

"No," said Wangero. "I don't want those. They are stitched around the borders by machine."

"That'll make them last better," I said.

"That's not the point," said Wangero. "These are all pieces of dresses Grandma used to wear. She did all this stitching by hand.

extending beyond the text

This quilt, known as the "Pine Burr Quilt," was created by artist Lucy Mingo in 1995. Now hanging in the Saint Louis Art Museum, it is one of many from the Gee's Bend area, a rural riverside community in Alabama established by African Americans after the end of the Civil War. Quilting became a central part of many women's lives in Gee's Bend, and remains so today. While completing the back of a quilt and assembling the pieces were occasionally communal endeavors, the design and piecing of the top of the quilt was always an individual effort meant to highlight a quilter's personal artistic expression.

UPI Photo/St. Louis Art Museum/Alamy

1. **What do you find most visually striking about this quilt? What emotions does it evoke in the viewer?**
2. **In light of the increased recognition quilting has gained, was Dee ahead of her time? How does the treatment of quilts such as this one inform your understanding of Dee's assertion that her family's heirlooms should be treated as art rather than being appropriate for everyday use?**
3. **Is it possible for something to be revered but put to "everyday use"? Use your perspective on this image and your interpretation of the story to support your response.**

extending beyond the text

The NAMES Project AIDS Memorial Quilt is a memorial to celebrate the lives of people lost to the disease. Conceived in 1985 by Cleve Jones, an American AIDS and LGBTQ+ rights activist, the quilt was first shown in 1987 as part of the National March on Washington, D.C. for Lesbian and Gay Rights. When it was unfolded on the National Mall for the first time, there were 1,920 panels, each representing one life lost; today, there are more than 48,000 panels. It is considered the largest example of community folk art in the world.

JOYCE NALTCHAYAN/AFP/Getty Images

1. **Why is a quilt a fitting memorial — and legacy — for those who lost their lives to AIDS?**
2. **How does this quilt reflect both a sense of community and shared grief?**
3. **Mama sees Dee's desire to hang the heirloom quilts on a wall as the antithesis of engaging with the past and her family's heritage. How might you use the example of the AIDS quilt to present an alternative view, even an opposing one, to Mama's?**

Imagine!" She held the quilts securely in her arms, stroking them.

"Some of the pieces, like those lavender ones, come from old clothes her mother handed down to her," I said, moving up to touch the quilts. Dee (Wangero) moved back just enough so that I couldn't reach the quilts. They already belonged to her.

"Imagine!" she breathed again, clutching them closely to her bosom.

"The truth is," I said, "I promised to give them quilts to Maggie, for when she marries John Thomas."

She gasped like a bee had stung her.

"Maggie can't appreciate these quilts!" she said. "She'd probably be backward enough to put them to everyday use."

"I reckon she would," I said. "God knows I been saving 'em for long enough with nobody using 'em. I hope she will!" I didn't want to bring up how I had offered Dee (Wangero) a quilt when she went away to college. Then she had told me they were old-fashioned, out of style.

"But they're *priceless*!" she was saying now, furiously; for she has a temper. "Maggie would put them on the bed and in five years they'd be in rags. Less than that!"

"She can always make some more," I said. "Maggie knows how to quilt."

Dee (Wangero) looked at me with hatred. 70 "You just will not understand. The point is these quilts, *these* quilts!"

"Well," I said, stumped. "What would *you* do with them?"

"Hang them," she said. As if that was the only thing you *could* do with quilts.

Maggie by now was standing in the door. I could almost hear the sound her feet made as they scraped over each other.

"She can have them, Mama," she said, like somebody used to never winning anything, or having anything reserved for her. "I can 'member Grandma Dee without the quilts."

I looked at her hard. She had filled her 75 bottom lip with checkerberry snuff and it gave her face a kind of dopey, hangdog look. It was Grandma Dee and Big Dee who taught her how to quilt herself. She stood there with her scarred hands hidden in the folds of her skirt. She looked at her sister with something like fear but she wasn't mad at her. This was Maggie's portion. This was the way she knew God to work.

When I looked at her like that something hit me in the top of my head and ran down to the soles of my feet. Just like when I'm in church and the spirit of God touches me and I get happy and shout. I did something I never had done before: hugged Maggie to me, then dragged her on into the room, snatched the quilts out of Miss Wangero's hands and dumped them into Maggie's lap. Maggie just sat there on my bed with her mouth open.

"Take one or two of the others," I said to Dee.

But she turned without a word and went out to Hakim-a-barber.

"You just don't understand," she said, as Maggie and I came out to the car.

"What don't I understand?" I wanted to 80 know.

"Your heritage," she said. And then she turned to Maggie, kissed her, and said, "You ought to try to make something of yourself, too, Maggie. It's really a new day for us. But from the way you and Mama still live you'd never know it."

She put on some sunglasses that hid everything above the tip of her nose and her chin.

Maggie smiled; maybe at the sunglasses. But a real smile, not scared. After we watched the car dust settle I asked Maggie to bring me a dip of snuff. And then the two of us sat there just enjoying, until it was time to go in the house and go to bed. ■

1973

Understanding and Interpreting

1. Mama recounts how she sometimes dreams about herself and Dee appearing in a heartwarming reunion on a television show. How accurate do you think Mama's dreams about being on television are? How do they prepare us as readers to meet Dee? Do they bias us against her? Explain.
2. The action of "Everyday Use" is quite contained: a visit back home for college-educated Dee. Yet Alice Walker expects us to understand that action in a larger context. What information about the past does Walker incorporate into the story's present? How does it affect our understanding of, or attitude toward, the three central characters?
3. Dee brings home a young man who introduces himself with an Islamic greeting and whose appearance Walker reports only through Mama's eyes: "a short, stocky man" whose "[h]air is

all over his head a foot long and hanging from his chin like a kinky mule tail" (par. 19). How does this minor character, referred to as "Hakim-a-barber," contribute to the development of the three central characters?

4. In many traditional African cultures, the tribe pools resources to finance the education of a promising young person, who is then expected to assist the community. How is this practice reflected in this Southern small town? What does Dee's disregard of the current practice or its origin say about her?
5. In college, Dee came into contact with people and ideas quite different from those with which she grew up. What values does the "new Dee" — Wangero — claim to embrace? How do these values conflict with her family's values? How might the two value systems overlap or complement each other?
6. How does Mama's view of family legacy and engagement with the "past" differ from that of Dee? Consider both the recent and remote past, as well as each character's perspective on their shared family heritage, in your response.
7. "Everyday Use" might boil down to one decision, one question: should Mama have given Dee the quilts she wanted? But is the more fundamental issue which daughter Mama favors? If so, how might she have resolved this family conflict more equitably, without stoking division? Cite passages from the story to support your viewpoint.

Analyzing Language, Style, and Structure

1. **Vocabulary in Context.** As they anticipate Dee's arrival, Maggie asks Mama how she looks. Walker writes that Maggie is "showing just enough of her thin body enveloped in pink skirt and red blouse for me to know she's there, almost hidden by the door" (par. 7). In this context, how does "enveloped" evoke a literal image to convey a figurative meaning? How do the connotations of the word add to its effectiveness?
2. The two opening paragraphs serve as a kind of exposition. What do these paragraphs tell you about Mama? How do they set up the conflicts explored in the rest of the story?
3. Walker gives the storytelling to Mama. Why? How would the story have been different with an omniscient narrator? Explain whether you think Mama's narration is the most effective way to convey Walker's purpose. Include consideration of whether Mama is a reliable narrator.
4. What role do names and the concept of naming play in the story? What is Walker's purpose in drawing attention to the differing degrees of knowledge about family names as well as Dee's choice to change her name?
5. How does Walker use clothing as one means of characterization for Mama, Maggie, and Dee? How does outer appearance reflect inner traits and values? How does it subvert our expectations for the characters?
6. Throughout the story, Walker frequently uses language that refers to sight. What symbolic meaning do these references take on? In your response, you may wish to consider the relationship between visibility, power, and resistance. Cite specific passages and examples to support your interpretation.
7. In the story, we gain information about the quilts — what they look like, who made them, how they are being used, different views on how they should be used. Like most symbols, the quilts have different meanings for different people. What do they symbolize to Dee? to Maggie? to Mama?

8. Where do you find irony in the story? How would you describe that irony: angry, gentle, playful, resigned, bitter, or something else? As you develop your response, consider whether you read the title as ironic.

Topics for Composing

1. **AP® FRQ Prose Fiction Analysis.** The following question refers to paragraphs 55–74 of Alice Walker's "Everyday Use," published in 1973. In this passage, Mama, the narrator, discusses her family's heirloom quilts with her two daughters: Dee, a college student, and Dee's younger sister, Maggie. Read the passage carefully. Then, in a well-written essay, analyze how Walker uses literary elements and techniques to convey conflicting values of the three characters.
2. **AP® FRQ Literary Argument.** A character's thoughts and actions in response to the resolution of a narrative often reveals important values. In "Everyday Use," Dee responds to her mother's decision to give the family heirloom quilts to Maggie, Dee's younger sister, with this comment as she puts on her sunglasses and turns to leave: "It's really a new day for us. But from the way you and Mama still live you'd never know it." In a well-written essay, analyze how Dee's response at the end of the story contributes to an interpretation of the work as a whole. Do not merely summarize the plot.
3. **AP® Literary Argumentation.** In "Everyday Use," the character of Dee/Wangero returns from college seemingly quite changed in both appearance and values from the girl who left her rural home. Yet, in the words of one critic, "Dee is a character at war not only with her mother and her culture, but with herself as well." How does Walker use literary elements to develop this characterization of Dee/Wangero?
4. **Speaking and Listening.** Education, particularly for those who are the first generation in their family to attend college, is a gateway to new perspectives; yet there are tradeoffs when postsecondary education is a new experience for the whole family. Working with a partner, discuss your interpretation of how Walker presents the benefits and obstacles presented by being the first in a family to attend college. How can a synergy develop between these two forces; how can they be successfully navigated? Consider how your viewpoint and that of your partner are influenced by personal experiences. Share your insights with the full class.
5. **Research.** Originating in a small, rural Black community in Alabama, the Gee's Bend Quilters began quilting in the 1800s. Since then, the practical task of sewing warm blankets has transformed into an art form as the quilters have passed down patterns and styles for generations. During the civil rights movement, the Freedom Quilting Bee became a means to achieve economic independence for the women in the community. After conducting more research into the Gee's Bend Quilters, discuss how your understanding of Walker's purpose in focusing in these material objects has expanded your interpretation of "Everyday Use."
6. **Creative Writing.** In "Everyday Use," Dee is an intelligent yet impressionable college student coming to terms with her identity. What will she be like ten years later? Create a dramatic monologue that imagines how Dee will interact with Mama and Maggie a decade after the close of the story.
7. **Connections.** Alice Walker's best-known work is *The Color Purple*, her 1982 Pulitzer Prize–winning novel that became a popular movie and a Broadway musical play. Either read the book or watch the movie, and consider its connections to "Everyday Use." What ideas, concerns, and themes does Walker explore in the story that she amplifies in *The Color Purple*?

Half a Day

Naguib Mahfouz

Micheline Pelletier/Getty Images

Naguib Mahfouz (1911–2006) grew up in Cairo and studied philosophy at Egyptian University (now Cairo University). He worked for much of his life as a civil servant, as did his father. A prolific writer, he published 34 novels, hundreds of short stories, and dozens of movie scripts in addition to numerous works of journalism. In 1988, he became the first Middle Eastern writer to be awarded the Nobel Prize for Literature. His work often explores the conflict between Egyptian and European traditions as well as other political and social topics that were sometimes controversial in Egypt. Several of his works were banned in Egypt, and in 1994, when he was 84, he survived an assassination attempt.

I proceeded alongside my father, clutching his right hand, running to keep up with the long strides he was taking. All my clothes were new: the black shoes, the green school uniform, and the red tarboosh.[1] My delight in my new clothes, however, was not altogether unmarred, for this was no feast day but the day on which I was to be cast into school for the first time.

My mother stood at the window watching our progress, and I would turn toward her from time to time, as though appealing for help. We walked along a street lined with gardens; on both sides were extensive fields planted with crops, prickly pears, henna trees, and a few date palms.

"Why school?" I challenged my father openly. "I shall never do anything to annoy you."

"I'm not punishing you," he said, laughing. "School's not a punishment. It's the factory that makes useful men out of boys. Don't you want to be like your father and brothers?"

5 I was not convinced. I did not believe there was really any good to be had in tearing me away from the intimacy of my home and throwing me into this building that stood at the end of the road like some huge, high-walled fortress, exceedingly stern and grim.

When we arrived at the gate we could see the courtyard, vast and crammed full of boys and girls. "Go in by yourself," said my father, "and join them. Put a smile on your face and be a good example to others."

I hesitated and clung to his hand, but he gently pushed me from him. "Be a man," he said. "Today you truly begin life. You will find me waiting for you when it's time to leave."

I took a few steps, then stopped and looked but saw nothing. Then the faces of boys and girls came into view. I did not know a single one of them, and none of them knew me. I felt I was a stranger who had lost his way. But glances of curiosity were directed toward me, and one boy approached and asked, "Who brought you?"

"My father," I whispered.

"My father's dead," he said quite simply. 10

I did not know what to say. The gate was closed, letting out a pitiable screech. Some of the children burst into tears. The bell rang. A lady came along, followed by a group of men. The men began sorting us into ranks. We were formed into an intricate pattern in the great courtyard surrounded on three sides by high buildings of several floors; from each floor we were overlooked by a long balcony roofed in wood.

"This is your new home," said the woman. "Here too there are mothers and fathers.

[1] A flat-topped brimless hat with a black tassel traditionally worn by Muslim men throughout the eastern Mediterranean region. — Eds.

Mark Kauzlarich/Bloomberg/Getty Images

Go, by Kehinde Wiley, is a hand-painted, stained-glass ceiling triptych created for the redesign of New York City's Penn Station, a metropolitan train hub. In this work, Wiley adapts the style of classical Renaissance fresco paintings that show religious figures ascending to heaven. **How does Wiley's reinterpretation of works from centuries ago capture the blurred boundaries between the real and the fantastical in "Half a Day"?**

Here there is everything that is enjoyable and beneficial to knowledge and religion. Dry your tears and face life joyfully."

We submitted to the facts, and this submission brought a sort of contentment. Living beings were drawn to other living beings, and from the first moments my heart made friends with such boys as were to be my friends and fell in love with such girls as I was to be in love with, so that it seemed my misgivings had had no basis. I had never imagined school would have this rich variety. We played all sorts of different games: swings, the vaulting horse, ball games. In the music room we chanted our first songs. We also had our first introduction to language. We saw a globe of the Earth, which revolved and showed the various continents and countries. We started learning the numbers. The story of the Creator of the universe was read to us, we were told of His present world and of His Hereafter, and we heard examples of what He said. We ate delicious food, took a little nap, and woke up to go on with friendship and love, play and learning.

As our path revealed itself to us, however, we did not find it as totally sweet and unclouded as we had presumed. Dust-laden winds and unexpected accidents came about suddenly, so we had to be watchful, at the ready, and very patient. It was not all a matter of playing and fooling around. Rivalries could bring about pain and hatred or give rise to fighting. And while the lady would sometimes smile, she would often scowl and scold. Even more frequently she would resort to physical punishment.

15 In addition, the time for changing one's mind was over and gone and there was no question of ever returning to the paradise of home. Nothing lay ahead of us but exertion, struggle, and perseverance. Those who were able took advantage of the opportunities for success and happiness that presented themselves amid the worries.

The bell rang announcing the passing of the day and the end of work. The throngs of children rushed toward the gate, which was opened again. I bade farewell to friends and sweethearts and passed through the gate. I peered around but found no trace of my father, who had promised to be there. I stepped aside to wait. When I had waited for a long time without avail, I decided to return home on my own. After I had taken a few steps, a middle-aged man passed by, and I realized at once that I knew him. He came toward me, smiling, and shook me by the hand, saying, "It's a long time since we last met—how are you?"

With a nod of my head, I agreed with him and in turn asked, "And you, how are you?"

"As you can see, not all that good, the Almighty be praised!"

This painting titled *Eyeing Time* (2000) by Egyptian artist Ahmed Morsi shows the interaction between a distorted figure and a distorted clock.
What does this image suggest about the relationship humans have with the passage of time? Is that relationship portrayed in a similar way in "Half a Day"? Explain why or why not.

Again he shook me by the hand and went off. I proceeded a few steps, then came to a startled halt. Good Lord! Where was the street lined with gardens? Where had it disappeared to? When did all these vehicles invade it? And when did all these hordes of humanity come to rest upon its surface? How did these hills of refuse come to cover its sides? And where were the fields that bordered it? High buildings had taken over, the street surged with children, and disturbing noises shook the air. At various points stood conjurers showing off their tricks and making snakes appear from baskets. Then there was a band announcing the opening of a circus, with clowns and weight lifters walking in front. A line of trucks carrying central security troops crawled majestically by. The siren of a fire engine shrieked, and it was not clear how the vehicle would cleave its way to reach the blazing fire. A battle raged between a taxi driver and his passenger, while the passenger's wife called out for help and no one answered. Good God! I was in a daze. My head spun. I almost went crazy. How could all this have happened in half a day, between early morning and sunset? I would find the answer at home with my father. But where was my home? I could see only tall buildings and hordes of people. I hastened on to the crossroads between the gardens and Abu Khoda. I had to cross Abu Khoda to reach my house, but the stream of cars would not let up. The fire engine's siren was shrieking at full pitch as it moved at a snail's pace, and I said to myself, "Let the fire take its pleasure in what it consumes." Extremely irritated, I wondered when I would be able to cross. I stood there a long time, until the young lad employed at the ironing shop on the corner came up to me. He stretched out his arm and said gallantly, "Grandpa, let me take you across." ■

1989

Understanding and Interpreting

1. Describe the narrator's relationship with his father and mother as depicted in the beginning of the story. What do each of his parents represent to him?
2. How does the narrator's perspective on school differ from that of his father's? What does the institution represent to each of them?
3. What does the father mean when he says, "Today you truly begin life" (par. 7)? What does this suggest about the narrator's life prior to entering school?

4. What are the narrator's "misgivings" about school at the beginning of the story? Why does he ultimately conclude that his "misgivings had had no basis" (par. 13)?
5. In paragraph 14, the narrator explains that some aspects of school are not "as totally sweet and unclouded as we had presumed." What problems arise at his school? How pervasive — and serious — are these issues?
6. Once the narrator leaves school, a middle-aged man he once knew responds to his greeting by saying, "'As you can see, not all that good […]'" (par. 18). How do you interpret this response? What might this man expect the narrator to notice about his appearance?
7. What does the story's final sentence reveal about the narrator and his experience at school? What details from the text align with this revelation?

Analyzing Language, Style, and Structure

1. **Vocabulary in Context.** When the school bell rings, "throngs of children rushed toward the gate" (par. 16) on their way home. What is a "throng," and what are the connotations of this word? What image does it paint of school?
2. What is the effect of the verb "cast" in paragraph 1? How does this word contribute to the narrator's perspective?
3. How does the narrator characterize the setting of the story in paragraph 2? What mood does this paragraph establish?
4. What is the function of the metaphor comparing school to a "factory" in paragraph 4? What does this metaphor suggest about the father's values?
5. When the narrator first enters school he says, "I felt I was a stranger who had lost his way" (par. 8). How does this metaphor apply to the narrator as he both enters and exits the school building?
6. What do the series of questions in paragraph 19 suggest about the relationship between the narrator and the story's setting?
7. How does the story's title function both literally and figuratively? How does the notion of "half a day" relate to the story's overall themes?

Topics for Composing

1. **AP® FRQ** **Prose Fiction Analysis.** The following question refers to paragraphs 1–14 of Naguib Mahfouz's "Half a Day," published in 1989. In this passage, the narrator recounts his departure from home and some of his experiences during his first day of school. Read the passage carefully. Then, in a well-written essay, analyze how Mahfouz uses literary elements and techniques to convey the narrator's complex attitude toward this new stage in his life.
2. **AP® FRQ** **Literary Argument.** Writers often manipulate time and pacing in their work to develop the overarching theme(s) of the narrative. In "Half a Day," time suddenly advances by decades without notice. In a well-written essay, analyze how the manipulation of time contributes to an interpretation of the work as a whole. Do not merely summarize the plot.
3. **AP® Literary Argumentation.** Look up various definitions of the term "allegory." How can we read the surface story of this boy who exits school to find a world transformed as an allegory? Explain your response with evidence from the story.
4. **Connections.** How has a particular place changed during the years you've spent at school? You can focus on your immediate surroundings, such as your home or neighborhood, or a

larger setting, such as a city or country. How do your observations inform your perspective on the "truth" of the boy's experiences in "Half a Day"? Explain.

5. **Speaking and Listening.** How does the narrator's perspective on school compare to your own? In small groups, discuss how you and your classmates first felt about school and how your opinions have evolved over time. You may also wish to discuss how the experience of going to school has shaped your relationship with the passage of time — for instance, do you count down to the end of the school day? Do you have enough time between classes to get to where you need to go?
6. **Research.** The world seems transformed once the narrator exits the school building at the end of "Half a Day." How do these changes align with those that occurred in Egypt during Naguib Mahfouz's lifetime (1911–2006)? Research the major social, political, and economic changes that took place in Egypt from the early twentieth to the early twenty-first centuries. How does your research enhance your understanding of the themes of "Half a Day"?
7. **Multimodal.** Create a digital collage that conveys the mood, tone, and thematic concerns of "Half a Day." Your collage should combine words from the text, images, and video recordings that capture the essence of Mahfouz's story.

We're Not Jews

Hanif Kureishi

Andrea Sabbadini/Alamy

Hanif Kureishi (b. 1954) is a British Pakistani playwright, screenwriter, filmmaker, and novelist. Born in Bromley, South London, to a Pakistani father and an English mother, he earned a degree in philosophy from King's College London. His first play, *Soaking the Heat* (1976), was performed at the Royal Court Theatre in London and was followed by *The Mother Country* (1980), for which he won the Thames Television Playwright Award. His screenplay for the film *My Beautiful Laundrette* (1985) was nominated for an Academy Award. Kureishi's first novel, *The Buddha of Suburbia* (1990), won the Whitbread Award and was made into a BBC television series. His most recent novel is *The Nothing* (2017).

KEY CONTEXT This story is set in London during the late 1950s. The text includes several racist and antisemitic epithets, which we have chosen to reprint in this textbook. We wish to accurately reflect both Kureishi's original intent as well as call attention to the racism and antisemitism of the time period depicted in the story. However, we also recognize that these terms have a long history as disrespectful and deeply hurtful. Be mindful of context, both Kureishi's and yours, as you read and discuss "We're Not Jews."

Azhar's mother led him to the front of the lower deck, sat him down with his satchel, hurried back to retrieve her shopping, and took her place beside him. As the bus pulled away Azhar spotted Big Billy and his son Little Billy racing alongside, yelling and waving at the driver. Azhar closed his eyes and hoped it was moving too rapidly for them to get on. But they not only flung themselves onto the platform, they charged up the almost empty vehicle hooting and panting as if they were on a fairground ride. They settled directly across the aisle from where they could stare at Azhar and his mother.

At this his mother made to rise. So did Big Billy. Little Billy sprang up. They would follow her and Azhar. With a sigh she sank back down. The conductor came, holding the arm of his ticket machine. He knew the Billys, and had a laugh with them. He let them ride for nothing.

Mother's grey perfumed glove took some pennies from her purse. She handed them to Azhar who held them up as she had shown him.

"One and a half to the Three Kings," he said.

"Please," whispered Mother, making a sign of exasperation.

"Please," he repeated.

The conductor passed over the tickets and went away.

"Hold onto them tightly," said Mother. "In case the inspector gets on."

Big Billy said, "Look, he's a big boy."

"Big boy," echoed Little Billy.

"So grown up he has to run to teacher," said Big Billy.

"Cry baby!" trumpeted Little Billy.

Mother was looking straight ahead, through the window. Her voice was almost normal, but subdued. "Pity we didn't have time to get to the library. Still, there's tomorrow. Are you still the best reader in the class?" She nudged him. "Are you?"

"S'pose so," he mumbled.

Every evening after school Mother took him to the tiny library nearby where he exchanged the previous day's books. Tonight, though, there hadn't been time. She didn't want Father asking why they were late. She wouldn't want him to know they had been in to complain.

Big Billy had been called to the headmistress's stuffy room and been sharply informed — so she told Mother — that she took a "dim view." Mother was glad. She had objected to Little Billy bullying her boy. Azhar had had Little Billy sitting behind him in class. For weeks Little Billy had called him names and clipped him round the head with his ruler. Now some of the other boys, mates of Little Billy, had also started to pick on Azhar.

"I eat nuts!"

Big Billy was hooting like an orang-utan, jumping up and down and scratching himself under the arms — one of the things Little Billy had been castigated for. But it didn't restrain his father. His face looked horrible.

Big Billy lived a few doors away from them. Mother had known him and his family since she was a child. They had shared the same air-raid shelter during the war. Big Billy had been a Ted[1] and still wore a drape coat and his hair in a sculpted quiff. He had black bitten-down fingernails and a smear of grease across his forehead. He was known as Motorbike Bill because he repeatedly built and rebuilt his Triumph. "Triumph of the Bill," Father liked to murmur as they passed. Sometimes numerous lumps of metal stood on rags around the skeleton of the bike, and in the late evening Big Bill revved up the machine while his record player balanced on the windowsill repeatedly blared out a 45 called "Rave On." Then everyone knew Big Billy was preparing for the annual bank holiday run to the coast. Mother and the other neighbours were forced to shut their windows to exclude the noise and fumes.

Mother had begun to notice not only Azhar's dejection but also his exhausted and dishevelled appearance on his return from school. He looked as if he'd been flung into a hedge and rolled in a puddle — which he had. Unburdening with difficulty, he confessed the abuse the boys gave him, Little Billy in particular.

At first Mother appeared amused by such pranks. She was surprised that Azhar took it so hard. He should ignore the childish remarks: a lot of children were cruel. Yet he couldn't make out what it was with him that made people say

[1] Short for "Teddy Boy," referring to young men in London in the 1950s who wore clothes inspired by the dandies, or well-groomed men, of the Edwardian period (1901–1910). — Eds.

such things, or why, after so many contented hours at home with his mother, such violence had entered his world.

Mother had taken Azhar's hand and instructed him to reply, "Little Billy, you're common — common as muck!"

Azhar held onto the words and repeated them continuously to himself. Next day, in a corner with his enemy's taunts going at him, he closed his eyes and hollered them out. "Muck, muck, muck — common as muck you!"

Little Billy was as perplexed as Azhar by the epithet. Like magic it shut his mouth. But the next day Little Billy came back with the renewed might of names new to Azhar: sambo, wog, little coon. Azhar returned to his mother for more words but they had run out.

Big Billy was saying across the bus, "Common! Why don't you say it out loud to me face, eh? Won't say it, eh?"

"Nah," said Little Billy. "Won't!"

"But we ain't as common as a slut who marries a darkie."

"Darkie, darkie," Little Billy repeated. "Monkey, monkey!"

Mother's look didn't deviate. But, perhaps anxious that her shaking would upset Azhar, she pulled her hand from his and pointed at a shop.

"Look."

"What?" said Azhar, distracted by Little Billy murmuring his name.

The instant Azhar turned his head, Big Billy called, "Hey! why don't you look at us, little lady?"

She twisted round and waved at the conductor standing on his platform. But a passenger got on and the conductor followed him upstairs. The few other passengers, sitting like statues, were unaware or unconcerned.

Mother turned back. Azhar had never seen her like this, ashen, with wet eyes, her body stiff as a tree. Azhar sensed what an effort she was making to keep still. When she wept at home she threw herself on the bed, shook convulsively and thumped the pillow. Now all that moved was a bulb of snot shivering on the end of her nose. She sniffed determinedly, before opening her bag and extracting the scented handkerchief with which she usually wiped Azhar's face, or, screwing up a corner, dislodged any stray eyelashes around his eye. She blew her nose vigorously but he heard a sob.

Now she knew what went on and how it felt. How he wished he'd said nothing and protected her, for Big Billy was using her name: "Yvonne, Yvonne, hey, Yvonne, didn't I give you a good time that time?"

"Evie, a good time, right?" sang Little Billy.

Big Billy smirked. "Thing is," he said, holding his nose, "there's a smell on this bus."

"Pooh!"

"How many of them are there living in that flat, all squashed together like, and stinkin' the road out, eatin' curry and rice!"

There was no doubt that their flat was jammed. Grandpop, a retired doctor, slept in one bedroom, Azhar, his sister and parents in another, and two uncles in the living room. All day big pans of Indian food simmered in the kitchen so people could eat when they wanted. The kitchen wallpaper bubbled and cracked and hung down like ancient scrolls. But Mother always denied that they were "like that." She refused to allow the word "immigrant" to be used about Father, since in her eyes it applied only to illiterate tiny men with downcast eyes and mismatched clothes.

Mother's lips were moving but her throat must have been dry: no words came, until she managed to say, "We're not Jews."

There was a silence. This gave Big Billy an opportunity. "What you say?" He cupped his ear and his long dark sideburn. With his other hand he cuffed Little Billy, who had begun hissing. "Speak up. Hey, tart, we can't hear you!"

Mother repeated the remark but could make her voice no louder.

Azhar wasn't sure what she meant. In his confusion he recalled a recent conversation about South Africa, where his best friend's family had

This mixed media collage, by Pakistani artist Sophiya Khwaja (b. 1982), is entitled *Closed Minded*.

What does the image have to say about the effect of closed minds? Whose minds do you consider the most closed in "We're Not Jews"?

just emigrated. Azhar had asked why, if they were to go somewhere — and there had been such talk — they too couldn't choose Cape Town. Painfully she replied that there the people with white skins were cruel to the black and brown people who were considered inferior and were forbidden to go where the whites went. The coloureds had separate entrances and were prohibited from sitting with the whites.

This peculiar fact of living history, vertiginously irrational and not taught in his school, struck his head like a hammer and echoed through his dreams night after night. How could such a thing be possible? What did it mean? How then should he act?

"Nah," said Big Billy. "You no Yid,[2] Yvonne. You us. But worse. Goin' with the Paki[3]."

All the while Little Billy was hissing and twisting his head in imitation of a spastic.

Azhar had heard his father say that there had been "gassing" not long ago. Neighbour had slaughtered neighbour, and such evil hadn't died. Father would poke his finger at his wife, son and baby daughter, and state, "We're in the front line!"

These conversations were often a prelude to his announcing that they were going "home" to Pakistan. There they wouldn't have these problems. At this point Azhar's mother would become uneasy. How could she go "home" when she was at home already? Hot weather made her swelter; spicy food upset her stomach; being surrounded by people who didn't speak English made her feel lonely. As it was, Azhar's grandfather and uncle chattered away in Urdu, and when Uncle Asif's wife had been in the country, she had, without prompting, walked several paces behind them in the street. Not wanting to side with either camp, Mother had had to position herself, with Azhar, somewhere in the middle of this curious procession as it made its way to the shops.

Not that the idea of "home" didn't trouble Father. He himself had never been there. His family had lived in China and India; but since he'd left, the remainder of his family had moved, along with hundreds of thousands of others, to Pakistan. How could he know if the new country would suit him, or if he could succeed there? While Mother wailed, he would smack his hand against his forehead and cry "Oh God, I am trying to think in all directions at the same time!"

He had taken to parading about the flat in Wellington boots with a net curtain over his head, swinging his portable typewriter and saying he expected to be called to Vietnam as a war correspondent, and was preparing for jungle combat.

It made them laugh. For two years Father had been working as a packer in a factory that manufactured shoe polish. It was hard physical labour, which drained and infuriated him. He loved books and wanted to write them. He got

[2] An antisemitic epithet referring to Yiddish, a language spoken by many Ashkenazi Jewish people. — Eds.

[3] A racist epithet for people of South Asian descent. — Eds.

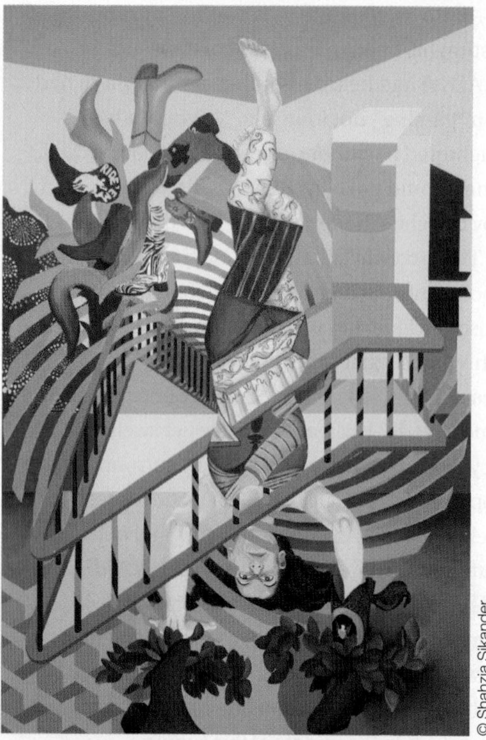

Pakistan American artist Shahzia Sikander (b. 1969) has said that she is inspired by "combining different religious and cultural references" in her work. This piece is entitled *Elusive Realities*.

What religious and cultural references do you recognize in this work? Where do you see overlap with some of the cultural and religious references in "We're Not Jews"? What "elusive realities" exist in the story?

up at five every morning; at night he wrote for as long as he could keep his eyes open. Even as they ate he scribbled over the backs of envelopes, rejection slips and factory stationery, trying to sell articles to magazines and newspapers. At the same time he was studying for a correspondence course on "How To Be A Published Author." The sound of his frenetic typing drummed into their heads like gunfire. They were forbidden to complain. Father was determined to make money from the articles on sport, politics and literature which he posted off most days, each accompanied by a letter that began, "Dear Sir, Please find enclosed . . ."

But Father didn't have a sure grasp of the English language which was his, but not entirely, being "Bombay variety, mish and mash." Their neighbour, a retired school-teacher, was kind enough to correct Father's spelling and grammar, suggesting that he sometimes used "the right words in the wrong place, and vice versa." His pieces were regularly returned in the self-addressed stamped envelope that the *Writers' and Artists' Yearbook* advised. Lately, when they plopped through the letter box, Father didn't open them, but tore them up, stamped on the pieces and swore in Urdu, cursing the English who, he was convinced, were barring him. Or were they? Mother once suggested he was doing something wrong and should study something more profitable. But this didn't get a good response.

In the morning now Mother sent Azhar out to intercept the postman and collect the returned manuscripts. The envelopes and parcels were concealed around the garden like an alcoholic's bottles, behind the dustbins, in the bike shed, even under buckets, where, mouldering in secret, they sustained hope and kept away disaster.

At every stop Azhar hoped someone might get on who would discourage or arrest the Billys. But no one did, and as they moved forward the bus emptied. Little Billy took to jumping up and twanging the bell, at which the conductor only laughed.

Then Azhar saw that Little Billy had taken a marble from his pocket, and, standing with his arm back, was preparing to fling it. When Big Billy noticed this even his eyes widened. He reached for Billy's wrist. But the marble was released: it cracked into the window between Azhar and mother's head, chipping the glass.

She was screaming. "Stop it, stop it! Won't anyone help! We'll be murdered!"

The noise she made came from hell or eternity. Little Billy blanched and shifted closer to his father; they went quiet.

Azhar got out of his seat to fight them but the conductor blocked his way.

Their familiar stop was ahead. Before the bus braked Mother was up, clutching her bags; she gave Azhar two carriers to hold, and nudged him towards the platform. As he went past he wasn't going to look at the Billys, but he did give them the eye, straight on, stare to stare, so he could see them and not be so afraid. They could hate him but he would know them. But if he couldn't fight them, what could he do with his anger?

They stumbled off and didn't need to check if the crêpe-soled Billys were behind, for they were already calling out, though not as loud as before.

As they approached the top of their street the retired teacher who assisted Father came out of his house, wearing a three-piece suit and trilby hat and leading his Scottie. He looked over his garden, picked up a scrap of paper which had blown over the fence, and sniffed the evening air. Azhar wanted to laugh: he resembled a phantom; in a deranged world the normal appeared the most bizarre. Mother immediately pulled Azhar towards his gate.

Their neighbour raised his hat and said in a friendly way, "How's it all going?"

At first Azhar didn't understand what his mother was talking about. But it was Father she was referring to. "They send them back, his writing, every day, and he gets so angry . . . so angry . . . Can't you help him?"

"I do help him, where I can," he replied.

"Make him stop, then!"

She choked into her handkerchief and shook her head when he asked what the matter was.

The Billys hesitated a moment and then passed on silently. Azhar watched them go. It was all right, for now. But tomorrow Azhar would be for it, and the next day, and the next. No mother could prevent it.

"He's a good little chap," the teacher was saying, of Father.

"But will he get anywhere?"

"Perhaps," he said. "Perhaps. But he may be a touch —" Azhar stood on tiptoe to listen. "Over hopeful. Over hopeful."

"Yes," she said, biting her lip.

"Tell him to read more Gibbon and Macaulay[4]," he said. "That should set him straight."

"Right."

"Are you feeling better?"

"Yes, yes," Mother insisted.

He said, concerned, "Let me walk you back."

"That's all right, thank you."

Instead of going home, mother and son went in the opposite direction. They passed a bomb site and left the road for a narrow path. When they could no longer feel anything firm beneath their feet, they crossed a nearby rutted muddy playing field in the dark. The strong wind, buffeting them sideways, nearly had them tangled in the slimy nets of a soccer goal. He had no idea she knew this place.

At last they halted outside a dismal shed, the public toilet, rife with spiders and insects, where he and his friends often played. He looked up but couldn't see her face. She pushed the door and stepped across the wet floor. When he hesitated she tugged him into the stall with her. She wasn't going to let him go now. He dug into the wall with his penknife and practised holding his breath until she finished, and wiped herself on the scratchy paper. Then she sat there with her eyes closed, as if she were saying a prayer. His teeth were clicking; ghosts whispered in his ears; outside there were footsteps; dead fingers seemed to be clutching at him.

---

[4] Edward Gibbon (1737–1794) was an English historian who openly critiqued organized religion. Thomas Babington Macaulay (1800–1859) was an English historian, essayist, critic, and politician most famous for his books on British history. — Eds.

This work, by Khaver Idrees, entitled *Bohemian Rhapsody*, was exhibited as part of a show of the best Pakistani contemporary art. The artist said that the layering of symbols over the British Union Jack flag "mirrored levels of integration" that she has felt living in England. **How does "We're Not Jews" layer symbols or markers of several cultures?**

For a long time she examined herself in the mirror, powdering her face, replacing her lipstick and combing her hair. There were no human voices, only rain on the metal roof, which dripped through onto their heads.

"Mum," he cried.

"Don't you whine!"

He wanted his tea. He couldn't wait to get away. Her eyes were scorching his face in the yellow light. He knew she wanted to tell him not to mention any of this. Recognising at last that it wasn't necessary, she suddenly dragged him by his arm, as if it had been his fault they were held up, and hurried him home without another word.

The flat was lighted and warm. Father, having worked the early shift, was home. Mother went into the kitchen and Azhar helped her unpack the shopping. She was trying to be normal, but the very effort betrayed her, and she didn't kiss Father as she usually did.

Now, beside Grandpop and Uncle Asif, Father was listening to the cricket commentary on the big radio, which had an illuminated panel printed with the names of cities they could never pick up, Brussels, Stockholm, Hilversum, Berlin, Budapest. Father's typewriter, with its curled paper tongue, sat on the table surrounded by empty beer bottles.

"Come, boy."

Azhar ran to his father who poured some beer into a glass for him, mixing it with lemonade.

The men were smoking pipes, peering into the ashy bowls, tapping them on the table, poking them with pipe cleaners, and relighting them. They were talking loudly in Urdu or Punjabi, using some English words but gesticulating and slapping one another in a way English people never did. Then one of them would suddenly leap up, clapping his hands and shouting, "Yes — out — out!"

Azhar was accustomed to being with his family while grasping only fragments of what they said. He endeavoured to decipher the gist of it, laughing, as he always did, when the men laughed, and silently moving his lips without knowing what the words meant, whirling, all the while, in incomprehension. ■

1995

Understanding and Interpreting

1. Describe the community in which Azhar and his family live. How does Azhar fit in? How is he both similar to and different from each of his parents?
2. Whom do you consider the central character of "We're Not Jews"? Explain.
3. How is Azhar's father characterized? What do you make of his obsession with journalism in a language that's not his first? Do you think he's intended to be a comic figure, or something else? Explain.
4. Identify the race, ethnicity, gender, and social class of each of the central characters. How do their backgrounds affect the way they interact with each other? How does that interaction create the conflict in the story?
5. Why do you think Azhar's mother doesn't want his father to know that they had "been in to complain" (par. 15)?
6. What do you see as the primary differences between Azhar and Little Billy? How does each one face his world? Based on their characterizations in this story, what kind of person will each grow up to be?
7. Why is Big Billy particularly hostile to Azhar's mother? Why do you think she has trouble standing up to him? Why does she finally say, "We're not Jews"?
8. What purpose does the "retired teacher" (pars. 63–80) serve? Think about both his appearance and what he says to Azhar and his mother. Why do you think the two Billys are silenced when they see him?
9. What is the reason for Azhar and his mother's visit to the public toilet before returning home at the end of the story? Why isn't it "necessary" for his mother to "tell him not to mention any of this" (par. 84)?

Analyzing Language, Style, and Structure

1. **Vocabulary in Context.** What is the meaning of "common" in paragraph 22? What is the effect of the insult "common as muck" supposed to be? Based on your interpretation of the story, does Azhar's choice to use it have the desired effect?
2. How does the setting establish the tone of the story? What does it signal to readers about England in the late 1950s, when the story takes place?
3. "We're Not Jews" contains many historical allusions, including references to World War II, the partition of India, and apartheid in South Africa. How do these allusions provide context for Azhar's particular experience? How do they inform your reading of the Billys' actions and Azhar's mother's reaction to them?
4. The narrator of "We're Not Jews" is a limited third-person narrator who is privy to Azhar's thoughts but not to those of the other characters. Why do you think Hanif Kureishi chose to tell the story from this point of view? How does Kureishi give his diverse cast of characters their voices?
5. Why do you think Kureishi set most of the story on a moving bus with a driver who ignores the passengers?
6. Azhar's father is described as not having a "sure grasp of the English language which was his, but not entirely, being 'Bombay variety, mish and mash'" (par. 53). How can the language be his but not entirely? What does this statement convey about the meaning of "home" for their family?

7. Why is what Azhar learns about South Africa referred to as a "peculiar fact of living history, vertiginously irrational and not taught in his school" (par. 45)? How, ultimately, does the story answer the question at the end of that paragraph: "How then should he act?"

Topics for Composing

1. AP® FRQ **Prose Fiction Analysis.** The following question refers to paragraphs 18–19 of Hanif Kureishi's "We're Not Jews," published in 1995. In this passage, the narrator describes Big Billy, the father of the boy who bullies Azhar, the young boy who is the story's protagonist. Read the passage carefully. Then, in a well-written essay, analyze how Kureishi uses literary elements and techniques to develop Big Billy's character as an antagonist on both a personal and a symbolic level.
2. AP® FRQ **Literary Argument.** Many works of literature comment on conflicts based on social status. "We're Not Jews" introduces several different determinants of social status, including race, gender identity, and class. In a well-written essay, analyze how the story's portrayal of the complex intersection of these concepts contributes to an interpretation of the work as a whole. Do not merely summarize the plot.
3. **AP® Literary Argumentation.** What does "We're Not Jews" say about the place of women? Consider how both Azhar's family and the Billys treat Azhar's mother.
4. **AP® Literary Argumentation.** In a review of *Love in a Blue Time*, the collection in which "We're Not Jews" appears, critic Laura Miller wrote that "Kureishi's love of the world has always been the heartbeat of his work." To what extent do you believe that statement applies to this story? Explain your answer, using specific details from the story to support your response.
5. **Connections.** After Little Billy throws a marble, Azhar tries to fight him, but is blocked by the conductor. As Azhar and his mother prepare to get off the bus, Azhar "wasn't going to look at the Billys, but he did give them the eye, straight on, stare to stare, so he could see them and not be so afraid. They could hate him but he would know them. But if he couldn't fight them, what could he do with his anger?" (par. 60). To what extent does Azhar's confrontation dampen the Billys' bullying? Does standing up to bullying help end it? If so, what type of resistance works best? If not, why not?
6. **Connections.** Hanif Kureishi has referred to himself as a "cultural translator." What culture(s) does Kureishi translate in "We're Not Jews"?
7. **Argument.** In an interview with the *Guardian*, Kureishi said, "If Britain is a cultural force in Europe . . . then that's because of multiculturalism and diversity. . . . Britain became a multicultural society by mistake. No one ever thought, 'How do we make a multicultural society?'. . . The racism of the 50s and 60s . . . was overt. You were made aware of your difference all the time. So you began to think, 'Where does this come from? What does it mean?'" How is Kureishi's observation illustrated in "We're Not Jews"? Does the story, written in the 1990s and taking place in the late 1950s, seem optimistic about Britain's future as a cultural force? Explain why or why not.

Elegy Written in a Country Churchyard

Thomas Gray

Lebrecht Music & Arts/Alamy

Born to a middle-class family in Cornhill, England, Thomas Gray (1716–1771) was the fifth of twelve children, and the only one to survive past infancy. He was educated at Eton and later Cambridge. Despite the success of many of his poems, he was very self-critical, often employing his lacerating wit at his own expense. He turned down the position of poet laureate of England, later saying that he feared his poems would be "mistaken for the words of a flea."

KEY CONTEXT This poem is an elegy, or a poem that mourns a death; Thomas Gray likely felt inspired to write it following the death of another poet. An epitaph, which is the title of the second part of the poem, is what is written on a person's headstone. Gray was buried in the churchyard of Stoke Poges, which is thought to be the setting of "Elegy," so he wrote it not only contemplating his own death but also imagining the very place he knew he would likely be buried.

The curfew[1] tolls the knell of parting day,
   The lowing herd wind slowly o'er the lea,[2]
The plowman homeward plods his weary way,
   And leaves the world to darkness and to me.

Now fades the glimmering landscape on the sight,
   And all the air a solemn stillness holds,
Save where the beetle wheels his droning flight,
   And drowsy tinklings lull the distant folds;

Save that from yonder ivy-mantled tower
   The moping owl does to the moon complain
Of such, as wandering near her secret bower,
   Molest her ancient solitary reign.

Beneath those rugged elms, that yew tree's shade,
   Where heaves the turf in many a moldering heap,
Each in his narrow cell forever laid,
   The rude[3] forefathers of the hamlet sleep

[1] Evening bell. — Eds.
[2] A field. — Eds.
[3] Humble. — Eds.

The breezy call of incense-breathing morn,
 The swallow twittering from the straw-built shed,
The cock's shrill clarion, or the echoing horn,
 No more shall rouse them from their lowly bed.

For them no more the blazing hearth shall burn,
 Or busy housewife ply her evening care;
No children run to lisp their sire's return,
 Or climb his knees the envied kiss to share.

Oft did the harvest to their sickle yield,
 Their furrow oft the stubborn glebe[4] has broke;
How jocund[5] did they drive their team afield!
 How bowed the woods beneath their sturdy stroke!

Let not Ambition mock their useful toil,
 Their homely joys, and destiny obscure;
Nor Grandeur hear with a disdainful smile
 The short and simple annals of the poor.

The boast of heraldry, the pomp of power,
 And all that beauty, all that wealth e'er gave,
Awaits alike the inevitable hour.
 The paths of glory lead but to the grave.

Nor you, ye proud, impute to these the fault,
 If memory o'er their tomb no trophies raise,
Where through the long-drawn aisle and fretted[6] vault
 The pealing anthem swells the note of praise.

Can storied urn or animated[7] bust
 Back to its mansion call the fleeting breath?
Can Honor's voice provoke the silent dust,
 Or Flattery soothe the dull cold ear of Death?

Perhaps in this neglected spot is laid
 Some heart once pregnant with celestial fire;
Hands that the rod of empire might have swayed,
 Or waked to ecstasy the living lyre.

---

[4] Soil. — Eds.
[5] Joyful. — Eds.
[6] Ornamented. — Eds.
[7] Lifelike. — Eds.

But Knowledge to their eyes her ample page
  Rich with the spoils of time did ne'er unroll;
Chill Penury repressed their noble rage,
  And froze the genial current of the soul.

Full many a gem of purest ray serene,
  The dark unfathomed caves of ocean bear.
Full many a flower is born to blush unseen,
  And waste its sweetness on the desert air.

Some village Hampden,[8] that with dauntless breast
  The little tyrant of his fields withstood;
Some mute inglorious Milton here may rest,
  Some Cromwell[9] guiltless of his country's blood.

The applause of listening senates to command,
  The threats of pain and ruin to despise,
To scatter plenty o'er a smiling land,
  And read their history in a nation's eyes,

Their lot forbade: nor circumscribed alone
  Their growing virtues, but their crimes confined;
Forbade to wade through slaughter to a throne,
  And shut the gates of mercy on mankind,

The struggling pangs of conscious truth to hide,
  To quench the blushes of ingenuous shame,
Or heap the shrine of Luxury and Pride
  With incense kindled at the Muse's flame.

Far from the madding crowd's ignoble strife,
  Their sober wishes never learned to stray;
Along the cool sequestered vale of life
  They kept the noiseless tenor of their way.

Yet even these bones from insult to protect
  Some frail memorial still erected nigh,
With uncouth rhymes and shapeless sculpture decked,
  Implores the passing tribute of a sigh.

---

[8] John Hampden (1594–1643) was a prominent figure in the English Civil War (1642–1651). He famously refused to pay a protection tax levied by King Charles I. — Eds.

[9] Oliver Cromwell (1599–1658), a Puritan, was a rebel leader in the English Civil War. — Eds.

Their name, their years, spelt by the unlettered Muse,
The place of fame and elegy supply:
And many a holy text around she strews,
That teach the rustic moralist to die.

For who to dumb Forgetfulness a prey,
This pleasing anxious being e'er resigned,
Left the warm precincts of the cheerful day,
Nor cast one longing lingering look behind?

On some fond breast the parting soul relies,
Some pious drops the closing eye requires;
Even from the tomb the voice of Nature cries,
Even in our ashes live their wonted fires.

For thee, who mindful of the unhonored dead
Dost in these lines their artless tale relate;
If chance, by lonely contemplation led,
Some kindred spirit shall inquire thy fate,

Haply some hoary-headed swain[10] may say,
"Oft have we seen him at the peep of dawn
Brushing with hasty steps the dews away
To meet the sun upon the upland lawn.

"There at the foot of yonder nodding beech
That wreathes its old fantastic roots so high,
His listless length at noontide would he stretch,
And pore upon the brook that babbles by.

"Hard by yon wood, now smiling as in scorn,
Muttering his wayward fancies he would rove,
Now drooping, woeful wan, like one forlorn,
Or crazed with care, or crossed in hopeless love.

"One morn I missed him on the customed hill,
Along the heath and near his favorite tree;
Another came; nor yet beside the rill,
Nor up the lawn, nor at the wood was he;

"The next with dirges due in sad array
Slow through the churchway path we saw him borne.
Approach and read (for thou canst read) the lay,
Graved on the stone beneath yon aged thorn."

---

[10] White-haired (elderly) shepherd. —Eds.

THE EPITAPH

Here rests his head upon the lap of Earth
A youth to fortune and to Fame unknown.
Fair Science[11] *frowned not on his humble birth,*
And Melancholy marked him for her own.

Large was his bounty, and his soul sincere,
Heaven did a recompense as largely send:
He gave to Misery all he had, a tear,
He gained from Heaven ('twas all he wished), a friend.

No farther seek his merits to disclose,
Or draw his frailties from their dread abode
(There they alike in trembling hope repose),
The bosom of his Father and his God. ■

1751

[11] Learning, education. — Eds.

Understanding and Interpreting

1. Who do you think is the speaker? Now, try to imagine the setting. Is the speaker literally in the churchyard? How do you know?
2. Whom does the speaker describe in line 20: "No more shall rouse them from their lowly bed"? What does he mean by this?
3. What "homely joys" (l. 30) does the speaker believe those buried in the churchyard once experienced? Why are such things important to the speaker?
4. How might line 36 ("The paths . . . to the grave") be the thesis of this poem?
5. Whom does the speaker address in line 37? What can you infer about the subject of this line?
6. In lines 45–48, what does the speaker suggest those buried in the churchyard might have accomplished? What does his statement convey about lost potential? How do lines 53–56 echo this sentiment?
7. Does the speaker use a critical tone or an admiring tone as he describes the men in lines 57–60? Explain.
8. How does the speaker honor simple folk in lines 61–76?
9. Stanza 24 (ll. 93–96) begins the lead-up to the epitaph, which comprises the last twelve lines of the poem. Who is speaking beginning in line 98, and what are they speaking about? Whose epitaph ends the poem?
10. What three things does the speaker believe would make someone "woeful wan" (l. 107)? Explain them using your own words.
11. Some scholars believe that "Elegy" was inspired by the fact that Gray was the only one of twelve siblings to survive until adulthood. How does this knowledge affect your reading of the poem?

Analyzing Language, Style, and Structure

1. **Vocabulary in Context.** While people do still use the word *ingenuous*, its antonym *disingenuous* will likely be a word you encounter more often today. Research the denotations and connotations of both words. To what extent do their emotional associations place them in opposition to each other? How does this inform your understanding of the "ingenuous shame" the speaker describes in line 70?
2. Notice the use of sound imagery in stanzas 1–3. How does the toll of the "knell of parting day" (l. 1) echo throughout those stanzas? In what context do you usually hear the word "knell"? What is its connotation, and how does that connotation contribute to the meaning of this section of the poem? How does this sound imagery introduce stanza 4?
3. Look carefully at stanza 2. How does Thomas Gray use the natural world to comment on the issue of tradition and progress?
4. The poem shifts in stanza 8. Analyze the stanza, looking carefully at Gray's diction and syntax choices, and explain how it works as a transition from one idea to another.
5. You may have noticed that the syntax changes in stanza 11 (ll. 41–44) as the speaker asks two questions. How does this shift affect the speaker's tone?
6. Stanza 13 (ll. 49–52) may be the poem's most famous. How does Gray use figurative language to mirror the stanza's meaning, that poverty may have forced talented people to remain unknown and unfulfilled?
7. If you read lines 61–65 grammatically — that is, as a complete sentence — you will find that the subject and verb do not appear until line 65, in a separate stanza from the object of the sentence. What is the effect of this delay? Why might Gray have considered the object worth introducing before the subject?
8. Gray's "Elegy" is considered one of the great poems, in part because of the seamless way structure, rhyme scheme, and imagery combine to communicate Gray's message that life is short. First consider each of these elements separately. How does each element connect to the poem's message? Then consider the way these elements work together to elevate this simple theme.

Topics for Composing

1. AP® FRQ **Poetry Analysis.** In Thomas Gray's "Elegy Written in a Country Churchyard," published in 1751, the speaker reflects on death's role as the great equalizer. He then contemplates his own epitaph in this elegy. Read the poem carefully. Then, in a well-written essay, analyze how Gray uses literary elements and techniques to portray the speaker's complex understanding of death and grief.
2. **Research.** Gray alludes to three famous Englishmen in his poem: John Hampden, Oliver Cromwell, and John Milton. Research two of these individuals to better understand the meaning of these allusions. Then, write an essay that analyzes how Gray illustrates his point in alluding to the two individuals you have chosen.
3. **Connections.** In 2011, Carol Rumens of the *Guardian* wrote that children should still memorize "Elegy Written in a Country Churchyard" in part because "its ideas about society and education are deeply relevant today." Write an essay in which you develop a position on Rumens's assertion.

4. **Speaking and Listening.** Discuss as a class how we honor the dead today. Are the customs and rituals you're familiar with similar to those Gray describes? Are you familiar with or part of cultures with mourning rituals that differ from those in the poem? Were Gray alive today, would he recognize the role anonymity and fame play in the ways we commemorate the dead?
5. **Creative Writing.** "Elegy Written in a Country Churchyard" is one of the most imitated, parodied, and quoted poems in the English language. Explore some of the imitations and parodies before writing one of your own.
6. **Research.** In many ways, "Elegy Written in a Country Churchyard" does not match the form and content of a traditional elegy. Research the elegy as a poetic form and read other elegies. Finally, compare and contrast Gray's poem with more traditional elegies to explain how and why Gray's use of the term "elegy" contributes to the meaning of the work.

London

William Blake

World History Archive/Alamy

Born in London and educated at home by parents who held nonconformist religious and political beliefs, William Blake (1757–1827) developed highly controversial views about spirituality, women's rights, and personal liberty that informed much of his work. On occasion, his views led to difficulties with the law, including an arrest in 1803 for "uttering seditious statements against the Crown." Following an apprenticeship to an engraver, Blake began experimenting with relief engraving — a technique he called "illuminated printing" — to illustrate both his own books and works such as Milton's *Paradise Lost* and Dante's *The Divine Comedy*. "London" comes from *Songs of Experience* (1794), a response to his earlier collection of poems, *Songs of Innocence* (1789).

I wander through each chartered[1] street,
Near where the chartered Thames[2] does flow,
And mark in every face I meet
Marks of weakness, marks of woe.

In every cry of every man,
In every Infant's cry of fear,
In every voice, in every ban,
The mind-forged manacles I hear.

How the Chimney-sweeper's cry
Every black'ning Church appalls;
And the hapless Soldier's sigh
Runs in blood down Palace walls.

---

[1] Defined by law. — Eds.

[2] A river that flows through Oxford and London in England. — Eds.

But most through midnight streets I hear
How the youthful Harlot's curse
Blasts the new-born Infant's tear,
And blights with plagues the Marriage hearse. ■

1794

Understanding and Interpreting

1. The last two stanzas introduce a series of exploited persons: chimney sweepers, soldiers, and prostitutes. Why do you think Blake saves the "youthful Harlot" (l. 14) for last?
2. What do you think the speaker means by "blights with plagues the Marriage hearse" in line 16? What is the significance of this line as the ending of the poem?
3. What is your interpretation of "mind-forged manacles" (l. 8)? How might that phrase comment on the overindustrialized world of London in the eighteenth century?
4. Why might Blake use the phrase "Every black'ning Church" (l. 10). What does "black'ning" suggest about the speaker's perspective on the church? How does it contribute to the tone of the poem?
5. "London," like many of Blake's poems, has been interpreted in different ways. Critic Camille Paglia, who writes about "London" in *Break, Blow, Burn*, sees it as part of Blake's "exposé of commercial society." What is your view? Why? Can you see another way the poem might be interpreted?

Analyzing Language, Style, and Structure

1. **Vocabulary in Context.** In line 8, the speaker refers to "mind-forged manacles" that he hears "[i]n every cry of every man, / In every Infant's cry of fear, / In every voice, in every ban" (ll. 5–7). What does the word "manacles" convey about the speaker's perception of these things? Who or what does it suggest is responsible for such limitations?
2. "London" takes the form of a walking tour through London. How does William Blake use visual and auditory imagery to both convey the atmosphere in the streets and create a sense of foreboding?
3. What do you make of the repetition of the words "mark" and "marks" in the first stanza? Blake uses "mark" in line 3 to mean "notice." Consider other possible meanings of the word.
4. The poem's third stanza is an acrostic; the first letters of the first words in each line spell out "HEAR." In addition, lines 8 and 13 both end with the word "hear." What does Blake want us to hear? Why is this technique effective in this part of the poem?
5. How does the poem shift in line 13? What does the word "But" emphasize about this shift?

Topics for Composing

1. AP® FRQ **Poetry Analysis.** In William Blake's "London," published in 1794, the speaker takes a walking tour through the city and narrates his experiences. Read the poem carefully. Then, in a well-written essay, analyze how Blake uses literary elements and techniques to convey the speaker's complex attitude toward the city of London.
2. **Research.** Due in part to industrialization, England changed dramatically throughout the late 1700s. Research how these changes affected the society of London as a city as well as its environmental conditions. How did such developments contribute to Blake's description of London in this poem?

3. **Connections.** In addition to writing poetry, Blake also created artwork to illustrate his work. Explore Blake's artwork, and choose a piece you interpret as sharing a theme with "London." Then, write a response in which you explain how these two works each illuminate meaning in the other.
4. **Speaking and Listening.** The Tate, an art museum in London, writes in its overview of its 2019–2020 William Blake exhibition that Blake was a "radical and rebellious" writer and artist whose "personal struggles in a period of political terror and oppression, his technical innovation, his vision and political commitment, have perhaps never been more pertinent." Discuss as a class the importance of those who are willing to be "radical and rebellious" as they fight "political terror and oppression." What responsibility do we have to take such risks ourselves — or at least to listen to those who do? Do you agree that such struggles have "never been more pertinent"? Why or why not?

The World Is Too Much with Us

William Wordsworth

IanDagnall Computing/Alamy

William Wordsworth (1770–1850), one of the most famous and influential Romantic poets, was widely known for his reverence of nature and the power of his lyrical verse. With Samuel Taylor Coleridge, he published *Lyrical Ballads* in 1798; the collection includes Wordsworth's "Lines Composed a Few Miles above Tintern Abbey." "The World Is Too Much with Us," written around 1802 and published in 1807, is one of his most famous works.

KEY CONTEXT This poem is a Petrarchan sonnet, a form made up of fourteen lines divided into an octet (eight lines) and a sestet (six lines). The octet rhymes *abba*, *abba*, and the sestet that follows can have a variety of different rhyme schemes: *cdcdcd*, *cdecde*, *cddcdd*. The first line of the sestet typically, but not always, provides the volta, a poetic shift.

The world is too much with us; late and soon,
Getting and spending, we lay waste our powers:
Little we see in Nature that is ours;
We have given our hearts away, a sordid boon!
This Sea that bares her bosom to the moon;
The winds that will be howling at all hours,
And are up-gathered now like sleeping flowers;
For this, for everything, we are out of tune;
It moves us not. — Great God! I'd rather be
A Pagan suckled in a creed outworn;
So might I, standing on this pleasant lea,
Have glimpses that would make me less forlorn;
Have sight of Proteus rising from the sea;
Or hear old Triton[1] blow his wreathèd horn. ■

1807

---

[1] In Greek mythology, both Proteus and Triton were gods of the sea and sons of Poseidon. — Eds.

Understanding and Interpreting

1. What do you think the speaker means by "the world is too much with us" (l. 1)? What about the world is "too much"? How does that statement contrast with "Little we see in Nature that is ours" (l. 3)?
2. What is meant by "late and soon" (l. 1)? How does it relate to the speaker's statement that "we lay waste our powers" (l. 2)?
3. To whom does the speaker think we have "given our hearts away" (l. 4)?
4. Why does the speaker feel that his sense of self is compromised? What does the speaker refer to when he says that "For this, for everything, we are out of tune" (l. 8)?
5. What "glimpses" would make the speaker less "forlorn" (l. 12)?

Analyzing Language, Style, and Structure

1. **Vocabulary in Context.** What is the meaning of "boon" in line 4? Why does the speaker state the boon here is "sordid"?
2. How does the rigid form of the Petrarchan sonnet enhance William Wordsworth's passionate message? Is his passion at all repressed by the sonnet form? Explain.
3. How does the poem's sestet answer the octet?
4. What shifts or transitions, besides the shift from the octet to the sestet, do you notice in the poem?
5. What effect does the speaker achieve by personifying the wind and the sea?
6. What effect do the references to mythology have? How are they connected to Wordsworth's conviction that materialism causes an estrangement from nature that may have dire results?
7. According to critic Camille Paglia, line 8's "we are out of tune" contains a "buried image": the body as Aeolian or wind harp, played upon and vibrated by nature. How does that image — and its related metaphor — add to Wordsworth's argument about the loss of self that results from "late and soon, / Getting and spending" (ll. 1–2)?

Topics for Composing

1. AP® FRQ **Poetry Analysis.** In William Wordsworth's "The World Is Too Much with Us," published in 1807, the speaker mourns a lack of connection to nature. Read the poem carefully. Then, in a well-written essay, analyze how Wordsworth uses literary elements and techniques to explore the causes and consequences of that disconnection.
2. **Research.** Wordsworth's work was part of an artistic movement called Romanticism, which began during the late eighteenth century and flourished during the first half of the nineteenth century. Do some research on the art and writing from this era. What qualities do Romantic works share? What makes "The World Is Too Much with Us" an exemplar of Romantic poetry?
3. **Connections.** How does Wordsworth's assertion about "Getting and spending" (l. 2) apply to the world today?
4. **Research.** Wordsworth was intrigued by the religious practices in pre-Christian England, and alludes to them in much of his work. Read about those practices and consider the vestiges of them in contemporary Britain, including physical remains such as Stonehenge.
5. **Creative Writing.** Update "The World Is Too Much with Us" for the digital age, and be sure to suggest that which might make us "less forlorn." For an extra challenge, try using or adapting the sonnet form in your version.

Julien Lienard/Contour/Getty Images

For Calling the Spirit Back from Wandering the Earth in Its Human Feet

Joy Harjo

A member of the Muscogee (Creek) Nation, Joy Harjo (b. 1951) was named the twenty-third Poet Laureate of the United States in 2019, the first time an American Indian has held that post. She has published numerous books of poetry, most recently *American Sunrise* (2019), and two memoirs: *Poet Warrior* (2021) and *Crazy Brave* (2012), winner of the American Book Award. Harjo has been the recipient of numerous literary awards and grants, including a Guggenheim Fellowship. In addition to writing, Harjo plays the saxophone and is a vocalist with her own band, Poetic Justice. She has released several albums of original music, notably *Red Dreams, a Trail Beyond Tears* (2010).

Put down that bag of potato chips, that white bread, that bottle of pop.

Turn off that cellphone, computer, and remote control.

Open the door, then close it behind you.

Take a breath offered by friendly winds. They travel the earth gathering essences of plants
to clean.

Give it back with gratitude.

If you sing it will give your spirit lift to fly to the stars' ears and back.

Acknowledge this earth who has cared for you since you were a dream planting itself
precisely within your parents' desire.

Let your moccasin feet take you to the encampment of the guardians who have known
you before time, who will be there after time. They sit before the fire that has been
there without time.

Let the earth stabilize your postcolonial insecure jitters.

Be respectful of the small insects, birds and animal people who accompany you.

Ask their forgiveness for the harm we humans have brought down upon them.

Don't worry.
The heart knows the way though there may be high-rises, interstates, checkpoints, armed
soldiers, massacres, wars, and those who will despise you because they despise
themselves.

The journey might take you a few hours, a day, a year, a few years, a hundred,
a thousand or even more.

Watch your mind. Without training it might run away and leave your heart for the immense human feast set by the thieves of time.

Do not hold regrets.

When you find your way to the circle, to the fire kept burning by the keepers of your soul, you will be welcomed.

You must clean yourself with cedar, sage, or other healing plant.

Cut the ties you have to failure and shame.

Let go the pain you are holding in your mind, your shoulders, your heart, all the way to your feet. Let go the pain of your ancestors to make way for those who are heading in our direction.

Ask for forgiveness.

Call upon the help of those who love you. These helpers take many forms: animal, element, bird, angel, saint, stone, or ancestor.

Call your spirit back. It may be caught in corners and creases of shame, judgment, and human abuse.

You must call in a way that your spirit will want to return.

Speak to it as you would to a beloved child.

Welcome your spirit back from its wandering. It may return in pieces, in tatters. Gather them together. They will be happy to be found after being lost for so long.

Your spirit will need to sleep awhile after it is bathed and given clean clothes.

Now you can have a party. Invite everyone you know who loves and supports you. Keep room for those who have no place else to go.

Make a giveaway, and remember, keep the speeches short.

Then, you must do this: help the next person find their way through the dark. ■

2015

Exploring the Text

1. Who is the speaker addressing in "For Calling the Spirit Back from Wandering the Earth in Its Human Feet"? Explain.
2. How do you characterize the advice given in the poem? What aspects of it are practical? What aspects are aspirational or even fantastical?
3. How would you describe the tone of the poem? What aspects of the poem contribute most to that tone?
4. Why do you think Joy Harjo places the spirit in "its human feet" in the title of the poem? What does that image suggest about how the speaker sees humans' relationship to nature?

5. What do you think the speaker means by "postcolonial insecure jitters" (l. 9)? How might the "earth stabilize" them?
6. How might this poem be used as a guide for meditation? What instructions does it give for mindfulness? How does it treat the connection between mind and body?
7. Why do you think Harjo uses an expansive form for this particular poem, rather than a traditional form such as the sonnet?

Making Connections

1. What are the similarities between "For Calling the Spirit Back from Wandering the Earth in Its Human Feet" and "The World Is Too Much with Us"? Can you match any of the lines from William Wordsworth's poem to lines in Joy Harjo's poem?
2. What parallel does Wordsworth's evocation of characters from mythology or the past have in Harjo's poem? What allusions to folklore or history do you find in "For Calling the Spirit Back from Wandering the Earth in Its Human Feet"?
3. List the suggestions each poet gives for living a better life. Which do you find most convincing? Explain.
4. Do the speakers in these poems share a similar perspective on how humanity treats the rest of the world? Use evidence from each poem to support your response.
5. Does Harjo's poem have elements of Romanticism in it? If so, identify them; if not, explain why.
6. In a 2020 interview with the *Chicago Review of Books*, Harjo commented:

   > Poetry holds a crucial role in society. Poetry can hold, in a very small container sometimes, what nothing else can hold. Poetry can hold grief so immense that there's nothing else [that] can contain it; poetry can hold stories that are dense or unspeakable; poetry can hold joy and awe; poetry can hold the contradictory parts of ourselves, the contradictory parts of the country.

   How do "The World Is Too Much with Us" and "For Calling the Spirit Back from Wandering the Earth in Its Human Feet" treat "the contradictory parts of ourselves"? What do these poems hold that "nothing else can hold"?

Mannahatta

Walt Whitman

Library of Congress, Prints & Photographs Division, [LC-DIG-ppmsca-57645]

Walt Whitman (1819–1892) was born on Long Island, New York. Early in his life, he worked as a country schoolteacher and printer and served as writer and editor for the *Brooklyn Eagle* newspaper. He continued in a variety of jobs, in newspapers and as a carpenter, and published his now famous *Leaves of Grass* in 1855. Regarded as controversial at the time, the poems celebrated individuality and the richness of life. During the Civil War, Whitman worked as an aide in army hospitals in Washington, D.C., caring first for his wounded brother and then for other soldiers, and published poems about his experiences in *Drum-Taps* in 1865. Whitman would continue to revise and add to *Leaves of Grass* until his death.

KEY CONTEXT Whitman is credited with the invention of American free verse, which is poetry that lacks a strict meter or rhyming sequence but is still recognizable as poetry because of its rhythmic cadence. Whitman used some conventional poetic techniques, such as iambic pentameter — the traditional meter of the sonnet — and anaphora — the repetition of the first word in a line — to achieve that cadence.

I was asking for something specific and perfect for my city,
Whereupon lo! upsprang the aboriginal name.

Now I see what there is in a name, a word, liquid, sane, unruly, musical, self-sufficient,
I see that the word of my city is that word from of old,
Because I see that word nested in nests of water-bays, superb,
Rich, hemm'd thick all around with sailships and steamships, an island sixteen
miles long, solid-founded,
Numberless crowded streets, high growths of iron, slender, strong, light, splendidly
uprising toward clear skies,
Tides swift and ample, well-loved by me, toward sundown,
The flowing sea-currents, the little islands, larger adjoining islands, the heights, the villas,
The countless masts, the white shore-steamers, the lighters, the ferry-boats, the black
sea-steamers well-model'd,
The down-town streets, the jobbers' houses of business, the houses of business of the
ship-merchants and money-brokers, the river-streets,
Immigrants arriving, fifteen or twenty thousand a week,
The carts hauling goods, the manly race of drivers of horses, the brown-faced sailors,
The summer air, the bright sun shining, and the sailing clouds aloft,
The winter snows, the sleigh-bells, the broken ice in the river, passing along up or
down with the flood-tide or ebb-tide,
The mechanics of the city, the masters, well-form'd, beautiful-faced, looking you
straight in the eyes,
Trottoirs[1] throng'd, vehicles, Broadway, the women, the shops and shows,
A million people — manners free and superb — open voices — hospitality — the most
courageous and friendly young men,
City of hurried and sparkling waters! city of spires and masts!
City nested in bays! my city! ■

1860

[1] Footpaths or sidewalks. — Eds.

Understanding and Interpreting

1. "Mannahatta" was the name given to Manhattan by the Lenape Indians who lived there before the Dutch settlers arrived. Why do you think Walt Whitman rhapsodizes about this early name?
2. Describe the speaker's persona in this poem. From what vantage point does he see the city? Is he an observer or a participant? Explain.
3. What particular qualities of the city does the speaker highlight in his description of Manhattan? From what you know, which of these exist still today?

Analyzing Language, Style, and Structure

1. **Vocabulary in Context.** What is the meaning of the word "aboriginal" in line 2? Consider different ways it can be used and how more than one use works in "Mannahatta."
2. How does Walt Whitman create the poem's pace? What is the connection between its pace and its subject?
3. Look at Whitman's punctuation choices. How do they help create the sense of activity in the poem?
4. What contrasts does "Mannahatta" set up? Look carefully at how Whitman invokes the past and the present.
5. While this poem was published in 1860, long before New York City became notable for its skyscrapers, Whitman manages to create a feeling of verticality. How does he accomplish that in "Mannahatta"?
6. Examine the cadence in "Mannahatta." Do you see any other techniques Whitman used to achieve it? What is its effect in the poem? How does the cadence help create the vivid setting that is the subject of the poem?

Topics for Composing

1. AP® FRQ **Poetry Analysis.** In Walt Whitman's "Mannahatta," published in 1860, the speaker celebrates a city he loves. Read the poem carefully. Then, in a well-written essay, analyze how Whitman uses literary elements and techniques to convey the qualities that make the city unique.
2. **Connections.** Whitman worked as a typesetter and was fascinated by the shapes of letters and words. How does the physical appearance of "Mannahatta" reflect its subject matter?
3. **Connections.** Whitman wrote this celebration of urban life at a time when many of his contemporaries, including American intellectuals such as Ralph Waldo Emerson and Henry David Thoreau, were praising the joys of nature, proselytizing for self-reliance, and protesting against the rise of urbanization. Read "Self-Reliance" by Emerson and an excerpt of your choice from *Walden* by Thoreau. How does "Mannahatta" argue for life in the metropolis? How do you think Emerson and Thoreau would respond to that argument?
4. **Multimodal.** It is possible to retrace many of Whitman's steps through Brooklyn, where he lived, and Manhattan, which he would have gotten to by crossing the East River on a ferry. Create a map of his wanderings. Illustrate it with photos and artwork from Whitman's time and images of what the city looks like now.

TALKBACK

Chicago

Library of Congress, Prints & Photographs Division, [LC-USZ62-115064]

Carl Sandburg

Carl Sandburg (1878–1967) was born in Galesburg, Illinois, the son of Swedish immigrants. He spent most of his life in the Midwest, working as a reporter and a writer of poetry, history, biography, fiction, children's books, and folk songs. He fought against fascism in the Spanish Civil War (1936–1939) and served as secretary to the mayor of Milwaukee, who was the country's first Socialist mayor. Sandburg and his wife raised their family in the suburbs of Chicago. Sandburg was awarded two Pulitzers, one for his biography *Abraham Lincoln: The War Years* (1939) and one for his collection *Complete Poems* (1950). The poem "Chicago" is one of the most famous literary descriptions of an American city.

Hog Butcher for the World,
Tool Maker, Stacker of Wheat,
Player with Railroads and the Nation's Freight Handler;
Stormy, husky, brawling,
City of the Big Shoulders:

They tell me you are wicked and I believe them, for I have seen your painted women under the gas lamps luring the farm boys.
And they tell me you are crooked and I answer: Yes, it is true I have seen the gunman kill and go free to kill again.
And they tell me you are brutal and my reply is: On the faces of women and children I have seen the marks of wanton hunger.
And having answered so I turn once more to those who sneer at this my city, and I give them back the sneer and say to them:
Come and show me another city with lifted head singing so proud to be alive and coarse and strong and cunning.
Flinging magnetic curses amid the toil of piling job on job, here is a tall bold slugger set vivid against the little soft cities;
Fierce as a dog with tongue lapping for action, cunning as a savage pitted against the wilderness,
Bareheaded,
Shoveling,
Wrecking,
Planning,
Building, breaking, rebuilding,
Under the smoke, dust all over his mouth, laughing with white teeth,
Under the terrible burden of destiny laughing as a young man laughs,

Laughing even as an ignorant fighter laughs who has never lost a battle,
Bragging and laughing that under his wrist is the pulse, and under his ribs the
heart of the people,
Laughing!
Laughing the stormy, husky, brawling laughter of Youth, half-naked, sweating,
proud to be Hog Butcher, Tool Maker, Stacker of Wheat, Player with Railroads
and Freight Handler to the Nation. ■

1916

Exploring the Text

1. Personification is the principal technique in "Chicago." Describe the persona Carl Sandburg creates for the city.
2. Sandburg also uses apostrophe, a figure of speech in which someone or something absent, dead, or inanimate is addressed as if the speaker expected a reply. What is the effect of addressing Chicago? What might it reply if it could answer?
3. Describe the poem's tone. How does Sandburg create it? How is Chicago honored through the poem's tone?
4. In lines 18–23, the words "laughs" and "laughing" are repeated over and over. Characterize the city's laughter. How does it both create an image and comment on Sandburg's Chicago?
5. Sandburg's work was inspired by Walt Whitman, especially his use of free verse. The poet Amy Lowell said that the ideal of free verse was to "copy new rhythms — as expressions of new moods — and not to copy old rhythms, which merely echo old moods." How does the rhythm of "Chicago" express "new moods"?
6. Nearly a third of the city burned down in the Chicago Fire of 1871; in the aftermath, the city underwent a period of rapid reconstruction and growth. What passages in the poem seem specifically to deal with this event? How does this part of Chicago history relate to the persona that Sandburg attributes to the city?

Making Connections

1. Both "Mannahatta" and "Chicago" have a cadence that is characteristic of free verse. What are the similarities and differences in their cadences?
2. Whitman was famous for his lists, a technique that is also evident in Sandburg's "Chicago." What is the effect of these lists? How do the poets use repetition without seeming repetitive?
3. What do the poems have in common in their descriptions of cities? What is different?
4. Compare and contrast the speakers in the two poems. What do they have in common? How are they different? How does each poet create the speaker's persona?
5. Read "Mannahatta" and "Chicago" aloud. Compare and contrast the way free verse imbues the two poems with energy and vigor. You might also look for videos on the internet in which filmmakers have combined images of New York City and Chicago with the poets' words.
6. "Mannahatta" and "Chicago" each praise the city in which it is set. Compare the speakers' pride in their cities and analyze the techniques the poets use to communicate and re-create the speakers' feelings.

Dover Beach

Matthew Arnold

GL Archive/Alamy

Poet, essayist, and critic Matthew Arnold (1822–1888) was brought up and educated at Rugby School, one of England's oldest boarding schools, where his father was headmaster. After graduating from Balliol College at Oxford, he became inspector of schools at Her Majesty's Inspectorate of Education to support his family. He held this position for thirty years, during which time he wrote the bulk of his poetry, including *Empedocles on Etna* (1852) and *Poems* (1853). Arnold was elected professor of poetry at Oxford in 1857 and 1862, and during this time he produced several collections of essays and literary, cultural, and religious criticism. In 1867, Arnold published "Dover Beach," his most famous work.

KEY CONTEXT Dover is the English port city from which most people traveled to France.

The sea is calm tonight.
The tide is full, the moon lies fair
Upon the straits; — on the French coast the light
Gleams and is gone; the cliffs of England stand,
Glimmering and vast, out in the tranquil bay.
Come to the window, sweet is the night-air!
Only, from the long line of spray
Where the sea meets the moon-blanched land,
Listen! you hear the grating roar
Of pebbles which the waves draw back, and fling,
At their return, up the high strand,
Begin, and cease, and then again begin,
With tremulous cadence slow, and bring
The eternal note of sadness in.

Sophocles[1] long ago
Heard it on the Aegean,[2] and it brought
Into his mind the turbid ebb and flow
Of human misery;[3] we
Find also in the sound a thought,
Hearing it by this distant northern sea.

The Sea of Faith
Was once, too, at the full, and round earth's shore
Lay like the folds of a bright girdle furled.

---

[1] Ancient Greek playwright (c. 497–406 B.C.E.) best known for *Antigone, Oedipus Rex, Electra,* and *Oedipus at Colonus.* — Eds.

[2] An extension of the Mediterranean Sea, located between Europe and Asia. — Eds.

[3] A reference to Sophocles's play *Antigone*: "the gods have rocked a house to its foundations / the ruin will never cease, cresting on and on / from one generation on throughout the race — / like a great mounting tide" (ll. 659–62). — Eds.

But now I only hear
Its melancholy, long, withdrawing roar,
Retreating, to the breath
Of the night-wind, down the vast edges drear
And naked shingles[4] of the world.

Ah, love, let us be true
To one another! for the world, which seems
To lie before us like a land of dreams,
So various, so beautiful, so new,
Hath really neither joy, nor love, nor light,
Nor certitude, nor peace, nor help for pain;
And we are here as on a darkling plain
Swept with confused alarms of struggle and flight,
Where ignorant armies clash by night. ■

1867

---

[4] Pebble beaches. — Eds.

Understanding and Interpreting

1. What do you think Arnold means by "The Sea of Faith" (l. 21)? What does he think has replaced it?
2. What crisis does the speaker seem to be experiencing in this poem? How does his connection to the physical world help him make sense of it?
3. What does the speaker mean when he says "[L]et us be true / To one another!" (ll. 29–30)? Why is "the world" (l. 30) the reason the speaker makes this request?
4. There is evidence that Arnold wrote "Dover Beach" on his honeymoon in 1851. How does that possibility change the meaning of the poem for you?

Analyzing Language, Style, and Structure

1. **Vocabulary in Context.** What is the meaning of the word "darkling" in line 35? Why is it a more evocative choice than any of its synonyms?
2. Analyze the series of vivid images of nighttime by the sea in the first stanza. To which senses do these images appeal? How do these images relate to the meaning of the poem? Why do you think Matthew Arnold highlights the auditory images, such as "Listen!" in line 9?
3. What do the consonance and caesura in lines 9–14 add to the imagery in those lines? How does that imagery help create the mood of sadness with which the stanza ends?
4. Many of the word choices and structural decisions in "Dover Beach" either directly depict or evoke the movement of the sea or tides. How do those choices connect to the speaker's thoughts about his faith?
5. You might notice that the last stanza of the poem is self-contradictory; it almost argues with itself. What are some of the competing ideas in the stanza?
6. How does the tone change over the course of the last stanza? How does this shift in tone highlight the stanza's mixed message?

7. Arnold develops several sets of contrasts in the poem. What are they and how do they set up the conflicts that are at the heart of "Dover Beach"?
8. The last four lines of the poem are rhymed couplets, the form traditionally used to conclude and resolve a sonnet. What is the effect of that form on the meaning of those lines? How does the stanza resolve, or fail to resolve, the problem introduced by the poem?

Topics for Composing

1. AP® FRQ **Poetry Analysis.** In Matthew Arnold's "Dover Beach," published in 1867, the speaker examines his faith as he visits the seaside in England. Read the poem carefully. Then, in a well-written essay, analyze how Arnold uses literary elements and techniques to convey his complex attitude toward his faith and the world he is facing.
2. **Connections.** In her Poem of the Week column for the *Guardian*, critic Carol Rumens writes, "Dover Beach fundamentally seems to be about a withdrawal into personal values. Historical pessimism moves in swiftly as a tide." Develop a position on this assertion using evidence from the poem as well as your own knowledge and reading.
3. **Research.** Do some research into the technological advances and economic changes in the United Kingdom during the mid-nineteenth century. To what extent do you think Arnold's spiritual crisis was caused by the scientific discoveries of his time?
4. **Connections.** Arnold's poetry is considered a bridge between Romanticism and modernism. Learn about the major features of work from both of these artistic movements — what qualities does this poem share with each? How does it form a bridge between the two?
5. **Research.** "Dover Beach" was written when England was the most powerful country in the world. Do some research on the United Kingdom's role in the world during the second half of the nineteenth century. How does Arnold's poem comment on this period in English history?

God's Grandeur

Gerard Manley Hopkins

The History Collection/Alamy

Torn between his obligations as a Jesuit and his love for poetry, Gerard Manley Hopkins (1844–1889) declined to seek an audience for his work during his lifetime; the bulk of his poems were published posthumously in 1916. Hopkins was born in Stratford, London, to a wealthy family. After converting to Catholicism near the end of his studies at Oxford, Hopkins entered the priesthood and, adhering to one of his vows, burned nearly all of his accumulated poems. He began to write again in 1875, when he was asked to commemorate the death of five Franciscan nuns who drowned in a shipwreck off the coast of England as they fled oppression in Germany. In the poem he wrote, entitled "Wreck of the Deutschland," Hopkins introduced what he called "sprung rhythm," a meter designed to imitate the rhythm of natural speech; this meter anticipated free verse and would influence new generations of poets. "God's Grandeur," written in 1877, makes occasional use of this unconventional rhythm and is representative of Hopkins's work in both subject and form.

KEY CONTEXT "God's Grandeur" follows the form of a Petrarchan sonnet, a form made up of fourteen lines divided into an octet (eight lines) and a sestet (six lines). The octet rhymes *abba*, *abba*, and the sestet that follows can have a variety of different rhyme schemes: *cdcdcd*, *cdecde*, *cddcdd*. The first line of the sestet typically, but not always, provides the volta, a poetic shift.

The world is charged with the grandeur of God.
  It will flame out, like shining from shook foil;
  It gathers to a greatness, like the ooze of oil
Crushed. Why do men then now not reck[1] his rod?[2]
Generations have trod, have trod, have trod;
  And all is seared with trade; bleared, smeared with toil;
  And wears man's smudge and shares man's smell: the soil
Is bare now, nor can foot feel, being shod.

And for all this, nature is never spent;
  There lives the dearest freshness deep down things;
And though the last lights off the black West went
  Oh, morning, at the brown brink eastward, springs —
Because the Holy Ghost over the bent
  World broods with warm breast and with ah! bright wings. ■

1877

[1] Mind, obey. — Eds.

[2] "Rod" here is a scepter, representing God's position as king of kings. — Eds.

Understanding and Interpreting

1. How do you interpret the meaning of lines 2–4? What contradictory elements of "God's Grandeur" do they capture?
2. What does "all" refer to in line 6, and what does the speaker suggest has happened to it? How does "all" in line 9 relate to "all" in line 6?
3. What does the speaker mean when he says that "all is seared with trade" (l. 6)? How does this state compare to that of past generations, according to the speaker?
4. What argument does "God's Grandeur" make? How does Hopkins present his evidence, including a counterargument? Which do you find more convincing, the argument or the counterargument?

Analyzing Language, Style, and Structure

1. **Vocabulary in Context.** What does the word "charged" suggest in line 1? Consider several possibilities.
2. How does style reinforce meaning in line 5? What other examples of the close connection between style and meaning do you see in "God's Grandeur"?
3. How is the sound of the poem created? Look especially at the internal rhymes. Try reading this poem aloud to hear how Gerard Manley Hopkins uses stressed syllables to create the poem's musical quality.

4. Consider the structure of "God's Grandeur," a Petrarchan sonnet. What question or problem is posed in the octet and answered or resolved in the sestet? How does the tone of the sestet contrast that of the octet?
5. What does the metaphor in the poem's last two lines evoke for you? Explain the metaphor, and how and why it affects you the way it does.

Topics for Composing

1. AP® FRQ **Poetry Analysis.** In Gerard Manley Hopkins's "God's Grandeur," published in 1877, the speaker contemplates God's presence in the world. Read the poem carefully. Then. in a well-written essay, analyze how Hopkins uses literary elements and techniques to convey the speaker's complex perspective on the connection between God, humankind, and nature.
2. **Speaking and Listening.** Do you think Hopkins's assertion that "nature is never spent" (l. 9) holds true today? Has it become more difficult — even impossible — for "the grandeur of God" (l. 1) to keep up with "man's smudge" and "man's smell" (l. 7)? Develop your position in preparation for a class discussion.
3. **Research.** Do some research into the technological advances and economic changes in the United Kingdom during the mid-nineteenth century. Then, write an essay in which you explain how the historical context of the Industrial Revolution influences Hopkins's argument in "God's Grandeur."
4. **Connections.** Read Hopkins's sonnet "The Starlight Night," which Hopkins originally published in the same collection as "God's Grandeur." How does Hopkins develop specific details in "The Starlight Night" that expand beyond the more general imagery in "God's Grandeur"?

Crumbling is not an instant's Act

Emily Dickinson

IanDagnall Computing/Alamy

Born into a prominent family in Amherst, Massachusetts, Emily Dickinson (1830–1886) received some formal education at Amherst Academy and Mount Holyoke Female Seminary (which became Mount Holyoke College). Dickinson was known as a shy and reclusive person, who preferred to remain within her close family circle, though some contemporary scholars have begun to question that characterization. Dickinson wrote nearly eighteen hundred poems, but only ten were published in her lifetime.

KEY CONTEXT This poem, published four years after Dickinson's death, demonstrates the terse and spare style for which she was known as she approaches philosophical questions.

Crumbling is not an instant's Act
    A fundamental pause
Dilapidation's processes
Are organized Decays.

'Tis first a Cobweb on the Soul
A Cuticle of Dust
A Borer in the Axis
An Elemental Rust —

Ruin is formal — Devil's work
Consecutive and slow —
Fail in an instant, no man did
Slipping — is Crash's law. ■

1890

Understanding and Interpreting

1. What is the tension in the poem between something sudden or instantaneous and a gradual progression? Why is the latter "Devil's work" (l. 9)?
2. What examples of "organized Decay" does the speaker name in the second stanza? How do they relate to the first stanza?
3. What do the examples drawn from the natural world suggest about the speaker's spiritual life or moral values?
4. What is "Crash's law" in the final stanza? How is it different from "[r]uin" (l. 9)?
5. Do you think Dickinson is talking only about personal crumbling, or does the poem have a wider application? Explain.

Analyzing Language, Style, and Structure

1. **Vocabulary in Context.** The speaker refers to "Dilapidation's processes" (l. 3). What is the meaning of "dilapidation" in this context? How is it different from "Crumbling" (l. 1) or "Decays" (l. 4)?
2. What choices of language and image does Dickinson make to emphasize the systematic, progressive nature of ruin or destruction that she describes?
3. Identify several examples of personification in "Crumbling is not an instant's Act." What is their effect on the poem's overall meaning? Pay careful attention to the way they help Emily Dickinson support the poem's argument that falling apart is a slow process.
4. What are the metaphors of natural decay in the second stanza? How does each one address a specific kind of decline? In your analysis, consider that "[c]uticle" was often used to mean an outer layer in Dickinson's time.
5. How would you characterize the tone of this poem? How does it change or intensify from stanza to stanza?

Topics for Composing

1. AP® FRQ **Poetry Analysis.** In Emily Dickinson's "Crumbling is not an instant's Act," published in 1890, the speaker describes the process of progressive decline. Read the poem carefully. Then, in a well-written essay, analyze how Dickinson uses literary elements and techniques to convey the complex process and consequences of decay.

2. **AP® Literary Argumentation.** In an article entitled "Vesuvius at Home," poet Adrienne Rich refers to "Crumbling is not an instant's Act" as being part of Dickinson's "poetry of danger." What is the nature of the "danger" in this poem? Is the speaker warning of specific dangers, predicting danger's inevitability, offering a way to avoid it, or something else?
3. **Connections.** What situation in contemporary society or in your personal experience shows the process of "crumbling" at work as Dickinson describes it in this poem? Explain the progressive movement — "Slipping" — that leads to "Ruin" in your chosen example.
4. **Multimodal.** Put together a visual interpretation of this poem by selecting or creating a sequence of at least one image per stanza. Consider both still images, such as photographs or fine art, and videos. Include the text of the poem as print or read it in a voice-over.

Mending Wall

Robert Frost

Library of Congress, Prints & Photographs Division, [LC-USZ62-120743]

Though Robert Frost (1874–1963) is considered the quintessential New England poet, he was born in San Francisco. After the death of his father when Frost was eleven years old, the family moved to Massachusetts. Frost attended Dartmouth College and Harvard University, but in both cases left early to support his family. He delivered newspapers, farmed, did factory work, and taught high school and college, but considered poetry to be his true calling. Frost won four Pulitzer Prizes for his collections *New Hampshire: A Poem with Notes and Grace Notes* (1924), *Collected Poems* (1931), *A Further Range* (1937), and *A Witness Tree* (1943), and in 1961 he spoke at the inauguration of President John F. Kennedy.

KEY CONTEXT Frost wrote this poem, which became one of his most popular, early in his career when he was living in rural New Hampshire.

Something there is that doesn't love a wall,
That sends the frozen-ground-swell under it,
And spills the upper boulders in the sun;
And makes gaps even two can pass abreast.
The work of hunters is another thing:
I have come after them and made repair
Where they have left not one stone on a stone,
But they would have the rabbit out of hiding,
To please the yelping dogs. The gaps I mean,
No one has seen them made or heard them made,
But at spring mending-time we find them there.
I let my neighbor know beyond the hill;
And on a day we meet to walk the line
And set the wall between us once again.
We keep the wall between us as we go.
To each the boulders that have fallen to each.

And some are loaves and some so nearly balls
We have to use a spell to make them balance:
"Stay where you are until our backs are turned!"
We wear our fingers rough with handling them.
Oh, just another kind of outdoor game,
One on a side. It comes to little more:
There where it is we do not need the wall:
He is all pine and I am apple orchard.
My apple trees will never get across
And eat the cones under his pines, I tell him.
He only says, "Good fences make good neighbors."
Spring is the mischief in me, and I wonder
If I could put a notion in his head:
"*Why* do they make good neighbors? Isn't it
Where there are cows? But here there are no cows.
Before I built a wall I'd ask to know
What I was walling in or walling out,
And to whom I was like to give offense.
Something there is that doesn't love a wall,
That wants it down." I could say "Elves" to him,
But it's not elves exactly, and I'd rather
He said it for himself. I see him there
Bringing a stone grasped firmly by the top
In each hand, like an old-stone savage armed.
He moves in darkness as it seems to me,
Not of woods only and the shade of trees.
He will not go behind his father's saying,
And he likes having thought of it so well
He says again, "Good fences make good neighbors." ■

1914

Understanding and Interpreting

1. What is the main conflict in this poem?
2. Overall, how would you characterize the perspectives of the speaker and his neighbor? How do you interpret the speaker's assertion that "He is all pine and I am apple orchard" (l. 24)?
3. What does the speaker mean by the "gaps" in line 4? Why is it important that "No one has seen them made or heard them made, / But at spring mending-time we find them there" (ll. 9–11)?
4. How do the speaker and his neighbor collaborate as they "walk the line" (l. 13) at the same time that they disagree?
5. To what extent do the speaker and his neighbor know what they are "walling in or walling out" (l. 33)?
6. Based on your interpretation of the poem, what is the "[s]omething" that "doesn't love a wall" (ll. 1, 35)?

Analyzing Language, Style, and Structure

1. **Vocabulary in Context.** In line 40, the speaker refers to his neighbor as being "like an old-stone savage." What does the word "savage," in this context, convey about the speaker's attitude toward his neighbor?
2. Contrast the inverted syntax of lines 1 and 35 — "Something there is that doesn't love a wall" — to the traditional subject-verb-object syntax of lines 27 and 45 — "Good fences make good neighbors." How does the difference help develop each of the poem's characters? What effect does the difference have on the poem's meaning?
3. Frost alludes to the myth of Sisyphus by description, although not by name. In Greek mythology, Sisyphus is condemned to roll a rock up to the top of a mountain, only to have the rock roll back down to the bottom every time he reaches the top. It has come to be associated with futile work that is never-ending. How does this allusion contribute to your interpretation of the poem?
4. Lines 13–18 lead up to the "spell" in line 18 that the two wall-menders use to keep the rocks from toppling. How are those lead-up lines a sort of incantation in themselves? How might they connect to the image in lines 39–40 of the speaker's neighbor "bringing a stone grasped firmly by the top / In each hand, like an old-stone savage armed"?
5. What is the literal and metaphorical "darkness" that is "not of woods only and the shade of trees" (l. 42)? How does this image inform your understanding of "Mending Wall"?
6. Why do you think Frost allows the neighbor to offer the proverb "Good fences make good neighbors" twice? Why do you think the neighbor gets the last word?
7. Frost believed that poetry should be a "reproduction of human speech." How is this evident in the diction, syntax, and structure of "Mending Wall"?

Topics for Composing

1. AP® FRQ **Poetry Analysis.** In Robert Frost's "Mending Wall," published in 1914, the speaker describes the different views he and his neighbor have toward a stone wall they repair each spring. Read the poem carefully. Then, in a well-written essay, analyze how Frost uses literary elements and techniques to develop the speaker's complex perspective on the meaning of the wall that separates him and his neighbor.
2. **AP® Literary Argumentation.** In a 2019 analysis of "Mending Wall," poet Austin Allen explains what he believes is the lasting allure of the poem: the speaker "does not denounce walls; he doubts them. Doubt is what makes 'Mending Wall' a poem and not an editorial—not the kind of writing with obvious applications. But it's also what makes 'Mending Wall' a subversive classic rather than a scrap of yesterday's news." Write an essay that examines doubt as a thematic concern throughout the poem. How is it a subversive force? How does it help craft a timeless message to readers?
3. **AP® Literary Argumentation.** Although "Mending Wall" is set in a specific place with two people engaging in a tangible task, Frost raises abstract philosophical issues about the necessity and meaning of walls, borders, and dividing lines in general. Do clear boundaries enhance human relationship or sow suspicion and doubt? Is the neighbor an old-fashioned inflexible person and the speaker a progressive thinker? Where do you think Frost leans in this meditative poem?
4. **Connections.** "Mending Wall" questions whether a wall that has no function in the modern world still fulfills a ritualistic need. When Frost was asked about the poem's meaning, he said his poems are "all set to trip the reader head foremost into the boundless." In what way does trying to answer the poem's question trip you "into the boundless"?

5. **Research.** "Mending Wall" has occasioned many discussions of physical walls or divisions, both historical and current — such as the Berlin Wall, the United States border wall, the Great Wall of China, Hadrian's Wall, the Wailing Wall, the Belfast Peace Walls, and more. Research one of these walls, or another of your choosing, and discuss how the questions "Mending Wall" raises might apply in that context. You might also consider places that are not named as "walls," per se, but are the result of political and military disputes, such as the border between North and South Korea, the Kashmir Line of Control, or the Russia-Ukraine border.
6. **Speaking and Listening.** When President Kennedy visited the Berlin Wall, he quoted the first line of "Mending Wall." His audience knew what he meant, of course. Later, when Frost visited Russia, he found that the Russian translation of the poem left off the first line. He said he could have done better for them by saying: "Something there is that doesn't love a wall, / Something there is that does." Working with a partner, discuss whether or how that potential change alters the meaning of the poem for you.

The Second Coming

William Butler Yeats

Library of Congress, Prints & Photographs Division, [LC-G432-0612-B]

William Butler Yeats (1865–1939) was born in Dublin to a middle-class Protestant family with strong connections to England. Yeats began as a playwright, founding the Irish Literary Theatre in 1899, and wrote several plays celebrating Irish cultural tradition. His early plays earned him the Nobel Prize for Literature in 1923. By 1912, he had turned to writing poetry. Profoundly influenced by William Blake, Yeats's poetry reflects Ireland's rich mythology and a fascination with the occult. His collections include *The Wild Swans at Coole* (1919), *Michael Robartes and the Dancer* (1921), *The Tower* (1928), and *The Winding Stair* (1933). Yeats's work spans the transition from the nineteenth century to the modernism of the twentieth century.

KEY CONTEXT William Butler Yeats wrote this poem in the aftermath of World War I (1914–1918) and near the end of the Irish War of Independence (1919–1921). The violence of this time period, along with Yeats's interest in mysticism and knowledge of Christian imagery, contribute to this modernist poem.

Turning and turning in the widening gyre[1]
The falcon cannot hear the falconer;
Things fall apart; the center cannot hold;
Mere anarchy is loosed upon the world,
The blood-dimmed tide is loosed, and everywhere
The ceremony of innocence is drowned;
The best lack all conviction, while the worst
Are full of passionate intensity.

Surely some revelation is at hand;
Surely the Second Coming is at hand.

[1] Widening spiral of a falcon's flight, used by Yeats to describe the cycles of history. — Eds.

The Second Coming! Hardly are those words out
When a vast image out of *Spiritus Mundi*[2]
Troubles my sight: somewhere in sands of the desert
A shape with lion body and the head of a man,
A gaze blank and pitiless as the sun,
Is moving its slow thighs, while all about it
Reel shadows of the indignant desert birds.
The darkness drops again; but now I know
That twenty centuries of stony sleep
Were vexed to nightmare by a rocking cradle,
And what rough beast, its hour come round at last,
Slouches towards Bethlehem to be born? ■

1921

---

[2] Soul of the world and a major component of Yeats's belief system. — Eds.

Understanding and Interpreting

1. What kind of scene does the speaker describe in lines 4–6?
2. What does the speaker mean by "The best lack all conviction" (l. 7)? How do they compare to the "worst" people?
3. What is the relationship between this "Second Coming" and the "revelation" to which the speaker refers in line 9?
4. Why do you think the poem ends with a question?
5. Based on your interpretation of the poem, what is the "rough beast" in the penultimate line? Why has "its hour come round at last"?

Analyzing Language, Style, and Structure

1. **Vocabulary in Context.** While the word *revelation* generally refers to a new understanding, it often carries religious connotations as well. How does Yeats use this word in line 9? How do the connotations of this word contribute to the overall mood of the poem?
2. Consider both the speaker and the imagery in the first eight lines. How do the images help create the persona of the speaker? How are the speaker and the imagery different in the last fourteen lines?
3. What do you think the falcon and the falconer (l. 2) symbolize? What do you think it means that the "falcon cannot hear the falconer"? How is that metaphor connected to the image in lines 14–17?
4. What is the effect of the repetition of "loosed" in lines 4 and 5, and "Surely" in lines 9 and 10?
5. What is ironic about the phrase "[m]ere anarchy" (l. 4)? What other instances of irony do you spot in the poem? What does this irony reveal about the speaker's worldview?
6. Describe the tone of the poem. How is it created?

Topics for Composing

1. **AP® FRQ Poetry Analysis.** In William Butler Yeats's "The Second Coming," published in 1921, the speaker conveys his perspective on a world marked by chaos and destruction. Read the poem carefully. Then, in a well-written essay, analyze how Yeats uses literary elements and techniques to convey the speaker's complex perspective on what the future will hold.
2. **Connections.** Adam Cohen, in an editorial in the *New York Times*, notes that phrases from "The Second Coming" are "irresistible to pundits" — analysts or commentators on politics or social policy — who find that lines such as "The best lack all conviction, while the worst / Are full of passionate intensity" (ll. 7–8) perfectly sum up any era in history. Cohen, however, believes that "The Second Coming" is "a powerful brief against punditry," a caution against confident predictions. Do you agree? Explain.
3. **Research.** Yeats wrote "The Second Coming" the year a truce was declared in the Irish War of Independence (1919–1921), which came on the heels of World War I. Do some research on Irish history from 1900 to 1930 and on the causes and effects of World War I. Then, write an essay in which you explain how the poem reflects the violence, anxiety, and rapid change of this historical period, particularly in Ireland.
4. **Connections.** The lyrics of Joni Mitchell's song "Slouching towards Bethlehem" closely follow Yeats's poem. Listen to Mitchell's song and read her lyrics. Why do you think she deviates from Yeats's poem in the way she does? How do Mitchell's additions build on the themes of the poem?
5. **Speaking and Listening.** A number of poems, songs, books, television shows, and movies have drawn from lines of "The Second Coming." Have a class discussion about how relevant the poem is today. How does Yeats's speaker's vision of the world apply to your generation?

Dedication

Czesław Miłosz

RDB/ullstein bild Dtl./Getty Images

Polish poet and essayist Czesław Miłosz (1911–2004) published his first book of poems when he was 21. He defected from communist Poland in 1951, eventually immigrating to the United States, where he became a professor at the University of California, Berkeley. He became an American citizen in 1970, and he received the Nobel Prize for Literature in 1980. Miłosz wrote in Polish, but he often translated his own works into English, as he did with "Dedication." This poem was part of his 1945 collection *Ocalenie* (*Rescue*), which included many poems that he wrote during the occupation of Poland.

KEY CONTEXT Warsaw, Poland, fell to Nazi Germany in late September of 1939 after weeks of heavy artillery bombardment. During the occupation, Nazis confined the city's large Jewish population in the Warsaw Ghetto before deporting them to extermination camps beginning in 1942 — although not without violent resistance. In 1943, a group of inhabitants of the ghetto staged the Warsaw Ghetto Uprising. Elsewhere in the city, non-Jewish Poles mounted their own underground resistance efforts, many of which Miłosz joined. In August 1944, a resistance group called the Home Army began an uprising against the Nazis that lasted sixty-three days and became the largest military action of any underground movement in World War II. Although the Home Army met with early success, they received little assistance from Allied nations and were ultimately defeated. The Nazis razed what was left of the city in an act of reprisal. Museums, libraries, parks, art galleries, churches, theaters, and many other important cultural and historic landmarks were completely destroyed. When Soviet forces liberated Warsaw in 1945, little of the city remained intact. Miłosz himself did not join the Home Army or fight in the uprising, in large part because he disagreed with the political views of its leadership and because he saw it as a "blameworthy, light-headed enterprise" doomed to fail.

You whom I could not save
Listen to me.
Try to understand this simple speech as I would be ashamed of another.
I swear, there is in me no wizardry of words.
I speak to you with silence like a cloud or a tree.

What strengthened me, for you was lethal.
You mixed up farewell to an epoch[1] with the beginning of a new one,
Inspiration of hatred with lyrical beauty;
Blind force with accomplished shape.

Here is a valley of shallow Polish rivers. And an immense bridge
Going into white fog. Here is a broken city;
And the wind throws the screams of gulls on your grave
When I am talking with you.

What is poetry which does not save
Nations or people?
A connivance with official lies,
A song of drunkards whose throats will be cut in a moment,
Readings for sophomore girls.
That I wanted good poetry without knowing it,
That I discovered, late, its salutary aim,
In this and only this I find salvation.

They used to pour millet on graves or poppy seeds
To feed the dead who would come disguised as birds.
I put this book here for you, who once lived
So that you should visit us no more.

Warsaw, 1945 ■

[1] An era. — Eds.

Understanding and Interpreting

1. To whom does the speaker address this poem? Why is he addressing this audience? Consider the final stanza in your response.
2. In line 3, the speaker claims he is using "simple speech as I would be ashamed of another." What seems to be the root of this shame?
3. What does the speaker mean when he says, "What strengthened me, for you was lethal" (l. 6)? What has been "mixed up" (l. 7)?
4. What does the speaker suggest is the "salutary aim" (l. 20) of poetry? How does the speaker characterize poetry that does not achieve this aim?
5. What helps the speaker find "salvation" (l. 21)? Why does he need it?
6. In a profile of Czesław Miłosz for the Poetry Foundation, Cynthia Haven writes that his "anguish and ambivalence allowed him to speak for generations that have been paralyzed and helpless before a century of holocausts — from the killing fields of Cambodia to the slaughter in Darfur." How does Miłosz acknowledge this anguish at the end of "Dedication"? What ambivalence does the speaker convey?

Analyzing Language, Style, and Structure

1. **Vocabulary in Context.** The connotation of "connivance" suggests a manipulation of the truth or a misrepresentation. How does Miłosz's use of this word in line 16 help convey the speaker's emotional state? What does it say about his perspective on himself and the world around him?
2. Describe the speaker's tone in lines 1–3 using a pair of words. To capture the nuanced tone in these lines, try using two adjectives with different denotations. How does this tone speak to the larger thematic concerns of the poem?
3. How do you interpret the simile in line 5? Does "silence like a cloud or a tree" differ from other kinds of silence? Explain.
4. Miłosz incorporates contrasting details in lines 8 and 9. What message do these juxtapositions convey? What is the speaker's attitude toward them?
5. Consider the imagery in stanza 3, including the contrasting details of the "shallow Polish rivers" and "an immense bridge" (l. 10) as well as "the wind throw[ing] the screams of gulls" (l. 12). How do such details develop the speaker's tone? What do they convey about the "broken city" (l. 11)?

Topics for Composing

1. AP® FRQ **Poetry Analysis.** In Czesław Miłosz's "Dedication," published in 1945, the speaker addresses those who died in Warsaw, Poland, during the Nazi occupation of the city. Read the poem carefully. Then, in a well-written essay, analyze how Miłosz uses literary elements and techniques to develop the complex relationship between the speaker and his intended audience.
2. **Research.** Do some research on the Nazi occupation of Poland, particularly Warsaw, and learn the details of the events described in the Key Context note for this poem. You might also do some research on the particulars of Miłosz's resistance activities. What do these details add to your understanding of the speaker's message in "Dedication"? How does this additional context affect your understanding of Miłosz's intended audience?

3. **Speaking and Listening.** How can poetry "save / Nations or people" (ll. 14–15)? Consider the way art historian Dr. Sarah Lewis explains "aesthetic force" in her book *The Rise* as an experience so powerful "it leaves us changed — stunned, dazzled, knocked out" in a way that "forces us to see our errors, collective failures, ones too large to ignore." What role can or should the arts play in activist or revolutionary causes?
4. **Connections.** Find a poem that has a great deal of meaning to you, and explain how it achieves the "salutary aim" of poetry Miłosz mentions in line 20. How does it avoid becoming "a connivance with official lies" (l. 16)?
5. **Creative Writing.** Imagine the perspective of a member of Miłosz's intended audience. Calling on that perspective and such a person's fictional voice, compose a poem or a letter to Miłosz in response to "Dedication."

Michelle Matiyow

Letter Beginning with Two Lines by Czesław Miłosz

Matthew Olzmann

Poet and educator Matthew Olzmann was born in Detroit, Michigan. He received his BA from the University of Michigan at Dearborn and his MFA from Warren Wilson College. He is the author of several books of poetry: *Mezzanines* (2013), *Contradictions in the Design* (2016) and *Constellation Route* (2022). He currently teaches at Dartmouth College and at Warren Wilson College.

KEY CONTEXT Matthew Olzmann described, in the *Columbia Tribune*, events that took place the day prior to the original publication of this poem: "[M]y workplace went on lockdown because a man with a rifle was sighted on campus. Later that evening, there was a mass shooting in California. When I wrote the first draft of this poem . . . I thought it was an elegy but realized quickly that it's less about mourning and more about anger — anger that this is normal; this is everyday, and our rhetoric around gun violence does not change." Content note: This poem contains references to gun violence.

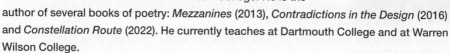

You whom I could not save,
Listen to me.

Can we agree Kevlar
backpacks shouldn't be needed

for children walking to school?
Those same children

also shouldn't require a suit
of armor when standing

on their front lawns, or snipers
to watch their backs

as they eat at McDonalds.
They shouldn't have to stop

to consider the speed
of a bullet or how it might

reshape their bodies. But
one winter, back in Detroit,

I had one student
who opened a door and died.

It was the front
door of his house, but

it could have been any door,
and the bullet could have written

any name. The shooter
was thirteen years old

and was aiming
at someone else. But

a bullet doesn't care
about "aim," it doesn't

distinguish between
the innocent and the innocent,

and how was the bullet
supposed to know this

child would open the door
at the exact wrong moment

because his friend
was outside and screaming

for help. Did I say
I had "one" student who

opened a door and died?
That's wrong.

There were many.
The classroom of grief

had far more seats
than the classroom for math

though every student
in the classroom for math

could count the names
of the dead.

A kid opens a door. The bullet
couldn't possibly know,

nor could the gun, because
"guns don't kill people," they don't

have minds to decide
such things, they don't choose

or have a conscience,
and when a man doesn't

have a conscience, we call him
a psychopath. This is how

we know what type of assault rifle
a man can be,

and how we discover
the hell that thrums inside

each of them. Today,
there's another

shooting with dead
kids everywhere. It was a school,

a movie theater, a parking lot.
The world

is full of doors.
And you, whom I cannot save,

you may open a door
and enter

a meadow or a eulogy.
And if the latter, you will be

mourned, then buried
in rhetoric.

There will be
monuments of legislation,

little flowers made
from red tape.

What should we do? we'll ask
again. The earth will close

like a door above you.
What should we do?

And that click you hear?
That's just our voices,

the deadbolt of discourse
sliding into place. ■

2017

Exploring the Text

1. Why might Matthew Olzmann have made his poem a "Letter"? To whom has it been written?
2. What does Olzmann place at the center of his argument in this poem?
3. Is "Letter Beginning with Two Lines by Czesław Miłosz" a political poem? Or does Olzmann avoid politics? Explain.
4. What is Olzmann's speaker's perspective on the phrase "'guns don't kill people'" (l. 52)? Why is it in quotation marks?
5. What is "the hell that thrums inside // each of them" (ll. 62–63)? Could the pronoun "them" refer to multiple antecedents? Explain.
6. What does "The world // is full of doors" (ll. 68–69) mean on a literal level? What figurative meaning does it take on in the context of the poem?
7. Whom does the speaker address in lines 70–76? What function does this shift serve?
8. Lines 74–80 juxtapose common responses to deaths in general with responses to deaths in war and deaths in mass-shooting events. How does Olzmann's use of figurative language in these lines speak to the larger themes of the poem?
9. What does the speaker mean by the metaphor of "the deadbolt of discourse" (l. 87)? What is the significance of the fact that it is "sliding into place" (l. 88)?

Making Connections

1. What function do Miłosz's lines serve at the beginning of Olzmann's poem? How does this epigraph contextualize the speaker's role in the poem and signal his perspective on the poem's subject?
2. Compare and contrast the purpose, style, and audience of each poem. Beyond the first two lines, which lines of Olzmann's poem demonstrate a connection to Miłosz's? Which indicate a divergence? How do the plights of the intended audiences compare?
3. What parallels can you draw between the setting of each poem? Do you think it is significant that neither poem goes into much detail in describing the specific setting of the events the speakers discuss? Explain why or why not.
4. How does each poem address the role of language — "words" in Milosz's poem; "discourse" in Olzmann's — in the tragic deaths at the center of each text? What power do they have — or lack — according to each speaker? How does the imperative "Listen to me" figure into the dialogue between the speaker and the audience in each poem?

Bogland

Seamus Heaney

PA Images/Alamy

Seamus Heaney (1939–2013) was born at Mossbawn, his family's farm, in Northern Ireland. Heaney was the eldest of nine children. Heaney lived on the farm until he was twelve and won a scholarship to St. Columb's College, a Catholic boarding school about forty miles away. At St. Columb's, Heaney learned Latin and Irish, and as a student at Queen's University in Belfast, he learned Anglo-Saxon; these languages resonate throughout his work. Heaney's works include the collections *Death of a Naturalist* (1966), *Door into the Dark* (1969), *North* (1975), *Station Island* (1984), *Opened Ground* (1998), and *Electric Light* (2001). He is also known for his translations — such as *Sweeney Astray* (1983), *Sweeney's Flight* (1992), and *Beowulf* (1999) — and the plays *The Cure at Troy* (1990) and *Burial at Thebes* (2004). He was awarded the Nobel Prize for Literature in 1995.

KEY CONTEXT T. P. Flanagan (1929–2011), to whom "Bogland" is dedicated, was an Irish landscape artist with whom Heaney shared a love for the bogs in Northern Ireland and other parts of northern Europe in which remains of ancient civilizations — including preserved bodies — have been found intact.

for T. P. Flanagan

We have no prairies
To slice a big sun at evening —
Everywhere the eye concedes to
Encroaching horizon,

Is wooed into the cyclops' eye
Of a tarn.[1] Our unfenced country
Is bog that keeps crusting
Between the sights of the sun.

They've taken the skeleton
Of the Great Irish Elk
Out of the peat, set it up
An astounding crate full of air.

Butter sunk under
More than a hundred years
Was recovered salty and white.
The ground itself is kind, black butter

Melting and opening underfoot,
Missing its last definition
By millions of years.
They'll never dig coal here,

Only the waterlogged trunks
Of great firs, soft as pulp.
Our pioneers keep striking
Inwards and downwards,

Every layer they strip
Seems camped on before.
The bogholes might be Atlantic seepage.
The wet centre is bottomless. ■

1969

[1] A small mountain lake. — Eds.

Understanding and Interpreting

1. The poem's first line is "We have no prairies." Imagine the next words are "But we have . . ." How would you finish that sentence? What might that imaginary second line say about Ireland in comparison to a country with prairies or a country that can "dig coal" (l. 20)?
2. What do you think it means that the "Encroaching horizon" is "wooed into the cyclops' eye / Of a tarn" (ll. 4–6)? How is it wooed, and why?
3. What is the speaker's attitude toward his country? What is his perspective on the passage of time?
4. What does "Bogland" have to say about living in the past? How might that be a comment on Ireland?

Analyzing Language, Style, and Structure

1. **Vocabulary in Context.** What is the meaning of the word "seepage" in line 27? Why does the speaker suggest that "[t]he bogholes might be Atlantic seepage"?
2. While the intact skeleton of an elk and unspoiled butter were, in fact, found in the bogs, "millions of years" (l. 19) and "bottomless" (l. 28) may be exaggerations. What do you think Seamus Heaney is saying about Ireland — and about history — in this mixture of artifacts and fiction?
3. How does the poem create a feeling of drilling downwards to the very last word, which is "bottomless" (l. 28)?
4. What words or images feel mythical in "Bogland," and what is their effect? What is the effect, for example, of describing a "tarn" (l. 6) as a "cyclops' eye" (l. 5)?
5. What aspects of visual art do you see in "Bogland"? What might Heaney have learned from the artist to whom the poem is dedicated?
6. How do Heaney's language choices re-create the waterlogged landscape that is the bogs in Ireland? What does that landscape reveal about Ireland and its history?

Topics for Composing

1. AP® FRQ **Poetry Analysis.** In Seamus Heaney's "Bogland," published in 1969, the speaker considers the bogs in Ireland from which intact artifacts of the very distant past have been retrieved. Read the poem carefully. Then, in a well-written essay, analyze how Heaney uses literary elements and techniques to portray his complex perspective on the relationship between the past and the present.
2. **Connections.** In a lecture entitled "Feeling into Words" (1974), Heaney said he "had been reading up about the frontier and the West as an important myth in the American consciousness, so [he] set up — or rather, laid down — the bog as an answering Irish myth." What do the bogs suggest about the Irish psyche? How does "Bogland" make a comparison with the American myth of the West?
3. **Research.** The publication of "Bogland" in 1969 coincided with an outbreak of violence in Northern Ireland. Heaney has said that at around that time the "problems of poetry moved from being simply a matter of achieving the satisfactory verbal icon to being a search for images and symbols adequate to our predicament." Do some research on the Troubles in Ireland, particularly during the 1960s and 1970s. What images and ideas does "Bogland" offer that help Heaney comment on these events?
4. **Connections.** *New York Times* critic Michiko Kakutani wrote about Heaney's "literary power to unearth from the Irish their gloriously gruesome relics of innocent death and sudden violence and the transcendent nurturing of present upon past that is revealed in the ancient murk of the boglands of Ireland and Jutland." How does "Boglands" illustrate Kakutani's observation?
5. **Multimodal.** Do some research on the people who have been recovered from the bogs in Europe, and prepare a presentation in which you combine images of them with "Bogland" as well as two other poems on the topic by Heaney. How do these poems characterize our connection to the past? What do the images add to your interpretation of Heaney's work?

The Eve of Rosh Hashanah

Yehuda Amichai

Translated from Hebrew by Chana Block and Stephen Mitchell

Sueddeutsche Zeitung Photo/Alamy

Yehuda Amichai (1924–2000) was an internationally renowned Israeli writer whose work has been translated into forty languages and has won numerous international awards. Born in Würtzburg, Germany, to an Orthodox Jewish family, Amichai immigrated with his family to Palestine at the age of eleven and then to Jerusalem the following year. He fought for the British army during World War II and the Israeli Defense Forces during the 1948 Arab-Israeli War. Amichai went on to study biblical and Hebrew literature at the Hebrew University of Jerusalem. He published his first book of poetry, *Now and in Other Days*, in 1955, and his first novel, *Not of This Time, Not of This Place*, in 1963.

KEY CONTEXT The beginning of the Jewish New Year, Rosh Hashanah translates as "head of the year." Like the secular New Year celebrated on January 1, Rosh Hashanah is a time to consider the year past and to make resolutions for the coming year.

The eve of Rosh Hashanah. At the house that's being built,
a man makes a vow: not to do anything wrong in it, only to love.
Sins that were green last spring
dried out over the summer. Now they're whispering.

So I washed my body and clipped my fingernails,
the last good deed a man can do for himself
while he's still alive.
What is man? In the daytime he untangles into words
what night turns into a heavy coil.
What do we do to one another —
a son to his father, a father to his son?

And between him and death there's nothing
but a wall of words
like a battery of agitated lawyers.

And whoever uses people as handles or as rungs of a ladder
will soon find himself hugging a stick of wood
and holding a severed hand and wiping his tears
with a potsherd.[1] ■

1976

[1] A piece of broken ceramic often found at an archaeological site. — Eds.

Understanding and Interpreting

1. What does the speaker of "The Eve of Rosh Hashanah" say about the year past? What resolutions does he make for the year to come?
2. What do you think the "house that's being built" (l. 1) means?
3. A potsherd (l. 19) is an artifact often found at an archaeological site. Why is "wiping his tears / with a potsherd" an appropriate fate for someone who uses people?
4. Who is the audience for this poem? Is there more than one? Is the speaker offering advice or reflecting on his own behavior — or both? Use evidence from the poem to support your interpretation.

Analyzing Language, Style, and Structure

1. **Vocabulary in Context.** What is "a *battery* of agitated lawyers" (l. 14)? Why is that an effective choice to convey the impact of "a wall of words" (l. 13)?
2. What does the figurative language in lines 3–4 suggest about the nature of sin?
3. What is the function of the rhetorical questions in lines 8 and 11?
4. How is the last stanza a fitting conclusion for the holy day — that is, the night before Rosh Hashanah? Consider the figurative language and the syntax in your analysis.

Topics for Composing

1. AP® FRQ **Poetry Analysis.** In Yehuda Amichai's "On the Eve of Rosh Hashanah," published in 1976, the speaker contemplates the start of a new year. Read the poem carefully. Then, in a well-written essay, analyze how Amichai uses literary elements and techniques to convey the speaker's complex perspective on what people owe to each other.
2. **AP® Literary Argumentation.** In Rosie Schaap's *New York Times* review of *The Poetry of Yehuda Amichai*, she cites "The Eve of Rosh Hashanah" as her personal favorite, because "[i]t reminds us . . . to treat one another with decency and care; to love, not to exploit." Do you agree that this is the poem's message? If not, what do you believe that message is? How do the poem's style elements and structure help convey its message to readers?
3. **Connections.** Yehuda Amichai believed that good poetry must be useful. Chana Kronfeld, a professor of comparative literature at UC Berkeley, discusses this belief in her book *The Full Severity of Compassion: The Poetry of Yehuda Amichai*: "Providing useful poetry was indeed something he was always proud of, especially when it was ordinary human beings, not the mechanisms of state or institutional religion, that would find some practical application for his words." In what ways is "The Eve of Rosh Hashanah" a *useful* poem?
4. **Connections.** Find and read at least three other poems that take the concept of the new year as their subject to compare and contrast with "On the Eve of Rosh Hashanah." You might look at Robert Burns's "Auld Lang Syne" (1788), William Cullen Bryant's "A Song for New Year's Eve" (1859), Ella Wheeler Wilcox's "The Year" (1910), or Naomi Shihab Nye's "Burning the Old Year" (1995) — but there are many, many more to choose from. What do these poems have in common with each other in terms of both style and theme? What makes each speaker unique?
5. **Speaking and Listening.** How does this poem refuse to see tradition and progress as binaries or as mutually exclusive choices? Working with a partner, discuss this question with a focus on the language of the poem in Amichai's references to "a vow," "whispering," and "words." Explain to the class how you came to consensus — or why you could not.

Gentrifier

Franny Choi

Jasmine Durhal

Franny Choi (b. 1989) is a writer of poems, essays, and plays. She earned a BA at Brown University and an MFA at the University of Michigan's Helen Zell Writers' Program. Born in the United States to a Korean immigrant family, Choi's writing focuses on identity, language, and power. She has published two poetry collections, edits for *Hyphen Magazine*, and is a Gaius Charles Bolin Fellow in English at Williams College. "Gentrifier" is from her collection *Floating, Brilliant, Gone*.

KEY CONTEXT Gentrification is a process in which a poor area (as of a city) experiences an influx of middle-class or wealthy people who renovate and rebuild homes and businesses and which often results in an increase in property values and the displacement of earlier, usually poorer residents. It is a controversial topic in politics and urban planning.

the new grocery store sells *real* cheese, edging out
the plastic bodega substitute. the new neighbors

know how to feed their children, treat themselves
to oysters sometimes. other times, to brunch. *finally,*

some good pastrami around these parts. new cafe
on broadway. new trees in the sidewalk. everyone

can breathe a little easier. neighborhood association
throws a block party. builds a dog park right

in the middle of the baseball field. crime watch listserv
snaps photos of suspicious natives. *how'd all these ghosts*

get in my yard? cop on speed dial. arrange flowers
as the radio croons orders. rubber on tar,

skin on steel. an army of macbook pros guarding
its french presses. revival pioneers. meanwhile,

white college grads curse their racist neighbors,
get drunk at olneyville[1] warehouse punk shows,

ride their bikes on the right side of the road, say *west end*
like a badge, while folks on the other side of cranston street[2]

[1] Olneyville is a working-class neighborhood in Providence, Rhode Island. — Eds.

[2] Cranston Street functions as a dividing line between the more affluent east side and the primarily working-class west side of Providence. —Eds.

shake their heads and laugh. interrogation lamps
burning down their stoops. banks gutting their houses.

i look more like the cambodian kids against that wall
than any of my roommates. but feel safest within two miles

of an espresso machine. look around at parties and think,
fresh saplings. revival pioneers. know folks look at me

on my bike and think, *ivy league. dog park. treat yourself*
to a neighborhood sometimes. none of this land is mine

but our footprints are everywhere. silent battlefront
we new settlers shove into our back pockets,

lump in our collective throat as we chase a new world,
sweep the foyer, promise we'll help clean up the mess. ■

2014

Understanding and Interpreting

1. Consider the title of the poem. What does it suggest about the speaker's perspective on the causes and effects of gentrification? How would your interpretation of or expectations for the poem be different if it were titled "Gentrification"?
2. How do the possessions of the gentrifiers characterize them? Identify at least four and discuss what associations they carry. What do these associations reveal about the speaker's attitude toward gentrifiers? Is she stereotyping them? Does she include herself among them?
3. What does the speaker mean in lines 26–27: "none of this land is mine / but our footprints are everywhere"? Is she just talking about her neighborhood? Explain.
4. How do you interpret the final lines of the poem? Who will "help clean up the mess"? What, in the speaker's eyes, is the "mess"?
5. Overall, what is the attitude of the speaker toward gentrifiers? In her eyes, who — or what — ultimately bears responsibility for gentrification?

Analyzing Language, Style, and Structure

1. **Vocabulary in Context.** In line 12, the speaker relates that "the radio croons orders." What connotations does the verb "croons" carry? What does the speaker convey by juxtaposing this word with "orders"?
2. How do the italicized words and phrases in the poem relate to the internal conflict the speaker feels?
3. How do the references to the people who are displaced from versus moving into the gentrified area characterize each group? Consider "suspicious natives," "revival pioneers," "ghosts," "white college grads," and "new settlers" in your analysis.
4. Consider the figurative language in lines 19–20: "interrogation lamps / burning down their stoops. banks gutting their houses." What is the effect of these language choices?

What does it suggest about the relationship between government, business, and neighborhood inhabitants?

5. How does the lack of capitalization throughout the poem contribute to the development of a central theme? How does this deviation from conventional grammar inform your analysis of the poem?
6. How do the formal elements of the poem support the idea of displacement and fragmentation Choi explores in "Gentrifier"? Consider rhythm, enjambment, and juxtaposition in your response.

Topics for Composing

1. AP® FRQ **Poetry Analysis.** In Franny Choi's "Gentrifier," published in 2014, the speaker describes gentrification, the controversial phenomenon of an impoverished community or neighborhood being populated by more affluent residents, thus displacing the original inhabitants. Read the poem carefully. Then, in a well-written essay, analyze how Choi uses literary elements and techniques to convey the speaker's complex perspective on the causes and effects of gentrification.
2. **AP® Literary Argumentation.** Of her work, Choi has said that "there's no time for poems that aren't invested in shaking something up, poems that have no stakes." How does "Gentrifier" "shak[e] something up"? What are the "stakes" in this poem?
3. **AP® Literary Argumentation.** In an interview, Choi referred to another poet's definition of "community" as "the people to whom you feel accountable, and who are (at least in some part) accountable to you." How is "Gentrifier" a poem about the loss or exploitation of community? What failure of accountability does it illustrate?
4. **Multimodal.** Develop a short video interpretation of "Gentrifier" that incorporates images, spoken word narrative, and/or musical accompaniment. Be prepared to lead a discussion with your classmates about your interpretation.
5. **Creative Writing.** Using the italicized words and phrases in "Gentrifier" as a jumping-off point, create a poem of your own about gentrification or a changing neighborhood. Feel free to switch the order around, but somehow incorporate Choi's language into your own work.

Why Whales Are Back in New York City

Rajiv Mohabir

Rajiv Mohabir

Rajiv Mohabir (b. 1981) is an Indo-Caribbean American poet and translator. He was born in London but grew up in Florida. He has numerous degrees in different fields: a BA in religious studies from the University of Florida; an MSEd in Teaching English to Speakers of Other Languages from Long Island University, Brooklyn; an MFA in poetry and literary translation from Queens College, City University of New York; and a PhD in English from the University of Hawai'i. He worked as public school teacher in New York and currently teaches at Emerson College. He is the author of two collections of poetry, *The Taxidermist's Cut* (2016) and *The Cowherd's Son* (2017), as well as a translation of Lalbihari Sharma's *I Even Regret Night: Holi Songs of Demerara* (2019) and a memoir, *Antiman* (2021).

KEY CONTEXT Prior to the federal ban on any new usage of polychlorinated-biphenyls, or PCBs, in 1979, this oily yellow substance had been used widely in the United States for decades in electrical equipment, lubricants, and hydraulic fluid things because PCBs are resistant to extreme temperatures. Given the longevity of PCBs, however, they can still be found in older products as well as in soil and waste. They have also been linked to a number of serious health conditions in humans and animals.

After a century, humpbacks migrate
again to Queens. They left
due to sewage and white froth

banking the shores from polychlorinated-
biphenyl-dumping into the Hudson
and winnowing menhaden[1] schools.

But now grace, dark bodies of song
return. Go to the seaside —

Hold your breath. Submerge.
A black fluke silhouetted
against the Manhattan skyline.

Now ICE[2] beats doors
down on Liberty Avenue
to deport. I sit alone on orange

A train seats, mouth sparkling
from Singh's,[3] no matter how
white supremacy gathers

at the sidewalks, flows down
the streets, we still beat our drums
wild. Watch their false-god statues

prostrate to black and brown hands.
They won't keep us out
though they send us back.

Our songs will pierce the dark
fathoms. Behold the miracle:

what was once lost now leaps before you. ■

2017

---

[1] A type of herring that is an important part of the diet of humpback whales. — Eds.

[2] Immigration and Customs Enforcement. — Eds.

[3] A West Indian restaurant in the New York City borough of Queens. — Eds.

Understanding and Interpreting

1. Describe the speaker (or speakers) of the poem. In your response, consider the shift to "us" and "our" in the final three stanzas.
2. What, according to the speaker, caused the century-long disappearance of whales around New York City? What connection does the speaker make between their return and his everyday life?
3. Based on the details in the poem, compare and contrast "now" (ll. 7, 12, and 26) with the past. How have circumstances changed? What does the speaker state or imply has remained the same?
4. What does the speaker mean in lines 20–21 by "Watch their false-god statues / prostrate to black and brown hands"?
5. How do you interpret lines 22–23: "They won't keep us out / though they send us back"? What does this statement have to do with the whales?

Analyzing Language, Style, and Structure

1. **Vocabulary in Context.** Look up the word "prostrate" to determine which of its definitions Rajiv Mohabir intends in line 21. How do the word's connotations and denotations help shape the speaker's tone in lines 20–21?
2. Beyond the obvious detriments of such pollution, what connotations do "sewage and white froth" (l. 3) convey?
3. What shift in tone occurs in line 12? How does this shift reveal the speaker's thematic concerns?
4. The final line of the poem subtly alludes to the hymn "Amazing Grace." How does this allusion help frame the speaker's attitude toward progress?
5. The speaker uses a series of imperatives in lines 8, 9, 20, and 25. To whom does the speaker give these commands? What effect do these syntax choices have on the speaker's tone?
6. How do enjambment and the structure of the stanzas help emphasize certain ideas in the poem?

Topics for Composing

1. **AP® FRQ Poetry Analysis.** In Rajiv Mohabir's "Why Whales Are Back in New York City," published in 2017, the speaker discusses the return of humpback whales to Hudson Bay following efforts to limit the pollution that drove them out a century prior. Read the poem carefully. Then, in a well-written essay, analyze how Mohabir uses literary elements and techniques to develop the complex connection between how humans treat nature and how they treat each other.
2. **Research.** Explore the history of humpback whales in Hudson Bay as well as the demographic makeup of those who live in the New York City borough of Queens. Then, explain how the diversity in Queens further develops the poem's meaning.
3. **Connections.** Have animal populations changed because of population or industrial growth in the place where you live? Write an informational overview of the ways industrialization and urban development have impacted your area. As an added challenge, compose a poem using the themes in Mohabir's poem for inspiration.

4. **Speaking and Listening.** To what extent do our interactions with the environment around us reflect or inform our interactions with each other? Does our treatment of animals and nature mirror the ways in which we treat our fellow humans? Determine your personal stance on these questions and gather evidence to support your position in preparation for a class discussion on the topic.
5. **Connections.** In his explanation of "Why Whales Are Back in New York City" for Poets.org, Rajiv Mohabir writes, "How beautiful that the whales, once threatened by a fouled environment, retreated and now come back that the waters are cleaner; we have so much work to do." What type of work does his poem suggest we have to do?

Pseudacris Crucifer

Terrance Hayes

Manny Carabel/Getty Images

Terrance Hayes (b. 1971) is an American poet and educator. Born in Columbia, South Carolina, he earned a BA from Coker College and an MFA at the University of Pittsburgh. Hayes is the author of six books of poetry: *Muscular Music* (1999), which won both a Whiting Award and the Kate Tufts Discovery Award; *Hip Logic* (2002), which won the National Poetry Series; *Wind in a Box* (2006); *Lighthead* (2010), which won a National Book Award; *How to Be Drawn* (2015); and *Sonnets for My Past and Future Assassin* (2018).

KEY CONTEXT Pseudacris is a genus of frogs found in North America ranging from the Pacific coastline to the Atlantic. The name comes from the Greek *pseudes* and *akris*, probably a reference to the repeated rasping trill of most chorus frogs. Please note that this poem references lynchings, which were not uncommon during the Jim Crow era in the South. In some instances, white communities gathered to witness them, even posing for photographs.

The father begins to make the sound a tree frog makes
When he comes with his son & daughter to a pail
Of tree frogs for sale in a Deep South flea market
Just before the last blood of dusk.
A tree frog is called a tree frog because it chirps
Like a bird in a tree, he tells his daughter
While her little brother, barely four years old,
Busies himself like a small blues piper
With a brand-new birthday harmonica.
A single tree frog can sound like a sleigh bell,
The father says. Several can sound like a choir
Of crickets. Once in high school, as I dissected
A frog, the frog opened its eyes to judge
Its deconstruction, its disassembly,
My scooping & poking at its soul.
And the little girl's eyes go wide as a tree frog's eyes.

Some call it the "spring peeper." In Latin
It's called *Pseudacris crucifer*. False locusts,
Toads with falsettos, their chimes issuing below
The low leaves & petals. The harmonica playing
Is so otherworldly, the boy blows with his eyes closed.
Some tree-frog species spend most every day underground.
They don't know what sunlight does at dusk.
They are nocturnal insectivores. No bigger than
A green thumb, they are the first frogs to call
In the spring. They may sound like crickets
Only because they eat so many crickets.
Tree frogs mostly sound like birds.
The tree frog overcomes its fear of birds by singing.
The harmonica playing is so bewitching,
The boy gathers a crowd in a flea market
In the Deep South. A bird may eat a frog.
A fox may eat the bird. A wolf may eat the fox.
And the wolf then may carry varieties of music
And cunning in its belly as it roams the countryside.
A wolf hungers because it cannot feel the good
In its body. The people clap & gather round
With fangs & smiles. The father lifts the son
To his shoulders so the boy's harmonics hover
Over varieties of affections, varieties of bodies
With their backs to a firmament burning & opening.
You can find damn near anything in a flea market:
Pets, weapons, flags, farm-fresh as well as farm-spoiled
Fruits & vegetables, varieties of old wardrobes,
A rusty old tin box with old postcards & old photos
Of lynchings dusted in the rust of the box.
You can feel it on the tips of your fingers,
This rust, which is almost as brown as the father
And the boy on his shoulders & the girl making
The sound a tree frog makes in a flea market
In the Deep South before the blood of dusk,
Just before the last blood of dusk. Just before the dusk. ■

2020

Understanding and Interpreting

1. What is the overall situation of this poem? Who is the speaker? What is the setting and occasion? Who does the speaker encounter? What time of day is it?
2. By the end of the poem, what information do you know about the tree frog? What is scientific, and what is speculative?

3. The poem pivots on surprises — unusual combinations, a jarring reference, a dramatic contrast. How do you respond to at least two of these "surprises"?
4. How do you interpret the connections and consequences in ll. 32–37? What does it mean that "A wolf hungers because it cannot feel the good / In its body"?
5. What associations do you have with the time of day known as dusk? In your response, consider the concept of "sundown towns": all-white communities that excluded nonwhite people through discriminatory laws or practices, often including violence. The term refers to the time at which all nonwhite people needed to be outside the town limits — in other words, it was a threat of violence. How does this information add to your understanding of the mood that dusk evokes?
6. Why do you think Terrance Hayes chose a scientific term for the tree frog as the title of his poem? What does this title imply about the speaker's relationship to, and perspective on, the items he encounters at the flea market? How does it relate to the main subject of the poem?

Analyzing Language, Style, and Structure

1. **Vocabulary in Context.** Hayes refers to "varieties of bodies / With their backs to a firmament burning and opening" (ll. 40–41). What is the meaning of "firmament," and what image does this meaning help evoke in context of the poem? What does the biblical allusion implicit in "firmament" add to the impact of this choice?
2. Who is the speaker of the poem? What perspective does he bring to the scene and commentary — or is the speaker detached, objective? Pay particular attention to ll. 12–15, in which the speaker recalls an experience in high school. What purpose do these lines serve?
3. How does repetition function in this poem? Consider how and why Hayes repeats essentially the same phrase but with slight differences, such as "a Deep South flea market" (l. 3) and "a flea market / In the Deep South" (ll. 50–51). Include "dusk" and its variant descriptions in your analysis. What is the overarching significance of these repeated words and phrases in slightly different forms?
4. How do word choices suggesting mystery — such as "otherworldly" (l. 21) and "bewitching" (l. 30) — contribute to your interpretation of the poem? What meaning does their contrast with the descriptions of wildlife convey?
5. Sound is central to "Pseudicris Crucifer" as Hayes interweaves the sound made by the frogs, the boy's harmonica, and the girl mimicking the frog's call. How does Hayes's sound-related word play (such as "piper" and "peeper") and his auditory images contribute to the larger meaning of the poem? In other words, why is the concept of sound so important to the speaker? What might it suggest about the past as echoing in the present?
6. How does Hayes use juxtaposition to dramatize unfairness or injustice in the poem? Cite at least three examples to support your analysis.

Topics for Composing

1. **AP® FRQ** **Poetry Analysis.** In Terrance Hayes's "Pseudacris Crucifer," published in 2020, the speaker observes people at a flea market at dusk. Read the poem carefully. Then, in a well-written essay, analyze how Hayes uses literary elements and techniques to convey the speaker's complex perspective on the relationship between the past and present.
2. **AP® Literary Argumentation.** Is "Pseudacris Crucifer" a protest poem? a political poem? a personal meditation? a warning? How does your interpretation of the poem reflect your view of the purpose Hayes wants to achieve?

3. **AP® Literary Argumentation.** In his novel *Requiem for a Nun*, Southern author William Faulkner wrote, "The past is never dead. It's not even past." How does this poem exemplify this statement? What resources of language does Hayes draw on to make this point?
4. **AP® Literary Argumentation.** The writer James Baldwin wrote in his essay "Stranger in the Village" (1955), "People are trapped in history, and history is trapped in them." How does this statement about the intersection of past and present illuminate the central themes of "Pseudacris Crucifer"?
5. **Speaking and Listening.** Develop a performance of the poem that involves several voices. Working with a small group, decide how you would divide the poem among the speakers — perhaps someone takes the natural world descriptions, another takes the flea market scene, and another takes the speaker's commentary on his descriptions — to best reflect your interpretation of the poem as a whole. You might add music to evoke emotions related to your interpretation.
6. **Connections.** The iconic jazz singer Billie Holiday recorded the song "Strange Fruit" in 1939. It originated as a poem written by Abel Meeropol, a teacher in the Bronx, as a protest against lynching. Although popular from the start, the song engendered significant controversy, resulting in efforts to ban its performance over the years. Yet in 2002, "Strange Fruit" was selected for preservation in the National Recording Registry by the Library of Congress as being "culturally, historically or aesthetically significant." After listening to at least two renditions of the song and analyzing the lyrics, explain why you think the song has endured. How does Hayes's use of literary elements in "Pseudacis Crucifer" parallel the techniques in "Strange Fruit"? How similar are the messages each poem conveys?
7. **Research.** Hayes concludes his poem with this image: "before the blood of dusk, / Just before the last blood of dusk. Just before the dusk." These lines could be read as an allusion to the 1923 poetic novel *Cane* by Harlem Renaissance writer Jean Toomer, who describes the mystery and beauty of set and dusk in the South along with the threat of brutality. Read some of the opening sections of *Cane*, and discuss how Hayes continues and amplifies the "historical present" that Toomer describes in his work.

i want to speak of unity

Juan Felipe Herrera

Chris Felver/Getty Images

Juan Felipe Herrera (b. 1948) is a poet, performer, writer, cartoonist, teacher, and activist. He was the U.S. Poet Laureate from 2015 to 2019. The son of farmworkers, Herrera grew up in California's San Joaquín and Salinas Valleys. He earned a BA in social anthropology from the University of California, Los Angeles, and an MFA from the Iowa Writers' Workshop. Herrera's publications include fifteen collections of poetry and eleven other books of prose, short stories, young adult novels, and picture books for children. His most recent book, *Every Day We Get More Illegal*, was published in 2020. He won the 2008 National Book Critics Circle Award in poetry for *Half the World in Light*. In 2012, Herrera was appointed California Poet Laureate. He currently holds the Tomás Rivera Endowed Chair in the Creative Writing Department at the University of California, Riverside, and directs the Art and Barbara Culver Center for the Arts in Riverside.

— i want to speak of unity that indescribable thing
we have been speaking of since '67 when I first stepped into LA
with a cardboard box luggage piece I was distracted by you
your dances askew & somersaults the kind you see at shopping centers
& automobile super sale events — the horns &
bayonets most of all
I wanted to pierce the density the elixirs of everything something
like Max Beckmann[1] did in that restaurant painting of '37 or '38[2]
exiled from Germany banned & blazing black jacket —
that everything
in a time of all things in collapse
that embrace that particular set of syllables of a sudden attack
or just a breath of a song
the one I would hear back in the early '50s
when I walked the barren earth with my mother & father
the sound
of One when Luz still lived & Felipe[3] still parted the red lands
& no one knew we existed in the fires
the flames that consume all of us
now ■

2020

[1] Max Beckmann (1884–1950) was a German artist who was labeled a "cultural Bolshevik," or communist, under Adolf Hitler's regime. In 1937 over five hundred of his paintings, deemed "degenerate art," were confiscated by the Nazi government. In response, Beckmann fled to the Netherlands, where he lived for the duration of World War II. — Eds.

[2] A reference to *Paris Society*, a painting Beckmann completed in 1931. — Eds.

[3] A reference to the author's parents, María de la Luz Quintana and Felipe Emilio Herrera. — Eds.

Understanding and Interpreting

1. Why might the speaker refer to unity as "that indescribable thing" (l. 1)? Consider the implications of it being "indescribable" as well as Juan Felipe Herrera's use of the word "thing."
2. When is the "time of all things in collapse" (l. 11)? How does it relate to the three other decades the speaker mentions by name?
3. The names in line 17 refer to Herrera's parents, María de la Luz Quintana and Felipe Emilio Herrera, both of whom were farmworkers in California. What does Herrera convey about his parents and his childhood in this poem? What might be "the sound / of One" (ll. 17–18)?
4. How do you interpret the final three lines of the poem? Cite evidence from the poem to support your response.

Analyzing Language, Style, and Structure

1. **Vocabulary in Context.** The word *elixirs* has multiple definitions, the most general of which is that of a cure-all. Historically, however, elixirs were substances that were believed to turn common metals into gold or to grant immortality. Which definition or definitions of "elixir" (l. 7) might Herrera be calling on in this poem?

2. Herrera plays with the words "everything" (ll. 7 and 10) and "something" (l. 7) and places each on its own line at different points in the poem. He also incorporates the word "thing" into lines 1, and 11. What does Herrera suggest is the philosophical relationship between "every" and "some" with these repetitions? How might this relationship help define "unity" as an "indescribable thing" (l. 1)?
3. What is the purpose of the allusion to Max Beckmann? How does it serve as a kind of evidence for the speaker's argument in this poem?
4. Herrera juxtaposes the phrase "that particular set of syllables of a sudden attack" (l. 12) with "just a breath of a song" (l. 13). What does this choice convey about the connection between memory and sound? How does the consonance of these two lines help emphasize the speaker's point?
5. Why might Herrera have placed "now" on the final line of the poem by itself? How does such an emphasis reflect the poem's larger meaning?
6. How does the overall structure of the poem relate to the concept of unity? Does it work against it or mirror it?
7. In her review of Herrera's book *Every Day We Get More Illegal* for *The Rumpus*, Barbara Berman writes that "Herrera has always been a masterful breaker of lines." How does Herrera use line breaks and enjambment in strategic ways to separate thoughts, images, and ideas in meaningful ways? How do these structural choices convey the speaker's message?
8. How might "the fires / the flames that consume all of us / now" in the final three lines symbolize something other than the destruction we normally associate with fire?

Topics for Composing

1. AP® FRQ **Poetry Analysis.** In Juan Felipe Herrera's "i want to speak of unity," published in 2020, the speaker attempts to capture the elusive nature of unity. Read the poem carefully. Then, in a well-written essay, analyze how Herrera uses literary elements and techniques to convey the complexity of the speaker's perspective on what unity means.
2. **Speaking and Listening.** What might unity look like in our society, and how might we know we have achieved it? Discuss these questions in a small group to come up with an explanation of the "indescribable thing" Herrera contemplates in his poem. Once you have a consensus, share your ideas in a larger class discussion.
3. **Research.** Do some research on the life and artwork of Max Beckmann. Pay particular attention to his 1931 painting *Paris Society*. In your research, explore specific elements of Beckmann's biography, themes you discover in Beckmann's artwork, and his experiences in the 1930s. How do all of these aspects of your research add layers of meaning to the allusion in Herrera's poem?
4. **Multimodal.** Write, draw, or otherwise construct a creative work, such as a collage or a mixed media piece, in which you capture what unity, the "indescribable thing" (l. 1), means to you.
5. **Connections.** In a 2015 interview at the Miami International Book Fair, Herrera talked about the importance of reflecting on the extreme violence occurring in our communities. He explained that "we can't be fully alive if we aren't thoughtful, if we don't respond to extreme violence with our own experiences and our own words." What response does this poem offer? What experiences does it convey that exemplify what it means to be thoughtful and fully alive?

AP® Multiple-Choice Practice

from Fences

August Wilson

ROSE I don't know why you want to get on talking about death.

TROY Ain't nothing wrong with talking about death. That's part of life. Everybody gonna die. You gonna die, I'm gonna die. Bono's gonna die. Hell, we all gonna die.

ROSE But you ain't got to talk about it. I don't like to talk about it.

TROY You the one brought it up. Me and Bono was talking about baseball . . . you tell me I'm gonna drink myself to death. Ain't that right, Bono? You know I don't drink this but one night out of the week. That's Friday night. I'm gonna drink just enough to where I can handle it. Then I cuts it loose. I leave it alone. So don't you worry about me drinking myself to death. 'Cause I ain't worried about Death. I done seen him. I done wrestled with him.

Look here, Bono . . . I looked up one day and Death was marching straight at me. Like Soldiers on Parade! The Army of Death was marching straight at me. The middle of July, 1941. It got real cold just like it be winter. It seem like Death himself reached out and touched me on the shoulder. He touch me just like I touch you. I got cold as ice and Death standing there grinning at me.

ROSE Troy, why don't you hush that talk.

TROY I say . . . what you want, Mr. Death? You be wanting me? You done brought your army to be getting me? I looked him dead in the eye. I wasn't fearing nothing. I was ready to tangle. Just like I'm ready to tangle now. The Bible say be ever vigilant. That's why I don't get but so drunk. I got to keep watch.

ROSE Troy was right down there in Mercy Hospital. You remember he had pneumonia? Laying there with a fever talking plumb out of his head.

TROY Death standing there staring at me . . . carrying that sickle in his hand. Finally he say, "You want bound over for another year?" See, just like that . . . "You want bound over for another year?" I told him, "Bound over hell! Let's settle this now!"

It seem like he kinda fell back when I said that, and all the cold went out of me. I reached down and grabbed that sickle and threw it just as far as I could throw it . . . and me and him commenced to wrestling.

We wrestled for three days and three nights. I can't say where I found the strength from. Every time it seemed like he was gonna get the best of me, I'd reach way down deep inside myself and find the strength to do him one better.

ROSE Every time Troy tell that story he find different ways to tell it. Different things to make up about it.

TROY I ain't making up nothing. I'm telling you the facts of what happened. I wrestled with Death for three days and three nights and I'm standing here to tell you about it. (*Pause.*) All right. At the end of the third night we done weakened each other to where we can't hardly move. Death stood up, throwed on his robe . . . had him a white robe with a hood on it. He throwed on that robe and went off to look for his sickle. Say, "I'll be back." Just like that. "I'll be back." I told him, say, "Yeah, but . . . you gonna have to find me!" I wasn't no fool. I wan't going looking for him. Death ain't nothing to play with. And I know he's gonna get me. I know I got to join his army . . . his camp followers. But as long as I keep my strength and see him coming . . . as long as I keep up my vigilance . . . he's gonna have to fight to get me. I ain't going easy. ■

AP® Multiple-Choice Questions

1. In this passage, Troy's descriptions align Death with all of the following EXCEPT a
   a. reaper
   b. soldier
   c. wrestler
   d. Ku Klux Klan member
   e. Major League Baseball player

2. In line 15, "Then I cuts it loose" means that Troy
   a. lets go of all his inhibitions
   b. dances with wild abandon
   c. stops drinking alcohol
   d. loses his fear of death
   e. walks out on his family

3. Which of the following is the best synonym for "bound over" in line 44?
   a. enslaved
   b. fettered
   c. beaten
   d. postponed
   e. tried

4. Which of the following best describes Rose's reaction in lines 57–59 to Troy's narration of his struggle with Death?
   a. ambiguity
   b. cynicism
   c. hostility
   d. trepidation
   e. veneration

5. Troy mentions a Bible verse in line 34 in order to
   a. convince Rose that he is a moral man
   b. convey the depth of his religious knowledge
   c. lend credence to his claim that he wrestled with Death
   d. explain why his drinking is never uncontrolled
   e. underscore why he drinks every Friday

6. The probable reason for including the stage direction to pause in line 63 is to
   a. allow time for the audience to absorb Troy's startling revelation that he has fought with Death
   b. signal that Troy is allowing a moment for his wife and friend to argue with him about what took place
   c. indicate that Troy is finally ready to reveal the truth about earlier versions of his story
   d. suggest that Troy is coming close to tears and must stop briefly to get his emotions under control
   e. underscore that Troy is growing increasingly angry, but composes himself and continues more calmly

7. From this passage, the reader can infer that
   a. Rose detests Bono and does not want Troy to spend time with him
   b. Troy suffered hallucinations as a result of pneumonia
   c. Troy served in the U.S. Army during World War II
   d. Troy is a compulsive liar who exhibits no remorse
   e. Bono is purposely ignoring Troy and Rose's argument

8. Troy's attitude toward Death might be characterized as
   a. amused
   b. irrational
   c. petrified
   d. undaunted
   e. welcoming

9. What is Rose's attitude toward death in this passage?
   a. fearless
   b. indifferent
   c. intrigued
   d. irreverent
   e. unnerved

10. The phrase "[Death's] army . . . his camp followers" (ll. 74–75) refers to those who
    a. defeat death
    b. elude death
    c. seek out death
    d. celebrate death
    e. succumb to death

from Frankenstein

Mary Shelley

It was on a dreary night of November, that I beheld the accomplishment of my toils. With an anxiety that almost amounted to agony, I collected the instruments of life around me, that I might infuse a spark of being into the lifeless thing that lay at my feet. It was already one in the morning; the rain pattered dismally against the panes, and my candle was nearly burnt out, when, by the glimmer of the half-extinguished light, I saw the dull yellow eye of the creature open; it breathed hard, and a convulsive motion agitated its limbs.

How can I describe my emotions at this catastrophe, or how delineate the wretch whom with such infinite pains and care I had endeavoured to form? His limbs were in proportion, and I had selected his features as beautiful. Beautiful! — Great God! His yellow skin scarcely covered the work of muscles and arteries beneath; his hair was of a lustrous black, and flowing; his teeth of a pearly whiteness; but these luxuriances only formed a more horrid contrast with his watery eyes, that seemed almost of the same colour as the dun white sockets in which they were set, his shriveled complexion and straight black lips.

The different accidents of life are not so changeable as the feelings of human nature. I had worked hard for nearly two years, for the sole purpose of infusing life into an inanimate body. For this I had deprived myself of rest and health. I had desired it with an ardour that far exceeded moderation; but now that I had finished, the beauty of the dream vanished, and breathless horror and disgust filled my heart. Unable to endure the aspect of the being I had created, I rushed out of the room, and continued a long time traversing my bedchamber, unable to compose my mind to sleep. At length lassitude succeeded to the tumult I had before endured; and I threw myself on the bed in my clothes, endeavouring to seek a few moments of forgetfulness. But it was in vain; I slept, indeed, but I was disturbed by the wildest dreams. I thought I saw Elizabeth, in the bloom of health, walking in the streets of Ingolstadt. Delighted and surprised, I embraced her; but as I imprinted the first kiss on her lips, they became livid with the hue of death; her features appeared to change, and I thought that I held the corpse of my dead mother in my arms; a shroud enveloped her form, and I saw the graveworms crawling in the folds of the flannel. I started from my sleep with horror; a cold dew covered my forehead, my teeth chattered, and every limb became convulsed; when, by the dim and yellow light of the moon, as it forced its way through the window shutters, I beheld the wretch — the miserable monster whom I had created. He held up the curtain of the bed; and his eyes, if eyes they may be called, were fixed on me. His jaws opened, and he muttered some inarticulate sounds, while a grin wrinkled his cheeks. He might have spoken, but I did not hear; one hand was stretched out, seemingly to detain me, but I escaped, and rushed down stairs. I took refuge in the courtyard belonging to the house which I inhabited; where I remained during the rest of the night, walking up and down in the greatest agitation, listening attentively, catching and fearing each sound as if it were to announce the approach of the demoniacal corpse to which I had so miserably given life.

Oh! no mortal could support the horror of that countenance. A mummy again endued with animation could not be so hideous as that wretch. I had gazed on him while unfinished; he was ugly then; but when those muscles and joints were rendered capable of motion, it became a thing such as even Dante[1] could not have conceived.

I passed the night wretchedly. Sometimes my pulse beat so quickly and hardly, that I felt the palpitation of every artery; at others, I nearly sank to the ground through languor and extreme weakness. Mingled with this horror, I felt the bitterness of disappointment; dreams that had been my food and pleasant rest for so long a space were now become a hell to me; and the change was so rapid, the overthrow so complete! ■

[1] A reference to *The Inferno,* the first part of the three-part fourteenth-century poem *The Divine Comedy* by Dante Alighieri (1265–1321). In it, Dante tells of fantastical punishments and their effects on the people he meets as he is guided through hell by the Roman poet Virgil. — Eds.

AP® Multiple-Choice Questions

1. Paragraph 2 indicates that the speaker

- **a.** immediately regrets reanimating the creature
- **b.** unintentionally reanimated the creature
- **c.** always intended to create a hideous monster
- **d.** is thrilled by his success but appalled at his creation
- **e.** needs to make a plan to hide his creation from others

2. All of the following happen in the speaker's dream in paragraph 3 EXCEPT

- **a.** he sees a young woman he once loved
- **b.** he realizes that Elizabeth has been reanimated
- **c.** he holds the corpse of another person
- **d.** Elizabeth seems to turn into his mother
- **e.** he is repulsed by worms and decaying flesh

3. In paragraph 5, the "dreams" in the last sentence of this passage most likely refer to

- **a.** seeing Elizabeth alive and well
- **b.** having a vision of the monster
- **c.** resurrecting the speaker's mother
- **d.** reanimating dead tissue
- **e.** escaping from the monster

4. According to this passage, the speaker is MOST surprised to discover that he is

- **a.** successful in reanimating a lifeless creature
- **b.** in danger of being killed by the monster
- **c.** horrified at the success of his experiment
- **d.** able to sleep after everything he has experienced
- **e.** having nightmares that stem from his anxiety

5. The setting, as depicted in paragraph 1, is best described as

- **a.** chaotic
- **b.** ominous
- **c.** passionate
- **d.** tropical
- **e.** unpredictable

6. Which word best describes the speaker's state of mind throughout the passage?

- **a.** "dreary" (par. 1)
- **b.** "horrid" (par. 2)
- **c.** "delighted" (par. 3)
- **d.** "disturbed" (par. 3)
- **e.** "hideous" (par. 4)

7. In context, the expression "demoniacal corpse" (par. 3) suggests that the speaker

- **a.** wishes to imbue faith into the soul of his creation
- **b.** used the bodies of evil men to create the monster
- **c.** recognizes the sinfulness of his experimentation
- **d.** lacks hope for the magnanimity of his creation
- **e.** believes he should destroy the monster

8. At the end of the passage, the speaker primarily feels

- **a.** satisfaction at having accomplished his goals
- **b.** despondent due to his new circumstances
- **c.** anxiety over his deteriorating health
- **d.** frailty due to his unsatiated hunger
- **e.** panic over his recurring nightmares

9. In context, the expression "my candle was nearly burnt out" (par. 1) emphasizes the

a. speaker's exhaustion
b. creature's lifeless body
c. late hour of the day
d. power of the rain
e. futility of his experiment

10. The ironies presented in paragraph 2 emphasize the

a. sinful nature of Victor's experiment
b. futility of Victor's plans for the creature
c. poor aesthetic sensibilities Victor possesses
d. difficulties of bestowing life to the creature
e. inadequacy of the resources available to Victor

Suggestions for Writing

Tradition and Progress

1. AP® FRQ **Literary Argument.** The tension between following and maintaining tradition and choosing to break with tradition in order to strike out in an uncertain path, though one with possibility, is the subject of much of classic and contemporary literature. In *Fences* by August Wilson, the main character, Troy, seems trapped by a tradition of racial discrimination that transcribes and stunts his life, yet he continues to react to it rather than take decisive action. In a well-written essay, analyze how the conflict between tradition and progress contributes to an interpretation of the work as a whole. Do not merely summarize the plot.
2. **Connections.** Nathaniel Hawthorne once wrote, "The world owes all its onward impulses to men ill at ease. The happy man inevitably confines himself within ancient limits." Using at least one of the works in this chapter to support your position, write an essay in which you agree or disagree with Hawthorne that the drive toward progress is made by those who are "ill at ease," while those who are happy embrace tradition.
3. **AP® Literary Argumentation.** The natural world provides the background for several of the works in this chapter. Choose a text from this chapter and write an essay in which you explore the way the writer uses the natural world to comment on the clash between tradition and progress.
4. **Connections.** Choose two poems from this chapter, one that criticizes progress and another that celebrates it. Write an essay in which you analyze the contrasting attitudes toward the subject. Include personal commentary on which view comes closer to your own.
5. **Speaking and Listening.** Choose one of the following statements, and prepare for a class discussion about why it fits your beliefs about tradition and progress. Use examples from at least two of the texts in this chapter to support your position.
   - **a.** "Discontent is the first step in the progress of a man or a nation." — Oscar Wilde
   - **b.** "A tradition without intelligence is not worth having." — T. S. Eliot
   - **c.** "Tradition is a guide and not a jailer." — W. Somerset Maugham
6. **Connections.** The short stories in this chapter examine racial or ethnic issues through conflicts in families or communities. Write an essay in which you analyze the racial or ethnic clashes in one or more of the stories.
7. **Connections.** Some of the poetry in this chapter — William Blake's "London," William Butler Yeats's "The Second Coming," Matthew Arnold's "Dover Beach," Seamus Heaney's "Bogland," and Terrance Hayes's "Pseudacris Crucifer," for example — convey serious criticism of society and politics. Write an essay in which you examine the poets' positions and evaluate their arguments in light of today's world.
8. **Connections.** The plots of both *Frankenstein* and "A Good Man Is Hard to Find" involve travel. Consider both texts, along with other works you've read, and write an essay in which you analyze the role of travel. Be sure to address the reasons you think the subject lends itself to a study of human behavior.
9. **Creative Writing.** Many of the works in this chapter concern a clash between cultures. Try writing your own story about a culture clash. You might use your family background or the diversity in your home or community as a starting point.

AP® English Literature Practice Exam

Section 1 / Multiple-Choice

Questions 1–11 refer to the passage.

The following passage is excerpted from Helena María Viramontes's "The Moths" (p. 958), a short story first published in 1985.

I was fourteen years old when Abuelita requested my help. And it seemed only fair. Abuelita had pulled me through the rages of scarlet fever by placing, removing and replacing potato slices on the temples of my forehead; she had seen me through several whippings, an arm broken by a dare jump off Tío Enrique's toolshed, puberty, and my first lie. Really, I told Amá, it was only fair.

Not that I was her favorite granddaughter or anything special. I wasn't even pretty or nice like my older sisters and I just couldn't do the girl things they could do. My hands were too big to handle the fineries of crocheting or embroidery and I always pricked my fingers or knotted my colored threads time and time again while my sisters laughed and called me bull hands with their cute waterlike voices. So I began keeping a piece of jagged brick in my sock to bash my sisters or anyone who called me bull hands. Once, while we all sat in the bedroom, I hit Teresa on the forehead, right above her eyebrow and she ran to Amá with her mouth open, her hand over her eye while blood seeped between her fingers. I was used to the whippings by then.

I wasn't respectful either. I even went so far as to doubt the power of Abuelita's slices, the slices she said absorbed my fever. "You're still alive, aren't you?" Abuelita snapped back, her pasty gray eye beaming at me and burning holes in my suspicions. Regretful that I had let secret questions drop out of my mouth, I couldn't look into her eyes. My hands began to fan out, grow like a liar's nose until they hung by my side like low weights. Abuelita made a balm out of dried moth wings and Vicks and rubbed my hands, shaped them back to size and it was the strangest feeling. Like bones melting. Like sun shining through the darkness of your eyelids. I didn't mind helping Abuelita after that, so Amá would always send me over to her.

In the early afternoon Amá would push her hair back, hand me my sweater and shoes, and tell me to go to Mama Luna's. This was to avoid another fight and another whipping, I knew. I would deliver one last direct shot on Marisela's arm and jump out of our house, the slam of the screen door burying her cries of anger, and I'd gladly go help Abuelita plant her wild lilies or jasmine or heliotrope or cilantro or hierbabuena[1] in red Hills Brothers coffee cans. Abuelita would wait for me at the top step of her porch holding a hammer and nail and empty coffee cans.

[1] Also yerba buena, or "good herb," a plant in the mint family that is steeped to make a tea-like beverage. — Eds.

1. The narrator's response to her grandmother's request for "help" (par. 1) is best understood as

a. accepting

b. confused

c. excited

d. perturbed

e. surprised

2. It can be inferred from the excerpt that the narrator

a. benefited from Abuelita's medical training

b. blamed Abuelita for her childhood problems

c. wished she had done more for Abuelita

d. appreciated Abuelita's efforts even when she was a teenager

e. recognized the value of Abuelita once she became an adult

3. The reference to the narrator's "bull hands" (par. 2) emphasizes her

a. aggressive temper

b. hatred for her family

c. lack of dexterity

d. physical deftness

e. troubled childhood

4. Paragraph 1 primarily serves to

a. summarize the narrator's conversation with Amá

b. catalog the highlights of the narrator's life

c. question Abuelita's impact on the narrator

d. lament the narrator's difficult childhood

e. provide a rationale for the narrator's decision

5. The narrator's reference to her sisters in paragraph 2 conveys her

a. desire to lash out at them

b. jovial relationship with them

c. begrudging respect for their femininity

d. indifference toward their comments

e. pride in her own manners

6. "Abuelita's slices" (par. 3) can be interpreted as symbols of her

a. compulsion to intervene in her family's lives

b. anger at the end of her life

c. adherence to bygone traditions

d. wish to protect her unhappy granddaughter

e. trepidation about her own future

7. The narrator refers to her sisters' "waterlike voices" (par. 2) to mock their

a. bitterness

b. raspiness

c. enviousness

d. sweetness

e. harshness

8. The tone of the expression "I was used to the whippings by then" (par. 2) conveys the narrator's

a. acceptance of the repercussions of her actions

b. sadness at the way she is treated by her family

c. awareness of the hardships of everyday life

d. regret at her infantile and violent behavior

e. whimsy while recollecting her childhood

9. The narrator perceives her "doubt" in paragraph 3 as emblematic of her

a. rebellious attitude

b. empirical nature

c. progressive ideas

d. repressed emotions

e. deliberate playfulness

10. Abuelita's balm symbolizes her

a. knowledge of witchcraft

b. desire to purify her granddaughter

c. ignorance of her granddaughter's antagonism

d. love and dedication toward the narrator

e. ability to protect her community

11. In paragraph 3, the focus on eyes is symbolic of the narrator's

a. fear of Abuelita's growing rage

b. understanding of Abuelita's perspective on her sisters' flaws

c. unwillingness to see her own faults

d. growing realization that Abuelita loves and accepts her

e. tendency to criticize every family member

Questions 12–22 refer to the passage.

The following is Ben Jonson's "On My First Son" (p. 984), a poem first published in 1616.

Farewell, thou child of my right hand,[1] and joy;
My sin was too much hope of thee, loved boy:
Seven years thou wert lent to me, and I thee pay,
Exacted by thy fate, on the just day.
O could I lose all father now! For why
Will man lament the state he should envy,
To have so soon 'scaped world's and flesh's rage,
And, if no other misery, yet age?
Rest in soft peace, and asked, say, "Here doth lie
Ben Jonson his best piece of poetry."
For whose sake henceforth all his vows be such
As what he loves may never like too much.

[1] Benjamin means "son of my right hand" in Hebrew. — Eds.

12. The poem's speaker directly addresses
- a. God
- b. his wife
- c. his child
- d. an unidentified audience
- e. any grieving parent

13. In line 2, the speaker acknowledges his
- a. transgressions
- b. affection
- c. fears
- d. joys
- e. doubts

14. The language of the metaphor in lines 3–4 primarily expresses the speaker's relationship to his son in terms of a(n)
- a. business transaction
- b. religious covenant
- c. historical feat
- d. political treaty
- e. astrological prediction

15. The question in lines 5–8 primarily asks why
- a. the speaker's son has died so young
- b. anyone should grieve someone's ascent to heaven
- c. people wish they had a different life
- d. rulers seek to increase the size of their empire
- e. some choose to live abroad after experiencing a loss

16. Which word best captures the speaker's view of life on earth?
- a. joy (l. 1)
- b. just (l. 4)
- c. rage (l. 7)
- d. peace (l. 9)
- e. loves (l. 12)

17. The speaker figuratively compares his son to
- a. sin (l. 2)
- b. fate (l. 4)
- c. misery (l. 8)
- d. poetry (l. 10)
- e. vows (l. 11)

18. Which of the following lines reiterates the theme of the line "O could I lose all father now" (l. 5)?

a. "My sin was too much hope of thee." (l. 2)

b. "Seven years thou wert lent to me." (l. 3)

c. "For why / Will man lament the state he should envy." (ll. 5–6)

d. " 'Here doth lie / Ben Jonson his best piece of poetry.' " (ll. 9–10)

e. "For whose sake henceforth all his vows be such / As what he loves may never like too much." (ll. 11–12)

19. The phrase "the just day" (l. 4) is best interpreted to mean

a. Judgment Day

b. time chosen by the speaker

c. fair and precise moment

d. beginning of a new day

e. day the speaker's son was born

20. The interjection "O" (l. 5) conveys the speaker's

a. anger

b. confusion

c. grief

d. realization

e. surprise

21. In the final heroic couplet, the speaker vows to

a. never love someone again

b. always love the memory of his son

c. temper the extent of his love

d. keep his feelings concealed

e. never focus on how others feel

22. The overall tone of this poem is best described as

a. composed

b. incensed

c. grateful

d. resentful

e. sorrowful

Questions 23–33 refer to the passage.

The following passage is excerpted from Tillie Olsen's "I Stand Here Ironing" (p. 950), a short story first published in 1961.

And when is there time to remember, to sift, to weigh, to estimate, to total? I will start and there will be an interruption and I will have to gather it all together again. Or I will become engulfed with all I did or did not do, with what should have been and what cannot be helped.

She was a beautiful baby. The first and only one of our five that was beautiful at birth. You do not guess how new and uneasy her tenancy in her now-loveliness. You did not know her all those years she was thought homely, or see her poring over her baby pictures, making me tell her over and over how beautiful she had been — and would be, I would tell her — and was now, to the seeing eye. But the seeing eyes were few or nonexistent. Including mine.

I nursed her. They feel that's important nowadays, I nursed all the children, but with her, with all the fierce rigidity of first motherhood, I did like the books then said. Though her cries battered me to trembling and my breasts ached with swollenness, I waited till the clock decreed.

Why do I put that first? I do not even know if it matters, or if it explains anything.

She was a beautiful baby. She blew shining bubbles of sound. She loved motion, loved light, loved color and music and textures. She would lie on the floor in her blue overalls patting the surface so hard in ecstasy her hands and feet would blur. She was a miracle to me, but when she was eight months old I had to leave her daytimes with the woman downstairs to whom she was no miracle at all, for I worked or looked for work and for Emily's father, who "could no longer endure" (he wrote in his good-bye note) "sharing want with us."

I was nineteen. It was the pre-relief, pre-WPA world of the depression. I would start running as soon as I got off the streetcar, running up the stairs, the place smelling sour, and awake or asleep to startle awake, when she saw me she would break into a clogged weeping that could not be comforted, a weeping I can hear yet.

After a while I found a job hashing at night so I could be with her days, and it was better. But it came to where I had to bring her to his family and leave her.

It took a long time to raise the money for her fare back. Then she got chicken pox and I had to wait longer. When she finally came, I hardly knew her, walking quick and nervous like her father, looking like her father, thin, and dressed in a shoddy red that yellowed her skin and glared at the pockmarks. All the baby loveliness gone.

She was two. Old enough for nursery school they said, and I did not know then what I know now — the fatigue of the long day, and the lacerations of group life in the kinds of nurseries that are only parking places for children.

Except that it would have made no difference 10
if I had known. It was the only place there was. It was the only way we could be together, the only way I could hold a job.

And even without knowing, I knew. I knew the teacher that was evil because all these years it has curdled into my memory, the little boy hunched in the corner, her rasp, "why aren't you outside, because Alvin hits you? that's no reason, go out, scaredy." I knew Emily hated it even if she did not clutch and implore "don't go Mommy" like the other children, mornings.

23. Which of the following statements best conveys what the narrator means in context when she references the time it takes "to remember, to sift, to weigh, to estimate, to total" (par. 1)?

a. The narrator is evaluating her daughter's shortcomings and accomplishments.

b. The narrator's decisions and actions as a mother can be objectively measured.

c. People evaluate each other's worthiness based on their accomplishments.

d. The narrator is considering the value of the sacrifices she made for Emily.

e. We should all take stock of our contributions to assess our role in society.

24. "You" (par. 5) most likely refers to

a. the reader

b. a childhood friend of Emily's

c. Emily's father

d. someone who barely knows Emily

e. Emily's nursery school teacher

25. The repetition of "She was a beautiful baby" in paragraphs 2 and 5 can be interpreted to emphasize all of the following EXCEPT

a. the narrator's disappointment in herself for later disliking Emily's looks

b. the contrast between Emily's appearance as a baby and later in life

c. the suggestion of the kind of physical toll Emily's early years had on her

d. the preoccupation Emily eventually develops with her appearance

e. the effect Emily's beauty had even on friends, neighbors, and caregivers

26. Within which paragraph does the narrator's tone shift?

a. paragraph 4

b. paragraph 6

c. paragraph 8

d. paragraph 9

e. paragraph 10

27. The phrase "She was a miracle to me" (par. 8) is best interpreted to mean that the baby

a. was unwanted by the narrator

b. was an unplanned interruption to her mother's life

c. had abilities that surprised those who met her

d. seemed unique and extraordinary to her mother

e. saved her parents' failing marriage

28. The phrase "sharing want" (par. 8) is best interpreted to mean

a. living together in poverty

b. having the same wishes

c. being forced to share possessions

d. desiring an adulterous affair

e. hoping that a business will become profitable

29. Why does the narrator include the statement "It was the pre-relief, pre-WPA world of the depression" (par. 9)?

a. To explain why she was unhappy

b. To rationalize why Emily cried so frequently

c. To indicate why she had to find a job

d. To elucidate the reference to the streetcar

e. To prove that she is not to blame for Emily's problems

30. The sentence that begins "I would start running" (par. 9) characterizes the narrator as

a. agitated and distressed

b. harried and sorrowful

c. panicky and horrified

d. nervous and fidgety

e. fervent and alarmed

31. In context, the phrase "the lacerations of group life" in paragraph 12 most likely indicates the nursery school was a(n)

a. strict environment with appropriate rules

b. overcrowded but well-staffed option for parents

c. emotionally unpleasant, scary place for children

d. place where children were punished physically

e. environment in which Emily made close friends

32. Throughout the passage, the narrator can best be described as

a. ruminating on all of her shortcomings as a single parent

b. alternating between self-reproach and pragmatic acceptance

c. reminiscing about the highlights of Emily's early childhood

d. focusing on why she abandoned her daughter as a baby

e. commenting on the lack of options for child care at the time

33. All of the following suggest that the narrator is thinking about "what should have been and what cannot be helped" (par. 4) EXCEPT

a. "[W]hen she was eight months old I had to leave her daytimes with the woman downstairs to whom she was no miracle at all, for I worked or looked for work" (par. 5)

b. "After a while I found a job hashing at night so I could be with her days, and it was better" (par. 10)

c. "But it came to where I had to bring her to his family and leave her" (par. 10)

d. "Except that it would have made no difference if I had known" (par. 13)

e. "I knew Emily hated it even if she did not clutch and implore 'don't go Mommy' like the other children, mornings" (par. 14)

Questions 34–44 refer to the passage.

The following passage is Molly Rose Quinn's "Dolorosa" (p. 307), a poem first published in 2013.

(The Chapel at St. Mary's School for Girls)

where the pillar falls at the edge of morning the teachers
beg us to tug down our skirts they offer their palms
for our gumballs and your god is here to say that beauty
is easy like cutting teeth and your legs and your legs
and yours and I in the pew wish to scrape down
to nothing cuff myself kneel better and what could be
worthier hair voice and loudly I beg for ascendancy
dear classmates your legs in neat rows pray as you do
with fists up and the sun in here bare pray for safety
the teen saint she is the girl to win it all for I beg my
mariology[1] as she sets the way that girl she never once
begged for sparing she begged for death like wine
she begged the best she supplicated she died this dying
begs for me I give it such pleasure and legs and the pew
and the alb[2] and the bread and all other objects beg to be
candles when you are a candle you can beg to be lit
each of you in the pew you beg to be lit I'll never shine
bigger as we know teenagers beg to be begged and we do
you girls you begged me to hold you begged me to take
what I took you beg bigger and better and for that
you'll be queens the chimes chime and bells bell
and dear god I know I can be the greatest girl ever
by anointing all alone and being loved the very best
and she says what is so good about anger god killed
my son for himself I suppose and this halo it's nothing
I asked for and of course she'll be lying and your legs
and your legs and yours tanned and the best thing all year.

[1] The study of the Virgin Mary. — Eds.

[2] A white garment worn by leaders in the several different church denominations; in this case the author is referencing the Episcopal church. — Eds.

34. The poem's structure suggests

a. the sound of multiple students arguing

b. a dialogue between teachers and students

c. the jumbled thoughts in the speaker's mind

d. a chorus of voices singing a hymn

e. a religious leader delivering a sermon

35. Throughout the poem, the words "beg" and "begged" suggest all of the following EXCEPT

a. displays of devotion

b. requests for charity

c. appeals to modesty

d. expressions of desires

e. acts of desperation

36. In context, "like cutting teeth" (l. 4) most likely refers to a(n)

a. hard, painful experience
b. ability that comes naturally
c. goal that requires sacrifice
d. unearned accolade
e. simple, repetitive process

37. Which of the following lines undermines the speaker's assertion, "I in the pew wish to scrape down / to nothing" (ll. 5–6)?

a. "loudly I beg for ascendancy" (l. 7)
b. "I beg my / mariology" (ll. 10–11)
c. "I give it such pleasure" (l. 14)
d. "I'll never shine / bigger" (ll. 17–18)
e. "it's nothing / I asked for" (ll. 25–26)

38. One effect of the shift in the speaker's focus in line 8 is to

a. emphasize the condescension she feels toward her classmates
b. imagine her classmates from the perspective of the school's teachers
c. demonstrate why she envies her classmates' religious devotion
d. mock her classmates' behavior as less sophisticated than her own
e. juxtapose her self-awareness with her enchantment with her classmates

39. The speaker's statement "she begged the best" (l. 13) can be inferred to be a(n)

a. comparison between the Virgin Mary and the school girls
b. claim that the Virgin Mary attracts exceptional followers
c. assertion that the Virgin Mary had high expectations
d. suggestion that the speaker has seen visions of the Virgin Mary
e. belief that the Virgin Mary asked to be queen

40. The speaker's tone can be described as

a. nonchalant but unsettling
b. proud but insecure
c. pleasant but frustrated
d. stubborn but inspirational
e. rebellious but weary

41. The speaker mentions "the pew / and the alb and the bread" (ll. 14–15) to

a. illustrate the insignificance of everyday items in a church
b. emphasize her boredom during the religious service
c. highlight the symbolism of the religious objects around her
d. introduce people unfamiliar with Christian symbolism to such objects
e. draw a comparison between the items and the schoolgirls

42. The phrase "beg to be lit" (l. 16) can be interpreted as a desire to do all of the following EXCEPT

a. burn and shine like a candle
b. embody a spiritual significance
c. provide literal and figurative light
d. serve a singular and finite purpose
e. transcend one's common existence

43. In line 24, "she says what is so good about anger" references

a. the speaker's internalized response to her own feelings
b. the Virgin Mary's rejection of the speaker's prayers
c. a response to "I know I can be the greatest girl ever" (l. 22)
d. the Virgin Mary's acknowledgment of the speaker's anger
e. a response to "she is the girl to win it all for" (l. 10)

44. Taken as a whole, the poem can best be described as an exploration of

a. the conflicting messages society sends teenage girls
b. the relevance of the Virgin Mary to Christian schoolgirls
c. the challenges of conformity and religious devotion
d. the speaker's confidence in what and whom she values
e. the unique experiences of Christian schoolgirls

Questions 45–55 refer to the passage.

The following passage is excerpted from Nathaniel Hawthorne's "Young Goodman Brown" (p. 216), a short story first published in 1835.

Young Goodman Brown came forth at sunset into the street of Salem village; but put his head back, after crossing the threshold, to exchange a parting kiss with his young wife. And Faith, as the wife was aptly named, thrust her own pretty head into the street, letting the wind play with the pink ribbons of her cap while she called to Goodman Brown.

"Dearest heart," whispered she, softly and rather sadly, when her lips were close to his ear, "prithee put off your journey until sunrise and sleep in your own bed to-night. A lone woman is troubled with such dreams and such thoughts that she's afeard of herself sometimes. Pray tarry with me this night, dear husband, of all nights in the year."

"My love and my Faith," replied young Goodman Brown, "of all nights in the year, this one night must I tarry away from thee. My journey, as thou callest it, forth and back again, must needs be done 'twixt now and sunrise. What, my sweet, pretty wife, dost thou doubt me already, and we but three months married?"

"Then God bless you!" said Faith, with the pink ribbons; "and may you find all well when you come back."

"Amen!" cried Goodman Brown. "Say thy prayers, dear Faith, and go to bed at dusk, and no harm will come to thee."

So they parted; and the young man pursued his way until, being about to turn the corner by the meeting-house, he looked back and saw the head of Faith still peeping after him with a melancholy air, in spite of her pink ribbons.

"Poor little Faith!" thought he, for his heart smote him. "What a wretch am I to leave her on such an errand! She talks of dreams, too. Methought as she spoke there was trouble in her face, as if a dream had warned her what work is to be done to-night. But no, no; 't would kill her to think it. Well, she's a blessed angel on earth; and after this one night I'll cling to her skirts and follow her to heaven."

With this excellent resolve for the future, Goodman Brown felt himself justified in making more haste on his present evil purpose. He had taken a dreary road, darkened by all the gloomiest trees of the forest, which barely stood aside to let the narrow path creep through, and closed immediately behind. It was all as lonely as could be; and there is this peculiarity in such a solitude, that the traveler knows not who may be concealed by the innumerable trunks and the thick boughs overhead; so that with lonely footsteps he may yet be passing through an unseen multitude.

"There may be a devilish Indian behind every tree," said Goodman Brown to himself; and he glanced fearfully behind him as he added, "What if the devil himself should be at my very elbow!"

His head being turned back, he passed a crook of the road, and, looking forward again, beheld the figure of a man, in grave and decent attire, seated at the foot of an old tree. He arose at Goodman Brown's approach and walked onward side by side with him.

"You are late, Goodman Brown," said he. "The clock of the Old South was striking as I came through Boston, and that is full fifteen minutes agone."

"Faith kept me back a while," replied the young man, with a tremor in his voice, caused by the sudden appearance of his companion, though not wholly unexpected.

It was now deep dusk in the forest, and deepest in that part of it where these two were journeying. As nearly as could be discerned, the second traveller was about fifty years old, apparently in the same rank of life as Goodman Brown, and bearing a considerable resemblance to him, though perhaps more in expression than features. Still they might have been taken for father and son. And yet, though the elder person was as simply clad as the younger, and as simple in manner too, he had an indescribable air of one who knew the world, and who would not have felt abashed at the governor's dinner table or in King William's court, were it possible that his affairs should call him thither. But the only thing about him that could be fixed upon as remarkable was his staff, which bore the likeness of a great black snake, so curiously wrought that it might almost be seen to twist and wriggle itself like a living serpent. This, of course, must have been an ocular deception, assisted by the uncertain light.

45. The narrator's perspective throughout the passage might best be described as that of

a. a resident of Salem village using first-person narrative perspective

b. a third-person narrator conveying Goodman Brown's perspective

c. a third-person narrator conveying multiple characters' perspectives

d. a third-person narrator conveying Faith's perspective

e. Goodman Brown using first-person narrative perspective

46. Which of the following statements best conveys the effect of the final sentence in paragraph 3 ("What, my sweet, pretty wife . . . we but three months married!")?

a. Faith believes in the innocence of her husband's errand.

b. Faith feels even more justified in doubting her husband.

c. Readers understand Goodman Brown can be trusted.

d. Goodman Brown's response shows him to be manipulative.

e. Goodman Brown establishes himself as a devoted husband.

47. In paragraphs 6–8, Goodman Brown can best be described as

a. cautious but determined

b. resolute but rash

c. tempted but resisting

d. doomed but defiant

e. unseemly but indecorous

48. Paragraph 7 suggests Goodman Brown wonders whether his wife is

a. trepidatious because of premonitions of evil

b. fortunate because she remains safe at home

c. apoplectic because she suspects infidelity

d. penitent because she is responsible for his safety

e. reluctant because she cannot bear the truth

49. The function of the adjectives "dreary," "darkened," and "gloomiest" in paragraph 8 is primarily to

a. contrast the forest with the Browns' home

b. develop the irony of the setting

c. contradict Goodman Brown's jovial nature

d. dissuade Goodman Brown from continuing

e. establish a foreboding atmosphere

50. Throughout the excerpt, Faith's pink ribbons can best be understood as symbols of her

a. normally ebullient nature

b. strict religious devotion

c. temporary dejected air

d. unusually keen perceptions

e. ironic ongoing doubt

51. The juxtaposition in paragraph 8 of an atmosphere "as lonely as could be" with a place in which one "may yet be passing through an unseen multitude" is most likely to emphasize the

a. lack of familiarity Goodman Brown has with the forest

b. many people who had previously taken this dangerous route

c. ironic reality that people can feel lonely in large crowds

d. unseen dangers into which Goodman Brown is walking

e. reality that we can never be "in such a solitude" (par. 8)

52. The interaction between Goodman Brown and the second traveler in paragraphs 11 and 12 ("'You are late, Goodman Brown' . . . though not wholly unexpected") conveys all of the following EXCEPT

a. an unequal power dynamic between the men

b. the defiance Goodman Brown wants to show

c. the uneasiness Goodman Brown experiences

d. the men's previous familiarity with each other

e. a desire of Goodman Brown to be forgiven

53. The narrator's tone in paragraph 13 ("It was now deep dusk . . . assisted by the uncertain light") is best described as

a. disturbed

b. inquisitive

c. uninterested

d. cautious

e. fascinated

54. In paragraph 13, "ocular deception" suggests the appearance of the second traveler's staff was a(n)

a. type of weapon

b. glowing stick

c. perfect replica

d. snake in actuality

e. optical illusion

55. The second traveler's appearance and demeanor differ from Goodman Brown's because the second traveler appears surprisingly

a. worldly

b. indifferent

c. extravagant

d. commonplace

e. innocent

Poetry Analysis (Question 1)

In Ada Limón's "The Raincoat," published in 2018, the speaker contemplates the protective role that parents play in their children's lives. Read the poem carefully. Then, in a well-written essay, analyze how Limón uses literary elements and techniques to develop the speaker's understanding of her complex relationship with her mother.

In your response you should do the following:

- Respond to the prompt with a thesis that presents a defensible interpretation.
- Select and use evidence to support the line of reasoning.
- Explain how the evidence supports the line of reasoning.
- Use appropriate grammar and punctuation in communicating the argument.

When the doctor suggested surgery
and a brace for all my youngest years,
my parents scrambled to take me
to massage therapy, deep tissue work,
osteopathy, and soon my crooked spine
unspooled a bit, I could breathe again,
and move more in a body unclouded
by pain. My mom would tell me to sing
songs to her the whole forty-five minute
drive to Middle Two Rock Road and forty-
five minutes back from physical therapy.
She'd say, even my voice sounded unfettered
by my spine afterward. So I sang and sang,
because I thought she liked it. I never
asked her what she gave up to drive me,
or how her day was before this chore. Today,
at her age, I was driving myself home from yet
another spine appointment, singing along
to some maudlin but solid song on the radio,
and I saw a mom take her raincoat off
and give it to her young daughter when
a storm took over the afternoon. My god,
I thought, my whole life I've been under her
raincoat thinking it was somehow a marvel
that I never got wet. ■

Prose Fiction Analysis (Question 2)

The following excerpt is from Paul Laurence Dunbar's novel *The Sport of the Gods*, published in 1902. In this passage, the narrator describes the first reactions Mrs. Hamilton and her children Joe and Kit have upon their move to New York City. Read the passage carefully. Then, in a well-written essay, analyze how Dunbar uses literary elements and techniques to portray the family's complex responses to their new environment.

In your response you should do the following:

- Respond to the prompt with a thesis that presents a defensible interpretation.
- Select and use evidence to support the line of reasoning.
- Explain how the evidence supports the line of reasoning.
- Use appropriate grammar and punctuation in communicating the argument.

With the first pause in the rush that they had experienced since starting away from home, Mrs. Hamilton began to have time for reflection, and their condition seemed to her much better as it was. Of course, it was hard to be away from home and among strangers, but the arrangement had this advantage, — that no one knew them or could taunt them with their past trouble. She was not sure that she was going to like New York. It had a great name and was really a great place, but the very bigness of it frightened her and made her feel alone, for she knew that there could not be so many people together without a deal of wickedness. She did not argue the complement of this, that the amount of good would also be increased, but this was because to her evil was the very present factor in her life.

Joe and Kit were differently affected by what they saw about them. The boy was wild with enthusiasm and with a desire to be a part of all that the metropolis meant. In the evening he saw the young fellows passing by dressed in their spruce clothes, and he wondered with a sort of envy where they could be going. Back home there had been no place much worth going to, except church and one or two people's houses. But these young fellows seemed to show by their manners that they were neither going to church nor a family visiting. In the moment that he recognized this, a revelation came to him, — the knowledge that his horizon had been very narrow, and he felt angry that it was so. Why should those fellows be different from him? Why should they walk the streets so knowingly, so independently, when he knew not whither to turn his steps? Well, he was in New York, and now he would learn. Some day some greenhorn from the South should stand at a window and look out envying him, as he passed, red-cravated, patent-leathered, intent on some goal. Was it not better, after all, that circumstances had forced them thither? Had it not been so, they might all have stayed home and stagnated. Well, thought he, it's an ill wind that blows nobody good, and somehow, with a guilty under-thought, he forgot to feel the natural pity for his father, toiling guiltless in the prison of his native State.

Whom the Gods wish to destroy they first make mad. The first sign of the demoralization of the provincial who comes to New York is his pride at his insensibility to certain impressions which used to influence him at home. First, he begins to scoff, and there is no truth in his views nor depth in his laugh. But by and by, from mere pretending, it becomes real. He grows callous. After that he goes to the devil very cheerfully.

No such radical emotions, however, troubled Kit's mind. She too stood at the windows and looked down into the street. There was a sort of complacent calm in the manner in which she viewed the girls' hats and dresses. Many of them were really pretty, she told herself, but for the most part they were not better than what she had had down home. There was a sound quality in the girl's make-up that helped her to see through the glamour of mere place and recognize worth for itself. Or it may have been the critical faculty, which is prominent in most women, that kept her from thinking a five-cent cheese-cloth any better in New York than it was at home. She had a certain self-respect which made her value herself and her own traditions higher than her brother did his.

Literary Argument (Question 3)

In many works of literature, characters believe that attaining a particular goal will ensure their happiness and satisfaction. Once attained, however, even the most sought-after goal can sometimes produce unintended consequences. These repercussions might challenge the merits of the original goal, teach characters valuable lessons, or even lead characters to establish a new goal.

Either from your own reading or from the list that follows, choose a character who must contend with unexpected consequences after attaining a sought-after goal. Then, in a well-written essay, analyze how struggling with this unexpected consequence contributes to an interpretation of the work as a whole. Do not merely summarize the plot.

In your response you should do the following:

- Respond to the prompt with a thesis that presents a defensible interpretation.
- Provide evidence to support the line of reasoning.
- Explain how the evidence supports the line of reasoning.
- Use appropriate grammar and punctuation in communicating the argument.

- Rudolfo Anaya, *Bless Me, Ultima*
- Charlotte Brontë, *Jane Eyre*
- Emily Brontë, *Wuthering Heights*
- Kate Chopin, *The Awakening*
- Charles Dickens, *Great Expectations*
- Ralph Ellison, *Invisible Man*
- William Faulkner, *Light in August*
- F. Scott Fitzgerald, *The Great Gatsby*
- Kaitlyn Greenidge, *Libertie*
- Zora Neale Hurston, *Their Eyes Were Watching God*
- Kazuo Ishiguro, *Never Let Me Go*
- Nella Larsen, *Passing* (p. 487)
- Arthur Miller, *Death of a Salesman*
- Toni Morrison, *Song of Solomon*
- Celeste Ng, *Little Fires Everywhere*
- Viet Thanh Nguyen, *The Sympathizer*
- Tommy Orange, *There There*
- William Shakespeare, *Hamlet* (p. 555)
- Mary Shelley, *Frankenstein* (p. 1093)
- Leslie Marmon Silko, *Ceremony*
- August Wilson, *Fences* (p. 1047)

Glossary / Glosario

English	Español
A	
abstract An abstract term is a general term that refers to a broad concept, as opposed to a term that refers to a specific, particular thing (e.g., *personhood* as opposed to *Seamus Heaney*); opposite of **concrete.**	**abstracto** Un término abstracto describe un concepto amplio, en contraste con un término concreto, que se refiere a una cosa específica y particular (por ejemplo, *persona* en contraste con *Seamus Heaney*); opuesto de **concreto.**
act The major subunit into which the action of a play is divided. The number of acts in a play typically ranges between one and five, and acts are usually further divided into scenes.	**acto** Subunidad principal en la que se divide la acción de una obra. El número de actos de una obra suele oscilar entre uno y cinco. Los actos suelen dividirse a su vez en escenas.
allegory A literary work that portrays abstract ideas concretely. Characters in an allegory are frequently personifications of abstract ideas and are given names that refer to these ideas.	**alegoría** Obra literaria que representa ideas abstractas de forma concreta. Los personajes de una alegoría suelen ser personificaciones de ideas abstractas y reciben nombres que hacen referencia a estas ideas.
alliteration The repetition of the same initial consonant sounds in a sequence of words or syllables.	**aliteración** Repetición de los mismos sonidos consonantes iniciales en una secuencia de palabras o sílabas.
allusion A reference to another work of literature, a piece of art, a famous person or place, history, or current events.	**alusión** Referencia a otra obra literaria, a una obra de arte, a un personaje o lugar famoso, o a eventos históricos o actuales.
analogy In literature, a comparison between two things that helps explain or illustrate one or both of them.	**analogía** En literatura, una comparación entre dos cosas que ayuda a explicar o ilustrar una o ambas.
anapest See **meter.**	**anapesto** Véase **métrica.**
anaphora Repetition of an initial word or words to add emphasis.	**anáfora** Repetición de una palabra o palabras iniciales para añadir énfasis.
annotation The act of noting observations directly on a text, especially anything striking or confusing, in order to record ideas and impressions for later analysis.	**anotación** Acto de apuntar observaciones directamente sobre un texto, especialmente aquello que resulta llamativo o confuso, con el fin de registrar ideas e impresiones para su posterior análisis.
antagonist Character in a story or play who opposes the protagonist; while not necessarily an enemy, the antagonist creates or intensifies a conflict for the protagonist. An evil antagonist is a villain.	**antagonista** Personaje de una historia u obra de teatro que se opone al protagonista. Aunque no es necesariamente un enemigo, el antagonista crea o intensifica un conflicto para el protagonista. Un antagonista malvado es un villano.
antithesis Contradictory ideas that are juxtaposed, often using parallel grammatical construction.	**antítesis** Ideas contradictorias que se yuxtaponen, generalmente utilizando construcciones gramaticales paralelas.

apostrophe A direct address to an abstraction (such as time), a thing (the wind), an animal, or an imaginary or absent person.

apóstrofe Interpelación directa a una abstracción (como el tiempo), una cosa (el viento), un animal o una persona imaginaria o ausente.

archaic language Words that were once common but that are no longer used.

lenguaje arcaico Palabras que antes eran comunes pero que ya no se usan.

archetype A cultural symbol that has become universally understood and recognized.

arquetipo Símbolo cultural universalmente comprendido y reconocido.

ars poetica Literally, "the art of poetry"; a form of poetry written about poetry.

ars poetica Literalmente, "el arte de la poesía"; una forma de poesía escrita sobre la poesía.

assonance The repetition of vowel sounds in a sequence of words.

asonancia Repetición de sonidos vocálicos en una secuencia de palabras.

atmosphere The feeling created for the reader by a work of literature. Atmosphere can be generated by many things but especially by **style**, **tone**, and **setting**. Similar to **mood**.

atmósfera La sensación que crea una obra literaria en el lector. Hay muchos elementos que generan atmósfera, pero especialmente el **estilo**, **tono** y **ambientación**. Es similar al **estado de ánimo**.

B

ballad Dating from the late Middle Ages, the ballad, often passed down orally from generation to generation, was a sung poem that recounted a dramatic story.

balada Poema cantado que narra una historia dramática y que solía transmitirse oralmente de generación en generación.

Beat movement A movement of American writers in the 1950s who saw society as oppressively conformist. These writers rejected mainstream values, seeking ways to escape through drugs, various forms of spirituality, and sexual experimentation. The writers of the Beat generation, among them Allen Ginsberg and Jack Kerouac, celebrated freedom of expression and held generally antiestablishment views about politics. Their writing, likewise, rejected conventional norms of structure and diction, and their books prompted several notorious obscenity trials, which helped reshape censorship laws in the United States.

movimiento Beat Movimiento de escritores estadounidenses de la década de 1950 que consideraban que la sociedad era opresiva y conformista. Estos escritores rechazaban los valores dominantes y buscaban formas de escapar a través de las drogas, la espiritualidad en sus diversas formas y la experimentación sexual. Los escritores de la generación Beat, entre ellos Allen Ginsberg y Jack Kerouac, celebraban la libertad de expresión y tenían opiniones generalmente contrarias al sistema político. Sus escritos también rechazaban las normas convencionales de estructura y dicción, y sus libros dieron lugar a varios juicios por obscenidad que contribuyeron a modificar las leyes de censura en Estados Unidos.

bildungsroman A novel that explores the maturation of the protagonist, with the narrative usually moving the main character from childhood into adulthood. Also called a coming-of-age story.

bildungsroman Novela que explora la maduración del protagonista a través de una narración que suele trasladar al personaje principal de la infancia a la edad adulta. También se conoce como historia de crecimiento o maduración personal.

blank verse Unrhymed iambic pentameter, blank verse is the most commonly used verse form in English because it comes closest to natural patterns of speaking. See also **iambic pentameter**.

verso blanco Verso con métrica regular pero sin rima. En inglés el verso blanco suele usar una métrica de pentámetro yámbico. Es la forma de verso más utilizada en inglés porque se acerca más a los patrones naturales del habla. Véase también **pentámetro yámbico**.

C

cadence Quality of spoken text formed from combining the text's rhythm with the rise and fall in the inflection of the speaker's voice.

cadencia Cualidad del texto hablado que se forma a partir de la combinación del ritmo del texto con el ascenso y descenso de la inflexión de la voz del orador.

caesura A pause within a line of poetry, sometimes punctuated, sometimes not, often mirroring natural speech.

cesura Pausa dentro de una línea de poesía, a veces puntuada, a veces no, que suele reflejar el habla natural.

caricature A character with features or traits that are exaggerated so that the character seems ridiculous. The term is usually applied to graphic depictions but can also be applied to written depictions.

caricatura Un personaje con características o rasgos que se exageran para que el personaje parezca ridículo. El término se suele usar para representaciones gráficas, pero también se puede aplicar a representaciones escritas.

carpe diem A widespread literary theme meaning "seize the day" in Latin and found especially in lyric poetry, carpe diem encourages readers to enjoy the present and make the most of their short lives.

carpe diem Un tema literiario muy conocido que significa "aprovechar el día" en latín y que se suele encontrar en la poesía lírica. Carpe diem anima al lector a disfrutar del presente y a aprovechar al máximo su corta vida.

catharsis The moment of emotional release that occurs when the major conflict(s) of a plot resolve. See also **resolution**.

catarsis El momento de descarga emocional que ocurre cuando se resuelve(n) el/los conflicto(s) principal(es) de una trama. Véase también **resolución**.

character A person depicted in a narrative. While this term generally refers to human beings, it can also include animals or inanimate objects that are given human characteristics. Several more specific terms are used to refer to types of characters:

dynamic character Also known as a round character, a character who exhibits a range of emotions and who evolves over the course of the story.

flat character A character embodying only one or two traits and who lacks character development; a flat character is also called a static character. Often such characters exist only to provide background or adequate motivation for a protagonist's actions.

secondary character A supporting character; while not as prominent or central as a main character, he or she is still important to the events of a story or play.

stock character A type of flat character based on a stereotype; one who falls into an immediately recognizable category or type — such as the absentminded professor or the town drunk — and thus resists unique characterization. Stock characters can be artfully used for humor or satire.

caricatura Personaje con rasgos o características exageradas, llevadas al punto del ridículo. El término suele aplicarse a representaciones gráficas, pero también puede aplicarse a representaciones escritas.

personaje dinámico También conocido como personaje redondo, es un personaje que presenta una serie de emociones y que evoluciona a lo largo de la historia.

personaje plano Personaje que encarna sólo uno o dos rasgos y que carece de desarrollo; un personaje plano también se denomina personaje estático. Por lo general, estos personajes existen sólo para proporcionar un trasfondo o una motivación adecuada para las acciones del protagonista.

personaje secundario Personaje de apoyo que, aunque no es tan destacado o central como un personaje principal, sigue siendo importante para los acontecimientos de una historia u obra de teatro.

personaje tipo Personaje plano basado en un estereotipo que cae en una categoría fácilmente reconocible –como el profesor distraído o el borracho del pueblo— y que, por tanto, se resiste a una caracterización única. Los personajes tipo pueden ser utilizados para el humor o la sátira.

characterization The method by which the author builds, or reveals, a character; it can be direct or indirect. Indirect characterization means that an author shows rather than tells readers what a character is like through what the character says, does, or thinks, or what others say about the character. Direct characterization occurs when a narrator tells the reader who a character is by describing the background, motivation, temperament, or appearance of that character.

caracterización Método mediante el cual el autor construye, o revela, un personaje; puede ser directa o indirecta. En la caracterización indirecta, el autor muestra a los lectores cómo es un personaje a través de lo que éste dice, hace o piensa, o de lo que otros dicen sobre él. La caracterización directa se produce cuando un narrador le dice explícitamente al lector cómo es un personaje describiendo sus antecedentes, su motivación, su temperamento o su aspecto.

chorus In drama, especially classical Greek drama, the chorus refers to a group of participants in a play who deliver commentary on the play's action. The role of the chorus is no longer a regular feature of modern drama, although it has been employed in a few prominent works, such as T. S. Eliot's *Murder in the Cathedral.*

coro En el teatro, especialmente en el teatro griego clásico, el coro se refiere a un grupo de participantes en una obra que comentan la acción de la obra. El papel del coro ya no suele utilizarse en el teatro moderno, aunque se ha empleado en algunas obras destacadas, como *Asesinato en la catedral* de T. S. Eliot.

claim A claim states the argument's main idea or position in an analytical essay. A claim differs from a topic or subject in that a claim has to be arguable.

declaración Es la idea o postura principal del argumento en un ensayo analítico. Una declaración se diferencia de un tema o asunto en que la declaración tiene que poderse argumentar.

climax The point in a story when the conflict reaches its highest intensity.

clímax Punto de una historia en el que el conflicto alcanza su máxima intensidad.

closed form See **form**.

forma cerrada Véase **forma.**

colloquial language/colloquialism An expression or language construction characteristic of casual, informal speaking or writing.

lenguaje coloquial/coloquialismo Expresión o construcción lingüística característica del habla o la escritura casual e informal.

comedy Usually used to refer to a dramatic work that, in contrast to tragedy, has a light, amusing plot, features a happy ending, centers around ordinary people, and is written and performed in the vernacular.

comedia Obra dramática que, a diferencia de la tragedia, tiene una trama ligera y divertida, presenta un final feliz, se centra en personas normales y está escrita y representada en lengua vernácula.

comedy of manners A satiric dramatic form that lampoons social conventions.

comedia costumbrista Forma dramática satírica que ridiculiza las convenciones sociales.

coming-of-age story See **bildungsroman**.

historia de maduración personal Véase **bildungsroman**.

complex sentence See **sentence**.

oración compleja Véase **oración**.

compound sentence See **sentence**.

oración compuesta Véase **oración**.

compound-complex sentence See **sentence**.

oración compuesta-compleja Véase **oración**.

conceit A complex comparison developed through the juxtaposition or association of unexpected or paradoxical ideas. Poets sometimes use a conceit to illustrate the complex relationship between the speaker and the natural world. See also **metaphysical conceit**.

presunción Comparación compleja desarrollada mediante la yuxtaposición o asociación de ideas inesperadas o paradójicas. A veces, los poetas se sirven de una idea para ilustrar la compleja relación entre el hablante y el mundo natural. Véase también **presunción metafísica**.

concrete A concrete term is one that refers to a specific, particular thing, as opposed to a term that refers to a broad concept (e.g., *Seamus Heaney* as opposed to *personhood*); opposite of **abstract**.	**concreto** Un término concreto se refiere a una cosa específica, particular, en contraste con un término abstracto que se refiere a un concepto general (por ejemplo, *Seamus Heaney* en contraste con *persona*); opuesto de **abstracto**.
conflict The tension, opposition, or struggle that drives a plot. External conflict is the opposition or tension between two characters or forces. Internal conflict occurs within a character. Conflict usually arises between the protagonist and the antagonist in a story.	**conflicto** La tensión, oposición o lucha que impulsa una trama. El conflicto externo es la oposición o tensión entre dos personajes o fuerzas. El conflicto interno se produce dentro de un personaje. El conflicto suele surgir entre el protagonista y el antagonista de una historia.
connotation Meanings or associations readers have with a word or an item beyond its dictionary definition, or denotation. Connotations may reveal another layer of meaning, affect the tone, or suggest symbolic resonance in a work of literature.	**connotación** Significados o asociaciones de una palabra o un elemento más allá de su definición de diccionario, o denotación. Las connotaciones pueden revelar otra capa de significado, afectar al tono o sugerir una resonancia simbólica en una obra literaria.
consonance Identical consonant sounds in nearby words. See also **rhyme**.	**consonancia** Sonidos consonantes idénticos en palabras cercanas. Véase también **rima**.
couplet See **stanza**.	**pareado** Ver **estrofa**.
critical lenses Different ways to approach interpreting a work of literature, also known as critical perspectives. Specific types of lenses discussed in this book include the following: **cultural lens** An interpretation of a text that examines how different races and ethnicities, social and economic class distinctions, and political ideologies influence the creation and interpretation of literature. Although the perspective of cultural criticism covers a broad landscape, it focuses on how dominant groups have silenced, devalued, misrepresented, or even demonized marginalized ones. **formalist lens** Also called New Criticism. An interpretation of a text that treats it as an independent and self-sufficient entity, focusing on style features such as diction, structure, figurative language, and syntax. **gendered lens** An interpretation of a text that explores its treatment of gender stereotypes, social mores and values based on gender, and the overall representation of the genders. **psychological lens** An interpretation of a text that considers the behavior and motivations of characters, exploring how both conscious and unconscious drives and desires influence their actions.	**lentes críticas** Distintas formas de abordar la interpretación de una obra literaria, también conocidas como perspectivas críticas. Los tipos específicos de lentes que se analizan en este libro son los siguientes: **lente cultural** Interpretación de un texto que estudia cómo las diferentes razas y etnias, distinciones de clase social y económica e ideologías políticas influyen en la creación e interpretación de la literatura. Aunque la perspectiva de la crítica cultural abarca un amplio panorama, se enfoca en cómo los grupos dominantes han silenciado, devaluado, tergiversado o incluso satanizado a los grupos marginados. **lente formalista** También llamada "Nueva crítica". Interpretación de un texto que lo aborda como una entidad independiente y autosuficiente, enfocándose en rasgos de estilo como la dicción, la estructura, el lenguaje figurado y la sintaxis. **lente de género** Interpretación de un texto que explora su tratamiento de representación de los géneros, los estereotipos de género, las costumbres sociales y los valores basados en el género. **lente psicológica** Interpretación de un texto que analiza el comportamiento y las motivaciones de los personajes, explorando cómo influyen en sus acciones los impulsos y deseo.

cultural lens See **critical lenses.**	**lente cultural** Véase **lentes críticas.**
cumulative sentence See **sentence.**	**oración acumulativa** Véase **oración.**

D

dactyl See **meter.**	**dáctilo** Véase **métrica.**
denotation The literal definition of a word, often referred to as the "dictionary definition."	**denotación** La definición literal de una palabra, también conocida como "definición del diccionario".
denouement Pronounced *day-noo-moh*, this literally means "untying the knot"; in this phase of a plot, the conflict has been resolved and balance is restored to the world of the story.	**desenlace** Fase de una trama en la que el conflicto se ha resuelto y se restablece el equilibrio en el mundo de la historia.
dialect Dialogue or narration written to simulate regional or cultural speech patterns.	**dialecto** Diálogo o narración escrita para simular patrones de habla regionales o culturales.
dialogue The written depiction of conversation between characters.	**diálogo** La representación escrita de una conversación entre los personajes.
diction A writer's choice of words. In addition to choosing words with precise denotations and connotations, an author must choose whether to use words that are abstract or concrete, formal or informal, or literal or figurative. See also **colloquial language.**	**dicción** Forma de emplear las palabras. Además de elegir palabras con denotaciones y connotaciones precisas, un autor debe elegir si utiliza palabras abstractas o concretas, formales o informales, literales o figurativas. Véase también **lenguaje coloquial.**
direct characterization See **characterization.**	**caracterización directa** Véase **caracterización.**
dramatic irony See **irony, dramatic.**	**ironía dramática** Véase **ironía dramática.**
dramatic monologue A poem written in the form of a speech of an individual character; it usually creates a single scene that reveals a sense of the speaker's history and provides psychological insight into the speaker's character.	**monólogo dramático** Poema escrito en forma de discurso de un personaje individual; suele crear una escena que revela la historia del orador y proporciona una visión psicológica de su personaje.
dynamic character See **character.**	**personaje dinámico** Véase **personaje.**

E

ekphrastic poetry A form of poetry that comments on a work of art in another genre, such as a painting or a piece of music.	**poesía ecfrástica** Forma de poesía que comenta una obra de arte de otro género, como una pintura o una pieza musical.
elegy A contemplative poem on death and mortality, often written for someone who has died.	**elegía** Poema contemplativo que aborda la muerte y la mortalidad, suele ser escrito para alguien que ha muerto.
end rhyme See **rhyme.**	**rima final** Véase **rima.**
end-stopped line An end-stopped line of poetry concludes with punctuation that marks a pause. The line is completely meaningful in itself, unlike run-on lines, which require the reader to move to the next line to grasp the poet's complete thought. See also **enjambment.**	**pausa versal** Cuando un verso concluye con un signo de puntuación que marca una pausa. El verso tiene pleno sentido en sí mismo, a diferencia de los versos encabalgados, que obligan al lector a pasar al siguiente verso para captar el pensamiento completo del poeta. Véase también **encabalgamiento.**

English sonnet See **sonnet**.

soneto inglés Véase **soneto**.

enjambment A poetic technique in which one line ends without a pause and must continue on to the next line to complete its meaning; also referred to as a "run-on line."

encabalgamiento Técnica poética en la que un verso termina sin pausa y debe continuar en el siguiente para completar su significado.

epigram A short, witty statement designed to surprise an audience or a reader.

epigrama Declaración breve e ingeniosa destinada a sorprender al público o al lector.

epigraph A quotation preceding a work of literature that helps set the text's mood or suggests its themes.

epígrafe Cita que precede a una obra literaria y que ayuda a ambientar el texto o a sugerir sus temas.

epiphany A character's transformative moment of realization. James Joyce, often credited with coining this as a literary term, defined it as the "sudden revelation of the whatness of a thing," the moment in which "the soul of the commonest object . . . seems to us radiant . . . a sudden spiritual manifestation [either] in the vulgarity of speech or of a gesture or in a memorable phrase of the mind itself."

epifanía Momento de transformación de un personaje. James Joyce, a quien suele atribuirse la acuñación de este término literario, lo definió como la "súbita revelación del qué de una cosa", el momento en que "el alma del objeto más común . . . nos parece radiante . . . una súbita manifestación espiritual [ya sea] en la vulgaridad de un discurso o de un gesto, o en una frase memorable de la propia mente".

eulogy A poem, a speech, or another work written in great praise of something or someone, usually a person no longer living.

elogio Poema, discurso u obra escrita en gran alabanza de algo o alguien, generalmente una persona que ha muerto.

evidence Support for the claims of an argument. In literary analysis, evidence is drawn from the text of the work of literature.

evidencia Apoyo a las afirmaciones de un argumento. En el análisis literario, las pruebas se extraen del texto literario.

exposition In a literary work, contextual and background information told to readers (rather than shown through action) about the characters, plot, setting, and situation.

exposición En una obra literaria, información contextual y de fondo sobre los personajes, la trama, el escenario y la situación que, en lugar de mostrarse a través de la acción, se cuenta explícitamente a los lectores.

extended metaphor A metaphor that continues over several lines or throughout an entire literary work, expanding the comparison through additional details. See also **metaphor**.

metáfora extendida Metáfora que se prolonga durante varias líneas o a lo largo de toda una obra literaria, ampliando la comparación a través de detalles adicionales. Véase también **metáfora**.

eye rhyme See **rhyme**.

rima visual Ver **rima**.

F

falling action In a plot diagram, this is the result (or fallout) of the climax or turning point. In this phase, the conflict is being resolved. See also **plot**.

acción descendente En un diagrama de trama, es el resultado, o las secuelas, del clímax o punto de inflexión. En esta fase se resuelve el conflicto. Véase también **trama**.

farce A dramatic form marked by wholly absurd situations, slapstick, raucous wordplay, and sometimes innuendo.

farsa Forma dramática caracterizada por situaciones totalmente absurdas, payasadas, juegos de palabras y, a veces, insinuaciones.

feet Combinations of patterns of stressed or unstressed syllables within a line of poetry.	**pie** Combinación de patrones de sílabas acentuadas y no acentuadas dentro de una línea de poesía.
figurative language Language that uses figures of speech; nonliteral language usually evoking strong images. Sometimes referred to as metaphorical language, most of its forms explain, clarify, or enhance an idea by comparing it to something else; the comparison can be explicit (simile) or implied (metaphor). Other forms of figurative language include **personification**, **paradox**, **overstatement (hyperbole)**, **understatement**, and **irony**.	**lenguaje figurado** Lenguaje que utiliza figuras retóricas; lenguaje no literal que suele evocar imágenes fuertes. A veces denominado lenguaje metafórico, la mayoría de sus formas explican, aclaran o realzan una idea comparándola con otra cosa; la comparación puede ser explícita (símil) o implícita (metáfora). Otras formas de lenguaje figurado son la **personificación**, la **paradoja**, la **exageración (hipérbole)**, la **subestimación** y la **ironía**.
figure of speech See **figurative language.**	**figura retórica** Véase **lenguaje figurado.**
first-person narrator See **narrator**.	**narrador en primera persona** Véase **narrador**.
flashback A scene in a narrative that is set in an earlier time than the main action.	**Analepsis** También conocida por el término en inglés *flashback*, es una escena dentro de una narración que se sitúa en un tiempo anterior al de la acción principal.
flat character See **character**.	**personaje plano** Véase **personaje**.
foil A contrasting character who allows the protagonist to stand out more distinctly.	**personaje complementario** Conocido también por el término en inglés *foil*, es un personaje de contraste que permite al protagonista destacarse más.
foot See **meter**.	**pies** Véase **pie**.
foreshadowing A plot device in which future events are hinted at.	**presagio** Dispositivo argumental en el que se insinúan acontecimientos futuros de la historia.
form Refers to the defining structural characteristics of a work, especially a poem (i.e., meter and rhyme scheme). Often poets work within closed forms, such as the sonnet or sestina, which require adherence to fixed conventions. Other poets work with open forms, which do not adhere to a traditional or conventional structure.	**forma** Las características estructurales que definen una obra, especialmente un poema (es decir, la métrica y el esquema de rima). A menudo los poetas trabajan con formas cerradas, como el soneto o la sextina, que exigen el cumplimiento de convenciones fijas. Otros poetas trabajan con formas abiertas que no se adhieren a una estructura tradicional o convencional.
formal diction See **diction**.	**dicción formal** Véase dicción.
formalist lens See **critical lenses**.	**lente formalista** Véase **lentes críticas**.
free verse A form of poetry that does not have a regular meter or rhyme scheme.	**verso libre** Forma de poesía que no tiene una métrica ni un esquema de rima regulares.

G

gendered lens See **critical lenses**.	**lente de género** Véase **lentes críticas**.

genre This term can refer broadly to the general category that a literary work falls into (drama or poetry, fiction or nonfiction) or more specifically to a certain subset of literary works grouped together on the basis of similar characteristics (science fiction, local color, western).

género Este término puede referirse a la categoría general en la que se inscribe una obra literaria (drama o poesía, ficción o no ficción) o, más específicamente, a un determinado subconjunto de obras literarias agrupadas en función de características similares (ciencia ficción, comedia romántica, *Western*).

ghazal A form that originated in Arabic poetry, consisting of rhyming couplets and a refrain. The second line of each couplet typically ends with the same word, and the penultimate words in the second line of each couplet also rhyme with each other.

ghazal Forma de poesía árabe compuesta por coplas que riman y un estribillo. La segunda línea de cada copla suele terminar con la misma palabra, y las penúltimas palabras de la segunda línea de cada copla también riman.

graphic organizer A pre-writing strategy that helps break a work into more manageable sections for close reading and analysis. Structuring close reading in this way helps move a reader beyond simply describing the author's language choices to analysis that connects style with its effect and meaning.

organizador gráfico Estrategia de pre-escritura que ayuda a dividir una obra en secciones más manejables para su lectura y análisis. Estructurar la lectura de este modo ayuda a que el lector vaya más allá de la simple descripción de las decisiones lingüísticas del autor y realice un análisis que relacione el estilo con su efecto y significado.

H

Harlem Renaissance A movement in the 1920s and 1930s marked by a great flowering of Black arts and culture centered in the Harlem neighborhood of New York City.

Renacimiento de Harlem Movimiento de las décadas de 1920 y 1930 caracterizado por un gran florecimiento de las artes y la cultura negras, y centrado en el barrio de Harlem de la ciudad de Nueva York.

historical lens See **critical lenses**.

lente histórica Véase **lentes críticas**.

hook An opening to a piece of writing designed to catch the reader's attention.

gancho narrativo Apertura de un texto diseñada para captar la atención del lector.

hubris An excessive level of pride that leads to the protagonist's downfall. See also **tragedy**.

hibris Nivel excesivo de orgullo que lleva a la caída del protagonista. Véase también **tragedia**.

hyperbole Deliberate exaggeration used for emphasis or to produce a comic or an ironic effect; an overstatement to make a point.

hipérbole Exageración deliberada utilizada para dar énfasis o producir un efecto cómico o irónico; uso de la exageración para demostrar algo.

I

iamb A poetic foot of two syllables with the stress, or accent, on the second, as in the word "again," or the phrase "by far." See also **meter**.

yambo Pie poético de dos sílabas con el acento en la segunda, como en la palabra "bastón", o la frase "sin más". Véase también **métrica**.

iambic hexameter A line of six iambic feet (twelve syllables) See also **meter**.

hexámetro yámbico Línea de seis pies yámbicos (doce sílabas) Véase también **métrica**.

iambic pentameter An iamb, the most common metrical foot in English poetry, is made up of an unstressed syllable followed by a stressed one. Iambic pentameter, then, is a rhythmic meter containing five iambs (ten syllables). Unrhymed iambic pentameter is called blank verse. See also **blank verse**; **meter**.

pentámetro yámbico Un yambo, el pie métrico más común en la poesía inglesa, está formado por una sílaba no acentuada seguida de otra acentuada. El pentámetro yámbico, por tanto, es una métrica rítmica que contiene cinco yambos (diez sílabas). El pentámetro yámbico no rimado se denomina verso blanco. Véase también **verso blanco**; **métrica**.

iambic tetrameter A line of four iambic feet (eight syllables) See also **meter**.

tetrámetro yámbico Línea de cuatro pies yámbicos (ocho sílabas) Véase también **métrica**.

imagery A description of how something looks, feels, tastes, smells, or sounds. The verbal expression of a sensory experience: visual (sight), auditory (sound), olfactory (scent), gustatory (taste), tactile (touch), or kinesthetic (movement/tension). Imagery may use literal or figurative language.

imaginería También llamada simplemente "imagen". En literatura, se refiere a la descripción de cómo algo se ve, se siente, sabe, huele o suena; la expresión verbal de una experiencia sensorial: visual (vista), auditiva (sonido), olfativa (olor), gustativa (sabor), táctil (tacto) o kinestésica (movimiento/tensión). La imaginería puede utilizar un lenguaje literal o figurado.

imagism A modernist literary movement that rejected overly sentimental, decorative language in favor of direct and succinct expression, often focusing an entire poem on a single image.

imagismo Movimiento literario modernista que rechaza el lenguaje excesivamente sentimental y decorativo en favor de la expresión directa y concisa. Muchas veces un poema completo se enfoca en una sola imagen.

imperative sentence See **sentence**.

oración imperativa Véase **oración**.

in medias res Latin for "in the middle of things," a technique in which a narrative begins in the middle of the action.

in medias res en latín significa "en medio de las cosas". Técnica en la que la narración comienza en medio de la acción.

indirect characterization See **characterization**.

caracterización indirecta Véase **caracterización**.

informal diction See **diction**.

dicción informal Véase **dicción**.

internal rhyme See **rhyme**.

rima interna Véase **rima**.

interrupted sentence See **sentence**.

frase interrumpida Véase **frase**.

inversion Also called an inverted sentence, it is created by alteration of the standard English word order of a subject (S) being followed by a verb (V) and its object (O) in a declarative sentence. It is often used to call attention to something, perhaps to emphasize a point or an idea by placing it in the initial position, or to slow the pace by choosing an unusual order. Sometimes it works in service of rhyme.

inversión También llamada frase invertida, se crea mediante la alteración del orden estándar de las palabras en inglés y español en el que una frase declarativa está compuesta por un sujeto (S) seguido de un verbo (V) y su objeto (O). Suele utilizarse para llamar la atención sobre algo, quizás para enfatizar una idea colocándola en la posición inicial, o para desacelerar el ritmo del texto eligiendo un orden inusual. A veces se utiliza para ayudar a crear una rima.

irony An incongruity between expectation and reality.

dramatic irony Tension created by the contrast between what a character says or thinks and what the audience or readers know to be true; as a result of this technique, some words and actions in a story or play take on a different meaning for the reader than they do for the characters.

situational irony A pointed discrepancy between what seems fitting or expected in a story and what actually happens.

verbal irony A figure of speech that occurs when a speaker or character says one thing but means something else or when what is said is the opposite of what is expected, creating a noticeable incongruity. **Sarcasm** is verbal irony used derisively.

ironía Incongruencia entre expectativa y realidad.

ironía dramática Tensión creada por el contraste entre lo que un personaje dice o piensa y lo que el público o los lectores saben que es verdad; como resultado de esta técnica, algunas palabras y acciones de una historia u obra de teatro adquieren un significado diferente para el lector que para los personajes.

ironía situacional Discrepancia puntual entre lo que parece adecuado o esperado en una historia y lo que sucede en realidad.

ironía verbal Figura retórica que se produce cuando un orador o personaje dice una cosa pero quiere decir otra, o cuando lo que se dice es lo contrario de lo que se espera, creando una incongruencia. El **sarcasmo** es una ironía verbal utilizada para burlarse.

Italian sonnet See **sonnet**.

soneto italiano Ver **soneto**.

J

juxtaposition Placing two things side by side for the sake of comparison or contrast. Authors sometimes use incongruous juxtapositions to produce **verbal irony**.

yuxtaposición Colocar dos cosas una junto a la otra para compararlas o contrastarlas. Los autores utilizan a veces yuxtaposiciones incongruentes para producir **ironía verbal**.

L

limited omniscient point of view See **point of view**.

punto de vista omnisciente limitado Ver **punto de vista**.

linear plot A plot that is arranged chronologically; it effectively builds tension and suspense and charts the growth of characters in a fairly straightforward way. See also **plot**.

trama lineal Trama ordenada cronológicamente, que crea tensión y suspenso de forma eficaz y traza el crecimiento de los personajes de forma directa. Véase también **trama**.

literary elements The components that together create a literary work. This term encompasses elements of style, such as imagery, syntax, figurative language, and tone, as well as storytelling elements, such as **plot**, **character**, **setting**, and **point of view**.

elementos literarios Componentes que, en conjunto, crean una obra literaria. Este término engloba elementos de estilo, como la imaginería, la sintaxis, el lenguaje figurado y el tono, así como elementos narrativos, como **trama**, **personaje**, **escenario** y **punto de vista**.

lyric A short poem expressing the personal feelings of a first-person speaker. The term comes from the Greek word *lyre*, and the form is descended from poems intended to be sung while accompanied by that instrument.

lírica Forma de poesía breve que expresa los sentimientos personales de un hablante en primera persona. El término proviene de la palabra griega "*lira*", y la forma desciende de los poemas que solían cantarse con acompañamiento de este instrumento.

M

metaphor A figure of speech that compares or equates two things without using *like* or *as*. See also **extended metaphor**. For comparisons made using *like* or *as*, see **simile**.

metáfora Figura retórica que compara o equipara dos cosas sin utilizar la palabra *como*. Véase también **metáfora ampliada**. Para las comparaciones realizadas con el uso de “como” o “cual”, véase **símil**.

metaphysical conceit A literary device that sets up a striking analogy between two entities that would not usually invite comparison, often drawing connections between the physical and the spiritual. This literary device is famously used by metaphysical poets, including John Donne and George Herbert. See also **conceit**.

presunción metafísica Recurso literario que establece una analogía sorprendente entre dos entidades que normalmente no invitan a la comparación, estableciendo conexiones entre lo físico y lo espiritual. Este recurso literario es muy usado entre los poetas metafísicos, como John Donne y George Herbert. Véase también **presunción**.

meter The formal, regular organization of stressed and unstressed syllables, measured in feet. A foot is distinguished by the number of syllables it contains and how stress is placed on the syllables — stressed (’) or unstressed (˘). There are five typical feet in English verse: iamb (˘’), trochee (’˘), anapest (˘˘’), dactyl (’˘˘), and spondee (’’). Some meters dictate the number of feet per line, the most common being tetrameter, pentameter, and hexameter, having four, five, and six feet, respectively. See also **iambic pentameter**.

métrica Organización formal y regular de las sílabas acentuadas y no acentuadas, medida en pies. Los pies se distinguen por el número de sílabas que contiene y por la forma en que se acentúan las sílabas: acentuadas (’) o no acentuadas (˘). Hay cinco pies típicos en el verso inglés: el yambo (˘’), el troqueo (’˘), el anapesto (˘˘’), el dáctilo (’˘˘) y el espondeo (’’). Algunas métricas dictan el número de pies por línea, siendo las más comunes el tetrámetro, el pentámetro y el hexámetro, que tienen cuatro, cinco y seis pies, respectivamente. Véase también **pentámetro yámbico**.

metonymy A figure of speech in which something is represented by another thing that is related to it. Compare to **synecdoche**; see also **metaphor**.

metonimia Figura retórica en la que algo es representado por otra cosa relacionada. Compárese con **sinécdoque**; véase también **metáfora**.

modernism In literature, modernism refers to a movement of writers who reached their apex between the 1920s and 1930s and expressed views of disillusionment with contemporary Western civilization, especially in the wake of World War I’s mindless brutality. Rejecting the conventions of the Victorian era, these writers experimented with form and took insights from recent writings by Sigmund Freud and Carl Jung about the unconscious. They viewed art as restorative and frequently ordered their writing around symbols and allusions. Representative modernist writers include T. S. Eliot, James Joyce, and Virginia Woolf.

modernismo En literatura, el modernismo se refiere a un movimiento de escritores que alcanzó su cúspide entre las décadas de 1920 y 1930 y expresó opiniones de desilusión con la civilización occidental contemporánea, especialmente tras la absurda brutalidad de la Primera Guerra Mundial. Estos escritores rechazaron las convenciones de la era victoriana, experimentaron con la forma y tomaron ideas de los recientes escritos de Sigmund Freud y Carl Jung sobre el inconsciente. Consideraban que el arte debía ser restaurativo y solían estructurar sus escritos en torno a símbolos y alusiones. Entre los escritores modernistas más representativos se encuentran T. S. Eliot, James Joyce y Virginia Woolf.

monologue In a play, a speech given by one person. See also **soliloquy**.

monólogo En una obra de teatro, discurso pronunciado por una sola persona. Véase también **soliloquio**.

mood Similar to **atmosphere**, mood is the feeling created for the reader by a work of literature. Many things can generate mood — especially **character**, **dialogue**, **setting**, **style**, and **tone** .

estado de ánimo Similar a la **atmósfera**, el estado de ánimo es la sensación que crea una obra literaria en el lector. Hay muchas cosas que pueden generar ese estado de ánimo, especialmente **personajes**, **diálogos**, **escenario**, **estilo** y **tono**.

motif A recurring pattern of images, words, or symbols that reveals a theme in a work of literature.

motivo Patrón recurrente de imágenes, palabras o símbolos que revela un tema en una obra literaria.

N

narrative A story. Narratives may be written either in prose or in verse, as in narrative poetry.

narrativa Una historia. Las narrativas pueden estar escritas en prosa o en verso, como en la poesía narrativa.

narrative frame Also known as a frame story, a narrative frame is a plot device in which the author places the main narrative of his or her work within another narrative — the narrative frame. This exterior narrative usually serves to explain the main narrative in some way.

narración enmarcada También conocida como relato-marco, una narración enmarcada es un recurso argumental en el que el autor sitúa la narración principal de su obra dentro de otra narración: el relato-marco. Esta narración exterior suele servir para explicar de algún modo la narración principal.

narrative perspective How narrators or characters see and experience their individual circumstances. See also **point of view**.

perspectiva narrativa Cómo los narradores o los personajes ven y experimentan sus circunstancias individuales. Véase también **punto de vista**.

narrator The character, or persona, that the author uses to tell a narrative, or story. Narrators may tell stories from several different points of view, including first person, second person (very rare), and third person. See also **point of view**. More specific terms are used to discuss the role a narrator plays in interpreting the events in a narrative:

> **objective narrator** Also known as a neutral narrator, a narrator who recounts only what characters say and do, offering no insight into their thinking or analysis of events. All interpretation is left to the reader.
>
> **unreliable narrator** A narrator who is biased and doesn't give a full or an accurate picture of events in a narrative. Narrators may be unreliable because of youth, inexperience, madness, intentional or unintentional bias, or even a lack of morals. Authors often use this technique to distinguish the character's point of view from their own. Sometimes an author will use an unreliable narrator to make an ironic point.

narrador Personaje que el autor utiliza para contar una historia. Los narradores pueden contar historias desde diferentes puntos de vista, como la primera persona, la segunda persona (muy rara vez) y la tercera persona. Véase también **punto de vista**. Se utilizan términos más específicos para hablar del papel que desempeña un narrador en la interpretación de los acontecimientos de una narración:

> **narrador objetivo** También conocido como narrador neutro, un narrador que sólo cuenta lo que los personajes dicen y hacen, sin ofrecer una mirada a su pensamiento ni un análisis de los acontecimientos. Toda la interpretación se deja al lector.
>
> **narrador sospechoso** También conocido como narrador falible o poco fiable, es un narrador parcial a los eventos de la historia, que no da una imagen completa o exacta de los acontecimientos en una narración. Los narradores pueden ser sospechosos debido a su juventud, inexperiencia, locura, parcialidad intencionada o no, o incluso falta de moral. Los autores suelen utilizar esta técnica para distinguir el punto de vista del personaje del suyo propio. A veces, el autor utiliza un narrador poco fiable para crear ironía.

near rhyme See **rhyme**.

rima imperfecta Véase **rima**.

nonlinear plot A plot that presents the events of a narrative out of chronological order or interrupts chronological order using techniques such as flashback, foreshadowing, and *in medias res*. See also **plot**.

trama no lineal Trama que presenta los acontecimientos de una narración fuera del orden cronológico, o que interrumpe el orden cronológico mediante técnicas como la analepsis o *flashback*, el presagio y el *in medias res*. Véase también **trama**.

non sequitur In literature, a reply or remark that does not have any relevance to what occasioned or preceded it; in rhetoric, a conclusion that does not logically follow from the premises.

non sequitur En literatura, respuesta u observación que no tiene ninguna relación con lo que la ha ocasionado o precedido; en retórica, conclusión que no se deduce lógicamente de las premisas.

novella A short novel, from the Italian word meaning "story."

novella Novela corta, de la palabra italiana que significa "historia".

O

objective narrator See **narrator**.

narrador objetivo Véase **narrador**.

objective point of view See **point of view**.

punto de vista objetivo Véase **punto de vista**.

octet See **stanza**.

octeto Véase **estrofa**.

ode A form of poetry used to meditate on or address a single object or condition. It originally followed strict rules of rhythm, meter, and rhyme, which by the romantic period had become more flexible.

oda Forma de poesía utilizada para abordar un único objeto o condición. Originalmente seguía reglas estrictas de ritmo, métrica y rima, que para la época romántica se habían vuelto más flexibles.

omniscient narrator An omniscient narrator gives readers access to what all the characters are thinking and feeling. This narrator sometimes remains objective, recounts only what characters say and do, and offers no analysis of events or insight into characters' thinking. As a result, all interpretations are left to the reader. Other omniscient narrators provide subjective interpretations in addition to relating events in the narrative. See also **narrator**.

narrador omnisciente Un narrador omnisciente permite a los lectores conocer lo que piensan y sienten todos los personajes. A veces, este narrador es objetivo: sólo cuenta lo que los personajes dicen y hacen, y no ofrece ningún análisis de los acontecimientos ni nos acerca al pensamiento de los personajes. En consecuencia, todas las interpretaciones quedan en manos del lector. Otros narradores omniscientes ofrecen interpretaciones subjetivas además de relatar los acontecimientos de la narración. Véase también **narrador**.

omniscient point of view See **point of view**.

punto de vista omnisciente Véase **punto de vista**.

onomatopoeia Use of words that refer to sound and whose pronunciations mimic those sounds.

onomatopeya Palabra que hace referencia a un sonido y cuya pronunciación imita este sonido.

open form See **form**.

forma abierta Véase **forma.**

overstatement See **hyperbole**.

exageración Véase **hipérbole**.

oxymoron A paradox made up of two seemingly contradictory words.

oxímoron Paradoja formada por dos conceptos aparentemente contradictorios.

P

parable A tale told explicitly to illustrate a moral lesson or conclusion. Parables can take the form of drama, poetry, or fiction.	**parábola** Cuento escrito explícitamente para ilustrar una lección moral. Las parábolas pueden encontrarse en forma de teatro, poesía y ficción.
paradox A statement that seems contradictory but actually reveals a surprising or hidden truth.	**paradoja** Afirmación que parece contradictoria pero que en realidad revela una verdad sorprendente u oculta.
parallel structure Also known as parallelism, this term refers to the repeated use of similar grammatical structures for the purpose of emphasis. Compare with **anaphora**, a type of parallel structure concerned only with the repetitions of an initial word or words.	**estructura paralela** También conocido como paralelismo, este término se refiere al uso repetido de estructuras gramaticales similares con el propósito de generar énfasis. Compárese con la **anáfora**, un tipo de estructura paralela que sólo consiste en repetir una palabra o palabras iniciales.
parody A comic or satiric imitation of a particular literary work or style. Parodies can run the gamut from light-hearted imitations to exaggerations intended to criticize, usually by making a work or literary style look ridiculous.	**parodia** Imitación cómica o satírica de una determinada obra o estilo literario. Las parodias pueden abarcar desde imitaciones ligeras hasta exageraciones cuya intención es criticar, y que generalmente llevan a una obra o un estilo literario al punto del ridículo.
passive voice A sentence employs passive voice when the subject doesn't act but is acted on.	**voz pasiva** Una oración emplea la voz pasiva cuando el sujeto no actúa, sino que algo más actúa sobre él.
pastoral Literature that employs a romanticized description of leisurely farm or rural life.	**pastoral** Literatura que describe la vida rural o de granja de una forma idealizada y romántica.
periodic sentence See **sentence**.	**oración periódica** Véase **oración**.
persona A voice and viewpoint that an author adopts in order to deliver a story or poem. See **narrator**.	**persona** Voz y punto de vista que adopta un autor para narrar una historia o un poema. Véase **narrador**.
personification A figure of speech in which an animal or inanimate object is imbued with human qualities.	**personificación** Figura retórica en la que se le otorgan cualidades humanas a un animal u objeto inanimado.
Petrarchan sonnet See **sonnet**.	**Soneto petrarquista** Véase **soneto**.

plot The arrangement of events in a narrative. Almost always, a conflict is central to a plot, and traditionally a plot develops in accordance with the following model: **exposition**, **rising action**, **climax**, **falling action**, **denouement**. There can be more than one sequence of events in a work, although typically there is one major sequence along with other minor sequences. These minor sequences are called subplots. The following terms refer to the chronological arrangement of events in a narrative:

linear plot A plot that is arranged chronologically; it effectively builds tension and suspense and charts the growth of characters in a fairly straightforward way.

nonlinear plot A plot that presents the events of a narrative either out of chronological order or interrupts that order using techniques such as flashback, foreshadowing, and *in medias res.*

trama Disposición de los acontecimientos en una narración. Casi siempre hay un conflicto al centro de la trama, que tradicionalmente se desarrolla según el siguiente modelo: **exposición**, **acción ascendente**, **clímax**, **acción descendente**, **desenlace**. Puede haber más de una secuencia de acontecimientos en una obra, aunque normalmente hay una secuencia principal junto con otras secuencias menores. Estas secuencias menores se denominan subtramas. Los siguientes términos se refieren a la disposición cronológica de los acontecimientos en una narración:

trama lineal Trama ordenada cronológicamente que crea tensión y suspenso de forma efectiva y que traza el crecimiento de los personajes de forma directa.

trama no lineal Trama que presenta los acontecimientos de una narración fuera del orden cronológico, o que interrumpe el orden cronológico mediante técnicas como la analepsis o *flashback*, el presagio y el *in medias res.*

poetic syntax Similar to syntax in prose, poetic syntax also includes the arrangement of words into lines — where they break or do not break, the use of enjambment or caesura, and line length/patterns. See also **syntax**.

sintaxis poética Al igual que la sintaxis en la prosa, la sintaxis poética también incluye la disposición de las palabras en las líneas –que pueden romperse o no– el uso del encabalgamiento o la cesura, y la longitud y patrones de las líneas. Véase también **sintaxis**.

point of view The position from which a narrator relates the events of a narrative. The most common points of view are:

first person A narrator who is a character in the story and who refers to him- or herself as "I." First-person narrators are sometimes **unreliable narrators**.

second person Though rare, some stories are told using second-person pronouns (*you*). This casts the reader as a character in the story.

third-person limited omniscient A narrator who relates the action using third-person pronouns (*he, she, it*). This narrator is usually privy to the thoughts and actions of only one character.

third-person omniscient A narrator using third-person pronouns. This narrator is privy to the thoughts and actions of all the characters in the story. See also **narrator**.

punto de vista Posición desde la que un narrador relata los acontecimientos de una narración. Los puntos de vista más comunes son:

primera persona El narrador es un personaje de la historia y que se refiere a sí mismo como "yo". Los narradores en primera persona a veces pueden ser **narradores sospechosos**.

segunda persona Aunque es poco frecuente, algunas historias se narran con pronombres de segunda persona (*tú*). De este modo, el lector se convierte en un personaje más de la historia.

omnisciente limitado en tercera persona Un narrador que relata la acción utilizando pronombres en tercera persona (*él, ella*). Este narrador suele conocer los pensamientos y acciones de un solo personaje.

omnisciente en tercera persona Un narrador que utiliza pronombres en tercera persona. Este narrador está al tanto de los pensamientos y acciones de todos los personajes de la historia. Véase también **narrador**.

postmodernism In literature, postmodernism refers to a loose grouping of writers in the post–World War II era who carry on the agenda of modernism, rejecting traditional literary conventions, embracing experimentation, and seeing contemporary life as bleak and fragmented. Rather than attempt to instill order through some literary device — as T. S. Eliot did with his use of allusions and myth or as William Butler Yeats did with his symbolic system — postmodern writers don't treat art as a corrective to modern malaises, and their writing celebrates or plays with the fragmentation of life instead of seeking to fix it. In addition, postmodern writers ignore the distinction between "high" and "low" art, and their writing engages with popular art forms like cartoons and television. Representative postmodern fiction writers include Don DeLillo, Thomas Pynchon, and Kurt Vonnegut; representative postmodern poets include John Ashbery, Ted Berrigan, Denise Levertov, and Frank O'Hara.

postmodernismo En literatura, el postmodernismo suele englobar a un grupo de escritores de la época posterior a la Segunda Guerra Mundial que continuaron con la agenda del modernismo, rechazaron las convenciones literarias tradicionales, recurrieron a la experimentación y consideraban que la vida contemporánea como algo sombrío y fragmentado. En lugar de intentar instaurar orden a través de algún recurso literario –como T. S. Eliot con su uso de alusiones y mitos o como William Butler Yeats con su sistema simbólico– los escritores posmodernos no tratan el arte como una cura a los males modernos, y sus escritos celebran o juegan con la fragmentación de la vida en lugar de intentar arreglarla. Además, los escritores posmodernos ignoran la distinción entre arte "culto" y "popular", y sus escritos abordan formas de arte popular como los dibujos animados y la televisión. Entre los escritores de ficción posmodernos más representativos se encuentran Don DeLillo, Thomas Pynchon y Kurt Vonnegut; entre los poetas posmodernos más representativos se encuentran John Ashbery, Ted Berrigan, Denise Levertov y Frank O'Hara.

prose poem A blending of prose and poetry, usually resembling prose in its use of sentences without line breaks and poetry in its use of poetic devices such as figurative language. See also **form**.

poema en prosa Mezcla de prosa y poesía, que suele parecerse a la prosa por el uso de frases sin saltos de línea y a la poesía por el uso de recursos poéticos como el lenguaje figurado. Véase también **forma**.

protagonist The main character in a work; often a hero or heroine, but not always.

protagonista El personaje principal de una obra. Muchas veces, pero no siempre, se trata de un héroe o una heroína.

psychological lens See **critical lenses**.

lente psicológica Ver **lentes críticas**.

pun A play on words that derives its humor from the replacement of one word with another that has a similar pronunciation or spelling but a different meaning. A pun can also derive humor from the use of a single word that has more than one meaning.

calambur Deriva su humor de la sustitución de una palabra por otra que tiene una pronunciación u ortografía similar pero un significado diferente. Un calambur también puede derivar su humor del uso de una sola palabra que tiene más de un significado.

Q

quatrain See **stanza**.

cuarteto Véase **estrofa**.

R

realism Describing a literary technique, the goal of which is to render work that feels true, immediate, natural, and realistic.

realismo Describe una técnica literaria cuyo objetivo es hacer que la obra parezca verdadera, inmediata, natural y realista.

refrain A line, lines, or a stanza in a poem that repeat(s) at intervals.	**estribillo** Línea, líneas o estrofas de un poema que se repiten a intervalos.
resolution The working out of a plot's conflicts, following the climax. See also **plot**.	**resolución** Parte de una trama posterior al clímax, en la que los conflictos se resuelven. Véase también **trama**.
reversal When, in a narrative, the protagonist's fortunes take an unforeseen turn. See also **plot**.	**inversión** Cuando, en una narración, la suerte del protagonista da un giro imprevisto. Véase también **trama**.
rhetorical question A question asked for stylistic effect and emphasis to make a point rather than to solicit an answer.	**pregunta retórica** Pregunta formulada con un efecto estilístico y de énfasis con la intención de demostrar un punto en lugar de solicitar una respuesta.
rhyme The repetition of the same (or similar) vowel or consonant sounds or constructions. A rhyme at the end of two or more lines of poetry is called an end rhyme. A rhyme that occurs within a line is called an internal rhyme. A rhyme that pairs sounds that are similar but not exactly the same is called a near rhyme or a slant rhyme. A rhyme that only works because the words look the same is called an eye rhyme or a sight rhyme. Rhyme often follows a pattern, called a rhyme scheme.	**rima** Repetición de sonidos vocálicos, consonánticos o construcciones iguales o similares. Una rima al final de dos o más versos se denomina rima final. Una rima que se produce dentro de un verso se denomina rima interna. Una rima que combina sonidos similares pero no exactamente iguales se denomina rima imperfecta. Una rima que sólo funciona porque las palabras se parecen se llama rima visual. La rima suele seguir un patrón llamado esquema de rima.
rhythm The general pattern of stressed and unstressed syllables. See also **meter**.	**ritmo** Patrón general de sílabas acentuadas y no acentuadas. Véase también **métrica**.
rising action The events, marked by increasing tension and conflict, that build up to a story's climax. See also **plot**.	**acción ascendente** Acontecimientos marcados por una tensión y un conflicto crecientes que se acumulan hasta el clímax de una historia. Véase también **trama**.
romanticism In literature, a late eighteenth- to early nineteenth-century movement that emphasized beauty for beauty's sake, the natural world, emotion, imagination, the value of a nation's past and its folklore, and the heroic roles of the individual and the artist. Some prominent romantic poets in this book include Percy Bysshe Shelley, Lord Byron, William Wordsworth, and John Keats.	**romanticismo** En literatura, un movimiento de finales del siglo XVIII a principios del XIX que se enfocaba en la belleza por la belleza misma, el mundo natural, la emoción, la imaginación, el valor del pasado de una nación y su folclore, y el papel heroico del individuo y el artista. Algunos de los poetas románticos más destacados en este libro son Percy Bysshe Shelley, Lord Byron, William Wordsworth y John Keats.
run-on line See **enjambment**.	**línea seguida** Véase **encabalgamiento**.

S

sarcasm See **irony**, **verbal**.	**sarcasmo** Véase **ironía verbal**.
satire A literary or an artistic work that uses irony, wit, and humor to critique society or an individual in an attempt to effect change.	**sátira** Obra literaria o artística que utiliza la ironía, el ingenio y el humor para criticar a la sociedad o a un individuo en una búsqueda por lograr un cambio.

scene A subdivision of an act in a play. Scenes usually break up the action into logical chunks. Many contemporary plays, however, contain only sequences of scenes, without an overarching act structure. See also **act**.

escena Subdivisión de un acto en una obra de teatro. Las escenas suelen dividir la acción en fragmentos lógicos. Sin embargo, muchas obras de teatro contemporáneas sólo contienen secuencias de escenas, sin una estructura general de actos. Véase también **acto**.

secondary character See **character**.

personaje secundario Véase **personaje**.

sentence Specific types of sentences discussed in this book include the following:

complex sentence A sentence containing an independent clause and one or more subordinate clauses (beginning with words such as *after*, *before*, *although*, *because*, *until*, *when*, *while*, and *if*).

compound sentence Two independent clauses joined by a coordinating conjunction (*and*, *but*, *or*, *nor*, *for*, *yet*, or *so*) or a semicolon.

compound-complex sentence A combination of a compound sentence and a complex sentence; it is often fairly long.

cumulative sentence A sentence in which an independent clause is followed by details, qualifications, or modifications in subordinate clauses or phrases.

imperative sentence A sentence that issues a command. The subject of an imperative sentence is often implied rather than explicit.

interrupted sentence A sentence of any pattern modified by interruptions that add descriptive details, state conditions, suggest uncertainty, voice possible alternative views, or present qualifications.

inverted sentence A sentence that deviates from the traditional subject-verb-object order; the verb may appear before the subject.

periodic sentence A sentence that begins with details, qualifications, or modifications, building toward the main clause.

simple sentence A sentence composed of one main clause without any subordinate clauses.

oración Los tipos de oraciones que se analizan en este libro son los siguientes:

oración compleja Oración que contiene una cláusula independiente y una o más cláusulas subordinadas (que comienzan con palabras como *posterior a*, *antes de*, *sin embargo*, *porque*, *hasta que*, *cuando*, *mientras* y *si*).

oración compuesta Dos cláusulas independientes unidas por una conjunción copulativa (*y*, *pero*, *o*, *ni*, *para*, *pues*, o *así*) o un punto y coma.

oración compuesta-compleja Combinación de una oración compuesta y una oración compleja; suele ser bastante larga.

oración acumulativa Oración en la que una cláusula independiente va seguida de detalles, calificaciones o modificaciones en cláusulas o frases subordinadas.

oración imperativa Oración que emite una orden. El sujeto de una oración imperativa suele ser implícito y no explícito.

oración interrumpida Oración de cualquier patrón modificada por interrupciones que añaden detalles descriptivos, indican condiciones, sugieren incertidumbre, expresan posibles puntos de vista alternativos o presentan calificativos.

oración invertida Oración que se desvía del orden tradicional sujeto-verbo-objeto; el verbo puede aparecer antes del sujeto.

oración periódica Oración que comienza con detalles, calificativos o modificaciones, construyendo hacia la cláusula principal.

oración simple Oración compuesta por una cláusula principal sin cláusulas subordinadas.

sestet See **stanza**.

sexteto Véase **estrofa**.

setting Where and when a story takes place.

ambientación El momento y lugar donde se desarrolla una historia.

social setting The manners, mores, customs, rituals, and codes of conduct in a work; an author may suggest approval or disapproval of any of these through a description of place.	**ambientación social** Los modales, costumbres, rituales y códigos de conducta en una obra; un autor puede sugerir su aprobación o desaprobación de cualquiera de ellos a través de descripciones.
Shakespearean sonnet See **sonnet**.	**Soneto shakespeariano** Véase **soneto**.
shift A point in a poem that indicates a change. It is most often a change in the speaker's perspective.	**giro** Punto de un poema que indica un cambio. La mayoría de las veces se trata de un cambio en la perspectiva del hablante.
sight rhyme See **rhyme**.	**rima visual** Ver **rima**.
simile A figure of speech used to explain or clarify an idea by comparing it explicitly to something else, using the words *like*, *as*, or *as though* to do so.	**símil** Figura retórica que se utiliza para explicar o aclarar una idea comparándola explícitamente con otra cosa, utilizando para ello las palabras *como* o *cual*.
simple sentence See **sentence**.	**oración simple** Véase **oración**.
slang See **colloquial language/colloquialism**.	**jerga** Véase **lenguaje coloquial/coloquialismo**.
slant rhyme See **rhyme**.	**rima imperfecta** Véase **rima**.
soliloquy In a play, a monologue in which a character, alone on the stage, reveals his or her thoughts or emotions.	**soliloquio** En una obra de teatro, monólogo en el que un personaje, solo en el escenario, revela sus pensamientos o emociones.
sonnet A poetic form composed of fourteen lines in iambic pentameter that adheres to a particular rhyme scheme. The two most common types are the following: **Petrarchan sonnet** Also known as the Italian sonnet, its fourteen lines are divided into an octet and a sestet. The octet rhymes *abba, abba*; the sestet that follows can have a variety of different rhyme schemes: *cdcdcd*, *cdecde*, *cddcdd*. **Shakespearean sonnet** Also known as the English sonnet, its fourteen lines are composed of three quatrains and a couplet, and its rhyme scheme is *abab, cdcd, efef, gg*.	**soneto** Forma poética compuesta por catorce versos en pentámetro yámbico, escrita en un esquema de rima determinado. Los dos tipos más comunes son los siguientes: **soneto petrarquista** También conocido como soneto italiano, sus catorce versos se dividen en un octeto y un sexteto. El octeto rima *abba*, *abba*; el sexteto que le sigue puede tener diferentes esquemas de rima: *cdcdcd*, *cdecde*, *cddcdd*. **soneto shakespeariano** También conocido como soneto inglés, sus catorce versos se componen de tres cuartetos y un pareado, y su esquema de rima es *abab*, *cdcd*, *efef*, *gg*.
sound The musical quality of poetry, as created through techniques such as **rhyme**, **enjambment**, **caesura**, **alliteration**, **assonance**, **consonance**, **onomatopoeia**, **rhythm**, and **cadence**.	**sonido** La cualidad musical de la poesía, creada mediante técnicas como **rima**, **encabalgamiento**, **cesura**, **aliteración**, **asonancia**, **consonancia**, **onomatopeya**, **ritmo** y **cadencia**.
speaker This term is most frequently used in the context of drama and poetry. In drama, the speaker is the character who is currently delivering lines. In poetry, the speaker is the person who is expressing a point of view in the poem, either the author or a persona created by the author. See also **narrator**; **persona**; **perspective**; **point of view**.	**orador** Este término se utiliza con mayor frecuencia en el contexto del teatro y la poesía. En el teatro, el orador es el personaje que pronuncia los versos en ese momento. En poesía, el orador es la persona que expresa un punto de vista en el poema, ya sea el autor o un personaje creado por el autor. Véase también **narrador**; **personaje**; **perspectiva**; **punto de vista**.

spondee See **meter**.	**espondeo** Véase **métrica**.
stage directions Any notes in the script of a play written by the author that set guidelines for the performance, explaining, for example, what the set should look like, how actors should move and deliver certain lines, and so on. They are generally italicized.	**instrucciones escénicas** Cualquier nota en el guión de una obra escrita por el autor que establece las directrices para su representación, explicando, por ejemplo, cómo debe ser la escenografía, cómo deben moverse los actores, cómo pronunciar ciertas líneas, etc. Suelen ir en cursiva.
stanza Lines in a poem that the poet has chosen to group together, usually separated from other lines by a space. Stanzas within a poem usually have repetitive forms, often sharing rhyme schemes or rhythmic structures. A number of frequently used stanza types have specific names: **couplet** A two-line, rhyming stanza. **tercet** A three-line stanza. **quatrain** A four-line stanza. **sestet** A six-line stanza. **octet** An eight-line stanza.	**estrofa** Líneas de un poema que el poeta ha decidido agrupar, normalmente separadas de otras líneas por un espacio. Las estrofas de un poema suelen tener formas repetitivas, y también suelen compartir esquemas de rima o estructuras rítmicas. Algunos tipos de estrofas de uso frecuente tienen nombres específicos: **pareado** También conocido como dístico. Estrofa de dos versos que rima. **terceto** Una estrofa de tres versos. **cuarteto** Una estrofa de cuatro versos. **sexteto** Una estrofa de seis versos. **octeto** Una estrofa de ocho versos.
stock character See **character.**	**personaje tipo** Véase **personaje**
stream of consciousness A technique in which prose follows the logic and flow of a character's (or multiple characters') thought processes — associations, tangents, seemingly strange transitions — rather than a more ordered narrative.	**flujo de conciencia** Técnica en la que la prosa sigue la lógica de los procesos de pensamiento de uno o varios personajes –asociaciones, tangentes, transiciones extrañas– en lugar de una narración más ordenada.
structure The organization of a work.	**estructura** La organización de una obra.
style The way a literary work is written. Style is produced by an author's choices in **diction**, **syntax**, **imagery**, **figurative language**, and other literary elements.	**estilo** Forma de escribir una obra literaria. El estilo se produce por las elecciones del autor en cuanto a **dicción**, **sintaxis**, **imágenes**, **lenguaje figurado** y otros elementos literarios.
suspense A literary device that uses tension to make the plot more exciting; it is the effect created by artful delays and selective dissemination of information.	**suspenso** Recurso literario que utiliza la tensión para hacer más emocionante la trama; efecto creado por los retrasos ingeniosos y la divulgación selectiva de la información.
symbol A setting, an object, or an event in a story that carries more than literal meaning and therefore represents something significant to understanding the meaning of a work of literature.	**símbolo** Ambientación, objeto o acontecimiento de una historia que conlleva algo más que un significado literal y, por tanto, representa algo significativo para comprender el sentido de una obra literaria.
synecdoche A figure of speech in which part of something is used to represent the whole. Compare to **metonymy**.	**sinécdoque** Figura retórica en la que se utiliza una parte de algo para representar el todo. Compárese con la **metonimia**.

syntax The arrangement of words into phrases, clauses, and sentences in a prose passage. This includes word order (subject-verb-object, for instance, or an inverted structure); the length and structure of sentences (simple, compound, or complex), phrases, and clauses; the chronology of passages; the preference of various parts of speech over others; the use of connectors between and within sentences; and more. See also **poetic syntax**.

sintaxis Disposición de las palabras en frases, cláusulas y oraciones en un pasaje en prosa. Incluye el orden de las palabras (sujeto-verbo-objeto, por ejemplo, o una estructura invertida); la longitud y la estructura de las oraciones (simples, compuestas o complejas), las frases y cláusulas; la cronología de los pasajes; la preferencia de varias partes de la oración sobre otras; el uso de conectores entre y dentro de las oraciones, etc. Véase también **sintaxis poética**.

T

tercet See **stanza**.

terceto Véase **estrofa**.

theatrical property Known more commonly as a **prop**, this is a term for any object used onstage by an actor in a play.

utilería Conocido también como **atrezzo**, es un término para cualquier objeto utilizado en el escenario por un actor en una obra.

theme Underlying issues or ideas of a work.

tema Asunto o ideas subyacentes de una obra.

thesis statement The chief claim that a writer makes in any argumentative piece of writing, usually stated in one sentence.

enunciado de tesis La afirmación principal que hace un escritor en cualquier escrito argumentativo, normalmente expresada en una oración.

tone A speaker's attitude or stance as exposed through style choices. (Tone is often confused with **mood**, another element of style that describes the feeling created by the work.) Along with mood, tone provides the emotional coloring of a work and is created by some combination of the other elements of style.

tono Actitud o postura del hablante expuesta a través de elecciones de estilo. El tono suele confundirse con el **estado de ánimo**, otro elemento de estilo que describe el sentimiento creado por la obra. Junto con el estado de ánimo, el tono proporciona el colorido emocional de una obra y es resultado de una combinación de los otros elementos de estilo.

tragedy A serious dramatic work in which the protagonist experiences a series of unfortunate reversals due to some character trait, referred to as a *tragic flaw*. The most common tragic flaw is hubris. *Hubris* comes from the Greek word *hybris*, which means pride. Modern tragedies tend to depart from some of the genre's classical conventions, portraying average rather than noble characters and attributing the protagonist's downfall to something other than a flaw in character — for example, to social circumstances.

tragedia Obra dramática seria en la que el protagonista se enfrenta a una serie de desafortunados eventos debido a algún rasgo de carácter denominado *error trágico*. El error trágico más común es la arrogancia. *Hibris* viene de la palabra griega *hybris*, que significa orgullo. Las tragedias modernas tienden a apartarse de algunas de las convenciones clásicas del género, representan a personajes normales en lugar de nobles y atribuyen la caída del protagonista a algo distinto a un error trágico, por ejemplo, a las circunstancias sociales.

tragic flaw See **tragedy**.

error trágico Véase **tragedia**.

tragic hero A character who possesses a flaw or commits an error in judgment that leads to his or her downfall and a reversal of fortune.

héroe trágico Personaje que posee un defecto o comete un error trágico que lleva a su caída y a un cambio de fortuna.

transcendental movement A reaction against both rationalism and empiricism in philosophy, as well as austere Calvinist doctrines about human nature, transcendentalism emphasized knowledge via mystical insight, the divine spark in each human being, and the immanence of God in nature. Beginning in Europe and drawing inspiration from European thinkers, among them Immanuel Kant and Samuel Taylor Coleridge, the transcendental movement flourished in the nineteenth-century United States, where it was linked with Christian Unitarianism. Key thinkers include Ralph Waldo Emerson and Henry David Thoreau.

movimiento trascendental Movimiento definido por su reacción contra el racionalismo y el empirismo en la filosofía, así como contra las austeras doctrinas calvinistas sobre la naturaleza humana. El trascendentalismo hizo énfasis en la adquisición de conocimiento a través de la percepción mística, la chispa divina en cada ser humano y la inmanencia de Dios en la naturaleza. Iniciado en Europa e inspirado por pensadores europeos, entre ellos Immanuel Kant y Samuel Taylor Coleridge, el movimiento trascendental floreció en Estados Unidos durante el siglo XIX, donde se vinculó con el unitarismo cristiano. Entre los pensadores clave se encuentran Ralph Waldo Emerson y Henry David Thoreau.

trochee See **meter**.

tróqueo Véase **métrica**.

U

understatement The presentation or framing of something as less important, urgent, awful, good, powerful, and so on than it actually is, often for satiric or comical effect; the opposite of hyperbole, it is often used along with this technique, and for similar effect.

subestimación Presentación o enmarcación de algo como menos importante, urgente, horrible, bueno, poderoso, etc. de lo que realmente es, generalmente para producir un efecto satírico o cómico. Aunque es el opuesto de la hipérbole, suele utilizarse junto con esta técnica para producir un efecto similar.

unreliable narrator See **narrator**.

narrador sospechoso Véase **narrador**.

V

verbal irony See **irony**.

ironía verbal Véase **ironía**.

verse A broad term, verse refers to a piece of writing that is metered and rhythmic. (Free verse is an exception to this, being a piece of writing grouped with verse rather than prose, even though it lacks a meter.) The term *verse* can also be used to refer to poetry in general. See also **meter; rhyme; rhythm**.

verso Término amplio para referirse a un escrito medido y rítmico. El verso libre es una excepción a esto, al ser un escrito agrupado con verso en lugar de prosa a pesar de que carece de métrica. El término *verso* también puede utilizarse para referirse a la poesía en general. Véase también **métrica**; **rima**; **ritmo**.

vignette A short narrative scene or description, often one in a series. If a story or novel is composed of a series of vignettes, it often relies on a thematic, rather than a plot-driven, structure.

viñeta Escena o descripción narrativa breve, que suele ser parte de una serie. Si una historia o novela se compone de una serie de viñetas, a menudo se basa en una estructura temática, más que argumental.

villanelle A form of poetry in which five tercets (rhyme scheme *aba*) are followed by a quatrain (rhyme scheme *abaa*). At the end of tercets two and four, the first line of tercet one is repeated. At the end of tercets three and five, the last line of tercet one is repeated. These two repeated lines, called *refrain lines*, are again repeated to conclude the quatrain. Much of the power of this form lies in its repeated lines and their subtly shifting sense or meaning over the course of the poem.

villanella Forma de poesía en la que cinco tercetos (esquema de rima *aba*) van seguidos de un cuarteto (esquema de rima *abaa*). Al final de los tercetos dos y cuatro se repite el primer verso del primer terceto. Al final de los tercetos tres y cinco, se repite el último verso del primer terceto. Estos dos versos repetidos, llamados *estribillos*, se repiten de nuevo para concluir el cuarteto. Gran parte de la fuerza de esta forma reside en la repetición de los versos y en su sutil cambio de sentido o significado a lo largo del poema.

volta Also known as a turn, the place in the poem where the speaker shifts his or her perspective in some way. See **shift**.

volta También conocido como giro, es el momento del poema en que el hablante cambia su perspectiva de alguna manera. Véase **giro**.

W

wordplay Techniques by which writers manipulate language for effect; examples include puns (the deliberate misuse of words that sound alike) or double entendres (expressions with two meanings).

juego de palabras Técnica por las que los escritores manipulan el lenguaje para conseguir un efecto; ejemplos de ello son los calambures (el mal uso deliberado de palabras que suenan igual) o el doble sentido (expresiones con dos significados).

Z

zeugma Pronounced *zoyg-muh*, a technique in which one verb is used with multiple (and often incongruous) objects, so that the definition of the verb is changed, complicated, or made both literal and figurative.

zeugma Técnica en la que un verbo se utiliza con múltiples objetos, a veces incongruentes, de modo que la definición del verbo cambia, se complica o se vuelve tanto literal como figurada.

MLA Guidelines for a List of Works Cited

Print Resources

1. A Book with One Author

A book with one author serves as a general model for most MLA citations. Include author, title, publisher, and date of publication.

Robinson, Marilynne. *Jack.* Farrar, Straus and Giroux, 2020.

2. A Book with Multiple Authors

King, Stephen, and Peter Straub. *Black House.* Random House, 2001.

3. Two or More Works by the Same Author

Multiple entries should be arranged alphabetically by title. The author's name appears at the beginning of the first entry, but is replaced by three hyphens and a period in all subsequent entries.

Ward, Jesmyn. *Sing, Unburied, Sing.* Scribner, 2017.

---. *Salvage the Bones.* Bloomsbury, 2011.

---. *Where the Line Bleeds.* Agate, 2008.

4. Author and Editor Both Named

Vidal, Gore. *The Selected Essays of Gore Vidal.* Edited by Jay Parini, Vintage Books, 2009.

Alternately, to cite the editor's contribution, start with the editor's name.

Parini, Jay, editor. *The Selected Essays of Gore Vidal.* By Gore Vidal, Vintage Books, 2009.

5. Anthology

Oates, Joyce Carol, editor. *Telling Stories: An Anthology for Writers.* W. W. Norton, 1997.

Selection from an anthology:

Irving, Washington. "Rip Van Winkle." *American Literature & Rhetoric,* edited by Robin Aufses, et al., Bedford, Freeman & Worth, 2021, pp. 494–509.

6. Translation

Ferrante, Elena. *My Brilliant Friend.* Translated by Ann Goldstein, Europa Editions, 2011.

7. Entry in a Reference Work

Because most reference works are alphabetized, you should omit page numbers.

Lounsberry, Barbara. "Joan Didion." *Encyclopedia of the Essay,* edited by Tracy Chevalier, Fitzroy, 1997.

For a well-known encyclopedia, use only the edition and year of publication. When an article is not attributed to an author, start the entry with article's title.

"Gilgamesh." *The Columbia Encyclopedia.* 5th ed., 1993.

8. Sacred Text

Unless a specific published edition is being cited, sacred texts should be omitted from the Works Cited list.

The New Testament. Translated by Richmond Lattimore, North Point Press, 1997.

9. Article in a Journal

The title of the journal should be followed by the volume, issue, and year of the journal's publication, as well as the page range of the article.

Marshall, Sarah. "Remote Control: Tonya Harding, Nancy Kerrigan, and the Spectacles of Female Power and Pain." *The Believer*, vol. 12, no. 1, 2014, pp. 1–10.

10. Article in a Magazine

In a weekly:

Schjeldahl, Peter. "A Pairing of Josef Albers and Giorgio Morandi. *The New Yorker*, 1 February 2021, pp. 76-77.

In a monthly:

Shulevitz, Judith. "The Brontës' Secret." *The Atlantic*, June 2016, pp. 38–41.

11. Article in a Newspaper

If you are citing a local paper that does not contain the city name in its title, add the city name in brackets after the newspaper title. When citing an article that does not appear on consecutive pages, list the first page followed by a plus sign. The edition only needs to be included if it is listed on the paper's masthead. For an opinion piece written by a named author, include the label "Op-ed" at the end of the entry if it is not clear from the title that it is an opinion piece.

Krugman, Paul. "The Economy Is About to Take Off." *The New York Times*, 28 May 2021, p. A19.

12. Review

In a weekly:

St. Félix, Doreen. "Social Contract." Review of *Mare of Easttown*, HBO Max, *The New Yorker*, 10 May 2021, p. 74.

In a monthly:

Simpson, Mona. "Imperfect Union." Review of *Mrs. Woolf and the Servants*, by Alison Light, *The Atlantic*, Jan./Feb. 2009, pp. 93–101.

Electronic Resources

13. Article from a Database Accessed through a Subscription Service

Apply the normal rules for citing a journal article, but include the name of the subscription service in italics and the digital object identifier (doi), if available.

Morano, Michele. "Boy Eats World." *Fourth Genre: Explorations in Nonfiction*, vol. 13, no. 2, 2011, pp. 31–35. *Project MUSE*, https://doi.org/10.1353/fge.2011.0029.

14. Article in an Online Magazine

Follow the author name and article title with the name of the magazine in italics, the date published, and the URL of the article.

Schuman, Rebecca. "This Giant Sculpture of Kafka's Head Perfectly Encapsulates His Strange Relationship to Prague." *Slate*, 24 May 2016, slate.com/blogs/browbeat/2016/05/24/this_giant_moving_sculpture_of_kafka_s_head_is_the_perfect_tribute_to_kafka.html.

15. Article in an Online Newspaper

Kelly, John. "The Secret to Keeping the Norwegian Royals Safe in World War II? The U.S. Secret Service." *The Washington Post*, 30 May 2020, www.washingtonpost.com/local/atlantic-crossing-secret-service/2021/05/29/862da36c-bfb7-11eb-83e3-0ca705a96ba4_story.html.

16. Online Review

Stevens, Dana. "The New *It* Has Too Much Insane Clown, Not Enough Posse." Review of *It*, directed by Andrés Muschietti. *Slate*, 16 Oct. 2017, slate.com/arts/2017/09/the-new-adaptation-of-stephen-kings-it-reviewed.html.

17. Entry in an Online Reference Work

"Eschatology." *Merriam-Webster*, 7 Apr. 2016, www.merriam-webster.com/dictionary/eschatology.

18. Work from a Website

"Wallace Stevens (1879–1955)." *Poetry Foundation*, 2015, www.poetryfoundation.org/bio/wallace-stevens.

19. Entire Website

Website with editor:

Dutton, Dennis, editor. *Arts and Letters Daily*. Chronicle of Higher Education, 2020, www.aldaily.com.

Website without editor:

Academy of American Poets. *poets.org*. 2021, www.poets.org/.

Personal website:

Valdez Quade, Kirstin. Home page, 2021, kirstinvaldezquade.com/.

20. Entire Web Log (Blog)

Benkkabou, Nagrisse, editor. *My Moroccan Food*. www.mymoroccanfood.com.

21. Social Media Post

List the author's full display name — that is, how it appears on their account, regardless of whether it's the person's real name — followed by the screen name or handle in brackets if it is significantly different from the display name. In the title position, use the caption of the post, the full text of the post (if it's brief), or the first few words of the post followed by an ellipsis (if it's long). Follow the capitalization and style of the post exactly and include any hashtags. If there is no text on the post, use a description of the photo or video as the title.

President Biden [@POTUS]. "I believe this is our moment to rebuild our economy from the bottom up and the middle out." *Twitter*, 27 May 2021, twitter.com/POTUS/status/1398062543466291200?s=20.

Brooklyn Nets [@brooklynnets]. Photo of James Harden, Game 3, Tonight 8:30pm. *Instagram*, 27 May 2020, www.instagram.com/p/CPaucADL1FR/?utm_source=ig_web_copy_link.

Lincoln Center [@lincolncenter] "BRB, watching this excerpt from Ballet Hispánico's "'CARMEN.maquia'" on repeat." 😍 #dancer #fyp #lincolncenter #ballet." *TikTok*, 7 May 2021, www.tiktok.com/@lincolncenter/video/6959623118910475526.

Richardson, Heather Cox. "Sunday, June 13, 2021." *Facebook*, 13 June 2021, www.facebook.com/heathercoxrichardson/posts/335806744581231.

22. Entry in a Wiki

"Pre-Raphaelite Brotherhood." *Wikipedia: The Free Encyclopedia*, Wikimedia Foundation, 25 Nov. 2013, en.wikipedia.org/wiki/Pre-Raphaelite_Brotherhood.

Other Sources

23. Film and Video

Follow the film title with the director, notable performers, the distribution company, and the date of release. For films viewed on the web, follow this with the URL of the website used to view the film. If citing a particular individual's work on the film, you may begin the entry with his or her name before the title.

Viewed in a theater:

The Hurt Locker. Directed by Kathryn Bigelow, performances by Jeremy Renner, Anthony Mackie, Guy Pearce, and Ralph Fiennes, Summit, 2009.

Viewed on the web (use original distributor and release date):

Fincher, David. "Mank." *Netflix*, 13 Nov. 2020, www.netflix.com.

24. Interview

Include the name of the interviewer if it is someone of note.

Personal interview:

Tripp, Lawrence. Personal interview, 14 Apr. 2014.

In print:

Dylan, Bob. "Who Is This Bob Dylan?" Interview by Tom Junod. *Esquire*, 23 Jan. 2014, pp. 124+.

On the radio:

Thompson, Ahmir. "Questlove." Interview by Terry Gross. *Fresh Air*, NPR, 27 Apr. 2016.

On the web:

Thompson, Ahmir. "Questlove." Interview by Terry Gross. *Fresh Air*, NPR, 27 Apr. 2016, www.npr.org/2016/04/27/475721555/questlove-on-prince-doo-wop-and-thefood-equivalent-of-the-mona-lisa.

25. Lecture or Speech

Viewed in person:

Smith, Anna Deavere. "On the Road: A Search for American Character." Jefferson Lecture in the Humanities, John F. Kennedy Center for the Performing Arts, Washington, 6 Apr. 2015. 44th Jefferson Lecture.

Viewed on the web:

Batuman, Elif. Lowell Humanities Series. Boston College. 13 Oct. 2010. www.frontrow.bc.edu/program/batuman.

26. Podcast

Hobbes, Michael, and Sarah Marshall. "Princess Diana Part 4, The Divorce." *You're Wrong About*, 2 Nov. 2020, podcasts.apple.com/us/podcast/princess-diana-part-4-the-divorce/id1380008439?i=1000497028549.

27. Work of Art or Photograph

In a museum:

Thomas, Mickalene. *A-E-I-O-U and Sometimes Y.* 2009, National Museum of Women in the Arts, Washington, D.C.

On the web:

Thiebaud, Wayne. *Three Machines.* 1963, De Young Museum, San Francisco, art.famsf.org/wayne-thiebaud/three-machines-199318.

In print:

Clark, Edward. *Navy CPO Graham Jackson Plays "Goin' Home."* 1945, *The Great LIFE Photographers*, Bulfinch, 2004, pp. 78–79.

28. Map or Chart

In print:

"U.S. Personal Savings Rate, 1929–1999." *Credit Card Nation: The Consequences of America's Addiction to Credit*, by Robert D. Manning, Basic, 2000, p. 100.

On the web:

"1914 New Balkan States and Central Europe Map." *National Geographic*, www.natgeomaps.com/hm-1914-new-balkan-states-and-central-europe.

29. Cartoon or Comic Strip

In print:

Flake, Emily. Cartoon. *The New Yorker*, 27 May 2021, p. 52.

On the web:

De Adder, Michael. "Doubling Down on Stupid," *The Washington Post*, 25 May 2021, www.washingtonpost.com/opinions/2021/05/25/doubling-down-stupid/.

30. Advertisement

In print:

Advertisement for Pittsburgh International Jazz Festival. *Jazz Times*, May 2021, p. 21.

On the web:

Advertisement for eBay authenticity guarantee. *Yahoo Sports*, 25 Nov. 2020, www.sports.yahoo.com.

Text Credits

Chimamanda Ngozi Adichie, "Apollo" by Chimamanda Adichie, first published in *The New Yorker.* Copyright © 2015 by Chimamanda Adichie, used by permission of The Wylie Agency LLC.

Anna Akhmatova, "The First Long-Range Artillery Shell in Leningrad" from ANNA AKHMATOVA: POEMS by Anna Akhmatova, translated by Lyn Coffin. Copyright © 1983 by Lyn Coffin. Used by permission of W. W. Norton & Company, Inc.

Brian Aldiss, "Super-Toys Last All Summer Long" by Brian Aldiss (St. Martin's Griffin). Copyright © 2001 by Brian Aldiss. Permission granted by the Estate of Brian Aldiss and his agent, Robin Straus Agency, Inc. All rights reserved.

Claribel Alegria, "Not yet" from *Woman of the River: Bilingual edition* by Claribel Alegria, translated by D. J. Flakoll, Copyright © 1989. Reprinted by permission of the University of Pittsburgh Press.

Threa Almontaser, "A Mother's Mouth Illuminated" from *The Wild Fox of Yemen.* Copyright © 2020, 2021 by Threa Almontaser. Reprinted with the permission of The Permissions Company, LLC on behalf of Graywolf Press, graywolfpress.org.

Amy Alvarez, "How to Date a White Boy," *Rattle*, #64, Summer 2019. Copyright © 2019 by Amy Alvarez. Used with permission.

Yehuda Amichai, "The Eve of Rosh Hashanah" from *The Selected Poetry of Yehuda Amichai,* edited and translated from the Hebrew by Chana Bloch and Stephen Mitchell, Copyright © 1986, 1996, 2013 by Chana Bloch and Stephen Mitchell. Published by the University of California Press.

Margaret Atwood, "Siren Song" from SELECTED POEMS 1965–1975 by Margaret Atwood. Copyright © 1976 by Margaret Atwood. Reprinted by permission of Houghton Mifflin Harcourt Publishing Company. Available in Canada in SELECTED POEMS, 1966–1984, published by Oxford University Press, © Margaret Atwood, 1990. All rights reserved. Reproduced with permission of Curtis Brown Group Ltd, London on behalf of Margaret Atwood. Copyright © Margaret Atwood, 1974.

David Baker, "Peril Sonnet," Copyright © 2019 by David Baker, from SWIFT: NEW AND SELECTED POEMS by David Baker. Used by permission of W. W. Norton & Company, Inc.

Amy Quan Barry, "loose strife ("Somebody says draw a map")" from *Loose Strife* by Amy Quan Barry. Copyright © 2015. Reprinted by permission of the University of Pittsburgh Press.

Amy Quan Barry, "Napalm" from the poem sequence entitled "child of the enemy" from *Asylum* by Amy Quan Barry, © 2001. Reprinted by permission of the University of Pittsburgh Press.

Elizabeth Bishop, "One Art" from POEMS by Elizabeth Bishop. Copyright © 2011 by The Alice H. Methfessel Trust. Publisher's Note and compilation copyright © 2011 by Farrar, Straus and Giroux. Reprinted by permission of Farrar, Straus and Giroux. All Rights Reserved.

Richard Blanco, "Mother Country." From *For All of Us, One Today* by Richard Blanco. Copyright © 2013 by Richard Blanco. Reprinted by permission of Beacon Press, Boston.

Kamau Brathwaite, "Ogun" (46 lines) from THE ARRIVANTS: A NEW WORLD TRILOGY by Brathwaite (1973). Copyright © Edward Brathwaite 1967, 1968, 1969, 1973 by permission of Oxford University Press. Reproduced with permission of the Licensor through PLSclear.

Julian Talamantez Brolaski, "What to Say Upon Being Asked to Be Friends" from *Advice for Lovers.* Copyright © 2012 by Julian Talamantez Brolaski. Reprinted with the permission of The Permissions Company, LLC on behalf of City Lights, www.citylights.com.

Gwendolyn Brooks, "We Real Cool." Copyright © Gwendolyn Brooks. Reprinted by consent of Brooks Permissions.

Jericho Brown, "Crossing" from *The Tradition.* Copyright © 2019 by Jericho Brown. All rights reserved. Used with the permission of The Permissions Company, Inc., on behalf of Copper Canyon Press.

Gladys Cardiff, "Combing" from *To Frighten a Storm.* Copyright © 1976 by Gladys Cardiff. Reprinted by permission of Copper Canyon Press.

C. P. Cavafy, republished with permission of Princeton University Press, from C. P. Cavafy, "Waiting for the Barbarians" from *C.P. Cavafy: Collected Poems.* Translated by Edmund Keeley and Philip Sherrard. Translation Copyright © 1975, 1992; permission conveyed through Copyright Clearance Center, Inc.

Chen Chen, "I invite my Parents to a Dinner Party." Copyright © 2018 by Chen Chen. Originally published in *Poem-a-Day* on April 19, 2018, by the Academy of American Poets.

Te-Ping Chen, "Lulu" from LAND OF BIG NUMBERS: Stories by Te-Ping Chen. Copyright © 2021 by Te-Ping Chen. Reprinted by permission of Houghton Mifflin Harcourt Publishing Company. All rights reserved.

Marilyn Chin, "Turtle Soup" from THE PHOENIX GONE, THE TERRACE EMPTY (Minneapolis: Milkwood Editions). Copyright © 2009 by Marilyn Chin. Reprinted with permission from Milkweed Editions. www.milkweed.org.

Franny Choi, "Gentrifier" from FLOATING, BRILLIANT, GONE by Franny Choi. Copyright © 2014 by Franny Choi. Used by permission of Write Bloody Publishing.

Maxine Clair, "The Creation," from *Rattlebone.* Copyright © 1994 by Maxine Clair.

"Poem to My Yellow Coat" copyright © 2020 by Lucille Clifton. Originally published by BOA Editions. Currently published in HOW TO CARRY WATER: SELECTED POEMS OF LUCILLE CLIFTON. Reprinted by permission of Curtis Brown, Ltd.

Billy Collins, "Weighing the Dog" from *Questions About Angels* by Billy Collins, copyright © 1995. Reprinted by permission of the University of Pittsburgh Press.

Kristiana Rae Colon, "a remix for remembrance," appeared in *Poetry*, April 2015. Copyright © 2015 by Kristiana Rae Colon. Used with permission.

Laura Da', "Passive Voice" From *Tributaries by Laura Da'*, © 2015 Laura Da'. Reprinted by permission of the University of Arizona Press.

Edwidge Danticat, "The Book of the Dead" from THE DEW BREAKER by Edwidge Danticat, copyright © 2004 by Edwidge Danticat. Used by permission of Alfred A. Knopf, an imprint of the Knopf Doubleday Publishing Group, a division of Penguin Random House LLC. All rights reserved.

Mahmoud Darwish, "Identity Card" by Mahmoud Darwish. Translated by Denys Johnson-Davies. Used by permission of Denys Johnson-Davies and Actes SUD SA.

"Blind Date" from THE COLLECTED STORIES OF LYDIA DAVIS by Lydia Davis. Copyright © 2009 by Lydia Davis. Reprinted by permission of Farrar, Straus and Giroux. All Rights Reserved.

Oliver de la Paz, "Diaspora Sonnet 40." Originally published in *Poem-a-Day* on July 3, 2018, by the Academy of American Poets. Copyright © 2018 by Oliver de la Paz. Used with permission.

Danielle DeTiberus, "The Artist Signs Her Masterpiece, Immodestly." Originally published in *Poem-a-Day* on January 7, 2020, by the Academy of American Poets. Copyright © 2020 by Danielle DeTiberus. Used with permission.

Natalie Diaz, "The Facts of Art" from *When My Brother Was an Aztec.* Copyright © 2012 by Natalie Diaz. Reprinted with the permission of The Permissions Company, LLC on behalf of Copper Canyon Press, www.coppercanyonpress.org.

Emily Dickinson, "Crumbling is not an instant's Act," "I'm Nobody! Who are you?" and "Much Madness is divinest Sense" from THE POEMS OF EMILY DICKINSON: VARIORUM EDITION, edited by Ralph W. Franklin, Cambridge, Mass.: The Belknap Press of Harvard University Press, Copyright © 1998 by the President and Fellows of Harvard College. Copyright © 1951, 1955 by the President and Fellows of Harvard College. Copyright © renewed 1979, 1983 by the President and Fellows of Harvard College. Copyright © 1914, 1918, 1919, 1924, 1929, 1930, 1932, 1935, 1937, 1942 by Martha Dickinson Bianchi. Copyright © 1952, 1957, 1958, 1963, 1965 by Mary L. Hampson.

Rita Dove, "Family Reunion." Copyright © 2007 by Rita Dove. Originally published in *Callaloo.* Used with the permission of the poet.

Carol Ann Duffy, "Penelope" from THE WORLD'S WIFE by Carol Ann Duffy. Copyright © 1999 by Carol Ann Duffy. Reprinted by permission of Farrar, Straus and Giroux, Pan Macmillan through PLSclear and permission of the author c/o Rogers, Coleridge & White Ltd., 20 Powis Mews, London W11 1JN. All Rights Reserved.

Ralph Ellison, "Boy on a Train" from FLYING HOME: AND OTHER STORIES by Ralph Ellison, edited by John F. Callahan, copyright © 1996 by Fanny Ellison. Used by permission of Random House, an imprint and division of Penguin Random House LLC. All rights reserved.

Heid E. Erdrich, "Intimate Detail" from The Mother's Tongue. Copyright © 2005 by Heid E. Erdich. Republished by permission of Author and with permission of Salt Publishing through PLSclear.

Louise Erdrich, "The Red Convertible" by Louise Erdrich. Copyright © 1984, 1993, 2009 by Louise Erdrich, used by permission of The Wylie Agency LLC.

William Faulkner, "A Rose for Emily." Copyright 1930 & renewed 1958 by William Faulkner, from COLLECTED STORIES OF WILLIAM FAULKNER by William Faulkner. Used by permission of Random House, an imprint and division of Penguin Random House LLC and W. W. Norton & Company, Inc. All rights reserved. Used by permission.

Nikky Finney, "A New Day Dawns" from *Love Child's Hotbed of Occasional Poetry.* Copyright © 2020 by Nikky Finney. Published 2020 by TriQuarterly Books/Northwestern University Press. All rights reserved.

Denice Frohman, "Lady Jordan," appeared in *The New York Times,* May 15, 2020. Copyright © 2020 by Denice Frohman. Used with permission.

Robert Frost, "Mending Wall" by Robert Frost from the book THE POETRY OF ROBERT FROST edited by Edward Connery Lathem. Copyright © 1930, 1939, 1969 by Henry Holt and Company. Copyright © 1958 by Robert Frost, copyright © 1967 by Lesley Frost Ballantine. Reprinted by permission of Henry Holt and Company. All rights reserved.

Marjorie Garber, "Hamlet: The Matter of Character" from SHAKESPEARE AND MODERN CULTURE by Marjorie Garber, copyright © 2008 by Marjorie Garber. Used by permission of Pantheon Books, an imprint of the Knopf Doubleday Publishing Group, a division of Penguin Random House LLC. All rights reserved.

Alexis Aceves García, "AQUÍ HAY TODO, MIJA," appeared in *Brooklyn Poets,* June 22–28, 2020. Copyright © 2020 by Alexis Aceves Garcia. Used with permission.

Ross Gay, "Say It" from *Bringing the Shovel Down* by Ross Gay, Copyright © 2011. Reprinted by permission of the University of Pittsburgh Press.

Hafizah Geter, "The Widower" from *Un-American.* Copyright © 2020 by Hafizah Geter. Published by Wesleyan University Press and reprinted with permission.

Allen Ginsberg, "Is About" from *Death & Fame* by Allen Ginsberg. Copyright © 1999 by The Allen Ginsberg Trust. Used by permission of HarperCollins Publishers.

Dana Gioia, "Summer Storm" originally appeared in *The New Criterion*, Volume 14, Number 10, page 32. Copyright © 2001 by Dana Gioia. All rights reserved. Used with permission.

Elisa Gonzalez, "Failed Essay on Privilege," *The New Yorker*, October 28, 2019. Copyright © 2019 by Conde Nast Publications, Inc. Used with permission.

Nadine Gordimer, "Homage" from *Loot and Other Stories*. Copyright © 2003 by Felix Licensing, B. V. Reprinted by permission of Farrar, Straus and Giroux. All Rights Reserved.

Stephen Jay Gould, "The Monster's Human Nature" from *Dinosaur in a Haystack: Reflections in Natural History,* copyright © 1995 by Stephen Jay Gould. Used by permission of Harmony Books, an imprint of Random House, a division of Penguin Random House LLC. All rights reserved.

Nathalie Handal, "Ways of Rebelling" from *The Republics* by Nathalie Handal. Copyright © 2015. Reprinted by permission of University of Pittsburgh Press.

Joy Harjo, "For Calling the Spirit Back from Wandering the Earth in Its Human Feet", from CONFLICT RESOLUTION FOR HOLY BEINGS: POEMS by Joy Harjo. Copyright © 2015 by Joy Harjo. Used by permission of W. W. Norton & Company, Inc.

Robert Hayden, "Those Winter Sundays." Copyright © 1966 by Robert Hayden, from COLLECTED POEMS OF ROBERT HAYDEN by Robert Hayden, edited by Frederick Glaysher. Used by permission of Liveright Publishing Corporation.

Terrance Hayes, "Pseudacris Crucifer," *The New Yorker*, August 10. 2020. Copyright © 2020 by Conde Nast Publications, Inc. Used with permission.

Terrance Hayes, "Wind in a Box — after Lorca" from WIND IN A BOX by Terrance Hayes, copyright © 2006 by Terrance Hayes. Used by permission of Penguin Books, an imprint of Penguin Publishing Group, a division of Penguin Random House LLC. All rights reserved.

Rebecca Hazelton Stafford, "My Husband." From BEST AMERICAN POETRY 2015. Used with permission of the author.

Seamus Heaney, "Bogland" and "Digging" from OPENED GROUND: SELECTED POEMS 1966–1996 by Seamus Heaney. Copyright © 1998 by Seamus Heaney. Reprinted by permission of Farrar, Straus and Giroux LLC. Canadian rights courtesy of Faber and Faber Ltd. All rights reserved.

Zbigniew Herbert, "Elegy of Fortinbras" from *The Collected Poems: 1956–1998.* Translated & edited by Alissa Valles.

Juan Felipe Herrera, "i want to speak of unity" from *Every Day We Get More Illegal.* Copyright © 2020 by Juan Felipe Herrera. Reprinted with the permission of The Permissions Company, LLC on behalf of City Lights, www.citylights.com.

Edward Hirsch, "My Own Acquaintance" from THE MAKING OF A SONNET: A NORTON ANTHOLOGY, edited by Edward Hirsch and Eavan Boland. Copyright © 2008 by Edward Hirsch and Eavan Boland. Used by permission of W. W. Norton & Company, Inc.

Sakinah Hofler, "Erasure," first published in *Kenyon Review Online*, May/June 2020. Copyright © 2020 by Sakinah Hofler. All rights reserved. Used with permission.

Amorak Huey, "We Were All Odysseus in Those Days." Copyright © 2019 by Amorak Huey. Originally published in *Poem-a-Day* on March 20, 2019, by the Academy of American Poets.

Langston Hughes, "I look at the world" from New Haven: Beinecke Library, Yale University. Reprinted by permission of Harold Ober Associates. Copyright by the Langston Hughes Estate.

Major Jackson, "Mighty Pawns" from ROLL DEEP: POEMS by Major Jackson. Copyright © 2015 by Major Jackson. Used by permission of W. W. Norton & Company, Inc.

Major Jackson, "Urban Renewal XVIII," from HOOPS by Major Jackson. Copyright © 2006 by Major Jackson. Used by permission of W. W. Norton & Company, Inc.

Taylor Johnson, "Trans Is Against Nostalgia," *Four Way Review*, November 15, 2018. Copyright © 2018 by Taylor Johnson. Used by permission.

Saeed Jones, "A Stranger," *The New Yorker*, July 13, 2020. Copyright © Saeed Jones 2020 — first published in *The New Yorker* in July 2020 and reprinted herewith by permission of the Charlotte Sheedy Literary Agency.

Edward P. Jones, "The First Day" from *Lost in the City* by Edward P. Jones. Copyright © 1992, 2005, 2012 by Edward P. Jones. Used by permission of HarperCollins Publishers.

Mohja Kahf, "My Grandmother Washes Her Feet in the Sink of the Bathroom at Sears" from *Emails from Scheherazad* by Mohja Kahf. Gainesville: University Press of Florida, 2003, pp. 26–28. Reprinted with permission of the University Press of Florida.

Jamaica Kincaid, "Girl" from AT THE BOTTOM OF THE RIVER by Jamaica Kincaid. Copyright © 1983 by Jamaica Kincaid. Reprinted by permission of Farrar, Straus and Giroux. All Rights Reserved.

Jamil Jan Kochai, "Playing Metal Gear Solid V: The Phantom Pain." Copyright © 2020 by Jamil Jan Kochai, used by permission of The Wylie Agency LLC.

Yusef Komunyakaa, "Between Days" from *Pleasure Dome: New and Collected Poems.* Copyright © 2001 by Yusef Komunyakaa. Published by Wesleyan University Press. Used with permission.

Maxine Kumin, "Woodchucks." Copyright © 1972, 1997 by Maxine Kumin, from SELECTED POEMS 1960–1990 by Maxine Kumin. Used by permission of W. W. Norton & Company, Inc.

Hanif Kureishi, "We're Not Jews" from LOVE IN A BLUE TIME by Hanif Kureishi. Copyright © 1997 by Hanif Kureishi. Reprinted with the permission of Scribner, a division of Simon & Schuster, Inc. All rights reserved.

Jhumpa Lahiri, "Interpreter of Maladies" from INTERPRETER OF MALADIES by Jhumpa Lahiri. Copyright © 1999 by Jhumpa Lahiri. Reproduced by permission of Houghton Mifflin Harcourt Publishing Company. All rights reserved.

Li-Young Lee, "The Hammock" from BOOK OF MY NIGHTS. Copyright © 2001 by Li-Young Lee. Reprinted with permission of The Permissions Company, Inc., on behalf of BOA Editions, Ltd. www.boaeditions.org.

Robin Coste Lewis, "Art & Craft" from VOYAGE OF THE SABLE VENUS: AND OTHER POEMS by Robin Coste Lewis, copyright © 2015 by Robin Coste Lewis. Used by permission of Alfred A. Knopf, an imprint of the Knopf Doubleday Publishing Group, a division of Penguin Random House LLC. All rights reserved.

C. S. Lewis, "Hamlet: The Prince or the Poem?" from *Selected Literary Essays* by C. S. Lewis Copyright © C. S. Lewis Pte Ltd 1969. Extract reprinted by permission.

Ada Limón, "The Raincoat" from *The Carrying.* Copyright © 2018 by Ada Limón. Reprinted with the permission of The Permissions Company LLC on behalf of Milkweed Editions, milkweed.org.

Naguib Mahfouz, "Half a Day," copyright © 1991 by American University in Cairo Press; from VOICES FROM THE OTHER WORLD: ANCIENT EGYPTIAN TALES by Naguib Mahfouz, Selected and Translated by Denys Johnson-Davies. Used by permission of Doubleday, an imprint of the Knopf Doubleday Publishing Group, a division of Penguin Random House LLC. All rights reserved.

Amit Majmudar, "True Believer," from *America Magazine*, March 16, 2015. with permission of America Press, Inc. Copyright © 2015. All rights reserved.

Jill McDonough, "Twelve-Hour Shifts" originally published in *Poem-a-Day*, September 30, 2015. Copyright © 2015 by Jill McDonough. All rights reserved. Used with permission.

Dunya Mikhail, "The War Works Hard" By Dunya Mikhail, translated by Elizabeth Winslow, from THE WAR WORKS HARD, copyright © 2005 by Dunya Mikhail. Reprinted by permission of New Directions Publishing Corp.

Czesław Miłosz, "Dedication" from *New and Collected Poems: 1931–2001* by Czesław Miłosz. Copyright © 1988, 1991, 1995, 2001 by Czesław Miłosz Royalties, Inc. Used by permission of HarperCollins Publishers.

Rajiv Mohabir, "Why Whales Are Back in New York City" from *The Cowherd's Sons.* Originally published in *Poem-a-Day* (October 16, 2017). Copyright © 2017 by Rajiv Mohabir. Reprinted with the permission of The Permissions Company, LLC on behalf of Tupelo Press, tupelopress.org.

Marianne Moore, "Part of a Novel, Part of a Poem, Part of a Play: The Steeple-Jack," Poetry: A Magazine of Verse, June 1932. Permission for the use of "Part of a Novel, Part of a Poem, Part of a Play: Steeplejack" is granted by the Literary Estate of Marianne C. Moore, David M. Moore, Esq., Successor Executor, Literary Estate of Marianne Moore. All rights reserved.

Scholastique Mukasonga, "Grief," from *Igifu*, translated by Jordan Stump, Archipelago Books, Copyright © 2020.

Bharati Mukherjee, "The Management of Grief" from THE MIDDLEMAN AND OTHER STORIES, copyright © 1988 by Bharati Mukherjee. Used by permission of Grove/Atlantic, Inc. Any third party use of this material, outside of this publication, is prohibited.

Harryette Mullen, "We Are Not Responsible" from *Sleeping with the Dictionary,* by Harryette Mullen, copyright © 2002 by The Regents of the University of California. Published by the University of California Press.

Marilyn Nelson, "The Century Quilt" from *Mama's Promises.* Copyright © 1985 by Louisiana State University Press. Used with permission.

Marilyn Nelson, "How I Discovered Poetry" from *The Fields of Praise: New and Selected Poems.* Copyright © 1997 by Louisiana State University Press. Used with permission.

Aimee Nezhukumatahil, "Chess" from *Poem-a-Day*, November 20, 2015. Copyright © 2015 by Aimee Nezhukumatahil. All rights reserved. Used with permission.

Viet Thanh Nguyen, "On True War Stories," Copyright © (Fall 2015): 140–145, originally published in "(Re)Collecting the Vietnam War," special issue of Asian American Literary Review 6.2. All rights reserved. Used with permission.

Bao Ninh, "Savage Winds," translated by Phun Huy Dong & Nina McPherson, Published by *Granta Magazine*, Copyright © Bao Ninh. Reproduced by permission of the author c/o Rogers, Coleridge & White Ltd., 20 Powis Mews, London W11 1 JN.

Naomi Shihab Nye, "For Mohammed Zeid of Gaza, Age 15" from *You & Yours.* Copyright © 2005 by Naomi Shihab Nye. Reprinted with the permission of The Permissions Company, LLC on behalf of BOA Editions, Ltd., www.boaeditions.org.

Frank O'Hara, "Having a Coke with You" from THE COLLECTED POEMS OF FRANK O'HARA by Frank O'Hara, copyright © 1971 by Maureen Granville-Smith, Administratrix of the Estate of Frank O'Hara, copyright renewed 1999 by Maureen O'Hara Granville-Smith and Donald Allen. Used by permission of Alfred A. Knopf, an imprint of the Knopf Doubleday Publishing Group, a division of Penguin Random House LLC. All rights reserved.

Tim O'Brien, "The Things they Carried" from THE THINGS THEY CARRIED by Tim O'Brien. Copyright © 1990 by Tim O'Brien. Reprinted by permission of Houghton Mifflin Harcourt Publishing Company. All rights reserved.

Flannery O'Connor, "A Good Man Is Hard to Find" from A GOOD MAN IS HARD TO FIND AND OTHER STORIES by Flannery O'Connor. Copyright 1953 by Flannery O'Connor. Copyright © renewed 1981 by Regina O'Connor. Reprinted by permission of Houghton Mifflin Harcourt Publishing Company. All rights reserved.

Joyce Carol Oates, "Where Are You Going, Where Have You Been?" from *High Lonesome* by Joyce Carol Oates. Copyright © 2006 by The Ontario Review, Inc. Used by permission of HarperCollins Publishers.

José Olivarez, "(Citizen) (Illegal)" from *Citizen Illegal.* Copyright © 2018 by José Olivarez. Used with permission from Haymarket Books.

Mary Oliver, "The Black Walnut Tree" from *Twelve Moons.* Copyright © 1979. Reprinted by permission of Little, Brown, an imprint of Hachette Book Group, Inc.

Tillie Olsen, "I Stand Here Ironing" from TELL ME A RIDDLE, REQUA 1, AND OTHER WORKS by Tillie Olsen. Reprinted by permission of the University of Nebraska Press. Copyright © 2013 by the Board of Regents of the University of Nebraska.

Matthew Olzmann, "Letter Beginning with Two Lines by Czeslaw Milosz." Originally appeared in *Poem-a-Day* on the Academy of American Poets website. Copyright © 2017 by Matthew Olzmann. Reprinted by permission of Matthew Olzmann.

Cynthai Ozick, "The Shawl" from THE SHAWL by Cynthia Ozick, copyright © 1980, 1983 by Cynthia Ozick. Used by permission of Alfred A. Knopf, an imprint of the Knopf Doubleday Publishing Group, a division of Penguin Random House LLC. All rights reserved.

Gregory Pardlo, "Written by Himself" from *Digest.* Copyright © 2014 by Gregory Pardlo. Reprinted with permission of The Permission Company, Inc., on behalf of Four Way Books, www.fourwaybooks.com. All rights reserved.

Hai-Dang Phan, "My Father's Norton Introduction to Literature, Third Edition (1981)" from Reenactments: Poems and Translations. Originally in Poetry (November 2015). Copyright © 2015, 2019 by Hai-Dang Phan. Reprinted with the permission of The Permissions Company, LLC on behalf of Sarabande Books, sarabandebooks.org. All rights reserved. Used with permission.

Kirstin Valdez Quade, "Jubilee," from NIGHT AT THE FIESTAS: STORIES by Kirstin Valdez Quade. Copyright © 2015 by Kirstin Valdez Quade. Used by permission of W. W. Norton & Company, Inc.

Molly Rose Quinn, "Dolorosa" first published in *Four Way Review* online. Reprinted by permission of the author.

Victoria Redel, "Bedecked" from *Swoon.* Copyright © 2003 by Victoria Redel. Published by University of Chicago Press. All rights reserved. Used with permission.

Henry Reed, "Naming of Parts" by Henry Reed, ed. John Stallworthy (*Collected Poems, 2007*) is reprinted here by kind permission of Carcanet Press Limited, Manchester, UK.

Paisley Rekdal, "Happiness" from *Animal Eye* by Paisley Rekdal, copyright © 2012. Reprinted by permission of the University of Pittsburgh Press.

Jason Reynolds, "Match." Originally published in *Poem-a-Day* on July 28, 2020, by the Academy of American Poets. Copyright © 2020 by Jason Reynolds.

Adrienne Rich, "A Valediction Forbidding Mourning." Copyright © 2016 by the Adrienne Rich Literary Trust. Copyright © 1971 by W. W. Norton & Company, Inc., from COLLECTED POEMS: 1950–2012 by Adrienne Rich. Used by permission of W. W. Norton & Company, Inc.

Rainer Maria Rilke, "Untitled [Do you still remember: falling stars]" from THE POETRY OF RILKE: BILINGUAL EDITION by Rainer Maria Rilke, translated and edited by Edward Snow. Translation © 2009 by Edward Snow. Reprinted by permission of North Point Press, a division of Farrar, Straus and Giroux. All Rights Reserved.

Peggy Robles-Alvarado, "When I Became La Promesa," Copyright © 2020 by Peggy Robles–Alvarado. Originally published in *Poem-a-Day* on October 6, 2020, by the Academy of American Poets.

Theodore Roethke, "My Papa's Waltz," copyright © 1942 by Hearst Magazines, Inc., from COLLECTED POEMS by Theodore Roethke. Used by permission of Doubleday, an imprint of the Knopf Doubleday Publishing Group, a division of Penguin Random House LLC. All rights reserved.

Anne Sexton, "Her Kind" from TO BEDLAM AND PART WAY BACK. Copyright © 1960 by Anne Sexton, renewed 1988 by Linda G. Sexton. Reprinted with permission of Houghton Mifflin Harcourt Publishing Company. All rights reserved. Electronic rights courtesy of SLL/Sterling Lord Literistic, Inc. Copyright by Linda Gray Sexton and Loring Conant, Jr. 1981.

William Shakespeare, "Hamlet, Prince of Denmark," glosses from *The Bedford Shakespeare*, Bedford/St. Martin's (2015). Copyright © 2015 by Cambridge University Press. Reproduced with permission of the Licensor through PLSclear.

Solmaz Sharif, "Reaching Guantánamo [Dear Salim/Love are you well?]" from *Look.* Originally published in *Paperbag Magazine* no. 1 (Summer 2010). Copyright © 2010, 2016 by Solmaz Sharif. Reprinted with the permission of The Permissions Company, LLC on behalf of Graywolf Press, graywolfpress.org.

Warsan Shire, "For Women Who Are Difficult to Love." Copyright © Warsan Shire.

Tracy K. Smith, "Wade in the Water" from *Wade in the Water.* Copyright © 2018 by Tracy K. Smith. Reprinted with the permission of The Permissions Company, LLC on behalf of Graywolf Press, graywolfpress.org.

Rivers Solomon, "Prudent Girls," appeared in *The New York Times*, July 7, 2020. Copyright © 2020 by Rivers Solomon. All rights reserved. Used with permission.

Edna St. Vincent Millay, "Love is not all: it is not meat nor drink" from *Collected Poems.* Copyright 1931, © 1958 by Edna St. Vincent Millay and Norma Millay Ellis. Reprinted with the permission of The Permissions Company, LLC on behalf of Holly Peppe, Literary Executor, The Edna St. Vincent Millay Society, www.millay.org.

A. E. Stallings, "The Wife of the Man of Many Wiles" from *Archaic Smile: Poems.* Copyright © 1999 by University of Evansville Press. Used with permission.

Ruth Stone, "Pokeberries" from *What Love Comes To: New & Selected Poems.* Copyright © 2008 by Ruth Stone. Reprinted with the permission of The Permissions Company, LLC on behalf of Copper Canyon Press, www.coppercanyonpress.org.

Adrienne Su, "Peaches" from *Peach State* by Adrienne Su, © 2021. Reprinted by permission of the University of Pittsburgh Press.

Wisława Szymborska, "The Terrorist, He Watches," from *Sounds, Feelings, Thoughts*, translated by Magnus J. Krynski and Robert A. Maguire. Copyright © 1981 by Princeton University Press. Republished with permission of Princeton University Press, Permission Conveyed through Copyright Clearance Center, Inc.

Dylan Thomas, "Do not go gentle into that good night," by Dylan Thomas, from THE POEMS OF DYLAN THOMAS, copyright © 1952 by Dylan Thomas. Reprinted by permission of New Directions Publishing Corp.

Nafissa Thompson-Spires, "Belles Lettres" from HEADS OF THE COLORED PEOPLE by Nafissa Thompson-Spires. Copyright © 2018 by Nafissa Thompson-Spires. Reprinted with the permission of 37 Ink, a division of Simon & Schuster, Inc. All rights reserved.

Paul Tran, "East Mountain View," Winter Tangerine, April 2017. Copyright © 2017 by Paul Tran. All rights reserved. Used with permission.

Deborah Treisman, "Jamil Jan Kochai on the Intimate Alienation of Video Games," *The New Yorker,* December 30, 2019. Copyright © 2019 by Conde Nast. All rights reserved. Used with permission.

Natasha Trethewey, "Southern History" from NATIVE GUARD: Poems by Natasha Trethewey. Copyright © 2006 by Natasha Trethewey. Reprinted by permission of Houghton Mifflin Harcourt Publishing Company. All rights reserved.

Brian Turner, "Sadiq" from *Here, Bullet*. Copyright © 2005 by Brian Turner. Reprinted with the permission of The Permissions Company, LLC on behalf of Alice James Books, www.alicejamesbooks.org.

Jon Turney, excerpt from *Frankenstein's Footsteps.* Copyright © 1969 by Yale University Press. All rights reserved. Used with permission.

Laura van den Berg, "Lessons" from THE ISLE OF YOUTH by Laura van den Berg. Copyright © 2013 by Laura van den Berg. Reprinted by permission of Farrar, Straus and Giroux. All Rights Reserved.

Helena María Viramontes, "The Moths" by Helena María Viramontes is reprinted with permission from Arte Público Press - University of Houston, the publisher of THE MOTHS AND OTHER STORIES/Las palomillas de la noche y otros relatos, copyright © 1985 by Helena María Viramontes, and protected by the Copyright Laws of the United States. All rights reserved. The printing, copying, redistribution, or retransmission of this Content without express permission is prohibited.

Alice Walker, "Everyday Use" from IN LOVE & TROUBLE: STORIES OF BLACK WOMEN by Alice Walker. Copyright © 1973, renewed 2001 by Alice Walker. Reprinted by permission of Houghton Mifflin Harcourt Publishing Company. All rights reserved. Electronic rights courtesy of the Joy Harris Literary Agency, Inc.

Weike Wang, "The Trip," appeared in *The New Yorker*, November 11, 2019. Copyright © 2019. Reprinted by permission of The Joy Harris Literary Agency, Inc.

Richard Wilbur, "The Writer" from THE MIND-READER by Richard Wilbur. Copyright © 1971 and renewed 1999 by Richard Wilbur. Reprinted by permission of Houghton Mifflin Harcourt Publishing Company. All rights reserved.

August Wilson, Entire Play from FENCES by August Wilson, copyright © 1986 by August Wilson. Used by permission of New American Library, an imprint of Penguin Publishing Group, a division of Penguin Random House LLC. All rights reserved.

Jamila Woods, "Ghazal for White Hen Pantry" first published in *Poetry Magazine*, Dec. 2015 issue is reprinted by permission of the author.

Index

C

D

E

F

G

J

K

L

M

N

O

P

U

V

W

Y

Z